10. Shipping Terms:

	FOB Shipping Point	FOB Destination
Ownership (title) passes to buyer when merchandise is...................	delivered to freight carrier	delivered to buyer
Transportation costs are paid by	buyer	seller

11. Format for Bank Reconciliation:

Cash balance according to bank statement		$xxx
Add: Additions by company not on bank statement	$xx	
Bank errors	xx	xx
		$xxx
Deduct: Deductions by company not on bank statement	$xx	
Bank errors	xx	xx
Adjusted balance..		$xxx
Cash balance according to company's records		$xxx
Add: Additions by bank not recorded by company ..	$xx	
Company errors..	xx	xx
		$xxx
Deduct: Deductions by bank not recorded by company...	$xx	
Company errors...	xx	xx
Adjusted balance..		$xxx

12. Inventory Costing Methods:

1. First-in, First-out (FIFO)
2. Last-in, First-out (LIFO)
3. Average Cost

13. Interest Computations:

$$\text{Interest} = \text{Face Amount (or Principal)} \times \text{Rate} \times \text{Time}$$

14. Methods of Determining Annual Depreciation:

$$\text{STRAIGHT-LINE:} \quad \frac{\text{Cost} - \text{Estimated Residual Value}}{\text{Estimated Life}}$$

DOUBLE-DECLINING-BALANCE: Rate* × Book Value at Beginning of Period

*Rate is commonly twice the straight-line rate (1/Estimated Life).

15. Adjustments to Net Income (Loss) Using the Indirect Method

	Increase (Decrease)
Net income (loss)	$ XXX
Adjustments to reconcile net income to net cash flow from operating activities:	
Depreciation of fixed assets	XXX
Amortization of intangible assets	XXX
Losses on disposal of assets	XXX
Gains on disposal of assets	(XXX)
Changes in current operating assets and liabilities:	
Increases in noncash current operating assets	(XXX)
Decreases in noncash current operating assets	XXX
Increases in current operating liabilities	XXX
Decreases in current operating liabilities	(XXX)
Net cash flow from operating activities	$ XXX
	or
	$(XXX)

16. Contribution Margin Ratio $= \dfrac{\text{Sales} - \text{Variable Costs}}{\text{Sales}}$

17. Break-Even Sales (Units) $= \dfrac{\text{Fixed Costs}}{\text{Unit Contribution Margin}}$

18. Sales (Units) $= \dfrac{\text{Fixed Costs} + \text{Target Profit}}{\text{Unit Contribution Margin}}$

19. Margin of Safety $= \dfrac{\text{Sales} - \text{Sales at Break-Even Point}}{\text{Sales}}$

20. Operating Leverage $= \dfrac{\text{Contribution Margin}}{\text{Income from Operations}}$

21. Variances

$$\text{Direct Materials Price Variance} = \begin{pmatrix}\text{Actual Price per Unit} - \\ \text{Standard Price}\end{pmatrix} \times \begin{pmatrix}\text{Actual Quantity} \\ \text{Used}\end{pmatrix}$$

$$\text{Direct Materials Quantity Variance} = \begin{pmatrix}\text{Actual Quantity Used} - \\ \text{Standard Quantity}\end{pmatrix} \times \begin{pmatrix}\text{Standard Price} \\ \text{per Unit}\end{pmatrix}$$

$$\text{Direct Labor Rate Variance} = \begin{pmatrix}\text{Actual Rate per Hour} - \\ \text{Standard Rate}\end{pmatrix} \times \begin{pmatrix}\text{Actual Hours} \\ \text{Worked}\end{pmatrix}$$

$$\text{Direct Labor Time Variance} = \begin{pmatrix}\text{Actual Hours Worked} - \\ \text{Standard Hours}\end{pmatrix} \times \begin{pmatrix}\text{Standard Rate} \\ \text{per Hour}\end{pmatrix}$$

$$\text{Variable Factory Overhead Controllable Variance} = \begin{pmatrix}\text{Actual} \\ \text{Factory} \\ \text{Overhead}\end{pmatrix} - \begin{pmatrix}\text{Budgeted Factory} \\ \text{Overhead for} \\ \text{Amount Produced}\end{pmatrix}$$

$$\text{Fixed Factory Overhead Volume Variance} = \begin{pmatrix}\text{Budgeted Factory} \\ \text{Overhead for} \\ \text{Amount Produced}\end{pmatrix} - \begin{pmatrix}\text{Applied} \\ \text{Factory} \\ \text{Overhead}\end{pmatrix}$$

22. Rate of Return on Investment (ROI) $= \dfrac{\text{Income from Operations}}{\text{Invested Assets}}$

Alternative ROI Computation:

$$\text{ROI} = \frac{\text{Income from Operations}}{\text{Sales}} \times \frac{\text{Sales}}{\text{Invested Assets}}$$

23. Capital Investment Analysis Methods:

1. Methods That Ignore Present Values:
   A. Average Rate of Return Method
   B. Cash Payback Method
2. Methods That Use Present Values:
   A. Net Present Value Method
   B. Internal Rate of Return Method

24. Average Rate of Return $= \dfrac{\text{Estimated Average Annual Income}}{\text{Average Investment}}$

25. Present Value Index $= \dfrac{\text{Total Present Value of Net Cash Flow}}{\text{Amount to Be Invested}}$

26. Present Value Factor for an Annuity of $1 $= \dfrac{\text{Amount to Be Invested}}{\text{Equal Annual Net Cash Flows}}$

WARREN   REEVE

FINANCIAL AND MANAGERIAL
ACCOUNTING

9E

CARL S. WARREN
Professor Emeritus of Accounting
University of Georgia, Athens

JAMES M. REEVE
Professor Emeritus of Accounting
University of Tennessee, Knoxville

THOMSON
———※———™
SOUTH-WESTERN

Australia · Brazil · Canada · Mexico · Singapore · Spain · United Kingdom · United States

THOMSON
————★————
SOUTH-WESTERN

Financial and Managerial Accounting, 9e
Carl S. Warren and James M. Reeve

VP/Editorial Director:
Jack W. Calhoun

Publisher:
Rob Dewey

Executive Editor:
Sharon Oblinger

Developmental Editor:
Steven E. Joos

Assistant Editor:
Erin Berger

Marketing Manager:
Robin Farrar

Sr. Content Project Manager:
Cliff Kallemeyn

Manager of Technology, Editorial:
Vicky True

Associate Manager of Technology:
John Barans

Sr. Technology Project Editors:
Sally Nieman and Robin Browning

Manufacturing Coordinator:
Doug Wilke

Editorial Assistant:
Kelly Somers

Production House:
LEAP Publishing Services, Inc.

Compositor:
GGS Book Services, Inc.

Printer:
RR Donnelley
Willard, OH

Art Director:
Bethany Casey

Infographic Illustrations:
Grannan Graphic Design, Ltd.

Internal Designer:
Grannan Graphic Design, Ltd.

Cover Designer:
Grannan Graphic Design, Ltd.

Cover Images:
Max Dereta/Jupiterimages

Photography Manager:
John Hill

Photo Researcher:
Rose Alcorn

Library of Congress Control Number:
2006934848

For more information about our products, contact us at:

Thomson Learning Academic Resource
Center

1-800-423-0563

Thomson Higher Education
5191 Natorp Boulevard
Mason, OH 45040
USA

Carl S. Warren

Dr. Carl S. Warren is Professor Emeritus of Accounting at the University of Georgia, Athens. For over 25 years, Professor Warren taught all levels of accounting classes. Professor Warren has taught classes at the University of Georgia, University of Iowa, Michigan State University, and University of Chicago. Professor Warren focused his teaching efforts on principles of accounting and auditing. Professor Warren received his doctorate degree (Ph.D.) from Michigan State University and his undergraduate (B.B.A) and masters (M.A.) degrees from the University of Iowa. During his career, Professor Warren published numerous articles in professional journals, including *The Accounting Review, Journal of Accounting Research, Journal of Accountancy, The CPA Journal*, and *Auditing: A Journal of Practice & Theory*. Professor Warren's outside interests include writing short stories and novels, oil painting, playing handball, golfing, skiing, backpacking, and fly-fishing.

James M. Reeve

Dr. James M. Reeve is Professor Emeritus of Accounting and Information Management at the University of Tennessee. Professor Reeve taught on the accounting faculty for 25 years, after graduating with his Ph.D. from Oklahoma State University. His teaching effort focused on undergraduate accounting principles and graduate education in the Master of Accountancy and Senior Executive MBA programs. Beyond this, Professor Reeve is also very active in the Supply Chain Certification program, which is a major executive education and research effort of the College. His research interests are varied and include work in managerial accounting, supply chain management, lean manufacturing, and information management. He has published over 40 articles in academic and professional journals, including the *Journal of Cost Management, Journal of Management Accounting Research, Accounting Review, Management Accounting Quarterly, Supply Chain Management Review*, and *Accounting Horizons*. He has consulted or provided training around the world for a wide variety of organizations, including Boeing, Procter and Gamble, Norfolk Southern, Hershey Foods, Coca-Cola, and Sony. When not writing books, Professor Reeve plays golf and is involved in faith-based activities.

For over 75 years, *Accounting* has been used effectively to teach generations of businessmen and women. As the most successful business textbook of all time, it continues to introduce students to accounting through a variety of time-tested ways. With this edition, we continue our quest to explore new ways to connect the modern student to accounting, a discipline that is challenging and rewarding.

With this quest in mind, we came to you, the teachers of accounting, and asked what works, what doesn't, and what needs improvement. For this edition, we employed many new methods to get closer to instructors who teach the course every day. As always, your responses were thorough and insightful, and through reviews, focus groups, and our ground-breaking Blue Sky Workshops, we've created a contemporary and efficient learning system for today's student and instructor. In fact, our Blue Sky Workshops brought together accounting teachers from all over the country to discuss content, chapter pedagogy, book design, and supplements. For the first time, instructors had input on every aspect of the project, and the effect of their input on this edition is clear. By connecting with those who use the book, *Financial and Managerial Accounting, 9e*, delivers everything students and instructors need, with nothing they don't.

The original author of *Accounting*, James McKinsey, could not have imagined the success and influence this text has enjoyed or that his original vision would continue to lead the market into the twenty-first century. As the current authors, we appreciate the responsibility of protecting and enhancing this vision, while continuing to refine it to meet the changing needs of students and instructors. Always in touch with a tradition of excellence but never satisfied with yesterday's success, this edition enthusiastically embraces a changing environment and continues to proudly lead the way. We sincerely thank our many colleagues who have helped to make it happen.

Carl S. Warren

"The teaching of accounting is no longer designed to train professional accountants only. With the growing complexity of business and the constantly increasing difficulty of the problems of management, it has become essential that everyone who aspires to a position of responsibility should have a knowledge of the fundamental principles of accounting."

— James O. McKinsey, Author, first edition, 1929

Connect to Course Content

As the clear leader in pedagogical innovation, *Financial and Managerial Accounting, 9e,* introduces the next step in the evolution of accounting textbooks. Through discussions at the Blue Sky Workshops and other instructor interactions, this edition is closer than ever to becoming the "perfect" accounting text.

(NEW!) Example Exercise

Based on extensive market feedback, we've developed new Example Exercises that reinforce concepts and procedures in a bold, new way. Like a teacher in a classroom, students follow the authors' example to see how to complete accounting applications as they are presented in the text. This feature also provides a list of Practice Exercises that parallel the Example Exercises, so students get the practice they need.

See the example of the application being presented.

Example Exercise 1-1

objective 2

On August 25, Gallatin Repair Service extended an offer of $125,000 for land that had been priced for sale at $150,000. On September 3, Gallatin Repair Service accepted the seller's counteroffer of $137,000. On October 20, the land was assessed at a value of $98,000 for property tax purposes. On December 4, Gallatin Repair Service was offered $160,000 for the land by a national retail chain. At what value should the land be recorded in Gallatin Repair Service's records?

Follow My Example 1-1

$137,000. Under the cost concept, the land should be recorded at the cost to Gallatin Repair Service.

For Practice: PE 1-1A, PE 1-1B

Follow along as the authors work through the example exercise.

Try these corresponding end-of-chapter exercises for practice!

Clear Objectives and Key Learning Outcomes

To help guide students, the authors revised and focused the chapter objectives and developed key learning outcomes related to each chapter objective. All aspects of the chapter content and end-of-chapter exercises and problems connect back to these objectives and related outcomes. In doing so, students can test their understanding and quickly locate concepts for review.

NEW! "At a Glance" Chapter Summary

The "At a Glance" summary grid ties everything together and helps students stay on track. First, the Key Points recap the chapter content for each chapter objective. Second, the related Key Learning Outcomes list all of the expected student performance capabilities that come from completing each objective. In case students need further practice on a specific outcome, the last two columns reference related Example Exercises and their corresponding Practice Exercises. Through this intuitive grid, all the chapter pedagogy links together in one cleanly integrated summary.

5. Describe the financial statements of a corporation and explain how they interrelate.			
Key Points	**Key Learning Outcomes**	**Example Exercises**	**Practice Exercises**
The principal financial statements of a corporation are the income statement, the retained earnings statement, the balance sheet, and the statement of cash flows. The income statement reports a period's net income or net loss, which also appears on the retained earnings statement. The ending retained earnings reported on the retained earnings statement is also reported on the balance sheet. The ending cash balance is reported on the balance sheet and the statement of cash flows.	• List and describe the financial statements of a corporation. • Prepare an income statement. • Prepare a retained earnings statement. • Prepare a balance sheet. • Prepare a statement of cash flows. • Explain how the financial statements of a corporation are interrelated.	**1-4** **1-5** **1-6** **1-7**	1-4A, 1-4B 1-5A, 1-5B 1-6A, 1-6B 1-7A, 1-7B

Provides a conceptual review of each objective.

Creates a checklist of skills to help review for a test.

Directs the student to this helpful new feature!

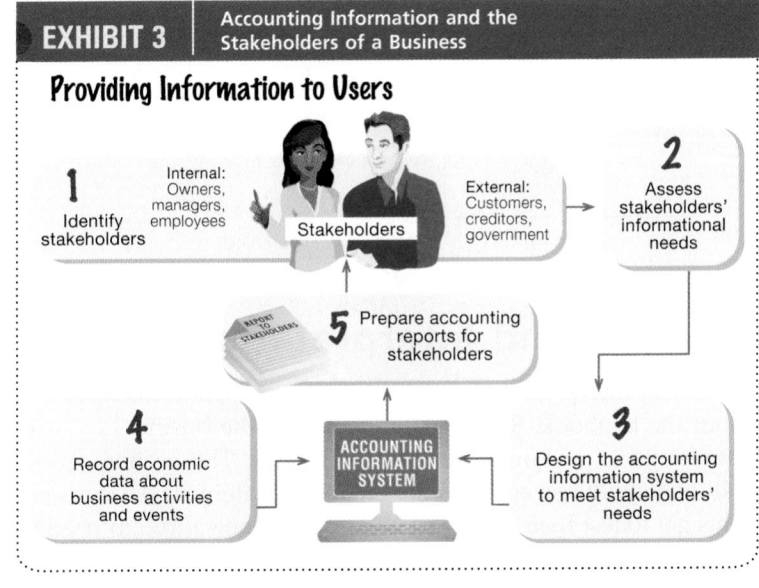

EXHIBIT 3 Accounting Information and the Stakeholders of a Business

Providing Information to Users

1 Identify stakeholders — Internal: Owners, managers, employees — Stakeholders — External: Customers, creditors, government

2 Assess stakeholders' informational needs

3 Design the accounting information system to meet stakeholders' needs

4 Record economic data about business activities and events — ACCOUNTING INFORMATION SYSTEM

5 Prepare accounting reports for stakeholders — REPORT TO STAKEHOLDERS

Modern, User-Friendly Design

The internal design has been modified to be both appealing and easy to navigate. Based on student testimonials of what they find most useful, this streamlined presentation includes a wealth of helpful resources without feeling cluttered. To update the look of the material, some Exhibits use computerized spreadsheets to better reflect the changing environment of business. Visual learners will appreciate the generous number of exhibits and illustrations used to convey concepts and procedures.

Always aware of the issues and changes in real world accounting, the colorful and dynamic *Financial and Managerial Accounting, 9e,* visually highlights coverage that is designed to help students make the connection between accounting concepts and business practices. Accounting doesn't occur in a vacuum, and the new and improved features found in each chapter make the content come to life.

Improved Chapter Openers

Building on the strengths of past editions, these openers continue to relate the accounting and business concepts in the chapter to the student's life. New for this edition, these openers now employ examples of real companies as well providing invaluable insight into real practice. The following companies are among those that have been incorporated into the chapter openers.

- Google
- Marvel Entertainment
- Fatburger
- Gold's Gym
- Electronic Arts
- The North Face

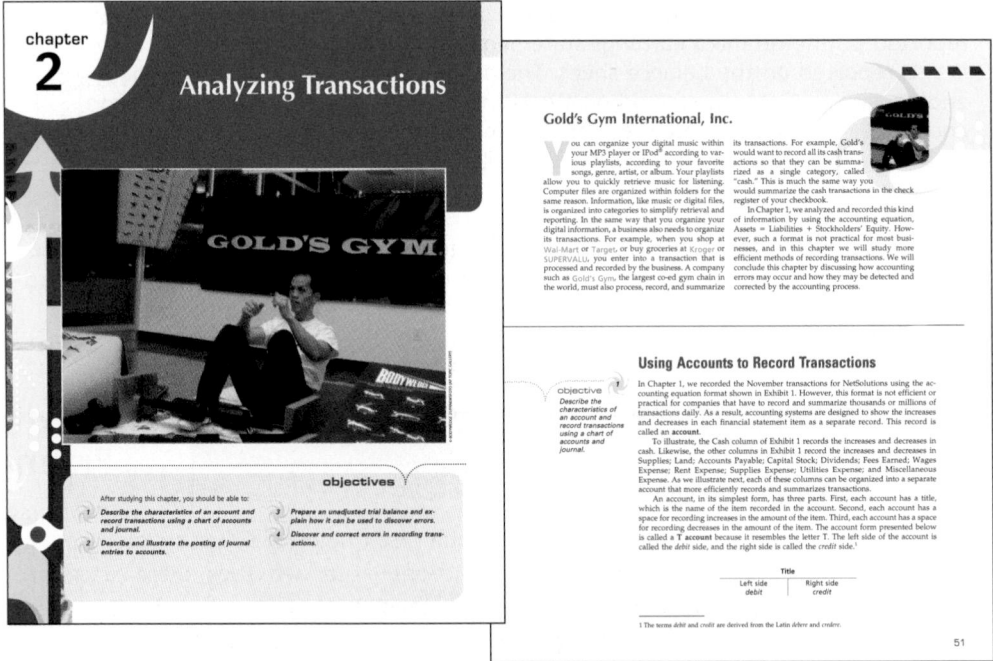

Financial Analysis and Interpretation

The Financial Analysis and Interpretation section in Chapters 5–14 introduces relevant, key ratios throughout the textbook. Students connect with the business environment as they learn how stakeholders will interpret financial reports. This section covers basic analysis tools that students will use again in the Financial Statement Analysis chapter. Furthermore, students get to test their proficiency with these tools through special activities and exercises in the end of the chapter. Both the section and related end-of-chapter material are indicated with a unique icon for a consistent presentation.

World Businesses

Roughly eight out of every ten workers in the United States are service providers.

Comprehensive Real World Notes

Students get a close-up look at how accounting operates in the marketplace through a variety of items in the margins and in the Business Connections boxed features throughout the book. In addition, a variety of end-of-chapter exercises and problems employ real world data to give students a feel for the material accountants see daily. No matter where they are found, elements that use material from real companies are indicated with a unique icon for a consistent presentation. The following companies are among those highlighted in the text.

- AT&T
- Campbell Soup Co.
- Mercedes-Benz
- J.C. Penney Co.
- Hewlett-Packard
- Delta Air Lines
- Ford Motor Co.
- Gillette
- General Electric

Business Connections

RAPID INVENTORY AT COSTCO

Costco Wholesale Corporation operates over 300 membership warehouses that offer members low prices on a limited selection of nationally branded and selected private label products. Costco emphasizes generating high sales volumes and rapid inventory turnover. This enables Costco to operate profitably at significantly lower gross margins than traditional wholesalers, discount retailers, and supermarkets. In addition, Costco's rapid turnover provides it the opportunity to conserve on its cash, as described below.

Because of its high sales volume and rapid inventory turnover, Costco generally has the opportunity to receive cash from the sale of a substantial portion of its inventory at mature warehouse operations before it is required to pay all its merchandise vendors, even though Costco takes advantage of early payment terms to obtain payment dis-

counts. As sales in a given warehouse increase and inventory turnover becomes more rapid, a greater percentage of the inventory is financed through payment terms provided by vendors rather than by working capital (cash).

© DON RYAN/ASSOCIATED PRESS

Integrity, Objectivity, and Ethics in Business

In each chapter, these cases help students develop their ethical compass. Often coupled with related end-of-chapter activities, these cases can be discussed in class or the students can consider them as they read the chapter. These are always indicated with a unique icon for a consistent presentation.

Integrity, Objectivity, and Ethics in Business

THE RESPONSIBLE BOARD

Recent accounting scandals, such as those involving Enron, WorldCom, and Fannie Mae, have highlighted the roles of boards of directors in executing their responsibilities. For example, eighteen of Enron's former directors and their insurance providers have settled shareholder litiga-

tion for $168 million, of which $13 million is to come from the directors' personal assets. Board members are now on notice that their directorship responsibilities are being taken seriously by stockholders.

Connect and Review

Though the presentation of this edition includes many new and improved elements, the traditional tools that have helped students for years remain an integral part of the book.

@netsolutions

Continuing Case Study: Students follow a fictitious company, NetSolutions, throughout Chapters 1–5 as the example company to demonstrate a variety of transactions. To help students connect to the world of accounting, the NetSolutions transactions in Chapters 1 and 2 are often paired with nonbusiness events to which students can easily relate.

Summaries: Within each chapter, these synopses draw special attention to important points and help clarify difficult concepts.

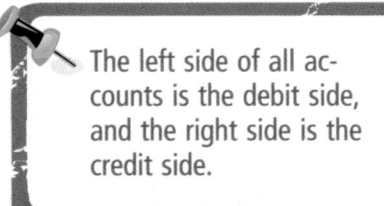

The left side of all accounts is the debit side, and the right side is the credit side.

In the preceding examples, you should observe that the left side of asset accounts is used for recording increases, and the right side is used for recording decreases. Also, the right side of liability and stockholders' equity accounts is used to record increases, and the left side of such accounts is used to record decreases. The left side of all accounts, whether asset, liability, or stockholders' equity, is the debit side, and the right side is the credit side. Thus, a debit may be either an increase or a decrease,

Key Terms: At the end of each chapter, this list of key terms provides page numbers for easy reference.

Self-Examination Questions: Five multiple-choice questions, with answers at the end of the chapter, help students review and retain chapter concepts.

Illustrative Problem and Solution: A solved problem models one or more of the chapter's assignment problems, so that students can apply the modeled procedures to end-of-chapter materials.

Illustrative Problem

J. F. Outz, M.D., has been practicing as a cardiologist for three years in a professional corporation known as Hearts, P.C. During April 2007, Hearts, P.C. completed the following transactions:

Apr. 1. Paid office rent for April, $800.
    3. Purchased equipment on account, $2,100.
    5. Received cash on account from patients, $3,150.
    8. Purchased X-ray film and other supplies on account, $245.
    9. One of the items of equipment purchased on April 3 was defective. It was returned with the permission of the supplier, who agreed to reduce the account for the amount charged for the item, $325.

Connect and Practice

Students need to practice accounting in order to understand and use it. To give your students the greatest possible advantages in the real world, *Financial and Managerial Accounting, 9e,* **goes beyond presenting theory and procedure with comprehensive, time-tested, end-of-chapter material.**

Eye Openers (formerly Discussion Questions): Contains quick concept review questions and single transaction exercises, which are ideal to help students break down concepts into basic parts, ensuring a solid foundation on which to build.

Example Exercises: For Practice Includes two parallel variations of the Example Exercise in the chapter, allowing students to practice the applications the authors illustrated earlier.

Exercises: Completely revised and accompanied by a general topic and a reference to chapter objective.

Problems Series A and B: Completely revised and accompanied by a general topic and a reference to chapter objective.

Special Activities: Focus on understanding and solving pertinent business and ethical issues. Some are presented as conversations in which students can "observe" and "participate" when they respond to the issue being discussed.

Comprehensive Problems: Located after Chapters 4, 5, 10, 14 and 22 to integrate and summarize chapter concepts and test students' comprehension.

Financial Statement Analysis Problem: Located in Chapter 15, this problem features the Williams-Sonoma, Inc., 2005 Annual Report, which allows students to engage current, real world data.

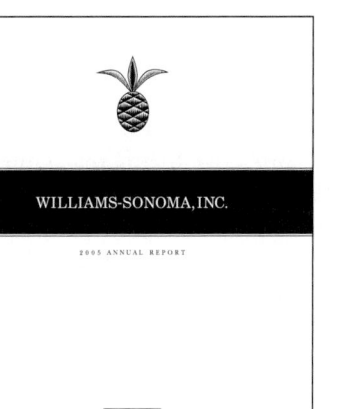

WILLIAMS-SONOMA, INC.

2005 ANNUAL REPORT

Annual Meeting of Shareholders
May 25, 2006

Williams-Sonoma, Inc., Problem

FINANCIAL STATEMENT ANALYSIS

The financial statements for Williams-Sonoma, Inc., are presented in Appendix E at the end of the text. The following additional information (in thousands) is available:

Accounts receivable at February 1, 2004	$ 31,573
Inventories at February 1, 2004	404,100
Total assets at February 1, 2004	1,470,735
Stockholders' equity at February 1, 2004	804,591

Instructions

1. Determine the following measures for the fiscal years ended January 29, 2006, and January 30, 2005, rounding to one decimal place.
   a. Working capital
   b. Current ratio
   c. Quick ratio
   d. Accounts receivable turnover
   e. Number of days' sales in receivables
   f. Inventory turnover

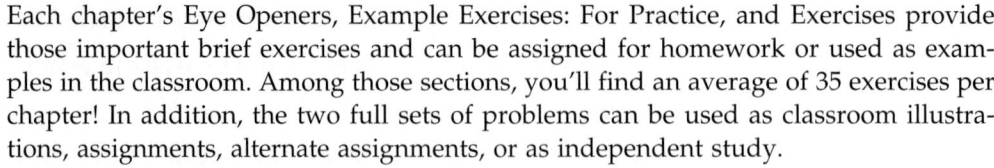

Connect and Practice

Each chapter's Eye Openers, Example Exercises: For Practice, and Exercises provide those important brief exercises and can be assigned for homework or used as examples in the classroom. Among those sections, you'll find an average of 35 exercises per chapter! In addition, the two full sets of problems can be used as classroom illustrations, assignments, alternate assignments, or as independent study.

While always tied to the chapter content, some of the end-of-chapter material covers special topics like those covered in the book features. Specifically, you'll see

Financial Analysis and Interpretation: After being introduced to key ratios of financial analysis and interpretation in the related section of Chapters 5–15, students get to test their proficiency through special activities and exercises that frequently feature real company data.

Ethical Dilemmas: Often paired with the scenario presented in the Integrity, Objectivity, and Ethics in Business feature, these exercises and activities put the student in the role of a decision maker faced with a problem to solve.

Real World Applications: These exercises and activities encourage students to speculate about the real-world effects of newly learned material.

In addition to content, the versatile end-of-chapter section also indicates

Communication Items: These activities help students develop communication skills that will be essential on the job, regardless of the fields they pursue.

EX 1-2
Professional ethics
obj. 1

A fertilizer manufacturing company wants to relocate to Collier County. A 13-year-old report from a fired researcher at the company says the company's product is releasing toxic by-products. The company has suppressed that report. A second report commissioned by the company shows there is no problem with the fertilizer.

➤ Should the company's chief executive officer reveal the context of the unfavorable report in discussions with Collier County representatives? Discuss.

Internet Projects: These activities acquaint students with the ever-expanding accounting-related areas of the Web.

Team Building: Group Learning Activities let students learn accounting and business concepts while building teamwork skills.

SA 4-4
Compare balance sheets

Group Project

Internet Project

In groups of three or four, compare the balance sheets of two different companies, and present to the class a summary of the similarities and differences of the two companies. You may obtain the balance sheets you need from one of the following sources:

1. Your school or local library.
2. The investor relations department of each company.
3. The company's Web site on the Internet.
4. EDGAR (Electronic Data Gathering, Analysis, and Retrieval), the electronic archives of financial statements filed with the Securities and Exchange Commission.

Your Time
Your Course
Your Way

Just what you need to know and do NOW.

ThomsonNOW for Accounting is a powerful, fully integrated online teaching and learning system that provides you with the ultimate in flexibility, ease of use, and efficient paths to success to deliver the results you want—NOW!

- Select from flexible choices and options to best meet the needs of you and your students.

- Test and grade student results based on AACSB and AICPA or IMA accreditation standards and a special set of principles of accounting course outcomes.

- Teach and reinforce chapter content through integrated eBooks and Personalized Study Plans.

- Save valuable time in planning and managing your course assignments.

- Students stay mobile with Lectures-to-Go. Available in both audio and video formats, these iPod-ready broadcasts can be downloaded for preparation before class or last-minute reviewing for a test.

- Students connect to real businesses through our Business Connections videos. This collection of films on accounting issues brings the subject alive. Most notably, the new Chapter 16, "Introduction to Managerial Accounting," incorporates a video of the manufacturing operation of Washburn Guitars, a producer of instruments used by many popular artists today.

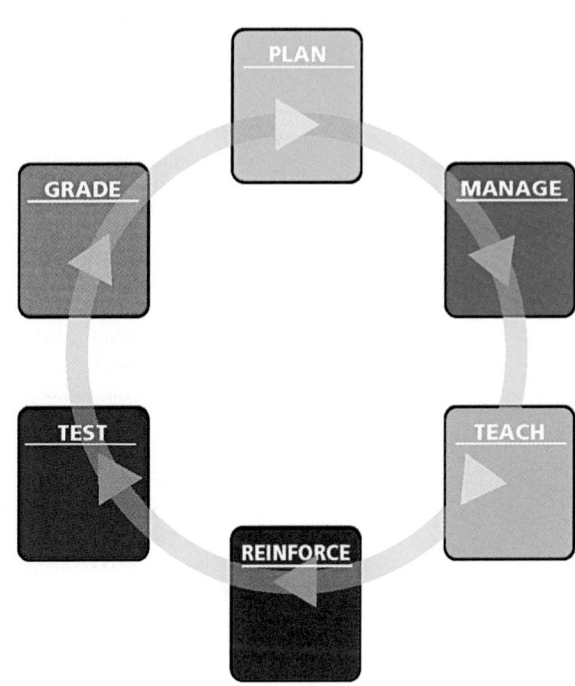

Chapter Changes

1. **Introduction to Accounting and Business**
   - New informational Exhibit 4 on accounting career paths with salary ranges gets students excited about the field.
   - Expanded section on ethical behavior in business accompanied by new Exhibit 2 outlining examples of fraud since 2000 emphasizes the importance of reporting accurate, reliable financial information.
   - A new horizontal format displays how transactions affect each account and facilitates the preparation of the financial statements.
   - New chapter opener features Google.

2. **Analyzing Transactions**
   - Opens with a new transition that ties the horizontal format of Chapter 1 into the use of accounts and the rules of debits and credits. Also, a new section describing how students should analyze and record transactions aids students with their homework.
   - New Exhibit 3 summarizes the rules of debit and credit along with normal balances of accounts so students can see how both guiding principles operate together.
   - New margin labels help guide students through transaction analysis.
   - New chapter opener features Gold's Gym.

3. **The Adjusting Process**
   - All adjusting entries now include explanations.
   - New Exhibits 1 and 2 illustrate the types of adjustments students will encounter as well as the affects of those adjustments on the Income Statement and Balance Sheet. Exhibit 1 focuses on prepaid expense and unearned revenue, and Exhibit 2 focuses on accrued revenue and accrued expense.
   - The terminology has been revised to be consistent with Chapter 2. That is, we now use the terms *prepaid expense* and *unearned revenue* instead of *deferred expense* and *deferred revenue*.
   - Exhibit 6 (formerly Exhibit 5) has been revised with adjusting entries from NetSolutions to clearly summarize the effect of adjustments on the financial statements.
   - New chapter opener features Marvel Entertainment, Inc.
   - New Integrity, Objectivity, and Ethics in Business discusses personal use of office supplies.

4. **Completing the Accounting Cycle**
   - Opens by illustrating the flow of accounting data from the unadjusted trial balance to the adjusted trial balance and financial statements using an end-of-period spreadsheet (work sheet). This is followed by the preparation of financial statements and closing entries for NetSolutions.
   - New Exhibit 8 clearly illustrates each step in the accounting cycle and the role of the accountant in the process.
   - New learning objective, Illustration of the Accounting Cycle, reviews and illustrates each step in the accounting cycle for Kelly Consulting. This illustration is a complete review of the accounting cycle and recaps what students have learned in Chapters 1–4.
   - To familiarize students with alternate formats, the end-of-period spreadsheet is presented in a computerized spreadsheet format.
   - Preparation of the end-of-period spreadsheet (work sheet) is included in an end of the chapter appendix. This appendix uses the NetSolutions chapter illustration. The chapter exercises and problems have been designed so that instructors have the option of requiring students prepare the end-of-period spreadsheet (work sheet).
   - New chapter opener features Electronic Arts, Inc.

5. **Accounting for Merchandising Businesses**
   - The chart of accounts for a merchandising business is now integrated with the discussion of merchandise transactions early in the chapter to help students transition from service businesses to merchandising business.
   - Nonbank Credit Card transactions such as American Express transactions are recorded in the same manner as MasterCard and VISA transactions. This better reflects the accounting for American Express transactions used by most retailers.
   - New appendix covers periodic inventory in a merchandising business and includes a new exhibit which compares the perpetual and periodic systems. This appendix also includes the closing entries under the periodic system.
   - The end-of-chapter exercises and problems have been designed so that instructors can assign exercises and problems using the perpetual system, the periodic inventory, or both systems.

- Transportation Out has been revised as Delivery Expense so that it is easier for students to identify it as an income statement account.
- New chapter opener features Whole Foods Market.

6. **Inventories** (formerly Chapter 8)
   - Based on reviewer and user feedback, inventories are now covered after merchandising businesses.
   - Objectives 3 and 4 now use the same data to draw a better comparison between perpetual (Objective 3) and periodic (Objective 4) inventory systems.
   - The periodic inventory discussion (Objective 4) has been reorganized to better reflect real world practice. Specifically, ending inventory is determined first and is then subtracted from merchandise available for sale to determine the cost of merchandise sold.
   - The prior edition's Objective 2, which focuses on reporting errors of inventory on the financial statements, has been moved to Objective 6 to improve the flow of the chapter. In addition, this discussion has been simplified.
   - New chapter opener features Best Buy.

7. **Sarbanes Oxley, Internal Controls, and Cash** (formerly Chapter 6)
   - The chapter begins with a discussion of the Sarbanes-Oxley Act that includes an example of a General Electric internal control report.
   - The coverage of cash now reflects modern banking practices, including new information about cash received by Electronic Funds Transfer, expanded information about bank statements in an electronic environment, and streamlined coverage of vouchers and manual forms.
   - The bank reconciliation form now appears in a vertical format to be consistent with practice. To simplify for students, "company" replaces "depositor" in the bank reconciliation form.
   - Petty Cash coverage is now covered as Special Purpose Cash Funds.
   - New chapter opener features Ebay.
   - Two new Integrity, Objectivity, and Ethics in Business discuss check fraud and bank errors.

8. **Receivables** (formerly Chapter 7)
   - The direct write-off method of accounting for uncollectible receivables now comes before the allowance method, so students can build from simple to complex concepts.
   - A T-account approach is used to illustrate the allowance method.
   - New comparison of the percent of sales and analysis of receivables estimation methods summarizes Objective 4.
   - New Objective 5 compares direct write-off and allowance methods.
   - New chapter opener features FedEx-Kinkos.

9. **Fixed Assets and Intangible Assets**
   - Declining-Balance Depreciation is now Double-Declining-Balance Depreciation.
   - New Exhibit 7 compares depreciation methods.
   - New Exhibit 8 presents revising depreciation estimates graphically.
   - Certain coverage has been streamlined for a clearer presentation. Specifically, capital and revenue expenditure is now covered as part of Objective 1, as is the discussion of leasing fixed assets.
   - Financial Analysis and Interpretation item now covers the Fixed Asset Turnover Ratio, as it is more relevant to the chapter.
   - New chapter opener features Fat Burger.

10. **Current Liabilities and Payroll**
    - Changes to the McGrath withholding table use the universal IRS Percentage Method. This change simplifies the calculation method in the text.
    - New chapter opener features Panera.
    - New Business Connections features a discussion on the condition of Social Security.

11. **Corporations: Organization, Capital Stock Transactions, and Dividends**
    - Based upon user and reviewer feedback, this chapter has been reorganized so that dividends are discussed immediately after the accounting for issuing of stock. The accounting for treasury stock, reporting stockholders' equity, and stock splits now follows the discussion of dividends.
    - New Exhibit 2 shows the advantages and disadvantages of corporate forms.
    - The discussion of preferred stock has now been simplified to focus only on nonparticipating preferred stock.
    - New chapter opener features Yankee Candle.
    - New Integrity, Objectivity, and Ethics in Business discusses not-for-profit organizations.

Chapter Changes

12. **Income Taxes, Unusual Income Items, and Investments in Stocks**
    - New classification scheme for unusual items: those that impact current periods and those that impact prior periods.
    - New section on Retroactive Restatements presented in Objective 2.
    - Cumulative change in accounting principle replaced with the restatement method per SFAS 154.
    - New graphic on three treatments for unusual items.
    - New chapter opener features Gaylord Entertainment, Inc.

13. **Bonds Payable and Investments in Bonds**
    - Objective 2 covers the characteristics and computation of bonds to improve the flow of the chapter.
    - New section covers the payment and redemption of bonds. Sinking funds are now covered here.
    - New chapter opener features Under Armor.
    - Business Connections feature on Bowie Bonds reflects the effect of recent events on these bonds.
    - New Integrity, Objectivity, and Ethics in Business discusses credit quality.

14. **Statement of Cash Flows**
    - Opening section orients the student to the Statement of Cash Flows by building on the discussion in Chapter 1. In addition, new Exhibit 1 examines the Statement of Cash Flows of NetSolutions.
    - New format for the indirect method reflects real world practice.
    - Expanded section on Cash Flows from Operating Activities includes new Exhibit 5 that outlines the adjustment to net income on cash flows and summarizes the affect of changes in current assets and current liabilities on net income as it pertains to cash flows.
    - New chapter opener features Jones Soda Company, as does Exercise 14-16.
    - New Business Connections features Microsoft and Dell's view of cash resources.
    - New Integrity, Objectivity, and Ethics in Business on collecting accounts features Overhill Flowers.
    - Financial Analysis and Interpretation item redefines free cash flows to leave out dividends, which could be considered discretionary, to simplify the presentation.

15. **Financial Statement Analysis**
    - Features Williams-Sonoma in the chapter opener and engages Williams-Sonoma's 2005 Annual Report in the end-of-chapter material.
    - Objective 4 on Corporate Annual Reports now discusses internal controls and other auditing issues.
    - New Integrity, Objectivity, and Ethics in Business discusses the results of a CEO survey about corporate ethics.
    - New Business Connections features different investing strategies.

16. **Introduction to Managerial Accounting**
    - New chapter introduction to Managerial Accounting begins with a description of managerial accounting that transitions students from financial accounting and outlines the role of the management accountant in the business world.
    - Comprehensive example featuring the Legend Guitar Company grounds the manufacturing processes and provides students with a framework to discuss managerial topics. Objective 2 covers the costs and terminology associated with a manufacturing business, while Objective 3 provides a set of sample financial statements with financial data similar to what students examined in financial accounting.
    - The chapter closes with a description of the other specific uses of managerial accounting information to complete the introduction.
    - New chapter opener features Washburn Guitar. A video tour of the manufacturing process for a specific Washburn Guitar is available through ThomsonNOW.
    - New Integrity, Objectivity, and Ethics in Business discusses developing an ethical framework.
    - New Business Connections discuss grocery plus cards and decisions that can be made from the data they collect.

17. **Job Order Cost Systems** (formerly part of Chapter 16)
    - This chapter continues the Legend Guitar Company from Chapter 18 to provide continuity in the presentation.

- Washburn Guitar is again featured in the opener with more detail about the manufacturing process of the custom Maya guitar.
- New Business Connections discusses contingent compensation in the movie industry.

18. **Process Cost Systems** (formerly Chapter 17)
- Objective 1 compares and contrasts Job Order and Process Costing to help transition students between the two concepts. New Exhibit 1 summarizes this comparison.
- New comprehensive text example features Frozen Delight Ice Cream Company. In addition, new Exhibit 2 provides a diagram of the ice cream making process, which helps students understand the processes and departments involved.
- The Example Exercises feature Rocky Springs Bottling Company and can be used in a progression throughout the chapter, providing another comprehensive example of process costing. Yet, they can be assigned independently of each other, providing flexibility in the chapter's coverage.
- New chapter opener features Dreyer's Grand Ice Cream. A video tour of the manufacturing process for Dreyer's is available through ThomsonNOW.
- New Integrity, Objectivity, and Ethics in Business discusses DuPont's advocacy for social responsibility.

19. **Cost Behavior and Cost-Volume-Profit Analysis** (formerly Chapter 18)
- Former objective on the assumption underlying cost-volume-profit analysis now concludes Objective 4 on using CVP and profit-volume chart to improve the flow of the chapter.
- New chapter opener features NetFlix.
- New Integrity, Objectivity, and Ethics in Business discusses how pharmaceutical companies create orphan drugs, which target rare diseases, in reference to break-even points.
- Business Connections features Sirius Satellite Radio's contract with Howard Stern in reference to break-even point.

20. **Variable Costing for Management Analysis** (formerly Chapter 19—Profit Reporting)
- New title is "Variable Costing for Management Analysis" to reflect the new focus of the chapter on the type of analysis rather than focusing on the method of reporting.
- A new definition of market segments better defines their characteristics.
- A new section on Analyzing Contribution Margins introduces Analyzing Market Segments for greater clarity.
- New Exhibit 11 on Contribution Margin Analysis illustrates the causes for difference between planned and actual contributions margins.
- New graphic conveys the discrepancy of actual versus planned for both quantity and price/unit cost factors.
- New chapter opener features Adobe Systems.

21. **Budgeting** (formerly Chapter 20)
- New Exhibit 2 examines human behavior and budgeting.
- Computerized budgeting discussion in Objective 2 reflects current business practices.
- New chapter opener features The North Face.
- New Business Connections discusses MP3 players.

22. **Performance Evaluation Using Variances from Standard Costs** (formerly Chapter 21)
- The Example Exercises feature Landon Awards Co., and can be used in a progression throughout the chapter, providing a comprehensive example of using variances. Yet, they can be assigned independently of each other, providing flexibility in the chapter's coverage.
- Direct Labor and Materials combined in new Objective 3 to integrate related topics. In addition, nonmanufacturing expenses are now covered with direct labor.
- New terminology is added to reflect other real world considerations. Specifically, nonfinancial performance measure is now defined as a performance measure expressed in unit other than dollars, such as yield, customer satisfaction, or percent on time.
- New chapter opener features Mini Cooper.
- New Business Connections contrasts performance evaluation in school with evaluation in the business world.

23. **Performance Evaluation for Decentralized Operations** (formerly Chapter 22)
- New chapter opener features K2.
- New Integrity, Objectivity, and Ethics in Business on Shifting Income through Transfer Prices features Glaxo Smith Kline.
- New Business Connections features Scripps Howard Company in its discussion of ROI.

24. **Differential Analysis and Product Pricing** (formerly Chapter 23)
    - New Exhibit 1 provides a template for using differential analysis to choose between alternatives.
    - The new example of XM Satellite Radio introduces differential analysis to students.
    - Chapter opener features Real Networks.

25. **Capital Investment Analysis** (formerly Chapter 24)
    - Chapter opener features XM Radio.

26. **Cost Allocation and Activity-Based Costing** (formerly Chapter 25)
    - The first three Example Exercises feature the fictitious Morris Company to provide a comprehensive example of the chapter content. They can be assigned in a series or independently.
    - New chapter opener features Coldstone Creamery.
    - Revised Business Connections feature discusses Market Segmentation and features Fidelity Investments.
    - New Integrity, Objectivity, and Ethics in Business feature discusses large government purchases and the use of the False Claims Act in instances where the government and a contractor disagree.
    - New Integrity, Objectivity, and Ethics in Business feature provides an example of students using ABC to help Sommerville, Massachusetts, employ the town's resources effectively.

27. **Cost Management for Just-in-Time Environments** (formerly Chapter 26)
    - Yamaha is now the example company in the section about emphasizing product-oriented layout.
    - Coverage of zero defects section now includes the "six-sigma" improvement system.
    - "Emphasizing Supplier Partnering" has been revised as "Emphasizing Supply Change Management" and covers more electronic means of relaying information about supplies, specifically radio frequency identification devices (RFID) and enterprise resource planning (ERP).
    - Nonfinancial performance usage table has been updated with the latest information.
    - Chapter opener features Precor.
    - Business Connections discusses eliminating nonvalue time and features Northrop Grunman's manufacturing of a B-2 bomber.
    - New Exercise 27-15 covers JIT journal entries.

Connect to Your Resources

When it comes to supporting instructors, South-Western is unsurpassed. *Financial and Managerial Accounting, 9e,* **continues the tradition with powerful printed materials along with the latest integrated classroom technology.**

Instructor's Manual: This manual contains a number of resources designed to aid instructors as they prepare lectures, assign homework, and teach in the classroom. For each chapter, the instructor is given a brief synopsis and a list of objectives. Then each objective is explored, including information on Key Terms, Ideas for Class Discussion, Lecture Aids, Demonstration Problems, Group Learning Activities, Exercises and Problems for Reinforcement, and Internet Activities. Also, Suggested Approaches are included that incorporate many of the teaching initiatives being stressed in higher education today, including active learning, collaborative learning, critical thinking, and writing across the curriculum. Other key features are the following:

- New informational grids relate the Key Learning Outcomes from the new At a Glance grid to the exercises and problems found in the end-of-chapter. These helpful resources ensure comprehensive homework assignments.

- Demonstration problems can be used in the classroom to illustrate accounting practices. Working through an accounting problem gives the instructor an opportunity to point out pitfalls that students should avoid.

- Group learning activities provide another opportunity to actively involve students in the learning process. These activities ask students to apply accounting topics by completing an assigned task in small groups of three to five students. Small group work is an excellent way to introduce variety into the accounting classroom and creates a more productive learning environment.

- Writing exercises provide an opportunity for students to develop good written communication skills essential to any businessperson. These exercises probe students' knowledge of conceptual issues related to accounting.

- Three to five Accounting Scenarios can be used as handouts.

The Teaching Transparency Masters can be made into acetate transparencies or can be duplicated and used as handouts.

Solutions Manual and Solutions Transparencies: The Solutions Manual contains answers to all exercises, problems, and activities that appear in the text. As always, the solutions are author-written and verified multiple times for numerical accuracy and consistency with the core text. New to this edition, there is an expanded end-of-chapter information chart, which includes correlations to chapter objective, level of difficulty, AACSB outcomes, AICPA or IMA competencies, time to completion and available software. Solutions transparencies are also available.

Test Bank: For each chapter, the Test Bank includes True/False questions, Multiple-Choice questions, and Problems, each marked with a difficulty level, chapter objective association, and a tie-in to standard course outcomes. Along with the normal update and upgrade of the 2,000 test bank questions, variations of the new Example Exercises have been added to this bank for further quizzing and better integration with the textbook. In addition, the bank provides a grid for each chapter that compiles the correlation of each question to the individual chapter's objectives, as well as a ranking of difficulty based on a clearly described categorization. Through this helpful grid, making a test that is comprehensive and well-balanced is a snap! Also included are blank Achievement Tests and Achievement Test Solutions.

ExamView® Pro Testing Software: This intuitive software allows you to easily customize exams, practice tests, and tutorials and deliver them over a network, on the Internet, or in printed form. In addition, ExamView comes with searching capabilities that make sorting the wealth of questions from the printed test bank easy. The software and files are found on the IRCD.

PowerPoint® and Presentation Transparencies: Each presentation, which is included on the IRCD and on the product support site, enhances lectures and simplifies class preparation. Each chapter contains objectives followed by a thorough outline of the chapter that easily provide an entire lecture model. Also, exhibits from the chapter, such as the new Example Exercises, have been recreated as colorful PowerPoint slides to create a powerful, customizable tool. Selections from the PowerPoint presentation are also available on transparency slides.

JoinIn on Turning Point: JoinIn™ on Turning Point™ is interactive PowerPoint® and is simply the best classroom response system available today! This lecture tool makes full use of the Instructor's PowerPoint® presentation but moves it to the next level with interactive questions that provide immediate feedback on the students' understanding of the topic at hand. As students are quizzed using clicker technology, instructors can use this instant feedback to lecture more efficiently. Adding to the already robust PowerPoint® presentation, JoinIn™ integrates 10–20 questions stemming from the textbook's Example Exercises and Eye Openers and includes a variety of newly created questions. Visit http://www.turningpoint.thomsonlearningconnections.com to find out more!

Instructor Excel® Templates: These templates provide the solutions for the problems and exercises that have Enhanced Excel® templates for students. Through these files, instructors can see the solutions in the same format as the students. All problems with accompanying templates are marked in the book with an icon and are listed in the information grid in the solutions manual. These templates are available for download on www.thomsonedu.com/accounting/warren or on the IRCD.

Tutorial and Telecourse Videos: Nothing brings accounting to life like these media-intensive videos. Each chapter comes alive in two half-hour features that reinforce the concepts presented in the text. Based on the Tutorial Videos, the high-broadcast-quality Telecourse Videos are designed for distributed learning courses.

Product Support Web Site: www.thomsonedu.com/accounting/warren Our instructor Web site provides a variety of password-protected, instructor resources. You'll find text-specific and other related resources organized by chapter and topic. Many are also available on the Instructor's Resource CD-ROM.

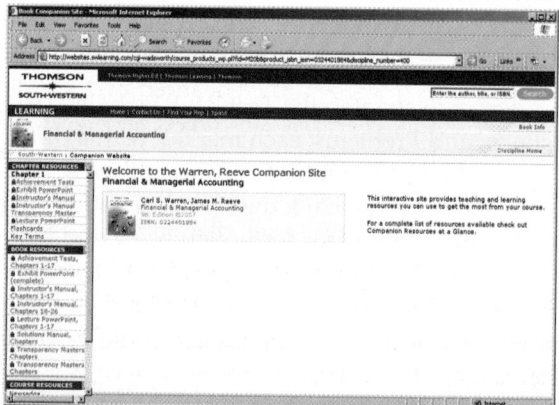

Students come to accounting with a variety of learning needs. *Financial and Managerial Accounting, 9e,* **offers a broad range of supplements in both printed form and easy-to-use technology. We've designed our entire supplement package around the comments instructors have provided about their courses and teaching needs. These comments have made this supplement package the best in the business.**

Study Guide: This author-written guide provides students Quiz and Test Hints, Matching questions, Fill-in-the-Blank questions (Parts A & B), Multiple-Choice questions, True/False questions, Exercises, and Problems for each chapter. Designed to assist students in comprehending the concepts and principles in the text, solutions for all of these items are available in the guide for quick reference.

Working Papers for Exercises and Problems: The traditional working papers include problem-specific forms for preparing solutions for Exercises, A & B Problems, the Continuing Problem, and the Comprehensive Problems from the textbook. These forms, with preprinted headings, provide a structure for the problems, which helps students get started and saves them time. Additional blank forms are included.

Working Papers Plus: This alternative to traditional working papers integrates selected Practice Exercises, Exercises, Problems, the Continuing Problem, and the Comprehensive Problems from the text together with the narrative and forms needed to complete the solutions. Because the problem narrative is integrated with the solution, the student's work is easy and quick to review—a real plus when preparing for an exam.

Blank Working Papers: These Working Papers are available for completing exercises and problems either from the text or prepared by the instructor. They have no preprinted headings.

Enhanced Excel® Templates: These templates are provided for selected long or complicated end-of-chapter exercises and problems and provide assistance to the student as they set up and work the problem. Certain cells are coded to display a red asterisk when an incorrect answer is entered, which helps students stay on track. Selected problems that can be solved using these templates are designated by an icon.

Klooster & Allen General Ledger Software: *(formerly P.A.S.S)* Prepared by Dale Klooster and Warren Allen, this best-selling, educational, general ledger package introduces students to the world of computerized accounting through a more intuitive, user-friendly system than the commercial software they'll use in the future. In addition, students have access to general ledger files with information based on problems from the textbook and practice sets. This context allows them to see the difference between manual and computerized accounting systems firsthand, while alleviating the stress of an empty screen. Also, the program is enhanced with a problem checker that enables students to determine if their entries are correct and emulates commercial general ledger packages more closely than other educational packages. Problems that can be used with Klooster/Allen are highlighted by an icon. The benefits of using Klooster/Allen are that:

- Errors are more easily corrected than in commercial software.
- After the course ends, students are prepared to use a variety of commercial products.
- The Inspector Disk allows instructors to grade students' work.

A free Network Version is available to schools whose students purchase Klooster/Allen GL.

Product Support Web Site: www.thomsonedu.com/accounting/warren. This site provides students with a wealth of introductory accounting resources, including limited quizzing and supplement downloads.

The textbook plays a vital role in the teaching/learning environment, which makes our collaboration with instructors invaluable. For this edition, accounting teachers discussed with us ways to create a more efficient presentation and connect more with students. The result of these discussions can be seen throughout the textbook.

The following instructors participated in our Blue Sky Workshops in 2005 and 2006.

Gilda M. Agacer
Monmouth Univ.

Rick Andrews
Sinclair Comm. College

Irene C. Bembenista
Davenport Univ.

Laurel L. Berry
Bryant & Stratton College

Bill Black
Raritan Valley Comm. College

Gregory Brookins
Santa Monica College

Rebecca Carr
Arkansas State Univ.

James L. Cieslak
Cuyahoga Comm. College

Sue Cook
Tulsa Comm. College

Ana M. Cruz
Miami Dade College

Terry Dancer
Arkansas State Univ.

David L. Davis
Tallahassee Comm. College

Walter DeAguero
Saddleback College

Robert Dunlevy
Montgomery County Comm. College

Richard Ellison
Middlesex County College

W. Michael Fagan
Raritan Valley Comm. College

Carol Flowers
Orange Coast College

Linda S. Flowers
Houston Comm. College

Mike Foland
Southwest Illinois College

Anthony Fortini
Camden Comm. College

Barbara M. Gershowitz
Nashville State Comm. College

Angelina Gincel
Middlesex County College

Lori Grady
Bucks County Comm. College

Joseph R. Guardino
Kingsborough Comm. College

Amy F. Haas
Kingsborough Comm. College

Betty Habershon
Prince George's Comm. College

Patrick A. Haggerty
Lansing Comm. College

Becky Hancock
El Paso Comm. College

Paul Harris
Camden County College

Patricia H. Holmes
Des Moines Area Comm. College

Shirly A. Kleiner
Johnson County Comm. College

Michael M. Landers
Middlesex College

Phillip Lee
Nashville State Comm. College

Denise Leggett
Middle Tennessee State Univ.

Lynne Luper
Ocean County College

Maria C. Mari
Miami Dade College

Thomas S. Marsh
Northern Virginia Comm. College—Annandale

Cynthia McCall
Des Moines Area Comm. College

Andrea Murowski
Brookdale Comm. College

Rachel Pernia
Essex County College

Dawn Peters
Southwest Illinois College

Gary J. Pieroni
Diablo Valley College

Debra Prendergast
Northwestern Business College

Renee A. Rigoni
Monroe Comm. College

Lou Rosamillia
Hudson Valley Comm. College

Eric Rothernburg
Kingsborough Comm. College

Richard Sarkisian
Camden Comm. College

Gerald Savage
Essex Comm. College

Janice Stoudemire
Midlands Technical College

Linda H. Tarrago
Hillsborough Comm. College

Judy Toland
Buck Comm. College

Bob Urell
Irvine Valley College

Carol Welsh
Rowan Univ.

Chris Widmer
Tidewater Comm. College

Gloria Worthy
Southwest Tennessee Comm. College

Lynnette Mayne Yerbury
Salt Lake Comm. College

The following instructors participated in our Adopter Advisory Board.

Lizabeth Austen
East Carolina Univ.

Robert Adkins
Clark State Comm. College

Candace S. Blankenship
Belmont Univ.

Patrick M. Borja
Citrus College and California State Univ.—Los Angeles

Gary Bower
Comm. College of Rhode Island

Gregory Brookins
Santa Monica College

Martha Cavalaris
Miami Dade Comm. College—North Campus

Sue Cook
Tulsa Comm. College

Leonard Cronin
Rochester Comm. and Technical College

Bruce England
Massasoit Comm. College

Robert T. Fahnestock
Univ. of West Florida

Michael J. Farina
Cerritos College

Brenda S. Fowler
Alamance Comm. College

Mark Fronke
Cerritos College

Marina Grau
Houston Comm. College

Paul C. Harris Jr.
Camden County College

James L. Haydon
East Los Angeles Comm. College

Brenda Hester
Volunteer State Comm. College

Cheryl Honoré
Riverside Comm. College

Calvin Hoy
County College of Morris

Frank D. Iazzetta
Long Beach City College

Anne C. Kenner
Brevard Comm. College

Satoshi K. Kojima
East Los Angeles College

Susan Logorda
Lehigh Carbon Comm. College

Don Lucy
Indian River Comm. College

Cathy Mallory
San Antonio College

Marjorie A. Marinovic
Univ. of Texas at El Paso

Patricia Norton
Northwest Mississippi Comm. College

Ken O'Brien
Farmington State Univ.

Craig Pence
Highland Comm. College

Rachel Pernia
Essex County College

Abe Qastin
Lakeland College

Paul Rivers
Bunker Hill Comm. College

Patrick D. Rogan
Cosumnes River College

Gary M. Rupp
Farmingdale State Univ.

Richard M. Sarkisian
Camden County College

Debra L. Schmidt
Cerritos Colzlege

Larry L. Simpson
Davenport Univ., Lansing Campus

Robert K. Smolin
Citrus College

Dawn W. Stevens
Northwest Mississippi Comm. College

John F. Templeton
Houston Comm. College

Kathryn Williams
St. Johns River Comm. College

Karen Wisniewski
County College of Morris

Wayne Yesbick
Darton College

The following instructors participated in the review process and in focus groups.

Heather Albinger
Concordia Univ.

Sylvia Allen
Los Angeles Valley College

Beverley Alleyne
Belmont Univ.

Felix Amenkhienan
Radford Univ.

Sheila Ammons
Austin Comm. College

Rick Andrews
Sinclair Comm. College

Joseph Aubert
Bemidji State Univ.

Elenita Ayuyao
Los Angeles City College

Progyan Basu
The Univ. of Georgia

Diane Bechtel
Northwest State Comm. College

Terry Bechtel
Northwestern State Univ. of Louisiana

Margaret A. Berezewski
Robert Morris College

Bernard Beatty
Wake Forest Univ.

Cynthia Birk
Univ. of Nevada—Reno

Kathy Blondell
St. Johns River Comm. College

Julio C. Borges
Miami Dade College

Carolyn Bottjer
Lehigh Carbon Comm. College

Angele Brill
Castleton State College

Rada Brooks
Univeristy of California—Berkeley

Rebecca F. Brown
Des Moines Area Comm. College

Charles I. Bunn Jr.
Wake Technical Comm. College

Janet Butler
Texas State Univ.—San Marcos

Robert Carpenter
Eastfield College

Bill Carter
Univ. of Virginia

Fonda L. Carter
Columbus State Univ.

Stanley Chu
Borough of Manhattan Comm. College

Marilyn G. Ciolino
Delgado Comm. College

Gretchen Charrier
The Univ. of Texas at Austin

Alexander Clifford
Kennebec Valley Comm. College

Weldon Terry
Dancer Arkansas State Univ.

Vaun C. Day
Central Arizona College

Stan Deal
Azusa Pacific Univ.

John E. Delaney
Southwestern Univ.

Beatrix DeMott
Park Univ.

Edward Douthett
George Mason Univ.

Richard Dugger
Kilgore College

Carol Dutchover
Eastern New Mexico Univ., Roswell

Steve Easter
Mineral Area College

Ronald Edward
Camp Trinity Valley Comm. College

Rafik Z. Elias
California State Univ.—Los Angeles

Carl Essig
Montgomery County Comm. College

Jack Fatica
Terra Comm. College

Kathleen Fitzpatrick
Univ. of Toledo

Daniel Fulks
Transylvania Univ.

Thurman Gardner
Harold Washington College

Caroline C. Garrett
The Victoria College

J. Rendall Garrett
Southern Nazarene Univ.

Earl Godfrey
Gardner—Webb Univ.

Saturnino Gonzalez
El Paso Comm. College

Edward Gordon
Triton College

Thomas Grant
Kutztown Univ.

Barbara Gregorio
Nassau Comm. College

Jeri W. Griego
Laramie County Comm. College

Kenneth Haling, Jr.
Gateway Technical College

Carolyn J. Hays
Mount San Jacinto College

Mark Henry
The Victoria College

Aleecia Hibbets
Univ. of Louisiana—Monroe

Linda Hischke
Northeast Wisconsin Technical College

Patricia H. Holmes
Des Moines Area Comm. College

Anita Hope
Tarrant County College

Allison Hubley
Davenport Univ.

Dawn A. Humburg
Iowa Central Comm. College

Marianne L. James
California State Univ.—Los Angeles

Bettye Bishop Johnson
Northwest Mississippi Comm. College

Tara Laken Joliet
Junior College

Becky Knickel
Brookhaven College

Larry W. Koch
Navarro College, Ellis County Campus

Ellen L. Landgraf
Loyola Univ. Chicago

Cathy X. Larson
Middlesex Comm. College

Brenda Lauer
Davenport Univ.—Kalamazoo Campus

Greg Lauer
North Iowa Area Comm. College

James Lukawitz
Univ. of Memphis

Terri Lukshaitis
Davenport Univ.

Debbie Luna
El Paso Comm. College

Diane Marker
Univ. of Toledo

Matthew Maron
Univ. of Bridgeport

John J. Masserwick
Farmingdale State Univ.

Robert McCutcheon
East Texas Baptist Univ.

Andrew M. McKee
North Country Comm. College

Michael McKittrick
Santa Fe Comm. College

Yaw Mensah
Rutgers Univ.

Leslie Michie
Big Bend Comm. College

Nancy Milleman
Central Ohio Technical College

Brian Moore
Davenport Univ.

Carol Moore
Northwest State Comm. College

Andrew Morgret
Univ. of Memphis

Tim Mulder
Davenport Univ.

Charles Murphy
Bunker Hill Comm. College

Gary Nelson
Normandale Comm. College

Patricia Norton
Northwest Mississippi Comm. College

Blanca R. Ortega
Miami Dade College

Kathy Otero
Univ. of Texas at El Paso

Carol Pace
Grayson County College

Vanda Pauwels
Lubbock Christian Univ.

John Perricone
Harper College

Timothy Prindle
Des Moines Area Comm. College

Paulette Ratliff-MIller
Arkansas State Univ.

Ronald Reed
Univ. of Northern Colordao

John Renza, Jr.
Comm. College of Rhode Island

Jenny Resnick
Santa Monica College

John C. Roberts, Jr.
St. Johns River Comm. College

Lawrence A. Roman
Cuyahoga Comm. College

Gary W. Ross
Harding Univ.

Ann Rowell
Central Piedmont Comm. College

Charles J. Russo
Bloomsburg Univ. of Pennsylvania

Maria Sanchez
Rider Univ.

Marcia A. Sandvold
Des Moines Area Comm. College

Tony Scott
Norwalk Comm. College

Bonnie Scrogham
Sullivan Univ.

Angela Seidel
Cambria-Rowe Business College

Sara Seyedin
Foothill College

Larry L. Simpson
Davenport Univ., Lansing Campus

Alice Sineath
Forsyth Technical Comm. College

Kimberly D. Smith
County College of Morris

Roberta Spigle
DuBois Business College

Mary Stevens
Univ. of Texas at El Paso

Norman Sunderman
Angelo State Univ.

Thomas Szczurek
Delaware County Comm. College

Kathy Tam
Tulsa Comm. College

Lynette E. Teal
Western Wisconsin Technical College

Wayne Thomas
Univ. of Oklahoma

Bill Townsend
Ferris State Univ.

Robin Turner
Rowan-Cabarrus Comm. College

Nancy Tyler
Dalton State College

Allan D. Unseth
Norfolk State Univ.

Bob Urell
Irvine Valley College

Michael Van Breda
Southern Methodist Univ.

Peter Vander Weyst
Edmonds Comm. College

Patricia Walczak
Lansing Comm. College

Scott Wang
Davenport Univ.

Luke A. Waller
Lindenwood Univ.

Jeffrey Waybright
Spokane Comm. College

Kimberly Webb
Texas Wesleyan Univ.

Clifford Weeks
Southwestern Michigan College

Karen Williamson
Rochester Comm. and Technical College

Judith Zander
Grossmont College

Brief Contents

Contents

Practice Set: Casa Bella
This set is a service and merchandising business operated as a corporation. It includes narrative for six months of transactions, which are to be recorded in a general journal. The set can be solved manually or with the Klooster/Allen software.

Practice Set: Wizard Computer Sales & Services
This set is a departmentalized merchandising business operated as a corporation. It includes a narrative of transactions, which are to be recorded in special journals. The set can be solved manually or with the Klooster/Allen software.

Practice Set: Kitchen Concepts, Inc.
This set is a manufacturing business operated as a corporation that uses a job order cost system. The set can be solved manually or with the Klooster/ Allen software.

Introduction to Accounting and Business

© PAUL SAKUMA/ASSOCIATED PRESS

objectives

After studying this chapter, you should be able to:

1 **Describe the nature of a business and the role of ethics and accounting in business.**

2 **Summarize the development of accounting principles and relate them to practice.**

3 **State the accounting equation and define each element of the equation.**

4 **Describe and illustrate how business transactions can be recorded in terms of the resulting change in the basic elements of the accounting equation.**

5 **Describe the financial statements of a corporation and explain how they interrelate.**

Google™

hen two teams pair up for a game of football, there is often a lot of noise. The band plays, the fans cheer, and fireworks light up the scoreboard. Obviously, the fans are committed and care about the outcome of the game. Just like fans at a football game, the owners of a business want their business to "win" against their competitors in the marketplace. While having our football team win can be a source of pride, winning in the marketplace goes beyond pride and has many tangible benefits. Companies that are winners are better able to serve customers, to provide good jobs for employees, and to make more money for the owners.

One such successful company is Google, one of the most visible companies on the Internet. Many of us cannot visit the Web without first stopping at Google to get a search listing. As one writer said, "Google is the closest thing the Web has to an ultimate answer machine."[1] And yet, Google is a free tool—no one asks for your credit card when you use any of Google's search tools. So, do you think Google has been a successful company? Does it make money? How would you know? Accounting helps to answer these questions. Google's accounting information tells us that Google is a very successful company that makes a lot of money, but not from you and me. Google makes its money from advertisers.

In this textbook, we will introduce you to accounting, the language of business. In this chapter, we begin by discussing what a business is, how it operates, and the role that accounting plays.

Nature of Business and Accounting

objective *1*

Describe the nature of a business and the role of ethics and accounting in business.

You can probably list some examples of companies like Google with which you have recently done business. Your examples might be large companies, such as The Coca-Cola Company, Dell Inc., or Amazon.com. They might be local companies, such as gas stations or grocery stores, or perhaps employers. They might be restaurants, law firms, or medical offices. What do all these examples have in common that identify them as businesses?

In general, a **business**[2] is an organization in which basic resources (inputs), such as materials and labor, are assembled and processed to provide goods or services (outputs) to customers. Businesses come in all sizes, from a local coffee house to a DaimlerChrysler, which sells several billion dollars' worth of cars and trucks each year. A business's customers are individuals or other businesses who purchase goods or services in exchange for money or other items of value. In contrast, a church is not a business, because those who receive its services are not legally obligated to pay for them.

The objective of most businesses is to maximize profits. **Profit** is the difference between the amounts received from customers for goods or services provided and the amounts paid for the inputs used to provide the goods or services. Some businesses operate with an objective other than to maximize profits. The objective of such not-for-profit businesses is to provide some benefit to society, such as medical research or conservation of natural resources. In other cases, governmental units such as cities operate water works or sewage treatment plants on a nonprofit basis. We will focus in this text on businesses operating to earn a profit. Keep in mind, though, that many of the same concepts and principles apply to not-for-profit businesses as well.

---

1 As quoted on Google's Web site.
2 A complete glossary of terms appears at the end of the text.

TYPES OF BUSINESSES

There are three different types of businesses that are operated for profit: service, merchandising, and manufacturing businesses. Each type of business has unique characteristics.

Service businesses provide services rather than products to customers. Examples of service businesses and the types of services they offer are shown below.

Service Business	Service
The Walt Disney Company	Entertainment
Delta Air Lines	Transportation
Marriott International, Inc.	Hospitality and lodging
Bank of America Corporation	Financial services
XM Satellite Radio	Satellite radio

Roughly eight out of every ten workers in the United States are service providers.

Merchandising businesses sell products they purchase from other businesses to customers. In this sense, merchandisers bring products and customers together. Examples of merchandising businesses and some of the products they sell are shown below.

Merchandising Business	Product
Wal-Mart	General merchandise
GameStop Corporation	Video games and accessories
Best Buy	Consumer electronics
Gap Inc.	Apparel
Amazon.com	Internet books, music, videos

Manufacturing businesses change basic inputs into products that are sold to individual customers. Examples of manufacturing businesses and some of their products are as follows:

Manufacturing Business	Product
General Motors Corporation	Cars, trucks, vans
Samsung	Cell phones
Dell Inc.	Personal computers
NIKE	Athletic shoes and apparel
The Coca-Cola Company	Beverages
Sony Corporation	Stereos and televisions

TYPES OF BUSINESS ORGANIZATIONS

The common forms of business organization are proprietorship, partnership, corporation, or limited liability company. Each of these forms and their major characteristics are listed below.

- A **proprietorship** is owned by one individual and
  - Comprises 70% of business organizations in the United States.
  - Cost of organizing is low.
  - Is limited to financial resources of the owner.
  - Is used by small businesses.
- A **partnership** is similar to a proprietorship except that it is owned by two or more individuals and
  - Comprises 10% of business organizations in the United States.
  - Combines the skills and resources of more than one person.
- A **corporation** is organized under state or federal statutes as a separate legal taxable entity and
  - Generates 90% of the total dollars of business receipts received.
  - Comprises 20% of the business organizations in the United States.

- Includes ownership divided into shares of stock, sold to shareholders (stockholders).
- Is able to obtain large amounts of resources by issuing stock.
- Is used by large businesses.

■ A **limited liability company (LLC)** combines attributes of a partnership and a corporation in that it is organized as a corporation. However, an LLC can elect to be taxed as a partnership and
- Is a popular alternative to a partnership.
- Has tax and liability advantages to the owners.

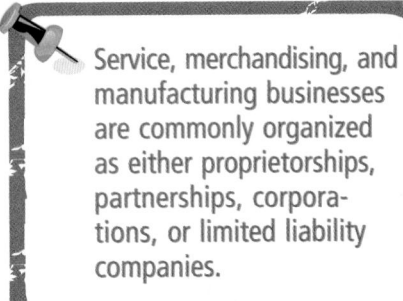

Service, merchandising, and manufacturing businesses are commonly organized as either proprietorships, partnerships, corporations, or limited liability companies.

The three types of businesses we discussed earlier—service, merchandising, and manufacturing—may be organized as either proprietorships, partnerships, corporations, or limited liability companies. Because of the large amount of resources required to operate a manufacturing business, most manufacturing businesses are corporations. Likewise, most large retailers such as Wal-Mart, Home Depot, and JCPenney are corporations.

BUSINESS STAKEHOLDERS

A **business stakeholder** is a person or entity that has an interest in the economic performance and well-being of a business. For example, owners, suppliers, customers, and employees are all stakeholders in a business. Business stakeholders can be classified into one of the four categories illustrated in Exhibit 1.

Capital market stakeholders provide the major financing for the business in order for the business to begin and continue its operations. Banks and other long-term creditors have an economic interest in recovering the amount they loaned the business plus interest. Owners want to maximize the economic value of their investments and thus also have an economic interest in the business.

Product or service market stakeholders include customers who purchase the business's products or services as well as the vendors who supply inputs to the business. Customers have an economic interest in the continued success of the business. For example, customers who purchase advance tickets from Southwest Airlines Co. have an economic interest in whether Southwest will stay in business. Similarly, suppliers are stakeholders in the continued success of their customers as a source of business.

REAL WORLD

The state of Alabama offered DaimlerChrysler millions of dollars in incentives to locate a Mercedes plant in Alabama.

Government stakeholders have an interest in the economic performance of businesses. As a result, city and state governments often provide incentives for businesses to locate in their jurisdictions. City, county, state, and federal governments collect taxes from businesses within their jurisdictions. In addition, workers are taxed on their wages. The better a business does, the more taxes the government can collect.

Internal stakeholders include individuals employed by the business. The managers are those individuals whom the owners have authorized to operate the business. Managers are primarily evaluated on the economic performance of the business. Thus, managers have an incentive to maximize the economic value of the business. Owners may offer managers salary contracts that are tied directly to how well the business performs. For example, a manager might receive a percentage of the profits or a percentage of the increase in profits. Employees provide services to the company they work for in exchange for pay. Thus, employees have an interest in the economic performance of the business because their jobs depend upon it.

ROLE OF ETHICS IN BUSINESS

The moral principles that guide the conduct of individuals are called **ethics**. Unfortunately, business managers can be pressured to violate personal ethics. Such was the case for a number of companies listed in Exhibit 2, on page 6, that engaged in fraudulent business practices and accounting coverups in the early 2000s.

EXHIBIT 1 Business Stakeholders

Business Stakeholder	Interest in the Business	Examples
Capital market stakeholders	Providers of major financing for the business	Banks and owners
Product or service market stakeholders	Buyers of products or services and vendors to the business	Customers and suppliers
Government stakeholders	Collect taxes and fees from the business and its employees	Federal, state, and local governments
Internal stakeholders	Individuals employed by the business	Employees and managers

Stakeholders

Employees/Managers

Customers

Suppliers

Bank and/or Owners

Business

Government

REAL WORLD

Most colleges and universities publish a Student Code of Conduct that sets forth the ethical conduct expected of students.

The companies listed in Exhibit 2 were caught in the midst of ethical lapses that led to fines, firings, and criminal and/or civil prosecution. The second column of Exhibit 2 identifies the nature of the scandal. The third column of the table identifies some of the results of these events. In most cases, senior and mid-level executives lost their jobs and were sued by upset investors. In some cases, the executives were also criminally prosecuted and are serving prison terms.

What went wrong for these companies and executives? The answer to this question involves the following three factors:

1. Individual character
2. Firm culture
3. Laws and enforcement

Individual Character An ethical businessperson displays character by embracing honesty, integrity, and fairness in the face of pressure to hide the truth. Executives often face pressures from senior managers to meet company and analysts' expectations. In many of the cases in Exhibit 2, executives initially justified small violations to avoid such pressures. However, these small lies became big lies as the company's financial problems became worse. By the time the abuses were discovered, the misstatements became sufficient to ruin businesses and wreck lives. For example, David Myers, the former controller

EXHIBIT 2   Accounting and Business Fraud in the 2000s

Company	Nature of Accounting or Business Fraud	Result
Adelphia Communications	Rigas family treated the company assets as their own.	Bankruptcy. Rigas family members found guilty of fraud and lost their investment in the company.
American International Group, Inc. (AIG)	Used sham accounting transactions to inflate performance.	CEO resigned. Executives indicted. AIG paid $126 million in fines.
America Online, Inc. and PurchasePro	Artificially inflated their financial results.	Civil charges filed against senior executives of both companies. $500 million fine.
Computer Associates International, Inc.	Fraudulently inflated its financial results.	CEO and senior executives indicted. Five executives plead guilty. $225 million fine.
Enron	Fraudulently inflated its financial results.	Bankrupcty. Criminal charges against senior executives, over $60 billion in stock market losses.
Fannie Mae	Improperly shifted financial performance between periods.	CEO and CFO fired. Company made a $9 billion correction to previously reported earnings.
HealthSouth	Overstated performance by $4 billion in false entries.	Senior executives criminally indicted.
Qwest Communications International, Inc.	Improperly recognized $3 billion in false receipts.	CEO and six other executives charged with "massive financial fraud." $250 million SEC fine.
Tyco International, Ltd.	Failed to disclose secret loans to executives that were subsequently forgiven.	CEO forced to resign and subjected to frozen asset order and criminal proceedings.
WorldCom	Misstated financial results by nearly $9 billion.	Bankruptcy. Criminal conviction of CEO and CFO. Over $100 billion in stock market losses. Directors forced to pay $18 million.
Xerox Corporation	Recognized $3 billion in revenue prior to when it should have been.	$10 million fine to SEC. Six executives forced to pay $22 million.

of WorldCom, in testifying about his recording of improper transactions, stated the following:

> *"I didn't think that it was the right thing to do, but I had been asked by Scott (Sullivan, the VP of Finance) to do it. . . ."*[3]

Nonetheless, David Myers was criminally convicted and was sentenced to prison.

Firm Culture   By their behavior and attitude, senior managers of a company set the firm culture. As explained by one author, when the leaders of a company are put on a pedestal, "they begin to believe they and their organizations are one-of-a-kind, that they're changing the face of the industry. They desire rewards and benefits beyond any other CEOs (chief executive officers)."[4] In most of the firms shown in Exhibit 2, the senior managers created a culture of greed and indifference to the truth. This

---

3 Susan Pulliam, "Crossing the Line: At Center of Fraud, WorldCom Official Sees Life Unravel," *The Wall Street Journal*, March 24, 2005, p. A1.
4 Tim Race, "New Economy Executives Are Smitten, and Undone by Their Own Images," *The New York Times*, July 7, 2002. Quote attributed to Professor Jay A. Conger.

Integrity, Objectivity, and Ethics in Business

DOING THE RIGHT THING

Time Magazine named three women as "Persons of the Year 2002." Each of these not-so-ordinary women had the courage, determination, and integrity to do the right thing. Each risked their personal careers to expose shortcomings in their organizations. Sherron Watkins, an Enron vice president, wrote a letter to Enron's chairman, Kenneth Lay, warning him of improper accounting that eventually led to Enron's collapse. Cynthia Cooper, an internal accountant, informed WorldCom's Board of Directors of phony accounting that allowed WorldCom to cover up over $3 billion in losses and forced WorldCom into bankruptcy. Coleen Rowley, an FBI staff attorney, wrote a memo to FBI Director Robert Mueller, exposing how the Bureau brushed off her pleas to investigate Zacarias Moussaoui, who was indicted as a co-conspirator in the September 11 terrorist attacks.

Stanley James Cardiges, the former top U.S. sales representative for American Honda, admitted to receiving $2 million to $5 million in illegal kickbacks from dealers. After being sentenced to five years in prison, he admitted to falling into a pattern of unethical behavior early in his career.

culture flowed down to lower-level managers, creating an environment of short cuts, greed, and lies that ultimately resulted in financial fraud.

Laws and Enforcement Many blamed the lack of laws and enforcement for contributing to the financial reporting abuses described in Exhibit 2. For example, Eliot Spitzer, the attorney general of New York, stated the following:

". . . a key lesson from the recent scandals is that the checks on the system simply have not worked. The honor code among CEOs didn't work. Board oversight didn't work. Self-regulation was a complete failure."[5]

As a result, new laws were enacted by Congress, and enforcement efforts have increased since the early 2000s. For example, the Sarbanes-Oxley Act of 2002 (SOX) was enacted. SOX established a new oversight body for the accounting profession called the Public Company Accounting Oversight Board (PCAOB). In addition, SOX established standards for independence, corporate responsibility, enhanced financial disclosures, and corporate accountability.

THE ROLE OF ACCOUNTING IN BUSINESS

What is the role of accounting in business? The simplest answer to this question is that accounting provides information for managers to use in operating the business. In addition, accounting provides information to other stakeholders to use in assessing the economic performance and condition of the business.

In a general sense, **accounting** can be defined as an information system that provides reports to stakeholders about the economic activities and condition of a business. As we indicated earlier in this chapter, we will focus our discussions on accounting and its role in business. However, many of the concepts in this text apply also to individuals, governments, and other types of organizations.

You may think of accounting as the "language of business." This is because accounting is the means by which business information is communicated to the stakeholders. For example, accounting reports summarizing the profitability of a new product help The Coca-Cola Company's management decide whether to continue selling the product. Likewise, financial analysts use accounting reports in deciding whether to recommend the purchase of Coca-Cola's stock. Banks use accounting reports in determining the amount

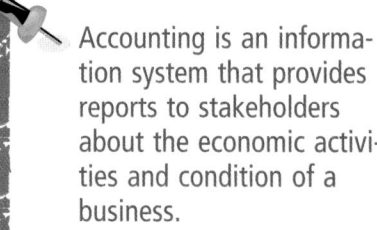

Accounting is an information system that provides reports to stakeholders about the economic activities and condition of a business.

---

5 Eliot Spitzer, "Strong Law Enforcement Is Good for the Economy," *The Wall Street Journal,* April 5, 2005, p. A18.

of credit to extend to Coca-Cola. Suppliers use accounting reports in deciding whether to offer credit for Coca-Cola's purchases of supplies and raw materials. State and federal governments use accounting reports as a basis for assessing taxes on Coca-Cola.

The process by which accounting provides information to business stakeholders is as follows:

1. Identify stakeholders.
2. Assess stakeholders' informational needs.
3. Design the accounting information system to meet stakeholders' needs.
4. Record economic data about business activities and events.
5. Prepare accounting reports for stakeholders.

As illustrated in Exhibit 3, stakeholders use accounting reports as a primary, although not the only, source of information on which they base their decisions. Stakeholders use other information as well. For example, in deciding whether to extend credit to a local retail store, a banker would not only use the store's accounting reports but might also visit the store and inquire about the owner's reputation in the business community.

EXHIBIT 3	Accounting Information and the Stakeholders of a Business

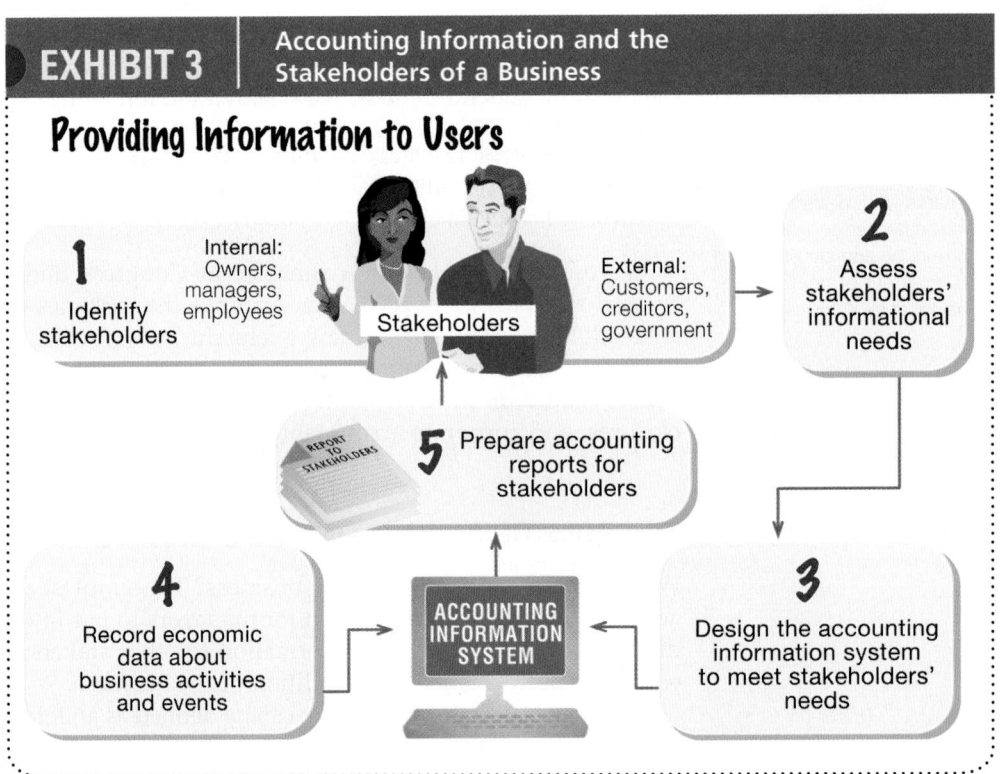

PROFESSION OF ACCOUNTING

You may think that all accounting is the same. However, you will find several specialized fields of accounting in practice. The two most common are financial accounting and managerial accounting. Other fields include cost accounting, environmental accounting, tax accounting, accounting systems, international accounting, not-for-profit accounting, and social accounting.

Financial accounting is primarily concerned with the recording and reporting of economic data and activities for a business. Although such reports provide useful information for managers, they are the primary reports for owners, creditors, governmental agencies, and the public. For example, if you wanted to buy some stock in PepsiCo, Inc., American Airlines, or McDonald's, how would you know in which company to invest? One way is to review financial reports and compare the financial performance and condition of each company. The purpose of financial accounting is to provide such reports.

Managerial accounting, or **management accounting**, uses both financial accounting and estimated data to aid management in running day-to-day operations and in planning future operations. Management accountants gather and report information that is relevant and timely to the decision-making needs of management. For example, management might need information on alternative ways to finance the construction of a new building. Alternatively, management might need information on whether to expand its operations into a new product line. Thus, reports to management can differ widely in form and content.

Whether they are engaged in financial accounting or managerial accounting, accountants are employed in either private accounting or public accounting as shown in Exhibit 4. Accountants employed by a business firm or a not-for-profit organization are said to be employed in **private accounting**. Accountants and their staff who provide services on a fee basis are said to be employed in **public accounting**.

Private accountants have a variety of possible career options inside the firm. Some of these career options are shown in Exhibit 4 along with their starting salaries. The phrase "audit services" may be new to you. Individuals who provide audit services, called auditors, verify the accuracy of financial records, accounts, and systems. Several private accounting careers have certification options. The Institute of Management Accountants (IMA) sponsors the **Certified Management Accountant (CMA)** program. The CMA certificate is evidence of competence in management accounting. Becoming a CMA requires a college degree, two years of experience, and successful completion of a two-day examination. Additional certifications in private accounting include the Certified Internal Auditor (CIA), sponsored by The Institute of Internal Auditors, the Certified Information Systems Auditor (CISA), sponsored by the Information Systems Audit and Control Association, and the Certified Payroll Professional (CPP), sponsored by the American Payroll Association.

EXHIBIT 4   Accounting Career Paths and Salaries

Accounting Career Track	Description	Career Options	Annual Starting Salaries[1]	Certification
Private Accounting	Accountants employed by companies, government, and not-for-profit entities.	Bookkeeper	$28,500	
		Payroll clerk	$30,875	Certified Payroll Professional (CPP)
		General accountant	$35,750	
		Budget analyst	$36,750	
		Cost accountant	$37,375	Certified Management Accountant (CMA)
		Internal auditor	$41,500	Certified Internal Auditor (CIA)
		Information technology auditor	$72,500	Certified Information Systems Auditor (CISA)
Public Accounting	Accountants employed individually or within a public accounting firm in tax or audit services.	Local firms	$36,625	Certified Public Accountant (CPA)
		National firms	$44,375	Certified Public Accountant (CPA)

Source: Robert Half 2006 Salary Guide (Finance and Accounting), Robert Half International, Inc.

[1]Median salaries of a reported range. Private accounting salaries are reported for large companies. Information technology auditor salary is for all company sizes and experience levels combined. Salaries may vary by region.

In public accounting, an accountant may practice as an individual or as a member of a public accounting firm. Public accountants who have met a state's education, experience, and examination requirements may become **Certified Public Accountants (CPAs)**. As can be seen in Exhibit 4, CPAs generally perform general accounting, audit, or tax services. CPAs have slightly better starting salaries than private accountants. Career statistics indicate, however, that these salary differences tend to disappear over time.

The requirements for obtaining a CPA certificate differ among the various states. All states require a college education in accounting, and most states require 150 semester hours of college credit. In addition, a candidate must pass an examination prepared by the American Institute of Certified Public Accountants (AICPA). Because all functions within a business use accounting information, experience in private or public accounting provides a solid foundation for a career. Many positions in industry and in government agencies are held by individuals with accounting backgrounds.

Generally Accepted Accounting Principles

objective **2**

Summarize the development of accounting principles and relate them to practice.

If a company's management could record and report financial data as it saw fit, comparisons among companies would be difficult, if not impossible. Thus, financial accountants follow **generally accepted accounting principles (GAAP)** in preparing reports. These reports allow investors and other stakeholders to compare one company to another.

To illustrate the importance of generally accepted accounting principles, assume that each sports conference in college football used different rules for counting touchdowns. For example, assume that the Pacific Athletic Conference (PAC 10) counted a touchdown as six points and the Atlantic Coast Conference (ACC) counted a touchdown as two points. It would be difficult to evaluate the teams under such different scoring systems. A standard set of rules and a standard scoring system help fans compare teams across conferences. Likewise, a standard set of generally accepted accounting principles allows for the comparison of financial performance and condition across companies.

Accounting principles and concepts develop from research, accepted accounting practices, and pronouncements of authoritative bodies. Currently, the **Financial Accounting Standards Board (FASB)** is the authoritative body having the primary responsibility for developing accounting principles. The FASB publishes *Statements of Financial Accounting Standards* as well as *Interpretations* of these Standards.

Because generally accepted accounting principles impact how companies report and what they report, all stakeholders are interested in the setting of these principles. Thus, standards are established according to a process that seeks and considers input from all affected parties. The standard-setting activities of the FASB are published and made available at **http://www.fasb.org.**

In this chapter and throughout this text, we emphasize accounting principles and concepts. It is through this emphasis on the "why" of accounting as well as the "how"

Integrity, Objectivity, and Ethics in Business

ETHICS

ACCOUNTING REFORM

The financial accounting and reporting failures of Enron, WorldCom, Tyco, Xerox, and others shocked the investing public. The disclosure that some of the nation's largest and best-known corporations had overstated profits and misled investors raised the question: Where were the CPAs?

In response, Congress passed the Investor Protection, Auditor Reform, and Transparency Act of 2002, called the Sarbanes-Oxley Act. The Act establishes a Public Company

Accounting Oversight Board to regulate the portion of the accounting profession that has public companies as clients. In addition, the Act prohibits auditors (CPAs) from providing certain types of nonaudit services, such as investment banking or legal services, to their clients, prohibits employment of auditors by clients for one year after they last audited the client, and increases penalties for the reporting of misleading financial statements.

that you will gain an understanding of the full significance of accounting. In the following paragraphs, we discuss the business entity concept and the cost concept.

BUSINESS ENTITY CONCEPT

The individual business unit is the business entity for which economic data are needed. This entity could be an automobile dealer, a department store, or a grocery store. The business entity must be identified, so that the accountant can determine which economic data should be analyzed, recorded, and summarized in reports.

> Under the business entity concept, the activities of a business are recorded separately from the activities of the stakeholders.

The **business entity concept** is important because it limits the economic data in the accounting system to data related directly to the activities of the business. In other words, the business is viewed as an entity separate from its owners, creditors, or other stakeholders. For example, the accountant for a business with one owner (a proprietorship) would record the activities of the business only, not the personal activities, property, or debts of the owner.

THE COST CONCEPT

If a building is bought for $150,000, that amount should be entered into the buyer's accounting records. The seller may have been asking $170,000 for the building up to the time of the sale. The buyer may have initially offered $130,000 for the building. The building may have been assessed at $125,000 for property tax purposes. The buyer may have received an offer of $175,000 for the building the day after it was acquired. These latter amounts have no effect on the accounting records because they did not result in an exchange of the building from the seller to the buyer. The **cost concept** is the basis for entering the *exchange price, or cost, of $150,000* into the accounting records for the building.

Continuing the illustration, the $175,000 offer received by the buyer the day after the building was acquired indicates that it was a bargain purchase at $150,000. To use $175,000 in the accounting records, however, would record an illusory or unrealized profit. If, after buying the building, the buyer accepts the offer and sells the building for $175,000, a profit of $25,000 is then realized and recorded. The new owner would record $175,000 as the cost of the building.

Using the cost concept involves two other important accounting concepts—objectivity and the unit of measure. The **objectivity concept** requires that the accounting records and reports be based upon objective evidence. In exchanges between a buyer and a seller, both try to get the best price. Only the final agreed-upon amount is objective enough for accounting purposes. If the amounts at which properties were recorded were constantly being revised upward and downward based on offers, appraisals, and opinions, accounting reports could soon become unstable and unreliable.

The **unit of measure concept** requires that economic data be recorded in dollars. Money is a common unit of measurement for reporting uniform financial data and reports.

Example Exercise 1-1   objective

On August 25, Gallatin Repair Service extended an offer of $125,000 for land that had been priced for sale at $150,000. On September 3, Gallatin Repair Service accepted the seller's counteroffer of $137,000. On October 20, the land was assessed at a value of $98,000 for property tax purposes. On December 4, Gallatin Repair Service was offered $160,000 for the land by a national retail chain. At what value should the land be recorded in Gallatin Repair Service's records?

Follow My Example 1-1

$137,000. Under the cost concept, the land should be recorded at the cost to Gallatin Repair Service.

For Practice: PE 1-1A, PE 1-1B

The Accounting Equation

objective **3**

State the accounting equation and define each element of the equation.

The resources owned by a business are its **assets**. Examples of assets include cash, land, buildings, and equipment. The rights or claims to the properties are normally divided into two principal types: (1) the rights of creditors and (2) the rights of owners. The rights of creditors represent debts of the business and are called **liabilities**. The rights of the owners are called **owner's equity**. The relationship between the two may be stated in the form of an equation, as follows:

$$\text{Assets} = \text{Liabilities} + \text{Owner's Equity}$$

This equation is known as the **accounting equation**. Liabilities usually are shown before owner's equity in the accounting equation because creditors have first rights to the assets. The claim of the owners is sometimes given greater emphasis by transposing liabilities to the other side of the equation, which yields:

$$\text{Assets} - \text{Liabilities} = \text{Owner's Equity}$$

To illustrate, if the assets owned by a business amount to $100,000 and the liabilities amount to $30,000, the owner's equity is equal to $70,000, as shown below.

Assets	**− Liabilities**	**= Owner's Equity**
$100,000	− $30,000	= $70,000

Example Exercise 1-2   objective **3**

John Joos is the owner and operator of You're A Star, a motivational consulting business. At the end of its accounting period, December 31, 2007, You're A Star has assets of $800,000 and liabilities of $350,000. Using the accounting equation, determine the following amounts:

a. Owner's equity, as of December 31, 2007.
b. Owner's equity, as of December 31, 2008, assuming that assets increased by $130,000 and liabilities decreased by $25,000 during 2008.

Follow My Example 1-2

a.
$$\text{Assets} = \text{Liabilities} + \text{Owner's Equity}$$
$$\$800,000 = \$350,000 + \text{Owner's Equity}$$
$$\text{Owner's Equity} = \$450,000$$

b. First, determine the change in Owner's Equity during 2008 as follows:

$$\text{Assets} = \text{Liabilities} + \text{Owner's Equity}$$
$$\$130,000 = -\$25,000 + \text{Owner's Equity}$$
$$\text{Owner's Equity} = \$155,000$$

Next, add the change in Owner's Equity on December 31, 2007, to arrive at Owner's Equity on December 31, 2008, as shown below:

$$\text{Owner's Equity on December 31, 2008} =$$
$$\$605,000 = \$450,000 + \$155,000$$

For Practice: PE 1-2A, PE 1-2B

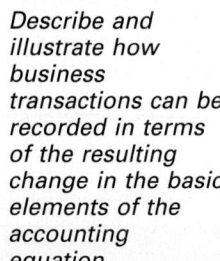

objective **4**

Describe and illustrate how business transactions can be recorded in terms of the resulting change in the basic elements of the accounting equation.

Business Transactions and the Accounting Equation

Paying a monthly telephone bill of $168 affects a business's financial condition because it now has less cash on hand. Such an economic event or condition that directly changes an entity's financial condition or directly affects its results of operations is a **business transaction**. For example, purchasing land for $50,000 is a business transaction. In contrast, a change in a business's credit rating does not directly affect cash or any other element of its financial condition.

Business Connections

REAL WORLD

THE ACCOUNTING EQUATION

The accounting equation serves as the basic foundation for the accounting systems of all companies. From the smallest business, such as the local convenience store, to the largest business, such as Ford Motor Company, com-

panies use the accounting equation. Some examples taken from recent financial reports of well-known companies are shown below.

Company	Assets*	=	Liabilities	+	Owner's Equity
The Coca-Cola Company	$ 31,327	=	$15,392	+	$15,935
Circuit City Stores, Inc.	3,709	=	1,795	+	1,914
Dell Inc.	22,874	=	18,053	+	4,821
eBay Inc.	9,626	=	1,599	+	8,027
Hilton Hospitality, Inc.	8,242	=	5,674	+	2,568
McDonald's	27,844	=	13,328	+	14,516
Microsoft Corporation	71,462	=	23,135	+	48,327
Southwest Airlines Co.	11,337	=	5,813	+	5,524
Wal-Mart	124,765	=	77,044	+	47,721

*Amounts are shown in millions of dollars.

All business transactions can be stated in terms of changes in the elements of the accounting equation. You will see how business transactions affect the accounting equation by studying some typical transactions. As a basis for illustration, we will use a business organized by Chris Clark.

Assume that on November 1, 2007, Chris Clark organizes a corporation that will be known as NetSolutions. The first phase of Chris's business plan is to operate NetSolutions as a service business that provides assistance to individuals and small businesses in developing Web pages and in configuring and installing application software. Chris expects this initial phase of the business to last one to two years. During this period, Chris will gather information on the software and hardware needs of customers. During the second phase of the business plan, Chris plans to expand NetSolutions into a personalized retailer of software and hardware for individuals and small businesses.

> All business transactions can be stated in terms of changes in the elements of the accounting equation.

Each transaction or group of similar transactions during NetSolutions' first month of operations is described in the following paragraphs. The effect of each transaction on the accounting equation is then shown.

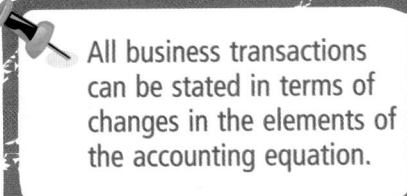
@netsolutions

Transaction a Chris Clark deposits $25,000 in a bank account in the name of NetSolutions in return for shares of stock in the corporation. Stock issued to owners (stockholders), such as Chris Clark, is referred to as **capital stock**. The owner's equity in a corporation is called **stockholders' equity**.

The effect of this transaction is to increase the asset (cash) on the left side of the equation by $25,000. To balance the equation, the stockholders' equity (capital stock) on the right side of the equation is increased by the same amount. The effect of this transaction on NetSolutions' accounting equation is shown below.

	Assets	=	Stockholders' Equity
	Cash	=	Capital Stock
a.	25,000		25,000

Note that the accounting equation shown above relates only to the business, NetSolutions. Under the business entity concept, Chris Clark's personal assets, such as a home or personal bank account, and personal liabilities are excluded from the equation.

Transaction b If you purchased this textbook by paying cash, you entered into a transaction in which you exchanged one asset for another. That is, you exchanged cash for the textbook. Businesses often enter into similar transactions. NetSolutions, for example, exchanged $20,000 cash for land. The land is located in a new business park with convenient access to transportation facilities. Chris Clark plans to rent office space and equipment during the first phase of the business plan. During the second phase, Chris plans to build an office and a warehouse on the land.

The purchase of the land changes the makeup of the assets but does not change the total assets. The items in the equation prior to this transaction and the effect of the transaction are shown next, as well as the new amounts, or *balances*, of the items.

	Assets			=	Stockholders' Equity
	Cash	+	Land		Capital Stock
Bal.	25,000				25,000
b.	−20,000		+20,000		
Bal.	5,000		20,000		25,000

Transaction c You have probably used a credit card to buy clothing or other merchandise. In this type of transaction, you received clothing for a promise to pay your credit card bill in the future. That is, you received an asset and incurred a liability to pay a future bill. During the month, NetSolutions entered into a similar transaction, buying supplies for $1,350 and agreeing to pay the supplier in the near future. This type of transaction is called a purchase *on account*. The liability created is called an **account payable**. Items such as supplies that will be used in the business in the future are called **prepaid expenses**, which are assets. The effect of this transaction is to increase assets and liabilities by $1,350, as follows:

Other examples of common prepaid expenses include insurance and rent. Businesses often report these assets together as a single item, prepaid expenses.

	Assets					=	Liabilities +	Stockholders' Equity
							Accounts	Capital
	Cash	+	Supplies	+	Land		Payable +	Stock
Bal.	5,000				20,000			25,000
c.			+1,350				+1,350	
Bal.	5,000		1,350		20,000		1,350	25,000

Transaction d You may have earned money by painting houses or mowing lawns. If so, you received money for rendering services to a customer. Likewise, a business earns money by selling goods or services to its customers. This amount is called **revenue**.

During its first month of operations, NetSolutions provided services to customers, earning fees of $7,500 and receiving the amount in cash. The receipt of cash increases NetSolutions' assets and also increases the stockholders' equity in the business. In order to aid in the preparation of financial statements, the revenues of $7,500 are recorded in a separate column to the right of Capital Stock. This is done so that the effects of revenues on stockholders' equity can be separately identified and summarized. Thus, this transaction is recorded as an increase in Cash and Fees Earned of $7,500 as shown below.

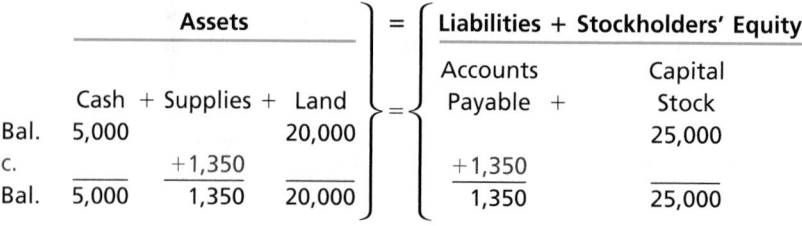

	Assets					=	Liabilities +	Stockholders' Equity	
							Accounts	Capital	Fees
	Cash	+	Supplies	+	Land		Payable +	Stock	+ Earned
Bal.	5,000		1,350		20,000		1,350	25,000	
d.	+7,500								+7,500
Bal.	12,500		1,350		20,000		1,350	25,000	7,500

Special terms may be used to describe certain kinds of revenue, such as **sales** for the sale of merchandise. Revenue from providing services is called **fees earned**. For example, a physician would record fees earned for services to patients. Other examples include **rent revenue** (money received for rent) and **interest revenue** (money received for interest).

Instead of requiring the payment of cash at the time services are provided or goods are sold, a business may accept payment at a later date. Such revenues are called *fees on account* or *sales on account*. In such cases, the firm has an **account receivable**, which is a claim against the customer. An account receivable is an asset, and the revenue is earned as if cash had been received. When customers pay their accounts, there is an exchange of one asset for another. Cash increases, while accounts receivable decreases.

Transaction e If you painted houses to earn money, you probably used your own ladders and brushes. NetSolutions also spent cash or used up other assets in earning revenue. The amounts used in this process of earning revenue are called **expenses**. Expenses include supplies used, wages of employees, and other assets and services used in operating the business.

NetSolutions paid the following expenses during the month: wages, $2,125; rent, $800; utilities, $450; and miscellaneous, $275. Miscellaneous expenses include small amounts paid for such items as postage, coffee, and magazine subscriptions. The effect of this group of transactions is the opposite of the effect of revenues. These transactions reduce cash and stockholders' equity. Like fees earned, the expenses are recorded in separate columns to the right of Capital Stock. However, since expenses reduce stockholders' equity, the expenses are entered as negative amounts.

	Assets			=	**Liabilities +**		**Stockholders' Equity**				
	Cash	+ Supplies +	Land	=	Accounts Payable +	Capital Stock +	Fees Earned	− Wages Expense	− Rent Expense	− Utilities Expense	− Misc. Expense
Bal.	12,500	1,350	20,000		1,350	25,000	7,500				
e.	−3,650							−2,125	−800	−450	−275
Bal.	8,850	1,350	20,000		1,350	25,000	7,500	−2,125	−800	−450	−275

Businesses usually record each revenue and expense transaction separately as it occurs. However, to simplify this illustration, we have summarized NetSolutions' revenues and expenses for the month in transactions (d) and (e).

Transaction f When you pay your monthly credit card bill, you decrease the cash in your checking account and also decrease the amount you owe to the credit card company. Likewise, when NetSolutions pays $950 to creditors during the month, it reduces both assets and liabilities, as shown below.

	Assets			=	**Liabilities +**		**Stockholders' Equity**				
	Cash	+ Supplies +	Land	=	Accounts Payable +	Capital Stock +	Fees Earned	− Wages Expense	− Rent Expense	− Utilities Expense	− Misc. Expense
Bal.	8,850	1,350	20,000		1,350	25,000	7,500	−2,125	−800	−450	−275
f.	−950				−950						
Bal.	7,900	1,350	20,000		400	25,000	7,500	−2,125	−800	−450	−275

You should note that paying an amount on account is different from paying an amount for an expense. The payment of an expense reduces stockholders' equity, as illustrated in transaction (e). Paying an amount on account reduces the amount owed on a liability.

Transaction g At the end of the month, the cost of the supplies on hand (not yet used) is $550. The remainder of the supplies ($1,350 − $550) was used in the operations of the business and is treated as an expense. This decrease of $800 in supplies and stockholders' equity is shown at the top of the following page.

	Assets			=	Liabilities +								Stockholders' Equity		
					Accounts	Capital	Fees	Wages	Rent	Supplies	Utilities	Misc.			
	Cash +	Supplies +	Land	=	Payable +	Stock	+ Earned −	Exp. −	Exp. −	Exp. −	Exp. −	Exp.			
Bal.	7,900	1,350	20,000		400	25,000	7,500	−2,125	−800		−450	−275			
g.		−800								−800					
Bal.	7,900	550	20,000		400	25,000	7,500	−2,125	−800	−800	−450	−275			

Transaction h At the end of the month, NetSolutions pays $2,000 to stockholders (Chris Clark) as dividends. **Dividends** are distributions of earnings to stockholders. The payment of dividends reduces both cash and stockholders' equity. Like expenses, dividends are recorded in a separate column to the right of Capital Stock. The effect of the payment of dividends of $2,000 is shown below.

	Assets			=	Liabilities +									Stockholders' Equity	
					Accounts	Capital		Fees	Wages	Rent	Supplies	Utilities	Misc.		
	Cash +	Supp. +	Land	=	Payable +	Stock	− Dividends	+ Earned −	Exp. −	Exp. −	Exp. −	Exp. −	Exp.		
Bal.	7,900	550	20,000		400	25,000		7,500	−2,125	−800	−800	−450	−275		
h.	−2,000						−2,000								
Bal.	5,900	550	20,000		400	25,000	−2,000	7,500	−2,125	−800	−800	−450	−275		

You should be careful not to confuse dividends with expenses. Dividends do not represent assets or services used in the process of earning revenues. Instead, dividends are considered a distribution of earnings to stockholders.

Summary The transactions of NetSolutions are summarized as follows. They are identified by letter, and the balance of each item is shown after each transaction.

	Assets			=	Liabilities +									Stockholders' Equity	
					Accounts	Capital		Fees	Wages	Rent	Supplies	Utilities	Misc.		
	Cash +	Supp. +	Land	=	Payable +	Stock	− Dividends	+ Earned −	Exp. −	Exp. −	Exp. −	Exp. −	Exp.		
a.	+25,000					+25,000									
b.	−20,000		+20,000												
Bal.	5,000		20,000			25,000									
c.		+1,350			+1,350										
Bal.	5,000	1,350	20,000		1,350	25,000									
d.	+ 7,500							+7,500							
Bal.	12,500	1,350	20,000		1,350	25,000		7,500							
e.	− 3,650								−2,125	−800		−450	−275		
Bal.	8,850	1,350	20,000		1,350	25,000		7,500	−2,125	−800		−450	−275		
f.	− 950				− 950										
Bal.	7,900	1,350	20,000		400	25,000		7,500	−2,125	−800		−450	−275		
g.		− 800									−800				
Bal.	7,900	550	20,000		400	25,000		7,500	−2,125	−800	−800	−450	−275		
h.	− 2,000						−2,000								
Bal.	5,900	550	20,000 =		400	25,000	−2,000	7,500	−2,125	−800	−800	−450	−275		

In reviewing the preceding summary, you should note the following, which apply to all types of businesses:

1. The effect of every transaction is *an increase or a decrease in one or more of the accounting equation elements*.
2. The two sides of the accounting equation are *always equal*.

3. The stockholders' equity (owner's equity) is increased by amounts invested by stockholders (capital stock).
4. The stockholders' equity (owner's equity) is increased by revenues and decreased by expenses.
5. The stockholders' equity (owner's equity) is decreased by dividends paid to stockholders.

As we discussed earlier, the owner's equity in a corporation is called stockholders' equity. Stockholders' equity is classified as either capital stock or retained earnings. Capital stock represents investments by the stockholders. **Retained earnings** represents stockholders' equity created from business operations through revenue and expense transactions. For NetSolutions, retained earnings of $3,050 were created by its November operations (revenue and expense transactions) as shown below.

NetSolutions
Retained Earnings
November Operations
(Revenue and Expense Transactions)

	Fees Earned	−	Wages Exp.	−	Rent Exp.	−	Supplies Exp.	−	Utilities Exp.	−	Misc. Exp.
Trans. d.	+7,500										
Trans. e.			−2,125		−800				−450		−275
Trans. g.							−800				
Balance, Nov. 30	7,500		−2,125		−800		−800		−450		−275

$3,050

Stockholders' equity created by investments by stockholders (Capital Stock) and by business operations (Retained Earnings) are reported separately to stakeholders. Since dividends are distributions of earnings to stockholders, dividends reduce retained earnings. The effects of these four types of transactions on stockholders' equity are illustrated in Exhibit 5.

Example Exercise 1-3 objective 4

Salvo Delivery Service is owned and operated by Joel Salvo. The following selected transactions were completed by Salvo Delivery Service during February:

1. Received cash from owner as additional investment in exchange for capital stock, $35,000.
2. Paid creditors on account, $1,800.
3. Billed customers for delivery services on account, $11,250.
4. Received cash from customers on account, $6,740.
5. Paid dividends, $1,000.

Indicate the effect of each transaction on the accounting equation elements (Assets, Liabilities, Stockholders' Equity, Dividends, Revenue, and Expense) by listing the numbers identifying the transactions, (1) through (5). Also, indicate the specific item within the accounting equation element that is affected. To illustrate, the answer to (1) is shown below.

(1) Asset (Cash) increases by $35,000; Stockholders' Equity (Capital Stock) increases by $35,000.

Follow My Example 1-3

(2) Asset (Cash) decreases by $1,800; Liability (Accounts Payable) decreases by $1,800.
(3) Asset (Accounts Receivable) increases by $11,250; Revenue (Delivery Service Fees) increases by $11,250.
(4) Asset (Cash) increases by $6,740; Asset (Accounts Receivable) decreases by $6,740.
(5) Asset (Cash) decreases by $1,000; Dividends increases by $1,000.

For Practice: PE 1-3A, PE 1-3B

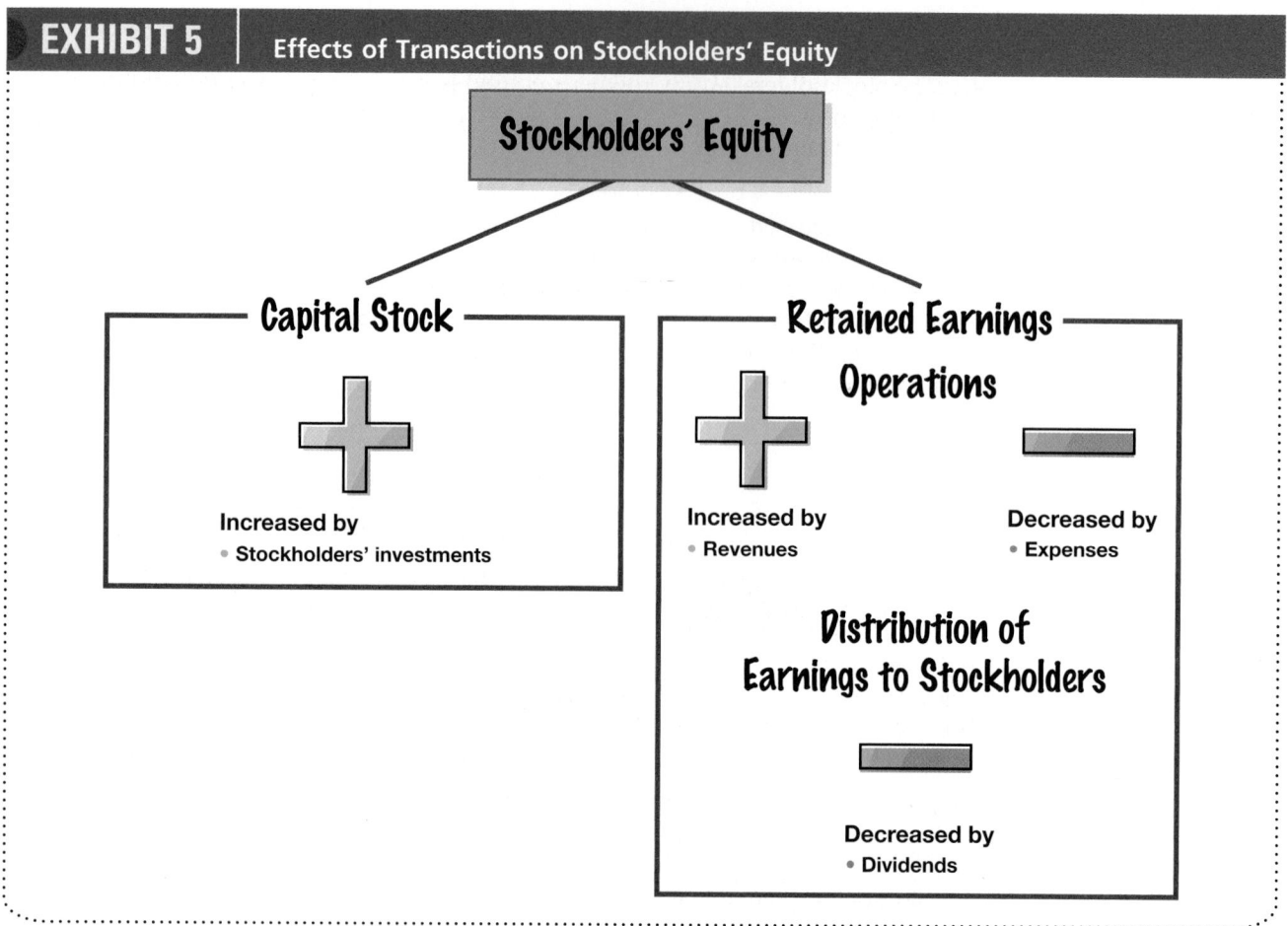

EXHIBIT 5 | **Effects of Transactions on Stockholders' Equity**

Financial Statements

After transactions have been recorded and summarized, reports are prepared for users. The accounting reports that provide this information are called **financial statements**. The principal financial statements of a corporation are the income statement, the retained earnings statement, the balance sheet, and the statement of cash flows. The order in which the statements are normally prepared and the nature of the data presented in each statement are as follows:

- **Income statement**—A summary of the revenue and expenses *for a specific period of time,* such as a month or a year.
- **Retained earnings statement**—A summary of the changes in the earnings retained in the corporation for *a specific period of time,* such as a month or a year.
- **Balance sheet**—A list of the assets, liabilities, and owner's equity *as of a specific date,* usually at the close of the last day of a month or a year.
- **Statement of cash flows**—A summary of the cash receipts and cash payments *for a specific period of time,* such as a month or a year.

The basic features of the four statements and their interrelationships are illustrated in Exhibit 6. The data for the statements were taken from the summary of transactions of NetSolutions.

All financial statements should be identified by the name of the business, the title of the statement, and the *date* or *period of time.* The data presented in the income statement, the retained earnings statement, and the statement of cash flows are for a period of time. The data presented in the balance sheet are for a specific date.

You should note the use of indents, captions, dollar signs, and rulings in the financial statements. They aid the reader by emphasizing the sections of the statements.

EXHIBIT 6

Financial Statements for NetSolutions

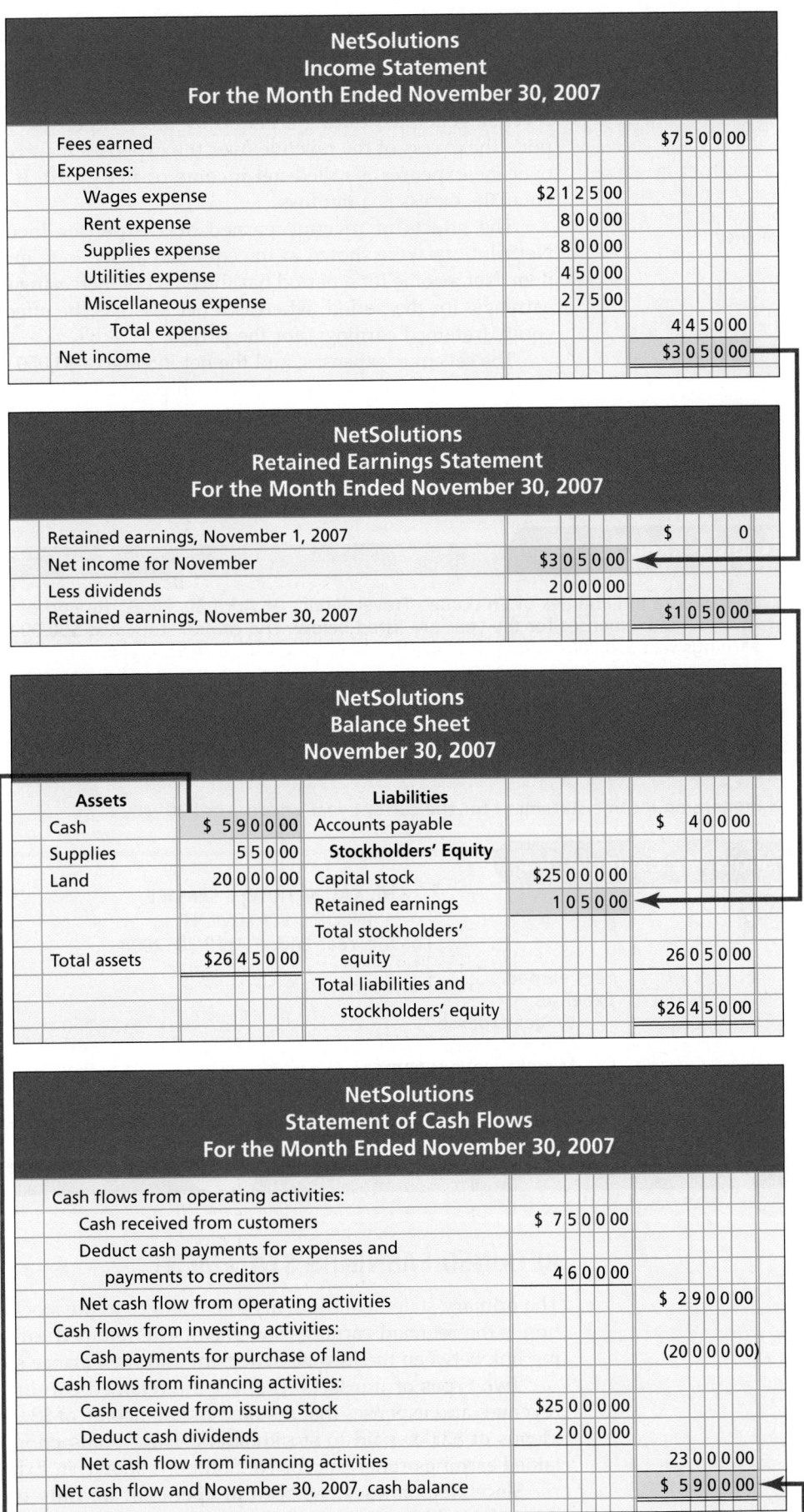

NetSolutions
Income Statement
For the Month Ended November 30, 2007

Fees earned		$7 5 0 0 00
Expenses:		
Wages expense	$2 1 2 5 00	
Rent expense	8 0 0 00	
Supplies expense	8 0 0 00	
Utilities expense	4 5 0 00	
Miscellaneous expense	2 7 5 00	
Total expenses		4 4 5 0 00
Net income		$3 0 5 0 00

NetSolutions
Retained Earnings Statement
For the Month Ended November 30, 2007

Retained earnings, November 1, 2007		$ 0
Net income for November	$3 0 5 0 00	
Less dividends	2 0 0 0 00	
Retained earnings, November 30, 2007		$1 0 5 0 00

NetSolutions
Balance Sheet
November 30, 2007

Assets		Liabilities		
Cash	$ 5 9 0 0 00	Accounts payable		$ 4 0 0 00
Supplies	5 5 0 00	**Stockholders' Equity**		
Land	20 0 0 0 00	Capital stock	$25 0 0 0 00	
		Retained earnings	1 0 5 0 00	
		Total stockholders'		
Total assets	$26 4 5 0 00	equity		26 0 5 0 00
		Total liabilities and		
		stockholders' equity		$26 4 5 0 00

NetSolutions
Statement of Cash Flows
For the Month Ended November 30, 2007

Cash flows from operating activities:		
Cash received from customers	$ 7 5 0 0 00	
Deduct cash payments for expenses and		
payments to creditors	4 6 0 0 00	
Net cash flow from operating activities		$ 2 9 0 0 00
Cash flows from investing activities:		
Cash payments for purchase of land		(20 0 0 0 00)
Cash flows from financing activities:		
Cash received from issuing stock	$25 0 0 0 00	
Deduct cash dividends	2 0 0 0 00	
Net cash flow from financing activities		23 0 0 0 00
Net cash flow and November 30, 2007, cash balance		$ 5 9 0 0 00

INCOME STATEMENT

The income statement reports the revenues and expenses for a period of time, based on the **matching concept**. This concept is applied by *matching* the expenses with the revenue generated during a period by those expenses. The income statement also reports the excess of the revenue over the expenses incurred. This excess of the revenue over the expenses is called **net income** or **net profit**. If the expenses exceed the revenue, the excess is a **net loss**.

The effects of revenue earned and expenses incurred during the month for NetSolutions were shown in the equation as separate increases and decreases in each item. Net income for a period has the effect of increasing stockholders' equity (retained earnings) for the period, whereas a net loss has the effect of decreasing stockholders' equity (retained earnings) for the period.

The revenue, expenses, and the net income of $3,050 for NetSolutions are reported in the income statement in Exhibit 6 on page 20. The order in which the expenses are listed in the income statement varies among businesses. One method is to list them in order of size, beginning with the larger items. Miscellaneous expense is usually shown as the last item, regardless of the amount.

Example Exercise 1-4

objective **5**

The assets and liabilities of Chickadee Travel Service at April 30, 2008, the end of the current year, and its revenue and expenses for the year are listed below. The capital stock was $50,000, and the retained earnings was $30,000 on May 1, 2007, the beginning of the current year.

Accounts payable	$ 12,200	Miscellaneous expense	$ 12,950
Accounts receivable	31,350	Office expense	63,000
Cash	53,050	Supplies	3,350
Fees earned	263,200	Wages expense	131,700
Land	80,000		

Prepare an income statement for the current year ended April 30, 2008.

Follow My Example 1-4

CHICKADEE TRAVEL SERVICE
INCOME STATEMENT
For the Year Ended April 30, 2008

Fees earned		$263,200
Expenses:		
Wages expense	$131,700	
Office expense	63,000	
Miscellaneous expense	12,950	
Total expenses		207,650
Net income		$ 55,550

For Practice: PE 1-4A, PE 1-4B

RETAINED EARNINGS STATEMENT

The primary statement for analyzing changes in the stockholders' equity of a corporation is the retained earnings statement. The retained earnings statement is a connecting link between the income statement and the balance sheet.

Two types of transactions affect the retained earnings during the month: (1) the revenues and expenses that resulted in net income of $3,050 for the month and (2) dividends of $2,000 paid to stockholders. These transactions are summarized in the retained earnings statement for NetSolutions shown in Exhibit 6.

Since NetSolutions has been in operation for only one month, it has no retained earnings at the beginning of November. For December, however, there is a beginning balance—the balance at the end of November. This balance of $1,050 is reported on the retained earnings statement. To illustrate, assume that NetSolutions earned net income of $4,155 and paid dividends of $2,000 during December. The retained earnings statement for NetSolutions for December is shown here.

NetSolutions Retained Earnings Statement For the Month Ended December 31, 2007			
Retained earnings, December 1, 2007			$1 0 5 0 00
Net income for the month	$4 1 5 5 00		
Less dividends	2 0 0 0 00		
Increase in retained earnings			2 1 5 5 00
Retained earnings, December 31, 2007			$3 2 0 5 00

Example Exercise 1-5 objective 5

Using the data for Chickadee Travel Service shown in Example Exercise 1-4, prepare a retained earnings statement for the current year ended April 30, 2008. Adam Cellini invested an additional $50,000 in exchange for capital stock in the business during the year and dividends of $30,000 were paid during the year.

Follow My Example 1-5

CHICKADEE TRAVEL SERVICE
RETAINED EARNINGS STATEMENT
For the Year Ended April 30, 2008

Retained earnings, May 1, 2007		$30,000
Net income for the year	$55,550	
Less dividends	30,000	
Increase in retained earnings		25,550
Retained earnings, April 30, 2008		$55,550

For Practice: PE 1-5A, PE 1-5B

BALANCE SHEET

The balance sheet in Exhibit 6 reports the amounts of NetSolutions' assets, liabilities, and stockholders' equity at the end of November. The asset, liability, and capital stock amounts are taken from the last line of the summary of transactions presented earlier. Retained earnings as of November 30, 2007, is taken from the retained earnings statement. The form of balance sheet shown in Exhibit 6 is called the **account form** because it resembles the basic format of the accounting equation, with assets on the left side and the liabilities and stockholders' equity sections on the right side. We illustrate an alternative form of balance sheet, called the **report form**, in a later chapter. It presents the liabilities and stockholders' equity sections below the assets section.

The assets section of the balance sheet normally presents assets in the order that they will be converted into cash or used in operations. Cash is presented first, followed by receivables, supplies, prepaid insurance, and other assets. The assets of a more permanent nature are shown next, such as land, buildings, and equipment.

In the liabilities section of the balance sheet in Exhibit 6, accounts payable is the only liability. When there are two or more categories of liabilities, each should be listed and the total amount of liabilities presented as follows:

Liabilities		
Accounts payable	$12,900	
Wages payable	2,570	
Total liabilities		$15,470

Example Exercise 1-6

Using the data for Chickadee Travel Service shown in Example Exercises 1-4 and 1-5, prepare the balance sheet as of April 30, 2008.

Follow My Example 1-6

CHICKADEE TRAVEL SERVICE
BALANCE SHEET
April 30, 2008

Assets		Liabilities	
Cash	$ 53,050	Accounts payable	$ 12,200
Accounts receivable	31,350		
Supplies	3,350	**Stockholders' Equity**	
Land	80,000	Capital stock $100,000	
		Retained earnings 55,550	
		Total stockholders' equity	155,550
Total assets	$167,750	Total liabilities and stockholders' equity	$167,750

For Practice: PE 1-6A, PE 1-6B

STATEMENT OF CASH FLOWS

The statement of cash flows consists of three sections, as we see in Exhibit 6: (1) operating activities, (2) investing activities, and (3) financing activities. Each of these sections is briefly described below.

Cash Flows from Operating Activities This section reports a summary of cash receipts and cash payments from operations. The net cash flow from operating activities will normally differ from the amount of net income for the period. In Exhibit 6, NetSolutions reported net cash flows from operating activities of $2,900 and net income of $3,050. This difference occurs because revenues and expenses may not be recorded at the same time that cash is received from customers or paid to creditors.

Cash Flows from Investing Activities This section reports the cash transactions for the acquisition and sale of relatively permanent assets. Exhibit 6 reports that NetSolutions paid $20,000 for the purchase of land during November.

Cash Flows from Financing Activities This section reports the cash transactions related to cash investments by stockholders, borrowings, and cash dividends. Exhibit 6 shows that Chris Clark invested $25,000 in the business in exchange for capital stock and dividends of $2,000 were paid during November.

Preparing the statement of cash flows requires that each of the November cash transactions for NetSolutions be classified as operating, investing, or financing activities. Using the summary of transactions shown on page 16, the November cash transactions for NetSolutions can be classified as follows:

Transaction	Amount	Cash Flow Activity
a.	$25,000	Financing (Issuance of capital stock)
b.	−20,000	Investing (Purchase of land)
d.	7,500	Operating (Fees earned)
e.	−3,650	Operating (Payment of expenses)
f.	−950	Operating (Payment of account payable)
h.	−2,000	Financing (Dividends)

Transactions (c) and (g) are not listed above since they did not involve a cash receipt or payment. In additon, the payment of accounts payable in transaction (f) is classified as an operating activity since the account payable arose from the purchase of supplies, which are used in operations. Using the preceding classifications of November cash transactions, the statement of cash flows is prepared as shown in Exhibit 6.[6]

The ending cash balance shown on the statement of cash flows also appears on the balance sheet as of the end of the period. To illustrate, the ending cash of $5,900 reported on the November statement of cash flows in Exhibit 6 also appears as the amount of cash on hand in the November 30, 2007, balance sheet.

Since November is NetSolutions' first period of operations, the net cash flow for November and the November 30, 2007, cash balance are the same amount, $5,900, as shown in Exhibit 6. In subsequent periods, NetSolutions will report in its statement of cash flows a beginning cash balance, an increase or a decrease in cash for the period, and an ending cash balance. For example, assume that for December NetSolutions has a decrease in cash of $3,835. The last three lines of NetSolutions' statement of cash flows for December appear as follows:

Decrease in cash	$3,835
Cash as of December 1, 2007	5,900
Cash as of December 31, 2007	$2,065

Example Exercise 1-7
objective 5

A summary of cash flows for Chickadee Travel Service for the year ended April 30, 2008, is shown below.

Cash receipts:	
Cash received from customers	$251,000
Cash received from issuing capital stock	50,000
Cash payments:	
Cash paid for expenses	210,000
Cash paid for land	80,000
Cash paid for dividends	30,000

The cash balance as of May 1, 2007, was $72,050.

Prepare a statement of cash flows for Chickadee Travel Service for the year ended April 30, 2008.

Follow My Example 1-7

CHICKADEE TRAVEL SERVICE
STATEMENT OF CASH FLOWS
For the Year Ended April 30, 2008

Cash flows from operating activities:		
Cash received from customers	$251,000	
Deduct cash payments for expenses	210,000	
Net cash flow from operating activities		$ 41,000
Cash flows from investing activities:		
Cash payments for purchase of land		(80,000)
Cash flows from financing activities:		
Cash received from issuing capital stock	$ 50,000	
Deduct cash dividends	30,000	
Net cash flow from financing activities		20,000
Net decrease in cash during year		$(19,000)
Cash as of May 1, 2007		72,050
Cash as of April 30, 2008		$ 53,050

For Practice: PE 1-7A, PE 1-7B

---

[6] This method of preparing the statement of cash flows is called the "direct method." This method and the indirect method are discussed further in Chapter 14.

INTERRELATIONSHIPS AMONG FINANCIAL STATEMENTS

As we mentioned earlier, financial statements are prepared in the order of the income statement, retained earnings statement, balance sheet, and statement of cash flows. Preparing them in this order is important because the financial statements are interrelated. Using the financial statements of NetSolutions as an example, these interrelationships are shown in Exhibit 6 as follows:[7]

1. The income statement and the retained earnings statement are interrelated. The net income or net loss appears on the income statement and also on the retained earnings statement—as either an addition (net income) to or deduction (net loss) from the beginning retained earnings. To illustrate, NetSolutions' net income of $3,050 for November is shown in the retained earnings statement in Exhibit 6.
2. The retained earnings statement and the balance sheet are interrelated. The retained earnings at the end of the period on the retained earnings statement also appears on the balance sheet. To illustrate, retained earnings of $1,050 as of November 30, 2007, on the retained earnings statement also appears on the November 30, 2007, balance sheet shown in Exhibit 6.
3. The balance sheet and the statement of cash flows are interrelated. The cash on the balance sheet also appears as the end-of-period cash on the statement of cash flows. To illustrate, the cash of $5,900 reported on NetSolutions' balance sheet as of November 30, 2007, is also reported on NetSolutions' November statement of cash flows as the end-of-period cash as shown in Exhibit 6.

The preceding interrelationships shown in Exhibit 6 are important in analyzing financial statements and the impact of transactions on a business. In addition, these interrelationships serve as a check on whether the financial statements have been prepared correctly. For example, if the ending cash on the statement of cash flows doesn't agree with the balance sheet cash, then an error has occurred.

---

7 Depending upon the method of preparing the cash flows from operating activities section of the statement of cash flows, net income (or net loss) may also appear on the statement of cash flows. This interrelationship or method of preparing the statement of cash flows, called the "indirect method," is described and illustrated in Chapter 14.

At a Glance

1. Describe the nature of a business and the role of ethics and accounting in business.

Key Points	Key Learning Outcomes	Example Exercises	Practice Exercises
A business provides goods or services (outputs) to customers with the objective of maximizing profits. Service, merchandising, and manufacturing businesses may be organized as proprietorships, partnerships, corporations, and limited liability companies. A business stakeholder is a person or entity (such as an owner, manager, employee, customer, creditor, or the government) who has an interest in the economic performance of the business. Ethics are moral principles that guide the conduct of individuals. Good ethical conduct depends upon individual character, firm culture, and laws and enforcement. Accounting, called the "language of business," is an information system that provides reports to stakeholders about the economic activities and condition of a business. Accountants are engaged in private accounting or public accounting.	• Distinguish among service, merchandising, and manufacturing businesses. • Describe the characteristics of a proprietorship, partnership, corporation, and limited liability company. • List business stakeholders. • Define ethics and list the three factors affecting good ethical conduct. • Describe the role of accounting in business and explain why accounting is called the "language of business." • Describe what private and public accounting means.		

2. Summarize the development of accounting principles and relate them to practice.

Key Points	Key Learning Outcomes	Example Exercises	Practice Exercises
Generally accepted accounting principles (GAAP) are used in preparing financial statements so that stakeholders can compare one company to another. Accounting principles and concepts develop from research, practice, and pronouncements of authoritative bodies such as the Financial Accounting Standards Board (FASB). The business entity concept views the business as an entity separate from its owners, creditors, or other stakeholders. The cost concept requires that properties and services bought by a business be recorded in terms of actual cost. The objectivity concept requires that the accounting records and reports be based upon objective evidence. The unit of measure concept requires that economic data be recorded in dollars.	• Explain what is meant by generally accepted accounting principles. • Describe how generally accepted accounting principles are developed. • Describe and give an example of what is meant by the business entity concept. • Describe and give an example of what is meant by the cost concept. • Describe and give an example of what is meant by the objectivity concept. • Describe and give an example of what is meant by the unit of measure concept.	1-1	1-1A, 1-1B

(continued)

3. State the accounting equation and define each element of the equation.

Key Points	Key Learning Outcomes	Example Exercises	Practice Exercises
The resources owned by a business and the rights or claims to these resources may be stated in the form of an equation, as follows: Assets = Liabilities + Owner's Equity	• State the accounting equation. • Define assets, liabilities, and owner's equity. • Given two elements of the accounting equation, solve for the third element.	**1-2**	1-2A, 1-2B

4. Describe and illustrate how business transactions can be recorded in terms of the resulting change in the basic elements of the accounting equation.

Key Points	Key Learning Outcomes	Example Exercises	Practice Exercises
All business transactions can be stated in terms of the change in one or more of the three elements of the accounting equation.	• Define a business transaction. • Using the accounting equation as a framework, record transactions.	**1-3**	1-3A, 1-3B

5. Describe the financial statements of a corporation and explain how they interrelate.

Key Points	Key Learning Outcomes	Example Exercises	Practice Exercises
The principal financial statements of a corporation are the income statement, the retained earnings statement, the balance sheet, and the statement of cash flows. The income statement reports a period's net income or net loss, which also appears on the retained earnings statement. The ending retained earnings reported on the retained earnings statement is also reported on the balance sheet. The ending cash balance is reported on the balance sheet and the statement of cash flows.	• List and describe the financial statements of a corporation. • Prepare an income statement. • Prepare a retained earnings statement. • Prepare a balance sheet. • Prepare a statement of cash flows. • Explain how the financial statements of a corporation are interrelated.	**1-4** **1-5** **1-6** **1-7**	1-4A, 1-4B 1-5A, 1-5B 1-6A, 1-6B 1-7A, 1-7B

Key Terms

account form (21)
account payable (14)
account receivable (15)
accounting (7)
accounting equation (12)
assets (12)
balance sheet (18)
business (2)
business entity concept (11)
business stakeholder (4)
business transaction (12)
capital stock (13)

Certified Management Accountant (CMA) (9)
Certified Public Accountant (CPA) (10)
corporation (3)
cost concept (11)
dividends (16)
ethics (4)
expenses (15)
fees earned (14)
financial accounting (8)

Financial Accounting Standards Board (FASB) (10)
financial statements (18)
generally accepted accounting principles (GAAP) (10)
income statement (18)
interest revenue (15)
liabilities (12)
limited liability company (LLC) (4)
management (or managerial) accounting (9)

manufacturing business (3)
matching concept (20)
merchandising business (3)
net income or net profit (20)
net loss (20)
objectivity concept (11)
owner's equity (12)
partnership (3)

prepaid expenses (14)
private accounting (9)
profit (2)
proprietorship (3)
public accounting (9)
rent revenue (15)
report form (21)
retained earnings (17)

retained earnings statement (18)
revenue (14)
sales (14)
service business (3)
statement of cash flows (18)
stockholders' equity (13)
unit of measure concept (11)

Illustrative Problem

Cecil Jameson, Attorney-at-Law, P.C. is organized as a professional corporation owned and operated by Cecil Jameson. On July 1, 2007, Cecil Jameson, Attorney-at-Law, P.C. has the following assets and liabilities: cash, $1,000; accounts receivable, $3,200; supplies, $850; land, $10,000; accounts payable, $1,530; capital stock, $10,000. Office space and office equipment are currently being rented, pending the construction of an office complex on land purchased last year. Business transactions during July are summarized as follows:

a. Received cash from clients for services, $3,928.
b. Paid creditors on account, $1,055.
c. Received cash from Cecil Jameson as an additional investment in exchange for capital stock, $3,700.
d. Paid office rent for the month, $1,200.
e. Charged clients for legal services on account, $2,025.
f. Purchased office supplies on account, $245.
g. Received cash from clients on account, $3,000.
h. Received invoice for paralegal services from Legal Aid Inc. for July (to be paid on August 10), $1,635.
i. Paid the following: wages expense, $850; answering service expense, $250; utilities expense, $325; and miscellaneous expense, $75.
j. Determined that the cost of office supplies on hand was $980; therefore, the cost of supplies used during the month was $115.
k. Paid dividends of $1,000.

Instructions
1. Determine the amount of retained earnings as of July 1, 2007.
2. State the assets, liabilities, and stockholders' equity as of July 1 in equation form similar to that shown in this chapter. In tabular form below the equation, indicate the increases and decreases resulting from each transaction and the new balances after each transaction.
3. Prepare an income statement for July, a retained earnings statement for July, and a balance sheet as of July 31, 2007.
4. (Optional). Prepare a statement of cash flows for July.

Solution
1. Assets − Liabilities = Stockholders' Equity
$15,050 − $1,530 = Capital Stock + Retained Earnings
$13,520 = $10,000 + Retained Earnings
$3,520 = Retained Earnings

(continued)

2.

	Cash +	Accts. Rec. +	Supp. +	Land =	Accts. Pay. +	Capital Stock +	Retained Earnings −	Dividends +	Fees Earned −	Paralegal Exp. −	Wages Exp. −	Rent Exp. −	Utilities Exp. −	Answering Service Exp. −	Supp. Exp. −	Misc. Exp.
Bal.	1,000	3,200	850	10,000	1,530	10,000	3,520									
a.	+3,928								3,928							
Bal.	4,928	3,200	850	10,000	1,530	10,000										
b.	−1,055				−1,055											
Bal.	3,873	3,200	850	10,000	475	10,000			3,928							
c.	+3,700					+3,700										
Bal.	7,573	3,200	850	10,000	475	13,700			3,928							
d.	−1,200											−1,200				
Bal.	6,373	3,200	850	10,000	475	13,700			3,928			−1,200				
e.		+2,025							+2,025							
Bal.	6,373	5,225	850	10,000	475	13,700			5,953			−1,200				
f.			+ 245		+ 245											
Bal.	6,373	5,225	1,095	10,000	720	13,700			5,953			−1,200				
g.	+3,000	−3,000														
Bal.	9,373	2,225	1,095	10,000	720	13,700			5,953			−1,200				
h.					+1,635					−1,635						
Bal.	9,373	2,225	1,095	10,000	2,355	13,700			5,953	−1,635		−1,200				
i.	−1,500										−850		−325	−250		−75
Bal.	7,873	2,225	1,095	10,000	2,355	13,700			5,953	−1,635	−850	−1,200	−325	−250		−75
j.			− 115												−115	
Bal.	7,873	2,225	980	10,000	2,355	13,700			5,953	−1,635	−850	−1,200	−325	−250	−115	−75
k.	−1,000							−1,000								
Bal.	6,873	2,225	980	10,000 =	2,355	13,700	3,520	−1,000	5,953	−1,635	−850	−1,200	−325	−250	−115	−75

3.

Cecil Jameson, Attorney-at-Law, P.C.
Income Statement
For the Month Ended July 31, 2007

Fees earned		$5,953
Expenses:		
Paralegal expense	$1,635	
Rent expense	1,200	
Wages expense	850	
Utilities expense	325	
Answering service expense	250	
Supplies expense	115	
Miscellaneous expense	75	
Total expenses		4,450
Net income		$1,503

Cecil Jameson, Attorney-at-Law, P.C.
Retained Earnings Statement
For the Month Ended July 31, 2007

Retained earnings, July 1, 2007		$3,520
Net income for the month	$1,503	
Less dividends	1,000	
Increase in retained earnings		503
Retained earnings, July 31, 2007		$4,023

Cecil Jameson, Attorney-at-Law, P.C.
Balance Sheet
July 31, 2007

Assets			Liabilities		
Cash	$ 6,873		Accounts payable		$ 2,355
Accounts receivable	2,225		**Stockholders' Equity**		
Supplies	980		Capital stock	$13,700	
Land	10,000		Retained earnings	4,023	
Total assets	$20,078		Total stockholders' equity		17,723
			Total liabilities and		
			stockholders' equity		$20,078

4. Optional.

Cecil Jameson, Attorney-at-Law, P.C.
Statement of Cash Flows
For the Month Ended July 31, 2007

Cash flows from operating activities:		
Cash received from customers	$6,928*	
Deduct cash payments for operating expenses	3,755**	
Net cash flow from operating activities		$3,173
Cash flows from investing activities		—
Cash flows from financing activities:		
Cash received from issuing capital stock	$3,700	
Deduct dividends	1,000	
Net cash flow from financing activities		2,700
Net increase in cash during year		$5,873
Cash as of July 1, 2007		1,000
Cash as of July 31, 2007		$6,873

*$6,928 = $3,928 + $3,000
**$3,755 = $1,055 + $1,200 + $1,500

Self-Examination Questions   (Answers at End of Chapter)

1. A profit-making business operating as a separate legal entity and in which ownership is divided into shares of stock is known as a:
   A. proprietorship.   C. partnership.
   B. service business.   D. corporation.

2. The resources owned by a business are called:
   A. assets.   C. the accounting equation.
   B. liabilities.   D. stockholders' equity.

3. A listing of a business entity's assets, liabilities, and stockholders' equity as of a specific date is a(n):
   A. balance sheet.
   B. income statement.
   C. retained earnings statement.
   D. statement of cash flows.

4. If total assets increased $20,000 during a period and total liabilities increased $12,000 during the same period, the amount and direction (increase or decrease) of the change in owner's equity for that period is a(n):
   A. $32,000 increase.   C. $8,000 increase.
   B. $32,000 decrease.   D. $8,000 decrease.

5. If revenue was $45,000, expenses were $37,500, and dividends were $10,000, the amount of net income or net loss would be:
   A. $45,000 net income.   C. $37,500 net loss.
   B. $7,500 net income.   D. $2,500 net loss.

Eye Openers

1. What is the objective of most businesses?
2. What is the difference between a manufacturing business and a service business? Is a restaurant a manufacturing business, a service business, or both?

(continued)

3. Why are most large companies like Microsoft, PepsiCo, Caterpillar, and AutoZone organized as corporations?
4. Who are normally included as the stakeholders of a business?
5. What is the role of accounting in business?
6. Rebecca Olson is the owner of Aquarius Delivery Service. Recently, Rebecca paid interest of $1,850 on a personal loan of $30,000 that she used to begin the business. Should Aquarius Delivery Service record the interest payment? Explain.
7. On February 3, Dependable Repair Service extended an offer of $80,000 for land that had been priced for sale at $90,000. On March 6, Dependable Repair Service accepted the seller's counteroffer of $88,000. Describe how Dependable Repair Service should record the land.
8. a. Land with an assessed value of $250,000 for property tax purposes is acquired by a business for $375,000. Seven years later, the plot of land has an assessed value of $400,000 and the business receives an offer of $725,000 for it. Should the monetary amount assigned to the land in the business records now be increased?
   b. Assuming that the land acquired in (a) was sold for $725,000, how would the various elements of the accounting equation be affected?
9. Describe the difference between an account receivable and an account payable.
10. A business had revenues of $420,000 and operating expenses of $565,000. Did the business (a) incur a net loss or (b) realize net income?
11. A business had revenues of $919,500 and operating expenses of $738,600. Did the business (a) incur a net loss or (b) realize net income?
12. What particular item of financial or operating data appears on both the income statement and the retained earnings statement? What item appears on both the balance sheet and the retained earnings statement? What item appears on both the balance sheet and the statement of cash flows?

Practice Exercises

PE 1-1A
Cost concept
obj. 2

On November 15, Johnson Repair Service extended an offer of $35,000 for land that had been priced for sale at $43,000. On December 8, Johnson Repair Service accepted the seller's counteroffer of $37,000. On December 30, the land was assessed at a value of $50,000 for property tax purposes. On April 1, Johnson Repair Service was offered $60,000 for the land by a national retail chain. At what value should the land be recorded in Johnson Repair Service's records?

PE 1-1B
Cost concept
obj. 2

On February 2, Duck Repair Service extended an offer of $90,000 for land that had been priced for sale at $115,000. On February 16, Duck Repair Service accepted the seller's counteroffer of $100,000. On April 29, the land was assessed at a value of $110,000 for property tax purposes. On August 30, Duck Repair Service was offered $130,000 for the land by a national retail chain. At what value should the land be recorded in Duck Repair Service's records?

PE 1-2A
Accounting equation
obj. 3

Daryl Wallin is the owner and operator of Pima LLC, a motivational consulting business. At the end of its accounting period, December 31, 2007, Pima has assets of $617,000 and liabilities of $382,000. Using the accounting equation, determine the following amounts:

a. Owner's equity, as of December 31, 2007.
b. Owner's equity, as of December 31, 2008, assuming that assets increased by $114,000 and liabilities decreased by $29,000 during 2008.

PE 1-2B
Accounting equation
obj. 3

Kristen Hagan is the owner and operator of You're Cool, a motivational consulting business. At the end of its accounting period, December 31, 2007, You're Cool has assets of $336,000 and liabilities of $172,500. Using the accounting equation, determine the following amounts:

a. Owner's equity, as of December 31, 2007.
b. Owner's equity, as of December 31, 2008, assuming that assets increased by $75,000 and liabilities increased by $15,000 during 2008.

PE 1-3A
Transactions
obj. 4

Mime Delivery Service is owned and operated by Pamela Kolp. The following selected transactions were completed by Mime Delivery Service during October:

1. Received cash in exchange for capital stock, $7,500.
2. Paid creditors on account, $815.
3. Billed customers for delivery services on account, $3,250.
4. Received cash from customers on account, $1,150.
5. Paid dividends, $500.

Indicate the effect of each transaction on the accounting equation elements (Assets, Liabilities, Stockholders' Equity, Dividends, Revenue, and Expense) by listing the numbers identifying the transactions, (1) through (5). Also, indicate the specific item within the accounting equation element that is affected. To illustrate, the answer to (1) is shown below.

(1) Asset (Cash) increases by $7,500; Stockholders' Equity (Capital Stock) increases by $7,500.

PE 1-3B
Transactions
obj. 4

Quicken Delivery Service is owned and operated by Zoey Tucker. The following selected transactions were completed by Quicken Delivery Service during July:

1. Received cash in exchange for capital stock, $9,000.
2. Paid advertising expense, $674.
3. Purchased supplies on account, $280.
4. Billed customers for delivery services on account, $4,800.
5. Received cash from customers on account, $1,150.

Indicate the effect of each transaction on the accounting equation elements (Assets, Liabilities, Stockholders' Equity, Dividends, Revenue, and Expense) by listing the numbers identifying the transactions, (1) through (5). Also, indicate the specific item within the accounting equation element that is affected. To illustrate, the answer to (1) is shown below.

(1) Asset (Cash) increases by $9,000; Stockholders' Equity (Capital Stock) increases by $9,000.

PE 1-4A
Income statement
obj. 5

The assets and liabilities of Herat Travel Service at June 30, 2008, the end of the current year, and its revenue and expenses for the year are listed below. The capital stock was $30,000 and the retained earnings was $45,000 on July 1, 2007, the beginning of the current year.

Accounts payable	$ 15,300	Miscellaneous expense	$ 3,150
Accounts receivable	24,350	Office expense	91,350
Cash	70,800	Supplies	5,350
Fees earned	378,200	Wages expense	181,500
Land	100,000		

Prepare an income statement for the current year ended June 30, 2008.

PE 1-4B
Income statement
obj. 5

The assets and liabilities of Leotard Travel Service at February 28, 2008, the end of the current year, and its revenue and expenses for the year are listed below. The capital stock was $80,000 and the retained earnings was $110,000 on March 1, 2007, the beginning of the current year.

Accounts payable	$ 21,000	Miscellaneous expense	$ 6,350
Accounts receivable	37,750	Office expense	156,650
Cash	22,700	Supplies	2,550
Fees earned	377,000	Wages expense	225,000
Land	145,000		

Prepare an income statement for the current year ended February 28, 2008.

PE 1-5A
Retained earnings statement
obj. 5

Using the data for Herat Travel Service shown in Practice Exercise 1-4A, prepare a retained earnings statement for the current year ended June 30, 2008. Lola Stahn invested an additional $20,000 in exchange for capital stock and dividends of $12,000 were paid during the year.

PE 1-5B
*Retained earnings
statement*
obj. 5

Using the data for Leotard Travel Service shown in Practice Exercise 1-4B, prepare a retained earnings statement for the current year ended February 28, 2008. Harry Thompson invested an additional $18,000 in exchange for capital stock and dividends of $10,000 were paid during the year.

PE 1-6A
Balance sheet
obj. 5

Using the data for Herat Travel Service shown in Practice Exercises 1-4A and 1-5A, prepare the balance sheet as of June 30, 2008.

PE 1-6B
Balance sheet
obj. 5

Using the data for Leotard Travel Service shown in Practice Exercises 1-4B and 1-5B, prepare the balance sheet as of February 28, 2008.

PE 1-7A
Statement of cash flows
obj. 5

A summary of cash flows for Herat Travel Service for the year ended June 30, 2008, is shown below.

Cash receipts:	
Cash received from customers	$350,000
Cash received from issuing capital stock	20,000
Cash payments:	
Cash paid for operating expenses	270,000
Cash paid for land	60,000
Cash paid for dividends	12,000

The cash balance as of July 1, 2007, was $42,800.
    Prepare a statement of cash flows for Herat Travel Service for the year ended June 30, 2008.

PE 1-7B
Statement of cash flows
obj. 5

A summary of cash flows for Leotard Travel Service for the year ended February 28, 2008, is shown below.

Cash receipts:	
Cash received from customers	$350,000
Cash received from issuing capital stock	18,000
Cash payments:	
Cash paid for operating expenses	365,000
Cash paid for land	27,000
Cash paid for dividends	10,000

The cash balance as of March 1, 2007, was $56,700.
    Prepare a statement of cash flows for Leotard Travel Service for the year ended February 28, 2008.

Exercises

EX 1-1
Types of businesses
obj. 1

Indicate whether each of the following companies is primarily a service, merchandise, or manufacturing business. If you are unfamiliar with the company, use the Internet to locate the company's home page or use the finance Web site of Yahoo.com.

1. H&R Block
2. eBay Inc.
3. Wal-Mart Stores, Inc.
4. Ford Motor Company
5. Citigroup
6. Boeing
7. First Union Corporation
8. Alcoa Inc.
9. Procter & Gamble
10. FedEx
11. Gap Inc.
12. Hilton Hospitality, Inc.
13. CVS
14. Caterpillar
15. The Dow Chemical Company

EX 1-2
Professional ethics
obj. 1

ETHICS

A fertilizer manufacturing company wants to relocate to Collier County. A 13-year-old report from a fired researcher at the company says the company's product is releasing toxic by-products. The company has suppressed that report. A second report commissioned by the company shows there is no problem with the fertilizer.

Should the company's chief executive officer reveal the context of the unfavorable report in discussions with Collier County representatives? Discuss.

EX 1-3
Business entity concept
obj. 2

Frontier Sports sells hunting and fishing equipment and provides guided hunting and fishing trips. Frontier Sports is owned and operated by Wally Schnee, a well-known sports enthusiast and hunter. Wally's wife, Helen, owns and operates Blue Sky Boutique, a women's clothing store. Wally and Helen have established a trust fund to finance their children's college education. The trust fund is maintained by First Bank in the name of the children, Anna and Conner.

For each of the following transactions, identify which of the entities listed should record the transaction in its records.

Entities

F	Frontier Sports
B	First Bank Trust Fund
S	Blue Sky Boutique
X	None of the above

1. Wally paid a breeder's fee for an English springer spaniel to be used as a hunting guide dog.
2. Helen paid her dues to the YWCA.
3. Helen purchased two dozen spring dresses from a Denver designer for a special spring sale.
4. Helen deposited a $3,500 personal check in the trust fund at First Bank.
5. Wally paid for an advertisement in a hunters' magazine.
6. Helen authorized the trust fund to purchase mutual fund shares.
7. Wally paid for dinner and a movie to celebrate their tenth wedding anniversary.
8. Helen donated several dresses from inventory for a local charity auction for the benefit of a women's abuse shelter.
9. Wally received a cash advance from customers for a guided hunting trip.
10. Wally paid a local doctor for his annual physical, which was required by the workmen's compensation insurance policy carried by Frontier Sports.

EX 1-4
Accounting equation
obj. 3

REAL WORLD

✓ Coca-Cola, $15,935

The total assets and total liabilities of Coca-Cola and PepsiCo are shown below.

	Coca-Cola (in millions)	PepsiCo (in millions)
Assets	$31,327	$27,987
Liabilities	15,392	14,415

Determine the stockholders' (owners') equity of each company.

EX 1-5
Accounting equation
obj. 3

REAL WORLD

✓ eBay, $6,728

The total assets and total liabilities of eBay and Google are shown below.

	eBay (in millions)	Google (in millions)
Assets	$7,991	$3,313
Liabilities	1,263	384

Determine the stockholders' (owners') equity of each company.

EX 1-6
Accounting equation
obj. **3**
✓ *a. $300,600*

Determine the missing amount for each of the following:

	Assets	=	Liabilities	+	Stockholders' (Owner's) Equity
a.	X	=	$85,000	+	$215,600
b.	$93,500	=	X	+	$6,150
c.	$42,500	=	$11,275	+	X

EX 1-7
Accounting equation
objs. **3, 4**
✓ *b. $710,000*

Hector Lopez is the sole stockholder and operator of Centillion, a motivational consulting business. At the end of its accounting period, December 31, 2007, Centillion has assets of $950,000 and liabilities of $300,000. Using the accounting equation and considering each case independently, determine the following amounts:

a. Stockholders' equity, as of December 31, 2007.
b. Stockholders' equity, as of December 31, 2008, assuming that assets increased by $150,000 and liabilities increased by $90,000 during 2008.
c. Stockholders' equity, as of December 31, 2008, assuming that assets decreased by $75,000 and liabilities increased by $27,000 during 2008.
d. Stockholders' equity, as of December 31, 2008, assuming that assets increased by $125,000 and liabilities decreased by $48,000 during 2008.
e. Net income (or net loss) during 2008, assuming that as of December 31, 2008, assets were $1,200,000, liabilities were $195,000, and no additional capital stock was issued nor dividends distributed.

EX 1-8
Asset, liability, stockholders' equity items
obj. **3**

Indicate whether each of the following is identified with (1) an asset, (2) a liability, or (3) stockholders' equity (retained earnings):

a. land
b. wages expense
c. accounts payable
d. fees earned
e. supplies
f. cash

EX 1-9
Effect of transactions on accounting equation
obj. **4**

Describe how the following business transactions affect the three elements of the accounting equation.

a. Purchased supplies on account.
b. Purchased supplies for cash.
c. Paid for utilities used in the business.
d. Received cash for services performed.
e. Invested cash in business.

EX 1-10
Effect of transactions on accounting equation
obj. **4**
✓ *a. (1) increase $70,000*

a. A vacant lot acquired for $75,000 is sold for $145,000 in cash. What is the effect of the sale on the total amount of the seller's (1) assets, (2) liabilities, and (3) stockholders' equity (retained earnings)?
b. Assume that the seller owes $40,000 on a loan for the land. After receiving the $145,000 cash in (a), the seller pays the $40,000 owed. What is the effect of the payment on the total amount of the seller's (1) assets, (2) liabilities, and (3) stockholders' equity (retained earnings)?

EX 1-11
Effect of transactions on stockholders' equity
obj. **4**

Indicate whether each of the following types of transactions will either (a) increase stockholders' equity or (b) decrease stockholders' equity:

1. revenues
2. expenses
3. stockholders' investments
4. dividends

EX 1-12
Transactions
obj. **4**

The following selected transactions were completed by Pilgrim Delivery Service during July:

1. Received cash from issuing capital stock, $115,000.
2. Received cash for providing delivery services, $58,000.
3. Paid advertising expense, $2,000.
4. Paid creditors on account, $4,800.
5. Billed customers for delivery services on account, $31,250.
6. Purchased supplies for cash, $800.

7. Paid rent for July, $3,000.
8. Received cash from customers on account, $10,740.
9. Determined that the cost of supplies on hand was $135; therefore, $665 of supplies had been used during the month.
10. Paid dividends, $1,500.

Indicate the effect of each transaction on the accounting equation by listing the numbers identifying the transactions, (1) through (10), in a column, and inserting at the right of each number the appropriate letter from the following list:

a. Increase in an asset, decrease in another asset.
b. Increase in an asset, increase in a liability.
c. Increase in an asset, increase in stockholders' equity.
d. Decrease in an asset, decrease in a liability.
e. Decrease in an asset, decrease in stockholders' equity.

EX 1-13
Nature of transactions
obj. **4**

✓ d. $26,500

Otto Egan operates his own catering service. Summary financial data for August are presented in equation form as follows. Each line designated by a number indicates the effect of a transaction on the equation.

	Assets			= Liabilities +		Stockholders' Equity			
	Cash	+ Supplies +	Land	= Accounts Payable +	Capital Stock +	Retained Earnings −	Dividends +	Fees Earned −	Expenses
Bal.	27,000	3,000	100,000	15,000	25,000	90,000			
1.	+45,000							45,000	
2.	−20,000		+20,000						
3.	−16,000								−16,000
4.		+3,000		+ 3,000					
5.	− 5,000						−5,000		
6.	−12,000			−12,000					
7.		−2,500							−2,500
Bal.	19,000	3,500	120,000 =	6,000	25,000	90,000	−5,000	45,000	−18,500

a. Describe each transaction.
b. What is the amount of net decrease in cash during the month?
c. What is the amount of net increase in stockholders' equity during the month?
d. What is the amount of the net income for the month?
e. How much of the net income for the month was retained in the business?

EX 1-14
Net income and dividends

obj. **5**

The income statement of a corporation for the month of July indicates a net income of $117,800. During the same period, $150,000 in cash dividends were paid.
Would it be correct to say that the business incurred a net loss of $32,200 during the month? Discuss.

EX 1-15
Net income and stockholders' equity for four businesses

obj. **5**

✓ Charlie: Net income, $180,000

Four different corporations, Alpha, Bravo, Charlie, and Delta, show the same balance sheet data at the beginning and end of a year. These data, exclusive of the amount of stockholders' equity, are summarized as follows:

	Total Assets	Total Liabilities
Beginning of the year	$1,350,000	$540,000
End of the year	2,160,000	900,000

On the basis of the above data and the following additional information for the year, determine the net income (or loss) of each company for the year. (*Hint:* First determine the amount of increase or decrease in stockholders' equity during the year.)

Alpha: No additional capital stock was issued and no dividends were paid.
Bravo: No additional capital stock was issued but dividends of $120,000 were paid.

(continued)

Charlie: Additional capital stock of $270,000 was issued and no dividends were paid.

Delta: Additional capital stock of $270,000 was issued and dividends of $120,000 were paid.

EX 1-16

Balance sheet items

obj. 5

From the following list of selected items taken from the records of Maya Appliance Service as of a specific date, identify those that would appear on the balance sheet:

1. Accounts Payable
2. Cash
3. Fees Earned
4. Capital Stock
5. Land
6. Supplies
7. Supplies Expense
8. Utilities Expense
9. Wages Expense
10. Wages Payable

EX 1-17

Income statement items

obj. 5

Based on the data presented in Exercise 1-16, identify those items that would appear on the income statement.

EX 1-18

Retained earnings statement

obj. 5

✓ *Retained earnings, June 30, 2008: $864,250*

Financial information related to Pickerel Company for the month ended June 30, 2008, is as follows:

Net income for June	$196,350
Dividends during June	15,000
Retained earnings, June 1, 2008	682,900

Prepare a retained earnings statement for the month ended June 30, 2008.

EX 1-19

Income statement

obj. 5

✓ *Net income: $91,330*

Giblet Services was organized on February 1, 2008. A summary of the revenue and expense transactions for February follows:

Fees earned	$479,280
Wages expense	310,600
Rent expense	60,000
Supplies expense	6,200
Miscellaneous expense	11,150

Prepare an income statement for the month ended February 28.

EX 1-20

Missing amounts from balance sheet and income statement data

obj. 5

✓ *(a) $117,225*

One item is omitted in each of the following summaries of balance sheet and income statement data for the following four corporations:

	Oscar	Papa	Quebec	Romeo
Beginning of the year:				
Assets	$540,000	$125,000	$200,000	(d)
Liabilities	324,000	65,000	152,000	$120,000
End of the year:				
Assets	670,500	175,000	180,000	248,000
Liabilities	292,500	55,000	160,000	136,000
During the year:				
Additional issuance of				
capital stock	(a)	25,000	20,000	40,000
Dividends	36,000	8,000	(c)	60,000
Revenue	177,975	(b)	230,000	112,000
Expenses	97,200	32,000	245,000	128,000

Determine the missing amounts, identifying them by letter. (*Hint:* First determine the amount of increase or decrease in stockholders' equity during the year.)

EX 1-21

Balance sheets, net income

obj. **5**

✓ b. $54,510

Financial information related to the proprietorship of Burst Interiors for March and April 2008 is as follows:

	March 31, 2008	April 30, 2008
Accounts payable	$18,480	$ 19,920
Accounts receivable	40,800	46,950
Capital stock	20,000	20,000
Retained earnings	?	?
Cash	72,000	122,400
Supplies	3,600	3,000

a. Prepare balance sheets for Burst Interiors as of March 31 and as of April 30, 2008.
b. Determine the amount of net income for April, assuming that no additional capital stock was issued and no dividends were paid during the month.
c. Determine the amount of net income for April, assuming that no additional capital stock was issued but dividends of $15,000 were paid during the month.

EX 1-22

Financial statements

obj. **5**

Each of the following items is shown in the financial statements of ExxonMobil Corporation. Identify the financial statement (balance sheet or income statement) in which each item would appear.

a. Accounts payable
b. Cash equivalents
c. Crude oil inventory
d. Equipment
e. Exploration expenses
f. Income taxes payable
g. Investments
h. Long-term debt

i. Marketable securities
j. Notes and loans payable
k. Notes receivable
l. Operating expenses
m. Prepaid taxes
n. Sales
o. Selling expenses

EX 1-23

Statement of cash flows

obj. **5**

Indicate whether each of the following activities would be reported on the statement of cash flows as (a) an operating activity, (b) an investing activity, or (c) a financing activity:

1. Cash received from issuance of capital stock
2. Cash received from fees earned
3. Cash paid for land
4. Cash paid for expenses

EX 1-24

Statement of cash flows

obj. **5**

A summary of cash flows for Webster Consulting Group for the year ended July 31, 2008, is shown below.

Cash receipts:
    Cash received from customers $495,000
    Cash received from additional issuance of capital stock 20,000
Cash payments:
    Cash paid for operating expenses 371,500
    Cash paid for land 40,000
    Cash paid for dividends 9,000

The cash balance as of August 1, 2007, was $46,750.
    Prepare a statement of cash flows for Webster Consulting Group for the year ended July 31, 2008.

EX 1-25

Financial statements

obj. **5**

Galaxy Realty, organized October 1, 2008, is owned and operated by Ora Tasker. How many errors can you find in the following financial statements for Galaxy Realty, prepared after its second month of operations?

✓ *Correct amount of total assets is $39,200*

Galaxy Realty
Income Statement
November 30, 2008

Sales commissions		$103,800
Expenses:		
Office salaries expense	$64,800	
Rent expense	22,000	
Automobile expense	5,000	
Miscellaneous expense	1,600	
Supplies expense	600	
Total expenses		94,000
Net income		$ 29,800

Ora Tasker
Retained Earnings Statement
November 30, 2007

Retained earnings, November 1, 2008	$20,800
Less dividends during November	4,000
	$16,800
Additional issuance of capital stock during November	5,000
	$21,800
Net income for the month	29,800
Retained earnings, November 30, 2008	$51,600

Balance Sheet
For the Month Ended November 30, 2008

Assets		Liabilities	
Cash	$ 6,600	Accounts receivable	$28,600
Accounts payable	7,600	Supplies	4,000
		Stockholders' Equity	
		Capital stock $10,000	
		Retained earnings 41,600	
		Total stockholders' equity	51,600
Total assets	$14,200	Total liabilities and stockholders' equity	$84,200

Problems Series A

PR 1-1A
Transactions
obj. 4

✓ *Cash bal. at end of June: $24,620*

On June 1 of the current year, Doni Gilmore established a business to manage rental property. She completed the following transactions during June:

a. Opened a business bank account with a deposit of $25,000 in exchange for capital stock.
b. Purchased supplies (pens, file folders, and copy paper) on account, $1,150.
c. Received cash from fees earned for managing rental property, $4,500.
d. Paid rent on office and equipment for the month, $1,500.
e. Paid creditors on account, $600.
f. Billed customers for fees earned for managing rental property, $2,250.
g. Paid automobile expenses (including rental charges) for month, $400, and miscellaneous expenses, $180.
h. Paid office salaries, $1,200.
i. Determined that the cost of supplies on hand was $380; therefore, the cost of supplies used was $770.
j. Paid dividends of $1,000.

Instructions
1. Indicate the effect of each transaction and the balances after each transaction, using the following tabular headings:

	Assets		= Liabilities +				Stockholders' Equity						
Cash	Accounts + Receivable	+ Supplies =	Accounts Payable	Capital + Stock	− Dividends	Fees + Earned	Rent − Expense	Salaries − Expense	Supplies − Expense	Auto − Expense	Misc. − Expense		

2. Briefly explain why the stockholders' investment and revenues increased stockholders' equity, while dividends and expenses decreased stockholders' equity.

PR 1-2A
Financial statements

obj. 5

✓ *1. Net income: $137,500*

Following are the amounts of the assets and liabilities of Pedigree Travel Agency at December 31, 2008, the end of the current year, and its revenue and expenses for the year. The capital stock was $40,000 and the retained earnings was $75,000 on January 1, 2008, the beginning of the current year. During the current year, dividends of $40,000 were paid.

Accounts payable	$ 12,500	Rent expense	$25,000
Accounts receivable	42,300	Supplies	2,700
Cash	180,000	Supplies expense	2,800
Fees earned	250,000	Utilities expense	18,200
Miscellaneous expense	1,500	Wages expense	65,000

Instructions
1. Prepare an income statement for the current year ended December 31, 2008.
2. Prepare a retained earnings statement for the current year ended December 31, 2008.
3. Prepare a balance sheet as of December 31, 2008.

PR 1-3A
Financial statements

obj. 5

✓ *1. Net income: $23,665*

Barry Kimm established Mariner Financial Services on January 1, 2008. Mariner Financial Services offers financial planning advice to its clients. The effect of each transaction and the balances after each transaction for January are shown at the bottom of the page.

Instructions
1. Prepare an income statement for the month ended January 31, 2008.
2. Prepare a retained earnings statement for the month ended January 31, 2008.
3. Prepare a balance sheet as of January 31, 2008.
4. (Optional). Prepare a statement of cash flows for the month ending January 31, 2008.

	Assets			= Liabilities +				Stockholders' Equity					
	Cash	Accounts + Receivable	+ Supplies =	Accounts Payable	Capital + Stock	− Dividends	Fees + Earned	Salaries − Expense	Rent − Expense	Auto − Expense	Supplies − Expense	Misc. − Expense	
a.	+25,000				+25,000								
b.			+1,180	+1,180									
Bal.	25,000		1,180	1,180	25,000								
c.	− 580			− 580									
Bal.	24,420		1,180	600	25,000								
d.	+42,000						+42,000						
Bal.	66,420		1,180	600	25,000		42,000						
e.	− 7,500								−7,500				
Bal.	58,920		1,180	600	25,000		42,000		−7,500				
f.	− 5,780									−4,500		−1,280	
Bal.	53,140		1,180	600	25,000		42,000		−7,500	−4,500		−1,280	
g.	−15,000							−15,000					
Bal.	38,140		1,180	600	25,000		42,000	−15,000	−7,500	−4,500		−1,280	
h.			− 455								−455		
Bal.	38,140		725	600	25,000		42,000	−15,000	−7,500	−4,500	−455	−1,280	
i.		+10,400					+10,400						
Bal.	38,140	10,400	725	600	25,000		52,400	−15,000	−7,500	−4,500	−455	−1,280	
j.	− 9,000					−9,000							
Bal.	29,140	10,400	725 =	600	25,000	−9,000	52,400	−15,000	−7,500	−4,500	−455	−1,280	

PR 1-4A

Transactions; financial statements

objs. **4, 5**

✓ *2. Net income: $16,850*

On March 1, 2008, Ginny Tyler established Seltzer Realty. Ginny completed the following transactions during the month of March:

a. Opened a business bank account with a deposit of $30,000 in exchange for capital stock.
b. Purchased supplies (pens, file folders, paper, etc.) on account, $2,650.
c. Paid creditor on account, $1,500.
d. Earned sales commissions, receiving cash, $36,750.
e. Paid rent on office and equipment for the month, $5,200.
f. Paid dividends of $8,000.
g. Paid automobile expenses (including rental charge) for month, $2,500, and miscellaneous expenses, $1,200.
h. Paid office salaries, $9,250.
i. Determined that the cost of supplies on hand was $900; therefore, the cost of supplies used was $1,750.

Instructions

1. Indicate the effect of each transaction and the balances after each transaction, using the following tabular headings:

Assets		=	Liabilities	+				Stockholders' Equity					
Cash	+ Supplies	=	Accounts Payable	+	Capital Stock	− Dividends	+ Sales Commissions	− Office Salaries Expense	− Rent Expense	− Auto Expense	− Supplies Expense	− Misc. Expense

2. Prepare an income statement for March, a retained earnings statement for March, and a balance sheet as of March 31.

PR 1-5A

Transactions; financial statements

objs. **4, 5**

✓ *3. Net income: $9,445*

Argon Dry Cleaners is owned and operated by Kerry Ulman. A building and equipment are currently being rented, pending expansion to new facilities. The actual work of dry cleaning is done by another company at wholesale rates. The assets and the liabilities of the business on July 1, 2008, are as follows: Cash, $8,500; Accounts Receivable, $15,500; Supplies, $1,600; Land, $18,000; Accounts Payable, $5,200; Capital Stock, $15,000. Business transactions during July are summarized as follows:

a. Kerry Ulman invested additional cash in the business with a deposit of $30,000 in exchange for capital stock.
b. Paid $22,000 for the purchase of land as a future building site.
c. Received cash from cash customers for dry cleaning sales, $17,900.
d. Paid rent for the month, $3,000.
e. Purchased supplies on account, $1,550.
f. Paid creditors on account, $4,950.
g. Charged customers for dry cleaning sales on account, $12,350.
h. Received monthly invoice for dry cleaning expense for July (to be paid on August 10), $7,880.
i. Paid the following: wages expense, $5,100; truck expense, $1,200; utilities expense, $800; miscellaneous expense, $950.
j. Received cash from customers on account, $13,200.
k. Determined that the cost of supplies on hand was $1,275; therefore, the cost of supplies used during the month was $1,875.
l. Paid dividends of $5,000.

Instructions

1. Determine the amount of retained earnings as of July 1 of the current year.
2. State the assets, liabilities, and stockholders' equity as of July 1 in equation form similar to that shown in this chapter. In tabular form below the equation, indicate increases and decreases resulting from each transaction and the new balances after each transaction.
3. Prepare an income statement for July, a retained earnings statement for July, and a balance sheet as of July 31.
4. (Optional). Prepare a statement of cash flows for July.

	Assets			= Liabilities +		Stockholders' Equity						
	Cash	+ Accounts Receivable	+ Supplies =	Accounts Payable	+ Capital Stock	− Dividends +	Fees Earned	− Salaries Expense	− Rent Expense	− Auto Expense	− Supplies Expense	− Misc. Expense
a.	+25,000				+25,000							
b.			+3,600	+3,600								
Bal.	25,000		3,600	3,600	25,000							
c.	+22,500						+22,500					
Bal.	47,500		3,600	3,600	25,000		22,500					
d.	− 9,000								−9,000			
Bal.	38,500		3,600	3,600	25,000		22,500		−9,000			
e.	− 1,250			−1,250								
Bal.	37,250		3,600	2,350	25,000		22,500		−9,000			
f.		+18,750					+18,750					
Bal.	37,250	18,750	3,600	2,350	25,000		41,250		−9,000			
g.	− 5,750									−3,875		−1,875
Bal.	31,500	18,750	3,600	2,350	25,000		41,250		−9,000	−3,875		−1,875
h.	−10,000							−10,000				
Bal.	21,500	18,750	3,600	2,350	25,000		41,250	−10,000	−9,000	−3,875		−1,875
i.			−1,625								−1,625	
Bal.	21,500	18,750	1,975	2,350	25,000		41,250	−10,000	−9,000	−3,875	−1,625	−1,875
j.	− 5,000					−5,000						
Bal.	16,500	18,750	1,975 =	2,350	25,000	−5,000	41,250	−10,000	−9,000	−3,875	−1,625	−1,875

PR 1-4B
Transactions; financial statements
objs. 4, 5

✓ *2. Net income: $12,990*

On April 1, 2008, Britt Quinn established Uptown Realty. Britt completed the following transactions during the month of April:

a. Opened a business bank account with a deposit of $30,000 in exchange for capital stock.
b. Paid rent on office and equipment for the month, $2,200.
c. Paid automobile expenses (including rental charge) for month, $1,200, and miscellaneous expenses, $650.
d. Purchased supplies (pens, file folders, and copy paper) on account, $200.
e. Earned sales commissions, receiving cash, $20,800.
f. Paid creditor on account, $150.
g. Paid office salaries, $3,600.
h. Paid dividends of $1,500.
i. Determined that the cost of supplies on hand was $40; therefore, the cost of supplies used was $160.

Instructions

1. Indicate the effect of each transaction and the balances after each transaction, using the following tabular headings:

	Assets		= Liabilities +		Stockholders' Equity						
	Cash	+ Supplies =	Accounts Payable	+ Capital Stock	− Dividends +	Sales Commissions	− Office Salaries Expense	− Rent Expense	− Auto Expense	− Supplies Expense	− Misc. Expense

2. Prepare an income statement for April, a retained earnings statement for April, and a balance sheet as of April 30.

PR 1-5B
Transactions; financial statements
objs. 4, 5

✓ *3. Net income: $2,320*

Skivvy Dry Cleaners is owned and operated by Jean Potts. A building and equipment are currently being rented, pending expansion to new facilities. The actual work of dry cleaning is done by another company at wholesale rates. The assets and the liabilities of the business on November 1, 2008, are as follows: Cash, $17,200; Accounts Receivable, $19,000; Supplies, $3,750; Land, $30,000; Accounts Payable, $8,200; Capital Stock, $25,000. Business transactions during November are summarized as follows:

a. Jean Potts invested additional cash in the business with a deposit of $50,000 in exchange for capital stock.

b. Purchased land for use as a parking lot, paying cash of $45,000.

c. Paid rent for the month, $4,500.

d. Charged customers for dry cleaning sales on account, $15,250.

e. Paid creditors on account, $5,800.

f. Purchased supplies on account, $3,200.

g. Received cash from cash customers for dry cleaning sales, $22,900.

h. Received cash from customers on account, $17,250.

i. Received monthly invoice for dry cleaning expense for November (to be paid on December 10), $16,380.

j. Paid the following: wages expense, $6,200; truck expense, $1,875; utilities expense, $1,575; miscellaneous expense, $850.

k. Determined that the cost of supplies on hand was $2,500; therefore, the cost of supplies used during the month was $4,450.

l. Paid dividends of $6,000.

Instructions

1. Determine the amount of retained earnings as of November 1.
2. State the assets, liabilities, and stockholders' equity as of November 1 in equation form similar to that shown in this chapter. In tabular form below the equation, indicate increases and decreases resulting from each transaction and the new balances after each transaction.
3. Prepare an income statement for November, a retained earnings statement for November, and a balance sheet as of November 30.
4. (Optional). Prepare a statement of cash flows for November.

PR 1-6B
Missing amounts from financial statements

obj. 5

✓ i. $62,100

The financial statements at the end of Harp Realty's first month of operations are shown below and on the next page.

Harp Realty
Income Statement
For the Month Ended April 30, 2008

Fees earned		$28,200
Expenses:		
Wages expense	$ (a)	
Rent expense	2,880	
Supplies expense	2,400	
Utilities expense	1,620	
Miscellaneous expense	990	
Total expenses		14,340
Net income		(b)

Harp Realty
Retained Earnings Statement
For the Month Ended April 30, 2008

Retained earnings, April 1, 2008		$ (c)
Net income for April	$ (d)	
Less dividends	(e)	
Increase in retained earnings		(f)
Retained earnings, April 30, 2008		(g)

Harp Realty
Balance Sheet
April 30, 2008

Assets			Liabilities		
Cash	$17,700		Accounts payable		$1,440
Supplies	1,200		**Stockholders' Equity**		
Land	(h)		Capital stock	$ (j)	
			Retained earnings	6,660	
			Total stockholders' equity		(k)
			Total liabilities and		
Total assets	(i)		stockholders' equity		(l)

Harp Realty
Statement of Cash Flows
For the Month Ended April 30, 2008

Cash flows from operating activities:		
Cash received from customers	$ (m)	
Deduct cash payments for expenses and		
payments to creditors	14,100	
Net cash flow from operating activities		$ (n)
Cash flows from investing activities:		
Cash payments for acquisition of land		(43,200)
Cash flows from financing activities:		
Cash received from issuing capital stock	$54,000	
Deduct cash dividends	7,200	
Net cash flow from financing activities		(o)
Net cash flow and April 30, 2008, cash balance		(p)

Instructions

By analyzing the interrelationships among the four financial statements, determine the proper amounts for (a) through (p).

Continuing Problem

✓ 2. Net income: $730

Kris Payne enjoys listening to all types of music and owns countless CDs and tapes. Over the years, Kris has gained a local reputation for knowledge of music from classical to rap and the ability to put together sets of recordings that appeal to all ages.

During the last several months, Kris served as a guest disc jockey on a local radio station. In addition, Kris has entertained at several friends' parties as the host deejay.

On April 1, 2008, Kris established a corporation known as Dancin Music. Using an extensive collection of CDs and tapes, Kris will serve as a disc jockey on a fee basis for weddings, college parties, and other events. During April, Kris entered into the following transactions:

April 1. Deposited $10,000 in a checking account in the name of Dancin Music in exchange for capital stock.

2. Received $2,500 from a local radio station for serving as the guest disc jockey for April.

2. Agreed to share office space with a local real estate agency, Cash Realty. Dancin Music will pay one-fourth of the rent. In addition, Dancin Music agreed to pay a portion of the salary of the receptionist and to pay one-fourth of the utilities. Paid $1,000 for the rent of the office.

4. Purchased supplies (blank CDs, poster board, extension cords, etc.) from Richt Office Supply Co. for $350. Agreed to pay $100 within 10 days and the remainder by May 3, 2008.

6. Paid $750 to a local radio station to advertise the services of Dancin Music twice daily for two weeks.

8. Paid $800 to a local electronics store for renting digital recording equipment.

12. Paid $300 (music expense) to Rocket Music for the use of its current music demos to make various music sets.

13. Paid Richt Office Supply Co. $100 on account.

16. Received $350 from a dentist for providing two music sets for the dentist to play for her patients.

22. Served as disc jockey for a wedding party. The father of the bride agreed to pay $1,350 the 1st of May.

25. Received $500 from a friend for serving as the disc jockey for a cancer charity ball hosted by the local hospital.

29. Paid $240 (music expense) to Score Music for the use of its library of music demos.

(continued)

April 30. Received $1,000 for serving as disc jockey for a local club's monthly dance.
    30. Paid Cash Realty $400 for Dancin Music's share of the receptionist's salary for April.
    30. Paid Cash Realty $350 for Dancin Music's share of the utilities for April.
    30. Determined that the cost of supplies on hand is $170. Therefore, the cost of supplies used during the month was $180.
    30. Paid for miscellaneous expenses, $150.
    30. Paid $800 royalties (music expense) to Federated Clearing for use of various artists' music during the month.
    30. Paid dividends of $300.

Instructions

1. Indicate the effect of each transaction and the balances after each transaction, using the following tabular headings:

Assets			=	Liabilities +					Stockholders' Equity							
Cash	+ Accounts Receivable	+ Supplies	=	Accounts Payable	+ Capital Stock	− Dividends	+ Fees Earned	− Music Expense	− Office Rent Expense	− Equipment Rent Expense	− Advertising Expense	− Wages Expense	− Utilities Expense	− Supplies Expense	− Misc. Expense

2. Prepare an income statement for Dancin Music for the month ended April 30, 2008.
3. Prepare a retained earnings statement for Dancin Music for the month ended April 30, 2008.
4. Prepare a balance sheet for Dancin Music as of April 30, 2008.

Special Activities

SA 1-1
Ethics and professional conduct in business

Group Project

ETHICS

Chester Hunter, president of Jackrabbit Enterprises, applied for a $250,000 loan from Belgrade National Bank. The bank requested financial statements from Jackrabbit Enterprises as a basis for granting the loan. Chester has told his accountant to provide the bank with a balance sheet. Chester has decided to omit the other financial statements because there was a net loss during the past year.

In groups of three or four, discuss the following questions:

1. Is Chester behaving in a professional manner by omitting some of the financial statements?
2. a. What types of information about their businesses would owners be willing to provide bankers? What types of information would owners not be willing to provide?
   b. What types of information about a business would bankers want before extending a loan?
   c. What common interests are shared by bankers and business owners?

SA 1-2
Net income

On July 7, 2007, Dr. Jennifer Dejong established Second Opinion, a medical practice organized as a professional corporation. The following conversation occurred in January between Dr. Dejong and a former medical school classmate, Dr. James Tomlin, at an American Medical Association convention in Paris.

Dr. Tomlin: Jennifer, good to see you again. Why didn't you call when you were in Chicago? We could have had dinner together.

Dr. Dejong: Actually, I never made it to Chicago this year. My husband and kids went up to our Aspen condo twice, but I got stuck in Boston. I opened a new consulting practice this July and haven't had any time for myself since.

Dr. Tomlin: I heard about it . . . Second . . . something . . . right?

Dr. Dejong: Yes, Second Opinion. My husband chose the name.

Dr. Tomlin: I've thought about doing something like that. Are you making any money? I mean, is it worth your time?

Dr. Dejong: You wouldn't believe it. I started by opening a bank account with $50,000, and my December bank statement has a balance of $140,000. Not bad for six months—all pure profit.

Dr. Tomlin: Maybe I'll try it in Chicago! Let's have breakfast together tomorrow and you can fill me in on the details.

~~~~▶ Comment on Dr. Dejong's statement that the difference between the opening bank balance ($50,000) and the December statement balance ($140,000) is pure profit.

SA 1-3
Transactions and financial statements

Kathy Hoss, a junior in college, has been seeking ways to earn extra spending money. As an active sports enthusiast, Kathy plays tennis regularly at the Racquet Club, where her family has a membership. The president of the club recently approached Kathy with the proposal that she manage the club's tennis courts. Kathy's primary duty would be to supervise the operation of the club's four indoor and six outdoor courts, including court reservations.

In return for her services, the club would pay Kathy $150 per week, plus Kathy could keep whatever she earned from lessons and the fees from the use of the ball machine. The club and Kathy agreed to a one-month trial, after which both would consider an arrangement for the remaining two years of Kathy's college career. On this basis, Kathy organized Advantage as a proprietorship.

Small businesses such as Advantage are often organized as proprietorships. The accounting for proprietorships is similar to that for a corporation, except for owner's equity. Instead of Capital Stock and Retained Earnings, an item entitled Kathy Hoss, Capital, is used to indicate owner's equity in the accounting equation. Withdrawals for personal use are handled similarly to dividends.

During June 2007, Kathy managed the tennis courts and entered into the following transactions:

a. Opened a business account by depositing $1,500.
b. Paid $250 for tennis supplies (practice tennis balls, etc.).
c. Paid $160 for the rental of videotape equipment to be used in offering lessons during June.
d. Arranged for the rental of two ball machines during June for $200. Paid $140 in advance, with the remaining $60 due July 1.
e. Received $1,600 for lessons given during June.
f. Received $350 in fees from the use of the ball machines during June.
g. Paid $600 for salaries of part-time employees who answered the telephone and took reservations while Kathy was giving lessons.
h. Paid $150 for miscellaneous expenses.
i. Received $600 from the club for managing the tennis courts during June.
j. Determined that the cost of supplies on hand at the end of the month totaled $150; therefore, the cost of supplies used was $100.
k. Withdrew $500 for personal use on June 30.

As a friend and accounting student, you have been asked by Kathy to aid her in assessing the venture.

1. Indicate the effect of each transaction and the balances after each transaction, using the following tabular headings:

Assets		= Liabilities +		Owner's Equity					
Cash + Supplies =		Accounts Payable +	Kathy Hoss, Capital –	Kathy Hoss, Drawing +	Service Revenue –	Salary Expense –	Rent Expense –	Supplies Expense –	Misc. Expense

2. Prepare an income statement for June.
3. Prepare a statement of owner's equity for June.
4. Prepare a balance sheet as of June 30.
5. a. Assume that Kathy Hoss could earn $8 per hour working 30 hours a week as a waitress. Evaluate which of the two alternatives, working as a waitress or operating Advantage, would provide Kathy with the most income per month.
   b. ~~~~▶ Discuss any other factors that you believe Kathy should consider before discussing a long-term arrangement with the Racquet Club.

SA 1-4
Certification requirements for accountants

By satisfying certain specific requirements, accountants may become certified as public accountants (CPAs), management accountants (CMAs), or internal auditors (CIAs). Find the certification requirements for one of these accounting groups by accessing the appropriate Internet site listed at the top of the following page.

Internet Project

Site	Description
http://www.ais-cpa.com	This site lists the address and/or Internet link for each state's board of accountancy. Find your state's requirements.
http://www.imanet.org	This site lists the requirements for becoming a CMA.
http://www.theiia.org	This site lists the requirements for becoming a CIA.

SA 1-5
Cash flows

Amazon.com, an Internet retailer, was incorporated and began operation in the mid-90s. On the statement of cash flows, would you expect Amazon.com's net cash flows from operating, investing, and financing activities to be positive or negative for its first three years of operations? Use the following format for your answers, and briefly explain your logic.

	First Year	Second Year	Third Year
Net cash flow from operating activities	negative		
Net cash flow from investing activities			
Net cash flow from financing activities			

SA 1-6
Financial analysis of Enron Corporation

Internet Project

The now defunct Enron Corporation, once headquartered in Houston, Texas, provided products and services for natural gas, electricity, and communications to wholesale and retail customers. Enron's operations were conducted through a variety of subsidiaries and affiliates that involved transporting gas through pipelines, transmitting electricity, and managing energy commodities. The following data were taken from Enron's financial statements:

	In millions
Total revenues	$100,789
Total costs and expenses	98,836
Operating income	1,953
Net income	979
Total assets	65,503
Total liabilities	54,033
Total stockholders' equity	11,470
Net cash flow from operating activities	4,779
Net cash flow from investing activities	(4,264)
Net cash flow from financing activities	571
Net increase in cash	1,086

The market price of Enron's stock was approximately $83 per share when the prior financial statement data were taken. However, eventually Enron's stock was selling for $0.22 per share. ▸ Review the preceding financial statement data and search the Internet for articles on Enron Corporation. Briefly explain why Enron's stock dropped so dramatically.

Answers to Self-Examination Questions

1. **D** A corporation, organized in accordance with state or federal statutes, is a separate legal entity in which ownership is divided into shares of stock (answer D). A proprietorship (answer A) is an unincorporated business owned by one individual. A service business (answer B) provides services to its customers. It can be organized as a proprietorship, partnership, corporation, or limited liability company. A partnership (answer C) is an unincorporated business owned by two or more individuals.

2. **A** The resources owned by a business are called assets (answer A). The debts of the business are called liabilities (answer B), and the equity of the owners is called stockholders' equity (answer D). The relationship between assets, liabilities, and owner's equity is expressed as the accounting equation (answer C).

3. **A** The balance sheet is a listing of the assets, liabilities, and stockholders' equity of a business at a specific date (answer A). The income statement (answer B) is a summary of the revenue and expenses of a business for a specific period of time. The retained earnings statement (answer C) summarizes the changes in retained earnings during a specific period of time. The statement of cash flows (answer D) summarizes the cash receipts and cash payments for a specific period of time.

4. **C**   The accounting equation is:

Assets = Liabilities + Owner's Equity

Therefore, if assets increased by $20,000 and liabilities increased by $12,000, owner's equity must have increased by $8,000 (answer C), as indicated in the following computation:

Assets	= Liabilities + Owner's Equity
+$20,000	= +$12,000 + Owner's Equity
+$20,000 − $12,000 =	Owner's Equity
+$8,000	= Owner's Equity

5. **B**   Net income is the excess of revenue over expenses, or $7,500 (answer B). If expenses exceed revenue, the difference is a net loss. Dividends are the opposite of the stockholders' investing in the business and do not affect the amount of net income or net loss.

Analyzing Transactions

© BODYWEDGE 21/PRNEWSFOTO (AP TOPIC GALLERY)

objectives

After studying this chapter, you should be able to:

1 Describe the characteristics of an account and record transactions using a chart of accounts and journal.

2 Describe and illustrate the posting of journal entries to accounts.

3 Prepare an unadjusted trial balance and explain how it can be used to discover errors.

4 Discover and correct errors in recording transactions.

Gold's Gym International, Inc.

You can organize your digital music within your MP3 player or IPod® according to various playlists, according to your favorite songs, genre, artist, or album. Your playlists allow you to quickly retrieve music for listening. Computer files are organized within folders for the same reason. Information, like music or digital files, is organized into categories to simplify retrieval and reporting. In the same way that you organize your digital information, a business also needs to organize its transactions. For example, when you shop at Wal-Mart or Target, or buy groceries at Kroger or SUPERVALU, you enter into a transaction that is processed and recorded by the business. A company such as Gold's Gym, the largest co-ed gym chain in the world, must also process, record, and summarize its transactions. For example, Gold's would want to record all its cash transactions so that they can be summarized as a single category, called "cash." This is much the same way you would summarize the cash transactions in the check register of your checkbook.

In Chapter 1, we analyzed and recorded this kind of information by using the accounting equation, Assets = Liabilities + Stockholders' Equity. However, such a format is not practical for most businesses, and in this chapter we will study more efficient methods of recording transactions. We will conclude this chapter by discussing how accounting errors may occur and how they may be detected and corrected by the accounting process.

Using Accounts to Record Transactions

objective **1**

Describe the characteristics of an account and record transactions using a chart of accounts and journal.

In Chapter 1, we recorded the November transactions for NetSolutions using the accounting equation format shown in Exhibit 1. However, this format is not efficient or practical for companies that have to record and summarize thousands or millions of transactions daily. As a result, accounting systems are designed to show the increases and decreases in each financial statement item as a separate record. This record is called an **account**.

To illustrate, the Cash column of Exhibit 1 records the increases and decreases in cash. Likewise, the other columns in Exhibit 1 record the increases and decreases in Supplies; Land; Accounts Payable; Capital Stock; Dividends; Fees Earned; Wages Expense; Rent Expense; Supplies Expense; Utilities Expense; and Miscellaneous Expense. As we illustrate next, each of these columns can be organized into a separate account that more efficiently records and summarizes transactions.

An account, in its simplest form, has three parts. First, each account has a title, which is the name of the item recorded in the account. Second, each account has a space for recording increases in the amount of the item. Third, each account has a space for recording decreases in the amount of the item. The account form presented below is called a **T account** because it resembles the letter T. The left side of the account is called the *debit* side, and the right side is called the *credit* side.[1]

Title	
Left side *debit*	Right side *credit*

---

[1] The terms *debit* and *credit* are derived from the Latin *debere* and *credere*.

EXHIBIT 1   NetSolutions November Transactions   @netsolutions

	Cash	+ Supp.	+ Land	= Accounts Payable	+ Capital Stock	− Dividends	+ Fees Earned	− Wages Exp.	− Rent Exp.	− Supplies Exp.	− Utilities Exp.	− Misc. Exp.
a.	+25,000				+25,000							
b.	−20,000		+20,000									
Bal.	5,000		20,000		25,000							
c.		+1,350		+1,350								
Bal.	5,000	1,350	20,000	1,350	25,000							
d.	+ 7,500						+7,500					
Bal.	12,500	1,350	20,000	1,350	25,000		7,500					
e.	− 3,650							−2,125	−800		−450	−275
Bal.	8,850	1,350	20,000	1,350	25,000		7,500	−2,125	−800		−450	−275
f.	− 950			− 950								
Bal.	7,900	1,350	20,000	400	25,000		7,500	−2,125	−800		−450	−275
g.		− 800								−800		
Bal.	7,900	550	20,000	400	25,000		7,500	−2,125	−800	−800	−450	−275
h.	− 2,000					−2,000						
Bal.	5,900	550	20,000 =	400	25,000	−2,000	7,500	−2,125	−800	−800	−450	−275

> Amounts entered on the left side of an account are debits, and amounts entered on the right side of an account are credits.

Amounts entered on the left side of an account, regardless of the account title, are called **debits** to the account. When debits are entered in an account, the account is said to be *debited*. Amounts entered on the right side of an account are called **credits**, and the account is said to be *credited*. Debits and credits are sometimes abbreviated as *Dr.* and *Cr.*

The cash account shown below illustrates how NetSolutions' November cash transactions shown in the first column of Exhibit 1 would be recorded in an account. Transactions involving receipts of cash are listed on the debit side of the account. For example, the receipt of $25,000 from Chris Clark in transaction (a) is entered on the debit side of the account. The letter or date of the transaction is also entered into the account. This is done so that if any questions later arise related to the entry, the entry can be traced back to the underlying transaction data. The transactions involving cash payments are listed on the credit side. For example, the payment of $20,000 to purchase land in transaction (b) is entered on the credit side of the account.

If at any time the total of the cash receipts is needed, the entries on the debit side of the account may be added. For NetSolutions, the total receipts is $32,500 ($25,000 + $7,500). Likewise, the total cash payments of $26,600 ($20,000 + $3,650 + $950 + $2,000) may be determined by adding the entries on the credit side of the account. Subtracting the smaller sum from the larger, $32,500 − $26,600, identifies the amount of cash on hand, $5,900. This amount is called the **balance of the account** and is inserted in the

Many times when accountants analyze complex transactions, they use T accounts to simplify the thought process. In the same way, you will find T accounts a useful device in this and later accounting courses.

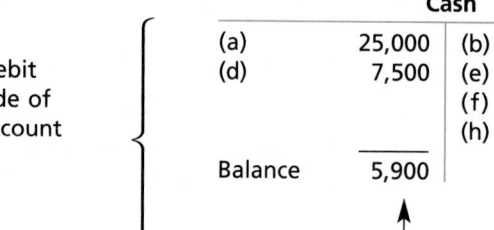

Cash

Debit side of account	(a)	25,000	(b)	20,000
	(d)	7,500	(e)	3,650
			(f)	950
			(h)	2,000
Balance		5,900		

Credit side of account

Balance of account

account in the debit column. In this way, the balance is identified as a debit balance.[2] This balance is reported on the balance sheet for NetSolutions as of November 30, 2007, shown in Exhibit 6 of Chapter 1. Each of the columns in Exhibit 1 can be converted into an account form in a similar manner as was done for the cash column of Exhibit 1. We illustrate each of these accounts later in this chapter.

CHART OF ACCOUNTS

A group of accounts for a business entity is called a **ledger**. A list of the accounts in the ledger is called a **chart of accounts**. The accounts are normally listed in the order in which they appear in the financial statements. The balance sheet accounts are usually listed first, in the order of assets, liabilities, and stockholders' equity. The income statement accounts are then listed in the order of revenues and expenses. Each of these major account classifications is briefly described below.

Assets are resources owned by the business entity. These resources can be physical items, such as cash and supplies, or intangibles that have value, such as patent rights. Some other examples of assets include accounts receivable, prepaid expenses (such as insurance), buildings, equipment, and land.

Liabilities are debts owed to outsiders (creditors). Liabilities are often identified on the balance sheet by titles that include the word *payable*. Examples of liabilities include accounts payable, notes payable, and wages payable. Cash received before services are delivered creates a liability to perform the services. These future service commitments are often called *unearned revenues*. Examples of unearned revenues are magazine subscriptions received by a publisher and tuition received by a college at the beginning of a term.

Stockholders' equity is the stockholders' right to the assets of the business. Stockholders' equity is represented by the balance of the capital stock and retained earnings accounts. A **dividends** account represents distributions of earnings to stockholders.

Revenues are increases in stockholders' equity (retained earnings) as a result of selling services or products to customers. Examples of revenues include fees earned, fares earned, commissions revenue, and rent revenue.

Expenses result from using up assets or consuming services in the process of generating revenues. Examples of typical expenses include wages expense, rent expense, utilities expense, supplies expense, and miscellaneous expense.

A chart of accounts is designed to meet the information needs of a company's managers and other users of its financial statements. The accounts within the chart of accounts are numbered for use as references. A flexible numbering system is normally used so that new accounts can be added without affecting other account numbers.

Exhibit 2 is NetSolutions' chart of accounts that we will be using in this chapter. Additional accounts will be introduced in later chapters. In Exhibit 2, each account number has two digits. The first digit indicates the major classification of the ledger in which the account is located. Accounts beginning with 1 represent assets; 2, liabilities; 3, stockholders' equity; 4, revenue; and 5, expenses. The second digit indicates the location of the account within its class. You should note that each of the columns in Exhibit 1 has been assigned an account number in the chart of accounts shown in Exhibit 2. In addition, we have added accounts for Accounts Receivable, Prepaid Insurance, Office Equipment, Unearned Rent, and Retained Earnings. These accounts will be used in recording NetSolutions' December transactions.

ANALYZING AND SUMMARIZING TRANSACTIONS IN ACCOUNTS

Every business transaction affects at least two accounts. To illustrate how transactions are analyzed and summarized in accounts, we will use the NetSolutions transactions from Chapter 1, with dates added. First, we illustrate how transactions (a), (b), (c), and

REAL WORLD

Procter & Gamble's account numbers have over 30 digits to reflect P&G's many different operations and regions.

---

2 The totals of the debit and credit columns may be shown separately in an account. When this is done, these amounts should be identified in some way so that they are not mistaken for entries or the ending balance of the account.

EXHIBIT 2   Analysis and Recording of Transactions Using Accounts

Balance Sheet Accounts	Income Statement Accounts
1. Assets	**4. Revenue**
11 Cash	41 Fees Earned
12 Accounts Receivable	**5. Expenses**
14 Supplies	51 Wages Expense
15 Prepaid Insurance	52 Rent Expense
17 Land	54 Utilities Expense
18 Office Equipment	55 Supplies Expense
2. Liabilities	59 Miscellaneous Expense
21 Accounts Payable	
23 Unearned Rent	
3. Stockholders' Equity	
31 Capital Stock	
32 Retained Earnings	
33 Dividends	

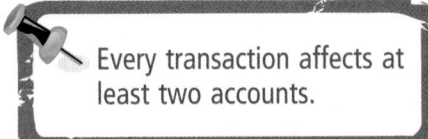

Every transaction affects at least two accounts.

(f) are analyzed and summarized in balance sheet accounts (assets, liabilities, and stockholders' equity). Next, we illustrate how transactions (d), (e), and (g) are analyzed and summarized in income statement accounts (revenues and expenses). Finally, we illustrate how the payment of dividends, transaction (h), is analyzed and summarized in the accounts.

Balance Sheet Accounts Chris Clark's first transaction, (a), was to deposit $25,000 in a bank account in the name of NetSolutions in exchange for capital stock. The effect of this November 1 transaction on the balance sheet is to increase assets and stockholders' equity, as shown below.

November 1 Transaction

NetSolutions Balance Sheet November 1, 2007			
Assets		**Stockholders' Equity**	
Cash	$25 0 0 0 00	Capital stock	$25 0 0 0 00

This transaction is initially entered in a record called a **journal**. The title of the account to be debited is listed first, followed by the amount to be debited. The title of the account to be credited is listed below and to the right of the debit, followed by the amount to be credited. This process of recording a transaction in the journal is called **journalizing**. This form of recording a transaction is called a **journal entry**.

The journal entry for transaction (a) is shown below.

		JOURNAL			Page 1	
	Date	**Description**	**Post. Ref.**	**Debit**	**Credit**	
1	2007 Nov. 1	Cash		25 0 0 0 00		1
2		Capital Stock			25 0 0 0 00	2
3		Issued capital stock for cash.				3

REAL WORLD

A journal can be thought of as being similar to an individual's diary of significant day-to-day life events.

The increase in the asset (Cash), which is reported on the left side of the balance sheet, is debited to the cash account. The increase in stockholders' equity, which is reported on the right side of the balance sheet, is credited to the capital stock account. As other assets are acquired, the increases are also recorded as debits to asset accounts. Likewise, other increases in stockholders' equity will be recorded as credits to stockholders' equity accounts.

The effects of this transaction are shown in the accounts by transferring the amount and date of the journal entry to the left (debit) side of Cash and to the right (credit) side of Capital Stock as follows:

Cash		Capital Stock	
Nov. 1	25,000	Nov. 1	25,000

November 5 Transaction

On November 5 [transaction (b)], NetSolutions bought land for $20,000, paying cash. This transaction increases one asset account and decreases another. It is entered in the journal as a $20,000 increase (debit) to Land and a $20,000 decrease (credit) to Cash, as shown below.

4				4
5	5	Land	20 0 0 0 00	5
6		Cash		20 0 0 0 00 6
7		Purchased land for building site.		7

The effect of this entry is shown in the accounts of NetSolutions as follows:

Cash		Land		Capital Stock	
Nov. 1 25,000	Nov. 5 20,000	Nov. 5 20,000			Nov. 1 25,000

November 10 Transaction

On November 10 [transaction (c)], NetSolutions purchased supplies on account for $1,350. This transaction increases an asset account and increases a liability account. It is entered in the journal as a $1,350 increase (debit) to Supplies and a $1,350 increase (credit) to Accounts Payable, as shown below. To simplify the illustration, the effect of entry (c) and the remaining journal entries for NetSolutions will be shown in the accounts later.

8				8
9	10	Supplies	1 3 5 0 00	9
10		Accounts Payable		1 3 5 0 00 10
11		Purchased supplies on account.		11

November 30 Transaction

On November 30 [transaction (f)], NetSolutions paid creditors on account, $950. This transaction decreases a liability account and decreases an asset account. It is entered in the journal as a $950 decrease (debit) to Accounts Payable and a $950 decrease (credit) to Cash, as shown below.

23				23
24	30	Accounts Payable	9 5 0 00	24
25		Cash		9 5 0 00 25
26		Paid creditors on account.		26

> The left side of all accounts is the debit side, and the right side is the credit side.

In the preceding examples, you should observe that the left side of asset accounts is used for recording increases, and the right side is used for recording decreases. Also, the right side of liability and stockholders' equity accounts is used to record increases, and the left side of such accounts is used to record decreases. The left side of all accounts, whether asset, liability, or stockholders' equity, is the debit side, and the right side is the credit side. Thus, a debit may be either an increase or a decrease, depending on the account affected. Likewise, a credit may be either an increase or a decrease, depending on the account.

The general rules of debit and credit for balance sheet accounts may be stated as follows:

	Debit	Credit
Asset accounts	Increase (+)	Decrease (−)
Liability accounts	Decrease (−)	Increase (+)
Stockholders' equity accounts	Decrease (−)	Increase (+)

The rules of debit and credit may also be stated in relationship to the accounting equation, as shown below. The side of the account for recording increases is shown in green.

Balance Sheet Accounts

ASSETS		LIABILITIES		STOCKHOLDERS' EQUITY	
Asset Accounts	=	Liability Accounts	+	Stockholders' Equity Accounts	
Debit for increases(+)	Credit for decreases(−)	Debit for decreases(−)	Credit for increases(+)	Debit for decreases(−)	Credit for increases(+)

Example Exercise 2-1   objective **1**

Prepare a journal entry for the purchase of a truck on June 3 for $42,500, paying $8,500 cash and the remainder on account.

Follow My Example 2-1

June 3	Truck	42,500	
	Cash		8,500
	Accounts Payable		34,000

For Practice: PE 2-1A, PE 2-1B

Income Statement Accounts   The analysis of revenue and expense transactions focuses on how each transaction affects stockholders' equity (retained earnings). Just as increases in capital stock are recorded as credits, so, too, are increases in retained earnings. Because revenue transactions increase retained earnings, increases in revenues are recorded as credits. Similarly, because expense transactions decrease retained earnings, increases in expenses are recorded as debits.

November 18 Transaction   We will use NetSolutions' transactions (d), (e), and (g) to illustrate the analysis of transactions and the rules of debit and credit for revenue and expense accounts. On November 18 [transaction (d)], NetSolutions received fees of $7,500 from customers for services provided. This transaction increases an asset account and increases a revenue account. It is entered in the journal as a $7,500 increase (debit) to Cash and a $7,500 increase (credit) to Fees Earned, as shown below [transaction (d)].

12					12
13	18	Cash	7 5 0 0 00		13
14		Fees Earned		7 5 0 0 00	14
15		Received fees from customers.			15

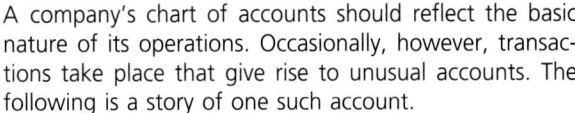

Business Connections

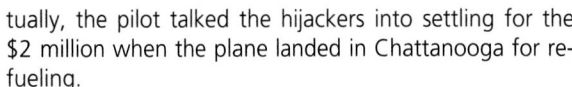

THE HIJACKING RECEIVABLE

A company's chart of accounts should reflect the basic nature of its operations. Occasionally, however, transactions take place that give rise to unusual accounts. The following is a story of one such account.

During the early 1970s, before strict airport security was implemented across the United States, several airlines experienced hijacking incidents. One such incident occurred on November 10, 1972, when a Southern Airways DC-9 en route from Memphis to Miami was hijacked during a stopover in Birmingham, Alabama. The three hijackers boarded the plane in Birmingham armed with handguns and hand grenades. At gunpoint, the hijackers took the plane, the plane's crew of four, and 27 passengers to nine American cities, Toronto, and eventually to Havana, Cuba.

During the long flight, the hijackers threatened to crash the plane into the Oak Ridge, Tennessee, nuclear facilities, insisted on talking with President Nixon, and demanded a ransom of $10 million. Southern Airways, however, was only able to come up with $2 million. Even-

tually, the pilot talked the hijackers into settling for the $2 million when the plane landed in Chattanooga for refueling.

Upon landing in Havana, the Cuban authorities arrested the hijackers and, after a brief delay, sent the plane, passengers, and crew back to the United States. The hijackers and $2 million stayed in Cuba.

How did Southern Airways account for and report the hijacking payment in its subsequent financial statements? As you might have analyzed, the initial entry credited Cash for $2 million. The debit was to an account entitled "Hijacking Payment." This account was reported as a type of receivable under "other assets" on Southern's balance sheet. The company maintained that it would be able to collect the cash from the Cuban government and that, therefore, a receivable existed. In fact, in August 1975, Southern Airways was repaid $2 million by the Cuban government, which was, at that time, attempting to improve relations with the United States.

November 30 Transaction Throughout the month, NetSolutions incurred the following expenses: wages, $2,125; rent, $800; utilities, $450; and miscellaneous, $275. To simplify the illustration, the entry to journalize the payment of these expenses is recorded on November 30 [transaction (e)], as shown below. This transaction increases various expense accounts and decreases an asset account.

16					16
17	30	Wages Expense	2 1 2 5 00		17
18		Rent Expense	8 0 0 00		18
19		Utilities Expense	4 5 0 00		19
20		Miscellaneous Expense	2 7 5 00		20
21		Cash		3 6 5 0 00	21
22		Paid expenses.			22

You should note that regardless of the number of accounts, the sum of the debits is always equal to the sum of the credits in a journal entry.

November 30 Transaction On November 30, NetSolutions recorded the amount of supplies used in the operations during the month [transaction (g)]. This transaction increases an expense account and decreases an asset account. The journal entry for transaction (g) is shown below.

27					27
28	30	Supplies Expense	8 0 0 00		28
29		Supplies		8 0 0 00	29
30		Supplies used during November.			30

The general rules of debit and credit for analyzing transactions affecting income statement accounts are stated as shown at the top of the following page.

	Debit	Credit
Revenue accounts	Decrease (−)	Increase (+)
Expense accounts	Increase (+)	Decrease (−)

The rules of debit and credit for income statement accounts may also be summarized in relationship to the accounting equation, stockholders' equity (retained earnings) accounts, and net income or net loss as shown below.

ASSETS   =   LIABILITIES   +   **STOCKHOLDERS' EQUITY**

Retained Earnings

Debit for decreases(−)	Credit for increases(+)

Income Statement Accounts

Revenue Accounts

Debit for decreases(−)	Credit for increases(+)

Less

Expense Accounts

Debit for increases(+)	Credit for decreases(−)

Equals

Net Income
Revenues exceed expenses
Increases stockholders' equity
(retained earnings)

or

Net Loss
Expenses exceed revenues
Decreases stockholders' equity
(retained earnings)

> The sum of the debits must always equal the sum of the credits.

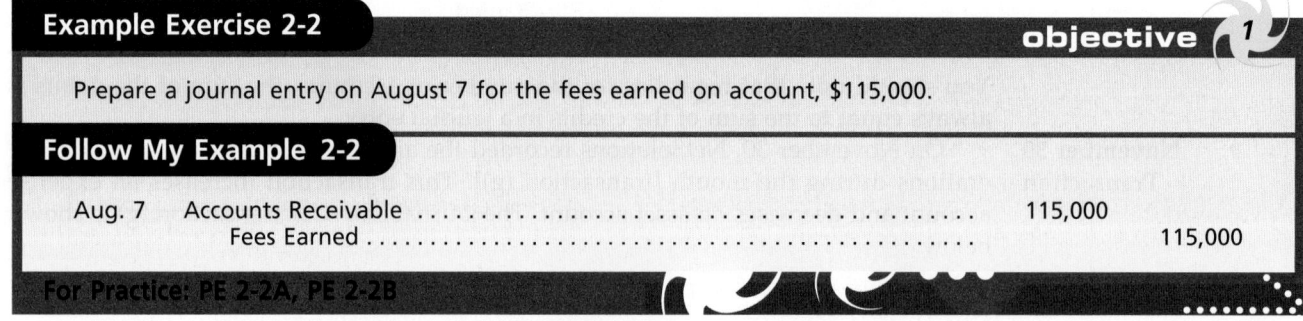

Example Exercise 2-2   objective 1

Prepare a journal entry on August 7 for the fees earned on account, $115,000.

Follow My Example 2-2

| Aug. 7 | Accounts Receivable .... | 115,000 | |
| | Fees Earned .... | | 115,000 |

For Practice: PE 2-2A, PE 2-2B

Dividends Account   Dividends are the distribution of earnings to stockholders. Since earnings (revenues minus expenses) increase retained earnings, the distribution of these earnings to stockholders decreases retained earnings. Because dividend transactions decrease retained earnings, increases in dividends are recorded as debits.

November 30 Transaction   In transaction (h), NetSolutions paid dividends of $2,000. The effect of this transaction is to increase the dividends account and decrease the cash account. The journal entry for transaction (h) is shown on the next page.

	2007					
1	Nov.	30	Dividends	2 0 0 0 00		1
2			Cash		2 0 0 0 00	2
3			Paid dividends to stockholders.			3

Example Exercise 2-3   objective 1

Prepare a journal entry on December 29 for the payment of dividends of $12,000.

Follow My Example 2-3

Dec. 29   Dividends   12,000
                 Cash   12,000

For Practice: PE 2-3A, PE 2-3B

NORMAL BALANCES OF ACCOUNTS

The sum of the increases recorded in an account is usually equal to or greater than the sum of the decreases recorded in the account. For this reason, the normal balances of all accounts are positive rather than negative. For example, the total debits (increases) in an asset account will ordinarily be greater than the total credits (decreases). Thus, asset accounts normally have debit balances.

The rules of debit and credit and the normal balances of the various types of accounts are summarized in Exhibit 3. In Exhibit 3, the side of the account for recording increases and the normal balance is shown in green.

When an account normally having a debit balance actually has a credit balance, or vice versa, an error may have occurred or an unusual situation may exist. For example, a credit balance in the office equipment account could result only from an error. On the other hand, a debit balance in an accounts payable account could result from an overpayment.

Example Exercise 2-4   objective 1

State for each account whether it is likely to have (a) debit entries only, (b) credit entries only, or (c) both debit and credit entries. Also, indicate its normal balance.

1. Dividends
2. Accounts Payable
3. Cash

4. Fees Earned
5. Supplies
6. Utilities Expense

Follow My Example 2-4

1. Debit entries only; normal debit balance
2. Debit and credit entries; normal credit balance
3. Debit and credit entries; normal debit balance

4. Credit entries only; normal credit balance
5. Debit and credit entries; normal debit balance
6. Debit entries only; normal debit balance

For Practice: PE 2-4A, PE 2-4B

Integrity, Objectivity, and Ethics in Business

ETHICS

WILL JOURNALIZING PREVENT FRAUD?

While journalizing transactions reduces the possibility of fraud, it by no means eliminates it. For example, embezzlement can be hidden within the double-entry bookkeeping system by creating fictitious suppliers to whom checks are issued.

EXHIBIT 3 | Rules of Debit and Credit, Normal Balances of Accounts

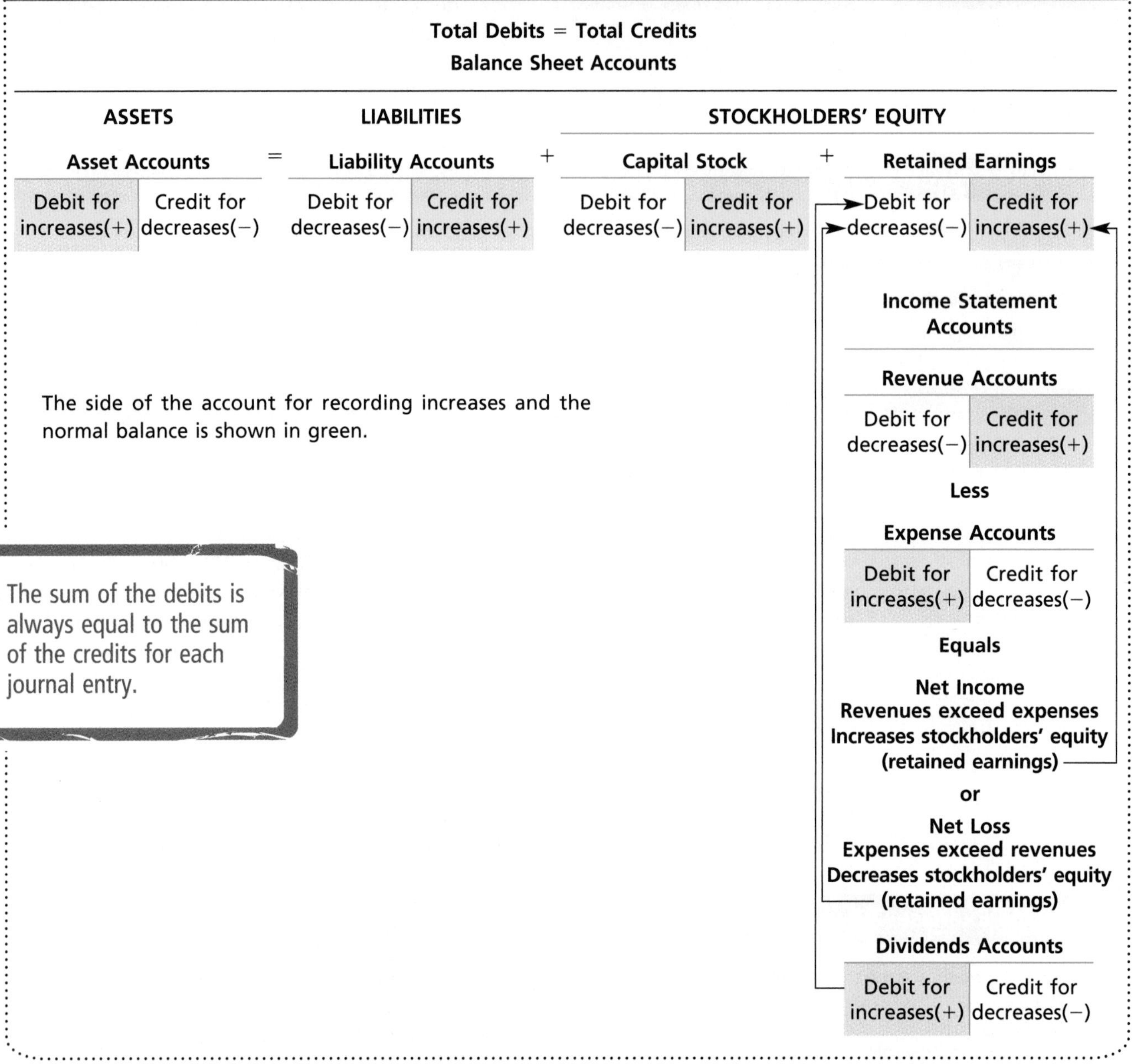

Total Debits = Total Credits

Balance Sheet Accounts

ASSETS			LIABILITIES			STOCKHOLDERS' EQUITY				
Asset Accounts		=	**Liability Accounts**		+	**Capital Stock**		+	**Retained Earnings**	
Debit for increases(+)	Credit for decreases(−)		Debit for decreases(−)	Credit for increases(+)		Debit for decreases(−)	Credit for increases(+)		Debit for decreases(−)	Credit for increases(+)

The side of the account for recording increases and the normal balance is shown in green.

Income Statement Accounts

Revenue Accounts

Debit for decreases(−)	Credit for increases(+)

Less

Expense Accounts

Debit for increases(+)	Credit for decreases(−)

Equals

Net Income
Revenues exceed expenses
Increases stockholders' equity
(retained earnings)

or

Net Loss
Expenses exceed revenues
Decreases stockholders' equity
(retained earnings)

Dividends Accounts

Debit for increases(+)	Credit for decreases(−)

> The sum of the debits is always equal to the sum of the credits for each journal entry.

Double-Entry Accounting System

In 1494, Luca Pacioli, a Franciscan monk, invented the double-entry accounting system that is still used today.

In the preceding paragraphs, we illustrated the rules of debit and credit for recording transactions in accounts using journal entries. In doing so, the sum of the debits is always equal to the sum of the credits for each journal entry. As shown in Exhibit 3, this equality of debits and credits for each transaction is built into the accounting equation: Assets = Liabilities + Stockholders' Equity. Because of this double equality, this system of recording transactions is called the **double-entry accounting system**.

As we illustrate in the remainder of this text, the double-entry accounting system is a very powerful tool in analyzing the effects of transactions. Using this system to analyze transactions is summarized below and in Exhibit 4.

1. Carefully read the description of the transaction to determine whether an asset, liability, capital stock, retained earnings, revenue, expense, or dividends account is affected by the transaction.

EXHIBIT 4 | Recording Transactions Using Double-Entry Accounting

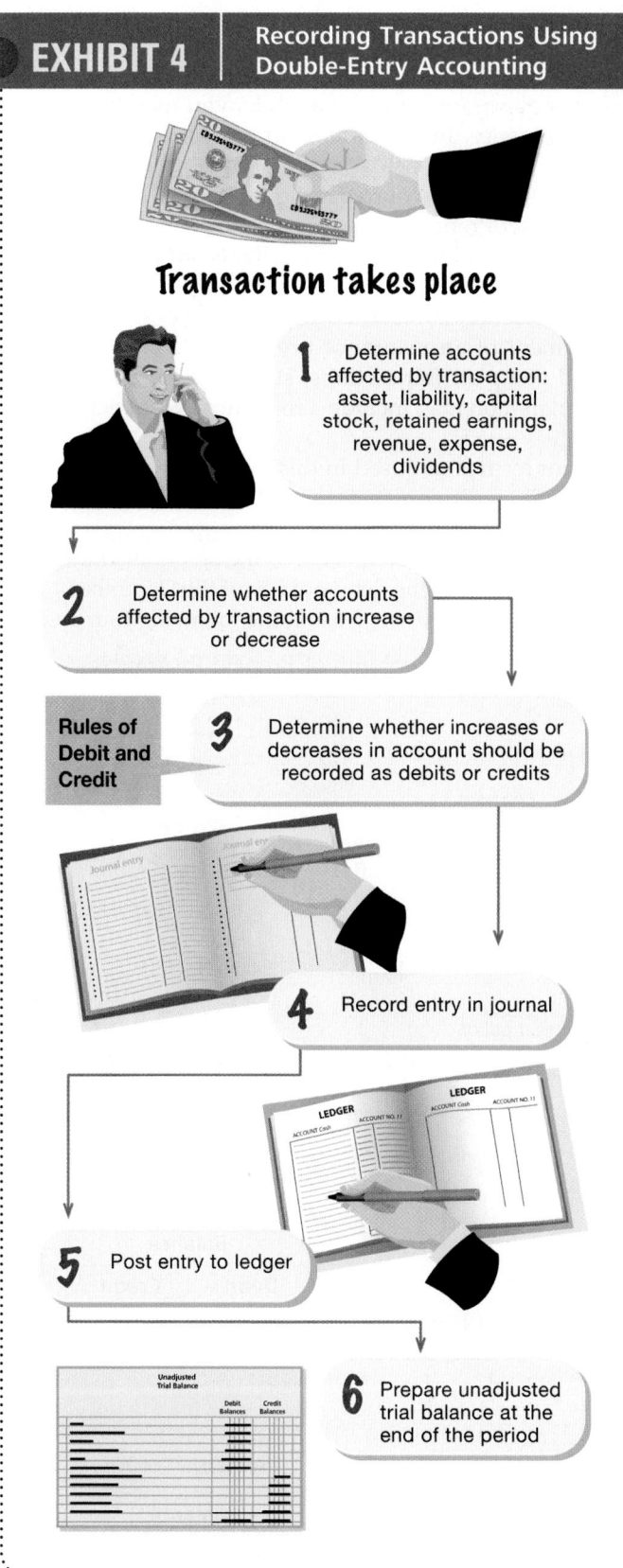

Transaction takes place

1 Determine accounts affected by transaction: asset, liability, capital stock, retained earnings, revenue, expense, dividends

2 Determine whether accounts affected by transaction increase or decrease

Rules of Debit and Credit

3 Determine whether increases or decreases in account should be recorded as debits or credits

4 Record entry in journal

5 Post entry to ledger

6 Prepare unadjusted trial balance at the end of the period

2. For each account affected by the transaction, determine whether the account increases or decreases.
3. Determine whether each increase or decrease should be recorded as a debit or a credit, following the rules of debit and credit shown in Exhibit 3.
4. Record the transaction using a journal entry.
5. Periodically post journal entries to the accounts in the ledger.
6. Prepare an unadjusted trial balance at the end of the period.

We have described and illustrated steps 1–4 in the preceding paragraphs. In the remainder of this chapter, we describe and illustrate steps 5 and 6.

2 objective

Describe and illustrate the posting of journal entries to accounts.

Posting Journal Entries to Accounts

As we discussed in the preceding section, a transaction is first recorded in a journal. Periodically, the journal entries are transferred to the accounts in the ledger (step 5 in Exhibit 4). The ledger is a history of transactions by account. The process of transferring the debits and credits from the journal entries to the accounts is called **posting**.

In practice, businesses use a variety of formats for recording journal entries. A business may use one all-purpose journal, sometimes called a **two-column journal**, or it may use several journals. In the latter case, each journal is used to record different types of transactions, such as cash receipts or cash payments. The journals may be part of either a manual accounting system or a computerized accounting system.[3]

As a review of the analysis and recording of transactions and to illustrate posting in a manual accounting system, we will use the December transactions of NetSolutions. The first transaction in December occurred on December 1.

---

3 The use of special journals and computerized accounting systems is discussed in Chapter 5, after the basics of accounting systems have been covered.

**December 1
Transaction**

NetSolutions paid a premium of $2,400 for a comprehensive insurance policy covering liability, theft, and fire. The policy covers a one-year period.

@netsolutions

Analysis   When you purchase insurance for your automobile, you may be required to pay the insurance premium in advance. In this case, your transaction is similar to NetSolutions. Advance payments of expenses such as insurance are prepaid expenses, which are assets. For NetSolutions, the asset acquired for the cash payment is insurance protection for 12 months. The asset Prepaid Insurance increases and is debited for $2,400. The asset Cash decreases and is credited for $2,400. The recording and posting of this transaction is shown in Exhibit 5.

Note where the date of the transaction is recorded in the journal. Also note that the entry is explained as the payment of an insurance premium. Such explanations should be brief. For unusual and complex transactions, such as a long-term rental arrangement, the journal entry explanation may include a reference to the rental agreement or other business document.

You will note that the T account form is not used in this illustration. Although the T account clearly separates debit and credit entries, in practice, the T account is usually replaced with the standard form shown in Exhibit 5.

The debits and credits for each journal entry are posted to the accounts in the order in which they occur in the journal. To illustrate, the debit portion of the December 1 journal entry is posted to the prepaid account in Exhibit 5 using the following four steps:

Step 1: The date (Dec. 1) is entered in the Date column of Prepaid Insurance;

EXHIBIT 5

Diagram of the
Recording and
Posting of a Debit
and a Credit

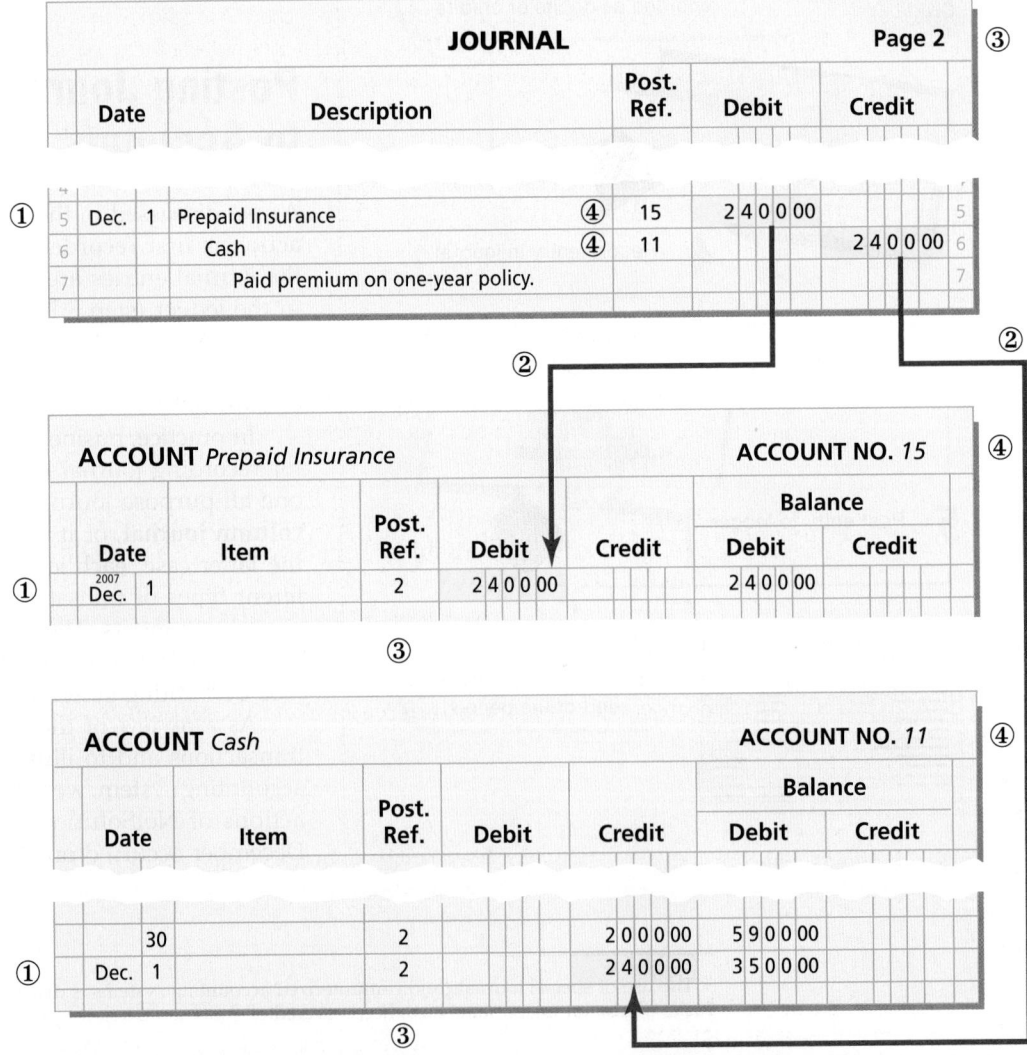

Step 2: The amount (2,400) is entered into the Debit column of Prepaid Insurance;

Step 3: The journal page number (2) is entered in the Posting Reference (Post. Ref.) column of Prepaid Insurance;

Step 4: The account number (15) is entered in the Posting Reference (Post. Ref.) column in the journal.

As shown in Exhibit 5, the credit portion of the December 1 journal entry is posted to the cash account in a similar manner.

The remaining December transactions for NetSolutions are analyzed in the following paragraphs. These transactions are posted to the ledger in Exhibit 6, shown later. To simplify and reduce repetition, some of the December transactions are stated in summary form. For example, cash received for services is normally recorded on a daily basis. In this example, however, only summary totals are recorded at the middle and end of the month. Likewise, all fees earned on account during December are recorded at the middle and end of the month. In practice, each fee earned is recorded separately.

December 1 Transaction   NetSolutions paid rent for December, $800. The company from which NetSolutions is renting its store space now requires the payment of rent on the first of each month, rather than at the end of the month.

Analysis   You may pay monthly rent on an apartment on the first of each month. Your rent transaction is similar to NetSolutions. The advance payment of rent is an asset, much like the advance payment of the insurance premium in the preceding transaction. Unlike the insurance premium, this prepaid rent will expire in one month. When an asset that is purchased will be used up in a short period of time, such as a month, it is normal to debit an expense account initially. This avoids having to transfer the balance from an asset account (Prepaid Rent) to an expense account (Rent Expense) at the end of the month. Thus, when the rent for December is prepaid at the beginning of the month, Rent Expense is debited for $800, and Cash is credited for $800.

9						9
10	1	Rent Expense	52	8 0 0 00		10
11		Cash	11		8 0 0 00	11
12		Paid rent for December.				12

December 1 Transaction   NetSolutions received an offer from a local retailer to rent the land purchased on November 5. The retailer plans to use the land as a parking lot for its employees and customers. NetSolutions agreed to rent the land to the retailer for three months, with the rent payable in advance. NetSolutions received $360 for three months' rent beginning December 1.

Analysis   By agreeing to rent the land and accepting the $360, NetSolutions has incurred an obligation (liability) to the retailer. This obligation is to make the land available for use for three months and not to interfere with its use. The liability created by receiving the cash in advance of providing the service is called **unearned revenue**. Thus, the $360 received is an increase in an asset and is debited to Cash. The liability account Unearned Rent increases and is credited for $360. As time passes, the unearned rent liability will decrease and will become revenue.

Magazines that receive subscriptions in advance must record the receipts as unearned revenues. Likewise, airlines that receive ticket payments in advance must record the receipts as unearned revenues until the passengers use the tickets.

13						13
14	1	Cash	11	3 6 0 00		14
15		Unearned Rent	23		3 6 0 00	15
16		Received advance payment for				16
17		three months' rent on land.				17

December 4 Transaction   NetSolutions purchased office equipment on account from Executive Supply Co. for $1,800.

Analysis   The asset account Office Equipment increases and is therefore debited for $1,800. The liability account Accounts Payable increases and is credited for $1,800.

18						18
19	4	Office Equipment	18	1 8 0 0 00		19
20		Accounts Payable	21		1 8 0 0 00	20
21		Purchased office equipment				21
22		on account.				22

December 6 Transaction   NetSolutions paid $180 for a newspaper advertisement.

Analysis   An expense increases and is debited for $180. The asset Cash decreases and is credited for $180. Expense items that are expected to be minor in amount are normally included as part of the miscellaneous expense. Thus, Miscellaneous Expense is debited for $180.

23						23
24	6	Miscellaneous Expense	59	1 8 0 00		24
25		Cash	11		1 8 0 00	25
26		Paid for newspaper ad.				26

December 11 Transaction   NetSolutions paid creditors $400.

Analysis   This payment decreases the liability account Accounts Payable, which is debited for $400. Cash also decreases and is credited for $400.

27						27
28	11	Accounts Payable	21	4 0 0 00		28
29		Cash	11		4 0 0 00	29
30		Paid creditors on account.				30

December 13 Transaction   NetSolutions paid a receptionist and a part-time assistant $950 for two weeks' wages.

Analysis   This transaction is similar to the December 6 transaction, where an expense account is increased and Cash is decreased. Thus, Wages Expense is debited for $950, and Cash is credited for $950.

In computerized accounting systems, some transactions may be automatically authorized and recorded when certain events occur. For example, the wages of employees may be paid automatically at the end of each pay period.

		JOURNAL				Page 3	
	Date	Description	Post. Ref.	Debit	Credit		
1	2007 Dec. 13	Wages Expense	51	9 5 0 00			1
2		Cash	11		9 5 0 00		2
3		Paid two weeks' wages.					3

December 16 Transaction   NetSolutions received $3,100 from fees earned for the first half of December.

Analysis   Cash increases and is debited for $3,100. The revenue account Fees Earned increases and is credited for $3,100.

4						4
5	16	Cash	11	3 1 0 0 00		5
6		Fees Earned	41		3 1 0 0 00	6
7		Received fees from customers.				7

December 16
Transaction

Fees earned on account totaled $1,750 for the first half of December.

Analysis Assume that you have agreed to take care of a neighbor's dog for a week for $100. At the end of the week, you agree to wait until the first of the next month to receive the $100. Like NetSolutions, you have provided services on account and thus have a right to receive the payment from your neighbor. When a business agrees that payment for services provided or goods sold can be accepted at a later date, the firm has an **account receivable**, which is a claim against the customer. The account receivable is an asset, and the revenue is earned even though no cash has been received. Thus, Accounts Receivable increases and is debited for $1,750. The revenue account Fees Earned increases and is credited for $1,750.

8				8
9	16	Accounts Receivable	12	1 7 5 0 00	9
10		Fees Earned	41		1 7 5 0 00	10
11		Recorded fees earned on account.				11

December 20
Transaction

NetSolutions paid $900 to Executive Supply Co. on the $1,800 debt owed from the December 4 transaction.

Analysis This is similar to the transaction of December 11.

12				12
13	20	Accounts Payable	21	9 0 0 00	13
14		Cash	11		9 0 0 00	14
15		Paid part of amount owed to				15
16		Executive Supply Co.				16

December 21
Transaction

NetSolutions received $650 from customers in payment of their accounts.

Analysis When customers pay amounts owed for services they have previously received, one asset increases and another asset decreases. Thus, Cash is debited for $650, and Accounts Receivable is credited for $650.

17				17
18	21	Cash	11	6 5 0 00	18
19		Accounts Receivable	12		6 5 0 00	19
20		Received cash from customers				20
21		on account.				21

December 23
Transaction

NetSolutions paid $1,450 for supplies.

Analysis The asset account Supplies increases and is debited for $1,450. The asset account Cash decreases and is credited for $1,450.

22				22
23	23	Supplies	14	1 4 5 0 00	23
24		Cash	11		1 4 5 0 00	24
25		Purchased supplies.				25

December 27
Transaction

NetSolutions paid the receptionist and the part-time assistant $1,200 for two weeks' wages.

Analysis This is similar to the transaction of December 13.

26								26
27		27	Wages Expense	51	1 2 0 0 00			27
28			Cash	11		1 2 0 0 00		28
29			Paid two weeks' wages.					29

December 31 Transaction   NetSolutions paid its $310 telephone bill for the month.

Analysis   You pay a telephone bill each month. Businesses, such as NetSolutions, also must pay monthly utility bills. Such transactions are similar to the transaction of December 6. The expense account Utilities Expense is debited for $310, and Cash is credited for $310.

30							30
31		31	Utilities Expense	54	3 1 0 00		31
32			Cash	11		3 1 0 00	32
33			Paid telephone bill.				33

December 31 Transaction   NetSolutions paid its $225 electric bill for the month.

Analysis   This is similar to the preceding transaction.

JOURNAL   Page 4

	Date		Description	Post. Ref.	Debit	Credit	
1	2007 Dec.	31	Utilities Expense	54	2 2 5 00		1
2			Cash	11		2 2 5 00	2
3			Paid electric bill.				3

December 31 Transaction   NetSolutions received $2,870 from fees earned for the second half of December.

Analysis   This is similar to the transaction of December 16.

4							4
5		31	Cash	11	2 8 7 0 00		5
6			Fees Earned	41		2 8 7 0 00	6
7			Received fees from customers.				7

December 31 Transaction   Fees earned on account totaled $1,120 for the second half of December.

Analysis   This is similar to the transaction of December 16.

8							8
9		31	Accounts Receivable	12	1 1 2 0 00		9
10			Fees Earned	41		1 1 2 0 00	10
11			Recorded fees earned on account.				11

December 31 Transaction   NetSolutions paid dividends of $2,000 to stockholders.

Analysis   This transaction resulted in an increase in the amount of dividends and is recorded by a $2,000 debit to Dividends. The decrease in business cash is recorded by a $2,000 credit to Cash.

12							12
13		31	Dividends	33	2 0 0 0 00		13
14			Cash	11		2 0 0 0 00	14
15			Paid dividends to stockholders.				15

Example Exercise 2-5  objective 2

On March 1, the cash account balance was $22,350. During March, cash receipts totaled $241,880 and the March 31 balance was $19,125. Determine the cash payments made during March.

Follow My Example 2-5

Using the following T account, solve for the amount of cash payments (indicated by ? below).

Cash

Mar. 1 Bal.	22,350	?	Cash payments
Cash receipts	241,880		
Mar. 31 Bal.	19,125		

$19,125 = $22,350 + $241,880 − Cash payments
Cash payments = $22,350 + $241,880 − $19,125 = $245,105

For Practice: PE 2-5A, PE 2-5B

The journal for NetSolutions since it was organized on November 1 is shown in Exhibit 6. Exhibit 6 also shows the ledger after the transactions for both November and December have been posted.

EXHIBIT 6

Journal and Ledger—
NetSolutions

	JOURNAL				Page 1	
	Date	**Description**	**Post. Ref.**	**Debit**	**Credit**	
1	2007 Nov. 1	Cash	11	25 0 0 0 00		1
2		Capital Stock	31		25 0 0 0 00	2
3		Issued capital stock for cash.				3
4						4
5	5	Land	17	20 0 0 0 00		5
6		Cash	11		20 0 0 0 00	6
7		Purchased land for building site.				7
8						8
9	10	Supplies	14	1 3 5 0 00		9
10		Accounts Payable	21		1 3 5 0 00	10
11		Purchased supplies on account.				11
12						12
13	18	Cash	11	7 5 0 0 00		13
14		Fees Earned	41		7 5 0 0 00	14
15		Received fees from customers.				15
16						16
17	30	Wages Expense	51	2 1 2 5 00		17
18		Rent Expense	52	8 0 0 00		18
19		Utilities Expense	54	4 5 0 00		19
20		Miscellaneous Expense	59	2 7 5 00		20
21		Cash	11		3 6 5 0 00	21
22		Paid expenses.				22
23						23
24	30	Accounts Payable	21	9 5 0 00		24
25		Cash	11		9 5 0 00	25
26		Paid creditors on account.				26
27						27
28	30	Supplies Expense	55	8 0 0 00		28
29		Supplies	14		8 0 0 00	29
30		Supplies used during November.				30

(continued)

EXHIBIT 6

	Date		Description	Post. Ref.	Debit	Credit	
1	2007 Nov.	30	Dividends	33	2 0 0 0 00		1
2			Cash	11		2 0 0 0 00	2
3			Paid dividends to stockholders.				3
4							4
5	Dec.	1	Prepaid Insurance	15	2 4 0 0 00		5
6			Cash	11		2 4 0 0 00	6
7			Paid premium on one-year policy.				7
8							8
9		1	Rent Expense	52	8 0 0 00		9
10			Cash	11		8 0 0 00	10
11			Paid rent for December.				11
12							12
13		1	Cash	11	3 6 0 00		13
14			Unearned Rent	23		3 6 0 00	14
15			Received advance payment for				15
16			three months' rent on land.				16
17							17
18		4	Office Equipment	18	1 8 0 0 00		18
19			Accounts Payable	21		1 8 0 0 00	19
20			Purchased office equipment				20
21			on account.				21
22							22
23		6	Miscellaneous Expense	59	1 8 0 00		23
24			Cash	11		1 8 0 00	24
25			Paid for newspaper ad.				25
26							26
27		11	Accounts Payable	21	4 0 0 00		27
28			Cash	11		4 0 0 00	28
29			Paid creditors on account.				29

JOURNAL   Page 2

(continued)

EXHIBIT 6

	Date		Description	Post. Ref.	Debit	Credit	
			JOURNAL			Page 3	
1	2007 Dec.	13	Wages Expense	51	9 5 0 00		1
2			Cash	11		9 5 0 00	2
3			Paid two weeks' wages.				3
4							4
5		16	Cash	11	3 1 0 0 00		5
6			Fees Earned	41		3 1 0 0 00	6
7			Received fees from customers.				7
8							8
9		16	Accounts Receivable	12	1 7 5 0 00		9
10			Fees Earned	41		1 7 5 0 00	10
11			Recorded fees earned on account.				11
12							12
13		20	Accounts Payable	21	9 0 0 00		13
14			Cash	11		9 0 0 00	14
15			Paid part of amount owed to				15
16			Executive Supply Co.				16
17							17
18		21	Cash	11	6 5 0 00		18
19			Accounts Receivable	12		6 5 0 00	19
20			Received cash from customers				20
21			on account.				21
22							22
23		23	Supplies	14	1 4 5 0 00		23
24			Cash	11		1 4 5 0 00	24
25			Purchased supplies.				25
26							26
27		27	Wages Expense	51	1 2 0 0 00		27
28			Cash	11		1 2 0 0 00	28
29			Paid two weeks' wages.				29
30							30
31		31	Utilities Expense	54	3 1 0 00		31
32			Cash	11		3 1 0 00	32
33			Paid telephone bill.				33

(continued)

EXHIBIT 6

	Date		Description	Post. Ref.	Debit	Credit	
1	2007 Dec.	31	Utilities Expense	54	2 2 5 00		1
2			Cash	11		2 2 5 00	2
3			Paid electric bill.				3
4							4
5		31	Cash	11	2 8 7 0 00		5
6			Fees Earned	41		2 8 7 0 00	6
7			Received fees from customers.				7
8							8
9		31	Accounts Receivable	12	1 1 2 0 00		9
10			Fees Earned	41		1 1 2 0 00	10
11			Recorded fees earned on account.				11
12							12
13		31	Dividends	33	2 0 0 0 00		13
14			Cash	11		2 0 0 0 00	14
15			Paid dividends to stockholders.				15

JOURNAL   Page 4

LEDGER

ACCOUNT *Cash*   **ACCOUNT NO.** *11*

Date		Item	Post. Ref.	Debit	Credit	Balance Debit	Balance Credit
2007 Nov.	1		1	25 0 0 0 00		25 0 0 0 00	
	5		1		20 0 0 0 00	5 0 0 0 00	
	18		1	7 5 0 0 00		12 5 0 0 00	
	30		1		3 6 5 0 00	8 8 5 0 00	
	30		1		9 5 0 00	7 9 0 0 00	
	30		2		2 0 0 0 00	5 9 0 0 00	
Dec.	1		2		2 4 0 0 00	3 5 0 0 00	
	1		2		8 0 0 00	2 7 0 0 00	
	1		2	3 6 0 00		3 0 6 0 00	
	6		2		1 8 0 00	2 8 8 0 00	
	11		2		4 0 0 00	2 4 8 0 00	
	13		3		9 5 0 00	1 5 3 0 00	
	16		3	3 1 0 0 00		4 6 3 0 00	
	20		3		9 0 0 00	3 7 3 0 00	
	21		3	6 5 0 00		4 3 8 0 00	
	23		3		1 4 5 0 00	2 9 3 0 00	
	27		3		1 2 0 0 00	1 7 3 0 00	
	31		3		3 1 0 00	1 4 2 0 00	
	31		4		2 2 5 00	1 1 9 5 00	
	31		4	2 8 7 0 00		4 0 6 5 00	
	31		4		2 0 0 0 00	2 0 6 5 00	

(continued)

EXHIBIT 6

ACCOUNT *Accounts Receivable*   **ACCOUNT NO.** *12*

Date	Item	Post. Ref.	Debit	Credit	Balance Debit	Balance Credit
2007 Dec. 16		3	1 7 5 0 00		1 7 5 0 00	
21		3		6 5 0 00	1 1 0 0 00	
31		4	1 1 2 0 00		2 2 2 0 00	

ACCOUNT *Supplies*   **ACCOUNT NO.** *14*

Date	Item	Post. Ref.	Debit	Credit	Balance Debit	Balance Credit
2007 Nov. 10		1	1 3 5 0 00		1 3 5 0 00	
30		1		8 0 0 00	5 5 0 00	
Dec. 23		3	1 4 5 0 00		2 0 0 0 00	

ACCOUNT *Prepaid Insurance*   **ACCOUNT NO.** *15*

Date	Item	Post. Ref.	Debit	Credit	Balance Debit	Balance Credit
2007 Dec. 1		2	2 4 0 0 00		2 4 0 0 00	

ACCOUNT *Land*   **ACCOUNT NO.** *17*

Date	Item	Post. Ref.	Debit	Credit	Balance Debit	Balance Credit
2007 Nov. 5		1	20 0 0 0 00		20 0 0 0 00	

ACCOUNT *Office Equipment*   **ACCOUNT NO.** *18*

Date	Item	Post. Ref.	Debit	Credit	Balance Debit	Balance Credit
2007 Dec. 4		2	1 8 0 0 00		1 8 0 0 00	

(continued)

EXHIBIT 6

ACCOUNT *Accounts Payable*   **ACCOUNT NO.** *21*

Date	Item	Post. Ref.	Debit	Credit	Balance Debit	Balance Credit
2007 Nov. 10		1		1 3 5 0 00		1 3 5 0 00
30		1	9 5 0 00			4 0 0 00
Dec. 4		2		1 8 0 0 00		2 2 0 0 00
11		2	4 0 0 00			1 8 0 0 00
20		3	9 0 0 00			9 0 0 00

ACCOUNT *Unearned Rent*   **ACCOUNT NO.** *23*

Date	Item	Post. Ref.	Debit	Credit	Balance Debit	Balance Credit
2007 Dec. 1		2		3 6 0 00		3 6 0 00

ACCOUNT *Capital Stock*   **ACCOUNT NO.** *31*

Date	Item	Post. Ref.	Debit	Credit	Balance Debit	Balance Credit
2007 Nov. 1		1		25 0 0 0 00		25 0 0 0 00

ACCOUNT *Dividends*   **ACCOUNT NO.** *33*

Date	Item	Post. Ref.	Debit	Credit	Balance Debit	Balance Credit
2007 Nov. 30		2	2 0 0 0 00		2 0 0 0 00	
Dec. 31		4	2 0 0 0 00		4 0 0 0 00	

ACCOUNT *Fees Earned*   **ACCOUNT NO.** *41*

Date	Item	Post. Ref.	Debit	Credit	Balance Debit	Balance Credit
2007 Nov. 18		1		7 5 0 0 00		7 5 0 0 00
Dec. 16		3		3 1 0 0 00		10 6 0 0 00
16		3		1 7 5 0 00		12 3 5 0 00
31		4		2 8 7 0 00		15 2 2 0 00
31		4		1 1 2 0 00		16 3 4 0 00

(continued)

EXHIBIT 6

ACCOUNT *Wages Expense*   **ACCOUNT NO.** *51*

Date		Item	Post. Ref.	Debit	Credit	Balance Debit	Balance Credit
2007 Nov.	30		1	2 1 2 5 00		2 1 2 5 00	
Dec.	13		3	9 5 0 00		3 0 7 5 00	
	27		3	1 2 0 0 00		4 2 7 5 00	

ACCOUNT *Rent Expense*   **ACCOUNT NO.** *52*

Date		Item	Post. Ref.	Debit	Credit	Balance Debit	Balance Credit
2007 Nov.	30		1	8 0 0 00		8 0 0 00	
Dec.	1		2	8 0 0 00		1 6 0 0 00	

ACCOUNT *Utilities Expense*   **ACCOUNT NO.** *54*

Date		Item	Post. Ref.	Debit	Credit	Balance Debit	Balance Credit
2007 Nov.	30		1	4 5 0 00		4 5 0 00	
Dec.	31		3	3 1 0 00		7 6 0 00	
	31		4	2 2 5 00		9 8 5 00	

ACCOUNT *Supplies Expense*   **ACCOUNT NO.** *55*

Date		Item	Post. Ref.	Debit	Credit	Balance Debit	Balance Credit
2007 Nov.	30		1	8 0 0 00		8 0 0 00	

ACCOUNT *Miscellaneous Expense*   **ACCOUNT NO.** *59*

Date		Item	Post. Ref.	Debit	Credit	Balance Debit	Balance Credit
2007 Nov.	30		1	2 7 5 00		2 7 5 00	
Dec.	6		2	1 8 0 00		4 5 5 00	

(concluded)

Trial Balance

How can you be sure that you have not made an error in posting the debits and credits to the ledger? One way is to determine the equality of the debits and credits in the ledger. This equality should be proved at the end of each accounting period, if not more often. Such a proof, called a **trial balance**, may be in the form of a computer printout or in the form shown in Exhibit 7.

The trial balance shown in Exhibit 7 is prepared by first listing the name of the company (NetSolutions), its title (Unadjusted Trial Balance), and the date it is prepared (December 31, 2007). The trial balance shown in Exhibit 7 is titled an unadjusted trial balance. This is to distinguish it from other trial balances that we will be preparing in later chapters. These other trial balances include an adjusted trial balance and a post-closing trial balance.[4]

The account balances in Exhibit 7 are taken from the ledger shown in Exhibit 6. Thus, before the trial balance can be prepared, each account balance in the ledger must be determined. When the standard account form is used, the balance of each account appears in the balance column on the same line as the last posting to the account.

EXHIBIT 7

Trial Balance

NetSolutions
Unadjusted Trial Balance
December 31, 2007

	Debit Balances	Credit Balances
Cash	2 0 6 5 00	
Accounts Receivable	2 2 2 0 00	
Supplies	2 0 0 0 00	
Prepaid Insurance	2 4 0 0 00	
Land	20 0 0 0 00	
Office Equipment	1 8 0 0 00	
Accounts Payable		9 0 0 00
Unearned Rent		3 6 0 00
Capital Stock		25 0 0 0 00
Dividends	4 0 0 0 00	
Fees Earned		16 3 4 0 00
Wages Expense	4 2 7 5 00	
Rent Expense	1 6 0 0 00	
Utilities Expense	9 8 5 00	
Supplies Expense	8 0 0 00	
Miscellaneous Expense	4 5 5 00	
	42 6 0 0 00	42 6 0 0 00

The trial balance does not provide complete proof of the accuracy of the ledger. It indicates only that the debits and the credits are equal. This proof is of value, however, because errors often affect the equality of debits and credits. If the two totals of a trial balance are not equal, an error has occurred. In the next section of this chapter, we will discuss procedures for discovering and correcting errors.

---

4 The adjusted trial balance is discussed in Chapter 3, and the post-closing trial balance is discussed in Chapter 4.

Example Exercise 2-6

objective **3**

For each of the following errors, considered individually, indicate whether the error would cause the trial balance totals to be unequal. If the error would cause the trial balance total to be unequal, indicate whether the debit or credit total is higher and by how much.

a. Payment of dividends of $5,600 was journalized and posted as a debit of $6,500 to Salary Expense and a credit of $6,500 to Cash.

b. A fee of $2,850 earned from a client was debited to Accounts Receivable for $2,580 and credited to Fees Earned for $2,850.

c. A payment of $3,500 to a creditor was posted as a debit of $3,500 to Accounts Payable and a debit of $3,500 to Cash.

Follow My Example 2-6

a. The totals are equal since both the debit and credit entries were journalized and posted for $6,500.

b. The totals are unequal. The credit total is higher by $270 ($2,850 − $2,580).

c. The totals are unequal. The debit total is higher by $7,000 ($3,500 + $3,500).

For Practice: PE 2-6A, PE 2-6B

Discovery and Correction of Errors

objective **4**

Discover and correct errors in recording transactions.

REAL WORLD

Many large corporations such as Microsoft and Quaker Oats round the figures in their financial statements to millions of dollars.

Errors will sometimes occur in journalizing and posting transactions. In some cases, however, an error might not be significant enough to affect the decisions of management or others. In such cases, the **materiality concept** implies that the error may be treated in the easiest possible way. For example, an error of a few dollars in recording an asset as an expense for a business with millions of dollars in assets would be considered immaterial, and a correction would not be necessary. In the remaining paragraphs, we assume that errors discovered are material and should be corrected.

DISCOVERY OF ERRORS

As mentioned previously, preparing the trial balance is one of the primary ways to discover errors in the ledger. However, it indicates only that the debits and credits are equal. If the two totals of the trial balance are not equal, it is probably due to one or more of the errors described in Exhibit 8.

Among the types of errors that will *not* cause the trial balance totals to be unequal are the following:

1. Failure to record a transaction or to post a transaction.
2. Recording the same erroneous amount for both the debit and the credit parts of a transaction.
3. Recording the same transaction more than once.
4. Posting a part of a transaction correctly as a debit or credit but to the wrong account.

It is obvious that care should be used in recording transactions in the journal and in posting to the accounts. The need for accuracy in determining account balances and reporting them on the trial balance is also evident.

Errors in the accounts may be discovered in various ways: (1) through audit procedures, (2) by looking at the trial balance, or (3) by chance. If the two trial balance totals are not equal, the amount of the difference between the totals should be determined before searching for the error.

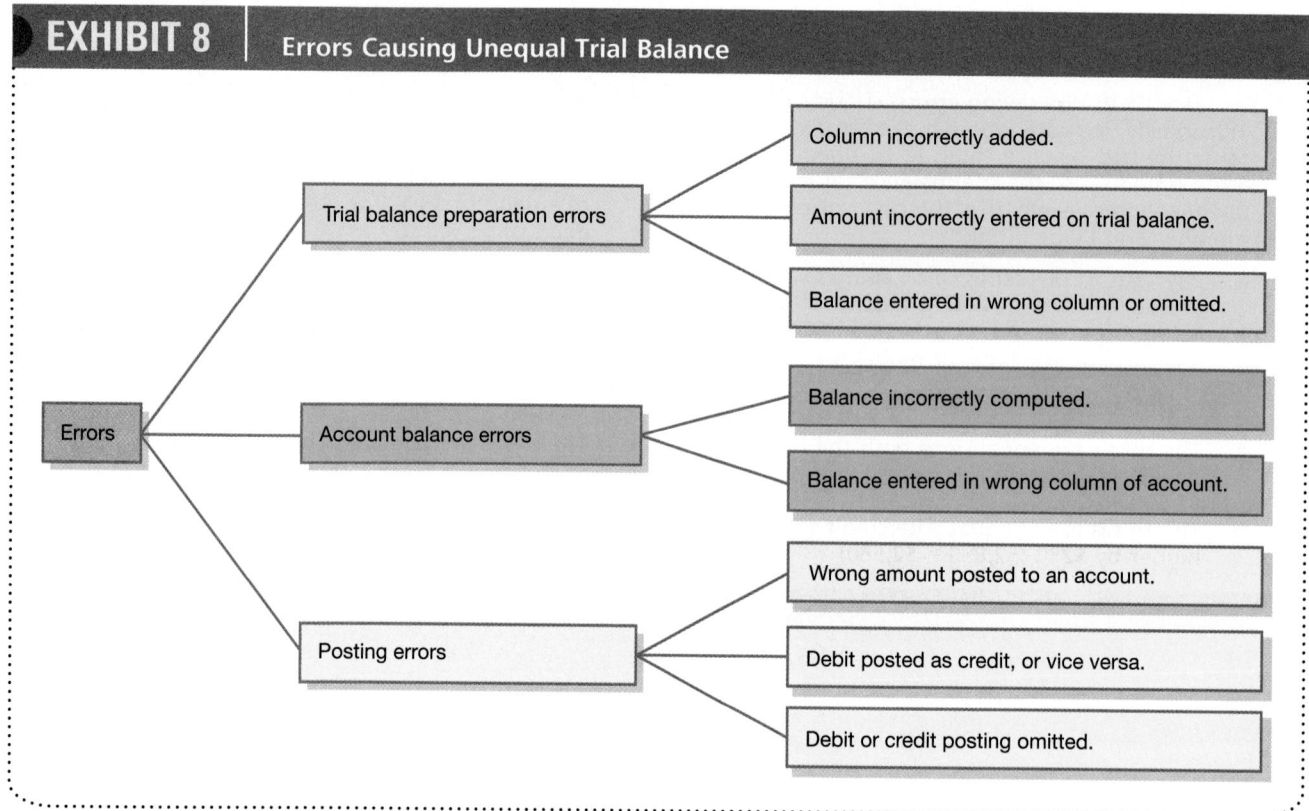

EXHIBIT 8 | Errors Causing Unequal Trial Balance

The amount of the difference between the two totals of a trial balance sometimes gives a clue as to the nature of the error or where it occurred. For example, a difference of 10, 100, or 1,000 between two totals is often the result of an error in addition. A difference between totals can also be due to omitting a debit or a credit posting. If the difference can be evenly divided by 2, the error may be due to the posting of a debit as a credit, or vice versa. For example, if the debit total is $20,640 and the credit total is $20,236, the difference of $404 may indicate that a credit posting of $404 was omitted or that a credit of $202 was incorrectly posted as a debit.

Two other common types of errors are known as transpositions and slides. A **transposition** occurs when the order of the digits is changed mistakenly, such as writing $542 as $452 or $524. In a **slide**, the entire number is mistakenly moved one or more spaces to the right or the left, such as writing $542.00 as $54.20 or $5,420.00. If an error of either type has occurred and there are no other errors, the difference between the two trial balance totals can be evenly divided by 9.

If an error is not revealed by the trial balance, the steps in the accounting process must be retraced, beginning with the last step and working back to the entries in the journal. Usually, errors causing the trial balance totals to be unequal will be discovered before all of the steps are retraced.

CORRECTION OF ERRORS

The procedures used to correct an error vary according to the nature of the error, when the error is discovered, and whether a manual or computerized accounting system is used. Oftentimes, an error is discovered as it is being journalized or posted. In such cases, the error is simply corrected. For example, computerized accounting systems automatically verify for each journal entry whether the total debits equal the total credits. If the totals are not equal, an error report is created and the computer program will not proceed until the journal entry is corrected.

Occasionally, however, an error is not discovered until after a journal entry has been recorded and posted to the accounts. Correcting this type of error is more complex. To illustrate, assume that on May 5 a $12,500 purchase of office equipment on account was incorrectly journalized and posted as a debit to Supplies and a credit to Accounts Payable for $12,500. This posting of the incorrect entry is shown in the following T accounts:

	Supplies			Accounts Payable	
Incorrect:	12,500				12,500

Before making a correcting entry, it is best to determine the debit(s) and credit(s) that should have been recorded. These are shown in the following T accounts:

	Office Equipment			Accounts Payable	
Correct:	12,500				12,500

Comparing the two sets of T accounts shows that the incorrect debit to Supplies may be corrected by debiting Office Equipment for $12,500 and crediting Supplies for $12,500. The following correcting entry is then journalized and posted:

Entry to Correct Error:

17							17
18	May	31	Office Equipment	18	12 5 0 0 00		18
19			Supplies	14		12 5 0 0 00	19
20			To correct erroneous debit				20
21			to Supplies on May 5. See invoice				21
22			from Bell Office Equipment Co.				22

Example Exercise 2-7   objective  4

The following errors took place in journalizing and posting transactions:

a. Dividends of $6,000 were recorded as a debit to Office Salaries Expense and a credit to Cash.
b. Utilities Expense of $4,500 paid for the current month was recorded as a debit to Miscellaneous Expense and a credit to Accounts Payable.

Journalize the entries to correct the errors. Omit explanations.

Follow My Example 2-7

a.	Dividends	6,000	
	Office Salaries Expense		6,000
b.	Accounts Payable	4,500	
	Miscellaneous Expense		4,500
	Utilities Expense	4,500	
	Cash		4,500

Note: The first entry in (b) reverses the incorrect entry, and the second entry records the correct entry. These two entries could also be combined into one entry; however, preparing two entries will make it easier for someone later to understand what had happened and why the entries were necessary.

For Practice: PE 2-7A, PE 2-7B

At a Glance

1. Describe the characteristics of an account and record transactions using a chart of accounts and journal.

Key Points	Key Learning Outcomes	Example Exercises	Practice Exercises
The record used for recording individual transactions is an account. A group of accounts is called a ledger. The system of accounts that make up a ledger is called a chart of accounts. Transactions are initially entered in a record called a journal.	• Prepare a chart of accounts for a corporation.		
	• Prepare journal entries.	2-1 2-2 2-3	2-1A, 2-1B 2-2A, 2-2B 2-3A, 2-3B
The simplest form of an account, a T account, has three parts: (1) a title; (2) a left side, called the debit side; and (3) a right side, called the credit side. Amounts entered on the left side of an account are called debits to the account. Amounts entered on the right side of an account are called credits. Periodically, the balance of the account is determined.	• Record entries in T accounts.		
The rules of debit and credit for recording increases or decreases in asset, liability, capital stock, retained earnings, revenue, expense, and dividends accounts are shown in Exhibit 3. Each transaction is recorded so that the sum of the debits is always equal to the sum of the credits. The normal balance of an account is the side of the account (debit or credit) in which increases are recorded.	• List the rules of debit and credit.	2-4	2-4A, 2-4B
	• Determine the normal balance for accounts.	2-4	2-4A, 2-4B

2. Describe and illustrate the posting of journal entries to accounts.

Key Points	Key Learning Outcomes	Example Exercises	Practice Exercises
The debits and credits for each journal entry are periodically posted to the accounts in the order in which they occur in the journal using the steps illustrated in Exhibit 5.	• Post journal entries to a standard account.		
	• Post journal entries to a T account.	2-5	2-5A, 2-5B

3. Prepare an unadjusted trial balance and explain how it can be used to discover errors.

Key Points	Key Learning Outcomes	Example Exercises	Practice Exercises
A trial balance is prepared by listing the accounts from the ledger and their balances. If the two totals of the trial balance are not equal, an error has occurred.	• Prepare an unadjusted trial balance.	2-6	2-6A, 2-6B

	Key Learning Outcomes	Example Exercises	Practice Exercises
4. Discover and correct errors in recording transactions.			
Key Points			
Errors may be discovered (1) by audit procedures, (2) by looking at the trial balance, or (3) by chance.	• Discover errors in journalizing, posting, or preparing the trial balance. • Prepare correcting entries for errors that have been journalized and posted.	2-7	2-7A, 2-7B

Key Terms

account (51)
account receivable (65)
assets (53)
balance of the account (52)
chart of accounts (53)
credits (52)
debits (52)
dividends (53)
double-entry accounting
    system (60)

expenses (53)
journal (54)
journal entry (54)
journalizing (54)
ledger (53)
liabilities (53)
materiality concept (75)
posting (61)

revenues (53)
slide (76)
stockholders' equity (53)
T account (51)
transposition (76)
trial balance (74)
two-column journal (61)
unearned revenue (63)

Illustrative Problem

J. F. Outz, M.D., has been practicing as a cardiologist for three years in a professional corporation known as Hearts, P.C. During April 2007, Hearts, P.C. completed the following transactions:

Apr. 1. Paid office rent for April, $800.
    3. Purchased equipment on account, $2,100.
    5. Received cash on account from patients, $3,150.
    8. Purchased X-ray film and other supplies on account, $245.
    9. One of the items of equipment purchased on April 3 was defective. It was returned with the permission of the supplier, who agreed to reduce the account for the amount charged for the item, $325.
  12. Paid cash to creditors on account, $1,250.
  17. Paid cash for renewal of a six-month property insurance policy, $370.
  20. Discovered that the balances of the cash account and the accounts payable account as of April 1 were overstated by $200. A payment of that amount to a creditor in March had not been recorded. Journalize the $200 payment as of April 20.
  24. Paid cash for laboratory analysis, $545.
  27. Paid dividends of $1,250.
  30. Recorded the cash received in payment of services (on a cash basis) to patients during April, $1,720.
  30. Paid salaries of receptionist and nurses, $1,725.
  30. Paid various utility expenses, $360.
  30. Recorded fees charged to patients on account for services performed in April, $5,145.
  30. Paid miscellaneous expenses, $132.

Hearts, P.C.'s account titles, numbers, and balances as of April 1 (all normal balances) are listed as follows: Cash, 11, $4,123; Accounts Receivable, 12, $6,725; Supplies, 13, $290; Prepaid Insurance, 14, $465; Equipment, 18, $19,745; Accounts Payable, 22, $765; Capital Stock, 31, $10,000; Retained Earnings, 32, $20,583; Dividends, 33; Professional Fees, 41; Salary Expense, 51; Rent Expense, 53; Laboratory Expense, 55; Utilities Expense, 56; Miscellaneous Expense, 59.

Instructions

1. Open a ledger of standard four-column accounts for Hearts, P.C. as of April 1. Enter the balances in the appropriate balance columns and place a check mark (✓) in the Posting Reference column. (*Hint:* Verify the equality of the debit and credit balances in the ledger before proceeding with the next instruction.)
2. Journalize each transaction in a two-column journal.
3. Post the journal to the ledger, extending the month-end balances to the appropriate balance columns after each posting.
4. Prepare an unadjusted trial balance as of April 30.

Solution

2. and **3.**

JOURNAL   Page 27

	Date		Description	Post. Ref.	Debit	Credit	
1	2007 Apr.	1	Rent Expense	53	8 0 0 00		1
2			Cash	11		8 0 0 00	2
3			Paid office rent for April.				3
4							4
5		3	Equipment	18	2 1 0 0 00		5
6			Accounts Payable	22		2 1 0 0 00	6
7			Purchased equipment on account.				7
8							8
9		5	Cash	11	3 1 5 0 00		9
10			Accounts Receivable	12		3 1 5 0 00	10
11			Received cash on account.				11
12							12
13		8	Supplies	13	2 4 5 00		13
14			Accounts Payable	22		2 4 5 00	14
15			Purchased supplies.				15
16							16
17		9	Accounts Payable	22	3 2 5 00		17
18			Equipment	18		3 2 5 00	18
19			Returned defective equipment.				19
20							20
21		12	Accounts Payable	22	1 2 5 0 00		21
22			Cash	11		1 2 5 0 00	22
23			Paid creditors on account.				23
24							24
25		17	Prepaid Insurance	14	3 7 0 00		25
26			Cash	11		3 7 0 00	26
27			Renewed six-month property policy.				27
28							28
29		20	Accounts Payable	22	2 0 0 00		29
30			Cash	11		2 0 0 00	30
31			Recorded March payment				31
32			to creditor.				32
33							33

			JOURNAL			Page 28		
	Date		Description	Post. Ref.	Debit	Credit		
1	2007 Apr.	24	Laboratory Expense	55	5 4 5 00			1
2			Cash	11		5 4 5 00		2
3			Paid for laboratory analysis.					3
4								4
5		27	Dividends	33	1 2 5 0 00			5
6			Cash	11		1 2 5 0 00		6
7			Paid dividends to stockholders.					7
8								8
9		30	Cash	11	1 7 2 0 00			9
10			Professional Fees	41		1 7 2 0 00		10
11			Received fees from patients.					11
12								12
13		30	Salary Expense	51	1 7 2 5 00			13
14			Cash	11		1 7 2 5 00		14
15			Paid salaries.					15
16								16
17		30	Utilities Expense	56	3 6 0 00			17
18			Cash	11		3 6 0 00		18
19			Paid utilities.					19
20								20
21		30	Accounts Receivable	12	5 1 4 5 00			21
22			Professional Fees	41		5 1 4 5 00		22
23			Recorded fees earned on account.					23
24								24
25		30	Miscellaneous Expense	59	1 3 2 00			25
26			Cash	11		1 3 2 00		26
27			Paid expenses.					27

1. and **3.**

ACCOUNT Cash							ACCOUNT NO. 11	
							Balance	
	Date	Item	Post. Ref.	Debit	Credit	Debit	Credit	
2007 Apr.	1	Balance	✓			4 1 2 3 00		
	1		27		8 0 0 00	3 3 2 3 00		
	5		27	3 1 5 0 00		6 4 7 3 00		
	12		27		1 2 5 0 00	5 2 2 3 00		
	17		27		3 7 0 00	4 8 5 3 00		
	20		27		2 0 0 00	4 6 5 3 00		
	24		28		5 4 5 00	4 1 0 8 00		
	27		28		1 2 5 0 00	2 8 5 8 00		
	30		28	1 7 2 0 00		4 5 7 8 00		
	30		28		1 7 2 5 00	2 8 5 3 00		
	30		28		3 6 0 00	2 4 9 3 00		
	30		28		1 3 2 00	2 3 6 1 00		

ACCOUNT *Accounts Receivable*   **ACCOUNT NO.** *12*

Date		Item	Post. Ref.	Debit	Credit	Balance Debit	Balance Credit
2007 Apr.	1	Balance	✓			6 7 2 5 00	
	5		27		3 1 5 0 00	3 5 7 5 00	
	30		28	5 1 4 5 00		8 7 2 0 00	

ACCOUNT *Supplies*   **ACCOUNT NO.** *13*

Date		Item	Post. Ref.	Debit	Credit	Balance Debit	Balance Credit
2007 Apr.	1	Balance	✓			2 9 0 00	
	8		27	2 4 5 00		5 3 5 00	

ACCOUNT *Prepaid Insurance*   **ACCOUNT NO.** *14*

Date		Item	Post. Ref.	Debit	Credit	Balance Debit	Balance Credit
2007 Apr.	1	Balance	✓			4 6 5 00	
	17		27	3 7 0 00		8 3 5 00	

ACCOUNT *Equipment*   **ACCOUNT NO.** *18*

Date		Item	Post. Ref.	Debit	Credit	Balance Debit	Balance Credit
2007 Apr.	1	Balance	✓			19 7 4 5 00	
	3		27	2 1 0 0 00		21 8 4 5 00	
	9		27		3 2 5 00	21 5 2 0 00	

ACCOUNT *Accounts Payable*   **ACCOUNT NO.** *22*

Date		Item	Post. Ref.	Debit	Credit	Balance Debit	Balance Credit
2007 Apr.	1	Balance	✓				7 6 5 00
	3		27		2 1 0 0 00		2 8 6 5 00
	8		27		2 4 5 00		3 1 1 0 00
	9		27	3 2 5 00			2 7 8 5 00
	12		27	1 2 5 0 00			1 5 3 5 00
	20		27	2 0 0 00			1 3 3 5 00

ACCOUNT *Capital Stock*   **ACCOUNT NO.** *31*

Date		Item	Post. Ref.	Debit	Credit	Balance Debit	Balance Credit
2007 Apr.	1	Balance	✓				10 0 0 0 00

ACCOUNT *Retained Earnings* ACCOUNT NO. *32*

Date	Item	Post. Ref.	Debit	Credit	Balance Debit	Balance Credit
2007 Apr. 1	Balance	✓				20 5 8 3 00

ACCOUNT *Dividends* ACCOUNT NO. *33*

Date	Item	Post. Ref.	Debit	Credit	Balance Debit	Balance Credit
2007 Apr. 27		28	1 2 5 0 00		1 2 5 0 00	

ACCOUNT *Professional Fees* ACCOUNT NO. *41*

Date	Item	Post. Ref.	Debit	Credit	Balance Debit	Balance Credit
2007 Apr. 30		28		1 7 2 0 00		1 7 2 0 00
30		28		5 1 4 5 00		6 8 6 5 00

ACCOUNT *Salary Expense* ACCOUNT NO. *51*

Date	Item	Post. Ref.	Debit	Credit	Balance Debit	Balance Credit
2007 Apr. 30		28	1 7 2 5 00		1 7 2 5 00	

ACCOUNT *Rent Expense* ACCOUNT NO. *53*

Date	Item	Post. Ref.	Debit	Credit	Balance Debit	Balance Credit
2007 Apr. 1		27	8 0 0 00		8 0 0 00	

ACCOUNT *Laboratory Expense* ACCOUNT NO. *55*

Date	Item	Post. Ref.	Debit	Credit	Balance Debit	Balance Credit
2007 Apr. 24		28	5 4 5 00		5 4 5 00	

ACCOUNT *Utilities Expense* ACCOUNT NO. *56*

Date	Item	Post. Ref.	Debit	Credit	Balance Debit	Balance Credit
2007 Apr. 30		28	3 6 0 00		3 6 0 00	

ACCOUNT *Miscellaneous Expense* ACCOUNT NO. *59*

Date	Item	Post. Ref.	Debit	Credit	Balance Debit	Balance Credit
2007 Apr. 30		28	1 3 2 00		1 3 2 00	

4.

Hearts, P.C.
Unadjusted Trial Balance
April 30, 2007

	Debit Balances	Credit Balances
Cash	2 3 6 1 00	
Accounts Receivable	8 7 2 0 00	
Supplies	5 3 5 00	
Prepaid Insurance	8 3 5 00	
Equipment	21 5 2 0 00	
Accounts Payable		1 3 3 5 00
Capital Stock		10 0 0 0 00
Retained Earnings		20 5 8 3 00
Dividends	1 2 5 0 00	
Professional Fees		6 8 6 5 00
Salary Expense	1 7 2 5 00	
Rent Expense	8 0 0 00	
Laboratory Expense	5 4 5 00	
Utilities Expense	3 6 0 00	
Miscellaneous Expense	1 3 2 00	
	38 7 8 3 00	38 7 8 3 00

Self-Examination Questions

(Answers at End of Chapter)

1. A debit may signify a(n):
   A. increase in an asset account.
   B. decrease in an asset account.
   C. increase in a liability account.
   D. increase in the capital stock account.

2. The type of account with a normal credit balance is:
   A. an asset.   C. a revenue.
   B. dividends.   D. an expense.

3. A debit balance in which of the following accounts would indicate a likely error?
   A. Accounts Receivable
   B. Cash
   C. Fees Earned
   D. Miscellaneous Expense

4. The receipt of cash from customers in payment of their accounts would be recorded by:
   A. a debit to Cash and a credit to Accounts Receivable.
   B. a debit to Accounts Receivable and a credit to Cash.
   C. a debit to Cash and a credit to Accounts Payable.
   D. a debit to Accounts Payable and a credit to Cash.

5. The form listing the titles and balances of the accounts in the ledger on a given date is the:
   A. income statement.
   B. balance sheet.
   C. retained earnings statement.
   D. trial balance.

Eye Openers

1. What is the difference between an account and a ledger?
2. Do the terms *debit* and *credit* signify increase or decrease or can they signify either? Explain.
3. Explain why the rules of debit and credit are the same for liability accounts and stockholders' equity accounts.

4. What is the effect (increase or decrease) of a debit to an expense account (a) in terms of retained earnings and (b) in terms of expense?
5. What is the effect (increase or decrease) of a credit to a revenue account (a) in terms of retained earnings and (b) in terms of revenue?
6. Rabun Company adheres to a policy of depositing all cash receipts in a bank account and making all payments by check. The cash account as of January 31 has a credit balance of $2,500, and there is no undeposited cash on hand. (a) Assuming no errors occurred during journalizing or posting, what caused this unusual balance? (b) Is the $2,500 credit balance in the cash account an asset, a liability, stockholders' equity, a revenue, or an expense?
7. Cortes Company performed services in February for a specific customer, for a fee of $6,000. Payment was received the following March. (a) Was the revenue earned in February or March? (b) What accounts should be debited and credited in (1) February and (2) March?
8. What proof is provided by a trial balance?
9. If the two totals of a trial balance are equal, does it mean that there are no errors in the accounting records? Explain.
10. Assume that a trial balance is prepared with an account balance of $21,360 listed as $21,630 and an account balance of $1,500 listed as $15,000. Identify the transposition and the slide.
11. Assume that when a purchase of supplies of $1,380 for cash was recorded, both the debit and the credit were journalized and posted as $1,830. (a) Would this error cause the trial balance to be out of balance? (b) Would the trial balance be out of balance if the $1,380 entry had been journalized correctly but the credit to Cash had been posted as $1,830?
12. Assume that Hahn Consulting erroneously recorded the payment of dividends of $5,000 as a debit to Salary Expense. (a) How would this error affect the equality of the trial balance? (b) How would this error affect the income statement, retained earnings statement, and balance sheet?
13. Assume that Hacienda Realty Co. borrowed $80,000 from Clinton Bank and Trust. In recording the transaction, Hacienda erroneously recorded the receipt as a debit to Cash, $80,000, and a credit to Fees Earned, $80,000. (a) How would this error affect the equality of the trial balance? (b) How would this error affect the income statement, retained earnings statement, and balance sheet?
14. In journalizing and posting the entry to record the purchase of supplies for cash, the accounts payable account was credited in error. What is the preferred procedure to correct this error?
15. Banks rely heavily upon customers' deposits as a source of funds. Demand deposits normally pay interest to the customer, who is entitled to withdraw at any time without prior notice to the bank. Checking and NOW (negotiable order of withdrawal) accounts are the most common form of demand deposits for banks. Assume that Peachtree Storage has a checking account at Buckhead Savings Bank. What type of account (asset, liability, stockholders' equity, revenue, expense, dividends) does the account balance of $18,750 represent from the viewpoint of (a) Peachtree Storage and (b) Buckhead Savings Bank?

Practice Exercises

PE 2-1A
Journal entry for purchase of office equipment
obj. 1

Prepare a journal entry for the purchase of office equipment on November 23 for $13,750, paying $5,000 cash and the remainder on account.

PE 2-1B
Journal entry for purchase of office supplies
obj. 1

Prepare a journal entry for the purchase of office supplies on March 13 for $6,500, paying $1,300 cash and the remainder on account.

PE 2-2A
Journal entry for fees earned on account
obj. 1

Prepare a journal entry on February 2 for fees earned on account, $6,300.

PE 2-2B
Journal entry for cash received for services rendered
obj. 1

Prepare a journal entry on January 21 for cash received for services rendered, $1,250.

PE 2-3A
Journal entry for dividends
obj. 1

Prepare a journal entry on October 31 for the payment of $4,500 of dividends.

PE 2-3B
Journal entry for dividends
obj. 1

Prepare a journal entry on July 31 for the payment of $7,250 of dividends.

PE 2-4A
Rules of debit and credit and normal balances
obj. 1

State for each account whether it is likely to have (a) debit entries only, (b) credit entries only, or (c) both debit and credit entries. Also, indicate its normal balance.

1. Notes Payable
2. Accounts Receivable
3. Wages Expense
4. Commissions Earned
5. Unearned Rent
6. Capital Stock

PE 2-4B
Rules of debit and credit and normal balances
obj. 1

State for each account whether it is likely to have (a) debit entries only, (b) credit entries only, or (c) both debit and credit entries. Also, indicate its normal balance.

1. Prepaid Insurance
2. Rent Revenue
3. Dividends
4. Miscellaneous Expense
5. Accounts Payable
6. Cash

PE 2-5A
Determining cash receipts
obj. 2

On April 1, the cash account balance was $18,750. During April, cash payments totaled $219,140, and the April 30 balance was $22,175. Determine the cash receipts during April.

PE 2-5B
Determining supplies expense
obj. 2

On January 1, the supplies account balance was $1,035. During January, supplies of $2,325 were purchased, and $786 of supplies were on hand as of January 31. Determine supplies expense for January.

PE 2-6A
Effect of errors on a trial balance
obj. 3

For each of the following errors, considered individually, indicate whether the error would cause the trial balance totals to be unequal. If the error would cause the trial balance total to be unequal, indicate whether the debit or credit total is higher and by how much.

a. A payment of $468 on account was debited to Accounts Payable for $486 and credited to Cash for $486.
b. A purchase of supplies of $1,130 was debited to Supplies for $1,130 and debited to Accounts Payable for $1,130.
c. The payment of an insurance premium of $2,450 for a two-year policy was debited to Prepaid Insurance for $2,450 and credited to Cash for $2,540.

PE 2-6B
Effect of errors on a trial balance
obj. 3

For each of the following errors, considered individually, indicate whether the error would cause the trial balance totals to be unequal. If the error would cause the trial balance total to be unequal, indicate whether the debit or credit total is higher and by how much.

a. The receipt of cash on account of $1,312 was recorded as a debit to Cash for $1,012 and a credit to Accounts Receivable for $1,312.
b. The payment of cash for the purchase of office equipment of $4,500 was debited to Land for $4,500 and credited to Cash for $4,500.
c. The payment of $1,420 on account was debited to Accounts Payable for $142 and credited to Cash for $1,420.

PE 2-7A
Correction of errors
obj. 4

The following errors took place in journalizing and posting transactions:

a. The payment of $3,125 from a customer on account was recorded as a debit to Cash and a credit to Accounts Payable.
b. Advertising expense of $1,500 paid for the current month was recorded as a debit to Miscellaneous Expense and a credit to Advertising Expense.

Journalize the entries to correct the errors. Omit explanations.

PE 2-7B
Correction of errors
obj. 4

The following errors took place in journalizing and posting transactions:

a. The purchase of supplies of $2,690 on account was recorded as a debit to Office Equipment and a credit to Supplies.
b. The receipt of $3,750 for services rendered was recorded as a debit to Accounts Receivable and a credit to Fees Earned.

Journalize the entries to correct the errors. Omit explanations.

Exercises

EX 2-1
Chart of accounts
obj. 1

The following accounts appeared in recent financial statements of Continental Airlines:

Accounts Payable	Flight Equipment
Air Traffic Liability	Landing Fees
Aircraft Fuel Expense	Passenger Revenue
Cargo and Mail Revenue	Purchase Deposits for Flight Equipment
Commissions	Spare Parts and Supplies

Identify each account as either a balance sheet account or an income statement account. For each balance sheet account, identify it as an asset, a liability, or stockholders' equity. For each income statement account, identify it as a revenue or an expense.

EX 2-2
Chart of accounts
obj. 1

Mandalay Interiors is owned and operated by Angie Stowe, an interior decorator. In the ledger of Mandalay Interiors, the first digit of the account number indicates its major account classification (1—assets, 2—liabilities, 3—stockholders' equity, 4—revenues, 5—expenses). The second digit of the account number indicates the specific account within each of the preceding major account classifications.

Match each account number with its most likely account in the list below. The account numbers are 11, 12, 13, 21, 31, 32, 33, 41, 51, 52, and 53.

Accounts Payable	Land
Accounts Receivable	Miscellaneous Expense
Capital Stock	Retained Earnings
Cash	Supplies Expense
Dividends	Wages Expense
Fees Earned	

EX 2-3
Chart of accounts
obj. 1

Dazzle School is a newly organized business that teaches people how to inspire and influence others. The list of accounts to be opened in the general ledger is as follows:

Accounts Payable	Equipment	Retained Earnings
Accounts Receivable	Fees Earned	Supplies
Capital Stock	Miscellaneous Expense	Supplies Expense
Cash	Prepaid Insurance	Unearned Rent
Dividends	Rent Expense	Wages Expense

List the accounts in the order in which they should appear in the ledger of Dazzle School and assign account numbers. Each account number is to have two digits: the first digit is to indicate the major classification (1 for assets, etc.), and the second digit is to identify the specific account within each major classification (11 for Cash, etc.).

EX 2-4
Identifying transactions
obj. 1

Eos Co. is a travel agency. The nine transactions recorded by Eos during March 2008, its first month of operations, are indicated in the following T accounts:

Cash		Equipment		Dividends	
(1) 30,000	(2) 1,800	(3) 24,000		(8) 2,500	
(7) 10,000	(3) 9,000				
	(4) 3,050				
	(6) 7,500				
	(8) 2,500				

Accounts Receivable		Accounts Payable		Service Revenue	
(5) 15,000	(7) 10,000	(6) 7,500	(3) 15,000		(5) 15,000

Supplies		Capital Stock		Operating Expenses	
(2) 1,800	(9) 1,050		(1) 30,000	(4) 3,050	
				(9) 1,050	

Indicate for each debit and each credit: (a) whether an asset, liability, capital stock, dividends, revenue, or expense account was affected and (b) whether the account was increased (+) or decreased (−). Present your answers in the following form, with transaction (1) given as an example:

	Account Debited		Account Credited	
Transaction	Type	Effect	Type	Effect
(1)	asset	+	capital stock	+

EX 2-5
Journal entries
objs. 1, 2

Based upon the T accounts in Exercise 2-4, prepare the nine journal entries from which the postings were made. Journal entry explanations may be omitted.

EX 2-6
Trial balance
obj. 3

✓ *Total Debit column:*
$52,500

Based upon the data presented in Exercise 2-4, prepare an unadjusted trial balance, listing the accounts in their proper order.

EX 2-7
Normal entries for accounts
obj. 1

During the month, Witherspoon Labs Co. has a substantial number of transactions affecting each of the following accounts. State for each account whether it is likely to have (a) debit entries only, (b) credit entries only, or (c) both debit and credit entries.

1. Accounts Payable
2. Accounts Receivable
3. Cash
4. Fees Earned

5. Insurance Expense
6. Dividends
7. Supplies Expense

EX 2-8
Normal balances of accounts
obj. 1

Identify each of the following accounts of Sydney Services Co. as asset, liability, stockholders' equity, revenue, or expense, and state in each case whether the normal balance is a debit or a credit.

a. Accounts Payable
b. Accounts Receivable
c. Capital Stock
d. Dividends
e. Cash

f. Fees Earned
g. Office Equipment
h. Rent Expense
i. Supplies
j. Wages Expense

EX 2-9
Rules of debit and credit
obj. 1

The following table summarizes the rules of debit and credit. For each of the items (a) through (l), indicate whether the proper answer is a debit or a credit.

	Increase	Decrease	Normal Balance
Balance sheet accounts:			
Asset	(a)	Credit	(b)
Liability	(c)	(d)	Credit
Stockholders' equity:			
Capital Stock	Credit	(e)	Credit
Retained Earnings	Credit	Debit	(f)
Dividends	(g)	(h)	Debit
Income statement accounts:			
Revenue	(i)	(j)	(k)
Expense	Debit	(l)	Debit

EX 2-10
Retained Earnings balance
obj. 1

As of January 1, Retained Earnings had a credit balance of $21,800. During the year, dividends totaled $1,500, and the business incurred a net loss of $24,000.

a. Calculate the balance of Retained Earnings as of the end of the year.
b. Assuming that there have been no recording errors, will the balance sheet prepared at December 31 balance? Explain.

EX 2-11
Cash account balance
obj. 1

During the month, Harpoon Co. received $479,250 in cash and paid out $312,380 in cash.

a. Do the data indicate that Harpoon Co. earned $166,870 during the month? Explain.
b. If the balance of the cash account is $241,925 at the end of the month, what was the Cash balance at the beginning of the month?

EX 2-12
Account balances
obj. 1

✔ *c. $5,100*

a. On June 1, the cash account balance was $11,150. During June, cash receipts totaled $72,300 and the June 30 balance was $15,750. Determine the cash payments made during June.

b. On July 1, the accounts receivable account balance was $25,500. During July, $115,000 was collected from customers on account. Assuming the July 31 balance was $27,500, determine the fees billed to customers on account during July.

c. During December, $60,500 was paid to creditors on account, and purchases on account were $77,700. Assuming the December 31 balance of Accounts Payable was $22,300, determine the account balance on December 1.

EX 2-13
Transactions
objs. 1, 2

The Boa Co. has the following accounts in its ledger: Cash; Accounts Receivable; Supplies; Office Equipment; Accounts Payable; Capital Stock; Retained Earnings; Dividends; Fees Earned; Rent Expense; Advertising Expense; Utilities Expense; Miscellaneous Expense.

Journalize the following selected transactions for October 2007 in a two-column journal. Journal entry explanations may be omitted.

Oct. 1. Paid rent for the month, $2,500.
      3. Paid advertising expense, $1,100.
      4. Paid cash for supplies, $725.
      6. Purchased office equipment on account, $7,500.
      10. Received cash from customers on account, $3,600.
      12. Paid creditor on account, $600.
      20. Paid dividends of $1,000.
      27. Paid cash for repairs to office equipment, $500.
      30. Paid telephone bill for the month, $195.
      31. Fees earned and billed to customers for the month, $20,150.
      31. Paid electricity bill for the month, $315.

EX 2-14
Journalizing and posting
objs. 1, 2

On July 27, 2008, Colorcast Co. purchased $1,875 of supplies on account. In Colorcast Co.'s chart of accounts, the supplies account is No. 15, and the accounts payable account is No. 21.

a. Journalize the July 27, 2008, transaction on page 38 of Colorcast Co.'s two-column journal. Include an explanation of the entry.

b. Prepare a four-column account for Supplies. Enter a debit balance of $735 as of July 1, 2008. Place a check mark (✔) in the Posting Reference column.

c. Prepare a four-column account for Accounts Payable. Enter a credit balance of $11,380 as of July 1, 2008. Place a check mark (✔) in the Posting Reference column.

d. Post the July 27, 2008, transaction to the accounts.

EX 2-15
Transactions and T accounts
objs. 1, 2

The following selected transactions were completed during August of the current year:

1. Billed customers for fees earned, $13,750.
2. Purchased supplies on account, $1,325.
3. Received cash from customers on account, $8,150.
4. Paid creditors on account, $800.

a. Journalize the above transactions in a two-column journal, using the appropriate number to identify the transactions. Journal entry explanations may be omitted.

b. Post the entries prepared in (a) to the following T accounts: Cash, Supplies, Accounts Receivable, Accounts Payable, Fees Earned. To the left of each amount posted in the accounts, place the appropriate number to identify the transactions.

EX 2-16
Trial balance
obj. 3

The accounts in the ledger of Matice Co. as of July 31, 2008, are listed in alphabetical order as follows. All accounts have normal balances. The balance of the cash account has been intentionally omitted.

Accounts Payable	$ 56,130	Notes Payable	$120,000
Accounts Receivable	112,500	Prepaid Insurance	9,000
Capital Stock	25,000	Rent Expense	180,000
Cash	?	Retained Earnings	234,920
Dividends	60,000	Supplies	6,300
Fees Earned	930,000	Supplies Expense	23,700
Insurance Expense	18,000	Unearned Rent	27,000
Land	255,000	Utilities Expense	124,500
Miscellaneous Expense	26,700	Wages Expense	525,000

✓ *Total Credit column:*
$1,393,050

Prepare an unadjusted trial balance, listing the accounts in their proper order and inserting the missing figure for cash.

EX 2-17
Effect of errors on trial balance
obj. 3

Indicate which of the following errors, each considered individually, would cause the trial balance totals to be unequal:

a. A fee of $2,350 earned and due from a client was not debited to Accounts Receivable or credited to a revenue account, because the cash had not been received.
b. A payment of $1,500 to a creditor was posted as a debit of $1,500 to Accounts Payable and a debit of $1,500 to Cash.
c. A payment of $6,000 for equipment purchased was posted as a debit of $600 to Equipment and a credit of $600 to Cash.
d. Payment of a cash dividend of $12,000 was journalized and posted as a debit of $21,000 to Salary Expense and a credit of $12,000 to Cash.
e. A receipt of $750 from an account receivable was journalized and posted as a debit of $750 to Cash and a credit of $750 to Fees Earned.

EX 2-18
Errors in trial balance
obj. 3

✓ *Total of Credit column: $363,200*

The following preliminary unadjusted trial balance of Awesome Co., a sports ticket agency, does not balance:

Awesome Co.
Unadjusted Trial Balance
December 31, 2008

	Debit Balances	Credit Balances
Cash	94,700	
Accounts Receivable	44,200	
Prepaid Insurance		16,000
Equipment	15,000	
Accounts Payable		25,960
Unearned Rent		5,800
Capital Stock	75,000	
Retained Earnings	89,840	
Dividends	20,000	
Service Revenue		167,500
Wages Expense		84,000
Advertising Expense	14,400	
Miscellaneous Expense		2,850
	353,140	302,110

When the ledger and other records are reviewed, you discover the following: (1) the debits and credits in the cash account total $94,700 and $67,950, respectively; (2) a billing of $5,000 to a customer on account was not posted to the accounts receivable account; (3) a payment of $3,600 made to a creditor on account was not posted to the accounts payable account; (4) the balance of the unearned rent account is $8,500; (5) the correct balance of the equipment account is $150,000; and (6) each account has a normal balance.

Prepare a corrected unadjusted trial balance.

EX 2-19
Effect of errors on trial balance

obj. **3**

The following errors occurred in posting from a two-column journal:

1. A credit of $5,125 to Accounts Payable was not posted.
2. A debit of $675 to Accounts Payable was posted as a credit.
3. A debit of $1,375 to Supplies was posted twice.
4. A debit of $3,575 to Wages Expense was posted as $3,557.
5. An entry debiting Accounts Receivable and crediting Fees Earned for $6,000 was not posted.
6. A credit of $350 to Cash was posted as $530.
7. A debit of $1,000 to Cash was posted to Miscellaneous Expense.

Considering each case individually (i.e., assuming that no other errors had occurred), indicate: (a) by "yes" or "no" whether the trial balance would be out of balance; (b) if answer to (a) is "yes," the amount by which the trial balance totals would differ; and (c) whether the Debit or Credit column of the trial balance would have the larger total. Answers should be presented in the following form, with error (1) given as an example:

Error	(a) Out of Balance	(b) Difference	(c) Larger Total
1.	yes	$5,125	debit

EX 2-20
Errors in trial balance

obj. **3**

✓ *Total of Credit column: $375,000*

Identify the errors in the following trial balance. All accounts have normal balances.

Hybrid Co.
Unadjusted Trial Balance
For the Month Ending October 31, 2008

	Debit Balances	Credit Balances
Cash	22,500	
Accounts Receivable		49,200
Prepaid Insurance	10,800	
Equipment	150,000	
Accounts Payable	5,550	
Salaries Payable		3,750
Capital Stock		15,000
Retained Earnings		114,600
Dividends		18,000
Service Revenue		236,100
Salary Expense	98,430	
Advertising Expense		21,600
Miscellaneous Expense	4,470	
	458,250	458,250

EX 2-21
Entries to correct errors

obj. **4**

The following errors took place in journalizing and posting transactions:

a. Dividends of $20,000 were recorded as a debit to Wages Expense and a credit to Cash.
b. Rent of $3,600 paid for the current month was recorded as a debit to Rent Expense and a credit to Prepaid Rent.

Journalize the entries to correct the errors. Omit explanations.

EX 2-22
Entries to correct errors

obj. **4**

The following errors took place in journalizing and posting transactions:

a. A $940 purchase of supplies for cash was recorded as a debit to Supplies Expense and a credit to Accounts Payable.
b. Cash of $2,750 received on account was recorded as a debit to Fees Earned and a credit to Cash.

Journalize the entries to correct the errors. Omit explanations.

Problems Series A

PR 2-1A
Entries into T accounts and trial balance

objs. 1, 2, 3

✔ *3. Total of Debit column: $51,200*

Hannah Knox, an architect, opened an office on July 1, 2008. During the month, she completed the following transactions connected with her professional corporation, Hannah Knox, Architect, P.C.:

a. Transferred cash from a personal bank account to an account to be used for the business in exchange for capital stock, $25,000.
b. Paid July rent for office and workroom, $2,000.
c. Purchased used automobile for $16,500, paying $1,500 cash and giving a note payable for the remainder.
d. Purchased office and computer equipment on account, $6,500.
e. Paid cash for supplies, $975.
f. Paid cash for annual insurance policies, $1,200.
g. Received cash from client for plans delivered, $3,750.
h. Paid cash for miscellaneous expenses, $240.
i. Paid cash to creditors on account, $2,500.
j. Paid installment due on note payable, $450.
k. Received invoice for blueprint service, due in August, $750.
l. Recorded fee earned on plans delivered, payment to be received in August, $3,150.
m. Paid salary of assistant, $1,500.
n. Paid gas, oil, and repairs on automobile for July, $280.

Instructions

1. Record the above transactions directly in the following T accounts, without journalizing: Cash; Accounts Receivable; Supplies; Prepaid Insurance; Automobiles; Equipment; Notes Payable; Accounts Payable; Capital Stock; Professional Fees; Rent Expense; Salary Expense; Automobile Expense; Blueprint Expense; Miscellaneous Expense. To the left of the amount entered in the accounts, place the appropriate letter to identify the transaction.
2. Determine account balances of the T accounts. Accounts containing a single entry only (such as Prepaid Insurance) do not need a balance.
3. Prepare an unadjusted trial balance for Hannah Knox, Architect, P.C. as of July 31, 2008.

PR 2-2A
Journal entries and trial balance

objs. 1, 2, 3

✔ *4. c. $6,425*

On March 1, 2008, Kara Frantz established Mudcat Realty, which completed the following transactions during the month:

a. Kara Frantz transferred cash from a personal bank account to an account to be used for the business in exchange for capital stock, $15,000.
b. Paid rent on office and equipment for the month, $2,500.
c. Purchased supplies on account, $850.
d. Paid creditor on account, $400.
e. Earned sales commissions, receiving cash, $15,750.
f. Paid automobile expenses (including rental charge) for month, $2,400, and miscellaneous expenses, $600.
g. Paid office salaries, $3,250.
h. Determined that the cost of supplies used was $575.
i. Paid dividends of $1,000.

Instructions

1. Journalize entries for transactions (a) through (i), using the following account titles: Cash; Supplies; Accounts Payable; Capital Stock; Dividends; Sales Commissions; Office Salaries Expense; Rent Expense; Automobile Expense; Supplies Expense; Miscellaneous Expense. Explanations may be omitted.
2. Prepare T accounts, using the account titles in (1). Post the journal entries to these accounts, placing the appropriate letter to the left of each amount to identify the transactions. Determine the account balances, after all posting is complete. Accounts containing only a single entry do not need a balance.
3. Prepare an unadjusted trial balance as of March 31, 2008.

(continued)

4. Determine the following:
   a. Amount of total revenue recorded in the ledger.
   b. Amount of total expenses recorded in the ledger.
   c. Amount of net income for March.

PR 2-3A
Journal entries and trial balance

objs. 1, 2, 3

✓ 3. Total of Credit column: $49,825

On June 1, 2008, Brooks Dodd established an interior decorating business, Coordinated Designs. During the month, Brooks completed the following transactions related to the business:

June   1. Brooks transferred cash from a personal bank account to an account to be used for the business in exchange for capital stock, $18,000.
       5. Paid rent for period of June 5 to end of month, $2,150.
       6. Purchased office equipment on account, $8,500.
       8. Purchased a used truck for $18,000, paying $10,000 cash and giving a note payable for the remainder.
      10. Purchased supplies for cash, $1,200.
      12. Received cash for job completed, $10,500.
      15. Paid annual premiums on property and casualty insurance, $2,400.
      23. Recorded jobs completed on account and sent invoices to customers, $5,950.
      24. Received an invoice for truck expenses, to be paid in July, $1,000.
      29. Paid utilities expense, $1,200.
      29. Paid miscellaneous expenses, $400.
      30. Received cash from customers on account, $3,200.
      30. Paid wages of employees, $2,900.
      30. Paid creditor a portion of the amount owed for equipment purchased on June 6, $2,125.
      30. Paid dividends of $1,750.

Instructions
1. Journalize each transaction in a two-column journal, referring to the following chart of accounts in selecting the accounts to be debited and credited. (Do not insert the account numbers in the journal at this time.) Explanations may be omitted.

11 Cash	31 Capital Stock
12 Accounts Receivable	33 Dividends
13 Supplies	41 Fees Earned
14 Prepaid Insurance	51 Wages Expense
16 Equipment	53 Rent Expense
18 Truck	54 Utilities Expense
21 Notes Payable	55 Truck Expense
22 Accounts Payable	59 Miscellaneous Expense

2. Post the journal to a ledger of four-column accounts, inserting appropriate posting references as each item is posted. Extend the balances to the appropriate balance columns after each transaction is posted.
3. Prepare an unadjusted trial balance for Coordinated Designs as of June 30, 2008.

PR 2-4A
Journal entries and trial balance

objs. 1, 2, 3

✓ 4. Total of Debit column: $430,650

Passport Realty acts as an agent in buying, selling, renting, and managing real estate. The unadjusted trial balance on October 31, 2008, is shown at the top of the following page.
   The following business transactions were completed by Passport Realty during November 2008:

Nov.   1. Paid rent on office for month, $5,000.
       2. Purchased office supplies on account, $1,750.
       5. Paid annual insurance premiums, $4,800.
      10. Received cash from clients on account, $52,000.
      15. Purchased land for a future building site for $90,000, paying $10,000 in cash and giving a note payable for the remainder.
      17. Paid creditors on account, $7,750.

Passport Realty
Unadjusted Trial Balance
October 31, 2008

		Debit Balances	Credit Balances
11	Cash	26,300	
12	Accounts Receivable	67,500	
13	Prepaid Insurance	3,000	
14	Office Supplies	1,800	
16	Land	—	
21	Accounts Payable		13,020
22	Unearned Rent		—
23	Notes Payable		—
31	Capital Stock		5,000
32	Retained Earnings		27,980
33	Dividends	2,000	
41	Fees Earned		260,000
51	Salary and Commission Expense	148,200	
52	Rent Expense	30,000	
53	Advertising Expense	17,800	
54	Automobile Expense	5,500	
59	Miscellaneous Expense	3,900	
		306,000	306,000

Nov. 20. Returned a portion of the office supplies purchased on November 2, receiving full credit for their cost, $250.
    23. Paid advertising expense, $2,100.
    27. Discovered an error in computing a commission; received cash from the salesperson for the overpayment, $700.
    28. Paid automobile expense (including rental charges for an automobile), $1,500.
    29. Paid miscellaneous expenses, $450.
    30. Recorded revenue earned and billed to clients during the month, $48,400.
    30. Paid salaries and commissions for the month, $25,000.
    30. Paid dividends of $8,000.
    30. Rented land purchased on November 15 to local merchants association for use as a parking lot in December and January, during a street rebuilding program; received advance payment of $2,500.

Instructions

1. Record the November 1, 2008, balance of each account in the appropriate balance column of a four-column account, write *Balance* in the item section, and place a check mark (✓) in the Posting Reference column.
2. Journalize the transactions for November in a two-column journal. Journal entry explanations may be omitted.
3. Post to the ledger, extending the account balance to the appropriate balance column after each posting.
4. Prepare an unadjusted trial balance of the ledger as of November 30, 2008.

PR 2-5A
Errors in trial balance

objs. 3, 4

✓ 7. Total of Debit
column: $43,338.10

If the working papers correlating with this textbook are not used, omit Problem 2-5A.

The following records of Mainstay TV Repair are presented in the working papers:

• Journal containing entries for the period July 1–31.
• Ledger to which the July entries have been posted.
• Preliminary trial balance as of July 31, which does not balance.

Locate the errors, supply the information requested, and prepare a corrected trial balance according to the following instructions. The balances recorded in the accounts as of July 1 and the entries in the journal are correctly stated. If it is necessary to correct any posted amounts in the ledger, a line should be drawn through the erroneous figure and the correct amount inserted above. Corrections or notations may be inserted on the preliminary trial balance in any manner desired. It is not necessary to complete all of the instructions if equal trial balance totals can be obtained earlier. However, the requirements of instructions (6) and (7) should be completed in any event.

Instructions

1. Verify the totals of the preliminary trial balance, inserting the correct amounts in the schedule provided in the working papers.
2. Compute the difference between the trial balance totals.
3. Compare the listings in the trial balance with the balances appearing in the ledger, and list the errors in the space provided in the working papers.
4. Verify the accuracy of the balance of each account in the ledger, and list the errors in the space provided in the working papers.
5. Trace the postings in the ledger back to the journal, using small check marks to identify items traced. Correct any amounts in the ledger that may be necessitated by errors in posting, and list the errors in the space provided in the working papers.
6. Journalize as of July 31 the payment of $125 for advertising expense. The bill had been paid on July 31 but was inadvertently omitted from the journal. Post to the ledger. (Revise any amounts necessitated by posting this entry.)
7. Prepare a new unadjusted trial balance.

PR 2-6A
Corrected trial balance
obj. **3**

✓ *1. Total of Debit
column: $200,000*

Iberian Carpet has the following unadjusted trial balance as of March 31, 2008:

Iberian Carpet
Unadjusted Trial Balance
March 31, 2008

	Debit Balances	Credit Balances
Cash	4,300	
Accounts Receivable	11,870	
Supplies	2,320	
Prepaid Insurance	880	
Equipment	56,000	
Notes Payable		26,100
Accounts Payable		7,900
Capital Stock		6,000
Retained Earnings		32,400
Dividends	14,500	
Fees Earned		122,700
Wages Expense	70,000	
Rent Expense	16,600	
Advertising Expense	720	
Miscellaneous Expense	1,450	
	178,640	195,100

The debit and credit totals are not equal as a result of the following errors:

a. The balance of cash was understated by $3,000.
b. A cash receipt of $4,500 was posted as a debit to Cash of $5,400.
c. A debit of $1,850 to Accounts Receivable was not posted.
d. A return of $350 of defective supplies was erroneously posted as a $530 credit to Supplies.
e. An insurance policy acquired at a cost of $175 was posted as a credit to Prepaid Insurance.
f. The balance of Notes Payable was understated by $7,500.
g. A credit of $900 in Accounts Payable was overlooked when determining the balance of the account.
h. A debit of $3,500 for dividends was posted as a credit to Retained Earnings.
i. The balance of $7,200 in Advertising Expense was entered as $720 in the trial balance.
j. Gas, Electricity, and Water Expense, with a balance of $6,900, was omitted from the trial balance.

Instructions
1. Prepare a corrected unadjusted trial balance as of March 31, 2008.
2. ▬▬▶ Does the fact that the unadjusted trial balance in (1) is balanced mean that there are no errors in the accounts? Explain.

Problems Series B

PR 2-1B
Entries into T accounts and trial balance

objs. 1, 2, 3

✓3. Total of Debit column: $47,800

Lynette Moss, an architect, opened an office on April 1, 2008. During the month, she completed the following transactions connected with her professional corporation, Lynette Moss, Architect, P.C.:

a. Transferred cash from a personal bank account to an account to be used for the business in exchange for capital stock, $22,500.
b. Purchased used automobile for $15,300, paying $4,000 cash and giving a note payable for the remainder.
c. Paid April rent for office and workroom, $2,500.
d. Paid cash for supplies, $1,200.
e. Purchased office and computer equipment on account, $5,200.
f. Paid cash for annual insurance policies on automobile and equipment, $1,600.
g. Received cash from a client for plans delivered, $6,500.
h. Paid cash to creditors on account, $1,800.
i. Paid cash for miscellaneous expenses, $300.
j. Received invoice for blueprint service, due in May, $800.
k. Recorded fee earned on plans delivered, payment to be received in May, $3,500.
l. Paid salary of assistant, $1,500.
m. Paid cash for miscellaneous expenses, $210.
n. Paid installment due on note payable, $200.
o. Paid gas, oil, and repairs on automobile for April, $250.

Instructions
1. Record the above transactions directly in the following T accounts, without journalizing: Cash; Accounts Receivable; Supplies; Prepaid Insurance; Automobiles; Equipment; Notes Payable; Accounts Payable; Capital Stock; Professional Fees; Rent Expense; Salary Expense; Blueprint Expense; Automobile Expense; Miscellaneous Expense. To the left of each amount entered in the accounts, place the appropriate letter to identify the transaction.
2. Determine account balances of the T accounts. Accounts containing a single entry only (such as Prepaid Insurance) do not need a balance.
3. Prepare an unadjusted trial balance for Lynette Moss, Architect, P.C. as of April 30, 2008.

PR 2-2B
Journal entries and trial balance

objs. 1, 2, 3

✓4. c. $5,575

On July 1, 2008, Bill Bonds established Genesis Realty, which completed the following transactions during the month:

a. Bill Bonds transferred cash from a personal bank account to an account to be used for the business in exchange for capital stock, $18,000.
b. Purchased supplies on account, $1,000.
c. Earned sales commissions, receiving cash, $14,600.
d. Paid rent on office and equipment for the month, $3,000.
e. Paid creditor on account, $600.
f. Paid dividends of $1,500.
g. Paid automobile expenses (including rental charge) for month, $2,000, and miscellaneous expenses, $500.
h. Paid office salaries, $2,800.
i. Determined that the cost of supplies used was $725.

Instructions
1. Journalize entries for transactions (a) through (i), using the following account titles: Cash; Supplies; Accounts Payable; Capital Stock; Dividends; Sales Commissions; Rent Expense; Office Salaries Expense; Automobile Expense; Supplies Expense; Miscellaneous Expense. Journal entry explanations may be omitted.

(continued)

2. Prepare T accounts, using the account titles in (1). Post the journal entries to these accounts, placing the appropriate letter to the left of each amount to identify the transactions. Determine the account balances, after all posting is complete. Accounts containing only a single entry do not need a balance.
3. Prepare an unadjusted trial balance as of July 31, 2008.
4. Determine the following:
   a. Amount of total revenue recorded in the ledger.
   b. Amount of total expenses recorded in the ledger.
   c. Amount of net income for July.

PR 2-3B
Journal entries and trial balance
objs. 1, 2, 3

✓ 3. Total of Credit column: $47,675

On October 1, 2008, Kristy Gomez established an interior decorating business, Ultimate Designs. During the month, Kristy Gomez completed the following transactions related to the business:

Oct. 1. Kristy transferred cash from a personal bank account to an account to be used for the business in exchange for capital stock, $20,000.
   3. Paid rent for period of October 3 to end of month, $1,600.
   10. Purchased a truck for $15,000, paying $5,000 cash and giving a note payable for the remainder.
   13. Purchased equipment on account, $4,500.
   14. Purchased supplies for cash, $1,100.
   15. Paid annual premiums on property and casualty insurance, $2,800.
   15. Received cash for job completed, $6,100.
   21. Paid creditor a portion of the amount owed for equipment purchased on October 13, $2,400.
   24. Recorded jobs completed on account and sent invoices to customers, $8,600.
   26. Received an invoice for truck expenses, to be paid in November, $875.
   27. Paid utilities expense, $900.
   27. Paid miscellaneous expenses, $315.
   29. Received cash from customers on account, $4,100.
   30. Paid wages of employees, $2,500.
   31. Paid dividends of $3,000.

Instructions
1. Journalize each transaction in a two-column journal, referring to the following chart of accounts in selecting the accounts to be debited and credited. (Do not insert the account numbers in the journal at this time.) Journal entry explanations may be omitted.

11 Cash	31 Capital Stock
12 Accounts Receivable	33 Dividends
13 Supplies	41 Fees Earned
14 Prepaid Insurance	51 Wages Expense
16 Equipment	53 Rent Expense
18 Truck	54 Utilities Expense
21 Notes Payable	55 Truck Expense
22 Accounts Payable	59 Miscellaneous Expense

2. Post the journal to a ledger of four-column accounts, inserting appropriate posting references as each item is posted. Extend the balances to the appropriate balance columns after each transaction is posted.
3. Prepare an unadjusted trial balance for Ultimate Designs as of October 31, 2008.

PR 2-4B
Journal entries and trial balance
objs. 1, 2, 3

✓ 4. Total of Debit column: $375,230

Equity Realty acts as an agent in buying, selling, renting, and managing real estate. The unadjusted trial balance on July 31, 2008, is shown at the top of the following page.
   The following business transactions were completed by Equity Realty during August 2008:

Aug. 1. Purchased office supplies on account, $1,500.
   2. Paid rent on office for month, $2,500.
   3. Received cash from clients on account, $28,720.
   5. Paid annual insurance premiums, $3,600.

Equity Realty
Unadjusted Trial Balance
July 31, 2008

		Debit Balances	Credit Balances
11	Cash	21,200	
12	Accounts Receivable	35,750	
13	Prepaid Insurance	4,500	
14	Office Supplies	1,000	
16	Land	—	
21	Accounts Payable		6,200
22	Unearned Rent		—
23	Notes Payable		—
31	Capital Stock		7,500
32	Retained Earnings		24,050
33	Dividends	16,000	
41	Fees Earned		220,000
51	Salary and Commission Expense	140,000	
52	Rent Expense	17,500	
53	Advertising Expense	14,300	
54	Automobile Expense	6,400	
59	Miscellaneous Expense	1,100	
		257,750	257,750

Aug. 9. Returned a portion of the office supplies purchased on August 1, receiving full credit for their cost, $250.

17. Paid advertising expense, $3,450.

23. Paid creditors on account, $2,670.

29. Paid miscellaneous expenses, $500.

30. Paid automobile expense (including rental charges for an automobile), $1,500.

31. Discovered an error in computing a commission; received cash from the salesperson for the overpayment, $1,000.

31. Paid salaries and commissions for the month, $17,400.

31. Recorded revenue earned and billed to clients during the month, $51,900.

31. Purchased land for a future building site for $75,000, paying $10,000 in cash and giving a note payable for the remainder.

31. Paid dividends of $5,000.

31. Rented land purchased on August 31 to a local university for use as a parking lot during football season (September, October, and November); received advance payment of $2,000.

Instructions

1. Record the August 1 balance of each account in the appropriate balance column of a four-column account, write *Balance* in the item section, and place a check mark (✓) in the Posting Reference column.

2. Journalize the transactions for August in a two-column journal. Journal entry explanations may be omitted.

3. Post to the ledger, extending the account balance to the appropriate balance column after each posting.

4. Prepare an unadjusted trial balance of the ledger as of August 31, 2008.

PR 2-5B
Errors in trial balance
objs. **3, 4**

If the working papers correlating with this textbook are not used, omit Problem 2-5B.

The following records of Mainstay TV Repair are presented in the working papers:

- Journal containing entries for the period July 1–31.
- Ledger to which the July entries have been posted.
- Preliminary trial balance as of July 31, which does not balance.

Locate the errors, supply the information requested, and prepare a corrected trial balance according to the following instructions. The balances recorded in the accounts as of July 1

✓ 7. Total of Credit
column: $43,338.10

and the entries in the journal are correctly stated. If it is necessary to correct any posted amounts in the ledger, a line should be drawn through the erroneous figure and the correct amount inserted above. Corrections or notations may be inserted on the preliminary trial balance in any manner desired. It is not necessary to complete all of the instructions if equal trial balance totals can be obtained earlier. However, the requirements of instructions (6) and (7) should be completed in any event.

Instructions

1. Verify the totals of the preliminary trial balance, inserting the correct amounts in the schedule provided in the working papers.
2. Compute the difference between the trial balance totals.
3. Compare the listings in the trial balance with the balances appearing in the ledger, and list the errors in the space provided in the working papers.
4. Verify the accuracy of the balance of each account in the ledger, and list the errors in the space provided in the working papers.
5. Trace the postings in the ledger back to the journal, using small check marks to identify items traced. Correct any amounts in the ledger that may be necessitated by errors in posting, and list the errors in the space provided in the working papers.
6. Journalize as of July 31 the payment of $110 for gas and electricity. The bill had been paid on July 31 but was inadvertently omitted from the journal. Post to the ledger. (Revise any amounts necessitated by posting this entry.)
7. Prepare a new unadjusted trial balance.

PR 2-6B
Corrected trial balance

obj. 3

✓ 1. Total of Debit
column: $234,000

Epic Video has the following unadjusted trial balance as of July 31, 2008:

Epic Video
Unadjusted Trial Balance
July 31, 2008

	Debit Balances	Credit Balances
Cash	6,250	
Accounts Receivable	12,520	
Supplies	2,232	
Prepaid Insurance	710	
Equipment	54,000	
Notes Payable		22,500
Accounts Payable		4,980
Capital Stock		2,500
Retained Earnings		27,900
Dividends	11,500	
Fees Earned		178,020
Wages Expense	102,000	
Rent Expense	20,850	
Advertising Expense	9,540	
Gas, Electricity, and Water Expense	5,670	
	225,272	235,900

The debit and credit totals are not equal as a result of the following errors:

a. The balance of cash was overstated by $5,000.
b. A cash receipt of $3,200 was posted as a credit to Cash of $2,300.
c. A debit of $2,780 to Accounts Receivable was not posted.
d. A return of $235 of defective supplies was erroneously posted as a $253 credit to Supplies.
e. An insurance policy acquired at a cost of $500 was posted as a credit to Prepaid Insurance.
f. The balance of Notes Payable was overstated by $4,500.
g. A credit of $600 in Accounts Payable was overlooked when the balance of the account was determined.

h. A debit of $2,000 for dividends was posted as a debit to Retained Earnings.

i. The balance of $9,450 in Advertising Expense was entered as $9,540 in the trial balance.

j. Miscellaneous Expense, with a balance of $2,520, was omitted from the trial balance.

Instructions

1. Prepare a corrected unadjusted trial balance as of July 31 of the current year.

2. ▬▬▶ Does the fact that the unadjusted trial balance in (1) is balanced mean that there are no errors in the accounts? Explain.

Continuing Problem

✓4. Total of Debit
column: $37,800

The transactions completed by Dancin Music during April 2008 were described at the end of Chapter 1. The following transactions were completed during May, the second month of the business's operations:

May 1. Kris Payne made an additional investment in Dancin Music by depositing $2,500 in Dancin Music's checking account in exchange for capital stock.

1. Instead of continuing to share office space with a local real estate agency, Kris decided to rent office space near a local music store. Paid rent for May, $1,600.

1. Paid a premium of $3,360 for a comprehensive insurance policy covering liability, theft, and fire. The policy covers a one-year period.

2. Received $1,350 on account.

3. On behalf of Dancin Music, Kris signed a contract with a local radio station, KPRG, to provide guest spots for the next three months. The contract requires Dancin Music to provide a guest disc jockey for 80 hours per month for a monthly fee of $2,400. Any additional hours beyond 80 will be billed to KPRG at $40 per hour. In accordance with the contract, Kris received $4,800 from KPRG as an advance payment for the first two months.

3. Paid $250 on account.

4. Paid an attorney $300 for reviewing the May 3rd contract with KPRG. (Record as Miscellaneous Expense.)

5. Purchased office equipment on account from One-Stop Office Mart, $5,000.

8. Paid for a newspaper advertisement, $180.

11. Received $750 for serving as a disc jockey for a college fraternity party.

13. Paid $500 to a local audio electronics store for rental of digital recording equipment.

14. Paid wages of $1,000 to receptionist and part-time assistant.

16. Received $1,500 for serving as a disc jockey for a wedding reception.

18. Purchased supplies on account, $750.

21. Paid $325 to Rocket Music for use of its current music demos in making various music sets.

22. Paid $800 to a local radio station to advertise the services of Dancin Music twice daily for the remainder of May.

23. Served as disc jockey for a party for $2,500. Received $750, with the remainder due June 4, 2008.

27. Paid electric bill, $560.

28. Paid wages of $1,000 to receptionist and part-time assistant.

29. Paid miscellaneous expenses, $150.

30. Served as a disc jockey for a charity ball for $1,500. Received $400, with the remainder due on June 9, 2008.

31. Received $2,800 for serving as a disc jockey for a party.

31. Paid $900 royalties (music expense) to Federated Clearing for use of various artists' music during May.

31. Paid dividends of $1,000.

Dancin Music's chart of accounts and the balance of accounts as of May 1, 2008 (all normal balances), are as follows:

11	Cash	$ 9,160	41	Fees Earned	$5,700
12	Accounts Receivable	1,350	50	Wages Expense	400
14	Supplies	170	51	Office Rent Expense	1,000
15	Prepaid Insurance	—	52	Equipment Rent Expense	800
17	Office Equipment	—	53	Utilities Expense	350
21	Accounts Payable	250	54	Music Expense	1,340
23	Unearned Revenue	—	55	Advertising Expense	750
31	Capital Stock	10,000	56	Supplies Expense	180
33	Dividends	300	59	Miscellaneous Expense	150

Instructions

1. Enter the May 1, 2008, account balances in the appropriate balance column of a four-column account. Write *Balance* in the Item column, and place a check mark (✓) in the Posting Reference column. (*Hint:* Verify the equality of the debit and credit balances in the ledger before proceeding with the next instruction.)
2. Analyze and journalize each transaction in a two-column journal, omitting journal entry explanations.
3. Post the journal to the ledger, extending the account balance to the appropriate balance column after each posting.
4. Prepare an unadjusted trial balance as of May 31, 2008.

Special Activities

SA 2-1
Ethics and professional conduct in business

ETHICS

At the end of the current month, Tomas Lott prepared a trial balance for AAA Rescue Service. The credit side of the trial balance exceeds the debit side by a significant amount. Tomas has decided to add the difference to the balance of the miscellaneous expense account in order to complete the preparation of the current month's financial statements by a 5 o'clock deadline. Tomas will look for the difference next week when he has more time.

⟶ Discuss whether Tomas is behaving in a professional manner.

SA 2-2
Account for revenue

Ennis College requires students to pay tuition each term before classes begin. Students who have not paid their tuition are not allowed to enroll or to attend classes.

What journal entry do you think Ennis College would use to record the receipt of the students' tuition payments? Describe the nature of each account in the entry.

SA 2-3
Record transactions

The following discussion took place between Mary Louden, the office manager of Zoomworks Data Company, and a new accountant, Allen Jarvis.

Allen: I've been thinking about our method of recording entries. It seems that it's inefficient.
Mary: In what way?
Allen: Well—correct me if I'm wrong—it seems like we have unnecessary steps in the process. We could easily develop a trial balance by posting our transactions directly into the ledger and bypassing the journal altogether. In this way, we could combine the recording and posting process into one step and save ourselves a lot of time. What do you think?
Mary: We need to have a talk.

⟶ What should Mary say to Allen?

SA 2-4
Debits and credits

Group Project

The following excerpt is from a conversation between Shelley Ryan, the president and chief operating officer of Diamond Construction Company, and her neighbor, Miguel Jimenez.

Miguel: Shelley, I'm taking a course in night school, "Intro to Accounting." I was wondering—could you answer a couple of questions for me?

Shelley: Well, I will if I can.

Miguel: Okay, our instructor says that it's critical we understand the basic concepts of accounting, or we'll never get beyond the first test. My problem is with those rules of debit and credit . . . you know, assets increase with debits, decrease with credits, etc.

Shelley: Yes, pretty basic stuff. You just have to memorize the rules. It shouldn't be too difficult.

Miguel: Sure, I can memorize the rules, but my problem is I want to be sure I understand the basic concepts behind the rules. For example, why can't assets be increased with credits and decreased with debits like revenue? As long as everyone did it that way, why not? It would seem easier if we had the same rules for all increases and decreases in accounts. Also, why is the left side of an account called the debit side? Why couldn't it be called something simple . . . like the "LE" for Left Entry? The right side could be called just "RE" for Right Entry. Finally, why are there just two sides to an entry? Why can't there be three or four sides to an entry?

In a group of four or five, select one person to play the role of Shelley and one person to play the role of Miguel.

1. ◖▬▬▶ After listening to the conversation between Shelley and Miguel, help Shelley answer Miguel's questions.
2. What information (other than just debit and credit journal entries) could the accounting system gather that might be useful to Shelley in managing Diamond Construction Company?

SA 2-5
Transactions and income statement

Shane Raburn is planning to manage and operate Birdie Caddy Service at Biloxi Golf and Country Club during June through August 2008. Shane will rent a small maintenance building from the country club for $500 per month and will offer caddy services, including cart rentals, to golfers. Shane has had no formal training in record keeping.

Shane keeps notes of all receipts and expenses in a shoe box. An examination of Shane's shoe box records for June revealed the following:

June 1. Withdrew $2,000 from personal bank account to be used to operate the caddy service.
   1. Paid rent to Biloxi Golf and Country Club, $500.
   2. Paid for golf supplies (practice balls, etc.), $650.
   3. Arranged for the rental of 40 regular (pulling) golf carts and 10 gasoline-driven carts for $1,500 per month. Paid $750 in advance, with the remaining $750 due June 20.
   7. Purchased supplies, including gasoline, for the golf carts on account, $350. Biloxi Golf and Country Club has agreed to allow Shane to store the gasoline in one of its fuel tanks at no cost.
  15. Received cash for services from June 1–15, $3,150.
  17. Paid cash to creditors on account, $350.
  20. Paid remaining rental on golf carts, $750.
  22. Purchased supplies, including gasoline, on account, $200.
  25. Accepted IOUs from customers on account, $850.
  28. Paid miscellaneous expenses, $180.
  30. Received cash for services from June 16–30, $3,200.
  30. Paid telephone and electricity (utilities) expenses, $160.
  30. Paid wages of part-time employees, $450.
  30. Received cash in payment of IOUs on account, $550.
  30. Determined the amount of supplies on hand at the end of June, $390.

Shane has asked you several questions concerning his financial affairs to date, and he has asked you to assist with his record keeping and reporting of financial data.

a. To assist Shane with his record keeping, prepare a chart of accounts that would be appropriate for Birdie Caddy Service. *Note:* Small businesses such as Birdie Caddy Service are often organized as proprietorships. The accounting for proprietorships is similar to that for a corporation, except that the owner's equity accounts differ. Specifically, instead of the account for Capital Stock, a capital account entitled Shane Raburn, Capital is used to record investments in the business. In addition, instead of a dividends account, withdrawals from the business are debited to Shane Raburn, Drawing. A proprietorship has no retained earnings account.

b. Prepare an income statement for June in order to help Shane assess the profitability of Birdie Caddy Service. For this purpose, the use of T accounts may be helpful in analyzing the effects of each June transaction.

c. Based on Shane's records of receipts and payments, calculate the amount of cash on hand on June 30. For this purpose, a T account for cash may be useful.

d. ▭▬▶ A count of the cash on hand on June 30 totaled $4,980. Briefly discuss the possible causes of the difference between the amount of cash computed in (c) and the actual amount of cash on hand.

SA 2-6
Opportunities for accountants

[Internet Project]

The increasing complexity of the current business and regulatory environment has created an increased demand for accountants who can analyze business transactions and interpret their effects on the financial statements. In addition, a basic ability to analyze the effects of transactions is necessary to be successful in all fields of business as well as in other disciplines, such as law. To better understand the importance of accounting in today's environment, search the Internet or your local newspaper for job opportunities. One possible Internet site is **http://www.monster.com**. Then do one of the following:

1. Print a listing of at least two ads for accounting jobs. Alternatively, bring to class at least two newspaper ads for accounting jobs.

2. Print a listing of at least two ads for nonaccounting jobs for which some knowledge of accounting is preferred or necessary. Alternatively, bring to class at least two newspaper ads for such jobs.

Answers to Self-Examination Questions

1. **A** A debit may signify an increase in an asset account (answer A) or a decrease in a liability or retained earnings account. A credit may signify a decrease in an asset account (answer B) or an increase in a liability or capital stock account (answers C and D).

2. **C** Liability, capital stock, retained earnings, and revenue (answer C) accounts have normal credit balances. Asset (answer A), dividends (answer B), and expense (answer D) accounts have normal debit balances.

3. **C** Accounts Receivable (answer A), Cash (answer B), and Miscellaneous Expense (answer D) would all normally have debit balances. Fees Earned should normally have a credit balance. Hence, a debit balance in Fees Earned (answer C) would indicate a likely error in the recording process.

4. **A** The receipt of cash from customers on account increases the asset Cash and decreases the asset Accounts Receivable, as indicated by answer A. Answer B has the debit and credit reversed, and answers C and D involve transactions with creditors (accounts payable) and not customers (accounts receivable).

5. **D** The trial balance (answer D) is a listing of the balances and the titles of the accounts in the ledger on a given date, so that the equality of the debits and credits in the ledger can be verified. The income statement (answer A) is a summary of revenue and expenses for a period of time. The balance sheet (answer B) is a presentation of the assets, liabilities, and stockholders' equity on a given date. The retained earnings statement (answer C) is a summary of the changes in retained earnings for a period of time.

The Adjusting Process

© JEFF KRAVITZ/ASSOCIATED PRESS

objectives

After studying this chapter, you should be able to:

1 *Describe the nature of the adjusting process.*

2 *Journalize entries for accounts requiring adjustment.*

3 *Summarize the adjustment process.*

4 *Prepare an adjusted trial balance.*

Marvel Entertainment, Inc.

Do you subscribe to any magazines? Most of us subscribe to one or more magazines such as *Cosmopolitan*, *Sports Illustrated*, *Golf Digest*, *Newsweek*, or *Rolling Stone*. Magazines usually require you to prepay the yearly subscription price before you receive any issues. When should the magazine company record revenue from the subscriptions? As we discussed in Chapter 2, sometimes revenues are earned and expenses are incurred at the point cash is received or paid. For transactions such as magazine subscriptions, the revenue is earned when the magazine is delivered, not when the cash is received. Most companies are required to account for revenues and expenses when the benefit is substantially provided or consumed, which may not be when cash is received or paid.

One company that records revenue from subscriptions is Marvel Entertainment, Inc. Marvel began in 1939 as a comic book publishing company, establishing such popular comic book characters as Spider-Man®, X-Men®, Fantastic Four®, and the Avengers®. From these humble beginnings, Marvel has grown into a full-line, multi-billion-dollar entertainment company. Marvel not only publishes comic books, but it has also added feature films, such as the *Spider-Man* movies, video games, and toys to its product offerings.

Most companies, like Marvel Entertainment, are required to update their accounting records for items such as revenues earned from magazine subscriptions before preparing their financial statements. In this chapter, we describe and illustrate this updating process.

Nature of the Adjusting Process

objective *1*

Describe the nature of the adjusting process.

REAL WORLD

American Airlines uses the accrual basis of accounting. Revenues are recognized when passengers take flights, not when the passenger makes the reservation or pays for the ticket.

When accountants prepare financial statements, they assume that the economic life of the business can be divided into time periods. Using this **accounting period concept**, accountants must determine in which period the revenues and expenses of the business should be reported. To determine the proper period, accountants use generally accepted accounting principles, which require the use of the accrual basis of accounting.

Under the **accrual basis of accounting**, revenues are reported in the income statement in the period in which they are earned. For example, revenue is reported when the services are provided to customers. Cash may or may not be received from customers during this period. The accounting concept that supports this reporting of revenues is called the **revenue recognition concept**.

Under the accrual basis, expenses are reported in the same period as the revenues to which they relate. For example, employee wages are reported as an expense in the period in which the employees provided services to customers, and not necessarily when the wages are paid. The accounting concept that supports reporting revenues and related expenses in the same period is called the **matching concept**, or **matching principle**. By matching revenues and expenses, net income or loss for the period will be properly reported on the income statement.

Although generally accepted accounting principles require the accrual basis of accounting, some businesses use the **cash basis of accounting**. Under the cash basis of accounting, revenues and expenses are reported in the income statement in the period in which cash is received or paid. For example, fees are recorded when cash is received from clients, and wages are recorded when cash is paid to employees. The net income (or net loss) is the difference between the cash receipts (revenues) and the cash payments (expenses).

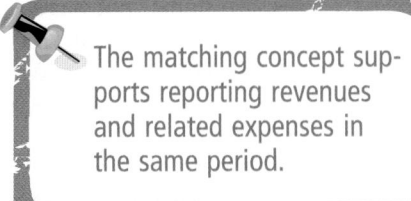

The matching concept supports reporting revenues and related expenses in the same period.

Small service businesses may use the cash basis, because they have few receivables and payables. For example, attorneys, physicians, and real estate agents often use the cash basis. For them, the cash basis will yield financial statements similar to those prepared under the accrual basis. For most large businesses, the cash basis will not provide accurate financial statements for user needs. For this reason, we will emphasize the accrual basis in this text.

THE ADJUSTING PROCESS

At the end of an accounting period, many of the balances of accounts in the ledger can be reported, without change, in the financial statements. For example, the balances of the cash and land accounts are normally the amount reported on the balance sheet.

Under the accrual basis, however, some accounts in the ledger require updating.[1] For example, the balances listed for prepaid expenses are normally overstated because the use of these assets is not recorded on a day-to-day basis. The balance of the supplies account usually represents the cost of supplies at the beginning of the period plus the cost of supplies acquired during the period. To record the daily use of supplies would require many entries with small amounts. In addition, the total amount of supplies is small relative to other assets, and managers usually do not require day-to-day information about supplies.

All adjusting entries affect at least one income statement account and one balance sheet account.

The analysis and updating of accounts at the end of the period before the financial statements are prepared is called the **adjusting process**. The journal entries that bring the accounts up to date at the end of the accounting period are called **adjusting entries**. All adjusting entries affect at least one income statement account and one balance sheet account. Thus, an adjusting entry will *always* involve a revenue or an expense account *and* an asset or a liability account. In the next section, we describe how to determine if an account needs adjusting.

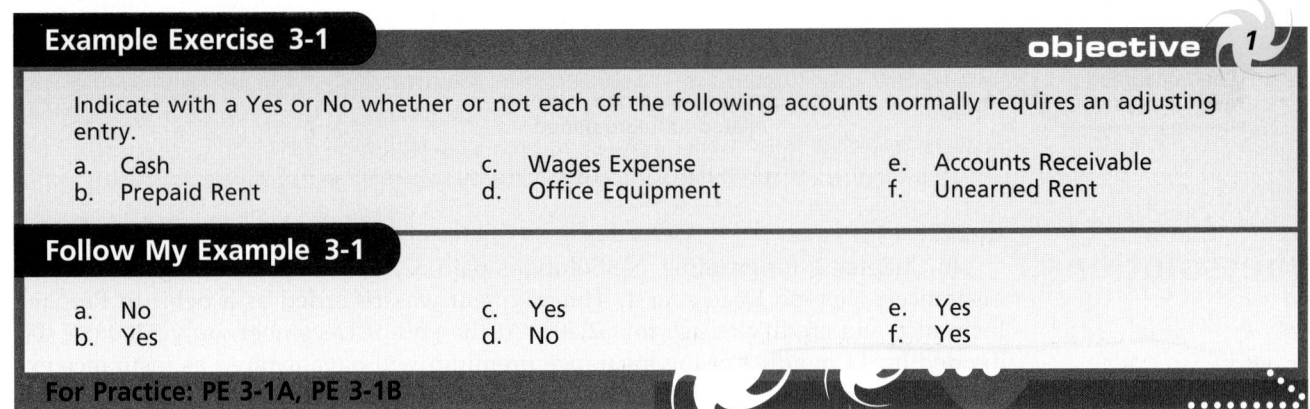

Example Exercise 3-1   objective 1

Indicate with a Yes or No whether or not each of the following accounts normally requires an adjusting entry.

a. Cash   c. Wages Expense   e. Accounts Receivable
b. Prepaid Rent   d. Office Equipment   f. Unearned Rent

Follow My Example 3-1

a. No   c. Yes   e. Yes
b. Yes   d. No   f. Yes

For Practice: PE 3-1A, PE 3-1B

TYPES OF ACCOUNTS REQUIRING ADJUSTMENT

Is there an easy way to know when an adjusting entry is needed? Yes, four basic types of accounts require adjusting entries. These accounts are prepaid expenses, unearned revenues, accrued revenues, and accrued expenses.

---

1 Under the cash basis of accounting, accounts do not require adjusting. This is because transactions are recorded only when cash is received or paid. Thus, the matching concept is not used under the cash basis.

Prepaid expenses, sometimes referred to as *deferred expenses*, are items that have been initially recorded as assets but are expected to become expenses over time or through the normal operations of the business. Supplies and prepaid insurance are two examples of prepaid expenses that may require adjustment at the end of an accounting period. Other examples include prepaid advertising and prepaid interest.

Unearned revenues, sometimes referred to as *deferred revenues*, are items that have been initially recorded as liabilities but are expected to become revenues over time or through the normal operations of the business. An example of unearned revenue is unearned rent. Other examples include tuition received in advance by a school, an annual retainer fee received by an attorney, premiums received in advance by an insurance company, and magazine subscriptions received in advance by a publisher.

Prepaid expenses and unearned revenues are created from transactions that involve the receipt or payment of cash. In both cases, the recording of the related expense or revenue is delayed until the end of the period or to a future period as illustrated in Exhibit 1.

EXHIBIT 1 | Type of Adjustments: Prepaid Expense and Unearned Revenue

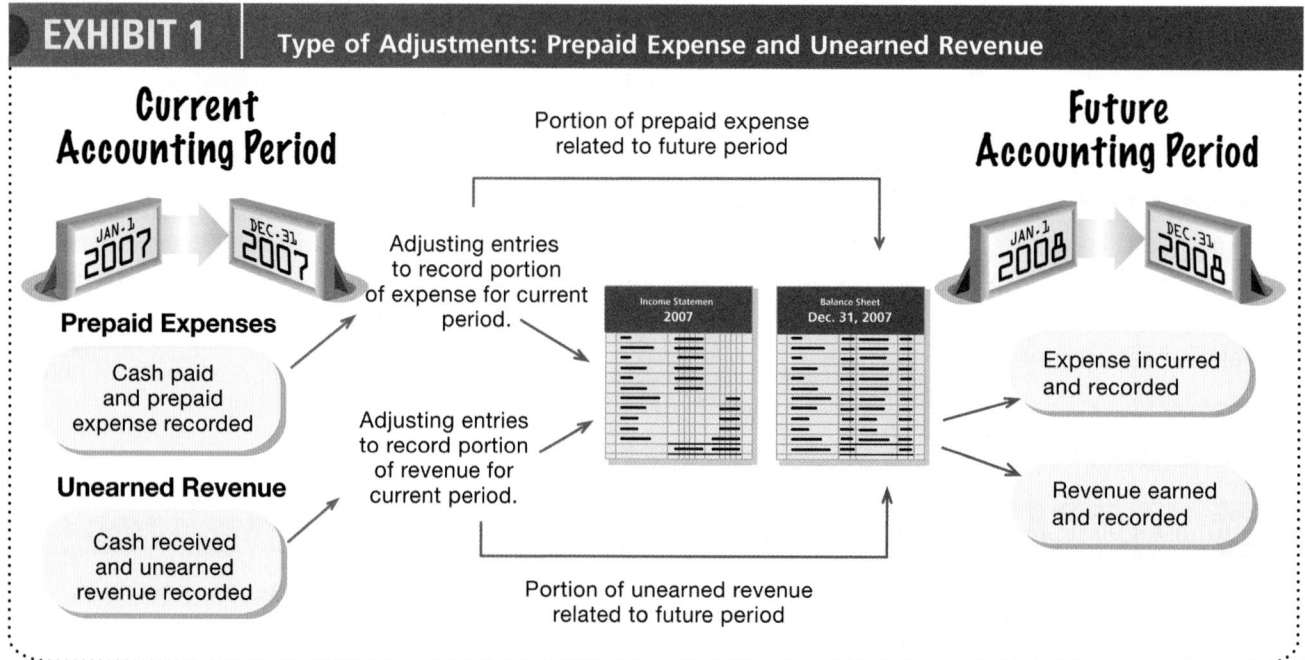

@netsolutions

In Chapter 2, for example, NetSolutions paid $2,400 as a premium on a one-year insurance policy on December 1. The payment was recorded as a debit to Prepaid Insurance and credit to Cash for $2,400. At the end of December, only $200 ($2,400 divided by 12 months) of the insurance premium will have expired as insurance expense, and the recording of the remaining $2,200 of insurance expense will be delayed to future periods. As we will see in the next section, the $200 insurance premium expiring in December will be recorded as insurance expense at the end of December, using an adjusting entry.

Accrued revenues, sometimes referred to as *accrued assets*, are revenues that have been earned but have not been recorded in the accounts. An example of an accrued revenue is fees for services that an attorney has provided but hasn't billed to the client at the end of the period. Other examples include unbilled commissions by a travel agent, accrued interest on notes receivable, and accrued rent on property rented to others.

Accrued expenses, sometimes referred to as *accrued liabilities*, are expenses that have been incurred but have not been recorded in the accounts. An example of an accrued expense is accrued wages owed to employees at the end of a period. Other examples include accrued interest on notes payable and accrued taxes.

Accrued revenues and expenses are created by an unrecorded revenue that has been earned or an unrecorded expense that has been incurred. For example, in the next section, we will record accrued revenues and accrued wages expense for NetSolutions at the end of December by using adjusting entries. Prior to recording the adjusting entries, neither accrued revenues nor accrued wages have been recorded. The nature of accrued revenues and expenses is illustrated in Exhibit 2.

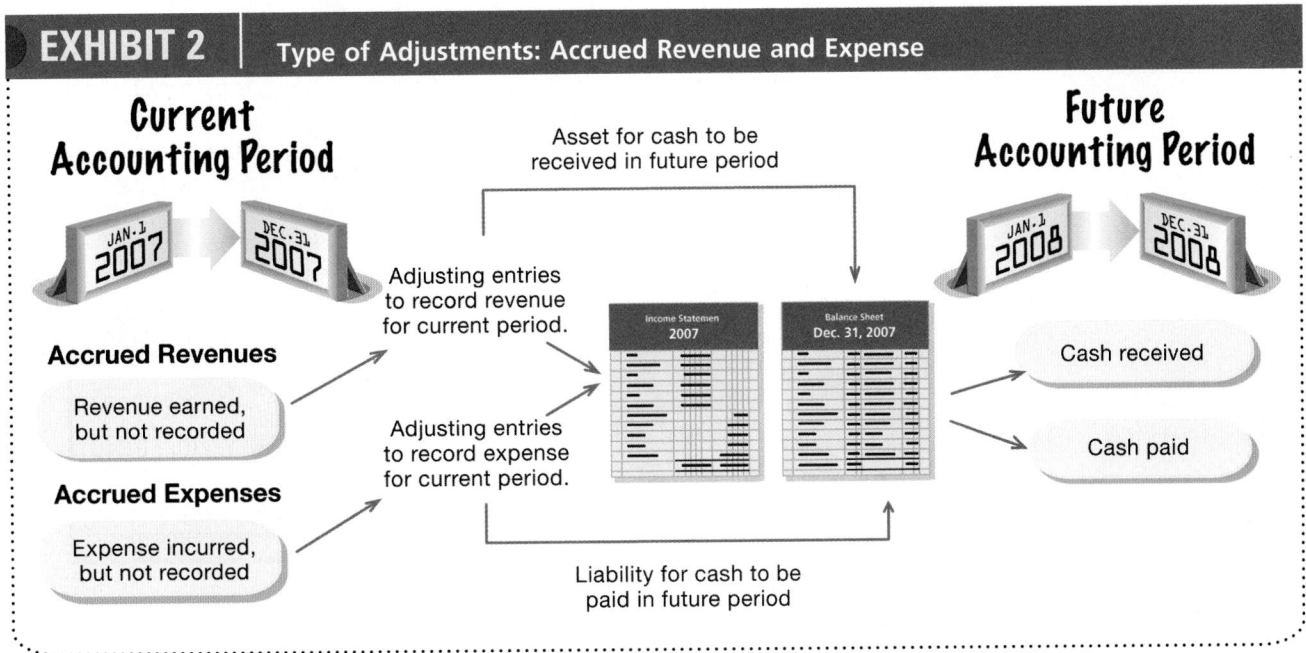

EXHIBIT 2 | Type of Adjustments: Accrued Revenue and Expense

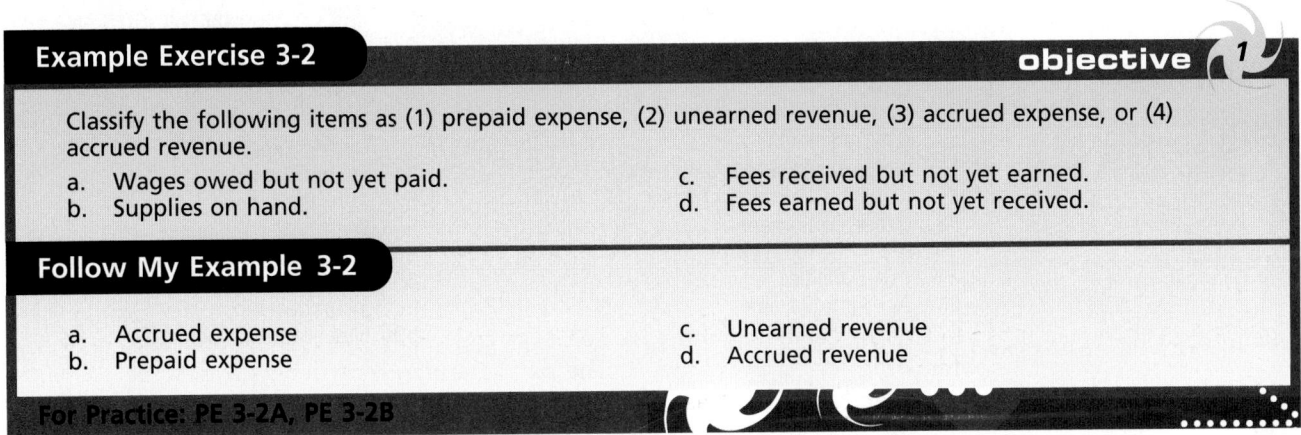

Example Exercise 3-2   objective ①

Classify the following items as (1) prepaid expense, (2) unearned revenue, (3) accrued expense, or (4) accrued revenue.

  a. Wages owed but not yet paid.   c. Fees received but not yet earned.
  b. Supplies on hand.   d. Fees earned but not yet received.

Follow My Example 3-2

  a. Accrued expense   c. Unearned revenue
  b. Prepaid expense   d. Accrued revenue

For Practice: PE 3-2A, PE 3-2B

Recording Adjusting Entries

objective ②

Journalize entries for accounts requiring adjustment.

The examples of adjusting entries in the following paragraphs are based on the ledger of NetSolutions as reported in the December 31, 2007, unadjusted trial balance in Exhibit 3.

An expanded chart of accounts for NetSolutions is shown in Exhibit 4. The additional accounts that will be used in this chapter are shown in color. In addition, the adjusting entries are shown in color in T accounts to separate them from other transactions.

EXHIBIT 3

Unadjusted Trial
Balance for
NetSolutions

@netsolutions

NetSolutions
Unadjusted Trial Balance
December 31, 2007

	Debit Balances	Credit Balances
Cash	2 0 6 5 00	
Accounts Receivable	2 2 2 0 00	
Supplies	2 0 0 0 00	
Prepaid Insurance	2 4 0 0 00	
Land	20 0 0 0 00	
Office Equipment	1 8 0 0 00	
Accounts Payable		9 0 0 00
Unearned Rent		3 6 0 00
Capital Stock		25 0 0 0 00
Dividends	4 0 0 0 00	
Fees Earned		16 3 4 0 00
Wages Expense	4 2 7 5 00	
Rent Expense	1 6 0 0 00	
Utilities Expense	9 8 5 00	
Supplies Expense	8 0 0 00	
Miscellaneous Expense	4 5 5 00	
	42 6 0 0 00	42 6 0 0 00

EXHIBIT 4   **Expanded Chart of Accounts for NetSolutions**

Balance Sheet Accounts	Income Statement Accounts
1. Assets	4. Revenue
11 Cash	41 Fees Earned
12 Accounts Receivable	42 Rent Revenue
14 Supplies	5. Expenses
15 Prepaid Insurance	51 Wages Expense
17 Land	52 Rent Expense
18 Office Equipment	53 Depreciation Expense
19 Accumulated Depreciation—Equipment	54 Utilities Expense
2. Liabilities	55 Supplies Expense
21 Accounts Payable	56 Insurance Expense
22 Wages Payable	59 Miscellaneous Expense
23 Unearned Rent	
3. Stockholders' Equity	
31 Capital Stock	
32 Retained Earnings	
33 Dividends	

PREPAID EXPENSES

The concept of adjusting accounting records was introduced in Chapters 1 and 2 in the illustration for NetSolutions. In that illustration, supplies were purchased on November 10 [transaction (c)]. The supplies used during November were recorded on November 30 [transaction (g)].

The balance in NetSolutions' supplies account on December 31 is $2,000. Some of these supplies (CDs, paper, envelopes, etc.) were used during December, and some are still on hand (not used). If either amount is known, the other can be determined. It is normally easier to determine the cost of the supplies on hand at the end of the month than it is to keep a daily record of those used. Assuming that on December 31 the amount of supplies on hand is $760, the amount to be transferred from the asset account to the expense account is $1,240, computed as follows:

Supplies available during December (balance of account)	$2,000
Supplies on hand, December 31	760
Supplies used (amount of adjustment)	$1,240

As we discussed in Chapter 2, increases in expense accounts are recorded as debits and decreases in asset accounts are recorded as credits. At the end of December, the supplies expense account should be debited for $1,240, and the supplies account should be credited for $1,240 to record the supplies used during December. The adjusting journal entry and T accounts for Supplies and Supplies Expense are as follows:

1					
2	2007 Dec.	31	Supplies Expense	55	1 2 4 0 00
3			Supplies	14	1 2 4 0 00
4			Supplies used ($2,000 − $760).		

Supplies

Bal.	2,000	Dec. 31	1,240
Adj. Bal.	760		

Supplies Expense

Bal.	800
Dec. 31	1,240
Adj. Bal.	2,040

After the adjustment has been recorded and posted, the supplies account has a debit balance of $760. This balance represents an asset that will become an expense in a future period.

The debit balance of $2,400 in NetSolutions' prepaid insurance account represents a December 1 prepayment of insurance for 12 months. At the end of December, the insurance expense account should be increased (debited), and the prepaid insurance account should be decreased (credited) by $200, the insurance for one month. The adjusting journal entry and T accounts for Prepaid Insurance and Insurance Expense are as follows:

5					
6		31	Insurance Expense	56	2 0 0 00
7			Prepaid Insurance	15	2 0 0 00
8			Insurance expired ($2,400/12).		

Prepaid Insurance

Bal.	2,400	Dec. 31	200
Adj. Bal.	2,200		

Insurance Expense

Dec. 31	200

Integrity, Objectivity, and Ethics in Business

ETHICS

FREE ISSUE

Office supplies are often available to employees on a "free issue" basis. This means that employees do not have to "sign" for the release of office supplies but merely obtain the necessary supplies from a local storage area as needed. Just because supplies are easily available, however, doesn't mean they can be taken for personal use. There are many instances where employees have been terminated for taking supplies home for personal use.

> The adjusted balance of a prepaid expense is an asset that will become an expense in a future period.

After the adjustment has been recorded and posted, the prepaid insurance account has a debit balance of $2,200. This balance represents an asset that will become an expense in future periods. The insurance expense account has a debit balance of $200, which is an expense of the current period.

What is the effect of omitting adjusting entries? If the preceding adjustments for supplies ($1,240) and insurance ($200) are not recorded, the financial statements prepared as of December 31 will be misstated. On the income statement, Supplies Expense and Insurance Expense will be understated by a total of $1,440, and net income will be overstated by $1,440. On the balance sheet, Supplies and Prepaid Insurance will be overstated by a total of $1,440. Since net income increases Retained Earnings, Stockholders' Equity will also be overstated by $1,440 on the balance sheet. The effects of omitting these adjusting entries on the income statement and balance sheet are as follows:

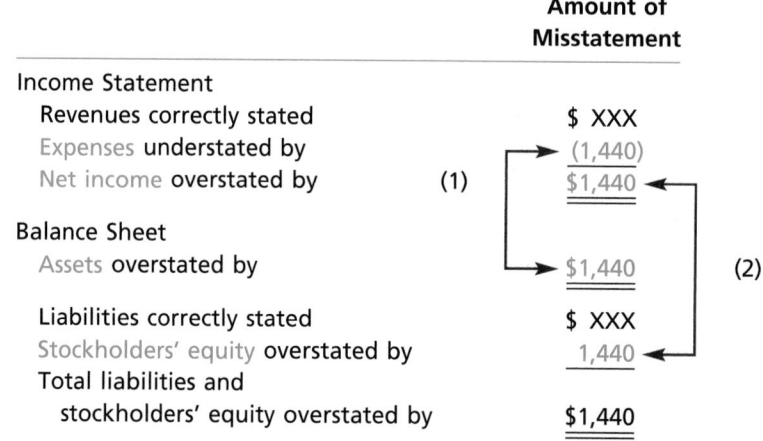

	Amount of Misstatement
Income Statement	
Revenues correctly stated	$ XXX
Expenses understated by	(1,440)
Net income overstated by (1)	$1,440
Balance Sheet	
Assets overstated by (2)	$1,440
Liabilities correctly stated	$ XXX
Stockholders' equity overstated by	1,440
Total liabilities and stockholders' equity overstated by	$1,440

Arrow (1) indicates the effect of the understated expenses on assets. Arrow (2) indicates the effect of the overstated net income on stockholders' equity.

Prepayments of expenses are sometimes made at the beginning of the period in which they will be *entirely consumed*. On December 1, for example, NetSolutions paid rent of $800 for the month. On December 1, the rent payment represents the asset prepaid rent. The prepaid rent expires daily, and at the end of December, the entire amount has become an expense (rent expense). In cases such as this, the initial payment is recorded as an expense rather than as an asset. Thus, if the payment is recorded as a debit to Rent Expense, no adjusting entry is needed at the end of the period.[2]

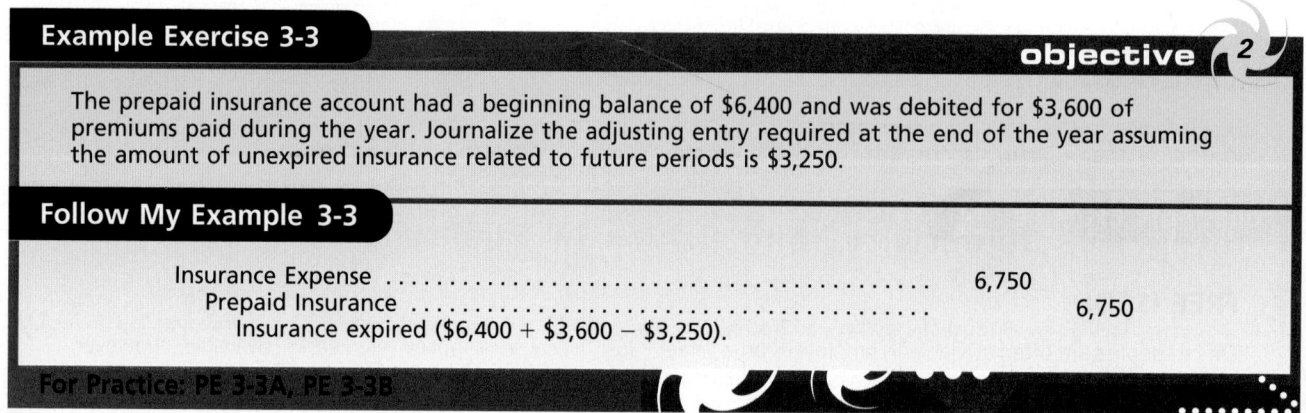

Example Exercise 3-3   objective 2

The prepaid insurance account had a beginning balance of $6,400 and was debited for $3,600 of premiums paid during the year. Journalize the adjusting entry required at the end of the year assuming the amount of unexpired insurance related to future periods is $3,250.

Follow My Example 3-3

Insurance Expense	6,750	
Prepaid Insurance		6,750
Insurance expired ($6,400 + $3,600 − $3,250).		

For Practice: PE 3-3A, PE 3-3B

---

2 This alternative treatment of recording the cost of supplies, rent, and other prepayments of expenses is discussed in an appendix that can be downloaded from the book's companion Web site.

UNEARNED REVENUES

According to NetSolutions' trial balance on December 31, the balance in the unearned rent account is $360. This balance represents the receipt of three months' rent on December 1 for December, January, and February. At the end of December, the unearned rent account should be decreased (debited) by $120, and the rent revenue account should be increased (credited) by $120. The $120 represents the rental revenue for one month ($360/3). The adjusting journal entry and T accounts are shown below.

REAL WORLD

Best Buy sells extended warranty contracts with terms between 12 and 36 months. The receipts from sales of these contracts are reported as unearned revenue on Best Buy's balance sheet. Revenue is recorded as the contracts expire.

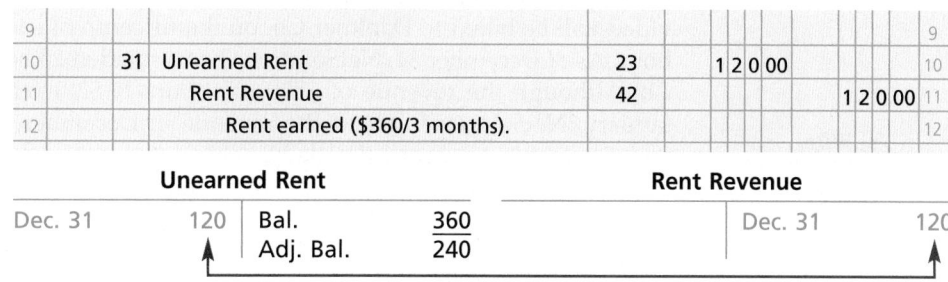

9						9
10	31	Unearned Rent	23	1 2 0 00		10
11		Rent Revenue	42		1 2 0 00	11
12		Rent earned ($360/3 months).				12

Unearned Rent					Rent Revenue		
Dec. 31	120	Bal.	360			Dec. 31	120
		Adj. Bal.	240				

After the adjustment has been recorded and posted, the unearned rent account, which is a liability, has a credit balance of $240. This amount represents a deferral that will become revenue in a future period. The rent revenue account has a balance of $120, which is revenue of the current period.[3]

If the preceding adjustment of unearned rent and rent revenue is not recorded, the financial statements prepared on December 31 will be misstated. On the income statement, Rent Revenue and the net income will be understated by $120. On the balance sheet, Unearned Rent will be overstated by $120, and Retained Earnings will be understated by $120. The effects of omitting this adjusting entry are shown below.

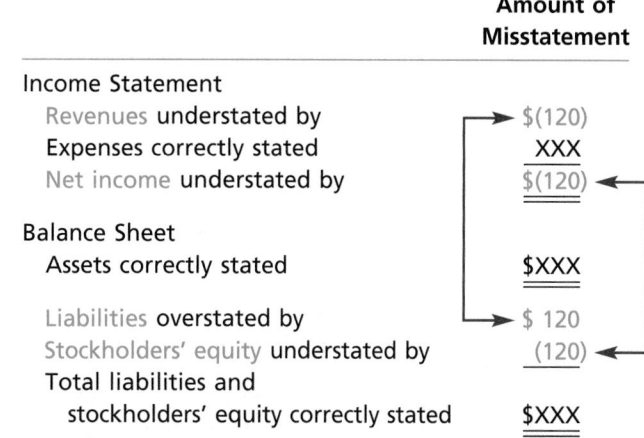

	Amount of Misstatement
Income Statement	
Revenues understated by	$(120)
Expenses correctly stated	XXX
Net income understated by	$(120)
Balance Sheet	
Assets correctly stated	$XXX
Liabilities overstated by	$ 120
Stockholders' equity understated by	(120)
Total liabilities and stockholders' equity correctly stated	$XXX

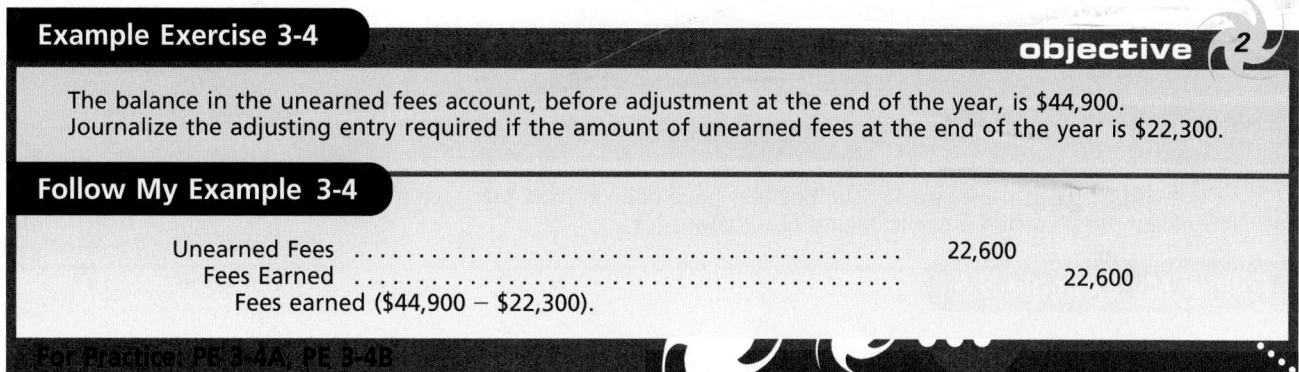

Example Exercise 3-4   objective 2

The balance in the unearned fees account, before adjustment at the end of the year, is $44,900. Journalize the adjusting entry required if the amount of unearned fees at the end of the year is $22,300.

Follow My Example 3-4

Unearned Fees	22,600	
Fees Earned		22,600
Fees earned ($44,900 − $22,300).		

For Practice: PE 3-4A, PE 3-4B

---

3 An alternative treatment of recording revenues received in advance of their being earned is discussed in an appendix that can be downloaded from the book's companion Web site (www.thomsonedu.com/accounting/warren).

ACCRUED REVENUES

During an accounting period, some revenues are recorded only when cash is received. Thus, at the end of an accounting period, there may be items of revenue that have been earned *but have not been recorded*. In such cases, the amount of the revenue should be recorded by debiting an asset account and crediting a revenue account.

To illustrate, assume that NetSolutions signed an agreement with Dankner Co. on December 15. The agreement provides that NetSolutions will be on call to answer computer questions and render assistance to Dankner Co.'s employees. The services provided will be billed to Dankner Co. on the fifteenth of each month at a rate of $20 per hour. As of December 31, NetSolutions had provided 25 hours of assistance to Dankner Co. Although the revenue of $500 (25 hours × $20) will be billed and collected in January, NetSolutions earned the revenue in December. The adjusting journal entry and T accounts to record the claim against the customer (an account receivable) and the fees earned in December are shown below.

REAL WORLD

RadioShack Corporation is engaged in consumer electronics retailing. RadioShack accrues revenue for finance charges, late charges, and returned check fees related to its credit operations.

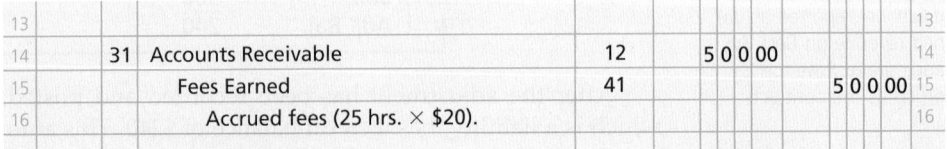

13						13
14	31	Accounts Receivable	12	5 0 0 00		14
15		Fees Earned	41		5 0 0 00	15
16		Accrued fees (25 hrs. × $20).				16

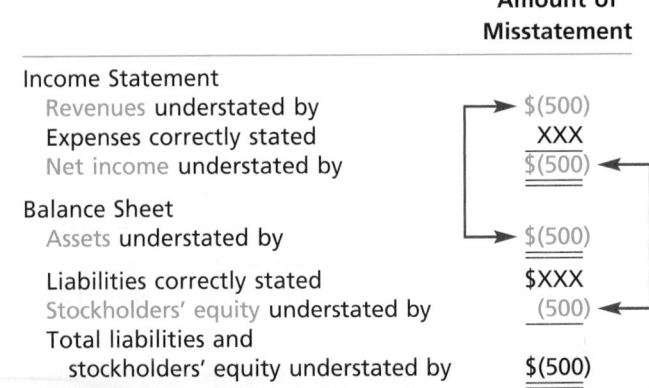

Accounts Receivable			Fees Earned	
Bal.	2,220		Bal.	16,340
Dec. 31	500		Dec. 31	500
Adj. Bal.	2,720		Adj. Bal.	16,840

If the adjustment for the accrued asset ($500) is not recorded, Fees Earned and the net income will be understated by $500 on the income statement. On the balance sheet, Accounts Receivable and Retained Earnings will be understated by $500. The effects of omitting this adjusting entry are shown below.

	Amount of Misstatement
Income Statement	
Revenues understated by	$(500)
Expenses correctly stated	XXX
Net income understated by	$(500)
Balance Sheet	
Assets understated by	$(500)
Liabilities correctly stated	$XXX
Stockholders' equity understated by	(500)
Total liabilities and stockholders' equity understated by	$(500)

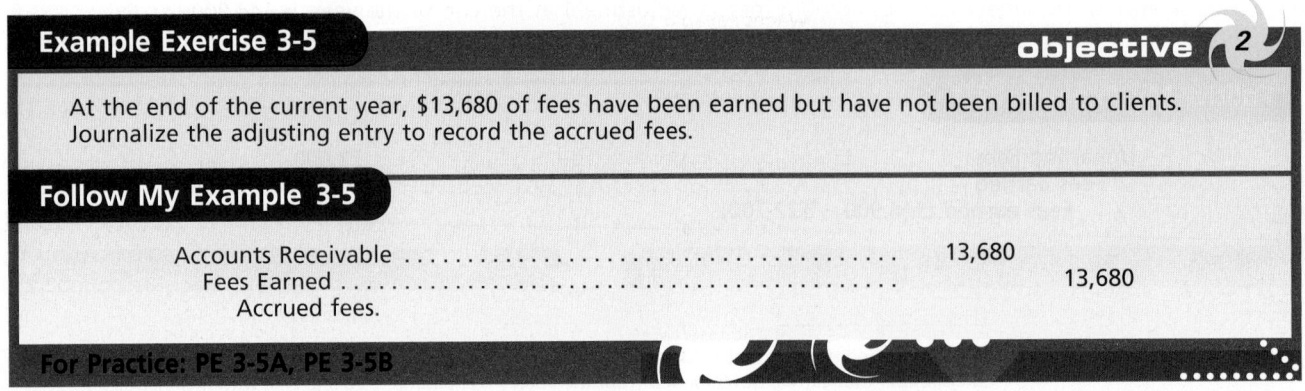

Example Exercise 3-5   objective 2

At the end of the current year, $13,680 of fees have been earned but have not been billed to clients. Journalize the adjusting entry to record the accrued fees.

Follow My Example 3-5

Accounts Receivable	13,680	
Fees Earned		13,680
Accrued fees.		

For Practice: PE 3-5A, PE 3-5B

ACCRUED EXPENSES

Some types of services, such as insurance, are normally paid for *before* they are used. These prepayments are deferrals. Other types of services are paid for *after* the service has been performed. For example, wages expense accumulates or *accrues* hour by hour and day by day, but payment may be made only weekly, biweekly, or monthly. The amount of such an accrued but unpaid item at the end of the accounting period is both an expense and a liability. In the case of wages expense, if the last day of a pay period is not the last day of the accounting period, the accrued wages expense and the related liability must be recorded in the accounts by an adjusting entry. This adjusting entry is necessary so that expenses are properly matched to the period in which they were incurred.

At the end of December, accrued wages for NetSolutions were $250. This amount is an additional expense of December and is debited to the wages expense account. It is also a liability as of December 31 and is credited to Wages Payable. The adjusting journal entry and T accounts are as follows:

18	31	Wages Expense	51	250 00	
19		Wages Payable	22		250 00
20		Accrued wages.			

Wages Expense

Bal.	4,275
Dec. 31	250
Adj. Bal.	4,525

Wages Payable

Dec. 31	250

REAL WORLD

Callaway Golf Company, a manufacturer of such innovative golf clubs as the "Big Bertha" driver, reports accrued warranty expense on its balance sheet.

After the adjustment has been recorded and posted, the debit balance of the wages expense account is $4,525, which is the wages expense for the two months, November and December. The credit balance of $250 in Wages Payable is the amount of the liability for wages owed as of December 31.

The accrual of the wages expense for NetSolutions is summarized in Exhibit 5, on page 116. Note that NetSolutions paid wages of $950 on December 13 and $1,200 on December 27. These payments covered the biweekly pay periods that ended on those days. The wages of $250 incurred for Monday and Tuesday, December 30 and 31, are accrued at December 31. The wages paid on January 10 totaled $1,275, which included the $250 accrued wages of December 31. The payment of the January 10 wages is recorded by debiting Wages Expense for $1,025, debiting Wages Payable for $250, and crediting Cash for $1,275, as shown below.[4]

22	Jan.	10	Wages Expense	1025 00		
23			Wages Payable	250 00		
24			Cash		1275 00	

What would be the effect on the financial statements if the adjustment for wages ($250) is not recorded? On the income statement, Wages Expense will be understated by $250, and the net income will be overstated by $250. On the balance sheet, Wages

---

4 To simplify the subsequent recording of the following period's transactions, some accountants use what is known as reversing entries for certain types of adjustments. Reversing entries are discussed and illustrated in an appendix at the end of the textbook.

EXHIBIT 5

Accrued Wages

1. Wages are paid on the second and fourth Fridays for the two-week periods ending on those Fridays. The payments were $950 on December 13 and $1,200 on December 27.

2. The wages accrued for Monday and Tuesday, December 30 and 31, are $250.

3. Wages paid on Friday, January 10, total $1,275.

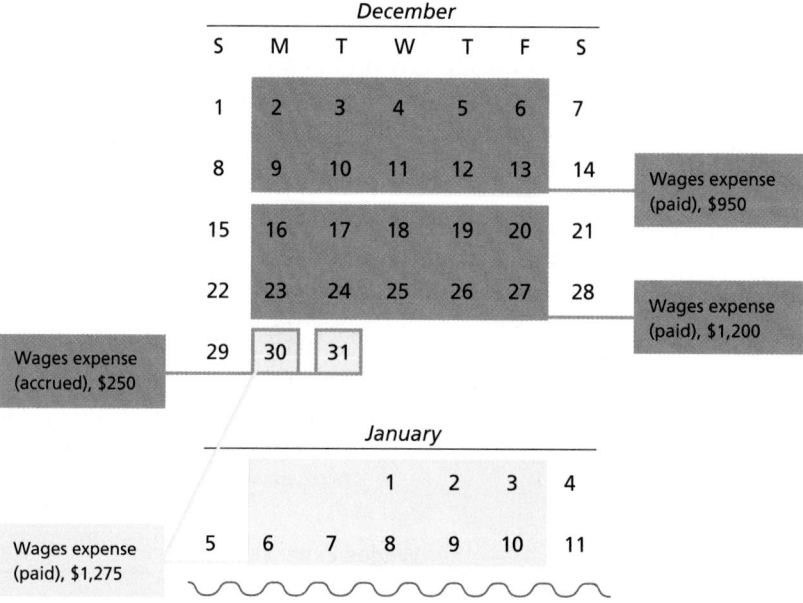

Payable will be understated by $250, and Retained Earnings will be overstated by $250. The effects of omitting this adjusting entry are shown as follows:

	Amount of Misstatement
Income Statement	
Revenues correctly stated	$XXX
Expenses understated by	(250)
Net income overstated by	$ 250
Balance Sheet	
Assets correctly stated	$XXX
Liabilities understated by	$(250)
Stockholders' equity overstated by	250
Total liabilities and stockholders' equity correctly stated	$XXX

Example Exercise 3-6

objective **2**

Sanregret Realty Co. pays weekly salaries of $12,500 on Friday for a five-day week ending on that day. Journalize the necessary adjusting entry at the end of the accounting period, assuming that the period ends on Thursday.

Follow My Example 3-6

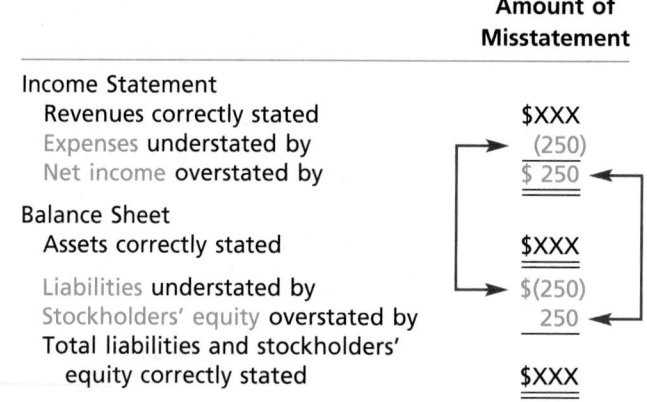

Salaries Expense	10,000	
Salaries Payable		10,000
Accrued salaries [($12,500/5 days) × 4 days].		

For Practice: PE 3-6A, PE 3-6B

DEPRECIATION EXPENSE

Physical resources that are owned and used by a business and are permanent or have a long life are called **fixed assets**, or **plant assets**. In a sense, fixed assets are a type of long-term prepaid expense. Because of their nature and long life, they are discussed separately from other prepaid expenses, such as supplies and prepaid insurance.

NetSolutions' fixed assets include office equipment, which is used much like supplies are used to generate revenue. Unlike supplies, however, there is no visible reduction in the quantity of the equipment. Instead, as time passes, the equipment loses its ability to provide useful services. This decrease in usefulness is called **depreciation**.

All fixed assets, except land, lose their usefulness. Decreases in the usefulness of assets that are used in generating revenue are recorded as expenses. However, such decreases for fixed assets are difficult to measure. For this reason, a portion of the cost of a fixed asset is recorded as an expense each year of its useful life. This periodic expense is called **depreciation expense**. Methods of computing depreciation expense are discussed and illustrated in a later chapter.

Lowe's Companies, Inc., reported land, buildings, and store equipment at a cost of over $18 billion and accumulated depreciation of over $4.1 billion.

The adjusting entry to record depreciation is similar to the adjusting entry for supplies used. The account debited is a depreciation expense account. However, the asset account Office Equipment is not credited because both the original cost of a fixed asset and the amount of depreciation recorded since its purchase are normally reported on the balance sheet. The account credited is an **accumulated depreciation** account. Accumulated depreciation accounts are called **contra accounts**, or **contra asset accounts**, because they are deducted from the related asset accounts on the balance sheet. The normal balance of a contra account is opposite to the account from which it is deducted. Thus, the normal balance for Accumulated Depreciation is a credit.

Normal titles for fixed asset accounts and their related contra asset accounts are as follows:

Fixed Asset	Contra Asset
Land	None—Land is not depreciated.
Buildings	Accumulated Depreciation—Buildings
Store Equipment	Accumulated Depreciation—Store Equipment
Office Equipment	Accumulated Depreciation—Office Equipment

The adjusting entry to record depreciation for December for NetSolutions is illustrated in the following journal entry and T accounts. The estimated amount of depreciation for the month is assumed to be $50.

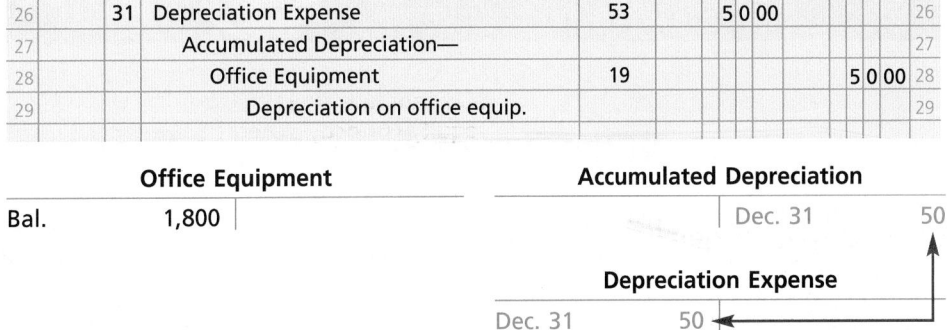

25						25
26	31	Depreciation Expense	53	5 0 00		26
27		Accumulated Depreciation—				27
28		Office Equipment	19		5 0 00	28
29		Depreciation on office equip.				29

Office Equipment		Accumulated Depreciation	
Bal. 1,800			Dec. 31 50

Depreciation Expense

Dec. 31   50

The $50 increase in the accumulated depreciation account is subtracted from the $1,800 cost recorded in the related fixed asset account. The difference between the two balances is the $1,750 cost that has not yet been depreciated. This amount ($1,750) is called the **book value of the asset** (or **net book value**), which may be presented on the balance sheet in the following manner:

Office equipment	$1,800	
Less accumulated depreciation	50	$1,750

You should note that the market value of a fixed asset usually differs from its book value. This is because depreciation is an *allocation* method, not a *valuation* method. That is, depreciation allocates the cost of a fixed asset to expense over its estimated life. Depreciation does not attempt to measure changes in market values, which may vary significantly from year to year.

If the previous adjustment for depreciation ($50) is not recorded, Depreciation Expense on the income statement will be understated by $50, and the net income will be overstated by $50. On the balance sheet, the book value of Office Equipment and Retained Earnings will be overstated by $50. The effects of omitting the adjustment for depreciation are shown below.

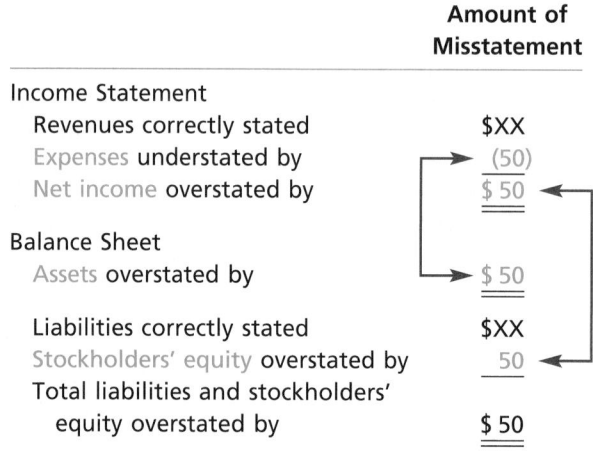

	Amount of Misstatement
Income Statement	
Revenues correctly stated	$XX
Expenses understated by	(50)
Net income overstated by	$ 50
Balance Sheet	
Assets overstated by	$ 50
Liabilities correctly stated	$XX
Stockholders' equity overstated by	50
Total liabilities and stockholders' equity overstated by	$ 50

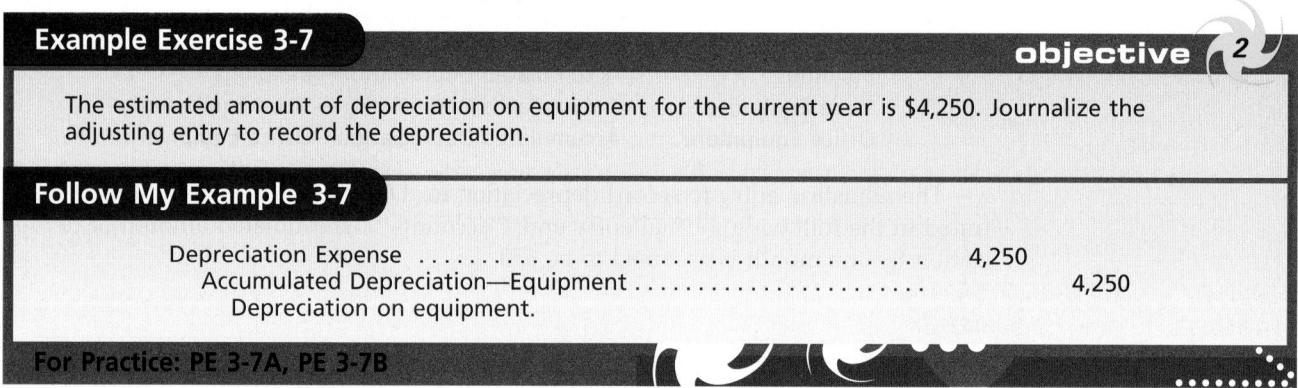

Example Exercise 3-7   objective 2

The estimated amount of depreciation on equipment for the current year is $4,250. Journalize the adjusting entry to record the depreciation.

Follow My Example 3-7

Depreciation Expense	4,250	
Accumulated Depreciation—Equipment		4,250
Depreciation on equipment.		

For Practice: PE 3-7A, PE 3-7B

Summary of Adjustment Process

objective 3

Summarize the adjustment process.

@netsolutions

We have described and illustrated the basic types of adjusting entries in the preceding section. A summary of these basic adjustments, including the type of adjustment, the adjusting entry, and the effect of the adjustment on the financial statements, is shown in Exhibit 6. As Exhibit 6 illustrates, each adjustment affects the income statement and balance sheet.

The adjusting entries for NetSolutions that we illustrated in this chapter are shown in Exhibit 7, on page 120. The adjusting entries are dated as of the last day of the period. However, because some time may be needed for collecting the adjustment information, the entries are usually recorded at a later date. Each adjusting entry is normally supported by an explanation. These adjusting entries have been posted to the ledger for NetSolutions shown in Exhibit 8, on pages 121–122. The adjustments are shown in color in Exhibit 8 to distinguish them from other transactions.

EXHIBIT 6   Summary of Adjustments

**Financial Statement Effect of Adjustment
Increase (Decrease)**

Type of Adjustment	Adjusting Entry			Income Statement			Balance Sheet		
				Revenues −	Expenses =	Net Income	Assets =	Liabilities +	Stockholders' Equity
Prepaid Expenses									
Supplies	Supplies Exp.	1,240			1,240	(1,240)			
	Supplies		1,240				(1,240)		(1,240)
Prepaid Insurance	Insurance Exp.	200			200	(200)			
	Prepaid Ins.		200				(200)		(200)
Unearned Revenue									
Unearned Rent	Unearned Rent	120						(120)	120
	Rent Revenue		120	120		120			
Accrued Revenue									
Accrued Fees	Accts. Receivable	500					500		500
	Fees Earned		500	500		500			
Accrued Expense									
Accrued Wages	Wages Expense	250			250	(250)			
	Wages Payable		250					250	(250)
Depreciation Expense									
Office Equipment	Depreciation Exp.	50			50	(50)			
	Acc. Dep.—								
	Office Equip.		50				(50)		(50)

Example Exercise 3-8   objective **3**

For the year ending December 31, 2008, Mann Medical Co. mistakenly omitted adjusting entries for (1) $8,600 of unearned revenue that was earned, (2) earned revenue that was not billed of $12,500, and (3) accrued wages of $2,900. Indicate the combined effect of the errors on (a) revenues, (b) expenses, and (c) net income for 2008.

Follow My Example 3-8

 a.   Revenues were understated by $21,100 ($8,600 + $12,500).
 b.   Expenses were understated by $2,900.
 c.   Net income was understated by $18,200 ($8,600 + $12,500 − $2,900).

For Practice: PE 3-8A, PE 3-8B

EXHIBIT 7

Adjusting Entries—
NetSolutions

	Date		Description	Post. Ref.	Debit	Credit	
1			Adjusting Entries				1
2	2007 Dec.	31	Supplies Expense	55	1 2 4 0 00		2
3			Supplies	14		1 2 4 0 00	3
4			Supplies used ($2,000 − $760).				4
5							5
6		31	Insurance Expense	56	2 0 0 00		6
7			Prepaid Insurance	15		2 0 0 00	7
8			Insurance expired ($2,400/12 months).				8
9							9
10		31	Unearned Rent	23	1 2 0 00		10
11			Rent Revenue	42		1 2 0 00	11
12			Rent earned ($360/3 months).				12
13							13
14		31	Accounts Receivable	12	5 0 0 00		14
15			Fees Earned	41		5 0 0 00	15
16			Accrued fees (25 hrs. × $20).				16
17							17
18		31	Wages Expense	51	2 5 0 00		18
19			Wages Payable	22		2 5 0 00	19
20			Accrued wages.				20
21							21
22		31	Depreciation Expense	53	5 0 00		22
23			Accum. Depr.—Office Equip.	19		5 0 00	23
24			Depreciation on office equip.				24
25							25

JOURNAL Page 5

One way for an accountant to check whether all adjustments have been made is to compare the current period's adjustments with those of the prior period.

Business Connections

Microsoft Corporation develops, manufactures, licenses, and supports a wide range of computer software products, including Windows XP®, Windows NT®, Word®, Excel®, and the Xbox® gaming system. When Microsoft sells its products, it incurs an obligation to support its software with technical support and periodic updates. As a result, not all the revenue is earned on the date of sale; some of the revenue on the date of sale is unearned. The portion of revenue related to support services, such as updates and technical support, is earned as time passes and support is provided to customers. Thus, each year Microsoft makes adjusting entries transferring some of its unearned revenue to revenue. The following excerpts were taken from Microsoft's 2005 financial statements.

> The percentage of revenue recorded as unearned . . . ranges from approximately 15% to 25% of the sales price for Windows XP Home, approximately 5% to 15% of the sales price for Windows XP Professional, and approximately 1% to 15% of the sales price for desktop applications . . .
>
> Unearned Revenue:

	June 30, 2005	June 30, 2004
Unearned revenue (in millions)	$9,167	$8,177

During the year ending June 30, 2006, Microsoft expects to record over $7,500 million of unearned revenue as revenue. At the same time, Microsoft will record additional unearned revenue from current period sales.

Source: Taken from Microsoft's June 30, 2005, annual report.

EXHIBIT 8   Ledger with Adjusting Entries—NetSolutions

ACCOUNT Cash   **ACCOUNT NO. 11**

Date	Item	Post. Ref.	Debit	Credit	Balance Debit	Balance Credit
2007 Nov. 1		1	25,000		25,000	
5		1		20,000	5,000	
18		1	7,500		12,500	
30		1		3,650	8,850	
30		1		950	7,900	
30		2		2,000	5,900	
Dec. 1		2		2,400	3,500	
1		2		800	2,700	
1		2	360		3,060	
6		2		180	2,880	
11		2		400	2,480	
13		3		950	1,530	
16		3	3,100		4,630	
20		3		900	3,730	
21		3	650		4,380	
23		3		1,450	2,930	
27		3		1,200	1,730	
31		3		310	1,420	
31		4		225	1,195	
31		4	2,870		4,065	
31		4		2,000	2,065	

ACCOUNT Accounts Receivable   **ACCOUNT NO. 12**

Date	Item	Post. Ref.	Debit	Credit	Balance Debit	Balance Credit
2007 Dec. 16		3	1,750		1,750	
21		3		650	1,100	
31		4	1,120		2,220	
31	Adjusting	5	500		2,720	

ACCOUNT Supplies   **ACCOUNT NO. 14**

Date	Item	Post. Ref.	Debit	Credit	Balance Debit	Balance Credit
2007 Nov. 10		1	1,350		1,350	
30		1		800	550	
Dec. 23		3	1,450		2,000	
31	Adjusting	5		1,240	760	

ACCOUNT Prepaid Insurance   **ACCOUNT NO. 15**

Date	Item	Post. Ref.	Debit	Credit	Balance Debit	Balance Credit
2007 Dec. 1		2	2,400		2,400	
31	Adjusting	5		200	2,200	

ACCOUNT Land   **ACCOUNT NO. 17**

Date	Item	Post. Ref.	Debit	Credit	Balance Debit	Balance Credit
2007 Nov. 5		1	20,000		20,000	

ACCOUNT Office Equipment   **ACCOUNT NO. 18**

Date	Item	Post. Ref.	Debit	Credit	Balance Debit	Balance Credit
2007 Dec. 4		2	1,800		1,800	

ACCOUNT Acc. Depr.—Equipment   **ACCOUNT NO. 19**

Date	Item	Post. Ref.	Debit	Credit	Balance Debit	Balance Credit
2007 Dec. 31	Adjusting	5		50		50

ACCOUNT Accounts Payable   **ACCOUNT NO. 21**

Date	Item	Post. Ref.	Debit	Credit	Balance Debit	Balance Credit
2007 Nov. 10		1		1,350		1,350
30		1	950			400
Dec. 4		2		1,800		2,200
11		2	400			1,800
20		3	900			900

ACCOUNT Wages Payable   **ACCOUNT NO. 22**

Date	Item	Post. Ref.	Debit	Credit	Balance Debit	Balance Credit
2007 Dec. 31	Adjusting	5		250		250

ACCOUNT Unearned Rent   **ACCOUNT NO. 23**

Date	Item	Post. Ref.	Debit	Credit	Balance Debit	Balance Credit
2007 Dec. 1		2		360		360
31	Adjusting	5	120			240

ACCOUNT Capital Stock   **ACCOUNT NO. 31**

Date	Item	Post. Ref.	Debit	Credit	Balance Debit	Balance Credit
2007 Nov. 1		1		25,000		25,000

(continued)

EXHIBIT 8

ACCOUNT *Dividends*   **ACCOUNT NO.** *33*

Date	Item	Post. Ref.	Debit	Credit	Balance Debit	Balance Credit
2007 Nov. 30		2	2,000		2,000	
Dec. 31		4	2,000		4,000	

ACCOUNT *Fees Earned*   **ACCOUNT NO.** *41*

Date	Item	Post. Ref.	Debit	Credit	Balance Debit	Balance Credit
2007 Nov. 18		1		7,500		7,500
Dec. 16		3		3,100		10,600
16		3		1,750		12,350
31		4		2,870		15,220
31		4		1,120		16,340
31	Adjusting	5		500		16,840

ACCOUNT *Rent Revenue*   **ACCOUNT NO.** *42*

Date	Item	Post. Ref.	Debit	Credit	Balance Debit	Balance Credit
2007 Dec. 31	Adjusting	5		120		120

ACCOUNT *Wages Expense*   **ACCOUNT NO.** *51*

Date	Item	Post. Ref.	Debit	Credit	Balance Debit	Balance Credit
2007 Nov. 30		1	2,125		2,125	
Dec. 13		3	950		3,075	
27		3	1,200		4,275	
31	Adjusting	5	250		4,525	

ACCOUNT *Rent Expense*   **ACCOUNT NO.** *52*

Date	Item	Post. Ref.	Debit	Credit	Balance Debit	Balance Credit
2007 Nov. 30		1	800		800	
Dec. 1		2	800		1,600	

ACCOUNT *Depreciation Expense*   **ACCOUNT NO.** *53*

Date	Item	Post. Ref.	Debit	Credit	Balance Debit	Balance Credit
2007 Dec. 31	Adjusting	5	50		50	

ACCOUNT *Utilities Expense*   **ACCOUNT NO.** *54*

Date	Item	Post. Ref.	Debit	Credit	Balance Debit	Balance Credit
2007 Nov. 30		1	450		450	
Dec. 31		3	310		760	
31		4	225		985	

ACCOUNT *Supplies Expense*   **ACCOUNT NO.** *55*

Date	Item	Post. Ref.	Debit	Credit	Balance Debit	Balance Credit
2007 Nov. 30		1	800		800	
Dec. 31	Adjusting	5	1,240		2,040	

ACCOUNT *Insurance Expense*   **ACCOUNT NO.** *56*

Date	Item	Post. Ref.	Debit	Credit	Balance Debit	Balance Credit
2007 Dec. 31	Adjusting	5	200		200	

ACCOUNT *Miscellaneous Expense*   **ACCOUNT NO.** *59*

Date	Item	Post. Ref.	Debit	Credit	Balance Debit	Balance Credit
2007 Nov. 30		1	275		275	
Dec. 6		2	180		455	

Adjusted Trial Balance

objective **4**

Prepare an adjusted trial balance.

After all the adjusting entries have been posted, another trial balance, called the **adjusted trial balance**, is prepared. The purpose of the adjusted trial balance is to verify the equality of the total debit balances and total credit balances before we prepare the financial statements. If the adjusted trial balance does not balance, an error has occurred. However, as we discussed in Chapter 2, errors may have occurred even though the adjusted trial balance totals agree. For example, the adjusted trial balance totals would agree if an adjusting entry has been omitted.

@netsolutions

Exhibit 9 shows the adjusted trial balance for NetSolutions as of December 31, 2007. In Chapter 4, we discuss how financial statements, including a classified balance sheet, can be prepared from an adjusted trial balance. We also discuss the use of an end-of-period spreadsheet (work sheet) as an aid in summarizing the data for preparing adjusting entries and financial statements.

EXHIBIT 9

Adjusted Trial Balance

NetSolutions Adjusted Trial Balance December 31, 2007	Debit Balances	Credit Balances
Cash	2 0 6 5 00	
Accounts Receivable	2 7 2 0 00	
Supplies	7 6 0 00	
Prepaid Insurance	2 2 0 0 00	
Land	20 0 0 0 00	
Office Equipment	1 8 0 0 00	
Accumulated Depreciation—Equipment		5 0 00
Accounts Payable		9 0 0 00
Wages Payable		2 5 0 00
Unearned Rent		2 4 0 00
Capital Stock		25 0 0 0 00
Dividends	4 0 0 0 00	
Fees Earned		16 8 4 0 00
Rent Revenue		1 2 0 00
Wages Expense	4 5 2 5 00	
Rent Expense	1 6 0 0 00	
Depreciation Expense	5 0 00	
Utilities Expense	9 8 5 00	
Supplies Expense	2 0 4 0 00	
Insurance Expense	2 0 0 00	
Miscellaneous Expense	4 5 5 00	
	43 4 0 0 00	43 4 0 0 00

Example Exercise 3-9   objective 4

For each of the following errors, considered individually, indicate whether the error would cause the adjusted trial balance totals to be unequal. If the error would cause the adjusted trial balance totals to be unequal, indicate whether the debit or credit total is higher and by how much.
a. The adjustment for accrued fees of $5,340 was journalized as a debit to Accounts Payable for $5,340 and a credit to Fees Earned of $5,340.
b. The adjustment for depreciation of $3,260 was journalized as a debit to Depreciation Expense for $3,620 and a credit to Accumulated Depreciation for $3,260.

Follow My Example 3-9

a. The totals are equal even though the debit should have been to Accounts Receivable instead of Accounts Payable.
b. The totals are unequal. The debit total is higher by $360 ($3,620 − $3,260).

For Practice: PE 3-9A, PE 3-9B

At a Glance

1. Describe the nature of the adjusting process.

Key Points	Key Learning Outcomes	Example Exercises	Practice Exercises
The accrual basis of accounting requires that revenues are reported in the period in which they are earned and expenses matched with the revenues they generate. The updating of accounts at the end of the accounting period is called the adjusting process. Each adjusting entry affects an income statement and balance sheet account. The four types of accounts requiring adjusting entries are prepaid expenses, unearned revenues, accrued revenues, and accrued expenses.	• Explain why accrual accounting requires adjusting entries. • List accounts that do and do NOT require adjusting entries at the end of the accounting period. • Give an example of a prepaid expense, unearned revenue, accrued revenue, and accrued expense.	3-1 3-2	3-1A, 3-1B 3-2A, 3-2B

2. Journalize entries for accounts requiring adjustment.

Key Points	Key Learning Outcomes	Example Exercises	Practice Exercises
Adjusting entries illustrated in this chapter include prepaid expenses, unearned revenues, accrued revenues, and accrued expenses. In addition, the adjusting entry necessary to record depreciation on fixed assets was illustrated.	• Prepare an adjusting entry for a prepaid expense. • Prepare an adjusting entry for an unearned revenue. • Prepare an adjusting entry for an accrued revenue. • Prepare an adjusting entry for an accrued expense. • Prepare an adjusting entry for depreciation expense.	3-3 3-4 3-5 3-6 3-7	3-3A, 3-3B 3-4A, 3-4B 3-5A, 3-5B 3-6A, 3-6B 3-7A, 3-7B

3. Summarize the adjustment process.

Key Points	Key Learning Outcomes	Example Exercises	Practice Exercises
A summary of adjustments, including the type of adjustment, the adjusting entry, and the effect of omitting an adjustment on the financial statements, is shown in Exhibit 6.	• Determine the effect on the income statement and balance sheet of omitting an adjusting entry for prepaid expense, unearned revenue, accrued revenue, accrued expense, and depreciation.	3-8	3-8A, 3-8B

4. Prepare an adjusted trial balance.

Key Points	Key Learning Outcomes	Example Exercises	Practice Exercises
After all the adjusting entries have been posted, the equality of the total debit balances and total credit balances is verified by an adjusted trial balance.	• Prepare an adjusted trial balance. • Determine the effect of errors on the equality of the adjusted trial balance.	3-9	3-9A, 3-9B

Key Terms

accounting period concept (106)
accrual basis of accounting (106)
accrued expenses (108)
accrued revenues (108)
accumulated depreciation (117)
adjusted trial balance (122)
adjusting entries (107)

adjusting process (107)
book value of the asset (or net book value) (117)
cash basis of accounting (106)
contra accounts (or contra asset accounts) (117)
depreciation (117)

depreciation expense (117)
fixed assets (or plant assets) (117)
matching concept (or matching principle) (106)
prepaid expenses (108)
revenue recognition concept (106)
unearned revenues (108)

Illustrative Problem

Three years ago, T. Roderick organized Harbor Realty Inc. At July 31, 2008, the end of the current year, the unadjusted trial balance of Harbor Realty appears as shown below.

Harbor Realty Inc.
Unadjusted Trial Balance
July 31, 2008

	Debit Balances	Credit Balances
Cash	3 4 2 5 00	
Accounts Receivable	7 0 0 0 00	
Supplies	1 2 7 0 00	
Prepaid Insurance	6 2 0 00	
Office Equipment	51 6 5 0 00	
Accumulated Depreciation		9 7 0 0 00
Accounts Payable		9 2 5 00
Wages Payable		0 00
Unearned Fees		1 2 5 0 00
Capital Stock		5 0 0 0 00
Retained Earnings		24 0 0 0 00
Dividends	5 2 0 0 00	
Fees Earned		59 1 2 5 00
Wages Expense	22 4 1 5 00	
Depreciation Expense	0 00	
Rent Expense	4 2 0 0 00	
Utilities Expense	2 7 1 5 00	
Supplies Expense	0 00	
Insurance Expense	0 00	
Miscellaneous Expense	1 5 0 5 00	
	100 0 0 0 00	100 0 0 0 00

The data needed to determine year-end adjustments are as follows:

a. Supplies on hand at July 31, 2008, $380.
b. Insurance premiums expired during the year, $315.
c. Depreciation of equipment during the year, $4,950.
d. Wages accrued but not paid at July 31, 2008, $440.
e. Accrued fees earned but not recorded at July 31, 2008, $1,000.
f. Unearned fees on July 31, 2008, $750.

Instructions
1. Prepare the necessary adjusting journal entries. Include journal entry explanations.
2. Determine the balance of the accounts affected by the adjusting entries, and prepare an adjusted trial balance.

Solution

1.

		JOURNAL			
	Date	Description	Post. Ref.	Debit	Credit
1	2008 July 31	Supplies Expense		8 9 0 00		1
2		Supplies			8 9 0 00	2
3		Supplies used ($1,270 − $380).				3
4						4
5	31	Insurance Expense		3 1 5 00		5
6		Prepaid Insurance			3 1 5 00	6
7		Insurance expired.				7
8						8
9	31	Depreciation Expense		4 9 5 0 00		9
10		Accumulated Depreciation			4 9 5 0 00	10
11		Depreciation expense.				11
12						12
13	31	Wages Expense		4 4 0 00		13
14		Wages Payable			4 4 0 00	14
15		Accrued wages.				15
16						16
17	31	Accounts Receivable		1 0 0 0 00		17
18		Fees Earned			1 0 0 0 00	18
19		Accrued fees.				19
20						20
21	31	Unearned Fees		5 0 0 00		21
22		Fees Earned			5 0 0 00	22
23		Fees earned ($1,250 − $750).				23

2.

Harbor Realty Inc.
Adjusted Trial Balance
July 31, 2008

	Debit Balances	Credit Balances
Cash	3 4 2 5 00	
Accounts Receivable	8 0 0 0 00	
Supplies	3 8 0 00	
Prepaid Insurance	3 0 5 00	
Office Equipment	51 6 5 0 00	
Accumulated Depreciation		14 6 5 0 00
Accounts Payable		9 2 5 00
Wages Payable		4 4 0 00
Unearned Fees		7 5 0 00
Capital Stock		5 0 0 0 00
Retained Earnings		24 0 0 0 00
Dividends	5 2 0 0 00	
Fees Earned		60 6 2 5 00
Wages Expense	22 8 5 5 00	
Depreciation Expense	4 9 5 0 00	
Rent Expense	4 2 0 0 00	
Utilities Expense	2 7 1 5 00	
Supplies Expense	8 9 0 00	
Insurance Expense	3 1 5 00	
Miscellaneous Expense	1 5 0 5 00	
	106 3 9 0 00	106 3 9 0 00

Self-Examination Questions
(Answers at End of Chapter)

1. Which of the following items represents a deferral?
   A. Prepaid insurance   C. Fees earned
   B. Wages payable   D. Accumulated depreciation

2. If the supplies account, before adjustment on May 31, indicated a balance of $2,250, and supplies on hand at May 31 totaled $950, the adjusting entry would be:
   A. debit Supplies, $950; credit Supplies Expense, $950.
   B. debit Supplies, $1,300; credit Supplies Expense, $1,300.
   C. debit Supplies Expense, $950; credit Supplies, $950.
   D. debit Supplies Expense, $1,300; credit Supplies, $1,300.

3. The balance in the unearned rent account for Jones Co. as of December 31 is $1,200. If Jones Co. failed to record the adjusting entry for $600 of rent earned during December, the effect on the balance sheet and income statement for December would be:
   A. assets understated $600; net income overstated $600.
   B. liabilities understated $600; net income understated $600.

C. liabilities overstated $600; net income understated $600.
D. liabilities overstated $600; net income overstated $600.

4. If the estimated amount of depreciation on equipment for a period is $2,000, the adjusting entry to record depreciation would be:
   A. debit Depreciation Expense, $2,000; credit Equipment, $2,000.
   B. debit Equipment, $2,000; credit Depreciation Expense, $2,000.
   C. debit Depreciation Expense, $2,000; credit Accumulated Depreciation, $2,000.
   D. debit Accumulated Depreciation, $2,000; credit Depreciation Expense, $2,000.

5. If the equipment account has a balance of $22,500 and its accumulated depreciation account has a balance of $14,000, the book value of the equipment would be:
   A. $36,500.   C. $14,000.
   B. $22,500.   D. $8,500.

Eye Openers

1. How are revenues and expenses reported on the income statement under (a) the cash basis of accounting and (b) the accrual basis of accounting?
2. Fees for services provided are billed to a customer during 2007. The customer remits the amount owed in 2008. During which year would the revenues be reported on the income statement under (a) the cash basis? (b) the accrual basis?
3. Employees performed services in 2007, but the wages were not paid until 2008. During which year would the wages expense be reported on the income statement under (a) the cash basis? (b) the accrual basis?
4. Is the matching concept related to (a) the cash basis of accounting or (b) the accrual basis of accounting?
5. Is the balance listed for cash on the trial balance, before the accounts have been adjusted, the amount that should normally be reported on the balance sheet? Explain.
6. Is the balance listed for supplies on the trial balance, before the accounts have been adjusted, the amount that should normally be reported on the balance sheet? Explain.
7. Why are adjusting entries needed at the end of an accounting period?
8. What is the difference between *adjusting entries* and *correcting entries*?
9. Identify the four different categories of adjusting entries frequently required at the end of an accounting period.
10. If the effect of the credit portion of an adjusting entry is to increase the balance of a liability account, which of the following statements describes the effect of the debit portion of the entry?
    a. Increases the balance of a revenue account.
    b. Increases the balance of an expense account.
    c. Increases the balance of an asset account.
11. If the effect of the debit portion of an adjusting entry is to increase the balance of an asset account, which of the following statements describes the effect of the credit portion of the entry?
    a. Increases the balance of a revenue account.
    b. Increases the balance of an expense account.
    c. Increases the balance of a liability account.

12. Does every adjusting entry have an effect on determining the amount of net income for a period? Explain.
13. What is the nature of the balance in the prepaid insurance account at the end of the accounting period (a) before adjustment? (b) after adjustment?
14. On October 1 of the current year, a business paid the October rent on the building that it occupies. (a) Do the rights acquired at October 1 represent an asset or an expense? (b) What is the justification for debiting Rent Expense at the time of payment?
15. (a) Explain the purpose of the two accounts: Depreciation Expense and Accumulated Depreciation. (b) What is the normal balance of each account? (c) Is it customary for the balances of the two accounts to be equal in amount? (d) In what financial statements, if any, will each account appear?

Practice Exercises

PE 3-1A
Accounts requiring adjustment
obj. 1

Indicate with a Yes or No whether or not each of the following accounts normally requires an adjusting entry.

a. Salaries Payable
b. Land
c. Dividends
d. Accumulated Depreciation
e. Unearned Rent
f. Supplies

PE 3-1B
Accounts requiring adjustment
obj. 1

Indicate with a Yes or No whether or not each of the following accounts normally requires an adjusting entry.

a. Capital Stock
b. Building
c. Prepaid Insurance
d. Cash
e. Interest Payable
f. Miscellaneous Expense

PE 3-2A
Type of adjustment
obj. 1

Classify the following items as (1) prepaid expense, (2) unearned revenue, (3) accrued revenue, or (4) accrued expense.

a. Cash received for services not yet rendered
b. Salaries owed but not yet paid
c. Insurance paid
d. Rent revenue earned but not received

PE 3-2B
Type of adjustment
obj. 1

Classify the following items as (1) prepaid expense, (2) unearned revenue, (3) accrued revenue, or (4) accrued expense.

a. Rent expense owed but not yet paid
b. Fees earned but not received
c. Supplies on hand
d. Cash received for use of land next month

PE 3-3A
Adjustment for supplies used
obj. 2

The supplies account had a beginning balance of $1,245 and was debited for $2,860 for supplies purchased during the year. Journalize the adjusting entry required at the end of the year assuming the amount of supplies on hand is $1,349.

PE 3-3B
Adjustment for insurance expired
obj. 2

The prepaid insurance account had a beginning balance of $4,800 and was debited for $5,850 of premiums paid during the year. Journalize the adjusting entry required at the end of the year assuming the amount of unexpired insurance related to future periods is $4,125.

PE 3-4A
*Adjustment for
unearned fees*
obj. 2

The balance in the unearned fees account, before adjustment at the end of the year, is $23,676. Journalize the adjusting entry required assuming the amount of unearned fees at the end of the year is $7,388.

PE 3-4B
*Adjustment for
unearned rent*
obj. 2

On August 1, 2007, Myopic Co. received $6,900 for the rent of land for 12 months. Journalize the adjusting entry required for unearned rent on December 31, 2007.

PE 3-5A
*Adjustment for accrued
fees*
obj. 2

At the end of the current year, $7,234 of fees have been earned but have not been billed to clients. Journalize the adjusting entry to record the accrued fees.

PE 3-5B
*Adjustment for accrued
fees*
obj. 2

At the end of the current year, $1,772 of fees have been earned but have not been billed to clients. Journalize the adjusting entry to record the accrued fees.

PE 3-6A
*Adjustment for salaries
payable*
obj. 2

Yarbrough Realty Co. pays weekly salaries of $11,875 on Friday for a five-day workweek ending on that day. Journalize the necessary adjusting entry at the end of the accounting period assuming that the period ends on Tuesday.

PE 3-6B
*Adjustment for salaries
payable*
obj. 2

Hobbs Realty Co. pays weekly salaries of $24,840 on Monday for a six-day workweek ending the preceding Saturday. Journalize the necessary adjusting entry at the end of the accounting period assuming that the period ends on Thursday.

PE 3-7A
*Adjustment for
depreciation*
obj. 2

The estimated amount of depreciation on equipment for the current year is $6,450. Journalize the adjusting entry to record the depreciation.

PE 3-7B
*Adjustment for
depreciation*
obj. 2

The estimated amount of depreciation on equipment for the current year is $1,820. Journalize the adjusting entry to record the depreciation.

PE 3-8A
*Effect of omitting
adjustments*
obj. 3

For the year ending February 28, 2007, Miracle Medical Co. mistakenly omitted adjusting entries for (1) depreciation of $2,276, (2) fees earned that were not billed of $9,638, and (3) accrued wages of $780. Indicate the combined effect of the errors on (a) revenues, (b) expenses, and (c) net income for the year ended February 28, 2007.

PE 3-8B
Effect of omitting adjustments
obj. **3**

For the year ending June 30, 2008, Ambulatory Medical Services Co. mistakenly omitted adjusting entries for (1) $1,034 of supplies that were used, (2) unearned revenue of $6,481 that was earned, and (3) insurance of $7,500 that expired. Indicate the combined effect of the errors on (a) revenues, (b) expenses, and (c) net income for the year ended June 30, 2008.

PE 3-9A
Effect of errors on adjusted trial balance
obj. **4**

For each of the following errors, considered individually, indicate whether the error would cause the adjusted trial balance totals to be unequal. If the error would cause the adjusted trial balance totals to be unequal, indicate whether the debit or credit total is higher and by how much.

a. The adjustment of depreciation of $3,500 was omitted from the end-of-period adjusting entries.

b. The adjustment of $2,565 for accrued fees earned was journalized as a debit to Accounts Receivable for $2,565 and a credit to Fees Earned for $2,556.

PE 3-9B
Effect of errors on adjusted trial balance
obj. **4**

For each of the following errors, considered individually, indicate whether the error would cause the adjusted trial balance totals to be unequal. If the error would cause the adjusted trial balance totals to be unequal, indicate whether the debit or credit total is higher and by how much.

a. The entry for $460 of supplies used during the period was journalized as a debit to Supplies Expense of $460 and a credit to Supplies of $640.

b. The adjustment for accrued wages of $1,240 was journalized as a debit to Wages Expense for $1,240 and a credit to Accounts Payable for $1,240.

Exercises

EX 3-1
Classifying types of adjustments
obj. **1**

Classify the following items as (a) prepaid expense, (b) unearned revenue, (c) accrued revenue, or (d) accrued expense.

1. Fees earned but not yet received.
2. Taxes owed but payable in the following period.
3. Utilities owed but not yet paid.
4. Salary owed but not yet paid.
5. Supplies on hand.
6. Fees received but not yet earned.
7. A two-year premium paid on a fire insurance policy.
8. Subscriptions received in advance by a magazine publisher.

EX 3-2
Classifying adjusting entries
obj. **1**

The following accounts were taken from the unadjusted trial balance of Hartford Co., a congressional lobbying firm. Indicate whether or not each account would normally require an adjusting entry. If the account normally requires an adjusting entry, use the following notation to indicate the type of adjustment:

AE—Accrued Expense
AR—Accrued Revenue
PE—Prepaid Expense
UR—Unearned Revenue

To illustrate, the answer for the first account is shown below.

Account	Answer
Accounts Receivable	Normally requires adjustment (AR).
Cash	
Dividends	
Interest Payable	
Interest Receivable	
Land	
Office Equipment	
Prepaid Rent	
Supplies	
Unearned Fees	
Wages Expense	

EX 3-3
Adjusting entry for supplies
obj. 2

The balance in the supplies account, before adjustment at the end of the year, is $2,975. Journalize the adjusting entry required if the amount of supplies on hand at the end of the year is $614.

EX 3-4
Determining supplies purchased
obj. 2

The supplies and supplies expense accounts at December 31, after adjusting entries have been posted at the end of the first year of operations, are shown in the following T accounts:

Supplies		Supplies Expense	
Bal.	279	Bal.	1,261

Determine the amount of supplies purchased during the year.

EX 3-5
Effect of omitting adjusting entry
obj. 2

At December 31, the end of the first month of operations, the usual adjusting entry transferring prepaid insurance expired to an expense account is omitted. Which items will be incorrectly stated, because of the error, on (a) the income statement for December and (b) the balance sheet as of December 31? Also indicate whether the items in error will be overstated or understated.

EX 3-6
Adjusting entries for prepaid insurance
obj. 2

The balance in the prepaid insurance account, before adjustment at the end of the year, is $6,175. Journalize the adjusting entry required under each of the following *alternatives* for determining the amount of the adjustment: (a) the amount of insurance expired during the year is $4,180; (b) the amount of unexpired insurance applicable to future periods is $1,995.

EX 3-7
Adjusting entries for prepaid insurance
obj. 2

The prepaid insurance account had a balance of $3,600 at the beginning of the year. The account was debited for $4,800 for premiums on policies purchased during the year. Journalize the adjusting entry required at the end of the year for each of the following situations: (a) the amount of unexpired insurance applicable to future periods is $2,950; (b) the amount of insurance expired during the year is $5,450.

EX 3-8
Adjusting entries for unearned fees
obj. 2
✓ *Amount of entry: $22,320*

The balance in the unearned fees account, before adjustment at the end of the year, is $49,500. Journalize the adjusting entry required if the amount of unearned fees at the end of the year is $27,180.

EX 3-9
*Effect of omitting
adjusting entry*
obj. 2

At the end of August, the first month of the business year, the usual adjusting entry transferring rent earned to a revenue account from the unearned rent account was omitted. Indicate which items will be incorrectly stated, because of the error, on (a) the income statement for August and (b) the balance sheet as of August 31. Also indicate whether the items in error will be overstated or understated.

EX 3-10
*Adjusting entry for
accrued fees*
obj. 2

At the end of the current year, $17,600 of fees have been earned but have not been billed to clients.

a. Journalize the adjusting entry to record the accrued fees.
b. If the cash basis rather than the accrual basis had been used, would an adjusting entry have been necessary? Explain.

EX 3-11
*Adjusting entries for
unearned and accrued
fees*
obj. 2

The balance in the unearned fees account, before adjustment at the end of the year, is $39,750. Of these fees, $12,300 have been earned. In addition, $7,100 of fees have been earned but have not been billed. Journalize the adjusting entries (a) to adjust the unearned fees account and (b) to record the accrued fees.

EX 3-12
*Effect on financial
statements of omitting
adjusting entry*
obj. 2

The adjusting entry for accrued fees was omitted at December 31, the end of the current year. Indicate which items will be in error, because of the omission, on (a) the income statement for the current year and (b) the balance sheet as of December 31. Also indicate whether the items in error will be overstated or understated.

EX 3-13
*Adjusting entries for
accrued salaries*
obj. 2

✓ *a. Amount of entry:
$12,375*

Ash Realty Co. pays weekly salaries of $20,625 on Friday for a five-day workweek ending on that day. Journalize the necessary adjusting entry at the end of the accounting period assuming that the period ends (a) on Wednesday and (b) on Thursday.

EX 3-14
Determining wages paid
obj. 2

The wages payable and wages expense accounts at March 31, after adjusting entries have been posted at the end of the first month of operations, are shown in the following T accounts:

Wages Payable			Wages Expense	
	Bal.	6,480	Bal.	72,150

Determine the amount of wages paid during the month.

EX 3-15
*Effect of omitting
adjusting entry*
obj. 2

Accrued salaries of $3,910 owed to employees for December 30 and 31 are not considered in preparing the financial statements for the year ended December 31. Indicate which items will be erroneously stated, because of the error, on (a) the income statement for the year and (b) the balance sheet as of December 31. Also indicate whether the items in error will be overstated or understated.

EX 3-16
*Effect of omitting
adjusting entry*
obj. 2

Assume that the error in Exercise 3-15 was not corrected and that the $3,910 of accrued salaries was included in the first salary payment in January. Indicate which items will be erroneously stated, because of failure to correct the initial error, on (a) the income statement for the month of January and (b) the balance sheet as of January 31.

EX 3-17
Adjusting entries for prepaid and accrued taxes

obj. 2

✔ b. $18,675

Pisces Financial Services was organized on April 1 of the current year. On April 2, Pisces prepaid $3,000 to the city for taxes (license fees) for the *next* 12 months and debited the pre-paid taxes account. Pisces is also required to pay in January an annual tax (on property) for the *previous* calendar year. The estimated amount of the property tax for the current year (April 1 to December 31) is $16,425.

a. Journalize the two adjusting entries required to bring the accounts affected by the two taxes up to date as of December 31, the end of the current year.
b. What is the amount of tax expense for the current year?

EX 3-18
Adjustment for depreciation

obj. 2

The estimated amount of depreciation on equipment for the current year is $3,275. Journalize the adjusting entry to record the depreciation.

EX 3-19
Determining fixed asset's book value

obj. 2

The balance in the equipment account is $678,950, and the balance in the accumulated depreciation—equipment account is $262,200.

a. What is the book value of the equipment?
b. Does the balance in the accumulated depreciation account mean that the equipment's loss of value is $262,200? Explain.

EX 3-20
Book value of fixed assets

objs. 2, 3

In a recent balance sheet, Microsoft Corporation reported *Property, Plant, and Equipment* of $6,078 million and *Accumulated Depreciation* of $3,855 million.

a. What was the book value of the fixed assets?
b. Would the book value of Microsoft Corporation's fixed assets normally approximate their fair market values?

EX 3-21
Effects of errors on financial statements

objs. 2, 3

For a recent period, Circuit City Stores, Inc., reported accrued expenses and other current liabilities of $228,966,000. For the same period, Circuit City reported earnings of $95,789,000 before income taxes. If accrued expenses and other current liabilities had not been recorded, what would have been the earnings (loss) before income taxes?

EX 3-22
Effects of errors on financial statements

objs. 2, 3

For a recent year, the balance sheet for The Campbell Soup Company includes accrued liabilities of $606,000,000. The income before taxes for The Campbell Soup Company for the year was $1,030,000,000.

a. If the accruals had not been recorded at the end of the year, by how much would income before taxes have been misstated?
b. What is the percentage of the misstatement in (a) to the reported income of $1,030,000,000? Round to one decimal place.

EX 3-23
Effects of errors on financial statements

objs. 2, 3

The accountant for Cyprus Medical Co., a medical services consulting firm, mistakenly omitted adjusting entries for (a) unearned revenue earned during the year ($12,450) and (b) accrued wages ($7,280). Indicate the effect of each error, considered individually, on the income statement for the current year ended August 31. Also indicate the effect of each error on the August 31 balance sheet. Set up a table similar to the following, and record your

✓1. a. Revenue
understated, $12,450

answers by inserting the dollar amount in the appropriate spaces. Insert a zero if the error does not affect the item.

	Error (a)		Error (b)	
	Over-stated	Under-stated	Over-stated	Under-stated
1. Revenue for the year would be	$ ____	$ ____	$ ____	$ ____
2. Expenses for the year would be	$ ____	$ ____	$ ____	$ ____
3. Net income for the year would be	$ ____	$ ____	$ ____	$ ____
4. Assets at August 31 would be	$ ____	$ ____	$ ____	$ ____
5. Liabilities at August 31 would be	$ ____	$ ____	$ ____	$ ____
6. Stockholders' equity at August 31 would be	$ ____	$ ____	$ ____	$ ____

EX 3-24
Effects of errors on financial statements
objs. 2, 3

If the net income for the current year had been $262,800 in Exercise 3-23, what would have been the correct net income if the proper adjusting entries had been made?

EX 3-25
Adjusting entries for depreciation; effect of error
objs. 2, 3

On December 31, a business estimates depreciation on equipment used during the first year of operations to be $18,100.

a. Journalize the adjusting entry required as of December 31.
b. If the adjusting entry in (a) were omitted, which items would be erroneously stated on (1) the income statement for the year and (2) the balance sheet as of December 31?

EX 3-26
Adjusting entries from trial balances
obj. 4

The unadjusted and adjusted trial balances for Tomahawk Services Co. on July 31, 2008, are shown below.

Tomahawk Services Co.
Trial Balance
July 31, 2008

	Unadjusted		Adjusted	
	Debit Balances	Credit Balances	Debit Balances	Credit Balances
Cash	48		48	
Accounts Receivable	114		126	
Supplies	36		27	
Prepaid Insurance	60		36	
Land	78		78	
Equipment	120		120	
Accumulated Depreciation—Equipment		24		39
Accounts Payable		78		78
Wages Payable		0		3
Capital Stock		100		100
Retained Earnings		176		176
Dividends	24		24	
Fees Earned		222		234
Wages Expense	72		75	
Rent Expense	24		24	
Insurance Expense	0		24	
Utilities Expense	12		12	
Depreciation Expense	0		15	
Supplies Expense	0		9	
Miscellaneous Expense	12		12	
	600	600	630	630

Journalize the five entries that adjusted the accounts at July 31, 2008. None of the accounts were affected by more than one adjusting entry.

EX 3-27
Adjusting entries from trial balances

obj. 4

✓ *Corrected trial balance totals, $310,950*

The accountant for Sweetwater Laundry prepared the following unadjusted and adjusted trial balances. Assume that all balances in the unadjusted trial balance and the amounts of the adjustments are correct. Identify the errors in the accountant's adjusting entries.

Sweetwater Laundry
Trial Balance
October 31, 2008

	Unadjusted		Adjusted	
	Debit Balances	Credit Balances	Debit Balances	Credit Balances
Cash	7,500		7,500	
Accounts Receivable	18,250		22,000	
Laundry Supplies	3,750		5,500	
Prepaid Insurance*	5,200		1,400	
Laundry Equipment	140,000		134,000	
Accumulated Depreciation		48,000		48,000
Accounts Payable		9,600		9,600
Wages Payable				1,200
Capital Stock		10,000		10,000
Retained Earnings		50,300		50,300
Dividends	28,775		28,775	
Laundry Revenue		182,100		182,100
Wages Expense	49,200		49,200	
Rent Expense	25,575		25,575	
Utilities Expense	18,500		18,500	
Depreciation Expense			6,000	
Laundry Supplies Expense			1,750	
Insurance Expense			800	
Miscellaneous Expense	3,250		3,250	
	300,000	300,000	304,250	301,200

*$3,800 of insurance expired during the year.

Problems Series A

PR 3-1A
Adjusting entries

obj. 2

On July 31, 2008, the following data were accumulated to assist the accountant in preparing the adjusting entries for Fremont Realty:

a. The supplies account balance on July 31 is $1,975. The supplies on hand on July 31 are $625.
b. The unearned rent account balance on July 31 is $3,750, representing the receipt of an advance payment on July 1 of three months' rent from tenants.
c. Wages accrued but not paid at July 31 are $1,000.
d. Fees accrued but unbilled at July 31 are $12,275.
e. Depreciation of office equipment is $850.

Instructions
1. Journalize the adjusting entries required at July 31, 2008.
2. Briefly explain the difference between adjusting entries and entries that would be made to correct errors.

PR 3-2A
Adjusting entries

obj. 2

Selected account balances before adjustment for Foxboro Realty at December 31, 2008, the end of the current year, are as follows:

	Debits	Credits
Accounts Receivable	$18,250	
Equipment	72,500	
Accumulated Depreciation		$ 11,900
Prepaid Rent	7,500	
Supplies	2,050	
Wages Payable		—
Unearned Fees		8,500
Fees Earned		187,950
Wages Expense	60,100	
Rent Expense	—	
Depreciation Expense	—	
Supplies Expense	—	

Data needed for year-end adjustments are as follows:

a. Unbilled fees at December 31, $1,650.
b. Supplies on hand at December 31, $200.
c. Rent expired, $5,000.
d. Depreciation of equipment during year, $1,150.
e. Unearned fees at December 31, $1,500.
f. Wages accrued but not paid at December 31, $3,150.

Instructions

Journalize the six adjusting entries required at December 31, based upon the data presented.

PR 3-3A
Adjusting entries
obj. 2

KLOOSTER
& ALLEN

Iron River Company, an electronics repair store, prepared the unadjusted trial balance at the end of its first year of operations shown below.

Iron River Company
Unadjusted Trial Balance
April 30, 2008

	Debit Balances	Credit Balances
Cash	3,450	
Accounts Receivable	22,500	
Supplies	5,400	
Equipment	113,700	
Accounts Payable		5,250
Unearned Fees		6,000
Capital Stock		25,000
Retained Earnings		53,000
Dividends	4,500	
Fees Earned		135,750
Wages Expense	31,500	
Rent Expense	24,000	
Utilities Expense	17,250	
Miscellaneous Expense	2,700	
	225,000	225,000

For preparing the adjusting entries, the following data were assembled:

a. Fees earned but unbilled on April 30 were $1,775.
b. Supplies on hand on April 30 were $1,200.
c. Depreciation of equipment was estimated to be $4,100 for the year.
d. The balance in unearned fees represented the April 1 receipt in advance for services to be provided. Only $1,750 of the services was provided between April 1 and April 30.
e. Unpaid wages accrued on April 30 were $600.

Instructions

Journalize the adjusting entries necessary on April 30, 2008.

PR 3-4A
Adjusting entries
objs. 2, 3, 4

Danville Company specializes in the repair of music equipment and is owned and operated by Harry Nagel. On April 30, 2008, the end of the current year, the accountant for Danville Company prepared the following trial balances:

Danville Company
Trial Balance
April 30, 2008

	Unadjusted		Adjusted	
	Debit Balances	Credit Balances	Debit Balances	Credit Balances
Cash	12,750		12,750	
Accounts Receivable	36,500		36,500	
Supplies	3,750		900	
Prepaid Insurance	4,750		1,500	
Equipment	120,150		120,150	
Accumulated Depreciation—Equipment		31,500		34,000
Automobiles	36,500		36,500	
Accumulated Depreciation—Automobiles		18,250		20,400
Accounts Payable		8,310		8,800
Salaries Payable		—		2,000
Unearned Service Fees		6,000		2,900
Capital Stock		40,000		40,000
Retained Earnings		91,340		91,340
Dividends	25,000		25,000	
Service Fees Earned		244,600		247,700
Salary Expense	172,300		174,300	
Rent Expense	18,000		18,000	
Supplies Expense	—		2,850	
Depreciation Expense—Equipment	—		2,500	
Depreciation Expense—Automobiles	—		2,150	
Utilities Expense	4,300		4,790	
Taxes Expense	2,725		2,725	
Insurance Expense	—		3,250	
Miscellaneous Expense	3,275		3,275	
	440,000	440,000	447,140	447,140

Instructions
Journalize the seven entries that adjusted the accounts at April 30. None of the accounts were affected by more than one adjusting entry.

PR 3-5A
Adjusting entries and adjusted trial balances
objs. 2, 3, 4

✓ *2. Total of Debit column: $765,000*

Cambridge Company is a small editorial services company owned and operated by Dave Maier. On December 31, 2008, the end of the current year, Cambridge Company's accounting clerk prepared the unadjusted trial balance shown at the top of the following page.
The data needed to determine year-end adjustments are as follows:

a. Unexpired insurance at December 31, $2,700.
b. Supplies on hand at December 31, $480.
c. Depreciation of building for the year, $1,600.
d. Depreciation of equipment for the year, $4,400.
e. Rent unearned at December 31, $3,250.
f. Accrued salaries and wages at December 31, $2,800.
g. Fees earned but unbilled on December 31, $6,200.

Instructions
1. Journalize the adjusting entries. Add additional accounts as needed.
2. Determine the balances of the accounts affected by the adjusting entries, and prepare an adjusted trial balance.

Cambridge Company
Unadjusted Trial Balance
December 31, 2008

	Debit Balances	Credit Balances
Cash	5,550	
Accounts Receivable	28,350	
Prepaid Insurance	7,200	
Supplies	1,980	
Land	112,500	
Building	212,250	
Accumulated Depreciation—Building		137,550
Equipment	135,300	
Accumulated Depreciation—Equipment		97,950
Accounts Payable		12,150
Unearned Rent		6,750
Capital Stock		60,000
Retained Earnings		141,000
Dividends	15,000	
Fees Earned		294,600
Salaries and Wages Expense	143,370	
Utilities Expense	42,375	
Advertising Expense	22,800	
Repairs Expense	17,250	
Miscellaneous Expense	6,075	
	750,000	750,000

PR 3-6A
Adjusting entries and errors
obj. 3

✓ 2. Corrected Net Income: $157,600

At the end of June, the first month of operations, the following selected data were taken from the financial statements of Teryse Weire, Attorney at Law, P.C.:

Net income for June	$155,000
Total assets at June 30	350,000
Total liabilities at June 30	120,000
Total stockholders' equity at June 30	230,000

In preparing the financial statements, adjustments for the following data were overlooked:

a. Supplies used during June, $1,800.
b. Unbilled fees earned at June 30, $11,600.
c. Depreciation of equipment for June, $4,950.
d. Accrued wages at June 30, $2,250.

Instructions

1. Journalize the entries to record the omitted adjustments.
2. Determine the correct amount of net income for June and the total assets, liabilities, and stockholders' equity at June 30. In addition to indicating the corrected amounts, indicate the effect of each omitted adjustment by setting up and completing a columnar table similar to the following. Adjustment (a) is presented as an example.

	Net Income	Total Assets	Total Liabilities	Total Stockholders' Equity
Reported amounts	$155,000	$350,000	$120,000	$230,000
Corrections:				
Adjustment (a)	−1,800	−1,800	0	−1,800
Adjustment (b)				
Adjustment (c)				
Adjustment (d)				
Corrected amounts				

Problems Series B

PR 3-1B
Adjusting entries
obj. 2

On October 31, 2008, the following data were accumulated to assist the accountant in preparing the adjusting entries for Twin Bluffs Realty:

a. Fees accrued but unbilled at October 31 are $11,385.
b. The supplies account balance on October 31 is $2,973. The supplies on hand at October 31 are $740.
c. Wages accrued but not paid at October 31 are $1,500.
d. The unearned rent account balance at October 31 is $9,450, representing the receipt of an advance payment on October 1 of three months' rent from tenants.
e. Depreciation of office equipment is $2,650.

Instructions
1. Journalize the adjusting entries required at October 31, 2008.
2. Briefly explain the difference between adjusting entries and entries that would be made to correct errors.

PR 3-2B
Adjusting entries
obj. 2

Selected account balances before adjustment for Green Lake Realty at August 31, 2008, the end of the current year, are shown below.

	Debits	Credits
Accounts Receivable	$38,250	
Accumulated Depreciation		$ 26,900
Depreciation Expense	—	
Equipment	90,500	
Fees Earned		275,500
Prepaid Rent	9,750	
Rent Expense	—	
Supplies	2,145	
Supplies Expense	—	
Unearned Fees		6,175
Wages Expense	81,500	
Wages Payable	—	

Data needed for year-end adjustments are as follows:

a. Supplies on hand at August 31, $500.
b. Depreciation of equipment during year, $1,375.
c. Rent expired during year, $4,525.
d. Wages accrued but not paid at August 31, $2,200.
e. Unearned fees at August 31, $1,500.
f. Unbilled fees at August 31, $6,780.

Instructions
Journalize the six adjusting entries required at August 31, based upon the data presented.

PR 3-3B
Adjusting entries
obj. 2

Lander Outfitters Co., an outfitter store for fishing treks, prepared the unadjusted trial balance shown on the following page at the end of its first year of operations.
    For preparing the adjusting entries, the following data were assembled:

a. Supplies on hand on June 30 were $300.
b. Fees earned but unbilled on June 30 were $2,310.
c. Depreciation of equipment was estimated to be $1,500 for the year.

d. Unpaid wages accrued on June 30 were $475.

e. The balance in unearned fees represented the June 1 receipt in advance for services to be provided. Only $1,000 of the services was provided between June 1 and June 30.

Lander Outfitters Co.
Unadjusted Trial Balance
June 30, 2008

	Debit Balances	Credit Balances
Cash	6,610	
Accounts Receivable	21,900	
Supplies	1,820	
Equipment	37,860	
Accounts Payable		3,050
Unearned Fees		4,800
Capital Stock		8,000
Retained Earnings		47,700
Dividends	2,500	
Fees Earned		71,450
Wages Expense	38,210	
Rent Expense	13,790	
Utilities Expense	10,050	
Miscellaneous Expense	2,260	
	135,000	135,000

Instructions
Journalize the adjusting entries necessary on June 30.

PR 3-4B
Adjusting entries
objs. 2, 3, 4

Elkton Company specializes in the maintenance and repair of signs, such as billboards. On July 31, 2008, the accountant for Elkton Company prepared the following trial balances:

Elkton Company
Trial Balance
July 31, 2008

	Unadjusted Debit Balances	Unadjusted Credit Balances	Adjusted Debit Balances	Adjusted Credit Balances
Cash	4,750		4,750	
Accounts Receivable	17,400		17,400	
Supplies	3,600		975	
Prepaid Insurance	5,650		1,200	
Land	50,000		50,000	
Buildings	120,000		120,000	
Accumulated Depreciation—Buildings		49,500		53,100
Trucks	75,000		75,000	
Accumulated Depreciation—Trucks		11,800		13,300
Accounts Payable		6,920		7,520
Salaries Payable		—		1,180
Unearned Service Fees		7,400		5,100
Capital Stock		35,000		35,000
Retained Earnings		111,700		111,700
Dividends	5,000		5,000	
Service Fees Earned		152,680		154,980
Salary Expense	73,600		74,780	
Depreciation Expense—Trucks	—		1,500	
Rent Expense	9,600		9,600	
Supplies Expense	—		2,625	
Utilities Expense	6,200		6,800	
Depreciation Expense—Buildings	—		3,600	
Taxes Expense	1,720		1,720	
Insurance Expense	—		4,450	
Miscellaneous Expense	2,480		2,480	
	375,000	375,000	381,880	381,880

Instructions

Journalize the seven entries that adjusted the accounts at July 31. None of the accounts were affected by more than one adjusting entry.

PR 3-5B
Adjusting entries and adjusted trial balances
objs. **2, 3, 4**

✓2. Total of Debit column: $285,150

Lincoln Service Co., which specializes in appliance repair services, is owned and operated by Molly Jordan. Lincoln Service Co.'s accounting clerk prepared the unadjusted trial balance at December 31, 2008, shown below.

Lincoln Service Co.
Unadjusted Trial Balance
December 31, 2008

	Debit Balances	Credit Balances
Cash	2,100	
Accounts Receivable	10,300	
Prepaid Insurance	3,000	
Supplies	1,725	
Land	50,000	
Building	80,750	
Accumulated Depreciation—Building		37,850
Equipment	44,000	
Accumulated Depreciation—Equipment		17,650
Accounts Payable		3,750
Unearned Rent		3,600
Capital Stock		26,000
Retained Earnings		57,550
Dividends	2,500	
Fees Earned		128,600
Salaries and Wages Expense	50,900	
Utilities Expense	14,100	
Advertising Expense	7,500	
Repairs Expense	6,100	
Miscellaneous Expense	2,025	
	275,000	275,000

The data needed to determine year-end adjustments are as follows:

a. Depreciation of building for the year, $3,500.
b. Depreciation of equipment for the year, $2,300.
c. Accrued salaries and wages at December 31, $1,100.
d. Unexpired insurance at December 31, $750.
e. Fees earned but unbilled on December 31, $3,250.
f. Supplies on hand at December 31, $525.
g. Rent unearned at December 31, $1,500.

Instructions

1. Journalize the adjusting entries. Add additional accounts as needed.
2. Determine the balances of the accounts affected by the adjusting entries and prepare an adjusted trial balance.

PR 3-6B
Adjusting entries and errors
obj. **3**

✓2. Corrected Net Income: $97,755

At the end of October, the first month of operations, the following selected data were taken from the financial statements of Lauren Powell, Attorney at Law, P.C.:

Net income for October	$ 99,480
Total assets at October 31	400,000
Total liabilities at October 31	100,000
Total stockholders' equity at October 31	300,000

In preparing the financial statements, adjustments for the following data were overlooked:

a. Unbilled fees earned at October 31, $8,000.
b. Depreciation of equipment for October, $5,500.
c. Accrued wages at October 31, $2,500.
d. Supplies used during October, $1,725.

Instructions

1. Journalize the entries to record the omitted adjustments.
2. Determine the correct amount of net income for October and the total assets, liabilities, and stockholders' equity at October 31. In addition to indicating the corrected amounts, indicate the effect of each omitted adjustment by setting up and completing a columnar table similar to the following. Adjustment (a) is presented as an example.

	Net Income	Total Assets	Total Liabilities	Total Stockholders' Equity
Reported amounts	$99,480	$400,000	$100,000	$300,000
Corrections:				
Adjustment (a)	+8,000	+8,000	0	+8,000
Adjustment (b)	___	___	___	___
Adjustment (c)	___	___	___	___
Adjustment (d)	___	___	___	___
Corrected amounts	___	___	___	___

Continuing Problem

✓ *3. Total of Debit column: $39,500*

The unadjusted trial balance that you prepared for Dancin Music at the end of Chapter 2 should appear as follows:

Dancin Music
Unadjusted Trial Balance
May 31, 2008

	Debit Balances	Credit Balances
Cash	12,085	
Accounts Receivable	2,850	
Supplies	920	
Prepaid Insurance	3,360	
Office Equipment	5,000	
Accounts Payable		5,750
Unearned Revenue		4,800
Capital Stock		12,500
Dividends	1,300	
Fees Earned		14,750
Wages Expense	2,400	
Office Rent Expense	2,600	
Equipment Rent Expense	1,300	
Utilities Expense	910	
Music Expense	2,565	
Advertising Expense	1,730	
Supplies Expense	180	
Miscellaneous Expense	600	
	37,800	37,800

The data needed to determine adjustments for the two-month period ending May 31, 2008, are as follows:

a. During May, Dancin Music provided guest disc jockeys for KPRG for a total of 115 hours. For information on the amount of the accrued revenue to be billed to KPRG, see the contract described in the May 3, 2008, transaction at the end of Chapter 2.
b. Supplies on hand at May 31, $160.
c. The balance of the prepaid insurance account relates to the May 1, 2008, transaction at the end of Chapter 2.
d. Depreciation of the office equipment is $100.

e. The balance of the unearned revenue account relates to the contract between Dancin Music and KPRG, described in the May 3, 2008, transaction at the end of Chapter 2.

f. Accrued wages as of May 31, 2008, were $200.

Instructions

1. Prepare adjusting journal entries. You will need the following additional accounts:

   18 Accumulated Depreciation—Office Equipment
   22 Wages Payable
   57 Insurance Expense
   58 Depreciation Expense

2. Post the adjusting entries, inserting balances in the accounts affected.
3. Prepare an adjusted trial balance.

Special Activities

SA 3-1
Ethics and professional conduct in business

ETHICS

Annette Kagel opened Harre Real Estate Co. on January 1, 2007. At the end of the first year, the business needed additional capital. On behalf of Harre Real Estate, Annette applied to Lake County State Bank for a loan of $200,000. Based on Harre Real Estate's financial statements, which had been prepared on a cash basis, the Lake County State Bank loan officer rejected the loan as too risky.

After receiving the rejection notice, Annette instructed her accountant to prepare the financial statements on an accrual basis. These statements included $31,500 in accounts receivable and $10,200 in accounts payable. Annette then instructed her accountant to record an additional $10,000 of accounts receivable for commissions on property for which a contract had been signed on December 28, 2007, but which would not be formally "closed" and the title transferred until January 5, 2008.

Annette then applied for a $200,000 loan from First National Bank, using the revised financial statements. On this application, Annette indicated that she had not previously been rejected for credit.

Discuss the ethical and professional conduct of Annette Kagel in applying for the loan from First National Bank.

SA 3-2
Accrued expense

REAL WORLD

On December 30, 2008, you buy a Ford Expedition. It comes with a three-year, 36,000-mile warranty. On March 5, 2009, you return the Expedition to the dealership for some basic repairs covered under the warranty. The cost of the repairs to the dealership is $1,560. In what year, 2008 or 2009, should Ford Motor Company recognize the cost of the warranty repairs as an expense?

SA 3-3
Accrued revenue

REAL WORLD

The following is an excerpt from a conversation between Sybil Towns and Greg Gibbs just before they boarded a flight to London on American Airlines. They are going to London to attend their company's annual sales conference.

Sybil: Greg, aren't you taking an introductory accounting course at college?

Greg: Yes, I decided it's about time I learned something about accounting. You know, our annual bonuses are based upon the sales figures that come from the accounting department.

Sybil: I guess I never really thought about it.

Greg: You should think about it! Last year, I placed a $500,000 order on December 28. But when I got my bonus, the $500,000 sale wasn't included. They said it hadn't been shipped until January 3, so it would have to count in next year's bonus.

Sybil: A real bummer!

Greg: Right! I was counting on that bonus including the $500,000 sale.

Sybil: Did you complain?

Greg: Yes, but it didn't do any good. Ashley, the head accountant, said something about matching revenues and expenses. Also, something about not recording revenues until the sale is final. I figure I'd take the accounting course and find out whether she's just jerking me around.

Sybil: I never really thought about it. When do you think American Airlines will record its revenues from this flight?

Greg: Mmm ... I guess it could record the revenue when it sells the ticket ... or ... when the boarding passes are taken at the door ... or ... when we get off the plane ... or when our company pays for the tickets ... or ... I don't know. I'll ask my accounting instructor.

Discuss when American Airlines should recognize the revenue from ticket sales to properly match revenues and expenses.

SA 3-4
Adjustments and financial statements

Several years ago, your brother opened Pomona Television Repair. He made a small initial investment and added money from his personal bank account as needed. He withdrew money for living expenses at irregular intervals. As the business grew, he hired an assistant. He is now considering adding more employees, purchasing additional service trucks, and purchasing the building he now rents. To secure funds for the expansion, your brother submitted a loan application to the bank and included the most recent financial statements (shown below) prepared from accounts maintained by a part-time bookkeeper.

Pomona Television Repair
Income Statement
For the Year Ended July 31, 2008

Service revenue		$90,000
Less: Rent paid	$30,000	
Wages paid	28,500	
Supplies paid	5,100	
Utilities paid	3,175	
Insurance paid	2,400	
Miscellaneous payments	3,600	72,775
Net income		$17,225

Pomona Television Repair
Balance Sheet
July 31, 2008

Assets

Cash	$10,600
Amounts due from customers	12,500
Truck	36,900
Total assets	$60,000

Equities

Stockholders' equity	$60,000

After reviewing the financial statements, the loan officer at the bank asked your brother if he used the accrual basis of accounting for revenues and expenses. Your brother responded that he did and that is why he included an account for "Amounts Due from Customers." The loan officer then asked whether or not the accounts were adjusted prior to the preparation of the statements. Your brother answered that they had not been adjusted.

a. Why do you think the loan officer suspected that the accounts had not been adjusted prior to the preparation of the statements?
b. Indicate possible accounts that might need to be adjusted before an accurate set of financial statements could be prepared.

SA 3-5
Codes of ethics

Group Project

ETHICS

Obtain a copy of your college or university's student code of conduct. In groups of three or four, answer the following questions.

1. Compare this code of conduct with the accountant's Codes of Professional Conduct, which is linked to the text Web site at **www.thomsonedu.com/accounting/warren**.
2. One of your classmates asks you for permission to copy your homework, which your instructor will be collecting and grading for part of your overall term grade. Although your instructor has not stated whether one student may or may not copy another student's homework, is it ethical for you to allow your classmate to copy your homework? Is it ethical for your classmate to copy your homework?

Answers to Self-Examination Questions

1. **A**   A deferral is the delay in recording an expense already paid, such as prepaid insurance (answer A). Wages payable (answer B) is considered an accrued expense or accrued liability. Fees earned (answer C) is a revenue item. Accumulated depreciation (answer D) is a contra account to a fixed asset.

2. **D**   The balance in the supplies account, before adjustment, represents the amount of supplies available. From this amount ($2,250) is subtracted the amount of supplies on hand ($950) to determine the supplies used ($1,300). Since increases in expense accounts are recorded by debits and decreases in asset accounts are recorded by credits, answer D is the correct entry.

3. **C**   The failure to record the adjusting entry debiting Unearned Rent, $600, and crediting Rent Revenue, $600, would have the effect of overstating liabilities by $600 and understating net income by $600 (answer C).

4. **C**   Since increases in expense accounts (such as depreciation expense) are recorded by debits and it is customary to record the decreases in usefulness of fixed assets as credits to accumulated depreciation accounts, answer C is the correct entry.

5. **D**   The book value of a fixed asset is the difference between the balance in the asset account and the balance in the related accumulated depreciation account, or $22,500 − $14,000, as indicated by answer D ($8,500).

chapter

4

Completing the Accounting Cycle

© ERIC RISBERG/ASSOCIATED PRESS

objectives

After studying this chapter, you should be able to:

1 Describe the flow of accounting information from the unadjusted trial balance into the adjusted trial balance and financial statements.

2 Prepare financial statements from adjusted account balances.

3 Prepare closing entries.

4 Describe the accounting cycle.

5 Illustrate the accounting cycle for one period.

6 Explain what is meant by the fiscal year and the natural business year.

Electronic Arts Inc.

Most of us have had to file a personal tax return. At the beginning of the year, you estimate your upcoming income and decide whether you need to increase your payroll tax withholdings or perhaps pay estimated taxes. During the year, you earn income and enter into tax-related transactions, such as making charitable contributions. At the end of the year, your employer sends you a tax withholding information form (W-2) form, and you collect the tax records needed for completing your yearly tax forms. As the next year begins, you start the cycle all over again.

Businesses also go through a cycle of activities. For example, Electronic Arts Inc., the world's largest developer and marketer of electronic game software, begins its cycle by developing new or revised game titles, such as Madden NFL Football®, Need for Speed®, Tiger Woods PGA Tour®, The Sims®, and The Lord of the Rings®. These games are marketed and sold throughout the year. During the year, operating transactions of the business are recorded. For Electronic Arts, such transactions include the salaries for game developers, advertising expenditures, costs for producing and packaging games, and game revenues. At the end of the year, financial statements are prepared that summarize the operating activities for the year. Electronic Arts publishes these statements on its Web site at **http://www.investor.ea.com**. Finally, before the start of the next year, the accounts are readied for recording the operations of the next year.

As we saw in Chapter 1, the initial cycle for NetSolutions began with Chris Clark's investment in the business on November 1, 2007. The cycle continued with recording NetSolutions' transactions for November and December, as we discussed and illustrated in Chapters 1 and 2. In Chapter 3, the cycle continued when the adjusting entries for the two months ending December 31, 2007, were recorded. In this chapter, we complete the cycle for NetSolutions by preparing financial statements and getting the accounts ready for recording transactions of the next period.

Flow of Accounting Information

The end-of-period process by which accounts are adjusted and the financial statements are prepared is one of the most important in accounting. Using our illustration of NetSolutions from Chapters 1–3, this process is summarized in spreadsheet form in Exhibit 1.

Exhibit 1 begins with the unadjusted trial balance as of the end of the period. The unadjusted trial balance serves as a control to verify that the total of the debit balances equals the total of the credit balances. If the trial balance totals are unequal, an error has occurred, which must be found and corrected before the end-of-period process can continue.

The adjustments that we explained and illustrated for NetSolutions in Chapter 3 are shown in the Adjustments columns of Exhibit 1. Cross-referencing (by letters) the debit and credit of each adjustment is useful in reviewing the impact of the adjustments on the unadjusted account balances. The order of the adjustments on the spreadsheet is not important, and the adjustments are normally entered in the order in which the data are assembled. When the titles of the accounts to be adjusted do not appear in the unadjusted trial balance, the accounts are inserted in the Account Title column, below the unadjusted trial balance totals. The total of the Adjustments columns is a control to verify the mathematical accuracy of the adjustment data and adjusting entries. The total of the Debit column must equal the total of the Credit column.

The adjustment data are added to or subtracted from the amounts in the Unadjusted Trial Balance columns to arrive at the Adjusted Trial Balance columns. In this way, the Adjusted Trial Balance columns of Exhibit 1 illustrate the impact of the adjusting entries

EXHIBIT 1   End-of-Period Spreadsheet (Work Sheet)

	A	B	C	D	E	F	G	H	I	J	K	
						NetSolutions						
						End-of-Period Spreadsheet (Work Sheet)						
						For the Two Months Ended December 31, 2007						
		Unadjusted Trial Balance		Adjustments		Adjusted Trial Balance		Income Statement		Balance Sheet		
	Account Title	Dr.	Cr.	Dr.	Cr.	Dr.	Cr.	Dr.	Cr.	Dr.	Cr.	
1	Cash	2,065				2,065				2,065		1
2	Accounts Receivable	2,220		(d) 500		2,720				2,720		2
3	Supplies	2,000			(a) 1,240	760				760		3
4	Prepaid Insurance	2,400			(b) 200	2,200				2,200		4
5	Land	20,000				20,000				20,000		5
6	Office Equipment	1,800				1,800				1,800		6
7	Accounts Payable		900				900				900	7
8	Unearned Rent		360	(c) 120			240				240	8
9	Capital Stock		25,000				25,000				25,000	9
10	Dividends	4,000				4,000				4,000		10
11	Fees Earned		16,340		(d) 500		16,840		16,840			11
12	Wages Expense	4,275		(e) 250		4,525		4,525				12
13	Rent Expense	1,600				1,600		1,600				13
14	Utilities Expense	985				985		985				14
15	Supplies Expense	800		(a) 1,240		2,040		2,040				15
16	Miscellaneous Expense	455				455		455				16
17		42,600	42,600									17
18	Insurance Expense			(b) 200		200		200				18
19	Rent Revenue				(c) 120		120		120			19
20	Wages Payable				(e) 250		250				250	20
21	Depreciation Expense			(f) 50		50		50				21
22	Accumulated Depreciation				(f) 50		50				50	22
23				2,360	2,360	43,400	43,400	9,855	16,960	33,545	26,440	23
24	Net income							7,105			7,105	24
25								16,960	16,960	33,545	33,545	25

on the unadjusted accounts. The totals of the Adjusted Trial Balance columns prove the equality of the totals of the debit and credit balances after adjustment.

Exhibit 1 also illustrates the flow of the accounts from the adjusted trial balance into the financial statements. The revenue and expense accounts are extended to the Income Statement columns. At the bottom of the Income Statement columns, the net income or net loss for the period is shown. For example, Exhibit 1 shows that NetSolutions had net income of $7,105 for the period. Likewise, the assets, liabilities, capital stock, retained earnings, and dividends accounts are extended to the Balance Sheet columns. Since net income increases stockholders' equity (retained earnings), NetSolutions' net income of $7,105 is also shown in the Balance Sheet Cr. column. As we will describe and illustrate in the next section, the financial statements can be prepared directly from Exhibit 1.

To summarize, Exhibit 1 illustrates the end-of-period process by which accounts are adjusted and how the adjusted accounts flow into the financial statements. The spreadsheet shown in Exhibit 1 is not a required part of the accounting process. However, many accountants prepare such a spreadsheet, often called a work sheet, in manual or electronic form, as part of their normal end-of-period process. The primary advantage in doing so is that it allows managers and accountants to see the impact of the adjustments on the financial statements. This is especially useful for adjustments that depend upon estimates. We discuss such estimates and their impact on the financial statements in later chapters.[1]

---

1 The appendix to this chapter describes and illustrates how to prepare the end-of-period spreadsheet (work sheet) shown in Exhibit 1.

Example Exercise 4-1

objective 1

The balances for the accounts listed below appear in the Adjusted Trial Balance columns of the end-of-period spreadsheet (work sheet). Indicate whether each balance should be extended to (a) an Income Statement column or (b) a Balance Sheet column.

1. Dividends
2. Utilities Expense
3. Accumulated Depreciation—Equipment
4. Unearned Rent

5. Fees Earned
6. Accounts Payable
7. Rent Revenue
8. Supplies

Follow My Example 4-1

1. Balance Sheet column
2. Income Statement column
3. Balance Sheet column
4. Balance Sheet column

5. Income Statement column
6. Balance Sheet column
7. Income Statement column
8. Balance Sheet column

For Practice: PE 4-1A, PE 4-1B

Financial Statements

objective 2

Prepare financial statements from adjusted account balances.

Using Exhibit 1, the financial statements for NetSolutions can be prepared. The income statement, the retained earnings statement, and the balance sheet are shown in Exhibit 2, on page 150. In the following paragraphs, we discuss each of these financial statements and how they are prepared.

INCOME STATEMENT

@netsolutions

The income statement is prepared directly from the Income Statement or Adjusted Trial Balance columns of Exhibit 1 beginning with fees earned of $16,840. The order of the expenses may change, however, from that listed in Exhibit 1. As we did in Chapter 1, we list the expenses in the income statement in Exhibit 2 in order of size, beginning with the larger items. Miscellaneous expense is the last item, regardless of its amount.

RETAINED EARNINGS STATEMENT

The first item normally presented on the retained earnings statement is the balance of the retained earnings account at the beginning of the period. Since NetSolutions began operations on November 1, this balance is zero in Exhibit 2. Then, the retained earnings statement shows the net income for the two months ended December 31, 2007. The amount of dividends is deducted from the net income to arrive at the retained earnings as of December 31, 2007.

Example Exercise 4-2

objective 2

In the Balance Sheet columns of the end-of-period spreadsheet (work sheet) for Dimple Consulting Co. for the current year, the Debit column total is $678,450, and the Credit column total is $599,750 before the amount for net income or net loss has been included. In preparing the income statement from the end-of-period spreadsheet (work sheet), what is the amount of net income or net loss?

Follow My Example 4-2

A net income of $78,700 ($678,450 − $599,750) would be reported. When the Debit column of the Balance Sheet columns is more than the Credit column, net income is reported. If the Credit column exceeds the Debit column, a net loss is reported.

For Practice: PE 4-2A, PE 4-2B

EXHIBIT 2   Financial Statements Prepared from Work Sheet

NetSolutions
Income Statement
For the Two Months Ended December 31, 2007

Fees earned	$16 8 4 0 00	
Rent revenue	1 2 0 00	
Total revenues		$16 9 6 0 00
Expenses:		
Wages expense	$ 4 5 2 5 00	
Supplies expense	2 0 4 0 00	
Rent expense	1 6 0 0 00	
Utilities expense	9 8 5 00	
Insurance expense	2 0 0 00	
Depreciation expense	5 0 00	
Miscellaneous expense	4 5 5 00	
Total expenses		9 8 5 5 00
Net income		$ 7 1 0 5 00

NetSolutions
Retained Earnings
For the Two Months Ended December 31, 2007

Retained earnings, November 1, 2007		$ 0
Net income for November and December	$7 1 0 5 00	
Less dividends	4 0 0 0 00	
Increase in retained earnings		3 1 0 5 00
Retained earnings, December 31, 2007		$3 1 0 5 00

NetSolutions
Balance Sheet
December 31, 2007

Assets			Liabilities		
Current assets:			Current liabilities:		
Cash	$ 2 0 6 5 00		Accounts payable	$ 9 0 0 00	
Accounts receivable	2 7 2 0 00		Wages payable	2 5 0 00	
Supplies	7 6 0 00		Unearned rent	2 4 0 00	
Prepaid insurance	2 2 0 0 00		Total liabilities		$ 1 3 9 0 00
Total current assets		$ 7 7 4 5 00			
Property, plant, and equipment:					
Land	$20 0 0 0 00		**Stockholders' Equity**		
Office equipment $1,800			Capital stock	$25 0 0 0 00	
Less accum. depr. 50	1 7 5 0 00		Retained earnings	3 1 0 5 00	
Total property, plant,			Total stockholders' equity		28 1 0 5 00
and equipment		21 7 5 0 00	Total liabilities and		
Total assets		$29 4 9 5 00	stockholders' equity		$29 4 9 5 00

Integrity, Objectivity, and Ethics in Business

 ETHICS

THE ROUND TRIP

A common type of fraud involves artificially inflating revenue. One fraudulent method of inflating revenue is called "round tripping." Under this scheme, a selling company (S) "lends" money to a customer company (C). The money is then used by C to purchase a product from S. Thus, S

sells product to C and is paid with the money just loaned to C! This looks like a sale in the accounting records, but in reality, S is shipping free product. The fraud is exposed when it is determined that there was no intent to repay the original loan.

For the following period, the beginning balance of retained earnings for NetSolutions is the ending balance that was reported for the previous period. For example, assume that during 2008, NetSolutions earned net income of $59,595 and paid dividends of $24,000. The retained earnings statement for the year ending December 31, 2008, for NetSolutions is as follows:

NetSolutions Retained Earnings Statement For the Month Ended December 31, 2008		
Retained earnings, January 1, 2008		$ 3 2 0 5 00
Net income for the year	$59 5 9 5 00	
Less dividends	24 0 0 0 00	
Increase in retained earnings		35 5 9 5 00
Retained earnings, December 31, 2008		$38 8 0 0 00

For NetSolutions, the amount of dividends was less than the net income. If the dividends had exceeded the net income, the order of the net income and the dividends could have been reversed. The difference between the two items would then be deducted from the beginning Retained Earnings balance. Other factors, such as a net loss, may also require some change in the form of the retained earnings statement, as shown in the following example:

Retained earnings, January 1, 20—		$45,000
Net loss for the year	$5,600	
Dividends	9,500	
Decrease in retained earnings		15,100
Retained earnings, December 31, 20—		$29,900

Some accountants prefer to debit dividends directly to Retained Earnings. When you are preparing a retained earnings statement and there is no dividends account in the ledger, you will need to refer to the retained earnings account to determine the beginning balance of Retained Earnings and the amount of the dividends paid during the period.

Example Exercise 4-3

objective **2**

Zack Gaddis owns and operates Gaddis Employment Services. On January 1, 2007, Retained Earnings had a balance of $186,000. During the year, an additional $40,000 of capital stock was issued for cash and dividends of $25,000 were paid. For the year ended December 31, 2007, Gaddis Employment Services reported a net income of $18,750. Prepare a retained earnings statement for the year ended December 31, 2007.

(continued)

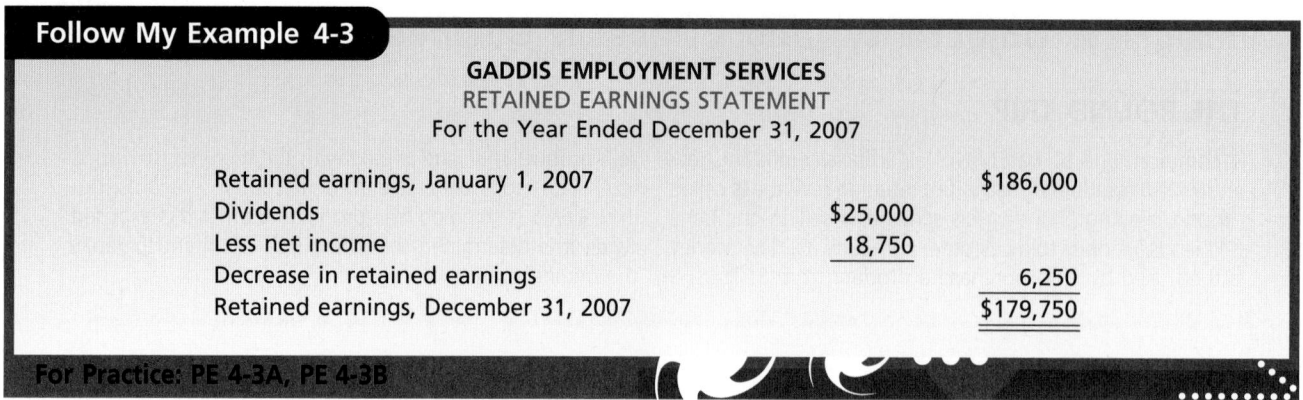

Follow My Example 4-3

GADDIS EMPLOYMENT SERVICES
RETAINED EARNINGS STATEMENT
For the Year Ended December 31, 2007

Retained earnings, January 1, 2007		$186,000
Dividends	$25,000	
Less net income	18,750	
Decrease in retained earnings		6,250
Retained earnings, December 31, 2007		$179,750

For Practice: PE 4-3A, PE 4-3B

BALANCE SHEET

The balance sheet is prepared directly from the Balance Sheet or Adjusted Trial Balance columns of Exhibit 1 beginning with Cash of $2,065.

The balance sheet in Exhibit 2 was expanded by adding subsections for current assets; property, plant, and equipment; and current liabilities. Such a balance sheet is a *classified balance sheet*. In the following paragraphs, we describe some of the sections and subsections that may be used in a balance sheet. We will introduce additional sections in later chapters.

> Two common classes of assets are current assets and property, plant, and equipment.

Assets   Assets are commonly divided into classes for presentation on the balance sheet. Two of these classes are (1) current assets and (2) property, plant, and equipment.

Current Assets   Cash and other assets that are expected to be converted to cash or sold or used up usually within one year or less, through the normal operations of the business, are called **current assets**. In addition to cash, the current assets usually owned by a service business are notes receivable, accounts receivable, supplies, and other prepaid expenses.

Notes receivable are amounts that customers owe. They are written promises to pay the amount of the note and possibly interest at an agreed-upon rate. Accounts receivable are also amounts customers owe, but they are less formal than notes and do not provide for interest. Accounts receivable normally result from providing services or selling merchandise on account. Notes receivable and accounts receivable are current assets because they will usually be converted to cash within one year or less.

Property, Plant, and Equipment   The **property, plant, and equipment** section may also be described as **fixed assets** or **plant assets**. These assets include equipment, machinery, buildings, and land. With the exception of land, as we discussed in Chapter 3, fixed assets depreciate over a period of time. The cost, accumulated depreciation, and book value of each major type of fixed asset are normally reported on the balance sheet or in accompanying notes.

> Two common classes of liabilities are current liabilities and long-term liabilities.

Liabilities   Liabilities are the amounts the business owes to creditors. The two most common classes of liabilities are (1) current liabilities and (2) long-term liabilities.

Current Liabilities   Liabilities that will be due within a short time (usually one year or less) and that are to be paid out of current assets are called **current liabilities**. The most common liabilities in this group are notes payable and accounts payable. Other current liability accounts commonly found in the ledger are Wages Payable, Interest Payable, Taxes Payable, and Unearned Fees.

Long-Term Liabilities   Liabilities that will not be due for a long time (usually more than one year) are called **long-term liabilities**. If NetSolutions had long-term liabilities, they would be reported below the current liabilities. As long-term liabilities come due and are to be paid within one year, they are classified as current liabilities. If they are to be renewed rather than paid, they would continue to be classified as long term. When an asset is pledged as security for a liability, the obligation may be called a *mortgage note payable* or a *mortgage payable*.

Stockholders' Equity The stockholders' right to the assets of the business is presented on the balance sheet below the liabilities section. The stockholders' equity consists of capital stock and retained earnings. The total stockholders' equity is added to the total liabilities, and this total must be equal to the total assets.

Example Exercise 4-4 — objective 2

The following accounts appear in an adjusted trial balance of Hindsight Consulting. Indicate whether each account would be reported in the (a) current asset; (b) property, plant, and equipment; (c) current liability; (d) long-term liability; or (e) stockholders' equity section of the December 31, 2007, balance sheet of Hindsight Consulting.

1. Capital Stock
2. Notes Receivable (due in 6 months)
3. Notes Payable (due in 2009)
4. Land
5. Cash
6. Unearned Rent (3 months)
7. Accumulated Depreciation—Equipment
8. Accounts Payable

Follow My Example 4-4

1. Stockholders' equity
2. Current asset
3. Long-term liability
4. Property, plant, and equipment
5. Current asset
6. Current liability
7. Property, plant, and equipment
8. Current liability

For Practice: PE 4-4A, PE 4-4B

Business Connections

REAL WORLD

INTERNATIONAL DIFFERENCES

Financial statements prepared under accounting practices in other countries often differ from those prepared under generally accepted accounting principles found in the United States. This is to be expected, since cultures and market structures differ from country to country.

To illustrate, **BMW Group** prepares its financial statements under German law and German accounting principles. In doing so, BMW's balance sheet reports fixed assets first, followed by current assets. It also reports stockholders' equity before the liabilities. In contrast, balance sheets prepared under U.S. accounting principles report current assets followed by fixed assets and current liabilities followed by long-term liabilities and stockholders'

equity. The U.S. form of balance sheet is organized to emphasize creditor interpretation and analysis. For example, current assets and current liabilities are presented first to facilitate their interpretation and analysis by creditors. Likewise, to emphasize their importance, liabilities are reported before stockholders' equity.

Regardless of these differences, the basic principles underlying the accounting equation and the double-entry accounting system are the same in Germany and the United States. Even though differences in recording and reporting exist, the accounting equation holds true: the total assets still equal the total liabilities and stockholders' equity.

Closing Entries

objective 3

Prepare closing entries.

@netsolutions

As we discussed in Chapter 3, the adjusting entries are recorded in the journal at the end of the accounting period. For NetSolutions, the adjusting entries are shown in Exhibit 7 of Chapter 3.

After the adjusting entries have been posted to NetSolutions' ledger, shown in Exhibit 6 (on pages 157–161), the ledger is in agreement with the data reported on the financial statements. The balances of the accounts reported on the balance sheet

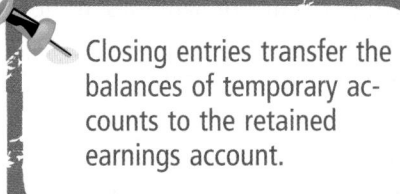

Closing entries transfer the balances of temporary accounts to the retained earnings account.

are carried forward from year to year. Because they are relatively permanent, these accounts are called **real accounts**. The balances of the accounts reported on the income statement are not carried forward from year to year. Likewise, the balance of the dividends account, which is reported on the retained earnings statement, is not carried forward. Because these accounts report amounts for only one period, they are called **temporary accounts** or **nominal accounts**.

To report amounts for only one period, temporary accounts should have zero balances at the beginning of a period. How are these balances converted to zero? The revenue and expense account balances are transferred to an account called **Income Summary**. The balance of Income Summary is then transferred to the retained earnings account. The balance of the dividends account is also transferred to the retained earnings account. The entries that transfer these balances are called **closing entries**. The transfer process is called the **closing process**. Exhibit 3 is a diagram of this process.

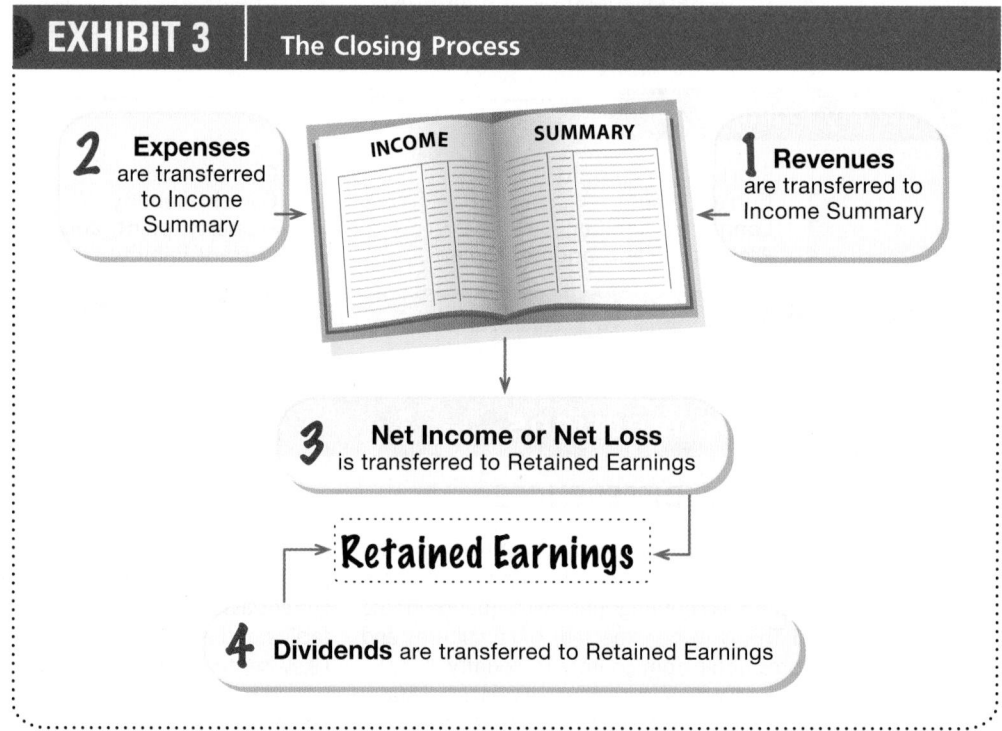

EXHIBIT 3 | **The Closing Process**

2 Expenses are transferred to Income Summary

INCOME   SUMMARY

1 Revenues are transferred to Income Summary

3 Net Income or Net Loss is transferred to Retained Earnings

Retained Earnings

4 Dividends are transferred to Retained Earnings

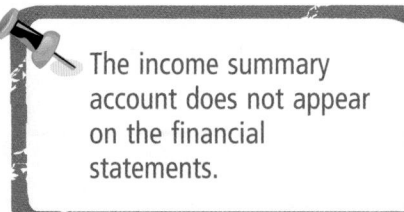

The income summary account does not appear on the financial statements.

You should note that Income Summary is used only at the end of the period. At the beginning of the closing process, Income Summary has no balance. During the closing process, Income Summary will be debited and credited for various amounts. At the end of the closing process, Income Summary will again have no balance. Because Income Summary has the effect of clearing the revenue and expense accounts of their balances, it is sometimes called a **clearing account**. Other titles used for this account include Revenue and Expense Summary, Profit and Loss Summary, and Income and Expense Summary.

It is possible to close the temporary revenue and expense accounts without using a clearing account such as Income Summary. In this case, the balances of the revenue and expense accounts are closed directly to the retained earnings account. This process is automatic in a computerized accounting system. In a manual system, the use of an income summary account aids in detecting and correcting errors.

JOURNALIZING AND POSTING CLOSING ENTRIES

Four closing entries are required at the end of an accounting period, as outlined in Exhibit 3. The account titles and balances needed in preparing these entries may be obtained from the end-of-period spreadsheet (work sheet), the adjusted trial balance, the income statement, the retained earnings statement, or the ledger.

A flowchart of the closing entries for NetSolutions is shown in Exhibit 4. The balances in the accounts are those shown in the Adjusted Trial Balance columns of the end-of-period spreadsheet (work sheet) shown in Exhibit 1.

EXHIBIT 4	Flowchart of Closing Entries for NetSolutions

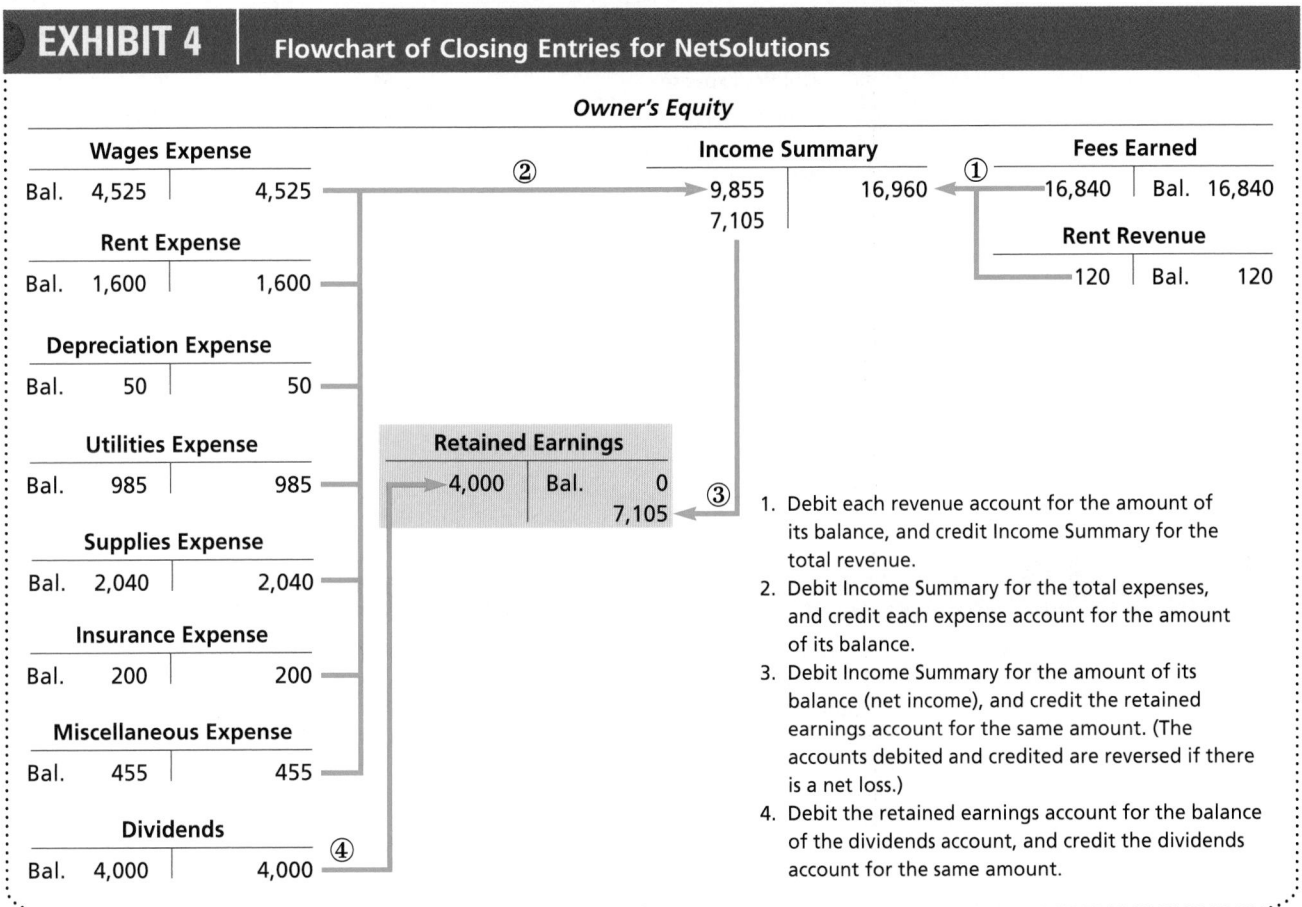

The closing entries for NetSolutions are shown in Exhibit 5. After the closing entries have been posted to the ledger, as shown in Exhibit 6 (on pages 157–161), the balance in the retained earnings account will agree with the amount reported on the retained earnings statement and the balance sheet. In addition, the revenue, expense, and dividends accounts will have zero balances.

After the entry to close an account has been posted, a line should be inserted in both balance columns opposite the final entry. The next period's transactions for the revenue, expense, and dividends accounts will be posted directly below the closing entry.

EXHIBIT 5

Closing Entries for NetSolutions

	Date		Description	Post. Ref.	Debit	Credit	
1			Closing Entries				1
2	2007 Dec.	31	Fees Earned	41	16 8 4 0 00		2
3			Rent Revenue	42	1 2 0 00		3
4			Income Summary	34		16 9 6 0 00	4
5							5
6		31	Income Summary	34	9 8 5 5 00		6
7			Wages Expense	51		4 5 2 5 00	7
8			Rent Expense	52		1 6 0 0 00	8
9			Depreciation Expense	53		5 0 00	9
10			Utilities Expense	54		9 8 5 00	10
11			Supplies Expense	55		2 0 4 0 00	11
12			Insurance Expense	56		2 0 0 00	12
13			Miscellaneous Expense	59		4 5 5 00	13
14							14
15		31	Income Summary	34	7 1 0 5 00		15
16			Retained Earnings	32		7 1 0 5 00	16
17							17
18		31	Retained Earnings	32	4 0 0 0 00		18
19			Dividends	33		4 0 0 0 00	19

JOURNAL — Page 6

Example Exercise 4-5

objective **3**

After the accounts have been adjusted at July 31, the end of the fiscal year, the following balances are taken from the ledger of Cabriolet Services Co.:

Retained Earnings	$615,850
Dividends	25,000
Fees Earned	380,450
Wages Expense	250,000
Rent Expense	65,000
Supplies Expense	18,250
Miscellaneous Expense	6,200

Journalize the four entries required to close the accounts.

Follow My Example 4-5

July	31	Fees Earned	380,450	
		Income Summary		380,450
	31	Income Summary	339,450	
		Wages Expense		250,000
		Rent Expense		65,000
		Supplies Expense		18,250
		Miscellaneous Expense		6,200
	31	Income Summary	41,000	
		Retained Earnings		41,000
	31	Retained Earnings	25,000	
		Dividends		25,000

For Practice: PE 4-5A, PE 4-5B

POST-CLOSING TRIAL BALANCE

The last accounting procedure for a period is to prepare a trial balance after the closing entries have been posted. The purpose of the **post-closing** (after closing) **trial balance** is to make sure that the ledger is in balance at the beginning of the next period. The accounts and amounts should agree exactly with the accounts and amounts listed on the balance sheet at the end of the period. The post-closing trial balance for NetSolutions is shown in Exhibit 7, on page 161.

Instead of preparing a formal post-closing trial balance, it is possible to list the accounts directly from the ledger, using a computer. The computer printout, in effect, becomes the post-closing trial balance.

EXHIBIT 6

Ledger for
NetSolutions

LEDGER

ACCOUNT *Cash*   **ACCOUNT NO.** *11*

Date		Item	Post. Ref.	Debit	Credit	Balance Debit	Balance Credit
2007 Nov.	1		1	25 000 00		25 000 00	
	5		1		20 000 00	5 000 00	
	18		1	7 500 00		12 500 00	
	30		1		3 650 00	8 850 00	
	30		1		950 00	7 900 00	
	30		2		2 000 00	5 900 00	
Dec.	1		2		2 400 00	3 500 00	
	1		2		800 00	2 700 00	
	1		2	360 00		3 060 00	
	6		2		180 00	2 880 00	
	11		2		400 00	2 480 00	
	13		3		950 00	1 530 00	
	16		3	3 100 00		4 630 00	
	20		3		900 00	3 730 00	
	21		3	650 00		4 380 00	
	23		3		1 450 00	2 930 00	
	27		3		1 200 00	1 730 00	
	31		3		310 00	1 420 00	
	31		4		225 00	1 195 00	
	31		4	2 870 00		4 065 00	
	31		4		2 000 00	2 065 00	

ACCOUNT *Accounts Receivable*   **ACCOUNT NO.** *12*

Date		Item	Post. Ref.	Debit	Credit	Balance Debit	Balance Credit
2007 Dec.	16		3	1 750 00		1 750 00	
	21		3		650 00	1 100 00	
	31		4	1 120 00		2 220 00	
	31	Adjusting	5	500 00		2 720 00	

(continued)

EXHIBIT 6

ACCOUNT *Supplies*   **ACCOUNT NO.** *14*

Date		Item	Post. Ref.	Debit	Credit	Balance Debit	Balance Credit
2007 Nov.	10		1	1 3 5 0 00		1 3 5 0 00	
	30		1		8 0 0 00	5 5 0 00	
	23		3	1 4 5 0 00		2 0 0 0 00	
Dec.	31	Adjusting	5		1 2 4 0 00	7 6 0 00	

ACCOUNT *Prepaid Insurance*   **ACCOUNT NO.** *15*

Date		Item	Post. Ref.	Debit	Credit	Balance Debit	Balance Credit
2007 Dec.	1		2	2 4 0 0 00		2 4 0 0 00	
	31	Adjusting	5		2 0 0 00	2 2 0 0 00	

ACCOUNT *Land*   **ACCOUNT NO.** *17*

Date		Item	Post. Ref.	Debit	Credit	Balance Debit	Balance Credit
2007 Nov.	5		1	20 0 0 0 00		20 0 0 0 00	

ACCOUNT *Office Equipment*   **ACCOUNT NO.** *18*

Date		Item	Post. Ref.	Debit	Credit	Balance Debit	Balance Credit
2007 Dec.	4		2	1 8 0 0 00		1 8 0 0 00	

ACCOUNT *Accumulated Depreciation*   **ACCOUNT NO.** *19*

Date		Item	Post. Ref.	Debit	Credit	Balance Debit	Balance Credit
2007 Dec.	31	Adjusting	5		5 0 00		5 0 00

ACCOUNT *Accounts Payable*   **ACCOUNT NO.** *21*

Date		Item	Post. Ref.	Debit	Credit	Balance Debit	Balance Credit
2007 Nov.	10		1		1 3 5 0 00		1 3 5 0 00
	30		1	9 5 0 00			4 0 0 00
Dec.	4		2		1 8 0 0 00		2 2 0 0 00
	11		2	4 0 0 00			1 8 0 0 00
	20		3	9 0 0 00			9 0 0 00

ACCOUNT *Wages Payable*   **ACCOUNT NO.** *22*

Date		Item	Post. Ref.	Debit	Credit	Balance Debit	Balance Credit
2007 Dec.	31	Adjusting	5		2 5 0 00		2 5 0 00

(continued)

EXHIBIT 6

ACCOUNT *Unearned Rent*   **ACCOUNT NO.** *23*

Date		Item	Post. Ref.	Debit	Credit	Balance Debit	Balance Credit
2007 Dec.	1		2		3 6 0 00		3 6 0 00
	31	Adjusting	5	1 2 0 00			2 4 0 00

ACCOUNT *Capital Stock*   **ACCOUNT NO.** *31*

Date		Item	Post. Ref.	Debit	Credit	Balance Debit	Balance Credit
2007 Nov.	1		1		25 0 0 0 00		25 0 0 0 00

ACCOUNT *Retained Earnings*   **ACCOUNT NO.** *32*

Date		Item	Post. Ref.	Debit	Credit	Balance Debit	Balance Credit
2007 Dec.	31	Closing	6		7 1 0 5 00		7 1 0 5 00
	31	Closing	6	4 0 0 0 00			3 1 0 5 00

ACCOUNT *Dividends*   **ACCOUNT NO.** *33*

Date		Item	Post. Ref.	Debit	Credit	Balance Debit	Balance Credit
2007 Nov.	30		2	2 0 0 0 00		2 0 0 0 00	
Dec.	31		4	2 0 0 0 00		4 0 0 0 00	
	31	Closing	6		4 0 0 0 00	—	—

ACCOUNT *Income Summary*   **ACCOUNT NO.** *34*

Date		Item	Post. Ref.	Debit	Credit	Balance Debit	Balance Credit
2007 Dec.	31	Closing	6		16 9 6 0 00		16 9 6 0 00
	31	Closing	6	9 8 5 5 00			7 1 0 5 00
	31	Closing	6	7 1 0 5 00		—	—

ACCOUNT *Fees Earned*   **ACCOUNT NO.** *41*

Date		Item	Post. Ref.	Debit	Credit	Balance Debit	Balance Credit
2007 Nov.	18		1		7 5 0 0 00		7 5 0 0 00
Dec.	16		3		3 1 0 0 00		10 6 0 0 00
	16		3		1 7 5 0 00		12 3 5 0 00
	31		4		2 8 7 0 00		15 2 2 0 00
	31		4		1 1 2 0 00		16 3 4 0 00
	31	Adjusting	5		5 0 0 00		16 8 4 0 00
	31	Closing	6	16 8 4 0 00		—	—

(continued)

EXHIBIT 6

ACCOUNT *Rent Revenue*   **ACCOUNT NO.** *42*

Date		Item	Post. Ref.	Debit	Credit	Balance Debit	Balance Credit
2007 Dec.	31	Adjusting	5		1 2 0 00		1 2 0 00
	31	Closing	6	1 2 0 00		—	—

ACCOUNT *Wages Expense*   **ACCOUNT NO.** *51*

Date		Item	Post. Ref.	Debit	Credit	Balance Debit	Balance Credit
2007 Nov.	30		1	2 1 2 5 00		2 1 2 5 00	
Dec.	13		3	9 5 0 00		3 0 7 5 00	
	27		3	1 2 0 0 00		4 2 7 5 00	
	31	Adjusting	5	2 5 0 00		4 5 2 5 00	
	31	Closing	6		4 5 2 5 00	—	—

ACCOUNT *Rent Expense*   **ACCOUNT NO.** *52*

Date		Item	Post. Ref.	Debit	Credit	Balance Debit	Balance Credit
2007 Nov.	30		1	8 0 0 00		8 0 0 00	
Dec.	1		2	8 0 0 00		1 6 0 0 00	
	31	Closing	6		1 6 0 0 00	—	—

ACCOUNT *Depreciation Expense*   **ACCOUNT NO.** *53*

Date		Item	Post. Ref.	Debit	Credit	Balance Debit	Balance Credit
2007 Dec.	31	Adjusting	5	5 0 00		5 0 00	
	31	Closing	6		5 0 00	—	—

ACCOUNT *Utilities Expense*   **ACCOUNT NO.** *54*

Date		Item	Post. Ref.	Debit	Credit	Balance Debit	Balance Credit
2007 Nov.	30		1	4 5 0 00		4 5 0 00	
Dec.	31		3	3 1 0 00		7 6 0 00	
	31		4	2 2 5 00		9 8 5 00	
	31	Closing	6		9 8 5 00	—	—

ACCOUNT *Supplies Expense*   **ACCOUNT NO.** *55*

Date		Item	Post. Ref.	Debit	Credit	Balance Debit	Balance Credit
2007 Nov.	30		1	8 0 0 00		8 0 0 00	
Dec.	31	Adjusting	5	1 2 4 0 00		2 0 4 0 00	
	31	Closing	6		2 0 4 0 00	—	—

(continued)

EXHIBIT 6

ACCOUNT *Insurance Expense*					ACCOUNT NO. 56	
Date	Item	Post. Ref.	Debit	Credit	Balance Debit	Balance Credit
2007 Dec. 31	Adjusting	5	2 0 0 00		2 0 0 00	
31	Closing	6		2 0 0 00	—	—

ACCOUNT *Miscellaneous Expense*					ACCOUNT NO. 59	
Date	Item	Post. Ref.	Debit	Credit	Balance Debit	Balance Credit
2007 Nov. 30		1	2 7 5 00		2 7 5 00	
Dec. 6		2	1 8 0 00		4 5 5 00	
31	Closing	6		4 5 5 00	—	—

(concluded)

EXHIBIT 7

Post-Closing Trial Balance

NetSolutions
Post-Closing Trial Balance
December 31, 2007

	Debit Balances	Credit Balances
Cash	2 0 6 5 00	
Accounts Receivable	2 7 2 0 00	
Supplies	7 6 0 00	
Prepaid Insurance	2 2 0 0 00	
Land	20 0 0 0 00	
Office Equipment	1 8 0 0 00	
Accumulated Depreciation		5 0 00
Accounts Payable		9 0 0 00
Wages Payable		2 5 0 00
Unearned Rent		2 4 0 00
Capital Stock		25 0 0 0 00
Retained Earnings		3 1 0 5 00
	29 5 4 5 00	29 5 4 5 00

Accounting Cycle

objective 4

Describe the accounting cycle.

The accounting process that begins with analyzing and journalizing transactions and ends with preparing the accounting records for the next period's transactions is called the **accounting cycle**. The steps in the accounting cycle are as follows:

1. Transactions are analyzed and recorded in the journal.
2. Transactions are posted to the ledger.
3. An unadjusted trial balance is prepared.
4. Adjustment data are assembled and analyzed.
5. An optional end-of-period spreadsheet (work sheet) is prepared.
6. Adjusting entries are journalized and posted to the ledger.
7. An adjusted trial balance is prepared.
8. Financial statements are prepared.
9. Closing entries are journalized and posted to the ledger.
10. A post-closing trial balance is prepared.[2]

2 Some accountants include the journalizing and posting of "reversing entries" as the last step in the accounting cycle. Because reversing entries are not required, we describe and illustrate them in Appendix B at the end of the book.

Exhibit 8 illustrates the accounting cycle in graphic form. In addition, Exhibit 8 illustrates how the accounting data beginning with the source documents for a transaction flow through the accounting system and into the financial statements. In the next section, we illustrate a comprehensive example of the accounting cycle.

EXHIBIT 8 | Accounting Cycle

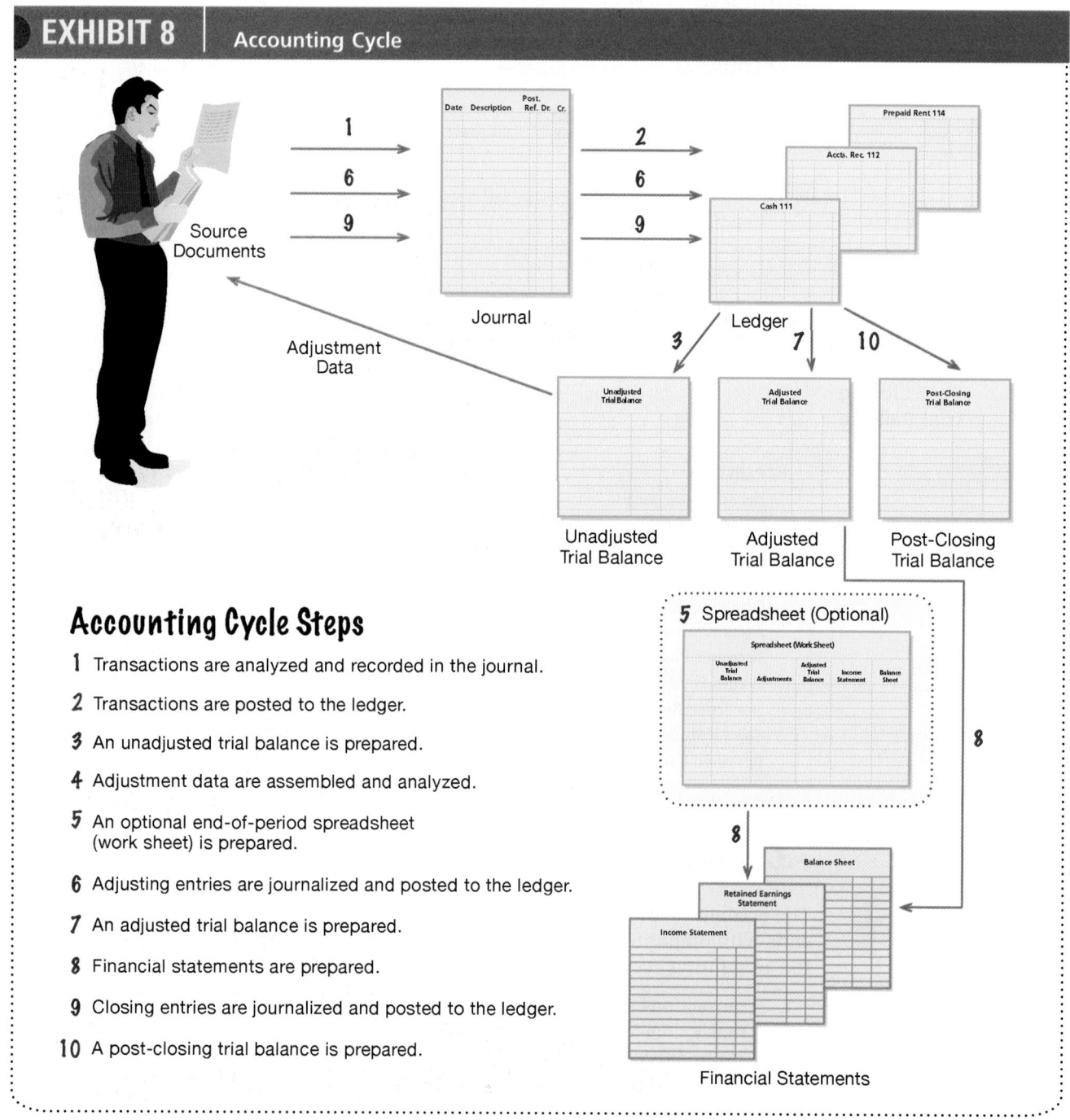

Accounting Cycle Steps

1 Transactions are analyzed and recorded in the journal.

2 Transactions are posted to the ledger.

3 An unadjusted trial balance is prepared.

4 Adjustment data are assembled and analyzed.

5 An optional end-of-period spreadsheet (work sheet) is prepared.

6 Adjusting entries are journalized and posted to the ledger.

7 An adjusted trial balance is prepared.

8 Financial statements are prepared.

9 Closing entries are journalized and posted to the ledger.

10 A post-closing trial balance is prepared.

Example Exercise 4-6

objective 4

From the following list of steps in the accounting cycle, identify what two steps are missing.

       a. Transactions are analyzed and recorded in the journal.
       b. Transactions are posted to the ledger.
       c. Adjustment data are assembled and analyzed.
       d. An optional end-of-period spreadsheet (work sheet) is prepared.
       e. Adjusting entries are journalized and posted to the ledger.
       f. Financial statements are prepared.
       g. Closing entries are journalized and posted to the ledger.
       h. A post-closing trial balance is prepared.

Follow My Example 4-6

The following two steps are missing: (1) the preparation of an unadjusted trial balance and (2) the preparation of the adjusted trial balance. The unadjusted trial balance should be prepared after step (b). The adjusted trial balance should be prepared after step (e).

For Practice: PE 4-6A, PE 4-6B

Illustration of the Accounting Cycle

objective 5

Illustrate the accounting cycle for one period.

In this section, we will illustrate the complete accounting cycle for one period. We assume that for several years Kelly Pitney has operated a part-time consulting business from her home. As of April 1, 2008, Kelly decided to move to rented quarters and to operate the business as a professional corporation, which will be known as Kelly Consulting, P.C., on a full-time basis. Kelly Consulting entered into the following transactions during April:

Apr. 1. The following assets were received from Kelly Pitney in exchange for capital stock: cash, $13,100; accounts receivable, $3,000; supplies, $1,400; and office equipment, $12,500. There were no liabilities received.

     1. Paid three months' rent on a lease rental contract, $4,800.

     2. Paid the premiums on property and casualty insurance policies, $1,800.

     4. Received cash from clients as an advance payment for services to be provided and recorded it as unearned fees, $5,000.

     5. Purchased additional office equipment on account from Office Station Co., $2,000.

     6. Received cash from clients on account, $1,800.

   10. Paid cash for a newspaper advertisement, $120.

   12. Paid Office Station Co. for part of the debt incurred on April 5, $1,200.

   12. Recorded services provided on account for the period April 1–12, $4,200.

   14. Paid part-time receptionist for two weeks' salary, $750.

   17. Recorded cash from cash clients for fees earned during the period April 1–16, $6,250.

   18. Paid cash for supplies, $800.

   20. Recorded services provided on account for the period April 13–20, $2,100.

   24. Recorded cash from cash clients for fees earned for the period April 17–24, $3,850.

   26. Received cash from clients on account, $5,600.

   27. Paid part-time receptionist for two weeks' salary, $750.

   29. Paid telephone bill for April, $130.

   30. Paid electricity bill for April, $200.

   30. Recorded cash from cash clients for fees earned for the period April 25–30, $3,050.

   30. Recorded services provided on account for the remainder of April, $1,500.

   30. Paid dividends of $6,000.

STEP 1. ANALYZING AND RECORDING TRANSACTIONS IN THE JOURNAL

The first step in the accounting cycle is to analyze and record transactions in the journal shown in Exhibit 9. As we illustrated in Chapter 2, the double-entry accounting system is a very powerful tool for analyzing transactions. In using this system to analyze transactions, we do the following:

1. Carefully read the description of the transaction to determine whether an asset, liability, capital stock, retained earnings, revenue, expense, or dividends account is affected by the transaction.
2. For each account affected by the transaction, determine whether the account increases or decreases.
3. Determine whether each increase or decrease should be recorded as a debit or a credit following the rules of debit and credit shown in Exhibit 3 of Chapter 2.
4. Record the transaction using a journal entry.

EXHIBIT 9

Journal Entries for April, Kelly Consulting, P.C.

JOURNAL   Page 1

	Date		Description	Post. Ref.	Debit	Credit	
1	2008 Apr.	1	Cash	11	13 1 0 0 00		1
2			Accounts Receivable	12	3 0 0 0 00		2
3			Supplies	14	1 4 0 0 00		3
4			Office Equipment	18	12 5 0 0 00		4
5			Capital Stock	31		3 0 0 0 0 00	5
6							6
7		1	Prepaid Rent	15	4 8 0 0 00		7
8			Cash	11		4 8 0 0 00	8
9							9
10		2	Prepaid Insurance	16	1 8 0 0 00		10
11			Cash	11		1 8 0 0 00	11
12							12
13		4	Cash	11	5 0 0 0 00		13
14			Unearned Fees	23		5 0 0 0 00	14
15							15
16		5	Office Equipment	18	2 0 0 0 00		16
17			Accounts Payable	21		2 0 0 0 00	17
18							18
19		6	Cash	11	1 8 0 0 00		19
20			Accounts Receivable	12		1 8 0 0 00	20
21							21
22		10	Miscellaneous Expense	59	1 2 0 00		22
23			Cash	11		1 2 0 00	23
24							24
25		12	Accounts Payable	21	1 2 0 0 00		25
26			Cash	11		1 2 0 0 00	26
27							27
28		12	Accounts Receivable	12	4 2 0 0 00		28
29			Fees Earned	41		4 2 0 0 00	29
30							30
31		14	Salary Expense	51	7 5 0 00		31
32			Cash	11		7 5 0 00	32
33							33

(continued)

The company's chart of accounts is useful in determining which accounts are affected by the transaction. The chart of accounts for Kelly Consulting is as follows:

11	Cash		32	Retained Earnings
12	Accounts Receivable		33	Dividends
14	Supplies		34	Income Summary
15	Prepaid Rent		41	Fees Earned
16	Prepaid Insurance		51	Salary Expense
18	Office Equipment		52	Rent Expense
19	Accumulated Depreciation		53	Supplies Expense
21	Accounts Payable		54	Depreciation Expense
22	Salaries Payable		55	Insurance Expense
23	Unearned Fees		59	Miscellaneous Expense
31	Capital Stock			

After analyzing each of Kelly Consulting's transactions for April, the journal entries are recorded as shown in Exhibit 9.

EXHIBIT 9

Continued

JOURNAL   Page 2

	Date		Description	Post. Ref.	Debit	Credit	
1	2008 Apr.	17	Cash	11	6 2 5 0 00		1
2			Fees Earned	41		6 2 5 0 00	2
3							3
4		18	Supplies	14	8 0 0 00		4
5			Cash	11		8 0 0 00	5
6							6
7		20	Accounts Receivable	12	2 1 0 0 00		7
8			Fees Earned	41		2 1 0 0 00	8
9							9
10		24	Cash	11	3 8 5 0 00		10
11			Fees Earned	41		3 8 5 0 00	11
12							12
13		26	Cash	11	5 6 0 0 00		13
14			Accounts Receivable	12		5 6 0 0 00	14
15							15
16		27	Salary Expense	51	7 5 0 00		16
17			Cash	11		7 5 0 00	17
18							18
19		29	Miscellaneous Expense	59	1 3 0 00		19
20			Cash	11		1 3 0 00	20
21							21
22		30	Miscellaneous Expense	59	2 0 0 00		22
23			Cash	11		2 0 0 00	23
24							24
25		30	Cash	11	3 0 5 0 00		25
26			Fees Earned	41		3 0 5 0 00	26
27							27
28		30	Accounts Receivable	12	1 5 0 0 00		28
29			Fees Earned	41		1 5 0 0 00	29
30							30
31		30	Dividends	33	6 0 0 0 00		31
32			Cash	11		6 0 0 0 00	32
33							33

STEP 2. POSTING TRANSACTIONS TO THE LEDGER

Periodically, the transactions recorded in the journal are posted to the accounts in the ledger. As we illustrated in Chapters 2 and 3, the posting process includes recording the date of the transaction, the debit or credit amount, and the journal reference in the account. In addition, account numbers are recorded in the Posting Reference column of the journal to indicate that the entry has been posted to the accounts in the ledger. The journal entries for Kelly Consulting have been posted to the ledger shown in Exhibit 17.

STEP 3. PREPARING AN UNADJUSTED TRIAL BALANCE

In order to determine whether any errors have been made in posting the debits and credits to the ledger, an unadjusted trial balance should be prepared. The unadjusted trial balance does not provide complete proof of the accuracy of the ledger. It indicates only that the debits and the credits are equal. This proof is of value, however, because errors often affect the equality of debits and credits. If the two totals of a trial balance are not equal, an error has occurred that must be discovered and corrected.

The unadjusted trial balance for Kelly Consulting is shown in Exhibit 10. The unadjusted account balances shown in Exhibit 10 were taken from Kelly Consulting's ledger shown in Exhibit 17, on pages 172–176, before any adjusting entries were recorded.

EXHIBIT 10

Unadjusted
Trial Balance,
Kelly Consulting, P.C.

Kelly Consulting, P.C.
Unadjusted Trial Balance
April 30, 2008

	Debit Balances	Credit Balances
Cash	22 1 0 0 00	
Accounts Receivable	3 4 0 0 00	
Supplies	2 2 0 0 00	
Prepaid Rent	4 8 0 0 00	
Prepaid Insurance	1 8 0 0 00	
Office Equipment	14 5 0 0 00	
Accumulated Depreciation		
Accounts Payable		8 0 0 00
Salaries Payable		
Unearned Fees		5 0 0 0 00
Capital Stock		30 0 0 0 00
Dividends	6 0 0 0 00	
Fees Earned		20 9 5 0 00
Salary Expense	1 5 0 0 00	
Rent Expense		
Supplies Expense		
Depreciation Expense		
Insurance Expense		
Miscellaneous Expense	4 5 0 00	
	56 7 5 0 00	56 7 5 0 00

STEP 4. ASSEMBLING AND ANALYZING ADJUSTMENT DATA

Before the financial statements can be prepared, the accounts must be updated. The four types of accounts that normally require adjustment include prepaid expenses, unearned revenue, accrued revenue, and accrued expenses. In addition, depreciation expense must be recorded for fixed assets other than land. The following data have been assembled on April 30, 2008, for analysis of possible adjustments for Kelly Consulting:

a. Insurance expired during April is $300.
b. Supplies on hand on April 30 are $1,350.
c. Depreciation of office equipment for April is $330.
d. Accrued receptionist salary on April 30 is $120.
e. Rent expired during April is $1,600.
f. Unearned fees on April 30 are $2,500.

STEP 5. PREPARING AN OPTIONAL END-OF-PERIOD SPREADSHEET (WORK SHEET)

Although an end-of-period spreadsheet (work sheet) is not required, it is useful in showing the flow of accounting information from the unadjusted trial balance to the adjusted trial balance and financial statements. In addition, an end-of-period spreadsheet (work sheet) is useful in analyzing the impact of proposed adjustments on the financial statements. The end-of-period spreadsheet (work sheet) for Kelly Consulting is shown in Exhibit 11.

EXHIBIT 11 End-of-Period Spreadsheet (Work Sheet)

Kelly Consulting, P.C.
End-of-Period Spreadsheet (Work Sheet)
For the Month Ended April 30, 2008

	Account Title	Unadjusted Trial Balance Dr.	Cr.	Adjustments Dr.	Cr.	Adjusted Trial Balance Dr.	Cr.	Income Statement Dr.	Cr.	Balance Sheet Dr.	Cr.	
1	Cash	22,100				22,100				22,100		1
2	Accounts Receivable	3,400				3,400				3,400		2
3	Supplies	2,200			(b) 850	1,350				1,350		3
4	Prepaid Rent	4,800			(e) 1,600	3,200				3,200		4
5	Prepaid Insurance	1,800			(a) 300	1,500				1,500		5
6	Office Equipment	14,500				14,500				14,500		6
7	Accum. Depreciation				(c) 330		330				330	7
8	Accounts Payable		800				800				800	8
9	Salaries Payable				(d) 120		120				120	9
10	Unearned Fees		5,000	(f) 2,500			2,500				2,500	10
11	Capital Stock		30,000				30,000				30,000	11
12	Dividends	6,000				6,000				6,000		12
13	Fees Earned		20,950		(f) 2,500		23,450		23,450			13
14	Salary Expense	1,500		(d) 120		1,620		1,620				14
15	Rent Expense			(e) 1,600		1,600		1,600				15
16	Supplies Expense			(b) 850		850		850				16
17	Depreciation Expense			(c) 330		330		330				17
18	Insurance Expense			(a) 300		300		300				18
19	Miscellaneous Expense	450				450		450				19
20		56,750	56,750	5,700	5,700	57,200	57,200	5,150	23,450	52,050	33,750	20
21	Net income							18,300			18,300	21
22								23,450	23,450	52,050	52,050	22

STEP 6. JOURNALIZNG AND POSTING ADJUSTING ENTRIES

Based upon the adjustment data shown in step 4, adjusting entries for Kelly Consulting are prepared. Each adjusting entry affects at least one income statement account and one balance sheet account. Explanations for each adjustment including any computations are normally included with each adjusting entry. The adjusting entries for Kelly Consulting are shown in Exhibit 12.

Each of the adjusting entries shown in Exhibit 12 is posted to Kelly Consulting's ledger shown in Exhibit 17. The adjusting entries are identified in the ledger as "Adjusting Entry."

EXHIBIT 12

Adjusting Entries, Kelly Consulting, P.C.

	JOURNAL		Page 3	
		Post. Ref.	Debit	Credit
Date				
	Adjusting Entries			
1	2008 Apr. 30	Insurance Expense	55	3 0 0 00		1
2		Prepaid Insurance	16		3 0 0 00	2
3		Expired insurance.				3
4						4
5	30	Supplies Expense	53	8 5 0 00		5
6		Supplies	14		8 5 0 00	6
7		Supplies used ($2,200 − $1,350).				7
8						8
9	30	Depreciation Expense	54	3 3 0 00		9
10		Accumulated Depreciation	19		3 3 0 00	10
11		Depreciation of office equipment.				11
12						12
13	30	Salary Expense	51	1 2 0 00		13
14		Salaries Payable	22		1 2 0 00	14
15		Accrued salary.				15
16						16
17	30	Rent Expense	52	1 6 0 0 00		17
18		Prepaid Rent	15		1 6 0 0 00	18
19		Rent expired during April.				19
20						20
21	30	Unearned Fees	23	2 5 0 0 00		21
22		Fees Earned	41		2 5 0 0 00	22
23		Fees earned ($5,000 − $2,500).				23

STEP 7. PREPARING AN ADJUSTED TRIAL BALANCE

After the adjustments have been journalized and posted, an adjusted trial balance is prepared to verify the equality of the total of the debit and credit balances. This is the last step before preparing the financial statements, and any errors arising from posting the adjusting entries must be found and corrected. The adjusted trial balance for Kelly Consulting as of April 30, 2008, is shown in Exhibit 13.

STEP 8. PREPARING THE FINANCIAL STATEMENTS

The most important outcome of the accounting cycle is the financial statements. The income statement is prepared first, followed by the retained earnings statement and then the balance sheet. The statements can be prepared directly from the adjusted trial balance, the end-of-period spreadsheet, or the ledger. The net income or net loss shown on the income statement is reported on the retained earnings statement along with any

EXHIBIT 13

Adjusted Trial Balance,
Kelly Consulting, P.C.

Kelly Consulting, P.C.
Adjusted Trial Balance
April 30, 2008

	Debit Balances	Credit Balances
Cash	22 1 0 0 00	
Accounts Receivable	3 4 0 0 00	
Supplies	1 3 5 0 00	
Prepaid Rent	3 2 0 0 00	
Prepaid Insurance	1 5 0 0 00	
Office Equipment	14 5 0 0 00	
Accumulated Depreciation		3 3 0 00
Accounts Payable		8 0 0 00
Salaries Payable		1 2 0 00
Unearned Fees		2 5 0 0 00
Capital Stock		30 0 0 0 00
Dividends	6 0 0 0 00	
Fees Earned		23 4 5 0 00
Salary Expense	1 6 2 0 00	
Rent Expense	1 6 0 0 00	
Supplies Expense	8 5 0 00	
Depreciation Expense	3 3 0 00	
Insurance Expense	3 0 0 00	
Miscellaneous Expense	4 5 0 00	
	57 2 0 0 00	57 2 0 0 00

dividends. The ending retained earnings is reported on the balance sheet. Total stockholders' equity is added with total liabilities to equal total assets.

The financial statements for Kelly Consulting are shown in Exhibit 14. Kelly Consulting earned net income of $18,300 for April. As of April 30, 2008, Kelly Consulting has total assets of $45,720, total liabilities of $3,420, and total stockholders' equity of $42,300.

EXHIBIT 14

Financial Statements,
Kelly Consulting, P.C.

Kelly Consulting, P.C.
Income Statement
For the Month Ended April 30, 2008

Fees earned		$23 4 5 0 00
Expenses:		
Salary expense	$1 6 2 0 00	
Rent expense	1 6 0 0 00	
Supplies expense	8 5 0 00	
Depreciation expense	3 3 0 00	
Insurance expense	3 0 0 00	
Miscellaneous expense	4 5 0 00	
Total expenses		5 1 5 0 00
Net income		$18 3 0 0 00

(continued)

EXHIBIT 14

Kelly Consulting, P.C.
Retained Earnings Statement
For the Month Ended April 30, 2008

Retained earnings, April 1, 2008			$ 0
Net income for the month	$18 3 0 0 00		
Less dividends	6 0 0 0 00		
Increase in retained earnings		12 3 0 0 00	
Retained earnings, April 30, 2008		$12 3 0 0 00	

Kelly Consulting, P.C.
Balance Sheet
April 30, 2008

Assets				Liabilities		
Current assets:				Current liabilities:		
Cash	$22 1 0 0 00			Accounts payable	$ 9 0 0 00	
Accounts receivable	3 4 0 0 00			Salaries payable	1 2 0 00	
Supplies	1 3 5 0 00			Unearned fees	2 5 0 0 00	
Prepaid rent	3 2 0 0 00			Total liabilities		$ 3 4 2 0 00
Prepaid insurance	1 5 0 0 00					
Total current assets		$31 5 5 0 00				
Property, plant, and equipment:				**Stockholders' Equity**		
Office equipment	$14 5 0 0 00			Capital stock	$30 0 0 0 00	
Less accumulated depr.	3 3 0 00			Retained earnings	12 3 0 0 00	
Total property, plant,				Total stockholders' equity		42 3 0 0 00
and equipment		14 1 7 0 00		Total liabilities and		
Total assets		$45 7 2 0 00		stockholders' equity		$45 7 2 0 00

STEP 9. JOURNALIZING AND POSTING CLOSING ENTRIES

As described earlier in this chapter, four closing entries are required at the end of an accounting period to ready the accounts for the next period. The first closing entry transfers the revenue account balances to Income Summary. The second closing entry transfers the expense account balances to Income Summary. The third entry transfers the balance of Income Summary to the retained earnings account. Finally, the fourth entry transfers any balance in the dividends account to the retained earnings account. The four closing entries for Kelly Consulting are shown in Exhibit 15.

After the closing entries have been posted to the ledger, the balance in the retained earnings account will agree with the amount reported on the retained earnings statement and the balance sheet. For Kelly Consulting, the ending balance of Retained Earnings is $12,300, as shown in Exhibit 17. In addition, as shown in Exhibit 17, after the closing entries are posted, all the revenue, expense, and dividends accounts have zero balances. The closing entries are identified in the ledger as "Closing."

STEP 10. PREPARING A POST-CLOSING TRIAL BALANCE

The last step in the accounting cycle is to prepare a post-closing trial balance. The purpose of the post-closing trial balance is to make sure that the ledger is in balance at the

EXHIBIT 15

Closing Entries,
Kelly Consulting, P.C.

	Date		Description	Post. Ref.	Debit	Credit	
			JOURNAL			**Page 4**	
			Closing Entries				
1	2008 Apr.	30	Fees Earned	41	23 4 5 0 00		1
2			Income Summary	34		23 4 5 0 00	2
3							3
4		30	Income Summary	34	5 1 5 0 00		4
5			Salary Expense	51		1 6 2 0 00	5
6			Rent Expense	52		1 6 0 0 00	6
7			Supplies Expense	53		8 5 0 00	7
8			Depreciation Expense	54		3 3 0 00	8
9			Insurance Expense	55		3 0 0 00	9
10			Miscellaneous Expense	59		4 5 0 00	10
11							11
12		30	Income Summary	34	18 3 0 0 00		12
13			Retained Earnings	32		18 3 0 0 00	13
14							14
15		30	Retained Earnings	32	6 0 0 0 00		15
16			Dividends	33		6 0 0 0 00	16

beginning of the next period. The accounts and amounts in the post-closing trial balance should agree exactly with the accounts and amounts listed on the balance sheet at the end of the period.

The post-closing trial balance for Kelly Consulting is shown in Exhibit 16. The balances shown in the post-closing trial balance are taken from the ending balances in the ledger shown in Exhibit 17. These balances agree with the amounts shown on Kelly Consulting's balance sheet in Exhibit 14.

EXHIBIT 16

Post-Closing
Trial Balance,
Kelly Consulting, P.C.

Kelly Consulting, P.C.
Post-Closing Trial Balance
April 30, 2008

	Debit Balances	Credit Balances
Cash	22 1 0 0 00	
Accounts Receivable	3 4 0 0 00	
Supplies	1 3 5 0 00	
Prepaid Rent	3 2 0 0 00	
Prepaid Insurance	1 5 0 0 00	
Office Equipment	14 5 0 0 00	
Accumulated Depreciation		3 3 0 00
Accounts Payable		8 0 0 00
Salaries Payable		1 2 0 00
Unearned Fees		2 5 0 0 00
Capital Stock		30 0 0 0 00
Retained Earnings		12 3 0 0 00
	46 0 5 0 00	46 0 5 0 00

EXHIBIT 17

Ledger,
Kelly Consulting, P.C.

LEDGER

ACCOUNT *Cash*   **ACCOUNT NO. 11**

Date		Item	Post. Ref.	Debit	Credit	Balance Debit	Balance Credit
2008 Apr.	1		1	13 1 0 0 00		13 1 0 0 00	
	1		1		4 8 0 0 00	8 3 0 0 00	
	2		1		1 8 0 0 00	6 5 0 0 00	
	4		1	5 0 0 0 00		11 5 0 0 00	
	6		1	1 8 0 0 00		13 3 0 0 00	
	10		1		1 2 0 00	13 1 8 0 00	
	12		1		1 2 0 0 00	11 9 8 0 00	
	14		1		7 5 0 00	11 2 3 0 00	
	17		2	6 2 5 0 00		17 4 8 0 00	
	18		2		8 0 0 00	16 6 8 0 00	
	24		2	3 8 5 0 00		20 5 3 0 00	
	26		2	5 6 0 0 00		26 1 3 0 00	
	27		2		7 5 0 00	25 3 8 0 00	
	29		2		1 3 0 00	25 2 5 0 00	
	30		2		2 0 0 00	25 0 5 0 00	
	30		2	3 0 5 0 00		28 1 0 0 00	
	30		2		6 0 0 0 00	22 1 0 0 00	

ACCOUNT *Accounts Receivable*   **ACCOUNT NO. 12**

Date		Item	Post. Ref.	Debit	Credit	Balance Debit	Balance Credit
2008 Apr.	1		1	3 0 0 0 00		3 0 0 0 00	
	6		1		1 8 0 0 00	1 2 0 0 00	
	12		1	4 2 0 0 00		5 4 0 0 00	
	20		2	2 1 0 0 00		7 5 0 0 00	
	26		2		5 6 0 0 00	1 9 0 0 00	
	30		2	1 5 0 0 00		3 4 0 0 00	

ACCOUNT *Supplies*   **ACCOUNT NO. 14**

Date		Item	Post. Ref.	Debit	Credit	Balance Debit	Balance Credit
2008 Apr.	1		1	1 4 0 0 00		1 4 0 0 00	
	18		2	8 0 0 00		2 2 0 0 00	
	30	Adjusting	3		8 5 0 00	1 3 5 0 00	

(continued)

EXHIBIT 17

ACCOUNT *Prepaid Rent*   **ACCOUNT NO.** *15*

Date		Item	Post. Ref.	Debit	Credit	Balance Debit	Balance Credit
2008 Apr.	1		1	4 8 0 0 00		4 8 0 0 00	
	30	Adjusting	3		1 6 0 0 00	3 2 0 0 00	

ACCOUNT *Prepaid Insurance*   **ACCOUNT NO.** *16*

Date		Item	Post. Ref.	Debit	Credit	Balance Debit	Balance Credit
2008 Apr.	2		1	1 8 0 0 00		1 8 0 0 00	
	30	Adjusting	3		3 0 0 00	1 5 0 0 00	

ACCOUNT *Office Equipment*   **ACCOUNT NO.** *18*

Date		Item	Post. Ref.	Debit	Credit	Balance Debit	Balance Credit
2008 Apr.	1		1	12 5 0 0 00		12 5 0 0 00	
	5		1	2 0 0 0 00		14 5 0 0 00	

ACCOUNT *Accumulated Depreciation*   **ACCOUNT NO.** *19*

Date		Item	Post. Ref.	Debit	Credit	Balance Debit	Balance Credit
2008 Apr.	30	Adjusting	3		3 3 0 00		3 3 0 00

ACCOUNT *Accounts Payable*   **ACCOUNT NO.** *21*

Date		Item	Post. Ref.	Debit	Credit	Balance Debit	Balance Credit
2008 Apr.	5	.	1		2 0 0 0 00		2 0 0 0 00
	12		1	1 2 0 0 00			8 0 0 00

(continued)

EXHIBIT 17

ACCOUNT *Salaries Payable*					ACCOUNT NO. *22*	
		Post.			Balance	
Date	Item	Ref.	Debit	Credit	Debit	Credit
2008 Apr. 30	Adjusting	3		1 2 0 00		1 2 0 00

ACCOUNT *Unearned Fees*					ACCOUNT NO. *23*	
		Post.			Balance	
Date	Item	Ref.	Debit	Credit	Debit	Credit
2008 Apr. 4		1		5 0 0 0 00		5 0 0 0 00
30	Adjusting	3	2 5 0 0 00			2 5 0 0 00

ACCOUNT *Capital Stock*					ACCOUNT NO. *31*	
		Post.			Balance	
Date	Item	Ref.	Debit	Credit	Debit	Credit
2008 Apr. 1		1		30 0 0 0 00		30 0 0 0 00

ACCOUNT *Retained Earnings*					ACCOUNT NO. *32*	
		Post.			Balance	
Date	Item	Ref.	Debit	Credit	Debit	Credit
2008 Apr. 30	Closing	4		18 3 0 0 00		18 3 0 0 00
30	Closing	4	6 0 0 0 00			12 3 0 0 00

ACCOUNT *Dividends*					ACCOUNT NO. *33*	
		Post.			Balance	
Date	Item	Ref.	Debit	Credit	Debit	Credit
2008 Apr. 30		2	6 0 0 0 00		6 0 0 0 00	
30	Closing	4		6 0 0 0 00	—	—

ACCOUNT *Income Summary*					ACCOUNT NO. *34*	
		Post.			Balance	
Date	Item	Ref.	Debit	Credit	Debit	Credit
2008 Apr. 30	Closing	4		23 4 5 0 00		23 4 5 0 00
30	Closing	4	5 1 5 0 00			18 3 0 0 00
30	Closing	4	18 3 0 0 00		—	—

(continued)

EXHIBIT 17

ACCOUNT *Fees Earned*   **ACCOUNT NO. 41**

Date		Item	Post. Ref.	Debit	Credit	Balance Debit	Balance Credit
2008 Apr.	12		1		4 2 0 0 00		4 2 0 0 00
	17		2		6 2 5 0 00		10 4 5 0 00
	20		2		2 1 0 0 00		12 5 5 0 00
	24		2		3 8 5 0 00		16 4 0 0 00
	30		2		3 0 5 0 00		19 4 5 0 00
	30		2		1 5 0 0 00		20 9 5 0 00
	30	Adjusting	3		2 5 0 0 00		23 4 5 0 00
	30	Closing	4	23 4 5 0 00		—	—

ACCOUNT *Salary Expense*   **ACCOUNT NO. 51**

Date		Item	Post. Ref.	Debit	Credit	Balance Debit	Balance Credit
2008 Apr.	14		1	7 5 0 00		7 5 0 00	
	27		2	7 5 0 00		1 5 0 0 00	
	30	Adjusting	3	1 2 0 00		1 6 2 0 00	
	30	Closing	4		1 6 2 0 00	—	—

ACCOUNT *Rent Expense*   **ACCOUNT NO. 52**

Date		Item	Post. Ref.	Debit	Credit	Balance Debit	Balance Credit
2008 Apr.	30	Adjusting	3	1 6 0 0 00		1 6 0 0 00	
	30	Closing	4		1 6 0 0 00	—	—

ACCOUNT *Supplies Expense*   **ACCOUNT NO. 53**

Date		Item	Post. Ref.	Debit	Credit	Balance Debit	Balance Credit
2008 Apr.	30	Adjusting	3	8 5 0 00		8 5 0 00	
	30	Closing	4		8 5 0 00	—	—

ACCOUNT *Depreciation Expense*   **ACCOUNT NO. 54**

Date		Item	Post. Ref.	Debit	Credit	Balance Debit	Balance Credit
2008 Apr.	30	Adjusting	3	3 3 0 00		3 3 0 00	
	30	Closing	4		3 3 0 00	—	—

(continued)

EXHIBIT 17

ACCOUNT *Insurance Expense*   **ACCOUNT NO.** 55

Date		Item	Post. Ref.	Debit	Credit	Balance	
						Debit	Credit
2008 Apr.	30	Adjusting	3	3 0 0 00		3 0 0 00	
	30	Closing	4		3 0 0 00	—	—

ACCOUNT *Miscellaneous Expense*   **ACCOUNT NO.** 59

Date		Item	Post. Ref.	Debit	Credit	Balance	
						Debit	Credit
2008 Apr.	10		1	1 2 0 00		1 2 0 00	
	29		2	1 3 0 00		2 5 0 00	
	30		2	2 0 0 00		4 5 0 00	
	30	Closing	4		4 5 0 00	—	—

(concluded)

Fiscal Year

objective **6**

Explain what is meant by the fiscal year and the natural business year.

The annual accounting period adopted by a business is known as its **fiscal year**. Fiscal years begin with the first day of the month selected and end on the last day of the following twelfth month. The period most commonly used is the calendar year. Other periods are not unusual, especially for businesses organized as corporations. For example, a corporation may adopt a fiscal year that ends when business activities have reached the lowest point in its annual operating cycle. Such a fiscal year is called the **natural business year**. At the low point in its operating cycle, a business has more time to analyze the results of operations and to prepare financial statements.

Percentage of Companies with Fiscal Years Ending in:			
January	5%	July	2%
February	1	August	2
March	3	September	7
April	2	October	3
May	3	November	2
June	7	December	63

Source: *Accounting Trends & Techniques,* 59th edition, 2005 (New York: American Institute of Certified Public Accountants).

Because companies with fiscal years often have highly seasonal operations, investors and others should be careful in interpreting partial-year reports for such companies. That is, you should expect the results of operations for these companies to vary significantly throughout the fiscal year.

The financial history of a business may be shown by a series of balance sheets and income statements for several fiscal years. If the life of a business is expressed by a line moving from left to right, the series of balance sheets and income statements may be graphed as follows:

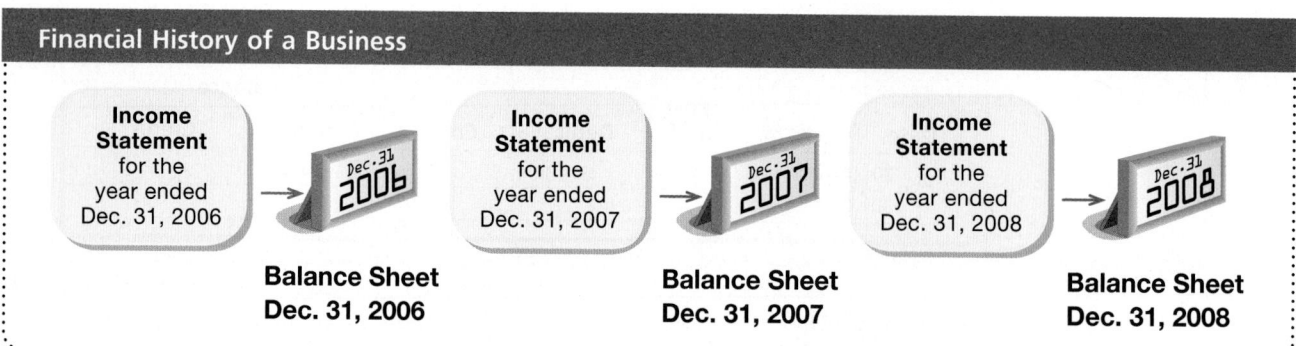

Financial History of a Business

You may think of the income statements, balance sheets, and financial history of a business as similar to the record of a college football team. The final score of each football game is similar to the net income reported on the income statement of a business. The team's season record after each game is similar to the balance sheet. At the end of the season, the final record of the team measures its success or failure. Likewise, at the end of a life of a business, its final balance sheet is a measure of its financial success or failure.

Appendix

End-of-Period Spreadsheet (Work Sheet)

Accountants often use working papers for collecting and summarizing data they need for preparing various analyses and reports. Such working papers are useful tools, but they are not considered a part of the formal accounting records. This is in contrast to the chart of accounts, the journal, and the ledger, which are essential parts of the accounting system. Working papers are usually prepared by using a spreadsheet program on a computer.

Ɡnetsolutions

The end-of-period spreadsheet (work sheet) shown in Exhibit 1 is a working paper that accountants can use to summarize adjusting entries and the account balances for the financial statements. In small companies with few accounts and adjustments, an end-of-period spreadsheet (work sheet) may not be necessary. For example, the financial statements for NetSolutions can be prepared directly from the adjusted trial balance in Exhibit 1. However, many accountants prefer to use an end-of-period spreadsheet (work sheet) as an aid to analyzing adjustment data and preparing the financial statements. We use Exhibits 18 through 21 on pages 178–182 to describe and illustrate how to prepare this type of end-of-period spreadsheet (work sheet).

UNADJUSTED TRIAL BALANCE COLUMNS

To begin the spreadsheet (work sheet), enter at the top the name of the business, the type of working paper, and the period of time, as shown in Exhibit 18. Next, enter the unadjusted trial balance directly on the spreadsheet. The spreadsheet in Exhibit 18 shows the unadjusted trial balance for NetSolutions at December 31, 2007.

ADJUSTMENTS COLUMNS

The adjustments that we explained and illustrated for NetSolutions in Chapter 3 are entered in the Adjustments columns, as shown in Exhibit 19. Cross-referencing (by letters) the debit and credit of each adjustment is useful in reviewing the spreadsheet (work sheet). It is also helpful for identifying the adjusting entries that need to be recorded in the journal.

The order in which the adjustments are entered on the spreadsheet (work sheet) is not important. Most accountants enter the adjustments in the order in which the data are assembled. If the titles of some of the accounts to be adjusted do not appear in the trial balance, they should be entered in the Account Title column, below the trial balance totals, as needed.

To review, the entries in the Adjustments columns of the work sheet are:

(a) **Supplies.** The supplies account has a debit balance of $2,000. The cost of the supplies on hand at the end of the period is $760. Therefore, the supplies expense for December is the difference between the two amounts, or $1,240. The adjustment is entered as (1) $1,240 in the Adjustments Debit column on the same line as Supplies Expense and (2) $1,240 in the Adjustments Credit column on the same line as Supplies.

EXHIBIT 18   Spreadsheet (Work Sheet) with Unadjusted Trial Balance Entered

	A	B	C	D	E	F	G	H	I	J	K	
		NetSolutions										
		End-of-Period Spreadsheet (Work Sheet)										
		For the Two Months Ended December 31, 2007										
		Unadjusted Trial Balance		Adjustments		Adjusted Trial Balance		Income Statement		Balance Sheet		
	Account Title	Dr.	Cr.	Dr.	Cr.	Dr.	Cr.	Dr.	Cr.	Dr.	Cr.	
1	Cash	2,065										1
2	Accounts Receivable	2,220										2
3	Supplies	2,000										3
4	Prepaid Insurance	2,400										4
5	Land	20,000										5
6	Office Equipment	1,800										6
7	Accounts Payable		900									7
8	Unearned Rent		360									8
9	Capital Stock		25,000									9
10	Dividends	4,000										10
11	Fees Earned		16,340									11
12	Wages Expense	4,275										12
13	Rent Expense	1,600										13
14	Utilities Expense	985										14
15	Supplies Expense	800										15
16	Miscellaneous Expense	455										16
17		42,600	42,600									17
18												18
19												19
20												20
21												21
22												22
23												23
24												24
25												25

> The spreadsheet (work sheet) is used for summarizing the effects of adjusting entries. It also aids in preparing financial statements.

(b) **Prepaid Insurance.** The prepaid insurance account has a debit balance of $2,400, which represents the prepayment of insurance for 12 months beginning December 1. Thus, the insurance expense for December is $200 ($2,400/12). The adjustment is entered as (1) $200 in the Adjustments Debit column on the same line as Insurance Expense and (2) $200 in the Adjustments Credit column on the same line as Prepaid Insurance.

(c) **Unearned Rent.** The unearned rent account has a credit balance of $360, which represents the receipt of three months' rent, beginning with December. Thus, the rent revenue for December is $120. The adjustment is entered as (1) $120 in the Adjustments Debit column on the same line as Unearned Rent and (2) $120 in the Adjustments Credit column on the same line as Rent Revenue.

(d) **Accrued Fees.** Fees accrued at the end of December but not recorded total $500. This amount is an increase in an asset and an increase in revenue. The adjustment is entered as (1) $500 in the Adjustments Debit column on the same line as Accounts Receivable and (2) $500 in the Adjustments Credit column on the same line as Fees Earned.

(e) **Wages.** Wages accrued but not paid at the end of December total $250. This amount is an increase in expenses and an increase in liabilities. The adjustment is entered as (1) $250 in the Adjustments Debit column on the same line as Wages Expense and (2) $250 in the Adjustments Credit column on the same line as Wages Payable.

(f) **Depreciation.** Depreciation of the office equipment is $50 for December. The adjustment is entered as (1) $50 in the Adjustments Debit column on the same line as Depreciation Expense and (2) $50 in the Adjustments Credit column on the same line as Accumulated Depreciation.

Total the Adjustments columns to verify the mathematical accuracy of the adjustment data. The total of the Debit column must equal the total of the Credit column.

ADJUSTED TRIAL BALANCE COLUMNS

The adjustment data are added to or subtracted from the amounts in the Unadjusted Trial Balance columns. The adjusted amounts are then extended to (placed in) the Adjusted Trial Balance columns, as shown in Exhibit 19. For example, the cash amount of $2,065 is extended to the Adjusted Trial Balance Debit column, since no adjustments affected Cash. Accounts Receivable has an initial balance of $2,220 and a debit adjustment (increase) of $500. The amount entered in the Adjusted Trial Balance Debit column is the debit balance of $2,720. The same procedure continues until all account balances are extended to the Adjusted Trial Balance columns. Total the columns of the Adjusted Trial Balance to verify the equality of debits and credits.

EXHIBIT 19 Spreadsheet (Work Sheet) with Unadjusted Trial Balance, Adjustments, and Adjusted Trial Balance Entered

	A	B	C	D	E	F	G	H	I	J	K	
		\multicolumn{10}{c}{NetSolutions}									
		End-of-Period Spreadsheet (Work Sheet)										
		For the Two Months Ended December 31, 2007										
		Unadjusted Trial Balance		Adjustments		Adjusted Trial Balance		Income Statement		Balance Sheet		
	Account Title	Dr.	Cr.	Dr.	Cr.	Dr.	Cr.	Dr.	Cr.	Dr.	Cr.	
1	Cash	2,065				2,065						1
2	Accounts Receivable	2,220		(d) 500		2,720						2
3	Supplies	2,000			(a) 1,240	760						3
4	Prepaid Insurance	2,400			(b) 200	2,200						4
5	Land	20,000				20,000						5
6	Office Equipment	1,800				1,800						6
7	Accounts Payable		900				900					7
8	Unearned Rent		360	(c) 120			240					8
9	Capital Stock		25,000				25,000					9
10	Dividends	4,000				4,000						10
11	Fees Earned		16,340		(d) 500		16,840					11
12	Wages Expense	4,275		(e) 250		4,525						12
13	Rent Expense	1,600				1,600						13
14	Utilities Expense	985				985						14
15	Supplies Expense	800		(a) 1,240		2,040						15
16	Miscellaneous Expense	455				455						16
17		42,600	42,600									17
18	Insurance Expense			(b) 200		200						18
19	Rent Revenue				(c) 120		120					19
20	Wages Payable				(e) 250		250					20
21	Depreciation Expense			(f) 50		50						21
22	Accumulated Depreciation				(f) 50		50					22
23				2,360	2,360	43,400	43,400					23
24												24
25												25

The adjustments on the spreadsheet (work sheet) are used in preparing the adjusting journal entries.

The adjusted trial balance amounts are determined by adding the adjustments to or subtracting the adjustments from the trial balance amounts. For example, the Wages Expense debit of $4,525 is the trial balance amount of $4,275 plus the $250 adjustment debit.

Accounts are added, as needed, to complete the adjustments.

INCOME STATEMENT AND BALANCE SHEET COLUMNS

The spreadsheet (work sheet) is completed by extending the adjusted trial balance amounts to the Income Statement and Balance Sheet columns. The amounts for revenues and expenses are extended to the Income Statement columns. The amounts for assets, liabilities, capital stock, retained earnings, and dividends are extended to the Balance Sheet columns.[3]

In the NetSolutions spreadsheet (work sheet), the first account listed is Cash, and the balance appearing in the Adjusted Trial Balance Debit column is $2,065. Cash is an asset, is listed on the balance sheet, and has a debit balance. Therefore, $2,065 is extended to the Balance Sheet Debit column. The Fees Earned balance of $16,840 is extended to the Income Statement Credit column. The same procedure continues until all account balances have been extended to the proper columns, as shown in Exhibit 20.

After all of the balances have been extended to the four statement columns, total each of these columns, as shown in Exhibit 21. The difference between the two Income Statement column totals is the amount of the net income or the net loss for the period. Likewise, the difference between the two Balance Sheet column totals is also the amount of the net income or net loss for the period.

If the Income Statement Credit column total (representing total revenue) is greater than the Income Statement Debit column total (representing total expenses), the difference is the net income. If the Income Statement Debit column total is greater than the Income Statement Credit column total, the difference is a net loss. For NetSolutions, the computation of net income is as follows:

Total of Credit column (revenues)	$16,960
Total of Debit column (expenses)	9,855
Net income (excess of revenues over expenses)	$ 7,105

As shown in Exhibit 21, enter the amount of the net income, $7,105, in the Income Statement Debit column and the Balance Sheet Credit column. Enter the term *Net income* in the Account Title column. If there was a net loss instead of net income, you would enter the amount in the Income Statement Credit column and the Balance Sheet Debit column and the term *Net loss* in the Account Title column. Entering the net income or net loss in the statement columns on the spreadsheet (work sheet) shows the effect of transferring the net balance of the revenue and expense accounts to the retained earnings account.

After the net income or net loss has been entered on the spreadsheet (work sheet), again total each of the four statement columns. The totals of the two Income Statement columns must now be equal. The totals of the two Balance Sheet columns must also be equal.

The spreadsheet (work sheet) is an aid in preparing the income statement, the retained earnings statement, and the balance sheet, which are presented in Exhibit 2. The income statement is normally prepared directly from the spreadsheet (work sheet). However, the order of the expenses may be changed. As we did in Chapter 1, we list the expenses in the income statement in Exhibit 2 in order of size, beginning with the larger items. Miscellaneous expense is the last item, regardless of its amount.

The first item normally presented on the retained earnings statement is the balance of the retained earnings account at the beginning of the period. This amount, along with the net income (or net loss) and the dividends amount shown in the spreadsheet (work sheet), is used to determine the ending retained earnings account balance. The balance sheet can be prepared directly from the spreadsheet (work sheet) columns ex-

---

3 The balances of the retained earnings and dividends accounts are also extended to the Balance Sheet columns because this spreadsheet (work sheet) does not provide for separate Retained Earnings Statement columns.

EXHIBIT 20 Spreadsheet (Work Sheet) with Amounts Extended to Income Statement and Balance Sheet Columns

NetSolutions
End-of-Period Spreadsheet (Work Sheet)
For the Two Months Ended December 31, 2007

	A	Unadjusted Trial Balance Dr.	Cr.	Adjustments Dr.	Cr.	Adjusted Trial Balance Dr.	Cr.	Income Statement Dr.	Cr.	Balance Sheet Dr.	Cr.	
	Account Title											
1	Cash	2,065				2,065				2,065		1
2	Accounts Receivable	2,220		(d) 500		2,720				2,720		2
3	Supplies	2,000			(a) 1,240	760				760		3
4	Prepaid Insurance	2,400			(b) 200	2,200				2,200		4
5	Land	20,000				20,000				20,000		5
6	Office Equipment	1,800				1,800				1,800		6
7	Accounts Payable		900				900				900	7
8	Unearned Rent		360	(c) 120			240				240	8
9	Capital Stock		25,000				25,000				25,000	9
10	Dividends	4,000				4,000				4,000		10
11	Fees Earned		16,340		(d) 500		16,840		16,840			11
12	Wages Expense	4,275		(e) 250		4,525		4,525				12
13	Rent Expense	1,600				1,600		1,600				13
14	Utilities Expense	985				985		985				14
15	Supplies Expense	800		(a) 1,240		2,040		2,040				15
16	Miscellaneous Expense	455				455		455				16
17		42,600	42,600									17
18	Insurance Expense			(b) 200		200		200				18
19	Rent Revenue				(c) 120		120		120			19
20	Wages Payable				(e) 250		250				250	20
21	Depreciation Expense			(f) 50		50		50				21
22	Accumulated Depreciation				(f) 50		50				50	22
23				2,360	2,360	43,400	43,400					23
24												24
25												25

The revenue and expense amounts are extended to (entered in) the Income Statement columns.

The asset, liability, capital stock, and dividends amounts are extended to (entered in) the Balance Sheet columns.

cept for the ending balance of retained earnings, which is taken from the retained earnings statement.

When a spreadsheet (work sheet) is used, the adjusting and closing entries are normally not journalized or posted until after the spreadsheet and financial statements have been prepared. The data for the adjusting entries are taken from the adjustments columns of the spreadsheet. The data for the first two closing entries are taken from the Income Statement columns of the spreadsheet. The amount for the closing third entry is the net income or net loss appearing at the bottom of the spreadsheet. The amount for the fourth closing entry is the dividends account balance that appears in the Balance Sheet Debit column of the spreadsheet.

EXHIBIT 21   Completed Spreadsheet (Work Sheet) with Net Income Shown

	A	B	C	D	E	F	G	H	I	J	K	
				NetSolutions								
				End-of-Period Spreadsheet (Work Sheet)								
				For the Two Months Ended December 31, 2007								
		Unadjusted Trial Balance		Adjustments		Adjusted Trial Balance		Income Statement		Balance Sheet		
	Account Title	Dr.	Cr.	Dr.	Cr.	Dr.	Cr.	Dr.	Cr.	Dr.	Cr.	
1	Cash	2,065				2,065				2,065		1
2	Accounts Receivable	2,220		(d) 500		2,720				2,720		2
3	Supplies	2,000			(a) 1,240	760				760		3
4	Prepaid Insurance	2,400			(b) 200	2,200				2,200		4
5	Land	20,000				20,000				20,000		5
6	Office Equipment	1,800				1,800				1,800		6
7	Accounts Payable		900				900				900	7
8	Unearned Rent		360	(c) 120			240				240	8
9	Capital Stock		25,000				25,000				25,000	9
10	Dividends	4,000				4,000				4,000		10
11	Fees Earned		16,340		(d) 500		16,840		16,840			11
12	Wages Expense	4,275		(e) 250		4,525		4,525				12
13	Rent Expense	1,600				1,600		1,600				13
14	Utilities Expense	985				985		985				14
15	Supplies Expense	800		(a) 1,240		2,040		2,040				15
16	Miscellaneous Expense	455				455		455				16
17		42,600	42,600									17
18	Insurance Expense			(b) 200		200		200				18
19	Rent Revenue				(c) 120		120		120			19
20	Wages Payable				(e) 250		250				250	20
21	Depreciation Expense			(f) 50		50		50				21
22	Accumulated Depreciation				(f) 50		50				50	22
23				2,360	2,360	43,400	43,400	9,855	16,960	33,545	26,440	23
24	Net income							7,105			7,105	24
25								16,960	16,960	33,545	33,545	25

The difference between the Income Statement column totals is the net income (or net loss) for the period. The difference between the Balance Sheet column totals is also the net income (or net loss) for the period.

At a Glance

1. Describe the flow of accounting information from the unadjusted trial balance into the adjusted trial balance and financial statements.

Key Points	Key Learning Outcomes	Example Exercises	Practice Exercises
Exhibit 1 illustrates the end-of-period process by which accounts are adjusted and how the adjusted accounts flow into the financial statements.	• Using an end-of-period spreadsheet (work sheet), describe how the unadjusted trial balance accounts are affected by adjustments and how the adjusted trial balance accounts flow into the income statement and balance sheet.	4-1	4-1A, 4-1B

2. Prepare financial statements from adjusted account balances.

Key Points	Key Learning Outcomes	Example Exercises	Practice Exercises
Using the end-of-period spreadsheet (work sheet) shown in Exhibit 1, the income statement and balance sheet for NetSolutions can be prepared. The retained earnings statement is prepared by listing the beginning balance of retained earnings, adding net income (subtracting a net loss), and deducting dividends. A classified balance sheet has sections for current assets; property, plant, and equipment; current liabilities; long-term liabilities; and stockholders' equity.	• Describe how the net income or net loss from the period can be determined from an end-of-period spreadsheet (work sheet).	4-2	4-2A, 4-2B
	• Prepare an income statement, retained earnings statement, and a balance sheet.	4-3	4-3A, 4-3B
	• Indicate how accounts would be reported in a classified balance sheet.	4-4	4-4A, 4-4B

3. Prepare closing entries.

Key Points	Key Learning Outcomes	Example Exercises	Practice Exercises
Four entries are required in closing the temporary accounts. The first entry closes the revenue accounts to Income Summary. The second entry closes the expense accounts to Income Summary. The third entry closes the balance of Income Summary (net income or net loss) to the retained earnings account. The fourth entry closes the dividends account to the retained earnings account. After the closing entries have been posted to the ledger, the balance in the retained earnings account agrees with the amount reported on the retained earnings statement and balance sheet. In addition, the revenue, expense, and dividends accounts will have zero balances.	• Prepare the closing entry for revenues.	4-5	4-5A, 4-5B
	• Prepare the closing entry for expenses.	4-5	4-5A, 4-5B
	• Prepare the closing entry for transferring the balance of Income Summary to the retained earnings account.	4-5	4-5A, 4-5B
	• Prepare the closing entry for the dividends account.	4-5	4-5A, 4-5B

(continued)

4. Describe the accounting cycle.

Key Points	Key Learning Outcomes	Example Exercises	Practice Exercises
The 10 basic steps of the accounting cycle are as follows: 1. Transactions are analyzed and recorded in the journal. 2. Transactions are posted to the ledger. 3. An unadjusted trial balance is prepared. 4. Adjustment data are assembled and analyzed. 5. An optional end-of-period spreadsheet (work sheet) is prepared. 6. Adjusting entries are journalized and posted to the ledger. 7. An adjusted trial balance is prepared. 8. Financial statements are prepared. 9. Closing entries are journalized and posted to the ledger. 10. A post-closing trial balance is prepared.	• List the 10 steps of the accounting cycle. • Determine whether any steps are out of order in a listing of accounting cycle steps. • Determine whether there are any missing steps in a listing of accounting cycle steps.	**4-6**	4-6A, 4-6B

5. Illustrate the accounting cycle for one period.

Key Points	Key Learning Outcomes	Example Exercises	Practice Exercises
The complete accounting for Kelly Consulting, P.C. for the month of April is described and illustrated on pages 163–176.	• Complete the accounting cycle for a period from beginning to end.		

6. Explain what is meant by the fiscal year and the natural business year.

Key Points	Key Learning Outcomes	Example Exercises	Practice Exercises
The annual accounting period adopted by a business is its fiscal year. A company's fiscal year that ends when business activities have reached the lowest point in its annual operating cycle is called the natural business year.	• Explain why companies use a fiscal year that is different from the calendar year.		

Key Terms

accounting cycle (161)
clearing account (154)
closing entries (154)
closing process (154)
current assets (152)
current liabilities (152)

fiscal year (176)
fixed (plant) assets (152)
Income Summary (154)
long-term liabilities (152)
natural business year (176)
notes receivable (152)

post-closing trial balance (157)
property, plant, and equipment (152)
real accounts (154)
temporary (nominal) accounts (154)

Illustrative Problem

Three years ago, T. Roderick organized Harbor Realty Inc. At July 31, 2008, the end of the current fiscal year, the following end-of-period spreadsheet (work sheet) was prepared:

	A	B	C	D	E	F	G	H	I	J	K	
		Harbor Realty Inc. End-of-Period Spreadsheet (Work Sheet) For the Year Ended July 31, 2008										
			Unadjusted Trial Balance		Adjustments		Adjusted Trial Balance		Income Statement		Balance Sheet	
	Account Title	Dr.	Cr.	Dr.	Cr.	Dr.	Cr.	Dr.	Cr.	Dr.	Cr.	
1	Cash	3,425				3,425				3,425		1
2	Accounts Receivable	7,000		(e) 1,000		8,000				8,000		2
3	Supplies	1,270			(a) 890	380				380		3
4	Prepaid Insurance	620			(b) 315	305				305		4
5	Office Equipment	51,650				51,650				51,650		5
6	Accum. Depreciation		9,700		(c) 4,950		14,650				14,650	6
7	Accounts Payable		925				925				925	7
8	Unearned Fees		1,250	(f) 500			750				750	8
9	Capital Stock		5,000				5,000				5,000	9
10	Retained Earnings		24,000				24,000				24,000	10
11	Dividends	5,200				5,200				5,200		11
12	Fees Earned		59,125		(e) 1,000		60,625		60,625			12
13					(f) 500							13
14	Wages Expense	22,415		(d) 440		22,855		22,855				14
15	Rent Expense	4,200				4,200		4,200				15
16	Utilities Expense	2,715				2,715		2,715				16
17	Miscellaneous Expense	1,505				1,505		1,505				17
18		100,000	100,000									18
19	Supplies Expense			(a) 890		890		890				19
20	Insurance Expense			(b) 315		315		315				20
21	Depreciation Expense			(c) 4,950		4,950		4,950				21
22	Wages Payable				(d) 440		440				440	22
23				8,095	8,095	106,390	106,390	37,430	60,625	68,960	45,765	23
24	Net income							23,195			23,195	24
25								60,625	60,625	68,960	68,960	25

Instructions

1. Prepare an income statement, a retained earnings statement, and a balance sheet.
2. On the basis of the data in the end-of-period spreadsheet (work sheet), journalize the closing entries.

Solution

1.

Harbor Realty Inc.
Income Statement
For the Year Ended July 31, 2008

Fees earned			$60 625 00
Expenses:			
Wages expense	$22 855 00		
Depreciation expense	4 950 00		
Rent expense	4 200 00		
Utilities expense	2 715 00		
Supplies expense	890 00		
Insurance expense	315 00		
Miscellaneous expense	1 505 00		
Total expenses		37 430 00	
Net income			$23 195 00

(continued)

Harbor Realty Inc.
Retained Earnings Statement
For the Year Ended July 31, 2008

Retained earnings, August 1, 2007		$24 0 0 0 00
Net income for the year	$23 1 9 5 00	
Less dividends	5 2 0 0 00	
Increase in retained earnings		17 9 9 5 00
Retained earnings, July 31, 2008		$41 9 9 5 00

Harbor Realty Inc.
Balance Sheet
July 31, 2008

Assets				Liabilities			
Current assets:				Current liabilities:			
Cash	$ 3 4 2 5 00			Accounts payable	$ 9 2 5 00		
Accounts receivable	8 0 0 0 00			Unearned fees	7 5 0 00		
Supplies	3 8 0 00			Wages payable	4 4 0 00		
Prepaid insurance	3 0 5 00			Total liabilities		$ 2 1 1 5 00	
Total current assets		$12 1 1 0 00					
Property, plant, and equipment:				Stockholders' Equity			
Office equipment	$51 6 5 0 00			Capital stock	$ 5 0 0 0 00		
Less accumulated depr.	14 6 5 0 00			Retained earnings	41 9 9 5 00		
Total property, plant,				Total stockholders' equity		46 9 9 5 00	
and equipment		37 0 0 0 00		Total liabilities and			
Total assets		$49 1 1 0 00		stockholders' equity		$49 1 1 0 00	

2.

JOURNAL
Page

	Date		Description	Post. Ref.	Debit	Credit	
1			Closing Entries				1
2	2008 July	31	Fees Earned		60 6 2 5 00		2
3			Income Summary			60 6 2 5 00	3
4							4
5		31	Income Summary		37 4 3 0 00		5
6			Wages Expense			22 8 5 5 00	6
7			Rent Expense			4 2 0 0 00	7
8			Utilities Expense			2 7 1 5 00	8
9			Miscellaneous Expense			1 5 0 5 00	9
10			Supplies Expense			8 9 0 00	10
11			Insurance Expense			3 1 5 00	11
12			Depreciation Expense			4 9 5 0 00	12
13							13
14		31	Income Summary		23 1 9 5 00		14
15			Retained Earnings			23 1 9 5 00	15
16							16
17		31	Retained Earnings		5 2 0 0 00		17
18			Dividends			5 2 0 0 00	18

Self-Examination Questions

(Answers at End of Chapter)

1. Which of the following accounts in the Adjusted Trial Balance columns of the end-of-period spreadsheet (work sheet) would be extended to the Balance Sheet columns?
   A. Utilities Expense   C. Dividends
   B. Rent Revenue   D. Miscellaneous Expense

2. Which of the following accounts would be classified as a current asset on the balance sheet?
   A. Office Equipment
   B. Land
   C. Accumulated Depreciation
   D. Accounts Receivable

3. Which of the following entries closes the dividends account at the end of the period?
   A. Debit the dividends account, credit the income summary account.
   B. Debit the retained earnings account, credit the dividends account.

C. Debit the income summary account, credit the dividends account.
D. Debit the dividends account, credit the retained earnings account.

4. Which of the following accounts would *not* be closed to the income summary account at the end of a period?
   A. Fees Earned
   B. Wages Expense
   C. Rent Expense
   D. Accumulated Depreciation

5. Which of the following accounts would *not* be included in a post-closing trial balance?
   A. Cash
   B. Fees Earned
   C. Accumulated Depreciation
   D. Capital Stock

Eye Openers

1. Why do some accountants prepare an end-of-period spreadsheet (work sheet)?
2. Is the end-of-period spreadsheet (work sheet) a substitute for the financial statements? Discuss.
3. In the Income Statement columns of the end-of-period spreadsheet (work sheet) for Allen Consulting Co. for the current year, the Debit column total is $262,250 and the Credit column total is $323,500 before the amount for net income or net loss has been included. In preparing the income statement from the end-of-period spreadsheet (work sheet), what is the amount of net income or net loss?
4. Describe the nature of the assets that compose the following sections of a balance sheet: (a) current assets, (b) property, plant, and equipment.
5. What is the difference between a current liability and a long-term liability?
6. What types of accounts are referred to as temporary accounts?
7. Why are closing entries required at the end of an accounting period?
8. What is the difference between adjusting entries and closing entries?
9. Describe the four entries that close the temporary accounts.
10. What is the purpose of the post-closing trial balance?
11. (a) What is the most important output of the accounting cycle? (b) Do all companies have an accounting cycle? Explain.
12. What is the natural business year?
13. Why might a department store select a fiscal year ending January 31, rather than a fiscal year ending December 31?
14. The fiscal years for several well-known companies are as follows:

Company	Fiscal Year Ending	Company	Fiscal Year Ending
Kmart	January 30	Toys "R" Us, Inc.	February 3
JCPenney	January 26	Federated Department Stores, Inc.	February 3
Target Corp.	January 28	The Limited, Inc.	February 2

What general characteristic shared by these companies explains why they do not have fiscal years ending December 31?

Practice Exercises

PE 4-1A
Flow of accounts into financial statements
obj. 1

The balances for the accounts listed below appear in the Adjusted Trial Balance columns of the end-of-period spreadsheet (work sheet). Indicate whether each balance should be extended to (a) an Income Statement column or (b) a Balance Sheet column.

1. Supplies Expense
2. Unearned Service Revenue
3. Accounts Payable
4. Rent Revenue
5. Wages Payable
6. Office Equipment
7. Depreciation Expense—Equipment
8. Capital Stock

PE 4-1B
Flow of accounts into financial statements
obj. 1

The balances for the accounts listed below appear in the Adjusted Trial Balance columns of the end-of-period spreadsheet (work sheet). Indicate whether each balance should be extended to (a) an Income Statement column or (b) a Balance Sheet column.

1. Cash
2. Insurance Expense
3. Prepaid Rent
4. Supplies
5. Commissions Earned
6. Accumulated Depreciation—Equipment
7. Dividends
8. Wages Expense

PE 4-2A
Determining net income from the end-of-period spreadsheet (work sheet)
obj. 2

In the Balance Sheet columns of the end-of-period spreadsheet (work sheet) for FreeLance Consulting Co. for the current year, the Debit column total is $247,690 and the Credit column total is $278,100 before the amount for net income or net loss has been included. In preparing the income statement from the end-of-period spreadsheet (work sheet), what is the amount of net income or net loss?

PE 4-2B
Determining net income from the end-of-period spreadsheet (work sheet)
obj. 2

In the Income Statement columns of the end-of-period spreadsheet (work sheet) for Irwin Consulting Co. for the current year, the Debit column total is $436,700 and the Credit column total is $523,550 before the amount for net income or net loss has been included. In preparing the income statement from the end-of-period spreadsheet (work sheet), what is the amount of net income or net loss?

PE 4-3A
Retained earnings statement
obj. 2

Jody Padget owns and operates Padget Advertising Services. On January 1, 2007, retained earnings had a balance of $550,600. During the year, Jody invested an additional $50,000 in exchange for capital stock and received dividends of $40,000. For the year ended December 31, 2007, Padget Advertising Services reported a net income of $68,150. Prepare a retained earnings statement for the year ended December 31, 2007.

PE 4-3B
Retained earnings statement
obj. 2

Ali Khalid owns and operates AAA Delivery Services. On January 1, 2007, retained earnings had a balance of $854,450. During the year, no additional capital stock was issued and dividends of $38,400 were paid. For the year ended December 31, 2007, AAA Delivery Services reported a net loss of $11,875. Prepare a retained earnings statement for the year ended December 31, 2007.

PE 4-4A
Reporting accounts on classified balance sheet
obj. 2

The following accounts appear in an adjusted trial balance of Ramrod Consulting. Indicate whether each account would be reported in the (a) current asset; (b) property, plant, and equipment; (c) current liability; (d) long-term liability; or (e) stockholders' equity section of the December 31, 2007, balance sheet of Ramrod Consulting.

1. Taxes Payable
2. Building
3. Supplies
4. Mortgage Payable (due in 2011)
5. Prepaid Rent
6. Salaries Payable
7. Unearned Service Fees
8. Capital Stock

PE 4-4B
Reporting accounts on classified balance sheet
obj. 2

The following accounts appear in an adjusted trial balance of Fastback Consulting. Indicate whether each account would be reported in the (a) current asset; (b) property, plant, and equipment; (c) current liability; (d) long-term liability; or (e) stockholders' equity section of the December 31, 2007, balance sheet of Fastback Consulting.

1. Accounts Payable
2. Accounts Receivable
3. Retained Earnings
4. Wages Payable
5. Note Payable (due in 2014)
6. Cash
7. Supplies
8. Accumulated Depreciation—Building

PE 4-5A
Closing entries with net loss
obj. 3

After the accounts have been adjusted at October 31, the end of the fiscal year, the following balances were taken from the ledger of Velocity Delivery Services Co.:

Capital Stock	$318,500
Dividends	36,000
Fees Earned	475,150
Wages Expense	390,000
Rent Expense	85,000
Supplies Expense	38,350
Miscellaneous Expense	12,675

Journalize the four entries required to close the accounts.

PE 4-5B
Closing entries with net income
obj. 3

After the accounts have been adjusted at April 30, the end of the fiscal year, the following balances were taken from the ledger of Magnolia Landscaping Co.:

Capital Stock	$528,900
Dividends	60,000
Fees Earned	690,500
Wages Expense	410,000
Rent Expense	75,000
Supplies Expense	48,650
Miscellaneous Expense	19,700

Journalize the four entries required to close the accounts.

PE 4-6A
Missing steps in the accounting cycle
obj. 4

From the following list of steps in the accounting cycle, identify what two steps are missing.

a. Transactions are analyzed and recorded in the journal.
b. An unadjusted trial balance is prepared.
c. Adjustment data are assembled and analyzed.
d. An optional end-of-period spreadsheet (work sheet) is prepared.
e. Adjusting entries are journalized and posted to the ledger.
f. An adjusted trial balance is prepared.
g. Closing entries are journalized and posted to the ledger.
h. A post-closing trial balance is prepared.

PE 4-6B
Missing steps in the accounting cycle
obj. 4

From the following list of steps in the accounting cycle, identify what two steps are missing.

a. Transactions are analyzed and recorded in the journal.
b. Transactions are posted to the ledger.
c. An unadjusted trial balance is prepared.
d. An optional end-of-period spreadsheet (work sheet) is prepared.
e. Adjusting entries are journalized and posted to the ledger.
f. An adjusted trial balance is prepared.
g. Financial statements are prepared.
h. A post-closing trial balance is prepared.

Exercises

EX 4-1
Extending account balances in an end-of-period spreadsheet (work sheet)
objs. 1, 2

The balances for the accounts listed below appear in the Adjusted Trial Balance columns of the end-of-period spreadsheet (work sheet). Indicate whether each balance should be extended to (a) an Income Statement column or (b) a Balance Sheet column.

1. Accounts Payable
2. Accounts Receivable
3. Capital Stock
4. Dividends
5. Fees Earned

6. Supplies
7. Unearned Fees
8. Utilities Expense
9. Wages Expense
10. Wages Payable

EX 4-2
Classifying accounts
objs. 1, 2

Balances for each of the following accounts appear in an adjusted trial balance. Identify each as (a) asset, (b) liability, (c) revenue, or (d) expense.

1. Accounts Receivable
2. Fees Earned
3. Insurance Expense
4. Land
5. Prepaid Advertising
6. Prepaid Insurance

7. Rent Revenue
8. Salary Expense
9. Salary Payable
10. Supplies
11. Supplies Expense
12. Unearned Rent

EX 4-3
Financial statements from the end-of-period spreadsheet (work sheet)
objs. 1, 2

Sandy Bottom Consulting is a consulting firm owned and operated by Dee Schofield. The end-of-period spreadsheet (work sheet) shown below was prepared for the year ended August 31, 2008.

	A	B	C	D	E	F	G	H	I	J	K	
				Sandy Bottom Consulting								
				End-of-Period Spreadsheet (Work Sheet)								
				For the Year Ended August 31, 2008								
		Unadjusted Trial Balance		Adjustments		Adjusted Trial Balance		Income Statement		Balance Sheet		
	Account Title	Dr.	Cr.	Dr.	Cr.	Dr.	Cr.	Dr.	Cr.	Dr.	Cr.	
1	Cash	10,000				10,000				10,000		1
2	Accounts Receivable	12,500				12,500				12,500		2
3	Supplies	2,200			(a) 1,750	450				450		3
4	Office Equipment	14,500				14,500				14,500		4
5	Accumulated Depreciation		2,500		(b) 1,200		3,700				3,700	5
6	Accounts Payable		6,100				6,100				6,100	6
7	Salaries Payable				(c) 800		800				800	7
8	Capital Stock		7,000				7,000				7,000	8
9	Retained Earnings		12,400				12,400				12,400	9
10	Dividends	2,700				2,700				2,700		10
11	Fees Earned		32,000				32,000		32,000			11
12	Salary Expense	16,250		(c) 800		17,050		17,050				12
13	Supplies Expense			(a) 1,750		1,750		1,750				13
14	Depreciation Expense			(b) 1,200		1,200		1,200				14
15	Miscellaneous Expense	1,850				1,850		1,850				15
16		60,000	60,000	3,750	3,750	62,000	62,000	21,850	32,000	40,150	30,000	16
17	Net income							10,150			10,150	17
18								32,000	32,000	40,150	40,150	18

Based upon the preceding spreadsheet, prepare an income statement, retained earnings statement, and balance sheet for Sandy Bottom Consulting.

EX 4-4
Financial statements from the end-of-period spreadsheet (work sheet)
objs. 1, 2

Rectifier Consulting is a consulting firm owned and operated by Adam Beauchamp. The following end-of-period spreadsheet (work sheet) was prepared for the year ended June 30, 2008.

	A	B	C	D	E	F	G	H	I	J	K	
		Rectifier Consulting										
		End-of-Period Spreadsheet (Work Sheet)										
		For the Year Ended June 30, 2008										
		Unadjusted Trial Balance		**Adjustments**		**Adjusted Trial Balance**		**Income Statement**		**Balance Sheet**		
	Account Title	Dr.	Cr.	Dr.	Cr.	Dr.	Cr.	Dr.	Cr.	Dr.	Cr.	
1	Cash	8,000				8,000				8,000		1
2	Accounts Receivable	15,500				15,500				15,500		2
3	Supplies	2,500			(a) 1,850	650				650		3
4	Office Equipment	24,500				24,500				24,500		4
5	Accumulated Depreciation		4,500		(b) 900		5,400				5,400	5
6	Accounts Payable		3,300				3,300				3,300	6
7	Salaries Payable				(c) 400		400				400	7
8	Capital Stock		5,000				5,000				5,000	8
9	Retained Earnings		20,200				20,200				20,200	9
10	Dividends	2,000				2,000				2,000		10
11	Fees Earned		51,750				51,750		51,750			11
12	Salary Expense	30,750		(c) 400		31,150		31,150				12
13	Supplies Expense			(a) 1,850		1,850		1,850				13
14	Depreciation Expense			(b) 900		900		900				14
15	Miscellaneous Expense	1,500				1,500		1,500				15
16		84,750	84,750	3,150	3,150	86,050	86,050	35,400	51,750	50,650	34,300	16
17	Net income							16,350			16,350	17
18								51,750	51,750	50,650	50,650	18

Based upon the preceding spreadsheet, prepare an income statement, retained earnings statement, and balance sheet for Rectifier Consulting.

EX 4-5
Income statement
obj. 2
✓ *Net income, $184,500*

The following account balances were taken from the adjusted trial balance for Admiral Messenger Service, a delivery service firm, for the current fiscal year ended April 30, 2008:

Depreciation Expense	$ 5,000	Rent Expense	$ 43,400
Fees Earned	375,500	Salaries Expense	125,600
Insurance Expense	1,500	Supplies Expense	2,750
Miscellaneous Expense	1,250	Utilities Expense	11,500

Prepare an income statement.

EX 4-6
Income statement; net loss
obj. 2
✓ *Net loss, $23,300*

The following revenue and expense account balances were taken from the ledger of Cup-cake Services Co. after the accounts had been adjusted on October 31, 2008, the end of the current fiscal year:

Depreciation Expense	$10,000	Service Revenue	$163,375
Insurance Expense	6,000	Supplies Expense	2,875
Miscellaneous Expense	4,750	Utilities Expense	18,750
Rent Expense	51,500	Wages Expense	92,800

Prepare an income statement.

EX 4-7
Income statement
obj. 2

Internet Project

✓ *a. Net income: $1,449*

FedEx Corporation had the following revenue and expense account balances (in millions) at its fiscal year-end of May 31, 2005:

Depreciation	$1,462	Purchased Transportation	$ 2,935
Fuel	2,317	Rentals and Landing Fees	2,314
Maintenance and Repairs	1,680	Revenues	29,363
Other Expenses	4,379	Salaries and Employee Benefits	11,963
Provision for Income Taxes	864		

a. Prepare an income statement.
b. ▬▬▬➤ Compare your income statement with the related income statement that is available at the FedEx Corporation Web site, which is linked to the text's Web site at **www.thomsonedu.com/accounting/warren**. What similarities and differences do you see?

EX 4-8
Retained earnings statement

obj. 2

✓ *Retained earnings, Aug. 31, 2008: $652,750*

Icon Systems Co. offers its services to residents in the Pasadena area. Selected accounts from the ledger of Icon Systems Co. for the current fiscal year ended August 31, 2008, are as follows:

Retained Earnings				Dividends		
Aug. 31	16,000	Sept. 1 (2007)	573,750	Nov. 30	4,000	Aug. 31	16,000
		Aug. 31	95,000	Feb. 28	4,000		
				May 31	4,000		
				Aug. 31	4,000		

Income Summary			
Aug. 31	380,000	Aug. 31	475,000
31	95,000		

Prepare a retained earnings statement for the year.

EX 4-9
Retained earnings statement; net loss

obj. 2

✓ *Retained earnings, June 30, 2008: $128,250*

Selected accounts from the ledger of Aspen Sports for the current fiscal year ended June 30, 2008, are as follows:

Retained Earnings				Dividends		
June 30	30,000	July 1 (2007)	190,800	Sept. 30	7,500	June 30	30,000
30	32,550			Dec. 31	7,500		
				May 31	7,500		
				June 30	7,500		

Income Summary			
June 30	348,150	June 30	315,600
		30	32,550

Prepare a retained earnings statement for the year.

EX 4-10
Classifying assets

obj. 2

Identify each of the following as (a) a current asset or (b) property, plant, and equipment:

1. Accounts receivable
2. Building
3. Cash
4. Equipment
5. Prepaid insurance
6. Supplies

EX 4-11
Balance sheet classification

obj. 2

At the balance sheet date, a business owes a mortgage note payable of $750,000, the terms of which provide for monthly payments of $15,000.

➤ Explain how the liability should be classified on the balance sheet.

EX 4-12
Balance sheet

obj. 2

✓ *Total assets: $375,000*

Healthy & Trim Co. offers personal weight reduction consulting services to individuals. After all the accounts have been closed on November 30, 2008, the end of the current fiscal year, the balances of selected accounts from the ledger of Healthy & Trim Co. are as follows:

Accounts Payable	$ 17,250	Prepaid Insurance	$ 9,600
Accounts Receivable	41,560	Prepaid Rent	6,000
Accumulated Depreciation—		Retained Earnings	296,000
Equipment	51,950	Salaries Payable	6,750
Capital Stock	50,000	Supplies	1,040
Cash	?	Unearned Fees	5,000
Equipment	350,000		

Prepare a classified balance sheet that includes the correct balance for Cash.

EX 4-13
Balance sheet

obj. 2

List the errors you find in the following balance sheet. Prepare a corrected balance sheet.

Eucalyptus Services Co.
Balance Sheet
For the Year Ended July 31, 2008

Assets			Liabilities		
Current assets:			Current liabilities:		
Cash	$ 5,280		Accounts receivable	$ 13,750	
Accounts payable	6,790		Accum. depr.—building	86,700	
Supplies	1,650		Accum. depr.—equipment	18,480	
Prepaid insurance	4,800		Net income	25,000	
Land	60,000		Total liabilities		$143,930
Total current assets		$ 78,520			
Property, plant, and			**Stockholders' Equity**		
equipment:			Wages payable	$ 1,340	
Building	$156,700		Capital stock	55,000	
Equipment	43,000		Retained earnings	116,870	
Total property, plant,			Total stockholders' equity		173,210
and equipmet		238,620	Total liabilities and		
Total assets		$317,140	stockholders' equity		$317,140

EX 4-14
*Identifying accounts to
be closed*
obj. 3

From the following list, identify the accounts that should be closed to Income Summary at the end of the fiscal year:

a. Accounts Receivable
b. Accumulated Depreciation—
Equipment
c. Depreciation Expense—Equipment
d. Equipment
e. Fees Earned
f. Capital Stock

g. Dividends
h. Land
i. Supplies
j. Supplies Expense
k. Wages Expense
l. Wages Payable

EX 4-15
Closing entries
obj. 3

Prior to its closing, Income Summary had total debits of $279,615 and total credits of $392,750.

➥ Briefly explain the purpose served by the income summary account and the nature of the entries that resulted in the $279,615 and the $392,750.

EX 4-16
*Closing entries with
net income*
obj. 3

After all revenue and expense accounts have been closed at the end of the fiscal year, Income Summary has a debit of $218,380 and a credit of $375,000. At the same date, Retained Earnings has a credit balance of $479,100, and Dividends has a balance of $18,000. (a) Journalize the entries required to complete the closing of the accounts. (b) Determine the amount of Retained Earnings at the end of the period.

EX 4-17
*Closing entries with net
loss*
obj. 3

Firefly Services Co. offers its services to individuals desiring to improve their personal images. After the accounts have been adjusted at October 31, the end of the fiscal year, the following balances were taken from the ledger of Firefly Services Co.

Capital Stock	$554,500	Rent Expense	$65,000
Dividends	20,000	Supplies Expense	3,150
Fees Earned	293,300	Miscellaneous Expense	7,100
Wages Expense	250,000		

Journalize the four entries required to close the accounts.

EX 4-18
*Identifying permanent
accounts*
obj. 3

Which of the following accounts will usually appear in the post-closing trial balance?

a. Accounts Payable
b. Accumulated Depreciation
c. Capital Stock
d. Cash
e. Depreciation Expense
f. Dividends

g. Fees Earned
h. Office Equipment
i. Salaries Expense
j. Salaries Payable
k. Supplies

EX 4-19
Post-closing trial balance

obj. 3

✓ *Correct column totals,*
$150,505

An accountant prepared the following post-closing trial balance:

Honest Sam's Repair Co.
Post-Closing Trial Balance
July 31, 2008

	Debit Balances	Credit Balances
Cash	12,915	
Accounts Receivable	46,620	
Supplies		2,770
Equipment		88,200
Accumulated Depreciation—Equipment	27,970	
Accounts Payable	15,750	
Salaries Payable		3,780
Unearned Rent	7,560	
Capital Stock	15,000	
Retained Earnings		80,445
	125,815	175,195

Prepare a corrected post-closing trial balance. Assume that all accounts have normal balances and that the amounts shown are correct.

EX 4-20
Steps in the accounting cycle

obj. 4

Rearrange the following steps in the accounting cycle in proper sequence:

a. An adjusted trial balance is prepared.
b. Financial statements are prepared.
c. A post-closing trial balance is prepared.
d. Transactions are analyzed and recorded in the journal.
e. An optional end-of-period spreadsheet (work sheet) is prepared.
f. Adjustment data are asssembled and analyzed.
g. Transactions are posted to the ledger.
h. Closing entries are journalized and posted to the ledger.
i. An unadjusted trial balance is prepared.
j. Adjusting entries are journalized and posted to the ledger.

EX 4-21
Appendix: Steps in completing an end-of-period spreadsheet (work sheet)

The steps performed in completing an end-of-period spreadsheet (work sheet) are listed below in random order.

a. Extend the adjusted trial balance amounts to the Income Statement columns and the Balance Sheet columns.
b. Enter the adjusting entries into the spreadsheet (work sheet), based upon the adjustment data.
c. Add the Debit and Credit columns of the Unadjusted Trial Balance columns of the spreadsheet (work sheet) to verify that the totals are equal.
d. Enter the amount of net income or net loss for the period in the proper Income Statement column and Balance Sheet column.
e. Add the Debit and Credit columns of the Balance Sheet and Income Statement columns of the spreadsheet (work sheet) to verify that the totals are equal.
f. Enter the unadjusted account balances from the general ledger into the Unadjusted Trial Balance columns of the spreadsheet (work sheet).
g. Add or deduct adjusting entry data to trial balance amounts, and extend amounts to the Adjusted Trial Balance columns.
h. Add the Debit and Credit columns of the Adjustments columns of the spreadsheet (work sheet) to verify that the totals are equal.
i. Add the Debit and Credit columns of the Balance Sheet and Income Statement columns of the spreadsheet (work sheet) to determine the amount of net income or net loss for the period.
j. Add the Debit and Credit columns of the Adjusted Trial Balance columns of the spreadsheet (work sheet) to verify that the totals are equal.

Indicate the order in which the preceding steps would be performed in preparing and completing a spreadsheet (work sheet).

EX 4-22
Appendix: Adjustment data on an end-of-period spreadsheet (work sheet)

✓ *Total debits of Adjustments column: $15*

Dakota Services Co. offers cleaning services to business clients. The trial balance for Dakota Services Co. has been prepared on the end-of-period spreadsheet (work sheet) for the year ended July 31, 2008, shown below.

Dakota Services Co.
End-of-Period Spreadsheet (Work Sheet)
For the Year Ended July 31, 2008

Account Title	Unadjusted Trial Balance Dr.	Cr.	Adjustments Dr.	Cr.	Adjusted Trial Balance Dr.	Cr.
Cash	4					
Accounts Receivable	25					
Supplies	4					
Prepaid Insurance	6					
Land	25					
Equipment	16					
Accum. Depr.—Equipment		1				
Accounts Payable		13				
Wages Payable		0				
Capital Stock		10				
Retained Earnings		46				
Dividends	4					
Fees Earned		30				
Wages Expense	8					
Rent Expense	4					
Insurance Expense	0					
Utilities Expense	3					
Depreciation Expense	0					
Supplies Expense	0					
Miscellaneous Expense	1					
	100	100				

The data for year-end adjustments are as follows:

a. Fees earned, but not yet billed, $5.
b. Supplies on hand, $1.
c. Insurance premiums expired, $4.
d. Depreciation expense, $2.
e. Wages accrued, but not paid, $1.

Enter the adjustment data, and place the balances in the Adjusted Trial Balance columns.

EX 4-23
Appendix: Completing an end-of-period spreadsheet (work sheet)

✓ *Net income: $9*

Dakota Services Co. offers cleaning services to business clients. Complete the following end-of-period spreadsheet (work sheet) for Dakota Services Co.

(continued)

Dakota Services Co.
End-of-Period Spreadsheet (Work Sheet)
For the Year Ended July 31, 2008

Account Title	Adjusted Trial Balance		Income Statement		Balance Sheet	
	Dr.	Cr.	Dr.	Cr.	Dr.	Cr.
Cash	4					
Accounts Receivable	30					
Supplies	1					
Prepaid Insurance	2					
Land	25					
Equipment	16					
Accum. Depr.—Equipment		3				
Accounts Payable		13				
Wages Payable		1				
Capital Stock		10				
Retained Earnings		46				
Dividends	4					
Fees Earned		35				
Wages Expense	9					
Rent Expense	4					
Insurance Expense	4					
Utilities Expense	3					
Depreciation Expense	2					
Supplies Expense	3					
Miscellaneous Expense	1					
	108	108				
Net income (loss)						

EX 4-24
Appendix: Financial statements from an end-of-period spreadsheet (work sheet)

✓ *Retained earnings, July 31, 2008: $51*

Based upon the data in Exercise 4-23, prepare an income statement, retained earnings statement, and balance sheet for Dakota Services Co.

EX 4-25
Appendix: Adjusting entries from an end-of-period spreadsheet (work sheet)

Based upon the data in Exercise 4-22, prepare the adjusting entries for Dakota Services Co.

EX 4-26
Appendix: Closing entries from an end-of-period spreadsheet (work sheet)

Based upon the data in Exercise 4-23, prepare the closing entries for Dakota Services Co.

Problems Series A

PR 4-1A
Financial statements and closing entries
objs. 1, 2, 3

Blink-On Company maintains and repairs warning lights, such as those found on radio towers and lighthouses. Blink-On Company prepared the end-of-period spreadsheet (work sheet) at the top of the following page at March 31, 2008, the end of the current fiscal year:

	A	B	C	D	E	F	G	H	I	J	K	
		\multicolumn{10}{c	}{**Blink-On Company**}	
		\multicolumn{10}{c	}{**End-of-Period Spreadsheet (Work Sheet)**}	
		\multicolumn{10}{c	}{**For the Year Ended March 31, 2008**}	
		Unadjusted Trial Balance		**Adjustments**		**Adjusted Trial Balance**		**Income Statement**		**Balance Sheet**		
	Account Title	Dr.	Cr.	Dr.	Cr.	Dr.	Cr.	Dr.	Cr.	Dr.	Cr.	
1	Cash	6,300				6,300				6,300		1
2	Accounts Receivable	18,900		(a) 3,500		22,400				22,400		2
3	Prepaid Insurance	4,200			(b) 2,800	1,400				1,400		3
4	Supplies	2,730			(c) 1,600	1,130				1,130		4
5	Land	98,000				98,000				98,000		5
6	Building	140,000				140,000				140,000		6
7	Acc. Depr.—Building		100,300		(d) 1,400		101,700				101,700	7
8	Equipment	100,500				100,500				100,500		8
9	Acc. Depr.—Equipment		85,100		(e) 3,200		88,300				88,300	9
10	Accounts Payable		5,700				5,700				5,700	10
11	Unearned Rent		2,100	(g) 1,200			900				900	11
12	Capital Stock		18,000				18,000				18,000	12
13	Retained Earnings		60,100				60,100				60,100	13
14	Dividends	5,600				5,600				5,600		14
15	Fees Revenue		253,700		(a) 3,500		257,200		257,200			15
16	Salaries & Wages Expense	102,500		(f) 1,800		104,300		104,300				16
17	Advertising Expense	21,700				21,700		21,700				17
18	Utilities Expense	11,400				11,400		11,400				18
19	Repairs Expense	8,850				8,850		8,850				19
20	Misc. Expense	4,320				4,320		4,320				20
21		525,000	525,000									21
22	Insurance Expense			(b) 2,800		2,800		2,800				22
23	Supplies Expense			(c) 1,600		1,600		1,600				23
24	Depr. Exp.—Building			(d) 1,400		1,400		1,400				24
25	Depr. Exp.—Equipment			(e) 3,200		3,200		3,200				25
26	Salaries & Wages Payable				(f) 1,800		1,800				1,800	26
27	Rent Revenue				(g) 1,200		1,200		1,200			27
28				15,500	15,500	534,900	534,900	159,570	258,400	375,330	276,500	28
29	Net income							98,830			98,830	29
30								258,400	258,400	375,330	375,330	30

Instructions

1. Prepare an income statement for the year ended March 31.
2. Prepare a retained earnings statement for the year ended March 31.
3. Prepare a balance sheet as of March 31.
4. Based upon the end-of-period spreadsheet (work sheet), journalize the closing entries.
5. Prepare a post-closing trial balance.

✓1. Net income: $98,830

PR 4-2A

Financial statements and closing entries

objs. 2, 3

✓1. Retained earnings, April 30: $117,800

The Nevus Company is an investigative services firm that is owned and operated by Stacey Vargas. On April 30, 2008, the end of the current fiscal year, the accountant for The Nevus Company prepared an end-of-period spreadsheet (work sheet), a part of which is shown at the top of the following page.

Instructions

1. Prepare an income statement, retained earnings statement, and a balance sheet.
2. Journalize the entries that were required to close the accounts at April 30.
3. If Retained Earnings decreased $35,000 after the closing entries were posted, and the dividends remained the same, what was the amount of net income or net loss?

(continued)

	A	H	I	J	K	
	The Nevus Company					
	End-of-Period Spreadsheet (Work Sheet)					
	For the Year Ended April 30, 2008					
		Income Statement		Balance Sheet		
1	Cash			9,000		1
2	Accounts Receivable			37,200		2
3	Supplies			3,500		3
4	Prepaid Insurance			4,800		4
5	Equipment			169,500		5
6	Accumulated Depreciation—Equipment				55,200	6
7	Accounts Payable				10,500	7
8	Salaries Payable				2,500	8
9	Unearned Rent				3,000	9
10	Capital Stock				35,000	10
11	Retained Earnings				107,800	11
12	Dividends			16,000		12
13	Service Fees		363,000			13
14	Rent Revenue		7,000			14
15	Salary Expense	270,000				15
16	Rent Expense	37,000				16
17	Supplies Expense	8,000				17
18	Depreciation Expense—Equipment	7,000				18
19	Utilities Expense	6,400				19
20	Repairs Expense	6,200				20
21	Insurance Expense	4,800				21
22	Miscellaneous Expense	4,600				22
23		344,000	370,000	240,000	214,000	23
24	Net income	26,000			26,000	24
25		370,000	370,000	240,000	240,000	25

PR 4-3A
T accounts, adjusting entries, financial statements, and closing entries; optional end-of-period spreadsheet (work sheet)

objs. 2, 3

✓ *2. Net income: $13,650*

The unadjusted trial balance of Iguana Laundromat at June 30, 2008, the end of the current fiscal year, is shown below.

Iguana Laundromat
Unadjusted Trial Balance
June 30, 2008

	Debit Balances	Credit Balances
Cash	5,500	
Laundry Supplies	9,450	
Prepaid Insurance	4,300	
Laundry Equipment	142,000	
Accumulated Depreciation		75,200
Accounts Payable		4,900
Capital Stock		7,500
Retained Earnings		46,300
Dividends	4,200	
Laundry Revenue		116,100
Wages Expense	52,000	
Rent Expense	19,650	
Utilities Expense	10,200	
Miscellaneous Expense	2,700	
	250,000	250,000

The data needed to determine year-end adjustments are as follows:

a. Laundry supplies on hand at June 30 are $1,500.
b. Insurance premiums expired during the year are $3,200.
c. Depreciation of equipment during the year is $6,000.
d. Wages accrued but not paid at June 30 are $750.

Instructions

1. For each account listed in the unadjusted trial balance, enter the balance in a T account. Identify the balance as "June 30 Bal." In addition, add T accounts for Wages Payable, Depreciation Expense, Laundry Supplies Expense, Insurance Expense, and Income Summary.
2. **Optional:** Enter the unadjusted trial balance on an end-of-period spreadsheet (work sheet) and complete the spreadsheet. Add the accounts listed in part (1) as needed.
3. Journalize and post the adjusting entries. Identify the adjustments by "Adj." and the new balances as "Adj. Bal."
4. Prepare an adjusted trial balance.
5. Prepare an income statement, a retained earnings statement, and a balance sheet.
6. Journalize and post the closing entries. Identify the closing entries by "Clos."
7. Prepare a post-closing trial balance.

PR 4-4A
Ledger accounts,
adjusting entries,
financial statements, and
closing entries;
optional end-of-period
spreadsheet (work sheet)

objs. 2, 3

✓ *4. Net income: $24,593*

If the working papers correlating with this textbook are not used, omit Problem 4-4A.

The ledger and trial balance of Wainscot Services Co. as of March 31, 2008, the end of the first month of its current fiscal year, are presented in the working papers.

Data needed to determine the necessary adjusting entries are as follows:

a. Service revenue accrued at March 31 is $1,750.
b. Supplies on hand at March 31 are $400.
c. Insurance premiums expired during March are $250.
d. Depreciation of the building during March is $400.
e. Depreciation of equipment during March is $200.
f. Unearned rent at March 31 is $1,000.
g. Wages accrued at March 31 are $500.

Instructions

1. **Optional:** Complete the end-of-period spreadsheet (work sheet) using the adjustment data shown above.
2. Journalize and post the adjusting entries, inserting balances in the accounts affected.
3. Prepare an adjusted trial balance.
4. Prepare an income statement, a retained earnings statement, and a balance sheet.
5. Journalize and post the closing entries. Indicate closed accounts by inserting a line in both Balance columns opposite the closing entry. Insert the new balance of the capital account.
6. Prepare a post-closing trial balance.

PR 4-5A
Ledger accounts,
adjusting entries,
financial statements,
and closing entries;
optional spreadsheet
(work sheet)

objs. 2, 3

✓ *5. Net income: $41,705*

The unadjusted trial balance of Quick Repairs at October 31, 2008, the end of the current year, is shown below.

Quick Repairs
Unadjusted Trial Balance
October 31, 2008

		Debit Balances	Credit Balances
11	Cash	2,950	
13	Supplies	12,295	
14	Prepaid Insurance	2,735	
16	Equipment	95,650	
17	Accumulated Depreciation—Equipment		21,209
18	Trucks	36,300	
19	Accumulated Depreciation—Trucks ...		7,400
21	Accounts Payable		4,015
31	Capital Stock		10,000
32	Retained Earnings		57,426
33	Dividends	6,000	
41	Service Revenue		99,950
51	Wages Expense	26,925	
53	Rent Expense	9,600	
55	Truck Expense	5,350	
59	Miscellaneous Expense	2,195	
		200,000	200,000

The data needed to determine year-end adjustments are as follows:

a. Supplies on hand at October 31 are $7,120.
b. Insurance premiums expired during year are $2,000.
c. Depreciation of equipment during year is $4,200.
d. Depreciation of trucks during year is $2,200.
e. Wages accrued but not paid at October 31 are $600.

Instructions

1. For each account listed in the trial balance, enter the balance in the appropriate Balance column of a four-column account and place a check mark (✔) in the Posting Reference column.
2. **Optional:** Enter the unadjusted trial balance on an end-of-period spreadsheet (work sheet) and complete the spreadsheet. Add the accounts listed in part (3) as needed.
3. Journalize and post the adjusting entries, inserting balances in the accounts affected. The following additional accounts from Quick Repair's chart of accounts should be used: Wages Payable, 22; Supplies Expense, 52; Depreciation Expense—Equipment, 54; Depreciation Expense—Trucks, 56; Insurance Expense, 57.
4. Prepare an adjusted trial balance.
5. Prepare an income statement, a retained earnings statement, and a balance sheet.
6. Journalize and post the closing entries. (Income Summary is account #34 in the chart of accounts.) Indicate closed accounts by inserting a line in both Balance columns opposite the closing entry.
7. Prepare a post-closing trial balance.

PR 4-6A
Complete accounting cycle

objs. 4, 5, 6

✔ *8. Net income: $17,250*

For the past several years, Dawn Lytle has operated a part-time consulting business from her home. As of October 1, 2008, Dawn decided to move to rented quarters and to operate the business as a professional corporation, which is to be known as Sky's-The-Limit Consulting, P.C., on a full-time basis. Sky's-The-Limit Consulting entered into the following transactions during October:

Oct. 1. The following assets were received from Dawn Lytle in exchange for capital stock: cash, $12,950; accounts receivable, $2,800; supplies, $1,500; and office equipment, $18,750. There were no liabilities received.
  1. Paid three months' rent on a lease rental contract, $3,600.
  2. Paid the premiums on property and casualty insurance policies, $2,400.
  4. Received cash from clients as an advance payment for services to be provided and recorded it as unearned fees, $4,150.
  5. Purchased additional office equipment on account from Office Station Co., $2,500.
  6. Received cash from clients on account, $1,900.
  10. Paid cash for a newspaper advertisement, $325.
  12. Paid Office Station Co. for part of the debt incurred on October 5, $1,250.
  12. Recorded services provided on account for the period October 1–12, $3,750.
  14. Paid part-time receptionist for two weeks' salary, $750.
  17. Recorded cash from cash clients for fees earned during the period October 1–17, $6,250.
  18. Paid cash for supplies, $600.
  20. Recorded services provided on account for the period October 13–20, $2,100.
  24. Recorded cash from cash clients for fees earned for the period October 17–24, $3,850.
  26. Received cash from clients on account, $4,450.
  27. Paid part-time receptionist for two weeks' salary, $750.
  29. Paid telephone bill for October, $250.
  31. Paid electricity bill for October, $300.
  31. Recorded cash from cash clients for fees earned for the period October 25–31, $2,975.
  31. Recorded services provided on account for the remainder of October, $1,500.
  31. Paid dividends of $5,000.

Instructions

1. Journalize each transaction in a two-column journal, referring to the following chart of accounts in selecting the accounts to be debited and credited. (Do not insert the account numbers in the journal at this time.)

11	Cash	31	Capital Stock
12	Accounts Receivable	32	Retained Earnings
14	Supplies	33	Dividends
15	Prepaid Rent	41	Fees Earned
16	Prepaid Insurance	51	Salary Expense
18	Office Equipment	52	Rent Expense
19	Accumulated Depreciation	53	Supplies Expense
21	Accounts Payable	54	Depreciation Expense
22	Salaries Payable	55	Insurance Expense
23	Unearned Fees	59	Miscellaneous Expense

2. Post the journal to a ledger of four-column accounts.
3. Prepare an unadjusted trial balance.
4. At the end of October, the following adjustment data were assembled. Analyze and use these data to complete parts (5) and (6).
   a. Insurance expired during October is $200.
   b. Supplies on hand on October 31 are $875.
   c. Depreciation of office equipment for October is $675.
   d. Accrued receptionist salary on October 31 is $150.
   e. Rent expired during October is $1,550.
   f. Unearned fees on October 31 are $1,150.
5. **Optional:** Enter the unadjusted trial balance on an end-of-period spreadsheet (work sheet) and complete the spreadsheet.
6. Journalize and post the adjusting entries.
7. Prepare an adjusted trial balance.
8. Prepare an income statement, a retained earnings statement, and a balance sheet.
9. Prepare and post the closing entries. (Income Summary is account #34 in the chart of accounts.) Indicate closed accounts by inserting a line in both the Balance columns opposite the closing entry.
10. Prepare a post-closing trial balance.

Problems Series B

PR 4-1B
Financial statements and closing entries
objs. 1, 2, 3

✓1. Net loss: $10,900

Last-Chance Company offers legal consulting advice to prison inmates. Last-Chance Company prepared the end-of-period spreadsheet (work sheet) at the top of the following page at November 30, 2008, the end of the current fiscal year.

Instructions

1. Prepare an income statement for the year ended November 30.
2. Prepare a retained earnings statement for the year ended November 30.
3. Prepare a balance sheet as of November 30.
4. On the basis of the end-of-period spreadsheet (work sheet), journalize the closing entries.
5. Prepare a post-closing trial balance.

	A	B	C	D	E	F	G	H	I	J	K	
		Last-Chance Company										
		End-of-Period Spreadsheet (Work Sheet)										
		For the Year Ended November 30, 2008										
		Unadjusted Trial Balance		Adjustments		Adjusted Trial Balance		Income Statement		Balance Sheet		
	Account Title	Dr.	Cr.	Dr.	Cr.	Dr.	Cr.	Dr.	Cr.	Dr.	Cr.	
1	Cash	4,800				4,800				4,800		1
2	Accounts Receivable	15,750		(a) 4,200		19,950				19,950		2
3	Prepaid Insurance	2,700			(b) 1,450	1,250				1,250		3
4	Supplies	2,025			(c) 1,525	500				500		4
5	Land	75,000				75,000				75,000		5
6	Building	205,000				205,000				205,000		6
7	Acc. Depr.—Building		76,000		(d) 2,000		78,000				78,000	7
8	Equipment	139,000				139,000				139,000		8
9	Acc. Depr.—Equipment		54,450		(e) 5,200		59,650				59,650	9
10	Accounts Payable		9,750				9,750				9,750	10
11	Unearned Rent		4,500	(g) 2,000			2,500				2,500	11
12	Capital Stock		80,000				80,000				80,000	12
13	Retained Earnings		238,800				238,800				238,800	13
14	Dividends	15,000				15,000				15,000		14
15	Fees Revenue		286,500		(a) 4,200		290,700		290,700			15
16	Salaries & Wages Expense	144,300		(f) 2,700		147,000		147,000				16
17	Advertising Expense	94,800				94,800		94,800				17
18	Utilities Expense	27,000				27,000		27,000				18
19	Travel Expense	18,750				18,750		18,750				19
20	Misc. Expense	5,875				5,875		5,875				20
21		750,000	750,000									21
22	Insurance Expense			(b) 1,450		1,450		1,450				22
23	Supplies Expense			(c) 1,525		1,525		1,525				23
24	Depr. Exp.—Building			(d) 2,000		2,000		2,000				24
25	Depr. Exp.—Equipment			(e) 5,200		5,200		5,200				25
26	Sal. & Wages Payable				(f) 2,700		2,700				2,700	26
27	Rent Revenue				(g) 2,000		2,000		2,000			27
28				19,075	19,075	764,100	764,100	303,600	292,700	460,500	471,400	28
29	Net loss								10,900	10,900		29
30								303,600	303,600	471,400	471,400	30

PR 4-2B

Financial statements and closing entries

objs. 2, 3

✓ *1. Retained earnings, July 31: $402,000*

The Ultra Services Company is a financial planning services firm owned and operated by Chad Tillman. As of July 31, 2008, the end of the current fiscal year, the accountant for The Ultra Services Company prepared an end-of-period spreadsheet (work sheet), part of which is shown at the top of the next page.

Instructions

1. Prepare an income statement, a retained earnings statement, and a balance sheet.
2. Journalize the entries that were required to close the accounts at July 31.
3. If the balance of Capital Stock decreased $40,000 after the closing entries were posted, and the dividends remained the same, what was the amount of net income or net loss?

	A	H	I	J	K	
	The Ultra Services Company					
	End-of-Period Spreadsheet (Work Sheet)					
	For the Year Ended July 31, 2008					
		Income Statement		Balance Sheet		
1	Cash			13,950		1
2	Accounts Receivable			41,880		2
3	Supplies			8,400		3
4	Prepaid Insurance			7,500		4
5	Land			180,000		5
6	Buildings			360,000		6
7	Accumulated Depreciation—Buildings				217,200	7
8	Equipment			258,270		8
9	Accumulated Depreciation—Equipment				122,700	9
10	Accounts Payable				33,300	10
11	Salaries Payable				3,300	11
12	Unearned Rent				1,500	12
13	Capital Stock				90,000	13
14	Retained Earnings				250,500	14
15	Dividends			30,000		15
16	Service Fees		525,000			16
17	Rent Revenue		4,500			17
18	Salary Expense	219,000				18
19	Depreciation Expense—Equipment	28,500				19
20	Rent Expense	25,500				20
21	Supplies Expense	22,950				21
22	Utilities Expense	15,900				22
23	Depreciation Expense—Buildings	15,600				23
24	Repairs Expense	12,450				24
25	Insurance Expense	3,000				25
26	Miscellaneous Expense	5,100				26
27		348,000	529,500	900,000	718,500	27
28	Net income	181,500			181,500	28
29		529,500	529,500	900,000	900,000	29

PR 4-3B

T accounts, adjusting entries, financial statements, and closing entries; optional end-of-period spreadsheet (work sheet)

objs. 2, 3

✓ 2. Net income: $12,300

The unadjusted trial balance of Best Laundry at March 31, 2008, the end of the current fiscal year, is shown below.

Best Laundry
Unadjusted Trial Balance
March 31, 2008

	Debit Balances	Credit Balances
Cash	1,450	
Laundry Supplies	3,750	
Prepaid Insurance	2,400	
Laundry Equipment	54,500	
Accumulated Depreciation		20,500
Accounts Payable		3,100
Capital Stock		4,000
Retained Earnings		14,900
Dividends	1,000	
Laundry Revenue		82,500
Wages Expense	35,750	
Rent Expense	18,000	
Utilities Expense	6,800	
Miscellaneous Expense	1,350	
	125,000	125,000

The data needed to determine year-end adjustments are as follows:

a. Wages accrued but not paid at March 31 are $600.
b. Depreciation of equipment during the year is $2,900.
c. Laundry supplies on hand at March 31 are $950.
d. Insurance premiums expired during the year are $2,000.

Instructions

1. For each account listed in the unadjusted trial balance, enter the balance in a T account. Identify the balance as "Mar. 31 Bal." In addition, add T accounts for Wages Payable, Depreciation Expense, Laundry Supplies Expense, Insurance Expense, and Income Summary.
2. **Optional:** Enter the unadjusted trial balance on an end-of-period spreadsheet (work sheet) and complete the spreadsheet. Add the accounts listed in part (1) as needed.
3. Journalize and post the adjusting entries. Identify the adjustments by "Adj." and the new balances as "Adj. Bal."
4. Prepare an adjusted trial balance.
5. Prepare an income statement, a retained earnings statement, and a balance sheet.
6. Journalize and post the closing entries. Identify the closing entries by "Clos."
7. Prepare a post-closing trial balance.

PR 4-4B

Ledger accounts, adjusting entries, financial statements, and closing entries; optional end-of-period spreadsheet (work sheet)

objs. 2, 3

✓ *4. Net income: $23,818*

If the working papers correlating with this textbook are not used, omit Problem 4-4B.

The ledger and trial balance of Wainscot Services Co. as of March 31, 2008, the end of the first month of its current fiscal year, are presented in the working papers.

Data needed to determine the necessary adjusting entries are as follows:

a. Service revenue accrued at March 31 is $2,000.
b. Supplies on hand at March 31 are $400.
c. Insurance premiums expired during March are $150.
d. Depreciation of the building during March is $625.
e. Depreciation of equipment during March is $200.
f. Unearned rent at March 31 is $1,800.
g. Wages accrued but not paid at March 31 are $600.

Instructions

1. **Optional:** Complete the end-of-period spreadsheet (work sheet) using the adjustment data shown above.
2. Journalize and post the adjusting entries, inserting balances in the accounts affected.
3. Prepare an adjusted trial balance.
4. Prepare an income statement, a retained earnings statement, and a balance sheet.
5. Journalize and post the closing entries. Indicate closed accounts by inserting a line in both Balance columns opposite the closing entry. Insert the new balance of the capital account.
6. Prepare a post-closing trial balance.

PR 4-5B

Ledger accounts, adjusting entries, financial statements, and closing entries; optional end-of-period spreadsheet (work sheet)

objs. 2, 3

✓ *5. Net income: $30,175*

The unadjusted trial balance of Reliable Repairs at December 31, 2008, the end of the current year, is shown at the top of the next page. The data needed to determine year-end adjustments are as follows:

a. Supplies on hand at December 31 are $6,500.
b. Insurance premiums expired during the year are $2,500.
c. Depreciation of equipment during the year is $4,800.
d. Depreciation of trucks during the year is $3,500.
e. Wages accrued but not paid at December 31 are $1,000.

Reliable Repairs
Unadjusted Trial Balance
December 31, 2008

		Debit Balances	Credit Balances
11	Cash	2,825	
13	Supplies	10,820	
14	Prepaid Insurance	7,500	
16	Equipment	54,200	
17	Accumulated Depreciation—Equipment		12,050
18	Trucks	50,000	
19	Accumulated Depreciation—Trucks		27,100
21	Accounts Payable		12,015
31	Capital Stock		3,000
32	Retained Earnings		29,885
33	Dividends	5,000	
41	Service Revenue		90,950
51	Wages Expense	28,010	
53	Rent Expense	8,100	
55	Truck Expense	6,350	
59	Miscellaneous Expense	2,195	
		175,000	175,000

Instructions
1. For each account listed in the unadjusted trial balance, enter the balance in the appropriate Balance column of a four-column account and place a check mark (✓) in the Posting Reference column.
2. **Optional:** Enter the unadjusted trial balance on an end-of-period spreadsheet (work sheet) and complete the spreadsheet. Add the accounts listed in part (3) as needed.
3. Journalize and post the adjusting entries, inserting balances in the accounts affected. The following additional accounts from Reliable's chart of accounts should be used: Wages Payable, 22; Supplies Expense, 52; Depreciation Expense—Equipment, 54; Depreciation Expense—Trucks, 56; Insurance Expense, 57.
4. Prepare an adjusted trial balance.
5. Prepare an income statement, a retained earnings statement, and a balance sheet.
6. Journalize and post the closing entries. (Income Summary is account #34 in the chart of accounts.) Indicate closed accounts by inserting a line in both Balance columns opposite the closing entry.
7. Prepare a post-closing trial balance.

PR 4-6B
Complete accounting cycle
objs. 4, 5, 6

✓ *8. Net income: $10,980*

For the past several years, Derrick Epstein has operated a part-time consulting business from his home. As of June 1, 2008, Derrick decided to move to rented quarters and to operate the business as a professional corporation, which is to be known as Luminary Consulting, P.C., on a full-time basis. Luminary Consulting entered into the following transactions during June:

June 1. The following assets were received from Derrick Epstein in exchange for capital stock: cash, $26,200; accounts receivable, $6,000; supplies, $2,800; and office equipment, $25,000. There were no liabilities received.
1. Paid three months' rent on a lease rental contract, $5,250.
2. Paid the premiums on property and casualty insurance policies, $2,100.
4. Received cash from clients as an advance payment for services to be provided and recorded it as unearned fees, $2,700.
5. Purchased additional office equipment on account from Office Station Co., $5,000.
6. Received cash from clients on account, $3,000.
10. Paid cash for a newspaper advertisement, $200.
12. Paid Office Station Co. for part of the debt incurred on June 5, $1,000.
12. Recorded services provided on account for the period June 1–12, $5,100.
14. Paid part-time receptionist for two weeks' salary, $800.
17. Recorded cash from cash clients for fees earned during the period June 1–16, $3,500.

(continued)

June 18. Paid cash for supplies, $750.

    20. Recorded services provided on account for the period June 13–20, $1,100.

    24. Recorded cash from cash clients for fees earned for the period June 17–24, $4,150.

    26. Received cash from clients on account, $4,900.

    27. Paid part-time receptionist for two weeks' salary, $800.

    29. Paid telephone bill for June, $150.

    30. Paid electricity bill for June, $400.

    30. Recorded cash from cash clients for fees earned for the period June 25–30, $1,500.

    30. Recorded services provided on account for the remainder of June, $1,000.

    30. Paid dividends of $8,000.

Instructions

1. Journalize each transaction in a two-column journal, referring to the following chart of accounts in selecting the accounts to be debited and credited. (Do not insert the account numbers in the journal at this time.)

11	Cash	31	Capital Stock
12	Accounts Receivable	32	Retained Earnings
14	Supplies	33	Dividends
15	Prepaid Rent	41	Fees Earned
16	Prepaid Insurance	51	Salary Expense
18	Office Equipment	52	Rent Expense
19	Accumulated Depreciation	53	Supplies Expense
21	Accounts Payable	54	Depreciation Expense
22	Salaries Payable	55	Insurance Expense
23	Unearned Fees	59	Miscellaneous Expense

2. Post the journal to a ledger of four-column accounts.
3. Prepare an unadjusted trial balance.
4. At the end of June, the following adjustment data were assembled. Analyze and use these data to complete parts (5) and (6).
   a. Insurance expired during June is $175.
   b. Supplies on hand on June 30 are $2,000.
   c. Depreciation of office equipment for June is $500.
   d. Accrued receptionist salary on June 30 is $120.
   e. Rent expired during June is $1,500.
   f. Unearned fees on June 30 are $1,875.
5. **Optional:** Enter the unadjusted trial balance on an end-of-period spreadsheet (work sheet) and complete the spreadsheet.
6. Journalize and post the adjusting entries.
7. Prepare an adjusted trial balance.
8. Prepare an income statement, a retained earnings statement, and a balance sheet.
9. Prepare and post the closing entries. (Income Summary is account #34 in the chart of accounts.) Indicate closed accounts by inserting a line in both the Balance columns opposite the closing entry.
10. Prepare a post-closing trial balance.

Continuing Problem

The unadjusted trial balance of Dancin Music as of May 31, 2008, along with the adjustment data for the two months ended May 31, 2008, are shown in Chapter 3.

    Based upon the adjustment data, the adjusted trial balance shown at the top of the following page was prepared.

Instructions

1. **Optional.** Using the data from Chapter 3, prepare an end-of-period spreadsheet (work sheet).
2. Prepare an income statement, a retained earnings statement, and a balance sheet.

✓ 2. Net income: $4,925

Dancin Music
Adjusted Trial Balance
May 31, 2008

	Debit Balances	Credit Balances
Cash	12,085	
Accounts Receivable	4,250	
Supplies	160	
Prepaid Insurance	3,080	
Office Equipment	5,000	
Accumulated Depreciation—Office Equipment		100
Accounts Payable		5,750
Wages Payable		200
Unearned Revenue		2,400
Capital Stock		12,500
Dividends	1,300	
Fees Earned		18,550
Wages Expense	2,600	
Office Rent Expense	2,600	
Equipment Rent Expense	1,300	
Utilities Expense	910	
Music Expense	2,565	
Advertising Expense	1,730	
Supplies Expense	940	
Insurance Expense	280	
Depreciation Expense	100	
Miscellaneous Expense	600	
	39,500	39,500

3. Journalize and post the closing entries. The income summary account is #34 in the ledger of Dancin Music. Indicate closed accounts by inserting a line in both Balance columns opposite the closing entry.
4. Prepare a post-closing trial balance.

Comprehensive Problem 1

✓ 8. Net income, $22,160

Kelly Pitney began her consulting business, Kelly Consulting, P.C., on April 1, 2008. The accounting cycle for Kelly Consulting for April, including financial statements, was illustrated on pages 163–176. During May, Kelly Consulting entered into the following transactions:

May 3. Received cash from clients as an advance payment for services to be provided and recorded it as unearned fees, $1,550.
5. Received cash from clients on account, $1,750.
9. Paid cash for a newspaper advertisement, $100.
13. Paid Office Station Co. for part of the debt incurred on April 5, $400.
15. Recorded services provided on account for the period May 1–15, $5,100.
16. Paid part-time receptionist for two weeks' salary including the amount owed on April 30, $750.
17. Recorded cash from cash clients for fees earned during the period May 1–16, $7,380.
20. Purchased supplies on account, $500.
21. Recorded services provided on account for the period May 16–20, $2,900.
25. Recorded cash from cash clients for fees earned for the period May 17–23, $4,200.
27. Received cash from clients on account, $6,600.
28. Paid part-time receptionist for two weeks' salary, $750.
30. Paid telephone bill for May, $150.
31. Paid electricity bill for May, $225.
31. Recorded cash from cash clients for fees earned for the period May 26–31, $2,875.
31. Recorded services provided on account for the remainder of May, $2,200.
31. Paid dividends of $7,500.

Instructions

1. The chart of accounts for Kelly Consulting is shown on page 165, and the post-closing trial balance as of April 30, 2008, is shown on page 171. For each account in the post-closing trial balance, enter the balance in the appropriate Balance column of a four-column account. Date the balances May 1, 2008, and place a check mark (✔) in the Posting Reference column. Journalize each of the May transactions in a two-column journal using Kelly Consulting's chart of accounts. (Do not insert the account numbers in the journal at this time.)

2. Post the journal to a ledger of four-column accounts.

3. Prepare an unadjusted trial balance.

4. At the end of May, the following adjustment data were assembled. Analyze and use these data to complete parts (5) and (6).
   a. Insurance expired during May is $300.
   b. Supplies on hand on May 31 are $950.
   c. Depreciation of office equipment for May is $330.
   d. Accrued receptionist salary on May 31 is $260.
   e. Rent expired during May is $1,600.
   f. Unearned fees on May 31 are $1,300.

5. **Optional:** Enter the unadjusted trial balance on an end-of-period spreadsheet (work sheet) and complete the spreadsheet.

6. Journalize and post the adjusting entries.

7. Prepare an adjusted trial balance.

8. Prepare an income statement, a retained earnings statement, and a balance sheet.

9. Prepare and post the closing entries. (Income Summary is account #34 in the chart of accounts.) Indicate closed accounts by inserting a line in both the Balance columns opposite the closing entry.

10. Prepare a post-closing trial balance.

Special Activities

SA 4-1
Ethics and professional conduct in business

ETHICS

Fantasy Graphics is a graphics arts design consulting firm. Terri Bierman, its treasurer and vice president of finance, has prepared a classified balance sheet as of January 31, 2008, the end of its fiscal year. This balance sheet will be submitted with Fantasy Graphics' loan application to Booneville Trust & Savings Bank.

In the current assets section of the balance sheet, Terri reported a $100,000 receivable from Kent Miles, the president of Fantasy Graphics, as a trade account receivable. Kent borrowed the money from Fantasy Graphics in November 2006 for a down payment on a new home. He has orally assured Terri that he will pay off the account receivable within the next year. Terri reported the $100,000 in the same manner on the preceding year's balance sheet.

▷ Evaluate whether it is acceptable for Terri Bierman to prepare the January 31, 2008, balance sheet in the manner indicated above.

SA 4-2
Financial statements

The following is an excerpt from a telephone conversation between Jan Young, president of Cupboard Supplies Co., and Steve Nisbet, owner of Nisbet Employment Co.:

Jan: Steve, you're going to have to do a better job of finding me a new computer programmer. That last guy was great at programming, but he didn't have any common sense.

Steve: What do you mean? The guy had a master's degree with straight A's.

Jan: Yes, well, last month he developed a new financial reporting system. He said we could do away with manually preparing an end-of-period spreadsheet (work sheet) and financial statements. The computer would automatically generate our financial statements with "a push of a button."

Steve: So what's the big deal? Sounds to me like it would save you time and effort.

Jan: Right! The balance sheet showed a minus for supplies!

Steve: Minus supplies? How can that be?

Jan: That's what I asked.

Steve: So, what did he say?

Jan: Well, after he checked the program, he said that it must be right. The minuses were greater than the pluses. . . .

Steve: Didn't he know that Supplies can't have a credit balance—it must have a debit balance?

Jan: He asked me what a debit and credit were.

Steve: I see your point.

1. ▭▭▸ Comment on (a) the desirability of computerizing Cupboard Supplies Co.'s financial reporting system, (b) the elimination of the end-of-period spreadsheet (work sheet) in a computerized accounting system, and (c) the computer programmer's lack of accounting knowledge.
2. ▭▭▸ Explain to the programmer why Supplies could not have a credit balance.

SA 4-3
Financial statements

Assume that you recently accepted a position with the First Security Bank as an assistant loan officer. As one of your first duties, you have been assigned the responsibility of evaluating a loan request for $80,000 from DiamondJewelry.com, a small corporation. In support of the loan application, Marion Zastrow, owner, submitted a "Statement of Accounts" (trial balance) for the first year of operations ended December 31, 2008.

DiamondJewelry.com
Statement of Accounts
December 31, 2008

Cash	2,050	
Billings Due from Others	15,070	
Supplies (chemicals, etc.)	7,470	
Trucks	26,370	
Equipment	8,090	
Amounts Owed to Others		2,850
Investment in Business		23,500
Service Revenue		73,650
Wages Expense	30,050	
Utilities Expense	7,330	
Rent Expense	2,400	
Insurance Expense	700	
Other Expenses	470	
	100,000	100,000

1. ▭▭▸ Explain to Marion Zastrow why a set of financial statements (income statement, retained earnings statement, and balance sheet) would be useful to you in evaluating the loan request.
2. In discussing the "Statement of Accounts" with Marion Zastrow, you discovered that the accounts had not been adjusted at December 31. Analyze the "Statement of Accounts" and indicate possible adjusting entries that might be necessary before an accurate set of financial statements could be prepared.
3. ▭▭▸ Assuming that an accurate set of financial statements will be submitted by Marion Zastrow in a few days, what other considerations or information would you require before making a decision on the loan request?

SA 4-4
Compare balance sheets

Group Project

Internet Project

In groups of three or four, compare the balance sheets of two different companies, and present to the class a summary of the similarities and differences of the two companies. You may obtain the balance sheets you need from one of the following sources:

1. Your school or local library.
2. The investor relations department of each company.
3. The company's Web site on the Internet.
4. EDGAR (Electronic Data Gathering, Analysis, and Retrieval), the electronic archives of financial statements filed with the Securities and Exchange Commission.

SEC documents can be retrieved using the EdgarScan™ service from Pricewaterhouse-Coopers at **http://edgarscan.pwcglobal.com**. To obtain annual report information, key in a company name in the appropriate space. EdgarScan will list the reports available to you for the company you've selected. Select the most recent annual report filing, identified as a 10-K or 10-K405. EdgarScan provides an outline of the report, including the separate financial statements, which can also be selected in an Excel® spreadsheet.

Answers to Self-Examination Questions

1. **C**   The dividends account (answer C) would be extended to the Balance Sheet columns of the work sheet. Utilities Expense (answer A), Rent Revenue (answer B), and Miscellaneous Expense (answer D) would all be extended to the Income Statement columns of the work sheet.

2. **D**   Cash or other assets that are expected to be converted to cash or sold or used up within one year or less, through the normal operations of the business, are classified as current assets on the balance sheet. Accounts Receivable (answer D) is a current asset, since it will normally be converted to cash within one year. Office Equipment (answer A), Land (answer B), and Accumulated Depreciation (answer C) are all reported in the property, plant, and equipment section of the balance sheet.

3. **B**   The entry to close the dividends account is to debit the retained earnings account and credit the dividends account (answer B).

4. **D**   Since all revenue and expense accounts are closed at the end of the period, Fees Earned (answer A), Wages Expense (answer B), and Rent Expense (answer C) would all be closed to Income Summary. Accumulated Depreciation (answer D) is a contra asset account that is not closed.

5. **B**   Since the post-closing trial balance includes only balance sheet accounts (all of the revenue, expense, and dividends accounts are closed), Cash (answer A), Accumulated Depreciation (answer C), and Capital Stock (answer D) would appear on the post-closing trial balance. Fees Earned (answer B) is a temporary account that is closed prior to preparing the post-closing trial balance.

Accounting for Merchandising Businesses

objectives

After studying this chapter, you should be able to:

1 *Distinguish between the activities and financial statements of service and merchandising businesses.*

2 *Describe and illustrate the financial statements of a merchandising business.*

3 Describe and illustrate the accounting for merchandise transactions including:
- sale of merchandise
- purchase of merchandise
- transportation costs, sales taxes, and trade discounts
- dual nature of merchandising transactions

4 *Describe the adjusting and closing process for a merchandising business.*

Whole Foods Market

When you buy groceries, textbooks, school supplies, or an automobile, you are doing business with either a retail or a merchandising business. One such merchandising business is Whole Foods Market, the world's leading retailer of natural and organic foods. Whole Foods obtains its products locally and around the world, with a unique commitment to sustainable agriculture. In addition, Whole Foods has distinguished itself by placing 15th on the Fortune ®100 Best Companies to Work For.

Assume you bought groceries at Whole Foods Market and received the receipt such as shown below.

```
             WHOLE
             FOODS
             M A R K E T

*      365 FRENCH ROAST 2      9.99 B
****  TAX    .39    BAL       10.38

      Cash                    20.00

      CHANGE                   9.62

TOTAL NUMBER OF ITEMS SOLD = 1
 2/24/06   3:32 PM 0713 10 0064 706

     Your cashier today is MAX
    Thank You For Shopping at
 Whole Foods Buckhead 404-324-4100
```

This receipt indicates that one item was purchased totaling $9.99, the sales tax was $0.39 (4%), the total due was $10.38, the clerk was given $20.00, and change of $9.62 was given back to the customer. The receipt also indicates that the sale was made by Buckhead Store of the Whole Foods Market chain, located in Atlanta, Georgia. The date and time of the sale and other data used internally by the store are also indicated.

As you may have guessed from the preceding receipt, the accounting for a merchandising business is more complex than that for a service business. For example, the accounting system for a merchandiser must be designed to record the receipt of goods for resale, keep track of the goods available for sale, and record the sale and cost of the merchandise sold.

In this chapter, we will focus on the accounting principles and concepts for merchandising businesses. We begin our discussion by highlighting the basic differences between the activities of merchandise and service businesses. We then describe and illustrate financial statements for merchandising businesses and purchases and sales transactions.

Nature of Merchandising Businesses

objective 1

Distinguish between the activities and financial statements of service and merchandising businesses.

@netsolutions

How do the activities of NetSolutions, an attorney, and an architect, which are service businesses, differ from those of Wal-Mart or Best Buy, which are merchandising businesses? These differences are best illustrated by focusing on the revenues and expenses in the following condensed income statements:

Service Business		Merchandising Business	
Fees earned	$XXX	Sales	$XXX
Operating expenses	−XXX	Cost of merchandise sold	−XXX
Net income	$XXX	Gross profit	$XXX
		Operating expenses	−XXX
		Net income	$XXX

The revenue activities of a service business involve providing services to customers. On the income statement for a service business, the revenues from services are reported as *fees earned*. The operating expenses incurred in providing the services are subtracted from the fees earned to arrive at *net income*.

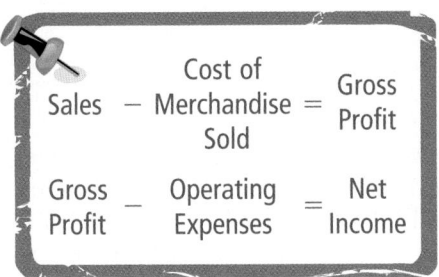

$$\text{Sales} - \begin{array}{c}\text{Cost of}\\ \text{Merchandise}\\ \text{Sold}\end{array} = \begin{array}{c}\text{Gross}\\ \text{Profit}\end{array}$$

$$\begin{array}{c}\text{Gross}\\ \text{Profit}\end{array} - \begin{array}{c}\text{Operating}\\ \text{Expenses}\end{array} = \begin{array}{c}\text{Net}\\ \text{Income}\end{array}$$

In contrast, the revenue activities of a merchandising business involve the buying and selling of merchandise. A merchandising business must first purchase merchandise to sell to its customers. When this merchandise is sold, the revenue is reported as sales, and its cost is recognized as an expense called the **cost of merchandise sold**. The cost of merchandise sold is subtracted from sales to arrive at gross profit. This amount is called **gross profit** because it is the profit *before* deducting operating expenses.

Merchandise on hand (not sold) at the end of an accounting period is called **merchandise inventory**. Merchandise inventory is reported as a current asset on the balance sheet.

In the remainder of this chapter, we illustrate merchandiser financial statements and transactions that affect the income statement (sales, cost of merchandise sold, and gross profit) and the balance sheet (merchandise inventory).

Example Exercise 5-1

objective 1

During the current year, merchandise is sold for $250,000 cash and for $975,000 on account. The cost of the merchandise sold is $735,000. What is the amount of the gross profit?

Follow My Example 5-1

The gross profit is $490,000 ($250,000 + $975,000 − $735,000).

For Practice: PE 5-1A, PE 5-1B

THE OPERATING CYCLE

The operations of a merchandising business involve the purchase of merchandise for sale (purchasing activity), the sale and distribution of the products to customers (sales activity), and the receipt of cash from customers (collection activity). This overall process is referred to as the *operating cycle*. Thus, the operating cycle begins with spending cash, and it ends with receiving cash from customers. The operating cycle for a merchandising business is shown below.

Operating cycles differ, depending upon the nature of the business and its operations. For example, the operating cycles for tobacco, distillery, and lumber industries are much longer than the operating cycles of the automobile, consumer electronics, and home furnishings industries. Likewise, the operating cycles for retailers are usually shorter than for manufacturers because retailers purchase goods in a form ready for sale to the customer. Of course, some retailers will have shorter operating cycles than others because of the nature of their products. For example, a jewelry store or an automobile dealer normally has a longer operating cycle than a consumer electronics store or a grocery store.

Businesses with longer operating cycles normally have higher profit margins on their products than businesses with shorter operating cycles. For example, it is not unusual for jewelry stores to price their jewelry at 30%–50% above cost. In contrast, grocery stores operate on very small profit margins, often below 5%. Grocery stores make up the difference by selling their products more quickly.

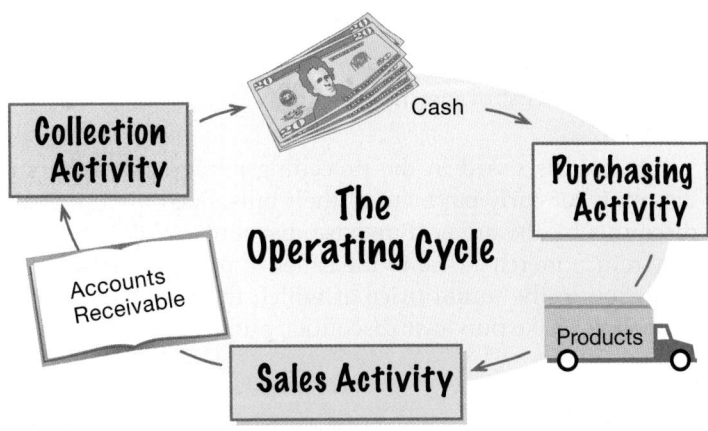

Financial Statements for a Merchandising Business

objective   **2**

Describe and illustrate the financial statements of a merchandising business.

@netsolutions

In this section, we illustrate the financial statements for NetSolutions after it becomes a retailer of computer hardware and software. During 2007, we assume that Chris Clark implemented the second phase of NetSolutions' business plan. Accordingly, Chris notified clients that beginning July 1, 2008, NetSolutions would be terminating its consulting services. Instead, it would become a personalized retailer.

NetSolutions' business strategy is to focus on offering personalized service to individuals and small businesses who are upgrading or purchasing new computer systems. NetSolutions' personal service before the sale will include a no-obligation, on-site assessment of the customer's computer needs. By providing tailor-made solutions, personalized service, and follow-up, Chris feels that NetSolutions can compete effectively against larger retailers, such as Best Buy or Office Depot, Inc.

MULTIPLE-STEP INCOME STATEMENT

The 2009 income statement for NetSolutions is shown in Exhibit 1.[1] This form of income statement, called a **multiple-step income statement**, contains several sections, subsections, and subtotals.

Sales is the total amount charged customers for merchandise sold, including cash sales and sales on account. Both sales returns and allowances and sales discounts are subtracted in arriving at net sales.

Sales returns and allowances are granted by the seller to customers for damaged or defective merchandise. For example, rather than have a buyer return merchandise, a seller may offer a $500 allowance to the customer as compensation for damaged merchandise. Sales returns and allowances are recorded when the merchandise is returned or when the allowance is granted by the seller.

Sales discounts are granted by the seller to customers for early payment of amounts owed. For example, a seller may offer a customer a 2% discount on a sale of $10,000 if the customer pays within 10 days. If the customer pays within the 10-day period, the seller receives cash of $9,800 and the buyer receives a discount of $200 ($10,000 × 2%). Sales discounts are recorded when the customer pays the bill.

Net sales is determined by subtracting sales returns and allowances and sales discounts from sales. Rather than reporting sales, sales returns and allowances, and sales discounts as shown in Exhibit 1, many companies report only net sales.

Cost of merchandise sold is the cost of the merchandise sold to customers. To illustrate the determination of the cost of merchandise sold, assume that NetSolutions purchased $340,000 of merchandise during the last half of 2008. If the inventory at December 31, 2008, the end of the year, is $59,700, the cost of the merchandise sold during 2007 is $280,300.

For many merchandising businesses, the cost of merchandise sold is usually the largest expense. For example, the approximate percentage of cost of merchandise sold to sales is 61% for JCPenney and 67% for The Home Depot.

Purchases	$340,000
Less merchandise inventory, December 31, 2008	59,700
Cost of merchandise sold	$280,300

As we discussed in the preceding paragraphs, sellers may offer customers sales discounts for early payment of their bills. Such discounts are referred to as **purchases discounts** by the buyer. Purchase discounts reduce the cost of merchandise. A buyer may return merchandise to the seller (a **purchase return**), or the buyer may receive a reduction in the initial price at which the merchandise was purchased (a **purchase allowance**). Like purchase discounts, purchases returns and allowances reduce the cost

---

1 We use the NetSolutions income statement for 2009 as a basis for illustration because, as will be shown, it allows us to better illustrate the computation of the cost of merchandise sold.

EXHIBIT 1 Multiple-Step Income Statement

NetSolutions
Income Statement
For the Year Ended December 31, 2009

Revenue from sales:			
Sales		$720 1 8 5 00	
Less: Sales returns and allowances	$ 6 1 4 0 00		
Sales discounts	5 7 9 0 00	11 9 3 0 00	
Net sales			$708 2 5 5 00
Cost of merchandise sold			525 3 0 5 00
Gross profit			$182 9 5 0 00
Operating expenses:			
Selling expenses:			
Sales salaries expense	$53 4 3 0 00		
Advertising expense	10 8 6 0 00		
Depr. expense—store equipment	3 1 0 0 00		
Delivery expense	2 8 0 0 00		
Miscellaneous selling expense	6 3 0 00		
Total selling expenses		$ 70 8 2 0 00	
Administrative expenses:			
Office salaries expense	$21 0 2 0 00		
Rent expense	8 1 0 0 00		
Depr. expense—office equipment	2 4 9 0 00		
Insurance expense	1 9 1 0 00		
Office supplies expense	6 1 0 00		
Misc. administrative expense	7 6 0 00		
Total administrative expenses		34 8 9 0 00	
Total operating expenses			105 7 1 0 00
Income from operations			$ 77 2 4 0 00
Other income and expense:			
Rent revenue		$ 6 0 0 00	
Interest expense		(2 4 4 0 00)	(1 8 4 0 00)
Net income			$ 75 4 0 0 00

of merchandise purchased during a period. In addition, transportation costs paid by the buyer for merchandise also increase the cost of merchandise purchased.

To continue the illustration, assume that during 2009 NetSolutions purchased additional merchandise of $521,980. It received credit for purchases returns and allowances of $9,100, took purchases discounts of $2,525, and paid transportation costs of $17,400. The purchases returns and allowances and the purchases discounts are deducted from the total purchases to yield the **net purchases**. The transportation costs, termed **transportation in**, are added to the net purchases to yield the **cost of merchandise purchased** of $527,755, as shown below.

Purchases		$521,980
Less: Purchases returns and allowances	$9,100	
Purchases discounts	2,525	11,625
Net purchases		$510,355
Add transportation in		17,400
Cost of merchandise purchased		$527,755

The ending inventory of NetSolutions on December 31, 2008, $59,700, becomes the beginning inventory for 2009. This beginning inventory is added to the cost of merchandise purchased to yield **merchandise available for sale**. The ending inventory, which is assumed to be $62,150, is then subtracted from the merchandise available for sale to yield the cost of merchandise sold of $525,305, as shown in Exhibit 2.

EXHIBIT 2   Cost of Merchandise Sold

Merchandise inventory, January 1, 2009			$ 59,700
Purchases		$521,980	
Less: Purchases returns and allowances	$9,100		
Purchases discounts	2,525	11,625	
Net purchases		$510,355	
Add transportation in		17,400	
Cost of merchandise purchased			527,755
Merchandise available for sale			$587,455
Less merchandise inventory, December 31, 2009 . .			62,150
Cost of merchandise sold			$525,305

The cost of merchandise sold was determined by deducting the merchandise on hand at the end of the period from the merchandise available for sale during the period. The merchandise on hand at the end of the period is determined by taking a physical count of inventory on hand. This method of determining the cost of merchandise sold and the amount of merchandise on hand is called the **periodic system** of accounting for merchandise inventory. Under the periodic system, the inventory records do not show the amount available for sale or the amount sold during the period. In contrast, under the **perpetual system** of accounting for merchandise inventory, each purchase and sale of merchandise is recorded in the inventory and the cost of merchandise sold accounts. As a result, the amount of merchandise available for sale and the amount sold are continuously (perpetually) disclosed in the inventory records.

Most large retailers and many small merchandising businesses use computerized perpetual inventory systems. Such systems normally use bar codes, such as the one on the back of this textbook. An optical scanner reads the bar code to record merchandise purchased and sold. Merchandise businesses using a perpetual inventory system report the cost of merchandise sold as a single line on the income statement, as shown in Exhibit 1 for NetSolutions. Merchandise businesses using the periodic inventory system report the cost of merchandise sold by using the format shown in Exhibit 2. Because of its wide use, we will use the perpetual inventory system throughout the remainder of this chapter. The periodic inventory system is described and illustrated in the appendix at the end of this chapter.

Gross profit is determined by subtracting the cost of merchandise sold from net sales. Exhibit 1 shows that NetSolutions reported gross profit of $182,950 in 2009. *Operating income*, sometimes called **income from operations**, is determined by subtracting operating expenses from gross profit. Most merchandising businesses classify operating expenses as either selling expenses or administrative expenses. Expenses that are incurred directly in the selling of merchandise are **selling expenses**. They include such expenses as salespersons' salaries, store supplies used, depreciation of store equipment, delivery expense, and advertising. Expenses incurred in the administration or general operations of the business are **administrative expenses** or *general expenses*. Examples of these expenses are office salaries, depreciation of office equipment, and office supplies used. Credit card expense is also normally classified as an administrative expense. Although selling and administrative expenses may be reported separately, many companies report operating expenses as a single item.

Retailers, such as Best Buy, Sears Holding Corporation, and Wal-Mart, and grocery store chains, such as Winn-Dixie Stores, Inc. and Kroger, use bar codes and optical scanners as part of their computerized inventory systems.

Other income and expense is reported on NetSolutions' income statement in Exhibit 1. Revenue from sources other than the primary operating activity of a business is classified as **other income**. In a merchandising business, these items include income from interest, rent, and gains resulting from the sale of fixed assets.

Expenses that cannot be traced directly to operations are identified as **other expense**. Interest expense that results from financing activities and losses incurred in the disposal of fixed assets are examples of these items.

Other income and other expense are offset against each other on the income statement, as shown in Exhibit 1. If the total of other income exceeds the total of other expense, the difference is added to income from operations to determine net income. If the reverse is true, the difference is subtracted from income from operations.

Example Exercise 5-2   objective 2

Based upon the following data, determine the cost of merchandise sold for May. Follow the format used in Exhibit 2.

Merchandise inventory, May 1	$121,200
Merchandise inventory, May 31	142,000
Purchases	985,000
Purchases returns and allowances	23,500
Purchases discounts	21,000
Transportation in	11,300

Follow My Example 5-2

Cost of merchandise sold:

Merchandise inventory, May 1			$ 121,200
Purchases		$985,000	
Less: Purchases returns and allowances	$23,500		
Purchases discounts	21,000	44,500	
Net purchases		$940,500	
Add transportation in		11,300	
Cost of merchandise purchased			951,800
Merchandise available for sale			$1,073,000
Less merchandise inventory, May 31			142,000
Cost of merchandise sold			$ 931,000

For Practice: PE 5-2A, PE 5-2B

SINGLE-STEP INCOME STATEMENT

An alternate form of income statement is the **single-step income statement**. As shown in Exhibit 3, the income statement for NetSolutions deducts the total of all expenses *in one step* from the total of all revenues.

The single-step form emphasizes total revenues and total expenses as the factors that determine net income. A criticism of the single-step form is that such amounts as gross profit and income from operations are not readily available for analysis.

RETAINED EARNINGS STATEMENT

The retained earnings statement for NetSolutions is shown in Exhibit 4. This statement is prepared in the same manner that we described previously for a service business.

BALANCE SHEET

As we discussed and illustrated in previous chapters, the balance sheet may be presented with assets on the left-hand side and the liabilities and stockholders' equity on

EXHIBIT 3

Single-Step Income Statement

NetSolutions Income Statement For the Year Ended December 31, 2009		
Revenues:		
Net sales		$708 255 00
Rent revenue		6 00 00
Total revenues		$708 855 00
Expenses:		
Cost of merchandise sold	$525 305 00	
Selling expenses	70 820 00	
Administrative expenses	34 890 00	
Interest expense	2 440 00	
Total expenses		633 455 00
Net income		$ 75 400 00

EXHIBIT 4

Retained Earnings Statement for Merchandising Business

NetSolutions Retained Earnings Statement For the Year Ended December 31, 2009		
Retained earnings, January 1, 2009		$128 800 00
Net income for year	$75 400 00	
Less dividends	18 000 00	
Increase in retained earnings		57 400 00
Retained earnings, December 31, 2009		$186 200 00

Business Connections

H&R BLOCK VERSUS THE HOME DEPOT

H&R Block is a service business that primarily offers tax planning and preparation to its customers. The Home Depot is the world's largest home improvement retailer and the second largest merchandise business in the United States. The differences in the operations of a service and merchandise business are illustrated in their income statements, as shown below.

As will be discussed in a later chapter, corporations are subject to income taxes. Thus, the income statements of H&R Block and Home Depot report "income taxes" as a deduction from "income before income taxes" in arriving at net income. This is in contrast to a proprietorship, which is not subject to income taxes.

H&R Block
Condensed Income Statement
For the Year Ending April 30, 2005
(in millions)

Revenue	$4,420
Operating expenses	3,368
Operating income	$1,052
Other income (expense)	(34)
Income before taxes	$1,018
Income taxes	382
Net income	$ 636

The Home Depot
Condensed Income Statement
For the Year Ending January 30, 2005
(in millions)

Net sales	$73,094
Cost of merchandise sold	48,664
Gross profit	$24,430
Operating expenses	16,504
Operating income	$ 7,926
Other income (expense)	(14)
Income before taxes	$ 7,912
Income taxes	2,911
Net income	$ 5,001

the right-hand side. This form of the balance sheet is called the **account form**. The balance sheet may also be presented in a downward sequence in three sections. This form of balance sheet is called the **report form**. The report form of balance sheet for Net-Solutions is shown in Exhibit 5. In this balance sheet, note that merchandise inventory at the end of the period is reported as a current asset and that the current portion of the note payable is $5,000.

EXHIBIT 5

Report Form of
Balance Sheet

NetSolutions
Balance Sheet
December 31, 2009

Assets				
Current assets:				
Cash			$ 52 9 5 0 00	
Accounts receivable			91 0 8 0 00	
Merchandise inventory			62 1 5 0 00	
Office supplies			4 8 0 00	
Prepaid insurance			2 6 5 0 00	
Total current assets				$209 3 1 0 00
Property, plant, and equipment:				
Land			$ 20 0 0 0 00	
Store equipment	$27 1 0 0 00			
Less accumulated depreciation	5 7 0 0 00		21 4 0 0 00	
Office equipment	$15 5 7 0 00			
Less accumulated depreciation	4 7 2 0 00		10 8 5 0 00	
Total property, plant, and equipment				52 2 5 0 00
Total assets				$261 5 6 0 00
Liabilities				
Current liabilities:				
Accounts payable			$ 22 4 2 0 00	
Note payable (current portion)			5 0 0 0 00	
Salaries payable			1 1 4 0 00	
Unearned rent			1 8 0 0 00	
Total current liabilities				$ 30 3 6 0 00
Long-term liabilities:				
Note payable (final payment due 2019)				20 0 0 0 00
Total liabilities				$ 50 3 6 0 00
Stockholders' Equity				
Capital stock			$ 25 0 0 0 00	
Retained earnings			186 2 0 0 00	
Total stockholders' equity				211 2 0 0 00
Total liabilities and stockholders' equity				$261 5 6 0 00

objective **3**

Describe and illustrate the accounting for merchandise transactions including:
- *sale of merchandise*
- *purchase of merchandise*
- *transportation costs, sales taxes, and trade discounts*
- *dual nature of merchandising transactions*

Merchandising Transactions

In the preceding section, we described and illustrated the financial statements of a merchandising business, NetSolutions. In this section, we describe and illustrate the recording of merchandise transactions including sales, purchases, transportation costs, and sales taxes. We also discuss trade discounts and the dual nature of merchandising transactions. As a basis for recording merchandise transactions, we begin by describing the chart of accounts for a merchandising business.

CHART OF ACCOUNTS FOR A MERCHANDISING BUSINESS

The chart of accounts for a merchandising business should reflect the elements of the financial statements we described and illustrated in the preceding section. The chart of

EXHIBIT 6

Chart of Accounts for NetSolutions' Merchandising Business

Balance Sheet Accounts	Income Statement Accounts
100 Assets	**400 Revenues**
110 Cash	410 Sales
112 Accounts Receivable	411 Sales Returns and Allowances
115 Merchandise Inventory	412 Sales Discounts
116 Office Supplies	**500 Costs and Expenses**
117 Prepaid Insurance	510 Cost of Merchandise Sold
120 Land	520 Sales Salaries Expense
123 Store Equipment	521 Advertising Expense
124 Accumulated Depreciation— Store Equipment	522 Depreciation Expense—Store Equipment
125 Office Equipment	523 Delivery Expense
126 Accumulated Depreciation— Office Equipment	529 Miscellaneous Selling Expense
	530 Office Salaries Expense
200 Liabilities	531 Rent Expense
210 Accounts Payable	532 Depreciation Expense—Office Equipment
211 Salaries Payable	533 Insurance Expense
212 Unearned Rent	534 Office Supplies Expense
215 Notes Payable	539 Misc. Administrative Expense
300 Stockholders' Equity	**600 Other Income**
310 Capital Stock	610 Rent Revenue
311 Retained Earnings	**700 Other Expense**
312 Dividends	710 Interest Expense
313 Income Summary	

accounts for NetSolutions is shown in Exhibit 6. The accounts related to merchandising transactions are shown in color.

NetSolutions is now using three-digit account numbers, which permits it to add new accounts as they are needed. The first digit indicates the major financial statement classification (1 for assets, 2 for liabilities, and so on). The second digit indicates the subclassification (e.g., 11 for current assets, 12 for noncurrent assets). The third digit identifies the specific account (e.g., 110 for Cash, 123 for Store Equipment).

NetSolutions is using a more complex numbering system because it has a greater variety of transactions. In addition, its growth creates a need for more detailed information for use in managing it. For example, a wages expense account was adequate for NetSolutions when it was a small service business with few employees. However, as a merchandising business, NetSolutions now uses two payroll accounts, one for Sales Salaries Expense and one for Office Salaries Expense. In the following paragraphs, we use the accounts appearing in Exhibit 6 to record various merchandising transactions of NetSolutions.

SALES TRANSACTIONS

Merchandise transactions are recorded in a journal and posted to the accounts, using the rules of debit and credit that we described and illustrated in earlier chapters. This simple manual system is often modified, however, to more efficiently record transactions. For example, as the number of suppliers increases, the ledger becomes unwieldy when a separate account for each supplier is included. Thus, individual accounts payable to suppliers may be placed in a separate ledger, called a **subsidiary ledger**. Similarly, individual accounts receivable from customers and individual items of merchandise inventory may be placed in a subsidiary ledger. Each subsidiary ledger is represented in the primary ledger (now called the **general ledger**) by a summarizing account, called a **controlling account**. The balance of this controlling account must equal the sum of the balances of the individual accounts in the subsidiary ledger. For example, the accounts payable controlling account must equal the sum of the balances of the accounts in the accounts payable subsidiary ledger.[2]

---

2 Subsidiary ledgers are further described and illustrated in Appendix C.

In this section, we illustrate the recording of sales transactions made for cash and on account. In addition, we describe and illustrate the recording of transactions involving sales discounts and sales returns and allowances.

Cash Sales A business may sell merchandise for cash. Cash sales are normally rung up (entered) on a cash register and recorded in the accounts. To illustrate, assume that on January 3, NetSolutions sells merchandise for $1,800. These cash sales can be recorded as follows:

			JOURNAL			Page 25
Date			Description	Post. Ref.	Debit	Credit
2009 Jan.	3	Cash			1 8 0 0 00	
			Sales			1 8 0 0 00
			To record cash sales.			

Under the perpetual inventory system, the cost of merchandise sold and the reduction in merchandise inventory should also be recorded. In this way, the merchandise inventory account will indicate the amount of merchandise on hand (not sold). To illustrate, assume that the cost of merchandise sold on January 3 was $1,200. The entry to record the cost of merchandise sold and the reduction in the merchandise inventory is as follows:

Jan.	3	Cost of Merchandise Sold			1 2 0 0 00	
		Merchandise Inventory				1 2 0 0 00
		To record the cost of merch. sold.				

In recent years, a large percentage of retail sales have been made to customers who use credit cards such as MasterCard or VISA. How do retailers record sales made with the use of credit cards? Such sales are recorded as cash sales. This is because the retailer normally receives payment within a few days of making the sale. Specifically, such sales are normally processed by a clearing-house that contacts the bank that issued the card. The issuing bank then electronically transfers cash directly to the retailer's bank account.[3] Thus, if the customers in the preceding sales had used MasterCards to pay for their purchases, the sales would be recorded exactly as shown above. Any processing fees charged by the clearing-house or issuing bank are periodically recorded as an expense as shown below.

Jan.	31	Credit Card Expense			4 8 00	
		Cash				4 8 00
		To record service charges on credit				
		card sales for the month.				

Instead of using MasterCard or VISA, a customer may use a credit card that is not issued by a bank, such as American Express or Discover. If the seller uses a clearing-house, the clearing-house will collect the receivable and transfer the cash to the retailer's bank account similar to the way it would have if the customer had used MasterCard or VISA. Large businesses, however, may not use a clearing-house. In such cases, nonbank credit card sales must first be reported to the card company before cash is received. Thus, a receivable is created with the nonbank credit card company.

---

3 CyberSource is one of the major credit card clearing-houses. For a more detailed description of how credit card sales are processed, see the following CyberSource Web page: **http://www.cybersource.com/products_and_services/electronic_payments/credit_card_processing/howitworks.xml.**

However, since most retailers use clearing-houses to process both bank and nonbank credit cards, we will record all credit card sales as cash sales.

Sales on Account   A business may sell merchandise on account. The seller records such sales as a debit to Accounts Receivable and a credit to Sales. An example of an entry for a NetSolutions sale on account of $510 follows. The cost of merchandise sold was $280.

Jan.	12	Accounts Receivable—Sims Co.	5 1 0 00	
		Sales		5 1 0 00
		Invoice No. 7172.		
	12	Cost of Merchandise Sold	2 8 0 00	
		Merchandise Inventory		2 8 0 00
		Cost of merch. sold on Invoice No. 7172.		

Sales Discounts   The terms of a sale are normally indicated on the **invoice** or bill that the seller sends to the buyer. An example of a sales invoice for NetSolutions is shown in Exhibit 7.

EXHIBIT 7   Invoice

106-8

netsolutions
Invoice

5101 Washington Ave.
Cincinnati, OH 45227-5101

Made in U.S.A.

SOLD TO	**CUSTOMER'S ORDER NO. & DATE**
Omega Technologies	412 Jan. 10, 2009
1000 Matrix Blvd.	
San Jose, CA 95116–1000	

DATE SHIPPED	**HOW SHIPPED AND ROUTE**	**TERMS**	**INVOICE DATE**
Jan. 12, 2009	US Express Trucking Co.	2/10, n/30	Jan. 12, 2009
FROM	**F.O.B.**		
Cincinnati	Cincinnati		

QUANTITY	**DESCRIPTION**	**UNIT PRICE**	**AMOUNT**
10	3COM Megahertz 10/100 Lan PC Card	150.00	1,500.00

The terms for when payments for merchandise are to be made, agreed on by the buyer and the seller, are called the **credit terms**. If payment is required on delivery, the terms are *cash* or *net cash*. Otherwise, the buyer is allowed an amount of time, known as the **credit period**, in which to pay.

The credit period usually begins with the date of the sale as shown on the invoice. If payment is due within a stated number of days after the date of the invoice, such as 30 days, the terms are *net 30 days*. These terms may be written as *n/30*.[4] If payment is due by the end of the month in which the sale was made, the terms are written as *n/eom*.

---

4 The word *net* as used here does not have the usual meaning of a number after deductions have been subtracted, as in *net income*.

As a means of encouraging the buyer to pay before the end of the credit period, the seller may offer a discount. For example, a seller may offer a 2% discount if the buyer pays within 10 days of the invoice date. If the buyer does not take the discount, the total amount is due within 30 days. These terms are expressed as *2/10, n/30* and are read as 2% *discount if paid within 10 days, net amount due within 30 days*. The credit terms of 2/10, n/30 are summarized in Exhibit 8, using the information from the invoice in Exhibit 7.

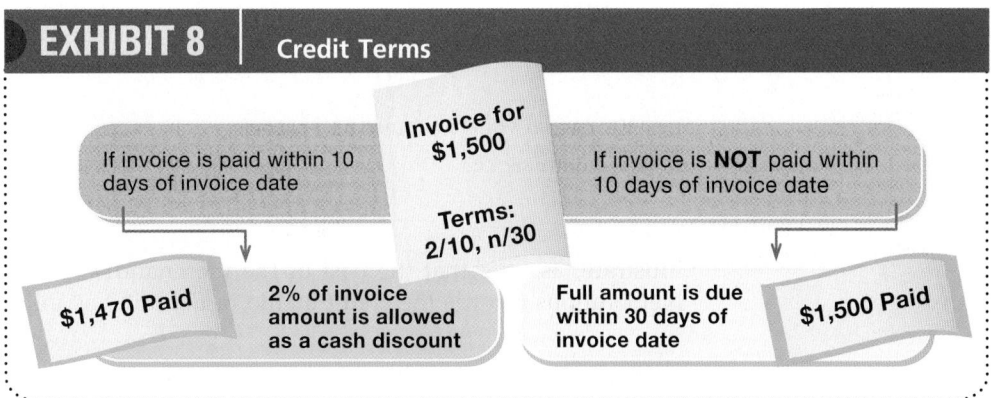

EXHIBIT 8 | **Credit Terms**

Invoice for $1,500

Terms: 2/10, n/30

If invoice is paid within 10 days of invoice date

$1,470 Paid

2% of invoice amount is allowed as a cash discount

If invoice is **NOT** paid within 10 days of invoice date

Full amount is due within 30 days of invoice date

$1,500 Paid

Discounts taken by the buyer for early payment are recorded as sales discounts by the seller. Since managers may want to know the amount of the sales discounts for a period, the seller normally records the sales discounts in a separate account. The sales discounts account is a *contra* (or *offsetting*) account to Sales. To illustrate, assume that cash is received within the discount period (10 days) from the credit sale of $1,500, shown on the invoice in Exhibit 7. NetSolutions would record the receipt of the cash as follows:

Jan.	22	Cash		1 4 7 0 00	
		Sales Discounts		3 0 00	
		Accounts Receivable—Omega Tech.			1 5 0 0 00
		Collection on Invoice No. 106-8, less			
		2% discount.			

Sales Returns and Allowances   Merchandise sold may be returned to the seller (**sales return**). In addition, because of defects or for other reasons, the seller may reduce the initial price at which the goods were sold (**sales allowance**). If the return or allowance is for a sale on account, the seller usually issues the buyer a **credit memorandum**. This memorandum shows the amount of and the reason for the seller's credit to an account receivable. A credit memorandum issued by NetSolutions is illustrated in Exhibit 9.

Like sales discounts, sales returns and allowances reduce sales revenue. They also result in additional shipping and other expenses. Since managers often want to know the amount of returns and allowances for a period, the seller records sales returns and allowances in a separate account. Sales Returns and Allowances is a *contra* (or *offsetting*) account to Sales.

The seller debits Sales Returns and Allowances for the amount of the return or allowance. If the original sale was on account, the seller credits Accounts Receivable. Since the merchandise inventory is kept up to date in a perpetual system, the seller adds the cost of the returned merchandise to the merchandise inventory account. The seller must also credit the cost of returned merchandise to the cost of merchandise sold account, since this account was debited when the original sale was recorded. To

REAL WORLD

Book publishers often experience large returns if a book is not immediately successful. For example, 35% of adult hardcover books shipped to retailers are returned to publishers, according to the Association of American Publishers.

EXHIBIT 9

Credit Memorandum

@netsolutions

No. 32

5101 Washington Ave.
Cincinnati, OH 45227–5101

CREDIT MEMORANDUM

TO	DATE
Krier Company	January 13, 2009
7608 Melton Avenue	
Los Angeles, CA 90025-3942	

WE CREDIT YOUR ACCOUNT AS FOLLOWS

1 Controller Kit	225.00

illustrate, assume that the cost of the merchandise returned in Exhibit 9 was $140. NetSolutions records the credit memo in Exhibit 9 as follows:

Jan.	13	Sales Returns and Allowances	2 2 5 00	
		Accounts Receivable—Krier Company		2 2 5 00
		Credit Memo No. 32.		

Jan.	13	Merchandise Inventory	1 4 0 00	
		Cost of Merchandise Sold		1 4 0 00
		Cost of merchandise returned, Credit		
		Memo No. 32.		

What if the buyer pays for the merchandise and the merchandise is later returned? In this case, the seller may issue a credit and apply it against other accounts receivable owed by the buyer, or the cash may be refunded. If the credit is applied against the buyer's other receivables, the seller records entries similar to those preceding. If cash is refunded for merchandise returned or for an allowance, the seller debits Sales Returns and Allowances and credits Cash.

Example Exercise 5-3   objective **3**

Journalize the following merchandise transactions:

a. Sold merchandise on account, $7,500 with terms 2/10, n/30. The cost of the merchandise sold was $5,625.
b. Received payment less the discount.

Follow My Example 5-3

a.	Accounts Receivable	7,500	
	Sales		7,500
	Cost of Merchandise Sold	5,625	
	Merchandise Inventory		5,625
b.	Cash	7,350	
	Sales Discounts	150	
	Accounts Receivable		7,500

For Practice: PE 5-3A, PE 5-3B

Integrity, Objectivity, and Ethics in Business

ETHICS

THE CASE OF THE FRAUDULENT PRICE TAGS

One of the challenges for a retailer is policing its sales return policy. There are many ways in which customers can unethically or illegally abuse such policies. In one case, a couple was accused of attaching Marshalls' store price tags to cheaper merchandise bought or obtained else- where. The couple then returned the cheaper goods and received the substantially higher refund amount. Company security officials discovered the fraud and had the couple arrested after they had allegedly bilked the company for over $1 million.

PURCHASE TRANSACTIONS

As we indicated earlier in this chapter, most large retailers and many small merchandising businesses use computerized perpetual inventory systems. Under the perpetual inventory system, cash purchases of merchandise are recorded as follows:

		JOURNAL			Page 24
Date		Description	Post. Ref.	Debit	Credit
2009 Jan.	3	Merchandise Inventory		2 5 1 0 00	
		Cash			2 5 1 0 00
		Purchased inventory from Bowen Co.			

Purchases of merchandise on account are recorded as follows:

Jan.	4	Merchandise Inventory		9 2 5 0 00	
		Accounts Payable—Thomas Corporation			9 2 5 0 00
		Purchased inventory on account.			

Purchases Discounts   Purchases discounts taken by the buyer for early payment of an invoice reduce the cost of the merchandise purchased. Most businesses design their accounting systems so that all available discounts are taken. Even if the buyer has to borrow to make the payment within a discount period, it is normally to the buyer's advantage to do so. To illustrate, assume that Alpha Technologies issues an invoice for $3,000 to NetSolutions, dated March 12, with terms 2/10, n/30. The last day of the discount period in which the $60 discount can be taken is March 22. Assume that in order to pay the invoice on March 22, NetSolutions borrows the money for the remaining 20 days of the credit period. If we assume an annual interest rate of 6% and a 360-day year, the interest on the loan of $2,940 ($3,000 − $60) is $9.80 ($2,940 × 6% × 20/360). The net savings to NetSolutions is $50.20, computed as follows:

Discount of 2% on $3,000	$60.00
Interest for 20 days at rate of 6% on $2,940	−9.80
Savings from borrowing	$50.20

The savings can also be seen by comparing the interest rate on the money *saved* by taking the discount and the interest rate on the money *borrowed* to take the discount. For NetSolutions, the interest rate on the money saved in this example is estimated by converting 2% for 20 days to a yearly rate, as follows:

$$2\% \times \frac{360 \text{ days}}{20 \text{ days}} = 2\% \times 18 = 36\%$$

If NetSolutions borrows the money to take the discount, it *pays* interest of 6%. If NetSolutions does not take the discount, it *pays* estimated interest of 36% for using the $2,940 for an additional 20 days.

Under the perpetual inventory system, the buyer initially debits the merchandise inventory account for the amount of the invoice. When paying the invoice, the buyer credits the merchandise inventory account for the amount of the discount. In this way, the merchandise inventory shows the *net* cost to the buyer. For example, NetSolutions would record the Alpha Technologies invoice and its payment at the end of the discount period as follows:

Mar.	12	Merchandise Inventory	3 0 0 0 00	
		Accounts Payable—Alpha Technologies		3 0 0 0 00
	22	Accounts Payable—Alpha Technologies	3 0 0 0 00	
		Cash		2 9 4 0 00
		Merchandise Inventory		6 0 00

If NetSolutions does not take the discount because it does not pay the invoice until April 11, it would record the payment as follows:

Apr.	11	Accounts Payable—Alpha Technologies	3 0 0 0 00	
		Cash		3 0 0 0 00

Purchases Returns and Allowances   When merchandise is returned (**purchases return**) or a price adjustment is requested (**purchases allowance**), the buyer (debtor) usually sends the seller a letter or a debit memorandum. A **debit memorandum**, shown in Exhibit 10, informs the seller of the amount the buyer proposes to *debit* to the account payable due the seller. It also states the reasons for the return or the request for a price reduction.

The buyer may use a copy of the debit memorandum as the basis for recording the return or allowance or wait for approval from the seller (creditor). In either case, the buyer must debit Accounts Payable and credit Merchandise Inventory. To illustrate,

EXHIBIT 10

Debit Memorandum

@netsolutions
5101 Washington Ave.
Cincinnati, OH 45227–5101

No. 18

DEBIT MEMORANDUM

TO	DATE
Maxim Systems	March 7, 2009
7519 East Willson Ave.	
Seattle, WA 98101–7519	

WE DEBIT YOUR ACCOUNT AS FOLLOWS

	@ 90.00	900.00
10 Server Network Interface Cards, your Invoice No. 7291, are being returned via parcel post. Our order specified No. 825X.		

NetSolutions records the return of the merchandise indicated in the debit memo in Exhibit 10 as follows:

Mar.	7	Accounts Payable—Maxim Systems	9 0 0 00	
		Merchandise Inventory		9 0 0 00
		Debit Memo No. 18.		

When a buyer returns merchandise or has been granted an allowance prior to paying the invoice, the amount of the debit memorandum is deducted from the invoice amount. The amount is deducted before the purchase discount is computed. For example, assume that on May 2, NetSolutions purchases $5,000 of merchandise from Delta Data Link, subject to terms 2/10, n/30. On May 4, NetSolutions returns $3,000 of the merchandise, and on May 12, NetSolutions pays the original invoice less the return. NetSolutions would record these transactions as follows:

May	2	Merchandise Inventory	5 0 0 0 00	
		Accounts Payable—Delta Data Link		5 0 0 0 00
		Purchased merchandise.		
	4	Accounts Payable—Delta Data Link	3 0 0 0 00	
		Merchandise Inventory		3 0 0 0 00
		Returned portion of merch. purchased.		
	12	Accounts Payable—Delta Data Link	2 0 0 0 00	
		Cash		1 9 6 0 00
		Merchandise Inventory		4 0 00
		Paid invoice [($5,000 − $3,000) × 2% = $40; $2,000 − $40 = $1,960].		

Example Exercise 5-4   objective **3**

Rofles Company purchased merchandise on account from a supplier for $11,500, terms 2/10, n/30. Rofles Company returned $3,000 of the merchandise and received full credit.

a.   If Rofles Company pays the invoice within the discount period, what is the amount of cash required for the payment?

b.   Under a perpetual inventory system, what account is credited by Rofles Company to record the return?

Follow My Example 5-4

a. $8,330. Purchase of $11,500 less the return of $3,000 less the discount of $170 [($11,500 − $3,000) × 2%].

b.   Merchandise Inventory

For Practice: PE 5-4A, PE 5-4B

TRANSPORTATION COSTS, SALES TAXES, AND TRADE DISCOUNTS

In the preceding two sections, we described and illustrated merchandise transactions involving sales and purchases. In this section, we discuss merchandise transactions involving transportation costs, sales taxes, and trade discounts.

REAL WORLD

Transportation Costs   The terms of a sale should indicate when the ownership (title) of the merchandise passes to the buyer. This point determines which party, the buyer or the seller, must pay the transportation costs.[5]

The ownership of the merchandise may pass to the buyer when the seller delivers the merchandise to the transportation company or freight carrier. For example, DaimlerChrysler records the sale and the transfer of ownership of its vehicles to dealers when the vehicles are shipped from the factory. In this case, the terms are said to be **FOB (free on board) shipping point**. This term means that the dealer pays the transportation costs from the shipping point (factory) to the final destination. Such costs are part of the dealer's total cost of purchasing inventory and should be added to the cost of the inventory by debiting Merchandise Inventory.

To illustrate, assume that on June 10, NetSolutions buys merchandise from Magna Data on account, $900, terms FOB shipping point, and pays the transportation cost of $50. NetSolutions records these two transactions as follows:

June	10	Merchandise Inventory		9 0 0 00	
		Accounts Payable—Magna Data			9 0 0 00
		Purchased merchandise, terms FOB			
		shipping point.			
	10	Merchandise Inventory		5 0 00	
		Cash			5 0 00
		Paid shipping cost on merchandise			
		purchased.			

The ownership of the merchandise may pass to the buyer when the buyer receives the merchandise. In this case, the terms are said to be **FOB (free on board) destination**. This term means that the seller delivers the merchandise to the buyer's final destination, free of transportation charges to the buyer. The seller thus pays the transportation costs to the final destination. The seller debits Delivery Expense or Transportation Out, which is reported on the seller's income statement as an expense.

To illustrate, assume that on June 15, NetSolutions sells merchandise to Kranz Company on account, $700, terms FOB destination. The cost of the merchandise sold is $480, and NetSolutions pays the transportation cost of $40. NetSolutions records the sale, the cost of the sale, and the transportation cost as follows:

June	15	Accounts Receivable—Kranz Company		7 0 0 00	
		Sales			7 0 0 00
		Sold merchandise, terms FOB			
		destination.			
	15	Cost of Merchandise Sold		4 8 0 00	
		Merchandise Inventory			4 8 0 00
		Recorded cost of merchandise sold to			
		Kranz Company.			
	15	Delivery Expense		4 0 00	
		Cash			4 0 00
		Paid shipping cost on merch. sold.			

---

5 The passage of title also determines whether the buyer or seller must pay other costs, such as the cost of insurance, while the merchandise is in transit.

As a convenience to the buyer, the seller may prepay the transportation costs, even though the terms are FOB shipping point. The seller will then add the transportation costs to the invoice. The buyer will debit Merchandise Inventory for the total amount of the invoice, including the transportation costs. Any discount terms would not apply to the prepaid transportation costs.

To illustrate, assume that on June 20, NetSolutions sells merchandise to Planter Company on account, $800, terms FOB shipping point. NetSolutions pays the transportation cost of $45 and adds it to the invoice. The cost of the merchandise sold is $360. NetSolutions records these transactions as follows:

June	20	Accounts Receivable—Planter Company		800 00	
		Sales			800 00
		Sold merch., terms FOB shipping point.			
	20	Cost of Merchandise Sold		360 00	
		Merchandise Inventory			360 00
		Recorded cost of merchandise sold to			
		Planter Company.			
	20	Accounts Receivable—Planter Company		45 00	
		Cash			45 00
		Prepaid shipping cost on merch. sold.			

Shipping terms, the passage of title, and whether the buyer or seller is to pay the transportation costs are summarized in Exhibit 11.

Example Exercise 5-5   objective 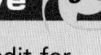 3

Determine the amount to be paid in full settlement of each of invoices (a) and (b), assuming that credit for returns and allowances was received prior to payment and that all invoices were paid within the discount period.

	Merchandise	Transportation Paid by Seller	Transportation Terms	Returns and Allowances
a.	$4,500	$200	FOB shipping point, 1/10, n/30	$ 800
b.	5,000	60	FOB destination, 2/10, n/30	2,500

Follow My Example 5-5

a. $3,863. Purchase of $4,500 less return of $800 less the discount of $37 [($4,500 − $800) × 1%] plus $200 of shipping.
b. $2,450. Purchase of $5,000 less return of $2,500 less the discount of $50 [($5,000 − $2,500) × 2%].

For Practice: PE 5-5A, PE 5-5B

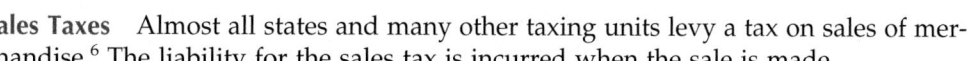

Sales Taxes   Almost all states and many other taxing units levy a tax on sales of merchandise.[6] The liability for the sales tax is incurred when the sale is made.

At the time of a cash sale, the seller collects the sales tax. When a sale is made on account, the seller charges the tax to the buyer by debiting Accounts Receivable. The seller credits the sales account for the amount of the sale and credits the tax to Sales

---

6 Businesses that purchase merchandise for resale to others are normally exempt from paying sales taxes on their purchases. Only final buyers of merchandise normally pay sales taxes.

EXHIBIT 11 | Transportation Terms

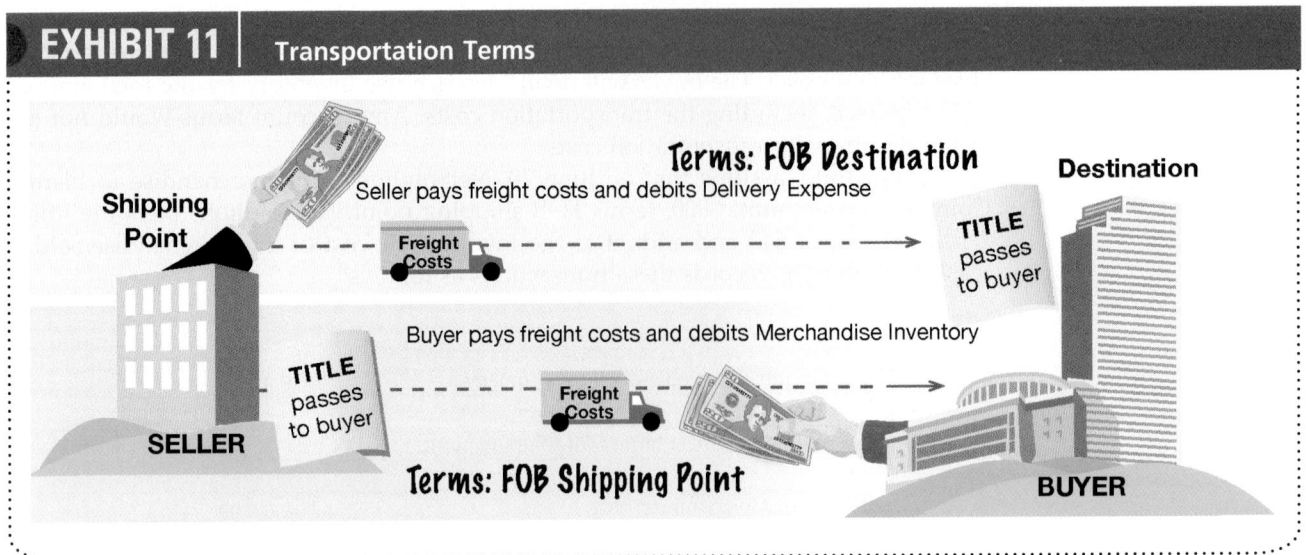

Tax Payable. For example, the seller would record a sale of $100 on account, subject to a tax of 6%, as follows:

Aug.	12	Accounts Receivable—Lemon Co.	1 0 6 00	
		Sales		1 0 0 00
		Sales Tax Payable		6 00
		Invoice No. 339.		

Normally on a regular basis, the seller pays to the taxing unit the amount of the sales tax collected. The seller records such a payment as follows:

Sept.	15	Sales Tax Payable	2 9 0 0 00	
		Cash		2 9 0 0 00
		Payment for sales taxes collected		
		during August.		

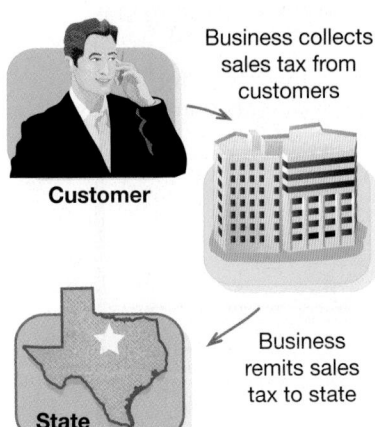

Trade Discounts   Wholesalers are businesses that sell merchandise to other businesses rather than to the general public. Many wholesalers publish catalogs. Rather than updating their catalogs frequently, wholesalers often publish price updates, which may involve large discounts from the list prices in their catalogs. In addition, wholesalers may offer special discounts to certain classes of buyers, such as government agencies or businesses that order large quantities. Such discounts are called **trade discounts**.

Sellers and buyers do not normally record the list prices of merchandise and the related trade discounts in their accounts. For example, assume that an item has a list price of $1,000 and a 40% trade discount. The seller records the sale of the item at $600 [$1,000 less the trade discount of $400 ($1,000 × 40%)]. Likewise, the buyer records the purchase at $600.

DUAL NATURE OF MERCHANDISE TRANSACTIONS

Each merchandising transaction affects a buyer and a seller. In the illustration on the next page, we show how the same transactions would be recorded by both the seller and the buyer. In this example, the seller is Scully Company and the buyer is Burton Co.

Transaction	Scully Company (Seller)			Burton Co. (Buyer)		

July 1. Scully Company sold merchandise on account to Burton Co., $7,500, terms FOB shipping point, n/45. The cost of the merchandise sold was $4,500.	Accounts Receivable—Burton Co.
	  Sales
		7,500	7,500	Merchandise Inventory
				  Accounts Payable—Scully Co.
					7,500	7,500

	Cost of Merchandise Sold Merchandise Inventory	4,500	4,500			
July 2. Burton Co. paid transportation charges of $150 on July 1 purchase from Scully Company.	No entry.			Merchandise Inventory Cash	150	150

July 5. Scully Company sold merchandise on account to Burton Co., $5,000, terms FOB destination, n/30. The cost of the merchandise sold was $3,500.	Accounts Receivable—Burton Co.
	  Sales
		5,000	5,000	Merchandise Inventory
				  Accounts Payable—Scully Co.
					5,000	5,000

	Cost of Merchandise Sold Merchandise Inventory	3,500	3,500			
July 7. Scully Company paid transportation costs of $250 for delivery of merchandise sold to Burton Co. on July 5.	Delivery Expense Cash	250	250	No entry.		

July 13. Scully Company issued Burton Co. a credit memorandum for merchandise returned, $1,000. The merchandise had been purchased by Burton Co. on account on July 5. The cost of the merchandise returned was $700.	Sales Returns and Allowances
	  Accounts Receivable—Burton Co.
		1,000	1,000	Accounts Payable—Scully Co.
				  Merchandise Inventory
					1,000	1,000

	Merchandise Inventory Cost of Merchandise Sold	700	700			

July 15. Scully Company received payment from Burton Co. for purchase of July 5.	Cash
	  Accounts Receivable—Burton Co.
		4,000	4,000	Accounts Payable—Scully Co.
				  Cash
					4,000	4,000

July 18. Scully Company sold merchandise on account to Burton Co., $12,000, terms FOB shipping point, 2/10, n/eom. Scully Company prepaid transportation costs of $500, which were added to the invoice. The cost of the merchandise sold was $7,200.	Accounts Receivable—Burton Co.
	  Sales
		12,000	12,000	Merchandise Inventory
				  Accounts Payable—Scully Co.
					12,500	12,500

	Accounts Receivable—Burton Co. Cash	500	500			
	Cost of Merchandise Sold Merchandise Inventory	7,200	7,200			

July 28. Scully Company received payment from Burton Co. for purchase of July 18, less discount (2% × $12,000).	Cash
	Sales Discounts
	  Accounts Receivable—Burton Co.
		12,260
		240
			12,500	Accounts Payable—Scully Co.
				  Merchandise Inventory
				  Cash
					12,500	240
						12,260

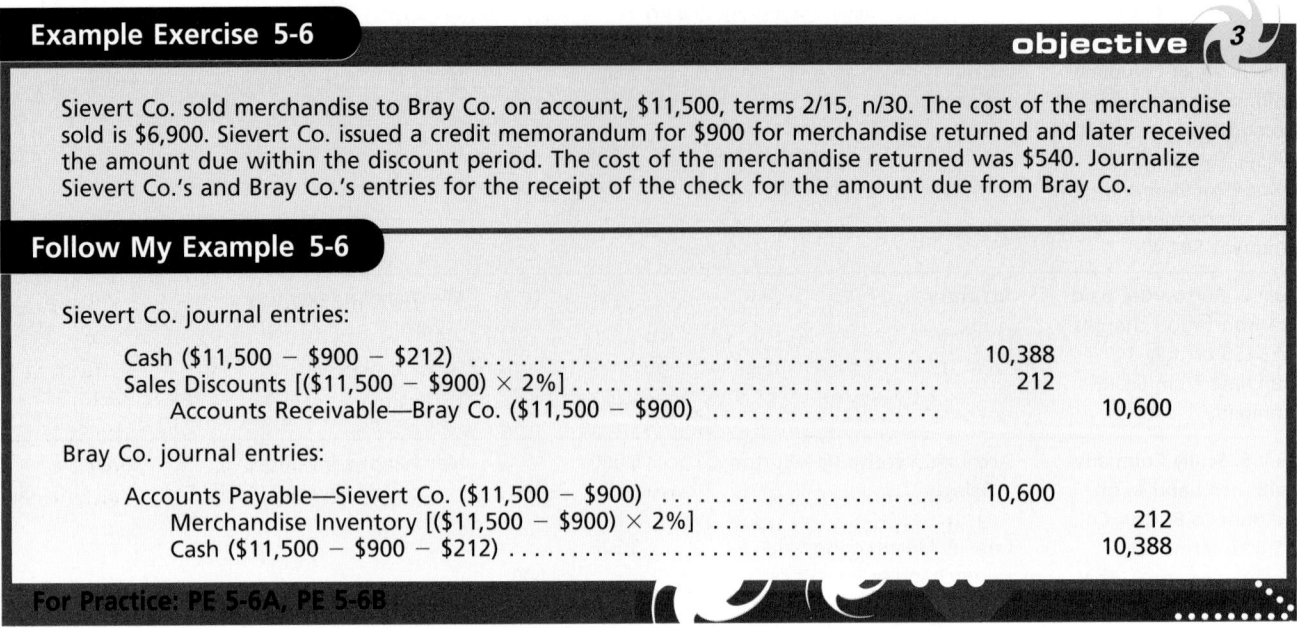

Example Exercise 5-6   objective **3**

Sievert Co. sold merchandise to Bray Co. on account, $11,500, terms 2/15, n/30. The cost of the merchandise sold is $6,900. Sievert Co. issued a credit memorandum for $900 for merchandise returned and later received the amount due within the discount period. The cost of the merchandise returned was $540. Journalize Sievert Co.'s and Bray Co.'s entries for the receipt of the check for the amount due from Bray Co.

Follow My Example 5-6

Sievert Co. journal entries:

Cash ($11,500 − $900 − $212)	10,388	
Sales Discounts [($11,500 − $900) × 2%]	212	
Accounts Receivable—Bray Co. ($11,500 − $900)		10,600

Bray Co. journal entries:

Accounts Payable—Sievert Co. ($11,500 − $900)	10,600	
Merchandise Inventory [($11,500 − $900) × 2%]		212
Cash ($11,500 − $900 − $212)		10,388

For Practice: PE 5-6A, PE 5-6B

The Adjusting and Closing Process

objective **4**

Describe the adjusting and closing process for a merchandising business.

@netsolutions

$62,150
Actual Inventory Per Physical Count

$1,800
Shrinkage

$63,950
Available For Sale Per Records

We have described and illustrated the chart of accounts and the analysis and recording of transactions for a merchandising business. We have also illustrated the preparation of financial statements for a merchandiser, NetSolutions. In the remainder of this chapter, we describe the adjusting and closing process for a merchandising business. In this discussion, we will focus primarily on the elements of the accounting cycle that are likely to differ from those of a service business.

ADJUSTING ENTRY FOR INVENTORY SHRINKAGE

Under the perpetual inventory system, a separate merchandise inventory account is maintained in the ledger. During the accounting period, this account shows the amount of merchandise for sale at any time. However, merchandising businesses may experience some loss of inventory due to shoplifting, employee theft, or errors in recording or counting inventory. As a result, the physical inventory taken at the end of the accounting period may differ from the amount of inventory shown in the inventory records. Normally, the amount of merchandise for sale, as indicated by the balance of the merchandise inventory account, is larger than the total amount of merchandise counted during the physical inventory. For this reason, the difference is often called **inventory shrinkage** or *inventory shortage*.

To illustrate, NetSolutions' inventory records indicate that $63,950 of merchandise should be available for sale on December 31, 2009. The physical inventory taken on December 31, 2009, however, indicates that only $62,150 of merchandise is actually available. Thus, the inventory shrinkage for the year ending December 31, 2009, is $1,800 ($63,950 − $62,150), as shown at the left. This amount is recorded by the following adjusting entry:

		Adjusting Entry			
Dec.	31	Cost of Merchandise Sold		1 8 0 0 00	
		Merchandise Inventory			1 8 0 0 00
		Inv. shrinkage ($63,950 − $62,150).			

Retailers lose an estimated $30 billion to inventory shrinkage. The primary causes of the shrinkage are employee theft and shoplifting.

After this entry has been recorded, the accounting records agree with the actual physical inventory at the end of the period. Since no system of procedures and safeguards can totally eliminate it, inventory shrinkage is often considered a normal cost of operations. If the amount of the shrinkage is abnormally large, it may be disclosed separately on the income statement. In such cases, the shrinkage may be recorded in a separate account, such as Loss from Merchandise Inventory Shrinkage.[7]

CLOSING ENTRIES

The closing entries for a merchandising business are similar to those for a service business. The first entry closes the temporary accounts with credit balances, such as Sales, to the income summary account. The second entry closes the temporary accounts with debit balances, including Sales Returns and Allowances, Sales Discounts, and Cost of Merchandise Sold, to the income summary account. The third entry closes the balance of the income summary account to the retained earnings account. The fourth entry closes the dividends account to the retained earnings account. The closing entries for NetSolutions are shown below.

		JOURNAL			Page 29
	Date	Item	Post. Ref.	Debit	Credit
1		Closing Entries				1
2	2009 Dec. 31	Sales	410	720 1 8 5 00		2
3		Rent Revenue	610	6 0 0 00		3
4		Income Summary	313		720 7 8 5 00	4
5						5
6	31	Income Summary	313	645 3 8 5 00		6
7		Sales Returns and Allowances	411		6 1 4 0 00	7
8		Sales Discounts	412		5 7 9 0 00	8
9		Cost of Merchandise Sold	510		525 3 0 5 00	9
10		Sales Salaries Expense	520		53 4 3 0 00	10
11		Advertising Expense	521		10 8 6 0 00	11
12		Depr. Expense—Store Equipment	522		3 1 0 0 00	12
13		Delivery Expense	523		2 8 0 0 00	13
14		Miscellaneous Selling Expense	529		6 3 0 00	14
15		Office Salaries Expense	530		21 0 2 0 00	15
16		Rent Expense	531		8 1 0 0 00	16
17		Depr. Expense—Office Equipment	532		2 4 9 0 00	17
18		Insurance Expense	533		1 9 1 0 00	18
19		Office Supplies Expense	534		6 1 0 00	19
20		Misc. Administrative Expense	539		7 6 0 00	20
21		Interest Expense	710		2 4 4 0 00	21
22						22
23	31	Income Summary	313	75 4 0 0 00		23
24		Retained Earnings	311		75 4 0 0 00	24
25						25
26	31	Retained Earnings	311	18 0 0 0 00		26
27		Dividends	312		18 0 0 0 00	27

The balance of Income Summary, after the first two closing entries have been posted, is the net income or net loss for the period. The third closing entry transfers

---

7 The adjusting process for a merchandising business may be aided by preparing an end-of-period spreadsheet (work sheet). An end-of-period spreadsheet (work sheet) for a merchandising business is described and illustrated in Appendix D.

this balance to the retained earnings account. NetSolutions' income summary account after the closing entries have been posted is as follows:

ACCOUNT *Income Summary*					ACCOUNT NO. *313*	
		Post.			Balance	
Date	Item	Ref.	Debit	Credit	Debit	Credit
2009 Dec. 31	Revenues	29		720 78 5 00		720 78 5 00
31	Expenses	29	645 38 5 00			75 40 0 00
31	Net income	29	75 40 0 00		—	—

After the closing entries have been prepared and posted to the accounts, a post-closing trial balance may be prepared to verify the debit-credit equality. The only accounts that should appear on the post-closing trial balance are the asset, contra asset, liability, and stockholders' equity accounts with balances. These are the same accounts that appear on the end-of-period balance sheet.

Example Exercise 5-7   objective  4

Pulmonary Company's perpetual inventory records indicate that $382,800 of merchandise should be on hand on March 31, 2008. The physical inventory indicates that $371,250 of merchandise is actually on hand. Journalize the adjusting entry for the inventory shrinkage for Pulmonary Company for the year ended March 31, 2008.

Follow My Example 5-7

Mar. 31	Cost of Merchandise Sold	11,550	
	Merchandise Inventory		11,550
	Inventory shrinkage ($382,800 − $371,250).		

For Practice: PE 5-7A, PE 5-7B

FINANCIAL ANALYSIS AND INTERPRETATION

The ratio of net sales to assets measures how effectively a business is using its assets to generate sales. A high ratio indicates an effective use of assets. The assets used in computing the ratio may be the total assets at the end of the year, the average of the total assets at the beginning and end of the year, or the average of the monthly assets. For our purposes, we will use the average of the total assets at the beginning and end of the year. The ratio is computed as follows:

$$\text{Ratio of Net Sales to Assets} = \frac{\text{Net Sales}}{\text{Average Total Assets}}$$

To illustrate the use of this ratio, the following data (in millions) are taken from annual reports of Sears Holding Corporation and JCPenney:

	Sears	JCPenney
Total revenues (net sales)	$19,701	$18,424
Total assets:		
Beginning of year	6,074	18,300
End of year	8,651	14,127

The ratio of net sales to assets for each company is as follows:

	Sears	JCPenney
Ratio of net sales to assets	2.68*	1.14**

*$19,701/[($6,074 + $8,651)/2]
**$18,424/[($18,300 + $14,127)/2]

Based on these ratios, Sears appears better than JCPenney in utilizing its assets to generate sales. Comparing this ratio over time for both Sears and JCPenney, as well as comparing it with industry averages, would provide a better basis for interpreting the financial performance of each company.

Integrity, Objectivity, and Ethics in Business

THE COST OF EMPLOYEE THEFT

One survey reported that the 27 largest U.S. retail store chains have lost over $4.7 billion to shoplifting and employee theft. Of this amount, only 2.74% of the losses resulted in any recovery. The stores apprehended over 750,000 shoplifters and dishonest employees. Approximately 1 out of every 28 employees was apprehended for theft from his or her employer. Each dishonest employee stole approximately 6.6 times the amount stolen by shoplifters ($671 vs. $102).

Source: Jack L. Hayes International, 17th Annual Retail Theft Survey, 2004.

Appendix

The Periodic Inventory System

Throughout this chapter, we have emphasized the perpetual inventory system of accounting for purchases and sales of merchandise. Not all merchandise businesses, however, use the perpetual inventory system. For example, some small merchandise businesses, such as locally owned hardware stores, use manual accounting systems. Because a manual perpetual inventory system is time consuming and costly to maintain, the periodic inventory system may be used in these cases. In this appendix, we describe and illustrate the use of the periodic inventory system for recording merchandise transactions.

COST OF MERCHANDISE SOLD USING THE PERIODIC INVENTORY SYSTEM

@netsolutions

Using the periodic inventory system, the revenues from sales are recorded when sales are made in the same manner as in the perpetual inventory system. However, no attempt is made on the date of sale to record the cost of the merchandise sold. Instead, as we illustrated earlier in this chapter for NetSolutions, cost of merchandise sold is determined as shown in Exhibit 12.

CHART OF ACCOUNTS UNDER THE PERIODIC INVENTORY SYSTEM

The chart of accounts under a periodic inventory system is shown in Exhibit 13. The accounts used to record transactions under the periodic inventory system are highlighted in Exhibit 13. We describe and illustrate how these accounts are used to record transactions under the periodic inventory system next.

> **EXHIBIT 12**
>
> Determining Cost of Merchandise Sold Using the Periodic System

Merchandise inventory, January 1, 2009 . . .			$ 59,700
Purchases		$521,980	
Less: Purchases returns and allowances	$9,100		
Purchases discounts	2,525	11,625	
Net purchases		$510,355	
Add transportation in		17,400	
Cost of merchandise purchased			527,755
Merchandise available for sale			$587,455
Less merchandise inventory, Dec. 31, 2009 . .			62,150
Cost of merchandise sold			$525,305

EXHIBIT 13

Chart of Accounts Under the Periodic Inventory System

Balance Sheet Accounts		Income Statement Accounts	
	100 Assets		**400 Revenues**
110	Cash	410	Sales
111	Notes Receivable	411	Sales Returns and Allowances
112	Accounts Receivable	412	Sales Discounts
115	Merchandise Inventory		
116	Office Supplies		**500 Costs and Expenses**
117	Prepaid Insurance	510	Purchases
120	Land	511	Purchases Returns and
123	Store Equipment		Allowances
124	Accumulated Depreciation—	512	Purchases Discounts
	Store Equipment	513	Transportation In
125	Office Equipment	520	Sales Salaries Expense
126	Accumulated Depreciation—	521	Advertising Expense
	Office Equipment	522	Depreciation Expense—Store
			Equipment
	200 Liabilities	523	Delivery Expense
210	Accounts Payable	529	Miscellaneous Selling Expense
211	Salaries Payable	530	Office Salaries Expense
212	Unearned Rent	531	Rent Expense
215	Notes Payable	532	Depreciation Expense—Office
			Equipment
	300 Stockholders' Equity	533	Insurance Expense
310	Capital Stock	534	Office Supplies Expense
311	Retained Earnings	539	Misc. Administrative Expense
312	Dividends		
313	Income Summary		**600 Other Income**
		610	Rent Revenue
			700 Other Expense
		710	Interest Expense

RECORDING MERCHANDISE TRANSACTIONS UNDER THE PERIODIC INVENTORY SYSTEM

Using the periodic inventory system, purchases of inventory are recorded in a *purchases* account rather than in a merchandise inventory account. No attempt is made to keep a detailed record of the amount of inventory on hand at any given time. Instead, at the end of the period, a physical count of merchandise inventory is taken. This physical count is then used to determine the cost of merchandise sold as shown in Exhibit 12.

The purchases account is debited for the amount of the invoice before considering any purchases discounts. Purchases discounts are normally recorded in a separate *purchases discounts* account. The balance of this account is reported as a deduction from the amount initially recorded in Purchases for the period. Thus, the purchases discounts account is viewed as a contra (or offsetting) account to Purchases.

Purchases returns and allowances are recorded in a similar manner as purchases discounts. A separate *purchases returns and allowances* account is used to keep a record of the amount of returns and allowances during a period. Purchases returns and allowances are reported as a deduction from the amount initially recorded as Purchases. Like Purchases Discounts, the purchases returns and allowances account is a contra (or offsetting) account to Purchases.

When merchandise is purchased FOB shipping point, the buyer is responsible for paying the freight charges. Under the periodic inventory system, freight charges paid when purchasing merchandise FOB shipping point are debited to *Transportation In*, *Freight In*, or a similarly titled account.

The preceding periodic inventory accounts and their effect on the cost of merchandise purchased are summarized on page 237.

Account	Entry to Increase (Decrease)	Normal Balance	Effect on Cost of Merchandise Purchased
Purchases	Debit	Debit	Increases
Purchases Discounts	Credit	Credit	Decreases
Purchases Returns and Allowances	Credit	Credit	Decreases
Transportation In	Debit	Debit	Increases

Exhibit 14 illustrates the recording of merchandise transactions using the periodic system. As a review, Exhibit 14 also illustrates how each transaction would have been recorded using the perpetual system.

EXHIBIT 14 Transactions Using the Periodic and Perpetual Inventory Systems

Transaction	Periodic Inventory System		Perpetual Inventory System	
June 5. Purchased $30,000 of merchandise on account, terms 2/10, n/30.	Purchases 　Accounts Payable	30,000 　30,000	Merchandise Inventory 　Accounts Payable	30,000 　30,000
June 8. Returned merchandise purchased on account on June 5, $500.	Accounts Payable 　Purchases Returns and Allowances	500 　500	Accounts Payable 　Merchandise Inventory	500 　500
June 15. Paid for purchase of June 5, less return of $500 and discount of $590 [($30,000 − $500) × 2%].	Accounts Payable 　Cash 　Purchases Discounts	29,500 　28,910 　590	Accounts Payable 　Cash 　Merchandise Inventory	29,500 　28,910 　590
June 18. Sold merchandise on account, $12,500, 1/10, n/30. The cost of the merchandise sold was $9,000.	Accounts Receivable 　Sales	12,500 　12,500	Accounts Receivable 　Sales Cost of Merchandise Sold 　Merchandise Inventory	12,500 　12,500 9,000 　9,000
June 21. Received merchandise returned on account, $4,000. The cost of the merchandise returned was $2,800.	Sales Returns and Allowances 　Accounts Receivable	4,000 　4,000	Sales Returns and Allowances 　Accounts Receivable Merchandise Inventory 　Cost of Merchandise Sold	4,000 　4,000 2,800 　2,800
June 22. Purchased merchandise, $15,000, terms FOB shipping point, 2/15, n/30, with prepaid transportation charges of $750 added to the invoice.	Purchases Transportation In 　Accounts Payable	15,000 750 　15,750	Merchandise Inventory 　Accounts Payable	15,750 　15,750
June 28. Received $8,415 as payment on account from June 18 sale less return of June 21 and less discount of $85 [($12,500 − $4,000) × 1%].	Cash Sales Discount 　Accounts Receivable	8,415 85 　8,500	Cash Sales Discounts 　Accounts Receivable	8,415 85 　8,500
June 29. Received $19,600 from cash sales. The cost of the merchandise sold was $13,800.	Cash 　Sales	19,600 　19,600	Cash 　Sales Cost of Merchandise Sold 　Merchandise Inventory	19,600 　19,600 13,800 　13,800

ADJUSTING PROCESS UNDER THE PERIODIC INVENTORY SYSTEM

The adjusting process is the same under the periodic and perpetual inventory systems except for the inventory shrinkage adjustment. Under both the periodic and perpetual inventory systems, the ending merchandise inventory is determined by a physical count. Under the perpetual inventory system, the ending inventory physical count is then compared to the amounts in the inventory ledger, and the amount of inventory shrinkage is determined. This inventory shrinkage is recorded as a debit to Cost of Merchandise Sold and a credit to Merchandise Inventory.

Under the periodic inventory system, a separate inventory ledger is not maintained during the year. Instead, purchases of inventory are recorded in the *purchases* account. As a result, the inventory shrinkage cannot be directly determined but is included indirectly in the cost of merchandise sold computation shown in Exhibit 12. This is done at the end of the year when the merchandise inventory account is increased or decreased to the ending physical merchandise inventory, which we will describe later. A primary disadvantage of the periodic inventory system is that the amount of inventory shrinkage is not separately determined.

FINANCIAL STATEMENTS UNDER THE PERIODIC INVENTORY SYSTEM

The financial statements are essentially the same under both the perpetual and periodic inventory systems. When a multiple-step income statement is reported, cost of merchandise sold may be reported as shown in Exhibit 12.

CLOSING ENTRIES UNDER THE PERIODIC INVENTORY SYSTEM

The closing entries differ in the periodic inventory system in that there is no cost of merchandise sold account to be closed to Income Summary. Instead, the purchases, purchases discounts, purchases returns and allowances, and transportation in accounts are closed to Income Summary. In addition, the merchandise inventory account is adjusted to the physical inventory count through the closing process. To illustrate, the closing entries for NetSolutions under the periodic inventory system are shown at the top of the following page.

In the closing entries, the periodic accounts are highlighted. Under the perpetual inventory system, these highlighted periodic inventory accounts are replaced by the cost of merchandise sold account. Also, you should note that in the first closing entry Merchandise Inventory is debited for $62,150 to increase it to the ending physical inventory count on December 31, 2009. In the second closing entry, Merchandise Inventory is credited for its January 1, 2009, balance of $59,700. Including beginning and ending balances of Merchandise Inventory in both entries highlights its importance in determining cost of merchandise sold as shown in Exhibit 12. After the closing entries are posted, Merchandise Inventory will have a balance of $62,150, which is the amount reported on the December 31, 2009, balance sheet.

JOURNAL

	Date		Item	Post. Ref.	Debit	Credit	
1			Closing Entries				1
2	2009 Dec.	31	Merchandise Inventory	115	62 1 5 0 00		2
3			Sales	410	720 1 8 5 00		3
4			Purchases Returns and Allowances	511	9 1 0 0 00		4
5			Purchases Discounts	512	2 5 2 5 00		5
6			Rent Revenue	610	6 0 0 00		6
7			Income Summary	313		794 5 6 0 00	7
8							8
9		31	Income Summary	313	719 1 6 0 00		9
10			Merchandise Inventory	115		59 7 0 0 00	10
11			Sales Returns and Allowances	411		6 1 4 0 00	11
12			Sales Discounts	412		5 7 9 0 00	12
13			Purchases	510		521 9 8 0 00	13
14			Transportation In	513		17 4 0 0 00	14
15			Sales Salaries Expense	520		53 4 3 0 00	15
16			Advertising Expense	521		10 8 6 0 00	16
17			Depreciation Expense—Store Equipment	522		3 1 0 0 00	17
18			Delivery Expense	523		2 8 0 0 00	18
19			Miscellaneous Selling Expense	529		6 3 0 00	19
20			Office Salaries Expense	530		21 0 2 0 00	20
21			Rent Expense	531		8 1 0 0 00	21
22			Depreciation Expense—Office Equipment	532		2 4 9 0 00	22
23			Insurance Expense	533		1 9 1 0 00	23
24			Office Supplies Expense	534		6 1 0 00	24
25			Miscellaneous Administrative Expense	539		7 6 0 00	25
26			Interest Expense	710		2 4 4 0 00	26
27							27
28		31	Income Summary	313	75 4 0 0 00		28
29			Retained Earnings	311		75 4 0 0 00	29
30							30
31		31	Retained Earnings	311	18 0 0 0 00		31
32			Dividends	312		18 0 0 0 00	32

At a Glance

1. Distinguish between the activities and financial statements of service and merchandising businesses.

Key Points	Key Learning Outcomes	Example Exercises	Practice Exercises
The primary differences between a service business and a merchandising business relate to revenue activities. Merchandising businesses purchase merchandise for selling to customers. On a merchandising business's income statement, revenue from selling merchandise is reported as sales. The cost of the merchandise sold is subtracted from sales to arrive at gross profit. The operating expenses are subtracted from gross profit to arrive at net income. Merchandise inventory, which is merchandise not sold, is reported as a current asset on the balance sheet.	• Describe how the activities of a service and a merchandising business differ. • Describe the differences between the income statements of a service and a merchandising business. • Compute gross profit. • Describe how merchandise inventory is reported on the balance sheet.	5-1	5-1A, 5-1B

2. Describe and illustrate the financial statements of a merchandising business.

Key Points	Key Learning Outcomes	Example Exercises	Practice Exercises
The multiple-step income statement of a merchandiser reports sales, sales returns and allowances, sales discounts, and net sales. The cost of the merchandise sold is subtracted from net sales to determine the gross profit. The cost of merchandise sold is determined by using either the periodic or perpetual system. Operating income is determined by subtracting operating expenses from gross profit. Operating expenses are normally classified as selling or administrative expenses. Net income is determined by adding or subtracting the net of other income and expense. The income statement may also be reported in a single-step form. The retained earnings statement is similar to that for a service business. The balance sheet reports merchandise inventory at the end of the period as a current asset.	• Prepare a multiple-step income statement for a merchandising business. • Describe how cost of merchandise sold is determined under a periodic inventory system. • Compute cost of merchandise sold under a periodic inventory system as shown in Exhibit 2. • Prepare a single-step income statement. • Prepare a retained earnings statement for a merchandising business. • Prepare a balance sheet for a merchandising business.	5-2	5-2A, 5-2B

3. **Describe and illustrate the accounting for merchandise transactions including:**
    - **sale of merchandise**
    - **purchase of merchandise**
    - **transportation costs, sales taxes, and trade discounts**
    - **dual nature of merchandising transactions**

Key Points	Key Learning Outcomes	Example Exercises	Practice Exercises
Sales of merchandise for cash or on account are recorded by crediting Sales. Under the perpetual inventory system, the cost of merchandise sold and the reduction in merchandise inventory are also recorded for the sale. For sales of merchandise on account, the credit terms may allow discounts for early payment. Such discounts are recorded by the seller as a debit to Sales Discounts. Sales discounts are reported as a deduction from the amount initially recorded in Sales. Likewise, when merchandise is returned or a price adjustment is granted, the seller debits Sales Returns and Allowances.	• Prepare journal entries to record sales of merchandise for cash or using a credit card.		
	• Prepare journal entries to record sales of merchandise on account.	5-3	5-3A, 5-3B
	• Prepare journal entries to record sales discounts and sales returns and allowances.	5-3	5-3A, 5-3B
Purchases of merchandise for cash or on account are recorded by debiting Merchandise Inventory. For purchases of merchandise on account, the credit terms may allow cash discounts for early payment. Such purchases discounts are viewed as a reduction in the cost of the merchandise purchased. When merchandise is returned or a price adjustment is granted, the buyer credits Merchandise Inventory.	• Prepare journal entries to record the purchase of merchandise for cash.		
	• Prepare journal entries to record the purchase of merchandise on account.	5-4	5-4A, 5-4B
	• Prepare journal entries to record purchases discounts and purchases returns and allowances.	5-4	5-4A, 5-4B
When merchandise is shipped FOB shipping point, the buyer pays the transportation costs and debits Merchandise Inventory. When merchandise is shipped FOB destination, the seller pays the transportation costs and debits Transportation Out or Delivery Expense. If the seller prepays transportation costs as a convenience to the buyer, the seller debits Accounts Receivable for the costs.	• Prepare journal entries for transportation costs from the point of view of the buyer and seller.		
	• Determine the total cost of the purchase of merchandise under differing transportation terms.	5-5	5-5A, 5-5B
The liability for sales tax is incurred when the sale is made and is recorded by the seller as a credit to the sales tax payable account. When the amount of the sales tax is paid to the taxing unit, Sales Tax Payable is debited and Cash is credited.	• Prepare journal entries for the collection and payment of sales taxes by the seller.		
Many wholesalers offer trade discounts, which are discounts off the list prices of merchandise. Normally, neither the seller nor the buyer records the list price and the related trade discount in the accounts.	• Determine the cost of merchandise purchased when a trade discount is offered by the seller.		
Each merchandising transaction affects a buyer and a seller. The illustration in this chapter shows how the same transactions would be recorded by both.	• Record the same merchandise transactions for the buyer and seller.	5-6	5-6A, 5-6B

4. Describe the adjusting and closing process for a merchandising business.

Key Points	Key Learning Outcomes	Example Exercises	Practice Exercises
The accounting cycle for a merchandising business is similar to that of a service business. However, a merchandiser is likely to experience inventory shrinkage, which must be recorded. The normal adjusting entry is to debit Cost of Merchandise Sold and credit Merchandise Inventory for the amount of the shrinkage.

The closing entries for a merchandising business are similar to those for a service business. The first entry closes sales and other revenue to Income Summary. The second entry closes cost of merchandise sold, sales discounts, sales returns and allowances, and other expenses to Income Summary. The third entry closes the balance of Income Summary (the net income or net loss) to the retained earnings account. The fourth entry closes the dividends account to the retained earnings account. | • Prepare the adjusting journal entry for inventory shrinkage.

• Prepare the closing entries for a merchandise business. | 5-7 | 5-7A, 5-7B |

Key Terms

account form (219)
administrative expenses (general expenses) (216)
controlling account (220)
cost of merchandise purchased (215)
cost of merchandise sold (213)
credit memorandum (223)
credit period (222)
credit terms (222)
debit memorandum (226)
FOB (free on board) destination (228)
FOB (free on board) shipping point (228)

general ledger (220)
gross profit (213)
income from operations (operating income) (216)
inventory shrinkage (232)
invoice (222)
merchandise available for sale (216)
merchandise inventory (213)
multiple-step income statement (214)
net purchases (215)
net sales (214)
other expense (217)
other income (217)

periodic system (216)
perpetual system (216)
purchase return or allowance (214)
purchases discounts (214)
report form (219)
sales (214)
sales discounts (214)
sales returns and allowances (214)
selling expenses (216)
single-step income statement (217)
subsidiary ledger (220)
trade discounts (230)
transportation in (215)

Illustrative Problem

The following transactions were completed by Montrose Company during May of the current year. Montrose Company uses a perpetual inventory system.

May 3. Purchased merchandise on account from Floyd Co., $4,000, terms FOB shipping point, 2/10, n/30, with prepaid transportation costs of $120 added to the invoice.

5. Purchased merchandise on account from Kramer Co., $8,500, terms FOB destination, 1/10, n/30.

6. Sold merchandise on account to C. F. Howell Co., list price $4,000, trade discount 30%, terms 2/10, n/30. The cost of the merchandise sold was $1,125.

May 8. Purchased office supplies for cash, $150.

10. Returned merchandise purchased on May 5 from Kramer Co., $1,300.

13. Paid Floyd Co. on account for purchase of May 3, less discount.

14. Purchased merchandise for cash, $10,500.

15. Paid Kramer Co. on account for purchase of May 5, less return of May 10 and discount.

16. Received cash on account from sale of May 6 to C. F. Howell Co., less discount.

19. Sold merchandise on MasterCard credit cards, $2,450. The cost of the merchandise sold was $980.

22. Sold merchandise on account to Comer Co., $3,480, terms 2/10, n/30. The cost of the merchandise sold was $1,400.

24. Sold merchandise for cash, $4,350. The cost of the merchandise sold was $1,750.

25. Received merchandise returned by Comer Co. from sale on May 22, $1,480. The cost of the returned merchandise was $600.

31. Paid a service processing fee of $140 for MasterCard sales.

Instructions

1. Journalize the preceding transactions.
2. Journalize the adjusting entry for merchandise inventory shrinkage, $3,750.

Solution

1.	May 3	Merchandise Inventory		4,120	
		Accounts Payable—Floyd Co.			4,120
	5	Merchandise Inventory		8,500	
		Accounts Payable—Kramer Co.			8,500
	6	Accounts Receivable—C. F. Howell Co.		2,800	
		Sales			2,800
		[$4,000 − (30% × $4,000)].			
	6	Cost of Merchandise Sold		1,125	
		Merchandise Inventory			1,125
	8	Office Supplies		150	
		Cash			150
	10	Accounts Payable—Kramer Co.		1,300	
		Merchandise Inventory			1,300
	13	Accounts Payable—Floyd Co.		4,120	
		Merchandise Inventory			80
		Cash			4,040
		[$4,000 − (2% × $4,000) + $120].			
	14	Merchandise Inventory		10,500	
		Cash			10,500
	15	Accounts Payable—Kramer Co.		7,200	
		Merchandise Inventory			72
		Cash			7,128
		[($8,500 − $1,300) × 1% = $72;			
		$8,500 − $1,300 − $72 = $7,128].			
	16	Cash		2,744	
		Sales Discounts		56	
		Accounts Receivable—C. F. Howell Co.			2,800
	19	Cash		2,450	
		Sales			2,450
	19	Cost of Merchandise Sold		980	
		Merchandise Inventory			980
	22	Accounts Receivable—Comer Co.		3,480	
		Sales			3,480
	22	Cost of Merchandise Sold		1,400	
		Merchandise Inventory			1,400
	24	Cash		4,350	
		Sales			4,350
	24	Cost of Merchandise Sold		1,750	
		Merchandise Inventory			1,750

	May 25	Sales Returns and Allowances	1,480	
		Accounts Receivable—Comer Co.		1,480
	25	Merchandise Inventory	600	
		Cost of Merchandise Sold		600
	31	Credit Card Expense	140	
		Cash		140
2.	May 31	Cost of Merchandise Sold	3,750	
		Merchandise Inventory		3,750
		Inventory shrinkage.		

Self-Examination Questions
(Answers at End of Chapter)

1. If merchandise purchased on account is returned, the buyer may inform the seller of the details by issuing a(n):
   A. debit memorandum.
   B. credit memorandum.
   C. invoice.
   D. bill.

2. If merchandise is sold on account to a customer for $1,000, terms FOB shipping point, 1/10, n/30, and the seller prepays $50 in transportation costs, the amount of the discount for early payment would be:
   A. $0.   C. $10.00.
   B. $5.00.   D. $10.50.

3. The income statement in which the total of all expenses is deducted from the total of all revenues is termed the:
   A. multiple-step form.   C. account form.
   B. single-step form.   D. report form.

4. On a multiple-step income statement, the excess of net sales over the cost of merchandise sold is called:
   A. operating income.
   B. income from operations.
   C. gross profit.
   D. net income.

5. Which of the following expenses would normally be classified as other expense on a multiple-step income statement?
   A. Depreciation expense—office equipment
   B. Sales salaries expense
   C. Insurance expense
   D. Interest expense

Eye Openers

1. What distinguishes a merchandising business from a service business?
2. Can a business earn a gross profit but incur a net loss? Explain.
3. In computing the cost of merchandise sold, does each of the following items increase or decrease that cost? (a) transportation costs, (b) beginning merchandise inventory, (c) purchase discounts, (d) ending merchandise inventory.
4. Describe how the periodic system differs from the perpetual system of accounting for merchandise inventory.
5. Differentiate between the multiple-step and the single-step forms of the income statement.
6. What are the major advantages and disadvantages of the single-step form of income statement compared to the multiple-step statement?
7. What type of revenue is reported in the other income section of the multiple-step income statement?
8. Name at least three accounts that would normally appear in the chart of accounts of a merchandising business but would not appear in the chart of accounts of a service business.
9. How are sales to customers using MasterCard and VISA recorded?
10. The credit period during which the buyer of merchandise is allowed to pay usually begins with what date?
11. What is the meaning of (a) 2/10, n/60; (b) n/30; (c) n/eom?
12. What is the nature of (a) a credit memorandum issued by the seller of merchandise, (b) a debit memorandum issued by the buyer of merchandise?

13. Who bears the transportation costs when the terms of sale are (a) FOB shipping point, (b) FOB destination?
14. Pembroke Office Equipment, which uses a perpetual inventory system, experienced a normal inventory shrinkage of $13,762. What accounts would be debited and credited to record the adjustment for the inventory shrinkage at the end of the accounting period?
15. Assume that Pembroke Office Equipment in Eye Opener 14 experienced an abnormal inventory shrinkage of $215,650. Pembroke Office Equipment has decided to record the abnormal inventory shrinkage so that it would be separately disclosed on the income statement. What account would be debited for the abnormal inventory shrinkage?

Practice Exercises

PE 5-1A
Determine gross profit
obj. 1

During the current year, merchandise is sold for $127,500 cash and $435,600 on account. The cost of the merchandise sold is $422,325. What is the amount of the gross profit?

PE 5-1B
Determine gross profit
obj. 1

During the current year, merchandise is sold for $17,500 cash and $141,750 on account. The cost of the merchandise sold is $127,400. What is the amount of the gross profit?

PE 5-2A
Computing cost of merchandise sold
obj. 2

Based upon the following data, determine the cost of merchandise sold for July:

Merchandise inventory, July 1	$ 88,370
Merchandise inventory, July 31	92,120
Purchases	681,400
Purchases returns and allowances	9,250
Purchases discounts	7,000
Transportation in	3,180

PE 5-2B
Computing cost of merchandise sold
obj. 2

Based upon the following data, determine the cost of merchandise sold for April:

Merchandise inventory, April 1	$128,120
Merchandise inventory, April 30	140,500
Purchases	983,400
Purchases returns and allowances	10,250
Purchases discounts	8,000
Transportation in	5,680

PE 5-3A
Entries for sales transactions
obj. 3

Journalize the following merchandise transactions:

a. Sold merchandise on account, $12,250 with terms 2/10, n/30. The cost of the merchandise sold was $7,400.
b. Received payment less the discount.

PE 5-3B
Entries for sales transactions
obj. 3

Journalize the following merchandise transactions:

a. Sold merchandise on account, $22,500 with terms 1/10, n/30. The cost of the merchandise sold was $14,150.
b. Received payment less the discount.

PE 5-4A
Purchase transactions
obj. 3

Wilder Company purchased merchandise on account from a supplier for $7,500, terms 2/10, n/30. Wilder Company returned $1,500 of the merchandise and received full credit.

a. If Wilder Company pays the invoice within the discount period, what is the amount of cash required for the payment?
b. Under a perpetual inventory system, what account is credited by Wilder Company to record the return?

PE 5-4B
Purchase transactions
obj. 3

Gupta Company purchased merchandise on account from a supplier for $13,200, terms 1/10, n/30. Gupta Company returned $1,700 of the merchandise and received full credit.

a. If Gupta Company pays the invoice within the discount period, what is the amount of cash required for the payment?
b. Under a perpetual inventory system, what account is debited by Gupta Company to record the return?

PE 5-5A
Payments under different transportation terms
obj. 3

Determine the amount to be paid in full settlement of each of invoices (a) and (b), assuming that credit for returns and allowances was received prior to payment and that all invoices were paid within the discount period.

	Merchandise	Transportation Paid by Seller	Transportation Terms	Returns and Allowances
a.	$6,000	$400	FOB shipping point, 1/10, n/30	$1,000
b.	2,500	150	FOB destination, 2/10, n/30	900

PE 5-5B
Payments under different transportation terms
obj. 3

Determine the amount to be paid in full settlement of each of invoices (a) and (b), assuming that credit for returns and allowances was received prior to payment and that all invoices were paid within the discount period.

	Merchandise	Transportation Paid by Seller	Transportation Terms	Returns and Allowances
a.	$ 8,150	$200	FOB destination, 2/10, n/30	$1,300
b.	12,750	625	FOB shipping point, 2/10, n/30	3,000

PE 5-6A
Recording transactions for buyer and seller
obj. 3

Stuckey Co. sold merchandise to Bullock Co. on account, $5,250, terms 2/15, n/30. The cost of the merchandise sold is $3,150. Stuckey Co. issued a credit memorandum for $650 for merchandise returned and later received the amount due within the discount period. The cost of the merchandise returned was $390. Journalize Stuckey Co.'s and Bullock Co.'s entries for the receipt of the check for the amount due from Bullock Co.

PE 5-6B
Recording transactions for buyer and seller
obj. 3

Sparks Co. sold merchandise to Boyt Co. on account, $8,500, terms FOB shipping point, 2/10, n/30. The cost of the merchandise sold is $5,100. Sparks Co. paid transportation charges of $225 and later received the amount due within the discount period. Journalize Sparks Co.'s and Boyt Co.'s entries for the receipt of the check for the amount due from Boyt Co.

PE 5-7A
Entry for inventory shrinkage
obj. 4

Triangle Company's perpetual inventory records indicate that $111,500 of merchandise should be on hand on September 30, 2008. The physical inventory indicates that $107,400 of merchandise is actually on hand. Journalize the adjusting entry for the inventory shrinkage for Triangle Company for the year ended September 30, 2008.

PE 5-7B
Entry for inventory shrinkage
obj. 4

Three Turtles Company's perpetual inventory records indicate that $543,735 of merchandise should be on hand on August 31, 2008. The physical inventory indicates that $520,250 of merchandise is actually on hand. Journalize the adjusting entry for the inventory shrinkage for Three Turtles Company for the year ended August 31, 2008.

Exercises

EX 5-1
Determining gross profit
obj. 1

During the current year, merchandise is sold for $2,850,750. The cost of the merchandise sold is $1,995,525.

a. What is the amount of the gross profit?
b. Compute the gross profit percentage (gross profit divided by sales).
c. Will the income statement necessarily report a net income? Explain.

EX 5-2
Determining cost of merchandise sold
obj. 1

REAL WORLD

In 2005, Best Buy reported revenue of $27,433 million. Its gross profit was $6,495 million. What was the amount of Best Buy's cost of merchandise sold?

EX 5-3
Identify items missing in determining cost of merchandise sold
obj. 2

For (a) through (d), identify the items designated by "X" and "Y."

a. Purchases − (X + Y) = Net purchases.
b. Net purchases + X = Cost of merchandise purchased.
c. Merchandise inventory (beginning) + Cost of merchandise purchased = X.
d. Merchandise available for sale − X = Cost of merchandise sold.

EX 5-4
Cost of merchandise sold and related items
obj. 2

✓ a. Cost of merchandise sold, $1,218,300

The following data were extracted from the accounting records of Meniscus Company for the year ended June 30, 2008:

Merchandise inventory, July 1, 2007	$ 183,250
Merchandise inventory, June 30, 2008	200,100
Purchases	1,279,600
Purchases returns and allowances	41,200
Purchases discounts	20,500
Sales	1,800,000
Transportation in	17,250

a. Prepare the cost of merchandise sold section of the income statement for the year ended June 30, 2008, using the periodic inventory system.
b. Determine the gross profit to be reported on the income statement for the year ended June 30, 2008.

EX 5-5
Cost of merchandise sold
obj. 2

✓ Correct cost of merchandise sold, $820,500

Identify the errors in the following schedule of cost of merchandise sold for the current year ended March 31, 2008:

Cost of merchandise sold:			
Merchandise inventory, March 31, 2008			$135,750
Purchases		$852,100	
Plus: Purchases returns and allowances	$10,500		
Purchases discounts	8,000	18,500	
Gross purchases		$870,600	
Less transportation in		7,500	
Cost of merchandise purchased			863,100
Merchandise available for sale			$998,850
Less merchandise inventory, April 1, 2007			115,150
Cost of merchandise sold			$883,700

EX 5-6
Income statement for merchandiser
obj. 2

For the fiscal year, sales were $4,125,800, sales discounts were $380,000, sales returns and allowances were $186,750, and the cost of merchandise sold was $2,475,500.

a. What was the amount of net sales?
b. What was the amount of gross profit?

EX 5-7
Income statement for merchandiser
obj. 2

The following expenses were incurred by a merchandising business during the year. In which expense section of the income statement should each be reported: (a) selling, (b) administrative, or (c) other?

1. Advertising expense.
2. Depreciation expense on store equipment.
3. Insurance expense on office equipment.
4. Interest expense on notes payable.
5. Rent expense on office building.
6. Salaries of office personnel.
7. Salary of sales manager.
8. Sales supplies used.

EX 5-8
Single-step income statement
obj. 2

✓ *Net income: $451,450*

Summary operating data for The Voodoo Company during the current year ended November 30, 2008, are as follows: cost of merchandise sold, $2,175,350; administrative expenses, $500,000; interest expense, $23,200; rent revenue, $30,000; net sales, $4,000,000; and selling expenses, $880,000. Prepare a single-step income statement.

EX 5-9
Multiple-step income statement
obj. 2

Identify the errors in the following income statement:

The Euclidian Company
Income Statement
For the Year Ended March 31, 2008

Revenue from sales:			
Sales		$7,127,500	
Add: Sales returns and allowances	$112,300		
Sales discounts	60,000	172,300	
Gross sales			$7,299,800
Cost of merchandise sold			4,175,100
Income from operations			$3,124,700
Expenses:			
Selling expenses		$ 710,000	
Administrative expenses		525,000	
Delivery expense		18,100	
Total expenses			1,253,100
			$1,871,600
Other expense:			
Interest revenue			80,000
Gross profit			$1,791,600

EX 5-10
Determining amounts for items omitted from income statement
obj. 2

✓ *a. $30,000*

✓ *h. $690,000*

Two items are omitted in each of the following four lists of income statement data. Determine the amounts of the missing items, identifying them by letter.

Sales	$400,000	$500,000	$1,000,000	$ (g)
Sales returns and allowances	(a)	15,000	(e)	30,500
Sales discounts	20,000	8,000	40,000	37,000
Net sales	350,000	(c)	910,000	(h)
Cost of merchandise sold	(b)	285,000	(f)	540,000
Gross profit	200,000	(d)	286,500	150,000

EX 5-11
Multiple-step income statement

obj. 2

✓ *a. Net income: $137,500*

On August 31, 2008, the balances of the accounts appearing in the ledger of The Bent Needle Company, a furniture wholesaler, are as follows:

Administrative Expenses	$125,000	Notes Payable	$ 25,000
Building	512,500	Office Supplies	10,600
Cash	48,500	Salaries Payable	3,220
Cost of Merchandise Sold	700,000	Sales	1,275,000
Interest Expense	7,500	Sales Discounts	20,000
Capital Stock	568,580	Sales Returns and Allowances	80,000
Dividends	25,000	Selling Expenses	205,000
Merchandise Inventory	130,000	Store Supplies	7,700

a. Prepare a multiple-step income statement for the year ended August 31, 2008.
b. Compare the major advantages and disadvantages of the multiple-step and single-step forms of income statements.

EX 5-12
Chart of accounts

obj. 3

Gemini Co. is a newly organized business with a list of accounts arranged in alphabetical order below.

Accounts Payable
Accounts Receivable
Accumulated Depreciation—Office Equipment
Accumulated Depreciation—Store Equipment
Advertising Expense
Capital Stock
Cash
Cost of Merchandise Sold
Delivery Expense
Depreciation Expense—Office Equipment
Depreciation Expense—Store Equipment
Dividends
Income Summary
Insurance Expense
Interest Expense
Land
Merchandise Inventory

Miscellaneous Administrative Expense
Miscellaneous Selling Expense
Notes Payable
Office Equipment
Office Salaries Expense
Office Supplies
Office Supplies Expense
Prepaid Insurance
Rent Expense
Retained Earnings
Salaries Payable
Sales
Sales Discounts
Sales Returns and Allowances
Sales Salaries Expense
Store Equipment
Store Supplies
Store Supplies Expense

Construct a chart of accounts, assigning account numbers and arranging the accounts in balance sheet and income statement order, as illustrated in Exhibit 6. Each account number is three digits: the first digit is to indicate the major classification ("1" for assets, and so on); the second digit is to indicate the subclassification ("11" for current assets, and so on); and the third digit is to identify the specific account ("110" for Cash, and so on).

EX 5-13
Sales-related transactions, including the use of credit cards

obj. 3

Journalize the entries for the following transactions:

a. Sold merchandise for cash, $12,150. The cost of the merchandise sold was $9,100.
b. Sold merchandise on account, $6,000. The cost of the merchandise sold was $4,000.
c. Sold merchandise to customers who used MasterCard and VISA, $30,780. The cost of the merchandise sold was $20,000.
d. Sold merchandise to customers who used American Express, $17,650. The cost of the merchandise sold was $10,500.
e. Received an invoice from National Credit Co. for $1,900, representing a service fee paid for processing MasterCard, VISA, and American Express sales.

EX 5-14
Sales returns and allowances

obj. 3

During the year, sales returns and allowances totaled $172,100. The cost of the merchandise returned was $100,300. The accountant recorded all the returns and allowances by debiting the sales account and crediting Cost of Merchandise Sold for $172,100.

Was the accountant's method of recording returns acceptable? Explain. In your explanation, include the advantages of using a sales returns and allowances account.

EX 5-15
Sales-related transactions
obj. 3

After the amount due on a sale of $18,500, terms 2/10, n/eom, is received from a customer within the discount period, the seller consents to the return of the entire shipment. The cost of the merchandise returned was $11,100. (a) What is the amount of the refund owed to the customer? (b) Journalize the entries made by the seller to record the return and the refund.

EX 5-16
Sales-related transactions
obj. 3

The debits and credits for three related transactions are presented in the following T accounts. Describe each transaction.

Cash		
(5)	9,310	

Sales		
		(1) 11,750

Accounts Receivable		
(1)	11,750	(3) 2,250
		(5) 9,500

Sales Discounts		
(5)	190	

Merchandise Inventory		
(4)	1,350	(2) 6,900

Sales Returns and Allowances		
(3)	2,250	

Cost of Merchandise Sold		
(2)	6,900	(4) 1,350

EX 5-17
Sales-related transactions
obj. 3
✓ d. $9,654

Merchandise is sold on account to a customer for $9,200, terms FOB shipping point, 2/10, n/30. The seller paid the transportation costs of $638. Determine the following: (a) amount of the sale, (b) amount debited to Accounts Receivable, (c) amount of the discount for early payment, and (d) amount due within the discount period.

EX 5-18
Purchase-related transaction
obj. 3

Hushpuppy Company purchased merchandise on account from a supplier for $6,750, terms 2/10, n/30. Hushpuppy Company returned $1,500 of the merchandise and received full credit.

a. If Hushpuppy Company pays the invoice within the discount period, what is the amount of cash required for the payment?
b. Under a perpetual inventory system, what account is credited by Hushpuppy Company to record the return?

EX 5-19
Purchase-related transactions
obj. 3

A retailer is considering the purchase of 100 units of a specific item from either of two suppliers. Their offers are as follows:

A: $375 a unit, total of $37,500, 2/10, n/30, plus transportation costs of $1,050.
B: $380 a unit, total of $38,000, 1/10, n/30, no charge for transportation.

Which of the two offers, A or B, yields the lower price?

EX 5-20
Purchase-related transactions
obj. 3

The debits and credits from four related transactions are presented in the following T accounts. Describe each transaction.

Cash		
		(2) 450
		(4) 10,780

Accounts Payable		
(3)	500	(1) 11,500
(4)	11,000	

Merchandise Inventory		
(1)	11,500	(3) 500
(2)	450	(4) 220

EX 5-21
Purchase-related
transactions
obj. 3
✓ *(c) Cash, cr. $7,350*

Madamé Co., a women's clothing store, purchased $10,000 of merchandise from a supplier on account, terms FOB destination, 2/10, n/30. Madamé Co. returned $2,500 of the merchandise, receiving a credit memorandum, and then paid the amount due within the discount period. Journalize Madamé Co.'s entries to record (a) the purchase, (b) the merchandise return, and (c) the payment.

EX 5-22
Purchase-related
transactions
obj. 3
✓ *(e) Cash, dr. $1,410*

Journalize entries for the following related transactions of La Paz Company:

a. Purchased $18,400 of merchandise from Harbin Co. on account, terms 2/10, n/30.
b. Paid the amount owed on the invoice within the discount period.
c. Discovered that $4,500 of the merchandise was defective and returned items, receiving credit.
d. Purchased $3,000 of merchandise from Harbin Co. on account, terms n/30.
e. Received a check for the balance owed from the return in (c), after deducting for the purchase in (d).

EX 5-23
Determining amounts to
be paid on invoices
obj. 3
✓ *a. $6,435*

Determine the amount to be paid in full settlement of each of the following invoices, assuming that credit for returns and allowances was received prior to payment and that all invoices were paid within the discount period.

	Merchandise	Transportation Paid by Seller		Returns and Allowances
a.	$ 8,000	—	FOB shipping point, 1/10, n/30	$1,500
b.	2,900	$125	FOB shipping point, 2/10, n/30	400
c.	3,850	—	FOB destination, 2/10, n/30	—
d.	15,000	—	FOB destination, n/30	2,500
e.	5,000	275	FOB shipping point, 2/10, n/30	1,000

EX 5-24
Sales tax
obj. 3
✓ *c. $12,932*

A sale of merchandise on account for $12,200 is subject to a 6% sales tax. (a) Should the sales tax be recorded at the time of sale or when payment is received? (b) What is the amount of the sale? (c) What is the amount debited to Accounts Receivable? (d) What is the title of the account to which the $732 ($12,200 × 6%) is credited?

EX 5-25
Sales tax transactions
obj. 3

Journalize the entries to record the following selected transactions:

a. Sold $15,750 of merchandise on account, subject to a sales tax of 8%. The cost of the merchandise sold was $9,450.
b. Paid $29,183 to the state sales tax department for taxes collected.

EX 5-26
Sales-related transactions
obj. 3

Sellers Co., a furniture wholesaler, sells merchandise to Beyer Co. on account, $14,500, terms 2/10, n/30. The cost of the merchandise sold is $8,800. Sellers Co. issues a credit memorandum for $3,750 for merchandise returned and subsequently receives the amount due within the discount period. The cost of the merchandise returned is $2,100. Journalize Sellers Co.'s entries for (a) the sale, including the cost of the merchandise sold, (b) the credit memorandum, including the cost of the returned merchandise, and (c) the receipt of the check for the amount due from Beyer Co.

EX 5-27
Purchase-related
transactions
obj. 3

Based on the data presented in Exercise 5-26, journalize Beyer Co.'s entries for (a) the purchase, (b) the return of the merchandise for credit, and (c) the payment of the invoice within the discount period.

EX 5-28
Normal balances of merchandise accounts
obj. **3**

What is the normal balance of the following accounts: (a) Sales, (b) Sales Discounts, (c) Sales Returns and Allowances, (d) Cost of Merchandise Sold, (e) Delivery Expense, (f) Merchandise Inventory, (g) Sales Tax Payable?

EX 5-29
Adjusting entry for merchandise inventory shrinkage
obj. **4**

Teramycin Inc.'s perpetual inventory records indicate that $715,275 of merchandise should be on hand on January 31, 2008. The physical inventory indicates that $698,150 of merchandise is actually on hand. Journalize the adjusting entry for the inventory shrinkage for Teramycin Inc. for the year ended January 31, 2008.

EX 5-30
Closing the accounts of a merchandiser
obj. **4**

From the following list, identify the accounts that should be closed to Income Summary at the end of the fiscal year under a perpetual inventory system: (a) Accounts Payable, (b) Advertising Expense, (c) Cost of Merchandise Sold, (d) Dividends, (e) Merchandise Inventory, (f) Sales, (g) Sales Discounts, (h) Sales Returns and Allowances, (i) Supplies, (j) Supplies Expense, (k) Wages Payable.

EX 5-31
Closing entries; net income
obj. **4**

Based on the data presented in Exercise 5-11, journalize the closing entries.

EX 5-32
Closing entries
obj. **4**

On October 31, 2008, the balances of the accounts appearing in the ledger of Kavanaugh Company, a furniture wholesaler, are as follows:

Accumulated Dep.—Building	$152,300	Notes Payable	$ 120,000
Administrative Expenses	326,500	Retained Earnings	605,775
Building	278,400	Salaries Payable	3,400
Capital Stock	100,000	Sales	1,567,700
Cash	44,200	Sales Discounts	90,000
Cost of Merchandise Sold	940,000	Sales Returns and Allow.	60,000
Dividends	39,750	Sales Tax Payable	24,500
Interest Expense	9,600	Selling Expenses	620,000
Merchandise Inventory	130,000	Store Supplies	22,900
		Store Supplies Exp.	12,325

Prepare the October 31, 2008, closing entries for Kavanaugh Company.

EX 5-33
Ratio of net sales to total assets

The Home Depot reported the following data (in millions) in its financial statements for 2005 and 2004:

	2005	2004
Net sales	$73,094	$64,816
Total assets at the end of the year	38,907	34,437
Total assets at the beginning of the year	34,437	30,011

a. Determine the ratio of net sales to average total assets for The Home Depot for 2005 and 2004. Round to two decimal places.
b. What conclusions can be drawn from these ratios concerning the trend in the ability of The Home Depot to effectively use its assets to generate sales?

EX 5-34
Ratio of net sales to total assets

Kroger, a national supermarket chain, reported the following data (in millions) in its financial statements for 2005:

Total revenue	$56,434
Total assets at end of year	20,491
Total assets at beginning of year	20,763

a. Compute the ratio of net sales to assets for 2005. Round to two decimal places.
b. ▄▄▄▄▶ Would you expect the ratio of net sales to assets for Kroger to be similar to or different from that of Tiffany & Co.? Tiffany is the large North American retailer of jewelry, with a ratio of net sales to average total assets of 0.87.

APPENDIX
EX 5-35
Accounts for periodic and perpetual inventory systems

Indicate which of the following accounts would be included in the chart of accounts of a merchandising company using either the (a) periodic inventory system or (b) perpetual inventory system. If the account would be included in the chart of accounts of a company using the periodic and perpetual systems, indicate (c) for both.

(1) Cost of Merchandise Sold	(6) Purchases Returns and Allowances
(2) Purchases Discounts	(7) Delivery Expense
(3) Sales	(8) Sales Returns and Allowances
(4) Merchandise Inventory	(9) Transportation In
(5) Sales Discounts	(10) Purchases

APPENDIX
EX 5-36
Rules of debit and credit for periodic inventory accounts

Complete the following table by indicating for (a) through (g) whether the proper answer is debit or credit.

Account	Increase	Decrease	Normal Balance
Purchases	(a)	credit	(b)
Purchases Discounts	credit	debit	(c)
Purchases Returns and Allowances	(d)	(e)	credit
Transportation In	(f)	credit	(g)

APPENDIX
EX 5-37
Journal entries using the periodic inventory system

The following selected transactions were completed by Lorimer Company during August of the current year. Lorimer Company uses the periodic inventory system.

Aug. 3. Purchased $24,500 of merchandise on account, FOB shipping point, terms 2/10, n/30.
   4. Paid transportation costs of $475 on the August 3 purchase.
   7. Returned $4,000 of the merchandise purchased on August 3.
   11. Sold merchandise on account, $12,700, FOB destination, 2/15, n/30. The cost of merchandise sold was $7,600.
   12. Paid transportation costs of $300 for the merchandise sold on August 11.
   13. Paid for the purchase of August 3 less the return and discount.
   26. Received payment on account for the sale of August 11 less the discount.

Journalize the entries to record the transactions of Lorimer Company.

APPENDIX
EX 5-38
Journal entries using perpetual inventory system

Using the data shown in Exercise 5-37, journalize the entries for the transactions assuming that Lorimer Company uses the perpetual inventory system.

APPENDIX
EX 5-39
Closing entries using periodic inventory system

Greenway Company is a small rug retailer owned and operated by Lorene Greenway. After the accounts have been adjusted on March 31, the following account balances were taken from the ledger:

Advertising Expense	$ 25,800
Depreciation Expense	5,100
Dividends	50,000
Merchandise Inventory, March 1	34,500
Merchandise Inventory, March 31	42,150
Miscellaneous Expense	6,350
Purchases	480,000
Purchases Discounts	2,000
Purchases Returns and Allowances	9,000
Sales	925,000
Sales Discounts	4,000
Sales Returns and Allowances	8,000
Salaries Expense	76,300
Transportation In	15,400

Journalize the closing entries on March 31.

Problems Series A

PR 5-1A
Multiple-step income statement and report form of balance sheet

obj. 2

✓1. Net income: $120,000

The following selected accounts and their current balances appear in the ledger of Magic Vinyl Co. for the fiscal year ended March 31, 2008:

Cash	$ 184,500	Sales	$1,542,000
Accounts Receivable	145,200	Sales Returns and Allowances	27,720
Merchandise Inventory	210,000	Sales Discounts	26,280
Office Supplies	6,720	Cost of Merchandise Sold	930,000
Prepaid Insurance	4,080	Sales Salaries Expense	207,840
Office Equipment	102,000	Advertising Expense	52,560
Accumulated Depreciation—		Depreciation Expense—	
Office Equipment	15,360	Store Equipment	7,680
Store Equipment	183,600	Miscellaneous Selling Expense	1,920
Accumulated Depreciation—		Office Salaries Expense	100,980
Store Equipment	41,040	Rent Expense	37,620
Accounts Payable	66,720	Depreciation Expense—	
Salaries Payable	2,880	Office Equipment	15,240
Note Payable		Insurance Expense	4,680
(final payment due 2018)	67,200	Office Supplies Expense	1,560
Capital Stock	75,000	Miscellaneous Administrative	
Retained Earnings	489,900	Expense	1,920
Dividends	42,000	Interest Expense	6,000

Instructions
1. Prepare a multiple-step income statement.
2. Prepare a retained earnings statement.
3. Prepare a report form of balance sheet, assuming that the current portion of the note payable is $9,000.
4. Briefly explain (a) how multiple-step and single-step income statements differ and (b) how report-form and account-form balance sheets differ.

PR 5-2A
Single-step income statement and account form of balance sheet

objs. 2, 4

✓3. Total assets: $779,700

Selected accounts and related amounts for Magic Vinyl Co. for the fiscal year ended March 31, 2008, are presented in Problem 5-1A.

Instructions
1. Prepare a single-step income statement in the format shown in Exhibit 3.
2. Prepare a retained earnings statement.
3. Prepare an account form of balance sheet, assuming that the current portion of the note payable is $9,000.
4. Prepare closing entries as of March 31, 2008.

PR 5-3A
Sales-related transactions
obj. 3

The following selected transactions were completed by Cardroom Supply Co., which sells office supplies primarily to wholesalers and occasionally to retail customers:

Jan. 2. Sold merchandise on account to Kibler Co., $10,000, terms FOB destination, 1/10, n/30. The cost of the merchandise sold was $6,500.
3. Sold merchandise for $12,000 plus 8% sales tax to cash customers. The cost of merchandise sold was $9,000.
4. Sold merchandise on account to Glickman Co., $5,600, terms FOB shipping point, n/eom. The cost of merchandise sold was $3,100.
5. Sold merchandise for $8,000 plus 8% sales tax to customers who used Master-Card. The cost of merchandise sold was $6,000.
12. Received check for amount due from Kibler Co. for sale on January 2.
14. Sold merchandise to customers who used American Express cards, $15,000. The cost of merchandise sold was $9,200.
16. Sold merchandise on account to Bryan Co., $12,000, terms FOB shipping point, 1/10, n/30. The cost of merchandise sold was $7,200.
18. Issued credit memorandum for $3,000 to Bryan Co. for merchandise returned from sale on January 16. The cost of the merchandise returned was $1,800.
19. Sold merchandise on account to Cooney Co., $15,750, terms FOB shipping point, 2/10, n/30. Added $400 to the invoice for transportation costs prepaid. The cost of merchandise sold was $9,500.
26. Received check for amount due from Bryan Co. for sale on January 16 less credit memorandum of January 18 and discount.
28. Received check for amount due from Cooney Co. for sale of January 19.
31. Received check for amount due from Glickman Co. for sale of January 4.
31. Paid Speedy Delivery Service $1,875 for merchandise delivered during January to customers under shipping terms of FOB destination.
Feb. 3. Paid First State Bank $1,150 for service fees for handling MasterCard and American Express sales during January.
15. Paid $1,600 to state sales tax division for taxes owed on sales.

Instructions
Journalize the entries to record the transactions of Cardroom Supply Co.

PR 5-4A
Purchase-related transactions
obj. 3

The following selected transactions were completed by Scat Trak Company during July of the current year:

July 1. Purchased merchandise from Kermit Co., $18,750, terms FOB destination, n/30.
3. Purchased merchandise from Basaway Co., $12,150, terms FOB shipping point, 2/10, n/eom. Prepaid transportation costs of $180 were added to the invoice.
4. Purchased merchandise from Phillips Co., $13,800, terms FOB destination, 2/10, n/30.
6. Issued debit memorandum to Phillips Co. for $1,900 of merchandise returned from purchase on July 4.
13. Paid Basaway Co. for invoice of July 3, less discount.
14. Paid Phillips Co. for invoice of July 4, less debit memorandum of July 6 and discount.
19. Purchased merchandise from Cleghorne Co., $18,000, terms FOB shipping point, n/eom.
19. Paid transportation charges of $500 on July 19 purchase from Cleghorne Co.
20. Purchased merchandise from Graham Co., $9,000, terms FOB destination, 1/10, n/30.
30. Paid Graham Co. for invoice of July 20, less discount.
31. Paid Kermit Co. for invoice of July 1.
31. Paid Cleghorne Co. for invoice of July 19.

Instructions
Journalize the entries to record the transactions of Scat Trak Company for July.

PR 5-5A
*Sales-related and
purchase-related
transactions*

obj. 3

The following were selected from among the transactions completed by Southmont Company during April of the current year:

Apr. 3. Purchased merchandise on account from Mandell Co., list price $30,000, trade discount 40%, terms FOB destination, 2/10, n/30.
   4. Sold merchandise for cash, $12,800. The cost of the merchandise sold was $7,600.
   5. Purchased merchandise on account from Quinn Co., $18,750, terms FOB shipping point, 2/10, n/30, with prepaid transportation costs of $715 added to the invoice.
   6. Returned $3,500 of merchandise purchased on April 3 from Mandell Co.
   11. Sold merchandise on account to Campo Co., list price $6,000, trade discount 20%, terms 1/10, n/30. The cost of the merchandise sold was $3,200.
   13. Paid Mandell Co. on account for purchase of April 3, less return of April 6 and discount.
   14. Sold merchandise on VISA, $52,700. The cost of the merchandise sold was $31,500.
   15. Paid Quinn Co. on account for purchase of April 5, less discount.
   21. Received cash on account from sale of April 11 to Campo Co., less discount.
   24. Sold merchandise on account to Elkins Co., $8,150, terms 1/10, n/30. The cost of the merchandise sold was $4,500.
   28. Paid VISA service fee of $1,500.
   30. Received merchandise returned by Elkins Co. from sale on April 24, $1,200. The cost of the returned merchandise was $900.

Instructions
Journalize the transactions.

PR 5-6A
*Sales-related and
purchase-related
transactions for seller
and buyer*

obj. 3

The following selected transactions were completed during August between Sellars Company and Beyer Co.:

Aug. 1. Sellars Company sold merchandise on account to Beyer Co., $17,850, terms FOB destination, 2/15, n/eom. The cost of the merchandise sold was $10,700.
   2. Sellars Company paid transportation costs of $140 for delivery of merchandise sold to Beyer Co. on August 1.
   5. Sellars Company sold merchandise on account to Beyer Co., $27,550, terms FOB shipping point, n/eom. The cost of the merchandise sold was $16,500.
   6. Beyer Co. returned $1,800 of merchandise purchased on account on August 1 from Sellars Company. The cost of the merchandise returned was $1,050.
   9. Beyer Co. paid transportation charges of $165 on August 5 purchase from Sellars Company.
   15. Sellars Company sold merchandise on account to Beyer Co., $32,000, terms FOB shipping point, 1/10, n/30. Sellars Company paid transportation costs of $1,243, which were added to the invoice. The cost of the merchandise sold was $19,200.
   16. Beyer Co. paid Sellars Company for purchase of August 1, less discount and less return of August 6.
   25. Beyer Co. paid Sellars Company on account for purchase of August 15, less discount.
   31. Beyer Co. paid Sellars Company on account for purchase of August 5.

Instructions
Journalize the August transactions for (1) Sellars Company and (2) Beyer Co.

**APPENDIX
PR 5-7A**
*Purchase-related
transactions using
periodic inventory
system*

Selected transactions for Scat Trak Company during July of the current year are listed in Problem 5-4A.

Instructions
Journalize the entries to record the transactions of Scat Trak Company for July using the periodic inventory system.

**APPENDIX
PR 5-8A**
*Sales-related and
purchase-related
transactions using
periodic inventory
system*

Selected transactions for Southmont Company during April of the current year are listed in Problem 5-5A.

Instructions
Journalize the entries to record the transactions of Southmont Company for April using the periodic inventory system.

**APPENDIX
PR 5-9A**
*Sales-related and
purchase-related
transactions for buyer
and seller using periodic
inventory system*

Selected transactions during August between Sellars Company and Beyer Co. are listed in Problem 5-6A.

Instructions
Journalize the entries to record the transactions for (1) Sellars Company and (2) Beyers Co. assuming that both companies use the periodic inventory system.

**APPENDIX
PR 5-10A**
*Periodic inventory
accounts, multiple-step
income statement,
closing entries*

✓2. Net income, $725,200

On July 31, 2008, the balances of the accounts appearing in the ledger of Odell Company are as follows:

Cash	$ 73,200	Sales Discounts	$ 37,500
Accounts Receivable	288,500	Purchases	2,146,000
Merchandise Inventory, Aug. 1, 2007	350,900	Purchases Returns and Allowances	24,000
Office Supplies	12,100	Purchases Discounts	18,000
Prepaid Insurance	18,000	Transportation In	43,600
Land	140,000	Sales Salaries Expense	625,000
Store Equipment	683,100	Advertising Expense	220,000
Accumulated Depreciation—		Delivery Expense	36,000
Store Equipment	223,600	Depreciation Expense—Store	
Office Equipment	314,000	Equipment	23,600
Accumulated Depreciation—		Miscellaneous Selling Expense	42,800
Office Equipment	65,000	Office Salaries Expense	400,000
Accounts Payable	111,300	Rent Expense	125,000
Salaries Payable	11,800	Insurance Expense	12,000
Unearned Rent	33,200	Office Supplies Expense	9,200
Notes Payable	50,000	Depreciation Expense—	
Capital Stock	100,000	Office Equipment	6,000
Retained Earnings	660,200	Miscellaneous Administrative Expense	23,400
Dividends	75,000	Rent Revenue	25,000
Sales	4,425,800	Interest Expense	3,000
Sales Returns and Allowances	40,000		

Instructions
1. Does Odell Company use the periodic or perpetual inventory system? Explain.
2. Prepare a multiple-step income statement for Odell Company for the year ended July 31, 2008. The merchandise inventory as of July 31, 2008, was $376,400.
3. Prepare the closing entries for Odell Company as of July 31, 2008.

Problems Series B

PR 5-1B
*Multiple-step income
statement and report
form of balance sheet*

obj. 2

✓1. Net income: $61,200

The following selected accounts and their current balances appear in the ledger of Hobbs' Co. for the fiscal year ended June 30, 2008:

Cash	$ 68,850	Accumulated Depreciation—	
Accounts Receivable	55,800	Office Equipment	$ 9,720
Merchandise Inventory	90,000	Store Equipment	105,750
Office Supplies	2,340	Accumulated Depreciation—	
Prepaid Insurance	6,120	Store Equipment	43,740
Office Equipment	57,600	Accounts Payable	24,300

continued

Salaries Payable	$ 1,800	Depreciation Expense—
Note Payable		Store Equipment	$ 4,140
(final payment due 2018)	27,000	Miscellaneous Selling Expense	990
Capital Stock	80,000	Office Salaries Expense	36,900
Retained Earnings	161,200	Rent Expense	19,935
Dividends	22,500	Insurance Expense	11,475
Sales	1,351,800	Depreciation Expense—
Sales Returns and Allowances	18,900	Office Equipment	8,100
Sales Discounts	9,900	Office Supplies Expense	810
Cost of Merchandise Sold	963,000	Miscellaneous Administrative
Sales Salaries Expense	189,000	Expense	1,080
Advertising Expense	25,470	Interest Expense	900

Instructions

1. Prepare a multiple-step income statement.
2. Prepare a retained earnings statement.
3. Prepare a report form of balance sheet, assuming that the current portion of the note payable is $2,250.
4. Briefly explain (a) how multiple-step and single-step income statements differ and (b) how report-form and account-form balance sheets differ.

PR 5-2B
Single-step income statement and account form of balance sheet
objs. 2, 4

✓ 3. Total assets: $333,000

Selected accounts and related amounts for Hobbs' Co. for the fiscal year ended June 30, 2008, are presented in Problem 5-1B.

Instructions

1. Prepare a single-step income statement in the format shown in Exhibit 3.
2. Prepare a retained earnings statement.
3. Prepare an account form of balance sheet, assuming that the current portion of the note payable is $2,250.
4. Prepare closing entries as of June 30, 2008.

PR 5-3B
Sales-related transactions
obj. 3

The following selected transactions were completed by Water Tech Supplies Co., which sells irrigation supplies primarily to wholesalers and occasionally to retail customers:

July 1. Sold merchandise on account to Upshaw Co., $8,000, terms FOB shipping point, n/eom. The cost of merchandise sold was $4,800.
      2. Sold merchandise for $15,000 plus 7% sales tax to cash customers. The cost of merchandise sold was $8,800.
      5. Sold merchandise on account to Westone Company, $16,000, terms FOB destination, 1/10, n/30. The cost of merchandise sold was $10,500.
      8. Sold merchandise for $11,500 plus 7% sales tax to customers who used VISA cards. The cost of merchandise sold was $7,000.
     13. Sold merchandise to customers who used MasterCard cards, $8,000. The cost of merchandise sold was $4,750.
     14. Sold merchandise on account to Tyler Co., $7,500, terms FOB shipping point, 1/10, n/30. The cost of merchandise sold was $4,000.
     15. Received check for amount due from Westone Company for sale on July 5.
     16. Issued credit memorandum for $800 to Tyler Co. for merchandise returned from sale on July 14. The cost of the merchandise returned was $360.
     18. Sold merchandise on account to Horton Company, $6,850, terms FOB shipping point, 2/10, n/30. Paid $210 for transportation costs and added them to the invoice. The cost of merchandise sold was $4,100.
     24. Received check for amount due from Tyler Co. for sale on July 14 less credit memorandum of July 16 and discount.
     28. Received check for amount due from Horton Company for sale of July 18.
     31. Paid Uptown Delivery Service $3,100 for merchandise delivered during July to customers under shipping terms of FOB destination.
     31. Received check for amount due from Upshaw Co. for sale of July 1.

Aug. 3. Paid First National Bank $780 for service fees for handling MasterCard and VISA sales during July.
10. Paid $1,855 to state sales tax division for taxes owed on sales.

Instructions
Journalize the entries to record the transactions of Water Tech Supplies Co.

PR 5-4B
Purchase-related transactions

obj. 3

The following selected transactions were completed by Bodyworks Co. during October of the current year:

Oct. 1. Purchased merchandise from Mantooth Co., $11,800, terms FOB shipping point, 2/10, n/eom. Prepaid transportation costs of $325 were added to the invoice.
5. Purchased merchandise from Hauck Co., $17,500, terms FOB destination, n/30.
10. Paid Mantooth Co. for invoice of October 1, less discount.
13. Purchased merchandise from Lieu Co., $7,500, terms FOB destination, 1/10, n/30.
14. Issued debit memorandum to Lieu Co. for $2,500 of merchandise returned from purchase on October 13.
18. Purchased merchandise from Fowler Company, $9,600, terms FOB shipping point, n/eom.
18. Paid transportation charges of $150 on October 18 purchase from Fowler Company.
19. Purchased merchandise from Hatcher Co., $9,750, terms FOB destination, 2/10, n/30.
23. Paid Lieu Co. for invoice of October 13, less debit memorandum of October 14 and discount.
29. Paid Hatcher Co. for invoice of October 19, less discount.
31. Paid Fowler Company for invoice of October 18.
31. Paid Hauck Co. for invoice of October 5.

Instructions
Journalize the entries to record the transactions of Bodyworks Co. for October.

PR 5-5B
Sales-related and purchase-related transactions

obj. 3

The following were selected from among the transactions completed by Theisen Company during December of the current year:

Dec. 3. Purchased merchandise on account from Shipley Co., list price $24,000, trade discount 25%, terms FOB shipping point, 2/10, n/30, with prepaid transportation costs of $615 added to the invoice.
5. Purchased merchandise on account from Kirch Co., $10,250, terms FOB destination, 2/10, n/30.
6. Sold merchandise on account to Murdock Co., list price $18,000, trade discount 35%, terms 2/10, n/30. The cost of the merchandise sold was $8,250.
7. Returned $1,800 of merchandise purchased on December 5 from Kirch Co.
13. Paid Shipley Co. on account for purchase of December 3, less discount.
15. Paid Kirch Co. on account for purchase of December 5, less return of December 7 and discount.
16. Received cash on account from sale of December 6 to Murdock Co., less discount.
19. Sold merchandise on MasterCard, $39,500. The cost of the merchandise sold was $23,700.
22. Sold merchandise on account to Milk River Co., $11,300, terms 2/10, n/30. The cost of the merchandise sold was $6,700.
23. Sold merchandise for cash, $17,680. The cost of the merchandise sold was $9,100.
28. Received merchandise returned by Milk River Co. from sale on December 22, $2,000. The cost of the returned merchandise was $1,100.
31. Paid MasterCard service fee of $1,050.

Instructions
Journalize the transactions.

PR 5-6B
Sales-related and purchase-related transactions for seller and buyer

obj. 3

The following selected transactions were completed during November between Sallis Company and Byce Company:

Nov. 2. Sallis Company sold merchandise on account to Byce Company, $12,500, terms FOB shipping point, 2/10, n/30. Sallis Company paid transportation costs of $425, which were added to the invoice. The cost of the merchandise sold was $7,500.

8. Sallis Company sold merchandise on account to Byce Company, $21,600, terms FOB destination, 1/15, n/eom. The cost of the merchandise sold was $13,000.

8. Sallis Company paid transportation costs of $879 for delivery of merchandise sold to Byce Company on November 8.

12. Byce Company returned $5,000 of merchandise purchased on account on November 8 from Sallis Company. The cost of the merchandise returned was $2,900.

12. Byce Company paid Sallis Company for purchase of November 2, less discount.

23. Byce Company paid Sallis Company for purchase of November 8, less discount and less return of November 12.

24. Sallis Company sold merchandise on account to Byce Company, $15,000, terms FOB shipping point, n/eom. The cost of the merchandise sold was $9,000.

26. Byce Company paid transportation charges of $400 on November 24 purchase from Sallis Company.

30. Byce Company paid Sallis Company on account for purchase of November 24.

Instructions
Journalize the November transactions for (1) Sallis Company and (2) Byce Company.

APPENDIX
PR 5-7B
Purchase-related transactions using periodic inventory system

Selected transactions for Bodyworks Co. during October of the current year are listed in Problem 5-4B.

Instructions
Journalize the entries to record the transactions of Bodyworks Co. for October using the periodic inventory system.

APPENDIX
PR 5-8B
Sales-related and purchase-related transactions using periodic inventory system

Selected transactions for Theisen Company during December of the current year are listed in Problem 5-5B.

Instructions
Journalize the entries to record the transactions of Theisen Company for December using the periodic inventory system.

APPENDIX
PR 5-9B
Sales-related and purchase-related transactions for buyer and seller using periodic inventory system

Selected transactions during November between Sallis Company and Byce Company are listed in Problem 5-6B.

Instructions
Journalize the entries to record the transactions for (1) Sallis Company and (2) Byce Company assuming that both companies use the periodic inventory system.

APPENDIX
PR 5-10B
Periodic inventory accounts, multiple-step income statement, closing entries

✓2. Net income, $181,300

On April 30, 2008, the balances of the accounts appearing in the ledger of Headwinds Company are as follows:

Cash	$ 18,300	Accumulated Depreciation—	
Accounts Receivable	72,125	Store Equipment	$55,900
Merchandise Inventory, May 1, 2007	87,725	Office Equipment	78,500
Office Supplies	3,025	Accumulated Depreciation—	
Prepaid Insurance	4,500	Office Equipment	16,250
Land	35,000	Accounts Payable	27,825
Store Equipment	170,775	Salaries Payable	2,950

Unearned Rent	$ 8,300	Delivery Expense	$ 9,000
Notes Payable	12,500	Depreciation Expense—	
Capital Stock	60,000	Store Equipment	5,900
Retained Earnings	130,050	Miscellaneous Selling Expense	10,700
Dividends	18,750	Office Salaries Expense	100,000
Sales	1,106,450	Rent Expense	31,250
Sales Returns and Allowances	10,000	Insurance Expense	3,000
Sales Discounts	9,375	Office Supplies Expense	2,300
Purchases	536,500	Depreciation Expense—	
Purchases Returns and Allowances	6,000	Office Equipment	1,500
Purchases Discounts	4,500	Miscellaneous Administrative Expense	5,850
Transportation In	10,900	Rent Revenue	6,250
Sales Salaries Expense	156,250	Interest Expense	750
Advertising Expense	55,000		

Instructions

1. Does Headwinds Company use a periodic or perpetual inventory system? Explain.
2. Prepare a multiple-step income statement for Headwinds Company for the year ended April 30, 2008. The merchandise inventory as of April 30, 2008, was $94,100.
3. Prepare the closing entries for Headwinds Company as of April 30, 2008.

Comprehensive Problem 2

✓ 8. Net income:
$231,962

World Boards Co. is a merchandising business. The account balances for World Boards Co. as of March 1, 2008 (unless otherwise indicated), are as follows:

110	Cash	$ 21,200
112	Accounts Receivable	51,300
115	Merchandise Inventory	200,800
116	Prepaid Insurance	5,600
117	Store Supplies	3,800
123	Store Equipment	156,500
124	Accumulated Depreciation—Store Equipment	18,900
210	Accounts Payable	32,200
211	Salaries Payable	—
310	Capital Stock	50,000
311	Retained Earnings, April 1, 2007	135,100
312	Dividends	45,000
313	Income Summary	—
410	Sales	1,073,700
411	Sales Returns and Allowances	30,900
412	Sales Discounts	19,800
510	Cost of Merchandise Sold	541,000
520	Sales Salaries Expense	111,600
521	Advertising Expense	27,000
522	Depreciation Expense	—
523	Store Supplies Expense	—
529	Miscellaneous Selling Expense	4,200
530	Office Salaries Expense	60,700
531	Rent Expense	27,900
532	Insurance Expense	—
539	Miscellaneous Administrative Expense	2,600

During March, the last month of the fiscal year, the following transactions were completed:

Mar. 1. Paid rent for March, $2,400.
 3. Purchased merchandise on account from Huisman Co., terms 2/10, n/30, FOB shipping point, $21,600.

Mar. 4. Paid transportation charges on purchase of March 3, $500.
6. Sold merchandise on account to Hillcrest Co., terms 2/10, n/30, FOB shipping point, $8,500. The cost of the merchandise sold was $5,000.
7. Received $8,900 cash from Foley Co. on account, no discount.
10. Sold merchandise for cash, $27,200. The cost of the merchandise sold was $16,000.
13. Paid for merchandise purchased on March 3, less discount.
14. Received merchandise returned on sale of March 6, $1,500. The cost of the merchandise returned was $900.
15. Paid advertising expense for last half of March, $2,600.
16. Received cash from sale of March 6, less return of March 14 and discount.
19. Purchased merchandise for cash, $11,800.
19. Paid $9,000 to Bakke Co. on account, no discount.
20. Sold merchandise on account to Wilts Co., terms 1/10, n/30, FOB shipping point, $22,300. The cost of the merchandise sold was $13,200.
21. For the convenience of the customer, paid shipping charges on sale of March 20, $1,100.
21. Received $17,600 cash from Owen Co. on account, no discount.
21. Purchased merchandise on account from Nye Co., terms 1/10, n/30, FOB destination, $19,900.
24. Returned $2,000 of damaged merchandise purchased on March 21, receiving credit from the seller.
26. Refunded cash on sales made for cash, $1,200. The cost of the merchandise returned was $700.
28. Paid sales salaries of $7,600 and office salaries of $4,800.
29. Purchased store supplies for cash, $800.
30. Sold merchandise on account to Whitetail Co., terms 2/10, n/30, FOB shipping point, $18,750. The cost of the merchandise sold was $11,250.
30. Received cash from sale of March 20, less discount, plus transportation paid on March 21.
31. Paid for purchase of March 21, less return of March 24 and discount.

Instructions

1. Enter the balances of each of the accounts in the appropriate balance column of a four-column account. Write *Balance* in the item section, and place a check mark (✓) in the Posting Reference column. Journalize the transactions for March.
2. Post the journal to the general ledger, extending the month-end balances to the appropriate Balance columns after all posting is completed. In this problem, you are not required to update or post to the accounts receivable and accounts payable subsidiary ledgers.
3. Prepare an unadjusted trial balance.
4. At the end of March, the following adjustment data were assembled. Analyze and use these data to complete (5) and (6).

a.	Merchandise inventory on March 31	$196,139
b.	Insurance expired during the year	1,875
c.	Store supplies on hand on March 31	1,500
d.	Depreciation for the current year	9,500
e.	Accrued salaries on March 31:	
	Sales salaries	$1,200
	Office salaries	800	2,000

5. **Optional:** Enter the unadjusted trial balance on a 10-column end-of-period spreadsheet (work sheet), and complete the spreadsheet. See Appendix D for how to prepare an end-of-period spreadsheet (work sheet) for a merchandising business.
6. Journalize and post the adjusting entries.
7. Prepare an adjusted trial balance.
8. Prepare an income statement, a retained earnings statement, and a balance sheet.
9. Prepare and post the closing entries. Indicate closed accounts by inserting a line in both the Balance columns opposite the closing entry. Insert the new balance in the retained earnings account.
10. Prepare a post-closing trial balance.

Special Activities

SA 5-1
Ethics and professional conduct in business

ETHICS

On February 24, 2008, Lawn Ranger Company, a garden retailer, purchased $40,000 of corn seed, terms 2/10, n/30, from Nebraska Farm Co. Even though the discount period had expired, Corey Gilbert subtracted the discount of $800 when he processed the documents for payment on March 25, 2008.

➤ Discuss whether Corey Gilbert behaved in a professional manner by subtracting the discount, even though the discount period had expired.

SA 5-2
Purchases discounts and accounts payable

The Eclipse Video Store Co. is owned and operated by Jared Helms. The following is an excerpt from a conversation between Jared Helms and Allison Fain, the chief accountant for The Eclipse Video Store:

Jared: Allison, I've got a question about this recent balance sheet.

Allison: Sure, what's your question?

Jared: Well, as you know, I'm applying for a bank loan to finance our new store in Winterville, and I noticed that the accounts payable are listed as $85,000.

Allison: That's right. Approximately $78,000 of that represents amounts due our suppliers, and the remainder is miscellaneous payables to creditors for utilities, office equipment, supplies, etc.

Jared: That's what I thought. But as you know, we normally receive a 2% discount from our suppliers for earlier payment, and we always try to take the discount.

Allison: That's right. I can't remember the last time we missed a discount.

Jared: Well, in that case, it seems to me the accounts payable should be listed minus the 2% discount. Let's list the accounts payable due suppliers as $76,440, rather than $78,000. Every little bit helps. You never know. It might make the difference between getting the loan and not.

➤ How would you respond to Jared Helms' request?

SA 5-3
Determining cost of purchases

The following is an excerpt from a conversation between Kate Fleming and Bob Dent. Kate is debating whether to buy a stereo system from Design Sound, a locally owned electronics store, or Big Sound Electronics, an online electronics company.

Kate: Bob, I don't know what to do about buying my new stereo.

Bob: What's the problem?

Kate: Well, I can buy it locally at Design Sound for $580.00. However, Big Sound Electronics has the same system listed for $599.99.

Bob: So what's the big deal? Buy it from Design Sound.

Kate: It's not quite that simple. Big Sound said something about not having to pay sales tax, since I was out-of-state.

Bob: Yes, that's a good point. If you buy it at Design Sound, they'll charge you 8% sales tax.

Kate: But Big Sound Electronics charges $18.99 for shipping and handling. If I have them send it next-day air, it'll cost $24.99 for shipping and handling.

Bob: I guess it is a little confusing.

Kate: That's not all. Design Sound will give an additional 1% discount if I pay cash. Otherwise, they will let me use my VISA, or I can pay it off in three monthly installments.

Bob: Anything else???

Kate: Well . . . Big Sound says I have to charge it on my VISA. They don't accept checks.

Bob: I am not surprised. Many online stores don't accept checks.

Kate: I give up. What would you do?

1. Assuming that Big Sound Electronics doesn't charge sales tax on the sale to Kate, which company is offering the best buy?
2. ➤ What might be some considerations other than price that might influence Kate's decision on where to buy the stereo system?

SA 5-4
Sales discounts

Your sister operates Emigrant Parts Company, an online boat parts distributorship that is in its third year of operation. The income statement shown below was recently prepared for the year ended July 31, 2008.

Emigrant Parts Company
Income Statement
For the Year Ended July 31, 2008

Revenues:		
Net sales		$800,000
Interest revenue		10,000
Total revenues		$810,000
Expenses:		
Cost of merchandise sold	$520,000	
Selling expenses	90,000	
Administrative expenses	48,550	
Interest expense	15,000	
Total expenses		673,550
Net income		$136,450

Your sister is considering a proposal to increase net income by offering sales discounts of 2/15, n/30, and by shipping all merchandise FOB shipping point. Currently, no sales discounts are allowed and merchandise is shipped FOB destination. It is estimated that these credit terms will increase net sales by 15%. The ratio of the cost of merchandise sold to net sales is expected to be 65%. All selling and administrative expenses are expected to remain unchanged, except for store supplies, miscellaneous selling, office supplies, and miscellaneous administrative expenses, which are expected to increase proportionately with increased net sales. The amounts of these preceding items for the year ended July 31, 2008, were as follows:

Store supplies expense	$12,000
Miscellaneous selling expense	3,000
Office supplies expense	2,000
Miscellaneous administrative expense	1,000

The other income and other expense items will remain unchanged. The shipment of all merchandise FOB shipping point will eliminate all delivery expense, which for the year ended July 31, 2008, were $18,750.

1. Prepare a projected single-step income statement for the year ending July 31, 2009, based on the proposal. Assume all sales are collected within the discount period.
2. a. ▭▬ Based on the projected income statement in (1), would you recommend the implementation of the proposed changes?
   b. Describe any possible concerns you may have related to the proposed changes described in (1).

SA 5-5
Shopping for a television

Group Project

Assume that you are planning to purchase a 50-inch Plasma television. In groups of three or four, determine the lowest cost for the television, considering the available alternatives and the advantages and disadvantages of each alternative. For example, you could purchase locally, through mail order, or through an Internet shopping service. Consider such factors as delivery charges, interest-free financing, discounts, coupons, and availability of warranty services. Prepare a report for presentation to the class.

Answers to Self-Examination Questions

1. **A**   A debit memorandum (answer A), issued by the buyer, indicates the amount the buyer proposes to debit to the accounts payable account. A credit memorandum (answer B), issued by the seller, indicates the amount the seller proposes to credit to the accounts receivable account. An invoice (answer C) or a bill (answer D), issued by the seller, indicates the amount and terms of the sale.

2. **C**   The amount of discount for early payment is $10 (answer C), or 1% of $1,000. Although the $50 of transportation costs paid by the seller is debited to the customer's account, the customer is not entitled to a discount on that amount.

3. **B**   The single-step form of income statement (answer B) is so named because the total of all expenses is deducted in one step from the total of all revenues. The multiple-step form (answer A) includes numerous sections and subsections with several subtotals. The account form (answer C) and the report form (answer D) are two common forms of the balance sheet.

4. **C**   Gross profit (answer C) is the excess of net sales over the cost of merchandise sold. Operating income (answer A) or income from operations (answer B) is the excess of gross profit over operating expenses. Net income (answer D) is the final figure on the income statement after all revenues and expenses have been reported.

5. **D**   Expenses such as interest expense (answer D) that cannot be associated directly with operations are identified as *other expense* or *nonoperating expense*. Depreciation expense—office equipment (answer A) is an administrative expense. Sales salaries expense (answer B) is a selling expense. Insurance expense (answer C) is a mixed expense with elements of both selling expense and administrative expense. For small businesses, insurance expense is usually reported as an administrative expense.

Inventories

© RYAN MCVAY/PHOTODISC/GETTY IMAGES

objectives

After studying this chapter, you should be able to:

1 **Describe the importance of control over inventory.**

2 **Describe three inventory cost flow assumptions and how they impact the income statement and balance sheet.**

3 **Determine the cost of inventory under the perpetual inventory system, using the FIFO, LIFO, and average cost methods.**

4 **Determine the cost of inventory under the periodic inventory system, using the FIFO, LIFO, and average cost methods.**

5 **Compare and contrast the use of the three inventory costing methods.**

6 **Describe and illustrate the reporting of merchandise inventory in the financial statements.**

7 **Estimate the cost of inventory, using the retail method and the gross profit method.**

Best Buy

Assume that in September you purchased a Philips HDTV plasma television from Best Buy. At the same time, you purchased a Sony surround sound system for $299.99. You liked your surround sound so well that in November you purchased an identical Sony system on sale for $249.99 for your bedroom TV. Over the holidays, you moved to a new apartment and in the process of unpacking discovered that one of the Sony surround sound systems was missing. Luckily, your renters/homeowners insurance policy will cover the theft, but the insurance company needs to know the cost of the system that was stolen.

The Sony systems were identical. However, to respond to the insurance company, you will need to identify which system was stolen. Was it the first system, which cost $299.99, or was it the second system, which cost $249.99? Whichever assumption you make may determine the amount that you receive from the insurance company.

Merchandising businesses such as Best Buy make similar assumptions when identical merchandise is purchased at different costs. For example, Best Buy may have purchased thousands of Sony surround sound systems over the past year at different costs. At the end of a period, some of the Sony systems will still be in inventory, and some will have been sold. But which costs relate to the sold systems, and which costs relate to the Sony systems still in inventory? Best Buy's assumption about inventory costs can involve large dollar amounts and, thus, can have a significant impact on the financial statements. For example, Best Buy reported $2,851,000,000 of inventory and net income of $984,000,000 for the year ending February 26, 2005.

In this chapter, we will discuss such issues as how to determine the cost of merchandise in inventory and the cost of merchandise sold. However, we begin this chapter by discussing the importance of control over inventory.

Control of Inventory

objective **1**

Describe the importance of control over inventory.

Best Buy uses scanners to screen customers as they leave the store for merchandise that has not been purchased. In addition, Best Buy stations greeters at the store's entrance to keep customers from bringing in bags that can be used to shoplift merchandise.

For companies such as Best Buy, good control over inventory must be maintained. Two primary objectives of control over inventory are safeguarding the inventory and properly reporting it in the financial statements.[1]

Control over inventory should begin as soon as the inventory is received. A *receiving report* should be completed by the company's receiving department in order to establish initial accountability for the inventory. To make sure the inventory received is what was ordered, the receiving report should agree with the company's original *purchase order* for the merchandise. A purchase order authorizes the purchase of an item from a vendor. Likewise, the price at which the inventory was ordered, as shown on the purchase order, should be compared to the price at which the vendor billed the company, as shown on the *vendor's invoice*. After the receiving report, purchase order, and vendor's invoice have been reconciled, the company should record the inventory and related account payable in the accounting records.

Controls for safeguarding inventory include developing and using security measures to prevent inventory damage or customer or employee theft. For example, inventory should be stored in a warehouse or other area to which access is restricted to authorized employees. When shopping, you may have noticed how retail stores protect inventory from customer theft. Retail stores often use such devices as two-way mirrors, cameras, and security guards. High-priced items are often displayed in locked cabinets. Retail clothing stores often place plastic alarm tags on valuable items such as leather coats. Sensors at the exit doors set off alarms if the tags have not been removed by the clerk. These controls are designed to prevent customers from shoplifting.

---

1 Additional controls used by businesses are described and illustrated in Chapter 7, "Sarbanes-Oxley, Internal Control, and Cash."

Using a perpetual inventory system for merchandise also provides an effective means of control over inventory. The amount of each type of merchandise is always readily available in a subsidiary *inventory ledger*. In addition, the subsidiary ledger can be an aid in maintaining inventory quantities at proper levels. Frequently, comparing balances with predetermined maximum and minimum levels allows for the timely re-ordering of merchandise and prevents the ordering of excess inventory.

To ensure the accuracy of the amount of inventory reported in the financial statements, a merchandising business should take a **physical inventory** (i.e., count the merchandise). In a perpetual inventory system, the physical inventory is compared to the recorded inventory in order to determine the amount of shrinkage or shortage. If the inventory shrinkage is unusually large, management can investigate further and take any necessary corrective action. Knowing that a physical inventory will be taken also helps prevent employee thefts or misuses of inventory.

Most companies take their physical inventories when their inventory levels are the lowest. For example, most retailers take their physical inventories in late January or early February, which is after the holiday selling season but before restocking for spring.

objective *2*

Describe three inventory cost flow assumptions and how they impact the income statement and balance sheet.

Inventory Cost Flow Assumptions

A major accounting issue arises when identical units of merchandise are acquired at different unit costs during a period. In such cases, when an item is sold, it is necessary to determine its unit cost using a cost flow assumption so that the proper accounting entry can be recorded. There are three common cost flow assumptions used in business. Each of these assumptions is identified with an inventory costing method, as shown below.

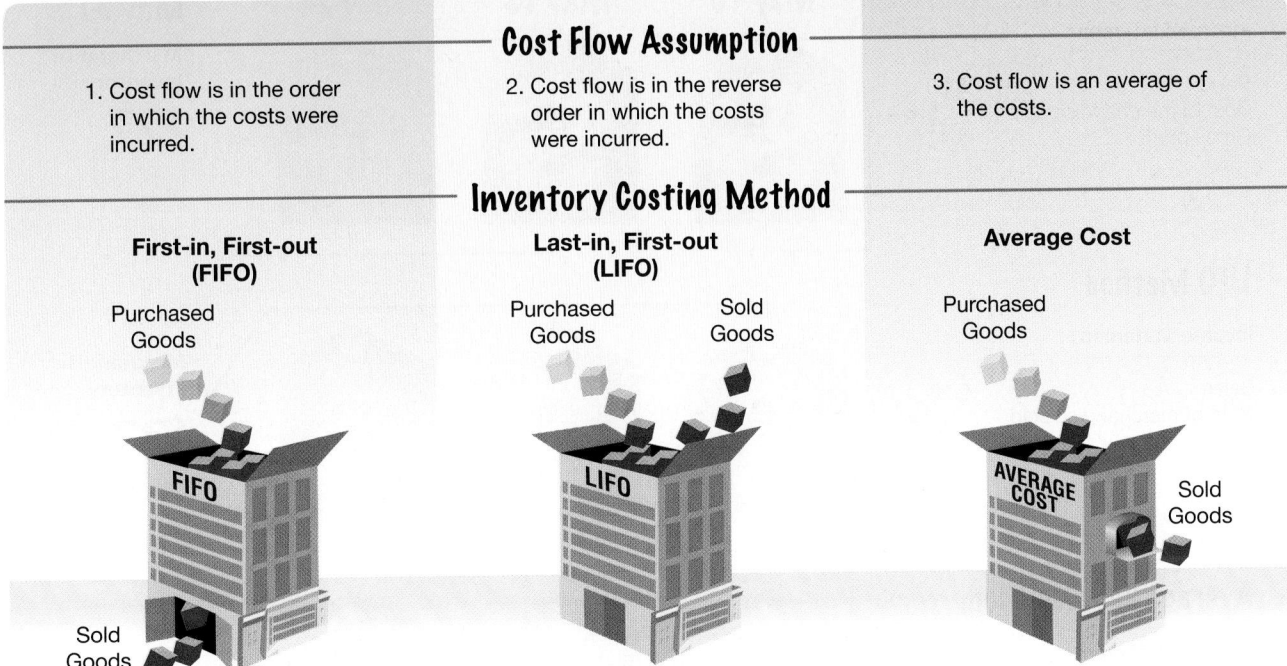

To illustrate, assume that three identical units of Item X are purchased during May, as shown at the top of page 270.

Assume that one unit is sold on May 30 for $20. If this unit can be identified with a specific purchase, the *specific identification method* can be used to determine the cost of the unit sold. For example, if the unit sold was purchased on May 18, the cost assigned to the unit is $13 and the gross profit is $7 ($20 − $13). If, however, the unit sold was purchased on May 10, the cost assigned to the unit is $9 and the gross profit is $11 ($20 − $9).

Item X		Units	Cost
May 10	Purchase	1	$ 9
18	Purchase	1	13
24	Purchase	1	14
Total		3	$36
Average cost per unit			$12

The specific identification method is normally used by automobile dealerships, jewelry stores, and art galleries.

The specific identification method is not practical unless each unit can be identified accurately. An automobile dealer, for example, may be able to use this method, since each automobile has a unique serial number. For many businesses, however, identical units cannot be separately identified, and a cost flow must be assumed. That is, which units have been sold and which units are still in inventory must be assumed using the first-in, first-out; last-in, first-out; or average cost method.

When the **first-in, first-out (FIFO) method** is used, the ending inventory is made up of the most recent costs. When the **last-in, first-out (LIFO) method** is used, the ending inventory is made up of the earliest costs. When the **average cost method** is used, the cost of the units in inventory is an average of the purchase costs.

To illustrate, we use the preceding example to prepare the income statement for May and the balance sheet as of May 31 for each of the cost flow methods, again assuming that one unit is sold. These financial statements are shown in Exhibit 1.

EXHIBIT 1 | **Effect of Inventory Costing Methods on Financial Statements**

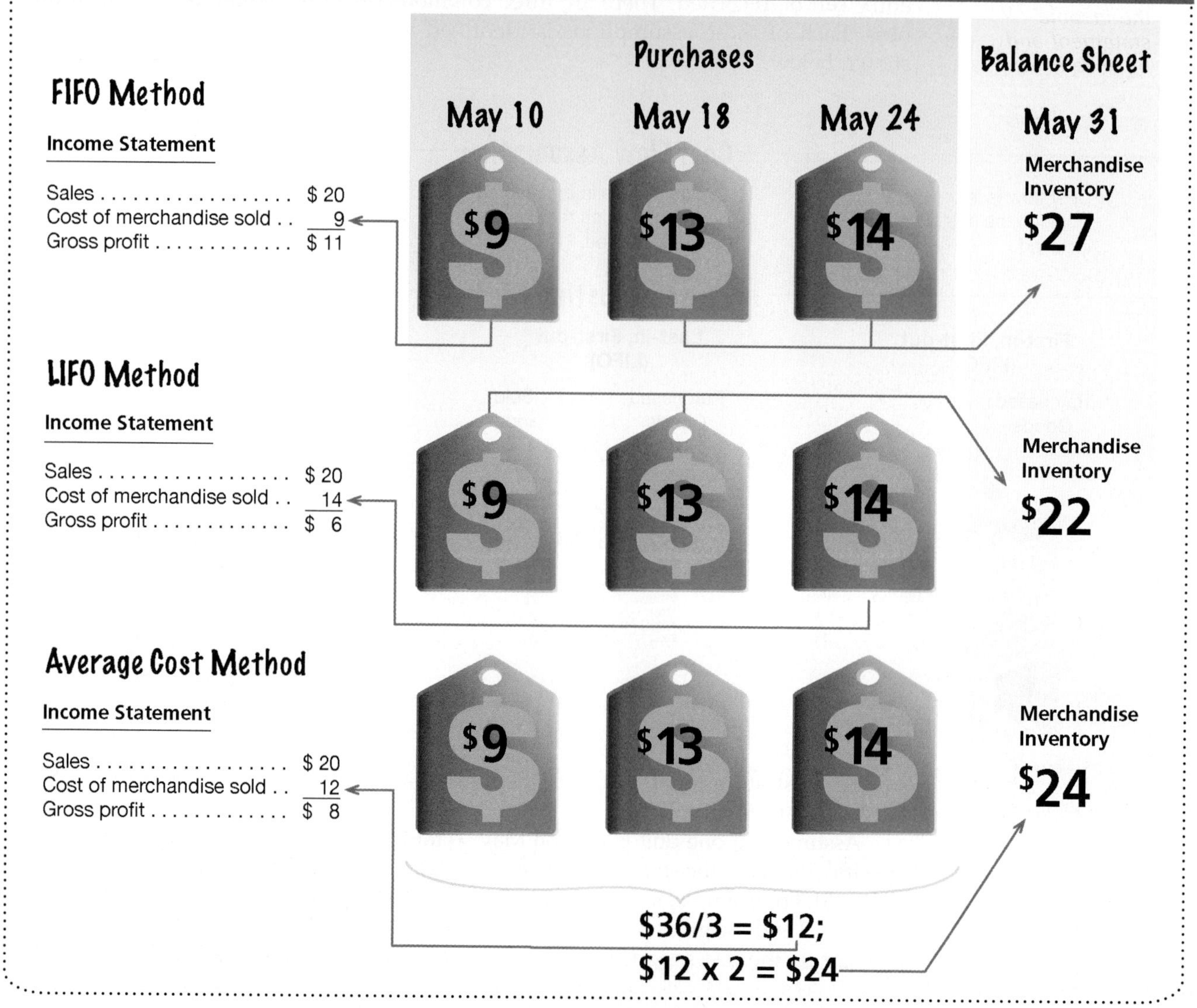

Purchases

Balance Sheet

FIFO Method

Income Statement

Sales	$ 20
Cost of merchandise sold . .	9
Gross profit	$ 11

May 10 **$9**   May 18 **$13**   May 24 **$14**

May 31

Merchandise Inventory

$27

LIFO Method

Income Statement

Sales	$ 20
Cost of merchandise sold . .	14
Gross profit	$ 6

$9   **$13**   **$14**

Merchandise Inventory

$22

Average Cost Method

Income Statement

Sales	$ 20
Cost of merchandise sold . .	12
Gross profit	$ 8

$9   **$13**   **$14**

Merchandise Inventory

$24

$36/3 = $12;
$12 x 2 = $24

As you can see, the selection of an inventory costing method can have a significant impact on the financial statements. For this reason, the selection has important implications for managers and others in analyzing and interpreting the financial statements. The chart in Exhibit 2 shows the frequency with which FIFO, LIFO, and the average methods are used in practice.

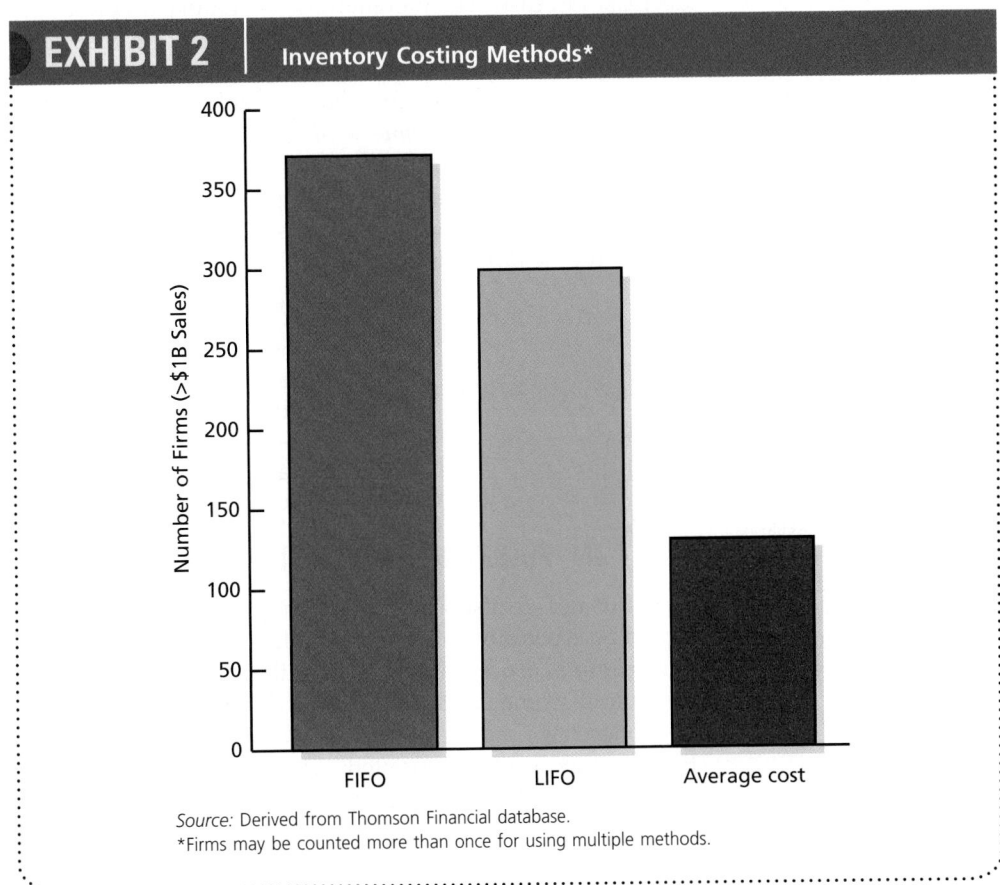

EXHIBIT 2 | **Inventory Costing Methods***

Source: Derived from Thomson Financial database.
*Firms may be counted more than once for using multiple methods.

Example Exercise 6-1
objective 2

Three identical units of Item QBM are purchased during February, as shown below.

Item QBM		Units	Cost
Feb. 8	Purchase	1	$ 45
15	Purchase	1	48
26	Purchase	1	51
Total		3	$144
Average cost per unit			$ 48 ($144/3 units)

Assume that one unit is sold on February 27 for $70.

Determine the gross profit for February and ending inventory on February 28 using the (a) first-in, first-out (FIFO); (b) last-in, first-out (LIFO); and (c) average cost methods.

Follow My Example 6-1

		Gross Profit	Ending Inventory
a.	First-in, first-out (FIFO)	$25 ($70 − $45)	$99 ($48 + $51)
b.	Last-in, first-out (LIFO)	$19 ($70 − $51)	$93 ($45 + $48)
c.	Average cost	$22 ($70 − $48)	$96 ($48 × 2)

For Practice: PE 6-1A, PE 6-1B

Inventory Costing Methods Under a Perpetual Inventory System

Determine the cost of inventory under the perpetual inventory system, using the FIFO, LIFO, and average cost methods.

Although e-tailers, such as eToys Direct, Inc., Amazon.com, and Furniture.com, Inc., don't have retail stores, they still take possession of inventory in warehouses. Thus, they must account for inventory as we are illustrating in this chapter.

In a perpetual inventory system, as we discussed in Chapter 5, all merchandise increases and decreases are recorded in a manner similar to recording increases and decreases in cash. The merchandise inventory account at the beginning of an accounting period indicates the merchandise in stock on that date. Purchases are recorded by debiting *Merchandise Inventory* and crediting *Cash* or *Accounts Payable*. On the date of each sale, the cost of the merchandise sold is recorded by debiting *Cost of Merchandise Sold* and crediting *Merchandise Inventory*.

As we illustrated in the preceding section, when identical units of an item are purchased at different unit costs during a period, a cost flow must be assumed. In such cases, the FIFO, LIFO, or average cost method is used. We illustrate each of these methods, using the data for Item 127B, shown below.

Item 127B		Units	Cost
Jan. 1	Inventory	100	$20
4	Sale	70	
10	Purchase	80	21
22	Sale	40	
28	Sale	20	
30	Purchase	100	22

FIRST-IN, FIRST-OUT METHOD

Most businesses dispose of goods in the order in which the goods are purchased. This would be especially true of perishables and goods whose styles or models often change. For example, grocery stores shelve their milk products by expiration dates. Likewise, men's and women's clothing stores display clothes by season. At the end of a season, they often have sales to clear their stores of off-season or out-of-style clothing. Thus, the FIFO method is often consistent with the *physical flow* or movement of merchandise. To the extent that this is the case, the FIFO method provides results that are about the same as those obtained by identifying the specific costs of each item sold and in inventory.

When the FIFO method of costing inventory is used, costs are included in the cost of merchandise sold in the order in which they were incurred. To illustrate, Exhibit 3

EXHIBIT 3   Entries and Perpetual Inventory Account (FIFO)

Jan. 4	Accounts Receivable	2,100	
	Sales		2,100
4	Cost of Merchandise Sold	1,400	
	Merchandise Inventory		1,400
10	Merchandise Inventory	1,680	
	Accounts Payable		1,680
22	Accounts Receivable	1,200	
	Sales		1,200
22	Cost of Merchandise Sold	810	
	Merchandise Inventory		810
28	Accounts Receivable	600	
	Sales		600
28	Cost of Merchandise Sold	420	
	Merchandise Inventory		420
30	Merchandise Inventory	2,200	
	Accounts Payable		2,200

Item 127B

	Purchases			Cost of Merchandise Sold			Inventory		
Date	Quantity	Unit Cost	Total Cost	Quantity	Unit Cost	Total Cost	Quantity	Unit Cost	Total Cost
Jan. 1							100	20	2,000
4				70	20	1,400	30	20	600
10	80	21	1,680				30	20	600
							80	21	1,680
22				30	20	600			
				10	21	210	70	21	1,470
28				20	21	420	50	21	1,050
30	100	22	2,200				50	21	1,050
							100	22	2,200
31	Balances					2,630			3,250

Cost of merchandise sold

January 31, inventory

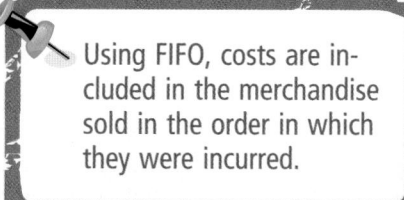

Using FIFO, costs are included in the merchandise sold in the order in which they were incurred.

shows the journal entries for purchases and sales and the inventory subsidiary ledger account for Item 127B. The number of units in inventory after each transaction, together with total costs and unit costs, are shown in the account. We assume that the units are sold on account for $30 each.

You should note that after the 70 units were sold on January 4, there was an inventory of 30 units at $20 each. The 80 units purchased on January 10 were acquired at a unit cost of $21, instead of $20. Therefore, the inventory after the January 10 purchase is reported on two lines, 30 units at $20 each and 80 units at $21 each. Next, note that the $810 cost of the 40 units sold on January 22 is made up of the remaining 30 units at $20 each and 10 unit at $21. At this point, 70 units are in inventory at a cost of $21 per unit. The remainder of the illustration is explained in a similar manner.

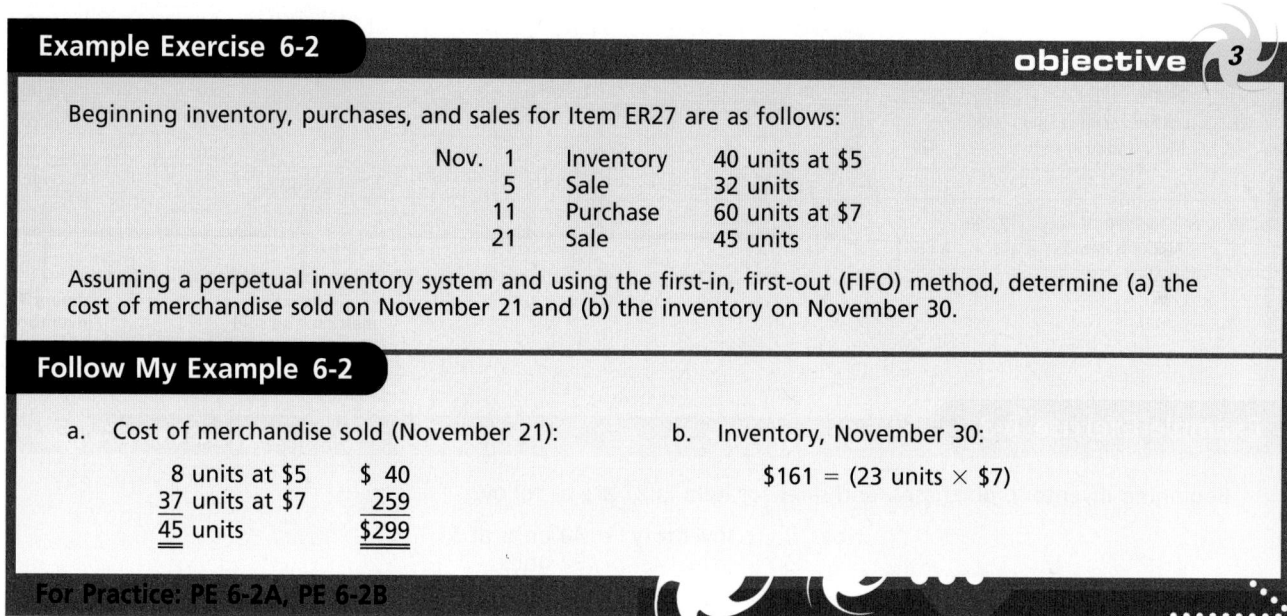

Example Exercise 6-2

objective **3**

Beginning inventory, purchases, and sales for Item ER27 are as follows:

Nov.	1	Inventory	40 units at $5
	5	Sale	32 units
	11	Purchase	60 units at $7
	21	Sale	45 units

Assuming a perpetual inventory system and using the first-in, first-out (FIFO) method, determine (a) the cost of merchandise sold on November 21 and (b) the inventory on November 30.

Follow My Example 6-2

a. Cost of merchandise sold (November 21):

8 units at $5	$ 40
37 units at $7	259
45 units	$299

b. Inventory, November 30:

$161 = (23 units × $7)

For Practice: PE 6-2A, PE 6-2B

LAST-IN, FIRST-OUT METHOD

When the LIFO method is used in a perpetual inventory system, the cost of the units sold is the cost of the most recent purchases. To illustrate, Exhibit 4 shows the journal entries for purchases and sales and the subsidiary ledger account for Item 127B, prepared on a LIFO basis.

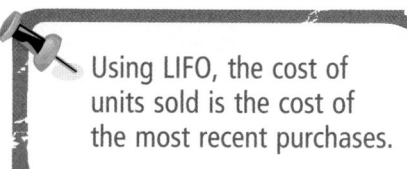

Using LIFO, the cost of units sold is the cost of the most recent purchases.

If you compare the ledger accounts for the FIFO perpetual system and the LIFO perpetual system, you should discover that the accounts are the same through the January 10 purchase. Using LIFO, however, the cost of the 40 units sold on January 22 is the cost of the units from the January 10 purchase ($21 per unit). The cost of the 70 units in inventory after the sale on January 22 is the cost of the 30 units remaining from the beginning inventory and the cost of the 40 units remaining from the January 10 purchase. The remainder of the LIFO illustration is explained in a similar manner.

When the LIFO method is used, the inventory ledger is sometimes maintained in units only. The units are converted to dollars when the financial statements are prepared at the end of the period.

The use of the LIFO method was originally limited to rare situations in which the units sold were taken from the most recently acquired goods. For tax reasons, which we will discuss later, its use has greatly increased during the past few decades. LIFO is now often used even when it does not represent the physical flow of goods.

EXHIBIT 4   Entries and Perpetual Inventory Account (LIFO)

Jan. 4 Accounts Receivable 2,100
         Sales   2,100

      4 Cost of Merchandise Sold 1,400
         Merchandise Inventory   1,400

     10 Merchandise Inventory   1,680
         Accounts Payable   1,680

     22 Accounts Receivable   1,200
         Sales   1,200

     22 Cost of Merchandise Sold   840
         Merchandise Inventory   840

     28 Accounts Receivable   600
         Sales   600

     28 Cost of Merchandise Sold   420
         Merchandise Inventory   420

     30 Merchandise Inventory   2,200
         Accounts Payable   2,200

Item 127B

	Purchases			Cost of Merchandise Sold			Inventory		
Date	Quantity	Unit Cost	Total Cost	Quantity	Unit Cost	Total Cost	Quantity	Unit Cost	Total Cost
Jan. 1							100	20	2,000
4				70	20	1,400	30	20	600
10	80	21	1,680				30	20	600
							80	21	1,680
22				40	21	840	30	20	600
							40	21	840
28				20	21	420	30	20	600
							20	21	420
30	100	22	2,200				30	20	600
							20	21	420
							100	22	2,200
31	Balances					2,660			3,220

↑ Cost of merchandise sold

↑ January 31, inventory

Beginning inventory, purchases, and sales for Item ER27 are as follows:

Nov.	1	Inventory	40 units at $5
	5	Sale	32 units
	11	Purchase	60 units at $7
	21	Sale	45 units

Assuming a perpetual inventory system and using the last-in, first-out (LIFO) method, determine (a) the cost of the merchandise sold on November 21 and (b) the inventory on November 30.

Follow My Example 6-3

a. Cost of merchandise sold (November 21):

    $315 = (45 units × $7)

b. Inventory, November 30:

    8 units at $5 $ 40
    15 units at $7   105
    23 units $145

For Practice: PE 6-3A, PE 6-3B

REAL WORLD

The FIFO, LIFO, and average cost flow assumptions also apply to other areas of business. For example, individuals and businesses often purchase marketable securities at different costs per share. When such investments are sold, the investor must either specifically identify which shares are sold or use the FIFO cost flow assumption.

AVERAGE COST METHOD

When the average cost method is used in a perpetual inventory system, an average unit cost for each type of item is computed each time a purchase is made. This unit cost is then used to determine the cost of each sale until another purchase is made and a new average is computed. This averaging technique is called a *moving average*. Since the average cost method is rarely used in a perpetual inventory system, we do not illustrate it in this chapter.

COMPUTERIZED PERPETUAL INVENTORY SYSTEMS

The records for a perpetual inventory system may be maintained manually. However, such a system is costly and time consuming for businesses with a large number of inventory items with many purchase and sales transactions. In most cases, the record keeping for perpetual inventory systems is computerized.

An example of using computers in maintaining perpetual inventory records for retail stores follows.

1. The relevant details for each inventory item, such as a description, quantity, and unit size, are stored in an inventory record. The individual inventory records make up the computerized inventory file, the total of which agrees with the balance of the inventory ledger account.
2. Each time an item is purchased or returned by a customer, the inventory data are entered into the computer's inventory records and files.
3. Each time an item is sold, a salesclerk scans the item's bar code with an optical scanner. The scanner reads the magnetic code and rings up the sale on the cash register. The inventory records and files are then updated for the cost of goods sold.
4. After a physical inventory is taken, the inventory count data are entered into the computer. These data are compared with the current balances, and a listing of the overages and shortages is printed. The inventory balances are then adjusted to the quantities determined by the physical count.

Wal-Mart, Target, and other retailers use bar code scanners as part of their perpetual inventory systems.

Such systems can be extended to aid managers in controlling and managing inventory quantities. For example, items that are selling fast can be reordered before the stock is depleted. Past sales patterns can be analyzed to determine when to mark down merchandise for sales and when to restock seasonal merchandise. In addition, such systems can provide managers with data for developing and fine-tuning their marketing strategies. For example, such data can be used to evaluate the effectiveness of advertising campaigns and sales promotions.

Inventory Costing Methods Under a Periodic Inventory System

objective **4**

Determine the cost of inventory under the periodic inventory system, using the FIFO, LIFO, and average cost methods.

When the periodic inventory system is used, only revenue is recorded each time a sale is made. No entry is made at the time of the sale to record the cost of the merchandise sold. At the end of the accounting period, a physical inventory is taken to determine the cost of the inventory and the cost of the merchandise sold.[2]

Like the perpetual inventory system, a cost flow assumption must be made when identical units are acquired at different unit costs during a period. In such cases, the FIFO, LIFO, or average cost method is used.

FIRST-IN, FIRST-OUT METHOD

To illustrate the use of the FIFO method in a periodic inventory system, we use the same data for Item 127B as in the perpetual inventory example. The beginning inventory entry and purchases of Item 127B in January are as follows:

Jan.	1	Inventory:	100 units at	$20	$2,000
	10	Purchase:	80 units at	21	1,680
	30	Purchase:	100 units at	22	2,200
Available for sale during month			280		$5,880

---

2 Determining the cost of merchandise sold using the periodic system was illustrated in Chapter 5.

The physical count on January 31 shows that 150 units are on hand. Using the FIFO method, the cost of the merchandise on hand at the end of the period is made up of the most recent costs. The cost of the 150 units in ending inventory on January 31 is determined as follows:

Most recent costs, January 30 purchase	100 units at	$22	$2,200
Next most recent costs, January 10 purchase	50 units at	$21	1,050
Inventory, January 31	150 units		$3,250

Deducting the cost of the January 31 inventory of $3,250 from the cost of merchandise available for sale of $5,880 yields the cost of merchandise sold of $2,630, as shown below.

Beginning inventory, January 1	$2,000
Purchases ($1,680 + $2,200)	3,880
Cost of merchandise available for sale in January	$5,880
Ending inventory, January 31	3,250
Cost of merchandise sold	$2,630

The $3,250 cost of the ending merchandise inventory on January 31 is made up of the most recent costs. The $2,630 cost of merchandise sold is made up of the beginning inventory and the earliest costs. Exhibit 5 shows the relationship of the cost of merchandise sold for January and the ending inventory on January 31.

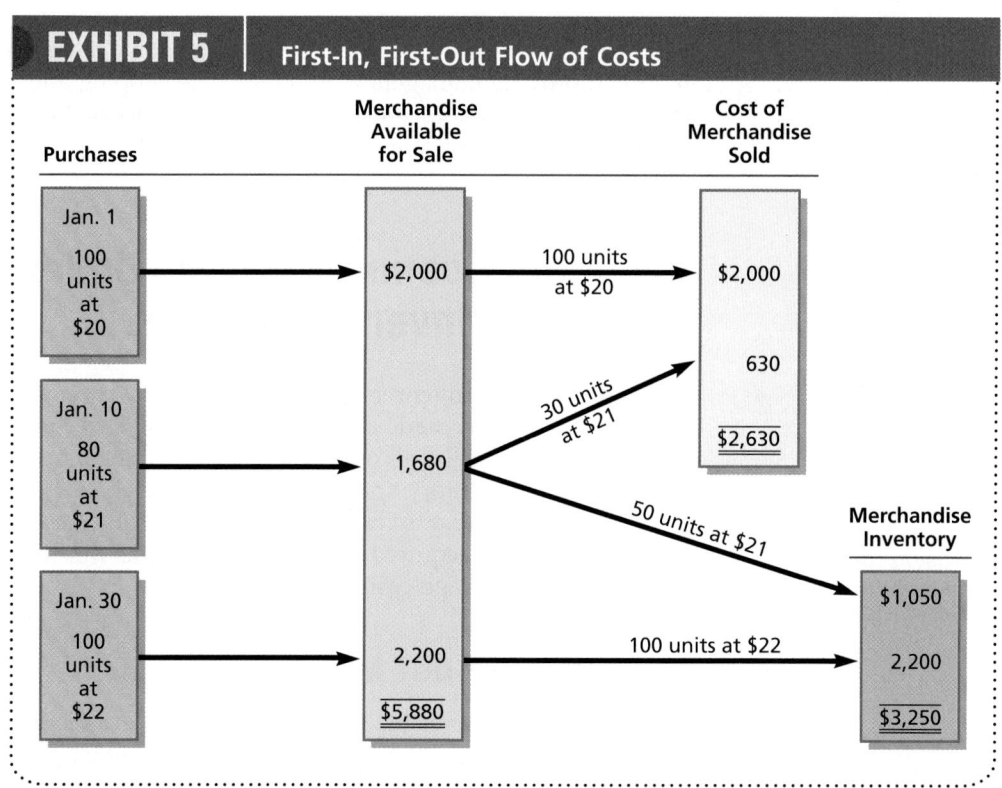

EXHIBIT 5 | **First-In, First-Out Flow of Costs**

LAST-IN, FIRST-OUT METHOD

When the LIFO method is used, the cost of merchandise on hand at the end of the period is made up of the earliest costs. Based upon the same data as in the FIFO example, the cost of the 150 units in ending inventory on January 31 is determined as follows:

Beginning inventory, January 1	100 units at	$20	$2,000
Next earliest costs, January 10	50 units at	$21	1,050
Inventory, January 31	150 units		$3,050

Deducting the cost of the January 31 inventory of $3,050 from the cost of merchandise available for sale of $5,880 yields the cost of merchandise sold of $2,830, as shown below.

Beginning inventory, January 1	$2,000
Purchases ($1,680 + $2,200)	3,880
Cost of merchandise available for sale in January	$5,880
Ending inventory, January 31	3,050
Cost of merchandise sold	$2,830

The $3,050 cost of the ending merchandise inventory on January 31 is made up of the earliest costs. The $2,830 cost of merchandise sold is made up of the most recent costs. Exhibit 6 shows the relationship of the cost of merchandise sold for January and the ending inventory on January 31.

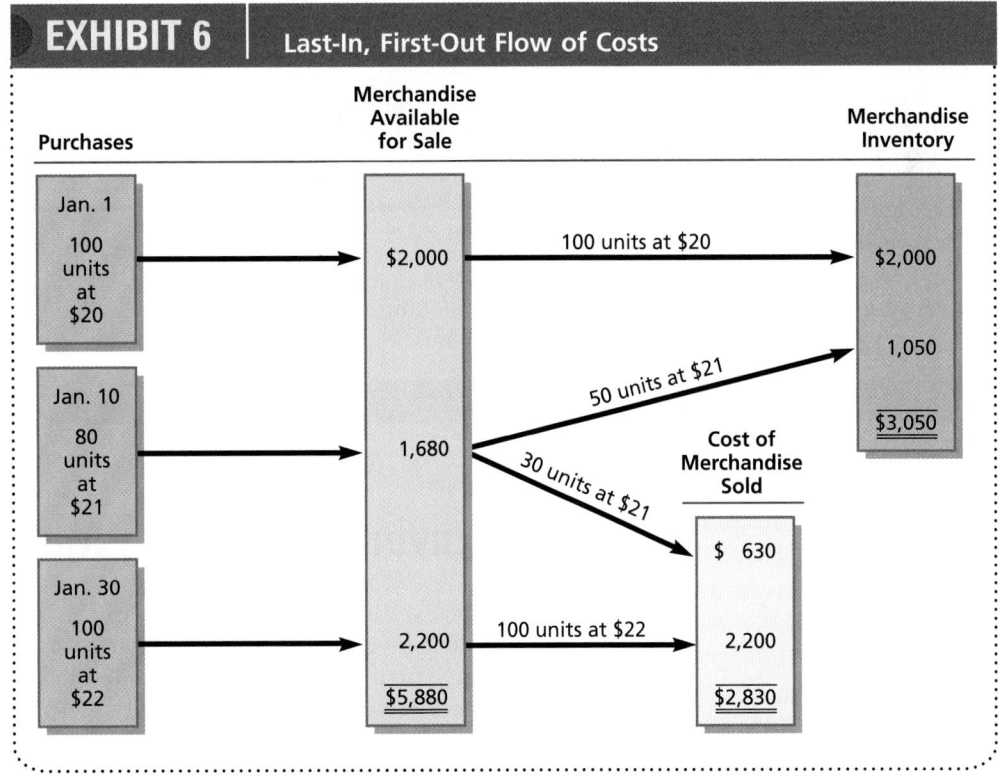

EXHIBIT 6 | **Last-In, First-Out Flow of Costs**

AVERAGE COST METHOD

The average cost method is sometimes called the *weighted average method*. When this method is used, costs are matched against revenue according to an average of the unit costs of the goods sold. The same weighted average unit costs are used in determining the cost of the merchandise inventory at the end of the period. For businesses in which merchandise sales may be made up of various purchases of identical units, the average cost method approximates the physical flow of goods.

The weighted average unit cost is determined by dividing the total cost of the units of each item available for sale during the period by the related number of units of that item. Using the same cost data as in the FIFO and LIFO examples, the average cost of the 280 units, $21, and the cost of 150 units in ending inventory, are determined as follows:

Average unit cost: $5,880/280 units = $21
Inventory, January 31: 150 units at $21 = $3,150

Deducting the cost of the January 31 inventory of $3,150 from the cost of merchandise available for sale of $5,880 yields the cost of merchandise sold of $2,730, as shown below.

Beginning inventory, January 1	$2,000
Purchases ($1,680 + $2,200)	3,880
Cost of merchandise available for sale in January	$5,880
Ending inventory, January 31	3,150
Cost of merchandise sold	$2,730

Example Exercise 6-4

 objective 4

The units of an item available for sale during the year were as follows:

Jan. 1	Inventory	6 units at $50	$ 300
Mar. 20	Purchase	14 units at $55	770
Oct. 30	Purchase	20 units at $62	1,240
	Available for sale	40 units	$2,310

There are 16 units of the item in the physical inventory at December 31. The periodic inventory system is used. Determine the inventory cost using (a) the first-in, first-out (FIFO) method, (b) the last-in, first-out (LIFO) method, and (c) the average cost method.

Follow My Example 6-4

a.   First-in, first-out (FIFO) method: $992 = (16 units × $62)
b.   Last-in, first-out (LIFO) method: $850 = (6 units × $50) + (10 units × $55)
c.   Average cost method: $924 (16 units × $57.75), where average cost = $57.75 = $2,310/40 units

 For Practice: PE 6-4A, PE 6-4B

Comparing Inventory Costing Methods

objective 5

Compare and contrast the use of the three inventory costing methods.

As we have illustrated, a different cost flow is assumed for each of the three alternative methods of costing inventories. You should note that if the cost of units had remained stable, all three methods would have yielded the same results. Since prices do change, however, the three methods will normally yield different amounts for (1) the cost of the merchandise sold for the period, (2) the gross profit (and net income) for the period, and (3) the ending inventory. Using the preceding examples for the periodic inventory system and sales of $3,900 (130 units × $30), the partial income statements, shown on page 279, indicate the effects of each method when prices are rising.[3]

As shown in the partial income statements, the FIFO method yielded the lowest amount for the cost of merchandise sold and the highest amount for gross profit (and net income). It also yielded the highest amount for the ending inventory. On the other hand, the LIFO method yielded the highest amount for the cost of merchandise sold, the lowest amount for gross profit (and net income), and the lowest amount for ending inventory. The average cost method yielded results that were between those of FIFO and LIFO.

---

3 Similar results would also occur when comparing inventory costing methods under a perpetual inventory system.

Partial Income Statements

	First-In, First-Out		Average Cost		Last-In, First-Out	
Net sales		$3,900		$3,900		$3,900
Cost of merchandise sold:						
Beginning inventory	$2,000		$2,000		$2,000	
Purchases	3,880		3,880		3,880	
Merchandise available for sale	$5,880		$5,880		$5,880	
Less ending inventory	3,250		3,150		3,050	
Cost of merchandise sold		2,630		2,730		2,830
Gross profit		$1,270		$1,170		$1,070

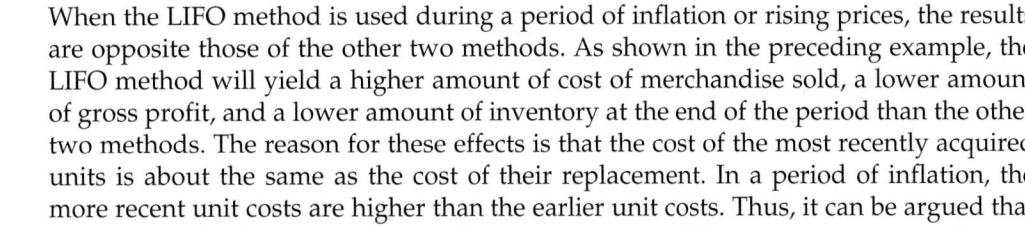

USE OF THE FIRST-IN, FIRST-OUT METHOD

When the FIFO method is used during a period of inflation or rising prices, the earlier unit costs are lower than the more recent unit costs, as shown in the preceding FIFO example. Thus, FIFO will show a larger gross profit. However, the inventory must be replaced at prices higher than indicated by the cost of merchandise sold. In fact, the balance sheet will report the ending merchandise inventory at an amount that is about the same as its current replacement cost. When the rate of inflation reaches double digits, as it did during the 1970s, the larger gross profits that result from the FIFO method are often called *inventory profits* or *illusory profits*. You should note that in a period of deflation or declining prices, the effect is just the opposite.

USE OF THE LAST-IN, FIRST-OUT METHOD

When the LIFO method is used during a period of inflation or rising prices, the results are opposite those of the other two methods. As shown in the preceding example, the LIFO method will yield a higher amount of cost of merchandise sold, a lower amount of gross profit, and a lower amount of inventory at the end of the period than the other two methods. The reason for these effects is that the cost of the most recently acquired units is about the same as the cost of their replacement. In a period of inflation, the more recent unit costs are higher than the earlier unit costs. Thus, it can be argued that the LIFO method more nearly matches current costs with current revenues.

During periods of rising prices, using LIFO offers an income tax savings. The income tax savings results because LIFO reports the lowest amount of net income of the three methods. During the double-digit inflationary period of the 1970s, many businesses changed from FIFO to LIFO for the tax savings. However, the ending inventory on the balance sheet may be quite different from its current replacement cost. In such cases, the financial statements normally include a note that states the estimated difference between the LIFO inventory and the inventory if FIFO had been used. Again, you should note that in a period of deflation or falling price levels, the effects are just the opposite.

USE OF THE AVERAGE COST METHOD

As you might have already reasoned, the average cost method of inventory costing is, in a sense, a compromise between FIFO and LIFO. The effect of price trends is averaged in determining the cost of merchandise sold and the ending inventory. For a series of purchases, the average cost will be the same, regardless of the direction of price trends. For example, a complete reversal of the sequence of unit costs presented in the preceding illustration would not affect the reported cost of merchandise sold, gross profit, or ending inventory.

Integrity, Objectivity, and Ethics in Business

ETHICS

WHERE'S THE BONUS?

Managers are often given bonuses based on reported earnings numbers. This can create a conflict. LIFO can improve the value of the company through lower taxes. However, LIFO also produces a lower earnings number and, therefore, lower management bonuses. Ethically, managers should select accounting procedures that will maximize the value of the firm, rather than their own compensation. Compensation specialists can help avoid this ethical dilemma by adjusting the bonus plan for the accounting procedure differences.

Reporting Merchandise Inventory in the Financial Statements

objective **6**

Describe and illustrate the reporting of merchandise inventory in the financial statements.

REAL WORLD

Dell Inc. recorded over $39.3 million of charges (expenses) in writing down its inventory of notebook computers. The remaining inventories of computers were then sold at significantly reduced prices.

As we indicated earlier, cost is the primary basis for valuing inventories. In some cases, however, inventory is valued at other than cost. Two such cases arise when (1) the cost of replacing items in inventory is below the recorded cost and (2) the inventory is not salable at normal sales prices. This latter case may be due to imperfections, shop wear, style changes, or other causes.

VALUATION AT LOWER OF COST OR MARKET

If the cost of replacing an item in inventory is lower than the original purchase cost, the **lower-of-cost-or-market (LCM) method** is used to value the inventory. *Market*, as used in *lower of cost or market*, is the cost to replace the merchandise on the inventory date. This market value is based on quantities normally purchased from the usual source of supply. In businesses where inflation is the norm, market prices rarely decline. In businesses where technology changes rapidly (e.g., microcomputers and televisions), market declines are common. The primary advantage of the lower-of-cost-or-market method is that gross profit (and net income) is reduced in the period in which the market decline occurred.

In applying the lower-of-cost-or-market method, the cost and replacement cost can be determined in one of three ways. Cost and replacement cost can be determined for (1) each item in the inventory, (2) major classes or categories of inventory, or (3) the inventory as a whole. In practice, the cost and replacement cost of each item are usually determined.

To illustrate, assume that there are 400 identical units of Item A in inventory, acquired at a unit cost of $10.25 each. If at the inventory date the item would cost $10.50 to replace, the cost price of $10.25 would be multiplied by 400 to determine the inventory value. On the other hand, if the item could be replaced at $9.50 a unit, the replacement cost of $9.50 would be used for valuation purposes.

Exhibit 7 illustrates a method of organizing inventory data and applying the lower-of-cost-or-market method to each inventory item. The amount of the market decline, $450 ($15,520 − $15,070), may be reported as a separate item on the income statement

EXHIBIT 7

Determining Inventory at Lower of Cost or Market

	A	B	C	D	E	F	G	
			Unit	Unit		Total		
		Inventory	Cost	Market			Lower	
	Commodity	Quantity	Price	Price	Cost	Market	of C or M	
1	A	400	$10.25	$ 9.50	$ 4,100	$ 3,800	$ 3,800	1
2	B	120	22.50	24.10	2,700	2,892	2,700	2
3	C	600	8.00	7.75	4,800	4,650	4,650	3
4	D	280	14.00	14.75	3,920	4,130	3,920	4
5	Total				$15,520	$15,472	$15,070	5

or included in the cost of merchandise sold. Regardless, net income will be reduced by the amount of the market decline.

Example Exercise 6-5

objective **6**

On the basis of the following data, determine the value of the inventory at the lower of cost or market. Apply lower of cost or market to each inventory item as shown in Exhibit 7.

Commodity	Inventory Quantity	Unit Cost Price	Unit Market Price
C17Y	10	$ 39	$40
B563	7	110	98

Follow My Example 6-5

	A	B	C	D	E	F	G	
			Unit	Unit	Total			
		Inventory	Cost	Market			Lower	
	Commodity	Quantity	Price	Price	Cost	Market	of C or M	
1	C17Y	10	$ 39	$ 40	$ 390	$ 400	$ 390	1
2	B563	7	110	98	770	686	686	2
3	Total				$1,160	$1,086	$1,076	3

For Practice: PE 6-5A, PE 6-5B

VALUATION AT NET REALIZABLE VALUE

REAL WORLD

Out-of-date merchandise is a major problem for many types of retailers. For example, you may have noticed the shelf-life dates of grocery products, such as milk, eggs, canned goods, and meat. Grocery stores often mark down the prices of products nearing the end of their shelf life to avoid having to dispose of the products as waste.

As you would expect, merchandise that is out of date, spoiled, or damaged or that can be sold only at prices below cost should be written down. Such merchandise should be valued at net realizable value. **Net realizable value** is the estimated selling price less any direct cost of disposal, such as sales commissions. For example, assume that damaged merchandise costing $1,000 can be sold for only $800, and direct selling expenses are estimated to be $150. This inventory should be valued at $650 ($800 − $150), which is its net realizable value.

For example, Digital Theater Systems Inc. provides digital entertainment technologies, products, and services to the motion picture, consumer electronics, and professional audio industries. In the notes to its recent financial statements, Digital Theater reported the following write-downs of its monochrome projector inventory:

Inventories are stated at the lower of cost or market. Cost is determined using the first-in, first-out method. The Company evaluates its ending inventories for estimated excess quantities and obsolescence. The Company's evaluation includes the analysis of future sales demand by product, within specific time horizons. Inventories in excess of projected future demand are written down to net realizable value. In addition, the Company assesses the impact of changing technology on inventory balances and writes down inventories that are considered obsolete. The Company recorded an inventory write-down of $3,871 (thousands) related to its monochrome projector inventory during the year ended December 31, 2004 due to declines in future demand and technological obsolescence.

REAL WORLD

General Motors Corporation uses the last-in, first-out (LIFO) method to account for all U.S. inventories other than those of Saturn Corporation. The cost of non-U.S., Saturn inventories is determined by using either first-in, first-out (FIFO) or average cost.

MERCHANDISE INVENTORY ON THE BALANCE SHEET

Merchandise inventory is usually presented in the Current Assets section of the balance sheet, following receivables. Both the method of determining the cost of the inventory (FIFO, LIFO, or average) and the method of valuing the inventory (cost or the lower of cost or market) should be shown. It is not unusual for large businesses with varied activities to use different costing methods for different segments of their inventories.

The details may be disclosed in parentheses on the balance sheet or in a note to the financial statements. Exhibit 8 shows how parentheses may be used.

A company may change its inventory costing methods for a valid reason. In such cases, the effect of the change and the reason for the change should be disclosed in the financial statements for the period in which the change occurred.

EXHIBIT 8　　Merchandise Inventory on the Balance Sheet

Metro Arts
Balance Sheet
December 31, 2008

Assets			
Current assets:			
Cash			$ 19 4 0 0 00
Accounts receivable	$80 0 0 0 00		
Less allowance for doubtful accounts	3 0 0 0 00	77 0 0 0 00	
Merchandise inventory—at lower of cost (first-in, first-out method) or market		216 3 0 0 00	

EFFECT OF INVENTORY ERRORS ON THE FINANCIAL STATEMENTS

Any errors in the merchandise inventory will affect both the balance sheet and the income statement. For example, an error in the physical inventory will misstate the ending inventory, current assets, and total assets on the balance sheet. In addition, an error in inventory will also affect the cost of merchandise sold and gross profit on the income statement.

To illustrate the effect of inventory errors on the financial statements, we use the following partial income statement of SysExpress Company. We will illustrate the effect of inventory errors using the periodic system. This is because it is easier to see the impact of inventory errors on the income statement using the periodic system.[4]

SysExpress Company
Income Statement
For the Year Ended December 31, 2008

Net sales		$980,000
Merchandise inventory, January 1, 2008	$ 55,000	
Purchases	650,000	
Merchandise available for sale	$705,000	
Less merchandise inventory, December 31, 2008	60,000	
Cost of merchandise sold		645,000
Gross profit		$335,000

Assume that in taking the physical inventory on December 31, 2008, SysExpress incorrectly records its physical inventory as $57,500 instead of the correct amount of $60,000. As a result, the merchandise inventory, current assets, and total assets reported on the December 31, 2008, balance sheet would be understated by $2,500 ($60,000 − $57,500). Because the ending physical inventory is understated, the cost of merchandise sold will be overstated by $2,500. Thus, the gross profit and the net income for the year will be understated by $2,500. Since the net income is closed to the retained earnings account at the end of the period, the stockholders' equity on the December 31, 2008, balance sheet will also be understated by $2,500. These effects on SysExpress's financial statements are summarized as follows:

---

4 The effect of inventory errors would be the same under the perpetual inventory system.

	Amount of Misstatement
Balance Sheet:	
Merchandise inventory understated	$(2,500)
Current assets understated	(2,500)
Total assets understated	(2,500)
Stockholders' equity understated	(2,500)
Income Statement:	
Cost of merchandise sold overstated	$ 2,500
Gross profit understated	(2,500)
Net income understated	(2,500)

Now assume that in the preceding example the physical inventory had been overstated on December 31, 2008, by $2,500. That is, SysExpress erroneously recorded its inventory as $62,500. In this case, the effects on the balance sheet and income statement would be just the opposite of those indicated above.

Inventory errors often arise from shipping terms and inventory held on consignment. As we discussed in Chapter 5, shipping terms determine when the title to merchandise passes. When goods are purchased or sold *FOB shipping point*, title passes to the buyer when the goods are shipped. When the terms are *FOB destination*, title passes to the buyer when the goods are delivered.

To illustrate inventory errors arising from shipping terms, assume that SysExpress orders $8,300 of merchandise FOB shipping point on December 27. Assume also that the supplier ships the merchandise on December 30. When SysExpress counts its physical inventory on December 31, the merchandise is still in transit. In such cases, it would be easy for SysExpress to overlook the inventory in transit and not include it in the December 31 physical inventory. Likewise, merchandise *sold* by SysExpress FOB destination is still SysExpress's inventory even if it is still in transit to the buyer on December 31.

Inventory errors also arise frequently from consigned inventory. Manufacturers sometimes ship merchandise to retailers who act as the manufacturer's agent when selling the merchandise. The manufacturer, called the *consignor*, retains title until the goods are sold. Such merchandise is said to be shipped on consignment to the retailer, called the *consignee*. The unsold merchandise is a part of the manufacturer's (consignor's) inventory, even though the merchandise is in the hands of the retailer (consignee). In taking its year-end physical inventory, the retailer (consignee) must be careful to not include any consigned inventory on hand as part of its physical inventory. Likewise, the manufacturer (consignor) must be careful to include consigned inventory in its physical inventory even though the inventory is not on hand.

Example Exercise 6-6   objective 6

Zula Repair Shop incorrectly counted its December 31, 2008, inventory as $250,000 instead of the correct amount of $220,000. Indicate the effect of the misstatement on Zula's December 31, 2008, balance sheet and income statement for the year ended December 31, 2008.

Follow My Example 6-6

	Amount of Misstatement Overstatement (Understatement)
Balance Sheet:	
Merchandise inventory overstated	$ 30,000
Current assets overstated	30,000
Total assets overstated	30,000
Stockholders' equity overstated	30,000
Income Statement:	
Cost of merchandise sold understated	$(30,000)
Gross profit overstated	30,000
Net income overstated	30,000

For Practice: PE 6-6A, PE 6-6B

Estimating Inventory Cost

objective   **7**

Estimate the cost of inventory, using the retail method and the gross profit method.

It may be necessary for a business to know the amount of inventory when perpetual inventory records are not maintained and it is impractical to take a physical inventory. For example, a business that uses a periodic inventory system may need monthly income statements, but taking a physical inventory each month may be too costly. Moreover, when a disaster such as a fire has destroyed the inventory, the amount of the loss must be determined. In this case, taking a physical inventory is impossible, and even if perpetual inventory records have been kept, the accounting records may also have been destroyed. In such cases, the inventory cost can be estimated by using (1) the retail method or (2) the gross profit method.

RETAIL METHOD OF INVENTORY COSTING

The **retail inventory method** of estimating inventory cost is based on the relationship of the cost of merchandise available for sale to the retail price of the same merchandise. To use this method, the retail prices of all merchandise are maintained and totaled. Next, the inventory at retail is determined by deducting sales for the period from the retail price of the goods that were available for sale during the period. The estimated inventory cost is then computed by multiplying the inventory at retail by the ratio of cost to selling (retail) price for the merchandise available for sale, as illustrated in Exhibit 9.

EXHIBIT 9

Determining Inventory by the Retail Method

	A	B Cost	C Retail	
1	Merchandise inventory, January 1	$19,400	$ 36,000	1
2	Purchases in January (net)	42,600	64,000	2
3	Merchandise available for sale	$62,000	$100,000	3
4	Ratio of cost to retail price: $\frac{\$62,000}{\$100,000} = 62\%$			4
5	Sales for January (net)		70,000	5
6	Merchandise inventory, January 31, at retail		$ 30,000	6
7	Merchandise inventory, January 31, at estimated cost			7
8	($30,000 × 62%)		$ 18,600	8

When estimating the percent of cost to selling price, we assume that the mix of the items in the ending inventory is the same as the entire stock of merchandise available for sale. In Exhibit 9, for example, it is unlikely that the retail price of every item was made up of exactly 62% cost and 38% gross profit. We assume, however, that the weighted average of the cost percentages of the merchandise in the inventory ($30,000) is the same as in the merchandise available for sale ($100,000).

When the inventory is made up of different classes of merchandise with very different gross profit rates, the cost percentages and the inventory should be developed for each class of inventory.

One of the major advantages of the retail method is that it provides inventory figures for preparing monthly or quarterly statements when the periodic system is used. Department stores and similar merchandisers like to determine gross profit and operating income each month but may take a physical inventory only once or twice a year. In addition, comparing the estimated ending inventory with the physical ending inventory, both at retail prices, will help identify inventory shortages resulting from shoplifting and other causes. Management can then take appropriate actions.

The retail method may also be used as an aid in taking a physical inventory. In this case, the items counted are recorded on the inventory sheets at their retail (selling) prices instead of their cost prices. The physical inventory at selling price is then converted to cost by applying the ratio of cost to selling (retail) price for the merchandise available for sale.

To illustrate, assume that the data in Exhibit 9 are for an entire fiscal year rather than for only January. If the physical inventory taken at the end of the year totaled $29,000, priced at retail, this amount rather than the $30,000 would be converted to cost. Thus, the inventory at cost would be $17,980 ($29,000 × 62%) instead of $18,600 ($30,000 × 62%). The $17,980 would be used for the year-end financial statements and for income tax purposes.

Example Exercise 6-7

objective 7

A business using the retail method of inventory costing determines that merchandise inventory at retail is $900,000. If the ratio of cost to retail price is 70%, what is the amount of inventory to be reported on the financial statements?

Follow My Example 6-7

$630,000 ($900,000 × 70%)

For Practice: PE 6-7A, PE 6-7B

GROSS PROFIT METHOD OF ESTIMATING INVENTORIES

The **gross profit method** uses the estimated gross profit for the period to estimate the inventory at the end of the period. The gross profit is usually estimated from the actual rate for the preceding year, adjusted for any changes made in the cost and sales prices during the current period. By using the gross profit rate, the dollar amount of sales for a period can be divided into its two components: (1) gross profit and (2) cost of merchandise sold. The latter amount may then be deducted from the cost of merchandise available for sale to yield the estimated cost of the inventory.

Exhibit 10 illustrates the gross profit method for estimating a company's inventory on January 31. In this example, the inventory on January 1 is assumed to be $57,000, the net purchases during the month are $180,000, and the net sales during the month are $250,000. In addition, the historical gross profit was 30% of net sales.

EXHIBIT 10

Estimating Inventory by Gross Profit Method

	A	B	C	
1	Merchandise inventory, January 1		$ 57,000	1
2	Purchases in January (net)		180,000	2
3	Merchandise available for sale		$237,000	3
4	Sales for January (net)	$250,000		4
5	Less estimated gross profit ($250,000 × 30%)	75,000		5
6	Estimated cost of merchandise sold		175,000	6
7	Estimated merchandise inventory, January 31		$ 62,000	7

The gross profit method is useful for estimating inventories for monthly or quarterly financial statements in a periodic inventory system. It is also useful in estimating the cost of merchandise destroyed by fire or other disasters.

Example Exercise 6-8   objective 7

Based upon the following data, estimate the cost of ending merchandise inventory:

Sales (net)	$1,250,000
Estimated gross profit rate	40%
Beginning merchandise inventory	$100,000
Purchases (net)	800,000
Merchandise available for sale	$900,000

Follow My Example 6-8

Merchandise available for sale	$900,000
Less cost of merchandise sold [$1,250,000 × (100% − 40%)]	750,000
Estimated ending merchandise inventory	$150,000

For Practice: PE 6-8A, PE 6-8B

Financial Analysis and Interpretation

A merchandising business should keep enough inventory on hand to meet the needs of its customers. A failure to do so may result in lost sales. At the same time, too much inventory reduces solvency by tying up funds that could be better used to expand or improve operations. In addition, excess inventory increases expenses such as storage, insurance, and property taxes. Finally, excess inventory increases the risk of losses due to price declines, damage, or changes in customers' buying patterns.

As with many types of financial analyses, it is possible to use more than one measure to analyze the efficiency and effectiveness by which a business manages its inventory. Two such measures are the inventory turnover and the number of days' sales in inventory.

Inventory turnover measures the relationship between the volume of goods (merchandise) sold and the amount of inventory carried during the period. It is computed as follows:

$$\text{Inventory Turnover} = \frac{\text{Cost of Merchandise Sold}}{\text{Average Inventory}}$$

To illustrate, the following data have been taken from recent annual reports for SUPERVALU Inc. and Zale Corporation:

	SUPERVALU	Zale
Cost of merchandise sold	$16,681,472,000	$1,157,226,000
Inventories:		
Beginning of year	$1,078,343,000	$826,824,000
End of year	$1,032,034,000	$853,580,000
Average	$1,055,188,500	$840,202,000
Inventory turnover	15.8	1.4

The inventory turnover is 15.8 for SUPERVALU and 1.4 for Zale. Generally, the larger the inventory turnover, the more efficient and effective the management of inventory. However, differences in companies and industries may be too great to allow specific statements as to what is a good inventory turnover. For example, SUPERVALU is a leading food distributor and the tenth largest food retailer in the United States. Because SUPERVALU's inventory is perishable, we would expect it to have a high inventory turnover. In contrast, Zale Corporation is the largest speciality retailer of fine jewelry in the United States. Thus, we would expect Zale to have a lower inventory turnover than SUPERVALU.

The **number of days' sales in inventory** is a rough measure of the length of time it takes to acquire, sell, and replace the inventory. It is computed as follows:

$$\text{Number of Days' Sales in Inventory} = \frac{\text{Average Inventory}}{\text{Average Daily Cost of Merchandise Sold}}$$

The average daily cost of merchandise sold is determined by dividing the cost of merchandise sold by 365. The number of days' sales in inventory for SUPERVALU and Zale is computed as shown below.

	SUPERVALU	Zale
Average daily cost of merchandise sold:		
$16,681,472,000/365	$45,702,663	
$1,157,226,000/365		$3,170,482
Average inventory	$1,055,188,500	$840,202,000
Number of days' sales in inventory	23.1 days	265.0 days

Generally, the lower the number of days' sales in inventory, the better. As with inventory turnover, we should expect differences among industries, such as those for SUPERVALU and Zale.

Business Connections

REAL WORLD

RAPID INVENTORY AT COSTCO

Costco Wholesale Corporation operates over 300 membership warehouses that offer members low prices on a limited selection of nationally branded and selected private label products. Costco emphasizes generating high sales volumes and rapid inventory turnover. This enables Costco to operate profitably at significantly lower gross margins than traditional wholesalers, discount retailers, and supermarkets. In addition, Costco's rapid turnover provides it the opportunity to conserve on its cash, as described below.

Because of its high sales volume and rapid inventory turnover, Costco generally has the opportunity to receive cash from the sale of a substantial portion of its inventory at mature warehouse operations before it is required to pay all its merchandise vendors, even though Costco takes advantage of early payment terms to obtain payment dis- counts. *As sales in a given warehouse increase and inventory turnover becomes more rapid, a greater percentage of the inventory is financed through payment terms provided by vendors rather than by working capital (cash).*

© DON RYAN/ASSOCIATED PRESS

At a Glance

1. Describe the importance of control over inventory.

Key Points	Key Learning Outcomes	Example Exercises	Practice Exercises
Two primary objectives of control over inventory are safeguarding the inventory and properly reporting it in the financial statements. The perpetual inventory system enhances control over inventory. In addition, a physical inventory count should be taken periodically to detect shortages as well as to deter employee thefts.	• Describe controls for safeguarding inventory. • Describe how a perpetual inventory system enhances control over inventory. • Describe why taking a physical inventory enhances control over inventory.		

2. Describe three inventory cost flow assumptions and how they impact the income statement and balance sheet.

Key Points	Key Learning Outcomes	Example Exercises	Practice Exercises
The three common cost flow assumptions used in business are the (1) first-in, first-out method (FIFO); (2) last-in, first-out method (LIFO); and (3) average cost method. The choice of a cost flow assumption directly affects the income statement and balance sheet.	• Describe the FIFO, LIFO, and average cost flow methods. • Describe how choice of a cost flow method affects the income statement and balance sheet.	6-1	6-1A, 6-1B

3. Determine the cost of inventory under the perpetual inventory system, using the FIFO, LIFO, and average cost methods.

Key Points	Key Learning Outcomes	Example Exercises	Practice Exercises
In a perpetual inventory system, the number of units and the cost of each type of merchandise are recorded in a subsidiary inventory ledger, with a separate account for each type of merchandise.	• Determine the cost of inventory and cost of merchandise sold using a perpetual inventory system under the FIFO method.	6-2	6-2A, 6-2B
	• Determine the cost of inventory and cost of merchandise sold using a perpetual inventory system under the LIFO method.	6-3	6-3A, 6-3B

4. Determine the cost of inventory under the periodic inventory system, using the FIFO, LIFO, and average cost methods.

Key Points	Key Learning Outcomes	Example Exercises	Practice Exercises
In a periodic inventory system, a physical inventory is taken to determine the cost of the inventory and the cost of merchandise sold.	• Determine the cost of inventory and cost of merchandise sold using a periodic inventory system under the FIFO method.	6-4	6-4A, 6-4B
	• Determine the cost of inventory and cost of merchandise sold using a periodic inventory system under the LIFO method.	6-4	6-4A, 6-4B
	• Determine the cost of inventory and cost of merchandise sold using a periodic inventory system under the average cost method.	6-4	6-4A, 6-4B

5. Compare and contrast the use of the three inventory costing methods.

Key Points	Key Learning Outcomes	Example Exercises	Practice Exercises
The three inventory costing methods will normally yield different amounts for (1) the ending inventory, (2) the cost of merchandise sold for the period, and (3) the gross profit (and net income) for the period.	• Indicate which inventory cost flow method will yield the highest and lowest ending inventory and net income under periods of increasing prices. • Indicate which inventory cost flow method will yield the highest and lowest ending inventory and net income under periods of decreasing prices.		

6. Describe and illustrate the reporting of merchandise inventory in the financial statements.

Key Points	Key Learning Outcomes	Example Exercises	Practice Exercises
The lower of cost or market is used to value inventory. Inventory that is out of date, spoiled, or damaged is valued at its net realizable value. Merchandise inventory is usually presented in the Current Assets section of the balance sheet, following receivables. The method of determining the cost and valuing the inventory is reported.	• Determine inventory using lower of cost or market. • Illustrate the use of net realizable value for spoiled or damaged inventory. • Prepare the Current Assets section of the balance sheet that includes inventory.	6-5	6-5A, 6-5B
Errors in reporting inventory based upon the physical inventory will affect the balance sheet and income statement.	• Determine the effect of inventory errors on the balance sheet and income statement.	6-6	6-6A, 6-6B

7. Estimate the cost of inventory, using the retail method and the gross profit method.

Key Points	Key Learning Outcomes	Example Exercises	Practice Exercises
The retail method of estimating inventory determines inventory at retail prices and then converts it to cost using the ratio of cost to selling (retail) price.	• Estimate ending inventory using the retail method.	6-7	6-7A, 6-7B
The gross profit method of estimating inventory deducts gross profit from the sales to determine the cost of merchandise sold. This amount is then deducted from the cost of merchandise available for sale to determine the ending inventory.	• Estimate ending inventory using the gross profit method.	6-8	6-8A, 6-8B

Key Terms

Illustrative Problem

Stewart Co.'s beginning inventory and purchases during the year ended December 31, 2008, were as follows:

		Units	Unit Cost	Total Cost
January 1	Inventory	1,000	$50.00	$ 50,000
March 10	Purchase	1,200	52.50	63,000
June 25	Sold 800 units			
August 30	Purchase	800	55.00	44,000
October 5	Sold 1,500 units			
November 26	Purchase	2,000	56.00	112,000
December 31	Sold 1,000 units			
	Total	5,000		$269,000

Instructions

1. Determine the cost of inventory on December 31, 2008, using the perpetual inventory system and each of the following inventory costing methods:
    a. first-in, first-out
    b. last-in, first-out
2. Determine the cost of inventory on December 31, 2008, using the periodic inventory system and each of the following inventory costing methods:
    a. first-in, first-out
    b. last-in, first-out
    c. average cost
3. Assume that during the fiscal year ended December 31, 2008, sales were $290,000 and the estimated gross profit rate was 40%. Estimate the ending inventory at December 31, 2008, using the gross profit method.

Solution

1. a. First-in, first-out method: $95,200 (shown on page 291)
    b. Last-in, first-out method: $91,000 ($35,000 + $56,000) (shown on page 291)
2. a. First-in, first-out method:
       1,700 units at $56 = $95,200
    b. Last-in, first-out method:

1,000 units at $50.00	$50,000
700 units at $52.50	36,750
1,700 units	$86,750

1. a. First-in, first-out method: $95,200

Date	Purchases			Cost of Merchandise Sold			Inventory		
	Quantity	Unit Cost	Total Cost	Quantity	Unit Cost	Total Cost	Quantity	Unit Cost	Total Cost
2008 Jan. 1							1,000	50.00	50,000
Mar. 10	1,200	52.50	63,000				1,000	50.00	50,000
							1,200	52.50	63,000
June 25				800	50.00	40,000	200	50.00	10,000
							1,200	52.50	63,000
Aug. 30	800	55.00	44,000				200	50.00	10,000
							1,200	52.50	63,000
							800	55.00	44,000
Oct. 5				200	50.00	10,000	700	55.00	38,500
				1,200	52.50	63,000			
				100	55.00	5,500			
Nov. 26	2,000	56.00	112,000				700	55.00	38,500
							2,000	56.00	112,000
Dec. 31				700	55.00	38,500	1,700	56.00	95,200
				300	56.00	16,800			
Balances						173,800			95,200

b. Last-in, first-out method: $91,000 ($35,000 + $56,000)

Date	Purchases			Cost of Merchandise Sold			Inventory		
	Quantity	Unit Cost	Total Cost	Quantity	Unit Cost	Total Cost	Quantity	Unit Cost	Total Cost
2008 Jan. 1							1,000	50.00	50,000
Mar. 10	1,200	52.50	63,000				1,000	50.00	50,000
							1,200	52.50	63,000
June 25				800	52.50	42,000	1,000	50.00	50,000
							400	52.50	21,000
Aug. 30	800	55.00	44,000				1,000	50.00	50,000
							400	52.50	21,000
							800	55.00	44,000
Oct. 5				800	55.00	44,000	700	50.00	35,000
				400	52.50	21,000			
				300	50.00	15,000			
Nov. 26	2,000	56.00	112,000				700	50.00	35,000
							2,000	56.00	112,000
Dec. 31				1,000	56.00	56,000	700	50.00	35,000
							1,000	56.00	56,000
Balances						178,000			91,000

c. Average cost method:

Average cost per unit: $269,000/5,000 units = $53.80

Inventory, December 31, 2008: 1,700 units at $53.80 = $91,460

3. Merchandise inventory, January 1, 2008 .... $ 50,000

Purchases (net) 219,000

Merchandise available for sale $269,000

Sales (net) $290,000

Less estimated gross profit ($290,000 × 40%) 116,000

Estimated cost of merchandise sold 174,000

Estimated merchandise inventory, December 31, 2008 .... $ 95,000

Self-Examination Questions

(Answers at End of Chapter)

1. The inventory costing method that is based on the assumption that costs should be charged against revenue in the order in which they were incurred is:
   A. FIFO.
   B. LIFO.
   C. average cost.
   D. perpetual inventory.

2. The following units of a particular item were purchased and sold during the period:

Beginning inventory	40 units at $20
First purchase	50 units at $21
Second purchase	50 units at $22
First sale	110 units
Third purchase	50 units at $23
Second sale	45 units

   What is the cost of the 35 units on hand at the end of the period as determined under the perpetual inventory system by the LIFO costing method?
   A. $715
   B. $705
   C. $700
   D. $805

3. The following units of a particular item were available for sale during the period:

Beginning inventory	40 units at $20
First purchase	50 units at $21
Second purchase	50 units at $22
Third purchase	50 units at $23

   What is the unit cost of the 35 units on hand at the end of the period as determined under the periodic inventory system by the FIFO costing method?
   A. $20   B. $21   C. $22   D. $23

4. If merchandise inventory is being valued at cost and the price level is steadily rising, the method of costing that will yield the highest net income is:
   A. LIFO.
   B. FIFO.
   C. average.
   D. periodic.

5. If the inventory at the end of the year is understated by $7,500, the error will cause an:
   A. understatement of cost of merchandise sold for the year by $7,500.
   B. overstatement of gross profit for the year by $7,500.
   C. overstatement of merchandise inventory for the year by $7,500.
   D. understatement of net income for the year by $7,500.

Eye Openers

1. Before inventory purchases are recorded, the receiving report should be reconciled to what documents?
2. What security measures may be used by retailers to protect merchandise inventory from customer theft?
3. Which inventory system provides the more effective means of controlling inventories (perpetual or periodic)? Why?
4. Why is it important to periodically take a physical inventory if the perpetual system is used?
5. Do the terms *FIFO* and *LIFO* refer to techniques used in determining quantities of the various classes of merchandise on hand? Explain.
6. Does the term *last-in* in the LIFO method mean that the items in the inventory are assumed to be the most recent (last) acquisitions? Explain.
7. If merchandise inventory is being valued at cost and the price level is steadily rising, which of the three methods of costing—FIFO, LIFO, or average cost—will yield (a) the highest inventory cost, (b) the lowest inventory cost, (c) the highest gross profit, and (d) the lowest gross profit?
8. Which of the three methods of inventory costing—FIFO, LIFO, or average cost—will in general yield an inventory cost most nearly approximating current replacement cost?
9. If inventory is being valued at cost and the price level is steadily rising, which of the three methods of costing—FIFO, LIFO, or average cost—will yield the lowest annual income tax expense? Explain.
10. Can a company change its method of costing inventory? Explain.
11. Because of imperfections, an item of merchandise cannot be sold at its normal selling price. How should this item be valued for financial statement purposes?
12. How is the method of determining the cost of the inventory and the method of valuing it disclosed in the financial statements?

13. The inventory at the end of the year was understated by $8,750. (a) Did the error cause an overstatement or an understatement of the gross profit for the year? (b) Which items on the balance sheet at the end of the year were overstated or understated as a result of the error?
14. Fargo Co. sold merchandise to Keepsakes Company on December 31, FOB shipping point. If the merchandise is in transit on December 31, the end of the fiscal year, which company would report it in its financial statements? Explain.
15. A manufacturer shipped merchandise to a retailer on a consignment basis. If the merchandise is unsold at the end of the period, in whose inventory should the merchandise be included?
16. What uses can be made of the estimate of the cost of inventory determined by the gross profit method?

Practice Exercises

PE 6-1A
Cost flow methods, gross profit, and ending inventory
obj. 2

Three identical units of Item T4W are purchased during July, as shown below.

Item T4W		Units	Cost
July 6	Purchase	1	$115
19	Purchase	1	118
24	Purchase	1	121
Total		3	$354
Average cost per unit			$118 ($354/3 units)

Assume that one unit is sold on July 28 for $150.

Determine the gross profit for July and ending inventory on July 31 using the (a) first-in, first-out (FIFO); (b) last-in, first-out (LIFO); and (c) average cost methods.

PE 6-1B
Cost flow methods, gross profit, and ending inventory
obj. 2

Three identical units of Item S77 are purchased during October, as shown below.

Item S77		Units	Cost
Oct. 6	Purchase	1	$ 88
19	Purchase	1	85
24	Purchase	1	82
Total		3	$255
Average cost per unit			$ 85 ($255/3 units)

Assume that one unit is sold on October 26 for $100.

Determine the gross profit for October and ending inventory on October 31 using the (a) first-in, first-out (FIFO); (b) last-in, first-out (LIFO); and (c) average cost methods.

PE 6-2A
Perpetual inventory using FIFO method
obj. 3

Beginning inventory, purchases, and sales for Item SJ68 are as follows:

Aug. 1	Inventory	28 units at $34
8	Sale	15 units
15	Purchase	22 units at $38
30	Sale	20 units

Assuming a perpetual inventory system and using the first-in, first-out (FIFO) method, determine (a) the cost of merchandise sold on August 30 and (b) the inventory on August 31.

PE 6-2B
Perpetual inventory using FIFO method
obj. **3**

Beginning inventory, purchases, and sales for Item FC33 are as follows:

Mar.	1	Inventory	23 units at $10
	8	Sale	18 units
	15	Purchase	57 units at $14
	29	Sale	40 units

Assuming a perpetual inventory system and using the first-in, first-out (FIFO) method, determine (a) the cost of merchandise sold on March 29 and (b) the inventory on March 31.

PE 6-3A
Perpetual inventory using LIFO method
obj. **3**

Beginning inventory, purchases, and sales for Item SJ68 are as follows:

Aug.	1	Inventory	28 units at $34
	8	Sale	15 units
	15	Purchase	22 units at $38
	30	Sale	20 units

Assuming a perpetual inventory system and using the last-in, first-out (LIFO) method, determine (a) the cost of merchandise sold on August 30 and (b) the inventory on August 31.

PE 6-3B
Perpetual inventory using LIFO method
obj. **3**

Beginning inventory, purchases, and sales for Item FC33 are as follows:

Mar.	1	Inventory	23 units at $10
	8	Sale	18 units
	15	Purchase	57 units at $14
	29	Sale	40 units

Assuming a perpetual inventory system and using the last-in, first-out (LIFO) method, determine (a) the cost of merchandise sold on March 29 and (b) the inventory on March 31.

PE 6-4A
Periodic inventory using FIFO, LIFO, average cost methods
obj. **4**

The units of an item available for sale during the year were as follows:

Jan. 1	Inventory	12 units at $25	$ 300
Apr. 20	Purchase	28 units at $30	840
Nov. 30	Purchase	40 units at $36	1,440
	Available for sale	80 units	$2,580

There are 20 units of the item in the physical inventory at December 31. The periodic inventory system is used. Determine the inventory cost using (a) the first-in, first-out (FIFO) method; (b) the last-in, first-out (LIFO) method; and (c) the average cost method.

PE 6-4B
Periodic inventory using FIFO, LIFO, average cost methods
obj. **4**

The units of an item available for sale during the year were as follows:

Jan. 1	Inventory	18 units at $300	$ 5,400
Apr. 20	Purchase	46 units at $275	12,650
Nov. 30	Purchase	36 units at $250	9,000
	Available for sale	100 units	$27,050

There are 38 units of the item in the physical inventory at December 31. The periodic inventory system is used. Determine the inventory cost using (a) the first-in, first-out (FIFO) method; (b) the last-in, first-out (LIFO) method; and (c) the average cost method.

PE 6-5A
Lower of cost or market
obj. **6**

On the basis of the following data, determine the value of the inventory at the lower of cost or market. Apply lower of cost or market to each inventory item as shown in Exhibit 7.

Commodity	Inventory Quantity	Unit Cost Price	Unit Market Price
TRP4	96	$29	$18
V555	200	13	14

PE 6-5B
Lower of cost or market
obj. 6

On the basis of the following data, determine the value of the inventory at the lower of cost or market. Apply lower of cost or market to each inventory item as shown in Exhibit 7.

Commodity	Inventory Quantity	Unit Cost Price	Unit Market Price
E662	215	$30	$28
C11R	741	22	26

PE 6-6A
Effect of inventory errors
obj. 6

During the taking of its physical inventory on December 31, 2008, Genesis Company incorrectly counted its inventory as $126,000 instead of the correct amount of $135,000. Indicate the effect of the misstatement on Genesis's December 31, 2008, balance sheet and income statement for the year ended December 31, 2008.

PE 6-6B
Effect of inventory errors
obj. 6

During the taking of its physical inventory on December 31, 2008, Poindexter Company incorrectly counted its inventory as $769,000 instead of the correct amount of $740,000. Indicate the effect of the misstatement on Poindexter's December 31, 2008, balance sheet and income statement for the year ended December 31, 2008.

PE 6-7A
Retail inventory method
obj. 7

A business using the retail method of inventory costing determines that merchandise inventory at retail is $675,000. If the ratio of cost to retail price is 80%, what is the amount of inventory to be reported on the financial statements?

PE 6-7B
Retail inventory method
obj. 7

A business using the retail method of inventory costing determines that merchandise inventory at retail is $280,000. If the ratio of cost to retail price is 65%, what is the amount of inventory to be reported on the financial statements?

PE 6-8A
Gross profit method
obj. 7

Based upon the following data, estimate the cost of ending merchandise inventory:

Sales (net)	$1,500,000
Estimated gross profit rate	35%
Beginning merchandise inventory	$ 180,000
Purchases (net)	1,200,000
Merchandise available for sale	$1,380,000

PE 6-8B
Gross profit method
obj. 7

Based upon the following data, estimate the cost of ending merchandise inventory:

Sales (net)	$800,000
Estimated gross profit rate	36%
Beginning merchandise inventory	$ 75,000
Purchases (net)	625,000
Merchandise available for sale	$700,000

Exercises

EX 6-1
Control of inventories
obj. 1

Handy Hardware Store currently uses a periodic inventory system. Peggy Yang, the owner, is considering the purchase of a computer system that would make it feasible to switch to a perpetual inventory system.

Peggy is unhappy with the periodic inventory system because it does not provide timely information on inventory levels. Peggy has noticed on several occasions that the store runs out of good-selling items, while too many poor-selling items are on hand.

Peggy is also concerned about lost sales while a physical inventory is being taken. Handy Hardware currently takes a physical inventory twice a year. To minimize distractions, the store is closed on the day inventory is taken. Peggy believes that closing the store is the only way to get an accurate inventory count.

▬▬▬▶ Will switching to a perpetual inventory system strengthen Handy Hardware's control over inventory items? Will switching to a perpetual inventory system eliminate the need for a physical inventory count? Explain.

EX 6-2
Control of inventories
obj. 1

PacTec Luggage Shop is a small retail establishment located in a large shopping mall. This shop has implemented the following procedures regarding inventory items:

a. Since the display area of the store is limited, only a sample of each piece of luggage is kept on the selling floor. Whenever a customer selects a piece of luggage, the salesclerk gets the appropriate piece from the store's stockroom. Since all salesclerks need access to the stockroom, it is not locked. The stockroom is adjacent to the break room used by all mall employees.

b. Whenever PacTec receives a shipment of new inventory, the items are taken directly to the stockroom. PacTec's accountant uses the vendor's invoice to record the amount of inventory received.

c. Since the shop carries mostly high-quality, designer luggage, all inventory items are tagged with a control device that activates an alarm if a tagged item is removed from the store.

▬▬▬▶ State whether each of these procedures is appropriate or inappropriate. If it is inappropriate, state why.

EX 6-3
Perpetual inventory using FIFO
objs. 2, 3

✓ *Inventory balance, November 30, $1,302*

Beginning inventory, purchases, and sales data for portable MP3 players are as follows:

Nov.	1	Inventory	70 units at $40
	5	Sale	52 units
	16	Purchase	30 units at $42
	21	Sale	24 units
	24	Sale	8 units
	30	Purchase	14 units at $45

The business maintains a perpetual inventory system, costing by the first-in, first-out method. Determine the cost of the merchandise sold for each sale and the inventory balance after each sale, presenting the data in the form illustrated in Exhibit 3.

EX 6-4
Perpetual inventory using LIFO
objs. 2, 3

✓ *Inventory balance, November 30, $1,270*

Assume that the business in Exercise 6-3 maintains a perpetual inventory system, costing by the last-in, first-out method. Determine the cost of merchandise sold for each sale and the inventory balance after each sale, presenting the data in the form illustrated in Exhibit 4.

EX 6-5
Perpetual inventory using LIFO
objs. 2, 3

✓ *Inventory balance, July 31, $1,764*

Beginning inventory, purchases, and sales data for cell phones for July are as follows:

Inventory		Purchases		Sales	
July 1	100 units at $30	July 3	80 units at $32	July 7	72 units
		21	60 units at $33	13	80 units
				31	32 units

Assuming that the perpetual inventory system is used, costing by the LIFO method, determine the cost of merchandise sold for each sale and the inventory balance after each sale, presenting the data in the form illustrated in Exhibit 4.

EX 6-6
Perpetual inventory using FIFO

objs. **2, 3**

✓ *Inventory balance, July 31, $1,848*

Assume that the business in Exercise 6-5 maintains a perpetual inventory system, costing by the first-in, first-out method. Determine the cost of merchandise sold for each sale and the inventory balance after each sale, presenting the data in the form illustrated in Exhibit 3.

EX 6-7
FIFO, LIFO costs under perpetual inventory system

objs. **2, 3**

✓ *a. $5,040*

The following units of a particular item were available for sale during the year:

Beginning inventory	100 units at $60
Sale	75 units at $112
First purchase	155 units at $65
Sale	135 units at $112
Second purchase	200 units at $72
Sale	175 units at $112

The firm uses the perpetual inventory system, and there are 70 units of the item on hand at the end of the year. What is the total cost of the ending inventory according to (a) FIFO, (b) LIFO?

EX 6-8
Periodic inventory by three methods

objs. **2, 4**

✓ *b. $1,410*

The units of an item available for sale during the year were as follows:

Jan. 1	Inventory	18 units at $40
Feb. 26	Purchase	36 units at $46
June 18	Purchase	42 units at $52
Dec. 29	Purchase	24 units at $55

There are 33 units of the item in the physical inventory at December 31. The periodic inventory system is used. Determine the inventory cost by (a) the first-in, first-out method, (b) the last-in, first-out method, and (c) the average cost method.

EX 6-9
Periodic inventory by three methods; cost of merchandise sold

objs. **2, 4**

✓ *a. Inventory, $9,760*

The units of an item available for sale during the year were as follows:

Jan. 1	Inventory	168 units at $60
Apr. 15	Purchase	232 units at $65
Sept. 3	Purchase	80 units at $68
Nov. 23	Purchase	120 units at $70

There are 140 units of the item in the physical inventory at December 31. The periodic inventory system is used. Determine the inventory cost and the cost of merchandise sold by three methods, presenting your answers in the following form:

	Cost	
Inventory Method	**Merchandise Inventory**	**Merchandise Sold**
a. First-in, first-out	$	$
b. Last-in, first-out		
c. Average cost		

EX 6-10
Comparing inventory methods

obj. **5**

Assume that a firm separately determined inventory under FIFO and LIFO and then compared the results.

1. In each space below, place the correct sign [less than (<), greater than (>), or equal (=)] for each comparison, assuming periods of rising prices.

a. FIFO inventory	_____	LIFO inventory
b. FIFO cost of goods sold	_____	LIFO cost of goods sold
c. FIFO net income	_____	LIFO net income
d. FIFO income tax	_____	LIFO income tax

2. Why would management prefer to use LIFO over FIFO in periods of rising prices?

EX 6-11
Lower-of-cost-or-market inventory
obj. 6

✓ *LCM: $10,473*

On the basis of the following data, determine the value of the inventory at the lower of cost or market. Assemble the data in the form illustrated in Exhibit 7.

Commodity	Inventory Quantity	Unit Cost Price	Unit Market Price
62CF3	10	$120	$131
41DH2	35	80	75
O3MQ3	10	275	260
23FH6	16	40	28
10KT4	40	90	94

EX 6-12
Merchandise inventory on the balance sheet
obj. 6

Based on the data in Exercise 6-11 and assuming that cost was determined by the FIFO method, show how the merchandise inventory would appear on the balance sheet.

EX 6-13
Effect of errors in physical inventory
obj. 6

Morena White Water Co. sells canoes, kayaks, whitewater rafts, and other boating supplies. During the taking of its physical inventory on December 31, 2008, Morena White Water incorrectly counted its inventory as $279,150 instead of the correct amount of $285,780.

a. State the effect of the error on the December 31, 2008, balance sheet of Morena White Water.
b. State the effect of the error on the income statement of Morena White Water for the year ended December 31, 2008.

EX 6-14
Effect of errors in physical inventory
obj. 6

Megan's Motorcycle Shop sells motorcycles, jet skis, and other related supplies and accessories. During the taking of its physical inventory on December 31, 2008, Megan's Motorcycle Shop incorrectly counted its inventory as $315,200 instead of the correct amount of $300,750.

a. State the effect of the error on the December 31, 2008, balance sheet of Megan's Motorcycle Shop.
b. State the effect of the error on the income statement of Megan's Motorcycle Shop for the year ended December 31, 2008.

EX 6-15
Error in inventory
obj. 6

During 2008, the accountant discovered that the physical inventory at the end of 2007 had been understated by $8,175. Instead of correcting the error, however, the accountant assumed that an $8,175 overstatement of the physical inventory in 2008 would balance out the error.

Are there any flaws in the accountant's assumption? Explain.

EX 6-16
Retail inventory method
obj. 7

A business using the retail method of inventory costing determines that merchandise inventory at retail is $1,260,000. If the ratio of cost to retail price is 74%, what is the amount of inventory to be reported on the financial statements?

EX 6-17
Retail inventory method
obj. 7

✓ *Inventory, September 30: $173,400*

On the basis of the following data, estimate the cost of the merchandise inventory at September 30 by the retail method:

		Cost	Retail
September 1	Merchandise inventory	$ 220,000	$ 320,000
September 1–30	Purchases (net)	1,718,000	2,530,000
September 1–30	Sales (net)		2,595,000

EX 6-18
Gross profit inventory method
obj. 7

The merchandise inventory was destroyed by fire on August 19. The following data were obtained from the accounting records:

Jan. 1		Merchandise inventory	$ 360,000
Jan. 1–Aug. 19		Purchases (net)	3,200,000
		Sales (net)	5,200,000
		Estimated gross profit rate	36%

a. Estimate the cost of the merchandise destroyed.
b. Briefly describe the situations in which the gross profit method is useful.

EX 6-19
Inventory turnover

The following data were taken from recent annual reports of Apple Computer, Inc., a manufacturer of personal computers and related products, and American Greetings Corporation, a manufacturer and distributor of greeting cards and related products:

	Apple	**American Greetings**
Cost of goods sold	$9,888,000,000	$905,201,000
Inventory, end of year	165,000,000	222,874,000
Inventory, beginning of the year	101,000,000	246,171,000

a. Determine the inventory turnover for Apple and American Greetings. Round to one decimal place.
b. Would you expect American Greetings' inventory turnover to be higher or lower than Apple's? Why?

EX 6-20
Inventory turnover and number of days' sales in inventory

✓ a. Albertson's, 40 days' sales in inventory

Kroger, Albertson's, Inc., and Safeway Inc. are the three largest grocery chains in the United States. Inventory management is an important aspect of the grocery retail business. Recent balance sheets for these three companies indicated the following merchandise inventory information:

	Merchandise Inventory	
	End of Year (in millions)	**Beginning of Year** (in millions)
Albertson's	$3,162	$3,104
Kroger	4,356	4,169
Safeway	2,741	2,642

The cost of goods sold for each company were:

	Cost of Goods Sold (in millions)
Albertson's	$28,711
Kroger	42,140
Safeway	25,228

a. Determine the number of days' sales in inventory and inventory turnover for the three companies. Round to the nearest day and one decimal place.
b. Interpret your results in (a).
c. If Albertson's had Kroger's number of days' sales in inventory, how much additional cash flow would have been generated from the smaller inventory relative to its actual average inventory position?

Problems Series A

PR 6-1A
FIFO perpetual inventory

The beginning inventory at Continental Office Supplies and data on purchases and sales for a three-month period are as follows:

objs. **2, 3**

✓3. $11,420

Date		Transaction	Number of Units	Per Unit	Total
Jan.	1	Inventory	50	$20.00	$1,000
	7	Purchase	200	22.00	4,400
	20	Sale	90	40.00	3,600
	30	Sale	110	40.00	4,400
Feb.	8	Sale	20	44.00	880
	10	Purchase	130	23.00	2,990
	27	Sale	90	42.00	3,780
	28	Sale	50	45.00	2,250
Mar.	5	Purchase	180	24.00	4,320
	13	Sale	90	50.00	4,500
	23	Purchase	100	26.00	2,600
	30	Sale	80	50.00	4,000

Instructions

1. Record the inventory, purchases, and cost of merchandise sold data in a perpetual inventory record similar to the one illustrated in Exhibit 3, using the first-in, first-out method.
2. Determine the total sales and the total cost of merchandise sold for the period. Journalize the entries in the sales and cost of merchandise sold accounts. Assume that all sales were on account.
3. Determine the gross profit from sales for the period.
4. Determine the ending inventory cost.

PR 6-2A
LIFO perpetual inventory
objs. **2, 3**

✓2. Gross profit, $11,180

The beginning inventory at Continental Office Supplies and data on purchases and sales for a three-month period are shown in Problem 6-1A.

Instructions

1. Record the inventory, purchases, and cost of merchandise sold data in a perpetual inventory record similar to the one illustrated in Exhibit 4, using the last-in, first-out method.
2. Determine the total sales, the total cost of merchandise sold, and the gross profit from sales for the period.
3. Determine the ending inventory cost.

PR 6-3A
Periodic inventory by three methods
objs. **2, 4**

✓1. $6,863

Del Mar Appliances uses the periodic inventory system. Details regarding the inventory of appliances at August 1, 2007, purchases invoices during the year, and the inventory count at July 31, 2008, are summarized as follows:

Model	Inventory, August 1	Purchases Invoices			Inventory Count, July 31
		1st	2nd	3rd	
T742	2 at $125	2 at $130	4 at $135	2 at $140	5
PM18	7 at 242	6 at 250	5 at 260	10 at 259	9
K21G	6 at 80	5 at 82	8 at 89	8 at 90	6
H60W	2 at 108	2 at 110	3 at 128	3 at 130	5
B153Z	8 at 88	4 at 79	3 at 85	6 at 92	8
J600T	5 at 160	4 at 170	4 at 175	7 at 180	8
C273W	—	4 at 75	4 at 100	4 at 101	5

Instructions

1. Determine the cost of the inventory on July 31, 2008, by the first-in, first-out method. Present data in columnar form, using the following headings:

Model	Quantity	Unit Cost	Total Cost

If the inventory of a particular model comprises one entire purchase plus a portion of another purchase acquired at a different unit cost, use a separate line for each purchase.
2. Determine the cost of the inventory on July 31, 2008, by the last-in, first-out method, following the procedures indicated in (1).

3. Determine the cost of the inventory on July 31, 2008, by the average cost method, using the columnar headings indicated in (1).
4. ▭▶ Discuss which method (FIFO or LIFO) would be preferred for income tax purposes in periods of (a) rising prices and (b) declining prices.

PR 6-4A
Lower-of-cost-or-market inventory
obj. 6
✓ *Total LCM, $43,703*

If the working papers correlating with this textbook are not used, omit Problem 6-4A.

Data on the physical inventory of Exchange Company as of December 31, 2008, are presented in the working papers. The quantity of each commodity on hand has been determined and recorded on the inventory sheet. Unit market prices have also been determined as of December 31 and recorded on the sheet. The inventory is to be determined at cost and also at the lower of cost or market, using the first-in, first-out method. Quantity and cost data from the last purchases invoice of the year and the next-to-the-last purchases invoice are summarized as follows:

Description	Last Purchases Invoice Quantity Purchased	Last Purchases Invoice Unit Cost	Next-to-the-Last Purchases Invoice Quantity Purchased	Next-to-the-Last Purchases Invoice Unit Cost
AC172	25	$ 60	30	$ 58
BE43	35	175	20	180
CJ9	18	130	25	128
E34	150	25	100	24
F17	10	565	10	560
G68	100	15	100	14
K41	10	385	5	384
Q79	500	6	500	6
RZ13	80	22	50	21
S60	5	250	4	260
W21	100	20	75	19
XR90	9	750	9	740

Instructions
Record the appropriate unit costs on the inventory sheet, and complete the pricing of the inventory. When there are two different unit costs applicable to an item, proceed as follows:

1. Draw a line through the quantity, and insert the quantity and unit cost of the last purchase.
2. On the following line, insert the quantity and unit cost of the next-to-the-last purchase.
3. Total the cost and market columns and insert the lower of the two totals in the Lower of C or M column. The first item on the inventory sheet has been completed as an example.

PR 6-5A
Retail method; gross profit method
obj. 7
✓ *1. $306,000*

Selected data on merchandise inventory, purchases, and sales for Hacienda Co. and San Lucas Co. are as follows:

	Cost	Retail
Hacienda Co.		
Merchandise inventory, June 1	$ 200,000	$ 290,000
Transactions during June:		
Purchases (net)	2,086,000	2,885,000
Sales		2,780,000
Sales returns and allowances		30,000
San Lucas Co.		
Merchandise inventory, November 1	$ 225,000	
Transactions during November and December:		
Purchases (net)	1,685,000	
Sales	2,815,000	
Sales returns and allowances	85,000	
Estimated gross profit rate	40%	

Instructions

1. Determine the estimated cost of the merchandise inventory of Hacienda Co. on June 30 by the retail method, presenting details of the computations.
2. a. Estimate the cost of the merchandise inventory of San Lucas Co. on December 31 by the gross profit method, presenting details of the computations.
   b. Assume that San Lucas Co. took a physical inventory on December 31 and discovered that $269,250 of merchandise was on hand. What was the estimated loss of inventory due to theft or damage during November and December?

Problems Series B

PR 6-1B
FIFO perpetual inventory
objs. 2, 3

✓ *3. $1,560,000*

The beginning inventory of merchandise at Citrine Co. and data on purchases and sales for a three-month period are as follows:

Date		Transaction	Number of Units	Per Unit	Total
March	1	Inventory	132	$1,500	$198,000
	8	Purchase	108	2,000	216,000
	11	Sale	72	4,800	345,600
	22	Sale	66	4,800	316,800
April	3	Purchase	96	2,300	220,800
	10	Sale	60	5,000	300,000
	21	Sale	30	5,000	150,000
	30	Purchase	120	2,350	282,000
May	5	Sale	120	5,250	630,000
	13	Sale	72	5,250	378,000
	21	Purchase	180	2,400	432,000
	28	Sale	90	5,400	486,000

Instructions

1. Record the inventory, purchases, and cost of merchandise sold data in a perpetual inventory record similar to the one illustrated in Exhibit 3, using the first-in, first-out method.
2. Determine the total sales and the total cost of merchandise sold for the period. Journalize the entries in the sales and cost of merchandise sold accounts. Assume that all sales were on account.
3. Determine the gross profit from sales for the period.
4. Determine the ending inventory cost.

PR 6-2B
LIFO perpetual inventory
objs. 2, 3

✓ *2. Gross profit,*
$1,527,600

The beginning inventory and data on purchases and sales for a three-month period are shown in Problem 6-1B.

Instructions

1. Record the inventory, purchases, and cost of merchandise sold data in a perpetual inventory record similar to the one illustrated in Exhibit 4, using the last-in, first-out method.
2. Determine the total sales, the total cost of merchandise sold, and the gross profit from sales for the period.
3. Determine the ending inventory cost.

PR 6-3B
Periodic inventory by three methods

Concord Appliances uses the periodic inventory system. Details regarding the inventory of appliances at January 1, 2008, purchases invoices during the year, and the inventory count at December 31, 2008, are summarized as follows:

objs. 2, 4

✓ 1. $11,108

Model	Inventory, January 1	Purchases Invoices 1st	Purchases Invoices 2nd	Purchases Invoices 3rd	Inventory Count, December 31
F10	5 at $ 60	6 at $ 65	2 at $ 65	2 at $ 70	3
J64	6 at 305	3 at 310	3 at 316	4 at 317	4
M13	2 at 520	2 at 527	2 at 530	2 at 535	4
Q73	6 at 520	8 at 531	4 at 549	6 at 542	7
144Z	9 at 213	7 at 215	6 at 222	6 at 225	11
Z120	—	4 at 222	4 at 232	—	2
W941	4 at 140	6 at 144	8 at 148	7 at 156	5

Instructions

1. Determine the cost of the inventory on December 31, 2008, by the first-in, first-out method. Present data in columnar form, using the following headings:

Model	Quantity	Unit Cost	Total Cost

   If the inventory of a particular model comprises one entire purchase plus a portion of another purchase acquired at a different unit cost, use a separate line for each purchase.
2. Determine the cost of the inventory on December 31, 2008, by the last-in, first-out method, following the procedures indicated in (1).
3. Determine the cost of the inventory on December 31, 2008, by the average cost method, using the columnar headings indicated in (1).
4. ▭▭▷ Discuss which method (FIFO or LIFO) would be preferred for income tax purposes in periods of (a) rising prices and (b) declining prices.

PR 6-4B
Lower-of-cost-or-market inventory

obj. 6

✓ Total LCM, $43,548

If the working papers correlating with this textbook are not used, omit Problem 6-4B.

Data on the physical inventory of Satchell Co. as of December 31, 2008, are presented in the working papers. The quantity of each commodity on hand has been determined and recorded on the inventory sheet. Unit market prices have also been determined as of December 31 and recorded on the sheet. The inventory is to be determined at cost and also at the lower of cost or market, using the first-in, first-out method. Quantity and cost data from the last purchases invoice of the year and the next-to-the-last purchases invoice are summarized as follows:

Description	Last Purchases Invoice Quantity Purchased	Last Purchases Invoice Unit Cost	Next-to-the-Last Purchases Invoice Quantity Purchased	Next-to-the-Last Purchases Invoice Unit Cost
AC172	30	$ 60	40	$ 59
BE43	25	175	15	180
CJ9	20	130	15	128
E34	150	25	100	27
F17	6	550	15	540
G68	75	14	100	13
K41	8	400	4	398
Q79	500	6	500	7
RZ13	65	22	50	21
S60	5	250	4	260
W21	120	20	115	17
XR90	10	750	8	740

Instructions

Record the appropriate unit costs on the inventory sheet, and complete the pricing of the inventory. When there are two different unit costs applicable to an item:

1. Draw a line through the quantity, and insert the quantity and unit cost of the last purchase.
2. On the following line, insert the quantity and unit cost of the next-to-the-last purchase.
3. Total the cost and market columns and insert the lower of the two totals in the Lower of C or M column. The first item on the inventory sheet has been completed as an example.

PR 6-5B

Retail method; gross profit method

obj. 7

✓ 1. $187,000

Selected data on merchandise inventory, purchases, and sales for Miramar Co. and Boyar's Co. are as follows:

	Cost	Retail
Miramar Co.		
Merchandise inventory, March 1	$ 185,000	$ 280,000
Transactions during March:		
Purchases (net)	2,246,000	3,295,000
Sales		3,360,000
Sales returns and allowances		60,000
Boyar's Co.		
Merchandise inventory, August 1	$ 425,000	
Transactions during August and September:		
Purchases (net)	2,980,000	
Sales	5,075,000	
Sales returns and allowances	75,000	
Estimated gross profit rate	40%	

Instructions

1. Determine the estimated cost of the merchandise inventory of Miramar Co. on March 31 by the retail method, presenting details of the computations.
2. a. Estimate the cost of the merchandise inventory of Boyar's Co. on September 30 by the gross profit method, presenting details of the computations.
   b. Assume that Boyar's Co. took a physical inventory on September 30 and discovered that $398,250 of merchandise was on hand. What was the estimated loss of inventory due to theft or damage during August and September?

Special Activities

SA 6-1

Ethics and professional conduct in business

ETHICS

Beeson Co. is experiencing a decrease in sales and operating income for the fiscal year ending December 31, 2008. Julia Faure, controller of Beeson Co., has suggested that all orders received before the end of the fiscal year be shipped by midnight, December 31, 2008, even if the shipping department must work overtime. Since Beeson Co. ships all merchandise FOB shipping point, it would record all such shipments as sales for the year ending December 31, 2008, thereby offsetting some of the decreases in sales and operating income.

▬▬▬▶ Discuss whether Julia Faure is behaving in a professional manner.

SA 6-2

LIFO and inventory flow

The following is an excerpt from a conversation between Jack O'Brien, the warehouse manager for Murrieta Wholesale Co., and its accountant, Carole Timmons. Murrieta Wholesale operates a large regional warehouse that supplies produce and other grocery products to grocery stores in smaller communities.

Jack: Carole, can you explain what's going on here with these monthly statements?

Carole: Sure, Jack. How can I help you?

Jack: I don't understand this last-in, first-out inventory procedure. It just doesn't make sense.

Carole: Well, what it means is that we assume that the last goods we receive are the first ones sold. So the inventory is made up of the items we purchased first.

Jack: Yes, but that's my problem. It doesn't work that way! We always distribute the oldest produce first. Some of that produce is perishable! We can't keep any of it very long or it'll spoil.

Carole: Jack, you don't understand. We only *assume* that the products we distribute are the last ones received. We don't actually have to distribute the goods in this way.

Jack: I always thought that accounting was supposed to show what really happened. It all sounds like "make believe" to me! Why not report what really happens?

▬▬▬▶ Respond to Jack's concerns.

SA 6-3
Costing inventory

Kowalski Company began operations in 2007 by selling a single product. Data on purchases and sales for the year were as follows:

Purchases:

Date	Units Purchased	Unit Cost	Total Cost
April 6	3,875	$12.20	$ 47,275
May 18	4,125	13.00	53,625
June 6	5,000	13.20	66,000
July 10	5,000	14.00	70,000
August 10	3,400	14.25	48,450
October 25	1,600	14.50	23,200
November 4	1,000	14.95	14,950
December 10	1,000	16.00	16,000
	25,000		$339,500

Sales:

April	2,000 units
May	2,000
June	2,500
July	3,000
August	3,500
September	3,500
October	2,250
November	1,250
December	1,000
Total units	21,000
Total sales	$325,000

On January 6, 2008, the president of the company, Jolly Zondra, asked for your advice on costing the 4,000-unit physical inventory that was taken on December 31, 2007. Moreover, since the firm plans to expand its product line, she asked for your advice on the use of a perpetual inventory system in the future.

1. Determine the cost of the December 31, 2007, inventory under the periodic system, using the (a) first-in, first-out method, (b) last-in, first-out method, and (c) average cost method.
2. Determine the gross profit for the year under each of the three methods in (1).
3. a. ▭▬▶ Explain varying viewpoints why each of the three inventory costing methods may best reflect the results of operations for 2007.
   b. ▭▬▶ Which of the three inventory costing methods may best reflect the replacement cost of the inventory on the balance sheet as of December 31, 2007?
   c. ▭▬▶ Which inventory costing method would you choose to use for income tax purposes? Why?
   d. ▭▬▶ Discuss the advantages and disadvantages of using a perpetual inventory system. From the data presented in this case, is there any indication of the adequacy of inventory levels during the year?

SA 6-4
Inventory ratios for Dell and HP

Dell Inc. and Hewlett-Packard Development Company, L.P. (HP) are both manufacturers of computer equipment and peripherals. However, the two companies follow two different strategies. Dell follows a build-to-order strategy, where the consumer orders the computer from a Web page. The order is then manufactured and shipped to the customer within days of the order. In contrast, HP follows a build-to-stock strategy, where the computer is first built for inventory, then sold from inventory to retailers, such as Best Buy. The two strategies can be seen in the difference between the inventory turnover and number of days' sales in inventory ratios for the two companies. The following financial statement information is provided for Dell and HP for a recent fiscal year (in millions):

	Dell	HP
Inventory, beginning of period	$ 327	$ 7,071
Inventory, end of period	459	6,877
Cost of goods sold	40,190	66,224

a. Determine the inventory turnover ratio and number of days' sales in inventory ratio for each company. Round to one decimal place.
b. ▭▬▶ Interpret the difference between the ratios for the two companies.

SA 6-5
Comparing inventory ratios for two companies

The Neiman Marcus Group, Inc., is a high-end specialty retailer, while Amazon.com uses its e-commerce services, features, and technologies to sell its products through the Internet. Recent balance sheet inventory disclosures for Neiman Marcus and Amazon.com are as follows:

	End-of-Period Inventory	Beginning-of-Period Inventory
Neiman Marcus Group, Inc.	$720,277,000	$687,062,000
Amazon.com	479,709,000	293,917,000

The cost of merchandise sold reported by each company was as follows:

	Neiman Marcus Group, Inc.	Amazon.com
Cost of merchandise sold	$2,321,110,000	$5,319,127,000

a. Determine the inventory turnover and number of days' sales in inventory for Neiman Marcus and Amazon.com.
b. Interpret your results.

SA 6-6
Comparing inventory ratios for three companies

The general merchandise retail industry has a number of segments represented by the following companies:

Company Name	Merchandise Concept
Costco Wholesale Corporation	Membership warehouse
Wal-Mart	Discount general merchandise
JCPenney	Department store

For a recent year, the following cost of merchandise sold and beginning and ending inventories have been provided from corporate annual reports for these three companies:

	Costco	Wal-Mart	JCPenney
Cost of merchandise sold	$42,092	$219,793	$11,285
Merchandise inventory, beginning	3,339	26,612	3,156
Merchandise inventory, ending	3,644	29,447	3,169

a. Determine the inventory turnover ratio for all three companies. Round to one decimal place.
b. Determine the number of days' sales in inventory for all three companies. Round to one decimal place.
c. Interpret these results based upon each company's merchandise concept.

Answers to Self-Examination Questions

1. **A** The FIFO method (answer A) is based on the assumption that costs are charged against revenue in the order in which they were incurred. The LIFO method (answer B) charges the most recent costs incurred against revenue, and the average cost method (answer C) charges a weighted average of unit costs of items sold against revenue. The perpetual inventory system (answer D) is a system and not a method of costing.

2. **A** The LIFO method of costing is based on the assumption that costs should be charged against revenue in the reverse order in which costs were incurred. Thus, the oldest costs are assigned to inventory. Thirty of the 35 units would be assigned a unit cost of $20 (since 10 of the beginning inventory units were sold on the first sale), and the remaining 5 units would be assigned a cost of $23, for a total of $715 (answer A).

3. **D** The FIFO method of costing is based on the assumption that costs should be charged against revenue in the order in which they were incurred (first-in, first-out). Thus, the most recent costs are assigned to inventory. The 35 units would be assigned a unit cost of $23 (answer D).

4. **B** When the price level is steadily rising, the earlier unit costs are lower than recent unit costs. Under the FIFO method (answer B), these earlier costs are matched against revenue to yield the highest possible net income. The periodic inventory system (answer D) is a system and not a method of costing.

5. **D** The understatement of inventory by $7,500 at the end of the year will cause the cost of merchandise sold for the year to be overstated by $7,500, the gross profit for the year to be understated by $7,500, the merchandise inventory to be understated by $7,500, and the net income for the year to be understated by $7,500 (answer D).

Sarbanes-Oxley, Internal Control, and Cash

© KEMIE GUAIDA/ISTOCKPHOTO INC.

objectives

After studying this chapter, you should be able to:

1 Describe the Sarbanes-Oxley Act of 2002 and its impact on internal controls and financial reporting.

2 Describe and illustrate the objectives and elements of internal control.

3 Describe and illustrate the application of internal controls to cash.

4 Describe the nature of a bank account and its use in controlling cash.

5 Describe and illustrate the use of a bank reconciliation in controlling cash.

6 Describe the accounting for special-purpose cash funds.

7 Describe and illustrate the reporting of cash and cash equivalents in the financial statements.

eBay Inc.

Controls are a part of your everyday life. At one extreme, laws are used to limit your behavior. For example, the speed limit is a control on your driving, designed for traffic safety. In addition, you are also affected by many nonlegal controls. For example, you can keep credit card receipts in order to compare your transactions to the monthly credit card statement. Comparing receipts to the monthly statement is a control designed to catch mistakes made by the credit card company. Likewise, recording checks in your checkbook is a control that you can use at the end of the month to verify the accuracy of your bank statement. In addition, banks give you a personal identification number (PIN) as a control against unauthorized access to your cash if you lose your automated teller machine (ATM) card. Dairies use freshness dating on their milk containers as a control to prevent the purchase or sale of soured milk. As you can see, you use and encounter controls every day.

Just as there are many examples of controls throughout society, businesses must also implement controls to help guide the behavior of their managers, employees, and customers. For example, eBay Inc. maintains an Internet-based marketplace for the sale of goods and services. Using eBay's online platform, buyers and sellers can browse, buy, and sell a wide variety of items, including antiques and used cars. However, in order to maintain the integrity and trust of its buyers and sellers, eBay must have controls to ensure that buyers pay for their items and sellers don't misrepresent their items or fail to deliver sales. One such control that eBay uses is the buyer's or seller's reputation based upon feedback from past transactions of the member. A prospective buyer or seller can view the member's reputation and feedback comments before completing a transaction. Dishonest or unfair trading can lead to a negative reputation and even suspension or cancellation of the member's ability to trade on eBay.

In this chapter, we will discuss controls that can be included in accounting systems to provide reasonable assurance that the financial statements are reliable. We also discuss controls over cash that you can use to determine whether your bank has made any errors in your account. We begin this chapter by discussing the Sarbanes-Oxley Act of 2002 and its impact on controls and financial reporting.

Sarbanes-Oxley Act of 2002

During the Enron, WorldCom, Tyco International, Ltd., Adelphia Communications, and other financial scandals of the early 2000s, stockholders, creditors, and other investors lost millions and in some cases billions of dollars.[1] The resulting public outcry led Congress to pass the **Sarbanes-Oxley Act of 2002**. This act, referred to simply as *Sarbanes-Oxley*, is considered one of the most important and significant laws affecting publicly held companies in recent history. Although Sarbanes-Oxley applies only to companies whose stock is traded on public exchanges, referred to as *publicly held companies*, it has highlighted the need to assess the financial controls and reporting of all companies.

Sarbanes-Oxley's purpose is to restore public confidence and trust in the financial statements of companies. In doing so, Sarbanes-Oxley emphasizes the importance of effective internal control.[2] **Internal control** is broadly defined as the procedures and processes used by a company to safeguard its assets, process information accurately, and ensure compliance with laws and regulations.

---

1 Exhibit 2 in Chapter 1 briefly summarizes these scandals.
2 Sarbanes-Oxley also has important implications for corporate governance and the regulation of the public accounting profession. In this chapter, we focus on the internal control implications of Sarbanes-Oxley.

Sarbanes-Oxley requires companies to maintain strong and effective internal controls over the recording of transactions and the preparing of financial statements. Such controls are important because they deter fraud and prevent misleading financial statements as shown in the following illustration:

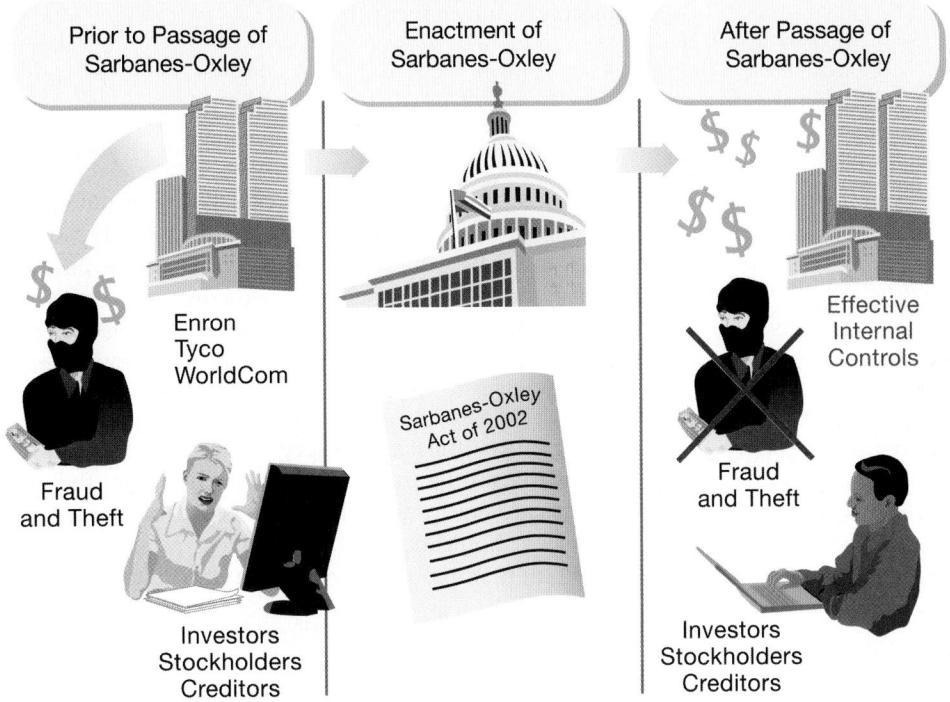

Prior to Passage of Sarbanes-Oxley
Enron Tyco WorldCom
Fraud and Theft
Investors Stockholders Creditors

Enactment of Sarbanes-Oxley
Sarbanes-Oxley Act of 2002

After Passage of Sarbanes-Oxley
Effective Internal Controls
Fraud and Theft
Investors Stockholders Creditors

REAL WORLD

It is estimated that companies spend millions each year to comply with the requirements of Sarbanes-Oxley.

Sarbanes-Oxley not only requires companies to maintain strong and effective internal controls, but it also requires companies and their independent accountants to report on the effectiveness of the company's internal controls.[3] These reports are required to be filed with the company's annual 10-K report with the Securities and Exchange Commission. The act also encourages companies to include these reports in their annual reports to stockholders. An example of such a report by the management of General Electric Company (GE) is shown in Exhibit 1.

EXHIBIT 1

Sarbanes-Oxley Report General Electric Company

> **Management's Annual Report on Internal Control over Financial Reporting**
>
> The management of General Electric Company is responsible for establishing and maintaining adequate internal control over financial reporting for the company. With the participation of the Chief Executive Officer and the Chief Financial Officer, our management conducted an evaluation of the effectiveness of our internal control over financial reporting based on the framework and criteria established in *Internal Control—Integrated Framework*, issued by the Committee of Sponsoring Organizations. . . . Based on this evaluation . . . our management has concluded that our internal control over financial reporting was effective. . . .
>
> General Electric Company's independent [accountant] auditor, KPMG LLP, a registered public accounting firm, has [also] issued an audit report on our management's assessment of our internal control over financial reporting.
>
> JEFFREY R. IMMELT   KEITH S. SHERIN
> Chairman of the Board   Senior Vice President, Finance
> and Chief Executive Officer   and Chief Financial Officer

---

3 These reporting requirements are required under Section 404 of the act. As a result, these requirements and reports are often referred to as 404 requirements and 404 reports.

GE based its assessment and evaluation of internal controls upon *Internal Control—Integrated Framework,* which was issued by the Committee of Sponsoring Organizations (COSO) of the Treadway Commission. This framework is the widely accepted standard by which companies design, analyze, and evaluate internal controls. For this reason, we use this framework in the next section of this chapter as a basis for our discussion of internal controls.

Internal Control

objective **2**

Describe and illustrate the objectives and elements of internal control.

As indicated in the prior section, effective internal controls are required by Sarbanes-Oxley. In addition, effective internal controls help businesses guide their operations and prevent theft and other abuses. For example, assume that you own and manage a lawn care service. Your business uses several employee teams, and you provide each team with vehicle and lawn equipment. What issues might you face as a manager in controlling the operations of this business? Below are some examples.

- Lawn care must be provided on time.
- The quality of lawn care services must meet customer expectations.
- Employees must provide work for the hours they are paid.
- Lawn care equipment should be used for business purposes only.
- Vehicles should be used for business purposes only.
- Customers must be billed and payments collected for services rendered.

How would you address these issues? You could, for example, develop a schedule at the beginning of each day and then inspect the work at the end of the day to verify that it was completed according to quality standards. You could have "surprise" inspections by arriving on site at random times to verify that the teams are working according to schedule. You could require employees to "clock in" at the beginning of the day and "clock out" at the end of the day to make sure that they are paid for hours worked. You could require the work teams to return the vehicles and equipment to a central location to prevent unauthorized use. You could keep a log of odometer readings at the end of each day to verify that the vehicles have not been used for "joy riding." You could bill customers after you have inspected the work and then monitor the collection of all receivables. All of these are examples of internal control.

In this section, we describe and illustrate internal control using the framework developed by the Committee of Sponsoring Organizations (COSO), which was formed by five major business associations. The committee's deliberations were published in *Internal Control—Integrated Framework.*[4] This framework, cited by GE in Exhibit 1, has become the standard by which companies design, analyze, and evaluate internal control. We describe and illustrate the framework by first describing the objectives of internal control and then showing how these objectives can be achieved through the five elements of internal control.

Information on *Internal Control—Integrated Framework* can be found on COSO's Web site at **http://www.coso.org/**.

OBJECTIVES OF INTERNAL CONTROL

The objectives of internal control are to provide reasonable assurance that (1) assets are safeguarded and used for business purposes, (2) business information is accurate, and (3) employees comply with laws and regulations. These objectives are illustrated on the following page.

Internal control can safeguard assets by preventing theft, fraud, misuse, or misplacement. One of the most serious breaches of internal control is employee fraud. **Employee fraud** is the intentional act of deceiving an employer for personal gain.

---

4 *Internal Control—Integrated Framework* by the Committee of Sponsoring Organizations of the Treadway Commission, 1992.

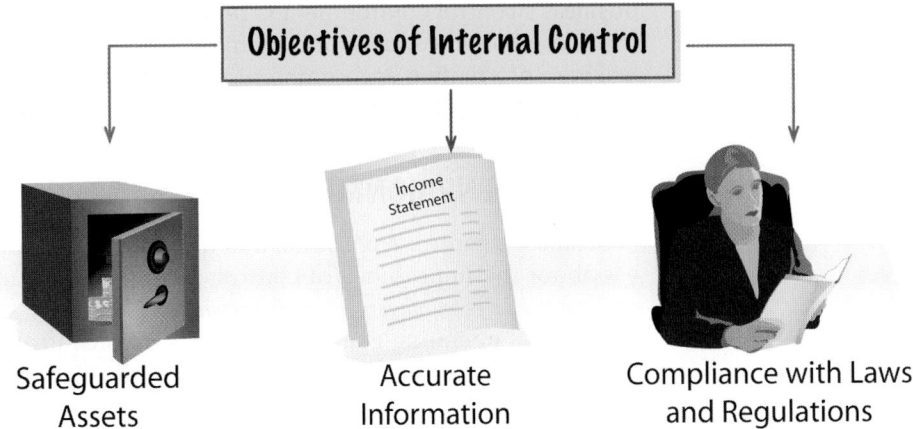

Safeguarded Assets   Accurate Information   Compliance with Laws and Regulations

The Association of Certified Fraud Examiners has estimated that businesses will lose over $660 billion, or around 6% of revenue, to employee fraud.

Source: *2004 Report to the Nation: Occupational Fraud and Abuse*, Association of Certified Fraud Examiners.

Such deception may range from purposely overstating expenses on a travel expense report to embezzling millions of dollars through complex schemes.

Accurate information is necessary for operating a business successfully. The safeguarding of assets and accurate information often go hand-in-hand. The reason is that employees attempting to defraud a business will also need to adjust the accounting records in order to hide the fraud.

Businesses must comply with applicable laws, regulations, and financial reporting standards. Examples of such standards and laws include environmental regulations, contract terms, safety regulations, and generally accepted accounting principles (GAAP).

ELEMENTS OF INTERNAL CONTROL

How does management achieve its internal control objectives? Management is responsible for designing and applying five **elements of internal control** to meet the three internal control objectives. These elements are (1) the control environment, (2) risk assessment, (3) control procedures, (4) monitoring, and (5) information and communication.[5]

The elements of internal control are illustrated in Exhibit 2. In this exhibit, these elements form an umbrella over the business to protect it from control threats. The

EXHIBIT 2 | **Elements of Internal Control**

---

5 Ibid., 12–14.

business's control environment is represented by the size of the umbrella. Risk assessment, control procedures, and monitoring are the fabric that keeps the umbrella from leaking. Information and communication link the umbrella to management. In the following paragraphs, we discuss each of these elements.

CONTROL ENVIRONMENT

A business's control environment is the overall attitude of management and employees about the importance of controls. One of the factors that influences the control environment is *management's philosophy and operating style*. A management that overemphasizes operating goals and deviates from control policies may indirectly encourage employees to ignore controls. For example, the pressure to achieve revenue targets may encourage employees to fraudulently record sham sales. On the other hand, a management that emphasizes the importance of controls and encourages adherence to control policies will create an effective control environment.

Control Environment

Management's Philosophy and Operating Style

CEO

Employees

Organizational Structure

Personnel Policies

How do companies discover fraud? Most fraud is discovered from tips by employees, customers, suppliers, or anonymous sources.

The business's *organizational structure*, which is the framework for planning and controlling operations, also influences the control environment. For example, a department store chain might organize each of its stores as separate business units. Each store manager has full authority over pricing and other operating activities. In such a structure, each store manager has the responsibility for establishing an effective control environment.

Personnel policies also affect the control environment. Personnel policies involve the hiring, training, evaluation, compensation, and promotion of employees. In addition, job descriptions, employee codes of ethics, and conflict-of-interest policies are part of the personnel policies. Such policies can enhance the internal control environment if they provide reasonable assurance that only competent, honest employees are hired and retained.

To illustrate the importance of the control environment, consider the case where the head of a bank's loan department perpetrated a fraud by accepting bribes from customers with poor credit ratings. As a result, the bank lost thousands of dollars from bad loans. After discovering the fraud, the bank president improved the bank's control environment by implementing a program that allowed employees to report suspicious conduct anonymously. In addition to encouraging employees to report suspicious conduct, the employees were warned that employee fraud might occur anywhere and involve anyone.

RISK ASSESSMENT

All organizations face risks. Examples of risk include changes in customer requirements, competitive threats, regulatory changes, changes in economic factors such as interest rates, and employee violations of company policies and procedures. Management should assess these risks and take necessary actions to control them, so that the objectives of internal control can be achieved.

Once risks are identified, they can be analyzed to estimate their significance, to assess their likelihood of occurring, and to determine actions that will minimize them. For example, the manager of a warehouse operation may analyze the risk of employee back injuries, which might give rise to lawsuits. If the manager determines that the risk is significant, the company may purchase back support braces for its warehouse employees and require them to wear the braces.

CONTROL PROCEDURES

Control procedures are established to provide reasonable assurance that business goals will be achieved, including the prevention of fraud. In the following paragraphs, we will briefly discuss control procedures that can be integrated throughout the accounting system. These procedures are listed in Exhibit 3.

EXHIBIT 3 | **Internal Control Procedures**

Control Threats

Control Procedures
Competent personnel, rotating duties, and mandatory vacations
Separating responsibilities for related operations
Separating operations, custody of assets, and accounting proofs and security measures

Management

Business

Competent Personnel, Rotating Duties, and Mandatory Vacations The successful operation of an accounting system requires procedures to ensure that people are able to perform the duties to which they are assigned. Hence, it is necessary that all accounting employees be adequately trained and supervised in performing their jobs. It may also be advisable to rotate duties of clerical personnel and mandate vacations for nonclerical personnel. These policies encourage employees to adhere to prescribed procedures. In addition, existing errors or fraud may be detected. For example, numerous cases of employee fraud have been discovered after a long-term employee, who never took vacations, missed work because of an illness or other unavoidable reasons.

To illustrate, consider the case where a bank officer who was not required to take vacations stole approximately $5 million over 16 years by printing fake certificates of deposit. The officer would then issue the fake certificate to the customer and pocket the customer's money. After discovering the theft, the bank began requiring all employees to take vacations.

Integrity, Objectivity, and Ethics in Business

ETHICS

TIPS ON PREVENTING EMPLOYEE FRAUD IN SMALL COMPANIES

- Do not have the same employee write company checks and keep the books. Look for payments to vendors you don't know or payments to vendors whose names appear to be misspelled.
- If your business has a computer system, restrict access to accounting files as much as possible. Also, keep a backup copy of your accounting files and store it at an off-site location.
- Be wary of anybody working in finance that declines to take vacations. They may be afraid that a replacement will uncover fraud.

- Require and monitor supporting documentation (such as vendor invoices) before signing checks.
- Track the number of credit card bills you sign monthly.
- Limit and monitor access to important documents and supplies, such as blank checks and signature stamps.
- Check W-2 forms against your payroll annually to make sure you're not carrying any fictitious employees.
- Rely on yourself, not on your accountant, to spot fraud.

Source: Steve Kaufman, "Embezzlement Common at Small Companies," Knight-Ridder Newspapers, reported in *Athens Daily News/Athens Banner-Herald*, March 10, 1996, p. 4D.

Many companies have "fraud hotlines" where employees can anonymously report suspicious or fraudulent activities.

Separating Responsibilities for Related Operations   To decrease the possibility of inefficiency, errors, and fraud, the responsibility for related operations should be divided among two or more persons. For example, the responsibilities for purchasing, receiving, and paying for computer supplies should be divided among three persons or departments. If the same person orders supplies, verifies the receipt of the supplies, and pays the supplier, the following abuses are possible:

1. Orders may be placed on the basis of friendship with a supplier, rather than on price, quality, and other objective factors.
2. The quantity and quality of supplies received may not be verified, thus causing payment for supplies not received or poor-quality supplies.
3. Supplies may be stolen by the employee.
4. The validity and accuracy of invoices may be verified carelessly, thus causing the payment of false or inaccurate invoices.

The "checks and balances" provided by dividing responsibilities among various departments requires no duplication of effort. The business documents prepared by one department are designed to coordinate with and support those prepared by other departments.

To illustrate, consider the case where an accounts payable clerk created false invoices and submitted them for payment. The clerk obtained the resulting checks, opened a bank account, and cashed the checks under an assumed name. The clerk was able to steal thousands of dollars because no one was required to approve the payments other than the accounts payable clerk.

An accounting clerk for the Grant County (Washington) Alcoholism Program was in charge of collecting money, making deposits, and keeping the records. While the clerk was away on maternity leave, the replacement clerk discovered a fraud: $17,800 in fees had been collected but had been hidden for personal gain.

Separating Operations, Custody of Assets, and Accounting   Control policies should establish the responsibilities for various business activities. To reduce the possibility of errors and fraud, the responsibilities for operations, custody of assets, and accounting should be separated. The accounting records then serve as an independent check on the individuals who have custody of the assets and who engage in the business operations. For example, the employees entrusted with handling cash receipts from credit customers should not record cash receipts in the accounting records. To do so would allow employees to borrow or steal cash and hide the theft in the records. Likewise, if those engaged in operating activities also record the results of operations, they could distort the accounting reports to show favorable results. For example, a store manager whose year-end bonus is based upon operating profits might be tempted to record fictitious sales in order to receive a larger bonus.

To illustrate, consider the case where a payroll clerk was responsible for preparing the payroll and distributing the payroll checks. The clerk stole almost $40,000 over two months by preparing duplicate payroll checks and checks for fictitious part-time employees. After the theft was detected, the duties of preparing payroll checks and distributing payroll checks were assigned to separate employees.

Proofs and Security Measures   Proofs and security measures should be used to safeguard assets and ensure reliable accounting data. This control procedure applies to many different techniques, such as authorization, approval, and reconciliation procedures. For example, employees who travel on company business may be required to obtain a department manager's approval on a travel request form.

Other examples of control procedures include the use of bank accounts and other measures to ensure the safety of cash and valuable documents. A cash register that displays the amount recorded for each sale and provides the customer a printed receipt can be an effective part of the internal control structure. An all-night convenience store could use the following security measures to deter robberies:

1. Locate the cash register near the door, so that it is fully visible from outside the store; have two employees work late hours; employ a security guard.
2. Deposit cash in the bank daily, before 5 p.m.
3. Keep only small amounts of cash on hand after 5 p.m. by depositing excess cash in a store safe that can't be opened by employees on duty.
4. Install cameras and alarm systems.

To illustrate, consider the case where someone stole thousands of dollars in parking fines from a small town. Citizens would pay their parking fines by placing money in ticket envelopes and putting them in a locked box outside the town hall. The key to the locked box was not safeguarded and was readily available to a variety of people. As a result, the person who stole the money was never discovered. The town later gave one person the responsibility of safeguarding the key and emptying the locked box.

MONITORING

Monitoring the internal control system locates weaknesses and improves control effectiveness. The internal control system can be monitored through either ongoing efforts by management or by separate evaluations. Ongoing monitoring efforts may include observing both employee behavior and warning signs from the accounting system. The indicators shown in Exhibit 4 may be clues to internal control problems.[6]

Separate monitoring evaluations are generally performed when there are major changes in strategy, senior management, business structure, or operations. In large businesses, internal auditors who are independent of operations normally are responsible for monitoring the internal control system. Internal auditors can report issues and concerns to an audit committee of the board of directors, who are independent of management. In addition, external auditors also evaluate internal control as a normal part of their annual financial statement audit.

INFORMATION AND COMMUNICATION

Information and communication are essential elements of internal control. Information about the control environment, risk assessment, control procedures, and monitoring is needed by management to guide operations and ensure compliance with reporting, legal, and regulatory requirements. Management can also use external information to assess events and conditions that impact decision making and external reporting. For example, management uses information from the Financial Accounting Standards Board (FASB) to assess the impact of possible changes in reporting standards.

---

6 Edwin C. Bliss, "Employee Theft," *Boardroom Reports,* July 15, 1994, pp. 5–6.

EXHIBIT 4 | Warning Signs of Internal Control Problems

Warning signs with regard to people

1. Abrupt change in lifestyle (without winning the lottery).
2. Close social relationships with suppliers.
3. Refusing to take a vacation.
4. Frequent borrowing from other employees.
5. Excessive use of alcohol or drugs.

Warning signs from the accounting system

1. Missing documents or gaps in transaction numbers (could mean documents are being used for fraudulent transactions).
2. An unusual increase in customer refunds (refunds may be phony).
3. Differences between daily cash receipts and bank deposits (could mean receipts are being pocketed before being deposited).
4. Sudden increase in slow payments (employee may be pocketing the payment).
5. Backlog in recording transactions (possibly an attempt to delay detection of fraud).

Example Exercise 7-1

objective **2**

Identify each of the following as relating to (a) the control environment, (b) risk assessment, or (c) control procedures.

1. Mandatory vacations
2. Personnel policies
3. Report of outside consultants on future market changes

Follow My Example 7-1

1. (c) control procedures
2. (a) the control environment
3. (b) risk assessment

For Practice: PE 7-1A, PE 7-1B

Cash Controls Over Receipts and Payments

Cash includes coins, currency (paper money), checks, money orders, and money on deposit that is available for unrestricted withdrawal from banks and other financial institutions. Normally, you can think of cash as anything that a bank would accept for deposit in your account. For example, a check made payable to you could normally be deposited in a bank and thus is considered cash.

We will assume in this chapter that a business maintains only *one* bank account, represented in the ledger as *Cash*. In practice, however, a business may have several bank accounts, such as one for general cash payments and another for payroll. For each of its bank accounts, the business will maintain a ledger account, one of which may be called *Cash in Bank—First Bank*, for example. It will also maintain separate ledger accounts for special-purpose cash funds, such as travel reimbursements. We will introduce some of these other cash accounts later in this chapter.

Because of the ease with which money can be transferred, cash is the asset most likely to be diverted and used improperly by employees. In addition, many transactions either directly or indirectly affect the receipt or the payment of cash. Businesses must therefore design and use controls that safeguard cash and control the authorization of cash transactions. In the following paragraphs, we will discuss these controls.

CONTROL OF CASH RECEIPTS

To protect cash from theft and misuse, a business must control cash from the time it is received until it is deposited in a bank. Businesses normally receive cash from two main sources: (1) customers purchasing products or services and (2) customers making payments on account. For example, fast-food restaurants, such as McDonald's, Wendy's International Inc., and Burger King Corporation, receive cash primarily from over-the-counter sales to customers. Mail-order and Internet retailers, such as Lands' End Inc., The Orvis Company, Inc., L.L. Bean, Inc., and Amazon.com, receive cash primarily through electronic funds transfers from credit card companies.

Cash Received from Cash Sales   Regardless of the source of cash receipts, every business must properly safeguard and record its cash receipts. One of the most important controls to protect cash received in over-the-counter sales is a cash register. When a clerk (cashier) enters the amount of a sale, the cash register normally displays the amount. This is a control to ensure that the clerk has charged you the correct amount. You also receive a receipt to verify the accuracy of the amount.

At the beginning of a work shift, each cash register clerk is given a cash drawer that contains a predetermined amount of cash for making change for customers. The amount in each drawer is sometimes called a *change fund*. At the end of the shift, the clerk and the supervisor count the cash in that clerk's cash drawer. The amount of cash in each drawer should equal the beginning amount of cash plus the cash sales for the day. However, errors in recording cash sales or errors in making change cause the amount of cash on hand to differ from this amount. Such differences are recorded in a **cash short and over account**.

At the end of the accounting period, a debit balance in the cash short and over account is included in Miscellaneous Expense in the income statement. A credit balance is included in the Other Income section. If a clerk consistently has significant cash short and over amounts, the supervisor may require the clerk to take additional training.

After a cash register clerk's cash has been counted and recorded on a memorandum form, the cash is then placed in a store safe in the Cashier's Department until it can be deposited in the bank. The supervisor forwards the clerk's cash register receipts to the Accounting Department, where they serve as the basis for recording the transactions for the day as shown on the following page.

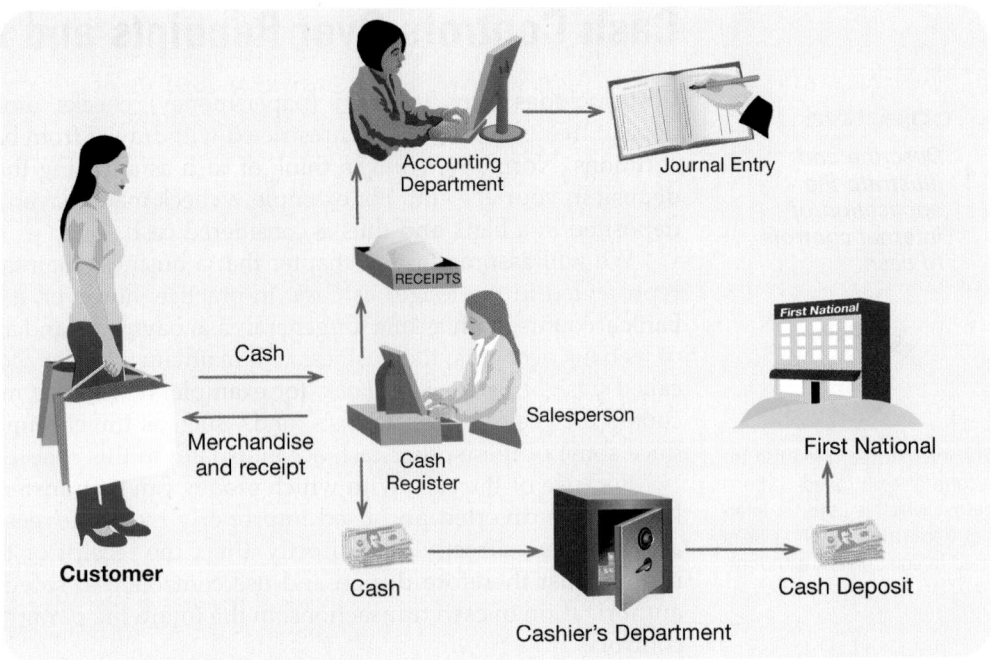

Some retail companies use debit card systems to transfer and record the receipt of cash. In a debit card system, a customer pays for goods at the time of purchase by presenting a plastic card. The card authorizes the electronic transfer of cash from the customer's checking account to the retailer's bank account.

Cash Received in the Mail   Cash is received in the mail when customers pay their bills. This cash is usually in the form of checks and money orders. Most companies' invoices are designed so that customers return a portion of the invoice, called a *remittance advice*, with their payment. The employee who opens the incoming mail should initially compare the amount of cash received with the amount shown on the remittance advice. If a customer does not return a remittance advice, an employee prepares one. Like the cash register, the remittance advice serves as a record of cash initially received. It also helps ensure that the posting to the customer's account is accurate. Finally, as a control, the employee opening the mail normally also stamps checks and money orders "For Deposit Only" in the bank account of the business.

All cash received in the mail is sent to the Cashier's Department. An employee there combines it with the receipts from cash sales and prepares a bank deposit ticket. The remittance advices and their summary totals are delivered to the Accounting Department. An accounting clerk then prepares the records of the transactions and posts them to the customer accounts.

When cash is deposited in the bank, the bank normally stamps a duplicate copy of the deposit ticket with the amount received. This bank receipt is returned to the Accounting Department, where a clerk compares the receipt with the total amount that should have been deposited. This control helps ensure that all the cash is deposited and that no cash is lost or stolen on the way to the bank. Any shortages are thus promptly detected.

Separating the duties of the Cashier's Department, which handles cash, and the Accounting Department, which records cash, is a control. If Accounting Department employees both handle and record cash, an employee could steal cash and change the accounting records to hide the theft.

Cash Received by EFT   Cash may also be received from customers through **electronic funds transfers (EFT)**. For example, customers may authorize automatic electronic transfers from their checking accounts to pay monthly bills for such items as cell phone, cable, Internet, and electric services. In such cases, the company sends the customer's bank a signed form from the customer authorizing the monthly electronic transfers from the customer's checking account to the company's bank account. Each month, the company electronically notifies the customer's bank of the amount of the transfer and the date the transfer should take place. On the due date, the company records the electronic transfer as a receipt of cash to its bank account and posts the amount paid to the customer's account.

Most companies encourage automatic electronic transfers by customers for several reasons. First, electronic transfers are less costly than receiving cash payments through the mail since the employee handling of cash is eliminated. Second, electronic transfers enhance internal controls over cash since the cash is received directly by the bank without the handling of cash by employees. Thus, potential theft of cash is eliminated. Finally, electronic transfers reduce late payments from customers and speed up the processing of cash receipts.

CONTROL OF CASH PAYMENTS

Howard Schultz & Associates (HS&A) specializes in reviewing cash payments for its clients. HS&A searches for errors, such as duplicate payments, failures to take discounts, and inaccurate computations. Amounts recovered for clients ranged from thousands to millions of dollars.

The control of cash payments should provide reasonable assurance that payments are made for only authorized transactions. In addition, controls should ensure that cash is used efficiently. For example, controls should ensure that all available discounts, such as purchase discounts, are taken.

In a small business, an owner/manager may authorize payments based upon personal knowledge of goods and services purchased. In a large business, however, the duties of purchasing goods, inspecting the goods received, and verifying the invoices are usually performed by different employees. These duties must be coordinated to ensure that checks for proper payments are made to creditors. One system used for this purpose is the voucher system.

Voucher System   A **voucher system** is a set of procedures for authorizing and recording liabilities and cash payments. A **voucher** is any document that serves as proof of authority to pay cash or issue an electronic funds transfer. For example, an invoice properly approved for payment could be considered a voucher. In many businesses, however, a voucher is a special form for recording relevant data about a liability and the details of its payment.

A voucher system may be either manual or computerized. In a manual system, a voucher is normally prepared after all necessary supporting documents have been received. For example, when a voucher is prepared for the purchase of goods, the voucher should be supported by the supplier's invoice, a purchase order, and a receiving report. After a voucher is prepared, it is submitted to the proper manager for approval. Once approved, the voucher is recorded in the accounts and filed by due date. Upon payment, the voucher is recorded in the same manner as the payment of an account payable.

In a computerized system, properly approved supporting documents (such as purchase orders and receiving reports) would be entered directly into computer files. At the due date, the checks would be automatically generated and mailed to creditors. At that time, the voucher would be electronically transferred to a paid voucher file.

Cash Paid by EFT   Cash can also be paid by electronic funds transfer systems by using computers rather than paper money or checks. For example, a company may pay its employees by means of EFT. Under such a system, employees may authorize the deposit of their payroll checks directly into checking accounts. Each pay period, the business electronically transfers the employees' net pay to their checking accounts through the use of computer systems and networks. Likewise, many companies are using EFT systems to pay their suppliers and other vendors.

Bank Accounts

objective **4**

Describe the nature of a bank account and its use in controlling cash.

Many businesses and individuals are now using Internet banking services, which provide for the payment of funds electronically.

Most of you are familiar with bank accounts. You probably have a checking account at a local bank, credit union, savings and loan association, or other financial institution. In this section, we discuss the use of bank accounts by businesses. We then discuss the use of bank accounts as an additional control over cash.

USE OF BANK ACCOUNTS

A business often maintains several bank accounts. For example, a business with several branches or retail outlets such as Sears Holdings, Inc. or Gap Inc. will often maintain a bank account for each location. In addition, businesses usually maintain a separate bank account for payroll and other special purposes.

A major reason that businesses use bank accounts is for control purposes. Use of bank accounts reduces the amount of cash on hand at any one time. For example, many merchandise businesses deposit cash receipts twice daily to reduce the amount of cash on hand that is susceptible to theft. Likewise, using a payroll account allows for paying employees by check or electronic funds transfer rather than by distributing a large amount of cash each payroll period.

In addition to reducing the amount of cash on hand, bank accounts provide an independent recording of cash transactions that can be used as a verification of the business's recording of transactions. That is, the use of bank accounts provides a double recording of cash transactions. The company's cash account corresponds to the bank's liability (deposit) account for the company. As we will discuss and illustrate in the next section, this double recording of cash transactions allows for a reconciliation of the cash account on the company's records with the cash balance recorded by the bank.

Finally, the use of bank accounts facilitates the transfer of funds. For example, electronic funds transfer systems require bank accounts for the transfer of funds between companies. Within a company, cash can be transferred between bank accounts through the use of wire transfers. In addition, online banking allows companies to transfer funds and pay bills electronically as well as monitor their cash balances on a real-time basis.

BANK STATEMENT

Banks usually maintain a record of all checking account transactions. A summary of all transactions, called a **bank statement**, is mailed to the depositor or made available online, usually each month. Like any account with a customer or a creditor, the bank statement shows the beginning balance, additions, deductions, and the balance at the end of the period. A typical bank statement is shown in Exhibit 5.

The depositor's checks or copies of the checks received by the bank during the period may accompany the bank statement, arranged in order of payment. If paid checks are returned, they are stamped "Paid," together with the date of payment. Many banks no longer return checks or check copies with bank statements. Instead, the check payment information is available online. Other entries that the bank has made in the depositor's account are described as debit or credit memorandums on the statement.

The depositor's checking account balance *in the bank records* is a liability; thus, in the bank's records, the depositor's account has a credit balance. Since the bank statement is prepared from the bank's point of view, a credit memorandum entry on the bank statement indicates an increase (a credit) in the depositor's account. Likewise, a debit memorandum entry on the bank statement indicates a decrease (a debit) in the depositor's account. This relationship is shown at the bottom of page 321.

A bank makes credit entries (issues credit memoranda) for deposits made by electronic funds transfer, for collections of note receivable for the depositor, for proceeds for a loan to the depositor, for interest earned on the depositor's account, and to correct bank errors. A bank makes debit entries (issues debit memoranda) for payments made by electronic funds transfer, for service charges, for customers' checks returned for not sufficient funds, and to correct bank errors.

EXHIBIT 5

Bank Statement

MEMBER FDIC

PAGE   1

VALLEY NATIONAL BANK OF LOS ANGELES

LOS ANGELES, CA 90020-4253   (310)555-5151

ACCOUNT NUMBER   1627042

FROM 6/30/07   TO 7/31/07

BALANCE   4,218.60

22 DEPOSITS   13,749.75

52 WITHDRAWALS   14,698.57

3 OTHER DEBITS
  AND CREDITS   90.00CR

NEW BALANCE   3,359.78

POWER NETWORKING
1000 Belkin Street
Los Angeles, CA 90014 -1000

* - - CHECKS AND OTHER DEBITS - - -		* - - - DEPOSITS - -	* - - DATE - -	* - - BALANCE - - *
819.40	122.54	585.75	07/01	3,862.41
369.50	732.26	20.15	421.53	07/02	3,162.03
600.00	190.70	52.50	781.30	07/03	3,100.13
25.93	160.00	662.50	07/05	3,576.70
921.20	NSF 300.00	503.18	07/07	2,858.68

32.26	535.09	ACH 932.00	07/29	3,404.40
21.10	126.20	705.21	07/30	3,962.31
	SC 18.00	MS 408.00	07/30	4,352.31
26.12	ACH 1,615.13	648.72	07/31	3,359.78

EC — ERROR CORRECTION   ACH — AUTOMATED CLEARING HOUSE

MS — MISCELLANEOUS

NSF — NOT SUFFICIENT FUNDS   SC — SERVICE CHARGE

* * *   * * *   * * *

THE RECONCILEMENT OF THIS STATEMENT WITH YOUR RECORDS IS ESSENTIAL.
ANY ERROR OR EXCEPTION SHOULD BE REPORTED IMMEDIATELY.

Customers' checks returned for not sufficient funds, called *NSF checks*, are checks that were initially deposited but were not paid when they were presented to the customer's bank for payment. Since the bank initially credited the check to the depositor's account when it was deposited, the bank debits (issues a debit memorandum) when

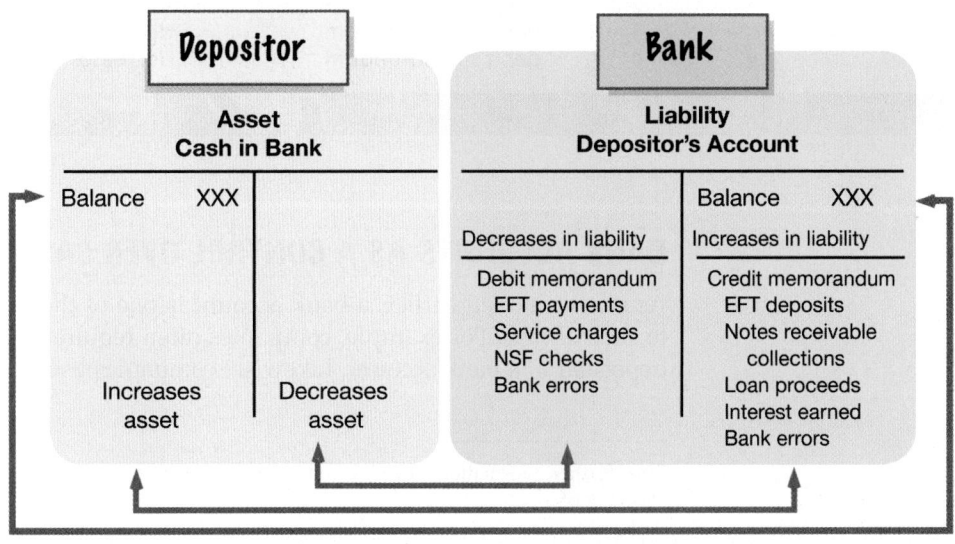

the check is returned without payment. We discuss the accounting for NSF checks later in this chapter.

The reason for a credit or debit memorandum entry is indicated on the bank statement. For example, Exhibit 5 identifies the following types of credit and debit memorandum entries:

EC: Error correction to correct bank error.
NSF: Not sufficient funds check.
SC: Service charge.
ACH: Automated Clearing House entry for electronic funds transfer.
MS: Miscellaneous item such as collection of a note receivable on behalf of the depositor or receipt of loan proceeds by the depositor from the bank.

In the preceding list, we have included the notation "ACH" for electronic funds transfers. ACH is a network for clearing electronic funds transfers among individuals, companies, and banks.[7] Because electronic funds transfers may be either deposits or payments, ACH entries may indicate either a debit or credit entry to the depositor's account. Likewise, entries to correct bank errors and miscellaneous items may indicate a debit or credit entry to the depositor's account.

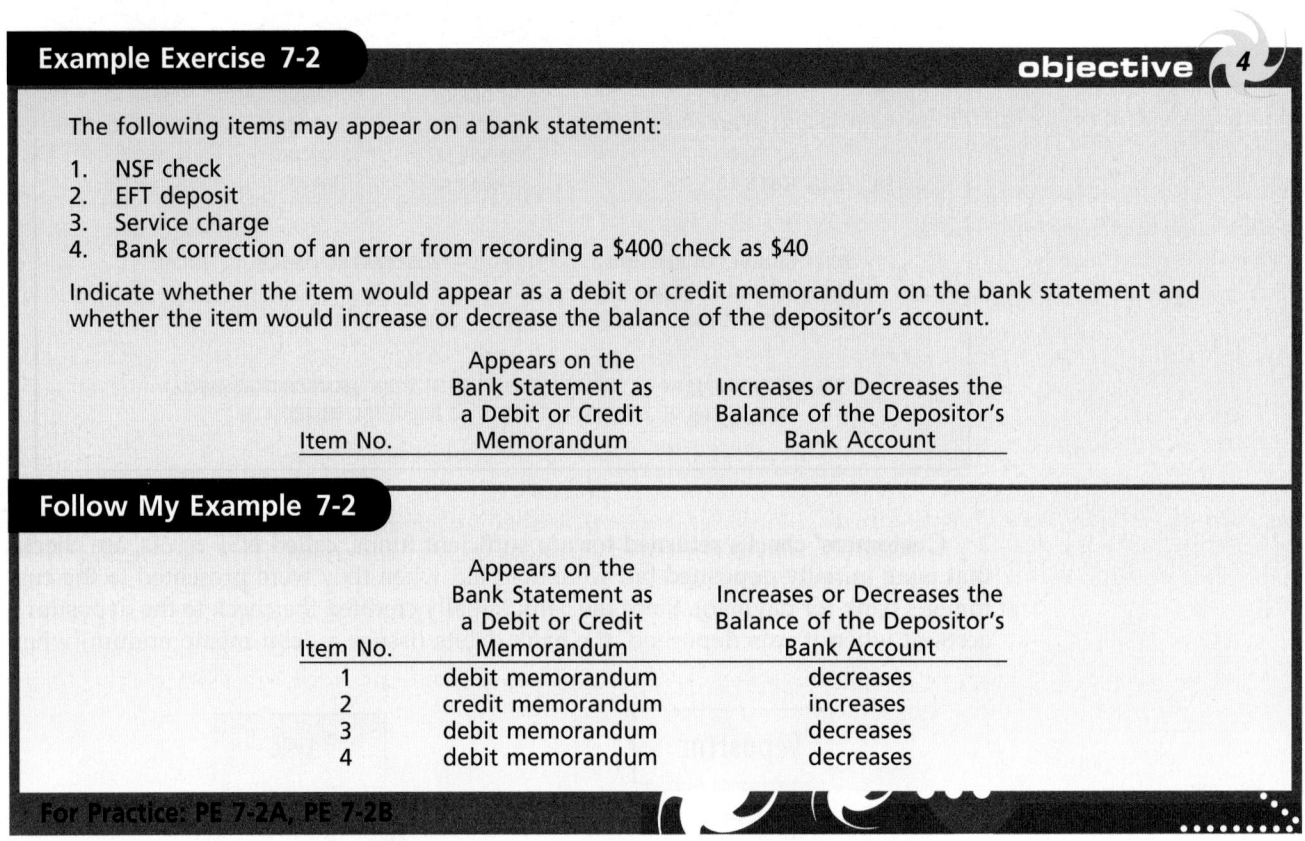

Example Exercise 7-2   **objective** 4

The following items may appear on a bank statement:

1. NSF check
2. EFT deposit
3. Service charge
4. Bank correction of an error from recording a $400 check as $40

Indicate whether the item would appear as a debit or credit memorandum on the bank statement and whether the item would increase or decrease the balance of the depositor's account.

Item No.	Appears on the Bank Statement as a Debit or Credit Memorandum	Increases or Decreases the Balance of the Depositor's Bank Account

Follow My Example 7-2

Item No.	Appears on the Bank Statement as a Debit or Credit Memorandum	Increases or Decreases the Balance of the Depositor's Bank Account
1	debit memorandum	decreases
2	credit memorandum	increases
3	debit memorandum	decreases
4	debit memorandum	decreases

For Practice: PE 7-2A, PE 7-2B

BANK ACCOUNTS AS A CONTROL OVER CASH

As we mentioned earlier, a bank account is one of the primary tools a company uses to control cash. For example, companies often require that all cash receipts be initially deposited in a bank account. Likewise, companies usually use checks or bank account

---

7 For further information on ACH, go to **http://www.nacha.org**/. Click on "About Us," and then click on "What is ACH?"

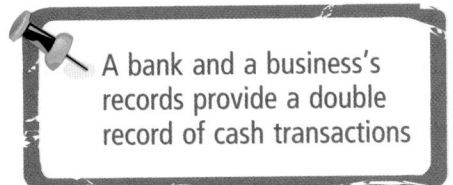

A bank and a business's records provide a double record of cash transactions

transfers to make all cash payments, except for very small amounts. When such a system is used, there is a double record of cash transactions—one by the company and the other by the bank.

A company can use a bank statement to compare the cash transactions recorded in its accounting records to those recorded by the bank. The cash balance shown by a bank statement is usually different from the cash balance shown in the accounting records of the company, as shown in Exhibit 6.

EXHIBIT 6

Power Networking's Records and Bank Statement

Bank Statement		
Beginning balance		$ 4,218.60
Additions:		
Deposits	$13,749.75	
Miscellaneous	408.00	14,157.75
Deductions:		
Checks	$14,698.57	
NSF check	300.00	
Service charge	18.00	15,016.57
Ending balance		$ 3,359.78

Power Networking Records	
Beginning balance	$ 4,227.60
Deposits	14,565.95
Checks	16,243.56
Ending balance	$ 2,549.99

Power Networking should determine the reason for the difference in these two amounts.

This difference may be the result of a delay by either party in recording transactions. For example, there is a time lag of one day or more between the date a check is written and the date that it is presented to the bank for payment. If the company mails deposits to the bank or uses the night depository, a time lag between the date of the deposit and the date that it is recorded by the bank is also probable. The bank may also debit or credit the company's account for transactions about which the company will not be informed until later.

The difference may be the result of errors made by either the company or the bank in recording transactions. For example, the company may incorrectly post to Cash a check written for $4,500 as $450. Likewise, a bank may incorrectly record the amount of a check.

Integrity, Objectivity, and Ethics in Business

ETHICS

CHECK FRAUD

Check fraud involves counterfeiting, altering, or otherwise manipulating the information on checks in order to fraudulently cash a check. According to the National Check Fraud Center, check fraud and counterfeiting are among the fastest growing problems affecting the financial system, generating over $10 billion in losses annually. Criminals perpetrate the fraud by taking blank checks from your checkbook, finding a canceled check in the garbage, or removing a check you have mailed to pay bills. Consumers can prevent check fraud by carefully storing blank checks, placing outgoing mail in postal mailboxes, and shredding canceled checks.

Bank Reconciliation

objective 5

Describe and illustrate the use of a bank reconciliation in controlling cash.

For effective control, the reasons for the difference between the cash balance on the bank statement and the cash balance in the accounting records should be analyzed by preparing a bank reconciliation. A **bank reconciliation** is an analysis of the items and amounts that cause the cash balance reported in the bank statement to differ from the balance of the cash account in the ledger in order to determine the adjusted cash balance.

A bank reconciliation is usually divided into two sections. The first section, referred to as the bank section, begins with the cash balance according to the bank statement and ends with the adjusted balance. The second section, referred to as the company section, begins with the cash balance according to the company's records and ends with the adjusted balance. The two amounts designated as the adjusted balance must be equal. The content of the bank reconciliation is shown below.

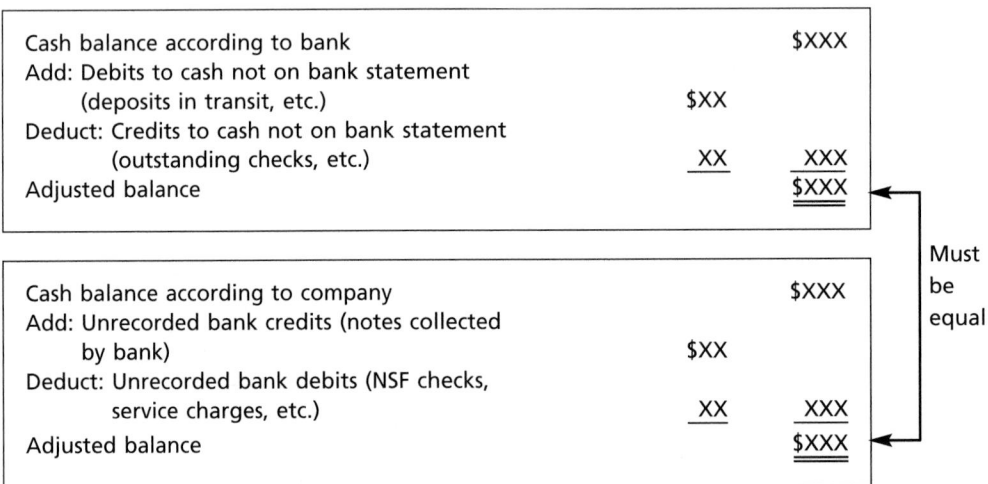

The following steps are useful in finding the reconciling items and determining the adjusted balance of Cash:

1. Compare each deposit listed on the bank statement with unrecorded deposits appearing in the preceding period's reconciliation and with the current period's deposits. *Add deposits not recorded by the bank to the balance according to the bank statement.*

2. Compare paid checks with outstanding checks appearing on the preceding period's reconciliation and with recorded checks. *Deduct checks outstanding that have not been paid by the bank from the balance according to the bank statement.*

3. Compare bank credit memorandums to entries in the journal. For example, a bank would issue a credit memorandum for a note receivable and interest that it collected for a company. *Add credit memorandums that have not been recorded to the balance according to the company's records.*

4. Compare bank debit memorandums to entries recording cash payments. For example, a bank normally issues debit memorandums for service charges and check printing charges. A bank also issues debit memorandums for not sufficient funds checks. NSF checks are normally charged back to the customer as an account receivable. *Deduct debit memorandums that have not been recorded from the balance according to the company's records.*

5. List any errors discovered during the preceding steps. For example, if an amount has been recorded incorrectly by the company, the amount of the error should be added to or deducted from the cash balance according to the company's records. Similarly, errors by the bank should be added to or deducted from the cash balance according to the bank statement.

To illustrate a bank reconciliation, we will use the bank statement for Power Networking in Exhibit 5. This bank statement shows a balance of $3,359.78 as of July 31. The cash balance in Power Networking's ledger as of the same date is $2,549.99. The following reconciling items are revealed by using the steps outlined above:

Deposit of July 31, not recorded on bank statement	$ 816.20
Checks outstanding: No. 812, $1,061.00; No. 878, $435.39;	
No. 883, $48.60	1,544.99
Note plus interest of $8 collected by bank (credit memorandum), not	
recorded in the journal	408.00
Check from customer (Thomas Ivey) returned by bank because of	
insufficient funds (NSF)	300.00
Bank service charges (debit memorandum), not recorded in the journal	18.00
Check No. 879 for $732.26 to Taylor Co. on account, recorded	
in the journal as $723.26	9.00

The bank reconciliation, based on the bank statement and the reconciling items, is shown in Exhibit 7.

EXHIBIT 7

Bank Reconciliation for Power Networking

Power Networking
Bank Reconciliation
July 31, 2007

Cash balance according to bank statement			$3 3 5 9 78
Add deposit of July 31, not recorded by bank			8 1 6 20
			$4 1 7 5 98
Deduct outstanding checks:			
No. 812	$1 0 6 1 00		
No. 878	4 3 5 39		
No. 883	4 8 60	1 5 4 4 99	
Adjusted balance			$2 6 3 0 99
Cash balance according to Power Networking records			$2 5 4 9 99
Add note and interest collected by bank			4 0 8 00
			$2 9 5 7 99
Deduct: Check returned because of insufficient funds	$ 3 0 0 00		
Bank service charge	1 8 00		
Error in recording Check No. 879	9 00	3 2 7 00	
Adjusted balance			$2 6 3 0 99

No entries are necessary on the company's records as a result of the information included in the bank section of the reconciliation. This section begins with the cash balance according to the bank statement. However, the bank should be notified of any errors that need to be corrected on its records.

Any items in the company's section of the bank reconciliation must be recorded in the company's accounts. For example, journal entries should be made for any unrecorded bank memorandums and any company errors. The journal entries for Power Networking, based on the preceding bank reconciliation, are as follows:

July	31	Cash		4 0 8 00	
		Notes Receivable			4 0 0 00
		Interest Revenue			8 00
	31	Accounts Receivable—Thomas Ivey		3 0 0 00	
		Miscellaneous Expense		1 8 00	
		Accounts Payable—Taylor Co.		9 00	
		Cash			3 2 7 00

After the entries above have been posted, the cash account will have a debit balance of $2,630.99. This balance agrees with the adjusted cash balance shown on the bank reconciliation. This is the amount of cash available as of July 31 and the amount that would be reported on Power Networking's July 31 balance sheet.

Although businesses may reconcile their bank accounts in a slightly different format from what we described here, the objective is the same: to control cash by reconciling the company's records to the records of an independent outside source, the bank. In doing so, any errors or misuse of cash may be detected.

For effective control, the bank reconciliation should be prepared by an employee who does not take part in or record cash transactions. When these duties are not properly separated, mistakes are likely to occur, and it is more likely that cash will be stolen or otherwise misapplied. For example, an employee who takes part in all of these duties could prepare and cash an unauthorized check, omit it from the accounts, and omit it from the reconciliation.

A bank reconciliation is also appropriate in a computerized environment where the deposits and checks are stored in electronic files and records. In some systems, the computer determines the difference between the ending bank balance and the balance per the company's records and then adjusts for deposits in transit and outstanding checks. Any remaining differences are reported for further analysis.

Example Exercise 7-3   objective 5

The following data were gathered to use in reconciling the bank account of Photo Op:

Balance per bank	$14,500
Balance per company records	13,875
Bank service charges	75
Deposit in transit	3,750
NSF check	800
Outstanding checks	5,250

a. What is the adjusted balance on the bank reconciliation?
b. Journalize any necessary entries for Photo Op based upon the bank reconciliation.

Follow My Example 7-3

a. $13,000, as shown below.

Bank section of reconciliation: $14,500 + $3,750 − $5,250 = $13,000
Company section of reconciliation: $13,875 − $75 − $800 = $13,000

b. Accounts Receivable   800
     Miscellaneous Expense   75
          Cash   875

For Practice: PE 7-3A, PE 7-3B

Integrity, Objectivity, and Ethics in Business

ETHICS

BANK ERROR IN YOUR FAVOR

You may sometime have a bank error in your favor, such as a misposted deposit. Such errors are not a case of "found money," as in the Monopoly® game. Bank con- trol systems quickly discover most errors and make auto- matic adjustments. Even so, you have a legal responsibil- ity to report the error and return the money to the bank.

Special-Purpose Cash Funds

objective **6**

Describe the accounting for special-purpose cash funds.

It is usually not practical for a business to write checks to pay small amounts, such as postage. Yet, these small payments may occur often enough to add up to a significant total amount. Thus, it is desirable to control such payments. For this purpose, a spe- cial cash fund, called a **petty cash fund**, is used.

A petty cash fund is established by first estimating the amount of cash needed for payments from the fund during a period, such as a week or a month. After necessary approvals, a check is written and cashed for this amount. The money obtained from cashing the check is then given to an employee, called the petty cash custodian, who is authorized to disburse monies from the fund. For control purposes, the company may place restrictions on the maximum amount and the types of payments that can be made from the fund. Each time monies are paid from petty cash, the custodian records the details of the payment on a petty cash receipt form.

The petty cash fund is normally replenished at periodic intervals or when it is depleted or reaches a minimum amount. When a petty cash fund is replenished, the accounts debited are determined by summarizing the petty cash receipts. A check is then written for this amount, payable to petty cash.

To illustrate normal petty cash fund entries, assume that a petty cash fund of $500 is established on August 1. The entry to record this transaction is as follows:

Aug.	1	Petty Cash		5 0 0 00	
		Cash			5 0 0 00

At the end of August, the petty cash receipts indicate expenditures for the follow- ing items: office supplies, $380; postage (office supplies), $22; store supplies, $35; and miscellaneous administrative expense, $30. The entry to replenish the petty cash fund on August 31 is as follows:

Aug.	31	Office Supplies		4 0 2 00	
		Store Supplies		3 5 00	
		Miscellaneous Administrative Expense		3 0 00	
		Cash			4 6 7 00

Replenishing the petty cash fund restores it to its original amount of $500. You should note that there is no entry in Petty Cash when the fund is replenished. Petty Cash is debited only when the fund is initially set up or when the amount of the fund is increased at a later time. Petty Cash is credited if it is being decreased.

In addition, businesses often use other cash funds to meet special needs, such as payroll or travel expenses for salespersons. Such funds are called **special-purpose**

funds. For example, each salesperson might be given $200 for travel-related expenses. Periodically, the salesperson submits a detailed expense report and the travel funds are replenished. Also, as we discussed earlier in this chapter, retail businesses use change funds for making change for customers. Finally, most businesses use a payroll bank account to pay employees.

A special-purpose cash fund is initially established by first estimating the amount of cash needed for payments from the fund during a period, such as a week or a month. After necessary approvals, cash is transferred to the special-purpose fund. The employee responsible for disbursing monies from the fund, called the custodian, approves all diburements from the fund. For control purposes, the company may place restrictions on the maximum amount and types of payments that can be made from the fund. Periodically, an independent employee reviews disbursements from the fund, the disbursements are recorded, and the fund is replenished.

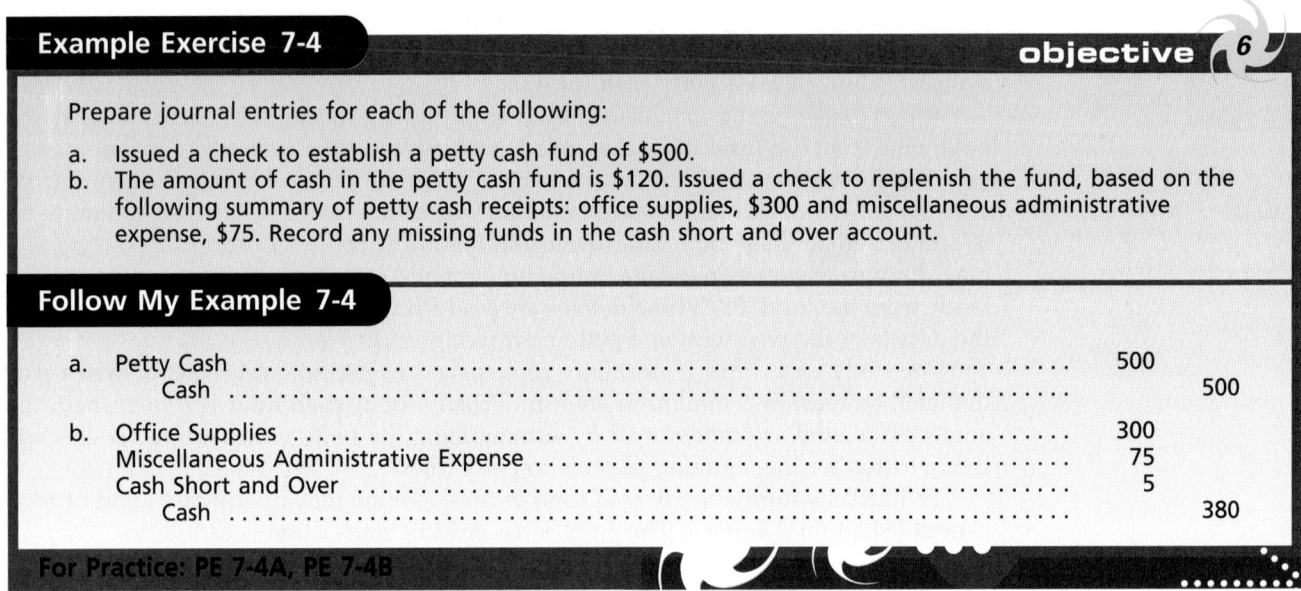

Example Exercise 7-4   **objective** 6

Prepare journal entries for each of the following:

a. Issued a check to establish a petty cash fund of $500.
b. The amount of cash in the petty cash fund is $120. Issued a check to replenish the fund, based on the following summary of petty cash receipts: office supplies, $300 and miscellaneous administrative expense, $75. Record any missing funds in the cash short and over account.

Follow My Example 7-4

a.	Petty Cash	500	
	Cash		500
b.	Office Supplies	300	
	Miscellaneous Administrative Expense	75	
	Cash Short and Over	5	
	Cash		380

For Practice: PE 7-4A, PE 7-4B

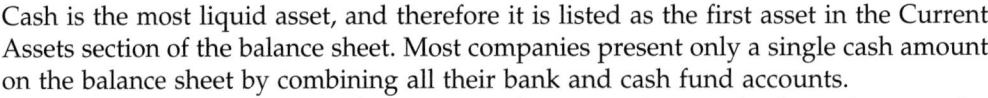

Financial Statement Reporting of Cash

objective 7

Describe and illustrate the reporting of cash and cash equivalents in the financial statements.

Cash is the most liquid asset, and therefore it is listed as the first asset in the Current Assets section of the balance sheet. Most companies present only a single cash amount on the balance sheet by combining all their bank and cash fund accounts.

A company may have cash in excess of its operating needs. In such cases, the company normally invests in highly liquid investments in order to earn interest. These investments are called **cash equivalents**.[8] Examples of cash equivalents include U.S. Treasury Bills, notes issued by major corporations (referred to as commercial paper), and money market funds. Companies that have invested excess cash in cash equivalents usually report *Cash and cash equivalents* as one amount on the balance sheet.

Banks may require depositors to maintain minimum cash balances in their bank accounts. Such a balance is called a **compensating balance**. This requirement is often imposed by the

In the United Kingdom, the statement of cash flows is prepared using a narrower definition of "cash" than in the United States. Specifically, the United Kingdom does not include cash equivalents, such as certificates of deposit, in its definition of cash as does the United States.

---

8 To be classified a cash equivalent, according to FASB Statement 95, the investment is expected to be converted to cash within 90 days.

bank as a part of a loan agreement or line of credit. A *line of credit* is a preapproved amount the bank is willing to lend to a customer upon request. Compensating balance requirements should be disclosed in notes to the financial statements.

Business Connections

REAL WORLD

MICROSOFT CORPORATION

Microsoft Corporation develops, manufactures, licenses, and supports software products for computing devices. Microsoft software products include computer operating systems, such as Windows, and application software, such as Microsoft Word™ and Excel.™ Microsoft is actively in-

volved in the video game market through its Xbox and is also involved in online products and services.

Microsoft is known for its strong cash position. Microsoft's June 30, 2005, balance sheet reported almost $38 billion of cash and short-term investments, as shown below.

Balance Sheet June 30, 2005 (In millions) Assets	
Current assets:	
Cash and equivalents	$ 4,851
Short-term investments	32,900
Total cash and short-term investments	$37,751

© RENE MACURO/ASSOCIATED PRESS

The cash and cash equivalents of $4,851 million are further described in the notes to the financial statements, as shown below.

Cash and equivalents:	
Cash	$1,911
Commercial paper	1,570
Certificates of deposit	453
Money market mutual funds	817
Corporate notes and bonds	80
Municipal securities	20
Total cash and equivalents	$4,851

Financial Analysis and Interpretation

For companies that are either starting up or in financial distress, cash is critical for their survival. In their first few years of operations, startup companies often report losses and negative net cash flows. In these cases, the ratio of cash to monthly cash expenses (negative cash flow for operating activities) is useful for assessing how long a company can continue to operate without additional financing or without generating positive cash flows from operations. Likewise, this ratio can be used to assess how long a business may continue to operate when experiencing financial distress. In computing cash to monthly cash expenses, the amount of cash on hand can be taken from the balance sheet, while the monthly cash expenses can be estimated from the operating activities section of the statement of cash flows.

The ratio of cash to monthly cash expenses is computed by first determining the monthly cash expenses. The monthly cash expenses are determined as follows:

$$\text{Monthly Cash Expenses} = \frac{\text{Negative Cash Flows from Operations}}{12}$$

The ratio of cash to monthly cash expenses can then be computed as follows:

$$\text{Ratio of Cash to Monthly Cash Expenses} = \frac{\text{Cash and Cash Equivalents as of Year-End}}{\text{Monthly Cash Expenses}}$$

To illustrate these ratios, we use Northwest Airlines Corporation, a major carrier of passengers and cargo with service to approximately 900 cities in 160 countries. For the year ending December 31, 2005, Northwest Airlines reported the following data (in millions):

Negative cash flows from operations	$ (436)
Cash and cash equivalents as of December 31, 2005	1,284

Based upon the preceding data, the monthly cash expenses, sometimes referred to as cash burn, were $36.3 million per month ($436/12). Thus, as of December 31, 2005, the cash to monthly cash expenses ratio was 35.4 ($1,284/$36.3). That is, as of December 31, 2005, Northwest would run out of cash in less than three years unless it changes its operations, sells investments, or raises additional financing. In September 2005, Northwest Airlines filed for voluntary reorganization under Chapter 11 of the U.S. Bankruptcy Code.

At a Glance

1. Describe the Sarbanes-Oxley Act of 2002 and its impact on internal controls and financial reporting.

Key Points	Key Learning Outcomes	Example Exercises	Practice Exercises
The purpose of the Sarbanes-Oxley Act of 2002 is to restore public confidence and trust in the financial statements of companies. Sarbanes-Oxley requires companies to maintain strong and effective internal controls and to report on the effectiveness of the internal controls.	• Describe why Congress passed Sarbanes-Oxley. • Describe the purpose of Sarbanes-Oxley. • Define *internal control*.		

2. Describe and illustrate the objectives and elements of internal control.

Key Points	Key Learning Outcomes	Example Exercises	Practice Exercises
The objectives of internal control are to provide reasonable assurance that (1) assets are safeguarded and used for business purposes, (2) business information is accurate, and (3) laws and regulations are complied with. The elements of internal control are the control environment, risk assessment, control procedures, monitoring, and information and communication.	• List the objectives of internal control. • List the elements of internal control. • Describe each element of internal control and factors influencing each element.	7-1	7-1A, 7-1B

3. Describe and illustrate the application of internal controls to cash.

Key Points	Key Learning Outcomes	Example Exercises	Practice Exercises
A cash register is one of the most important controls to protect cash received in over-the-counter sales. A remittance advice is a control for cash received through the mail. Separating the duties of handling cash and recording cash is also a control. A voucher system is a control system for cash payments that uses a set of procedures for authorizing and recording liabilities and cash payments. Many companies use electronic funds transfers to enhance their control over cash receipts and cash payments.	• Describe and give examples of controls for cash received from cash sales, cash received in the mail, and cash received by EFT. • Describe and give examples of controls for cash payments made using a voucher system and cash payments made by EFT.		

4. Describe the nature of a bank account and its use in controlling cash.

Key Points	Key Learning Outcomes	Example Exercises	Practice Exercises
Bank accounts help control cash by reducing the amount of cash on hand and facilitating the transfer of cash between businesses and locations. In addition, the bank statement allows a business to reconcile the cash transactions recorded in the accounting records to those recorded by the bank.	• Describe how the use of bank accounts helps control cash. • Describe a bank statement and provide examples of items that appear on a bank statement as debit and credit memoranda.	7-2	7-2A, 7-2B

(continued)

5. Describe and illustrate the use of a bank reconciliation in controlling cash.

Key Points	Key Learning Outcomes	Example Exercises	Practice Exercises
The bank reconciliation begins with the cash balance according to the bank statement. This balance is adjusted for the company's changes in cash that do not appear on the bank statement and for any bank errors. The second section begins with the cash balance according to the company's records. This balance is adjusted for the bank's changes in cash that do not appear on the company's records and for any company errors. The adjusted balances for the two sections must be equal. The items in the company section must be journalized on the company's records.	• Describe a bank reconciliation. • Prepare a bank reconciliation. • Journalize any necessary entries on the company's records based upon the bank reconciliation.	7-3 7-3 7-3	7-3A, 7-3B 7-3A, 7-3B 7-3A, 7-3B

6. Describe the accounting for special-purpose cash funds.

Key Points	Key Learning Outcomes	Example Exercises	Practice Exercises
Special-purpose cash funds, such as a petty cash fund or travel funds, are used by businesses to meet specific needs. Each fund is established by cashing a check for the amount of cash needed. At periodic intervals, the fund is replenished and the disbursements recorded.	• Describe the use of special-purpose cash funds. • Journalize the entry to establish a petty cash fund. • Journalize the entry to replenish a petty cash fund.	 7-4 7-4	 7-4A, 7-4B 7-4A, 7-4B

7. Describe and illustrate the reporting of cash and cash equivalents in the financial statements.

Key Points	Key Learning Outcomes	Example Exercises	Practice Exercises
Cash is listed as the first asset in the Current Assets section of the balance sheet. Companies that have invested excess cash in highly liquid investments usually report *Cash and cash equivalents* on the balance sheet.	• Describe the reporting of cash and cash equivalents in the financial statements. • Illustrate the reporting of cash and cash equivalents in the financial statements.		

Key Terms

bank reconciliation (324)
bank statement (320)
cash (317)
cash equivalents (328)
cash short and over account (317)
compensating balance (328)

electronic funds transfer (EFT) (318)
elements of internal control (311)
employee fraud (310)
internal control (308)
petty cash fund (327)

Sarbanes-Oxley Act of 2002 (308)
special-purpose fund (327)
voucher (319)
voucher system (319)

Illustrative Problem

The bank statement for Urethane Company for June 30, 2007, indicates a balance of $9,143.11. All cash receipts are deposited each evening in a night depository, after banking hours. The accounting records indicate the following summary data for cash receipts and payments for June:

Cash balance as of June 1	$ 3,943.50
Total cash receipts for June	28,971.60
Total amount of checks issued in June	28,388.85

Comparing the bank statement and the accompanying canceled checks and memoranda with the records reveals the following reconciling items:

a. The bank had collected for Urethane Company $1,030 on a note left for collection. The face amount of the note was $1,000.
b. A deposit of $1,852.21, representing receipts of June 30, had been made too late to appear on the bank statement.
c. Checks outstanding totaled $5,265.27.
d. A check drawn for $139 had been incorrectly charged by the bank as $157.
e. A check for $30 returned with the statement had been recorded in the company's records as $240. The check was for the payment of an obligation to Avery Equipment Company for the purchase of office supplies on account.
f. Bank service charges for June amounted to $18.20.

Instructions
1. Prepare a bank reconciliation for June.
2. Journalize the entries that should be made by Urethane Company.

Solution
1.

Urethane Company
Bank Reconciliation
June 30, 2007

Cash balance according to bank statement			$ 9,143.11
Add: Deposit of June 30 not recorded by bank	$1,852.21		
Bank error in charging check as $157			
instead of $139		18.00	1,870.21
			$11,013.32
Deduct: Outstanding checks			5,265.27
Adjusted balance			$ 5,748.05
Cash balance according to company's records			$ 4,526.25 *
Add: Proceeds of note collected by bank,			
including $30 interest	$1,030.00		
Error in recording check	210.00		1,240.00
			$ 5,766.25
Deduct: Bank service charges			18.20
Adjusted balance			$ 5,748.05
*$3,943.50 + $28,971.60 − $28,388.85			

(continued)

2.

June	30	Cash		1 2 4 0 00	
		Notes Receivable			1 0 0 0 00
		Interest Revenue			3 0 00
		Accounts Payable—Avery Equipment Company			2 1 0 00
	30	Miscellaneous Administrative Expense		1 8 20	
		Cash			1 8 20

Self-Examination Questions
(Answers at End of Chapter)

1. Which of the following is *not* an element of internal control?
   A. Control environment
   B. Monitoring
   C. Compliance with laws and regulations
   D. Control procedures

2. The bank erroneously charged Tropical Services' account for $450.50 for a check that was correctly written and recorded by Tropical Services as $540.50. To reconcile the bank account of Tropical Services at the end of the month, you would:
   A. add $90 to the cash balance according to the bank statement.
   B. add $90 to the cash balance according to Tropical Services' records.
   C. deduct $90 from the cash balance according to the bank statement.
   D. deduct $90 from the cash balance according to Tropical Services' records.

3. In preparing a bank reconciliation, the amount of checks outstanding would be:
   A. added to the cash balance according to the bank statement.
   B. deducted from the cash balance according to the bank statement.
   C. added to the cash balance according to the company's records.
   D. deducted from the cash balance according to the company's records.

4. Journal entries based on the bank reconciliation are required for:
   A. additions to the cash balance according to the company's records.
   B. deductions from the cash balance according to the company's records.
   C. both A and B.
   D. neither A nor B.

5. A petty cash fund is:
   A. used to pay relatively small amounts.
   B. established by estimating the amount of cash needed for disbursements of relatively small amounts during a specified period.
   C. reimbursed when the amount of money in the fund is reduced to a predetermined minimum amount.
   D. all of the above.

Eye Openers

1. (a) Why did Congress pass the Sarbanes-Oxley Act of 2002? (b) What was the purpose of the Sarbanes-Oxley Act of 2002?
2. Define *internal control*.
3. (a) Name and describe the five elements of internal control. (b) Is any one element of internal control more important than another?
4. How does a policy of rotating clerical employees from job to job aid in strengthening the control procedures within the control environment? Explain.
5. Why should the responsibility for a sequence of related operations be divided among different persons? Explain.
6. Why should the employee who handles cash receipts not have the responsibility for maintaining the accounts receivable records? Explain.
7. In an attempt to improve operating efficiency, one employee was made responsible for all purchasing, receiving, and storing of supplies. Is this organizational change wise from an internal control standpoint? Explain.
8. The ticket seller at a movie theater doubles as a ticket taker for a few minutes each day while the ticket taker is on a break. Which control procedure of a business's system of internal control is violated in this situation?

9. Why should the responsibility for maintaining the accounting records be separated from the responsibility for operations? Explain.
10. Assume that Julee Shiver, accounts payable clerk for Galaxy Inc., stole $110,000 by paying fictitious invoices for goods that were never received. The clerk set up accounts in the names of the fictitious companies and cashed the checks at a local bank. Describe a control procedure that would have prevented or detected the fraud.
11. Before a voucher for the purchase of merchandise is approved for payment, supporting documents should be compared to verify the accuracy of the liability. Give an example of supporting documents for the purchase of merchandise.
12. The accounting clerk pays all obligations by prenumbered checks. What are the strengths and weaknesses in the internal control over cash payments in this situation?
13. The balance of Cash is likely to differ from the bank statement balance. What two factors are likely to be responsible for the difference?
14. What is the purpose of preparing a bank reconciliation?
15. Do items reported as credits on the bank statement represent (a) additions made by the bank to the company's balance or (b) deductions made by the bank from the company's balance? Explain.
16. Spectacle Inc. has a petty cash fund of $2,000. (a) Since the petty cash fund is only $2,000, should Spectacle Inc. implement controls over petty cash? (b) What controls, if any, could be used for the petty cash fund?
17. (a) How are cash equivalents reported in the financial statements? (b) What are some examples of cash equivalents?

Practice Exercises

PE 7-1A
Internal control elements
obj. 2

Identify each of the following as relating to (a) the control environment, (b) control procedures, or (c) information and communication.

1. Separating related operations
2. Report of internal auditors
3. Management's philosophy and operating style

PE 7-1B
Internal control elements
obj. 2

Identify each of the following as relating to (a) the control environment, (b) control procedures, or (c) monitoring.

1. Personnel policies
2. Safeguarding inventory in a locked warehouse
3. Hiring of external auditors to review the adequacy of controls

PE 7-2A
Effect of items on depositor's bank account
obj. 4

The following items may appear on a bank statement:

1. Service charge
2. Note collected for depositor
3. Bank correction of an error from recording a $2,100 deposit as $1,200
4. EFT payment

Using the format shown below, indicate whether each item would appear as a debit or credit memorandum on the bank statement and whether the item would increase or decrease the balance of your account.

Item No.	Appears on the Bank Statement as a Debit or Credit Memorandum	Increases or Decreases the Balance of the Depositor's Bank Account

PE 7-2B
Effect of items on depositor's bank account
obj. 4

The following items may appear on a bank statement:

1. Bank correction of an error from posting another customer's check to your account
2. Loan proceeds
3. NSF check
4. EFT deposit

Using the format shown below, indicate whether each item would appear as a debit or credit memorandum on the bank statement and whether the item would increase or decrease the balance of your account.

Item No.	Appears on the Bank Statement as a Debit or Credit Memorandum	Increases or Decreases the Balance of the Depositor's Bank Account

PE 7-3A
Adjusted balance and entries from bank account reconciliation

obj. 5

The following data were gathered to use in reconciling the bank account of Cards Company:

Balance per bank	$9,200
Balance per company records	9,335
Bank service charges	40
Deposit in transit	2,800
NSF check	475
Outstanding checks	3,180

a. What is the adjusted balance on the bank reconciliation?
b. Journalize any necessary entries for Cards Company based upon the bank reconciliation.

PE 7-3B
Adjusted balance and entries from bank account reconciliation

obj. 5

The following data were gathered to use in reconciling the bank account of DRW Company:

Balance per bank	$28,100
Balance per company records	9,155
Bank service charges	80
Deposit in transit	3,100
Note collected by bank with $225 interest	15,225
Outstanding checks	6,900

a. What is the adjusted balance on the bank reconciliation?
b. Journalize any necessary entries for DRW Company based upon the bank reconciliation.

PE 7-4A
Entries for petty cash fund

obj. 6

Prepare journal entries for each of the following:

a. Issued a check to establish a petty cash fund of $600.
b. The amount of cash in the petty cash fund is $175. Issued a check to replenish the fund, based on the following summary of petty cash receipts: repair expense, $350 and miscellaneous selling expense, $55. Record any missing funds in the cash short and over account.

PE 7-4B
Entries for petty cash fund

obj. 6

Prepare journal entries for each of the following:

a. Issued a check to establish a petty cash fund of $400.
b. The amount of cash in the petty cash fund is $85. Issued a check to replenish the fund, based on the following summary of petty cash receipts: store supplies, $180 and miscellaneous selling expense, $110. Record any missing funds in the cash short and over account.

Exercises

EX 7-1
Sarbanes-Oxley internal control report

obj. 1

Locate a copy of the Sarbanes-Oxley Act of 2002 on the Web. Scan the Act and read Section 404.

➤ What does Section 404 require of management's internal control report?

EX 7-2
Internal controls
objs. 2, 3

Tyler Kirsch has recently been hired as the manager of Dark Canyon Coffee. Dark Canyon Coffee is a national chain of franchised coffee shops. During his first month as store manager, Tyler encountered the following internal control situations:

a. Dark Canyon Coffee has one cash register. Prior to Tyler's joining the coffee shop, each employee working on a shift would take a customer order, accept payment, and then prepare the order. Tyler made one employee on each shift responsible for taking orders and accepting the customer's payment. Other employees prepare the orders.

b. Since only one employee uses the cash register, that employee is responsible for counting the cash at the end of the shift and verifying that the cash in the drawer matches the amount of cash sales recorded by the cash register. Tyler expects each cashier to balance the drawer to the penny *every* time—no exceptions.

c. Tyler caught an employee putting a box of 100 single-serving tea bags in his car. Not wanting to create a scene, Tyler smiled and said, "I don't think you're putting those tea bags on the right shelf. Don't they belong inside the coffee shop?" The employee returned the tea bags to the stockroom.

State whether you agree or disagree with Tyler's method of handling each situation and explain your answer.

EX 7-3
Internal controls
objs. 2, 3

Rare Earth Clothing is a retail store specializing in women's clothing. The store has established a liberal return policy for the holiday season in order to encourage gift purchases. Any item purchased during November and December may be returned through January 31, with a receipt, for cash or exchange. If the customer does not have a receipt, cash will still be refunded for any item under $100. If the item is more than $100, a check is mailed to the customer.

Whenever an item is returned, a store clerk completes a return slip, which the customer signs. The return slip is placed in a special box. The store manager visits the return counter approximately once every two hours to authorize the return slips. Clerks are instructed to place the returned merchandise on the proper rack on the selling floor as soon as possible.

This year, returns at Rare Earth Clothing have reached an all-time high. There are a large number of returns under $100 without receipts.

a. How can sales clerks employed at Rare Earth Clothing use the store's return policy to steal money from the cash register?

b. What internal control weaknesses do you see in the return policy that make cash thefts easier?

c. Would issuing a store credit in place of a cash refund for all merchandise returned without a receipt reduce the possibility of theft? List some advantages and disadvantages of issuing a store credit in place of a cash refund.

d. Assume that Rare Earth Clothing is committed to the current policy of issuing cash refunds without a receipt. What changes could be made in the store's procedures regarding customer refunds in order to improve internal control?

EX 7-4
Internal controls for bank lending
objs. 2, 3

First Capone Bank provides loans to businesses in the community through its Commercial Lending Department. Small loans (less than $125,000) may be approved by an individual loan officer, while larger loans (greater than $125,000) must be approved by a board of loan officers. Once a loan is approved, the funds are made available to the loan applicant under agreed-upon terms. The president of First Capone Bank has instituted a policy whereby she has the individual authority to approve loans up to $4,000,000. The president believes that this policy will allow flexibility to approve loans to valued clients much quicker than under the previous policy.

As an internal auditor of First Capone Bank, how would you respond to this change in policy?

EX 7-5
Internal controls
objs. 2, 3

One of the largest fraud losses in history involved a securities trader for the Singapore office of Barings Bank, a British merchant bank. The trader established an unauthorized account number that was used to hide $1.4 billion in losses. Even after Barings' internal auditors noted that the trader both executed trades and recorded them, management did not take action. As a result, a lone individual in a remote office bankrupted an internationally recognized firm overnight.

What general weaknesses in Barings' internal controls contributed to the occurrence and size of the fraud?

EX 7-6
Internal controls
objs. 2, 3

An employee of JHT Holdings, Inc., a trucking company, was responsible for resolving roadway accident claims under $25,000. The employee created fake accident claims and wrote settlement checks of between $5,000 and $25,000 to friends or acquaintances acting as phony "victims." One friend recruited subordinates at his place of work to cash some of the checks. Beyond this, the JHT employee also recruited lawyers, who he paid to represent both the trucking company and the fake victims in the bogus accident settlements. When the lawyers cashed the checks, they allegedly split the money with the corrupt JHT employee. This fraud went undetected for two years.

Why would it take so long to discover such a fraud?

EX 7-7
Internal controls
objs. 2, 3

Quality Sound Co. discovered a fraud whereby one of its front office administrative employees used company funds to purchase goods, such as computers, digital cameras, compact disk players, and other electronic items for her own use. The fraud was discovered when employees noticed an increase in delivery frequency from vendors and the use of unusual vendors. After some investigation, it was discovered that the employee would alter the description or change the quantity on an invoice in order to explain the cost on the bill.

What general internal control weaknesses contributed to this fraud?

EX 7-8
Financial statement fraud
objs. 2, 3

A former chairman, CFO, and controller of Donnkenny, Inc., an apparel company that makes sportswear for Pierre Cardin and Victoria Jones, pleaded guilty to financial statement fraud. These managers used false journal entries to record fictitious sales, hid inventory in public warehouses so that it could be recorded as "sold," and required sales orders to be backdated so that the sale could be moved back to an earlier period. The combined effect of these actions caused $25 million out of $40 million in quarterly sales to be phony.

a. Why might control procedures listed in this chapter be insufficient in stopping this type of fraud?
b. How could this type of fraud be stopped?

EX 7-9
Internal control of cash receipts
objs. 2, 3

The procedures used for over-the-counter receipts are as follows. At the close of each day's business, the sales clerks count the cash in their respective cash drawers, after which they determine the amount recorded by the cash register and prepare the memorandum cash form, noting any discrepancies. An employee from the cashier's office counts the cash, compares the total with the memorandum, and takes the cash to the cashier's office.

a. Indicate the weak link in internal control.
b. How can the weakness be corrected?

EX 7-10
Internal control of cash receipts
objs. 2, 3

Amber Meehan works at the drive-through window of Jackpot Burgers. Occasionally, when a drive-through customer orders, Amber fills the order and pockets the customer's money. She does not ring up the order on the cash register.

Identify the internal control weaknesses that exist at Jackpot Burgers, and discuss what can be done to prevent this theft.

EX 7-11
Internal control of cash receipts
objs. 2, 3

The mailroom employees send all remittances and remittance advices to the cashier. The cashier deposits the cash in the bank and forwards the remittance advices and duplicate deposit slips to the Accounting Department.

a. Indicate the weak link in internal control in the handling of cash receipts.
b. How can the weakness be corrected?

EX 7-12
Entry for cash sales; cash short
objs. 2, 3

The actual cash received from cash sales was $21,099.75, and the amount indicated by the cash register total was $21,114.26. Journalize the entry to record the cash receipts and cash sales.

EX 7-13
Entry for cash sales; cash over
objs. 2, 3

The actual cash received from cash sales was $8,374.58, and the amount indicated by the cash register total was $8,351.14. Journalize the entry to record the cash receipts and cash sales.

EX 7-14
Internal control of cash payments
objs. 2, 3

Paul's Rama Co. is a medium-size merchandising company. An investigation revealed that in spite of a sufficient bank balance, a significant amount of available cash discounts had been lost because of failure to make timely payments. In addition, it was discovered that the invoices for several purchases had been paid twice.

Outline procedures for the payment of vendors' invoices, so that the possibilities of losing available cash discounts and of paying an invoice a second time will be minimized.

EX 7-15
Internal control of cash payments
objs. 2, 3

Clear Voice Company, a communications equipment manufacturer, recently fell victim to a fraud scheme developed by one of its employees. To understand the scheme, it is necessary to review Clear Voice's procedures for the purchase of services.

The purchasing agent is responsible for ordering services (such as repairs to a photocopy machine or office cleaning) after receiving a service requisition from an authorized manager. However, since no tangible goods are delivered, a receiving report is not prepared. When the Accounting Department receives an invoice billing Clear Voice for a service call, the accounts payable clerk calls the manager who requested the service in order to verify that it was performed.

The fraud scheme involves Dana Foley, the manager of plant and facilities. Dana arranged for her uncle's company, Foley Industrial Supply and Service, to be placed on Clear Voice's approved vendor list. Dana did not disclose the family relationship.

On several occasions, Dana would submit a requisition for services to be provided by Foley Industrial Supply and Service. However, the service requested was really not needed, and it was never performed. Foley would bill Clear Voice for the service and then split the cash payment with Dana.

Explain what changes should be made to Clear Voice's procedures for ordering and paying for services in order to prevent such occurrences in the future.

EX 7-16
Bank reconciliation
obj. 5

Identify each of the following reconciling items as: (a) an addition to the cash balance according to the bank statement, (b) a deduction from the cash balance according to the bank statement, (c) an addition to the cash balance according to the company's records, or (d) a deduction from the cash balance according to the company's records. (None of the transactions reported by bank debit and credit memoranda have been recorded by the company.)

1. Bank service charges, $48.
2. Outstanding checks, $8,125.50.
3. Deposit in transit, $12,200.
4. Note collected by bank, $8,750.
5. Check drawn by company for $150 but incorrectly recorded as $510.
6. Check for $200 incorrectly charged by bank as $2,000.
7. Check of a customer returned by bank to company because of insufficient funds, $1,200.

EX 7-17
Entries based on bank reconciliation
obj. 5

Which of the reconciling items listed in Exercise 7-16 require an entry in the company's accounts?

EX 7-18
Bank reconciliation

obj. 5

✓ *Adjusted balance:*
$8,506.50

The following data were accumulated for use in reconciling the bank account of Spectrum Co. for July:

a. Cash balance according to the company's records at July 31, $8,346.50.
b. Cash balance according to the bank statement at July 31, $9,066.35.
c. Checks outstanding, $3,175.25.
d. Deposit in transit, not recorded by bank, $2,615.40.
e. A check for $240 in payment of an account was erroneously recorded in the check register as $420.
f. Bank debit memorandum for service charges, $20.00.

Prepare a bank reconciliation, using the format shown in Exhibit 7.

EX 7-19
Entries for bank reconciliation

obj. 5

Using the data presented in Exercise 7-18, journalize the entry or entries that should be made by the company.

EX 7-20
Entries for note collected by bank

obj. 5

Accompanying a bank statement for Bionics Company is a credit memorandum for $17,750, representing the principal ($15,000) and interest ($2,750) on a note that had been collected by the bank. The depositor had been notified by the bank at the time of the collection, but had made no entries. Journalize the entry that should be made by the depositor to bring the accounting records up to date.

EX 7-21
Bank reconciliation

obj. 5

✓ *Adjusted balance:*
$15,175.60

An accounting clerk for Lock-It Co. prepared the following bank reconciliation:

Lock-It Co.
Bank Reconciliation
October 31, 2008

Cash balance according to company's records		$ 9,305.60
Add: Outstanding checks	$ 7,115.35	
Error by Lock-It Co. in recording Check		
No. 1007 as $4,715 instead of $4,175	540.00	
Note for $5,000 collected by bank, including interest	5,375.00	13,030.35
		$22,335.95
Deduct: Deposit in transit on October 31	$13,690.45	
Bank service charges	45.00	13,735.45
Cash balance according to bank statement		$ 8,600.50

a. From the data in the above bank reconciliation, prepare a new bank reconciliation for Lock-It Co., using the format shown in the illustrative problem.
b. If a balance sheet were prepared for Lock-It Co. on October 31, 2008, what amount should be reported for cash?

EX 7-22
Bank reconciliation

obj. 5

✓ *Corrected adjusted balance: $9,000.00*

Identify the errors in the following bank reconciliation:

Mkabe Co.
Bank Reconciliation
For the Month Ended June 30, 2008

Cash balance according to bank statement		$ 7,560.14
Add outstanding checks:		
No. 315	$ 717.42	
360	617.11	
364	906.15	
365	1,501.50	3,742.18
		$11,302.32
Deduct deposit of June 30, not recorded by bank		5,182.04
Adjusted balance		$ 7,120.28

(continued)

Cash balance according to company's records			$ 3,735.70
Add: Proceeds of note collected by bank:			
Principal	$6,000.00		
Interest	180.00	$6,180.00	
Service charges		27.00	6,207.00
			$ 9,942.70
Deduct: Check returned because of			
insufficient funds		$1,158.70	
Error in recording June 15			
deposit of $3,960 as $3,690		270.00	1,428.70
Adjusted balance			$ 8,514.00

EX 7-23
Using bank reconciliation to determine cash receipts stolen

obj. 5

Argonaut Co. records all cash receipts on the basis of its cash register tapes. Argonaut Co. discovered during November 2008 that one of its sales clerks had stolen an undetermined amount of cash receipts when she took the daily deposits to the bank. The following data have been gathered for November:

Cash in bank according to the general ledger	$12,510.45
Cash according to the November 30, 2008, bank statement	22,060.65
Outstanding checks as of November 30, 2008	6,381.42
Bank service charge for November	35.00
Note receivable, including interest collected by bank in November	7,140.00

No deposits were in transit on November 30, which fell on a Sunday.

a. Using bank reconciliation, determine the amount of cash receipts stolen by the sales clerk.
b. What accounting controls would have prevented or detected this theft?

EX 7-24
Petty cash fund entries

obj. 6

Journalize the entries to record the following:

a. Check No. 6172 is issued to establish a petty cash fund of $1,000.
b. The amount of cash in the petty cash fund is now $239.16. Check No. 6319 is issued to replenish the fund, based on the following summary of petty cash receipts: office supplies, $379.10; miscellaneous selling expense, $216.25; miscellaneous administrative expense, $143.06. (Since the amount of the check to replenish the fund plus the balance in the fund do not equal $1,000, record the discrepancy in the cash short and over account.)

EX 7-25
Variation in cash flows

obj. 7

Mattel, Inc., designs, manufactures, and markets toy products worldwide. Mattel's toys include Barbie™ fashion dolls and accessories, Hot Wheels™, and Fisher-Price brands. For a recent year, Mattel reported the following net cash flows from operating activities (in thousands):

First quarter ending March 31, 2005	$(374,933)
Second quarter ending June 30, 2005	(551,080)
Third quarter ending September 30, 2005	(629,006)
Year ending December 31, 2005	466,677

Explain how Mattel can report negative net cash flows from operating activities during the first three quarters yet report net positive cash flows on December 31.

EX 7-26
Cash to monthly cash expenses ratio

FAI

During 2007, Kinetic Inc. has monthly cash expenses of $175,000. On December 31, 2007, the cash balance is $1,575,000.

a. Compute the ratio of cash to monthly cash expenses.
b. Based upon (a), what are the implications for Kinetic Inc.?

EX 7-27
Cash to monthly cash expenses ratio

Delta Air Lines is one of the major airlines in the United States and the world. It provides passengers and cargo services for over 200 domestic U.S. cities as well as 70 international cities. It operates a fleet of over 800 aircraft and is headquartered in Atlanta, Georgia.

Delta reported the following financial data (in millions) for the year ended December 31, 2004:

Net cash flows from operating activities	$(1,123)
Cash, December 31, 2004	1,811

a. Determine the monthly cash expenses. Round to one decimal place.
b. Determine the ratio of cash to monthly expenses. Round to one decimal place.
c. Based upon your analysis, do you believe that Delta will remain in business?

EX 7-28
Cash to monthly cash expenses ratio

Hyperspace Communications, Inc., engages in the development, manufacture, and marketing of network acceleration and data compression software worldwide. Its software products speed up the delivery of information over computer networks, including the Internet, wireless, broadband, private, and dial-up networks. Hyperspace reported the following data (in thousands) for the years ending December 31:

	2005	2004
Net cash flows from operating activities	$(7,827)	$(2,558)
Cash, December 31	3,897	5,875

a. Determine the monthly cash expenses for 2005 and 2004. Round to one decimal place.
b. Determine the ratio of cash to monthly expenses for December 31, 2005 and 2004. Round to one decimal place.
c. Based upon (a) and (b), what are the implications for Hyperspace?

Problems Series A

PR 7-1A
Evaluating internal control of cash

objs. 2, 3

The following procedures were recently installed by Sacha's Company:

a. The accounts payable clerk prepares a voucher for each disbursement. The voucher along with the supporting documentation is forwarded to the treasurer's office for approval.
b. After necessary approvals have been obtained for the payment of a voucher, the treasurer signs and mails the check. The treasurer then stamps the voucher and supporting documentation as paid and returns the voucher and supporting documentation to the accounts payable clerk for filing.
c. Along with petty cash expense receipts for postage, office supplies, etc., several post-dated employee checks are in the petty cash fund.
d. At the end of the day, cash register clerks are required to use their own funds to make up any cash shortages in their registers.
e. All mail is opened by the mail clerk, who forwards all cash remittances to the cashier. The cashier prepares a listing of the cash receipts and forwards a copy of the list to the accounts receivable clerk for recording in the accounts.
f. At the end of each day, any deposited cash receipts are placed in the bank's night depository.
g. At the end of each day, an accounting clerk compares the duplicate copy of the daily cash deposit slip with the deposit receipt obtained from the bank.
h. The bank reconciliation is prepared by the cashier, who works under the supervision of the treasurer.

Instructions
Indicate whether each of the procedures of internal control over cash represents (1) a strength or (2) a weakness. For each weakness, indicate why it exists.

PR 7-2A
*Transactions for petty
cash, cash short and over*

objs. 3, 6

Ivan's Restoration Company completed the following selected transactions during October 2008:

Oct. 1. Established a petty cash fund of $750.
15. The cash sales for the day, according to the cash register records, totaled $9,702.38. The actual cash received from cash sales was $9,752.38.
31. Petty cash on hand was $40.75. Replenished the petty cash fund for the following disbursements, each evidenced by a petty cash receipt:

    Oct. 4. Store supplies, $217.30.
        8. Express charges on merchandise sold, $150 (Delivery Expense).
        9. Office supplies, $13.75.
      18. Office supplies, $27.80.
      19. Postage stamps, $11.70 (Office Supplies).
      21. Repair to office file cabinet lock, $50.00 (Miscellaneous Administrative Expense).
      23. Postage due on special delivery letter, $21.95 (Miscellaneous Administrative Expense).
      24. Express charges on merchandise sold, $165 (Delivery Expense).
      29. Office supplies, $26.85.
31. The cash sales for the day, according to the cash register records, totaled $10,125.95. The actual cash received from cash sales was $10,123.05.
31. Increased the petty cash fund by $150.

Instructions
Journalize the transactions.

PR 7-3A
*Bank reconciliation and
entries*

obj. 5

✓ *1. Adjusted balance:
$12,110.30*

The cash account for Bonita Medical Co. at September 30, 2008, indicated a balance of $5,335.30. The bank statement indicated a balance of $5,604.60 on September 30, 2008. Comparing the bank statement and the accompanying canceled checks and memoranda with the records revealed the following reconciling items:

a. Checks outstanding totaled $4,790.45.
b. A deposit of $9,226.15, representing receipts of September 30, had been made too late to appear on the bank statement.
c. The bank had collected $7,725 on a note left for collection. The face of the note was $7,500.
d. A check for $4,315 returned with the statement had been incorrectly recorded by Bonita Medical Co. as $3,415. The check was for the payment of an obligation to Rowe Co. for the purchase of office equipment on account.
e. A check drawn for $230 had been erroneously charged by the bank as $2,300.
f. Bank service charges for September amounted to $50.

Instructions
1. Prepare a bank reconciliation.
2. Journalize the necessary entries. The accounts have not been closed.

PR 7-4A
*Bank reconciliation and
entries*

obj. 5

✓ *1. Adjusted balance:
$9,175.15*

The cash account for Cabrillo Co. at March 1, 2008, indicated a balance of $10,676.67. During March, the total cash deposited was $39,146.38, and checks written totaled $42,918.40. The bank statement indicated a balance of $10,960.06 on March 31. Comparing the bank statement, the canceled checks, and the accompanying memoranda with the records revealed the following reconciling items:

a. Checks outstanding totaled $11,008.25.
b. A deposit of $8,773.34, representing receipts of March 31, had been made too late to appear on the bank statement.
c. The bank had collected for Cabrillo Co. $3,710 on a note left for collection. The face of the note was $3,500.
d. A check for $380 returned with the statement had been incorrectly charged by the bank as $830.

e. A check for $419 returned with the statement had been recorded by Cabrillo Co. as $149. The check was for the payment of an obligation to Graven Co. on account.

f. Bank service charges for March amounted to $40.

g. A check for $1,129.50 from Kane-Miller Co. was returned by the bank because of insufficient funds.

Instructions

1. Prepare a bank reconciliation as of March 31.
2. Journalize the necessary entries. The accounts have not been closed.

PR 7-5A

Bank reconciliation and entries

obj. 5

✓ *1. Adjusted balance: $12,822.02*

Pacific Furniture Company deposits all cash receipts each Wednesday and Friday in a night depository after banking hours. The data required to reconcile the bank statement as of June 30 have been taken from various documents and records and are reproduced as follows. The sources of the data are printed in capital letters. All checks were written for payments on account.

JUNE BANK STATEMENT:

		MEMBER FDIC		PAGE 1
A N B **AMERICAN NATIONAL BANK OF DETROIT**			ACCOUNT NUMBER	
DETROIT, MI 48201-2500 (313)933-8547			FROM 6/01/20– TO 6/30/20–	
			BALANCE	9,447.20
			9 DEPOSITS	8,691.77
			20 WITHDRAWALS	7,345.91
PACIFIC FURNITURE COMPANY			4 OTHER DEBITS AND CREDITS	2,298.70CR
			NEW BALANCE	13,091.76

–––CHECKS AND OTHER DEBITS–––				*––DEPOSITS––*	*–DATE–*	*––BALANCE––*
No.731	162.15	No.738	251.40	690.25	6/01	9,723.90
No.739	60.55	No.740	237.50	1,080.50	6/02	10,506.35
No.741	495.15	No.742	501.90	854.17	6/04	10,363.47
No.743	671.30	No.744	506.88	840.50	6/09	10,025.79
No.745	117.25	No.746	298.66	MS 2,500.00	6/09	12,109.88
No.748	450.90	No.749	640.13	MS 125.00	6/09	11,143.85
No.750	276.77	No.751	299.37	896.61	6/11	11,464.32
No.752	537.01	No.753	380.95	882.95	6/16	11,429.31
No.754	449.75	No.756	113.95	1,606.74	6/18	12,472.35
No.757	407.95	No.760	486.39	897.34	6/23	12,475.35
				942.71	6/25	13,418.06
			NSF 291.90		6/28	13,126.16
			SC 34.40		6/30	13,091.76

EC — ERROR CORRECTION	OD — OVERDRAFT
MS — MISCELLANEOUS	PS — PAYMENT STOPPED
NSF — NOT SUFFICIENT FUNDS	SC — SERVICE CHARGE

* * *   * * *   * * *

THE RECONCILEMENT OF THIS STATEMENT WITH YOUR RECORDS IS ESSENTIAL. ANY ERROR OR EXCEPTION SHOULD BE REPORTED IMMEDIATELY.

CASH ACCOUNT:
Balance as of June 1 $9,317.40

CASH RECEIPTS FOR MONTH OF JUNE $9,565.31

DUPLICATE DEPOSIT TICKETS:
Date and amount of each deposit in June:

Date	Amount	Date	Amount	Date	Amount
June 1	$1,080.50	June 10	$ 896.61	June 22	$ 897.34
3	854.17	15	882.95	24	942.71
8	840.50	17	1,660.47	30	1,510.06

CHECKS WRITTEN:
Number and amount of each check issued in June:

Check No.	Amount	Check No.	Amount	Check No.	Amount
740	$237.50	747	Void	754	$ 449.75
741	495.15	748	$450.90	755	272.75
742	501.90	749	640.31	756	113.95
743	671.30	750	276.77	757	407.95
744	506.88	751	299.37	758	259.60
745	117.25	752	537.01	759	901.50
746	298.66	753	380.95	760	486.39

Total amount of checks issued in June	$8,305.84

BANK RECONCILIATION FOR PRECEDING MONTH:

Pacific Furniture Company
Bank Reconciliation
May 31, 20—

Cash balance according to bank statement		$ 9,447.20
Add deposit for May 31, not recorded by bank		690.25
		$10,137.45
Deduct outstanding checks:		
No. 731	$162.15	
736	345.95	
738	251.40	
739	60.55	820.05
Adjusted balance		$ 9,317.40
Cash balance according to depositor's records		$ 9,352.50
Deduct service charges		35.10
Adjusted balance		$ 9,317.40

Instructions
1. Prepare a bank reconciliation as of June 30. If errors in recording deposits or checks are discovered, assume that the errors were made by the company. Assume that all deposits are from cash sales. All checks are written to satisfy accounts payable.
2. Journalize the necessary entries. The accounts have not been closed.
3. What is the amount of Cash that should appear on the balance sheet as of June 30?
4. ▭▬▶ Assume that a canceled check for $390 has been incorrectly recorded by the bank as $930. Briefly explain how the error would be included in a bank reconciliation and how it should be corrected.

Problems Series B

PR 7-1B
Evaluate internal control of cash

objs. 2, 3

The following procedures were recently installed by The Insideout Company:

a. All sales are rung up on the cash register, and a receipt is given to the customer. All sales are recorded on a record locked inside the cash register.
b. Vouchers and all supporting documents are perforated with a PAID designation after being paid by the treasurer.

c. Checks received through the mail are given daily to the accounts receivable clerk for recording collections on account and for depositing in the bank.

d. At the end of a shift, each cashier counts the cash in his or her cash register, unlocks the cash register record, and compares the amount of cash with the amount on the record to determine cash shortages and overages.

e. Each cashier is assigned a separate cash register drawer to which no other cashier has access.

f. Disbursements are made from the petty cash fund only after a petty cash receipt has been completed and signed by the payee.

g. The bank reconciliation is prepared by the accountant.

Instructions

Indicate whether each of the procedures of internal control over cash represents (1) a strength or (2) a weakness. For each weakness, indicate why it exists.

PR 7-2B
Transactions for petty cash, cash short and over

objs. 3, 6

Avalanche Company completed the following selected transactions during April 2008:

Apr. 1. Established a petty cash fund of $900.
4. The cash sales for the day, according to the cash register records, totaled $12,099.69. The actual cash received from cash sales was $12,115.42.
30. Petty cash on hand was $118.40. Replenished the petty cash fund for the following disbursements, each evidenced by a petty cash receipt:

Apr. 4. Store supplies, $62.18.
9. Express charges on merchandise purchased, $116.30 (Merchandise Inventory).
12. Office supplies, $42.80.
15. Office supplies, $119.82.
19. Postage stamps, $78.00 (Office Supplies).
20. Repair to fax, $205.00 (Miscellaneous Administrative Expense).
21. Repair to office door lock, $51.50 (Miscellaneous Administrative Expense).
22. Postage due on special delivery letter, $24.10 (Miscellaneous Administrative Expense).
27. Express charges on merchandise purchased, $75.40 (Merchandise Inventory).

30. The cash sales for the day, according to the cash register records, totaled $13,800.60. The actual cash received from cash sales was $13,774.90.
30. Decreased the petty cash fund by $100.

Instructions
Journalize the transactions.

PR 7-3B
Bank reconciliation and entries

obj. 5

✓1. Adjusted balance: $19,278.13

The cash account for Turbocharged Systems at February 29, 2008, indicated a balance of $8,608.13. The bank statement indicated a balance of $17,877.63 on February 29, 2008. Comparing the bank statement and the accompanying canceled checks and memoranda with the records reveals the following reconciling items:

a. Checks outstanding totaled $9,652.40.

b. A deposit of $11,322.90, representing receipts of February 29, had been made too late to appear on the bank statement.

c. The bank had collected $10,250 on a note left for collection. The face of the note was $10,000.

d. A check for $2,380 returned with the statement had been incorrectly recorded by Turbocharged Systems as $2,830. The check was for the payment of an obligation to Yanni Co. for the purchase of office supplies on account.

e. A check drawn for $960 had been incorrectly charged by the bank as $690.

f. Bank service charges for February amounted to $30.

Instructions
1. Prepare a bank reconciliation.
2. Journalize the necessary entries. The accounts have not been closed.

PR 7-4B
Bank reconciliation and entries

obj. 5

✓*1. Adjusted balance: $29,615.50*

The cash account for Black Diamond Sports Co. on November 1, 2008, indicated a balance of $23,326.69. During November, the total cash deposited was $118,125.41, and checks written totaled $115,650.10. The bank statement indicated a balance of $24,226.75 on November 30, 2008. Comparing the bank statement, the canceled checks, and the accompanying memoranda with the records revealed the following reconciling items:

a. Checks outstanding totaled $12,673.40.
b. A deposit of $18,332.15, representing receipts of November 30, had been made too late to appear on the bank statement.
c. A check for $850 had been incorrectly charged by the bank as $580.
d. A check for $39.30 returned with the statement had been recorded by Black Diamond Sports Co. as $393.00. The check was for the payment of an obligation to Locke & Son on account.
e. The bank had collected for Black Diamond Sports Co. $4,590 on a note left for collection. The face of the note was $4,500.
f. Bank service charges for November amounted to $50.
g. A check for $1,080.20 from Kalina Co. was returned by the bank because of insufficient funds.

Instructions
1. Prepare a bank reconciliation as of November 30.
2. Journalize the necessary entries. The accounts have not been closed.

PR 7-5B
Bank reconciliation and entries

obj. 5

✓*1. Adjusted balance: $12,644.09*

Vintage Interiors deposits all cash receipts each Wednesday and Friday in a night depository after banking hours. The data required to reconcile the bank statement as of July 31 have been taken from various documents and records and are reproduced as follows. The sources of the data are printed in capital letters. All checks were written for payments on account.

BANK RECONCILIATION FOR PRECEDING MONTH (DATED JUNE 30):

Cash balance according to bank statement		$ 9,422.80
Add deposit of June 30, not recorded by bank		780.80
		$10,203.60
Deduct outstanding checks:		
No. 580	$310.10	
No. 602	85.50	
No. 612	92.50	
No. 613	137.50	625.60
Adjusted balance		$ 9,578.00
Cash balance according to company's records		$ 9,605.70
Deduct service charges		27.70
Adjusted balance		$ 9,578.00

CASH ACCOUNT:
Balance as of July 1 $9,578.00

CHECKS WRITTEN:
Number and amount of each check issued in July:

Check No.	Amount	Check No.	Amount	Check No.	Amount
614	$243.50	621	$309.50	628	$ 837.70
615	350.10	622	Void	629	329.90
616	279.90	623	Void	630	882.80
617	395.50	624	707.01	631	1,081.56
618	435.40	625	518.63	632	62.40
619	320.10	626	550.03	633	310.08
620	238.87	627	318.73	634	503.30

Total amount of checks issued in July $8,675.01

JULY BANK STATEMENT:

```
                                    MEMBER FDIC                        PAGE    1
 A                                              ACCOUNT NUMBER
 N  B   AMERICAN NATIONAL BANK
        OF DETROIT                              FROM   7/01/20-   TO   7/31/20-

   DETROIT, MI 48201-2500    (313)933-8547      BALANCE              9,422.80

                                             9  DEPOSITS             6,086.35

                                            20  WITHDRAWALS          7,514.11

         VINTAGE INTERIORS                   4  OTHER DEBITS
                                                AND CREDITS          5,150.50CR

                                                NEW BALANCE         13,145.54
```

* – – – – – CHECKS AND OTHER DEBITS – – – – – *				– DEPOSITS – * – – DATE – * – – BALANCE– *		
No.580	310.10	No.612	92.50	780.80	07/01	9,801.00
No.613	137.50	No.614	243.50	569.50	07/03	9,989.50
No.615	350.10	No.616	279.90	701.80	07/06	10,061.30
No.617	395.50	No.618	435.40	819.24	07/11	10,049.64
No.619	320.10	No.620	238.87	580.70	07/13	10,071.37
No.621	309.50	No.624	707.01	MS 5,000.00	07/14	14,054.86
No.625	158.63	No.626	550.03	MS 400.00	07/14	13,746.20
No.627	318.73	No.629	329.90	600.10	07/17	13,697.67
No.630	882.80	No.631	1,081.56 NSF 225.40		07/20	11,507.91
No.632	62.40	No.633	310.08	701.26	07/21	11,836.69
				731.45	07/24	12,568.14
				601.50	07/28	13,169.64
		SC	24.10		07/31	13,145.54

```
      EC — ERROR CORRECTION              OD — OVERDRAFT
      MS — MISCELLANEOUS                 PS — PAYMENT STOPPED
      NSF — NOT SUFFICIENT FUNDS         SC — SERVICE CHARGE

 * * *                      * * *                        * * *

      THE RECONCILEMENT OF THIS STATEMENT WITH YOUR RECORDS IS ESSENTIAL.
         ANY ERROR OR EXCEPTION SHOULD BE REPORTED IMMEDIATELY.
```

CASH RECEIPTS FOR MONTH OF JULY $6,230.10

DUPLICATE DEPOSIT TICKETS:
   Date and amount of each deposit in July:

Date	Amount	Date	Amount	Date	Amount
July 2	$569.50	July 12	$580.70	July 23	$731.45
5	701.80	16	600.10	26	601.00
9	819.24	19	701.26	31	925.05

Instructions

1. Prepare a bank reconciliation as of July 31. If errors in recording deposits or checks are discovered, assume that the errors were made by the company. Assume that all deposits are from cash sales. All checks are written to satisfy accounts payable.
2. Journalize the necessary entries. The accounts have not been closed.
3. What is the amount of Cash that should appear on the balance sheet as of July 31?
4. ▆▆▆➤ Assume that a canceled check for $2,680 has been incorrectly recorded by the bank as $6,280. Briefly explain how the error would be included in a bank reconciliation and how it should be corrected.

Special Activities

SA 7-1
Ethics and professional conduct in business

ETHICS

During the preparation of the bank reconciliation for Colonial Co., Javier Frailey, the assistant controller, discovered that El Camino National Bank incorrectly recorded an $819 check written by Colonial Co. as $189. Javier has decided not to notify the bank but wait for the bank to detect the error. Javier plans to record the $630 error as Other Income if the bank fails to detect the error within the next three months.

➤ Discuss whether Javier is behaving in a professional manner.

SA 7-2
Internal controls

The following is an excerpt from a conversation between two sales clerks, Fred Loya and Steph Gillespie. Both Fred and Steph are employed by Wireless Electronics, a locally owned and operated electronics retail store.

Fred: Did you hear the news?
Steph: What news?
Fred: Alice and John were both arrested this morning.
Steph: What? Arrested? You're putting me on!
Fred: No, really! The police arrested them first thing this morning. Put them in handcuffs, read them their rights—the whole works. It was unreal!
Steph: What did they do?
Fred: Well, apparently they were filling out merchandise refund forms for fictitious customers and then taking the cash.
Steph: I guess I never thought of that. How did they catch them?
Fred: The store manager noticed that returns were twice that of last year and seemed to be increasing. When he confronted Alice, she became flustered and admitted to taking the cash, apparently over $5,000 in just three months. They're going over the last six months' transactions to try to determine how much John stole. He apparently started stealing first.

➤ Suggest appropriate control procedures that would have prevented or detected the theft of cash.

SA 7-3
Internal controls

The following is an excerpt from a conversation between the store manager of Trader Sam's Grocery Stores, Jennings Maloy, and Sam Burley, president of Trader Sam's Grocery Stores.

Sam: Jennings, I'm concerned about this new scanning system.
Jennings: What's the problem?
Sam: Well, how do we know the clerks are ringing up all the merchandise?
Jennings: That's one of the strong points about the system. The scanner automatically rings up each item, based on its bar code. We update the prices daily, so we're sure that the sale is rung up for the right price.
Sam: That's not my concern. What keeps a clerk from pretending to scan items and then simply not charging his friends? If his friends were buying 10-15 items, it would be easy for the clerk to pass through several items with his finger over the bar code or just pass the merchandise through the scanner with the wrong side showing. It would look normal for anyone observing. In the old days, we at least could hear the cash register ringing up each sale.
Jennings: I see your point.

➤ Suggest ways that Trader Sam's Grocery Stores could prevent or detect the theft of merchandise as described.

SA 7-4
Ethics and professional conduct in business

ETHICS

Pete Harsh and Sara Alper are both cash register clerks for Farmers' Markets. Gina Majed is the store manager for Farmers' Markets. The following is an excerpt of a conversation between Pete and Sara:

Pete: Sara, how long have you been working for Farmers' Markets?
Sara: Almost five years this July. You just started two weeks ago . . . right?

Pete: Yes. Do you mind if I ask you a question?

Sara: No, go ahead.

Pete: What I want to know is, have they always had this rule that if your cash register is short at the end of the day, you have to make up the shortage out of your own pocket?

Sara: Yes, as long as I've been working here.

Pete: Well, it's the pits. Last week I had to pay in almost $50.

Sara: It's not that big a deal. I just make sure that I'm not short at the end of the day.

Pete: How do you do that?

Sara: I just short-change a few customers early in the day. There are a few jerks that deserve it anyway. Most of the time, their attention is elsewhere and they don't think to check their change.

Pete: What happens if you're over at the end of the day?

Sara: Majed lets me keep it as long as it doesn't get to be too large. I've not been short in over a year. I usually clear about $50 to $80 extra per day.

> Discuss this case from the viewpoint of proper controls and professional behavior.

SA 7-5

Bank reconciliation and internal control

The records of Filippi's Company indicate a March 31 cash balance of $10,806.05, which includes undeposited receipts for March 30 and 31. The cash balance on the bank statement as of March 31 is $7,004.95. This balance includes a note of $3,000 plus $120 interest collected by the bank but not recorded in the journal. Checks outstanding on March 31 were as follows: No. 670, $1,129.16; No. 679, $830; No. 690, $525.90; No. 2148, $127.40; No. 2149, $520; and No. 2151, $851.50.

On March 3, the cashier resigned, effective at the end of the month. Before leaving on March 31, the cashier prepared the following bank reconciliation:

Cash balance per books, March 31		$10,806.05
Add outstanding checks:		
No. 2148	$127.40	
2149	520.00	
2151	851.50	1,198.90
		$12,004.95
Less undeposited receipts		5,000.00
Cash balance per bank, March 31		$ 7,004.95
Deduct unrecorded note with interest		3,120.00
True cash, March 31		$ 3,884.95

> *Calculator Tape of Outstanding Checks:*
> 0.00 *
> 127.40 +
> 520.00 +
> 851.50 +
> 1,198.90 *

Subsequently, the owner of Filippi's Company discovered that the cashier had stolen an unknown amount of undeposited receipts, leaving only $5,000 to be deposited on March 31. The owner, a close family friend, has asked your help in determining the amount that the former cashier has stolen.

1. Determine the amount the cashier stole from Filippi's. Show your computations in good form.
2. How did the cashier attempt to conceal the theft?
3. a. Identify two major weaknesses in internal controls, which allowed the cashier to steal the undeposited cash receipts.
   b. > Recommend improvements in internal controls, so that similar types of thefts of undeposited cash receipts can be prevented.

SA 7-6
Observe internal controls over cash

Group Project

Select a business in your community and observe its internal controls over cash receipts and cash payments. The business could be a bank or a bookstore, restaurant, department store, or other retailer. In groups of three or four, identify and discuss the similarities and differences in each business's cash internal controls.

SA 7-7
Cash to monthly cash expenses ratio

OccuLogix, Inc., provides treatments for eye diseases, including age-related macular degeneration (AMD). The company's treatment system, called the RHEO system, consists of an Octonova pump and disposable treatment sets that improve microcirculation in the eye by filtering high molecular weight proteins and other macromolecules from the patient's plasma. OccuLogix reported the following data (in thousands) for the years ending December 31, 2005, 2004, and 2003:

	2005	2004	2003
Cash as of December 31*	$ 41,268	$60,040	$ 1,239
Net cash flows from operating activities	(18,710)	(5,382)	(2,375)

*Includes cash equivalents and short-term investments.

1. Determine the monthly cash expenses for 2005, 2004, and 2003. Round to one decimal place.
2. Determine the ratio of cash to monthly expenses as of December 31, 2005, 2004, and 2003. Round to one decimal place.
3. ▭▭▭▶ Based upon (1) and (2), comment on OccuLogix's ratio of cash to monthly operating expenses for 2005, 2004, and 2003.

SA 7-8
Cash to monthly cash expenses ratio

Acusphere, Inc., is a specialty pharmaceutical company that develops new drugs and improved formulations of existing drugs using its proprietary microparticle technology. Currently, the company has three products in development in the areas of cardiology, oncology, and asthma. Acusphere reported the following data (in thousands) for the years ending December 31, 2005, 2004, and 2003.

	2005	2004	2003
Cash as of December 31*	$ 51,112	$ 45,180	$ 54,562
Net cash flows from operating activities	(30,683)	(19,319)	(15,507)

*Includes cash equivalents and short-term investments.

1. Determine the monthly cash expenses for 2005, 2004, and 2003. Round to one decimal place.
2. Determine the ratio of cash to monthly expenses as of December 31, 2005, 2004, and 2003. Round to one decimal place.
3. ▭▭▭▶ Based upon (1) and (2), comment on Acusphere's ratio of cash to monthly operating expenses for 2005, 2004, and 2003.

Answers to Self-Examination Questions

1. **C** Compliance with laws and regulations (answer C) is an objective, not an element, of internal control. The control environment (answer A), monitoring (answer B), control procedures (answer D), risk assessment, and information and communication are the five elements of internal control.
2. **C** The error was made by the bank, so the cash balance according to the bank statement needs to be adjusted.

Since the bank deducted $90 ($540.50 − $450.50) too little, the error of $90 should be deducted from the cash balance according to the bank statement (answer C).

3. **B** On any specific date, the cash account in a company's ledger may not agree with the account in the bank's ledger because of delays and/or errors by either party in recording transactions. The purpose of a bank reconciliation, therefore, is to determine the reasons for

any differences between the two account balances. All errors should then be corrected by the company or the bank, as appropriate. In arriving at the adjusted cash balance according to the bank statement, outstanding checks must be deducted (answer B) to adjust for checks that have been written by the company but that have not yet been presented to the bank for payment.

4. **C** All reconciling items that are added to and deducted from the cash balance according to the company's records on the bank reconciliation (answer C) require that journal entries be made by the company to correct errors made in recording transactions or to bring the cash account up to date for delays in recording transactions.

5. **D** To avoid the delay, annoyance, and expense that is associated with paying all obligations by check, relatively small amounts (answer A) are paid from a petty cash fund. The fund is established by estimating the amount of cash needed to pay these small amounts during a specified period (answer B), and it is then reimbursed when the amount of money in the fund is reduced to a predetermined minimum amount (answer C).

Receivables

© JOHN M. HARRIS/ASSOCIATED PRESS

objectives

After studying this chapter, you should be able to:

1 *Describe the common classifications of receivables.*

2 *Describe the nature of and the accounting for uncollectible receivables.*

3 *Describe the direct write-off method of accounting for uncollectible receivables.*

4 *Describe the allowance method of accounting for uncollectible receivables.*

5 *Compare the direct write-off and allowance methods of accounting for uncollectible accounts.*

6 *Describe the nature, characteristics, and accounting for notes receivable.*

7 *Describe the reporting of receivables on the balance sheet.*

FedEx Kinko's

The sale and purchase of merchandise involves the exchange of goods for money. The point at which the merchandise and the money changes hands, however, can vary depending on the transaction. Consider transactions with FedEx Kinko's, a division of FedEx consisting of a nationwide chain of copy shops. If you were to purchase class notes or other copy services, you would pay at the same time they are received. FedEx Kinko's also provides services to businesses prior to receiving payment. Because FedEx Kinko's has a history with its business partners, it allows these customers to purchase goods and services "on account." In the same way, you, as an individual, might be able to purchase goods or services on account with some businesses, such as a copy store, coffee shop, or bar, after establishing trust from a history of cash basis transactions.

Trust is a large part of business. Trust allows companies to avoid cash transactions and use trade credit. Trade credit gives rise to accounts receivable for the seller, which is often a significant current asset for many businesses. In this chapter, we will discuss common classifications of receivables, how to account for uncollectible receivables, and the reporting of receivables on the balance sheet.

Classification of Receivables

objective **1**

Describe the common classifications of receivables.

An annual report of La-Z-Boy Incorporated reported that receivables made up over 48% of La-Z-Boy's current assets.

Many companies sell on credit in order to sell more services or products. The receivables that result from such sales are normally classified as accounts receivable or notes receivable. The term **receivables** includes all money claims against other entities, including people, business firms, and other organizations. These receivables are usually a significant portion of the total current assets.

ACCOUNTS RECEIVABLE

The most common transaction creating a receivable is selling merchandise or services on credit. The receivable is recorded as a debit to the accounts receivable account. Such **accounts receivable** are normally expected to be collected within a relatively short period, such as 30 or 60 days. They are classified on the balance sheet as a current asset.

NOTES RECEIVABLE

If you have purchased an automobile on credit, you probably signed a note. From your viewpoint, the note is a note payable. From the creditor's viewpoint, the note is a note receivable.

Notes receivable are amounts that customers owe for which a formal, written instrument of credit has been issued. As long as notes receivable are expected to be collected within a year, they are normally classified on the balance sheet as a current asset.

Notes are often used for credit periods of more than 60 days. For example, a furniture dealer may require a down payment at the time of sale and accept a note or a series of notes for the remainder. Such arrangements usually provide for monthly payments. For example, if you have purchased furniture on credit, you probably signed a note. From your viewpoint, the note is a note payable. From the creditor's viewpoint, the note is a note receivable.

Notes may be used to settle a customer's account receivable. Notes and accounts receivable that result from sales transactions are sometimes called *trade receivables*. Unless stated otherwise, we will assume that all notes and accounts receivable in this chapter are from sales transactions.

OTHER RECEIVABLES

Other receivables are normally listed separately on the balance sheet. If they are expected to be collected within one year, they are classified as current assets. If collection is expected beyond one year, they are classified as noncurrent assets and reported under the caption *Investments*. *Other receivables* include interest receivable, taxes receivable, and receivables from officers or employees.

Uncollectible Receivables

objective   2

Describe the nature of and the accounting for uncollectible receivables.

In addition to their own credit departments, many businesses use external credit agencies, such as Dun & Bradstreet, to evaluate credit customers.

Adams, Stevens & Bradley, Ltd. is a collection agency that operates on a contingency basis. That is, its fees are based upon what it collects.

In prior chapters, we described and illustrated the accounting for transactions involving sales of merchandise or services on credit. A major issue that we have not yet discussed is that some customers will not pay their accounts. That is, some accounts receivable will be uncollectible.

Many retail businesses may shift the risk of uncollectible receivables to other companies. For example, some retailers do not accept sales on account but will accept only cash or credit cards. Such policies shift the risk to the credit card companies.

Companies may also sell their receivables to other companies. This is often the case when a company issues its own credit card. For example, Macy's, Sears Holdings Corp., and JCPenney issue their own credit cards. Selling receivables is called *factoring* the receivables, and the buyer of the receivables is called a *factor*. An advantage of factoring is that the company selling its receivables receives immediate cash for operating and other needs. In addition, depending upon the factoring agreement, some of the risk of uncollectible accounts may be shifted to the factor.

Regardless of the care used in granting credit and the collection procedures used, a part of the credit sales will not be collectible. The operating expense recorded from uncollectible receivables is called **Bad debt expense**, *Uncollectible accounts expense*, or *Doubtful accounts expense*.

When does an account or a note become uncollectible? There is no general rule for determining when an account is uncollectible. Once a receivable is past due, a company should first notify the customer and try to collect the account. If after repeated attempts the customer doesn't pay, the company may turn the account over to a collection agency. After the collection agency attempts collection, any remaining balance in the account is considered worthless. One of the most significant indications of partial or complete uncollectibility occurs when the debtor goes into bankruptcy. Other indications include the closing of the customer's business and an inability to locate or contact the customer.

There are two methods of accounting for receivables that appear to be uncollectible: the direct write-off method and the allowance method. The **direct write-off method** records bad debt expense only when an account is judged to be worthless. The **allowance method** records bad debt expense by estimating uncollectible accounts at the end of the accounting period.

In the next sections of this chapter, we describe and illustrate the accounting for bad debt expense using the direct write-off method and the allowance method. We begin by describing and illustrating the direct write-off method since it is simpler and easier to understand. The direct write-off method is used by smaller companies and by companies with few receivables.[1] Generally accepted accounting principles, however, require companies with a large amount of receivables to use the allowance method.

---

1 The direct write-off method is also required for federal income tax purposes.

Direct Write-Off Method for Uncollectible Accounts

objective ③

Describe the direct write-off method of accounting for uncollectible receivables.

Under the direct write-off method, Bad Debt Expense is not recorded until the customer's account is determined to be worthless. At that time, the customer's account receivable is written off. To illustrate, assume that a $4,200 account receivable from D. L. Ross has been determined to be uncollectible. The entry to write off the account is as follows:

May	10	Bad Debt Expense	4 2 0 0 00	
		Accounts Receivable—D. L. Ross		4 2 0 0 00

What happens if an account receivable that has been written off is later collected? In such cases, the account is reinstated by an entry that reverses the write-off entry. The cash received in payment is then recorded as a receipt on account.

To illustrate, assume that the D. L. Ross account of $4,200 written off on May 10 in the preceding entry is later collected on November 21. The reinstatement and receipt of cash is recorded as follows:

Nov.	21	Accounts Receivable—D. L. Ross	4 2 0 0 00	
		Bad Debt Expense		4 2 0 0 00
	21	Cash	4 2 0 0 00	
		Accounts Receivable—D. L. Ross		4 2 0 0 00

The direct write-off method is used by businesses that sell most of their goods or services for cash and accept only MasterCard or VISA, which are recorded as cash sales. In such cases, receivables are a small part of the current assets and any bad debt expense would be small. Examples of such businesses are a restaurant, a convenience store, and a small retail store.

Example Exercise 8-1

objective ③

Journalize the following transactions using the direct write-off method of accounting for uncollectible receivables:

July 9.   Received $1,200 from Jay Burke and wrote off the remainder owed of $3,900 as uncollectible.
Oct. 11.   Reinstated the account of Jay Burke and received $3,900 cash in full payment.

Follow My Example 8-1

July	9	Cash	1,200	
		Bad Debt Expense	3,900	
		Accounts Receivable—Jay Burke		5,100
Oct.	11	Accounts Receivable—Jay Burke	3,900	
		Bad Debt Expense		3,900
	11	Cash	3,900	
		Accounts Receivable—Jay Burke		3,900

For Practice: PE 8-1A, PE 8-1B

Allowance Method for Uncollectible Accounts

objective **4**

Describe the allowance method of accounting for uncollectible receivables.

As we mentioned earlier, the allowance method is required by generally accepted accounting principles for companies with large accounts receivable. As a result, most well-known companies such as General Electric Company, PepsiCo, Inc., Intel Corporation, and FedEx use the allowance method.

As discussed in the preceding section, the direct write-off method records bad debt expense only when an account is determined to be worthless. In contrast, the allowance method estimates the accounts receivable that will not be collected and records bad debt expense for this estimate at the end of each accounting period. Based upon this estimate, Bad Debt Expense is then recorded by an adjusting entry.

To illustrate, assume that ExTone Company began operations in August and chose to use the calendar year as its fiscal year. As of December 31, 2007, ExTone Company has an accounts receivable balance of $1,000,000 that includes some accounts that are past due. However, ExTone doesn't know which customer accounts will be uncollectible. Based upon industry data, ExTone estimates that $40,000 of its accounts receivable will be uncollectible. Using this estimate, the following adjusting entry is made on December 31:

Dec.	31	Bad Debt Expense	40 0 0 0 00	
		Allowance for Doubtful Accounts		40 0 0 0 00
		Uncollectible accounts estimate.		

> The adjusting entry reduces receivables to their net realizable value and matches the uncollectible expense with revenues.

Since the $40,000 reduction in accounts receivable is an estimate, specific customer accounts cannot be reduced or credited. Instead, a contra asset account entitled **Allowance for Doubtful Accounts** is credited.

As with all adjustments, the preceding adjusting entry affects the balance sheet and income statement. First, the adjusting entry records $40,000 of Bad Debt Expense, which will be matched against the related revenues of the period on the income statement. Second, the adjusting entry reduces the value of the receivables to the amount of cash expected to be realized in the future. This amount, $960,000 ($1,000,000 − $40,000), is called the **net realizable value** of the receivables. The net realizable value of the receivables is reported on the balance sheet.

You should note that after the preceding adjusting entry has been recorded, Accounts Receivable still has a debit balance of $1,000,000. This balance represents the total amount owed by customers on account and is supported by the individual customer accounts in the accounts receivable subsidiary ledger. The accounts receivable contra account, Allowance for Doubtful Accounts, has a credit balance of $40,000.

Integrity, Objectivity, and Ethics in Business

ETHICS

SELLER BEWARE

A company in financial distress will still try to purchase goods and services on account. In these cases, rather than "buyer beware," it is more like "seller beware." Sellers must be careful in advancing credit to such companies, because trade creditors have low priority for cash payments in the event of bankruptcy. To help suppliers, third-party services specialize in evaluating financially distressed customers. These services analyze credit risk for these firms by evaluating recent management payment decisions (who is getting paid and when), court actions (if in bankruptcy), and other supplier credit tightening or suspension actions. Such information helps a supplier monitor and tune trade credit amounts and terms with the financially distressed customer.

WRITE-OFFS TO THE ALLOWANCE ACCOUNT

When a customer's account is identified as uncollectible, it is written off against the allowance account. This requires the company to remove the specific accounts receivable and an equal amount from the allowance account. For example, on January 21, 2008, John Parker's account of $6,000 with ExTone Company is written off as follows:

Jan.	21	Allowance for Doubtful Accounts	6 0 0 0 00	
		Accounts Receivable—John Parker		6 0 0 0 00

At the end of a period, the Allowance for Doubtful Accounts will normally have a balance. This is because the Allowance for Doubtful Accounts is based upon an estimate. As a result, the total write-offs to the allowance account during the period will rarely equal the balance of the account at the beginning of the period. The allowance account will have a credit balance at the end of the period if the write-offs during the period are less than the beginning balance. It will have a debit balance if the write-offs exceed the beginning balance.

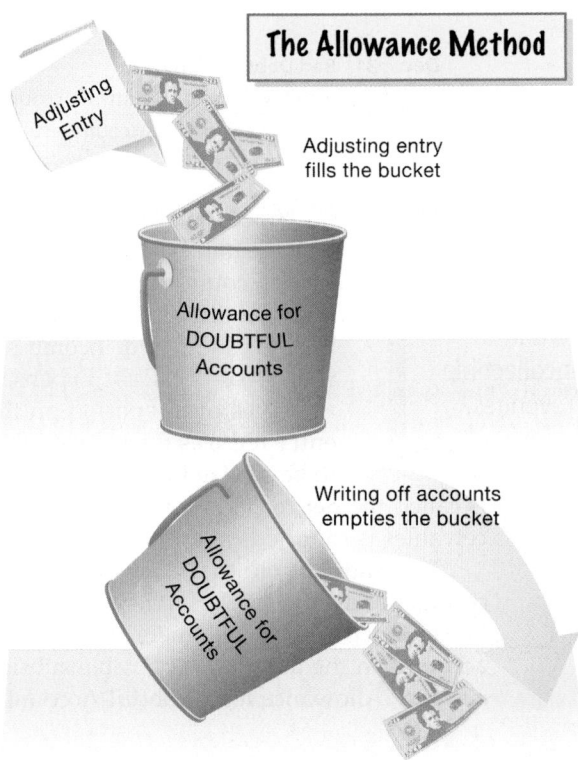

The Allowance Method

Adjusting Entry

Adjusting entry fills the bucket

Allowance for DOUBTFUL Accounts

Writing off accounts empties the bucket

Allowance for DOUBTFUL Accounts

To illustrate, assume that during 2008 ExTone Company writes off $36,750 of uncollectible accounts, including the $6,000 account of John Parker recorded on January 21. The Allowance for Doubtful Accounts will have a credit balance of $3,250 ($40,000 − $36,750), as shown below.

ALLOWANCE FOR DOUBTFUL ACCOUNTS

			Jan. 1, 2008 Balance	40,000
	Jan. 21	6,000		
	Feb. 2	3,900		
Total accounts written off $36,750	.	.		
	.	.		
			Dec. 31, 2008 Unadjusted balance	3,250

If ExTone Company had written off $44,100 in accounts receivable during 2008, the Allowance for Doubtful Accounts would have a debit balance of $4,100, as shown below.

ALLOWANCE FOR DOUBTFUL ACCOUNTS

				Jan. 1, 2008 Balance	40,000
	Jan. 21	6,000			
	Feb. 2	3,900			
Total accounts	.	.			
written off $44,100	.	.			
Dec. 31, 2008 Unadjusted balance	4,100				

You should note that the allowance account balances (credit balance of $3,250 and debit balance of $4,100) in the preceding illustrations are *before* the end-of-period adjusting entry. After the end-of-period adjusting entry is recorded, Allowance for Doubtful Accounts should always have a credit balance.

What happens if an account receivable that has been written off against the allowance account is later collected? Like the direct write-off method, the account is reinstated by an entry that reverses the write-off entry. The cash received in payment is then recorded as a receipt on account.

To illustrate, assume that Nancy Smith's account of $5,000 which was written off on April 2 is later collected on June 10. ExTone Company records the reinstatement and the collection as follows:

June	10	Accounts Receivable—Nancy Smith	5 0 0 0 00	
		Allowance for Doubtful Accounts		5 0 0 0 00
	10	Cash	5 0 0 0 00	
		Accounts Receivable—Nancy Smith		5 0 0 0 00

Example Exercise 8-2   objective 4

Journalize the following transactions using the allowance method of accounting for uncollectible receivables.

July 9. Received $1,200 from Jay Burke and wrote off the remainder owed of $3,900 as uncollectible.
Oct. 11. Reinstated the account of Jay Burke and received $3,900 cash in full payment.

Follow My Example 8-2

July 9	Cash	1,200	
	Allowance for Doubtful Accounts	3,900	
	Accounts Receivable—Jay Burke		5,100
Oct. 11	Accounts Receivable—Jay Burke	3,900	
	Allowance for Doubtful Accounts		3,900
11	Cash	3,900	
	Accounts Receivable—Jay Burke		3,900

For Practice: PE 8-2A, PE 8-2B

ESTIMATING UNCOLLECTIBLES

As we indicated earlier in this section, the allowance method estimates bad debt expense at the end of the period. How is the amount of uncollectible accounts estimated? The estimate of uncollectibles at the end of a fiscal period is based on past experience and forecasts of the future. When the general economy is doing well, the estimate of bad debt expense is normally less than it would be when the economy is doing poorly.

Two methods are commonly used to estimate uncollectible accounts receivable at the end of the period. The estimate may be based upon (1) a percent of sales or (2) an analysis of the receivables. We describe and illustrate each method next.

Estimate Based on Percent of Sales   Since accounts receivable are created by credit sales, bad debt expense can be estimated as a percent of credit sales. To illustrate, assume that on December 31, 2008, the Allowance for Doubtful Accounts for ExTone Company has a credit balance of $3,250. In addition, ExTone estimates that $1\frac{1}{2}$% of 2008 credit sales will be uncollectible. If credit sales for the year are $3,000,000, the adjusting entry for uncollectible accounts on December 31 is as follows:

The percentage of uncollectible accounts will vary across companies and industries. For example, in their recent annual reports, JCPenney reported 1.7% of its receivables as uncollectible, Deere & Company (manufacturer of John Deere tractors, etc.) reported only 1.0% of its dealer receivables as uncollectible, and HCA Inc., a hospital management company, reported 42% of its receivables as uncollectible.

Dec.	31	Bad Debt Expense	45 0 0 0 00	
		Allowance for Doubtful Accounts		45 0 0 0 00
		Uncollectible accounts estimate.		
		($3,000,000 × 0.015 = $45,000)		

After the preceding adjusting entry is posted to the ledger, Bad Debt Expense will have a balance of $45,000, and the Allowance for Doubtful Accounts will have a balance of $48,250, as shown below.

BAD DEBT EXPENSE

Dec. 31	Adjusting entry	45,000
Dec. 31	Adjusted balance	45,000

ALLOWANCE FOR DOUBTFUL ACCOUNTS

			Jan. 1, 2008	Balance	40,000
	Jan. 21	6,000			
Total accounts	Feb. 2	3,900			
written off $36,750	.	.	Dec. 31	Unadjusted balance	3,250
	.	.	Dec. 31	Adjusting entry	45,000
	.	___	Dec. 31	Adjusted balance	48,250

As shown above, after the adjusting entry is recorded, the Allowance for Doubtful Accounts has a credit balance of $48,250. If there had been a debit balance of $4,100 in the allowance account before the year-end adjustment, the amount of the adjustment would still have been $45,000. However, the December 31 ending balance of the allowance account would have been $40,900 ($45,000 − $4,100). In other words, under the percent of sales method, the amount of the adjusting entry for Bad Debt Expense is credited to whatever balance exists in the Allowance for Doubtful Accounts.

> The estimate based on sales is added to any balance in Allowance for Doubtful Accounts.

Example Exercise 8-3   objective **4**

At the end of the current year, Accounts Receivable has a balance of $800,000; Allowance for Doubtful Accounts has a credit balance of $7,500; and net sales for the year total $3,500,000. Bad debt expense is estimated at $\frac{1}{2}$ of 1% of net sales.

Determine (a) the amount of the adjusting entry for uncollectible accounts; (b) the adjusted balances of Accounts Receivable, Allowance for Doubtful Accounts, and Bad Debt Expense; and (c) the net realizable value of accounts receivable.

(continued)

Follow My Example 8-3

a. $17,500 ($3,500,000 × 0.005)

		Adjusted Balance
b.	Accounts Receivable	$800,000
	Allowance for Doubtful Accounts ($7,500 + $17,500)	25,000
	Bad Debt Expense	17,500

c. $775,000 ($800,000 − $25,000)

For Practice: PE 8-3A, PE 8-3B

Estimate Based on Analysis of Receivables The longer an account receivable is outstanding, the less likely that it will be collected. Thus, we can base the estimate of uncollectible accounts on how long specific accounts have been outstanding. For this purpose, we can use a process called **aging the receivables**.

Receivables are aged by preparing a schedule that classifies each customer's receivable by its due date. The number of days an account is past due is the number of days between the due date of the account and the date the aging schedule is prepared. To illustrate, assume that Rodriguez Company is preparing an aging schedule for its accounts receivable of $86,300 as of August 31, 2008. The $160 account receivable for Saxon Woods Company was due on May 29. As of August 31, Saxon's account is 94 days past due, as shown below.

Number of days past due in May	2 days	(31 − 29)
Number of days past due in June	30 days	
Number of days past due in July	31 days	
Number of days past due in August	31 days	
Total number of days past due	94 days	

A portion of the aging schedule for Rodriguez Company is shown in Exhibit 1. The schedule shows the total amount of receivables in each aging class.

EXHIBIT 1

Aging of Accounts Receivable

	A	B	C	D	E	F	G	H	I	
			Not		Days Past Due					
			Past						Over	
	Customer	Balance	Due	1–30	31–60	61–90	91–180	181–365	365	
1	Ashby & Co.	$ 150			$ 150					1
2	B. T. Barr	610					$ 350	$260		2
3	Brock Co.	470	$ 470							3
21										21
22	Saxon Woods Co.	160					160			22
23	Total	$86,300	$75,000	$4,000	$3,100	$1,900	$1,200	$800	$300	23

The estimate based on receivables is compared to the balance in the allowance account to determine the amount of the adjusting entry.

Rodriguez Company uses a sliding scale of percentages, based on industry or company experience, to estimate the amount of uncollectibles in each aging class. As shown in Exhibit 2, the percent estimated as uncollectible increases the longer the account is past due. For accounts not past due, the percent is 2%, while for accounts over 365 days past due, the percent is 80%. The total of these amounts is the desired end-of-period balance for the Allowance for Doubtful Accounts. For Rodriguez Company, the desired August 31 balance of the Allowance for Doubtful Accounts is $3,390.

Comparing the estimate of $3,390 with the unadjusted balance of the allowance account determines the amount of the adjustment for Bad Debt

EXHIBIT 2

Estimate of
Uncollectible
Accounts

	A	B	C	D	
			Estimated Uncollectible Accounts		
	Age Interval	Balance	Percent	Amount	
1	Not past due	$75,000	2%	$1,500	1
2	1–30 days past due	4,000	5	200	2
3	31–60 days past due	3,100	10	310	3
4	61–90 days past due	1,900	20	380	4
5	91–180 days past due	1,200	30	360	5
6	181–365 days past due	800	50	400	6
7	Over 365 days past due	300	80	240	7
8	Total	$86,300		$3,390	8

Expense. For example, assume that the unadjusted balance of the allowance account is a credit balance of $510. The amount to be added to this balance is therefore $2,880 ($3,390 − $510), and the adjusting entry is as follows:

Aug.	31	Bad Debt Expense		2 8 8 0 00	
		Allowance for Doubtful Accounts			2 8 8 0 00
		Uncollectible accounts estimate.			
		($3,390 − $510)			

After the preceding adjusting entry is posted to the ledger, Bad Debt Expense will have a balance of $2,880, and the Allowance for Doubtful Accounts will have a balance of $3,390, as shown below.

BAD DEBT EXPENSE

Aug. 31	Adjusting entry	2,880
Aug. 31	Adjusted balance	2,880

ALLOWANCE FOR DOUBTFUL ACCOUNTS

	Aug. 31	Unadusted balance	510
	Aug. 31	Adjusting entry	2,880
	Aug. 31	Adjusted balance	3,390

The Commercial Collection Agency Section of the Commercial Law League of America reported the following collection rates by number of months past due:

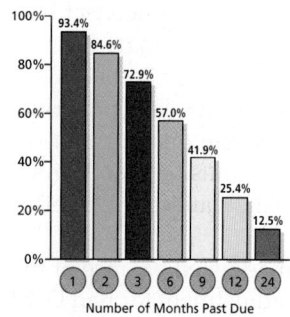

As shown above, after the adjustment is recorded, the balance of the bad debt expense account is $2,880, and the balance of the allowance account is $3,390. The net realizable value of the receivables is $82,910 ($86,300 − $3,390).

If the unadjusted balance of the allowance account had been a debit balance of $300, the amount of the adjustment would have been $3,690 ($3,390 + $300). In this case, the bad debt expense account would have a $3,690 balance, but the balance of the allowance account would still have been $3,390, as shown below.

BAD DEBT EXPENSE

Aug. 31	Adjusting entry	3,690
Aug. 31	Adjusted balance	3,690

ALLOWANCE FOR DOUBTFUL ACCOUNTS

Aug. 31	Unadjusted balance	300			
			Aug. 31	Adjusting entry	3,690
			Aug. 31	Adjusted balance	3,390

Example Exercise 8-4 objective 4

At the end of the current year, Accounts Receivable has a balance of $800,000; Allowance for Doubtful Accounts has a credit balance of $7,500; and net sales for the year total $3,500,000. Using the aging method, the balance of Allowance for Doubtful Accounts is estimated as $30,000.

Determine (a) the amount of the adjusting entry for uncollectible accounts; (b) the adjusted balances of Accounts Receivable, Allowance for Doubtful Accounts, and Bad Debt Expense; and (c) the net realizable value of accounts receivable.

Follow My Example 8-4

a. $22,500 ($30,000 − $7,500)

	Adjusted Balance
b. Accounts Receivable	$800,000
Allowance for Doubtful Accounts	30,000
Bad Debt Expense	22,500

c. $770,000 ($800,000 − $30,000)

For Practice: PE 8-4A, PE 8-4B

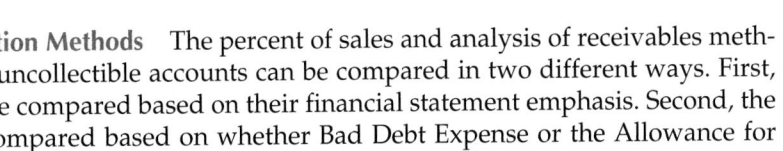

Comparing Estimation Methods The percent of sales and analysis of receivables methods of estimating uncollectible accounts can be compared in two different ways. First, the methods can be compared based on their financial statement emphasis. Second, the methods can be compared based on whether Bad Debt Expense or the Allowance for Doubtful Accounts is the focus of the estimate.

The percent of sales method emphasizes the matching of bad debt expense with the related credit sales of the period. In doing so, the percent of sales method places more emphasis on the income statement. The analysis of receivables method emphasizes the end-of-period net realizable value of the receivables and the related balance of the allowance account. Thus, the analysis of receivables method places more emphasis on the balance sheet.

Under the percent of sales method, Bad Debt Expense is the focus of the estimation process. In other words, the percent of sales method emphasizes obtaining the best estimate for Bad Debt Expense for the period. The ending balance for Allowance for Doubtful Accounts is the result of estimating bad debt expense. For example, in the ExTone Company illustration, bad debt expense was estimated as $45,000 ($3,000,000 × 1½%) and thus, $45,000 was credited to the Allowance for Doubtful Accounts. Since the Allowance for Doubtful Accounts had an unadjusted credit balance of $3,250, its ending balance became a credit balance of $48,250.

Under the analysis of receivables method, Allowance for Doubtful Accounts is the focus of the estimation process. Bad Debt Expense becomes the end result of estimating Allowance for Doubtful Accounts. For example, in the Rodriguez Company illustration, the adjusted balance for the Allowance for Doubtful Accounts was estimated using the aging method as $3,390. Since the Allowance for Doubtful Accounts had an unadjusted credit balance of $510, it was credited for $2,880 ($3,390 − $510). The related debit of $2,880 was to Bad Debt Expense. Thus, the ending balance of Bad Debt Expense became $2,880.

The following table summarizes the differences between the percent of sales and the analysis of receivables methods.

	Percent of Sales Method	Analysis of Receivables Method
Financial statement emphasis	Income statement	Balance sheet
Focus of estimate	Bad Debt Expense	Allowance for Doubtful Accounts
End result of estimate	Allowance for Doubtful Accounts	Bad Debt Expense

Comparing Direct Write-Off and Allowance Methods

objective **5**

Compare the direct write-off and allowance methods of accounting for uncollectible accounts.

In this section, we will illustrate and compare the journal entries for the direct write-off and allowance methods. As a basis for our illustration, we will use the following selected transactions, taken from the records of Hobbs Company for the year ending December 31, 2007:

Mar. 1. Wrote off account of C. York, $3,650.

Apr. 12. Received $2,250 as partial payment on the $5,500 account of Cary Bradshaw. Wrote off the remaining balance as uncollectible.

June 22. Received the $3,650 from C. York, which had been written off on March 1. Reinstated the account and recorded the cash receipt.

Sept. 7. Wrote off the following accounts as uncollectible (record as one journal entry):

Jason Bigg	$1,100	Stanford Noonan	$1,360
Steve Bradey	2,220	Aiden Wyman	990
Samantha Neeley	775		

Dec. 31. Hobbs Company uses the percent of credit sales method of estimating uncollectible expenses. Based upon past history and industry averages, 1.25% of credit sales are expected to be uncollectible. Hobbs recorded $3,400,000 of credit sales during 2007.

Exhibit 3 illustrates the journal entries that would have been recorded for Hobbs Company using the direct write-off method and the allowance method. Using the direct write-off method, there is no adjusting entry on December 31 for uncollectible accounts. In contrast, the allowance method records an adjusting entry for estimated uncollectible accounts of $42,500.

EXHIBIT 3   Comparing Direct Write-Off and Allowance Methods

	Direct Write-Off Method			Allowance Method		
Mar. 1	Bad Debt Expense	3,650		Allowance for Doubtful Accounts	3,650	
	Accounts Receivable—C. York		3,650	Accounts Receivable—C. York		3,650
Apr. 12	Cash	2,250		Cash	2,250	
	Bad Debt Expense	3,250		Allowance for Doubtful Accounts	3,250	
	Accounts Receivable—Cary Bradshaw		5,500	Accounts Receivable—Cary Bradshaw		5,500
June 22	Accounts Receivable—C. York	3,650		Accounts Receivable—C. York	3,650	
	Bad Debt Expense		3,650	Allowance for Doubtful Accounts		3,650
22	Cash	3,650		Cash	3,650	
	Accounts Receivable—C. York		3,650	Accounts Receivable—C. York		3,650
Sept. 7	Bad Debt Expense	6,445		Allowance for Doubtful Accounts	6,445	
	Accounts Receivable—Jason Bigg		1,100	Accounts Receivable—Jason Bigg		1,100
	Accounts Receivable—Steve Bradey		2,220	Accounts Receivable—Steve Bradey		2,220
	Accounts Receivable—Samantha Neeley		775	Accounts Receivable—Samantha Neeley		775
	Accounts Receivable—Stanford Noonan		1,360	Accounts Receivable—Stanford Noonan		1,360
	Accounts Receivable—Aiden Wyman		990	Accounts Receivable—Aiden Wyman		990
Dec. 31	No Entry			Bad Debt Expense	42,500	
				Allowance for Doubtful Accounts		42,500
				Uncollectible accounts estimate.		
				($3,400,000 × 0.0125 = $42,500)		

The primary differences between these two methods are summarized in the table below.

COMPARING THE DIRECT WRITE-OFF AND ALLOWANCE METHODS

	Direct Write-Off Method	Allowance Method
Amount of bad debt expense recorded	When the actual accounts receivable are determined to be uncollectible.	Using estimate based on either (1) a percent of sales or (2) an analysis of receivables.
Allowance account	No allowance account is used.	The allowance account is used.
Primary users	Small companies and companies with relatively few receivables.	Large companies and those with a large amount of receivables.

Integrity, Objectivity, and Ethics in Business

ETHICS

RECEIVABLES FRAUD

Financial reporting frauds are often tied to accounts receivable, because receivables allow companies to record revenue before cash is received. Take, for example, the case of entrepreneur Michael Weinstein, who acquired Coated Sales, Inc., with the dream of growing the small specialty company into a major corporation. To acquire funding that would facilitate this growth, Weinstein had to artificially boost the company's sales. He accomplished this by adding millions in false accounts receivable to existing customer accounts.

The company's auditors began to sense a problem when they called one of the company's customers to confirm a large order. When the customer denied placing the order, the auditors began to investigate the company's receivables more closely. Their analysis revealed a fraud which overstated profits by $55 million and forced the company into bankruptcy, costing investors and creditors over $160 million.

Source: Joseph T. Wells, "Follow Fraud to the Likely Perpetrator," *The Journal of Accountancy*, March 2001.

Notes Receivable

objective 6

Describe the nature, characteristics, and accounting for notes receivable.

A claim supported by a note has some advantages over a claim in the form of an account receivable. By signing a note, the debtor recognizes the debt and agrees to pay it according to the terms listed. A note is thus a stronger legal claim.

CHARACTERISTICS OF NOTES RECEIVABLE

A note receivable, or promissory note, is a written promise to pay a sum of money (face amount) on demand or at a definite time. It can be payable either to an individual or a business, or to the bearer or holder of the note. It is signed by the person or firm that makes the promise. The one to whose order the note is payable is called the *payee*, and the one making the promise is called the *maker*.

The date a note is to be paid is called the *due date* or *maturity date*. The period of time between the issuance date and the due date of a short-term note may be stated in either days or months. When the term of a note is stated in days, the due date is the specified number of days after its issuance. To illustrate, the due date of a 90-day note dated March 16 is June 14, as shown at the top of the following page.

The term of a note may be stated as a certain number of months after the issuance date. In such cases, the due date is determined by counting the number of months from the issuance date. For example, a three-month note dated June 5 would be due on September 5. A two-month note dated July 31 would be due on September 30.

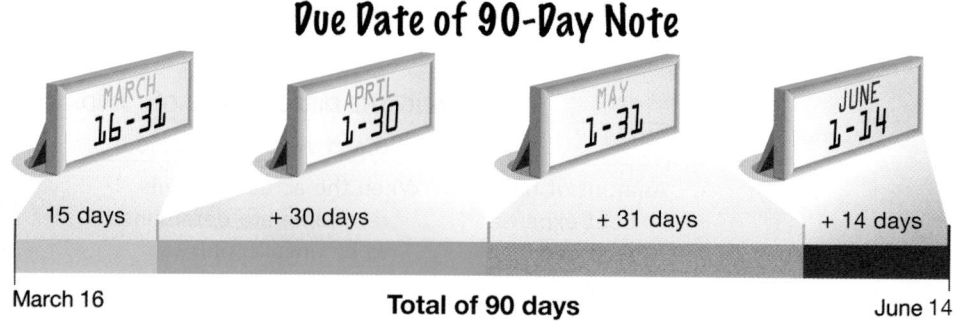

Due Date of 90-Day Note

MARCH 16-31	APRIL 1-30	MAY 1-31	JUNE 1-14
15 days	+ 30 days	+ 31 days	+ 14 days

March 16   **Total of 90 days**   June 14

REAL WORLD

Your credit card balances that are not paid at the end of the month incur an interest charge expressed as a percent per month. Interest charges of $1\frac{1}{2}\%$ per month are common. Such charges approximate an annual interest rate of 18% per year ($1\frac{1}{2}\% \times 12$). Thus, if you can borrow money at less than 18%, you are better off borrowing the money to pay off the credit card balance.

A note normally specifies that interest be paid for the period between the issuance date and the due date.[2] Notes covering a period of time longer than one year normally provide for interest to be paid annually, semiannually, quarterly, or monthly. When the term of the note is less than one year, the interest is usually payable at the time the note is paid.

The interest rate on notes is normally stated in terms of a year, regardless of the actual period of time involved. Thus, the interest on $2,000 for one year at 12% is $240 (12% × $2,000). The interest on $2,000 for 90 days at 12% is $60 ($2,000 × 12% × 90/360). To simplify computations, we will use 360 days per year. In practice, companies such as banks and mortgage companies use the exact number of days in a year, 365.

The amount that is due at the maturity or due date of a note receivable is its **maturity value**. The maturity value of a note is the sum of the face amount and the interest. For example, the maturity value of a $25,000, 9%, 120-day note receivable is $25,750 [$25,000 + ($25,000 × 9% × 120/360)].

ACCOUNTING FOR NOTES RECEIVABLE

A customer may use a note to replace an account receivable. To illustrate, assume that a company accepts a 30-day, 12% note dated November 21, 2008, in settlement of the account of W. A. Bunn Co., which is past due and has a balance of $6,000. The company records the receipt of the note as follows:

Nov.	21	Notes Receivable—W. A. Bunn Co.	6 0 0 0 00	
		Accounts Receivable—W. A. Bunn Co.		6 0 0 0 00

When the note matures, the company records the receipt of $6,060 ($6,000 principal plus $60 interest) as follows:

Dec.	21	Cash	6 0 6 0 00	
		Notes Receivable—W. A. Bunn Co.		6 0 0 0 00
		Interest Revenue		6 0 00

If the maker of a note fails to pay the debt on the due date, the note is a **dishonored note receivable**. A company that holds a dishonored note transfers the face value of the note plus any interest due back to an accounts receivable account. For example, assume that the $6,000, 30-day, 12% note received from W. A. Bunn Co. and recorded on November 21 is dishonored at maturity. The company holding the note transfers the note and interest back to the customer's account as follows:

---

2 You may occasionally see references to non-interest-bearing notes receivable. Such notes are not widely used and carry an assumed or implicit interest rate.

Dec.	21	Accounts Receivable—W. A. Bunn Co.	6 0 6 0 00	
		Notes Receivable—W. A. Bunn Co.		6 0 0 0 00
		Interest Revenue		6 0 00

The company has earned the interest of $60, even though the note is dishonored. If the account receivable is uncollectible, the company will write off $6,060 against the Allowance for Doubtful Accounts.

If a note matures in a later fiscal period, the company holding the note records an adjustment for the interest accrued in the period in which the note is received. For example, assume that Crawford Company uses a 90-day, 12% note dated December 1, 2008, to settle its account, which has a balance of $4,000. Assuming that the accounting period ends on December 31, the holder of the note records the transactions as follows:

2008 Dec.	1	Notes Receivable—Crawford Company	4 0 0 0 00	
		Accounts Receivable—Crawford Company		4 0 0 0 00
	31	Interest Receivable	4 0 00	
		Interest Revenue		4 0 00
		Accrued interest		
		($4,000 × 12% × 30/360).		
2009 Mar.	1	Cash	4 1 2 0 00	
		Notes Receivable—Crawford Company		4 0 0 0 00
		Interest Receivable		4 0 00
		Interest Revenue		8 0 00
		Total interest of $120		
		($4,000 × 12% × 90/360).		

The interest revenue account is closed at the end of each accounting period. The amount of interest revenue is normally reported in the Other Income section of the income statement.

Example Exercise 8-5 — objective 6

Same Day Surgery Center received a 120-day, 6% note for $40,000, dated March 14 from a patient on account.

a. Determine the due date of the note.
b. Determine the maturity value of the note.
c. Journalize the entry to record the receipt of the payment of the note at maturity.

Follow My Example 8-5

a. The due date of the note is July 12, determined as follows:

March	17 days (31 – 14)
April	30 days
May	31 days
June	30 days
July	12 days
Total	120 days

b. $40,800 [$40,000 + ($40,000 × 6% × 120/360)]

c. July 12 Cash 40,800
  Note Receivable 40,000
  Interest Revenue 800

For Practice: PE 8-5A, PE 8-5B

Reporting Receivables on the Balance Sheet

objective   7

Describe the reporting of receivables on the balance sheet.

All receivables that are expected to be realized in cash within a year are presented in the Current Assets section of the balance sheet. It is normal to list the assets in the order of their liquidity. This is the order in which they are expected to be converted to cash during normal operations. An example of the presentation of receivables is shown in the partial balance sheet for Crabtree Co. in Exhibit 4.

> **EXHIBIT 4**
>
> **Receivables on Balance Sheet**

Crabtree Co. Balance Sheet December 31, 2008		
Assets		
Current assets:		
Cash		$119 5 0 0 00
Notes receivable		250 0 0 0 00
Accounts receivable	$445 0 0 0 00	
Less allowance for doubtful accounts	15 0 0 0 00	430 0 0 0 00
Interest receivable		14 5 0 0 00

The balances of Crabtree's notes receivable, accounts receivable, and interest receivable accounts are reported in Exhibit 4. The allowance for doubtful accounts is subtracted from the accounts receivable. Alternatively, the accounts receivable may be listed on the balance sheet at its net realizable value of $430,000, with a note showing the amount of the allowance. If the allowance account includes provisions for doubtful notes as well as accounts, it should be deducted from the total of Notes Receivable and Accounts Receivable.

Other disclosures related to receivables are presented either on the face of the financial statements or in the accompanying notes. Such disclosures include the market (fair) value of the receivables. In addition, if unusual credit risks exist within the receivables, the nature of the risks should be disclosed. For example, if the majority of

---

Business Connections

REAL WORLD

DELTA AIR LINES

Delta Air Lines is a major air carrier that services over 144 cities in 47 states within the United States and 59 cities in 41 countries throughout the world. In its operations, Delta generates accounts receivable as reported in the following note to its financial statements:

Our accounts receivable are generated largely from the sale of passenger airline tickets and cargo transportation services. The majority of these sales are processed through major credit card companies, re- sulting in accounts receivable which are generally short-term in duration. We also have receivables from the sale of mileage credits to partners, such as credit card com-

panies, hotels and car rental agencies, that participate in our SkyMiles program. We believe that the credit risk associated with these receivables is minimal and that the allowance for uncollectible accounts that we have provided is appropriate.

In its December 31, 2004, balance sheet, Delta reported the following accounts receivable (in millions):

	2005	2004
Current Assets:		
. . .		
Accounts receivable, net of an allowance for uncollectible accounts of $41 at 12/31/05 and 12/31/04	819	696

© RIC FELD/ASSOCIATED PRESS

the receivables are due from one customer or are due from customers located in one area of the country or one industry, these facts should be disclosed.[3]

Financial Analysis and Interpretation

Two financial measures that are especially useful in evaluating efficiency in collecting receivables are (1) the accounts receivable turnover and (2) the number of days' sales in receivables.

The **accounts receivable turnover** measures how frequently during the year the accounts receivable are being converted to cash. For example, with credit terms of 2/10, n/30, the accounts receivable should turn over more than 12 times per year. The accounts receivable turnover is computed as follows:[4]

$$\text{Accounts Receivable Turnover} = \frac{\text{Net Sales}}{\text{Average Accounts Receivable}}$$

The average accounts receivable can be determined by using monthly data or by simply adding the beginning and ending accounts receivable balances and dividing by two. For example, using the following financial data (in millions) for FedEx, the 2005 and 2004 accounts receivable turnover is computed as 7.5 and 7.4, respectively.

	2005	2004	2003
Net sales	$19,364	$17,383	—
Accounts receivable	2,703	2,475	$2,199
Average accounts receivable	2,589 [($2,703 + $2,475)/2]	2,337 [($2,475 + $2,199)/2]	
Accounts receivable turnover	7.5 ($19,364/$2,589)	7.4 ($17,383/$2,337)	

Comparing 2005 and 2004 indicates that the accounts receivable turnover has increased from 7.4 to 7.5. Thus, FedEx's management of accounts receivable has improved slightly in 2005.

The **number of days' sales in receivables** is an estimate of the length of time the accounts receivable have been outstanding. With credit terms of 2/10, n/30, the number of days' sales in receivables should be less than 20 days. It is computed as follows:

$$\text{Number of Days' Sales in Receivables} = \frac{\text{Average Accounts Receivable}}{\text{Average Daily Sales}}$$

Average daily sales are determined by dividing net sales by 365 days. For example, using the preceding data for FedEx, the number of days' sales in receivables is 48.8 and 49.1 for 2005 and 2004, respectively, as shown below.

	2005	2004
Net sales	$19,364	$17,383
Average accounts receivable	2,589 [($2,703 + $2,475)/2]	2,337 [($2,475 + $2,199)/2]
Average daily sales	53.1 ($19,364/365)	47.6 ($17,383/365)
Days' sales in receivables	48.8 ($2,589/53.1)	49.1 ($2,337/47.6)

The number of days' sales in receivables confirms a slight improvement in managing accounts receivable during 2005. That is, the efficiency in collecting accounts receivable has improved when the number of days' sales in receivables decreases. However, these measures should also be compared with similar companies within the industry.

---

3 *Statement of Financial Accounting Standards No. 105*, "Disclosures of Information about Financial Instruments with Off-Balance Sheet Risk and Financial Instruments with Concentrations of Credit Risk," and *No. 107*, "Disclosures about Fair Value of Financial Instruments" (Norwalk, CT: Financial Accounting Standards Board).

4 If known, credit sales can be used in the numerator. However, because credit sales are not normally disclosed to external users, most analysts use net sales in the numerator.

Discounting Notes Receivable

Although it is not a common transaction, a company may endorse its notes receivable by transferring them to a bank in return for cash. The bank transfers cash (the *proceeds*) to the company after deducting a *discount* (interest) that is computed on the maturity value of the note for the discount period. The discount period is the time that the bank must hold the note before it becomes due.

To illustrate, assume that a 90-day, 12%, $1,800 note receivable from Pryor & Co., dated April 8, is discounted at the payee's bank on May 3 at the rate of 14%. The data used in determining the effect of the transaction are as follows:

Face value of note dated April 8	$1,800.00
Interest on note (90 days at 12%)	54.00
Maturity value of note due July 7	$1,854.00
Discount on maturity value (65 days from	
May 3 to July 7, at 14%)	46.87
Proceeds	$1,807.13

The endorser records as interest revenue the excess of the proceeds from discounting the note, $1,807.13, over its face value, $1,800, as follows:

May	3	Cash	1 8 0 7 13		
		Notes Receivable		1 8 0 0 00	
		Interest Revenue			7 13
		Discounted $1,800, 90-day, 12% note			
		at 14%.			

What if the proceeds from discounting a note receivable are less than the face value? When this situation occurs, the endorser records the excess of the face value over the proceeds as interest expense. The length of the discount period and the difference between the interest rate and the discount rate determine whether interest expense or interest revenue will result from discounting.

Without a statement limiting responsibility, the endorser of a note is committed to paying the note if the maker defaults. This potential liability is called a *contingent liability*. Thus, the endorser of a note that has been discounted has a contingent liability until the due date. If the maker pays the promised amount at maturity, the contingent liability is removed without any action on the part of the endorser. If, on the other hand, the maker dishonors the note and the endorser is notified according to legal requirements, the endorser's liability becomes an actual one.

When a discounted note receivable is dishonored, the bank notifies the endorser and asks for payment. In some cases, the bank may charge a *protest fee* for notifying the endorser that a note has been dishonored. The entire amount paid to the bank by the endorser, including the interest and protest fee, should be debited to the account receivable of the maker. For example, assume that the $1,800, 90-day, 12% note discounted on May 3 is dishonored at maturity by the maker, Pryor & Co. The bank charges a protest fee of $12. The endorser's entry to record the payment to the bank is as follows:

July	7	Accounts Receivable—Pryor & Co.	1 8 6 6 00	
		Cash		1 8 6 6 00
		Paid dishonored, discounted note		
		(maturity value of $1,854 plus protest		
		fee of $12).		

At a Glance

1. Describe the common classifications of receivables.

Key Points	Key Learning Outcomes	Example Exercises	Practice Exercises
The term *receivables* includes all money claims against other entities, including people, business firms, and other organizations. Receivables are normally classified as accounts receivable, notes receivable, or other receivables.	• Define the term *receivables*. • List some common classifications of receivables.		

2. Describe the nature of and the accounting for uncollectible receivables.

Key Points	Key Learning Outcomes	Example Exercises	Practice Exercises
Regardless of the care used in granting credit and the collection procedures used, a part of the credit sales will not be collectible. The operating expense recorded from uncollectible receivables is called *bad debt expense*. The two methods of accounting for uncollectible receivables are the direct write-off method and the allowance method.	• Describe how a company may shift the risk of uncollectible receivables to other companies. • List factors that indicate an account receivable is uncollectible. • Describe two methods of accounting for uncollectible accounts receivable.		

3. Describe the direct write-off method of accounting for uncollectible receivables.

Key Points	Key Learning Outcomes	Example Exercises	Practice Exercises
Under the direct write-off method, the entry to write off an account debits Bad Debt Expense and credits Accounts Receivable. Neither an allowance account nor an adjusting entry is needed at the end of the period.	• Prepare journal entries to write off an account using the direct method. • Prepare journal entries for the reinstatement and collection of an account previously written off.	8-1 8-1	8-1A, 8-1B 8-1A, 8-1B

(continued)

4. Describe the allowance method of accounting for uncollectible receivables.

Key Points	Key Learning Outcomes	Example Exercises	Practice Exercises
Under the allowance method, an adjusting entry is made for uncollectible accounts. When an account is determined to be uncollectible, it is written off against the allowance account. The allowance account normally has a credit balance after the adjusting entry has been posted and is a contra asset account.	• Prepare journal entries to write off an account using the allowance method.	8-2	8-2A, 8-2B
	• Prepare journal entries for the reinstatement and collection of an account previously written off.	8-2	8-2A, 8-2B
The estimate of uncollectibles may be based on a percent of sales or an analysis of receivables. Using the percent of sales, the adjusting entry is made without regard to the balance of the allowance account. Using the analysis of receivables, the adjusting entry is made so that the balance of the allowance account will equal the estimated uncollectibles at the end of the period.	• Determine the adjustment, bad debt expense, and net realizable value of accounts receivable using the percent of sales method.	8-3	8-3A, 8-3B
	• Determine the adjustment, bad debt expense, and net realizable value of accounts receivable using the analysis of receivables.	8-4	8-4A, 8-4B

5. Compare the direct write-off and allowance methods of accounting for uncollectible accounts.

Key Points	Key Learning Outcomes	Example Exercises	Practice Exercises
The direct write-off and allowance methods of accounting for uncollectible accounts are recorded differently in the accounts and presented differently in the financial statements. Exhibit 3 illustrates both methods of accounting for uncollectible accounts.	• Describe the differences in accounting for uncollectible accounts under the direct write-off and allowance methods.		
	• Record journal entries using the direct write-off and allowance methods.		

6. Describe the nature, characteristics, and accounting for notes receivable.

Key Points	Key Learning Outcomes	Example Exercises	Practice Exercises
A note received in settlement of an account receivable is recorded as a debit to Notes Receivable and a credit to Accounts Receivable. When a note matures, Cash is debited, Notes Receivable is credited, and Interest Revenue is credited. If the maker of a note fails to pay the debt on the due date, the dishonored note is recorded by debiting an accounts receivable account for the amount of the claim against the maker of the note.	• Describe the characteristics of a note receivable.		
	• Determine the due date and maturity value of a note receivable.	8-5	8-5A, 8-5B
	• Prepare journal entries for the receipt of the payment of a note receivable.	8-5	8-5A, 8-5B
	• Prepare a journal entry for the dishonored note receivable.		

7. Describe the reporting of receivables on the balance sheet.

Key Points	Key Learning Outcomes	Example Exercises	Practice Exercises
All receivables that are expected to be realized in cash within a year are reported in the Current Assets section of the balance sheet in the order in which they can be converted to cash in normal operations. In addition to the allowance for doubtful accounts, additional receivable disclosures include the market (fair) value and unusual credit risks.	• Describe how receivables are reported in the Current Assets section of the balance sheet. • Describe disclosures related to receivables that should be reported in the financial statements.		

Key Terms

accounts receivable (354)
accounts receivable turnover (369)
aging the receivables (361)
allowance for doubtful accounts (357)

allowance method (355)
bad debt expense (355)
direct write-off method (355)
dishonored note receivable (366)
maturity value (366)

net realizable value (357)
notes receivable (354)
number of days' sales in receivables (369)
receivables (354)

Illustrative Problem

Ditzler Company, a construction supply company, uses the allowance method of accounting for uncollectible accounts receivable. Selected transactions completed by Ditzler Company are as follows:

Feb. 1 Sold merchandise on account to Ames Co., $8,000. The cost of the merchandise sold was $4,500.

Mar. 15 Accepted a 60-day, 12% note for $8,000 from Ames Co. on account.

Apr. 9 Wrote off a $2,500 account from Dorset Co. as uncollectible.

21 Loaned $7,500 cash to Jill Klein, receiving a 90-day, 14% note.

May 14 Received the interest due from Ames Co. and a new 90-day, 14% note as a renewal of the loan. (Record both the debit and the credit to the notes receivable account.)

June 13 Reinstated the account of Dorset Co., written off on April 9, and received $2,500 in full payment.

July 20 Jill Klein dishonored her note.

Aug. 12 Received from Ames Co. the amount due on its note of May 14.

19 Received from Jill Klein the amount owed on the dishonored note, plus interest for 30 days at 15%, computed on the maturity value of the note.

Dec. 16 Accepted a 60-day, 12% note for $12,000 from Global Company on account.

31 It is estimated that 3% of the credit sales of $1,375,000 for the year ended December 31 will be uncollectible.

Instructions

1. Journalize the transactions.
2. Journalize the adjusting entry to record the accrued interest on December 31 on the Global Company note.

Solution

1.

Feb.	1	Accounts Receivable—Ames Co.		8 0 0 0 00	
		Sales			8 0 0 0 00
	1	Cost of Merchandise Sold		4 5 0 0 00	
		Merchandise Inventory			4 5 0 0 00
Mar.	15	Notes Receivable—Ames Co.		8 0 0 0 00	
		Accounts Receivable—Ames Co.			8 0 0 0 00
Apr.	9	Allowance for Doubtful Accounts		2 5 0 0 00	
		Accounts Receivable—Dorset Co.			2 5 0 0 00
	21	Notes Receivable—Jill Klein		7 5 0 0 00	
		Cash			7 5 0 0 00
May	14	Notes Receivable—Ames Co.		8 0 0 0 00	
		Cash		1 6 0 00	
		Notes Receivable—Ames Co.			8 0 0 0 00
		Interest Revenue			1 6 0 00
June	13	Accounts Receivable—Dorset Co.		2 5 0 0 00	
		Allowance for Doubtful Accounts			2 5 0 0 00
	13	Cash		2 5 0 0 00	
		Accounts Receivable—Dorset Co.			2 5 0 0 00
July	20	Accounts Receivable—Jill Klein		7 7 6 2 50	
		Notes Receivable—Jill Klein			7 5 0 0 00
		Interest Revenue			2 6 2 50
Aug.	12	Cash		8 2 8 0 00	
		Notes Receivable—Ames Co.			8 0 0 0 00
		Interest Revenue			2 8 0 00
Aug.	19	Cash		7 8 5 9 53	
		Accounts Receivable—Jill Klein			7 7 6 2 50
		Interest Revenue			9 7 03
		($7,762.50 × 15% × 30/360).			
Dec.	16	Notes Receivable—Global Company		12 0 0 0 00	
		Accounts Receivable—Global Company			12 0 0 0 00
	31	Bad Debt Expense		41 2 5 0 00	
		Allowance for Doubtful Accounts			41 2 5 0 00
		Uncollectible accounts estimate.			
		($1,375,000 × 3%)			

2.

Dec.	31	Interest Receivable		6 0 00	
		Interest Revenue			6 0 00
		Accrued interest			
		($12,000 × 12% × 15/360).			

Self-Examination Questions

(Answers at End of Chapter)

1. At the end of the fiscal year, before the accounts are adjusted, Accounts Receivable has a balance of $200,000 and Allowance for Doubtful Accounts has a credit balance of $2,500. If the estimate of uncollectible accounts determined by aging the receivables is $8,500, the amount of bad debt expense is:
   A. $2,500.
   B. $6,000.
   C. $8,500.
   D. $11,000.

2. At the end of the fiscal year, Accounts Receivable has a balance of $100,000 and Allowance for Doubtful Accounts has a balance of $7,000. The expected net realizable value of the accounts receivable is:
   A. $7,000.
   B. $93,000.
   C. $100,000.
   D. $107,000.

3. What is the maturity value of a 90-day, 12% note for $10,000?
   A. $8,800
   B. $10,000
   C. $10,300
   D. $11,200

4. What is the due date of a $12,000, 90-day, 8% note receivable dated August 5?
   A. October 31
   B. November 2
   C. November 3
   D. November 4

5. When a note receivable is dishonored, Accounts Receivable is debited for what amount?
   A. The face value of the note
   B. The maturity value of the note
   C. The maturity value of the note less accrued interest
   D. The maturity value of the note plus accrued interest

Eye Openers

1. What are the three classifications of receivables?
2. What types of transactions give rise to accounts receivable?
3. In what section of the balance sheet should a note receivable be listed if its term is (a) 120 days, (b) six years?
4. Give two examples of other receivables.
5. Wilson's Hardware is a small hardware store in the rural township of Struggleville that rarely extends credit to its customers in the form of an account receivable. The few customers that are allowed to carry accounts receivable are long-time residents of Struggleville and have a history of doing business at Wilson's. What method of accounting for uncollectible receivables should Wilson's Hardware use? Why?
6. Which of the two methods of accounting for uncollectible accounts provides for the recognition of the expense at the earlier date?
7. What kind of an account (asset, liability, etc.) is Allowance for Doubtful Accounts, and is its normal balance a debit or a credit?
8. After the accounts are adjusted and closed at the end of the fiscal year, Accounts Receivable has a balance of $783,150 and Allowance for Doubtful Accounts has a balance of $41,694. Describe how the accounts receivable and the allowance for doubtful accounts are reported on the balance sheet.
9. A firm has consistently adjusted its allowance account at the end of the fiscal year by adding a fixed percent of the period's net sales on account. After five years, the balance in Allowance for Doubtful Accounts has become very large in relationship to the balance in Accounts Receivable. Give two possible explanations.
10. Which of the two methods of estimating uncollectibles provides for the most accurate estimate of the current net realizable value of the receivables?
11. For a business, what are the advantages of a note receivable in comparison to an account receivable?
12. Tecan Company issued a note receivable to Bauer Company. (a) Who is the payee? (b) What is the title of the account used by Bauer Company in recording the note?
13. If a note provides for payment of principal of $75,000 and interest at the rate of 8%, will the interest amount to $6,000? Explain.
14. The maker of a $6,000, 10%, 120-day note receivable failed to pay the note on the due date of April 30. What accounts should be debited and credited by the payee to record the dishonored note receivable?
15. The note receivable dishonored in Eye Opener 14 is paid on May 30 by the maker, plus interest for 30 days, 9%. What entry should be made to record the receipt of the payment?
16. Under what section should accounts receivable be reported on the balance sheet?

Practice Exercises

PE 8-1A
Entries for uncollectible accounts using direct write-off method
obj. 3

Journalize the following transactions using the direct write-off method of accounting for uncollectible receivables:

Feb. 12. Received $750 from Manning Wingard and wrote off the remainder owed of $2,000 as uncollectible.
June 30. Reinstated the account of Manning Wingard and received $2,000 cash in full payment.

PE 8-1B
Entries for uncollectible accounts using direct write-off method
obj. 3

Journalize the following transactions using the direct write-off method of accounting for uncollectible receivables:

Aug. 7. Received $175 from Roosevelt McLair and wrote off the remainder owed of $400 as uncollectible.
Nov. 23. Reinstated the account of Roosevelt McLair and received $400 cash in full payment.

PE 8-2A
Entries for uncollectible accounts using allowance method
obj. 4

Journalize the following transactions using the allowance method of accounting for uncollectible receivables:

Feb. 12. Received $750 from Manning Wingard and wrote off the remainder owed of $2,000 as uncollectible.
June 30. Reinstated the account of Manning Wingard and received $2,000 cash in full payment.

PE 8-2B
Entries for uncollectible accounts using allowance method
obj. 4

Journalize the following transactions using the allowance method of accounting for uncollectible receivables:

Aug. 7. Received $175 from Roosevelt McLair and wrote off the remainder owed of $400 as uncollectible.
Nov. 23. Reinstated the account of Roosevelt McLair and received $400 cash in full payment.

PE 8-3A
Percent of sales method of estimating uncollectible accounts
obj. 4

At the end of the current year, Accounts Receivable has a balance of $500,000; Allowance for Doubtful Accounts has a credit balance of $4,000; and net sales for the year total $2,800,000. Bad debt expense is estimated at 1/4 of 1% of net sales.

Determine (1) the amount of the adjusting entry for uncollectible accounts; (2) the adjusted balances of Accounts Receivable, Allowance for Doubtful Accounts, and Bad Debt Expense; and (3) the net realizable value of accounts receivable.

PE 8-3B
Percent of sales method of estimating uncollectible accounts
obj. 4

At the end of the current year, Accounts Receivable has a balance of $1,200,000; Allowance for Doubtful Accounts has a debit balance of $5,000; and net sales for the year total $6,200,000. Bad debt expense is estimated at 1/2 of 1% of net sales.

Determine (1) the amount of the adjusting entry for uncollectible accounts; (2) the adjusted balances of Accounts Receivable, Allowance for Doubtful Accounts, and Bad Debt Expense; and (3) the net realizable value of accounts receivable.

PE 8-4A
Aging method of estimating uncollectible accounts
obj. 4

At the end of the current year, Accounts Receivable has a balance of $500,000; Allowance for Doubtful Accounts has a credit balance of $4,000; and net sales for the year total $2,800,000. Using the aging method, the balance of Allowance for Doubtful Accounts is estimated as $16,000.

Determine (1) the amount of the adjusting entry for uncollectible accounts; (2) the adjusted balances of Accounts Receivable, Allowance for Doubtful Accounts, and Bad Debt Expense; and (3) the net realizable value of accounts receivable.

PE 8-4B
*Aging method of
estimating uncollectible
accounts*

obj. 4

At the end of the current year, Accounts Receivable has a balance of $1,200,000; Allowance for Doubtful Accounts has a debit balance of $5,000; and net sales for the year total $6,200,000. Using the aging method, the balance of Allowance for Doubtful Accounts is estimated as $34,500.

Determine (1) the amount of the adjusting entry for uncollectible accounts; (2) the adjusted balances of Accounts Receivable, Allowance for Doubtful Accounts, and Bad Debt Expense; and (3) the net realizable value of accounts receivable.

PE 8-5A
*Note receivable due date,
maturity value, and entry*

obj. 6

Mountain Supply received a 90-day, 8% note for $25,000, dated August 10 from a customer on account.

a. Determine the due date of the note.
b. Determine the maturity value of the note.
c. Journalize the entry to record the receipt of the payment of the note at maturity.

PE 8-5B
*Note receivable due date,
maturity value, and entry*

obj. 6

Mountain Supply received a 60-day, 7% note for $120,000, dated April 2 from a customer on account.

a. Determine the due date of the note.
b. Determine the maturity value of the note.
c. Journalize the entry to record the receipt of the payment of the note at maturity.

Exercises

EX 8-1
*Classifications of
receivables*

obj. 1

Boeing is one of the world's major aerospace firms, with operations involving commercial aircraft, military aircraft, missiles, satellite systems, and information and battle management systems. As of December 31, 2005, Boeing had $2,620 million of receivables involving U.S. government contracts and $1,155 million of receivables involving commercial aircraft customers, such as Delta Air Lines and United Airlines.

➤ Should Boeing report these receivables separately in the financial statements, or combine them into one overall accounts receivable amount? Explain.

EX 8-2
*Nature of uncollectible
accounts*

obj. 2

✓ a. 5.4%

Mandalay Resort Group owns and operates casinos at several of its hotels, located primarily in Nevada. At the end of one fiscal year, the following accounts and notes receivable were reported (in thousands):

Hotel accounts and notes receivable	$31,724	
Less: Allowance for doubtful accounts	1,699	
		$30,025
Casino accounts receivable	$44,139	
Less: Allowance for doubtful accounts	12,300	
		31,839

a. Compute the percentage of the allowance for doubtful accounts to the gross hotel accounts and notes receivable for the end of the fiscal year.
b. Compute the percentage of the allowance for doubtful accounts to the gross casino accounts receivable for the end of the fiscal year.
c. ➤ Discuss possible reasons for the difference in the two ratios computed in (a) and (b).

EX 8-3
*Entries for uncollectible
accounts, using direct
write-off method*

obj. 3

Journalize the following transactions in the accounts of Simmons Co., a medical equipment company that uses the direct write-off method of accounting for uncollectible receivables:

Feb. 10. Sold merchandise on account to Dr. Pete Baker, $21,400. The cost of the merchandise sold was $12,600.
July 9. Received $13,000 from Dr. Pete Baker and wrote off the remainder owed on the sale of February 10 as uncollectible.
Oct. 27. Reinstated the account of Dr. Pete Baker that had been written off on July 9 and received $8,400 cash in full payment.

EX 8-4

Entries for uncollectible receivables, using allowance method

obj. 4

Journalize the following transactions in the accounts of Simply Yummy Company, a restaurant supply company that uses the allowance method of accounting for uncollectible receivables:

June   2.   Sold merchandise on account to Lynn Berry, $16,000. The cost of the merchandise sold was $9,400.

Oct.   15.   Received $4,000 from Lynn Berry and wrote off the remainder owed on the sale of June 2 as uncollectible.

Dec.   30.   Reinstated the account of Lynn Berry that had been written off on October 15 and received $12,000 cash in full payment.

EX 8-5

Entries to write off accounts receivable

objs. 3, 4

Jadelis Resources, a computer consulting firm, has decided to write off the $12,500 balance of an account owed by a customer. Journalize the entry to record the write-off, assuming that (a) the direct write-off method is used and (b) the allowance method is used.

EX 8-6

Providing for doubtful accounts

obj. 4

✓ a. $13,750

✓ b. $12,900

At the end of the current year, the accounts receivable account has a debit balance of $650,000, and net sales for the year total $5,500,000. Determine the amount of the adjusting entry to provide for doubtful accounts under each of the following assumptions:

a. The allowance account before adjustment has a credit balance of $3,175. Bad debt expense is estimated at ¼ of 1% of net sales.

b. The allowance account before adjustment has a credit balance of $4,600. An aging of the accounts in the customer ledger indicates estimated doubtful accounts of $17,500.

c. The allowance account before adjustment has a debit balance of $8,100. Bad debt expense is estimated at ½ of 1% of net sales.

d. The allowance account before adjustment has a debit balance of $8,100. An aging of the accounts in the customer ledger indicates estimated doubtful accounts of $24,650.

EX 8-7

Number of days past due

obj. 4

✓ Ben's Pickup Shop, 52 days

Chuck's Auto Supply distributes new and used automobile parts to local dealers throughout the Southeast. Chuck's credit terms are n/30. As of the end of business on July 31, the following accounts receivable were past due:

Account	Due Date	Amount
Ben's Pickup Shop	June 9	$5,000
Bumper Auto	July 10	4,500
Downtown Repair	March 18	2,000
Jake's Auto Repair	May 19	1,800
Like New	June 18	750
Sally's	April 12	2,800
Uptown Auto	May 8	1,500
Yellowstone Repair & Tow	April 15	3,100

Determine the number of days each account is past due.

EX 8-8

Aging-of-receivables schedule

obj. 4

The accounts receivable clerk for Vandalay Industries prepared the following partially completed aging-of-receivables schedule as of the end of business on November 30:

	A	B	C	D	E	F	G	
			Not		Days Past Due			
			Past				Over	
	Customer	Balance	Due	1–30	31–60	61–90	90	
1	Aaron Brothers Inc.	2,000	2,000					1
2	Abell Company	1,500		1,500				2
								3
21	Zollo Company	5,000			5,000			21
22	Subtotals	772,500	440,000	180,000	78,500	42,300	31,700	22

The following accounts were unintentionally omitted from the aging schedule and not included in the subtotals above:

Customer	Balance	Due Date
Tamika Industries	$25,000	August 24
Ruppert Company	8,500	September 3
Welborne Inc.	35,000	October 17
Kristi Company	6,500	November 5
Simrill Company	12,000	December 3

a. Determine the number of days past due for each of the preceding accounts.
b. Complete the aging-of-receivables schedule by including the omitted accounts.

EX 8-9
Estimating allowance for doubtful accounts
obj. **4**

✓ $75,290

Vandalay Industries has a past history of uncollectible accounts, as shown below. Estimate the allowance for doubtful accounts, based on the aging-of-receivables schedule you completed in Exercise 8-8.

Age Class	Percent Uncollectible
Not past due	3%
1–30 days past due	5
31–60 days past due	15
61–90 days past due	25
Over 90 days past due	40

EX 8-10
Adjustment for uncollectible accounts
obj. **4**

Using data in Exercise 8-9, assume that the allowance for doubtful accounts for Vandalay Industries has a credit balance of $6,150 before adjustment on November 30. Journalize the adjusting entry for uncollectible accounts as of November 30.

EX 8-11
Estimating doubtful accounts
obj. **4**

Renegade Co. is a wholesaler of motorcycle supplies. An aging of the company's accounts receivable on December 31, 2008, and a historical analysis of the percentage of uncollectible accounts in each age category are as follows:

Age Interval	Balance	Percent Uncollectible
Not past due	$400,000	1%
1–30 days past due	80,000	2
31–60 days past due	18,000	5
61–90 days past due	12,500	10
91–180 days past due	6,000	70
Over 180 days past due	2,500	90
	$519,000	

Estimate what the proper balance of the allowance for doubtful accounts should be as of December 31, 2008.

EX 8-12
Entry for uncollectible accounts
obj. **4**

Using the data in Exercise 8-11, assume that the allowance for doubtful accounts for Renegade Co. had a debit balance of $3,500 as of December 31, 2008.

Journalize the adjusting entry for uncollectible accounts as of December 31, 2008.

EX 8-13
Entries for bad debt expense under the direct write-off and allowance methods
obj. **5**

The following selected transactions were taken from the records of Shaw Company for the first year of its operations ending December 31, 2008:

Jan. 31. Wrote off account of B. Roberts, $2,400.
Mar. 26. Received $1,500 as partial payment on the $3,500 account of Carol Castellino. Wrote off the remaining balance as uncollectible.

(continued)

✓ c. $8,325 higher

July 7. Received $2,400 from B. Roberts, which had been written off on January 31. Reinstated the account and recorded the cash receipt.

Oct. 12. Wrote off the following accounts as uncollectible (record as one journal entry):

Julie Lindley	$1,350
Mark Black	950
Jennifer Kerlin	525
Beth Chalhoub	1,125
Allison Fain	725

Dec. 31. Shaw Company uses the percent of credit sales method of estimating uncollectible accounts expense. Based upon past history and industry averages, 2% of credit sales are expected to be uncollectible. Shaw recorded $750,000 of credit sales during 2008.

a. Journalize the transactions for 2008 under the direct write-off method.
b. Journalize the transactions for 2008 under the allowance method.
c. How much higher (lower) would Shaw's 2008 net income have been under the direct write-off method than under the allowance method?

EX 8-14
Entries for bad debt expense under the direct write-off and allowance methods
obj. 5
✓ c. $3,675 higher

The following selected transactions were taken from the records of Kemper Company for the year ending December 31, 2008:

Feb. 2. Wrote off account of L. Armstrong, $7,250.
May 10. Received $4,150 as partial payment on the $8,500 account of Jill Knapp. Wrote off the remaining balance as uncollectible.
Aug. 12. Received the $7,250 from L. Armstrong, which had been written off on February 2. Reinstated the account and recorded the cash receipt.
Sept. 27. Wrote off the following accounts as uncollectible (record as one journal entry):

Kim Whalen	$4,400
Brad Johnson	2,210
Angelina Quan	1,375
Tammy Newsome	2,850
Donna Short	1,690

Dec. 31. The company prepared the following aging schedule for its accounts receivable:

Aging Class (Number of Days Past Due)	Receivables Balance on December 31	Estimated Percent of Uncollectible Accounts
0–30 days	$160,000	3%
31–60 days	40,000	10
61–90 days	18,000	20
91–120 days	11,000	40
More than 120 days	6,500	75
Total receivables	$235,500	

a. Journalize the transactions for 2008 under the direct write-off method.
b. Journalize the transactions for 2008 under the allowance method, assuming that the allowance account had a beginning balance of $18,000 on January 1, 2008, and the company uses the analysis of receivables method.
c. How much higher (lower) would Kemper's 2008 net income have been under the direct write-off method than under the allowance method?

EX 8-15
Effect of doubtful accounts on net income
obj. 5

During its first year of operations, West Plumbing Supply Co. had net sales of $1,800,000, wrote off $51,000 of accounts as uncollectible using the direct write-off method, and reported net income of $125,000. Determine what the net income would have been if the allowance method had been used, and the company estimated that 3% of net sales would be uncollectible.

EX 8-16
Effect of doubtful accounts on net income
obj. 5
✓ b. $7,500 credit balance

Using the data in Exercise 8-15, assume that during the second year of operations West Plumbing Supply Co. had net sales of $2,200,000, wrote off $61,500 of accounts as uncollectible using the direct write-off method, and reported net income of $143,500.

a. Determine what net income would have been in the second year if the allowance method (using 3% of net sales) had been used in both the first and second years.
b. Determine what the balance of the allowance for doubtful accounts would have been at the end of the second year if the allowance method had been used in both the first and second years.

EX 8-17
Entries for bad debt expense under the direct write-off and allowance methods
obj. 5
✓ c. $15,000 higher

Becker Company wrote off the following accounts receivable as uncollectible for the first year of its operations ending December 31, 2008:

Customer	Amount
Skip Simon	$20,000
Clarence Watson	13,500
Bill Jacks	7,300
Matt Putnam	4,200
Total	$45,000

a. Journalize the write-offs for 2008 under the direct write-off method.
b. Journalize the write-offs for 2008 under the allowance method. Also, journalize the adjusting entry for uncollectible accounts. The company recorded $2,000,000 of credit sales during 2008. Based on past history and industry averages, 3% of credit sales are expected to be uncollectible.
c. How much higher (lower) would Becker Company's 2008 net income have been under the direct write-off method than under the allowance method?

EX 8-18
Entries for bad debt expense under the direct write-off and allowance methods
obj. 5

Hazard Company wrote off the following accounts receivable as uncollectible for the year ending December 31, 2008:

Customer	Amount
Boss Hogg	$ 5,000
Daisy Duke	3,500
Bo Duke	6,300
Luke Duke	4,200
Total	$19,000

The company prepared the following aging schedule for its accounts receivable on December 31, 2008:

Aging Class (Number of Days Past Due)	Receivables Balance on December 31	Estimated Percent of Uncollectible Accounts
0–30 days	$380,000	2%
31–60 days	70,000	5
61–90 days	30,000	15
91–120 days	25,000	25
More than 120 days	10,000	50
Total receivables	$515,000	

a. Journalize the write-offs for 2008 under the direct write-off method.
b. Journalize the write-offs and the year-end adjusting entry for 2008 under the allowance method, assuming that the allowance account had a beginning balance of $18,000 on January 1, 2008, and the company uses the analysis of receivables method.

EX 8-19
Determine due date and interest on notes

obj. 6

✓ a. May 5, $225

Determine the due date and the amount of interest due at maturity on the following notes:

	Date of Note	Face Amount	Interest Rate	Term of Note
a.	March 6	$15,000	9%	60 days
b.	May 20	8,000	10	60 days
c.	June 2	5,000	12	90 days
d.	August 30	18,000	10	120 days
e.	October 1	10,500	12	60 days

EX 8-20
Entries for notes receivable

obj. 6

✓ b. $30,675

Holsten Interior Decorators issued a 90-day, 9% note for $30,000, dated May 20, to Maderia Furniture Company on account.

a. Determine the due date of the note.
b. Determine the maturity value of the note.
c. Journalize the entries to record the following: (1) receipt of the note by Maderia Furniture and (2) receipt of payment of the note at maturity.

EX 8-21
Entries for notes receivable

obj. 6

The series of seven transactions recorded in the following T accounts were related to a sale to a customer on account and the receipt of the amount owed. Briefly describe each transaction.

CASH		
(7)	26,446	

NOTES RECEIVABLE			
(5)	26,000	(6)	26,000

ACCOUNTS RECEIVABLE			
(1)	29,500	(3)	3,500
(6)	26,226	(5)	26,000
		(7)	26,226

SALES RETURNS AND ALLOWANCES		
(3)	3,500	

MERCHANDISE INVENTORY			
(4)	2,100	(2)	17,700

COST OF MERCHANDISE SOLD			
(2)	17,700	(4)	2,100

SALES		
	(1)	29,500

INTEREST REVENUE		
	(6)	226
	(7)	220

EX 8-22
Entries for notes receivable, including year-end entries

obj. 6

The following selected transactions were completed by Cactus Co., a supplier of velcro for clothing:

2007
Dec. 13. Received from Lady Ann's Co., on account, a $60,000, 90-day, 9% note dated December 13.
     31. Recorded an adjusting entry for accrued interest on the note of December 13.
2008
Mar. 12. Received payment of note and interest from Lady Ann's Co.

Journalize the transactions.

EX 8-23
Entries for receipt and dishonor of note receivable

obj. 6

Journalize the following transactions of Theres Productions:

May 3. Received a $150,000, 90-day, 8% note dated May 3 from Xpedx Company on account.
Aug. 1. The note is dishonored by Xpedx Company.
     31. Received the amount due on the dishonored note plus interest for 30 days at 10% on the total amount charged to Xpedx Company on August 1.

EX 8-24
Entries for receipt and dishonor of notes receivable

objs. 4, 6

Journalize the following transactions in the accounts of Powerplay Co., which operates a riverboat casino:

Mar. 1. Received a $45,000, 60-day, 6% note dated March 1 from Pynn Co. on account.
18. Received a $24,000, 60-day, 9% note dated March 18 from Abode Co. on account.
Apr. 30. The note dated March 1 from Pynn Co. is dishonored, and the customer's account is charged for the note, including interest.
May 17. The note dated March 18 from Abode Co. is dishonored, and the customer's account is charged for the note, including interest.
July 29. Cash is received for the amount due on the dishonored note dated March 1 plus interest for 90 days at 8% on the total amount debited to Pynn Co. on April 30.
Aug. 23. Wrote off against the allowance account the amount charged to Abode Co. on May 17 for the dishonored note dated March 18.

EX 8-25
Receivables on the balance sheet

obj. 7

List any errors you can find in the following partial balance sheet.

Mishkie Company
Balance Sheet
December 31, 2008

Assets

Current assets:		
Cash		$127,500
Notes receivable	$400,000	
Less interest receivable	24,000	376,000
Accounts receivable	$529,200	
Plus allowance for doubtful accounts	42,000	571,200

EX 8-26
Accounts receivable turnover and days' sales in receivables

✓ a. 2005: 6.7

Polo Ralph Lauren Corporation designs, markets, and distributes a variety of apparel, home decor, accessory, and fragrance products. The company's products include such brands as Polo by Ralph Lauren, Ralph Lauren Purple Label, Ralph Lauren, Polo Jeans Co., and Chaps. Polo Ralph Lauren reported the following (in thousands):

	For the Period Ending	
	April 2, 2005	**April 3, 2004**
Net sales	$3,305,415	$2,649,654
Accounts receivable	530,503	463,289

Assume that accounts receivable (in thousands) were $391,558 at the beginning of the 2004 fiscal year.

a. Compute the accounts receivable turnover for 2005 and 2004. Round to one decimal place.
b. Compute the days' sales in receivables for 2005 and 2004. Round to one decimal place.
c. ▭▭▶ What conclusions can be drawn from these analyses regarding Ralph Lauren's efficiency in collecting receivables?

EX 8-27
Accounts receivable turnover and days' sales in receivables

✓ a. 2005: 8.2

H.J. Heinz Company was founded in 1869 at Sharpsburg, Pennsylvania, by Henry J. Heinz. The company manufactures and markets food products throughout the world, including ketchup, condiments and sauces, frozen food, pet food, soups, and tuna. For the fiscal years 2005 and 2004, H.J. Heinz reported the following (in thousands):

	Year Ending	
	April 27, 2005	**April 28, 2004**
Net sales	$8,912,297	$8,414,538
Accounts receivable	1,092,394	1,093,155

Assume that the accounts receivable (in thousands) were $1,165,460 at the beginning of 2004.

a. Compute the accounts receivable turnover for 2005 and 2004. Round to one decimal place.

b. Compute the days' sales in receivables at the end of 2005 and 2004. Round to one decimal place.

c. What conclusions can be drawn from these analyses regarding Heinz's efficiency in collecting receivables?

EX 8-28

Accounts receivable turnover and days' sales in receivables

The Limited, Inc., sells women's and men's clothing through specialty retail stores, including The Limited, Express, and Lane Bryant. The Limited sells women's intimate apparel and personal care products through Victoria's Secret and Bath & Body Works stores. The Limited reported the following (in millions):

	For the Period Ending	
	Jan. 31, 2006	**Jan. 29, 2005**
Net sales	$9,699	$9,408
Accounts receivable	182	128

Assume that accounts receivable (in millions) were $110 on February 1, 2004.

a. Compute the accounts receivable turnover for 2006 and 2005. Round to one decimal place.

b. Compute the day's sales in receivables for 2006 and 2005. Round to one decimal place.

c. What conclusions can be drawn from these analyses regarding The Limited's efficiency in collecting receivables?

EX 8-29

Accounts receivable turnover

Use the data in Exercises 8-27 and 8-28 to analyze the accounts receivable turnover ratios of H.J. Heinz Company and The Limited, Inc.

a. Compute the average accounts receivable turnover ratio for The Limited, Inc., and H.J. Heinz Company for the years shown in Exercises 8-27 and 8-28.

b. Does The Limited or H.J. Heinz Company have the higher average accounts receivable turnover ratio?

c. Explain the logic underlying your answer in (b).

APPENDIX EX 8-30

Discounting notes receivable

✓ a. $82,400

Alpine Co., a building construction company, holds a 120-day, 9% note for $80,000, dated July 23, which was received from a customer on account. On September 21, the note is discounted at the bank at the rate of 12%.

a. Determine the maturity value of the note.

b. Determine the number of days in the discount period.

c. Determine the amount of the discount.

d. Determine the amount of the proceeds.

e. Journalize the entry to record the discounting of the note on September 21.

APPENDIX EX 8-31

Entries for receipt and discounting of note receivable and dishonored notes

Journalize the following transactions in the accounts of Monarch Theater Productions:

Aug. 1. Received a $100,000, 90-day, 8% note dated August 1 from Elk Horn Company on account.

Sept. 1. Discounted the note at National Credit Bank at 10%.

Oct. 30. The note is dishonored by Elk Horn Company; paid the bank the amount due on the note, plus a protest fee of $500.

Nov. 29. Received the amount due on the dishonored note plus interest for 30 days at 12% on the total amount charged to Elk Horn Company on October 30.

Problems Series A

PR 8-1A
Entries related to uncollectible accounts

obj. 4

✓ 3. $798,490

The following transactions were completed by Clark Management Company during the current fiscal year ended December 31:

July   5. Received 70% of the $21,000 balance owed by Dockins Co., a bankrupt business, and wrote off the remainder as uncollectible.
Sept. 21. Reinstated the account of Bart Tiffany, which had been written off in the preceding year as uncollectible. Journalized the receipt of $4,875 cash in full payment of Tiffany's account.
Oct. 19. Wrote off the $6,275 balance owed by Ski Time Co., which has no assets.
Nov.   6. Reinstated the account of Kirby Co., which had been written off in the preceding year as uncollectible. Journalized the receipt of $4,750 cash in full payment of the account.
Dec. 31. Wrote off the following accounts as uncollectible (compound entry): Maxie Co., $2,150; Kommers Co., $3,600; Helena Distributors, $5,500; Ed Ballantyne, $1,750.
      31. Based on an analysis of the $815,240 of accounts receivable, it was estimated that $16,750 will be uncollectible. Journalized the adjusting entry.

Instructions

1. Record the January 1 credit balance of $12,550 in a T account for Allowance for Doubtful Accounts.
2. Journalize the transactions. Post each entry that affects the following selected T accounts and determine the new balances:

   Allowance for Doubtful Accounts
   Bad Debt Expense

3. Determine the expected net realizable value of the accounts receivable as of December 31.
4. Assuming that instead of basing the provision for uncollectible accounts on an analysis of receivables, the adjusting entry on December 31 had been based on an estimated expense of ¼ of 1% of the net sales of $7,126,000 for the year, determine the following:
   a. Bad debt expense for the year.
   b. Balance in the allowance account after the adjustment of December 31.
   c. Expected net realizable value of the accounts receivable as of December 31.

PR 8-2A
Aging of receivables; estimating allowance for doubtful accounts

obj. 4

✓ 3. $76,171

Steelhead Company supplies flies and fishing gear to sporting goods stores and outfitters throughout the western United States. The accounts receivable clerk for Steelhead prepared the following partially completed aging-of-receivables schedule as of the end of business on December 31, 2007:

	A	B	C	D	E	F	G	H	
			Not		Days Past Due				
			Past						
	Customer	Balance	Due	1–30	31–60	61–90	91–120	Over 120	
1	Alexandra Fishery	15,000	15,000						1
2	Cutthroat Sports	5,500			5,500				2
2									3
30	Yellowstone Sports	2,900		2,900					30
31	Subtotals	880,000	448,600	247,250	98,750	33,300	29,950	22,150	31

The following accounts were unintentionally omitted from the aging schedule.

Customer	Due Date	Balance
Baitfish Sports & Flies	June 21, 2007	$1,750
Kiwi Flies	Sept. 9, 2007	650
Adams Co.	Sept. 30, 2007	1,500
Bailey Sports	Oct. 17, 2007	600
Prince Sports	Nov. 18, 2007	950
Cahill Co.	Nov. 28, 2007	2,000
Winston Company	Dec. 1, 2007	2,250
Goofus Bug Sports	Jan. 6, 2008	6,200

Steelhead Company has a past history of uncollectible accounts by age category, as follows:

Age Class	Percent Uncollectible
Not past due	2%
1–30 days past due	5
31–60 days past due	10
61–90 days past due	25
91–120 days past due	45
Over 120 days past due	90

Instructions

1. Determine the number of days past due for each of the preceding accounts.
2. Complete the aging-of-receivables schedule.
3. Estimate the allowance for doubtful accounts, based on the aging-of-receivables schedule.
4. Assume that the allowance for doubtful accounts for Steelhead Company has a debit balance of $3,199 before adjustment on December 31, 2007. Journalize the adjusting entry for uncollectible accounts.

PR 8-3A
Compare two methods of accounting for uncollectible receivables
objs. 3, 4, 5

✓ *1. Year 4: Balance of allowance account, end of year, $17,150*

Pegasus Company, a telephone service and supply company, has just completed its fourth year of operations. The direct write-off method of recording bad debt expense has been used during the entire period. Because of substantial increases in sales volume and the amount of uncollectible accounts, the firm is considering changing to the allowance method. Information is requested as to the effect that an annual provision of $3/4\%$ of sales would have had on the amount of bad debt expense reported for each of the past four years. It is also considered desirable to know what the balance of Allowance for Doubtful Accounts would have been at the end of each year. The following data have been obtained from the accounts:

Year	Sales	Uncollectible Accounts Written Off	1st	2nd	3rd	4th
				Year of Origin of Accounts Receivable Written Off as Uncollectible		
1st	$ 910,000	$ 3,500	$3,500			
2nd	1,064,000	4,130	2,660	$1,470		
3rd	1,330,000	7,980	980	5,600	$1,400	
4th	2,520,000	10,920		1,680	3,570	$5,670

Instructions

1. Assemble the desired data, using the following column headings:

Year	Bad Debt Expense			Balance of Allowance Account, End of Year
	Expense Actually Reported	Expense Based on Estimate	Increase (Decrease) in Amount of Expense	

2. ▭▭▷ Experience during the first four years of operations indicated that the receivables were either collected within two years or had to be written off as uncollectible. Does the estimate of $3/4\%$ of sales appear to be reasonably close to the actual experience with uncollectible accounts originating during the first two years? Explain.

PR 8-4A
Details of notes receivable and related entries
obj. 6

✓ *1. Note 2: Due date, July 15; Interest due at maturity, $190*

Gentry Co. wholesales bathroom fixtures. During the current fiscal year, Gentry Co. received the following notes:

	Date	Face Amount	Term	Interest Rate
1.	Mar. 3	$27,000	60 days	8%
2.	June 15	19,000	30 days	12
3.	Aug. 20	10,800	120 days	6
4.	Oct. 31	36,000	60 days	9
5.	Nov. 23	15,000	60 days	6
6.	Dec. 27	27,000	30 days	12

Instructions

1. Determine for each note (a) the due date and (b) the amount of interest due at maturity, identifying each note by number.
2. Journalize the entry to record the dishonor of Note (3) on its due date.
3. Journalize the adjusting entry to record the accrued interest on Notes (5) and (6) on December 31.
4. Journalize the entries to record the receipt of the amounts due on Notes (5) and (6) in January.

PR 8-5A
Notes receivable entries
obj. 6

The following data relate to notes receivable and interest for Generic Optic Co., a cable manufacturer and supplier. (All notes are dated as of the day they are received.)

June 12. Received a $20,000, 9%, 60-day note on account.
July 13. Received a $36,000, 10%, 120-day note on account.
Aug. 11. Received $20,300 on note of June 12.
Sept. 4. Received a $15,000, 9%, 60-day note on account.
Nov. 3. Received $15,225 on note of September 4.
       5. Received a $24,000, 7%, 30-day note on account.
      10. Received $37,200 on note of July 13.
      30. Received a $15,000, 10%, 30-day note on account.
Dec. 5. Received $24,140 on note of November 5.
      30. Received $15,125 on note of November 30.

Instructions
Journalize entries to record the transactions.

PR 8-6A
Sales and notes receivable transactions
obj. 6

The following were selected from among the transactions completed by Hunter Co. during the current year. Hunter Co. sells and installs home and business security systems.

Jan. 15. Loaned $6,000 cash to Dan Hough, receiving a 90-day, 8% note.
Feb. 6. Sold merchandise on account to Kent and Son, $16,000. The cost of the merchandise sold was $9,000.
      13. Sold merchandise on account to Centennial Co., $30,000. The cost of merchandise sold was $15,750.
Mar. 5. Accepted a 60-day, 6% note for $16,000 from Kent and Son on account.
      14. Accepted a 60-day, 12% note for $30,000 from Centennial Co. on account.
Apr. 15. Received the interest due from Dan Hough and a new 90-day, 10% note as a renewal of the loan of January 15. (Record both the debit and the credit to the notes receivable account.)
May   4. Received from Kent and Son the amount due on the note of March 5.
      13. Centennial Co. dishonored its note dated March 14.
June 12. Received from Centennial Co. the amount owed on the dishonored note, plus interest for 30 days at 12% computed on the maturity value of the note.
July 14. Received from Dan Hough the amount due on his note of April 15.
Aug. 10. Sold merchandise on account to Conover Co., $10,000. The cost of the merchandise sold was $6,500.
      20. Received from Conover Co. the amount of the invoice of August 10, less 1% discount.

Instructions
Journalize the transactions.

Problems Series B

PR 8-1B
Entries related to uncollectible accounts

obj. 4

✓ 3. $842,750

The following transactions were completed by The Corion Gallery during the current fiscal year ended December 31:

Mar. 21. Reinstated the account of Tony Marshal, which had been written off in the preceding year as uncollectible. Journalized the receipt of $4,050 cash in full payment of Marshal's account.

Apr. 18. Wrote off the $5,500 balance owed by Crossroads Co., which is bankrupt.

Aug. 17. Received 25% of the $10,000 balance owed by Raven Co., a bankrupt business, and wrote off the remainder as uncollectible.

Oct. 10. Reinstated the account of Elden Hickman, which had been written off two years earlier as uncollectible. Recorded the receipt of $2,400 cash in full payment.

Dec. 31. Wrote off the following accounts as uncollectible (compound entry): Buffalo Co., $13,275; Combs Co., $4,000; Nash Furniture, $6,150; Tony DePuy, $1,720.

31. Based on an analysis of the $900,750 of accounts receivable, it was estimated that $58,000 will be uncollectible. Journalized the adjusting entry.

Instructions

1. Record the January 1 credit balance of $41,500 in a T account for Allowance for Doubtful Accounts.

2. Journalize the transactions. Post each entry that affects the following T accounts and determine the new balances:

    Allowance for Doubtful Accounts
    Bad Debt Expense

3. Determine the expected net realizable value of the accounts receivable as of December 31.

4. Assuming that instead of basing the provision for uncollectible accounts on an analysis of receivables, the adjusting entry on December 31 had been based on an estimated expense of ½ of 1% of the net sales of $10,380,000 for the year, determine the following:

    a. Bad debt expense for the year.
    b. Balance in the allowance account after the adjustment of December 31.
    c. Expected net realizable value of the accounts receivable as of December 31.

PR 8-2B
Aging of receivables; estimating allowance for doubtful accounts

obj. 4

✓ 3. $61,266

Looks Good Wigs Company supplies wigs and hair care products to beauty salons throughout California and the Pacific Northwest. The accounts receivable clerk for Looks Good prepared the following partially completed aging-of-receivables schedule as of the end of business on December 31, 2007:

	A	B	C	D	E	F	G	H	
			Not		Days Past Due				
			Past						
	Customer	Balance	Due	1–30	31–60	61–90	91–120	Over 120	
1	Daytime Beauty	20,000	20,000						1
2	Blount Wigs	11,000			11,000				2
⌇									3
30	Zabka's	2,900		2,900					30
31	Subtotals	780,000	398,600	197,250	98,750	33,300	29,950	22,150	31

The following accounts were unintentionally omitted from the aging schedule:

Customer	Due Date	Balance
Uniquely Yours	July 1, 2007	$1,200
Paradise Beauty Store	Sept. 29, 2007	1,050
Morgan's Hair Products	Oct. 17, 2007	800
Hairy's Hair Care	Oct. 31, 2007	2,000
Superior Images	Nov. 18, 2007	700
Oh The Hair	Nov. 30, 2007	3,500
Mountain Coatings	Dec. 1, 2007	1,000
Theatrical Images	Jan. 3, 2008	6,200

Looks Good Wigs has a past history of uncollectible accounts by age category, as follows:

Age Class	Percent Uncollectible
Not past due	2%
1–30 days past due	4
31–60 days past due	10
61–90 days past due	15
91–120 days past due	35
Over 120 days past due	80

Instructions
1. Determine the number of days past due for each of the preceding accounts.
2. Complete the aging-of-receivables schedule.
3. Estimate the allowance for doubtful accounts, based on the aging-of-receivables schedule.
4. Assume that the allowance for doubtful accounts for Looks Good Wigs has a credit balance of $9,550 before adjustment on December 31, 2007. Journalize the adjustment for uncollectible accounts.

PR 8-3B
Compare two methods of accounting for uncollectible receivables

objs. 3, 4, 5

✓ *1. Year 4: Balance of allowance account, end of year, $5,050*

Baron Company, which operates a chain of 30 electronics supply stores, has just completed its fourth year of operations. The direct write-off method of recording bad debt expense has been used during the entire period. Because of substantial increases in sales volume and the amount of uncollectible accounts, the firm is considering changing to the allowance method. Information is requested as to the effect that an annual provision of ½% of sales would have had on the amount of bad debt expense reported for each of the past four years. It is also considered desirable to know what the balance of Allowance for Doubtful Accounts would have been at the end of each year. The following data have been obtained from the accounts:

Year	Sales	Uncollectible Accounts Written Off	Year of Origin of Accounts Receivable Written Off as Uncollectible			
			1st	2nd	3rd	4th
1st	$ 500,000	$ 600	$ 600			
2nd	750,000	1,500	700	$ 800		
3rd	1,150,000	6,500	1,900	1,500	$3,100	
4th	2,100,000	8,850		2,000	3,050	$3,800

Instructions
1. Assemble the desired data, using the following column headings:

	Bad Debt Expense			
Year	Expense Actually Reported	Expense Based on Estimate	Increase (Decrease) in Amount of Expense	Balance of Allowance Account, End of Year

2. ▬▬▶ Experience during the first four years of operations indicated that the receivables were either collected within two years or had to be written off as uncollectible.

(continued)

Does the estimate of ½% of sales appear to be reasonably close to the actual experience with uncollectible accounts originating during the first two years? Explain.

PR 8-4B
*Details of notes
receivable and related
entries*
obj. 6

✓ *1. Note 2: Due date,
Sept. 7; Interest due at
maturity, $200*

Abdou Co. produces advertising videos. During the last six months of the current fiscal year, Abdou Co. received the following notes:

	Date	Face Amount	Term	Interest Rate
1.	May 17	$12,000	45 days	9%
2.	July 9	15,000	60 days	8
3.	Aug. 1	18,000	90 days	7
4.	Sept. 4	20,000	90 days	6
5.	Nov. 26	54,000	60 days	8
6.	Dec. 16	36,000	60 days	13

Instructions
1. Determine for each note (a) the due date and (b) the amount of interest due at maturity, identifying each note by number.
2. Journalize the entry to record the dishonor of Note (3) on its due date.
3. Journalize the adjusting entry to record the accrued interest on Notes (5) and (6) on December 31.
4. Journalize the entries to record the receipt of the amounts due on Notes (5) and (6) in January and February.

PR 8-5B
Notes receivable entries
obj. 6

The following data relate to notes receivable and interest for Vidovich Co., a financial services company. (All notes are dated as of the day they are received.)

Mar. 6. Received an $18,000, 9%, 60-day note on account.
      25. Received a $10,000, 8%, 90-day note on account.
May   5. Received $18,270 on note of March 6.
      16. Received a $40,000, 7%, 90-day note on account.
      31. Received a $12,000, 8%, 30-day note on account.
June 23. Received $10,200 on note of March 25.
      30. Received $12,080 on note of May 31.
July   1. Received a $5,000, 12%, 30-day note on account.
      31. Received $5,050 on note of July 1.
Aug. 14. Received $40,700 on note of May 16.

Instructions
Journalize the entries to record the transactions.

PR 8-6B
*Sales and notes
receivable transactions*
obj. 6

The following were selected from among the transactions completed during the current year by Hackworth Co., an appliance wholesale company:

Jan. 12. Sold merchandise on account to Dewit Co., $12,300. The cost of merchandise sold was $6,800.
Mar. 12. Accepted a 60-day, 8% note for $12,300 from Dewit Co. on account.
May 11. Received from Dewit Co. the amount due on the note of March 12.
June 3. Sold merchandise on account to Kihl's for $15,000. The cost of merchandise sold was $10,750.
      5. Loaned $18,000 cash to Michele Hobson, receiving a 30-day, 6% note.
     13. Received from Kihl's the amount due on the invoice of June 3, less 2% discount.
July 5. Received the interest due from Michele Hobson and a new 60-day, 9% note as a renewal of the loan of June 5. (Record both the debit and the credit to the notes receivable account.)
Sept. 3. Received from Michele Hobson the amount due on her note of July 5.
     17. Sold merchandise on account to Wood Co., $9,000. The cost of merchandise sold was $6,250.
Oct. 4. Accepted a 60-day, 6% note for $9,000 from Wood Co. on account.

Dec. 3. Wood Co. dishonored the note dated October 4.
　　29. Received from Wood Co. the amount owed on the dishonored note, plus interest for 26 days at 6% computed on the maturity value of the note.

Instructions
Journalize the transactions.

Special Activities

SA 8-1
Ethics and professional conduct in business

ETHICS

Neka Kiser, vice president of operations for Mountain National Bank, has instructed the bank's computer programmer to use a 365-day year to compute interest on depository accounts (payables). Neka also instructed the programmer to use a 360-day year to compute interest on loans (receivables).

　▶ Discuss whether Neka is behaving in a professional manner.

SA 8-2
Estimate uncollectible accounts

For several years, sales have been on a "cash only" basis. On January 1, 2005, however, Litespeed Co. began offering credit on terms of n/30. The amount of the adjusting entry to record the estimated uncollectible receivables at the end of each year has been ¼ of 1% of credit sales, which is the rate reported as the average for the industry. Credit sales and the year-end credit balances in Allowance for Doubtful Accounts for the past four years are as follows:

Year	Credit Sales	Allowance for Doubtful Accounts
2005	$8,160,000	$ 8,520
2006	8,400,000	15,840
2007	8,520,000	22,680
2008	8,700,000	32,820

Ursula Sykes, president of Litespeed Co., is concerned that the method used to account for and write off uncollectible receivables is unsatisfactory. She has asked for your advice in the analysis of past operations in this area and for recommendations for change.

1. Determine the amount of (a) the addition to Allowance for Doubtful Accounts and (b) the accounts written off for each of the four years.
2. a. ▶ Advise Ursula Sykes as to whether the estimate of ¼ of 1% of credit sales appears reasonable.
　b. ▶ Assume that after discussing (a) with Ursula Sykes, she asked you what action might be taken to determine what the balance of Allowance for Doubtful Accounts should be at December 31, 2008, and what possible changes, if any, you might recommend in accounting for uncollectible receivables. How would you respond?

SA 8-3
Accounts receivable turnover and days' sales in receivables

Best Buy is a specialty retailer of consumer electronics, including personal computers, entertainment software, and appliances. Best Buy operates retail stores in addition to the Best Buy, Media Play, On Cue, and Magnolia Hi-Fi Web sites. For the years ending February 26, 2005, and February 28, 2004, Best Buy reported the following (in millions):

	Year Ending	
	Feb. 26, 2005	Feb. 28, 2004
Net sales	$27,433	$24,548
Accounts receivable at end of year	375	343

Assume that the accounts receivable (in millions) were $312 at the beginning of the year ending February 28, 2004.

1. Compute the accounts receivable turnover for 2005 and 2004. Round to one decimal place.
2. Compute the days' sales in receivables at the end of 2005 and 2004.

(continued)

3. ━━▶ What conclusions can be drawn from (1) and (2) regarding Best Buy's efficiency in collecting receivables?

4. ━━▶ For its years ending in 2005 and 2004, Circuit City Stores, Inc., has an accounts receivable turnover of 61.0 and 56.3, respectively. Compare Best Buy's efficiency in collecting receivables with that of Circuit City.

5. ━━▶ What assumption did we make about sales for the Circuit City and Best Buy ratio computations that might distort the two company ratios and therefore cause the ratios not to be comparable?

SA 8-4
Accounts receivable turnover and days' sales in receivables

Apple Computer, Inc., designs, manufactures, and markets personal computers and related personal computing and communicating solutions for sale primarily to education, creative, consumer, and business customers. Substantially all of the company's net sales over the last five years are from sales of its Apple Macintosh line of personal computers and related software and peripherals. For the fiscal years ending September 24, 2005 and September 25, 2004, Apple reported the following (in millions):

	Year Ending	
	Sept. 24, 2005	**Sept. 25, 2004**
Net sales	$13,931	$8,279
Accounts receivable at end of year	895	774

Assume that the accounts receivable (in millions) were $766 at the beginning of 2004.

1. Compute the accounts receivable turnover for 2005 and 2004. Round to one decimal place.
2. Compute the days' sales in receivables at the end of 2005 and 2004.
3. ━━▶ What conclusions can be drawn from (1) and (2) regarding Apple's efficiency in collecting receivables?
4. ━━▶ Using the Internet, access the Apple September 25, 2004, 10-K filing with the Securities and Exchange Commission. You can use the PricewaterhouseCoopers Web site at **http://edgarscan.pwcglobal.com** to search for company filings by name. Search the 10-K filing for the term "receivable." Identify one company that had accounts receivable with Apple at the end of fiscal years 2005 and 2004.

SA 8-5
Accounts receivable turnover and days' sales in receivables

EarthLink, Inc., is a nationwide Internet Service Provider (ISP). Earthlink provides a variety of services to its customers, including narrowband access, broadband or high-speed access, and Web hosting services. For the years ending December 31, 2005 and 2004, Earthlink reported the following (in thousands):

	Year Ending	
	Dec. 31, 2005	**Dec. 31, 2004**
Net sales	$1,290,072	$1,382,202
Accounts receivable at end of year	36,033	30,733

Assume that the accounts receivable (in thousands) were $35,585 at January 1, 2004.

1. Compute the accounts receivable turnover for 2005 and 2004. Round to one decimal place.
2. Compute the days' sales in receivables at the end of 2005 and 2004.
3. ━━▶ What conclusions can be drawn from (1) and (2) regarding EarthLink's efficiency in collecting receivables?
4. ━━▶ Given the nature of EarthLink's operations, do you believe EarthLink's accounts receivable turnover ratio would be higher or lower than a typical manufacturing company, such as Boeing or Kellogg Company? Explain.

SA 8-6
Accounts receivable turnover

The accounts receivable turnover ratio will vary across companies, depending upon the nature of the company's operations. For example, an accounts receivable turnover of 6 for an Internet Services Provider is unacceptable but might be excellent for a manufacturer of specialty milling equipment. A list of well-known companies follows.

Alcoa Inc.	The Coca-Cola Company	Kroger
AutoZone, Inc.	Delta Air Lines	Procter & Gamble
Barnes & Noble, Inc.	The Home Depot	Wal-Mart
Caterpillar	IBM	Whirlpool Corporation

1. Using the PricewaterhouseCoopers Web site, **http://edgarscan.pwcglobal.com**, look up each company by entering its name. Click on each company's name and then scroll down to the bottom of the page to "Set Preferences." Select "Receivables Turnover" in the Ratios list. Then click "Save Preferences."
2. Categorize each of the preceding companies as to whether its turnover ratio is above or below 15.
3. ▭▷ Based upon (2), identify a characteristic of companies with accounts receivable turnover ratios above 15.

Answers to Self-Examination Questions

1. **B** The estimate of uncollectible accounts, $8,500 (answer C), is the amount of the desired balance of Allowance for Doubtful Accounts after adjustment. The amount of the current provision to be made for uncollectible accounts expense is thus $6,000 (answer B), which is the amount that must be added to the Allowance for Doubtful Accounts credit balance of $2,500 (answer A) so that the account will have the desired balance of $8,500.

2. **B** The amount expected to be realized from accounts receivable is the balance of Accounts Receivable, $100,000, less the balance of Allowance for Doubtful Accounts, $7,000, or $93,000 (answer B).

3. **C** Maturity value is the amount that is due at the maturity or due date. The maturity value of $10,300 (answer C) is determined as follows:

Face amount of note	$10,000
Plus interest ($10,000 × 0.12 × 90/360)	300
Maturity value of note	$10,300

4. **C** November 3 is the due date of a $12,000, 90-day, 8% note receivable dated August 5 [26 days in August (31 days − 5 days) + 30 days in September + 31 days in October + 3 days in November].

5. **B** If a note is dishonored, Accounts Receivable is debited for the maturity value of the note (answer B). The maturity value of the note is its face value (answer A) plus the accrued interest. The maturity value of the note less accrued interest (answer C) is equal to the face value of the note. The maturity value of the note plus accrued interest (answer D) is incorrect, since the interest would be added twice.

Fixed Assets and Intangible Assets

© W.A. HAREWOOD/ASSOCIATED PRESS

objectives

After studying this chapter, you should be able to:

1 Define, classify, and account for the cost of fixed assets.

2 Compute depreciation, using the following methods: straight-line method, units-of-production method, and double-declining-balance method.

3 Journalize entries for the disposal of fixed assets.

4 Compute depletion and journalize the entry for depletion.

5 Describe the accounting for intangible assets, such as patents, copyrights, and goodwill.

6 Describe how depreciation expense is reported in an income statement and prepare a balance sheet that includes fixed assets and intangible assets.

FATBURGER Corporation

Do you remember purchasing your first car? You probably didn't buy your first car like you would buy a CD. A used or new car is expensive and will affect your life for years to come. Typically, you would spend hours considering different makes and models, safety ratings, warranties, and operating costs before deciding on the final purchase.

Like buying her first car, Lovie Yancey spent a lot of time before deciding to open her first restaurant. In 1952, she created the biggest, juiciest hamburger that anyone had ever seen. She called it a Fatburger. The restaurant initially started as a 24-hour operation to cater to the schedules of professional musicians. As a fan of popular music and its performers, Yancey played rhythm and blues, jazz, and blues recordings for her customers. Fatburger's popularity with entertainers was illustrated when its name was used in a 1992 rap by Ice Cube. "Two in the mornin' got the Fatburger," Cube said, in "It Was a Good Day," a track on his *Predator* album.

The demand for this incredible burger was such that, in 1980, Ms. Yancey decided to offer Fatburger franchise opportunities. In 1990, with the goal of expanding Fatburger throughout the world, the Fatburger Corporation purchased the business from Ms. Yancey. Today, Fatburger has grown to a multi-restaurant chain with owners and investors such as talk show host Montel Williams, Cincinnati Bengal's tackle Willie Anderson, comedian David Spade, and musicians Cher, Janet Jackson, and Pharrell.

So, how much would it cost you to open a Fatburger restaurant? The total investment ranges from $491,500 to $818,000 per restaurant. Thus, in starting a Fatburger restaurant, you would be making a significant investment that would affect your life for years to come. In this chapter, we discuss the accounting for investments in fixed assets such as those used to open a Fatburger restaurant. We also explain how to determine the portion of the fixed asset that becomes an expense over time. Finally, we discuss the accounting for the disposal of fixed assets and accounting for intangible assets such as patents and copyrights.

http://www.fatburger.net

Nature of Fixed Assets

objective 1

Define, classify, and account for the cost of fixed assets.

Businesses purchase and use a variety of fixed assets, such as equipment, furniture, tools, machinery, buildings, and land. **Fixed assets** are long-term or relatively permanent assets. They are *tangible assets* because they exist physically. They are owned and used by the business and are not offered for sale as part of normal operations. Other descriptive titles for these assets are *plant assets* or *property, plant, and equipment*.

The fixed assets of a business can be a significant part of the total assets. Exhibit 1 shows the percent of fixed assets to total assets for some select companies, divided between service, manufacturing, and merchandising firms. As you can see, the fixed assets for most firms comprise a significant proportion of their total assets. In contrast, Computer Associates International, Inc., is a consulting firm that relies less on fixed assets to deliver value to customers.

CLASSIFYING COSTS

Exhibit 2 displays questions that help classify costs. If the purchased item is long-lived, then it should be *capitalized*, which means it should appear on the balance sheet as an asset. Otherwise, the cost should be reported as an expense on the income statement. Capitalized costs are normally expected to last more than a year. If the asset is also used for a productive purpose, which involves a repeated use or benefit, then it should

	Fixed Assets as a Percent of Total Assets
Service Firms:	
Computer Associates International, Inc.	6%
Marriott International, Inc.	31
Verizon Communications	45
Manufacturing Firms:	
Alcoa Inc.	40%
Ford Motor Company	35
ExxonMobil Corporation	60
Merchandising Firms:	
Kroger	55%
Walgreen Co.	46
Wal-Mart	53

be classified as a fixed asset, such as land, buildings, or equipment. An asset does not need to be used regularly to be a fixed asset. For example, standby equipment for use in the event of a breakdown of regular equipment or for use only during peak periods is included in fixed assets. Fixed assets that have been abandoned or are no longer used should not be classified as fixed assets.

EXHIBIT 2

Classifying Costs

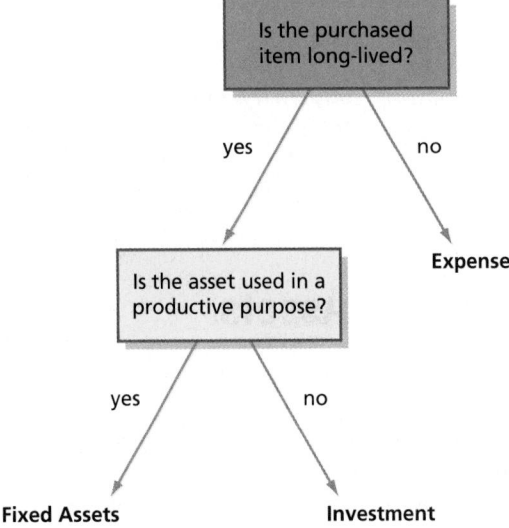

Fixed assets are owned and used by the business and are not offered for resale. Long-lived assets held for resale are not classified as fixed assets but should be listed on the balance sheet in a section entitled *Investments*. For example, undeveloped land acquired as an investment for resale would be classified as an investment, not land.

THE COST OF FIXED ASSETS

The costs of acquiring fixed assets include all amounts spent to get the asset in place and ready for use. For example, freight costs and the costs of installing equipment are included as part of the asset's total cost. The direct costs associated with new construction, such as labor and materials, should be debited to a "construction in progress" asset account. When the construction is complete, the costs should be reclassified by

Intel Corporation recently reported almost $2 billion of construction in progress, which was 5% of its total fixed assets.

crediting the construction in progress account and debiting the appropriate fixed asset account. For growing companies, construction in progress can be significant.

Exhibit 3 summarizes some of the common costs of acquiring fixed assets. These costs should be recorded by debiting the related fixed asset account, such as Land,[1] Building, Land Improvements, or Machinery and Equipment.

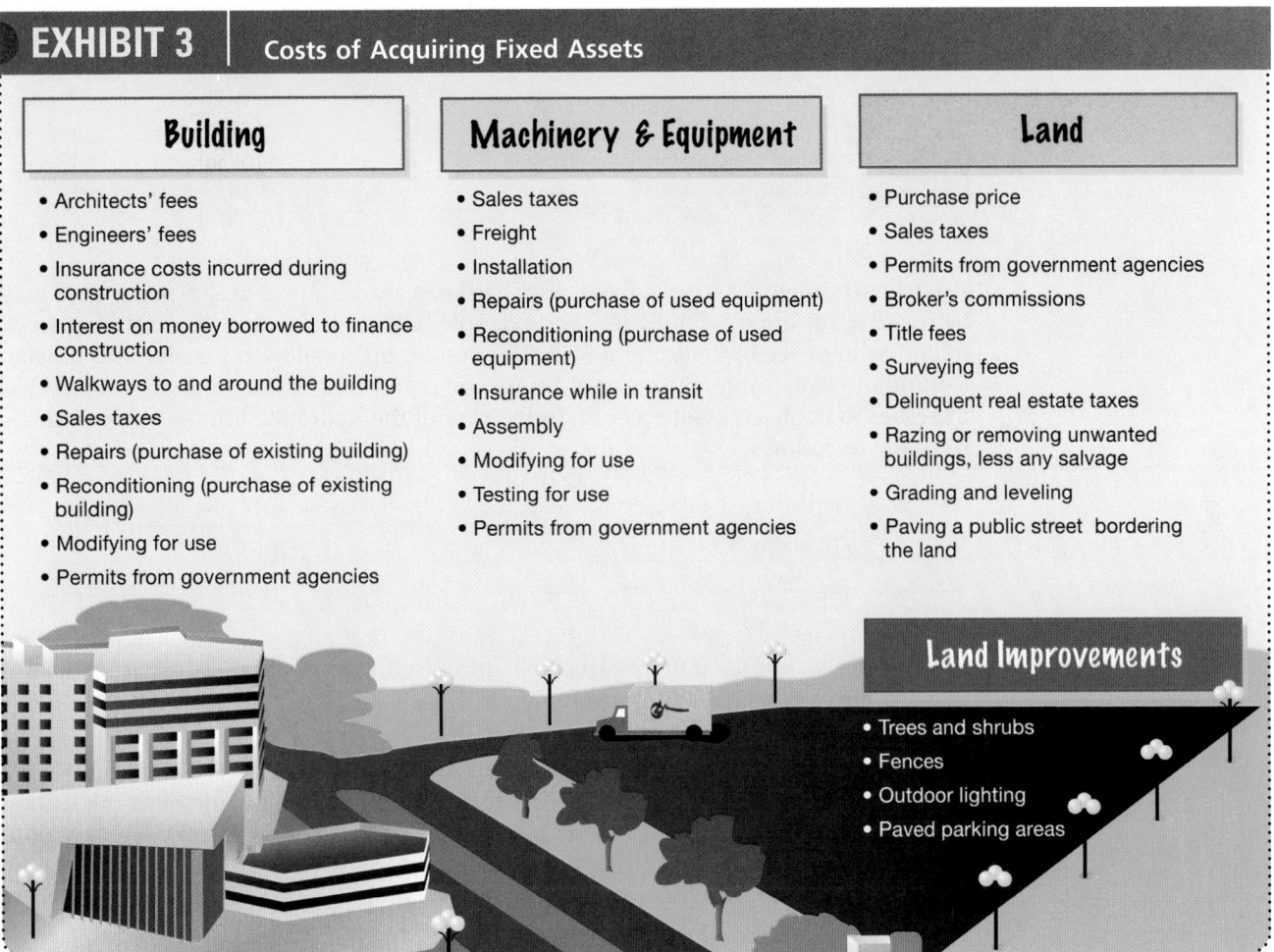

EXHIBIT 3 | **Costs of Acquiring Fixed Assets**

Building
- Architects' fees
- Engineers' fees
- Insurance costs incurred during construction
- Interest on money borrowed to finance construction
- Walkways to and around the building
- Sales taxes
- Repairs (purchase of existing building)
- Reconditioning (purchase of existing building)
- Modifying for use
- Permits from government agencies

Machinery & Equipment
- Sales taxes
- Freight
- Installation
- Repairs (purchase of used equipment)
- Reconditioning (purchase of used equipment)
- Insurance while in transit
- Assembly
- Modifying for use
- Testing for use
- Permits from government agencies

Land
- Purchase price
- Sales taxes
- Permits from government agencies
- Broker's commissions
- Title fees
- Surveying fees
- Delinquent real estate taxes
- Razing or removing unwanted buildings, less any salvage
- Grading and leveling
- Paving a public street bordering the land

Land Improvements
- Trees and shrubs
- Fences
- Outdoor lighting
- Paved parking areas

Only costs necessary for preparing a long-lived asset for use should be included as a cost of the asset. Unnecessary costs that do not increase the asset's usefulness are recorded as an expense. For example, the following costs are included as an expense:

- Vandalism
- Mistakes in installation
- Uninsured theft
- Damage during unpacking and installing
- Fines for not obtaining proper permits from governmental agencies

REVENUE AND CAPITAL EXPENDITURES

Once a fixed asset has been acquired and placed in service, expenditures may be incurred for ordinary maintenance and repairs. In addition, expenditures may be incurred

1 As discussed here, land is assumed to be used only as a location or site and not for its mineral deposits or other natural resources.

for improving an asset or for extraordinary repairs that extend the asset's useful life. Expenditures that benefit only the current period are called **revenue expenditures**. Expenditures that improve the asset or extend its useful life are **capital expenditures**.

Ordinary Maintenance and Repairs   Expenditures related to the ordinary maintenance and repairs of a fixed asset are recorded as an expense of the current period. Such expenditures are *revenue expenditures* and are recorded as increases to Repairs and Maintenance Expense. For example, $300 paid for a tune-up of a delivery truck would be recorded as follows:

	Repairs and Maintenance Expense	3 0 0 00	
	Cash		3 0 0 00

Asset Improvements   After a fixed asset has been placed in service, expenditures may be incurred to improve an asset. For example, the service value of a delivery truck might be improved by adding a $5,500 hydraulic lift to allow for easier and quicker loading of heavy cargo. Such expenditures are *capital expenditures* and are recorded as increases to the fixed asset account. In the case of the hydraulic lift, the expenditure is recorded as follows:

	Delivery Truck	5 5 0 0 00	
	Cash		5 5 0 0 00

Because the cost of the delivery truck has increased, depreciation for the truck would also change over its remaining useful life.

Extraordinary Repairs   After a fixed asset has been placed in service, expenditures may be incurred to extend the asset's useful life. For example, the engine of a forklift that is near the end of its useful life may be overhauled at a cost of $4,500, which would extend its useful life by eight years. Such expenditures are *capital expenditures* and are recorded as a decrease in an accumulated depreciation account. In the case of the forklift, the expenditure is recorded as follows:

	Accumulated Depreciation—Forklift	4 5 0 0 00	
	Cash		4 5 0 0 00

Because the forklift's remaining useful life has changed, depreciation for the forklift would also change based upon the new book value of the forklift.

Integrity, Objectivity, and Ethics in Business

ETHICS

CAPITAL CRIME

One of the largest alleged accounting frauds in history involved the improper accounting for capital expenditures. WorldCom, the second largest telecommunications company in the United States, improperly treated maintenance expenditures on its telecommunications network as capital expenditures. As a result, the company had to restate its prior years' earnings downward by nearly $4 billion to correct this error. The company declared bankruptcy within months of disclosing the error, and the CEO was sentenced to 25 years in prison.

The accounting for revenue and capital expenditures is summarized below.

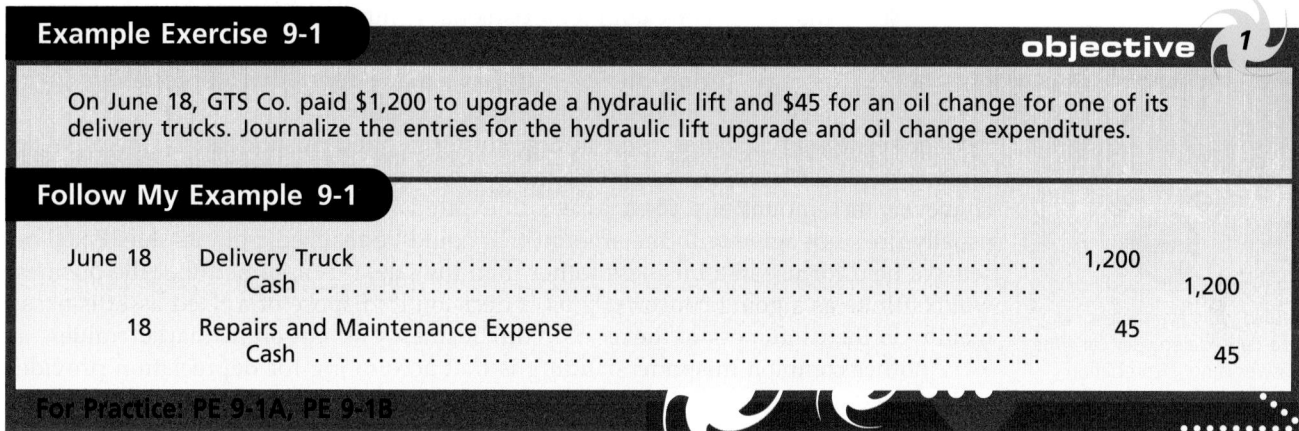

LEASING FIXED ASSETS

You are probably familiar with leases. A *lease* is a contract for the use of an asset for a stated period of time. Leases are frequently used in business. For example, automobiles, computers, medical equipment, buildings, and airplanes are often leased.

The two parties to a lease contract are the lessor and the lessee. The *lessor* is the party who owns the asset. The *lessee* is the party to whom the rights to use the asset are granted by the lessor. The lessee is obligated to make periodic rent payments for the lease term. All leases are classified by the lessee as either capital leases or operating leases.

A **capital lease** is accounted for as if the lessee has, in fact, purchased the asset. The lessee debits an asset account for the fair market value of the asset and credits a long-term lease liability account. The asset is then written off as expense (amortized) over the life of the capital lease. The accounting for capital leases and the criteria that a capital lease must satisfy are discussed in more advanced accounting texts.

A lease that is not classified as a capital lease for accounting purposes is classified as an **operating lease**. The lessee records the payments under an operating lease by debiting *Rent Expense* and crediting *Cash*. Neither future lease obligations nor the

future rights to use the leased asset are recognized in the accounts. However, the lessee must disclose future lease commitments in notes to the financial statements.

The asset rentals described in earlier chapters of this text were accounted for as operating leases. To simplify, we will continue to treat asset leases as operating leases.

Accounting for Depreciation

As we have discussed in earlier chapters, land has an unlimited life and therefore can provide unlimited services. On the other hand, other fixed assets such as equipment, buildings, and land improvements lose their ability, over time, to provide services. As a result, the costs of equipment, buildings, and land improvements should be transferred to expense accounts in a systematic manner during their expected useful lives. This periodic transfer of cost to expense is called **depreciation**.

The adjusting entry to record depreciation is usually made at the end of each month or at the end of the year. This entry debits *Depreciation Expense* and credits a *contra asset* account entitled *Accumulated Depreciation* or *Allowance for Depreciation*. The use of a contra asset account allows the original cost to remain unchanged in the fixed asset account.

> The adjusting entry to record depreciation debits Depreciation Expense and credits Accumulated Depreciation.

Factors that cause a decline in the ability of a fixed asset to provide services may be identified as physical depreciation or functional depreciation. *Physical depreciation* occurs from wear and tear while in use and from the action of the weather. *Functional depreciation* occurs when a fixed asset is no longer able to provide services at the level for which it was intended. For example, a personal computer made in the 1980s would not be able to provide an Internet connection. Such advances in technology during this century have made functional depreciation an increasingly important cause of depreciation.

The term *depreciation* as used in accounting is often misunderstood because the same term is also used in business to mean a decline in the market value of an asset. However, the amount of a fixed asset's unexpired cost reported in the balance sheet usually does not agree with the amount that could be realized from its sale. Fixed assets are held for use in a business rather than for sale. It is assumed that the business will continue as a going concern. Thus, a decision to dispose of a fixed asset is based mainly on the usefulness of the asset to the business and not on its market value.

Another common misunderstanding is that accounting for depreciation provides cash needed to replace fixed assets as they wear out. This misunderstanding probably occurs because depreciation, unlike most expenses, does not require an outlay of cash in the period in which it is recorded. The cash account is neither increased nor decreased by the periodic entries that transfer the cost of fixed assets to depreciation expense accounts.

FACTORS IN COMPUTING DEPRECIATION EXPENSE

Three factors are considered in determining the amount of depreciation expense to be recognized each period. These three factors are (a) the fixed asset's initial cost, (b) its expected useful life, and (c) its estimated value at the end of its useful life. This third factor is called the *residual value, scrap value, salvage value,* or *trade-in value.*

A fixed asset's **residual value** at the end of its expected useful life must be estimated at the time the asset is placed in service. If a fixed asset is expected to have little or no residual value when it is taken out of service, then its initial cost should be spread over its expected useful life as depreciation expense. If, however, a fixed asset is expected to have a significant residual value, the difference between its initial cost and its residual value, called the asset's *depreciable cost,* is the amount that is spread over the asset's useful life as depreciation expense. Exhibit 4 shows the relationship among the three factors and the periodic depreciation expense.

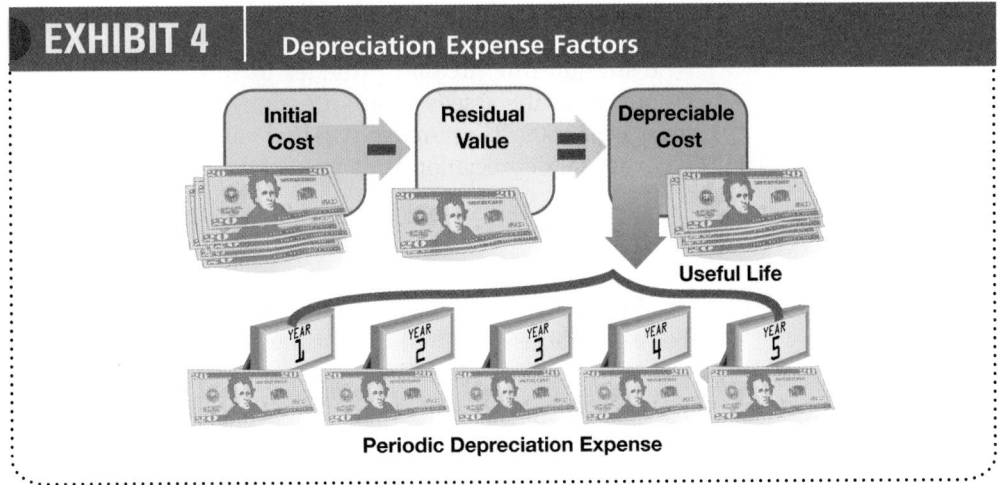

EXHIBIT 4 | **Depreciation Expense Factors**

A fixed asset's *expected useful life* must also be estimated at the time the asset is placed in service. Estimates of expected useful lives are available from various trade associations and other publications. For federal income tax purposes, the Internal Revenue Service has established guidelines for useful lives. These guidelines may also be helpful in determining depreciation for financial reporting purposes. However, it is common for different companies to use a different useful life for similar assets.

In practice, many businesses use the guideline that all assets placed in or taken out of service during the first half of a month are treated as if the event occurred on the first day of *that* month. That is, these businesses compute depreciation on these assets for the entire month. Likewise, all fixed asset additions and deductions during the second half of a month are treated as if the event occurred on the first day of the *next* month. We will follow this practice in this chapter.

It is not necessary that a business use a single method of computing depreciation for all its depreciable assets. The methods used in the accounts and financial statements may also differ from the methods used in determining income taxes and property taxes. The three methods used most often are (1) straight-line, (2) units-of-production, and (3) double-declining-balance.[2] Exhibit 5 shows the extent of the use of these methods in financial statements.

EXHIBIT 5

Use of Depreciation Methods

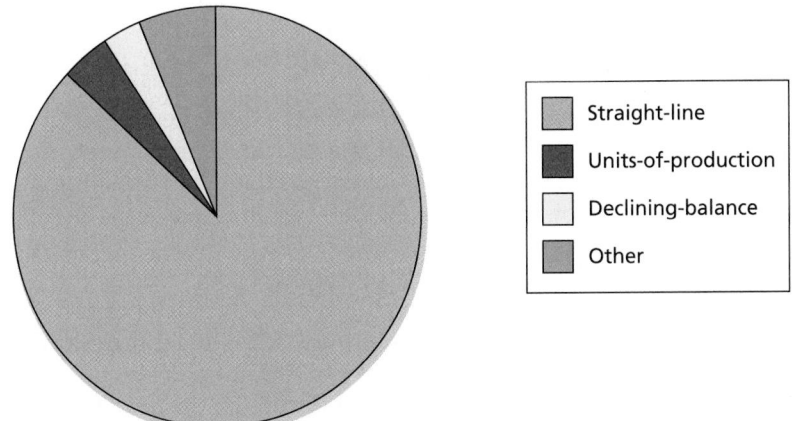

- Straight-line
- Units-of-production
- Declining-balance
- Other

Source: Accounting Trends & Techniques, 59th ed., American Institute of Certified Public Accountants, New York, 2005.

---

2 Another method not often used today, called the *sum-of-the-years-digits method*, is described and illustrated in the appendix at the end of this chapter.

STRAIGHT-LINE METHOD

The **straight-line method** provides for the same amount of depreciation expense for each year of the asset's useful life. For example, assume that the cost of a depreciable asset is $24,000, its estimated residual value is $2,000, and its estimated life is five years. The annual depreciation is computed as follows:

$$\frac{\$24{,}000 \text{ cost} - \$2{,}000 \text{ estimated residual value}}{5 \text{ years estimated life}} = \$4{,}400 \text{ annual depreciation}$$

When an asset is used for only part of a year, the annual depreciation is prorated. For example, assume that the fiscal year ends on December 31 and that the asset in the above example is placed in service on October 1. The depreciation for the first fiscal year of use would be $1,100 ($4,400 × 3/12).

For ease in applying the straight-line method, the annual depreciation may be converted to a percentage of the depreciable cost. This percentage is determined by dividing 100% by the number of years of useful life. For example, a useful life of 20 years converts to a 5% rate (100%/20), 8 years converts to a 12.5% rate (100%/8), and so on.[3] In the above example, the annual depreciation of $4,400 can be computed by multiplying the depreciable cost of $22,000 by 20% (100%/5).

The straight-line method is simple and is widely used. It provides a reasonable transfer of costs to periodic expense when the asset's use and the related revenues from its use are about the same from period to period.

Example Exercise 9-2   objective 2

Equipment acquired at the beginning of the year at a cost of $125,000 has an estimated residual value of $5,000 and an estimated useful life of 10 years. Determine (a) the depreciable cost, (b) the straight-line rate, and (c) the annual straight-line depreciation.

Follow My Example 9-2

a. $120,000 ($125,000 − $5,000)
b. 10% = 1/10
c. $12,000 ($120,000 × 10%), or ($120,000/10 years)

For Practice: PE 9-2A, PE 9-2B

UNITS-OF-PRODUCTION METHOD

How would you depreciate a fixed asset when its service is related to use rather than time? When the amount of use of a fixed asset varies from year to year, the units-of-production method is more appropriate than the straight-line method. In such cases, the units-of-production method better matches the depreciation expense with the related revenue.

The **units-of-production method** provides for the same amount of depreciation expense for each unit produced or each unit of capacity used by the asset. To apply this method, the useful life of the asset is expressed in terms of units of productive capacity such as hours or miles. The total depreciation expense for each accounting period is then determined by multiplying the unit depreciation by the number of units produced or used during the period. For example, assume that a machine with a cost of $24,000 and an estimated residual value of $2,000 is expected to have an estimated

Norfolk Southern Corporation depreciates its train engines based upon hours of operation.

---

3 The depreciation rate may also be expressed as a fraction. For example, the annual straight-line rate for an asset with a three-year useful life is 1/3.

life of 10,000 operating hours. The depreciation for a unit of one hour is computed as follows:

$$\frac{\$24,000 \text{ cost} - \$2,000 \text{ estimated residual value}}{10,000 \text{ estimated hours}} = \$2.20 \text{ hourly depreciation}$$

Assuming that the machine was in operation for 2,100 hours during a year, the depreciation for that year would be \$4,620 (\$2.20 × 2,100 hours).

Example Exercise 9-3   objective 2

Equipment acquired at a cost of \$180,000 has an estimated residual value of \$10,000, has an estimated useful life of 40,000 hours, and was operated 3,600 hours during the year. Determine (a) the depreciable cost, (b) the depreciation rate, and (c) the units-of-production depreciation for the year.

Follow My Example 9-3

a. \$170,000 (\$180,000 − \$10,000)
b. \$4.25 per hour (\$170,000/40,000 hours)
c. \$15,300 (3,600 hours × \$4.25)

For Practice: PE 9-3A, PE 9-3B

DOUBLE-DECLINING-BALANCE METHOD

The **double-declining-balance method** provides for a declining periodic expense over the estimated useful life of the asset. In using this method, a double-declining-balance rate is determined by doubling the straight-line rate. To illustrate, assume that an asset has a useful life of five years. The double-declining-balance rate of 40% is determined as shown below.

$$\text{Double-Declining-Balance Rate} = \text{Straight-Line Rate} \times 2$$
$$= (1/5) \times 2 = 20\% \times 2$$
$$= 40\%$$

For the first year of use, the cost of the asset is multiplied by the double-declining-balance rate. After the first year, the declining **book value** (cost minus accumulated depreciation) of the asset is multiplied by this rate. To illustrate, the annual double-declining-balance depreciation for an asset with an estimated five-year life and a cost of \$24,000 is shown below.

Year	Cost	Accum. Depr. at Beginning of Year	Book Value at Beginning of Year	Double-Declining-Balance Rate	Depreciation for Year	Book Value at End of Year
1	\$24,000		\$24,000.00	× 40%	\$9,600.00	\$14,400.00
2	24,000	\$ 9,600.00	14,400.00	× 40%	5,760.00	8,640.00
3	24,000	15,360.00	8,640.00	× 40%	3,456.00	5,184.00
4	24,000	18,816.00	5,184.00	× 40%	2,073.60	3,110.40
5	24,000	20,889.60	3,110.40	—	1,110.40	2,000.00

You should note that when the double-declining-balance method is used, the estimated residual value is *not* considered in determining the depreciation rate. It is also ignored in computing the periodic depreciation. However, the asset should not be depreciated below its estimated residual value. In the above example, the estimated residual value was \$2,000. Therefore, the depreciation for the fifth year is \$1,110.40 (\$3,110.40 − \$2,000.00) instead of \$1,244.16 (40% × \$3,110.40).

In the example, we assumed that the first use of the asset occurred at the beginning of the fiscal year. This is normally not the case in practice, however, and depreciation for the first partial year of use must be computed. For example, assume that the asset above was in service at the end of the *third* month of the fiscal year. In this case, only a portion (9/12) of the first full year's depreciation of $9,600 is allocated to the first fiscal year. Thus, depreciation of $7,200 (9/12 × $9,600) is allocated to the first partial year of use. The depreciation for the second fiscal year would then be $6,720 [40% × ($24,000 − $7,200)].

Example Exercise 9-4

objective **2**

Equipment acquired at the beginning of the year at a cost of $125,000 has an estimated residual value of $5,000 and an estimated useful life of 10 years. Determine (a) the depreciable cost, (b) the double-declining-balance rate, and (c) the double-declining-balance depreciation for the first year.

Follow My Example 9-4

a. $120,000 ($125,000 − $5,000)
b. 20% [(1/10) × 2]
c. $25,000 ($125,000 × 20%)

For Practice: PE 9-4A, PE 9-4B

COMPARING DEPRECIATION METHODS

The differences among the three depreciation methods are summarized in Exhibit 6. All three methods assign a portion of the total cost of an asset to an accounting period, while never depreciating an asset below its residual value.

	Method	Useful Life	Depreciable Cost	Depreciation Rate	Depreciation Expense
EXHIBIT 6 **Summary of Depreciation Methods**	Straight-line	Years	Cost less residual value	Straight-line rate*	Constant
	Units-of-production	Total estimated units of production	Cost less residual value	(Cost − Residual value)/Total estimated units of production	Variable
	Double-declining-balance	Years	Declining book value, but not below residual value	Straight-line rate* × 2	Declining

*Straight-line rate = (1/Useful life)

The straight-line method provides for the same periodic amounts of depreciation expense over the life of the asset. The units-of-production method provides for periodic amounts of depreciation expense that vary, depending upon the amount the asset is used.

The double-declining-balance method provides for a higher depreciation amount in the first year of the asset's use, followed by a gradually declining amount. For this reason, the double-declining-balance method is called an **accelerated depreciation method**. It is most appropriate when the decline in an asset's productivity or earning power is greater in the early years of its use than in later years. Further, using this method is often justified because repairs tend to increase with the age of an asset. The reduced amounts of depreciation in later years are thus offset to some extent by increased repair expenses.

The periodic depreciation amounts for the straight-line method and the double-declining-balance method are compared in Exhibit 7. This comparison is based on an asset cost of $24,000, an estimated life of five years, and an estimated residual value of $2,000.

EXHIBIT 7

Comparing
Depreciation Methods

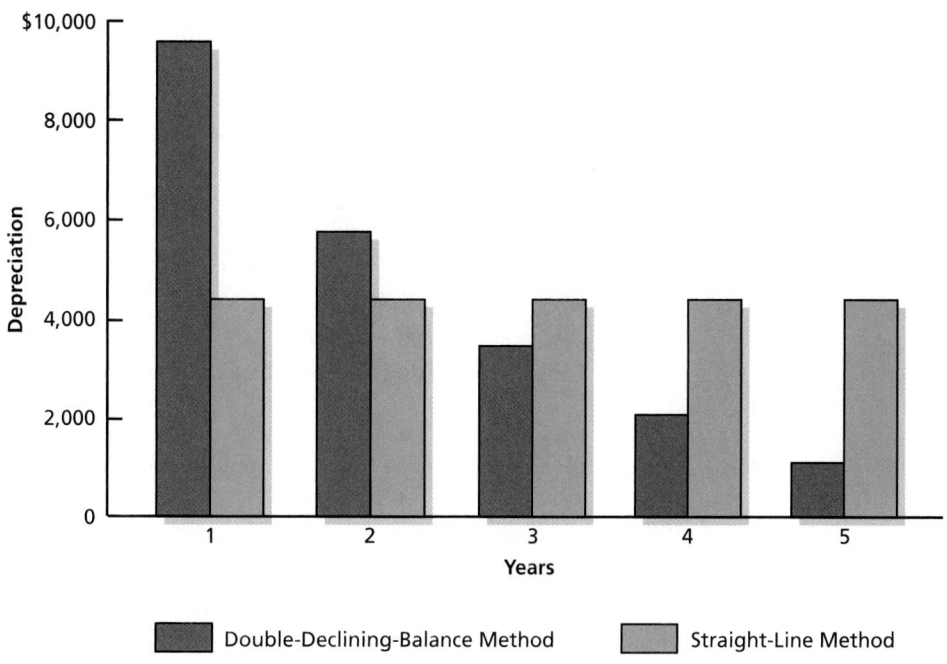

Double-Declining-Balance Method   Straight-Line Method

DEPRECIATION FOR FEDERAL INCOME TAX

The Internal Revenue Code specifies the *Modified Accelerated Cost Recovery System (MACRS)* for use by businesses in computing depreciation for tax purposes. MACRS specifies eight classes of useful life and depreciation rates for each class. The two most common classes, other than real estate, are the five-year class and the seven-year class.[4] The five-year class includes automobiles and light-duty trucks, and the seven-year class includes most machinery and equipment. The depreciation deduction for these two classes is similar to that computed using the double-declining-balance method.

In using the MACRS rates, residual value is ignored, and all fixed assets are assumed to be put in and taken out of service in the middle of the year. For the five-year-class assets, depreciation is spread over six years, as shown in the following MACRS schedule of depreciation rates:

Tax Code Section 179 allows a business to deduct up to $100,000 of the cost of qualified property in the year it is placed in service.

Year	5-Year-Class Depreciation Rates
1	20.0%
2	32.0
3	19.2
4	11.5
5	11.5
6	5.8
	100.0%

---

4 Real estate is in either a 27½ year or a 31½ year class and is depreciated by the straight-line method.

To simplify its record keeping, a business will sometimes use the MACRS method for both financial statement and tax purposes. This is acceptable if MACRS does not result in significantly different amounts than would have been reported using one of the three depreciation methods discussed earlier in this chapter.

REVISING DEPRECIATION ESTIMATES

Revising the estimates of the residual value and the useful life is normal. When these estimates are revised, they are used to determine the depreciation expense in future periods. They do not affect the amounts of depreciation expense recorded in earlier years.[5]

To illustrate, assume that a fixed asset purchased for $140,000 was originally estimated to have a useful life of five years and a residual value of $10,000. The asset has been depreciated for two years by the straight-line method at a rate of $26,000 per year [($140,000 − $10,000)/5 years]. At the end of two years, the asset's book value (undepreciated cost) is $88,000, determined as follows:

Asset cost	$140,000
Less accumulated depreciation ($26,000 per year × 2 years)	52,000
Book value (undepreciated cost), end of second year	$ 88,000

During the third year, the company estimates that the remaining useful life is eight years (instead of three) and that the residual value is $8,000 (instead of $10,000). The depreciation expense for each of the remaining eight years is $10,000, computed as follows:

Book value (undepreciated cost), end of second year	$88,000
Less revised estimated residual value	8,000
Revised remaining depreciable cost	$80,000
Revised annual depreciation expense ($80,000 ÷ 8 years)	$10,000

Exhibit 8 shows the book value of the asset over its original and revised lives. Notice that the book value declines at a slower rate beginning at the end of year 2 and continuing until it reaches the residual value of $8,000 at the end of year 10, which is the revised end of the asset's useful life.

St. Paul Companies recently shortened the useful life of its application software at its data center.

5 *Statement of Financial Accounting Standards No. 154,* "Accounting Changes and Error Corrections" (Financial Accounting Standards Board, Norwalk, CT: 2005).

EXHIBIT 8

Book Value of Asset with Change in Estimate

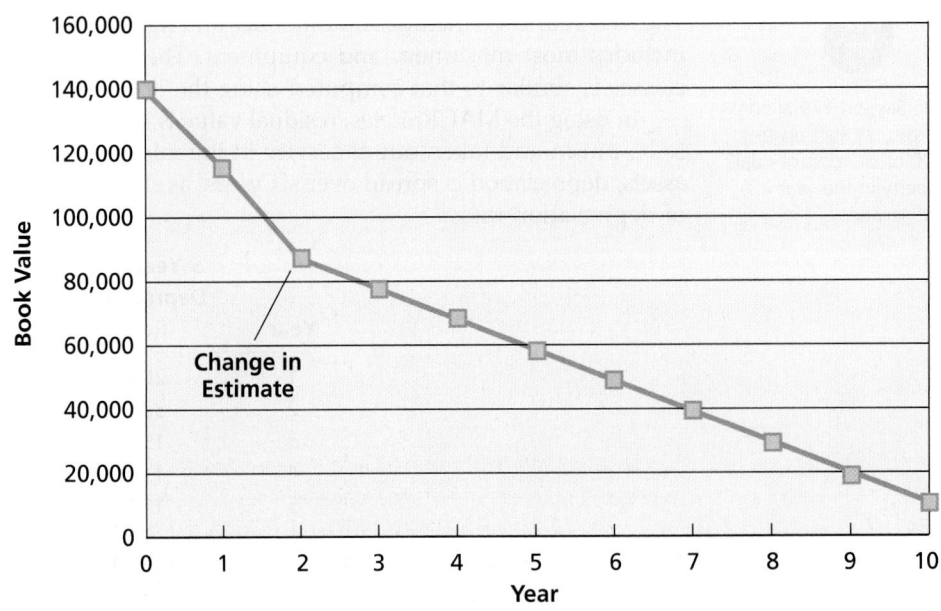

Example Exercise 9-5

objective 2

A warehouse with a cost of $500,000 has an estimated residual value of $120,000, has an estimated useful life of 40 years, and is depreciated by the straight-line method. (a) Determine the amount of the annual depreciation. (b) Determine the book value at the end of the twentieth year of use. (c) Assuming that at the start of the twenty-first year the remaining life is estimated to be 25 years and the residual value is estimated to be $150,000, determine the depreciation expense for each of the remaining 25 years.

Follow My Example 9-5

a. $9,500 [($500,000 − $120,000)/40]
b. $310,000 [$500,000 − ($9,500 × 20)]
c. $6,400 [($310,000 − $150,000)/25]

For Practice: PE 9-5A, PE 9-5B

Disposal of Fixed Assets

objective 3

Journalize entries for the disposal of fixed assets.

Fixed assets that are no longer useful may be discarded, sold, or traded for other fixed assets. The details of the entry to record a disposal will vary. In all cases, however, the book value of the asset must be removed from the accounts. The entry for this purpose debits the asset's accumulated depreciation account for its balance on the date of disposal and credits the asset account for the cost of the asset.

A fixed asset should not be removed from the accounts only because it has been fully depreciated. If the asset is still used by the business, the cost and accumulated depreciation should remain in the ledger. This maintains accountability for the asset in the ledger. If the book value of the asset was removed from the ledger, the accounts would contain no evidence of the continued existence of the asset. In addition, the cost and the accumulated depreciation data on such assets are often needed for property tax and income tax reports.

> The entry to record the disposal of a fixed asset removes the cost of the asset and its accumulated depreciation from the accounts.

DISCARDING FIXED ASSETS

When fixed assets are no longer useful to the business and have no residual or market value, they are discarded. To illustrate, assume that an item of equipment acquired at a cost of $25,000 is fully depreciated at December 31, the end of the preceding fiscal year. On February 14, the equipment is discarded. The entry to record this is as follows:

Feb.	14	Accumulated Depreciation—Equipment	25 0 0 0 00	
		Equipment		25 0 0 0 00
		To write off equipment discarded.		

If an asset has not been fully depreciated, depreciation should be recorded prior to removing it from service and from the accounting records. To illustrate, assume that equipment costing $6,000 with no estimated residual value is depreciated at an annual straight-line rate of 10%. In addition, assume that on December 31 of the preceding fiscal year, the accumulated depreciation balance, after adjusting entries, is $4,750. Finally, assume that the asset is removed from service on the following March 24. The entry to record the depreciation for the three months of the current period prior to the asset's removal from service is as follows:

Mar.	24	Depreciation Expense—Equipment		1 5 0 00		
		Accumulated Depreciation—Equipment			1 5 0 00	
		To record current depreciation on				
		equipment discarded ($600 × ³/₁₂).				

The discarding of the equipment is then recorded by the following entry:

Mar.	24	Accumulated Depreciation—Equipment		4 9 0 0 00		
		Loss on Disposal of Fixed Assets		1 1 0 0 00		
		Equipment			6 0 0 0 00	
		To write off equipment discarded.				

The loss of $1,100 is recorded because the balance of the accumulated depreciation account ($4,900) is less than the balance in the equipment account ($6,000). Losses on the discarding of fixed assets are nonoperating items and are normally reported in the Other Expense section of the income statement.

SELLING FIXED ASSETS

The entry to record the sale of a fixed asset is similar to the entries illustrated above, except that the cash or other asset received must also be recorded. If the selling price is more than the book value of the asset, the transaction results in a gain. If the selling price is less than the book value, there is a loss.

To illustrate, assume that equipment is acquired at a cost of $10,000 with no estimated residual value and is depreciated at an annual straight-line rate of 10%. The equipment is sold for cash on October 12 of the eighth year of its use. The balance of the accumulated depreciation account as of the preceding December 31 is $7,000. The entry to update the depreciation for the nine months of the current year is as follows:

Oct.	12	Depreciation Expense—Equipment		7 5 0 00		
		Accumulated Depreciation—Equipment			7 5 0 00	
		To record current depreciation on				
		equipment sold ($10,000 × ¾ × 10%).				

After the current depreciation is recorded, the book value of the asset is $2,250 ($10,000 − $7,750). The entries to record the sale, assuming three different selling prices, are as follows:

Sold at book value, for $2,250. No gain or loss.

Oct.	12	Cash		2 2 5 0 00		
		Accumulated Depreciation—Equipment		7 7 5 0 00		
		Equipment			10 0 0 0 00	

Sold below book value, for $1,000. Loss of $1,250.

Oct.	12	Cash		1 0 0 0 00		
		Accumulated Depreciation—Equipment		7 7 5 0 00		
		Loss on Disposal of Fixed Assets		1 2 5 0 00		
		Equipment			10 0 0 0 00	

Sold above book value, for $2,800. Gain of $550.	Oct.	12	Cash	2 8 0 0 00	
			Accumulated Depreciation—Equipment	7 7 5 0 00	
			Equipment		10 0 0 0 00
			Gain on Disposal of Fixed Assets		5 5 0 00

Example Exercise 9-6   objective ③

Equipment was acquired at the beginning of the year at a cost of $91,000. The equipment was depreciated using the straight-line method based upon an estimated useful life of nine years and an estimated residual value of $10,000.

a. What was the depreciation for the first year?
b. Assuming the equipment was sold at the end of the second year for $78,000, determine the gain or loss on sale of the equipment.
c. Journalize the entry to record the sale.

Follow My Example 9-6

a. $9,000 [($91,000 − $10,000)/9]
b. $5,000 gain {$78,000 − [$91,000 − ($9,000 × 2)]}

c. Cash 78,000
Accumulated Depreciation—Equipment 18,000
    Equipment 91,000
    Gain on Sale of Equipment 5,000

For Practice: PE 9-6A, PE 9-6B

EXCHANGING SIMILAR FIXED ASSETS

Old equipment is often traded in for new equipment having a similar use. In such cases, the seller allows the buyer an amount for the old equipment traded in.[6] This amount, called the **trade-in allowance**, may be either greater or less than the book value of the old equipment. The remaining balance—the amount owed—is either paid in cash or recorded as a liability. It is normally called **boot**, which is its tax name.

Gains on Exchanges   Gains on exchanges of similar fixed assets are not recognized for financial reporting purposes.[7] This is based on the theory that revenue occurs from the production and sale of goods produced by fixed assets and not from the exchange of similar fixed assets.

Gains on exchanges of similar fixed assets are also not recognized for federal income tax purposes.

When the trade-in allowance exceeds the book value of an asset traded in and no gain is recognized, the cost recorded for the new asset can be determined in either of two ways:

1. Cost of new asset = List price of new asset − Unrecognized gain

or

2. Cost of new asset = Cash given (or liability assumed) + Book value of old asset

---

6 We assume that exchanges of equipment having similar use will not significantly change the company's future cash flows. As a result, such exchanges are said be to lacking in commercial substance as defined by *Statement of Financial Accounting Standards No. 153*, "Exchanges of Nonmonetary Assets" (Financial Accounting Standards Board, Norwalk, CT: 2004).
7 Gains on exchanges of similar fixed assets are recognized if cash (boot) is received. This topic is discussed in advanced accounting texts.

To illustrate, assume the following exchange:

Similar equipment acquired (new):

List price of new equipment	$5,000
Trade-in allowance on old equipment	1,100
Cash paid at June 19, date of exchange	$3,900

Equipment traded in (old):

Cost of old equipment	$4,000
Accumulated depreciation at date of exchange	3,200
Book value at June 19, date of exchange	$ 800

Recorded cost of new equipment:

Method One:

List price of new equipment		$5,000
Trade-in allowance	$1,100	
Book value of old equipment	800	
Unrecognized gain on exchange		(300)
Cost of new equipment		$4,700

Method Two:

Book value of old equipment	$ 800
Cash paid at date of exchange	3,900
Cost of new equipment	$4,700

The entry to record this exchange and the payment of cash is as follows:

June	19	Accumulated Depreciation—Equipment	3 2 0 0 00	
		Equipment (new equipment)	4 7 0 0 00	
		Equipment (old equipment)		4 0 0 0 00
		Cash		3 9 0 0 00
		To record exchange of equipment.		

Not recognizing the $300 gain ($1,100 trade-in allowance minus $800 book value) at the time of the exchange reduces future depreciation expense. That is, the depreciation expense for the new asset is based on a cost of $4,700 rather than on the list price of $5,000. In effect, the unrecognized gain of $300 reduces the total amount of depreciation taken during the life of the equipment by $300.

Losses on exchanges of similar fixed assets are *not* recognized for federal income tax purposes.

Losses on Exchanges   For financial reporting purposes, losses are recognized on exchanges of similar fixed assets if the trade-in allowance is less than the book value of the old equipment. When there is a loss, the cost recorded for the new asset should be the market (list) price. To illustrate, assume the following exchange:

Similar equipment acquired (new):

List price of new equipment	$10,000
Trade-in allowance on old equipment	2,000
Cash paid at September 7, date of exchange	$ 8,000

Equipment traded in (old):

Cost of old equipment	$ 7,000
Accumulated depreciation at date of exchange	4,600
Book value at September 7, date of exchange	$ 2,400
Trade-in allowance on old equipment	2,000
Loss on exchange	$ 400

The entry to record the exchange is as follows:

Sept.	7	Accumulated Depreciation—Equipment	4 6 0 0 00		
		Equipment	10 0 0 0 00		
		Loss on Disposal of Fixed Assets	4 0 0 00		
		Equipment		7 0 0 0 00	
		Cash		8 0 0 0 00	
		To record exchange of equipment,			
		with loss.			

Review of Accounting for Exchanges of Similar Fixed Assets   Exhibit 9 reviews the accounting for exchanges of similar fixed assets, using the following data:

List price of new equipment acquired	$15,000
Cost of old equipment traded in	$12,500
Accumulated depreciation at date of exchange	10,100
Book value at date of exchange	$ 2,400

EXHIBIT 9

Summary Illustration— Accounting for Exchanges of Similar Fixed Assets

---

CASE ONE (GAIN): Trade-in allowance is more than book value of asset traded in.

Trade-in allowance, $3,000; cash paid, $12,000 ($15,000 – $3,000)

Cost of new asset	List price of new asset acquired, less unrecognized gain: $14,400 [$15,000 – ($3,000 – $2,400)] or Cash paid plus book value of asset traded in: $14,400 ($12,000 + $2,400)
Gain recognized	None
Entry	Equipment 14,400
	Accumulated Depreciation 10,100
	Equipment 12,500
	Cash 12,000

CASE TWO (LOSS): Trade-in allowance is less than book value of asset traded in.

Trade-in allowance, $2,000; cash paid, $13,000 ($15,000 – $2,000)

Cost of new asset	List price of new asset acquired: $15,000
Loss recognized	$400
Entry	Equipment 15,000
	Accumulated Depreciation 10,100
	Loss on Disposal of Fixed Assets 400
	Equipment 12,500
	Cash 13,000

Example Exercise 9-7   objective **3**

On the first day of the fiscal year, a delivery truck with a list price of $75,000 was acquired in exchange for an old delivery truck and $63,000 cash. The old truck had a cost of $50,000 and accumulated depreciation of $39,500.

a. Determine the cost of the new truck for financial reporting purposes.
b. Journalize the entry to record the exchange.

(continued)

Follow My Example 9-7

a. $73,500

List price of new truck		$75,000
Trade-in allowance on old truck ($75,000 − $63,000)	$12,000	
Book value of old truck ($50,000 − $39,500)	10,500	
Unrecognized gain on exchange		(1,500)
Cost of new truck		$73,500

or

Book value of old truck ($50,000 − $39,500)	$10,500
Plus cash paid at date of exchange	63,000
Cost of new truck	$73,500

b.
Truck (new)	73,500	
Accumulated Depreciation—Truck (old)	39,500	
Truck (old)		50,000
Cash		63,000

For Practice: PE 9-7A, PE 9-7B

Natural Resources

The fixed assets of some businesses include timber, metal ores, minerals, or other natural resources. As these businesses harvest or mine and then sell these resources, a portion of the cost of acquiring them must be debited to an expense account. This process of transferring the cost of natural resources to an expense account is called **depletion**. The amount of depletion is determined by multiplying the quantity extracted during the period by the depletion rate. This rate is computed by dividing the cost of the mineral deposit by its estimated size.

Computing depletion is similar to computing units-of-production depreciation. To illustrate, assume that a business paid $400,000 for the mining rights to a mineral deposit estimated at 1,000,000 tons of ore. The depletion rate is $0.40 per ton ($400,000/1,000,000 tons). If 90,000 tons are mined during the year, the periodic depletion is $36,000 (90,000 tons × $0.40). The adjusting entry to record the depletion is shown below.

Dec.	31	Depletion Expense	36 0 0 0 00	
		Accumulated Depletion		36 0 0 0 00
		Depletion of mineral deposit.		

Like the accumulated depreciation account, Accumulated Depletion is a *contra asset* account. It is reported on the balance sheet as a deduction from the cost of the mineral deposit.

Example Exercise 9-8

Earth's Treasures Mining Co. acquired mineral rights for $45,000,000. The mineral deposit is estimated at 50,000,000 tons. During the current year, 12,600,000 tons were mined and sold.

a. Determine the depletion rate.
b. Determine the amount of depletion expense for the current year.
c. Journalize the adjusting entry on December 31 to recognize the depletion expense.

Follow My Example 9-8

a. $0.90 per ton = $45,000,000/50,000,000 tons
b. $11,340,000 = (12,600,000 tons × $0.90 per ton)

c. Dec. 31   Depletion Expense 11,340,000
                  Accumulated Depletion   11,340,000
                  Depletion of mineral deposit.

For Practice: PE 9-8A, PE 9-8B

Intangible Assets

objective 5

Describe the accounting for intangible assets, such as patents, copyrights, and goodwill.

Patents, copyrights, trademarks, and goodwill are long-lived assets that are useful in the operations of a business and are not held for sale. These assets are called **intangible assets** because they do not exist physically.

The basic principles of accounting for intangible assets are like those described earlier for fixed assets. The major concerns are determining (1) the initial cost and (2) the **amortization**—the amount of cost to transfer to expense. Amortization results from the passage of time or a decline in the usefulness of the intangible asset.

PATENTS

Apple Computer, Inc., amortizes intangible assets over 3–10 years.

Manufacturers may acquire exclusive rights to produce and sell goods with one or more unique features. Such rights are granted by **patents**, which the federal government issues to inventors. These rights continue in effect for 20 years. A business may purchase patent rights from others, or it may obtain patents developed by its own research and development efforts.

The initial cost of a purchased patent, including any related legal fees, is debited to an asset account. This cost is written off, or amortized, over the years of the patent's expected usefulness. This period of time may be less than the remaining legal life of the patent. The estimated useful life of the patent may also change as technology or consumer tastes change.

The straight-line method is normally used to determine the periodic amortization. When the amortization is recorded, it is debited to an expense account and credited directly to the patents account. A separate contra asset account is usually *not* used for intangible assets.

To illustrate, assume that at the beginning of its fiscal year, a business acquires patent rights for $100,000. The patent had been granted six years earlier by the Federal Patent Office. Although the patent will not expire for 14 years, its remaining useful life is estimated as five years. The adjusting entry to amortize the patent at the end of the year is as follows:

Dec.	31	Amortization Expense—Patents	20 0 0 0 00	
		Patents		20 0 0 0 00
		Patent amortization ($100,000/5).		

Rather than purchase patent rights, a business may incur significant costs in developing patents through its own research and development efforts. Such *research and development costs* are usually accounted for as current operating expenses in the period in which they are incurred. Expensing research and development costs is justified because the future benefits from research and development efforts are highly uncertain.

COPYRIGHTS AND TRADEMARKS

The exclusive right to publish and sell a literary, artistic, or musical composition is granted by a **copyright**. Copyrights are issued by the federal government and extend for 70 years beyond the author's death. The costs of a copyright include all costs of creating the work plus any administrative or legal costs of obtaining the copyright. A copyright that is purchased from another should be recorded at the price paid for it. Copyrights are amortized over their estimated useful lives. For example, Sony Corporation of America states the following amortization policy with respect to its artistic and music intangible assets:

> *Intangibles, which mainly consist of artist contracts and music catalogs, are being amortized on a straight-line basis principally over 16 years and 21 years, respectively.*

Coke® is one of the world's most recognizable trademarks. As stated in *LIFE*, "Two-thirds of the earth is covered by water; the rest is covered by Coke. If the French are known for wine and the Germans for beer, America achieved global beverage dominance with fizzy water and caramel color."

A **trademark** is a name, term, or symbol used to identify a business and its products. For example, The Coca-Cola Company's distinctive red-and-white Coke logo is an example of a trademark. Most businesses identify their trademarks with ® in their advertisements and on their products. Under federal law, businesses can protect against others using their trademarks by registering them for 10 years and renewing the registration for 10-year periods thereafter. Like a copyright, the legal costs of registering a trademark with the federal government are recorded as an asset. Thus, even though the Coca-Cola trademarks are extremely valuable, they are not shown on the balance sheet, because the legal costs for establishing these trademarks are immaterial. If, however, a trademark is purchased from another business, the cost of its purchase is recorded as an asset. The cost of a trademark is in most cases considered to have an indefinite useful life. Thus, trademarks are not amortized over a useful life, as are the previously discussed intangible assets. Rather, trademarks should be tested periodically for impaired value. When a trademark is impaired from competitive threats or other circumstances, the trademark should be written down and a loss recognized.

Integrity, Objectivity, and Ethics in Business

21ST CENTURY PIRATES

Pirated software is a major concern of software companies. For example, during a recent global sweep, Microsoft Corporation seized nearly five million units of counterfeit Microsoft software with an estimated retail value of $1.7 billion. U.S. copyright laws and practices are sometimes ignored or disputed in other parts of the world.

Businesses must honor the copyrights held by software companies by eliminating pirated software from cor-

porate computers. The Business Software Alliance (BSA) represents the largest software companies in campaigns to investigate illegal use of unlicensed software by businesses. The BSA estimates software industry losses of nearly $12 billion annually from software piracy. Employees using pirated software on business assets risk bringing legal penalties to themselves and their employers.

GOODWILL

In business, **goodwill** refers to an intangible asset of a business that is created from such favorable factors as location, product quality, reputation, and managerial skill. Goodwill allows a business to earn a rate of return on its investment that is often in excess of the normal rate for other firms in the same business.

Generally accepted accounting principles permit goodwill to be recorded in the accounts only if it is objectively determined by a transaction. An example of such a transaction is the purchase of a business at a price in excess of the net assets (assets − liabilities) of the acquired business. The excess is recorded as goodwill and reported as an intangible asset. Unlike patents and copyrights, goodwill is not amortized. However, a loss should be recorded if the business prospects of the acquired firm become significantly impaired. This loss would normally be disclosed in the Other Expense section of the income statement. To illustrate, Time Warner recorded one of the largest losses in corporate history (nearly $54 billion) for the write-down of goodwill associated with the AOL and Time Warner merger. The entry is recorded as follows:

Loss from Impaired Goodwill	54 0 0 0 0 0 0 0 0 0 00		
Goodwill		54 0 0 0 0 0 0 0 0 0 00	
Impaired goodwill.			

Exhibit 10 shows the frequency of intangible asset disclosures for a sample of 600 large firms. As you can see, goodwill is the most frequently reported intangible asset. This is because goodwill arises from merger transactions, which are common.

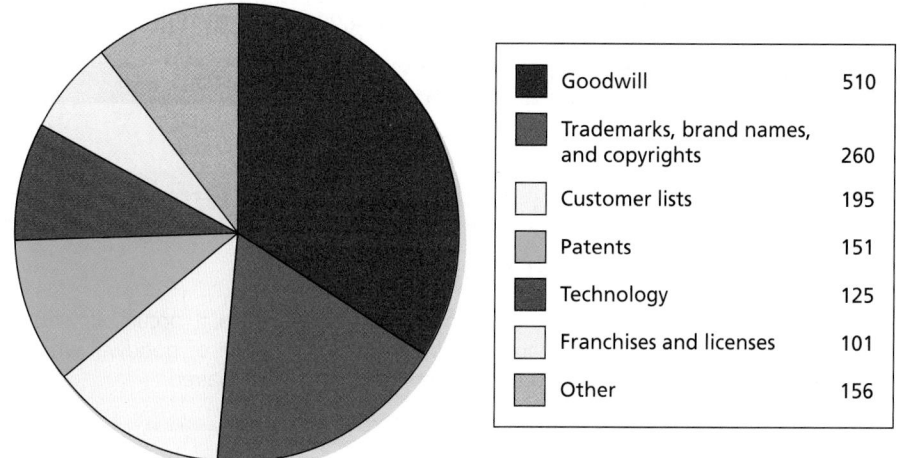

EXHIBIT 10

Frequency of
Intangible Asset
Disclosures for
600 Firms

■	Goodwill	510
■	Trademarks, brand names, and copyrights	260
□	Customer lists	195
▨	Patents	151
■	Technology	125
□	Franchises and licenses	101
▨	Other	156

Source: Accounting Trends & Techniques, 59th ed., American Institute of Certified Public Accountants, New York, 2005.
Note: Some firms have multiple disclosures.

Exhibit 11 summarizes the characteristics of intangible assets discussed in this section. Patents and copyrights are examples of intangible assets with finite lives and are thus subject to periodic amortization based upon their estimated useful lives. Trademarks and goodwill are examples of intangible assets with indefinite lives and are thus not subject to periodic amortization. Rather, intangible assets with indefinite lives are tested periodically for impairment. If the intangible asset is impaired, then the intangible asset's carrying value is written down, and an impairment loss is recognized for the period.

EXHIBIT 11

Comparison of
Intangible Assets

Intangible Asset	Description	Amortization Period	Periodic Expense
Patent	Exclusive right to benefit from an innovation.	Estimated useful life not to exceed legal life.	Amortization expense.
Copyright	Exclusive right to benefit from a literary, artistic, or musical composition.	Estimated useful life not to exceed legal life.	Amortization expense.
Trademark	Exclusive use of a name, term, or symbol.	None	Impairment loss if fair value less than carrying value (impaired).
Goodwill	Excess of purchase price of a business over its net assets.	None	Impairment loss if fair value less than carrying value (impaired).

Example Exercise 9-9

objective **5**

On December 31, it was estimated that goodwill of $40,000 was impaired. In addition, a patent with an estimated useful economic life of 12 years was acquired for $84,000 on July 1.

a. Journalize the adjusting entry on December 31 for the impaired goodwill.
b. Journalize the adjusting entry on December 31 for the amortization of the patent rights.

Follow My Example 9-9

a.	Dec. 31	Loss from Impaired Goodwill	40,000	
		Goodwill		40,000
		Impaired goodwill.		
b.	Dec. 31	Amortization Expense—Patents	3,500	
		Patents		3,500
		Amortized patent rights [($84,000/12) × (6/12)].		

For Practice: PE 9-9A, PE 9-9B

Integrity, Objectivity, and Ethics in Business

ETHICS

WHEN DOES GOODWILL BECOME WORTHLESS?

The timing and amount of goodwill write-offs can be very subjective. Managers and their accountants should fairly estimate the value of goodwill and record goodwill impairment when it occurs. It would be unethical to delay a write-down of goodwill when it is determined that the asset is impaired.

Financial Reporting for Fixed Assets and Intangible Assets

objective **6**

Describe how depreciation expense is reported in an income statement and prepare a balance sheet that includes fixed assets and intangible assets.

How should fixed assets and intangible assets be reported in the financial statements? The amount of depreciation and amortization expense of a period should be reported separately in the income statement or disclosed in a note. A general description of the method or methods used in computing depreciation should also be reported.

The amount of each major class of fixed assets should be disclosed in the balance sheet or in notes. The related accumulated depreciation should also be disclosed, either by major class or in total. The fixed assets may be shown at their *book value* (cost less accumulated depreciation), which can also be described as their *net* amount. To illustrate, the net book value of office equipment originally costing $125,750 with accumulated depreciation of $86,300 is shown below.

Office equipment	$125,750
Less accumulated depreciation	86,300
Net book value	$ 39,450

If there are too many classes of fixed assets, a single amount may be presented in the balance sheet, supported by a separate detailed listing. Fixed assets are normally presented under the more descriptive caption of *property, plant, and equipment*.

The cost of mineral rights or ore deposits is normally shown as part of the Fixed Assets section of the balance sheet. The related accumulated depletion should also be disclosed. In some cases, the mineral rights are shown net of depletion on the face of the balance sheet, accompanied by a note that discloses the amount of the accumulated depletion.

Intangible assets are usually reported in the balance sheet in a separate section immediately following fixed assets. The balance of each major class of intangible assets should be disclosed at an amount net of amortization taken to date. Exhibit 12 is a partial balance sheet that shows the reporting of fixed assets and intangible assets.

EXHIBIT 12

Fixed Assets and
Intangible Assets in
the Balance Sheet

Discovery Mining Co.
Balance Sheet
December 31, 2008

Assets

	Cost	Accum. Depr.	Book Value		
Total current assets					$ 462,500
Property, plant, and equipment:					
Land	$ 30,000	—	$ 30,000		
Buildings	110,000	$ 26,000	84,000		
Factory equipment	650,000	192,000	458,000		
Office equipment	120,000	13,000	107,000		
	$ 910,000	$ 231,000		$679,000	
	Cost	Accum. Depl.	Book Value		
Mineral deposits:					
Alaska deposit	$1,200,000	$ 800,000	$400,000		
Wyoming deposit	750,000	200,000	550,000		
	$1,950,000	$1,000,000		950,000	
Total property, plant, and equipment					1,629,000
Intangible assets:					
Patents				$ 75,000	
Goodwill				50,000	
Total intangible assets					125,000

Business Connections

REAL WORLD

HUB-AND-SPOKE OR POINT-TO-POINT?

Southwest Airlines Co. uses a simple fare structure, featuring low, unrestricted, unlimited, everyday coach fares. These fares are made possible by Southwest's use of a point-to-point, rather than hub-and-spoke, business approach. United Airlines, Inc., Delta Air Lines, and American Airlines employ a hub-and-spoke approach in which an airline establishes major hubs that serve as connecting links to other cities. For example, Delta has established major connecting hubs in Atlanta, Cincinnati, and Salt Lake City. In contrast, Southwest focuses on point-to-point service between selected cities with over 300 one-way, nonstop city pairs with an average length of 500 miles and average fly-ing time of 1.5 hours. As a result, Southwest minimizes connections, delays, and total trip time. Southwest also focuses on serving conveniently located satellite or downtown airports, such as Dallas Love Field, Houston Hobby, and Chicago Midway. Because these airports are normally less congested than hub airports, Southwest is better able to maintain high employee productivity and reliable ontime performance. This operating approach permits the company to achieve high utilization of its fixed assets, such as its 737 aircraft. For example, aircraft are scheduled to spend only 25 minutes at the gate, thereby reducing the number of aircraft and gate facilities that would otherwise be required.

© MATT SLOCUM/ASSOCIATED PRESS

Financial Analysis and Interpretation

Fixed assets can be evaluated by their ability to generate revenue. One measure of the revenue-generating efficiency of fixed assets is the fixed asset turnover ratio. The **fixed asset turnover ratio** measures the number of dollars of revenue earned per dollar of fixed assets and is computed as follows:

$$\text{Fixed Asset Turnover Ratio} = \frac{\text{Revenue}}{\text{Average Book Value of Fixed Assets}}$$

To illustrate, the following fixed asset balance sheet information is used for Marriott International, Inc.:

	December 31, 2005 (in millions)	January 2, 2005 (in millions)
Property and equipment (net)	$2,341	$2,389

Marriott reported revenue of $11,550 million for 2005. Thus, the fixed asset turnover ratio is calculated as follows:

$$\text{Fixed Asset Turnover Ratio} = \frac{\$11,550}{(\$2,341 + \$2,389)/2} = 4.88$$

For every dollar of fixed assets, Marriott earns $4.88 of revenue. The larger this ratio, the more efficiently a business is using its fixed assets. This ratio can be compared across time within a single firm or to other companies in the industry to evaluate overall fixed asset turnover performance. For example, the fixed asset turnover ratios for Starwood Hotels & Resorts Worldwide, Inc. and Choice Hotels International, Inc. are 0.76 and 8.4, respectively. Marriott is operating its hotel assets at an efficiency level between that of Starwood and Choice.

The fixed asset turnover ratio for a number of different businesses is shown below. The smaller ratios are associated with companies that require large fixed asset investments. The larger fixed asset turnover ratios are associated with firms that are more labor-intensive and require smaller fixed asset investments.

Company (industry)	Fixed Asset Turnover Ratio
Comcast Corporation (cable)	1.00
Computer Associates International, Inc. (consulting)	5.00
Google (Internet)	12.15
Manpower Inc. (temporary employment)	65.15
Norfolk Southern Corporation (railroad)	0.35
Ruby Tuesday, Inc. (restaurant)	1.47
Southwest Airlines Co. (airline)	0.84

Appendix

Sum-of-the-Years-Digits Depreciation

A recent edition of *Accounting Trends & Techniques* reported that only 1%–2% of the surveyed companies now use this method for financial reporting purposes.

At one time, the sum-of-the-years-digits method of depreciation was used by many businesses. However, tax law changes limited its use for tax purposes.

Under the *sum-of-the-years-digits method*, depreciation expense is determined by multiplying the original cost of the asset less its estimated residual value by a smaller fraction each year. Thus, the sum-of-the-years-digits method is similar to the double-declining-balance method in that the depreciation expense declines each year.

The denominator of the fraction used in determining the depreciation expense is the sum of the digits of the years of the asset's useful life. For example, an asset with a useful life of five years would have a denominator of 15 (5 + 4 + 3 + 2 + 1).[8] The

---

8 The denominator can also be determined from the following formula: $S = N[(N + 1)/2]$, where S = sum of the digits and N = number of years of estimated life.

numerator of the fraction is the number of years of useful life remaining at the beginning of each year for which depreciation is being computed. Thus, the numerator decreases each year by 1. For a useful life of five years, the numerator is 5 the first year, 4 the second year, 3 the third year, and so on.

The following depreciation schedule illustrates the sum-of-the-years-digits method for an asset with a cost of $24,000, an estimated residual value of $2,000, and an estimated useful life of five years:

Year	Cost Less Residual Value	Rate	Depreciation for Year	Accum. Depr. at End of Year	Book Value at End of Year
1	$22,000	$5/15$	$7,333.33	$ 7,333.33	$16,666.67
2	22,000	$4/15$	5,866.67	13,200.00	10,800.00
3	22,000	$3/15$	4,400.00	17,600.00	6,400.00
4	22,000	$2/15$	2,933.33	20,533.33	3,466.67
5	22,000	$1/15$	1,466.67	22,000.00	2,000.00

What if the fixed asset is not placed in service at the beginning of the year? When the date an asset is first put into service is not the beginning of a fiscal year, each full year's depreciation must be allocated between the two fiscal years benefited. To illustrate, assume that the asset in the above example was put into service at the beginning of the fourth month of the first fiscal year. The depreciation for that year would be $5,500 ($9/12 \times 5/15 \times $22,000$). The depreciation for the second year would be $6,233.33, computed as follows:

$3/12 \times 5/15 \times$ $22,000	$1,833.33
$9/12 \times 4/15 \times$ $22,000	4,400.00
Total depreciation for second fiscal year	$6,233.33

At a Glance

1. Define, classify, and account for the cost of fixed assets.

Key Points	Key Learning Outcomes	Example Exercises	Practice Exercises
Fixed assets are long-term tangible assets that are owned by the business and are used in the normal operations of the business such as equipment, buildings, and land. The initial cost of a fixed asset includes all amounts spent to get the asset in place and ready for use. Once an asset is placed into service, revenue and capital expenditures may be incurred. Revenue expenditures include ordinary repairs and maintenance. Capital expenditures include asset improvements and extraordinary repairs. Fixed assets may also be leased and accounted for as capital or operating leases.	• Define *fixed assets*. • List types of costs that should and should not be included in the cost of a fixed asset. • Provide examples of ordinary repairs, asset improvements, and extraordinary repairs. • Prepare journal entries for ordinary repairs, asset improvements, and extraordinary repairs.	9-1	9-1A, 9-1B

(continued)

2. Compute depreciation, using the following methods: straight-line method, units-of-production method, and double-declining-balance method.

Key Points	Key Learning Outcomes	Example Exercises	Practice Exercises
All fixed assets except land lose their ability to provide services and should be depreciated over time. Three factors are considered in determining depreciation: (1) the fixed asset's initial cost, (2) the useful life of the asset, and (3) the residual value of the asset.	• Define and describe *depreciation*. • List the factors used in determining depreciation.		
The straight-line method spreads the initial cost less the residual value equally over the useful life. The units-of-production method spreads the initial cost less the residual value equally over the units expected to be produced by the asset during its useful life. The double-declining-balance method is applied by multiplying the declining book value of the asset by twice the straight-line rate.	• Compute straight-line depreciation. • Compute units-of-production depreciation. • Compute double-declining-balance depreciation.	9-2 9-3 9-4	9-2A, 9-2B 9-3A, 9-3B 9-4A, 9-4B
Depreciation may be revised for changes in an asset's useful life or residual value. Such changes affect future depreciation.	• Compute revised depreciation for a change in an asset's useful life and residual value.	9-5	9-5A, 9-5B

3. Journalize entries for the disposal of fixed assets.

Key Points	Key Learning Outcomes	Example Exercises	Practice Exercises
To record disposals of fixed assets, any depreciation for the current period should be recorded, and the book value of the asset is then removed from the accounts. For assets discarded from service, a loss may be recorded for any remaining book value of the asset.	• Prepare the journal entry for discarding a fixed asset.		
When a fixed asset is sold, the book value is removed, and the cash or other asset received is recorded. If the selling price is more than the book value of the asset, the transaction results in a gain. If the selling price is less than the book value, there is a loss.	• Prepare journal entries for the sale of a fixed asset.	9-6	9-6A, 9-6B
When a fixed asset is exchanged for another of similar nature, no gain is recognized on the exchange. The acquired asset's cost is adjusted for any gains. A loss on an exchange of similar assets is recorded.	• Prepare journal entries for the exchange of similar fixed assets.	9-7	9-7A, 9-7B

4. Compute depletion and journalize the entry for depletion.

Key Points	Key Learning Outcomes	Example Exercises	Practice Exercises
The amount of periodic depletion is computed by multiplying the quantity of minerals extracted during the period by a depletion rate. The depletion rate is computed by dividing the cost of the mineral deposit by its estimated size. The entry to record depletion debits a depletion expense account and credits an accumulated depletion account.	• Define and describe *depletion*. • Compute a depletion rate. • Prepare the journal entry to record depletion.	 9-8 9-8	 9-8A, 9-8B 9-8A, 9-8B

5. Describe the accounting for intangible assets, such as patents, copyrights, and goodwill.

Key Points	Key Learning Outcomes	Example Exercises	Practice Exercises
Long-term assets such as patents, copyrights, trademarks, and goodwill that are without physical attributes but are used in the business are intangible assets. The initial cost of an intangible asset should be debited to an asset account. The cost of patents and copyrights should be amortized over the years of the asset's expected usefulness by debiting an expense account and crediting the intangible asset account. Trademarks and goodwill are not amortized but are written down only upon impairment.	• Define, describe, and provide examples of intangible assets. • Prepare a journal entry for the purchase of an intangible asset. • Prepare a journal entry to amortize the costs of patents and copyrights. • Prepare the journal entry to record the impairment of goodwill.	9-9 9-9	9-9A, 9-9B 9-9A, 9-9B

6. Describe how depreciation expense is reported in an income statement and prepare a balance sheet that includes fixed assets and intangible assets.

Key Points	Key Learning Outcomes	Example Exercises	Practice Exercises
The amount of depreciation expense and the method or methods used in computing depreciation should be disclosed in the financial statements. In addition, each major class of fixed assets should be disclosed, along with the related accumulated depreciation. Intangible assets are usually presented in the balance sheet in a separate section immediately following fixed assets. Each major class of intangible assets should be disclosed at an amount net of the amortization recorded to date.	• Describe and illustrate how fixed assets are reported on the income statement and balance sheet. • Describe and illustrate how intangible assets are reported on the income statement and balance sheet.		

Key Terms

accelerated depreciation method (404)
amortization (413)
book value (403)
boot (409)
capital expenditures (398)
capital lease (399)
copyright (414)

depletion (412)
depreciation (400)
double-declining-balance method (403)
fixed asset turnover ratio (418)
fixed assets (395)
goodwill (414)
intangible assets (413)

operating lease (399)
patents (413)
residual value (400)
revenue expenditures (398)
straight-line method (402)
trade-in allowance (409)
trademark (414)
units-of-production method (402)

Illustrative Problem

McCollum Company, a furniture wholesaler, acquired new equipment at a cost of $150,000 at the beginning of the fiscal year. The equipment has an estimated life of five years and an estimated residual value of $12,000. Ellen McCollum, the president, has requested information regarding alternative depreciation methods.

Instructions

1. Determine the annual depreciation for each of the five years of estimated useful life of the equipment, the accumulated depreciation at the end of each year, and the book value of the equipment at the end of each year by (a) the straight-line method and (b) the double-declining-balance method.
2. Assume that the equipment was depreciated under the double-declining-balance method. In the first week of the fifth year, the equipment was traded in for similar equipment priced at $175,000. The trade-in allowance on the old equipment was $10,000, and cash was paid for the balance. Journalize the entry to record the exchange.

Solution

1.

	Year	Depreciation Expense	Accumulated Depreciation, End of Year	Book Value, End of Year
a.	1	$27,600*	$ 27,600	$122,400
	2	27,600	55,200	94,800
	3	27,600	82,800	67,200
	4	27,600	110,400	39,600
	5	27,600	138,000	12,000

*$27,600 = ($150,000 − $12,000) ÷ 5

	Year	Depreciation Expense	Accumulated Depreciation, End of Year	Book Value, End of Year
b.	1	$60,000**	$ 60,000	$ 90,000
	2	36,000	96,000	54,000
	3	21,600	117,600	32,400
	4	12,960	130,560	19,440
	5	7,440***	138,000	12,000

**$60,000 = $150,000 × 40%
***The asset is not depreciated below the estimated residual value of $12,000.

2.

Accumulated Depreciation—Equipment	130 5 6 0 00		
Equipment	175 0 0 0 00		
Loss on Disposal of Fixed Assets	9 4 4 0 00		
Equipment		150 0 0 0 00	
Cash		165 0 0 0 00	

Self-Examination Questions   (Answers at End of Chapter)

1. Which of the following expenditures incurred in connection with acquiring machinery is a proper charge to the asset account?
   A. Freight
   B. Installation costs
   C. Both A and B
   D. Neither A nor B

2. What is the amount of depreciation, using the double-declining-balance method for the second year of use for equipment costing $9,000, with an estimated residual value of $600 and an estimated life of three years?
   A. $6,000
   B. $3,000
   C. $2,000
   D. $400

3. An example of an accelerated depreciation method is:
   A. straight-line.
   B. double-declining-balance.
   C. units-of-production.
   D. depletion.

4. A fixed asset priced at $100,000 is acquired by trading in a similar asset that has a book value of $25,000. Assuming that the trade-in allowance is $30,000 and that $70,000 cash is paid for the new asset, what is the cost of the new asset for financial reporting purposes?
   A. $100,000
   B. $95,000
   C. $70,000
   D. $30,000

5. Which of the following is an example of an intangible asset?
   A. Patents
   B. Goodwill
   C. Copyrights
   D. All of the above

Eye Openers

1. Which of the following qualities are characteristic of fixed assets? (a) tangible, (b) capable of repeated use in the operations of the business, (c) held for sale in the normal course of business, (d) used rarely in the operations of the business, (e) long-lived.

2. Office Outfitters Co. has a fleet of automobiles and trucks for use by salespersons and for delivery of office supplies and equipment. Westgate Auto Sales Co. has automobiles and trucks for sale. Under what caption would the automobiles and trucks be reported on the balance sheet of (a) Office Outfitters Co., (b) Westgate Auto Sales Co.?

3. Design Space Co. acquired an adjacent vacant lot with the hope of selling it in the future at a gain. The lot is not intended to be used in Design Space's business operations. Where should such real estate be listed in the balance sheet?

4. Triplent Company solicited bids from several contractors to construct an addition to its office building. The lowest bid received was for $750,000. Triplent Company decided to construct the addition itself at a cost of $590,000. What amount should be recorded in the building account?

5. Distinguish between the accounting for capital expenditures and revenue expenditures.

6. Immediately after a used truck is acquired, a new motor is installed and the tires are replaced at a total cost of $4,150. Is this a capital expenditure or a revenue expenditure?

7. How does the accounting for a capital lease differ from the accounting for an operating lease?

8. Are the amounts at which fixed assets are reported in the balance sheet their approximate market values as of the balance sheet date? Discuss.

9. a. Does the recognition of depreciation in the accounts provide a special cash fund for the replacement of fixed assets? Explain.
   b. Describe the nature of depreciation as the term is used in accounting.

10. Emporium Company purchased a machine that has a manufacturer's suggested life of 20 years. The company plans to use the machine on a special project that will last 13 years. At the completion of the project, the machine will be sold. Over how many years should the machine be depreciated?

11. Is it necessary for a business to use the same method of computing depreciation (a) for all classes of its depreciable assets, (b) in the financial statements and in determining income taxes?

12. a. Under what conditions is the use of an accelerated depreciation method most appropriate?
    b. Why is an accelerated depreciation method often used for income tax purposes?
    c. What is the Modified Accelerated Cost Recovery System (MACRS), and under what conditions is it used?

13. A company revised the estimated useful lives of its fixed assets, which resulted in an increase in the remaining lives of several assets. Can the company include, as income of the current period, the cumulative effect of the changes, which reduces the depreciation expense of past periods? Discuss.

14. For some of the fixed assets of a business, the balance in Accumulated Depreciation is exactly equal to the cost of the asset. (a) Is it permissible to record additional depreciation on the assets if they are still useful to the business? Explain. (b) When should an entry be made to remove the cost and the accumulated depreciation from the accounts?

15. a. Over what period of time should the cost of a patent acquired by purchase be amortized?
    b. In general, what is the required accounting treatment for research and development costs?
    c. How should goodwill be amortized?

Practice Exercises

PE 9-1A
Capital and revenue expenditure entries
obj. 1

On February 13, Scandia Co. paid $1,650 to install a hydraulic lift and $25 for an air filter for one of its delivery trucks. Journalize the entries for the new lift and air filter expenditures.

PE 9-1B
Capital and revenue expenditure entries
obj. 1

On August 30, Stop Shop Co. paid $1,325 to repair the transmission on one of its delivery vans. In addition, Stop Shop paid $1,100 to install a GPS system in its van. Journalize the entries for the transmission and GPS system expenditures.

PE 9-2A
Straight-line depreciation
obj. 2

Equipment acquired at the beginning of the year at a cost of $88,000 has an estimated residual value of $6,000 and an estimated useful life of five years. Determine (a) the depreciable cost, (b) the straight-line rate, and (c) the annual straight-line depreciation.

PE 9-2B
Straight-line depreciation
obj. 2

A building acquired at the beginning of the year at a cost of $316,000 has an estimated residual value of $48,000 and an estimated useful life of 40 years. Determine (a) the depreciable cost, (b) the straight-line rate, and (c) the annual straight-line depreciation.

PE 9-3A
Units-of-production depreciation
obj. 2

A tractor acquired at a cost of $120,000 has an estimated residual value of $5,000, has an estimated useful life of 50,000 hours, and was operated 4,200 hours during the year. Determine (a) the depreciable cost, (b) the depreciation rate, and (c) the units-of-production depreciation for the year.

PE 9-3B
Units-of-production depreciation
obj. 2

A truck acquired at a cost of $90,000 has an estimated residual value of $18,000, has an estimated useful life of 200,000 miles, and was driven 40,000 miles during the year. Determine (a) the depreciable cost, (b) the depreciation rate, and (c) the units-of-production depreciation for the year.

PE 9-4A
Double-declining-balance depreciation
obj. 2

Equipment acquired at the beginning of the year at a cost of $88,000 has an estimated residual value of $6,000 and an estimated useful life of five years. Determine (a) the depreciable cost, (b) the double-declining-balance rate, and (c) the double-declining-balance depreciation for the first year.

PE 9-4B
Double-declining-balance depreciation
obj. 2

A building acquired at the beginning of the year at a cost of $316,000 has an estimated residual value of $48,000 and an estimated useful life of 40 years. Determine (a) the depreciable cost, (b) the double-declining-balance rate, and (c) the double-declining-balance depreciation for the first year.

PE 9-5A
Revision of depreciation estimates
obj. 2

A truck with a cost of $90,000 has an estimated residual value of $15,000, has an estimated useful life of eight years, and is depreciated by the straight-line method. (a) Determine the amount of the annual depreciation. (b) Determine the book value at the end of the fourth year of use. (c) Assuming that at the start of the fifth year the remaining life is estimated to be five years and the residual value is estimated to be $12,500, determine the depreciation expense for each of the remaining five years.

PE 9-5B
Revision of depreciation estimates
obj. 2

Equipment with a cost of $189,000 has an estimated residual value of $24,000, has an estimated useful life of 15 years, and is depreciated by the straight-line method. (a) Determine the amount of the annual depreciation. (b) Determine the book value at the end of the ninth year of use. (c) Assuming that at the start of the tenth year the remaining life is estimated to be eight years and the residual value is estimated to be $6,000, determine the depreciation expense for each of the remaining eight years.

PE 9-6A
Sale of equipment
obj. 3

Equipment was acquired at the beginning of the year at a cost of $158,000. The equipment was depreciated using the straight-line method based upon an estimated useful life of 10 years and an estimated residual value of $28,000.

a. What was the depreciation for the first year?
b. Assuming the equipment was sold at the end of the fifth year for $86,000, determine the gain or loss on the sale of the equipment.
c. Journalize the entry to record the sale.

PE 9-6B
Sale of equipment
obj. 3

Equipment was acquired at the beginning of the year at a cost of $250,000. The equipment was depreciated using the double-declining-balance method based upon an estimated useful life of 10 years and an estimated residual value of $45,000.

a. What was the depreciation for the first year?
b. Assuming the equipment was sold at the end of the second year for $142,000, determine the gain or loss on the sale of the equipment.
c. Journalize the entry to record the sale.

PE 9-7A
Exchange of similar fixed assets
obj. 3

On the first day of the fiscal year, equipment with a list price of $160,000 was acquired in exchange for similar equipment and $136,000 cash. The old equipment had a cost of $99,000 and accumulated depreciation of $79,000.

a. Determine the cost of the new truck for financial reporting purposes.
b. Journalize the entry to record the exchange.

PE 9-7B
Exchange of similar fixed assets
obj. 3

On the first day of the fiscal year, a delivery truck with a list price of $90,000 was acquired in exchange for an old delivery truck and $74,500 cash. The old truck had a cost of $60,000 and accumulated depreciation of $42,000.

a. Determine the cost of the new truck for financial reporting purposes.
b. Journalize the entry to record the exchange.

PE 9-8A
Entry for depletion of mineral rights
obj. 4

Butte Mining Co. acquired mineral rights for $36,000,000. The mineral deposit is estimated at 75,000,000 tons. During the current year, 29,350,000 tons were mined and sold.

a. Determine the depletion rate.
b. Determine the amount of depletion expense for the current year.
c. Journalize the adjusting entry on December 31 to recognize the depletion expense.

PE 9-8B
Entry for depletion of mineral rights
obj. 4

Rocky Mountain Mining Co. acquired mineral rights for $88,000,000. The mineral deposit is estimated at 110,000,000 tons. During the current year, 33,800,000 tons were mined and sold.

a. Determine the depletion rate.
b. Determine the amount of depletion expense for the current year.
c. Journalize the adjusting entry on December 31 to recognize the depletion expense.

PE 9-9A
Entries for impaired goodwill and amortization of patent
obj. 5

On December 31, it was estimated that goodwill of $100,000 was impaired. In addition, a patent with an estimated useful economic life of 12 years was acquired for $450,000 on June 1.

a. Journalize the adjusting entry on December 31 for the impaired goodwill.
b. Journalize the adjusting entry on December 31 for the amortization of the patent rights.

PE 9-9B
Entries for impaired goodwill and amortization of patent
obj. 5

On December 31, it was estimated that goodwill of $375,000 was impaired. In addition, a patent with an estimated useful economic life of 10 years was acquired for $600,000 on October 1.

a. Journalize the adjusting entry on December 31 for the impaired goodwill.
b. Journalize the adjusting entry on December 31 for the amortization of the patent rights.

Exercises

EX 9-1
Costs of acquiring fixed assets
obj. 1

Kelly Melnik owns and operates Aaladin Print Co. During July, Aaladin Print Co. incurred the following costs in acquiring two printing presses. One printing press was new, and the other was used by a business that recently filed for bankruptcy.

Costs related to new printing press:

1. Sales tax on purchase price
2. Insurance while in transit
3. Freight
4. Special foundation
5. Fee paid to factory representative for installation
6. New parts to replace those damaged in unloading

Costs related to used printing press:

7. Fees paid to attorney to review purchase agreement
8. Installation
9. Repair of vandalism during installation
10. Replacement of worn-out parts
11. Freight
12. Repair of damage incurred in reconditioning the press

a. Indicate which costs incurred in acquiring the new printing press should be debited to the asset account.
b. Indicate which costs incurred in acquiring the used printing press should be debited to the asset account.

EX 9-2
Determine cost of land
obj. 1

Serenity Ski Co. has developed a tract of land into a ski resort. The company has cut the trees, cleared and graded the land and hills, and constructed ski lifts. (a) Should the tree cutting, land clearing, and grading costs of constructing the ski slopes be debited to the land account? (b) If such costs are debited to Land, should they be depreciated?

EX 9-3
Determine cost of land
obj. 1
✓ *$224,650*

Next Day Delivery Company acquired an adjacent lot to construct a new warehouse, paying $25,000 and giving a short-term note for $175,000. Legal fees paid were $1,200, delinquent taxes assumed were $10,850, and fees paid to remove an old building from the land were $15,000. Materials salvaged from the demolition of the building were sold for $2,400. A contractor was paid $760,000 to construct a new warehouse. Determine the cost of the land to be reported on the balance sheet.

EX 9-4
Capital and revenue expenditures
obj. 1

Thare Co. incurred the following costs related to trucks and vans used in operating its delivery service:

1. Changed the oil and greased the joints of all the trucks and vans.
2. Installed security systems on four of the newer trucks.
3. Changed the radiator fluid on a truck that had been in service for the past four years.
4. Installed a hydraulic lift to a van.
5. Removed a two-way radio from one of the trucks and installed a new radio with a greater range of communication.
6. Overhauled the engine on one of the trucks that had been purchased three years ago.
7. Tinted the back and side windows of one of the vans to discourage theft of contents.
8. Repaired a flat tire on one of the vans.
9. Rebuilt the transmission on one of the vans that had been driven 40,000 miles. The van was no longer under warranty.
10. Replaced the trucks' suspension system with a new suspension system that allows for the delivery of heavier loads.

Classify each of the costs as a capital expenditure or a revenue expenditure.

EX 9-5
Capital and revenue expenditures
obj. 1

Felix Little owns and operates Big Sky Transport Co. During the past year, Felix incurred the following costs related to his 18-wheel truck:

1. Replaced a headlight that had burned out.
2. Replaced fog and cab light bulbs.
3. Installed a television in the sleeping compartment of the truck.
4. Removed the old CB radio and replaced it with a newer model with a greater range.
5. Replaced a shock absorber that had worn out.
6. Installed a wind deflector on top of the cab to increase fuel mileage.
7. Replaced the old radar detector with a newer model that detects the KA frequencies now used by many of the state patrol radar guns. The detector is wired directly into the cab, so that it is partially hidden. In addition, Felix fastened the detector to the truck with a locking device that prevents its removal.
8. Changed engine oil.
9. Replaced the hydraulic brake system that had begun to fail during his latest trip through the Rocky Mountains.
10. Modified the factory-installed turbo charger with a special-order kit designed to add 50 more horsepower to the engine performance.

Classify each of the costs as a capital expenditure or a revenue expenditure.

EX 9-6
Capital and revenue expenditures
obj. 1

Load All Company made the following expenditures on one of its delivery trucks:

Feb. 22. Replaced transmission at a cost of $2,300.
Mar. 20. Paid $900 for installation of a hydraulic lift.
Nov. 2. Paid $67 to change the oil and air filter.

Prepare journal entries for each expenditure.

EX 9-7
Nature of depreciation
obj. 2

Armored Metal Co. reported $975,600 for equipment and $600,000 for accumulated depreciation—equipment on its balance sheet.
➤ Does this mean (a) that the replacement cost of the equipment is $975,600 and (b) that $600,000 is set aside in a special fund for the replacement of the equipment? Explain.

EX 9-8
Straight-line depreciation rates
obj. 2
✓ a. 50%

Convert each of the following estimates of useful life to a straight-line depreciation rate, stated as a percentage, assuming that the residual value of the fixed asset is to be ignored: (a) 2 years, (b) 8 years, (c) 10 years, (d) 20 years, (e) 25 years, (f) 40 years, (g) 50 years.

EX 9-9
Straight-line depreciation
obj. 2
✓ $11,200

A refrigerator used by a meat processor has a cost of $198,500, an estimated residual value of $30,500, and an estimated useful life of 15 years. What is the amount of the annual depreciation computed by the straight-line method?

EX 9-10
Depreciation by units-of-production method
obj. 2
✓ $893

A diesel-powered tractor with a cost of $215,000 and estimated residual value of $27,000 is expected to have a useful operating life of 80,000 hours. During October, the generator was operated 380 hours. Determine the depreciation for the month.

EX 9-11
Depreciation by units-of-production method
obj. 2

Prior to adjustment at the end of the year, the balance in Trucks is $225,900 and the balance in Accumulated Depreciation—Trucks is $87,010. Details of the subsidiary ledger are as follows:

✓ *a. Truck #1, credit*
Accumulated
Depreciation, $15,120

Truck No.	Cost	Estimated Residual Value	Estimated Useful Life	Accumulated Depreciation at Beginning of Year	Miles Operated During Year
1	$75,000	$12,000	150,000 miles	$19,110	36,000 miles
2	72,900	9,900	300,000	59,850	18,000
3	38,000	3,000	200,000	8,050	36,000
4	40,000	4,000	120,000	—	16,000

a. Determine the depreciation rates per mile and the amount to be credited to the accumulated depreciation section of each of the subsidiary accounts for the miles operated during the current year.
b. Journalize the entry to record depreciation for the year.

EX 9-12
Depreciation by two methods
obj. 2
✓ *a. $2,800*

A John Deere tractor acquired on January 5 at a cost of $44,800 has an estimated useful life of 16 years. Assuming that it will have no residual value, determine the depreciation for each of the first two years (a) by the straight-line method and (b) by the double-declining-balance method. Round to the nearest dollar.

EX 9-13
Depreciation by two methods
obj. 2
✓ *a. $9,500*

A storage tank acquired at the beginning of the fiscal year at a cost of $86,000 has an estimated residual value of $10,000 and an estimated useful life of eight years. Determine the following: (a) the amount of annual depreciation by the straight-line method and (b) the amount of depreciation for the first and second year computed by the double-declining-balance method.

EX 9-14
Partial-year depreciation
obj. 2
✓ *a. First year, $1,250*

Sandblasting equipment acquired at a cost of $68,000 has an estimated residual value of $18,000 and an estimated useful life of 10 years. It was placed in service on October 1 of the current fiscal year, which ends on December 31. Determine the depreciation for the current fiscal year and for the following fiscal year by (a) the straight-line method and (b) the double-declining-balance method.

EX 9-15
Revision of depreciation
obj. 2
✓ *a. $12,500*

A building with a cost of $750,000 has an estimated residual value of $300,000, has an estimated useful life of 36 years, and is depreciated by the straight-line method. (a) What is the amount of the annual depreciation? (b) What is the book value at the end of the twentieth year of use? (c) If at the start of the twenty-first year it is estimated that the remaining life is 20 years and that the residual value is $200,000, what is the depreciation expense for each of the remaining 20 years?

EX 9-16
Capital expenditure and depreciation
objs. 1, 2
✓ *b. Depreciation Expense, $2,400*

Sime Company purchased and installed carpet in its new general offices on March 29 for a total cost of $48,000. The carpet is estimated to have a 15-year useful life and no residual value.

a. Prepare the journal entries necessary for recording the purchase of the new carpet.
b. Record the December 31 adjusting entry for the partial-year depreciation expense for the carpet, assuming that Sime Company uses the straight-line method.

EX 9-17
Entries for sale of fixed asset
obj. 3

Equipment acquired on January 3, 2005, at a cost of $360,000, has an estimated useful life of 12 years, has an estimated residual value of $30,000, and is depreciated by the straight-line method.

a. What was the book value of the equipment at December 31, 2008, the end of the year?
b. Assuming that the equipment was sold on April 1, 2009, for $220,000, journalize the entries to record (1) depreciation for the three months until the sale date, and (2) the sale of the equipment.

EX 9-18
Disposal of fixed asset
obj. 3
✓ b. $98,750

Equipment acquired on January 3, 2005, at a cost of $147,500, has an estimated useful life of eight years and an estimated residual value of $17,500.

a. What was the annual amount of depreciation for the years 2005, 2006, and 2007, using the straight-line method of depreciation?
b. What was the book value of the equipment on January 1, 2008?
c. Assuming that the equipment was sold on January 2, 2008, for $95,000, journalize the entry to record the sale.
d. Assuming that the equipment had been sold on January 2, 2008, for $100,000 instead of $95,000, journalize the entry to record the sale.

EX 9-19
Asset traded for similar asset
obj. 3
✓ a. $200,000

A printing press priced at $280,000 is acquired by trading in a similar press and paying cash for the difference between the trade-in allowance and the price of the new press.

a. Assuming that the trade-in allowance is $80,000, what is the amount of cash given?
b. Assuming that the book value of the press traded in is $78,750, what is the cost of the new press for financial reporting purposes?

EX 9-20
Asset traded for similar asset
obj. 3
✓ a. $200,000

Assume the same facts as in Exercise 9-19, except that the book value of the press traded in is $103,250. (a) What is the amount of cash given? (b) What is the cost of the new press for financial reporting purposes?

EX 9-21
Entries for trade of fixed asset
obj. 3

On October 1, Clear Springs Co., a water distiller, acquired new bottling equipment with a list price of $288,750. Clear Springs received a trade-in allowance of $60,000 on the old equipment of a similar type, paid cash of $28,750, and gave a series of five notes payable for the remainder. The following information about the old equipment is obtained from the account in the equipment ledger: cost, $210,000; accumulated depreciation on December 31, the end of the preceding fiscal year, $137,500; annual depreciation, $12,500. Journalize the entries to record (a) the current depreciation of the old equipment to the date of trade-in and (b) the exchange transaction on October 1 for financial reporting purposes.

EX 9-22
Entries for trade of fixed asset
obj. 3

On April 1, Senorita's Delivery Services acquired a new truck with a list price of $75,000. Senorita's received a trade-in allowance of $15,000 on an old truck of similar type, paid cash of $10,000, and gave a series of five notes payable for the remainder. The following information about the old truck is obtained from the account in the equipment ledger: cost, $48,000; accumulated depreciation on December 31, the end of the preceding fiscal year, $32,000; annual depreciation, $8,000. Journalize the entries to record (a) the current depreciation of the old truck to the date of trade-in and (b) the transaction on April 1 for financial reporting purposes.

EX 9-23
Depreciable cost of asset acquired by exchange
obj. 3

On the first day of the fiscal year, a delivery truck with a list price of $86,500 was acquired in exchange for an old delivery truck and $75,000 cash. The old truck had a book value of $15,675 at the date of the exchange.

a. Determine the depreciable cost for financial reporting purposes.
b. Assuming that the book value of the old delivery truck was $6,000, determine the depreciable cost for financial reporting purposes.

EX 9-24
Depletion entries
obj. 4
✓ a. $4,500,000

Rainbow Mining Co. acquired mineral rights for $30,000,000. The mineral deposit is estimated at 75,000,000 tons. During the current year, 11,250,000 tons were mined and sold.

a. Determine the amount of depletion expense for the current year.
b. Journalize the adjusting entry to recognize the depletion expense.

EX 9-25
Amortization entries
obj. 5

✓ a. $52,850

Venture Company acquired patent rights on January 3, 2005, for $661,500. The patent has a useful life equal to its legal life of 15 years. On January 5, 2008, Venture successfully defended the patent in a lawsuit at a cost of $105,000.

a. Determine the patent amortization expense for the current year ended December 31, 2008.
b. Journalize the adjusting entry to recognize the amortization.

EX 9-26
Book value of fixed assets
obj. 6

Apple Computer, Inc., designs, manufactures, and markets personal computers and related software. Apple also manufactures and distributes music players (Ipod) along with related accessories and services, including the on-line distribution of third-party music. The following information was taken from a recent annual report of Apple:

Property, Plant, and Equipment (in millions):

	Current Year	Preceding Year
Land and buildings	$361	$351
Machinery, equipment, and internal-use software	494	422
Office furniture and equipment	81	79
Other fixed assets related to leases	545	446
Accumulated depreciation and amortization	664	591

a. Compute the book value of the fixed assets for the current year and the preceding year and explain the differences, if any.
b. 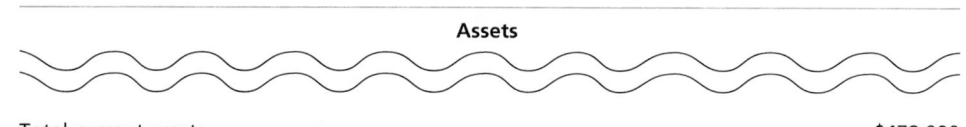 Would you normally expect the book value of fixed assets to increase or decrease during the year?

EX 9-27
Balance sheet presentation
obj. 6

List the errors you find in the following partial balance sheet:

Planet Bronze Company
Balance Sheet
December 31, 2008

Assets

Total current assets $478,000

	Replacement Cost	Accumulated Depreciation	Book Value
Property, plant, and equipment:			
Land	$ 80,000	$ 16,000	$ 64,000
Buildings	208,000	60,800	147,200
Factory equipment	440,000	233,600	206,400
Office equipment	96,000	64,000	32,000
Patents	64,000	—	64,000
Goodwill	36,000	4,000	32,000
Total property, plant, and equipment	$924,000	$378,400	545,600

EX 9-28
Fixed asset turnover ratio

Verizon Communications is a major telecommunications company in the United States. Verizon's balance sheet disclosed the following information regarding fixed assets:

	Dec. 31, 2005 (in millions)	Dec. 31, 2004 (in millions)
Plant, property, and equipment	$193,610	$185,522
Less accumulated depreciation	118,305	111,398
	$ 75,305	$ 74,124

Verizon's revenue for 2005 was $75,112 million. The fixed asset turnover for the telecommunications industry averages 1.10.

a. Determine Verizon's fixed asset turnover ratio. Round to two decimal places.
b. ▭▬▶ Interpret Verizon's fixed asset turnover ratio.

EX 9-29
Fixed asset turnover ratio

The following table shows the revenue and average net fixed assets (in millions) for a recent fiscal year for Best Buy and Circuit City Stores, Inc.:

	Revenue	Average Net Fixed Assets
Best Buy	$27,433	$2,354
Circuit City Stores, Inc.	10,472	662

a Compute the fixed asset turnover for each company. Round to two decimal places.
b. ▭▬▶ Which company uses its fixed assets more efficiently? Explain.

APPENDIX EX 9-30
Sum-of-the-years-digits depreciation

✓ First year: $5,271

Based on the data in Exercise 9-12, determine the depreciation for the John Deere tractor for each of the first two years, using the sum-of-the-years-digits depreciation method. Round to the nearest dollar.

APPENDIX EX 9-31
Sum-of-the-years-digits depreciation

✓ First year: $16,889

Based on the data in Exercise 9-13, determine the depreciation for the storage tank for each of the first two years, using the sum-of-the-years-digits depreciation method. Round to the nearest dollar.

APPENDIX EX 9-32
Partial-year depreciation

✓ First year: $2,273

Based on the data in Exercise 9-14, determine the depreciation for the sandblasting equipment for each of the first two years, using the sum-of-the-years-digits depreciation method. Round to the nearest dollar.

Problems Series A

PR 9-1A
Allocate payments and receipts to fixed asset accounts

obj. 1

✓ Land $443,200

The following payments and receipts are related to land, land improvements, and buildings acquired for use in a wholesale ceramic business. The receipts are identified by an asterisk.

a. Fee paid to attorney for title search .... $ 3,000
b. Cost of real estate acquired as a plant site: Land 325,000
                                                    Building 75,000
c. Delinquent real estate taxes on property, assumed by purchaser 10,000
d. Special assessment paid to city for extension of water main to the
   property 12,800
e. Cost of razing and removing building 3,900
f. Proceeds from sale of salvage materials from old building 4,000*
g. Cost of filling and grading land 17,500
h. Architect's and engineer's fees for plans and supervision 40,000
i. Premium on one-year insurance policy during construction 4,800
j. Cost of trees and shrubbery planted 9,000
k. Money borrowed to pay building contractor 800,000*
l. Cost of paving parking lot to be used by customers 15,000
m. Cost of repairing windstorm damage during construction 2,000

(continued)

n. Cost of repairing vandalism damage during construction . . . . $ 2,500

o. Cost of floodlights installed on parking lot   1,100

p. Interest incurred on building loan during construction   42,000

q. Payment to building contractor for new building   915,000

r. Proceeds from insurance company for windstorm and vandalism damage . .   4,000*

s. Refund of premium on insurance policy (i) canceled after 11 months 400*

Instructions

1. Assign each payment and receipt to Land (unlimited life), Land Improvements (limited life), Building, or Other Accounts. Indicate receipts by an asterisk. Identify each item by letter and list the amounts in columnar form, as follows:

Item	Land	Land Improvements	Building	Other Accounts

2. Determine the amount debited to Land, Land Improvements, and Building.

3. ◀▬▬▶ The costs assigned to the land, which is used as a plant site, will not be depreciated, while the costs assigned to land improvements will be depreciated. Explain this seemingly contradictory application of the concept of depreciation.

PR 9-2A

Compare three depreciation methods

obj. 2

✓ *a. 2006: straight-line depreciation, $28,000*

Air Pack Company purchased packaging equipment on January 3, 2006, for $90,000. The equipment was expected to have a useful life of three years, or 21,000 operating hours, and a residual value of $6,000. The equipment was used for 8,000 hours during 2006, 7,500 hours in 2007, and 5,500 hours in 2008.

Instructions

Determine the amount of depreciation expense for the years ended December 31, 2006, 2007, and 2008, by (a) the straight-line method, (b) the units-of-production method, and (c) the double-declining-balance method. Also determine the total depreciation expense for the three years by each method. The following columnar headings are suggested for recording the depreciation expense amounts:

	Depreciation Expense		
Year	Straight-Line Method	Units-of-Production Method	Double-Declining-Balance Method

---

PR 9-3A

Depreciation by three methods; partial years

obj. 2

✓ *a. 2006: $1,255*

Covershot Company purchased plastic laminating equipment on July 1, 2006, for $7,830. The equipment was expected to have a useful life of three years, or 10,040 operating hours, and a residual value of $300. The equipment was used for 1,600 hours during 2006, 3,800 hours in 2007, 3,400 hours in 2008, and 1,240 hours in 2009.

Instructions

Determine the amount of depreciation expense for the years ended December 31, 2006, 2007, 2008, and 2009, by (a) the straight-line method, (b) the units-of-production method, and (c) the double-declining-balance method. Round to the nearest dollar.

PR 9-4A

Depreciation by two methods; trade of fixed asset

objs. 2, 3

✓ *1. b. Year 1: $70,000 depreciation expense*

✓ *2. $237,680*

New lithographic equipment, acquired at a cost of $175,000 at the beginning of a fiscal year, has an estimated useful life of five years and an estimated residual value of $15,000. The manager requested information regarding the effect of alternative methods on the amount of depreciation expense each year. On the basis of the data presented to the manager, the double-declining-balance method was selected.

    In the first week of the fifth year, the equipment was traded in for similar equipment priced at $240,000. The trade-in allowance on the old equipment was $25,000, cash of $15,000 was paid, and a note payable was issued for the balance.

Instructions

1. Determine the annual depreciation expense for each of the estimated five years of use, the accumulated depreciation at the end of each year, and the book value of the equipment at the end of each year by (a) the straight-line method and (b) the double-declining-balance method. The following columnar headings are suggested for each schedule:

Year	Depreciation Expense	Accumulated Depreciation, End of Year	Book Value, End of Year

2. For financial reporting purposes, determine the cost of the new equipment acquired in the exchange.
3. Journalize the entry to record the exchange.
4. Journalize the entry to record the exchange, assuming that the trade-in allowance was $18,000 instead of $25,000.

PR 9-5A

Transactions for fixed assets, including trade

objs. 1, 2, 3

The following transactions, adjusting entries, and closing entries were completed by Willow Run Furniture Co. during a three-year period. All are related to the use of delivery equipment. The double-declining-balance method of depreciation is used.

2006

Jan. 9. Purchased a used delivery truck for $32,000, paying cash.
Sept. 24. Paid garage $470 for miscellaneous repairs to the truck.
Dec. 31. Recorded depreciation on the truck for the year. The estimated useful life of the truck is four years, with a residual value of $4,500 for the truck.

2007

Jan. 1. Purchased a new truck for $57,500, paying cash.
June 30. Sold the used truck for $13,500. (Record depreciation to date in 2007 for the truck.)
Nov. 23. Paid garage $550 for miscellaneous repairs to the truck.
Dec. 31. Recorded depreciation on the truck. It has an estimated residual value of $12,000 and an estimated life of five years.

2008

July 1. Purchased a new truck for $60,000, paying cash.
Oct. 1. Sold the truck purchased January 1, 2007, for $22,000. (Record depreciation for the year.)
Dec. 31. Recorded depreciation on the remaining truck. It has an estimated residual value of $15,000 and an estimated useful life of eight years.

Instructions

Journalize the transactions and the adjusting entries.

PR 9-6A

Amortization and depletion entries

objs. 4, 5

✓1. a. $216,000

Data related to the acquisition of timber rights and intangible assets during the current year ended December 31 are as follows:

a. Timber rights on a tract of land were purchased for $648,000 on July 5. The stand of timber is estimated at 3,600,000 board feet. During the current year, 1,200,000 board feet of timber were cut and sold.
b. Goodwill in the amount of $27,000,000 was purchased on January 7.
c. Governmental and legal costs of $780,000 were incurred on October 4 in obtaining a patent with an estimated economic life of 12 years. Amortization is to be for one-fourth year.

Instructions

1. Determine the amount of the amortization or depletion expense for the current year for each of the foregoing items.
2. Journalize the adjusting entries required to record the amortization or depletion for each item.

Problems Series B

PR 9-1B
*Allocate payments and
receipts to fixed asset
accounts*

obj. 1

✓ *Land: $322,400*

The following payments and receipts are related to land, land improvements, and buildings acquired for use in a wholesale apparel business. The receipts are identified by an
asterisk.

a. Finder's fee paid to real estate agency	$ 7,500
b. Cost of real estate acquired as a plant site: Land	210,000
Building	50,000
c. Fee paid to attorney for title search	2,500
d. Delinquent real estate taxes on property, assumed by purchaser	20,650
e. Cost of razing and removing building	16,250
f. Cost of filling and grading land	12,500
g. Proceeds from sale of salvage materials from old building	5,000*
h. Architect's and engineer's fees for plans and supervision	36,000
i. Special assessment paid to city for extension of water main to the	
property	8,000
j. Premium on one-year insurance policy during construction	3,600
k. Money borrowed to pay building contractor	900,000*
l. Cost of trees and shrubbery planted	18,000
m. Cost of repairing windstorm damage during construction	3,000
n. Cost of repairing vandalism damage during construction	4,200
o. Cost of paving parking lot to be used by customers	15,000
p. Proceeds from insurance company for windstorm and vandalism	
damage	7,000*
q. Interest incurred on building loan during construction	54,000
r. Payment to building contractor for new building	1,000,000
s. Refund of premium on insurance policy (j) canceled after 10 months	600*

Instructions

1. Assign each payment and receipt to Land (unlimited life), Land Improvements (limited
   life), Building, or Other Accounts. Indicate receipts by an asterisk. Identify each item by
   letter and list the amounts in columnar form, as follows:

Item	Land	Land Improvements	Building	Other Accounts

2. Determine the amount debited to Land, Land Improvements, and Building.
3. ▭▶ The costs assigned to the land, which is used as a plant site, will not be depreciated, while the costs assigned to land improvements will be depreciated. Explain this
   seemingly contradictory application of the concept of depreciation.

PR 9-2B
*Compare three
depreciation methods*

obj. 2

✓ *a. 2007: straight-line
depreciation, $107,500*

Seal Coatings Company purchased waterproofing equipment on January 2, 2007, for
$475,000. The equipment was expected to have a useful life of four years, or 21,500 operat-
ing hours, and a residual value of $45,000. The equipment was used for 7,600 hours dur-
ing 2007, 6,800 hours in 2008, 5,100 hours in 2009, and 2,000 hours in 2010.

Instructions

Determine the amount of depreciation expense for the years ended December 31, 2007, 2008,
2009, and 2010, by (a) the straight-line method, (b) the units-of-production method, and (c)
the double-declining-balance method. Also determine the total depreciation expense for the
four years by each method. The following columnar headings are suggested for recording
the depreciation expense amounts:

	Depreciation Expense		
Year	Straight-Line Method	Units-of-Production Method	Double-Declining-Balance Method

PR 9-3B

Depreciation by three methods; partial years

obj. 2

✓ *a. 2006, $15,200*

E-Sharp Company purchased tool sharpening equipment on July 1, 2006, for $97,200. The equipment was expected to have a useful life of three years, or 22,800 operating hours, and a residual value of $6,000. The equipment was used for 3,650 hours during 2006, 8,000 hours in 2007, 7,850 hours in 2008, and 3,300 hours in 2009.

Instructions

Determine the amount of depreciation expense for the years ended December 31, 2006, 2007, 2008, and 2009, by (a) the straight-line method, (b) the units-of-production method, and (c) the double-declining-balance method.

PR 9-4B

Depreciation by two methods; trade of fixed asset

objs. 2, 3

✓ *1. b. Year 1, $120,000 depreciation expense*

✓ *2. $310,000*

New tire retreading equipment, acquired at a cost of $240,000 at the beginning of a fiscal year, has an estimated useful life of four years and an estimated residual value of $18,000. The manager requested information regarding the effect of alternative methods on the amount of depreciation expense each year. On the basis of the data presented to the manager, the double-declining-balance method was selected.

In the first week of the fourth year, the equipment was traded in for similar equipment priced at $325,000. The trade-in allowance on the old equipment was $45,000, cash of $10,000 was paid, and a note payable was issued for the balance.

Instructions

1. Determine the annual depreciation expense for each of the estimated four years of use, the accumulated depreciation at the end of each year, and the book value of the equipment at the end of each year by (a) the straight-line method and (b) the double-declining-balance method. The following columnar headings are suggested for each schedule:

Year	Depreciation Expense	Accumulated Depreciation, End of Year	Book Value, End of Year

2. For financial reporting purposes, determine the cost of the new equipment acquired in the exchange.
3. Journalize the entry to record the exchange.
4. Journalize the entry to record the exchange, assuming that the trade-in allowance was $25,000 instead of $45,000.

PR 9-5B

Transactions for fixed assets, including trade

objs. 1, 2, 3

The following transactions, adjusting entries, and closing entries were completed by Crown Furniture Co. during a three-year period. All are related to the use of delivery equipment. The double-declining-balance method of depreciation is used.

2006

Jan. 9. Purchased a used delivery truck for $38,000, paying cash.

Mar. 15. Paid garage $180 for changing the oil, replacing the oil filter, and tuning the engine on the delivery truck.

Dec. 31. Recorded depreciation on the truck for the fiscal year. The estimated useful life of the truck is eight years, with a residual value of $7,000 for the truck.

2007

Jan. 3. Purchased a new truck for $62,500, paying cash.

Feb. 20. Paid garage $150 to tune the engine and make other minor repairs on the used truck.

Apr. 30. Sold the used truck for $25,000. (Record depreciation to date in 2007 for the truck.)

Dec. 31. Recorded depreciation on the truck. It has an estimated trade-in value of $12,000 and an estimated life of 10 years.

2008

July 1. Purchased a new truck for $70,000, paying cash.

Oct. 6. Sold the truck purchased January 3, 2007, for $43,900. (Record depreciation for the year.)

Dec. 31. Recorded depreciation on the remaining truck. It has an estimated residual value of $4,500 and an estimated useful life of 10 years.

Instructions

Journalize the transactions and the adjusting entries.

PR 9-6B
Amortization and depletion entries
objs. 4, 5

✓ *1. b. $23,750*

Data related to the acquisition of timber rights and intangible assets during the current year ended December 31 are as follows:

a. Goodwill in the amount of $15,000,000 was purchased on January 11.
b. Governmental and legal costs of $475,000 were incurred on June 30 in obtaining a patent with an estimated economic life of 10 years. Amortization is to be for one-half year.
c. Timber rights on a tract of land were purchased for $900,000 on April 6. The stand of timber is estimated at 6,000,000 board feet. During the current year, 800,000 board feet of timber were cut and sold.

Instructions

1. Determine the amount of the amortization or depletion expense for the current year for each of the foregoing items.
2. Journalize the adjusting entries to record the amortization or depletion expense for each item.

Special Activities

SA 9-1
Ethics and professional conduct in business

ETHICS

Leah Corbin, CPA, is an assistant to the controller of Beartooth Consulting Co. In her spare time, Leah also prepares tax returns and performs general accounting services for clients. Frequently, Leah performs these services after her normal working hours, using Beartooth Consulting Co.'s computers and laser printers. Occasionally, Leah's clients will call her at the office during regular working hours.

Discuss whether Leah is performing in a professional manner.

SA 9-2
Financial vs. tax depreciation

The following is an excerpt from a conversation between two employees of Resource Technologies, Haley Eubanks and Clay Hamon. Haley is the accounts payable clerk, and Clay is the cashier.

Haley: Clay, could I get your opinion on something?
Clay: Sure, Haley.
Haley: Do you know Amber, the fixed assets clerk?
Clay: I know who she is, but I don't know her real well. Why?
Haley: Well, I was talking to her at lunch last Monday about how she liked her job, etc. You know, the usual . . . and she mentioned something about having to keep two sets of books . . . one for taxes and one for the financial statements. That can't be good accounting, can it? What do you think?
Clay: Two sets of books? It doesn't sound right.
Haley: It doesn't seem right to me either. I was always taught that you had to use generally accepted accounting principles. How can there be two sets of books? What can be the difference between the two?

How would you respond to Clay and Haley if you were Amber?

SA 9-3
Effect of depreciation on net income

Cowboy Construction Co. specializes in building replicas of historic houses. Tom Askew, president of Cowboy Construction, is considering the purchase of various items of equipment on July 1, 2006, for $150,000. The equipment would have a useful life of five years and no residual value. In the past, all equipment has been leased. For tax purposes, Tom is considering depreciating the equipment by the straight-line method. He discussed the matter with his CPA and learned that, although the straight-line method could be elected, it was to his advantage to use the Modified Accelerated Cost Recovery System (MACRS) for tax purposes. He asked for your advice as to which method to use for tax purposes.

1. Compute depreciation for each of the years (2006, 2007, 2008, 2009, 2010, and 2011) of useful life by (a) the straight-line method and (b) MACRS. In using the straight-line method, one-half year's depreciation should be computed for 2006 and 2011. Use the MACRS rates presented in the chapter.

2. Assuming that income before depreciation and income tax is estimated to be $300,000 uniformly per year and that the income tax rate is 30%, compute the net income for each of the years 2006, 2007, 2008, 2009, 2010, and 2011, if (a) the straight-line method is used and (b) MACRS is used.
3. ▭▬▶ What factors would you present for Tom's consideration in the selection of a depreciation method?

SA 9-4
Shopping for a delivery truck

Group Project

You are planning to acquire a delivery truck for use in your business for three years. In groups of three or four, explore a local dealer's purchase and leasing options for the truck. Summarize the costs of purchasing versus leasing, and list other factors that might help you decide whether to buy or lease the truck.

SA 9-5
Applying for patents, copyrights, and trademarks

Internet Project

Go to the Internet and review the procedures for applying for a patent, a copyright, and a trademark. One Internet site that is useful for this purpose is **idresearch.com**, which is linked to the text's Web site at **http://www.thomsonedu.com/accounting/warren**. Prepare a written summary of these procedures.

SA 9-6
Fixed asset turnover: three industries

The following table shows the revenues and average net fixed assets for a recent fiscal year for three different companies from three different industries: retailing, manufacturing, and communications.

	Revenues (in millions)	Average Net Fixed Assets (in millions)
Wal-Mart	$258,681	$51,686
Alcoa Inc.	21,504	12,333
Comcast Corporation	18,348	18,427

a. For each company, determine the fixed asset turnover ratio. Round to two decimal places.
b. Explain Wal-Mart's ratio relative to the other two companies.

Answers to Self-Examination Questions

1. **C** All amounts spent to get a fixed asset (such as machinery) in place and ready for use are proper charges to the asset account. In the case of machinery acquired, the freight (answer A) and the installation costs (answer B) are both (answer C) proper charges to the machinery account.

2. **C** The periodic charge for depreciation under the double-declining-balance method for the second year is determined by first computing the depreciation charge for the first year. The depreciation for the first year of $6,000 (answer A) is computed by multiplying the cost of the equipment, $9,000, by 2/3 (the straight-line rate of 1/3 multiplied by 2). The depreciation for the second year of $2,000 (answer C) is then determined by multiplying the book value at the end of the first year, $3,000 (the cost of $9,000 minus the first-year depreciation of $6,000), by 2/3. The third year's depreciation is $400 (answer D). It is determined by multiplying the book value at the end of the second year, $1,000, by 2/3, thus yielding $667. However, the equipment cannot be depreciated below its residual value

of $600; thus, the third-year depreciation is $400 ($1,000 − $600).

3. **B** A depreciation method that provides for a higher depreciation amount in the first year of the use of an asset and a gradually declining periodic amount thereafter is called an accelerated depreciation method. The double-declining-balance method (answer B) is an example of such a method.

4. **B** The acceptable method of accounting for an exchange of similar assets in which the trade-in allowance ($30,000) exceeds the book value of the old asset ($25,000) requires that the cost of the new asset be determined by adding the amount of cash given ($70,000) to the book value of the old asset ($25,000), which totals $95,000. Alternatively, the unrecognized gain ($5,000) can be subtracted from the list price ($100,000).

5. **D** Long-lived assets that are useful in operations, not held for sale, and without physical qualities are called intangible assets. Patents, goodwill, and copyrights are examples of intangible assets (answer D).

Current Liabilities and Payroll

objectives

After studying this chapter, you should be able to:

1   **Describe and illustrate current liabilities related to accounts payable, current portion of long-term debt, and notes payable.**

2   **Determine employer liabilities for payroll, including liabilities arising from employee earnings and deductions from earnings.**

3   **Describe payroll accounting systems that use a payroll register, employee earnings records, and a general journal.**

4   **Journalize entries for employee fringe benefits, including vacation pay and pensions.**

5   **Describe the accounting treatment for contingent liabilities and journalize entries for product warranties.**

Panera Bread

anks and other financial institutions provide loans or credit to buyers for purchases of various items. Using credit to purchase items is probably as old as commerce itself. In fact, the Babylonians were lending money to support trade as early as 1300 B.C. The use of credit provides *individuals* convenience and buying power. Credit cards provide individuals convenience over writing checks and make purchasing over the Internet easier. Credit cards also provide individuals control over cash by providing documentation of their purchases through receipt of monthly credit card statements and by allowing them to avoid carrying large amounts of cash and purchase items before they are paid.

Short-term credit is also used by *businesses* to provide convenience in purchasing items for manufacture or resale. More importantly, short-term credit gives a business control over the payment for goods and services. For example, Panera Bread, a chain of bakery-cafés located throughout the United States, uses short-term trade credit, or accounts payable, to purchase ingredients for making bread products in its bakeries. Short-term trade credit gives Panera control over cash payments by separating the purchase function from the payment function. Thus, the employee responsible for purchasing the bakery ingredients is separated from the employee responsible for paying for the purchase. This separation of duties can help prevent unauthorized purchases or payments.

In addition to accounts payable, a business like Panera Bread can also have current liabilities related to payroll, payroll taxes, employee benefits, short-term notes, unearned revenue, and contingencies. We will discuss each of these types of current liabilities in this chapter.

Current Liabilities

objective 1

Describe and illustrate current liabilities related to accounts payable, current portion of long-term debt, and notes payable.

When a business or a bank advances *credit*, it is making a loan. In these circumstances, it is called a *creditor* (or *lender*). Individuals or businesses that receive the credit are called *debtors* (or *borrowers*). Debt is an obligation that is recorded as a liability. *Long-term liabilities* are obligations due for a period of time greater than one year. Thus, a 30-year mortgage taken out to purchase property would be an example of a long-term liability. In contrast, *current liabilities* are obligations that will be paid out of current assets and are due within a short time, usually within one year.

Three types of current liabilities will be discussed in this section—accounts payable, current portion of long-term debt, and notes payable.

ACCOUNTS PAYABLE

Accounts payable arise from purchasing goods or services for use in a company's operations or for purchasing merchandise for resale. We have described and illustrated accounts payable transactions in earlier chapters. For most businesses, this is often the largest current liability. Exhibit 1 illustrates the size of the accounts payable balance as a percent of total current liabilities for a number of different companies. The average percent of accounts payable to total current liabilities for large companies is 35.7%.[1]

---

1 Determined from analysis of public companies exceeding $10 billion in sales.

Accounts Payable as a Percent of Total Current Liabilities

Company	Accounts Payable as a Percent of Total Current Liabilities
Alcoa Inc.	39%
BellSouth Corp.	16
Gap Inc.	47
IBM	22
Nissan Motor Co. Ltd.	25
Rite Aid Corp.	51
ChevronTexaco	54

CURRENT PORTION OF LONG-TERM DEBT

Long-term liabilities are often paid back in periodic payments, called *installments*, much like a car loan. Long-term liability installments that are due *within* the coming year must be classified as a current liability. The total amount of the installments due *after* the coming year is classified as a long-term liability. To illustrate, Starbucks Corporation reported the following scheduled debt payments in the notes to its September 30, 2005, annual report to shareholders:

Fiscal year ending	
2006	$ 748,000
2007	762,000
2008	775,000
2009	790,000
2010	337,000
Thereafter	206,000
Total principal payments	$3,618,000

The debt of $748,000 due in 2006 would be reported as a current liability on the September 30, 2005, balance sheet. The remaining debt of $2,870,000 ($3,618,000 − $748,000) would be reported as a long-term liability on the balance sheet, which we will discuss in a later chapter.

SHORT-TERM NOTES PAYABLE

Notes may be issued when merchandise or other assets are purchased. They may also be issued to creditors to temporarily satisfy an account payable created earlier. For example, assume that a business issues a 90-day, 12% note for $1,000, dated August 1, 2007, to Murray Co. for a $1,000 overdue account. The entry to record the issuance of the note is as follows:

Aug.	1	Accounts Payable—Murray Co.	1 0 0 0 00	
		Notes Payable		1 0 0 0 00
		Issued a 90-day, 12% note on account.		

When the note matures, the entry to record the payment of $1,000 principal plus $30 interest ($1,000 × 12% × 90/360) is as follows:

Oct.	30	Notes Payable	1 0 0 0 00	
		Interest Expense	3 0 00	
		Cash		1 0 3 0 00
		Paid principal and interest due on note.		

The interest expense is reported in the Other expense section of the income statement for the year ended December 31, 2007. The interest expense account is closed at December 31.

The preceding entries for notes payable are similar to those we discussed in Chapter 9 for notes receivable. Notes payable entries are presented from the viewpoint of the borrower, while notes receivable entries are presented from the viewpoint of the creditor or lender. To illustrate, the following entries are journalized for a borrower (Bowden Co.), who issues a note payable to a creditor (Coker Co.):

	Bowden Co. (Borrower)			Coker Co. (Creditor)		

May 1. Bowden Co. purchased merchandise on account from Coker Co., $10,000, 2/10, n/30. The merchandise cost Coker Co. $7,500.	Merchandise Inventory
	  Accounts Payable
		10,000	10,000	Accounts Receivable
				  Sales
				
				Cost of Merchandise Sold
				  Merchandise Inventory
					10,000
					
					7,500
						10,000
						
						7,500

May 31. Bowden Co. issued a 60-day, 12% note for $10,000 to Coker Co. on account.	Accounts Payable
	  Notes Payable
		10,000	10,000	Notes Receivable
				  Accounts Receivable
					10,000	10,000

July 30. Bowden Co. paid Coker Co. the amount due on the note of May 31. Interest: $10,000 × 12% × 60/360.	Notes Payable
	Interest Expense
	  Cash
		10,000
		200
			10,200	Cash
				  Interest Revenue
				  Notes Receivable
					10,200	200
						10,000

Notes may also be issued when money is borrowed from banks. Although the terms may vary, many banks would accept from the borrower an interest-bearing note for the amount of the loan. For example, assume that on September 19 a firm borrows $4,000 from First National Bank by giving the bank a 90-day, 15% note. The entry to record the receipt of cash and the issuance of the note is as follows:

Sept.	19	Cash		4 0 0 0 00	
		Notes Payable			4 0 0 0 00
		Issued a 90-day, 15% note to the bank.			

On the due date of the note (December 18), the borrower owes $4,000, the principal of the note, plus interest of $150 ($4,000 × 15% × 90/360). The entry to record the payment of the note is as follows:

Dec.	18	Notes Payable		4 0 0 0 00	
		Interest Expense		1 5 0 00	
		Cash			4 1 5 0 00
		Paid principal and interest due on note.			

The U.S. Treasury issues short-term treasury bills to investors at a discount.

Sometimes a borrower will issue a discounted note rather than an interest-bearing note. Although such a note does not specify an interest rate, the creditor sets a rate of interest and deducts the interest from the face amount of the note. This interest is called the **discount**. The rate used in computing the discount is called the **discount rate**. The borrower is given the remainder, called the **proceeds**.

To illustrate, assume that on August 10, Cary Company issues a $20,000, 90-day note to Rock Company in exchange for inventory. Rock discounts the note at a rate of 15%. The amount of the discount, $750, is debited to *Interest Expense*. The proceeds, $19,250, are debited to *Merchandise Inventory*. *Notes Payable* is credited for the face amount of the note, which is also its maturity value. The entry for Cary Company is shown at the top of the following page.

Aug.	10	Merchandise Inventory		19 2 5 0 00	
		Interest Expense		7 5 0 00	
		Notes Payable			20 0 0 0 00
		Issued a 90-day note to Rock Company,			
		discounted at 15%.			

When the note is paid, the following entry is recorded:[2]

Nov.	8	Notes Payable		20 0 0 0 00	
		Cash			20 0 0 0 00
		Paid note due.			

Additional current liabilities include accrued expenses, unearned revenue, and interest payable, which we have discussed in previous chapters. We have also discussed wages and salaries payable earlier. However, the accounting for wages and salaries, termed *payroll accounting,* is important to every business. Thus, we will discuss payroll accounting in detail in the next two sections.

Example Exercise 10-1   objective 1

On July 1, Bella Salon Company issued a 60-day note with a face amount of $60,000 to Delilah Hair Products Company for merchandise inventory.

a. Determine the proceeds of the note, assuming the note carries an interest rate of 6%.
b. Determine the proceeds of the note, assuming the note is discounted at 6%.

Follow My Example 10-1

a. $60,000.
b. $59,400. [$60,000 − ($60,000 × 6% × 60/360)]

For Practice: PE 10-1A, PE 10-1B

Payroll and Payroll Taxes

objective 2

Determine employer liabilities for payroll, including liabilities arising from employee earnings and deductions from earnings.

We are all familiar with the term *payroll.* In accounting, the term **payroll** refers to the amount paid to employees for the services they provide during a period. A business's payroll is usually significant for several reasons. First, employees are sensitive to payroll errors and irregularities. Maintaining good employee morale requires that the payroll be paid on a timely, accurate basis. Second, the payroll is subject to various federal and state regulations. Finally, the payroll and related payroll taxes have a significant effect on the net income of most businesses. Although the amount of such expenses varies widely, it is not unusual for a business's payroll and payroll-related expenses to equal nearly one-third of its revenue.

---

2 If the accounting period ends before a discounted note is paid, an adjusting entry should record the prepaid (deferred) interest that is not yet an expense. This deferred interest would be deducted from Notes Payable in the Current Liabilities section of the balance sheet.

LIABILITY FOR EMPLOYEE EARNINGS

Salaries and wages paid to employees are an employer's labor expenses. The term *salary* usually refers to payment for managerial, administrative, or similar services. The rate of salary is normally expressed in terms of a month or a year. The term *wages* usually refers to payment for manual labor, both skilled and unskilled. The rate of wages is normally stated on an hourly or a weekly basis. In practice, the terms salary and wages are often used interchangeably.

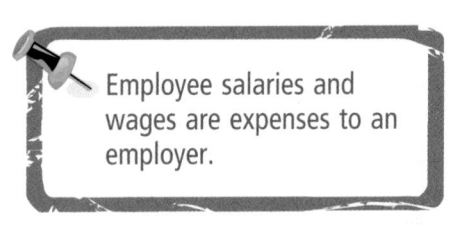

Employee salaries and wages are expenses to an employer.

The basic salary or wage of an employee may be increased by commissions, profit sharing, or cost-of-living adjustments. Many businesses pay managers an annual bonus in addition to a basic salary. The amount of the bonus is often based on some measure of productivity, such as income or profit of the business. Although payment is usually made by check or in cash, it may be in the form of securities, notes, lodging, or other property or services. Generally, the form of payment has no effect on how salaries and wages are treated by either the employer or the employee.

Information on average salaries for a variety of professions can be found at the *Economic Research Institute's* Web site, which is **http://www.erieri.com**.

Salary and wage rates are determined by agreement between the employer and the employees. Businesses engaged in interstate commerce must follow the requirements of the Fair Labor Standards Act. Employers covered by this legislation, which is commonly called the Federal Wage and Hour Law, are required to pay a minimum rate of $1\frac{1}{2}$ times the regular rate for all hours worked in excess of 40 hours per week. Exemptions are provided for executive, administrative, and certain supervisory positions. Premium rates for overtime or for working at night, holidays, or other less desirable times are fairly common, even when not required by law. In some cases, the premium rates may be as much as twice the base rate.

To illustrate computing an employee's earnings, assume that John T. McGrath is a salesperson employed by McDermott Supply Co. at the rate of $34 per hour. Any hours in excess of 40 hours per week are paid at a rate of $1\frac{1}{2}$ times the normal rate, or $51 ($34 + $17) per hour. For the week ended December 27, McGrath's time card indicates that he worked 42 hours. His earnings for that week are computed as follows:

Earnings at base rate (40 × $34)	$1,360
Earnings at overtime rate (2 × $51)	102
Total earnings	$1,462

DEDUCTIONS FROM EMPLOYEE EARNINGS

Professional athletes must pay local taxes in each location in which they play their sport.

The total earnings of an employee for a payroll period, including bonuses and overtime pay, are called **gross pay**. From this amount is subtracted one or more *deductions* to arrive at the net pay. **Net pay** is the amount the employer must pay the employee. The deductions for federal taxes are usually the largest deduction. Deductions may also be required for state or local income taxes. Other deductions may be made for medical insurance, contributions to pensions, and for items authorized by individual employees.

Income Taxes   Except for certain types of employment, all employers must withhold a portion of employee earnings for payment of the employees' federal income tax. As a basis for determining the amount to be withheld, each employee completes and submits to the employer an "Employee's Withholding Allowance Certificate," often called a W-4. Exhibit 2 is an example of a completed W-4 form.

You may recall filling out a W-4 form. On the W-4, an employee indicates marital status, the number of withholding allowances, and whether any additional withholdings are authorized. A single employee may claim one withholding allowance. A married employee may claim an additional allowance for a spouse. An employee may also claim an allowance for each dependent other than a spouse. Each allowance claimed reduces the amount of federal income tax withheld from the employee's check.

EXHIBIT 2

Employee's
Withholding
Allowance Certificate
(W-4 Form)

Cut here and give Form W-4 to your employer. Keep the top part for your records. ---

Form **W-4**	**Employee's Withholding Allowance Certificate**	OMB No. 1545-0074
Department of the Treasury Internal Revenue Service	► Whether you are entitled to claim a certain number of allowances or exemption from withholding is subject to review by the IRS. Your employer may be required to send a copy of this form to the IRS.	20**06**

1 Type or print your first name and middle initial. John T.	Last name McGrath	2 Your social security number 381 ¦48¦ 9120

Home address (number and street or rural route)
1830 4ᵗʰ Street

3 ☒ Single ☐ Married ☐ Married, but withhold at higher Single rate.
Note. If married, but legally separated, or spouse is a nonresident alien, check the "Single" box.

City or town, state, and ZIP code
Clinton, Iowa 52732-6142

4 If your last name differs from that shown on your social security card, check here. You must call 1-800-772-1213 for a new card. ► ☐

5	Total number of allowances you are claiming (from line **H** above **or** from the applicable worksheet on page 2)	5	1
6	Additional amount, if any, you want withheld from each paycheck	6	$
7	I claim exemption from withholding for **2006**, and I certify that I meet **both** of the following conditions for exemption.		

• Last year I had a right to a refund of **all** federal income tax withheld because I had **no** tax liability **and**
• This year I expect a refund of **all** federal income tax withheld because I expect to have **no** tax liability.

If you meet both conditions, write "Exempt" here . . . . ► | 7 |

Under penalties of perjury, I declare that I have examined this certificate and to the best of my knowledge and belief, it is true, correct, and complete.

Employee's signature
(Form is not valid
unless you sign it.) ► *John T. McGrath*   Date ► June 2, 2006

8 Employer's name and address (Employer: Complete lines 8 and 10 only if sending to the IRS.)	9 Office code (optional)	10 Employer identification number (EIN)

Cat. No. 10220Q   Form **W-4** (2006)

The amount that must be withheld for income tax differs, depending upon each employee's gross pay and completed W-4. Most employers use wage bracket withholding tables furnished by the Internal Revenue Service (IRS) to determine the amount to be withheld.

Exhibit 3 is an example of an IRS wage bracket withholding table for a single person who is paid weekly.[3] Each row represents a person's wages after subtracting a standard IRS withholding allowance. The standard IRS withholding allowance is determined annually by the IRS. For a single person paid weekly, we assume the standard withholding allowance is $63.[4]

To illustrate, John T. McGrath made $1,462 for the week ended December 27. Thus, the wages used in determining McGrath's withholding for the week are $1,399 ($1,462 − $63). If McGrath had declared two withholding allowances, the total amount deducted would have been $126, and the wages used in determining McGrath's withholding for the week would have been $1,336 ($1,462 − $126).

EXHIBIT 3

Wage Bracket
Withholding Table

**Table for Percentage Method of Withholding
WEEKLY Payroll Period**

(a) SINGLE person (including head of household)—

If the amount of wages (after subtracting withholding allowances) is:	The amount of income tax to withhold is:
Not over $51	$0

Over—	But not over—			of excess over—
$51	—$192	.	10%	—$51
$192	—$620	.	$14.10 plus 15%	—$192
$620	—$1,409	.	$78.30 plus 25%	—$620	◄— McGrath wage bracket
$1,409	—$3,013	.	$275.55 plus 28%	—$1,409
$3,013	—$6,508	.	$724.67 plus 33%	—$3,013
$6,508	. . . . .		$1,878.02 plus 35%	—$6,508

Source: Publication 15, *Employer's Tax Guide*, Internal Revenue Service, 2006.

After the person's withholding wage bracket has been computed, the amount of federal income tax withheld is determined using Exhibit 3 as follows:

1. Locate the proper withholding wage bracket. Since McGrath's wages after deducting one standard IRS withholding allowance is $1,399, the proper wage bracket for McGrath is $620 − $1,409.

---

3 IRS withholding tables are also available for married employees and for pay periods other than weekly.
4 The actual IRS standard withholding allowance changes every year and was $63.46 for 2006.

2. Compute the withholding for the proper wage bracket using the directions in the two right-hand columns of Exhibit 3. For McGrath's wage bracket, Exhibit 3 indicates that the withholding should be "$78.30 plus 25% of the excess over $620." Thus, the withholding for McGrath is $273.05, as shown below.

Initial withholding from wage bracket in Exhibit 3	$ 78.30
Plus additional withholding: 25% of excess over $620	194.75*
Total withholding	$273.05

*($1,399 − $620) × 25%

In addition to the federal income tax, employees may also be required to pay a state income tax and a city income tax. State and city taxes are withheld from employees' earnings and paid to state and city governments.

Example Exercise 10-2   objective 2

Karen Dunn's weekly gross earnings for the present week were $2,250. Dunn has two exemptions. Using the wage bracket withholding table in Exhibit 3 with a $63 standard withholding allowance for each exemption, what is Dunn's federal income tax withholding?

Follow My Example 10-2

Total wage payment		$2,250
One allowance (provided by IRS)	$63	
Multiplied by allowances claimed on Form W-4	× 2	126
Amount subject to withholding		$2,124
Initial withholding from wage bracket in Exhibit 3		$275.55
Plus additional withholding: 28% of excess over $1,409		200.20*
Federal income tax withholding		$475.75

*28% × ($2,124 − $1,409)

For Practice: PE 10-2A, PE 10-2B

FICA Tax Most of us have FICA tax withheld from our payroll checks by our employers. Employers are required by the Federal Insurance Contributions Act (FICA) to withhold a portion of the earnings of each of the employees. The amount of **FICA tax** withheld is the employees' contribution to two federal programs. Tax is withheld separately under each program. The first program, called *social security*, is for old age, survivors, and disability insurance (OASDI). The second program, called *Medicare*, is health insurance for senior citizens.

The amount of tax that employers are required to withhold from each employee is normally based on the amount of earnings paid in the *calendar* year. Although both the schedule of future tax rates and the maximum amount subject to tax are revised often by Congress, such changes have little effect on the basic payroll system. In this text, we will use a social security rate of 6% on the first $100,000 of annual earnings and a Medicare rate of 1.5% on all annual earnings.

To illustrate, assume that John T. McGrath's annual earnings prior to the current payroll period total $99,038. Assume also that the current period earnings are $1,462. The total FICA tax of $79.65 is determined as follows:

Earnings subject to 6% social security tax		
($100,000 − $99,038)	$ 962	
Social security tax rate	× 6%	
Social security tax		$57.72
Earnings subject to 1.5% Medicare tax	$1,462	
Medicare tax rate	× 1.5%	
Medicare tax		21.93
Total FICA tax		$79.65

Other Deductions   Neither the employer nor the employee has any choice in deducting taxes from gross earnings. However, employees may choose to have additional amounts deducted for other purposes. For example, you as an employee may authorize deductions for retirement savings, for contributions to charitable organizations, or for premiums on employee insurance. A union contract may also require the deduction of union dues.

COMPUTING EMPLOYEE NET PAY

Gross earnings less payroll deductions equals the amount to be paid to an employee for the payroll period. This amount is the *net pay*, which is often called the *take-home pay*. Assuming that John T. McGrath authorized deductions for retirement savings and for a United Fund contribution, the amount to be paid McGrath for the week ended December 27 is $1,084.30, as shown below.

Gross earnings for the week		$1,462.00
Deductions:		
Social security tax	$ 57.72	
Medicare tax	21.93	
Federal income tax	273.05	
Retirement savings	20.00	
United Fund	5.00	
Total deductions		377.70
Net pay		$1,084.30

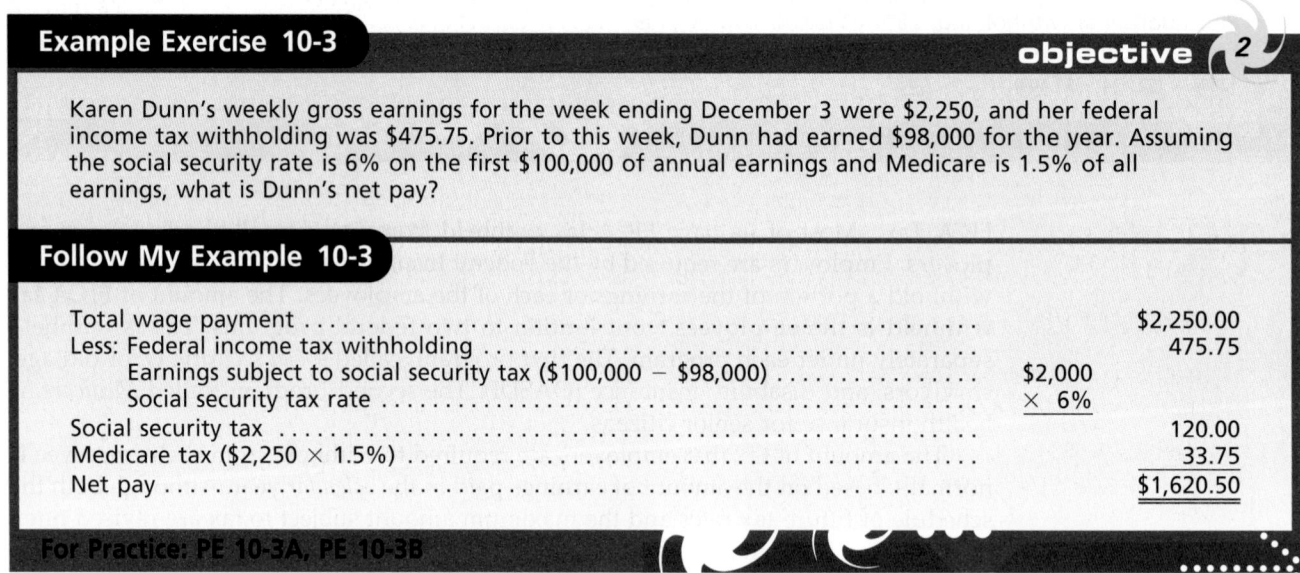

Example Exercise 10-3   objective 2

Karen Dunn's weekly gross earnings for the week ending December 3 were $2,250, and her federal income tax withholding was $475.75. Prior to this week, Dunn had earned $98,000 for the year. Assuming the social security rate is 6% on the first $100,000 of annual earnings and Medicare is 1.5% of all earnings, what is Dunn's net pay?

Follow My Example 10-3

Total wage payment		$2,250.00
Less: Federal income tax withholding		475.75
Earnings subject to social security tax ($100,000 − $98,000)	$2,000	
Social security tax rate	× 6%	
Social security tax		120.00
Medicare tax ($2,250 × 1.5%)		33.75
Net pay		$1,620.50

For Practice: PE 10-3A, PE 10-3B

LIABILITY FOR EMPLOYER'S PAYROLL TAXES

So far, we have discussed the payroll taxes that are withheld from the employees' earnings. Most employers are also subject to federal and state payroll taxes based on the amount paid their employees. Such taxes are an operating expense of the business. Exhibit 4 summarizes the responsibility for employee and employer payroll taxes.

FICA Tax   Employers are required to contribute to the social security and Medicare programs for each employee. The employer must match the employee's contribution to each program.

EXHIBIT 4 | **Responsibility for Tax Payments**

Employee
Social security tax
Medicare tax
Federal withholding tax

Government

Social security tax
Medicare tax
Federal unemployment compensation tax
State unemployment compensation tax

Business

Federal Unemployment Compensation Tax The Federal Unemployment Tax Act (FUTA) provides for temporary payments to those who become unemployed as a result of layoffs due to economic causes beyond their control. Types of employment subject to this program are similar to those covered by FICA taxes. A tax of 6.2% is levied on employers only, rather than on both employers and employees.[5] It is applied to only the first $7,000 of the earnings of each covered employee during a calendar year. Congress often revises the rate and maximum earnings subject to federal unemployment compensation tax. The funds collected by the federal government are not paid directly to the unemployed but are allocated among the states for use in state programs.

State Unemployment Compensation Tax State Unemployment Tax Acts (SUTA) also provide for payments to unemployed workers. The amounts paid as benefits are obtained, for the most part, from a tax levied upon employers only. A few states require employee contributions also. The rates of tax and the tax bases vary. In most states, employers who provide stable employment for their employees are granted reduced rates. The employment experience and the status of each employer's tax account are reviewed annually, and the tax rates are adjusted accordingly.[6]

Business Connections

REAL WORLD

THE MOST YOU WILL EVER PAY

In 1936, the Social Security Board described how the tax was expected to affect a worker's pay, as follows:

The taxes called for in this law will be paid both by your employer and by you. For the next 3 years you will pay maybe 15 cents a week, maybe 25 cents a week, maybe 30 cents or more, according to what you earn. That is to say, during the next 3 years, beginning January 1, 1937, you will pay 1 cent for every dollar you earn, and at the same time your employer will pay 1 cent for every dollar you earn, up to $3,000 a year. . . .

. . . Beginning in 1940 you will pay, and your employer will pay, 1 1/2 cents for each dollar you earn, up to $3,000 a year . . . and then beginning in 1943, you will

pay 2 cents, and so will your employer, for every dollar you earn for the next three years. After that, you and your employer will each pay half a cent more for 3 years, and finally, beginning in 1949, . . . you and your employer will each pay 3 cents on each dollar you earn, up to $3,000 a year. That is the most you will ever pay.

The rate on January 1, 2006, was 7.65 cents per dollar earned (7.65%). The social security portion was 6.20% on the first $94,200 of earnings. The Medicare portion was 1.45% on all earnings.

Source: Arthur Lodge, "That Is the Most You Will Ever Pay," *Journal of Accountancy,* October 1985, p. 44.

---

5 This rate may be reduced to 0.8% for credits for state unemployment compensation tax.
6 As of January 1, 2006, the maximum state rate credited against the federal unemployment rate was 5.4% of the first $7,000 of each employee's earnings during a calendar year.

Integrity, Objectivity, and Ethics in Business

ETHICS

RESUMÉ PADDING

Misrepresenting your accomplishments on your resumé could come back to haunt you. In one case, the chief financial officer (CFO) of Veritas Software was forced to resign his position when it was discovered that he had lied about earning an MBA from Stanford University, when in actuality he had earned only an undergraduate degree from Idaho State University.

Source: Reuters News Service, October 4, 2002.

Accounting Systems for Payroll and Payroll Taxes

objective *3*

Describe payroll accounting systems that use a payroll register, employee earnings records, and a general journal.

In designing payroll systems, the requirements of various federal, state, and local agencies for payroll data are considered. Payroll data must also be maintained accurately for each payroll period and for each employee. Periodic reports using payroll data must be submitted to government agencies. The payroll data itself must be retained for possible inspection by the various agencies.

Payroll systems must be designed to pay employees on a timely basis. Payroll systems should also be designed to provide useful data for management decision-making needs. Such needs might include settling employee grievances and negotiating retirement or other benefits with employees.

Although payroll systems differ among businesses, the major elements common to most payroll systems are the payroll register, employee's earnings record, and payroll checks. We discuss and illustrate each of these elements next. We have kept the illustrations relatively simple, and they may be modified in practice to meet the needs of each individual business.

PAYROLL REGISTER

The **payroll register** is a multicolumn report used for summarizing the data for each payroll period. Its design varies according to the number and classes of employees and the extent to which computers are used. Exhibit 5 illustrates a payroll register suitable for a small number of employees.

The nature of the data appearing in the payroll register is evident from the column headings. The number of hours worked and the earnings and deduction data are inserted in their proper columns. The sum of the deductions for each employee is then

EXHIBIT 5

Payroll Register

	Employee Name	Total Hours	Earnings			
			Regular	Overtime	Total	
1	Abrams, Julie S.	40	500.00		500.00	1
2	Elrod, Fred G.	44	392.00	58.80	450.80	2
3	Gomez, Jose C.	40	840.00		840.00	3
4	McGrath, John T.	42	1,360.00	102.00	1,462.00	4
25	Wilkes, Glenn K.	40	480.00		480.00	25
26	Zumpano, Michael W.	40	600.00		600.00	26
27	Total		13,328.00	574.00	13,902.00	27
28						28

subtracted from the total earnings to yield the amount to be paid. The check numbers are recorded in the payroll register as evidence of payment.

The last two columns of the payroll register are used to accumulate the total wages or salaries to be debited to the various expense accounts. This process is usually called *payroll distribution*.

Recording Employees' Earnings   The column totals of the payroll register support the journal entry for payroll. The entry based on the payroll register in Exhibit 5 follows.

Dec.	27	Sales Salaries Expense	11 1 2 2 00	
		Office Salaries Expense	2 7 8 0 00	
		Social Security Tax Payable		6 4 3 07
		Medicare Tax Payable		2 0 8 53
		Employees Federal Income Tax Payable		3 3 3 2 00
		Retirement Savings Deductions Payable		6 8 0 00
		United Fund Deductions Payable		4 7 0 00
		Accounts Receivable—Fred G. Elrod (emp.)		5 0 00
		Salaries Payable		8 5 1 8 40
		Payroll for week ended December 27.		

Example Exercise 10-4   objective 3

The payroll register of Chen Engineering Services indicates $900 of social security withheld and $225 of Medicare tax withheld on total salaries of $15,000 for the period. Federal income tax withholding for the period totaled $2,925.

Provide the journal entry for the period's payroll.

Follow My Example 10-4

Salaries Expense	15,000	
Social Security Tax Payable		900
Medicare Tax Payable		225
Employees Federal Income Tax Payable		2,925
Salaries Payable		10,950

For Practice: PE 10-4A, PE 10-4B

EXHIBIT 5   (Concluded)

	Deductions						Paid		Accounts Debited		
	Social Security Tax	Medicare Tax	Federal Income Tax	Retirement Savings	Misc.		Total	Net Amount	Check No.	Sales Salaries Expense	Office Salaries Expense	
1	30.00	7.50	74.00	20.00	UF	10.00	141.50	358.50	6857	500.00		1
2	27.05	6.76	62.00		AR	50.00	145.81	304.99	6858		450.80	2
3	50.40	12.60	131.00	25.00	UF	10.00	229.00	611.00	6859	840.00		3
4	57.72	21.93	273.05	20.00	UF	5.00	377.70	1,084.30	6860	1,462.00		4
25	28.80	7.20	69.00	10.00			115.00	365.00	6880	480.00		25
26	36.00	9.00	79.00	5.00	UF	2.00	131.00	469.00	6881		600.00	26
27	643.07	208.53	3,332.00	680.00	UF	470.00	5,383.60	8,518.40		11,122.00	2,780.00	27
28					AR	50.00						28

Miscellaneous Deductions: UF—United Fund; AR—Accounts Receivable

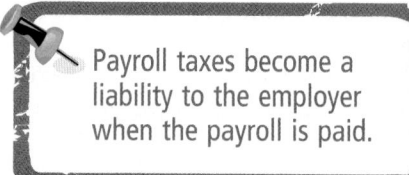

Payroll taxes become a liability to the employer when the payroll is paid.

Recording and Paying Payroll Taxes The employer's payroll taxes become liabilities when the related payroll is *paid* to employees. In addition, employers are required to compute and report payroll taxes on a *calendar-year* basis, even if a different fiscal year is used for financial reporting and income tax purposes.

To illustrate, assume that Everson Company's fiscal year ends on April 30. Also, assume that Everson Company owes its employees $26,000 of wages on December 31. The following portions of the $26,000 of wages are subject to payroll taxes on December 31:

	Earnings Subject to Payroll Taxes
Social security tax (6.0%)	$18,000
Medicare tax (1.5%)	26,000
State and federal unemployment compensation tax	1,000

If the payroll is paid on December 31, the payroll taxes will be based on the preceding amounts. If the payroll is paid on January 2, however, the *entire* $26,000 will be subject to *all* payroll taxes. This is because the maximum earnings limitation for determining social security and unemployment taxes will not be exceeded at the beginning of the calendar year.

The payroll register for McDermott Supply Co. in Exhibit 5 indicates that the amount of social security tax withheld is $643.07 and Medicare tax withheld is $208.53. Since the employer must match the employees' FICA contributions, the employer's social security payroll tax will also be $643.07, and the Medicare tax will be $208.53. Further, assume that the earnings subject to state and federal unemployment compensation taxes are $2,710. Multiplying this amount by the state (5.4%) and federal (0.8%) rates yields the unemployment compensation taxes shown in the following payroll tax computation:

Social security tax	$ 643.07
Medicare tax	208.53
State unemployment compensation tax (5.4% × $2,710)	146.34
Federal unemployment compensation tax (0.8% × $2,710)	21.68
Total payroll tax expense	$1,019.62

The entry to journalize the payroll tax expense for the week and the liability for the taxes accrued is shown below.

Dec.	27	Payroll Tax Expense			1 0 1 9 62		
		Social Security Tax Payable				6 4 3 07
		Medicare Tax Payable				2 0 8 53
		State Unemployment Tax Payable				1 4 6 34
		Federal Unemployment Tax Payable				2 1 68
		Payroll taxes for week ended				
		December 27.				

Example Exercise 10-5

objective 3

The payroll register of Chen Engineering Services indicates $900 of social security withheld and $225 of Medicare tax withheld on total salaries of $15,000 for the period. Assume earnings subject to state and federal unemployment compensation taxes are $5,250, at the federal rate of 0.8% and the state rate of 5.4%.

Provide the journal entry to record the payroll tax expense for the period.

(continued)

EMPLOYEE'S EARNINGS RECORD

The amount of each employee's earnings to date must be available at the end of each payroll period. This cumulative amount is required in order to compute each employee's social security and Medicare tax withholding and the employer's payroll taxes. It is essential, therefore, that a detailed payroll record be maintained for each employee. This record is called an **employee's earnings record**.

Exhibit 6, on the following pages, shows a portion of the employee's earnings record for John T. McGrath. The relationship between this record and the payroll register can be seen by tracing the amounts entered on McGrath's earnings record for December 27 back to its source—the fourth line of the payroll register in Exhibit 5.

In addition to spaces for recording data for each payroll period and the cumulative total of earnings, the employee's earnings record has spaces for quarterly totals and the yearly total. These totals are used in various reports for tax, insurance, and other purposes. One such report is the Wage and Tax Statement, commonly called a *Form W-2*. You may recall receiving a W-2 form for use in preparing your individual tax return. This form must be provided annually to each employee as well as to the Social Security Administration. The amounts reported in the Form W-2 shown below were taken from McGrath's employee's earnings record.

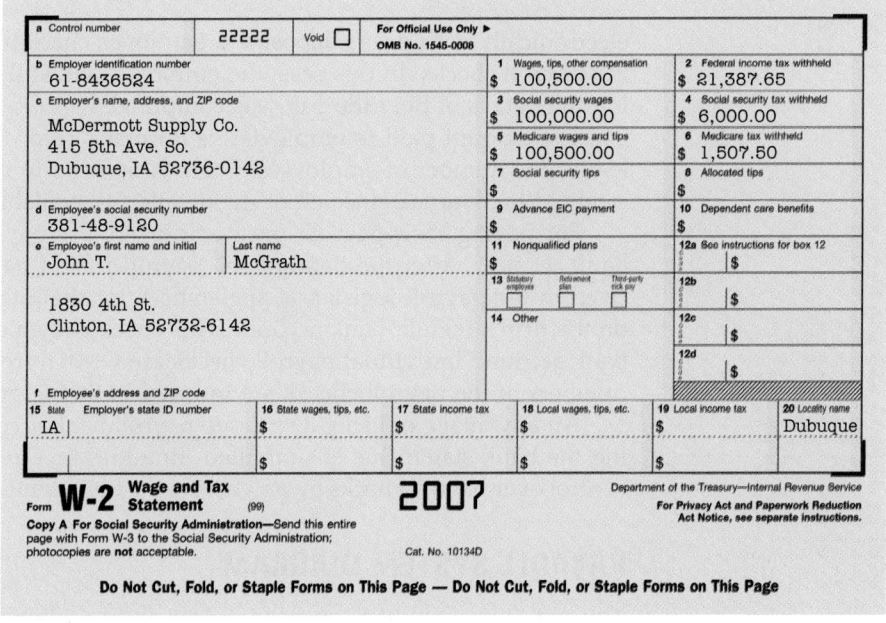

PAYROLL CHECKS

At the end of each pay period, *payroll checks* are prepared. Each check includes a detachable statement showing the details of how the net pay was computed. Exhibit 7, on page 454, is a payroll check for John T. McGrath. Many businesses pay their employees

EXHIBIT 6	Employee's Earnings Record

John T. McGrath
1830 4th Street
Clinton, IA 52732-6142   PHONE: 555-3148

SINGLE	NUMBER OF WITHHOLDING ALLOWANCES: 1	PAY RATE:	$1,360.00 Per Week

OCCUPATION:	Salesperson	EQUIVALENT HOURLY RATE: $34

	Period Ending	Total Hours	Earnings				
			Regular Earnings	Overtime Earnings	Total Earnings	Cumulative Total	
42	SEP. 27	53	1,360.00	663.00	2,023.00	75,565.00	42
43	THIRD QUARTER		17,680.00	7,605.00	25,285.00		43
44	OCT. 4	51	1,360.00	561.00	1,921.00	77,486.00	44
50	NOV. 15	50	1,360.00	510.00	1,870.00	89,382.00	50
51	NOV. 22	53	1,360.00	663.00	2,023.00	91,405.00	51
52	NOV. 29	47	1,360.00	357.00	1,717.00	93,122.00	52
53	DEC. 6	53	1,360.00	663.00	2,023.00	95,145.00	53
54	DEC.13	52	1,360.00	612.00	1,972.00	97,117.00	54
55	DEC. 20	51	1,360.00	561.00	1,921.00	99,038.00	55
56	DEC. 27	42	1,360.00	102.00	1,462.00	100,500.00	56
57	FOURTH QUARTER		17,680.00	7,255.00	24,935.00		57
58	YEARLY TOTAL		70,720.00	29,780.00	100,500.00		58

electronically with direct deposits to employee checking accounts, rather than preparing payroll checks. In this case, the employee will still receive a statement summarizing the details of how the pay was computed.

The amount paid to employees is normally recorded as a single amount, regardless of the number of employees. There is no need to record each payroll check separately in the journal, since all of the details are available in the payroll register.

For paying their payroll, most employers use payroll checks drawn on a special bank account. After the data for the payroll period have been recorded and summarized in the payroll register, a single check for the total amount to be paid is written on the firm's regular bank account. This check is then deposited in the special payroll bank account. Individual payroll checks are written from the payroll account, and the numbers of the payroll checks are inserted in the payroll register.

An advantage of using a separate payroll bank account is that the task of reconciling the bank statements is simplified. In addition, a payroll bank account establishes control over payroll checks by preventing the theft or misuse of uncashed payroll checks.

PAYROLL SYSTEM DIAGRAM

You may find Exhibit 8, on page 454, useful in following the flow of data within the payroll segment of an accounting system. The diagram indicates the relationships among the primary components of the payroll system we described in this chapter.

Our focus in the preceding discussion has been on the outputs of a payroll system: the payroll register, payroll checks, the employees' earnings records, and tax and other reports. As shown in the diagram in Exhibit 8, the inputs into a payroll system may be classified as either constants or variables.

EXHIBIT 6   (Concluded)

| SOC. SEC. NO.: 381-48-9120 | | | | | | | | EMPLOYEE NO.: 814 | |

| DATE OF BIRTH: February 15, 1982 | | | | | | | | | |
| DATE EMPLOYMENT TERMINATED: | | | | | | | | | |

| | Deductions | | | | | | | Paid | |
	Social Security Tax	Medicare Tax	Federal Income Tax	Retirement Savings	Other		Total	Net Amount	Check No.
42	121.38	30.35	429.83	20.00			601.56	1,421.44	6175
43	1,517.10	379.28	5,391.71	260.00	UF	40.00	7,588.09	17,696.91	
44	115.26	28.82	401.27	20.00			565.35	1,355.65	6225
50	112.20	28.05	386.99	20.00			547.24	1,322.76	6530
51	121.38	30.35	429.83	20.00			601.56	1,421.44	6582
52	103.02	25.76	344.15	20.00			492.93	1,224.07	6640
53	121.38	30.35	429.83	20.00	UF	5.00	606.56	1,416.44	6688
54	118.32	29.58	415.55	20.00			583.45	1,388.55	6743
55	115.26	28.82	401.27	20.00			565.35	1,355.65	6801
56	57.72	21.93	273.05	20.00	UF	5.00	377.70	1,084.30	6860
57	1,466.10	374.03	5,293.71	260.00	UF	15.00	7,408.84	17,526.16	
58	6,000.00	1,507.50	21,387.65	1,040.00	UF	100.00	30,035.15	70,464.85	

REAL WORLD

Many computerized payroll systems are offered on the Internet for a monthly fee. Internet-based payroll systems have the advantage of maintaining current federal and state tax rates.

Constants are data that remain unchanged from payroll to payroll and thus do not need to be entered into the system each pay period. Examples of constants include such data as each employee's name and social security number, marital status, number of income tax withholding allowances, rate of pay, payroll category (office, sales, etc.), and department where employed. The FICA tax rates and various tax tables are also constants that apply to all employees. In a computerized accounting system, constants are stored within a payroll file.

Variables are data that change from payroll to payroll and thus must be entered into the system each pay period. Examples of variables include such data as the number of hours or days worked for each employee during the payroll period, days of sick leave with pay, vacation credits, and cumulative earnings and taxes withheld. If salespersons are paid commissions, the amount of their sales would also vary from period to period.

Most companies use computerized payroll systems that maintain an electronic payroll register and employee earnings record, similar to those discussed in this section. Payroll system outputs, such as employee checks and tax records, are automatically produced by the software.

INTERNAL CONTROLS FOR PAYROLL SYSTEMS

Payroll processing, as we discussed above, requires the input of a large amount of data, along with numerous and sometimes complex computations. These factors, combined with the large dollar amounts involved, require controls to ensure that payroll payments are timely and accurate. In addition, the system must also provide adequate safeguards against theft or other misuse of funds.

EXHIBIT 7

Payroll Check

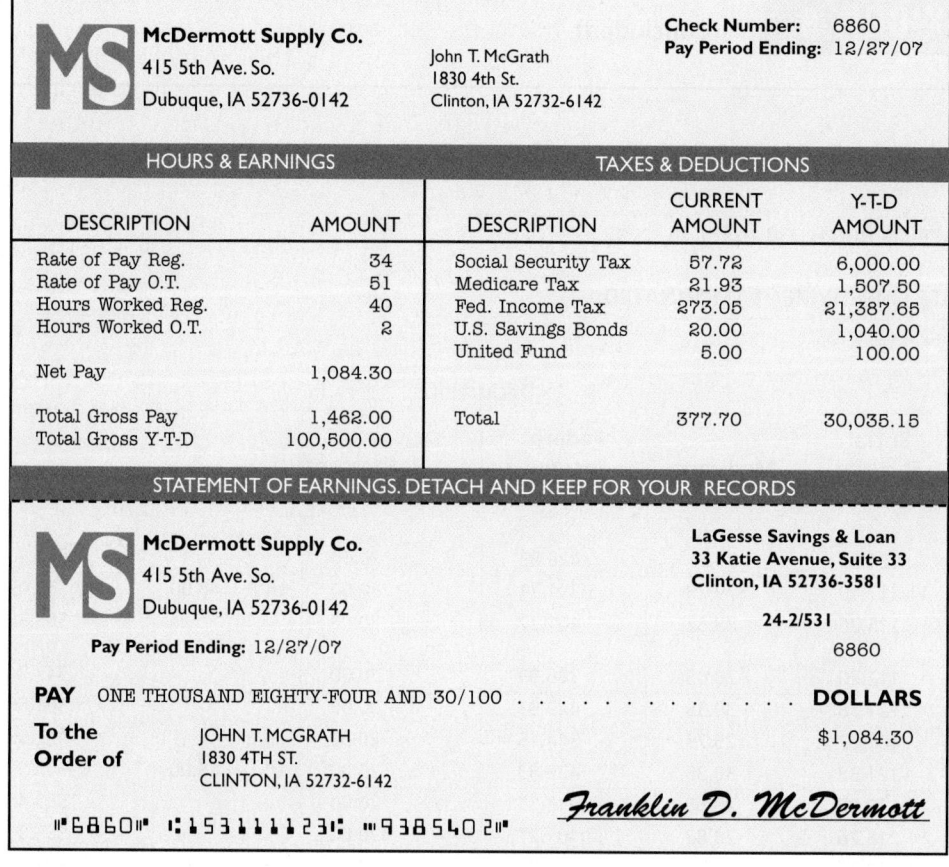

The cash payment controls we discussed in the cash chapter also apply to payrolls. Thus, it is normally desirable to use a system that includes procedures for proper authorization and approval of payroll. When a check-signing machine is used, it is

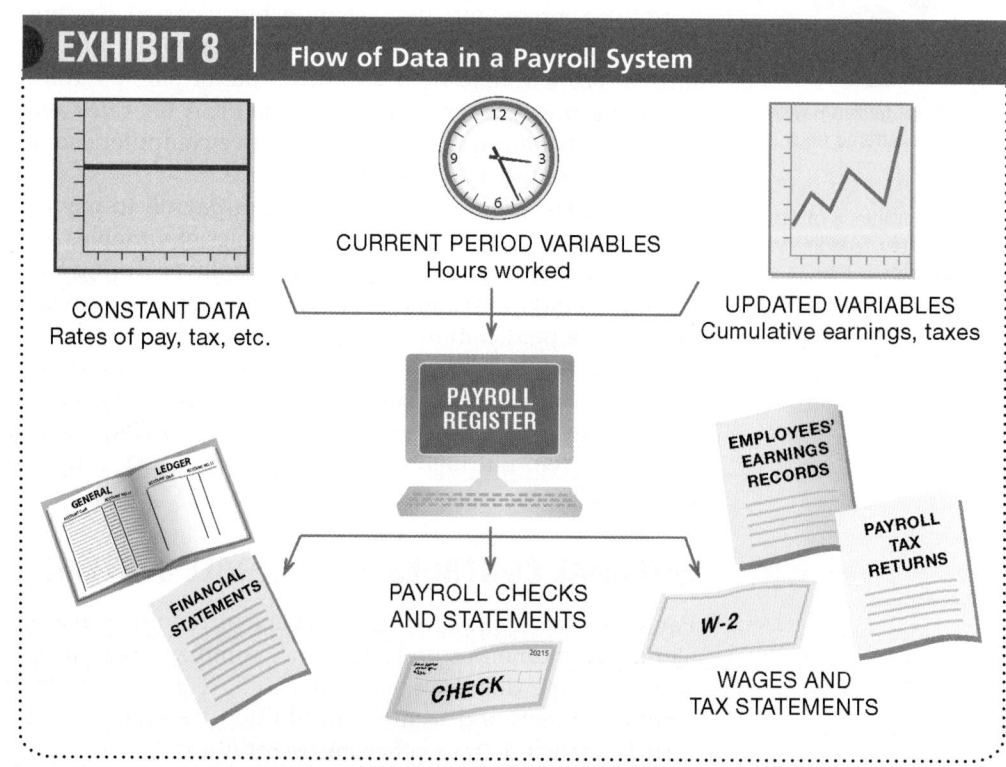

important that blank payroll checks and access to the machine be carefully controlled to prevent the theft or misuse of payroll funds.

It is especially important to authorize and approve in writing employee additions and deletions and changes in pay rates. For example, numerous payroll frauds have involved a supervisor adding fictitious employees to the payroll. The supervisor then cashes the fictitious employees' checks. Similar frauds have occurred where employees have been fired, but the Payroll Department is not notified. As a result, payroll checks to the fired employees are prepared and cashed by a supervisor.

To prevent or detect frauds such as those we described above, employees' attendance records should be controlled. For example, employee arrival and departure times for computing pay are often determined from a time clock stamp or from the scan of an employee identification card or badge. A Payroll Department employee may be stationed near the time clock or scanning device to verify that authorized employees are "clocking in" only once and only for themselves. When payroll checks are distributed, employee identification cards may be used to deter one employee from picking up another's check.

Other controls include verifying and approving all payroll rate changes. In addition, in a computerized system, all program changes should be properly approved and tested by employees who are independent of the payroll system. The use of a special payroll bank account, as we discussed earlier in this chapter, also enhances control over payroll.

Integrity, Objectivity, and Ethics in Business

ETHICS

$8 MILLION FOR 18 MINUTES OF WORK

Computer system controls can be very important in issuing payroll checks. In one case, a Detroit schoolteacher was paid $4,015,625 after deducting $3,884,375 in payroll deductions for 18 minutes of overtime work. The error was caused by a computer glitch when the teacher's employee identification number was substituted incorrectly in the "hourly wage" field and wasn't caught by the payroll software. After six days, the error was discovered and the money was returned. "One of the things that came with (the software) is a fail-safe that prevents that. It doesn't work," a financial officer said. The district has since installed a program to flag any paycheck exceeding $10,000.

Source: Associated Press, September 27, 2002.

Employees' Fringe Benefits

objective **4**

Journalize entries for employee fringe benefits, including vacation pay and pensions.

Many companies provide their employees a variety of benefits in addition to salary and wages earned. Such **fringe benefits** may take many forms, including vacations, medical, and postretirement benefits, such as pension plans. The U.S. Chamber of Commerce has estimated that fringe benefits, excluding FICA, average approximately 33% of gross wages. Exhibit 9 shows the three major categories of fringe benefits as a percent of total payroll costs as reported from the same survey.[7]

When the employer pays part or all of the cost of the fringe benefits, these costs must be recognized as expenses. To properly match revenues and expenses, the estimated cost of these benefits should be recorded as an expense during the period in which the employee earns the benefit, as we will illustrate in the next section for vacation pay.

VACATION PAY

Most employers grant vacation rights, sometimes called *compensated absences*, to their employees. Such rights give rise to a liability. The liability for employees' vacation

7 *2005 Employee Benefits Study*, U.S. Chamber of Commerce, 2006.

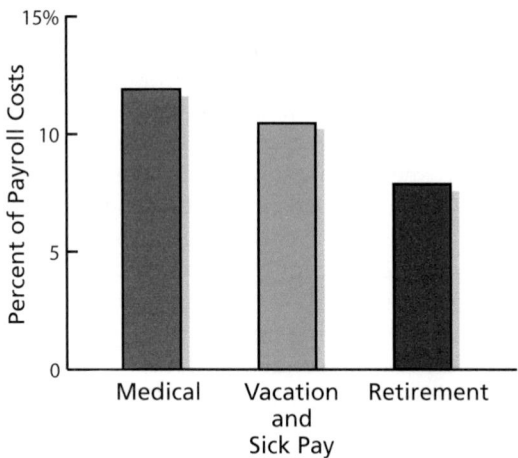

EXHIBIT 9

Benefit Dollars as a Percent of Payroll Costs

pay should be accrued as a liability as the vacation rights are earned. The entry to accrue vacation pay may be recorded in total at the end of each fiscal year, or it may be recorded at the end of each pay period. To illustrate this latter case, assume that employees earn one day of vacation for each month worked during the year. Assume also that the estimated vacation pay for the payroll period ending May 5 is $2,000. The entry to record the accrued vacation pay for this pay period is shown as follows:

> Vacation pay becomes the employer's liability as the employee earns vacation rights.

May	5	Vacation Pay Expense	2 0 0 0 00	
		Vacation Pay Payable		2 0 0 0 00
		Vacation pay for week ended May 5.		

If employees are required to take all their vacation time within one year, the vacation pay payable is reported on the balance sheet as a current liability. If employees are allowed to accumulate their vacation time, the estimated vacation pay liability that is applicable to time that will *not* be taken within one year is a long-term liability.

When payroll is prepared for the period in which employees have taken vacations, the vacation pay payable is reduced. The entry debits *Vacation Pay Payable* and credits *Salaries Payable* and the other related accounts for taxes and withholdings.

PENSIONS

A *pension* represents a cash payment to retired employees. Rights to pension payments are earned by employees during their working years, based on the pension plan established by the employer. One of the fundamental characteristics of such a plan is whether it is a defined contribution plan or a defined benefit plan.

Investment professionals advise employees to diversify their 401k investments and avoid concentrating investments in their employer's common stock so that they won't risk losing their retirement savings if their employer enters bankruptcy.

Defined Contribution Plan   In a **defined contribution plan**, a fixed amount of money is invested on the employee's behalf during the employee's working years. It is common for the employee and employer to make contributions. There is no promise of future pension benefit payments. The amount of the final pension depends on the total contributions and investment returns earned on those contributions over the employee's working years. The employee bears the investment risk under defined contribution plans.

One of the more popular defined contribution plans is the 401k plan. Under this plan, employees may contribute a limited part of their income to investments, such as mutual funds. A 401k plan offers employees two advantages: (1) the contribution is deducted, before taxes, from current period income, and (2) the contributions and future investment earnings are tax deferred until withdrawn at retirement. In addition, in 90% of the

401k plans, the employer matches some portion of the employee's contribution. These advantages are why nearly 70% of eligible employees elect to enroll in a 401k.[8]

The employer's cost of a defined contribution plan is debited to *Pension Expense*. To illustrate, assume that the pension plan of Heaven Scent Perfumes Company requires an employer contribution of 10% of employee monthly salaries, paid at the end of the month to the employee's plan administrator. The journal entry to record the transaction, assuming $500,000 of monthly salaries, is as follows:

Dec.	31	Pension Expense	50 000 00	
		Cash		50 000 00
		Contributed 10% of monthly salaries to		
		pension plan.		

Defined Benefit Plan Employers may choose to promise employees a fixed annual pension benefit at retirement, based on years of service and compensation levels. An example would be a promise to pay an annual pension based on a formula, such as the following:

1.5% × Years of Service × Average Salary for Most Recent 3 Years Prior to Retirement

Pension benefits based on a formula are termed a **defined benefit plan**. Unlike a defined contribution plan, the employer bears the investment risk in funding a future retirement income benefit. As a result, many companies are replacing their defined benefit plans with defined contribution plans.

The accounting for defined benefit plans is usually very complex due to the uncertainties of projecting future pension obligations. These obligations depend upon such factors as employee life expectancies, employee turnover, expected employee compensation levels, and investment income on pension contributions.

The pension cost of a defined benefit plan is debited to *Pension Expense*. The amount funded is credited to *Cash*. Any unfunded amount is credited to *Unfunded Pension Liability*. For example, assume that the pension plan of Hinkle Co. requires an annual pension cost of $80,000, based on an estimate of the future benefit obligation. Further assume that Hinkle Co. pays $60,000 to the pension fund. The entry to record this transaction is as follows:

Dec.	31	Pension Expense	80 000 00	
		Cash		60 000 00
		Unfunded Pension Liability		20 000 00
		To record annual pension cost and		
		contribution to pension plan.		

If the unfunded pension liability is to be paid within one year, it will be classified as a current liability. That portion of the liability to be paid beyond one year is a long-term liability.

Example Exercise 10-6 objective 4

Manfield Services Company provides its employees vacation benefits and a defined contribution pension plan. Employees earned vacation pay of $44,000 for the period. The pension plan requires a contribution to the plan administrator equal to 8% of employee salaries. Salaries were $450,000 during the period. Provide the journal entry for the (a) vacation pay and (b) pension benefit.

(continued)

---

8 "Employees Sluggish in Interacting with 401k Plans," Hewitt Associates, December 26, 2005.

Follow My Example 10-6

a.	Vacation Pay Expense	44,000	
	Vacation Pay Payable		44,000
	Vacation pay accrued for the period.		
b.	Pension Expense	36,000	
	Cash		36,000
	Pension contribution, 8% of $450,000 salary.		

For Practice: PE 10-6A, PE 10-6B

REAL WORLD

Twenty-one percent of private industry uses defined benefit plans, while 42% uses defined contribution plans.

Source: Bureau of Labor Statistics, "Employee Benefits in Private Industry," 2005.

POSTRETIREMENT BENEFITS OTHER THAN PENSIONS

In addition to the pension benefits described above, employees may earn rights to other *postretirement benefits* from their employer. Such benefits may include dental care, eye care, medical care, life insurance, tuition assistance, tax services, and legal services for employees or their dependents. The amount of the annual benefits expense is based upon health statistics of the workforce. This amount is recorded by debiting *Postretirement Benefits Expense*. *Cash* is credited for the same amount if the benefits are fully funded. If the benefits are not fully funded, a postretirement benefits plan liability account is credited. Thus, the accounting for postretirement health benefits is very similar to that of defined benefit pension plans.

A business's financial statements should fully disclose the nature of its postretirement benefit obligations. These disclosures are usually included as notes to the financial statements. The complex nature of accounting for postretirement benefits is described in more advanced accounting courses.

Contingent Liabilities

objective 5

Describe the accounting treatment for contingent liabilities and journalize entries for product warranties.

Some past transactions will result in liabilities if certain events occur in the future. These potential obligations are called *contingent liabilities*. For example, Ford Motor Company would have a contingent liability for the estimated costs associated with warranty work on new car sales. The obligation is contingent upon a *future event*, namely, a customer requiring warranty work on a vehicle. The obligation is the result of a *past transaction*, which is the original sale of the vehicle.

If a contingent liability is *probable* and the amount of the liability can be *reasonably estimated*, it should be recorded in the accounts. Ford Motor Company's vehicle warranty costs are an example of a *recordable* contingent liability. The warranty costs are *probable* because it is known that warranty repairs will be required on some vehicles. In addition, the costs can be *estimated* from past warranty experience.

To illustrate, assume that during June a company sells a product for $60,000 on which there is a 36-month warranty for repairing defects. Past experience indicates that the average cost to repair defects is 5% of the sales price over the warranty period. The entry to record the estimated product warranty expense for June is as follows:

June	30	Product Warranty Expense	3 0 0 0 00		
		Product Warranty Payable		3 0 0 0 00	
		Warranty expense for June, 5% × $60,000.			

This transaction matches revenues and expenses properly by recording warranty costs in the same period in which the sale is recorded. When the defective product is

DO YOU WANT TO BE A MILLIONAIRE?

A recent survey found that 66% of individuals believe that their standard of living at retirement will be the same or higher than during their current working years. Yet, nearly 30% of these respondents don't have a formal savings plan for retirement. One-fourth of these respondents believe that they will need to save only $100,000 in order to maintain their lifestyle in retirement. However, experts believe that today's 25-year-old will need savings of $750,000 to $1 million to support a basic retirement, given increased life expectancies and inflation. How do you save this much money? The two keys to savings success are (1) save regularly, such as monthly or quarterly, even if it's a small amount, and (2) start early. For example, to have the same retirement income as a 25-year-old saving $100 per month, a 30-year-old would need to save $200 per month. Waiting until you are 35 years old would require saving $400 per month. Every five years of delay requires doubling the necessary contribution. This is the power of compound interest. Therefore, the worst strategy is to begin retirement saving at middle age.

So how much would a 25-year-old need to save monthly to reach the $1 million mark? There are many assumptions that go into such a calculation. Let's assume that an individual begins saving $150 per month at the age of 25, earns 8% on these savings, increases the amount contributed by 5% per year (to match salary increases), and retires at the age of 65. Under these assumptions, the individual would accumulate $975,000 by age 65.

repaired, the repair costs are recorded by debiting *Product Warranty Payable* and crediting *Cash, Supplies, Wages Payable*, or other appropriate accounts. Thus, if a customer required a $200 part replacement on August 16, the entry would be as follows:

Aug.	16	Product Warranty Payable	2 0 0 00	
		Supplies		2 0 0 00
		Replaced defective part under warranty.		

If a contingent liability is probable but cannot be *reasonably estimated* or is only *possible*, then the nature of the contingent liability should be disclosed in the notes to the financial statements. Professional judgment is required in distinguishing between contingent liabilities that are probable versus those that are only possible.

Common examples of contingent liabilities disclosed in notes to the financial statements are litigation, environmental matters, guarantees, and contingencies from the sale of receivables. The following is an example of a contingency disclosure related to litigation from a recent annual report of Google Inc., the popular Internet search engine provider:

Certain entities have also filed copyright claims against us, alleging that certain of our products, including Google Web Search, Google News, Google Image Search, and Google Book Search, infringe their rights. Adverse results in these lawsuits may include awards of damages and may also result in, or even compel, a change in our business practices, which could result in a loss of revenue for us or otherwise harm our business.

Although the results of litigation and claims cannot be predicted with certainty, we believe that the final outcome of the matters discussed above will not have a material adverse effect on our business. . . .

The accounting treatment of contingent liabilities is summarized in Exhibit 10.

EXHIBIT 10   Accounting Treatment of Contingent Liabilities

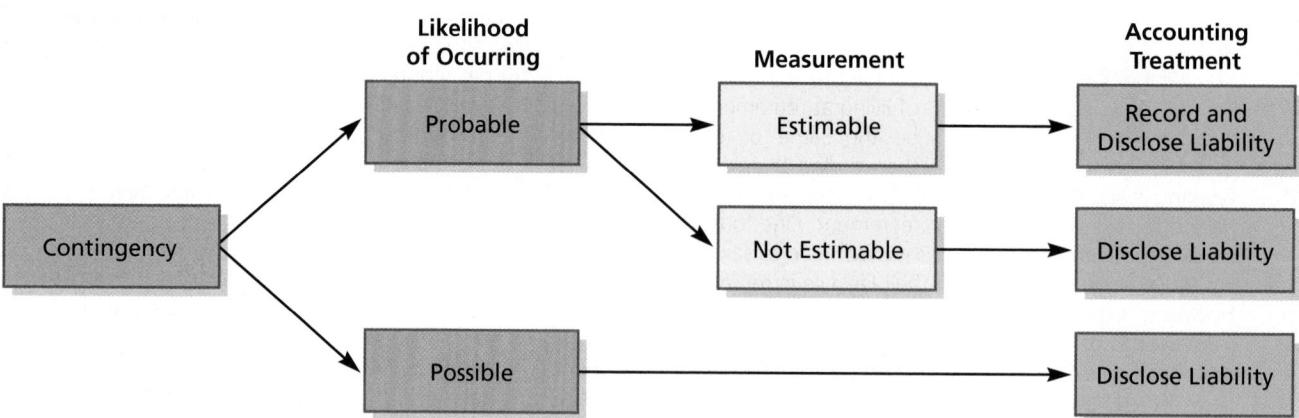

Likelihood of Occurring	Measurement	Accounting Treatment

Contingency → Probable → Estimable → Record and Disclose Liability

Probable → Not Estimable → Disclose Liability

Contingency → Possible → Disclose Liability

Example Exercise 10-7

Cook-Rite Co. sold $140,000 of kitchen appliances during August under a six-month warranty. The cost to repair defects under the warranty is estimated at 6% of the sales price. On September 11, a customer required a $200 part replacement, plus $90 of labor under the warranty.

    Provide the journal entry for (a) the estimated warranty expense on August 31 and (b) the September 11 warranty work.

Follow My Example 10-7

a.	Product Warranty Expense	8,400	
	Product Warranty Payable		8,400
	To record warranty expense for August, 6% × $140,000.		
b.	Product Warranty Payable	290	
	Supplies		200
	Wages Payable		90
	Replaced defective part under warranty.		

For Practice: PE 10-7A, PE 10-7B

Integrity, Objectivity, and Ethics in Business

ETHICS

TODAY'S MISTAKES CAN BE TOMORROW'S LIABILITY

Environmental and public health claims are quickly growing into some of the largest contingent liabilities facing companies. For example, tobacco, asbestos, and environmental cleanup claims have reached billions of dollars and have led to a number of corporate bankruptcies. Managers must be careful that today's decisions do not become tomorrow's nightmare.

Financial Analysis and Interpretation

The Current Assets and Current Liabilities sections of the balance sheet for Noble Co. and Hart Co. are illustrated as follows:

	Noble Co.	Hart Co.
Current assets:		
Cash	$147,000	$120,000
Accounts receivable (net)	84,000	472,000
Inventory	150,000	200,000
Total	$381,000	$792,000
Current liabilities:		
Accounts payable	$ 75,000	$227,000
Wages payable	30,000	193,000
Notes payable	115,000	320,000
Total	$220,000	$740,000

We can use this information to evaluate Noble's and Hart's ability to pay their current liabilities within a short period of time, using the **quick ratio** or *acid-test ratio*. The quick ratio is computed as follows:

$$\text{Quick Ratio} = \frac{\text{Quick Assets}}{\text{Current Liabilities}}$$

The quick ratio measures the "instant" debt-paying ability of a company, using quick assets. **Quick assets** are cash, receivables, and other current assets that can quickly be converted into cash. It is often considered desirable to have a quick ratio exceeding 1.0. A ratio less than 1.0 would indicate that current liabilities cannot be covered by cash and "near cash" assets.

To illustrate, the quick ratios for both companies would be:

$$\text{Noble Co:} \quad \frac{\$147,000 + \$84,000}{\$220,000} = 1.05$$

$$\text{Hart Co:} \quad \frac{\$120,000 + \$472,000}{\$740,000} = 0.80$$

As you can see, Noble Co. has quick assets in excess of current liabilities, or a quick ratio of 1.05. The ratio exceeds 1.0, indicating that the quick assets should be sufficient to meet current liabilities. Hart Co., however, has a quick ratio of 0.8. Its quick assets will not be sufficient to cover the current liabilities. Hart could solve this problem by working with a bank to convert its short-term debt of $320,000 into a long-term obligation. This would remove the notes payable from current liabilities. If Hart did this, then its quick ratio would improve to 1.4 ($592,000/$420,000), which would be sufficient for quick assets to cover current liabilities.

At a Glance

1. Describe and illustrate current liabilities related to accounts payable, current portion of long-term debt, and notes payable.

Key Points	Key Learning Outcomes	Example Exercises	Practice Exercises
Current liabilities are obligations that are to be paid out of current assets and are due within a short time, usually within one year. The three primary types of current liabilities are accounts payable, notes payable, and current portion of long-term debt.	• Identify and define the most frequently reported current liabilities on the balance sheet. • Determine the interest from interest-bearing and discounted notes payable.	10-1	10-1A, 10-1B

2. Determine employer liabilities for payroll, including liabilities arising from employee earnings and deductions from earnings.

Key Points	Key Learning Outcomes	Example Exercises	Practice Exercises
An employer's liability for payroll is determined from employee total earnings, including overtime pay. From this amount, employee deductions are subtracted to arrive at the net pay to be paid to each employee. Most employers also incur liabilities for payroll taxes, such as social security tax, Medicare tax, federal unemployment compensation tax, and state unemployment compensation tax.	• Calculate the federal withholding tax from a wage bracket withholding table. • Compute employee net pay, including deductions for social security and Medicare tax.	10-2 10-3	10-2A, 10-2B 10-3A, 10-3B

3. Describe payroll accounting systems that use a payroll register, employee earnings records, and a general journal.

Key Points	Key Learning Outcomes	Example Exercises	Practice Exercises
The payroll register is used in assembling and summarizing the data needed for each payroll period. The payroll register is supported by a detailed payroll record for each employee, called an *employee's earnings record*.	• Journalize the employee's earnings, net pay, and payroll liabilities from the payroll register. • Journalize the payroll tax expense. • Describe elements of a payroll system, including the employee's earnings record, payroll checks, and internal controls.	10-4 10-5	10-4A, 10-4B 10-5A, 10-5B

4. Journalize entries for employee fringe benefits, including vacation pay and pensions.

Key Points	Key Learning Outcomes	Example Exercises	Practice Exercises
Fringe benefits are expenses of the period in which the employees earn the benefits. Fringe benefits are recorded by debiting an expense account and crediting a liability account.	• Journalize vacation pay. • Distinguish and journalize defined contribution and defined benefit pension plans.	10-6 10-6	10-6A, 10-6B 10-6A, 10-6B

5. Describe the accounting treatment for contingent liabilities and journalize entries for product warranties.

Key Points	Key Learning Outcomes	Example Exercises	Practice Exercises
A contingent liability is a potential obligation that results from a past transaction but depends on a future event. If the contingent liability is both probable and estimable, the liability should be recorded.	• Describe the accounting for contingent liabilities. • Journalize estimated warranty obligations and services granted under warranty.	10-7	10-7A, 10-7B

Key Terms

defined benefit plan (457)
defined contribution plan (456)
discount (441)
discount rate (441)
employee's earnings record (451)

FICA tax (445)
fringe benefits (455)
gross pay (443)
net pay (443)
payroll (442)

payroll register (448)
proceeds (441)
quick assets (461)
quick ratio (461)

Illustrative Problem

Selected transactions of Taylor Company, completed during the fiscal year ended December 31, are as follows:

Mar. 1. Purchased merchandise on account from Kelvin Co., $20,000.

Apr. 10. Issued a 60-day, 12% note for $20,000 to Kelvin Co. on account.

June 9. Paid Kelvin Co. the amount owed on the note of April 10.

Aug. 1. Issued a $50,000, 90-day note to Harold Co. in exchange for a building. Harold Co. discounted the note at 15%.

Oct. 30. Paid Harold Co. the amount due on the note of August 1.

Dec. 27. Journalized the entry to record the biweekly payroll. A summary of the payroll record follows:

Salary distribution:		
Sales	$63,400	
Officers	36,600	
Office	10,000	$110,000
Deductions:		
Social security tax	$ 5,050	
Medicare tax	1,650	
Federal income tax withheld	17,600	
State income tax withheld	4,950	
Savings bond deductions	850	
Medical insurance deductions	1,120	31,220
Net amount		$ 78,780

27. Journalized the entry to record payroll taxes for social security and Medicare from the biweekly payroll.

30. Issued a check in payment of liabilities for employees' federal income tax of $17,600, social security tax of $10,100, and Medicare tax of $3,300.

31. Issued a check for $9,500 to the pension fund trustee to fully fund the pension cost for December.

(continued)

Dec. 31. Journalized an entry to record the employees' accrued vacation pay, $36,100.
    31. Journalized an entry to record the estimated accrued product warranty liability, $37,240.

Instructions
Journalize the preceding transactions.

Solution

Date		Account	Debit	Credit
Mar.	1	Merchandise Inventory	20 0 0 0 00	
		Accounts Payable—Kelvin Co.		20 0 0 0 00
Apr.	10	Accounts Payable—Kelvin Co.	20 0 0 0 00	
		Notes Payable		20 0 0 0 00
June	9	Notes Payable	20 0 0 0 00	
		Interest Expense	4 0 0 00	
		Cash		20 4 0 0 00
Aug.	1	Building	48 1 2 5 00	
		Interest Expense	1 8 7 5 00	
		Notes Payable		50 0 0 0 00
Oct.	30	Notes Payable	50 0 0 0 00	
		Cash		50 0 0 0 00
Dec.	27	Sales Salaries Expense	63 4 0 0 00	
		Officers Salaries Expense	36 6 0 0 00	
		Office Salaries Expense	10 0 0 0 00	
		Social Security Tax Payable		5 0 5 0 00
		Medicare Tax Payable		1 6 5 0 00
		Employees Federal Income Tax Payable		17 6 0 0 00
		Employees State Income Tax Payable		4 9 5 0 00
		Bond Deductions Payable		8 5 0 00
		Medical Insurance Payable		1 1 2 0 00
		Salaries Payable		78 7 8 0 00
	27	Payroll Tax Expense	6 7 0 0 00	
		Social Security Tax Payable		5 0 5 0 00
		Medicare Tax Payable		1 6 5 0 00
	30	Employees Federal Income Tax Payable	17 6 0 0 00	
		Social Security Tax Payable	10 1 0 0 00	
		Medicare Tax Payable	3 3 0 0 00	
		Cash		31 0 0 0 00
	31	Pension Expense	9 5 0 0 00	
		Cash		9 5 0 0 00
	31	Vacation Pay Expense	36 1 0 0 00	
		Vacation Pay Payable		36 1 0 0 00
	31	Product Warranty Expense	37 2 4 0 00	
		Product Warranty Payable		37 2 4 0 00

Self-Examination Questions

(Answers at End of Chapter)

1. A business issued a $5,000, 60-day, 12% note to the bank. The amount due at maturity is:
   A. $4,900.   C. $5,100.
   B. $5,000.   D. $5,600.

2. A business issued a $5,000, 60-day note to a supplier, which discounted the note at 12%. The proceeds are:
   A. $4,400.   C. $5,000.
   B. $4,900.   D. $5,100.

3. Which of the following taxes are employers usually not required to withhold from employees?
   A. Federal income tax
   B. Federal unemployment compensation tax
   C. Medicare tax
   D. State and local income tax

4. An employee's rate of pay is $40 per hour, with time and a half for all hours worked in excess of 40 during a week. The social security rate is 6.0% on the first $100,000 of annual earnings, and the Medicare rate is 1.5% on all earnings. The following additional data are available:

Hours worked during current week	45
Year's cumulative earnings prior to current week	$99,400
Federal income tax withheld	$450

   Based on these data, the amount of the employee's net pay for the current week is:
   A. $1,307.50.   C. $1,450.00.
   B. $1,405.00.   D. $1,385.50.

5. Within limitations on the maximum earnings subject to the tax, employers do not incur an expense for which of the following payroll taxes?
   A. Social security tax
   B. Federal unemployment compensation tax
   C. State unemployment compensation tax
   D. Employees' federal income tax

Eye Openers

1. Does a discounted note payable provide credit without interest? Discuss.
2. Employees are subject to taxes withheld from their paychecks.
   a. List the federal taxes withheld from most employee paychecks.
   b. Give the title of the accounts credited by amounts withheld.
3. For each of the following payroll-related taxes, indicate whether there is a ceiling on the annual earnings subject to the tax: (a) federal income tax, (b) Medicare tax, (c) social security tax, (d) federal unemployment compensation tax.
4. Why are deductions from employees' earnings classified as liabilities for the employer?
5. Taylor Company, with 20 employees, is expanding operations. It is trying to decide whether to hire one full-time employee for $25,000 or two part-time employees for a total of $25,000. Would any of the employer's payroll taxes discussed in this chapter have a bearing on this decision? Explain.
6. For each of the following payroll-related taxes, indicate whether they generally apply to (a) employees only, (b) employers only, or (c) both employees and employers:
   1. Federal income tax
   2. Medicare tax
   3. Social security tax
   4. Federal unemployment compensation tax
   5. State unemployment compensation tax
7. What are the principal reasons for using a special payroll checking account?
8. In a payroll system, what types of input data are referred to as (a) constants and (b) variables?
9. Explain how a payroll system that is properly designed and operated tends to ensure that (a) wages paid are based on hours actually worked and (b) payroll checks are not issued to fictitious employees.
10. To match revenues and expenses properly, should the expense for employee vacation pay be recorded in the period during which the vacation privilege is earned or during the period in which the vacation is taken? Discuss.
11. Identify several factors that influence the future pension obligation of an employer under a defined benefit pension plan.

12. When should the liability associated with a product warranty be recorded? Discuss.
13. General Motors Corporation reported $8.8 billion of product warranties in the Current Liabilities section of a recent balance sheet. How would costs of repairing a defective product be recorded?
14. The "Questions and Answers Technical Hotline" in the *Journal of Accountancy* included the following question:

Several years ago, Company B instituted legal action against Company A. Under a memorandum of settlement and agreement, Company A agreed to pay Company B a total of $17,500 in three installments—$5,000 on March 1, $7,500 on July 1, and the remaining $5,000 on December 31. Company A paid the first two installments during its fiscal year ended September 30. Should the unpaid amount of $5,000 be presented as a current liability at September 30?

How would you answer this question?

Practice Exercises

PE 10-1A
Calculate proceeds from notes payable
obj. 1

On September 1, Klondike Co. issued a 90-day note with a face amount of $120,000 to Arctic Apparel Co. for merchandise inventory.

a. Determine the proceeds of the note, assuming the note carries an interest rate of 8%.
b. Determine the proceeds of the note, assuming the note is discounted at 8%.

PE 10-1B
Calculate proceeds from notes payable
obj. 1

On February 1, Electronic Warehouse Co. issued a 30-day note with a face amount of $50,000 to Yamura Products Co. for cash.

a. Determine the proceeds of the note, assuming the note carries an interest rate of 6%.
b. Determine the proceeds of the note, assuming the note is discounted at 6%.

PE 10-2A
Calculate federal income tax withholding
obj. 2

Don Truett's weekly gross earnings for the present week were $1,680. Truett has three exemptions. Using the wage bracket withholding table in Exhibit 3 with a $63 standard withholding allowance for each exemption, what is Truett's federal income tax withholding?

PE 10-2B
Calculate federal income tax withholding
obj. 2

Leah Wilson's weekly gross earnings for the present week were $600. Wilson has one exemption. Using the wage bracket withholding table in Exhibit 3 with a $63 standard withholding allowance for each exemption, what is Wilson's federal income tax withholding?

PE 10-3A
Calculate employee net pay
obj. 2

Don Truett's weekly gross earnings for the week ending December 18 were $1,680, and his federal income tax withholding was $298.51. Prior to this week, Truett had earned $99,000 for the year. Assuming the social security rate is 6% on the first $100,000 of annual earnings and Medicare is 1.5% of all earnings, what is Truett's net pay?

PE 10-3B
Calculate employee net pay
obj. 2

Leah Wilson's weekly gross earnings for the week ending September 5 were $600, and her federal income tax withholding was $65.85. Prior to this week, Wilson had earned $21,500 for the year. Assuming the social security rate is 6% on the first $100,000 of annual earnings and Medicare is 1.5% of all earnings, what is Wilson's net pay?

PE 10-4A
Journalize period payroll
obj. 3

The payroll register of Lowry Landscaping Co. indicates $1,260 of social security withheld and $315 of Medicare tax withheld on total salaries of $21,000 for the period. Federal income tax withholding for the period totaled $3,822.
Provide the journal entry for the period's payroll.

PE 10-4B
Journalize period payroll
obj. 3

The payroll register of Tri-State Construction Co. indicates $25,650 of social security withheld and $6,750 of Medicare tax withheld on total salaries of $450,000 for the period. Retirement savings withheld from employee paychecks were $27,000 for the period. Federal income tax withholding for the period totaled $89,100.

Provide the journal entry for the period's payroll.

PE 10-5A
Journalize period payroll tax
obj. 3

The payroll register of Lowry Landscaping Co. indicates $1,260 of social security withheld and $315 of Medicare tax withheld on total salaries of $21,000 for the period. Assume earnings subject to state and federal unemployment compensation taxes are $6,540, at the federal rate of 0.8% and the state rate of 5.4%.

Provide the journal entry to record the payroll tax expense for the period.

PE 10-5B
Journalize period payroll tax
obj. 3

The payroll register of Tri-State Construction Co. indicates $25,650 of social security withheld and $6,750 of Medicare tax withheld on total salaries of $450,000 for the period. Assume earnings subject to state and federal unemployment compensation taxes are $12,550, at the federal rate of 0.8% and the state rate of 5.4%.

Provide the journal entry to record the payroll tax expense for the period.

PE 10-6A
Journalize vacation pay and pension benefits
obj. 4

Kirby Company provides its employees with vacation benefits and a defined contribution pension plan. Employees earned vacation pay of $17,500 for the period. The pension plan requires a contribution to the plan administrator equal to 7% of employee salaries. Salaries were $180,000 during the period.

Provide the journal entry for the (a) vacation pay and (b) pension benefit.

PE 10-6B
Journalize vacation pay and pension benefits
obj. 4

Lyon Capital Company provides its employees vacation benefits and a defined benefit pension plan. Employees earned vacation pay of $52,300 for the period. The pension formula calculated a pension cost of $123,000. Only $100,000 was contributed to the pension plan administrator.

Provide the journal entry for the (a) vacation pay and (b) pension benefit.

PE 10-7A
Journalize estimated warranty liability
obj. 5

EZ Equipment Co. sold $870,000 of equipment during March under a one-year warranty. The cost to repair defects under the warranty is estimated at 4.5% of the sales price. On October 4, a customer required a $420 part replacement, plus $100 of labor under the warranty.

Provide the journal entry for (a) the estimated warranty expense on March 31 and (b) the October 4 warranty work.

PE 10-7B
Journalize estimated warranty liability
obj. 5

Tower Electronics sold $480,000 of consumer electronics during June under a nine-month warranty. The cost to repair defects under the warranty is estimated at 5% of the sales price. On August 16, a customer was given $90 cash under terms of the warranty.

Provide the journal entry for (a) the estimated warranty expense on June 30 and (b) the August 16 cash payment.

Exercises

EX 10-1
Current liabilities
obj. 1

✓ Total current liabilities, $348,250

Rock On Magazine Co. sold 11,400 annual subscriptions of *Rock On* for $35 during December 2008. These new subscribers will receive monthly issues, beginning in January 2009. In addition, the business had taxable income of $140,000 during the first calendar quarter of 2009. The federal tax rate is 35%. A quarterly tax payment will be made on April 7, 2009.

Prepare the Current Liabilities section of the balance sheet for Rock On Magazine Co. on March 31, 2009.

EX 10-2
Entries for discounting notes payable

obj. 1

Home Center Warehouse issues a 90-day note for $250,000 to Gem Lighting Co. for merchandise inventory. Gem Lighting Co. discounts the note at 5%.

a. Journalize Home Center Warehouse's entries to record:
   1. the issuance of the note.
   2. the payment of the note at maturity.
b. Journalize Gem Lighting Co.'s entries to record:
   1. the receipt of the note.
   2. the receipt of the payment of the note at maturity.

EX 10-3
Evaluate alternative notes

obj. 1

A borrower has two alternatives for a loan: (1) issue a $120,000, 90-day, 6% note or (2) issue a $120,000, 90-day note that the creditor discounts at 6%.

a. Calculate the amount of the interest expense for each option.
b. Determine the proceeds received by the borrower in each situation.
c. ▸ Which alternative is more favorable to the borrower? Explain.

EX 10-4
Entries for notes payable

obj. 1

A business issued a 60-day, 7% note for $15,000 to a creditor on account. Journalize the entries to record (a) the issuance of the note and (b) the payment of the note at maturity, including interest.

EX 10-5
Entries for discounted note payable

obj. 1

A business issued a 90-day note for $80,000 to a creditor on account. The note was discounted at 8%. Journalize the entries to record (a) the issuance of the note and (b) the payment of the note at maturity.

EX 10-6
Fixed asset purchases with note

obj. 1

On June 30, Mystic Mountain Game Company purchased land for $250,000 and a building for $690,000, paying $240,000 cash and issuing an 8% note for the balance, secured by a mortgage on the property. The terms of the note provide for 20 semiannual payments of $35,000 on the principal plus the interest accrued from the date of the preceding payment. Journalize the entry to record (a) the transaction on June 30, (b) the payment of the first installment on December 31, and (c) the payment of the second installment the following June 30.

EX 10-7
Current portion of long-term debt

obj. 1

WD-40 Company, the manufacturer and marketer of WD-40® lubricant, reported the following information about its long-term debt in the notes to a recent financial statement:

Long-term debt is comprised of the following:

	August 31,	
	---	---
	2005	**2004**
Notes payable	$ 75,000,000	$ 85,000,000
Less current portion	(10,714,000)	(10,000,000)
Long-term debt	$ 64,286,000	$ 75,000,000

a. How much of the notes payable was disclosed as a current liability on the August 31, 2005, balance sheet?
b. How much did the total current liabilities change between 2004 and 2005 as a result of the current portion of long-term debt?
c. If WD-40 did not issue additional notes payable during 2006, what would be the total notes payable on August 31, 2006?

EX 10-8
Calculate payroll

obj. 2

An employee earns $22 per hour and 1½ times that rate for all hours in excess of 40 hours per week. Assume that the employee worked 50 hours during the week, and that the gross pay prior to the current week totaled $42,710. Assume further that the social security tax

✓ b. Net pay, $883.25

rate was 6.0% (on earnings up to $100,000), the Medicare tax rate was 1.5%, and federal income tax to be withheld was $236.

a. Determine the gross pay for the week.
b. Determine the net pay for the week.

EX 10-9
Calculate payroll
obj. 2

✓ *Administrator net pay, $829.32*

Strategem Business Consultants has three employees—a consultant, a computer programmer, and an administrator. The following payroll information is available for each employee:

	Consultant	Computer Programmer	Administrator
Regular earnings rate	$2,400 per week	$40 per hour	$22 per hour
Overtime earnings rate	Not applicable	1½ times hourly rate	1½ times hourly rate
Gross pay prior to current pay period	$115,200	$98,600	$43,100
Number of withholding allowances	1	0	3

For the current pay period, the computer programmer worked 48 hours and the administrator worked 45 hours. The federal income tax withheld for all three employees, who are single, can be determined from the wage bracket withholding table in Exhibit 3 in the chapter. Assume further that the social security tax rate was 6.0% on the first $100,000 of annual earnings, the Medicare tax rate was 1.5%, and one withholding allowance is $63.

Determine the gross pay and the net pay for each of the three employees for the current pay period.

EX 10-10
Summary payroll data
objs. 2, 3

✓ *a. (3) Total earnings, $260,000*

In the following summary of data for a payroll period, some amounts have been intentionally omitted:

Earnings:	
1. At regular rate	?
2. At overtime rate	$ 39,480
3. Total earnings	?
Deductions:	
4. Social security tax	15,250
5. Medicare tax	3,900
6. Income tax withheld	46,590
7. Medical insurance	7,775
8. Union dues	?
9. Total deductions	76,000
10. Net amount paid	184,000
Accounts debited:	
11. Factory Wages	138,900
12. Sales Salaries	?
13. Office Salaries	59,200

a. Calculate the amounts omitted in lines (1), (3), (8), and (12).
b. Journalize the entry to record the payroll accrual.
c. Journalize the entry to record the payment of the payroll.
d. ▭▭▭▶ From the data given in this exercise and your answer to (a), would you conclude that this payroll was paid sometime during the first few weeks of the calendar year? Explain.

EX 10-11
Payroll tax entries
obj. 3

According to a summary of the payroll of Glitz Publishing Co., $350,000 was subject to the 6.0% social security tax and $420,000 was subject to the 1.5% Medicare tax. Also, $14,000 was subject to state and federal unemployment taxes.

a. Calculate the employer's payroll taxes, using the following rates: state unemployment, 4.3%; federal unemployment, 0.8%.
b. Journalize the entry to record the accrual of payroll taxes.

EX 10-12
Payroll entries
obj. 3

The payroll register for Hillsdale Company for the week ended December 14 indicated the following:

Salaries	$690,000
Social security tax withheld	32,700
Medicare tax withheld	10,350
Federal income tax withheld	138,700

In addition, federal and state unemployment taxes were calculated at the rate of 0.8% and 5.2%, respectively, on $26,000 of salaries.

a. Journalize the entry to record the payroll for the week of December 14.
b. Journalize the entry to record the payroll tax expense incurred for the week of December 14.

EX 10-13
Payroll entries
obj. 3

Dowling Company had gross wages of $356,000 during the week ended December 6. The amount of wages subject to social security tax was $285,000, while the amount of wages subject to federal and state unemployment taxes was $18,000. Tax rates are as follows:

Social security	6.0%
Medicare	1.5%
State unemployment	5.4%
Federal unemployment	0.8%

The total amount withheld from employee wages for federal taxes was $66,900.

a. Journalize the entry to record the payroll for the week of December 6.
b. Journalize the entry to record the payroll tax expense incurred for the week of December 6.

EX 10-14
Payroll internal control procedures
obj. 3

Nashville Sounds is a retail store specializing in the sale of country music. The store employs 3 full-time and 10 part-time workers. The store's weekly payroll averages $2,500 for all 13 workers.

Nashville Sounds uses a personal computer to assist in preparing paychecks. Each week, the store's accountant collects employee time cards and enters the hours worked into the payroll program. The payroll program calculates each employee's pay and prints a paycheck. The accountant uses a check-signing machine to sign the paychecks. Next, the store's manager authorizes the transfer of funds from the store's regular bank account to the payroll account.

For the week of May 10, the accountant accidentally recorded 400 hours worked instead of 40 hours for one of the full-time employees.

Does Nashville Sounds have internal controls in place to catch this error? If so, how will this error be detected?

EX 10-15
Internal control procedures
obj. 3

Handyman's Helper is a small manufacturer of home workshop power tools. The company employs 30 production workers and 10 administrative persons. The following procedures are used to process the company's weekly payroll:

a. All employees are required to record their hours worked by clocking in and out on a time clock. Employees must clock out for lunch break. Due to congestion around the time clock area at lunch time, management has not objected to having one employee clock in and out for an entire department.
b. Whenever a salaried employee is terminated, Personnel authorizes Payroll to remove the employee from the payroll system. However, this procedure is not required when an hourly worker is terminated. Hourly employees only receive a paycheck if their time cards show hours worked. The computer automatically drops an employee from the payroll system when that employee has six consecutive weeks with no hours worked.
c. Whenever an employee receives a pay raise, the supervisor must fill out a wage adjustment form, which is signed by the company president. This form is used to change the employee's wage rate in the payroll system.

d. Handyman's Helper maintains a separate checking account for payroll checks. Each week, the total net pay for all employees is transferred from the company's regular bank account to the payroll account.

e. Paychecks are signed by using a check-signing machine. This machine is located in the main office so that it can be easily accessed by anyone needing a check signed.

⬛▬▶ State whether each of the procedures is appropriate or inappropriate after considering the principles of internal control. If a procedure is inappropriate, describe the appropriate procedure.

EX 10-16
Payroll procedures
obj. 3

The fiscal year for Super Sale Stores Co. ends on June 30. In addition, the company computes and reports payroll taxes on a fiscal-year basis. Thus, it applies social security and FUTA maximum earnings limitations to the fiscal-year payroll.

⬛▬▶ What is wrong with these procedures for accounting for payroll taxes?

EX 10-17
Accrued vacation pay
obj. 4

A business provides its employees with varying amounts of vacation per year, depending on the length of employment. The estimated amount of the current year's vacation pay is $54,960. Journalize the adjusting entry required on January 31, the end of the first month of the current year, to record the accrued vacation pay.

EX 10-18
Pension plan entries
obj. 4

Precious Images Co. operates a chain of photography stores. The company maintains a defined contribution pension plan for its employees. The plan requires quarterly installments to be paid to the funding agent, Safeguard Funds, by the fifteenth of the month following the end of each quarter. Assuming that the pension cost is $87,500 for the quarter ended December 31, journalize entries to record (a) the accrued pension liability on December 31 and (b) the payment to the funding agent on January 15.

EX 10-19
Defined benefit pension plan terms
obj. 4

In a recent year's financial statements, Procter & Gamble showed an unfunded pension liability of $2,096 million and a periodic pension cost of $268 million.

Explain the meaning of the $2,096 million unfunded pension liability and the $268 million periodic pension cost.

EX 10-20
Accrued product warranty
obj. 5

Audio-Wave Company warrants its products for one year. The estimated product warranty is 2% of sales. Assume that sales were $85,000 for January. In February, a customer received warranty repairs requiring $210 of parts and $135 of labor.

a. Journalize the adjusting entry required at January 31, the end of the first month of the current year, to record the accrued product warranty.

b. Journalize the entry to record the warranty work provided in February.

EX 10-21
Accrued product warranty
obj. 5

Ford Motor Company disclosed estimated product warranty payable for comparative years as follows:

	(in millions)	
	12/31/05	**12/31/04**
Current estimated product warranty payable	$12,953	$14,082
Noncurrent estimated product warranty payable	7,359	7,728
Total	$20,312	$21,810

Ford's sales were $147,128 million in 2004 and increased to $153,503 million in 2005. Assume that the total paid on warranty claims during 2005 was $12,000 million.

a. ⬛▬▶ Why are short- and long-term estimated warranty liabilities separately disclosed?

b. Provide the journal entry for the 2005 product warranty expense.

EX 10-22
Contingent liabilities
obj. 5

Several months ago, Rainbow Paint Company experienced a hazardous materials spill at one of its plants. As a result, the Environmental Protection Agency (EPA) fined the company $560,000. The company is contesting the fine. In addition, an employee is seeking $275,000 damages related to the spill. Lastly, a homeowner has sued the company for $190,000. The homeowner lives 25 miles from the plant but believes that the incident has reduced the home's resale value by $190,000.

Rainbow's legal counsel believes that it is probable that the EPA fine will stand. In addition, counsel indicates that an out-of-court settlement of $150,000 has recently been reached with the employee. The final papers will be signed next week. Counsel believes that the homeowner's case is much weaker and will be decided in favor of Rainbow. Other litigation related to the spill is possible, but the damage amounts are uncertain.

a. Journalize the contingent liabilities associated with the hazardous materials spill. Use the account "Damage Awards and Fines" to recognize the expense for the period.
b. ▰▰▰▶ Prepare a note disclosure relating to this incident.

EX 10-23
Quick ratio

✓ *a. 2008: 1.0*

Urban-Wear Clothes Co. had the following current assets and liabilities for two comparative years:

	Dec. 31, 2008	Dec. 31, 2007
Current assets:		
Cash	$140,000	$205,000
Accounts receivable	250,000	245,000
Inventory	300,000	180,000
Total current assets	$690,000	$630,000
Current liabilities:		
Current portion of long-term debt	$ 50,000	$ 50,000
Accounts payable	200,000	190,000
Accrued expenses payable	140,000	135,000
Total current liabilities	$390,000	$375,000

a. Determine the quick ratio for December 31, 2008 and 2007.
b. ▰▰▰▶ Interpret the change in the quick ratio between the two balance sheet dates.

EX 10-24
Quick ratio

The current assets and current liabilities for Apple Computer, Inc., and Dell Inc. are shown as follows at the end of a recent fiscal period:

	Apple Computer, Inc. (In millions) Sept. 24, 2005	Dell Inc. (In millions) Feb. 3, 2006
Current assets:		
Cash and cash equivalents	$ 3,491	$ 7,042
Short-term investments	4,770	2,016
Accounts receivable	895	4,089
Inventories	165	576
Other current assets*	979	3,983
Total current assets	$10,300	$17,706
Current liabilities:		
Accounts payable	$ 1,779	$ 9,840
Accrued and other current liabilities	1,705	6,087
Total current liabilities	$ 3,484	$15,927

*These represent prepaid expense and other nonquick current assets.

a. Determine the quick ratio for both companies.
b. ▰▰▰▶ Interpret the quick ratio difference between the two companies.

Problems Series A

PR 10-1A
Liability transactions
objs. 1, 5

The following items were selected from among the transactions completed by Sounds and Sight Stores during the current year:

Apr. 7. Borrowed $36,000 from First Financial Company, issuing a 60-day, 8% note for that amount.

May 10. Purchased equipment by issuing a $125,000, 120-day note to Milford Equipment Co., which discounted the note at the rate of 6%.

June 6. Paid First Financial Company the interest due on the note of April 7 and renewed the loan by issuing a new 30-day, 9% note for $36,000. (Record both the debit and credit to the notes payable account.)

July 6. Paid First Financial Company the amount due on the note of June 6.

Aug. 3. Purchased merchandise on account from Hamilton Co., $15,000, terms, n/30.

Sept. 2. Issued a 60-day, 6% note for $15,000 to Hamilton Co., on account.

7. Paid Milford Equipment Co. the amount due on the note of May 10.

Nov. 1. Paid Hamilton Co. the amount owed on the note of September 2.

15. Purchased store equipment from Merchandising Systems Co. for $150,000, paying $55,500 and issuing a series of seven 8% notes for $13,500 each, coming due at 30-day intervals.

Dec. 15. Paid the amount due Merchandising Systems Co. on the first note in the series issued on November 15.

21. Settled a personal injury lawsuit with a customer for $30,000, to be paid in January. Sounds and Sight Stores accrued the loss in a litigation claims payable account.

Instructions
1. Journalize the transactions.
2. Journalize the adjusting entry for each of the following accrued expenses at the end of the current year:
   a. Product warranty cost, $8,400.
   b. Interest on the six remaining notes owed to Merchandising Systems Co.

PR 10-2A
Entries for payroll and payroll taxes
objs. 2, 3

✓1. (b) Dr. Payroll Tax
Expense, $37,650

The following information about the payroll for the week ended December 30 was obtained from the records of Greenfield Co.:

Salaries:		Deductions:	
Sales salaries	$320,000	Income tax withheld	$109,760
Warehouse salaries	84,500	Social security tax withheld	28,560
Office salaries	155,500	Medicare tax withheld	8,400
	$560,000	U.S. savings bonds	16,400
		Group insurance	24,690
			$187,810

Tax rates assumed:
  Social security, 6% on first $100,000 of employee annual earnings
  Medicare, 1.5%
  State unemployment (employer only), 3.8%
  Federal unemployment (employer only), 0.8%

Instructions
1. Assuming that the payroll for the last week of the year is to be paid on December 31, journalize the following entries:
   a. December 30, to record the payroll.
   b. December 30, to record the employer's payroll taxes on the payroll to be paid on December 31. Of the total payroll for the last week of the year, $15,000 is subject to unemployment compensation taxes.
2. Assuming that the payroll for the last week of the year is to be paid on January 4 of the following fiscal year, journalize the following entries:
   a. December 30, to record the payroll.
   b. January 4, to record the employer's payroll taxes on the payroll to be paid on January 4.

PR 10-3A
Wage and tax statement data and employer FICA tax

objs. 2, 3

✓ 2. (e) $30,987.60

Bristol Distribution Company began business on January 2, 2007. Salaries were paid to employees on the last day of each month, and social security tax, Medicare tax, and federal income tax were withheld in the required amounts. An employee who is hired in the middle of the month receives half the monthly salary for that month. All required payroll tax reports were filed, and the correct amount of payroll taxes was remitted by the company for the calendar year. Early in 2008, before the Wage and Tax Statements (Form W-2) could be prepared for distribution to employees and for filing with the Social Security Administration, the employees' earnings records were inadvertently destroyed.

None of the employees resigned or were discharged during the year, and there were no changes in salary rates. The social security tax was withheld at the rate of 6.0% on the first $100,000 of salary and Medicare tax at the rate of 1.5% on salary. Data on dates of employment, salary rates, and employees' income taxes withheld, which are summarized as follows, were obtained from personnel records and payroll records.

Employee	Date First Employed	Monthly Salary	Monthly Income Tax Withheld
Arnold	June 2	$6,400	$1,408
Charles	Jan. 2	8,600	2,064
Gillam	Mar. 1	5,000	950
Nelson	Jan. 2	3,800	684
Quinn	Nov. 15	4,400	814
Ramirez	Apr. 15	3,200	560
Wu	Jan. 16	9,200	2,300

Instructions
1. Calculate the amounts to be reported on each employee's Wage and Tax Statement (Form W-2) for 2007, arranging the data in the following form:

Employee	Gross Earnings	Federal Income Tax Withheld	Social Security Tax Withheld	Medicare Tax Withheld

2. Calculate the following employer payroll taxes for the year: (a) social security; (b) Medicare; (c) state unemployment compensation at 3.8% on the first $9,000 of each employee's earnings; (d) federal unemployment compensation at 0.8% on the first $9,000 of each employee's earnings; (e) total.

PR 10-4A
Payroll register

objs. 2, 3

✓ 3. Dr. Payroll Tax Expense, $664.92

If the working papers correlating with this textbook are not used, omit Problem 10-4A.

The payroll register for Govi Guitar Co. for the week ended December 12, 2008, is presented in the working papers.

Instructions
1. Journalize the entry to record the payroll for the week.
2. Journalize the entry to record the issuance of the checks to employees.
3. Journalize the entry to record the employer's payroll taxes for the week. Assume the following tax rates: state unemployment, 3.2%; federal unemployment, 0.8%. Of the earnings, $1,200 is subject to unemployment taxes.
4. Journalize the entry to record a check issued on December 15 to Second National Bank in payment of employees' income taxes, $1,402.06, social security taxes, $987.06, and Medicare taxes, $246.78.

PR 10-5A
Payroll register

objs. 2, 3

The following data for Iris Publishing Co. relate to the payroll for the week ended December 7, 2008:

✓1. Total net amount
payable, $6,508.96

Employee	Hours Worked	Hourly Rate	Weekly Salary	Federal Income Tax	U.S. Savings Bonds	Accumulated Earnings, Nov. 30
A	38	$16		$109.44		$ 29,184
B	44	25		241.50	$20	47,400
C	46	30		338.10	20	70,800
D	40	12		81.60	35	30,700
E	30	10		36.00	10	14,400
F			$1,100.00	242.00		4,400
G	41	24		199.20		41,500
H			2,200.00	550.00	90	105,600
I	48	18		187.20	10	43,200

Employees F and H are office staff, and all of the other employees are sales personnel. All sales personnel are paid $1\frac{1}{2}$ times the regular rate for all hours in excess of 40 hours per week. The social security tax rate is 6.0% on the first $100,000 of each employee's annual earnings, and Medicare tax is 1.5% of each employee's annual earnings. The next payroll check to be used is No. 981.

Instructions

1. Prepare a payroll register for Iris Publishing Co. for the week ended December 7, 2008. Use the following columns for the payroll register: Total Hours Worked, Regular Hours, Overtime Hours, Social Security Tax, Medicare Tax, Federal Income Tax, U.S. Savings Bonds, Total Deductions, Net Pay, Ck. No., Salaries Expense, and Office Salaries Expense.
2. Journalize the entry to record the payroll for the week.

PR 10-6A
Payroll accounts and year-end entries

objs. **2, 3, 4**

The following accounts, with the balances indicated, appear in the ledger of Yosemite Outdoor Equipment Company on December 1 of the current year:

211	Salaries Payable	—	218	Bond Deductions Payable	$ 2,000
212	Social Security Tax Payable	$5,888	219	Medical Insurance Payable	2,400
213	Medicare Tax Payable	1,550	611	Sales Salaries Expense	685,900
214	Employees Federal Income Tax Payable	9,555	711	Officers Salaries Expense	326,400
215	Employees State Income Tax Payable	9,297	712	Office Salaries Expense	124,000
216	State Unemployment Tax Payable	1,000	719	Payroll Tax Expense	88,858
217	Federal Unemployment Tax Payable	280			

The following transactions relating to payroll, payroll deductions, and payroll taxes occurred during December:

Dec. 1. Issued Check No. 728 to Pico Insurance Company for $2,400, in payment of the semiannual premium on the group medical insurance policy.
2. Issued Check No. 729 to First National Bank for $16,993, in payment for $5,888 of social security tax, $1,550 of Medicare tax, and $9,555 of employees' federal income tax due.
3. Issued Check No. 730 for $2,000 to First National Bank to purchase U.S. savings bonds for employees.
14. Journalized the entry to record the biweekly payroll. A summary of the payroll record follows:

Salary distribution:
Sales	$31,000	
Officers	14,800	
Office	5,600	$51,400

Deductions:
Social security tax	$ 2,827	
Medicare tax	771	
Federal income tax withheld	9,149	
State income tax withheld	2,313	
Savings bond deductions	1,000	
Medical insurance deductions	400	16,460
Net amount		$34,940

(continued)

Dec. 14. Issued Check No. 738 in payment of the net amount of the biweekly payroll.

14. Journalized the entry to record payroll taxes on employees' earnings of December 14: social security tax, $2,827; Medicare tax, $771; state unemployment tax, $250; federal unemployment tax, $55.

17. Issued Check No. 744 to First National Bank for $16,345, in payment for $5,654 of social security tax, $1,542 of Medicare tax, and $9,149 of employees' federal income tax due.

28. Journalized the entry to record the biweekly payroll. A summary of the payroll record follows:

Salary distribution:		
Sales	$31,500	
Officers	15,000	
Office	5,500	$52,000
Deductions:		
Social security tax	$ 2,808	
Medicare tax	780	
Federal income tax withheld	9,256	
State income tax withheld	2,340	
Savings bond deductions	1,000	16,184
Net amount		$35,816

28. Issued Check No. 782 for the net amount of the biweekly payroll.

28. Journalized the entry to record payroll taxes on employees' earnings of December 28: social security tax, $2,808; Medicare tax, $780; state unemployment tax, $120; federal unemployment tax, $30.

30. Issued Check No. 791 for $13,950 to First National Bank, in payment of employees' state income tax due on December 31.

30. Issued Check No. 792 to First National Bank for $2,000 to purchase U.S. savings bonds for employees.

31. Paid $55,700 to the employee pension plan. The annual pension cost is $65,000. (Record both the payment and the unfunded pension liability.)

Instructions

1. Journalize the transactions.
2. Journalize the following adjusting entries on December 31:
   a. Salaries accrued: sales salaries, $3,150; officers salaries, $1,500; office salaries, $550. The payroll taxes are immaterial and are not accrued.
   b. Vacation pay, $13,200.

Problems Series B

PR 10-1B
Liability transactions
objs. 1, 5

The following items were selected from among the transactions completed by Silver Mountain Stores Co. during the current year:

Feb. 15. Purchased merchandise on account from Ranier Co., $120,000, terms n/30.

Mar. 17. Issued a 30-day, 5% note for $120,000 to Ranier Co., on account.

Apr. 16. Paid Ranier Co. the amount owed on the note of March 17.

July 15. Borrowed $180,000 from United Bank, issuing a 90-day, 6% note.

25. Purchased tools by issuing a $135,000, 120-day note to Sun Supply Co., which discounted the note at the rate of 7%.

Oct. 13. Paid United Bank the interest due on the note of July 15 and renewed the loan by issuing a new 30-day, 9% note for $180,000. (Journalize both the debit and credit to the notes payable account.)

Nov. 12. Paid United Bank the amount due on the note of October 13.

22. Paid Sun Supply Co. the amount due on the note of July 25.

Dec. 1. Purchased office equipment from Valley Equipment Co. for $40,000, paying $10,000 and issuing a series of ten 6% notes for $3,000 each, coming due at 30-day intervals.

17. Settled a product liability lawsuit with a customer for $56,000, payable in January. Silver Mountain accrued the loss in a litigation claims payable account.

Dec. 31. Paid the amount due Valley Equipment Co. on the first note in the series issued on December 1.

Instructions
1. Journalize the transactions.
2. Journalize the adjusting entry for each of the following accrued expenses at the end of the current year: (a) product warranty cost, $21,410; (b) interest on the nine remaining notes owed to Valley Equipment Co.

PR 10-2B
Entries for payroll and payroll taxes

objs. 2, 3

✓ *1. (b) Dr. Payroll Tax Expense, $21,450*

The following information about the payroll for the week ended December 30 was obtained from the records of Plumb Line Supply Co.:

Salaries:		Deductions:	
Sales salaries	$162,400	Income tax withheld	$52,800
Warehouse salaries	54,200	Social security tax withheld	16,200
Office salaries	83,400	Medicare tax withheld	4,500
	$300,000	U.S. savings bonds	6,500
		Group insurance	5,600
			$85,600

Tax rates assumed:
Social security, 6% on first $100,000 of employee annual earnings
Medicare, 1.5%
State unemployment (employer only), 4.2%
Federal unemployment (employer only), 0.8%

Instructions
1. Assuming that the payroll for the last week of the year is to be paid on December 31, journalize the following entries:
   a. December 30, to record the payroll.
   b. December 30, to record the employer's payroll taxes on the payroll to be paid on December 31. Of the total payroll for the last week of the year, $15,000 is subject to unemployment compensation taxes.
2. Assuming that the payroll for the last week of the year is to be paid on January 5 of the following fiscal year, journalize the following entries:
   a. December 30, to record the payroll.
   b. January 5, to record the employer's payroll taxes on the payroll to be paid on January 5.

PR 10-3B
Wage and tax statement data on employer FICA tax

objs. 2, 3

✓ *2. (e) $27,397*

Daisy Dairy Co. began business on January 2, 2007. Salaries were paid to employees on the last day of each month, and social security tax, Medicare tax, and federal income tax were withheld in the required amounts. An employee who is hired in the middle of the month receives half the monthly salary for that month. All required payroll tax reports were filed, and the correct amount of payroll taxes was remitted by the company for the calendar year. Early in 2008, before the Wage and Tax Statements (Form W-2) could be prepared for distribution to employees and for filing with the Social Security Administration, the employees' earnings records were inadvertently destroyed.

None of the employees resigned or were discharged during the year, and there were no changes in salary rates. The social security tax was withheld at the rate of 6.0% on the first $100,000 of salary and Medicare tax at the rate of 1.5% on salary. Data on dates of employment, salary rates, and employees' income taxes withheld, which are summarized as follows, were obtained from personnel records and payroll records.

Employee	Date First Employed	Monthly Salary	Monthly Income Tax Withheld
Alvarez	Jan. 16	$9,600	$2,400
Collins	Nov. 1	2,500	375
Felix	Jan. 2	3,000	480
Lydall	July 16	4,400	792
Penn	Jan. 2	8,800	2,112
Song	May 1	5,100	918
Walker	Feb. 16	2,000	240

Instructions

1. Calculate the amounts to be reported on each employee's Wage and Tax Statement (Form W-2) for 2007, arranging the data in the following form:

Employee	Gross Earnings	Federal Income Tax Withheld	Social Security Tax Withheld	Medicare Tax Withheld

2. Calculate the following employer payroll taxes for the year: (a) social security; (b) Medicare; (c) state unemployment compensation at 4.8% on the first $7,000 of each employee's earnings; (d) federal unemployment compensation at 0.8% on the first $7,000 of each employee's earnings; (e) total.

PR 10-4B
Payroll register

objs. 2, 3

✓ *3. Dr. Payroll Tax Expense, $654.32*

If the working papers correlating with this textbook are not used, omit Problem 10-4B.

The payroll register for Irish Heritage Stores Co. for the week ended December 12, 2008, is presented in the working papers.

Instructions

1. Journalize the entry to record the payroll for the week.
2. Journalize the entry to record the issuance of the checks to employees.
3. Journalize the entry to record the employer's payroll taxes for the week. Assume the following tax rates: state unemployment, 3.6%; federal unemployment, 0.8%. Of the earnings, $850 is subject to unemployment taxes.
4. Journalize the entry to record a check issued on December 15 to Second National Bank in payment of employees' income taxes, $1,402.06, social security taxes, $987.06, and Medicare taxes, $246.78.

PR 10-5B
Payroll register

objs. 2, 3

✓ *1. Total net amount payable, $7,503.36*

The following data for Center Pointe Co. relate to the payroll for the week ended December 7, 2008:

Employee	Hours Worked	Hourly Rate	Weekly Salary	Federal Income Tax	U.S. Savings Bonds	Accumulated Earnings, Nov. 30
M	52	$36.00		$480.24	$50	$ 82,600
N			$1,200.00	258.00		57,600
O	38	16.00		115.52	25	29,184
P	44	18.50		178.71		38,700
Q	40	20.00		168.00	15	40,500
R			2,400.00	576.00	100	115,200
S	32	22.00		105.60		12,600
T	46	28.00		301.84	40	64,200
U	40	18.00		144.00	20	35,600

Employees N and R are office staff, and all of the other employees are sales personnel. All sales personnel are paid 1½ times the regular rate for all hours in excess of 40 hours per week. The social security tax rate is 6.0% on the first $100,000 of each employee's annual earnings, and Medicare tax is 1.5% of each employee's annual earnings. The next payroll check to be used is No. 818.

Instructions

1. Prepare a payroll register for Center Pointe Co. for the week ended December 7, 2008. Use the following columns for the payroll register: Total Hours Worked, Regular Hours, Overtime Hours, Social Security Tax, Medicare Tax, Federal Income Tax, U.S. Savings Bonds, Total Deductions, Net Pay, Ck. No., Salaries Expense, and Office Salaries Expense.
2. Journalize the entry to record the payroll for the week.

PR 10-6B
Payroll accounts and year-end entries

objs. 2, 3, 4

The following accounts, with the balances indicated, appear in the ledger of Bonnie's Gifts Co. on December 1 of the current year:

211	Salaries Payable	—	218	Bond Deductions Payable	$ 3,000
212	Social Security Tax Payable	$ 8,032	219	Medical Insurance Payable	24,000
213	Medicare Tax Payable	2,114	611	Operations Salaries Expense	850,000
214	Employees Federal Income Tax Payable	13,035	711	Officers Salaries Expense	560,000
215	Employees State Income Tax Payable	12,682	712	Office Salaries Expense	140,000
216	State Unemployment Tax Payable	1,400	719	Payroll Tax Expense	121,506
217	Federal Unemployment Tax Payable	400			

The following transactions relating to payroll, payroll deductions, and payroll taxes occurred during December:

Dec. 2. Issued Check No. 728 for $3,000 to First National Bank to purchase U.S. savings bonds for employees.

3. Issued Check No. 729 to First National Bank for $23,181, in payment of $8,032 of social security tax, $2,114 of Medicare tax, and $13,035 of employees' federal income tax due.

14. Journalized the entry to record the biweekly payroll. A summary of the payroll record follows:

Salary distribution:		
Operations	$38,500	
Officers	25,500	
Office	6,200	$70,200
Deductions:		
Social security tax	$ 3,931	
Medicare tax	1,053	
Federal income tax withheld	12,496	
State income tax withheld	3,159	
Savings bond deductions	1,500	
Medical insurance deductions	4,000	26,139
Net amount		$44,061

14. Issued Check No. 738 in payment of the net amount of the biweekly payroll.

14. Journalized the entry to record payroll taxes on employees' earnings of December 14: social security tax, $3,931; Medicare tax, $1,053; state unemployment tax, $290; federal unemployment tax, $84.

17. Issued Check No. 744 to First National Bank for $22,464, in payment of $7,862 of social security tax, $2,106 of Medicare tax, and $12,496 of employees' federal income tax due.

18. Issued Check No. 750 to Pico Insurance Company for $24,000, in payment of the semiannual premium on the group medical insurance policy.

28. Journalized the entry to record the biweekly payroll. A summary of the payroll record follows:

Salary distribution:		
Operations	$39,000	
Officers	26,000	
Office	6,400	$71,400
Deductions:		
Social security tax	$ 3,856	
Medicare tax	1,071	
Federal income tax withheld	12,709	
State income tax withheld	3,213	
Savings bond deductions	1,500	22,349
Net amount		$49,051

28. Issued Check No. 782 in payment of the net amount of the biweekly payroll.

(continued)

Dec. 28. Journalized the entry to record payroll taxes on employees' earnings of December 28: social security tax, $3,856; Medicare tax, $1,071; state unemployment tax, $155; federal unemployment tax, $38.

30. Issued Check No. 791 to First National Bank for $3,000 to purchase U.S. savings bonds for employees.

30. Issued Check No. 792 for $19,054 to First National Bank in payment of employees' state income tax due on December 31.

31. Paid $43,000 to the employee pension plan. The annual pension cost is $45,000. (Record both the payment and unfunded pension liability.)

Instructions

1. Journalize the transactions.
2. Journalize the following adjusting entries on December 31:
   a. Salaries accrued: operations salaries, $3,900; officers salaries, $2,600; office salaries, $640. The payroll taxes are immaterial and are not accrued.
   b. Vacation pay, $12,650.

Comprehensive Problem 3

✓ 5. Total assets, $1,423,535

Selected transactions completed by Hirata Company during its first fiscal year ending December 31 were as follows:

Jan. 2. Issued a check to establish a petty cash fund of $1,400.

Mar. 1. Replenished the petty cash fund, based on the following summary of petty cash receipts: office supplies, $678; miscellaneous selling expense, $389; miscellaneous administrative expense, $245.

Apr. 5. Purchased $12,000 of merchandise on account, terms 1/10, n/30. The perpetual inventory system is used to account for inventory.

May 5. Paid the invoice of April 5 after the discount period had passed.

10. Received cash from daily cash sales for $7,755. The amount indicated by the cash register was $7,775.

June 2. Received a 60-day, 8.4% note for $60,000 on the Stevens account.

Aug. 1. Received amount owed on June 2 note, plus interest at the maturity date.

3. Received $2,300 on the Jacobs account and wrote off the remainder owed on a $2,500 accounts receivable balance. (The allowance method is used in accounting for uncollectible receivables.)

28. Reinstated the Jacobs account written off on August 3 and received $200 cash in full payment.

Sept. 2. Purchased land by issuing a $250,000, 90-day note to Ace Development Co., which discounted it at 8%.

Oct. 2. Sold office equipment in exchange for $55,000 cash plus receipt of a $25,000, 120-day, 6% note. The equipment had cost $96,000 and had accumulated depreciation of $10,000 as of October 1.

Nov. 30. Journalized the monthly payroll for November, based on the following data:

Salaries		Deductions	
Sales salaries	$58,200	Income tax withheld	$15,804
Office salaries	29,600	Social security tax	
	$87,800	withheld	5,120
		Medicare tax withheld	1,317

Unemployment tax rates:	
State unemployment	3.8%
Federal unemployment	0.8%
Amount subject to unemployment taxes:	
State unemployment	$2,000
Federal unemployment	2,000

Nov. 30. Journalized the employer's payroll taxes on the payroll.

Dec. 1. Journalized the payment of the September 2 note at maturity.

30. The pension cost for the year was $65,000, of which $57,450 was paid to the pension plan trustee.

Instructions

1. Journalize the selected transactions.

2. Based on the following data, prepare a bank reconciliation for December of the current year:
   a. Balance according to the bank statement at December 31, $123,200.
   b. Balance according to the ledger at December 31, $108,680.
   c. Checks outstanding at December 31, $27,450.
   d. Deposit in transit, not recorded by bank, $12,450.
   e. Bank debit memorandum for service charges, $280.
   f. A check for $330 in payment of an invoice was incorrectly recorded in the accounts as $130.

3. Based on the bank reconciliation prepared in (2), journalize the entry or entries to be made by Hirata Company.

4. Based on the following selected data, journalize the adjusting entries as of December 31 of the current year:
   a. Estimated uncollectible accounts at December 31, $6,490, based on an aging of accounts receivable. The balance of Allowance for Doubtful Accounts at December 31 was $600 (debit).
   b. The physical inventory on December 31 indicated an inventory shrinkage of $1,320.
   c. Prepaid insurance expired during the year, $9,850.
   d. Office supplies used during the year, $1,580.
   e. Depreciation is computed as follows:

Asset	Cost	Residual Value	Acquisition Date	Useful Life in Years	Depreciation Method Used
Buildings	$380,000	$ 0	January 2	50	Straight-line
Office Equip.	90,000	14,000	October 2	5	Straight-line
Store Equip.	45,000	10,000	January 3	8	Double-declining-balance (at twice the straight-line rate)

   f. A patent costing $18,600 when acquired on January 2 has a remaining legal life of nine years and is expected to have value for six years.
   g. The cost of mineral rights was $185,000. Of the estimated deposit of 333,000 tons of ore, 22,500 tons were mined during the year.
   h. Vacation pay expense for December, $4,400.
   i. A product warranty was granted beginning December 1 and covering a one-year period. The estimated cost is 2.5% of sales, which totaled $796,000 in December.
   j. Interest was accrued on the note receivable received on October 2.

5. Based on the following information and the post-closing trial balance shown on the following page, prepare a balance sheet in report form at December 31 of the current year.

The merchandise inventory is stated at cost by the LIFO method.

The product warranty payable is a current liability.

Vacation pay payable:
   Current liability $3,000
   Long-term liability   1,400

The unfunded pension liability is a long-term liability.

Notes payable:
   Current liability $25,000
   Long-term liability   75,000

Hirata Company
Post-Closing Trial Balance
December 31, 2007

	Debit Balances	Credit Balances
Petty Cash	1,400	
Cash	108,200	
Notes Receivable	25,000	
Accounts Receivable	202,300	
Allowance for Doubtful Accounts		6,490
Merchandise Inventory	140,600	
Interest Receivable	375	
Prepaid Insurance	19,700	
Office Supplies	7,100	
Land	245,000	
Buildings	380,000	
Accumulated Depreciation—Buildings		7,600
Office Equipment	90,000	
Accumulated Depreciation—Office Equipment		3,800
Store Equipment	45,000	
Accumulated Depreciation—Store Equipment		11,250
Mineral Rights	185,000	
Accumulated Depletion		12,500
Patents	15,500	
Social Security Tax Payable		9,910
Medicare Tax Payable		2,700
Employees Federal Income Tax Payable		15,887
State Unemployment Tax Payable		42
Federal Unemployment Tax Payable		9
Salaries Payable		90,000
Accounts Payable		125,300
Interest Payable		3,000
Product Warranty Payable		19,900
Vacation Pay Payable		4,400
Unfunded Pension Liability		7,550
Notes Payable		100,000
Capital Stock		300,000
Retained Earnings		744,837
	1,465,175	1,465,175

6. On February 7 of the following year, the merchandise inventory was destroyed by fire. Based on the following data obtained from the accounting records, estimate the cost of the merchandise destroyed:

Jan. 1 Merchandise inventory	$140,600
Jan. 1–Feb. 7 Purchases (net)	38,000
Jan. 1–Feb. 7 Sales (net)	68,000
Estimated gross profit rate	40%

Special Activities

SA 10-1
Ethics and professional conduct in business

ETHICS

Dan Lanier is a certified public accountant (CPA) and staff accountant for Baker and Lin, a local CPA firm. It had been the policy of the firm to provide a holiday bonus equal to two weeks' salary to all employees. The firm's new management team announced on November 25 that a bonus equal to only one week's salary would be made available to employees this year. Dan thought that this policy was unfair because he and his coworkers planned on the full two-week bonus. The two-week bonus had been given for 10 straight years, so it seemed as though the firm had breached an implied commitment. Thus, Dan decided that he would make up the lost bonus week by working an extra six hours of overtime per week over the next five weeks until the end of the year. Baker and Lin's policy is to pay overtime at 150% of straight time.

Dan's supervisor was surprised to see overtime being reported, since there is generally very little additional or unusual client service demands at the end of the calendar year. However, the overtime was not questioned, since firm employees are on the "honor system" in reporting their overtime.

➤ Discuss whether the firm is acting in an ethical manner by changing the bonus. Is Dan behaving in an ethical manner?

SA 10-2
Recognizing pension expense

The annual examination of Eclipse Company's financial statements by its external public accounting firm (auditors) is nearing completion. The following conversation took place between the controller of Eclipse Company (Greg) and the audit manager from the public accounting firm (Latiffah).

Latiffah: You know, Greg, we are about to wrap up our audit for this fiscal year. Yet, there is one item still to be resolved.

Greg: What's that?

Latiffah: Well, as you know, at the beginning of the year, Eclipse began a defined benefit pension plan. This plan promises your employees an annual payment when they retire, using a formula based on their salaries at retirement and their years of service. I believe that a pension expense should be recognized this year, equal to the amount of pension earned by your employees.

Greg: Wait a minute. I think you have it all wrong. The company doesn't have a pension expense until it actually pays the pension in cash when the employee retires. After all, some of these employees may not reach retirement, and if they don't, the company doesn't owe them anything.

Latiffah: You're not really seeing this the right way. The pension is earned by your employees during their working years. You actually make the payment much later—when they retire. It's like one long accrual—much like incurring wages in one period and paying them in the next. Thus, I think that you should recognize the expense in the period the pension is earned by the employees.

Greg: Let me see if I've got this straight. I should recognize an expense this period for something that may or may not be paid to the employees in 20 or 30 years, when they finally retire. How am I supposed to determine what the expense is for the current year? The amount of the final retirement depends on many uncertainties: salary levels, employee longevity, mortality rates, and interest earned on investments to fund the pension. I don't think that an amount can be determined, even if I accepted your arguments.

➤ Evaluate Latiffah's position. Is she right or is Greg correct?

SA 10-3
Executive bonuses and accounting methods

Troy Rogers, the owner of Rogers Trucking Company, initiated an executive bonus plan for his chief executive officer (CEO). The new plan provides a bonus to the CEO equal to 3% of the income before taxes. Upon learning of the new bonus arrangement, the CEO issued instructions to change the company's accounting for trucks. The CEO has asked the controller to make the following two changes:

a. Change from the double-declining-balance method to the straight-line method of depreciation.
b. Add 50% to the useful lives of all trucks.

➤ Why did the CEO ask for these changes? How would you respond to the CEO's request?

SA 10-4
Ethics and professional conduct in business

ETHICS

Connor Lang was discussing summer employment with Jarrod McIntyre, president of Azalea Landscaping Service:

Jarrod: I'm glad that you're thinking about joining us for the summer. We could certainly use the help.

(continued)

Connor: Sounds good. I enjoy outdoor work, and I could use the money to help with next year's school expenses.

Jarrod: I've got a plan that can help you out on that. As you know, I'll pay you $12 per hour, but in addition, I'd like to pay you with cash. Since you're only working for the summer, it really doesn't make sense for me to go to the trouble of formally putting you on our payroll system. In fact, I do some jobs for my clients on a strictly cash basis, so it would be easy to just pay you that way.

Connor: Well, that's a bit unusual, but I guess money is money.

Jarrod: Yeah, not only that, it's tax-free!

Connor: What do you mean?

Jarrod: Didn't you know? Any money that you receive in cash is not reported to the IRS on a W-2 form; therefore, the IRS doesn't know about the income—hence, it's the same as tax-free earnings.

a. ▭▶ Why does Jarrod McIntyre want to conduct business transactions using cash (not check or credit card)?

b. ▭▶ How should Connor respond to Jarrod's suggestion?

SA 10-5
Payroll forms

Group Project

Internet Project

Payroll accounting involves the use of government-supplied forms to account for payroll taxes. Three common forms are the W-2, Form 940, and Form 941. Form a team with three of your classmates and retrieve copies of each of these forms. They may be obtained from a local IRS office, a library, or downloaded from the Internet at **http://www.irs.gov** (go to forms and publications).

▭▶ Briefly describe the purpose of each of the three forms.

SA 10-6
Contingent liabilities

Internet Project

Altria Group, Inc., has over eight pages dedicated to describing contingent liabilities in the notes to recent financial statements. These pages include extensive descriptions of multiple contingent liabilities. Use the Internet to research Altria Group, Inc., at **http://www.altria.com**.

a. What are the major business units of Altria Group?

b. Based on your understanding of this company, why would Altria Group require eight pages of contingency disclosure?

Answers to Self-Examination Questions

1. **C** The maturity value is $5,100, determined as follows:

Face amount of note	$5,000
Plus interest ($5,000 × 12% × 60/360)	100
Maturity value	$5,100

2. **B** The net amount available to a borrower from discounting a note payable is called the proceeds. The proceeds of $4,900 (answer B) is determined as follows:

Face amount of note	$5,000
Less discount ($5,000 × 12% × 60/360)	100
Proceeds	$4,900

3. **B** Employers are usually required to withhold a portion of their employees' earnings for payment of federal income taxes (answer A), Medicare tax (answer C), and state and local income taxes (answer D). Generally, federal unemployment compensation taxes (answer B) are levied against the employer only and thus are not deducted from employee earnings.

4. **D** The amount of net pay of $1,385.50 (answer D) is determined as follows:

Gross pay:			
40 hours at $40		$1,600.00	
5 hours at $60		300.00	$1,900.00
Deductions:			
Federal income tax withheld		$ 450.00	
FICA:			
Social security tax ($600 × 0.06)	$36.00		
Medicare tax ($1,900 × 0.015)	28.50	64.50	514.50
			$1,385.50

5. **D** The employer incurs an expense for social security tax (answer A), federal unemployment compensation tax (answer B), and state unemployment compensation tax (answer C). The employees' federal income tax (answer D) is not an expense of the employer. It is withheld from the employees' earnings.

Corporations: Organization, Stock Transactions, and Dividends

© MATTHEW CAVANAUGH/ASSOCIATED PRESS

objectives

After studying this chapter, you should be able to:

1 **Describe the nature of the corporate form of organization.**

2 **Describe and illustrate the characteristics of stock, classes of stock, and entries for issuing stock.**

3 **Journalize the entries for cash dividends and stock dividends.**

4 **Journalize the entries for treasury stock transactions.**

5 **Describe and illustrate the reporting of stockholders' equity.**

6 **Describe the effect of stock splits on corporate financial statements.**

The Yankee Candle Company, Inc.

I f you purchased 100 shares of The Yankee Candle Company, Inc., you would own a small interest in the company. Thus, you would own a small amount of the future financial prospects of a company that makes and sells over 80 million candles each year. Yankee's candle products come in hundreds of fragrances, styles, and sizes, including Housewarmer® jar candles, Samplers® votive candles, Tarts® wax potpourri, designer pillars, tapers, and scented tea lights.

How did Yankee Candle begin? Yankee Candle began in 1969 when teenager Mike Kittredge made his first candle with melted crayons in his South Hadley, Massachusetts, family home as a Christmas gift for his mother. A neighbor saw the candle, wanted to buy it, and Yankee Candle was born. Family, friends, and neighbors raved about Mike's candles and kept buying them as fast as he could make them. Mike operated first out of his parent's kitchen, basement, and garage. In 1971, Mike opened his first retail store; in 1974, he moved his candle making to an abandoned mill building; in 1994, Mike moved Yankee Candle to a 294,000-square-foot manufacturing plant in South Deerfield, Massachusetts. In 1998, Mike sold Yankee Candle, which today is traded on the New York Stock Exchange (symbol YCC) with sales of over $550 million and net income of over $82 million.

Before buying your 100 shares of Yankee Candle, you would want to study the financial statements and management's plans for the future. You would want to know whether management planned to issue additional shares of stock that might impact the value of your stock. You would want to know whether Yankee Candle planned to continue paying its semiannual cash dividend of $0.125. You might visit Yankee Candle's Web site (**http://www.yankeecandle.com**). Finally, you would explore other sources of investor information, such as whether financial analysts recommend Yankee Candle stock as a buy or sell.

In this chapter, we describe and illustrate the nature of corporations including the accounting for stock and dividends. This discussion will aid you in making decisions such as whether or not to buy Yankee Candle stock.

Nature of a Corporation

objective 1

Describe the nature of the corporate form of organization.

In the preceding chapters, we mentioned that more than 70% of all businesses are proprietorships and 10% are partnerships. Most of these businesses are small businesses. The remaining 20% of businesses are corporations. Many corporations are large and, as a result, they generate more than 90% of the total business dollars in the United States.

CHARACTERISTICS OF A CORPORATION

A *corporation* is a legal entity, distinct and separate from the individuals who create and operate it. As a legal entity, a corporation may acquire, own, and dispose of property in its own name. It may also incur liabilities and enter into contracts. Most importantly, it can sell shares of ownership, called **stock**. This characteristic gives corporations the ability to raise large amounts of capital.

The **stockholders** or *shareholders* who own the stock own the corporation. They can buy and sell stock without affecting the corporation's operations or continued existence. Corporations whose shares of stock are traded in public markets are called *public corporations*. Corporations whose shares are not traded publicly are usually owned by a small group of investors and are called *nonpublic* or *private corporations*.

The stockholders of a corporation have *limited liability*. This means that a corporation's creditors usually may not go beyond the assets of the corporation to satisfy

REAL WORLD

A corporation was defined in the Dartmouth College case of 1819, in which Chief Justice Marshall of the United States Supreme Court stated: "A corporation is an artificial being, invisible, intangible, and existing only in contemplation of the law."

The Coca-Cola Company is a well-known public corporation. Mars, Incorporated, which is owned by family members, is a well-known private corporation.

their claims. Thus, the financial loss that a stockholder may suffer is limited to the amount invested. This feature has contributed to the rapid growth of the corporate form of business.

The stockholders control a corporation by electing a *board of directors*. This board meets periodically to establish corporate policies. It also selects the chief executive officer (CEO) and other major officers to manage the corporation's day-to-day affairs. Exhibit 1 shows the organizational structure of a corporation.

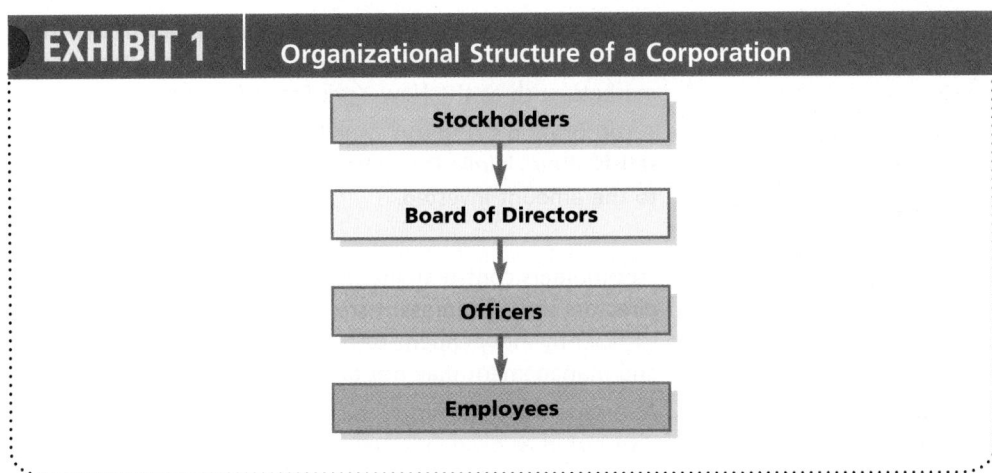

EXHIBIT 1 | Organizational Structure of a Corporation

Stockholders → Board of Directors → Officers → Employees

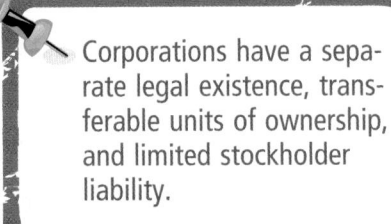

Corporations have a separate legal existence, transferable units of ownership, and limited stockholder liability.

As a separate entity, a corporation is subject to taxes. For example, corporations must pay federal income taxes on their income.[1] Thus, corporate income that is distributed to stockholders in the form of *dividends* has already been taxed. In turn, stockholders must pay income taxes on the dividends they receive. This *double taxation* of corporate earnings is a major disadvantage of the corporate form.[2] The advantages and disadvantages of the corporate form are listed in Exhibit 2.

Integrity, Objectivity, and Ethics in Business

THE RESPONSIBLE BOARD

Recent accounting scandals, such as those involving Enron, WorldCom, and Fannie Mae, have highlighted the roles of boards of directors in executing their responsibilities. For example, eighteen of Enron's former directors and their insurance providers have settled shareholder litigation for $168 million, of which $13 million is to come from the directors' personal assets. Board members are now on notice that their directorship responsibilities are being taken seriously by stockholders.

FORMING A CORPORATION

The first step in forming a corporation is to file an *application of incorporation* with the state. State incorporation laws differ, and corporations often organize in those states with the more favorable laws. For this reason, more than half of the largest companies

---

1 A majority of states also require corporations to pay income taxes.
2 Dividends presently receive a preferential individual tax rate of 15% to reduce the impact of double taxation.

EXHIBIT 2	Advantages and Disadvantages of the Corporate Form

Advantages	Explanation
Separate legal existence	A corporation exists separately from its owners.
Continuous life	A corporation's life is separate from its owners; therefore, it exists indefinitely.
Raising large amounts of capital	The corporate form is suited for raising large amounts of money from shareholders.
Ownership rights are easily transferable	A corporation sells shares of ownership, called *stock*. The stockholders of a public company can transfer their shares of stock to other stockholders through stock markets, such as the New York Stock Exchange.
Limited liability	A corporation's creditors usually may not go beyond the assets of the corporation to satisfy their claims. Thus, the financial loss that a stockholder may suffer is limited to the amount invested.

Disadvantages	
Owner is separate from management	Stockholders control management through a board of directors. The board of directors should represent shareholder interests; however, when the board is not sufficiently independent of management, it is possible that the board of directors and management may not always behave in the best interests of stockholders.
Double taxation of dividends	As a separate legal entity, a corporation is subject to taxation. Thus, net income distributed as dividends will be taxed once at the corporation level, and then again at the individual level.
Regulatory costs	Corporations must satisfy many requirements such as those required by the Sarbanes-Oxley Act of 2002.

A Financial Executives International survey estimated that Sarbanes-Oxley costs the average public company over $3 million per year.

are incorporated in Delaware. Exhibit 3 lists some corporations that you may be familiar with, their states of incorporation, and the location of their headquarters.

After the application of incorporation has been approved, the state grants a *charter* or *articles of incorporation*. The articles of incorporation formally create the corporation.[3] The corporate management and board of directors then prepare a set of *bylaws*, which are the rules and procedures for conducting the corporation's affairs.

EXHIBIT 3	Examples of Corporations and Their States of Incorporation

Corporation	State of Incorporation	Headquarters
Caterpillar	Delaware	Peoria, Ill.
Delta Air Lines	Delaware	Atlanta, Ga.
The Dow Chemical Company	Delaware	Midland, Mich.
General Electric Company	New York	Fairfield, Conn.
The Home Depot	Delaware	Atlanta, Ga.
Kellogg Company	Delaware	Battle Creek, Mich.
3M	Delaware	St. Paul, Minn.
R.J. Reynolds Tobacco Company	Delaware	Winston-Salem, N.C.
Starbucks Corporation	Washington	Seattle, Wash.
Sun Microsystems, Inc.	Delaware	Palo Alto, Calif.
The Washington Post Company	Delaware	Washington, D.C.
Whirlpool Corporation	Delaware	Benton Harbor, Mich.

---

3 The articles of incorporation may also restrict a corporation's activities in certain areas, such as owning certain types of real estate, conducting certain types of business activities, or purchasing its own stock.

Costs may be incurred in organizing a corporation. These costs include legal fees, taxes, state incorporation fees, license fees, and promotional costs. Such costs are debited to an expense account entitled *Organizational Expenses*. To illustrate, the recording of a corporation's organizing costs of $8,500 on January 5 is shown below.

Jan.	5	Organizational Expenses		8 5 0 0 00	
		Cash			8 5 0 0 00
		Paid costs of organizing the corporation.			

Integrity, Objectivity, and Ethics in Business

NOT-FOR-PROFIT, OR NOT?

Corporations can be formed for not-for-profit purposes by making a request to the Internal Revenue Service under *Internal Revenue Code* section 501(c)3. Such corporations, such as the Sierra Club and the National Audubon Society, are exempt from federal taxes. Forming businesses inside a 501(c)3 exempt organization that competes with profit-making (and hence, tax-paying) businesses is very controversial. For example, should the local YMCA receive a tax exemption for providing similar services as the local health club business? The IRS is now challenging such businesses and is withholding 501(c)3 status to many organizations due to this issue.

Paid-In Capital from Issuing Stock

objective **2**

Describe and illustrate the characteristics of stock, classes of stock, and entries for issuing stock.

As we discussed and illustrated in earlier chapters, the two main sources of stockholders' equity are paid-in capital (or contributed capital) and retained earnings. The main source of paid-in capital is from issuing stock. In the following paragraphs, we discuss the characteristics of stock, the classes of stock, and entries for recording the issuance of stock.

CHARACTERISTICS OF STOCK

The number of shares of stock that a corporation is *authorized* to issue is stated in its charter. The term *issued* refers to the shares issued to the stockholders. A corporation may, under circumstances we discuss later in this chapter, reacquire some of the stock that it has issued. The stock remaining in the hands of stockholders is then called **outstanding stock**. The relationship between authorized, issued, and outstanding stock is shown in the graphic at the left.

Shares of stock are often assigned a monetary amount, called **par**. Corporations may issue *stock certificates* to stockholders to document their ownership. Printed on a stock certificate is the par value of the stock, the name of the stockholder, and the number of shares owned. Stock may also be issued without par, in which case it is called *no-par stock*. Some states require the board of directors to assign a **stated value** to no-par stock.

Because corporations have limited liability, creditors have no claim against the personal assets of stockholders. However, some state laws require that corporations maintain a minimum stockholder contribution to protect creditors. This minimum amount is called *legal capital*. The amount of required legal capital varies among the states, but it usually includes the amount of par or stated value of the shares of stock issued.

The major rights that accompany ownership of a share of stock are listed at the top of page 490:

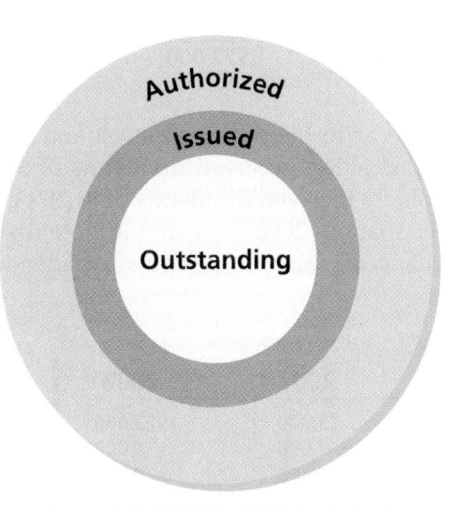

Number of shares authorized, issued, and outstanding

Some corporations have stopped issuing stock certificates except on special request. In these cases, the corporation maintains records of ownership.

1. The right to vote in matters concerning the corporation.
2. The right to share in distributions of earnings.
3. The right to share in assets on liquidation.

As we discuss next, these stock rights normally vary with the class of stock.

CLASSES OF STOCK

The two primary classes of paid-in capital are common stock and preferred stock.

When only one class of stock is issued, it is called **common stock**. In this case, each share of common stock has equal rights. To appeal to a broader investment market, a corporation may issue one or more classes of stock with various preference rights. A common example of such a right is the preference to dividends. Such a stock is generally called a **preferred stock**.

The dividend rights of preferred stock are usually stated in monetary terms or as a percent of par. For example, $4 *preferred stock* has a right to an annual $4 per share dividend. If the par value of the preferred stock were $50, the same right to dividends could be stated as *8% ($4/$50) preferred stock.*[4]

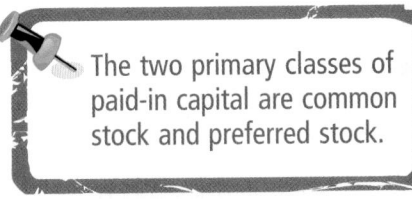

The board of directors of a corporation has the sole authority to distribute dividends to the stockholders. When such action is taken, the directors are said to *declare* a dividend. Since dividends are normally based on earnings, a corporation cannot guarantee dividends even to preferred stockholders. However, because they have first rights to any dividends, the preferred stockholders have a greater chance of receiving regular dividends than do the common stockholders.

To illustrate, assume that a corporation has 1,000 shares of $4 preferred stock and 4,000 shares of common stock outstanding. Also assume that the net income, amount of earnings retained, and the amount of earnings distributed by the board of directors for the first three years of operations are as follows:

	2006	2007	2008
Net income	$20,000	$9,000	$62,000
Amount retained	10,000	6,000	40,000
Amount distributed	$10,000	$3,000	$22,000

Exhibit 4 shows the earnings distributed each year to the preferred stock and the common stock. In this example, the preferred stockholders received dividends of $4, $3, and $4 per share. In contrast, common stockholders received dividends of $1.50 per share in 2006, no dividends in 2007, and $4.50 per share in 2008. You should note that although preferred stockholders have a greater chance of receiving a regular dividend,

EXHIBIT 4

Dividends to Preferred and Common Stock

	2006	2007	2008
Amount distributed	$10,000	$3,000	$22,000
Preferred dividend (1,000 shares)	4,000	3,000	4,000
Common dividend (4,000 shares)	$ 6,000	$ 0	$18,000
Dividends per share:			
Preferred stock	$ 4.00	$ 3.00	$ 4.00
Common stock	$ 1.50	none	$ 4.50

---

4 In some cases, preferred stock may receive additional dividends if certain conditions are met. Such stock, called *participating preferred stock*, is not often used.

common stockholders have a greater chance of receiving larger dividends than do the preferred stockholders.[5]

In addition to dividend preference, preferred stock may be given preferences to assets if the corporation goes out of business and is liquidated. However, claims of creditors must be satisfied first. Preferred stockholders are next in line to receive any remaining assets, followed by the common stockholders.

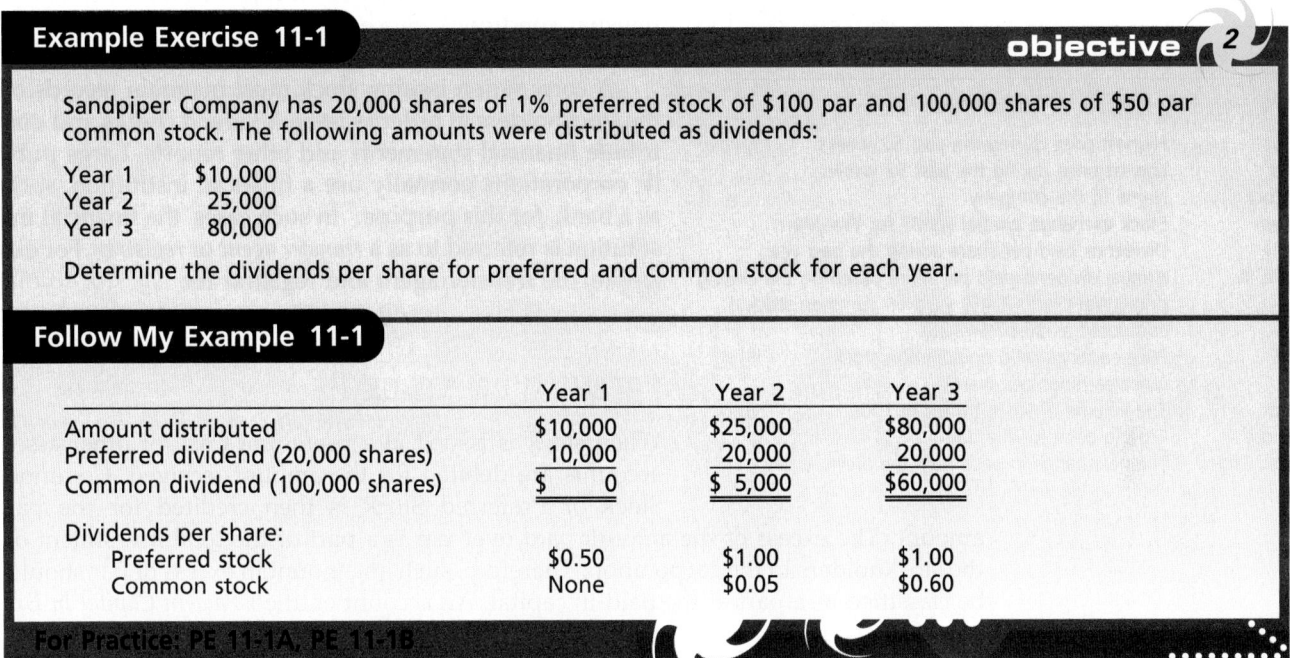

Example Exercise 11-1

objective 2

Sandpiper Company has 20,000 shares of 1% preferred stock of $100 par and 100,000 shares of $50 par common stock. The following amounts were distributed as dividends:

Year 1 $10,000
Year 2   25,000
Year 3   80,000

Determine the dividends per share for preferred and common stock for each year.

Follow My Example 11-1

	Year 1	Year 2	Year 3
Amount distributed	$10,000	$25,000	$80,000
Preferred dividend (20,000 shares)	10,000	20,000	20,000
Common dividend (100,000 shares)	$ 0	$ 5,000	$60,000
Dividends per share:			
Preferred stock	$0.50	$1.00	$1.00
Common stock	None	$0.05	$0.60

For Practice: PE 11-1A, PE 11-1B

ISSUING STOCK

A separate account is used for recording the amount of each class of stock issued to investors in a corporation. For example, assume that a corporation is authorized to issue 10,000 shares of $100 par preferred stock and 100,000 shares of $20 par common stock. One-half of each class of authorized shares is issued at par for cash. The corporation's entry to record the stock issue is as follows:[6]

Cash		1,500 00 0 00	
Preferred Stock			500 0 0 0 00
Common Stock			1,000 0 0 0 00
Issued preferred stock and common			
stock at par for cash.			

Stock is often issued by a corporation at a price other than its par. This is because the par value of a stock is simply its legal capital. The price at which stock can be sold by a corporation depends on a variety of factors, such as:

1. The financial condition, earnings record, and dividend record of the corporation.
2. Investor expectations of the corporation's potential earning power.
3. General business and economic conditions and prospects.

---

5 In some cases, preferred stock has the right to receive regular dividends that were not paid (not declared) in prior years before any common stock dividends are paid. Such preferred stock, called *cumulative preferred stock,* is described and illustrated in intermediate accounting textbooks.

6 The accounting for investments in stocks from the point of view of the investor is discussed in a later chapter.

The following stock quotation for Wal-Mart is taken from *The Wall Street Journal* from May 12, 2006:

NEW YORK STOCK EXCHANGE

| 52 Weeks | | Stock | Sym | Div | Yld % | PE | Vol 100s | Close | Net Chg |
Hi	Lo								
50.87	42.31	WalMart	WMT	.67	1.4	18	108,765	47.25	−.53

The preceding quotation is interpreted as follows:

Hi	Highest price during the past 52 weeks
Lo	Lowest price during the past 52 weeks
Stock	Name of the company
Sym	Stock exchange symbol (WMT for Wal-Mart)
Div	Dividends paid per share during the past year
Yld %	Annual dividend yield per share based on the closing price (Wal-Mart's 1.4% yield on common stock is computed as $0.67/$47.25)
PE	Price-earnings ratio on common stock (price/earnings per share)
Vol	The volume of stock traded in 100s
Close	Closing price for the day
Net Chg	The net change in price from the previous day

When stock is issued for a price that is more than its par, the stock has sold at a **premium**. When stock is issued for a price that is less than its par, the stock has sold at a **discount**. Thus, if stock with a par of $50 is issued for a price of $60, the stock has sold at a premium of $10. If the same stock is issued for a price of $45, the stock has sold at a discount of $5. Many states do not permit stock to be issued at a discount. In others, it may be done only under unusual conditions. Since issuing stock at a discount is rare, we will not illustrate it.

A corporation issuing stock must maintain records of the stockholders in order to issue dividend checks and distribute financial statements and other reports. Large public corporations normally use a financial institution, such as a bank, for this purpose.[7] In such cases, the financial institution is referred to as a *transfer agent* or *registrar*. For example, the transfer agent and registrar for The Coca-Cola Company is First Chicago Trust Company of New York.

PREMIUM ON STOCK

When stock is issued at a premium, Cash or other asset accounts are debited for the amount received. Common Stock or Preferred Stock is then credited for the par amount. The excess of the amount paid over par is a part of the total investment of the stockholders in the corporation. Therefore, such an amount in excess of par should be classified as a part of the paid-in capital. An account entitled *Paid-In Capital in Excess of Par* is usually credited for this amount.

To illustrate, assume that Caldwell Company issues 2,000 shares of $50 par preferred stock for cash at $55. The entry to record this transaction is as follows:

Cash		110 000 00		
	Preferred Stock		100 000 00	
	Paid-In Capital in Excess of Par—			
	Preferred Stock			10 000 00
	Issued $50 par preferred stock at $55.			

When stock is issued in exchange for assets other than cash, such as land, buildings, and equipment, the assets acquired should be recorded at their fair market value. If this value cannot be objectively determined, the fair market price of the stock issued may be used.

To illustrate, assume that a corporation acquired land for which the fair market value cannot be determined. In exchange, the corporation issued 10,000 shares of its $10 par common. Assuming that the stock has a current market price of $12 per share, this transaction is recorded as follows:

Land		120 000 00		
	Common Stock		100 000 00	
	Paid-In Capital in Excess of Par		20 000 00	
	Issued $10 par common stock, valued			
	at $12 per share, for land.			

---

7 Small corporations may use a subsidiary ledger, called a *stockholders ledger*. In this case, the stock accounts (Preferred Stock and Common Stock) are controlling accounts for the subsidiary ledger.

Business Connections

CISCO SYSTEMS, INC.

Cisco Systems, Inc., manufactures and sells networking and communications products worldwide.

The company's technology products include home networking products, which enable users to share Internet access, printers, music, movies, and games. Cisco Systems is incorporated in California and has its headquarters in San Jose, California. Some excerpts from its bylaws are shown below.

ARTICLE 2
SHAREHOLDERS' MEETINGS
Section 2.01 Annual Meetings. The annual meeting of the shareholders of the Corporation . . . shall be held each year on the second Thursday in November at 10:00 a.m. . .

ARTICLE 3
BOARD OF DIRECTORS
Section 3.02 Number and Qualification of Directors. The number of authorized directors of this Corporation shall be not less than eight (8) nor more than fifteen (15), the exact number of directors to be (determined) by a . . . resolution of the Board of Directors or shareholders.

Section 3.04 Special Meetings. Special meetings of the Board of Directors may be called at any time by the Chairman of the Board, the President of the Corporation or any two (2) directors.

Section 3.11 Removal. The Board of Directors may declare vacant the office of a director who has been declared of unsound mind by an order of court or who has been convicted of a felony.

ARTICLE 4
OFFICERS
Section 4.01 Number and Term. The officers of the Corporation shall include a President, a Secretary and a Chief Financial Officer, all of which shall be chosen by the Board of Directors. . . .

Section 4.03 Removal and Resignation. Any officer chosen by the Board of Directors may be removed at any time, with or without cause, by the affirmative vote of a majority of all the members of the Board of Directors.

Section 4.05 Chairman of the Board. The Chairman of the Board shall preside at all meetings of the Board of Directors.

Section 4.06 President. The President shall be the general manager and chief executive officer of the Corporation, subject to the control of the Board of Directors, . . . shall preside at all meetings of shareholders, shall have general supervision of the affairs of the Corporation. . . .

Section 4.08 Secretary. The Secretary shall see that notices for all meetings are given in accordance with the provisions of these Bylaws and as required by law, shall keep minutes of all meetings, shall have charge of the seal and the corporate books, and shall have all such other authority . . . as may be delegated or assigned from time to time by the President or by the Board of Directors.

Section 4.10 Treasurer. The Treasurer shall have custody of all moneys and securities of the Corporation and shall keep regular books of account. . . .

Section 4.13 Approval of Loans to Directors and Officers. The Corporation may, upon the approval of the Board of Directors alone, make loans of money or property to, or guarantee the obligations of, any director or officer of the Corporation or its parent or subsidiary, . . . provided that (i) the Board of Directors determines that such a loan or guaranty or plan may reasonably be expected to benefit the Corporation . . . and (iii) the approval of the Board of Directors is by a vote sufficient without counting the vote of any interested director or directors.

Section 5.04 Fiscal Year. The fiscal year of the Corporation shall end on the last Saturday of July.

NO-PAR STOCK

In most states, both preferred and common stock may be issued without a par value. When no-par stock is issued, the entire proceeds are credited to the stock account. This is true even though the issue price varies from time to time. For example, assume that a corporation issues 10,000 shares of no-par common stock at $40 a share and at a later date issues 1,000 additional shares at $36. The entries to record the no-par stock are as follows:

Cash			400 0 0 0 00	
Common Stock				400 0 0 0 00
Issued 10,000 shares of no-par				
common at $40.				
Cash			36 0 0 0 00	
Common Stock				36 0 0 0 00
Issued 1,000 shares of no-par				
common at $36.				

Some states require that the entire proceeds from the issue of no-par stock be recorded as legal capital. In this case, the preceding entries would be proper. In other states, no-par stock may be assigned a *stated value per share*. The stated value is recorded like a par value, and the excess of the proceeds over the stated value. To illustrate, assume that in the preceding example the no-par common stock is assigned a stated value of $25. The issuance of the stock would be recorded as follows:

Cash			400 0 0 0 00	
Common Stock				250 0 0 0 00
Paid-In Capital in Excess of Stated Value				150 0 0 0 00
Issued 10,000 shares of no-par common				
at $40; stated value, $25.				
Cash			36 0 0 0 00	
Common Stock				25 0 0 0 00
Paid-In Capital in Excess of Stated Value				11 0 0 0 00
Issued 1,000 shares of no-par common				
at $36; stated value, $25.				

Example Exercise 11-2   objective 2

On March 6, Limerick Corporation issued for cash 15,000 shares of no-par common stock at $30. On April 13, Limerick issued at par 1,000 shares of 4%, $40 par preferred stock for cash. On May 19, Limerick issued for cash 15,000 shares of 4%, $40 par preferred stock at $42.
    Journalize the entries to record the March 6, April 13, and May 19 transactions.

Follow My Example 11-2

Mar. 6	Cash	450,000	
	Common Stock		450,000
	(15,000 shares × $30).		
Apr. 13	Cash	40,000	
	Preferred Stock		40,000
	(1,000 shares × $40).		
May 19	Cash	630,000	
	Preferred Stock		600,000
	Paid-In Capital in Excess of Par		30,000
	(15,000 shares × $42)		

For Practice: PE 11-2A, PE 11-2B

Accounting for Dividends

objective **3**

Journalize the entries for cash dividends and stock dividends.

When a board of directors declares a cash dividend, it authorizes the distribution of a portion of the corporation's cash to stockholders. When a board of directors declares a stock dividend, it authorizes the distribution of a portion of its stock. In both cases, the declaration of a dividend reduces the retained earnings of the corporation.[8]

CASH DIVIDENDS

A cash distribution of earnings by a corporation to its shareholders is called a **cash dividend**. Although dividends may be paid in the form of other assets, cash dividends are the most common form.

There are usually three conditions that a corporation must meet to pay a cash dividend:

1. Sufficient retained earnings
2. Sufficient cash
3. Formal action by the board of directors

A large amount of retained earnings does not always mean that a corporation is able to pay dividends. As we indicated earlier in the chapter, the balances of the cash and retained earnings accounts are often unrelated. Thus, a large retained earnings account does not mean that there is cash available to pay dividends.

A corporation's board of directors is not required by law to declare dividends. This is true even if both retained earnings and cash are large enough to justify a dividend. However, many corporations try to maintain a stable dividend record in order to make their stock attractive to investors. Although dividends may be paid once a year or semiannually, most corporations pay dividends quarterly. In years of high profits, a corporation may declare a *special* or *extra* dividend.

You may have seen announcements of dividend declarations in financial newspapers or investor services. An example of such an announcement is shown below.

Board of Directors takes action to declare dividends.

ENTRY:
Debit *Cash Dividends*

Credit *Cash Dividends Payable*

Ownership of shares determines who receives dividend (no entry required).

Dividend is paid.

ENTRY:
Debit *Cash Dividends Payable*

Credit *Cash*

On June 26, the board of directors of The Campbell Soup Company *declared a quarterly cash dividend of $0.225 per common share to stockholders of record as of the close of business on July 8, payable on July 31.*

This announcement includes three important dates: the *date of declaration* (June 26), the *date of record* (July 8), and the *date of payment* (July 31). During the period of time between the record date and the payment date, the stock price is usually quoted as selling *ex-dividends*. This means that since the date of record has passed, a new investor will not receive the dividend.

To illustrate, assume that on *December 1* the board of directors of Hiber Corporation declares the following quarterly cash dividends. The date of record is *December 10*, and the date of payment is *January 2*.

	Dividend per Share	Total Dividends
Preferred stock, $100 par, 5,000 shares outstanding	$2.50	$12,500
Common stock, $10 par, 100,000 shares outstanding	$0.30	30,000
Total		$42,500

---

8 In rare cases, when a corporation is reducing its operations or going out of business, a dividend may be a distribution of paid-in capital. Such a dividend is called a *liquidating dividend*.

Hiber Corporation records the $42,500 liability for the dividends on December 1, the declaration date, as follows:

Dec.	1	Cash Dividends	42 5 0 0 00	
		Cash Dividends Payable		42 5 0 0 00
		Declared cash dividend.		

No entry is required on the date of record, December 10, since this date merely determines which stockholders will receive the dividend. On the date of payment, January 2, the corporation records the $42,500 payment of the dividends as follows:

Jan.	2	Cash Dividends Payable	42 5 0 0 00	
		Cash		42 5 0 0 00
		Paid cash dividend.		

If Hiber Corporation's fiscal year ends December 31, the balance in Cash Dividends will be transferred to Retained Earnings as a part of the closing process by debiting Retained Earnings and crediting Cash Dividends. Cash Dividends Payable will be listed on the December 31 balance sheet as a current liability.

Example Exercise 11-3   objective 3

The important dates in connection with a cash dividend of $75,000 on a corporation's common stock are February 26, March 30, and April 2. Journalize the entries required on each date.

Follow My Example 11-3

Feb. 26	Cash Dividends	75,000	
	Cash Dividends Payable		75,000
Mar. 30	No entry required.		
Apr. 2	Cash Dividends Payable	75,000	
	Cash		75,000

For Practice: PE 11-3A, PE 11-3B

Integrity, Objectivity, and Ethics in Business

ETHICS

THE PROFESSOR WHO KNEW TOO MUCH

A major Midwestern university released a quarterly "American Customer Satisfaction Index" based upon its research of customers of popular U.S. products and services. Before the release of the index to the public, the professor in charge of the research bought and sold stocks of some of the companies being reported upon. The professor was quoted as saying that he thought it was important to test his theories of customer satisfaction with "real" [his own] money.

Is this proper or ethical? Apparently, the dean of the Business School didn't think so. In a statement to the press,

the dean stated: "I have instructed anyone affiliated with the (index) not to make personal use of information gathered in the course of producing the quarterly index, prior to the index's release to the general public, and they [the researchers] have agreed."

Sources: Jon E. Hilsenrath and Dan Morse, "Researcher Uses Index to Buy, Short Stocks," *The Wall Street Journal*, February 18, 2003; and Jon E. Hilsenrath, "Satisfaction Theory: Mixed Results," *The Wall Street Journal*, February 19, 2003.

STOCK DIVIDENDS

A distribution of shares of stock to stockholders is called a **stock dividend**. Usually, such distributions are in common stock and are issued to holders of common stock. Stock dividends are different from cash dividends in that there is no distribution of cash or other assets to stockholders.

The effect of a stock dividend on the stockholders' equity of the issuing corporation is to transfer retained earnings to paid-in capital. For public corporations, the amount transferred from retained earnings to paid-in capital is normally the *fair value* (market price) of the shares issued in the stock dividend.[9] To illustrate, assume that the stockholders' equity accounts of Hendrix Corporation as of December 15 are as follows:

Common Stock, $20 par (2,000,000 shares issued)	$40,000,000
Paid-In Capital in Excess of Par—Common Stock	9,000,000
Retained Earnings	26,600,000

On December 15, the board of directors declares a stock dividend of 5% or 100,000 shares (2,000,000 shares × 5%) to be issued on January 10 to stockholders of record on December 31. The market price of the stock on the declaration date is $31 a share. The entry to record the declaration is as follows:

Dec.	15	Stock Dividends	3,100 0 0 0 00	
		Stock Dividends Distributable		2,000 0 0 0 00
		Paid-In Capital in Excess of Par—		
		Common Stock		1,100 0 0 0 00
		Declared 5% (100,000 shares) stock		
		dividend on $20 par common stock		
		with a market price of $31 per share.		

The $3,100,000 balance in Stock Dividends is closed to Retained Earnings on December 31. The stock dividends distributable account is listed in the Paid-In Capital section of the balance sheet. Thus, the effect of the stock dividend is to transfer $3,100,000 of retained earnings to paid-in capital.

On January 10, the number of shares outstanding is increased by 100,000 by the following entry to record the issue of the stock:

Jan.	10	Stock Dividends Distributable	2,000 0 0 0 00	
		Common Stock		2,000 0 0 0 00
		Issued stock for the stock dividend.		

A stock dividend does not change the assets, liabilities, or total stockholders' equity of the corporation. Likewise, it does not change a stockholder's proportionate interest (equity) in the corporation. For example, if a stockholder owned 1,000 of a corporation's 10,000 shares outstanding, the stockholder owns 10% (1,000/10,000) of the corporation. After declaring a 6% stock dividend, the corporation will issue 600 additional shares (10,000 shares × 6%), and the total shares outstanding will be 10,600. The stockholder of 1,000 shares will receive 60 additional shares and will now own 1,060 shares, which is still a 10% equity interest.

---

9 The use of fair market value is justified as long as the number of shares issued for the stock dividend is small (less than 25% of the shares outstanding).

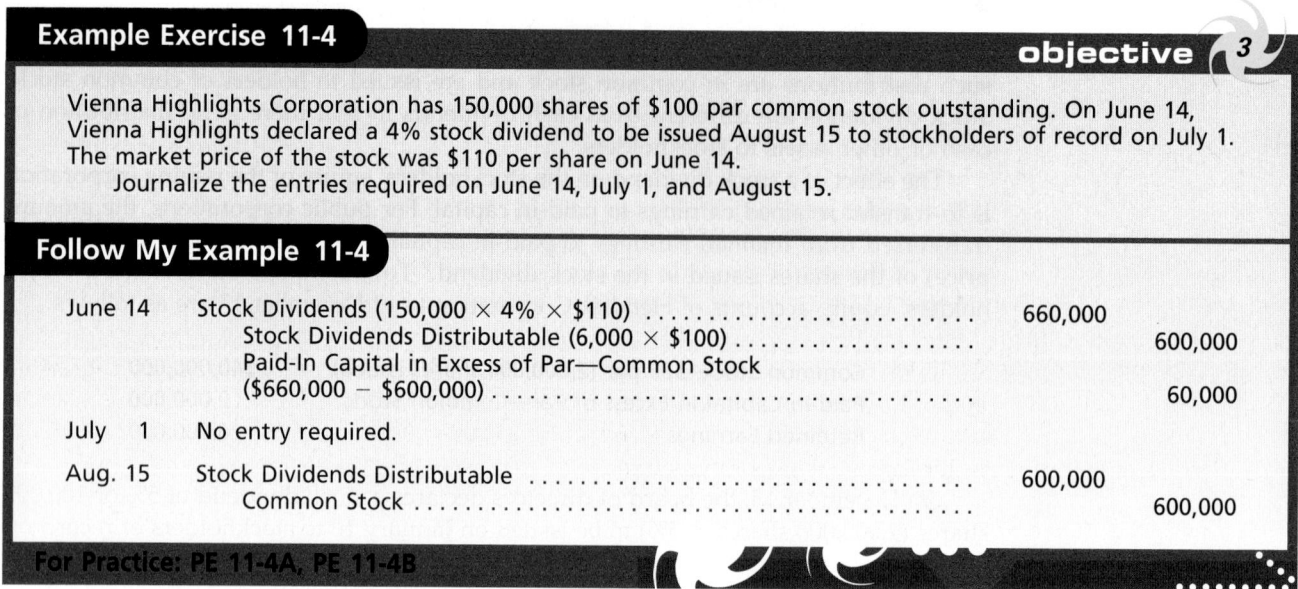

Example Exercise 11-4

objective **3**

Vienna Highlights Corporation has 150,000 shares of $100 par common stock outstanding. On June 14, Vienna Highlights declared a 4% stock dividend to be issued August 15 to stockholders of record on July 1. The market price of the stock was $110 per share on June 14.
Journalize the entries required on June 14, July 1, and August 15.

Follow My Example 11-4

June 14	Stock Dividends (150,000 × 4% × $110)	660,000	
	Stock Dividends Distributable (6,000 × $100)		600,000
	Paid-In Capital in Excess of Par—Common Stock		
	($660,000 − $600,000)		60,000
July 1	No entry required.		
Aug. 15	Stock Dividends Distributable	600,000	
	Common Stock		600,000

For Practice: PE 11-4A, PE 11-4B

Treasury Stock Transactions

objective **4**

Journalize the entries for treasury stock transactions.

REAL WORLD

The 2005 edition of *Accounting Trends & Techniques* indicated that over 66% of the companies surveyed reported treasury stock.

A corporation may buy its own stock to provide shares for resale to employees, for reissuing as a bonus to employees, or for supporting the market price of the stock. For example, General Motors Corporation bought back its common stock and stated that two primary uses of this stock would be for incentive compensation plans and employee savings plans. Such stock that a corporation has once issued and then reacquires is called **treasury stock**.

A commonly used method of accounting for the purchase and resale of treasury stock is the *cost method*.[10] When the stock is purchased by the corporation, paid-in capital is reduced by debiting *Treasury Stock* for its cost (the price paid for it). The par value and the price at which the stock was originally issued are ignored. In addition, no dividends are paid on stock held as treasury stock. To do so would place the corporation in the position of earning income through dealing with itself.

When the stock is resold, Treasury Stock is credited for its cost, and any difference between the cost and the selling price is normally debited or credited to *Paid-In Capital from Sale of Treasury Stock*.

To illustrate, assume that the paid-in capital of a corporation is as follows:

Common stock, $25 par (20,000 shares authorized and issued)	$500,000	
Excess of issue price over par	150,000	$650,000

The purchase and sale of the treasury stock are recorded as follows:

	Treasury Stock	45 0 0 0 00	
	Cash		45 0 0 0 00
	Purchased 1,000 shares of treasury		
	stock at $45.		

(continued)

---

10 Another method that is infrequently used, called the *par value method*, is discussed in advanced accounting texts.

Cash		12 0 0 0 00	
Treasury Stock			9 0 0 0 00
Paid-In Capital from Sale of Treasury Stock			3 0 0 0 00
Sold 200 shares of treasury stock at $60.			
Cash		8 0 0 0 00	
Paid-In Capital from Sale of Treasury Stock		1 0 0 0 00	
Treasury Stock			9 0 0 0 00
Sold 200 shares of treasury stock at $40.			

As shown above, a sale of treasury stock may result in a decrease in paid-in capital. To the extent that Paid-In Capital from Sale of Treasury Stock has a credit balance, it should be debited for any decrease. Any remaining decrease should then be debited to the retained earnings account.

Example Exercise 11-5
objective 4

On May 3, Buzz Off Corporation reacquired 3,200 shares of its common stock at $42 per share. On July 22, Buzz Off sold 2,000 of the reacquired shares at $47 per share. On August 30, Buzz Off sold the remaining shares at $40 per share.
 Journalize the transactions of May 3, July 22, and August 30.

Follow My Example 11-5

May 3	Treasury Stock (3,200 × $42)	134,400	
	Cash		134,400
July 22	Cash (2,000 × $47)	94,000	
	Treasury Stock (2,000 × $42)		84,000
	Paid-In Capital from Sale of Treasury Stock		
	[2,000 × ($47 − $42)]		10,000
Aug. 30	Cash (1,200 × $40)	48,000	
	Paid-In Capital from Sale of Treasury Stock [1,200 × ($42 − $40)]	2,400	
	Treasury Stock (1,200 × $42)		50,400

For Practice: PE 11-5A, PE 11-5B

Reporting Stockholders' Equity

objective 5

Describe and illustrate the reporting of stockholders' equity.

We discussed and illustrated simple Stockholders' Equity sections of balance sheets in earlier chapters. However, as with other sections of the balance sheet, alternative terms and formats may be used in reporting stockholders' equity. In addition, the significant changes in the sources of stockholders' equity—retained earnings and paid-in capital—may be reported in separate statements or notes that support the balance sheet.

STOCKHOLDERS' EQUITY IN THE BALANCE SHEET

Two alternatives for reporting stockholders' equity for the December 31, 2008, balance sheet for Telex Inc. are shown in Exhibit 5. In the first example, each class of stock is listed first, followed by its related paid-in capital accounts. In the second example, the stock accounts are listed first. The other paid-in capital accounts are listed as a single item described as *Additional paid-in capital*. These combined accounts could also be described as *Capital in excess of par (or stated value) of shares* or a similar title.

EXHIBIT 5

Stockholders' Equity
Section of a Balance
Sheet

Telex Inc.
Balance Sheet
December 31, 2008

Stockholders' Equity

Paid-in capital:
  Preferred 10% stock, $50 par
    (2,000 shares authorized and issued) $100,000
    Excess of issue price over par . . . .   10,000 $ 110,000
  Common stock, $20 par
    (50,000 shares authorized,
    45,000 shares issued) $900,000
    Excess of issue price over par   190,000   1,090,000
    From sale of treasury stock   2,000
      Total paid-in capital $1,202,000
  Retained earnings   350,000
    Total $1,552,000
  Deduct treasury stock (600 shares at cost)   27,000
  Total stockholders' equity $1,525,000

Telex Inc.
Balance Sheet
December 31, 2008

Stockholders' Equity

Contributed capital:
  Preferred 10% stock, $50 par
    (2,000 shares authorized and issued) $100,000
  Common stock, $20 par
    (50,000 shares authorized,
    45,000 shares issued)   900,000
    Additional paid-in capital   202,000
      Total contributed capital $1,202,000
  Retained earnings   350,000
    Total $1,552,000
  Deduct treasury stock (600 shares at cost)   27,000
  Total stockholders' equity $1,525,000

Significant changes in stockholders' equity during a period may be presented either in a *statement of stockholders' equity* or in notes to the financial statements. We illustrate the statement of stockholders' equity later in this section. In addition, relevant rights and privileges of the various classes of stock outstanding must be disclosed.[11] Examples of types of information that must be disclosed include dividend and liquidation preferences, conversion rights, and redemption rights. Such information may be disclosed on the face of the balance sheet or in the accompanying notes.

---

11 *Statement of Financial Accounting Standards No. 129*, "Disclosure Information about Capital Structure" (Financial Accounting Standards Board, Norwalk, CT: 1997).

Example Exercise 11-6

objective 5

Using the following accounts and balances, prepare the Stockholders' Equity section of the balance sheet. Forty thousand shares of common stock are authorized, and 5,000 shares have been reacquired.

Common Stock, $50 par	$1,500,000
Paid-In Capital in Excess of Par	160,000
Paid-In Capital from Sale of Treasury Stock	44,000
Retained Earnings	4,395,000
Treasury Stock	120,000

Follow My Example 11-6

Stockholders' Equity

Paid-in capital:		
Common stock, $50 par		
(40,000 shares authorized, 30,000 shares issued)	$1,500,000	
Excess of issue price over par	160,000	$1,660,000
From sale of treasury stock		44,000
Total paid-in capital		$1,704,000
Retained earnings		4,395,000
Total		$6,099,000
Deduct treasury stock (5,000 shares at cost)		120,000
Total stockholders' equity		$5,979,000

For Practice: PE 11-6A, PE 11-6B

The 2005 edition of *Accounting Trends & Techniques* indicated that 0.8% of the companies surveyed presented a separate statement of retained earnings, 0.5% presented a combined income and retained earnings statement, and 1.3% presented changes in retained earnings in the notes to the financial statements. The other 97% of the companies presented changes in retained earnings in a statement of stockholders' equity.

REPORTING RETAINED EARNINGS

A corporation may report changes in retained earnings by preparing a separate retained earnings statement, a combined income and retained earnings statement, or a statement of stockholders' equity.

When a separate **retained earnings statement** is prepared, as illustrated in earlier chapters, the beginning balance of retained earnings is reported. The net income is then added (or net loss is subtracted) and any dividends are subtracted to arrive at the ending retained earnings for the period. An example of a such a statement for Telex Inc. is shown in Exhibit 6.

An alternative format for presenting the retained earnings statement is to combine it with the income statement. An advantage of the combined format is that it emphasizes net income as the connecting link between the income statement and the retained earnings portion of stockholders' equity. Since the combined form is not often used, we do not illustrate it.

Restrictions The retained earnings available for use as dividends may be limited by action of a corporation's board of directors. These amounts, called **restrictions** or

---

EXHIBIT 6

Retained Earnings Statement

Telex Inc.
Retained Earnings Statement
For the Year Ended December 31, 2008

Retained earnings, January 1, 2008			$245,000
Net income		$180,000	
Less dividends:			
Preferred stock	$10,000		
Common stock	65,000	75,000	
Increase in retained earnings			105,000
Retained earnings, December 31, 2008			$350,000

appropriations, remain part of the retained earnings. However, they must be disclosed, usually in the notes to the financial statements.

Restrictions may be classified as either legal, contractual, or discretionary. The board of directors may be legally required to restrict retained earnings because of state laws. For example, some state laws require that retained earnings be restricted by the amount of treasury stock purchased, so that legal capital will not be used for dividends. The board may also be required to restrict retained earnings because of contractual requirements. For example, the terms of a bank loan may require restrictions, so that money for repaying the loan will not be used for dividends. Finally, the board may restrict retained earnings voluntarily. For example, the board may limit dividend distributions so that more money is available for expanding the business.

Prior Period Adjustments   Material errors in a prior period's net income may arise from mathematical mistakes and from mistakes in applying accounting principles. The effect of material errors that are not discovered within the same fiscal period in which they occurred should not be included in determining net income for the current period. Instead, corrections of such errors, called **prior period adjustments**, are reported in the retained earnings statement. These adjustments are reported as an adjustment to the retained earnings balance at the beginning of the period in which the error is discovered and corrected.[12]

Example Exercise 11-7

objective **5**

Dry Creek Cameras Inc. reported the following results for the year ending March 31, 2008:

Retained earnings, April 1, 2007	$3,338,500
Net income	461,500
Cash dividends declared	80,000
Stock dividends declared	120,000

Prepare a retained earnings statement for the fiscal year ended March 31, 2008.

Follow My Example 11-7

DRY CREEK CAMERAS INC.
RETAINED EARNINGS STATEMENT
For the Year Ended March 31, 2008

Retained earnings, April 1, 2007		$3,338,500
Net income	$461,500	
Less dividends declared	200,000	
Increase in retained earnings		261,500
Retained earnings, March 31, 2008		$3,600,000

For Practice: PE 11-7A, PE 11-7B

STATEMENT OF STOCKHOLDERS' EQUITY

Significant changes in stockholders' equity should be reported for the period in which they occur. When the only change in stockholders' equity is due to net income or net loss and dividends, a retained earnings statement is sufficient. However, when a corporation also has changes in stock and other paid-in capital accounts, a **statement of stockholders' equity** is normally prepared. This statement is often prepared in a columnar format, where each column represents a major stockholders' equity classification. Changes in each classification are then described in the left-hand column. Exhibit 7 illustrates a statement of stockholders' equity for Telex Inc.

---

12 Prior period adjustments are illustrated in advanced texts.

EXHIBIT 7   Statement of Stockholders' Equity

			Additional			
Telex Inc. Statement of Stockholders' Equity For the Year Ended December 31, 2008						
	Preferred Stock	Common Stock	Paid-In Capital	Retained Earnings	Treasury Stock	Total
Balance, January 1, 2008	$100,000	$850,000	$177,000	$245,000	$(17,000)	$1,355,000
Net income				180,000		180,000
Dividends on preferred stock				(10,000)		(10,000)
Dividends on common stock				(65,000)		(65,000)
Issuance of additional common stock		50,000	25,000			75,000
Purchase of treasury stock					(10,000)	(10,000)
Balance, December 31, 2008	$100,000	$900,000	$202,000	$350,000	$(27,000)	$1,525,000

Stock Splits

Corporations sometimes reduce the par or stated value of their common stock and issue a proportionate number of additional shares. When this is done, a corporation is said to have *split* its stock, and the process is called a **stock split**.

When stock is split, the reduction in par or stated value applies to all shares, including the unissued, issued, and treasury shares. A major objective of a stock split is to reduce the market price per share of the stock. This, in turn, should attract more investors to enter the market for the stock and broaden the types and numbers of stockholders.

To illustrate a stock split, assume that Rojek Corporation has 10,000 shares of $100 par common stock outstanding with a current market price of $150 per share. The board of directors declares a 5-for-1 stock split, reduces the par to $20, and increases the number of shares to 50,000. The amount of common stock outstanding is $1,000,000 both before and after the stock split. Only the number of shares and the par per share are changed. Each Rojek Corporation shareholder owns the same total par amount of stock before and after the stock split. For example, a stockholder who owned 4 shares of $100 par stock before the split (total par of $400) would own 20 shares of $20 par stock after the split (total par of $400).

Since there are more shares outstanding after the stock split, we would expect that the market price of the stock would fall. For example, in the preceding example, there would be 5 times as many shares outstanding after the split. Thus, we would expect the market price of the stock to fall from $150 to approximately $30 ($150/5).

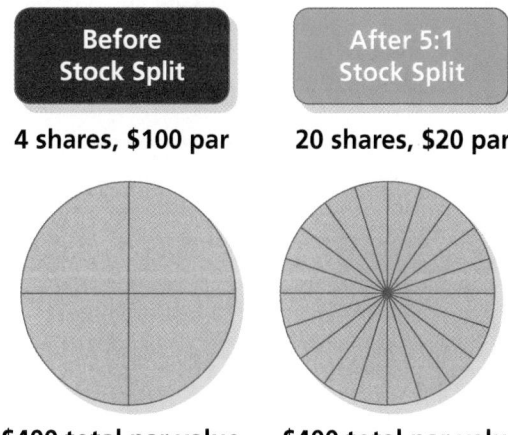

Before Stock Split	After 5:1 Stock Split
4 shares, $100 par	20 shares, $20 par
$400 total par value	$400 total par value

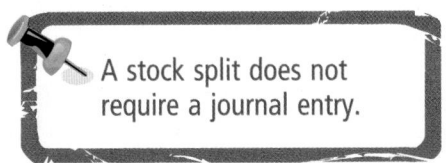

A stock split does not require a journal entry.

Since a stock split changes only the par or stated value and the number of shares outstanding, it is not recorded by a journal entry. Although the accounts are not affected, the details of stock splits are normally disclosed in the notes to the financial statements.

Financial Analysis and Interpretation

The **dividend yield** indicates the rate of return to stockholders in terms of cash dividend distributions. Although the dividend yield can be computed for both preferred and common stock, it is most often computed for common stock. This is because most preferred stock has a stated dividend rate or amount. In contrast, the amount of common stock dividends normally varies with the profitability of the corporation.

The dividend yield is computed by dividing the annual dividends paid per share of common stock by the market price per share at a specific date, as shown below.

$$\text{Dividend Yield} = \frac{\text{Dividends per Share of Common Stock}}{\text{Market Price per Share of Common Stock}}$$

To illustrate, the market price of Mattel, Inc., common stock was $18.89 as of the close of business, January 10, 2005. During the past year, Mattel had paid dividends of $0.45 per share. Thus, the dividend yield of Mattel's common stock is 2.38% ($0.45/$18.89). Because the market price of a corporation's stock will vary from day to day, its dividend yield will also vary from day to day. Fortunately, the dividend yield is provided with newspaper listings of market prices and most Internet quotation services, such as from Yahoo's Finance Web site.

The recent dividend yields for some selected companies are as follows:

Company	Dividend Yield (%)
AT&T Corporation	5.06
Duke Energy Corporation	4.46
General Motors Corporation	8.10
Hewlett-Packard Development Company, LP	1.05
The Home Depot	0.82
Oracle	None
The Coca-Cola Company	1.00

As can be seen, the dividend yield varies widely across firms. Growth companies often do not pay dividends, but instead, reinvest their earnings in research and development, such as with Oracle.

At a Glance

1. Describe the nature of the corporate form of organization.

Key Points	Key Learning Outcomes	Example Exercises	Practice Exercises
Corporations have a separate legal existence, transferable units of stock, unlimited life, and limited stockholders' liability. The advantages and disadvantages of the corporate form are summarized in Exhibit 2. Costs incurred in organizing a corporation are debited to Organizational Expense.	• Describe the characteristics of corporations. • List the advantages and disadvantages of the corporate form. • Prepare a journal entry for the costs of organizing a corporation.		

2. Describe and illustrate the characteristics of stock, classes of stock, and entries for issuing stock.

Key Points	Key Learning Outcomes	Example Exercises	Practice Exercises
The main source of paid-in capital is from issuing common and preferred stock. Stock issued at par is recorded by debiting Cash and crediting the class of stock issued for its par amount. Stock issued for more than par is recorded by debiting Cash and crediting Paid-In Capital in Excess of Par for the difference between the cash received and the par value of the stock. When stock is issued in exchange for assets other than cash, the assets acquired are recorded at their fair market value. When no-par stock is issued, the entire proceeds are credited to the stock account. No-par stock may be assigned a stated value per share, and the excess of the proceeds over the stated value may be credited to Paid-In Capital in Excess of Stated Value.	• Describe the characteristics of common and preferred stock, including rights to dividends. • Journalize the entry for common and preferred stock issued at par. • Journalize the entry for common and preferred stock issued at more than par. • Journalize the entry for issuing no-par stock.	11-1 11-2 11-2 11-2	11-1A, 11-1B 11-2A, 11-2B 11-2A, 11-2B 11-2A, 11-2B

3. Journalize the entries for cash dividends and stock dividends.

Key Points	Key Learning Outcomes	Example Exercises	Practice Exercises
The entry to record a declaration of cash dividends debits Dividends and credits Dividends Payable. When a stock dividend is declared, Stock Dividends is debited for the fair value of the stock to be issued. Stock Dividends Distributable is credited for the par or stated value of the common stock to be issued. The difference between the fair value of the stock and its par or stated value is credited to Paid-In Capital in Excess of Par—Common Stock. When the stock is issued on the date of payment, Stock Dividends Distributable is debited and Common Stock is credited for the par or stated value of the stock issued.	• Journalize the entries for the declaration and payment of cash dividends. • Journalize the entries for the declaration and payment of stock dividends.	11-3 11-4	11-3A, 11-3B 11-4A, 11-4B

4. Journalize the entries for treasury stock transactions.

Key Points	Key Learning Outcomes	Example Exercises	Practice Exercises
When a corporation buys its own stock, the cost method of accounting is normally used. Treasury Stock is debited for its cost, and Cash is credited. If the stock is resold, Treasury Stock is credited for its cost and any difference between the cost and the selling price is normally debited or credited to Paid-In Capital from Sale of Treasury Stock.	• Define *treasury stock*. • Describe the accounting for treasury stock. • Journalize entries for the purchase and sale of treasury stock.	**11-5**	11-5A, 11-5B

5. Describe and illustrate the reporting of stockholders' equity.

Key Points	Key Learning Outcomes	Example Exercises	Practice Exercises
Two alternatives for reporting stockholders' equity are shown in Exhibit 5. Changes in retained earnings are reported in a retained earnings statement, as shown in Exhibit 6. Restrictions to retained earnings should be disclosed. Any prior period adjustments are reported in the retained earnings statement. Changes in stockholders' equity may be reported on a statement of stockholders' equity, as shown in Exhibit 7.	• Prepare the Stockholders' Equity section of the balance sheet. • Prepare a retained earnings statement. • Describe retained earnings restrictions and prior period adjustments. • Prepare a statement of stockholders' equity.	**11-6** **11-7**	11-6A, 11-6B 11-7A, 11-7B

6. Describe the effect of stock splits on corporate financial statements.

Key Points	Key Learning Outcomes	Example Exercises	Practice Exercises
When a corporation reduces the par or stated value of its common stock and issues a proportionate number of additional shares, a stock split has occurred. There are no changes in the balances of any accounts, and no entry is required for a stock split.	• Define and give an example of a stock split. • Describe the accounting for and effects of a stock split on the financial statements.		

Key Terms

cash dividend (495)
common stock (490)
discount (492)
dividend yield (504)
outstanding stock (489)
par (489)
preferred stock (490)

premium (492)
prior period adjustments (502)
restrictions (501)
retained earnings statement (501)
stated value (489)
statement of stockholders' equity (502)

stock (486)
stock dividend (497)
stock split (503)
stockholders (486)
treasury stock (498)

Illustrative Problem

Altenburg Inc. is a lighting fixture wholesaler located in Arizona. During its current fiscal year, ended December 31, 2008, Altenburg Inc. completed the following selected transactions:

Feb. 3. Purchased 2,500 shares of its own common stock at $26, recording the stock at cost. (Prior to the purchase, there were 40,000 shares of $20 par common stock outstanding.)

May 1. Declared a semiannual dividend of $1 on the 10,000 shares of preferred stock and a 30¢ dividend on the common stock to stockholders of record on May 31, payable on June 15.

June 15. Paid the cash dividends.

Sept. 23. Sold 1,000 shares of treasury stock at $28, receiving cash.

Nov. 1. Declared semiannual dividends of $1 on the preferred stock and 30¢ on the common stock. In addition, a 5% common stock dividend was declared on the common stock outstanding, to be capitalized at the fair market value of the common stock, which is estimated at $30.

Dec. 1. Paid the cash dividends and issued the certificates for the common stock dividend.

Instructions

Journalize the entries to record the transactions for Altenburg Inc.

Solution

2008					
Feb.	3	Treasury Stock		65 0 0 0 00	
		Cash			65 0 0 0 00
May	1	Cash Dividends		21 2 5 0 00	
		Cash Dividends Payable			21 2 5 0 00
		(10,000 × $1) + [(40,000 − 2,500)			
		× $0.30].			
June	15	Cash Dividends Payable		21 2 5 0 00	
		Cash			21 2 5 0 00
Sept.	23	Cash		28 0 0 0 00	
		Treasury Stock			26 0 0 0 00
		Paid-In Capital from Sale of Treasury Stock			2 0 0 0 00
Nov.	1	Cash Dividends		21 5 5 0 00	
		Cash Dividends Payable			21 5 5 0 00
		(10,000 × $1) + [(40,000 − 1,500)			
		× $0.30].			
	1	Stock Dividends		57 7 5 0 00 *	
		Stock Dividends Distributable			38 5 0 0 00
		Paid-In Capital in Excess of			
		Par—Common Stock			19 2 5 0 00
		*(40,000 − 1,500) × 5% × $30.			
Dec.	1	Cash Dividends Payable		21 5 5 0 00	
		Stock Dividends Distributable		38 5 0 0 00	
		Cash			21 5 5 0 00
		Common Stock			38 5 0 0 00

Self-Examination Questions

(Answers at End of Chapter)

1. Which of the following is a disadvantage of the corporate form of organization?
   A. Limited liability
   B. Continuous life
   C. Owner is separate from management
   D. Ability to raise capital

2. Paid-in capital for a corporation may arise from which of the following sources?
   A. Issuing preferred stock
   B. Issuing common stock
   C. Selling the corporation's treasury stock
   D. All of the above

3. The Stockholders' Equity section of the balance sheet may include:
   A. Common Stock.
   B. Stock Dividends Distributable.
   C. Preferred Stock.
   D. All of the above.

4. If a corporation reacquires its own stock, the stock is listed on the balance sheet in the:
   A. Current Assets section.
   B. Long-Term Liabilities section.
   C. Stockholders' Equity section.
   D. Investments section.

5. A corporation has issued 25,000 shares of $100 par common stock and holds 3,000 of these shares as treasury stock. If the corporation declares a $2 per share cash dividend, what amount will be recorded as cash dividends?
   A. $22,000   C. $44,000
   B. $25,000   D. $50,000

Eye Openers

1. Describe the stockholders' liability to creditors of a corporation.
2. Why are most large businesses organized as corporations?
3. Of two corporations organized at approximately the same time and engaged in competing businesses, one issued $150 par common stock, and the other issued $1 par common stock. Do the par designations provide any indication as to which stock is preferable as an investment? Explain.
4. A stockbroker advises a client to "buy preferred stock. . . . With that type of stock, . . . [you] will never have to worry about losing the dividends." Is the broker right?
5. What are some of the factors that influence the market price of a corporation's stock?
6. When a corporation issues stock at a premium, is the premium income? Explain.
7. (a) What are the three conditions for the declaration and the payment of a cash dividend? (b) The dates in connection with the declaration of a cash dividend are February 6, March 9, and April 5. Identify each date.
8. A corporation with both preferred stock and common stock outstanding has a substantial credit balance in its retained earnings account at the beginning of the current fiscal year. Although net income for the current year is sufficient to pay the preferred dividend of $250,000 each quarter and a common dividend of $610,000 each quarter, the board of directors declares dividends only on the preferred stock. Suggest possible reasons for passing the dividends on the common stock.
9. An owner of 200 shares of Felt Company common stock receives a stock dividend of 4 shares. (a) What is the effect of the stock dividend on the stockholder's proportionate interest (equity) in the corporation? (b) How does the total equity of 204 shares compare with the total equity of 200 shares before the stock dividend?
10. a. Where should a declared but unpaid cash dividend be reported on the balance sheet?
    b. Where should a declared but unissued stock dividend be reported on the balance sheet?
11. a. In what respect does treasury stock differ from unissued stock?
    b. How should treasury stock be presented on the balance sheet?
12. A corporation reacquires 8,000 shares of its own $10 par common stock for $120,000, recording it at cost. (a) What effect does this transaction have on revenue or expense of the period? (b) What effect does it have on stockholders' equity?

13. The treasury stock in Eye Opener 12 is resold for $158,000. (a) What is the effect on the corporation's revenue of the period? (b) What is the effect on stockholders' equity?
14. What is the primary advantage of combining the retained earnings statement with the income statement?
15. What are the three classifications of restrictions of retained earnings, and how are such restrictions normally reported in the financial statements?
16. Indicate how prior period adjustments would be reported on the financial statements presented only for the current period.
17. When is a statement of stockholders' equity normally prepared?
18. What is the primary purpose of a stock split?

Practice Exercises

PE 11-1A
Dividends per share
obj. 2

Golf-Easy Company has 10,000 shares of 3% preferred stock of $50 par and 25,000 shares of $100 par common stock. The following amounts were distributed as dividends:

Year 1	$ 40,000
Year 2	10,000
Year 3	120,000

Determine the dividends per share for preferred and common stock for each year.

PE 11-1B
Dividends per share
obj. 2

Marsala Company has 5,000 shares of 2% preferred stock of $75 par and 10,000 shares of $150 par common stock. The following amounts were distributed as dividends:

Year 1	$20,000
Year 2	4,000
Year 3	40,000

Determine the dividends per share for preferred and common stock for each year.

PE 11-2A
Entries for issuing stock
obj. 2

On August 3, Waterways Corporation issued for cash 45,000 shares of no-par common stock (with a stated value of $100) at $128. On September 22, Waterways issued at par 2,000 shares of 1%, $75 par preferred stock for cash. On November 4, Waterways issued for cash 3,000 shares of 1%, $75 par preferred stock at $80.
  Journalize the entries to record the August 3, September 22, and November 4 transactions.

PE 11-2B
Entries for issuing stock
obj. 2

On July 6, Istanbul Artifacts Corporation issued for cash 800,000 shares of no-par common stock at $1.20. On August 30, Istanbul Artifacts issued at par 10,000 shares of 2%, $50 par preferred stock for cash. On October 14, Istanbul Artifacts issued for cash 7,500 shares of 2%, $50 par preferred stock at $54.
  Journalize the entries to record the July 6, August 30, and October 14 transactions.

PE 11-3A
Entries for cash dividends
obj. 3

The important dates in connection with a cash dividend of $48,000 on a corporation's common stock are July 16, August 15, and September 30. Journalize the entries required on each date.

PE 11-3B
Entries for cash dividends
obj. 3

The important dates in connection with a cash dividend of $90,000 on a corporation's common stock are October 1, November 1, and December 24. Journalize the entries required on each date.

PE 11-4A
Entries for stock dividends
obj. 3

Stonehenge Corporation has 300,000 shares of $40 par common stock outstanding. On February 13, Stonehenge Corporation declared a 3% stock dividend to be issued April 30 to stockholders of record on March 14. The market price of the stock was $63 per share on February 13.

Journalize the entries required on February 13, March 14, and April 30.

PE 11-4B
Entries for stock dividends
obj. 3

Big Ben Corporation has 250,000 shares of $50 par common stock outstanding. On May 10, Big Ben Corporation declared a 2% stock dividend to be issued August 1 to stockholders of record on June 9. The market price of the stock was $60 per share on May 10.

Journalize the entries required on May 10, June 9, and August 1.

PE 11-5A
Entries for treasury stock
obj. 4

On January 24, Thunderstorm Inc. reacquired 6,000 shares of its common stock at $18 per share. On March 15, Thunderstorm sold 4,500 of the reacquired shares at $21 per share. On June 2, Thunderstorm sold the remaining shares at $17 per share.

Journalize the transactions of January 24, March 15, and June 2.

PE 11-5B
Entries for treasury stock
obj. 4

On October 2, Baja Clothing Inc. reacquired 12,000 shares of its common stock at $6 per share. On November 15, Baja Clothing sold 8,400 of the reacquired shares at $9 per share. On December 22, Baja Clothing sold the remaining shares at $5 per share.

Journalize the transactions of October 2, November 15, and December 22.

PE 11-6A
Stockholders' Equity section of balance sheet
obj. 5

Using the following accounts and balances, prepare the Stockholders' Equity section of the balance sheet. Thirty thousand shares of common stock are authorized, and 2,000 shares have been reacquired.

Common Stock, $80 par	$2,000,000
Paid-In Capital in Excess of Par	315,000
Paid-In Capital from Sale of Treasury Stock	33,000
Retained Earnings	1,112,000
Treasury Stock	180,000

PE 11-6B
Stockholders' Equity section of balance sheet
obj. 5

Using the following accounts and balances, prepare the Stockholders' Equity section of the balance sheet. Fifty thousand shares of common stock are authorized, and 5,000 shares have been reacquired.

Common Stock, $75 par	$3,375,000
Paid-In Capital in Excess of Par	485,000
Paid-In Capital from Sale of Treasury Stock	18,000
Retained Earnings	1,452,000
Treasury Stock	420,000

PE 11-7A
Retained earnings statement
obj. 5

Dynamic Leaders Inc. reported the following results for the year ending July 31, 2008:

Retained earnings, August 1, 2007	$988,500
Net income	325,000
Cash dividends declared	35,000
Stock dividends declared	90,000

Prepare a retained earnings statement for the fiscal year ended July 31, 2008.

PE 11-7B
Retained earnings statement
obj. 5

Maxima Retractors Inc. reported the following results for the year ending October 31, 2008:

Retained earnings, November 1, 2007	$2,906,000
Net income	553,000
Cash dividends declared	100,000
Stock dividends declared	200,000

Prepare a retained earnings statement for the fiscal year ended October 31, 2008.

Exercises

EX 11-1
Dividends per share
obj. 2

✓ *Preferred stock,*
1st year: $0.80

Electro-Rad Inc., a developer of radiology equipment, has stock outstanding as follows: 50,000 shares of 2%, preferred stock of $50 par, and 100,000 shares of $25 par common. During its first four years of operations, the following amounts were distributed as dividends: first year, $40,000; second year, $98,000; third year, $120,000; fourth year, $195,000. Calculate the dividends per share on each class of stock for each of the four years.

EX 11-2
Dividends per share
obj. 2

✓ *Preferred stock,*
1st year: $0.15

CompuLead Inc., a software development firm, has stock outstanding as follows: 40,000 shares of 1%, preferred stock of $25 par, and 50,000 shares of $75 par common. During its first four years of operations, the following amounts were distributed as dividends: first year, $6,000; second year, $26,000; third year, $4,000; fourth year, $60,000. Calculate the dividends per share on each class of stock for each of the four years.

EX 11-3
Entries for issuing par stock
obj. 2

On February 4, Cinderella Rocks Inc., a marble contractor, issued for cash 30,000 shares of $20 par common stock at $64, and on March 31, it issued for cash 18,000 shares of $75 par preferred stock at $90.

a. Journalize the entries for February 4 and March 31.
b. What is the total amount invested (total paid-in capital) by all stockholders as of March 31?

EX 11-4
Entries for issuing no-par stock
obj. 2

On July 17, America Carpet Inc., a carpet wholesaler, issued for cash 150,000 shares of no-par common stock (with a stated value of $5) at $36, and on September 20, it issued for cash 10,000 shares of $50 par preferred stock at $80.

a. Journalize the entries for July 17 and September 20, assuming that the common stock is to be credited with the stated value.
b. What is the total amount invested (total paid-in capital) by all stockholders as of September 20?

EX 11-5
Issuing stock for assets other than cash
obj. 2

On November 10, Craddock's Corporation, a wholesaler of hydraulic lifts, acquired land in exchange for 15,000 shares of $8 par common stock with a current market price of $32. Journalize the entry to record the transaction.

EX 11-6
Selected stock transactions
obj. 2

Country Sounds Corp., an electric guitar retailer, was organized by Julie Arnold, Joe Harris, and Scott Pickens. The charter authorized 500,000 shares of common stock with a par of $12. The following transactions affecting stockholders' equity were completed during the first year of operations:

a. Issued 20,000 shares of stock at par to Julie Arnold for cash.
b. Issued 500 shares of stock at par to Scott Pickens for promotional services provided in connection with the organization of the corporation, and issued 18,000 shares of stock at par to Scott Pickens for cash.
c. Purchased land and a building from Joe Harris. The building is mortgaged for $200,000 for 25 years at 7%, and there is accrued interest of $2,200 on the mortgage note at the time of the purchase. It is agreed that the land is to be priced at $75,000 and the building at $240,000, and that Joe Harris's equity will be exchanged for stock at par. The corporation agreed to assume responsibility for paying the mortgage note and the accrued interest.

Journalize the entries to record the transactions.

EX 11-7
Issuing stock
obj. 2

Angel Creek Nursery, with an authorization of 40,000 shares of preferred stock and 150,000 shares of common stock, completed several transactions involving its stock on August 15, the first day of operations. The trial balance at the close of the day follows:

Cash	450,000	
Land	100,000	
Buildings	80,000	
Preferred 2% Stock, $80 par		160,000
Paid-In Capital in Excess of Par—Preferred Stock		20,000
Common Stock, $50 par		400,000
Paid-In Capital in Excess of Par—Common Stock		50,000
	630,000	630,000

All shares within each class of stock were sold at the same price. The preferred stock was issued in exchange for the land and buildings.

Journalize the two entries to record the transactions summarized in the trial balance.

EX 11-8
Issuing stock
obj. 2

Heritage Products Inc., a wholesaler of office products, was organized on February 19 of the current year, with an authorization of 60,000 shares of 3% preferred stock, $40 par and 300,000 shares of $75 par common stock. The following selected transactions were completed during the first year of operations:

Feb. 19. Issued 20,000 shares of common stock at par for cash.
    27. Issued 100 shares of common stock at par to an attorney in payment of legal fees for organizing the corporation.
Mar. 13. Issued 6,000 shares of common stock in exchange for land, buildings, and equipment with fair market prices of $80,000, $350,000, and $45,000, respectively.
May 6. Issued 5,000 shares of preferred stock at $46 for cash.

Journalize the transactions.

EX 11-9
Entries for cash dividends
obj. 3

The dates of importance in connection with a cash dividend of $275,000 on a corporation's common stock are July 2, August 1, and September 1. Journalize the entries required on each date.

EX 11-10
Entries for stock dividends
obj. 3

✓ b. (1) $34,500,000
   (3) $85,100,000

Earthworks Health Co. is an HMO for 12 businesses in the St. Louis area. The following account balances appear on the balance sheet of Earthworks Health Co.: Common stock (400,000 shares authorized), $100 par, $30,000,000; Paid-in capital in excess of par—common stock, $4,500,000; and Retained earnings, $50,600,000. The board of directors declared a 2% stock dividend when the market price of the stock was $120 a share. Earthworks Health Co. reported no income or loss for the current year.

a. Journalize the entries to record (1) the declaration of the dividend, capitalizing an amount equal to market value, and (2) the issuance of the stock certificates.
b. Determine the following amounts before the stock dividend was declared: (1) total paid-in capital, (2) total retained earnings, and (3) total stockholders' equity.
c. Determine the following amounts after the stock dividend was declared and closing entries were recorded at the end of the year: (1) total paid-in capital, (2) total retained earnings, and (3) total stockholders' equity.

EX 11-11
Treasury stock transactions
obj. 4

✓ b. $9,000 credit

Mountain Springs Inc. bottles and distributes spring water. On May 2 of the current year, Mountain Springs reacquired 3,000 shares of its common stock at $72 per share. On August 14, Mountain Springs sold 2,500 of the reacquired shares at $76 per share. The remaining 500 shares were sold at $70 per share on November 7.

a. Journalize the transactions of May 2, August 14, and November 7.
b. What is the balance in Paid-In Capital from Sale of Treasury Stock on December 31 of the current year?
c. ▭▭▭▭ For what reasons might Mountain Springs have purchased the treasury stock?

EX 11-12
Treasury stock transactions
objs. 4, 5
✓ b. $36,900 credit

Azalea Gardens Inc. develops and produces spraying equipment for lawn maintenance and industrial uses. On September 9 of the current year, Azalea Gardens Inc. reacquired 12,000 shares of its common stock at $89 per share. On October 31, 10,500 of the reacquired shares were sold at $92 per share, and on December 4, 900 of the reacquired shares were sold at $95.

a. Journalize the transactions of September 9, October 31, and December 4.
b. What is the balance in Paid-In Capital from Sale of Treasury Stock on December 31 of the current year?
c. What is the balance in Treasury Stock on December 31 of the current year?
d. How will the balance in Treasury Stock be reported on the balance sheet?

EX 11-13
Treasury stock transactions
objs. 4, 5
✓ b. $12,000 credit

Tacoma Inc. bottles and distributes spring water. On June 12 of the current year, Tacoma Inc. reacquired 15,000 shares of its common stock at $48 per share. On August 10, Tacoma Inc. sold 9,000 of the reacquired shares at $50 per share. The remaining 6,000 shares were sold at $47 per share on December 20.

a. Journalize the transactions of June 12, August 10, and December 20.
b. What is the balance in Paid-In Capital from Sale of Treasury Stock on December 31 of the current year?
c. Where will the balance in Paid-In Capital from Sale of Treasury Stock be reported on the balance sheet?
d. ▉▉▉▶ For what reasons might Tacoma Inc. have purchased the treasury stock?

EX 11-14
Reporting paid-in capital
obj. 5
✓ Total paid-in capital, $2,494,500

The following accounts and their balances were selected from the unadjusted trial balance of Sailors Inc., a freight forwarder, at August 31, the end of the current fiscal year:

Preferred 3% Stock, $100 par	$1,500,000
Paid-In Capital in Excess of Par—Preferred Stock	180,000
Common Stock, no par, $10 stated value	675,000
Paid-In Capital in Excess of Stated Value—Common Stock	125,000
Paid-In Capital from Sale of Treasury Stock	14,500
Retained Earnings	2,106,500

Prepare the Paid-In Capital portion of the Stockholders' Equity section of the balance sheet. There are 500,000 shares of common stock authorized and 50,000 shares of preferred stock authorized.

EX 11-15
Stockholders' Equity section of balance sheet
obj. 5
✓ Total stockholders' equity, $4,020,000

The following accounts and their balances appear in the ledger of Heart and Saul Inc. on April 30 of the current year:

Common Stock, $50 par	$ 900,000
Paid-In Capital in Excess of Par	110,000
Paid-In Capital from Sale of Treasury Stock	42,000
Retained Earnings	3,178,000
Treasury Stock	210,000

Prepare the Stockholders' Equity section of the balance sheet as of April 30. Twenty-five thousand shares of common stock are authorized, and 3,500 shares have been reacquired.

EX 11-16
Stockholders' Equity section of balance sheet
obj. 5
✓ Total stockholders' equity, $4,726,500

Sports Car Inc. retails racing products for BMWs, Porsches, and Ferraris. The following accounts and their balances appear in the ledger of Sports Car Inc. on November 30, the end of the current year:

Common Stock, $5 par	$ 875,000
Paid-In Capital in Excess of Par—Common Stock	700,000
Paid-In Capital in Excess of Par—Preferred Stock	25,000
Paid-In Capital from Sale of Treasury Stock—Common	16,000
Preferred 3% Stock, $75 par	937,500
Retained Earnings	2,338,000
Treasury Stock—Common	165,000

Twenty thousand shares of preferred and 400,000 shares of common stock are authorized. There are 22,000 shares of common stock held as treasury stock.

Prepare the Stockholders' Equity section of the balance sheet as of November 30, the end of the current year.

EX 11-17
Retained earnings statement

obj. 5

✓ *Retained earnings, August 31, $1,950,000*

Stillwater Corporation, a manufacturer of industrial pumps, reports the following results for the year ending August 31, 2008:

Retained earnings, September 1, 2007	$1,752,000
Net income	378,000
Cash dividends declared	80,000
Stock dividends declared	100,000

Prepare a retained earnings statement for the fiscal year ended August 31, 2008.

EX 11-18
Stockholders' Equity section of balance sheet

obj. 5

✓ *Corrected total stockholders' equity, $5,439,000*

List the errors in the following Stockholders' Equity section of the balance sheet prepared as of the end of the current year.

Stockholders' Equity

Paid-in capital:			
Preferred 1% stock, $75 par			
(8,000 shares authorized and issued)		$ 600,000	
Excess of issue price over par		56,000	$ 656,000
Retained earnings			1,278,000
Treasury stock (4,000 shares at cost)			320,000
Dividends payable			18,000
Total paid-in capital			$2,272,000
Common stock, $50 par (100,000 shares			
authorized, 60,000 shares issued)			3,900,000
Organizing costs			75,000
Total stockholders' equity			$6,247,000

EX 11-19
Statement of stockholders' equity

obj. 5

✓ *Total stockholders' equity, Dec. 31, $3,529,000*

The stockholders' equity T accounts of Family Greeting Cards Inc. for the current fiscal year ended December 31, 2008, are as follows. Prepare a statement of stockholders' equity for the fiscal year ended December 31, 2008.

COMMON STOCK

	Jan.	1	Balance	600,000
	Apr.	9	Issued	
			50,000 shares	150,000
	Dec.	31	Balance	750,000

PAID-IN CAPITAL IN EXCESS OF PAR

	Jan.	1	Balance	350,000
	Apr.	9	Issued	
			50,000 shares	100,000
	Dec.	31	Balance	450,000

TREASURY STOCK

Aug. 7 Purchased		
6,000 shares	24,000	

RETAINED EARNINGS

June 30 Dividend	40,000	Jan.	1	Balance	2,108,000
Dec. 30 Dividend	40,000	Dec.	31	Closing	
				(net income)	325,000
		Dec.	31	Balance	2,353,000

EX 11-20
Effect of stock split
obj. 6

Rolling Pin Corporation wholesales ovens and ranges to restaurants throughout the Midwest. Rolling Pin Corporation, which had 50,000 shares of common stock outstanding, declared a 3-for-1 stock split (2 additional shares for each share issued).

a. What will be the number of shares outstanding after the split?
b. If the common stock had a market price of $180 per share before the stock split, what would be an approximate market price per share after the split?

EX 11-21
Effect of cash dividend and stock split
objs. 3, 6

Indicate whether the following actions would (+) increase, (−) decrease, or (0) not affect Indigo Inc.'s total assets, liabilities, and stockholders' equity:

	Assets	Liabilities	Stockholders' Equity
(1) Declaring a cash dividend	_____	_____	_____
(2) Paying the cash dividend declared in (1)	_____	_____	_____
(3) Authorizing and issuing stock certificates in a stock split	_____	_____	_____
(4) Declaring a stock dividend	_____	_____	_____
(5) Issuing stock certificates for the stock dividend declared in (4)	_____	_____	_____

EX 11-22
Selected dividend transactions, stock split
objs. 3, 6

Selected transactions completed by NuCraft Boating Supply Corporation during the current fiscal year are as follows:

Mar. 5. Split the common stock 4 for 1 and reduced the par from $100 to $25 per share. After the split, there were 800,000 common shares outstanding.
May 15. Declared semiannual dividends of $2 on 15,000 shares of preferred stock and $0.12 on the common stock to stockholders of record on June 14, payable on July 14.
July 14. Paid the cash dividends.
Nov. 15. Declared semiannual dividends of $2 on the preferred stock and $0.14 on the common stock (before the stock dividend). In addition, a 1% common stock dividend was declared on the common stock outstanding. The fair market value of the common stock is estimated at $30.
Dec. 15. Paid the cash dividends and issued the certificates for the common stock dividend.

Journalize the transactions.

EX 11-23
Dividend yield

At the market close on May 12, 2006, Bank of America Corporation had a closing stock price of $49.69. In addition, Bank of America had earnings per share of $4.05 and dividend per share was $1.95. Determine Bank of America's dividend yield. Round to one decimal place.

EX 11-24
Dividend yield

General Electric Company had earnings per share of $1.72 for 2005 and $1.56 for 2004. In addition, the dividends per share were $0.91 for 2005 and $0.82 for 2004. The market price of GE's stock closed at $35.05 and $36.50 on December 31, 2005 and 2004, respectively.

a. Determine the dividend yield for General Electric on December 31, 2005 and 2004. Round percentages to two decimal places.
b. ●━━━▶ Interpret these measures.

EX 11-25
Dividend yield

eBay Inc. developed a Web-based marketplace at **http://www.ebay.com**, in which individuals can buy and sell a variety of items. eBay also acquired PayPal, an online payments system that allows businesses and individuals to send and receive online payments securely. In a recent annual report, eBay published the following dividend policy:

We have never paid cash dividends on our stock, and currently anticipate that we will continue to retain any future earnings to finance the growth of our business.

→ Given eBay's dividend policy, why would an investor be attracted to its stock?

Problems Series A

PR 11-1A
Dividends on preferred and common stock
obj. 2

✓1. Common dividends in 2004: $20,000

Olympic Theatre Inc. owns and operates movie theaters throughout Texas and California. Olympic Theatre has declared the following annual dividends over a six-year period: 2003, $21,000; 2004, $50,000; 2005, $15,000; 2006, $80,000; 2007, $90,000; and 2008, $140,000. During the entire period, the outstanding stock of the company was composed of 10,000 shares of 4% preferred stock, $75 par, and 100,000 shares of common stock, $10 par.

Instructions

1. Calculate the total dividends and the per-share dividends declared on each class of stock for each of the six years. Summarize the data in tabular form, using the following column headings:

Year	Total Dividends	Preferred Dividends		Common Dividends	
		Total	Per Share	Total	Per Share
2003	$ 21,000				
2004	50,000				
2005	15,000				
2006	80,000				
2007	90,000				
2008	140,000				

2. Calculate the average annual dividend per share for each class of stock for the six-year period.
3. Assuming that the preferred stock was sold at $80 and common stock was sold at par at the beginning of the six-year period, calculate the average annual percentage return on initial shareholders' investment, based on the average annual dividend per share (a) for preferred stock and (b) for common stock.

PR 11-2A
Stock transactions for corporate expansion
obj. 2

KLOOSTER & ALLEN

On January 31 of the current year, the following accounts and their balances appear in the ledger of Gargantuan Corp., a meat processor:

Preferred 3% Stock, $25 par (50,000 shares authorized, 30,000 shares issued)	$ 750,000
Paid-In Capital in Excess of Par—Preferred Stock	90,000
Common Stock, $30 par (400,000 shares authorized, 120,000 shares issued)	3,600,000
Paid-In Capital in Excess of Par—Common Stock	300,000
Retained Earnings	5,794,000

At the annual stockholders' meeting on April 2, the board of directors presented a plan for modernizing and expanding plant operations at a cost of approximately $2,550,000. The plan provided (a) that a building, valued at $1,200,000, and the land on which it is located, valued at $300,000, be acquired in accordance with preliminary negotiations by the issuance of 45,000 shares of common stock, (b) that 15,000 shares of the unissued preferred stock be issued through an underwriter, and (c) that the corporation borrow $500,000. The plan was approved by the stockholders and accomplished by the following transactions:

June 6. Issued 45,000 shares of common stock in exchange for land and a building, according to the plan.
      14. Issued 15,000 shares of preferred stock, receiving $36 per share in cash.
      30. Borrowed $500,000 from Mt. Baker National Bank, giving a 7% mortgage note.

No other transactions occurred during June.

Instructions
Journalize the entries to record the foregoing transactions.

PR 11-3A
*Selected stock
transactions*

objs. **2, 3, 4**

f. Cash dividends, $86,500

The following selected accounts appear in the ledger of Clear Skies Environmental Corporation on July 1, 2008, the beginning of the current fiscal year:

Preferred 2% Stock, $100 par (25,000 shares authorized,	
18,000 shares issued)	$1,800,000
Paid-In Capital in Excess of Par—Preferred Stock	216,000
Common Stock, $40 par (100,000 shares authorized,	
70,000 shares issued)	2,800,000
Paid-In Capital in Excess of Par—Common Stock	700,000
Retained Earnings	3,200,000

During the year, the corporation completed a number of transactions affecting the stockholders' equity. They are summarized as follows:

a. Issued 12,000 shares of common stock at $62, receiving cash.
b. Sold 5,000 shares of preferred 2% stock at $124.
c. Purchased 10,000 shares of treasury common for $580,000.
d. Sold 7,500 shares of treasury common for $457,500.
e. Sold 1,500 shares of treasury common for $82,500.
f. Declared cash dividends of $2 per share on preferred stock and $0.50 per share on common stock.
g. Paid the cash dividends.

Instructions
Journalize the entries to record the transactions. Identify each entry by letter.

PR 11-4A
*Entries for selected
corporate transactions*

objs. **2, 3, 4, 5**

✓ *4. Total stockholders'
equity, $9,869,000*

Eureka Enterprises Inc. manufactures bathroom fixtures. The stockholders' equity accounts of Eureka Enterprises Inc., with balances on January 1, 2008, are as follows:

Common Stock, $10 stated value (500,000 shares authorized,	
380,000 shares issued)	$3,800,000
Paid-In Capital in Excess of Stated Value	760,000
Retained Earnings	4,390,000
Treasury Stock (25,000 shares, at cost)	500,000

The following selected transactions occurred during the year:

Jan. 10. Paid cash dividends of $0.20 per share on the common stock. The dividend had been properly recorded when declared on December 30 of the preceding fiscal year for $71,000.

Mar. 3. Issued 20,000 shares of common stock for $460,000.

May 21. Sold all of the treasury stock for $650,000.

July 1. Declared a 3% stock dividend on common stock, to be capitalized at the market price of the stock, which is $30 per share.

Aug. 15. Issued the certificates for the dividend declared on July 1.

Sept. 30. Purchased 10,000 shares of treasury stock for $230,000.

Dec. 27. Declared a $0.25-per-share dividend on common stock.

31. Closed the credit balance of the income summary account, $639,500.

31. Closed the two dividends accounts to Retained Earnings.

Instructions
1. Enter the January 1 balances in T accounts for the stockholders' equity accounts listed. Also prepare T accounts for the following: Paid-In Capital from Sale of Treasury Stock; Stock Dividends Distributable; Stock Dividends; Cash Dividends.
2. Journalize the entries to record the transactions, and post to the eight selected accounts.
3. Prepare a retained earnings statement for the year ended December 31, 2008.
4. Prepare the Stockholders' Equity section of the December 31, 2008, balance sheet.

PR 11-5A
*Entries for selected
corporate transactions*

objs. 2, 3, 4, 6

✓ *Nov. 15, cash dividends,
$82,800*

Selected transactions completed by Oceano Boating Corporation during the current fiscal year are as follows:

Jan.   3.   Split the common stock 2 for 1 and reduced the par from $50 to $25 per share. After the split, there were 400,000 common shares outstanding.

Feb. 20.   Purchased 50,000 shares of the corporation's own common stock at $32, recording the stock at cost.

May   1.   Declared semiannual dividends of $0.80 on 30,000 shares of preferred stock and $0.14 on the common stock to stockholders of record on May 15, payable on June 1.

June   1.   Paid the cash dividends.

Aug.   5.   Sold 42,000 shares of treasury stock at $39, receiving cash.

Nov. 15.   Declared semiannual dividends of $0.80 on the preferred stock and $0.15 on the common stock (before the stock dividend). In addition, a 2% common stock dividend was declared on the common stock outstanding. The fair market value of the common stock is estimated at $40.

Dec. 31.   Paid the cash dividends and issued the certificates for the common stock dividend.

Instructions
Journalize the transactions.

Problems Series B

PR 11-1B
*Dividends on preferred
and common stock*

obj. 2

✓ *1. Common dividends
in 2003: $40,000*

Rainer Bike Corp. manufactures mountain bikes and distributes them through retail outlets in Oregon and Washington. Rainer Bike Corp. has declared the following annual dividends over a six-year period: 2003, $60,000; 2004, $8,000; 2005, $30,000; 2006, $40,000; 2007, $80,000; and 2008, $115,000. During the entire period, the outstanding stock of the company was composed of 40,000 shares of 2% preferred stock, $25 par, and 50,000 shares of common stock, $1 par.

Instructions
1. Determine the total dividends and the per-share dividends declared on each class of stock for each of the six years. Summarize the data in tabular form, using the following column headings:

Year	Total Dividends	Preferred Dividends		Common Dividends	
		Total	Per Share	Total	Per Share
2003	$ 60,000				
2004	8,000				
2005	30,000				
2006	40,000				
2007	80,000				
2008	115,000				

2. Determine the average annual dividend per share for each class of stock for the six-year period.
3. Assuming that the preferred stock was sold at par and common stock was sold at $18.75 at the beginning of the six-year period, calculate the average annual percentage return on initial shareholders' investment, based on the average annual dividend per share (a) for preferred stock and (b) for common stock.

PR 11-2B
*Stock transactions for
corporate expansion*

obj. 2

I-Can-See Optics produces medical lasers for use in hospitals. The accounts and their balances appear in the ledger of I-Can-See Optics on November 30 of the current year at the top of the following page.

Preferred 2% Stock, $80 par (40,000 shares authorized,	
25,000 shares issued)	$ 2,000,000
Paid-In Capital in Excess of Par—Preferred Stock	120,000
Common Stock, $100 par (500,000 shares authorized,	
50,000 shares issued)	5,000,000
Paid-In Capital in Excess of Par—Common Stock	300,000
Retained Earnings	12,794,000

At the annual stockholders' meeting on December 10, the board of directors presented a plan for modernizing and expanding plant operations at a cost of approximately $3,800,000. The plan provided (a) that the corporation borrow $900,000, (b) that 10,000 shares of the un-issued preferred stock be issued through an underwriter, and (c) that a building, valued at $1,675,000, and the land on which it is located, valued at $250,000, be acquired in accordance with preliminary negotiations by the issuance of 16,000 shares of common stock. The plan was approved by the stockholders and accomplished by the following transactions:

Jan. 6. Borrowed $900,000 from City National Bank, giving a 6% mortgage note.
      15. Issued 10,000 shares of preferred stock, receiving $95 per share in cash.
      31. Issued 16,000 shares of common stock in exchange for land and a building, according to the plan.

No other transactions occurred during January.

Instructions
Journalize the entries to record the foregoing transactions.

PR 11-3B
Selected stock transactions
objs. 2, 3, 4

✓ *f. Cash dividends, $123,900*

Buellton Welding Corporation sells and services pipe welding equipment in California. The following selected accounts appear in the ledger of Buellton Welding Corporation on January 1, 2008, the beginning of the current fiscal year:

Preferred 2% Stock, $50 par (100,000 shares authorized,	
50,000 shares issued)	$ 2,500,000
Paid-In Capital in Excess of Par—Preferred Stock	180,000
Common Stock, $15 par (900,000 shares authorized,	
600,000 shares issued)	9,000,000
Paid-In Capital in Excess of Par—Common Stock	1,500,000
Retained Earnings	13,100,000

During the year, the corporation completed a number of transactions affecting the stockholders' equity. They are summarized as follows:

a. Purchased 25,000 shares of treasury common for $650,000.
b. Sold 18,000 shares of treasury common for $576,000.
c. Sold 10,000 shares of preferred 2% stock at $80.
d. Issued 40,000 shares of common stock at $30, receiving cash.
e. Sold 6,000 shares of treasury common for $150,000.
f. Declared cash dividends of $1 per share on preferred stock and $0.10 per share on common stock.
g. Paid the cash dividends.

Instructions
Journalize the entries to record the transactions. Identify each entry by letter.

PR 11-4B
Entries for selected corporate transactions
objs. 2, 3, 4, 5

✓ *4. Total stockholders' equity, $11,160,300*

GPS Enterprises Inc. produces aeronautical navigation equipment. The stockholders' equity accounts of GPS Enterprises Inc., with balances on January 1, 2008, are as follows:

Common Stock, $20 stated value (250,000 shares authorized,	
150,000 shares issued)	$3,000,000
Paid-In Capital in Excess of Stated Value	600,000
Retained Earnings	6,175,000
Treasury Stock (10,000 shares, at cost)	280,000

The following selected transactions occurred during the year:

Jan. 12. Paid cash dividends of $0.25 per share on the common stock. The dividend had been properly recorded when declared on December 28 of the preceding fiscal year for $35,000.

Feb. 19. Sold all of the treasury stock for $360,000.

Apr.   3. Issued 40,000 shares of common stock for $1,600,000.

July 30. Declared a 2% stock dividend on common stock, to be capitalized at the market price of the stock, which is $45 per share.

Aug. 30. Issued the certificates for the dividend declared on July 30.

Nov.   7. Purchased 15,000 shares of treasury stock for $600,000.

Dec. 30. Declared a $0.25-per-share dividend on common stock.

      31. Closed the credit balance of the income summary account, $350,000.

      31. Closed the two dividends accounts to Retained Earnings.

Instructions

1. Enter the January 1 balances in T accounts for the stockholders' equity accounts listed. Also prepare T accounts for the following: Paid-In Capital from Sale of Treasury Stock; Stock Dividends Distributable; Stock Dividends; Cash Dividends.
2. Journalize the entries to record the transactions, and post to the eight selected accounts.
3. Prepare a retained earnings statement for the year ended December 31, 2008.
4. Prepare the Stockholders' Equity section of the December 31, 2008, balance sheet.

PR 11-5B

Entries for selected corporate transactions

objs. 2, 3, 4, 6

✓ *Sept. 1, Cash dividends, $169,100*

Moro Bay Corporation manufactures and distributes leisure clothing. Selected transactions completed by Moro Bay during the current fiscal year are as follows:

Jan. 10. Split the common stock 4 for 1 and reduced the par from $20 to $5 per share. After the split, there were 500,000 common shares outstanding.

Mar.   1. Declared semiannual dividends of $1 on 125,000 shares of preferred stock and $0.12 on the 500,000 shares of $5 par common stock to stockholders of record on March 31, payable on April 30.

Apr. 30. Paid the cash dividends.

July   9. Purchased 40,000 shares of the corporation's own common stock at $16, recording the stock at cost.

Aug. 29. Sold 30,000 shares of treasury stock at $21, receiving cash.

Sept. 1. Declared semiannual dividends of $1 on the preferred stock and $0.09 on the common stock (before the stock dividend). In addition, a 1% common stock dividend was declared on the common stock outstanding, to be capitalized at the fair market value of the common stock, which is estimated at $22.

Oct. 31. Paid the cash dividends and issued the certificates for the common stock dividend.

Instructions

Journalize the transactions.

Special Activities

SA 11-1

Board of directors' actions

Bernie Ebbers, the CEO of WorldCom, a major telecommunications company, was having personal financial troubles. Ebbers pledged a large stake of his WorldCom stock as security for some personal loans. As the price of WorldCom stock sank, Ebbers' bankers threatened to sell his stock in order to protect their loans. To avoid having his stock sold, Ebbers asked the board of directors of WorldCom to loan him nearly $400 million of corporate assets at 2.5% interest to pay off his bankers. The board agreed to lend him the money.

▬▬▶ Comment on the decision of the board of directors in this situation.

SA 11-2
Ethics and professional conduct in business

ETHICS

Gigi Liken and Ron Bobo are organizing Gold Unlimited Inc. to undertake a high-risk gold-mining venture in Canada. Gigi and Ron tentatively plan to request authorization for 75,000,000 shares of common stock to be sold to the general public. Gigi and Ron have decided to establish par of $1 per share in order to appeal to a wide variety of potential investors. Gigi and Ron feel that investors would be more willing to invest in the company if they received a large quantity of shares for what might appear to be a "bargain" price.

➤ Discuss whether Gigi and Ron are behaving in a professional manner.

SA 11-3
Issuing stock

Las Animas Inc. began operations on January 2, 2008, with the issuance of 100,000 shares of $50 par common stock. The sole stockholders of Las Animas Inc. are Cindy Stern and Dr. Kassay Heyen, who organized Las Animas Inc. with the objective of developing a new flu vaccine. Dr. Heyen claims that the flu vaccine, which is nearing the final development stage, will protect individuals against 80% of the flu types that have been medically identified. To complete the project, Las Animas Inc. needs $5,000,000 of additional funds. The local banks have been unwilling to loan the funds because of the lack of sufficient collateral and the riskiness of the business.

The following is a conversation between Cindy Stern, the chief executive officer of Las Animas Inc., and Dr. Kassay Heyen, the leading researcher.

Stern: What are we going to do? The banks won't loan us any more money, and we've got to have $5 million to complete the project. We are so close! It would be a disaster to quit now. The only thing I can think of is to issue additional stock. Do you have any suggestions?

Heyen: I guess you're right. But if the banks won't loan us any more money, how do you think we can find any investors to buy stock?

Stern: I've been thinking about that. What if we promise the investors that we will pay them 2% of net sales until they have received an amount equal to what they paid for the stock?

Heyen: What happens when we pay back the $5 million? Do the investors get to keep the stock? If they do, it'll dilute our ownership.

Stern: How about, if after we pay back the $5 million, we make them turn in their stock for $100 per share? That's twice what they paid for it, plus they would have already gotten all their money back. That's a $100 profit per share for the investors.

Heyen: It could work. We get our money, but don't have to pay any interest, dividends, or the $50 until we start generating net sales. At the same time, the investors could get their money back plus $50 per share.

Stern: We'll need current financial statements for the new investors. I'll get our accountant working on them and contact our attorney to draw up a legally binding contract for the new investors. Yes, this could work.

In late 2008, the attorney and the various regulatory authorities approved the new stock offering, and 100,000 shares of common stock were privately sold to new investors at the stock's par of $50.

In preparing financial statements for 2008, Cindy Stern and Debra Allen, the controller for Las Animas Inc., have the following conversation:

Allen: Cindy, I've got a problem.

Stern: What's that, Debra?

Allen: Issuing common stock to raise that additional $5 million was a great idea. But . . .

Stern: But what?

Allen: I've got to prepare the 2008 annual financial statements, and I am not sure how to classify the common stock.

Stern: What do you mean? It's common stock.

Allen: I'm not so sure. I called the auditor and explained how we are contractually obligated to pay the new stockholders 2% of net sales until $50 per share is paid. Then, we may be obligated to pay them $100 per share.

Stern: So . . .

Allen: So the auditor thinks that we should classify the additional issuance of $5 million as debt, not stock! And, if we put the $5 million on the balance sheet as debt, we will violate our other loan agreements with the banks. And, if these agreements are violated, the banks may call in all our debt immediately. If they do that, we are in deep trouble. We'll probably have to file for bankruptcy. We just don't have the cash to pay off the banks.

1. ▭▷ Discuss the arguments for and against classifying the issuance of the $5 million of stock as debt.
2. ▭▷ What do you think might be a practical solution to this classification problem?

SA 11-4
Interpret stock exchange listing

The Wall Street Journal reported the following May 11, 2006 market information for General Electric Company's (GE) common stock:

52 Weeks		Stock	Sym	Div	Yld%	PE	Vol 100s	LAST	Net Chg
Hi	Lo								
37³⁴	32²¹	GenElec	GE	1.00	2.9	22	227,456	34⁵¹	−.19

a. If you owned 500 shares of GE, what amount would you receive as a quarterly dividend?
b. Calculate and prove the dividend yield. Round to two decimal places.
c. What is GE's percentage change in market price from the May 11, 2006, close? Round to one decimal place.
d. If you bought 500 shares of GE at the close price on May 11, 2006, how much would it cost, and who gets the money?

SA 11-5
Dividends

Sentinel Inc. has paid quarterly cash dividends since 1995. These dividends have steadily increased from $0.05 per share to the latest dividend declaration of $0.40 per share. The board of directors would like to continue this trend and is hesitant to suspend or decrease the amount of quarterly dividends. Unfortunately, sales dropped sharply in the fourth quarter of 2008 because of worsening economic conditions and increased competition. As a result, the board is uncertain as to whether it should declare a dividend for the last quarter of 2008.

On November 1, 2008, Sentinel Inc. borrowed $800,000 from American National Bank to use in modernizing its retail stores and to expand its product line in reaction to its competition. The terms of the 10-year, 6% loan require Sentinel Inc. to:

a. Pay monthly interest on the last day of the month.
b. Pay $80,000 of the principal each November 1, beginning in 2009.
c. Maintain a current ratio (current assets/current liabilities) of 2.
d. Maintain a minimum balance (a compensating balance) of $40,000 in its American National Bank account.

On December 31, 2008, $200,000 of the $800,000 loan had been disbursed in modernization of the retail stores and in expansion of the product line. Sentinel Inc.'s balance sheet as of December 31, 2008, is shown at the top of the following page.

The board of directors is scheduled to meet January 6, 2009, to discuss the results of operations for 2008 and to consider the declaration of dividends for the fourth quarter of 2008. The chairman of the board has asked for your advice on the declaration of dividends.

1. ▭▷ What factors should the board consider in deciding whether to declare a cash dividend?
2. ▭▷ The board is considering the declaration of a stock dividend instead of a cash dividend. Discuss the issuance of a stock dividend from the point of view of (a) a stockholder and (b) the board of directors.

Sentinel Inc.
Balance Sheet
December 31, 2008

Assets

Current assets:			
Cash		$ 64,000	
Marketable securities		600,000	
Accounts receivable	$ 146,400		
Less allowance for doubtful accounts	10,400	136,000	
Merchandise inventory		200,000	
Prepaid expenses		7,200	
Total current assets			$1,007,200
Property, plant, and equipment:			
Land		$ 240,000	
Buildings	$1,520,000		
Less accumulated depreciation	344,000	1,176,000	
Equipment	$ 736,000		
Less accumulated depreciation	176,000	560,000	
Total property, plant, and equipment			1,976,000
Total assets			$2,983,200

Liabilities

Current liabilities:			
Accounts payable		$ 114,880	
Notes payable (American National Bank)		80,000	
Salaries payable		5,120	
Total current liabilities		$ 200,000	
Long-term liabilities:			
Notes payable (American National Bank)		720,000	
Total liabilities			$ 920,000

Stockholders' Equity

Paid-in capital:			
Common stock, $20 par (50,000 shares			
authorized, 40,000 shares issued)		$ 800,000	
Excess of issue price over par		64,000	
Total paid-in capital		$ 864,000	
Retained earnings		1,199,200	
Total stockholders' equity			2,063,200
Total liabilities and stockholders' equity			$2,983,200

SA 11-6
Profiling a corporation

Group Project

Internet Project

Select a public corporation you are familiar with or which interests you. Using the Internet, your school library, and other sources, develop a short (1 to 2 pages) profile of the corporation. Include in your profile the following information:

1. Name of the corporation.
2. State of incorporation.
3. Nature of its operations.
4. Total assets for the most recent balance sheet.
5. Total revenues for the most recent income statement.
6. Net income for the most recent income statement.
7. Classes of stock outstanding.
8. Market price of the stock outstanding.
9. High and low price of the stock for the past year.
10. Dividends paid for each share of stock during the past year.

In groups of three or four, discuss each corporate profile. Select one of the corporations, assuming that your group has $100,000 to invest in its stock. Summarize why your group selected the corporation it did and how financial accounting information may have affected your decision. Keep track of the performance of your corporation's stock for the remainder of the term.

Note: Most major corporations maintain "home pages" on the Internet. This home page provides a variety of information on the corporation and often includes the corporation's financial statements. In addition, the New York Stock Exchange Web site (**http://www.nyse .com**) includes links to the home pages of many listed companies. Financial statements can also be accessed using EDGAR, the electronic archives of financial statements filed with the Securities and Exchange Commission (SEC).

SEC documents can also be retrieved using the EdgarScan™ service from Pricewater-houseCoopers at **http://edgarscan.pwcglobal.com**. To obtain annual report information, key in a company name in the appropriate space. EdgarScan will list the reports available to you for the company you've selected. Select the most recent annual report filing, identified as a 10-K or 10-K405. EdgarScan provides an outline of the report, including the separate financial statements, which can also be selected in an Excel® spreadsheet.

Answers to Self-Examination Questions

1. **C** The separation of the owner from management (answer C) is a disadvantage of the corporate form of organization. This is because management may not always behave in the best interests of the owners. Limited liability (answer A), continuous life (answer B), and the ability to raise capital (answer D) are all advantages of the corporate form of organization.

2. **D** Paid-in capital is one of the two major subdivisions of the stockholders' equity of a corporation. It may result from many sources, including the issuance of preferred stock (answer A), issuing common stock (answer B), or the sale of a corporation's treasury stock (answer C).

3. **D** The Stockholders' Equity section of corporate balance sheets is divided into two principal subsections: (1) investments contributed by the stockholders and others and (2) net income retained in the business.

Included as part of the investments by stockholders and others is the par of common stock (answer A), stock dividends distributable (answer B), and the par of preferred stock (answer C).

4. **C** Reacquired stock, known as *treasury stock*, should be listed in the Stockholders' Equity section (answer C) of the balance sheet. The price paid for the treasury stock is deducted from the total of all the stockholders' equity accounts.

5. **C** If a corporation that holds treasury stock declares a cash dividend, the dividends are not paid on the treasury shares. To do so would place the corporation in the position of earning income through dealing with itself. Thus, the corporation will record $44,000 (answer C) as cash dividends [(25,000 shares issued less 3,000 shares held as treasury stock) × $2 per share dividend].

Income Taxes, Unusual Income Items, and Investments in Stocks

© NEIL BRAKE/ASSOCIATED PRESS

objectives

After studying this chapter, you should be able to:

1 *Journalize the entries for corporate income taxes, including deferred income taxes.*

2 *Describe and illustrate the reporting of unusual items on the income statement.*

3 *Prepare an income statement reporting earnings per share data.*

4 *Describe the concept and the reporting of comprehensive income.*

5 *Describe the accounting for investments in stocks.*

Gaylord Entertainment Co.

I f you apply for a bank loan, you will be required to list your assets and liabilities on a loan application. In addition, you will be asked to indicate your monthly income. Assume that the day you fill out the application, you win $4,000 in the state lottery. The $4,000 lottery winnings increase your assets by $4,000. Should you also show your lottery winnings as part of your monthly income?

The answer, of course, is no. Winning the lottery is an unusual event and, for most of us, a nonrecurring event. In determining whether to grant the loan, the bank is interested in your ability to make monthly loan payments. Such payments depend upon your recurring monthly income.

Businesses also experience unusual and nonrecurring events that affect their financial statements. Such events should be clearly disclosed in the financial statements so that stakeholders in the business will not misinterpret the financial effects of the events.

Gaylord Entertainment Co. is an example of such a company. Gaylord has pioneered the self-contained "all-in-one-place" hotel and resort concept, with the Gaylord Opryland, Gaylord Texan, and Gaylord Palms resorts. In addition, Gaylord owns ResortQuest and Ryman Auditorim (the original Grand Ole Opry) in Nashville, Tennessee. While Gaylord's operating income is positive, it has continued to report net losses over a number of recent years, due to losses from discontinued operations. Such unusual items are identified on Gaylord's income statement to alert users of the nonrecurring nature of some of its activities.

In this chapter, we discuss unusual items that affect income statements, such as those for Gaylord Entertainment, and illustrate how such items should be reported. We also discuss other specialized accounting and reporting topics, including accounting for income taxes, comprehensive income, and investments.

Corporate Income Taxes

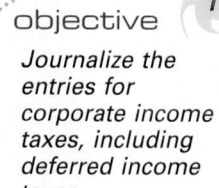

objective **1**

Journalize the entries for corporate income taxes, including deferred income taxes.

Under the U.S. tax code, corporations are taxable entities that must pay federal income taxes.[1] Depending upon where it is located, a corporation may also be required to pay state and local income taxes. Although we limit our discussion to federal income taxes, the basic concepts also apply to other income taxes.

PAYMENT OF INCOME TAXES

Most corporations are required to pay estimated federal income taxes in four installments throughout the year. For example, assume that a corporation with a calendar-year accounting period estimates its income tax expense for the year as $84,000. The entry to record the first of the four estimated tax payments of $21,000 (1/4 of $84,000) is as follows:

Individuals pay quarterly estimated taxes if the amount of tax withholding is not sufficient to pay their taxes at the end of the year. This usually occurs when a significant portion of an individual's income is from self-employment, rent, dividends, or interest.

Apr.	15	Income Tax Expense		21 0 0 0 00	
		Cash			21 0 0 0 00

---

1 Limited liability companies (LLCs) are not separate taxable entities and thus are not subject to federal (and most state) income taxes. For this reason, the material in this section would not generally apply to an LLC.

At year-end, the actual taxable income and the related tax are determined.[2] If additional taxes are owed, the additional liability is recorded. If the total estimated tax payments are greater than the tax liability based on actual taxable income, the overpayment should be debited to a receivable account and credited to *Income Tax Expense*.[3]

Income taxes are normally disclosed as a deduction at the bottom of the income statement in determining net income, as shown below, in an excerpt from an income statement for Procter & Gamble.

Year Ended June 30, 2005	(Amounts in Millions)
Net Sales	**$56,741**
Cost of products sold	27,804
Marketing, research, and administrative expenses	18,010
Income from Operations	**$10,927**
Interest expense	(834)
Other income, net	346
Earnings Before Income Taxes	**$10,439**
Income taxes	3,182
Net Earnings	**$ 7,257**

The ratio of reported income tax expense to earnings before taxes is shown for selected industries, as follows:

Industry	Percent of Reported Income Tax Expense to Earnings before Taxes
Automobiles	33%
Banking	35
Computers	23
Food	35
Integrated oil	39
Pharmaceuticals	30
Retail	39
Telecommunication	37
Transportation	38

As you can see, the reported income tax expense is normally between 30%–40% of earnings before tax. Therefore, taxes are a significant expense for most companies and must be considered when analyzing a company. Differences in tax rates between industries can be due to tax regulations unique to certain industries.

ALLOCATING INCOME TAXES

The **taxable income** of a corporation is determined according to the tax laws and is reported to taxing authorities on the corporation's tax return.[4] It is often different from the income before income taxes reported in the income statement according to

---

2 A corporation's income tax returns and supporting records are subject to audits by taxing authorities, who may assess additional taxes. Because of this possibility, the liability for income taxes is sometimes described in the balance sheet as *Estimated income tax payable*.

3 Another common term used for income taxes on the income statement and note disclosures is *Provision for income taxes*.

4 Accounting for deferred income taxes is a complex topic that is treated in greater detail in advanced accounting texts. The treatment here provides a general overview and conceptual understanding of the topic.

generally accepted accounting principles. As a result, the *income tax based on taxable income* usually differs from the *income tax based on income before taxes*. This difference may need to be allocated between various financial statement periods, depending on the nature of the items causing the differences.

Some differences between taxable income and income before income taxes are created because items are recognized in one period for tax purposes and in another period for income statement purposes. Such differences, called **temporary differences**, reverse or turn around in later years. Some examples of items that create temporary differences are listed below.

1. *Revenues or gains are taxed **after** they are reported in the income statement.* Example: In some cases, companies that make sales under an installment plan recognize revenue for financial reporting purposes when a sale is made but defer recognizing revenue for tax purposes until cash is collected.
2. *Expenses or losses are deducted in determining taxable income **after** they are reported in the income statement.* Example: Product warranty expense estimated and reported in the year of the sale for financial statement reporting is deducted for tax reporting when paid.
3. *Revenues or gains are taxed **before** they are reported in the income statement.* Example: Cash received in advance for magazine subscriptions is included in taxable income when received but included in the income statement only when earned in a future period.
4. *Expenses or losses are deducted in determining taxable income **before** they are reported in the income statement.* Example: MACRS depreciation is used for tax purposes, and the straight-line method is used for financial reporting purposes.

Since temporary differences reverse in later years, they do not change or reduce the total amount of taxable income over the life of a business. Exhibit 1 illustrates the reversing nature of temporary differences in which a business uses MACRS depreciation for tax purposes and straight-line depreciation for financial statement purposes. Exhibit 1 assumes that MACRS recognizes more depreciation in the early years and less depreciation in the later years. The total depreciation expense is the same for both methods over the life of the asset.

As Exhibit 1 illustrates, temporary differences affect only the timing of when revenues and expenses are recognized for tax purposes. As a result, the total amount of taxes paid does not change. Only the timing of the payment of taxes is affected. As shown in Exhibit 1, most managers use tax-planning techniques so that temporary differences delay or defer the payment of taxes to later years. As a result, at the end of

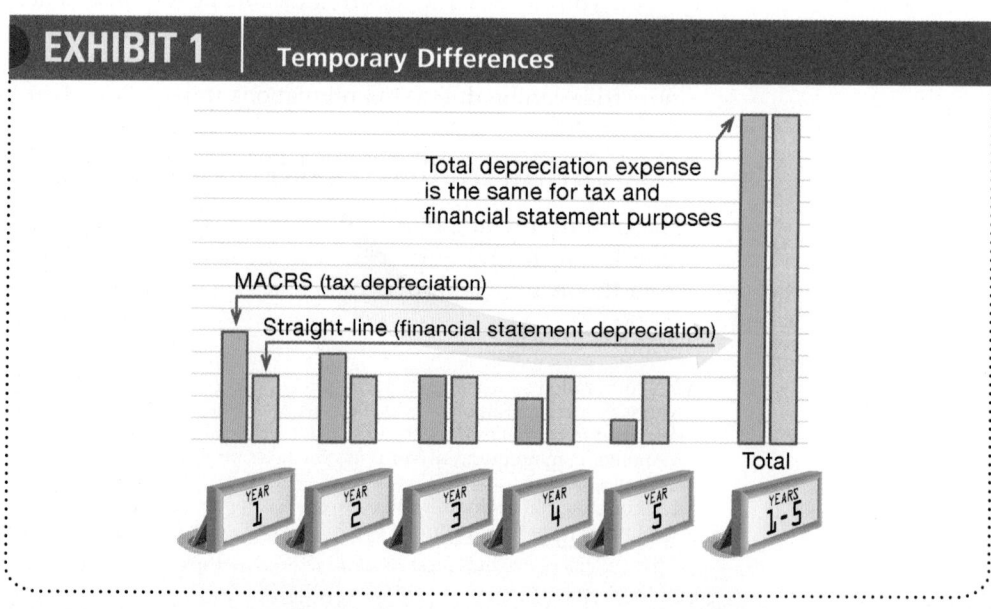

EXHIBIT 1 | **Temporary Differences**

each year the amount of the current tax liability and the postponed (deferred) liability must be recorded.

To illustrate, assume that at the end of the first year of operations a corporation reports $300,000 income before income taxes on its income statement. If we assume an income tax rate of 40%, the income tax expense reported on the income statement is $120,000 ($300,000 × 40%).[5] However, to reduce the amount owed for current income taxes, the corporation uses tax planning to reduce the taxable income to $100,000. Thus, the income tax actually due for the year is only $40,000 ($100,000 × 40%). The $80,000 ($120,000 − $40,000) difference between the two tax amounts is created by temporary differences in recognizing revenue. This amount is deferred to future years. The example is summarized below.

Income tax expense based on $300,000 reported income at 40%	$120,000
Income tax payable based on $100,000 taxable income at 40%	40,000
Income tax deferred to future years	$ 80,000

To match the current year's expenses (including income tax) against the current year's revenue on the income statement, income tax is allocated between periods, using the following journal entry:

Income Tax Expense	120 0 0 0 00	
Income Tax Payable		40 0 0 0 00
Deferred Income Tax Payable		80 0 0 0 00

The income tax expense reported on the income statement is the total tax, $120,000, expected to be paid on the income for the year. In future years, the $80,000 in *Deferred Income Tax Payable* will be transferred to *Income Tax Payable* as the temporary differences reverse and the taxes become due. For example, if $48,000 of the deferred tax reverses and becomes due in the second year, the following journal entry would be made in the second year:

Deferred Income Tax Payable	48 0 0 0 00	
Income Tax Payable		48 0 0 0 00

REPORTING AND ANALYZING TAXES

The balance of *Deferred Income Tax Payable* at the end of a year is reported as a liability.[6] The amount due within one year is classified as a current liability. The remainder is classified as a long-term liability or reported in a Deferred Credits section following the Long-Term Liabilities section.[7]

Interest from investments in municipal bonds is also tax exempt for individual taxpayers.

Differences between taxable income and income (before taxes) reported on the income statement may also arise because certain revenues are exempt from tax and certain expenses are not deductible in determining taxable income. Such differences, which will not reverse with the passage of time, are sometimes called **permanent differences**. For example, interest income on municipal bonds may be exempt from taxation. Such differences create no special financial reporting problems, since the amount of income tax determined according to the tax laws is the *same* amount reported on the income statement.

---

5 For purposes of illustration, the 40% rate is assumed to include all federal, state, and local income taxes.
6 In some cases, a deferred tax asset may arise for tax benefits to be received in the future. Such deferred tax assets are reported as either current or long-term assets, depending on when the benefits are expected to be realized.
7 Additional note disclosures for deferred income taxes are also required. These are discussed in advanced accounting texts.

Example Exercise 12-1   objective ① 1

A corporation has $200,000 of income before income taxes, a 40% tax rate, and $130,000 of taxable income. Provide the journal entry for the current year's taxes.

Follow My Example 12-1

Income Tax Expense	80,000	
Income Tax Payable		52,000
Deferred Income Tax Payable		28,000

Income tax expense based on $200,000 reported income at 40%	$80,000
Income tax payable based on $130,000 taxable income at 40%	52,000
Income tax deferred to future years	$28,000

For Practice: PE 12-1A, PE 12-1B

Reporting Unusual Items on the Income Statement

objective ② 2

Describe and illustrate the reporting of unusual items on the income statement.

Generally accepted accounting principles require that certain unusual items be reported separately on the current or prior period's income statement. These items can be classified into items affecting the current period income statement and those affecting prior period income statements as shown below.

> Unusual Items Affecting the Current Period's Income Statement
>   Fixed asset impairments
>   Restructuring charges
>   Discontinued operations
>   Extraordinary item
>
> Unusual Items Affecting the Prior Period's Income Statement
>   Errors
>   Change in accounting principles

The first category of unusual items affects the current period's income statement. However, the location of the disclosure on the income statement is different among these items. Fixed asset impairment and restructuring charges are reported above income from continuing operations as shown in item 1 of Exhibit 2. That is, fixed asset impairment and restructuring charges are subtracted in arriving at income from continuing operations. Although discontinued operations and extraordinary items affect net income, they are reported below income from continuing operations as shown in item 2 of Exhibit 2.

In the following paragraphs, we first describe and illustrate unusual items affecting the current period's income statement. We then discuss unusual items affecting prior period income statements as shown in item 3 of Exhibit 2.

UNUSUAL ITEMS AFFECTING THE CURRENT PERIOD'S INCOME STATEMENT

Unusual items affecting the current period's income statement include fixed asset impairments, restructuring charges, discontinued operations, and extraordinary items. Fixed asset impairments and restructuring charges, sometimes termed *special charges* when combined, will be discussed first. Following these, we will discuss discontinued operations and extraordinary items.

EXHIBIT 2

Reporting of Unusual Items on the Income Statement

1. Unusual items subtracted from gross profit in determining income from continuing operations.

2. Unusual items that adjust income from continuing operations in determining net income.

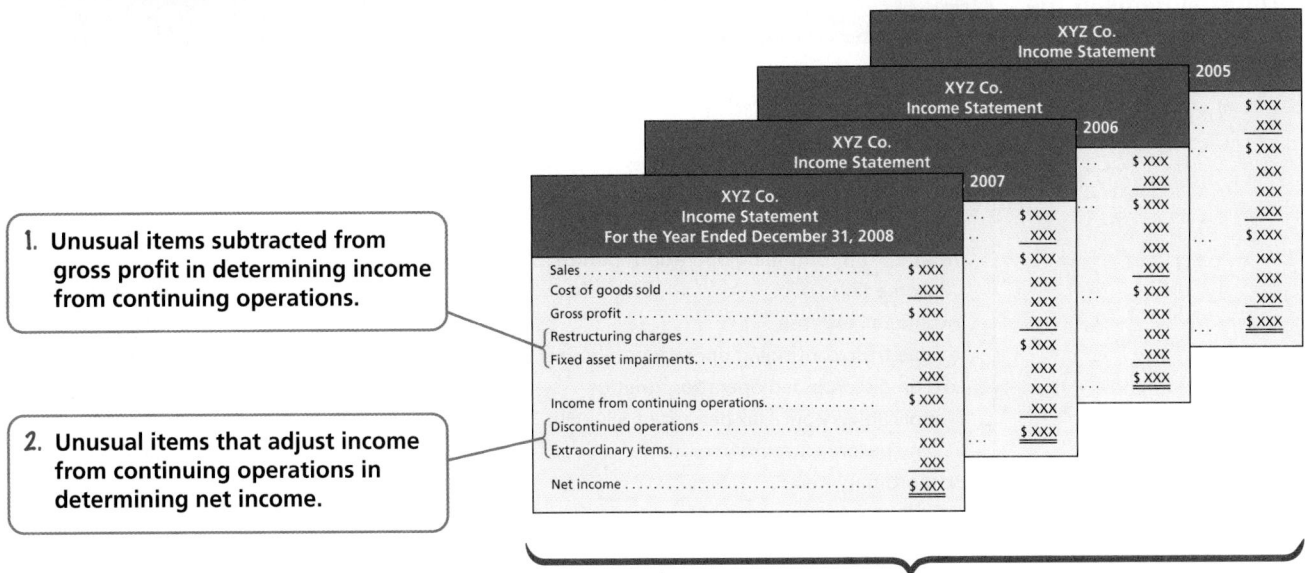

3. Unusual items affecting prior period income statements.

Fixed Asset Impairments   A **fixed asset impairment** occurs when the fair value of a fixed asset falls below its book value (cost less accumulated depreciation) and is not expected to recover.[8] Examples of events that might cause an asset impairment are (1) decreases in the market price of fixed assets, (2) significant changes in the business or regulations related to fixed assets, (3) adverse conditions affecting the use of fixed assets, or (4) expected cash flow losses from using fixed assets.[9] For example, on March 1, assume that Jones Corporation consolidates operations by closing a factory. As a result of the closing, plant and equipment is impaired by $750,000. The journal entry to record the impairment is as follows:

Mar.	1	Loss on Fixed Asset Impairment	750 0 0 0 00	
		Equipment		750 0 0 0 00

The loss on fixed asset impairment is reported as a separate expense item deducted from gross profit in determining income from continuing operations, as illustrated for Jones Corporation in Exhibit 3. In addition, note disclosure should describe the nature of the asset impaired and the cause of the impairment.

The loss reduces the book value of the fixed asset and thus reduces the depreciation expense for future periods. If the asset is later sold, the gain or loss on the sale would be based on the lower book value. Thus, asset impairment accounting recognizes the loss when it is first identified, rather than when the asset is later sold.

---

8 Fixed assets that are discontinued components, such as an operating segment, subsidiary, or asset group, should be treated as discontinued items, as discussed in a later section.
9 *Statement of Financial Accounting Standards No. 144*, "Accounting for the Impairment or Disposal of Long-Lived Assets" (Norwalk, CT: Financial Accounting Standards Board, 2001).

EXHIBIT 3

Unusual Items in the
Income Statement

Jones Corporation
Income Statement
For the Year Ended December 31, 2008

Net sales		$12,350,000
Cost of merchandise sold		5,800,000
Gross profit		$ 6,550,000
Selling and administrative expenses	$3,490,000	
Loss from asset impairment	750,000	
Restructuring charge	1,000,000	5,240,000
Income from continuing operations before		
income tax		$ 1,310,000
Income tax expense		620,000
Income from continuing operations		$ 690,000
Loss on discontinued operations (net of		
applicable income tax benefit of $50,000)		100,000
Income before extraordinary items		$ 590,000
Extraordinary item:		
Gain on condemnation of land (net of applicable		
income tax of $65,000)		150,000
Net income		$ 740,000

Integrity, Objectivity, and Ethics in Business

ETHICS

WHEN IS AN ASSET IMPAIRED?

The asset impairment principle is designed to reduce the subjectivity of timing asset write-downs. That is, write-downs should occur when the impairment is deemed permanent. In practice, however, judgment is still needed in determining when such impairment has occurred. Ethical managers will recognize asset write-downs when they occur, not when it is most convenient. For example, the SEC investigated Avon Products, Inc., for delaying the write-off of a computer software project. In settling the formal investigation, Avon had to restate its earnings to reflect the earlier write-off date.

Restructuring Charges   **Restructuring charges** are costs incurred with actions such as canceling contracts, laying off or relocating employees, and combining operations. Often, these events incur initial one-time costs in order to obtain long-term savings. For example, terminated employees often receive a one-time termination or severance benefit at the time of their dismissal. Employee termination benefits are normally the most significant restructuring charges; thus, they will be the focus of this section.

Employee termination benefits arise when a plan specifying the number of terminated employees, the benefit, and the benefit timing has been authorized by senior management and communicated to the employees.[10] To illustrate, assume that the management of Jones Corporation communicates a plan to terminate 200 employees from the closed manufacturing plant on March 1. The plan calls for a termination benefit of $5,000 per employee. Once the plan is communicated to employees, they have the legal right to work for 60 days but may elect to leave the firm earlier. That is, employees may be paid severance at the end of 60 days or at any time in between.

---

10 *Statement of Financial Accounting Standards No. 146*, "Accounting for Costs Associated with Exit or Disposal Activities" (Norwalk, CT: Financial Accounting Standards Board, 2002).

The expense and liability to provide employee benefits should be recognized at fair value on the plan communication date.[11] The fair value of this plan would be $1,000,000 (200 employees × $5,000), which is the aggregate expected cost of terminating the employees. Thus, the $1,000,000 restructuring charge would be recorded as follows:

Mar.	1	Restructuring Charge	1000 0 0 0 00	
		Employee Termination Obligation		1000 0 0 0 00

The restructuring charge is reported as a separate expense deducted from gross profit in determining income from continuing operations, as shown in Exhibit 3. The employee termination obligation would be shown as a current liability. If the plan called for expected severance payments beyond one year, then a long-term liability would be recognized. In addition, a note should disclose the nature and cause of the restructuring event and the costs associated with the type of restructuring event.

The actual benefits paid to terminated employees should be debited to the liability as employees leave the firm. For example, assume that 25 employees find other employment and leave the company on March 25. The entry to record the severance payment to these employees would be as follows:

Mar.	25	Employee Termination Obligation	125 0 0 0 00	
		Cash		125 0 0 0 00

Example Exercise 12-2

objective 2

On December 20 of the current year, Torre Corporation determined that equipment had been impaired so that the book value of the equipment was reduced by $180,000. In addition, the senior management of the company communicated an employee severance plan whereby 80 employees could receive a termination benefit of $7,000 per employee. Provide the journal entry for the asset impairment and the restructuring charge.

Follow My Example 12-2

Dec. 20	Loss on Fixed Asset Impairment	180,000	
	Equipment		180,000
	Restructuring Charge	560,000*	
	Employee Termination Obligation		560,000

*80 employees × $7,000

For Practice: PE 12-2A, PE 12-2B

Discontinued Operations   A gain or loss from disposing of a business segment or component of an entity is reported on the income statement as a gain or loss from **discontinued operations**. The term *business segment* refers to a major line of business for a company, such as a division, department, or certain class of customer. A *component* of an entity is the lowest level at which the operations and cash flows can be clearly distinguished, operationally and for financial reporting purposes, from the rest of the

---

11 For long-term severance agreements, present value concepts may be required to determine fair value. We will assume short-term agreements where the time value of money is assumed to be immaterial. Present value concepts are discussed in Chapter 13.

entity.[12] Examples would be a store for a retailer, a territory for a sales organization, or a product category for a consumer products company.

To illustrate the disclosure, assume that Jones Corporation has separate divisions that produce electrical products, hardware supplies, and lawn equipment. Jones sells its electrical products division at a loss. As shown in Exhibit 3 on page 532, this loss is deducted from Jones's income from continuing operations (income from its hardware and lawn equipment divisions). In addition, a note should disclose the identity of the segment sold, the disposal date, a description of the segment's assets and liabilities, and the manner of disposal.

Extraordinary Items   An **extraordinary item** results from events and transactions that (1) are significantly different (unusual) from the typical or the normal operating activities of the business *and* (2) occur infrequently. The gains and losses resulting from natural disasters that occur infrequently, such as floods, earthquakes, and fires, are extraordinary items. Gains or losses from condemning land or buildings for public use are also extraordinary. Such gains and losses, other than those from disposing of a business segment, should be reported in the income statement as extraordinary items, as shown in Exhibit 3.

Sometimes, extraordinary items result in unusual financial results. For example, Delta Air Lines once reported an extraordinary gain of over $5.5 million as the result of the crash of one of its 727s. The plane that crashed was insured for $6.5 million, but its book value in Delta's accounting records was $962,000. Gains and losses on the disposal of fixed assets are *not* extraordinary items. This is because (1) they are not unusual and (2) they recur from time to time in the normal operations of a business. Likewise, gains and losses from the sale of investments are usual and recurring for most businesses.

UNUSUAL ITEMS AFFECTING THE PRIOR PERIOD'S INCOME STATEMENT

In addition to unusual items impacting the income statement, there are two major items that require a retroactive restatement of prior period earnings. These two items are:

1. Errors in the recognition, measurement, presentation, or disclosure of financial statements, and
2. Changes from one generally accepted accounting principle to another generally accepted accounting principle.[13]

A retroactive restatement requires previously issued financial statements to be adjusted for the impact of errors and changes in accounting principle. If an error is discovered that impacts a prior period financial statement, the prior period statement, and all following statements, should be restated to reflect the correction. If there is a change from one generally accepted accounting principle to another generally accepted accounting principle, then the change is applied to prior period financial statements. That is, the prior period financial statements are restated as if the new accounting principle had always been used.[14] Thus, in both cases, these changes do *not* impact current period earnings but will impact the earnings reported in past periods. As a result, the present Retained Earnings and other balance sheet accounts will be restated to reflect these prior period changes. Illustrations of these types of adjustments are provided in advanced accounting courses.

---

12 *Statement of Financial Accounting Standards No. 144*, op. cit., par. 41.
13 *Statement of Financial Accounting Standards No. 154*, "Accounting Changes and Error Corrections" (Norwalk, CT: Financial Accounting Standards Board, 2005).
14 Changes from one acceptable depreciation method to another acceptable depreciation method are an exception to this general rule and are to be treated prospectively as a change in estimate, as discussed in Chapter 9.

Earnings per Common Share

objective **3**

Prepare an income statement reporting earnings per share data.

The amount of net income is often used by investors and creditors in evaluating a company's profitability. However, net income by itself is difficult to use in comparing companies of different sizes. Also, trends in net income may be difficult to evaluate, using only net income, if there have been significant changes in a company's stockholders' equity. Thus, the profitability of companies is often expressed as earnings per share. **Earnings per common share (EPS)**, sometimes called *basic earnings per share*, is the net income per share of common stock outstanding during a period.

Because of its importance, earnings per share is reported in the financial press and by various investor services, such as Moody's and Standard & Poor's. Changes in earnings per share can lead to significant changes in the price of a corporation's stock in the marketplace. For example, the stock of eBay Inc. fell by over 19% to $83 per share after the company announced earnings per share of 33¢ as compared to Wall Street analysts' estimate of 34¢ per share.

Corporations whose stock is traded in a public market must report earnings per common share on their income statements.[15] If no preferred stock is outstanding, the earnings per common share is calculated as follows:

$$\text{Earnings per Common Share} = \frac{\text{Net Income}}{\text{Number of Common Shares Outstanding}}$$

When the number of common shares outstanding has changed during the period, a weighted average number of shares outstanding is used. If a company has preferred stock outstanding, the net income must be reduced by the amount of any preferred dividends, as shown below.

$$\text{Earnings per Common Share} = \frac{\text{Net Income} - \text{Preferred Stock Dividends}}{\text{Number of Common Shares Outstanding}}$$

Comparing the earnings per share of two or more years, based on only the net incomes of those years, could be misleading. For example, assume that Jones Corporation, whose partial income statement was presented in Exhibit 3, reported $700,000 net income for 2007. Also assume that no extraordinary or other unusual items were reported in 2007. Jones has no preferred stock outstanding and has 200,000 common shares outstanding in 2007 and 2008. The earnings per common share is $3.50 ($700,000/200,000 shares) for 2007 and $3.70 ($740,000/200,000 shares) for 2008. Comparing the two earnings per share amounts suggests that operations have improved. However, the 2008 earnings per share comparable to the $3.50 is $3.45, which is the income from continuing operations of $690,000 divided by 200,000 shares. The latter amount indicates a slight downturn in normal earnings.

When unusual items reported *below* income from continuing operations exist, earnings per common share should be reported for those items. To illustrate, a partial income statement for Jones Corporation, showing earnings per common share, is shown in Exhibit 4. In this income statement, Jones reports all the earnings per common share amounts on the face of the income statement. However, only earnings per share amounts for income from continuing operations and net income are required to be presented on the face of the statement. The other per share amounts may be presented in the notes to the financial statements.[16]

In the preceding paragraphs, we have assumed a simple capital structure with only common stock or common stock and preferred stock outstanding. Often, however, corporations have complex capital structures with various types of securities outstanding, such as convertible preferred stock, options, warrants, and contingently

---

15 *Statement of Financial Accounting Standards No. 128*, "Earnings per Share" (Norwalk, CT: Financial Accounting Standards Board, 1997).
16 Ibid., pars. 36 and 37.

EXHIBIT 4

Income Statement
with Earnings
per Share

Jones Corporation	
Income Statement	
For the Year Ended December 31, 2008	

Earnings per common share:	
Income from continuing operations	$ 3.45
Loss on discontinued operations (net of $50,000 tax benefit)	0.50
Income before extraordinary items	$ 2.95
Extraordinary item:	
Gain on condemnation of land (net of applicable income	
tax of $65,000)	0.75
Net income	$ 3.70

issuable shares. In such cases, the possible effects of converting such securities to common stock must be calculated and reported as *earnings per common share assuming dilution* or *diluted earnings per share*.[17] This topic is discussed further in advanced accounting texts.

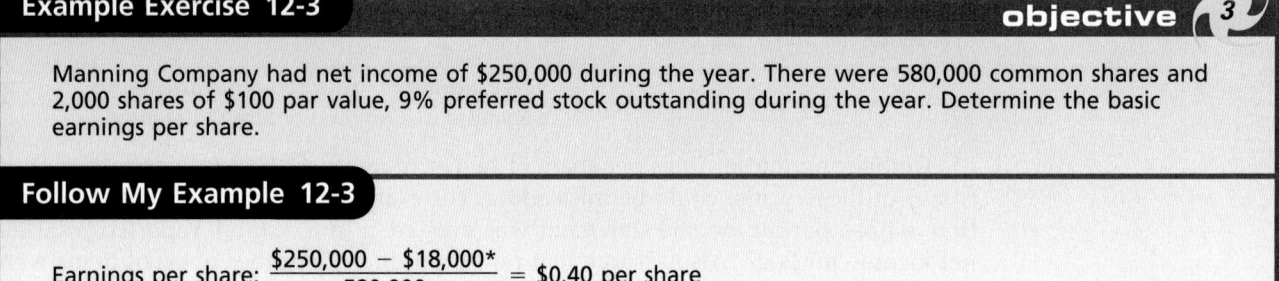

Example Exercise 12-3   objective **3**

Manning Company had net income of $250,000 during the year. There were 580,000 common shares and 2,000 shares of $100 par value, 9% preferred stock outstanding during the year. Determine the basic earnings per share.

Follow My Example 12-3

Earnings per share: $\dfrac{\$250{,}000 - \$18{,}000^*}{580{,}000} = \$0.40$ per share

*2,000 shares × $100 par value × 9% = $18,000

For Practice: PE 12-3A, PE 12-3B

Comprehensive Income

objective **4**

Describe the concept and the reporting of comprehensive income.

Comprehensive income is defined as all changes in stockholders' equity during a period, except those resulting from dividends and stockholders' investments. Companies must report traditional net income plus or minus other comprehensive income items to arrive at comprehensive income.

Other comprehensive income items include foreign currency items, pension liability adjustments, and unrealized gains and losses on investments. Generally accepted accounting principles (GAAP) require these items to be disclosed separately from earnings. To the extent that other comprehensive income items give rise to tax effects, the taxes should be allocated to these items similar to that illustrated in Exhibit 4 for extraordinary items. The cumulative effects of other comprehensive income items must be reported separately from retained earnings and paid-in capital, on the balance sheet, as **accumulated other comprehensive income**. When other comprehen-

17 Ibid., pars. 11–39.

In the 2005 edition of *Accounting Trends & Techniques*, over 95% of the surveyed companies reported other comprehensive income, and the majority of these companies disclosed it in the statement of stockholders' equity.

sive income items are not present, the income statement and balance sheet formats are similar to those we have illustrated in this and preceding chapters.

Companies may report comprehensive income on the income statement, in a separate statement of comprehensive income, or in the statement of stockholders' equity. In addition, companies may use terms other than comprehensive income, such as "total nonowner changes in equity."

To illustrate reporting for comprehensive income, assume that Triple-A Enterprises Inc. reported comprehensive income on a separate statement, called the *statement of comprehensive income*, as follows:

Triple-A Enterprises Inc. Statement of Comprehensive Income For the Year Ended December 31, 2008	
Net income	$8 5 0 0 00
Other comprehensive income, net of tax	9 0 00
Total comprehensive income	$8 5 9 0 00

The Stockholders' Equity section of the balance sheet for Triple-A Enterprises is as follows:

Triple-A Enterprises Inc. Stockholders' Equity December 31, 2008 and 2007		
	2008	**2007**
Stockholders' equity:		
Common stock	$ 20 0 0 0 00	$ 20 0 0 0 00
Paid-in capital in excess of par	36 0 0 0 00	36 0 0 0 00
Retained earnings	165 5 0 0 00	157 0 0 0 00
Accumulated other comprehensive income	1 2 9 0 00	1 2 0 0 00
Total stockholders' equity	$222 7 9 0 00	$214 2 0 0 00

Accumulated other comprehensive income is the cumulative effect of other comprehensive income items. Thus, the additional other comprehensive income of $90 for 2008 is added to the accumulated other comprehensive income on December 31, 2007, to yield the December 31, 2008, balance of $1,290.

You should note that comprehensive income does not affect net income or retained earnings. In the next section, we will illustrate the determination of other comprehensive income, using unrealized gains and losses on investments.

Example Exercise 12-4   objective 4

Myers Company had a net income of $74,000 and other comprehensive income of $12,500 for 2008. On January 1, 2008, the Retained Earnings balance was $425,000, and the Accumulated Other Comprehensive Income balance was $57,000. Determine the (a) comprehensive income for 2008, (b) Retained Earnings balance on December 31, 2008, and (c) Accumulated Other Comprehensive Income balance on December 31, 2008.

(continued)

Accounting for Investments in Stocks

Corporations not only issue stock, but they also purchase stocks of other companies for investment purposes. Like individuals, businesses have a variety of reasons for investing in stocks, called **equity securities**. A business may purchase stocks as a means of earning a return (income) on excess cash that it does not need for its normal operations. Such investments are usually for a short period of time. In other cases, a business may purchase the stock of another company as a long-term investment. Such investments can be as a means of developing or maintaining business relationships with another company. Sometimes, a business will purchase most, if not all, of the common stock of another company for purposes of owning and controlling another entity. This is termed a *business combination*. In this section, we will discuss short-term investments in equity securities, long-term investments in equity securities, sales of investments, and business combinations. First, however, we will introduce two major equity security classifications according to generally accepted accounting principles.

The equity securities in which a business invests may be classified as trading securities or available-for-sale securities. **Trading securities** are securities that management intends to actively trade for profit. Businesses holding trading securities are those whose normal operations involve buying and selling securities. Examples of such businesses include banks and insurance companies. **Available-for-sale securities** are securities that management expects to sell in the future but which are not actively traded for profit. For example, Warren Buffett, one of the wealthiest men in the world, invests through a public company called Berkshire Hathaway Inc. In a recent annual report, Berkshire Hathaway reported over $35 billion of equity investment holdings listed on its balance sheet as available-for-sale securities. Some of these investments include The Coca-Cola Company, McDonald's, and American Express Company. In this section, we describe and illustrate the accounting for available-for-sale equity securities. The accounting for trading securities is described and illustrated in advanced accounting texts.

SHORT-TERM INVESTMENTS IN STOCKS

Rather than allow excess cash to be idle until it is needed, a business may invest in available-for-sale securities. These investments are classified as **temporary investments** or *marketable securities*. Although such investments may be retained for several years,

Integrity, Objectivity, and Ethics in Business

WHAT DOES IT TAKE TO SUCCEED IN LIFE?

The answer to this question, according to Warren Buffett, the noted investment authority, is three magic ingredients: intelligence, energy, and integrity. According to Buffett, "If you lack the third ingredient, the other two will kill you." In other words, without integrity, your intelligence and energy may very well misguide you.

Source: Eric Clifford, *University of Tennessee Torchbearer,* Summer 2002.

they continue to be classified as temporary, provided they meet two conditions. First, the securities are readily marketable and can be sold for cash at any time. Second, management intends to sell the securities when the business needs cash for operations.

Temporary investments in available-for-sale securities are recorded in a current asset account, *Marketable Securities*, at their cost. This cost includes all amounts spent to acquire the securities, such as brokers' commissions. Any dividends received on the investment are recorded as a debit to *Cash* and a credit to *Dividend Revenue*.[18]

To illustrate, assume that on June 1 Crabtree Co. purchased 2,000 shares of Inis Corporation common stock at $89.75 per share plus a brokerage fee of $500. On October 1, Inis declared a $0.90 per share cash dividend payable on November 30. Crabtree's entries to record the stock purchase and the receipt of the dividend are as follows:

June	1	Marketable Securities	180 0 0 0 00	
		Cash		180 0 0 0 00
		Purchased 2,000 shares of Inis Corporation common stock [($89.75 × 2,000 shares) + $500].		
Nov.	30	Cash	1 8 0 0 00	
		Dividend Revenue		1 8 0 0 00
		Received dividend on Inis Corporation common stock (2,000 shares × $0.90).		

On the balance sheet, temporary investments are reported at their fair market value. Market values are normally available from stock quotations in financial newspapers, such as *The Wall Street Journal*. Any difference between the fair market values of the securities and their cost is an **unrealized holding gain or loss**. This gain or loss is termed "unrealized" because a transaction (the sale of the securities) is necessary before a gain or loss becomes real (realized).

To illustrate, assume that Crabtree Co.'s portfolio of temporary investments was purchased during 2008 and has the following fair market values and unrealized gains and losses on December 31, 2008:

Common Stock	Cost	Market	Unrealized Gain (Loss)
Edwards Inc.	$150,000	$190,000	$ 40,000
SWS Corp.	200,000	200,000	—
Inis Corporation	180,000	210,000	30,000
Bass Co.	160,000	150,000	(10,000)
Total	$690,000	$750,000	$ 60,000

If income taxes of $18,000 are allocated to the unrealized gain, Crabtree's temporary investments should be reported at their total cost of $690,000, plus the unrealized gain (net of applicable income tax) of $42,000 ($60,000 − $18,000), as shown in Exhibit 5.

The unrealized gain (net of applicable taxes) of $42,000 should also be reported as an *other comprehensive income item*, as we mentioned in the preceding section. For example, assume that Crabtree Co. has net income of $720,000 for the year ended December 31, 2008. Crabtree elects to report comprehensive income in the *statement of comprehensive income*, as shown in Exhibit 6. In addition, the accumulated other comprehensive income on the balance sheet would also be $42,000, representing the beginning balance of zero plus other comprehensive income of $42,000, as shown in Exhibit 5.

---

18 Stock dividends received on an investment are not journalized, since they have no effect on the investor's assets and revenues.

EXHIBIT 5

Temporary Investments on the Balance Sheet

Crabtree Co.
Balance Sheet (selected items)
December 31, 2008

Assets

Current assets:

Cash		$119,500
Temporary investments in marketable		
securities at cost	$690,000	
Unrealized gain (net of applicable		
income tax of $18,000)	42,000	732,000

Stockholders' Equity

Accumulated other comprehensive income		$ 42,000

EXHIBIT 6

Statement of Comprehensive Income

Crabtree Co.
Statement of Comprehensive Income
For the Year Ended December 31, 2008

Net income		$720,000
Other comprehensive income:		
Unrealized gain on temporary investments in marketable		
securities (net of applicable income tax of $18,000)		42,000
Comprehensive income		$762,000

Unrealized losses are reported in a similar manner. Unrealized gains and losses are reported as other comprehensive income items until the related securities are sold. When temporary securities are sold, the unrealized gains or losses become realized and are included in determining net income.

Example Exercise 12-5   objective **5**

Drew Company began operations on January 1, 2008, and purchased temporary investments in marketable securities during the year at a cost of $75,000. The end-of-period market value for these investments was $110,000. Net income was $180,000 for 2008. Determine (a) the reported amount of marketable securities on the December 31, 2008, balance sheet and (b) the comprehensive income for 2008. Assume a tax rate of 40%.

Follow My Example 12-5

a.	Initial cost		$ 75,000
	Unrealized gain ($110,000 − $75,000)	$35,000	
	Less: Tax on unrealized gain ($35,000 × 40%)	14,000	
	Unrealized gain, net of tax		21,000
	Reported amount of marketable securities		$ 96,000
b.	Net income		$180,000
	Unrealized gain ($110,000 − $75,000)	$35,000	
	Less: Tax on unrealized gain ($35,000 × 40%)	14,000	
	Other comprehensive income, net of tax		21,000
	Comprehensive income		$201,000

For Practice: PE 12-5A, PE 12-5B

LONG-TERM INVESTMENTS IN STOCKS

Long-term investments in stocks are not intended as a source of cash in the normal operations of the business. Rather, such investments are often held for their income, long-term gain potential, or influence over another business entity. They are reported in the balance sheet under the caption **Investments**, which usually follows the Current Assets section.

Accounting for Long-Term Stock Investments

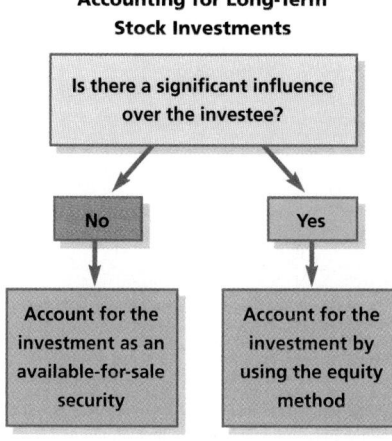

Long-term investments in stock are treated as available-for-sale securities, as we illustrated previously for short-term available-for-sale securities. Thus, a long-term investment treated as an available-for-sale security is recorded at cost and reported at fair market value net of any applicable income tax effects. In addition, any unrealized gains and losses are reported as part of the comprehensive income.[19] For example, Delta Air Lines disclosed investments in Priceline.com preferred stock as a noncurrent investment at the appraised fair market value.

However, if the investor (the buyer of the stock) has significant influence over the operating and financing activities of the investee (company whose stock is owned), the **equity method** is used. When the equity method is used, a stock purchase is recorded at cost, as shown previously. Evidence of significant influence includes the percentage of ownership, the existence of intercompany transactions, and the interchange of managerial personnel. Generally, if the investor owns 20% or more of the voting stock of the investee, it is assumed that the investor has significant influence over the investee.

Under the equity method, the investment is *not* subsequently adjusted to fair value. Rather, the book value of the investment is adjusted as follows:

1. The investor's share of the periodic net income of the investee is recorded as an *increase in the investment account* and as *income for the period*. Likewise, the investor's share of an investee's net loss is recorded as a *decrease in the investment account* and as a *loss for the period*.
2. The investor's share of cash dividends from the investee is recorded as an *increase in the cash account* and a *decrease in the investment account*.

To illustrate, assume that on January 2, Hally Inc. pays cash of $350,000 for 40% of the common stock and net assets of Brock Corporation. Assume also that, for the year ending December 31, Brock Corporation reports net income of $105,000 and declares and pays $45,000 in dividends. Using the equity method, Hally Inc. (the investor) records these transactions as follows:

REAL WORLD

The 2005 edition of *Accounting Trends & Techniques* indicated that over 50% of the companies surveyed used the equity method to account for investments.

Jan.	2	Investment in Brock Corporation Stock	350 000 00	
		Cash		350 000 00
		Purchased 40% of Brock Corporation stock.		
Dec.	31	Investment in Brock Corporation Stock	42 000 00	
		Income of Brock Corporation		42 000 00
		Recorded 40% share of Brock Corporation		
		net income of $105,000.		
Dec.	31	Cash	18 000 00	
		Investment in Brock Corporation Stock		18 000 00
		Recorded 40% share of Brock Corporation		
		dividends.		

---

19 An exception to reporting unrealized gains and losses as part of comprehensive income is made if the decrease in the market value for a stock is considered permanent. In this case, the cost of the individual stock is written down (decreased), and the amount of the write-down is included in net income.

The combined effect of recording 40% of Brock Corporation's net income and dividends is to increase Hally's interest in the net assets of Brock by $24,000 ($42,000 − $18,000), as shown below.

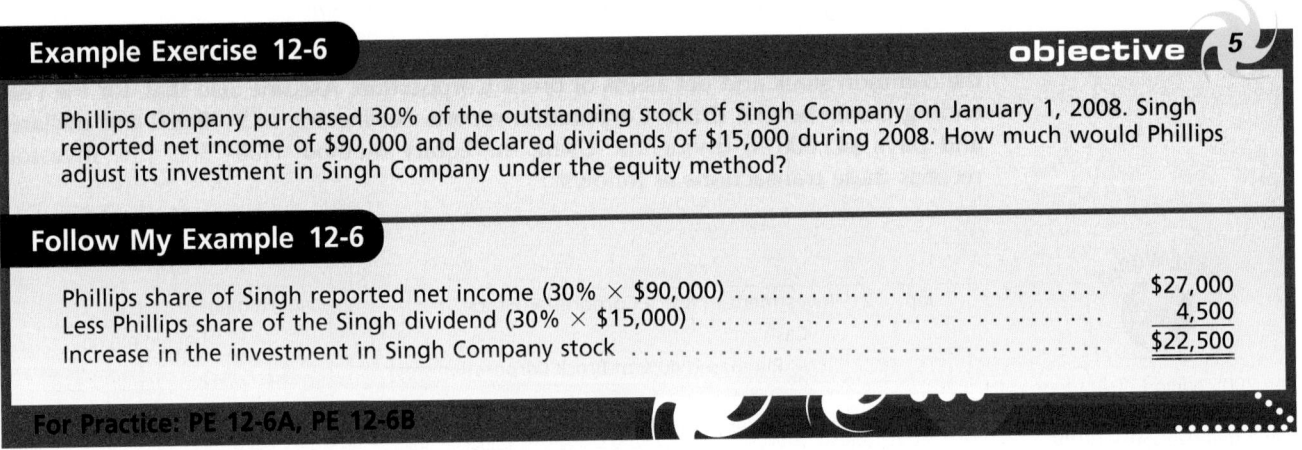

Investment and Dividends

The equity method causes the investment account to mirror the proportional changes in the book value of the investee. Thus, Brock Corporation's book value increased by $60,000 ($105,000 − $45,000), while the investment in Brock Corporation stock account increased by Hally's proportional share of that increase, or $24,000 ($60,000 × 40%). Thus, both the book value of Brock Corporation and Hally's investment in Brock increased at the same rate from the original cost.

Example Exercise 12-6   objective 5

Phillips Company purchased 30% of the outstanding stock of Singh Company on January 1, 2008. Singh reported net income of $90,000 and declared dividends of $15,000 during 2008. How much would Phillips adjust its investment in Singh Company under the equity method?

Follow My Example 12-6

Phillips share of Singh reported net income (30% × $90,000)	$27,000
Less Phillips share of the Singh dividend (30% × $15,000)	4,500
Increase in the investment in Singh Company stock	$22,500

For Practice: PE 12-6A, PE 12-6B

SALE OF INVESTMENTS IN STOCKS

Accounting for the sale of stock is the same for both short- and long-term investments. When shares of stock are sold, the investment account is credited for the carrying amount (book value) of the shares sold. The cash or receivables account is debited for the proceeds (sales price less commission and other selling costs). Any difference between the proceeds and the carrying amount is recorded as a gain or loss on the sale and is included in determining net income.

To illustrate, assume that an investment in Drey Inc. stock has a carrying amount of $15,700 when it is sold on March 1. If the proceeds from the sale of the stock are $17,500, the entry to record the transaction is as follows:

Mar.	1	Cash		17 5 0 0 00	
		Investment in Drey Inc. Stock			15 7 0 0 00
		Gain on Sale of Investments			1 8 0 0 00

BUSINESS COMBINATIONS

A business may make an investment in another business by acquiring a controlling share, often greater than 50%, of the outstanding voting stock of another corporation by paying cash or exchanging stock. This is termed a **business combination**. Businesses may combine in order to produce more efficiently, diversify product lines, expand geographically, or acquire know-how.

A corporation owning all or a majority of the voting stock of another corporation is called a **parent company**. The corporation that is controlled is called the **subsidiary company**. For example, PayPal became a subsidiary of eBay Inc. when eBay exchanged eBay common stock for all the outstanding common stock of PayPal. Although parent and subsidiary corporations may operate as a single economic unit, they continue to maintain separate accounting records and prepare their own periodic financial statements.

At the end of the year, the financial statements of the parent and subsidiary are combined and reported as a single company.[20] These combined financial statements are called **consolidated financial statements**. Such statements are usually identified by adding "and subsidiary(ies)" to the name of the parent corporation or by adding "consolidated" to the statement title. For example, eBay's income statement is titled, "Consolidated Statement of Income." To the stockholders of the parent company, consolidated financial statements are more meaningful than separate statements for each corporation. This is because the parent company, in substance, controls the subsidiaries, even though the parent and its subsidiaries are separate entities. Accounting for business combinations and preparing consolidated financial statements are discussed in greater detail in advanced accounting courses.

Business Connections

REAL WORLD

1 + 1 = 3

Companies merge in order to create synergy, which occurs when the value of the companies as a single unit is greater than their value as separate companies. How do mergers create synergy? The four basic strategies for creating value in a merger are explained below.

1. *Reduce costs:* When two companies combine, they may be able to eliminate duplicate administrative expenses. For example, the combined company does not need two CEOs or two CFOs, or the company can run on a single computer system or distribution network. Hewlett-Packard Company identified cost savings such as these in justifying its acquisition of Compaq Computer Corporation.

2. *Replace management:* If the target company has been suffering from mismanagement, the acquirer can purchase the target for a low price and replace the target company's management.

3. *Horizontal integration:* The acquirer may purchase the target company because it has a complementary product line, territory, or customer base to its own. The new combined entity is able to serve customers with a broader reach than were two separate entities. For example, The Walt Disney Company purchased Pixar in order to reestablish its presence as the premier animation movie studio in the era of digital animation.

4. *Vertical integration:* A vertical integration occurs when a business acquires a supplier or customer. Acquiring a supplier may provide a more stable source of supply of a strategic resource and reduce coordination costs. For example, Delta Air Lines acquired Comair Holdings Inc., a regional jet carrier, to supply passengers from smaller cities into its large city hub system.

---

20 When a parent company owns less than 100% of the subsidiary stock, the amount owned by the outsiders is often termed a minority interest and is reported immediately following the consolidated total liabilities. Accounting for the minority interest is covered in advanced accounting texts.

Financial Analysis and Interpretation

A firm's growth potential and future earnings prospects are indicated by how much the market is willing to pay per dollar of a company's earnings. This ratio, called the **price-earnings ratio**, or *P/E ratio*, is commonly included in stock market quotations reported by the financial press. A high P/E ratio indicates that the market expects high growth and earnings in the future. Likewise, a low P/E ratio indicates lower growth and earnings expectations.

The price-earnings ratio on common stock is computed by dividing the stock's market price per share at a specific date by the company's annual earnings per share, as shown below.

$$\text{Price-Earnings Ratio} = \frac{\text{Market Price per Share of Common Stock}}{\text{Earnings per Share of Common Stock}}$$

Investors that invest in high price-earnings ratio companies are often referred to as *growth* investors. Growth investors pay a high price for shares because they expect the company to grow and provide a superior return. That is, high price-earnings ratios can be related to investor optimism. Examples of growth companies are Google (P/E 87), eBay Inc. (P/E 54), and Genentech, Inc. (P/E 72). Growth companies are considered risky because high growth expectations are already reflected in the market price. Thus, if the company's high growth expectations are not realized, the stock price will likely fall.

In contrast, investors in low price-earnings ratio companies are often referred to as *value* investors. Value investors invest in companies with stable and predictable earnings. The value investor believes that the low price-earnings ratio investment is safer than a high price-earnings investment, since the stock is priced at a "bargain" level. Value investing is generally considered the "tortoise" strategy to the growth investor's "hare" strategy. Examples of value stocks are Bank of America Corporation (P/E 11), H.J. Heinz Company (P/E 16), and Ford Motor Company (P/E 9).

To illustrate the calculation of the price-earnings ratio, assume that Harper Inc. reported earnings per share of $1.64 in 2008 and $1.35 in 2007. The market prices per common share are $24.60 at the end of 2008 and $16.20 at the end of 2007. The price-earnings ratio on this stock is computed as follows:

Price-Earnings Ratio

Year 2008	15 ($24.60/$1.64)
Year 2007	12 ($16.20/$1.35)

The price-earnings ratio indicates that a share of Harper Inc.'s common stock was selling for 12 times the amount of earnings per share at the end of 2007. At the end of 2008, the common stock was selling for 15 times the amount of earnings per share. These results would indicate a generally improving expectation of growth and earnings for Harper Inc. However, a prospective investor should also consider the price-earnings ratios for competing firms in the same industry.

At a Glance

1. Journalize the entries for corporate income taxes, including deferred income taxes.

Key Points	Key Learning Outcomes	Example Exercises	Practice Exercises
Corporations are subject to income tax and are required to make estimated payments throughout the year. The effects of temporary differences between taxable income and income before income taxes must be allocated between periods.	• Journalize estimated tax payments. • Journalize and interpret temporary differences that give rise to deferred taxes.	12-1	12-1A, 12-1B

2. Describe and illustrate the reporting of unusual items on the income statement.

Key Points	Key Learning Outcomes	Example Exercises	Practice Exercises
Fixed asset impairments and restructuring charges are separately disclosed and deducted as part of operating expenses in determining income from continuing operations. The gain or loss from disposal of a business and gains and losses from unusual and infrequent (extraordinary) events are disclosed separately below income from continuing operations. Errors and changes from one generally accepted accounting method to another are treated as restatements of prior period financial statements.	• Identify, journalize, and report fixed asset impairments and restructuring charges. • Identify and report gains and losses from discontinued operations and extraordinary items. • Describe unusual items affecting prior period financial statements.	**12-2**	12-2A, 12-2B

3. Prepare an income statement reporting earnings per share data.

Key Points	Key Learning Outcomes	Example Exercises	Practice Exercises
Earnings per share is a required disclosure. Basic earnings per share removes preferred dividends in the numerator of the calculation. Earnings per share should be separately disclosed for discontinued operations and extraordinary items.	• Calculate basic earnings per share. • Prepare earnings per share disclosures for discontinued operations and extraordinary items.	**12-3**	12-3A, 12-3B

4. Describe the concept and the reporting of comprehensive income.

Key Points	Key Learning Outcomes	Example Exercises	Practice Exercises
Comprehensive income is all the changes in stockholders' equity during a period except those resulting from dividends and stockholders' investments. Total comprehensive income includes other comprehensive income, which consists of items excluded from net income, such as unrealized gains and losses on certain investments in debt or equity securities. Accumulated other comprehensive income is separately reported in the Stockholders' Equity section of the balance sheet.	• Prepare a statement of comprehensive income. • Determine and report accumulated other comprehensive income.	**12-4** **12-4**	12-4A, 12-4B 12-4A, 12-4B

5. Describe the accounting for investments in stocks.

Key Points	Key Learning Outcomes	Example Exercises	Practice Exercises
Short- and long-term investments in marketable securities may be accounted for as available-for-sale securities. Available-for-sale securities are recognized at fair value on the balance sheet, with changes in fair value being recognized as other comprehensive income. Long-term investments in equity securities in which there is a significant influence are accounted for under the equity method. Investments as the result of a business combination are accounted for as consolidations.	• Identify, journalize, and report changes in market value for available-for-sale securities. • Identify, journalize, and report investments under the equity method. • Define and describe the accounting for a business combination.	**12-5** **12-6**	12-5A, 12-5B 12-6A, 12-6B

Key Terms

accumulated other comprehensive income (536)

available-for-sale securities (538)

business combination (543)

comprehensive income (536)

consolidated financial statements (543)

discontinued operations (533)

earnings per common share (EPS) (535)

equity method (541)

equity securities (538)

extraordinary item (534)

fixed asset impairment (531)

investments (541)

other comprehensive income items (536)

parent company (543)

permanent differences (529)

price-earnings ratio (544)

restructuring charges (532)

subsidiary company (543)

taxable income (527)

temporary differences (528)

temporary investments (538)

trading securities (538)

unrealized holding gain or loss (539)

Illustrative Problem

The following data were selected from the records of Botanica Greenhouses Inc. for the current fiscal year ended August 31:

Administrative expenses	$ 82,200
Cost of merchandise sold	750,000
Fixed asset impairment	115,000
Gain on condemnation of land	25,000
Income tax:	
Applicable to continuing operations	27,200
Applicable to gain on condemnation of land	10,000
Applicable to loss on discontinued operations (reduction)	24,000
Interest expense	15,200
Loss on discontinued operations	60,200
Restructuring charge	40,000
Sales	1,252,500
Selling expenses	182,100

Instructions

Prepare a multiple-step income statement, concluding with a section for earnings per share in the form illustrated in this chapter. There were 10,000 shares of common stock (no preferred) outstanding throughout the year. Assume that the gain on condemnation of land is an extraordinary item.

Solution

Botanica Greenhouses Inc.
Income Statement
For the Year Ended August 31, 2008

Sales..		$1,252,500
Cost of merchandise sold...........................		750,000
Gross profit.......................................		$ 502,500
Operating expenses:		
Selling expenses...............................	$182,100	
Administrative expenses.........................	82,200	
Fixed asset impairment..........................	115,000	
Restructuring charge	40,000	
Total operating expenses.........................		419,300
Income from operations............................		$ 83,200
Other expense:		
Interest expense		15,200
Income from continuing operations before		
income tax....................................		$ 68,000
Income tax expense................................		27,200
Income from continuing operations		$ 40,800
Loss on discontinued operations	$ 60,200	
Less applicable income tax	24,000	36,200
Income before extraordinary item...................		$ 4,600
Extraordinary item:		
Gain on condemnation of land...................	$ 25,000	
Less applicable income tax	10,000	15,000
Net income		$ 19,600
Earnings per share:		
Income from continuing operations		$4.08
Loss on discontinued operations..................		3.62
Income before extraordinary item		$0.46
Extraordinary item		1.50
Net income		$1.96

Self-Examination Questions

(Answers at End of Chapter)

1. During its first year of operations, a corporation elected to use the straight-line method of depreciation for financial reporting purposes and MACRS in determining taxable income. If the income tax rate is 40% and the amount of depreciation expense is $60,000 under the straight-line method and $100,000 under MACRS, what is the amount of income tax deferred to future years?
   A. $16,000
   B. $24,000
   C. $40,000
   D. $60,000

2. A material gain resulting from condemning land for public use would be reported on the income statement as a(n):
   A. extraordinary item.
   B. other income item.
   C. restructuring charge.
   D. fixed asset impairment.

3. Gwinnett Corporation's temporary investments cost $100,000 and have a market value of $120,000 at the end of the accounting period. Assuming a tax rate of

40%, the difference between the cost and market value would be reported as a:

A. $12,000 realized gain.
B. $12,000 unrealized gain.
C. $20,000 realized gain.
D. $20,000 unrealized gain.

4. Cisneros Corporation owns 75% of Harrell Inc. During the current year, Harrell Inc. reported net income of $150,000 and declared dividends of $40,000. How much would Cisneros Corporation increase Investment in Harrell Inc. Stock for the current year?

A. $0　　　　　　　C. $82,500
B. $30,000　　　　D. $112,500

5. Harkin Company has a market price of $60 per share on December 31. The total stockholders' equity is $2,400,000, and the net income is $800,000. There are 200,000 shares outstanding. Preferred dividends are $50,000. The price-earnings ratio would be:

A. 3.
B. 15.
C. 16.
D. 20.

Eye Openers

1. How would the amount of deferred income tax payable be reported in the balance sheet if (a) it is payable within one year and (b) it is payable beyond one year?
2. Darnell Company owns plant and equipment that has a book value of $120 million. Due to a permanent decline in consumer demand for the products produced by this plant, the market value of the plant and equipment is appraised at $20 million. Describe the accounting treatment for this impairment.
3. How should the severance costs of terminated employees be accounted for?
4. During the current year, 40 acres of land that cost $200,000 were condemned for construction of an interstate highway. Assuming that an award of $320,000 in cash was received and that the applicable income tax on this transaction is 40%, how would this information be presented in the income statement?
5. Mann Corporation realized a material gain when its facilities at a designated floodway were acquired by the urban renewal agency. How should the gain be reported in the income statement?
6. An annual report of Ford Motor Company disclosed the sale of its ownership interest in Visteon Corporation, a major automotive components manufacturer. The estimated after-tax loss on disposal of these operations was $2.3 billion. Indicate how the loss from discontinued operations should be reported by Ford on its income statement.
7. How is the change from one acceptable accounting principle to another acceptable accounting principle shown on the income statement?
8. A corporation reports earnings per share of $1.38 for the most recent year and $1.10 for the preceding year. The $1.38 includes a $0.40-per-share gain from insurance proceeds related to a fully depreciated asset that was destroyed by fire.
   a. Should the composition of the $1.38 be disclosed in the financial reports?
   b. On the basis of the limited information presented, would you conclude that operations had improved or declined?
9. a. List some examples of other comprehensive income items.
   b. Does the reporting of other comprehensive income affect the determination of net income and retained earnings?
10. Why might a business invest in another company's stock?
11. How are temporary investments in marketable securities reported on the balance sheet?
12. How are unrealized gains and losses on temporary investments in marketable securities reported on the statement of comprehensive income?
13. a. What method of accounting is used for long-term investments in stock in which there is significant influence over the investee?
    b. Under what caption are long-term investments in stock reported on the balance sheet?
14. Glover Inc. received a $0.20-per-share cash dividend on 50,000 shares of Gestalt Corporation common stock, which Glover Inc. carries as a long-term investment. Assuming that Glover Inc. uses the equity method of accounting for its investment in Gestalt Corporation, what account would be credited for the receipt of the $10,000 dividend?

15. An annual report of The Campbell Soup Company reported on its income statement $2.4 million as "equity in earnings of affiliates." Journalize the entry that Campbell would have made to record this equity in earnings of affiliates.

16. How is an investment as the result of a business combination reported?

Practice Exercises

PE 12-1A
Deferred tax entries
obj. 1

A corporation has $540,000 of income before income taxes, a 35% tax rate, and $480,000 of taxable income. Provide the journal entry for the current year's taxes.

PE 12-1B
Deferred tax entries
obj. 1

Bismark Corp. has $90,000 of income before income taxes, a 40% tax rate, and $76,000 of taxable income. Provide the journal entry for the current year's taxes.

PE 12-2A
Journalize fixed asset impairment and restructuring charge
obj. 2

On December 15 of the current year, Adams Corporation determined that equipment had been impaired so that the book value of the equipment was reduced by $46,000. In addition, the senior management of the company communicated an employee severance plan whereby 15 employees could receive a termination benefit of $4,000 per employee. Provide the journal entry for the asset impairment and the restructuring charge.

PE 12-2B
Journalize fixed asset impairment and restructuring charge
obj. 2

On December 23 of the current year, Dallas Corporation determined that land had been impaired so that the book value of the land was reduced by $320,000. In addition, the senior management of the company communicated an employee severance plan whereby 45 employees could receive a termination benefit of $9,000 per employee. Provide the journal entry for the asset impairment and the restructuring charge.

PE 12-3A
Calculate earnings per share
obj. 3

Wyoming Company had net income of $2,430,000 during the year. There were 240,000 common shares and 30,000 shares of $100 par value, 9% preferred stock outstanding during the year. Determine the basic earnings per share.

PE 12-3B
Calculate earnings per share
obj. 3

Broad Plain Inc. had net income of $350,000 during the year. There were 420,000 common shares and 5,000 shares of $100 par value, 7% preferred stock outstanding during the year. Determine the basic earnings per share.

PE 12-4A
Comprehensive income
obj. 4

Zorba Company had a net income of $104,000 and other comprehensive income of $13,400 for 2008. On January 1, 2008, the Retained Earnings balance was $565,000, and the Accumulated Other Comprehensive Income balance was $71,000. Determine the (a) comprehensive income for 2008, (b) Retained Earnings balance on December 31, 2008, and (c) Accumulated Other Comprehensive Income balance on December 31, 2008.

PE 12-4B
Comprehensive income
obj. 4

Manitoba Company had a net income of $856,000 and other comprehensive income of $123,500 for 2008. On January 1, 2008, the Retained Earnings balance was $3,460,000, and the Accumulated Other Comprehensive Income balance was $624,000. Determine the (a) comprehensive income for 2008, (b) Retained Earnings balance on December 31, 2008, and (c) Accumulated Other Comprehensive Income balance on December 31, 2008.

PE 12-5A
Temporary investments
obj. 5

Mansfield Company began operations on January 1, 2008, and purchased temporary investments in marketable securities during the year at a cost of $123,000. The end-of-period market value for these investments was $137,000. Net income was $151,000 for 2008. Determine (a) the reported amount of marketable securities on the December 31, 2008, balance sheet and (b) the comprehensive income for 2008. Assume a tax rate of 40%.

PE 12-5B
Temporary investments
obj. 5

Aaron Company began operations on January 1, 2008, and purchased temporary investments in marketable securities during the year at a cost of $56,000. The end-of-period market value for these investments was $49,700. Net income was $97,500 for 2008. Determine (a) the reported amount of marketable securities on the December 31, 2008, balance sheet and (b) the comprehensive income for 2008. Assume a tax rate of 35%.

PE 12-6A
Equity method
obj. 5

Gilliam Company purchased 35% of the outstanding stock of Forrester Company on January 1, 2008. Forrester reported net income of $675,000 and declared dividends of $155,000 during 2008. How much would Gilliam adjust its investment in Forrester Company under the equity method?

PE 12-6B
Equity method
obj. 5

Miranda Company purchased 25% of the outstanding stock of Orson Company on January 1, 2008. Orson reported a net loss of $300,000 and declared dividends of $40,000 during 2008. How much would Miranda adjust its investment in Orson Company under the equity method?

Exercises

EX 12-1
Income tax entries
obj. 1

Journalize the entries to record the following selected transactions of Lone Star Leather Co.:

Apr. 15. Paid the first installment of the estimated income tax for the current fiscal year ending December 31, $90,000. No entry had been made to record the liability.
June 15. Paid the second installment of $90,000.
Sept. 15. Paid the third installment of $90,000.
Dec. 31. Recorded the estimated income tax liability for the year just ended and the deferred income tax liability, based on the transactions above and the following data:

Income tax rate	40%
Income before income tax	$950,000
Taxable income according to tax return	$800,000

Jan. 15. Paid the fourth installment of $50,000.

EX 12-2
Deferred income taxes
obj. 1

Storage Systems Inc. recognized service revenue of $420,000 on its financial statements in 2007. Assume, however, that the Tax Code requires this amount to be recognized for tax purposes in 2008. The taxable income for 2007 and 2008 is $2,600,000 and $3,000,000, respectively. Assume a tax rate of 40%.

Prepare the journal entries to record the tax expense, deferred taxes, and taxes payable for 2007 and 2008, respectively.

EX 12-3
Deferred income taxes
obj. 1

Eason Company began operations on January 1, 2007, and reported net income of $260,000 during the year. Eason had a taxable income of $350,000 for 2007. The difference between the reported net income and taxable income will reverse in 2008. The reported net income for 2008 was $405,000. There were no other temporary differences. The tax rate is 35% for both years. Prepare the journal entries to record the tax expense, deferred taxes, and taxes payable for 2007 and 2008, respectively.

EX 12-4
Fixed asset impairment

obj. 2

✓ a. $74,000,000

Laser Pulse Communications Inc. spent $90 million expanding its fiber optic communication network between Chicago and Los Angeles during 2006. The fiber optic network was assumed to have a 10-year life, with a $10 million salvage value, when it was put into service on January 1, 2007. The network is depreciated using the straight-line method. At the end of 2008, the expected traffic volume on the fiber optic network was only 60% of what was originally expected. The reduced traffic volume caused the fair market value of the asset to be estimated at $50 million on December 31, 2008. The loss is not expected to be recoverable.

a. Determine the book value of the network on December 31, 2008, prior to the impairment adjustment.
b. Provide the journal entry to record the fixed asset impairment on December 31, 2008.
c. Provide the balance sheet disclosure for fixed assets on December 31, 2008.

EX 12-5
Fixed asset impairment

obj. 2

Harmony Resorts Inc. owns and manages resort properties. On January 15, 2008, one of its properties was found to be adjacent to a toxic chemical disposal site. As a result of the negative publicity, this property's bookings dropped 40% during 2008. On December 31, 2008, the accounts of the company showed the following details regarding the impaired property:

Land	$ 30,000,000
Buildings and improvements (net)	120,000,000
Equipment (net)	25,000,000
Total	$175,000,000

Management decides that closing the resort is the only option. As a result, it is estimated that the buildings and improvements will be written off completely. The land can be sold for other uses for $17 million, while the equipment can be disposed of for $6 million, net of disposal costs.

a. Provide the journal entry to record the asset impairment on December 31, 2008.
b. ▭▬▶ Provide the note disclosure for the impairment.

EX 12-6
Restructuring charge

obj. 2

✓ a. Restructuring charge,
$4,680,000

Morton Company's board of directors approved and communicated an employee severance plan in response to a decline in demand for the company's products. The plan called for the elimination of 180 headquarters positions by providing a severance equal to 5% of the annual salary multiplied by the number of years of service. The average annual salary of the eliminated positions is $65,000. The average tenure of terminated employees is eight years. The plan was communicated to employees on November 1, 2008. Actual termination notices will be distributed over the period between December 1, 2008, and April 1, 2009. On December 21, 2008, 50 employees received a lay-off notice and were terminated with severance.

a. Provide the appropriate journal entry for the restructuring charge.
b. Provide the journal entry to record the severance payment on December 21, 2008, assuming that the actual tenure and salary of terminated employees were consistent with the overall average.
c. Provide the balance sheet and note disclosures on December 31, 2008.

EX 12-7
Restructuring charge

obj. 2

✓ a. Restructuring charge,
$3,774,000

Kiwi Juice Company has been suffering a downturn in its juice business due to adverse publicity regarding the caffeine content of its drink products. As a result, the company has been required to restructure operations. The board of directors approved and communicated a plan on July 1, 2008, calling for the following actions:

1. Close a juice plant on October 15, 2008. Closing, equipment relocation, and employee relocation costs are expected to be $600,000 during October.
2. Eliminate 300 plant positions. A severance will be paid to the terminated employees equal to 400% of their estimated monthly earnings payable in four quarterly installments on October 15, 2008; January 15, 2009; April 15, 2009; and July 15, 2009.

3. Terminate a juice supply contract, activating a $150,000 cancellation penalty, payable upon notice of termination. The notice will be formally delivered to the supplier on August 15, 2008.

   The 300 employees earn an average of $14 per hour. The average employee works 180 hours per month.

a. Determine the total restructuring charge for 2008.
b. Provide the journal entry for the restructuring charge on July 1, 2008. (*Note:* Use Restructuring Obligation as the liability account, since the charges involve more than just employee terminations.)
c. Provide the journal entry for the October 15, 2008, employee severance payment.
d. Provide the balance sheet disclosure for December 31, 2008.
e. ▬▬➤ Provide a note disclosure for December 31, 2008.

EX 12-8
Restructuring charges and asset impairments
obj. 2

✓ *a. Severance restructuring charge, $780,000*

TransCo Inc. has suffered losses due to increased competition in its service market from low-cost independent truckers. As a result, on December 31, 2008, the board of directors of the company approved and communicated a restructuring plan that calls for selling 50 tractor-trailers out of a fleet of 400. In addition, the plan calls for the elimination of 50 driver positions and 15 staff support positions. The market price for used tractor-trailers is depressed due to general overcapacity in the transportation industry. As a result, the market value of tractor-trailers is estimated to be only 60% of the book value of these assets. It is not believed that the impairment in fixed assets is recoverable. The cost and accumulated depreciation of the total tractor-trailer fleet on December 31 are $48 million and $14 million, respectively. The restructuring plan will provide a severance to the drivers and staff totaling $12,000 per employee, payable on March 14, 2009, which is the expected employee termination date.

a. Provide the journal entries on December 31, 2008, for the fixed asset impairment and the employee severance costs.
b. ▬▬➤ Provide the balance sheet and note disclosure on December 31, 2008.
c. Provide the journal entry for March 14, 2009.

EX 12-9
Extraordinary item
obj. 2

A company received life insurance proceeds on the death of its president before the end of its fiscal year. It intends to report the amount in its income statement as an extraordinary item.

▬▬➤ Would this reporting be in conformity with generally accepted accounting principles? Discuss.

EX 12-10
Extraordinary item
obj. 2

REAL WORLD

For the year ended December 31, 2002, Delta Air Lines provided the following note to its financial statements:

> *On September 22, 2001, the Air Transportation Safety and System Stabilization Act (Stabilization Act) became effective. The Stabilization Act is intended to preserve the viability of the U.S. air transportation system following the terrorist attacks on September 11, 2001 by, among other things, (1) providing for payments from the U.S. Government totaling $5 billion to compensate U.S. air carriers for losses incurred from September 11, 2001, through December 31, 2001, as a result of the September 11 terrorist attacks and (2) permitting the Secretary of Transportation to sell insurance to U.S. air carriers.*
>
> *Our allocated portion of compensation under the Stabilization Act was $668 million. Due to uncertainties regarding the U.S. government's calculation of compensation, we recognized $634 million of this amount in our 2001 Consolidated Statement of Operations. We recognized the remaining $34 million of compensation in our 2002 Consolidated Statement of Operations. We received $112 million and $556 million in cash for the years ended December 31, 2002 and 2001, respectively, under the Stabilization Act.*

▬▬➤ Do you believe that the income related to the Stabilization Act should be reported as an extraordinary item on the income statement of Delta Air Lines?

EX 12-11
Extraordinary items
obj. 2

Below are three separate historical incidents giving rise to losses for three different companies.

a. In 1980, Weyerhaeuser, a major wood products company, lost $36 million in timber, logs, and building equipment as a result of the volcanic eruption of Mount St. Helens in the state of Washington.

b. In 2001, Dow Jones & Company, Inc., the publisher of *The Wall Street Journal*, suffered $1.7 million in losses due to damage in its headquarters building as a result of the 9/11 terrorist incident.

c. In 2005, Northrop Grumman Corporation, a major defense contractor, reported significant losses in its shipbuilding yards along the Gulf Coast as a result of Hurricane Katrina. The losses were sufficient to cut its projected earnings in half for the year.

In each case, identify whether the loss should be reported as extraordinary.

EX 12-12
Identifying extraordinary items
obj. 2

Assume that the amount of each of the following items is material to the financial statements. Classify each item as either normally recurring (NR) or extraordinary (E).

a. Restructuring charge related to employee termination benefits.
b. Loss on sale of fixed assets.
c. Uninsured flood loss. (Flood insurance is unavailable because of periodic flooding in the area.)
d. Interest revenue on notes receivable.
e. Loss on disposal of equipment considered to be obsolete because of development of new technology.
f. Uninsured loss on building due to hurricane damage. The firm was organized in 1920 and had not previously incurred hurricane damage.
g. Uncollectible accounts expense.
h. Gain on sale of land condemned for public use.

EX 12-13
Income statement
objs. 2, 3

✓ *Net income, $126,600*

Wind Surfer Inc. produces and distributes equipment for sailboats. On the basis of the following data for the current fiscal year ended June 30, 2008, prepare a multiple-step income statement for Wind Surfer, including an analysis of earnings per share in the form illustrated in this chapter. There were 20,000 shares of $150 par common stock outstanding throughout the year.

Administrative expenses	$ 104,000
Cost of merchandise sold	467,500
Gain on condemnation of land (extraordinary item)	58,000
Income tax applicable to gain on condemnation of land	23,200
Income tax reduction applicable to loss from discontinued operations	32,000
Income tax applicable to income from continuing operations	93,200
Loss on discontinued operations	80,000
Loss from fixed asset impairment	120,000
Restructuring charge	50,000
Sales	1,100,000
Selling expenses	125,500

EX 12-14
Income statement
objs. 2, 3

✓ *Correct EPS for net income, $0.47*

Audio Affection Inc. sells automotive and home stereo equipment. It has 50,000 shares of $100 par common stock outstanding and 10,000 shares of $2, $100 par cumulative preferred stock outstanding as of December 31, 2008. List the errors you find in the following income statement for the year ended December 31, 2008.

(continued)

Audio Affection Inc.
Income Statement
For the Year Ended December 31, 2008

Net sales		$967,000
Cost of merchandise sold		578,000
Gross profit		$389,000
Operating expenses:		
Selling expenses	$127,000	
Administrative expenses	142,000	269,000
Income from continuing operations before income tax		$120,000
Income tax expense		48,000
Income from continuing operations		$ 72,000
Fixed asset impairment		(24,000)
Income before condemnation of land, restructuring charge,		
and discontinued operations		$ 48,000
Extraordinary items:		
Gain on condemnation of land, net of applicable		
income tax of $20,000		30,000
Restructuring charge, net of applicable income tax of $8,000		(12,000)
Loss on discontinued operations (net of applicable		
income tax of $15,000)		(22,500)
Net income		$ 43,500
Earnings per common share:		
Income from continuing operations		$ 1.44
Fixed asset impairment		(0.48)
Income before extraordinary item and discontinued operations		$ 0.96
Extraordinary items:		
Gain on condemnation of land		0.60
Restructuring charge		(0.24)
Loss on discontinued operations		(0.45)
Net income		$ 0.87

EX 12-15
Earnings per share with preferred stock
obj. **3**

FirstLight Lighting Company had earnings for 2008 of $150,600. The company had 90,000 shares of common stock outstanding during the year. In addition, the company issued 2,000 shares of $100 par value preferred stock on January 5, 2008. The preferred stock has a dividend of $6 per share. There were no transactions in either common or preferred stock during 2008.

Determine the basic earnings per share for FirstLight.

EX 12-16
Comprehensive income
obj. **4**
a. $1,693,000

The statement of comprehensive income for Lancaster Company was as follows:

Lancaster Company
Statement of Comprehensive Income
For the Year Ended December 31, 2008

Net income	$460,000
Other comprehensive income:	
Unrealized loss on temporary investments in marketable	
equity securities (net of $25,000 tax benefit)	(45,000)
Total comprehensive income	$415,000

The balance sheet dated December 31, 2007, showed a Retained Earnings balance of $1,483,000 and an Accumulated Other Comprehensive Income balance of $171,000. The company paid $250,000 in dividends during 2008.

a. Determine the December 31, 2008, Retained Earnings balance.
b. Determine the December 31, 2008, Accumulated Other Comprehensive Income (Loss) balance.

EX 12-17
Comprehensive income and temporary investments

objs. 4, 5

✓ c. $84,000

The statement of comprehensive income for the years ended December 31, 2008 and 2009, plus selected items from comparative balance sheets of Johnson Wholesalers Inc. are as follows:

Johnson Wholesalers Inc.
Statement of Comprehensive Income
For the Years Ended December 31, 2008 and 2009

	2008	2009
Net income	a.	$100,000
Other comprehensive income (loss), net of tax	b.	4,000
Total comprehensive income	c.	e.

Johnson Wholesalers Inc.
Selected Balance Sheet Items
December 31, 2007, 2008, and 2009

	Dec. 31, 2007	Dec. 31, 2008	Dec. 31, 2009
Temporary investments in marketable securities at fair market value, net of taxes on unrealized gains or losses	$ 32,000	d.	f.
Retained earnings	175,000	$250,000	g.
Accumulated other comprehensive income or (loss)	(8,000)	1,000	h.

There were no dividends or purchases or sales of temporary investments. Other comprehensive items included only after-tax unrealized gains and losses on investments. Determine the missing lettered items.

EX 12-18
Comprehensive income and temporary investments

objs. 4, 5

✓ a. Total comprehensive income, $205,000

During 2008, Mango Corporation held a portfolio of available-for-sale securities having a cost of $260,000. There were no purchases or sales of investments during the year. The market values after adjusting for the impact of taxes, at the beginning and end of the year, were $215,000 and $270,000, respectively. The net income for 2008 was $150,000, and no dividends were paid during the year. The Stockholders' Equity section of the balance sheet was as follows on December 31, 2007:

Mango Corporation
Stockholders' Equity
December 31, 2007

Common stock	$ 35,000
Paid-in capital in excess of par value	350,000
Retained earnings	435,000
Accumulated other comprehensive loss	(45,000)
Total	$775,000

a. Prepare a statement of comprehensive income for 2008.
b. Prepare the Stockholders' Equity section of the balance sheet for December 31, 2008.

EX 12-19
Temporary investments and other comprehensive income

objs. 4, 5

✓ a. 2009 unrealized gain, $54,000

The temporary investments of Catalyst Inc. only include 10,000 shares of Bristol Inc. common stock purchased on January 10, 2008, for $20 per share. As of the December 31, 2008, balance sheet date, assume that the share price declined to $16 per share. As of the December 31, 2009, balance sheet date, assume that the share price rose to $25 per share. The investment was held through December 31, 2009. Assume a tax rate of 40%.

a. Determine the net after-tax unrealized gain or loss from holding the Bristol common stock for 2008 and 2009.
b. What is the balance of Accumulated Other Comprehensive Income or Loss for December 31, 2008, and December 31, 2009?
c. Where is Accumulated Other Comprehensive Income or Deficit disclosed on the financial statements?

EX 12-20
Temporary investments in marketable securities

obj. **5**

During 2008, its first year of operations, Geo-Metrics Corporation purchased the following securities as a temporary investment:

Security	Shares Purchased	Cost	Cash Dividends Received
M-Labs Inc.	1,000	$19,000	$ 750
Spectrum Corp.	2,500	38,000	1,400

a. Record the purchase of the temporary investments for cash.
b. Record the receipt of the dividends.

EX 12-21
Financial statement reporting of temporary investments

objs. **4, 5**

✓b. Comprehensive income, $101,800

Using the data for Geo-Metrics Corporation in Exercise 12-20, assume that as of December 31, 2008, the M-Labs Inc. stock had a market value of $25 per share and the Spectrum Corp. stock had a market value of $14 per share. For the year ending December 31, 2008, Geo-Metrics Corporation had net income of $100,000. Its tax rate is 40%.

a. Prepare the balance sheet presentation for the temporary investments.
b. Prepare a statement of comprehensive income presentation for the temporary investments.

EX 12-22
Entries for investment in stock, receipt of dividends, and sale of shares

obj. **5**

On February 27, Ball Corporation acquired 4,000 shares of the 50,000 outstanding shares of Bat Co. common stock at 40.75 plus commission charges of $200. On July 8, a cash dividend of $1.75 per share and a 2% stock dividend were received. On December 7, 1,000 shares were sold at 53, less commission charges of $65. Record the entries to record (a) the purchase of the stock, (b) the receipt of dividends, and (c) the sale of the 1,000 shares.

EX 12-23
Entries using equity method for stock investment

obj. **5**

At a total cost of $1,960,000, Turner Corporation acquired 70,000 shares of May Corp. common stock as a long-term investment. Turner Corporation uses the equity method of accounting for this investment. May Corp. has 280,000 shares of common stock outstanding, including the shares acquired by Turner Corporation. Journalize the entries by Turner Corporation to record the following information:

a. May Corp. reports net income of $3,000,000 for the current period.
b. A cash dividend of $3.80 per common share is paid by May Corp. during the current period.

EX 12-24
Equity method for stock investment

obj. **5**

Sweet Company's balance sheet disclosed its long-term investment in Sour Company for comparative years as follows:

	Dec. 31, 2008	Dec. 31, 2007
Investment in Sour Company stock (in millions)	$146	$135

In addition, the 2008 Sweet Company income statement disclosed equity earnings in the Sour Company investment as $15 million. Sweet Company neither purchased nor sold Sour Company stock during 2008. The market value of Sour Company stock on December 31, 2008, was $154.

▬▬▶ Explain the change in the Investment in Sour Company Stock from December 31, 2007, to December 31, 2008.

EX 12-25
Price-earnings ratio

Goodman Company had a net income of $672,000 for 2008. Goodman Company's balance sheet disclosed the stockholders' equity on December 31, 2008, as follows:

Preferred stock, 8,000 shares of $100 par value, 6% stock	$ 800,000
Common stock, 120,000 shares of $1 par value stock issued and outstanding	120,000
Paid-in capital in excess of par value	2,400,000
Total stockholders' equity	$3,320,000

The price of Goodman common stock was $72.80 per share on December 31, 2008. Determine the price-earnings ratio for Goodman Company.

EX 12-26
Price-earnings ratio calculations

✓ a. 2005: 9.7

ExxonMobil Corporation is one of the largest companies in the world. The company explores, develops, refines, and markets petroleum products. The basic earnings per share for three comparative years were as follows:

	Years Ended Dec. 31,		
	2005	**2004**	**2003**
Basic earnings per share	$5.76	$3.91	$3.24

The market prices at the end of each year were $56, $51, and $41 for December 31, 2005, 2004, and 2003, respectively.

a. Determine the price-earnings ratio for 2005, 2004, and 2003, using end-of-year prices. Round to one decimal place.
b. ▭▭▭▶ Interpret your results over the three years.

Problems Series A

PR 12-1A
Income tax allocation

obj. 1

✓ 1. Year-end balance, 3rd year, $12,000

Differences between the accounting methods applied to accounts and financial reports and those used in determining taxable income yielded the following amounts for the first four years of a corporation's operations:

	First Year	Second Year	Third Year	Fourth Year
Income before income taxes	$250,000	$300,000	$500,000	$400,000
Taxable income	200,000	280,000	540,000	430,000

The income tax rate for each of the four years was 40% of taxable income, and each year's taxes were promptly paid.

Instructions
1. Determine for each year the amounts described by the following captions, presenting the information in the form indicated:

Year	Income Tax Deducted on Income Statement	Income Tax Payments for the Year	Deferred Income Tax Payable	
			Year's Addition (Deduction)	Year-End Balance

2. Total the first three amount columns.

PR 12-2A
Income tax; income statement

objs. 2, 3, 4

✓ Net income, $34,300

The following data were selected from the records of Xtreme World Inc. for the current fiscal year ended June 30, 2008:

Advertising expense	$ 57,000
Cost of merchandise sold	345,000
Depreciation expense—office equipment	16,000
Depreciation expense—store equipment	45,000
Gain on discontinued operations	38,000
Income tax:	
Applicable to continuing operations	10,500
Applicable to gain on disposal of business segment	11,400
Applicable to loss on condemnation of land (reduction)	7,200
Insurance expense	9,000
Interest expense	18,000
Loss from condemnation of land	24,000

(continued)

Loss from fixed asset impairment	$ 40,000
Miscellaneous administrative expense	11,000
Miscellaneous selling expense	14,000
Office salaries expense	70,000
Rent expense	25,000
Restructuring charge	50,000
Sales	865,000
Sales commissions expense	130,000
Unrealized gain on temporary investments	35,000

Instructions

Prepare a multiple-step income statement, concluding with a section for earnings per share in the form illustrated in this chapter. There were 5,000 shares of common stock (no preferred) outstanding throughout the year. Assume that the loss on the condemnation of land is an extraordinary item.

PR 12-3A
Income statement; retained earnings statement; balance sheet

objs. **1, 2, 3, 4**

✓ *Net income, $67,200*

The following data were taken from the records of Amana Bread Corporation for the year ended October 31, 2008:

Income statement data:

Administrative expenses	$ 80,000
Cost of merchandise sold	458,000
Gain on condemnation of land	80,000
Income tax:	
Applicable to continuing operations	36,800
Applicable to loss from discontinued business segment	24,000
Applicable to gain on condemnation of land	32,000
Interest expense	5,000
Interest revenue	4,000
Loss from discontinued operations	60,000
Loss from fixed asset impairment	35,000
Restructuring charge	65,000
Sales	955,000
Selling expenses	224,000

Retained earnings and balance sheet data:

Accounts payable	$ 47,800
Accounts receivable	185,000
Accumulated depreciation	465,000
Accumulated other comprehensive loss	28,000
Allowance for doubtful accounts	5,400
Cash	165,300
Common stock, $1 par (100,000 shares authorized; 82,000 shares issued)	82,000
Deferred income taxes payable (current portion, $5,400)	28,300
Dividends:	
Cash dividends for common stock	35,000
Cash dividends for preferred stock	16,000
Stock dividends for common stock	12,000
Dividends payable	12,750
Employee termination obligation (current)	45,000
Equipment	1,958,000
Income tax payable	11,200
Interest receivable	2,500
Merchandise inventory (October 31, 2008), at lower of cost (FIFO) or market	122,000
Notes receivable	42,500
Paid-in capital from sale of treasury stock	16,000
Paid-in capital in excess of par—common stock	451,000
Paid-in capital in excess of par—preferred stock	8,000
Patents	14,000
Preferred 8% stock, $100 par (10,000 shares authorized; 2,000 shares issued)	200,000
Prepaid expenses	2,600
Retained earnings, November 1, 2007	1,277,250
Temporary investment in marketable equity securities	122,000
Treasury stock (2,000 shares of common stock at cost of $20 per share)	40,000
Unrealized loss on temporary equity securities (net of taxes)	28,000

Instructions

1. Prepare a multiple-step income statement for the year ended October 31, 2008, concluding with earnings per share. In computing earnings per share, assume that the average number of common shares outstanding was 80,000 and preferred dividends were $16,000. Assume that the gain on condemnation of land is an extraordinary item.
2. Prepare a retained earnings statement for the year ended October 31, 2008.
3. Prepare a balance sheet in report form as of October 31, 2008.

PR 12-4A
Entries for investments in stock
obj. 5

Samson Company is a wholesaler of men's hair products. The following transactions relate to certain securities acquired by Samson Company, which has a fiscal year ending on December 31:

2006

Jan. 3. Purchased 4,000 shares of the 100,000 outstanding common shares of Nichols Corporation at 55 plus commission and other costs of $480.

July 2. Received the regular cash dividend of $1.25 a share on Nichols Corporation stock.

Dec. 5. Received the regular cash dividend of $1.25 a share plus an extra dividend of $0.10 a share on Nichols Corporation stock.

(Assume that all intervening transactions have been recorded properly and that the number of shares of stock owned have not changed from December 31, 2006, to December 31, 2008.)

2009

Jan. 2. Purchased controlling interest in Telico Inc. for $540,000 by purchasing 32,000 shares directly from the estate of the founder of Telico. There are 128,000 shares of Telico Inc. stock outstanding.

July 6. Received the regular cash dividend of $1.25 a share and a 4% stock dividend on the Nichols Corporation stock.

Oct. 23. Sold 800 shares of Nichols Corporation stock at 68. The broker deducted commission and other costs of $140, remitting the balance.

Dec. 10. Received a cash dividend at the new rate of $1.50 a share on the Nichols Corporation stock.

31. Received $38,000 of cash dividends on Telico Inc. stock. Telico Inc. reported net income of $260,000 in 2009. Samson uses the equity method of accounting for its investment in Telico Inc.

Instructions

Record the entries for the preceding transactions.

Problems Series B

PR 12-1B
Income tax allocation
obj. 1

✓ 1. Year-end balance, 3rd year, $4,200

Differences between the accounting methods applied to accounts and financial reports and those used in determining taxable income yielded the following amounts for the first four years of a corporation's operations:

	First Year	Second Year	Third Year	Fourth Year
Income before income taxes	$50,000	$65,000	$90,000	$100,000
Taxable income	35,000	60,000	98,000	112,000

The income tax rate for each of the four years was 35% of taxable income, and each year's taxes were promptly paid.

Instructions

1. Determine for each year the amounts described by the following captions, presenting the information in the form indicated:

(continued)

Year	Income Tax Deducted on Income Statement	Income Tax Payments for the Year	Deferred Income Tax Payable	
			Year's Addition (Deduction)	Year-End Balance

2. Total the first three amount columns.

PR 12-2B

Income tax; income statement

objs. 2, 3, 4

✓ *Net income, $203,000*

ATV Inc. sells off-road motorcycles and vehicles. The following data were selected from the records of ATV Inc. for the current fiscal year ended March 31, 2008:

Advertising expense	$ 36,000
Cost of merchandise sold	1,640,000
Depreciation expense—office equipment	32,000
Depreciation expense—store equipment	145,000
Gain on condemnation of land	54,000
Income tax:	
Applicable to continuing operations	94,200
Applicable to loss from discontinued operations (reduction)	23,400
Applicable to gain on condemnation of land	16,200
Interest revenue	25,000
Loss from disposal of business segment	78,000
Loss from fixed asset impairment	32,000
Miscellaneous administrative expense	41,000
Miscellaneous selling expense	25,000
Office salaries expense	230,000
Rent expense	100,000
Restructuring charge	70,000
Sales	2,800,000
Sales salaries expense	160,000
Unrealized loss on temporary investments	40,000

Instructions

Prepare a multiple-step income statement, concluding with a section for earnings per share in the form illustrated in this chapter. There were 20,000 shares of common stock (no preferred) outstanding throughout the year. Assume that the gain on the condemnation of land is an extraordinary item.

PR 12-3B

Income statement; retained earnings statement; balance sheet

objs. 1, 2, 3, 4

✓ *Net income, $128,700*

The following data were taken from the records of Disk N' Dat Corporation for the year ended August 31, 2008:

Income statement data:

Administrative expenses	$ 23,000
Cost of merchandise sold	232,000
Gain on condemnation of land	75,000
Income tax:	
Applicable to continuing operations	70,200
Applicable to loss from discontinued operation	14,400
Applicable to gain on condemnation of land	30,000
Interest expense	3,000
Interest revenue	2,500
Loss from disposal of discontinued operation	36,000
Loss from fixed asset impairment	14,000
Restructuring charge	45,000
Sales	550,000
Selling expenses	60,000

Retained earnings and balance sheet data:

Accounts payable	$ 12,000
Accounts receivable	28,000
Accumulated depreciation	145,000

Accumulated other comprehensive income	$	9,000
Allowance for doubtful accounts		2,500
Cash		87,500
Common stock, $1 par (100,000 shares authorized; 46,000 shares issued)		46,000
Deferred income taxes payable (current portion, $4,700)		12,800
Dividends:		
Cash dividends for common stock		21,000
Cash dividends for preferred stock		9,000
Stock dividends for common stock		5,000
Dividends payable		7,500
Employee termination obligation (current)		30,000
Equipment		1,350,000
Income tax payable		21,450
Interest receivable		500
Merchandise inventory (August 31, 2008), at lower of cost (FIFO) or market		87,000
Paid-in capital from sale of treasury stock		5,000
Paid-in capital in excess of par—common stock		820,000
Paid-in capital in excess of par—preferred stock		20,000
Patents		40,000
Preferred 6% stock, $100 par (30,000 shares authorized; 1,500 shares issued)		150,000
Prepaid expenses		15,900
Retained earnings, September 1, 2007		397,950
Temporary investments in marketable equity securities (at cost)		125,000
Treasury stock (1,000 shares of common stock at cost of $30 per share)		30,000
Unrealized gain on marketable equity securities		9,000

Instructions

1. Prepare a multiple-step income statement for the year ended August 31, 2008, concluding with earnings per share. In computing earnings per share, assume that the average number of common shares outstanding was 45,000 and preferred dividends were $9,000. Assume that the gain on the condemnation of land is an extraordinary item.
2. Prepare a retained earnings statement for the year ended August 31, 2008.
3. Prepare a balance sheet in report form as of August 31, 2008.

PR 12-4B
Entries for investments in stock
obj. 5

Encore Design Inc. produces and sells theater set designs and costumes. The following transactions relate to certain securities acquired by Encore Design Inc., which has a fiscal year ending on December 31:

2006

Feb. 10. Purchased 8,000 shares of the 150,000 outstanding common shares of Mode Corporation at 36 plus commission and other costs of $864.

July 15. Received the regular cash dividend of $1.10 a share on Mode Corporation stock.

Dec. 15. Received the regular cash dividend of $1.10 a share plus an extra dividend of $0.05 a share on Mode Corporation stock.

(Assume that all intervening transactions have been recorded properly and that the number of shares of stock owned have not changed from December 31, 2006, to December 31, 2008.)

2009

Jan. 3. Purchased controlling interest in Applause Inc. for $675,000 by purchasing 30,000 shares directly from the estate of the founder of Applause. There are 100,000 shares of Applause Inc. stock outstanding.

Apr. 14. Received the regular cash dividend of $1.10 a share and a 2% stock dividend on the Mode Corporation stock.

July 26. Sold 1,000 shares of Mode Corporation stock at 32. The broker deducted commission and other costs of $125, remitting the balance.

Dec. 15. Received a cash dividend at the new rate of $1.20 a share on the Mode Corporation stock.

    31. Received $12,500 of cash dividends on Applause Inc. stock. Applause Inc. reported net income of $325,000 in 2009. Encore Design uses the equity method of accounting for its investment in Applause Inc.

Instructions
Journalize the entries for the preceding transactions.

Special Activities

SA 12-1
Equity method disclosure

The following note to the consolidated financial statements for Goodyear Tire & Rubber Company relates to the principles of consolidation used in preparing the financial statements:

> *The Company's investments in 20% to 50% owned companies in which it has the ability to exercise significant influence over operating and financial policies are accounted for by the equity method. Accordingly, the Company's share of the earnings of these companies is included in consolidated net income.*

➤ Is it a requirement that Goodyear use the equity method in this situation? Explain.

SA 12-2
Special charges analysis

The two-year comparative income statements and a note disclosure for Mercury Shoes Inc. were as follows:

Income Statement
Mercury Shoes Inc.
For the Years Ended December 31, 2008 and 2007

	2008	2007
Sales	$510,000	$430,000
Cost of merchandise sold	224,400	193,500
Gross profit	$285,600	$236,500
Selling and administrative expenses	122,400	107,500
Loss on fixed asset impairment	127,500	—
Income from operations	$ 35,700	$129,000
Income tax expense	14,280	51,600
Net income	$ 21,420	$ 77,400

Note: A fixed asset impairment of $127,500 was recognized in 2008 as the result of abandoning an order management software system. The system project was started in early 2007 and ran into significant delays and performance problems throughout 2008. It was determined that there was no incremental benefit from completing the system. Thus, the accumulated costs associated with the system were written off.

1. Divide each amount in the 2008 and 2007 income statements by total sales for the given year.
2. ➤ Interpret the performance of the company in 2008.

SA 12-3
Comprehensive income

The Stockholders' Equity section of Yum! Brands, Inc., the operator of Pizza Hut, KFC, and Taco Bell restaurants, for two recent comparative dates was as follows:

Yum! Brands, Inc.
Stockholders' Equity (selected items)
December 31, 2005 and December 31, 2004
(in millions)

	Dec. 31, 2005	Dec. 31, 2004
Common stock, no par value	$ 0	$ 659
Retained earnings	1,619	1,067
Accumulated other comprehensive income (loss)	(170)	(131)
Total stockholders' equity	$1,449	$1,595

1. What is the "other" comprehensive income or loss for the year ended December 31, 2005?
2. ➤ Explain the concept of other comprehensive income.

SA 12-4
Ethics and professional conduct in business

ETHICS

Dillon Osborn is the president and chief operating officer of Dollars N' Sense Corporation, a developer of personal financial planning software. During the past year, Dollars N' Sense Corporation was forced to sell 10 acres of land to the city of Houston for expansion of a freeway exit. The corporation fought the sale; but after condemnation hearings, a judge ordered it to sell the land. Because of the land's location and the fact that Dollars N' Sense Corporation had purchased the land over 15 years ago, the corporation recorded a $0.20-per-share gain on the sale. Always looking to turn a negative into a positive, Dillon has decided to announce the corporation's earnings per share of $1.05, without identifying the $0.20 impact of selling the land. Although he will retain majority ownership, Dillon plans on selling 20,000 of his shares in the corporation sometime within the next month.

Are Dillon's plans to announce earnings per share of $1.05 without mentioning the $0.20 impact of selling the land ethical and professional?

SA 12-5
Reporting extraordinary item

Sunshine Fruit Co. is in the process of preparing its annual financial statements. Sunshine Fruit is a large citrus grower located in central Florida. The following is a discussion between Curtis Kirk, the controller, and Liz Gwinn, the chief executive officer and president of Sunshine Fruit Co.

Liz: Curtis, I've got a question about your rough draft of this year's income statement.
Curtis: Sure, Liz. What's your question?
Liz: Well, your draft shows a net loss of $750,000.
Curtis: That's right. We'd have had a profit, except for this year's frost damage. I figured that the frost destroyed over 30% of our crop. We had a good year otherwise.
Liz: That's my concern. I estimated that if we eliminate the frost damage, we'd show a profit of . . . let's see . . . about $250,000.
Curtis: That sounds about right.
Liz: This income statement seems misleading. Why can't we show the loss on the frost damage separately? That way the bank and our outside investors will be able to see that this year's loss is just temporary. I'd hate to get them upset over nothing.
Curtis: Maybe we can do something. I recall from my accounting courses something about showing unusual items separately. Let's see . . . yes, I remember. They're called extraordinary items.
Liz: Well, we haven't had any frost damage in over five years. This year's damage is certainly extraordinary. Let's do it!

Discuss the appropriateness of revising Sunshine Fruit's income statement to report the frost damage separately as an extraordinary item.

SA 12-6
Extraordinary items and discontinued operations

REAL WORLD

Group Project

Internet Project

In groups of three or four, search company annual reports, news releases, or the Internet for extraordinary items and announcements of discontinued operations. Identify the most unusual extraordinary item in your group. Also, select a discontinued operation of a well-known company that might be familiar to other students or might interest them.

Prepare a brief analysis of the earnings per share impact of both the extraordinary item and the discontinued operation. Estimate the *potential* impact on the company's market price by multiplying the current price-earnings ratio by the earnings per share amount of each item.

One Internet site that has annual reports is EDGAR (Electronic Data Gathering, Analysis, and Retrieval), the electronic archives of financial statements filed with the Securities and Exchange Commission. SEC documents can be retrieved using the EdgarScan service from PricewaterhouseCoopers at **http://edgarscan.pwcglobal.com**.

To obtain annual report information, type in a company name in the appropriate space. EdgarScan will list the reports available to you for the company you've selected. Select the most recent annual report filing, identified as a 10-K or 10-K405. EdgarScan provides an outline of the report, including the separate financial statements. You can double click the income statement and balance sheet for the selected company into an Excel™ spreadsheet for further analysis.

Answers to Self-Examination Questions

1. **A**   The amount of income tax deferred to future years is $16,000 (answer A), determined as follows:

Depreciation expense, MACRS	$100,000
Depreciation expense, straight-line method	60,000
Excess expense in determining taxable income	$ 40,000
Income tax rate	× 40%
Income tax deferred to future years	$ 16,000

2. **A**   Events and transactions that are distinguished by their unusual nature and by the infrequency of their occurrence, such as a gain on condemning land for public use, are reported in the income statement as extraordinary items (answer A). A restructuring charge (answer C) and fixed asset impairment (answer D) are unusual items that are related to different accounting events than land condemnation.

3. **B**   The difference between the cost of temporary investments held as available-for-sale securities and their market value is reported as an unrealized gain, net of applicable income taxes, as shown below.

Market value of investments	$120,000
Cost of investments	100,000
	$ 20,000
Applicable taxes (40%)	8,000
Unrealized gain, net of taxes	$ 12,000

The unrealized gain of $12,000 (answer B) is reported on the balance sheet as an addition to the cost of the investments and as part of other comprehensive income.

4. **C**   Under the equity method of accounting for investments in stocks, Cisneros Corporation records its share of both net income and dividends of Harrell Inc. in Investment in Harrell Inc. Stock. Thus, Investment in Harrell Inc. Stock would increase by $82,500 [($150,000 × 75%) − ($40,000 × 75%)] for the current year. $30,000 (answer B) is only Cisneros Corporation's share of Harrell's dividends for the current year. $112,500 (answer D) is only Cisneros Corporation's share of Harrell's net income for the year.

5. **C**   Price-Earnings Ratio =

$$\frac{\text{Market Price per Common Share}}{\text{Earnings per Share}}, \text{ or}$$

$$\frac{\$60}{(\$800,000 - \$50,000)/200,000} = 16$$

Bonds Payable and Investments in Bonds

© UNDER ARMOUR®/*PRNEWSFOTO (AP TOPIC GALLERY)*

objectives

After studying this chapter, you should be able to:

1 *Compute the potential impact of long-term borrowing on earnings per share.*

2 *Describe the characteristics, terminology, and pricing of bonds payable.*

3 *Journalize entries for bonds payable.*

4 *Describe and illustrate the payment and redemption of bonds payable.*

5 *Journalize entries for the purchase, interest, discount and premium amortization, and sale of bond investments.*

6 *Prepare a corporation balance sheet.*

Under Armour®

Most of us don't have enough money in our bank accounts to buy a house or a car by simply writing a check. Just imagine if you had to save the complete purchase price of a house before you could buy it! To help us make these types of purchases, banks will typically lend us the money, as long as we agree to repay the loan along with interest in smaller payments in the future. Loans such as this, or long-term debt, allow us to purchase assets such as houses and cars today, which benefit us over the long term.

The use of debt can also help a business reach its objectives. Most businesses have to borrow money in order to acquire assets that they will use to generate income. For example, Under Armour®, a maker of performance athletic clothing, uses debt to acquire assets that it needs to manufacture and sell its prod-

ucts. Since it began in 1995, the company has used long-term debt to transform itself from a small business to a leading athletic wear company. The company now sells products in over 8,000 retail stores across the world. In addition, Under Armour® products are used by a number of teams in the National Football League, Major League Baseball, the National Hockey League, and in Olympic sports.

While debt can help companies like Under Armour® grow to achieve financial success, too much debt can be a financial burden that may even lead to bankruptcy. Just like individuals, businesses must manage debt wisely. In this chapter, we will discuss the nature of, accounting for, analysis of, and investments in long-term debt.

Financing Corporations

objective **1**

Compute the potential impact of long-term borrowing on earnings per share.

REAL WORLD

Bonds of major corporations are actively traded on bond exchanges. You can purchase bonds through a financial services firm, such as Merrill Lynch & Co. Inc., A. G. Edwards & Sons, Inc., or Edward Jones.

As discussed above, both individuals and corporations use debt to purchase assets or resources today that they might otherwise be unable to afford. Corporations often finance their operations by purchasing on credit and issuing notes or bonds. We have discussed accounts payable and notes payable in earlier chapters. A **bond** is simply a form of an interest-bearing note. Like a note, a bond requires periodic interest payments, and the face amount must be repaid at the maturity date. Bondholders are creditors of the issuing corporation, and their claims on the assets of the corporation rank ahead of stockholders.

One of the many factors that influence the decision to issue debt or equity is the effect of each alternative on earnings per share. To illustrate the possible effects, assume that a corporation's board of directors is considering the following alternative plans for financing a $4,000,000 company:

	Plan 1	Plan 2	Plan 3
Issue 12% bonds	—	—	$2,000,000
Issue 9% preferred stock, $50 par value	—	$2,000,000	1,000,000
Issue common stock, $10 par value	$4,000,000	2,000,000	1,000,000
	$4,000,000	$4,000,000	$4,000,000

In each case, we assume that the stocks or bonds are issued at their par or face amount. The corporation is expecting to earn $800,000 annually, before deducting interest on the bonds and income taxes estimated at 40% of income. Exhibit 1 shows the effect of the three plans on the income of the corporation and the earnings per share on common stock.

EXHIBIT 1

Effect of Alternative Financing Plans— $800,000 Earnings

	Plan 1	Plan 2	Plan 3
12% bonds	—	—	$2,000,000
Preferred 9% stock, $50 par	—	$2,000,000	1,000,000
Common stock, $10 par	$4,000,000	2,000,000	1,000,000
Total	$4,000,000	$4,000,000	$4,000,000
Earnings before interest and income tax ...	$ 800,000	$ 800,000	$ 800,000
Deduct interest on bonds	—	—	240,000
Income before income tax	$ 800,000	$ 800,000	$ 560,000
Deduct income tax	320,000	320,000	224,000
Net income	$ 480,000	$ 480,000	$ 336,000
Dividends on preferred stock	—	180,000	90,000
Available for dividends on common stock ..	$ 480,000	$ 300,000	$ 246,000
Shares of common stock outstanding	÷ 400,000	÷ 200,000	÷ 100,000
Earnings per share on common stock	$ 1.20	$ 1.50	$ 2.46

When interest rates are low, corporations usually finance their operations with debt. For example, as interest rates fell in recent years, corporations issued large amounts of new debt.

Exhibit 1 indicates that Plan 3 yields the highest earnings per share on common stock and is thus the most attractive for common stockholders. If the estimated earnings are more than $800,000, the difference between the earnings per share to common stockholders under Plan 1 and Plan 3 is even greater.[1] However, if smaller earnings occur, Plans 2 and 3 become less attractive to common stockholders. To illustrate, the effect of earnings of $440,000 rather than $800,000 is shown in Exhibit 2.

In addition to the effect on earnings per share, the board of directors should consider other factors in deciding whether to issue debt or equity. For example, once bonds are issued, periodic interest payments and repayment of the face value of the bonds are beyond the control of the corporation. That is, if these payments are not made, the bondholders could seek court action and force the company into bankruptcy. In contrast, a corporation is not legally obligated to pay dividends.

EXHIBIT 2

Effect of Alternative Financing Plans— $440,000 Earnings

	Plan 1	Plan 2	Plan 3
12% bonds	—	—	$2,000,000
Preferred 9% stock, $50 par	—	$2,000,000	1,000,000
Common stock, $10 par	$4,000,000	2,000,000	1,000,000
Total	$4,000,000	$4,000,000	$4,000,000
Earnings before interest and income tax ...	$ 440,000	$ 440,000	$ 440,000
Deduct interest on bonds	—	—	240,000
Income before income tax	$ 440,000	$ 440,000	$ 200,000
Deduct income tax	176,000	176,000	80,000
Net income	$ 264,000	$ 264,000	$ 120,000
Dividends on preferred stock	—	180,000	90,000
Available for dividends on common stock ..	$ 264,000	$ 84,000	$ 30,000
Shares of common stock outstanding	÷ 400,000	÷ 200,000	÷ 100,000
Earnings per share on common stock	$ 0.66	$ 0.42	$ 0.30

1 The higher earnings per share under Plan 3 is due to a finance concept known as *leverage*. This concept is discussed further in a later chapter.

Example Exercise 13-1

objective **1**

Gonzales Co. is considering the following alternative plans for financing its company:

	Plan 1	Plan 2
Issue 10% bonds (at face value)	—	$2,000,000
Issue common stock, $10 par	$3,000,000	1,000,000

Income tax is estimated at 40% of income.

Determine the earnings per share of common stock under the two alternative financing plans, assuming income before bond interest and income tax is $750,000.

Follow My Example 13-1

	Plan 1	Plan 2
Earnings before bond interest and income tax	$750,000	$750,000
Bond interest	0	200,000[2]
Balance	$750,000	$550,000
Income tax	300,000[1]	220,000[3]
Net income	$450,000	$330,000
Dividends on preferred stock	0	0
Earnings available for common stock	$450,000	$330,000
Number of common shares	/300,000	/100,000
Earnings per share on common stock	$ 1.50	$ 3.30

[1]$750,000 × 40%   [2]$2,000,000 × 10%   [3]$550,000 × 40%

For Practice: PE 13-1A, PE 13-1B

Characteristics, Terminology, and Pricing of Bonds Payable

objective **2**

Describe the characteristics, terminology, and pricing of bonds payable.

In addition to their face values, interest rates, interest payment dates, and maturity dates, bonds may differ in a variety of ways. In this section, we describe the common characteristics of bonds and how bonds may differ from one another. In doing so, we introduce common terms used to describe types of bonds. In addition, we describe and illustrate how the price investors are willing to pay for a bond is determined.

BOND CHARACTERISTICS AND TERMINOLOGY

A corporation that issues bonds enters into a contract, called a **bond indenture** or *trust indenture*, with the bondholders. A bond issue is normally divided into a number of individual bonds. Usually, the face value of each bond, called the *principal*, is $1,000 or a multiple of $1,000. The interest on bonds may be payable annually, semiannually, or quarterly. Most bonds pay interest semiannually.

The prices of bonds are quoted as a percentage of the bonds' face value. Thus, investors could purchase or sell Wal-Mart bonds quoted at 113.84 for $1,138.40. Likewise, bonds quoted at 109 could be purchased or sold for $1,090.

When all bonds of an issue mature at the same time, they are called *term bonds*. If the maturities are spread over several dates, they are called *serial bonds*. For example, one-tenth of an issue of $1,000,000 bonds, or $100,000, may mature 16 years from the issue date, another $100,000 in the 17th year, and so on, until the final $100,000 matures in the 25th year.

Bonds that may be exchanged for other securities, such as common stock, are called *convertible bonds*. Bonds that a corporation reserves the right to redeem before their maturity are called *callable bonds*. Bonds issued on the basis of the general credit of the corporation are called *debenture bonds*.

REAL WORLD

Time Inc. 7.625% bonds maturing in 2031 were listed as selling for 112.1081 on January 24, 2006.

PRICING OF BONDS PAYABLE

When a corporation issues bonds, the price that buyers are willing to pay for the bonds depends upon the following three factors:

1. The face amount of the bonds, which is the amount due at the maturity date.
2. The periodic interest to be paid on the bonds.
3. The market rate of interest.

Market = Contract Rate

Selling price of bond = $1,000

$1,000 BOND

Market Rate > Contract Rate

Selling price of bond < $1,000

$1,000 BOND — Discount

Market Rate < Contract Rate

Selling price of bond > $1,000

$1,000 BOND + Premium

The face amount and the periodic interest to be paid on the bonds are identified in the bond indenture. The periodic interest is expressed as a percentage of the face amount of the bond. This percentage or rate of interest is called the **contract rate** or *coupon rate*.

The *market* or **effective rate of interest** is determined by transactions between buyers and sellers of similar bonds. The market rate of interest is affected by a variety of factors, including investors' assessment of current economic conditions as well as future expectations.

If the contract rate of interest equals the market rate of interest, the bonds will sell at their face amount. If the market rate is higher than the contract rate, the bonds will sell at a **discount**, or less than their face amount. Why is this the case? Buyers are not willing to pay the face amount for bonds whose contract rate is lower than the market rate. The discount, in effect, represents the amount necessary to make up for the difference in the market and the contract interest rates. In contrast, if the market rate is lower than the contract rate, the bonds will sell at a **premium**, or more than their face amount. In this case, buyers are willing to pay more than the face amount for bonds whose contract rate is higher than the market rate.

The face amount of the bonds and the periodic interest on the bonds represent cash to be received by the buyer in the future. The buyer determines how much to pay for the bonds by computing the present value of these future cash receipts, using the market rate of interest. The concept of present value is based on the time value of money.

The time value of money concept recognizes that an amount of cash to be received today is worth more than the same amount of cash to be received in the future. For example, what would you rather have: $100 today or $100 one year from now? You would rather have the $100 today because it could be invested to earn income. For example, if the $100 could be invested to earn 10% per year, the $100 will accumulate to $110 ($100 plus $10 earnings) in one year. In this sense, you can think of the $100 in hand today as the **present value** of $110 to be received a year from today. This present value is illustrated in the following time line:

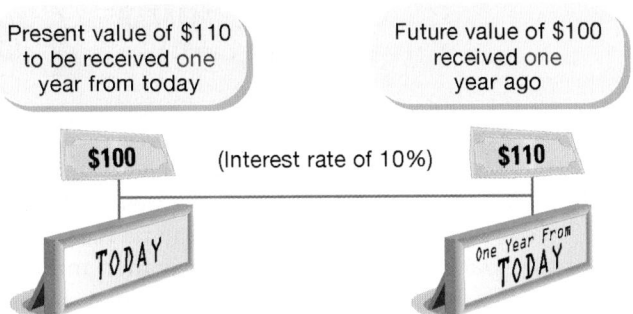

Present value of $110 to be received one year from today

Future value of $100 received one year ago

$100 (Interest rate of 10%) $110

TODAY

One Year From TODAY

A related concept to present value is **future value**. In the preceding illustration, the $110 to be received a year from today is the future value of $100 today, assuming an interest rate of 10%.

Present Value of the Face Amount of Bonds The present value of the face amount of bonds is the value today of the amount to be received at a future maturity date. For

Integrity, Objectivity, and Ethics in Business

ETHICS

CREDIT QUALITY

The market rate of interest for a corporate bond is influenced by a number of factors, including the credit quality of the issuer. In June 2002, WorldCom disclosed a massive accounting fraud within the company, prompting credit-rating agencies and bond investors to drastically lower their assessment of the company's credit quality. As a result, the price of WorldCom's $30 billion in bond debt dropped to 15 cents on the dollar, or $4.5 billion in a few short weeks.

example, assume that you are to receive the face value of a $1,000 bond in one year. If the market rate of interest is 10%, the present value of the face value of the $1,000 bond is $909.09 ($1,000/1.10). This present value is illustrated in the following time line:

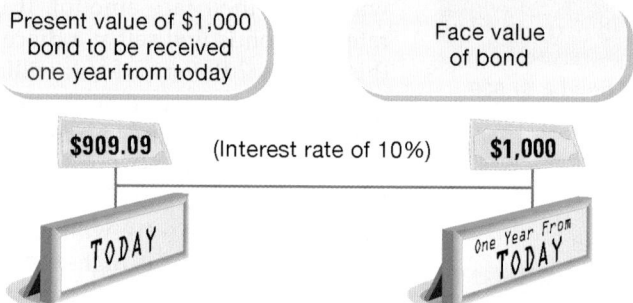

If you are to receive the face value of a $1,000 bond in two years, with interest of 10% compounded at the end of the first year, the present value is $826.45 ($909.09/1.10).[2] We illustrate this present value in the following time line:

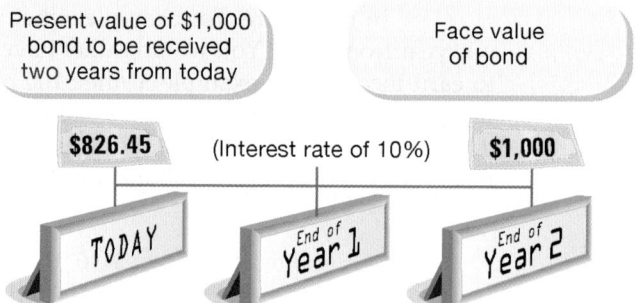

REAL WORLD

Spreadsheet software with built-in present value functions can be used to calculate present values.

You can determine the present value of the face amount of bonds to be received in the future by a time line and a series of divisions. In practice, however, it is easier to use a table of present values. The *present value of $1 table* can be used to find the present value factor for $1 to be received after a number of periods in the future. The face amount of the bonds is then multiplied by this factor to determine its present value. Exhibit 3 is a partial table of the present value of $1.[3]

---

2 Note that the future value of $826.45 in two years, at an interest rate of 10% compounded annually, is $1,000.

3 To simplify the illustrations and homework assignments, the tables presented in this chapter are limited to 10 periods for a small number of interest rates, and the amounts are carried to only five decimal places. Computer programs are available for determining present value factors for any number of interest rates, decimal places, or periods. More complete interest tables are presented in Appendix A.

EXHIBIT 3 — Present Value of $1 at Compound Interest

Periods	5%	5½%	6%	6½%	7%	10%	11%	12%	13%	14%
1	0.95238	0.94787	0.94340	0.93897	0.93458	0.90909	0.90090	0.89286	0.88496	0.87719
2	0.90703	0.89845	0.89000	0.88166	0.87344	0.82645	0.81162	0.79719	0.78315	0.76947
3	0.86384	0.85161	0.83962	0.82785	0.81630	0.75132	0.73119	0.71178	0.69305	0.67497
4	0.82270	0.80722	0.79209	0.77732	0.76290	0.68301	0.65873	0.63552	0.61332	0.59208
5	0.78353	0.76513	0.74726	0.72988	0.71299	0.62092	0.59345	0.56743	0.54276	0.51937
6	0.74622	0.72525	0.70496	0.68533	0.66634	0.56447	0.53464	0.50663	0.48032	0.45559
7	0.71068	0.68744	0.66506	0.64351	0.62275	0.51316	0.48166	0.45235	0.42506	0.39964
8	0.67684	0.65160	0.62741	0.60423	0.58201	0.46651	0.43393	0.40388	0.37616	0.35056
9	0.64461	0.61763	0.59190	0.56735	0.54393	0.42410	0.39092	0.36061	0.33288	0.30751
10	0.61391	0.58543	0.55840	0.53273	0.50835	0.38554	0.35218	0.32197	0.29459	0.26974

Exhibit 3 indicates that the present value of $1 to be received in two years with a market rate of interest of 10% a year is 0.82645. Multiplying the $1,000 face amount of the bond in the preceding example by 0.82645 yields $826.45.

In Exhibit 3, the Periods column represents the number of compounding periods, and the percentage columns represent the compound interest rate per period. For example, 10% for two years compounded *annually*, as in the preceding example, is 10% for two periods. Likewise, 10% for two years compounded *semiannually* would be 5% (10% per year/2 semiannual periods) for four periods (2 years × 2 semiannual periods). Similarly, 10% for three years compounded semiannually would be 5% (10%/2) for six periods (3 years × 2 semiannual periods).

Example Exercise 13-2 — objective 2

Using Exhibit 3, what is the present value of $4,000 to be received in five years, if the market rate of interest is 10% compounded annually?

Follow My Example 13-2

$2,483.68. [$4,000 × 0.62092 (Present value of $1 for 5 periods at 10%)]

For Practice: PE 13-2A, PE 13-2B

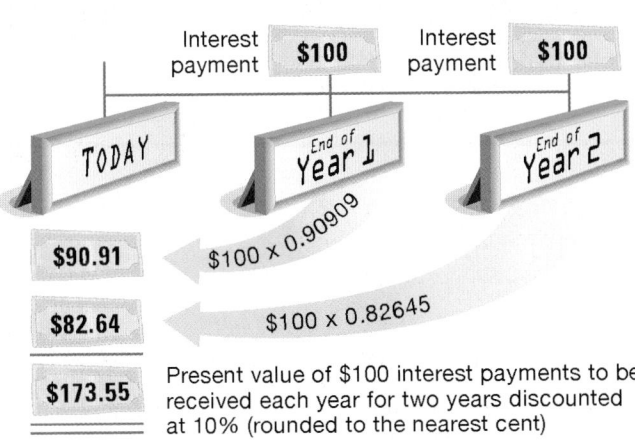

Interest payment $100   Interest payment $100

TODAY   End of Year 1   End of Year 2

$90.91 $100 × 0.90909

$82.64 $100 × 0.82645

$173.55

Present value of $100 interest payments to be received each year for two years discounted at 10% (rounded to the nearest cent)

Present Value of the Periodic Bond Interest Payments The present value of the periodic bond interest payments is the value today of the amount of interest to be received at the end of each interest period. Such a series of equal cash payments at fixed intervals is called an **annuity**.

The **present value of an annuity** is the sum of the present values of each cash flow. To illustrate, assume that the $1,000 bond in the preceding example pays interest of 10% annually and that the market rate of interest is also 10%. In addition, assume that the bond matures at the end of two years. The present value of the two interest payments of $100 ($1,000 × 10%) is $173.55, as shown in the time line to the left. It can be determined by using the present value table shown in Exhibit 3.

Instead of using present value of amount tables, such as Exhibit 3, separate present value tables are normally used for annuities. Exhibit 4 is a partial table of the *present value of an annuity of $1* at compound interest. It shows the present value of $1 to be received at the end of each period for various compound rates of interest. For example, the present value of $100 to be received at the end of each of the next two years at 10% compound interest per period is $173.55 ($100 × 1.73554). This amount is the same amount that we computed previously.

EXHIBIT 4   **Present Value of Annuity of $1 at Compound Interest**

Periods	5%	5½%	6%	6½%	7%	10%	11%	12%	13%	14%
1	0.95238	0.94787	0.94340	0.93897	0.93458	0.90909	0.90090	0.89286	0.88496	0.87719
2	1.85941	1.84632	1.83339	1.82063	1.80802	1.73554	1.71252	1.69005	1.66810	1.64666
3	2.72325	2.69793	2.67301	2.64848	2.62432	2.48685	2.44371	2.40183	2.36115	2.32163
4	3.54595	3.50515	3.46511	3.42580	3.38721	3.16987	3.10245	3.03735	2.97447	2.91371
5	4.32948	4.27028	4.21236	4.15568	4.10020	3.79079	3.69590	3.60478	3.51723	3.43308
6	5.07569	4.99553	4.91732	4.84101	4.76654	4.35526	4.23054	4.11141	3.99755	3.88867
7	5.78637	5.68297	5.58238	5.48452	5.38929	4.86842	4.71220	4.56376	4.42261	4.28830
8	6.46321	6.33457	6.20979	6.08875	5.97130	5.33493	5.14612	4.96764	4.79677	4.63886
9	7.10782	6.95220	6.80169	6.65610	6.51523	5.75902	5.53705	5.32825	5.13166	4.94637
10	7.72174	7.53763	7.36009	7.18883	7.02358	6.14457	5.88923	5.65022	5.42624	5.21612

As we stated earlier, the amount buyers are willing to pay for a bond is the sum of the present value of the face value and the periodic interest payments, calculated by using the market rate of interest. In our example, this calculation is as follows:

Present value of face value of $1,000 due in 2 years,
  at 10% compounded annually: $1,000 × 0.82645
  (present value factor of $1 for 2 periods at 10%) .... $ 826.45
Present value of 2 annual interest payments of $100,
  at 10% compounded annually: $100 × 1.73554
  (present value of annuity of $1 for 2 periods at 10%) 173.55
Total present value of bonds $1,000.00

In this example, the market rate and the contract rate of interest are the same. Thus, the present value is the same as the face value.

Example Exercise 13-3   objective **2**

Calculate the present value of a $20,000, 5%, five-year bond that pays $1,000 ($20,000 × 5%) interest annually, if the market rate of interest is 5%. Use Exhibits 3 and 4 for computing present values.

Follow My Example 13-3

Present value of face amount of $20,000 due in 5 years,
  at 5% compounded annually: $20,000 × 0.78353
  (present value factor of $1 for 5 periods at 5%) $15,671*

Present value of 5 annual interest payments of $1,000,
  at 5% interest compounded annually: $1,000 × 4.32948
  (present value of annuity of $1 for 5 periods at 5%) 4,329*
Total present value of bonds $20,000

*Rounded to the nearest dollar.

For Practice: PE 13-3A, PE 13-3B

Accounting for Bonds Payable

objective **3**

Journalize entries for bonds payable.

In the preceding section, we described and illustrated how present value concepts are used in determining how much buyers are willing to pay for bonds. In this section, we describe and illustrate how corporations record the issuance of bonds and the payment of bond interest.

BONDS ISSUED AT FACE AMOUNT

To illustrate the journal entries for issuing bonds, assume that on January 1, 2007, a corporation issues for cash $100,000 of 12%, five-year bonds, with interest of $6,000 payable *semiannually*. The market rate of interest at the time the bonds are issued is 12%. Since the contract rate and the market rate of interest are the same, the bonds will sell at their face amount. This amount is the sum of (1) the present value of the face amount of $100,000 to be repaid in five years and (2) the present value of 10 *semi-annual* interest payments of $6,000 each. This computation and a time line are shown below.

Present value of face amount of $100,000 due in 5 years,
    at 12% compounded semiannually: $100,000 × 0.55840
    (present value of $1 for 10 periods at 6%) .... $ 55,840
Present value of 10 semiannual interest payments of $6,000,
    at 12% compounded semiannually: $6,000 × 7.36009
    (present value of annuity of $1 for 10 periods at 6%) 44,160*
Total present value of bonds $100,000

*Because the present value tables are rounded to five decimal places, minor rounding differences may appear in the illustrations.

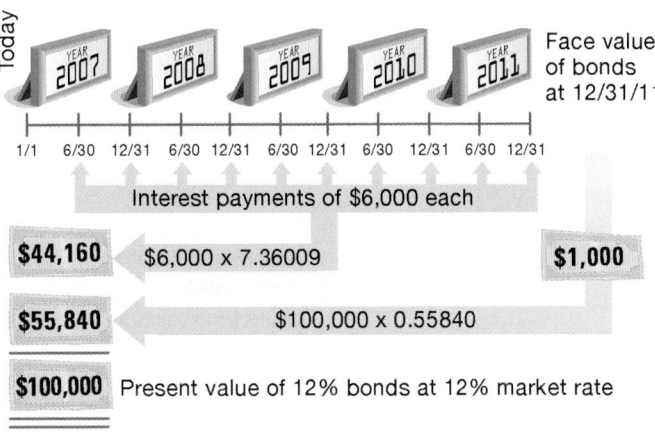

The following entry records the issuing of the $100,000 bonds at their face amount:

2007 Jan.	1	Cash		100 0 0 0 00	
		Bonds Payable			100 0 0 0 00
		Issued $100,000 bonds payable at			
		face amount.			

Every six months after the bonds have been issued, interest payments of $6,000 are made. The first interest payment is recorded as shown at the top of the following page.

June	30	Interest Expense		6 0 0 0 00	
		Cash			6 0 0 0 00
		Paid six months' interest on bonds.			

At the maturity date, the payment of the principal of $100,000 is recorded as follows:

2011 Dec.	31	Bonds Payable		100 0 0 0 00	
		Cash			100 0 0 0 00
		Paid bond principal at maturity date.			

BONDS ISSUED AT A DISCOUNT

What if the market rate of interest is higher than the contract rate of interest? If the market rate of interest is 13% and the contract rate is 12% on the five-year, $100,000 bonds, the bonds will sell at a discount. The present value of these bonds is calculated as follows:

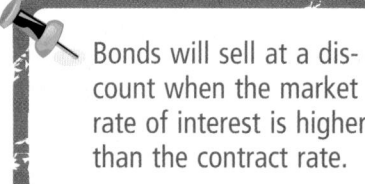

Bonds will sell at a discount when the market rate of interest is higher than the contract rate.

Present value of face amount of $100,000 due in 5 years,
  at 13% compounded semiannually: $100,000 × 0.53273
  (present value of $1 for 10 periods at 6½%) $53,273
Present value of 10 semiannual interest payments of $6,000,
  at 13% compounded semiannually: $6,000 × 7.18883
  (present value of an annuity of $1 for 10 periods at 6½%) 43,133
Total present value of bonds $96,406

The two present values that make up the total are both less than the related amounts in the preceding example. This is because the market rate of interest was 12% in the first example, while the market rate of interest is 13% in this example. The present value of a future amount becomes less and less as the interest rate used to compute the present value increases.

The entry to record the issuing of the $100,000 bonds at a discount is shown below.

2007 Jan.	1	Cash		96 4 0 6 00	
		Discount on Bonds Payable		3 5 9 4 00	
		Bonds Payable			100 0 0 0 00
		Issued $100,000 bonds at discount.			

The $3,594 discount may be viewed as the amount that is needed to entice investors to accept a contract rate of interest that is below the market rate. You may think of the discount as the market's way of adjusting a bond's contract rate of interest to the higher market rate of interest. Using this logic, generally accepted accounting principles require that bond discounts be amortized as interest expense over the life of the bond.

Example Exercise 13-4   objective 3

On the first day of the fiscal year, a company issues a $1,000,000, 6%, five-year bond that pays semiannual interest of $30,000 ($1,000,000 × 6% × ½), receiving cash of $845,562. Journalize the entry to record the issuance of the bonds.

(continued)

AMORTIZING A BOND DISCOUNT

There are two methods of amortizing a bond discount: (1) the *straight-line method* and (2) the **effective interest rate method**, often called the *interest method*. Both methods amortize the same total amount of discount over the life of the bonds. The interest method is required by generally accepted accounting principles. However, the straight-line method is acceptable if the results obtained do not materially differ from the results that would be obtained by using the interest method. Because the straight-line method illustrates the basic concept of amortizing discounts and is simpler, we will use it in this chapter. We illustrate the interest method in an appendix to this chapter.

The straight-line method of amortizing a bond discount provides for amortization in equal periodic amounts. Applying this method to the preceding example yields amortization of $\frac{1}{10}$ of $3,594, or $359.40, each half year. The amount of the interest expense on the bonds is the same, $6,359.40 ($6,000 + $359.40), for each half year. The entry to record the first interest payment and the amortization of the related discount follows.

2007					
June	30	Interest Expense	6 3 5 9 40		
		Discount on Bonds Payable		3 5 9 40	
		Cash		6 0 0 0 00	
		Paid semiannual interest and			
		amortized $\frac{1}{10}$ of bond discount.			

BONDS ISSUED AT A PREMIUM

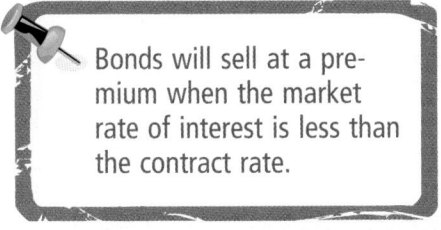
Bonds will sell at a premium when the market rate of interest is less than the contract rate.

If the market rate of interest is 11% and the contract rate is 12% on the five-year, $100,000 bonds, the bonds will sell at a premium. The present value of these bonds is computed as shown at the top of the following page.

Present value of face amount of $100,000 due in 5 years,
  at 11% compounded semiannually: $100,000 × 0.58543
  (present value of $1 for 10 periods at 5½%) .... $ 58,543
Present value of 10 semiannual interest payments of $6,000,
  at 11% compounded semiannually: $6,000 × 7.53763
  (present value of an annuity of $1 for 10 periods at 5½%) 45,226
Total present value of bonds $103,769

The entry to record the issuing of the bonds is as follows:

2007 Jan.	1	Cash	103 7 6 9 00	
		Bonds Payable		100 0 0 0 00
		Premium on Bonds Payable		3 7 6 9 00
		Issued $100,000 bonds at a premium.		

Example Exercise 13-6

objective **3**

A company issues a $2,000,000, 12%, five-year bond that pays semiannual interest of $120,000 ($2,000,000 × 12% × ½), receiving cash of $2,154,435. Journalize the bond issuance.

Follow My Example 13-6

Cash 2,154,435
  Bonds Payable 2,000,000
  Premium on Bonds Payable 154,435

For Practice: PE 13-6A, PE 13-6B

AMORTIZING A BOND PREMIUM

The amortization of bond premiums is basically the same as that for bond discounts, except that interest expense is decreased. In the above example, the straight-line method yields amortization of ¹⁄₁₀ of $3,769, or $376.90, each half year. The entry to record the first interest payment and the amortization of the related premium is as follows:

2007 June	30	Interest Expense	5 6 2 3 10	
		Premium on Bonds Payable	3 7 6 90	
		Cash		6 0 0 0 00
		Paid semiannual interest and		
		amortized ¹⁄₁₀ of bond premium.		

Example Exercise 13-7

objective **3**

Using the bond from Example Exercise 13-6, journalize the first interest payment and the amortization of the related bond premium.

Follow My Example 13-7

Interest Expense 104,556
Premium on Bonds Payable 15,444
  Cash 120,000
    Paid interest and amortized the bond premium ($154,435/10).

For Practice: PE 13-7A, PE 13-7B

ZERO-COUPON BONDS

Some corporations issue bonds that provide for only the payment of the face amount at the maturity date. Such bonds are called *zero-coupon bonds*. Because they do not provide for interest payments, these bonds sell at a large discount. For example, Merrill Lynch & Co. Inc.'s zero-coupon bonds maturing in 2028 were selling for 21.50.

The issuing price of zero-coupon bonds is the present value of their face amount. To illustrate, if the market rate of interest is 13%, the present value of $100,000 zero-coupon, five-year bonds is calculated as follows:

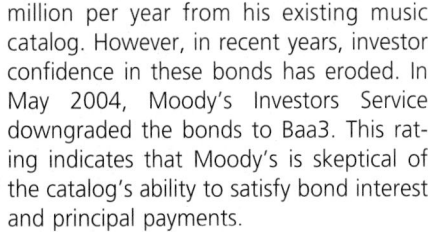

Some bonds with high contract rates, as well as some zero-coupon bonds, are issued by weak companies. Because such bonds are high-risk bonds, they are called **junk bonds**.

> Present value of $100,000 due in 5 years, at 13%
> compounded semiannually: $100,000 × 0.53273
> (present value of $1 for 10 periods at 6½%) $53,273

The accounting for zero-coupon bonds is similar to that for interest-bearing bonds that have been sold at a discount. The discount is amortized as interest expense over the life of the bonds. The entry to record the issuing of the bonds is as follows:

2007 Jan.	1	Cash		53 2 7 3 00	
		Discount on Bonds Payable		46 7 2 7 00	
		Bonds Payable			100 0 0 0 00
		Issued $100,000 zero-coupon			
		bonds.			

Business Connections

CH-CH-CH-CHANGES IN BOND TRENDS

How would you like to tune into some of the royalties from your favorite rock star or song? In the past decade, several well-known rock stars have offered bonds backed by future royalties from their hit songs and albums. These include rock icons like James Brown, Rod Stewart, and Iron Maiden.

The trend toward linking music royalties to bonds began when rock star David Bowie packaged royalties from his 25-album catalog of over 300 songs as a $55 million bond issue. These "Bowie Bonds" had an average maturity of 10 years and paid 7.9% annual interest. On the issue date, Moody's Investors Service gave the bonds its highest rating, AAA. Potential investors were confident in the bonds, knowing that Bowie never sold fewer than

a million albums a year prior to the bond issuance. In addition, Bowie reportedly had a steady cash flow of $1 million per year from his existing music catalog. However, in recent years, investor confidence in these bonds has eroded. In May 2004, Moody's Investors Service downgraded the bonds to Baa3. This rating indicates that Moody's is skeptical of the catalog's ability to satisfy bond interest and principal payments.

While Bowie Bonds have fallen on hard times in recent years, they did give rise to a variety of similar bonds that were backed by the future earnings of intellectual property. These include intangibles like copyrights from music and films, patents from prescription drugs and technology, trade secrets, and Internet Web site names.

Payment and Redemption of Bonds Payable

objective 4

Describe and illustrate the payment and redemption of bonds payable.

The face value of bonds payable should be paid at the maturity date of the bonds. The entry to record the payment of bonds at their maturity date is a debit to Bonds Payable and a credit to Cash.

The bond indenture may require that funds for the payment of the face value of the bonds at maturity be set aside over the life of the bond issue. A bond indenture may restrict dividend payments to stockholders as a means of increasing the likelihood that the bonds will be paid at maturity. Finally, the bond indenture may allow for the early payment or redemption of the bond issue.

BOND SINKING FUNDS

Since the payment of bonds normally involves a large amount of cash, a bond indenture may require that cash be periodically transferred into a special cash fund over the life of the bond issue. Doing so ensures that an adequate amount of cash will be available at the maturity date for the payment of the face amount of the bonds. This special type of cash fund is called a **sinking fund**.

When cash is transferred to the sinking fund, it is recorded in an account called *Sinking Fund Cash*. When investments are purchased with the sinking fund cash, they are recorded in an account called *Sinking Fund Investments*. As income (interest or dividends) is received, it is recorded in an account called *Sinking Fund Revenue*.

Sinking fund revenue represents earnings of the corporation and is reported in the income statement as other income. The cash and the securities making up the sinking fund are reported in the balance sheet as investments, immediately below the Current Assets section.

A bond indenture may restrict dividend payments to stockholders as a means of increasing the likelihood that the bonds will be paid at maturity. In addition to or instead of this restriction, the bond indenture may require that funds for the payment of the face value of the bonds at maturity be set aside over the life of the bond issue. The amounts set aside are kept separate from other assets in the sinking fund.

BOND REDEMPTION

Pacific Bell issued 7.5% bonds, maturing in 2033 but callable in 2023.

A corporation may call or redeem bonds before they mature. This is often done if the market rate of interest declines significantly after the bonds have been issued. In this situation, the corporation may sell new bonds at a lower interest rate and use the funds to redeem the original bond issue. The corporation can thus save on future interest expenses.

A corporation often issues callable bonds to protect itself against significant declines in future interest rates. However, callable bonds are more risky for investors, who may not be able to replace the called bonds with investments paying an equal amount of interest.

Callable bonds can be redeemed by the issuing corporation within the period of time and at the price stated in the bond indenture. Normally, the call price is above the face value. A corporation may also redeem its bonds by purchasing them on the open market.

A corporation usually redeems its bonds at a price different from that of the carrying amount (or book value) of the bonds. The **carrying amount** of bonds payable is the balance of the bonds payable account (face amount of the bonds) less any unamortized discount or plus any unamortized premium. If the price paid for redemption is below the bond carrying amount, the difference in these two amounts is recorded as a gain. If the price paid for the redemption is above the carrying amount, a loss is recorded. Gains and losses on the redemption of bonds are reported in the Other Income and Expense section of the income statement.

To illustrate, assume that on June 30 a corporation has a bond issue of $100,000 outstanding, on which there is an unamortized premium of $4,000. Assuming that the corporation purchases one-fourth ($25,000) of the bonds for $24,000 on June 30, the entry to record the redemption is as follows:

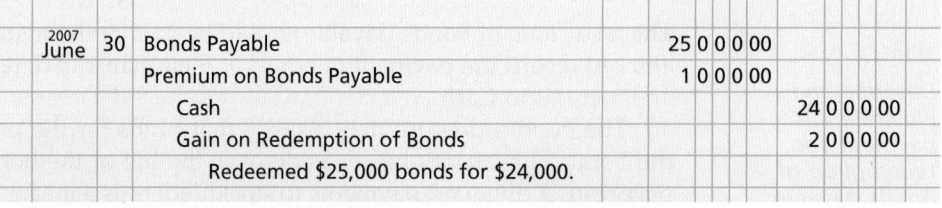

2007 June	30	Bonds Payable		25 0 0 0 00		
		Premium on Bonds Payable		1 0 0 0 00		
		Cash			24 0 0 0 00	
		Gain on Redemption of Bonds			2 0 0 0 00	
		Redeemed $25,000 bonds for $24,000.				

In the preceding entry, only a portion of the premium relating to the redeemed bonds is written off. The difference between the carrying amount of the bonds purchased, $26,000 ($25,000 + $1,000), and the price paid for the redemption, $24,000, is recorded as a gain.

If the corporation calls the entire bond issue for $105,000 on June 30, the entry to record the redemption is as follows:

2007 June	30	Bonds Payable		100 0 0 0 00	
		Premium on Bonds Payable		4 0 0 0 00	
		Loss on Redemption of Bonds		1 0 0 0 00	
		Cash			105 0 0 0 00
		Redeemed $100,000 bonds for $105,000.			

Example Exercise 13-8 — objective 4

A $500,000 bond issue on which there is an unamortized discount of $40,000 is redeemed for $475,000. Journalize the redemption of the bonds.

Follow My Example 13-8

Bonds Payable	500,000	
Loss on Redemption of Bonds	15,000	
Discount on Bonds Payable		40,000
Cash		475,000

For Practice: PE 13-8A, PE 13-8B

Investments in Bonds

objective 5

Journalize entries for the purchase, interest, discount and premium amortization, and sale of bond investments.

The Walt Disney Company's 5.875% bonds maturing in 2017 were listed as selling for 103.375 on January 20, 2006.

Throughout this chapter, we have discussed bonds and the related transactions of the issuing corporation (the debtor). However, these transactions also affect investors. In this section, we discuss the accounting for bonds from the point of view of investors, and assume that the investor uses the cost principle to account for these investments.

ACCOUNTING FOR BOND INVESTMENTS—PURCHASE, INTEREST, AND AMORTIZATION

Bonds may be purchased either directly from the issuing corporation or through an organized bond exchange. Bond exchanges publish daily bond quotations. These quotations normally include the bond interest rate, maturity date, volume of sales, and the high, low, and closing prices for each corporation's bonds traded during the day. Prices for bonds are quoted as a percentage of the face amount. Thus, the price of a $1,000 bond quoted at 99.5 would be $995, while the price of a bond quoted at 104.25 would be $1,042.50.

As with other assets, the cost of a bond investment includes all costs related to the purchase. For example, for bonds purchased through an exchange, the amount paid as a broker's commission should be included as part of the cost of the investment.

When bonds are purchased between interest dates, the buyer normally pays the seller the interest accrued from the last interest payment date to the date of purchase. The amount of the interest paid is normally debited to *Interest Revenue*, since it is an offset against the amount that will be received at the next interest date.

To illustrate, assume that an investor purchases a $1,000 bond at 102 plus a brokerage fee of $5.30 and accrued interest of $10.20. The investor records the transaction as shown at the top of the following page.

	2007 Apr.	2	Investment in Lewis Co. Bonds	10 2 5 30	
			Interest Revenue	10 20	
			Cash		1 03 5 50

> A premium or discount on a bond investment is recorded in the investment account and is amortized over the remaining life of the bonds.

The cost of the bond is recorded in a single investment account. The face amount of the bond and the premium (or discount) are normally not recorded in separate accounts. This is different from the accounting for bonds payable. Separate premium and discount accounts are usually not used by investors, because they usually do not hold bond investments until the bonds mature.

When bonds held as long-term investments are purchased at a price other than the face amount, the premium or discount should be amortized over the remaining life of the bonds. The amortization of premiums and discounts affects the investment and interest accounts as shown below.

Premium Amortization:			Discount Amortization:		
Interest Revenue	XXX		Investment in Bonds	XXX	
Investment in Bonds		XXX	Interest Revenue		XXX

The amount of the amortization can be determined by using either the straight-line or interest methods. Unlike bonds payable, the amortization of premiums and discounts on bond investments is usually recorded at the end of the period, rather than when interest is received.

To illustrate the accounting for bond investments, assume that on July 1, 2007, Crenshaw Inc. purchases $50,000 of 8% bonds of Deitz Corporation, due in $8\frac{3}{4}$ years. Crenshaw Inc. purchases the bonds directly from Deitz Corporation to yield an effective interest rate of 11%. The purchase price is $41,706 plus interest of $1,000 ($50,000 × 8% × $\frac{3}{12}$) accrued from April 1, 2007, the date of the last semiannual interest payment. Entries in the accounts of Crenshaw Inc. at the time of purchase and for the remainder of the fiscal period ending December 31, 2007, are as follows:

Calculations:

Cost of $50,000 of Deitz
    Corporation bonds $41,706
Interest accrued
    ($50,000 × 8% × $\frac{3}{12}$)   1,000
Total $42,706

$50,000 × 8% × $\frac{6}{12}$ = $2,000

$50,000 × 8% × $\frac{3}{12}$ = $1,000

Face value of bonds $50,000
Cost of bond invest.   41,706
Discount on bond
   investment $ 8,294

Number of months
  to maturity
  ($8\frac{3}{4}$ years × 12)   105 months
Monthly amortization
  ($8,294/105 months,
  rounded to nearest
  dollar) $79 per mo.
Amortization for
  6 months ($79 × 6) $474

	2007 July	1	Investment in Deitz Corporation Bonds	41 7 0 6 00	
			Interest Revenue	1 0 0 0 00	
			Cash		42 7 0 6 00
			Purchased investment in bonds, plus		
			accrued interest.		
	Oct.	1	Cash	2 0 0 0 00	
			Interest Revenue		2 0 0 0 00
			Received semiannual interest for		
			April 1 to October 1.		
	Dec.	31	Interest Receivable	1 0 0 0 00	
			Interest Revenue		1 0 0 0 00
			Accrued interest from October 1		
			to December 31.		
		31	Investment in Deitz Corporation Bonds	4 7 4 00	
			Interest Revenue		4 7 4 00
			Amortization of discount from July 1		
			to December 31.		

The effect of these entries on the interest revenue account is shown below.

Interest Revenue

July 1	1,000	Oct. 1	2,000
		Dec. 31 Adj.	1,000
		31 Adj.	474
		Adj. Bal.	2,474

ACCOUNTING FOR BOND INVESTMENTS—SALE

Many long-term investments in bonds are sold before their maturity date. When this occurs, the seller receives the sales price (less commissions and other selling costs) plus any accrued interest since the last interest payment date. Before recording the cash proceeds, the seller should amortize any discount or premium for the current period up to the date of sale. Any gain or loss on the sale is then recorded when the cash proceeds are recorded. Such gains and losses are normally reported in the Other Income and Expense section of the income statement.

To illustrate, assume that the Deitz Corporation bonds in the preceding example are sold for $47,350 plus accrued interest on June 30, 2014. The *carrying amount* of the bonds (cost plus amortized discount) as of January 1, 2014 (78 months after their purchase) is $47,868 [$41,706 + ($79 per month × 78 months)]. The entries to amortize the discount for the current year and to record the sale of the bonds are as follows:

Calculations:

$79 × 6 months

Carrying amount of
bonds on
Jan. 1, 2014 $47,868
Discount amortized,
Jan. 1 to
June 30, 2014   474
Carrying amount of
bonds on
June 30, 2014 $48,342
Proceeds of sale   47,350
Loss on sale $ 992

2014 June	30	Investment in Deitz Corporation Bonds		4 7 4 00	
		Interest Revenue			4 7 4 00
		Amortized discount for current year.			
	30	Cash		48 3 5 0 00	
		Loss on Sale of Investments		9 9 2 00	
		Interest Revenue			1 0 0 0 00
		Investment in Deitz Corporation Bonds			48 3 4 2 00
		Received interest and proceeds			
		from sale of bonds.			
		Interest for April 1 to June 30 =			
		$50,000 × 8% × ³/₁₂ = $1,000			

Example Exercise 13-9   objective **5**

On October 1, 2008, Viewtec Corporation purchases $10,000 of 6% bonds of Watson Corporation, due in 9¼ years. The bonds were purchased at a price of $8,341 plus interest of $150 ($10,000 × 6% × ³/₁₂) accrued from July 1, 2008, the date of the last semiannual interest payment.

a. Journalize the purchase of the bonds plus accrued interest.
b. Journalize the entry to record the amortization of the discount on December 31. (Round to the nearest dollar.)

Follow My Example 13-9

a. 2008
    Oct. 1   Investment in Watson Corporation Bonds   8,341
                Interest Revenue   150
                    Cash   8,491
b. 2008   Investment in Watson Corporation Bonds 42*
    Dec. 1   Interest Revenue   42
          *[($10,000 − $8,341)/111 months] × 3 months

For Practice: PE 13-9A, PE 13-9B

Corporation Balance Sheet

objective   **6**

Prepare a corporation balance sheet.

In previous chapters, we illustrated the income statement and retained earnings statement for a corporation. The consolidated balance sheet in Exhibit 5 illustrates the presentation of many of the items discussed in this and preceding chapters. These items include bond sinking funds, investments in bonds, goodwill, deferred income taxes, and bonds payable and unamortized discount.

BALANCE SHEET PRESENTATION OF BONDS PAYABLE

In Exhibit 5, Escoe Corporation's bonds payable are reported as long-term liabilities. If there were two or more bond issues, the details of each would be reported on the balance sheet or in a supporting schedule or note. Separate accounts are normally maintained for each bond issue.

When the balance sheet date is within one year of the maturity date of the bonds, the bonds may be classified as a current liability. This would be the case if the bonds are to be paid out of current assets. If the bonds are to be paid from a sinking fund or if they are to be refinanced with another bond issue, they should remain in the noncurrent category. In this case, the details of the retirement of the bonds are normally disclosed in a note to the financial statements.

The balance in Escoe's discount on bonds payable account is reported as a *deduction* from the bonds payable. Conversely, the balance in a bond premium account would be reported as an *addition* to the related bonds payable. Either on the face of the financial statements or in accompanying notes, a description of the bonds (terms, due date, and effective interest rate) and other relevant information such as sinking fund requirements should be disclosed.[4] Finally, the market (fair) value of the bonds payable should also be disclosed.

BALANCE SHEET PRESENTATION OF BOND INVESTMENTS

Investments in bonds or other debt securities that management intends to hold to their maturity are called **held-to-maturity securities**. Such securities are classified as long-term investments under the caption Investments. These investments are reported at their cost less any amortized premium or plus any amortized discount. In addition, the market (fair) value of the bond investments should be disclosed, either on the face of the balance sheet or in an accompanying note.

---

4 *Statement of Financial Accounting Standards No. 129*, "Disclosure Information About Capital Structure," Financial Accounting Standards Board (Norwalk, Connecticut: 1997).

EXHIBIT 5	Balance Sheet of a Corporation

Escoe Corporation and Subsidiaries
Consolidated Balance Sheet
December 31, 2008

Assets

Current assets:			
Cash and cash equivalents		$ 407,500	
Accounts and notes receivable	$ 722,000		
Less allowance for doubtful receivables	37,000	685,000	
Inventories, at lower of cost (first-in, first-out) or market		917,500	
Prepaid expenses		70,000	
Total current assets			$2,080,000
Investments:			
Bond sinking fund (market value, $473,000)		$ 422,500	
Investment in bonds of Dalton (market value, $231,000)		240,000	
Total investments			662,500

	Cost	Accumulated Depreciation	Book Value	
Property, plant, and equipment				
(depreciated by the straight-line method):				
Land	$ 250,000	—	$ 250,000	
Buildings	920,000	$ 379,955	540,045	
Machinery and equipment	2,764,400	766,200	1,998,200	
Total property, plant, and equipment	$3,934,400	$1,146,155		2,788,245
Intangible assets:				
Goodwill				350,000
Total assets				$5,880,745

Liabilities

Current liabilities:			
Accounts payable		$ 623,810	
Income tax payable		120,500	
Dividends payable		94,000	
Accrued liabilities		81,400	
Deferred income tax payable		10,000	
Total current liabilities			$ 929,710
Long-term liabilities:			
Debenture 8% bonds payable, due December 31, 2026			
(market value, $950,000)		$1,000,000	
Less unamortized discount		60,000	
Total long-term liabilities			940,000
Deferred credits:			
Deferred income tax payable			85,500
Total liabilities			$1,955,210

Stockholders' Equity

Paid-in capital:			
Common stock, $20 par (250,000 shares authorized,			
100,000 shares issued)		$2,000,000	
Excess of issue price over par		320,000	
Total paid-in capital		$2,320,000	
Retained earnings		1,605,535	
Total stockholders' equity			3,925,535
Total liabilities and stockholders' equity			$5,880,745

Financial Analysis and Interpretation

Analysts often assess the relative risk of the bondholders in terms of the **number of times interest charges are earned** during the year. The higher the ratio, the greater the chance that interest payments will continue to be made if earnings decrease.

The amount available to make interest payments is not affected by taxes on income. This is because interest is deductible in determining taxable income. To illustrate, the following data were taken from the 2005 annual report of Briggs & Stratton Corporation:

Interest expense	$36,883,000
Income before income tax	$174,315,000

The number of times interest charges are earned, 5.73, is calculated below.

$$\frac{\text{Number of Times}}{\text{Interest Charges Are Earned}} = \frac{\text{Income Before Income Tax} + \text{Interest Expense}}{\text{Interest Expense}}$$

$$\frac{\text{Number of Times}}{\text{Interest Charges Are Earned}} = \frac{\$174,315,000 + \$36,883,000}{\$36,883,000} = 5.73$$

The number of times interest charges are earned indicates that the debtholders of Briggs & Stratton Corporation have adequate protection against a potential drop in earnings jeopardizing their receipt of interest payments. However, a final assessment should include a review of trends of past years and a comparison with industry averages.

Appendix

Effective Interest Rate Method of Amortization

The effective interest rate method of amortizing discounts and premiums provides for a constant rate of interest on the carrying amount of the bonds at the beginning of each period. This is in contrast to the straight-line method, which provides for a constant amount of interest expense.

The interest rate used in the interest method of amortization is the market rate on the date the bonds are issued. The carrying amount of the bonds to which the interest rate is applied is the face amount of the bonds minus any unamortized discount or plus any unamortized premium. Under the interest method, the interest expense to be reported on the income statement is computed by multiplying the effective interest rate by the carrying amount of the bonds. The difference between the interest expense computed in this way and the periodic interest payment is the amount of discount or premium to be amortized for the period.

AMORTIZATION OF DISCOUNT BY THE INTEREST METHOD

To illustrate the interest method for amortizing bond discounts, we assume the following data from the chapter illustration of issuing $100,000 bonds at a discount:

Face value of 12%, 5-year bonds, interest compounded semiannually	$100,000
Present value of bonds at effective (market) rate of interest of 13%	96,406
Discount on bonds payable	$ 3,594

Applying the interest method to these data yields the amortization table in Exhibit 6. You should note the following items in this table:

1. The interest paid (Column A) remains constant at 6% of $100,000, the face amount of the bonds.
2. The interest expense (Column B) is computed at $6\frac{1}{2}\%$ of the bond carrying amount at the beginning of each period. This results in an increasing interest expense each period.
3. The excess of the interest expense over the interest payment of $6,000 is the amount of discount to be amortized (Column C).
4. The unamortized discount (Column D) decreases from the initial balance, $3,594, to a zero balance at the maturity date of the bonds.
5. The carrying amount (Column E) increases from $96,406, the amount received for the bonds, to $100,000 at maturity.

EXHIBIT 6   **Amortization of Discount on Bonds Payable**

Interest Payment	A Interest Paid (6% of Face Amount)	B Interest Expense (6½% of Bond Carrying Amount)	C Discount Amortization (B − A)	D Unamortized Discount (D − C)	E Bond Carrying Amount ($100,000 − D)
				$3,594	$ 96,406
1	$6,000	$6,266 (6½% of $96,406)	$266	3,328	96,672
2	6,000	6,284 (6½% of $96,672)	284	3,044	96,956
3	6,000	6,302 (6½% of $96,956)	302	2,742	97,258
4	6,000	6,322 (6½% of $97,258)	322	2,420	97,580
5	6,000	6,343 (6½% of $97,580)	343	2,077	97,923
6	6,000	6,365 (6½% of $97,923)	365	1,712	98,288
7	6,000	6,389 (6½% of $98,288)	389	1,323	98,677
8	6,000	6,414 (6½% of $98,677)	414	909	99,091
9	6,000	6,441 (6½% of $99,091)	441	468	99,532
10	6,000	6,470 (6½% of $99,532)	468*	—	100,000

*Cannot exceed unamortized discount.

The entry to record the first interest payment on June 30, 2007, and the related discount amortization is as follows:

2007 June	30	Interest Expense	6 2 6 6 00	
		Discount on Bonds Payable		2 6 6 00
		Cash		6 0 0 0 00
		Paid semiannual interest and amortized		
		bond discount for ½ year.		

If the amortization is recorded only at the end of the year, the amount of the discount amortized on December 31 would be $550. This is the sum of the first two semiannual amortization amounts ($266 and $284) from Exhibit 6.

AMORTIZATION OF PREMIUM BY THE INTEREST METHOD

To illustrate the interest method for amortizing bond premiums, we assume the following data from the chapter illustration of issuing $100,000 bonds at a premium:

Present value of bonds at effective (market) rate of interest of 11%	$103,769
Face value of 12%, 5-year bonds, interest compounded semiannually	100,000
Premium on bonds payable	$ 3,769

Using the interest method to amortize the above premium yields the amortization table in Exhibit 7. You should note the following items in this table:

1. The interest paid (Column A) remains constant at 6% of $100,000, the face amount of the bonds.
2. The interest expense (Column B) is computed at $5\frac{1}{2}$% of the bond carrying amount at the beginning of each period. This results in a decreasing interest expense each period.
3. The excess of the periodic interest payment of $6,000 over the interest expense is the amount of premium to be amortized (Column C).
4. The unamortized premium (Column D) decreases from the initial balance, $3,769, to a zero balance at the maturity date of the bonds.
5. The carrying amount (Column E) decreases from $103,769, the amount received for the bonds, to $100,000 at maturity.

EXHIBIT 7   Amortization of Premium on Bonds Payable

Interest Payment	A Interest Paid (6% of Face Amount)	B Interest Expense (5½% of Bond Carrying Amount)	C Premium Amortization (A − B)	D Unamortized Premium (D − C)	E Bond Carrying Amount ($100,000 + D)
				$3,769	$103,769
1	$6,000	$5,707 (5½% of $103,769)	$293	3,476	103,476
2	6,000	5,691 (5½% of $103,476)	309	3,167	103,167
3	6,000	5,674 (5½% of $103,167)	326	2,841	102,841
4	6,000	5,656 (5½% of $102,841)	344	2,497	102,497
5	6,000	5,637 (5½% of $102,497)	363	2,134	102,134
6	6,000	5,617 (5½% of $102,134)	383	1,751	101,751
7	6,000	5,596 (5½% of $101,751)	404	1,347	101,347
8	6,000	5,574 (5½% of $101,347)	426	921	100,921
9	6,000	5,551 (5½% of $100,921)	449	472	100,472
10	6,000	5,526 (5½% of $100,472)	472*	—	100,000

*Cannot exceed unamortized premium.

The entry to record the first interest payment on June 30, 2007, and the related premium amortization is as follows:

2007 June	30	Interest Expense		5 7 0 7 00	
		Premium on Bonds Payable		2 9 3 00	
		Cash			6 0 0 0 00
		Paid semiannual interest and amortized bond premium for ½ year.			

If the amortization is recorded only at the end of the year, the amount of the premium amortized on December 31, 2007, would be $602. This is the sum of the first two semiannual amortization amounts ($293 and $309) from Exhibit 7.

At a Glance

1. Compute the potential impact of long-term borrowing on earnings per share.

Key Points	Key Learning Outcomes	Example Exercises	Practice Exercises
Corporations can finance their operations by issuing bonds or additional equity. A bond is simply a form of an interest-bearing note. One of the many factors that influence a corporation's decision on whether it should issue debt or equity is the effect each alternative has on earnings per share.	• Define the concept of a bond. • Calculate and compare the effect of alternative financing plans on earnings per share.	13-1	13-1A, 13-1B

2. Describe the characteristics, terminology, and pricing of bonds payable.

Key Points	Key Learning Outcomes	Example Exercises	Practice Exercises
A corporation that issues bonds enters into a contract, or bond indenture. The characteristics of a bond depend on the type of bonds issued by a corporation. When a corporation issues bonds, the price that buyers are willing to pay for the bonds depends upon (1) the face amount of the bonds, (2) the periodic interest to be paid on the bonds, and (3) the market rate of interest. The price that a buyer is willing to pay for a bond is the sum of (1) the present value of the face amount and (2) the present value of the periodic interest payments.	• Define the characteristics of a bond. • Describe the various types of bonds. • Describe the factors that determine the price of a bond. • Define a bond discount or premium. • Calculate the present value of the face amount of a bond. • Calculate the present value of the periodic bond interest payments.	13-2 13-3	13-2A, 13-2B 13-3A, 13-3B

3. Journalize entries for bonds payable.

Key Points	Key Learning Outcomes	Example Exercises	Practice Exercises
The journal entry for issuing bonds payable debits Cash for the proceeds received and credits Bonds Payable for the face amount of the bonds. Any difference between the face amount of the bonds and the proceeds is debited to Discount on Bonds Payable or credited to Premium on Bonds Payable. A discount or premium on bonds payable is amortized to interest expense over the life of the bonds.	• Calculate the price of a bond. • Journalize the issuance of bonds at face value and the payment of periodic interest. • Journalize the issuance of bonds at a discount. • Journalize the amortization of a bond discount or premium. • Journalize the issuance of bonds at a premium. • Journalize the amortization of a bond premium.	13-4 13-5 13-6 13-7	13-4A, 13-4B 13-5A, 13-5B 13-6A, 13-6B 13-7A, 13-7B

(continued)

4. Describe and illustrate the payment and redemption of bonds payable.

Key Points	Key Learning Outcomes	Example Exercises	Practice Exercises
At the maturity date, the entry to record the payment at face value of a bond is a debit to Bonds Payable and a credit to Cash. Since the payment of bonds normally involves a large amount of cash, a bond indenture may require that cash be periodically transferred into a sinking fund. When a corporation redeems bonds, Bonds Payable is debited for the face amount of the bonds, the premium (discount) on bonds payable account is debited (credited) for its balance, Cash is credited, and any gain or loss on the redemption is recorded.	• Explain bond redemptions. • Journalize the redemption of bonds payable.	13-8	13-8A, 13-8B

5. Journalize entries for the purchase, interest, discount and premium amortization, and sale of bond investments.

Key Points	Key Learning Outcomes	Example Exercises	Practice Exercises
A long-term investment in bonds is recorded by debiting Investments in Bonds. When bonds are purchased between interest dates, the amount of interest paid should be debited to Interest Revenue. Any discount or premium on bond investments should be amortized, using the straight-line or effective interest rate methods. When bonds held as long-term investments are sold, any discount or premium for the current period should first be amortized.	• Journalize the purchase of bond investments. • Prepare the journal entry to record the receipt of periodic interest from bond investments. • Prepare the adjusting journal entry to accrue interest on bond investments and amortization of discounts and premiums on bond investments. • Journalize the sale of bond investments.	13-9	13-9A, 13-9B

6. Prepare a corporation balance sheet.

Key Points	Key Learning Outcomes	Example Exercises	Practice Exercises
Bonds payable are usually reported as long-term liabilities. A discount on bonds should be reported as a deduction from the related bonds payable. A premium on bonds should be reported as an addition to related bonds payable. Investments in bonds that are held-to-maturity securities are reported as investments at cost less any amortized premium or plus any amortized discount.	• Illustrate the balance sheet presentation of bond investments and bonds payable.		

Key Terms

annuity (571)
bond (566)
bond indenture (568)
carrying amount (578)
contract rate (569)
discount (569)

effective interest rate method (575)
effective rate of interest (569)
future value (569)
held-to-maturity securities (582)
number of times interest charges
    are earned (584)

premium (569)
present value (569)
present value of an annuity (571)
sinking fund (578)

Illustrative Problem

The fiscal year of Russell Inc., a manufacturer of acoustical supplies, ends December 31. Selected transactions for the period 2007 through 2014, involving bonds payable issued by Russell Inc., are as follows:

2007
June 30. Issued $2,000,000 of 25-year, 7% callable bonds dated June 30, 2007, for cash of $1,920,000. Interest is payable semiannually on June 30 and December 31.
Dec. 31. Paid the semiannual interest on the bonds.
    31. Recorded straight-line amortization of $1,600 of discount on the bonds.
    31. Closed the interest expense account.

2008
June 30. Paid the semiannual interest on the bonds.
Dec. 31. Paid the semiannual interest on the bonds.
    31. Recorded straight-line amortization of $3,200 of discount on the bonds.
    31. Closed the interest expense account.

2014
June 30. Recorded the redemption of the bonds, which were called at 101.5. The balance in the bond discount account is $57,600 after the payment of interest and amortization of discount have been recorded. (Record the redemption only.)

Instructions

1. Journalize entries to record the preceding transactions.
2. Determine the amount of interest expense for 2007 and 2008.
3. Determine the carrying amount of the bonds as of December 31, 2008.

Solution

1.

2007				
June	30	Cash	1,920 0 0 0 00	
		Discount on Bonds Payable	80 0 0 0 00	
		Bonds Payable		2,000 0 0 0 00
Dec.	31	Interest Expense	70 0 0 0 00	
		Cash		70 0 0 0 00
	31	Interest Expense	1 6 0 0 00	
		Discount on Bonds Payable		1 6 0 0 00
		Amortization of discount from July 1		
		to December 31.		
	31	Income Summary	71 6 0 0 00	
		Interest Expense		71 6 0 0 00

(continued)

2008 June	30	Interest Expense		70 0 0 0 00	
		Cash			70 0 0 0 00
Dec.	31	Interest Expense		70 0 0 0 00	
		Cash			70 0 0 0 00
	31	Interest Expense		3 2 0 0 00	
		Discount on Bonds Payable			3 2 0 0 00
		Amortization of discount from			
		January 1 to December 31.			
	31	Income Summary		143 2 0 0 00	
		Interest Expense			143 2 0 0 00
2014 June	30	Bonds Payable		2,000 0 0 0 00	
		Loss on Redemption of Bonds Payable		87 6 0 0 00	
		Discount on Bonds Payable			57 6 0 0 00
		Cash			2,030 0 0 0 00

2. a. 2007—$71,600
   b. 2008—$143,200

3.
Initial carrying amount of bonds	$1,920,000
Discount amortized on December 31, 2007	1,600
Discount amortized on December 31, 2008	3,200
Carrying amount of bonds, December 31, 2008	$1,924,800

Self-Examination Questions

(Answers at End of Chapter)

1. If a corporation plans to issue $1,000,000 of 12% bonds at a time when the market rate for similar bonds is 10%, the bonds can be expected to sell at:
   A. their face amount.
   B. a premium.
   C. a discount.
   D. a price below their face amount.

2. If the bonds payable account has a balance of $900,000 and the discount on bonds payable account has a balance of $72,000, what is the carrying amount of the bonds?
   A. $828,000   C. $972,000
   B. $900,000   D. $580,000

3. The cash and securities that make up the sinking fund established for the payment of bonds at maturity are classified on the balance sheet as:

   A. current assets.   C. long-term liabilities.
   B. investments.   D. current liabilities.

4. If a firm purchases $150,000 of bonds of X Company at 101 plus accrued interest of $2,000 and pays broker's commissions of $50, the amount debited to Investment in X Company Bonds would be:
   A. $150,000.   C. $153,500.
   B. $151,550.   D. $153,550.

5. The balance in the discount on bonds payable account would usually be reported in the balance sheet in the:
   A. Current Assets section.
   B. Current Liabilities section.
   C. Long-Term Liabilities section.
   D. Investments section.

Eye Openers

1. Describe the two distinct obligations incurred by a corporation when issuing bonds.
2. Explain the meaning of each of the following terms as they relate to a bond issue: (a) convertible, (b) callable, and (c) debenture.

3. What is meant by the phrase "time value of money"?
4. What has the higher present value: (a) $18,000 to be received at the end of two years, or (b) $9,000 to be received at the end of each of the next two years?
5. If you asked your broker to purchase for you a 9% bond when the market interest rate for such bonds was 10%, would you expect to pay more or less than the face amount for the bond? Explain.
6. A corporation issues $5,000,000 of 7% bonds to yield interest at the rate of 5%. (a) Was the amount of cash received from the sale of the bonds greater or less than $5,000,000? (b) Identify the following terms related to the bond issue: (1) face amount, (2) market or effective rate of interest, (3) contract rate of interest, and (4) maturity amount.
7. If bonds issued by a corporation are sold at a premium, is the market rate of interest greater or less than the contract rate?
8. The following data relate to a $2,000,000, 8% bond issue for a selected semiannual interest period:

Bond carrying amount at beginning of period	$2,125,000
Interest paid during period	160,000
Interest expense allocable to the period	148,750

(a) Were the bonds issued at a discount or at a premium? (b) What is the unamortized amount of the discount or premium account at the beginning of the period? (c) What account was debited to amortize the discount or premium?
9. Assume that Smith Co. amortizes premiums and discounts on bonds payable at the end of the year rather than when interest is paid. What accounts would be debited and credited to record (a) the amortization of a discount on bonds payable and (b) the amortization of a premium on bonds payable?
10. Would a zero-coupon bond ever sell for its face amount?
11. What is the purpose of a bond sinking fund?
12. Assume that two 30-year, 10% bond issues are identical, except that one bond issue is callable at its face amount at the end of five years. Which of the two bond issues do you think will sell for a lower value?
13. Bonds Payable has a balance of $500,000, and Discount on Bonds Payable has a balance of $22,000. If the issuing corporation redeems the bonds at 97, is there a gain or loss on the bond redemption?
14. Where are investments in bonds that are classified as held-to-maturity securities reported on the balance sheet?
15. At what amount are held-to-maturity investments in bonds reported on the balance sheet?

Practice Exercises

PE 13-1A
Determining the effect of alternative financing plans on earnings per share

obj. 1

Wilkinson Co. is considering the following alternative financing plans.

	Plan 1	Plan 2
Issue 12% bonds (at face value)	$1,000,000	$500,000
Issue preferred $2 stock, $10 per share	—	700,000
Issue common stock, $10 par	1,000,000	800,000

Income tax is estimated at 40% of income.
Determine the earnings per share of common stock, assuming income before bond interest and income tax is $400,000.

PE 13-1B
Determining the effect of alternative financing plans on earnings per share

obj. 1

Knight Co. is considering the following alternative financing plans.

	Plan 1	Plan 2
Issue 9% bonds (at face value)	$3,000,000	$2,400,000
Issue preferred $2.50 stock, $25 per share	—	1,200,000
Issue common stock, $20 par	3,000,000	2,400,000

Income tax is estimated at 40% of income.

Determine the earnings per share of common stock, assuming income before bond interest and income tax is $500,000.

PE 13-2A
Determine the present value of a future amount
obj. 2

Using Exhibit 3, what is the present value of $7,000 to be received in 10 years, if the market rate of interest is 7% compounded annually?

PE 13-2B
Determine the present value of a future amount
obj. 2

Using Exhibit 3, what is the present value of $3,000 to be received in seven years, if the market rate of interest is 12% compounded annually?

PE 13-3A
Determine the present value of a bond
obj. 2

Calculate the present value of a $150,000, 7%, 10-year bond that pays $10,500 ($150,000 × 7%) interest annually, if the market rate of interest is 7%. Use Exhibits 3 and 4 for computing present values.

PE 13-3B
Determine the present value of a bond
obj. 2

Calculate the present value of an $80,000, 10%, five-year bond that pays $8,000 ($80,000 × 10%) interest annually, if the market rate of interest is 10%. Use Exhibits 3 and 4 for computing present values.

PE 13-4A
Record the issuance of bonds payable
obj. 3

On the first day of the fiscal year, a company issues a $500,0000, 10%, 10-year bond that pays semiannual interest of $25,000 ($500,000 × 10% × ½), receiving cash of $463,202. Journalize the bond issuance.

PE 13-4B
Record the issuance of bonds payable
obj. 3

On the first day of the fiscal year, a company issues a $1,500,000, 8%, five-year bond that pays semiannual interest of $60,000 ($1,500,000 × 8% × ½), receiving cash of $1,330,403. Journalize the bond issuance.

PE 13-5A
Record the interest for bonds payable
obj. 3

Using the bond from Practice Exercise 13-4A, journalize the first interest payment and the amortization of the related bond discount.

PE 13-5B
Record the interest for bonds payable
obj. 3

Using the bond from Practice Exercise 15-4B, journalize the first interest payment and the amortization of the related bond discount.

PE 13-6A
Record the issuance of bonds payable
obj. 3

A company issues a $2,000,000, 12%, five-year bond that pays semiannual interest of $120,000 ($2,000,000 × 12% × ½), receiving cash of $2,154,429. Journalize the bond issuance.

PE 13-6B
Record the issuance of bonds payable
obj. 3

A company issues a $1,000,000, 10%, 10-year bond that pays semiannual interest of $50,000 ($1,000,000 × 10% × ½), receiving cash of $1,065,040. Journalize the bond issuance.

PE 13-7A
Record the interest for bonds payable
obj. 3

Using the bond from Practice Exercise 13-6A, journalize the first interest payment and the amortization of the related bond premium.

PE 13-7B
Record the interest for bonds payable
obj. 3

Using the bond from Practice Exercise 13-6B, journalize the first interest payment and the amortization of the related bond premium.

PE 13-8A
Record the redemption of bonds payable
obj. 4

A $700,000 bond issue on which there is an unamortized discount of $60,000 is redeemed for $685,000. Journalize the redemption of the bonds.

PE 13-8B
Record the redemption of bonds payable
obj. 4

A $250,000 bond issue on which there is an unamortized premium of $20,000 is redeemed for $245,000. Journalize the redemption of the bonds.

PE 13-9A
Record the purchase of a bond investment
obj. 5

On September 1, 2008, Wilkerson Corporation purchases $70,000 of 8% bonds of Maxtech Corporation, due in 9¼ years. The bonds were purchased at a price of $56,000 plus interest of $1,400 ($70,000 × 8% × ³⁄₁₂) accrued from June 1, 2008, the date of the last semiannual interest payment. (a) Journalize the purchase of the bonds plus accrued interest. (b) Journalize the entry to record the amortization of the discount on December 31.

PE 13-9B
Record the purchase of a bond investment
obj. 5

On March 1, 2008, Gordon Corporation purchases $50,000 of 10% bonds of PUA-Tech Corporation, due in 9¼ years. The bonds were purchased at a price of $40,000 plus interest of $1,250 ($50,000 × 10% × ³⁄₁₂) accrued from December 1, 2007, the date of the last semiannual interest payment. (a) Journalize the purchase of the bonds plus accrued interest. (b) Journalize the entry to record the amortization of the discount on December 31.

Exercises

EX 13-1
Effect of financing on earnings per share
obj. 1
✓ a. $0.68

Bliss Co., which produces and sells skiing equipment, is financed as follows:

Bonds payable, 6% (issued at face amount)	$4,000,000
Preferred $2 stock (nonparticipating), $25 par	4,000,000
Common stock, $20 par	4,000,000

Income tax is estimated at 40% of income.

Determine the earnings per share of common stock, assuming that the income before bond interest and income tax is (a) $1,000,000, (b) $1,800,000, and (c) $3,200,000.

EX 13-2
Evaluate alternative financing plans
obj. 1

Based upon the data in Exercise 13-1, discuss factors other than earnings per share that should be considered in evaluating such financing plans.

EX 13-3
Corporate financing
obj. 1

The financial statements for Williams-Sonoma, Inc., are presented in Appendix E at the end of the text. What is the major source of financing for Williams-Sonoma?

EX 13-4
Present value of amounts due

obj. 2

Determine the present value of $200,000 to be received in three years, using an interest rate of 7%, compounded annually, as follows:

a. By successive divisions. (Round to the nearest dollar.)
b. By using the present value table in Exhibit 3.

EX 13-5
Present value of an annuity

obj. 2

Determine the present value of $75,000 to be received at the end of each of four years, using an interest rate of 5%, compounded annually, as follows:

a. By successive computations, using the present value table in Exhibit 3.
b. By using the present value table in Exhibit 4.

EX 13-6
Present value of an annuity

obj. 2

✓ *$24,924,420*

On January 1, 2008, you win $40,000,000 in the state lottery. The $40,000,000 prize will be paid in equal installments of $2,000,000 over 20 years. The payments will be made on December 31 of each year, beginning on December 31, 2008. If the current interest rate is 5%, determine the present value of your winnings. Use the present value tables in Appendix A.

EX 13-7
Present value of an annuity

obj. 2

Assume the same data as in Exercise 13-6, except that the current interest rate is 10%. Will the present value of your winnings using an interest rate of 10% be one-half the present value of your winnings using an interest rate of 5%? Why or why not?

EX 13-8
Present value of bonds payable; discount

objs. 2, 3

Caps Co. produces and sells bottle capping equipment for soft drink and spring water bottlers. To finance its operations, Caps Co. issued $20,000,000 of five-year, 9% bonds with interest payable semiannually at an effective interest rate of 10%. Determine the present value of the bonds payable, using the present value tables in Exhibits 3 and 4. Round to the nearest dollar.

EX 13-9
Present value of bonds payable; premium

objs. 2, 3

✓ *$15,565,317*

Clowney Co. issued $15,000,000 of five-year, 12% bonds with interest payable semiannually, at an effective interest rate of 11%. Determine the present value of the bonds payable, using the present value tables in Exhibits 3 and 4. Round to the nearest dollar.

EX 13-10
Bond price

objs. 2, 3

McDonald's 6.375% bonds due in 2028 were reported as selling for 108.89. Were the bonds selling at a premium or at a discount? Explain.

EX 13-11
Entries for issuing bonds

obj. 3

Wolfe Co. produces and distributes fiber optic cable for use by telecommunications companies. Wolfe Co. issued $12,000,000 of 10-year, 8% bonds on May 1 of the current year, with interest payable on May 1 and November 1. The fiscal year of the company is the calendar year. Journalize the entries to record the following selected transactions for the current year:

May   1. Issued the bonds for cash at their face amount.
Nov. 1. Paid the interest on the bonds.
Dec. 31. Recorded accrued interest for two months.

EX 13-12
Entries for issuing bonds and amortizing discount by straight-line method

obj. 3

On the first day of its fiscal year, Ellis Company issued $12,000,000 of five-year, 10% bonds to finance its operations of producing and selling home improvement products. Interest is payable semiannually. The bonds were issued at an effective interest rate of 12%, resulting in Ellis Company receiving cash of $11,116,854.

✓b. $1,376,629

a. Journalize the entries to record the following:
  1. Sale of the bonds.
  2. First semiannual interest payment. (Amortization of discount is to be recorded annually.)
  3. Second semiannual interest payment.
  4. Amortization of discount at the end of the first year, using the straight-line method. (Round to the nearest dollar.)
b. Determine the amount of the bond interest expense for the first year.

EX 13-13
Computing bond proceeds, entries for issuing bonds and amortizing premium by straight-line method
objs. 2, 3

Hemby Corporation wholesales oil and grease products to equipment manufacturers. On March 1, 2008, Hemby Corporation issued $4,000,000 of five-year, 13% bonds at an effective interest rate of 11%. Interest is payable semiannually on March 1 and September 1. Journalize the entries to record the following:

a. Sale of bonds on March 1, 2008. (Use the tables of present values in Exhibits 3 and 4 to determine the bond proceeds. Round to the nearest dollar.)
b. First interest payment on September 1, 2008, and amortization of bond premium for six months, using the straight-line method. (Round to the nearest dollar.)

EX 13-14
Entries for issuing and calling bonds; loss
objs. 3, 4

Farrar Corp., a wholesaler of office furniture, issued $7,000,000 of 20-year, 9% callable bonds on April 1, 2008, with interest payable on April 1 and October 1. The fiscal year of the company is the calendar year. Journalize the entries to record the following selected transactions:

2008
Apr. 1. Issued the bonds for cash at their face amount.
Oct. 1. Paid the interest on the bonds.

2012
Oct. 1. Called the bond issue at 103, the rate provided in the bond indenture. (Omit entry for payment of interest.)

EX 13-15
Entries for issuing and calling bonds; gain
objs. 3, 4

Rolfes Corp. produces and sells designer clothing. To finance its operations, Rolfes Corp. issued $4,000,000 of 30-year, 7% callable bonds on January 1, 2008, with interest payable on January 1 and July 1. The fiscal year of the company is the calendar year. Journalize the entries to record the following selected transactions:

2008
Jan. 1. Issued the bonds for cash at their face amount.
July 1. Paid the interest on the bonds.

2014
July 1. Called the bond issue at 96, the rate provided in the bond indenture. (Omit entry for payment of interest.)

EX 13-16
Reporting bonds
objs. 4, 6

At the beginning of the current year, two bond issues (X and Y) were outstanding. During the year, bond issue X was redeemed and a significant loss on the redemption of bonds was reported as an extraordinary item on the income statement. At the end of the year, bond issue Y was reported as a current liability because its maturity date was early in the following year. A sinking fund of cash and securities sufficient to pay the series Y bonds was reported in the balance sheet as *Investments*.

➤ Identify the flaws in the reporting practices related to the two bond issues.

EX 13-17
Amortizing discount on bond investment
obj. 5

A company purchased a $5,000, 25-year zero-coupon bond for $820 to yield 8.5% to maturity. How is the interest revenue computed?

EX 13-18
Entries for purchase and sale of investment in bonds; loss

obj. **5**

Nanotech Innovations Co. sells orthopedic supplies to hospitals. Journalize the entries to record the following selected transactions of Nanotech Innovations Co.:

a. Purchased for cash $600,000 of Sanhueza Co. 7% bonds at 102 plus accrued interest of $10,500.
b. Received first semiannual interest.
c. At the end of the first year, amortized $960 of the bond premium.
d. Sold the bonds at 98 plus accrued interest of $3,500. The bonds were carried at $606,720 at the time of the sale.

EX 13-19
Entries for purchase and sale of investment in bonds; gain

obj. **5**

Burtard Company develops and sells graphics software for use by architects. Journalize the entries to record the following selected transactions of Burtard Company:

a. Purchased for cash $450,000 of Blaga Co. 8% bonds at 97 plus accrued interest of $9,000.
b. Received first semiannual interest.
c. Amortized $1,080 of the bond investment at the end of the first year.
d. Sold the bonds at 101 plus accrued interest of $3,000. The bonds were carried at $442,440 at the time of the sale.

EX 13-20
Number of times interest charges earned

The following data were taken from recent annual reports of Southwest Airlines, which operates a low-fare airline service to over 50 cities in the United States.

	Current Year	Preceding Year
Interest expense	$ 88,000,000	$ 91,000,000
Income before income tax	489,000,000	708,000,000

a. Determine the number of times interest charges were earned for the current and preceding years. Round to one decimal place.
b. ━━━▶ What conclusions can you draw?

APPENDIX EX 13-21
Amortize discount by interest method

✓ b. $1,179,806

On the first day of its fiscal year, Pedro Dynamite Company issued $11,000,000 of five-year, 9% bonds to finance its operations of producing and selling home electronics equipment. Interest is payable semiannually. The bonds were issued at an effective interest rate of 12%, resulting in Pedro Dynamite Company receiving cash of $9,785,645.

a. Journalize the entries to record the following:
   1. Sale of the bonds.
   2. First semiannual interest payment. (Amortization of discount is to be recorded annually.)
   3. Second semiannual interest payment.
   4. Amortization of discount at the end of the first year, using the interest method. (Round to the nearest dollar.)
b. Compute the amount of the bond interest expense for the first year.

APPENDIX EX 13-22
Amortize premium by interest method

✓ b. $294,923

Jarhead Corporation wholesales oil and grease products to equipment manufacturers. On March 1, 2008, Jarhead Corporation issued $2,500,000 of five-year, 13% bonds at an effective interest rate of 11%, receiving cash of $2,688,440. Interest is payable semiannually on March 1 and September 1. Jarhead Corporation's fiscal year begins on March 1.

a. Journalize the entries to record the following:
   1. Sale of the bonds.
   2. First interest payment on September 1, 2008. (Amortization of premium is to be recorded annually.)
   3. Second interest payment on March 1, 2009.
   4. Amortization of premium at the end of the first year, using the interest method. (Round to the nearest dollar.)
b. Determine the bond interest expense for the first year.

APPENDIX EX 13-23
Compute bond proceeds, amortizing premium by interest method, and interest expense

✓ a. $24,487,410

✓ c. $203,818

Ti-Pod Co. produces and sells advanced electronic equipment. On the first day of its fiscal year, Ti-Pod Co. issued $22,000,000 of five-year, 14% bonds at an effective interest rate of 11%, with interest payable semiannually. Compute the following, presenting figures used in your computations.

a. The amount of cash proceeds from the sale of the bonds. (Use the tables of present values in Exhibits 3 and 4. Round to the nearest dollar.)
b. The amount of premium to be amortized for the first semiannual interest payment period, using the interest method. (Round to the nearest dollar.)
c. The amount of premium to be amortized for the second semiannual interest payment period, using the interest method. (Round to the nearest dollar.)
d. The amount of the bond interest expense for the first year.

APPENDIX EX 13-24
Compute bond proceeds, amortizing discount by interest method, and interest expense

✓ a. $25,376,439

✓ b. $168,822

Little Chicken Co. produces and sells restaurant equipment. On the first day of its fiscal year, Little Chicken Co. issued $27,500,000 of five-year, 8% bonds at an effective interest rate of 10%, with interest payable semiannually. Compute the following, presenting figures used in your computations.

a. The amount of cash proceeds from the sale of the bonds. (Use the tables of present values in Exhibits 3 and 4.)
b. The amount of discount to be amortized for the first semiannual interest payment period, using the interest method. (Round to the nearest dollar.)
c. The amount of discount to be amortized for the second semiannual interest payment period, using the interest method. (Round to the nearest dollar.)
d. The amount of the bond interest expense for the first year.

Problems Series A

PR 13-1A
Effect of financing on earnings per share

obj. 1

✓ 1. Plan 3: $10.64

Three different plans for financing a $30,000,000 corporation are under consideration by its organizers. Under each of the following plans, the securities will be issued at their par or face amount, and the income tax rate is estimated at 40% of income.

	Plan 1	Plan 2	Plan 3
8% bonds	—	—	$20,000,000
Preferred $2 stock, $50 par	—	$20,000,000	10,000,000
Common stock, $10 par	$40,000,000	20,000,000	10,000,000
Total	$40,000,000	$40,000,000	$40,000,000

Instructions
1. Determine for each plan the earnings per share of common stock, assuming that the income before bond interest and income tax is $20,000,000.
2. Determine for each plan the earnings per share of common stock, assuming that the income before bond interest and income tax is $2,600,000.
3. ▬▬▶ Discuss the advantages and disadvantages of each plan.

PR 13-2A
Present value; bond premium; entries for bonds payable transactions

objs. 2, 3

✓ 3. $53,796

Atlantis Inc. produces and sells voltage regulators. On July 1, 2007, Atlantis Inc. issued $800,000 of 10-year, 14% bonds at an effective interest rate of 13%. Interest on the bonds is payable semiannually on December 31 and June 30. The fiscal year of the company is the calendar year.

Instructions
1. Journalize the entry to record the amount of the cash proceeds from the sale of the bonds. Use the tables of present values in Appendix A to compute the cash proceeds, rounding to the nearest dollar.

(continued)

2. Journalize the entries to record the following:
   a. The first semiannual interest payment on December 31, 2007, including the amorti-
      zation of the bond premium, using the straight-line method. (Round to the nearest
      dollar.)
   b. The interest payment on June 30, 2008, and the amortization of the bond premium,
      using the straight-line method. (Round to the nearest dollar.)
3. Determine the total interest expense for 2007.
4. ◀▬▬▶ Will the bond proceeds always be greater than the face amount of the bonds
   when the contract rate is greater than the market rate of interest? Explain.

PR 13-3A

*Present value; bond
discount; entries for
bonds payable
transactions*

objs. 2, 3

✓3. $723,347

On July 1, 2007, Iaket Equipment Inc. issued $12,500,000 of 10-year, 11% bonds at an effec-
tive interest rate of 12%. Interest on the bonds is payable semiannually on December 31 and
June 30. The fiscal year of the company is the calendar year.

Instructions

1. Journalize the entry to record the amount of the cash proceeds from the sale of the bonds.
   Use the tables of present values in Appendix A to compute the cash proceeds, rounding
   to the nearest dollar.
2. Journalize the entries to record the following:
   a. The first semiannual interest payment on December 31, 2007, and the amortization of
      the bond discount, using the straight-line method. (Round to the nearest dollar.)
   b. The interest payment on June 30, 2008, and the amortization of the bond discount,
      using the straight-line method. (Round to the nearest dollar.)
3. Determine the total interest expense for 2007.
4. ◀▬▬▶ Will the bond proceeds always be less than the face amount of the bonds when
   the contract rate is less than the market rate of interest? Explain.

PR 13-4A

*Entries for bonds payable
transactions*

objs. 3, 4

✓2. a. $1,005,659

Kornet Co. produces and sells graphite for golf clubs. The following transactions were completed by Kornet Co., whose fiscal year is the calendar year:

2007
July   1.   Issued $19,000,000 of seven-year, 12% callable bonds dated July 1, 2007, at an
             effective rate of 10%, receiving cash of $20,880,780. Interest is payable semi-
             annually on December 31 and June 30.
Dec. 31.   Paid the semiannual interest on the bonds.
      31.   Recorded bond premium amortization of $134,341, which was determined by
             using the straight-line method.
      31.   Closed the interest expense account.

2008
June 30.   Paid the semiannual interest on the bonds.
Dec. 31.   Paid the semiannual interest on the bonds.
Dec. 31.   Recorded bond premium amortization of $268,682, which was determined by
             using the straight-line method.
      31.   Closed the interest expense account.

2009
July   1.   Recorded the redemption of the bonds, which were called at 101.5. The balance
             in the bond premium account is $1,343,416 after the payment of interest and
             amortization of premium have been recorded. (Record the redemption only.)

Instructions

1. Journalize the entries to record the foregoing transactions.
2. Indicate the amount of the interest expense in (a) 2007 and (b) 2008.
3. Determine the carrying amount of the bonds as of December 31, 2008.

PR 13-5A

*Entries for bond
investments*

obj. 5

The following selected transactions relate to certain securities acquired by Wildflower
Blueprints Inc., whose fiscal year ends on December 31:

2007
Sept.   1.   Purchased $600,000 of Wilson Company 20-year, 10% bonds dated July 1, 2007,
             directly from the issuing company, for $578,580 plus accrued interest of $10,000.

Dec. 31. Received the semiannual interest on the Wilson Company bonds.
    31. Recorded bond discount amortization of $360 on the Wilson Company bonds. The amortization amount was determined by using the straight-line method.

(Assume that all intervening transactions and adjustments have been properly recorded and that the number of bonds owned has not changed from December 31, 2007, to December 31, 2011.)

2012
June 30. Received the semiannual interest on the Wilson Company bonds.
Oct. 31. Sold one-half of the Wilson Company bonds at 97 plus accrued interest. The broker deducted $400 for commission, etc., remitting the balance. Prior to the sale, $450 of discount on one-half of the bonds was amortized, reducing the carrying amount of those bonds to $292,080.
Dec. 31. Received the semiannual interest on the Wilson Company bonds.
    31. Recorded bond discount amortization of $540 on the Wilson Company bonds.

Instructions
Journalize the entries to record the foregoing transactions.

APPENDIX PR 13-6A
Entries for bonds payable transactions; interest method of amortizing bond premium

✓ 2. $54,865

Atlantis Inc. produces and sells voltage regulators. On July 1, 2007, Atlantis Inc. issued $800,000 of 10-year, 14% bonds at an effective interest rate of 13%, receiving proceeds of $844,077. Interest on the bonds is payable semiannually on December 31 and June 30. The fiscal year of the company is the calendar year.

Instructions
1. Journalize the entries to record the following:
   a. The first semiannual interest payment on December 31, 2007, and the amortization of the bond premium, using the interest method. (Round to the nearest dollar.)
   b. The interest payment on June 30, 2008, and the amortization of the bond premium, using the interest method. (Round to the nearest dollar.)
2. Determine the total interest expense for 2007.

APPENDIX PR 13-7A
Entries for bonds payable transactions; interest method of amortizing bond discount

✓ 2. $706,984

On July 1, 2007, Iaket Equipment Inc. issued $12,500,000 of 10-year, 11% bonds at an effective interest rate of 12%, receiving proceeds of $11,783,070. Interest on the bonds is payable semiannually on December 31 and June 30. The fiscal year of the company is the calendar year.

Instructions
1. Journalize the entries to record the following:
   a. The first semiannual interest payment on December 31, 2007, and the amortization of the bond discount, using the interest method.
   b. The interest payment on June 30, 2008, and the amortization of the bond discount, using the interest method.
2. Determine the total interest expense for 2007.

Problems Series B

PR 13-1B
Effect of financing on earnings per share

obj. 1

✓ 1. Plan 3: $9.06

Three different plans for financing a $30,000,000 corporation are under consideration by its organizers. Under each of the following plans, the securities will be issued at their par or face amount, and the income tax rate is estimated at 40% of income.

	Plan 1	Plan 2	Plan 3
8% bonds	—	—	$15,000,000
Preferred $4 stock, $100 par	—	$15,000,000	7,500,000
Common stock, $4 par	$30,000,000	15,000,000	7,500,000
Total	$30,000,000	$30,000,000	$30,000,000

Instructions

1. Determine for each plan the earnings per share of common stock, assuming that the income before bond interest and income tax is $30,000,000.
2. Determine for each plan the earnings per share of common stock, assuming that the income before bond interest and income tax is $1,800,000.
3. ▰▰▰▰▶ Discuss the advantages and disadvantages of each plan.

PR 13-2B
Present value; bond premium; entries for bonds payable transactions

objs. 2, 3

✓ 3. $870,307

Bobblehead Corporation produces and sells basketball jerseys. On July 1, 2008, Bobblehead Corporation issued $16,000,000 of seven-year, 13% bonds at an effective interest rate of 10%. Interest on the bonds is payable semiannually on December 31 and June 30. The fiscal year of the company is the calendar year.

Instructions

1. Journalize the entry to record the amount of the cash proceeds from the sale of the bonds. Use the tables of present values in Appendix A to compute the cash proceeds, rounding to the nearest dollar.
2. Journalize the entries to record the following:
   a. The first semiannual interest payment on December 31, 2008, and the amortization of the bond premium, using the straight-line method. (Round to the nearest dollar.)
   b. The interest payment on June 30, 2009, and the amortization of the bond premium, using the straight-line method. (Round to the nearest dollar.)
3. Determine the total interest expense for 2008.
4. ▰▰▰▰▶ Will the bond proceeds always be greater than the face amount of the bonds when the contract rate is greater than the market rate of interest? Explain.

PR 13-3B
Present value; bond discount; entries for bonds payable transactions

objs. 2, 3

✓ 3. $1,251,378

On July 1, 2007, Austin Corporation, a wholesaler of electronic circuits, issued $22,000,000 of 20-year, 11% bonds at an effective interest rate of 12%. Interest on the bonds is payable semiannually on December 31 and June 30. The fiscal year of the company is the calendar year.

Instructions

1. Journalize the entry to record the amount of the cash proceeds from the sale of the bonds. Use the tables of present values in Appendix A to compute the cash proceeds, rounding to the nearest dollar.
2. Journalize the entries to record the following:
   a. The first semiannual interest payment on December 31, 2007, and the amortization of the bond discount, using the straight-line method. (Round to the nearest dollar.)
   b. The interest payment on June 30, 2008, and the amortization of the bond discount, using the straight-line method. (Round to the nearest dollar.)
3. Determine the total interest expense for 2007.
4. ▰▰▰▰▶ Will the bond proceeds always be less than the face amount of the bonds when the contract rate is less than the market rate of interest? Explain.

PR 13-4B
Entries for bonds payable transactions

objs. 3, 4

✓ 2. a. $577,386

The following transactions were completed by Michura Inc., whose fiscal year is the calendar year:

2007
July   1. Issued $12,000,000 of 10-year, 9% callable bonds dated July 1, 2007, at an effective rate of 11%, receiving cash of $11,252,273. Interest is payable semiannually on December 31 and June 30.
Dec. 31. Paid the semiannual interest on the bonds.
     31. Recorded bond discount amortization of $37,386, which was determined by using the straight-line method.
     31. Closed the interest expense account.

2008
June 30. Paid the semiannual interest on the bonds.
Dec. 31. Paid the semiannual interest on the bonds.
     31. Recorded bond discount amortization of $74,772, which was determined by using the straight-line method.
     31. Closed the interest expense account.

2009

June 30. Recorded the redemption of the bonds, which were called at 98. The balance in the bond discount account is $598,183 after payment of interest and amortization of discount have been recorded. (Record the redemption only.)

Instructions
1. Journalize the entries to record the foregoing transactions.
2. Indicate the amount of the interest expense in (a) 2007 and (b) 2008.
3. Determine the carrying amount of the bonds as of December 31, 2008.

PR 13-5B
Entries for bond investments

obj. 5

Valent Inc. leases motor vehicles. The following selected transactions relate to certain securities acquired as a long-term investment by Valent Inc., whose fiscal year ends on December 31:

2007

Sept. 1. Purchased $800,000 of Ivan Company 10-year, 9% bonds dated July 1, 2007, directly from the issuing company, for $853,100 plus accrued interest of $12,000.
Dec. 31. Received the semiannual interest on the Ivan Company bonds.
       31. Recorded bond premium amortization of $1,800 on the Ivan Company bonds. The amortization amount was determined by using the straight-line method.

(Assume that all intervening transactions and adjustments have been properly recorded and that the number of bonds owned has not changed from December 31, 2007, to December 31, 2012.)

2013

June 30. Received the semiannual interest on the Ivan Company bonds.
Aug. 31. Sold one-half of the Ivan Company bonds at 102 plus accrued interest. The broker deducted $500 for commission, etc., remitting the balance. Prior to the sale, $1,800 of premium on one-half of the bonds is to be amortized, reducing the carrying amount of those bonds to $405,600.
Dec. 31. Received the semiannual interest on the Ivan Company bonds.
       31. Recorded bond premium amortization of $2,700 on the Ivan Company bonds.

Instructions
Journalize the entries to record the foregoing transactions.

APPENDIX PR 13-6B
Entries for bonds payable transactions; interest method of amortizing bond premium

✓ *2. $918,785*

Bobblehead Corporation produces and sells basketball jerseys. On July 1, 2008, Bobblehead Corporation issued $16,000,000 of seven-year, 13% bonds at an effective interest rate of 10%, receiving proceeds of $18,375,706. Interest on the bonds is payable semiannually on December 31 and June 30. The fiscal year of the company is the calendar year.

Instructions
1. Journalize the entries to record the following:
   a. The first semiannual interest payment on December 31, 2008, and the amortization of the bond premium, using the interest method. (Round to the nearest dollar.)
   b. The interest payment on June 30, 2009, and the amortization of the bond premium, using the interest method. (Round to the nearest dollar.)
2. Determine the total interest expense for 2008.

APPENDIX PR 13-7B
Entries for bonds payable transactions; interest method of amortizing bond discount

✓ *2. $1,220,692*

On July 1, 2007, Austin Corporation, a wholesaler of electronic circuits, issued $22,000,000 of 20-year, 11% bonds at an effective interest rate of 12%, receiving proceeds of $20,344,863. Interest on the bonds is payable semiannually on December 31 and June 30. The fiscal year of the company is the calendar year.

Instructions
1. Journalize the entries to record the following:
   a. The first semiannual interest payment on December 31, 2007, and the amortization of the bond discount, using the interest method. (Round to the nearest dollar.)
   b. The interest payment on June 30, 2008, and the amortization of the bond discount, using the interest method. (Round to the nearest dollar.)
2. Determine the total interest expense for 2007.

Comprehensive Problem 4

✔ *2.a. Net income,*
$229,000

Selected transactions completed by Delhome Products Inc. during the fiscal year ending July 31, 2008, were as follows:

a. Issued 12,500 shares of $30 par common stock at $65, receiving cash.

b. Issued 10,000 shares of $125 par preferred 8% stock at $160, receiving cash.

c. Issued $15,000,000 of 10-year, 12% bonds at an effective interest rate of 10%, with interest payable semiannually. Use the present value tables in Appendix A to determine the bond proceeds. (Round to the nearest dollar.)

d. Declared a dividend of $0.25 per share on common stock and $2.50 per share on preferred stock. On the date of record, 125,000 shares of common stock were outstanding, no treasury shares were held, and 18,750 shares of preferred stock were outstanding.

e. Paid the cash dividends declared in (d).

f. Redeemed $500,000 of eight-year, 15% bonds at 101. The balance in the bond premium account is $6,150 after the payment of interest and amortization of premium have been recorded. (Record only the redemption of the bonds payable.)

g. Purchased 6,250 shares of treasury common stock at $62.50 per share.

h. Declared a 2% stock dividend on common stock and a $2.50 cash dividend per share on preferred stock. On the date of declaration, the market value of the common stock was $63.75 per share. On the date of record, 125,000 shares of common stock had been issued, 6,250 shares of treasury common stock were held, and 18,750 shares of preferred stock had been issued. (Round to the nearest dollar.)

i. Issued the stock certificates for the stock dividends declared in (h) and paid the cash dividends to the preferred stockholders.

j. Purchased $150,000 of Lewis Sports Inc. 10-year, 15% bonds, directly from the issuing company, for $145,500 plus accrued interest of $5,625.

k. Sold, at $72.50 per share, 3,750 shares of treasury common stock purchased in (g).

l. Recorded the payment of semiannual interest on the bonds issued in (c) and the amortization of the premium for six months. The amortization was determined using the straight-line method. (Round the amortization to the nearest dollar.)

m. Accrued interest for four months on the Lewis Sports Inc. bonds purchased in (j). Also recorded amortization of $120.

Instructions

1. Journalize the selected transactions.

2. After all of the transactions for the year ended July 31, 2008, had been posted [including the transactions recorded in (1) and all adjusting entries], the data below and on the following page were taken from the records of Delhome Products Inc.

   a. Prepare a multiple-step income statement for the year ended July 31, 2008, concluding with earnings per share. In computing earnings per share, assume that the average number of common shares outstanding was 125,000 and preferred dividends were $131,250. (Round earnings per share to the nearest cent.)

   b. Prepare a retained earnings statement for the year ended July 31, 2008.

   c. Prepare a balance sheet in report form as of July 31, 2008.

Income statement data:	
Advertising expense	$ 150,000
Cost of merchandise sold	3,498,750
Delivery expense	27,000
Depreciation expense—office buildings and equipment	25,000
Depreciation expense—store buildings and equipment	90,000
Gain on redemption of bonds	1,150

Income tax:

Applicable to continuing operations	$ 247,509
Applicable to loss from discontinued operations	100,000
Applicable to gain from redemption of bonds	150
Interest expense	778,266
Interest revenue	2,025
Loss from disposal of discontinued operations	250,000
Loss from fixed asset impairment	187,500
Miscellaneous administrative expenses	7,500
Miscellaneous selling expenses	13,750
Office rent expense	50,000
Office salaries expense	170,000
Office supplies expense	10,000
Restructuring charges	93,750
Sales	6,300,000
Sales commissions	195,000
Sales salaries expense	360,000
Store supplies expense	20,000
Retained earnings and balance sheet data:	
Accounts payable	212,000
Accounts receivable	562,500
Accumulated depreciation—office buildings and equipment	1,670,650
Accumulated depreciation—store buildings and equipment	4,428,750
Allowance for doubtful accounts	43,750
Bonds payable, 11%, due 2018	14,500,000
Cash	250,000
Common stock, $30 par (400,000 shares authorized;	
124,875 shares outstanding)	3,746,250
Deferred income tax payable (current portion, $17,500)	51,375
Dividends:	
Cash dividends for common stock	122,815
Cash dividends for preferred stock	187,500
Stock dividends for common stock	151,406
Dividends payable	37,500
Employee termination obligation (current)	81,250
Goodwill	540,000
Income tax payable	40,000
Interest receivable	7,500
Investment in Lewis Sports Inc. bonds (long-term)	145,620
Merchandise inventory (July 31, 2008), at lower of	
cost (fifo) or market	850,000
Notes receivable	156,250
Office buildings and equipment	7,412,500
Paid-in capital from sale of treasury stock	37,500
Paid-in capital in excess of par—common stock	700,000
Paid-in capital in excess of par—preferred stock	300,000
Preferred 8% stock, $125 par (30,000 shares authorized;	
18,750 shares issued)	2,343,750
Premium on bonds payable	1,769,722
Prepaid expenses	31,250
Retained earnings, August 1, 2007	2,302,970
Store buildings and equipment	21,920,876
Treasury stock (2,500 shares of common stock at cost	
of $62.50 per share)	156,250

Special Activities

SA 13-1
General Electric bond issuance

General Electric Capital, a division of General Electric, uses long-term debt extensively. In early 2002, GE Capital issued $11 billion in long-term debt to investors, then within days filed legal documents to prepare for another $50 billion long-term debt issue. As a result of the $50 billion filing, the price of the initial $11 billion offering declined (due to higher risk of more debt).

> Bill Gross, a manager of a bond investment fund, "denounced a 'lack in candor' related to GE's recent debt deal. 'It was the most recent and most egregious example of how bondholders are mistreated.' Gross argued that GE was not forthright when GE Capital recently issued $11 billion in bonds, one of the largest issues ever from a U.S. corporation. What bothered Gross is that three days after the issue the company announced its intention to sell as much as $50 billion in additional debt, warrants, preferred stock, guarantees, letters of credit and promissory notes at some future date."

In your opinion, did GE Capital act unethically by selling $11 billion of long-term debt without telling those investors that a few days later it would be filing documents to prepare for another $50 billion debt offering?

Source: Jennifer Ablan, "Gross Shakes the Bond Market; GE Calms It, a Bit," *Barron's*, March 25, 2002.

SA 13-2
Ethics and professional conduct in business

Jenkins Pharmaceuticals develops and produces prescription medications primarily for use in hospitals. The company has an outstanding $100,000,000, 30-year, 12% bond issued dated July 1, 2001. The bond issue is due June 30, 2031. The bond indenture requires a bond sinking fund, which has a balance of $12,000,000 as of July 1, 2007. The company is currently experiencing a shortage of funds due to a recent acquisition. Bob Snapple, the company's treasurer, is considering using the funds from the bond sinking fund to cover payroll and other bills that are coming due at the end of the month. Bob's brother-in-law fo the a trustee sinking fund, has indicated willingness to allow Bob to use the funds from the sinking fund to temporarily meet the company's cash needs.

Discuss whether Bob's proposal is appropriate.

SA 13-3
Present values

Kristen Nash recently won the jackpot in the New Jersey lottery while she was visiting her parents. When she arrived at the lottery office to collect her winnings, she was offered the following three payout options:

a. Receive $5,000,000 in cash today.
b. Receive $2,000,000 today and $600,000 per year for 10 years, with the first $600,000 payment being received one year from today.
c. Receive $1,000,000 per year for 10 years, with the first payment being received one year from today.

Assuming that the effective rate of interest is 9%, which payout option should Kristen select? Explain your answer and provide any necessary supporting calculations.

SA 13-4
Preferred stock vs. bonds

Beacon Inc. has decided to expand its operations to owning and operating long-term health care facilities. The following is an excerpt from a conversation between the chief executive officer, Terry Clark, and the vice president of finance, Frank Mills.

Terry: Frank, have you given any thought to how we're going to finance the acquisition of St. Seniors Health Care?

Frank: Well, the two basic options, as I see it, are to issue either preferred stock or bonds. The equity market is a little depressed right now. The rumor is that the Federal Reserve Bank's going to increase the interest rates either this month or next.

Terry: Yes, I've heard the rumor. The problem is that we can't wait around to see what's going to happen. We'll have to move on this next week if we want any chance to complete the acquisition of St. Seniors.

Frank: Well, the bond market is strong right now. Maybe we should issue debt this time around.

Terry: That's what I would have guessed as well. St. Seniors's financial statements look pretty good, except for the volatility of its income and cash flows. But that's characteristic of the industry.

Discuss the advantages and disadvantages of issuing preferred stock versus bonds.

SA 13-5
Investing in bonds

REAL WORLD

Group Project

During fiscal year 2004, Georgia-Pacific called the following bond issuances:

$243 million	9.875% bonds	due November 1, 2021
$250 million	9.625% bonds	due March 15, 2022
$250 million	9.500% bonds	due May 15, 2022
$240 million	9.125% bonds	due July 1, 2022
$250 million	8.250% bonds	due March 1, 2023
$250 million	8.125% bonds	due June 15, 2023

In groups of three or four:

1. Identify the face value, coupon rate, and maturity of each bond issue.
2. Discuss some of the potential reasons that Georgia-Pacific may have had for deciding to call these bond issues early.

SA 13-6
Investing in bonds

REAL WORLD

Group Project

Select a bond from listings that appear daily in *The Wall Street Journal*, and summarize the information related to the bond you select. Include the following information in your summary:

1. Contract rate of interest
2. Year when the bond matures
3. Current yield (effective rate of interest)
4. Closing price of bond (indicate date)
5. Other information noted about the bond, such as whether it is a zero-coupon bond (see the Explanatory Notes to the listings)

In groups of three or four, share the information you developed about the bond you selected. As a group, select one bond to invest $100,000 in and prepare a justification for your choice for presentation to the class. For example, your justification should include a consideration of risk and return.

SA 13-7
Financing business expansion

You hold a 25% common stock interest in the family-owned business, a vending machine company. Your sister, who is the manager, has proposed an expansion of plant facilities at an expected cost of $5,000,000. Two alternative plans have been suggested as methods of financing the expansion. Each plan is briefly described as follows:

Plan 1. Issue $5,000,000 of 20-year, 7% bonds at face amount.
Plan 2. Issue an additional 87,500 shares of $5 par common stock at $20 per share, and $3,250,000 of 20-year, 7% bonds at face amount.

(continued)

The balance sheet as of the end of the previous fiscal year is as follows:

Vendco, Inc.
Balance Sheet
December 31, 2008

Assets

Current assets	$2,350,000
Property, plant, and equipment	5,150,000
Total assets	$7,500,000

Liabilities and Stockholders' Equity

Liabilities	$2,000,000
Common stock, $5	800,000
Paid-in capital in excess of par	80,000
Retained earnings	4,620,000
Total liabilities and stockholders' equity	$7,500,000

Net income has remained relatively constant over the past several years. The expansion program is expected to increase yearly income before bond interest and income tax from $500,000 in the previous year to $700,000 for this year. Your sister has asked you, as the company treasurer, to prepare an analysis of each financing plan.

1. Prepare a table indicating the expected earnings per share on the common stock under each plan. Assume an income tax rate of 40%. Round to the nearest cent.
2. a. Discuss the factors that should be considered in evaluating the two plans.
   b. Which plan offers the greater benefit to the present stockholders? Give reasons for your opinion.

SA 13-8
Bond ratings

REAL WORLD

Internet Project

Moody's Investors Service maintains a Web site at **http://www.Moodys.com**. One of the services offered at this site is a listing of announcements of recent bond rating changes. Visit this site and read over some of these announcements. Write down several of the reasons provided for rating downgrades and upgrades. If you were a bond investor or bond issuer, would you care if Moody's changed the rating on your bonds? Why or why not?

SA 13-9
Bonds payable in the financial statements

FAI

Refer to the financial statements of Williams-Sonoma, Inc., given in Appendix E at the end of this book.

1. How much interest expense did Williams-Sonoma record in 2003, 2004, and 2005?
2. What is the number of times interest charges are earned for Williams-Sonoma in 2003, 2004, and 2005? Evaluate this ratio for Williams-Sonoma. (Round your answer to one decimal place.)

Answers to Self-Examination Questions

1. **B** Since the contract rate on the bonds is higher than the prevailing market rate, a rational investor would be willing to pay more than the face amount, or a premium (answer B), for the bonds. If the contract rate and the market rate were equal, the bonds could be expected to sell at their face amount (answer A). Likewise, if the market rate is higher than the contract rate, the bonds would sell at a price below their face amount (answer D) or at a discount (answer C).

2. **A** The bond carrying amount is the face amount plus unamortized premium or less unamortized discount. For this question, the carrying amount is $900,000 less $72,000, or $828,000 (answer A).

3. **B** Although the sinking fund may consist of cash as well as securities, the fund is listed on the balance sheet as an investment (answer B) because it is to be used to pay the long-term liability at maturity.

4. **B** The amount debited to the investment account is the cost of the bonds, which includes the amount paid to the seller for the bonds (101% × $150,000) plus broker's commissions ($50), or $151,550 (answer B). The $2,000 of accrued interest that is paid to the seller should be debited to Interest Revenue, since it is an offset against the amount that will be received as interest at the next interest date.

5. **C** The balance of Discount on Bonds Payable is usually reported as a deduction from Bonds Payable in the Long-Term Liabilities section (answer C) of the balance sheet. Likewise, a balance in a premium on bonds payable account would usually be reported as an addition to Bonds Payable in the Long-Term Liabilities section of the balance sheet.

Statement of Cash Flows

© ELAINE THOMPSON/ASSOCIATED PRESS

objectives

After studying this chapter, you should be able to:

1 *Summarize the types of cash flow activities reported in the statement of cash flows.*

2 *Prepare a statement of cash flows, using the indirect method.*

3 *Prepare a statement of cash flows, using the direct method.*

Jones Soda Co.

S uppose you were to receive $100 as a result of some event. Would it make a difference what the event was? Yes, it would! If you received $100 for your birthday, then it's a gift. If you received $100 as a result of working part time for a week, then it's the result of your effort. If you received $100 as a loan, then it's money that you will have to pay back in the future. If you received $100 as a result of selling your CD player, then it's the result of giving up something tangible. Thus, the same $100 received can be associated with different types of events, and these events have different meanings to you. You would much rather receive a $100 gift than take out a $100 loan. Likewise, company stakeholders would also view events such as these differently.

Companies are required to report information about the events causing a change in cash over a period of time. This information is reported in the statement of cash flows. One such company is Jones Soda Co. Jones began in the late 1980s as an alternative beverage company, known for its customer provided labels, unique flavors, and support for extreme sports. You have probably seen Jones Soda at Barnes & Noble, Panera Bread, or Starbucks, or maybe sampled some of its unique flavors, such as Fufu Berry®, Blue Bubblegum®, or Lemon Drop®. As with any company, cash is important to Jones Soda. Without cash, Jones would be unable to expand its brands, distribute its product, support extreme sports, or provide a return for its owners. Thus, its managers are concerned about the sources and uses of cash.

In previous chapters, we have used the income statement, balance sheet, retained earnings statement, and other information to analyze the effects of management decisions on a business's financial position and operating performance. In this chapter, we focus on the events causing a change in cash by presenting the preparation and use of the statement of cash flows.

Reporting Cash Flows

In Chapter 1, we introduced the statement of cash flows as one of the basic financial statements of a business. The **statement of cash flows** reports a firm's major cash inflows and outflows for a period.[1] It provides useful information about a firm's ability to generate cash from operations, maintain and expand its operating capacity, meet its financial obligations, and pay dividends. As a result, it is used by managers in evaluating past operations and in planning future investing and financing activities. It is also used by investors, creditors, and others in assessing a firm's profit potential. In addition, it is a basis for assessing the firm's ability to pay its maturing debt.

The statement of cash flows reports cash flows by three types of activities:

1. **Cash flows from operating activities** are cash flows from transactions that affect net income. Examples of such transactions include the purchase and sale of merchandise by a retailer.
2. **Cash flows from investing activities** are cash flows from transactions that affect the investments in noncurrent assets. Examples of such transactions include the sale and purchase of fixed assets, such as equipment and buildings.
3. **Cash flows from financing activities** are cash flows from transactions that affect the debt and equity of the business. Examples of such transactions include issuing or retiring equity and debt securities.

---

1 As used in this chapter, *cash* refers to cash and cash equivalents. Examples of cash equivalents include short-term, highly liquid investments, such as money market funds, certificates of deposit, and commercial paper.

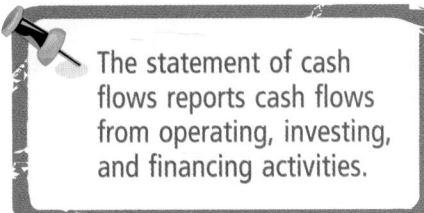

The statement of cash flows reports cash flows from operating, investing, and financing activities.

The cash flows from operating activities are normally presented first, followed by the cash flows from investing activities and financing activities. The total of the net cash flow from these activities is the net increase or decrease in cash for the period. The cash balance at the beginning of the period is added to the net increase or decrease in cash, resulting in the cash balance at the end of the period. The ending cash balance on the statement of cash flows equals the cash reported on the balance sheet. Exhibit 1 illustrates a simple statement of cash flows that is reproduced from Chapter 1 (Exhibit 6) for NetSolutions.

> ### EXHIBIT 1
>
> Statement of Cash Flows—NetSolutions

NetSolutions Statement of Cash Flows For the Month Ended November 30, 2007		
Cash flows from operating activities:		
Cash received from customers	$ 7,500	
Deduct cash payments for expenses and		
payments to creditors	4,600	
Net cash flow from operating activities		$ 2,900
Cash flows from investing activities:		
Cash payments for purchase of land		(20,000)
Cash flows from financing activities:		
Cash received from issuing stock	$25,000	
Deduct cash dividends	2,000	
Net cash flow provided by financing activities		23,000
Net cash flow and November 30, 2007, cash balance		$ 5,900

We have not discussed the statement of cash flows since introducing the statement in Chapter 1. We did this because a more complete understanding of operating, investing, and financing activities is helpful prior to developing and interpreting this statement. Previous chapters have introduced and described these activities so that you now have a foundation for the discussion that follows.

Exhibit 2 shows the major sources and uses of cash according to the three cash flow activities reported in the statement of cash flows. A *source* of cash causes the cash flow to increase, also called a *cash inflow*. For example, in Exhibit 1, the $25,000 cash received from issuing stock is a financing activity that is a source of cash. A *use* of cash causes cash flow to decrease, also called a *cash outflow*. In Exhibit 1, Net-Solutions' $20,000 cash payment for purchase of land is a use of cash. By reporting cash flows by operating, investing, and financing activities, significant relationships within and among the activities can be evaluated. For example, the cash receipts from issuing bonds can be related to repayments of borrowings when both are reported as financing activities. Also, the impact of each of the three activities (operating, investing, and financing) on cash flows can be identified. This allows investors and creditors to evaluate the effects of a firm's profits on cash flows and its ability to generate cash flows for dividends and for paying debts.

CASH FLOWS FROM OPERATING ACTIVITIES

The most important cash flows of a business often relate to operating activities. There are two alternative methods for reporting cash flows from operating activities in the statement of cash flows. These methods are (1) the direct method and (2) the indirect method.

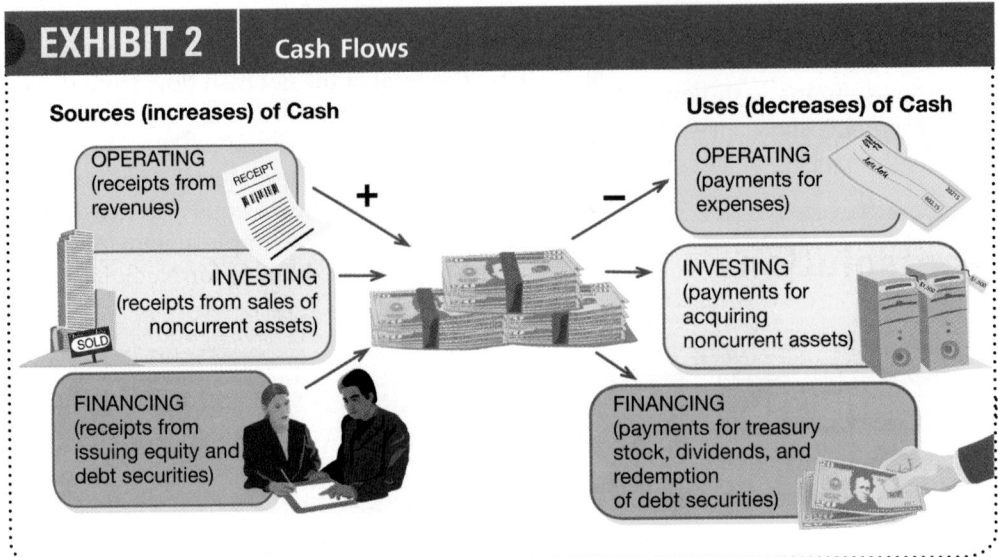

EXHIBIT 2 | Cash Flows

Sources (increases) of Cash

OPERATING (receipts from revenues)

INVESTING (receipts from sales of noncurrent assets)

FINANCING (receipts from issuing equity and debt securities)

Uses (decreases) of Cash

OPERATING (payments for expenses)

INVESTING (payments for acquiring noncurrent assets)

FINANCING (payments for treasury stock, dividends, and redemption of debt securities)

Cash Flows from Operating Activities

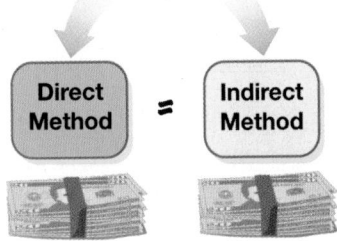

Direct Method **=** Indirect Method

The **direct method** reports the sources of operating cash and the uses of operating cash. The major source of operating cash is cash received from customers. The major uses of operating cash include cash paid to suppliers for merchandise and services and cash paid to employees for wages. The difference between these operating cash receipts and cash payments is the net cash flow from operating activities. The direct method is illustrated in Exhibit 1 for NetSolutions.

The primary advantage of the direct method is that it reports the sources and uses of operating cash flows in the statement of cash flows. Its primary disadvantage is that the necessary data may not be readily available and may be costly to gather.

The **indirect method** reports the operating cash flows by beginning with net income and adjusting it for revenues and expenses that do not involve the receipt or payment of cash. In other words, accrual net income is adjusted to determine the net amount of cash flows from operating activities.

A major advantage of the indirect method is that it focuses on the differences between net income and cash flows from operations. Thus, it shows the relationship between the income statement, the balance sheet, and the statement of cash flows. Because the data are readily available, the indirect method is normally less costly to use than the direct method. Because of these advantages, over 99% of all firms use the indirect method to report cash flows from operations.[2] We have not discussed the indirect method until this point, because it assumes an understanding of the accrual accounting concepts discussed in the prior chapters.

Exhibit 3 illustrates the cash flows from operating activities section of the statement of cash flows under the direct and indirect methods. Both statements are for NetSolutions for the month ended November 2007. The methods show the same amount of net cash flow from operating activities, regardless of the method. We will illustrate both methods in detail later in this chapter.

CASH FLOWS FROM INVESTING ACTIVITIES

Cash inflows from investing activities normally arise from selling fixed assets, investments, and intangible assets. Cash outflows normally include payments to acquire fixed assets, investments, and intangible assets.

The Walt Disney Company recently invested $1.4 billion in parks, resorts, and other properties, including the development of Hong Kong Disneyland.

2 *Accounting Trends & Techniques*, AICPA, 2005 edition.

EXHIBIT 3   Cash Flow from Operations: Direct and Indirect Methods—NetSolutions

Direct Method (from Exhibit 1)	
Cash flows from operating activities:	
Cash received from customers	$7,500
Deduct cash payments for expenses and payments to creditors	4,600
Net cash flow from operating activities	$2,900

Indirect Method	
Cash flows from operating activities:	
Net income	$3,050
Add increase in accounts payable	400
	$3,450
Deduct increase in supplies	550
Net cash flow from operating activities	$2,900

the same

Cash flows from investing activities are reported on the statement of cash flows by first listing the cash inflows. The cash outflows are then presented. If the inflows are greater than the outflows, *net cash flow provided by investing activities* is reported. If the inflows are less than the outflows, *net cash flow used for investing activities* is reported.

The cash flows from investing activities section in the statement of cash flows for NetSolutions from Exhibit 1 is shown below.

> Cash flows from investing activities:
> Cash payments for purchase of land .... $(20,000)

CASH FLOWS FROM FINANCING ACTIVITIES

Cash inflows from financing activities normally arise from issuing debt or equity securities. Examples of such inflows include issuing bonds, notes payable, and preferred and common stocks. Cash outflows from financing activities include paying cash dividends, repaying debt, and acquiring treasury stock.

Cash flows from financing activities are reported on the statement of cash flows by first listing the cash inflows. The cash outflows are then presented. If the inflows are greater than the outflows, *net cash flow provided by financing activities* is reported. If the inflows are less than the outflows, *net cash flow used for financing activities* is reported.

The cash flows from financing activities section in the statement of cash flows for NetSolutions from Exhibit 1 is shown below.

> Cash flows from financing activities:
> Cash received from issuing stock $25,000
> Deduct cash dividends   2,000
> Net cash flow provided by financing activities $23,000

NONCASH INVESTING AND FINANCING ACTIVITIES

A business may enter into investing and financing activities that do not directly involve cash. For example, it may issue common stock to retire long-term debt. Such a transaction does not have a direct effect on cash. However, the transaction does eliminate the need for future cash payments to pay interest and retire the bonds. Thus, because of their future effect on cash flows, such transactions should be reported to readers of the financial statements.

When noncash investing and financing transactions occur during a period, their effect is reported in a separate schedule. This schedule usually appears at the bottom of the statement of cash flows. For example, in such a schedule Google recently disclosed the issuance of over $25 million in common stock for business acquisitions. Other examples of noncash investing and financing transactions include acquiring fixed assets by issuing bonds or capital stock and issuing common stock in exchange for convertible preferred stock.

Business Connections

TOO MUCH CASH!

Is it possible to have too much cash? Clearly, most of us would answer no. However, a business views cash differently than an individual. Naturally, a business needs cash to develop and launch new products, expand markets, purchase plant and equipment, and acquire other businesses. However, some businesses have built up huge cash balances beyond even these needs. For example, both Microsoft Corporation and Dell Inc. have accumulated billions of dollars in cash and temporary investments, totaling in excess of 60% of their total assets. Such large cash balances can lower the return on total assets. As stated by one analyst, "When a company sits on cash (which earns 1% or 2%) and leaves equity outstanding . . . , it is tantamount to taking a loan at 15% and investing in a passbook savings account that earns 2%—it destroys value." So while having too much cash is a good problem to have, companies like Microsoft, Cisco Systems, Inc., IBM, Apple Computer Inc., and Dell are under pressure to pay dividends or repurchase common stock. For example, Microsoft recently declared a $32 billion special dividend to return cash to its shareholders.

NO CASH FLOW PER SHARE

The term *cash flow per share* is sometimes reported in the financial press. Often, the term is used to mean "cash flow from operations per share." Such reporting may be misleading to users of the financial statements. For example, users might interpret cash flow per share as the amount available for dividends. This would not be the case if most of the cash generated by operations is required for repaying loans or for reinvesting in the business. Users might also think that cash flow per share is equivalent or perhaps superior to earnings per share. For these reasons, the financial statements, including the statement of cash flows, should not report cash flow per share.

Example Exercise 14-1   objective 1

Identify whether each of the following would be reported as an operating, investing, or financing activity in the statement of cash flows.

a. Purchase of patent
b. Payment of cash dividend
c. Disposal of equipment

d. Cash sales
e. Purchase of treasury stock
f. Payment of wages expense

Follow My Example 14-1

a. Investing
b. Financing
c. Investing

d. Operating
e. Financing
f. Operating

For Practice: PE 14-1A, PE 14-1B

Statement of Cash Flows—The Indirect Method

objective 2

Prepare a statement of cash flows, using the indirect method.

The indirect method of reporting cash flows from operating activities is normally less costly and more efficient than the direct method. In addition, when the direct method is used, the indirect method must also be used in preparing a supplemental reconciliation of net income with cash flows from operations. The 2005 edition of *Accounting Trends & Techniques* reported that 99% of the companies surveyed used the indirect method. For these reasons, we will first discuss the indirect method of preparing the statement of cash flows.

To collect the data for the statement of cash flows, all the cash receipts and cash payments for a period could be analyzed. However, this procedure is expensive and time consuming. A more efficient approach is to analyze the changes in the noncash balance sheet accounts. The logic of this approach is that a change in any balance sheet account (including cash) can be analyzed in terms of changes in the other balance sheet accounts. To illustrate, the accounting equation is rewritten below to focus on the cash account.

$$\text{Assets} = \text{Liabilities} + \text{Stockholders' Equity}$$
$$\text{Cash} + \text{Noncash Assets} = \text{Liabilities} + \text{Stockholders' Equity}$$
$$\text{Cash} = \text{Liabilities} + \text{Stockholders' Equity} - \text{Noncash Assets}$$

Any change in the cash account results in a change in one or more noncash balance sheet accounts. That is, if the cash account changes, then a liability, stockholders' equity, or noncash asset account must also change.

Additional data are also obtained by analyzing the income statement accounts and supporting records. For example, since the net income or net loss for the period is closed to *Retained Earnings*, a change in the retained earnings account can be partially explained by the net income or net loss reported on the income statement.

There is no order in which the noncash balance sheet accounts must be analyzed. However, it is usually more efficient to analyze the accounts in the reverse order in which they appear on the balance sheet. Thus, the analysis of retained earnings provides the starting point for determining the cash flows from operating activities, which is the first section of the statement of cash flows.

The comparative balance sheet for Rundell Inc. on December 31, 2008 and 2007, is used to illustrate the indirect method. This balance sheet is shown in Exhibit 4. Selected ledger accounts and other data are presented as needed.[3]

RETAINED EARNINGS

The comparative balance sheet for Rundell Inc. shows that retained earnings increased $80,000 during the year. Analyzing the entries posted to the retained earnings account indicates how this change occurred. The retained earnings account for Rundell Inc. is shown below.

ACCOUNT Retained Earnings				ACCOUNT NO.		
					Balance	
Date	**Item**	**Debit**	**Credit**	**Debit**	**Debit**	**Credit**
2008 Jan. 1	Balance					202 3 0 0 00
Dec. 31	Net income		108 0 0 0 00			310 3 0 0 00
31	Cash dividends	28 0 0 0 00				282 3 0 0 00

The retained earnings account must be carefully analyzed because some of the entries to retained earnings may not affect cash. For example, a decrease in retained earnings resulting from issuing a stock dividend does not affect cash. Such transactions are not reported on the statement of cash flows.

For Rundell Inc., the retained earnings account indicates that the $80,000 change resulted from net income of $108,000 and cash dividends declared of $28,000. The effect of each of these items on cash flows is discussed in the following sections.

CASH FLOWS FROM OPERATING ACTIVITIES—INDIRECT METHOD

The net income of $108,000 reported by Rundell Inc. normally is not equal to the amount of cash generated from operations during the period. This is because net income is determined using the accrual method of accounting.

---

3 An appendix that discusses using a spreadsheet (work sheet) as an aid in assembling data for the statement of cash flows is presented at the end of this chapter. This appendix illustrates the use of this spreadsheet in reporting cash flows from operating activities using the indirect method.

EXHIBIT 4	Rundell Inc.			
Comparative Balance Sheet	Comparative Balance Sheet			
	December 31, 2008 and 2007			

Assets	2008	2007	Increase Decrease*
Cash.	$ 97,500	$ 26,000	$ 71,500
Accounts receivable (net).	74,000	65,000	9,000
Inventories.	172,000	180,000	8,000*
Land.	80,000	125,000	45,000*
Building.	260,000	200,000	60,000
Accumulated depreciation—building.	(65,300)	(58,300)	7,000
Total assets.	$618,200	$537,700	$ 80,500
Liabilities			
Accounts payable (merchandise			
creditors).	$ 43,500	$ 46,700	$ 3,200*
Accrued expenses payable			
(operating expenses).	26,500	24,300	2,200
Income taxes payable.	7,900	8,400	500*
Dividends payable.	14,000	10,000	4,000
Bonds payable.	100,000	150,000	50,000*
Total liabilities.	$191,900	$239,400	$ 47,500*
Stockholders' Equity			
Common stock ($2 par).	$ 24,000	$ 16,000	$ 8,000
Paid-in capital in excess of par.	120,000	80,000	40,000
Retained earnings.	282,300	202,300	80,000
Total stockholders' equity.	$426,300	$298,300	$128,000
Total liabilities and stockholders' equity. . . .	$618,200	$537,700	$ 80,500

Under the accrual method of accounting, revenues and expenses are recorded at different times from when cash is received or paid. For example, merchandise may be sold on account and the cash received at a later date. Likewise, insurance expense represents the amount of insurance expired during the period. The premiums for the insurance may have been paid in a prior period.

Under the indirect method, these differences are used to reconcile the net income to cash flows from operating activities. The typical adjustments to net income under the indirect method are reported in the statement of cash flows, as shown in Exhibit 5.[4]

In practice, the list of adjustments often begins with expenses that do not affect cash. Common examples are depreciation of fixed assets and amortization of intangible assets. Thus, in Exhibit 5, these two items are *added* to net income in determining cash flows from operating activities.

Typically, the next adjustments to net income are for gains and losses from disposal of assets. These adjustments arise because cash flows from operating activities should not include investing or financing transactions. For example, assume that land costing $50,000 was sold for $90,000 (a gain of $40,000). The sale should be reported as an investing activity: "Cash receipts from the sale of land, $90,000." However, the $40,000 gain on the disposal of the land is included in net income on the income statement. Thus, the $40,000 gain is *deducted* from net income in determining cash flows from operations to

---

4 Other items that also require adjustments to net income to obtain cash flows from operating activities include amortization of bonds payable discounts (add), losses on debt retirement (add), amortization of bonds payable premium (deduct), and gains on retirement of debt (deduct).

EXHIBIT 5		Increase (Decrease)
Adjustments to Net Income (Loss) Using the Indirect Method	Net income (loss)	$ XXX
	Adjustments to reconcile net income to net cash flow from operating activities:	
	Depreciation of fixed assets	XXX
	Amortization of intangible assets	XXX
	Losses on disposal of assets	XXX
	Gains on disposal of assets	(XXX)
	Changes in current operating assets and liabilities:	
	Increases in noncash current operating assets	(XXX)
	Decreases in noncash current operating assets	XXX
	Increases in current operating liabilities	XXX
	Decreases in current operating liabilities	(XXX)
	Net cash flow from operating activities	$ XXX or $(XXX)

Subtract	Add
Increases in accounts receivable	Decreases in accounts receivable
Increases in inventory	Decreases in inventory
Increases in prepaid expenses	Decreases in prepaid expenses
Decreases in accounts payable	Increases in accounts payable
Decreases in accrued expenses payable	Increases in accrued expenses payable

avoid "double counting" the cash flow from the gain. Likewise, losses from the disposal of fixed assets are *added* to net income in determining cash flows from operations.

Net income is also adjusted for changes in noncash current assets and current liabilities that support operations. Under the indirect method, these items are often listed last as "changes in current operating assets and liabilities." Under this heading, current assets are listed first, followed by current liabilities. Changes in noncash current assets and current liabilities are the result of revenue or expense transactions that may or may not affect cash flow. For example, a sale of $10,000 on account increases accounts receivable by $10,000. However, cash is not affected. Thus, the increase in accounts receivable of $10,000 between two balance sheet dates is *deducted* from net income in arriving at cash flows from operating activities. In contrast, a decrease in accounts receivable indicates the collection of cash that may have been reported as revenues in a prior period. Thus, a decrease in accounts receivable is added to net income in arriving at cash flows from operating activities.

Similar adjustments to net income are required for the changes in the other current asset and liability accounts supporting operations, such as inventory, prepaid expenses, accounts payable, and other accrued expenses. The direction of the adjustment is shown at the bottom of Exhibit 5. For example, an increase in accounts payable from the beginning to the end of the period would be added to net income in determining cash flows from operating activities.

The effect of dividends payable, though a current liability, is not included in the operating activity section of the statement of cash flows. Dividends payable is omitted from Exhibit 5 because dividends are not an operating activity that affects net income. Later in the chapter, we will discuss how dividends are reported in the statement of cash flows as a part of financing activities. In the following paragraphs, we will discuss each of the adjustments that convert Rundell Inc.'s net income to "Cash flows from operating activities."

Depreciation The comparative balance sheet in Exhibit 4 indicates that Accumulated Depreciation—Building increased by $7,000. As shown at the top of the following page, this account indicates that depreciation for the year was $7,000 for the building.

ACCOUNT *Accumulated Depreciation—Building*   ACCOUNT NO.

Date		Item	Debit	Credit	Balance Debit	Balance Credit
2008 Jan.	1	Balance				58 3 0 0 00
Dec.	31	Depreciation for year		7 0 0 0 00		65 3 0 0 00

The $7,000 of depreciation expense reduced net income but did not require an outflow of cash. Thus, the $7,000 is added to net income in determining cash flows from operating activities, as follows:

Cash flows from operating activities:
Net income $108,000
Add depreciation   7,000 $115,000

Gain on Sale of Land   The ledger or income statement of Rundell Inc. indicates that the sale of land resulted in a gain of $12,000. As we discussed previously, the sale proceeds, which include the gain and the carrying value of the land, are included in cash flows from investing activities.[5] The gain is also included in net income. Thus, to avoid double reporting, the gain of $12,000 is deducted from net income in determining cash flows from operating activities, as shown below.

Cash flows from operating activities:
Net income $108,000
Deduct gain on sale of land   12,000

Example Exercise 14-2   objective 2

Omni Corporation's accumulated depreciation increased by $12,000, while patents decreased by $3,400 between balance sheet dates. There were no purchases or sales of depreciable or intangible assets during the year. In addition, the income statement showed a gain of $4,100 from the sale of land. Reconcile a net income of $50,000 to net cash flow from operating activities.

Follow My Example 14-2

Net income $50,000
Adjustments to reconcile net income to net cash flow from operating activities:
   Depreciation   12,000
   Amortization   3,400
   Gain from sale of land . . . .   (4,100)
Net cash flow from operating activities $61,300

For Practice: PE 14-2A, PE 14-2B

Changes in Current Operating Assets and Liabilities   As shown in Exhibit 5, decreases in noncash current assets and increases in current liabilities are added to net income. In contrast, increases in noncash current assets and decreases in current liabilities are deducted from net income. The current asset and current liability accounts of Rundell Inc. are as follows:

---

5 The reporting of the proceeds (cash flows) from the sale of land as part of investing activities is discussed later in this chapter.

| Accounts | December 31 | | Increase |
	2008	2007	Decrease*
Accounts receivable (net)	$ 74,000	$ 65,000	$9,000
Inventories	172,000	180,000	8,000*
Accounts payable (merchandise creditors)	43,500	46,700	3,200*
Accrued expenses payable (operating expenses) ..	26,500	24,300	2,200
Income taxes payable	7,900	8,400	500*

REAL WORLD

Continental Airlines had a net loss of $363 million but a positive cash flow from operating activities of $373 million. This difference was mostly due to $414 million of depreciation expenses and $417 million from changes in operating assets and liabilities.

As discussed previously, the $9,000 increase in *accounts receivable* indicates that the sales on account during the year are $9,000 more than collections from customers on account. The amount reported as sales on the income statement therefore includes $9,000 that did not result in a cash inflow during the year. Thus, $9,000 is deducted from net income.

The $8,000 decrease in *inventories* indicates that the merchandise sold exceeds the cost of the merchandise purchased by $8,000. The amount deducted as cost of merchandise sold on the income statement therefore includes $8,000 that did not require a cash outflow during the year. Thus, $8,000 is added to net income.

The $3,200 decrease in *accounts payable* indicates that the amount of cash payments for merchandise exceeds the merchandise purchased on account by $3,200. The amount reported on the income statement for cost of merchandise sold therefore excludes $3,200 that required a cash outflow during the year. Thus, $3,200 is deducted from net income.

The $2,200 increase in *accrued expenses payable* indicates that the amount incurred during the year for operating expenses exceeds the cash payments by $2,200. The amount reported on the income statement for operating expenses therefore includes $2,200 that did not require a cash outflow during the year. Thus, $2,200 is added to net income.

The $500 decrease in *income taxes payable* indicates that the amount paid for taxes exceeds the amount incurred during the year by $500. The amount reported on the income statement for income tax therefore is less than the amount paid by $500. Thus, $500 is deducted from net income.

Example Exercise 14-3 **objective** **2**

Victor Corporation's comparative balance sheet for current assets and liabilities was as follows:

	Dec. 31, 2009	Dec. 31, 2008
Accounts receivable	$ 6,500	$ 4,900
Inventory	12,300	15,000
Accounts payable	4,800	5,200
Dividends payable	5,000	4,000

Adjust net income of $70,000 for changes in operating assets and liabilities to arrive at cash flows from operating activities.

Follow My Example 14-3

Net income	$70,000
Adjustments to reconcile net income to net cash flow from operating activities:	
Changes in current operating assets and liabilities:	
Increase in accounts receivable	(1,600)
Decrease in inventory	2,700
Decrease in accounts payable	(400)
Net cash flow from operating activities	$70,700

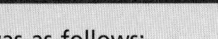

For Practice: PE 14-3A, PE 14-3B

Integrity, Objectivity, and Ethics in Business

CREDIT POLICY AND CASH FLOW

One would expect customers to pay for products and services sold on account. Unfortunately, that is not always the case. Collecting accounts receivable efficiently is the key to turning a current asset into positive cash flow. Most entrepreneurs would rather think about the exciting aspects of their business—such as product development, marketing, sales, and advertising—rather than credit collection. This can be a mistake. Hugh McHugh of Overhill Flowers, Inc., decided that he would have no more trade accounts after dealing with Christmas orders that weren't

paid for until late February, or sometimes not paid at all. As stated by one collection service, "One thing business owners always tell me is that they never thought about [collections] when they started their own business." To small business owners, the collected receivable is often their paycheck, so it pays to pay attention.

Source: Paulette Thomas, "Making Them Pay: The Last Thing Most Entrepreneurs Want to Think About Is Bill Collection; It Should Be One of the First Things," *The Wall Street Journal*, September 19, 2005, p. R6.

Reporting Cash Flows from Operating Activities   We have now presented all the necessary adjustments to convert the net income to cash flows from operating activities for Rundell Inc. These adjustments are summarized in Exhibit 6 for the statement of cash flows.

EXHIBIT 6   Cash Flows from Operating Activities—Indirect Method

Cash flows from operating activities:		
Net income		$108,000
Adjustments to reconcile net income to net cash flow from operating activities:		
Depreciation		7,000
Gain on sale of land		(12,000)
Changes in current operating assets and liabilities:		
Increase in accounts receivable		(9,000)
Decrease in inventory		8,000
Decrease in accounts payable		(3,200)
Increase in accrued expenses		2,200
Decrease in income taxes payable		(500)
Net cash flow from operating activities		$100,500

Example Exercise 14-4 objective 2

Omicron Inc. reported the following data:

Net income	$120,000
Depreciation expense	12,000
Loss on disposal of equipment	15,000
Increase in accounts receivable	5,000
Decrease in accounts payable	2,000

Prepare the cash flows from operating activities section of the statement of cash flows using the indirect method.

(continued)

Follow My Example 14-4

Cash flows from operating activities:	
Net income	$120,000
Adjustments to reconcile net income to net cash flow from operating activities:	
Depreciation	12,000
Loss from disposal of equipment	15,000
Changes in current operating assets and liabilities:	
Increase in accounts receivable	(5,000)
Decrease in accounts payable	(2,000)
Net cash flow from operating activities	$140,000

For Practice: PE 14-4A, PE 14-4B

CASH FLOWS USED FOR PAYMENT OF DIVIDENDS

According to the retained earnings account of Rundell Inc., shown earlier in the chapter, cash dividends of $28,000 were declared during the year. However, the dividends payable account, shown below, indicates that dividends of only $24,000 were paid during the year.

					Balance	
ACCOUNT Dividends Payable					**ACCOUNT NO.**	
Date		Item	Debit	Credit	Debit	Credit
2008 Jan.	1	Balance				10 0 0 0 00
	10	Cash paid	10 0 0 0 00		—	—
June	20	Dividends declared		14 0 0 0 00		14 0 0 0 00
July	10	Cash paid	14 0 0 0 00		—	—
Dec.	20	Dividends declared		14 0 0 0 00		14 0 0 0 00

The $24,000 of dividend payments represents a cash outflow that is reported in the financing activities section as follows:

Cash flows from financing activities:	
Cash paid for dividends	$24,000

COMMON STOCK

The common stock account increased by $8,000, and the paid-in capital in excess of par—common stock account increased by $40,000, as shown below. These increases result from issuing 4,000 shares of common stock for $12 per share.

					Balance	
ACCOUNT Common Stock					**ACCOUNT NO.**	
Date		Item	Debit	Credit	Debit	Credit
2008 Jan.	1	Balance				16 0 0 0 00
Nov.	1	4,000 shares issued for cash		8 0 0 0 00		24 0 0 0 00

					Balance	
ACCOUNT Paid-In Capital in Excess of Par—Common Stock					**ACCOUNT NO.**	
Date		Item	Debit	Credit	Debit	Credit
2008 Jan.	1	Balance				80 0 0 0 00
Nov.	1	4,000 shares issued for cash		40 0 0 0 00		120 0 0 0 00

This cash inflow is reported in the financing activities section as follows:

Cash flows from financing activities:
    Cash received from sale of common stock $48,000

BONDS PAYABLE

The bonds payable account decreased by $50,000, as shown below. This decrease results from retiring the bonds by a cash payment for their face amount.

ACCOUNT Bonds Payable				ACCOUNT NO.	
				Balance	
Date	Item	Debit	Credit	Debit	Credit
2008 Jan. 1	Balance				150 0 0 0 00
June 30	Retired by payment of cash				
	at face amount	50 0 0 0 00			100 0 0 0 00

This cash outflow is reported in the financing activities section as follows:

Cash flows from financing activities:
    Cash paid to retire bonds payable $50,000

BUILDING

The building account increased by $60,000, and the accumulated depreciation—building account increased by $7,000, as shown below.

ACCOUNT Building				ACCOUNT NO.	
				Balance	
Date	Item	Debit	Credit	Debit	Credit
2008 Jan. 1	Balance			200 0 0 0 00	
Dec. 27	Purchased for cash	60 0 0 0 00		260 0 0 0 00	

ACCOUNT Accumulated Depreciation—Building				ACCOUNT NO.	
				Balance	
Date	Item	Debit	Credit	Debit	Credit
2008 Jan. 1	Balance				58 3 0 0 00
Dec. 31	Depreciation for the year		7 0 0 0 00		65 3 0 0 00

The purchase of a building for cash of $60,000 is reported as an outflow of cash in the investing activities section, as follows:

Cash flows from investing activities:
    Cash paid for purchase of building $60,000

The credit in the accumulated depreciation—building account, shown earlier, represents depreciation expense for the year. This depreciation expense of $7,000 on the building has already been considered as an addition to net income in determining cash flows from operating activities, as reported in Exhibit 6.

LAND

The $45,000 decline in the land account resulted from two separate transactions, as shown below.

ACCOUNT *Land*				ACCOUNT NO.	
				Balance	
Date	Item	Debit	Credit	Debit	Credit
2008 Jan. 1	Balance			125 0 0 0 00	
June 8	Sold for $72,000 cash		60 0 0 0 00	65 0 0 0 00	
Oct. 12	Purchased for $15,000 cash	15 0 0 0 00		80 0 0 0 00	

The first transaction is the sale of land with a cost of $60,000 for $72,000 in cash. The $72,000 proceeds from the sale are reported in the investing activities section, as follows:

> Cash flows from investing activities:
> Cash received from sale of land (includes
> $12,000 gain reported in net income) $72,000

The proceeds of $72,000 include the $12,000 gain on the sale of land and the $60,000 cost (book value) of the land. As shown in Exhibit 6, the $12,000 gain is also deducted from net income in the cash flows from operating activities section. This is necessary so that the $12,000 cash inflow related to the gain is not included twice as a cash inflow.

The second transaction is the purchase of land for cash of $15,000. This transaction is reported as an outflow of cash in the investing activities section, as follows:

> Cash flows from investing activities:
> Cash paid for purchase of land $15,000

Example Exercise 14-5   **objective** (2)

Alpha Corporation purchased land for $125,000. Later in the year, the company sold land with a book value of $165,000 for $200,000. How are the effects of these transactions reported on the statement of cash flows?

Follow My Example 14-5

The gain on sale of land is deducted from net income as shown below:
Gain on sale of land . . . . $ (35,000)

The purchase and sale of land is reported as part of cash flows from investing activities as shown below:
Cash received for sale of land   200,000
Cash paid for purchase of land . . . .   (125,000)

For Practice: PE 14-5A, PE 14-5B

PREPARING THE STATEMENT OF CASH FLOWS

The statement of cash flows for Rundell Inc. is prepared from the data assembled and analyzed above, using the indirect method. Exhibit 7 shows the statement of cash flows prepared by Rundell Inc. The statement indicates that the cash position increased by $71,500 during the year. The most significant increase in net cash flows, $100,500, was from operating activities. The most significant use of cash, $26,000, was for financing activities.

EXHIBIT 7

Statement of Cash
Flows—Indirect
Method

Rundell Inc.
Statement of Cash Flows
For the Year Ended December 31, 2008

Cash flows from operating activities:		
Net income	$108,000	
Adjustments to reconcile net income to net cash flow from operating activities:		
Depreciation	7,000	
Gain on sale of land	(12,000)	
Changes in current operating assets and liabilities:		
Increase in accounts receivable	(9,000)	
Decrease in inventory	8,000	
Decrease in accounts payable	(3,200)	
Increase in accrued expenses.	2,200	
Decrease in income taxes payable	(500)	
Net cash flow from operating activities		$100,500
Cash flows from investing activities:		
Cash from sale of land	$ 72,000	
Less: Cash paid to purchase land $15,000		
Cash paid for purchase of building 60,000	75,000	
Net cash flow used for investing activities		(3,000)
Cash flows from financing activities:		
Cash received from sale of common stock	$ 48,000	
Less: Cash paid to retire bonds payable $50,000		
Cash paid for dividends 24,000	74,000	
Net cash flow used for financing activities		(26,000)
Increase in cash		$ 71,500
Cash at the beginning of the year		26,000
Cash at the end of the year		$ 97,500

Statement of Cash Flows—The Direct Method

objective **3**

Prepare a
statement of cash
flows, using the
direct method.

As we discussed previously, the manner of reporting cash flows from investing and financing activities is the same under the direct and indirect methods. In addition, the direct method and the indirect method will report the same amount of cash flows from operating activities. However, the methods differ in how the cash flows from operating activities data are obtained, analyzed, and reported.

To illustrate the direct method, we will use the comparative balance sheet and the income statement for Rundell Inc. In this way, we can compare the statement of cash flows under the direct method and the indirect method.

Exhibit 8 shows the changes in the current asset and liability account balances for Rundell Inc. The income statement in Exhibit 8 shows additional data for Rundell Inc.

The direct method reports cash flows from operating activities by major classes of operating cash receipts and operating cash payments. The difference between the major classes of total operating cash receipts and total operating cash payments is the net cash flow from operating activities.

CASH RECEIVED FROM CUSTOMERS

The $1,180,000 of sales for Rundell Inc. is reported by using the accrual method. To determine the cash received from sales to customers, the $1,180,000 must be adjusted.

EXHIBIT 8

Balance Sheet and
Income Statement
Data for Direct
Method

Rundell Inc.
Schedule of Changes in Current Accounts

Accounts	December 31		Increase Decrease*
	2008	2007	
Cash	$ 97,500	$ 26,000	$71,500
Accounts receivable (net)	74,000	65,000	9,000
Inventories	172,000	180,000	8,000*
Accounts payable (merchandise creditors)	43,500	46,700	3,200*
Accrued expenses payable (operating expenses)	26,500	24,300	2,200
Income taxes payable	7,900	8,400	500*
Dividends payable	14,000	10,000	4,000

Rundell Inc.
Income Statement
For the Year Ended December 31, 2008

Sales		$1,180,000
Cost of merchandise sold		790,000
Gross profit		$ 390,000
Operating expenses:		
Depreciation expense	$ 7,000	
Other operating expenses	196,000	
Total operating expenses		203,000
Income from operations		$ 187,000
Other income:		
Gain on sale of land	$ 12,000	
Other expense:		
Interest expense	8,000	4,000
Income before income tax		$ 191,000
Income tax expense		83,000
Net income		$ 108,000

The adjustment necessary to convert the sales reported on the income statement to the cash received from customers is summarized below.

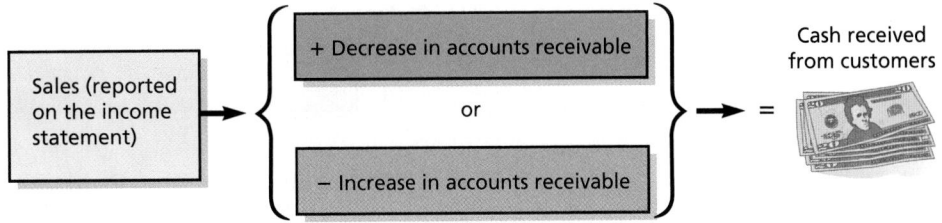

For Rundell Inc., the cash received from customers is $1,171,000, as shown below.

Sales	$1,180,000
Less increase in accounts receivable	9,000
Cash received from customers	$1,171,000

The additions to *accounts receivable* for sales on account during the year were $9,000 more than the amounts collected from customers on account. Sales reported on the income statement therefore included $9,000 that did not result in a cash inflow during the year. In other words, the increase of $9,000 in accounts receivable during 2008 indicates that sales on account exceeded cash received from customers by $9,000. Thus, $9,000 is deducted from sales to determine the cash received from customers. The $1,171,000 of cash received from customers is reported in the cash flows from operating activities section of the cash flow statement.

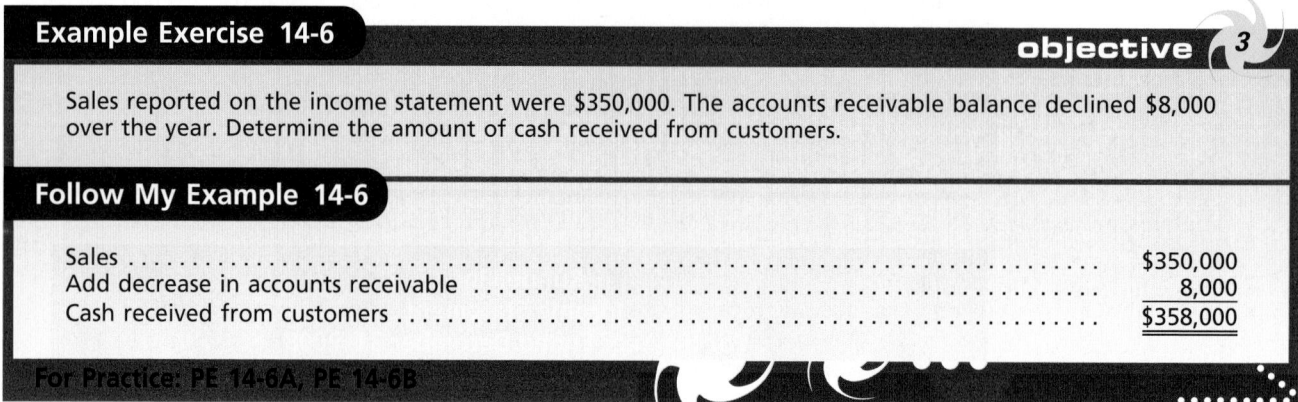

Example Exercise 14-6   objective 3

Sales reported on the income statement were $350,000. The accounts receivable balance declined $8,000 over the year. Determine the amount of cash received from customers.

Follow My Example 14-6

Sales	$350,000
Add decrease in accounts receivable	8,000
Cash received from customers	$358,000

For Practice: PE 14-6A, PE 14-6B

CASH PAYMENTS FOR MERCHANDISE

The $790,000 of cost of merchandise sold is reported on the income statement for Rundell Inc. using the accrual method. The adjustments necessary to convert the cost of merchandise sold to cash payments for merchandise during 2008 are summarized below.

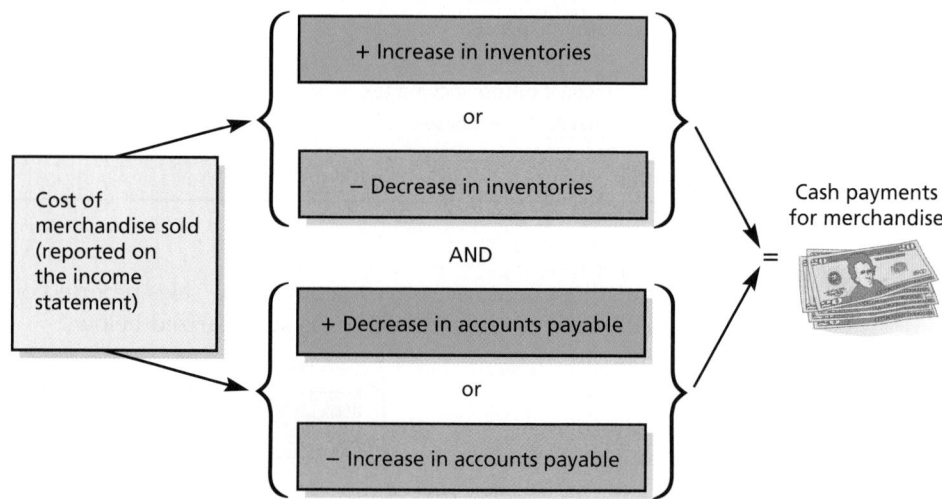

For Rundell Inc., the amount of cash payments for merchandise is $785,200, as determined below.

Cost of merchandise sold	$790,000
Deduct decrease in inventories	(8,000)
Add decrease in accounts payable	3,200
Cash payments for merchandise	$785,200

The $8,000 decrease in *inventories* indicates that the merchandise sold exceeded the cost of the merchandise purchased by $8,000. The amount reported on the income statement for cost of merchandise sold therefore includes $8,000 that did not require a cash outflow during the year. Thus, $8,000 is deducted from the cost of merchandise sold in determining the cash payments for merchandise.

The $3,200 decrease in *accounts payable* (merchandise creditors) indicates a cash outflow that is excluded from cost of merchandise sold. That is, the decrease in accounts payable indicates that cash payments for merchandise were $3,200 more than the purchases on account during 2008. Thus, $3,200 is added to the cost of merchandise sold in determining the cash payments for merchandise.

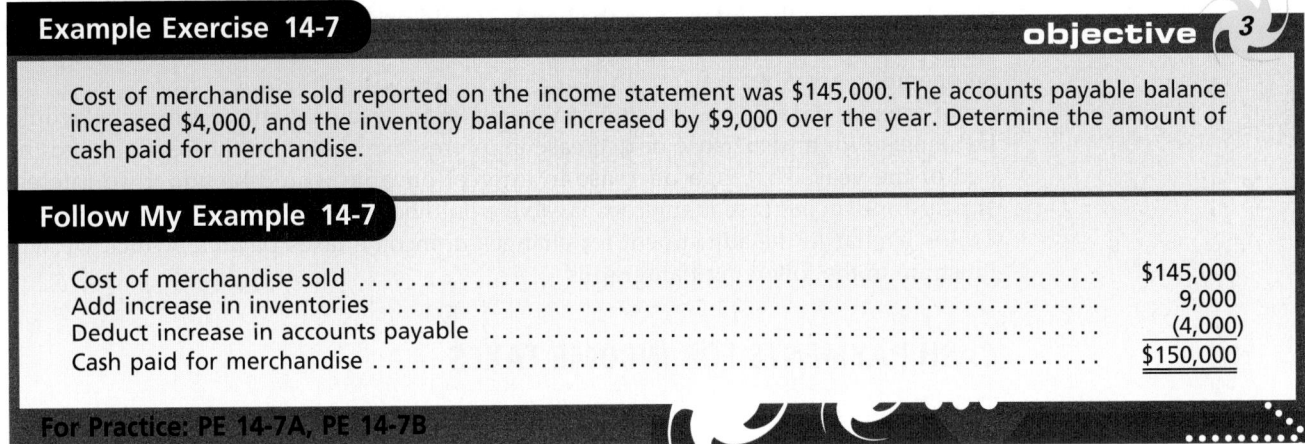

Example Exercise 14-7   objective 3

Cost of merchandise sold reported on the income statement was $145,000. The accounts payable balance increased $4,000, and the inventory balance increased by $9,000 over the year. Determine the amount of cash paid for merchandise.

Follow My Example 14-7

Cost of merchandise sold	$145,000
Add increase in inventories	9,000
Deduct increase in accounts payable	(4,000)
Cash paid for merchandise	$150,000

For Practice: PE 14-7A, PE 14-7B

CASH PAYMENTS FOR OPERATING EXPENSES

The $7,000 of depreciation expense reported on the income statement did not require a cash outflow. Thus, under the direct method, it is not reported on the statement of cash flows. The $196,000 reported for other operating expenses is adjusted to reflect the cash payments for operating expenses, as summarized below.

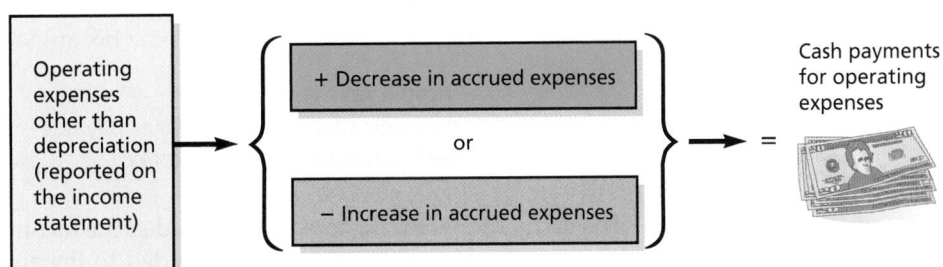

For Rundell Inc., the amount of cash payments for operating expenses is $193,800, determined as follows:

Operating expenses other than depreciation	$196,000
Deduct increase in accrued expenses	2,200
Cash payments for operating expenses	$193,800

The increase in *accrued expenses* (operating expenses) indicates that operating expenses include $2,200 for which there was no cash outflow (payment) during the year. That is, the increase in accrued expenses indicates that the cash payments for operating expenses were $2,200 less than the amount reported as an expense during the year. Thus, $2,200 is deducted from the operating expenses on the income statement in determining the cash payments for operating expenses.

GAIN ON SALE OF LAND

The income statement for Rundell Inc. in Exhibit 8 reports a gain of $12,000 on the sale of land. As we discussed previously, the gain is included in the proceeds from the sale of land, which is reported as part of the cash flows from investing activities.

INTEREST EXPENSE

The income statement for Rundell Inc. in Exhibit 8 reports interest expense of $8,000. The interest expense is related to the bonds payable that were outstanding during the year. We assume that interest on the bonds is paid on June 30 and December 31. Thus, $8,000 cash outflow for interest expense is reported on the statement of cash flows as an operating activity.

If interest payable had existed at the end of the year, the interest expense would be adjusted for any increase or decrease in interest payable from the beginning to the end of the year. That is, a decrease in interest payable would be added to interest expense and an increase in interest payable would be subtracted from interest expense. This is similar to the adjustment for changes in income taxes payable, which we will illustrate in the following paragraphs.

CASH PAYMENTS FOR INCOME TAXES

The adjustment to convert the income tax reported on the income statement to the cash basis is summarized below.

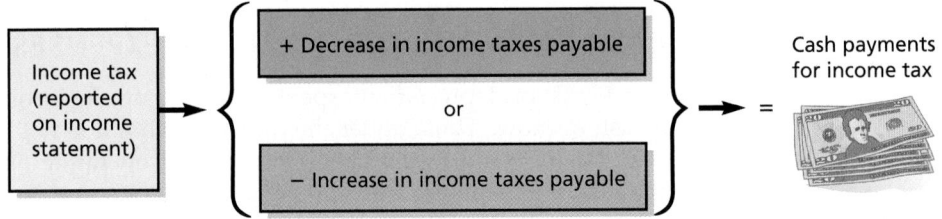

For Rundell Inc., cash payments for income tax are $83,500, determined as follows:

Income tax	$83,000
Add decrease in income taxes payable	500
Cash payments for income tax	$83,500

The cash outflow for income taxes exceeded the income tax deducted as an expense during the period by $500. Thus, $500 is added to the amount of income tax reported on the income statement in determining the cash payments for income tax.

REPORTING CASH FLOWS FROM OPERATING ACTIVITIES—DIRECT METHOD

Exhibit 9 is a complete statement of cash flows for Rundell Inc., using the direct method for reporting cash flows from operating activities. The portions of this statement that differ from the indirect method are highlighted in color. Exhibit 9 also includes the separate schedule reconciling net income and net cash flow from operating activities. This schedule must accompany the statement of cash flows when the direct method is used. This schedule is similar to the cash flows from operating activities section of the statement of cash flows prepared using the indirect method.

EXHIBIT 9

Statement of Cash
Flows—Direct Method

Rundell Inc.
Statement of Cash Flows
For the Year Ended December 31, 2008

Cash flows from operating activities:			
Cash received from customers		$1,171,000	
Deduct: Cash payments for merchandise	$785,200		
Cash payments for operating expenses	193,800		
Cash payments for interest	8,000		
Cash payments for income taxes	83,500	1,070,500	
Net cash flow from operating activities			$100,500
Cash flows from investing activities:			
Cash from sale of land		$ 72,000	
Less: Cash paid to purchase land	$ 15,000		
Cash paid for purchase of building	60,000	75,000	
Net cash flow used for investing activities			(3,000)
Cash flows from financing activities:			
Cash received from sale of common stock		$ 48,000	
Less: Cash paid to retire bonds payable	$ 50,000		
Cash paid for dividends	24,000	74,000	
Net cash flow used for financing activities			(26,000)
Increase in cash			$ 71,500
Cash at the beginning of the year			26,000
Cash at the end of the year			$ 97,500

**Schedule Reconciling Net Income with Cash
Flows from Operating Activities:**

Cash flows from operating activities:	
Net income	$108,000
Adjustments to reconcile net income to net cash flow from operating activities:	
Depreciation	7,000
Gain on sale of land	(12,000)
Changes in current operating assets and liabilities:	
Increase in accounts receivable	(9,000)
Decrease in inventory	8,000
Decrease in accounts payable	(3,200)
Increase in accrued expenses	2,200
Decrease in income taxes payable	(500)
Net cash flow from operating activities	$100,500

Financial Analysis and Interpretation

A valuable tool for evaluating the cash flows of a business is free cash flow. **Free cash flow** is a measure of operating cash flow available for corporate purposes after providing sufficient fixed asset additions to maintain current productive capacity and dividends. Thus, free cash flow can be calculated as follows:

Cash flow from operating activities	$XXX
Less: Investments in fixed assets to maintain current production	XXX
Free cash flow	$XXX

Analysts often use free cash flow, rather than cash flows from operating activities, to measure the financial strength of a business. Many high-technology firms must aggressively reinvest in new technology to remain competitive. This can reduce free cash flow. For example, Motorola Inc.'s free cash flow is less than 10% of the cash flow from operating activities. In contrast, The Coca-Cola Company's free cash flow is approximately 75% of the cash flow from operating activities. The top three nonfinancial companies with the largest free cash flows for a recent year were as follows:

	Free Cash Flow (in millions)
General Electric Company	$25,598
ExxonMobil Corporation	18,705
Microsoft Corporation	14,289

To illustrate, the cash flow from operating activities for Intuit Inc., the developer of TurboTax®, was $590 million in a recent fiscal year. The statement of cash flows indicated that the cash invested in property, plant, and equipment was $38 million. Assuming that the amount invested in property, plant, and equipment maintained existing operations, free cash flow would be calculated as follows (in millions):

Cash flow from operating activities	$590
Less: Investments in fixed assets to maintain current production	38
Free cash flow	$552

During this period, Intuit generated free cash flow in excess of $500 million, which was 94% of cash flows from operations and over 27% of sales.

Positive free cash flow is considered favorable. A company that has free cash flow is able to fund internal growth, retire debt, pay dividends, and enjoy financial flexibility. A company with no free cash flow is unable to maintain current productive capacity. Lack of free cash flow can be an early indicator of liquidity problems. As stated by one analyst, "Free cash flow gives the company firepower to reduce debt and ultimately generate consistent, actual income."[6]

Source: "CFO Free Cash Flow Scorecard," *CFO Magazine*, January 1, 2005.

Appendix

Spreadsheet (Work Sheet) for Statement of Cash Flows—The Indirect Method

A spreadsheet (work sheet) may be useful in assembling data for the statement of cash flows. Whether or not a spreadsheet (work sheet) is used, the concepts of cash flow and the statements of cash flows presented in this chapter are not affected. In this appendix, we will describe and illustrate use of the spreadsheet (work sheet) for the indirect method.

6 Jill Krutick, *Fortune*, March 30, 1998, p. 106.

We will use the data for Rundell Inc., presented in Exhibit 4, as a basis for illustrating the spreadsheet (work sheet) for the indirect method. The procedures used in preparing this spreadsheet (work sheet), shown in Exhibit 10, are outlined below.

1. List the title of each balance sheet account in the Accounts column. For each account, enter its balance as of December 31, 2007, in the first column and its balance as of December 31, 2008, in the last column. Place the credit balances in parentheses. The column totals should equal zero, since the total of the debits in a column should equal the total of the credits in a column.
2. Analyze the change during the year in each account to determine the net increase (decrease) in cash and the cash flows from operating activities, investing activities, financing activities, and the noncash investing and financing activities. Show the effect of the change on cash flows by making entries in the Transactions columns.

ANALYZING ACCOUNTS

An efficient method of analyzing cash flows is to determine the type of cash flow activity that led to changes in balance sheet accounts during the period. As we analyze each noncash account, we will make entries on the spreadsheet (work sheet) for specific types of cash flow activities related to the noncash accounts. After we have analyzed all the noncash accounts, we will make an entry for the increase (decrease) in cash during the period. These entries, however, are not posted to the ledger. They only aid in assembling the data on the spreadsheet.

The order in which the accounts are analyzed is unimportant. However, it is more efficient to begin with the retained earnings account and proceed upward in the account listing.

RETAINED EARNINGS

The spreadsheet (work sheet) shows a Retained Earnings balance of $202,300 at December 31, 2007, and $282,300 at December 31, 2008. Thus, Retained Earnings increased $80,000 during the year. This increase resulted from two factors: (1) net income of $108,000 and (2) declaring cash dividends of $28,000. To identify the cash flows by activity, we will make two entries on the spreadsheet. These entries also serve to account for or explain, in terms of cash flows, the increase of $80,000.

In closing the accounts at the end of the year, the retained earnings account was credited for the net income of $108,000. The $108,000 is reported on the statement of cash flows as "cash flows from operating activities." The following entry is made in the Transactions columns on the spreadsheet. This entry (1) accounts for the credit portion of the closing entry (to Retained Earnings) and (2) identifies the cash flow in the bottom portion of the spreadsheet.

(a)	Operating Activities—Net Income	108,000	
	Retained Earnings		108,000

In closing the accounts at the end of the year, the retained earnings account was debited for dividends declared of $28,000. The $28,000 is reported as a financing activity on the statement of cash flows. The following entry on the spreadsheet (1) accounts for the debit portion of the closing entry (to Retained Earnings) and (2) identifies the cash flow in the bottom portion of the spreadsheet.

(b)	Retained Earnings	28,000	
	Financing Activities—Declared Cash Dividends		28,000

The $28,000 of declared dividends will be adjusted later for the actual amount of cash dividends paid during the year.

EXHIBIT 10   End-of-Period Spreadsheet (Work Sheet) for Statement of Cash Flows—Indirect Method

Rundell Inc.
End-of-Period Spreadsheet (Work Sheet) for Statement of Cash Flows
For the Year Ended December 31, 2008

	Accounts	Balance, Dec. 31, 2007		Debit		Credit	Balance, Dec. 31, 2008	
1	Cash	26,000	(o)	71,500			97,500	1
2	Accounts receivable (net)	65,000	(n)	9,000			74,000	2
3	Inventories	180,000			(m)	8,000	172,000	3
4	Land	125,000	(k)	15,000	(l)	60,000	80,000	4
5	Building	200,000	(j)	60,000			260,000	5
6	Accumulated depreciation—building	(58,300)			(i)	7,000	(65,300)	6
7	Accounts payable (merchandise creditors)	(46,700)	(h)	3,200			(43,500)	7
8	Accrued expenses payable (operating expenses)	(24,300)			(g)	2,200	(26,500)	8
9	Income taxes payable	(8,400)	(f)	500			(7,900)	9
10	Dividends payable	(10,000)			(e)	4,000	(14,000)	10
11	Bonds payable	(150,000)	(d)	50,000			(100,000)	11
12	Common stock	(16,000)			(c)	8,000	(24,000)	12
13	Paid-in capital in excess of par	(80,000)			(c)	40,000	(120,000)	13
14	Retained earnings	(202,300)	(b)	28,000	(a)	108,000	(282,300)	14
15	Totals	0		237,200		237,200	0	15
16	Operating activities:							16
17	Net income		(a)	108,000				17
18	Depreciation of building		(i)	7,000				18
19	Gain on sale of land				(l)	12,000		19
20	Increase in accounts receivable				(n)	9,000		20
21	Decrease in inventories		(m)	8,000				21
22	Decrease in accounts payable				(h)	3,200		22
23	Increase in accrued expenses		(g)	2,200				23
24	Decrease in income taxes payable				(f)	500		24
25	Investing activities:							25
26	Sale of land		(l)	72,000				26
27	Purchase of land				(k)	15,000		27
28	Purchase of building				(j)	60,000		28
29	Financing activities:							29
30	Issued common stock		(c)	48,000				30
31	Retired bonds payable				(d)	50,000		31
32	Declared cash dividends				(b)	28,000		32
33	Increase in dividends payable		(e)	4,000				33
34	Net increase in cash				(o)	71,500		34
35	Totals			249,200		249,200		35

OTHER ACCOUNTS

The entries for the other accounts are made in the spreadsheet in a manner similar to entries (a) and (b). A summary of these entries is as follows:

(c)	Financing Activities—Issued Common Stock	48,000	
	Common Stock		8,000
	Paid-In Capital in Excess of Par—Common Stock		40,000
(d)	Bonds Payable	50,000	
	Financing Activities—Retired Bonds Payable		50,000
(e)	Financing Activities—Increase in Dividends Payable	4,000	
	Dividends Payable		4,000
(f)	Income Taxes Payable	500	
	Operating Activities—Decrease in Income Taxes Payable		500

(g)	Operating Activities—Increase in Accrued Expenses	2,200	
	Accrued Expenses Payable		2,200
(h)	Accounts Payable	3,200	
	Operating Activities—Decrease in Accounts Payable		3,200
(i)	Operating Activities—Depreciation of Building	7,000	
	Accumulated Depreciation—Building		7,000
(j)	Building	60,000	
	Investing Activities—Purchase of Building		60,000
(k)	Land	15,000	
	Investing Activities—Purchase of Land		15,000
(l)	Investing Activities—Sale of Land	72,000	
	Operating Activities—Gain on Sale of Land		12,000
	Land		60,000
(m)	Operating Activities—Decrease in Inventories	8,000	
	Inventories		8,000
(n)	Accounts Receivable	9,000	
	Operating Activities—Increase in Accounts Receivable		9,000
(o)	Cash	71,500	
	Net Increase in Cash		71,500

After we have analyzed all the balance sheet accounts and made the entries on the spreadsheet (work sheet), all the operating, investing, and financing activities are identified in the bottom portion of the spreadsheet. The accuracy of the spreadsheet entries is verified by the equality of each pair of the totals of the debit and credit Transactions columns.

PREPARING THE STATEMENT OF CASH FLOWS

The statement of cash flows prepared from the spreadsheet is identical to the statement in Exhibit 7. The data for the three sections of the statement are obtained from the bottom portion of the spreadsheet.

At a Glance

1. Summarize the types of cash flow activities reported in the statement of cash flows.

Key Points	Key Learning Outcomes	Example Exercises	Practice Exercises
The statement of cash flows reports cash receipts and cash payments by three types of activities: operating activities, investing activities, and financing activities. Investing and financing for a business may be affected by transactions that do not involve cash. The effect of such transactions should be reported in a separate schedule accompanying the statement of cash flows.	• Classify transactions that either provide or use cash into either operating, investing, or financing activities.	**14-1**	14-1A, 14-1B

(continued)

2. Prepare a statement of cash flows, using the indirect method.

Key Points	Key Learning Outcomes	Example Exercises	Practice Exercises
The changes in the noncash balance sheet accounts are used to develop the statement of cash flows, beginning with the cash flows from operating activities.			
Determine the cash flows from operating activities using the indirect method by adjusting net income for expenses that do not require cash and for gains and losses from disposal of fixed assets.	• Adjust net income for non-cash expenses and gains and losses from asset disposals under the indirect method.	**14-2**	14-2A, 14-2B
Determine the cash flows from operating activities using the indirect method by adjusting net income for changes in current operating assets and liabilities.	• Adjust net income for changes in current operating assets and liabilities under the indirect method.	**14-3**	14-3A, 14-3B
Report cash flows from operating activities under the indirect method.	• Prepare the cash flows from operating activities under the indirect method in proper form.	**14-4**	14-4A, 14-4B
Report investing and financing activities on the statement of cash flows.	• Prepare the remainder of the statement of cash flows by reporting investing and financing activities.	**14-5**	14-5A, 14-5B

3. Prepare a statement of cash flows, using the direct method.

Key Points	Key Learning Outcomes	Example Exercises	Practice Exercises
The direct method reports cash flows from operating activities by major classes of operating cash receipts and cash payments. The difference between the major classes of total operating cash receipts and total operating cash payments is the net cash flow from operating activities. The investing and financing activities sections of the statement are the same as under the indirect method.	• Prepare the cash flows from operating activities and the remainder of the statement of cash flows under the direct method.	**14-6** **14-7**	14-6A, 14-6B 14-7A, 14-7B

Key Terms

cash flows from financing activities (610)
cash flows from investing activities (610)
cash flows from operating activities (610)
direct method (612)
free cash flow (630)
indirect method (612)
statement of cash flows (610)

Illustrative Problem

The comparative balance sheet of Dowling Company for December 31, 2008 and 2007, is as follows:

Dowling Company
Comparative Balance Sheet
December 31, 2008 and 2007

Assets	2008	2007
Cash	$ 140,350	$ 95,900
Accounts receivable (net)	95,300	102,300
Inventories	165,200	157,900
Prepaid expenses	6,240	5,860
Investments (long-term)	35,700	84,700
Land	75,000	90,000
Buildings	375,000	260,000
Accumulated depreciation—buildings	(71,300)	(58,300)
Machinery and equipment	428,300	428,300
Accumulated depreciation—machinery and equipment	(148,500)	(138,000)
Patents	58,000	65,000
Total assets	$1,159,290	$1,093,660

Liabilities and Stockholders' Equity	2008	2007
Accounts payable (merchandise creditors)	$ 43,500	$ 46,700
Accrued expenses (operating expenses)	14,000	12,500
Income taxes payable	7,900	8,400
Dividends payable	14,000	10,000
Mortgage note payable, due 2019	40,000	0
Bonds payable	150,000	250,000
Common stock, $30 par	450,000	375,000
Excess of issue price over par—common stock	66,250	41,250
Retained earnings	373,640	349,810
Total liabilities and stockholders' equity	$1,159,290	$1,093,660

The income statement for Dowling Company is shown below.

Dowling Company
Income Statement
For the Year Ended December 31, 2008

Sales		$1,100,000
Cost of merchandise sold		710,000
Gross profit		$ 390,000
Operating expenses:		
Depreciation expense	$ 23,500	
Patent amortization	7,000	
Other operating expenses	196,000	
Total operating expenses		226,500
Income from operations		$ 163,500
Other income:		
Gain on sale of investments	$ 11,000	
Other expense:		
Interest expense	26,000	(15,000)
Income before income tax		$ 148,500
Income tax expense		50,000
Net income		$ 98,500

An examination of the accounting records revealed the following additional information applicable to 2008:

a. Land costing $15,000 was sold for $15,000.
b. A mortgage note was issued for $40,000.
c. A building costing $115,000 was constructed.
d. 2,500 shares of common stock were issued at 40 in exchange for the bonds payable.
e. Cash dividends declared were $74,670.

Instructions

1. Prepare a statement of cash flows, using the indirect method of reporting cash flows from operating activities.
2. Prepare a statement of cash flows, using the direct method of reporting cash flows from operating activities.

Solution

1.

Dowling Company
Statement of Cash Flows—Indirect Method
For the Year Ended December 31, 2008

Cash flows from operating activities:			
Net income		$ 98,500	
Adjustments to reconcile net income to net			
cash flow from operating activities:			
Depreciation		23,500	
Amortization of patents		7,000	
Gain on sale of investments		(11,000)	
Changes in current operating assets and			
liabilities:			
Decrease in accounts receivable		7,000	
Increase in inventories		(7,300)	
Increase in prepaid expenses		(380)	
Decrease in accounts payable		(3,200)	
Increase in accrued expenses		1,500	
Decrease in income taxes payable		(500)	
Net cash flow from operating activities			$115,120
Cash flows from investing activities:			
Cash received from sale of:			
Investments	$60,000		
Land	15,000	$ 75,000	
Less: Cash paid for construction of building		115,000	
Net cash flow used for investing activities			(40,000)
Cash flows from financing activities:			
Cash received from issuing mortgage note			
payable		$ 40,000	
Less: Cash paid for dividends		70,670	
Net cash flow used for financing activities			(30,670)
Increase in cash			$ 44,450
Cash at the beginning of the year			95,900
Cash at the end of the year			$140,350
Schedule of Noncash Investing and			
Financing Activities:			
Issued common stock to retire bonds payable . .			$100,000

2.

Dowling Company
Statement of Cash Flows—Direct Method
For the Year Ended December 31, 2008

Cash flows from operating activities:

Cash received from customers[1]		$1,107,000	
Deduct: Cash paid for merchandise[2]	$720,500		
Cash paid for operating expenses[3]	194,880		
Cash paid for interest expense	26,000		
Cash paid for income tax[4]	50,500	991,880	
Net cash flow from operating activities			$115,120
Cash flows from investing activities:			
Cash received from sale of:			
Investments	$ 60,000		
Land	15,000	$ 75,000	
Less: Cash paid for construction of building . . .		115,000	
Net cash flow used for investing activities			(40,000)
Cash flows from financing activities:			
Cash received from issuing mortgage			
note payable		$ 40,000	
Less: Cash paid for dividends[5]		70,670	
Net cash flow used for financing activities			(30,670)
Increase in cash			$ 44,450
Cash at the beginning of the year			95,900
Cash at the end of the year			$140,350

Schedule of Noncash Investing and
Financing Activities:

Issued common stock to retire bonds payable . .	$100,000

Schedule Reconciling Net Income with Cash Flows
from Operating Activities[6]

Computations:
[1]$1,100,000 + $7,000 = $1,107,000
[2]$710,000 + $3,200 + $7,300 = $720,500
[3]$196,000 + $380 − $1,500 = $194,880
[4]$50,000 + $500 = $50,500

[5]$74,670 + $10,000 − $14,000 = $70,670
[6]The content of this schedule is the same as the operating activities section of part (1) of this solution and is not reproduced here for the sake of brevity.

Self-Examination Questions

(Answers at End of Chapter)

1. An example of a cash flow from an operating activity is:
   A. receipt of cash from the sale of stock.
   B. receipt of cash from the sale of bonds.
   C. payment of cash for dividends.
   D. receipt of cash from customers on account.

2. An example of a cash flow from an investing activity is:
   A. receipt of cash from the sale of equipment.
   B. receipt of cash from the sale of stock.
   C. payment of cash for dividends.
   D. payment of cash to acquire treasury stock.

3. An example of a cash flow from a financing activity is:
   A. receipt of cash from customers on account.
   B. receipt of cash from the sale of equipment.

   C. payment of cash for dividends.
   D. payment of cash to acquire land.

4. Which of the following methods of reporting cash flows from operating activities adjusts net income for revenues and expenses not involving the receipt or payment of cash?
   A. Direct method   C. Reciprocal method
   B. Purchase method   D. Indirect method

5. The net income reported on the income statement for the year was $55,000, and depreciation of fixed assets for the year was $22,000. The balances of the current asset and current liability accounts at the beginning and end of the year are shown at the top of the following page.

	End	Beginning
Cash	$ 65,000	$ 70,000
Accounts receivable	100,000	90,000
Inventories	145,000	150,000
Prepaid expenses	7,500	8,000
Accounts payable		
(merchandise creditors)	51,000	58,000

The total amount reported for cash flows from operating activities in the statement of cash flows, using the indirect method, is:

A. $33,000.   C. $65,500.
B. $55,000.   D. $77,000.

Eye Openers

1. What is the principal disadvantage of the direct method of reporting cash flows from operating activities?
2. What are the major advantages of the indirect method of reporting cash flows from operating activities?
3. A corporation issued $300,000 of common stock in exchange for $300,000 of fixed assets. Where would this transaction be reported on the statement of cash flows?
4. a. What is the effect on cash flows of declaring and issuing a stock dividend?
   b. Is the stock dividend reported on the statement of cash flows?
5. A retail business, using the accrual method of accounting, owed merchandise creditors (accounts payable) $290,000 at the beginning of the year and $315,000 at the end of the year. How would the $25,000 increase be used to adjust net income in determining the amount of cash flows from operating activities by the indirect method? Explain.
6. If salaries payable was $75,000 at the beginning of the year and $60,000 at the end of the year, should $15,000 be added to or deducted from income to determine the amount of cash flows from operating activities by the indirect method? Explain.
7. A long-term investment in bonds with a cost of $75,000 was sold for $84,000 cash. (a) What was the gain or loss on the sale? (b) What was the effect of the transaction on cash flows? (c) How should the transaction be reported in the statement of cash flows if cash flows from operating activities are reported by the indirect method?
8. A corporation issued $4,000,000 of 20-year bonds for cash at 105. How would the transaction be reported on the statement of cash flows?
9. Fully depreciated equipment costing $65,000 was discarded. What was the effect of the transaction on cash flows if (a) $12,000 cash is received, (b) no cash is received?
10. For the current year, Bearings Company decided to switch from the indirect method to the direct method for reporting cash flows from operating activities on the statement of cash flows. Will the change cause the amount of net cash flow from operating activities to be (a) larger, (b) smaller, or (c) the same as if the indirect method had been used? Explain.
11. Name five common major classes of operating cash receipts or operating cash payments presented on the statement of cash flows when the cash flows from operating activities are reported by the direct method.
12. In a recent annual report, eBay Inc. reported that during the year it issued stock of $128 million for acquisitions. How would this be reported on the statement of cash flows?

Practice Exercises

PE 14-1A
Classifying cash flows
obj. 1

Identify whether each of the following would be reported as an operating, investing, or financing activity in the statement of cash flows.

a. Issuance of bonds payable
b. Collection of accounts receivable
c. Purchase of investments

d. Disposal of equipment
e. Payment for selling expenses
f. Cash sales

PE 14-1B
Classifying cash flows
obj. 1

Identify whether each of the following would be reported as an operating, investing, or financing activity in the statement of cash flows.

a. Payment for administrative expenses

b. Retirement of bonds payable

c. Purchase of land

d. Issuance of common stock

e. Cash received from customers

f. Payment of accounts payable

PE 14-2A
Adjustments to net income—indirect method
obj. 2

Zale Corporation's accumulated depreciation—equipment increased by $8,000, while patents decreased by $5,200 between balance sheet dates. There were no purchases or sales of depreciable or intangible assets during the year. In addition, the income statement showed a loss of $6,000 from the sale of investments. Reconcile a net income of $90,000 to net cash flow from operating activities.

PE 14-2B
Adjustments to net income—indirect method
obj. 2

Nordic Corporation's accumulated depreciation—furniture increased by $3,500, while patents decreased by $1,800 between balance sheet dates. There were no purchases or sales of depreciable or intangible assets during the year. In addition, the income statement showed a gain of $12,500 from the sale of land. Reconcile a net income of $125,000 to net cash flow from operating activities.

PE 14-3A
Changes in current operating assets and liabilities—indirect method
obj. 2

Sage Corporation's comparative balance sheet for current assets and liabilities was as follows:

	Dec. 31, 2008	Dec. 31, 2007
Accounts receivable	$12,000	$14,000
Inventory	9,000	6,500
Accounts payable	8,500	7,200
Dividends payable	24,000	26,000

Adjust net income of $110,000 for changes in operating assets and liabilities to arrive at cash flows from operating activities.

PE 14-3B
Changes in current operating assets and liabilities—indirect method
obj. 2

Lanier Corporation's comparative balance sheet for current assets and liabilities was as follows:

	Dec. 31, 2008	Dec. 31, 2007
Accounts receivable	$32,500	$25,000
Inventory	69,000	48,000
Accounts payable	51,500	32,000
Dividends payable	15,000	16,400

Adjust net income of $290,000 for changes in operating assets and liabilities to arrive at cash flows from operating activities.

PE 14-4A
Reporting cash flows from operating activities—indirect method
obj. 2

Texas Holdem Inc. reported the following data:

Net income	$85,000
Depreciation expense	14,000
Gain on disposal of equipment	10,500
Decrease in accounts receivable	6,000
Decrease in accounts payable	1,800

Prepare the cash flows from operating activities section of the statement of cash flows using the indirect method.

PE 14-4B
Reporting cash flows from operating activities—indirect method
obj. 2

Pier Inc. reported the following data:

Net income	$150,000
Depreciation expense	25,000
Loss on disposal of equipment	14,300
Increase in accounts receivable	9,400
Increase in accounts payable	4,300

Prepare the cash flows from operating activities section of the statement of cash flows using the indirect method.

PE 14-5A
*Reporting land
transactions on the
statement of cash flows*
obj. 2

Gamma Corporation purchased land for $200,000. Later in the year, the company sold land with a book value of $105,000 for $90,000. How are the effects of these transactions reported on the statement of cash flows?

PE 14-5B
*Reporting land
transactions on the
statement of cash flows*
obj. 2

Sunrise Corporation purchased land for $500,000. Later in the year, the company sold land with a book value of $320,000 for $375,000. How are the effects of these transactions reported on the statement of cash flows?

PE 14-6A
*Cash received from
customers—direct
method*
obj. 3

Sales reported on the income statement were $623,000. The accounts receivable balance increased $48,000 over the year. Determine the amount of cash received from customers.

PE 14-6B
*Cash received from
customers—direct
method*
obj. 3

Sales reported on the income statement were $58,400. The accounts receivable balance decreased $2,100 over the year. Determine the amount of cash received from customers.

PE 14-7A
*Cash payments for
merchandise—direct
method*
obj. 3

Cost of merchandise sold reported on the income statement was $568,000. The accounts payable balance decreased $28,000, and the inventory balance decreased by $39,000 over the year. Determine the amount of cash paid for merchandise.

PE 14-7B
*Cash payments for
merchandise—direct
method*
obj. 3

Cost of merchandise sold reported on the income statement was $111,000. The accounts payable balance increased $5,700, and the inventory balance increased by $8,400 over the year. Determine the amount of cash paid for merchandise.

Exercises

EX 14-1
*Cash flows from
operating activities—net
loss*
obj. 1

On its income statement for a recent year, Northwest Airlines Corporation reported a net *loss* of $862 million from operations. On its statement of cash flows, it reported $271 million of cash flows from operating activities.

⟶ Explain this apparent contradiction between the loss and the positive cash flows.

EX 14-2
*Effect of transactions on
cash flows*
obj. 1
✓ *b. Cash receipt, $36,000*

State the effect (cash receipt or payment and amount) of each of the following transactions, considered individually, on cash flows:

a. Sold 5,000 shares of $30 par common stock for $90 per share.
b. Sold equipment with a book value of $42,500 for $36,000.
c. Purchased land for $250,000 cash.
d. Purchased 5,000 shares of $30 par common stock as treasury stock at $60 per share.
e. Sold a new issue of $100,000 of bonds at 98.
f. Paid dividends of $1.50 per share. There were 40,000 shares issued and 5,000 shares of treasury stock.

g. Retired $500,000 of bonds, on which there was $2,500 of unamortized discount, for $500,500.

h. Purchased a building by paying $40,000 cash and issuing a $90,000 mortgage note payable.

EX 14-3
Classifying cash flows
obj. 1

Identify the type of cash flow activity for each of the following events (operating, investing, or financing):

a. Issued preferred stock.

b. Net income.

c. Sold equipment.

d. Purchased treasury stock.

e. Purchased buildings.

f. Purchased patents.

g. Issued bonds.

h. Issued common stock.

i. Sold long-term investments.

j. Paid cash dividends.

k. Redeemed bonds.

EX 14-4
Cash flows from operating activities—indirect method
obj. 2

Indicate whether each of the following would be added to or deducted from net income in determining net cash flow from operating activities by the indirect method:

a. Gain on retirement of long-term debt

b. Increase in merchandise inventory

c. Amortization of patent

d. Decrease in accounts receivable

e. Depreciation of fixed assets

f. Decrease in prepaid expenses

g. Decrease in salaries payable

h. Increase in notes receivable due in 90 days from customers

i. Decrease in accounts payable

j. Loss on disposal of fixed assets

k. Increase in notes payable due in 90 days to vendors

EX 14-5
Cash flows from operating activities—indirect method
obj. 2

✓ *Net cash flow from operating activities, $111,700*

The net income reported on the income statement for the current year was $92,000. Depreciation recorded on store equipment for the year amounted to $18,600. Balances of the current asset and current liability accounts at the beginning and end of the year are as follows:

	End of Year	Beginning of Year
Cash	$46,700	$44,200
Accounts receivable (net)	32,300	31,100
Merchandise inventory	54,800	56,700
Prepaid expenses	4,000	3,500
Accounts payable (merchandise creditors)	46,000	42,900
Wages payable	21,400	23,600

Prepare the cash flows from operating activities section of the statement of cash flows, using the indirect method.

EX 14-6
Cash flows from operating activities—indirect method
objs. 1, 2

✓ *a. Cash flows from operating activities, $203,100*

The net income reported on the income statement for the current year was $165,300. Depreciation recorded on equipment and a building amounted to $46,700 for the year. Balances of the current asset and current liability accounts at the beginning and end of the year are as follows:

	End of Year	Beginning of Year
Cash	$ 42,000	$ 43,500
Accounts receivable (net)	65,400	69,200
Inventories	125,900	115,100
Prepaid expenses	5,800	6,400
Accounts payable (merchandise creditors)	61,400	64,200
Salaries payable	8,300	8,000

a. Prepare the cash flows from operating activities section of the statement of cash flows, using the indirect method.

b. ▭▬▶ If the direct method had been used, would the net cash flow from operating activities have been the same? Explain.

EX 14-7
Cash flows from operating activities—indirect method
objs. 1, 2

The income statement disclosed the following items for 2008:

Depreciation expense	$ 24,500
Gain on disposal of equipment	10,200
Net income	186,000

Balances of the current assets and current liability accounts changed between December 31, 2007, and December 31, 2008, as follows:

Accounts receivable	$4,400
Inventory	2,000*
Prepaid insurance	800*
Accounts payable	2,700*
Income taxes payable	900
Dividends payable	500

*Decrease

Prepare the cash flows from operating activities section of the statement of cash flows, using the indirect method.

EX 14-8
Determining cash payments to stockholders
obj. 2

The board of directors declared cash dividends totaling $120,000 during the current year. The comparative balance sheet indicates dividends payable of $35,000 at the beginning of the year and $30,000 at the end of the year. What was the amount of cash payments to stockholders during the year?

EX 14-9
Reporting changes in equipment on statement of cash flows
obj. 2

An analysis of the general ledger accounts indicates that office equipment, which cost $60,000 and on which accumulated depreciation totaled $15,000 on the date of sale, was sold for $41,000 during the year. Using this information, indicate the items to be reported on the statement of cash flows.

EX 14-10
Reporting changes in equipment on statement of cash flows
obj. 2

An analysis of the general ledger accounts indicates that delivery equipment, which cost $45,000 and on which accumulated depreciation totaled $32,000 on the date of sale, was sold for $15,000 during the year. Using this information, indicate the items to be reported on the statement of cash flows.

EX 14-11
Reporting land transactions on statement of cash flows
obj. 2

On the basis of the details of the following fixed asset account, indicate the items to be reported on the statement of cash flows:

ACCOUNT *Land*   **ACCOUNT NO.**

Date		Item	Debit	Credit	Balance Debit	Balance Credit
2008						
Jan.	1	Balance			900,000	
Feb.	5	Purchased for cash	400,000		1,300,000	
Oct.	30	Sold for $365,000		250,000	1,050,000	

EX 14-12
Reporting stockholders' equity items on statement of cash flows
obj. 2

On the basis of the following stockholders' equity accounts, indicate the items, exclusive of net income, to be reported on the statement of cash flows. There were no unpaid dividends at either the beginning or the end of the year.

ACCOUNT *Common Stock, $10 par*   **ACCOUNT NO.**

Date		Item	Debit	Credit	Balance Debit	Balance Credit
2008						
Jan.	1	Balance, 70,000 shares				700,000
Feb.	11	16,000 shares issued for cash		160,000		860,000
June	30	4,100-share stock dividend		41,000		901,000

ACCOUNT *Paid-In Capital in Excess of Par—Common Stock*					ACCOUNT NO.
2008					
Jan.	1	Balance			140,000
Feb.	11	16,000 shares issued for cash		336,000	476,000
June	30	Stock dividend		102,500	578,500

ACCOUNT *Retained Earnings*					ACCOUNT NO.
2008					
Jan.	1	Balance			1,000,000
June	30	Stock dividend	143,500		856,500
Dec.	30	Cash dividend	124,000		732,500
	31	Net income		630,000	1,362,500

EX 14-13
Reporting land acquisition for cash and mortgage note on statement of cash flows
obj. 2

On the basis of the details of the following fixed asset account, indicate the items to be reported on the statement of cash flows:

ACCOUNT *Land*					ACCOUNT NO.	
					Balance	
Date		**Item**	**Debit**	**Credit**	**Debit**	**Credit**
2008						
Jan.	1	Balance			160,000	
Feb.	10	Purchased for cash	326,000		486,000	
Nov.	20	Purchased with long-term mortgage note	400,000		886,000	

EX 14-14
Reporting issuance and retirement of long-term debt
obj. 2

On the basis of the details of the following bonds payable and related discount accounts, indicate the items to be reported in the financing section of the statement of cash flows, assuming no gain or loss on retiring the bonds:

ACCOUNT *Bonds Payable*					ACCOUNT NO.	
					Balance	
Date		**Item**	**Debit**	**Credit**	**Debit**	**Credit**
2008						
Jan.	1	Balance				150,000
Jan.	3	Retire bonds	70,000			80,000
July	30	Issue bonds		350,000		430,000

ACCOUNT *Discount on Bonds Payable*					ACCOUNT NO.	
2008						
Jan.	1	Balance			12,000	
Jan.	3	Retire bonds		5,600	6,400	
July	30	Issue bonds	20,000		26,400	
Dec.	31	Amortize discount		1,600	24,800	

EX 14-15
Determining net income from net cash flow from operating activities
obj. 2

Emerald Golf Inc. reported a net cash flow from operating activities of $86,700 on its statement of cash flows for the year ended December 31, 2008. The following information was reported in the cash flows from operating activities section of the statement of cash flows, using the indirect method:

Decrease in income taxes payable	$2,000
Decrease in inventories	5,600
Depreciation	8,500
Gain on sale of investments	3,400
Increase in accounts payable	1,200
Increase in prepaid expenses	700
Increase in accounts receivable	4,300

Determine the net income reported by Emerald Golf Inc. for the year ended December 31, 2008.

EX 14-16
Cash flows from operating activities— indirect method

obj. 2

✓ *Net cash flow used in operating activities, ($773)*

Selected data derived from the income statement and balance sheet of Jones Soda Co. for a recent year are as follows:

Income statement data (in thousands):	
Net earnings	$1,330
Depreciation expense	193
Stock-based compensation expense (noncash)	20
Balance sheet data (in thousands):	
Increase in accounts receivable	$1,328
Increase in inventory	1,550
Increase in prepaid expenses	124
Increase in accounts payable	686

a. Prepare the cash flows from operating activities section of the statement of cash flows using the indirect method for Jones Soda Co. for the year.
b. Interpret your results in part (a).

EX 14-17
Statement of cash flows—indirect method

obj. 2

✓ *Net cash flow from operating activities, $50*

The comparative balance sheet of Alliance Structures Inc. for December 31, 2008 and 2007, is as follows (amounts in thousands):

	Dec. 31, 2008	Dec. 31, 2007
Assets		
Cash	$ 90	$ 23
Accounts receivable (net)	30	27
Inventories	24	21
Land	35	55
Equipment	32	22
Accumulated depreciation—equipment	(9)	(5)
Total	$202	$143
Liabilities and Stockholders' Equity		
Accounts payable (merchandise creditors)	$ 17	$ 10
Dividends payable	1	—
Common stock, $1 par	6	3
Paid-in capital in excess of par—common stock	30	10
Retained earnings	148	120
Total	$202	$143

The following additional information is taken from the records (all amounts in thousands):

a. Land was sold for $15.
b. Equipment was acquired for cash.
c. There were no disposals of equipment during the year.
d. The common stock was issued for cash.
e. There was a $40 credit to Retained Earnings for net income.
f. There was a $12 debit to Retained Earnings for cash dividends declared.

Prepare a statement of cash flows, using the indirect method of presenting cash flows from operating activities.

EX 14-18
Statement of cash flows—indirect method

obj. 2

List the errors you find in the following statement of cash flows. The cash balance at the beginning of the year was $83,600. All other amounts are correct, except the cash balance at the end of the year.

Whole Life Nutrition Products Inc.
Statement of Cash Flows
For the Year Ended December 31, 2008

Cash flows from operating activities:			
Net income		$123,400	
Adjustments to reconcile net income to net cash flow			
from operating activities:			
Depreciation		35,000	
Gain on sale of investements		6,000	
Changes in current operating assets and liabilities:			
Increase in accounts receivable		9,500	
Increase in inventories		(12,300)	
Increase in accounts payable		(3,700)	
Decrease in accrued expenses		(900)	
Net cash flow from operating activities			$157,000
Cash flows from investing activities:			
Cash received from sale of investments		$ 85,000	
Less: Cash paid for purchase of land	$ 90,000		
Cash paid for purchase of equipment	150,100	240,100	
Net cash flow used for investing activities			(155,100)
Cash flows from financing activities:			
Cash received from sale of common stock		$107,000	
Cash paid for dividends		45,000	
Net cash flow provided by financing activities			152,000
Increase in cash			$153,900
Cash at the end of the year			105,300
Cash at the beginning of the year			$259,200

EX 14-19
Cash flows from operating activities—direct method
obj. 3
✓ *a. $471,000*

The cash flows from operating activities are reported by the direct method on the statement of cash flows. Determine the following:

a. If sales for the current year were $450,000 and accounts receivable decreased by $21,000 during the year, what was the amount of cash received from customers?

b. If income tax expense for the current year was $35,000 and income tax payable decreased by $3,100 during the year, what was the amount of cash payments for income tax?

EX 14-20
Cash paid for merchandise purchases
obj. 3

The cost of merchandise sold for Kohl's Corporation for a recent year was $8,639 million. The balance sheet showed the following current account balances (in millions):

	Balance, End of Year	Balance, Beginning of Year
Merchandise inventories	$2,238	$1,947
Accounts payable	830	705

Determine the amount of cash payments for merchandise.

EX 14-21
Determining selected amounts for cash flows from operating activities—direct method
obj. 3
✓ *b. $59,900*

Selected data taken from the accounting records of Extravaganza Inc. for the current year ended December 31 are as follows:

	Balance, December 31	Balance, January 1
Accrued expenses (operating expenses)	$ 4,300	$ 4,700
Accounts payable (merchandise creditors)	32,100	35,400
Inventories	59,500	64,700
Prepaid expenses	2,500	3,000

During the current year, the cost of merchandise sold was $345,000, and the operating expenses other than depreciation were $60,000. The direct method is used for presenting the cash flows from operating activities on the statement of cash flows.

Determine the amount reported on the statement of cash flows for (a) cash payments for merchandise and (b) cash payments for operating expenses.

EX 14-22
Cash flows from operating activities—direct method

obj. 3

✔ *Net cash flow from operating activities, $87,200*

The income statement of Country Kitchen Bakeries Inc. for the current year ended June 30 is as follows:

Sales		$456,000
Cost of merchandise sold		259,000
Gross profit		$197,000
Operating expenses:		
Depreciation expense	$35,000	
Other operating expenses	92,400	
Total operating expenses		127,400
Income before income tax		$ 69,600
Income tax expense		19,300
Net income		$ 50,300

Changes in the balances of selected accounts from the beginning to the end of the current year are as follows:

	Increase Decrease*
Accounts receivable (net)	$10,500*
Inventories	3,500
Prepaid expenses	3,400*
Accounts payable (merchandise creditors)	7,200*
Accrued expenses (operating expenses)	1,100
Income tax payable	2,400*

Prepare the cash flows from operating activities section of the statement of cash flows, using the direct method.

EX 14-23
Cash flows from operating activities—direct method

obj. 3

✔ *Net cash flow from operating activities, $47,600*

The income statement for Wholly Bagel Company for the current year ended June 30 and balances of selected accounts at the beginning and the end of the year are as follows:

Sales		$184,000
Cost of merchandise sold		67,000
Gross profit		$117,000
Operating expenses:		
Depreciation expense	$14,500	
Other operating expenses	49,000	
Total operating expenses		63,500
Income before income tax		$ 53,500
Income tax expense		15,400
Net income		$ 38,100

	End of Year	Beginning of Year
Accounts receivable (net)	$14,800	$12,900
Inventories	38,100	33,100
Prepaid expenses	6,000	6,600
Accounts payable (merchandise creditors)	27,900	25,900
Accrued expenses (operating expenses)	7,900	8,600
Income tax payable	1,500	1,500

Prepare the cash flows from operating activities section of the statement of cash flows, using the direct method.

EX 14-24
Free cash flow

Mediterranean Tile Company has cash flows from operating activities of $120,000. Cash flows used for investments in property, plant, and equipment totaled $45,000, of which 60% of this investment was used to replace existing capacity.

Determine the free cash flow for Mediterranean Tile Company.

EX 14-25
Free cash flow

The financial statements for Williams-Sonoma, Inc., are provided in Appendix E at the end of the text.

Determine the free cash flow for the year ended January 29, 2006. Assume that 70% of purchases of property and equipment were for new store openings, and the remaining was for remodeling and updating existing stores.

Problems Series A

PR 14-1A
Statement of cash flows—indirect method

obj. 2

✓ Net cash flow from operating activities, $72,200

The comparative balance sheet of Oak and Tile Flooring Co. for June 30, 2008 and 2007, is as follows:

	June 30, 2008	June 30, 2007
Assets		
Cash	$ 34,700	$ 23,500
Accounts receivable (net)	101,600	92,300
Inventories	146,300	142,100
Investments	0	50,000
Land	145,000	0
Equipment	215,000	175,500
Accumulated depreciation	(48,600)	(41,300)
	$594,000	$442,100
Liabilities and Stockholders' Equity		
Accounts payable (merchandise creditors)	$100,900	$ 95,200
Accrued expenses (operating expenses)	15,000	13,200
Dividends payable	12,500	10,000
Common stock, $1 par	56,000	50,000
Paid-in capital in excess of par—common stock	220,000	100,000
Retained earnings	189,600	173,700
	$594,000	$442,100

The following additional information was taken from the records of Oak and Tile Flooring Co.:

a. Equipment and land were acquired for cash.
b. There were no disposals of equipment during the year.
c. The investments were sold for $45,000 cash.
d. The common stock was issued for cash.
e. There was a $65,900 credit to Retained Earnings for net income.
f. There was a $50,000 debit to Retained Earnings for cash dividends declared.

Instructions
Prepare a statement of cash flows, using the indirect method of presenting cash flows from operating activities.

PR 14-2A
Statement of cash flows—indirect method

obj. 2

The comparative balance sheet of Portable Luggage Company at December 31, 2008 and 2007, is as follows:

✓ *Net cash flow from operating activities, $221,700*

	Dec. 31, 2008	Dec. 31, 2007
Assets		
Cash	$ 175,900	$ 143,200
Accounts receivable (net)	264,100	235,000
Inventories	352,300	405,800
Prepaid expenses	12,500	10,000
Land	120,000	120,000
Buildings	680,000	450,000
Accumulated depreciation—buildings	(185,000)	(164,500)
Machinery and equipment	310,000	310,000
Accumulated depreciation—machinery & equipment	(85,000)	(76,000)
Patents	42,500	48,000
	$1,687,300	$1,481,500
Liabilities and Stockholders' Equity		
Accounts payable (merchandise creditors)	$ 332,300	$ 367,900
Dividends payable	13,000	10,000
Salaries payable	30,200	34,600
Mortgage note payable, due 2015	90,000	—
Bonds payable	—	154,000
Common stock, $1 par	24,000	20,000
Paid-in capital in excess of par—common stock	200,000	50,000
Retained earnings	997,800	845,000
	$1,687,300	$1,481,500

An examination of the income statement and the accounting records revealed the following additional information applicable to 2008:

a. Net income, $204,800.
b. Depreciation expense reported on the income statement: buildings, $20,500; machinery and equipment, $9,000.
c. Patent amortization reported on the income statement, $5,500.
d. A building was constructed for $230,000.
e. A mortgage note for $90,000 was issued for cash.
f. 4,000 shares of common stock were issued at $38.50 in exchange for the bonds payable.
g. Cash dividends declared, $52,000.

Instructions

Prepare a statement of cash flows, using the indirect method of presenting cash flows from operating activities.

PR 14-3A
Statement of cash flows—indirect method
obj. 2

✓ *Net cash flow from operating activities, $4,100*

The comparative balance sheet of Reston Supply Co. at December 31, 2008 and 2007, is as follows:

	Dec. 31, 2008	Dec. 31, 2007
Assets		
Cash	$ 45,500	$ 51,200
Accounts receivable (net)	106,700	92,400
Inventories	139,200	131,200
Prepaid expenses	2,800	4,000
Land	150,000	210,000
Buildings	300,000	150,000
Accumulated depreciation—buildings	(60,200)	(55,500)
Equipment	100,100	80,300
Accumulated depreciation—equipment	(20,200)	(24,500)
	$763,900	$639,100
Liabilities and Stockholders' Equity		
Accounts payable (merchandise creditors)	$ 90,000	$ 95,600
Income tax payable	4,000	3,200
Bonds payable	50,000	0
Common stock, $1 par	33,000	30,000
Paid-in capital in excess of par—common stock	180,000	120,000
Retained earnings	406,900	390,300
	$763,900	$639,100

The noncurrent asset, noncurrent liability, and stockholders' equity accounts for 2008 are as follows:

ACCOUNT *Land* ACCOUNT NO.

Date		Item	Debit	Credit	Balance Debit	Balance Credit
2008						
Jan.	1	Balance			210,000	
Apr.	20	Realized $69,000 cash from sale		60,000	150,000	

ACCOUNT *Buildings* ACCOUNT NO.

Date		Item	Debit	Credit	Debit	Credit
2008						
Jan.	1	Balance			150,000	
Apr.	20	Acquired for cash	150,000		300,000	

ACCOUNT *Accumulated Depreciation—Buildings* ACCOUNT NO.

Date		Item	Debit	Credit	Debit	Credit
2008						
Jan.	1	Balance				55,500
Dec.	31	Depreciation for year		4,700		60,200

ACCOUNT *Equipment* ACCOUNT NO.

Date		Item	Debit	Credit	Debit	Credit
2008						
Jan.	1	Balance			80,300	
	26	Discarded, no salvage		10,000	70,300	
Aug.	11	Purchased for cash	29,800		100,100	

ACCOUNT *Accumulated Depreciation—Equipment* ACCOUNT NO.

Date		Item	Debit	Credit	Debit	Credit
2008						
Jan.	1	Balance				24,500
	26	Equipment discarded	10,000			14,500
Dec.	31	Depreciation for year		5,700		20,200

ACCOUNT *Bonds Payable* ACCOUNT NO.

Date		Item	Debit	Credit	Debit	Credit
2008						
May	1	Issued 20-year bonds		50,000		50,000

ACCOUNT *Common Stock, $1 par* ACCOUNT NO.

Date		Item	Debit	Credit	Debit	Credit
2008						
Jan.	1	Balance				30,000
Dec.	7	Issued 3,000 shares of common stock for $21 per share		3,000		33,000

ACCOUNT *Paid-In Capital in Excess of Par—Common Stock* ACCOUNT NO.

Date		Item	Debit	Credit	Debit	Credit
2008						
Jan.	1	Balance				120,000
Dec.	7	Issued 3,000 shares of common stock for $21 per share		60,000		180,000

ACCOUNT *Retained Earnings* ACCOUNT NO.

Date		Item	Debit	Credit	Debit	Credit
2008						
Jan.	1	Balance				390,300
Dec.	31	Net income		28,600		418,900
	31	Cash dividends	12,000			406,900

Instructions
Prepare a statement of cash flows, using the indirect method of presenting cash flows from operating activities.

PR 14-4A
Statement of cash flows—direct method

obj. 3

✓ *Net cash flow from operating activities, $107,900*

The comparative balance sheet of Green Earth Lawn and Garden Inc. for December 31, 2008 and 2009, is as follows:

	Dec. 31, 2009	Dec. 31, 2008
Assets		
Cash	$ 137,900	$142,300
Accounts receivable (net)	206,800	190,500
Inventories	290,500	284,100
Investments	0	90,000
Land	200,000	0
Equipment	255,000	205,000
Accumulated depreciation	(100,300)	(76,700)
	$ 989,900	$835,200
Liabilities and Stockholders' Equity		
Accounts payable (merchandise creditors)	$ 224,900	$201,400
Accrued expenses (operating expenses)	14,100	16,500
Dividends payable	21,000	19,000
Common stock, $1 par	10,000	8,000
Paid-in capital in excess of par—common stock	200,000	100,000
Retained earnings	519,900	490,300
	$ 989,900	$835,200

The income statement for the year ended December 31, 2009, is as follows:

Sales		$940,000
Cost of merchandise sold		489,300
Gross profit		$450,700
Operating expenses:		
Depreciation expense	$ 23,600	
Other operating expenses	278,900	
Total operating expenses		302,500
Operating income		$148,200
Other income:		
Gain on sale of investments		32,000
Income before income tax		$180,200
Income tax expense		62,300
Net income		$117,900

The following additional information was taken from the records:

a. Equipment and land were acquired for cash.
b. There were no disposals of equipment during the year.
c. The investments were sold for $122,000 cash.
d. The common stock was issued for cash.
e. There was a $88,300 debit to Retained Earnings for cash dividends declared.

Instructions
Prepare a statement of cash flows, using the direct method of presenting cash flows from operating activities.

PR 14-5A
Statement of cash flows—direct method applied to PR 14-1A

obj. 3

✓ *Net cash flow from operating activities, $72,200*

The comparative balance sheet of Oak and Tile Flooring Co. for June 30, 2008 and 2007, is as follows:

	June 30, 2008	June 30, 2007
Assets		
Cash	$ 34,700	$ 23,500
Accounts receivable (net)	101,600	92,300
Inventories	146,300	142,100
Investments	0	50,000
Land	145,000	0
Equipment	215,000	175,500
Accumulated depreciation	(48,600)	(41,300)
	$594,000	$442,100

Liabilities and Stockholders' Equity

Accounts payable (merchandise creditors)	$100,900	$ 95,200
Accrued expenses (operating expenses)	15,000	13,200
Dividends payable	12,500	10,000
Common stock, $1 par	56,000	50,000
Paid-in capital in excess of par—common stock	220,000	100,000
Retained earnings	189,600	173,700
	$594,000	$442,100

The income statement for the year ended June 30, 2008, is as follows:

Sales		$963,400
Cost of merchandise sold		662,100
Gross profit		$301,300
Operating expenses:		
Depreciation expense	$ 7,300	
Other operating expenses	195,000	
Total operating expenses		202,300
Operating income		$ 99,000
Other expenses:		
Loss on sale of investments		(5,000)
Income before income tax		$ 94,000
Income tax expense		28,100
Net income		$ 65,900

The following additional information was taken from the records:

a. Equipment and land were acquired for cash.
b. There were no disposals of equipment during the year.
c. The investments were sold for $45,000 cash.
d. The common stock was issued for cash.
e. There was a $50,000 debit to Retained Earnings for cash dividends declared.

Instructions

Prepare a statement of cash flows, using the direct method of presenting cash flows from operating activities.

Problems Series B

PR 14-1B
Statement of cash flows—indirect method

obj. 2

✓ *Net cash flow from operating activities, $61,900*

The comparative balance sheet of Gold Medal Sporting Goods Inc. for December 31, 2008 and 2007, is shown as follows:

	Dec. 31, 2008	Dec. 31, 2007
Assets		
Cash	$ 391,100	$ 366,200
Accounts receivable (net)	142,400	130,600
Inventories	401,100	385,700
Investments	0	150,000
Land	205,000	0
Equipment	440,700	345,700
Accumulated depreciation—equipment	(104,000)	(92,500)
	$1,476,300	$1,285,700
Liabilities and Stockholders' Equity		
Accounts payable (merchandise creditors)	$ 267,800	$ 253,100
Accrued expenses (operating expenses)	26,400	32,900
Dividends payable	15,000	12,000
Common stock, $10 par	80,000	60,000
Paid-in capital in excess of par—common stock	300,000	175,000
Retained earnings	787,100	752,700
	$1,476,300	$1,285,700

The following additional information was taken from the records:

a. The investments were sold for $175,000 cash.
b. Equipment and land were acquired for cash.
c. There were no disposals of equipment during the year.
d. The common stock was issued for cash.
e. There was a $94,400 credit to Retained Earnings for net income.
f. There was a $60,000 debit to Retained Earnings for cash dividends declared.

Instructions
Prepare a statement of cash flows, using the indirect method of presenting cash flows from operating activities.

PR 14-2B
Statement of cash flows—indirect method
obj. 2

✓ *Net cash flow from operating activities, $108,500*

The comparative balance sheet of Air Glide Athletic Apparel Co. at December 31, 2008 and 2007, is as follows:

	Dec. 31, 2008	Dec. 31, 2007
Assets		
Cash	$ 45,800	$ 56,200
Accounts receivable (net)	70,200	75,600
Merchandise inventory	100,500	93,500
Prepaid expenses	4,200	3,000
Equipment	204,700	167,800
Accumulated depreciation—equipment	(53,400)	(41,300)
	$372,000	$354,800
Liabilities and Stockholders' Equity		
Accounts payable (merchandise creditors)	$ 78,200	$ 74,300
Mortgage note payable	0	105,000
Common stock, $1 par	15,000	10,000
Paid-in capital in excess of par—common stock	180,000	100,000
Retained earnings	98,800	65,500
	$372,000	$354,800

Additional data obtained from the income statement and from an examination of the accounts in the ledger for 2008 are as follows:

a. Net income, $81,300.
b. Depreciation reported on the income statement, $26,100.
c. Equipment was purchased at a cost of $50,900, and fully depreciated equipment costing $14,000 was discarded, with no salvage realized.
d. The mortgage note payable was not due until 2011, but the terms permitted earlier payment without penalty.
e. 5,000 shares of common stock were issued at $17 for cash.
f. Cash dividends declared and paid, $48,000.

Instructions
Prepare a statement of cash flows, using the indirect method of presenting cash flows from operating activities.

PR 14-3B
Statement of cash flows—indirect method
obj. 2

✓ *Net cash flow from operating activities, ($68,400)*

The comparative balance sheet of Rise N' Shine Juice Co. at December 31, 2008 and 2007, is as follows:

	Dec. 31, 2008	Dec. 31, 2007
Assets		
Cash	$ 392,300	$ 412,300
Accounts receivable (net)	354,200	325,600
Inventories	542,100	497,000
Prepaid expenses	12,500	15,000
Land	135,000	205,000
Buildings	625,000	385,000
Accumulated depreciation—buildings	(174,600)	(163,400)
Equipment	218,900	194,300
Accumulated depreciation—equipment	(60,400)	(67,800)
	$2,045,000	$1,803,000

Liabilities and Stockholders' Equity

Accounts payable (merchandise creditors)	$ 394,200	$ 409,500
Bonds payable	115,000	0
Common stock, $1 par	58,000	50,000
Paid-in capital in excess of par—common stock	400,000	240,000
Retained earnings	1,077,800	1,103,500
	$2,045,000	$1,803,000

The noncurrent asset, noncurrent liability, and stockholders' equity accounts for 2008 are as follows:

ACCOUNT *Land*   **ACCOUNT NO.**

Date		Item	Debit	Credit	Balance Debit	Balance Credit
2008						
Jan.	1	Balance			205,000	
Apr.	20	Realized $64,000 cash from sale		70,000	135,000	

ACCOUNT *Buildings*   **ACCOUNT NO.**

Date		Item	Debit	Credit	Balance Debit	Balance Credit
2008						
Jan.	1	Balance			385,000	
Apr.	20	Acquired for cash	240,000		625,000	

ACCOUNT *Accumulated Depreciation—Buildings*   **ACCOUNT NO.**

Date		Item	Debit	Credit	Balance Debit	Balance Credit
2008						
Jan.	1	Balance				163,400
Dec.	31	Depreciation for year		11,200		174,600

ACCOUNT *Equipment*   **ACCOUNT NO.**

Date		Item	Debit	Credit	Balance Debit	Balance Credit
2008						
Jan.	1	Balance			194,300	
	26	Discarded, no salvage		20,000	174,300	
Aug.	11	Purchased for cash	44,600		218,900	

ACCOUNT *Accumulated Depreciation—Equipment*   **ACCOUNT NO.**

Date		Item	Debit	Credit	Balance Debit	Balance Credit
2008						
Jan.	1	Balance				67,800
	26	Equipment discarded	20,000			47,800
Dec.	31	Depreciation for year		12,600		60,400

ACCOUNT *Bonds Payable*   **ACCOUNT NO.**

Date		Item	Debit	Credit	Balance Debit	Balance Credit
2008						
May	1	Issued 20-year bonds		115,000		115,000

ACCOUNT *Common Stock, $1 par*   **ACCOUNT NO.**

Date		Item	Debit	Credit	Balance Debit	Balance Credit
2008						
Jan.	1	Balance				50,000
Dec.	7	Issued 8,000 shares of common stock for $21 per share		8,000		58,000

ACCOUNT *Paid-In Capital in Excess of Par—Common Stock*   **ACCOUNT NO.**

Date		Item	Debit	Credit	Balance Debit	Balance Credit
2008						
Jan.	1	Balance				240,000
Dec.	7	Issued 8,000 shares of common stock for $21 per share		160,000		400,000

(continued)

ACCOUNT Retained Earnings					ACCOUNT NO.	
Date		Item	Debit	Credit	Balance	
					Debit	Credit
2008						
Jan.	1	Balance				1,103,500
Dec.	31	Net loss	11,700			1,091,800
	31	Cash dividends	14,000			1,077,800

Instructions
Prepare a statement of cash flows, using the indirect method of presenting cash flows from operating activities.

PR 14-4B
Statement of cash flows—direct method
obj. 3

✓ *Net cash flow from operating activities, $193,600*

The comparative balance sheet of Home and Hearth Inc. for December 31, 2009 and 2008, is as follows:

	Dec. 31, 2009	Dec. 31, 2008
Assets		
Cash	$ 402,100	$ 424,600
Accounts receivable (net)	354,200	342,100
Inventories	631,900	614,200
Investments	0	150,000
Land	325,000	0
Equipment	550,000	425,000
Accumulated depreciation	(152,700)	(125,300)
	$2,110,500	$1,830,600
Liabilities and Stockholders' Equity		
Accounts payable (merchandise creditors)	$ 482,400	$ 467,800
Accrued expenses (operating expenses)	39,600	44,200
Dividends payable	5,500	4,000
Common stock, $1 par	24,000	20,000
Paid-in capital in excess of par—common stock ..	260,000	120,000
Retained earnings	1,299,000	1,174,600
	$2,110,500	$1,830,600

The income statement for the year ended December 31, 2009, is as follows:

Sales		$3,745,700
Cost of merchandise sold		1,532,500
Gross profit		$2,213,200
Operating expenses:		
Depreciation expense	$ 27,400	
Other operating expenses	1,936,800	
Total operating expenses		1,964,200
Operating income		$ 249,000
Other expense:		
Loss on sale of investments		(40,000)
Income before income tax		$ 209,000
Income tax expense		63,000
Net income		$ 146,000

The following additional information was taken from the records:

a. Equipment and land were acquired for cash.
b. There were no disposals of equipment during the year.
c. The investments were sold for $110,000 cash.
d. The common stock was issued for cash.
e. There was a $21,600 debit to Retained Earnings for cash dividends declared.

Instructions

Prepare a statement of cash flows, using the direct method of presenting cash flows from operating activities.

PR 14-5B
Statement of cash flows—direct method applied to PR 14-1B

obj. 3

✓ *Net cash flow from operating activities, $61,900*

The comparative balance sheet of Gold Medal Sporting Goods Inc. for December 31, 2008 and 2007, is as follows:

	Dec. 31, 2008	Dec. 31, 2007
Assets		
Cash	$ 391,100	$ 366,200
Accounts receivable (net)	142,400	130,600
Inventories	401,100	385,700
Investments	0	150,000
Land	205,000	0
Equipment	440,700	345,700
Accumulated depreciation—equipment	(104,000)	(92,500)
	$1,476,300	$1,285,700
Liabilities and Stockholders' Equity		
Accounts payable (merchandise creditors)	$ 267,800	$ 253,100
Accrued expenses (operating expenses)	26,400	32,900
Dividends payable	15,000	12,000
Common stock, $10 par	80,000	60,000
Paid-in capital in excess of par—common stock	300,000	175,000
Retained earnings	787,100	752,700
	$1,476,300	$1,285,700

The income statement for the year ended December 31, 2008, is as follows:

Sales		$1,632,500
Cost of merchandise sold		908,300
Gross profit		$ 724,200
Operating expenses:		
Depreciation expense	$ 11,500	
Other operating expenses	609,000	
Total operating expenses		620,500
Operating income		$ 103,700
Other income:		
Gain on sale of investments		25,000
Income before income tax		$ 128,700
Income tax expense		34,300
Net income		$ 94,400

The following additional information was taken from the records:

a. The investments were sold for $175,000 cash.
b. Equipment and land were acquired for cash.
c. There were no disposals of equipment during the year.
d. The common stock was issued for cash.
e. There was a $60,000 debit to Retained Earnings for cash dividends declared.

Instructions

Prepare a statement of cash flows, using the direct method of presenting cash flows from operating activities.

Special Activities

SA 14-1
Ethics and professional conduct in business

ETHICS

Linda Stern, president of Venician Fashions Inc., believes that reporting operating cash flow per share on the income statement would be a useful addition to the company's just completed financial statements. The following discussion took place between Linda Stern and Venician Fashions' controller, Ben Trotter, in January, after the close of the fiscal year.

Linda: I have been reviewing our financial statements for the last year. I am disappointed that our net income per share has dropped by 10% from last year. This is not going to look good to our shareholders. Isn't there anything we can do about this?

Ben: What do you mean? The past is the past, and the numbers are in. There isn't much that can be done about it. Our financial statements were prepared according to generally accepted accounting principles, and I don't see much leeway for significant change at this point.

Linda: No, no. I'm not suggesting that we "cook the books." But look at the cash flow from operating activities on the statement of cash flows. The cash flow from operating activities has increased by 20%. This is very good news—and, I might add, useful information. The higher cash flow from operating activities will give our creditors comfort.

Ben: Well, the cash flow from operating activities is on the statement of cash flows, so I guess users will be able to see the improved cash flow figures there.

Linda: This is true, but somehow I feel that this information should be given a much higher profile. I don't like this information being "buried" in the statement of cash flows. You know as well as I do that many users will focus on the income statement. Therefore, I think we ought to include an operating cash flow per share number on the face of the income statement—someplace under the earnings per share number. In this way users will get the complete picture of our operating performance. Yes, our earnings per share dropped this year, but our cash flow from operating activities improved! And all the information is in one place where users can see and compare the figures. What do you think?

Ben: I've never really thought about it like that before. I guess we could put the operating cash flow per share on the income statement, under the earnings per share. Users would really benefit from this disclosure. Thanks for the idea—I'll start working on it.

Linda: Glad to be of service.

How would you interpret this situation? Is Ben behaving in an ethical and professional manner?

SA 14-2
Using the statement of cash flows

You are considering an investment in a new start-up company, Aspen Technologies Inc., an Internet service provider. A review of the company's financial statements reveals a negative retained earnings. In addition, it appears as though the company has been running a negative cash flow from operating activities since the company's inception.

How is the company staying in business under these circumstances? Could this be a good investment?

SA 14-3
Analysis of cash flow from operations

The Retailing Division of Bargain Buyer Inc. provided the following information on its cash flow from operations:

Net income	$ 450,000
Increase in accounts receivable	(540,000)
Increase in inventory	(600,000)
Decrease in accounts payable	(90,000)
Depreciation	100,000
Cash flow from operating activities	$(680,000)

The manager of the Retailing Division provided the accompanying memo with this report:

From: Senior Vice President, Retailing Division

I am pleased to report that we had earnings of $450,000 over the last period. This resulted in a return on invested capital of 10%, which is near our targets for this division. I have been aggressive in building the revenue volume in the division. As a result, I am happy to report that we have increased the number of new credit card customers as a result of an aggressive marketing campaign. In addition, we have found some excellent merchandise opportunities. Some of our suppliers have made some of their apparel merchandise available at a deep discount. We have purchased as much of these goods as possible in order to improve profitability. I'm also happy to report that our vendor payment problems have improved. We are nearly caught up on our overdue payables balances.

Comment on the senior vice president's memo in light of the cash flow information.

SA 14-4
Analysis of statement of cash flows

Jabari Daniels is the president and majority shareholder of Cabinet Craft Inc., a small retail store chain. Recently, Daniels submitted a loan application for Cabinet Craft Inc. to Montvale National Bank. It called for a $200,000, 9%, 10-year loan to help finance the construction of a building and the purchase of store equipment, costing a total of $250,000, to enable Cabinet Craft Inc. to open a store in Montvale. Land for this purpose was acquired last year. The bank's loan officer requested a statement of cash flows in addition to the most recent income statement, balance sheet, and retained earnings statement that Daniels had submitted with the loan application.

As a close family friend, Daniels asked you to prepare a statement of cash flows. From the records provided, you prepared the following statement:

Cabinet Craft Inc.
Statement of Cash Flows
For the Year Ended December 31, 2008

Cash flows from operating activities:		
Net income		$ 94,500
Adjustments to reconcile net income to net cash flow from operating activities:		
Depreciation		26,000
Gain on sale of investments		(8,000)
Changes in current operating assets and liabilities:		
Decrease in accounts receivable		5,000
Increase in inventories		(12,000)
Increase in accounts payable		8,500
Decrease in accrued expenses		(1,200)
Net cash flow from operating activities		$112,800
Cash flows from investing activities:		
Cash received from investments sold	$ 50,000	
Less cash paid for purchase of store equipment	(30,000)	
Net cash flow provided by investing activities		20,000
Cash flows from financing activities:		
Cash paid for dividends	$ 35,000	
Net cash flow used for financing activities		(35,000)
Increase in cash		$ 97,800
Cash at the beginning of the year		34,800
Cash at the end of the year		$132,600

Schedule of Noncash Financing and Investing Activities:	
Issued common stock for land	$ 75,000

After reviewing the statement, Daniels telephoned you and commented, "Are you sure this statement is right?" Daniels then raised the following questions:

1. "How can depreciation be a cash flow?"
2. "Issuing common stock for the land is listed in a separate schedule. This transaction has nothing to do with cash! Shouldn't this transaction be eliminated from the statement?"

(continued)

3. "How can the gain on sale of investments be a deduction from net income in determining the cash flow from operating activities?"

4. "Why does the bank need this statement anyway? They can compute the increase in cash from the balance sheets for the last two years."

   After jotting down Daniels' questions, you assured him that this statement was "right." However, to alleviate Daniels' concern, you arranged a meeting for the following day.

a. ▬▬▶ How would you respond to each of Daniels' questions?

b. ▬▬▶ Do you think that the statement of cash flows enhances the chances of Cabinet Craft Inc. receiving the loan? Discuss.

SA 14-5
Statement of cash flows

Group Project

Internet Project

This activity will require two teams to retrieve cash flow statement information from the Internet. One team is to obtain the most recent year's statement of cash flows for Johnson & Johnson, and the other team the most recent year's statement of cash flows for AMR Corp. (American Airlines).

The statement of cash flows is included as part of the annual report information that is a required disclosure to the Securities and Exchange Commission (SEC). The SEC, in turn, provides this information online through its EDGAR service. EDGAR (Electronic Data Gathering, Analysis, and Retrieval) is the electronic archive of financial statements filed with the Securities and Exchange Commission (SEC). SEC documents can be retrieved using the EdgarScan service from PricewaterhouseCoopers at **http://edgarscan.pwcglobal.com**.

To obtain annual report information, type in a company name in the appropriate space. EdgarScan will list the reports available to you for the company you've selected. Select the most recent annual report filing, identified as a 10-K or 10-K405. EdgarScan provides an outline of the report, including the separate financial statements. You can double-click the income statement and balance sheet for the selected company into an Excel™ spreadsheet for further analysis.

As a group, compare the two statements of cash flows.

a. How are Johnson & Johnson and AMR similar or different regarding cash flows?

b. Compute and compare the free cash flow for each company, assuming additions to property, plant, and equipment replace current capacity.

Answers to Self-Examination Questions

1. **D**   Cash flows from operating activities affect transactions that enter into the determination of net income, such as the receipt of cash from customers on account (answer D). Receipts of cash from the sale of stock (answer A) and the sale of bonds (answer B) and payments of cash for dividends (answer C) are cash flows from financing activities.

2. **A**   Cash flows from investing activities include receipts from the sale of noncurrent assets, such as equipment (answer A), and payments to acquire noncurrent assets. Receipts of cash from the sale of stock (answer B) and payments of cash for dividends (answer C) and to acquire treasury stock (answer D) are cash flows from financing activities.

3. **C**   Payment of cash for dividends (answer C) is an example of a financing activity. The receipt of cash from customers on account (answer A) is an operating activity. The receipt of cash from the sale of equipment (answer B) is an investing activity. The payment of cash to acquire land (answer D) is an example of an investing activity.

4. **D**   The indirect method (answer D) reports cash flows from operating activities by beginning with net income and adjusting it for revenues and expenses not involving the receipt or payment of cash.

5. **C**   The cash flows from operating activities section of the statement of cash flows would report net cash flow from operating activities of $65,500, determined as follows:

Cash flows from operating activities:	
Net income	$ 55,000
Adjustments to reconcile net income to net cash flow from operating activities:	
Depreciation	22,000
Changes in current operating assets and liabilities:	
Increase in accounts receivable	(10,000)
Decrease in inventories	5,000
Decrease in prepaid expenses	500
Decrease in accounts payable	(7,000)
Net cash flow from operating activities	$65,500

Financial Statement Analysis

© CHITOSE SUZUKI/ASSOCIATED PRESS

objectives

After studying this chapter, you should be able to:

1. **List basic financial statement analytical procedures.**

2. **Apply financial statement analysis to assess the solvency of a business.**

3. **Apply financial statement analysis to assess the profitability of a business.**

4. **Describe the contents of corporate annual reports.**

Williams-Sonoma, Inc.

During a recent year, Williams-Sonoma, Inc., reported revenues of over $3.1 billion and net income of over $190 million. The common stock of Williams-Sonoma is traded on the New York Stock Exchange (symbol WSM) and closed on February 17, 2006, at $39.80 per share. Based upon current market values, Williams-Sonoma is worth almost $4.6 billion. Do you wish you could have invested in Williams-Sonoma 15 years ago?

Williams-Sonoma is a specialty retailer in the United States, well-known for its home furnishings. The company began in 1956, when owner Chuck Williams opened a store selling restaurant-quality cookware from France in Sonoma, California. The business expanded quickly, and Williams soon moved his store to Sutter Street in San Francisco. From there, the company expanded into catalogs, the Internet, and additional brands, such as Pottery Barn.

The success of Williams-Sonoma shows that reputation and the popularity of a company's product are important indicators of success. However, these are not the *only* factors that determine a company's success. A business needs to combine product offerings with proper financial, marketing, and sales strategies to be successful. Clearly, Williams-Sonoma has accomplished this. If you had invested in its common stock back in 1990, the stock price would have risen from $3 per share to nearly $40 per share today.

How, then, should you select companies in which to invest? Like any significant purchase, you should do some research to guide your investment decision. If you were buying a car, for example, you might go to Edmunds.com to obtain reviews, ratings, prices, specifications, options, and fuel economy across a number of vehicle alternatives. In deciding whether to invest in a company, you can use financial analysis to gain insight into a company's past performance and future prospects. This chapter describes and illustrates common financial data that can be analyzed to assist you in making investment decisions such as whether or not to invest in Williams-Sonoma stock. The contents of corporate annual reports are also discussed.

Source: Walter Nicholls, "The 90-Year-Old Pioneer Behind Williams-Sonoma," *The Seattle Times*, October 5, 2005.

Basic Analytical Procedures

objective **1**

List basic financial statement analytical procedures.

The basic financial statements provide much of the information users need to make economic decisions about businesses. In this chapter, we illustrate how to perform a complete analysis of these statements by integrating individual analytical measures.

Analytical procedures may be used to compare items on a current statement with related items on earlier statements. For example, cash of $150,000 on the current balance sheet may be compared with cash of $100,000 on the balance sheet of a year earlier. The current year's cash may be expressed as 1.5 or 150% of the earlier amount, or as an increase of 50% or $50,000.

Analytical procedures are also widely used to examine relationships within a financial statement. To illustrate, assume that cash of $50,000 and inventories of $250,000 are included in the total assets of $1,000,000 on a balance sheet. In relative terms, the cash balance is 5% of the total assets, and the inventories are 25% of the total assets.

In this chapter, we will illustrate a number of common analytical measures. The measures are not ends in themselves. They are only guides in evaluating financial and operating data. Many other factors, such as trends in the industry and general economic conditions, should also be considered.

HORIZONTAL ANALYSIS

The percentage analysis of increases and decreases in related items in comparative financial statements is called **horizontal analysis**. The amount of each item on the most recent statement is compared with the related item on one or more earlier statements. The amount of increase or decrease in the item is listed, along with the percent of increase or decrease.

Horizontal analysis may compare two statements. In this case, the earlier statement is used as the base. Horizontal analysis may also compare three or more statements. In this case, the earliest date or period may be used as the base for comparing all later dates or periods. Alternatively, each statement may be compared to the immediately preceding statement. Exhibit 1 is a condensed comparative balance sheet for two years for Lincoln Company, with horizontal analysis.

EXHIBIT 1

Comparative Balance Sheet—Horizontal Analysis

Lincoln Company
Comparative Balance Sheet
December 31, 2008 and 2007

	2008	2007	Increase (Decrease) Amount	Percent
Assets				
Current assets	$ 550,000	$ 533,000	$ 17,000	3.2%
Long-term investments	95,000	177,500	(82,500)	(46.5%)
Property, plant, and				
equipment (net)	444,500	470,000	(25,500)	(5.4%)
Intangible assets	50,000	50,000	—	—
Total assets	$1,139,500	$1,230,500	$ (91,000)	(7.4%)
Liabilities				
Current liabilities	$ 210,000	$ 243,000	$ (33,000)	(13.6%)
Long-term liabilities	100,000	200,000	(100,000)	(50.0%)
Total liabilities	$ 310,000	$ 443,000	$(133,000)	(30.0%)
Stockholders' Equity				
Preferred 6% stock, $100 par . . .	$ 150,000	$ 150,000	—	—
Common stock, $10 par	500,000	500,000	—	—
Retained earnings	179,500	137,500	$ 42,000	30.5%
Total stockholders' equity	$ 829,500	$ 787,500	$ 42,000	5.3%
Total liabilities and				
stockholders' equity	$1,139,500	$1,230,500	$ (91,000)	(7.4%)

We cannot fully evaluate the significance of the various increases and decreases in the items shown in Exhibit 1 without additional information. Although total assets at the end of 2008 were $91,000 (7.4%) less than at the beginning of the year, liabilities were reduced by $133,000 (30%), and stockholders' equity increased $42,000 (5.3%). It appears that the reduction of $100,000 in long-term liabilities was achieved mostly through the sale of long-term investments.

The balance sheet in Exhibit 1 may be expanded to include the details of the various categories of assets and liabilities. An alternative is to present the details in separate schedules. Exhibit 2 is a supporting schedule with horizontal analysis.

The decrease in accounts receivable may be due to changes in credit terms or improved collection policies. Likewise, a decrease in inventories during a period of increased sales may indicate an improvement in the management of inventories.

EXHIBIT 2

Comparative Schedule
of Current Assets—
Horizontal Analysis

			Increase (Decrease)	
Lincoln Company Comparative Schedule of Current Assets December 31, 2008 and 2007				
	2008	**2007**	**Amount**	**Percent**
Cash	$ 90,500	$ 64,700	$ 25,800	39.9%
Marketable securities	75,000	60,000	15,000	25.0%
Accounts receivable (net)	115,000	120,000	(5,000)	(4.2%)
Inventories	264,000	283,000	(19,000)	(6.7%)
Prepaid expenses	5,500	5,300	200	3.8%
Total current assets	$550,000	$533,000	$ 17,000	3.2%

The changes in the current assets in Exhibit 2 appear favorable. This assessment is supported by the 24.8% increase in net sales shown in Exhibit 3.

EXHIBIT 3

Comparative Income
Statement—
Horizontal Analysis

			Increase (Decrease)	
Lincoln Company Comparative Income Statement For the Years Ended December 31, 2008 and 2007				
	2008	**2007**	**Amount**	**Percent**
Sales	$1,530,500	$1,234,000	$296,500	24.0%
Sales returns and allowances . . .	32,500	34,000	(1,500)	(4.4%)
Net sales	$1,498,000	$1,200,000	$298,000	24.8%
Cost of goods sold	1,043,000	820,000	223,000	27.2%
Gross profit	$ 455,000	$ 380,000	$ 75,000	19.7%
Selling expenses	$ 191,000	$ 147,000	$ 44,000	29.9%
Administrative expenses	104,000	97,400	6,600	6.8%
Total operating expenses	$ 295,000	$ 244,400	$ 50,600	20.7%
Income from operations	$ 160,000	$ 135,600	$ 24,400	18.0%
Other income	8,500	11,000	(2,500)	(22.7%)
	$ 168,500	$ 146,600	$ 21,900	14.9%
Other expense (interest)	6,000	12,000	(6,000)	(50.0%)
Income before income tax	$ 162,500	$ 134,600	$ 27,900	20.7%
Income tax expense	71,500	58,100	13,400	23.1%
Net income	$ 91,000	$ 76,500	$ 14,500	19.0%

An increase in net sales may not have a favorable effect on operating performance. The percentage increase in Lincoln Company's net sales is accompanied by a greater percentage increase in the cost of goods (merchandise) sold.[1] This has the effect of reducing gross profit as a percentage of sales. Selling expenses increased significantly, and administrative expenses increased slightly. Overall, operating expenses increased by 20.7%, whereas gross profit increased by only 19.7%.

The increase in income from operations and in net income is favorable. However, a study of the expenses and additional analyses and comparisons should be made before reaching a conclusion as to the cause.

Exhibit 4 illustrates a comparative retained earnings statement with horizontal analysis. It reveals that retained earnings increased 30.5% for the year. The increase is due to net income of $91,000 for the year, less dividends of $49,000.

---

1 The term *cost of goods sold* is often used in practice in place of *cost of merchandise sold*. Such usage is followed in this chapter.

EXHIBIT 4

Comparative Retained
Earnings Statement—
Horizontal Analysis

Lincoln Company
Comparative Retained Earnings Statement
December 31, 2008 and 2007

	2008	2007	Increase (Decrease) Amount	Percent
Retained earnings, January 1	$137,500	$100,000	$37,500	37.5%
Net income for the year	91,000	76,500	14,500	19.0%
Total	$228,500	$176,500	$52,000	29.5%
Dividends:				
On preferred stock	$ 9,000	$ 9,000	—	—
On common stock	40,000	30,000	$10,000	33.3%
Total	$ 49,000	$ 39,000	$10,000	25.6%
Retained earnings, December 31 . . .	$179,500	$137,500	$42,000	30.5%

Example Exercise 15-1   **objective** 1

The comparative cash and accounts receivable balances for a company are provided below.

	2008	2007
Cash	$62,500	$50,000
Accounts receivable (net)	74,400	80,000

Based on this information, what is the amount and percentage of increase or decrease that would be shown in a balance sheet with horizontal analysis?

Follow My Example 15-1

Cash $12,500 increase ($62,500 − $50,000), or 25%
Accounts receivable $5,600 decrease ($74,400 − $80,000), or −7%

For Practice: PE 15-1A, PE 15-1B

VERTICAL ANALYSIS

A percentage analysis may also be used to show the relationship of each component to the total within a single statement. This type of analysis is called **vertical analysis**. Like horizontal analysis, the statements may be prepared in either detailed or condensed form. In the latter case, additional details of the changes in individual items may be presented in supporting schedules. In such schedules, the percentage analysis may be based on either the total of the schedule or the statement total. Although vertical analysis is limited to an individual statement, its significance may be improved by preparing comparative statements.

In vertical analysis of the balance sheet, each asset item is stated as a percent of the total assets. Each liability and stockholders' equity item is stated as a percent of the total liabilities and stockholders' equity. Exhibit 5 is a condensed comparative balance sheet with vertical analysis for Lincoln Company.

The major percentage changes in Lincoln Company's assets are in the current asset and long-term investment categories. Current assets increased from 43.3% to 48.3% of total assets, and long-term investments decreased from 14.4% to 8.3% of total assets. In the Liabilities and Stockholders' Equity sections of the balance sheet, the greatest percentage changes are in long-term liabilities and retained earnings. Stockholders' equity increased from 64% to 72.8% of total liabilities and stockholders' equity in 2008. There is a comparable decrease in liabilities.

EXHIBIT 5

Comparative Balance
Sheet—Vertical
Analysis

Lincoln Company
Comparative Balance Sheet
December 31, 2008 and 2007

	2008		2007	
	Amount	Percent	Amount	Percent
Assets				
Current assets	$ 550,000	48.3%	$ 533,000	43.3%
Long-term investments	95,000	8.3	177,500	14.4
Property, plant, and				
equipment (net)	444,500	39.0	470,000	38.2
Intangible assets	50,000	4.4	50,000	4.1
Total assets	$1,139,500	100.0%	$1,230,500	100.0%
Liabilities				
Current liabilities	$ 210,000	18.4%	$ 243,000	19.7%
Long-term liabilities	100,000	8.8	200,000	16.3
Total liabilities	$ 310,000	27.2%	$ 443,000	36.0%
Stockholders' Equity				
Preferred 6% stock, $100 par	$ 150,000	13.2%	$ 150,000	12.2%
Common stock, $10 par	500,000	43.9	500,000	40.6
Retained earnings	179,500	15.7	137,500	11.2
Total stockholders' equity	$ 829,500	72.8%	$ 787,500	64.0%
Total liabilities and				
stockholders' equity	$1,139,500	100.0%	$1,230,500	100.0%

In a vertical analysis of the income statement, each item is stated as a percent of net sales. Exhibit 6 is a condensed comparative income statement with vertical analysis for Lincoln Company.

EXHIBIT 6

Comparative Income
Statement—Vertical
Analysis

Lincoln Company
Comparative Income Statement
For the Years Ended December 31, 2008 and 2007

	2008		2007	
	Amount	Percent	Amount	Percent
Sales	$1,530,500	102.2%	$1,234,000	102.8%
Sales returns and allowances	32,500	2.2	34,000	2.8
Net sales	$1,498,000	100.0%	$1,200,000	100.0%
Cost of goods sold	1,043,000	69.6	820,000	68.3
Gross profit	$ 455,000	30.4%	$ 380,000	31.7%
Selling expenses	$ 191,000	12.8%	$ 147,000	12.3%
Administrative expenses	104,000	6.9	97,400	8.1
Total operating expenses	$ 295,000	19.7%	$ 244,400	20.4%
Income from operations	$ 160,000	10.7%	$ 135,600	11.3%
Other income	8,500	0.6	11,000	0.9
	$ 168,500	11.3%	$ 146,600	12.2%
Other expense (interest)	6,000	0.4	12,000	1.0
Income before income tax	$ 162,500	10.9%	$ 134,600	11.2%
Income tax expense	71,500	4.8	58,100	4.8
Net income	$ 91,000	6.1%	$ 76,500	6.4%

We must be careful when judging the significance of differences between percentages for the two years. For example, the decline of the gross profit rate from 31.7% in 2007 to 30.4% in 2008 is only 1.3 percentage points. In terms of dollars of potential gross profit, however, it represents a decline of approximately $19,500 (1.3% × $1,498,000).

COMMON-SIZE STATEMENTS

Horizontal and vertical analyses with both dollar and percentage amounts are useful in assessing relationships and trends in financial conditions and operations of a business. Vertical analysis with both dollar and percentage amounts is also useful in comparing one company with another or with industry averages. Such comparisons are easier to make with the use of common-size statements. In a **common-size statement**, all items are expressed in percentages.

Common-size statements are useful in comparing the current period with prior periods, individual businesses, or one business with industry percentages. Industry data are often available from trade associations and financial information services. Exhibit 7 is a comparative common-size income statement for two businesses.

Exhibit 7 indicates that Lincoln Company has a slightly higher rate of gross profit than Madison Corporation. However, this advantage is more than offset by Lincoln Company's higher percentage of selling and administrative expenses. As a result, the income from operations of Lincoln Company is 10.7% of net sales, compared with 14.4% for Madison Corporation—an unfavorable difference of 3.7 percentage points.

EXHIBIT 7

Common-Size Income Statement

Lincoln Company and Madison Corporation
Condensed Common-Size Income Statement
For the Year Ended December 31, 2008

	Lincoln Company	Madison Corporation
Sales	102.2%	102.3%
Sales returns and allowances	2.2	2.3
Net sales	100.0%	100.0%
Cost of goods sold	69.6	70.0
Gross profit	30.4%	30.0%
Selling expenses	12.8%	11.5%
Administrative expenses	6.9	4.1
Total operating expenses	19.7%	15.6%
Income from operations	10.7%	14.4%
Other income	0.6	0.6
	11.3%	15.0%
Other expense (interest)	0.4	0.5
Income before income tax	10.9%	14.5%
Income tax expense	4.8	5.5
Net income	6.1%	9.0%

OTHER ANALYTICAL MEASURES

In addition to the preceding analyses, other relationships may be expressed in ratios and percentages. Often, these items are taken from the financial statements and thus are a type of vertical analysis. Comparing these items with items from earlier periods is a type of horizontal analysis.

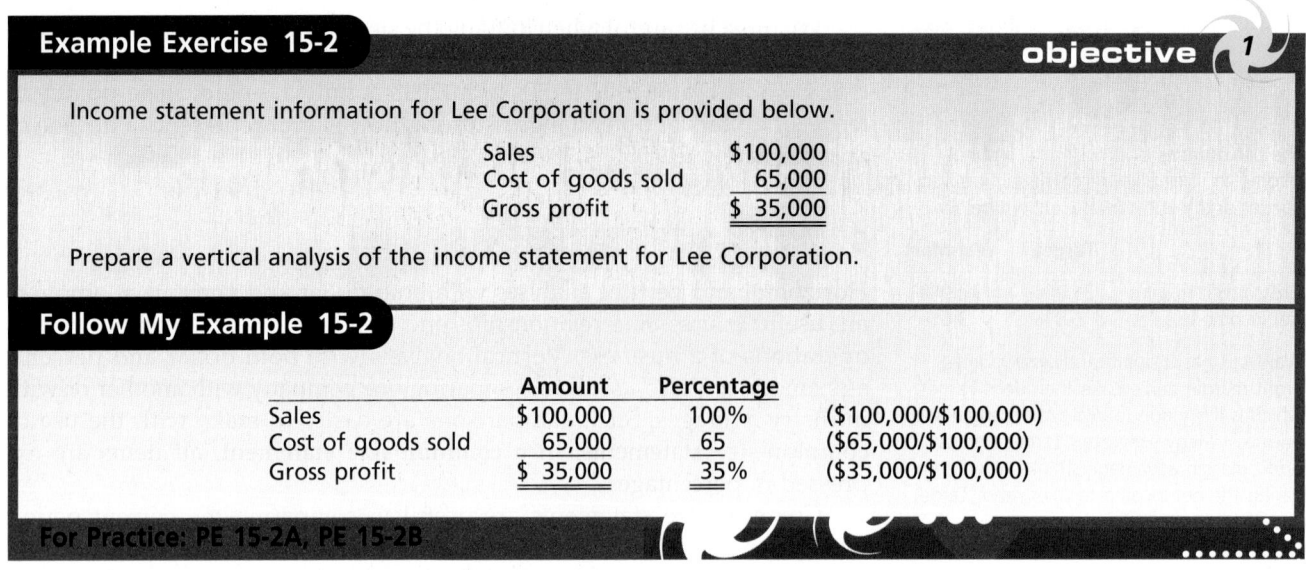

Example Exercise 15-2   objective 1

Income statement information for Lee Corporation is provided below.

Sales	$100,000
Cost of goods sold	65,000
Gross profit	$ 35,000

Prepare a vertical analysis of the income statement for Lee Corporation.

Follow My Example 15-2

	Amount	Percentage	
Sales	$100,000	100%	($100,000/$100,000)
Cost of goods sold	65,000	65	($65,000/$100,000)
Gross profit	$ 35,000	35%	($35,000/$100,000)

For Practice: PE 15-2A, PE 15-2B

Solvency Analysis

objective **2**

Apply financial statement analysis to assess the solvency of a business.

Some aspects of a business's financial condition and operations are of greater importance to some users than others. However, all users are interested in the ability of a business to pay its debts as they are due and to earn income. The ability of a business to meet its financial obligations (debts) is called **solvency**. The ability of a business to earn income is called **profitability**.

The factors of solvency and profitability are interrelated. A business that cannot pay its debts on a timely basis may experience difficulty in obtaining credit. A lack of available credit may, in turn, lead to a decline in the business's profitability. Eventually, the business may be forced into bankruptcy. Likewise, a business that is less profitable than its competitors is likely to be at a disadvantage in obtaining credit or new capital from stockholders.

In the following paragraphs, we discuss various types of financial analyses that are useful in evaluating the solvency of a business. In the next section, we discuss various types of profitability analyses. The examples in both sections are based on Lincoln Company's financial statements presented earlier. In some cases, data from Lincoln Company's financial statements of the preceding year and from other sources are also used. These historical data are useful in assessing the past performance of a business and in forecasting its future performance. The results of financial analyses may be even more useful when they are compared with those of competing businesses and with industry averages.

Solvency analysis focuses on the ability of a business to pay or otherwise satisfy its current and noncurrent liabilities. It is normally assessed by examining balance sheet relationships, using the following major analyses:

1. Current position analysis
2. Accounts receivable analysis
3. Inventory analysis
4. The ratio of fixed assets to long-term liabilities
5. The ratio of liabilities to stockholders' equity
6. The number of times interest charges are earned

REAL WORLD

Two popular printed sources for industry ratios are *Annual Statement Studies* from Robert Morris Associates and *Industry Norms & Key Business Ratios* from Dun's Analytical Services. Online analysis is available from Zacks Investment Research site or Market Guide's site, both of which are linked to the text's Web site at **www.thomson edu.com/accounting/warren**.

CURRENT POSITION ANALYSIS

To be useful in assessing solvency, a ratio or other financial measure must relate to a business's ability to pay or otherwise satisfy its liabilities. Using measures to assess a

> Solvency analysis focuses on the ability of a business to pay or otherwise satisfy its current and noncurrent liabilities.

business's ability to pay its current liabilities is called *current position analysis*. Such analysis is of special interest to short-term creditors.

An analysis of a firm's current position normally includes determining the working capital, the current ratio, and the quick ratio. The current and quick ratios are most useful when analyzed together and compared to previous periods and other firms in the industry.

Working Capital   The excess of the current assets of a business over its current liabilities is called *working capital*. The working capital is often used in evaluating a company's ability to meet currently maturing debts. It is especially useful in making monthly or other period-to-period comparisons for a company. However, amounts of working capital are difficult to assess when comparing companies of different sizes or in comparing such amounts with industry figures. For example, working capital of $250,000 may be adequate for a small kitchenware store, but it would be inadequate for all of Williams-Sonoma, Inc.

Current Ratio   Another means of expressing the relationship between current assets and current liabilities is the **current ratio**. This ratio is sometimes called the *working capital ratio* or *bankers' ratio*. The ratio is computed by dividing the total current assets by the total current liabilities. For Lincoln Company, working capital and the current ratio for 2008 and 2007 are as follows:

	2008	2007
a. Current assets	$550,000	$533,000
b. Current liabilities	210,000	243,000
Working capital (a − b)	$340,000	$290,000
Current ratio (a/b)	2.6	2.2

Microsoft Corporation maintains a high current ratio—4.7 for a recent year. Microsoft's stable and profitable software business has allowed it to develop a strong cash position coupled with no short-term notes payable.

The current ratio is a more reliable indicator of solvency than is working capital. To illustrate, assume that as of December 31, 2008, the working capital of a competitor is much greater than $340,000, but its current ratio is only 1.3. Considering these facts alone, Lincoln Company, with its current ratio of 2.6, is in a more favorable position to obtain short-term credit than the competitor, which has the greater amount of working capital.

Quick Ratio   The working capital and the current ratio do not consider the makeup of the current assets. To illustrate the importance of this consideration, the current position data for Lincoln Company and Jefferson Corporation as of December 31, 2008, are as follows:

	Lincoln Company	Jefferson Corporation
Current assets:		
Cash	$ 90,500	$ 45,500
Marketable securities	75,000	25,000
Accounts receivable (net)	115,000	90,000
Inventories	264,000	380,000
Prepaid expenses	5,500	9,500
a. Total current assets	$550,000	$550,000
b. Current liabilities	210,000	210,000
Working capital (a − b)	$340,000	$340,000
Current ratio (a/b)	2.6	2.6

Both companies have a working capital of $340,000 and a current ratio of 2.6. But the ability of each company to pay its current debts is significantly different. Jefferson Corporation has more of its current assets in inventories. Some of these inventories must be sold and the receivables collected before the current liabilities can be paid in full. Thus, a large amount of time may be necessary to convert these inventories into cash. Declines in market prices and a reduction in demand could also impair its ability to pay current liabilities. In contrast, Lincoln Company has cash and current assets (marketable securities and accounts receivable) that can generally be converted to cash rather quickly to meet its current liabilities.

A ratio that measures the "instant" debt-paying ability of a company is called the **quick ratio** or *acid-test ratio*. It is the ratio of the total quick assets to the total current liabilities. **Quick assets** are cash and other current assets that can be quickly converted to cash. Quick assets normally include cash, marketable securities, and receivables. The quick ratio data for Lincoln Company are as follows:

	2008	2007
Quick assets:		
Cash	$ 90,500	$ 64,700
Marketable securities	75,000	60,000
Accounts receivable (net)	115,000	120,000
a. Total quick assets	$280,500	$244,700
b. Current liabilities	$210,000	$243,000
Quick ratio (a/b)	1.3	1.0

Example Exercise 15-3   objective 2

The following items are reported on a company's balance sheet:

Cash	$300,000
Marketable securities	100,000
Accounts receivable (net)	200,000
Inventory	200,000
Accounts payable	400,000

Determine (a) the current ratio and (b) the quick ratio.

Follow My Example 15-3

a. Current Ratio = Current Assets/Current Liabilities
   Current Ratio = ($300,000 + $100,000 + $200,000 + $200,000)/$400,000
   Current Ratio = 2.0

b. Quick Ratio = Quick Assets/Current Liabilities
   Quick Ratio = ($300,000 + $100,000 + $200,000)/$400,000
   Quick Ratio = 1.5

For Practice: PE 15-3A, PE 15-3B

ACCOUNTS RECEIVABLE ANALYSIS

The size and makeup of accounts receivable change constantly during business operations. Sales on account increase accounts receivable, whereas collections from customers decrease accounts receivable. Firms that grant long credit terms usually have larger accounts receivable balances than those granting short credit terms. Increases or decreases in the volume of sales also affect the balance of accounts receivable.

It is desirable to collect receivables as promptly as possible. The cash collected from receivables improves solvency. In addition, the cash generated by prompt collections from customers may be used in operations for such purposes as purchasing merchandise in large quantities at lower prices. The cash may also be used for payment of dividends to stockholders or for other investing or financing purposes. Prompt collection also lessens the risk of loss from uncollectible accounts.

Accounts Receivable Turnover   The relationship between sales and accounts receivable may be stated as the **accounts receivable turnover**. This ratio is computed by dividing net sales by the average net accounts receivable.[2] It is desirable to base the average on monthly balances, which allows for seasonal changes in sales. When such data are not available, it may be necessary to use the average of the accounts receivable balance at the beginning and the end of the year. If there are trade notes receivable as well as accounts, the two may be combined. The accounts receivable turnover data for Lincoln Company are as follows.

	2008	2007
a. Net sales	$1,498,000	$1,200,000
Accounts receivable (net):		
Beginning of year	$ 120,000	$ 140,000
End of year	115,000	120,000
Total	$ 235,000	$ 260,000
b. Average accounts receivable (Total/2)	$ 117,500	$ 130,000
Accounts receivable turnover (a/b)	12.7	9.2

The increase in the accounts receivable turnover for 2008 indicates that there has been an improvement in the collection of receivables. This may be due to a change in the granting of credit or in collection practices or both.

Number of Days' Sales in Receivables   Another measure of the relationship between sales and accounts receivable is the **number of days' sales in receivables**. This ratio is computed by dividing the average accounts receivable by the average daily sales. Average daily sales is determined by dividing net sales by 365 days. The number of days' sales in receivables is computed for Lincoln Company as follows:

	2008	2007
a. Average accounts receivable (Total/2)	$ 117,500	$ 130,000
Net sales	$1,498,000	$1,200,000
b. Average daily sales (Sales/365)	$4,104	$3,288
Number of days' sales in receivables (a/b)	28.6	39.5

The number of days' sales in receivables is an estimate of the length of time (in days) the accounts receivable have been outstanding. Comparing this measure with the credit terms provides information on the efficiency in collecting receivables. For example, assume that the number of days' sales in receivables for Grant Inc. is 40. If Grant Inc.'s credit terms are n/45, then its collection process appears to be efficient. On the other hand, if Grant Inc.'s credit terms are n/30, its collection process does not appear to be efficient. A comparison with other firms in the same industry and with prior years also provides useful information. Such comparisons may indicate efficiency of collection procedures and trends in credit management.

---

2 If known, *credit* sales should be used in the numerator. Because credit sales are not normally known by external users, we use net sales in the numerator.

Example Exercise 15-4   **objective**

A company reports the following:

Net sales	$960,000
Average accounts receivable (net)	48,000

Determine (a) the accounts receivable turnover and (b) the number of days' sales in receivables. Round to one decimal place.

Follow My Example 15-4

a. Accounts Receivable Turnover = Sales/Average Accounts Receivable
    Accounts Receivable Turnover = $960,000/$48,000
    Accounts Receivable Turnover = 20.0

b. Number of Days' Sales in Receivables = Average Accounts Receivable/Average Daily Sales
    Number of Days' Sales in Receivables = $48,000/($960,000/365) = $48,000/$2,630
    Number of Days' Sales in Receivables = 18.3 days

For Practice: PE 15-4A, PE 15-4B

INVENTORY ANALYSIS

A business should keep enough inventory on hand to meet the needs of its customers and its operations. At the same time, however, an excessive amount of inventory reduces solvency by tying up funds. Excess inventories also increase insurance expense, property taxes, storage costs, and other related expenses. These expenses further reduce funds that could be used elsewhere to improve operations. Finally, excess inventory also increases the risk of losses because of price declines or obsolescence of the inventory. Two measures that are useful for evaluating the management of inventory are the inventory turnover and the number of days' sales in inventory.

Inventory Turnover   The relationship between the volume of goods (merchandise) sold and inventory may be stated as the **inventory turnover**. It is computed by dividing the cost of goods sold by the average inventory. If monthly data are not available, the average of the inventories at the beginning and the end of the year may be used. The inventory turnover for Lincoln Company is computed as follows:

	2008	2007
a. Cost of goods sold	$1,043,000	$820,000
Inventories:		
Beginning of year	$ 283,000	$311,000
End of year	264,000	283,000
Total	$ 547,000	$594,000
b. Average inventory (Total/2)	$ 273,500	$297,000
Inventory turnover (a/b)	3.8	2.8

The inventory turnover improved for Lincoln Company because of an increase in the cost of goods sold and a decrease in the average inventories. Differences across inventories, companies, and industries are too great to allow a general statement on what is a good inventory turnover. For example, a firm selling food should have a higher turnover than a firm selling furniture or jewelry. Likewise, the perishable foods department of a supermarket should have a higher turnover than the soaps and cleansers department. However, for each business or each department within a business, there is a reasonable turnover rate. A turnover lower than this rate could mean that inventory is not being managed properly.

Number of Days' Sales in Inventory   Another measure of the relationship between the cost of goods sold and inventory is the **number of days' sales in inventory**. This measure is computed by dividing the average inventory by the average daily cost of goods sold (cost of goods sold divided by 365). The number of days' sales in inventory for Lincoln Company is computed as follows:

	2008	2007
a. Average inventory (Total/2)	$ 273,500	$297,000
Cost of goods sold	$1,043,000	$820,000
b. Average daily cost of goods sold (COGS/365 days)	$2,858	$2,247
Number of days' sales in inventory (a/b)	95.7	132.2

The number of days' sales in inventory is a rough measure of the length of time it takes to acquire, sell, and replace the inventory. For Lincoln Company, there is a major improvement in the number of days' sales in inventory during 2008. However, a comparison with earlier years and similar firms would be useful in assessing Lincoln Company's overall inventory management.

Example Exercise 15-5

objective 2

A company reports the following:

Cost of goods sold	$560,000
Average inventory	112,000

Determine (a) the inventory turnover and (b) the number of days' sales in inventory. Round to one decimal place.

Follow My Example 15-5

a. Inventory Turnover = Cost of Goods Sold/Average Inventory
    Inventory Turnover = $560,000/$112,000
    Inventory Turnover = 5.0

b. Number of Days' Sales in Inventory = Average Inventory/Average Daily Cost of Goods Sold
    Number of Days' Sales in Inventory = $112,000/($560,000/365) = $112,000/$1,534
    Number of Days' Sales in Inventory = 73.0 days

For Practice: PE 15-5A, PE 15-5B

RATIO OF FIXED ASSETS TO LONG-TERM LIABILITIES

Long-term notes and bonds are often secured by mortgages on fixed assets. The **ratio of fixed assets to long-term liabilities** is a solvency measure that indicates the margin of safety of the noteholders or bondholders. It also indicates the ability of the business to borrow additional funds on a long-term basis. The ratio of fixed assets to long-term liabilities for Lincoln Company is as follows:

	2008	2007
a. Fixed assets (net)	$444,500	$470,000
b. Long-term liabilities	$100,000	$200,000
Ratio of fixed assets to long-term liabilities (a/b)	4.4	2.4

The major increase in this ratio at the end of 2008 is mainly due to liquidating one-half of Lincoln Company's long-term liabilities. If the company needs to borrow additional funds on a long-term basis in the future, it is in a strong position to do so.

RATIO OF LIABILITIES TO STOCKHOLDERS' EQUITY

REAL WORLD

The ratio of liabilities to stock-holders' equity varies across industries. For example, recent annual reports of some selected companies showed the following ratio of liabilities to stock-holders' equity:

Continental Airlines	66.8
Procter & Gamble	2.5
Circuit City Stores, Inc.	0.8

The airline industry generally uses more debt financing than the consumer product or retail industries. Thus, the airline in-dustry is generally considered more risky.

Claims against the total assets of a business are divided into two groups: (1) claims of creditors and (2) claims of owners. The relationship between the total claims of the creditors and owners—the **ratio of liabilities to stockholders' equity**—is a solvency measure that indicates the margin of safety for creditors. It also indicates the ability of the business to withstand adverse business conditions. When the claims of creditors are large in relation to the equity of the stockholders, there are usually significant in-terest payments. If earnings decline to the point where the company is unable to meet its interest payments, the business may be taken over by the creditors.

The relationship between creditor and stockholder equity is shown in the vertical analysis of the balance sheet. For example, the balance sheet of Lincoln Company in Exhibit 5 indicates that on December 31, 2008, liabilities represented 27.2% and stock-holders' equity represented 72.8% of the total liabilities and stockholders' equity (100.0%). Instead of expressing each item as a percent of the total, this relationship may be expressed as a ratio of one to the other, as follows:

	2008	2007
a. Total liabilities	$310,000	$443,000
b. Total stockholders' equity	$829,500	$787,500
Ratio of liabilities to stockholders' equity (a/b)	0.4	0.6

The balance sheet of Lincoln Company shows that the major factor affecting the change in the ratio was the $100,000 decrease in long-term liabilities during 2008. The ratio at the end of both years shows a large margin of safety for the creditors.

Example Exercise 15-6   objective 2

The following information was taken from Acme Company's balance sheet:

Fixed assets (net)	$1,400,000
Long-term liabilities	400,000
Total liabilities	560,000
Total stockholders' equity	1,400,000

Determine the company's (a) ratio of fixed assets to long-term liabilities and (b) ratio of liabilities to total stockholders' equity.

Follow My Example 15-6

a. Ratio of Fixed Assets to Long-Term Liabilities = Fixed Assets/Long-Term Liabilities
    Ratio of Fixed Assets to Long-Term Liabilities = $1,400,000/$400,000
    Ratio of Fixed Assets to Long-Term Liabilities = 3.5

b. Ratio of Liabilities to Total Stockholders' Equity = Total Liabilities/Total Stockholders' Equity
    Ratio of Liabilities to Total Stockholders' Equity = $560,000/$1,400,000
    Ratio of Liabilities to Total Stockholders' Equity = 0.4

For Practice: PE 15-6A, PE 15-6B

NUMBER OF TIMES INTEREST CHARGES EARNED

Corporations in some industries, such as airlines, normally have high ratios of debt to stockholders' equity. For such corporations, the relative risk of the debtholders is normally measured as the **number of times interest charges are earned**, sometimes called the *fixed charge coverage ratio*, during the year. The higher the ratio, the lower the risk that interest payments will not be made if earnings decrease. In other words, the higher the ratio, the greater the assurance that interest payments will be made on a continuing basis. This measure also indicates the general financial strength of the busi-ness, which is of interest to stockholders and employees as well as creditors.

The amount available to meet interest charges is not affected by taxes on income. This is because interest is deductible in determining taxable income. Thus, the number of times interest charges are earned for Lincoln Company is computed as shown below, rounded to one decimal place.

	2008	2007
Income before income tax	$162,500	$134,600
a. Add interest expense	6,000	12,000
b. Amount available to meet interest charges	$168,500	$146,600
Number of times interest charges earned (b/a)	28.1	12.2

These calculations indicate Lincoln Company has very high coverage of its interest charges for both years. Analysis such as this can also be applied to dividends on preferred stock. In such a case, net income is divided by the amount of preferred dividends to yield the *number of times preferred dividends are earned*. This measure indicates the risk that dividends to preferred stockholders may not be paid.

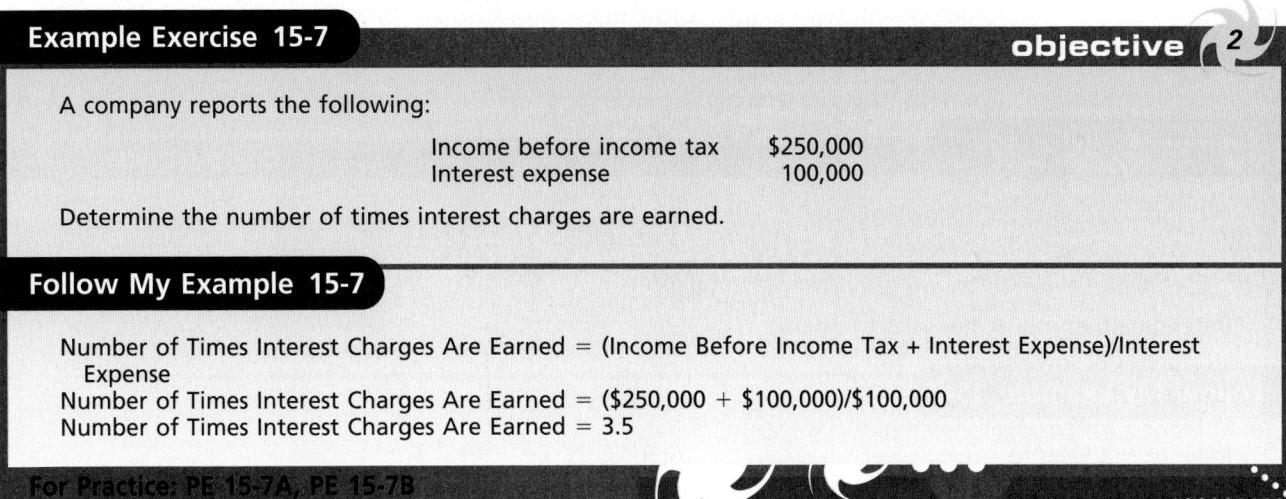

Example Exercise 15-7

objective 2

A company reports the following:

Income before income tax	$250,000
Interest expense	100,000

Determine the number of times interest charges are earned.

Follow My Example 15-7

Number of Times Interest Charges Are Earned = (Income Before Income Tax + Interest Expense)/Interest Expense

Number of Times Interest Charges Are Earned = ($250,000 + $100,000)/$100,000

Number of Times Interest Charges Are Earned = 3.5

For Practice: PE 15-7A, PE 15-7B

Profitability Analysis

objective 3

Apply financial statement analysis to assess the profitability of a business.

The ability of a business to earn profits depends on the effectiveness and efficiency of its operations as well as the resources available to it. Profitability analysis, therefore, focuses primarily on the relationship between operating results as reported in the income statement and resources available to the business as reported in the balance sheet. Major analyses used in assessing profitability include the following:

1. Ratio of net sales to assets
2. Rate earned on total assets
3. Rate earned on stockholders' equity
4. Rate earned on common stockholders' equity
5. Earnings per share on common stock
6. Price-earnings ratio
7. Dividends per share
8. Dividend yield

> Profitability analysis focuses on the relationship between operating results and the resources available to a business.

RATIO OF NET SALES TO ASSETS

The ratio of net sales to assets is a profitability measure that shows how effectively a firm utilizes its assets. For example, two competing businesses have equal amounts of assets. If the sales of one are twice the sales of the other, the business with the higher sales is making better use of its assets.

In computing the ratio of net sales to assets, any long-term investments are excluded from total assets, because such investments are unrelated to normal operations involving the sale of goods or services. Assets may be measured as the total at the end of the year, the average at the beginning and end of the year, or the average of monthly totals. The basic data and the computation of this ratio for Lincoln Company are as follows:

	2008	2007
a. Net sales	$1,498,000	$1,200,000
Total assets (excluding long-term investments):		
Beginning of year	$1,053,000	$1,010,000
End of year	1,044,500	1,053,000
Total	$2,097,500	$2,063,000
b. Average (Total/2)	$1,048,750	$1,031,500
Ratio of net sales to assets (a/b)	1.4	1.2

This ratio improved during 2008, primarily due to an increase in sales volume. A comparison with similar companies or industry averages would be helpful in assessing the effectiveness of Lincoln Company's use of its assets.

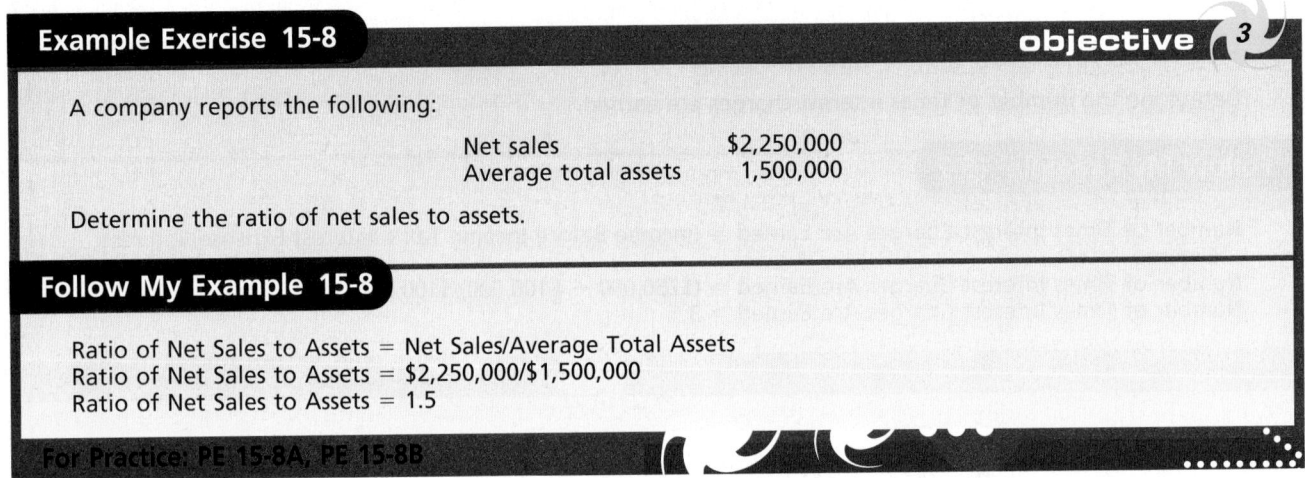

Example Exercise 15-8   objective 3

A company reports the following:

Net sales	$2,250,000
Average total assets	1,500,000

Determine the ratio of net sales to assets.

Follow My Example 15-8

Ratio of Net Sales to Assets = Net Sales/Average Total Assets
Ratio of Net Sales to Assets = $2,250,000/$1,500,000
Ratio of Net Sales to Assets = 1.5

For Practice: PE 15-8A, PE 15-8B

RATE EARNED ON TOTAL ASSETS

The **rate earned on total assets** measures the profitability of total assets without considering how the assets are financed. This rate is therefore not affected by whether the assets are financed primarily by creditors or stockholders.

The rate earned on total assets is computed by adding interest expense to net income and dividing this sum by the average total assets. Adding interest expense to net income eliminates the effect of whether the assets are financed by debt or equity. The rate earned by Lincoln Company on total assets is computed as follows:

	2008	2007
Net income	$ 91,000	$ 76,500
Plus interest expense	6,000	12,000
a. Total	$ 97,000	$ 88,500
Total assets:		
Beginning of year	$1,230,500	$1,187,500
End of year	1,139,500	1,230,500
Total	$2,370,000	$2,418,000
b. Average (Total/2)	$1,185,000	$1,209,000
Rate earned on total assets (a/b)	8.2%	7.3%

The rate earned on total assets of Lincoln Company during 2008 improved over that of 2007. A comparison with similar companies and industry averages would be useful in evaluating Lincoln Company's profitability on total assets.

Sometimes it may be desirable to compute the *rate of income from operations to total assets*. This is especially true if significant amounts of nonoperating income and expense are reported on the income statement. In this case, any assets related to the nonoperating income and expense items should be excluded from total assets in computing the rate. In addition, using income from operations (which is before tax) has the advantage of eliminating the effects of any changes in the tax structure on the rate of earnings. When evaluating published data on rates earned on assets, you should be careful to determine the exact nature of the measure that is reported.

Example Exercise 15-9   **objective** 3

A company reports the following income statement and balance sheet information for the current year:

Net income	$ 125,000
Interest expense	25,000
Average total assets	2,000,000

Determine the rate earned on total assets.

Follow My Example 15-9

Rate Earned on Total Assets = (Net Income + Interest Expense)/Average Total Assets
Rate Earned on Total Assets = ($125,000 + $25,000)/$2,000,000
Rate Earned on Total Assets = $150,000/$2,000,000
Rate Earned on Total Assets = 7.5%

For Practice: PE 15-9A, PE 15-9B

RATE EARNED ON STOCKHOLDERS' EQUITY

Another measure of profitability is the **rate earned on stockholders' equity**. It is computed by dividing net income by average total stockholders' equity. In contrast to the rate earned on total assets, this measure emphasizes the rate of income earned on the amount invested by the stockholders.

The total stockholders' equity may vary throughout a period. For example, a business may issue or retire stock, pay dividends, and earn net income. If monthly amounts are not available, the average of the stockholders' equity at the beginning and the end of the year is normally used to compute this rate. For Lincoln Company, the rate earned on stockholders' equity is computed as follows:

	2008	2007
a. Net income	$ 91,000	$ 76,500
Stockholders' equity:		
Beginning of year	$ 787,500	$ 750,000
End of year	829,500	787,500
Total	$1,617,000	$1,537,500
b. Average (Total/2)	$ 808,500	$ 768,750
Rate earned on stockholders' equity (a/b)	11.3%	10.0%

The rate earned by a business on the equity of its stockholders is usually higher than the rate earned on total assets. This occurs when the amount earned on assets acquired with creditors' funds is more than the interest paid to creditors. This difference in the rate on stockholders' equity and the rate on total assets is called **leverage**.

Lincoln Company's rate earned on stockholders' equity for 2008, 11.3%, is greater than the rate of 8.2% earned on total assets. The leverage of 3.1% (11.3% − 8.2%) for 2008 compares favorably with the 2.7% (10.0% − 7.3%) leverage for 2007. Exhibit 8 shows the 2008 and 2007 leverages for Lincoln Company.

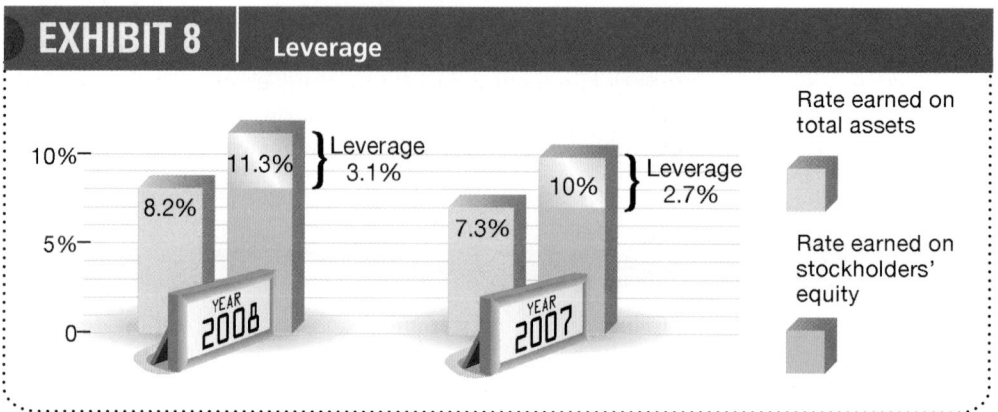

EXHIBIT 8 | **Leverage**

The approximate rates earned on assets and stockholders' equity for Molson Coors Brewing Company and Anheuser-Busch Companies, Inc., for a recent fiscal year are shown below.

	Molson Coors	Anheuser-Busch
Rate earned on assets	4%	15%
Rate earned on stockholders' equity	12%	83%

Anheuser-Busch has been more profitable and has benefited from a greater use of leverage than has Molson Coors.

RATE EARNED ON COMMON STOCKHOLDERS' EQUITY

A corporation may have both preferred and common stock outstanding. In this case, the common stockholders have the residual claim on earnings. The **rate earned on common stockholders' equity** focuses only on the rate of profits earned on the amount invested by the common stockholders. It is computed by subtracting preferred dividend requirements from the net income and dividing by the average common stockholders' equity.

Lincoln Company has $150,000 of 6% nonparticipating preferred stock outstanding on December 31, 2008 and 2007. Thus, the annual preferred dividend requirement is $9,000 ($150,000 × 6%). The common stockholders' equity equals the total stockholders' equity, including retained earnings, less the par of the preferred stock ($150,000). The basic data and the rate earned on common stockholders' equity for Lincoln Company are as follows:

	2008	2007
Net income	$ 91,000	$ 76,500
Preferred dividends	9,000	9,000
a. Remainder—identified with common stock	$ 82,000	$ 67,500
Common stockholders' equity:		
Beginning of year	$ 637,500	$ 600,000
End of year	679,500	637,500
Total	$1,317,000	$1,237,500
b. Average (Total/2)	$ 658,500	$ 618,750
Rate earned on common stockholders' equity (a/b)	12.5%	10.9%

The rate earned on common stockholders' equity differs from the rates earned by Lincoln Company on total assets and total stockholders' equity. This occurs if there are borrowed funds and also preferred stock outstanding, which rank ahead of the common shares in their claim on earnings. Thus, the concept of leverage, as we discussed in the preceding section, can also be applied to the use of funds from the sale of preferred stock as well as borrowing. Funds from both sources can be used in an attempt to increase the return on common stockholders' equity.

Example Exercise 15-10

objective **3**

A company reports the following:

Net income	$ 125,000
Preferred dividends	5,000
Average stockholders' equity	1,000,000
Average common stockholders' equity	800,000

Determine (a) the rate earned on stockholders' equity and (b) the rate earned on common stockholders' equity.

Follow My Example 15-10

a. Rate Earned on Stockholders' Equity = Net Income/Average Stockholders' Equity
    Rate Earned on Stockholders' Equity = $125,000/$1,000,000
    Rate Earned on Stockholders' Equity = 12.5%

b. Rate Earned on Common Stockholders' Equity = (Net Income − Preferred Dividends)/Average
                                                 Common Stockholders' Equity
    Rate Earned on Common Stockholders' Equity = ($125,000 − $5,000)/$800,000
    Rate Earned on Common Stockholders' Equity = 15%

For Practice: PE 15-10A, PE 15-10B

EARNINGS PER SHARE ON COMMON STOCK

One of the profitability measures often quoted by the financial press is **earnings per share (EPS) on common stock**. It is also normally reported in the income statement in corporate annual reports. If a company has issued only one class of stock, the earnings per share is computed by dividing net income by the number of shares of stock outstanding. If preferred and common stock are outstanding, the net income is first reduced by the amount of preferred dividend requirements.[3]

The data on the earnings per share of common stock for Lincoln Company are as follows:

	2008	2007
Net income	$91,000	$76,500
Preferred dividends	9,000	9,000
a. Remainder—identified with common stock	$82,000	$67,500
b. Shares of common stock outstanding	50,000	50,000
Earnings per share on common stock (a/b)	$1.64	$1.35

PRICE-EARNINGS RATIO

Another profitability measure quoted by the financial press is the **price-earnings (P/E) ratio** on common stock. The price-earnings ratio is an indicator of a firm's future earnings prospects. It is computed by dividing the market price per share of common stock at a specific date by the annual earnings per share. To illustrate, assume that the market prices per common share are $41 at the end of 2008 and $27 at the end of 2007. The price-earnings ratio on common stock of Lincoln Company is computed as follows:

	2008	2007
Market price per share of common stock	$41.00	$27.00
Earnings per share on common stock	÷ 1.64	÷ 1.35
Price-earnings ratio on common stock	25	20

---

3 Additional details related to earnings per share were discussed in Chapter 12.

The price-earnings ratio indicates that a share of common stock of Lincoln Company was selling for 20 times the amount of earnings per share at the end of 2007. At the end of 2008, the common stock was selling for 25 times the amount of earnings per share.

Example Exercise 15-11

objective **3**

A company reports the following:

Net income	$250,000
Preferred dividends	$15,000
Shares of common stock outstanding	20,000
Market price per share of common stock	$35.00

a. Determine the company's earnings per share on common stock.
b. Determine the company's price-earnings ratio. Round to one decimal place.

Follow My Example 15-11

a. Earnings per Share on Common Stock = (Net Income − Preferred Dividends)/Shares of Common Stock Outstanding
Earnings per Share = ($250,000 − $15,000)/20,000
Earnings per Share = $11.75

b. Price-Earnings Ratio = Market Price per Share of Common Stock/Earnings per Share on Common Stock
Price-Earnings Ratio = $35.00/$11.75
Price-Earnings Ratio = 3.0

For Practice: PE 15-11A, PE 15-11B

The dividend per share, dividend yield, and P/E ratio of a common stock are normally quoted on the daily listing of stock prices in *The Wall Street Journal* and on Yahoo!'s finance Web site.

DIVIDENDS PER SHARE AND DIVIDEND YIELD

Since the primary basis for dividends is earnings, dividends per share and earnings per share on common stock are commonly used by investors in assessing alternative stock investments. The dividends per share for Lincoln Company were $0.80 ($40,000/50,000 shares) for 2008 and $0.60 ($30,000/50,000 shares) for 2007.

Dividends per share can be reported with earnings per share to indicate the relationship between dividends and earnings. Comparing these two per share amounts indicates the extent to which the corporation is retaining its earnings for use in operations. Exhibit 9 shows these relationships for Lincoln Company.

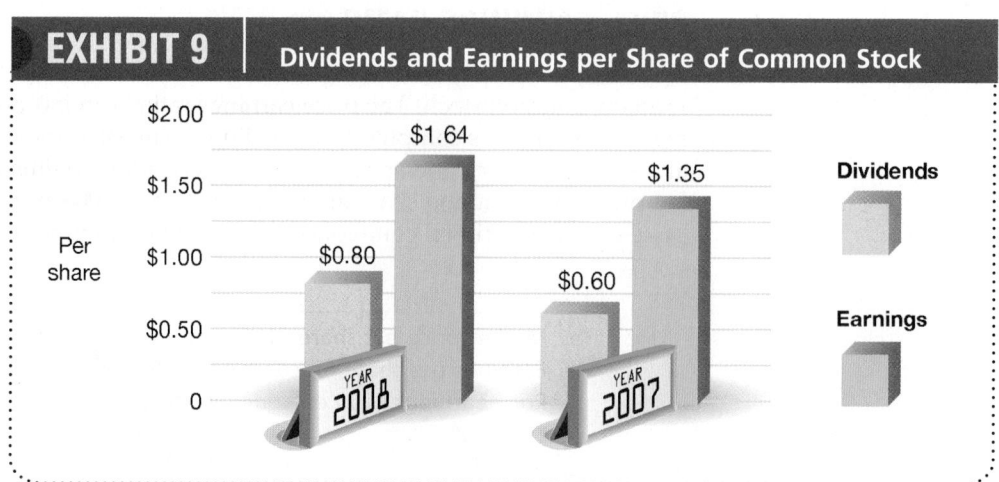

EXHIBIT 9   Dividends and Earnings per Share of Common Stock

The **dividend yield** on common stock is a profitability measure that shows the rate of return to common stockholders in terms of cash dividends. It is of special interest to investors whose main investment objective is to receive current returns (dividends) on an investment rather than an increase in the market price of the investment. The dividend yield is computed by dividing the annual dividends paid per share of common stock by the market price per share on a specific date. To illustrate, assume that the market price was $41 at the end of 2008 and $27 at the end of 2007. The dividend yield on common stock of Lincoln Company is as follows:

	2008	2007
Dividends per share of common stock	$ 0.80	$ 0.60
Market price per share of common stock	÷ 41.00	÷ 27.00
Dividend yield on common stock	2.0%	2.2%

SUMMARY OF ANALYTICAL MEASURES

Exhibit 10 presents a summary of the analytical measures that we have discussed. These measures can be computed for most medium-size businesses. Depending on the specific business being analyzed, some measures might be omitted or additional measures could be developed. The type of industry, the capital structure, and the diversity of the business's operations usually affect the measures used. For example, analysis for an airline might include revenue per passenger mile and cost per available seat as measures. Likewise, analysis for a hotel might focus on occupancy rates.

Percentage analyses, ratios, turnovers, and other measures of financial position and operating results are useful analytical measures. They are helpful in assessing a business's past performance and predicting its future. They are not, however, a substitute for sound judgment. In selecting and interpreting analytical measures, conditions peculiar to a business or its industry should be considered. In addition, the influence of the general economic and business environment should be considered.

In determining trends, the interrelationship of the measures used in assessing a business should be carefully studied. Comparable indexes of earlier periods should also be studied. Data from competing businesses may be useful in assessing the efficiency of operations for the firm under analysis. In making such comparisons, however, the effects of differences in the accounting methods used by the businesses should be considered.

EXHIBIT 10   Summary of Analytical Measures

	Method of Computation	Use
Solvency measures:		
Working Capital	Current Assets − Current Liabilities	To indicate the ability to meet currently maturing obligations
Current Ratio	$\dfrac{\text{Current Assets}}{\text{Current Liabilities}}$	
Quick Ratio	$\dfrac{\text{Quick Assets}}{\text{Current Liabilities}}$	To indicate instant debt-paying ability
Accounts Receivable Turnover	$\dfrac{\text{Net Sales}}{\text{Average Accounts Receivable}}$	To assess the efficiency in collecting receivables and in the management of credit
Numbers of Days' Sales in Receivables	$\dfrac{\text{Average Accounts Receivable}}{\text{Average Daily Sales}}$	
Inventory Turnover	$\dfrac{\text{Cost of Goods Sold}}{\text{Average Inventory}}$	To assess the efficiency in the management of inventory
Number of Days' Sales in Inventory	$\dfrac{\text{Average Inventory}}{\text{Average Daily Cost of Goods Sold}}$	
Ratio of Fixed Assets to Long-Term Liabilities	$\dfrac{\text{Fixed Assets (net)}}{\text{Long-Term Liabilities}}$	To indicate the margin of safety to long-term creditors
Ratio of Liabilities to Stockholders' Equity	$\dfrac{\text{Total Liabilities}}{\text{Total Stockholders' Equity}}$	To indicate the margin of safety to creditors
Number of Times Interest Charges Earned	$\dfrac{\text{Income Before Income Tax + Interest Expense}}{\text{Interest Expense}}$	To assess the risk to debtholders in terms of number of times interest charges were earned
Profitability measures:		
Ratio of Net Sales to Assets	$\dfrac{\text{Net Sales}}{\text{Average Total Assets (excluding long-term investments)}}$	To assess the effectiveness in the use of assets
Rate Earned on Total Assets	$\dfrac{\text{Net Income + Interest Expense}}{\text{Average Total Assets}}$	To assess the profitability of the assets
Rate Earned on Stockholders' Equity	$\dfrac{\text{Net Income}}{\text{Average Total Stockholders' Equity}}$	To assess the profitability of the investment by stockholders
Rate Earned on Common Stockholders' Equity	$\dfrac{\text{Net Income − Preferred Dividends}}{\text{Average Common Stockholders' Equity}}$	To assess the profitability of the investment by common stockholders
Earnings per Share on Common Stock	$\dfrac{\text{Net Income − Preferred Dividends}}{\text{Shares of Common Stock Outstanding}}$	
Price-Earnings Ratio	$\dfrac{\text{Market Price per Share of Common Stock}}{\text{Earnings per Share of Common Stock}}$	To indicate future earnings prospects, based on the relationship between market value of common stock and earnings
Dividends per Share of Common Stock	$\dfrac{\text{Dividends}}{\text{Shares of Common Stock Outstanding}}$	To indicate the extent to which earnings are being distributed to common stockholders
Dividend Yield	$\dfrac{\text{Dividends per Share of Common Stock}}{\text{Market Price per Share of Common Stock}}$	To indicate the rate of return to common stockholders in terms of dividends

Integrity, Objectivity, and Ethics in Business

ETHICS

ONE BAD APPLE

A recent survey by *CFO* magazine reported that 47% of chief financial officers have been pressured by the chief executive officer to use questionable accounting. In addition, only 38% of those surveyed feel less pressure to use aggressive accounting today than in years past, while 20% believe there is more pressure. Perhaps more troublesome is the chief financial officers' confidence in the quality of financial information, with only 27% being "very confident" in the quality of financial information presented by public companies.

Source: D. Durfee, "It's Better (and Worse) Than You Think," *CFO*, May 3, 2004.

Corporate Annual Reports

objective 4

Describe the contents of corporate annual reports.

Public corporations are required to issue annual reports to their stockholders and other interested parties. Such reports summarize the corporation's operating activities for the past year and plans for the future. There are many variations in the order and form for presenting the major sections of annual reports. However, one section of the annual report is devoted to the financial statements, including the accompanying notes. In addition, annual reports usually include the following sections:

1. Management discussion and analysis
2. Report on adequacy of internal control
3. Report on fairness of financial statements

In the following paragraphs, we describe these sections. Each section, as well as the financial statements, is illustrated in the annual report for Williams-Sonoma, Inc., in Appendix E.

MANAGEMENT DISCUSSION AND ANALYSIS

A required disclosure in the annual report filed with the Securities and Exchange Commission is the **Management's Discussion and Analysis (MD&A)**. The MD&A provides critical information in interpreting the financial statements and assessing the future of the company.

The MD&A includes an analysis of the results of operations and discusses management's opinion about future performance. It compares the prior year's income statement with the current year's to explain changes in sales, significant expenses, gross profit, and income from operations. For example, an increase in sales may be explained by referring to higher shipment volume or stronger prices.

The MD&A also includes an analysis of the company's financial condition. It compares significant balance sheet items between successive years to explain changes in liquidity and capital resources. In addition, the MD&A discusses significant risk exposure.

A new subsection of the MD&A required by the Sarbanes-Oxley Act must now include a section describing any "off-balance-sheet" arrangements. Such arrangements are discussed in advanced accounting courses.

REPORT ON ADEQUACY OF INTERNAL CONTROL

As discussed in Chapter 7, the Sarbanes-Oxley Act of 2002 requires management to provide a report stating their responsibility for establishing and maintaining internal control. In addition, the report must state management's conclusion concerning the effectiveness of internal controls over financial reporting. The act also requires a public accounting firm to examine and verify management's conclusions regarding internal control. Thus, public companies must provide two reports, one by management and one by a public accounting firm, certifying the management report as accurate. In some situations, the auditor may combine these reports into a single report. The combined report for Williams-Sonoma, Inc., is included in the annual report in Appendix E.

REPORT ON FAIRNESS OF FINANCIAL STATEMENTS

In addition to a public accounting firm's internal control report, all publicly held corporations are also required to have an independent audit (examination) of their financial statements. For the financial statements of most companies, the CPAs who conduct the audit render an opinion on the fairness of the statements. An opinion stating that the financial statements fairly represent the financial condition of a public company is said to be an unqualified, or "clean," opinion. The Independent Auditors' Report for Williams-Sonoma, Inc., is an unqualified opinion.

Business Connections

REAL WORLD

INVESTING STRATEGIES

How do people make investment decisions? Investment decisions, like any major purchase, must meet the needs of the buyer. For example, if you have a family of five and are thinking about buying a new car, you probably wouldn't buy a two-seat sports car. It just wouldn't meet your objectives or fit your lifestyle. Alternatively, if you are a young single person, a minivan might not meet your immediate needs. Investors buy stocks in the same way, buying stocks that match their investment style and their financial needs. Two common approaches are value and growth investing.

Value Investing

Value investors search for undervalued stocks. That is, the investor tries to find companies whose value is not reflected in their stock price. These are typically quiet, "boring" companies with excellent financial performance that are temporarily out of favor in the stock market. This investment approach assumes that the stock's price will eventually rise to match the company's value. The most successful investor of all time, Warren Buffett, uses this approach almost exclusively. Naturally, the key to successful value investing is to accurately determine a stock's value. This will often include analyzing a company's financial ratios, as discussed in this chapter, compared to target ratios and industry norms. For example,

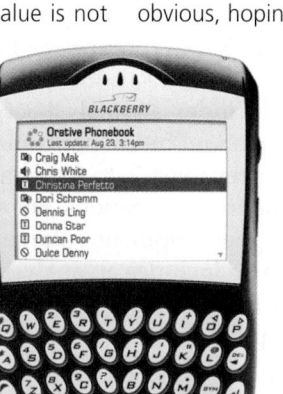

the stock of Darden Restaurants, the operator of restaurant chains including Olive Garden and Red Lobster, was selling for $18.35 on May 25, 2003, a value relative to its earnings per share of $1.36. Over the next three years, the company's stock price more than doubled, reaching $41.44 on February 17, 2006.

Growth Investing

The growth investor tries to identify companies that have the potential to grow sales and earnings through new products, markets, or opportunities. Growth companies are often newer companies that are still unproven but that possess unique technologies or capabilities. The strategy is to purchase these companies before their potential becomes obvious, hoping to profit from relatively large increases in the company's stock price. This approach, however, carries the risk that the growth may not occur. Growth investors use many of the ratios discussed in this chapter to identify high-potential growth companies. For example, in March 2003, Research in Motion Limited, maker of the popular BlackBerry® handheld mobile device, reported earnings per share of −$0.96, and the company's stock price was trading near $5 per share. In the following two years, the company's sales increased by 340%, earnings increased to $1.14 per share, and the company's stock price rose above $75 per share.

At a Glance

1. List basic financial statement analytical procedures.

Key Points	Key Learning Outcomes	Example Exercises	Practice Exercises
The basic financial statements provide much of the information users need to make economic decisions. Analytical procedures are used to compare items on a current financial statement with related items on earlier statements, or to examine relationships within a financial statement.	• Prepare a horizontal analysis from a company's financial statements. • Prepare a vertical analysis from a company's financial statements.	15-1	15-1A, 15-1B
	• Prepare common-size financial statements.	15-2	15-2A, 15-2B

2. Apply financial statement analysis to assess the solvency of a business.

Key Points	Key Learning Outcomes	Example Exercises	Practice Exercises
All users of financial statements are interested in the ability of a business to pay its debts (solvency) and earn income (profitability). Solvency and profitability are interrelated. Solvency analysis is normally assessed by examining the following balance sheet relationships: (1) current position analysis, (2) accounts receivable analysis, (3) inventory analysis, (4) the ratio of fixed assets to long-term liabilities, (5) the ratio of liabilities to stockholders' equity, and (6) the number of times interest charges are earned.	• Determine working capital. • Calculate and interpret the current ratio.	15-3	15-3A, 15-3B
	• Calculate and interpret the quick ratio.	15-3	15-3A, 15-3B
	• Calculate and interpret accounts receivable turnover.	15-4	15-4A, 15-4B
	• Calculate and interpret number of days' sales in receivables.	15-4	15-4A, 15-4B
	• Calculate and interpret inventory turnover.	15-5	15-5A, 15-5B
	• Calculate and interpret number of days' sales in inventory.	15-5	15-5A, 15-5B
	• Calculate and interpret the ratio of fixed assets to long-term liabilities.	15-6	15-6A, 15-6B
	• Calculate and interpret the ratio of liabilities to stockholders' equity.	15-6	15-6A, 15-6B
	• Calculate and interpret the number of times interest charges are earned.	15-7	15-7A, 15-7B

(continued)

3. Apply financial statement analysis to assess the profitability of a business.

Key Points	Key Learning Outcomes	Example Exercises	Practice Exercises
Profitability analysis focuses mainly on the relationship between operating results (income statement) and resources available (balance sheet). Major analyses include (1) the ratio of net sales to assets, (2) the rate earned on total assets, (3) the rate earned on stockholders' equity, (4) the rate earned on common stockholders' equity, (5) earnings per share on common stock, (6) the price-earnings ratio, (7) dividends per share, and (8) dividend yield.	• Calculate and interpret the ratio of net sales to assets.	15-8	15-8A, 15-8B
	• Calculate and interpret the rate earned on total assets.	15-9	15-9A, 15-9B
	• Calculate and interpret the rate earned on stockholders' equity.	15-10	15-10A, 15-10B
	• Calculate and interpret the rate earned on common stockholders' equity.	15-10	15-10A, 15-10B
	• Calculate and interpret the earnings per share on common stock.	15-11	15-11A, 15-11B
	• Calculate and interpret the price-earnings ratio.	15-11	15-11A, 15-11B
	• Calculate and interpret the dividends per share and dividend yield.		
	• Describe the uses and limitations of analytical measures.		

4. Describe the contents of corporate annual reports.

Key Points	Key Learning Outcomes	Example Exercises	Practice Exercises
Corporations normally issue annual reports to their stockholders and other interested parties. Such reports summarize the corporation's operating activities for the past year and plans for the future.	• Describe the elements of a corporate annual report.		

Key Terms

accounts receivable turnover (669)
common-size statement (665)
current ratio (667)
dividend yield (679)
earnings per share (EPS) on common stock (677)
horizontal analysis (660)
inventory turnover (670)
leverage (675)
Management's Discussion and Analysis (MD&A) (681)
number of days' sales in inventory (671)

number of days' sales in receivables (669)
number of times interest charges are earned (672)
price-earnings (P/E) ratio (677)
profitability (666)
quick assets (668)
quick ratio (668)
rate earned on common stockholders' equity (676)
rate earned on stockholders' equity (675)
rate earned on total assets (674)

ratio of fixed assets to long-term liabilities (671)
ratio of liabilities to stockholders' equity (672)
solvency (666)
vertical analysis (663)

Illustrative Problem

Rainbow Paint Co.'s comparative financial statements for the years ending December 31, 2008 and 2007, are as follows. The market price of Rainbow Paint Co.'s common stock was $30 on December 31, 2007, and $25 on December 31, 2008.

Rainbow Paint Co.
Comparative Income Statement
For the Years Ended December 31, 2008 and 2007

	2008	2007
Sales	$5,125,000	$3,257,600
Sales returns and allowances	125,000	57,600
Net sales	$5,000,000	$3,200,000
Cost of goods sold	3,400,000	2,080,000
Gross profit	$1,600,000	$1,120,000
Selling expenses	$ 650,000	$ 464,000
Administrative expenses	325,000	224,000
Total operating expenses	$ 975,000	$ 688,000
Income from operations	$ 625,000	$ 432,000
Other income	25,000	19,200
	$ 650,000	$ 451,200
Other expense (interest)	105,000	64,000
Income before income tax	$ 545,000	$ 387,200
Income tax expense	300,000	176,000
Net income	$ 245,000	$ 211,200

Rainbow Paint Co.
Comparative Retained Earnings Statement
For the Years Ended December 31, 2008 and 2007

	2008	2007
Retained earnings, January 1	$723,000	$581,800
Add net income for year	245,000	211,200
Total	$968,000	$793,000
Deduct dividends:		
On preferred stock	$ 40,000	$ 40,000
On common stock	45,000	30,000
Total	$ 85,000	$ 70,000
Retained earnings, December 31	$883,000	$723,000

(continued)

	2008	**2007**
Rainbow Paint Co.		
Comparative Balance Sheet		
December 31, 2008 and 2007		
Assets		
Current assets:		
Cash	$ 175,000	$ 125,000
Marketable securities	150,000	50,000
Accounts receivable (net)	425,000	325,000
Inventories	720,000	480,000
Prepaid expenses	30,000	20,000
Total current assets	$1,500,000	$1,000,000
Long-term investments.	250,000	225,000
Property, plant, and equipment (net)	2,093,000	1,948,000
Total assets	$3,843,000	$3,173,000
Liabilities		
Current liabilities	$ 750,000	$ 650,000
Long-term liabilities:		
Mortgage note payable, 10%, due 2011	$ 410,000	—
Bonds payable, 8%, due 2014	800,000	$ 800,000
Total long-term liabilities	$1,210,000	$ 800,000
Total liabilities	$1,960,000	$1,450,000
Stockholders' Equity		
Preferred 8% stock, $100 par	$ 500,000	$ 500,000
Common stock, $10 par	500,000	500,000
Retained earnings	883,000	723,000
Total stockholders' equity	$1,883,000	$1,723,000
Total liabilities and stockholders' equity	$3,843,000	$3,173,000

Instructions

Determine the following measures for 2008:

1. Working capital
2. Current ratio
3. Quick ratio
4. Accounts receivable turnover
5. Number of days' sales in receivables
6. Inventory turnover
7. Number of days' sales in inventory
8. Ratio of fixed assets to long-term liabilities
9. Ratio of liabilities to stockholders' equity
10. Number of times interest charges earned
11. Number of times preferred dividends earned
12. Ratio of net sales to assets
13. Rate earned on total assets
14. Rate earned on stockholders' equity
15. Rate earned on common stockholders' equity
16. Earnings per share on common stock
17. Price-earnings ratio
18. Dividends per share of common stock
19. Dividend yield

Solution
(Ratios are rounded to the nearest single digit after the decimal point.)

1. Working capital: $750,000
    $1,500,000 − $750,000

2. Current ratio: 2.0
    $1,500,000/$750,000

3. Quick ratio: 1.0
    $750,000/$750,000

4. Accounts receivable turnover: 13.3
    $5,000,000/[($425,000 + $325,000)/2]

5. Number of days' sales in receivables: 27.4 days
    $5,000,000/365 = $13,699
    $375,000/$13,699

6. Inventory turnover: 5.7
    $3,400,000/[($720,000 + $480,000)/2]

7. Number of days' sales in inventory: 64.4 days
    $3,400,000/365 = $9,315
    $600,000/$9,315

8. Ratio of fixed assets to long-term liabilities: 1.7
    $2,093,000/$1,210,000

9. Ratio of liabilities to stockholders' equity: 1.0
    $1,960,000/$1,883,000

10. Number of times interest charges earned: 6.2
    ($545,000 + $105,000)/$105,000

11. Number of times preferred dividends earned: 6.1
    $245,000/$40,000

12. Ratio of net sales to assets: 1.5
    $5,000,000/[($3,593,000 + $2,948,000)/2]

13. Rate earned on total assets: 10.0%
    ($245,000 + $105,000)/[($3,843,000 + $3,173,000)/2]

14. Rate earned on stockholders' equity: 13.6%
    $245,000/[($1,883,000 + $1,723,000)/2]

15. Rate earned on common stockholders' equity: 15.7%
    ($245,000 − $40,000)/[($1,383,000 + $1,223,000)/2]

16. Earnings per share on common stock: $4.10
    ($245,000 − $40,000)/50,000

17. Price-earnings ratio: 6.1
    $25/$4.10

18. Dividends per share of common stock: $0.90
    $45,000/50,000 shares

19. Dividend yield: 3.6%
    $0.90/$25

Self-Examination Questions

1. What type of analysis is indicated by the following?

	Amount	Percent
Current assets	$100,000	20%
Property, plant, and equipment	400,000	80
Total assets	$500,000	100%

  A. Vertical analysis   C. Profitability analysis
  B. Horizontal analysis   D. Contribution margin
  analysis

2. Which of the following measures indicates the ability of a firm to pay its current liabilities?
  A. Working capital   C. Quick ratio
  B. Current ratio   D. All of the above

3. The ratio determined by dividing total current assets by total current liabilities is:
  A. current ratio.   C. bankers' ratio.
  B. working capital ratio.   D. all of the above.

4. The ratio of the quick assets to current liabilities, which indicates the "instant" debt-paying ability of a firm, is the:
  A. current ratio.   C. quick ratio.
  B. working capital ratio.   D. bankers' ratio.

5. A measure useful in evaluating efficiency in the management of inventories is the:
  A. working capital ratio.
  B. quick ratio.
  C. number of days' sales in inventory.
  D. ratio of fixed assets to long-term liabilities.

Eye Openers

1. What is the difference between horizontal and vertical analysis of financial statements?
2. What is the advantage of using comparative statements for financial analysis rather than statements for a single date or period?
3. The current year's amount of net income (after income tax) is 20% larger than that of the preceding year. Does this indicate an improved operating performance? Discuss.
4. How would you respond to a horizontal analysis that showed an expense increasing by over 80%?
5. How would the current and quick ratios of a service business compare?
6. For Lindsay Corporation, the working capital at the end of the current year is $8,000 less than the working capital at the end of the preceding year, reported as follows:

	Current Year	Preceding Year
Current assets:		
Cash, marketable securities, and receivables	$35,000	$36,000
Inventories	55,000	42,000
Total current assets	$90,000	$78,000
Current liabilities	50,000	30,000
Working capital	$40,000	$48,000

  Has the current position improved? Explain.
7. Why would the accounts receivable turnover ratio be different between Wal-Mart and Procter & Gamble?
8. A company that grants terms of n/45 on all sales has a yearly accounts receivable turnover, based on monthly averages, of 5. Is this a satisfactory turnover? Discuss.
9. a. Why is it advantageous to have a high inventory turnover?
   b. Is it possible for the inventory turnover to be too high? Discuss.
   c. Is it possible to have a high inventory turnover and a high number of days' sales in inventory? Discuss.
10. What do the following data taken from a comparative balance sheet indicate about the company's ability to borrow additional funds on a long-term basis in the current year as compared to the preceding year?

	Current Year	Preceding Year
Fixed assets (net)	$300,000	$300,000
Total long-term liabilities	100,000	120,000

11. a. How does the rate earned on total assets differ from the rate earned on stockholders' equity?
    b. Which ratio is normally higher? Explain.
12. a. Why is the rate earned on stockholders' equity by a thriving business ordinarily higher than the rate earned on total assets?
    b. Should the rate earned on common stockholders' equity normally be higher or lower than the rate earned on total stockholders' equity? Explain.
13. The net income (after income tax) of Choi Inc. was $15 per common share in the latest year and $60 per common share for the preceding year. At the beginning of the latest year, the number of shares outstanding was doubled by a stock split. There were no other changes in the amount of stock outstanding. What were the earnings per share in the preceding year, adjusted for comparison with the latest year?
14. The price-earnings ratio for the common stock of Cotter Company was 10 at December 31, the end of the current fiscal year. What does the ratio indicate about the selling price of the common stock in relation to current earnings?
15. Why would the dividend yield differ significantly from the rate earned on common stockholders' equity?
16. Favorable business conditions may bring about certain seemingly unfavorable ratios, and unfavorable business operations may result in apparently favorable ratios. For example, Trivec Company increased its sales and net income substantially for the current year, yet the current ratio at the end of the year is lower than at the beginning of the year. Discuss some possible causes of the apparent weakening of the current position, while sales and net income have increased substantially.

Practice Exercises

PE 15-1A
Horizontal analysis
obj. 1

The comparative marketable securities and inventory balances for a company are provided below.

	2008	2007
Marketable securities	$68,200	$55,000
Inventory	63,700	65,000

Based on this information, what is the amount and percentage of increase or decrease that would be shown in a balance sheet with horizontal analysis?

PE 15-1B
Horizontal analysis
obj. 1

The comparative accounts payable and long-term debt balances of a company are provided below.

	2008	2007
Accounts payable	$141,600	$120,000
Long-term debt	150,000	125,000

Based on this information, what is the amount and percentage of increase or decrease that would be shown in a balance sheet with horizontal analysis?

PE 15-2A
Common-size financial statements
obj. 1

Income statement information for Washburn Corporation is provided below.

Sales	$400,000
Cost of goods sold	340,000
Gross profit	$ 60,000

Prepare a vertical analysis of the income statement for Washburn Corporation.

PE 15-2B
Common-size financial statements
obj. 1

Income statement information for Lewis Corporation is provided below.

Sales	$250,000
Gross profit	100,000
Net income	50,000

Prepare a vertical analysis of the income statement for Lewis Corporation.

PE 15-3A
Current position analysis
obj. 2

The following items are reported on a company's balance sheet:

Cash	$125,000
Marketable securities	40,000
Accounts receivable (net)	30,000
Inventory	120,000
Accounts payable	150,000

Determine (a) the current ratio and (b) the quick ratio. Round to one decimal place.

PE 15-3B
Current position analysis
obj. 2

The following items are reported on a company's balance sheet:

Cash	$275,000
Marketable securities	200,000
Accounts receivable (net)	625,000
Inventory	300,000
Accounts payable	800,000

Determine (a) the current ratio and (b) the quick ratio. Round to one decimal place.

PE 15-4A
Accounts receivable analysis
obj. 2

A company reports the following:

Net sales	$450,000
Average accounts receivable (net)	37,500

Determine (a) the accounts receivable turnover and (b) the number of days' sales in receivables. Round to one decimal place.

PE 15-4B
Accounts receivable analysis
obj. 2

A company reports the following:

Net sales	$225,000
Average accounts receivable (net)	25,000

Determine (a) the accounts receivable turnover and (b) the number of days' sales in receivables. Round to one decimal place.

PE 15-5A
Inventory analysis
obj. 2

A company reports the following:

Cost of goods sold	$465,000
Average inventory	71,500

Determine (a) the inventory turnover and (b) the number of days' sales in inventory. Round to one decimal place.

PE 15-5B
Inventory analysis
obj. 2

A company reports the following:

Cost of goods sold	$330,000
Average inventory	55,000

Determine (a) the inventory turnover and (b) the number of days' sales in inventory. Round to one decimal place.

PE 15-6A
Ratio of fixed assets to long-term liabilities and ratio of liabilities to stockholders' equity
obj. 2

The following information was taken from Straub Company's balance sheet:

Fixed assets (net)	$700,000
Long-term liabilities	218,750
Total liabilities	235,000
Total stockholders' equity	940,000

Determine the company's (a) ratio of fixed assets to long-term liabilities and (b) ratio of liabilities to stockholders' equity.

PE 15-6B
Ratio of fixed assets to long-term liabilities and ratio of liabilities to stockholders' equity
obj. 2

The following information was taken from Tristar Company's balance sheet:

Fixed assets (net)	$900,000
Long-term liabilities	625,000
Total liabilities	850,000
Total stockholders' equity	500,000

Determine the company's (a) ratio of fixed assets to long-term liabilities and (b) ratio of liabilities to stockholders' equity.

PE 15-7A
Number of times interest charges are earned
obj. 2

A company reports the following:

Income before income tax	$375,000
Interest expense	120,000

Determine the number of times interest charges are earned.

PE 15-7B
Number of times interest charges are earned
obj. 2

A company reports the following:

Income before income tax	$625,000
Interest expense	160,000

Determine the number of times interest charges are earned.

PE 15-8A
Ratio of net sales to assets
obj. 3

A company reports the following:

Net sales	$1,170,000
Average total assets	650,000

Determine the ratio of net sales to assets.

PE 15-8B
Ratio of net sales to assets
obj. 3

A company reports the following:

Net sales	$1,520,000
Average total assets	950,000

Determine the ratio of net sales to assets.

PE 15-9A
Rate earned on total assets
obj. 3

A company reports the following income statement and balance sheet information for the current year:

Net income	$ 225,000
Interest expense	20,000
Average total assets	3,250,000

Determine the rate earned on total assets.

PE 15-9B
Rate earned on total assets
obj. 3

A company reports the following income statement and balance sheet information for the current year:

Net income	$ 115,000
Interest expense	10,000
Average total assets	1,250,000

Determine the rate earned on total assets.

PE 15-10A
Rate earned on stockholders' equity and rate earned on common stockholders' equity

obj. 3

A company reports the following:

Net income	$ 225,000
Preferred dividends	20,000
Average stockholders' equity	1,750,000
Average common stockholders' equity	1,000,000

Determine (a) the rate earned on stockholders' equity and (b) the rate earned on common stockholders' equity. Round to one decimal place.

PE 15-10B
Rate earned on stockholders' equity and rate earned on common stockholders' equity

obj. 3

A company reports the following:

Net income	$115,000
Preferred dividends	10,000
Average stockholders' equity	850,000
Average common stockholders' equity	750,000

Determine (a) the rate earned on stockholders' equity and (b) the rate earned on common stockholders' equity.

PE 15-11A
Earnings per share on common stock and price-earnings ratio

obj. 3

A company reports the following:

Net income	$115,000
Preferred dividends	$15,000
Shares of common stock outstanding	20,000
Market price per share of common stock	$65.00

a. Determine the company's earnings per share on common stock.
b. Determine the company's price-earnings ratio.

PE 15-11B
Earnings per share on common stock and price-earnings ratio

obj. 3

A company reports the following:

Net income	$525,000
Preferred dividends	$25,000
Shares of common stock outstanding	50,000
Market price per share of common stock	$75.00

a. Determine the company's earnings per share on common stock.
b. Determine the company's price-earnings ratio.

Exercises

EX 15-1
Vertical analysis of income statement

obj. 1

✓a. 2008 net income:
$37,500; 5% of sales

Revenue and expense data for Jazz-Tech Communications Co. are as follows:

	2008	2007
Sales	$750,000	$600,000
Cost of goods sold	450,000	312,000
Selling expenses	120,000	126,000
Administrative expenses	105,000	84,000
Income tax expense	37,500	30,000

a. Prepare an income statement in comparative form, stating each item for both 2008 and 2007 as a percent of sales. Round to one decimal place.

b. Comment on the significant changes disclosed by the comparative income statement.

EX 15-2
Vertical analysis of income statement
obj. 1

✓ *a. Fiscal year 2004 income from continuing operations, 26.7% of revenues*

The following comparative income statement (in thousands of dollars) for the fiscal years 2003 and 2004 was adapted from the annual report of Speedway Motorsports, Inc., owner and operator of several major motor speedways, such as the Atlanta, Texas, and Las Vegas Motor Speedways.

	Fiscal Year 2004	Fiscal Year 2003
Revenues:		
Admissions	$156,718	$150,253
Event-related revenue	137,074	127,055
NASCAR broadcasting revenue	110,016	90,682
Other operating revenue	42,711	36,539
Total revenue	$446,519	$404,529
Expenses and other:		
Direct expense of events	$ 81,432	$ 77,962
NASCAR purse and sanction fees	78,473	69,691
Other direct expenses	102,053	101,408
General and administrative	65,152	58,698
Total expenses and other	$327,110	$307,759
Income from continuing operations	$119,409	$ 96,770

a. Prepare a comparative income statement for fiscal years 2003 and 2004 in vertical form, stating each item as a percent of revenues. Round to one decimal place.

b. Comment on the significant changes.

EX 15-3
Common-size income statement
obj. 1

✓ *a. Jaribo net income: $85,000; 6.8% of sales*

Revenue and expense data for the current calendar year for Jaribo Communications Company and for the communications industry are as follows. The Jaribo Communications Company data are expressed in dollars. The communications industry averages are expressed in percentages.

	Jaribo Communications Company	Communications Industry Average
Sales	$1,265,000	101.0%
Sales returns and allowances	15,000	1.0
Cost of goods sold	450,000	41.0
Selling expenses	525,000	38.0
Administrative expenses	143,750	10.5
Other income	22,500	1.2
Other expense (interest)	18,750	1.7
Income tax expense	50,000	4.0

a. Prepare a common-size income statement comparing the results of operations for Jaribo Communications Company with the industry average. Round to one decimal place.

b. As far as the data permit, comment on significant relationships revealed by the comparisons.

EX 15-4
Vertical analysis of balance sheet
obj. 1

Balance sheet data for the Dover Hot Tub Company on December 31, the end of the fiscal year, are shown at the top of the following page.

✓ *Retained earnings,*
Dec. 31, 2008, 47.5%

	2008	2007
Current assets	$768,000	$250,000
Property, plant, and equipment	336,000	650,000
Intangible assets	96,000	100,000
Current liabilities	270,000	175,000
Long-term liabilities	300,000	255,000
Common stock	60,000	70,000
Retained earnings	570,000	500,000

Prepare a comparative balance sheet for 2008 and 2007, stating each asset as a percent of total assets and each liability and stockholders' equity item as a percent of the total liabilities and stockholders' equity. Round to one decimal place.

EX 15-5
Horizontal analysis of the income statement

obj. **1**

✓ *a. Net income decrease,*
53.3%

Income statement data for Web-pics Company for the years ended December 31, 2008 and 2007, are as follows:

	2008	2007
Sales	$117,000	$150,000
Cost of goods sold	56,000	70,000
Gross profit	$ 61,000	$ 80,000
Selling expenses	$ 36,000	$ 37,500
Administrative expenses	12,500	10,000
Total operating expenses	$ 48,500	$ 47,500
Income before income tax	$ 12,500	$ 32,500
Income tax expense	2,000	10,000
Net income	$ 10,500	$ 22,500

a. Prepare a comparative income statement with horizontal analysis, indicating the increase (decrease) for 2008 when compared with 2007. Round to one decimal place.
b. ▭▭▭▶ What conclusions can be drawn from the horizontal analysis?

EX 15-6
Current position analysis

obj. **2**

✓ *a. 2008 working capital,*
$1,265,000

The following data were taken from the balance sheet of Outdoor Suppliers Company:

	Dec. 31, 2008	Dec. 31, 2007
Cash	$325,000	$300,000
Marketable securities	270,000	256,000
Accounts and notes receivable (net)	440,000	430,000
Inventories	675,000	557,000
Prepaid expenses	130,000	81,000
Accounts and notes payable (short-term)	425,000	450,000
Accrued liabilities	150,000	130,000

a. Determine for each year (1) the working capital, (2) the current ratio, and (3) the quick ratio. Round ratios to one decimal place.
b. ▭▭▭▶ What conclusions can be drawn from these data as to the company's ability to meet its currently maturing debts?

EX 15-7
Current position analysis

obj. **2**

✓ *a. (1) Dec. 25, 2004,*
current ratio, 1.2

PepsiCo, Inc., the parent company of Frito-Lay snack foods and Pepsi beverages, had the following current assets and current liabilities at the end of two recent years:

	Dec. 31, 2005	Dec. 25, 2004
	(in millions)	(in millions)
Cash and cash equivalents	$1,716	$1,280
Short-term investments, at cost	3,166	2,165
Accounts and notes receivable, net	3,261	2,999
Inventories	1,693	1,541
Prepaid expenses and other current assets	618	654
Short-term obligations	2,889	1,054
Accounts payable and other current liabilities	5,971	5,999
Income taxes payable	546	99

a. Determine the (1) current ratio and (2) quick ratio for both years. Round to one decimal place.

b. What conclusions can you draw from these data?

EX 15-8
Current position analysis
obj. 2

The bond indenture for the 20-year, 11% debenture bonds dated January 2, 2007, required working capital of $560,000, a current ratio of 1.5, and a quick ratio of 1.2 at the end of each calendar year until the bonds mature. At December 31, 2008, the three measures were computed as follows:

1. Current assets:

Cash	$190,000
Marketable securities	95,000
Accounts and notes receivable (net)	171,000
Inventories	20,000
Prepaid expenses	4,500
Intangible assets	55,000
Property, plant, and equipment	65,000
Total current assets (net)	$600,500
Current liabilities:	
Accounts and short-term notes payable	$250,000
Accrued liabilities	150,000
Total current liabilities	400,000
Working capital	$200,500

2. Current Ratio = 1.50 ($600,500/$400,000)
3. Quick Ratio = 2.04 ($511,000/$250,000)

a. List the errors in the determination of the three measures of current position analysis.

b. Is the company satisfying the terms of the bond indenture?

EX 15-9
Accounts receivable analysis
obj. 2

✓ *a. Accounts receivable turnover, 2008, 6.9*

The following data are taken from the financial statements of Creekside Technology Inc. Terms of all sales are 2/10, n/60.

	2008	2007	2006
Accounts receivable, end of year	$ 75,452	$ 85,500	$81,624
Monthly average accounts receivable (net)	78,261	80,645	—
Net sales	540,000	500,000	—

a. Determine for each year (1) the accounts receivable turnover and (2) the number of days' sales in receivables. Round to nearest dollar and one decimal place.

b. What conclusions can be drawn from these data concerning accounts receivable and credit policies?

EX 15-10
Accounts receivable analysis
obj. 2

REAL WORLD

✓ *a. (1) May's accounts receivable turnover, 7.1*

The May Department Stores Company (Marshall Field's, Hecht's, Lord & Taylor) and Federated Department Stores, Inc. (Macy's and Bloomingdale's) are two of the largest department store chains in the United States. Both companies offer credit to their customers through their own credit card operations. Information from the financial statements for both companies for two recent years is as follows (all numbers are in millions):

	May	Federated
Merchandise sales	$14,441	$15,630
Credit card receivables—beginning	2,294	3,418
Credit card receivables—ending	1,788	3,213

a. Determine the (1) accounts receivable turnover and (2) the number of days' sales in receivables for both companies. Round to one decimal place.

b. Compare the two companies with regard to their credit card policies.

EX 15-11
Inventory analysis

obj. 2

✓ a. *Inventory turnover, current year, 7.5*

The following data were extracted from the income statement of Clear View Systems Inc.:

	Current Year	Preceding Year
Sales	$756,000	$950,760
Beginning inventories	67,200	44,000
Cost of goods sold	492,000	528,200
Ending inventories	64,000	67,200

a. Determine for each year (1) the inventory turnover and (2) the number of days' sales in inventory. Round to nearest dollar and one decimal place.
b. ▭▬▶ What conclusions can be drawn from these data concerning the inventories?

EX 15-12
Inventory analysis

obj. 2

REAL WORLD

✓ a. *Dell inventory turnover, 88.2*

Dell Inc. and Hewlett-Packard Company (HP) compete with each other in the personal computer market. Dell's strategy is to assemble computers to customer orders, rather than for inventory. Thus, for example, Dell will build and deliver a computer within four days of a customer entering an order on a Web page. Hewlett-Packard, on the other hand, builds some computers prior to receiving an order, then sells from this inventory once an order is received. Below is selected financial information for both companies from a recent year's financial statements (in millions):

	Dell Inc.	Hewlett-Packard Company
Sales	$55,908	$86,696
Cost of goods sold	45,620	66,440
Inventory, beginning of period	459	7,071
Inventory, end of period	576	6,877

a. Determine for both companies (1) the inventory turnover and (2) the number of days' sales in inventory. Round to one decimal place.
b. ▭▬▶ Interpret the inventory ratios by considering Dell's and Hewlett-Packard's operating strategies.

EX 15-13
Ratio of liabilities to stockholders' equity and number of times interest charges earned

obj. 2

✓ a. *Ratio of liabilities to stockholders' equity, Dec. 31, 2008, 0.5*

The following data were taken from the financial statements of Quality Construction Inc. for December 31, 2008 and 2007:

	December 31, 2008	December 31, 2007
Accounts payable	$ 240,000	$ 224,000
Current maturities of serial bonds payable	320,000	320,000
Serial bonds payable, 10%, issued 2004, due 2014	1,600,000	1,920,000
Common stock, $1 par value	160,000	160,000
Paid-in capital in excess of par	800,000	800,000
Retained earnings	3,404,800	2,560,000

The income before income tax was $844,800 and $537,600 for the years 2008 and 2007, respectively.

a. Determine the ratio of liabilities to stockholders' equity at the end of each year. Round to one decimal place.
b. Determine the number of times the bond interest charges are earned during the year for both years. Round to one decimal place.
c. ▭▬▶ What conclusions can be drawn from these data as to the company's ability to meet its currently maturing debts?

EX 15-14
Ratio of liabilities to stockholders' equity and number of times interest charges earned

obj. 2

Hasbro and Mattel, Inc., are the two largest toy companies in North America. Condensed liabilities and stockholders' equity from a recent balance sheet are shown for each company as follows:

✓a. Hasbro, 1.0

	Hasbro	Mattel, Inc.
Current liabilities	$1,148,611,000	$1,727,171,000
Long-term debt	302,698,000	400,000,000
Deferred liabilities	149,627,000	243,509,000
Total liabilities	$1,600,936,000	$2,370,680,000
Shareholders' equity:		
Common stock, $0.50 par value	$ 104,847,000	$ 441,369,000
Additional paid-in capital	380,745,000	1,594,332,000
Retained earnings	1,721,209,000	1,093,288,000
Accumulated other comprehensive loss and other equity items	82,290,000	(269,828,000)
Treasury stock, at cost	(649,367,000)	(473,349,000)
Total stockholders' equity	$1,639,724,000	$2,385,812,000
Total liabilities and stockholders' equity	$3,240,660,000	$4,756,492,000

The income from operations and interest expense from the income statement for both companies were as follows:

	Hasbro	Mattel, Inc.
Income from operations	$293,012,000	$730,817,000
Interest expense	31,698,000	77,764,000

a. Determine the ratio of liabilities to stockholders' equity for both companies. Round to one decimal place.
b. Determine the number of times interest charges are earned for both companies. Round to one decimal place.
c. ▭▭▶ Interpret the ratio differences between the two companies.

EX 15-15
Ratio of liabilities to stockholders' equity and ratio of fixed assets to long-term liabilities

obj. 2

✓a. H.J. Heinz, 3.1

Recent balance sheet information for two companies in the food industry, H.J. Heinz Company and The Hershey Company, are as follows (in thousands of dollars):

	H.J. Heinz	Hershey
Net property, plant, and equipment	$2,163,938	$1,659,138
Current liabilities	2,587,068	1,518,223
Long-term debt	4,121,984	942,755
Other liabilities (pensions, deferred taxes)	1,266,093	813,182
Stockholders' equity	2,602,573	1,021,076

a. Determine the ratio of liabilities to stockholders' equity for both companies. Round to one decimal place.
b. Determine the ratio of fixed assets to long-term liabilities for both companies. Round to one decimal place.
c. ▭▭▶ Interpret the ratio differences between the two companies.

EX 15-16
Ratio of net sales to assets

obj. 3

✓a. YRC Worldwide, 1.9

Three major segments of the transportation industry are motor carriers, such as YRC Worldwide; railroads, such as Union Pacific; and transportation arrangement services, such as C.H. Robinson Worldwide Inc. Recent financial statement information for these three companies is shown as follows (in thousands of dollars):

	YRC Worldwide	Union Pacific	C.H. Robinson Worldwide
Net sales	$6,767,485	$12,215,000	$4,341,538
Average total assets	3,545,199	34,041,500	994,423

a. Determine the ratio of net sales to assets for all three companies. Round to one decimal place.
b. ▭▭▶ Assume that the ratio of net sales to assets for each company represents their respective industry segment. Interpret the differences in the ratio of net sales to assets in terms of the operating characteristics of each of the respective segments.

EX 15-17
Profitability ratios

obj. 3

✓ *a. Rate earned on total assets, 2008, 11.6%*

The following selected data were taken from the financial statements of Berry Group Inc. for December 31, 2008, 2007, and 2006:

	December 31, 2008	December 31, 2007	December 31, 2006
Total assets	$1,160,000	$1,040,000	$880,000
Notes payable (10% interest)	150,000	150,000	150,000
Common stock	360,000	360,000	360,000
Preferred $8 stock, $100 par			
(no change during year)	160,000	160,000	160,000
Retained earnings	426,900	327,200	205,000

The 2008 net income was $112,500, and the 2007 net income was $135,000. No dividends on common stock were declared between 2006 and 2008.

a. Determine the rate earned on total assets, the rate earned on stockholders' equity, and the rate earned on common stockholders' equity for the years 2007 and 2008. Round to one decimal place.

b. ▨▨▨▨▶ What conclusions can be drawn from these data as to the company's profitability?

EX 15-18
Profitability ratios

obj. 3

✓ *a. 2005 rate earned on total assets, 6.0%*

Ann Taylor Retail, Inc., sells professional women's apparel through company-owned retail stores. Recent financial information for Ann Taylor is provided below (all numbers in thousands):

	Fiscal Year Ended	
	Jan. 28, 2006	Jan. 29, 2005
Net income	$81,872	$63,276
Interest expense	2,083	3,641

	Jan. 28, 2006	Jan. 29, 2005	Jan. 31, 2004
Total assets	$1,492,906	$1,327,338	$1,256,397
Total stockholders' equity	1,034,482	926,744	818,856

Assume the apparel industry average rate earned on total assets is 8.2%, and the average rate earned on stockholders' equity is 16.7% for fiscal 2005.

a. Determine the rate earned on total assets for Ann Taylor for the fiscal years ended January 28, 2006, and January 29, 2005. Round to one digit after the decimal place.

b. Determine the rate earned on stockholders' equity for Ann Taylor for the fiscal years ended January 28, 2006, and January 29, 2005. Round to one decimal place.

c. ▨▨▨▨▶ Evaluate the two-year trend for the profitability ratios determined in (a) and (b).

d. ▨▨▨▨▶ Evaluate Ann Taylor's profit performance relative to the industry.

EX 15-19
Six measures of solvency or profitability

objs. 2, 3

✓ *c. Ratio of net sales to assets, 1.5*

The following data were taken from the financial statements of Bendax Enterprises Inc. for the current fiscal year. Assuming that long-term investments totaled $240,000 throughout the year and that total assets were $2,525,000 at the beginning of the year, determine the following: (a) ratio of fixed assets to long-term liabilities, (b) ratio of liabilities to stockholders' equity, (c) ratio of net sales to assets, (d) rate earned on total assets, (e) rate earned on stockholders' equity, and (f) rate earned on common stockholders' equity. Round to one decimal place.

Property, plant, and equipment (net)		$1,200,000
Liabilities:		
Current liabilities	$ 60,000	
Mortgage note payable, 8%, issued 1997, due 2013	825,000	
Total liabilities		$ 885,000

Stockholders' equity:

Preferred $9 stock, $100 par (no change during year) . . .		$ 250,000
Common stock, $20 par (no change during year)		800,000

Retained earnings:

Balance, beginning of year	$600,000		
Net income	216,000	$816,000	
Preferred dividends	$ 22,500		
Common dividends	57,600	80,100	
Balance, end of year			735,900
Total stockholders' equity			$1,785,900
Net sales			$3,600,000
Interest expense			$ 66,000

EX 15-20
Six measures of solvency or profitability
objs. 2, 3

✓d. Price-earnings ratio, 16.1

The balance sheet for Chaney Resources Inc. at the end of the current fiscal year indicated the following:

Bonds payable, 10% (issued in 1995, due in 2015)	$2,250,000
Preferred $25 stock, $200 par	500,000
Common stock, $10 par	2,500,000

Income before income tax was $625,000, and income taxes were $175,000 for the current year. Cash dividends paid on common stock during the current year totaled $125,000. The common stock was selling for $25 per share at the end of the year. Determine each of the following: (a) number of times bond interest charges are earned, (b) number of times preferred dividends are earned, (c) earnings per share on common stock, (d) price-earnings ratio, (e) dividends per share of common stock, and (f) dividend yield. Round to one decimal place except earnings per share, which should be rounded to two decimal places.

EX 15-21
Earnings per share, price-earnings ratio, dividend yield
obj. 3

✓b. Price-earnings ratio, 14.8

The following information was taken from the financial statements of Royer Medical Inc. for December 31 of the current fiscal year:

Common stock, $5 par value (no change during the year)	$1,500,000
Preferred $5 stock, $50 par (no change during the year)	450,000

The net income was $450,000, and the declared dividends on the common stock were $75,000 for the current year. The market price of the common stock is $20 per share.

For the common stock, determine (a) the earnings per share, (b) the price-earnings ratio, (c) the dividends per share, and (d) the dividend yield. Round to one decimal place except earnings per share, which should be rounded to two decimal places.

EX 15-22
Earnings per share
obj. 3

✓b. Earnings per share on common stock, $3.00

The net income reported on the income statement of Ground Hog Co. was $1,250,000. There were 250,000 shares of $40 par common stock and 50,000 shares of $10 preferred stock outstanding throughout the current year. The income statement included two extraordinary items: a $360,000 gain from condemnation of land and a $235,000 loss arising from flood damage, both after applicable income tax. Determine the per share figures for common stock for (a) income before extraordinary items and (b) net income.

EX 15-23
Price-earnings ratio; dividend yield
obj. 3

The table below shows the stock price, earnings per share, and dividends per share for three companies as of February 10, 2006:

	Price	Earnings per Share	Dividends per Share
Bank of America Corporation	$44.47	$4.15	$2.00
eBay Inc.	41.60	0.78	0.00
The Coca-Cola Company	41.19	2.04	1.12

a. Determine the price-earnings ratio and dividend yield for the three companies. Round to one decimal place.

b. ▬▬▬▶ Explain the differences in these ratios across the three companies.

Problems Series A

PR 15-1A
Horizontal analysis for income statement

obj. 1

✓1. Net sales, 25.1% increase

For 2008, Doane Inc. reported its most significant increase in net income in years. At the end of the year, Jeff Newton, the president, is presented with the following condensed comparative income statement:

Doane Inc.
Comparative Income Statement
For the Years Ended December 31, 2008 and 2007

	2008	2007
Sales	$91,500	$73,200
Sales returns and allowances	1,440	1,200
Net sales	$90,060	$72,000
Cost of goods sold	50,400	42,000
Gross profit	$39,660	$30,000
Selling expenses	$16,560	$14,400
Administrative expenses	10,800	9,600
Total operating expenses	$27,360	$24,000
Income from operations	$12,300	$ 6,000
Other income	600	600
Income before income tax	$12,900	$ 6,600
Income tax expense	2,880	1,440
Net income	$10,020	$ 5,160

Instructions
1. Prepare a comparative income statement with horizontal analysis for the two-year period, using 2007 as the base year. Round to one decimal place.
2. ▬▬▬▶ To the extent the data permit, comment on the significant relationships revealed by the horizontal analysis prepared in (1).

PR 15-2A
Vertical analysis for income statement

obj. 1

✓1. Net income, 2007, 8.0%

For 2008, Dusan Water Supplies Inc. initiated a sales promotion campaign that included the expenditure of an additional $21,000 for advertising. At the end of the year, Ivana Novatna, the president, is presented with the following condensed comparative income statement:

Dusan Water Supplies Inc.
Comparative Income Statement
For the Years Ended December 31, 2008 and 2007

	2008	2007
Sales	$255,000	$214,000
Sales returns and allowances	5,000	4,000
Net sales	$250,000	$210,000
Cost of goods sold	142,500	121,800
Gross profit	$107,500	$ 88,200
Selling expenses	$100,000	$ 50,400
Administrative expenses	20,000	16,800
Total operating expenses	$120,000	$ 67,200
Income from operations	$ (12,500)	$ 21,000
Other income	6,250	4,200
Income before income tax	$ (6,250)	$ 25,200
Income tax expense (benefit)	(2,500)	8,400
Net income (loss)	$ (3,750)	$ 16,800

Instructions

1. Prepare a comparative income statement for the two-year period, presenting an analysis of each item in relationship to net sales for each of the years. Round to one decimal place.
2. ■■■■➤ To the extent the data permit, comment on the significant relationships revealed by the vertical analysis prepared in (1).

PR 15-3A
Effect of transactions on current position analysis
obj. 2

✓*1. c. Quick ratio, 1.4*

Data pertaining to the current position of Tsali Industries, Inc., are as follows:

Cash	$195,000
Marketable securities	92,500
Accounts and notes receivable (net)	293,000
Inventories	357,500
Prepaid expenses	15,000
Accounts payable	295,000
Notes payable (short-term)	92,000
Accrued expenses	42,500

Instructions

1. Compute (a) the working capital, (b) the current ratio, and (c) the quick ratio. Round to one decimal place.
2. List the following captions on a sheet of paper:

Transaction	Working Capital	Current Ratio	Quick Ratio

Compute the working capital, the current ratio, and the quick ratio after each of the following transactions, and record the results in the appropriate columns. Consider each transaction separately and assume that only that transaction affects the data given above. Round to one decimal place.

a. Sold marketable securities at no gain or loss, $37,500.
b. Paid accounts payable, $84,000.
c. Purchased goods on account, $55,000.
d. Paid notes payable, $32,500.
e. Declared a cash dividend, $38,000.
f. Declared a common stock dividend on common stock, $21,500.
g. Borrowed cash from bank on a long-term note, $185,000.
h. Received cash on account, $93,500.
i. Issued additional shares of stock for cash, $175,000.
j. Paid cash for prepaid expenses, $15,000.

PR 15-4A
Nineteen measures of solvency and profitability
objs. 2, 3

✓*9. Ratio of liabilities to stockholders' equity, 0.5*

The comparative financial statements of Triad Images Inc. are as follows. The market price of Triad Images Inc. common stock was $55 on December 31, 2008.

Triad Images Inc.
Comparative Retained Earnings Statement
For the Years Ended December 31, 2008 and 2007

	Dec. 31, 2008	Dec. 31, 2007
Retained earnings, January 1	$1,006,500	$ 781,500
Add net income for year	430,000	277,500
Total	$1,436,500	$1,059,000
Deduct dividends:		
On preferred stock	$ 12,500	$ 12,500
On common stock	40,000	40,000
Total	$ 52,500	$ 52,500
Retained earnings, December 31	$1,384,000	$1,006,500

(continued)

Triad Images Inc.
Comparative Income Statement
For the Years Ended December 31, 2008 and 2007

	2008	2007
Sales	$3,395,000	$3,062,500
Sales returns and allowances	35,000	22,500
Net sales	$3,360,000	$3,040,000
Cost of goods sold	1,500,000	1,437,500
Gross profit	$1,860,000	$1,602,500
Selling expenses	$ 726,000	$ 718,750
Administrative expenses	486,000	475,000
Total operating expenses	$1,212,000	$1,193,750
Income from operations	$ 648,000	$ 408,750
Other income	48,000	37,500
	$ 696,000	$ 446,250
Other expense (interest)	98,000	50,000
Income before income tax	$ 598,000	$ 396,250
Income tax expense	168,000	118,750
Net income	$ 430,000	$ 277,500

Triad Images Inc.
Comparative Balance Sheet
December 31, 2008 and 2007

	Dec. 31, 2008	Dec. 31, 2007
Assets		
Current assets:		
Cash	$ 132,000	$ 120,000
Marketable securities	387,000	157,500
Accounts receivable (net)	260,000	196,500
Inventories	425,000	332,500
Prepaid expenses	27,500	35,000
Total current assets	$1,231,500	$ 841,500
Long-term investments	319,500	250,000
Property, plant, and equipment (net)	2,575,000	2,000,000
Total assets	$4,126,000	$3,091,500
Liabilities		
Current liabilities	$ 342,000	$ 285,000
Long-term liabilities:		
Mortgage note payable, 8%, due 2013	$ 600,000	—
Bonds payable, 10%, due 2017	500,000	$ 500,000
Total long-term liabilities	$1,100,000	$ 500,000
Total liabilities	$1,442,000	$ 785,000
Stockholders' Equity		
Preferred $2.50 stock, $100 par	$ 500,000	$ 500,000
Common stock, $20 par	800,000	800,000
Retained earnings	1,384,000	1,006,500
Total stockholders' equity	$2,684,000	$2,306,500
Total liabilities and stockholders' equity	$4,126,000	$3,091,500

Instructions

Determine the following measures for 2008, rounding to one decimal place:

1. Working capital
2. Current ratio
3. Quick ratio
4. Accounts receivable turnover
5. Number of days' sales in receivables
6. Inventory turnover
7. Number of days' sales in inventory
8. Ratio of fixed assets to long-term liabilities

9. Ratio of liabilities to stockholders' equity
10. Number of times interest charges earned
11. Number of times preferred dividends earned
12. Ratio of net sales to assets
13. Rate earned on total assets
14. Rate earned on stockholders' equity
15. Rate earned on common stockholders' equity
16. Earnings per share on common stock
17. Price-earnings ratio
18. Dividends per share of common stock
19. Dividend yield

PR 15-5A
Solvency and profitability trend analysis
objs. 2, 3

Shore Company has provided the following comparative information:

	2008	2007	2006	2005	2004
Net income	$ 42,000	$ 70,000	$ 140,000	$ 210,000	$ 210,000
Interest expense	142,800	133,000	119,000	112,000	105,000
Income tax expense	12,600	21,000	42,000	63,000	63,000
Total assets (ending balance)	2,240,000	2,100,000	1,890,000	1,680,000	1,400,000
Total stockholders' equity (ending balance)	812,000	770,000	700,000	560,000	350,000
Average total assets	2,170,000	1,995,000	1,785,000	1,540,000	1,260,000
Average stockholders' equity	791,000	735,000	630,000	455,000	315,000

You have been asked to evaluate the historical performance of the company over the last five years.

Selected industry ratios have remained relatively steady at the following levels for the last five years:

	2004–2008
Rate earned on total assets	14%
Rate earned on stockholders' equity	20%
Number of times interest charges earned	3.0
Ratio of liabilities to stockholders' equity	2.0

Instructions
1. Prepare four line graphs with the ratio on the vertical axis and the years on the horizontal axis for the following four ratios (rounded to one decimal place):
   a. Rate earned on total assets
   b. Rate earned on stockholders' equity
   c. Number of times interest charges earned
   d. Ratio of liabilities to stockholders' equity
   Display both the company ratio and the industry benchmark on each graph. That is, each graph should have two lines.
2. ▭▭▭▷ Prepare an analysis of the graphs in (1).

Problems Series B

PR 15-1B
Horizontal analysis for income statement
obj. 1

For 2008, Phoenix Technology Company reported its most significant decline in net income in years. At the end of the year, Hai Chow, the president, is presented with the following condensed comparative income statement:

✓ *1. Net sales, 11.8% increase*

Phoenix Technology Company
Comparative Income Statement
For the Years Ended December 31, 2008 and 2007

	2008	2007
Sales	$385,000	$343,200
Sales returns and allowances	4,800	3,200
Net sales	$380,200	$340,000
Cost of goods sold	180,000	144,000
Gross profit	$200,200	$196,000
Selling expenses	$ 87,400	$ 76,000
Administrative expenses	30,000	24,000
Total operating expenses	$117,400	$100,000
Income from operations	$ 82,800	$ 96,000
Other income	1,600	1,600
Income before income tax	$ 84,400	$ 97,600
Income tax expense	36,800	32,000
Net income	$ 47,600	$ 65,600

Instructions

1. Prepare a comparative income statement with horizontal analysis for the two-year period, using 2007 as the base year. Round to one decimal place.
2. ▷ To the extent the data permit, comment on the significant relationships revealed by the horizontal analysis prepared in (1).

PR 15-2B
Vertical analysis for income statement

obj. 1

✓ *1. Net income, 2008, 20.0%*

For 2008, Acedia Technology Company initiated a sales promotion campaign that included the expenditure of an additional $10,000 for advertising. At the end of the year, Gordon Kincaid, the president, is presented with the following condensed comparative income statement:

Acedia Technology Company
Comparative Income Statement
For the Years Ended December 31, 2008 and 2007

	2008	2007
Sales	$755,000	$676,000
Sales returns and allowances	5,000	6,000
Net sales	$750,000	$670,000
Cost of goods sold	292,500	274,700
Gross profit	$457,500	$395,300
Selling expenses	$172,500	$160,800
Administrative expenses	82,500	80,400
Total operating expenses	$255,000	$241,200
Income from operations	$202,500	$154,100
Other income	7,500	6,700
Income before income tax	$210,000	$160,800
Income tax expense	60,000	53,600
Net income	$150,000	$107,200

Instructions

1. Prepare a comparative income statement for the two-year period, presenting an analysis of each item in relationship to net sales for each of the years. Round to one decimal place.
2. ▷ To the extent the data permit, comment on the significant relationships revealed by the vertical analysis prepared in (1).

PR 15-3B
Effect of transactions on current position analysis

obj. 2

✓ *1. b. Current ratio, 2.1*

Data pertaining to the current position of Spruce Pine Medical Company are as follows:

Cash	$384,000
Marketable securities	176,000
Accounts and notes receivable (net)	608,000
Inventories	792,000
Prepaid expenses	48,000
Accounts payable	624,000
Notes payable (short-term)	240,000
Accrued expenses	80,000

Instructions

1. Compute (a) the working capital, (b) the current ratio, and (c) the quick ratio. Round to one decimal place.
2. List the following captions on a sheet of paper:

Transaction	Working Capital	Current Ratio	Quick Ratio

Compute the working capital, the current ratio, and the quick ratio after each of the following transactions, and record the results in the appropriate columns. Consider each transaction separately and assume that only that transaction affects the data given above. Round to one decimal place.

a. Sold marketable securities at no gain or loss, $65,000.
b. Paid accounts payable, $90,000.
c. Purchased goods on account, $120,000.
d. Paid notes payable, $65,000.
e. Declared a cash dividend, $32,500.
f. Declared a common stock dividend on common stock, $34,000.
g. Borrowed cash from bank on a long-term note, $160,000.
h. Received cash on account, $125,000.
i. Issued additional shares of stock for cash, $425,000.
j. Paid cash for prepaid expenses, $16,000.

PR 15-4B
Nineteen measures of solvency and profitability

objs. 2, 3

✓ *5. Number of days' sales in receivables, 50.8*

The comparative financial statements of Dental Innovations Inc. are as follows. The market price of Dental Innovations Inc. common stock was $15 on December 31, 2008.

Dental Innovations Inc.
Comparative Retained Earnings Statement
For the Years Ended December 31, 2008 and 2007

	Dec. 31, 2008	Dec. 31, 2007
Retained earnings, January 1	$265,000	$ 31,000
Add net income for year	321,500	244,000
Total	$586,500	$275,000
Deduct dividends:		
On preferred stock	$ 10,000	$ 5,000
On common stock	7,000	5,000
Total	$ 17,000	$ 10,000
Retained earnings, December 31	$569,500	$265,000

Dental Innovations Inc.
Comparative Income Statement
For the Years Ended December 31, 2008 and 2007

	2008	2007
Sales	$1,055,000	$966,000
Sales returns and allowances	5,000	6,000
Net sales	$1,050,000	$960,000
Cost of goods sold	300,000	312,000
Gross profit	$ 750,000	$648,000
Selling expenses	$ 202,500	$220,000
Administrative expenses	146,250	132,000
Total operating expenses	$ 348,750	$352,000
Income from operations	$ 401,250	$296,000
Other income	15,000	12,000
	$ 416,250	$308,000
Other expense (interest)	64,000	40,000
Income before income tax	$ 352,250	$268,000
Income tax expense	30,750	24,000
Net income	$ 321,500	$244,000

(continued)

Dental Innovations Inc.
Comparative Balance Sheet
December 31, 2008 and 2007

	Dec. 31, 2008	Dec. 31, 2007
Assets		
Current assets:		
Cash	$ 165,000	$ 101,500
Marketable securities	335,000	205,500
Accounts receivable (net)	160,000	132,000
Inventories	67,500	41,500
Prepaid expenses	27,000	14,500
Total current assets	$ 754,500	$ 495,000
Long-term investments	310,000	160,000
Property, plant, and equipment (net)	950,000	610,000
Total assets	$2,014,500	$1,265,000
Liabilities		
Current liabilities	$ 225,000	$ 200,000
Long-term liabilities:		
Mortgage note payable, 10%, due 2013	$ 240,000	—
Bonds payable, 8%, due 2017	500,000	$ 500,000
Total long-term liabilities	$ 740,000	$ 500,000
Total liabilities	$ 965,000	$ 700,000
Stockholders' Equity		
Preferred $2.50 stock, $50 par	$ 200,000	$ 100,000
Common stock, $10 par	280,000	200,000
Retained earnings	569,500	265,000
Total stockholders' equity	$1,049,500	$ 565,000
Total liabilities and stockholders' equity	$2,014,500	$1,265,000

Instructions

Determine the following measures for 2008, rounding to one decimal place:

1. Working capital
2. Current ratio
3. Quick ratio
4. Accounts receivable turnover
5. Number of days' sales in receivables
6. Inventory turnover
7. Number of days' sales in inventory
8. Ratio of fixed assets to long-term liabilities
9. Ratio of liabilities to stockholders' equity
10. Number of times interest charges earned
11. Number of times preferred dividends earned
12. Ratio of net sales to assets
13. Rate earned on total assets
14. Rate earned on stockholders' equity
15. Rate earned on common stockholders' equity
16. Earnings per share on common stock
17. Price-earnings ratio
18. Dividends per share of common stock
19. Dividend yield

PR 15-5B

Solvency and profitability trend analysis

objs. 2, 3

Van DeKamp Company has provided the following comparative information:

	2008	2007	2006	2005	2004
Net income	$1,815,000	$1,200,000	$ 900,000	$ 600,000	$ 450,000
Interest expense	271,800	234,000	202,500	162,000	135,000
Income tax expense	635,250	420,000	315,000	210,000	157,500
Total assets (ending balance)	9,035,000	6,800,000	5,250,000	3,900,000	3,000,000
Total stockholders' equity (ending balance)	6,015,000	4,200,000	3,000,000	2,100,000	1,500,000
Average total assets	7,917,500	6,025,000	4,575,000	3,450,000	2,700,000
Average stockholders' equity	5,107,500	3,600,000	2,550,000	1,800,000	1,350,000

You have been asked to evaluate the historical performance of the company over the last five years.

Selected industry ratios have remained relatively steady at the following levels for the last five years:

	2004–2008
Rate earned on total assets	13%
Rate earned on stockholders' equity	20%
Number of times interest charges earned	4.0
Ratio of liabilities to stockholders' equity	1.3

Instructions

1. Prepare four line graphs with the ratio on the vertical axis and the years on the horizontal axis for the following four ratios (rounded to one decimal place):
   a. Rate earned on total assets
   b. Rate earned on stockholders' equity
   c. Number of times interest charges earned
   d. Ratio of liabilities to stockholders' equity
   Display both the company ratio and the industry benchmark on each graph. That is, each graph should have two lines.
2. ✎ Prepare an analysis of the graphs in (1).

Williams-Sonoma, Inc., Problem

FINANCIAL STATEMENT ANALYSIS

The financial statements for Williams-Sonoma, Inc., are presented in Appendix E at the end of the text. The following additional information (in thousands) is available:

Accounts receivable at February 1, 2004	$ 31,573
Inventories at February 1, 2004	404,100
Total assets at February 1, 2004	1,470,735
Stockholders' equity at February 1, 2004	804,591

Instructions

1. Determine the following measures for the fiscal years ended January 29, 2006, and January 30, 2005, rounding to one decimal place.
   a. Working capital
   b. Current ratio
   c. Quick ratio
   d. Accounts receivable turnover
   e. Number of days' sales in receivables
   f. Inventory turnover
   g. Number of days' sales in inventory
   h. Ratio of liabilities to stockholders' equity
   i. Ratio of net sales to average total assets
   j. Rate earned on average total assets
   k. Rate earned on average common stockholders' equity
   l. Price-earnings ratio, assuming that the market price was $40.62 per share on January 29, 2006, and $34.53 on January 30, 2005.
   m. Percentage relationship of net income to net sales
2. ✎ What conclusions can be drawn from these analyses?

Special Activities

SA 15-1
Analysis of financing corporate growth

Assume that the president of Ice Mountain Brewery made the following statement in the Annual Report to Shareholders:

"The founding family and majority shareholders of the company do not believe in using debt to finance future growth. The founding family learned from hard experience during Prohibition and the Great Depression that debt can cause loss of flexibility and eventual loss of corporate control. The company will not place itself at such risk. As such, all future growth will be financed either by stock sales to the public or by internally generated resources."

➤ As a public shareholder of this company, how would you respond to this policy?

SA 15-2
Receivables and inventory turnover

Roan Mountain Fitness Company has completed its fiscal year on December 31, 2008. The auditor, Steve Berry, has approached the CFO, Tony Brubaker, regarding the year-end receivables and inventory levels of Roan Mountain Fitness. The following conversation takes place:

Steve: We are beginning our audit of Roan Mountain Fitness and have prepared ratio analyses to determine if there have been significant changes in operations or financial position. This helps us guide the audit process. This analysis indicates that the inventory turnover has decreased from 4.5 to 2.1, while the accounts receivable turnover has decreased from 10 to 6. I was wondering if you could explain this change in operations.

Tony: There is little need for concern. The inventory represents computers that we were unable to sell during the holiday buying season. We are confident, however, that we will be able to sell these computers as we move into the next fiscal year.

Steve: What gives you this confidence?

Tony: We will increase our advertising and provide some very attractive price concessions to move these machines. We have no choice. Newer technology is already out there, and we have to unload this inventory.

Steve: . . . and the receivables?

Tony: As you may be aware, the company is under tremendous pressure to expand sales and profits. As a result, we lowered our credit standards to our commercial customers so that we would be able to sell products to a broader customer base. As a result of this policy change, we have been able to expand sales by 35%.

Steve: Your responses have not been reassuring to me.

Tony: I'm a little confused. Assets are good, right? Why don't you look at our current ratio? It has improved, hasn't it? I would think that you would view that very favorably.

➤ Why is Steve concerned about the inventory and accounts receivable turnover ratios and Tony's responses to them? What action may Steve need to take? How would you respond to Tony's last comment?

SA 15-3
Vertical analysis

The condensed income statements through income from operations for Dell Inc. and Apple Computer, Inc., are reproduced below for recent fiscal years (numbers in millions of dollars).

	Dell Inc.	Apple Computer, Inc.
Sales (net)	$55,908	$13,931
Cost of sales	45,958	9,888
Gross profit	$ 9,950	$ 4,043
Selling, general, and administrative expenses	$ 5,140	$ 1,859
Research and development	463	534
Operating expenses	$ 5,603	$ 2,393
Income from operations	$ 4,347	$ 1,650

━━━━ Prepare comparative common-size statements, rounding percents to one decimal place. Interpret the analyses.

SA 15-4
Profitability and stockholder ratios

REAL WORLD

Ford Motor Company is the second largest automobile and truck manufacturer in the United States. In addition to manufacturing motor vehicles, Ford also provides vehicle-related financing, insurance, and leasing services. Historically, people purchase automobiles when the economy is strong and delay automobile purchases when the economy is faltering. For this reason, Ford is considered a cyclical company. This means that when the economy does well, Ford usually prospers, and when the economy is down, Ford usually suffers.

The following information is available for three recent years (in millions except per-share amounts):

	2005	2004	2003
Net income (loss)	$2,024	$3,487	$495
Preferred dividends	$0	$0	$0
Shares outstanding for computing earnings per share	1,846	1,830	1,832
Cash dividend per share	$0.40	$0.40	$0.40
Average total assets	$287,669	$308,032	$293,678
Average stockholders' equity	$14,501	$13,848	$8,532
Average stock price per share	$11.22	$14.98	$11.95

1. Calculate the following ratios for each year:
   a. Rate earned on total assets
   b. Rate earned on stockholders' equity
   c. Earnings per share
   d. Dividend yield
   e. Price-earnings ratio
2. What is the ratio of average liabilities to average stockholders' equity for 2005?
3. ━━━━ Why does Ford have so much leverage?
4. ━━━━ Explain the direction of the dividend yield and price-earnings ratio in light of Ford's profitability trend.

SA 15-5
Projecting financial statements

REAL WORLD

Internet Project

Go to Microsoft Corporation's Web site at **http://www.microsoft.com** and click on the "Investor Relations" area under "About Microsoft." Select the menu item "Stock Info and Analysis." Select the "What-if?" tool. With this tool, use horizontal and vertical information to create a full-year projection of the Microsoft income statement. Make the following assumptions:

Revenue growth	12%
Cost of goods sold as a percent of revenue	15%
Research and development growth	10%
Sales and marketing as a percent of sales	18%
General and administrative as a percent of sales	6%
Tax rate	32%
Diluted shares outstanding	12,000

SA 15-6
Comprehensive profitability and solvency analysis

REAL WORLD

Marriott International, Inc., and Hilton Hotels Corporation are two major owners and managers of lodging and resort properties in the United States. Abstracted income statement information for the two companies is as follows for a recent year:

(continued)

	Marriott (in millions)	Hilton (in millions)
Operating profit before other expenses and interest	$ 477	$ 658
Other income (expenses)	318	(19)
Interest expense	(99)	(274)
Income before income taxes	$ 696	$ 365
Income tax expense	100	127
Net income	$ 596	$ 238

Balance sheet information is as follows:

	Marriott (in millions)	Hilton (in millions)
Total liabilities	$4,587	$5,674
Total stockholders' equity	4,081	2,568
Total liabilties and stockholders' equity	$8,668	$8,242

The average liabilities, stockholders' equity, and total assets were as follows:

	Marriott	Hilton
Average total liabilities	$4,210	$5,809
Average total stockholders' equity	3,960	2,404
Average total assets	8,423	8,213

1. Determine the following ratios for both companies (round to one decimal place after the whole percent):
   a. Rate earned on total assets
   b. Rate earned on total stockholders' equity
   c. Number of times interest charges are earned
   d. Ratio of liabilities to stockholders' equity
2. ▭▭▭▶ Analyze and compare the two companies, using the information in (1).

Answers to Self-Examination Questions

1. **A** Percentage analysis indicating the relationship of the component parts to the total in a financial statement, such as the relationship of current assets to total assets (20% to 100%) in the question, is called vertical analysis (answer A). Percentage analysis of increases and decreases in corresponding items in comparative financial statements is called horizontal analysis (answer B). An example of horizontal analysis would be the presentation of the amount of current assets in the preceding balance sheet, along with the amount of current assets at the end of the current year, with the increase or decrease in current assets between the periods expressed as a percentage. Profitability analysis (answer C) is the analysis of a firm's ability to earn income. Contribution margin analysis (answer D) is discussed in a later managerial accounting chapter.

2. **D** Various solvency measures, categorized as current position analysis, indicate a firm's ability to meet currently maturing obligations. Each measure contributes to the analysis of a firm's current position and is most useful when viewed with other measures and when compared with similar measures for other periods and for other firms. Working capital (answer A) is the excess of current assets over current liabilities; the current ratio (answer B) is the ratio of current assets to current liabilities; and the quick ratio (answer C) is the ratio of the sum of cash, receivables, and marketable securities to current liabilities.

3. **D** The ratio of current assets to current liabilities is usually called the current ratio (answer A). It is sometimes called the working capital ratio (answer B) or bankers' ratio (answer C).

4. **C** The ratio of the sum of cash, receivables, and marketable securities (sometimes called quick assets) to current liabilities is called the quick ratio (answer C) or acid-test ratio. The current ratio (answer A), working capital ratio (answer B), and bankers' ratio (answer D) are terms that describe the ratio of current assets to current liabilities.

5. **C** The number of days' sales in inventory (answer C), which is determined by dividing the average inventory by the average daily cost of goods sold, expresses the relationship between the cost of goods sold and inventory. It indicates the efficiency in the management of inventory. The working capital ratio (answer A) indicates the ability of the business to meet currently maturing obligations (debt). The quick ratio (answer B) indicates the "instant" debt-paying ability of the business. The ratio of fixed assets to long-term liabilities (answer D) indicates the margin of safety for long-term creditors.

Managerial Accounting Concepts and Principles

© GREG BROWN/WATERLOO COURIER/ASSOCIATED PRESS

objectives

After studying this chapter, you should be able to:

1 **Describe managerial accounting and the role of managerial accounting in a business.**

2 **Describe and illustrate the following costs: direct and indirect, direct materials, direct labor, factory overhead, and product and period costs.**

3 **Describe and illustrate the statement of cost of goods manufactured, income statement, and balance sheet for a manufacturing business.**

4 **Describe the uses of managerial accounting information.**

Washburn Guitars

Dan Donnegan, guitarist for the rock band *Disturbed*, captivates millions of fans each year playing his guitar. His guitar was built by quality craftsmen at Washburn Guitars in Chicago. Washburn Guitars is no stranger to the music business. The company has been in business for over 120 years and is the guitar maker of choice for professional and amateur musicians.

Staying in business for 120 years requires a thorough understanding of how to manufacture high-quality guitars. In addition, it requires knowledge of how to account for the costs of making guitars. For example, how much should Washburn charge for its guitars? The purchase price must be greater than the cost of producing the guitar, but how is the cost of producing the guitar determined? Moreover, how many guitars does the company have to sell in a year to cover its costs? Would a new production facility be a good investment? How many employees should the company have working on each stage of the guitar manufacturing process?

All of these questions can be answered with the aid of managerial accounting information. In this chapter, we introduce cost concepts used in managerial accounting, which help answer questions like those above. We begin this chapter by describing managerial accounting and its relationship to financial accounting. Following this overview, we will describe the management process and the role of managerial accounting. We will also discuss characteristics of managerial accounting reports, various managerial accounting terms, and some of the uses of managerial accounting information.

Managerial Accounting

objective 1

Describe managerial accounting and the role of managerial accounting in a business.

Managing a business isn't easy. Managers must make numerous decisions in operating a business efficiently and in preparing for the future. Managerial accounting provides much of the information used by managers in running a business. The following sections discuss the differences between financial and managerial accounting and the role of the managerial accountant in an organization. The remaining chapters of this text are dedicated to examining the various types of managerial accounting information that managers use in operating a business.

THE DIFFERENCES BETWEEN MANAGERIAL AND FINANCIAL ACCOUNTING

Although economic information can be classified in many ways, accountants often divide information into two types: financial and managerial. The diagram in Exhibit 1 illustrates the relationship between financial accounting and managerial accounting. Understanding this relationship is useful in understanding the information needs of management.

Financial accounting information is reported in statements that are useful for stakeholders, such as creditors, who are "outside" or external to the organization. Examples of such stakeholders include:

- Shareholders,
- Creditors,
- Government agencies, and
- The general public.

The management of a company also uses the financial statements in directing current operations and planning future operations. In planning future operations, management often begins by evaluating the results of past activities as reported in the financial state-

EXHIBIT 1

Financial Accounting
and Managerial
Accounting

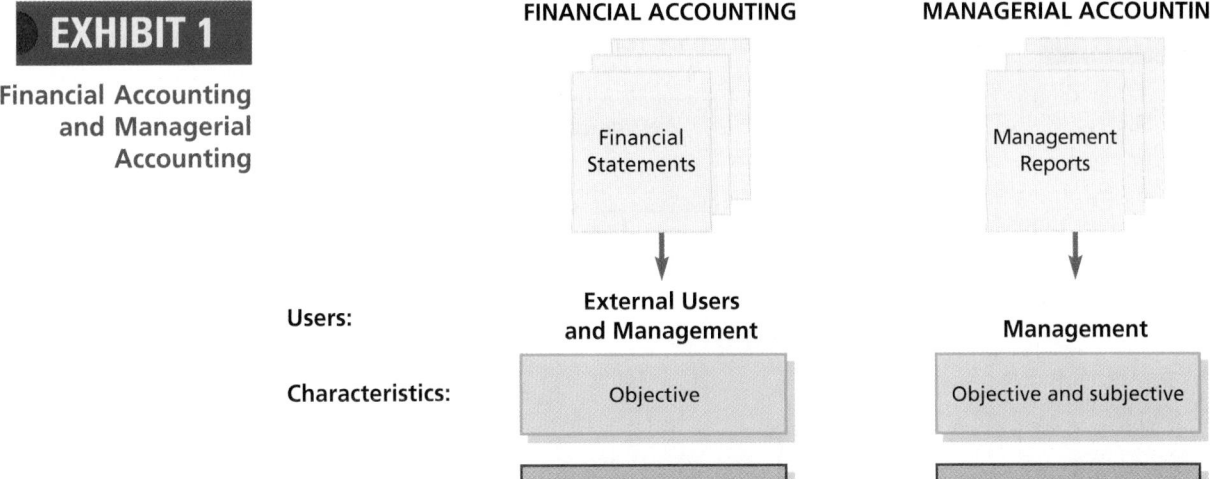

FINANCIAL ACCOUNTING	MANAGERIAL ACCOUNTING
Financial Statements	Management Reports

Users: External Users and Management | Management

Characteristics:

Objective	Objective and subjective
Prepared according to GAAP	Prepared according to management needs
Prepared periodically	Prepared periodically, or as needed
Business entity	Business entity or segment

ments. The financial statements objectively report the results of past operations at fixed periods and the financial condition of the business according to generally accepted accounting principles (GAAP).

Managerial accounting information meets the specific needs of a company's management. This information includes:

■ Historical data, which provide objective measures of past operations, and
■ Estimated data, which provide subjective estimates about future decisions.

Management uses both types of information in conducting daily operations, planning future operations, and developing overall business strategies. For example, subjective estimates in managerial accounting reports assist management in responding to business opportunities.

Unlike financial accounting statements, managerial accounting reports:

■ Are not prepared according to generally accepted accounting principles since only management uses the information;
■ Are prepared periodically, or at any time management needs information; and
■ Are prepared for the business entity as a whole or a segment of the entity, such as a division, product, project, or territory.

THE MANAGEMENT ACCOUNTANT IN THE ORGANIZATION

In most large organizations, departments or similar units are assigned responsibilities for specific functions or activities. This operating structure of an organization can be shown in an organization chart. Exhibit 2 is a partial organization chart for Callaway Golf Company, the manufacturer and distributor of Big Bertha® golf clubs.

The individual reporting units in an organization can be viewed as having either (1) line responsibilities or (2) staff responsibilities. A **line department** or unit is one directly involved in the basic objectives of the organization. For Callaway Golf, the

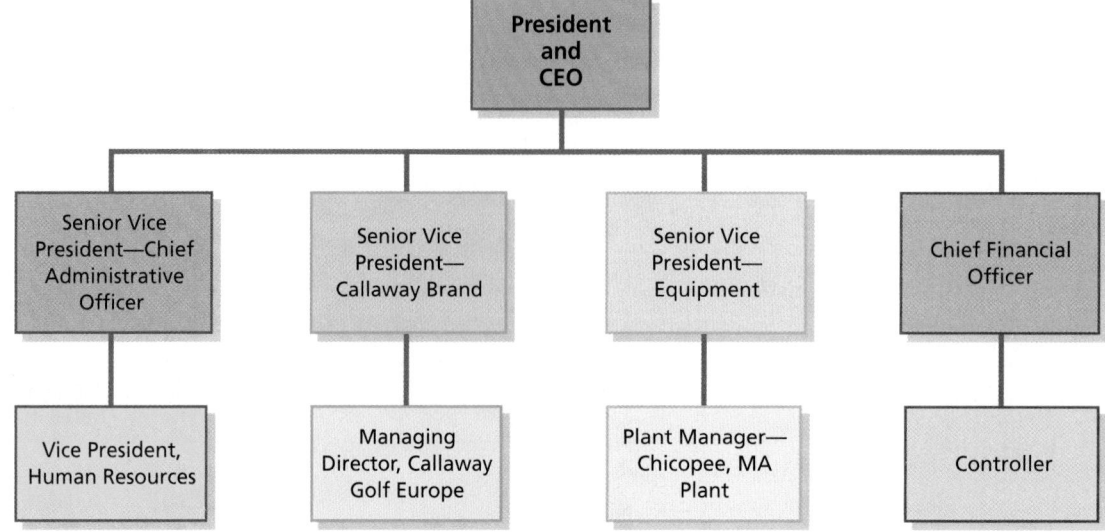

EXHIBIT 2   Partial Organizational Chart for Callaway Golf Company

The terms *line* and *staff* may be applied to service organizations. For example, the line positions in a hospital would be the nurses, doctors, and other caregivers. Staff positions would include admissions and records. The line positions for a professional basketball team, such as the Boston Celtics, would be the basketball players and coaches, since they are directly involved in the basic objectives of the organization—playing professional basketball. Staff positions would include public relations, player development and recruiting, legal staff, and accounting. These positions serve and advise the players and coaches.

senior vice president of equipment and the manager of the Chicopee, Massachusetts, plant occupy line positions because they are responsible for manufacturing Callaway's products. Likewise, the senior vice president of the Callaway Brand and other sales managers are in line positions because they are directly responsible for generating revenues.

A **staff department** or unit is one that provides services, assistance, and advice to the departments with line or other staff responsibilities. A staff department has no direct authority over a line department. For example, the senior vice president—chief administrative officer and vice president of human resources are staff positions supporting the organization. In addition, the chief financial officer (sometimes called the vice president of finance) occupies a staff position, to which the controller reports. In most business organizations, the **controller** is the chief management accountant.

The controller's staff often consists of several management accountants. Each accountant is responsible for a specialized accounting function, such as systems and procedures, general accounting, budgets and budget analysis, special reports and analysis, taxes, and cost accounting.

Experience in managerial accounting is often an excellent training ground for senior management positions. This is not surprising, since accounting and finance bring an individual into contact with all phases of operations.

MANAGERIAL ACCOUNTING IN THE MANAGEMENT PROCESS

In its role as a staff department, managerial accounting supports management and the management process. The **management process** has five basic phases:

1. Planning
2. Directing
3. Controlling
4. Improving
5. Decision making

As shown in Exhibit 3, the five phases interact with each other as the basis for a company's strategies and operations. Management's actions in the management process are, to some extent, measured by the company's operating results.

EXHIBIT 3 | The Management Process

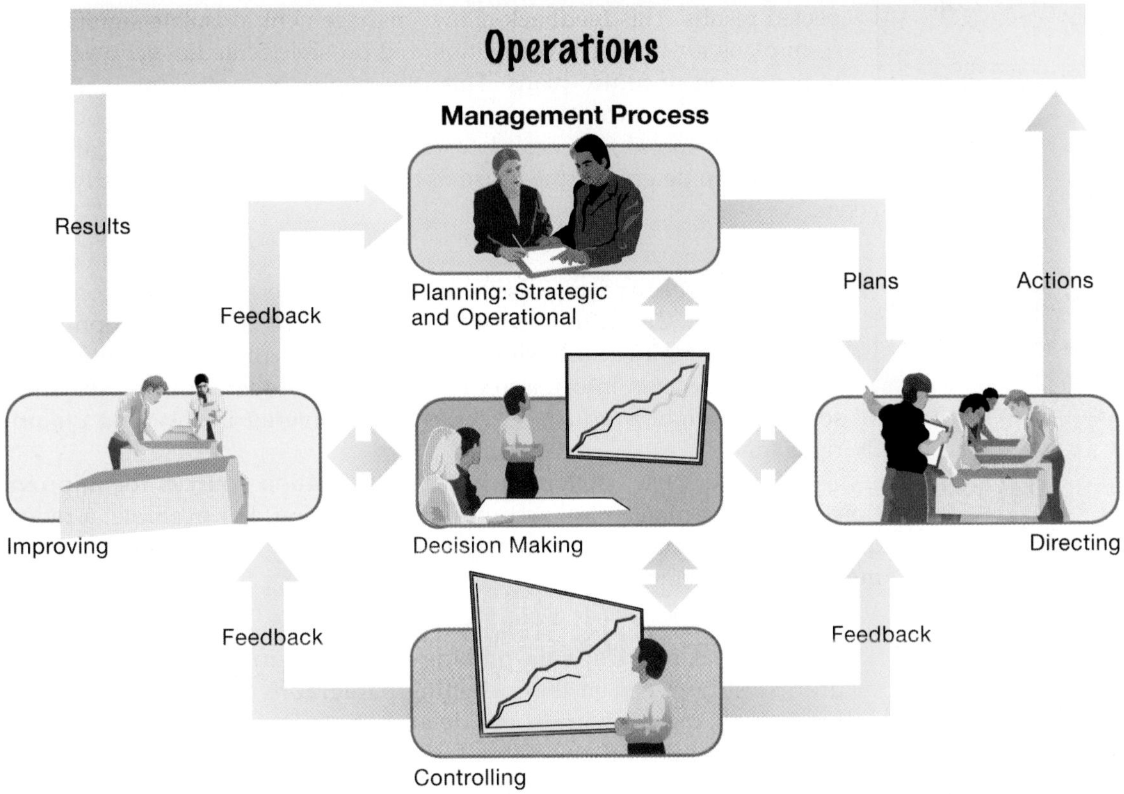

Operations

Management Process

Results

Feedback

Planning: Strategic and Operational

Plans

Actions

Improving

Decision Making

Directing

Feedback

Controlling

Feedback

Planning **Planning** is used by management to develop the company's **objectives (goals)** and to translate these objectives into courses of actions. For example, a company, as part of the planning process, may set objectives to increase market share by 15% and introduce three new products. The courses of action, or means, for achieving these objectives must be established. In this example, the company may decide to follow three courses of action: increase the advertising budget, open a new sales territory, and increase the research and development budget.

Planning can be categorized as either strategic planning or operational planning. **Strategic planning** is developing long-range courses of action to achieve goals. Long-range courses of action, called **strategies**, can often involve periods ranging from 5 to 10 years. **Operational planning** develops short-term courses of action to manage the day-to-day operations of a business.

Directing **Directing** is the process by which managers, given their assigned level of responsibilities, run day-to-day operations. Examples of directing include a production supervisor's efforts to keep the production line moving smoothly throughout a work shift and the credit manager's efforts to assess the credit standing of potential customers.

Managerial accounting aids managers in directing a business by providing reports that allow managers to adjust operations for changing conditions. For example, reports on the cost of defective material by vendors may aid managers in making vendor selections or improvements. In addition, managerial accounting reports are used by management to estimate the appropriate staffing and resources necessary for achieving plans.

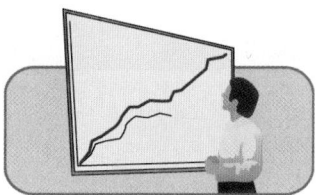

Controlling   Once managers have planned goals and directed the action, they must monitor how well the plan is working. **Controlling** consists of monitoring the operating results of implemented plans and comparing the actual results with the expected results. This **feedback** allows management to isolate significant departures from plans for further investigation and possible remedial action. It may also lead to a revision of future plans. This philosophy of controlling is sometimes called **management by exception**. For example, if actual departmental costs incurred in maintaining a process significantly exceed expected costs, then an investigation may be conducted to determine the cause of the difference so that corrective action may be taken.

Improving   Feedback can also be used by managers to support continuous process improvement. **Continuous process improvement** is the philosophy of continually improving employees, business processes, and products. Continuous improvement uses process information to eliminate the *source* of problems in a process, so that the right products (services) are delivered in the right quantities at the right time.

Managers use a wide variety of information sources for improving operations, including managerial accounting information. For example, a report identifying the cost of process inefficiency can be used by management to prioritize and monitor improvements.

Decision Making   **Decision making** is inherent in each of the four management processes described in the preceding paragraphs. For example, in developing a future plan, managers must decide among alternative courses of action to achieve long-range goals and objectives. Likewise, in directing operations, managers must decide on an operating structure, procedures, training, staffing, and other aspects of day-to-day operations. In controlling and improving, managers must decide how to respond to unfavorable performance.

Example Exercise 16-1

objective

Three phases of the management process are planning, controlling, and improving. Match the following descriptions to the proper phase.

Phase of management process	Description
Planning	a. Monitoring the operating results of implemented plans and comparing the actual results with expected results.
Controlling	b. Rejects solving individual problems with temporary solutions that fail to address the root cause of the problem.
Continuous improvement	c. Used by management to develop the company's objectives.

Follow My Example 16-1

Phase of management process

Planning (c)
Controlling (a)
Continuous improvement (b)

For Practice: PE 16-1A, PE 16-1B

Integrity, Objectivity, and Ethics in Business

ETHICS

ENVIRONMENTAL ACCOUNTING

In recent years, the environmental impact of a business has become an increasingly important issue. Multinational agreements such as the Montreal Protocol and Kyoto Protocol have acknowledged the impact that society has on the environment and raised public awareness of the impact that businesses have on the environment. As a result, environmental issues have become an important operational issue for most businesses. Managers must now consider the environmental impact of their decisions in the same way that they would consider other operational issues.

To help managers understand the environmental impact of their business decisions, new managerial accounting measures are being developed. The emerging field of environmental management accounting focuses on developing various measures of the environmental-related costs of a business. These measures can evaluate a variety of issues, including the volume and level of emissions, the estimated costs of different levels of emissions, and the impact that environmental costs have on product cost. Thus, environmental managerial accounting can provide managers with important information to help them more clearly consider the environmental effects of their decisions.

A Tour of Manufacturing Operations: Costs and Terminology

objective **2**

Describe and illustrate the following costs: direct and indirect, direct materials, direct labor, factory overhead, and product and period costs.

The operations of a business can be classified as service, merchandising, or manufacturing. Most of the managerial accounting concepts and terms described in the remaining chapters of this text apply to all three types of businesses. As an example, we focus primarily upon managerial concepts as they apply to manufacturing businesses in this textbook. We begin with a tour of a guitar manufacturer, Legend Guitars.

Like Washburn Guitars, Legend Guitars manufactures high-quality guitars that combine innovation with high-quality craftsmanship. Exhibit 4 provides an overview of Legend's guitar manufacturing operations. The process begins when a customer places an order for a custom-made guitar. Once the order is received, the production process is started by employees who cut the body and neck of the guitar out of raw lumber using a computerized saw. Once the wood is cut, the body and neck of the guitar are assembled. When the assembly is complete, the guitar is painted and finished.

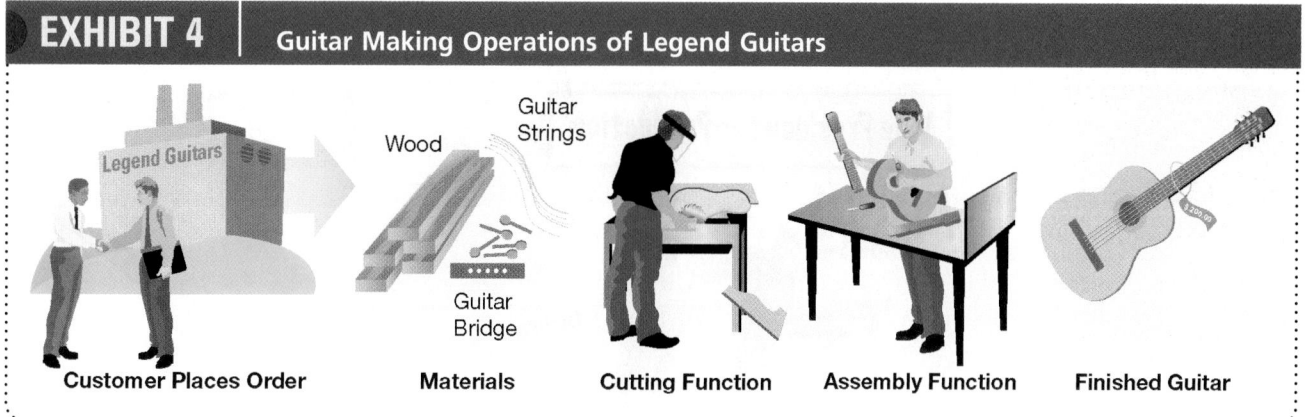

EXHIBIT 4 | **Guitar Making Operations of Legend Guitars**

Customer Places Order   Materials   Cutting Function   Assembly Function   Finished Guitar

Next, we introduce the common cost terms associated with manufacturing operations using Legend Guitars. We begin by defining *cost*. A **cost** is a payment of cash or the commitment to pay cash in the future for the purpose of generating revenues. For example, cash (or credit) used to purchase equipment is the cost of the equipment. If equipment is purchased by exchanging assets other than cash, the current market value of the assets given up is the cost of the equipment purchased.

Costs may be classified in a number of ways. Understanding these classifications provides a basis for later discussions and illustrations of managerial decision making.

DIRECT AND INDIRECT COSTS

For management's use in making decisions, costs are often classified in terms of how they relate to an object or segment of operations, often called a **cost object**. A cost object may be a product, a sales territory, a department, or some activity, such as research and development. Costs are identified with cost objects as either **direct costs** or **indirect costs**.

Direct costs are specifically attributed to the cost object. For example, if Legend Guitars is assigning costs to guitars that are produced, the cost of materials used in the guitar would be a direct cost of the guitar.

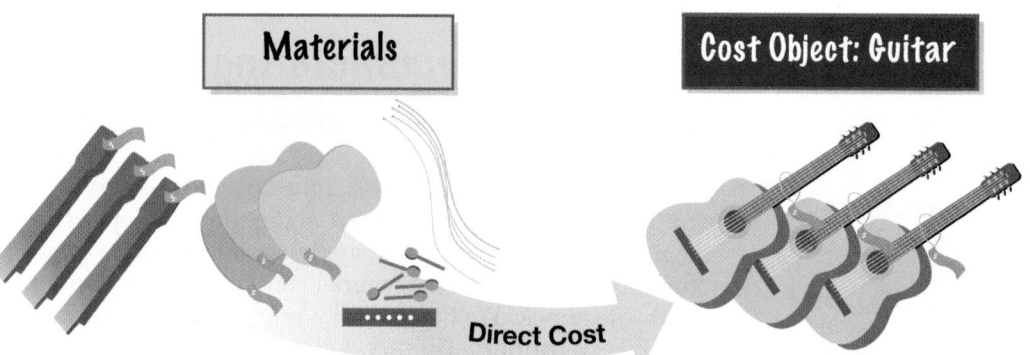

Indirect costs cannot be identified directly with a cost object. For example, the salary of the vice president of production is an indirect cost of the guitars produced by Legend Guitars. While the vice president provides an important contribution to the production of guitars produced by Legend, his salary cannot be directly identified or traced to the individual guitars produced. However, the salary of the vice president of production would be a direct cost to the overall production process. Thus, the salary of the production supervisor can be either an indirect cost (when the cost object is the guitar) or a direct cost (when the cost object is the overall production process).

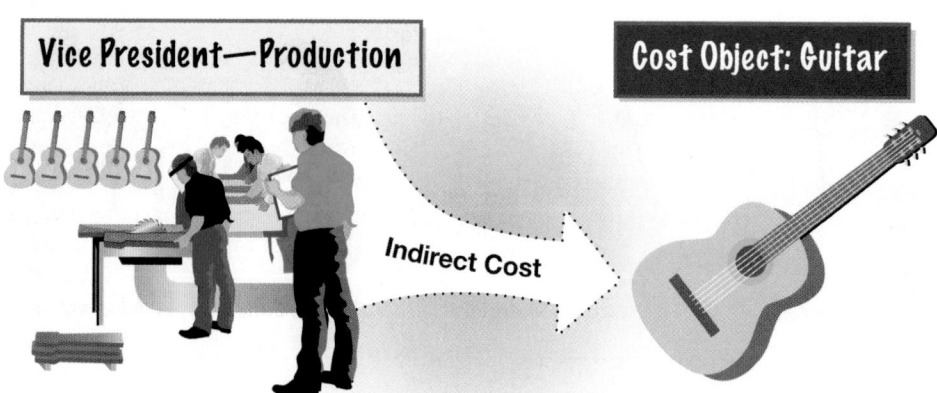

The process of classifying a cost as direct or indirect is illustrated in Exhibit 5.

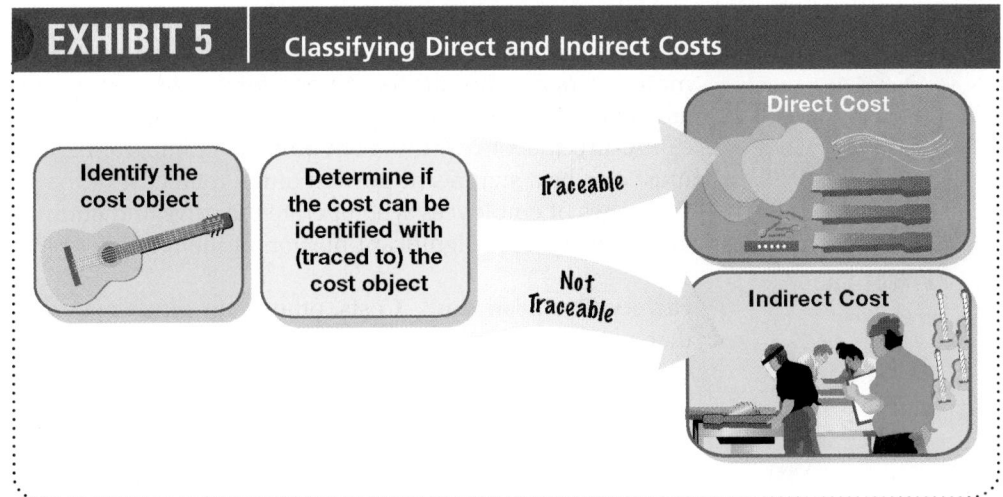

| **EXHIBIT 5** | Classifying Direct and Indirect Costs |

MANUFACTURING COSTS

The cost of a manufactured product includes the cost of materials used in making the product, as well as the costs incurred in converting the materials into a finished product. For example, Legend Guitars uses employees, machines, and other inputs to convert wood and other materials into the finished product, guitars. The finished guitar is the cost object, and the cost of the finished guitars includes direct materials cost, direct labor cost, and factory overhead cost.

Direct Materials Cost Manufactured products convert raw materials into finished products. For example, Legend Guitars uses raw materials such as wood, guitar strings, and guitar bridges and converts them into a finished guitar. The cost of any material that is an integral part of the final guitar is classified as a **direct materials cost**. Other examples of direct materials costs are the cost of electronic components for a TV manufacturer, lumber for a furniture manufacturer, silicon wafers for a producer of microcomputer chips, and tires for an automobile manufacturer.

As a practical matter, a direct materials cost must not only be an integral part of the finished product, but it must also be a significant portion of the total cost of the product. For Legend Guitars, the cost of wood used in the body and neck is a significant portion of the total cost of each guitar.

Direct Labor Cost Most manufacturing processes need employees to convert materials into the final product. For example, Legend Guitars uses employees to assemble guitars by gluing together the neck and body and installing the guitar bridge and strings. The wages of each employee who is directly involved in converting materials

Direct Labor

Factory Overhead

As manufacturing processes have become more automated, direct labor costs have become so small that they are often included as part of factory overhead.

into the final guitar are classified as a **direct labor cost**. Other examples of direct labor costs are carpenters' wages for a construction contractor, mechanics' wages in an automotive repair shop, machine operators' wages in a tool manufacturing plant, and assemblers' wages in a computer assembly plant.

A direct labor cost must not only be an integral part of the finished product, but it must also be a significant portion of the total cost of the product. For Legend Guitars, the wages of employees who operate the saws and cutting machines and assemble the guitars make up a significant portion of the total cost of each guitar.

Factory Overhead Cost   Costs, other than direct materials cost and direct labor cost, that are incurred in the manufacturing process are combined and classified as **factory overhead cost**. Factory overhead is sometimes called **manufacturing overhead** or **factory burden**. All factory overhead costs are indirect costs and include the costs of:

- ■ Heating and lighting the factory,
- ■ Repairing and maintaining factory equipment,
- ■ Property taxes,
- ■ Insurance, and
- ■ Depreciation on factory plant and equipment.

Factory overhead cost also includes materials and labor costs that do not enter directly into the finished product. Examples include the cost of oil used to lubricate machinery and the wages of janitorial and supervisory employees. If the costs of direct materials or direct labor are not a significant portion of the total product cost, these costs may be classified as factory overhead.

In Legend Guitars, the costs of sandpaper, buffing compound, and glue used in the assembly of guitars enter directly into the manufacture of each guitar. However, because these costs are a small cost of each guitar, they are classified as factory overhead. Other overhead costs for Legend Guitars would include the power to run the machines, the depreciation of machines, and the salary of production supervisors (including the vice president of production).

Example Exercise 16-2   objective 2

Identify the following costs as direct materials (DM), direct labor (DL), or factory overhead (FO) for a baseball glove manufacturer.

a. Leather used to make a baseball glove
b. Coolants for machines that sew baseball gloves
c. Wages of assembly line employees
d. Ink used to print a player's autograph on a baseball glove

Follow My Example 16-2

a. DM
b. FO
c. DL
d. FO

For Practice: PE 16-2A, PE 16-2B

Prime Costs and Conversion Costs   Direct materials, direct labor, and factory overhead costs are often grouped together for analysis and reporting purposes. Two common groupings of these costs are prime costs and conversion costs. Exhibit 6 summarizes the classification of manufacturing costs into prime costs and conversion costs.

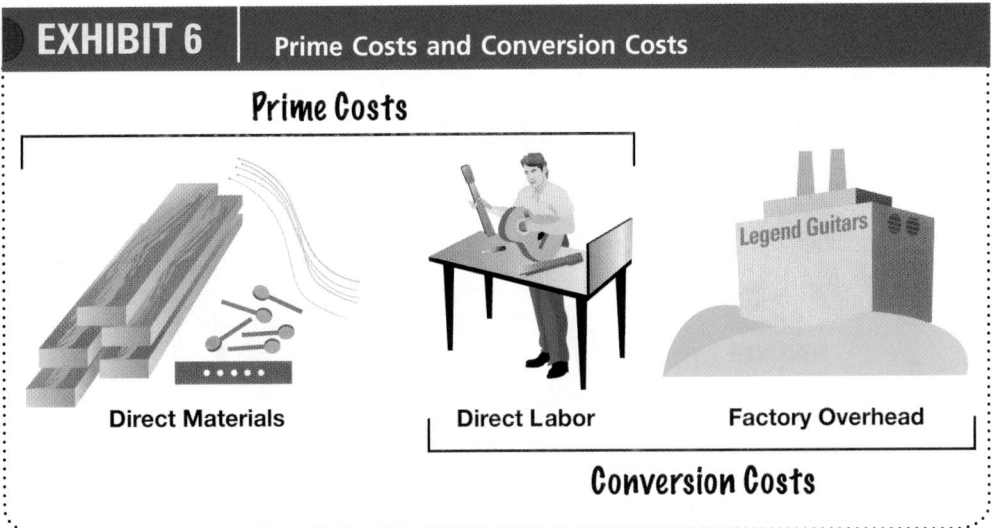

EXHIBIT 6 | Prime Costs and Conversion Costs

Prime Costs

Direct Materials — Direct Labor — Factory Overhead

Conversion Costs

Prime costs consist of direct materials and direct labor costs. **Conversion costs** consist of direct labor and factory overhead costs. Conversion costs are the costs of converting the materials into a finished product. As shown in Exhibit 6, direct labor is both a prime cost and a conversion cost.

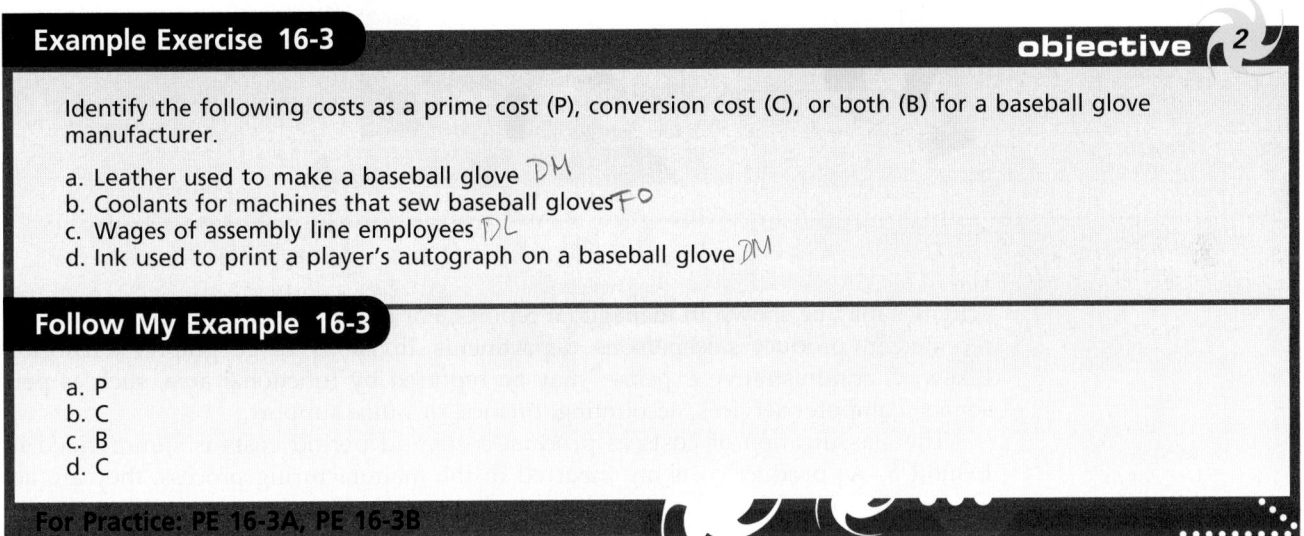

Example Exercise 16-3 objective 2

Identify the following costs as a prime cost (P), conversion cost (C), or both (B) for a baseball glove manufacturer.

a. Leather used to make a baseball glove *DM*
b. Coolants for machines that sew baseball gloves *FO*
c. Wages of assembly line employees *DL*
d. Ink used to print a player's autograph on a baseball glove *DM*

Follow My Example 16-3

a. P
b. C
c. B
d. C

For Practice: PE 16-3A, PE 16-3B

Product Costs and Period Costs For financial reporting purposes, costs are often classified as either product costs or period costs. **Product costs** consist of the three elements of manufacturing cost: direct materials, direct labor, and factory overhead. **Period costs** are generally classified into two categories: selling and administrative. Selling expenses are incurred in marketing the product and delivering the sold product to customers. Administrative expenses are incurred in the administration of the business and are not directly related to the manufacturing or selling functions. Examples of product costs and period costs for Legend Guitars are presented in Exhibit 7.

Classifying period costs as selling or administrative expenses assists management in controlling the costs of these two activities. Different levels of responsibility for these

EXHIBIT 7	Examples of Product Costs and Period Costs—Legend Guitars

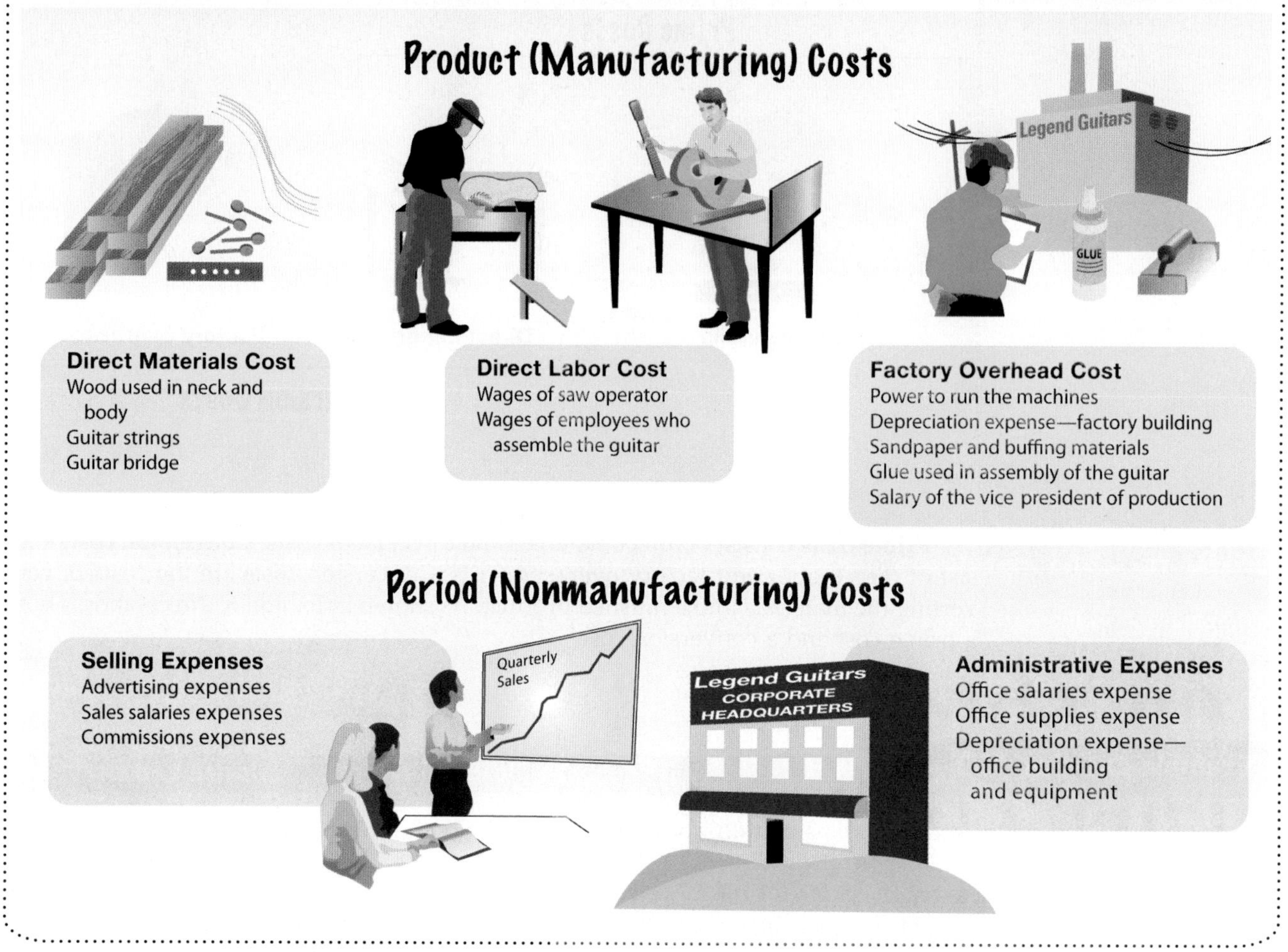

Product (Manufacturing) Costs

Direct Materials Cost
Wood used in neck and
  body
Guitar strings
Guitar bridge

Direct Labor Cost
Wages of saw operator
Wages of employees who
  assemble the guitar

Factory Overhead Cost
Power to run the machines
Depreciation expense—factory building
Sandpaper and buffing materials
Glue used in assembly of the guitar
Salary of the vice president of production

Period (Nonmanufacturing) Costs

Selling Expenses
Advertising expenses
Sales salaries expenses
Commissions expenses

Quarterly
Sales

Legend Guitars
CORPORATE
HEADQUARTERS

Administrative Expenses
Office salaries expense
Office supplies expense
Depreciation expense—
  office building
  and equipment

activities may be shown in managerial reports. For example, selling expenses may be reported by product, salespersons, departments, divisions, or geographic territories. Likewise, administrative expenses may be reported by functional area, such as personnel, computer services, accounting, finance, or office support.

The classification of costs as product costs and period costs is summarized in Exhibit 8. As product costs are incurred in the manufacturing process, they are accounted for as assets and reported on the balance sheet as inventory. When the in-

EXHIBIT 8	
Product Costs and Period Costs	

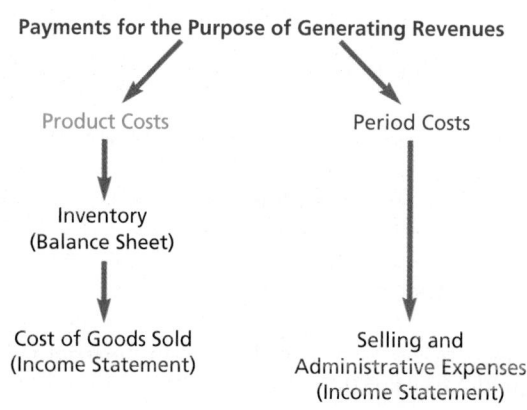

Payments for the Purpose of Generating Revenues

Product Costs → Inventory (Balance Sheet) → Cost of Goods Sold (Income Statement)

Period Costs → Selling and Administrative Expenses (Income Statement)

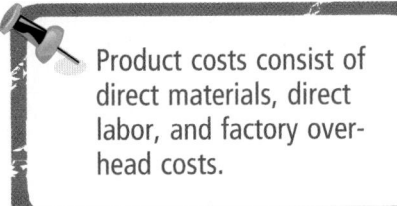

Product costs consist of direct materials, direct labor, and factory overhead costs.

ventory is sold, the direct materials, direct labor, and factory overhead costs are reported as cost of goods sold on the income statement. Period costs do not appear on the balance sheet. They are recognized as expenses in the period in which they are incurred. In the next section, we illustrate the reporting of product costs and period costs in the financial statements of manufacturing businesses.

Example Exercise 16-4   **objective 2**

Identify the following costs as a product cost or a period cost for a baseball glove manufacturer.

a. Leather used to make a baseball glove
b. Cost of endorsement from a professional baseball player
c. Office supplies used at the company headquarters
d. Ink used to print a player's autograph on the baseball glove

Follow My Example 16-4

a. Product cost
b. Period cost
c. Period cost
d. Product cost

For Practice: PE 16-4A, PE 16-4B

Financial Statements for a Manufacturing Business

objective 3

Describe and illustrate the statement of cost of goods manufactured, income statement, and balance sheet for a manufacturing business.

The financial statements for a manufacturing business are more complex than those for service and merchandising businesses. This is because a manufacturer makes the products that it sells. As a result, manufacturing costs must be properly accounted for and reported in the financial statements. These manufacturing costs primarily affect the preparation of the balance sheet and the income statement. The retained earnings and cash flow statements for merchandising and manufacturing businesses are similar to those in service and merchandising businesses. For this reason, we focus only upon the balance sheet and income statement.

BALANCE SHEET FOR A MANUFACTURING BUSINESS

A manufacturing business reports the following three types of inventory on its balance sheet:

1. **Materials inventory** (sometimes called raw materials inventory)
   - Consists of the costs of the direct and indirect materials that have not yet entered the manufacturing process.
   - For Legend Guitars, wood used to make the body and neck of the guitar is part of the materials inventory.

2. **Work in process inventory**
   - Consists of the direct materials costs, the direct labor costs, and the factory overhead costs that have entered the manufacturing process but are associated with products that have not been completed.

- For Legend Guitars, the unassembled guitars for which the neck and body have been produced are "in process" because they have not yet been put together into a finished guitar. Thus, the cost of the direct materials, direct labor, and factory overhead incurred during the period to create any in-process guitars is part of the work in process inventory.

3. **Finished goods inventory**
   - Consists of *completed* (or finished) products that have not been sold.
   - For Legend Guitars, finished goods inventory contains all of the costs incurred to manufacture the completed, but not yet sold, guitars.

Exhibit 9 compares the balance sheet presentation of inventory for a manufacturing company, Legend Guitars, to that of a merchandising company, MusicLand Stores, Inc. In both balance sheets, inventory is shown in the Current Assets section.

EXHIBIT 9

Balance Sheet Presentation of Inventory in Manufacturing and Merchandising Companies

Legend Guitars
Balance Sheet
December 31, 2008

Current assets:		
Cash		$ 21,000
Accounts receivable (net)		120,000
Inventories:		
Finished goods	$62,500	
Work in process	24,000	
Materials	35,000	121,500
Supplies		2,000
Total current assets		$264,500

MusicLand Stores, Inc.
Balance Sheet
December 31, 2008

Current assets:	
Cash	$ 25,000
Accounts receivable (net)	85,000
Merchandise inventory	142,000
Supplies	10,000
Total current assets	$262,000

INCOME STATEMENT FOR A MANUFACTURING COMPANY

The major difference in the income statements for merchandising and manufacturing businesses is in the reporting of cost of products sold during the period. A merchandising business purchases merchandise (products) in a finished state for resale to customers. The cost of products sold is called the **cost of merchandise sold**.

A manufacturer makes the products it sells, using direct materials, direct labor, and factory overhead. The cost of the product sold is generally called the cost of goods sold. For a manufacturer, the total cost of making and finishing the product is called the **cost**

of goods manufactured. This is very similar to the cost of merchandise available for sale in a merchandising business.

The income statement of manufacturing companies is supported by a **statement of cost of goods manufactured**, which provides the details of the cost of goods manufactured. To illustrate the flow of manufacturing costs to the income statement for Legend Guitars, assume the following data for 2008:

Inventories	January 1	December 31
Materials	$65,000	$35,000
Work in process	30,000	24,000
Finished goods	60,000	62,500

Materials purchased during the year		$100,000
Direct labor incurred in production		110,000
Factory overhead incurred in production:		
Indirect labor	$24,000	
Depreciation on factory equipment	10,000	
Factory supplies and utility costs	10,000	
Total		44,000
Selling expenses		20,000
Administrative expenses		15,000
Sales		366,000

The manufacturing costs for Legend Guitars would flow to the financial statements as shown in Exhibit 10.

EXHIBIT 10 Flow of Manufacturing Costs

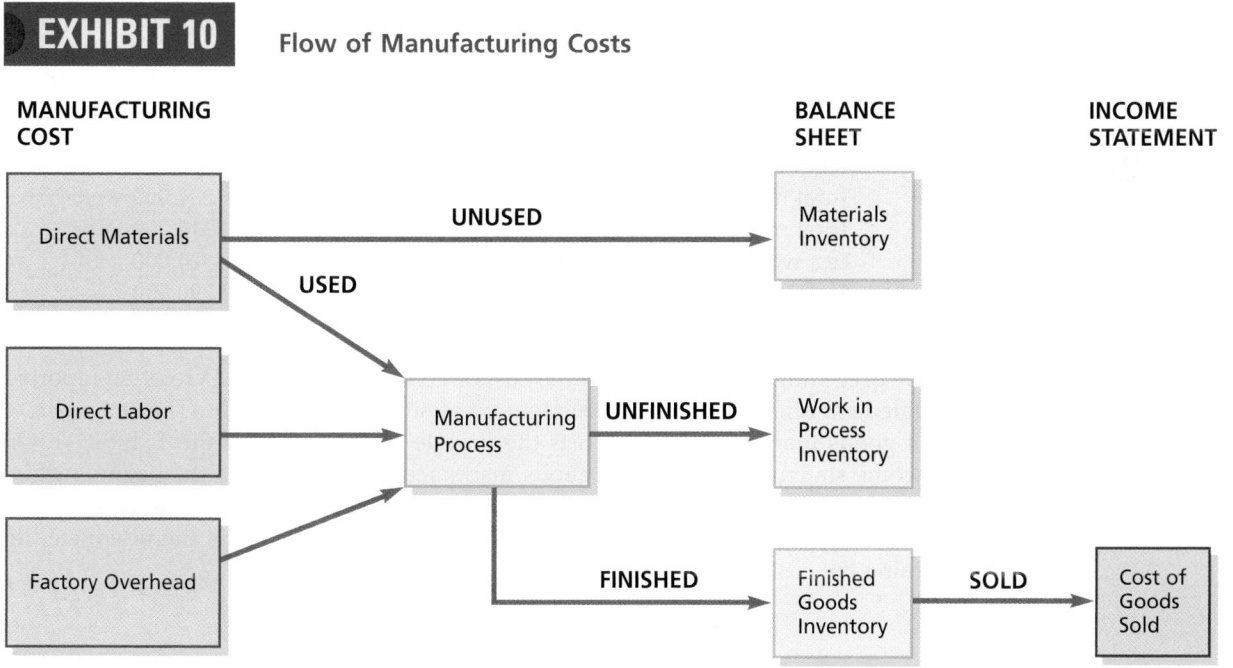

As discussed previously, three calculation steps are required to determine the cost of goods manufactured.

The cost of goods manufactured is determined by first computing the cost of direct materials used in the year as follows:

Materials inventory, January 1, 2008	$ 65,000
Add: Materials purchased during the year	100,000
Cost of materials available for use	$165,000
Less: Materials inventory, December 31, 2008	35,000
Cost of direct materials used in production	$130,000

Adding the beginning (January 1) materials inventory of $65,000 to the cost of materials purchased during the period, $100,000, yields the total cost of materials that are available for use during the period of $165,000. Deducting the ending December 31 materials inventory of $35,000 equals the cost of direct materials used in production during the year.

The total manufacturing costs incurred during the year of $284,000 is determined as follows:

Direct materials used during the year	$130,000
Direct labor	110,000
Factory overhead	44,000
Total manufacturing costs incurred during the year	$284,000

To determine the cost of goods manufactured during the year, the beginning work in process inventory of $30,000 is added to the total manufacturing costs incurred during the year of $284,000 to yield the total manufacturing costs of $314,000. The ending work in process of $24,000 is then deducted to determine the cost of goods manufactured during the year as follows:

Work in process inventory, January 1, 2008	$ 30,000
Total manufacturing costs incurred during the year	284,000
Total manufacturing costs	$314,000
Less work in process inventory, December 31, 2008	24,000
Cost of goods manufactured during the year	$290,000

The preceding computations of the cost of goods manufactured are often reported in a statement of cost of goods manufactured as shown in Exhibit 11. The statement of cost of goods manufactured supports the income statement shown in Exhibit 11. On the income statement, the cost of goods manufactured is added to the beginning finished goods inventory of $60,000 to determine the cost of finished goods available for sale of $350,000. The ending finished goods inventory of $62,500 is then deducted to determine the cost of goods sold of $287,500.

EXHIBIT 11

Manufacturing Company—Income Statement with Statement of Cost of Goods Manufactured

Legend Guitars
Income Statement
For the Year Ended December 31, 2008

Sales		$366,000
Cost of goods sold:		
Finished goods inventory, January 1, 2008	$ 60,000	
Cost of goods manufactured	290,000	
Cost of finished goods available for sale	$350,000	
Less finished goods inventory, December 31, 2008	62,500	
Cost of goods sold		287,500
Gross profit		$ 78,500
Operating expenses:		
Selling expenses	$ 20,000	
Administrative expenses	15,000	
Total operating expenses		35,000
Net income		$ 43,500

* Doesn't reflect finished goods →

Legend Guitars
Statement of Cost of Goods Manufactured
For the Year Ended December 31, 2008

Work in process inventory, January 1, 2008			$ 30,000
Direct materials:			
Materials inventory, January 1, 2008	$ 65,000		
Purchases	100,000		
Cost of materials available for use	$165,000		
Less materials inventory, December 31, 2008	35,000		
Cost of direct materials used in production		$130,000	
Direct labor		110,000	
Factory overhead:			
Indirect labor	$ 24,000		
Depreciation on factory equipment	10,000		
Factory supplies and utility costs	10,000		
Total factory overhead		44,000	
Total manufacturing costs incurred during the year			284,000
Total manufacturing costs			$314,000
Less work in process inventory, December 31, 2008			24,000
Cost of goods manufactured			$290,000

- the beginning fin. goods inv.   60,000
- the ending fin. goods inv.   —
  COGS =   287,500

Example Exercise 16-5

objective **3**

Gauntlet Company has the following information for January:

Cost of direct materials used in production	$25,000
Direct labor	35,000
Factory overhead	20,000
Work in process inventory, January 1	30,000
Work in process inventory, January 31	25,000
Finished goods inventory, January 1	15,000
Finished goods inventory, January 31	12,000

For January, determine (a) the cost of goods manufactured and (b) the cost of goods sold.

Follow My Example 16-5

a.	Work in process inventory, January 1		$ 30,000
	Cost of direct materials used in production	$ 25,000	
	Direct labor	35,000	
	Factory overhead	20,000	
	Total manufacturing costs incurred during January		80,000
	Total manufacturing costs		$110,000
	Less: Work in process inventory, January 31		25,000
	Cost of goods manufactured		$ 85,000
b.	Finished goods inventory, January 1		$ 15,000
	Cost of goods manufactured		85,000
	Cost of finished goods available for sale		$100,000
	Less: Finished goods inventory, January 31		12,000
	Cost of goods sold		$ 88,000

For Practice: PE 16-5A, PE 16-5B

Uses of Managerial Accounting

objective **4**

Describe the uses of managerial accounting information.

As discussed in the first part of this chapter, managers need information to guide their decision making. Managerial accounting provides information and reports that help managers run the day-to-day operations of their businesses. For example, Legend Guitars uses managerial information to determine the cost of manufacturing each guitar. This cost can then be used to set the selling price of guitars. In addition, comparing the costs of guitars over time can aid managers in monitoring and controlling the cost of direct materials, direct labor, and factory overhead.

Managerial reports also help managers evaluate the performance of a company's operations. Managerial accounting can be used to evaluate the efficiency in using raw materials or direct labor in the manufacturing process. For example, Legend Guitars can use performance reports to identify the cause for large amounts of unusable wood remaining after the cutting process. Managers can then use this information to make the cutting process more efficient.

Companies also use managerial accounting information to support long-term planning decisions, such as investment decisions. For example, Legend Guitars management may consider buying a new computerized saw to speed up the production process while providing higher quality cuts. Managerial accounting information can help management determine if this is a good investment.

Managerial accounting data can be used to help managers understand how many guitars need to be sold in a month in order to cover recurring monthly costs. Such information can be used to set monthly selling targets.

As these examples illustrate, managerial accounting information can be used for a variety of purposes. In the remaining chapters of this text, we examine these and other areas of managerial accounting in greater detail and discuss how this information is used to aid managerial decision making.

Business Connections

REAL WORLD

NAVIGATING THE INFORMATION HIGHWAY

Dell Inc. follows a build-to-order manufacturing process, where each computer is manufactured based on a specific customer order. In a build-to-order manufacturing process like this, customers select the features they want on their computer from the company's Web site. Once the order is submitted, the manufacturing process begins. The parts required for each feature are removed from inventory, and the computer is manufactured and shipped within days of the order. Inventory items are scanned as they are removed from inventory to keep accurate track of inventory levels and help the manufacturer determine when to reorder.

But calculating the amount of materials to reorder is not the only use of these data. Data on which parts are included in each order are placed in the company's database. This information can then be used to track manufacturing patterns such as the type of features that are frequently ordered together and seasonal changes in the features that are ordered.

In recent years, information systems have become more sophisticated, making it easier and less expensive for companies to gather large amounts of data on their manufacturing processes and customers. If used effectively, these new data sources can help a business like Dell decide what features to offer for its products, what features to discontinue, and how to combine features into a package. For example, manufacturing data might indicate that the demand for DVD drives on computers increases significantly each summer right before school starts. A

© 1999–2006 DELL INC.

build-to-order manufacturer like Dell might use this information to realign the manufacturing process during that time of year, or to offer certain packages of features in July and August.

However, the ability to generate value from this information depends on a company's ability to merge these new data with existing accounting information in a meaningful manner. The managerial accountant must now be prepared to analyze and evaluate a broader set of information and determine how it will affect a company's operational performance and profitability.

Source: "Delivering Strategic Business Value: Business Intelligence Can Help Management Accounting Reclaim Its Relevance and Rightful Role," Steve Williams, *Strategic Finance,* August 2004.

At a Glance

1. Describe managerial accounting and the role of managerial accounting in a business.

Key Points	Key Learning Outcomes	Example Exercises	Practice Exercises
Managerial accounting is a staff function that supports the management process by providing reports to aid management in planning, directing, controlling, improving, and decision making. This differs from financial accounting, which provides information to stakeholders outside of the organization. Managerial accounting reports are designed to meet the specific needs of management and aid management in planning long-term strategies and running the day-to-day operations.	• Describe the differences between financial accounting and managerial accounting. • Describe the role of the management accountant in the organization. • Describe the role of managerial accounting in the management process.	16-1	16-1A, 16-1B

(continued)

2. Describe and illustrate the following costs: direct and indirect, direct materials, direct labor, factory overhead, and product and period costs.

Key Points	Key Learning Outcomes	Example Exercises	Practice Exercises
Manufacturing companies use machinery and labor to convert materials into a finished product. A direct cost can be directly traced to a finished product, while an indirect cost cannot. The cost of a finished product is made up of three components: (1) the cost of materials that are directly identifiable with the final product, (2) the wages of employees that directly convert materials to a finished product, and (3) factory overhead. Costs incurred in the manufacturing process other than direct materials and direct labor are classified as factory overhead costs. These three manufacturing costs can be categorized into prime costs (direct material and direct labor) or conversion costs (direct labor and factory overhead). Product costs consist of the elements of manufacturing cost—direct materials, direct labor, and factory overhead—while period costs consist of selling and administrative expenses.	• Describe a cost object. • Classify a cost as a direct or indirect cost for a cost object. • Describe direct materials cost. • Describe direct labor cost. • Describe factory overhead cost. • Describe prime costs and conversion costs. • Describe product costs and period costs.	**16-2** **16-2** **16-2** **16-3** **16-4**	16-2A, 16-2B 16-2A, 16-2B 16-2A, 16-2B 16-3A, 16-3B 16-4A, 16-4B

3. Describe and illustrate the statement of cost of goods manufactured, income statement, and balance sheet for a manufacturing business.

Key Points	Key Learning Outcomes	Example Exercises	Practice Exercises
The financial statements of manufacturing companies differ from those of merchandising companies. Manufacturing company balance sheets report three types of inventory: materials, work in process, and finished goods. The income statement of manufacturing companies reports cost of goods sold, which is the total manufacturing cost of the goods sold. The income statement is supported by the statement of cost of goods manufactured, which provides the details of the cost of goods manufactured during the period.	• Describe materials inventory. • Describe work in process inventory. • Describe finished goods inventory. • Describe the differences between merchandising and manufacturing company balance sheets. • Prepare a statement of cost of goods manufactured. • Prepare an income statement for a manufacturing company.	**16-5** **16-5**	16-5A, 16-5B 16-5A, 16-5B

4. Describe the uses of managerial accounting information.

Key Points	Key Learning Outcomes	Example Exercises	Practice Exercises
Managers need information to guide their decision making. Managerial accounting provides a variety of information and reports that help managers run the operations of their businesses.	• Describe examples of how managerial accounting aids managers in decision making.		

Key Terms

continuous process improvement (718)

controller (716)

controlling (718)

conversion costs (723)

cost (719)

cost object (720)

cost of goods manufactured (726)

cost of merchandise sold (726)

decision making (718)

direct costs (720)

direct labor cost (722)

direct materials cost (721)

directing (717)

factory burden (722)

factory overhead cost (722)

feedback (718)

financial accounting (714)

finished goods inventory (726)

indirect costs (720)

line department (715)

management by exception (718)

management process (716)

managerial accounting (715)

manufacturing overhead (722)

materials inventory (725)

objectives (goals) (717)

operational planning (717)

period costs (723)

planning (717)

prime costs (723)

product costs (723)

staff department (716)

statement of cost of goods manufactured (727)

strategic planning (717)

strategies (717)

work in process inventory (725)

Illustrative Problem

The following is a list of costs that were incurred in producing this textbook:

a. Insurance on the factory building and equipment
b. Salary of the vice president of finance
c. Hourly wages of printing press operators during production
d. Straight-line depreciation on the printing presses used to manufacture the text
e. Electricity used to run the presses during the printing of the text
f. Sales commissions paid to textbook representatives for each text sold
g. Paper on which the text is printed
h. Book covers used to bind the pages
i. Straight-line depreciation on an office building
j. Salaries of staff used to develop artwork for the text
k. Glue used to bind pages to cover

Instructions

With respect to the manufacture and sale of this text, classify each cost as either a product cost or a period cost. Indicate whether each product cost is a direct materials cost, a direct labor cost, or a factory overhead cost. Indicate whether each period cost is a selling expense or an administrative expense.

Solution

	Product Cost			Period Cost	
Cost	Direct Materials Cost	Direct Labor Cost	Factory Overhead Cost	Selling Expense	Administrative Expense
a.			X		
b.					X
c.		X			
d.			X		
e.			X		
f.				X	
g.	X				
h.	X				
i.					X
j.			X		
k.			X		

Self-Examination Questions

1. Which of the following best describes the difference between financial and managerial accounting?
   A. Managerial accounting provides information to support decisions, while financial accounting does not.
   B. Managerial accounting is not restricted to generally accepted accounting principles (GAAP), while financial accounting is restricted to GAAP.
   C. Managerial accounting does not result in financial reports, while financial accounting does result in financial reports.
   D. Managerial accounting is concerned solely with the future and does not record events from the past, while financial accounting records only events from past transactions.

2. Which of the following is *not* one of the five basic phases of the management process?
   A. Planning   C. Decision making
   B. Controlling   D. Operating

3. Which of the following is *not* considered a cost of manufacturing a product?
   A. Direct materials cost
   B. Factory overhead cost
   C. Sales salaries
   D. Direct labor cost

4. Which of the following costs would be included as part of the factory overhead costs of a microcomputer manufacturer?
   A. The cost of memory chips
   B. Depreciation of testing equipment
   C. Wages of microcomputer assemblers
   D. The cost of disk drives

5. For the month of May, Latter Company has beginning finished goods inventory of $50,000, ending finished goods inventory of $35,000, and cost of goods manufactured of $125,000. What is the cost of goods sold for May?
   A. $90,000   C. $140,000
   B. $110,000   D. $170,000

Eye Openers

1. What are the major differences between managerial accounting and financial accounting?
2. a. Differentiate between a department with line responsibility and a department with staff responsibility.
   b. In an organization that has a Sales Department and a Personnel Department, among others, which of the two departments has (1) line responsibility and (2) staff responsibility?
3. a. What is the role of the controller in a business organization?
   b. Does the controller have a line or staff responsibility?
4. What are the five basic phases of the management process?
5. What is the term for a plan that encompasses a period ranging from five or more years and that serves as a basis for long-range actions?
6. What is the process by which management runs day-to-day operations?
7. What is the process by which management assesses how well a plan is working?
8. Describe what is meant by *management by exception*.
9. What term describes a payment in cash or the commitment to pay cash in the future for the purpose of generating revenues?
10. For a company that produces desktop computers, would memory chips be considered a direct or an indirect cost of each microcomputer produced?
11. What three costs make up the cost of manufacturing a product?
12. What manufacturing cost term is used to describe the cost of materials that are an integral part of the manufactured end product?
13. If the cost of wages paid to employees who are directly involved in converting raw materials into a manufactured end product is not a significant portion of the total product cost, how would the wages cost be classified as to type of manufacturing cost?
14. Distinguish between prime costs and conversion costs.
15. What is the difference between a product cost and a period cost?
16. Name the three inventory accounts for a manufacturing business, and describe what each balance represents at the end of an accounting period.

17. In what order should the three inventories of a manufacturing business be presented on the balance sheet?
18. What are the three categories of manufacturing costs included in the cost of finished goods and the cost of work in process?
19. For a manufacturer, what is the description of the amount that is comparable to a merchandising business's cost of merchandise sold?
20. For June, Fosina Company had beginning materials inventory of $25,000, ending materials inventory of $30,000, and materials purchases of $140,000. What is the cost of direct materials used in production?
21. How does the cost of goods sold section of the income statement differ between merchandising and manufacturing companies?
22. Describe how an automobile manufacturer might use managerial accounting information to (a) evaluate the performance of the company and (b) make strategic decisions.

Practice Exercises

PE 16-1A
Managerial accounting in the management process
obj. 1

Three phases of the management process are planning, directing, and controlling (management by exception). One type of planning is strategic planning. Match the following descriptions to the proper phase.

Phase of management process	Description
Strategic planning	a. Isolating significant departures from plans for further investigation and possible remedial action. It may lead to a revision of future plans.
Directing	b. Process by which managers, given their assigned levels of responsibilities, run day-to-day operations.
Management by exception	c. Developing long-range courses of action to achieve goals.

PE 16-1B
Managerial accounting in the management process
obj. 1

Three phases of the management process are controlling, strategies, and decision making. Match the following descriptions to the proper phase.

Phase of management process	Description
Controlling	a. Inherent in planning, directing, controlling, and improving.
Strategies	b. Monitoring the operating results of implemented plans and comparing the actual results with expected results.
Decision making	c. Long-range courses of action.

PE 16-2A
Direct materials, direct labor, and factory overhead
obj. 2

Identify the following costs as direct materials (DM), direct labor (DL), or factory overhead (FO) for a textbook publisher.

a. Maintenance on printing machines
b. Glue used to bind books
c. Wages of printing machine employees
d. Paper used to make a textbook

PE 16-2B
Direct materials, direct labor, and factory overhead
obj. 2

Identify the following costs as direct materials (DM), direct labor (DL), or factory overhead (FO) for an automobile manufacturer.

a. Wages of employees that operate painting equipment
b. Steel
c. Wages of the plant manager
d. Oil used for assembly line machinery

PE 16-3A
Prime costs vs. conversion costs
obj. 2

Identify the following costs as a prime cost (P), conversion cost (C), or both (B) for a textbook publisher.

a. Maintenance on printing machines
b. Glue used to bind books
c. Wages of printing machine employees
d. Paper used to make a textbook

PE 16-3B
Prime costs vs. conversion costs
obj. 2

Identify the following costs as a prime cost (P), conversion cost (C), or both (B) for an automobile manufacturer.

a. Wages of employees that operate painting equipment
b. Steel
c. Wages of the plant manager
d. Oil used for assembly line machinery

PE 16-4A
Product costs vs. period costs
obj. 2

Identify the following costs as a product cost or a period cost for a textbook publisher.

a. Maintenance on printing machines
b. Sales salaries
c. Depreciation expense—corporate headquarters
d. Paper used to make a textbook

PE 16-4B
Product costs vs. period costs
obj. 2

Identify the following costs as a product cost or a period cost for an automobile manufacturer.

a. Wages of employees that operate painting equipment
b. Steel
c. Accounting staff salaries
d. Rent on office building

PE 16-5A
Cost of goods sold, cost of goods manufactured
obj. 3

Nantahala Company has the following information for August:

Cost of direct materials used in production	$30,000
Direct labor	45,000
Factory overhead	22,000
Work in process inventory, August 1	10,000
Work in process inventory, August 31	8,000
Finished goods inventory, August 1	18,000
Finished goods inventory, August 31	10,000

For August, determine (a) the cost of goods manufactured and (b) the cost of goods sold.

PE 16-5B
Cost of goods sold, cost of goods manufactured
obj. 3

Tsali Company has the following information for February:

Cost of direct materials used in production	$18,000
Direct labor	54,000
Factory overhead	36,000
Work in process inventory, February 1	50,000
Work in process inventory, February 28	57,000
Finished goods inventory, February 1	22,000
Finished goods inventory, February 28	26,000

For February, determine (a) the cost of goods manufactured and (b) the cost of goods sold.

Exercises

EX 16-1
Classifying costs as materials, labor, or factory overhead
obj. 2

Indicate whether each of the following costs of an airplane manufacturer would be classified as direct materials cost, direct labor cost, or factory overhead cost:

a. Steel used in landing gear
b. Controls for flight deck
c. Welding machinery lubricants
d. Salary of test pilot
e. Wages of assembly line worker
f. Tires
g. Aircraft engines
h. Depreciation of welding equipment

EX 16-2
Classifying costs as materials, labor, or factory overhead
obj. 2

Indicate whether the following costs of Colgate-Palmolive Company would be classified as direct materials cost, direct labor cost, or factory overhead cost:

a. Packaging materials
b. Depreciation on production machinery
c. Salary of process engineers
d. Depreciation on the Clarksville, Indiana, soap plant
e. Scents and fragrances
f. Wages of Marketing Department employees
g. Resins for soap and shampoo products
h. Plant manager salary for the Morristown, Tennessee, toothpaste plant
i. Maintenance supplies
j. Wages paid to Packaging Department employees

EX 16-3
Classifying costs as factory overhead
obj. 2

Which of the following items are properly classified as part of factory overhead for Caterpillar?

a. Vice president of finance's salary
b. Interest expense on debt
c. Plant manager's salary at Aurora, Illinois, manufacturing plant
d. Consultant fees for a study of production line employee productivity
e. Factory supplies used in the Morganton, North Carolina, engine parts plant
f. Amortization of patents on new assembly process
g. Steel plate
h. Depreciation on Peoria, Illinois, headquarters building
i. Property taxes on the Danville, Kentucky, tractor tread plant
j. Sales incentive fees to dealers

EX 16-4
Classifying costs as product or period costs
obj. 2

For apparel manufacturer Ann Taylor, Inc., classify each of the following costs as either a product cost or a period cost:

a. Factory janitorial supplies
b. Depreciation on office equipment
c. Advertising expenses
d. Fabric used during production
e. Depreciation on sewing machines
f. Property taxes on factory building and equipment
g. Sales commissions
h. Wages of sewing machine operators
i. Repairs and maintenance costs for sewing machines
j. Salary of production quality control supervisor
k. Factory supervisors' salaries
l. Oil used to lubricate sewing machines

(continued)

m. Travel costs of salespersons

n. Corporate controller's salary

o. Utility costs for office building

p. Research and development costs

q. Salaries of distribution center personnel

EX 16-5
Concepts and terminology
objs. 1, 2

From the choices presented in parentheses, choose the appropriate term for completing each of the following sentences:

a. Feedback is often used to (improve, direct) operations.

b. A product, sales territory, department, or activity to which costs are traced is called a (direct cost, cost object).

c. Payments of cash or the commitment to pay cash in the future for the purpose of generating revenues are (costs, expenses).

d. The balance sheet of a manufacturer would include an account for (cost of goods sold, work in process inventory).

e. Factory overhead costs combined with direct labor costs are called (prime, conversion) costs.

f. Advertising costs are usually viewed as (period, product) costs.

g. The implementation of automatic, robotic factory equipment normally (increases, decreases) the direct labor component of product costs.

EX 16-6
Concepts and terminology
objs. 1, 2

From the choices presented in parentheses, choose the appropriate term for completing each of the following sentences:

a. Direct materials costs combined with direct labor costs are called (prime, conversion) costs.

b. The wages of an assembly worker are normally considered a (period, product) cost.

c. The phase of the management process that uses process information to eliminate the source of problems in a process so that the process delivers the correct product in the correct quantities is called (directing, improving).

d. Short-term plans are called (strategic, operational) plans.

e. The plant manager's salary would be considered (direct, indirect) to the product.

f. Materials for use in production are called (supplies, materials inventory).

g. An example of factory overhead is (sales office depreciation, plant depreciation).

EX 16-7
Classifying costs in a service company
obj. 2

A partial list of the costs for Mountain Lakes Railroad, a short hauler of freight, is provided below. Classify each cost as either indirect or direct. For purposes of classifying each cost as direct or indirect, use the train as the cost object.

a. Cost to lease (rent) train locomotives.

b. Wages of switch and classification yard personnel

c. Wages of train engineers

d. Cost to lease (rent) railroad cars

e. Maintenance costs of right of way, bridges, and buildings

f. Fuel costs

g. Payroll clerk salaries

h. Safety training costs

i. Salaries of dispatching and communications personnel

j. Costs of accident cleanup

k. Cost of track and bed (ballast) replacement

l. Depreciation of terminal facilities

EX 16-8
Classifying costs
objs. 2, 3

The following report was prepared for evaluating the performance of the plant manager of Miss-Take Inc. Evaluate and correct this report.

Miss-Take Inc.
Manufacturing Costs
For the Quarter Ended March 31, 2008

Direct labor (including $80,000 maintenance salaries)	$ 430,000
Materials used in production (including	
$40,000 of indirect materials)	680,000
Factory overhead:	
Supervisor salaries	610,000
Heat, light, and power	140,000
Sales salaries	270,000
Promotional expenses	310,000
Insurance and property taxes—plant	160,000
Insurance and property taxes—corporate offices	210,000
Depreciation—plant and equipment	80,000
Depreciation—corporate offices	100,000
Total	$2,990,000

EX 16-9
Financial statements of a manufacturing firm

obj. 3

✓ *a. Net income, $55,000*

The following events took place for Gantt Manufacturing Company during March, the first month of its operations as a producer of digital clocks:

a. Purchased $65,000 of materials.
b. Used $50,000 of direct materials in production.
c. Incurred $75,000 of direct labor wages.
d. Incurred $105,000 of factory overhead.
e. Transferred $175,000 of work in process to finished goods.
f. Sold goods with a cost of $140,000.
g. Earned revenues of $310,000.
h. Incurred $80,000 of selling expenses.
i. Incurred $35,000 of administrative expenses.

a. Prepare the March income statement for Gantt Manufacturing Company.
b. Determine the inventory balances at the end of the first month of operations.

EX 16-10
Manufacturing company balance sheet

obj. 3

Partial balance sheet data for Ellison Company at December 31, 2008, are as follows:

Finished goods inventory	$12,500
Prepaid insurance	6,000
Accounts receivable	25,000
Work in process inventory	45,000
Supplies	15,000
Materials inventory	24,000
Cash	32,000

Prepare the Current Assets section of Ellison Company's balance sheet at December 31, 2008.

EX 16-11
Cost of direct materials used in production for a manufacturing company

obj. 3

Guzman Manufacturing Company reported the following materials data for the month ending October 31, 2008:

Materials purchased	$175,000
Materials inventory, October 1	45,000
Materials inventory, October 31	30,000

Determine the cost of direct materials used in production by Guzman during the month ended October 31, 2008.

EX 16-12
Cost of goods manufactured for a manufacturing company

obj. 3

✓ e. $4,000

Two items are omitted from each of the following three lists of cost of goods manufactured statement data. Determine the amounts of the missing items, identifying them by letter.

Work in process inventory, December 1	$ 1,000	$ 10,000	(e)
Total manufacturing costs incurred during December	12,000	(c)	60,000
Total manufacturing costs	(a)	$120,000	$64,000
Work in process inventory, December 31	2,000	20,000	(f)
Cost of goods manufactured	(b)	(d)	$58,000

EX 16-13
Cost of goods manufactured for a manufacturing company

obj. 3

The following information is available for Applebaum Manufacturing Company for the month ending January 31, 2008:

Cost of direct materials used in production	$165,000
Direct labor	145,000
Work in process inventory, January 1	70,000
Work in process inventory, January 31	125,000
Total factory overhead	65,000

Determine Applebaum's cost of goods manufactured for the month ended January 31, 2008.

EX 16-14
Income statement for a manufacturing company

obj. 3

✓ d. $190,000

Two items are omitted from each of the following three lists of cost of goods sold data from a manufacturing company income statement. Determine the amounts of the missing items, identifying them by letter.

Finished goods inventory, November 1	$ 25,000	$ 40,000	(e)
Cost of goods manufactured	160,000	(c)	350,000
Cost of finished goods available for sale	(a)	$250,000	$400,000
Finished goods inventory, November 30	30,000	60,000	(f)
Cost of goods sold	(b)	(d)	$335,000

EX 16-15
Statement of cost of goods manufactured for a manufacturing company

obj. 3

✓ a. Total manufacturing costs, $622,000

Cost data for T. Clark Manufacturing Company for the month ending April 30, 2008, are as follows:

Inventories	April 1	April 30
Materials	$125,000	$110,000
Work in process	85,000	95,000
Finished goods	65,000	75,000

Direct labor	$225,000
Materials purchased during April	240,000
Factory overhead incurred during April:	
Indirect labor	24,000
Machinery depreciation	14,000
Heat, light, and power	5,000
Supplies	4,000
Property taxes	3,500
Miscellaneous cost	6,500

a. Prepare a cost of goods manufactured statement for April 2008.
b. Determine the cost of goods sold for April 2008.

EX 16-16
Cost of goods sold, profit margin, and net income for a manufacturing company

obj. 3

✓ a. Cost of goods sold, $270,000

The following information is available for Renteria Manufacturing Company for the month ending March 31, 2008:

Cost of goods manufactured	$265,000
Selling expenses	85,000
Administrative expenses	45,000
Sales	540,000
Finished goods inventory, March 1	60,000
Finished goods inventory, March 31	55,000

For the month ended March 31, 2008, determine Renteria's (a) cost of goods sold, (b) gross profit, and (c) net income.

EX 16-17
Cost flow relationships
obj. 3

✓ a. $250,000

The following information is available for the first month of operations of Brown Company, a manufacturer of mechanical pencils:

Sales	$600,000
Gross profit	350,000
Cost of goods manufactured	300,000
Indirect labor	130,000
Factory depreciation	20,000
Materials purchased	185,000
Total manufacturing costs for the period	345,000
Materials inventory	25,000

Using the above information, determine the following missing amounts:

a. Cost of goods sold
b. Finished goods inventory
c. Direct materials cost
d. Direct labor cost
e. Work in process inventory

Problems Series A

PR 16-1A
Classifying costs
obj. 2

The following is a list of costs that were incurred in the production and sale of boats:

a. Commissions to sales representatives, based upon the number of boats sold.
b. Cost of boat for "grand prize" promotion in local bass tournament.
c. Memberships for key executives in the Bass World Association.
d. Cost of electrical wiring for boats.
e. Cost of normal scrap from defective hulls.
f. Cost of metal hardware for boats, such as ornaments and tie-down grasps.
g. Cost of paving the employee parking lot.
h. Hourly wages of assembly line workers.
i. Annual bonus paid to top executives of the company.
j. Straight-line depreciation on factory equipment.
k. Wood paneling for use in interior boat trim.
l. Steering wheels.
m. Special advertising campaign in *Bass World*.
n. Masks for use by sanders in smoothing boat hulls.
o. Power used by sanding equipment.
p. Yearly cost maintenance contract for robotic equipment.
q. Oil to lubricate factory equipment.
r. Canvas top for boats.
s. Executive end-of-year bonuses.
t. Salary of shop supervisor.
u. Decals for boat hull.
v. Annual fee to pro-fisherman Jim Bo Wilks to promote the boats.
w. Paint for boats.
x. Legal department costs for the year.
y. Fiberglass for producing the boat hull.
z. Salary of president of company.

Instructions
Classify each cost as either a product cost or a period cost. Indicate whether each product cost is a direct materials cost, a direct labor cost, or a factory overhead cost. Indicate whether

each period cost is a selling expense or an administrative expense. Use the following tabular headings for your answer, placing an "X" in the appropriate column.

	Product Costs			Period Costs	
Cost	Direct Materials Cost	Direct Labor Cost	Factory Overhead Cost	Selling Expense	Administrative Expense

PR 16-2A
Classifying costs
obj. 2

The following is a list of costs incurred by several businesses:

a. Cost of dyes used by a clothing manufacturer.
b. Salary of the vice president of manufacturing logistics.
c. Wages of a machine operator on the production line.
d. Travel costs of marketing executives to annual sales meeting.
e. Cost of sewing machine needles used by a shirt manufacturer.
f. Depreciation of microcomputers used in the factory to coordinate and monitor the production schedules.
g. Pens, paper, and other supplies used by the Accounting Department in preparing various managerial reports.
h. Electricity used to operate factory machinery.
i. Factory janitorial supplies.
j. Fees paid to lawn service for office grounds upkeep.
k. Wages of computer programmers for production of microcomputer software.
l. Depreciation of copying machines used by the Marketing Department.
m. Telephone charges by president's office.
n. Cost of plastic for a telephone being manufactured.
o. Oil lubricants for factory plant and equipment.
p. Cost of a 30-second television commercial.
q. Depreciation of robot used to assemble a product.
r. Wages of production quality control personnel.
s. Maintenance and repair costs for factory equipment.
t. Depreciation of tools used in production.
u. Rent for a warehouse used to store finished products.
v. Maintenance costs for factory equipment.
w. Fees charged by collection agency on past-due customer accounts.
x. Charitable contribution to United Fund.

Instructions
Classify each of the preceding costs as product costs or period costs. Indicate whether each product cost is a direct materials cost, a direct labor cost, or a factory overhead cost. Indicate whether each period cost is a selling expense or an administrative expense. Use the following tabular headings for preparing your answer, placing an "X" in the appropriate column.

	Product Costs			Period Costs	
Cost	Direct Materials Cost	Direct Labor Cost	Factory Overhead Cost	Selling Expense	Administrative Expense

PR 16-3A
*Cost classifications—
service company*
obj. 2

A partial list of Highland Medical Center's costs is provided below.

a. Depreciation of X-ray equipment.
b. Cost of drugs used for patients.
c. Nurses' salaries.
d. Cost of new heart wing.
e. Overtime incurred in the Records Department due to a computer failure.

f. Cost of patient meals.
g. General maintenance of the hospital.
h. Salary of the nutritionist.
i. Cost of maintaining the staff and visitors' cafeteria.
j. Training costs for nurses.
k. Operating room supplies used on patients (catheters, sutures, etc.).
l. Utility costs of the hospital.
m. Cost of intravenous solutions.
n. Cost of blood tests.
o. Cost of improvements on the employee parking lot.
p. Cost of laundry services for operating room personnel.
q. Depreciation on patient rooms.
r. Cost of advertising hospital services on television.
s. Cost of X-ray test.
t. Salary of intensive care personnel.
u. Doctor's fee.

Instructions
1. What would be Highland's most logical definition for the final cost object?
2. Identify how each of the costs is to be classified as either direct or indirect. Define direct costs in terms of a patient as a cost object.

PR 16-4A
Manufacturing income statement, statement of cost of goods manufactured

objs. 2, 3

✓ *1. c. Vinston, $301,000*

Several items are omitted from each of the following income statement and cost of goods manufactured statement data for the month of December 2008:

	Vinston Company	Turkun Company
Materials inventory, December 1	$ 25,000	$ 32,000
Materials inventory, December 31	(a)	15,000
Materials purchased	105,000	(a)
Cost of direct materials used in production	120,000	(b)
Direct labor	145,000	95,000
Factory overhead	56,000	42,000
Total manufacturing costs incurred in December	(b)	249,000
Total manufacturing costs	336,000	283,000
Work in process inventory, December 1	45,000	34,000
Work in process inventory, December 31	65,000	(c)
Cost of goods manufactured	(c)	252,000
Finished goods inventory, December 1	84,000	44,000
Finished goods inventory, December 31	74,000	(d)
Sales	425,000	320,000
Cost of goods sold	(d)	254,000
Gross profit	(e)	(e)
Operating expenses	44,000	(f)
Net income	(f)	27,000

Instructions
1. Determine the amounts of the missing items, identifying them by letter.
2. Prepare a statement of cost of goods manufactured for Vinston Company.
3. Prepare an income statement for Vinston Company.

PR 16-5A
Statement of cost of goods manufactured and income statement for a manufacturing company

objs. 2, 3

The following information is available for Sano Instrument Manufacturing Company for 2008:

Inventories	January 1	December 31
Materials	$ 85,000	$105,000
Work in process	120,000	105,000
Finished goods	125,000	110,000

Advertising expense	$ 75,000
Depreciation expense—Office equipment	25,000
Depreciation expense—Factory equipment	16,000
Direct labor	205,000
Heat, light, and power—Factory	6,500
Indirect labor	26,000
Materials purchased during 2008	135,000
Office salaries expense	85,000
Property taxes—Factory	4,500
Property taxes—Headquarters building	15,000
Rent expense—Factory	7,500
Sales	950,000
Sales salaries expense	150,000
Supplies—Factory	3,500
Miscellaneous cost—Factory	4,500

Instructions

1. Prepare the 2008 statement of cost of goods manufactured.
2. Prepare the 2008 income statement.

Problems Series B

PR 16-1B

Classifying costs

obj. 2

The following is a list of costs that were incurred in the production and sale of lawn mowers:

a. Payroll taxes on hourly assembly line employees.
b. Filter for spray gun used to paint the lawn mowers.
c. Cost of boxes used in packaging lawn mowers.
d. Premiums on insurance policy for factory buildings.
e. Gasoline engines used for lawn mowers.
f. Salary of factory supervisor.
g. Tires for lawn mowers.
h. Cost of advertising in a national magazine.
i. Plastic for outside housing of lawn mowers.
j. Salary of quality control supervisor who inspects each lawn mower before it is shipped.
k. Steering wheels for lawn mowers.
l. Cash paid to outside firm for janitorial services for factory.
m. Engine oil used in mower engines prior to shipment.
n. Attorney fees for drafting a new lease for headquarters offices.
o. Maintenance costs for new robotic factory equipment, based upon hours of usage.
p. Straight-line depreciation on the robotic machinery used to manufacture the lawn mowers.
q. License fees for use of patent for lawn mower blade, based upon the number of lawn mowers produced.
r. Telephone charges for controller's office.
s. Paint used to coat the lawn mowers.
t. Steel used in producing the lawn mowers.
u. Commissions paid to sales representatives, based upon the number of lawn mowers sold.
v. Electricity used to run the robotic machinery.
w. Factory cafeteria cashier's wages.
x. Property taxes on the factory building and equipment.
y. Salary of vice president of marketing.
z. Hourly wages of operators of robotic machinery used in production.

Instructions

Classify each cost as either a product cost or a period cost. Indicate whether each product cost is a direct materials cost, a direct labor cost, or a factory overhead cost. Indicate whether each period cost is a selling expense or an administrative expense. Use the following tabular headings for your answer, placing an "X" in the appropriate column.

	Product Costs			Period Costs	
Cost	Direct Materials Cost	Direct Labor Cost	Factory Overhead Cost	Selling Expense	Administrative Expense

PR 16-2B
Classifying costs
obj. 2

The following is a list of costs incurred by several businesses:

a. Packing supplies for products sold.
b. Tires for an automobile manufacturer.
c. Costs for television advertisement.
d. Disk drives for a microcomputer manufacturer.
e. Executive bonus for vice president of marketing.
f. Seed for grain farmer.
g. Wages of a machine operator on the production line.
h. Wages of controller's secretary.
i. Factory operating supplies.
j. First-aid supplies for factory workers.
k. Depreciation of factory equipment.
l. Salary of quality control supervisor.
m. Sales commissions.
n. Maintenance and repair costs for factory equipment.
o. Cost of hogs for meat processor.
p. Health insurance premiums paid for factory workers.
q. Lumber used by furniture manufacturer.
r. Paper used by commercial printer.
s. Hourly wages of warehouse laborers.
t. Paper used by Computer Department in processing various managerial reports.
u. Costs of operating a research laboratory.
v. Entertainment expenses for sales representatives.
w. Cost of telephone operators for a toll-free hotline to help customers operate products.
x. Protective glasses for factory machine operators.

Instructions

Classify each of the preceding costs as product costs or period costs. Indicate whether each product cost is a direct materials cost, a direct labor cost, or a factory overhead cost. Indicate whether each period cost is a selling expense or an administrative expense. Use the following tabular headings for preparing your answer. Place an "X" in the appropriate column.

	Product Costs			Period Costs	
Cost	Direct Materials Cost	Direct Labor Cost	Factory Overhead Cost	Selling Expense	Administrative Expense

PR 16-3B
Cost classifications—service company
obj. 2

A partial list of Heartland Hotel's costs is provided below.

a. Salary of the hotel president.
b. Depreciation of the hotel.
c. Cost of new carpeting.
d. Cost of soaps and shampoos for rooms.
e. Cost of food.
f. Wages of desk clerks.
g. Cost to paint lobby.
h. Cost of advertising in local newspaper.
i. Utility cost.
j. Cost of valet service.
k. General maintenance supplies.
l. Wages of maids.
m. Wages of bellhops.
n. Wages of convention setup employees.
o. Pay-for-view rental costs (in rooms).

(continued)

p. Cost of room minibar supplies.
q. Guest room telephone costs for long-distance calls.
r. Wages of kitchen employees.
s. Cost of laundering towels and bedding.
t. Cost to replace lobby furniture.
u. Training for hotel restaurant servers.
v. Cost to mail a customer survey.
w. Champagne for guests.

Instructions

1. What would be Heartland's most logical definition for the final cost object?
2. Identify how each of the costs is to be classified as either direct or indirect. Define direct costs in terms of a hotel guest as the cost object.

PR 16-4B

Manufacturing income statement, statement of cost of goods manufactured

objs. 2, 3

✓ *1. c. Washington, $515,000*

Several items are omitted from each of the following income statement and cost of goods manufactured statement data for the month of December 2008:

	Washington Company	Lee Company
Materials inventory, December 1	$ 65,000	$ 85,000
Materials inventory, December 31	(a)	95,000
Materials purchased	165,000	190,000
Cost of direct materials used in production	174,000	(a)
Direct labor	245,000	(b)
Factory overhead	76,000	95,000
Total manufacturing costs incurred during December	(b)	550,000
Total manufacturing costs	620,000	755,000
Work in process inventory, December 1	125,000	205,000
Work in process inventory, December 31	105,000	(c)
Cost of goods manufactured	(c)	545,000
Finished goods inventory, December 1	110,000	95,000
Finished goods inventory, December 31	115,000	(d)
Sales	950,000	850,000
Cost of goods sold	(d)	551,000
Gross profit	(e)	(e)
Operating expenses	125,000	(f)
Net income	(f)	189,000

Instructions

1. Determine the amounts of the missing items, identifying them by letter.
2. Prepare a statement of cost of goods manufactured for Lee Company.
3. Prepare an income statement for Lee Company.

PR 16-5B

Statement of cost of goods manufactured and income statement for a manufacturing company

objs. 2, 3

The following information is available for Earp Corporation for 2008:

Inventories	January 1	December 31
Materials	$125,000	$155,000
Work in process	225,000	210,000
Finished goods	215,000	210,000

Advertising expense	$ 105,000
Depreciation expense—Office equipment	15,000
Depreciation expense—Factory equipment	20,000
Direct labor	240,000
Heat, light, and power—Factory	8,000
Indirect labor	28,000
Materials purchased during 2008	235,000
Office salaries expense	82,000
Property taxes—Factory	6,500
Property taxes—Office building	13,500
Rent expense—Factory	11,000
Sales	1,100,000
Sales salaries expense	135,000
Supplies—Factory	5,500
Miscellaneous cost—Factory	3,400

Instructions
1. Prepare the 2008 statement of cost of goods manufactured.
2. Prepare the 2008 income statement.

Special Activities

SA 16-1
Ethics and professional conduct in business

ETHICS

Farrar Manufacturing Company allows employees to purchase, at cost, manufacturing materials, such as metal and lumber, for personal use. To purchase materials for personal use, an employee must complete a materials requisition form, which must then be approved by the employee's immediate supervisor. Peggy Carron, an assistant cost accountant, charges the employee an amount based on Farrar's net purchase cost.

Peggy Carron is in the process of replacing a deck on her home and has requisitioned lumber for personal use, which has been approved in accordance with company policy. In computing the cost of the lumber, Peggy reviewed all the purchase invoices for the past year. She then used the lowest price to compute the amount due the company for the lumber.

➤ Discuss whether Peggy behaved in an ethical manner.

SA 16-2
Financial vs. managerial accounting

The following statement was made by the vice president of finance of Haberman Inc.: "The managers of a company should use the same information as the shareholders of the firm. When managers use the same information in guiding their internal operations as shareholders use in evaluating their investments, the managers will be aligned with the stockholders' profit objectives."

➤ Respond to the vice president's statement.

SA 16-3
Managerial accounting in the management process

For each of the following managers, describe how managerial accounting could be used to satisfy strategic or operational objectives:

1. ➤ The vice president of the Information Systems Division of a bank.
2. ➤ A hospital administrator.
3. ➤ The chief executive officer of a food company. The food company is divided into three divisions: Nonalcoholic Beverages, Snack Foods, and Fast-Food Restaurants.
4. ➤ The manager of the local campus copy shop.

SA 16-4
Classifying costs

On-Time Computer Repairs provides computer repair services for the community. Laurie Estes's computer was not working, and she called On-Time for a home repair visit. The On-Time technician arrived at 2:00 P.M. to begin work. By 4:00 P.M. the problem was diagnosed as a failed circuit board. Unfortunately, the technician did not have a new circuit board in the truck, since the technician's previous customer had the same problem, and a board was used on that visit. Replacement boards were available back at the On-Time shop. Therefore, the technician drove back to the shop to retrieve a replacement board. From 4:00 to 5:00 P.M., the On-Time technician drove the round trip to retrieve the replacement board from the shop.

At 5:00 P.M. the technician was back on the job at Laurie's home. The replacement procedure is somewhat complex, since a variety of tests must be performed once the board is installed. The job was completed at 6:00 P.M.

Laurie's repair bill showed the following:

Circuit board	$ 80
Labor charges	190
Total	$270

Laurie was surprised at the size of the bill and asked for some greater detail supporting the calculations. On-Time responded with the following explanations:

Cost of materials:

Purchase price of circuit board	$60
Markup on purchase price to cover storage and handling	20
Total materials charge	$80

The labor charge per hour is detailed as follows:

2:00–3:00 P.M.	$ 40
3:00–4:00 P.M.	35
4:00–5:00 P.M.	45
5:00–6:00 P.M.	70
Total labor charge	$190

Further explanations in the differences in the hourly rates are as follows:

First hour:

Base labor rate	$20
Fringe benefits	7
Overhead (other than storage and handling)	8
Total base labor rate	$35
Additional charge for first hour of any job to cover the cost of vehicle depreciation, fuel, and employee time in transit. A 30-minute transit time is assumed.	5
	$40

Third hour:

Base labor rate	$35
The trip back to the shop includes vehicle depreciation and fuel; therefore, a charge was added to the hourly rate to cover these costs. The round trip took an hour.	10
	$45

Fourth hour:

Base labor rate	$35
Overtime premium for time worked in excess of an eight-hour day (starting at 5:00 P.M.) is equal to the base rate.	35
	$70

1. If you were in Laurie's position, how would you respond to the bill? Are there parts of the bill that appear incorrect to you? If so, what argument would you employ to convince On-Time that the bill is too high?
2. Use the headings below to construct a table. Fill in the table by first listing the costs identified in the activity in the left-hand column. For each cost, place a check mark in the appropriate column identifying the correct cost classification. Assume that each service call is a job.

Cost	Direct Materials	Direct Labor	Overhead

SA 16-5
Using managerial accounting information

The following situations describe decision scenarios that could use managerial accounting information:

1. The manager of Taco Castle wishes to determine the price to charge for various lunch plates.
2. By evaluating the cost of leftover materials, the plant manager of a precision machining facility wishes to determine how effectively the plant is being run.
3. The division controller needs to determine the cost of products left in inventory.
4. The manager of the Maintenance Department wishes to plan next year's anticipated expenditures.

For each situation, discuss how managerial accounting information could be used.

SA 16-6
Classifying costs

Group Project

With a group of students, visit a local copy and graphics shop or a pizza restaurant. As you observe the operation, consider the costs associated with running the business. As a group, identify as many costs as you can and classify them according to the following table headings:

Cost	Direct Materials	Direct Labor	Overhead	Selling Expenses

Answers to Self-Examination Questions

1. **B** Managerial accounting is not restricted to generally accepted accounting principles, as is financial accounting (answer B). Both financial and managerial accounting support decision making (answer A). Financial accounting is mostly concerned with the decision making of external users, while managerial accounting supports decision making of management. Both financial and managerial accounting can result in financial reports (answer C). Managerial accounting reports are developed for internal use by managers at various levels in the organization. Both managerial and financial accounting record events from the past (answer D); however, managerial accounting can also include information about the future in the form of budgets and cash flow projections.

2. **D** The five basic phases of the management process are planning (answer A), directing (not listed), controlling (answer B), improving (not listed), and decision making (answer C). Operating (answer D) is not one of the five basic phases, but operations are the object of managers' attention.

3. **C** Sales salaries (answer C) is a selling expense and is not considered a cost of manufacturing a product. Direct materials cost (answer A), factory overhead cost (answer B), and direct labor cost (answer D) are costs of manufacturing a product.

4. **B** Depreciation of testing equipment (answer B) is included as part of the factory overhead costs of the microcomputer manufacturer. The cost of memory chips (answer A) and the cost of disk drives (answer D) are both considered a part of direct materials cost. The wages of microcomputer assemblers (answer C) are part of direct labor costs.

5. **C** Cost of goods sold is calculated as follows:

Beginning finished goods inventory	$ 50,000
Add: Cost of goods manufactured	125,000
Less: Ending finished goods inventory	35,000
Cost of goods sold	$140,000

Job Order Cost Systems

©2005 Washburn Guitars

Disturbed | Dan Donegan plays a
Chicago | **Washburn Maya** guitar.
www.washburn.com/donegan

© WASHBURN GUITARS

objectives

After studying this chapter, you should be able to:

1 *Describe accounting systems used by manufacturing businesses.*

2 *Describe and prepare summary journal entries for a job order cost accounting system.*

3 *Use job order cost information for decision making.*

4 *Diagram the flow of costs for a service business that uses a job order cost accounting system.*

Dan Donegan's Guitar

As we discussed in the previous chapter, Dan Donegan of the rock band Disturbed uses a custom-made guitar purchased from Washburn Guitars. In fact, Dan Donegan designed his guitar in partnership with Washburn Guitars, which contributed to Washburn's Maya Series of guitars. The Maya guitar is a precision instrument for which amateurs and professionals are willing to pay between $1,400 and $7,000. In order for Washburn to stay in business, the purchase price of the guitar must be greater than the cost of producing the guitar. So, how does Washburn determine the cost of producing a guitar?

Costs associated with creating a guitar include materials such as wood and strings, the salaries of employees who build the guitar, and factory overhead. To determine the purchase price of Dan's Maya, Washburn identifies and records the costs that go into the guitar during each step of the manufacturing process. As the guitar moves through the production process, the costs of direct materials, direct labor, and factory overhead are recorded. When the guitar is complete, the costs that have been recorded are added up to determine the cost of Dan's unique Maya Series guitar. The company then prices the guitar to achieve a level of profit over the cost of the guitar. In this chapter, we will introduce you to the principles of accounting systems that accumulate costs in the same manner as they were for Dan Donegan's guitar.

Cost Accounting System Overview

objective **1**

Describe accounting systems used by manufacturing businesses.

Managerial accounting provides useful information to managers for planning and controlling operations. For manufacturing operations, developing accurate information on product cost is a primary focus of the managerial accounting system. As described and illustrated in the previous chapter for Legend Guitars, product cost consists of direct materials, direct labor, and factory overhead. These components of product cost and their related inventories for Legend Guitars are summarized in Exhibit 1.

Cost accounting systems accumulate manufacturing costs for the goods that are produced. This product cost information is used by managers to establish product prices, control operations, and develop financial statements. In addition, the cost accounting system improves control by supplying data on the costs incurred by each manufacturing department or process.

There are two main types of cost accounting systems for manufacturing operations: job order cost systems and process cost systems. Each of the two systems is widely used, and any one manufacturer may use more than one type. In this chapter, we will illustrate the job order cost system. In the next chapter, we will illustrate the process cost system.

A **job order cost system** provides a separate record for the cost of each quantity of product that passes through the factory. A particular quantity of product is termed a *job*. A job order cost system is best suited to industries that manufacture custom goods to fill special orders from customers or that produce a wide variety of products for stock. Manufacturers that use a job order cost system are sometimes called *job shops*. An example of a job shop would be an apparel manufacturer, such as Levi Strauss & Co.

Many service firms also use job order cost systems to accumulate the costs associated with providing client services. For example, an accounting firm will accumulate all of the costs associated with a particular client engagement, such as accountant time, copying charges, and travel costs. Recording costs in this manner helps the accounting firm control costs during a client engagement and determines client billing and profitability.

EXHIBIT 1 | Manufacturing Costs and Inventories for Legend Guitars

Product Costs

Direct materials cost	Includes the cost of any material that is an integral part of the final product. For Legend Guitars, this includes the cost of wood used in the neck and body.
Direct labor cost	Includes the wages of each employee who is directly involved in converting materials into the finished product. For Legend Guitars, this includes the costs of wages of employees who assemble the guitars.
Factory overhead cost	Includes costs other than direct materials and direct labor costs that are incurred in the manufacturing process. For Legend Guitars, this includes the costs of sandpaper, buffing compound, glue, and factory utilities.

Inventories

Materials inventory	Includes the materials that have not yet entered the manufacturing process. For Legend Guitars, this includes the product costs; of wood used to make the body and neck of the guitar.
Work in process inventory	Includes the product costs of units that have entered the manufacturing process but have not been completed at the end of the period. For Legend Guitars, this includes the product costs assigned to guitars for which the neck and body have been produced but have not been assembled.
Finished goods inventory	Includes the cost of completed (or finished) products that have not been sold. For Legend Guitars, this includes the product costs assigned to completed guitars that have not yet been sold.

Under a **process cost system**, costs are accumulated for each of the departments or processes within the factory. A process system is best suited for manufacturers of units of product that are not distinguishable from each other during a continuous production process. Examples would be oil refineries, paper producers, chemical processors, aluminum smelters, and food processors.

Job Order Cost Systems for Manufacturing Businesses

objective   2

Describe and prepare summary journal entries for a job order cost accounting system.

In this section, we illustrate the job order cost system for Legend Guitars whose manufacturing process we described and illustrated in the prior chapter. The job order system accumulates manufacturing costs by jobs. At any point in time, some jobs will still be in the process of being manufactured while some jobs will have been completed. For example, although the materials for Jobs 71 and 72 have been added, they are still in the production process and are in Work in Process Inventory as shown in Exhibit 2. In contrast, Jobs 69 and 70 have been completed and are included in Finished Goods Inventory as shown in Exhibit 2. When finished guitars are sold to music stores, their costs are recorded as cost of goods sold.

In a job order cost accounting system, perpetual inventory controlling accounts and subsidiary ledgers are maintained for materials, work in process, and finished goods inventories. Each inventory account is debited for all additions and is credited for all deductions. The balance of each account thus represents the balance on hand.

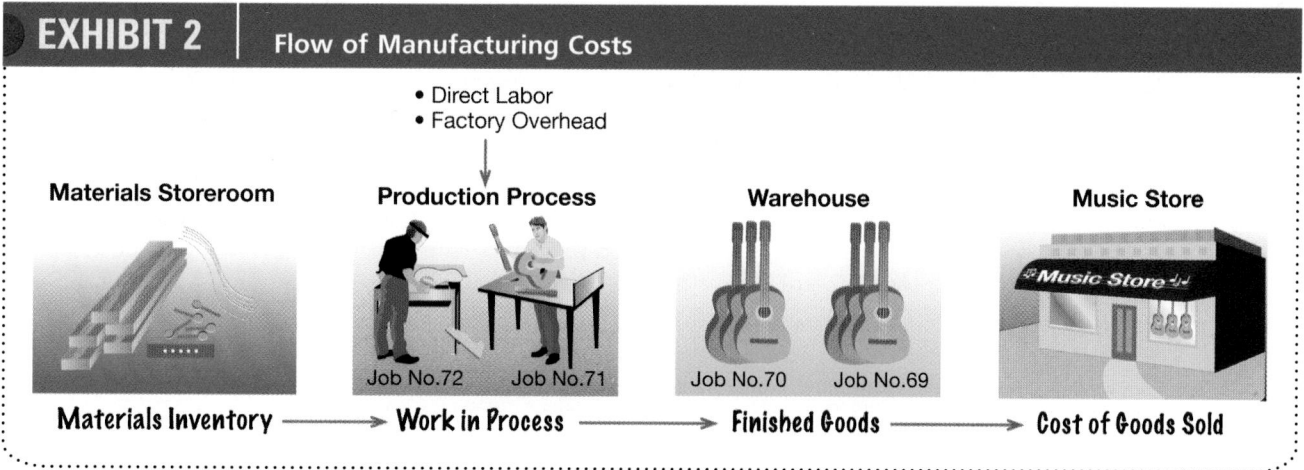

EXHIBIT 2 | Flow of Manufacturing Costs

MATERIALS

The procedures used to purchase, store, and issue materials to production often differ among manufacturers. Exhibit 3 shows the basic information and cost flows for the wood received and issued to production by Legend Guitars.

EXHIBIT 3

Materials Information and Cost Flows

Receiving Report No. 196 ← Supplier Invoice $10,500

MATERIALS LEDGER ACCOUNT

a.

MATERIAL: No. 8 Wood—Maple　　　　ORDER POINT: 500 ft.

RECEIVED			ISSUED			BALANCE			
Rec. Report No.	Quantity	Amount	Mat. Req. No.	Quantity	Amount	Date	Quantity	Amount	Unit Price
						Dec. 1	600	$ 6,000	$10.00
			672	200	$ 2,000	4	400	4,000	10.00
196	750	$10,500				8	400	4,000	10.00
							750	10,500	14.00
			704	900	11,000	12	250	3,500	14.00

Materials Requisitions

b.

MATERIALS REQUISITION

REQUISITION NO.: 672
JOB NO.: 71

Description	Quantity Issued	Unit Price	Amount
No. 8 Wood—Maple	200	$10.00	$2,000
Total Issued			$2,000

b.

MATERIALS REQUISITION

REQUISITION NO.: 704
JOB NO.: 72

Description	Quantity Issued	Unit Price	Amount
No. 8 Wood—Maple	400	$10.00	$ 4,000
No. 8 Wood—Maple	500	14.00	7,000
Total Issued			$11,000

Job Cost Sheets

b.

Job 71
20 units of Jazz Series guitars

Balance, Dec. 1　　　　$3,000

Direct Materials　　　2,000
Direct Labor
Factory Overhead

b.

Job 72
60 units of American Series guitars

Direct Materials　　　$11,000
Direct Labor
Factory Overhead

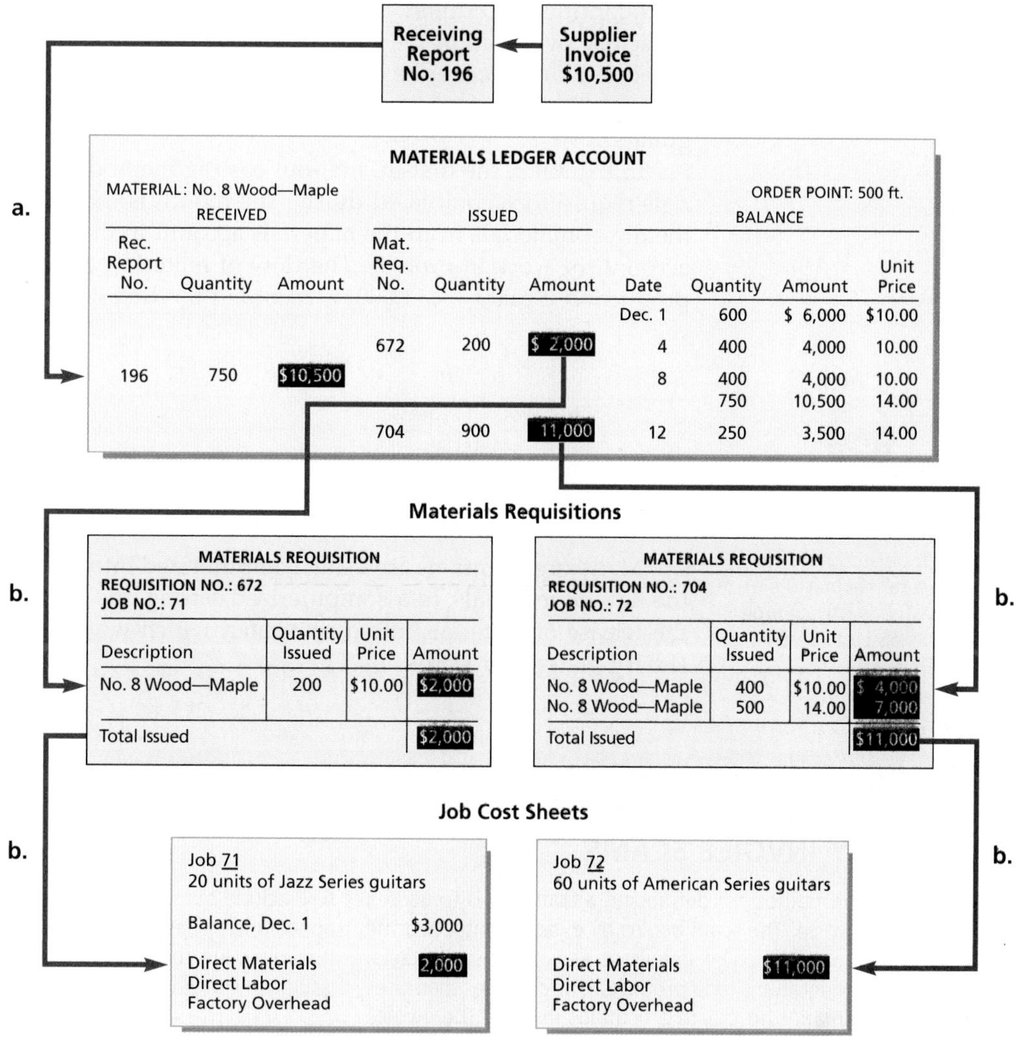

Purchased materials are first received and inspected by the Receiving Department. The Receiving Department personnel prepare a **receiving report**, showing the quantity received and its condition. Some organizations now use bar code scanning devices in place of receiving reports to record and electronically transmit incoming materials data. The receiving information and invoice are used to record the receipt and control the payment for purchased items. The journal entry to record Receiving Report No. 196 in Exhibit 3 is:

a.	Materials		10 5 0 0 00		
	Accounts Payable			10 5 0 0 00	
	Materials purchased during				
	December.				

The materials account in the general ledger is a controlling account. A separate account for each type of material is maintained in a subsidiary **materials ledger**. Details as to the quantity and cost of materials received are recorded in the materials ledger on the basis of the receiving reports. A typical form of a materials ledger account is illustrated in Exhibit 3.

Materials are released from the storeroom to the factory in response to **materials requisitions** from the Production Department. An illustration of a materials requisition is in Exhibit 3. The completed requisition for each job serves as the basis for posting quantities and dollar data to the job cost sheets in the case of direct materials or to factory overhead in the case of indirect materials. **Job cost sheets**, which are illustrated in Exhibit 3, are the work in process subsidiary ledger. For Legend Guitars, Job 71 is for 20 units of Jazz Series guitars, while Job 72 is for 60 units of American Series guitars.

In Exhibit 3, the first-in, first-out costing method is used. A summary of the materials requisitions completed during the month is the basis for transferring the cost of the direct materials from the materials account in the general ledger to the controlling account for work in process. The flow of materials from the materials storeroom into production ($2,000 + $11,000) is recorded by the following entry:

For many manufacturing firms, the direct materials cost can be greater than 50% of the total cost to manufacture a product. This is why controlling materials costs is very important.

b.	Work in Process		13 0 0 0 00		
	Materials			13 0 0 0 00	
	Materials requisitioned to jobs.				

Many organizations are using computerized information processes that account for the flow of materials. In a computerized setting, the storeroom manager would record the release of materials into a computer, which would automatically update the subsidiary materials records.

Integrity, Objectivity, and Ethics in Business

ETHICS

PHONY INVOICE SCAMS

A popular method for defrauding a company is to issue a phony invoice. The scam begins by initially contacting the target firm to discover details of key business contacts, business operations, and products. The swindler then uses this information to create a fictitious invoice. The invoice will include names, figures, and other details to give it the appearance of legitimacy. This type of scam can be avoided if invoices are matched with receiving documents prior to issuing a check.

Example Exercise 17-1

objective **2**

On March 5, Hatch Company purchased 400 units of raw materials at $14 per unit. On March 10, raw materials were requisitioned for production as follows: 200 units for Job 101 at $12 per unit and 300 units for Job 102 at $14 per unit. Journalize the entry on March 5 to record the purchase and on March 10 to record the requisition from the materials storeroom.

Follow My Example 17-1

Mar. 5	Materials	5,600	
	Accounts Payable		5,600
	$5,600 = 400 × $14.		
10	Work in Process	6,600*	
	Materials		6,600

*Job 101 $2,400 = 200 × $12
 Job 102 <u>4,200</u> = 300 × $14
 Total   <u>$6,600</u>

For Practice: PE 17-1A, PE 17-1B

FACTORY LABOR

There are two primary objectives in accounting for factory labor. One objective is to determine the correct amount to be paid each employee for each payroll period. A second objective is to properly allocate factory labor costs to factory overhead and individual job orders.

The amount of time spent by an employee in the factory is usually recorded on *clock cards* or *in-and-out cards*. The amount of time spent by each employee and the labor cost incurred for each individual job are recorded on **time tickets**. Exhibit 4 shows typical time ticket forms and cost flows for direct labor for Legend Guitars.

A summary of the time tickets at the end of each month is the basis for recording the direct and indirect labor costs incurred in production. Direct labor is posted to each job cost sheet, while indirect labor is debited to Factory Overhead.[1] Legend Guitars incurred 350 direct labor hours on Job 71 and 500 direct labor hours on Job 72 during December. The total direct labor costs were $11,000, divided into $3,500 for Job 71 and $7,500 for Job 72. The labor costs that flow into production are recorded by the following summary entry to the work in process controlling account:

c.	Work in Process		11 0 0 0 00	
	Wages Payable			11 0 0 0 00
	Factory labor used in production			
	of jobs.			

As with recording direct materials, many organizations are automating the labor recording process. Employees may log their time directly into computer terminals at their workstations. Alternatively, employees may be issued magnetic cards, much like credit cards, to log in and out of work assignments that are spread across a wide geographical area. For example, Shell Group uses a magnetic card system to track the work of maintenance crews in its refinery operations.

---

1 There are a variety of methods for recording direct labor costs. In the approach illustrated in this chapter, we assume that labor costs are automatically recorded to jobs or factory overhead when incurred. Alternatively, wages could first be debited to Factory Labor when incurred and then later distributed to jobs and factory overhead.

EXHIBIT 4

Labor Information
and Cost Flows

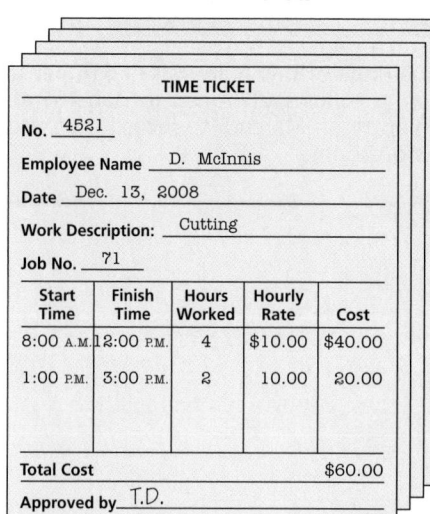

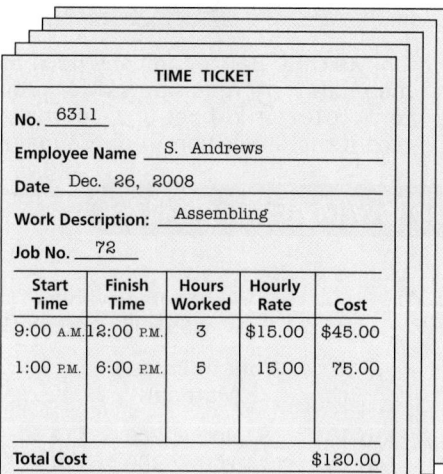

	December Job 71 Hours	350		December Job 72 Hours	500
	December Job 71 Labor Costs:	**$3,500**		December Job 72 Labor Costs:	**$7,500**

Job Cost Sheets

c.

Job 71	
20 units of Jazz Series guitars	
Balance	$3,000
Direct Materials	2,000
Direct Labor	**3,500**
Factory Overhead	

c.

Job 72	
60 units of American Series guitars	
Direct Materials	$11,000
Direct Labor	**7,500**
Factory Overhead	

Example Exercise 17-2   objective 2

During March, Hatch Company accumulated 800 hours of direct labor costs on Job 101 and 600 hours on Job 102. The total direct labor was incurred at a rate of $16 per direct labor hour for Job 101, and $12 per direct labor hour for Job 102. Journalize the entry to record the flow of labor costs into production during March.

Follow My Example 17-2

Work in Process 20,000*
    Wages Payable   20,000

*Job 101 $12,800 = 800 hrs. × $16
 Job 102   7,200 = 600 hrs. × $12
 Total $20,000

For Practice: PE 17-2A, PE 17-2B

Integrity, Objectivity, and Ethics in Business

ETHICS

GHOST EMPLOYEES

Companies must guard against the fraudulent creation and cashing of payroll checks. Numerous payroll frauds involve supervisors adding fictitious employees to the payroll or failing to remove departing employees from the payroll and then cashing the checks. Requiring proper authorization and approval of employee additions, removals, or changes in pay rates can minimize this type of fraud.

FACTORY OVERHEAD COST

Factory overhead includes all manufacturing costs except direct materials and direct labor. Debits to Factory Overhead come from various sources, such as indirect materials, indirect labor, factory power, and factory depreciation. For example, the factory overhead of $4,600 incurred in December for Legend Guitars would be recorded as follows:

d.	Factory Overhead	4 6 0 0 00	
	Materials		5 0 0 00
	Wages Payable		2 0 0 0 00
	Utilities Payable		9 0 0 00
	Accumulated Depreciation		1 2 0 0 00
	Factory overhead incurred in		
	production.		

Example Exercise 17-3
objective 2

During March, Hatch Company incurred factory overhead costs as follows: indirect materials, $800; indirect labor, $3,400; utilities cost, $1,600; and depreciation, $2,500. Journalize the entry to record the factory overhead incurred during March.

Follow My Example 17-3

Factory Overhead	8,300	
Materials...		800
Wages Payable		3,400
Utilities Payable		1,600
Accumulated Depreciation		2,500

For Practice: PE 17-3A, PE 17-3B

Allocating Factory Overhead Factory overhead is much different from direct labor and direct materials because it is indirectly related to the jobs. How, then, do the jobs get assigned a portion of overhead costs? The answer is through **cost allocation**, which is the process of assigning factory overhead costs to a cost object, such as a job. The factory overhead costs are assigned to the jobs on the basis of some known measure about each job. The measure used to allocate factory overhead is frequently called an **activity base**, *allocation base,* or *activity driver.* The estimated activity base should be a measure that reflects the consumption or use of factory overhead cost. For example, the direct labor is recorded for each job using time tickets. Thus, direct labor (hours or cost) could be used to allocate production-related factory overhead costs to each job. Likewise, direct materials costs are known about each job through the materials requisitions. Thus, materials-related factory overhead, such as Purchasing Department salaries, could logically be allocated to the job on the basis of direct materials cost.

Predetermined Factory Overhead Rate To provide current job costs, factory overhead may be allocated or applied to production using a **predetermined factory overhead rate**. The predetermined factory overhead rate is calculated by dividing the estimated amount of factory overhead for the forthcoming year by the estimated activity base, such as machine hours, direct materials costs, direct labor costs, or direct labor hours.

To illustrate calculating a predetermined overhead rate, assume that Legend Guitars estimates the total factory overhead cost to be $50,000 for the year and the activity base to be 10,000 direct labor hours. The predetermined factory overhead rate would be calculated as $5 per direct labor hour, as follows:

$$\text{Predetermined Factory Overhead Rate} = \frac{\text{Estimated Total Factory Overhead Costs}}{\text{Estimated Activity Base}}$$

$$\text{Predetermined Factory Overhead Rate} = \frac{\$50,000}{10,000 \text{ direct labor hours}} = \$5 \text{ per direct labor hour}$$

Why is the predetermined overhead rate calculated from estimated numbers at the beginning of the period? The answer is to ensure timely information. If a company waited until the end of an accounting period when all overhead costs are known, the allocated factory overhead would be accurate but not timely. If the cost system is to have maximum usefulness, cost data should be available as each job is completed, even though there may be a small sacrifice in accuracy. Only through timely reporting can management make needed adjustments in pricing or in manufacturing methods and achieve the best possible combination of revenue and cost on future jobs.

A number of companies are using a new product-costing approach called activity-based costing. **Activity-based costing** is a method of accumulating and allocating factory overhead costs to products, using many overhead rates. Each rate is related to separate factory activities, such as inspecting, moving, and machining. Activity-based costing is discussed and illustrated in a later chapter of this textbook.

Applying Factory Overhead to Work in Process As factory overhead costs are incurred, they are debited to the factory overhead account, as shown previously in transaction (d). For Legend Guitars, factory overhead costs are applied to production at the rate of $5 per direct labor hour. The amount of factory overhead applied to each job would be recorded in the job cost sheets as shown in Exhibit 5. For example, the 850 direct labor hours used in Legend's December operations would all be traced to individual jobs. Job 71 used 350 labor hours, so $1,750 (350 × $5) of factory overhead would be applied to Job 71. Similarly, $2,500 (500 × $5) of factory overhead would be applied to Job 72.

The factory overhead costs applied to production are periodically debited to the work in process account and credited to the factory overhead account. The summary entry to apply the $4,250 ($1,750 + $2,500) of factory overhead is as follows:

e.	Work in Process		4 2 5 0 00	
	Factory Overhead			4 2 5 0 00
	Factory overhead applied to jobs			
	according to the predetermined			
	overhead rate.			

The factory overhead costs applied and the actual factory overhead costs incurred during a period will usually differ. If the amount applied exceeds the actual costs incurred, the factory overhead account will have a credit balance. This credit is described as **overapplied** or overabsorbed **factory overhead**. If the amount applied is less than the actual costs incurred, the account will have a debit balance. This debit is described as **underapplied** or underabsorbed **factory overhead**. Both cases are illustrated in the following account for Legend Guitars:

ACCOUNT Factory Overhead					ACCOUNT NO.	
Date	Item	Post. Ref.	Debit	Credit	Balance Debit	Balance Credit
Dec. 1	Balance					2 0 0 00
31	Factory overhead cost incurred		4 6 0 0 00		4 4 0 0 00	
31	Factory overhead cost applied			4 2 5 0 00	1 5 0 00	

Underapplied balance
Overapplied balance

EXHIBIT 5

Assigning Factory
Overhead to Jobs

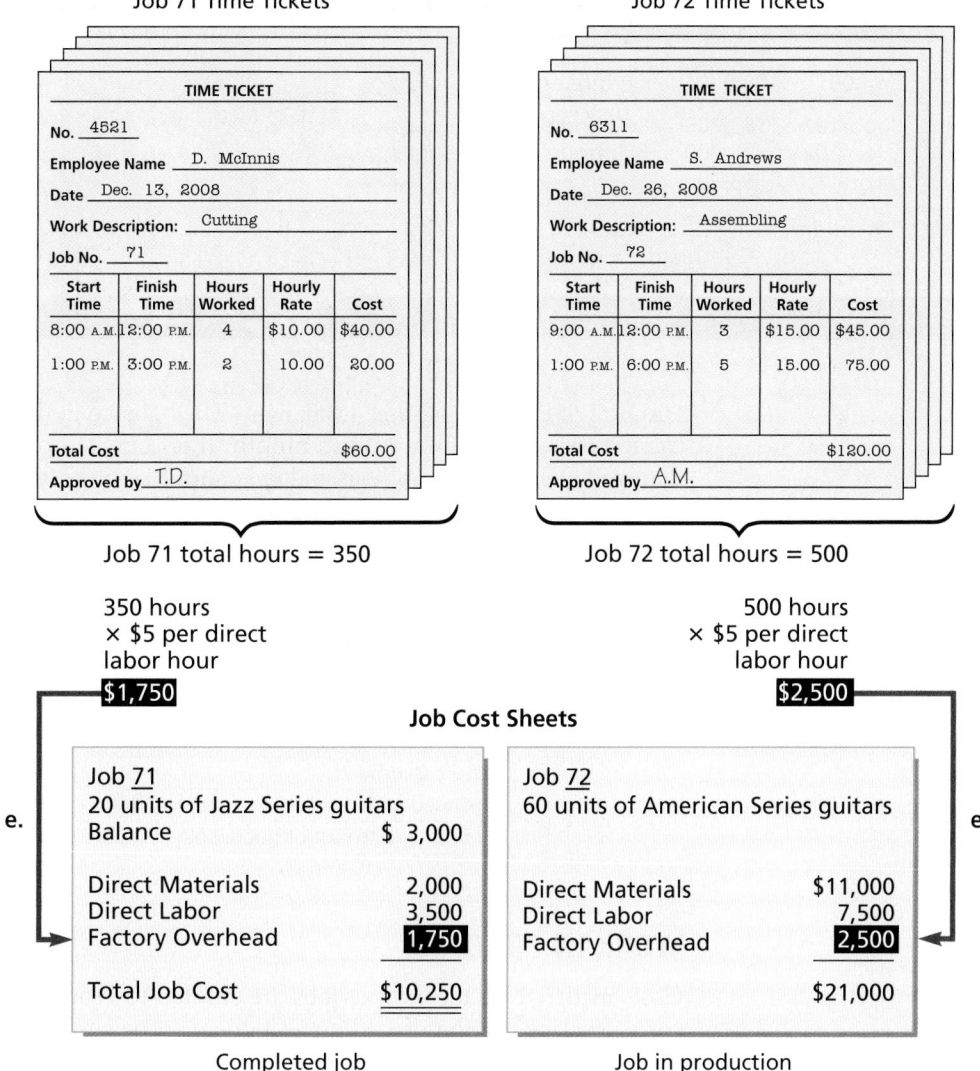

Job 71 Time Tickets

TIME TICKET

No. 4521

Employee Name D. McInnis

Date Dec. 13, 2008

Work Description: Cutting

Job No. 71

Start Time	Finish Time	Hours Worked	Hourly Rate	Cost
8:00 A.M.	12:00 P.M.	4	$10.00	$40.00
1:00 P.M.	3:00 P.M.	2	10.00	20.00
Total Cost				$60.00

Approved by T.D.

Job 71 total hours = 350

350 hours
× $5 per direct
labor hour
$1,750

Job 72 Time Tickets

TIME TICKET

No. 6311

Employee Name S. Andrews

Date Dec. 26, 2008

Work Description: Assembling

Job No. 72

Start Time	Finish Time	Hours Worked	Hourly Rate	Cost
9:00 A.M.	12:00 P.M.	3	$15.00	$45.00
1:00 P.M.	6:00 P.M.	5	15.00	75.00
Total Cost				$120.00

Approved by A.M.

Job 72 total hours = 500

500 hours
× $5 per direct
labor hour
$2,500

Job Cost Sheets

e.

Job 71	
20 units of Jazz Series guitars	
Balance	$ 3,000
Direct Materials	2,000
Direct Labor	3,500
Factory Overhead	1,750
Total Job Cost	$10,250

Completed job

e.

Job 72	
60 units of American Series guitars	
Direct Materials	$11,000
Direct Labor	7,500
Factory Overhead	2,500
	$21,000

Job in production

If the underapplied or overapplied balance increases in only one direction and it becomes large, the balance and the overhead rate should be investigated. For example, if a large balance is caused by changes in manufacturing methods or in production goals, the factory overhead rate should be revised. On the other hand, a large underapplied balance may indicate a serious control problem caused by inefficiencies in production methods, excessive costs, or a combination of factors.

Example Exercise 17-4

objective **2**

Hatch Company estimates that total factory overhead costs will be $100,000 for the year. Direct labor hours are estimated to be 25,000. For Hatch Company, (a) determine the predetermined factory overhead rate, (b) determine the amount of factory overhead applied to Jobs 101 and 102 in March using the data on direct labor hours from Example Exercise 17-2, and (c) prepare the journal entry to apply factory overhead to both jobs in March according to the predetermined overhead rate.

(continued)

a. $4.00 = $100,000/25,000 direct labor hours

b.   Job 101 $3,200 = 800 hours × $4.00 per hour
     Job 102   2,400 = 600 hours × $4.00 per hour
     Total $5,600

c.   Work in Process   5,600
        Factory Overhead   5,600

For Practice: PE 17-4A, PE 17-4B

Disposal of Factory Overhead Balance   The balance in the factory overhead account is carried forward from month to month. It is reported on interim balance sheets as a deferred debit or credit. This balance should not be carried over to the next year, however, since it applies to the operations of the year just ended.

One approach for disposing of the balance of factory overhead at the end of the year is to transfer the entire balance to the cost of goods sold account.[2] To illustrate, the journal entry to eliminate Legend Guitars' underapplied overhead balance of $150 at the end of the calendar year would be as follows:

f.	Cost of Goods Sold		1 5 0 00	
	Factory Overhead			1 5 0 00
	Closed underapplied factory			
	overhead to cost of goods sold.			

WORK IN PROCESS

Costs incurred for the various jobs are debited to Work in Process. Legend Guitars' job costs described in the preceding sections may be summarized as follows:

■ **Direct materials, $13,000**—Work in Process debited and Materials credited [transaction (b)]; data obtained from summary of materials requisitions.

■ **Direct labor, $11,000**—Work in Process debited and Wages Payable credited [transaction (c)]; data obtained from summary of time tickets.

■ **Factory overhead, $4,250**—Work in Process debited and Factory Overhead credited [transaction (e)]; data obtained from summary of time tickets.

The details concerning the costs incurred on each job order are accumulated in the job cost sheets. Exhibit 6 illustrates the relationship between the job cost sheets and the work in process controlling account.

In this example, Job 71 was started in November and completed in December. The beginning December balance for Job 71 represents the costs carried over from the end of November. Job 72 was started in December but was not yet completed at the end of the month. Thus, the balance of the incomplete Job 72, or $21,000, will be shown on the balance sheet on December 31 as work in process inventory.

When Job 71 was completed, the direct materials costs, the direct labor costs, and the factory overhead costs were totaled and divided by the number of units produced to determine the cost per unit. If we assume that 20 units of Jazz Series guitars were produced for Job 71, then the unit cost would be $512.50 ($10,250/20).

---

2 Alternatively, the balance may be allocated among the work in process, finished goods, and cost of goods sold balances. This approach brings the accounts into agreement with the costs actually incurred. Since this approach is a more complex calculation that adds little additional accuracy, it will not be used in this text.

Job Cost Sheets

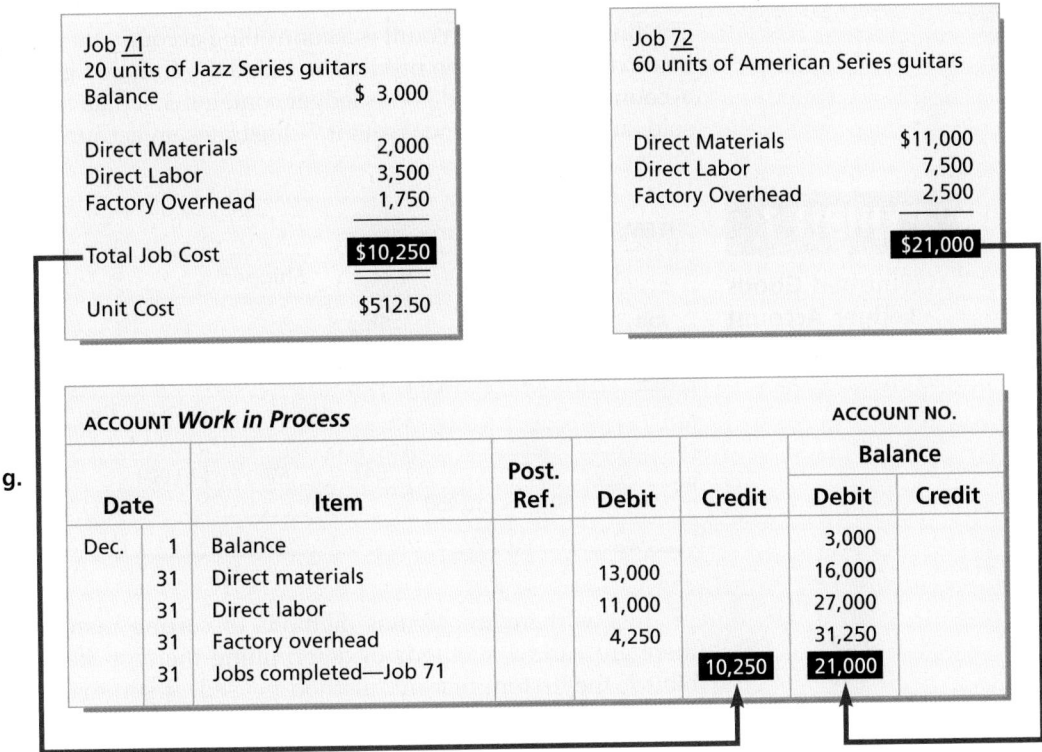

EXHIBIT 6

Job Cost Sheets and
the Work in Process
Controlling Account

Upon completing Job 71, the job cost sheet was removed from the cost ledger and filed for future reference. At the end of the accounting period (December), the total costs for all completed jobs during the period are determined, and the following entry is made:

		Debit	Credit
g.	Finished Goods	10 2 5 0 00	
	Work in Process		10 2 5 0 00
	Job 71 completed in December.		

Example Exercise 17-5   objective 2

At the end of March, Hatch Company had completed Jobs 101 and 102. Job 101 is for 500 units, and Job 102 is for 1,000 units. Using the data from Example Exercises 17-1, 17-2, and 17-4, determine (a) the balance on the job cost sheets for Jobs 101 and 102 at the end of March and (b) the cost per unit for Jobs 101 and 102 at the end of March.

Follow My Example 17-5

a.

	Job 101	Job 102
Direct materials	$ 2,400	$ 4,200
Direct labor	12,800	7,200
Factory overhead	3,200	2,400
Total costs	$18,400	$13,800

b. Job 101 $36.80 = $18,400/500 units
    Job 102 $13.80 = $13,800/1,000 units

For Practice: PE 17-5A, PE 17-5B

FINISHED GOODS AND COST OF GOODS SOLD

The finished goods account is a controlling account. Its related subsidiary ledger, which has an account for each product, is called the **finished goods ledger** or *stock ledger*. Each account in the finished goods ledger contains cost data for the units manufactured, units sold, and units on hand. Exhibit 7 illustrates an account in the finished goods ledger.

EXHIBIT 7

Finished Goods
Ledger Account

ITEM: *Jazz Series guitars*

Manufactured			Shipped			Balance			
Job Order No.	Quantity	Amount	Ship Order No.	Quantity	Amount	Date	Quantity	Amount	Unit Cost
						Dec. 1	40	$20,000	$500.00
			643	40	$20,000	9	—	—	—
71	20	$10,250				31	20	10,250	512.50

Just as there are various methods of costing materials entering into production, there are various methods of determining the cost of the finished goods sold. In Exhibit 7, the first-in, first-out method is used. A summary of the cost data for the units shipped ($20,000) becomes the basis for the following entry:

h.	Cost of Goods Sold		20 0 0 0 00	
	Finished Goods			20 0 0 0 00
	Cost of 40 Jazz Series guitars sold.			

SALES

The selling price of the goods sold is recorded by debiting Accounts Receivable (or Cash) and crediting Sales. To illustrate, assume that Legend Guitars sold the 40 Jazz Series guitars during December for $850 per unit. The entry to the accounts receivable controlling account would be:

i.	Accounts Receivable		34 0 0 0 00	
	Sales			34 0 0 0 00
	Revenue received from guitars sold.			

PERIOD COSTS

In addition to product costs (direct materials, direct labor, and factory overhead), businesses also have period costs. Recall from the previous chapter that **period costs** are expenses that are used in generating revenue during the current period and are not involved in the manufacturing process. Period costs are generally classified into two categories: selling and administrative. *Selling expenses* are incurred in marketing the product and delivering the sold product to customers. *Administrative expenses* are incurred in the administration of the business and are not related to the manufacturing or selling functions.

For Legend Guitars, the following selling and administrative expenses were recorded for December:

j.	Sales Salaries Expense		2 0 0 0 00	
	Office Salaries Expense		1 5 0 0 00	
	Salaries Payable			3 5 0 0 00
	Recorded December period costs.			

SUMMARY OF COST FLOWS FOR LEGEND GUITARS

Exhibit 8, on page 764, shows the cost flow through the manufacturing accounts, together with summary details of the subsidiary ledgers for Legend Guitars. Entries in the accounts are identified by letters that refer to the summary journal entries introduced in the preceding section.

The balances of the general ledger controlling accounts are supported by their respective subsidiary ledgers. The balances of the three inventory accounts—Finished Goods, Work in Process, and Materials—represent the respective ending inventories of December 31 on the balance sheet. These balances are as follows:

Materials	$ 3,500
Work in process	21,000
Finished goods	10,250

The income statement for Legend Guitars would be as shown in Exhibit 9.

EXHIBIT 9

Income Statement of Legend Guitars

Legend Guitars Income Statement For the Month Ended December 31, 2008		
Sales		$34,000
Cost of goods sold		20,150
Gross profit		$13,850
Selling and administrative expenses:		
Sales salaries expense	$2,000	
Office salaries expense	1,500	
Total selling and administrative expenses		3,500
Income from operations		$10,350

EXHIBIT 8   Flow of Manufacturing Costs for Legend Guitars

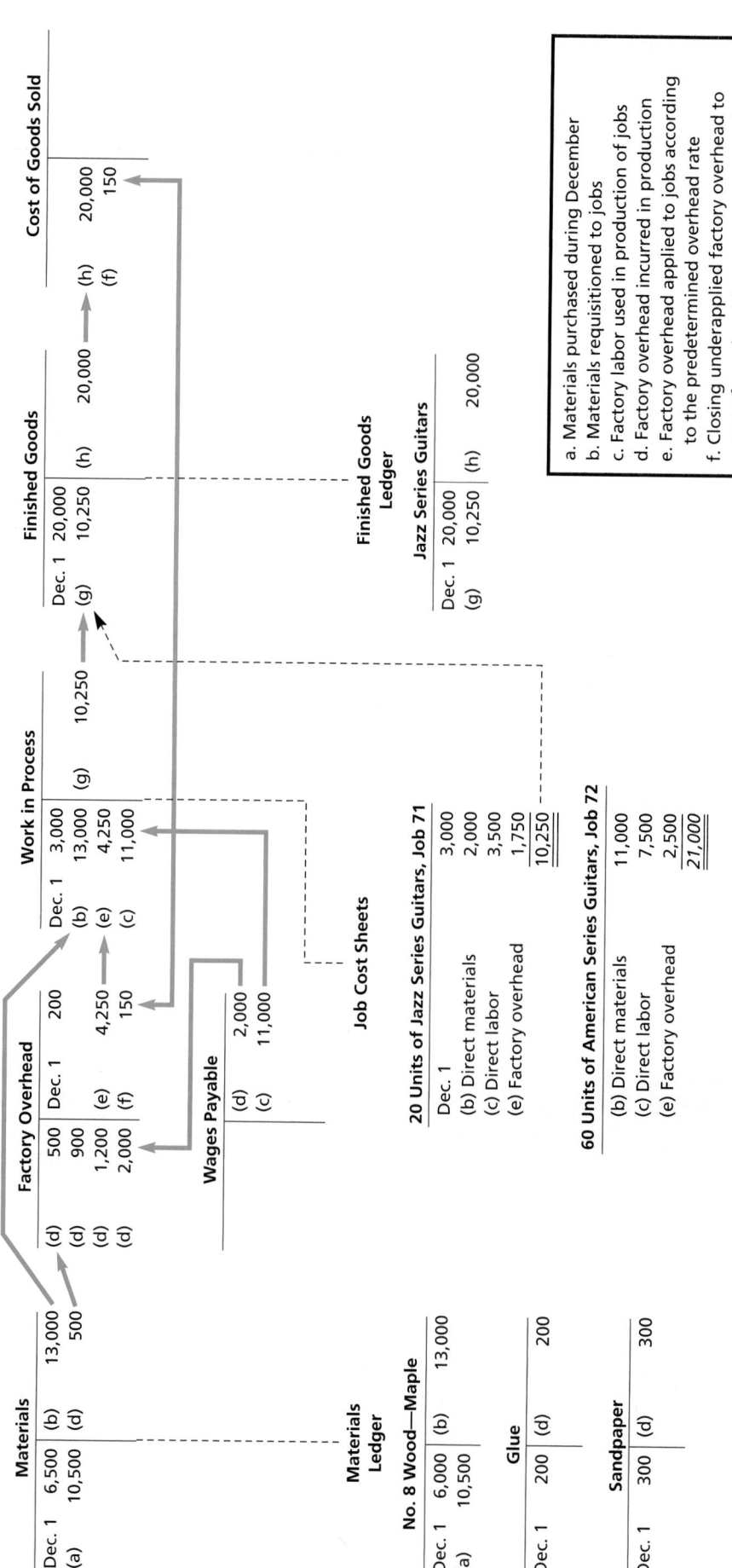

a. Materials purchased during December
b. Materials requisitioned to jobs
c. Factory labor used in production of jobs
d. Factory overhead incurred in production
e. Factory overhead applied to jobs according to the predetermined overhead rate
f. Closing underapplied factory overhead to cost of goods sold
g. Job 71 completed in December
h. Cost of 40 units of Jazz Series guitars sold

Job Order Costing for Decision Making

objective 3

Use job order cost information for decision making.

Major electric utilities such as Tennessee Valley Authority, Consolidated Edison Inc., and Pacific Gas and Electric Company use job order accounting to control the costs associated with major repairs and overhauls that occur during maintenance shutdowns.

The job order cost system that we developed in the previous sections can be used to evaluate an organization's cost performance. The unit costs for similar jobs can be compared over time to determine if costs are staying within expected ranges. If costs increase for some unexpected reason, the details in the job cost sheets can help discover the reasons.

To illustrate, Exhibit 10 shows the direct materials on the job cost sheets for Jobs 54 and 63 for Legend Guitars. The wood used in manufacturing guitars is measured in board feet. Since both job cost sheets refer to the same type and number of guitars, the direct materials cost per unit should be about the same. However, the materials cost per guitar for Job 54 is $100, while for Job 63 it is $125. The materials costs have increased since the guitars were produced for Job 54.

Job cost sheets can be used to investigate possible reasons for the increased cost. First, you should note that the price for direct materials did not change. Thus, the cost increase is not related to increasing prices. What about the wood consumption? This tells us a different story. The quantity of wood used to produce 40 guitars in Job 54 is 400 board feet. However, Job 63 required 500 board feet for the same number of guitars. How can this be explained? Any one of the following explanations is possible and could be investigated further:

1. There was a new employee that was not adequately trained for cutting the wood for guitars. As a result, the employee improperly cut and scrapped many pieces.
2. The lumber was of poor quality. As a result, the cutting operator ended up using and scrapping additional pieces of lumber.
3. The cutting tools were in need of repair. As a result, the cutting operators miscut and scrapped many pieces of wood.
4. The operator was careless. As a result of poor work, many pieces of cut wood had to be scrapped.
5. The instructions attached to the job were incorrect. The operator cut wood according to the instructions but discovered that the pieces would not fit. As a result, many pieces had to be scrapped.

You should note that many of these explanations are not necessarily related to operator error. Poor cost performance may be the result of root causes that are outside the control of the operator.

EXHIBIT 10

Comparing Data from Job Cost Sheets

Job 54
Item: 40 Jazz Series guitars

	Materials Quantity (board feet)	Materials Price	Materials Amount
Direct materials:			
No. 8 Wood—Maple	400	$10.00	$4,000
Direct materials per guitar			$100

Job 63
Item: 40 Jazz Series guitars

	Materials Quantity (board feet)	Materials Price	Materials Amount
Direct materials:			
No. 8 Wood—Maple	500	$10.00	$5,000
Direct materials per guitar			$125

Job Order Cost Systems for Professional Service Businesses

objective *4*

Diagram the flow of costs for a service business that uses a job order cost accounting system.

A job order cost accounting system may be useful to the management of a professional service business in planning and controlling operations. For example, an advertising agency, an attorney, and a physician all share the common characteristic of providing services to individual customers, clients, or patients. In such cases, the customer, client, or patient can be viewed as an individual job for which costs are accumulated.

Since the "product" of a service business is service, management's focus is on direct labor and overhead costs. The cost of any materials or supplies used in rendering services for a client is usually small and is normally included as part of the overhead.

The direct labor and overhead costs of rendering services to clients are accumulated in a work in process account. This account is supported by a cost ledger. A job cost sheet is used to accumulate the costs for each client's job. When a job is completed and the client is billed, the costs are transferred to a cost of services account. This account is similar to the cost of merchandise sold account for a merchandising business or the cost of goods sold account for a manufacturing business. A finished goods account and related finished goods ledger are not necessary, since the revenues associated with the services are recorded after the services have been provided. The flow of costs through a service business using a job order cost accounting system is shown in Exhibit 11.

EXHIBIT 11   Flow of Costs Through a Service Business

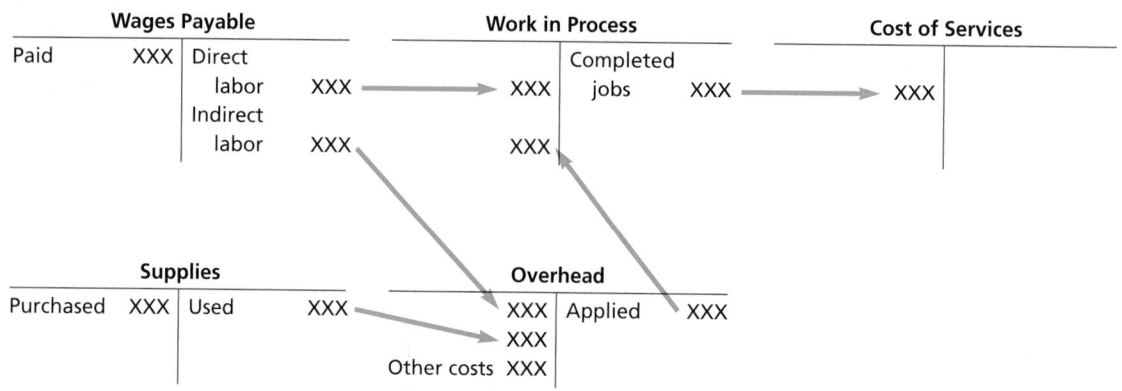

In practice, additional accounting considerations unique to service businesses may need to be considered. For example, a service business may bill clients on a weekly or monthly basis rather than waiting until a job is completed. In these situations, a portion of the costs related to each billing should be transferred from the work in process account to the cost of services account. A service business may also have advance billings that would be accounted for as deferred revenue until the services have been completed.

Business Connections

MAKING MONEY IN THE MOVIE BUSINESS

Movie making is a high risk venture. The movie must be produced and marketed before one dollar is received from the box office. If the movie is a hit, then all is well; but if the movie is a bomb, money will be lost. This is termed a "Blockbuster" business strategy and is common in businesses that have large up-front costs in the face of uncertain follow-up revenues, such as pharmaceuticals, video games, and publishing.

The profitability of a movie depends on its revenue and cost. A movie's cost is determined using job order costing; however, how costs are assigned to a movie is often complex and may be subject to disagreement. For example, in Hollywood's competitive environment, studios often negotiate payments to producers and actors based on a percentage of the film's

gross revenues. This is termed "contingent compensation." As movies become hits, compensation costs increase in proportion to the movie's revenues, which eats into a hit's profitability.

As the dollars involved get bigger, disagreements often develop between movie studios and actors or producers over the amount of contingent compensation. For example, the producer of the 2002 hit movie *Chicago* sued Miramax Film Corp. for failing to include foreign receipts and DVD sales in the revenue that was used to determine his payments. The controversial nature of contingent compensation is illustrated by the suit's claim that the accounting for contingent compensation leads to confusing and meaningless results.

At a Glance

1. Describe accounting systems used by manufacturing businesses.

Key Points	Key Learning Outcomes	Example Exercises	Practice Exercises
A cost accounting system accumulates product costs. Management uses cost accounting systems to determine product cost, establish product prices, control operations, and develop financial statements. The two primary cost accounting systems are job order and process cost systems. Job order cost systems accumulate costs for each quantity of product that passes through the factory. Process cost systems accumulate costs for each department or process within the factory.	• Describe a cost accounting system. • Describe a job order cost system. • Describe a process cost system.		

(continued)

2. Describe and prepare summary journal entries for a job order cost accounting system.

Key Points	Key Learning Outcomes	Example Exercises	Practice Exercises
A job order cost system accumulates costs for each quantity of product, or "job," that passes through the factory. Direct materials, direct labor, and factory overhead are accumulated on the job cost sheet, which is the subsidiary cost ledger for each job. Direct materials and direct labor are assigned to individual jobs based on the quantity used. Factory overhead costs are assigned to each job based on an activity base that reflects the use of factory overhead costs. As a job is finished, its costs are transferred to the finished goods ledger. When goods are sold, the cost is transferred from finished goods inventory to cost of goods sold.	• Describe the flow of materials and how materials costs are assigned in a job order cost system.		
	• Prepare the journal entry to record materials used in production.	17-1	17-1A, 17-1B
	• Describe how factory labor hours are recorded and how labor costs are assigned in a job order cost system.		
	• Prepare the journal entry to record factory labor used in production.	17-2	17-2A, 17-2B
	• Describe and illustrate how factory overhead costs are accumulated and assigned in a job order cost system.	17-3 17-4	17-3A, 17-3B 17-4A, 17-4B
	• Compute the predetermined overhead rate.	17-4	17-4A, 17-4B
	• Describe and illustrate how to dispose of the balance in the factory overhead account.		
	• Describe and illustrate how costs are accumulated for work in process and finished goods inventory and assigned to cost of goods sold in a job order cost system.	17-5 17-6	17-5A, 17-5B 17-6A, 17-6B
	• Describe and illustrate the flow of costs in a job order cost system.		

3. Use job order cost information for decision making.

Key Points	Key Learning Outcomes	Example Exercises	Practice Exercises
Job order cost systems can be used to evaluate cost performance. Unit costs can be compared over time to determine if product costs are staying within expected ranges.	• Describe and illustrate how job cost sheets can be used to investigate possible reasons for increased product costs.		

4. Diagram the flow of costs for a service business that uses a job order cost accounting system.

Key Points	Key Learning Outcomes	Example Exercises	Practice Exercises
Job order cost accounting systems can be used by service businesses to plan and control operations. Since the product is a service, the focus is on direct labor and overhead costs. The costs of providing a service are accumulated in a work in process account and transferred to a cost of services account upon completion.	• Describe how service businesses use a job order cost system.		

Key Terms

activity base (757)
activity-based costing (758)
cost accounting system (751)
cost allocation (757)
finished goods ledger (762)
job cost sheet (754)
job order cost system (751)

materials ledger (754)
materials requisitions (754)
overapplied factory overhead (758)
period costs (763)
predetermined factory overhead rate (757)

process cost system (752)
receiving report (754)
time tickets (755)
underapplied factory overhead (758)

Illustrative Problem

Derby Music Company specializes in producing and packaging compact discs (CDs) for the music recording industry. Derby uses a job order cost system. The following data summarize the operations related to production for March, the first month of operations:

a. Materials purchased on account, $15,500.
b. Materials requisitioned and labor used:

	Materials	Factory Labor
Job No. 100	$2,650	$1,770
Job No. 101	1,240	650
Job No. 102	980	420
Job No. 103	3,420	1,900
Job No. 104	1,000	500
Job No. 105	2,100	1,760
For general factory use	450	650

c. Factory overhead costs incurred on account, $2,700.
d. Depreciation of machinery, $1,750.
e. Factory overhead is applied at a rate of 70% of direct labor cost.
f. Jobs completed: Nos. 100, 101, 102, 104.
g. Jobs 100, 101, and 102 were shipped, and customers were billed for $8,100, $3,800, and $3,500, respectively.

Instructions

1. Journalize the entries to record the transactions identified above.
2. Determine the account balances for Work in Process and Finished Goods.
3. Prepare a schedule of unfinished jobs to support the balance in the work in process account.
4. Prepare a schedule of completed jobs on hand to support the balance in the finished goods account.

Solution

1. a.	Materials		15,500	
	Accounts Payable			15,500
b.	Work in Process		11,390	
	Materials			11,390
	Work in Process		7,000	
	Wages Payable			7,000
	Factory Overhead		1,100	
	Materials			450
	Wages Payable			650

(continued)

c.	Factory Overhead		2,700	
	Accounts Payable			2,700
d.	Factory Overhead		1,750	
	Accumulated Depreciation—Machinery			1,750
e.	Work in Process		4,900	
	Factory Overhead (70% of $7,000)			4,900
f.	Finished Goods		11,548	
	Work in Process			11,548

Computation of the cost of jobs finished:

Job	Direct Materials	Direct Labor	Factory Overhead	Total
Job No. 100	$2,650	$1,770	$1,239	$ 5,659
Job No. 101	1,240	650	455	2,345
Job No. 102	980	420	294	1,694
Job No. 104	1,000	500	350	1,850
				$11,548

g.	Accounts Receivable		15,400	
	Sales			15,400
	Cost of Goods Sold		9,698	
	Finished Goods			9,698

Cost of jobs sold computation:

Job No. 100	$5,659
Job No. 101	2,345
Job No. 102	1,694
	$9,698

2. Work in Process: $11,742 ($11,390 + $7,000 + $4,900 − $11,548)
Finished Goods: $1,850 ($11,548 − $9,698)

3.   **Schedule of Unfinished Jobs**

Job	Direct Materials	Direct Labor	Factory Overhead	Total
Job No. 103	$3,420	$1,900	$1,330	$ 6,650
Job No. 105	2,100	1,760	1,232	5,092
Balance of Work in Process, March 31				$11,742

4.   **Schedule of Completed Jobs**

Job No. 104:

Direct materials	$1,000
Direct labor	500
Factory overhead	350
Balance of Finished Goods, March 31	$1,850

Self-Examination Questions

(Answers at End of Chapter)

1. For which of the following would the job order cost system be appropriate?
   A. Antique furniture repair shop
   B. Rubber manufacturer
   C. Coal manufacturer
   D. Computer chip manufacturer

2. The journal entry to record the requisition of materials to the factory in a job order cost system is a debit to:
   A. Materials.
   B. Accounts Payable.
   C. Work in Process.
   D. Cost of Goods Sold.

3. Job order cost sheets accumulate all of the following costs *except* for:
   A. direct materials.
   B. indirect materials.
   C. direct labor.
   D. factory overhead applied.

4. A company estimated $420,000 of factory overhead cost and 16,000 direct labor hours for the period. During the period, a job was completed with $4,500 of direct materials and $3,000 of direct labor. The direct labor rate was $15 per hour. What is the factory overhead applied to this job?
   A. $2,100   C. $78,750
   B. $5,250   D. $420,000

5. If the factory overhead account has a credit balance, factory overhead is said to be:
   A. underapplied.   C. underabsorbed.
   B. overapplied.   D. in error.

Eye Openers

1. How is product cost information used by managers?
2. a. Name two principal types of cost accounting systems.
   b. Which system provides for a separate record of each particular quantity of product that passes through the factory?
   c. Which system accumulates the costs for each department or process within the factory?
3. What kind of firm would use a job order cost system?

4. Hewlett-Packard Company assembles ink jet printers in which a high volume of standardized units are assembled and tested. Is the job order cost system appropriate in this situation?
5. Which account is used in the job order cost system to accumulate direct materials, direct labor, and factory overhead applied to production costs for individual jobs?
6. How does the use of the materials requisition help control the issuance of materials from the storeroom?
7. What document is the source for (a) debiting the accounts in the materials ledger and (b) crediting the accounts in the materials ledger?
8. What is a job cost sheet?
9. a. Differentiate between the clock card and the time ticket.
   b. Why should the total time reported on an employee's time tickets for a payroll period be compared with the time reported on the employee's clock cards for the same period?
10. Describe the source of the data for debiting Work in Process for (a) direct materials, (b) direct labor, and (c) factory overhead.
11. Discuss how the predetermined factory overhead rate can be used in job order cost accounting to assist management in pricing jobs.
12. a. How is a predetermined factory overhead rate calculated?
    b. Name three common bases used in calculating the rate.
13. a. What is (1) overapplied factory overhead and (2) underapplied factory overhead?
    b. If the factory overhead account has a debit balance, was factory overhead underapplied or overapplied?
    c. If the factory overhead account has a credit balance at the end of the first month of the fiscal year, where will the amount of this balance be reported on the interim balance sheet?
14. At the end of the fiscal year, there was a relatively minor balance in the factory overhead account. What procedure can be used for disposing of the balance in the account?
15. What account is the controlling account for (a) the materials ledger, (b) the job cost sheets, and (c) the finished goods ledger?
16. How can job cost information be used to identify cost improvement opportunities?
17. Describe how a job order cost system can be used for professional service businesses.

Practice Exercises

PE 17-1A
Cost of materials issuances
obj. 2

On November 7, Taylor Company purchased 24,000 units of raw materials at $10 per unit. On November 11, raw materials were requisitioned for production as follows: 1,600 units for Job 80 at $8 per unit and 1,250 units for Job 82 at $10 per unit. Journalize the entry on November 7 to record the purchase and on November 11 to record the requisition from the materials storeroom.

PE 17-1B
Cost of materials issuances
obj. 2

On October 12, Blakely Company purchased 8,000 units of raw materials at $6 per unit. On October 21, raw materials were requisitioned for production as follows: 750 units for Job 50 at $4 per unit and 600 units for Job 51 at $6 per unit. Journalize the entry on October 12 to record the purchase and on October 21 to record the requisition from the materials storeroom.

PE 17-2A
Entry for factory labor costs
obj. 2

During November, Taylor Company accumulated 1,000 hours of direct labor costs on Job 80 and 800 hours on Job 82. The total direct labor was incurred at a rate of $14 per direct labor hour for Job 80 and $12 per direct labor hour for Job 82. Journalize the entry to record the flow of labor costs into production during November.

PE 17-2B
Entry for factory labor costs
obj. 2

During October, Blakely Company accumulated 1,500 hours of direct labor costs on Job 50 and 1,250 hours on Job 51. The total direct labor was incurred at a rate of $20 per direct labor hour for Job 50 and $16 per direct labor hour for Job 51. Journalize the entry to record the flow of labor costs into production during October.

PE 17-3A
Entry for factory overhead costs
obj. 2

During November, Taylor Company incurred factory overhead costs as follows: indirect materials, $6,500; indirect labor, $8,000; utilities cost, $3,500; and depreciation, $2,800. Journalize the entry to record the factory overhead incurred during November.

PE 17-3B
Entry for factory overhead costs
obj. 2

During October, Blakely Company incurred factory overhead costs as follows: indirect materials, $4,000; indirect labor, $4,700; utilities cost, $2,000; and depreciation $2,600. Journalize the entry to record the factory overhead incurred during October.

PE 17-4A
Predetermined factory overhead rate and applying factory overhead
obj. 2

Taylor Company estimates that total factory overhead costs will be $250,000 for the year. Direct labor hours are estimated to be 50,000. For Taylor Company, (a) determine the predetermined factory overhead rate, (b) determine the amount of factory overhead applied to Jobs 80 and 82 in November using the data on direct labor hours from Practice Exercise 17-2A, and (c) prepare the journal entry to apply factory overhead to both jobs in November according to the predetermined overhead rate.

PE 17-4B
Predetermined factory overhead rate and applying factory overhead
obj. 2

Blakely Company estimates that total factory overhead costs will be $160,000 for the year. Direct labor hours are estimated to be 20,000. For Blakely Company (a) determine the predetermined factory overhead rate, (b) determine the amount of factory overhead applied to Jobs 50 and 51 in October using the data on direct labor hours from Practice Exercise 17-2B, and (c) prepare the journal entry to apply factory overhead to both jobs in October according to the predetermined overhead rate.

PE 17-5A
Job costs
obj. 2

At the end of November, Taylor Company had completed Jobs 80 and 82. Job 80 is for 600 units, and Job 82 is for 900 units. Using the data from Practice Exercises 17-1A, 17-2A, and 17-4A, determine (a) the balance on the job cost sheets for Jobs 80 and 82 at the end of November and (b) the cost per unit for Jobs 80 and 82 at the end of November.

PE 17-5B
Job costs
obj. 2

At the end of October, Blakely Company had completed Jobs 50 and 51. Job 50 is for 1,500 units, and Job 51 is for 1,200 units. Using the data from Practice Exercises 17-1B, 17-2B, and 17-4B, determine (a) the balance on the job cost sheets for Jobs 50 and 51 at the end of October and (b) the cost per unit for Jobs 50 and 51 at the end of October.

PE 17-6A
Cost of goods sold
obj. 2

Venson Company completed 40,000 units during the year at a cost of $500,000. The beginning finished goods inventory was 5,000 units at $100,000. Determine the cost of goods sold for 30,000 units, assuming a FIFO cost flow.

PE 17-6B
Cost of goods sold
obj. 2

Berlin Company completed 90,000 units during the year at a cost of $900,000. The beginning finished goods inventory was 10,000 units at $75,000. Determine the cost of goods sold for 70,000 units, assuming a FIFO cost flow.

Exercises

EX 17-1
Transactions in a job order cost system
obj. 2

Five selected transactions for the current month are indicated by letters in the following T accounts in a job order cost accounting system:

Materials	
	(a)

Work in Process	
(a)	(d)
(b)	
(c)	

Wages Payable	
	(b)

Finished Goods	
(d)	(e)

Factory Overhead	
(a)	(c)
(b)	

Cost of Goods Sold	
(e)	

Describe each of the five transactions.

EX 17-2
Cost flow relationships
obj. 2
✓ c. $271,500

The following information is available for the first month of operations of Korv Inc., a manufacturer of art and craft items:

Sales	$775,000
Gross profit	265,000
Indirect labor	63,000
Indirect materials	32,000
Other factory overhead	17,500
Materials purchased	303,000
Total manufacturing costs for the period	620,000
Materials inventory, end of period	35,000

Using the above information, determine the following missing amounts:

a. Cost of goods sold
b. Direct materials cost
c. Direct labor cost

EX 17-3
*Cost of materials
issuances under the
FIFO method*

obj. 2

✓ b. $2,400

An incomplete subsidiary ledger of wire cable for August is as follows:

RECEIVED			ISSUED			BALANCE			
Receiving Report Number	Quantity	Unit Price	Materials Requisition Number	Quantity	Amount	Date	Quantity	Amount	Unit Price
						Aug. 1	200	$3,200	$16.00
110	240	$18.00				Aug. 3			
			108	300		Aug. 5			
139	160	20.00				Aug. 19			
			120	180		Aug. 25			

a. Complete the materials issuances and balances for the wire cable subsidiary ledger under FIFO.
b. Determine the balance of wire cable at the end of August.
c. Journalize the summary entry to transfer materials to work in process.
d. ▭▭▶ Explain how the materials ledger might be used as an aid in maintaining inventory quantities on hand.

EX 17-4
*Entry for issuing
materials*

obj. 2

Materials issued for the current month are as follows:

Requisition No.	Material	Job No.	Amount
811	Aluminum	511	$10,400
812	Steel	514	18,650
813	Plastic	526	875
814	Abrasives	Indirect	325
815	Titanium alloy	533	42,300

Journalize the entry to record the issuance of materials.

EX 17-5
Entries for materials

obj. 2

✓ c. Fabric, $31,700

Combes Furniture Company manufactures furniture. Combes uses a job order cost system. Balances on November 1 from the materials ledger are as follows:

Fabric	$ 33,500
Polyester filling	8,100
Lumber	107,400
Glue	1,600

The materials purchased during November are summarized from the receiving reports as follows:

Fabric	$549,900
Polyester filling	104,200
Lumber	969,500
Glue	14,200

Materials were requisitioned to individual jobs as follows:

	Fabric	Polyester Filling	Lumber	Glue	Total
Job 11	$362,200	$64,500	$611,300		$1,038,000
Job 12	121,700	13,900	198,600		334,200
Job 13	67,800	10,300	182,400		260,500
Factory overhead—indirect materials				$11,700	11,700
Total	$551,700	$88,700	$992,300	$11,700	$1,644,400

The glue is not a significant cost, so it is treated as indirect materials (factory overhead).

a. Journalize the entry to record the purchase of materials in November.
b. Journalize the entry to record the requisition of materials in November.
c. Determine the November 30 balances that would be shown in the materials ledger accounts.

EX 17-6
Entry for factory labor costs
obj. 2

A summary of the time tickets for the current month follows:

Job No.	Amount	Job No.	Amount
101	$1,620	141	$ 1,780
122	1,590	Indirect labor	13,400
133	760	143	3,330
139	5,210	147	1,080

Journalize the entry to record the factory labor costs.

EX 17-7
Entry for factory labor costs
obj. 2

The weekly time tickets indicate the following distribution of labor hours for three direct labor employees:

	Hours			
	Job 111	Job 112	Job 113	Process Improvement
Johnny Daniels	18	10	5	7
Jack Walker	7	8	23	2
Jim Morgan	8	12	16	4

The direct labor rate earned by the three employees is as follows:

Daniels	$11.40
Walker	13.50
Morgan	11.75

The process improvement category includes training, quality improvement, housekeeping, and other indirect tasks.

a. Journalize the entry to record the factory labor costs for the week.
b. Assume that Jobs 111 and 112 were completed but not sold during the week and that Job 113 remained incomplete at the end of the week. How would the direct labor costs for all three jobs be reflected on the financial statements at the end of the week?

EX 17-8
Entries for direct labor and factory overhead
obj. 2

Chasse Homes Inc. manufactures mobile homes. Chasse uses a job order cost system. The time tickets from October jobs are summarized below.

Job 502	$2,352
Job 503	1,440
Job 504	960
Job 505	1,320
Factory supervision	2,760

Factory overhead is applied to jobs on the basis of a predetermined overhead rate of $20 per direct labor hour. The direct labor rate is $12 per hour.

a. Journalize the entry to record the factory labor costs.
b. Journalize the entry to apply factory overhead to production for October.

EX 17-9
Factory overhead rates, entries, and account balance
obj. 2

✓ b. $13.00 per direct labor hour

Staten Island Turbine operates two factories. The company applies factory overhead to jobs on the basis of machine hours in Factory 1 and on the basis of direct labor hours in Factory 2. Estimated factory overhead costs, direct labor hours, and machine hours are as follows:

	Factory 1	Factory 2
Estimated factory overhead cost for fiscal year beginning May 1	$236,800	$118,300
Estimated direct labor hours for year		9,100
Estimated machine hours for year	12,800	
Actual factory overhead costs for May	$23,200	$11,625
Actual direct labor hours for May		885
Actual machine hours for May	1,270	

a. Determine the factory overhead rate for Factory 1.
b. Determine the factory overhead rate for Factory 2.
c. Journalize the entries to apply factory overhead to production in each factory for May.
d. Determine the balances of the factory accounts for each factory as of May 31, and indicate whether the amounts represent overapplied or underapplied factory overhead.

EX 17-10
Predetermined factory overhead rate
obj. 2

The Engine Shop uses a job order cost system to determine the cost of performing engine repair work. Estimated costs and expenses for the coming period are as follows:

Engine parts	$ 650,750
Shop direct labor	520,625
Shop and repair equipment depreciation	12,800
Shop supervisor salaries	93,125
Shop property tax	22,300
Shop supplies	12,650
Advertising expense	18,100
Administrative office salaries	61,600
Administrative office depreciation expense	8,050
Total costs and expenses	$1,400,000

The average shop direct labor rate is $17 per hour.
Determine the predetermined shop overhead rate per direct labor hour.

EX 17-11
Predetermined factory overhead rate
obj. 2

✓ a. $175 per hour

San Jose Medical Center has a single operating room that is used by local physicians to perform surgical procedures. The cost of using the operating room is accumulated by each patient procedure and includes the direct materials costs (drugs and medical devices), physician surgical time, and operating room overhead. On August 1 of the current year, the annual operating room overhead is estimated to be:

Disposable supplies	$116,700
Depreciation expense	18,000
Utilities	11,200
Nurse salaries	164,000
Technician wages	57,600
Total operating room overhead	$367,500

The overhead costs will be assigned to procedures based on the number of surgical room hours. The Medical Center expects to use the operating room an average of seven hours per day, six days per week. In addition, the operating room will be shut down two weeks per year for general repairs.

a. Determine the predetermined operating room overhead rate for the year.
b. Allison Mann had a 5-hour procedure on August 10. How much operating room overhead would be charged to her procedure, using the rate determined in part (a)?
c. During August, the operating room was used 182 hours. The actual overhead costs incurred for August were $30,700. Determine the overhead under- or overapplied for the period.

EX 17-12
*Entry for jobs completed;
cost of unfinished jobs*

obj. 2

✓ b. $5,800

The following account appears in the ledger after only part of the postings have been completed for January:

Work in Process	
Balance, January 1	$15,500
Direct materials	86,200
Direct labor	64,300
Factory overhead	93,700

Jobs finished during January are summarized as follows:

Job 320	$57,600	Job 327	$26,100
Job 326	75,400	Job 350	94,800

a. Journalize the entry to record the jobs completed.
b. Determine the cost of the unfinished jobs at January 31.

EX 17-13
*Entries for factory costs
and jobs completed*

obj. 2

✓ d. $18,340

Tobias Printing Inc. began printing operations on July 1. Jobs 101 and 102 were completed during the month, and all costs applicable to them were recorded on the related cost sheets. Jobs 103 and 104 are still in process at the end of the month, and all applicable costs except factory overhead have been recorded on the related cost sheets. In addition to the materials and labor charged directly to the jobs, $725 of indirect materials and $6,380 of indirect labor were used during the month. The cost sheets for the four jobs entering production during the month are as follows, in summary form:

Job 101			Job 102	
Direct materials	6,800		Direct materials	3,000
Direct labor	1,560		Direct labor	880
Factory overhead	3,900		Factory overhead	2,200
Total	12,260		Total	6,080

Job 103			Job 104	
Direct materials	8,700		Direct materials	1,500
Direct labor	1,350		Direct labor	500
Factory overhead			Factory overhead	

Journalize the summary entry to record each of the following operations for July (one entry for each operation):

a. Direct and indirect materials used.
b. Direct and indirect labor used.
c. Factory overhead applied (a single overhead rate is used based on direct labor cost).
d. Completion of Jobs 101 and 102.

EX 17-14
*Financial statements of a
manufacturing firm*

obj. 2

✓ a. Income from
operations, $47,600

The following events took place for Wreckin Ronnie Inc. during July 2008, the first month of operations as a producer of road bikes:

• Purchased $165,800 of materials.
• Used $147,600 of direct materials in production.
• Incurred $96,250 of direct labor wages.
• Applied factory overhead at a rate of 80% of direct labor cost.
• Transferred $302,900 of work in process to finished goods.
• Sold goods with a cost of $301,300.
• Sold goods for $520,000.
• Incurred $119,000 of selling expenses.
• Incurred $52,100 of administrative expenses.

a. Prepare the July income statement for Wreckin Ronnie. Assume that Wreckin Ronnie uses the perpetual inventory method.
b. Determine the inventory balances at the end of the first month of operations.

EX 17-15
Decision making with job order costs
obj. **3**

Bronx Machinery Inc. is a job shop. The management of Bronx Machinery uses the cost information from the job sheets to assess its cost performance. Information on the total cost, product type, and quantity of items produced is as follows:

Date	Job No.	Quantity	Product	Amount
Jan. 2	101	450	105X	$10,350
Jan. 24	125	1,500	205B	16,500
Feb. 18	144	750	205B	9,000
Mar. 4	162	500	105X	10,000
Mar. 28	173	1,100	120T	6,600
May 20	190	1,250	120T	11,250
June 10	201	450	105X	6,750
Aug. 9	210	1,900	120T	22,800
Sept. 16	215	500	205B	5,500
Nov. 11	227	650	105X	7,800
Dec. 9	238	1,050	120T	16,800

a. Develop a graph for *each* product (three graphs), with Job No. (in date order) on the horizontal axis and unit cost on the vertical axis. Use this information to determine Bronx Machinery's cost performance over time for the three products.

b. What additional information would you require to investigate Bronx Machinery's cost performance more precisely?

EX 17-16
Decision making with job order costs
obj. **3**

Sharp Trophies Inc. uses a job order cost system for determining the cost to manufacture award products (plaques and trophies). Among the company's products is an engraved plaque that is awarded to participants who complete an executive education program at a local university. The company sells the plaque to the university for $75 each.

Each plaque has a brass plate engraved with the name of the participant. Engraving requires approximately 6 minutes per name. Improperly engraved names must be redone. The plate is screwed to a walnut backboard. This assembly takes approximately 3 minutes per unit. Improper assembly must be redone using a new walnut backboard.

During the first half of the year, the university had two separate executive education classes. The job cost sheets for the two separate jobs indicated the following information:

Job 103	March 4		
	Cost per Unit	Units	Job Cost
Direct materials:			
Wood	$20.00/unit	30 units	$ 600.00
Brass	18.00/unit	30 units	540.00
Engraving labor	40.00/hr.	3 hrs.	120.00
Assembly labor	28.00/hr.	1.5 hrs.	42.00
Factory overhead	30.00/hr.	6 hrs.	180.00
			$1,482.00
Plaques shipped			/ 30
Cost per plaque			$ 49.40

Job 116	April 15		
	Cost per Unit	Units	Job Cost
Direct materials:			
Wood	$20.00/unit	25 units	$ 500.00
Brass	18.00/unit	25 units	450.00
Engraving labor	40.00/hr.	4 hrs.	160.00
Assembly labor	28.00/hr.	2 hrs.	56.00
Factory overhead	30.00/hr.	4 hrs.	120.00
			$1,286.00
Plaques shipped			/ 20
Cost per plaque			$ 64.30

a. Why did the cost per plaque increase from $49.40 to $64.30?
b. What improvements would you recommend for Sharp Trophies Inc.?

EX 17-17
Job order cost accounting entries for a service business
obj. **4**

The consulting firm of Reznick and Fedder accumulates costs associated with individual cases, using a job order cost system. The following transactions occurred during May:

May 7 Charged 440 hours of professional (lawyer) time to the Daley Co. breech of contract suit to prepare for the trial, at a rate of $175 per hour.

   11 Reimbursed travel costs to employees for depositions related to the Daley case, $24,000.

   22 Charged 225 hours of professional time for the Daley trial at a rate of $250 per hour.

   25 Received invoice from consultants Rucker and Putnam for $47,000 for expert testimony related to the Daley trial.

   30 Applied office overhead at a rate of $45 per professional hour charged to the Daley case.

   31 Paid secretarial and administrative salaries of $20,000 for the month.

   31 Used office supplies for the month, $6,000.

   31 Paid professional salaries of $55,000 for the month.

   31 Billed Daley $260,000 for successful defense of the case.

a. Provide the journal entries for each of the above transactions.
b. How much office overhead is over- or underapplied?
c. Determine the gross profit on the Daley case, assuming that over- or underapplied office overhead is closed annually to cost of services.

EX 17-18
Job order cost accounting entries for a service business
obj. **4**

✓ *d. Dr. Cost of Services, $609,800*

Tec Trends Inc. provides advertising services for clients across the nation. Tec Trends is presently working on four projects, each for a different client. Tec Trends accumulates costs for each account (client) on the basis of both direct costs and allocated indirect costs. The direct costs include the charged time of professional personnel and media purchases (air time and ad space). Overhead is allocated to each project as a percentage of media purchases. The predetermined overhead rate is 40% of media purchases.

On July 1, the four advertising projects had the following accumulated costs:

	July 1 Balances
Spitzer Hotel	$120,000
Gonzalez Bank	15,000
Gulliani Beverage	66,000
Koch Rentals	18,000

During July, Tec Trends Inc. incurred the following direct labor and media purchase costs related to preparing advertising for each of the four accounts:

	Direct Labor	Media Purchases
Spitzer Hotel	$ 42,000	$154,000
Gonzalez Bank	17,000	143,000
Gulliani Beverage	81,000	128,000
Koch Rentals	107,000	83,000
Total	$247,000	$508,000

At the end of July, both the Spitzer Hotel and Gonzalez Bank campaigns were completed. The costs of completed campaigns are debited to the cost of services account.

Journalize the summary entry to record each of the following for the month:

a. Direct labor costs
b. Media purchases
c. Overhead applied
d. Completion of Spitzer Hotel and Gonzalez Bank campaigns

Problems Series A

PR 17-1A
Entries for costs in a job order cost system

obj. 2

Goldberg Apparel Company uses a job order cost system. The following data summarize the operations related to production for March:

a. Materials purchased on account, $233,000.
b. Materials requisitioned, $208,300, of which $5,600 was for general factory use.
c. Factory labor used, $190,500, of which $62,500 was indirect.
d. Other costs incurred on account were for factory overhead, $89,300; selling expenses, $64,000; and administrative expenses, $37,800.
e. Prepaid expenses expired for factory overhead were $7,500; for selling expenses, $1,300; and for administrative expenses, $1,250.
f. Depreciation of factory equipment was $18,900; of office equipment, $14,700; and of store equipment, $2,600.
g. Factory overhead costs applied to jobs, $190,000.
h. Jobs completed, $583,300.
i. Cost of goods sold, $577,700.

Instructions
Journalize the entries to record the summarized operations.

PR 17-2A
Entries and schedules for unfinished jobs and completed jobs

obj. 2

✓3. Work in Process
balance, $131,975

291,600
53,600
─────────
238,000

Godwin Fixtures Co. uses a job order cost system. The following data summarize the operations related to production for April 2008, the first month of operations:

a. Materials purchased on account, $137,000.
b. Materials requisitioned and factory labor used:

Job	Materials	Factory Labor
No. 601	$18,100	$17,000
No. 602	20,000	25,500
No. 603	13,050	9,700
No. 604	34,500	33,550
No. 605	15,700	14,800
No. 606	17,800	18,300
For general factory use	6,600	47,000

125,750 + 165,850 = 291,600
6,600 + 47,000 = 53,600

c. Factory overhead costs incurred on account, $4,950.
d. Depreciation of machinery and equipment, $3,700.
e. The factory overhead rate is $53 per machine hour. Machine hours used:

Job	Machine Hours
No. 601	215
No. 602	230
No. 603	175
No. 604	300
No. 605	198
No. 606	225
Total	1,343

f. Jobs completed: 601, 602, 603, and 605.
g. Jobs were shipped and customers were billed as follows: Job 601, $72,750; Job 602, $88,780; Job 605, $74,500.

Instructions
1. Journalize the entries to record the summarized operations.
2. Post the appropriate entries to T accounts for Work in Process and Finished Goods, using the identifying letters as dates. Insert memorandum account balances as of the end of the month.

3. Prepare a schedule of unfinished jobs to support the balance in the work in process account.
4. Prepare a schedule of completed jobs on hand to support the balance in the finished goods account.

PR 17-3A
Job order cost sheet

objs. 2, 3

If the working papers correlating with the textbook are not used, omit Problem 17-3A.

Nu-Life Furniture Company refinishes and reupholsters furniture. Nu-Life uses a job order cost system. When a prospective customer asks for a price quote on a job, the estimated cost data are inserted on an unnumbered job cost sheet. If the offer is accepted, a number is assigned to the job, and the costs incurred are recorded in the usual manner on the job cost sheet. After the job is completed, reasons for the variances between the estimated and actual costs are noted on the sheet. The data are then available to management in evaluating the efficiency of operations and in preparing quotes on future jobs. On July 1, 2008, an estimate of $1,512.64 for reupholstering two chairs and a couch was given to Ed Douthett. The estimate was based on the following data:

Estimated direct materials:	
17 meters at $23 per meter	$ 391.00
Estimated direct labor:	
24 hours at $14 per hour	336.00
Estimated factory overhead (65% of direct labor cost)	218.40
Total estimated costs	$ 945.40
Markup (60% of production costs)	567.24
Total estimate	$1,512.64

On July 4, the chairs and couch were picked up from the residence of Ed Douthett, 411 Austin Lane, Alexandria, with a commitment to return them on September 13. The job was completed on September 10.

The related materials requisitions and time tickets are summarized as follows:

Materials Requisition No.	Description	Amount
3480	7 meters at $23	$161
3492	11 meters at $23	253

Time Ticket No.	Description	Amount
H143	13 hours at $14	$182
H151	15 hours at $14	210

Instructions
1. Complete that portion of the job order cost sheet that would be prepared when the estimate is given to the customer.
2. Assign number 00-10-23 to the job, record the costs incurred, and complete the job order cost sheet. Comment on the reasons for the variances between actual costs and estimated costs. For this purpose, assume that two meters of materials were spoiled, the factory overhead rate has been proved to be satisfactory, and an inexperienced employee performed the work.

PR 17-4A
Analyzing manufacturing cost accounts

obj. 2

✓ 1. G. $245,250

Dupont Fishing Equipment Company manufactures fishing rods in a wide variety of lengths and weights. The following incomplete ledger accounts refer to transactions that are summarized for November:

		Materials			
Nov. 1	Balance	10,000	Nov. 30	Requisitions	(A)
31	Purchases	120,000			

(continued)

Work in Process

Nov. 1	Balance	(B)	Nov. 30	Completed jobs	(F)
30	Materials	(C)			
30	Direct labor	(D)			
30	Factory overhead applied	(E)			

Finished Goods

Nov. 1	Balance	0	Nov. 30	Cost of goods sold	(G)
30	Completed jobs	(F)			

Wages Payable

		Nov. 30	Wages incurred	130,000

Factory Overhead

Nov. 1	Balance	2,500	Nov. 30	Factory overhead applied	(E)
30	Indirect labor	(H)			
30	Indirect materials	3,000			
30	Other overhead	60,000			

In addition, the following information is available:

a. Materials and direct labor were applied to six jobs in November:

Job No.	Style	Quantity	Direct Materials	Direct Labor
No. 111	DL-8	70	$ 15,000	$ 12,000
No. 112	DL-18	100	23,000	18,000
No. 113	DL-11	120	27,500	25,000
No. 114	SL-101	100	11,000	12,500
No. 115	SL-110	175	28,000	27,500
No. 116	DL-14	80	15,000	14,500
Total		645	$119,500	$109,500

b. Factory overhead is applied to each job at a rate of 75% of direct labor cost.
c. The November 1 Work in Process balance consisted of two jobs, as follows:

Job No.	Style	Work in Process, November 1
Job 111	DL-8	$20,000
Job 112	DL-18	30,000
Total		$50,000

d. Customer jobs completed and units sold in November were as follows:

Job No.	Style	Completed in November	Units Sold in November
Job 111	DL-8	X	60
Job 112	DL-18	X	100
Job 113	DL-11	X	80
Job 114	SL-101		0
Job 115	SL-110	X	150
Job 116	DL-14		0

Instructions

1. Determine the missing amounts associated with each letter. Provide supporting calculations by completing a table with the following headings:

Job No.	Quantity	Nov. 1 Work in Process	Direct Materials	Direct Labor	Factory Overhead	Total Cost	Unit Cost	Units Sold	Cost of Goods Sold

2. Determine the November 30 balances for each of the inventory accounts and factory overhead.

PR 17-5A
Flow of costs and income statement

obj. 2

✓1. Income from operations, $2,998,000

Outdoor Software Inc. is a designer, manufacturer, and distributor of software for microcomputers. A new product, *Landscape 2008*, was released for production and distribution in early 2008. In January, $700,000 was spent to design print advertisement. For the first six months of 2008, the company spent $2,500,000 promoting *Landscape 2008* in trade magazines. The product was ready for manufacture on January 10, 2008.

Outdoor uses a job order cost system to accumulate costs associated with each software title. Direct materials unit costs are:

Blank CD	$ 4.50
Packaging	8.00
Manual	11.00
Total	$23.50

The actual production process for the software product is fairly straightforward. First, blank CDs are brought to a CD copying machine. The copying machine requires 1 hour per 1,500 CDs.

After the program is copied onto the CD, the CD is brought to assembly, where assembly personnel pack the CD and manual for shipping. The direct labor cost for this work is $0.75 per unit.

The completed packages are then sold to retail outlets through a sales force. The sales force is compensated by a 10% commission on the wholesale price for all sales.

Total completed production was 45,000 units during the year. Other information is as follows:

Number of software units sold in 2008	40,000
Wholesale price per unit	$200

Factory overhead cost is applied to jobs at the rate of $1,200 per copy machine hour. There were an additional 1,000 copied CDs, packaging, and manuals waiting to be assembled on December 31, 2008.

Instructions
1. Prepare an annual income statement for the *Landscape 2008* product, including supporting calculations, from the information above.
2. Determine the balances in the finished goods and work in process inventory for the *Landscape 2008* product on December 31, 2008.

Problems Series B

PR 17-1B
Entries for costs in a job order cost system

obj. 2

Robinson Parts Co. uses a job order cost system. The following data summarize the operations related to production for June:

a. Materials purchased on account, $705,000.
b. Materials requisitioned, $527,000, of which $45,000 was for general factory use.
c. Factory labor used, $417,800, of which $95,000 was indirect.
d. Other costs incurred on account were for factory overhead, $340,500; selling expenses, $215,000; and administrative expenses, $128,500.
e. Prepaid expenses expired for factory overhead were $23,000; for selling expenses, $15,000; and for administrative expenses, $9,000.
f. Depreciation of office building was $39,000; of office equipment, $19,700; and of warehouse equipment, $12,300.
g. Factory overhead costs applied to jobs, $579,600.
h. Jobs completed, $1,643,700.
i. Cost of goods sold, $1,650,000.

Instructions
Journalize the entries to record the summarized operations.

PR 17-2B
Entries and schedules for unfinished jobs and completed jobs

obj. 2

✓ *3. Work in Process balance, $6,800*

Hillman Tool Company uses a job order cost system. The following data summarize the operations related to production for May 2008, the first month of operations:

a. Materials purchased on account, $9,400.
b. Materials requisitioned and factory labor used:

Job	Materials	Factory Labor
No. 101	$ 875	$ 750
No. 102	1,275	985
No. 103	660	500
No. 104	2,200	1,765
No. 105	1,300	1,350
No. 106	925	790
For general factory use	270	1,000

c. Factory overhead costs incurred on account, $405.
d. Depreciation of machinery and equipment, $520.
e. The factory overhead rate is $35 per machine hour. Machine hours used:

Job	Machine Hours
No. 101	6
No. 102	10
No. 103	8
No. 104	25
No. 105	11
No. 106	7
Total	67

f. Jobs completed: 101, 102, 103, and 105.
g. Jobs were shipped and customers were billed as follows: Job 101, $4,350; Job 102, $4,800; Job 103, $2,350.

Instructions
1. Journalize the entries to record the summarized operations.
2. Post the appropriate entries to T accounts for Work in Process and Finished Goods, using the identifying letters as dates. Insert memorandum account balances as of the end of the month.
3. Prepare a schedule of unfinished jobs to support the balance in the work in process account.
4. Prepare a schedule of completed jobs on hand to support the balance in the finished goods account.

PR 17-3B
Job order cost sheet

objs. 2, 3

If the working papers correlating with the textbook are not used, omit Problem 17-3B.

Asheville Furniture Company refinishes and reupholsters furniture. Asheville uses a job order cost system. When a prospective customer asks for a price quote on a job, the estimated cost data are inserted on an unnumbered job cost sheet. If the offer is accepted, a number is assigned to the job, and the costs incurred are recorded in the usual manner on the job cost sheet. After the job is completed, reasons for the variances between the estimated and actual costs are noted on the sheet. The data are then available to management in evaluating the efficiency of operations and in preparing quotes on future jobs. On July 10, 2008, an estimate of $805.20 for reupholstering a chair and couch was given to Ed Stone. The estimate was based on the following data:

Estimated direct materials:	
12 meters at $20 per meter	$240.00
Estimated direct labor:	
15 hours at $13 per hour	195.00
Estimated factory overhead (35% of direct labor cost)	68.25
Total estimated costs	$503.25
Markup (60% of production costs)	301.95
Total estimate	$805.20

On July 16, the chair and couch were picked up from the residence of Ed Stone, 10 Pub-lishers Lane, New York, with a commitment to return it on August 16. The job was com-pleted on August 11.

The related materials requisitions and time tickets are summarized as follows:

Materials Requisition No.	Description	Amount
U642	6 meters at $20	$120
U651	8 meters at $20	160

Time Ticket No.	Description	Amount
1519	10 hours at $12	$120
1520	8 hours at $12	96

Instructions

1. Complete that portion of the job order cost sheet that would be prepared when the es-timate is given to the customer.
2. ▬▬▶ Assign number 00-8-38 to the job, record the costs incurred, and complete the job order cost sheet. Comment on the reasons for the variances between actual costs and estimated costs. For this purpose, assume that two meters of materials were spoiled, the factory overhead rate has been proved to be satisfactory, and an inexperienced employee performed the work.

PR 17-4B
Analyzing manufacturing cost accounts
obj. 2

✓1. G. $163,272

Alpine Bliss Ski Company manufactures snow skis in a wide variety of lengths and styles. The following incomplete ledger accounts refer to transactions that are summarized for October:

Materials

Oct. 1	Balance	20,000	Oct. 31	Requisitions	(A)
31	Purchases	100,000			

Work in Process

Oct. 1	Balance	(B)	Oct. 31	Completed jobs	(F)
31	Materials	(C)			
31	Direct labor	(D)			
31	Factory overhead applied	(E)			

Finished Goods

Oct. 1	Balance	0	Oct. 31	Cost of goods sold	(G)
31	Completed jobs	(F)			

Wages Payable

			Oct. 31	Wages incurred	76,000

Factory Overhead

Oct. 1	Balance	5,000	Oct. 31	Factory overhead applied	(E)
31	Indirect labor	(H)			
31	Indirect materials	2,500			
31	Other overhead	57,500			

In addition, the following information is available:

a. Materials and direct labor were applied to six jobs in October:

Job No.	Style	Quantity	Direct Materials	Direct Labor
No. 51	V-100	175	$ 17,000	$13,000
No. 52	V-200	375	28,000	17,000
No. 53	V-500	175	10,000	4,500
No. 54	A-200	200	27,500	11,000
No. 55	V-400	150	18,000	10,500
No. 56	A-100	100	5,000	3,700
Total		1,175	$105,500	$59,700

b. Factory overhead is applied to each job at a rate of 140% of direct labor cost.
c. The October 1 Work in Process balance consisted of two jobs, as follows:

Job No.	Style	Work in Process, October 1
Job 51	V-100	$ 5,000
Job 52	V-200	11,000
Total		$16,000

d. Customer jobs completed and units sold in October were as follows:

Job No.	Style	Completed in October	Units Sold in October
Job 51	V-100	X	150
Job 52	V-200	X	215
Job 53	V-500		0
Job 54	A-200	X	160
Job 55	V-400	X	100
Job 56	A-100		0

Instructions

1. Determine the missing amounts associated with each letter. Provide supporting calculations by completing a table with the following headings:

Job No.	Quantity	Oct. 1 Work in Process	Direct Materials	Direct Labor	Factory Overhead	Total Cost	Unit Cost	Units Sold	Cost of Goods Sold

2. Determine the October 31 balances for each of the inventory accounts and factory overhead.

PR 17-5B

Flow of costs and income statement

obj. 2

✓ 1. Income from operations, $1,800,000

New Music Inc. is in the business of developing, promoting, and selling musical talent on compact disc (CD). The company signed a new musical act, called *The Sound*, on January 1, 2008. For the first six months of 2008, the company spent $3,500,000 on a media campaign for *The Sound* and $800,000 in legal costs. The CD production began on February 1, 2008.

New Music uses a job order cost system to accumulate costs associated with a CD title. The unit direct materials cost for the CD is:

Blank CD	$3.00
Jewel case	1.00
Song lyric insert	0.50

The production process is straightforward. First, the blank CDs are brought to a production area where the digital soundtrack is copied onto the CD. The copying machine requires one hour per 2,000 CDs.

After the CDs are copied, they are brought to an assembly area where an employee packs the CD with a jewel case and song lyric insert. The direct labor cost is $0.50 per unit.

The CDs are sold to record stores. Each record store is given promotional materials, such as posters and aisle displays. Promotional materials cost $30 per record store. In addition, shipping costs average $0.15 per CD.

Total completed production was 1,500,000 units during the year. Other information is as follows:

Number of customers (record stores)	50,000
Number of CDs sold	1,000,000
Wholesale price (to record store) per CD	$13

Factory overhead cost is applied to jobs at the rate of $500 per copy machine hour. There were an additional 20,000 copied CDs, packages, and inserts waiting to be assembled on December 31, 2008.

Instructions
1. Prepare an annual income statement for New Music Inc. for *The Sound* CD, including supporting calculations from the preceeding information.
2. Determine the balances in the work in process and finished goods inventory for the *The Sound* CD on December 31, 2008.

Special Activities

SA 17-1
Managerial analysis

The controller of the plant of Commercial Plumbing Supplies prepared a graph of the unit costs from the job cost reports for Product QQQ. The graph appeared as follows:

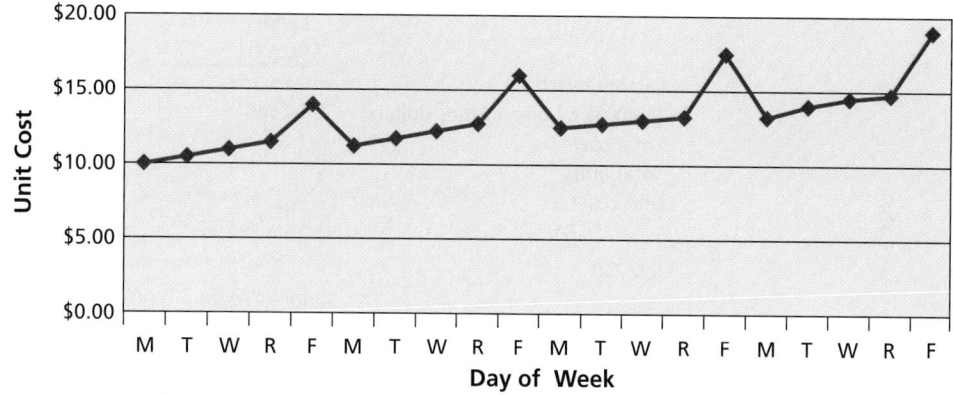

How would you interpret this information? What further information would you request?

SA 17-2
Factory overhead rate

Machine-Tech Inc., a specialized tool manufacturer, uses a job order costing system. The overhead is allocated to jobs on the basis of direct labor hours. The overhead rate is now $1,500 per direct labor hour. The design engineer thinks that this is illogical. The design engineer has stated the following:

Our accounting system doesn't make any sense to me. It tells me that every labor hour carries an additional burden of $1,500. This means that direct labor makes up only 5% of our total product cost, yet it drives all our costs. In addition, these rates give my design engineers incentives to "design out" direct labor by using machine technology. Yet, over the past years as we have had less and less direct labor, the overhead rate keeps going up and up. I won't be surprised if next year the rate is $2,000 per direct labor hour. I'm also concerned because small errors in our estimates of the direct labor content can have a large impact on our estimated costs. Just a 30-minute error in our estimate of assembly time is worth $750. Small mistakes in our direct labor time estimates really swing our bids around. I think this puts us at a disadvantage when we are going after business.

1. What is the engineer's concern about the overhead rate going "up and up"?
2. What did the engineer mean about the large overhead rate being a disadvantage when placing bids and seeking new business?
3. What do you think is a possible solution?

SA 17-3
Job order decision making and rate deficiencies

Kazaa Company makes attachments, such as backhoes and grader and bulldozer blades, for construction equipment. The company uses a job order cost system. Management is concerned about cost performance and evaluates the job cost sheets to learn more about the cost effectiveness of the operations. To facilitate a comparison, the cost sheet for Job 500 (15 Type Z bulldozer blades completed in March) was compared with Job 750, which was for 25 Type Z bulldozer blades completed in September. The two job cost sheets follow.

Job 500

Item: 15 Type Z bulldozer blades

Materials:	Direct Materials Quantity	×	Direct Materials Price	=	Amount
Steel (tons)	30		$800.00		$24,000
Steel components (pieces)	225		3.00		675
Total materials					$24,675

Direct labor	Direct Labor Hours	×	Direct Labor Rate	=	Amount
Foundry	180.0		$ 14.00		$ 2,520
Welding	120.0		16.00		1,920
Shipping	22.5		10.00		225
Total direct labor	322.5				$ 4,665

	Direct Total Labor Cost	×	Factory Overhead Rate	=	Amount
Factory overhead (400% of direct labor dollars)	$4,665	×	400%		$18,660
Total cost					$48,000
Total units					/ 15
Unit cost					$ 3,200

Job 750

Item: 25 Type Z bulldozer blades

Materials:	Direct Materials Quantity	×	Direct Materials Price	=	Amount
Steel (tons)	58		$750.00		$43,500
Steel components (pieces)	375		3.00		1,125
Total materials					$44,625

Direct labor	Direct Labor Hours	×	Direct Labor Rate	=	Amount
Foundry	325.0		$ 14.00		$ 4,550
Welding	250.0		16.00		4,000
Shipping	37.5		10.00		375
Total direct labor	612.5				$ 8,925

	Direct Total Labor Cost	×	Factory Overhead Rate	=	Amount
Factory overhead (400% of direct labor dollars)	$8,925	×	400%		$35,700
Total cost					$89,250
Total units					/ 25
Unit cost					$ 3,570

Management is concerned with the increase in unit costs over the months from March to September. To understand what has occurred, management interviewed the purchasing manager and quality manager.

Purchasing Manager: Prices have been holding steady for our raw materials during the first half of the year. I found a new supplier for our bulk steel that was willing to offer a better price than we received in the past. I saw these lower steel prices and jumped at them, knowing that a reduction in steel prices would have a very favorable impact on our costs.

Quality Manager: Something happened around midyear. All of a sudden, we were experiencing problems with respect to the quality of our steel. As a result, we've been having all sorts of problems on the shop floor in our foundry and welding operation.

1. Analyze the two job cost sheets, and identify why the unit costs have changed for the Type Z bulldozer blades. Complete the following schedule to help you in your analysis:

Item	Input Quantity per Unit—Job 500	Input Quantity per Unit—Job 750
Steel		
Foundry labor		
Welding labor		

2. ▭▬▶ How would you interpret what has happened in light of your analysis and the interviews?

SA 17-4
Recording manufacturing costs

Jake Nash just began working as a cost accountant for Marvel Industries Inc., which manufactures gift items. Jake is preparing to record summary journal entries for the month. Jake begins by recording the factory wages as follows:

Wages Expense	30,000	
Wages Payable		30,000

Then the factory depreciation:

Depreciation Expense—Factory Machinery	8,000	
Accumulated Depreciation—Factory Machinery		8,000

Jake's supervisor, Ronnie Berry, walks by and notices the entries. The following conversation takes place.

Ronnie: That's a very unusual way to record our factory wages and depreciation for the month.
Jake: What do you mean? This is exactly the way we were taught to record wages and depreciation in school. You know, debit an expense and credit Cash or payables, or in the case of depreciation, credit Accumulated Depreciation.
Ronnie: Well, it's not the credits I'm concerned about. It's the debits—I don't think you've recorded the debits correctly. I wouldn't mind if you were recording the administrative wages or office equipment depreciation this way, but I've got real questions about recording factory wages and factory machinery depreciation this way.
Jake: Now I'm really confused. You mean this is correct for administrative costs, but not for factory costs? Well, what am I supposed to do—and why?

1. ▭▬▶ Play the role of Ronnie and answer Jake's questions.
2. Why would Ronnie accept the journal entries if they were for administrative costs?

SA 17-5
Predetermined overhead rates

As an assistant cost accountant for Lovett Industries, you have been assigned to review the activity base for the predetermined factory overhead rate. The president, Calvin Adler, has expressed concern that the over- or underapplied overhead has fluctuated excessively over the years.

An analysis of the company's operations and use of the current overhead rate (direct materials usage) has narrowed the possible alternative overhead bases to direct labor cost and machine hours. For the past five years, the following data have been gathered:

	2008	2007	2006	2005	2004
Actual overhead	$ 590,000	$ 918,000	$ 450,000	$ 566,000	$ 501,000
Applied overhead	582,000	928,000	460,000	575,000	480,000
(Over-) underapplied overhead	$ 8,000	$ (10,000)	$ (10,000)	$ (9,000)	$ 21,000
Direct labor cost	$2,150,000	$3,350,000	$1,630,000	$2,040,000	$1,830,000
Machine hours	50,000	75,000	35,000	48,000	42,000

1. Calculate a predetermined factory overhead rate for each alternative base, assuming that rates would have been determined by relating the amount of factory overhead for the past five years to the base.
2. For each of the past five years, determine the over- or underapplied overhead, based on the two predetermined overhead rates developed in part (1).
3. ▭▬▶ Which predetermined overhead rate would you recommend? Discuss the basis for your recommendation.

Answers to Self-Examination Questions

1. **A**   Job order cost systems are best suited to businesses manufacturing special orders from customers, such as would be the case for a repair shop for antique furniture (answer A). A process cost system is best suited for manufacturers of similar units of products such as rubber manufacturers (answer B), coal manufacturers (answer C), and computer chip manufacturers (answer D).

2. **C**   The journal entry to record the requisition of materials to the factory in a job order cost system is a debit to Work in Process and a credit to Materials.

3. **B**   The job cost sheet accumulates the cost of materials (answer A), direct labor (answer C), and factory overhead applied (answer D). Indirect materials are *not* accumulated on the job order cost sheets, but are included as part of factory overhead applied.

4. **B**

$$\text{Predetermined Factory Overhead Rate} = \frac{\text{Estimated Total Factory Overhead Costs}}{\text{Estimated Activity Base}}$$

$$\text{Predetermined Factory Overhead Rate} = \frac{\$420,000}{16,000 \text{ dlh}} = \$26.25$$

$$\text{Hours applied to the job:} \quad \frac{\$3,000}{\$15 \text{ per hour}} = 200 \text{ hours}$$

Factory overhead applied to the job: 200 hours $\times$ \$26.25 = \$5,250

5. **B**   If the amount of factory overhead applied during a particular period exceeds the actual overhead costs, the factory overhead account will have a credit balance and is said to be overapplied (answer B) or overabsorbed. If the amount applied is less than the actual costs, the account will have a debit balance and is said to be underapplied (answer A) or underabsorbed (answer C). Since an "estimated" predetermined overhead rate is used to apply overhead, a credit balance does not necessarily represent an error (answer D).

Process Cost Systems

© MICHAEL STRAUCH @ STREETCARMIKE.COM

objectives

After studying this chapter, you should be able to:

1   **Explain and illustrate the characteristics and cost flows for a process manufacturer.**

2   **Prepare a cost of production report, accounting for completed and partially completed units under the FIFO method.**

3   **Prepare journal entries for transactions of a process manufacturer.**

4   **Use cost of production reports for decision making.**

5   **Contrast just-in-time processing with conventional manufacturing practices.**

Dreyer's Grand Ice Cream, Inc.

To make ice cream, you would need to gather ingredients, including milk, cream, sugar, and flavoring. Next, these ingredients would be added to an electric ice cream maker to be mixed. The ingredients must be cooled during mixing so the ice cream maker would be packed with ice and salt. Finally, you would turn on the electricity to begin the mixing. After mixing for half of the required mixing time, would you have ice cream? Of course not, because you'd need to mix for a longer time before the ice cream would freeze.

Now, assume that you ask the question, "What costs have I incurred so far in making ice cream, now that it is halfway through the mixing time?" The answer requires that you begin by separating the ingredients and the electricity costs. These two costs are incurred in the process at different rates so it is convenient to identify them separately. The ingredient costs have all been incurred, since all the ingredients were introduced at the beginning of the process. The electricity costs, however, are different. Since the mixing is only 50% complete, only 50% of the electricity costs used in operating the ice cream maker have been incurred in the mixing process. Therefore, the answer to the question is that *all* the materials costs and *half* the electricity costs have been incurred in the mixing process after half of the mixing time is completed.

These same costing concepts would apply for a much larger ice cream process, like that of Dreyer's Grand Ice Cream, Inc., manufacturer of the Häagen-Dazs®, Edys®, Dreyer's®, and Nestlé® ice cream brands. Dreyer's mixes ingredients in 3,000-gallon vats in much the same way that you would mix ice cream at home. It would also account for its costs by measuring the ingredients, electricity, labor, and other factory overhead costs consumed in making ice cream.

In this chapter, we apply these concepts to manufacturers that use a process cost system. After introducing process costing, we discuss decision making with process cost system reports. We conclude the chapter with a brief discussion of just-in-time cost systems.

Overview of Process Manufacturers and Process Costing

As we discussed in the previous chapter, the job order cost system is best suited to industries that make special orders for customers. Industries that use job order cost systems include special-order printing, custom-made tailoring, furniture manufacturing, shipbuilding, aircraft building, custom-made musical instruments, movie studios, and construction. **Process manufacturers** typically use large machines to process a flow of raw materials into a finished state. For example, a petrochemical business processes crude oil through numerous refining steps to produce higher grades of oil until gasoline is produced. A distinguishing feature of process manufacturers is that products produced are the same. This means that one unit of product cannot be distinguished from another. Thus, in a petrochemical business one barrel of gasoline cannot be distinguished from another barrel. This is in contrast to a printing company, where one print job is not the same as another. Other examples of process manufacturers are as follows:

Industry	Example Company
Beverages	The Coca-Cola Company
Chemicals	The Dow Chemical Company
Computer chips	Intel Corporation
Food	The Hershey Foods Corporation

Industry	Example Company
Forest and paper products	Georgia-Pacific
Metals	Alcoa Inc.
Petroleum refining	ExxonMobil Corporation
Pharmaceuticals	Merck & Co., Inc.
Soap and cosmetics	Procter & Gamble

The cost accounting system used by process manufacturers is called the **process cost system**.

Integrity, Objectivity, and Ethics in Business

ETHICS

SAFETY FIRST

Chemical processors must be concerned with safety, health, and the environment. Minimizing chemical spills, unwanted emissions, and equipment hazards are concerns in this industry. E. I. du Pont de Nemours and Company (DuPont) is widely regarded as one of the strongest advocates for social responsibility and one of the safest manufacturing businesses in which to work. As a result, DuPont publicly reports that its recorded workplace-related injuries or illnesses have been less than 40% of the chemical industry average and less than 20% of all manufacturing companies. Moreover, that rate has declined every year for the last 10 years. DuPont reports its community and employee safety and health performance on its Web site at **http://www2.dupont.com/Social_Commitment/en_us/.**

Source: "Recordable Injuries per 200,000 Hours Worked," DuPont Company, 2005.

COMPARING JOB ORDER AND PROCESS COST SYSTEMS

Job order and process costing systems are similar in many ways. For example, both systems:

1. Accumulate product costs.
2. Categorize manufacturing costs into direct materials, direct labor, and factory overhead.
3. Allocate costs to products.
4. Maintain perpetual materials, work in process, and finished goods inventory records.
5. Use product cost data for decision making.

The primary differences of job order and process costing systems reflect the underlying nature of the manufacturing systems. These differences influence the methods for accumulating and allocating costs. For example, the primary differences between job order and process cost systems are listed below.

1. Manufacturing costs are accumulated to departments, rather than jobs.
2. Manufacturing costs are allocated to products based on units of production.
3. Manufacturing costs are accumulated and transferred between departments.
4. Work in process inventory consists of partially completed production within a department, rather than the sum of job cost sheets of partially completed jobs.

Exhibit 1 illustrates the main differences between the job order and process cost systems. In a job order cost system, product costs are accumulated by job and are summarized on job cost sheets. The job cost sheets provide unit cost information and can be used by management for product pricing, cost control, and inventory valuation. The process manufacturer does not manufacture according to "jobs." Rather, costs are accumulated in work in process accounts by *department*. For example, the departments that accumulate costs for an ice cream manufacturer would be the Mixing Department and the Packaging Department. These employees are assigned to departments to monitor process equipment, load and unload product, and clean process equipment

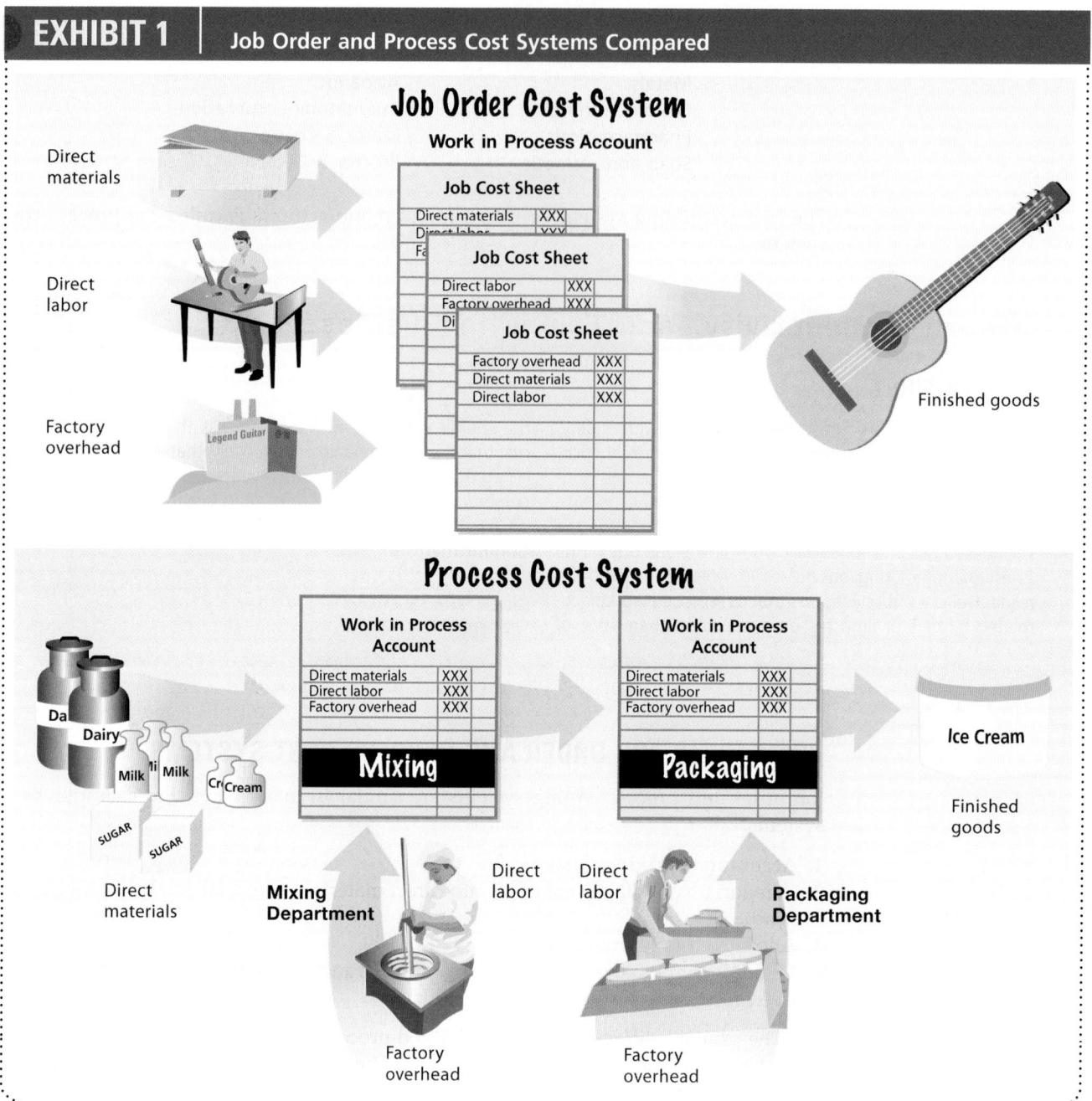

EXHIBIT 1 | **Job Order and Process Cost Systems Compared**

between product runs. Thus, the direct labor is more associated with the process department, than with the product.

Each unit of product that passes through the department is similar. Thus, the production costs reported by each department can be allocated to the product based upon the units produced within the department. The costs of one department can be transferred to a subsequent department. In this way, the cost of the product accumulates across the complete production process. For example, the costs of completed production in the Mixing Department become the costs transferred into the Packaging Department. The departmental unit cost information as well as the final unit cost information can be used by management for cost control. In a job order cost system, the work in process inventory at the end of the accounting period is the sum of the job cost sheets for partially completed jobs. In a process cost system, the amount of work in process inventory is determined by allocating costs between completed and partially completed units within a department.

Example Exercise 18-1

objective **1**

Which of the following industries would normally use job order costing systems, and which would normally use process costing systems?

Home construction	Computer chips
Beverages	Cookies
Military aircraft	Video game design and production

Follow My Example 18-1

Home construction	Job order
Beverages	Process
Military aircraft	Job order
Computer chips	Process
Cookies	Process
Video game design and production	Job order

For Practice: PE 18-1A, PE 18-1B

COST FLOWS FOR A PROCESS MANUFACTURER

Materials costs are a large portion of the costs for most process manufacturers. Often, the materials costs can be as high as 70% of the total manufacturing costs. Thus, accounting for materials costs is very important for process operations.

Exhibit 2 illustrates the physical flow of materials for an ice cream processor. Ice cream is made in a manufacturing plant much the same way as it would be made at home, except on a much larger scale. Direct materials in the form of milk, cream, and sugar are placed into a mixing vessel in the Mixing Department. This vessel is refrigerated to a very cold temperature while the material is mixed with large automated paddles called *agitators*. The Mixing Department uses direct labor and factory overhead (conversion costs) during the mixing process. Direct labor employees prepare the vessel for material, perform vessel cleaning, and set refrigeration temperature and mix speed. Factory overhead includes power and equipment depreciation.

EXHIBIT 2	Physical Flows for a Process Manufacturer

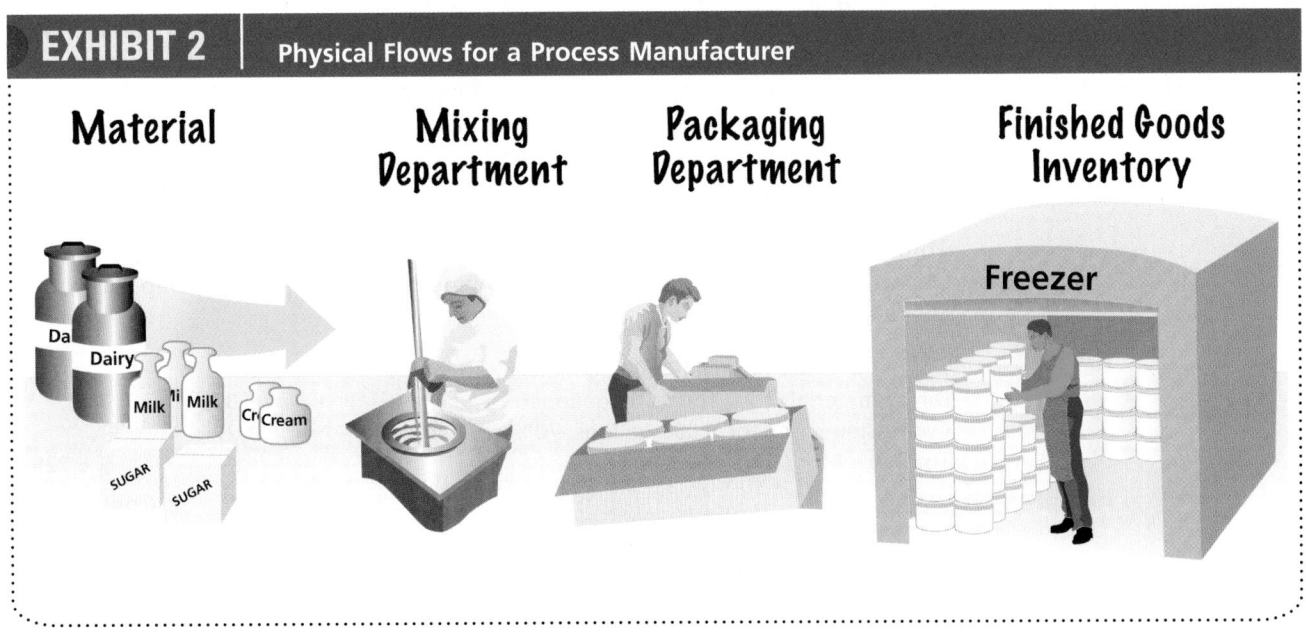

The soft ice cream is then transferred to the Packaging Department, where it is packaged into one-gallon containers. The Packaging Department also uses conversion costs during the packaging process. The ice cream is then transferred to the finished goods inventory for final freezing, prior to shipment to stores.

The cost flows in a process cost system reflect the physical material flows and are illustrated in Exhibit 3. Direct materials, direct labor, and applied factory overhead are debited to the departmental work in process accounts. Completed product is credited to the departmental work in process account and transferred to the next step in the process.

EXHIBIT 3   **Cost Flows for a Process Manufacturer**

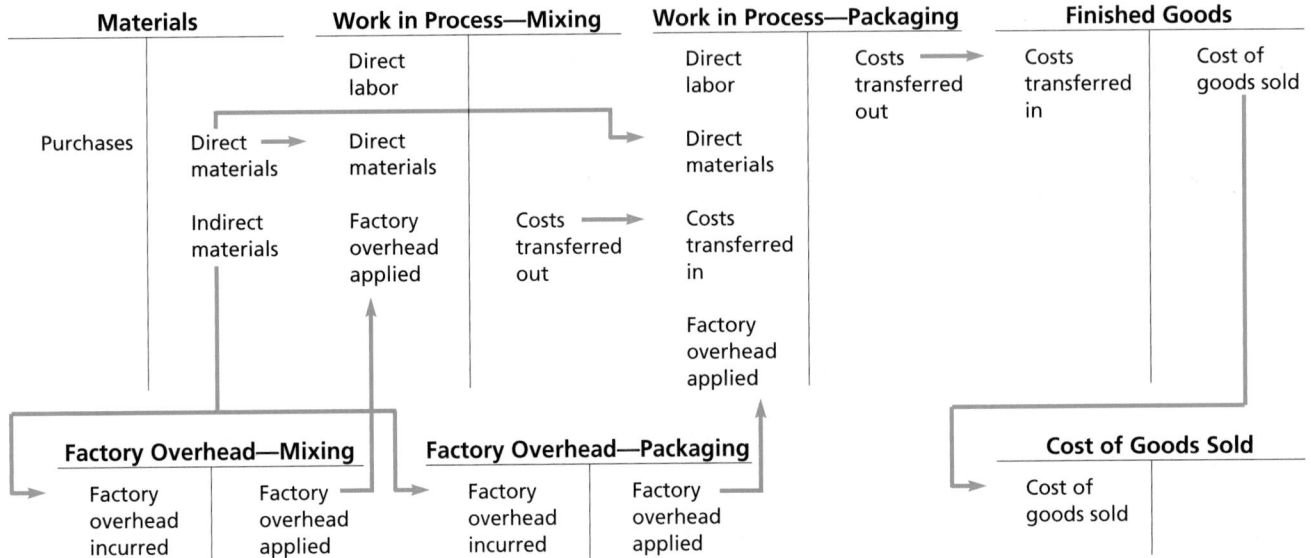

The First-In, First-Out (FIFO) Method

objective   **2**

Prepare a cost of production report, accounting for completed and partially completed units under the FIFO method.

In a process cost system, the accountant determines the cost transferred out and thus the amount remaining in inventory for each department. To determine this cost, the accountant must make a cost flow assumption. Like merchandise inventory, costs can be assumed to flow through the manufacturing process using the first-in, first-out (FIFO), last in, first-out (LIFO), or average cost methods. Because the **first-in, first-out (FIFO) method** is often the same as the physical flow of units, we use the FIFO method in this chapter.[1]

Most process manufacturers have more than one department. In the illustrations that follow, Frozen Delight Ice Cream Company has two departments, Mixing and Packaging. Frozen Delight mixes milk, cream, and sugar in a refrigerated vessel, and then pumps the soft ice cream to the Packaging Department for filling one-gallon containers.

To illustrate the first-in, first-out method, we will simplify by using only the Mixing Department of Frozen Delight. The following data for the Mixing Department are for July 2008:

Inventory in process, July 1, 5,000 gallons:		
Direct materials cost, for 5,000 gallons	$5,000	
Conversion costs, for 5,000 gallons, 70% completed	1,225	
Total inventory in process, July 1		$ 6,225

(continued)

---

1 The average cost method is illustrated in an appendix to this chapter.

Direct materials cost for July, 60,000 gallons	$66,000
Direct labor cost for July	10,500
Factory overhead applied for July	7,275
Total production costs to account for	$90,000
Goods transferred to Packaging in July (includes units in process on July 1), 62,000 gallons	?
Inventory in process, July 31, 3,000 gallons, 25% completed as to conversion costs	?

We assume that all materials used in the department are added at the beginning of the process, and conversion costs (direct labor and factory overhead) are incurred evenly throughout the mixing process. The objective is to determine the cost of goods completed and the ending inventory valuation, which are represented by the question marks. We determine these amounts by using the following four steps:

1. Determine the units to be assigned costs.
2. Compute equivalent units of production.
3. Determine the cost per equivalent unit.
4. Allocate costs to transferred and partially completed units.

STEP 1: DETERMINE THE UNITS TO BE ASSIGNED COSTS

The first step in our illustration is to determine the units to be assigned costs. A unit can be any measure of completed production, such as tons, gallons, pounds, barrels, or cases. We use gallons as the units for Frozen Delight.

Frozen Delight had 65,000 gallons of direct materials charged to production in the Mixing Department for July, as shown below.

Total gallons charged to production:	
In process, July 1	5,000 gallons
Received from materials storage	60,000
Total units accounted for by the Mixing Department	65,000 gallons

There are three categories of units to be assigned costs for an accounting period: **(A)** units in beginning in-process inventory, **(B)** units started and completed during the period, and **(C)** units in ending in-process inventory. Exhibit 4 illustrates these categories in the Mixing Department for July. The 5,000-gallon beginning inventory **(A)** was completed and transferred to the Packaging Department. Frozen Delight started another 60,000 gallons of material into the process during July. Of the 60,000 gallons introduced in July, 3,000 gallons were left incomplete at the end of the month **(C)**. Thus, only 57,000 of the 60,000 gallons were actually started and completed in July **(B)**.

The total units (gallons) to be assigned costs for Frozen Delight is summarized below.

(A)	Inventory in process, July 1, completed in July	5,000 gallons
(B)	Started and completed in July	57,000
	Transferred out to the Packaging Department in July	62,000 gallons
(C)	Inventory in process, July 31	3,000
	Total gallons to be assigned costs	65,000 gallons

Note that the total gallons to be assigned costs equals the total gallons accounted for by the department. The three unit categories (**A**, **B**, and **C**) are used in the remaining steps to determine the cost transferred to the Packaging Department and the cost remaining in the Mixing Department work in process inventory at the end of the period.

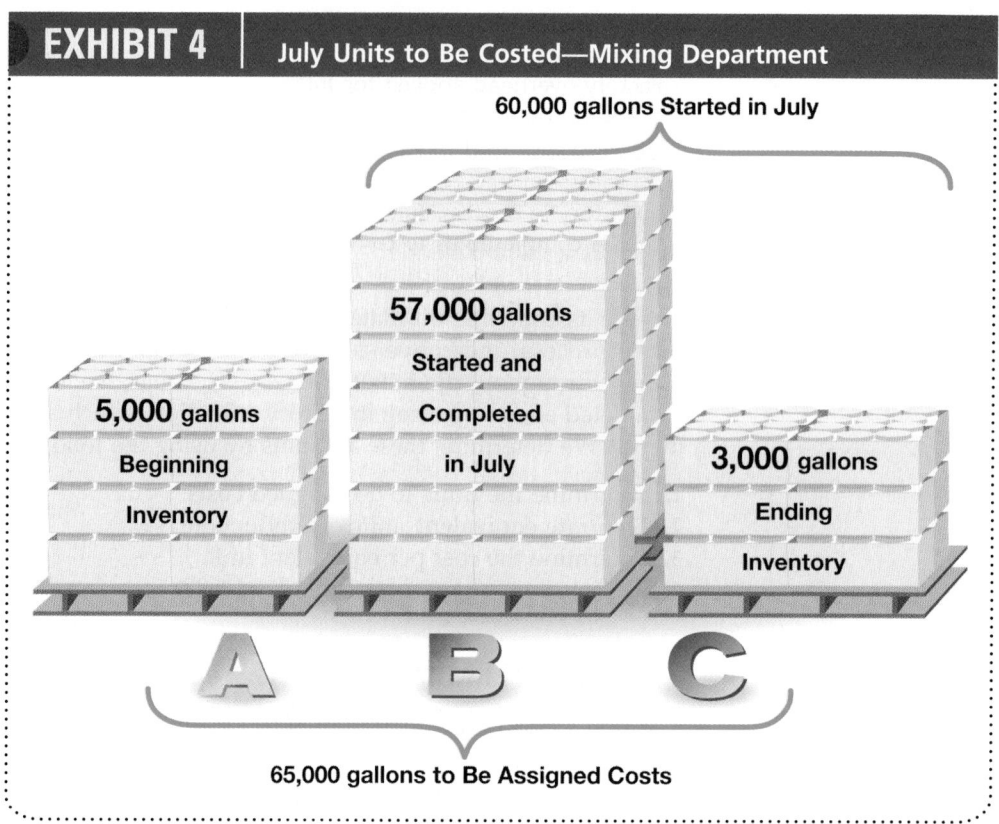

EXHIBIT 4 | July Units to Be Costed—Mixing Department

60,000 gallons Started in July

57,000 gallons Started and Completed in July

5,000 gallons Beginning Inventory

3,000 gallons Ending Inventory

A B C

65,000 gallons to Be Assigned Costs

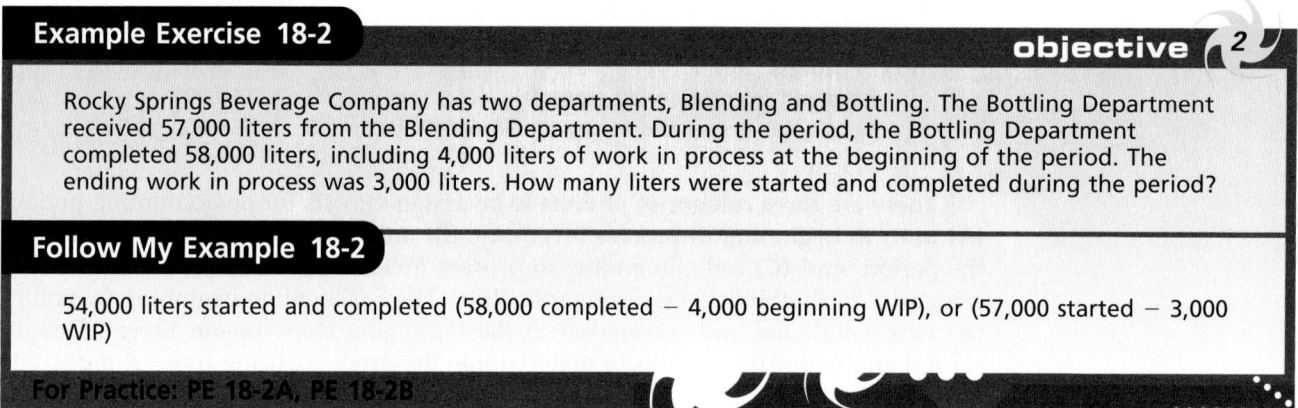

Example Exercise 18-2

objective 2

Rocky Springs Beverage Company has two departments, Blending and Bottling. The Bottling Department received 57,000 liters from the Blending Department. During the period, the Bottling Department completed 58,000 liters, including 4,000 liters of work in process at the beginning of the period. The ending work in process was 3,000 liters. How many liters were started and completed during the period?

Follow My Example 18-2

54,000 liters started and completed (58,000 completed − 4,000 beginning WIP), or (57,000 started − 3,000 WIP)

For Practice: PE 18-2A, PE 18-2B

STEP 2: COMPUTE EQUIVALENT UNITS OF PRODUCTION

Process manufacturers often have some partially processed materials remaining in production at the end of a period. For example, Frozen Delight might end its accounting period when a batch of ice cream is still in a vessel being mixed. In this case, the costs of production must be allocated between the units that have been completed and transferred to the next process (or finished goods), and those that are only partially completed and remain within the department. This allocation is determined using whole units and equivalent units of production.

Whole units are the number of units in production during a period, whether completed or not. **Equivalent units of production** are the portion of whole units that were completed with respect to either materials or conversion costs within a given accounting period. For example, assume that a 1,000-gallon batch (vessel) of ice cream is only 40% complete in the mixing process at the end of the period. In this case, the amount of conversion effort, such as power cost, for that batch is also only 40% complete.

Equivalent units for materials and conversion costs are usually determined separately because they are often introduced at different times or at different rates in the production process. In contrast, direct labor and factory overhead are normally combined together as conversion costs because they are often incurred in production at the same time and rate.

Materials Equivalent Units   To allocate materials costs between the completed and partially completed units, it is necessary to determine how materials are added during the manufacturing process. In the case of Frozen Delight, the materials are added at the beginning of the mixing process. In other words, the mixing process cannot begin without the ice cream ingredients. The equivalent unit computation for materials in July is as follows:

	Total Whole Units	Percent Materials Added in July	Equivalent Units for Direct Materials
Inventory in process, July 1	5,000	0%	0
Started and completed in July (62,000 − 5,000)	57,000	100%	57,000
Transferred out to Packaging Department in July	62,000	—	57,000
Inventory in process, July 31	3,000	100%	3,000
Total gallons to be assigned cost	65,000		60,000

The whole units from step 1 are multiplied by the percentage of materials that are added in July for the in-process inventories and units started and completed. The equivalent units for direct materials are illustrated in Exhibit 5.

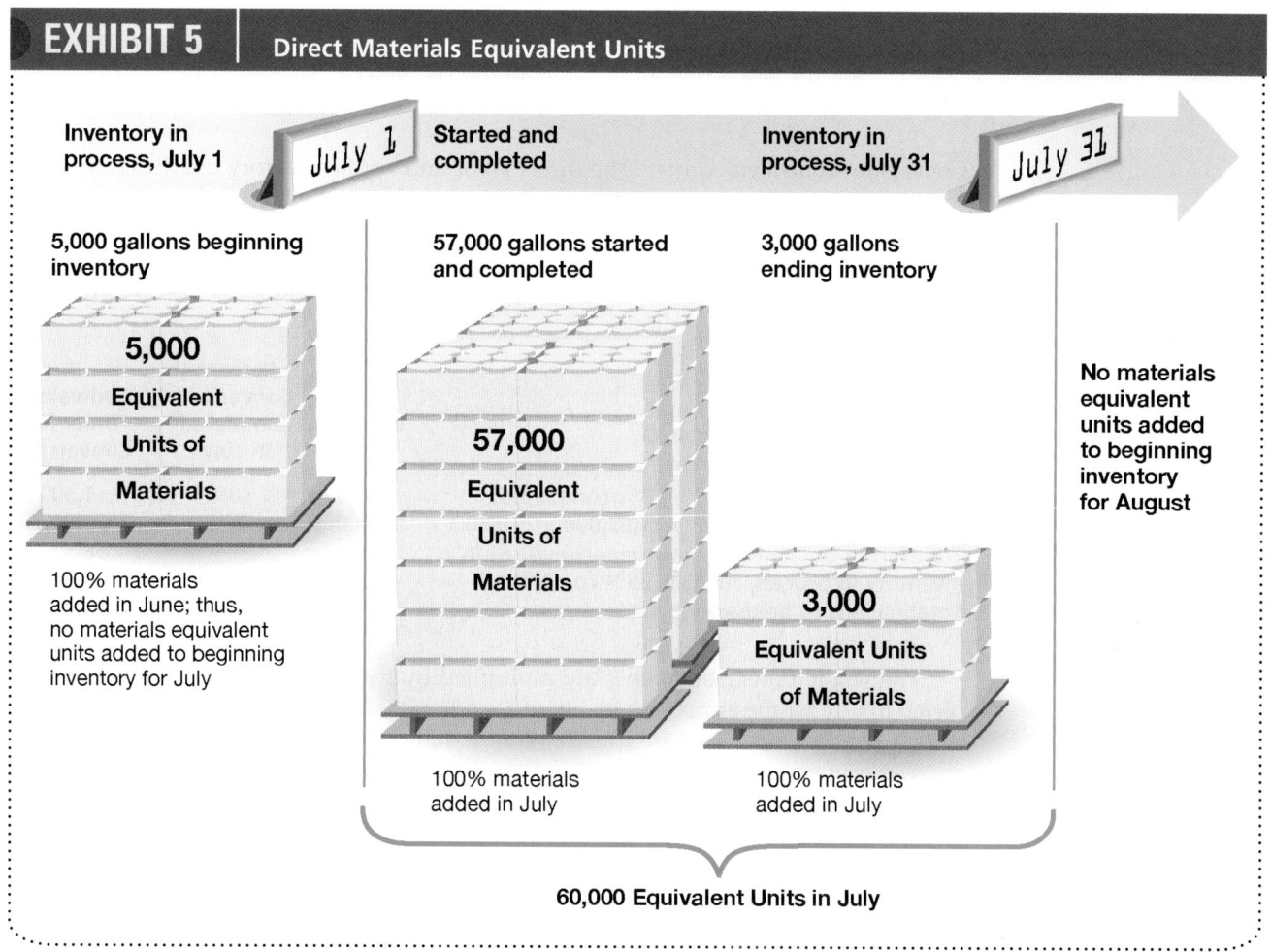

EXHIBIT 5 | **Direct Materials Equivalent Units**

Inventory in process, July 1 — July 1 — Started and completed — Inventory in process, July 31 — July 31

5,000 gallons beginning inventory

5,000 Equivalent Units of Materials

100% materials added in June; thus, no materials equivalent units added to beginning inventory for July

57,000 gallons started and completed

57,000 Equivalent Units of Materials

100% materials added in July

3,000 gallons ending inventory

3,000 Equivalent Units of Materials

100% materials added in July

No materials equivalent units added to beginning inventory for August

60,000 Equivalent Units in July

The direct materials for the 5,000 gallons of July 1 in-process inventory were introduced in June. Thus, no materials units were added in July for the inventory in process on July 1. All of the 57,000 gallons started and completed in July were 100% complete with respect to materials. Thus, 57,000 equivalent units of materials were added in July. All the materials for the July 31 in-process inventory were introduced at the beginning of the process. Thus, 3,000 equivalent units of material for the July 31 in-process inventory were added in July.

Example Exercise 18-3   objective ② 2

The Bottling Department of Rocky Springs Beverage Company had 4,000 liters in beginning work in process inventory (30% complete). During the period, 58,000 liters were completed. The ending work in process inventory was 3,000 liters (60% complete). What are the total equivalent units for direct materials if materials are added at the beginning of the process?

Follow My Example 18-3

	Total Whole Units	Percent Materials Added in Period	Equivalent Units for Direct Materials
Inventory in process, beginning of period	4,000	0%	0
Started and completed during the period	54,000*	100%	54,000
Transferred out of Bottling (completed)	58,000	—	54,000
Inventory in process, end of period	3,000	100%	3,000
Total units to be assigned costs	61,000		57,000

*(58,000 − 4,000)

For Practice: PE 18-3A, PE 18-3B

Conversion Equivalent Units   The direct labor and applied factory overhead are often combined as conversion costs because they are both usually incurred evenly throughout a process. For example, direct labor, utilities, and machine depreciation are usually used uniformly during processing. Thus, the conversion equivalent units are added in July in direct relation to the percentage of processing completed in July. The computations for July are as follows:

	Total Whole Units	Percent Conversion Completed in July	Equivalent Units for Conversion
Inventory in process, July 1 (70% completed)	5,000	30%	1,500
Started and completed in July (62,000 − 5,000)	57,000	100%	57,000
Transferred out to Packaging Department in July	62,000	—	58,500
Inventory in process, July 31 (25% completed)	3,000	25%	750
Total gallons to be assigned cost	65,000		59,250

The whole units from step 1 are multiplied by the percentage of conversion completed in July for the in-process inventories and units started and completed. The equivalent units for conversion are illustrated in Exhibit 6.

The conversion equivalent units of the July 1 in-process inventory are 30% of the 5,000 gallons, or 1,500 equivalent units. Since 70% of the conversion had been completed on July 1, only 30% of the conversion effort for these gallons was incurred in July. All the units started and completed used converting effort in July. Thus, conversion equivalent units are 100% of these gallons. The equivalent units for the July 31 in-process inventory are 25% of the 3,000 gallons because only 25% of the converting has been completed with respect to these gallons in July.

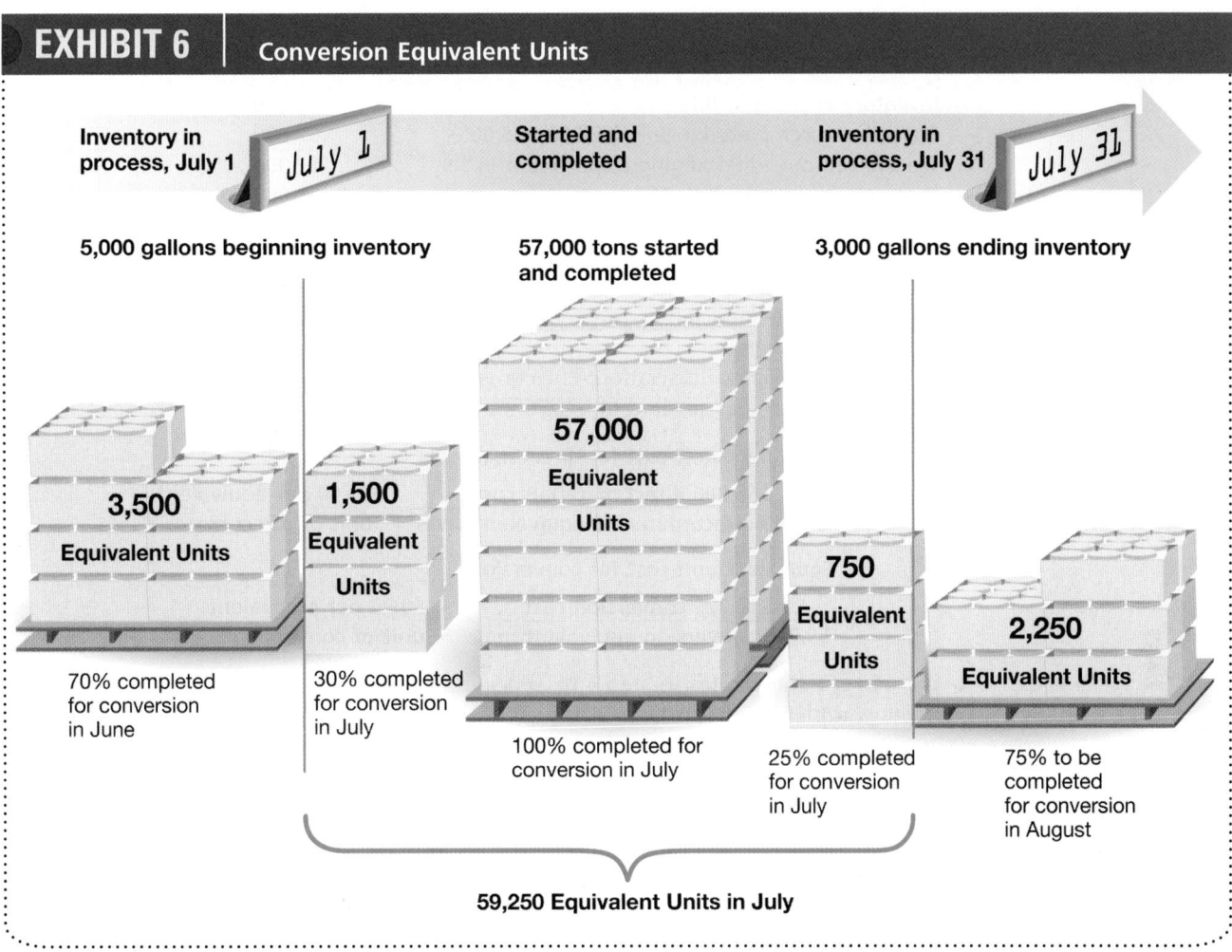

EXHIBIT 6 | Conversion Equivalent Units

5,000 gallons beginning inventory

57,000 tons started and completed

3,000 gallons ending inventory

3,500 Equivalent Units — 70% completed for conversion in June

1,500 Equivalent Units — 30% completed for conversion in July

57,000 Equivalent Units — 100% completed for conversion in July

750 Equivalent Units — 25% completed for conversion in July

2,250 Equivalent Units — 75% to be completed for conversion in August

59,250 Equivalent Units in July

Example Exercise 18-4
objective 2

The Bottling Department of Rocky Springs Beverage Company had 4,000 liters in beginning work in process inventory (30% complete). During the period, 58,000 liters were completed. The ending work in process inventory was 3,000 liters (60% complete). What are the total equivalent units for conversion costs?

Follow My Example 18-4

	Total Whole Units	Percent Conversion Completed in Period	Equivalent Units for Conversion
Inventory in process, beginning of period	4,000	70%	2,800
Started and completed during the period	54,000*	100%	54,000
Transferred out of Bottling (completed)	58,000	—	56,800
Inventory in process, end of period	3,000	60%	1,800
Total units to be assigned costs	61,000		58,600

*(58,000 − 4,000)

For Practice: PE 18-4A, PE 18-4B

STEP 3: DETERMINE THE COST PER EQUIVALENT UNIT

In step 3, we compute the cost per equivalent unit. The July direct materials and conversion cost equivalent unit totals for Frozen Delight's Mixing Department are reproduced from step 2 as follows:

	Equivalent Units	
	Direct Materials	**Conversion**
Inventory in process, July 1	0	1,500
Started and completed in July (62,000 − 5,000)	57,000	57,000
Transferred out to Packaging Department in July	57,000	58,500
Inventory in process, July 31	3,000	750
Total gallons to be assigned cost	60,000	59,250

The **cost per equivalent unit** is determined by dividing the direct materials and conversion costs incurred in July by the respective total equivalent units for direct materials and conversion costs. The direct materials and conversion costs were given at the beginning of this illustration. The conversion cost is the direct labor of $10,500 plus the factory overhead applied of $7,275, or $17,775. These calculations are as follows:

Equivalent unit cost for direct materials:

$$\frac{\$66,000 \text{ direct materials cost}}{60,000 \text{ direct materials equivalent units}} = \frac{\$1.10 \text{ per equivalent}}{\text{unit of direct materials}}$$

Equivalent unit cost for conversion:

$$\frac{\$17,775 \text{ conversion cost}}{59,250 \text{ conversion equivalent units}} = \frac{\$0.30 \text{ per equivalent}}{\text{unit of conversion}}$$

We will use these rates in step 4 to allocate the direct materials and conversion costs to the completed and partially completed units.

Example Exercise 18-5

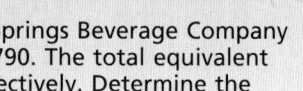 objective 2

The cost of direct materials transferred into the Bottling Department of Rocky Springs Beverage Company is $22,800. The conversion cost for the period in the Bottling Department is $8,790. The total equivalent units for direct materials and conversion are 57,000 liters and 58,600 liters, respectively. Determine the direct materials and conversion cost per equivalent unit.

Follow My Example 18-5

Equivalent units of direct materials: $\dfrac{\$22,800}{57,000 \text{ liters}} = \$0.40 \text{ per liter}$

Equivalent units of conversion: $\dfrac{\$8,790}{58,600 \text{ liters}} = \$0.15 \text{ per liter}$

For Practice: PE 18-5A, PE 18-5B

STEP 4: ALLOCATE COSTS TO TRANSFERRED AND PARTIALLY COMPLETED UNITS

In step 4, we multiply the equivalent unit rates by their respective equivalent units of production in order to determine the cost of transferred and partially completed units. The cost of the July 1 in-process inventory, completed and transferred out to the Packaging Department, is determined as follows:

	Direct Materials Costs	Conversion Costs	Total Costs
Inventory in process, July 1 balance			$6,225
Equivalent units for completing the July 1 in-process inventory	0	1,500	
Equivalent unit cost	×$1.10	×$0.30	
Cost of completed July 1 in-process inventory	0	$ 450	450
Cost of July 1 in-process inventory transferred to Packaging Department			$6,675

The July 1 in-process inventory cost of $6,225 is carried over from June and will be transferred to Packaging. The cost required to finish the July 1 in-process inventory is $450, which consists of conversion costs required to complete the remaining 30% of the processing. This total does not include direct materials costs, since these costs were added at the beginning of the process in June. The conversion costs required to complete the beginning inventory are added to the balance carried over from the previous month to yield a total cost of the completed July 1 in-process inventory of $6,675.

The 57,000 units started and completed in July receive 100% of their direct materials and conversion costs in July. The costs associated with the units started and completed are determined by multiplying the equivalent units in step 2 by the unit costs in step 3, as follows:

	Direct Materials Costs	Conversion Costs	Total Costs
Units started and completed in July	57,000	57,000	
Equivalent unit cost	× $1.10	× $0.30	
Cost to complete the units started and completed in July	$62,700	$17,100	$79,800

The total cost transferred to the Packaging Department is the sum of the beginning inventory cost from the previous period ($6,225), the additional costs incurred in July to complete the beginning inventory ($450), and the costs incurred for the units started and completed in July ($79,800). Thus, the total cost transferred to Packaging is $86,475 ($6,225 + $450 + $79,800).

The units of ending inventory have not been transferred, so they must be valued at July 31. The costs associated with the partially completed units in the ending inventory are determined by multiplying the equivalent units in step 2 by the unit costs in step 3, as follows:

	Direct Materials Costs	Conversion Costs	Total Costs
Equivalent units in ending inventory	3,000	750	
Equivalent unit cost	×$1.10	×$0.30	
Cost of ending inventory	$ 3,300	$ 225	$3,525

The units in the ending work in process inventory have received 100% of their materials in July. Thus, the materials cost incurred in July for the ending inventory is $3,300, or 3,000 equivalent units of materials multiplied by $1.10. The conversion cost incurred in July for the ending inventory is $225, which is 750 equivalent units of conversion (3,000 units, 25% complete) for the ending inventory multiplied by $0.30. Summing the conversion and materials costs, the total ending inventory cost is $3,525.

Example Exercise 18-6 objective ⟨2⟩

The cost per equivalent unit of direct materials and conversion in the Bottling Department of Rocky Springs Beverage Company is $0.40 and $0.15, respectively. The equivalent units to be assigned costs are as follows:

	Equivalent Units	
	Direct Materials	Conversion
Inventory in process, beginning of period	0	2,800
Started and completed during the period	54,000	54,000
Transferred out of Bottling (completed)	54,000	56,800
Inventory in process, end of period	3,000	1,800
Total units to be assigned costs	57,000	58,600

The beginning work in process inventory had a cost of $1,860. Determine the cost of completed and transferred-out production and the ending work in process inventory.

(continued)

Follow My Example 18-6

	Direct Materials Costs	Conversion Costs	Total Costs
Inventory in process, balance			$ 1,860
Inventory in process, beginning of period	0 +	2,800 × $0.15	420
Started and completed during the period	54,000 × $0.40 +	54,000 × $0.15	29,700
Transferred out of Bottling (completed)			$31,980
Inventory in process, end of period	3,000 × $0.40 +	1,800 × $0.15	1,470
Total costs assigned by the Bottling Department			$33,450

Completed and transferred out of production	$31,980
Inventory in process, ending	$1,470

For Practice: PE 18-6A, PE 18-6B

BRINGING IT ALL TOGETHER: THE COST OF PRODUCTION REPORT

A **cost of production report** is normally prepared for each processing department at periodic intervals. The July cost of production report for Frozen Delight's Mixing Department is shown in Exhibit 7. As can be seen on the report, the two question marks from page 797 can now be determined. The cost of goods transferred to the Packaging Department in July was $86,475, while the cost of the ending work in process in the Mixing Department on July 31 is $3,525.

The report summarizes the four previous steps by providing the following production quantity and cost data:

1. The units for which the department is accountable and the disposition of those units.
2. The production costs incurred by the department and the allocation of those costs between completed and partially completed units.

The cost of production report is also used to control costs. Each department manager is responsible for the units entering production and the costs incurred in the department. Any failure to account for all costs and any significant differences in unit product costs from one month to another should be investigated.

For example, the cost per equivalent unit for June can be compared with the cost per equivalent unit from the July cost of production report. The cost per equivalent unit for June can be determined from the beginning inventory. The Frozen Delight data on page 796 indicated that the July 1 inventory in process consisted of the following:

Direct materials cost, 5,000 gallons	$5,000
Conversion costs, 5,000 gallons, 70% completed	1,225
Total inventory in process, July 1	$6,225

Thus, the cost per equivalent unit incurred in June can be determined by dividing the direct material and conversion cost by their respective equivalent units in the beginning inventory as follows:

Direct materials cost per equivalent unit (June):

$$\frac{\$5,000}{5,000 \text{ equivalent units of materials}} = \$1.00 \text{ per equivalent unit}$$

Conversion cost per equivalent unit (June):

$$\frac{\$1,225}{(5,000 \times 70\%) \text{ equivalent units of conversion cost}} = \$0.35 \text{ per equivalent unit}$$

Thus, the cost per equivalent unit for materials increased, while the cost per equivalent unit for conversion costs decreased between June and July, as shown at the bottom of the next page.

EXHIBIT 7	Cost of Production Report for Frozen Delight's Mixing Department—FIFO

	A	B	C	D	E	
		Frozen Delight Ice Cream Company				
		Cost of Production Report—Mixing Department				
		For the Month Ended July 31, 2008				
		Step 1	Step 2			
		Whole Units	Equivalent Units			
	UNITS		Direct Materials	Conversion		
1	Units charged to production:					1
2	Inventory in process, July 1	5,000				2
3	Received from materials storeroom	60,000				3
4	Total units accounted for by the Mixing Department	65,000				4
5						5
6	Units to be assigned costs:					6
7	Inventory in process, July 1 (70% completed)	5,000	0	1,500		7
8	Started and completed in July	57,000	57,000	57,000		8
9	Transferred to Packaging Department in July	62,000	57,000	58,500		9
10	Inventory in process, July 31 (25% completed)	3,000	3,000	750		10
11	Total units to be assigned costs	65,000	60,000	59,250		11
12						12
13			Costs			13
14	**COSTS**		Direct Materials	Conversion	Total	14
15	**Step 3**					15
16	Costs per equivalent unit:					16
17	Total costs for July in Mixing Department		$ 66,000	$ 17,775		17
18	Total equivalent units (from step 2 above)		/ 60,000	/ 59,250		18
19	Cost per equivalent unit		$ 1.10	$ 0.30		19
20						20
21	Costs assigned to production:					21
22	Inventory in process, July 1				$ 6,225	22
23	Costs incurred in July				83,775[a]	23
24	Total costs accounted for by the Mixing Department				$90,000	24
25						25
26	**Step 4**					26
27	Cost allocated to completed and partially					27
28	completed units:					28
29	Inventory in process, July 1—balance				$ 6,225	29
30	To complete inventory in process, July 1		$ 0 +	$ 450[b] =	450	30
31	Started and completed in July		62,700[c] +	17,100[d] =	79,800	31
32	Transferred to Packaging Department in July				$86,475	32
33	Inventory in process, July 31		$ 3,300[e] +	$ 225[f] =	3,525	33
34	Total costs assigned by the Mixing Department				$90,000	34

[a]$66,000 + $10,500 + $7,275 = $83,775   [b]1,500 units × $0.30 = $450   [c]57,000 units × $1.10 = $62,700   [d]57,000 units × $0.30 = $17,100
[e]3,000 units × $1.10 = $3,300   [f]750 units × $0.30 = $225

	Inventory in process, July 1	July Cost of Production Report	Difference
Cost per equivalent unit— direct materials	$1.00	$1.10	$0.10 Increase
Cost per equivalent unit— conversion costs	$0.35	$0.30	$0.05 Decrease

This information would be used by Frozen Delight's management to identify cost changes requiring further investigation, such as the increase in the direct materials cost per equivalent unit.

Journal Entries for a Process Cost System

objective   **3**

Prepare journal entries for transactions of a process manufacturer.

To illustrate the journal entries to record the cost flows in a process costing system, we will use the July transactions for Frozen Delight. The entries in summary form for these transactions are shown here and on the following page. In practice, transactions would be recorded daily.

a.   Purchased materials, including milk, cream, sugar, packaging, and indirect materials on account, $88,000.

	Materials		88 0 0 0 00	
	Accounts Payable			88 0 0 0 00

b.   The Mixing Department requisitioned milk, cream, and sugar, $66,000. This is the amount originally indicated on page 797. Another $8,000 of packaging materials was requisitioned by the Packaging Department. Indirect materials for the Mixing and Packaging departments were $4,125 and $3,000, respectively.

	Work in Process—Mixing		66 0 0 0 00	
	Work in Process—Packaging		8 0 0 0 00	
	Factory Overhead—Mixing		4 1 2 5 00	
	Factory Overhead—Packaging		3 0 0 0 00	
	Materials			81 1 2 5 00

c.   Incurred direct labor in the Mixing and Packaging departments of $10,500 (from page 797) and $12,000, respectively.

	Work in Process—Mixing		10 5 0 0 00	
	Work in Process—Packaging		12 0 0 0 00	
	Wages Payable			22 5 0 0 00

d.   Recognized equipment depreciation for the Mixing and Packaging departments of $3,350 and $1,000, respectively.

	Factory Overhead—Mixing		3 3 5 0 00	
	Factory Overhead—Packaging		1 0 0 0 00	
	Accumulated Depreciation—Equipment			4 3 5 0 00

e.   Applied factory overhead to Mixing and Packaging departments of $7,275 (from page 797) and $3,500, respectively.

	Work in Process—Mixing		7 2 7 5 00	
	Work in Process—Packaging		3 5 0 0 00	
	Factory Overhead—Mixing			7 2 7 5 00
	Factory Overhead—Packaging			3 5 0 0 00

f.   Transferred costs of $86,475 from the Mixing Department to the Packaging Department per the cost of production report in Exhibit 7.

	Work in Process—Packaging		86 4 7 5 00	
	Work in Process—Mixing			86 4 7 5 00

g. Transferred goods of $106,000 out of the Packaging Department to Finished Goods according to the Packaging Department cost of production report (not illustrated).

Finished Goods—Ice Cream	106 000 00	
Work in Process—Packaging		106 000 00

h. Recorded cost of goods sold out of the finished goods inventory of $107,000.

Cost of Goods Sold	107 000 00	
Finished Goods—Ice Cream		107 000 00

Exhibit 8 shows the flow of costs for each transaction. Note that the highlighted amounts in Exhibit 8 were determined from assigning the costs charged to production in the Mixing Department. These amounts were computed and are shown at the bottom of the cost of production report for the Mixing Department in Exhibit 7. Likewise, the amount transferred out of the Packaging Department to Finished Goods would have also been determined from a cost of production report for the Packaging Department.

EXHIBIT 8 Frozen Delight's Cost Flows

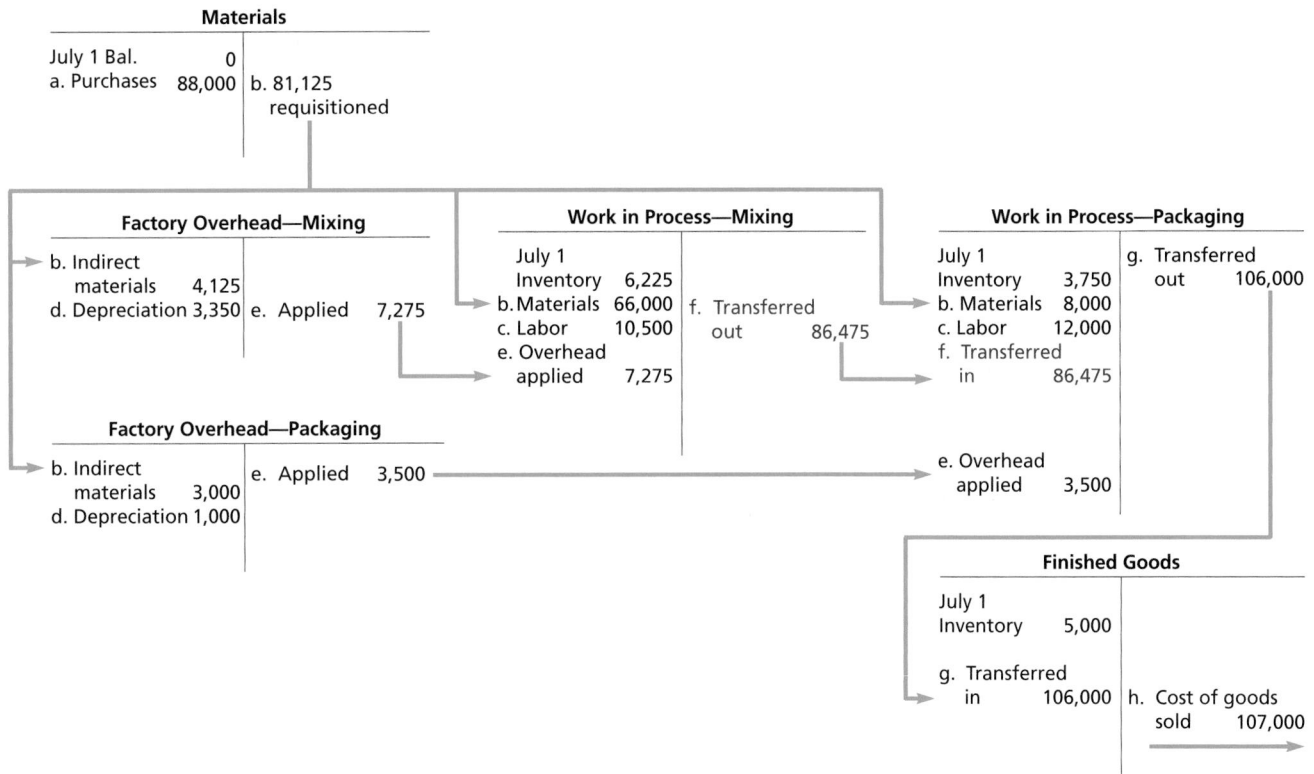

The ending inventories for Frozen Delight would be reported on the July 31 balance sheet as follows:

Materials	$ 6,875
Work in Process—Mixing Department	3,525
Work in Process—Packaging Department	7,725
Finished Goods	4,000
Total inventories	$22,125

The $3,525 of Work in Process—Mixing Department is the amount determined from the bottom of the cost of production report in Exhibit 7.

Example Exercise 18-7

The cost of materials transferred into the Bottling Department of Rocky Springs Beverage Company is $22,800, including $20,000 from the Blending Department and $2,800 from the materials storeroom. The conversion cost for the period in the Bottling Department is $8,790 ($3,790 factory overhead applied and $5,000 direct labor). The total cost transferred to Finished Goods for the period was $31,980. The Bottling Department had a beginning inventory of $1,860.

a. Journalize (1) the cost of transferred-in materials, (2) conversion costs, and (3) the costs transferred out to Finished Goods.
b. Determine the balance of Work in Process—Bottling at the end of the period.

Follow My Example 18-7

a.	1. Work in Process—Bottling	22,800	
	Work in Process—Blending		20,000
	Materials		2,800
	2. Work in Process—Bottling	8,790	
	Factory Overhead—Bottling		3,790
	Wages Payable		5,000
	3. Finished Goods	31,980	
	Work in Process—Bottling		31,980
b.	$1,470 ($1,860 + $22,800 + $8,790 − $31,980)		

For Practice: PE 18-7A, PE 18-7B

Using the Cost of Production Report for Decision Making

The cost of production report is one source of information that may be used by managers to control and improve operations. A cost of production report will normally list costs in greater detail than in Exhibit 7. This greater detail helps management isolate problems and opportunities. To illustrate, assume that the Blending Department of Holland Beverage Company prepared cost of production reports for April and May. In addition, assume that the Blending Department had no beginning or ending work in process inventory either month. Thus, in this simple case, there is no need to determine equivalent units of production for allocating costs between completed and partially completed units. The cost of production reports for April and May in the Blending Department are as follows:

	A	B	C	D	
	Cost of Production Reports				
	Holland Beverage Company—Blending Department				
	For the Months Ended April 30 and May 31, 2008				
		April	**May**		
1	Direct materials	$ 20,000	$ 40,600		1
2	Direct labor	15,000	29,400		2
3	Energy	8,000	20,000		3
4	Repairs	4,000	8,000		4
5	Tank cleaning	3,000	8,000		5
6	Total	$ 50,000	$106,000		6
7	Units completed	/ 100,000	/ 200,000		7
8	Cost per unit	$ 0.50	$ 0.53		8

Note that the preceding reports provide more cost detail than simply reporting direct materials and conversion costs. The May results indicate that total unit costs have increased from $0.50 to $0.53, or 6% from the previous month. What caused this in-

Middle Tennessee Lumber Co., Inc., purchased new computer and sawing technology that improved the cutting yield by approximately 10%. The new equipment scans the rough-cut lumber with a laser beam. The scanned information is input to a software program that calculates the optimum cutting pattern for minimizing trim waste.

crease? To determine the possible causes for this increase, the cost of production report may be restated in per-unit terms by dividing all the cost information by the number of units completed, as shown below.

	A	B	C	D	
	Blending Department Per-Unit Expense Comparisons				
		April	May	% Change	
1	Direct materials	$0.200	$0.203	1.50%	1
2	Direct labor	0.150	0.147	−2.00%	2
3	Energy	0.080	0.100	25.00%	3
4	Repairs	0.040	0.040	0.00%	4
5	Tank cleaning	0.030	0.040	33.33%	5
6	Total	$0.500	$0.530	6.00%	6

Both energy and tank cleaning per-unit costs have increased dramatically in May. Further investigation should focus on these costs. For example, an increasing trend in energy may indicate that the machines are losing fuel efficiency, thereby requiring the company to purchase an increasing amount of fuel. This unfavorable trend could motivate management to repair the machines. The tank cleaning costs could be investigated in a similar fashion.

In addition to unit production cost trends, managers of process manufacturers are also concerned about yield trends. **Yield** is the ratio of the materials output quantity to the input quantity. A yield less than one occurs when the output quantity is less than the input quantity due to materials losses during the process. For example, if 1,000 pounds of sugar entered the packing operation, and only 980 pounds of sugar were packed, the yield would be 98%. Two percent or 20 pounds of sugar were lost or spilled during the packing process.

Example Exercise 18-8   objective **4**

The cost of energy consumed in producing good units in the Bottling Department of Rocky Springs Beverage Company was $4,200 and $3,700 for March and April, respectively. The number of equivalent units produced in March and April was 70,000 liters and 74,000 liters, respectively. Evaluate the cost of energy between the two months.

Follow My Example 18-8

Energy cost per liter, March: $\dfrac{\$4,200}{70,000 \text{ liters}} = \$0.06$

Energy cost per liter, April: $\dfrac{\$3,700}{74,000 \text{ liters}} = \$0.05$

The cost of energy has appeared to improve by 1 cent per liter between March and April.

For Practice: PE 18-8A, PE 18-8B

Just-in-Time Processing

objective **5**

Contrast just-in-time processing with conventional manufacturing practices.

The objective of many companies is to produce products with high quality, low cost, and instant availability. One approach to achieving this objective is to implement just-in-time processing. **Just-in-time processing (JIT)** is a philosophy that focuses on reducing time and cost and eliminating poor quality. A JIT system achieves production efficiencies and flexibility by reorganizing the traditional production process.

In a traditional production process (illustrated in Exhibit 9), a product moves from process to process as each function or step is completed. Each worker is assigned a

EXHIBIT 9 | Traditional Production Line

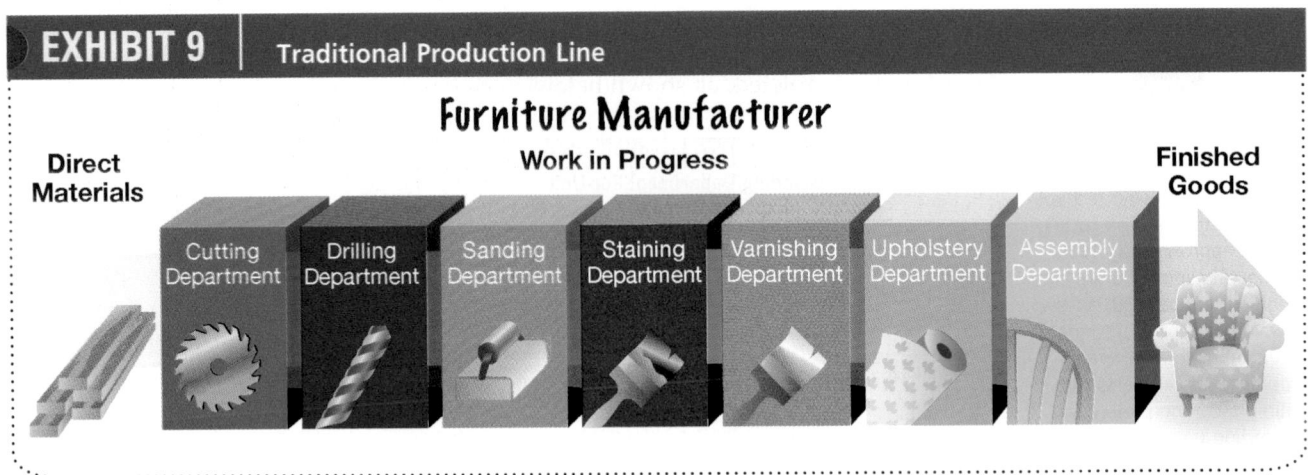

specific job, which is performed repeatedly as unfinished products are received from the preceding department. For example, a furniture manufacturer might use seven production departments to perform the operating functions necessary to manufacture furniture, as shown in the diagram in Exhibit 9.

For the furniture maker in the illustration, manufacturing would begin in the Cutting Department, where the wood would be cut to design specifications. Next, the Drilling Department would perform the drilling function, after which the Sanding Department would sand the wood, the Staining Department would stain the furniture, and the Varnishing Department would apply varnish and other protective coatings. Then, the Upholstery Department would add fabric and other materials. Finally, the Assembly Department would assemble the furniture to complete the process.

In the traditional production process, production supervisors attempt to enter enough materials into the process to keep all the manufacturing departments operating. Some departments, however, may process materials more rapidly than others. In addition, if one department stops production because of machine breakdowns, for example, the preceding departments usually continue production in order to avoid idle time. This may result in a build-up of work in process inventories in some departments.

In a just-in-time system, processing functions are combined into work centers, sometimes called **manufacturing cells**. For example, the seven departments illustrated above for the furniture manufacturer might be reorganized into three work centers. As shown in the diagram in Exhibit 10, Work Center One would perform the cutting, drilling, and sanding functions, Work Center Two would perform the staining and varnishing functions, and Work Center Three would perform the upholstery and assembly functions.

The Internet complements a just-in-time processing strategy. Ford Motor Company states that the impact of the Internet is the equivalent of "the moving assembly line of the 21st Century." This is because the Internet will connect the whole supply chain—from customers to suppliers—to create a fast and efficient manufacturing system.

EXHIBIT 10 | Just-in-Time Production Line

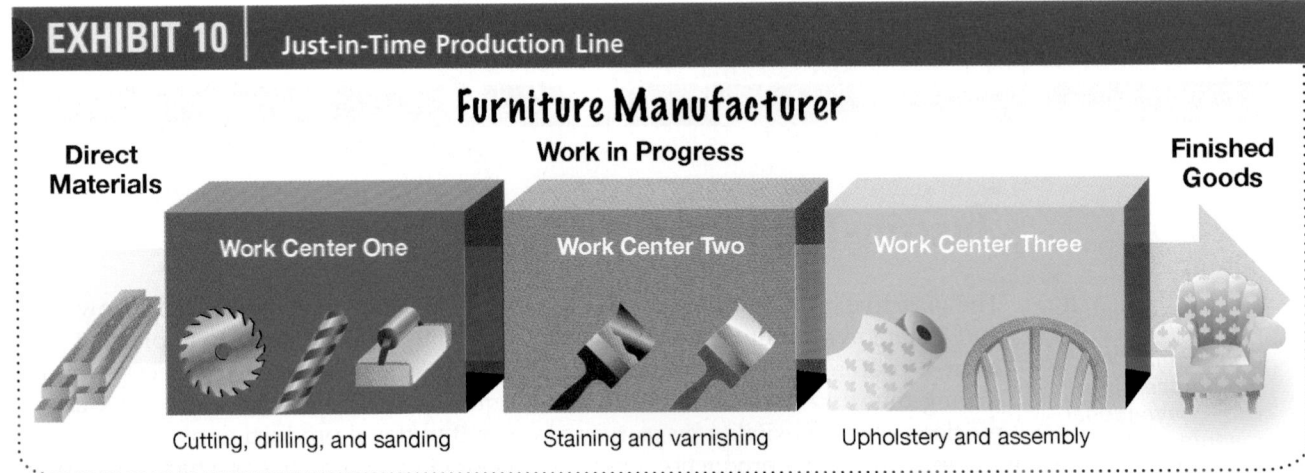

In the traditional production line, a worker typically performs only one function. However, in a work center in which several functions take place, the workers are often cross-trained to perform more than one function. Research has indicated that workers who perform several manufacturing functions identify better with the end product. This creates pride in the product and improves quality and productivity.

Implementing JIT may also result in reorganizing service activities. Specifically, the service activities may be assigned to individual work centers, rather than to centralized service departments. For example, each work center may be assigned the responsibility for the repair and maintenance of its machinery and equipment. Accepting this responsibility creates an environment in which workers gain a better understanding of the production process and the machinery. In turn, workers tend to take better care of the machinery, which decreases repairs and maintenance costs, reduces machine downtime, and improves product quality.

In a JIT system, wasted motion from moving the product and materials is reduced. The product is often placed on a movable carrier that is centrally located in the work center. After the workers in a work center have completed their activities with the product, the entire carrier and any additional materials are moved just in time to satisfy the demand or need of the next work center. In this sense, the product is said to be "pulled through." Each work center is connected to other work centers through information contained on Kanbans, which is a Japanese term for cards.

The experience of Caterpillar illustrates the impact of JIT. Before implementing JIT, an average transmission would travel 10 miles through the factory and require 1,000 pieces of paper for materials, labor, and movement transactions. After implementing JIT, Caterpillar improved manufacturing so that an average transmission traveled only 200 feet and required only 10 pieces of paper.

In summary, the primary benefit of JIT systems is the increased efficiency of operations, which is achieved by eliminating waste and simplifying the production process. At the same time, JIT systems emphasize continuous improvement in the manufacturing process and the improvement of product quality.

Business Connections

REAL WORLD

P&G'S "PIT STOPS"

What do Procter & Gamble and Formula One racing have in common? The answer begins with P&G's Packing Department, which is where detergents and other products are filled on a "pack line." Containers move down the pack line and are filled with products from a packing machine. When it was time to change from a 36-oz. to a 54-oz. *Tide* box, for example, the changeover involved stopping the line, adjusting guide rails, retrieving items from the tool room, placing items back in the tool room, changing and cleaning the pack heads, and performing routine maintenance. Changing the pack line could be a very difficult process and typically took up to eight hours.

Management realized that it was important to reduce this time significantly in order to become more flexible and cost efficient in packing products. Where could they learn how to do changeovers faster? They turned to Formula One racing, reasoning that a pit stop was much like a changeover. As a result, P&G videotaped actual Formula One pit stops. These videos were used to form the following principles for conducting a fast changeover:

- Position the tools near their point of use on the line prior to stopping the line, to reduce time going back and forth to the tool room.
- Arrange the tools in the exact order of work, so that no time is wasted looking for a tool.
- Have each employee perform a very specific task during the changeover.
- Design the workflow so that employees don't interfere with each other.
- Have each employee in position at the moment the line is stopped.
- Train each employee, and practice, practice, practice.
- Put a stop watch on the changeover process.
- Plot improvements over time on a visible chart.

As a result of these changes, P&G was able to reduce pack-line changeover time from eight hours to 20 minutes. This allowed it to produce a much larger variety of products every day and to improve the cost performance of the Packing Department.

Average Cost Method

A manufacturer uses a cost flow assumption in determining the costs flowing into, flowing out of, and remaining in each manufacturing department. In this chapter, we illustrated the first-in, first-out cost flow assumption for the Mixing Department of Frozen Delight Ice Cream Company. In this appendix, we illustrate the average cost flow method for S&W Ice Cream Company.

DETERMINING COSTS UNDER THE AVERAGE COST METHOD

S&W's operations are similar to those of Frozen Delight's in that S&W mixes cream and milk in refrigerated vessels and then fills containers with ice cream. Like Frozen Delight, S&W has two manufacturing departments, Mixing and Packaging. To illustrate the average cost method, we simplify by using only the Mixing Department of S&W. The manufacturing data for the Mixing Department for July 2008 are as follows:

Work in process inventory, July 1, 5,000 gallons (70% completed)	$ 6,200
Direct materials cost incurred in July, 60,000 gallons	66,000
Direct labor cost incurred in July	10,500
Factory overhead applied in July	6,405
Total production costs to account for	$89,105
Cost of goods transferred to Packaging in July (includes units in process on July 1), 62,000 gallons	?
Cost of work in process inventory, July 31, 3,000 gallons, 25% completed as to conversion costs	?

Using the average cost method, our objective is to allocate the total costs of production of $89,105 to the 62,000 gallons completed and transferred to the Packaging Department and the costs of the remaining 3,000 gallons in the ending work in process inventory. These costs are represented in the preceding table by two question marks. We determine these amounts by using the following four steps:

1. Determine the units to be assigned costs.
2. Compute equivalent units of production.
3. Determine the cost per equivalent unit.
4. Allocate costs to transferred and partially completed units.

Step 1: Determine the Units to Be Assigned Costs The first step in our illustration is to determine the units to be assigned costs. A unit can be any measure of completed production, such as tons, gallons, pounds, barrels, or cases. We use gallons as the units for S&W.

S&W's Mixing Department had 65,000 gallons of direct materials to account for during July, as shown here:

Total gallons to account for:	
Work in process, July 1	5,000 gallons
Received from materials storeroom	60,000
Total units to account for by the Packaging Department	65,000 gallons

There are two categories of units to be assigned costs for the period: (1) units completed and transferred out and (2) units in the ending work in process inventory. During July, the Mixing Department completed and transferred 62,000 gallons to the

Packaging Department. Of the 60,000 gallons started in July, 57,000 (60,000 − 3,000) gallons were completed and transferred to the Packaging Department. Thus, the ending work in process inventory consists of 3,000 gallons.

The total units (gallons) to be assigned costs for S&W can be summarized as follows:

(1) Transferred out to the Packaging Department in July	62,000 gallons
(2) Work in process inventory, July 31	3,000
Total gallons to be assigned costs	65,000 gallons

Note that the total units (gallons) to be assigned costs (65,000 gallons) equal the total units to account for (65,000 gallons).

Step 2: Compute Equivalent Units of Production S&W has 3,000 gallons of whole units in the work in process inventory for the Mixing Department on July 31. Since these units are 25% complete, the number of equivalent units in process in the Mixing Department on July 31 is 750 gallons (3,000 gallons × 25%). Since the units transferred to the Packaging Department have been completed, the whole units (62,000 gallons) transferred are the same as the equivalent units transferred.

The total equivalent units of production for the Mixing Department is determined by adding the equivalent units in the ending work in process inventory to the units transferred and completed during the period as shown here:

Equivalent units completed and transferred to the Packaging Department during July	62,000 gallons
Equivalent units in ending work in process, July 31	750
Total equivalent units	62,750 gallons

Step 3: Determine the Cost per Equivalent Unit Materials and conversion costs are often combined in computing cost per equivalent unit under the average cost method. In doing so, the cost per equivalent unit is determined by dividing the total production costs by the total equivalent units of production as follows:

$$\text{Cost per Equivalent Unit} = \frac{\text{Total Production Costs}}{\text{Total Equivalent Units}} = \frac{\$89,105}{62,750 \text{ gallons}} = \$1.42$$

We use the cost per equivalent unit in step 4 to allocate the production costs to the completed and partially completed units.

Step 4: Allocate Costs to Transferred and Partially Completed Units In step 4, we multiply the cost per equivalent unit by the equivalent units of production to determine the cost of transferred and partially completed units. For the Mixing Department, these costs are determined as follows:

(1) Transferred out to the Packaging Department (62,000 gallons × $1.42)	$88,040
(2) Work in process inventory, July 31 (3,000 gallons × 25% complete × $1.42)	1,065
Total production costs assigned	$89,105

THE COST OF PRODUCTION REPORT

The July cost of production report for S&W's Mixing Department is shown in Exhibit 11. The cost of production report in Exhibit 11 summarizes the following:

1. The units for which the department is accountable and the disposition of those units.
2. The production costs incurred by the department and the allocation of those costs between completed and partially completed units.

EXHIBIT 11

Cost of Production
Report for S&W's
Mixing Department

	A	B	C	
	S&W Ice Cream Company			
	Cost of Production Report—Mixing Department			
	For the Month Ended July 31, 2008			
UNITS		Step 1	Step 2	
		Whole Units	Equivalent Units of Production	
1 Units to account for during production:				1
2 Work in process inventory, July 1		5,000		2
3 Received from materials storeroom		60,000		3
4 Total units accounted for by the Mixing Department		65,000		4
5				5
6 Units to be assigned costs:				6
7 Transferred to Packaging Department in July		62,000	62,000	7
8 Inventory in process, July 31 (25% completed)		3,000	750	8
9 Total units to be assigned costs		65,000	62,750	9
10				10
11 COSTS				11
12 Step 3				12
13 Cost per equivalent unit:				13
14 Total production costs for July in Mixing Department			$89,105	14
15 Total equivalent units (from step 2 above)			/62,750	15
16 Cost per equivalent unit			$ 1.42	16
17				17
18 Costs assigned to production:				18
19 Inventory in process, July 1			$ 6,200	19
20 Direct materials, direct labor, and factory overhead incurred in July			82,905	20
21 Total costs accounted for by the Mixing Department			$89,105	21
22				22
23 Step 4				23
24 Costs allocated to completed and partially completed units:				24
25 Transferred to Packaging Department in July (62,000 gallons × $1.42)			$88,040	25
26 Inventory in process, July 31 (3,000 gallons × 25% × $1.42)			1,065	26
27 Total costs assigned by the Mixing Department			$89,105	27

At a Glance

1. Explain and illustrate the characteristics and cost flows for a process manufacturer.

Key Points	Key Learning Outcomes	Example Exercises	Practice Exercises
The process cost system is best suited for industries that mass produce identical units of a product. Costs are charged to processing departments, rather than to jobs as with the job order cost system. These costs are transferred from one department to the next until production is completed.	• Identify the characteristics of a process manufacturer. • Compare and contrast the job order cost system with the process cost system. • Describe the physical and cost flows of a process manufacturer.	18-1	18-1A, 18-1B

2. Prepare a cost of production report, accounting for completed and partially completed units under the FIFO method.

Key Points	Key Learning Outcomes	Example Exercises	Practice Exercises
Manufacturing costs must be allocated between the units that have been completed and those that remain within the department. This allocation is accomplished by allocating costs using equivalent units of production during the period for the beginning inventory, units started and completed, and the ending inventory.	• Determine the whole units charged to production and to be assigned costs.	18-2	18-2A, 18-2B
	• Compute the equivalent units with respect to materials.	18-3	18-3A, 18-3B
	• Compute the equivalent units with respect to conversion.	18-4	18-4A, 18-4B
	• Compute the costs per equivalent unit.	18-5	18-5A, 18-5B
	• Allocate the costs to beginning inventory, units started and completed, and ending inventory.	18-6	18-6A, 18-6B
	• Prepare a cost of production report.		

3. Prepare journal entries for transactions of a process manufacturer.

Key Points	Key Learning Outcomes	Example Exercises	Practice Exercises
Prepare the summary journal entries for materials, labor, applied factory overhead, and transferred costs incurred in production.	• Prepare journal entries for process costing transactions.	18-7	18-7A, 18-7B
	• Summarize cost flows in T account form.		
	• Compute the ending inventory balances.		

4. Use cost of production reports for decision making.

Key Points	Key Learning Outcomes	Example Exercises	Practice Exercises
The cost of production report provides information for controlling and improving operations. The report(s) can provide details of a department for a single period, or over a period of time.	• Prepare and evaluate a report showing the change in costs per unit by cost element for comparative periods.	18-8	18-8A, 18-8B

5. Contrast just-in-time processing with conventional manufacturing practices.

Key Points	Key Learning Outcomes	Example Exercises	Practice Exercises
The just-in-time processing philosophy focuses on reducing time, cost, and poor quality within the process.	• Identify the characteristics of a just-in-time process.		

Key Terms

Illustrative Problem

Southern Aggregate Company manufactures concrete by a series of four processes. All materials are introduced in Crushing. From Crushing, the materials pass through Sifting, Baking, and Mixing, emerging as finished concrete. All inventories are costed by the first-in, first-out method.

The balances in the accounts Work in Process—Mixing and Finished Goods were as follows on May 1, 2008:

Work in Process—Mixing (2,000 units, 1/4 completed)	$13,700
Finished Goods (1,800 units at $8.00 a unit)	14,400

The following costs were charged to Work in Process—Mixing during May:

Direct materials transferred from Baking:	
15,200 units at $6.50 a unit	$98,800
Direct labor	17,200
Factory overhead	11,780

During May, 16,000 units of concrete were completed, and 15,800 units were sold. Inventories on May 31 were as follows:

Work in Process—Mixing: 1,200 units, 1/2 completed
Finished Goods: 2,000 units

Instructions

1. Prepare a cost of production report for the Mixing Department.
2. Determine the cost of goods sold (indicate number of units and unit costs).
3. Determine the finished goods inventory, May 31, 2008.

Solution

1.

	A	B	C	D	E	
	Southern Aggregate Company					
	Cost of Production Report—Mixing Department					
	For the Month Ended May 31, 2008					
				Equivalent Units		
	UNITS	Whole Units	Direct Materials	Conversion		
1	Units charged to production:					1
2	Inventory in process, May 1	2,000				2
3	Received from Baking	15,200				3
4	Total units accounted for by the Mixing Department	17,200				4
5						5
6	Units to be assigned costs:					6
7	Inventory in process, May 1 (25% completed)	2,000	0	1,500		7
8	Started and completed in May	14,000	14,000	14,000		8
9	Transferred to finished goods in May	16,000	14,000	15,500		9
10	Inventory in process, May 31 (50% completed)	1,200	1,200	600		10
11	Total units to be assigned costs	17,200	15,200	16,100		11
12						12

13			Costs		13
14	**COSTS**		Direct Materials	Conversion	Total	14
15	Unit costs:					15
16	Total costs for May in Mixing		$ 98,800	$ 28,980		16
17	Total equivalent units (row 11)		/ 15,200	/ 16,100		17
18	Cost per equivalent unit		$ 6.50	$ 1.80		18
19						19
20	Costs assigned to production:					20
21	Inventory in process, May 1				$ 13,700	21
22	Costs incurred in May				127,780	22
23	Total costs accounted for by the Mixing Department				$141,480	23
24						24
25	Cost allocated to completed and partially					25
26	completed units:					26
27	Inventory in process, May 1—balance				$ 13,700	27
28	To complete inventory in process, May 1		$ 0	$ 2,700[a]	2,700	28
29	Started and completed in May		91,000[b]	25,200[c]	116,200	29
30	Transferred to finished goods in May				$132,600	30
31	Inventory in process, May 31		$ 7,800[d]	$ 1,080[e]	8,880	31
32	Total costs assigned by the Mixing Department				$141,480	32

[a]1,500 × $1.80 = $2,700 [b]14,000 × $6.50 = $91,000 [c]14,000 × $1.80 = $25,200 [d]1,200 × $6.50 = $7,800
[e]600 × $1.80 = $1,080

2. Cost of goods sold:

1,800 units at $8.00	$ 14,400	(from finished goods beginning inventory)
2,000 units at $8.20*	16,400	(from work in process beginning inventory)
12,000 units at $8.30**	99,600	(from May production started and completed)
15,800 units	$130,400	

*($13,700 + $2,700)/2,000
**$116,200/14,000

3. Finished goods inventory, May 31:

2,000 units at $8.30 $16,600

Self-Examination Questions

(Answers at End of Chapter)

1. For which of the following businesses would the process cost system be most appropriate?
   A. Custom furniture manufacturer
   B. Commercial building contractor
   C. Crude oil refinery
   D. Automobile repair shop

2. There were 2,000 pounds in process at the beginning of the period in the Packing Department. Packing received 24,000 pounds from the Blending Department during the month, of which 3,000 pounds were in process at the end of the month. How many pounds were completed and transferred to finished goods from the Packing Department?
   A. 23,000
   B. 21,000
   C. 26,000
   D. 29,000

3. Information relating to production in Department A for May is as follows:

May	1	Balance, 1,000 units, ¾ completed	$22,150
	31	Direct materials, 5,000 units	75,000
	31	Direct labor	32,500
	31	Factory overhead	16,250

If 500 units were one-fourth completed at May 31, 5,500 units were completed during May, and inventories are costed by the first-in, first-out method, what was the number of equivalent units of production with respect to conversion costs for May?
   A. 4,500
   B. 4,875
   C. 5,500
   D. 6,000

4. Based on the data presented in Question 3, what is the conversion cost per equivalent unit?
   A. $10
   B. $15
   C. $25
   D. $32

5. Information from the accounting system revealed the following:

	Day 1	Day 2	Day 3	Day 4	Day 5
Materials	$ 20,000	$18,000	$ 22,000	$ 20,000	$ 20,000
Electricity	2,500	3,000	3,500	4,000	4,700
Maintenance	4,000	3,750	3,400	3,000	2,800
Total costs	$ 26,500	$24,750	$ 28,900	$ 27,000	$ 27,500
Pounds produced	÷10,000	÷9,000	÷11,000	÷10,000	÷10,000
Cost per unit	$ 2.65	$ 2.75	$ 2.63	$ 2.70	$ 2.75

Which of the following statements best interprets this information?
A. The total costs are out of control.
B. The product costs have steadily increased because of higher electricity costs.
C. Electricity costs have steadily increased because of lack of maintenance.
D. The unit costs reveal a significant operating problem.

Eye Openers

1. Which type of cost system, process or job order, would be best suited for each of the following: (a) TV assembler, (b) building contractor, (c) automobile repair shop, (d) paper manufacturer, (e) custom jewelry manufacturer? Give reasons for your answers.
2. In job order cost accounting, the three elements of manufacturing cost are charged directly to job orders. Why is it not necessary to charge manufacturing costs in process cost accounting to job orders?
3. In a job order cost system, direct labor and factory overhead applied are debited to individual jobs. How are these items treated in a process cost system and why?
4. What are transferred-out materials?
5. What are the four steps for determining the cost of goods completed and the ending inventory?
6. What is meant by the term *equivalent units?*
7. Why is the cost per equivalent unit often determined separately for direct materials and conversion costs?
8. What is the purpose for determining the cost per equivalent unit?
9. Rameriz Company is a process manufacturer with two production departments, Blending and Filling. All direct materials are introduced in Blending from the materials store area. What is included in the cost transferred to Filling?
10. How is actual factory overhead accounted for in a process manufacturer?
11. What is the most important purpose of the cost of production report?
12. How are cost of production reports used for controlling and improving operations?
13. How is "yield" determined for a process manufacturer?
14. What is just-in-time processing?
15. How does just-in-time processing differ from the conventional manufacturing process?

Practice Exercises

PE 18-1A
Job order vs. process costing
obj. **1**

Which of the following industries would typically use job order costing, and which would typically use process costing?

Aluminum production	Papermaking
Gasoline refining	Print shop
Movie studio	Web designer

PE 18-1B
Job order vs. process costing
obj. **1**

Which of the following industries would typically use job order costing, and which would typically use process costing?

Apparel manufacturing	Automobile repair
Business consulting	Plastic manufacturing
CD manufacture	Steel manufacturing

PE 18-2A
Determine the units to be assigned costs
obj. 2

Keystone Personal Care Company consists of two departments, Blending and Filling. The Filling Department received 532,000 ounces from the Blending Department. During the period, the Filling Department completed 545,000 ounces, including 32,000 ounces of work in process at the beginning of the period. The ending work in process inventory was 19,000 ounces. How many ounces were started and completed during the period?

PE 18-2B
Determine the units to be assigned costs
obj. 2

Mohawk Valley Steel Company has two departments, Casting and Rolling. In the Rolling Department, ingots from the Casting Department are rolled into steel sheet. The Rolling Department received 83,680 tons from the Casting Department. During the period, the Rolling Department completed 81,450 tons, including 3,450 tons of work in process at the beginning of the period. The ending work in process inventory was 5,680 tons. How many tons were started and completed during the period?

PE 18-3A
Determine the equivalent units of materials
obj. 2

The Filling Department of Keystone Personal Care Company had 32,000 ounces in beginning work in process inventory (40% complete). During the period, 545,000 ounces were completed. The ending work in process inventory was 19,000 ounces (75% complete). What are the total equivalent units for direct materials if materials are added at the beginning of the process?

PE 18-3B
Determine the equivalent units of materials
obj. 2

The Rolling Department of Mohawk Valley Steel Company had 3,450 tons in beginning work in process inventory (20% complete). During the period, 81,450 tons were completed. The ending work in process inventory was 5,680 tons (25% complete). What are the total equivalent units for direct materials if materials are added at the beginning of the process?

PE 18-4A
Determine the equivalent units of conversion cost
obj. 2

The Filling Department of Keystone Personal Care Company had 32,000 ounces in beginning work in process inventory (40% complete). During the period, 545,000 ounces were completed. The ending work in process inventory was 19,000 ounces (75% complete). What are the total equivalent units for conversion costs?

PE 18-4B
Determine the equivalent units of conversion cost
obj. 2

The Rolling Department of Mohawk Valley Steel Company had 3,450 tons in beginning work in process inventory (20% complete). During the period, 81,450 tons were completed. The ending work in process inventory was 5,680 tons (25% complete). What are the total equivalent units for conversion costs?

PE 18-5A
Determine the cost per equivalent unit
obj. 2

The cost of direct materials transferred into the Filling Department of Keystone Personal Care Company is $170,240. The conversion cost for the period in the Filling Department is $87,432. The total equivalent units for direct materials and conversion are 532,000 ounces and 546,450 ounces, respectively. Determine the direct materials and conversion cost per equivalent unit.

PE 18-5B
Determine the cost per equivalent unit
obj. 2

The cost of direct materials transferred into the Rolling Department of Mohawk Valley Steel Company is $4,895,280. The conversion cost for the period in the Rolling Department is $953,288. The total equivalent units for direct materials and conversion are 83,680 tons and 82,180 tons, respectively. Determine the direct materials and conversion cost per equivalent unit.

PE 18-6A
Determine the cost of completed production and the ending work in process balance
obj. 2

The cost per equivalent unit of direct materials and conversion in the Filling Department of Keystone Personal Care Company is $0.32 and $0.16, respectively. The equivalent units to be assigned costs are as follows:

	Equivalent Units	
	Direct Materials	**Conversion**
Inventory in process, beginning of period	0	19,200
Started and completed during the period	513,000	513,000
Transferred out of Filling (completed)	513,000	532,200
Inventory in process, end of period	19,000	14,250
Total units to be assigned costs	532,000	546,450

The beginning work in process inventory had a cost of $12,500. Determine the cost of completed and transferred-out production and the ending work in process inventory.

PE 18-6B
Determine the cost of completed production and the ending work in process balance
obj. 2

The cost per equivalent unit of direct materials and conversion in the Rolling Department of Mohawk Valley Steel Company is $58.50 and $11.60, respectively. The equivalent units to be assigned costs are as follows:

	Equivalent Units	
	Direct Materials	Conversion
Inventory in process, beginning of period	0	2,760
Started and completed during the period	78,000	78,000
Transferred out of Rolling (completed)	78,000	80,760
Inventory in process, end of period	5,680	1,420
Total units to be assigned costs	83,680	82,180

The beginning work in process inventory had a cost of $209,000. Determine the cost of completed and transferred-out production and the ending work in process inventory.

PE 18-7A
Journalize process costing transactions
obj. 3

The cost of materials transferred into the Filling Department of Keystone Personal Care Company is $170,240, including $50,100 from the Blending Department and $120,140 from the materials storeroom. The conversion cost for the period in the Filling Department is $87,432 ($35,432 factory overhead applied and $52,000 direct labor). The total cost transferred to Finished Goods for the period was $261,812. The Filling Department had a beginning inventory of $12,500.

a. Journalize (1) the cost of transferred-in materials, (2) conversion costs, and (3) the costs transferred out to Finished Goods.
b. Determine the balance of Work in Process—Filling at the end of the period.

PE 18-7B
Journalize process costing transactions
obj. 3

The cost of materials transferred into the Rolling Department of Mohawk Valley Steel Company is $4,895,280 from the Casting Department. The conversion cost for the period in the Rolling Department is $953,288 ($553,038 factory overhead applied and $400,250 direct labor). The total cost transferred to Finished Goods for the period was $5,708,816. The Rolling Department had a beginning inventory of $209,000.

a. Journalize (1) the cost of transferred-in materials, (2) conversion costs, and (3) the costs transferred out to Finished Goods.
b. Determine the balance of Work in Process—Rolling at the end of the period.

PE 18-8A
Decision making
obj. 4

The cost of materials consumed in producing good units in the Forming Department was $88,000 and $80,500 for July and August, respectively. The number of equivalent units produced in July and August was 400 tons and 350 tons, respectively. Evaluate the cost of materials between the two months.

PE 18-8B
Decision making
obj. 4

The cost of energy consumed in producing good units in the Baking Department was $150,000 and $154,000 for October and November, respectively. The number of equivalent units produced in October and November was 500,000 pounds and 550,000 pounds, respectively. Evaluate the cost of energy between the two months.

Exercises

EX 18-1
Entries for materials cost flows in a process cost system
objs. 1, 3

The Hershey Foods Company manufactures chocolate confectionery products. The three largest raw materials are cocoa beans, sugar, and dehydrated milk. These raw materials first go into the Blending Department. The blended product is then sent to the Molding Department, where the bars of candy are formed. The candy is then sent to the Packing Department, where the bars are wrapped and boxed. The boxed candy is then sent to the distribution center, where it is eventually sold to food brokers and retailers.

Show the accounts debited and credited for each of the following business events:

a. Materials used by the Blending Department.
b. Transfer of blended product to the Molding Department.
c. Transfer of chocolate to the Packing Department.
d. Transfer of boxed chocolate to the distribution center.
e. Sale of boxed chocolate.

EX 18-2
Flowchart of accounts related to service and processing departments
obj. 1

Alcoa Inc. is the world's largest producer of aluminum products. One product that Alcoa manufactures is aluminum sheet products for the aerospace industry. The entire output of the Smelting Department is transferred to the Rolling Department. Part of the fully processed goods from the Rolling Department are sold as rolled sheet, and the remainder of the goods are transferred to the Converting Department for further processing into sheared sheet.

Prepare a chart of the flow of costs from the processing department accounts into the finished goods accounts and then into the cost of goods sold account. The relevant accounts are as follows:

Cost of Goods Sold	Finished Goods—Rolled Sheet
Materials	Finished Goods—Sheared Sheet
Factory Overhead—Smelting Department	Work in Process—Smelting Department
Factory Overhead—Rolling Department	Work in Process—Rolling Department
Factory Overhead—Converting Department	Work in Process—Converting Department

---

EX 18-3
Entries for flow of factory costs for process cost system
objs. 1, 3

Domino Foods, Inc., manufactures a sugar product by a continuous process, involving three production departments—Refining, Sifting, and Packing. Assume that records indicate that direct materials, direct labor, and applied factory overhead for the first department, Refining, were $355,000, $132,000, and $93,600, respectively. Also, work in process in the Refining Department at the beginning of the period totaled $25,500, and work in process at the end of the period totaled $31,200.

Journalize the entries to record (a) the flow of costs into the Refining Department during the period for (1) direct materials, (2) direct labor, and (3) factory overhead, and (b) the transfer of production costs to the second department, Sifting.

EX 18-4
Factory overhead rate, entry for applying factory overhead, and factory overhead account balance
objs. 1, 3
✓ *a. 140%*

The chief cost accountant for Crystal Spring Beverage Co. estimated that total factory overhead cost for the Blending Department for the coming fiscal year beginning March 1 would be $455,000, and total direct labor costs would be $325,000. During March, the actual direct labor cost totaled $27,000, and factory overhead cost incurred totaled $36,000.

a. What is the predetermined factory overhead rate based on direct labor cost?
b. Journalize the entry to apply factory overhead to production for March.
c. What is the March 31 balance of the account Factory Overhead—Blending Department?
d. Does the balance in part (c) represent overapplied or underapplied factory overhead?

EX 18-5
Equivalent units of production
obj. 2
✓ *Direct materials, 15,640 units*

The Converting Department of Stay-Soft Napkin Company had 760 units in work in process at the beginning of the period, which were 75% complete. During the period, 15,400 units were completed and transferred to the Packing Department. There were 1,000 units in process at the end of the period, which were 30% complete. Direct materials are placed into the process at the beginning of production. Determine the number of equivalent units of production with respect to direct materials and conversion costs.

EX 18-6
Equivalent units of production
obj. 2

✓ a. Conversion, 68,220 units

Units of production data for the two departments of Global Cable and Wire Company for June of the current fiscal year are as follows:

	Drawing Department	Winding Department
Work in process, June 1	6,200 units, 30% completed	1,500 units, 60% completed
Completed and transferred to next processing department during June	68,000 units	67,700 units
Work in process, June 30	3,200 units, 65% completed	1,800 units, 25% completed

If all direct materials are placed in process at the beginning of production, determine the direct materials and conversion equivalent units of production for June for (a) the Drawing Department and (b) the Winding Department.

EX 18-7
Equivalent units of production
obj. 2

✓ b. Conversion, 124,600

The following information concerns production in the Extruding Department for August. All direct materials are placed in process at the beginning of production.

ACCOUNT *Work in Process—Extruding Department*					ACCOUNT NO.	
					Balance	
Date		Item	Debit	Credit	Debit	Credit
Aug.	1	Bal., 12,000 units, ²/₅ completed			26,000	
	31	Direct materials, 125,000 units	237,500		263,500	
	31	Direct labor	68,000		331,500	
	31	Factory overhead	37,910		369,410	
	31	Goods finished, 118,000 units		323,620	45,790	
	31	Bal.—units, ³/₅ completed			45,790	

a. Determine the number of units in work in process inventory at the end of the month.
b. Determine the equivalent units of production for direct materials and conversion costs in August.

EX 18-8
Costs per equivalent unit
obj. 2

✓ a. 2. Conversion cost per equivalent unit, $0.85

a. Based upon the data in Exercise 18-7, determine the following:
   1. Direct materials cost per equivalent unit.
   2. Conversion cost per equivalent unit.
   3. Cost of the beginning work in process completed during August.
   4. Cost of units started and completed during August.
   5. Cost of the ending work in process.
b. Assuming that the direct materials cost is the same for July and August, did the conversion cost per equivalent unit increase, decrease, or remain the same in August?

EX 18-9
Equivalent units of production
obj. 2

REAL WORLD

Kellogg Company manufactures cold cereal products, such as *Frosted Flakes*. Assume that the inventory in process on October 1 for the Packing Department included 2,250 pounds of cereal in the packing machine hopper. In addition, there were 1,500 empty 24-oz. boxes held in the package carousel of the packing machine. During October, 26,500 boxes of 24-oz. cereal were packaged. Conversion costs are incurred when a box is filled with cereal. On October 31, the packing machine hopper held 900 pounds of cereal, and the package carousel held 600 empty 24-oz. (1¹/₂ -pound) boxes. Assume that once a box is filled with cereal, it is immediately transferred to the finished goods warehouse.

Determine the equivalent units of production for cereal, boxes, and conversion costs for October. An equivalent unit is defined as "pounds" for cereal and "24-oz. boxes" for boxes and conversion costs.

EX 18-10
Costs per equivalent unit
obj. 2

✓ c. $2.90

Pacific Products Inc. completed and transferred 150,000 particle board units of production from the Pressing Department. There was no beginning inventory in process in the department. The ending in-process inventory was 14,000 units, which were ³/₅ complete as to conversion cost. All materials are added at the beginning of the process. Direct materials cost incurred was $475,600, direct labor cost incurred was $69,720, and factory overhead applied was $25,320.

Determine the following for the Pressing Department:

a. Total conversion cost
b. Conversion cost per equivalent unit
c. Direct materials cost per equivalent unit

EX 18-11
Equivalent units of production and related costs

obj. 2

✓a. 7,500 units

The charges to Work in Process—Assembly Department for a period, together with information concerning production, are as follows. All direct materials are placed in process at the beginning of production.

Work in Process—Assembly Department

Bal., 3,000 units, 40% completed	8,550	To Finished Goods, 62,500 units	?
Direct materials, 67,000 units @ $1.55	103,850		
Direct labor	145,300		
Factory overhead	56,860		
Bal. _?_ units, 25% completed	?		

Determine the following:

a. The number of units in work in process inventory at the end of the period.
b. Equivalent units of production for direct materials and conversion.
c. Costs per equivalent unit for direct materials and conversion.
d. Cost of the units started and completed during the period.

EX 18-12
Cost of units completed and in process

obj. 2

✓a. 1. $14,310

a. Based upon the data in Exercise 18-11, determine the following:
   1. Cost of beginning work in process inventory completed this period.
   2. Cost of units transferred to finished goods during the period.
   3. Cost of ending work in process inventory.
   4. Cost per unit of beginning work in process completed during the period.
b. Did the production costs change from the preceding period? Explain.
c. Assuming that the direct materials cost per unit did not change from the preceding period, did the conversion costs per equivalent unit increase, decrease, or remain the same for the current period?

EX 18-13
Errors in equivalent unit computation

obj. 2

Louisiana Oil Refining Company processes gasoline. At June 1 of the current year, 4,500 units were $^{3}/_{5}$ completed in the Blending Department. During June, 20,000 units entered the Blending Department from the Refining Department. During June, the units in process at the beginning of the month were completed. Of the 20,000 units entering the department, all were completed except 6,200 units that were $^{1}/_{5}$ completed. The equivalent units for conversion costs for June for the Blending Department were computed as follows:

Equivalent units of production in June:	
To process units in inventory on June 1:	
4,500 × $^{3}/_{5}$	2,700
To process units started and completed in June:	
20,000 − 4,500	15,500
To process units in inventory on June 30:	
6,200 × $^{1}/_{5}$	1,240
Equivalent units of production	19,440

List the errors in the computation of equivalent units for conversion costs for the Blending Department for June.

EX 18-14
Cost per equivalent unit

obj. 2

✓a. 54,000 units

The following information concerns production in the Forging Department for November. All direct materials are placed into the process at the beginning of production, and conversion costs are incurred evenly throughout the process. The beginning inventory consists of $105,750 of direct materials.

(continued)

ACCOUNT *Work in Process—Forging Department*   ACCOUNT NO.

Date		Item	Debit	Credit	Balance Debit	Balance Credit
Nov.	1	Bal., 9,000 units, 60% completed			127,350	
	30	Direct materials, 50,000 units	580,000		707,350	
	30	Direct labor	78,970		786,320	
	30	Factory overhead	125,415		911,735	
	30	Goods transferred, _?_ units		?	?	
	30	Bal., 5,000 units, 25% completed			?	

a. Determine the number of units transferred to the next department.
b. Determine the cost per equivalent unit of direct materials and conversion.
c. Determine the cost of units started and completed in November.

EX 18-15
Costs per equivalent unit and production costs
obj. 2
✓ a. $142,110

Based upon the data in Exercise 18-14, determine the following:

a. Cost of beginning work in process inventory completed in November.
b. Cost of units transferred to the next department during November.
c. Cost of ending work in process inventory on November 30.
d. Cost per equivalent unit of direct materials and conversion included in the November 1 beginning work in process.
e. The November increase or decrease in cost per equivalent unit for direct materials and conversion.

EX 18-16
Cost of production report
obj. 2

✓ d. $26,676

The debits to Work in Process—Cooking Department for Yankee Bean Company for March 2008, together with information concerning production, are as follows:

Work in process, March 1, 3,000 pounds, 30% completed $ 14,160*
    *Direct materials (3,000 × $4.00) $12,000
    Conversion (3,000 × 30% × $2.40)   2,160
                         $14,160

Beans added during March, 85,900 pounds   352,190
Conversion costs during March   194,242
Work in process, March 31, 5,700 pounds, 25% completed   ?
Goods finished during March, 83,200 pounds   ?

All direct materials are placed in process at the beginning of production. Prepare a cost of production report, presenting the following computations:

a. Direct materials and conversion equivalent units of production for March.
b. Direct materials and conversion cost per equivalent unit for March.
c. Cost of goods finished during March.
d. Cost of work in process at March 31, 2008.

EX 18-17
Cost of production report
obj. 2

✓ Conversion rate, $5.20

Prepare a cost of production report for the Cutting Department of Aladdin Carpet Company for May 2008, using the following data and assuming that all materials are added at the beginning of the process:

Work in process, May 1, 5,000 units, 75% completed $ 49,800*
    *Direct materials (5,000 × $6.00) $30,000
    Conversion (5,000 × 75% × $5.28)   19,800
                      $49,800

Materials added during May from Weaving Department, 186,000 units   1,134,600
Direct labor for May   405,600
Factory overhead for May   540,436
Goods finished during May (includes goods in process, May 1), 183,400 units   —
Work in process, May 31, 7,600 units, 30% completed   —

EX 18-18

Cost of production and journal entries

objs. 1, 2, 3

✓ b. $31,100

Titanium Metals Inc. casts blades for turbine engines. Within the Casting Department, alloy is first melted in a crucible, then poured into molds to produce the castings. On October 1, there were 700 pounds of alloy in process, which were 60% complete as to conversion. The Work in Process balance for these 700 pounds was $45,920, determined as follows:

Direct materials (700 × $47)	$32,900
Conversion (700 × 60% × $31)	13,020
	$45,920

During October, the Casting Department was charged $441,000 for 9,000 pounds of alloy and $108,000 for direct labor. Factory overhead is applied to the department at a rate of 150% of direct labor. The department transferred out 9,200 pounds of finished castings to the Machining Department. The October 31 inventory in process was 44% complete as to conversion.

a. Prepare the following October journal entries for the Casting Department:
  1. The materials charged to production.
  2. The conversion costs charged to production.
  3. The completed production transferred to the Machining Department.
b. Determine the Work in Process—Casting Department October 31 balance.

EX 18-19

Cost of production and journal entries

objs. 1, 2, 3

✓ b. $49,800

Papyrus Paper Company manufactures newsprint. The product is manufactured in two departments, Papermaking and Converting. Pulp is first placed into a vessel at the beginning of papermaking production. The following information concerns production in the Papermaking Department for July.

ACCOUNT *Work in Process—Papermaking Department*   **ACCOUNT NO.**

Date		Item	Debit	Credit	Balance Debit	Balance Credit
July	1	Bal., 5,000 units, 20% completed			24,500	
	31	Direct materials, 68,000 units	306,000		330,500	
	31	Direct labor	100,000		430,500	
	31	Factory overhead	61,000		491,500	
	31	Goods transferred, 65,000 units		?	?	
	31	Bal., 8,000 units, 75% completed			?	

a. Prepare the following July journal entries for the Papermaking Department:
  1. The materials charged to production.
  2. The conversion costs charged to production.
  3. The completed production transferred to the Converting Department.
b. Determine the Work in Process—Papermaking Department July 31 balance.

EX 18-20

Decision making

obj. 4

Oasis Bottling Company bottles popular beverages in the Bottling Department. The beverages are produced by blending concentrate with water and sugar. The concentrate is purchased from a concentrate producer. The concentrate producer sets higher prices for the more popular concentrate flavors. Below is a simplified Bottling Department cost of production report separating the cost of bottling the four flavors.

	A	B Orange	C Cola	D Lemon-Lime	E Root Beer	
1	Concentrate	$ 5,400	$110,000	$ 63,000	$1,800	1
2	Water	1,800	30,000	18,000	600	2
3	Sugar	3,000	50,000	30,000	1,000	3
4	Bottles	6,600	110,000	66,000	2,200	4
5	Flavor changeover	3,000	6,000	3,600	3,000	5
6	Conversion cost	2,400	25,000	15,000	800	6
7	Total cost transferred to finished goods	$22,200	$331,000	$195,600	$9,400	7
8	Number of cases	3,000	50,000	30,000	1,000	8

Beginning and ending work in process inventories are negligible, so are omitted from the cost of production report. The flavor changeover cost represents the cost of cleaning the bottling machines between production runs of different flavors.

➤ Prepare a memo to the production manager analyzing this comparative cost information. In your memo, provide recommendations for further action, along with supporting schedules showing the total cost per case and cost per case by cost element.

EX 18-21
Decision making

obj. **4**

Instant Memories Inc. produces film products for cameras. One of the processes for this operation is a coating (solvent spreading) operation, where chemicals are coated on to film stock. There has been some concern about the cost performance of this operation. As a result, you have begun an investigation. You first discover that all input prices have not changed for the last six months. If there is a problem, it is related to the quantity of input. You have discovered three possible problems from some of the operating personnel whose quotes follow:

Operator 1: "I've been keeping an eye on my operating room instruments. I feel as though our energy consumption is becoming less efficient."

Operator 2: "Every time the coating machine goes down, we produce waste on shutdown and subsequent startup. It seems like during the last half year we have had more unscheduled machine shutdowns than in the past. Thus, I feel as though our yields must be dropping."

Operator 3: "My sense is that our coating costs are going up. It seems to me like we are spreading a thicker coating than we should. Perhaps the coating machine needs to be recalibrated."

The Coating Department had no beginning or ending inventories for any month during the study period. The following data from the cost of production report are made available:

	A	B	C	D	E	F	G	
		January	February	March	April	May	June	
1	Materials	$54,880	$68,600	$61,740	$51,450	$54,880	$68,600	1
2	Coating cost	$15,680	$21,560	$22,050	$20,580	$22,736	$31,360	2
3	Conversion cost (incl. energy)	$39,200	$49,000	$44,100	$36,750	$39,200	$49,000	3
4	Pounds input to the process	80,000	100,000	90,000	75,000	80,000	100,000	4
5	Pounds transferred out	78,400	98,000	88,200	73,500	78,400	98,000	5

a. Prepare a table showing the materials cost per output pound, coating cost per output pound, conversion cost per output pound, and yield for each month.
b. Interpret your table results.

EX 18-22
Just-in-time manufacturing

obj. **5**

The following are some quotes provided by a number of managers at Mesa Machining Company regarding the company's planned move toward a just-in-time manufacturing system:

Director of Sales: *I'm afraid we'll miss some sales if we don't keep a large stock of items on hand just in case demand increases. It only makes sense to me to keep large inventories in order to assure product availability for our customers.*

Director of Purchasing: *I'm very concerned about moving to a just-in-time system for materials. What would happen if one of our suppliers were unable to make a shipment? A supplier could fall behind in production or have a quality problem. Without some safety stock in our materials, our whole plant would shut down.*

Director of Manufacturing: *If we go to just-in-time, I think our factory output will drop. We need in-process inventory in order to "smooth out" the inevitable problems that occur during manufacturing. For example, if a machine that is used to process a product breaks down, I would starve the next machine if I don't have in-process inventory between the two machines. If I have in-process inventory, then I can keep the next operation busy while I fix the broken machine. Thus, the in-process inventories give me a safety valve that I can use to keep things running when things go wrong.*

➤ How would you respond to these managers?

APPENDIX EX 18-23

Equivalent units of production: average cost method

✓ a. 25,400

The Converting Department of Kwan Napkin Company uses the average cost method and had 1,500 units in work in process that were 60% complete at the beginning of the period. During the period, 24,500 units were completed and transferred to the Packing Department. There were 900 units in process that were 40% complete at the end of the period.

a. Determine the number of whole units to be accounted for and to be assigned costs for the period.
b. Determine the number of equivalent units of production for the period.

APPENDIX EX 18-24

Equivalent units of production: average cost method

✓ a. 94,500 units to be accounted for

Units of production data for the two departments of Frontier Cable and Wire Company for March of the current fiscal year are as follows:

	Drawing Department	Winding Department
Work in process, March 1	1,700 units, 50% completed	1,000 units, 30% completed
Completed and transferred to next processing department during March	92,000 units	90,400 units
Work in process, March 31	2,500 units, 65% completed	2,600 units, 25% completed

Each department uses the average cost method.

a. Determine the number of whole units to be accounted for and to be assigned costs and the equivalent units of production for the Drawing Department.
b. Determine the number of whole units to be accounted for and to be assigned costs and the equivalent units of production for the Winding Department.

APPENDIX EX 18-25

Equivalent units of production: average cost method

✓ a. 9,000

The following information concerns production in the Finishing Department for March. The Finishing Department uses the average cost method.

ACCOUNT *Work in Process—Finishing Department*   **ACCOUNT NO.**

Date		Item	Debit	Credit	Balance Debit	Balance Credit
Mar.	1	Bal., 12,000 units, 40% completed			22,320	
	31	Direct materials, 125,000 units	325,000		347,320	
	31	Direct labor	174,500		521,820	
	31	Factory overhead	93,200		615,020	
	31	Goods transferred, 128,000 units		586,240	28,780	
	31	Bal., _?_ units, 70% completed			28,780	

a. Determine the number of units in work in process inventory at the end of the month.
b. Determine the number of whole units to be accounted for and to be assigned costs and the equivalent units of production for March.

APPENDIX EX 18-26

Equivalent units of production and related costs

✓ b. 82,720 units

The charges to Work in Process—Baking Department for a period as well as information concerning production are as follows. The Baking Department uses the average cost method, and all direct materials are placed in process during production.

Work in Process—Baking Department

Bal., 5,000 units, 70% completed	10,000	To Finished Goods, 81,100 units	?
Direct materials, 81,500 units	195,700		
Direct labor	123,036		
Factory overhead	89,000		
Bal., 5,400 units, 30% completed	?		

Determine the following:

a. The number of whole units to be accounted for and to be assigned costs.
b. The number of equivalent units of production.   *(continued)*

c. The cost per equivalent unit.
d. The cost of the units transferred to Finished Goods.
e. The cost of ending Work in Process.

**APPENDIX
EX 18-27**
*Cost per equivalent unit:
average cost method*

✓a. $20.00

The following information concerns production in the Forging Department for April. The Forging Department uses the average cost method.

ACCOUNT *Work in Process—Forging Department*   ACCOUNT NO.

Date		Item	Debit	Credit	Balance Debit	Balance Credit
Apr.	1	Bal., 3,000 units, 40% completed			24,000	
	30	Direct materials, 28,500 units	355,800		379,800	
	30	Direct labor	128,200		508,000	
	30	Factory overhead	100,500		608,500	
	30	Goods transferred, 27,200 units		?	?	
	30	Bal., 4,300 units, 75% completed			?	

a. Determine the cost per equivalent unit.
b. Determine the cost of the units transferred to Finished Goods.
c. Determine the cost of ending Work in Process.

**APPENDIX
EX 18-28**
*Cost of production report:
average cost method*

✓ *Cost per equivalent
unit, $2.15*

The increases to Work in Process—Cooking Department for Boston Beans Company for January 2008 as well as information concerning production are as follows:

Work in process, January 1, 1,000 pounds, 40% completed	$ 900
Beans added during January, 58,200 pounds	92,400
Conversion costs during January	33,593
Work in process, January 31, 600 pounds, 70% completed	—
Goods finished during January, 58,600 pounds	—

Prepare a cost of production report, using the average cost method.

**APPENDIX
EX 18-29**
*Cost of production report:
average cost method*

✓ *Cost per equivalent
unit, $5.98*

Prepare a cost of production report for the Cutting Department of North Georgia Carpet Company for May 2008. Use the average cost method with the following data:

Work in process, May 1, 13,000 units, 75% completed	$ 58,000
Materials added during May from Weaving Department, 205,000 units	914,780
Direct labor for May	158,600
Factory overhead for May	100,500
Goods finished during May (includes goods in process, May 1), 202,000 units	—
Work in process, May 31, 16,000 units, 25% completed	—

Problems Series A

PR 18-1A
*Entries for process cost
system*
objs. 1, 3

✓ *2. Materials October
31 balance, $47,400*

Living Decor Carpet Company manufactures carpets. Fiber is placed in process in the Spinning Department, where it is spun into yarn. The output of the Spinning Department is transferred to the Tufting Department, where carpet backing is added at the beginning of the process and the process is completed. On October 1, Living Decor Carpet Company had the following inventories:

Finished Goods	$56,900
Work in Process—Spinning Department	7,900
Work in Process—Tufting Department	21,400
Materials	36,200

Departmental accounts are maintained for factory overhead, and both have zero balances on October 1.

Manufacturing operations for October are summarized as follows:

a. Materials purchased on account	$810,900
b. Materials requisitioned for use:	
Fiber—Spinning Department	$532,400
Carpet backing—Tufting Department	201,800
Indirect materials—Spinning Department	50,700
Indirect materials—Tufting Department	14,800
c. Labor used:	
Direct labor—Spinning Department	$224,100
Direct labor—Tufting Department	178,900
Indirect labor—Spinning Department	134,200
Indirect labor—Tufting Department	115,500
d. Depreciation charged on fixed assets:	
Spinning Department	$56,200
Tufting Department	33,000
e. Expired prepaid factory insurance:	
Spinning Department	$10,000
Tufting Department	8,000
f. Applied factory overhead:	
Spinning Department	$244,600
Tufting Department	173,200
g. Production costs transferred from Spinning Department to Tufting Department	$946,700
h. Production costs transferred from Tufting Department to Finished Goods	$1,400,500
i. Cost of goods sold during the period	$1,395,800

Instructions

1. Journalize the entries to record the operations, identifying each entry by letter.
2. Compute the October 31 balances of the inventory accounts.
3. Compute the October 31 balances of the factory overhead accounts.

PR 18-2A

Entries for process cost system

objs. 1, 3

Appalachian Bakery Company manufactures cookies. Materials are placed in production in the Baking Department and after processing are transferred to the Packing Department, where packing materials are added. The finished products emerge from the Packing Department.

There were no inventories of work in process at the beginning or at the end of August 2008. Finished goods inventory at August 1 was 900 cases of cookies at a total cost of $40,500.

Transactions related to manufacturing operations for August are summarized as follows:

a. Materials purchased on account, $425,000.
b. Materials requisitioned for use: Baking Department, $345,500 ($334,500 entered directly into the product); Packing Department, $73,500 ($72,000 entered directly into the product).
c. Labor costs incurred: Baking Department, $168,000 ($154,300 entered directly into the product); Packing Department, $127,000 ($119,600 entered directly into the product).
d. Miscellaneous costs and expenses incurred on account: Baking Department, $16,300; Packing Department, $6,300.
e. Depreciation charged on fixed assets: Baking Department, $22,400; Packing Department, $11,900.
f. Expiration of various prepaid expenses: Baking Department, $4,700; Packing Department, $2,300.
g. Factory overhead applied to production, based on machine hours: $67,500 for Baking and $30,700 for Packing.
h. Output of Baking Department: 17,000 cases.
i. Output of Packing Department: 17,000 cases of cookies.
j. Sales on account: 17,600 cases of cookies at $90. Credits to the finished goods account are to be made according to the first-in, first-out method.

Instructions

Journalize the entries to record the transactions, identifying each by letter. Include as an explanation for entry (j) the number of cases and the cost per case of cookies sold.

PR 18-3A
Cost of production report
obj. 2

✓1. Conversion cost per
equivalent unit, $3.60

Mountain Air Coffee Company roasts and packs coffee beans. The process begins by placing coffee beans into the Roasting Department. From the Roasting Department, coffee beans are then transferred to the Packing Department. The following is a partial work in process account of the Roasting Department at October 31, 2008:

ACCOUNT **Work in Process—Roasting Department**   ACCOUNT NO.

Date		Item	Debit	Credit	Balance Debit	Balance Credit
Oct.	1	Bal., 12,000 units, ²/₅ completed			84,600	
	31	Direct materials, 285,000 units	1,624,500		1,709,100	
	31	Direct labor	568,900		2,278,000	
	31	Factory overhead	428,480		2,706,480	
	31	Goods finished, 276,800 units		?		
	31	Bal. _?_ units, ¼ completed			?	

Instructions
1. Prepare a cost of production report, and identify the missing amounts for Work in Process—Roasting Department.
2. Assuming that the October 1 Work in Process inventory includes $67,800 of direct materials, determine the increase or decrease in the cost per equivalent unit for direct materials and conversion between September and October.

PR 18-4A
Equivalent units and related costs; cost of production report; entries
objs. 2, 3

✓2. Transferred to
Packaging Dept.,
$1,079,400

Blanco Flour Company manufactures flour by a series of three processes, beginning with wheat grain being introduced in the Milling Department. From the Milling Department, the materials pass through the Sifting and Packaging departments, emerging as packaged refined flour.

The balance in the account Work in Process—Sifting Department was as follows on May 1, 2008:

Work in Process—Sifting Department (20,000 units, 80% completed):
Direct materials (20,000 × $1.37) $27,400
Conversion (20,000 × 80% × $0.55)   8,800
                                       $36,200

The following costs were charged to Work in Process—Sifting Department during May:

Direct materials transferred from Milling Department:
 560,000 units at $1.40 a unit $784,000
Direct labor   179,000
Factory overhead   101,200

During May, 568,000 units of flour were completed. Work in Process—Sifting Department on May 31 was 12,000 units, 70% completed.

Instructions
1. Prepare a cost of production report for the Sifting Department for May.
2. Journalize the entries for costs transferred from Milling to Sifting and the costs transferred from Sifting to Packaging.
3. Determine the increase or decrease in the cost per equivalent unit from April to May for direct materials and conversion costs.
4. ▬▬▶ Discuss the uses of the cost of production report and the results of part (3).

PR 18-5A
Work in process account data for two months; cost of production reports
objs. 1, 2, 3

Won-Ton Soup Co. uses a process cost system to record the costs of processing soup, which requires a series of three processes. The inventory of Work in Process—Filling on July 1 and debits to the account during July 2008 were as follows:

Bal., 2,000 units, 30% completed:	
Direct materials (2,000 × $3.20)	$6,400
Conversion (2,000 × 30% × $1.25)	750
	$7,150
From Cooking Department, 126,000 units	$409,500
Direct labor	93,345
Factory overhead	71,950

During July, 2,000 units in process on July 1 were completed, and of the 126,000 units entering the department, all were completed except 2,500 units that were 90% completed.

Charges to Work in Process—Filling for August were as follows:

From Cooking Department, 138,000 units	$455,400
Direct labor	101,480
Factory overhead	77,578

During August, the units in process at the beginning of the month were completed, and of the 138,000 units entering the department, all were completed except 4,000 units that were 35% completed.

Instructions

1. Enter the balance as of July 1, 2008, in a four-column account for Work in Process—Filling. Record the debits and the credits in the account for July. Construct a cost of production report, and present computations for determining (a) equivalent units of production for materials and conversion, (b) equivalent costs per unit, (c) cost of goods finished, differentiating between units started in the prior period and units started and finished in July, and (d) work in process inventory.
2. Provide the same information for August by recording the August transactions in the four-column work in process account. Construct a cost of production report, and present the August computations (a through d) listed in part (1).
3. ▭▭▭➤ Comment on the change in cost per equivalent unit for June through August for direct materials and conversion costs.

APPENDIX
PR 18-6A
Cost of production report: average cost method

Arabica Coffee Company roasts and packs coffee beans. The process begins in the Roasting Department. From the Roasting Department, the coffee beans are transferred to the Packing Department. The following is a partial work in process account of the Roasting Department at March 31, 2008:

ACCOUNT *Work in Process—Roasting Department*					ACCOUNT NO.	
					Balance	
Date		Item	Debit	Credit	Debit	Credit
Mar.	1	Bal., 12,500 units, 60% completed			92,500	
	31	Direct materials, 215,400 units	1,345,900		1,438,400	
	31	Direct labor	365,766		1,804,166	
	31	Factory overhead	284,800		2,088,966	
	31	Goods finished, 219,700 units		?	?	
	31	Bal. _?_ units, 60% completed			?	

Instructions

Prepare a cost of production report, using the average cost method, and identify the missing amounts for Work in Process—Roasting Department.

APPENDIX
PR 18-7A
Equivalent units and related costs; cost of production report: average cost method

Snowflake Flour Company manufactures flour by a series of three processes, beginning in the Milling Department. From the Milling Department, the materials pass through the Sifting and Packaging departments, emerging as packaged refined flour.

(continued)

✓*Transferred to Packaging Dept., $1,976,620*

The balance in the account Work in Process—Sifting Department was as follows on July 1, 2008:

Work in Process—Sifting Department (19,600 units, 75% completed) $66,000

The following costs were charged to Work in Process—Sifting Department during July:

Direct materials transferred from Milling Department: 426,800 units	$1,435,000
Direct labor	375,925
Factory overhead	118,900

During July, 429,700 units of flour were completed. Work in Process—Sifting Department on July 31 was 16,700 units, 25% completed.

Instructions

Prepare a cost of production report for the Sifting Department for July, using the average cost method.

Problems Series B

PR 18-1B
Entries for process cost system
objs. 1, 3

✓*2. Materials December 31 balance, $8,720*

G&P Soap Company manufactures powdered detergent. Phosphate is placed in process in the Making Department, where it is turned into granulars. The output of Making is transferred to the Packing Department, where packaging is added at the beginning of the process. On December 1, G&P Soap Company had the following inventories:

Finished Goods	$14,500
Work in Process—Making	5,670
Work in Process—Packing	7,230
Materials	3,200

Departmental accounts are maintained for factory overhead, which both have zero balances on December 1.

Manufacturing operations for December are summarized as follows:

a. Materials purchased on account	$167,900
b. Materials requisitioned for use:	
Phosphate—Making Department	$114,200
Packaging—Packing Department	42,500
Indirect materials—Making Department	4,100
Indirect materials—Packing Department	1,580
c. Labor used:	
Direct labor—Making Department	$79,400
Direct labor—Packing Department	53,200
Indirect labor—Making Department	15,000
Indirect labor—Packing Department	26,900
d. Depreciation charged on fixed assets:	
Making Department	$14,800
Packing Department	11,300
e. Expired prepaid factory insurance:	
Making Department	$3,000
Packing Department	1,200
f. Applied factory overhead:	
Making Department	$37,500
Packing Department	40,100
g. Production costs transferred from Making Department to Packing Department	$215,800
h. Production costs transferred from Packing Department to Finished Goods	$351,200
i. Cost of goods sold during the period	$354,800

Instructions

1. Journalize the entries to record the operations, identifying each entry by letter.
2. Compute the December 31 balances of the inventory accounts.
3. Compute the December 31 balances of the factory overhead accounts.

PR 18-2B
Entries for process cost system
objs. 1, 3

Ozark Refining Company processes gasoline. Petroleum is placed in production in the Refining Department and, after processing, is transferred to the Blending Department, where detergents are added. The finished blended gasoline emerges from the Blending Department.

There were no inventories of work in process at the beginning or at the end of December 2008. Finished goods inventory at December 1 was 8,000 barrels of gasoline at a total cost of $296,000.

Transactions related to manufacturing operations for December are summarized as follows:

a. Materials purchased on account, $682,400.
b. Materials requisitioned for use: Refining, $580,200 ($567,800 entered directly into the product); Blending, $98,400 ($92,200 entered directly into the product).
c. Labor costs incurred: Refining, $165,100 ($134,200 entered directly into the product); Blending, $80,200 ($57,800 entered directly into the product).
d. Miscellaneous costs and expenses incurred on account: Refining, $21,100; Blending, $7,000.
e. Expiration of various prepaid expenses: Refining, $5,000; Blending, $3,000.
f. Depreciation charged on plant assets: Refining, $43,500; Blending, $19,200.
g. Factory overhead applied to production, based on processing hours: $111,900 for Refining and $58,100 for Blending.
h. Output of Refining: 28,000 barrels.
i. Output of Blending: 28,000 barrels of gasoline.
j. Sales on account: 30,000 barrels of gasoline at $60 per barrel. Credits to the finished goods account are to be made according to the first-in, first-out method.

Instructions
Journalize the entries to record the transactions, identifying each by letter. Include as an explanation for entry (j) the number of barrels and the cost per barrel of gasoline sold.

PR 18-3B
Cost of production report
obj. 2

✓ *1. Conversion cost per equivalent unit, $0.75*

Belgian Delight Chocolate Company processes chocolate into candy bars. The process begins by placing direct materials (raw chocolate, milk, and sugar) into the Blending Department. All materials are placed into production at the beginning of the blending process. After blending, the milk chocolate is then transferred to the Molding Department, where the milk chocolate is formed into candy bars. The following is a partial work in process account of the Blending Department at March 31, 2008:

ACCOUNT *Work in Process—Blending Department*   **ACCOUNT NO.**

Date		Item	Debit	Credit	Balance Debit	Balance Credit
Mar.	1	Bal., 9,000 units, 20% completed			28,260	
	31	Direct materials, 300,000 units	870,000		898,260	
	31	Direct labor	128,450		1,026,710	
	31	Factory overhead	100,300		1,127,010	
	31	Goods finished, 305,000 units		?		
	31	Bal. _?_ units, 45% completed			?	

Instructions
1. Prepare a cost of production report, and identify the missing amounts for Work in Process—Blending Department.
2. Assuming that the March 1 Work in Process inventory includes direct materials of $27,000, determine the increase or decrease in the cost per equivalent unit for direct materials and conversion between February and March.

PR 18-4B
Equivalent units and related costs; cost of production report; entries
objs. 2, 3

Delaware Chemical Company manufactures specialty chemicals by a series of three processes, all materials being introduced in the Distilling Department. From the Distilling Department, the materials pass through the Reaction and Filling departments, emerging as finished chemicals.

✓ *2. Transferred to finished goods, $929,819*

The balance in the account Work in Process—Filling was as follows on December 1, 2008:

Work in Process—Filling Department
(2,200 units, 10% completed):

Direct materials (2,200 × $12.10)	$26,620
Conversion (2,200 × 10% × $8.65)	1,903
	$28,523

The following costs were charged to Work in Process—Filling during December:

Direct materials transferred from Reaction Department: 44,400 units at $12.20 a unit	$541,680
Direct labor	105,600
Factory overhead	292,425

During December, 44,500 units of specialty chemicals were completed. Work in Process—Filling Department on December 31 was 2,100 units, 70% completed.

Instructions

1. Prepare a cost of production report for the Filling Department for December.
2. Journalize the entries for costs transferred from Reaction to Filling and the cost transferred from Filling to Finished Goods.
3. Determine the increase or decrease in the cost per equivalent unit from November to December for direct materials and conversion costs.
4. ▭▭▭▭▶ Discuss the uses of the cost of production report and the results of part (3).

PR 18-5B
Work in process account data for two months; cost of production reports

objs. 1, 2, 3

✓ *1. c. Transferred to finished goods in September, $7,975,700*

Dayton Aluminum Company uses a process cost system to record the costs of manufacturing rolled aluminum, which requires a series of four processes. The inventory of Work in Process—Rolling on September 1, 2008, and debits to the account during September were as follows:

Bal., 4,000 units, 1/4 completed:

Direct materials (4,000 × $41.00)	$ 164,000
Conversion (4,000 × 1/4 × $12.30)	12,300
	$ 176,300

From Smelting Department, 150,000 units	$6,195,000
Direct labor	773,780
Factory overhead	1,138,900

During September, 4,000 units in process on September 1 were completed, and of the 150,000 units entering the department, all were completed except 6,000 units that were ⁴/₅ completed.

Charges to Work in Process—Rolling for October were as follows:

From Smelting Department, 165,000 units	$6,930,000
Direct labor	824,500
Factory overhead	1,242,530

During October, the units in process at the beginning of the month were completed, and of the 165,000 units entering the department, all were completed except 6,800 units that were ²/₅ completed.

Instructions

1. Enter the balance as of September 1, 2008, in a four-column account for Work in Process—Rolling. Record the debits and the credits in the account for September. Construct a cost of production report and present computations for determining (a) equivalent units of production for materials and conversion, (b) equivalent costs per unit, (c) cost of goods finished, differentiating between units started in the prior period and units started and finished in September, and (d) work in process inventory.
2. Provide the same information for October by recording the October transactions in the four-column work in process account. Construct a cost of production report, and present the October computations (a through d) listed in part (1).
3. ▭▭▭▭▶ Comment on the change in cost per equivalent unit for August through October for direct materials and conversion cost.

APPENDIX PR 18-6B

Cost of production report: average cost method

✓ Cost per equivalent unit, $4.00

Robusta Coffee Company roasts and packs coffee beans. The process begins in the Roasting Department. From the Roasting Department, the coffee beans are transferred to the Packing Department. The following is a partial work in process account of the Roasting Department at July 31, 2008:

ACCOUNT *Work in Process—Roasting Department*					ACCOUNT NO.	
					Balance	
Date		**Item**	**Debit**	**Credit**	**Debit**	**Credit**
July	1	Bal., 18,000 units, 25% completed			18,450	
	31	Direct materials, 345,000 units	968,750		987,200	
	31	Direct labor	229,000		1,216,200	
	31	Factory overhead	203,600		1,419,800	
	31	Goods finished, 340,000 units		?	?	
	31	Bal. _?_ units, 65% completed			?	

Instructions

Prepare a cost of production report, using the average cost method, and identify the missing amounts for Work in Process—Roasting Department.

APPENDIX PR 18-7B

Equivalent units and related costs; cost of production report: average cost method

✓ Transferred to Packaging Dept., $865,060

Blue Ribbon Flour Company manufactures flour by a series of three processes, beginning in the Milling Department. From the Milling Department, the materials pass through the Sifting and Packaging departments, emerging as packaged refined flour.

The balance in the account Work in Process—Sifting Department was as follows on October 1, 2008:

Work in Process—Sifting Department (15,000 units, 75% completed) $42,000

The following costs were charged to Work in Process—Sifting Department during October:

Direct materials transferred from Milling Department: 235,800 units	$632,600
Direct labor	160,735
Factory overhead	76,900

During October, 233,800 units of flour were completed. Work in Process—Sifting Department on October 31 was 17,000 units, 75% completed.

Instructions

Prepare a cost of production report for the Sifting Department for October, using the average cost method.

Special Activities

SA 18-1

Ethics and professional conduct in business

ETHICS

Assume you are the division controller for Prairie Cookie Company. Prairie has introduced a new chocolate chip cookie called Full of Chips, and it is a success. As a result, the product manager responsible for the launch of this new cookie was promoted to division vice president and became your boss. A new product manager, Davis, has been brought in to replace the promoted manager. Davis notices that the Full of Chips cookie uses a lot of chips, which increases the cost of the cookie. As a result, Davis has ordered that the amount of chips used in the cookies be reduced by 10%. The manager believes that a 10% reduction in chips will not adversely affect sales, but will reduce costs, and hence improve margins. The increased margins would help Davis meet profit targets for the period.

You are looking over some cost of production reports segmented by cookie line. You notice that there is a drop in the materials costs for Full of Chips. On further investigation, you discover why the chip costs have declined (fewer chips). Both you and Davis report to the division vice president, who was the original product manager for Full of Chips. You are trying to decide what to do, if anything.

➡ Discuss the options you might consider.

SA 18-2
Accounting for materials costs

In papermaking operations for companies such as International Paper Company, wet pulp is fed into paper machines, which press and dry pulp into a continuous sheet of paper. The paper is formed at very high speeds (60 mph). Once the paper is formed, the paper is rolled onto a reel at the back end of the paper machine. One of the characteristics of papermaking is the creation of "broke" paper. Broke is paper that fails to satisfy quality standards and is therefore rejected for final shipment to customers. Broke is recycled back to the beginning of the process by combining the recycled paper with virgin (new) pulp material. The combination of virgin pulp and recycled broke is sent to the paper machine for papermaking. Broke is fed into this recycle process continuously from all over the facility.

In this industry, it is typical to charge the papermaking operation with the cost of direct materials, which is a mixture of virgin materials and broke. Broke has a much lower cost than does virgin pulp. Therefore, the more broke in the mixture, the lower the average cost of direct materials to the department. Papermaking managers will frequently comment on the importance of broke for keeping their direct materials costs down.

a. ▬▬▶ How do you react to this accounting procedure?
b. ▬▬▶ What "hidden costs" are not considered when accounting for broke as described above?

SA 18-3
Analyzing unit costs

Natcan Inc. manufactures cans for the canned food industry. The operations manager of a can manufacturing operation wants to conduct a cost study investigating the relationship of tin content in the material (can stock) to the energy cost for enameling the cans. The enameling was necessary to prepare the cans for labeling. A higher percentage of tin content in the can stock increases the cost of material. The operations manager believed there was a relationship between the tin content and energy costs for enameling. During the analysis period, the amount of tin content in the steel can stock was increased for every month, from April to September. The following operating reports were available from the controller:

	A	B	C	D	E	F	G	
		April	May	June	July	August	September	
1	Energy	$ 13,000	$ 28,800	$ 24,200	$ 14,000	$ 16,200	$ 15,000	1
2	Materials	12,000	30,000	28,600	18,900	25,200	29,000	2
3	Total cost	$ 25,000	$ 58,800	$ 52,800	$ 32,900	$ 41,400	$ 44,000	3
4	Units produced	/50,000	/120,000	/110,000	/70,000	/90,000	/100,000	4
5	Cost per unit	$ 0.50	$ 0.49	$ 0.48	$ 0.47	$ 0.46	$ 0.44	5

Differences in materials unit costs were entirely related to the amount of tin content.
▬▬▶ Interpret this information and report to the operations manager your recommendations with respect to tin content.

SA 18-4
Decision making

Lane Anderson, plant manager of Willow Run Paper Company's papermaking mill, was looking over the cost of production reports for July and August for the Papermaking Department. The reports revealed the following:

	July	August
Pulp and chemicals	$300,000	$307,000
Conversion cost	150,000	153,000
Total cost	$450,000	$460,000
Number of tons	/ 1,250	/ 1,150
Cost per ton	$ 360	$ 400

Lane was concerned about the increased cost per ton from the output of the department. As a result, he asked the plant controller to perform a study to help explain these results. The controller, Sarah Nold, began the analysis by performing some interviews of key plant personnel in order to understand what the problem might be. Excerpts from an interview with Jake Bennick, a paper machine operator, follow:

Jake: We have two papermaking machines in the department. I have no data, but I think paper machine 1 is applying too much pulp, and thus is wasting both conversion and materials resources. We haven't had repairs on paper machine 1 in a while. Maybe this is the problem.

Sarah: How does too much pulp result in wasted resources?

Jake: Well, you see, if too much pulp is applied, then we will waste pulp material. The customer will not pay for the extra weight. Thus, we just lose that amount of material. Also, when there is too much pulp, the machine must be slowed down in order to complete the drying process. This results in a waste of conversion costs.

Sarah: Do you have any other suspicions?

Jake: Well, as you know, we have two products—green paper and yellow paper. They are identical except for the color. The color is added to the papermaking process in the paper machine. I think that during August these two color papers have been behaving very differently. I don't have any data, but it just seems as though the amount of waste associated with the green paper has increased.

Sarah: Why is this?

Jake: I understand that there has been a change in specifications for the green paper, starting near the beginning of August. This change could be causing the machines to run poorly when making green paper. If this is the case, the cost per ton would increase for green paper.

Sarah also asked for a computer printout providing greater detail on August's operating results.

Computer run: 09085   September 9   Requested by: Sarah Nold

Papermaking Department—August detail

	A	B	C	D	E	F	
	Production Run Number	**Paper Machine**	**Color**	**Material Costs**	**Conversion Costs**	**Tons**	
1	1	1	Green	41,800	20,400	160	1
2	2	1	Yellow	41,700	21,200	140	2
3	3	1	Green	44,600	22,500	150	3
4	4	1	Yellow	36,100	18,100	120	4
5	5	2	Green	38,300	18,800	160	5
6	6	2	Yellow	35,300	16,900	150	6
7	7	2	Green	35,600	18,100	130	7
8	8	2	Yellow	33,600	17,000	140	8
9		Total		307,000	153,000	1,150	9

Assuming that you're Sarah Nold, write a memo to Lane Anderson with a recommendation to management. You should analyze the August data to determine whether the paper machine or the paper color explains the increase in the unit cost from July. Include any supporting schedules that are appropriate.

SA 18-5

Process costing companies

Group Project

Internet Project

The following categories represent typical process manufacturing industries:

Beverages   Metals
Chemicals   Petroleum refining
Food   Pharmaceuticals
Forest and paper products   Soap and cosmetics

In each category, identify one company (following your instructor's specific instructions) and determine the following:

1. Typical products manufactured by the selected company, including brand names.
2. Typical raw materials used by the selected company.
3. Types of processes used by the selected company.

Use annual reports, the Internet, or library resources in doing this activity.

Answers to Self-Examination Questions

1. **C** The process cost system is most appropriate for a business where manufacturing is conducted by continuous operations and involves a series of uniform production processes, such as the processing of crude oil (answer C). The job order cost system is most appropriate for a business where the product is made to customers' specifications, such as custom furniture manufacturing (answer A), commercial building construction (answer B), or automobile repair shop (answer D).

2. **A** The total pounds transferred to finished goods (23,000) are the 2,000 in-process pounds at the beginning of the period plus the number of pounds started and completed during the month, 21,000 (24,000 − 3,000). Answer B incorrectly assumes that the beginning inventory is not transferred during the month. Answer C assumes that all 24,000 pounds started during the month are transferred to finished goods, instead of only the portion started and completed. Answer D incorrectly adds all the numbers together.

3. **B** The number of units that could have been produced from start to finish during a period is termed equivalent units. The 4,875 equivalent units (answer B) is determined as follows:

To process units in inventory on May 1 (1,000 × ¼)	250
To process units started and completed in May (5,500 units − 1,000 units)	4,500
To process units in inventory on May 31 (500 units × ¼)	125
Equivalent units of production in May	4,875

4. **A** The conversion costs (direct labor and factory overhead) totaling $48,750 are divided by the number of equivalent units (4,875) to determine the unit conversion cost of $10 (answer A).

5. **C** The electricity costs have increased, and maintenance costs have decreased. Answer C would be a reasonable explanation for these results. The total costs, materials costs, and costs per unit do not reveal any type of pattern over the time period. In fact, the materials costs have stayed at exactly $2.00 per pound over the time period. This demonstrates that aggregated numbers can sometimes hide underlying information that can be used to improve the process.

Cost Behavior and Cost-Volume-Profit Analysis

objectives

After studying this chapter, you should be able to:

1 *Classify costs by their behavior as variable costs, fixed costs, or mixed costs.*

2 *Compute the contribution margin, the contribution margin ratio, and the unit contribution margin, and explain how they may be useful to managers.*

3 *Using the unit contribution margin, determine the break-even point and the volume necessary to achieve a target profit.*

4 *Using a cost-volume-profit chart and a profit-volume chart, determine the break-even point and the volume necessary to achieve a target profit.*

5 *Compute the break-even point for a business selling more than one product, the operating leverage, and the margin of safety.*

Netflix

How do you decide whether you are going to buy or rent a video game? It probably depends on how much you think you are going to use the game. If you are going to play the game a lot, you are probably better off buying the game than renting. The one-time cost of buying the game would be much less expensive than the cost of multiple rentals. If, on the other hand, you are uncertain about how frequently you are going to play the game, it may be less expensive to rent. The cost of an individual rental is much less than the cost of purchase. Understanding how the costs of rental and purchase behave is an important element of your decision.

Understanding how costs behave is also important to companies like Netflix, an online DVD movie rental service. For a fixed monthly fee, Netflix customers can select DVDs from the convenience of their own computers and have the DVDs delivered to their homes along with a prepaid return envelope. Customers can keep the DVDs as long as they want but must return the DVDs before they rent additional movies. The number of DVDs that members can check out at one time varies between one and three, depending on their subscription plans.

In order to entice customers to subscribe, Netflix had to invest in a well-stocked library of DVD titles and build a warehouse to hold and distribute these titles. These costs do not change with the number of subscriptions. But how many subscriptions does Netflix need in order to make a profit? That depends on the price of each subscription, the costs incurred with each DVD rental, and the costs associated with maintaining the DVD library.

As with Netflix, understanding how costs behave, and the relationship between costs, profits, and volume is important for all businesses. In this chapter, we discuss commonly used methods for classifying costs according to how they change. We also discuss techniques that management can use to evaluate costs in order to make sound business decisions.

Cost Behavior

objective   **1**

Classify costs by their behavior as variable costs, fixed costs, or mixed costs.

Knowing how costs behave is useful to management for a variety of purposes. For example, knowing how costs behave allows managers to predict profits as sales and production volumes change. Knowing how costs behave is also useful for estimating costs. Estimated costs, in turn, affect a variety of management decisions, such as whether to use excess machine capacity to produce and sell a product at a reduced price.

Cost behavior refers to the manner in which a cost changes as a related activity changes. To understand cost behavior, two factors must be considered. First, we must identify the activities that are thought to relate to the cost incurred. Such activities are called **activity bases** (or *activity drivers*). Second, we must specify the range of activity over which the changes in the cost are of interest. This range of activity is called the **relevant range**.

To illustrate, hospital administrators must plan and control hospital food costs. Why and how food costs change can be evaluated in terms of an activity base. The number of patients *treated* by the hospital would not be a good activity base, since some patients are outpatients who do not stay in the hospital. The number of patients who *stay* in the hospital, however, is a good activity base for studying food costs. Once the proper activity base is identified, food costs can then be analyzed over the range of the number of patients who normally stay in the hospital (the relevant range).

Three of the most common classifications of cost behavior are variable costs, fixed costs, and mixed costs.

VARIABLE COSTS

When the level of activity is measured in units produced, direct materials and direct labor costs are generally classified as variable costs. **Variable costs** are costs that vary in proportion to changes in the level of activity. For example, assume that Jason Inc. produces stereo sound systems under the brand name of J-Sound. The parts for the stereo systems are purchased from outside suppliers for $10 per unit and are assembled in Jason Inc.'s Waterloo plant. The direct materials costs for Model JS-12 for the relevant range of 5,000 to 30,000 units of production are shown below.

Number of Units of Model JS-12 Produced	Direct Materials Cost per Unit	Total Direct Materials Cost
5,000 units	$10	$ 50,000
10,000	10	100,000
15,000	10	150,000
20,000	10	200,000
25,000	10	250,000
30,000	10	300,000

Variable costs are the same per unit, while the total variable cost changes in proportion to changes in the activity base. For Model JS-12, for example, the direct materials cost for 10,000 units ($100,000) is twice the direct materials cost for 5,000 units ($50,000). The total direct materials cost varies in proportion to the number of units produced because the direct materials cost per unit ($10) is the same for all levels of production. Thus, producing 20,000 additional units of JS-12 will increase the direct materials cost by $200,000 (20,000 × $10), producing 25,000 additional units will increase the materials cost by $250,000, and so on.

Exhibit 1 illustrates how the variable costs for direct materials for Model JS-12 behave in total and on a per-unit basis as production changes.

EXHIBIT 1　　Variable Cost Graphs

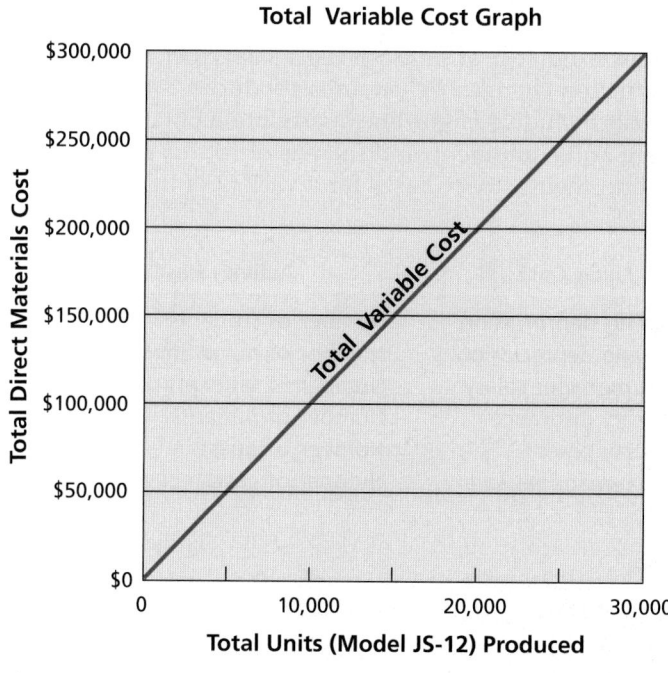

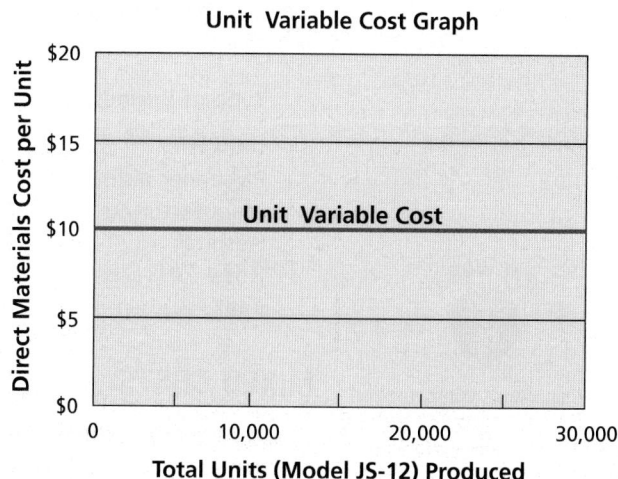

There are a variety of activity bases used by managers for evaluating cost behavior. The following list provides some examples of variable costs, along with their related activity bases for various types of businesses.

Type of Business	Cost	Activity Base
University	Instructor salaries	Number of classes
Passenger airline	Fuel	Number of miles flown
Manufacturing	Direct materials	Number of units produced
Hospital	Nurse wages	Number of patients
Hotel	Maid wages	Number of guests
Bank	Teller wages	Number of banking transactions

FIXED COSTS

Fixed costs are costs that remain the same in total dollar amount as the level of activity changes. To illustrate, assume that Minton Inc. manufactures, bottles, and distributes La Fleur Perfume at its Los Angeles plant. The production supervisor at the Los Angeles plant is Jane Sovissi, who is paid a salary of $75,000 per year. The relevant range of activity for a year is 50,000 to 300,000 bottles of perfume. Sovissi's salary is a fixed cost that does not vary with the number of units produced. Regardless of the number of bottles produced within the range of 50,000 to 300,000 bottles, Sovissi receives a salary of $75,000.

Although the total fixed cost remains the same as the number of bottles produced changes, the fixed cost per bottle changes. As more bottles are produced, the total fixed costs are spread over a larger number of bottles, and thus the fixed cost per bottle decreases. This relationship is shown below for Jane Sovissi's $75,000 salary.

Number of Bottles of Perfume Produced	Total Salary for Jane Sovissi	Salary per Bottle of Perfume Produced
50,000 bottles	$75,000	$1.500
100,000	75,000	0.750
150,000	75,000	0.500
200,000	75,000	0.375
250,000	75,000	0.300
300,000	75,000	0.250

Exhibit 2 illustrates how the fixed cost of Jane Sovissi's salary behaves in total and on a per-unit basis as production changes. When units produced is the measure of activity, examples of fixed costs include straight-line depreciation of factory equipment, insurance on factory plant and equipment, and salaries of factory supervisors. Other examples of fixed costs and their activity bases for a variety of businesses are as follows:

Type of Business	Fixed Cost	Activity Base
University	Building depreciation	Number of students
Passenger airline	Airplane depreciation	Number of miles flown
Manufacturing	Plant manager salary	Number of units produced
Hospital	Property insurance	Number of patients
Hotel	Property taxes	Number of guests
Bank	Branch manager salary	Number of customer accounts

A salesperson's compensation can be a mixed cost comprised of a salary (fixed portion) plus a commission as a percent of sales (variable portion).

MIXED COSTS

A **mixed cost** has characteristics of both a variable and a fixed cost. For example, over one range of activity, the total mixed cost may remain the same. It thus behaves as a fixed cost. Over another range of activity, the mixed cost may change in proportion to

EXHIBIT 2   Fixed Cost Graphs

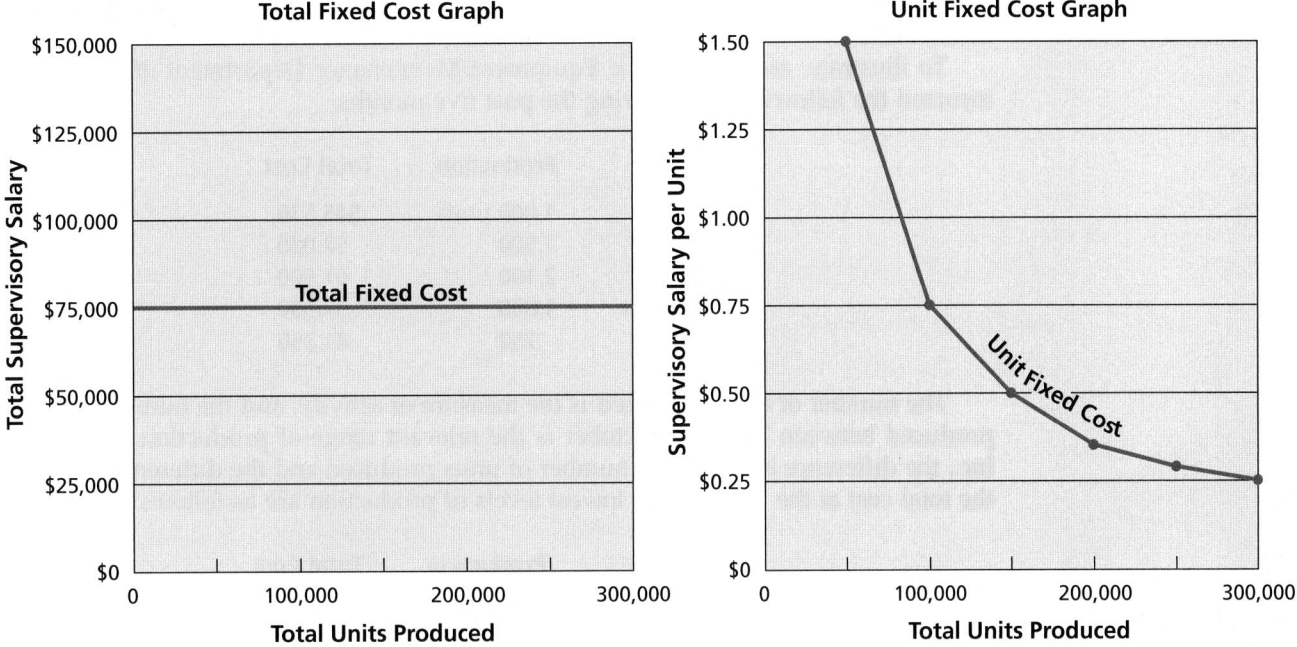

changes in the level of activity. It thus behaves as a variable cost. Mixed costs are some-times called *semivariable* or *semifixed* costs.

To illustrate, assume that Simpson Inc. manufactures sails, using rented machin-ery. The rental charges are $15,000 per year, plus $1 for each machine hour used over 10,000 hours. If the machinery is used 8,000 hours, the total rental charge is $15,000. If the machinery is used 20,000 hours, the total rental charge is $25,000 [$15,000 + (10,000 hours × $1)], and so on. Thus, if the level of activity is measured in machine hours and the relevant range is 0 to 40,000 hours, the rental charges are a fixed cost up to 10,000 hours and a variable cost thereafter. This mixed cost behavior is shown graphically in Exhibit 3.

EXHIBIT 3

Mixed Costs

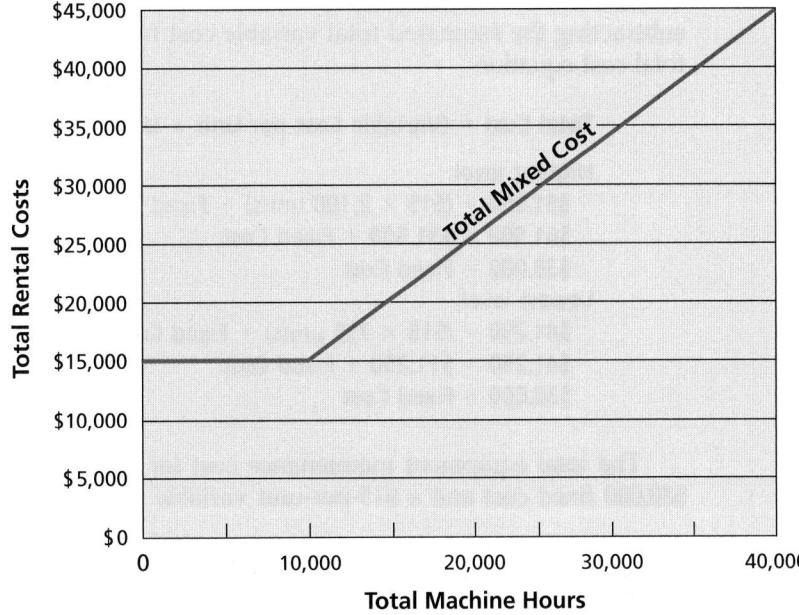

In analyses, mixed costs are usually separated into their fixed and variable components. The **high-low method** is a cost estimation technique that may be used for this purpose.[1] The high-low method uses the highest and lowest activity levels and their related costs to estimate the variable cost per unit and the fixed cost component of mixed costs.

To illustrate, assume that the Equipment Maintenance Department of Kason Inc. incurred the following costs during the past five months:

	Production	Total Cost
June	1,000 units	$45,550
July	1,500	52,000
August	2,100	61,500
September	1,800	57,500
October	750	41,250

The number of units produced is the measure of activity, and the number of units produced between June and October is the relevant range of production. For Kason Inc., the difference between the number of units produced and the difference between the total cost at the highest and lowest levels of production are as follows:

	Production	Total Cost
Highest level	2,100 units	$61,500
Lowest level	750	41,250
Difference	1,350 units	$20,250

Since the total fixed cost does not change with changes in volume of production, the $20,250 difference in the total cost is the change in the total variable cost. Hence, dividing the difference in the total cost by the difference in production provides an estimate of the variable cost per unit. For Kason Inc., this estimate is $15, as shown below.

$$\text{Variable Cost per Unit} = \frac{\text{Difference in Total Cost}}{\text{Difference in Production}}$$

$$\text{Variable Cost per Unit} = \frac{\$20,250}{1,350 \text{ units}} = \$15$$

The fixed cost will be the same at both the highest and the lowest levels of production. Thus, the fixed cost can be estimated at either of these levels. This is done by subtracting the estimated total variable cost from the total cost, using the following total cost equation:

Total Cost = (Variable Cost per Unit × Units of Production) + Fixed Cost

Highest level:
$61,500 = ($15 × 2,100 units) + Fixed Cost
$61,500 = $31,500 + Fixed Cost
$30,000 = Fixed Cost

Lowest level:
$41,250 = ($15 × 750 units) + Fixed Cost
$41,250 = $11,250 + Fixed Cost
$30,000 = Fixed Cost

The total equipment maintenance cost for Kason Inc. can thus be analyzed as a $30,000 fixed cost and a $15-per-unit variable cost. Using these amounts in the total

---

1 Other methods of estimating costs, such as the scattergraph method and the least squares method, are discussed in cost accounting textbooks.

cost equation, the total equipment maintenance cost at other levels of production can be estimated.

Example Exercise 19-1

objective

The manufacturing costs of Alex Industries for the first three months of the year are provided below.

	Total Cost	Production
January	$ 80,000	1,000 units
February	125,000	2,500
March	100,000	1,800

Using the high-low method, determine (a) the variable cost per unit and (b) the total fixed cost.

Follow My Example 19-1

a. $30 per unit = ($125,000 − $80,000)/(2,500 − 1,000)
b. $50,000 = $125,000 − ($30 × 2,500) or $80,000 − ($30 × 1,000)

For Practice: PE 19-1A, PE 19-1B

SUMMARY OF COST BEHAVIOR CONCEPTS

The following table summarizes the cost behavior attributes of variable costs and fixed costs:

Effect of Changing Activity Level

Cost	Total Amount	Per-Unit Amount
Variable	Increases and decreases proportionately with activity level.	Remains the same regardless of activity level.
Fixed	Remains the same regardless of activity level.	Increases and decreases inversely with activity level.

Examples of common variable, fixed, and mixed costs when the number of units produced is the activity base are:

Variable Cost	Fixed Cost	Mixed Cost
Direct materials	Depreciation expense	Quality Control Department salaries
Direct labor	Property taxes	Purchasing Department salaries
Electricity expense	Officer salaries	Maintenance expenses
Sales commissions	Insurance expense	Warehouse expenses

Mixed costs contain a fixed cost component that is incurred even if nothing is produced. For analyses, the fixed and variable cost components of mixed costs should be separated. Separating costs into their variable and fixed components for reporting purposes can be useful for decision making. One method of reporting variable and fixed costs is called **variable costing** or *direct costing*. Under variable costing, only the variable manufacturing costs (direct materials, direct labor, and variable factory overhead) are included in the product cost. The fixed factory overhead is an expense of the period in which it is incurred.[2]

---

2 The variable costing concept is discussed more fully in the next chapter.

Cost-Volume-Profit Relationships

After costs have been classified as fixed and variable, their effect on revenues, volume, and profits can be studied by using cost-volume-profit analysis. **Cost-volume-profit analysis** is the systematic examination of the relationships among selling prices, sales and production volume, costs, expenses, and profits.

Cost-volume-profit analysis provides management with useful information for decision making. For example, cost-volume-profit analysis may be used in setting selling prices, selecting the mix of products to sell, choosing among marketing strategies, and analyzing the effects of changes in costs on profits. In today's business environment, management must make such decisions quickly and accurately. As a result, the importance of cost-volume-profit analysis has increased in recent years.

CONTRIBUTION MARGIN CONCEPT

One relationship among cost, volume, and profit is the contribution margin. The **contribution margin** is the excess of sales revenues over variable costs. The contribution margin concept is especially useful in business planning because it gives insight into the profit potential of a firm. To illustrate, the income statement of Lambert Inc. in Exhibit 4 has been prepared in a contribution margin format.

EXHIBIT 4	
Contribution Margin Income Statement	

Sales	$1,000,000
Variable costs	600,000
Contribution margin	$ 400,000
Fixed costs	300,000
Income from operations	$ 100,000

The contribution margin of $400,000 is available to cover the fixed costs of $300,000. Once the fixed costs are covered, any remaining amount adds directly to the income from operations of the company. Consider the graphic to the left. The fixed costs are a bucket and the contribution margin is water filling the bucket. Once the bucket is filled, the overflow represents income from operations. Up until the point of overflow, however, the contribution margin contributes to fixed costs (filling the bucket).

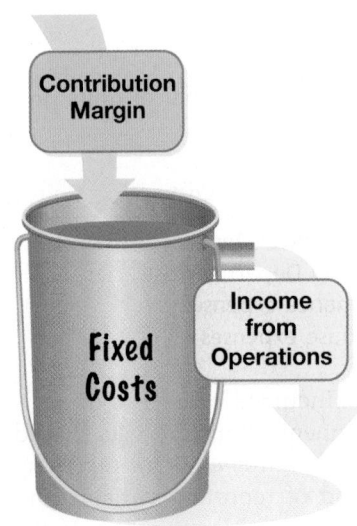

Contribution Margin Ratio   The contribution margin can also be expressed as a percentage. The **contribution margin ratio**, sometimes called the *profit-volume ratio,* indicates the percentage of each sales dollar available to cover the fixed costs and to provide income from operations. For Lambert Inc., the contribution margin ratio is 40%, as computed below.

$$\text{Contribution Margin Ratio} = \frac{\text{Sales} - \text{Variable Costs}}{\text{Sales}}$$

$$\text{Contribution Margin Ratio} = \frac{\$1,000,000 - \$600,000}{\$1,000,000} = 40\%$$

The contribution margin ratio measures the effect of an increase or a decrease in sales volume on income from operations. For example, assume that the management of Lambert Inc. is studying the effect of adding $80,000 in sales orders. Multiplying the contribution margin ratio (40%) by the change in sales volume ($80,000) indicates that income from operations will increase $32,000 if the additional orders are obtained. The validity of this analysis is illustrated by the following contribution margin income statement of Lambert Inc.:

Sales	$1,080,000
Variable costs ($1,080,000 × 60%)	648,000
Contribution margin ($1,080,000 × 40%)	$ 432,000
Fixed costs	300,000
Income from operations	$ 132,000

Variable costs as a percentage of sales are equal to 100% minus the contribution margin ratio. Thus, in the above income statement, the variable costs are 60% (100% − 40%) of sales, or $648,000 ($1,080,000 × 60%). The total contribution margin, $432,000, can also be computed directly by multiplying the sales by the contribution margin ratio ($1,080,000 × 40%).

In using the contribution margin ratio in analysis, factors other than sales volume, such as variable cost per unit and sales price, are assumed to remain constant. If such factors change, their effect must be considered.

The contribution margin ratio is also useful in setting business policy. For example, if the contribution margin ratio of a firm is large and production is at a level below 100% capacity, a large increase in income from operations can be expected from an increase in sales volume. A firm in such a position might decide to devote more effort to sales promotion because of the large change in income from operations that will result from changes in sales volume. In contrast, a firm with a small contribution margin ratio will probably want to give more attention to reducing costs before attempting to promote sales.

UNIT CONTRIBUTION MARGIN

The unit contribution margin is also useful for analyzing the profit potential of proposed projects. The **unit contribution margin** is the sales price less the variable cost per unit. For example, if Lambert Inc.'s unit selling price is $20 and its unit variable cost is $12, the unit contribution margin is $8 ($20 − $12).

The *contribution margin ratio* is most useful when the increase or decrease in sales volume is measured in sales *dollars*. The *unit contribution margin* is most useful when the increase or decrease in sales volume is measured in sales *units* (quantities). To illustrate, assume that Lambert Inc. sold 50,000 units. Its income from operations is $100,000, as shown in the following contribution margin income statement:

Sales (50,000 units × $20)	$1,000,000
Variable costs (50,000 units × $12)	600,000
Contribution margin (50,000 units × $8)	$ 400,000
Fixed costs	300,000
Income from operations	$ 100,000

A $350-per-night room at The Ritz-Carlton Hotel may have a variable cost, including maids' salaries, laundry, soap, and utilities, of only $40 per night and thus a high unit contribution margin per room. The high contribution margin per unit is necessary to cover the high fixed costs for the hotel.

If Lambert Inc.'s sales could be increased by 15,000 units, from 50,000 units to 65,000 units, its income from operations would increase by $120,000 (15,000 units × $8), as shown below.

Sales (65,000 units × $20)	$1,300,000
Variable costs (65,000 units × $12)	780,000
Contribution margin (65,000 units × $8)	$ 520,000
Fixed costs	300,000
Income from operations	$ 220,000

Unit contribution margin analyses can provide useful information for managers. The preceding illustration indicates, for example, that Lambert could spend up to $120,000 for special advertising or other product promotions to increase sales by 15,000 units.

Example Exercise 19-2   **objective** **2**

Molly Company sells 20,000 units at $12 per unit. Variable costs are $9 per unit, and fixed costs are $25,000. Determine the (a) contribution margin ratio, (b) unit contribution margin, and (c) income from operations.

Follow My Example 19-2

a. 25% = ($12 − $9)/$12 or ($240,000 − $180,000)/$240,000
b. $3 per unit = $12 − $9

c.

Sales	$240,000	(20,000 units × $12 per unit)
Variable costs	180,000	(20,000 units × $9 per unit)
Contribution margin	$ 60,000	[20,000 units × ($12 − $9)]
Fixed costs	25,000	
Income from operations	$ 35,000	

For Practice: PE 19-2A, PE 19-2B

Mathematical Approach to Cost-Volume-Profit Analysis

objective **3**

Using the unit contribution margin, determine the break-even point and the volume necessary to achieve a target profit.

Accountants use various approaches for expressing the relationship of costs, sales (volume), and income from operations (operating profit). The mathematical approach is one approach that is used often in practice.

The mathematical approach to cost-volume-profit analysis uses equations (1) to determine the units of sales necessary to achieve the break-even point in operations or (2) to determine the units of sales necessary to achieve a target or desired profit. We will next describe and illustrate these equations and their use by management in profit planning.

BREAK-EVEN POINT

The **break-even point** is the level of operations at which a business's revenues and expired costs are exactly equal. At break-even, a business will have neither an income nor a loss from operations. The break-even point is useful in business planning, especially when expanding or decreasing operations.

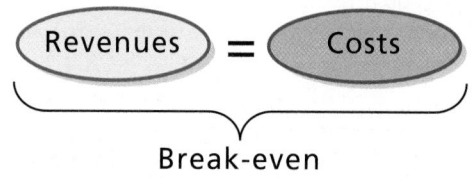

To illustrate the computation of the break-even point, assume that the fixed costs for Barker Corporation are estimated to be $90,000. The unit selling price, unit variable cost, and unit contribution margin for Barker Corporation are as follows:

Unit selling price	$25
Unit variable cost	15
Unit contribution margin	$10

The break-even point is 9,000 units, which can be computed by using the following equation:

$$\text{Break-Even Sales (units)} = \frac{\text{Fixed Costs}}{\text{Unit Contribution Margin}}$$

$$\text{Break-Even Sales (units)} = \frac{\$90,000}{\$10} = 9,000 \text{ units}$$

The following income statement verifies the preceding computation:

Sales (9,000 units × $25)	$225,000
Variable costs (9,000 units × $15)	135,000
Contribution margin	$ 90,000
Fixed costs	90,000
Income from operations	$ 0

The break-even point is affected by changes in the fixed costs, unit variable costs, and the unit selling price. Next, we will briefly describe the effect of each of these factors on the break-even point.

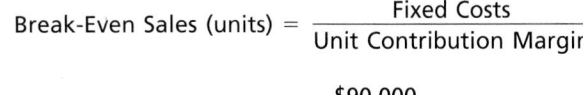
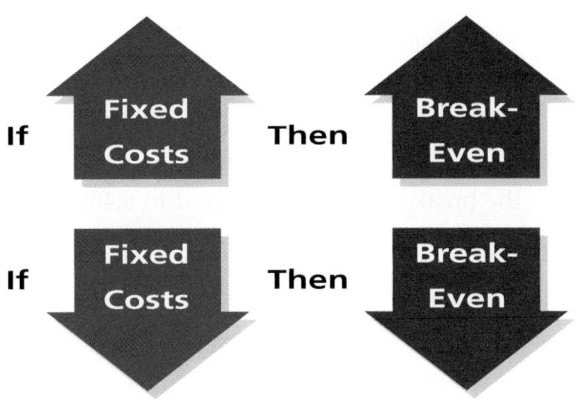

If Fixed Costs ↑ **Then** Break-Even ↑

If Fixed Costs ↓ **Then** Break-Even ↓

Effect of Changes in Fixed Costs Although fixed costs do not change in total with changes in the level of activity, they may change because of other factors. For example, changes in property tax rates or factory supervisors' salaries change fixed costs. Increases in fixed costs will raise the break-even point. Likewise, decreases in fixed costs will lower the break-even point.

To illustrate, assume that Bishop Co. is evaluating a proposal to budget an additional $100,000 for advertising. Fixed costs before the additional advertising are estimated at $600,000, and the unit contribution margin is $20. The break-even point before the additional expense is 30,000 units, computed as follows:

$$\text{Break-Even Sales (units)} = \frac{\text{Fixed Costs}}{\text{Unit Contribution Margin}}$$

$$\text{Break-Even Sales (units)} = \frac{\$600,000}{\$20} = 30,000 \text{ units}$$

If the additional amount is spent, the fixed costs will increase by $100,000 and the break-even point will increase to 35,000 units, computed as follows:

$$\text{Break-Even Sales (units)} = \frac{\text{Fixed Costs}}{\text{Unit Contribution Margin}}$$

$$\text{Break-Even Sales (units)} = \frac{\$700,000}{\$20} = 35,000 \text{ units}$$

The $100,000 increase in the fixed costs requires an additional 5,000 units ($100,000/$20) of sales to break even. In other words, an increase in sales of 5,000 units is required in order to generate an additional $100,000 of total contribution margin (5,000 units × $20) to cover the increased fixed costs.

Effect of Changes in Unit Variable Costs Although unit variable costs are not affected by changes in volume of activity, they may be affected by other factors. For example, changes in the price of direct materials and the wages for factory workers providing direct labor will change unit variable costs. Increases in unit variable costs will raise the break-even point. Likewise, decreases in unit variable costs will lower the break-even point. For example, when fuel prices rise or decline, there is a direct impact on the break-even freight load for the Union Pacific railroad.

To illustrate, assume that Park Co. is evaluating a proposal to pay an additional 2% commission on sales to its salespeople as an incentive to increase sales. Fixed costs are estimated at $840,000, and the unit selling price, unit variable cost, and unit contribution margin before the additional 2% commission are as follows:

Unit selling price	$250
Unit variable cost	145
Unit contribution margin	$105

The break-even point is 8,000 units, computed as follows:

$$\text{Break-Even Sales (units)} = \frac{\text{Fixed Costs}}{\text{Unit Contribution Margin}}$$

$$\text{Break-Even Sales (units)} = \frac{\$840,000}{\$105} = 8,000 \text{ units}$$

If the sales commission proposal is adopted, variable costs will increase by $5 per unit ($250 × 2%). This increase in the variable costs will decrease the unit contribution margin by $5 (from $105 to $100). Thus, the break-even point is raised to 8,400 units, computed as follows:

$$\text{Break-Even Sales (units)} = \frac{\text{Fixed Costs}}{\text{Unit Contribution Margin}}$$

$$\text{Break-Even Sales (units)} = \frac{\$840,000}{\$100} = 8,400 \text{ units}$$

At the original break-even point of 8,000 units, the new unit contribution margin of $100 would provide only $800,000 to cover fixed costs of $840,000. Thus, an additional 400 units of sales will be required in order to provide the additional $40,000 (400 units × $100) contribution margin necessary to break even.

Effect of Changes in Unit Selling Price   Increases in the unit selling price will lower the break-even point, while decreases in the unit selling price will raise the break-even point. To illustrate, assume that Graham Co. is evaluating a proposal to increase the unit selling price of its product from $50 to $60. The following data have been gathered:

	Current	Proposed
Unit selling price	$50	$60
Unit variable cost	30	30
Unit contribution margin	$20	$30
Total fixed costs	$600,000	$600,000

The break-even point based on the current selling price is 30,000 units, computed as follows:

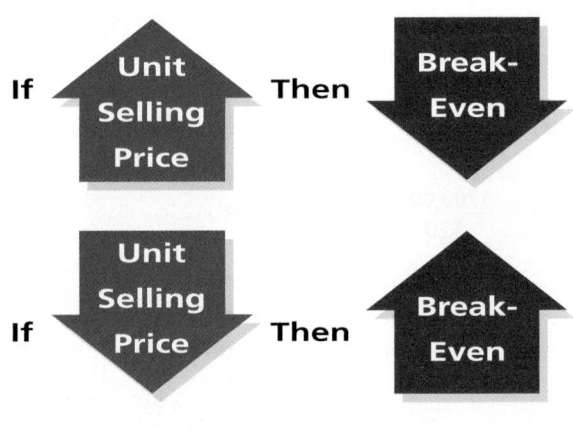

$$\text{Break-Even Sales (units)} = \frac{\text{Fixed Costs}}{\text{Unit Contribution Margin}}$$

$$\text{Break-Even Sales (units)} = \frac{\$600,000}{\$20} = 30,000 \text{ units}$$

If the selling price is increased by $10 per unit, the break-even point is decreased to 20,000 units, computed as follows:

$$\text{Break-Even Sales (units)} = \frac{\text{Fixed Costs}}{\text{Unit Contribution Margin}}$$

$$\text{Break-Even Sales (units)} = \frac{\$600,000}{\$30} = 20,000 \text{ units}$$

The increase of $10 per unit in the selling price increases the unit contribution margin by $10. Thus, the break-even point decreases by 10,000 units (from 30,000 units to 20,000 units).

Summary of Effects of Changes on Break-Even Point The break-even point in sales (units) moves in the same direction as changes in the variable cost per unit and fixed costs. In contrast, the break-even point in sales (units) moves in the opposite direction to changes in the sales price per unit. A summary of the impact of these changes on the break-even point in sales (units) is shown below.

Type of Change	Direction of Change	Effect of Change on Break-Even Sales (Units)
Fixed cost	Increase	Increase
	Decrease	Decrease
Variable cost per unit	Increase	Increase
	Decrease	Decrease
Unit sales price	Increase	Decrease
	Decrease	Increase

Business Connections

BREAKING EVEN ON HOWARD STERN

Satellite radio, one of the fastest growing forms of entertainment, has seen remarkable growth in recent years. Customers are able to choose from a variety of types of music and talk radio and listen from just about anywhere in the country with limited commercials. The satellite radio market is dominated by two companies, XM Satellite Radio and SIRIUS Satellite Radio. XM is the older of the two companies and has the largest market share. However, in 2005, Sirius tripled its customer base by diversifying its product line and signing high profile talk personalities. As part of this strategy, Sirius signed a five-year $500 million contract with radio "shock jock" Howard Stern. But how did Sirius determine that adding the self-proclaimed "King of All Media" to its play list was worth such a large amount of money? It used break-even analy-sis. Prior to signing with Sirius, 12 million listeners tuned in to Stern's show on Infinity Broadcasting Corporation. At the time the contract was signed, Sirius had about 600,000 subscribers. The company estimated that it would need 1 million of Stern's fans to subscribe to Sirius in order to break even on the $500 million fixed cost of the contract. Initial projections estimated that Stern's show would attract as many as 10 million listeners. It appears that the company's strategy is beginning to work, as Sirius's subscriber base had grown to 3.3 million customers by the end of 2005.

TARGET PROFIT

At the break-even point, sales and costs are exactly equal. However, the break-even point is not the goal of most businesses. Rather, managers seek to maximize profits. By modifying the break-even equation, the sales volume required to earn a target or desired amount of profit may be estimated. For this purpose, target profit is added to the break-even equation as shown below.

$$\text{Sales (units)} = \frac{\text{Fixed Costs} + \text{Target Profit}}{\text{Unit Contribution Margin}}$$

To illustrate, assume that fixed costs are estimated at $200,000, and the desired profit is $100,000. The unit selling price, unit variable cost, and unit contribution margin are as follows:

Unit selling price	$75
Unit variable cost	45
Unit contribution margin	$30

The sales volume necessary to earn the target profit of $100,000 is 10,000 units, computed as follows:

$$\text{Sales (units)} = \frac{\text{Fixed Costs} + \text{Target Profit}}{\text{Unit Contribution Margin}}$$

$$\text{Sales (units)} = \frac{\$200,000 + \$100,000}{\$30} = 10,000 \text{ units}$$

The following income statement verifies this computation:

Sales (10,000 units × $75)		$750,000
Variable costs (10,000 units × $45)		450,000
Contribution margin (10,000 units × $30)		$300,000
Fixed costs		200,000
Income from operations		$100,000	← Target profit

Follow My Example 19-4

a. 3,000 units = $240,000/($140 − $60)
b. 3,625 units = ($240,000 + $50,000)/($140 − $60)

For Practice: PE 19-4A, PE 19-4B

Integrity, Objectivity, and Ethics in Business

ETHICS

ORPHAN DRUGS

Each year, pharmaceutical companies develop new drugs that cure a variety of physical conditions. In order to be profitable, drug companies must sell enough of a product to exceed break-even for a reasonable selling price. Break-even points, however, create a problem for drugs targeted at rare diseases, called "orphan drugs." These drugs are typically expensive to develop and have low sales volumes, making it impossible to achieve break-even. To ensure that orphan drugs are not overlooked, Congress passed the Orphan Drug Act that provides incentives for pharmaceutical companies to develop drugs for rare diseases that might not generate enough sales to reach break-even. The program has been a great success. Since 1982, over 200 orphan drugs have come to market, including Jacobus Pharmaceuticals Company, Inc.'s drug for the treatment of tuberculosis and Novartis AG's drug for the treatment of Paget's disease.

Graphic Approach to Cost-Volume-Profit Analysis

objective 4

Using a cost-volume-profit chart and a profit-volume chart, determine the break-even point and the volume necessary to achieve a target profit.

Cost-volume-profit analysis can be presented graphically as well as in equation form. Many managers prefer the graphic format because the income or loss from operations (operating profit or loss) for different levels of sales can readily be determined. Next, we describe two graphic approaches that managers find useful.

COST-VOLUME-PROFIT (BREAK-EVEN) CHART

A **cost-volume-profit chart**, sometimes called a *break-even chart*, may assist management in understanding relationships among costs, sales, and operating profit or loss. To illustrate, the cost-volume-profit chart in Exhibit 5 is based on the following data:

Unit selling price	$50
Unit variable cost	30
Unit contribution margin	$20
Total fixed costs	$100,000

We constructed the cost-volume-profit chart in Exhibit 5 as follows:

A. Volume expressed in units of sales is indicated along the horizontal axis. The range of volume shown on the horizontal axis should reflect the *relevant range* in which the business expects to operate. Dollar amounts representing total sales and costs are indicated along the vertical axis.

B. A sales line is plotted by beginning at zero on the left corner of the graph. A second point is determined by multiplying any units of sales on the horizontal axis by the unit sales price of $50. For example, for 10,000 units of sales, the total sales would be $500,000 (10,000 units × $50). The sales line is drawn upward to the right from zero through the $500,000 point.

C. A cost line is plotted by beginning with total fixed costs, $100,000, on the vertical axis. A second point is determined by multiplying any units of sales on the horizontal axis by the unit variable costs and adding the fixed costs. For example, for 10,000 units of sales, the total estimated costs would be $400,000 [(10,000 units × $30) + $100,000]. The cost line is drawn upward to the right from $100,000 on the vertical axis through the $400,000 point.

EXHIBIT 5

Cost-Volume-Profit Chart

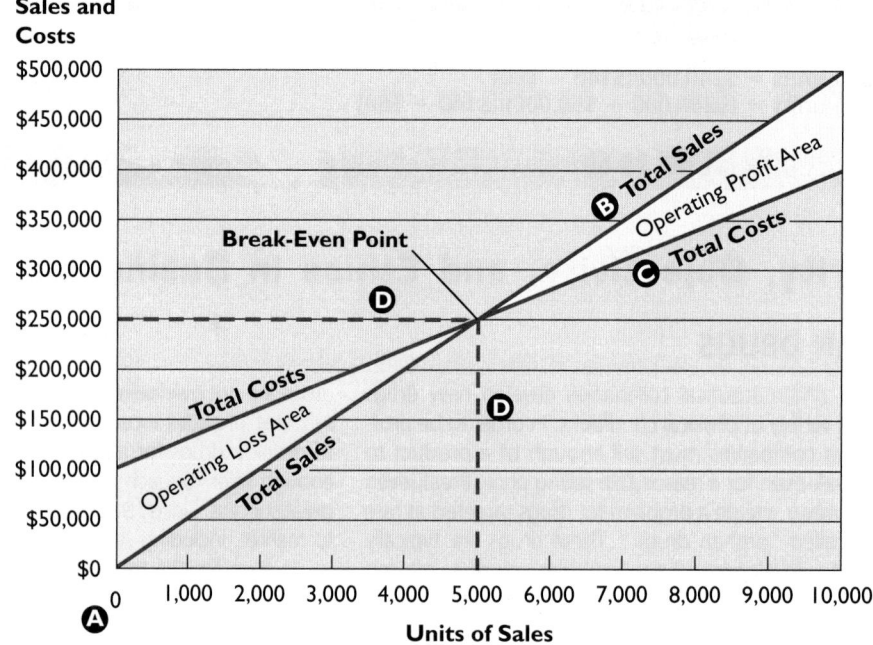

EXHIBIT 6

Revised Cost-Volume-Profit Chart

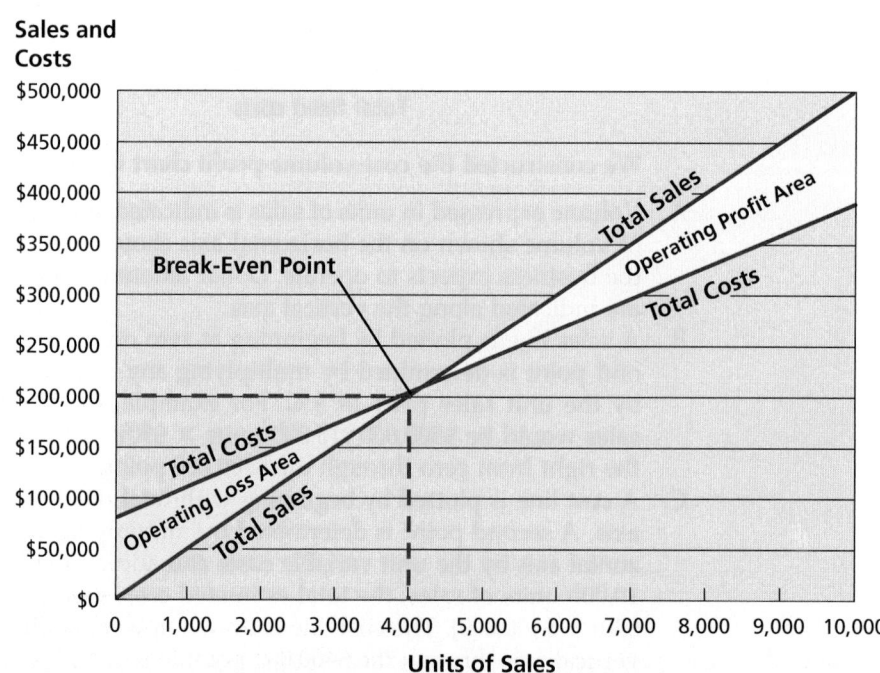

D. Horizontal and vertical lines are drawn at the intersection point of the sales and cost lines, which is the break-even point, and the areas representing operating profit and operating loss are identified.

In Exhibit 5, the dotted lines drawn from the intersection point of the total sales line and the total cost line identify the break-even point in total sales dollars and units. The break-even point is $250,000 of sales, which represents a sales volume of 5,000 units. Operating profits will be earned when sales levels are to the right of the break-even point (operating profit area). Operating losses will be incurred when sales levels are to the left of the break-even point (operating loss area).

Changes in the unit selling price, total fixed costs, and unit variable costs can be analyzed by using a cost-volume-profit chart. Using the data in Exhibit 5, assume that a proposal to reduce fixed costs by $20,000 is to be evaluated. In this case, the total fixed costs would be $80,000 ($100,000 − $20,000). As shown in Exhibit 6, the total cost line should be redrawn, starting at the $80,000 point (total fixed costs) on the vertical axis. A second point is determined by multiplying any units of sales on the horizontal axis by the unit variable costs and adding the fixed costs. For example, for 10,000 units of sales, the total estimated costs would be $380,000 [(10,000 units × $30) + $80,000]. The cost line is drawn upward to the right from $80,000 on the vertical axis through the $380,000 point. The revised cost-volume-profit chart in Exhibit 6 indicates that the break-even point decreases to $200,000 or 4,000 units of sales.

PROFIT-VOLUME CHART

Another graphic approach to cost-volume-profit analysis, the **profit-volume chart**, focuses on profits. This is in contrast to the cost-volume-profit chart, which focuses on sales and costs. The profit-volume chart plots only the difference between total sales and total costs (or profits). In this way, the profit-volume chart allows managers to determine the operating profit (or loss) for various levels of operations.

To illustrate, assume that the profit-volume chart in Exhibit 7 is based on the same data as used in Exhibit 5. These data are as follows:

Unit selling price	$50
Unit variable cost	30
Unit contribution margin	$20
Total fixed costs	$100,000

EXHIBIT 7

Profit-Volume Chart

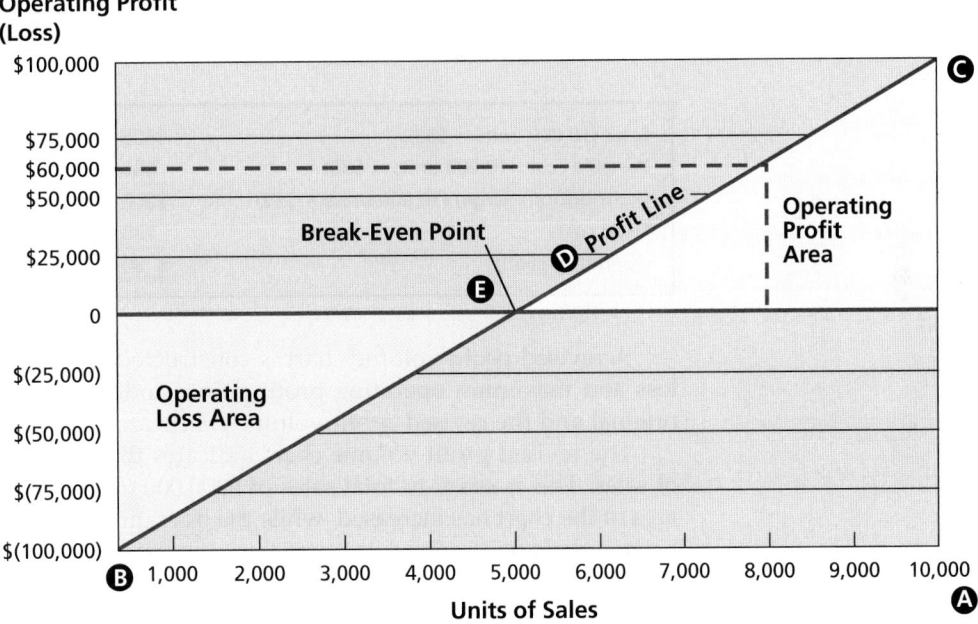

The maximum operating loss is equal to the fixed costs of $100,000. Assuming that the maximum unit sales within the relevant range is 10,000 units, the maximum operating profit is $100,000, computed as follows:

Sales (10,000 units × $50)	$500,000
Variable costs (10,000 units × $30)	300,000
Contribution margin (10,000 units × $20)	$200,000
Fixed costs	100,000
Operating profit	$100,000	← Maximum profit

We constructed the profit-volume chart in Exhibit 7 as follows:

A. Volume expressed in units of sales is indicated along the horizontal axis. The range of volume shown on the horizontal axis should reflect the *relevant range* in which the business expects to operate. In this illustration, the maximum number of sales units within the relevant range is assumed to be 10,000 units. Dollar amounts indicating operating profits and losses are shown along the vertical axis.

B. A point representing the maximum operating loss is plotted on the vertical axis at the left. This loss is equal to the total fixed costs at the zero level of sales.

C. A point representing the maximum operating profit within the relevant range is plotted on the right.

D. A diagonal profit line is drawn connecting the maximum operating loss point with the maximum operating profit point.

E. The profit line intersects the horizontal zero operating profit line at the break-even point expressed in units of sales, and the areas indicating operating profit and loss are identified.

In Exhibit 7, the break-even point is 5,000 units of sales, which is equal to total sales of $250,000 (5,000 units × $50). Operating profit will be earned when sales levels are to the right of the break-even point (operating profit area). Operating losses will be incurred when sales levels are to the left of the break-even point (operating loss area). For example, at sales of 8,000 units, an operating profit of $60,000 will be earned, as shown in Exhibit 7.

The effect of changes in the unit selling price, total fixed costs, and unit variable costs on profit can be analyzed using a profit-volume chart. To illustrate, using the data in Exhibit 7, we will evaluate the effect on profit of an increase of $20,000 in fixed costs. In this case, the total fixed costs would be $120,000 ($100,000 + $20,000), and the maximum operating loss would also be $120,000. If the maximum sales within the relevant range is 10,000 units, the maximum operating profit would be $80,000, computed as follows:

Sales (10,000 units × $50)	$500,000
Variable costs (10,000 units × $30)	300,000
Contribution margin (10,000 units × $20)	$200,000
Fixed costs	120,000
Operating profit	$ 80,000	← Revised maximum profit

A revised profit-volume chart is constructed by plotting the maximum operating loss and maximum operating profit points and drawing the revised profit line. The original and the revised profit-volume charts are shown in Exhibit 8.

The revised profit-volume chart indicates that the break-even point is 6,000 units of sales. This is equal to total sales of $300,000 (6,000 units × $50). The operating loss area of the chart has increased, while the operating profit area has decreased under the proposed change in fixed costs.

USE OF COMPUTERS IN COST-VOLUME-PROFIT ANALYSIS

With computers, the graphic approach and the mathematical approach to cost-volume-profit analysis are easy to use. Managers can vary assumptions regarding selling prices, costs, and volume and can immediately see the effects of each change on the break-even point and profit. Such an analysis is called a *"what if"* analysis or *sensitivity analysis*.

ASSUMPTIONS OF COST-VOLUME-PROFIT ANALYSIS

The reliability of cost-volume-profit analysis depends upon the validity of several assumptions. The primary assumptions are as follows:

1. Total sales and total costs can be represented by straight lines.
2. Within the relevant range of operating activity, the efficiency of operations does not change.

EXHIBIT 8

Original Profit-Volume
Chart and Revised
Profit-Volume Chart

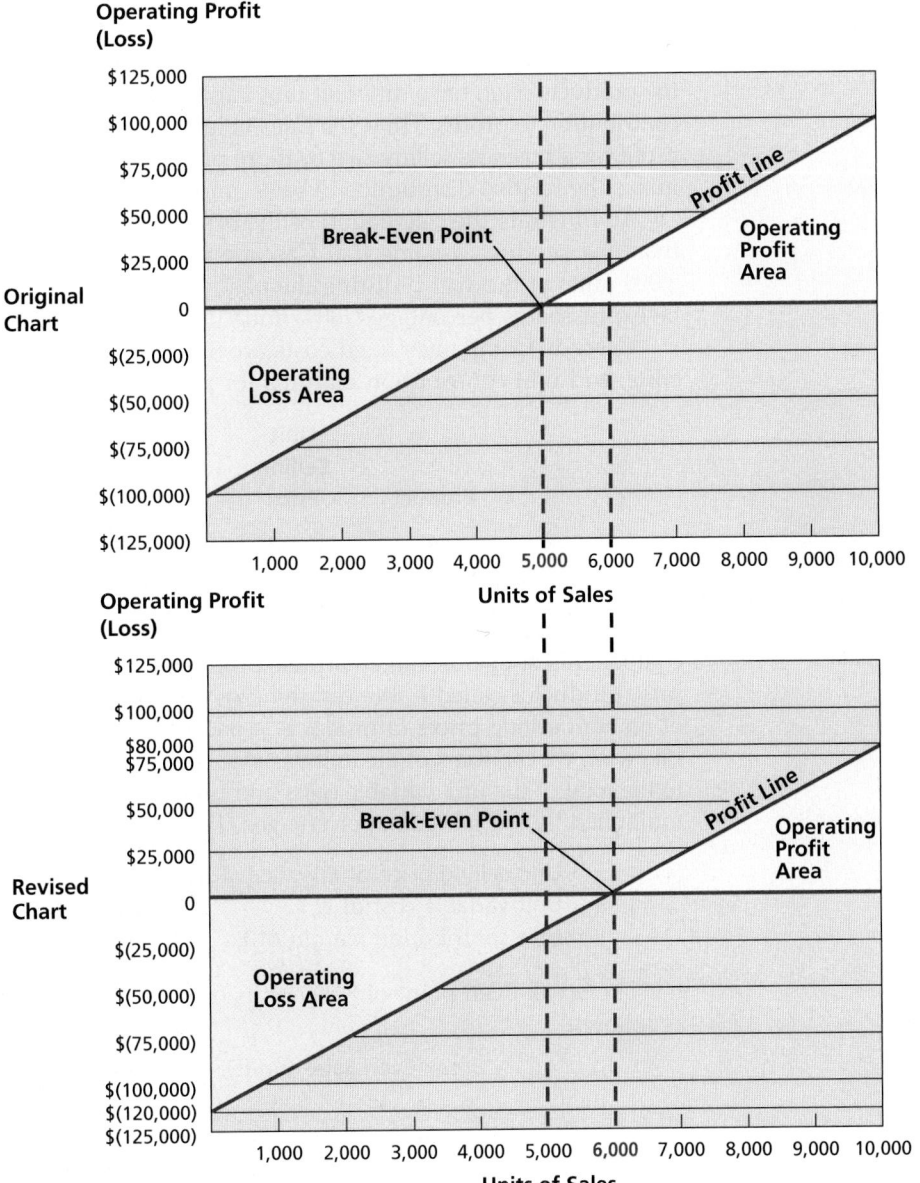

3. Costs can be accurately divided into fixed and variable components.
4. The sales mix is constant.
5. There is no change in the inventory quantities during the period.

These assumptions simplify cost-volume-profit analysis. Since they are often valid for the relevant range of operations, cost-volume-profit analysis is useful to decision making.[3]

Special Cost-Volume-Profit Relationships

objective   **5**

Compute the break-even point for a business selling more than one product, the operating leverage, and the margin of safety.

Cost-volume-profit analysis can also be used in a variety of ways other than those already illustrated in this chapter. These include the use of break-even analysis when a company sells several products with different costs and prices. In addition, operating leverage and the margin of safety are useful in summarizing important cost-volume-profit relationships.

---

3 The impact of violating these assumptions is discussed in advanced accounting texts.

SALES MIX CONSIDERATIONS

In most businesses, more than one product is sold at varying selling prices. In addition, the products often have different unit variable costs, and each product makes a different contribution to profits. Thus, the sales volume necessary to break even or to earn a target profit for a business selling two or more products depends upon the sales mix. The **sales mix** is the relative distribution of sales among the various products sold by a business.

To illustrate the calculation of the break-even point for a company that sells more than one product, assume that Cascade Company sold 8,000 units of Product A and 2,000 units of Product B during the past year. The sales mix for products A and B can be expressed as percentages (80% and 20%) or as a ratio (80:20).

Cascade Company's fixed costs are $200,000. The unit selling prices, unit variable costs, and unit contribution margins for products A and B are as follows:

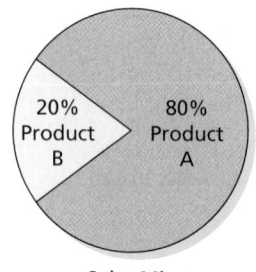

Sales Mix

Product	Unit Selling Price	Unit Variable Cost	Unit Contribution Margin
A	$ 90	$70	$20
B	140	95	45

In computing the break-even point, it is useful to think of the individual products as components of one overall enterprise product. For Cascade Company, this overall enterprise product is called E. We can think of the unit selling price of E as equal to the total of the unit selling prices of products A and B, multiplied by their sales mix percentages. Likewise, we can think of the unit variable cost and unit contribution margin of E as equal to the total of the unit variable costs and unit contribution margins of products A and B, multiplied by the sales mix percentages. These computations are as follows:

Unit selling price of E:	($90 × 0.8) + ($140 × 0.2) = $100
Unit variable cost of E:	($70 × 0.8) + ($ 95 × 0.2) = 75
Unit contribution margin of E:	= $ 25

The break-even point of 8,000 units of E can be determined in the normal manner as follows:

$$\text{Break-Even Sales (units)} = \frac{\text{Fixed Costs}}{\text{Unit Contribution Margin}}$$

$$\text{Break-Even Sales (units)} = \frac{\$200,000}{\$25} = 8,000 \text{ units}$$

Since the sales mix for products A and B is 80% and 20%, respectively, the break-even quantity of A is 6,400 units (8,000 units × 80%) and B is 1,600 units (8,000 units × 20%). This analysis can be verified in the following income statement:

The daily break-even attendance at Universal Studios theme areas depends on how many tickets were sold at an advance purchase discount rate vs. the full gate rate. Likewise, the break-even point for an overseas flight of Delta Air Lines will be influenced by the number of first class, business class, and economy class tickets sold for the flight.

	Product A	Product B	Total
Sales:			
6,400 units × $90	$576,000		$576,000
1,600 units × $140		$224,000	224,000
Total sales	$576,000	$224,000	$800,000
Variable costs:			
6,400 units × $70	$448,000		$448,000
1,600 units × $95		$152,000	152,000
Total variable costs	$448,000	$152,000	$600,000
Contribution margin	$128,000	$ 72,000	$200,000
Fixed costs			200,000
Income from operations		$ 0	← Break-even point

The effects of changes in the sales mix on the break-even point can be determined by repeating this analysis, assuming a different sales mix.

Example Exercise 19-5

objective 5

Megan Company has fixed costs of $180,000. The unit selling price, variable cost per unit, and contribution margin per unit for the company's two products are provided below.

Product	Selling Price	Variable Cost per Unit	Contribution Margin per Unit
Q	$160	$100	$60
Z	100	80	20

The sales mix for products Q and Z is 75% and 25%, respectively. Determine the break-even point in units of Q and Z.

Follow My Example 19-5

Unit Selling Price of E: $[(\$160 \times 0.75) + (\$100 \times 0.25)] = \$145$
Unit Variable Cost of E: $[(\$100 \times 0.75) + (\$80 \times 0.25)] = \underline{\quad 95}$
Unit Contribution Margin of E: $\underline{\$\ 50}$

Break-Even Sales (units) = 3,600 units = $180,000/$50

For Practice: PE 19-5A, PE 19-5B

OPERATING LEVERAGE

The relative mix of a business's variable costs and fixed costs is measured by the **operating leverage**. It is computed as follows:

$$\text{Operating Leverage} = \frac{\text{Contribution Margin}}{\text{Income from Operations}}$$

One type of business that has high operating leverage is what is called a "network" business—one in which service is provided over a network that moves either goods or information. Examples of network businesses include American Airlines, Verizon Communications, Yahoo!, and Google.

Since the difference between contribution margin and income from operations is fixed costs, companies with large amounts of fixed costs will generally have a high operating leverage. Thus, companies in capital-intensive industries, such as the airline and automotive industries, will generally have a high operating leverage. A low operating leverage is normal for companies in industries that are labor-intensive, such as professional services.

Managers can use operating leverage to measure the impact of changes in sales on income from operations. A high operating leverage indicates that a small increase in sales will yield a large percentage increase in income from operations. In contrast, a low operating leverage indicates that a large increase in sales is necessary to significantly increase income from operations. To illustrate, assume the following operating data for Jones Inc. and Wilson Inc.:

	Jones Inc.	Wilson Inc.
Sales	$400,000	$400,000
Variable costs	300,000	300,000
Contribution margin	$100,000	$100,000
Fixed costs	80,000	50,000
Income from operations	$ 20,000	$ 50,000

Both companies have the same sales, the same variable costs, and the same contribution margin. Jones Inc. has larger fixed costs than Wilson Inc. and, as a result, a lower income from operations and a higher operating leverage. The operating leverage for each company is computed as follows:

Jones Inc.

$$\text{Operating Leverage} = \frac{\$100,000}{\$20,000} = 5$$

Wilson Inc.

$$\text{Operating Leverage} = \frac{\$100,000}{\$50,000} = 2$$

Jones Inc.'s operating leverage indicates that, for each percentage point change in sales, income from operations will change five times that percentage. In contrast, for each percentage point change in sales, the income from operations of Wilson Inc. will change only two times that percentage. For example, if sales increased by 10% ($40,000) for each company, income from operations will increase by 50% (10% × 5), or $10,000 (50% × $20,000), for Jones Inc. The sales increase of $40,000 will increase income from operations by only 20% (10% × 2), or $10,000 (20% × $50,000), for Wilson Inc. The validity of this analysis is shown as follows:

	Jones Inc.	Wilson Inc.
Sales	$440,000	$440,000
Variable costs	330,000	330,000
Contribution margin	$110,000	$110,000
Fixed costs	80,000	50,000
Income from operations	$ 30,000	$ 60,000

For Jones Inc., even a small increase in sales will generate a large percentage increase in income from operations. Thus, Jones's managers may be motivated to think of ways to increase sales. In contrast, Wilson's managers might attempt to increase operating leverage by reducing variable costs and thereby change the cost structure.

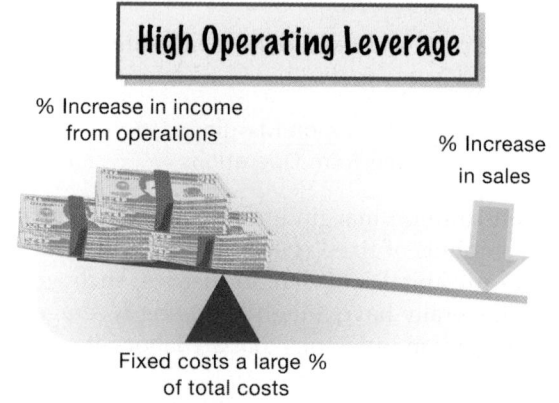

High Operating Leverage

% Increase in income from operations

% Increase in sales

Fixed costs a large % of total costs

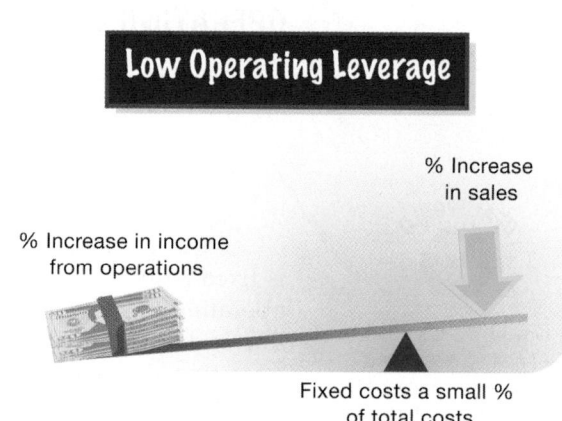

Low Operating Leverage

% Increase in sales

% Increase in income from operations

Fixed costs a small % of total costs

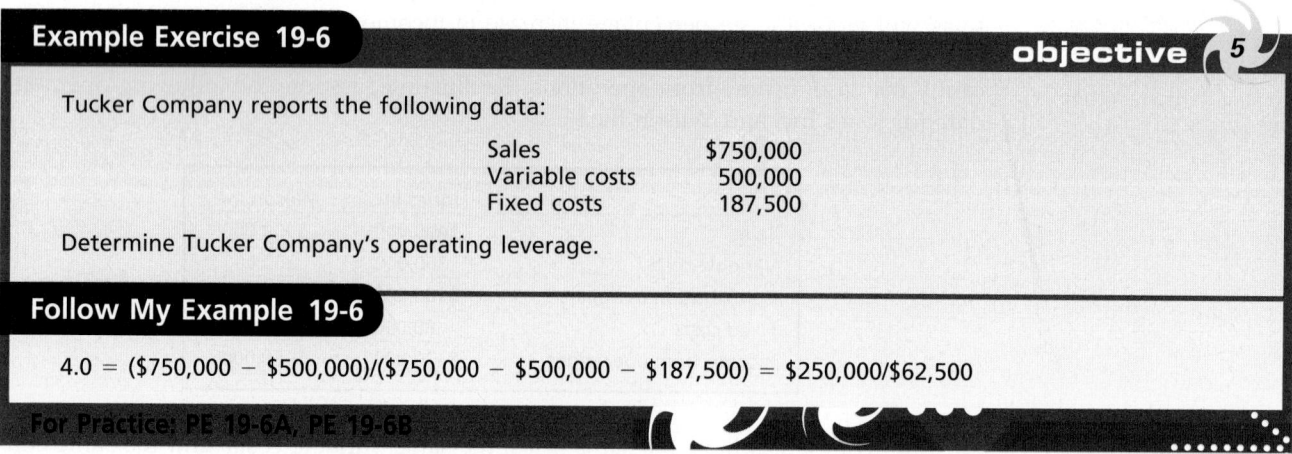

Example Exercise 19-6

objective 5

Tucker Company reports the following data:

Sales	$750,000
Variable costs	500,000
Fixed costs	187,500

Determine Tucker Company's operating leverage.

Follow My Example 19-6

4.0 = ($750,000 − $500,000)/($750,000 − $500,000 − $187,500) = $250,000/$62,500

For Practice: PE 19-6A, PE 19-6B

MARGIN OF SAFETY

The difference between the current sales revenue and the sales revenue at the break-even point is called the **margin of safety**. It indicates the possible decrease in sales that may occur before an operating loss results. For example, if the margin of safety is low, even a small decline in sales revenue may result in an operating loss.

If sales are $250,000, the unit selling price is $25, and sales at the break-even point are $200,000, the margin of safety is 20%, computed as follows:

$$\text{Margin of Safety} = \frac{\text{Sales} - \text{Sales at Break-Even Point}}{\text{Sales}}$$

$$\text{Margin of Safety} = \frac{\$250,000 - \$200,000}{\$250,000} = 20\%$$

The margin of safety may also be stated in terms of units. In this illustration, for example, the margin of safety of 20% is equivalent to $50,000 ($250,000 × 20%). In units, the margin of safety is 2,000 units ($50,000/$25). Thus, the current sales of $250,000 may decline $50,000 or 2,000 units before an operating loss occurs.

Example Exercise 19-7   objective 5

The Rachel Company has sales of $400,000, and the break-even point in sales dollars is $300,000. Determine the company's margin of safety.

Follow My Example 19-7

25% = ($400,000 − $300,000)/$400,000

For Practice: PE 19-7A, PE 19-7B

At a Glance

1. Classify costs by their behavior as variable costs, fixed costs, or mixed costs.

Key Points	Key Learning Outcomes	Example Exercises	Practice Exercises
Cost behavior refers to the manner in which costs change as a related activity changes. Variable costs vary in proportion to changes in the level of activity. Fixed costs remain the same in total dollar amount as the level of activity changes. Mixed costs are comprised of both fixed and variable costs.	• Describe variable costs. • Describe fixed costs. • Describe mixed costs. • Separate mixed costs using the high-low method.	 19-1	 19-1A, 19-1B

2. Compute the contribution margin, the contribution margin ratio, and the unit contribution margin, and explain how they may be useful to managers.

Key Points	Key Learning Outcomes	Example Exercises	Practice Exercises
Contribution margin is the excess of sales revenue over variable costs and can be expressed as a ratio (contribution margin ratio) or a dollar amount (unit contribution margin). The contribution margin concept is useful for business planning because it provides insight into the profit potential of the firm.	• Describe contribution margin. • Compute the contribution margin ratio. • Compute the unit contribution margin.	 19-2 19-2	 19-2A, 19-2B 19-2A, 19-2B

(continued)

3. **Using the unit contribution margin, determine the break-even point and the volume necessary to achieve a target profit.**

Key Points	Key Learning Outcomes	Example Exercises	Practice Exercises
The break-even point is the point at which a business's revenues exactly equal expired costs. The mathematical approach to cost-volume-profit analysis uses the unit contribution margin concept and mathematical equations to determine the break-even point and the volume necessary to achieve a target profit for a business.	• Compute the break-even point in units. • Describe how changes in fixed costs affect the break-even point. • Describe how changes in unit variable costs affect the break-even point.	**19-3**	19-3A, 19-3B
	• Describe how a change in the unit selling price affects the break-even point.	**19-3**	19-3A, 19-3B
	• Compute the break-even point to earn a target profit.	**19-4**	19-4A, 19-4B

4. **Using a cost-volume-profit chart and a profit-volume chart, determine the break-even point and the volume necessary to achieve a target profit.**

Key Points	Key Learning Outcomes	Example Exercises	Practice Exercises
Graphical methods can be used to determine the break-even point and the volume necessary to achieve a target profit. A cost-volume-profit chart focuses on the relationship among costs, sales, and operating profit or loss. The profit-volume chart focuses on profits rather than on revenues and costs.	• Describe how to construct a cost-volume-profit chart. • Determine the break-even point using a cost-volume-profit chart. • Describe how to construct a profit-volume chart. • Determine the break-even point using a profit-volume chart. • Describe factors affecting the reliability of cost-volume-profit analysis.		

5. **Compute the break-even point for a business selling more than one product, the operating leverage, and the margin of safety.**

Key Points	Key Learning Outcomes	Example Exercises	Practice Exercises
Cost-volume-profit relationships can be used for analyzing (1) sales mix, (2) operating leverage, and (3) margin of safety. Sales mix computes the break-even point for a business selling more than one product. Operating leverage measures the impact of changes in sales on income from operations. The margin of safety measures the possible decrease in sales that may occur before an operating loss results.	• Compute the break-even point for more than one product.	**19-5**	19-5A, 19-5B
	• Compute operating leverage.	**19-6**	19-6A, 19-6B
	• Compute the margin of safety.	**19-7**	19-7A, 19-7B

Key Terms

activity bases (drivers) (840)
break-even point (848)
contribution margin (846)
contribution margin ratio (846)
cost behavior (840)
cost-volume-profit analysis (846)

cost-volume-profit chart (853)
fixed costs (842)
high-low method (844)
margin of safety (860)
mixed cost (842)
operating leverage (859)

profit-volume chart (855)
relevant range (840)
sales mix (858)
unit contribution margin (847)
variable costing (845)
variable costs (841)

Illustrative Problem

Wyatt Inc. expects to maintain the same inventories at the end of the year as at the beginning of the year. The estimated fixed costs for the year are $288,000, and the estimated variable costs per unit are $14. It is expected that 60,000 units will be sold at a price of $20 per unit. Maximum sales within the relevant range are 70,000 units.

Instructions

1. What is (a) the contribution margin ratio and (b) the unit contribution margin?
2. Determine the break-even point in units.
3. Construct a cost-volume-profit chart, indicating the break-even point.
4. Construct a profit-volume chart, indicating the break-even point.
5. What is the margin of safety?

Solution

1. a. $\text{Contribution Margin Ratio} = \dfrac{\text{Sales} - \text{Variable Costs}}{\text{Sales}}$

$\text{Contribution Margin Ratio} = \dfrac{(60,000 \text{ units} \times \$20) - (60,000 \text{ units} \times \$14)}{(60,000 \text{ units} \times \$20)}$

$\text{Contribution Margin Ratio} = \dfrac{\$1,200,000 - \$840,000}{\$1,200,000} = \dfrac{\$360,000}{\$1,200,000}$

$\text{Contribution Margin Ratio} = 30\%$

b. Unit Contribution Margin = Unit Selling Price − Unit Variable Costs
Unit Contribution Margin = $20 − $14 = $6

2. $\text{Break-Even Sales (units)} = \dfrac{\text{Fixed Costs}}{\text{Unit Contribution Margin}}$

$\text{Break-Even Sales (units)} = \dfrac{\$288,000}{\$6} = 48,000 \text{ units}$

3. Sales and Costs

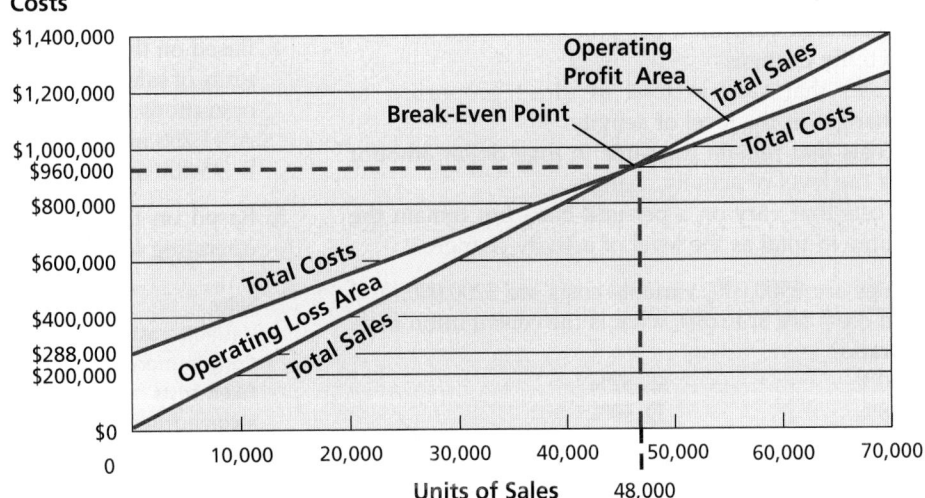

4. Operating Profit (Loss)

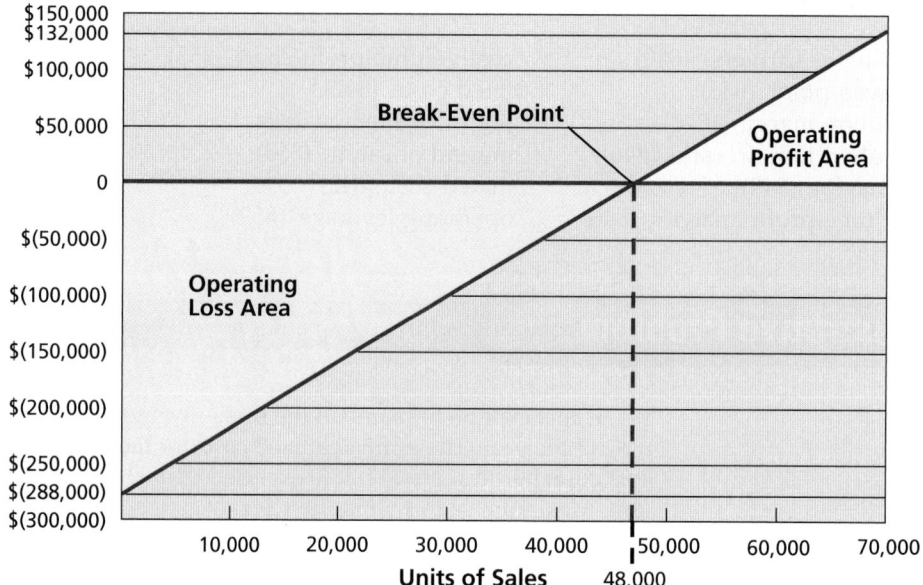

5. Margin of safety:

Expected sales (60,000 units × $20)	$1,200,000
Break-even point (48,000 units × $20)	960,000
Margin of safety	$ 240,000

or

$$\text{Margin of Safety} = \frac{\text{Sales} - \text{Sales at Break-Even Point}}{\text{Sales}}$$

$$\text{Margin of Safety} = \frac{\$240,000}{\$1,200,000} = 20\%$$

Self-Examination Questions   (Answers at End of Chapter)

1. Which of the following statements describes variable costs?
   A. Costs that vary on a per-unit basis as the level of activity changes.
   B. Costs that vary in total in direct proportion to changes in the level of activity.
   C. Costs that remain the same in total dollar amount as the level of activity changes.
   D. Costs that vary on a per-unit basis but remain the same in total as the level of activity changes.

2. If sales are $500,000, variable costs are $200,000, and fixed costs are $240,000, what is the contribution margin ratio?
   A. 40%   C. 52%
   B. 48%   D. 60%

3. If the unit selling price is $16, the unit variable cost is $12, and fixed costs are $160,000, what are the break-even sales (units)?

   A. 5,714 units   C. 13,333 units
   B. 10,000 units   D. 40,000 units

4. Based on the data presented in Question 3, how many units of sales would be required to realize income from operations of $20,000?
   A. 11,250 units   C. 40,000 units
   B. 35,000 units   D. 45,000 units

5. Based on the following operating data, what is the operating leverage?

Sales	$600,000
Variable costs	240,000
Contribution margin	$360,000
Fixed costs	160,000
Income from operations	$200,000

   A. 0.8   C. 1.8
   B. 1.2   D. 4.0

Eye Openers

1. Describe how total variable costs and unit variable costs behave with changes in the level of activity.
2. How would each of the following costs be classified if units produced is the activity base?
   a. Direct labor costs
   b. Direct materials costs
   c. Electricity costs of $0.35 per kilowatt hour
3. Describe the behavior of (a) total fixed costs and (b) unit fixed costs as the level of activity increases.
4. How would each of the following costs be classified if units produced is the activity base?
   a. Straight-line depreciation of plant and equipment
   b. Salary of factory supervisor ($70,000 per year)
   c. Property insurance premiums of $4,000 per month on plant and equipment
5. In cost analyses, how are mixed costs treated?
6. Which of the following graphs illustrates how total variable costs behave with changes in total units produced?

(a) 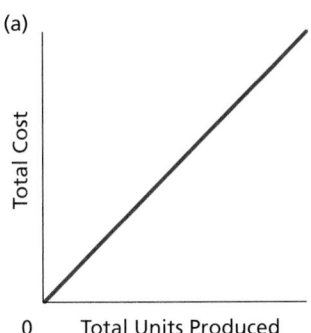   (b)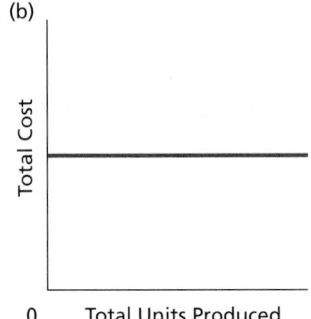

7. Which of the following graphs illustrates how unit variable costs behave with changes in total units produced?

(a) 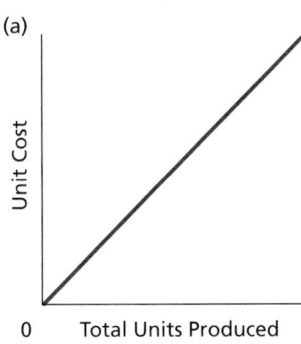   (b)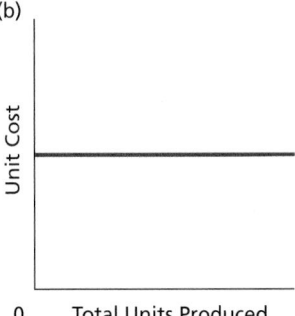

8. Which of the following graphs best illustrates fixed costs per unit as the activity base changes?

(a) 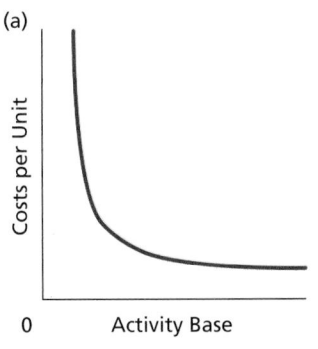   (b)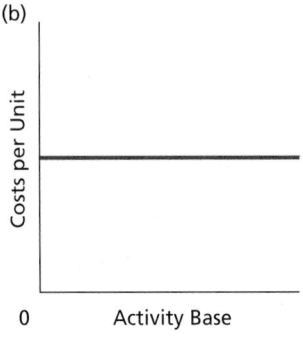

9. In applying the high-low method of cost estimation, how is the total fixed cost estimated?

10. If fixed costs increase, what would be the impact on the (a) contribution margin? (b) income from operations?

11. An examination of the accounting records of Mulgrew Company disclosed a high contribution margin ratio and production at a level below maximum capacity. Based on this information, suggest a likely means of improving income from operations. Explain.

12. If the unit cost of direct materials is decreased, what effect will this change have on the break-even point?

13. If insurance rates are increased, what effect will this change in fixed costs have on the break-even point?

14. Both Stratton Company and Callahan Company had the same sales, total costs, and income from operations for the current fiscal year; yet Stratton Company had a lower break-even point than Callahan Company. Explain the reason for this difference in break-even points.

15. The reliability of cost-volume-profit (CVP) analysis depends on several key assumptions. What are those primary assumptions?

16. How does the sales mix affect the calculation of the break-even point?

17. What does operating leverage measure, and how is it computed?

Practice Exercises

PE 19-1A
High-low method
obj. **1**

The manufacturing costs of Jake Industries for the first three months of the year are provided below.

	Total Costs	Production
January	$180,000	2,500 units
February	250,000	5,000
March	145,000	3,200

Using the high-low method, determine (a) the variable cost per unit and (b) the total fixed cost.

PE 19-1B
High-low method
obj. **1**

The manufacturing costs of Big T Enterprises for the first three months of the year are provided below.

	Total Costs	Production
January	$ 80,000	800 units
February	140,000	1,600
March	105,000	1,100

Using the high-low method, determine (a) the variable cost per unit and (b) the total fixed cost.

PE 19-2A
Contribution margin ratio
obj. **2**

Skinny Company sells 15,000 units at $20 per unit. Variable costs are $18 per unit, and fixed costs are $10,000. Determine (a) the contribution margin ratio, (b) the unit contribution margin, and (c) income from operations.

PE 19-2B
Contribution margin ratio
obj. **2**

Thorup Company sells 5,000 units at $40 per unit. Variable costs are $34 per unit, and fixed costs are $10,000. Determine (a) the contribution margin ratio, (b) the unit contribution margin, and (c) income from operations.

PE 19-3A
Break-even sales
obj. **3**

Frankel Enterprises sells a product for $25 per unit. The variable cost is $20 per unit, while fixed costs are $25,000. Determine (a) the break-even point in sales units and (b) the break-even point if the selling price were increased to $28 per unit.

PE 19-3B
Break-even sales
obj. 3

Barts Inc. sells a product for $120 per unit. The variable cost is $100 per unit, while fixed costs are $40,000. Determine (a) the break-even point in sales units and (b) the break-even point if the selling price were decreased to $110 per unit.

PE 19-4A
Break-even sales and sales to realize target profit
obj. 3

Melka Inc. sells a product for $80 per unit. The variable cost is $70 per unit, and fixed costs are $25,000. Determine (a) the break-even point in sales units and (b) the break-even point in sales units if the company desires a target profit of $25,000.

PE 19-4B
Break-even sales and sales to realize target profit
obj. 3

Averill Company sells a product for $100 per unit. The variable cost is $80 per unit, and fixed costs are $140,000. Determine (a) the break-even point in sales units and (b) the break-even point in sales units if the company desires a target profit of $30,000.

PE 19-5A
Sales mix and break-even sales
obj. 5

Simon Inc. has fixed costs of $150,000. The unit selling price, variable cost per unit, and contribution margin per unit for the company's two products are provided below.

Product	Selling Price	Variable Cost per Unit	Contribution Margin per Unit
X	$100	$ 60	$40
Y	140	125	15

The sales mix for products X and Y is 60% and 40%, respectively. Determine the break-even point in units of X and Y.

PE 19-5B
Sales mix and break-even sales
obj. 5

Brubaker Company has fixed costs of $120,000. The unit selling price, variable cost per unit, and contribution margin per unit for the company's two products are provided below.

Product	Selling Price	Variable Cost per Unit	Contribution Margin per Unit
Q	$90	$70	$20
Z	75	65	10

The sales mix for products Q and Z is 20% and 80%, respectively. Determine the break-even point in units of Q and Z.

PE 19-6A
Operating leverage
obj. 5

Ross Enterprises reports the following data:

Sales	$600,000
Variable costs	250,000
Fixed costs	100,000

Determine Ross Enterprises's operating leverage.

PE 19-6B
Operating leverage
obj. 5

EmilyCo reports the following data:

Sales	$900,000
Variable costs	400,000
Fixed costs	250,000

Determine EmilyCo's operating leverage.

PE 19-7A
Margin of safety
obj. 5

Miller Inc. has sales of $1,000,000, and the break-even point in sales dollars is $800,000. Determine the company's margin of safety.

PE 19-7B
Margin of safety
obj. 5

Ribisl Company has sales of $200,000, and the break-even point in sales dollars is $140,000. Determine the company's margin of safety.

Exercises

EX 19-1
Classify costs
obj. 1

Following is a list of various costs incurred in producing frozen pizzas. With respect to the production and sale of frozen pizzas, classify each cost as either variable, fixed, or mixed.

1. Property insurance premiums, $1,500 per month plus $0.005 for each dollar of property over $3,000,000
2. Packaging
3. Hourly wages of inspectors
4. Pension cost, $0.50 per employee hour on the job
5. Hourly wages of machine operators
6. Rent on warehouse, $5,000 per month plus $5 per square foot of storage used
7. Refrigerant used in refrigeration equipment
8. Pepperoni
9. Dough
10. Tomato paste
11. Property taxes, $50,000 per year on factory building and equipment
12. Electricity costs, $0.08 per kilowatt hour
13. Salary of plant manager
14. Straight-line depreciation on the production equipment
15. Janitorial costs, $3,000 per month

EX 19-2
Identify cost graphs
obj. 1

The following cost graphs illustrate various types of cost behavior:

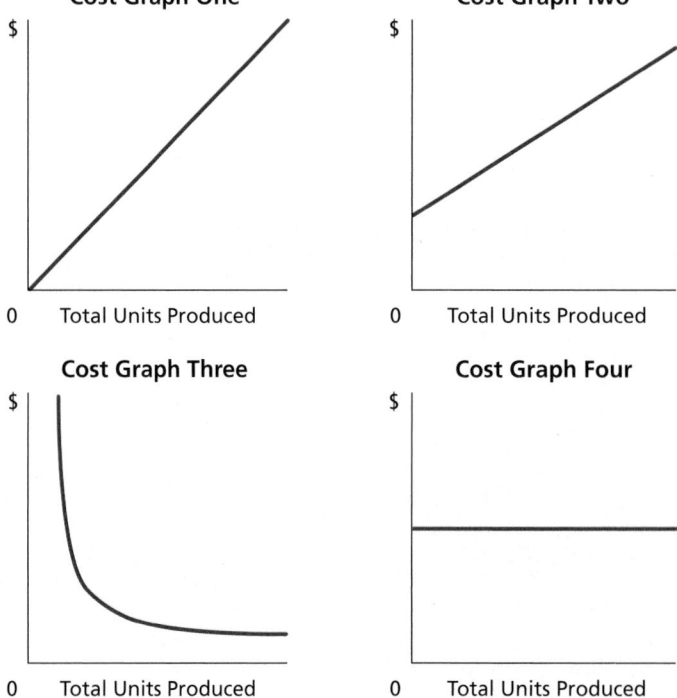

For each of the following costs, identify the cost graph that best illustrates its cost behavior as the number of units produced increases.

a. Per-unit direct labor cost

b. Salary of quality control supervisor, $5,000 per month
c. Total direct materials cost
d. Electricity costs of $3,000 per month plus $0.05 per kilowatt hour
e. Per-unit cost of straight-line depreciation on factory equipment

---

EX 19-3
Identify activity bases
obj. 1

For a major university, match each cost in the following table with the activity base most appropriate to it. An activity base may be used more than once, or not used at all.

Cost:
1. Financial aid office salaries
2. Instructor salaries
3. Housing personnel wages
4. Admissions office salaries
5. School supplies
6. Record office salaries

Activity Base:
a. Number of enrolled students and alumni
b. Student credit hours
c. Number of student/athletes
d. Number of enrollment applications
e. Number of students living on campus
f. Number of financial aid applications

EX 19-4
Identify activity bases
obj. 1

From the following list of activity bases for an automobile dealership, select the base that would be most appropriate for each of these costs: (1) preparation costs (cleaning, oil, and gasoline costs) for each car received, (2) salespersons' commission of 3% of the sales price for each car sold, and (3) administrative costs for ordering cars.

a. Dollar amount of cars on hand
b. Dollar amount of cars received
c. Dollar amount of cars sold
d. Dollar amount of cars ordered

e. Number of cars ordered
f. Number of cars sold
g. Number of cars on hand
h. Number of cars received

EX 19-5
Identify fixed and variable costs
obj. 1

Intuit Inc. develops and sells software products for the personal finance market, including popular titles such as Quicken® and TurboTax®. Classify each of the following costs and expenses for this company as either variable or fixed to the number of units produced and sold:

a. Straight-line depreciation of computer equipment
b. Sales commissions
c. Advertising
d. Packaging costs
e. CDs
f. Shipping expenses
g. Salaries of customer support personnel
h. Salaries of software developers
i. Wages of telephone order assistants
j. User's guides
k. President's salary
l. Property taxes on general offices

EX 19-6
Relevant range and fixed and variable costs
obj. 1
✓ a. $0.40

Laser Tex Inc. manufactures low-end computer components within a relevant range of 100,000 to 140,000 disks per year. Within this range, the following partially completed manufacturing cost schedule has been prepared:

CDs produced	100,000	120,000	140,000
Total costs:			
Total variable costs	$ 40,000	(d)	(j)
Total fixed costs	84,000	(e)	(k)
Total costs	$124,000	(f)	(l)
Cost per unit:			
Variable cost per unit	(a)	(g)	(m)
Fixed cost per unit	(b)	(h)	(n)
Total cost per unit	(c)	(i)	(o)

Complete the cost schedule, identifying each cost by the appropriate letter (a) through (o).

EX 19-7
High-low method
obj. 1
✓ *a. $10.00 per unit*

W & O Inc. has decided to use the high-low method to estimate the total cost and the fixed and variable cost components of the total cost. The data for various levels of production are as follows:

Units Produced	Total Costs
10,000	$750,000
22,500	845,000
30,000	950,000

a. Determine the variable cost per unit and the fixed cost.
b. Based on part (a), estimate the total cost for 25,000 units of production.

EX 19-8
High-low method for service company
obj. 1
✓ *Fixed cost, $250,000*

Great Plains Railroad decided to use the high-low method and operating data from the past six months to estimate the fixed and variable components of transportation costs. The activity base used by Great Plains Railroad is a measure of railroad operating activity, termed "gross-ton miles," which is the total number of tons multiplied by the miles moved.

	Transportation Costs	Gross-Ton Miles
January	$1,050,000	285,000
February	1,150,000	325,000
March	1,350,000	400,000
April	1,000,000	250,000
May	1,225,000	375,000
June	1,600,000	450,000

Determine the variable cost per gross-ton mile and the fixed cost.

EX 19-9
Contribution margin ratio
obj. 2
✓ *a. 55%*

a. Spock Company budgets sales of $840,000, fixed costs of $378,000, and variable costs of $378,000. What is the contribution margin ratio for Spock Company?
b. If the contribution margin ratio for Kirk Company is 34%, sales were $600,000, and fixed costs were $175,000, what was the income from operations?

EX 19-10
Contribution margin and contribution margin ratio
obj. 2

✓ *b. 34.00%*

For a recent year, McDonald's had the following sales and expenses (in millions):

Sales	$15,352
Food and packaging	$ 5,204
Payroll	4,040
Occupancy (rent, depreciation, etc.)	1,022
General, selling, and administrative expenses	2,220
	$12,486
Income from operations	$ 2,866

Assume that the variable costs consist of food and packaging, payroll, and 40% of the general, selling, and administrative expenses.

a. What is McDonald's contribution margin? Round to the nearest million.
b. What is McDonald's contribution margin ratio? Round to two decimal places.
c. How much would income from operations increase if same-store sales increased by $450 million for the coming year, with no change in the contribution margin ratio or fixed costs?

EX 19-11
Break-even sales and sales to realize income from operations
obj. 3
✓ *b. 20,435 units*

For the current year ending March 31, Zing Company expects fixed costs of $425,750, a unit variable cost of $40, and a unit selling price of $65.

a. Compute the anticipated break-even sales (units).
b. Compute the sales (units) required to realize income from operations of $85,125.

EX 19-12
Break-even sales
obj. 3

REAL WORLD

✓ a. 74,884,566 barrels

Anheuser-Busch Companies, Inc., reported the following operating information for a recent year (in millions):

Net sales	$14,935
Cost of goods sold	$ 8,983
Marketing and distribution	2,590
	$11,573
Income from operations	$ 3,362*

*Before special items

In addition, Anheuser-Busch sold 136 million barrels of beer during the year. Assume that variable costs were 70% of the cost of goods sold and 45% of marketing and distribution expenses. Assume that the remaining costs are fixed. For the following year, assume that Anheuser-Busch expects pricing, variable costs per barrel, and fixed costs to remain constant, except that new distribution and general office facilities are expected to increase fixed costs by $133 million.

Rounding to the nearest cent:

a. Compute the break-even sales (barrels) for the current year.
b. Compute the anticipated break-even sales (barrels) for the following year.

EX 19-13
Break-even sales
obj. 3

✓ a. 9,600 units

Currently, the unit selling price of a product is $300, the unit variable cost is $225, and the total fixed costs are $720,000. A proposal is being evaluated to increase the unit selling price to $345.

a. Compute the current break-even sales (units).
b. Compute the anticipated break-even sales (units), assuming that the unit selling price is increased and all costs remain constant.

EX 19-14
Break-even analysis
obj. 3

The Junior League of Tampa, Florida, collected recipes from members and published a cookbook entitled *Life of the Party*. The book will sell for $22 per copy. The chairwoman of the cookbook development committee estimated that the league needed to sell 16,000 books to break even on its $140,000 investment. What is the variable cost per unit assumed in the Junior League's analysis? Round to the nearest cent.

EX 19-15
Break-even analysis
obj. 3

REAL WORLD

The America Online division of Time Warner has fueled its growth by using aggressive promotion strategies. One of these strategies is to send compact disk software to potential customers, offering free AOL service for a period of time. Assume that during a given promotional campaign, AOL mailed 3,200,000 disks to potential customers, offering three months' free service. In addition, assume the following information:

Cost per disk (including mailing)	$1.50
Number of months an average new customer stays with the service (including the three free months)	30 months
Revenue per month per customer account	$10.00
Variable cost per month per customer account	$1.00

Determine the number of new customer accounts needed to break even on the cost of the promotional campaign. In forming your answer, (1) treat the cost of mailing the disk as a fixed cost, and (2) treat the revenue less variable cost per account for the service period as the unit contribution margin.

EX 19-16
Break-even analysis
obj. 3

REAL WORLD

Sprint Nextel is one of the largest digital wireless service providers in the United States. In a recent year, it had 39.7 million direct subscribers (accounts) that generated revenue of $14,647 million. Costs and expenses for the year were as follows (in millions):

(continued)

Cost of revenue	$6,091
Selling, general, and administrative expenses	4,411
Depreciation	2,557

Assume that 70% of the cost of revenue and 40% of the selling, general, and administrative expenses are variable to the number of direct subscribers (accounts).

a. What is Sprint Nextel's break-even number of accounts, using the data and assumptions above? Round units to the nearest million.
b. How much revenue per account would be sufficient for Sprint Nextel to break even if the number of accounts remained constant?

EX 19-17
Cost-volume-profit chart

obj. **4**

✓ b. $500,000

For the coming year, Knight Inc. anticipates fixed costs of $200,000, a unit variable cost of $15, and a unit selling price of $25. The maximum sales within the relevant range are $1,000,000.

a. Construct a cost-volume-profit chart.
b. Estimate the break-even sales (dollars) by using the cost-volume-profit chart constructed in part (a).
c. ▭▭▭▶ What is the main advantage of presenting the cost-volume-profit analysis in graphic form rather than equation form?

EX 19-18
Profit-volume chart

obj. **4**

✓ b. $200,000

Using the data for Knight Inc. in Exercise 19-17, (a) determine the maximum possible operating loss, (b) compute the maximum possible income from operations, (c) construct a profit-volume chart, and (d) estimate the break-even sales (units) by using the profit-volume chart constructed in part (c).

EX 19-19
Break-even chart

obj. **4**

Name the following chart, and identify the items represented by the letters (a) through (f).

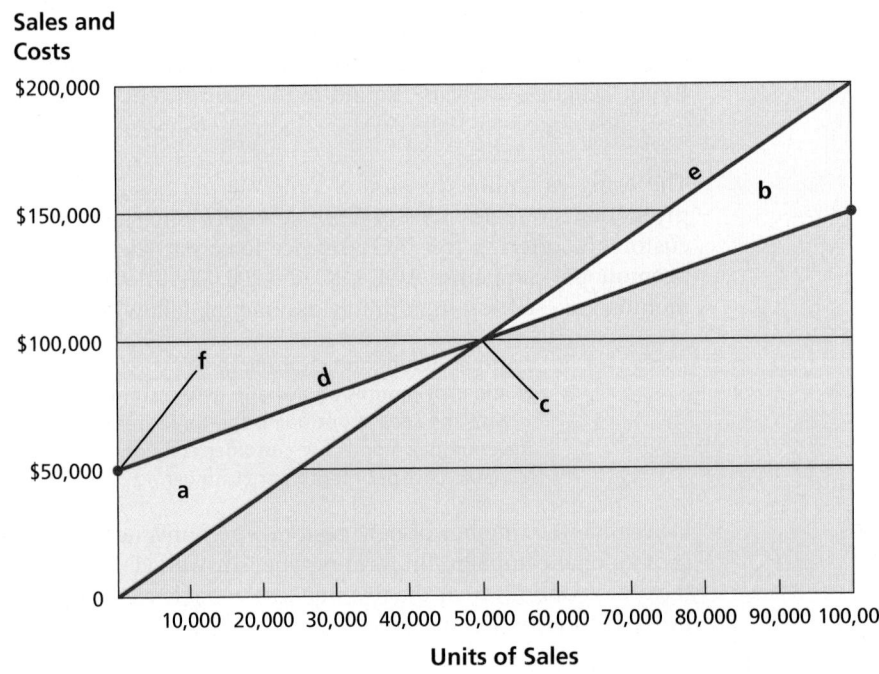

EX 19-20
Break-even chart

obj. **4**

Name the following chart, and identify the items represented by the letters (a) through (f).

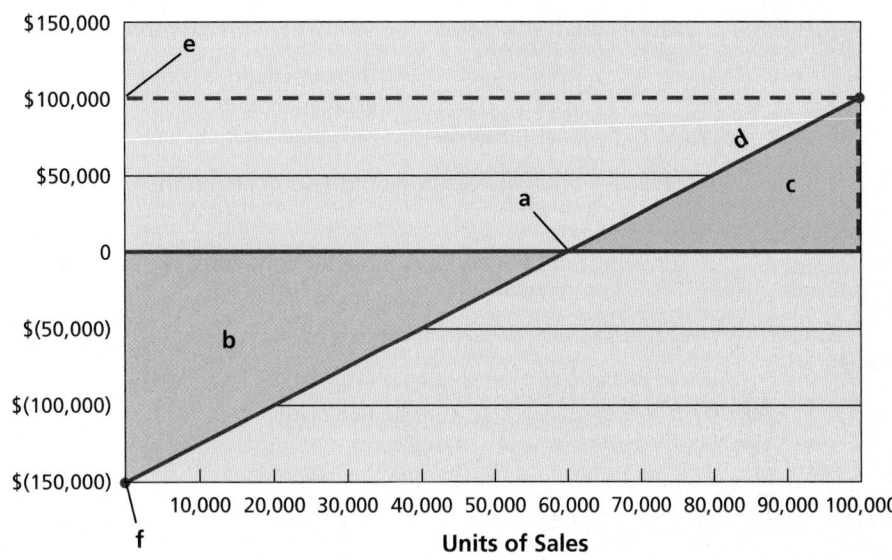

Operating Profit (Loss)

Units of Sales

EX 19-21
Sales mix and break-even sales

obj. **5**

✓ a. 280,000 units

Candies Inc. manufactures and sells two products, marshmallow bunnies and jelly beans. The fixed costs are $350,000, and the sales mix is 70% marshmallow bunnies and 30% jelly beans. The unit selling price and the unit variable cost for each product are as follows:

Products	Unit Selling Price	Unit Variable Cost
Marshmallow bunnies	$2.40	$1.00
Jelly beans	1.80	0.90

a. Compute the break-even sales (units) for the overall product, E.
b. How many units of each product, marshmallow bunnies and jelly beans, would be sold at the break-even point?

EX 19-22
Break-even sales and sales mix for a service company

obj. **5**

✓ a. 65 seats

Fly-by-Night Airways provides air transportation services between New York and Miami. A single New York to Miami round-trip flight has the following operating statistics:

Fuel	$3,540
Flight crew salaries	7,310
Airplane depreciation	2,995
Variable cost per passenger—business class	45
Variable cost per passenger—tourist class	35
Round-trip ticket price—business class	350
Round-trip ticket price—tourist class	225

It is assumed that the fuel, crew salaries, and airplane depreciation are fixed, regardless of the number of seats sold for the round-trip flight.

a. Compute the break-even number of seats sold on a single round-trip flight for the overall product. Assume that the overall product is 20% business class and 80% tourist class tickets.
b. How many business class and tourist class seats would be sold at the break-even point?

EX 19-23
Margin of safety

obj. **5**

✓ a. (2) 10%

a. If Larker Company, with a break-even point at $450,000 of sales, has actual sales of $500,000, what is the margin of safety expressed (1) in dollars and (2) as a percentage of sales?
b. If the margin of safety for Porter Company was 20%, fixed costs were $600,000, and variable costs were 70% of sales, what was the amount of actual sales (dollars)? (*Hint:* Determine the break-even in sales dollars first.)

EX 19-24
Break-even and margin of safety relationships
obj. 5

At a recent staff meeting, the management of Hom Technology Products was considering discontinuing the Hercules line of laptop computers from the product line. The chief financial analyst reported the following current monthly data for the Hercules:

Units of sales	32,000
Break-even units	36,800
Margin of safety in units	4,800

For what reason would you question the validity of these data?

EX 19-25
Operating leverage
obj. 5

✓ a. Juras, 3.00

Juras Inc. and Hinson Inc. have the following operating data:

	Juras	Hinson
Sales	$160,000	$215,000
Variable costs	130,000	115,000
Contribution margin	$ 30,000	$100,000
Fixed costs	20,000	75,000
Income from operations	$ 10,000	$ 25,000

a. Compute the operating leverage for Juras Inc. and Hinson Inc.
b. How much would income from operations increase for each company if the sales of each increased by 10%?
c. Why is there a difference in the increase in income from operations for the two companies? Explain.

Problems Series A

PR 19-1A
Classify costs
obj. 1

New Age Furniture Company manufactures sofas for distribution to several major retail chains. The following costs are incurred in the production and sale of sofas:

a. Springs
b. Consulting fee of $25,000 paid to efficiency specialists
c. Sewing supplies
d. Electricity costs of $0.10 per kilowatt hour
e. Fabric for sofa coverings
f. Salary of production vice president
g. Salesperson's salary, $20,000 plus 5% of the selling price of each sofa sold
h. Janitorial supplies, $15 for each sofa produced
i. Employer's FICA taxes on controller's salary of $150,000
j. Rent on experimental equipment, $35 for every sofa produced
k. Wood for framing the sofas
l. Insurance premiums on property, plant, and equipment, $10,000 per year plus $15 per $10,000 of insured value over $15,000,000
m. Hourly wages of sewing machine operators
n. Salary of designers
o. Property taxes on property, plant, and equipment
p. Legal fees paid to attorneys in defense of the company in a patent infringement suit, $15,000 plus $175 per hour
q. Cartons used to ship sofas
r. Rental costs of warehouse, $15,000 per month
s. Straight-line depreciation on factory equipment
t. Foam rubber for cushion fillings

Instructions
Classify the preceding costs as either fixed, variable, or mixed. Use the following tabular headings and place an "X" in the appropriate column. Identify each cost by letter in the Cost column.

Cost	Fixed Cost	Variable Cost	Mixed Cost

PR 19-2A
Break-even sales under present and proposed conditions

objs. 2, 3

✓ *3. 13,250 units*

French Broad Inc., operating at full capacity, sold 25,125 units at a price of $75 per unit during 2008. Its income statement for 2008 is as follows:

Sales		$1,884,375
Cost of goods sold		1,100,000
Gross profit		$ 784,375
Expenses:		
Selling expenses	$125,000	
Administrative expenses	125,000	
Total expenses		250,000
Income from operations		$ 534,375

The division of costs between fixed and variable is as follows:

	Fixed	Variable
Cost of sales	40%	60%
Selling expenses	50%	50%
Administrative expenses	75%	25%

Management is considering a plant expansion program that will permit an increase of $487,500 in yearly sales. The expansion will increase fixed costs by $135,000, but will not affect the relationship between sales and variable costs.

Instructions
1. Determine for 2008 the total fixed costs and the total variable costs.
2. Determine for 2008 (a) the unit variable cost and (b) the unit contribution margin.
3. Compute the break-even sales (units) for 2008.
4. Compute the break-even sales (units) under the proposed program.
5. Determine the amount of sales (units) that would be necessary under the proposed program to realize the $534,375 of income from operations that was earned in 2008.
6. Determine the maximum income from operations possible with the expanded plant.
7. If the proposal is accepted and sales remain at the 2008 level, what will the income or loss from operations be for 2009?
8. ⬤➤ Based on the data given, would you recommend accepting the proposal? Explain.

PR 19-3A
Break-even sales and cost-volume-profit chart

objs. 3, 4

✓ *1. 17,500 units*

For the coming year, Wisconsin Products Inc. anticipates a unit selling price of $72, a unit variable cost of $34, and fixed costs of $665,000.

Instructions
1. Compute the anticipated break-even sales (units).
2. Compute the sales (units) required to realize income from operations of $95,000.
3. Construct a cost-volume-profit chart, assuming maximum sales of 40,000 units within the relevant range.
4. Determine the probable income (loss) from operations if sales total 29,000 units.

PR 19-4A
Break-even sales and cost-volume-profit chart

objs. 3, 4

✓ *1. 1,500 units*

Last year, Pocket PC Co. had sales of $430,000, based on a unit selling price of $215. The variable cost per unit was $155, and fixed costs were $90,000. The maximum sales within Pocket PC's relevant range are 3,000 units. Pocket PC is considering a proposal to spend an additional $24,000 on billboard advertising during the current year in an attempt to increase sales and utilize unused capacity.

Instructions
1. Construct a cost-volume-profit chart indicating the break-even sales for last year. Verify your answer, using the break-even equation.
2. Using the cost-volume-profit chart prepared in part (1), determine (a) the income from operations for last year and (b) the maximum income from operations that could have been realized during the year. Verify your answers arithmetically.
3. Construct a cost-volume-profit chart indicating the break-even sales for the current year, assuming that a noncancelable contract is signed for the additional billboard advertising. No changes are expected in the selling price or other costs. Verify your answer, using the break-even equation.

(continued)

4. Using the cost-volume-profit chart prepared in part (3), determine (a) the income from operations if sales total 2,500 units and (b) the maximum income from operations that could be realized during the year. Verify your answers arithmetically.

PR 19-5A
Sales mix and break-even sales

obj. **5**

✓1. 52,200 units

Data related to the expected sales of two types of decorative flower pots for Boyeva Flower Pots, Inc. for the current year, which is typical of recent years, are as follows:

Products	Unit Selling Price	Unit Variable Cost	Sales Mix
Decorative Indoor Flower Pot	$ 9.00	$3.60	25%
Rugged Outdoor Flower Pot	12.00	5.40	75%

The estimated fixed costs for the current year are $328,860.

Instructions
1. Determine the estimated units of sales of the overall product necessary to reach the break-even point for the current year.
2. Based on the break-even sales (units) in part (1), determine the unit sales of both the Decorative Indoor Flower Pot and Rugged Outdoor Flower Pot for the current year.
3. ⬤━━▷ Assume that the sales mix was 50% Decorative Indoor Flower Pot and 50% Rugged Outdoor Flower Pot. Compare the break-even point with that in part (1). Why is it so different?

PR 19-6A
Contribution margin, break-even sales, cost-volume-profit chart, margin of safety, and operating leverage

objs. **2, 3, 4, 5**

✓2. 40.0%

Aspen Co. expects to maintain the same inventories at the end of 2008 as at the beginning of the year. The total of all production costs for the year is therefore assumed to be equal to the cost of goods sold. With this in mind, the various department heads were asked to submit estimates of the costs for their departments during 2008. A summary report of these estimates is as follows:

	Estimated Fixed Cost	Estimated Variable Cost (per unit sold)
Production costs:		
Direct materials	—	$ 8.90
Direct labor	—	3.80
Factory overhead	$ 80,200	2.10
Selling expenses:		
Sales salaries and commissions	41,200	1.70
Advertising	13,200	—
Travel	2,700	—
Miscellaneous selling expense	5,400	1.50
Administrative expenses:		
Office and officers' salaries	81,500	—
Supplies	4,700	0.70
Miscellaneous administrative expense	10,500	2.30
Total	$239,400	$21.00

It is expected that 19,000 units will be sold at a price of $35 a unit. Maximum sales within the relevant range are 30,000 units.

Instructions
1. Prepare an estimated income statement for 2008.
2. What is the expected contribution margin ratio?
3. Determine the break-even sales in units.
4. Construct a cost-volume-profit chart indicating the break-even sales.
5. What is the expected margin of safety?
6. Determine the operating leverage.

Problems Series B

PR 19-1B
Classify costs
obj. 1

Montana Jeans Inc. manufactures blue jeans for distribution to several major retail chains. The following costs are incurred in the production and sale of blue jeans:

a. Brass buttons
b. Janitorial supplies, $1,000 per month
c. Legal fees paid to attorneys in defense of the company in a patent infringement suit, $30,000 plus $150 per hour
d. Straight-line depreciation on sewing machines
e. Salary of production vice president
f. Leather for patches identifying each jean style
g. Salary of designers
h. Supplies
i. Denim fabric
j. Insurance premiums on property, plant, and equipment, $20,000 per year plus $2 per $10,000 of insured value over $7,000,000
k. Hourly wages of machine operators
l. Property taxes on property, plant, and equipment
m. Salesperson's salary, $15,000 plus 2% of the total sales
n. Rental costs of warehouse, $3,000 per month plus $2 per square foot of storage used
o. Electricity costs of $0.12 per kilowatt hour
p. Rent on experimental equipment, $30,000 per year
q. Thread
r. Blue dye
s. Shipping boxes used to ship orders
t. Consulting fee of $70,000 paid to industry specialist for marketing advice

Instructions

Classify the preceding costs as either fixed, variable, or mixed. Use the following tabular headings and place an "X" in the appropriate column. Identify each cost by letter in the cost column.

Cost	Fixed Cost	Variable Cost	Mixed Cost

PR 19-2B
Break-even sales under present and proposed conditions
objs. 2, 3

✓ 2. (a) $30.75

Castellino Company, operating at full capacity, sold 80,000 units at a price of $70.75 per unit during 2008. Its income statement for 2008 is as follows:

Sales	$5,660,000
Cost of goods sold	2,100,000
Gross profit	$3,560,000
Expenses:	
Selling expenses $1,500,000	
Administrative expenses 900,000	
Total expenses	2,400,000
Income from operations	$1,160,000

The division of costs between fixed and variable is as follows:

	Fixed	Variable
Cost of sales	50%	50%
Selling expenses	30%	70%
Administrative expenses	60%	40%

Management is considering a plant expansion program that will permit an increase of $884,375 in yearly sales. The expansion will increase fixed costs by $265,000 but will not affect the relationship between sales and variable costs.

Instructions

1. Determine for 2008 the total fixed costs and the total variable costs.
2. Determine for 2008 (a) the unit variable cost and (b) the unit contribution margin.
3. Compute the break-even sales (units) for 2008.
4. Compute the break-even sales (units) under the proposed program.
5. Determine the amount of sales (units) that would be necessary under the proposed program to realize the $1,160,000 of income from operations that was earned in 2008.
6. Determine the maximum income from operations possible with the expanded plant.
7. If the proposal is accepted and sales remain at the 2008 level, what will the income or loss from operations be for 2009?
8. ▰▰▰▶ Based on the data given, would you recommend accepting the proposal? Explain.

PR 19-3B
Break-even sales and cost-volume-profit chart
objs. 3, 4
✓1. 7,600 units

For the coming year, Baker Company anticipates a unit selling price of $450, a unit variable cost of $325, and fixed costs of $950,000.

Instructions

1. Compute the anticipated break-even sales (units).
2. Compute the sales (units) required to realize income from operations of $175,000.
3. Construct a cost-volume-profit chart, assuming maximum sales of 16,000 units within the relevant range.
4. Determine the probable income (loss) from operations if sales total 8,000 units.

PR 19-4B
Break-even sales and cost-volume-profit chart
objs. 3, 4
✓1. 5,000 units

Last year, Taylor Inc. had sales of $100,000, based on a unit selling price of $20. The variable cost per unit was $10, and fixed costs were $50,000. The maximum sales within Taylor's relevant range are 10,000 units. Taylor is considering a proposal to spend an additional $20,000 on billboard advertising during the current year in an attempt to increase sales and utilize unused capacity.

Instructions

1. Construct a cost-volume-profit chart indicating the break-even sales for last year. Verify your answer, using the break-even equation.
2. Using the cost-volume-profit chart prepared in part (1), determine (a) the income from operations for last year and (b) the maximum income from operations that could have been realized during the year. Verify your answers arithmetically.
3. Construct a cost-volume-profit chart indicating the break-even sales for the current year, assuming that a noncancelable contract is signed for the additional billboard advertising. No changes are expected in the unit selling price or other costs. Verify your answer, using the break-even equation.
4. Using the cost-volume-profit chart prepared in part (3), determine (a) the income from operations if sales total 8,000 units and (b) the maximum income from operations that could be realized during the year. Verify your answers arithmetically.

PR 19-5B
Sales mix and break-even sales
obj. 5

✓1. 73,700 units

Data related to the expected sales of lacrosse sticks and hockey sticks for Athletics Inc. for the current year, which is typical of recent years, are as follows:

Products	Unit Selling Price	Unit Variable Cost	Sales Mix
Lacrosse sticks	$52.00	$28.00	70%
Hockey sticks	64.00	36.00	30%

The estimated fixed costs for the current year are $1,857,240.

Instructions

1. Determine the estimated units of sales of the overall product necessary to reach the break-even point for the current year.
2. Based on the break-even sales (units) in part (1), determine the unit sales of both lacrosse sticks and hockey sticks for the current year.
3. ▰▰▰▶ Assume that the sales mix was 30% lacrosse sticks and 70% hockey sticks. Compare the break-even point with that in part (1). Why is it so different?

PR 19-6B
Contribution margin, break-even sales, cost-volume-profit chart, margin of safety, and operating leverage

objs. 2, 3, 4, 5

✓2. 45%

Loumis Home Care Products Inc. expects to maintain the same inventories at the end of 2008 as at the beginning of the year. The total of all production costs for the year is therefore assumed to be equal to the cost of goods sold. With this in mind, the various department heads were asked to submit estimates of the costs for their departments during 2008. A summary report of these estimates is as follows:

	Estimated Fixed Cost	Estimated Variable Cost (per unit sold)
Production costs:		
Direct materials	—	$137.70
Direct labor	—	116.40
Factory overhead	$232,000	27.20
Selling expenses:		
Sales salaries and commissions	356,225	9.15
Advertising	67,500	—
Travel	42,500	—
Miscellaneous selling expense	22,250	2.25
Administrative expenses:		
Office and officers' salaries	235,000	—
Supplies	15,525	6.30
Miscellaneous administrative expense	19,000	3.50
Total	$990,000	$302.50

It is expected that 5,000 units will be sold at a price of $550 a unit. Maximum sales within the relevant range are 10,000 units.

Instructions
1. Prepare an estimated income statement for 2008.
2. What is the expected contribution margin ratio?
3. Determine the break-even sales in units.
4. Construct a cost-volume-profit chart indicating the break-even sales.
5. What is the expected margin of safety?
6. Determine the operating leverage.

Special Activities

SA 19-1
Ethics and professional conduct in business

ETHICS

Paul Hambel is a financial consultant to Tecau Properties Inc., a real estate syndicate. Tecau Properties Inc. finances and develops commercial real estate (office buildings). The completed projects are then sold as limited partnership interests to individual investors. The syndicate makes a profit on the sale of these partnership interests. Paul provides financial information for the offering prospectus, which is a document that provides the financial and legal details of the limited partnership offerings. In one of the projects, the bank has financed the construction of a commercial office building at a rate of 7% for the first four years, after which time the rate jumps to 12% for the remaining 21 years of the mortgage. The interest costs are one of the major ongoing costs of a real estate project. Paul has reported prominently in the prospectus that the break-even occupancy for the first four years is 70%. This is the amount of office space that must be leased to cover the interest and general upkeep costs over the first four years. The 70% break-even is very low and thus communicates a low risk to potential investors. Paul uses the 70% break-even rate as a major marketing tool in selling the limited partnership interests. Buried in the fine print of the prospectus is additional information that would allow an astute investor to determine that the break-even occupancy will jump to 90% after the fourth year because of the contracted increase in the mortgage interest rate. Paul believes prospective investors are adequately informed as to the risk of the investment.

➤ Comment on the ethical considerations of this situation.

SA 19-2
Break-even sales,
contribution margin

"For a student, a grade of 65 percent is nothing to write home about. But for the airline . . . [industry], filling 65 percent of the seats . . . is the difference between profit and loss.

   The [economy] might be just strong enough to sustain all the carriers on a cash basis, but not strong enough to bring any significant profitability to the industry. . . . For the airlines . . . , the emphasis will be on trying to consolidate routes and raise ticket prices. . . ."

▰▰▰▶ The airline industry is notorious for boom and bust cycles. Why is airline profitability very sensitive to these cycles? Do you think that during a down cycle the strategy to consolidate routes and raise ticket prices is reasonable? What would make this strategy succeed or fail? Why?

   Source: Edwin McDowell, "Empty Seats, Empty Beds, Empty Pockets," *The New York Times*, January 6, 1992, p. C3.

SA 19-3
Break-even analysis

Southern Video Games Inc. has finished a new video game, *Olympic Competition Bobsledding*. Management is now considering its marketing strategies. The following information is available:

Anticipated sales price per unit	$30
Variable cost per unit*	$15
Anticipated volume	500,000
Production costs	$5,000,000
Anticipated advertising	$2,500,000

*The cost of the video game, packaging, and copying costs.

Two managers, Molly Smith and Alex Clarke, had the following discussion of ways to increase the profitability of this new offering.

Molly: I think we need to think of some way to increase our profitability. Do you have any ideas?
Alex: Well, I think the best strategy would be to become aggressive on price.
Molly: How aggressive?
Alex: If we drop the price to $22 per unit and maintain our advertising budget at $2,500,000, I think we will generate sales of 1,400,000 units.
Molly: I think that's the wrong way to go. You're giving too much up on price. Instead, I think we need to follow an aggressive advertising strategy.
Alex: How aggressive?
Molly: If we increase our advertising to a total of $5,000,000, we should be able to increase sales volume to 1,250,000 units without any change in price.
Alex: I don't think that's reasonable. We'll never cover the increased advertising costs.

▰▰▰▶ Which strategy is best: Do nothing? Follow the advice of Alex Clarke? Or follow Molly Smith's strategy?

SA 19-4
Variable costs and
activity bases in decision
making

The owner of Banner-Tech, a printing company, is planning direct labor needs for the upcoming year. The owner has provided you with the following information for next year's plans:

	One Color	Two Color	Three Color	Four Color	Total
Number of banners	100	150	200	400	850

Each color on the banner must be printed one at a time. Thus, for example, a four-color banner will need to be run through the printing operation four separate times. The total production volume last year was 425 banners, as shown below.

	One Color	Two Color	Three Color	Total
Number of banners	100	125	200	425

As you can see, the four-color banner is a new product offering for the upcoming year. The owner believes that the expected 425-unit increase in volume from last year means that direct labor expenses should increase by 100% (425/425). What do you think?

SA 19-5
Variable costs and activity bases in decision making

Sales volume has been dropping at Winona Publishing Company. During this time, however, the Shipping Department manager has been under severe financial constraints. The manager knows that most of the Shipping Department's effort is related to pulling inventory from the warehouse for each order and performing the paperwork. The paperwork involves preparing shipping documents for each order. Thus, the pulling and paperwork effort associated with each sales order is essentially the same, regardless of the size of the order. The Shipping Department manager has discussed the financial situation with senior management. Senior management has responded by pointing out that sales volume has been dropping, so that the amount of work in the Shipping Department should be dropping. Thus, senior management told the Shipping Department manager that costs should be decreasing in the department.

The Shipping Department manager prepared the following information:

Month	Sales Volume	Number of Customer Orders	Sales Volume per Order
January	$152,000	800	190
February	147,600	820	180
March	144,500	850	170
April	144,000	960	150
May	143,550	990	145
June	136,000	1,000	136
July	130,650	1,005	130
August	128,000	1,024	125

Given this information, how would you respond to senior management?

SA 19-6
Break-even analysis

Group Project

Break-even analysis is one of the most fundamental tools for managing any kind of business unit. Consider the management of your school. In a group, brainstorm some applications of break-even analysis at your school. Identify three areas where break-even analysis might be used. For each area, identify the revenues, variable costs, and fixed costs that would be used in the calculation.

Answers to Self-Examination Questions

1. **B** Variable costs vary in total in direct proportion to changes in the level of activity (answer B). Costs that vary on a per-unit basis as the level of activity changes (answer A) or remain constant in total dollar amount as the level of activity changes (answer C), or both (answer D), are fixed costs.

2. **D** The contribution margin ratio indicates the percentage of each sales dollar available to cover the fixed costs and provide income from operations and is determined as follows:

$$\text{Contribution Margin Ratio} = \frac{\text{Sales} - \text{Variable Costs}}{\text{Sales}}$$

$$\text{Contribution Margin Ratio} = \frac{\$500,000 - \$200,000}{\$500,000}$$

$$= 60\%$$

3. **D** The break-even sales of 40,000 units (answer D) is computed as follows:

$$\text{Break-Even Sales (units)} = \frac{\text{Fixed Costs}}{\text{Unit Contribution Margin}}$$

$$\text{Break-Even Sales (units)} = \frac{\$160,000}{\$4} = 40,000 \text{ units}$$

4. **D** Sales of 45,000 units are required to realize income from operations of $20,000, computed as follows:

$$\text{Sales (units)} = \frac{\text{Fixed Costs} + \text{Target Profit}}{\text{Unit Contribution Margin}}$$

$$\text{Sales (units)} = \frac{\$160,000 + \$20,000}{\$4} = 45,000 \text{ units}$$

5. **C** The operating leverage is 1.8, computed as follows:

$$\text{Operating Leverage} = \frac{\text{Contribution Margin}}{\text{Income from Operations}}$$

$$\text{Operating Leverage} = \frac{\$360,000}{\$200,000} = 1.8$$

Variable Costing for Management Analysis

© PAUL SAKURA/ASSOCIATED PRESS

objectives

After studying this chapter, you should be able to:

1 Describe and illustrate income reporting under variable costing and absorption costing.

2 Describe and illustrate income analysis under variable costing and absorption costing.

3 Describe and illustrate management's use of variable costing and absorption costing for controlling costs, pricing products, planning production, analyzing contribution margins, and analyzing market segments.

4 Use variable costing for analyzing market segments, including product, territories, and salespersons segments.

5 Use variable costing for analyzing and explaining changes in contribution margin as a result of quantity and price factors.

6 Describe and illustrate the use of variable costing for service firms.

Adobe Systems, Inc.

Assume that you are interested in obtaining a temporary job during the summer and that you have three different job options. How would you evaluate these options? Naturally, there are many things to consider, including how much income each job would provide.

Determining the income from each job may not be as simple as comparing the rates of pay per hour. For example, a job as an office clerk at a local company pays $7 per hour. A job delivering pizza pays $10 per hour (including estimated tips), although you must use your own transportation. Another job working in a store located in a beach resort over 500 miles away from your home pays $8 per hour. All three jobs offer work for 40 hours per week for the whole summer. If these options were ranked according to their pay per hour, the pizza delivery job would be the most attractive. However, the costs associated with each job must also be evaluated. For example, the office job may require that you pay for downtown parking and purchase office clothes. The pizza delivery job will require you to pay for gas and maintenance for your car. The resort job will require you to move to the resort city and incur additional living costs. Only by considering the costs for each job will you be able to determine which job will provide you with the most income.

Just as you should evaluate the relative income of various choices, so must a business evaluate the income earned from its choices. Important choices include the products offered and the geographical regions to be served. Thus, a company will often evaluate the profitability of products and regions. For example, Adobe Systems Inc., one of the largest software companies in the world, determines the income earned from their various product lines, such as Acrobat®, Photoshop®, Premier®, and Dreamweaver® software. Adobe uses this information to establish product line pricing, as well as sales, support, and development effort. Likewise, Adobe evaluates the income earned in the geographic regions it serves, such as the United States, Europe, and Asia. Again, such information aids management in managing revenue and expenses within the regions.

In this chapter we will discuss how businesses measure profitability, using absorption costing and variable costing. After illustrating and comparing these concepts, we discuss how businesses use them for controlling costs, pricing products, planning production, analyzing market segments, and analyzing contribution margins.

The Income Statement Under Variable Costing and Absorption Costing

objective 1

Describe and illustrate income reporting under variable costing and absorption costing.

One of the most important items affecting a manufacturing business's net income is the cost of goods sold. In many cases, the cost of goods sold is larger than all of the other expenses combined. The cost of goods sold can be determined under either the absorption costing or variable costing concept.

Under **absorption costing**, all manufacturing costs are included in finished goods and remain there as an asset until the goods are sold. Absorption costing is necessary in determining historical costs for financial reporting to external users and for tax reporting.

Variable costing may be more useful to management in making decisions. In **variable costing**, which is also called *direct costing*, the cost of goods manufactured is composed only of *variable* manufacturing costs—costs that increase or decrease as the volume of production rises or falls. These costs are the direct materials, direct labor, and only those factory overhead costs that vary with the rate of production. The remaining factory overhead costs, which are fixed or nonvariable costs, are generally related to the productive capacity of the manufacturing plant and are not affected by changes in the quantity of product manufactured. For example, depreciation on the

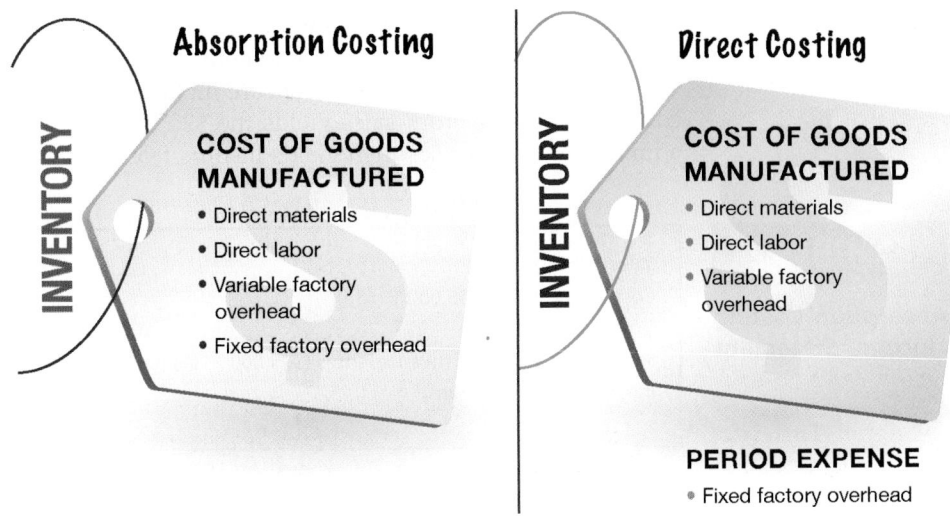

factory building is a cost that does not change with changes in the rate of production. Thus, the fixed factory overhead does not become a part of the cost of goods manufactured but is treated as an expense of the period in which it is incurred.

To illustrate the difference between the variable costing income statement and the absorption costing income statement, assume that Belling Co. manufactured 15,000 units at the following costs:

A	B	C	D	
	Total Cost	**Number of Units**	**Unit Cost**	
1 Manufacturing costs:				1
2 Variable	$375,000	15,000	$25	2
3 Fixed	150,000	15,000	10	3
4 Total	$525,000		$35	4
5 Selling and administrative expenses:				5
6 Variable ($5 per unit sold)	$ 75,000			6
7 Fixed	50,000			7
8 Total	$125,000			8

The units sell at a price of $50, as shown in the variable costing income statement for Belling Co. in Exhibit 1. In this income statement, variable costs are separated from fixed costs. The variable cost of goods sold, which includes the variable manufacturing costs, is deducted from sales to yield the **manufacturing margin** of $375,000. The variable selling and administrative expenses of $75,000 are deducted from the manufacturing margin to yield the contribution margin of $300,000. Thus, the **contribution margin** is sales less variable costs, as we defined in the previous chapter. The income from operations of $100,000 is then determined by deducting fixed costs of $200,000 from the contribution margin.

> The variable costing income statement includes only variable manufacturing costs in the cost of goods sold.

EXHIBIT 1

Variable Costing Income Statement

Sales (15,000 × $50)		$750,000
Variable cost of goods sold (15,000 × $25)		375,000
Manufacturing margin		$375,000
Variable selling and administrative expenses		75,000
Contribution margin		$300,000
Fixed costs:		
Fixed manufacturing costs	$150,000	
Fixed selling and administrative expenses	50,000	200,000
Income from operations		$100,000

Exhibit 2 shows the absorption costing income statement prepared for Belling Co. The absorption costing income statement does not distinguish between variable and fixed costs. All manufacturing costs are included in the cost of goods sold. Deducting cost of goods sold from sales yields the $225,000 gross profit. Deducting selling and administrative expenses then yields income from operations of $100,000.

EXHIBIT 2

Absorption Costing Income Statement

Sales (15,000 × $50)	$750,000
Cost of goods sold (15,000 × $35)	525,000
Gross profit	$225,000
Selling and administrative expenses ($75,000 + $50,000)	125,000
Income from operations	$100,000

Example Exercise 20-1

objective 1

Leone Company has the following information for March:

Sales	$450,000
Variable cost of goods sold	220,000
Fixed manufacturing costs	80,000
Variable selling and administrative expenses	50,000
Fixed selling and administrative expenses	35,000

Determine (a) the manufacturing margin, (b) the contribution margin, and (c) income from operations for Leone Company for the month of March.

Follow My Example 20-1

a. $230,000 ($450,000 − $220,000)
b. $180,000 ($230,000 − $50,000)
c. $65,000 ($180,000 − $80,000 − $35,000)

For Practice: PE 20-1A, PE 20-1B

INCOME FROM OPERATIONS WHEN UNITS MANUFACTURED EQUAL UNITS SOLD

In Exhibits 1 and 2, 15,000 units were manufactured and sold. Both the variable and the absorption costing income statements reported the same income from operations of $100,000. Thus, when the number of units manufactured equals the number of units sold, income from operations will be the same under both methods.

INCOME FROM OPERATIONS WHEN UNITS MANUFACTURED EXCEED UNITS SOLD

When the number of units manufactured exceeds the number of units sold, the variable costing income from operations will be *less* than the absorption costing income from operations. To illustrate, assume that in the preceding example only 12,000 units of the 15,000 units manufactured were sold. Exhibit 3 shows the two income statements that result.

The $30,000 difference ($70,000 − $40,000) in the amount of income from operations is due to the different treatment of the fixed manufacturing costs. The entire amount of the $150,000 of fixed manufacturing costs is included as an expense of the period in the variable costing statement. The ending inventory in the absorption costing statement includes $30,000 (3,000 units × $10) of fixed manufacturing costs.

EXHIBIT 3

Units Manufactured
Exceed Units Sold

Variable Costing Income Statement		
Sales (12,000 × $50)		$600,000
Variable cost of goods sold:		
Variable cost of goods manufactured (15,000 × $25)	$375,000	
Less ending inventory (3,000 × $25)	75,000	
Variable cost of goods sold		300,000
Manufacturing margin		$300,000
Variable selling and administrative expenses (12,000 × $5)		60,000
Contribution margin		$240,000
Fixed costs:		
Fixed manufacturing costs	$150,000	
Fixed selling and administrative expenses	50,000	200,000
Income from operations		$ 40,000

Absorption Costing Income Statement		
Sales (12,000 × $50)		$600,000
Cost of goods sold:		
Cost of goods manufactured (15,000 × $35)	$525,000	
Less ending inventory (3,000 × $35)	105,000	
Cost of goods sold		420,000
Gross profit		$180,000
Selling and administrative expenses ($60,000 + $50,000)		110,000
Income from operations		$ 70,000

This $30,000 is excluded from the current cost of goods sold in the absorption costing statement and is thus deferred to a future period.

Example Exercise 20-2

objective 1

Fixed manufacturing costs are $40 per unit, and variable manufacturing costs are $120 per unit. Production was 125,000 units, while sales were 120,000 units. Determine (a) whether variable costing income from operations is less than or greater than absorption costing income from operations, and (b) the difference in variable costing and absorption costing income from operations.

Follow My Example 20-2

a. Variable costing income from operations is less than absorption costing income from operations.
b. $200,000 ($40 per unit × 5,000 units)

For Practice: PE 20-2A, PE 20-2B

INCOME FROM OPERATIONS WHEN UNITS MANUFACTURED ARE LESS THAN UNITS SOLD

When the number of units manufactured is less than the number of units sold, the variable costing income from operations will be *greater* than the absorption costing income from operations. To illustrate, assume that 5,000 units of inventory were on hand at the beginning of a period, 10,000 units were manufactured during the period, and 15,000 units were sold (10,000 units manufactured during the period plus the 5,000 units on hand at the beginning of the period) at $50 per unit. The manufacturing costs and selling and administrative expenses are as follows. Exhibit 4 shows the two income statements prepared from this information.

	A	B	C	D	
			Number	Unit	
		Total Cost	of Units	Cost	
1	Beginning inventory:				1
2	Manufacturing costs:				2
3	Variable	$125,000	5,000	$25	3
4	Fixed	50,000	5,000	10	4
5	Total	$175,000		$35	5
6	Current period:				6
7	Manufacturing costs:				7
8	Variable	$250,000	10,000	$25	8
9	Fixed	150,000	10,000	15	9
10	Total	$400,000		$40	10
11	Selling and administrative expenses:				11
12	Variable ($5 per unit sold)	$ 75,000			12
13	Fixed	50,000			13
14	Total	$125,000			14

EXHIBIT 4

**Units Manufactured
Are Less than
Units Sold**

Variable Costing Income Statement

Sales (15,000 × $50).		$750,000
Variable cost of goods sold:		
Beginning inventory (5,000 × $25)	$125,000	
Variable cost of goods manufactured (10,000 × $25)	250,000	
Variable cost of goods sold		375,000
Manufacturing margin		$375,000
Variable selling and administrative expenses (15,000 × $5)		75,000
Contribution margin		$300,000
Fixed costs:		
Fixed manufacturing costs	$150,000	
Fixed selling and administrative expenses	50,000	200,000
Income from operations		$100,000

Absorption Costing Income Statement

Sales (15,000 × $50).		$750,000
Cost of goods sold:		
Beginning inventory (5,000 × $35)	$175,000	
Cost of goods manufactured (10,000 × $40)	400,000	
Cost of goods sold		575,000
Gross profit		$175,000
Selling and administrative expenses ($75,000 + $50,000)		125,000
Income from operations		$ 50,000

The $50,000 difference ($100,000 − $50,000) in the income from operations is caused by the different treatment of the fixed manufacturing costs. The beginning inventory in the absorption costing income statement includes $50,000 (5,000 units × $10) of fixed manufacturing costs incurred in the preceding period. By being included in the beginning inventory, this $50,000 is included in the cost of goods sold for the current period. Under variable costing, however, this $50,000 was included as an expense in an income statement of a prior period. Therefore, none of it is included as an expense in the current income statement.

Example Exercise 20-3   **objective** 1

The beginning inventory is 8,000 units. All of the units were manufactured during the period and 6,000 units of the beginning inventory were sold. The beginning inventory fixed manufacturing costs are $60 per unit, and variable manufacturing costs are $300 per unit. Determine (a) whether variable costing income from operations is less than or greater than absorption costing income from operations, and (b) the difference in variable costing and absorption costing income from operations.

Follow My Example 20-3

a. Variable costing income from operations is greater than absorption costing income from operations.
b. $360,000 ($60 per unit × 6,000 units)

For Practice: PE 20-3A, PE 20-3B

COMPARING INCOME FROM OPERATIONS UNDER THE TWO CONCEPTS

The two preceding examples illustrate the effects of the variable costing and absorption costing concepts on income from operations when the number of units sold do *not* equal the number of units produced. These effects are summarized below.

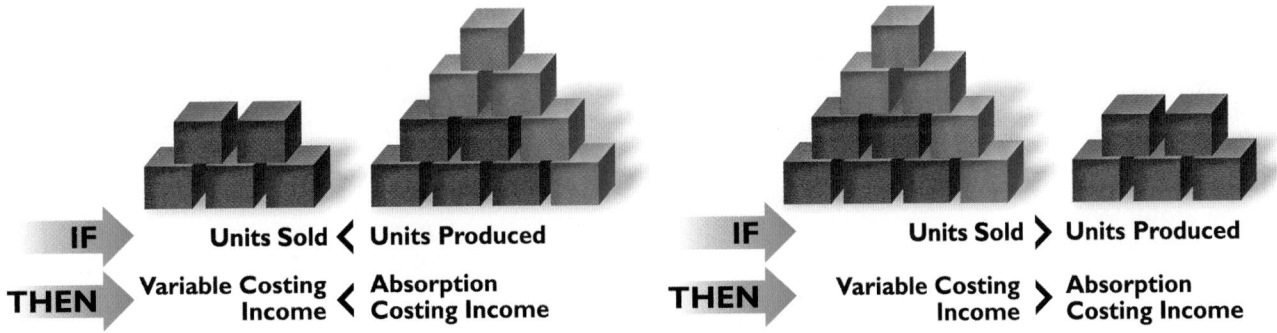

IF → Units Sold < Units Produced

THEN → Variable Costing Income < Absorption Costing Income

IF → Units Sold > Units Produced

THEN → Variable Costing Income > Absorption Costing Income

Income Analysis Under Variable Costing and Absorption Costing

objective 2

Describe and illustrate income analysis under variable costing and absorption costing.

As we have illustrated, the income from operations under variable costing can differ from the income from operations under absorption costing. This difference results from changes in the quantity of the finished goods inventory, which are caused by differences in the levels of sales and production. In analyzing and evaluating operations, management should be aware of the possible effects of changing inventory levels under the two concepts. To illustrate, assume that Frand Manufacturing Company has no beginning inventory and sales are estimated to be 20,000 units at $75 per unit, regardless of production levels. Assume further that the following two proposed production levels are being evaluated by the management of Frand Manufacturing Company:

	A	B	C	D	
	Proposal 1: 20,000 Units to Be Manufactured and Sold				
			Number	**Unit**	
		Total Cost	**of Units**	**Cost**	
1	Manufacturing costs:				1
2	Variable	$ 700,000	20,000	$35	2
3	Fixed	400,000	20,000	20	3
4	Total costs	$1,100,000		$55	4
5	Selling and administrative expenses:				5
6	Variable ($5 per unit sold)	$ 100,000			6
7	Fixed	100,000			7
8	Total expenses	$ 200,000			8

	A	B	C	D	
	Proposal 2: 25,000 Units to Be Manufactured: 20,000 Units to Be Sold				
			Number	**Unit**	
		Total Cost	**of Units**	**Cost**	
1	Manufacturing costs:				1
2	Variable	$ 875,000	25,000	$35	2
3	Fixed	400,000	25,000	16	3
4	Total costs	$1,275,000		$51	4
5	Selling and administrative expenses:				5
6	Variable ($5 per unit sold)	$ 100,000			6
7	Fixed	100,000			7
8	Total expenses	$ 200,000			8

If Frand Manufacturing Company manufactures 20,000 units, which is an amount equal to the estimated sales, income from operations under absorption costing would be $200,000. However, the income from operations could be increased by $80,000 by manufacturing 25,000 units and adding 5,000 units to the finished goods inventory. The absorption costing income statements illustrating this effect are shown in Exhibit 5.

EXHIBIT 5

Absorption Costing
Income Statements for
Two Production Levels

Frand Manufacturing Company
Absorption Costing Income Statements

	20,000 Units Manufactured	25,000 Units Manufactured
Sales (20,000 units × $75)	$1,500,000	$1,500,000
Cost of goods sold:		
Cost of goods manufactured:		
(20,000 units × $55)	$1,100,000	
(25,000 units × $51)		$1,275,000
Less ending inventory:		
(5,000 units × $51)		255,000
Cost of goods sold	$1,100,000	$1,020,000
Gross profit	$ 400,000	$ 480,000
Selling and administrative expenses		
($100,000 + $100,000)	200,000	200,000
Income from operations	$ 200,000	$ 280,000

The $80,000 increase in income from operations would be caused by allocating the fixed manufacturing costs of $400,000 over a greater number of units of production. Specifically, an increase in production from 20,000 units to 25,000 units meant that the fixed manufacturing costs per unit decreased from $20 ($400,000/20,000 units) to $16 ($400,000/25,000 units). Thus, the cost of goods sold when 25,000 units are manufactured would be $4 per unit less, or $80,000 less in total (20,000 units sold × $4). Since the cost of goods sold is less, income from operations is $80,000 more when 25,000 units rather than 20,000 units are manufactured.

Under variable costing, income from operations would have been $200,000, regardless of the amount by which units manufactured exceeded sales, because no fixed manufacturing costs are allocated to the units manufactured. To illustrate, Exhibit 6 presents the variable costing income statements for Frand Manufacturing Company for the production of 20,000 units, 25,000 units, and 30,000 units. In each case, the income from operations is $200,000.

EXHIBIT 6

Variable Costing Income Statements for Three Production Levels

Frand Manufacturing Company
Variable Costing Income Statements

	Level 1 20,000 Units Manufactured	Level 2 25,000 Units Manufactured	Level 3 30,000 Units Manufactured
Sales (20,000 units × $75)........	$1,500,000	$1,500,000	$1,500,000
Variable cost of goods sold:			
Variable cost of goods manufactured:			
(20,000 units × $35).......	$ 700,000		
(25,000 units × $35).......		$ 875,000	
(30,000 units × $35).......			$1,050,000
Less ending inventory:			
(0 units × $35)	0		
(5,000 units × $35)........		175,000	
(10,000 units × $35).......			350,000
Variable cost of goods sold....	$ 700,000	$ 700,000	$ 700,000
Manufacturing margin..........	$ 800,000	$ 800,000	$ 800,000
Variable selling and administrative			
expenses...................	100,000	100,000	100,000
Contribution margin...........	$ 700,000	$ 700,000	$ 700,000
Fixed costs:			
Fixed manufacturing costs	$ 400,000	$ 400,000	$ 400,000
Fixed selling and administrative			
expenses	100,000	100,000	100,000
Total fixed costs	$ 500,000	$ 500,000	$ 500,000
Income from operations.........	$ 200,000	$ 200,000	$ 200,000

As illustrated, if absorption costing is used, management should be careful in analyzing income from operations when large changes in inventory levels occur. Managers could misinterpret increases or decreases in income from operations, due to mere changes in inventory levels, to be the result of business events, such as changes in sales volume, prices, or costs.

Many accountants believe that variable costing should be used for evaluating operating performance because absorption costing encourages management to produce inventory. This is because producing inventory absorbs fixed costs and causes the income from operations to appear higher, as we have illustrated previously. In the long run, building inventory without the promise of future sales may lead to higher handling, storage, financing, and obsolescence costs.

Example Exercise 20-4   objective 2

Variable manufacturing costs are $100 per unit, and fixed manufacturing costs are $50,000. Sales are estimated to be 4,000 units.

a.   How much would absorption costing income from operations differ between a plan to produce 4,000 units and a plan to produce 5,000 units?
b.   How much would variable costing income from operations differ between the two production plans?

Follow My Example 20-4

a. $10,000 greater in producing 5,000 units. 4,000 units × ($12.50 − $10.00), or [1,000 units × ($50,000/5,000 units)].
b.   There would be no difference in variable costing income from operations between the two plans.

For Practice: PE 20-4A, PE 20-4B

Integrity, Objectivity, and Ethics in Business   ETHICS

TAKING AN "ABSORPTION HIT"

Aligning production to demand is a critical decision in business. Managers must not allow the temporary benefits of excess production through higher absorption of fixed costs to guide their decisions. Likewise, if demand falls, production should be dropped and inventory liquidated to match the new demand level, even though earnings will be penalized. The following interchange provides an example of an appropriate response to lowered demand for H.J. Heinz Company:

Analyst's question: *Could you talk for a moment about manufacturing costs during the quarter? You had highlighted that they were up and that gross margins at Heinz USA were down. Why was that the case?*

Heinz executive's response: *Yeah. The manufacturing costs were somewhat up . . . as we improve our inventory position, obviously you've got less inventory to spread your fixed costs over, so you'll take what accountants would call an absorption hit as we reduce costs. And that will be something that as we pull down inventory over the years, that will be an additional P&L cost hurdle that we need to overcome.*

Management operating with integrity will seek the tangible benefits of reducing inventory, even though there may be an adverse impact on published financial statements caused by absorption costing.

Management's Use of Variable Costing and Absorption Costing

objective **3**

Describe and illustrate management's use of variable costing and absorption costing for controlling costs, pricing products, planning production, analyzing contribution margins, and analyzing market segments.

Managerial accountants should carefully analyze each situation in evaluating whether variable costing or absorption costing reports would be more useful to management. In many situations, preparing reports under both concepts provides useful insights. In the following paragraphs, we discuss such reports and their advantages and disadvantages to management in making decisions related to the items identified in Exhibit 7.

CONTROLLING COSTS

All costs are controllable in the long run by someone within a business, but they are not all controllable at the same level of management. For example, plant supervisors, as members of operating management, are responsible for controlling the use of direct materials in their departments. They have no control, however, of insurance costs related to the buildings housing their departments. For a specific level of management, **controllable costs** are costs that can be influenced by management at that level, and **noncontrollable costs** are costs that another level of management controls. This distinction is useful in fixing the responsibility for incurring costs and for reporting costs to those responsible for their control.

EXHIBIT 7 | Accounting Reports and Management Decisions

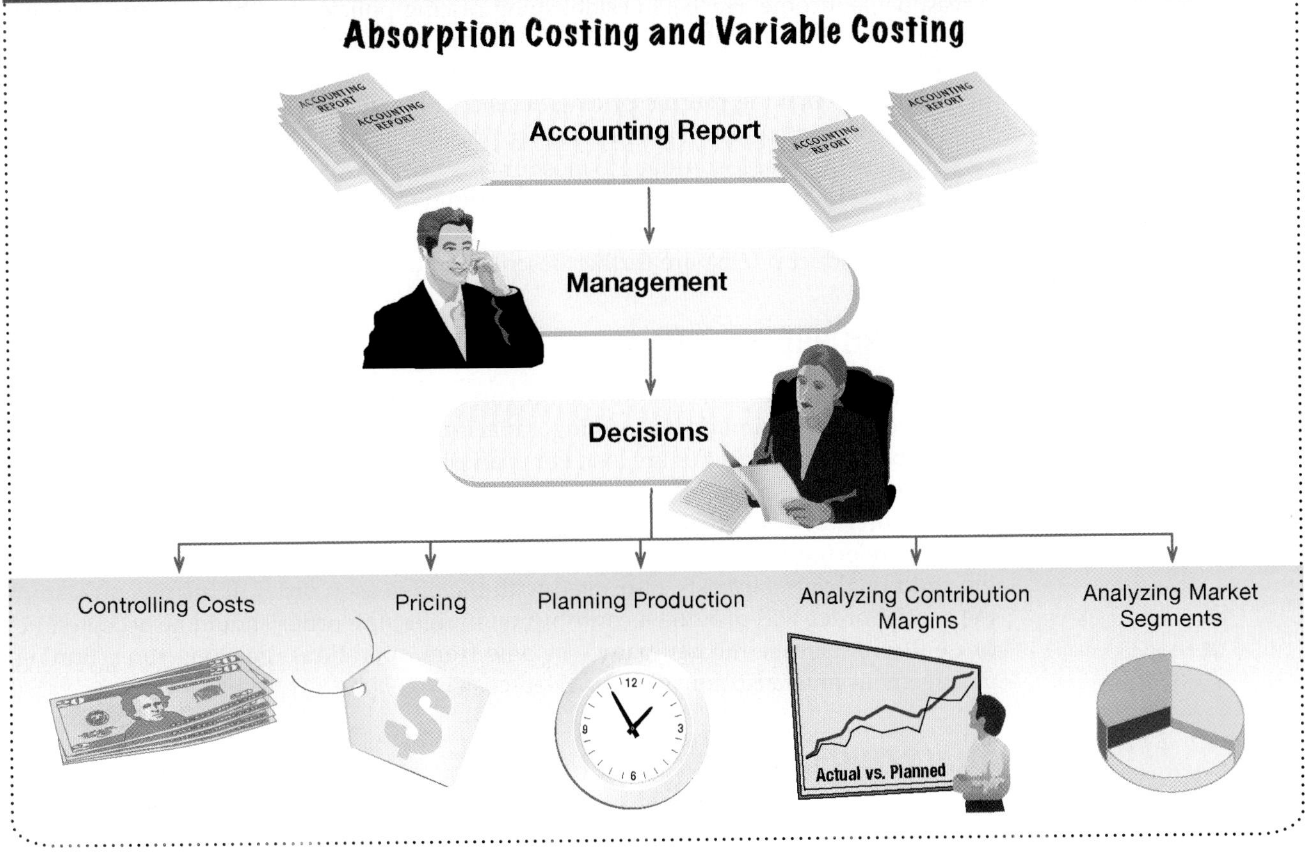

Absorption Costing and Variable Costing

Accounting Report → Management → Decisions → Controlling Costs | Pricing | Planning Production | Analyzing Contribution Margins (Actual vs. Planned) | Analyzing Market Segments

Most chemical companies, such as Union Carbide or Dow Chemical, use variable costing to evaluate the profitability of their operations. These approaches prevent fixed costs outside of managers' control to be used for evaluation purposes.

Variable manufacturing costs are controlled at the operating level. If the product's cost includes only variable manufacturing costs, the cost can be controlled by operating management. The fixed factory overhead costs are normally the responsibility of a higher level of management. When the fixed factory overhead costs are reported as a separate item in the variable costing income statement, they are easier to identify and control than when they are spread among units of product, as they are under absorption costing.

As in the case with the fixed and variable manufacturing costs, the control of the variable and fixed operating expenses is usually the responsibility of different levels of management. Under variable costing, the variable selling and administrative expenses are reported separately from the fixed selling and administrative expenses. Because they are reported in this manner, both types of operating expenses are easier to identify and control than is the case under absorption costing.

PRICING PRODUCTS

Many factors enter into determining the selling price of a product. The cost of making the product is clearly significant. Microeconomic theory states that income is maximized by expanding output to the volume where the revenue realized by the sale of an additional unit (marginal revenue) equals the cost of that unit (marginal cost). Although the degree of accuracy assumed in economic theory is rarely achieved, the concepts of marginal revenue and marginal cost are useful in setting selling prices.

In the short run, a business is committed to its existing manufacturing facilities. The pricing decision should be based upon making the best use of such capacity. The fixed costs cannot be avoided, but the variable costs can be eliminated if the company does not manufacture the product. The selling price of a product, therefore, should at least be equal to the variable costs of making and selling it. Any price above this minimum selling price contributes an amount toward covering fixed costs and providing income. Variable costing procedures yield data that emphasize these relationships.

In the long run, plant capacity can be increased or decreased. If a business is to continue operating, the selling prices of its products must cover all costs and provide a reasonable income. Hence, in establishing pricing policies for the long run, information provided by absorption costing procedures is needed.

The results of a research study indicated that the companies studied used absorption costing in making routine pricing decisions. However, these companies regularly used variable costing as a basis for setting prices in many short-run situations.

There are no simple solutions to most pricing problems. Consideration must be given to many factors of varying importance. Accounting can contribute by preparing analyses of various pricing plans for both the short run and the long run. Additional analyses useful for product pricing are further described and illustrated in a later chapter.

PLANNING PRODUCTION

Planning production also has both short-run and long-run implications. In the short run, production is limited to existing capacity. Operating decisions must be made quickly before opportunities are lost. For example, a company manufacturing products with a seasonal demand may have an opportunity to obtain an off-season order that will not interfere with its production schedule nor reduce the sales of its other products. The relevant factors for such a short-run decision are the additional revenues and the additional variable costs associated with the off-season order. If the revenues from the special order will provide a contribution margin, the order should be accepted because it will increase the company's income from operations. For long-run planning, management must also consider the fixed costs.

ANALYZING CONTRIBUTION MARGINS

Managers can plan and control operations by evaluating the differences between planned and actual contribution margins. For example, an increase in the price of gasoline due to market factors would have a positive impact on the planned contribution margin of a gasoline refiner. Such analyses are discussed in a separate section to follow.

ANALYZING MARKET SEGMENTS

Market analysis is performed by the sales and marketing function in order to determine the profit contributed by market segments. A **market segment** is a portion of a business that can be analyzed using sales, costs, and expenses to determine its profitability. Often the profitability of market segments can provide insight to business direction and performance. Examples of market segments include sales territories, products, salespersons, and customers. Variable costing can aid decision making regarding such segments. We will illustrate variable cost reporting for market segments in the next section.

Variable Costing in Analyzing Market Segments

As we illustrated earlier in this chapter, businesses can use income reporting under absorption or variable costing. Operating income defined under absorption costing can be used to evaluate market segments for long-term analyses. This type of analysis is illustrated in a later chapter using activity-based costing. For a short-term analysis, management often evaluates market segment profitability using variable costing. For example, variable costing can be used by managers to support short-term price decisions, evaluate cost changes, and plan volume changes. In this section, we will illustrate segment profitability reporting using variable costing.

Most companies develop profitability reports for products, since product pricing and retention decisions are influenced by their relative profitability. In addition to product segments, managers may evaluate the profitability of geographic, customer, distribution channel, or salesperson. A distribution channel is the method for placing a product with the customer. For example, Borders Group Inc. evaluates the profitability of its Internet and retail store distribution channels. In contrast, McDonald's Corporation evaluates geographic segments. Geographic segments are more meaningful for McDonald's than are customer segments. It is difficult, and probably meaningless, to try to distinguish McDonald's customers. However, McDonald's geographic segments are unique. For example, the operating results of restaurants in the United States are different from those in Asia or Europe.

To illustrate variable costing for analyzing market segments, assume the following data for March 2008 for Camelot Fragrance Company. Camelot Fragrance Company manufactures and sells the Gwenevere perfume line for women and the Lancelot cologne line for men. For simplicity, we assume that the inventories are negligible and are thus disregarded in the reports that follow.

	Northern Territory	Southern Territory	Total
Sales:			
Gwenevere	$60,000	$30,000	$ 90,000
Lancelot	20,000	50,000	70,000
Total territory sales	$80,000	$80,000	$160,000
Variable production costs:			
Gwenevere (12% of sales)	$ 7,200	$ 3,600	$ 10,800
Lancelot (12% of sales)	2,400	6,000	8,400
Total variable production cost by territory	$ 9,600	$ 9,600	$ 19,200
Promotion costs:			
Gwenevere (variable at 30% of sales)	$18,000	$ 9,000	$ 27,000
Lancelot (variable at 20% of sales)	4,000	10,000	14,000
Total promotion cost by territory	$22,000	$19,000	$ 41,000
Sales commissions:			
Gwenevere (variable at 20% of sales)	$12,000	$ 6,000	$ 18,000
Lancelot (variable at 10% of sales)	2,000	5,000	7,000
Total sales commissions by territory	$14,000	$11,000	$ 25,000

This information can be used by Camelot Fragrance Company to prepare a sales territory, product, and salesperson profitability analysis. Each of these is discussed on the following pages.

SALES TERRITORY PROFITABILITY ANALYSIS

An income statement presenting the contribution margin by sales territories is often useful to management in evaluating past performance and in directing future sales efforts. Sales territory profitability analysis may lead management to reduce costs in lower-profit sales territories or to increase sales effort in higher-profit territories. For example, The Coca-Cola Company earns over 75% of its total corporate profits outside of the United States. This information motivates the Coca-Cola management to continue expanding operations and sales efforts around the world.

There are many possible explanations for profit differences between territories, including differences in pricing, sales unit volumes, media rates, selling costs, and the types of products sold. To illustrate the analysis of profit differences by sales territory,

Exhibit 8 shows the contribution margin by sales territory for Camelot Fragrance Company.

EXHIBIT 8

Contribution Margin by Sales Territory Report

Camelot Fragrance Company Contribution Margin by Sales Territory For the Month Ended March 31, 2008				
	Northern Territory		**Southern Territory**	
Sales		$80,000		$80,000
Variable cost of goods sold . . .		9,600		9,600
Manufacturing margin		$70,400		$70,400
Variable selling expenses:				
Promotion costs	$22,000		$19,000	
Sales commissions	14,000	36,000	11,000	30,000
Contribution margin		$34,400		$40,400
Contribution margin ratio		43%		50.5%

The contribution margin for each territory consists of the sales less the variable costs associated with producing and selling products in each territory. In addition to the contribution margin, the contribution margin ratio (contribution margin divided by sales) for each territory is useful in evaluating sales territories and directing operations toward more profitable activities. For the Northern Territory, the contribution margin ratio is 43% ($34,400/$80,000), and for the Southern Territory, the ratio is 50.5% ($40,400/$80,000). Although each territory had the same sales, the contribution margin ratios are different. Why is this?

In this case, the difference in territory profit performance can be explained by the difference in sales mix between the two territories. **Sales mix**, sometimes referred to as *product mix*, is defined as the relative distribution of sales among the various products sold. From the assumed information, the Southern Territory had a higher relative proportion of Lancelot sales than did the Northern Territory. If the Lancelot line is more profitable than the Gwenevere line, then we would expect the Southern Territory's overall profitability to be higher than the Northern Territory's, as shown in Exhibit 8. To verify the difference between the profitabilities of the two products, product profitability analysis may be performed.

PRODUCT PROFITABILITY ANALYSIS

Management should focus its sales efforts on those products that will provide the maximum total contribution margin. An income statement presenting the contribution margin by products is often used by management to guide product-related sales and promotional efforts. For example, Ford's F Series pickups are one of its most profitable product lines. Ford uses this information to motivate higher production levels and promotion effort for this brand.

Some products are more profitable than others due to differences with respect to pricing, manufacturing costs, advertising support, or salesperson support. To illustrate the analysis of these differences, Exhibit 9 shows the contribution margin by product for Camelot Fragrance Company.

As you can see, Lancelot's contribution margin ratio is greater than Gwenevere's, even though both product lines have the same manufacturing margin as a percent of sales (88%). The higher contribution margin ratio is the result of Lancelot's lower promotion costs and sales commissions as a percent of sales. The sales territory profitability analysis and the product profitability analysis both indicate the superior profit performance of the Lancelot line. Thus, management should emphasize the Lancelot product line in its marketing plans, try to reduce the promotion and sales commission expenses associated with Gwenevere sales, or increase the price of Gwenevere.

EXHIBIT 9

Contribution Margin
by Product Line Report

Camelot Fragrance Company
Contribution Margin by Product Line
For the Month Ended March 31, 2008

	Gwenevere		Lancelot	
Sales		$90,000		$70,000
Variable cost of goods sold . . .		10,800		8,400
Manufacturing margin		$79,200		$61,600
Variable selling expenses:				
Promotion costs	$27,000		$14,000	
Sales commissions	18,000	45,000	7,000	21,000
Contribution margin		$34,200		$40,600
Contribution margin ratio		38%		58%

SALESPERSON PROFITABILITY ANALYSIS

In addition to the sales territory and product profitability analyses, sales managers may wish to evaluate the performance of salespersons. This may be done with a salesperson profitability analysis.

A report to management for use in evaluating the sales performance of each salesperson could include total sales, variable cost of goods sold, variable selling expenses, contribution margin, and contribution margin ratio. Exhibit 10 illustrates such a report for three salespersons in the Northern Territory of Camelot Fragrance Company.

EXHIBIT 10

Contribution Margin
by Salesperson Report

Camelot Fragrance Company
Contribution Margin by Salesperson—Northern Territory
For the Month Ended March 31, 2008

	Inez Rodriguez	Tom Ginger	Beth Williams	Northern Territory— Total
Sales	$20,000	$20,000	$40,000	$80,000
Variable cost of goods sold . . .	2,400	2,400	4,800	9,600
Manufacturing margin	$17,600	$17,600	$35,200	$70,400
Variable selling expenses:				
Promotion costs	$ 5,000	$ 5,000	$12,000	$22,000
Sales commissions	3,000	3,000	8,000	14,000
	$ 8,000	$ 8,000	$20,000	$36,000
Contribution margin	$ 9,600	$ 9,600	$15,200	$34,400
Contribution margin ratio	48%	48%	38%	43%
Sales mix (% Lancelot sales) . .	50%	50%	0	25%

The additional information provided on the total sales and costs of all three salespersons agrees with the total sales and costs for the Northern Territory in Exhibit 8. Thus, this report provides the Northern Territory manager with a more detailed analysis of the territory's performance. The report indicates that Beth Williams produced the greatest contribution margin for the company but had the lowest contribution margin ratio. Beth Williams sold $40,000 of product, which is twice as much product as the other two salespersons. However, Beth Williams sold only the Gwenevere product line, which has the lowest contribution margin ratio (from Exhibit 9). The other two salespersons sold equal amounts of Gwenevere and Lancelot. These two salespersons had higher contribution margin ratios because of the sales of the higher-margin Lancelot line. The territory manager could use this report to encourage Rodriguez and Ginger to sell more total product, while encouraging Williams to place more selling effort on the Lancelot line.

Business Connections

MCDONALD'S CORPORATION
CONTRIBUTION MARGIN BY STORE

McDonald's Corporation is the largest restaurant company in the world, representing 2.5% of the restaurants and 7.3% of the sales of all restaurants in the United States. McDonald's annual report identifies revenues and costs for its company-owned restaurants separately from its franchised restaurants. Assume that the food, paper, payroll, and benefit costs are variable and that occupancy and other operating expenses are fixed. A contribution margin and income from operations can be constructed for the company-owned restaurants as follows:

McDonald's Corporation
Company-Owned Restaurant Contribution Margin
and Income from Operations (estimated)
For the Year Ended December 31, 2005 (in millions)

Sales		$15,352
Variable restaurant expenses:		
Food and paper	$5,207	
Payroll and employee benefits	4,039	
Total variable restaurant operating costs		9,246
Contribution margin		$ 6,106
Occupancy and other operating expenses		3,868
Income from operations		$ 2,238

The annual report also indicates that McDonald's has 9,238 company-owned restaurants. Dividing the numbers above by 9,283 yields the contribution margin and income from operations *per restaurant* as follows:

Sales	$1,653,776
Variable restaurant expenses	996,014
Contribution margin	$ 657,762
Occupancy and other operating expenses	416,676
Income from operations	$ 241,086

In addition, McDonald's segments this information by its major operating regions, such as the United States, Europe, Latin America, Canada, and Asia. McDonald's can use this information for pricing products; evaluating the sensitivity of store profitability to changes in sales volume, prices, and costs; analyzing profitability by geographic segments; and evaluating the contribution of the company-owned stores to overall corporate profitability.

Other factors should also be considered in evaluating salespersons' performance. For example, sales growth rates, years of experience, customer service, territory size, and actual performance compared to budgeted performance may also be important.

Example Exercise 20-5

objective **4**

The following data are for Moss Creek Apparel:

	East	West
Sales volume (units):		
Shirts	6,000	5,000
Shorts	4,000	8,000
Sales price:		
Shirts	$12	$13
Shorts	$16	$18
Variable cost per unit:		
Shirts	$7	$7
Shorts	$10	$10

Determine the contribution margin for (a) Shorts and (b) the West Region.

(continued)

Contribution Margin Analysis

objective 5

Use variable costing for analyzing and explaining changes in contribution margin as a result of quantity and price factors.

The contribution margin concept can be used to assist managers in planning and controlling operations by focusing on the differences between planned and actual contribution margins. These differences, as well as the causes of the differences, can be systematically explained using **contribution margin analysis**.

Since contribution margin is the excess of sales over variable costs, a difference between the planned and actual contribution margin can be caused by (1) an increase or decrease in the amount of sales or (2) an increase or decrease in the amount of variable costs. An increase or decrease in either element may in turn be due to (1) an increase or decrease in the number of units sold or (2) an increase or decrease in the unit sales price or unit cost, as shown in Exhibit 11. The effect of these two factors on either sales or variable costs may be stated as follows:

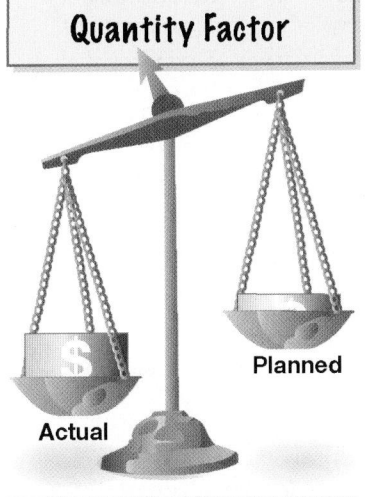

Quantity Factor

Actual

Planned

Price / Unit Cost Factor

$ Actual

$ Planned

1. **Quantity factor**—the effect of a difference in the number of units sold, assuming no change in unit sales price or unit cost. The quantity factor is the difference between the actual quantity sold and the planned quantity sold, multiplied by the planned unit sales price or unit cost.
2. Unit **price factor** or *unit cost factor*—the effect of a difference in unit sales price or unit cost on the number of units sold. The unit price or unit cost factor is the difference between the actual unit price or unit cost and the planned unit price or unit cost, multiplied by the actual quantity sold.

We will use the following data for Noble Inc. for the year ended December 31, 2008, as a basis for illustrating contribution margin analysis. For the sake of simplicity, we will assume a single commodity. The analysis would be more complex if several different commodities were sold, but the basic principles would not be affected.

	A	B	C	D	
		Actual	Planned	Increase or (Decrease)	
1	Sales	$937,500	$800,000	$137,500	1
2	Less: Variable cost of goods sold	$425,000	$350,000	$ 75,000	2
3	Variable selling and administrative expenses	162,500	125,000	37,500	3
4	Total	$587,500	$475,000	$112,500	4
5	Contribution margin	$350,000	$325,000	$ 25,000	5
6	Number of units sold	125,000	100,000		6
7					7
8	Per unit:				8
9	Sales price	$7.50	$8.00		9
10	Variable cost of goods sold	3.40	3.50		10
11	Variable selling and administrative expenses	1.30	1.25		11

The analysis of these data in Exhibit 12 shows that the favorable increase of $25,000 in the contribution margin was due in large part to an increase in the number of units sold. This increase was partially offset by a decrease in the unit sales price and an increase in the unit cost for variable selling and administrative expenses. The decrease in the unit cost for the variable cost of goods sold was an additional favorable result of 2008 operations.

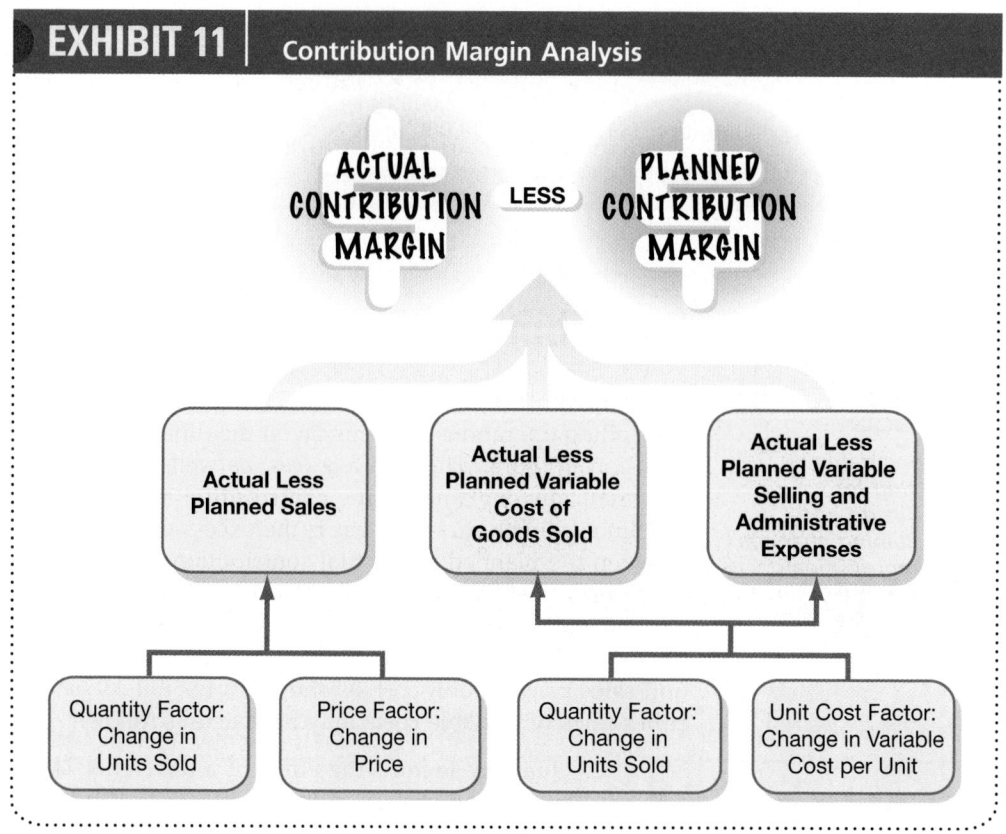

EXHIBIT 11 | **Contribution Margin Analysis**

EXHIBIT 12   **Contribution Margin Analysis Report**

	A	B	C	D	
	Noble Inc.				
	Contribution Margin Analysis				
	For the Year Ended December 31, 2008				
1	Increase in amount of sales attributed to:				1
2	Quantity factor:				2
3	Increase in number of units sold in 2008		25,000		3
4	Planned sales price in 2008		× $8.00	$200,000	4
5	Price factor:				5
6	Decrease in unit sales price in 2008		$(0.50)		6
7	Number of units sold in 2008		× 125,000	(62,500)	7
8	Net increase in amount of sales			$137,500	8
9	Increase in amount of variable cost of goods sold attributed to:				9
10	Quantity factor:				10
11	Increase in number of units sold in 2008	25,000			11
12	Planned unit cost in 2008	× $3.50	$ 87,500		12
13	Unit cost factor:				13
14	Decrease in unit cost in 2008	$(0.10)			14
15	Number of units sold in 2008	× 125,000	(12,500)		15
16	Net increase in amount of variable cost of goods sold		$ 75,000		16
17	Increase in amount of variable selling and administrative expenses attributed to:				17
18	Quantity factor:				18
19	Increase in number of units sold in 2008	25,000			19
20	Planned unit cost in 2008	× $1.25	$ 31,250		20
21	Unit cost factor:				21
22	Increase in unit cost in 2008	$0.05			22
23	Number of units sold in 2008	× 125,000	6,250		23
24	Net increase in the amount of variable selling and administrative expenses		$ 37,500		24
25	Net increase in amount of variable costs			112,500	25
26	Increase in contribution margin			$ 25,000	26

The information presented in the contribution margin analysis report is useful to management in evaluating past performance and in planning future operations. For example, the impact of the $0.50 reduction in the unit sales price on the number of units sold and on the total sales for the year is useful information that management can use in determining whether further price reductions might be desirable. The contribution margin analysis report also highlights the impact of changes in unit variable costs and expenses. For example, the $0.05 increase in the unit variable selling and administrative expenses might be a result of increased advertising expenditures. If so, the increase in the number of units sold in 2008 could be attributed to both the $0.50 price reduction and the increased advertising.

Example Exercise 20-6 objective 5

The actual price for a product was $48 per unit, while the planned price was $40 per unit. The volume increased by 5,000 units to 60,000 actual total units. Determine (a) the quantity factor and (b) the price factor for sales.

Follow My Example 20-6

a. $200,000 increase in sales (5,000 units × $40 per unit)
b. $480,000 increase in sales [($48 − $40) × 60,000 units]

For Practice: PE 20-6A, PE 20-6B

Variable Costing for Service Firms

objective 6

Describe and illustrate the use of variable costing for service firms.

The previous section illustrated the use of variable costing concepts for manufacturing firms. Service firms also use variable costing reports for contribution margin and segment analyses.

VARIABLE COSTING INCOME STATEMENT—SERVICE FIRM

Unlike a manufacturing firm, a service firm does not make a product for sale. As a result, service firms do not have inventory and thus do not allocate fixed costs to inventory using absorption costing concepts. In addition, most service firms do not have cost of goods sold. Thus, the variable costing reports of service firms will not report a manufacturing margin. Service firms can, however, report and analyze contribution margin as the difference between revenues and variable costs.

To illustrate, Blue Skies Airlines Inc. operates a small commercial airline. The fixed and variable costs associated with operating Blue Skies are shown in Exhibit 13.

EXHIBIT 13

Costs of Blue Skies Airlines

Cost	Amount	Cost Behavior	Activity Base
Depreciation expense	$3,600,000	Fixed	
Food and beverage service expense	444,000	Variable	Number of passengers
Fuel expense	4,080,000	Variable	Number of miles flown
Rental expense	800,000	Fixed	
Selling expense	3,256,000	Variable	Number of passengers
Wages expense	6,120,000	Variable	Number of miles flown

As discussed in the prior chapter, a cost is fixed or variable by defining its behavior relative to changes in an activity base. The activity base in a manufacturing firm is often the number of units produced and sold. A service firm, however, may have multiple activity bases. For example, some airline costs, such as food and beverage costs, vary with the number of passengers. An airline also has costs that vary with the number of miles flown, such as fuel and wage costs. As a result, it is important to identify the proper activity base. For example, if an airline increases the average number of passengers flown per flight, called the *load factor*, but not the number of flights, then only the selling and food and beverage costs will increase. However, the fuel and wage costs will not change because the number of miles flown is unchanged.[1]

The variable costing income statement for Blue Skies, assuming revenue of $19,238,000, is shown in Exhibit 14. In comparing this report to the variable costing income statement for a manufacturing firm (Exhibit 6), you will notice that there are no cost of goods sold, inventory, or manufacturing margin. However, as shown in Exhibit 14, contribution margin is reported separately from income from operations.

EXHIBIT 14

Variable Costing Income Statement

Blue Skies Airlines Inc.
Variable Costing Income Statement
For the Month Ended April 30, 2008

Revenue		$19,238,000
Variable costs:		
Fuel expense	$4,080,000	
Wages expense	6,120,000	
Food and beverage service expense	444,000	
Selling expenses	3,256,000	
Total variable costs		13,900,000
Contribution margin		$ 5,338,000
Fixed costs:		
Depreciation expense	$3,600,000	
Rental expense	800,000	
Total fixed costs		4,400,000
Income from operations		$ 938,000

MARKET SEGMENT ANALYSIS—SERVICE FIRM

As is the case with a manufacturing firm, the contribution margin report for service firms can be prepared to evaluate the contribution margin of market segments. The following table illustrates typical segments used in various service industries:

Service Industry	Market Segments
Electric power	Regions, customer types (industrial, consumer)
Banking	Customer types (commercial, retail), products (loans, savings accounts)
Airlines	Products (passengers, cargo), routes
Railroads	Products (commodity type), routes
Hotels	Hotel properties
Telecommunications	Customer type (commercial, retail), service type (voice, data)
Health care	Procedure, payment type (Medicare, insured)

1 Fuel costs may increase somewhat due to added passenger weight, traffic volume, or weather. Our examples are simplified to focus only on the dominant cost behavior patterns.

The contribution margin report for Blue Skies Airlines can be segmented by the various routes (city pairs) flown by the airline. Management would use such a report to evaluate the relative contribution to profitability of the various city pairs served by the airline. To illustrate, assume that Blue Skies serves three city pairs: Chicago/Atlanta, Atlanta/Los Angeles, and Los Angeles/Chicago. The contribution margin report is constructed by identifying the revenues and variable costs for each of the segments. The following information was determined from corporate records for the month of April for each route:

	Chicago/Atlanta	Atlanta/LA	LA/Chicago
Average ticket price per passenger	$400	$1,075	$805
Total passengers served	16,000	7,000	6,600
Total miles flown	56,000	88,000	60,000

The variable costs per unit are as follows:

Fuel	$ 20 per mile
Wages	30 per mile
Food and beverage service	15 per passenger
Selling	110 per passenger

A contribution margin report by segment is illustrated in Exhibit 15. You should note that the sum of the segment contribution margins in Exhibit 15 is equal to the total contribution margin shown in Exhibit 14.

As can be seen from the report, the Chicago/Atlanta route has the lowest contribution margin ratio, while the Atlanta/Los Angeles route has the highest contribution margin ratio. We discuss the implications of Exhibit 15 for management decision making next.

EXHIBIT 15   Contribution Margin by Segment Report—Service Firm

Blue Skies Airlines Inc.
Contribution Margin by Route
For the Month Ended April 30, 2008

	Chicago/ Atlanta	Atlanta/ Los Angeles	Los Angeles/ Chicago	Total
Revenue				
(Ticket price × No. of passengers)	$ 6,400,000	$ 7,525,000	$ 5,313,000	$19,238,000
Aircraft fuel				
($20 × No. of miles flown)	(1,120,000)	(1,760,000)	(1,200,000)	(4,080,000)
Wages and benefits				
($30 × No. of miles flown)	(1,680,000)	(2,640,000)	(1,800,000)	(6,120,000)
Food and beverage service				
($15 × No. of passengers)	(240,000)	(105,000)	(99,000)	(444,000)
Selling expenses				
($110 × No. of passengers)	(1,760,000)	(770,000)	(726,000)	(3,256,000)
Contribution margin	$ 1,600,000	$ 2,250,000	$ 1,488,000	$ 5,338,000
Contribution margin ratio*	25%	30%	28%	28%

*Contribution margin/revenue

CONTRIBUTION MARGIN ANALYSIS

The management of Blue Skies is concerned about the low contribution margin ratio on the Chicago/Atlanta route. To improve the contribution margin of this route, management decreased the ticket price from $400 to $380 in May. The price reduction increased the number of tickets sold (passengers) on the existing flights from 16,000 to 20,000. That is, the load factor increased. In addition, the price for fuel increased, causing the cost per mile to increase from $20 to $22. The following data were used for the contribution margin analysis for the month of May, assuming planned results in May were as in April:

	A	B	C	D	
		Chicago/Atlanta Route			
				Increase	
		Actual, May	Planned, May	(Decrease)	
1	Revenue	$7,600,000	$6,400,000	$1,200,000	1
2	Less variable expenses:				2
3	Aircraft fuel	$1,232,000	$1,120,000	$ 112,000	3
4	Wages and benefits	1,680,000	1,680,000	—	4
5	Food and beverage service	300,000	240,000	60,000	5
6	Selling expenses and commissions	2,200,000	1,760,000	440,000	6
7	Total	$5,412,000	$4,800,000	$ 612,000	7
8	Contribution margin	$2,188,000	$1,600,000	$ 588,000	8
9	Contribution margin ratio	29%	25%		9
10					10
11	Number of miles flown	56,000	56,000		11
12	Number of passengers flown	20,000	16,000		12
13	Per unit:				13
14	Ticket price	$380	$400		14
15	Fuel expense	22	20		15
16	Wages expense	30	30		16
17	Food and beverage service expense	15	15		17
18	Selling expenses	110	110		18

The highlighted numbers indicate the actual changes from the planned May results. The data can be used to develop a contribution margin analysis report similar to our previous example for a manufacturing firm in Exhibit 12. The analysis in Exhibit 16 provides the various quantity and price factors that are impacted by the changes.

EXHIBIT 16

Contribution Margin Analysis Report—Service Firm

	A	B	C	D	
	Blue Skies Airlines Inc.				
	Contribution Margin Analysis				
	For the Month Ended May 31, 2008				
1	Increase in revenue attributed to:				1
2	Quantity factor:				2
3	Increase in the number of passengers in May	4,000			3
4	Planned price	× $400	$1,600,000		4
5	Price factor:				5
6	Decrease in the ticket price in May	$(20)			6
7	Number of passengers in May	× 20,000	(400,000)		7
8	Net increase in revenue			$1,200,000	8
9	Increase in fuel costs attributed to:				9
10	Unit cost factor:				10
11	Increase in per mile cost in May	$2.00			11
12	Number of miles flown	× 56,000			12
13	Net increase in fuel costs		112,000		13
14	Increase in food and beverage service attributed to:				14
15	Quantity factor:				15
16	Increase in the number of passengers in May	4,000			16
17	Planned per passenger cost in May	× $15.00			17
18	Net increase in food and beverage service costs		60,000		18
19	Increase in selling costs and commissions attributed to:				19
20	Quantity factor:				20
21	Increase in the number of passengers in May	4,000			21
22	Planned per passenger cost in May	× $110			22
23	Increase in variable cost		612,000		23
24	Net increase in selling costs			440,000	24
25	Increase in contribution margin			$ 588,000	25

The contribution margin analysis indicates that the decrease in price generated an additional $1,200,000 in revenue. This amount consists of $1,520,000 from an increased number of passengers and a $320,000 revenue reduction from the reduced ticket price. The increased fuel costs (by $2 per mile) reduced the contribution margin by $112,000. The increased number of passengers also increased the food and beverage service costs by $60,000 and the selling costs by $440,000. The net increase in contribution margin from management's actions is $588,000, indicating that their actions were successful.

At a Glance

1. Describe and illustrate income reporting under variable costing and absorption costing.

Key Points	Key Learning Outcomes	Example Exercises	Practice Exercises
Under absorption costing, direct materials, direct labor, and factory overhead become part of the cost of goods manufactured. Under variable costing, the cost of goods manufactured is composed of only variable costs—the direct materials, direct labor, and only those factory overhead costs that vary with the rate of production. The fixed factory overhead costs do not become a part of the cost of goods manufactured but are considered an expense of the period.	• Describe the difference between absorption and variable costing.		
Deducting the variable cost of goods sold from sales in the variable costing income statement yields the manufacturing margin. Deducting the variable selling and administrative expenses from the manufacturing margin yields the contribution margin. Deducting the fixed costs from the contribution margin yields the income from operations.	• Prepare a variable costing income statement for a manufacturer.	20-1	20-1A, 20-1B
	• Evaluate the difference between the variable and absorption costing income statements when production exceeds sales.	20-2	20-2A, 20-2B
	• Evaluate the difference between the variable and absorption costing income statements when sales exceed production.	20-3	20-3A, 20-3B

2. Describe and illustrate income analysis under variable costing and absorption costing.

Key Points	Key Learning Outcomes	Example Exercises	Practice Exercises
Management should be aware of the effects of changes in inventory levels on income from operations reported under variable costing and absorption costing. If absorption costing is used, managers could misinterpret increases or decreases in income from operations due to changes in inventory levels to be the result of operating efficiencies or inefficiencies.	• Determine absorption costing and variable costing income under different planned levels of production for a given sales level.	20-4	20-4A, 20-4B

(continued)

3. Describe and illustrate management's use of variable costing and absorption costing for controlling costs, pricing products, planning production, analyzing contribution margins, and analyzing market segments.

Key Points	Key Learning Outcomes	Example Exercises	Practice Exercises
Variable costing is especially useful at the operating level of management because the amount of variable manufacturing costs are controllable at this level. The fixed factory overhead costs are ordinarily controllable by a higher level of management. In the short run, variable costing may be useful in establishing the selling price of a product. This price should be at least equal to the variable costs of making and selling the product. In the long run, however, absorption costing is useful in establishing selling prices because all costs must be covered and a reasonable amount of operating income must be earned.	• Describe the management's use of variable and absorption costing for controlling costs, pricing products, planning production, analyzing contribution margins, and analyzing market segments.		

4. Use variable costing for analyzing market segments, including product, territories, and salespersons segments.

Key Points	Key Learning Outcomes	Example Exercises	Practice Exercises
Variable costing can support management decision making in analyzing and evaluating market segments, such as territories, products, salespersons, and customers. Contribution margin reports by segment can be used by managers to support price decisions, evaluate cost changes, and plan volume changes.	• Describe management's uses of contribution margin reports by segment. • Prepare a contribution margin report by sales territory. • Prepare a contribution margin report by product. • Prepare a contribution margin report by salesperson.	20-5	20-5A, 20-5B

5. Use variable costing for analyzing and explaining changes in contribution margin as a result of quantity and price factors.

Key Points	Key Learning Outcomes	Example Exercises	Practice Exercises
Contribution margin analysis is the systematic examination of differences between planned and actual contribution margins. These differences can be caused by an increase/decrease in the amount of sales or variable costs, which can be caused by changes in the amount of units sold, unit sales price, or unit cost.	• Prepare a contribution margin analysis identifying changes between actual and planned contribution margin by price/cost and quantity factors.	20-6	20-6A, 20-6B

6. Describe and illustrate the use of variable costing for service firms.

Key Points	Key Learning Outcomes	Example Exercises	Practice Exercises
Service firms will not have inventories, manufacturing margin, or cost of goods sold. Service firms can prepare variable costing income statements and contribution margin reports for market segments. In addition, service firms can use contribution margin analysis to plan and control operations.	• Prepare a variable costing income statement for a service firm. • Prepare contribution margin reports by market segments for a service firm. • Prepare a contribution margin analysis for a service firm.		

Key Terms

absorption costing (884)
contribution margin (885)
contribution margin analysis (899)
controllable cost (892)

manufacturing margin (885)
market segment (894)
noncontrollable cost (892)
price factor (899)

quantity factor (899)
sales mix (896)
variable costing (884)

Illustrative Problem

During the current period, McLaughlin Company sold 60,000 units of product at $30 per unit. At the beginning of the period, there were 10,000 units in inventory and McLaughlin Company manufactured 50,000 units during the period. The manufacturing costs and selling and administrative expenses were as follows:

	Total Cost	Number of Units	Unit Cost
Beginning inventory:			
Direct materials	$ 67,000	10,000	$ 6.70
Direct labor	155,000	10,000	15.50
Variable factory overhead	18,000	10,000	1.80
Fixed factory overhead	20,000	10,000	2.00
Total	$ 260,000		$26.00
Current period costs:			
Direct materials	$ 350,000	50,000	$ 7.00
Direct labor	810,000	50,000	16.20
Variable factory overhead	90,000	50,000	1.80
Fixed factory overhead	100,000	50,000	2.00
Total	$1,350,000		$27.00
Selling and administrative expenses:			
Variable	$ 65,000		
Fixed	45,000		
Total	$ 110,000		

Instructions

1. Prepare an income statement based on the variable costing concept.
2. Prepare an income statement based on the absorption costing concept.
3. Give the reason for the difference in the amount of income from operations in 1 and 2.

Solution

1.

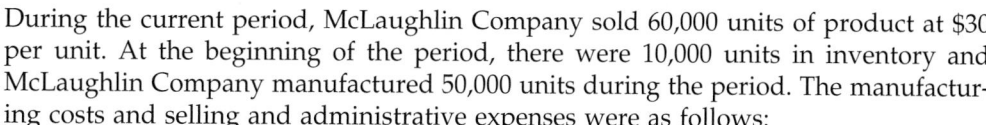

Variable Costing Income Statement

Sales (60,000 × $30)		$1,800,000
Variable cost of goods sold:		
Beginning inventory (10,000 × $24)	$ 240,000	
Variable cost of goods manufactured (50,000 × $25)	1,250,000	
Variable cost of goods sold		1,490,000
Manufacturing margin		$ 310,000
Variable selling and administrative expenses		65,000
Contribution margin		$ 245,000
Fixed costs:		
Fixed manufacturing costs	$ 100,000	
Fixed selling and administrative expenses	45,000	145,000
Income from operations		$ 100,000

(continued)

2.

Absorption Costing Income Statement		
Sales (60,000 × $30)		$1,800,000
Cost of goods sold:		
Beginning inventory (10,000 × $26)	$ 260,000	
Cost of goods manufactured (50,000 × $27)	1,350,000	
Cost of goods sold		1,610,000
Gross profit		$ 190,000
Selling and administrative expenses ($65,000 + $45,000)		110,000
Income from operations		$ 80,000

3. The difference of $20,000 ($100,000 − $80,000) in the amount of income from operations is attributable to the different treatment of the fixed manufacturing costs. The beginning inventory in the absorption costing income statement includes $20,000 (10,000 units × $2) of fixed manufacturing costs incurred in the preceding period. This $20,000 was included as an expense in a variable costing income statement of a prior period. Therefore, none of it is included as an expense in the current period variable costing income statement.

Self-Examination Questions

(Answers at End of Chapter)

1. Sales were $750,000, the variable cost of goods sold was $400,000, the variable selling and administrative expenses were $90,000, and fixed costs were $200,000. The contribution margin was:
   A. $60,000
   B. $260,000
   C. $350,000
   D. none of the above

2. During a year in which the number of units manufactured exceeded the number of units sold, the income from operations reported under the absorption costing concept would be:
   A. larger than the income from operations reported under the variable costing concept.
   B. smaller than the income from operations reported under the variable costing concept.
   C. the same as the income from operations reported under the variable costing concept.
   D. none of the above.

3. The beginning inventory consists of 6,000 units, all of which are sold during the period. The beginning inventory fixed costs are $20 per unit, and variable costs are $90 per unit. What is the difference in income from operations between variable and absorption costing?
   A. Variable costing income from operations is $540,000 less than under absorption costing.

   B. Variable costing income from operations is $660,000 greater than under absorption costing.
   C. Variable costing income from operations is $120,000 less than under absorption costing.
   D. Variable costing income from operations is $120,000 greater than under absorption costing.

4. Variable costs are $70 per unit and fixed costs are $150,000. Sales are estimated to be 10,000 units. How much would absorption costing income from operations differ between a plan to produce 10,000 units and 12,000 units?
   A. $150,000 greater for 12,000 units
   B. $150,000 less for 12,000 units
   C. $25,000 greater for 12,000 units
   D. $25,000 less for 12,000 units

5. If actual sales totaled $800,000 for the current year (80,000 units at $10 each) and planned sales were $765,000 (85,000 units at $9 each), the difference between actual and planned sales due to the quantity factor is:
   A. a $50,000 increase   C. a $45,000 decrease
   B. a $35,000 increase   D. none of the above

Eye Openers

1. What types of costs are customarily included in the cost of manufactured products under (a) the absorption costing concept and (b) the variable costing concept?

2. Which type of manufacturing cost (direct materials, direct labor, variable factory overhead, fixed factory overhead) is included in the cost of goods manufactured under the absorption costing concept but is excluded from the cost of goods manufactured under the variable costing concept?

3. Which of the following costs would be included in the cost of a manufactured product according to the variable costing concept: (a) rent on factory building, (b) direct materials, (c) property taxes on factory building, (d) electricity purchased to operate factory equipment, (e) salary of factory supervisor, (f) depreciation on factory building, (g) direct labor?

4. In the following equations, based on the variable costing income statement, identify the items designated by X:
   a. Net sales − X = manufacturing margin
   b. Manufacturing margin − X = contribution margin
   c. Contribution margin − X = income from operations

5. In the variable costing income statement, how are the fixed manufacturing costs reported and how are the fixed selling and administrative expenses reported?

6. If the quantity of the ending inventory is larger than that of the beginning inventory, will the amount of income from operations determined by absorption costing be more than or less than the amount determined by variable costing? Explain.

7. Since all costs of operating a business are controllable, what is the significance of the term *noncontrollable cost*?

8. Discuss how financial data prepared on the basis of variable costing can assist management in the development of short-run pricing policies.

9. How might management analyze sales territory profitability?

10. Why might management analyze product profitability?

11. Explain why rewarding sales personnel on the basis of total sales might not be in the best interests of a business whose goal is to maximize profits.

12. Discuss the two factors affecting both sales and variable costs to which a change in contribution margin can be attributed.

13. How is the quantity factor for an increase or decrease in the amount of sales computed in using contribution margin analysis?

14. How is the unit cost factor for an increase or decrease in the amount of variable cost of goods sold computed in using contribution margin analysis?

15. Provide examples of market segments for an entertainment company, such as The Walt Disney Co.

Practice Exercises

PE 20-1A
Variable costing income statement
obj. 1

Banner Company has the following information for October:

Sales	$150,000
Variable cost of goods sold	55,000
Fixed manufacturing costs	35,000
Variable selling and administrative expenses	12,000
Fixed selling and administrative expenses	10,000

Determine (a) the manufacturing margin, (b) the contribution margin, and (c) income from operations for Banner Company for the month of October.

PE 20-1B
Variable costing income statement
obj. 1

Mendoza Company has the following information for June:

Sales	$780,000
Variable cost of goods sold	400,000
Fixed manufacturing costs	70,000
Variable selling and administrative expenses	200,000
Fixed selling and administrative expenses	45,000

Determine (a) the manufacturing margin, (b) the contribution margin, and (c) income from operations for Mendoza Company for the month of June.

PE 20-2A
Variable costing difference—production exceeds sales
obj. 1

Fixed manufacturing costs are $90 per unit, and variable manufacturing costs are $175 per unit. Production was 200,000 units, while sales were 180,000 units. Determine (a) whether variable costing income from operations is less than or greater than absorption costing income from operations, and (b) the difference in variable costing and absorption costing income from operations.

PE 20-2B
Variable costing difference—production exceeds sales
obj. 1

Fixed manufacturing costs are $12 per unit, and variable manufacturing costs are $28 per unit. Production was 12,000 units, while sales were 9,000 units. Determine (a) whether variable costing income from operations is less than or greater than absorption costing income from operations, and (b) the difference in variable costing and absorption costing income from operations.

PE 20-3A
Variable costing difference—sales exceed production
obj. 1

The beginning inventory is 6,000 units. All of the units were manufactured during the period and 2,000 units of the beginning inventory were sold. The beginning inventory fixed manufacturing costs are $19 per unit, and variable manufacturing costs are $54 per unit. Determine (a) whether variable costing income from operations is less than or greater than absorption costing income from operations, and (b) the difference in variable costing and absorption costing income from operations.

PE 20-3B
Variable costing difference—sales exceed production
obj. 1

The beginning inventory is 54,000 units. All of the units were manufactured during the period and 31,000 units of the beginning inventory were sold. The beginning inventory fixed manufacturing costs are $4.20 per unit, and variable manufacturing costs are $8.50 per unit. Determine (a) whether variable costing income from operations is less than or greater than absorption costing income from operations, and (b) the difference in variable costing and absorption costing income from operations.

PE 20-4A
Income analysis under absorption and variable costing
obj. 2

Variable manufacturing costs are $14 per unit, and fixed manufacturing costs are $60,000. Sales are estimated to be 12,000 units.

a. How much would absorption costing income from operations differ between a plan to produce 12,000 units and a plan to produce 12,500 units?
b. How much would variable costing income from operations differ between the two production plans?

PE 20-4B
Income analysis under absorption and variable costing
obj. 2

Variable manufacturing costs are $26 per unit, and fixed manufacturing costs are $120,000. Sales are estimated to be 6,000 units.

a. How much would absorption costing income from operations differ between a plan to produce 6,000 units and a plan to produce 8,000 units?
b. How much would variable costing income from operations differ between the two production plans?

PE 20-5A
Contribution margin by segment
obj. 4

The following information is for Green Jacket Golf, Inc.:

	North	South
Sales volume (units):		
Ballistic	10,000	24,000
Pro Ballistic	9,500	28,000
Sales price:		
Ballistic	$20	$22
Pro Ballistic	$28	$32
Variable cost per unit:		
Ballistic	$9	$9
Pro Ballistic	$10	$10

Determine the contribution margin for (a) Ballistic golf balls and (b) North Region.

PE 20-5B
Contribution margin by segment
obj. 4

The following information is for RAM Technologies, Inc.:

	Northern California	Southern California
Sales volume (units):		
Palm Pod Basic	2,500	4,000
Palm Pod Executive	6,500	15,000
Sales price:		
Palm Pod Basic	$125	$110
Palm Pod Executive	$180	$175
Variable cost per unit:		
Palm Pod Basic	$45	$45
Palm Pod Executive	$55	$55

Determine the contribution margin for (a) Palm Pod Executive hand-held data organizer and (b) Southern California Region.

PE 20-6A
Contribution margin analysis of sales
obj. 5

The actual price for a product was $12 per unit, while the planned price was $10.50 per unit. The volume decreased by 15,000 units to 340,000 actual total units. Determine (a) the quantity factor and (b) the price factor for sales.

PE 20-6B
Contribution margin analysis of variable cost of goods sold
obj. 5

The actual variable cost of goods sold for a product was $245 per unit, while the planned variable cost of goods sold was $236 per unit. The volume increased by 900 units to 6,800 actual total units. Determine (a) the quantity factor and (b) the price factor for variable cost of goods sold.

Exercises

EX 20-1
Inventory valuation under absorption costing and variable costing
obj. 1
✓b. Inventory, $104,625

At the end of the first year of operations, 2,700 units remained in the finished goods inventory. The unit manufacturing costs during the year were as follows:

Direct materials	$24.00
Direct labor	11.60
Fixed factory overhead cost	3.90
Variable factory overhead cost	3.15

Determine the cost of the finished goods inventory reported on the balance sheet under (a) the absorption costing concept and (b) the variable costing concept.

EX 20-2
Income statements under absorption costing and variable costing
obj. 1
✓a. Income from operations, $281,600

Dillon Sounds Inc. assembles and sells CD players. The company began operations on May 1, 2008, and operated at 100% of capacity during the first month. The following data summarize the results for May:

Sales (12,000 units)		$2,160,000
Production costs (14,000 units):		
Direct materials	$896,000	
Direct labor	448,000	
Variable factory overhead	235,200	
Fixed factory overhead	145,600	1,724,800
Selling and administrative expenses:		
Variable selling and administrative expenses	$300,000	
Fixed selling and administrative expenses	100,000	400,000

(continued)

a. Prepare an income statement according to the absorption costing concept.
b. Prepare an income statement according to the variable costing concept.
c. What is the reason for the difference in the amount of income from operations reported in (a) and (b)?

EX 20-3
Income statements under absorption costing and variable costing

obj. 1

✓*b. Income from operations, $974,000*

Runway Fashions Inc. manufactures and sells women's clothes. The company began operations on August 1, 2009, and operated at 100% of capacity (35,000 units) during the first month, creating an ending inventory of 2,500 units. During September, the company produced 32,500 garments during the month but sold 35,000 units at $115 per unit. The September manufacturing costs and selling and administrative expenses were as follows:

	Total Cost	Number of Units Produced	Unit Cost
Manufacturing costs in Sept. beginning inventory:			
Variable	$ 115,000	2,500	$46.00
Fixed	32,500	2,500	13.00
Total	$ 147,500		$59.00
September manufacturing costs:			
Variable	$1,495,000	32,500	$46.00
Fixed	455,000	32,500	14.00
Total	$1,950,000		$60.00
Selling and administrative expenses:			
Variable ($21.60 per unit sold)	$ 756,000		
Fixed	230,000		
Total	$ 986,000		

a. Prepare an income statement according to the absorption costing concept for September.
b. Prepare an income statement according to the variable costing concept for September.
c. What is the reason for the difference in the amount of income from operations reported in (a) and (b)?

EX 20-4
Cost of goods manufactured, using variable costing and absorption costing

obj. 1

✓*b. Unit cost of goods manufactured, $36,625*

On July 31, the end of the first year of operations, Myatt Equipment Company manufactured 800 units and sold 700 units. The following income statement was prepared, based on the variable costing concept:

Myatt Equipment Company
Variable Costing Income Statement
For the Year Ended July 31, 2009

Sales		$36,400,000
Variable cost of goods sold:		
Variable cost of goods manufactured	$20,000,000	
Less inventory, August 31	2,500,000	
Variable cost of goods sold		17,500,000
Manufacturing margin		$18,900,000
Variable selling and administrative expenses		4,300,000
Contribution margin		$14,600,000
Fixed costs:		
Fixed manufacturing costs	$ 9,300,000	
Fixed selling and administrative expenses	2,800,000	12,100,000
Income from operations		$ 2,500,000

Determine the unit cost of goods manufactured, based on (a) the variable costing concept and (b) the absorption costing concept.

EX 20-5
Variable costing income statement

obj. 1

On June 30, the end of the first month of operations, Lone Star Petroleum Company prepared the following income statement, based on the absorption costing concept:

✓ Income from
operations, $7,450

Lone Star Petroleum Company
Absorption Costing Income Statement
For the Month Ended June 30, 2009

Sales (3,600 units)		$90,000
Cost of goods sold:		
Cost of goods manufactured (4,200 units)	$67,200	
Less inventory, June 30 (600 units)	9,600	
Cost of goods sold		57,600
Gross profit		$32,400
Selling and administrative expenses		22,550
Income from operations		$ 9,850

If the fixed manufacturing costs were $16,800 and the variable selling and administrative expenses were $7,600, prepare an income statement according to the variable costing concept.

EX 20-6
Absorption costing income statement
obj. 1
✓ Income from
operations, $251,870

On April 30, the end of the first month of operations, Country Manor Furniture Company prepared the following income statement, based on the variable costing concept:

Country Manor Furniture Company
Variable Costing Income Statement
For the Month Ended April 30, 2008

Sales (9,000 units)		$1,080,000
Variable cost of goods sold:		
Variable cost of goods manufactured	$540,000	
Less inventory, April 30 (1,800 units)	90,000	
Variable cost of goods sold		450,000
Manufacturing margin		$ 630,000
Variable selling and administrative expenses		245,000
Contribution margin		$ 385,000
Fixed costs:		
Fixed manufacturing costs	$108,000	
Fixed selling and administrative expenses	43,130	151,130
Income from operations		$ 233,870

Prepare an income statement under absorption costing.

EX 20-7
Variable costing income statement
obj. 1
✓ a. Income from
operations, $10,469

The following data were adapted from a recent income statement of Procter & Gamble Company:

	(in millions)
Net sales	$56,741
Operating costs:	
Cost of products sold	$27,872
Marketing, administrative, and other expenses	18,400
Total operating costs	$46,272
Income from operations	$10,469

Assume that the variable amount of each category of operating costs is as follows:

	(in millions)
Cost of products sold	$16,000
Marketing, administrative, and other expenses	7,300

a. Based on the above data, prepare a variable costing income statement for Procter & Gamble Company, assuming that the company maintained constant inventory levels during the period.
b. If Procter & Gamble reduced its inventories during the period, what impact would that have on the income from operations determined under absorption costing?

EX 20-8

Estimated income statements, using absorption and variable costing

objs. 1, 2

✓ a. 1. Income from operations, $17,950 (9,000 units)

Prior to the first month of operations ending March 31, 2009, Power Storage Inc. estimated the following operating results:

Sales (9,000 × $86)	$774,000
Manufacturing costs (9,000 units):	
Direct materials	486,000
Direct labor	121,500
Variable factory overhead	58,050
Fixed factory overhead	54,000
Fixed selling and administrative expenses	11,900
Variable selling and administrative expenses	24,600

The company is evaluating a proposal to manufacture 10,000 units instead of 9,000 units, thus creating an ending inventory of 1,000 units. Manufacturing the additional units will not change sales, unit variable factory overhead costs, total fixed factory overhead cost, or total selling and administrative expenses.

a. Prepare an estimated income statement, comparing operating results if 9,000 and 10,000 units are manufactured in (1) the absorption costing format and (2) the variable costing format.

b. What is the reason for the difference in income from operations reported for the two levels of production by the absorption costing income statement?

EX 20-9

Variable and absorption costing

obj. 1

✓ a. Contribution margin, $4,525

Whirlpool Corporation had the following abbreviated income statement for a recent year:

	(in millions)
Net sales	$14,317
Cost of goods sold	$11,269
Selling, administrative, and other expenses	2,256
Total expenses	$13,525
Income from operations	$ 792

Assume that there were $2,900 million fixed manufacturing costs and $800 million fixed selling, administrative, and other costs for the year.

    The finished goods inventories at the beginning and end of the year from the balance sheet were as follows:

January 1	$1,701 million
December 31	$1,591 million

Assume that 30% of the beginning and ending inventory consists of fixed costs. Assume work in process and materials inventory were unchanged during the period.

a. Prepare an income statement according to the variable costing concept for Whirlpool Corporation for the recent year.

b. Explain the difference between the amount of income from operations reported under the absorption costing and variable costing concepts.

EX 20-10

Variable and absorption costing—three products

objs. 2, 3

Tahoe Boot Company manufactures and sells three types of boots. The income statements prepared under the absorption costing method for the three boots are as follows:

Tahoe Boot Company
Product Income Statements—Absorption Costing
For the Year Ended December 31, 2008

	Hiking Boots	Fishing Boots	Ski Boots
Revenues	$580,000	$490,000	$420,000
Cost of goods sold	300,000	240,000	280,000
Gross profit	$280,000	$250,000	$140,000
Selling and administrative expenses	240,000	180,000	235,000
Income from operations	$ 40,000	$ 70,000	$ (95,000)

In addition, you have determined the following information with respect to allocated fixed costs:

	Hiking Boots	Fishing Boots	Ski Boots
Fixed costs:			
Cost of goods sold	$90,000	$65,000	$80,000
Selling and administrative expenses	70,000	60,000	80,000

These fixed costs are used to support all three product lines. In addition, you have determined that the inventory is negligible.

The management of the company has deemed the profit performance of the ski boot line as unacceptable. As a result, it has decided to eliminate the ski boot line. Management does not expect to be able to increase sales in the other two lines. However, as a result of eliminating the ski boot line, management expects the profits of the company to increase by $95,000.

a. Do you agree with management's decision and conclusions?
b. Prepare a variable costing income statement for the three products.
c. Use the report in (b) to determine the profit impact of eliminating the ski boot line, assuming no other changes.

EX 20-11
Change in sales mix and contribution margin
obj. **4**

Signature Pen Company manufactures ballpoint and fountain pens and is operating at less than full capacity. Market research indicates that 6,000 additional ballpoint pens and 8,500 additional fountain pens could be sold. The income from operations by unit of product is as follows:

	Ballpoint Pen	Fountain Pen
Sales price	$5.50	$15.00
Variable cost of goods sold	2.80	8.30
Manufacturing margin	$2.70	$ 6.70
Variable selling and administrative expenses	1.10	2.80
Contribution margin	$1.60	$ 3.90
Fixed manufacturing costs	0.50	1.00
Income from operations	$1.10	$ 2.90

Prepare an analysis indicating the increase or decrease in total profitability if 6,000 additional ballpoint pens and 8,500 additional fountain pens are produced and sold, assuming that there is sufficient capacity for the additional production.

EX 20-12
Product profitability analysis
obj. **4**

✔ *a. Plasma contribution margin, $131,200*

ViewPoint Video Inc. manufactures and sells two styles of televisions, LCD panel and plasma, from a single manufacturing facility. The manufacturing facility operates at 100% of capacity. The following per unit information is available for the two products:

	LCD Panel	Plasma
Sales price	$640	$500
Variable cost of goods sold	405	350
Manufacturing margin	$235	$150
Variable selling expenses	115	68
Contribution margin	$120	$ 82
Fixed expenses	70	32
Income from operations	$ 50	$ 50

In addition, the following unit volume information for the period is as follows:

	LCD Panel	Plasma
Sales unit volume	2,500	1,600

a. Prepare a contribution margin by product report. Calculate the contribution margin ratio for each product as a whole percent, rounded to two decimal places.

(continued)

b. What advice would you give to the management of ViewPoint Video Inc. regarding the relative profitability of the two products?

EX 20-13
Territory and product profitability analysis
obj. 4

✓*a. France contribution margin, $1,060,000*

PedalSport Inc. manufactures and sells two styles of bicycles, touring and mountain. These bicycles are sold in two countries, the Netherlands and France. Information about the two bicycles is as follows:

	Touring Bike	Mountain Bike
Sales price	$625	$415
Variable cost of goods sold per unit	230	205
Manufacturing margin per unit	$395	$210
Variable selling expense per unit	260	80
Contribution margin per unit	$135	$130

The sales unit volume for the territories and products for the period is as follows:

	Netherlands	France
Touring Bike	8,000	4,000
Mountain Bike	0	4,000

a. Prepare a contribution margin by sales territory report. Calculate the contribution margin ratio for each territory as a whole percent, rounded to one decimal place.
b. What advice would you give to the management of PedalSport Inc. regarding the relative profitability of the two territories?

EX 20-14
Sales territory and salesperson profitability analysis
obj. 4

✓*a. Raul A. contribution margin, $173,880*

Handy Hardware Company manufactures and sells a wide variety of hardware products to retailers in the Northern and Southern regions. There are two salespersons assigned to each territory. Higher commission rates go to the most experienced salespersons. The following sales statistics are available for each salesperson:

	Northern		Southern	
	Sarah M.	Raul A.	Benson L.	Tamara T.
Average per unit:				
Sales price	$80.00	$70.00	$90.00	$65.00
Variable cost of goods sold	$48.00	$28.00	$54.00	$26.00
Commission rate	10%	14%	14%	10%
Units sold	6,200	5,400	5,000	8,000
Manufacturing margin ratio	40%	60%	40%	60%

a. 1. Prepare a contribution margin by salesperson report. Calculate the contribution margin ratio for each salesperson.
   2. Interpret the report.
b. 1. Prepare a contribution margin by territory report. Calculate the contribution margin for each territory as a whole percent, rounded to one decimal place.
   2. Interpret the report.

EX 20-15
Segment profitability analysis
obj. 4

✓*a. North America contribution margin, $3,495.20*

Provided below are the marketing segment sales for Caterpillar, Inc., for a recent year.

Caterpillar, Inc.
Machinery and Engines Marketing Segment Sales
(in millions)

	Asia/Pacific	Europe/Africa/ Middle East (EAME)	Latin America	Power Products	North America
Sales	$2,462	$4,441	$2,275	$4,669	$10,998

The Power Products segment designs, manufactures, and markets engines. The geographic segments sell Caterpillar equipment to their respective regions.

Assume the following information:

	Asia/Pacific	Europe/Africa/ Middle East (EAME)	Latin America	Power Products	North America
Variable cost of goods sold as a percent of sales	50%	60%	45%	60%	52%
Dealer commissions as a percent of sales	8%	12%	8%	5%	8%
Variable promotion expenses (in millions)	$400	$450	$300	$750	$900

a. Use the sales information and the additional assumed information to prepare a contribution margin by segment report. Calculate the contribution margin ratio for each segment as a whole percent, rounded to one decimal place.

b. Prepare a table showing the manufacturing margin, dealer commissions, and variable promotion expenses as a percent of sales for each segment. Round whole percents to one decimal place.

c. Use the information in (a) and (b) to interpret the segment performance.

EX 20-16
Segment contribution margin analysis
objs. 4, 6

REAL WORLD

✓ a. Film, $8,889.75, 75%

The operating revenues of the four largest business segments for Time Warner, Inc., for a recent year are shown below. Each segment includes a number of businesses, examples of which are indicated in parentheses.

Time Warner, Inc.
Segment Revenues
(in millions)

AOL	$ 8,692
Cable (TWC, Inc.)	8,484
Filmed Entertainment (Warner Bros.)	11,853
Networks (CNN, HBO, WB)	9,054
Publishing (*Time, People, Sports Illustrated*)	5,565

Assume that the variable costs as a percent of sales for each segment are as follows:

AOL	15%
Cable	15%
Filmed Entertainment	25%
Networks	20%
Publishing	75%

a. Determine the contribution margin and contribution margin ratio for each segment from the above information.

b. Why is the contribution margin ratio for the publishing segment smaller than for the other segments?

c. Does your answer to (b) mean that the other segments are more profitable businesses than the publishing segment?

EX 20-17
Contribution margin analysis—sales
obj. 4

Back Beat Music Company sells recorded CD music. Management decided early in the year to reduce the price of the CD in order to increase sales volume. As a result, for the year ended December 31, 2009, the sales increased by $27,000 from the planned level of $171,000. The following information is available from the accounting records for the year ended December 31, 2009:

	Actual	Planned	Difference— Increase (Decrease)
Sales	$198,000	$171,000	$27,000
Number of units sold	12,000	9,500	2,500
Sales price	$16.50	$18.00	$(1.50)
Variable cost per unit	$8.00	$8.00	0

(continued)

a. Prepare an analysis of the sales quantity and price factors.
b. Did the price decrease generate sufficient volume to result in a net increase in contribution margin if the actual variable cost per unit was $8, as planned?

EX 20-18
Contribution margin analysis—sales
obj. 4

✓ *Sales quantity factor, $(82,500)*

The following data for Aesthetic Products Inc. are available:

For the Year Ended December 31, 2008	Actual	Planned	Difference—Increase or (Decrease)
Sales	$2,537,500	$2,475,000	$ 62,500
Less:			
Variable cost of goods sold	$1,334,000	$1,305,000	$ 29,000
Variable selling and administrative expenses	261,000	292,500	(31,500)
Total variable costs	$1,595,000	$1,597,500	$ (2,500)
Contribution margin	$ 942,500	$ 877,500	$ 65,000
Number of units sold	14,500	15,000	
Per unit:			
Sales price	$175.00	$165.00	
Variable cost of goods sold	92.00	87.00	
Variable selling and administrative expenses	18.00	19.50	

Prepare an analysis of the sales quantity and price factors.

EX 20-19
Contribution margin analysis—variable costs
obj. 4

✓ *Variable cost of goods sold unit cost factor, $72,500*

Based upon the data in Exercise 20-18, prepare a contribution analysis of the variable costs for Aesthetic Products Inc. for the year ended December 31, 2008.

EX 20-20
Variable costing income statement—service company
objs. 4, 6

Atlantic Railroad Company transports commodities among three routes (city-pairs): Atlanta/Baltimore, Baltimore/Pittsburgh, and Pittsburgh/Atlanta. Significant costs, their cost behavior, and activity rates for August 2008 are as follows:

Cost	Amount	Cost Behavior	Activity Rate
Labor costs for loading and unloading railcars	$275,600	Variable	$53 per railcar
Fuel costs	602,000	Variable	14 per train-mile
Train crew labor costs	344,000	Variable	8 per train-mile
Switchyard labor costs	187,200	Variable	36 per railcar
Track and equipment depreciation	225,000	Fixed	
Maintenance	150,000	Fixed	

Operating statistics from the management information system reveal the following for August:

	Atlanta/ Baltimore	Baltimore/ Pittsburgh	Pittsburgh/ Atlanta	Total
Number of train-miles	15,100	11,900	16,000	43,000
Number of railcars	600	2,975	1,625	5,200
Revenue per railcar	$640	$320	$510	

a. Prepare a contribution margin by route report for Atlantic Railroad Company for the month of August. Calculate the contribution margin ratio in whole percents, rounded to one decimal place.
b. Evaluate the route performance of the railroad using the report in (a).

EX 20-21
Contribution margin reporting and analysis—service company
objs. 5, 6

The management of Atlantic Railroad Company introduced in Exercise 20-20 improved the profitability of the Atlanta/Baltimore route in September by reducing the price of a railcar from $640 to $580. This price reduction increased the demand for rail services. Thus, the number of railcars increased by 200 railcars to a total of 800 railcars. This was accomplished by increasing the size of each train but not the number of trains. Thus, the number of train-miles was unchanged. All the activity rates remained unchanged.

a. Prepare a contribution margin report for the Atlanta/Baltimore route for September. Calculate the contribution margin ratio in percentage terms to one decimal place.
b. Prepare a contribution margin analysis to evaluate management's actions in September. Assume that the September planned quantity, price, and unit cost was the same as August.

EX 20-22
Variable costing income statement and contribution margin analysis—service company
objs. 5, 6

The actual and planned data for Sage University for the Fall term 2008 were as follows:

	Actual	Planned
Enrollment	4,700	4,300
Tuition per credit hour	$125	$140
Credit hours	63,000	45,000
Registration, records, and marketing cost per enrolled student	$290	$290
Instructional costs per credit hour	$66	$62
Depreciation on classrooms and equipment	$860,000	$860,000

Registration, records, and marketing costs vary by the number of enrolled students, while instructional costs vary by the number of credit hours. Depreciation is a fixed cost.

a. Prepare a variable costing income statement showing the contribution margin and income from operations for the Fall 2008 term.
b. Prepare a contribution margin analysis report comparing planned with actual performance for the Fall 2008 term.

Problems Series A

PR 20-1A
Absorption and variable costing income statements
objs. 1, 2

✓ *2. Contribution margin, $170,275*

During the first month of operations ended September 30, 2008, Zap Electronics Inc. manufactured 7,400 modems, of which 6,950 were sold. Operating data for the month are summarized as follows:

Sales		$764,500
Manufacturing costs:		
Direct materials	$362,600	
Direct labor	111,000	
Variable manufacturing cost	96,200	
Fixed manufacturing cost	48,100	617,900
Selling and administrative expenses:		
Variable	$ 59,075	
Fixed	27,800	86,875

Instructions
1. Prepare an income statement based on the absorption costing concept.
2. Prepare an income statement based on the variable costing concept.
3. Explain the reason for the difference in the amount of income from operations reported in (1) and (2).

PR 20-2A
Income statements under absorption costing and variable costing
objs. 1, 2

The demand for shampoo, one of numerous products manufactured by Venus Beauty Products Inc., has dropped sharply because of recent competition from a similar product. The company's chemists are currently completing tests of various new formulas, and it is anticipated that the manufacture of a superior product can be started on March 1, one month hence. No changes will be needed in the present production facilities to manufacture the new product because only the mixture of the various materials will be changed.

✓ *2. Contribution*
margin, $193,375

The controller has been asked by the president of the company for advice on whether to continue production during February or to suspend the manufacture of shampoo until March 1. The controller has assembled the following pertinent data:

Venus Beauty Products Inc.
Income Statement—Shampoo
For the Month Ended January 31, 2008

Sales (70,000 units)	$868,000
Cost of goods sold	708,500
Gross profit	$159,500
Selling and administrative expenses	155,000
Income from operations..	$ 4,500

The production costs and selling and administrative expenses, based on production of 70,000 units in January, are as follows:

Direct materials	$ 2.30 per unit
Direct labor	2.85 per unit
Variable manufacturing cost	1.40 per unit
Variable selling and administrative expenses	1.60 per unit
Fixed manufacturing costs	250,000 for January
Fixed selling and administrative expenses	43,000 for January

Sales for February are expected to drop about 35% below those of the preceding month. No significant changes are anticipated in the fixed costs or variable costs per unit. No extra costs will be incurred in discontinuing operations in the portion of the plant associated with shampoo. The inventory of shampoo at the beginning and end of February is expected to be inconsequential.

Instructions

1. Prepare an estimated income statement in absorption costing form for February for shampoo, assuming that production continues during the month.
2. Prepare an estimated income statement in variable costing form for February for shampoo, assuming that production continues during the month.
3. What would be the estimated loss in income from operations if the shampoo production were temporarily suspended for February?
4. ▭▬▸ What advice should the controller give to management?

PR 20-3A
Absorption and variable costing income statements for two months and analysis

objs. 1, 2

✓ *2. a. Manufacturing margin, $18,560*

During the first month of operations ended October 31, 2008, Sweet Occasions Inc. baked 3,200 cakes, of which 2,900 were sold. Operating data for the month are summarized as follows:

Sales		$36,250
Baking costs:		
Direct materials	$11,200	
Direct labor	5,440	
Variable manufacturing cost	2,880	
Fixed manufacturing cost	3,840	23,360
Selling and administrative expenses:		
Variable	$ 2,900	
Fixed	1,305	4,205

During November, Sweet Occasions Inc. baked 2,600 cakes and sold 2,900 cakes. Operating data for November are summarized as follows:

Sales		$36,250
Baking costs:		
Direct materials	$9,100	
Direct labor	4,420	
Variable manufacturing cost	2,340	
Fixed manufacturing cost	3,840	19,700
Selling and administrative expenses:		
Variable	$2,900	
Fixed	1,305	4,205

Instructions

1. Using the absorption costing concept, prepare income statements for (a) October and (b) November.
2. Using the variable costing concept, prepare income statements for (a) October and (b) November.
3. a. ▭▬▶ Explain the reason for the differences in the amount of income from operations in (1) and (2) for October.
   b. ▭▬▶ Explain the reason for the differences in the amount of income from operations in (1) and (2) for November.
4. Based upon your answers to (1) and (2), did Sweet Occasions Inc. operate more profitably in October or in November? Explain.

PR 20-4A
Salespersons' report and analysis
obj. 4

✓ 1. Michel contribution margin ratio, 29.5%

Tumbleweed Western Wear Inc. employs seven salespersons to sell and distribute its product throughout the state. Data taken from reports received from the salespersons during the year ended June 30, 2008, are as follows:

Salesperson	Total Sales	Variable Cost of Goods Sold	Variable Selling Expenses
Corso	$360,000	$180,000	$ 74,880
Eastwood	470,000	211,500	82,250
Lassiter	510,000	260,100	122,400
Michel	490,000	230,300	115,150
Ng	430,000	202,100	116,100
Ramon	490,000	235,200	88,200
Wayne	480,000	232,800	105,600

Instructions

1. Prepare a table indicating contribution margin, variable cost of goods sold as a percent of sales, variable selling expenses as a percent of sales, and contribution margin ratio by salesperson (round whole percent to one digit after decimal point).
2. Which salesperson generated the highest contribution margin ratio for the year and why?
3. Briefly list factors other than contribution margin that should be considered in evaluating the performance of salespersons.

PR 20-5A
Variable costing income statement and effect on income of change in operations
obj. 4

✓ 3. Income from operations, $99,750

Portable Seating Company manufactures three sizes of folding chairs—small (S), medium (M), and large (L). The income statement has consistently indicated a net loss for the M size, and management is considering three proposals: (1) continue Size M, (2) discontinue Size M and reduce total output accordingly, or (3) discontinue Size M and conduct an advertising campaign to expand the sales of Size S so that the entire plant capacity can continue to be used.

If Proposal 2 is selected and Size M is discontinued and production curtailed, the annual fixed production costs and fixed operating expenses could be reduced by $150,000 and $30,000, respectively. If Proposal 3 is selected, it is anticipated that an additional annual expenditure of $90,000 for the salary of an assistant brand manager (classified as a fixed operating expense) would yield an increase of 125% in Size S sales volume. It is also assumed that the increased production of Size S would utilize the plant facilities released by the discontinuance of Size M.

The sales and costs have been relatively stable over the past few years, and they are expected to remain so for the foreseeable future. The income statement for the past year ended January 31, 2009, is as follows:

	Size			
	S	M	L	Total
Sales	$1,050,000	$1,150,000	$1,000,000	$3,200,000
Cost of goods sold:				
Variable costs	$ 570,000	$ 760,000	$ 600,000	$1,930,000
Fixed costs	255,000	305,000	265,000	825,000
Total cost of goods sold	$ 825,000	$1,065,000	$ 865,000	$2,755,000
Gross profit	$ 225,000	$ 85,000	$ 135,000	$ 445,000

(continued)

	Size			
	S	**M**	**L**	**Total**
Less operating expenses:				
Variable expenses	$ 125,000	$ 115,000	$ 90,000	$ 330,000
Fixed expenses	34,000	45,000	15,000	94,000
Total operating expenses	$ 159,000	$ 160,000	$ 105,000	$ 424,000
Income from operations	$ 66,000	$ (75,000)	$ 30,000	$ 21,000

Instructions

1. Prepare an income statement for the past year in the variable costing format. Use the following headings:

Size

S   M   L   Total

   Data for each style should be reported through contribution margin. The fixed costs should be deducted from the total contribution margin, as reported in the "Total" column, to determine income from operations.
2. Based on the income statement prepared in (1) and the other data presented above, determine the amount by which total annual income from operations would be reduced below its present level if Proposal 2 is accepted.
3. Prepare an income statement in the variable costing format, indicating the projected annual income from operations if Proposal 3 is accepted. Use the following headings:

Size

S   L   Total

   Data for each style should be reported through contribution margin. The fixed costs should be deducted from the total contribution margin as reported in the "Total" column. For purposes of this problem, the additional expenditure of $90,000 for the assistant brand manager's salary can be added to the fixed operating expenses.
4. By how much would total annual income increase above its present level if Proposal 3 is accepted? Explain.

PR 20-6A
Contribution margin analysis
obj. 5

✓ *1. Sales price factor, $(26,000)*

Bay Company manufactures only one product. For the year ended December 31, 2008, the contribution margin increased by $2,000 from the planned level of $258,000. The president of Bay Company has expressed serious concern about such a small increase and has requested a follow-up report.

   The following data have been gathered from the accounting records for the year ended December 31, 2008:

	Actual	**Planned**	**Difference— Increase or (Decrease)**
Sales	$773,500	$738,000	$35,500
Less:			
Variable cost of goods sold	$396,500	$384,000	$12,500
Variable selling and administrative expenses	117,000	96,000	21,000
Total	$513,500	$480,000	$33,500
Contribution margin	$260,000	$258,000	$ 2,000
Number of units sold	6,500	6,000	
Per unit:			
Sales price	$119.00	$123.00	
Variable cost of goods sold	61.00	64.00	
Variable selling and administrative expenses	18.00	16.00	

Instructions

1. Prepare a contribution margin analysis report for the year ended December 31, 2008.

2. ▰▰▱▸ At a meeting of the board of directors on January 30, 2009, the president, after reviewing the contribution margin analysis report, made the following comment:

"It looks as if the price decrease of $4.00 had the effect of increasing sales. However, we lost control over the variable cost of goods sold and variable selling and administrative expenses. Let's look into these expenses and get them under control! Also, let's consider decreasing the sales price to $110 to increase sales further."

Do you agree with the president's comment? Explain.

Problems Series B

PR 20-1B
Absorption and variable costing income statements

objs. 1, 2

✓ *2. Income from operations, $156,200*

During the first month of operations ended May 31, 2008, Frost Zone Appliance Company manufactured 1,540 refrigerators, of which 1,430 were sold. Operating data for the month are summarized as follows:

Sales		$972,400
Manufacturing costs:		
Direct materials	$385,000	
Direct labor	161,700	
Variable manufacturing cost	61,600	
Fixed manufacturing cost	115,500	723,800
Selling and administrative expenses:		
Variable	$ 92,950	
Fixed	42,900	135,850

Instructions
1. Prepare an income statement based on the absorption costing concept.
2. Prepare an income statement based on the variable costing concept.
3. ▰▰▱▸ Explain the reason for the difference in the amount of income from operations reported in (1) and (2).

PR 20-2B
Income statements under absorption costing and variable costing

objs. 1, 2

✓ *2. Contribution margin, $79,776*

The demand for solvent, one of numerous products manufactured by Erie Products Inc., has dropped sharply because of recent competition from a similar product. The company's chemists are currently completing tests of various new formulas, and it is anticipated that the manufacture of a superior product can be started on May 1, one month hence. No changes will be needed in the present production facilities to manufacture the new product because only the mixture of the various materials will be changed.

The controller has been asked by the president of the company for advice on whether to continue production during April or to suspend the manufacture of solvent until May 1. The controller has assembled the following pertinent data:

Erie Products Inc.
Income Statement—Solvent
For the Month Ended March 31, 2009

Sales (3,600 units)	$360,000
Cost of goods sold	295,080
Gross profit	$ 64,920
Selling and administrative expenses	59,700
Income from operations	$ 5,220

The production costs and selling and administrative expenses, based on production of 3,600 units in March, are as follows:

Direct materials	$ 39.00 per unit
Direct labor	13.50 per unit
Variable manufacturing cost	12.80 per unit
Variable selling and administrative expenses	7.00 per unit
Fixed manufacturing costs	60,000 for March
Fixed selling and administrative expenses	34,500 for March

Sales for April are expected to drop about 20% below those of the preceding month. No significant changes are anticipated in the fixed costs or variable costs per unit. No extra costs will be incurred in discontinuing operations in the portion of the plant associated with solvent. The inventory of solvent at the beginning and end of April is expected to be inconsequential.

Instructions

1. Prepare an estimated income statement in absorption costing form for April for solvent, assuming that production continues during the month.
2. Prepare an estimated income statement in variable costing form for April for solvent, assuming that production continues during the month.
3. What would be the estimated loss in income from operations if the solvent production were temporarily suspended for April?
4. ▭▬▶ What advice should the controller give to management?

PR 20-3B

Absorption and variable costing income statements for two months and analysis

objs. 1, 2

✓1. b. Income from operations, $30,600

During the first month of operations ended July 31, 2009, Buzz T-Shirt Company produced 42,000 T-shirts, of which 39,000 were sold. Operating data for the month are summarized as follows:

Sales		$448,500
Manufacturing costs:		
Direct materials	$268,800	
Direct labor	71,400	
Variable manufacturing cost	33,600	
Fixed manufacturing cost	31,500	405,300
Selling and administrative expenses:		
Variable	$ 21,450	
Fixed	15,600	37,050

During August, Buzz T-Shirt Company produced 36,000 T-shirts and sold 39,000 shirts. Operating data for August are summarized as follows:

Sales		$448,500
Manufacturing costs:		
Direct materials	$230,400	
Direct labor	61,200	
Variable manufacturing cost	28,800	
Fixed manufacturing cost	31,500	351,900
Selling and administrative expenses:		
Variable	$ 21,450	
Fixed	15,600	37,050

Instructions

1. Using the absorption costing concept, prepare income statements for (a) July and (b) August.
2. Using the variable costing concept, prepare income statements for (a) July and (b) August.
3. a. ▭▬▶ Explain the reason for the differences in the amount of income from operations in (1) and (2) for July.
   b. ▭▬▶ Explain the reason for the differences in the amount of income from operations in (1) and (2) for August.
4. Based upon your answers to (1) and (2), did Buzz T-Shirt Company operate more profitably in July or in August? Explain.

PR 20-4B

Salespersons' report and analysis

obj. 4

Gabriel Horn Company employs seven salespersons to sell and distribute its product throughout the state. Data taken from reports received from the salespersons during the year ended December 31, 2008, are as follows:

✓1. Severinsen
contribution margin
ratio, 25%

Salesperson	Total Sales	Variable Cost of Goods Sold	Variable Selling Expenses
Armstrong	$550,000	$330,000	$110,000
Brown	550,000	330,000	119,900
Davis	450,000	271,000	80,000
Driscoll	500,000	200,000	100,000
Marsalis	525,000	300,300	99,750
Morrison	680,000	265,000	109,000
Severinsen	490,000	277,500	90,000

Instructions

1. Prepare a table indicating contribution margin, variable cost of goods sold as a percent of sales, variable selling expenses as a percent of sales, and contribution margin ratio by salesperson. Round whole percents to a single digit.
2. Which salesperson generated the highest contribution margin ratio for the year and why?
3. Briefly list factors other than contribution margin that should be considered in evaluating the performance of salespersons.

PR 20-5B
Segment variable costing income statement and effect on income of change in operations
obj. 4

✓1. Income from operations, $75,000

Canadian Coat Company manufactures three sizes of winter coats—small (S), medium (M), and large (L). The income statement has consistently indicated a net loss for the M size, and management is considering three proposals: (1) continue Size M, (2) discontinue Size M and reduce total output accordingly, or (3) discontinue Size M and conduct an advertising campaign to expand the sales of Size S so that the entire plant capacity can continue to be used.

If Proposal 2 is selected and Size M is discontinued and production curtailed, the annual fixed production costs and fixed operating expenses could be reduced by $40,000 and $28,000, respectively. If Proposal 3 is selected, it is anticipated that an additional annual expenditure of $30,000 for the rental of additional warehouse space would yield an increase of 125% in Size S sales volume. It is also assumed that the increased production of Size S would utilize the plant facilities released by the discontinuance of Size M.

The sales and costs have been relatively stable over the past few years, and they are expected to remain so for the foreseeable future. The income statement for the past year ended June 30, 2008, is as follows:

	S	M	L	Total
		Size		
Sales	$580,000	$640,000	$830,000	$2,050,000
Cost of goods sold:				
Variable costs	$260,000	$310,000	$380,000	$ 950,000
Fixed costs	65,000	120,000	150,000	335,000
Total cost of goods sold	$325,000	$430,000	$530,000	$1,285,000
Gross profit	$255,000	$210,000	$300,000	$ 765,000
Less operating expenses:				
Variable expenses	$115,000	$135,000	$170,000	$ 420,000
Fixed expenses	80,000	90,000	100,000	270,000
Total operating expenses	$195,000	$225,000	$270,000	$ 690,000
Income from operations	$ 60,000	$ (15,000)	$ 30,000	$ 75,000

Instructions

1. Prepare an income statement for the past year in the variable costing format. Use the following headings:

S	M	L	Total
		Size	

Data for each style should be reported through contribution margin. The fixed costs should be deducted from the total contribution margin, as reported in the "Total" column, to determine income from operations.

(continued)

2. Based on the income statement prepared in (1) and the other data presented, determine the amount by which total annual income from operations would be reduced below its present level if Proposal 2 is accepted.
3. Prepare an income statement in the variable costing format, indicating the projected annual income from operations if Proposal 3 is accepted. Use the following headings:

	Size	
S	L	Total

Data for each style should be reported through contribution margin. The fixed costs should be deducted from the total contribution margin as reported in the "Total" column. For purposes of this problem, the expenditure of $30,000 for the rental of additional warehouse space can be added to the fixed operating expenses.
4. By how much would total annual income increase above its present level if Proposal 3 is accepted? Explain.

PR 20-6B

Contribution margin analysis

obj. 5

1. Sales quantity factor, $(38,000)

Lyon Industries Inc. manufactures only one product. For the year ended December 31, 2008, the contribution margin decreased by $10,000 from the planned level of $110,000. The president of Lyon Industries Inc. has expressed some concern about this decrease and has requested a follow-up report.

The following data have been gathered from the accounting records for the year ended December 31, 2008:

	Actual	Planned	Difference—Increase (Decrease)
Sales	$430,000	$418,000	$ 12,000
Less:			
Variable cost of goods sold	190,000	198,000	(8,000)
Variable selling and administrative expense	140,000	110,000	30,000
Total	$330,000	$308,000	$ 22,000
Contribution margin	$100,000	$110,000	$(10,000)
Number of units sold	10,000	11,000	
Per unit:			
Sales price	$43.00	$38.00	
Variable cost of goods sold	19.00	18.00	
Variable selling and administrative expenses	14.00	10.00	

Instructions

1. Prepare a contribution margin analysis report for the year ended December 31, 2008.
2. ▬▬▬► At a meeting of the board of directors on January 30, 2009, the president, after reviewing the contribution margin analysis report, made the following comment:

It looks as if the price increase of $5.00 had the effect of decreasing sales volume. However, this was a favorable tradeoff. The variable cost of goods sold was less than planned. Apparently, we are efficiently managing our variable cost of goods sold. However, the variable selling and administrative expenses appear out of control. Let's look into these expenses and get them under control! Also, let's consider increasing the sales price to $50 and continue this favorable tradeoff between higher price and lower volume.

Do you agree with the president's comment? Explain.

Special Activities

SA 20-1

Ethics and professional conduct in business

The Sporting Goods Division of Star Brands Inc. uses absorption costing for profit reporting. The general manager of the Sporting Goods Division is concerned about meeting the income objectives of the division. At the beginning of the reporting period, the division had an adequate supply of inventory. The general manager has decided to increase production of goods in the plant in order to allocate fixed manufacturing cost over a greater number of units. Unfortunately, the increased production cannot be sold and will increase the inventory. However, the impact on earnings will be positive because the lower cost per unit will be matched against sales. The general manager has come to Blaine Thompson, the controller, to determine exactly how much additional production is required in order to increase net income enough to meet the division's profit objectives. Thompson analyzes the data and determines that the inventory will need to be increased by 30% in order to absorb enough fixed costs and meet the income objective. Thompson reports this information to the division manager.

Discuss whether Thompson is acting in an ethical manner.

SA 20-2
Inventories under absorption costing

Circle-D manufactures control panels for the electronics industry and has just completed its first year of operations. The following discussion took place between the controller, Nelson Driver, and the company president, Emily Prince:

Emily: I've been looking over our first year's performance by quarters. Our earnings have been increasing each quarter, even though our sales have been flat and our prices and costs have not changed. Why is this?

Nelson: Our actual sales have stayed even throughout the year, but we've been increasing the utilization of our factory every quarter. By keeping our factory utilization high, we will keep our costs down by allocating the fixed plant costs over a greater number of units. Naturally, this causes our cost per unit to be lower than it would be otherwise.

Emily: Yes, but what good is this if we have been unable to sell everything that we make? Our inventory is also increasing.

Nelson: This is true. However, our unit costs are lower because of the additional production. When these lower costs are matched against sales, it has a positive impact on our earnings.

Emily: Are you saying that we are able to create additional earnings merely by building inventory? Can this be true?

Nelson: Well, I've never thought about it quite that way . . . but I guess so.

Emily: And another thing. What will happen if we begin to reduce our production in order to liquidate the inventory? Don't tell me our earnings will go down even though our production effort drops!

Nelson: Well . . .

Emily: There must be a better way. I'd like our quarterly income statements to reflect what's really going on. I don't want our income reports to reward building inventory and penalize reducing inventory.

Nelson: I'm not sure what I can do—we have to follow generally accepted accounting principles.

1. Why does reporting income under generally accepted accounting principles "reward" building inventory and "penalize" reducing inventory?
2. ➤ What advice would you give to Nelson in responding to Emily's concern about the present method of profit reporting?

SA 20-3
Segmented contribution margin analysis

ACD Inc. manufactures and sells devices used in cardiovascular surgery. The company has two salespersons, Harken and King.

A contribution margin by salesperson report was prepared as follows:

ACD Inc.
Contribution Margin by Salesperson

	Harken	King
Sales	$180,000	$200,000
Variable cost of goods sold	81,000	130,000
Manufacturing margin	$ 99,000	$ 70,000
Variable promotion expenses	$ 52,200	$ 18,000
Variable sales commission expenses	19,800	22,000
	$ 72,000	$ 40,000
Contribution margin	$ 27,000	$ 30,000
Manufacturing margin as a percent of sales (manufacturing margin ratio)	55.00%	35.00%
Contribution margin ratio	15.00%	15.00%

▰▰▰▰▶ Interpret the report, and provide recommendations to the two salespersons for improving profitability.

SA 20-4
Margin analysis

Empire Equipment Inc. manufactures and sells kitchen cooking products throughout the state. The company employs four salespersons. The following contribution margin by salesperson analysis was prepared:

Empire Equipment Inc.
Contribution Margin Analysis by Salesperson

	Borland	Chow	Juarez	Mann
Sales	$130,000	$150,000	$140,000	$100,000
Variable cost of goods sold	52,000	90,000	84,000	60,000
Manufacturing margin	$ 78,000	$ 60,000	$ 56,000	$ 40,000
Variable selling expenses:				
Commissions	$ 6,000	$ 7,500	$ 7,000	$ 5,000
Promotion expenses	39,500	37,500	35,000	25,000
Total variable selling expenses	$ 45,500	$ 45,000	$ 42,000	$ 30,000
Contribution margin	$ 32,500	$ 15,000	$ 14,000	$ 10,000

1. Calculate the manufacturing margin as a percent of sales and the contribution margin ratio for each salesperson.
2. ▰▰▰▶ Explain the results of the analysis.

SA 20-5
Contribution margin analysis

Picasso Art Supply Company sells artistic supplies to retailers in three different states—North Carolina, Tennessee, and Virginia. The following profit analysis by state was prepared by the company:

	North Carolina	Tennessee	Virginia
Revenue	$400,000	$350,000	$420,000
Cost of goods sold	200,000	190,000	200,000
Gross profit	$200,000	$160,000	$220,000
Selling expenses	130,000	120,000	150,000
Income from operations	$ 70,000	$ 40,000	$ 70,000

The following fixed costs have also been provided:

	North Carolina	Tennessee	Virginia
Fixed manufacturing costs	$40,000	$80,000	$45,000
Fixed selling expenses	30,000	48,000	40,400

In addition, assume that inventories have been negligible.

Management believes it could increase state sales by 20%, without increasing any of the fixed costs, by spending an additional $15,000 per state on advertising.

1. Prepare a contribution margin by state report for Picasso Art Supply Company.
2. Determine how much state operating profit will be generated for an additional $15,000 per state on advertising.
3. Which state will provide the greatest profit return for a $15,000 increase in advertising? Why?

SA 20-6
Absorption costing

Goll Company is a family-owned business in which you own 20% of the common stock and your brothers and sisters own the remaining shares. The employment contract of Goll's new president, Glen Nash, stipulates a base salary of $150,000 per year plus 7% of income from operations in excess of $800,000. Nash uses the absorption costing method of reporting income from operations, which has averaged approximately $1,000,000 for the past several years.

Sales for 2008, Nash's first year as president of Goll Company, are estimated at 100,000 units at a selling price of $60 per unit. To maximize the use of Goll's productive capacity,

Nash has decided to manufacture 150,000 units, rather than the 100,000 units of estimated sales. The beginning inventory at January 1, 2008, is insignificant in amount, and the manufacturing costs and selling and administrative expenses for the production of 100,000 and 150,000 units are as follows:

100,000 Units to Be Manufactured

	Total Cost	Number of Units	Unit Cost
Manufacturing costs:			
Variable	$3,200,000	100,000	$32
Fixed	900,000	100,000	9
Total	$4,100,000		$41
Selling and administrative expenses:			
Variable	$ 900,000		
Fixed	300,000		
Total	$1,200,000		

150,000 Units to Be Manufactured

	Total Cost	Number of Units	Unit Cost
Manufacturing costs:			
Variable	$4,800,000	150,000	$32
Fixed	900,000	150,000	6
Total	$5,700,000		$38
Selling and administrative expenses:			
Variable	$ 900,000		
Fixed	300,000		
Total	$1,200,000		

1. In one group, prepare an absorption costing income statement for the year ending December 31, 2008, based upon sales of 100,000 units and the manufacture of 100,000 units. In the other group, conduct the same analysis, assuming production of 150,000 units.
2. Explain the difference in the income from operations reported in (1).
3. Compute Nash's total salary for the year 2008, based on sales of 100,000 units and the manufacture of 100,000 units (Group 1) and 150,000 units (Group 2). Compare your answers.
4. In addition to maximizing the use of Goll Company's productive capacity, why might Nash wish to manufacture 150,000 units rather than 100,000 units?
5. Can you suggest an alternative way in which Nash's salary could be determined, using a base salary of $150,000 and 7% of income from operations in excess of $800,000, so that the salary could not be increased by simply manufacturing more units?

Answers to Self-Examination Questions

1. **B** The contribution margin of $260,000 (answer B) is determined by deducting all of the variable costs ($400,000 + $90,000) from sales ($750,000).
2. **A** In a period in which the number of units manufactured exceeds the number of units sold, the income from operations reported under the absorption costing concept is larger than the income from operations reported under the variable costing concept (answer A). This is because a portion of the fixed manufacturing costs are deferred when the absorption costing concept is used. This deferment has the effect of excluding a portion of the fixed manufacturing costs from the current cost of goods sold.
3. **D** (6,000 units × $20 per unit). Answer A incorrectly calculates the difference in income from operations using the variable cost per unit, while Answer B incorrectly calculates the difference in income from operations using the total cost per unit. Answer C is incorrect because variable costing income from operations will be greater than absorption costing income from operations when units manufactured is less than units sold.

4. **C** [2,000 units × ($150,000/12,000 units)]. Answers A and B incorrectly calculate the difference in income from operations using variable cost per unit. When production exceeds sales, absorption costing will include fixed costs in the ending inventory, which causes cost of goods sold to decline and income from operations to increase. Thus, income from operations would not decline (answer D) for a production level of 12,000 units.

5. **C** A difference between planned and actual sales can be attributed to a unit price factor. The $45,000 decrease (answer C) attributed to the quantity factor is determined as follows:

Decrease in number of units sold	5,000
Planned unit sales price	× $9
Quantity factor—decrease	$45,000

The unit price factor can be determined as follows:

Increase in unit sales price	$1
Actual number of units sold	× 80,000
Price factor—increase	$80,000

The increase of $80,000 attributed to the price factor less the decrease of $45,000 attributed to the quantity factor accounts for the $35,000 increase in total sales.

Budgeting

objectives

After studying this chapter, you should be able to:

1. *Describe budgeting, its objectives, and its impact on human behavior.*

2. *Describe the basic elements of the budget process, the two major types of budgeting, and the use of computers in budgeting.*

3. *Describe the master budget for a manufacturing business.*

4. *Prepare the basic income statement budgets for a manufacturing business.*

5. *Prepare balance sheet budgets for a manufacturing business.*

The North Face

Y ou may have financial goals for your life. To achieve these goals, it is necessary to plan for future expenses. For example, you may consider taking a part-time job to save money for school expenses for the coming school year. How much money would you need to earn and save in order to pay these expenses? One way to find an answer to this question would be to prepare a budget. For example, a budget would show an estimate of your expenses associated with school, such as tuition, fees, and books. In addition, you would have expenses for day-to-day living, such as rent, food, and clothing. You might also have expenses for travel and entertainment. Once the school year begins, you can use the budget as a tool for guiding your spending priorities during the year.

The budget is used in businesses in much the same way as it can be used in personal life. For example, The North Face sponsors mountain climbing expeditions throughout the year for professional and amateur climbers. These events require budgeting to plan for the trip expenses, much like you might use a budget to plan a vacation.

Budgeting is also used by The North Face to plan the manufacturing costs associated with its outdoor clothing and equipment production. For example, budgets would be used to determine the number of coats to be produced, number of people to be employed, and amount of material to be purchased. The budget provides the company a "game plan" for the year. In this chapter, you will see how budgets can be used for financial planning and control.

Nature and Objectives of Budgeting

objective **1**

Describe budgeting, its objectives, and its impact on human behavior.

If you were driving across the country, you might plan your trip with the aid of a road map. The road map would lay out your route across the country, identify stopovers, and reduce your chances of getting lost. In the same way, a **budget** charts a course for a business by outlining the plans of the business in financial terms. Like the road map, the budget can help a company navigate through the year and reach the destination, while minimizing bad results.

Although budgets are normally associated with profit-making businesses, they also play an important role in operating most units of government. For example, budgets are important in managing rural school districts and small villages as well as agencies of the federal government. Budgets are also important for managing the operations of churches, hospitals, and other nonprofit institutions. Individuals and families also use budgeting techniques in managing their financial affairs. In this chapter, we emphasize the principles of budgeting in the context of a business organized for profit.

OBJECTIVES OF BUDGETING

Budgeting involves (1) establishing specific goals, (2) executing plans to achieve the goals, and (3) periodically comparing actual results with the goals. These goals include both the overall business goals as well as the specific goals for the individual units within the business. Establishing specific goals for future operations is part of the *planning* function of management, while executing

The chart below shows the estimated portion of your total monthly income that should be budgeted for various living expenses.

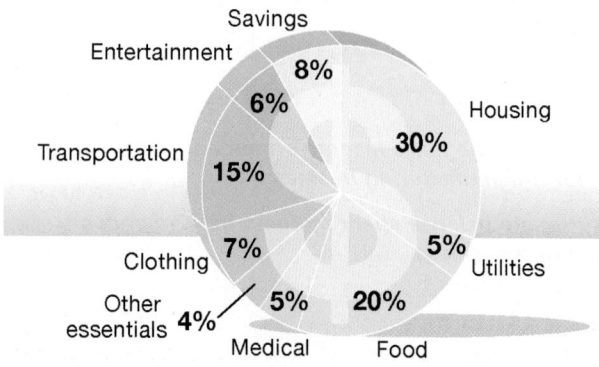

- Savings 8%
- Entertainment 6%
- Housing 30%
- Transportation 15%
- Clothing 7%
- Utilities 5%
- Other essentials 4%
- Medical 5%
- Food 20%

Source: Consumer Credit Counseling Service.

actions to meet the goals is the *directing* function of management. Periodically comparing actual results with these goals and taking appropriate action is the *controlling* function of management. The relationships of these functions are illustrated in Exhibit 1.

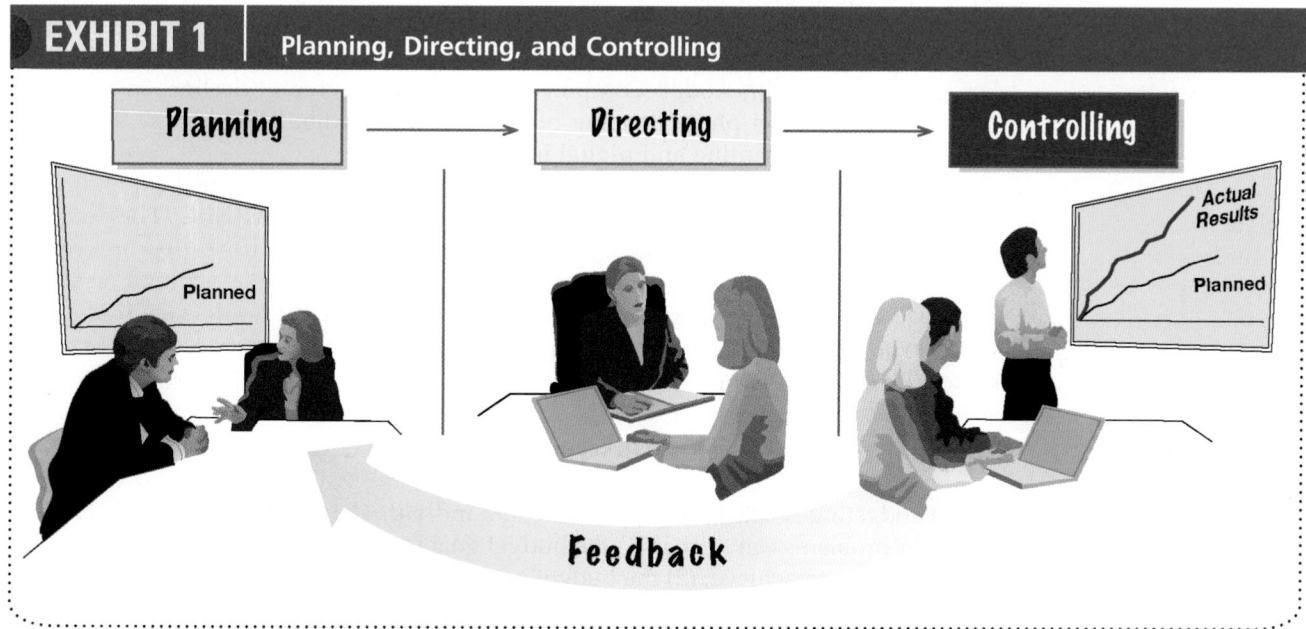

EXHIBIT 1 | Planning, Directing, and Controlling

Planning is also an important part of personal finances. Visa offers an online budget calculator and other helpful personal financial information at **http://www.practical moneyskills.com**.

Planning   A set of goals is often necessary to guide and focus individual and group actions. For example, students set academic goals, athletes set athletic goals, employees set career goals, and businesses set financial goals. In the same way, budgeting supports the planning process by requiring all organizational units to establish their goals for the upcoming period. These goals, in turn, motivate individuals and groups to perform at high levels. For example, General Motors Corporation is using its budget process to plan and execute a reduction of 25,000 manufacturing jobs through 2008 in order to better align its manufacturing capacity with the demand for vehicles.

Planning not only motivates employees to attain goals but also improves overall decision making. During the planning phase of the budget process, all viewpoints are considered, options identified, and cost reduction opportunities assessed. This effort leads to better decision making for the organization. As a result, the budget process may reveal opportunities or threats that were not known prior to the budget planning process. For example, the financial planning process helped Microsoft Corporation plan its expansion into the home and entertainment market with Xbox 360®.

Directing   Once the budget plans are in place, they can be used to direct and coordinate operations in order to achieve the stated goals. For example, your goal to receive an "A" in a course would result in certain activities, such as reading the book, completing assignments, participating in class, and studying for exams. Such actions are fairly easy to direct and coordinate. A business, however, is much more complex and requires more formal direction and coordination. The budget is one way to direct and coordinate business activities and units to achieve stated goals. The budgetary units of an organization are called **responsibility centers**. Each responsibility center is led by a manager who has the authority over and responsibility for the unit's performance.

If there is a change in the external environment, the budget process can also be used by unit managers to readjust the operations. For example, S-K-I Limited uses weather information to plan expenditures at its Killington and Mt. Snow ski resorts in Vermont. When the weather is forecasted to turn cold and dry, the company increases expenditures in snow-making activities and adds to the staff in order to serve a greater number of skiers.

Controlling   As time passes, the actual performance of an operation can be compared against the planned goals. This provides prompt feedback to employees about their performance. If necessary, employees can use such *feedback* to adjust their activities in the future. For example, a salesperson may be given a quota to achieve $100,000 in sales for the period. If the actual sales are only $75,000, the salesperson can use this feedback about underperformance to change sales tactics and improve future sales. Feedback is not only helpful to individuals, but it can also redirect a complete organization. For example, Eastman Kodak Company is responding to recent declines in the traditional chemical-based photo imaging business with an ambitious strategy to expand on-demand photo printing and digital image solutions.

Comparing actual results to the plan also helps prevent unplanned expenditures. The budget encourages employees to establish their spending priorities. For example, departments in universities have budgets to support faculty travel to conferences and meetings. The travel budget communicates to the faculty the upper limit on travel. Often, desired travel exceeds the budget. Thus, the budget requires the faculty to prioritize travel-related opportunities. In the next chapter, we will discuss comparing actual costs with budgeted costs in greater detail.

HUMAN BEHAVIOR AND BUDGETING

In the budgeting process, business, team, and individual goals are established. Human behavior problems can arise if (1) the budget goal is too tight and thus is very hard for the employees to achieve, (2) the budget goal is too loose and thus is very easy for the employees to achieve, or (3) the budget goals of the business conflict with the objectives of the employees. This is illustrated in Exhibit 2.

EXHIBIT 2 | Human Behavior Problems in Budgeting

Budget Goals Too Tight   Budget Goals Too Loose   Conflicting Budget Goals

Setting Budget Goals Too Tightly   People can become discouraged if performance expectations are set too high. For example, would you be inspired or discouraged by a guitar instructor expecting you to play like Eric Clapton after only a few lessons? You'd probably be discouraged. This same kind of problem can occur in businesses if employees view budget goals as unrealistic or unachievable. In such a case, the budget discourages employees from achieving the goals. On the other hand, aggressive but attainable goals are likely to inspire employees to achieve the goals. Therefore, it is important that employees (managers and nonmanagers) be involved in establishing reasonable budget estimates.

Involving all employees encourages cooperation both within and among departments. It also increases awareness of each department's importance to the overall objectives of the company. Employees view budgeting more positively when they have an opportunity to participate in the budget-setting process. This is because employees with a greater sense of control over the budget process will have a greater commitment to achieving its goals. In such cases, budgets are valuable planning tools that increase the possibility of achieving business goals.

Loose budgets may be appropriate in settings involving high uncertainty, such as research and development. The loose budget acts as a "shock absorber," giving managers maneuvering room to minimize work disruptions.

Setting Budget Goals Too Loosely Although it is desirable to establish attainable goals, it is undesirable to plan lower goals than may be possible. Such budget "padding" is termed **budgetary slack**. An example of budgetary slack is including spare employees in the plan. Managers may plan slack in the budget in order to provide a "cushion" for unexpected events or improve the appearance of operations. Budgetary slack can be avoided if lower- and mid-level managers are required to support their spending requirements with operational plans.

Slack budgets can cause employees to develop a "spend it or lose it" mentality. This often occurs at the end of the budget period when actual spending is less than the budget. Employees may attempt to spend the remaining budget (purchase equipment, hire consultants, purchase supplies) in order to avoid having the budget cut next period.

The state of Illinois' budget process requires unspent budget monies to be returned to the state when the fiscal year ends. According to the state comptroller, this encourages "an orgy of spending" at the end of a fiscal year.

Setting Conflicting Budget Goals **Goal conflict** occurs when individual self-interest differs from business objectives or when different departments are given conflicting objectives. Often, such conflicts are subtle. For example, the Sales Department manager may be given a sales goal, while the Manufacturing Department manager may be given a cost reduction goal. It is possible for both goals to conflict. The Sales Department may increase sales by promising customers small product deviations that are difficult and unprofitable to make. This would increase sales at the expense of Manufacturing's expense reduction goal and impact the overall profitability objectives of the firm. Likewise, Manufacturing may schedule the plant for maximum manufacturing efficiency with little regard for actual customer product demand. This would reduce manufacturing costs at the expense of the sales goal and reduce the overall profitability of the firm. Goal conflict can be avoided if budget goals are carefully designed for consistency across all areas of the organization.

Integrity, Objectivity, and Ethics in Business

BUDGET GAMES

The budgeting system is designed to plan and control a business. However, it is common for the budget to be "gamed" by its participants. For example, managers may pad their budgets with excess resources. In this way, the managers have additional resources for unexpected events during the period. If the budget is being used to establish the incentive plan, then sales managers have incentives to understate the sales potential of a territory in order to ensure hitting their quotas. Other times, managers engage in "land grabbing," which occurs when they overstate the sales potential of a territory in order to guarantee access to resources. If managers believe that unspent resources will not roll over to future periods, then they may be encouraged to "spend it or lose it," causing wasteful expenditures. These types of problems can be partially overcome by separating the budget into planning and incentive components. This is why many organizations have two budget processes, one for resource planning and another, more challenging budget, for motivating managers.

Budgeting Systems

Budgeting systems vary among businesses because of such factors as organizational structure, complexity of operations, and management philosophy. Differences in budget systems are even more significant among different types of businesses, such as manufacturers and service businesses. The details of a budgeting system used by an automobile manufacturer such as Ford Motor Company would obviously differ from a service company such as American Airlines. However, the basic budgeting concepts illustrated in the following paragraphs apply to all types of businesses and organizations.

The budgetary period for operating activities normally includes the fiscal year of a business. A year is short enough that future operations can be estimated fairly accurately, yet long enough that the future can be viewed in a broad context. However, to achieve effective control, the annual budgets are usually subdivided into shorter time periods, such as quarters of the year, months, or weeks.

A variation of fiscal-year budgeting, called **continuous budgeting**, maintains a 12-month projection into the future. The 12-month budget is continually revised by removing the data for the period just ended and adding estimated budget data for the same period next year, as shown in Exhibit 3.

Developing budgets for the next fiscal year usually begins several months prior to the end of the current year. This responsibility is normally assigned to a budget committee. Such a committee often consists of the budget director and such high-level executives as the controller, the treasurer, the production manager, and the sales manager. Once the budget has been approved, the budget process is monitored and summarized by the Accounting Department, which reports to the committee.

There are several methods of developing budget estimates. One method, termed **zero-based budgeting**, requires managers to estimate sales, production, and other operating data as though operations are being started for the first time. This approach has the benefit of taking a fresh view of operations each year. A more common approach is to start with last year's budget and revise it for actual results and expected changes for the coming year. Two major budgets using this approach are the static budget and the flexible budget.

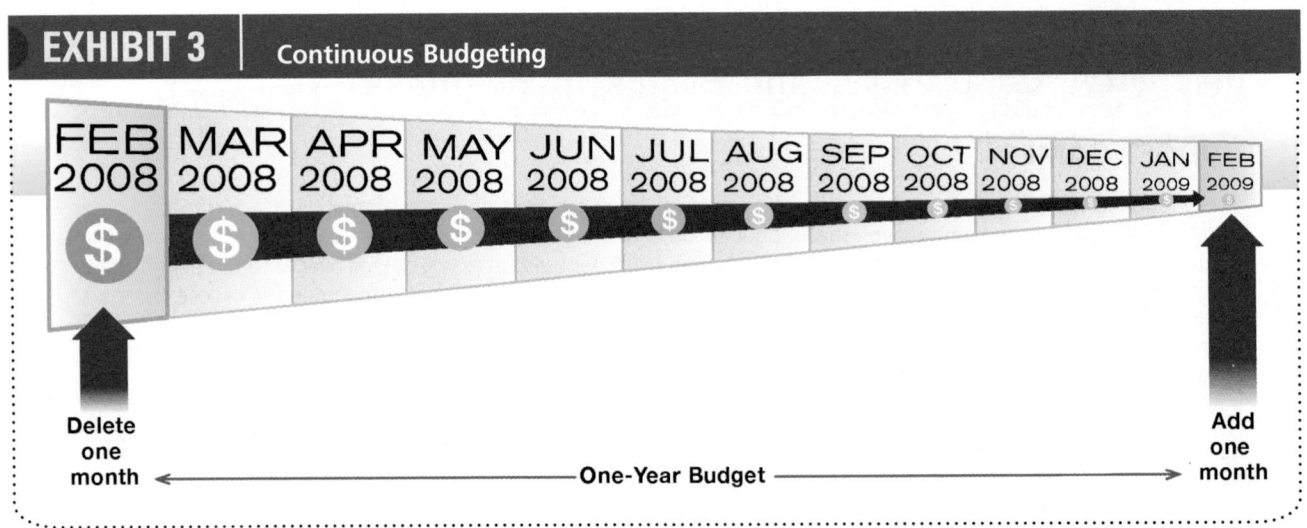

EXHIBIT 3 | **Continuous Budgeting**

FEB 2008 · MAR 2008 · APR 2008 · MAY 2008 · JUN 2008 · JUL 2008 · AUG 2008 · SEP 2008 · OCT 2008 · NOV 2008 · DEC 2008 · JAN 2009 · FEB 2009

Delete one month ← One-Year Budget → Add one month

STATIC BUDGET

A **static budget** shows the expected results of a responsibility center for only one activity level. Once the budget has been determined, it is not changed, even if the activity changes. Static budgeting is used by many service companies and for some administrative functions of manufacturing companies, such as purchasing, engineering, and accounting. For example, the Assembly Department manager for Colter Manufacturing Company prepared the static budget for the upcoming year, shown in Exhibit 4.

EXHIBIT 4

Static Budget

	A	B	
	Colter Manufacturing Company		
	Assembly Department Budget		
	For the Year Ending July 31, 2008		
1	Direct labor	$40,000	1
2	Electric power	5,000	2
3	Supervisor salaries	15,000	3
4	Total department costs	$60,000	4

A disadvantage of static budgets is that they do not adjust for changes in activity levels. For example, assume that the actual amounts spent by the Assembly Department of Colter Manufacturing totaled $72,000, which is $12,000 or 20% ($12,000/$60,000) more than budgeted. Is this good news or bad news? At first you might think that this is a bad result. However, this conclusion may not be valid, since static budget results may be difficult to interpret. To illustrate, assume that the assembly manager developed the budget based on plans to assemble *8,000* units during the year. However, if *10,000* units were actually produced, should the additional $12,000 in spending in excess of the budget be considered "bad news"? Maybe not. The Assembly Department provided 25% (2,000 units/8,000 units) more output for only 20% more cost.

Business Connections

BUILD VERSUS HARVEST

Budgeting systems are not "one size fits all" solutions but must adapt to the underlying business conditions. For example, a business can adopt either a build strategy or a harvest strategy. A *build* strategy is one where the business is designing, launching, and growing new products and markets. Build strategies often require short-term profit sacrifice in order to grow market share. Apple Computer, Inc.'s iPod® is an example of a product managed under a build strategy. A *harvest* strategy is often employed for business units with mature products enjoying high market share in low-growth industries. Harvest strategies maximize short-term earnings and cash flow, sometimes at the expense of market share. Often the term "cash cow" is used to describe a product managed under a harvest strategy. H.J. Heinz Company's Ketchup® and Ivory soap are examples of such products. Compared to the harvest strategy, a build strategy often has greater uncertainty, unpredictability, and change. The differences between build and harvest strategies imply different budgeting approaches.

The build strategy should employ a budget approach that is flexible to the uncertainty of the business. Thus, budgets should adapt to changing conditions by allowing periodic revisions and flexible targets. Often the managers controlled by the budget will participate in setting budget targets, so that all uncertainties are considered. In addition, the budget will complement other, more subjective, evaluation criteria. Overall, the budget serves as a short-term planning tool to guide management in executing an uncertain and evolving product market strategy.

Under the harvest strategy, the business is often much more stable and is managed to maximize profitability and cash flow. Cost control is much more important in a harvest strategy; thus, the budget is used to restrict the actions of managers. In addition, the managers controlled by the budget often do not participate in its development. Rather, the budget is imposed. In a harvest business, the budget is the major control tool and is often not supplemented with other more subjective performance measures.

FLEXIBLE BUDGET

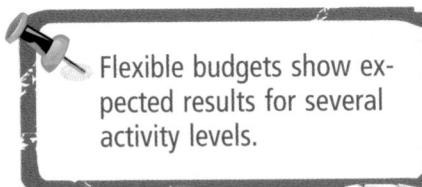

Flexible budgets show expected results for several activity levels.

Unlike static budgets, **flexible budgets** show the expected results of a responsibility center for several activity levels. You can think of a flexible budget as a series of static budgets for different levels of activity. Such budgets are especially useful in estimating and controlling factory costs and operating expenses. Exhibit 5 is a flexible budget for the annual manufacturing expense in the Assembly Department of Colter Manufacturing Company.

EXHIBIT 5

Flexible Budget

	A	B	C	D	
	Colter Manufacturing Company				
	Assembly Department Budget				
	For the Year Ending July 31, 2008				
		Level 1	Level 2	Level 3	
1	Units of production	8,000	9,000	10,000	1
2	Variable cost:				2
3	Direct labor ($5 per unit)	$40,000	$45,000	$50,000	3
4	Electric power ($0.50 per unit)	4,000	4,500	5,000	4
5	Total variable cost	$44,000	$49,500	$55,000	5
6	Fixed cost:				6
7	Electric power	$ 1,000	$ 1,000	$ 1,000	7
8	Supervisor salaries	15,000	15,000	15,000	8
9	Total fixed cost	$16,000	$16,000	$16,000	9
10	Total department costs	$60,000	$65,500	$71,000	10

Many hospitals use flexible budgeting to plan the number of nurses for patient floors. These budgets use a measure termed "relative value units," which is a measure of nursing effort. The more patients and the more severe their illnesses, the higher the total relative value units, and thus the higher the staffing budget.

When constructing a flexible budget, we first identify the relevant activity levels. In Exhibit 5, these are 8,000, 9,000, and 10,000 units of production. Alternative activity bases, such as machine hours or direct labor hours, may be used in measuring the volume of activity. Second, we identify the fixed and variable cost components of the costs being budgeted. For example, in Exhibit 5, the electric power cost is separated into its fixed cost ($1,000 per year) and variable cost ($0.50 per unit). Lastly, we prepare the budget for each activity level by multiplying the variable cost per unit by the activity level and then adding the monthly fixed cost.

With a flexible budget, the department manager can be evaluated by comparing actual expenses to the budgeted amount for actual activity. For example, if Colter Manufacturing Company's Assembly Department actually spent $72,000 to produce 10,000 units, the manager would be considered over budget by $1,000 ($72,000 − $71,000). Under the static budget in Exhibit 4, the department was $12,000 over budget. Exhibit 6

Example Exercise 21-1   objective **2**

At the beginning of the period, the Assembly Department budgeted direct labor of $45,000 and supervisor salaries of $30,000 for 5,000 hours of production. The department actually completed 6,000 hours of production. Determine the budget for the department, assuming that it uses flexible budgeting.

Follow My Example 21-1

Variable cost:	
Direct labor (6,000 hours × $9* per hour)	$54,000
Fixed cost:	
Supervisor salaries	30,000
Total department costs	$84,000

*$45,000/5,000 hours

For Practice: PE 21-1A, PE 21-1B

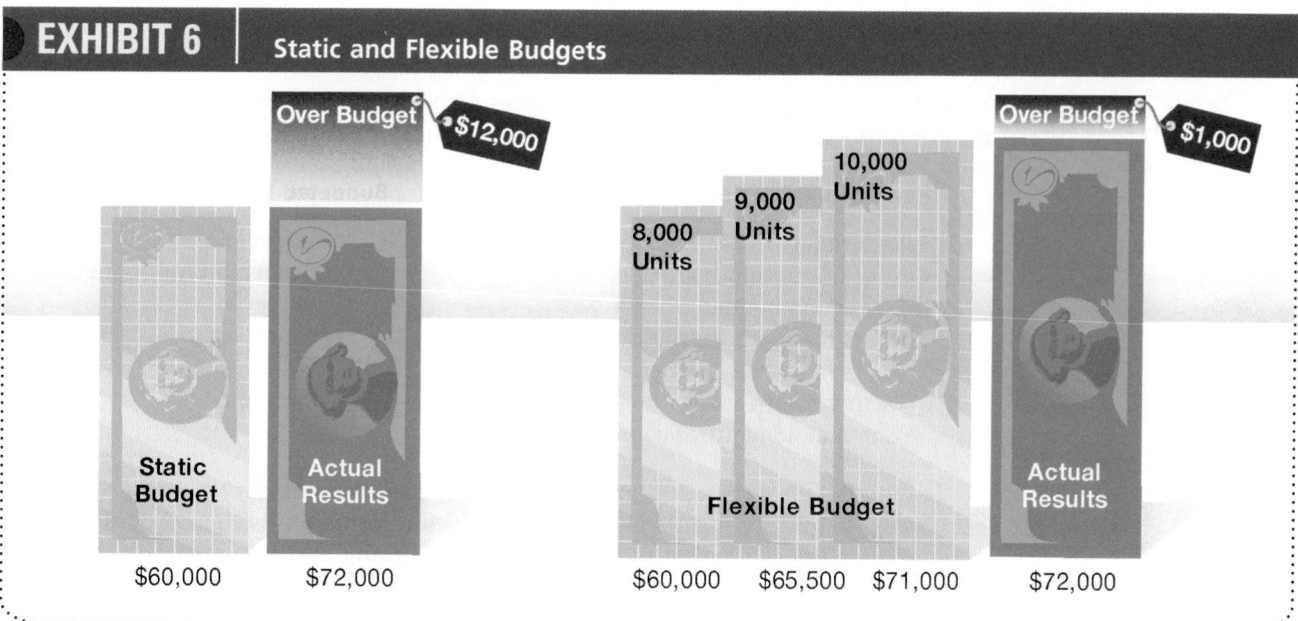

EXHIBIT 6 | **Static and Flexible Budgets**

illustrates this comparison. The flexible budget for the Assembly Department is much more accurate than the static budget, because budget amounts adjust for changes in activity.

COMPUTERIZED BUDGETING SYSTEMS

In developing budgets, firms use a variety of computerized approaches. A recent survey reported that 67% of the respondents relied on spreadsheets for budgeting and planning.[1] The remaining firms use integrated computerized budget and planning (B&P) systems. Such systems speed up and reduce the cost of preparing the budget. This is especially true when large quantities of data need to be processed. The same survey reported that companies relying on spreadsheets required 30 more days to prepare the budget than those relying on integrated B&P systems. For example, Fujitsu, a major Japanese technology company, used B&P software to streamline its budgeting process from 6 to 8 weeks down to 10 to 15 days.

Integrated B&P software is also useful in continuous budgeting. The newest B&P systems are accomplishing this by using Web-based applications to link thousands of employees together. With these systems, employees can input budget information onto the Web pages that are automatically aggregated and summarized throughout the organization. In this way, an organization can link the top-level strategy to the lower-level operational goals—and do so quickly and consistently across the organization. The use of Web-based B&P systems is moving companies closer to the real-time budget, wherein the budget is being "rolled" every day and represents the best assumptions at any moment in time.[2]

Managers often use computer spreadsheets or simulation models to represent the operating and budget relationships. By using computer simulation models, the impact of various operating alternatives on the budget can be assessed. For example, the budget can be revised to show the impact of a proposed change in indirect labor wage rates. Likewise, the budgetary effect of a proposed product line can be determined. In the next section, we illustrate how a company ties its budgets together, using a master budget.

---

1 Tim Reason, "Budgeting in the Real World," *CFO Magazine*, July 1, 2005.
2 Janet Kersnar, "Rolling Along," *CFO Europe*, September 14, 2004.

Master Budget

Manufacturing operations require a series of budgets that are linked together in a **master budget**. The major parts of the master budget are as follows:

Budgeted Income Statement	Budgeted Balance Sheet
Sales budget	Cash budget
Cost of goods sold budget:	Capital expenditures budget
Production budget	
Direct materials purchases budget	
Direct labor cost budget	
Factory overhead cost budget	
Selling and administrative expenses budget	

Exhibit 7 shows the relationship among the income statement budgets. The budget process begins by estimating sales. The sales information is then provided to the various units for estimating the production and selling and administrative expenses budgets. The production budgets are used to prepare the direct materials purchases, direct labor cost, and factory overhead cost budgets. These three budgets are used to develop the cost of goods sold budget. Once these budgets and the selling and administrative expenses budget have been completed, the budgeted income statement can be prepared, as we illustrate in the following section.

EXHIBIT 7

Income Statement
Budgets

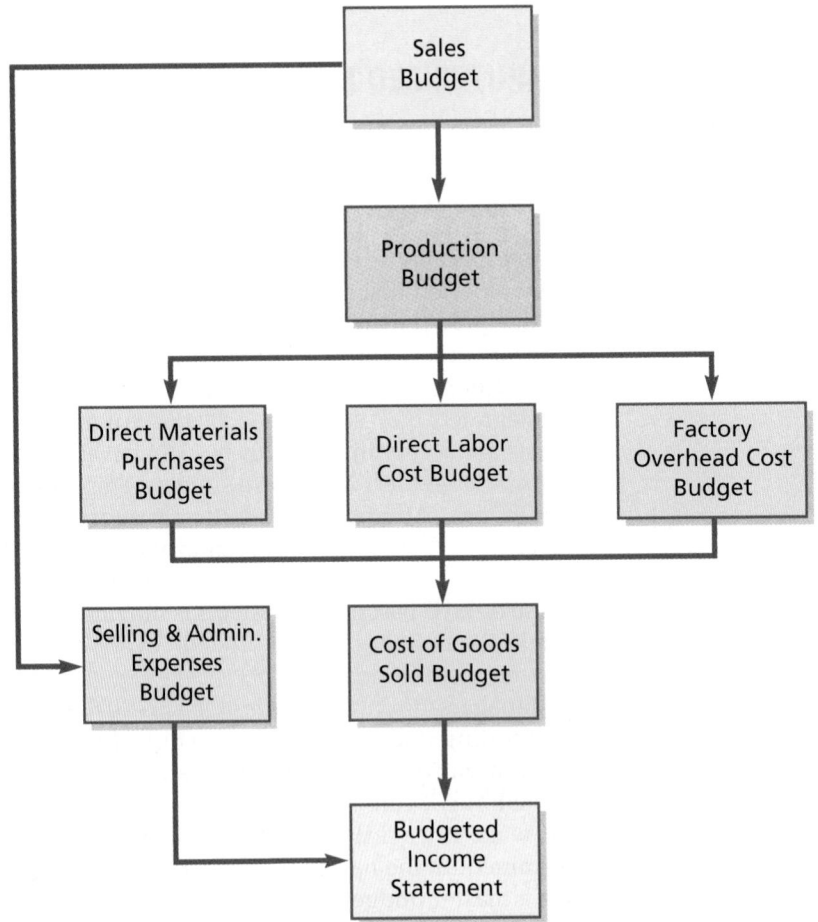

After the budgeted income statement has been developed, the budgeted balance sheet can be prepared. Two major budgets comprising the budgeted balance sheet are the cash budget and the capital expenditures budget, which we illustrate later.

Income Statement Budgets

In the following sections, we will illustrate the major elements of the income statement budget. We will use a small manufacturing business, Elite Accessories Inc., as the basis for our illustration.

SALES BUDGET

The **sales budget** normally indicates for each product (1) the quantity of estimated sales and (2) the expected unit selling price. These data are often reported by regions or by sales representatives.

In estimating the quantity of sales for each product, past sales volumes are often used as a starting point. These amounts are revised for factors that are expected to affect future sales, such as the factors listed below.

- backlog of unfilled sales orders
- planned advertising and promotion
- expected industry and general economic conditions
- productive capacity
- projected pricing policy
- findings of market research studies

Once an estimate of the sales volume is obtained, the expected sales revenue can be determined by multiplying the volume by the expected unit sales price. Exhibit 8 is the sales budget for Elite Accessories Inc.

EXHIBIT 8

Sales Budget

	A	B	C	D	
	Elite Accessories Inc.				
	Sales Budget				
	For the Year Ending December 31, 2008				
	Product and Region	Unit Sales Volume	Unit Selling Price	Total Sales	
1	Wallet:	287,000	$12.00	$ 3,444,000	1
2	East	241,000	12.00	2,892,000	2
3	West	528,000		$ 6,336,000	3
4	Total				4
5					5
6	Handbag:				6
7	East	156,400	$25.00	$ 3,910,000	7
8	West	123,600	25.00	3,090,000	8
9	Total	280,000		$ 7,000,000	9
10					10
11	Total revenue from sales			$13,336,000	11

For control purposes, management can compare actual sales and budgeted sales by product, region, or sales representative. Management would investigate any significant differences and take possible corrective actions.

PRODUCTION BUDGET

Production should be carefully coordinated with the sales budget to ensure that production and sales are kept in balance during the period. The number of units to be manufactured to meet budgeted sales and inventory needs for each product is set forth in the **production budget**. The budgeted volume of production is determined as follows:

Expected units to be sold
+ Desired units in ending inventory
− Estimated units in beginning inventory
Total units to be produced

Exhibit 9 is the production budget for Elite Accessories Inc.

EXHIBIT 9

Production Budget

	A	B	C	
	Elite Accessories Inc.			
	Production Budget			
	For the Year Ending December 31, 2008			
		Units		
		Wallet	Handbag	
1	Expected units to be sold (from Exhibit 8)	528,000	280,000	1
2	Plus desired ending inventory, December 31, 2008	80,000	60,000	2
3	Total	608,000	340,000	3
4	Less estimated beginning inventory, January 1, 2008	88,000	48,000	4
5	Total units to be produced	520,000	292,000	5

Example Exercise 21-2   objective 4

Landon Awards Co. projected sales of 45,000 brass plaques for 2008. The estimated January 1, 2008, inventory is 3,000 units, and the desired December 31, 2008, inventory is 5,000 units. What is the budgeted production (in units) for 2008?

Follow My Example 21-2

Expected units to be sold 45,000
Plus desired ending inventory, December 31, 2008 5,000
  Total 50,000
Less estimated beginning inventory, January 1, 2008 3,000
  Total units to be produced 47,000

For Practice: PE 21-2A, PE 21-2B

DIRECT MATERIALS PURCHASES BUDGET

The production budget is the starting point for determining the estimated quantities of direct materials to be purchased. Multiplying these quantities by the expected unit purchase price determines the total cost of direct materials to be purchased.

> Materials required for production
> + Desired ending materials inventory
> − Estimated beginning materials inventory
> Direct materials to be purchased

In Elite Accessories Inc.'s production operations, leather and lining are required for wallets and handbags. The quantity of direct materials expected to be used for each unit of product is as follows:

Wallet:
Leather: 0.30 square yard per unit
Lining: 0.10 square yard per unit

Handbag:
Leather: 1.25 square yards per unit
Lining: 0.50 square yard per unit

Based on these data and the production budget, the **direct materials purchases budget** is prepared. As shown in the budget in Exhibit 10, for Elite Accessories Inc. to produce 520,000 wallets, 156,000 square yards (520,000 units × 0.30 square yard per unit) of leather are needed. Likewise, to produce 292,000 handbags, 365,000 square yards (292,000 units × 1.25 square yards per unit) of leather are needed. We can compute the needs for lining in a similar manner. Then adding the desired ending inventory for each material and deducting the estimated beginning inventory determines the

EXHIBIT 10

Direct Materials
Purchases Budget

	A	B	C	D	E	
		Elite Accessories Inc.				
		Direct Materials Purchases Budget				
		For the Year Ending December 31, 2008				
			Direct Materials			
			Leather	Lining	Total	
1	Square yards required for production:					1
2	Wallet (Note A)		156,000	52,000		2
3	Handbag (Note B)		365,000	146,000		3
4	Plus desired inventory, December 31, 2008		20,000	12,000		4
5	Total		541,000	210,000		5
6	Less estimated inventory, January 1, 2008		18,000	15,000		6
7	Total square yards to be purchased		523,000	195,000		7
8	Unit price (per square yard)		× $4.50	× $1.20		8
9	Total direct materials to be purchased		$2,353,500	$234,000	$2,587,500	9
10						10
11	Note A:	Leather: 520,000 units × 0.30 sq. yd. per unit = 156,000 sq. yds.				11
12		Lining: 520,000 units × 0.10 sq. yd. per unit = 52,000 sq. yds.				12
13						13
14	Note B:	Leather: 292,000 units × 1.25 sq. yds. per unit = 365,000 sq. yds.				14
15		Lining: 292,000 units × 0.50 sq. yd. per unit = 146,000 sq. yds.				15

amount of each material to be purchased. Multiplying these amounts by the estimated cost per square yard yields the total materials purchase cost.

The direct materials purchases budget helps management maintain inventory levels within reasonable limits. For this purpose, the timing of the direct materials purchases should be coordinated between the purchasing and production departments.

Example Exercise 21-3   objective 4

Landon Awards Co. budgeted production of 47,000 brass plaques in 2008. Brass sheet is required to produce a brass plaque. Assume 96 square inches of brass sheet are required for each brass plaque. The estimated January 1, 2008, brass sheet inventory is 240,000 square inches. The desired December 31, 2008, brass sheet inventory is 200,000 square inches. If brass sheet costs $0.12 per square inch, determine the direct materials purchases budget for 2008.

Follow My Example 21-3

Square inches required for production:	
Brass sheet (47,000 × 96 sq. in.)	4,512,000
Plus desired ending inventory, December 31, 2008	200,000
Total	4,712,000
Less estimated beginning inventory, January 1, 2008	240,000
Total square inches to be purchased	4,472,000
Unit price (per square inch)	× $0.12
Total direct materials to be purchased	$ 536,640

For Practice: PE 21-3A, PE 21-3B

DIRECT LABOR COST BUDGET

The production budget also provides the starting point for preparing the direct labor cost budget. For Elite Accessories Inc., the labor requirements for each unit of product are estimated as follows:

Wallet:
    Cutting Department: 0.10 hour per unit
    Sewing Department: 0.25 hour per unit

Handbag:
    Cutting Department: 0.15 hour per unit
    Sewing Department: 0.40 hour per unit

Based on these data and the production budget, Elite Accessories Inc. prepares the direct labor budget. As shown in the budget in Exhibit 11, for Elite Accessories Inc. to produce 520,000 wallets, 52,000 hours (520,000 units × 0.10 hour per unit) of labor in the Cutting Department are required. Likewise, to produce 292,000 handbags, 43,800 hours (292,000 units × 0.15 hour per unit) of labor in the Cutting Department are required. In a similar manner, we can determine the direct labor hours needed in the Sewing Department to meet the budgeted production. Multiplying the direct labor hours for each department by the estimated department hourly rate yields the total direct labor cost for each department.

EXHIBIT 11

Direct Labor Cost Budget

	A	B	C	D	E	
			Elite Accessories Inc.			
			Direct Labor Cost Budget			
			For the Year Ending December 31, 2008			
			Cutting	Sewing	Total	
1	Hours required for production:					1
2	Wallet (Note A)		52,000	130,000		2
3	Handbag (Note B)		43,800	116,800		3
4	Total		95,800	246,800		4
5	Hourly rate		× $12.00	× $15.00		5
6	Total direct labor cost		$1,149,600	$3,702,000	$4,851,600	6
7						7
8	Note A: Cutting Department: 520,000 units × 0.10 hour per unit = 52,000 hours					8
9	Sewing Department: 520,000 units × 0.25 hour per unit = 130,000 hours					9
10						10
11	Note B: Cutting Department: 292,000 units × 0.15 hour per unit = 43,800 hours					11
12	Sewing Department: 292,000 units × 0.40 hour per unit = 116,800 hours					12

The direct labor needs should be coordinated between the production and personnel departments. This ensures that there will be enough labor available for production.

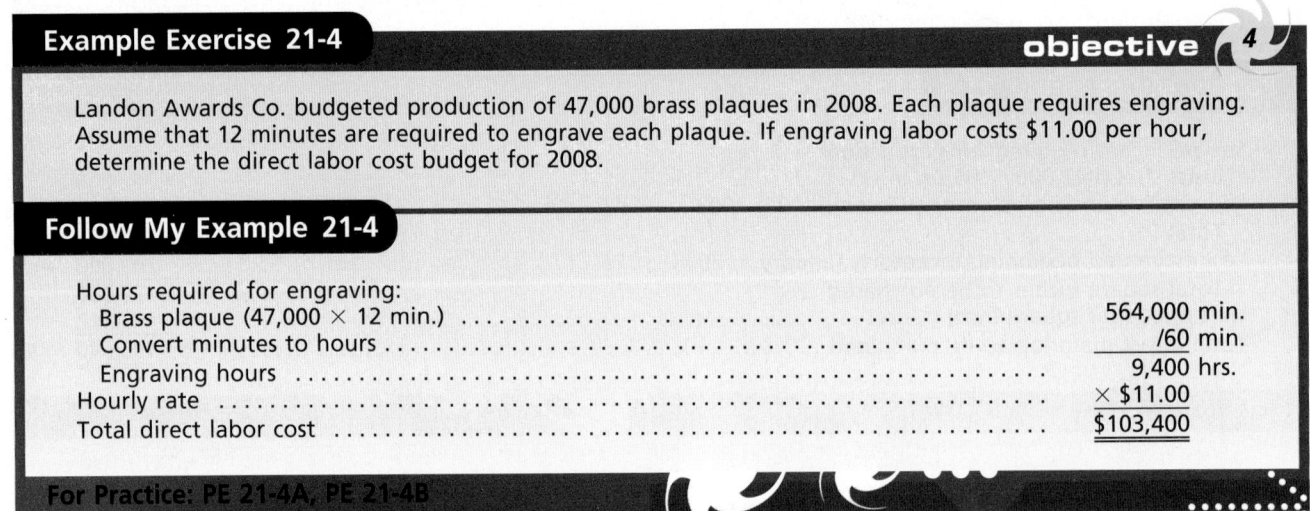

Example Exercise 21-4   objective **4**

Landon Awards Co. budgeted production of 47,000 brass plaques in 2008. Each plaque requires engraving. Assume that 12 minutes are required to engrave each plaque. If engraving labor costs $11.00 per hour, determine the direct labor cost budget for 2008.

Follow My Example 21-4

Hours required for engraving:
Brass plaque (47,000 × 12 min.) . . . .   564,000 min.
Convert minutes to hours . . . .   /60 min.
Engraving hours . . . .   9,400 hrs.
Hourly rate . . . .   × $11.00
Total direct labor cost $103,400

For Practice: PE 21-4A, PE 21-4B

FACTORY OVERHEAD COST BUDGET

The estimated factory overhead costs necessary for production make up the factory overhead cost budget. This budget usually includes the total estimated cost for each item of factory overhead, as shown in Exhibit 12.

A business may prepare supporting departmental schedules, in which the factory overhead costs are separated into their fixed and variable cost elements. Such schedules

EXHIBIT 12

Factory Overhead
Cost Budget

	A	B	
	Elite Accessories Inc. **Factory Overhead Cost Budget** **For the Year Ending December 31, 2008**		
1	Indirect factory wages	$ 732,800	1
2	Supervisor salaries	360,000	2
3	Power and light	306,000	3
4	Depreciation of plant and equipment	288,000	4
5	Indirect materials	182,800	5
6	Maintenance	140,280	6
7	Insurance and property taxes	79,200	7
8	Total factory overhead cost	$2,089,080	8

enable department managers to direct their attention to those costs for which they are responsible and to evaluate performance.

COST OF GOODS SOLD BUDGET

The direct materials purchases budget, direct labor cost budget, and factory overhead cost budget are the starting point for preparing the **cost of goods sold budget**. To illustrate, these data are combined with the desired ending inventory and the estimated beginning inventory data below to determine the budgeted cost of goods sold shown in Exhibit 13.

Estimated inventories on January 1, 2008:
    Finished goods $1,095,600
    Work in process 214,400

Desired inventories on December 31, 2008:
    Finished goods $1,565,000
    Work in process 220,000

EXHIBIT 13

Cost of Goods
Sold Budget

	A	B	C	D	E	F	
		Elite Accessories Inc. **Cost of Goods Sold Budget** **For the Year Ending December 31, 2008**					
1	Finished goods inventory, January 1, 2008					$ 1,095,600	1
2	Work in process inventory, January 1, 2008				$ 214,400		2
3	Direct materials:						3
4	Direct materials inventory,						4
5	January 1, 2008 (Note A)			$ 99,000			5
6	Direct materials purchases (from Exhibit 10)			2,587,500			6
7	Cost of direct materials available for use			$2,686,500			7
8	Less direct materials inventory,						8
9	December 31, 2008 (Note B)			104,400			9
10	Cost of direct materials placed in production			$2,582,100			10
11	Direct labor (from Exhibit 11)			4,851,600			11
12	Factory overhead (from Exhibit 12)			2,089,080			12
13	Total manufacturing costs				9,522,780		13
14	Total work in process during period				$9,737,180		14
15	Less work in process inventory,						15
16	December 31, 2008				220,000		16
17	Cost of goods manufactured					9,517,180	17
18	Cost of finished goods available for sale					$10,612,780	18
19	Less finished goods inventory,						19
20	December 31, 2008					1,565,000	20
21	Cost of goods sold					$ 9,047,780	21
22							22
23	Note A: Leather:		18,000 sq. yds. × $4.50 per sq. yd.			$ 81,000	23
24	Lining:		15,000 sq. yds. × $1.20 per sq. yd.			18,000	24
25	Direct materials inventory, January 1, 2008					$ 99,000	25
26	Note B: Leather:		20,000 sq. yds. × $4.50 per sq. yd.			$ 90,000	26
27	Lining:		12,000 sq. yds. × $1.20 per sq. yd.			14,400	27
28	Direct materials inventory, December 31, 2008					$104,400	28

Direct materials purchases budget

Direct labor cost budget

Factory overhead cost budget

Example Exercise 21-5

objective ④

Prepare a cost of goods sold budget for Landon Awards Co. using the information in Example Exercises 21-3 and 21-4. Assume the estimated inventories on January 1, 2008, for finished goods and work in process were $54,000 and $47,000, respectively. Also assume the desired inventories on December 31, 2008, for finished goods and work in process were $50,000 and $49,000, respectively. Factory overhead was budgeted for $126,000.

Follow My Example 21-5

Finished goods inventory, January 1, 2008			$ 54,000
Work in process inventory, January 1, 2008		$ 47,000	
Direct materials:			
Direct materials inventory, January 1, 2008 (240,000 × $0.12, from EE 21-3)	$ 28,800		
Direct materials purchases (from EE 21-3)	536,640		
Cost of direct materials available for use	$565,440		
Less direct materials inventory, December 31, 2008 (200,000 × $0.12, from EE 21-3)	24,000		
Cost of direct materials placed in production	$541,440		
Direct labor (from EE 21-4)	103,400		
Factory overhead	126,000		
Total manufacturing costs		770,840	
Total work in process during period		$817,840	
Less work in process inventory, December 31, 2008		49,000	
Cost of goods manufactured			768,840
Cost of finished goods available for sale			$822,840
Less finished goods inventory, December 31, 2008			50,000
Cost of goods sold			$772,840

For Practice: PE 21-5A, PE 21-5B

SELLING AND ADMINISTRATIVE EXPENSES BUDGET

The sales budget is often used as the starting point for estimating the selling and administrative expenses. For example, a budgeted increase in sales may require more advertising. Exhibit 14 is a selling and administrative expenses budget for Elite Accessories Inc.

Detailed supporting schedules are often prepared for major items in the selling and administrative expenses budget. For example, an advertising expense schedule for the Marketing Department should include the advertising media to be used (newspaper, direct mail, television), quantities (column inches, number of pieces, minutes), and the cost per unit. Attention to such details results in realistic budgets. Effective control results from assigning responsibility for achieving the budget to department supervisors.

EXHIBIT 14

Selling and Administrative Expenses Budget

	A	B	C	
	Elite Accessories Inc.			
	Selling and Administrative Expenses Budget			
	For the Year Ending December 31, 2008			
1	Selling expenses:			1
2	Sales salaries expense	$715,000		2
3	Advertising expense	360,000		3
4	Travel expense	115,000		4
5	Total selling expenses		$1,190,000	5
6	Administrative expenses:			6
7	Officers' salaries expense	$360,000		7
8	Office salaries expense	258,000		8
9	Office rent expense	34,500		9
10	Office supplies expense	17,500		10
11	Miscellaneous administrative expenses	25,000		11
12	Total administrative expenses		695,000	12
13	Total selling and administrative expenses		$1,885,000	13

BUDGETED INCOME STATEMENT

The budgets for sales, cost of goods sold, and selling and administrative expenses, combined with the data on other income, other expense, and income tax, are used to prepare the budgeted income statement. Exhibit 15 is a budgeted income statement for Elite Accessories Inc.

EXHIBIT 15

Budgeted Income Statement

	A	B	C	
	Elite Accessories Inc.			
	Budgeted Income Statement			
	For the Year Ending December 31, 2008			
1	Revenue from sales (from Exhibit 8)		$13,336,000	Sales budget
2	Cost of goods sold (from Exhibit 13)		9,047,780	Cost of goods sold budget
3				3
4	Gross profit		$ 4,288,220	4
5	Selling and administrative expenses:			5
6	Selling expenses (from Exhibit 14)	$1,190,000		6 Selling and administrative expenses budget
7				7
8	Administrative expenses (from Exhibit 14)	695,000		8
9	Total selling and administrative expenses		1,885,000	9
10	Income from operations		$ 2,403,220	10
11	Other income:			11
12	Interest revenue	$ 98,000		12
13	Other expenses:			13
14	Interest expense	90,000	8,000	14
15	Income before income tax		$ 2,411,220	15
16	Income tax		600,000	16
17	Net income		$ 1,811,220	17

The budgeted income statement summarizes the estimates of all phases of operations. This allows management to assess the effects of the individual budgets on profits for the year. If the budgeted net income is too low, management could review and revise operating plans in an attempt to improve income.

Balance Sheet Budgets

objective **5**

Prepare balance sheet budgets for a manufacturing business.

Balance sheet budgets are used by managers to plan financing, investing, and cash objectives for the firm. The balance sheet budgets illustrated for Elite Accessories Inc. in the following sections are the cash budget and the capital expenditures budget.

CASH BUDGET

The **cash budget** is one of the most important elements of the budgeted balance sheet. The cash budget presents the expected receipts (inflows) and payments (outflows) of cash for a period of time.

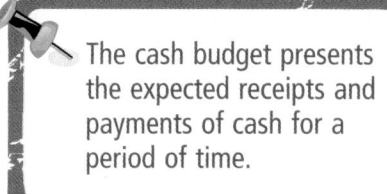

The cash budget presents the expected receipts and payments of cash for a period of time.

Information from the various operating budgets, such as the sales budget, the direct materials purchases budget, and the selling and administrative expenses budget, affects the cash budget. In addition, the capital expenditures budget, dividend policies, and plans for equity or long-term debt financing also affect the cash budget.

We illustrate the monthly cash budget for January, February, and March 2008, for Elite Accessories Inc. We begin by developing the estimated cash receipts and estimated cash payments portion of the cash budget.

Estimated Cash Receipts   Estimated cash receipts are planned additions to cash from sales and other sources, such as issuing securities or collecting interest. A supporting schedule can be used in determining the collections from sales. To illustrate this schedule, assume the following information for Elite Accessories Inc.:

Accounts receivable, January 1, 2008 . . . . $370,000

	January	February	March
Budgeted sales	$1,080,000	$1,240,000	$970,000

Elite Accessories Inc. expects to sell 10% of its merchandise for cash. Of the remaining 90% of the sales on account, 60% are expected to be collected in the month of the sale and the remainder in the next month. Thus, all of the accounts receivable are expected to be collectible.

Using this information, we prepare the schedule of collections from sales, shown in Exhibit 16. The cash receipts from sales on account are determined by adding the amounts collected from credit sales earned in the current period (60%) and the amounts accrued from sales in the previous period as accounts receivable (40%).

EXHIBIT 16

Schedule of Collections from Sales

	A	B	C	D	E	
		Elite Accessories Inc.				
		Schedule of Collections from Sales				
		For the Three Months Ending March 31, 2008				
			January	February	March	
1	Receipts from cash sales:					1
2	Cash sales (10% × current month's sales—					2
3	Note A)		$108,000	$ 124,000	$ 97,000	3
4						4
5	Receipts from sales on account:					5
6	Collections from prior month's sales (40% of					6
7	previous month's credit sales—Note B)		$370,000	$ 388,800	$446,400	7
8	Collections from current month's sales (60%					8
9	of current month's credit sales—Note C)		583,200	669,600	523,800	9
10	Total receipts from sales on account		$953,200	$1,058,400	$970,200	10
11						11
12	Note A: $108,000 = $1,080,000 × 10%					12
13	$124,000 = $1,240,000 × 10%					13
14	$ 97,000 = $ 970,000 × 10%					14
15						15
16	Note B: $370,000, given as January 1, 2008, Accounts Receivable balance					16
17	$388,800 = $1,080,000 × 90% × 40%					17
18	$446,400 = $1,240,000 × 90% × 40%					18
19						19
20	Note C: $583,200 = $1,080,000 × 90% × 60%					20
21	$669,600 = $1,240,000 × 90% × 60%					21
22	$523,800 = $ 970,000 × 90% × 60%					22

Estimated Cash Payments   Estimated cash payments are planned reductions in cash from manufacturing costs, selling and administrative expenses, capital expenditures, and other sources, such as buying securities or paying interest or dividends. A supporting schedule can be used in estimating the cash payments for manufacturing costs. To illustrate, the schedule shown in Exhibit 17 is based on the following information for Elite Accessories:

Accounts payable, January 1, 2008 . . . . $190,000

	January	February	March
Manufacturing costs	$840,000	$780,000	$812,000

EXHIBIT 17

Schedule of Payments
for Manufacturing
Costs

	A	B	C	D	E	
		Elite Accessories Inc.				
		Schedule of Payments for Manufacturing Costs				
		For the Three Months Ending March 31, 2008				
			January	February	March	
1	Payments of prior month's manufacturing costs					1
2	{[25% × previous month's manufacturing costs					2
3	(less depreciation)]—Note A}		$190,000	$204,000	$189,000	3
4	Payments of current month's manufacturing costs					4
5	{[75% × current month's manufacturing costs					5
6	(less depreciation)]—Note B}		612,000	567,000	591,000	6
7	Total payments		$802,000	$771,000	$780,000	7
8						8
9	Note A:	$190,000, given as January 1, 2008, Accounts Payable balance				9
10		$204,000 = ($840,000 − $24,000) × 25%				10
11		$189,000 = ($780,000 − $24,000) × 25%				11
12						12
13	Note B:	$612,000 = ($840,000 − $24,000) × 75%				13
14		$567,000 = ($780,000 − $24,000) × 75%				14
15		$591,000 = ($812,000 − $24,000) × 75%				15

Depreciation expense on machines is estimated to be $24,000 per month and is included in the manufacturing costs. The accounts payable were incurred for manufacturing costs. Elite Accessories Inc. expects to pay 75% of the manufacturing costs in the month in which they are incurred and the balance in the next month.

In Exhibit 17, the cash payments are determined by adding the amounts paid from costs incurred in the current period (75%) and the amounts accrued as a liability from costs in the previous period (25%). The $24,000 of depreciation must be excluded from all calculations, since depreciation is a noncash expense that should not be included in the cash budget.

Completing the Cash Budget To complete the cash budget for Elite Accessories Inc., as shown in Exhibit 18, assume that Elite Accessories Inc. is expecting the following:

Cash balance on January 1	$280,000
Quarterly taxes paid on March 31	150,000
Quarterly interest expense paid on January 10	22,500
Quarterly interest revenue received on March 21	24,500
Sewing equipment purchased in February	274,000

In addition, monthly selling and administrative expenses, which are paid in the month incurred, are estimated as follows:

	January	February	March
Selling and administrative expenses	$160,000	$165,000	$145,000

We can compare the estimated cash balance at the end of the period with the minimum balance required by operations. Assuming that the minimum cash balance for Elite Accessories Inc. is $340,000, we can determine any expected excess or deficiency.

The minimum cash balance protects against variations in estimates and for unexpected cash emergencies. For effective cash management, much of the minimum cash balance should be deposited in income-producing securities that can be readily converted to cash. U.S. Treasury Bills or Notes are examples of such securities.

EXHIBIT 18   Cash Budget

	A	C	D	E	
	Elite Accessories Inc.				
	Cash Budget				
	For the Three Months Ending March 31, 2008				
		January	February	March	
1	Estimated cash receipts from:				1
2	Cash sales (from Exhibit 16)	$ 108,000	$ 124,000	$ 97,000	2
3	Collections of accounts receivable				3
4	(from Exhibit 16)	953,200	1,058,400	970,200	4
5	Interest revenue			24,500	5
6	Total cash receipts	$1,061,200	$1,182,400	$1,091,700	6
7	Estimated cash payments for:				7
8	Manufacturing costs (from Exhibit 17)	$ 802,000	$ 771,000	$ 780,000	8
9	Selling and administrative expenses	160,000	165,000	145,000	9
10	Capital additions		274,000		10
11	Interest expense	22,500			11
12	Income taxes			150,000	12
13	Total cash payments	$ 984,500	$1,210,000	$1,075,000	13
14	Cash increase (decrease)	$ 76,700	$ (27,600)	$ 16,700	14
15	Cash balance at beginning of month	280,000	356,700	329,100	15
16	Cash balance at end of month	$ 356,700	$ 329,100	$ 345,800	16
17	Minimum cash balance	340,000	340,000	340,000	17
18	Excess (deficiency)	$ 16,700	$ (10,900)	$ 5,800	18

Schedule of collections from sales

Schedule of cash payments for manufacturing costs

Example Exercise 21-6   **objective 5**

Landon Awards Co. collects 25% of its sales on account in the month of the sale and 75% in the month following the sale. If sales on account are budgeted to be $100,000 for March and $126,000 for April, what are the budgeted cash receipts from sales on account for April?

Follow My Example 21-6

	April
Collections from March sales (75% × $100,000)	$ 75,000
Collections from April sales (25% × $126,000)	31,500
Total receipts from sales on account	$106,500

For Practice: PE 21-6A, PE 21-6B

CAPITAL EXPENDITURES BUDGET

The **capital expenditures budget** summarizes plans for acquiring fixed assets. Such expenditures are necessary as machinery and other fixed assets wear out, become obsolete, or for other reasons need to be replaced. In addition, expanding plant facilities may be necessary to meet increasing demand for a company's product.

The useful life of many fixed assets extends over long periods of time. In addition, the amount of the expenditures for such assets may vary from year to year. It is normal to project the plans for a number of periods into the future in preparing the capital expenditures budget. Exhibit 19 is a five-year capital expenditures budget for Elite Accessories Inc.

The capital expenditures budget should be considered in preparing the other operating budgets. For example, the estimated depreciation of new equipment affects the factory overhead cost budget and the selling and administrative expenses budget. The plans for financing the capital expenditures may also affect the cash budget.

EXHIBIT 19

Capital Expenditures
Budget

	A	B	C	D	E	F	
	Elite Accessories Inc.						
	Capital Expenditures Budget						
	For the Five Years Ending December 31, 2012						
	Item	2008	2009	2010	2011	2012	
1	Machinery—Cutting Department	$400,000			$280,000	$360,000	1
2	Machinery—Sewing Department	274,000	$260,000	$560,000	200,000		2
3	Office equipment		90,000			60,000	3
4	Total	$674,000	$350,000	$560,000	$480,000	$420,000	4

BUDGETED BALANCE SHEET

The budgeted balance sheet estimates the financial condition at the end of a budget period. The budgeted balance sheet assumes that all operating budgets and financing plans are met. It is similar to a balance sheet based on actual data in the accounts. For this reason, we do not illustrate a budgeted balance sheet for Elite Accessories Inc. If the budgeted balance sheet indicates a weakness in financial position, revising the financing plans or other plans may be necessary. For example, a large amount of long-term debt in relation to stockholders' equity might require revising financing plans for capital expenditures. Such revisions might include issuing equity rather than debt.

At a Glance

1. Describe budgeting, its objectives, and its impact on human behavior.

Key Points	Key Learning Outcomes	Example Exercises	Practice Exercises
Budgeting involves (1) establishing plans (planning), (2) directing operations (directing), and (3) evaluating performance (controlling). In addition, budgets should be established to avoid human behavior problems.	• Describe the planning, directing, controlling, and feedback elements of the budget process. • Describe the behavioral issues associated with tight goals, loose goals, and goal conflict.		

2. Describe the basic elements of the budget process, the two major types of budgeting, and the use of computers in budgeting.

Key Points	Key Learning Outcomes	Example Exercises	Practice Exercises
The budget process is often initiated by the budget committee. The budget estimates received by the committee should be carefully studied, analyzed, revised, and integrated. The static and continuous budgets are two major budgeting approaches. Computers can be used to make the budget process more efficient and organizationally integrated.	• Describe a static budget and explain when it might be used. • Describe and prepare a flexible budget and explain when it might be used. • Describe the role of computers in the budget process.	21-1	21-1A, 21-1B

(continued)

3. Describe the master budget for a manufacturing business.

Key Points	Key Learning Outcomes	Example Exercises	Practice Exercises
The master budget consists of the budgeted income statement and budgeted balance sheet.	• Illustrate the connection between the major income statement and balance sheet budgets.		

4. Prepare the basic income statement budgets for a manufacturing business.

Key Points	Key Learning Outcomes	Example Exercises	Practice Exercises
The basic income statement budgets are the sales budget, production budget, direct materials purchases budget, direct labor cost budget, factory overhead cost budget, cost of goods sold budget, and selling and administrative expenses budget.	• Prepare a sales budget. • Prepare a production budget. • Prepare a direct materials purchases budget. • Prepare a direct labor cost budget. • Prepare a factory overhead cost budget. • Prepare a cost of goods sold budget. • Prepare a selling and administrative expenses budget.	21-2 21-3 21-4 21-5	21-2A, 21-2B 21-3A, 21-3B 21-4A, 21-4B 21-5A, 21-5B

5. Prepare balance sheet budgets for a manufacturing business.

Key Points	Key Learning Outcomes	Example Exercises	Practice Exercises
The cash budget and capital expenditures budget can be used in preparing the budgeted balance sheet.	• Prepare cash receipts and cash payments budgets. • Prepare a capital expenditures budget.	21-6	21-6A, 21-6B

Key Terms

budget (932)
budgetary slack (935)
capital expenditures budget (950)
cash budget (947)
continuous budgeting (936)
cost of goods sold budget (945)

direct materials purchases budget (942)
flexible budget (938)
goal conflict (935)
master budget (940)
production budget (941)

responsibility center (933)
sales budget (941)
static budget (937)
zero-based budgeting (936)

Illustrative Problem

Selected information concerning sales and production for Cabot Co. for July 2008 are summarized as follows:

a. Estimated sales:

   Product K: 40,000 units at $30.00 per unit
   Product L: 20,000 units at $65.00 per unit

b. Estimated inventories, July 1, 2008:

Material A: 4,000 lbs.	Product K: 3,000 units at $17 per unit	$ 51,000
Material B: 3,500 lbs.	Product L: 2,700 units at $35 per unit	94,500
	Total	$145,500

   There were no work in process inventories estimated for July 1, 2008.

c. Desired inventories at July 31, 2008:

Material A: 3,000 lbs.	Product K: 2,500 units at $17 per unit	$ 42,500
Material B: 2,500 lbs.	Product L: 2,000 units at $35 per unit	70,000
	Total	$112,500

   There were no work in process inventories desired for July 31, 2008.

d. Direct materials used in production:

	Product K	Product L
Material A:	0.7 lb. per unit	3.5 lbs. per unit
Material B:	1.2 lbs. per unit	1.8 lbs. per unit

e. Unit costs for direct materials:

   Material A: $4.00 per lb.
   Material B: $2.00 per lb.

f. Direct labor requirements:

	Department 1	Department 2
Product K	0.4 hour per unit	0.15 hour per unit
Product L	0.6 hour per unit	0.25 hour per unit

g.

	Department 1	Department 2
Direct labor rate	$12.00 per hour	$16.00 per hour

h. Estimated factory overhead costs for July:

Indirect factory wages	$200,000
Depreciation of plant and equipment	40,000
Power and light	25,000
Indirect materials	34,000
Total	$299,000

Instructions

1. Prepare a sales budget for July.
2. Prepare a production budget for July.
3. Prepare a direct materials purchases budget for July.
4. Prepare a direct labor cost budget for July.
5. Prepare a cost of goods sold budget for July.

Solution

1.

	A	B	C	D	
		Cabot Co.			
		Sales Budget			
		For the Month Ending July 31, 2008			
	Product	Unit Sales Volume	Unit Selling Price	Total Sales	
1	Product K	40,000	$30.00	$1,200,000	1
2	Product L	20,000	65.00	1,300,000	2
3	Total revenue from sales			$2,500,000	3

2.

	A	C	D	
		Cabot Co.		
		Production Budget		
		For the Month Ending July 31, 2008		
		Units		
		Product K	Product L	
1	Sales	40,000	20,000	1
2	Plus desired inventories at July 31, 2008	2,500	2,000	2
3	Total	42,500	22,000	3
4	Less estimated inventories, July 1, 2008	3,000	2,700	4
5	Total production	39,500	19,300	5

3.

	A	B	C	D	E	F	G	
			Cabot Co.					
			Direct Materials Purchases Budget					
			For the Month Ending July 31, 2008					
			Direct Materials					
			Material A		Material B		Total	
1	Units required for production:							1
2	Product K (39,500 × lbs. per unit)		27,650	lbs.*	47,400	lbs.*		2
3	Product L (19,300 × lbs. per unit)		67,550	**	34,740	**		3
4	Plus desired units of inventory,							4
5	July 31, 2008		3,000		2,500			5
6	Total		98,200	lbs.	84,640	lbs.		6
7	Less estimated units of inventory,							7
8	July 1, 2008		4,000		3,500			8
9	Total units to be purchased		94,200	lbs.	81,140	lbs.		9
10	Unit price		× $4.00		× $2.00			10
11	Total direct materials purchases		$376,800		$162,280		$539,080	11
12								12
13	*27,650 = 39,500 × 0.7 47,400 = 39,500 × 1.2							13
14	**67,550 = 19,300 × 3.5 34,740 = 19,300 × 1.8							14

4.

	A	B	C	D	E	F	G	
			Cabot Co.					
			Direct Labor Cost Budget					
			For the Month Ending July 31, 2008					
			Department 1		Department 2		Total	
1	Hours required for production:							1
2	Product K (39,500 × hours per unit)		15,800	*	5,925	*		2
3	Product L (19,300 × hours per unit)		11,580	**	4,825	**		3
4	Total		27,380		10,750			4
5	Hourly rate		× $12.00		× $16.00			5
6	Total direct labor cost		$328,560		$172,000		$500,560	6
7								7
8	*15,800 = 39,500 × 0.4 5,925 = 39,500 × 0.15							8
9	**11,580 = 19,300 × 0.6 4,825 = 19,300 × 0.25							9

5.

	A	B	C	D	
	Cabot Co.				
	Cost of Goods Sold Budget				
	For the Month Ending July 31, 2008				
1	Finished goods inventory, July 1, 2008			$ 145,500	1
2	Direct materials:				2
3	Direct materials inventory, July 1, 2008—(Note A)		$ 23,000		3
4	Direct materials purchases		539,080		4
5	Cost of direct materials available for use		$562,080		5
6	Less direct materials inventory, July 31, 2008—(Note B)		17,000		6
7	Cost of direct materials placed in production		$545,080		7
8	Direct labor		500,560		8
9	Factory overhead		299,000		9
10	Cost of goods manufactured			1,344,640	10
11	Cost of finished goods available for sale			$1,490,140	11
12	Less finished goods inventory, July 31, 2008			112,500	12
13	Cost of goods sold			$1,377,640	13
14					14
15	Note A:				15
16	Material A 4,000 lbs. at $4.00 per lb.	$16,000			16
17	Material B 3,500 lbs. at $2.00 per lb.	7,000			17
18	Direct materials inventory, July 1, 2008	$23,000			18
19					19
20	Note B:				20
21	Material A 3,000 lbs. at $4.00 per lb.	$12,000			21
22	Material B 2,500 lbs. at $2.00 per lb.	5,000			22
23	Direct materials inventory, July 31, 2008	$17,000			23

Self-Examination Questions

(Answers at End of Chapter)

1. A tight budget may create:
   A. budgetary slack.
   B. discouragement.
   C. a flexible budget.
   D. a "spend it or lose it" mentality.

2. The first step of the budget process is:
   A. plan.   C. control.
   B. direct.   D. feedback.

3. Static budgets are often used by:
   A. production departments.
   B. administrative departments.
   C. responsibility centers.
   D. capital projects.

4. The total estimated sales for the coming year is 250,000 units. The estimated inventory at the beginning of the year is 22,500 units, and the desired inventory at the end of the year is 30,000 units. The total production indicated in the production budget is:
   A. 242,500 units.   C. 280,000 units.
   B. 257,500 units.   D. 302,500 units.

5. Dixon Company expects $650,000 of credit sales in March and $800,000 of credit sales in April. Dixon historically collects 70% of its sales in the month of sale and 30% in the following month. How much cash does Dixon expect to collect in April?
   A. $800,000   C. $755,000
   B. $560,000   D. $1,015,000

Eye Openers

1. What are the three major objectives of budgeting?
2. What is the manager's role in a responsibility center?
3. Briefly describe the type of human behavior problems that might arise if budget goals are set too tightly.
4. Why should all levels of management and all departments participate in preparing and submitting budget estimates?

5. Give an example of budgetary slack.
6. What behavioral problems are associated with setting a budget too loosely?
7. What behavioral problems are associated with establishing conflicting goals within the budget?
8. When would a company use zero-based budgeting?
9. Under what circumstances would a static budget be appropriate?
10. How do computerized budgeting systems aid firms in the budgeting process?
11. What is the first step in preparing a master budget?
12. Why should the production requirements set forth in the production budget be carefully coordinated with the sales budget?
13. Why should the timing of direct materials purchases be closely coordinated with the production budget?
14. In preparing the budget for the cost of goods sold, what are the three budgets from which data on relevant estimates of quantities and costs are combined with data on estimated inventories?
15. a. Discuss the purpose of the cash budget.
    b. If the cash for the first quarter of the fiscal year indicates excess cash at the end of each of the first two months, how might the excess cash be used?
16. How does a schedule of collections from sales assist in preparing the cash budget?
17. Give an example of how the capital expenditures budget affects other operating budgets.

Practice Exercises

PE 21-1A
Flexible budgeting
obj. 2

At the beginning of the period, the Assembly Department budgeted direct labor of $110,500 and property taxes of $50,000 for 8,500 hours of production. The department actually completed 10,000 hours of production. Determine the budget for the department, assuming that it uses flexible budgeting.

PE 21-1B
Flexible budgeting
obj. 2

At the beginning of the period, the Fabricating Department budgeted direct labor of $18,400 and equipment depreciation of $14,000 for 800 hours of production. The department actually completed 700 hours of production. Determine the budget for the department, assuming that it uses flexible budgeting.

PE 21-2A
Production budget
obj. 4

OnTime Publishers Inc. projected sales of 220,000 schedule planners for 2008. The estimated January 1, 2008, inventory is 15,000 units, and the desired December 31, 2008, inventory is 11,000 units. What is the budgeted production (in units) for 2008?

PE 21-2B
Production budget
obj. 4

New England Candle Co. projected sales of 95,000 candles for 2008. The estimated January 1, 2008, inventory is 2,400 units, and the desired December 31, 2008, inventory is 3,000 units. What is the budgeted production (in units) for 2008?

PE 21-3A
Direct materials purchases budget
obj. 4

OnTime Publishers Inc. budgeted production of 216,000 schedule planners in 2008. Paper is required to produce a planner. Assume 90 square feet of paper are required for each planner. The estimated January 1, 2008, paper inventory is 100,000 square feet. The desired December 31, 2008, paper inventory is 160,000 square feet. If paper costs $0.08 per square foot, determine the direct materials purchases budget for 2008.

PE 21-3B
Direct materials purchases budget
obj. 4

New England Candle Co. budgeted production of 95,600 candles in 2008. Wax is required to produce a candle. Assume 8 ounces (one half of a pound) of wax is required for each candle. The estimated January 1, 2008, wax inventory is 1,400 pounds. The desired December 31, 2008, wax inventory is 1,100 pounds. If candle wax costs $3.60 per pound, determine the direct materials purchases budget for 2008.

EX 21-11
Direct labor cost budget

obj. 4

✓ *Total direct labor cost, Assembly, $186,225*

Match Point Racket Company manufactures two types of tennis rackets, the Junior and Pro Striker models. The production budget for March for the two rackets is as follows:

	Junior	Pro Striker
Production budget	7,300 units	18,400 units

Both rackets are produced in two departments, Forming and Assembly. The direct labor hours required for each racket are estimated as follows:

	Forming Department	Assembly Department
Junior	0.25 hour per unit	0.45 hour per unit
Pro Striker	0.40 hour per unit	0.60 hour per unit

The direct labor rate for each department is as follows:

Forming Department	$18.00 per hour
Assembly Department	$13.00 per hour

Prepare the direct labor cost budget for March 2008.

EX 21-12
Direct labor budget— service business

obj. 4

✓ *Average weekday total, $1,696*

Night Rest Inn Inc. operates a downtown hotel property that has 240 rooms. On average, 75% of Night Rest's rooms are occupied on weekdays, and 50% are occupied during the weekend. The manager has asked you to develop a direct labor budget for the housekeeping and restaurant staff for weekdays and weekends. You have determined that the housekeeping staff requires 45 minutes to clean each occupied room. The housekeeping staff is paid $8 per hour. The restaurant has five full-time staff (eight-hour day) on duty, regardless of occupancy. However, for every 30 occupied rooms, an additional person is brought in to work in the restaurant for the eight-hour day. The restaurant staff is paid $7 per hour.

Determine the estimated housekeeping and restaurant direct labor cost for an average weekday and weekend day. Format the budget in two columns, labeled as weekday and weekend day.

EX 21-13
Production and direct labor cost budgets

obj. 4

✓ *a. Total production of 501 Jeans, 47,000*

Levi Strauss & Co. manufactures slacks and jeans under a variety of brand names, such as Dockers® and 501 Jeans®. Slacks and jeans are assembled by a variety of different sewing operations. Assume that the sales budget for Dockers and 501 Jeans shows estimated sales of 23,800 and 46,200 pairs, respectively, for March 2008. The finished goods inventory is assumed as follows:

	Dockers	501 Jeans
March 1 estimated inventory	320	1,230
March 31 desired inventory	520	2,030

Assume the following direct labor data per 10 pairs of Dockers and 501 Jeans for four different sewing operations:

	Direct Labor per 10 Pairs	
	Dockers	501 Jeans
Inseam	18 minutes	12 minutes
Outerseam	22	15
Pockets	7	9
Zipper	10	6
Total	57 minutes	42 minutes

a. Prepare a production budget for March. Prepare the budget in two columns: Dockers® and 501 Jeans®.
b. Prepare the March direct labor cost budget for the four sewing operations, assuming a $12 wage per hour for the inseam and outerseam sewing operations and a $14 wage per hour for the pocket and zipper sewing operations. Prepare the direct labor cost budget in four columns: inseam, outerseam, pockets, and zipper.

EX 21-14
Factory overhead cost budget

obj. **4**

✓ *Total variable factory overhead costs, $243,000*

Fresh Mint Candy Company budgeted the following costs for anticipated production for July 2008:

Advertising expenses	$275,000	Production supervisor wages	$125,000
Manufacturing supplies	14,000	Production control salaries	33,000
Power and light	42,000	Executive officer salaries	205,000
Sales commissions	290,000	Materials management salaries	29,000
Factory insurance	23,000	Factory depreciation	17,000

Prepare a factory overhead cost budget, separating variable and fixed costs. Assume that factory insurance and depreciation are the only factory fixed costs.

EX 21-15
Cost of goods sold budget

obj. **4**

✓ *Cost of goods sold, $1,269,300*

Dover Chemical Company uses oil to produce two types of plastic products, P1 and P2. Dover budgeted 30,000 barrels of oil for purchase in June for $28 per barrel. Direct labor budgeted in the chemical process was $150,000 for June. Factory overhead was budgeted $275,000 during June. The inventories on June 1 were estimated to be:

Oil	$15,300
P1	8,700
P2	9,200
Work in process	11,800

The desired inventories on June 30 were:

Oil	$12,200
P1	8,300
P2	9,500
Work in process	10,700

Use the preceding information to prepare a cost of goods sold budget for June.

EX 21-16
Cost of goods sold budget

obj. **4**

✓ *Cost of goods sold, $397,320*

The controller of Moravian Ceramics Inc. wishes to prepare a cost of goods sold budget for April. The controller assembled the following information for constructing the cost of goods sold budget:

Direct materials:	Enamel	Paint	Porcelain	Total
Total direct materials purchases budgeted for April	$32,450	$4,730	$114,240	$151,420
Estimated inventory, April 1, 2008	1,150	2,800	4,330	8,280
Desired inventory, April 30, 2008	2,500	2,050	6,000	10,550

Direct labor cost:	Kiln Department	Decorating Department	Total
Total direct labor cost budgeted for April	$37,500	$134,400	$171,900

Finished goods inventories:	Dish	Bowl	Figurine	Total
Estimated inventory, April 1, 2008	$4,280	$2,970	$2,470	$ 9,720
Desired inventory, April 30, 2008	3,350	4,150	3,700	11,200

Work in process inventories:

Estimated inventory, April 1, 2008	$2,800
Desired inventory, April 30, 2008	1,750

Budgeted factory overhead costs for April:

Indirect factory wages	$55,500
Depreciation of plant and equipment	12,600
Power and light	4,900
Indirect materials	3,700
Total	$76,700

Use the preceding information to prepare a cost of goods sold budget for April 2008.

EX 21-17
Schedule of cash collections of accounts receivable

obj. 5

✓ *Total cash collected in May, $535,700*

Happy Tails Wholesale Inc., a pet wholesale supplier, was organized on March 1, 2008. Projected sales for each of the first three months of operations are as follows:

March	$450,000
April	520,000
May	560,000

The company expects to sell 10% of its merchandise for cash. Of sales on account, 50% are expected to be collected in the month of the sale, 40% in the month following the sale, and the remainder in the second month following the sale.

Prepare a schedule indicating cash collections from sales for March, April, and May.

EX 21-18
Schedule of cash collections of accounts receivable

obj. 5

✓ *Total cash collected in January, $307,600*

Office Warehouse Supplies Inc. has "cash and carry" customers and credit customers. Office Warehouse estimates that 40% of monthly sales are to cash customers, while the remaining sales are to credit customers. Of the credit customers, 30% pay their accounts in the month of sale, while the remaining 70% pay their accounts in the month following the month of sale. Projected sales for the first three months of 2008 are as follows:

January	$220,000
February	275,000
March	260,000

The Accounts Receivable balance on December 31, 2007, was $180,000.

Prepare a schedule of cash collections from sales for January, February, and March.

EX 21-19
Schedule of cash payments

obj. 5

✓ *Total cash payments in August, $107,875*

A+ Learning Systems Inc. was organized on May 31, 2009. Projected selling and administrative expenses for each of the first three months of operations are as follows:

June	$114,800
July	124,500
August	129,000

Depreciation, insurance, and property taxes represent $20,000 of the estimated monthly expenses. The annual insurance premium was paid on May 31, and property taxes for the year will be paid in December. Three-fourths of the remainder of the expenses are expected to be paid in the month in which they are incurred, with the balance to be paid in the following month.

Prepare a schedule indicating cash payments for selling and administrative expenses for June, July, and August.

EX 21-20
Schedule of cash payments

obj. 5

✓ *Total cash payments in December, $128,720*

Total Flex Physical Therapy Inc. is planning its cash payments for operations for the fourth quarter (October–December), 2009. The Accrued Expenses Payable balance on October 1 is $22,600. The budgeted expenses for the next three months are as follows:

	October	November	December
Salaries	$ 58,200	$ 63,500	$ 74,500
Utilities	5,300	5,600	7,100
Other operating expenses	44,700	52,800	62,700
Total	$108,200	$121,900	$144,300

Other operating expenses include $10,500 of monthly depreciation expense and $600 of monthly insurance expense that was prepaid for the year on March 1 of the current year. Of the remaining expenses, 80% are paid in the month in which they are incurred, with the remainder paid in the following month. The Accrued Expenses Payable balance on October 1 relates to the expenses incurred in September.

Prepare a schedule of cash payments for operations for October, November, and December.

EX 21-21
Capital expenditures budget

obj. 5

✓ *Total capital expenditures in 2008, $7,000,000*

On January 1, 2008, the controller of Garden Master Tools Inc. is planning capital expenditures for the years 2008–2011. The following interviews helped the controller collect the necessary information for the capital expenditures budget.

Director of Facilities: A construction contract was signed in late 2007 for the construction of a new factory building at a contract cost of $12,000,000. The construction is scheduled to begin in 2008 and be completed in 2009.

Vice President of Manufacturing: Once the new factory building is finished, we plan to purchase $1.5 million in equipment in late 2009. I expect that an additional $300,000 will be needed early in the following year (2010) to test and install the equipment before we can begin production. If sales continue to grow, I expect we'll need to invest another million in equipment in 2011.

Vice President of Marketing: We have really been growing lately. I wouldn't be surprised if we need to expand the size of our new factory building in 2011 by at least 40%. Fortunately, we expect inflation to have minimal impact on construction costs over the next four years.

Director of Information Systems: We need to upgrade our information systems to wireless network technology. It doesn't make sense to do this until after the new factory building is completed and producing product. During 2010, once the factory is up and running, we should equip the whole facility with wireless technology. I think it would cost us $1,600,000 today to install the technology. However, prices have been dropping by 25% per year, so it should be less expensive at a later date.

President: I am excited about our long-term prospects. My only short-term concern is financing the $7,000,000 of construction costs on the portion of the new factory building scheduled to be completed in 2008.

Use the interview information above to prepare a capital expenditures budget for Garden Master Tools Inc. for the years 2008–2011.

Problems Series A

PR 21-1A
Forecast sales volume and sales budget

obj. 4

✓ *3. Total revenue from sales, $1,869,918*

Rembrandt Frame Company prepared the following sales budget for the current year:

Rembrandt Frame Company
Sales Budget
For the Year Ending December 31, 2008

Product and Area	Unit Sales Volume	Unit Selling Price	Total Sales
8" × 10" Frame:			
East	29,000	$14.00	$ 406,000
Central	22,000	14.00	308,000
West	31,500	14.00	441,000
Total	82,500		$1,155,000
12" × 16" Frame:			
East	16,000	$24.00	$ 384,000
Central	10,500	24.00	252,000
West	15,000	24.00	360,000
Total	41,500		$ 996,000
Total revenue from sales			$2,151,000

At the end of December 2008, the following unit sales data were reported for the year:

	Unit Sales	
	8" × 10" Frame	12" × 16" Frame
East	29,725	16,480
Central	22,770	10,710
West	30,240	14,325

For the year ending December 31, 2009, unit sales are expected to follow the patterns established during the year ending December 31, 2008. The unit selling price for the 8" × 10" frame is expected to change to $12, and the unit selling price for the 12" × 16" frame is expected to change to $21, effective January 1, 2009.

Instructions

1. Compute the increase or decrease of actual unit sales for the year ended December 31, 2008, over budget. Place your answers in a columnar table with the following format:

	Unit Sales, Year Ended 2008		Increase (Decrease) Actual Over Budget	
	Budget	Actual Sales	Amount	Percent
8" × 10" Frame:				
East				
Central				
West				
12" × 16" Frame:				
East				
Central				
West				

2. Assuming that the trend of sales indicated in part (1) is to continue in 2009, compute the unit sales volume to be used for preparing the sales budget for the year ending December 31, 2009. Place your answers in a columnar table similar to that in part (1) above but with the following column heads. Round budgeted units to the nearest unit.

2008 Actual Units	Percentage Increase (Decrease)	2009 Budgeted Units (rounded)

3. Prepare a sales budget for the year ending December 31, 2009.

PR 21-2A
Sales, production, direct materials purchases, and direct labor cost budgets

obj. 4

✓ *3. Total direct materials purchases, $9,806,650*

The budget director of Outdoor Chef Grill Company requests estimates of sales, production, and other operating data from the various administrative units every month. Selected information concerning sales and production for October 2008 is summarized as follows:

a. Estimated sales for October by sales territory:

Maine:
    Backyard Chef ....   4,500 units at $800 per unit
    Master Chef ....   1,600 units at $1,600 per unit
Vermont:
    Backyard Chef ....   3,800 units at $900 per unit
    Master Chef ....   1,700 units at $1,450 per unit
New Hampshire:
    Backyard Chef ....   4,200 units at $850 per unit
    Master Chef ....   1,800 units at $1,700 per unit

b. Estimated inventories at October 1:

Direct materials:		Finished products:	
Grates	1,200 units	Backyard Chef	1,600 units
Stainless steel	2,300 lbs.	Master Chef	500 units
Burner subassemblies	650 units		
Shelves	500 units		

c. Desired inventories at October 31:

Direct materials:		Finished products:	
Grates	900 units	Backyard Chef	1,300 units
Stainless steel	2,000 lbs.	Master Chef	600 units
Burner subassemblies	800 units		
Shelves	450 units		

d. Direct materials used in production:

In manufacture of Backyard Chef:

Grates	3 units per unit of product
Stainless steel	25 lbs. per unit of product
Burner subassemblies	2 units per unit of product
Shelves	5 units per unit of product

In manufacture of Master Chef:

Grates	6 units per unit of product
Stainless steel	50 lbs. per unit of product
Burner subassemblies	4 units per unit of product
Shelves	6 units per unit of product

e. Anticipated purchase price for direct materials:

Grates	$18 per unit	Burner subassemblies	$115 per unit
Stainless steel	$5 per lb.	Shelves	$6 per unit

f. Direct labor requirements:

Backyard Chef:

Stamping Department	0.60 hour at $15 per hour
Forming Department	0.80 hour at $12 per hour
Assembly Department	1.50 hours at $9 per hour

Master Chef:

Stamping Department	0.80 hour at $15 per hour
Forming Department	1.60 hours at $12 per hour
Assembly Department	2.50 hours at $9 per hour

Instructions

1. Prepare a sales budget for October.
2. Prepare a production budget for October.
3. Prepare a direct materials purchases budget for October.
4. Prepare a direct labor cost budget for October.

PR 21-3A
Budgeted income statement and supporting budgets
obj. **4**

✓ *4. Total direct labor cost in Fabrication Dept., $282,170*

The budget director of Backyard Habitat Inc., with the assistance of the controller, treasurer, production manager, and sales manager, has gathered the following data for use in developing the budgeted income statement for December 2008:

a. Estimated sales for December:

Bird House	34,500 units at $40 per unit
Bird Feeder	25,800 units at $70 per unit

b. Estimated inventories at December 1:

Direct materials:		Finished products:	
Wood	2,600 ft.	Bird House	4,900 units at $25 per unit
Plastic	3,200 lbs.	Bird Feeder	2,500 units at $35 per unit

c. Desired inventories at December 31:

Direct materials:		Finished products:	
Wood	3,500 ft.	Bird House	5,300 units at $24 per unit
Plastic	2,800 lbs.	Bird Feeder	2,100 units at $36 per unit

d. Direct materials used in production:

In manufacture of Bird House:		In manufacture of Bird Feeder:	
Wood	0.80 ft. per unit of product	Wood	1.20 ft. per unit of product
Plastic	0.50 lb. per unit of product	Plastic	0.75 lb. per unit of product

e. Anticipated cost of purchases and beginning and ending inventory of direct materials:

Wood	$6.50 per ft.	Plastic	$0.90 per lb.

f. Direct labor requirements:

Bird House:
Fabrication Department	0.25 hour at $14 per hour
Assembly Department	0.30 hour at $10 per hour

Bird Feeder:
Fabrication Department	0.45 hour at $14 per hour
Assembly Department	0.35 hour at $10 per hour

g. Estimated factory overhead costs for December:

Indirect factory wages	$650,000	Power and light	$42,000
Depreciation of plant and equipment	165,000	Insurance and property tax	15,400

h. Estimated operating expenses for December:

Sales salaries expense	$675,000
Advertising expense	148,600
Office salaries expense	214,800
Depreciation expense—office equipment	4,900
Telephone expense—selling	5,200
Telephone expense—administrative	1,700
Travel expense—selling	39,200
Office supplies expense	3,500
Miscellaneous administrative expense	5,000

i. Estimated other income and expense for December:

Interest revenue	$16,900
Interest expense	10,600

j. Estimated tax rate: 35%

Instructions
1. Prepare a sales budget for December.
2. Prepare a production budget for December.
3. Prepare a direct materials purchases budget for December.
4. Prepare a direct labor cost budget for December.
5. Prepare a factory overhead cost budget for December.
6. Prepare a cost of goods sold budget for December. Work in process at the beginning of December is estimated to be $27,000, and work in process at the end of December is estimated to be $32,400.
7. Prepare a selling and administrative expenses budget for December.
8. Prepare a budgeted income statement for December.

PR 21-4A
Cash budget
obj. **5**

[X]

✓*1. October deficiency, $64,500*

The controller of Santa Fe Housewares Inc. instructs you to prepare a monthly cash budget for the next three months. You are presented with the following budget information:

	August	September	October
Sales	$630,000	$715,000	$845,000
Manufacturing costs	350,000	360,000	410,000
Selling and administrative expenses	170,000	205,000	235,000
Capital expenditures			150,000

The company expects to sell about 10% of its merchandise for cash. Of sales on account, 70% are expected to be collected in full in the month following the sale and the remainder the following month. Depreciation, insurance, and property tax expense represent $25,000 of the estimated monthly manufacturing costs. The annual insurance premium is paid in July, and the annual property taxes are paid in November. Of the remainder of the manufacturing costs, 80% are expected to be paid in the month in which they are incurred and the balance in the following month.

Current assets as of August 1 include cash of $50,000, marketable securities of $85,000, and accounts receivable of $635,000 ($500,000 from July sales and $135,000 from June sales). Sales on account for June and July were $450,000 and $500,000, respectively. Current liabilities as of August 1 include a $100,000, 15%, 90-day note payable due October 20 and $65,000 of accounts payable incurred in July for manufacturing costs. All selling and administrative expenses are paid in cash in the period they are incurred. It is expected that $1,800 in dividends will be received in August. An estimated income tax payment of $39,000 will be made in September. Santa Fe's regular quarterly dividend of $12,000 is expected to be declared in September and paid in October. Management desires to maintain a minimum cash balance of $40,000.

Instructions

1. Prepare a monthly cash budget and supporting schedules for August, September, and October.
2. On the basis of the cash budget prepared in part (1), what recommendation should be made to the controller?

PR 21-5A
Budgeted income statement and balance sheet

objs. 4, 5

✓ *1. Budgeted net income, $175,850*

As a preliminary to requesting budget estimates of sales, costs, and expenses for the fiscal year beginning January 1, 2009, the following tentative trial balance as of December 31, 2008, is prepared by the Accounting Department of Coconut Grove Soap Co.:

Cash	$ 90,000	
Accounts Receivable	108,600	
Finished Goods	72,400	
Work in Process	27,500	
Materials	49,700	
Prepaid Expenses	3,400	
Plant and Equipment	350,000	
Accumulated Depreciation—Plant and Equipment		$130,400
Accounts Payable		57,000
Common Stock, $10 par		185,000
Retained Earnings		329,200
	$701,600	$701,600

Factory output and sales for 2009 are expected to total 215,000 units of product, which are to be sold at $4.60 per unit. The quantities and costs of the inventories at December 31, 2009, are expected to remain unchanged from the balances at the beginning of the year.

Budget estimates of manufacturing costs and operating expenses for the year are summarized as follows:

	Estimated Costs and Expenses	
	Fixed (Total for Year)	Variable (Per Unit Sold)
Cost of goods manufactured and sold:		
Direct materials	—	$0.80
Direct labor	—	0.45
Factory overhead:		
Depreciation of plant and equipment	$45,000	—
Other factory overhead	7,000	0.30
Selling expenses:		
Sales salaries and commissions	40,000	0.35
Advertising	55,000	—
Miscellaneous selling expense	4,500	0.15
Administrative expenses:		
Office and officers salaries	67,100	0.17
Supplies	3,000	0.06
Miscellaneous administrative expense	2,000	0.09

Balances of accounts receivable, prepaid expenses, and accounts payable at the end of the year are not expected to differ significantly from the beginning balances. Federal income tax of $80,000 on 2009 taxable income will be paid during 2009. Regular quarterly cash dividends of $0.80 a share are expected to be declared and paid in March, June, September, and December. It is anticipated that fixed assets will be purchased for $60,000 cash in May.

Instructions

1. Prepare a budgeted income statement for 2009.
2. Prepare a budgeted balance sheet as of December 31, 2009, with supporting calculations.

Problems Series B

PR 21-1B
Forecast sales volume and sales budget
obj. **4**

✓ *3. Total revenue from sales, $33,161,100*

Detect and Secure Devices Inc. prepared the following sales budget for the current year:

Detect and Secure Devices Inc.
Sales Budget
For the Year Ending December 31, 2008

Product and Area	Unit Sales Volume	Unit Selling Price	Total Sales
Home Alert System:			
United States	26,400	$240	$ 6,336,000
Europe	7,100	240	1,704,000
Asia	5,200	240	1,248,000
Total	38,700		$ 9,288,000
Business Alert System:			
United States	13,500	$850	$11,475,000
Europe	5,800	850	4,930,000
Asia	3,700	850	3,145,000
Total	23,000		$19,550,000
Total revenue from sales			$28,838,000

At the end of December 2008, the following unit sales data were reported for the year:

	Unit Sales	
	Home Alert System	Business Alert System
United States	27,720	14,040
Europe	6,816	5,916
Asia	5,356	3,589

For the year ending December 31, 2009, unit sales are expected to follow the patterns established during the year ending December 31, 2008. The unit selling price for the Home Alert System is expected to increase to $290, and the unit selling price for the Business Alert System is expected to be increased to $880, effective January 1, 2009.

Instructions

1. Compute the increase or decrease of actual unit sales for the year ended December 31, 2008, over budget. Place your answers in a columnar table with the following format:

	Unit Sales, Year Ended 2008		Increase (Decrease) Actual Over Budget	
	Budget	Actual Sales	Amount	Percent
Home Alert System:				
United States				
Europe				
Asia				

(continued)

	Unit Sales, Year Ended 2008		Increase (Decrease) Actual Over Budget	
	Budget	Actual Sales	Amount	Percent
Business Alert System:				
United States				
Europe				
Asia				

2. Assuming that the trend of sales indicated in part (1) is to continue in 2009, compute the unit sales volume to be used for preparing the sales budget for the year ending December 31, 2009. Place your answers in a columnar table similar to that in part (1) above but with the following column heads. Round budgeted units to the nearest unit.

2008 Actual Units	Percentage Increase (Decrease)	2009 Budgeted Units (rounded)

3. Prepare a sales budget for the year ending December 31, 2009.

PR 21-2B
Sales, production, direct materials purchases, and direct labor cost budgets

obj. 4

✓ 3. Total direct materials purchases, $6,679,381

The budget director of Kingdom Furniture Company requests estimates of sales, production, and other operating data from the various administrative units every month. Selected information concerning sales and production for May 2008 is summarized as follows:

a. Estimated sales of King and Prince chairs for May by sales territory:

Northern Domestic:
King .... 5,800 units at $650 per unit
Prince .... 6,700 units at $420 per unit

Southern Domestic:
King .... 3,500 units at $590 per unit
Prince .... 3,800 units at $480 per unit

International:
King .... 1,200 units at $700 per unit
Prince .... 1,000 units at $530 per unit

b. Estimated inventories at May 1:

Direct materials:
Fabric .... 5,000 sq. yds.
Wood .... 6,500 lineal ft.
Filler .... 3,000 cu. ft.
Springs .... 7,250 units

Finished products:
King .... 920 units
Prince .... 260 units

c. Desired inventories at May 31:

Direct materials:
Fabric .... 4,400 sq. yds.
Wood .... 5,800 lineal ft.
Filler .... 3,100 cu. ft.
Springs .... 7,500 units

Finished products:
King .... 800 units
Prince .... 400 units

d. Direct materials used in production:

In manufacture of King:
Fabric .... 4.6 sq. yds. per unit of product
Wood .... 35 lineal ft. per unit of product
Filler .... 3.8 cu. ft. per unit of product
Springs .... 14 units per unit of product

In manufacture of Prince:
Fabric .... 3 sq. yds. per unit of product
Wood .... 25 lineal ft. per unit of product
Filler .... 3.2 cu. ft. per unit of product
Springs .... 10 units per unit of product

e. Anticipated purchase price for direct materials:

Fabric	$8.00 per square yard		Filler	$3.50 per cubic foot
Wood	7.00 per lineal foot		Springs	4.50 per unit

f. Direct labor requirements:

King:
    Framing Department . . . . . .   2.5 hours at $12 per hour
    Cutting Department . . . .   1.5 hours at $9 per hour
    Upholstery Department . . . .   2.0 hours at $15 per hour
Prince:
    Framing Department . . . . . .   1.8 hours at $12 per hour
    Cutting Department . . . .   0.5 hour at $9 per hour
    Upholstery Department . . . .   2.3 hours at $15 per hour

Instructions

1. Prepare a sales budget for May.
2. Prepare a production budget for May.
3. Prepare a direct materials purchases budget for May.
4. Prepare a direct labor cost budget for May.

PR 21-3B
Budgeted income statement and supporting budgets

obj. 4

✓ *4. Total direct labor cost in Assembly Dept., $73,548*

The budget director of Safety Athletic Inc., with the assistance of the controller, treasurer, production manager, and sales manager, has gathered the following data for use in developing the budgeted income statement for January 2008:

a. Estimated sales for January:

Batting helmet	3,500 units at $65 per unit
Football helmet	6,800 units at $130 per unit

b. Estimated inventories at January 1:

Direct materials:			Finished products:	
Plastic	900 lbs.		Batting helmet	270 units at $32 per unit
Foam lining	490 lbs.		Football helmet	400 units at $52 per unit

c. Desired inventories at January 31:

Direct materials:			Finished products:	
Plastic	1,240 lbs.		Batting helmet	240 units at $34 per unit
Foam lining	470 lbs.		Football helmet	360 units at $55 per unit

d. Direct materials used in production:

In manufacture of batting helmet:
    Plastic . . . .   1.20 lbs. per unit of product
    Foam lining . . . .   0.50 lb. per unit of product
In manufacture of football helmet:
    Plastic . . . .   2.80 lbs. per unit of product
    Foam lining . . . .   1.40 lbs. per unit of product

e. Anticipated cost of purchases and beginning and ending inventory of direct materials:

Plastic	$7.00 per lb.
Foam lining	$4.00 per lb.

f. Direct labor requirements:

Batting helmet:
    Molding Department . . . .   0.20 hour at $14 per hour
    Assembly Department . . . .   0.50 hour at $12 per hour
Football helmet:
    Molding Department . . . .   0.30 hour at $14 per hour
    Assembly Department . . . .   0.65 hour at $12 per hour

g. Estimated factory overhead costs for January:

Indirect factory wages	$105,000	Power and light	$16,000
Depreciation of plant and equipment	30,000	Insurance and property tax	8,700

h. Estimated operating expenses for January:

Sales salaries expense	$265,800
Advertising expense	135,600
Office salaries expense	84,300
Depreciation expense—office equipment	5,200
Telephone expense—selling	3,500
Telephone expense—administrative	700
Travel expense—selling	43,100
Office supplies expense	4,900
Miscellaneous administrative expense	5,200

i. Estimated other income and expense for January:

Interest revenue	$14,500
Interest expense	18,700

j. Estimated tax rate: 30%

Instructions

1. Prepare a sales budget for January.
2. Prepare a production budget for January.
3. Prepare a direct materials purchases budget for January.
4. Prepare a direct labor cost budget for January.
5. Prepare a factory overhead cost budget for January.
6. Prepare a cost of goods sold budget for January. Work in process at the beginning of January is estimated to be $12,500, and work in process at the end of January is desired to be $13,500.
7. Prepare a selling and administrative expenses budget for January.
8. Prepare a budgeted income statement for January.

PR 21-4B
Cash budget
obj. 5

✓ *1. June deficiency,*
$10,000

The controller of Swift Shoes Inc. instructs you to prepare a monthly cash budget for the next three months. You are presented with the following budget information:

	April	May	June
Sales	$100,000	$150,000	$180,000
Manufacturing costs	40,000	50,000	54,000
Selling and administrative expenses	32,000	38,000	45,000
Capital expenditures	—	—	30,000

The company expects to sell about 10% of its merchandise for cash. Of sales on account, 60% are expected to be collected in full in the month following the sale and the remainder the following month. Depreciation, insurance, and property tax expense represent $18,000 of the estimated monthly manufacturing costs. The annual insurance premium is paid in July, and the annual property taxes are paid in November. Of the remainder of the manufacturing costs, 80% are expected to be paid in the month in which they are incurred and the balance in the following month.

Current assets as of April 1 include cash of $40,000, marketable securities of $65,000, and accounts receivable of $117,800 ($85,000 from March sales and $32,800 from February sales). Sales on account in February and March were $82,000 and $85,000, respectively. Current liabilities as of April 1 include a $50,000, 12%, 90-day note payable due June 20 and $29,000 of accounts payable incurred in March for manufacturing costs. All selling and administrative expenses are paid in cash in the period they are incurred. It is expected that $3,500 in dividends will be received in April. An estimated income tax payment of $34,000 will be made in May. Swift Shoes' regular quarterly dividend of $8,000 is expected to be declared in May and paid in June. Management desires to maintain a minimum cash balance of $35,000.

Instructions

1. Prepare a monthly cash budget and supporting schedules for April, May, and June 2008.
2. ➤ On the basis of the cash budget prepared in part (1), what recommendation should be made to the controller?

PR 21-5B
Budgeted income statement and balance sheet

objs. 4, 5

✓ *1. Budgeted net income, $619,800*

As a preliminary to requesting budget estimates of sales, costs, and expenses for the fiscal year beginning January 1, 2009, the following tentative trial balance as of December 31, 2008, is prepared by the Accounting Department of Cornerstone Publishing Co.:

Cash	$ 122,500	
Accounts Receivable	246,700	
Finished Goods	157,800	
Work in Process	37,800	
Materials	57,800	
Prepaid Expenses	4,500	
Plant and Equipment	620,000	
Accumulated Depreciation—Plant and Equipment		$ 267,000
Accounts Payable		184,500
Common Stock, $15 par		450,000
Retained Earnings		345,600
	$1,247,100	$1,247,100

Factory output and sales for 2009 are expected to total 30,000 units of product, which are to be sold at $110 per unit. The quantities and costs of the inventories at December 31, 2009, are expected to remain unchanged from the balances at the beginning of the year.

Budget estimates of manufacturing costs and operating expenses for the year are summarized as follows:

	Estimated Costs and Expenses	
	Fixed (Total for Year)	**Variable** (Per Unit Sold)
Cost of goods manufactured and sold:		
Direct materials	—	$26.00
Direct labor	—	8.50
Factory overhead:		
Depreciation of plant and equipment	$ 40,000	—
Other factory overhead	12,000	5.00
Selling expenses:		
Sales salaries and commissions	118,000	14.00
Advertising	114,200	—
Miscellaneous selling expense	10,500	2.15
Administrative expenses:		
Office and officers salaries	83,600	6.50
Supplies	4,400	1.25
Miscellaneous administrative expense	2,000	1.45

Balances of accounts receivable, prepaid expenses, and accounts payable at the end of the year are not expected to differ significantly from the beginning balances. Federal income tax of $350,000 on 2009 taxable income will be paid during 2009. Regular quarterly cash dividends of $1.75 a share are expected to be declared and paid in March, June, September, and December. It is anticipated that fixed assets will be purchased for $180,000 cash in May.

Instructions

1. Prepare a budgeted income statement for 2009.
2. Prepare a budgeted balance sheet as of December 31, 2009, with supporting calculations.

Special Activities

SA 21-1
Ethics and professional conduct in business

ETHICS

The director of marketing for Mobile Computer Co., Sheri Keller, had the following discussion with the company controller, Isaiah Johnson, on July 26 of the current year:

Sheri: Isaiah, it looks like I'm going to spend much less than indicated on my July budget.
Isaiah: I'm glad to hear it.
Sheri: Well, I'm not so sure it's good news. I'm concerned that the president will see that I'm under budget and reduce my budget in the future. The only reason that I look good is that we've delayed an advertising campaign. Once the campaign hits in September, I'm sure my actual expenditures will go up. You see, we are also having our sales convention in September. Having the advertising campaign and the convention at the same time is going to kill my September numbers.
Isaiah: I don't think that's anything to worry about. We all expect some variation in actual spending month to month. What's really important is staying within the budgeted targets for the year. Does that look as if it's going to be a problem?
Sheri: I don't think so, but just the same, I'd like to be on the safe side.
Isaiah: What do you mean?
Sheri: Well, this is what I'd like to do. I want to pay the convention-related costs in advance this month. I'll pay the hotel for room and convention space and purchase the airline tickets in advance. In this way, I can charge all these expenditures to July's budget. This would cause my actual expenses to come close to budget for July. Moreover, when the big advertising campaign hits in September, I won't have to worry about expenditures for the convention on my September budget as well. The convention costs will already be paid. Thus, my September expenses should be pretty close to budget.
Isaiah: I can't tell you when to make your convention purchases, but I'm not too sure that it should be expensed on July's budget.
Sheri: What's the problem? It looks like "no harm, no foul" to me. I can't see that there's anything wrong with this—it's just smart management.

How should Isaiah Johnson respond to Sheri Keller's request to expense the advanced payments for convention-related costs against July's budget?

SA 21-2
Evaluating budgeting systems

REAL WORLD

Children's Hospital of the King's Daughters Health System in Norfolk, Virginia, introduced a new budgeting method that allowed the hospital's annual plan to be updated for changes in operating plans. For example, if the budget was based on 400 patient-days (number of patients × number of days in the hospital) and the actual count rose to 450 patient-days, the variable costs of staffing, lab work, and medication costs could be adjusted to reflect this change. The budget manager stated, "I work with hospital directors to turn data into meaningful information and effect change before the month ends."

a. What budgeting methods are being used under the new approach?
b. Why are these methods superior to the former approaches?

SA 21-3
Service company static decision making

A bank manager of Citizens Bank Inc. uses the managerial accounting system to track the costs of operating the various departments within the bank. The departments include Cash Management, Trust Commercial Loans, Mortgage Loans, Operations, Credit Card, and Branch Services. The budget and actual results for the Operations Department are as follows:

Resources	Budget	Actual
Salaries	$150,000	$150,000
Benefits	30,000	30,000
Supplies	45,000	42,000
Travel	20,000	30,000
Training	25,000	35,000
Overtime	25,000	20,000
Total	$295,000	$307,000
Excess of actual over budget	$ 12,000	

a. ▭➤ What information is provided by the budget? Specifically, what questions can the bank manager ask of the Operations Department manager?

b. ▭➤ What information does the budget fail to provide? Specifically, could the budget information be presented differently to provide even more insight for the bank manager?

SA 21-4
Objectives of the master budget

Domino's Pizza L.L.C. operates pizza delivery and carryout restaurants. The annual report describes its business as follows:

> We offer a focused menu of high-quality, value priced pizza with three types of crust (Hand-Tossed, Thin Crust, and Deep Dish), along with buffalo wings, bread sticks, cheesy bread, CinnaStix®, and Coca-Cola® products. Our hand-tossed pizza is made from fresh dough produced in our regional distribution centers. We prepare every pizza using real cheese, pizza sauce made from fresh tomatoes, and a choice of high-quality meat and vegetable toppings in generous portions. Our focused menu and use of premium ingredients enable us to consistently and efficiently produce the highest-quality pizza.
>
> Over the 41 years since our founding, we have developed a simple, cost-efficient model. We offer a limited menu, our stores are designed for delivery and carry-out, and we do not generally offer dine-in service. As a result, our stores require relatively small, lower-rent locations and limited capital expenditures.

▭➤ How would a master budget support planning, directing, and control for Domino's?

SA 21-5
Integrity and evaluating budgeting systems

The city of Westwood has an annual budget cycle that begins on July 1 and ends on June 30. At the beginning of each budget year, an annual budget is established for each department. The annual budget is divided by 12 months to provide a constant monthly static budget. On June 30, all unspent budgeted monies for the budget year from the various city departments must be "returned" to the General Fund. Thus, if department heads fail to use their budget by year-end, they will lose it. A budget analyst prepared a chart of the difference between the monthly actual and budgeted amounts for the recent fiscal year. The chart was as follows:

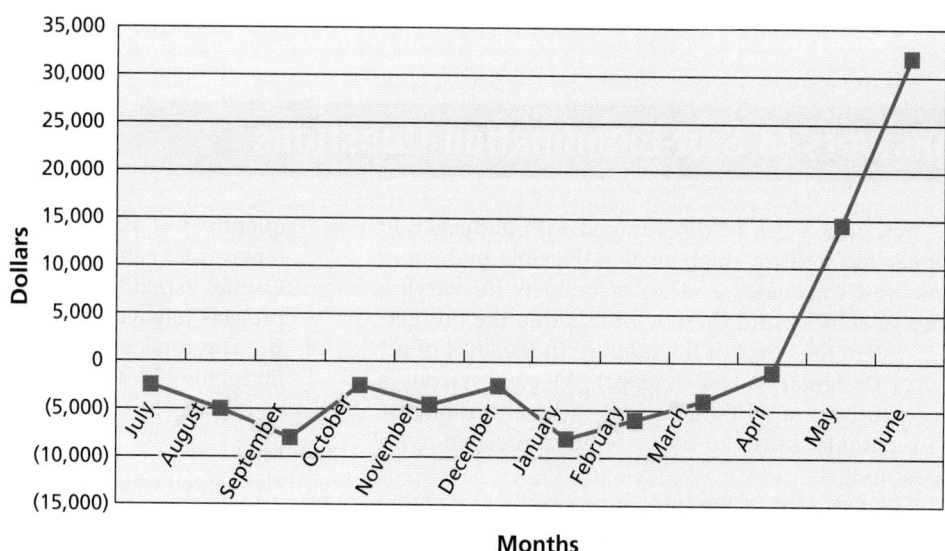

a. ▭➤ Interpret the chart.

b. ▭➤ Suggest an improvement in the budget system.

SA 21-6
Objectives of budgeting

At the beginning of the year, Kevin Frey decided to prepare a cash budget for the year, based upon anticipated cash receipts and payments. The estimates in the budget represent a "best guess." The budget is as follows:

Expected annual cash receipts:		
Salary from part-time job	$10,500	
Salary from summer job	5,000	
Total receipts		$15,500
Expected annual cash payments:		
Tuition	$ 5,000	
Books	400	
Rent	4,200	
Food	2,500	
Utilities	900	
Entertainment	4,000	
Total payments		17,000
Net change in cash		$ (1,500)

1. ▭▶ What does this budget suggest? In what ways is this information useful to Kevin?
2. a. ▭▶ Some items in the budget are more certain than are others. Which items are the most certain? Which items are the most uncertain? What are the implications of these different levels of certainty to Kevin's planning?
   b. ▭▶ Some payment items are more controllable than others. Assuming that Kevin plans to go to school, classify the items as controllable, partially controllable, or not controllable. What are the implications of controllable items to planning?
3. ▭▶ What actions could Kevin take in order to avoid having the anticipated shortfall of $1,500 at the end of the year?
4. ▭▶ What does this budget fail to consider, and what are the implications of these omissions to Kevin's planning?

SA 21-7
Budget for a state government

Group Project

Internet Project

In a group, find the home page of the state in which you presently live. The home page will be of the form *statename.gov*. At the home page site, search for annual budget information.

1. What are the budgeted sources of revenue and their percentage breakdown?
2. What are the major categories of budgeted expenditures (or appropriations) and their percentage breakdown?
3. Is the projected budget in balance?

Answers to Self-Examination Questions

1. **B** Individuals can be discouraged with budgets that appear too tight or unobtainable. Flexible budgeting (answer C) provides a series of budgets for varying rates of activity and thereby builds into the budgeting system the effect of fluctuations in the level of activity. Budgetary slack (answer A) comes from a loose budget, not a tight budget. A "spend it or lose it" mentality (answer D) is often associated with loose budgets.
2. **A** The first step of the budget process is to develop a plan. Once plans are established, management may direct actions (answer B). The results of actions can be controlled (answer C) by comparing them to the plan. This feedback (answer D) can be used by management to change plans or redirect actions.
3. **B** Administrative departments (answer B), such as Purchasing or Human Resources, will often use static budgeting. Production departments (answer A) fre-

quently use flexible budgets. Responsibility centers (answer C) can use either static or flexible budgeting. Capital expenditures budgets are used to plan capital projects (answer D).

4. **B** The total production indicated in the production budget is 257,500 units (answer B), which is computed as follows:

Sales	250,000 units
Plus desired ending inventory	30,000 units
Total	280,000 units
Less estimated beginning inventory	22,500 units
Total production	257,500 units

5. **C** Dixon expects to collect 70% of April sales ($560,000) plus 30% of the March sales ($195,000) in April, for a total of $755,000 (answer C). Answer A is 100% of April sales. Answer B is 70% of April sales. Answer D adds 70% of both March and April sales.

Performance Evaluation Using Variances from Standard Costs

1959-2000

© ALASTAIR GRANT/ASSOCIATED PRESS

objectives

After studying this chapter, you should be able to:

1 Describe the types of standards and how they are established for businesses.

2 Explain and illustrate how standards are used in budgeting.

3 Compute and interpret direct materials and direct labor variances.

4 Compute and interpret factory overhead controllable and volume variances.

5 Journalize the entries for recording standards in the accounts and prepare an income statement that includes variances from standard.

6 Explain and provide examples of nonfinancial performance measures.

BMW Group—Mini Cooper

When you play a sport, you are evaluated with respect to how well you perform compared to a standard or to a competitor. In bowling, for example, your score is compared to a perfect score of 300 or to the scores of your competitors. In this class, you are compared to performance standards. These standards are often described in terms of letter grades, which provide a measure of how well you achieved the class objectives. On your job, you are also evaluated according to performance standards.

Just as your class performance is evaluated, managers are evaluated according to goals and plans. For example, BMW Group uses manufacturing standards at its automobile assembly plants to guide performance. The Mini Cooper, a BMW Group car, is manufactured in a modern facility in Oxford, England. There are a number of performance targets applied in this plant. For example, the combined energy use in manufacturing a car has declined throughout this decade. The bodyshell is welded by over 250 robots so as to be two to three times stiffer than rival cars. In addition, the bodyshell dimensions are tested to the accuracy of the width of a human hair. Such performance standards are not surprising given the automotive racing background of John W. Cooper, the designer of the original Mini Cooper.

Performance is often measured as the difference between actual results and planned results. In this chapter, we will discuss and illustrate the ways in which business performance is evaluated.

If you want to take an online tour of the Oxford plant to see how a Mini Cooper is manufactured, go to **http://www.mini.com/com/en/manufacturing/index.jsp**.

Standards

objective 1

Describe the types of standards and how they are established for businesses.

What are standards? *Standards* are performance goals. Service, merchandising, and manufacturing businesses may all use standards to evaluate and control operations. For example, drivers for United Parcel Service, Inc., are expected to drive a standard distance per day. Salespersons for The Limited, Inc., are expected to meet sales standards.

Manufacturers normally use standard costs for each of the three manufacturing costs: direct materials, direct labor, and factory overhead. Accounting systems that use standards for these costs are called **standard cost systems**. These systems enable management to determine how much a product should cost (**standard cost**), how much it does cost (actual cost), and the causes of any difference (**cost variances**). When actual costs are compared with standard costs, only the exceptions or variances are reported for cost control. This reporting by the *principle of exceptions* allows management to focus on correcting the variances. Thus, using standard costs assists management in controlling costs and in motivating employees to focus on costs.

Standard cost systems are commonly used with job order and process systems. Automated manufacturing operations may also integrate standard cost data with the computerized system that directs operations. Such systems detect and report variances automatically and make adjustments to operations in progress.

SETTING STANDARDS

Setting standards is both an art and a science. The standard-setting process normally requires the joint efforts of accountants, engineers, and other management personnel. The accountant plays an essential role by expressing in dollars and cents the results of judgments and studies. Engineers contribute to the standard-setting process by identifying the materials, labor, and machine requirements needed to produce the product. For example, engineers determine the direct materials requirements by studying the materials specifications for products and estimating normal spoilage in production. Time and motion studies may be used to determine the time and direct labor required for each manufacturing operation. Engineering studies may also be used to determine standards for factory overhead, such as the amount of power needed to operate machinery.

Setting standards often begins with analyzing past operations. However, standards are not just an extension of past costs, and caution must be used in relying on past cost data. For example, inefficiencies may be contained within past costs. In addition, changes in technology, machinery, or production methods may make past costs irrelevant for future operations.

TYPES OF STANDARDS

Standards imply an acceptable level of production efficiency. One of the major objectives in setting standards is to motivate workers to achieve efficient operations.

Like the budgets we discussed earlier, tight, unrealistic standards may have a negative impact on performance. This is because workers may become frustrated with an inability to meet the standards and may give up trying to do their best. Such standards can be achieved only under perfect operating conditions, such as no idle time, no machine breakdowns, and no materials spoilage. These standards are called **ideal standards** or *theoretical standards*. Although ideal standards are not widely used, a few firms use ideal standards to motivate changes and improvement. Such an approach is termed "Kaizen costing." Kaizen is a Japanese term meaning "continuous improvement."

Standards that are too loose might not motivate employees to perform at their best. This is because the standard level of performance can be reached too easily. As a result, operating performance may be lower than what could be achieved.

Most companies use **currently attainable standards** (sometimes called *normal standards*). These standards can be attained with reasonable effort. Such standards allow for normal production difficulties and mistakes, such as materials spoilage and machine breakdowns. When reasonable standards are used, employees become more focused on cost and are more likely to put forth their best efforts.

An example from the game of golf illustrates the distinction between ideal and normal standards. In golf, "par" is an *ideal* standard for most players. Each player's USGA (United States Golf Association) handicap is the player's *normal* standard. The motivation of average players is to beat their handicaps because they may view beating par as unrealistic. Normal and ideal standards are illustrated as follows:

Mohawk Forest Products had a normal standard cost for a premium grade paper of $2,900 per ton, while the ideal cost was $1,342 per ton. The company used the ideal standard to motivate cost improvement. The resulting improvements allowed the company to reduce the normal standard cost to $1,738 per ton.

Currently attainable (personal best)   Ideal (world record)

REVIEWING AND REVISING STANDARDS

Standard costs should be continuously reviewed and should be revised when they no longer reflect operating conditions. Inaccurate standards may distort management decision making and may weaken management's ability to plan and control operations.

Business Connections

MAKING THE GRADE IN THE REAL WORLD—THE 360-DEGREE REVIEW

When you leave school and take your first job, you will likely be subject to an employee evaluation and feedback. These reviews provide feedback on performance that is often very detailed, providing insights to strengths and weaknesses that often go beyond mere grades.

One feedback trend is the 360-degree review. As stated by the human resources consulting firm Towers Perrin, the 360-degree review "is a huge wave that's just hitting—not only here, but all over the world." In a 360-

degree review, six to twelve evaluators who encircle an employee's sphere of influence, such as superiors, peers, and subordinates, are selected to fill out anonymous questionnaires. These questionnaires rate the employee on various criteria including the ability to work in groups, form a consensus, make timely decisions, motivate employees, and achieve objectives. The results are summarized and used to identify and strengthen weaknesses.

For example, one individual at Intel Corporation was very vocal during team meetings. In the 360-degree review, the manager thought this behavior was "refreshing." However, the employee's peers thought the vocal behavior monopolized conversations. Thus, what the manager viewed as a positive, the peer group viewed as a negative. The 360-degree review provided valuable information to both the manager and the employee to adjust behavior. Without the 360-degree feedback, the manager might have been blind to the group's reaction to the vocal behavior and reinforced behavior that was actually harmful to the group.

Sources: Llana DeBare, "360-Degrees of Evaluation: More Companies Turning to Full-Circle Job Reviews," *San Francisco Chronicle*, May 5, 1997; Francie Dalton, "Using 360 Degree Feedback Mechanisms," *Occupational Health and Safety*, Vol. 74, Issue 7, 2005.

Standards should not be revised, however, just because they differ from actual costs. They should be revised only when they no longer reflect the operating conditions that they were intended to measure. For example, the direct labor standard would not be revised simply because workers were unable to meet properly determined standards. On the other hand, standards should be revised when prices, product designs, labor rates, or manufacturing methods change. For example, when aluminum beverage cans were redesigned to taper slightly at the top of the can, manufacturers reduced the standard amount of aluminum per can because less aluminum was required for the top piece of the tapered can.

Using standards for performance evaluation has been criticized by some. Critics believe the following:

- Standards limit operating improvements by discouraging improvement beyond the standard.
- Standards are too difficult to maintain in a dynamic manufacturing environment, resulting in "stale standards."
- Standards can cause workers to lose sight of the larger objectives of the organization by focusing only on efficiency improvement.
- Standards can cause workers to unduly focus on their own operations to the possible harm of other operations that rely on them.

These critics believe that operating performance is more complex than just improving a single performance target. Advocates of standards would respond that standards are only part of the performance measurement system and that standards combined with other nonperformance measures, as discussed later in this chapter, can overcome these objections. Regardless of these criticisms, standards are widely used. Most managers strongly support standard cost systems and regard standards as critical for running large businesses efficiently.

Integrity, Objectivity, and Ethics in Business

COMPANY REPUTATION: THE BEST AND THE WORST

Harris Interactive annually ranks American corporations in terms of reputation. The ranking is based upon how respondents rate corporations on 20 attributes in six major areas. The six areas are emotional appeal, products and services, financial performance, workplace environment, social responsibility, and vision and leadership. What are the five highest and lowest ranked companies in its 2005 survey? The five highest (best) ranked companies were Johnson & Johnson, The Coca-Cola Company, Google, United Parcel Service of America, Inc. (UPS), and 3M. The five lowest (worst) companies were United Airlines, Haliburton Company, Adelphia Communications, MCI, and Enron. Not surprisingly, these latter companies are involved in either corporate scandal, financial distress, or bankruptcy.

Source: Harris Interactive, November 2005.

Budgetary Performance Evaluation

objective **2**

Explain and illustrate how standards are used in budgeting.

As we discussed in the previous chapter, the master budget assists a company in planning, directing, and controlling performance. In the remainder of this chapter, we will discuss using the master budget for control purposes. The control function, or budgetary performance evaluation, compares the actual performance against the budget.

We illustrate budget performance evaluation using Western Rider Inc., a manufacturer of blue jeans. Western Rider Inc. uses standard manufacturing costs in its budgets. The standards for direct materials, direct labor, and factory overhead are separated into two components: (1) a price standard and (2) a quantity standard. Multiplying these two elements together yields the standard cost per unit for a given manufacturing cost category, as shown for style XL jeans in Exhibit 1.

> **EXHIBIT 1**
>
> **Standard Cost for XL Jeans**

Manufacturing Costs	Standard Price	×	Standard Quantity per Pair	=	Standard Cost per Pair of XL Jeans
Direct materials	$5.00 per square yard		1.5 square yards		$ 7.50
Direct labor	$9.00 per hour		0.80 hour per pair		7.20
Factory overhead	$6.00 per hour		0.80 hour per pair		4.80
Total standard cost per pair					$19.50

The standard price and quantity are separated because the means of controlling them are normally different. For example, the direct materials price per square yard is controlled by the Purchasing Department, and the direct materials quantity per pair is controlled by the Production Department.

As we illustrated in the previous chapter, the budgeted costs at planned volumes are included in the master budget at the beginning of the period. The standard amounts budgeted for materials purchases, direct labor, and factory overhead are determined by multiplying the standard costs per unit by the *planned* level of production. At the end of the month, the standard costs per unit are multiplied by the *actual* production and compared to the actual costs.

To illustrate, assume that Western Rider produced and sold 5,000 pairs of XL jeans. It incurred direct materials costs of $40,150, direct labor costs of $38,500, and factory overhead costs of $22,400. The **budget performance report** shown in Exhibit 2 summarizes the actual costs, the standard amounts for the actual level of production achieved, and the differences between the two amounts. These differences are called

EXHIBIT 2

Budget Performance
Report

Western Rider Inc.
Budget Performance Report
For the Month Ended June 30, 2008

Manufacturing Costs	Actual Costs	Standard Cost at Actual Volume (5,000 pairs of XL Jeans)*	Cost Variance— (Favorable) Unfavorable
Direct materials	$ 40,150	$37,500	$ 2,650
Direct labor	38,500	36,000	2,500
Factory overhead	22,400	24,000	(1,600)
Total manufacturing costs	$101,050	$97,500	$ 3,550

*5,000 pairs × $7.50 per pair = $37,500
5,000 pairs × $7.20 per pair = $36,000
5,000 pairs × $4.80 per pair = $24,000

cost variances. A *favorable* cost variance occurs when the actual cost is less than the standard cost (at actual volumes). An *unfavorable* variance occurs when the actual cost exceeds the standard cost (at actual volumes).

Based on the information in the budget performance report, management can investigate major differences and take corrective action. In Exhibit 2, for example, the direct materials cost variance is an unfavorable $2,650. There are two possible explanations for this variance: (1) the amount of blue denim used per pair of blue jeans was different than expected, and/or (2) the purchase price of blue denim was different than expected. In the next sections, we will illustrate how to separate the price and quantity variances for direct materials, the rate and time variances for direct labor, and the controllable and volume variances for factory overhead.

The relationship of these variances to the total manufacturing cost variance is shown below.

> Favorable cost variance:
> Actual cost < Standard cost at actual volumes
>
> Unfavorable cost variance:
> Actual cost > Standard cost at actual volumes

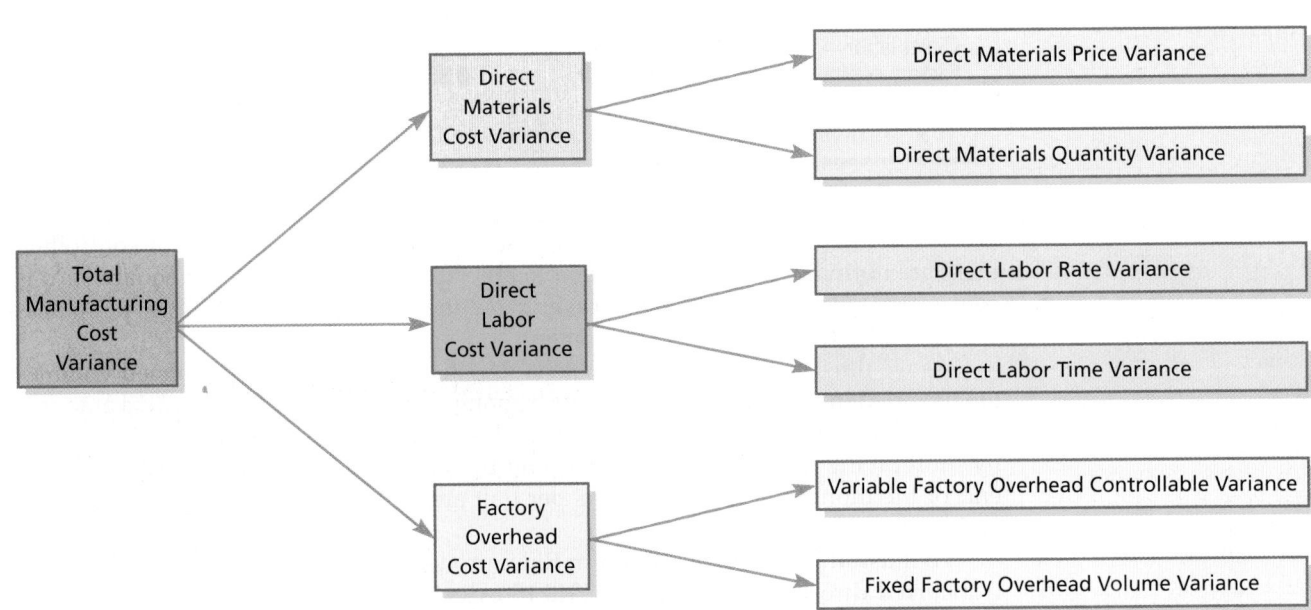

Direct Materials and Direct Labor Variances

The total cost of most goods or services is based on price multiplied by quantity. For example, your power bill is determined by multiplying the price per kilowatt hour by the number of kilowatt hours used during the month. Direct materials are determined by multiplying price by quantity, while direct labor is determined by multiplying the direct labor rate by time. Thus, the total cost variance for direct materials and direct labor can be separated into the portion of a cost variance that is caused by price (rate) differences and the portion that is caused by quantity (time) differences. These are illustrated next.

DIRECT MATERIALS VARIANCES

What caused Western Rider Inc.'s unfavorable materials variance of $2,650? Recall that the direct materials standards from Exhibit 1 are as follows:

> Price standard: $5.00 per square yard
> Quantity standard: 1.5 square yards per pair of XL jeans

To determine the number of standard square yards of denim budgeted, multiply the actual production for June 2008 (5,000 pairs) by the quantity standard (1.5 square yards per pair). Then multiply the standard square yards by the standard price per square yard ($5.00) to determine the *standard* budgeted cost at the actual volume. The calculation is shown as follows:

Standard square yards per pair of jeans	1.5 sq. yards
Actual units produced	× 5,000 pairs of XL jeans
Standard square yards of denim budgeted for actual production	7,500 sq. yards
Standard price per square yard	× $5.00
Standard direct materials cost at actual production (same as Exhibit 2)	$37,500

This calculation assumes that there is no change in the beginning and ending materials inventories. Thus, the amount of materials budgeted for production equals the amount purchased.

Assume that the *actual* total cost for denim used during June 2008 was as follows:

Actual quantity of denim used in production	7,300 sq. yards
Actual price per square yard	× $5.50
Total actual direct materials cost (same as Exhibit 2)	$40,150

The total unfavorable cost variance of $2,650 ($40,150 − $37,500) results from an excess price per square yard of $0.50 ($5.50 − $5.00) and using 200 (7,300 sq. yards − 7,500 sq. yards) fewer square yards of denim. These two reasons can be reported as two separate variances, as shown in the next sections.

Direct Materials Price Variance The **direct materials price variance** is the difference between the actual price per unit ($5.50) and the standard price per unit ($5.00), multiplied by the actual quantity used (7,300 square yards). If the actual price per unit exceeds the standard price per unit, the variance is unfavorable, as shown for Western Rider Inc. If the actual price per unit is less than the standard price per unit, the variance is favorable. The calculation for Western Rider Inc. is as follows:

Price variance:	
Actual price per unit	$5.50 per square yard
Standard price per unit	5.00 per square yard
Price variance—unfavorable	$0.50 per square yard × actual qty., 7,300 sq. yds. = $3,650 U

5,000
× 1.5
‾‾‾‾‾
7,500

Direct Materials Quantity Variance ~~The~~ **direct materials quantity variance** is the difference between the actual quantity used (7,300 square yards) and the standard quantity at actual production (7,500 square yards), multiplied by the standard price per unit ($5.00). If the actual quantity of materials used exceeds the standard quantity budgeted, the variance is unfavorable. If the actual quantity of materials used is less than the standard quantity, the variance is favorable, as shown for Western Rider Inc.:

Quantity variance:

Actual quantity	7,300 square yards
Standard quantity at	
actual production	7,500
Quantity variance—favorable	(200) square yards × standard price, $5.00 = ($1,000) F

Direct Materials Variance Relationships The direct materials variances can be illustrated by making the three calculations shown in Exhibit 3.

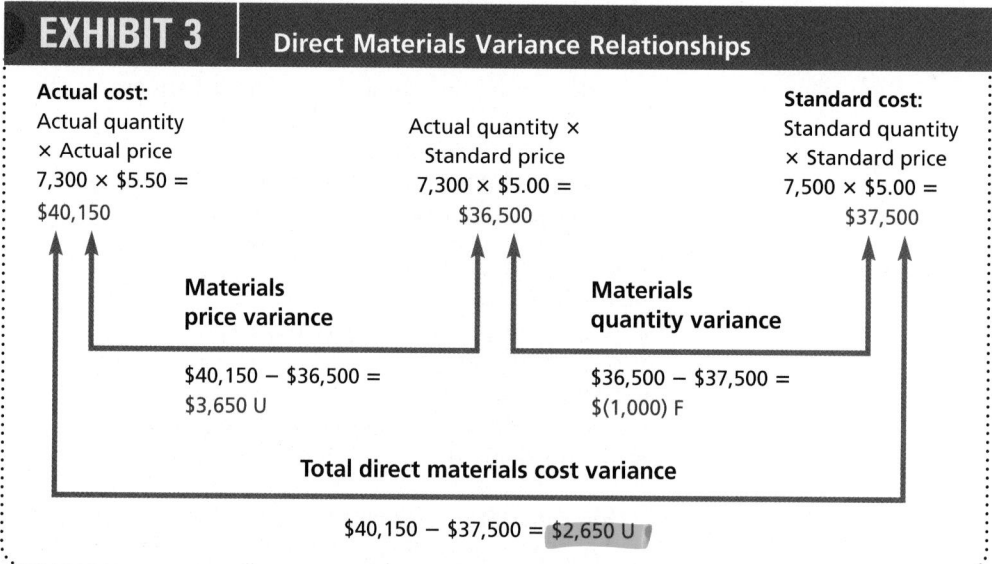

EXHIBIT 3 | **Direct Materials Variance Relationships**

Actual cost:
Actual quantity
× Actual price
7,300 × $5.50 =
$40,150

Actual quantity ×
Standard price
7,300 × $5.00 =
$36,500

Standard cost:
Standard quantity
× Standard price
7,500 × $5.00 =
$37,500

Materials price variance

$40,150 − $36,500 =
$3,650 U

Materials quantity variance

$36,500 − $37,500 =
$(1,000) F

Total direct materials cost variance

$40,150 − $37,500 = $2,650 U

Reporting Direct Materials Variances The direct materials quantity variance should be reported to the proper operating management level for corrective action. For example, an unfavorable quantity variance might have been caused by malfunctioning equipment that has not been properly maintained or operated. However, unfavorable materials quantity variances are not always caused by operating departments. For example, the excess materials usage may be caused by purchasing inferior raw materials. In this case, the Purchasing Department should be held responsible for the variance.

The materials price variance should normally be reported to the Purchasing Department, which may or may not be able to control this variance. If materials of the same quality could have been purchased from another supplier at the standard price, the variance was controllable. On the other hand, if the variance resulted from a marketwide price increase, the variance may not be controllable.

Example Exercise 22-1

objective **3**

Tip Top Corp. produces a product that requires six standard pounds per unit. The standard price is $4.50 per pound. If 3,000 units required 18,500 pounds, which were purchased at $4.35 per pound, what is the direct materials (a) price variance, (b) quantity variance, and (c) cost variance?

(continued)

Follow My Example 22-1

a. Direct materials price variance (favorable)	($2,775) [($4.35 − $4.50) × 18,500 pounds]
b. Direct materials quantity variance (unfavorable)	$2,250 [(18,500 pounds − 18,000 pounds*) × $4.50]
c. Direct materials cost variance (favorable)	($525) [($2,775) + $2,250] or [($4.35 × 18,500 pounds) − ($4.50 × 18,000 pounds)] = $80,475 − $81,000

*3,000 units × 6 pounds

For Practice: PE 22-1A, PE 22-1B

DIRECT LABOR VARIANCES

Western Rider Inc.'s direct labor cost variance can also be separated into two parts. Recall that the direct labor standards from Exhibit 1 are as follows:

Rate standard: $9.00 per hour
Time standard: 0.80 hour per pair of XL jeans

The actual production (5,000 pairs) is multiplied by the time standard (0.80 hour per pair) to determine the number of standard direct labor hours budgeted. The standard direct labor hours are then multiplied by the standard rate per hour ($9.00) to determine the *standard* direct labor cost at actual volumes. These calculations are shown below.

Standard direct labor hours per pair of XL jeans	0.80 direct labor hours
Actual units produced	× 5,000 pairs of jeans
Standard direct labor hours budgeted for actual production	4,000 direct labor hours
Standard rate per direct labor hour	× $9.00
Standard direct labor cost at actual production (same as Exhibit 2)	$36,000

Assume that the *actual* total cost for direct labor during June 2008 was as follows:

Actual direct labor hours used in production	3,850 direct labor hours
Actual rate per direct labor hour	× $10.00
Total actual direct labor cost (same as Exhibit 2)	$ 38,500

The total unfavorable cost variance $2,500 ($38,500 − $36,000) results from an excess rate of $1.00 ($10.00 − $9.00) per direct labor hour and using 150 (3,850 hours − 4,000 hours) fewer direct labor hours. These two reasons can be reported as two separate variances, as we discuss next.

Direct Labor Rate Variance The **direct labor rate variance** is the difference between the actual rate per hour ($10.00) and the standard rate per hour ($9.00), multiplied by the actual hours worked (3,850 hours). If the actual rate per hour is less than the standard rate per hour, the variance is favorable. If the actual rate per hour exceeds the standard rate per hour, the variance is unfavorable, as shown below for Western Rider Inc.

Rate variance:	
Actual rate	$10.00 per hour
Standard rate	9.00
Rate variance—unfavorable	$ 1.00 per hour × actual time, 3,850 hours = $3,850 U

Direct Labor Time Variance The **direct labor time variance** is the difference between the actual hours worked (3,850 hours) and the standard hours at actual production (4,000 hours), multiplied by the standard rate per hour ($9.00). If the actual hours worked exceed the standard hours, the variance is unfavorable. If the actual hours worked are less than the standard hours, the variance is favorable, as shown at the top of the next page for Western Rider Inc.

Time variance:

Actual hours	3,850 direct labor hours
Standard hours at actual production	4,000
Time variance—favorable	(150) direct labor hours × standard rate, $9.00 = ($1,350) F

Direct Labor Variance Relationships   The direct labor variances can be illustrated by making the three calculations shown in Exhibit 4.

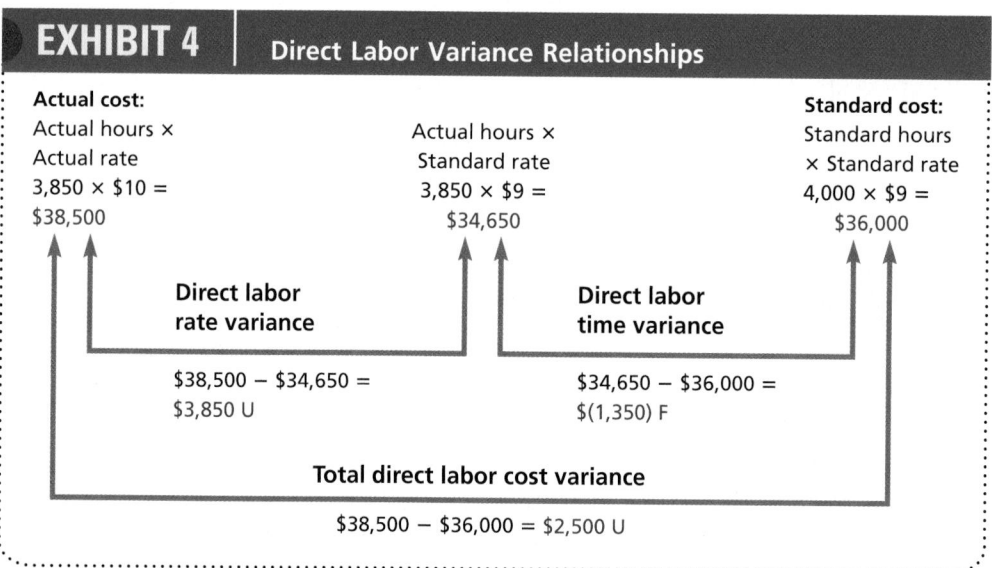

EXHIBIT 4 | **Direct Labor Variance Relationships**

Actual cost:
Actual hours ×
Actual rate
3,850 × $10 =
$38,500

Actual hours ×
Standard rate
3,850 × $9 =
$34,650

Standard cost:
Standard hours
× Standard rate
4,000 × $9 =
$36,000

Direct labor rate variance

$38,500 − $34,650 =
$3,850 U

Direct labor time variance

$34,650 − $36,000 =
$(1,350) F

Total direct labor cost variance

$38,500 − $36,000 = $2,500 U

Reporting Direct Labor Variances   Controlling direct labor cost is normally the responsibility of the production supervisors. To aid them, reports analyzing the cause of any direct labor variance may be prepared. Differences between standard direct labor hours and actual direct labor hours can be investigated. For example, a time variance may be incurred because of the shortage of skilled workers. Such variances may be uncontrollable unless they are related to high turnover rates among employees, in which case the cause of the high turnover should be investigated.

Likewise, differences between the rates paid for direct labor and the standard rates can be investigated. For example, unfavorable rate variances may be caused by the improper scheduling and use of workers. In such cases, skilled, highly paid workers may be used in jobs that are normally performed by unskilled, lower-paid workers. In this case, the unfavorable rate variance should be reported for corrective action to the managers who schedule work assignments.

Hospitals use time standards, termed *standard treatment protocols*, to evaluate the efficiency of performing hospital procedures.

Direct Labor Standards for Nonmanufacturing Activities   Direct labor time standards can also be applied to nonmanufacturing administrative, selling, and service activities, which are repetitive and produce a common output. In these cases, the use of standards is similar to that described in this section for a manufactured product. For example, standards can be applied to the work of customer service personnel who process sales orders. A standard time for processing a sales order (the output) could be developed. The variance between the actual time of processing a volume of sales orders and the standard time could then be used to control sales order processing costs. Other nonmanufacturing activities that have been used in conjunction with standards are help desk operations, warehouse operations, nursing care, and insurance application processing.

However, when nonmanufacturing activities are not repetitive, direct labor time standards are less commonly used. This occurs when the time to perform nonmanufacturing activities is not directly related to a unit of output. For example, the time associated with the work of a senior executive or the work of a research and development scientist is not easily related to a measurable output. In these cases, nonmanufacturing expenses are normally controlled by using static budgets.

Example Exercise 22-2   **objective 3**

Tip Top Corp. produces a product that requires 2.5 standard hours per unit at a standard hourly rate of $12 per hour. If 3,000 units required 7,420 hours at an hourly rate of $12.30 per hour, what is the direct labor (a) rate variance, (b) time variance, and (c) cost variance?

Follow My Example 22-2

a. Direct labor rate variance (unfavorable) $2,226 [($12.30 − $12.00) × 7,420 hours]
b. Direct labor time variance (favorable)   ($960) [(7,420 hours − 7,500 hours*) × $12.00]
c. Direct labor cost variance (unfavorable) $1,266 [$2,226 + ($960)] or [($12.30 × 7,420 hours) −
                                                   ($12.00 × 7,500 hours)] = $91,266 − $90,000

*3,000 units × 2.5 hours

For Practice: PE 22-2A, PE 22-2B

Factory Overhead Variances

objective 4

Compute and interpret factory overhead controllable and volume variances.

Factory overhead costs are more difficult to manage than are direct labor and materials costs. This is because the relationship between production volume and indirect costs is not easy to determine. For example, when production is increased, the direct materials will increase. But what about the Engineering Department overhead? The relationship between production volume and cost is less clear for the Engineering Department. Companies normally respond to this difficulty by separating factory overhead into variable and fixed costs. For example, manufacturing supplies are considered variable to production volume, whereas straight-line plant depreciation is considered fixed. In the following sections, we discuss the approaches used to budget and control factory overhead by separating overhead into fixed and variable components.

THE FACTORY OVERHEAD FLEXIBLE BUDGET

A flexible budget may be used to determine the impact of changing production on fixed and variable factory overhead costs. The standard overhead rate is determined by dividing the budgeted factory overhead costs by the standard amount of productive activity, such as direct labor hours. Exhibit 5 is a flexible factory overhead budget for Western Rider Inc.

In Exhibit 5, the standard factory overhead cost rate is $6.00. It is determined by dividing the total budgeted cost of 100% of normal capacity (6,250 units produced) by the standard hours required at 100% of normal capacity, or $30,000/5,000 hours = $6.00 per hour. This rate can be subdivided into $3.60 per hour for variable factory overhead ($18,000/5,000 hours) and $2.40 per hour for fixed factory overhead ($12,000/5,000 hours).

Variances from standard for factory overhead cost result from:

1. Actual variable factory overhead cost greater or less than budgeted variable factory overhead for actual production.
2. Actual production at a level above or below 100% of normal capacity.

The first factor results in the controllable variance for variable overhead costs. The second factor results in a volume variance for fixed overhead costs. We will discuss each of these variances next.

EXHIBIT 5

Factory Overhead Cost
Budget Indicating
Standard Factory
Overhead Rate

	A	B	C	D	E	
	Western Rider Inc.					
	Factory Overhead Cost Budget					
	For the Month Ending June 30, 2008					
1	Percent of normal capacity	80%	90%	100%	110%	1
2	Units produced	5,000	5,625	6,250	6,875	2
3	Direct labor hours (0.80 hour per unit)	4,000	4,500	5,000	5,500	3
4	Budgeted factory overhead:					4
5	Variable costs:					5
6	Indirect factory wages	$ 8,000	$ 9,000	$10,000	$11,000	6
7	Power and light	4,000	4,500	5,000	5,500	7
8	Indirect materials	2,400	2,700	3,000	3,300	8
9	Total variable cost	$14,400	$16,200	$18,000	$19,800	9
10	Fixed costs:					10
11	Supervisory salaries	$ 5,500	$ 5,500	$ 5,500	$ 5,500	11
12	Depreciation of plant					12
13	and equipment	4,500	4,500	4,500	4,500	13
14	Insurance and property taxes	2,000	2,000	2,000	2,000	14
15	Total fixed cost	$12,000	$12,000	$12,000	$12,000	15
16	Total factory overhead cost	$26,400	$28,200	$30,000	$31,800	16
17						17
18	Factory overhead rate per direct labor hour, $30,000/5,000 hours = $6.00					18

VARIABLE FACTORY OVERHEAD CONTROLLABLE VARIANCE

The variable factory overhead **controllable variance** is the difference between the actual variable overhead incurred and the budgeted variable overhead for actual production. The controllable variance measures the *efficiency* of using variable overhead resources. Thus, if the actual variable overhead is less than the budgeted variable overhead, the variance is favorable. If the actual variable overhead exceeds the budgeted variable overhead, the variance is unfavorable.

To illustrate, recall that Western Rider Inc. produced 5,000 pairs of XL jeans in June. Each pair requires 0.80 standard labor hour for production. As a result, Western Rider Inc. had 4,000 standard hours at actual production (5,000 jeans × 0.80 hour). This represents 80% of normal productive capacity (4,000 hours/5,000 hours). The standard variable overhead at 4,000 hours worked, according to the budget in Exhibit 5, was $14,400 (4,000 direct labor hours × $3.60). The following actual factory overhead costs were incurred in June:

Actual costs:	
Variable factory overhead	$10,400
Fixed factory overhead	12,000
Total actual factory overhead	$22,400

The controllable variance can be calculated as follows:

Controllable variance:	
Actual variable factory overhead	$10,400
Budgeted variable factory overhead for	
actual amount produced (4,000 hrs. × $3.60)	14,400
Variance—favorable	$ (4,000) F

The variable factory overhead controllable variance indicates management's ability to keep the factory overhead costs within the budget limits. Since variable factory overhead costs are normally controllable at the department level, responsibility for controlling this variance usually rests with department supervisors.

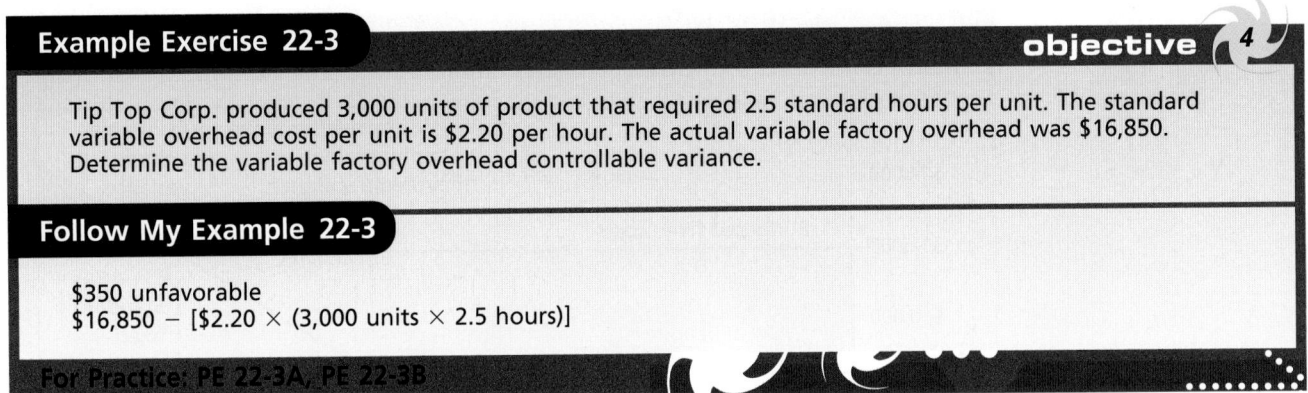

Example Exercise 22-3   **objective 4**

Tip Top Corp. produced 3,000 units of product that required 2.5 standard hours per unit. The standard variable overhead cost per unit is $2.20 per hour. The actual variable factory overhead was $16,850. Determine the variable factory overhead controllable variance.

Follow My Example 22-3

$350 unfavorable
$16,850 − [$2.20 × (3,000 units × 2.5 hours)]

For Practice: PE 22-3A, PE 22-3B

FIXED FACTORY OVERHEAD VOLUME VARIANCE

Using currently attainable standards, Western Rider Inc. set its budgeted normal capacity at 5,000 direct labor hours. This is the amount of expected capacity that management believes will be used under normal business conditions. You should note that this amount may be much less than the total available capacity if management believes demand will be low.

The fixed factory overhead **volume variance** is the difference between the budgeted fixed overhead at 100% of normal capacity and the standard fixed overhead for the actual production achieved during the period. The volume variance measures the use of fixed overhead resources. If the standard fixed overhead exceeds the budgeted overhead at 100% of normal capacity, the variance is favorable. Thus, the firm used its plant and equipment more than would be expected under normal operating conditions. If the standard fixed overhead is less than the budgeted overhead at 100% of normal capacity, the variance is unfavorable. Thus, the company used its plant and equipment less than would be expected under normal operating conditions.

The volume variance for Western Rider Inc. is shown in the following calculation:

100% of normal capacity (6,250 units produced)	5,000 direct labor hours
Standard hours at actual production	4,000
Capacity not used	1,000 direct labor hours
Standard fixed overhead rate	× $2.40
Volume variance—unfavorable	$ 2,400 U

Exhibit 6 illustrates the volume variance graphically. For Western Rider Inc., the budgeted fixed overhead is $12,000 at all levels. The standard fixed overhead at 5,000 hours is also $12,000. This is the point at which the standard fixed overhead line intersects the budgeted fixed cost line. For actual volume greater than 100% of normal capacity, the volume variance is favorable. For volume at less than 100% of normal volume, the volume variance is unfavorable. For Western Rider Inc., the volume variance is unfavorable because the actual production is 4,000 standard hours, or 80% of normal volume. The amount of the volume variance, $2,400, can be viewed as the cost of the unused capacity (1,000 hours).

An unfavorable volume variance may be due to such factors as failure to maintain an even flow of work, machine breakdowns, repairs causing work stoppages, and failure to obtain enough sales orders to keep the factory operating at normal capacity. Management should determine the causes of the unfavorable variance and consider taking corrective action. A volume variance caused by an uneven flow of work, for example, can be remedied by changing operating procedures. Volume variances caused by lack of sales orders may be corrected through increased advertising or other sales effort.

EXHIBIT 6 | Graph of Fixed Overhead Volume Variance

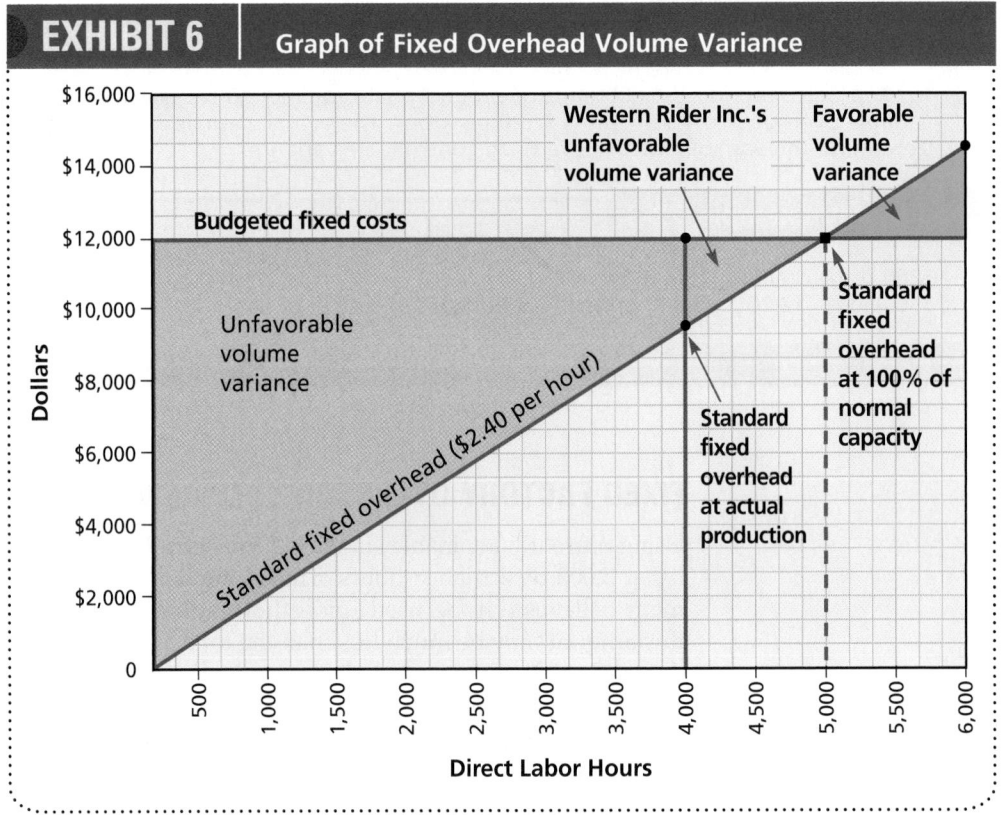

Volume variances tend to encourage manufacturing managers to run the factory above the normal capacity. This is favorable when the additional production can be sold. However, if the additional production cannot be sold and must be stored as inventory, favorable volume variances may actually be harmful. For example, one paper company ran paper machines above normal volume in order to create favorable volume variances. Unfortunately, this created a six months' supply of finished goods inventory that had to be stored in public warehouses. The "savings" from the favorable volume variances were exceeded by the additional inventory carrying costs. By creating incentives for manufacturing managers to overproduce, the volume variances produced *goal conflicts*, as we described in the preceding chapter.

Many companies develop customized variances to fit their business. For example, Parker Hannifin Corp. reports a "standard run quantity variance" (which measures the difference between actual lot size and ideal lot size), "material substitution variance" (which measures the financial impact of substituted material), and "method variance" (which measures the financial impact of a change in processing methods).

Example Exercise 22-4   objective 4

Tip Top Corp. produced 3,000 units of product that required 2.5 standard hours per unit. The standard fixed overhead cost per unit is $0.90 per hour at 8,000 hours, which is 100% of normal capacity. Determine the fixed factory overhead volume variance.

Follow My Example 22-4

$450 unfavorable
$0.90 × [8,000 hours − (3,000 units × 2.5 hours)]

For Practice: PE 22-4A, PE 22-4B

REPORTING FACTORY OVERHEAD VARIANCES

The total factory overhead cost variance is the difference between the actual factory overhead and the total overhead applied to production. This calculation is as follows:

Total actual factory overhead	$22,400
Factory overhead applied (4,000 hours × $6.00 per hour)	24,000
Total factory overhead cost variance—favorable	$ (1,600) F

The factory overhead cost variance may be broken down by each variable factory overhead cost and fixed factory overhead cost element in a *factory overhead cost variance report*. Such a report, which is useful to management in controlling costs, is shown in Exhibit 7. The report indicates both the controllable variance and the volume variance.

EXHIBIT 7

Factory Overhead
Cost Variance Report

	A	B	C	D	E	
		Western Rider Inc.				
		Factory Overhead Cost Variance Report				
		For the Month Ending June 30, 2008				
1	Productive capacity for the month (100% of normal)	5,000 hours				1
2	Actual production for the month	4,000 hours				2
3						3
4		**Budget**				4
5		(at Actual		**Variances**		5
6		Production)	**Actual**	Favorable	Unfavorable	6
7	Variable factory overhead costs:					7
8	Indirect factory wages	$ 8,000	$ 5,100	$2,900		8
9	Power and light	4,000	4,200		$ 200	9
10	Indirect materials	2,400	1,100	1,300		10
11	Total variable factory					11
12	overhead cost	$14,400	$10,400			12
13	Fixed factory overhead costs:					13
14	Supervisory salaries	$ 5,500	$ 5,500			14
15	Depreciation of plant and					15
16	equipment	4,500	4,500			16
17	Insurance and property taxes	2,000	2,000			17
18	Total fixed factory					18
19	overhead cost	$12,000	$12,000			19
20	Total factory overhead cost	$26,400	$22,400			20
21	Total controllable variances			$4,200	$ 200	21
22						22
23						23
24	Net controllable variance—favorable				$4,000	24
25	Volume variance—unfavorable:					25
26	Capacity not used at the standard rate for fixed					26
27	factory overhead—1,000 × $2.40				2,400	27
28	Total factory overhead cost variance—favorable				$1,600	28

FACTORY OVERHEAD VARIANCES AND THE FACTORY OVERHEAD ACCOUNT

At the end of the period, the factory overhead account normally has a balance. As we discussed in an earlier chapter, a debit balance in Factory Overhead is underapplied overhead, while a credit balance is overapplied overhead. This end-of-period balance, which represents the difference between actual overhead incurred and applied overhead, is also the total factory overhead variance for the period. A debit balance, underapplied overhead, represents an unfavorable total factory overhead variance, while a credit balance, overapplied overhead, is a favorable variance.

To illustrate, the factory overhead account for Western Rider Inc. for the month ending June 30, 2008, is shown below.

Factory Overhead

Actual factory overhead	22,400	24,000	Applied factory overhead
($10,400 + $12,000)			(4,000 hrs. × $6.00 per hr.)
		Bal., June 30 1,600	Overapplied factory overhead

The $1,600 overapplied factory overhead is the favorable total factory cost variance shown in Exhibit 7. The variable factory overhead controllable variance and the volume variance can be computed using the factory overhead account and comparing it with the budgeted total overhead for the actual amount produced. As shown below, the difference between the actual overhead incurred and the budgeted overhead is the controllable variance. The difference between the applied overhead and the budgeted overhead is the volume variance.

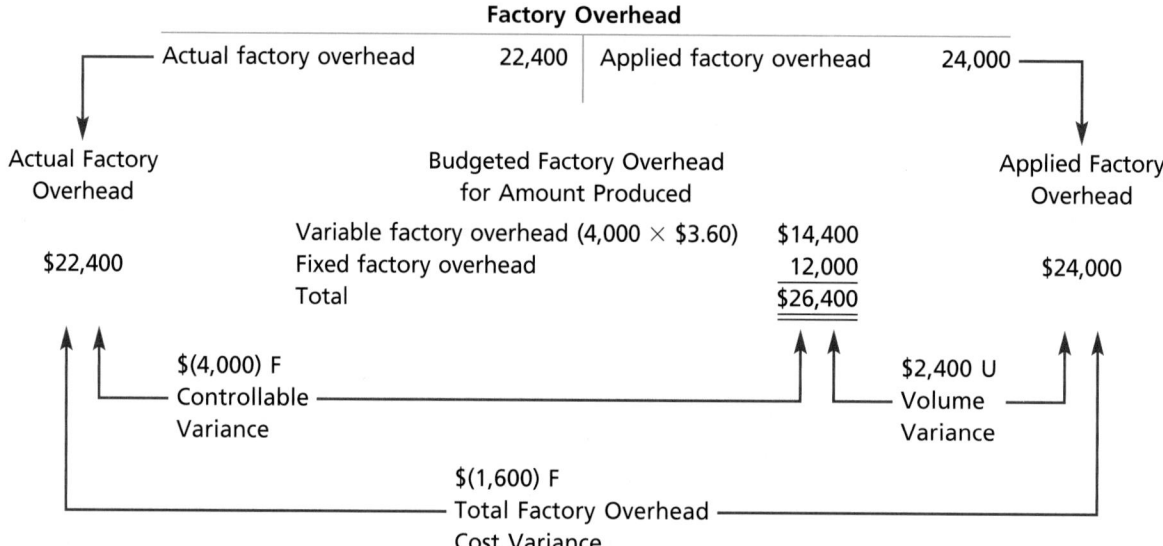

If the actual factory overhead exceeds (is less than) the budgeted factory overhead, the controllable variance is unfavorable (favorable). In contrast, if the applied factory overhead is less than (exceeds) the budgeted factory overhead, the volume variance is unfavorable (favorable). This is because, when the applied overhead is less than the budgeted overhead, the company has operated at less than normal capacity, and thus the volume variance is unfavorable.

It is also possible to break down many of the individual factory overhead cost variances into quantity and price variances, similar to direct materials and direct labor. For example, the indirect factory wages variance may include both time and rate variances. Likewise, the indirect materials variance may include both a quantity variance and a price variance. Such variances are illustrated in advanced textbooks.

objective 5

Journalize the entries for recording standards in the accounts and prepare an income statement that includes variances from standard.

Recording and Reporting Variances from Standards

Standard costs can be used solely as a management tool separate from the accounts in the general ledger. However, many companies include both standard costs and variances, in addition to actual costs, in their accounts. In doing so, one approach is to record the standard costs and variances at the same time the actual manufacturing costs are recorded in the accounts. To illustrate, assume that Western Rider Inc. purchased, on account, the 7,300 square yards of blue denim used at $5.50 per square yard. The standard price for direct materials is $5.00 per square yard. The entry to record the purchase and the unfavorable direct materials price variance is as follows:

Materials (7,300 sq. yds. × $5.00)	36 5 0 0 00		
Direct Materials Price Variance	3 6 5 0 00		
Accounts Payable (7,300 sq. yds. × $5.50)		40 1 5 0 00	

The materials account is debited for the actual quantity purchased at the standard price, $36,500 (7,300 square yards × $5.00). Accounts Payable is credited for the $40,150 actual cost. The unfavorable direct materials price variance is $3,650 [($5.50 actual price per square yard − $5.00 standard price per square yard) × 7,300 square yards purchased]. It is recorded by debiting Direct Materials Price Variance. If the variance had been favorable, Direct Materials Price Variance would have been credited for the amount of the variance.

The direct materials quantity variance is recorded in a similar manner. For example, Western Rider Inc. used 7,300 square yards of blue denim to produce 5,000 pairs of XL jeans, compared to a standard of 7,500 square yards. The entry to record the materials used is as follows:

Work in Process (7,500 sq. yds. × $5.00)	37 5 0 0 00		
Direct Materials Quantity Variance		1 0 0 0 00	
Materials (7,300 sq. yds. × $5.00)		36 5 0 0 00	

The work in process account is debited for the standard price of the standard amount of direct materials required, $37,500 (7,500 square yards × $5.00). Materials is credited for the actual amount of materials used at the standard price, $36,500 (7,300 square yards × $5.00). The favorable direct materials quantity variance of $1,000 [(7,500 standard square yards − 7,300 actual square yards) × $5.00 standard price per square yard] is credited to Direct Materials Quantity Variance. If the variance had been unfavorable, Direct Materials Quantity Variance would have been debited for the amount of the variance.

Example Exercise 22-5   objective 5

Tip Top Corp. produced 3,000 units that require six standard pounds per unit at $4.50 standard price per pound. The company actually used 18,500 pounds in production. Journalize the entry to record the standard direct materials used in production.

Follow My Example 22-5

Work in Process (18,000* pounds × $4.50)	81,000	
Direct Materials Quantity Variance [(18,500 pounds − 18,000 pounds) × $4.50]	2,250	
Materials (18,500 pounds × $4.50)		83,250

*3,000 units × 6 pounds per unit = 18,000 standard pounds for units produced

For Practice: PE 22-5A, PE 22-5B

The entries for direct labor are recorded in a manner similar to direct materials. Thus, the work in process account is debited for the standard cost of direct labor and the wages payable account credited for the actual direct labor cost. Direct labor rate and time variances would be either debited (unfavorable) or credited (favorable) as appropriate. Factory overhead would be treated in a similar manner as illustrated with the factory overhead T account in the previous section. As goods are completed, the work in process account is credited for the standard cost of the product transferred, and the finished goods account is debited.

In a given period, it is possible to have both favorable and unfavorable variances. At the end of the period, the balances of the variance accounts will indicate the net favorable or unfavorable variance for the period.

Variances from standard costs are usually not reported to stockholders and others outside the business. If standards are recorded in the accounts, however, the variances may be reported in income statements prepared for management's use. Exhibit 8 is an example of such an income statement prepared for Western Rider Inc.'s internal use. In this exhibit, we assume a sales price of $28 per pair of jeans, selling expenses of $14,500, and administrative expenses of $11,225.

At the end of the fiscal year, the variances from standard are usually transferred to the cost of goods sold account. However, if the variances are significant or if many of the products manufactured are still in inventory, the variances should be allocated to the work in process, finished goods, and cost of goods sold accounts. Such an allocation converts these account balances from standard cost to actual cost.

EXHIBIT 8		
	Western Rider Inc.	
	Income Statement	
Variances from	**For the Month Ended June 30, 2008**	
Standards in Income		
Statement		

Western Rider Inc.
Income Statement
For the Month Ended June 30, 2008

		Favorable	Unfavorable	
Sales				$140,000[1]
Cost of goods sold—at standard				97,500[2]
Gross profit—at standard				$ 42,500
Less variances from standard cost:				
Direct materials price			$ 3,650	
Direct materials quantity		$1,000		
Direct labor rate			3,850	
Direct labor time		1,350		
Factory overhead controllable		4,000		
Factory overhead volume			2,400	3,550
Gross profit				$ 38,950
Operating expenses:				
Selling expenses			$14,500	
Administrative expenses			11,225	25,725
Income before income tax				$ 13,225

[1]5,000 × $28
[2]$37,500 + $36,000 + $24,000 (from Exhibit 2),
  or 5,000 × $19.50 (from Exhibit 1)

Example Exercise 22-6   objective **5**

Prepare an income statement for the year ended December 31, 2008, through gross profit for Tip Top Corp. using the variance data in Example Exercises 22-1 through 22-4. Assume Tip Top sold 3,000 units at $100 per unit.

(continued)

Follow My Example 22-6

TIP TOP CORP.
INCOME STATEMENT THROUGH GROSS PROFIT
For the Year Ended December 31, 2008

Sales (3,000 units × $100)				$300,000
Cost of goods sold—at standard				194,250*
Gross profit—at standard				$105,750
		Favorable	Unfavorable	
Less variances from standard cost:				
Direct materials price (EE22-1)		$2,775		
Direct materials quantity (EE22-1)			$2,250	
Direct labor rate (EE22-2)			2,226	
Direct labor time (EE22-2)		960		
Factory overhead controllable (EE22-3)			350	
Factory overhead volume (EE22-4)			450	1,541
Gross profit—actual				$104,209

*Direct materials (3,000 units × 6 pounds × $4.50)	$ 81,000	
Direct labor (3,000 units × 2.5 hours × $12.00)	90,000	
Factory overhead [3,000 units × 2.5 hours × ($2.20 + $0.90)]	23,250	
Cost of goods sold at standard	$194,250	

For Practice: PE 22-6A, PE 22-6B

Nonfinancial Performance Measures

objective   6

Explain and provide examples of nonfinancial performance measures.

Many managers believe that financial performance measures, such as variances from standard, should be supplemented with nonfinancial performance measures. A **nonfinancial performance measure** is a performance measure expressed in units other than dollars. Nonfinancial performance measures are often used to evaluate the time, quality, or quantity of a business activity. Examples of nonfinancial performance measures from the airline industry are on-time performance, percent of bags lost, and number of customer complaints.

Measuring both financial and nonfinancial performance helps employees consider multiple, and sometimes conflicting, performance objectives. For example, one company had a machining operation that was measured according to a direct labor time standard. Employees did their work quickly in order to create favorable direct labor time variances. Unfortunately, the fast work resulted in poor quality that, in turn, created difficulty in the assembly operation. The company decided to use both a labor time standard and a quality standard in order to encourage employees to consider both the speed and quality of their work.

In the preceding example, nonfinancial performance measures brought additional perspectives, such as quality of work, to evaluating performance. Some additional examples of nonfinancial performance measures are as follows:

Nonfinancial Performance Measures

Inventory turnover
Percent on-time delivery
Elapsed time between a customer order and product delivery
Customer preference rankings compared to competitors
Response time to a service call
Time to develop new products
Employee satisfaction
Number of customer complaints

Nonfinancial measures can be linked to either the inputs or outputs of an activity or process. A **process** is a sequence of activities linked together for performing a particular task. For example, the fast food service process consists of the "food preparation" and "counter service" activities that are performed in providing fast food. The relationship between a process or activity and its inputs and outputs is shown as follows:

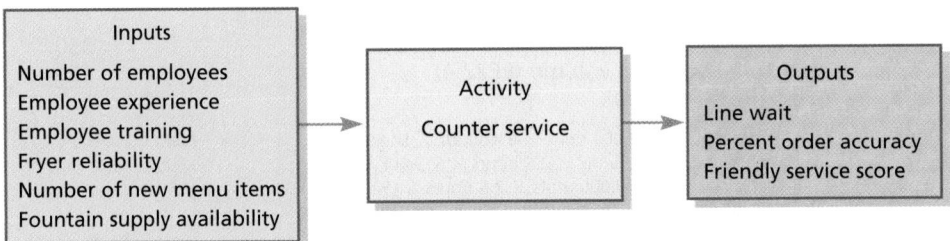

To illustrate nonfinancial measures for a single activity, consider the counter service activity of a fast food restaurant. The following input/output relationship could be identified:

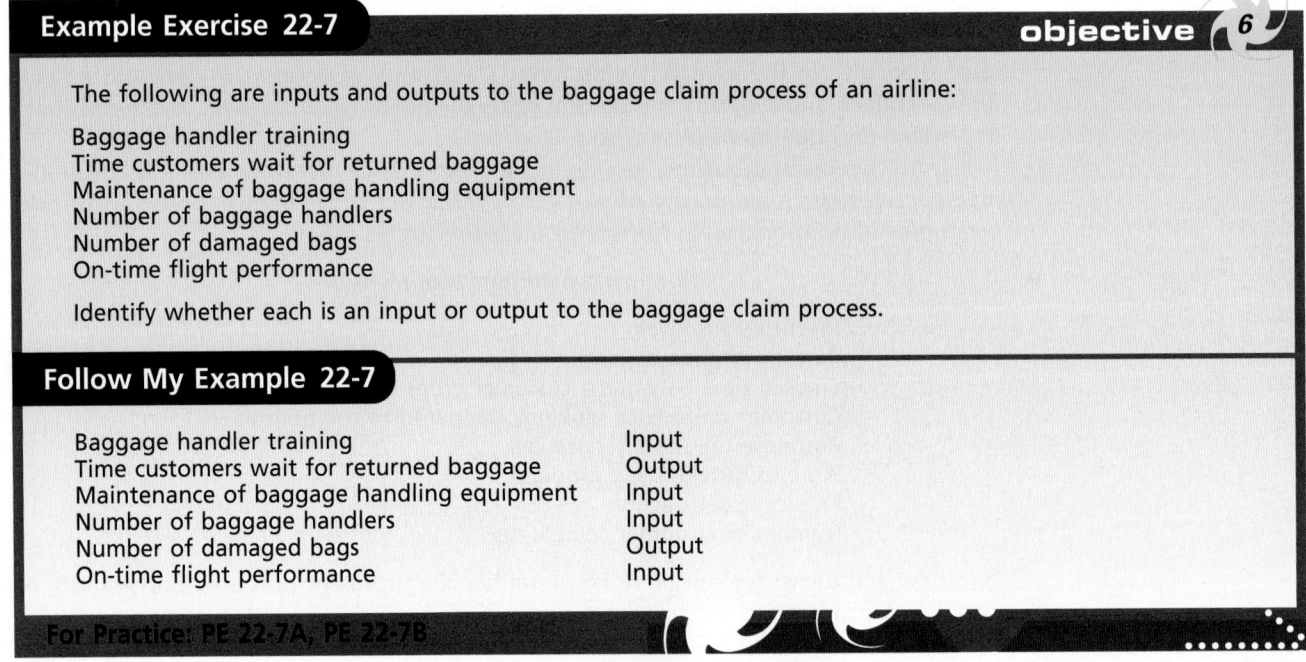

The outputs of the counter service activity include the customer line wait, order accuracy, and service experience. The inputs that impact these outputs include the number of employees, level of employee experience and training, reliability of the french fryer, menu complexity, fountain drink supply, and the like. Also, note that the inputs for one activity could be the outputs of another.

To illustrate, fryer reliability is an input to the counter service activity, but is an output of the french frying activity. Moving back, fryer maintenance would be an input to the french frying activity. Thus, a chain of inputs and outputs can be developed between a set of connected activities or processes. The fast food restaurant can develop a set of linked nonfinancial performance measures across the chain of inputs and outputs. The output measures tell management how the activity is performing, such as keeping the line wait to a minimum. The input measures are the *levers* that impact the activity's performance. Thus, if the fast food restaurant line wait is too long, then the input measures might indicate a need for more training, more employees, or better fryer reliability.

Example Exercise 22-7   objective 6

The following are inputs and outputs to the baggage claim process of an airline:

Baggage handler training
Time customers wait for returned baggage
Maintenance of baggage handling equipment
Number of baggage handlers
Number of damaged bags
On-time flight performance

Identify whether each is an input or output to the baggage claim process.

Follow My Example 22-7

Baggage handler training	Input
Time customers wait for returned baggage	Output
Maintenance of baggage handling equipment	Input
Number of baggage handlers	Input
Number of damaged bags	Output
On-time flight performance	Input

For Practice: PE 22-7A, PE 22-7B

At a Glance

1. Describe the types of standards and how they are established for businesses.

Key Points	Key Learning Outcomes	Example Exercises	Practice Exercises
Standards represent performance benchmarks that can be compared to actual results in evaluating performance. Standards are established so that they are neither too high nor too low, but are attainable.	• Define *ideal* and *normal standards* and explain how they are used in setting standards. • Describe some of the criticisms of the use of standards.		

2. Explain and illustrate how standards are used in budgeting.

Key Points	Key Learning Outcomes	Example Exercises	Practice Exercises
Budgets are prepared by multiplying the standard cost per unit by the planned production. To measure performance, the standard cost per unit is multiplied by the actual number of units produced, and the actual results are compared with the standard cost at actual volumes (cost variance).	• Compute the standard cost per unit of production for materials, labor, and factory overhead. • Compute the direct labor, direct materials, and factory overhead cost variances. • Prepare a budget performance report.		

3. Compute and interpret direct materials and direct labor variances.

Key Points	Key Learning Outcomes	Example Exercises	Practice Exercises
The direct materials cost variance can be separated into direct materials price and quantity variances. The direct labor cost variance can be separated into direct labor rate and time variances.	• Compute and interpret direct materials price and quantity variances. • Compute and interpret direct labor rate and time variances. • Describe and illustrate how time standards are used in nonmanufacturing settings.	**22-1** **22-2**	22-1A, 22-1B 22-2A, 22-2B

4. Compute and interpret factory overhead controllable and volume variances.

Key Points	Key Learning Outcomes	Example Exercises	Practice Exercises
The factory overhead cost variance can be separated into a variable factory overhead controllable variance and a fixed factory overhead volume variance.	• Prepare a factory overhead flexible budget. • Compute and interpret the variable factory overhead controllable variance. • Compute and interpret the fixed factory overhead volume variance. • Prepare a factory overhead cost variance report. • Evaluate factory overhead variances using a T account.	**22-3** **22-4**	22-3A, 22-3B 22-4A, 22-4B

(continued)

5. Journalize the entries for recording standards in the accounts and prepare an income statement that includes variances from standard.

Key Points	Key Learning Outcomes	Example Exercises	Practice Exercises
Standard costs and variances can be recorded in the accounts at the same time the manufacturing costs are recorded in the accounts. Work in Process is debited at standard. Under a standard cost system, the cost of goods sold will be reported at standard cost. Manufacturing variances can be disclosed on the income statement to adjust the gross profit at standard to the actual gross profit.	• Journalize the entries to record the purchase and use of direct materials at standard, recording favorable or unfavorable variances.	22-5	22-5A, 22-5B
	• Prepare an income statement, disclosing favorable and unfavorable direct materials, direct labor, and factory overhead variances.	22-6	22-6A, 22-6B

6. Explain and provide examples of nonfinancial performance measures.

Key Points	Key Learning Outcomes	Example Exercises	Practice Exercises
Many companies use a combination of financial and nonfinancial measures in order for multiple perspectives to be incorporated in evaluating performance. Nonfinancial measures are often used in conjunction with the inputs or outputs of a process or an activity.	• Define, provide the rationale for, and provide examples of nonfinancial performance measures. • Identify nonfinancial inputs and outputs to an activity.	22-7	22-7A, 22-7B

Key Terms

budget performance report (981)
controllable variance (988)
cost variance (978)
currently attainable standards (979)
direct labor rate variance (985)
direct labor time variance (985)

direct materials price variance (983)
direct materials quantity variance (984)
ideal standards (979)
nonfinancial performance measure (995)

process (995)
standard cost (978)
standard cost systems (978)
volume variance (989)

Illustrative Problem

Hawley Inc. manufactures woven baskets for national distribution. The standard costs for the manufacture of Folk Art style baskets were as follows:

	Standard Costs	Actual Costs
Direct materials	1,500 pounds at $35	1,600 pounds at $32
Direct labor	4,800 hours at $11	4,500 hours at $11.80
Factory overhead	Rates per labor hour, based on 100% of normal capacity of 5,500 labor hours:	
	Variable cost, $2.40	$12,300 variable cost
	Fixed cost, $3.50	$19,250 fixed cost

Instructions

1. Determine the quantity variance, price variance, and total direct materials cost variance for the Folk Art style baskets.
2. Determine the time variance, rate variance, and total direct labor cost variance for the Folk Art style baskets.
3. Determine the controllable variance, volume variance, and total factory overhead cost variance for the Folk Art style baskets.

Solution

1.

Direct Materials Cost Variance

Quantity variance:		
Actual quantity	1,600 pounds	
Standard quantity	1,500	
Variance—unfavorable	100 pounds × standard price, $35	$ 3,500
Price variance:		
Actual price	$32.00 per pound	
Standard price	35.00	
Variance—favorable	$ (3.00) per pound × actual quantity, 1,600	(4,800)
Total direct materials cost variance—favorable		$(1,300)

2.

Direct Labor Cost Variance

Time variance:		
Actual time	4,500 hours	
Standard time	4,800 hours	
Variance—favorable	(300) hours × standard rate, $11	$(3,300)
Rate variance:		
Actual rate	$11.80	
Standard rate	11.00	
Variance—unfavorable	$ 0.80 per hour × actual time, 4,500 hrs.	3,600
Total direct labor cost variance—unfavorable		$ 300

3.

Factory Overhead Cost Variance

Variable factory overhead—controllable variance:		
Actual variable factory overhead cost incurred	$12,300	
Budgeted variable factory overhead for 4,800 hours	11,520*	
Variance—unfavorable		$ 780
Fixed factory overhead—volume variance:		
Budgeted hours at 100% of normal capacity	5,500 hours	
Standard hours for actual production	4,800	
Productive capacity not used	700 hours	
Standard fixed factory overhead cost rate	× $3.50 per hour	
Variance—unfavorable		2,450
Total factory overhead cost variance—unfavorable		$3,230

*4,800 hrs. × $2.40 = $11,520

Self-Examination Questions

(Answers at End of Chapter)

1. The actual and standard direct materials costs for producing a specified quantity of product are as follows:

Actual:	51,000 pounds at $5.05	$257,550
Standard:	50,000 pounds at $5.00	$250,000

The direct materials price variance is:
A. $50 unfavorable.   C. $2,550 unfavorable.
B. $2,500 unfavorable. D. $7,550 unfavorable.

2. Bower Company produced 4,000 units of product. Each unit requires 0.5 standard hour. The standard labor rate is $12 per hour. Actual direct labor for the period was $22,000 (2,200 hours × $10 per hour). The direct labor time variance is:
A. 200 hours unfavorable.   C. $4,000 favorable.
B. $2,000 unfavorable.   D. $2,400 unfavorable.

(continued)

3. The actual and standard factory overhead costs for producing a specified quantity of product are as follows:

Actual: Variable factory overhead $72,500
          Fixed factory overhead   40,000 $112,500
Standard: 19,000 hours at $6
          ($4 variable and $2 fixed)   114,000

If 1,000 hours were unused, the fixed factory overhead volume variance would be:
A. $1,500 favorable.   C. $4,000 unfavorable.
B. $2,000 unfavorable.   D. $6,000 unfavorable.

4. Ramathan Company produced 6,000 units of Product Y, which is 80% of capacity. Each unit required 0.25 standard machine hour for production. The standard variable factory overhead rate is $5.00 per machine hour. The actual variable factory overhead incurred during the period was $8,000. The variable factory overhead controllable variance is:
A. $500 favorable.   C. $1,875 favorable.
B. $500 unfavorable.   D. $1,875 unfavorable.

5. Applegate Company has a normal budgeted capacity of 200 machine hours. Applegate produced 600 units. Each unit requires a standard 0.2 machine hour to complete. The standard fixed factory overhead is $12.00 per hour, determined at normal capacity. The fixed factory overhead volume variance is:
A. $4,800 unfavorable.   C. $960 favorable.
B. $4,800 favorable.   D. $960 unfavorable.

Eye Openers

1. What are the basic objectives in the use of standard costs?
2. How can standards be used by management to help control costs?
3. What is meant by reporting by the "principle of exceptions," as the term is used in reference to cost control?
4. How often should standards be revised?
5. How are standards used in budgetary performance evaluation?
6. a. What are the two variances between the actual cost and the standard cost for direct materials?
   b. Discuss some possible causes of these variances.
7. The materials cost variance report for Nickols Inc. indicates a large favorable materials price variance and a significant unfavorable materials quantity variance. What might have caused these offsetting variances?
8. a. What are the two variances between the actual cost and the standard cost for direct labor?
   b. Who generally has control over the direct labor cost?
9. A new assistant controller recently was heard to remark: "All the assembly workers in this plant are covered by union contracts, so there should be no labor variances." Was the controller's remark correct? Discuss.
10. Would the use of standards be appropriate in a nonmanufacturing setting, such as a fast food restaurant?
11. a. Describe the two variances between the actual costs and the standard costs for factory overhead.
    b. What is a factory overhead cost variance report?
12. What are budgeted fixed costs at normal volume?
13. If variances are recorded in the accounts at the time the manufacturing costs are incurred, what does a debit balance in Direct Materials Price Variance represent?
14. If variances are recorded in the accounts at the time the manufacturing costs are incurred, what does a credit balance in Direct Materials Quantity Variance represent?
15. Briefly explain why firms might use nonfinancial performance measures.

Practice Exercises

PE 22-1A
Direct materials variances
obj. **3**

Brewster Company produces a product that requires four standard pounds per unit. The standard price is $6.80 per pound. If 1,500 units required 6,400 pounds, which were purchased at $6.50 per pound, what is the direct materials (a) price variance, (b) quantity variance, and (c) cost variance?

PE 22-1B
Direct materials variances
obj. 3

Tipton Company produces a product that requires eight standard gallons per unit. The standard price is $12.40 per gallon. If 800 units required 6,200 gallons, which were purchased at $12.75 per gallon, what is the direct materials (a) price variance, (b) quantity variance, and (c) cost variance?

PE 22-2A
Direct labor variances
obj. 3

Brewster Company produces a product that requires 1.5 standard hours per unit at a standard hourly rate of $15 per hour. If 1,500 units required 2,100 hours at an hourly rate of $15.50 per hour, what is the direct labor (a) rate variance, (b) time variance, and (c) cost variance?

PE 22-2B
Direct labor variances
obj. 3

Tipton Company produces a product that requires four standard hours per unit at a standard hourly rate of $10 per hour. If 800 units required 3,380 hours at an hourly rate of $9.60 per hour, what is the direct labor (a) rate variance, (b) time variance, and (c) cost variance?

PE 22-3A
Factory overhead controllable variance
obj. 4

Brewster Company produced 1,500 units of product that required 1.5 standard hours per unit. The standard variable overhead cost per unit is $1.70 per hour. The actual variable factory overhead was $3,900. Determine the variable factory overhead controllable variance.

PE 22-3B
Factory overhead controllable variance
obj. 4

Tipton Company produced 800 units of product that required four standard hours per unit. The standard variable overhead cost per unit is $4.50 per hour. The actual variable factory overhead was $14,100. Determine the variable factory overhead controllable variance.

PE 22-4A
Factory overhead volume variance
obj. 4

Brewster Company produced 1,500 units of product that required 1.5 standard hours per unit. The standard fixed overhead cost per unit is $0.50 per hour at 2,500 hours, which is 100% of normal capacity. Determine the fixed factory overhead volume variance.

PE 22-4B
Factory overhead volume variance
obj. 4

Tipton Company produced 800 units of product that required four standard hours per unit. The standard fixed overhead cost per unit is $1.20 per hour at 3,000 hours, which is 100% of normal capacity. Determine the fixed factory overhead volume variance.

PE 22-5A
Standard cost journal entries
obj. 5

Brewster Company produced 1,500 units that require four standard pounds per unit at $6.80 standard price per pound. The company actually used 6,400 pounds in production. Journalize the entry to record the standard direct materials used in production.

PE 22-5B
Standard cost journal entries
obj. 5

Tipton Company produced 800 units that require eight standard gallons per unit at $12.40 standard price per gallon. The company actually used 6,200 gallons in production. Journalize the entry to record the standard direct materials used in production.

PE 22-6A
Standard cost income statement with variances from standard
obj. 5

Prepare an income statement through gross profit for Brewster Company using the variance data in Practice Exercises 22-1A, 22-2A, 22-3A, and 22-4A. Assume Brewster sold 1,500 units at $80 per unit.

PE 22-6B
Standard cost income statement with variances from standard
obj. 5

Prepare an income statement through gross profit for Tipton Company using the variance data in Practice Exercises 22-1B, 22-2B, 22-3B, and 22-4B. Assume Tipton sold 800 units at $200 per unit.

PE 22-7A
Identify activity inputs and outputs
obj. 6

The following are inputs and outputs to the copying process of a copy shop:

Copy machine downtime (broken)
Number of customer complaints
Number of employee errors
Number of pages copied per hour
Number of times paper supply runs out
Percent jobs done on time

Identify whether each is an input or output to the copying process.

PE 22-7B
Identify activity inputs and outputs
obj. 6

The following are inputs and outputs to the cooking process of a restaurant:

Number of customer complaints
Number of hours kitchen equipment is down for repairs
Number of server order mistakes
Number of times ingredients are missing
Number of unexpected cook absences
Percent of meals prepared on time

Identify whether each is an input or output to the cooking process.

Exercises

EX 22-1
Standard direct materials cost per unit
obj. 2

Sweet Swiss Chocolate Company produces chocolate bars. The primary materials used in producing chocolate bars are cocoa, sugar, and milk. The standard costs for a batch of chocolate (1,000 bars) are as follows:

Ingredient	Quantity	Price
Cocoa	465 pounds	$0.30 per pound
Sugar	168 pounds	$0.50 per pound
Milk	110 gallons	$1.15 per gallon

Determine the standard direct materials cost per bar of chocolate.

EX 22-2
Standard product cost
obj. 2

Carolina Furniture Company manufactures unfinished oak furniture. Carolina uses a standard cost system. The direct labor, direct materials, and factory overhead standards for an unfinished dining room table are as follows:

Direct labor:	standard rate	$17.00 per hour
	standard time per unit	3 hours
Direct materials (oak):	standard price	$8.60 per board foot
	standard quantity	16 board feet
Variable factory overhead:	standard rate	$2.60 per direct labor hour
Fixed factory overhead:	standard rate	$1.20 per direct labor hour

Determine the standard cost per dining room table.

EX 22-3
Budget performance report
obj. 2

✓b. Direct labor cost variance, $120 F

Vernon Bottle Company (VBC) manufactures plastic two-liter bottles for the beverage industry. The cost standards per 100 two-liter bottles are as follows:

Cost Category	Standard Cost per 100 Two-Liter Bottles
Direct labor	$1.28
Direct materials	5.21
Factory overhead	0.42
Total	$6.91

At the beginning of August, VBC management planned to produce 620,000 bottles. The actual number of bottles produced for August was 650,000 bottles. The actual costs for August of the current year were as follows:

Cost Category	Actual Cost for the Month Ended August 31, 2008
Direct labor	$ 8,200
Direct materials	34,500
Factory overhead	2,800
Total	$45,500

a. Prepare the August manufacturing standard cost budget (direct labor, direct materials, and factory overhead) for VBC, assuming planned production.
b. Prepare a budget performance report for manufacturing costs, showing the total cost variances for direct materials, direct labor, and factory overhead for August.
c. ▭▭▭ Interpret the budget performance report.

EX 22-4
Direct materials variances
obj. 3

✓ *a. Price variance, $26,048 F*

The following data relate to the direct materials cost for the production of 4,000 automobile tires:

Actual:	130,240 pounds at $1.65	$214,896
Standard:	128,760 pounds at $1.85	$238,206

a. Determine the price variance, quantity variance, and total direct materials cost variance.
b. ▭▭▭ To whom should the variances be reported for analysis and control?

EX 22-5
Standard direct materials cost per unit from variance data
objs. 2, 3

The following data relating to direct materials cost for March of the current year are taken from the records of Top Toys Inc., a manufacturer of plastic toys:

Quantity of direct materials used	40,000 pounds
Actual unit price of direct materials	$1.48 per pound
Units of finished product manufactured	7,600 units
Standard direct materials per unit of finished product	5 pounds
Direct materials quantity variance—unfavorable	$2,700
Direct materials price variance—unfavorable	$5,200

Determine the standard direct materials cost per unit of finished product, assuming that there was no inventory of work in process at either the beginning or the end of the month.

EX 22-6
Standard product cost, direct materials variance
objs. 2, 3

H.J. Heinz Company uses standards to control its materials costs. Assume that a batch of ketchup (1,500 pounds) has the following standards:

	Standard Quantity	Standard Price
Whole tomatoes	2,400 pounds	$0.40 per pound
Vinegar	130 gallons	2.50 per gallon
Corn syrup	10 gallons	8.00 per gallon
Salt	54 pounds	2.50 per pound

The actual materials in a batch may vary from the standard due to tomato characteristics. Assume that the actual quantities of materials for batch W196 were as follows:

2,500 pounds of tomatoes
115 gallons of vinegar
13 gallons of corn syrup
53 pounds of salt

a. Determine the standard unit materials cost per pound for a standard batch.
b. Determine the direct materials quantity variance for batch W196.

EX 22-7
Direct labor variances
obj. 3

The following data relate to labor cost for production of 12,500 cellular telephones:

✓a. Rate variance,
$2,040 U

Actual:	13,600 hours at $16.15	$219,640
Standard:	13,725 hours at $16.00	$219,600

a. Determine the rate variance, time variance, and total direct labor cost variance.
b. ▬▬▬▶ Discuss what might have caused these variances.

EX 22-8
Direct labor variances
obj. 3

✓a. Time variance,
$1,281 F

Blue Ridge Bicycle Company manufactures mountain bikes. The following data for May of the current year are available:

Quantity of direct labor used	1,400 hours
Actual rate for direct labor	$16.15 per hour
Bicycles completed in May	280
Standard direct labor per bicycle	5.30 hours
Standard rate for direct labor	$15.25 per hour
Planned bicycles for May	210

a. Determine the direct labor rate and time variances.
b. How much direct labor should be debited to Work in Process?

EX 22-9
Direct labor variances
obj. 3

✓a. Cutting Department
time variance, $4,400
unfavorable

The Lifestyle Clothes Company produced 24,000 units during April of the current year. The Cutting Department used 4,000 direct labor hours at an actual rate of $11.20 per hour. The Sewing Department used 8,000 direct labor hours at an actual rate of $10.50 per hour. Assume there were no work in process inventories in either department at the beginning or end of the month. The standard labor rate is $11.00. The standard labor time for the Cutting and Sewing departments is 0.15 hour and 0.35 hour per unit, respectively.

a. Determine the direct labor rate and time variance for the (1) Cutting Department and (2) Sewing Department.
b. ▬▬▬▶ Interpret your results.

EX 22-10
*Direct labor standards
for nonmanufacturing
expenses*
obj. 3

✓a. $2,520

Midlands Hospital began using standards to evaluate its Admissions Department. The standard was broken into two types of admissions as follows:

Type of Admission	Standard Time to Complete Admission Record
Unscheduled admission	60 minutes
Scheduled admission	40 minutes

The unscheduled admission took longer, since name, address, and insurance information needed to be determined at the time of admission. Information was collected on scheduled admissions prior to the admissions, which was less time consuming.

The Admissions Department employs three full-time people (40 productive hours per week, with no overtime) at $21 per hour. For the most recent week, the department handled 48 unscheduled and 150 scheduled admissions.

a. How much was actually spent on labor for the week?
b. What are the standard hours for the actual volume for the week? Round to one decimal place.
c. Calculate a time variance, and report how well the department performed for the week.

EX 22-11
*Direct labor standards
for nonmanufacturing
operations*
objs. 2, 3

One of the operations in the U.S. Post Office is a mechanical mail sorting operation. In this operation, letter mail is sorted at a rate of one letter per second. The letter is mechanically sorted from a three-digit code input by an operator sitting at a keyboard. The manager of the mechanical sorting operation wishes to determine the number of temporary employees to hire for December. The manager estimates that there will be an additional 32,400,000 pieces of mail in December, due to the upcoming holiday season.

Assume that the sorting operators are temporary employees. The union contract requires that temporary employees be hired for one month at a time. Each temporary employee is hired to work 150 hours in the month.

a. How many temporary employees should the manager hire for December?
b. If each employee earns a standard $16 per hour, what would be the labor time variance if the actual number of letters sorted in December was 32,814,000?

EX 22-12
Direct materials and direct labor variances

objs. 2, 3

✓ *Direct materials quantity variance, $400 F*

At the beginning of July, Commercial Printers Company budgeted 14,000 books to be printed in July at standard direct materials and direct labor costs as follows:

Direct materials	$28,000
Direct labor	24,500
Total	$52,500

The standard materials price is $0.80 per pound. The standard direct labor rate is $14 per hour. At the end of July, the actual direct materials and direct labor costs were as follows:

Actual direct materials	$31,200
Actual direct labor	28,400
Total	$59,600

There were no direct materials price or direct labor rate variances for July. In addition, assume no changes in the direct materials inventory balances in July. Commercial Printers Company actually produced 15,800 units during July.

Determine the direct materials quantity and direct labor time variances.

EX 22-13
Flexible overhead budget

obj. 4

✓ *Total factory overhead, 12,000 hrs.: $139,400*

Pine Knoll Wood Products Company prepared the following factory overhead cost budget for the Press Department for February 2008, during which it expected to require 10,000 hours of productive capacity in the department:

Variable overhead cost:		
Indirect factory labor	$28,000	
Power and light	4,500	
Indirect materials	22,000	
Total variable cost		$ 54,500
Fixed overhead cost:		
Supervisory salaries	$36,000	
Depreciation of plant and equipment	30,000	
Insurance and property taxes	8,000	
Total fixed cost		74,000
Total factory overhead cost		$128,500

Assuming that the estimated costs for March are the same as for February, prepare a flexible factory overhead cost budget for the Press Department for March for 8,000, 10,000, and 12,000 hours of production.

EX 22-14
Flexible overhead budget

obj. 4

Kompton Company has determined that the variable overhead rate is $2.10 per direct labor hour in the Fabrication Department. The normal production capacity for the Fabrication Department is 14,000 hours for the month. Fixed costs are budgeted at $54,600 for the month.

a. Prepare a monthly factory overhead flexible budget for 13,000, 14,000, and 15,000 hours of production.
b. How much overhead would be applied to production if 15,000 hours were used in the department during the month?

EX 22-15
Factory overhead cost variances

obj. 4

✓ *Volume variance, $28,080 U*

The following data relate to factory overhead cost for the production of 25,000 computers:

Actual:	Variable factory overhead	$650,000
	Fixed factory overhead	78,000
Standard:	32,000 hours at $21	672,000

If productive capacity of 100% was 50,000 hours and the factory overhead cost budgeted at the level of 32,000 standard hours was $700,080, determine the variable factory overhead controllable variance, fixed factory overhead volume variance, and total factory overhead cost variance. The fixed factory overhead rate was $1.56 per hour.

EX 22-16
Factory overhead cost variances
obj. 4

✓ a. $4,850 F

Banner Textiles Corporation began January with a budget for 28,000 hours of production in the Weaving Department. The department has a full capacity of 36,000 hours under normal business conditions. The budgeted overhead at the planned volumes at the beginning of January was as follows:

Variable overhead	$ 78,400
Fixed overhead	54,000
Total	$132,400

The actual factory overhead was $135,250 for January. The actual fixed factory overhead was as budgeted. During January, the Weaving Department had standard hours at actual production volume of 30,750 hours.

a. Determine the variable factory overhead controllable variance.
b. Determine the fixed factory overhead volume variance.

EX 22-17
Factory overhead variance corrections
obj. 4

The data related to Osage Sporting Goods Company's factory overhead cost for the production of 60,000 units of product are as follows:

Actual:	Variable factory overhead	$274,500
	Fixed factory overhead	224,000
Standard:	76,000 hours at $6.30 ($3.50 for variable factory overhead)	478,800

Productive capacity at 100% of normal was 80,000 hours, and the factory overhead cost budgeted at the level of 76,000 standard hours was $490,000. Based upon these data, the chief cost accountant prepared the following variance analysis:

Variable factory overhead controllable variance:		
Actual variable factory overhead cost incurred	$274,500	
Budgeted variable factory overhead for 76,000 hours	266,000	
Variance—unfavorable		$ 8,500
Fixed factory overhead volume variance:		
Normal productive capacity at 100%	80,000 hours	
Standard for amount produced	76,000	
Productive capacity not used	4,000 hours	
Standard variable factory overhead rate	× $6.30	
Variance—unfavorable		25,200
Total factory overhead cost variance—unfavorable		$33,700

Identify the errors in the factory overhead cost variance analysis.

EX 22-18
Factory overhead cost variance report
obj. 4

✓ Net controllable variance, $450 U

Form Fit Molded Products Inc. prepared the following factory overhead cost budget for the Trim Department for October 2008, during which it expected to use 20,000 hours for production:

Variable overhead cost:		
Indirect factory labor	$49,000	
Power and light	12,000	
Indirect materials	32,000	
Total variable cost		$ 93,000
Fixed overhead cost:		
Supervisory salaries	$35,000	
Depreciation of plant and equipment	28,400	
Insurance and property taxes	21,600	
Total fixed cost		85,000
Total factory overhead cost		$178,000

Form Fit Molded Products has available 34,000 hours of monthly productive capacity in the Trim Department under normal business conditions. During October, the Trim Department actually used 24,000 hours for production. The actual fixed costs were as budgeted. The actual variable overhead for October was as follows:

Actual variable factory overhead cost:	
Indirect factory labor	$ 58,300
Power and light	15,000
Indirect materials	38,750
Total variable cost	$112,050

Construct a factory overhead cost variance report for the Trim Department for October.

EX 22-19
Recording standards in accounts
obj. 5

Thexton Manufacturing Company incorporates standards in its accounts and identifies variances at the time the manufacturing costs are incurred. Journalize the entries to record the following transactions:

a. Purchased 1,400 units of copper tubing on account at $49.50 per unit. The standard price is $45.00 per unit.
b. Used 870 units of copper tubing in the process of manufacturing 110 air conditioners. Eight units of copper tubing are required, at standard, to produce one air conditioner.

EX 22-20
Recording standards in accounts
obj. 5

The Assembly Department produced 1,600 units of product during June. Each unit required 1.4 standard direct labor hours. There were 2,200 actual hours used in the Assembly Department during June at an actual rate of $12.00 per hour. The standard direct labor rate is $12.50 per hour. Assuming direct labor for a month is paid on the fifth day of the following month, journalize the direct labor in the Assembly Department on June 30.

EX 22-21
Income statement indicating standard cost variance
obj. 5

✓ Income before income tax, $75,500

The following data were taken from the records of Nomad Company for March 2008:

Administrative expenses	$ 58,000
Cost of goods sold (at standard)	885,500
Direct materials price variance—favorable	1,800
Direct materials quantity variance—unfavorable	2,250
Direct labor rate variance—favorable	900
Direct labor time variance—unfavorable	3,950
Variable factory overhead controllable variance—favorable	4,625
Fixed factory overhead volume variance—unfavorable	11,000
Interest expense	1,800
Sales	1,150,000
Selling expenses	119,325

Prepare an income statement for presentation to management.

EX 22-22
Nonfinancial performance measures
obj. 6

Windytrail.com is an Internet retailer of sporting good products. Customers order sporting goods from the company, using an online catalog. The company processes these orders and delivers the requested product from its warehouse. The company wants to provide customers with an excellent purchase experience in order to expand the business through favorable word-of-mouth advertising and to drive repeat business. To help monitor performance, the company developed a set of performance measures for its order placement and delivery process.

Average computer response time to customer "clicks"
Dollar amount of returned goods
Elapsed time between customer order and product delivery
Maintenance dollars divided by hardware investment
Number of customer complaints divided by the number of orders
Number of misfilled orders
Number of orders per warehouse employee
Number of page faults or errors due to software programming errors
Server (computer) downtime
System capacity divided by customer demands
Training dollars per programmer

Identify the input and output measures related to the "order placement and delivery" process.

EX 22-23
Nonfinancial performance measures

obj. 6

Metro College wishes to monitor the efficiency and quality of its course registration process.

a. Identify three input and three output measures for this process.
b. Why would Metro College use nonfinancial measures for monitoring this process?

Problems Series A

PR 22-1A
Direct materials and direct labor variance analysis

objs. 2, 3

✓c. Rate variance, $48 U

Dresses by Melissa Inc. manufactures dresses in a small manufacturing facility. Manufacturing has 15 employees. Each employee presently provides 32 hours of productive labor per week. Information about a production week is as follows:

Standard wage per hour	$10.40
Standard labor time per dress	15 minutes
Standard number of yards of fabric per dress	4.2 yards
Standard price per yard of fabric	$2.65
Actual price per yard of fabric	$2.70
Actual yards of fabric used during the week	7,200 yards
Number of dresses produced during the week	1,900
Actual wage per hour	$10.50
Actual hours per week	480 hours

Instructions
Determine (a) the standard cost per dress for direct materials and direct labor; (b) the price variance, quantity variance, and total direct materials cost variance; and (c) the rate variance, time variance, and total direct labor cost variance.

PR 22-2A
Flexible budgeting and variance analysis

objs. 2, 3

✓1. a. Direct materials quantity variance, $4,540 U

Koko Chocolate Company makes dark chocolate and light chocolate. Both products require cocoa and sugar. The following planning information has been made available:

| | Standard Quantity | | |
	Dark Chocolate	Light Chocolate	Standard Price per Pound
Cocoa	14 lbs.	9 lbs.	$8.80
Sugar	12 lbs.	15 lbs.	1.40
Standard labor time	0.30 hr.	0.45 hr.	
Planned production	3,200 cases	4,600 cases	
Standard labor rate	$16.40 per hour	$16.20 per hour	

Koko Chocolate does not expect there to be any beginning or ending inventories of cocoa or sugar. At the end of the budget year, Koko Chocolate had the following actual results:

	Dark Chocolate	Light Chocolate
Actual production (cases)	2,500	4,500

	Actual Price per Pound	Actual Pounds Purchased and Used
Cocoa	$8.50	74,250
Sugar	1.65	108,600

	Actual Labor Rate	Actual Labor Hours Used
Dark chocolate	$16.50	760
Light chocolate	16.50	2,000

Instructions

1. Prepare the following variance analyses, based on the actual results and production levels at the end of the budget year:
   a. Direct materials price, quantity, and total variance.
   b. Direct labor rate, time, and total variance.
2. ━━━▶ Why are the standard amounts in part (1) based on the actual production for the year instead of the planned production for the year?

PR 22-3A
Direct materials, direct labor, and factory overhead cost variance analysis

objs. 3, 4

✓ *c. Controllable variance, $155 F*

Gulf Coast Resins Company processes a base chemical into plastic. Standard costs and actual costs for direct materials, direct labor, and factory overhead incurred for the manufacture of 2,600 units of product were as follows:

	Standard Costs	Actual Costs
Direct materials	6,850 pounds at $6.40	7,000 pounds at $6.35
Direct labor	2,050 hours at $19.80	2,100 hours at $20.20
Factory overhead	Rates per direct labor hour, based on 100% of normal capacity of 1,950 direct labor hours:	
	Variable cost, $2.50	$4,970 variable cost
	Fixed cost, $4.50	$8,775 fixed cost

Each unit requires 0.6 hour of direct labor.

Instructions

Determine (a) the price variance, quantity variance, and total direct materials cost variance; (b) the rate variance, time variance, and total direct labor cost variance; and (c) variable factory overhead controllable variance, the fixed factory overhead volume variance, and total factory overhead cost variance.

PR 22-4A
Standard factory overhead variance report

objs. 4, 6

✓ *Controllable variance, $300 F*

Power Equipment Inc., a manufacturer of construction equipment, prepared the following factory overhead cost budget for the Welding Department for July 2008. The company expected to operate the department at 100% of normal capacity of 4,800 hours.

Variable costs:		
Indirect factory wages	$14,160	
Power and light	7,680	
Indirect materials	8,880	
Total variable cost		$30,720
Fixed costs:		
Supervisory salaries	$16,000	
Depreciation of plant and equipment	43,500	
Insurance and property taxes	6,740	
Total fixed cost		66,240
Total factory overhead cost		$96,960

During July, the department operated at 5,000 standard hours, and the factory overhead costs incurred were indirect factory wages, $14,000; power and light, $9,250; indirect materials, $8,450; supervisory salaries, $16,000; depreciation of plant and equipment, $43,500; and insurance and property taxes, $6,740.

Instructions

Prepare a factory overhead cost variance report for July. To be useful for cost control, the budgeted amounts should be based on 5,000 hours.

PR 22-5A
Standards for nonmanufacturing expenses

objs. 3, 6

✓ *3. $640 U*

Elite Technologies Inc. does software development. One important activity in software development is writing software code. The manager of the WritePro Development Team determined that the average software programmer could write 45 lines of code in an hour. The plan for the first week in May called for 6,840 lines of code to be written on the WritePro product. The WritePro Team has four programmers. Each programmer is hired from an employment firm that requires temporary employees to be hired for a minimum of a 40-hour week. Programmers are paid $32.00 per hour. The manager offered a bonus if the team could generate more than 7,200 lines for the week, without overtime. Due to a project emergency, the programmers wrote more code in the first week of May than planned. The actual amount of code written in the first week of May was 7,650 lines, without overtime. As a result, the bonus caused the average programmer's hourly rate to increase to $36.00 per hour during the first week in May.

Instructions

1. If the team generated 6,840 lines of code according to the original plan, what would have been the labor time variance?
2. What was the actual labor time variance as a result of generating 7,650 lines of code?
3. What was the labor rate variance as a result of the bonus?
4. The manager is trying to determine if a better decision would have been to hire a temporary programmer to meet the higher programming demand in the first week of May, rather than paying out the bonus. If another employee was hired from the employment firm, what would have been the labor time variance in the first week?
5. ▭▬▶ Which decision is better, paying the bonus or hiring another programmer?
6. ▭▬▶ Are there any performance-related issues that the labor time and rate variances fail to consider? Explain.

Problems Series B

PR 22-1B
Direct materials and direct labor variance analysis

objs. 2, 3

✓c. Direct labor time variance, $1,680 F

AtHome Fixtures Company manufactures faucets in a small manufacturing facility. The faucets are made from zinc. Manufacturing has 80 employees. Each employee presently provides 36 hours of labor per week. Information about a production week is as follows:

Standard wage per hour	$14.00
Standard labor time per faucet	15 minutes
Standard number of pounds of zinc	1.8 lbs.
Standard price per pound of zinc	$9.50
Actual price per pound of zinc	$9.20
Actual pounds of zinc used during the week	21,900 lbs.
Number of faucets produced during the week	12,000
Actual wage per hour	$14.50
Actual hours per week	2,880 hours

Instructions

Determine (a) the standard cost per unit for direct materials and direct labor; (b) the price variance, quantity variance, and total direct materials cost variance; and (c) the rate variance, time variance, and total direct labor cost variance.

PR 22-2B
Flexible budgeting and variance analysis

objs. 2, 3

✓1. a. Price variance, $9,000 F

Arctic Coat Company makes women's and men's coats. Both products require filler and lining material. The following planning information has been made available:

	Standard Quantity		
	Women's Coats	Men's Coats	Standard Price per Unit
Filler	2.5 lbs.	4.0 lbs.	$29.00
Liner	6.0 yds.	8.5 yds.	5.00
Standard labor time	0.40 hr.	0.60 hr.	
Planned production	2,500 units	4,000 units	
Standard labor rate	$12.80 per hour	$15.50 per hour	

Arctic Coat does not expect there to be any beginning or ending inventories of filler and lining material. At the end of the budget year, Arctic Coat experienced the following actual results:

	Women's Coats	Men's Coats
Actual production	2,300	3,500

	Actual Price per Unit	Actual Quantity Purchased and Used
Filler	$27.50	20,400
Liner	5.50	43,200

	Actual Labor Rate	Actual Labor Hours Used
Women's Coats	$12.00	1,050
Men's Coats	15.80	1,980

The expected beginning inventory and desired ending inventory were realized.

Instructions

1. Prepare the following variance analyses, based on the actual results and production levels at the end of the budget year:
   a. Direct materials price, quantity, and total variance.
   b. Direct labor rate, time, and total variance.
2. Why are the standard amounts in part (1) based on the actual production at the end of the year instead of the planned production at the beginning of the year?

PR 22-3B
Direct materials, direct labor, and factory overhead cost variance analysis

objs. 3, 4

✓ a. Price variance,
$28,840 U

SureGrip Tire Co. manufactures automobile tires. Standard costs and actual costs for direct materials, direct labor, and factory overhead incurred for the manufacture of 39,000 tires were as follows:

	Standard Costs	Actual Costs
Direct materials	68,000 pounds at $4.80	72,100 pounds at $5.20
Direct labor	15,600 hours at $16.00	15,400 hours at $15.70
Factory overhead	Rates per direct labor hour, based on 100% of normal capacity of 21,000 direct labor hours:	
	Variable cost, $2.70	$41,650 variable cost
	Fixed cost, $3.65	$76,650 fixed cost

Each tire requires 0.40 hour of direct labor.

Instructions
Determine (a) the price variance, quantity variance, and total direct materials cost variance; (b) the rate variance, time variance, and total direct labor cost variance; and (c) variable factory overhead controllable variance, the fixed factory overhead volume variance, and total factory overhead cost variance.

PR 22-4B
Standard factory overhead variance report

objs. 4, 6

✓ Controllable variance,
$6,900 F

Med-Tech Company, a manufacturer of disposable medical supplies, prepared the following factory overhead cost budget for the Assembly Department for August 2008. The company expected to operate the department at 100% of normal capacity of 28,000 hours.

Variable costs:		
Indirect factory wages	$246,400	
Power and light	179,200	
Indirect materials	44,800	
Total variable cost		$470,400
Fixed costs:		
Supervisory salaries	$130,000	
Depreciation of plant and equipment	105,000	
Insurance and property taxes	22,600	
Total fixed cost		257,600
Total factory overhead cost		$728,000

During August, the department operated at 25,250 hours, and the factory overhead costs incurred were indirect factory wages, $216,500; power and light, $162,600; indirect materials, $38,200; supervisory salaries, $130,000; depreciation of plant and equipment, $105,000; and insurance and property taxes, $22,600.

Instructions

Prepare a factory overhead cost variance report for August. To be useful for cost control, the budgeted amounts should be based on 25,250 hours.

PR 22-5B
Standards for nonmanufacturing expenses
objs. 3, 6

✓2. $150 F

The Radiology Department provides imaging services for Memorial Medical Center. One important activity in the Radiology Department is transcribing tape-recorded analyses of images into a written report. The manager of the Radiology Department determined that the average transcriptionist could type 800 lines of a report in an hour. The plan for the first week in July called for 60,000 typed lines to be written. The Radiology Department has two transcriptionists. Each transcriptionist is hired from an employment firm that requires temporary employees to be hired for a minimum of a 40-hour week. Transcriptionists are paid $15.00 per hour. The manager offered a bonus if the department could type more than 70,000 lines for the week, without overtime. Due to high service demands, the transcriptionists typed more lines in the first week of July than planned. The actual amount of lines typed in the first week of July was 72,000 lines, without overtime. As a result, the bonus caused the average transcriptionist hourly rate to increase to $18.00 per hour during the first week in July.

Instructions

1. If the department typed 60,000 lines according to the original plan, what would have been the labor time variance?
2. What was the labor time variance as a result of typing 72,000 lines?
3. What was the labor rate variance as a result of the bonus?
4. The manager is trying to determine if a better decision would have been to hire a temporary transcriptionist to meet the higher typing demands in the first week of July, rather than paying out the bonus. If another employee was hired from the employment firm, what would have been the labor time variance in the first week?
5. ▭▭▭▶ Which decision is better, paying the bonus or hiring another transcriptionist?
6. ▭▭▭▶ Are there any performance-related issues that the labor time and rate variances fail to consider? Explain.

Comprehensive Problem 5

Royal Essentials, Inc. began operations on January 1, 2008. The company produces a hand and body lotion in an eight-ounce bottle called *Eternal Beauty*. The lotion is sold wholesale in 12-bottle cases for $80 per case. There is a selling commission of $16 per case. The January direct materials, direct labor, and factory overhead costs are as follows:

DIRECT MATERIALS

	Cost Behavior	Units per Case	Cost per Unit	Direct Materials Cost per Case
Cream base	Variable	72 ozs.	$0.015	$ 1.08
Natural oils	Variable	24 ozs.	0.250	6.00
Bottle (8-oz.)	Variable	12 bottles	0.400	4.80
				$11.88

DIRECT LABOR

Department	Cost Behavior	Time per Case	Labor Rate per Hour	Direct Labor Cost per Case
Mixing	Variable	16.80 min.	$15.00	$4.20
Filling	Variable	4.20 min.	12.00	0.84
		21.00 min.		$5.04

FACTORY OVERHEAD

	Cost Behavior	Total Cost
Utilities	Mixed	$ 230
Facility lease	Fixed	9,694
Equipment depreciation	Fixed	3,600
Supplies	Fixed	600
		$14,124

Part A—Break-Even Analysis

The management of Royal Essentials, Inc., wishes to determine the number of cases required to break even per month. The utilities cost, which is part of factory overhead, is a mixed cost. The following information was gathered from the first six months of operation regarding this cost:

2008	Case Production	Utility Total Cost
January	300	$230
February	600	265
March	1,000	300
April	900	292
May	750	275
June	825	280

Instructions

1. Determine the fixed and variable portion of the utility cost using the high-low method.
2. Determine the contribution margin per case.
3. Determine the fixed costs per month, including the utility fixed cost from part (1).
4. Determine the break-even number of cases per month.

Part B—Variable versus Absorption Costing Income Statements

There was no finished goods inventory on July 1, 2008, for Royal Essentials. The company operated the manufacturing facility at 100% of capacity during July. The following data summarize the results for Royal Essentials Inc. for July:

Sales (1,350 cases × $80 per case)		$108,000
Production costs (1,500 cases):		
Direct materials	$18,000	
Direct labor	7,500	
Variable factory overhead	150	
Fixed factory overhead	14,100	39,750
Variable selling expenses (1,350 cases × $16 per case)		21,600

Instructions

5. Prepare an income statement according to the absorption costing concept.
6. Prepare an income statement according to the variable costing concept.
7. What is the reason for the difference in the amount of income from operations reported in (5) and (6)?

Part C—August Budgets

During July of the current year, the management of Royal Essentials, Inc., asked the controller to prepare August manufacturing and income statement budgets. Demand was expected to be 1,200 cases at $80 per case for August. Inventory planning information is provided as follows:

Finished Goods Inventory:

	Cases	Cost
Estimated finished goods inventory, August 1, 2008	150	$3,160
Desired finished goods inventory, August 31, 2008	100	2,100

Materials Inventory:

	Cream Base (ozs.)	Oils (ozs.)	Bottles (bottles)
Estimated materials inventory, August 1, 2008	500	260	500
Desired materials inventory, August 31, 2008	700	300	400

There was negligible work in process inventory assumed for either the beginning or end of the month; thus, none was assumed. In addition, there was no change in the cost per unit or estimated units per case operating data from January.

Instructions

8. Prepare the August production budget.
9. Prepare the August direct materials purchases budget.
10. Prepare the August direct labor budget.
11. Prepare the August factory overhead budget.
12. Prepare the August budgeted income statement, including selling expenses.

Part D—August Variance Analysis

During September of the current year, the controller was asked to perform variance analyses for August. The January operating data provided the standard prices, rates, times, and quantities per case. There were 1,200 actual cases produced during August, which was 50 more cases than planned at the beginning of the month. Actual data for August were as follows:

	Actual Direct Materials Price per Case	Actual Direct Materials Quantity per Case
Cream base	$1.00 (for 72 ozs.)	75 ozs.
Natural oils	6.20 (for 24 ozs.)	25 ozs.
Bottle (8-oz.)	4.50 (for 12 bottles)	12.2 bottles

	Actual Direct Labor Rate	Actual Direct Labor Time per Case
Mixing	$15.25	16.50 min.
Filling	11.50	4.50 min.
Actual variable overhead	$125.00	
Normal volume	1,500 cases	

The prices of the materials were different than standard due to fluctuations in market prices. Specifically, the prices of the cream base and bottles were below the standard price, while the price of natural oils was above the standard price. The standard quantity of materials used per case was an ideal standard. The Mixing Department used a higher grade labor classification during the month, thus causing the actual labor rate to exceed standard. The Filling Department used a lower grade labor classification during the month, thus causing the actual labor rate to be less than standard.

Instructions

13. Determine and interpret the direct materials price and quantity variances for the three materials.
14. Determine and interpret the direct labor rate and time variances for the two departments.
15. Determine and interpret the factory overhead controllable variance.
16. Determine and interpret the factory overhead volume variance.
17. Why are the standard direct labor and direct materials costs in the calculations for parts (13) and (14) based on the actual 1,200-case production volume rather than the planned 1,150 cases of production used in the budgets for parts (9) and (10)?

Special Activities

SA 22-1
Ethics and professional conduct in business using nonmanufacturing standards

ETHICS

Trey McIntyre is a cost analyst with Global Insurance Company. Global is applying standards to its claims payment operation. Claims payment is a repetitive operation that could be evaluated with standards. Trey used time and motion studies to identify an ideal standard of 36 claims processed per hour. The Claims Processing Department manager, Carol Mann, has rejected this standard and has argued that the standard should be 30 claims processed per hour. Carol and Trey were unable to agree, so they decided to discuss this matter openly at a joint meeting with the vice president of operations, who would arbitrate a final decision. Prior to the meeting, Trey wrote the following memo to the VP.

> To: T. J. Logan, Vice President of Operations
> From: Trey McIntyre
> Re: Standards in the Claims Processing Department
>
> As you know, Carol and I are scheduled to meet with you to discuss our disagreement with respect to the appropriate standards for the Claims Processing Department. I have conducted time and motion studies and have determined that the ideal standard is 36 claims processed per hour. Carol argues that 30 claims processed per hour would be more appropriate. I believe she is trying to "pad" the budget with some slack. I'm not sure what she is trying to get away with, but I believe a tight standard will drive efficiency up in her area. I hope you will agree when we meet with you next week.

➤ Discuss the ethical and professional issues in this situation.

SA 22-2
Nonfinancial performance measures

The senior management of Lannigan Company has proposed the following three performance measures for the company:

1. Net income as a percent of stockholders' equity
2. Revenue growth
3. Employee satisfaction

Management believes these three measures combine both financial and nonfinancial measures and are thus superior to using just financial measures.

➤ What advice would you give Lannigan Company for improving its performance measurement system?

SA 22-3
Nonfinancial performance measures

REAL WORLD

At the Soladyne Division of Rogers Corporation, a manufacturer of specialty materials for the electronics industry, the controller used a number of measures to provide managers information about the performance of a just-in-time (JIT) manufacturing operation. Three measures used by the company are:

- Scrap Index: The sales dollar value of scrap for the period.
- Orders Past Due: Sales dollar value of orders that were scheduled for shipment, but were not shipped during the period.
- Buyer's Misery Index: Number of different customers that have orders that are late (scheduled for shipment, but not shipped).

1. ➤ Why do you think the scrap index is measured at sales dollar value, rather than at cost?
2. ➤ How is the "orders past due" measure different from the "buyer's misery index," or are the two measures just measuring the same thing?

SA 22-4
Variance interpretation

You have been asked to investigate some cost problems in the Assembly Department of Digital Life Electronics Co., a consumer electronics company. To begin your investigation, you have obtained the following budget performance report for the department for the last quarter:

Digital Life Electronics Co.—Assembly Department
Quarterly Budget Performance Report

	Standard Quantity at Standard Rates	Actual Quantity at Standard Rates	Quantity Variances
Direct labor	$ 78,750	$113,750	$35,000 U
Direct materials	148,750	192,500	43,750 U
Total	$227,500	$306,250	$78,750 U

The following reports were also obtained:

Digital Life Electronics Co.—Purchasing Department
Quarterly Budget Performance Report

	Actual Quantity at Standard Rates	Actual Quantity at Actual Rates	Price Variance
Direct materials	$218,750	$192,500	$26,250 F

Digital Life Electronics Co.—Fabrication Department
Quarterly Budget Performance Report

	Standard Quantity at Standard Rates	Actual Quantity at Standard Rates	Quantity Variances
Direct labor	$122,500	$101,500	$21,000 F
Direct materials	70,000	70,000	0
Total	$192,500	$171,500	$21,000 F

You also interviewed the Assembly Department supervisor. Excerpts from the interview follow.

Q: *What explains the poor performance in your department?*
A: *Listen, you've got to understand what it's been like in this department recently. Lately, it seems no matter how hard we try, we can't seem to make the standards. I'm not sure what is going on, but we've been having a lot of problems lately.*
Q: *What kind of problems?*
A: *Well, for instance, all this quarter we've been requisitioning purchased parts from the material storeroom, and the parts just didn't fit together very well. I'm not sure what is going on, but during most of this quarter we've had to scrap and sort purchased parts—just to get our assemblies put together. Naturally, all this takes time and material. And that's not all.*
Q: *Go on.*
A: *All this quarter, the work that we've been receiving from the Fabrication Department has been shoddy. I mean, maybe around 20% of the stuff that comes in from Fabrication just can't be assembled. The fabrication is all wrong. As a result, we've had to scrap and rework a lot of the stuff. Naturally, this has just shot our quantity variances.*

Interpret the variance reports in light of the comments by the Assembly Department supervisor.

SA 22-5
Variance interpretation

Sound Sensation Inc. is a small manufacturer of electronic musical instruments. The plant manager received the following variable factory overhead report for the period:

	Actual	Budgeted Variable Factory Overhead at Actual Production
Supplies	$28,000	$26,520
Power and light	35,000	33,990
Indirect factory wages	26,112	20,400
Total	$89,112	$80,910

Actual units produced: 10,200 (85% of practical capacity)

The plant manager is not pleased with the $8,202 unfavorable variable factory overhead controllable variance and has come to discuss the matter with the controller. The following discussion occurred:

Plant Manager: I just received this factory report for the latest month of operation. I'm not very pleased with these figures. Before these numbers go to headquarters, you and I will need to reach an understanding.

Controller: Go ahead, what's the problem?

Plant Manager: What's the problem? Well, everything. Look at the variance. It's too large. If I understand the accounting approach being used here, you are assuming that my costs are variable to the units produced. Thus, as the production volume declines, so should these costs. Well, I don't believe that these costs are variable at all. I think they are fixed costs. As a result, when we operate below capacity, the costs really don't go down at all. I'm being penalized for costs I have no control over at all. I need this report to be redone to reflect this fact. If anything, the difference between actual and budget is essentially a volume variance. Listen, I know that you're a team player. You really need to reconsider your assumptions on this one.

➤ If you were in the controller's position, how would you respond to the plant manager?

SA 22-6
Nonmanufacturing performance measures—government

Group Project

Internet Project

Municipal governments are discovering that you can control only what you measure. As a result, many municipal governments are introducing nonfinancial performance measures to help improve municipal services. In a group, use the Google search engine to perform a search for "municipal government performance measurement." Google will provide a list of Internet sites that outline various city efforts in using nonfinancial performance measures. As a group, report on the types of measures used by one of the cities from the search.

Answers to Self-Examination Questions

1. **C** The unfavorable direct materials price variance of $2,550 is determined as follows:

Actual price	$5.05 per pound
Standard price	5.00
Price variance—unfavorable	$0.05 per pound

$0.05 × 51,000 actual pounds = $2,550

2. **D** The unfavorable direct labor time variance of $2,400 is determined as follows:

Actual direct labor time	2,200
Standard direct labor time	2,000
Direct labor time variance—unfavorable	200 × $12 standard rate = $2,400

3. **B** The unfavorable factory overhead volume variance of $2,000 is determined as follows:

Productive capacity not used	1,000 hours
Standard fixed factory overhead cost rate	× $2
Factory overhead volume variance—unfavorable	$2,000

4. **B** The controllable variable factory overhead variance is determined as follows:

6,000 units × 0.25 hour = 1,500 hours
1,500 hours × $5.00 per hour = $7,500

Actual variable overhead	$8,000
Less: Budgeted variable overhead at actual volume	7,500
Unfavorable controllable variance	$ 500

5. **D** The fixed factory overhead volume variance can be determined as follows:

Actual production in standard hours:
600 units × 0.2 machine hour = 120 machine hours

Practical capacity	200 machine hours
Standard hours at actual production	120
Idle capacity	80 machine hours

80 hours × $12.00 = $960 unfavorable volume variance

Performance Evaluation for Decentralized Operations

© INDIANHEAD MOUNTAIN SKI RESORT/PRNEWSFOTO (AP TOPIC GALLERY)

objectives

After studying this chapter, you should be able to:

1 List and explain the advantages and disadvantages of decentralized operations.

2 Prepare a responsibility accounting report for a cost center.

3 Prepare responsibility accounting reports for a profit center.

4 Compute and interpret the rate of return on investment, the residual income, and the balanced scorecard for an investment center.

5 Explain how the market price, negotiated price, and cost price approaches to transfer pricing may be used by decentralized segments of a business.

K2 Sports

Have you ever wondered why large retail stores like Wal-Mart, The Home Depot, and Sports Authority are divided into departments? Dividing into departments allows these retailers to provide products and expertise in specialized areas, while still offering a broad line of products. Departments allow companies to assign and follow financial performance. This information can be used to make product decisions, evaluate operations, and guide company strategy. Strong performance in a department might be attributed to a good department manager, who might be rewarded with a promotion. Poor departmental performance might lead to a change in the mix of products that the department sells.

Like retailers, most large businesses organize into operational units, such as divisions and depart-ments. For example, K2 Sports, a lead-ing maker of athletic and outdoor equipment, manages its business across four primary business segments: Marine and Outdoor, Action Sports, Team Sports, and Footwear and Apparel. These segments are fur-ther broken down into individual product lines, such as K2 skis, Rawlings athletic equipment, Marmot outdoor products, and WGP Paintball. Managers are responsible for running the operations of their re-spective segment of the business. Each segment is evaluated based on operating profit, and this infor-mation is used to plan and control K2's operations. In this chapter, we will discuss the role of account-ing in assisting managers in planning and control-ling organizational units, such as departments, divisions, and stores.

Centralized and Decentralized Operations

objective 1

List and explain the advantages and disadvantages of decentralized operations.

In 2006, Wachovia Corpora-tion, a national bank, decen-tralized decisions about how the bank does business over the Internet. Each business unit independently decides how it will conduct business over the Internet. For exam-ple, the Mortgage Loan Divi-sion allows customers to check current mortgage rates and apply for mortgages online.

A *centralized* business is one in which all major planning and operating decisions are made by top management. For example, a one-person, owner/manager-operated busi-ness is centralized because all plans and decisions are made by one person. In a small owner/manager-operated business, centralization may be desirable. This is because the owner/manager's close supervision ensures that the business will be operated in the way the owner/manager wishes.

Separating a business into **divisions** or operating units and delegating responsi-bility to unit managers is called **decentralization.** In a decentralized business, the unit managers are responsible for planning and controlling the operations of their units.

Divisions are often structured around common functions, products, customers, or regions. For example, Delta Air Lines is organized around *functions*, such as the Flight Operations Division. Procter & Gamble is organized around common *products*, such as the Soap Division, which sells a wide array of cleaning products. Norfolk Southern Corporation decentralizes its railroad operations into Eastern, Western, and Northern regional divisions.

There is no one best amount of decentralization for all businesses. In some com-panies, division managers have authority over all operations, including fixed asset acquisitions and retirements. In other companies, division managers have authority over profits but not fixed asset acquisitions and retirements. The proper amount of decentralization for a company depends on its advantages and disadvantages for the company's unique circumstances.

ADVANTAGES OF DECENTRALIZATION

As a business grows, it becomes more difficult for top management to maintain close daily contact with all operations. In such cases, delegating authority to managers closest to the operations usually results in better decisions. These managers often anticipate and react to operating data more quickly than could top management. In addition, as a company expands into a wide range of products and services, it becomes more difficult for top management to maintain operating expertise in all product lines and services. Decentralization allows managers to focus on acquiring expertise in their areas of responsibility. For example, in a company that maintains operations in insurance, banking, and health care, managers could become "experts" in their area of operation and responsibility.

Decentralized decision making also provides excellent training for managers. This may be a factor in helping a company retain quality managers. Since the art of management is best acquired through experience, delegating responsibility allows managers to acquire and develop managerial expertise early in their careers.

Businesses that work closely with customers, such as hotels, are often decentralized. This helps managers create good customer relations by responding quickly to customers' needs. In addition, because managers of decentralized operations tend to identify with customers and with operations, they are often more creative in suggesting operating and product improvements.

REAL WORLD

The Walt Disney Company is a multinational entertainment company that is decentralized into four major divisions. Media Networks owns numerous television stations and operates the ABC and ESPN broadcasting networks. Parks and Resorts operates the company's theme parks, including Disneyland® and Disneyworld®. Studio Entertainment includes the motion picture studios that have produced films including *Pirates of the Caribbean* and *Chronicles of Narnia*. Consumer Products licenses the company's brand name and its characters to manufacturers, publishers, and retailers.

DISADVANTAGES OF DECENTRALIZATION

A primary disadvantage of decentralized operations is that decisions made by one manager may negatively affect the profitability of the entire company. For example, the Pizza Hut chain added chicken to its menu and ended up taking business away from KFC. Then KFC retaliated with a blistering ad campaign against Pizza Hut. This happened even though both chains are part of the same company, Yum! Brands, Inc.

Another potential disadvantage of decentralized operations is duplicating assets and costs in operating divisions. For example, each manager of a product line might have a separate sales force and administrative office staff. Centralizing these personnel could save money. For example, in 2003, Hewlett-Packard Company announced that it would merge its consulting division with the division that sells business equipment in order to simplify its operations following the acquisition of Compaq. Advantages and disadvantages of decentralization are summarized in Exhibit 1.

EXHIBIT 1

Advantages and Disadvantages of Decentralized Operations

Advantages of Decentralization

- Lets managers closest to the operations make decisions.
- Allows managers to acquire expertise in their areas of responsibility.
- Provides excellent training opportunity for managers.
- Helps retain quality managers.
- Improves customer relations in businesses that work closely with customers, such as hotels.

Disadvantages of Decentralization

- Decisions made by one manager may negatively affect the profitability of the entire company.
- Assets and costs may be duplicated.

RESPONSIBILITY ACCOUNTING

In a decentralized business, an important function of accounting is to assist unit managers in evaluating and controlling their areas of responsibility, called *responsibility centers*. **Responsibility accounting** is the process of measuring and reporting operating data by responsibility center. Three common types of responsibility centers are cost centers, profit centers, and investment centers. These three responsibility centers differ in their scope of responsibility, as shown at the top of the following page.

Cost Center	Profit Center	Investment Center
Cost	Revenue − Cost ――― Profit	Revenue − Cost ――― Profit Investment in assets

Responsibility Accounting for Cost Centers

objective **2**

Prepare a responsibility accounting report for a cost center.

In a **cost center,** the unit manager has responsibility and authority for controlling the costs incurred. For example, the supervisor of the Power Department has responsibility for the costs incurred in providing power. A cost center manager does not make decisions concerning sales or the amount of fixed assets invested in the center.

Cost centers may vary in size from a small department to an entire manufacturing plant. In addition, cost centers may exist within other cost centers. For example, we could view an entire university as a cost center, and each college and department within the university could also be a cost center, as shown in Exhibit 2.

EXHIBIT 2 | Cost Centers in a University

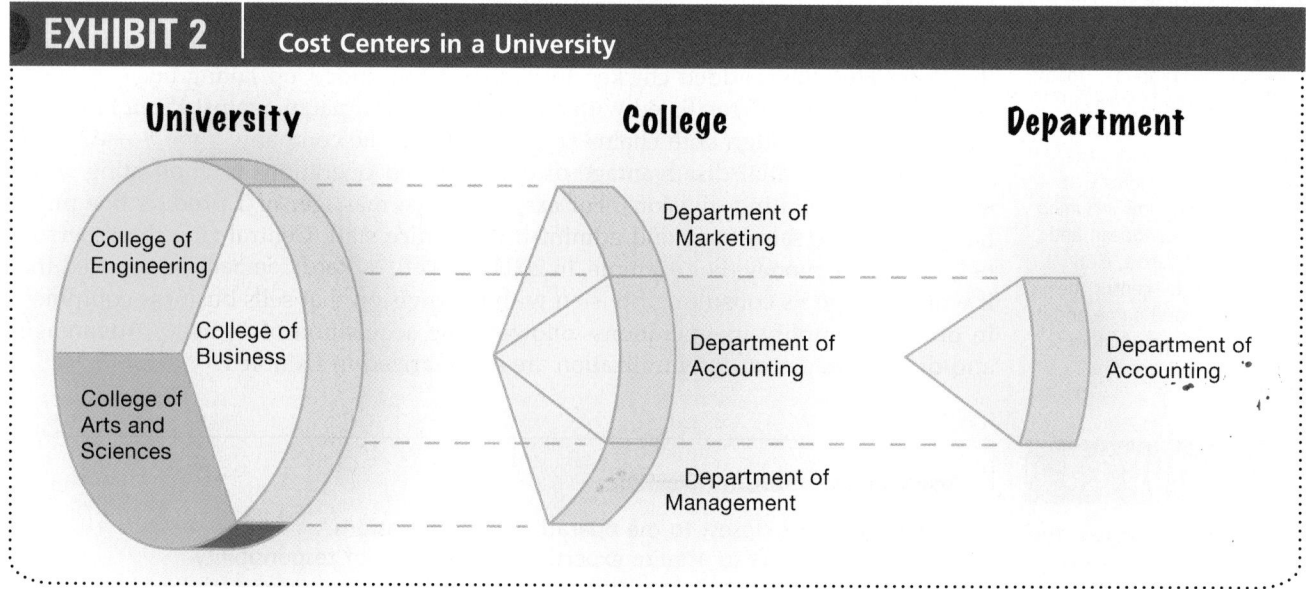

Since managers of cost centers have responsibility and authority over costs, responsibility accounting for cost centers focuses on costs. To illustrate, the budget performance reports in Exhibit 3 are part of a responsibility accounting system. These reports aid the managers in controlling costs.

In Exhibit 3, the reports prepared for the department supervisors show the budgeted and actual manufacturing costs for their departments. The supervisors can use these reports to focus on areas of significant difference, such as the difference between the budgeted and actual materials cost. The supervisor of Department 1 in Plant A may use additional information from a scrap report to determine why materials are over budget. Such a report might show that materials were scrapped as a result of machine malfunctions, improper use of machines by employees, or low quality materials.

For higher levels of management, responsibility accounting reports are usually more summarized than for lower levels of management. In Exhibit 3, for example, the budget performance report for the plant manager summarizes budget and actual cost data for the departments under the manager's supervision. This report enables the plant manager to identify the department supervisors responsible for major differences. Likewise, the report for the vice president of production summarizes the cost data for each plant. The plant managers can thus be held responsible for major differences in budgeted and actual costs in their plants.

EXHIBIT 3

Responsibility
Accounting Reports
for Cost Centers

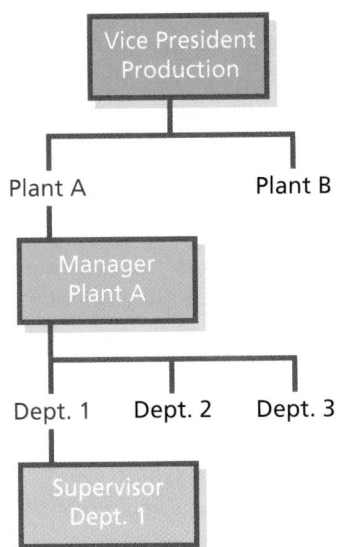

Reports
More
Summarized
as we
go up

Budget Performance Report
Vice President, Production
For the Month Ended October 31, 2008

	Budget	Actual	Over Budget	Under Budget
Administration	$ 19,500	$ 19,700	$ 200	
Plant A	467,475	470,330	2,855 ←	
Plant B	395,225	394,300		$925
	$882,200	$884,330	$3,055	$925

Budget Performance Report
Manager, Plant A
For the Month Ended October 31, 2008

	Budget	Actual	Over Budget	Under Budget
Administration	$ 17,500	$ 17,350		$150
Department 1	109,725	111,280 →	$1,555	
Department 2	190,500	192,600	2,100	
Department 3	149,750	149,100		650
	$467,475	$470,330	$3,655 ←	$800

Budget Performance Report
Supervisor, Department 1—Plant A
For the Month Ended October 31, 2008

	Budget	Actual	Over Budget	Under Budget
Factory wages	$ 58,100	$ 58,000		$100
Materials	32,500	34,225	$1,725	
Supervisory salaries	6,400	6,400		
Power and light	5,750	5,690		60
Depreciation of plant and equipment	4,000	4,000		
Maintenance	2,000	1,990		10
Insurance and property taxes	975	975		
	$109,725	$111,280	$1,725 →	$170

Example Exercise 23-1

objective **2**

Nuclear Power Company's costs were over budget by $24,000. The company is divided into North and South regions. The North Region's costs were under budget by $2,000. Determine the amount that the South Region's costs were over or under budget.

(continued)

Follow My Example 23-1

$26,000 over budget ($24,000 + $2,000)

For Practice: PE 23-1A, PE 23-1B

Responsibility Accounting for Profit Centers

objective **3**

Prepare responsibility accounting reports for a profit center.

In a **profit center,** the unit manager has the responsibility and the authority to make decisions that affect both costs and revenues (and thus profits). Profit centers may be divisions, departments, or products. For example, a consumer products company might organize its brands (product lines) as divisional profit centers. The manager of each brand could have responsibility for product cost and decisions regarding revenues, such as setting sales prices. The manager of a profit center does not make decisions concerning the fixed assets invested in the center. For example, the brand manager of a consumer products company does not make the decision to expand the plant capacity for the brand.

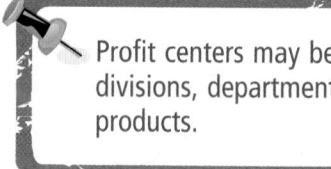

Profit centers may be divisions, departments, or products.

Profit centers are often viewed as an excellent training assignment for new managers. For example, Lester B. Korn, chairman and chief executive officer of Korn/Ferry International, offered the following strategy for young executives en route to top management positions:

Get Profit-Center Responsibility—Obtain a position where you can prove yourself as both a specialist with particular expertise and a generalist who can exercise leadership, authority, and inspire enthusiasm among colleagues and subordinates.

Responsibility accounting reports usually show the revenues, expenses, and income from operations for the profit center. The profit center income statement should include only revenues and expenses that are controlled by the manager. *Controllable revenues* are revenues earned by the profit center. **Controllable expenses** are costs that can be influenced (controlled) by the decisions of profit center managers. For example, the manager of the Men's Department at Nordstrom Inc. most likely controls the salaries of department personnel, but does not control the property taxes of the store.

SERVICE DEPARTMENT CHARGES

We will illustrate profit center income reporting for the Nova Entertainment Group (NEG). Assume that NEG is a diversified entertainment company with two operating divisions organized as profit centers: the Theme Park Division and the Movie Production Division. The revenues and operating expenses for the two divisions are shown below. The operating expenses consist of the direct expenses, such as the wages and salaries of a division's employees.

	Theme Park Division	Movie Production Division
Revenues	$6,000,000	$2,500,000
Operating expenses	2,495,000	405,000

In addition to direct expenses, divisions may also have expenses for services provided by internal centralized *service departments.* These service departments are often more efficient at providing service than are outside service providers. Examples of such service departments include the following:

■ Research and Development
■ Government Relations
■ Telecommunications
■ Publications and Graphics
■ Facilities Management

- Purchasing
- Information Systems
- Payroll Accounting
- Transportation
- Personnel Administration

A profit center's income from operations should reflect the cost of any internal services used by the center. To illustrate, assume that NEG established a Payroll Accounting Department. The costs of the payroll services, called **service department charges**, are charged to NEG's profit centers, as shown in Exhibit 4.

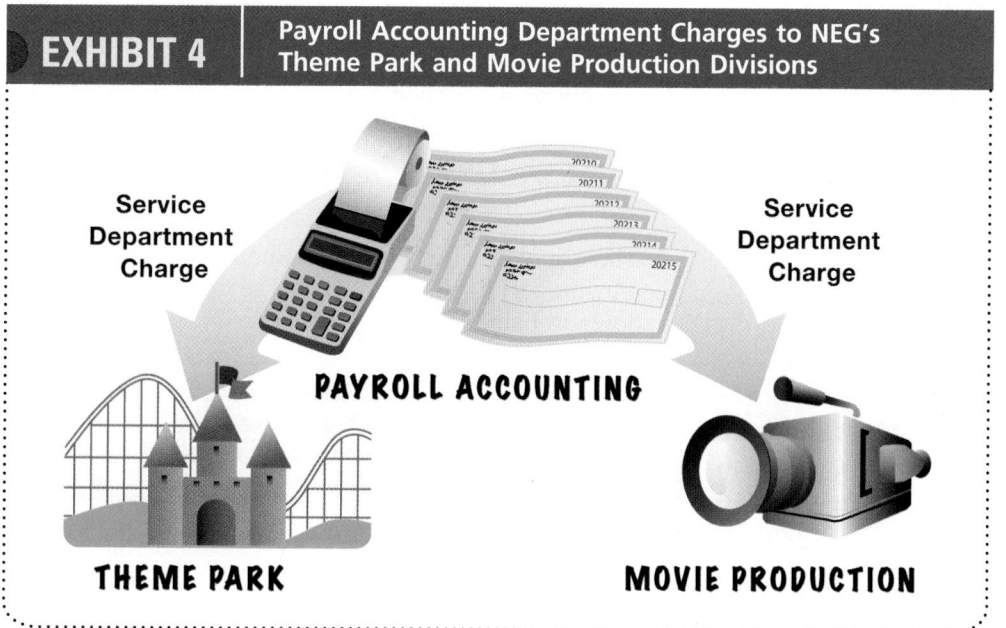

EXHIBIT 4	Payroll Accounting Department Charges to NEG's Theme Park and Movie Production Divisions

Service department charges are *indirect expenses* to a profit center. They are similar to the expenses that would be incurred if the profit center had purchased the services from a source outside the company. A profit center manager has control over such expenses if the manager is free to choose *how much* service is used from the service department.

To illustrate service department charges, assume that NEG has two other service departments—Purchasing and Legal, in addition to Payroll Accounting. The expenses for the year ended December 31, 2008, for each service department are as follows:

Purchasing	$400,000
Payroll Accounting	255,000
Legal	250,000
Total	$905,000

An *activity base* for each service department is used to charge service department expenses to the Theme Park and Movie Production divisions. The activity base for each service department is a measure of the services performed. For NEG, the service department activity bases are as follows:

Department	Activity Base
Purchasing	Number of purchase requisitions
Payroll Accounting	Number of payroll checks
Legal	Number of billed hours

The use of services by the Theme Park and Movie Production divisions is as follows:

Employees of IBM speak of "green money" and "blue money." Green money comes from customers. Blue money comes from providing services to other IBM departments via service department charges. IBM employees note that blue money is easier to earn than green money; yet from the stockholders' perspective, green money is the only money that counts.

	Service Usage		
	Purchasing	Payroll Accounting	Legal
Theme Park Division	25,000 purchase requisitions	12,000 payroll checks	100 billed hrs.
Movie Production Division	15,000	3,000	900
Total	40,000 purchase requisitions	15,000 payroll checks	1,000 billed hrs.

The rates at which services are charged to each division are called *service department charge rates*. These rates are determined by dividing each service department's expenses by the total service usage as follows:

$$\text{Purchasing: } \frac{\$400,000}{40,000 \text{ purchase requisitions}} = \$10 \text{ per purchase requisition}$$

$$\text{Payroll Accounting: } \frac{\$255,000}{15,000 \text{ payroll checks}} = \$17 \text{ per payroll check}$$

$$\text{Legal: } \frac{\$250,000}{1,000 \text{ hours}} = \$250 \text{ per hour}$$

The use of services by the Theme Park and Movie Production divisions is multiplied by the service department charge rates to determine the charges to each division, as shown in Exhibit 5.

EXHIBIT 5

Service Department Charges to NEG Divisions

Nova Entertainment Group
Service Department Charges to NEG Divisions
For the Year Ended December 31, 2008

Service Department	Theme Park Division	Movie Production Division
Purchasing (Note A)	$250,000	$150,000
Payroll Accounting (Note B)	204,000	51,000
Legal (Note C)	25,000	225,000
Total service department charges	$479,000	$426,000

Note A:
25,000 purchase requisitions × $10 per purchase requisition = $250,000
15,000 purchase requisitions × $10 per purchase requisition = $150,000

Note B:
12,000 payroll checks × $17 per check = $204,000
3,000 payroll checks × $17 per check = $51,000

Note C:
100 hours × $250 per hour = $25,000
900 hours × $250 per hour = $225,000

The Theme Park Division employs many temporary and part-time employees who are paid weekly. This is in contrast to the Movie Production Division, which has a more permanent payroll that is paid on a monthly basis. As a result, the Theme Park Division requires 12,000 payroll checks. This results in a large service charge from Payroll Accounting to the Theme Park Division. In contrast, the Movie Production Division uses many legal services for contract negotiations. Thus, there is a large service charge from Legal to the Movie Production Division.

PROFIT CENTER REPORTING

The divisional income statements for NEG are presented in Exhibit 6. These statements show the service department charges to the divisions.

Example Exercise 23-2

objective **3**

The centralized legal department of Johnson Company has expenses of $60,000. The department has provided a total of 2,000 hours of service for the period. The East Division has used 500 hours of legal service during the period, and the West Division has used 1,500 hours. How much should it be charged for legal services?

Follow My Example 23-2

East Division Service Charge for Legal Department:
$15,000 = 500 billed hours × ($60,000/2,000 hours)

West Division Service Charge for Legal Department:
$45,000 = 1,500 billed hours × ($60,000/2,000 hours)

For Practice: PE 23-2A, PE 23-2B

EXHIBIT 6

Divisional Income
Statements—NEG

Nova Entertainment Group
Divisional Income Statements
For the Year Ended December 31, 2008

	Theme Park Division	Movie Production Division
Revenues*	$6,000,000	$2,500,000
Operating expenses	2,495,000	405,000
Income from operations before service department charges	$3,505,000	$2,095,000
Less service department charges:		
Purchasing	$ 250,000	$ 150,000
Payroll Accounting	204,000	51,000
Legal	25,000	225,000
Total service department charges	$ 479,000	$ 426,000
Income from operations	$3,026,000	$1,669,000

*For a profit center that sells products, the income statement would show: Net sales − Cost of goods sold = Gross profit. The operating expenses would be deducted from the gross profit to get the income from operations before service department charges.

The **income from operations** is a measure of a manager's performance. In evaluating the profit center manager, the income from operations should be compared over time to a budget. It should not be compared across profit centers, since the profit centers are usually different in terms of size, products, and customers.

Example Exercise 23-3

objective **3**

Using the data for Johnson Company from Example Exercise 23-2 along with the data given below, determine the divisional income from operations for the East and West divisions.

	East Division	West Division
Sales	$300,000	$800,000
Cost of goods sold	165,000	420,000
Selling expenses	85,000	185,000

(continued)

Follow My Example 23-3

	East Division	West Division
Revenues	$300,000	$800,000
Operating expenses	250,000*	605,000**
Income from operations before		
service department charges	$ 50,000	$195,000
Service department charges	15,000	45,000
Income from operations	$ 35,000	$150,000

*$165,000 + $85,000
**$420,000 + $185,000

For Practice: PE 23-3A, PE 23-3B

Responsibility Accounting for Investment Centers

objective **4**

Compute and interpret the rate of return on investment, the residual income, and the balanced scorecard for an investment center.

In an **investment center**, the unit manager has the responsibility and the authority to make decisions that affect not only costs and revenues but also the assets invested in the center. Investment centers are widely used in highly diversified companies organized by divisions.

The manager of an investment center has more authority and responsibility than the manager of a cost center or a profit center. The manager of an investment center occupies a position similar to that of a chief operating officer or president of a company and is evaluated in much the same way.

Since investment center managers have responsibility for revenues and expenses, income from operations is an important part of investment center reporting. In addition, because the manager has responsibility for the assets invested in the center, two additional measures of performance are often used. These measures are the rate of return on investment and residual income. Top management often compares these measures across investment centers to reward performance and assess investment in the centers.

To illustrate, assume that DataLink Inc. is a cellular phone company that has three regional divisions, Northern, Central, and Southern. Condensed divisional income statements for the investment centers are shown in Exhibit 7.

EXHIBIT 7

Divisional Income Statements— DataLink Inc.

		DataLink Inc. Divisional Income Statements For the Year Ended December 31, 2008	
	Northern Division	Central Division	Southern Division
Revenues	$560,000	$672,000	$750,000
Operating expenses	336,000	470,400	562,500
Income from operations			
before service			
department charges	$224,000	$201,600	$187,500
Service department			
charges	154,000	117,600	112,500
Income from operations	$ 70,000	$ 84,000	$ 75,000

Using only income from operations, the Central Division is the most profitable division. However, income from operations does not reflect the amount of assets invested in each center. For example, a manager responsible for more assets should earn more income from operations than a manager responsible for fewer assets.

RATE OF RETURN ON INVESTMENT

Since investment center managers also control the amount of assets invested in their centers, they should be held accountable for the use of these assets. One measure that considers the amount of assets invested is the **rate of return on investment (ROI)** or *rate of return on assets*. It is one of the most widely used measures for investment centers and is computed as follows:

$$\text{Rate of Return on Investment (ROI)} = \frac{\text{Income from Operations}}{\text{Invested Assets}}$$

The rate of return on investment is useful because the three factors subject to control by divisional managers (revenues, expenses, and invested assets) are used in its computation. By measuring profitability relative to the amount of assets invested in each division, the rate of return on investment can be used to compare divisions. The higher the rate of return on investment, the better the division utilizes its assets to generate income. To illustrate, the rate of return on investment for each division of DataLink Inc., based on the book value of invested assets, is as follows:

	Northern Division	Central Division	Southern Division
Income from operations	$70,000	$84,000	$75,000
Invested assets	$350,000	$700,000	$500,000
Rate of return on investment	20%	12%	15%

Although the Central Division generated the largest income from operations, its rate of return on investment (12%) is the lowest. Hence, relative to the assets invested, the Central Division is the least profitable division. In comparison, the rate of return on investment of the Northern Division is 20% and the Southern Division is 15%. One way to analyze these differences is by using an expanded formula, called the DuPont formula, for the rate of return on investment.

The **DuPont formula**, created by a financial executive of E.I. du Pont de Nemours and Company in 1919, states that the rate earned on total assets is the product of two factors. The first factor is the ratio of income from operations to sales, often called the **profit margin**. The second factor is the ratio of sales to invested assets, often called the **investment turnover**. In the illustration at the left, profits can be earned by either increasing the investment turnover (turning the crank faster), by increasing the profit margin (increasing the size of the opening), or both.

Using the DuPont formula yields the same rate of return on investment for the Northern Division, 20%, as computed previously.

$$\begin{aligned}\text{Rate of Return on Investment (ROI)} &= \text{Profit Margin} \times \text{Investment Turnover}\end{aligned}$$

$$\text{Rate of Return on Investment (ROI)} = \frac{\text{Income from Operations}}{\text{Sales}} \times \frac{\text{Sales}}{\text{Invested Assets}}$$

$$\text{ROI} = \frac{\$70,000}{\$560,000} \times \frac{\$560,000}{\$350,000}$$

$$\text{ROI} = 12.5\% \times 1.6$$
$$\text{ROI} = 20\%$$

The DuPont formula for the rate of return on investment is useful in evaluating and controlling divisions. This is because the profit margin and the investment turnover focus on the underlying operating relationships of each division.

The profit margin component focuses on profitability by indicating the rate of profit earned on each sales dollar. If a division's profit margin increases, and all other factors

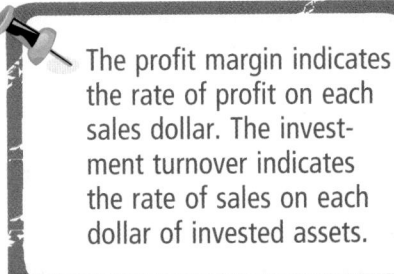

The profit margin indicates the rate of profit on each sales dollar. The investment turnover indicates the rate of sales on each dollar of invested assets.

remain the same, the division's rate of return on investment will increase. For example, a division might add more profitable products to its sales mix and thereby increase its overall profit margin and rate of return on investment.

The investment turnover component focuses on efficiency in using assets and indicates the rate at which sales are generated for each dollar of invested assets. The more sales per dollar invested, the greater the efficiency in using the assets. If a division's investment turnover increases, and all other factors remain the same, the division's rate of return on investment will increase. For example, a division might attempt to increase sales through special sales promotions or reduce inventory assets by using just-in-time principles, either of which would increase investment turnover.

The rate of return on investment, using the DuPont formula for each division of DataLink Inc., is summarized as follows:

$$\text{Rate of Return on Investment (ROI)} = \frac{\text{Income from Operations}}{\text{Sales}} \times \frac{\text{Sales}}{\text{Invested Assets}}$$

$$\text{Northern Division (ROI)} = \frac{\$70,000}{\$560,000} \times \frac{\$560,000}{\$350,000}$$

$$\text{ROI} = 12.5\% \times 1.6$$
$$\text{ROI} = 20\%$$

$$\text{Central Division (ROI)} = \frac{\$84,000}{\$672,000} \times \frac{\$672,000}{\$700,000}$$

$$\text{ROI} = 12.5\% \times 0.96$$
$$\text{ROI} = 12\%$$

$$\text{Southern Division (ROI)} = \frac{\$75,000}{\$750,000} \times \frac{\$750,000}{\$500,000}$$

$$\text{ROI} = 10\% \times 1.5$$
$$\text{ROI} = 15\%$$

Although the Northern and Central divisions have the same profit margins, the Northern Division investment turnover (1.6) is larger than that of the Central Division (0.96). Thus, by using its invested assets more efficiently, the Northern Division's rate of return on investment is higher than the Central Division's. The Southern Division's profit margin of 10% and investment turnover of 1.5 are lower than those of the Northern Division. The product of these factors results in a return on investment of 15% for the Southern Division, compared to 20% for the Northern Division.

To determine possible ways of increasing the rate of return on investment, the profit margin and investment turnover for a division may be analyzed. For example, if the Northern Division is in a highly competitive industry in which the profit margin cannot be easily increased, the division manager might focus on increasing the investment turnover. To illustrate, assume that the revenues of the Northern Division could be increased by $56,000 through increasing operating expenses, such as advertising, to $385,000. The Northern Division's income from operations will increase from $70,000 to $77,000, as shown below.

Revenues ($560,000 + $56,000)	$616,000
Operating expenses	385,000
Income from operations before service department charges	$231,000
Service department charges	154,000
Income from operations	$ 77,000

The rate of return on investment for the Northern Division, using the DuPont formula, is recomputed as follows:

$$\text{Rate of Return on Investment (ROI)} = \frac{\text{Income from Operations}}{\text{Sales}} \times \frac{\text{Sales}}{\text{Invested Assets}}$$

$$\text{Northern Division Revised ROI} = \frac{\$77,000}{\$616,000} \times \frac{\$616,000}{\$350,000}$$

$$\text{ROI} = 12.5\% \times 1.76$$
$$\text{ROI} = 22\%$$

Although the Northern Division's profit margin remains the same (12.5%), the investment turnover has increased from 1.6 to 1.76, an increase of 10% (0.16 ÷ 1.6). The 10% increase in investment turnover also increases the rate of return on investment by 10% (from 20% to 22%).

In addition to using it as a performance measure, the rate of return on investment may assist management in other ways. For example, in considering a decision to expand the operations of DataLink Inc., management might consider giving priority to the Northern Division because it earns the highest rate of return on investment. If the current rates of return on investment are maintained in the future, an investment in the Northern Division will return 20 cents (20%) on each dollar invested. In contrast, investments in the Central Division will earn only 12 cents per dollar invested, and investments in the Southern Division will return only 15 cents per dollar.

A disadvantage of the rate of return on investment as a performance measure is that it may lead divisional managers to reject new investments that could be profitable for the company as a whole. For example, the Northern Division of DataLink Inc. has an overall rate of return on investment of 20%. Assume the top management establishes

Business Connections

REAL WORLD

RETURN ON INVESTMENT

The annual reports of public companies must provide segment disclosure information identifying revenues, income from operations, and total assets. This information can be used to compute the return on investment for the segments of a company. For example, The E.W. Scripps Company, a media company, operates four major segments:

1. Newspapers: Owns and operates daily and community newspapers in 19 markets in the United States.
2. Scripps Networks: Owns and operates five national television networks: Home and Garden Television, Food Network, DIY Network, Fine Living, and Great American Country.
3. Broadcast Television: Owns and operates several local televisions in various markets.
4. Shop at Home: Markets a range of consumer goods to television viewers and visitors to its Internet site.

The DuPont formulas for these segments, as derived from a recent annual report, are as follows:

	Segment Profit Margin	×	Investment Turnover	=	Return on Investment
Newspapers	34.9%		0.55		19.2%
Scripps Networks	42.0%		0.67		28.1%
Broadcast Television	31.6%		0.69		21.8%
Shop at Home	−7.5%		0.80		−6.0%

As can be seen from the data, E.W. Scripps' three business segments (Newspapers, Scripps Networks, and Broadcast Television) have relatively low investment turnover, with all three being slightly above 0.50. Each of these segments also had very strong profit margins, ranging from 31.6% to 42.0%. Multiplying the profit margin by the investment turnover yields the ROI. The ROI is strong for the three primary business segments. The Shop at Home segment, however, is not performing as well. While this segment has a stronger investment turnover than the other three segments, it operates at a negative profit. This is the newest segment of the company and represents a relatively small portion of the company's total revenues. As the segment grows, the company should be careful to control costs to ensure that this segment attains a level of profitability consistent with the company's other segments.

a minimal acceptable rate of return of 10%. Assume further the manager of the Northern Division has the opportunity to invest in a new project that is estimated to earn a 14% rate of return. If the manager of the Northern Division invests in the project, however, the Northern Division's overall rate of return will decrease from 20% due to averaging. Thus, the division manager might decide to reject the project, even though the investment would exceed DataLink's minimum acceptable rate of return on investment. The CFO of Millennium Chemicals referred to a similar situation by stating: "We had too many divisional executives who failed to spend money on capital projects with more than satisfactory returns because those projects would have lowered the average return on assets of their particular business."

Example Exercise 23-4   objective 4

Campbell Company has income from operations of $35,000, invested assets of $140,000, and sales of $437,500. Use the DuPont formula to compute the rate of return on investment and show (a) the profit margin, (b) the investment turnover, and (c) the rate of return on investment.

Follow My Example 23-4

a. Profit margin = $35,000/$437,500 = 8%
b. Investment turnover = $437,500/$140,000 = 3.125
c. Rate of return on investment = 8% × 3.125 = 25%

For Practice: PE 23-4A, PE 23-4B

RESIDUAL INCOME

An additional measure of evaluating divisional performance—residual income—is useful in overcoming some of the disadvantages associated with the rate of return on investment. **Residual income**[1] is the excess of income from operations over a minimum acceptable income from operations, as illustrated below.

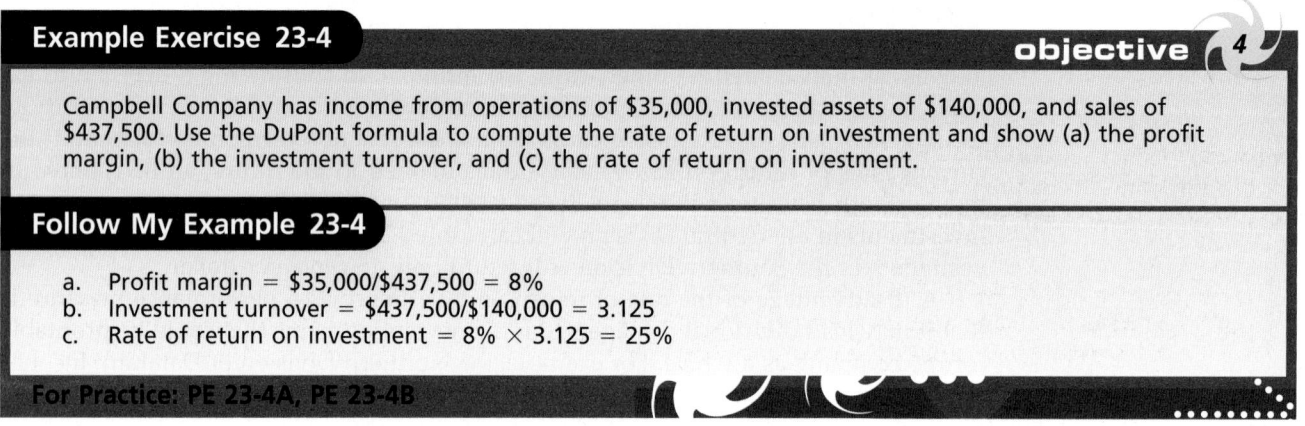

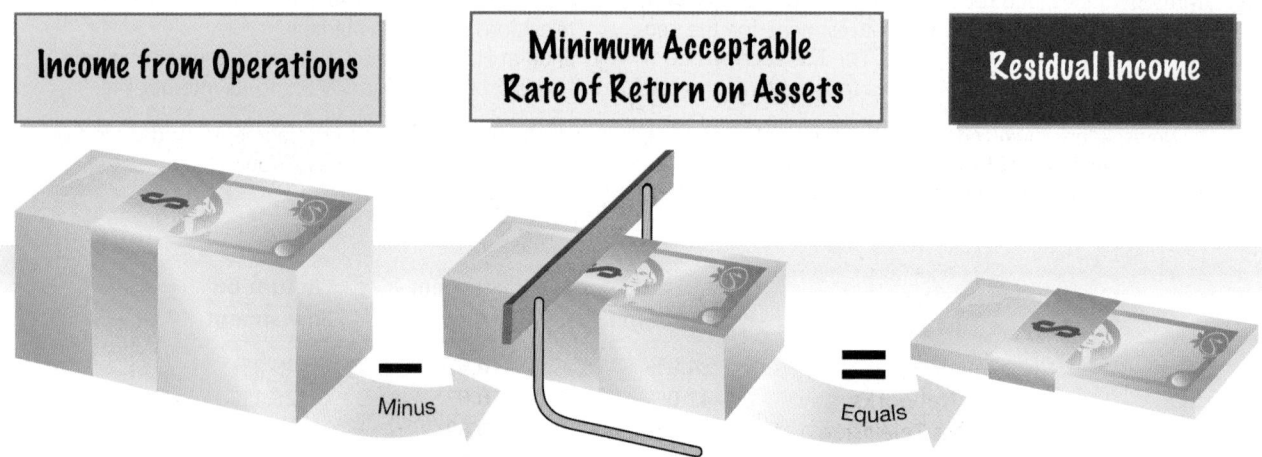

The minimum acceptable income from operations is normally computed by multiplying a minimum rate of return by the amount of divisional assets. The minimum rate is set by top management, based on such factors as the cost of financing the business operations. To illustrate, assume that DataLink Inc. has established 10% as the mini-

---

1 Another popular term for residual income is economic value added (EVA), which has been trademarked by the consulting firm Stern Stewart & Co.

mum acceptable rate of return on divisional assets. The residual incomes for the three divisions are as follows:

	Northern Division	Central Division	Southern Division
Income from operations	$70,000	$84,000	$75,000
Minimum acceptable income from operations as a percent of assets:			
$350,000 × 10%	35,000		
$700,000 × 10%		70,000	
$500,000 × 10%			50,000
Residual income	$35,000	$14,000	$25,000

The Northern Division has more residual income than the other divisions, even though it has the least amount of income from operations. This is because the assets on which to earn a minimum acceptable rate of return are less for the Northern Division than for the other divisions.

The major advantage of residual income as a performance measure is that it considers both the minimum acceptable rate of return and the total amount of the income from operations earned by each division. Residual income encourages division managers to maximize income from operations in excess of the minimum. This provides an incentive to accept any project that is expected to have a rate of return in excess of the minimum. Thus, the residual income number supports both divisional and overall company objectives.

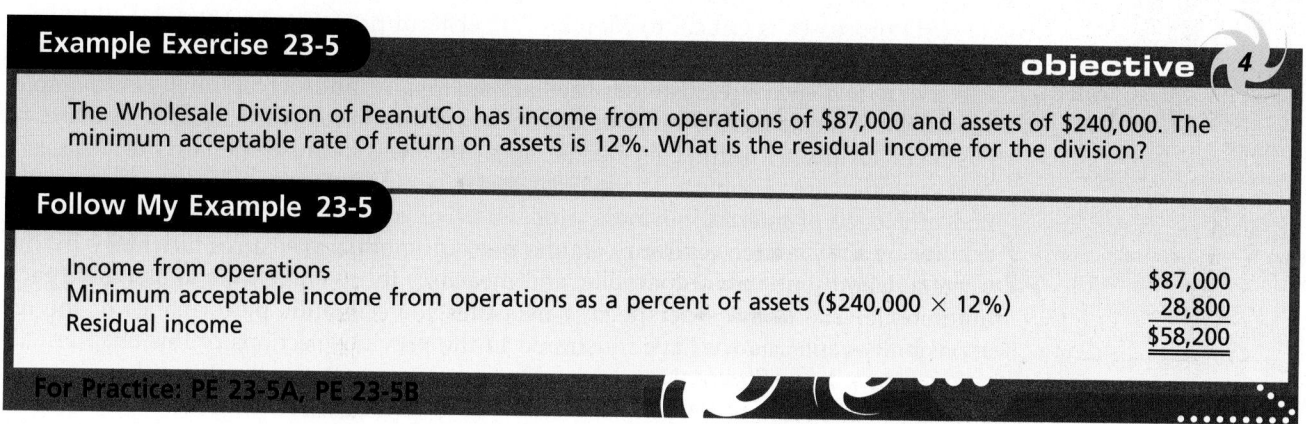

Example Exercise 23-5

objective 4

The Wholesale Division of PeanutCo has income from operations of $87,000 and assets of $240,000. The minimum acceptable rate of return on assets is 12%. What is the residual income for the division?

Follow My Example 23-5

Income from operations	$87,000
Minimum acceptable income from operations as a percent of assets ($240,000 × 12%)	28,800
Residual income	$58,200

For Practice: PE 23-5A, PE 23-5B

THE BALANCED SCORECARD[2]

In addition to financial divisional performance measures, many companies are also relying on nonfinancial divisional measures. One popular evaluation approach is the **balanced scorecard**. The balanced scorecard is a set of financial and nonfinancial measures that reflect multiple performance dimensions of a business. A common balanced scorecard design measures performance in the innovation and learning, customer, internal, and financial dimensions of a business. These four areas can be diagrammed as shown in Exhibit 8.

The *innovation and learning* perspective measures the amount of innovation in an organization. For example, a drug company, such as Merck & Co., Inc., would measure the number of drugs in its FDA (Food and Drug Administration) approval pipeline,

2 The balanced scorecard was developed by R. S. Kaplan and D. P. Norton and explained in *The Balanced Scorecard: Translating Strategy into Action* (Cambridge: Harvard Business School Press, 1996).

EXHIBIT 8

The Balanced
Scorecard

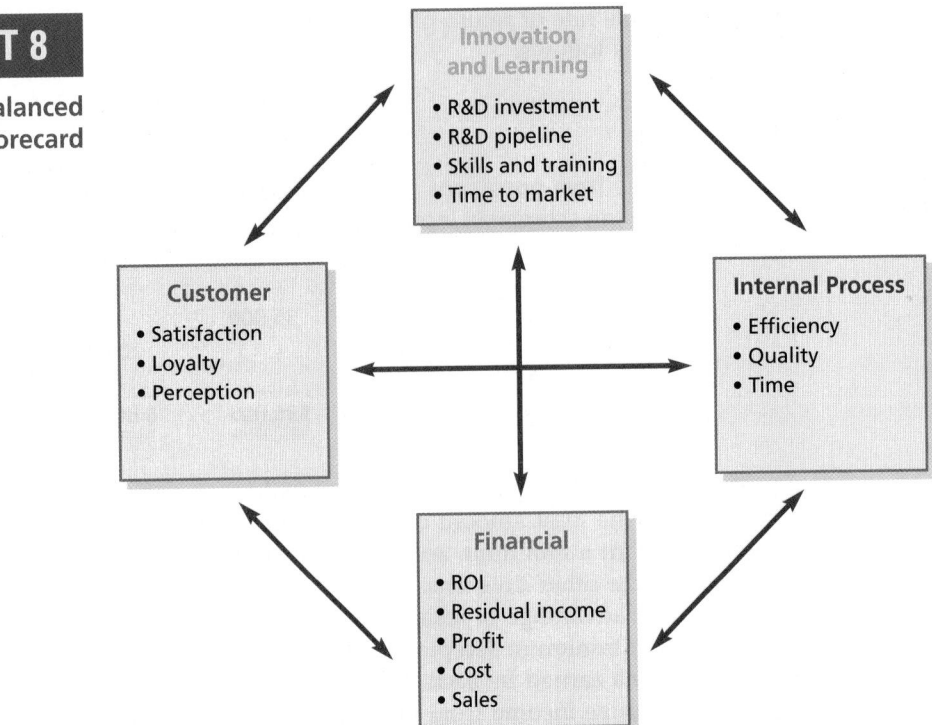

Hilton Hotels Corporation
was one of the first major
companies to develop a balanced scorecard. It used a
scorecard to measure em-
ployee satisfaction, customer
loyalty, and financial performance. These measures helped
the company improve its relationship with its employees,
customer service, and financial performance for its shareholders.

the amount of research and development (R&D) spending per period, and the length of time it takes to turn ideas into marketable products. Managing the performance of its R&D processes is critical to Merck's longer-term prospects and thus would be an additional performance perspective beyond the financial numbers. The *customer* perspective would measure customer satisfaction, loyalty, and perceptions. For example, Amazon.com measures the number of repeat visitors to its Web site as a measure of customer loyalty. Amazon.com needs repeat business because the costs to acquire a new customer are very high. The *internal process* perspective measures the effectiveness and efficiency of internal business processes. For example, DaimlerChrysler measures quality by the average warranty claims per automobile, measures efficiency by the average labor hours per automobile, and measures the average time to assemble each automobile. The *financial* perspective measures the economic performance of the responsibility center as we have illustrated in the previous sections of this chapter. All companies will use financial measures. The measures most commonly used are income from operations as a percent of sales and rate of return on investment.

The balanced scorecard is designed to reveal the underlying nonfinancial drivers, or causes, of financial performance. For example, if a business improves customer satisfaction, this will likely lead to improved financial performance. In addition, the balanced scorecard helps managers consider trade-offs between short- and long-term performance. For example, additional investment in research and development (R&D) would penalize the short-term financial perspective, because R&D is an expense that reduces income from operations. However, the innovation perspective would measure additional R&D expenditures favorably, because current R&D expenditures will lead to future profits from new products. The balanced scorecard will motivate the manager to invest in new R&D, even though it is recognized as a current period expense. A survey by Bain & Co., a consulting firm, indicated that 57% of large companies use the balanced scorecard.[3] Thus, the balanced scorecard is gaining acceptance because of its ability to reveal the underlying causes of financial performance, while helping managers consider the short- and long-term implications of their decisions.

---

3 Bain & Co., "Management Tools 2005."

Transfer Pricing

objective 5

Explain how the market price, negotiated price, and cost price approaches to transfer pricing may be used by decentralized segments of a business.

When divisions transfer products or render services to each other, a **transfer price** is used to charge for the products or services. Since transfer prices affect the goals for both divisions, setting these prices is a sensitive matter for division managers.

Transfer prices should be set so that overall company income is increased when goods are transferred between divisions. As we will illustrate, however, transfer prices may be misused in such a way that overall company income suffers.

In the following paragraphs, we discuss various approaches to setting transfer prices. Exhibit 9 shows the range of prices that results from common approaches to setting transfer prices.[4] Transfer prices can be set as low as the variable cost per unit or as high as the market price. Often, transfer prices are negotiated at some point between variable cost per unit and market price.

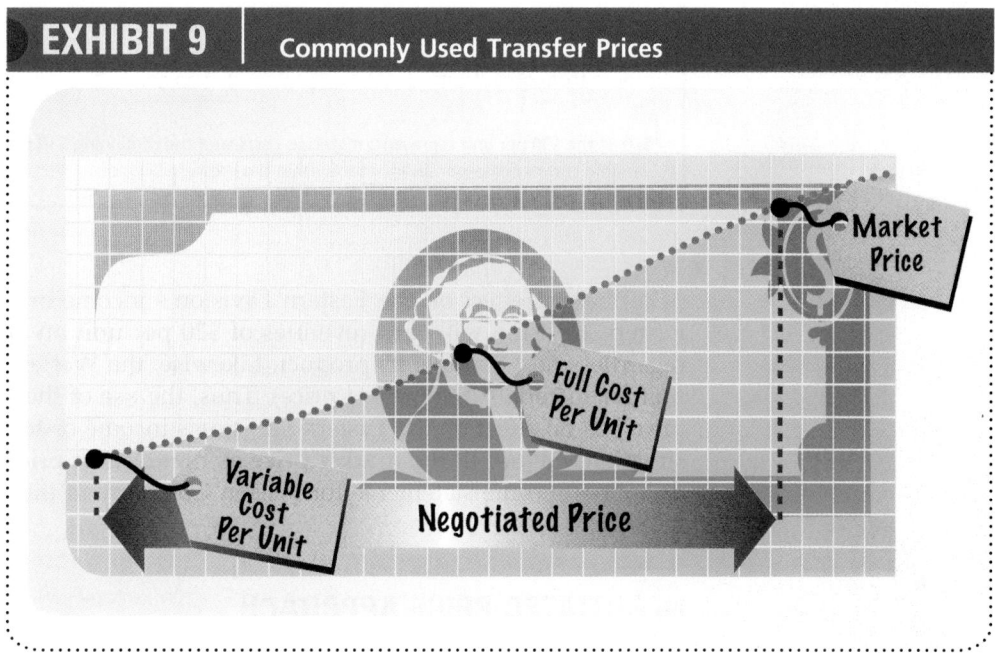

EXHIBIT 9 | Commonly Used Transfer Prices

Transfer prices may be used when decentralized units are organized as cost, profit, or investment centers. To illustrate, we will use a packaged snack food company (Wilson Company) with no service departments and two operating divisions (Eastern and Western) organized as investment centers. Condensed divisional income statements for Wilson Company, assuming no transfers between divisions, are shown in Exhibit 10.

MARKET PRICE APPROACH

Using the **market price approach,** the transfer price is the price at which the product or service transferred could be sold to outside buyers. If an outside market exists for the product or service transferred, the current market price may be a proper transfer price.

To illustrate, assume that materials used by Wilson Company in producing snack food in the Western Division are currently purchased from an outside supplier at $20 per unit. The same materials are produced by the Eastern Division. The Eastern Division is operating at full capacity of 50,000 units and can sell all it produces to either the Western Division or to outside buyers. A transfer price of $20 per unit (the market

---

4 The discussion in this chapter highlights the essential concepts of transfer pricing. In-depth discussion of transfer pricing can be found in advanced texts.

EXHIBIT 10

Income Statements—
No Transfers Between
Divisions

**Wilson Company
Divisional Income Statements
For the Year Ended December 31, 2008**

	Eastern Division	Western Division	Total
Sales:			
50,000 units × $20 per unit	$1,000,000		$1,000,000
20,000 units × $40 per unit		$800,000	800,000
			$1,800,000
Expenses:			
Variable:			
50,000 units × $10 per unit . . .	$ 500,000		$ 500,000
20,000 units × $30* per unit . .		$600,000	600,000
Fixed	300,000	100,000	400,000
Total expenses	$ 800,000	$700,000	$1,500,000
Income from operations	$ 200,000	$100,000	$ 300,000

*$20 of the $30 per unit represents materials costs, and the remaining $10 per unit represents other variable conversion expenses incurred within the Western Division.

price) has no effect on the Eastern Division's income or total company income. The Eastern Division will earn revenues of $20 per unit on all its production and sales, regardless of who buys its product. Likewise, the Western Division will pay $20 per unit for materials (the market price). Thus, the use of the market price as the transfer price has no effect on the Eastern Division's income or total company income. In this situation, the use of the market price as the transfer price is proper. The condensed divisional income statements for Wilson Company in this case are also shown in Exhibit 10.

NEGOTIATED PRICE APPROACH

If unused or excess capacity exists in the supplying division (the Eastern Division), and the transfer price is equal to the market price, total company profit may not be maximized. This is because the manager of the Western Division will be indifferent toward purchasing materials from the Eastern Division or from outside suppliers. Thus, the Western Division may purchase the materials from outside suppliers. If, however, the Western Division purchases the materials from the Eastern Division, the difference between the market price of $20 and the variable costs of the Eastern Division can cover fixed costs and contribute to company profits. When the negotiated price approach is used in this situation, the manager of the Western Division is encouraged to purchase the materials from the Eastern Division.

The **negotiated price approach** allows the managers of decentralized units to agree (negotiate) among themselves as to the transfer price. The only constraint on the negotiations is that the transfer price be less than the market price but greater than the supplying division's variable costs per unit.

To illustrate the use of the negotiated price approach, assume that instead of a capacity of 50,000 units, the Eastern Division's capacity is 70,000 units. In addition, assume that the Eastern Division can continue to sell only 50,000 units to outside buyers. A transfer price less than $20 would encourage the manager of the Western Division to purchase from the Eastern Division. This is because the Western Division's materials cost per unit would decrease, and its income from operations would increase. At the same time, a transfer price above the Eastern Division's variable costs per unit of $10 (from Exhibit 10) would encourage the manager of the Eastern Division to use the excess capacity to supply materials to the Western Division. In doing so, the Eastern Division's income from operations would increase.

We continue the illustration with the aid of Exhibit 11, assuming that Wilson Company's division managers agree to a transfer price of $15 for the Eastern Division's product. By purchasing from the Eastern Division, the Western Division's materials cost would be $5 per unit less. At the same time, the Eastern Division would increase its sales by $300,000 (20,000 units × $15 per unit) and increase its income by $100,000 ($300,000 sales − $200,000 variable costs). The effect of reducing the Western Division's materials cost by $100,000 (20,000 units × $5 per unit) is to increase its income by $100,000. Therefore, Wilson Company's income is increased by $200,000 ($100,000 reported by the Eastern Division and $100,000 reported by the Western Division), as shown in the condensed income statements in Exhibit 11.

EXHIBIT 11

Income Statements—
Negotiated Transfer
Price

Wilson Company
Divisional Income Statements
For the Year Ended December 31, 2008

	Eastern Division	Western Division	Total
Sales:			
50,000 units × $20 per unit	$1,000,000		$1,000,000
20,000 units × $15 per unit	300,000		300,000
20,000 units × $40 per unit		$800,000	800,000
	$1,300,000	$800,000	$2,100,000
Expenses:			
Variable:			
70,000 units × $10 per unit . . .	$ 700,000		$ 700,000
20,000 units × $25* per unit . .		$500,000	500,000
Fixed	300,000	100,000	400,000
Total expenses	$1,000,000	$600,000	$1,600,000
Income from operations	$ 300,000	$200,000	$ 500,000

*$10 of the $25 represents variable conversion expenses incurred solely within the Western Division, and $15 per unit represents the transfer price per unit from the Eastern Division.

In this illustration, any transfer price less than the market price of $20 but greater than the Eastern Division's unit variable costs of $10 would increase each division's income. In addition, overall company profit would increase by $200,000. By establishing a range of $20 to $10 for the transfer price, each division manager has an incentive to negotiate the transfer of the materials.

Example Exercise 23-6

objective **5**

The materials used by the Winston-Salem Division of Fox Company are currently purchased from outside suppliers at $30 per unit. These same materials are produced by Fox's Flagstaff Division. The Flagstaff Division can produce the materials needed by the Winston-Salem Division at a variable cost of $15 per unit. The division is currently producing 70,000 units and has capacity of 100,000 units. The two divisions have recently negotiated a transfer price of $22 per unit for 30,000 units. By how much will each division's income increase as a result of this transfer?

(continued)

Follow My Example 23-6

Winston-Salem Division

Change in sales	$ 0
Decrease in variable costs [30,000 units × ($30 − $22)]	(240,000)
Increase in income	$240,000

Flagstaff Division

Increase in sales (30,000 units × $22)	$660,000
Increase in variable costs (30,000 units × $15)	450,000
Increase in income	$210,000

For Practice: PE 23-6A, PE 23-6B

COST PRICE APPROACH

Under the **cost price approach**, cost is used to set transfer prices. With this approach, a variety of cost concepts may be used. For example, cost may refer to either total product cost per unit or variable product cost per unit. If total product cost per unit is used, direct materials, direct labor, and factory overhead are included in the transfer price. If variable product cost per unit is used, the fixed factory overhead component of total product cost is excluded from the transfer price.

Either actual costs or standard (budgeted) costs may be used in applying the cost price approach. If actual costs are used, inefficiencies of the producing division are transferred to the purchasing division. Thus, there is little incentive for the producing division to control costs carefully. For this reason, most companies use standard costs in the cost price approach. In this way, differences between actual and standard costs remain with the producing division for cost control purposes.

When division managers have responsibility for cost centers, the cost price approach to transfer pricing is proper and is often used. The cost price approach may not be proper, however, for decentralized operations organized as profit or investment centers. In profit and investment centers, division managers have responsibility for both revenues and expenses. The use of cost as a transfer price ignores the supplying division manager's responsibility for revenues. When a supplying division's sales are all intracompany transfers, for example, using the cost price approach prevents the supplying division from reporting any income from operations. A cost-based transfer price may therefore not motivate the division manager to make intracompany transfers, even though they are in the best interests of the company.

Integrity, Objectivity, and Ethics in Business

ETHICS

SHIFTING INCOME THROUGH TRANSFER PRICES

Transfer prices allow companies to minimize taxes by shifting taxable income from countries with high tax rates to countries with low taxes. For example, GlaxoSmithKline, a British company, and the second biggest drug maker in the world, has been in a dispute with the U.S. Internal Revenue Service (IRS) over international transfer prices since the early 1990s. The company pays U.S. taxes on income from its U.S. Division and British taxes on income from the British Division. The IRS claims that the transfer prices on sales from the British Division to the U.S. Division were too high, which reduced profits and taxes in the U.S. Division. In January 2005, the company received a new tax bill from the IRS for almost $1.9 billion related to the transfer pricing issue, raising the total bill to almost $5 billion. The company has filed suit in the U.S. Tax Court to dispute the IRS assessment.

Source: J. Whalen, "Glaxo Gets New IRS Bill Seeking Another $1.9 Billion in Back Tax," *The Wall Street Journal*, January 27, 2005.

At a Glance

1. List and explain the advantages and disadvantages of decentralized operations.

Key Points	Key Learning Outcomes	Example Exercises	Practice Exercises
In a centralized business, all major planning and operating decisions are made by top management. In a decentralized business, these responsibilities are delegated to unit managers. Decentralization may allow a company to be more effective because operational decisions are made by the managers closest to the operations, allowing top management to focus on strategic issues.	• Describe the advantages of decentralization. • Describe the disadvantages of decentralization. • Describe the common types of responsibility centers and the role of responsibility accounting.		

2. Prepare a responsibility accounting report for a cost center.

Key Points	Key Learning Outcomes	Example Exercises	Practice Exercises
Cost centers limit the responsibility and authority of managers to decisions related to the costs of their unit. The primary accounting tool for planning and controlling costs for a cost center are budgets and budget performance reports.	• Describe cost centers. • Describe the responsibility reporting for a cost center. • Compute the over (under) budgeted costs for a cost center.	23-1	23-1A, 23-1B

3. Prepare responsibility accounting reports for a profit center.

Key Points	Key Learning Outcomes	Example Exercises	Practice Exercises
In a profit center, managers have the responsibility and authority to make decisions that affect both revenues and costs. Responsibility reports for a profit center usually show income from operations for the unit.	• Describe profit centers. • Determine how service department charges are allocated to profit centers.	23-2	23-2A, 23-2B
	• Describe the responsibility reporting for a profit center. • Compute income from operations for a profit center.	23-3	23-3A, 23-3B

4. Compute and interpret the rate of return on investment, the residual income, and the balanced scorecard for an investment center.

Key Points	Key Learning Outcomes	Example Exercises	Practice Exercises
In an investment center, the unit manager has the responsibility and authority to make decisions that affect the unit's revenues, expenses, and assets invested in the center. Three measures are commonly used to assess investment center performance: return on investment (ROI), residual income, and the balanced scorecard. These measures are often used to compare and assess investment center performance.	• Describe investment centers. • Describe the responsibility reporting for an investment center. • Compute the rate of return on investment (ROI). • Compute residual income. • Describe the balanced scorecard approach.	23-4 23-5	23-4A, 23-4B 23-5A, 23-5B

5. Explain how the market price, negotiated price, and cost price approaches to transfer pricing may be used by decentralized segments of a business.

Key Points	Key Learning Outcomes	Example Exercises	Practice Exercises
When divisions within a company transfer products or provide services to each other, a transfer price is used to charge for the products or services. Transfer prices should be set so that the overall company income is increased when goods are transferred between divisions. One of three common approaches is typically used to establish transfer prices: market price, negotiated price, or cost price.	• Describe how companies determine the price used to transfer products or services between divisions. • Determine transfer prices using the market price approach. • Determine transfer prices using the negotiated price approach. • Describe the cost price approach to determining transfer price.	23-6	23-6A, 23-6B

Key Terms

balanced scorecard (1033)
controllable expenses (1024)
cost center (1022)
cost price approach (1038)
decentralization (1020)
division (1020)
DuPont formula (1029)

income from operations (1027)
investment center (1028)
investment turnover (1029)
market price approach (1035)
negotiated price approach (1036)
profit center (1024)
profit margin (1029)

rate of return on investment (ROI) (1029)
residual income (1032)
responsibility accounting (1021)
service department charges (1025)
transfer price (1035)

Illustrative Problem

Quinn Company has two divisions, Domestic and International. Invested assets and condensed income statement data for each division for the past year ended December 31 are as follows:

	Domestic Division	International Division
Revenues	$675,000	$480,000
Operating expenses	450,000	372,400
Service department charges	90,000	50,000
Invested assets	600,000	384,000

Instructions

1. Prepare condensed income statements for the past year for each division.
2. Using the DuPont formula, determine the profit margin, investment turnover, and rate of return on investment for each division.
3. If management's minimum acceptable rate of return is 10%, determine the residual income for each division.

Solution

1.

Quinn Company
Divisional Income Statements
For the Year Ended December 31, 2008

	Domestic Division	International Division
Revenues	$675,000	$480,000
Operating expenses	450,000	372,400
Income from operations before		
service department charges	$225,000	$107,600
Service department charges	90,000	50,000
Income from operations	$135,000	$ 57,600

2.

$$\frac{\text{Rate of Return on}}{\text{Investment (ROI)}} = \text{Profit Margin} \times \text{Investment Turnover}$$

$$\frac{\text{Rate of Return on}}{\text{Investment (ROI)}} = \frac{\text{Income from Operations}}{\text{Sales}} \times \frac{\text{Sales}}{\text{Invested Assets}}$$

$$\text{Domestic Division: ROI} = \frac{\$135,000}{\$675,000} \times \frac{\$675,000}{\$600,000}$$

$$\text{ROI} = 20\% \times 1.125$$
$$\text{ROI} = 22.5\%$$

$$\text{International Division: ROI} = \frac{\$57,600}{\$480,000} \times \frac{\$480,000}{\$384,000}$$

$$\text{ROI} = 12\% \times 1.25$$
$$\text{ROI} = 15\%$$

3. Domestic Division: $75,000 [$135,000 − (10% × $600,000)]
   International Division: $19,200 [$57,600 − (10% × $384,000)]

Self-Examination Questions

(Answers at End of Chapter)

1. When the manager has the responsibility and authority to make decisions that affect costs and revenues but no responsibility for or authority over assets invested in the department, the department is called a(n):
   A. cost center.
   B. profit center.
   C. investment center.
   D. service department.

2. The Accounts Payable Department has expenses of $600,000 and makes 150,000 payments to the various vendors who provide products and services to the divisions. Division A has income from operations of $900,000, before service department charges, and requires 60,000 payments to vendors. If the Accounts Payable Department is treated as a service department, what is Division A's income from operations?
   A. $300,000
   B. $900,000
   C. $660,000
   D. $540,000

3. Division A of Kern Co. has sales of $350,000, cost of goods sold of $200,000, operating expenses of $30,000, and invested assets of $600,000. What is the rate of return on investment for Division A?
   A. 20%
   B. 25%
   C. 33%
   D. 40%

4. Division L of Liddy Co. has a rate of return on investment of 24% and an investment turnover of 1.6. What is the profit margin?
   A. 6%
   B. 15%
   C. 24%
   D. 38%

5. Which approach to transfer pricing uses the price at which the product or service transferred could be sold to outside buyers?
   A. Cost price approach
   B. Negotiated price approach
   C. Market price approach
   D. Standard cost approach

Eye Openers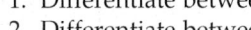

1. Differentiate between a cost center and a profit center.
2. Differentiate between a profit center and an investment center.
3. In what major respect would budget performance reports prepared for the use of plant managers of a manufacturing business with cost centers differ from those prepared for the use of the various department supervisors who report to the plant managers?
4. For what decisions is the manager of a cost center *not* responsible?
5. Weyerhaeuser developed a system that assigns service department expenses to user divisions on the basis of actual services consumed by the division. Here are a number of Weyerhaeuser's activities in its central Financial Services Department:

   * Payroll
   * Accounts payable
   * Accounts receivable
   * Database administration—report preparation

   For each activity, identify an output measure that could be used to charge user divisions for service.
6. What is the major shortcoming of using income from operations as a performance measure for investment centers?
7. Why should the factors under the control of the investment center manager (revenues, expenses, and invested assets) be considered in computing the rate of return on investment?
8. In a decentralized company in which the divisions are organized as investment centers, how could a division be considered the least profitable even though it earned the largest amount of income from operations?
9. How does using the rate of return on investment facilitate comparability between divisions of decentralized companies?
10. The rates of return on investment for Kardin Co.'s three divisions, East, Central, and West, are 22%, 18%, and 16%, respectively. In expanding operations, which of Kardin Co.'s divisions should be given priority? Explain.
11. Why would a firm use a balanced scorecard in evaluating divisional performance?
12. What is the objective of transfer pricing?
13. When is the negotiated price approach preferred over the market price approach in setting transfer prices?
14. Why would standard cost be a more appropriate transfer cost between cost centers than actual cost?
15. When using the negotiated price approach to transfer pricing, within what range should the transfer price be established?

Practice Exercises

PE 23-1A
Budgetary performance
obj. 2

Wizard Company's costs were under budget by $100,000. The company is divided into North and South regions. The North Region's costs were over budget by $20,000. Determine the amount that the South Region's costs were over or under budget.

PE 23-1B
Budgetary performance
obj. 2

Quick Start Company's costs were over budget by $42,000. The company is divided into Southwest and Northeast regions. The Southwest Region's costs were under budget by $8,000. Determine the amount that the Northeast Region's costs were over or under budget.

PE 23-2A
Service department charges
obj. 3

The centralized employee Travel Department of Wilson Company has expenses of $150,000. The department has serviced a total of 2,500 travel reservations for the period. The Midwest Division has made 1,000 reservations during the period, and the Southeast Division has made 1,500 reservations. How much should each division be charged for travel services?

PE 23-2B
Service department charges
obj. 3

The centralized Help Desk of Exton Company has expenses of $120,000. The department has provided a total of 12,000 hours of service for the period. The Fabrication Division has used 5,000 hours of Help Desk service during the period, and the Assembly Division has used 7,000 hours of Help Desk service. How much should each division be charged for travel services?

PE 23-3A
Income from operations
obj. 3

Using the data for the Wilson Company from Practice Exercise 23-2A along with the data provided below, determine the divisional income from operations for the Midwest and Southeast divisions.

	Midwest Division	Southeast Division
Sales	$600,000	$750,000
Cost of goods sold	315,000	450,000
Selling expenses	138,750	165,000

PE 23-3B
Income from operations
obj. 3

Using the data for the Exton Company from Practice Exercise 23-2B along with the data provided below, determine the divisional income from operations for the Fabrication and Assembly divisions.

	Fabrication Division	Assembly Division
Sales	$1,080,000	$1,200,000
Cost of goods sold	567,000	740,000
Selling expenses	249,750	230,000

PE 23-4A
Profit margin, investment turnover, and rate of return on investment
obj. 4

Fain Company has income from operations of $31,500, invested assets of $84,000, and sales of $262,500. Use the DuPont formula to compute the rate of return on investment and show (a) the profit margin, (b) the investment turnover, and (c) the rate of return on investment.

PE 23-4B
Profit margin, investment turnover, and rate of return on investment
obj. 4

Felton Company has income from operations of $51,250, invested assets of $280,000, and sales of $644,000. Use the DuPont formula to compute the rate of return on investment and show (a) the profit margin, (b) the investment turnover, and (c) the rate of return on investment.

PE 23-5A
Residual income
obj. 4

The Distribution Division has income from operations of $75,000 and assets of $500,000. The minimum acceptable rate of return on assets is 10%. What is the residual income for the division?

PE 23-5B
Residual income
obj. 4

The Consumer Division has income from operations of $45,000 and assets of $425,000. The minimum acceptable rate of return on assets is 9%. What is the residual income for the division?

PE 23-6A
Transfer pricing
obj. 5

The materials used by the Toms River Division of Jadelis Company are currently purchased from outside suppliers at $35 per unit. These same materials are produced by Jadelis's Racine Division. The Racine Division can produce the materials needed by the Toms River Division at a variable cost of $22 per unit. The division is currently producing 60,000 units and has capacity of 80,000 units. The two divisions have recently negotiated a transfer price of $28 per unit for 20,000 units. By how much will each division's income increase as a result of this transfer?

PE 23-6B
Transfer pricing
obj. 5

The materials used by the Colorado Division of the Soprano Company are currently purchased from outside suppliers at $40 per unit. These same materials are produced by the Florida Division. The Florida Division can produce the materials needed by the Colorado Division at a variable cost of $25 per unit. The division is currently producing 160,000 units and has capacity of 200,000 units. The two divisions have recently negotiated a transfer price of $33 per unit for 40,000 units. By how much will each division's income increase as a result of this transfer?

Exercises

EX 23-1
Budget performance reports for cost centers
obj. 2
✓ a. (c) $2,310

Partially completed budget performance reports for Qual-Tech Company, a manufacturer of air conditioners, are provided below.

Qual-Tech Company
Budget Performance Report—Vice President, Production
For the Month Ended April 30, 2008

Plant	Budget	Actual	Over Budget	Under Budget
North Region	$362,460	$360,920		$1,540
Central Region	259,980	258,580		1,400
South Region	(g)	(h)	$ (i)	
	$ (j)	$ (k)	$ (l)	$2,940

Qual-Tech Company
Budget Performance Report—Manager, South Region Plant
For the Month Ended April 30, 2008

Department	Budget	Actual	Over Budget	Under Budget
Chip Fabrication	$ (a)	$ (b)	$ (c)	
Electronic Assembly	74,480	75,460	980	
Final Assembly	119,980	119,560		$420
	$ (d)	$ (e)	$ (f)	$420

Qual-Tech Company
Budget Performance Report—Supervisor, Chip Fabrication
For the Month Ended April 30, 2008

Costs	Budget	Actual	Over Budget	Under Budget
Factory wages	$ 21,560	$ 23,100	$1,540	
Materials	60,900	60,480		$420
Power and light	3,360	3,990	630	
Maintenance	5,880	6,440	560	
	$ 91,700	$ 94,010	$2,730	$420

a. Complete the budget performance reports by determining the correct amounts for the lettered spaces.
b. ▭▶ Compose a memo to Dana Johnson, vice president of production for Qual-Tech Company, explaining the performance of the production division for April.

EX 23-2
Divisional income statements
obj. 3

The following data were summarized from the accounting records for Huggins Construction Company for the year ended June 30, 2008:

Cost of goods sold:		Service department charges:	
Residential Division	$300,800	Residential Division	$ 54,240
Industrial Division	167,840	Industrial Division	24,960

✓ *Residential Division income from operations, $80,640*

Administrative expenses:		Net sales:	
Residential Division	$80,320	Residential Division	$516,000
Industrial Division	66,560	Industrial Division	321,920

Prepare divisional income statements for Huggins Construction Company.

EX 23-3
Service department charges and activity bases
obj. 3

For each of the following service departments, identify an activity base that could be used for charging the expense to the profit center.

a. Accounts receivable
b. Electronic data processing
c. Central purchasing

d. Legal
e. Telecommunications
f. Duplication services

EX 23-4
Activity bases for service department charges
obj. 3

For each of the following service departments, select the activity base listed that is most appropriate for charging service expenses to responsible units.

Service Department	Activity Base
a. Training	1. Number of conference attendees
b. Employee Travel	2. Number of computers
c. Payroll Accounting	3. Number of employees trained
d. Accounts Receivable	4. Number of telephone lines
e. Conferences	5. Number of purchase requisitions
f. Telecommunications	6. Number of sales invoices
g. Computer Support	7. Number of payroll checks
h. Central Purchasing	8. Number of travel claims

EX 23-5
Service department charges
obj. 3

✓ *b. Commercial payroll, $9,960*

In divisional income statements prepared for Franklin Electrical Company, the Payroll Department costs are charged back to user divisions on the basis of the number of payroll checks, and the Purchasing Department costs are charged back on the basis of the number of purchase requisitions. The Payroll Department had expenses of $44,010, and the Purchasing Department had expenses of $18,720 for the year. The following annual data for Residential, Commercial, and Government Contract divisions were obtained from corporate records:

	Residential	Commercial	Government Contract
Sales	$420,000	$500,000	$1,800,000
Number of employees:			
Weekly payroll (52 weeks per year)	144	72	108
Monthly payroll	25	20	18
Number of purchase requisitions per year	1,800	1,530	1,350

a. Determine the total amount of payroll checks and purchase requisitions processed per year by each division.
b. Using the activity base information in (a), determine the annual amount of payroll and purchasing costs charged back to the Residential, Commercial, and Government Contract divisions from payroll and purchasing services.
c. ➤ Why does the Residential Division have a larger service department charge than the other two divisions, even though its sales are lower?

EX 23-6
Service department charges and activity bases
obj. 3

✓ *b. Help desk, $28,800*

Harris Corporation, a manufacturer of electronics and communications systems, uses a service department charge system to charge profit centers with Computing and Communications Services (CCS) service department costs. The following table identifies an abbreviated list of service categories and activity bases used by the CCS department. The table also includes some assumed cost and activity base quantity information for each service for October.

CCS Service Category	Activity Base	Assumed Cost	Assumed Activity Base Quantity
Help desk	Number of calls	$ 73,600	2,300
Network center	Number of devices monitored	614,250	9,450
Electronic mail	Number of user accounts	53,550	6,300
Local voice support	Number of phone extensions	127,238	8,775

One of the profit centers for Harris Corporation is the Communication Systems (COMM) sector. Assume the following information for the COMM sector:

- The sector has 4,000 employees, of whom 50% are office employees.
- All the office employees have a phone, and 90% of them have a computer on the network.
- Ninety percent of the employees with a computer also have an e-mail account.
- The average number of help desk calls for October was 0.50 call per individual with a computer.
- There are 300 additional printers, servers, and peripherals on the network beyond the personal computers.

a. Determine the service charge rate for the four CCS service categories for October.
b. Determine the charges to the COMM sector for the four CCS service categories for October.

EX 23-7
Divisional income statements with service department charges
obj. 3

✓ *Consumer income from operations, $1,154,650*

Waverunner Watersports Company has two divisions, Commercial and Consumer, and two corporate service departments, Tech Support and Accounts Payable. The corporate expenses for the year ended December 31, 2008, are as follows:

Tech Support Department	$ 588,000
Accounts Payable Department	231,000
Other corporate administrative expenses	343,000
Total corporate expense	$1,162,000

The other corporate administrative expenses include officers' salaries and other expenses required by the corporation. The Tech Support Department charges the divisions for services rendered, based on the number of computers in the department, and the Accounts Payable Department charges divisions for services, based on the number of checks issued. The usage of service by the two divisions is as follows:

	Tech Support	Accounts Payable
Commercial Division	252 computers	5,880 checks
Consumer Division	168	10,920
Total	420 computers	16,800 checks

The service department charges of the Tech Support Department and the Accounts Payable Department are considered controllable by the divisions. Corporate administrative expenses are not considered controllable by the divisions. The revenues, cost of goods sold, and operating expenses for the two divisions are as follows:

	Commerical	Consumer
Revenues	$5,600,000	$4,760,000
Cost of goods sold	2,940,000	2,240,000
Operating expenses	1,050,000	980,000

Prepare the divisional income statements for the two divisions.

EX 23-8
Corrections to service department charges
obj. 3

Worldwide Air, Inc., has two divisions organized as profit centers, the Passenger Division and the Cargo Division. The following divisional income statements were prepared:

✓b. Income from operations, Cargo Division, $255,000

Worldwide Air, Inc.
Divisional Income Statements
For the Year Ended July 31, 2008

	Passenger Division		Cargo Division	
Revenues		$600,000		$600,000
Operating expenses		300,000		250,000
Income from operations before service department charges		$300,000		$350,000
Less service department charges:				
Training	$50,000		$50,000	
Trip scheduling	60,000		60,000	
Reservations	80,000	190,000	80,000	190,000
Income from operations		$110,000		$160,000

The service department charge rate for the service department costs was based on revenues. Since the revenues of the two divisions were the same, the service department charges to each division were also the same.

The following additional information is available:

	Passenger Division	Cargo Division	Total
Number of personnel trained	40	10	50
Number of trips	30	50	80
Number of reservations requested	4,000	—	4,000

a. Does the income from operations for the two divisions accurately measure performance?
b. Correct the divisional income statements, using the activity bases provided above in revising the service department charges.

EX 23-9
Profit center responsibility reporting
objs. 3, 5

✓ Income from operations, Winter Sports Division, $11,700

Outdoor Athletic Equipment Co. operates two divisions—the Winter Sports Division and the Summer Sports Division. The following income and expense accounts were provided from the trial balance as of June 30, 2008, the end of the current fiscal year, after all adjustments, including those for inventories, were recorded and posted:

Sales—Winter Sports (WS) Division	$ 950,000
Sales—Summer Sports (SS) Division	1,437,500
Cost of Goods Sold—Winter Sports (WS) Division	512,500
Cost of Goods Sold—Summer Sports (SS) Division	687,500
Sales Expense—Winter Sports (WS) Division	150,000
Sales Expense—Summer Sports (SS) Division	205,000
Administrative Expense—Winter Sports (WS) Division	97,000
Administrative Expense—Summer Sports (SS) Division	128,000
Advertising Expense	64,500
Transportation Expense	100,700
Accounts Receivable Collection Expense	58,100
Warehouse Expense	120,000

The bases to be used in allocating expenses, together with other essential information, are as follows:

a. Advertising expense—incurred at headquarters, charged back to divisions on the basis of usage: Winter Sports Division, $28,000; Summer Sports Division, $36,500.
b. Transportation expense—charged back to divisions at a transfer price of $7.60 per bill of lading: Winter Sports Division, 6,000 bills of lading; Summer Sports Division, 7,250 bills of lading.
c. Accounts receivable collection expense—incurred at headquarters, charged back to divisions at a transfer price of $5.60 per invoice: Winter Sports Division, 4,500 sales invoices; Summer Sports Division, 5,875 sales invoices.
d. Warehouse expense—charged back to divisions on the basis of floor space used in storing division products: Winter Sports Division, 25,000 square feet; Summer Sports Division, 12,500 square feet.

Prepare a divisional income statement with two column headings: Winter Sports Division and Summer Sports Division. Provide supporting schedules for determining service department charges.

EX 23-10
Rate of return on investment
obj. 4
✓ a. Textbook Division, 26%

The income from operations and the amount of invested assets in each division of Deacon Publishing Company are as follows:

	Income from Operations	Invested Assets
Magazine Division	$ 96,000	$ 800,000
Textbook Division	166,400	640,000
Business Publishing Division	260,400	1,240,000

a. Compute the rate of return on investment for each division.
b. Which division is the most profitable per dollar invested?

EX 23-11
Residual income
obj. 4
✓ a. Magazine Division, $0

Based on the data in Exercise 23-10, assume that management has established a 12% minimum acceptable rate of return for invested assets.

a. Determine the residual income for each division.
b. Which division has the most residual income?

EX 23-12
Determining missing items in rate of return computation
obj. 4
✓ d. 2.0

One item is omitted from each of the following computations of the rate of return on investment:

Rate of Return on Investment	=	Profit Margin	×	Investment Turnover
24%	=	15%	×	(a)
(b)	=	8%	×	2.50
12%	=	(c)	×	0.80
24%	=	12%	×	(d)
(e)	=	10%	×	1.60

Determine the missing items, identifying each by the appropriate letter.

EX 23-13
Profit margin, investment turnover, and rate of return on investment
obj. 4
✓ a. ROI, 11%

The condensed income statement for the European Division of Cougar Motors Inc. is as follows (assuming no service department charges):

Sales	$875,000
Cost of goods sold	400,000
Gross profit	$475,000
Administrative expenses	282,500
Income from operations	$192,500

The manager of the European Division is considering ways to increase the rate of return on investment.

a. Using the DuPont formula for rate of return on investment, determine the profit margin, investment turnover, and rate of return on investment of the European Division, assuming that $1,750,000 of assets have been invested in the European Division.
b. If expenses could be reduced by $52,500 without decreasing sales, what would be the impact on the profit margin, investment turnover, and rate of return on investment for the European Division?

EX 23-14
Rate of return on investment
obj. 4

REAL WORLD

✓ a. Media Networks ROI, 10.1%

The Walt Disney Company has four major sectors, described as follows:

• **Media Networks:** The ABC television and radio network, Disney channel, ESPN, A&E, E!, and Disney.com.
• **Parks and Resorts:** Walt Disney World Resort, Disneyland, Disney Cruise Line, and other resort properties.
• **Studio Entertainment:** Walt Disney Pictures, Touchstone Pictures, Hollywood Pictures, Miramax Films, and Buena Vista Theatrical Productions.
• **Consumer Products:** Character merchandising, Disney stores, books, and magazines.

Disney recently reported sector income from operations, revenue, and invested assets (in millions) as follows:

	Income from Operations	Revenue	Invested Assets
Media Networks	$2,749	$13,027	$26,926
Parks and Resorts	1,178	9,023	15,807
Studio Entertainment	207	7,587	5,965
Consumer Products	520	2,157	877

a. Use the DuPont formula to determine the rate of return on investment for the four Disney sectors. Round whole percents to one decimal place and investment turnover to one decimal place.
b. ▬▬▶ How do the four sectors differ in their profit margin, investment turnover, and return on investment?

EX 23-15
Determining missing items in rate of return and residual income computations
obj. 4
✓c. $38,625

Data for Grobe Products Company is presented in the following table of rates of return on investment and residual incomes:

Invested Assets	Income from Operations	Rate of Return on Investment	Minimum Rate of Return	Minimum Acceptable Income from Operations	Residual Income
$643,750	$115,875	(a)	12%	(b)	(c)
$418,750	(d)	(e)	(f)	$62,813	$16,750
$275,000	(g)	12%	(h)	$44,000	(i)
$600,000	$84,000	(j)	10%	(k)	(l)

Determine the missing items, identifying each item by the appropriate letter.

EX 23-16
Determining missing items from computations
obj. 4
✓a. (e) $500,000

Data for the North, East, South, and West divisions of Tor Max Semiconductor Communication Company are as follows:

	Sales	Income from Operations	Invested Assets	Rate of Return on Investment	Profit Margin	Investment Turnover
North	$425,000	(a)	(b)	20%	10%	(c)
East	(d)	$50,000	(e)	(f)	8%	1.25
South	$400,000	(g)	$125,000	12%	(h)	(i)
West	$750,000	$180,000	$1,250,000	(j)	(k)	(l)

a. Determine the missing items, identifying each by the letters (a) through (l).
b. Determine the residual income for each division, assuming that the minimum acceptable rate of return established by management is 9%.
c. Which division is the most profitable in terms of (1) return on investment and (2) residual income?

EX 23-17
Rate of return on investment, residual income
obj. 4

REAL WORLD

Hilton Hotels Corporation provides lodging services around the world. The company is separated into three major divisions:

• **Hotel Ownership:** Hotels owned and operated by Hilton.
• **Managing and Franchising:** Hotels franchised to others or managed for others.
• **Timeshare:** Resort properties managed for timeshare vacation owners.

Financial information for each division, from a recent annual report, is as follows (in millions):

	Hotel Ownership	Managing and Franchising	Timeshare
Revenues	$2,215	$1,510	$421
Income from operations	394	343	99
Total assets	4,825	2,112	507

a. Use the DuPont formula to determine the return on investment for each of the Hilton business divisions. Round whole percents to one decimal place and investment turnover to one decimal place.

b. Determine the residual income for each division, assuming a minimum acceptable income of 14% of total assets. Round minimal acceptable return to the nearest million dollars.

c. ▬▬▶ Interpret your results.

EX 23-18
Balanced scorecard
obj. 4

American Express Company is a major financial services company, noted for its American Express® card. Below are some of the performance measures used by the company in its balanced scorecard.

Average cardmember spending	Number of merchant signings
Cards in force	Number of card choices
Earnings growth	Number of new card launches
Hours of credit consultant training	Return on equity
Investment in information technology	Revenue growth
Number of Internet features	

For each measure, identify whether the measure best fits the innovation, customer, internal process, or financial dimension of the balanced scorecard.

EX 23-19
Balanced scorecard
obj. 4

Several years ago, United Parcel Service (UPS) believed that the Internet was going to change the parcel delivery market and would require UPS to become a more nimble and customer-focused organization. As a result, UPS replaced its old measurement system, which was 90% oriented toward financial performance, with a balanced scorecard. The scorecard emphasized four "point of arrival" measures, which were:

1. Customer satisfaction index—a measure of customer satisfaction.
2. Employee relations index—a measure of employee sentiment and morale.
3. Competitive position—delivery performance relative to competition.
4. Time in transit—the time from order entry to delivery.

a. ▬▬▶ Why did UPS introduce a balanced scorecard and nonfinancial measures in its new performance measurement system?

b. ▬▬▶ Why do you think UPS included a factor measuring employee sentiment?

EX 23-20
Decision on transfer pricing
obj. 5

✓ a. $1,000,000

Materials used by the Industrial Division of Crow Manufacturing are currently purchased from outside suppliers at a cost of $120 per unit. However, the same materials are available from the Materials Division. The Materials Division has unused capacity and can produce the materials needed by the Industrial Division at a variable cost of $95 per unit.

a. If a transfer price of $105 per unit is established and 40,000 units of materials are transferred, with no reduction in the Materials Division's current sales, how much would Crow Manufacturing's total income from operations increase?

b. How much would the Industrial Division's income from operations increase?

c. How much would the Materials Division's income from operations increase?

EX 23-21
Decision on transfer pricing
obj. 5

✓ b. $400,000

Based on Crow Manufacturing's data in Exercise 23–20, assume that a transfer price of $110 has been established and that 40,000 units of materials are transferred, with no reduction in the Materials Division's current sales.

a. How much would Crow Manufacturing's total income from operations increase?

b. How much would the Industrial Division's income from operations increase?

c. How much would the Materials Division's income from operations increase?

d. ▬▬▶ If the negotiated price approach is used, what would be the range of acceptable transfer prices and why?

Problems Series A

PR 23-1A
Budget performance report for a cost center
obj. 2

The Southwest District of Pop Soft Drinks, Inc., is organized as a cost center. The budget for the Southwest District of Pop Soft Drinks, Inc., for the month ended May 31, 2008, is as follows:

Sales salaries	$406,725
System support salaries	222,300
Customer relations salaries	75,975
Accounting salaries	48,975
Repair and service	134,625
Depreciation of plant and equipment	45,750
Insurance and property taxes	20,475
Total	$954,825

During May, the costs incurred in the Southwest District were as follows:

Sales salaries	$406,200
System support salaries	222,075
Customer relations salaries	89,025
Accounting salaries	48,675
Repair and service	135,375
Depreciation of plant and equipment	45,750
Insurance and property taxes	20,550
Total	$967,650

Instructions
1. Prepare a budget performance report for the manager of the Southwest District of Pop Soft Drinks for the month of May.
2. ➤ For which costs might the supervisor be expected to request supplemental reports?

PR 23-2A
Profit center responsibility reporting
obj. 3

✓ 1. Income from operations, South Region, $280,800

Cross-Country Transport Company organizes its three divisions, the Southeast, East, and South regions, as profit centers. The chief executive officer (CEO) evaluates divisional performance, using income from operations as a percent of revenues. The following quarterly income and expense accounts were provided from the trial balance as of December 31, 2008:

Revenues—SE Region	$1,740,000
Revenues—E Region	2,820,000
Revenues—S Region	2,340,000
Operating Expenses—SE Region	1,134,400
Operating Expenses—E Region	2,097,300
Operating Expenses—S Region	1,721,700
Corporate Expenses—Dispatching	500,000
Corporate Expenses—Equipment	525,000
Corporate Expenses—Treasurer's	375,000
General Corporate Officers' Salaries	710,000

The company operates three service departments: the Dispatching Department, the Equipment Management Department, and the Treasurer's Department. The Dispatching Department manages the scheduling and releasing of completed trains. The Equipment Management Department manages the railroad cars inventories. It makes sure the right freight cars are at the right place at the right time. The Treasurer's Department conducts a variety of services for the company as a whole. The following additional information has been gathered:

	Southeast	East	South
Number of scheduled trains	400	680	520
Number of railroad cars in inventory	4,800	6,400	5,600

Instructions

1. Prepare quarterly income statements showing income from operations for the three regions. Use three column headings: Southeast, East, and South.
2. Identify the most successful region according to the profit margin.
3. ▭▬▶ Provide a recommendation to the CEO for a better method for evaluating the performance of the regions. In your recommendation, identify the major weakness of the present method.

PR 23-3A

Divisional income statements and rate of return on investment analysis

obj. **4**

✓2. Retail Division ROI, 16%

Hi-Growth Investments Inc. is a diversified investment company with three operating divisions organized as investment centers. Condensed data taken from the records of the three divisions for the year ended June 30, 2008, are as follows:

	Retail Division	Electronic Brokerage Division	Investment Banking Division
Fee revenue	$1,250,000	$750,000	$1,500,000
Operating expenses	750,000	682,500	1,170,000
Invested assets	3,125,000	250,000	2,000,000

The management of Hi-Growth Investments Inc. is evaluating each division as a basis for planning a future expansion of operations.

Instructions

1. Prepare condensed divisional income statements for the three divisions, assuming that there were no service department charges.
2. Using the DuPont formula for rate of return on investment, compute the profit margin, investment turnover, and rate of return on investment for each division.
3. ▭▬▶ If available funds permit the expansion of operations of only one division, which of the divisions would you recommend for expansion, based on parts (1) and (2)? Explain.

PR 23-4A

Effect of proposals on divisional performance

obj. **4**

✓3. Proposal 3 ROI, 13.6%

A condensed income statement for the Paintball Division of Outdoor Games Inc. for the year ended January 31, 2008, is as follows:

Sales	$900,000
Cost of goods sold	500,000
Gross profit	$400,000
Operating expenses	274,000
Income from operations	$126,000

Assume that the Paintball Division received no charges from service departments.

The president of Outdoor Games Inc. has indicated that the division's rate of return on a $720,000 investment must be increased to at least 20% by the end of the next year if operations are to continue. The division manager is considering the following three proposals:

Proposal 1: Transfer equipment with a book value of $120,000 to other divisions at no gain or loss and lease similar equipment. The annual lease payments would be less than the amount of depreciation expense on the old equipment by $18,000. This decrease in expense would be included as part of the cost of goods sold. Sales would remain unchanged.

Proposal 2: Reduce invested assets by discontinuing a product line. This action would eliminate sales of $75,000, cost of goods sold of $35,000, and operating expenses of $37,750. Assets of $32,500 would be transferred to other divisions at no gain or loss.

Proposal 3: Purchase new and more efficient machinery and thereby reduce the cost of goods sold by $27,000. Sales would remain unchanged, and the old machinery, which has no remaining book value, would be scrapped at no gain or loss. The new machinery would increase invested assets by $405,000 for the year.

Instructions

1. Using the DuPont formula for rate of return on investment, determine the profit margin, investment turnover, and rate of return on investment for the Paintball Division for the past year.

2. Prepare condensed estimated income statements and compute the invested assets for each proposal.
3. Using the DuPont formula for rate of return on investment, determine the profit margin, investment turnover, and rate of return on investment for each proposal.
4. Which of the three proposals would meet the required 20% rate of return on investment?
5. If the Paintball Division were in an industry where the profit margin could not be increased, how much would the investment turnover have to increase to meet the president's required 20% rate of return on investment? Round to two decimal places.

PR 23-5A
Divisional performance analysis and evaluation
obj. 4

✓2. Personal Computing Division ROI, 32%

The vice president of operations of I4 Computers Inc. is evaluating the performance of two divisions organized as investment centers. Invested assets and condensed income statement data for the past year for each division are as follows:

	Personal Computing Division	Business Computing Division
Sales	$800,000	$1,200,000
Cost of goods sold	460,000	780,000
Operating expenses	180,000	156,000
Invested assets	500,000	2,000,000

Instructions
1. Prepare condensed divisional income statements for the year ended December 31, 2008, assuming that there were no service department charges.
2. Using the DuPont formula for rate of return on investment, determine the profit margin, investment turnover, and rate of return on investment for each division.
3. If management's minimum acceptable rate of return is 15%, determine the residual income for each division.
4. ▭▭▭▶ Discuss the evaluation of the two divisions, using the performance measures determined in parts (1), (2), and (3).

PR 23-6A
Transfer pricing
obj. 5

✓3. Navigational Systems Division, $195,200

Goho Manufacturing Company is a diversified aerospace company, including two operating divisions, Specialized Semiconductors and Navigational Systems Divisions. Condensed divisional income statements, which involve no intracompany transfers and which include a breakdown of expenses into variable and fixed components, are as follows:

Goho Manufacturing Company
Divisional Income Statements
For the Year Ended December 31, 2008

	Specialized Semi-conductors Division	Navigational Systems Division	Total
Sales:			
640 units × $1,320 per unit	$844,800		$ 844,800
1,000 units × $1,984 per unit		$1,984,000	1,984,000
			$2,828,800
Expenses:			
Variable:			
640 units × $776 per unit	$496,640		$ 496,640
1,000 units × $1,560* per unit		$1,560,000	1,560,000
Fixed	195,200	254,400	449,600
Total expenses	$691,840	$1,814,400	$2,506,240
Income from operations	$152,960	$ 169,600	$ 322,560

*$1,320 of the $1,560 per unit represents materials costs, and the remaining $240 per unit represents other variable conversion expenses incurred within the Navigational Systems Division.

The Specialized Semiconductors Division is presently producing 640 units out of a total capacity of 800 units. Materials used in producing the Navigational Systems Division's product are currently purchased from outside suppliers at a price of $1,320 per unit. The Specialized Semiconductors Division is able to produce the components used by the

Navigational Systems Division. Except for the possible transfer of materials between divisions, no changes are expected in sales and expenses.

Instructions

1. ▭▭▶ Would the market price of $1,320 per unit be an appropriate transfer price for Goho Manufacturing Company? Explain.
2. ▭▭▶ If the Navigational Systems Division purchases 160 units from the Specialized Semiconductors Division, rather than externally, at a negotiated transfer price of $1,160 per unit, how much would the income from operations of each division and total company income from operations increase?
3. Prepare condensed divisional income statements for Goho Manufacturing Company, based on the data in part (2).
4. ▭▭▶ If a transfer price of $880 per unit is negotiated, how much would the income from operations of each division and total company income from operations increase?
5. a. ▭▭▶ What is the range of possible negotiated transfer prices that would be acceptable for Goho Manufacturing Company?
   b. Assuming that the managers of the two divisions cannot agree on a transfer price, what price would you suggest as the transfer price?

Problems Series B

PR 23-1B
Budget performance report for a cost center

obj. **2**

The Furnishings Company sells furnishings and fixtures over the Internet. The International Division is organized as a cost center. The budget for the International Division for the month ended October 31, 2008, is as follows (in millions):

Customer service salaries	$ 119
Insurance and property taxes	32
Distribution salaries	238
Marketing salaries	336
Engineer salaries	217
Warehouse wages	147
Equipment depreciation	45
Total	$1,134

During October, the costs incurred in the International Division were as follows:

Customer service salaries	$ 153
Insurance and property taxes	31
Distribution salaries	235
Marketing salaries	377
Engineer salaries	213
Warehouse wages	141
Equipment depreciation	45
Total	$1,195

Instructions

1. Prepare a budget performance report for the director of the International Division for the month of October.
2. For which costs might the director be expected to request supplemental reports?

PR 23-2B
Profit center responsibility reporting

obj. **3**

Diversified Railroad has three regional divisions organized as profit centers. The chief executive officer (CEO) evaluates divisional performance, using income from operations as a percent of revenues. The following quarterly income and expense accounts were provided from the trial balance as of December 31, 2008:

✓1. Income from
operations, Metro Division,
$283,200

Revenues—East Division	$500,000
Revenues—West Division	690,000
Revenues—Metro Division	944,000
Operating Expenses—East Division	303,000
Operating Expenses—West Division	399,600
Operating Expenses—Metro Division	536,000
Corporate Expenses—Shareholder Relations	75,000
Corporate Expenses—Customer Support	192,000
Corporate Expenses—Legal	102,000
General Corporate Officers' Salaries	180,000

The company operates three service departments: Shareholder Relations, Customer Support, and Legal. The Shareholder Relations Department conducts a variety of services for shareholders of the company. The Customer Support Department is the company's point of contact for new service, complaints, and requests for repair. The department believes that the number of customer contacts is an activity base for this work. The Legal Department provides reports for division management. The department believes that the number of hours billed is an activity base for this work. The following additional information has been gathered:

	East	West	Metro
Number of customer contacts	3,200	3,680	5,920
Number of hours billed	640	1,120	960

Instructions
1. Prepare quarterly income statements showing income from operations for the three divisions. Use three column headings: East, West, and Metro.
2. Identify the most successful division according to the profit margin.
3. ▭▭▶ Provide a recommendation to the CEO for a better method for evaluating the performance of the divisions. In your recommendation, identify the major weakness of the present method.

PR 23-3B
*Divisional income
statements and rate of
return on investment
analysis*

obj. 4

✓2. Bread Division, ROI,
12.8%

Fresh Tracks Baking Company is a diversified food products company with three operating divisions organized as investment centers. Condensed data taken from the records of the three divisions for the year ended June 30, 2008, are as follows:

	Bread Division	Snack Cake Division	Retail Bakeries Division
Sales	$1,450,000	$1,750,000	$1,000,000
Cost of goods sold	950,000	1,125,000	650,000
Operating expenses	268,000	380,000	170,000
Invested assets	1,812,500	2,187,500	800,000

The management of Fresh Tracks Baking Company is evaluating each division as a basis for planning a future expansion of operations.

Instructions
1. Prepare condensed divisional income statements for the three divisions, assuming that there were no service department charges.
2. Using the DuPont formula for rate of return on investment, compute the profit margin, investment turnover, and rate of return on investment for each division.
3. ▭▭▶ If available funds permit the expansion of operations of only one division, which of the divisions would you recommend for expansion, based on parts (1) and (2)? Explain.

PR 23-4B
*Effect of proposals on
divisional performance*

obj. 4

A condensed income statement for the Turbine Division of Mega Engines Inc. for the year ended December 31, 2008, is as follows:

✓ 1. ROI, 12%

Sales	$600,000
Cost of goods sold	338,000
Gross profit	$262,000
Operating expenses	190,000
Income from operations	$ 72,000

Assume that the Turbine Division received no charges from service departments. The president of Mega Engines has indicated that the division's rate of return on a $600,000 investment must be increased to at least 20% by the end of the next year if operations are to continue. The division manager is considering the following three proposals:

Proposal 1: Transfer equipment with a book value of $120,000 to other divisions at no gain or loss and lease similar equipment. The annual lease payments would exceed the amount of depreciation expense on the old equipment by $18,000. This increase in expense would be included as part of the cost of goods sold. Sales would remain unchanged.

Proposal 2: Purchase new and more efficient machining equipment and thereby reduce the cost of goods sold by $48,000. Sales would remain unchanged, and the old equipment, which has no remaining book value, would be scrapped at no gain or loss. The new equipment would increase invested assets by an additional $150,000 for the year.

Proposal 3: Reduce invested assets by discontinuing an engine line. This action would eliminate sales of $180,000, cost of goods sold of $133,200, and operating expenses of $42,000. Assets of $300,000 would be transferred to other divisions at no gain or loss.

Instructions

1. Using the DuPont formula for rate of return on investment, determine the profit margin, investment turnover, and rate of return on investment for the Turbine Division for the past year.
2. Prepare condensed estimated income statements and compute the invested assets for each proposal.
3. Using the DuPont formula for rate of return on investment, determine the profit margin, investment turnover, and rate of return on investment for each proposal.
4. Which of the three proposals would meet the required 20% rate of return on investment?
5. If the Turbine Division were in an industry where the profit margin could not be increased, how much would the investment turnover have to increase to meet the president's required 20% rate of return on investment?

PR 23-5B
Divisional performance analysis and evaluation
obj. 4

✓ 2. Road Bike Division ROI, 25%

The vice president of operations of Cantor-Simmons Cycle Company is evaluating the performance of two divisions organized as investment centers. Invested assets and condensed income statement data for the past year for each division are as follows:

	Road Bike Division	Mountain Bike Division
Sales	$750,000	$ 950,000
Cost of goods sold	412,500	560,000
Operating expenses	187,500	181,000
Invested assets	600,000	1,187,500

Instructions

1. Prepare condensed divisional income statements for the year ended December 31, 2008, assuming that there were no service department charges.
2. Using the DuPont formula for rate of return on investment, determine the profit margin, investment turnover, and rate of return on investment for each division.
3. If management desires a minimum acceptable rate of return of 18%, determine the residual income for each division.
4. ▬▬▬▶ Discuss the evaluation of the two divisions, using the performance measures determined in parts (1), (2), and (3).

PR 23-6B
Transfer pricing
obj. 5

Hi-Tech Electronics, Inc. manufactures electronic products, with two operating divisions, the Specialized Electronic Component and MP3 Player divisions. Condensed divisional income statements, which involve no intracompany transfers and which include a breakdown of expenses into variable and fixed components, are as follows:

✓3. Total income from operations, $1,146,000

Hi-Tech Electronics, Inc.
Divisional Income Statements
For the Year Ended December 31, 2008

	Specialized Electronic Component Division	MP3 Player Division	Total
Sales:			
12,000 units × $126 per unit	$1,512,000		$1,512,000
18,000 units × $228 per unit		$4,104,000	4,104,000
			$5,616,000
Expenses:			
Variable:			
12,000 units × $86 per unit	$1,032,000		$1,032,000
18,000 units × $162* per unit		$2,916,000	2,916,000
Fixed	186,000	432,000	618,000
Total expenses	$1,218,000	$3,348,000	$4,566,000
Income from operations	$ 294,000	$ 756,000	$1,050,000

*$126 of the $162 per case represents materials costs, and the remaining $36 per case represents other variable conversion expenses incurred within the MP3 Player Division.

The Specialized Electronic Component Division is presently producing 12,000 units out of a total capacity of 14,400 units. Materials used in producing the MP3 Player Division's product are currently purchased from outside suppliers at a price of $126 per unit. The Specialized Electronic Component Division is able to produce the materials used by the MP3 Player Division. Except for the possible transfer of materials between divisions, no changes are expected in sales and expenses.

Instructions
1. ▆▆▆▶ Would the market price of $126 per unit be an appropriate transfer price for Hi-Tech Electronics, Inc.? Explain.
2. ▆▆▆▶ If the MP3 Player Division purchases 2,400 units from the Specialized Electronic Component Division, rather than externally, at a negotiated transfer price of $96 per unit, how much would the income from operations of each division and the total company income from operations increase?
3. Prepare condensed divisional income statements for Hi-Tech Electronics, Inc., based on the data in part (2).
4. ▆▆▆▶ If a transfer price of $120 per unit is negotiated, how much would the income from operations of each division and the total company income from operations increase?
5. a. ▆▆▆▶ What is the range of possible negotiated transfer prices that would be acceptable for Hi-Tech Electronics, Inc.?
   b. Assuming that the managers of the two divisions cannot agree on a transfer price, what price would you suggest as the transfer price?

Special Activities

SA 23-1
Ethics and professional conduct in business

ETHICS

Micro Tech Company has two divisions, the Semiconductor Division and the PC Division. The PC Division may purchase semiconductors from the Semiconductor Division or from outside suppliers. The Semiconductor Division sells semiconductor products both internally and externally. The market price for semiconductors is $250 per 100 semiconductors. Michael Blount is the controller of the PC Division, and Lynn Williams is the controller of the Semiconductor Division. The following conversation took place between Michael and Lynn:

Michael: I hear you are having problems selling semiconductors out of your division. Maybe I can help.
Lynn: You've got that right. We're producing and selling at about 80% of our capacity to outsiders. Last year we were selling 100% of capacity. Would it be possible for your division to pick up some of our excess capacity? After all, we are part of the same company.
Michael: What kind of price could you give me?
Lynn: Well, you know as well as I that we are under strict profit responsibility in our divisions, so I would expect to get market price, $250 for 100 semiconductors.

Michael: I'm not so sure we can swing that. I was expecting a price break from a "sister" division.

Lynn: Hey, I can only take this "sister" stuff so far. If I give you a price break, our profits will fall from last year's levels. I don't think I could explain that. I'm sorry, but I must remain firm—market price. After all, it's only fair—that's what you would have to pay from an external supplier.

Michael: Fair or not, I think we'll pass. Sorry we couldn't have helped.

➤ Was Michael behaving ethically by trying to force the Semiconductor Division into a price break? Comment on Lynn's reactions.

SA 23-2
Service department charges

The Customer Service Department of Grand Lakes Technologies asked the Publications Department to prepare a brochure for its training program. The Publications Department delivered the brochures and charged the Customer Service Department a rate that was 25% higher than could be obtained from an outside printing company. The policy of the company required the Customer Service Department to use the internal publications group for brochures. The Publications Department claimed that it had a drop in demand for its services during the fiscal year, so it had to charge higher prices in order to recover its payroll and fixed costs.

➤ Should the cost of the brochure be transferred to the Customer Service Department in order to hold the department head accountable for the cost of the brochure? What changes in policy would you recommend?

SA 23-3
Evaluating divisional performance

The three divisions of Monster Foods are Snack Goods, Cereal, and Frozen Foods. The divisions are structured as investment centers. The following responsibility reports were prepared for the three divisions for the prior year:

	Snack Goods	Cereal	Frozen Foods
Revenues	$1,050,000	$2,450,000	$ 875,000
Operating expenses	420,000	1,400,000	175,000
Income from operations before service department charges	$ 630,000	$1,050,000	$ 700,000
Service department charges:			
Promotion	$ 175,000	$ 350,000	$ 308,000
Legal	87,500	70,000	140,000
	$ 262,500	$ 420,000	$ 448,000
Income from operations	$ 367,500	$ 630,000	$ 252,000
Invested assets	$2,100,000	$4,200,000	$1,260,000

1. Which division is making the best use of invested assets and thus should be given priority for future capital investments?
2. ➤ Assuming that the minimum acceptable rate of return on new projects is 12%, would all investments that produce a return in excess of 12% be accepted by the divisions?
3. ➤ Can you identify opportunities for improving the company's financial performance?

SA 23-4
Evaluating division performance over time

The Truck Division of Yang Motors Inc. has been experiencing revenue and profit growth during the years 2006–2008. The divisional income statements are provided below.

Yang Motors Inc.
Divisional Income Statements, Truck Division
For the Years Ended December 31, 2006–2008

	2006	2007	2008
Sales	$756,000	$972,000	$1,170,000
Cost of goods sold	475,200	558,000	616,500
Gross profit	$280,800	$414,000	$ 553,500
Operating expenses	167,400	209,880	261,000
Income from operations	$113,400	$204,120	$ 292,500

Assume that there are no charges from service departments. The vice president of the division, Terry Clark, is proud of his division's performance over the last three years. The president of Yang Motors Inc., Billy Clark, is discussing the division's performance with Terry, as follows:

Terry: As you can see, we've had a successful three years in the Truck Division.
Billy: I'm not too sure.
Terry: What do you mean? Look at our results. Our income from operations has nearly tripled, while our profit margins are improving.
Billy: I am looking at your results. However, your income statements fail to include one very important piece of information; namely, the invested assets. You have been investing a great deal of assets into the division. You had $315,000 in invested assets in 2006, $810,000 in 2007, and $1,950,000 in 2008.
Terry: You are right. I've needed the assets in order to upgrade our technologies and expand our operations. The additional assets are one reason we have been able to grow and improve our profit margins. I don't see that this is a problem.
Billy: The problem is that we must maintain a 20% rate of return on invested assets.

1. Determine the profit margins for the Truck Division for 2006–2008.
2. Compute the investment turnover for the Truck Division for 2006–2008.
3. Compute the rate of return on investment for the Truck Division for 2006–2008.
4. ✏ Evaluate the division's performance over the 2006–2008 time period. Why was Billy concerned about the performance?

SA 23-5
Evaluating division performance

Casual Living Furniture Inc. is a privately held diversified company with five separate divisions organized as investment centers. A condensed income statement for the Outdoor Division for the past year, assuming no service department charges, is as follows:

Casual Living Furniture Inc.—Outdoor Division
Income Statement
For the Year Ended December 31, 2007

Sales	$12,800,000
Cost of goods sold	8,080,000
Gross profit	$ 4,720,000
Operating expenses	1,520,000
Income from operations	$ 3,200,000

The manager of the Outdoor Division was recently presented with the opportunity to add an additional product line, which would require invested assets of $11,000,000. A projected income statement for the new product line is as follows:

New Product Line
Projected Income Statement
For the Year Ended December 31, 2008

Sales	$6,000,000
Cost of goods sold	3,360,000
Gross profit	$2,640,000
Operating expenses	1,680,000
Income from operations	$ 960,000

The Outdoor Division currently has $20,000,000 in invested assets, and Casual Living Furniture Inc.'s overall rate of return on investment, including all divisions, is 8%. Each division manager is evaluated on the basis of divisional rate of return on investment, and a bonus equal to $12,000 for each percentage point by which the division's rate of return on investment exceeds the company average is awarded each year.

The president is concerned that the manager of the Outdoor Division rejected the addition of the new product line, when all estimates indicated that the product line would be profitable and would increase overall company income. You have been asked to analyze the possible reasons why the Outdoor Division manager rejected the new product line.

1. Determine the rate of return on investment for the Outdoor Division for the past year.

(continued)

2. Determine the Outdoor Division manager's bonus for the past year.
3. Determine the estimated rate of return on investment for the new product line. Round whole percents to one decimal place.
4. ▭▭▭ Why might the manager of the Outdoor Division decide to reject the new product line? Support your answer by determining the projected rate of return on investment for 2008, assuming that the new product line was launched in the Outdoor Division, and 2008 actual operating results were similar to those of 2007.
5. ▭▭▭ Can you suggest an alternative performance measure for motivating division managers to accept new investment opportunities that would increase the overall company income and rate of return on investment?

SA 23-6
The balanced scorecard and EVA

REAL WORLD

Internet Project

Group Project

Divide responsibilities between two groups, with one group going to the home page of Balanced Scorecard Collaborative at **http://www.bscol.com**, and the second group going to the home page of Stern Stewart & Co. at **http://www.eva.com**. Balanced Scorecard Collaborative is a consulting firm that helped develop the balanced scorecard concept. Stern Stewart & Co. is a consulting firm that developed the concept of economic value added (EVA), another method of measuring corporate and divisional performance, similar to residual income.

After reading about the balanced scorecard at the bscol.com site, prepare a brief report describing the balanced scorecard and its claimed advantages. In the Stern group, use links in the home page of Stern Stewart & Co. to learn about EVA. After reading about EVA, prepare a brief report describing EVA and its claimed advantages. After preparing these reports, both groups should discuss their research and prepare a brief analysis comparing and contrasting these two approaches to corporate and divisional performance measurement.

Answers to Self-Examination Questions

1. **B**   The manager of a profit center (answer B) has responsibility for and authority over costs and revenues. If the manager has responsibility for only costs, the department is called a cost center (answer A). If the responsibility and authority extend to the investment in assets as well as costs and revenues, it is called an investment center (answer C). A service department (answer D) provides services to other departments. A service department could be a cost center, a profit center, or an investment center.

2. **C** $600,000/150,000 = $4 per payment. Division A anticipates 60,000 payments or $240,000 (60,000 × $4) in service department charges from the Accounts Payable Department. Income from operations is thus $900,000 − $240,000, or $660,000. Answer A assumes that all of the service department overhead is assigned to Division A, which would be incorrect, since Division A does not use all of the accounts payable service. Answer B incorrectly assumes that there are no service department charges from Accounts Payable. Answer D incorrectly determines the accounts payable transfer rate from Division A's income from operations.

3. **A**   The rate of return on investment for Division A is 20% (answer A), computed as follows:

$$\text{Rate of Return on Investment (ROI)} = \frac{\text{Income from Operations}}{\text{Invested Assets}}$$

$$\text{ROI} = \frac{\$350,000 - \$200,000 - \$30,000}{\$600,000} = 20\%$$

4. **B**   The profit margin for Division L of Liddy Co. is 15% (answer B), computed as follows:

$$\text{Rate of Return on Investment (ROI)} = \text{Profit Margin} \times \text{Investment Turnover}$$

$$24\% = \text{Profit Margin} \times 1.6$$
$$15\% = \text{Profit Margin}$$

5. **C**   The market price approach (answer C) to transfer pricing uses the price at which the product or service transferred could be sold to outside buyers. The cost price approach (answer A) uses cost as the basis for setting transfer prices. The negotiated price approach (answer B) allows managers of decentralized units to agree (negotiate) among themselves as to the proper transfer price. The standard cost approach (answer D) is a version of the cost price approach that uses standard costs in setting transfer prices.

Differential Analysis and Product Pricing

© KEVIN P. CASEY/ASSOCIATED PRESS

objectives

After studying this chapter, you should be able to:

1 *Prepare a differential analysis report for decisions involving leasing or selling equipment, discontinuing an unprofitable segment, manufacturing or purchasing a needed part, replacing usable fixed assets, processing further or selling an intermediate product, or accepting additional business at a special price.*

2 *Determine the selling price of a product, using the total cost, product cost, and variable cost concepts.*

3 *Compute the relative profitability of products in bottleneck production environments.*

RealNetworks, Inc.

Many of the decisions that you make depend on comparing the estimated costs of alternatives. The payoff from such comparisons is described in the following report from a University of Michigan study.

Richard Nisbett and two colleagues quizzed Michigan faculty members and university seniors on such questions as how often they walk out on a bad movie, refuse to finish a bad meal, start over on a weak term paper, or abandon a research project that no longer looks promising. They believe that people who cut their losses this way are following sound economic rules: calculating the net benefits of alternative courses of action, writing off past costs that can't be recovered, and weighing the opportunity to use future time and effort more profitably elsewhere.

Among students, those who have learned to use cost-benefit analysis frequently are apt to have far better grades than their Scholastic Aptitude Test scores would have predicted. Again, the more economics courses the students have, the more likely they are to apply cost-benefit analysis outside the classroom.

Dr. Nisbett concedes that for many Americans, cost-benefit rules often appear to conflict with such traditional principles as "never give up" and "waste not, want not."

Managers must also apply cost-benefit rules in making decisions affecting their business. RealNetworks, Inc., the Internet-based music and game company, like most companies must choose between alternatives. Examples of decisions faced by this company include whether it should expand or discontinue services, such as its recent decision to Mac-enable its digital music service, Rhapsody®. Another decision is whether to accept business at special prices, such as special pricing on its Helix Media Delivery System®. Other decisions include whether to replace network equipment, develop its own software, or buy software from others.

In this chapter, we discuss differential analysis, which reports the effects of decisions on total revenues and costs. We also describe and illustrate practical approaches to setting product prices. Finally, we discuss how production bottlenecks influence product mix and pricing decisions.

Source: Alan L. Otten, "Economic Perspective Produces Steady Yields," from People Patterns, *The Wall Street Journal*, March 31, 1992, p. B1.

Differential Analysis

objective **1**

Prepare a differential analysis report for decisions involving leasing or selling equipment, discontinuing an unprofitable segment, manufacturing or purchasing a needed part, replacing usable fixed assets, processing further or selling an intermediate product, or accepting additional business at a special price.

Planning for future operations involves decision making. For some decisions, revenue and cost data from the accounting records may be useful. However, the revenue and cost data for use in evaluating courses of future operations or choosing among competing alternatives are often not available in the accounting records and must be estimated. Consider:

- The decision by General Motors Corporation to purchase on-board communications products from Delphi Corporation instead of making them internally.
- The decision by Marriott International, Inc., to accept a special price for a bid placed on Priceline.com Inc. for a room.
- The decision by Delta Air Lines to discontinue its low-fare Song Airline subsidiary.

In each of these decisions, the estimated revenues and costs were *relevant*. The relevant revenues and costs focus on the differences between each alternative. Costs that have been incurred in the past are not relevant to the decision. These costs are called **sunk costs**. For example, a couple who decides to walk out on a bad movie ignores the original cost of the tickets. In this case, the ticket cost is sunk and thus irrelevant to the decision to walk out early. We all make decisions everyday using relevant costs and benefits. Businesses make similar decisions by considering the differential revenues and costs.

Differential revenue is the amount of increase or decrease in revenue that is expected from a course of action as compared with an alternative. To illustrate, assume

that certain equipment is being used to manufacture calculators, which are expected to generate revenue of $150,000. If the equipment could be used to make digital clocks, which would generate revenue of $175,000, the differential revenue from making and selling digital clocks is $25,000.

Differential cost is the amount of increase or decrease in cost that is expected from a course of action as compared with an alternative. For example, if an increase in advertising expenditures from $100,000 to $150,000 is being considered, the differential cost of the action is $50,000.

Differential income or loss is the difference between the differential revenue and the differential costs. Differential income indicates that a particular decision is expected to be profitable, while a differential loss indicates the opposite.

Differential analysis focuses on the effect of alternative courses of action on the relevant revenues and costs, as illustrated in Exhibit 1. For example, if a manager must decide between two alternatives, differential analysis would involve comparing the differential revenues of the two alternatives with the differential costs.

EXHIBIT 1   Differential Analysis

Differential revenue from alternatives:		
Revenue from alternative A	$XXX	
Revenue from alternative B	XXX	
Differential revenue		$ XXX
Differential cost of alternatives:		
Cost of alternative A	$XXX	
Cost of alternative B	XXX	
Differential cost		XXX
Net differential income or loss from alternatives		**$XXX**

In this chapter, we will discuss the use of differential analysis in analyzing the following alternatives:

1. Leasing or selling equipment.
2. Discontinuing an unprofitable segment.
3. Manufacturing or purchasing a needed part.
4. Replacing usable fixed assets.
5. Processing further or selling an intermediate product.
6. Accepting additional business at a special price.

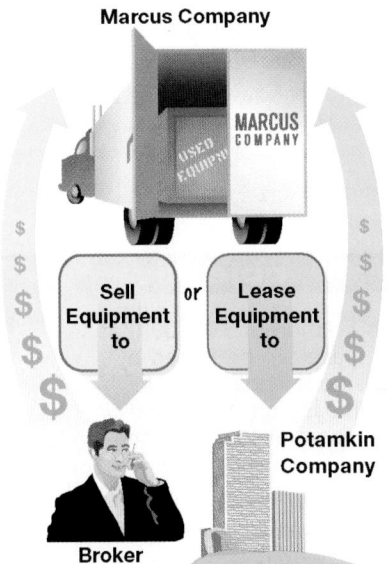

LEASE OR SELL

Management may have a choice between leasing or selling a piece of equipment that is no longer needed in the business. In deciding which option is best, management may use differential analysis. To illustrate, assume that Marcus Company is considering disposing of equipment that cost $200,000 and has $120,000 of accumulated depreciation to date. Marcus Company can sell the equipment through a broker for $100,000 less a 6% commission. Alternatively, Potamkin Company (the lessee) has offered to lease the equipment for five years for a total of $160,000. At the end of the fifth year of the lease, the equipment is expected to have no residual value. During the period of the lease, Marcus Company (the lessor) will incur repair, insurance, and property tax expenses estimated at $35,000. Exhibit 2 shows Marcus Company's analysis of whether to lease or sell the equipment.

Note that in Exhibit 2, the $80,000 book value ($200,000 − $120,000) of the equipment is a sunk cost and is not considered in the analysis. The $80,000 is a cost that resulted from a previous decision. It is not affected by the alternatives now being considered in leasing or selling the equipment. The relevant

EXHIBIT 2

Differential Analysis
Report—Lease or Sell

Proposal to Lease or Sell Equipment		
June 22, 2008		
Differential revenue from alternatives:		
Revenue from lease	$160,000	
Revenue from sale	100,000	
Differential revenue from lease		$60,000
Differential cost of alternatives:		
Repair, insurance, and property tax expenses	$ 35,000	
Commission expense on sale	6,000	
Differential cost of lease		29,000
Net differential income from the lease alternative . . .		**$31,000**

factors to be considered are the differential revenues and differential costs associated
with the lease or sell decision. This analysis is verified by the traditional analysis in
Exhibit 3.

EXHIBIT 3

Traditional Analysis

Lease or Sell			
Lease alternative:			
Revenue from lease		$160,000	
Depreciation expense for remaining five years	$80,000		
Repair, insurance, and property tax expenses	35,000	115,000	
Net gain			$45,000
Sell alternative:			
Sales price		$100,000	
Book value of equipment	$80,000		
Commission expense	6,000	86,000	
Net gain			14,000
Net differential income from the lease alternative			**$31,000**

Many companies that manu-
facture expensive equipment
give customers the choice of
leasing the equipment. For
example, construction equipment from Caterpillar can
either be purchased outright
or leased through Caterpillar's
financial services subsidiary.

    The alternatives presented in Exhibits 2 and 3 were relatively simple. However,
regardless of the complexity, the approach to differential analysis is basically the same.
Two additional factors that often need to be considered are (1) differential revenue from
investing the funds generated by the alternatives and (2) any income tax differential.
In Exhibit 2, there could be differential interest revenue related to investing the cash
flows from the two alternatives. Any income tax differential would be related to the
differences in the timing of the income from the alternatives and the differences in the
amount of investment income. In the next chapter, we will consider these factors on
management decisions.

Example Exercise 24-1   objective  1

Casper Company owns office space with a cost of $100,000 and accumulated depreciation of $30,000 that
can be sold for $150,000, less a 6% broker commission. Alternatively, the office space can be leased by
Casper Company for 10 years for a total of $170,000 at the end of which there is no salvage value. In
addition, repair, insurance, and property tax that would be incurred by Casper Company on the rented
office space would total $24,000 over the 10 years. Determine the differential income or loss from the
lease alternative for Casper Company.

(continued)

Follow My Example 24-1

Differential revenue from alternatives:		
Revenue from lease	$170,000	
Revenue from sale	150,000	
Differential revenue from lease		$20,000
Differential cost of alternatives:		
Repair, insurance, and property tax expenses	$ 24,000	
Commission expense on sale	9,000	
Differential cost of lease		15,000
Net differential income from the lease alternative		$ 5,000

For Practice: PE 24-1A, PE 24-1B

DISCONTINUE A SEGMENT OR PRODUCT

When a product or a department, branch, territory, or other segment of a business is generating losses, management may consider eliminating the product or segment. It is often assumed, sometimes in error, that the total income from operations of a business would be increased if the operating loss could be eliminated. Discontinuing the product or segment usually eliminates all of the product or segment's variable costs (direct materials, direct labor, sales commissions, and so on). However, if the product or segment is a relatively small part of the business, the fixed costs (depreciation, insurance, property taxes, and so on) may not be decreased by discontinuing it. It is possible in this case for the total operating income of a company to decrease rather than increase by eliminating the product or segment. To illustrate, the income statement for Battle Creek Cereal Co. presented in Exhibit 4 is for a normal year ending August 31, 2008.

Because Bran Flakes incurs annual losses, management is considering discontinuing it. Total annual operating income of $80,000 ($40,000 Toasted Oats + $40,000 Corn Flakes) might seem to be indicated by the income statement in Exhibit 4 if Bran Flakes is discontinued.

Discontinuing Bran Flakes, however, would actually decrease operating income by $15,000, to $54,000 ($69,000 − $15,000). This is shown by the differential analysis report in Exhibit 5, in which we assume that discontinuing Bran Flakes would have

EXHIBIT 4

Income (Loss) by Product

Battle Creek Cereal Co.
Condensed Income Statement
For the Year Ended August 31, 2008

	Corn Flakes	Toasted Oats	Bran Flakes	Total
Sales	$500,000	$400,000	$100,000	$1,000,000
Cost of goods sold:				
Variable costs	$220,000	$200,000	$ 60,000	$ 480,000
Fixed costs	120,000	80,000	20,000	220,000
Total cost of goods sold	$340,000	$280,000	$ 80,000	$ 700,000
Gross profit	$160,000	$120,000	$ 20,000	$ 300,000
Operating expenses:				
Variable expenses	$ 95,000	$ 60,000	$ 25,000	$ 180,000
Fixed expenses	25,000	20,000	6,000	51,000
Total operating expenses ...	$120,000	$ 80,000	$ 31,000	$ 231,000
Income (loss) from operations	$ 40,000	$ 40,000	$(11,000)	$ 69,000

EXHIBIT 5

Differential Analysis
Report—Discontinue
an Unprofitable
Segment

Proposal to Discontinue Bran Flakes September 29, 2008		
Differential revenue from annual sales of Bran Flakes:		
Revenue from sales		$100,000
Differential cost of annual sales of Bran Flakes:		
Variable cost of goods sold	$60,000	
Variable operating expenses	25,000	85,000
Annual differential income from sales of Bran Flakes . . .		**$ 15,000**

no effect on fixed costs and expenses. The traditional analysis in Exhibit 6 verifies the differential analysis in Exhibit 5.

In Exhibit 6, only the short-term (one year) effects of discontinuing Bran Flakes are considered. When eliminating a product or segment, management may also consider the long-term effects. For example, the plant capacity made available by discontinuing Bran Flakes might be eliminated. This could reduce fixed costs. Some employees may have to be laid off, and others may have to be relocated and retrained. Further, there may be a related decrease in sales of more profitable products to those customers who were attracted by the discontinued product.

EXHIBIT 6   **Traditional Analysis**

Proposal to Discontinue Bran Flakes September 29, 2008			
	Bran Flakes, Toasted Oats, and Corn Flakes	Discontinue Bran Flakes*	Toasted Oats and Corn Flakes
Sales	$1,000,000	$100,000	$900,000
Cost of goods sold:			
Variable costs	$ 480,000	$ 60,000	$420,000
Fixed costs	220,000	—	220,000
Total cost of goods sold	$ 700,000	$ 60,000	$640,000
Gross profit	$ 300,000	$ 40,000	$260,000
Operating expenses:			
Variable expenses	$ 180,000	$ 25,000	$155,000
Fixed expenses	51,000	—	51,000
Total operating expenses	$ 231,000	$ 25,000	$206,000
Income (loss) from operations	**$ 69,000**	**$ 15,000**	**$ 54,000**

*Fixed costs are assumed to remain unchanged with the discontinuance of Bran Flakes.

Example Exercise 24-2   objective 1

Product A has revenue of $65,000, variable cost of goods sold of $50,000, variable selling expenses of $12,000, and fixed costs of $25,000, creating a loss from operations of $22,000.

a.   Determine the differential income or loss from sales of Product A.
b.   Should Product A be discontinued?

(continued)

Follow My Example 24-2

a. Differential revenue from annual sales of Product A:

Revenue from sales		$65,000
Differential cost of annual sales of Product A:		
Variable cost of goods sold	$50,000	
Variable selling expenses	12,000	62,000
Annual differential income from sales of Product A		$ 3,000

b. Product A should not be discontinued.

For Practice: PE 24-2A, PE 24-2B

REAL WORLD

NIKE does not make shoes but buys 100% of its shoe manufacturing from outside suppliers. NIKE believes that its strengths are in designing, marketing, distributing, and selling athletic shoes, not in manufacturing shoes.

MAKE OR BUY

The assembly of many parts is often a major element in manufacturing some products, such as automobiles. These parts may be made by the product's manufacturer, or they may be purchased. For example, some of the parts for an automobile, such as the motor, may be produced by the automobile manufacturer. Other parts, such as tires, may be purchased from other manufacturers. In addition, in manufacturing motors, such items as spark plugs and nuts and bolts may be acquired from suppliers.

Management uses differential costs to decide whether to make or buy a part. For example, if a part is purchased, management has concluded that it is less costly to buy the part than to manufacture it. Make or buy options often arise when a manufacturer has excess productive capacity in the form of unused equipment, space, and labor.

The differential analysis is similar, whether management is considering making a part that is currently being purchased or purchasing a part that is currently being made. To illustrate, assume that an automobile manufacturer has been purchasing instrument panels for $240 a unit. The factory is currently operating at 80% of capacity, and no major increase in production is expected in the near future. The cost per unit of manufacturing an instrument panel internally, including fixed costs, is estimated as follows:

Direct materials	$ 80
Direct labor	80
Variable factory overhead	52
Fixed factory overhead	68
Total cost per unit	$280

If the *make* price of $280 is simply compared with the *buy* price of $240, the decision is to buy the instrument panel. However, if unused capacity could be used in manufacturing the part, there would be no increase in the total amount of fixed factory overhead costs. Thus, only the variable factory overhead costs need to be considered. The relevant costs are summarized in the differential report in Exhibit 7.

Other possible effects of a decision to manufacture the instrument panel should also be considered. For example, capacity committed to the instrument panel may not be available for more production opportunities in the future. This decision may affect employees. It may also affect future business relations with the instrument panel supplier, who may provide other essential parts. The company's decision to manufacture instrument panels might jeopardize the timely delivery of these other parts.

EXHIBIT 7

Differential Analysis Report—Make or Buy

Proposal to Manufacture Instrument Panels
February 15, 2008

Purchase price of an instrument panel		$240.00
Differential cost to manufacture:		
Direct materials	$80.00	
Direct labor	80.00	
Variable factory overhead	52.00	212.00
Cost savings from manufacturing an instrument panel		**$ 28.00**

Example Exercise 24-3

objective 1

A company manufactures a subcomponent of an assembly for $80 per unit, including fixed costs of $25 per unit. A proposal is offered to purchase the subcomponent from an outside source for $60 per unit, plus $5 per unit freight. Provide a differential analysis of the outside purchase proposal.

Follow My Example 24-3

Differential cost to purchase:		
Purchase price of the subcomponent	$60	
Freight for subcomponent	5	$65
Differential cost to manufacture:		
Variable manufacturing costs ($80 − $25 fixed costs)		55
Cost savings from manufacturing subcomponent		$10

For Practice: PE 24-3A, PE 24-3B

REPLACE EQUIPMENT

The usefulness of fixed assets may be reduced long before they are considered to be worn out. For example, equipment may no longer be efficient for the purpose for which it is used. On the other hand, the equipment may not have reached the point of complete inadequacy. Decisions to replace usable fixed assets should be based on relevant costs. The relevant costs are the future costs of continuing to use the equipment versus replacement. The book values of the fixed assets being replaced are sunk costs and are irrelevant.

Integrity, Objectivity, and Ethics in Business

ETHICS

RELATED-PARTY DEALS

The make-or-buy decision can be complicated if the purchase (buy) is being made by a related party. A related party is one in which there is direct or indirect control of one party over another or the presence of a family member in a transaction. Such dependence or familiarity may interfere with the appropriateness of the business transaction. One investor has said, "Related parties are akin to steroids used by athletes. If you're an athlete and you can cut the mustard, you don't need steroids to make your-

self stronger or faster. By the same token, if you're a good company, you don't need related parties or deals that don't make sense." While related-party transactions are legal, GAAP (FASB Statement No. 56) and the Sarbanes-Oxley Act require that they must be disclosed under the presumption that such transactions are less than arm's length.

Source: Herb Greenberg, "Poor Relations: The Problem with Related-Party Transactions," *Fortune Advisor* (February 5, 2001), p. 198.

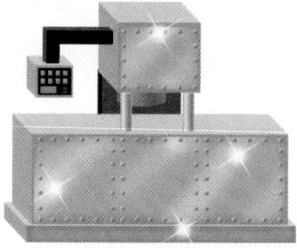

Estimated annual reduction
of costs of $75,000

(handwritten note) Doesn't matter that old equipt. is not fully depreciated

To illustrate, assume that a business is considering the disposal of several identical machines having a total book value of $100,000 and an estimated remaining life of five years. The old machines can be sold for $25,000. They can be replaced by a single high-speed machine at a cost of $250,000. The new machine has an estimated useful life of five years and no residual value. Analyses indicate an estimated annual reduction in variable manufacturing costs from $225,000 with the old machine to $150,000 with the new machine. No other changes in the manufacturing costs or the operating expenses are expected. The relevant costs are summarized in the differential report in Exhibit 8.

EXHIBIT 8 — Differential Analysis Report—Replace Equipment

Proposal to Replace Equipment
November 28, 2008

Annual variable costs—present equipment	$225,000	
Annual variable costs—new equipment	150,000	
Annual differential decrease in cost	$ 75,000	
Number of years applicable	× 5	
Total differential decrease in cost	$375,000	
Proceeds from sale of present equipment	25,000	$400,000
Cost of new equipment		250,000
Net differential decrease in cost, 5-year total		$150,000
Annual net differential decrease in cost—new equipment		**$ 30,000**

Other factors are often important in equipment replacement decisions. For example, differences between the remaining useful life of the old equipment and the estimated life of the new equipment could exist. In addition, the new equipment might improve the overall quality of the product, resulting in an increase in sales volume. Additional factors could include the time value of money and other uses for the cash needed to purchase the new equipment.[1]

The amount of income that is forgone from an alternative use of an asset, such as cash, is called an **opportunity cost**. For example, your opportunity cost of attending school is the income forgone from lost work hours. Although the opportunity cost does not appear as a part of historical accounting data, it is useful in analyzing alternative courses of action. To illustrate, assume that the cash outlay of $250,000 for the new equipment, less the $25,000 proceeds from the sale of the present equipment, could be invested to yield a 10% return. Thus, the annual opportunity cost related to the purchase of the new equipment is $22,500 (10% × $225,000).

Example Exercise 24-4 — objective 1

A machine with a book value of $32,000 has an estimated four-year life. A proposal is offered to sell the old machine for $10,000 and replace it with a new machine at a cost of $45,000. The new machine has a four-year life with no salvage value. The new machine would reduce annual direct labor costs by $11,000. Provide a differential analysis on the proposal to replace the machine.

(continued)

[1] The importance of the time value of money in equipment replacement decisions is discussed in the next chapter.

PROCESS OR SELL

When a product is manufactured, it progresses through various stages of production. Often a product can be sold at an intermediate stage of production, or it can be processed further and then sold. In deciding whether to sell a product at an intermediate stage or to process it further, differential analysis is useful. The differential revenues from further processing are compared to the differential costs of further processing. The costs of producing the intermediate product do not change, regardless of whether the intermediate product is sold or processed further. Thus, these costs are not differential costs and are irrelevant to the decision to process further.

To illustrate, assume that a business produces kerosene in batches of 4,000 gallons. Standard quantities of 4,000 gallons of direct materials are processed, which cost $0.60 per gallon. Kerosene can be sold without further processing for $0.80 per gallon. It can be processed further to yield gasoline, which can be sold for $1.25 per gallon. Gasoline requires additional processing costs of $650 per batch, and 20% of the gallons of kerosene will evaporate during production. Exhibit 9 summarizes the differential revenues and costs in deciding whether to process kerosene to produce gasoline.

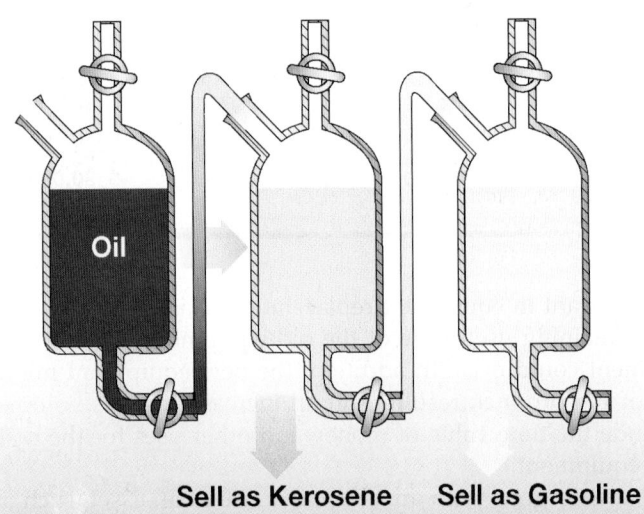

Sell as Kerosene   Sell as Gasoline

EXHIBIT 9

Differential Analysis Report—Process or Sell

Proposal to Process Kerosene Further
October 1, 2008

Differential revenue from further processing per batch:		
Revenue from sale of gasoline [(4,000 gallons − 800 gallons evaporation) × $1.25]	$4,000	
Revenue from sale of kerosene (4,000 gallons × $0.80)	3,200	
Differential revenue		$800
Differential cost per batch:		
Additional cost of producing gasoline		650
Differential income from further processing gasoline per batch		**$150**

The differential income from further processing kerosene into gasoline is $150 per batch. The initial cost of producing the intermediate kerosene, $2,400 (4,000 gallons × $0.60), is not considered in deciding whether to process kerosene further. This initial cost will be incurred, regardless of whether gasoline is produced.

Example Exercise 24-5 — objective 1

Product T is produced for $2.50 per gallon including a $1.00 per gallon fixed cost. Product T can be sold without additional processing for $3.50 per gallon, or processed further into Product V at an additional cost of $1.60 per gallon, including a $0.90 per gallon fixed cost. Product V can be sold for $4.00 per gallon. Provide a differential analysis for further processing into Product V.

Follow My Example 24-5

Differential revenue from further processing per gallon:
Revenue per gallon from sale of Product V $4.00
Revenue per gallon from sale of Product T 3.50
  Differential revenue $0.50
Differential cost per gallon:
Additional cost for producing Product V ($1.60 − $0.90) 0.70
Differential loss from further processing into Product V $0.20

For Practice: PE 24-5A, PE 24-5B

ACCEPT BUSINESS AT A SPECIAL PRICE

The Internet is forcing many companies to respond to "dynamic" pricing. For example, in Priceline.com Inc.'s "name your price" format, customers tell the company what they are willing to pay and then the company must decide if it is willing to sell at that price.

Order for 5,000 basketballs at $18 each

Differential analysis is also useful in deciding whether to accept additional business at a special price. The differential revenue that would be provided from the additional business is compared to the differential costs of producing and delivering the product to the customer. If the company is operating at full capacity, any additional production will increase both fixed and variable production costs. If, however, the normal production of the company is below full capacity, additional business may be undertaken without increasing fixed production costs. In this case, the differential costs of the additional production are the variable manufacturing costs. If operating expenses increase because of the additional business, these expenses should also be considered.

To illustrate, assume that the monthly capacity of a sporting goods business is 12,500 basketballs. Current sales and production are averaging 10,000 basketballs per month. The current manufacturing cost of $20 per unit consists of variable costs of $12.50 and fixed costs of $7.50. The normal selling price of the product in the domestic market is $30. The manufacturer receives from an exporter an offer for 5,000 basketballs at $18 each. Production can be spread over a three-month period without interfering with normal production or incurring overtime costs. Pricing policies in the domestic market will not be affected. Simply comparing the sales price of $18 with the present unit manufacturing cost of $20 indicates that the offer should be rejected. However, by focusing only on the differential cost, which in this case is the variable cost, the decision is different. Exhibit 10 shows the differential analysis report for this decision.

Proposals to sell a product in the domestic market at prices lower than the normal price may require additional considerations. For example, it may be unwise to increase sales volume in one territory by price reductions if

EXHIBIT 10

Differential Analysis Report—Sell at Special Price

Proposal to Sell Basketballs to Exporter
March 10, 2008

Differential revenue from accepting offer:
  Revenue from sale of 5,000 additional units at $18 .... $90,000
Differential cost of accepting offer:
  Variable costs of 5,000 additional units at $12.50 62,500
Differential income from accepting offer **$27,500**

sales volume is lost in other areas. Manufacturers must also conform to the Robinson-Patman Act, which prohibits price discrimination within the United States unless differences in prices can be justified by different costs of serving different customers.

Example Exercise 24-6   objective **1**

Product D is normally sold for $4.40 per unit. A special price of $3.60 is offered for the export market. The variable production cost is $3.00 per unit. An additional export tariff of 10% of revenue must be paid for all export products. Determine the differential income or loss per unit from selling Product D for export.

Follow My Example 24-6

Differential revenue from export:		
Revenue per unit from export sale		$3.60
Differential cost from export:		
Variable manufacturing costs	$3.00	
Export tariff (10% × $3.60)	0.36	3.36
Differential income from accepting export sale		$0.24

For Practice: PE 24-6A, PE 24-6B

Setting Normal Product Selling Prices

objective **2**

Determine the selling price of a product, using the total cost, product cost, and variable cost concepts.

Differential analysis may be useful in deciding to lower selling prices for special short-run decisions, such as whether to accept business at a price lower than the normal price. In such cases, the minimum short-run price is set high enough to cover all variable costs. Any price above this minimum price will improve profits in the short run. In the long run, however, the normal selling price must be set high enough to cover all costs and expenses (both fixed and variable) and provide a reasonable profit. Otherwise, the business may not survive.

The normal selling price can be viewed as the target selling price to be achieved in the long run. The basic approaches to setting this price are as follows:

Market Methods	Cost-Plus Methods
1. Demand-based methods	1. Total cost concept
2. Competition-based methods	2. Product cost concept
	3. Variable cost concept

Managers using the market methods refer to the external market to determine the price. Demand-based methods set the price according to the demand for the product. If there is high demand for the product, then the price may be set high, while lower demand may require the price to be set low. An example of setting different prices according to the demand for the product is found in the lodging industry, where rates are set low for weekends and high during business days according to the demand by business travelers.

Competition-based methods set the price according to the price offered by competitors. For example, if a competitor reduces the price, then management may be required to adjust the price to meet the competition. The market-based pricing approaches are discussed in greater detail in marketing courses, so we will not expand upon them here.

Managers using the cost-plus methods price the product in order to achieve a target profit. Managers add to the cost an amount called a **markup**, so that all costs plus a profit are included in the selling price. In the following paragraphs, we describe and illustrate the three cost concepts often used in applying the cost-plus approach: (1) total cost, (2) product cost, and (3) variable cost. A cost reduction method that uses market-method pricing, called target costing, is discussed later in this section.

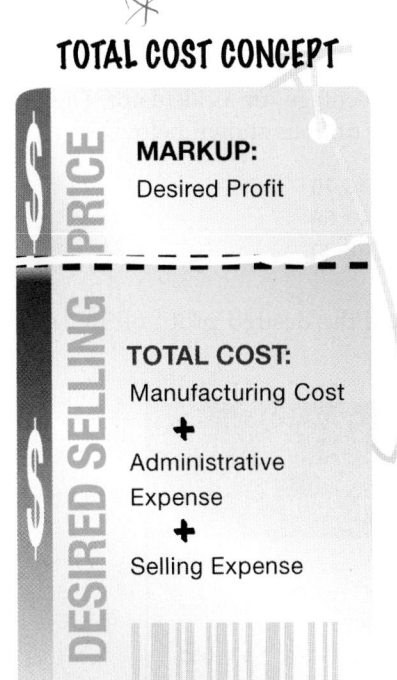

TOTAL COST CONCEPT

Using the **total cost concept**, all costs of manufacturing a product plus the selling and administrative expenses are included in the cost amount to which the markup is added. Since all costs and expenses are included in the cost amount, the dollar amount of the markup equals the desired profit.

The first step in applying the total cost concept is to determine the total cost of manufacturing the product. This cost includes the costs of direct materials, direct labor, and factory overhead and should be available from the accounting records. The next step is to add the estimated selling and administrative expenses to the total cost of manufacturing the product. The cost amount per unit is then computed by dividing the total costs by the total units expected to be produced and sold.

After the cost amount per unit has been determined, the dollar amount of the markup is determined. For this purpose, the markup is expressed as a percentage of cost. This percentage is then multiplied by the cost amount per unit. The dollar amount of the markup is then added to the cost amount per unit to arrive at the selling price.

The markup percentage for the total cost concept is determined by applying the following formula:

$$\text{Markup Percentage} = \frac{\text{Desired Profit}}{\text{Total Costs}}$$

The numerator of the formula is only the desired profit. This is because all costs and expenses are included in the cost amount to which the markup is added. The denominator of the formula is the total costs.

To illustrate, assume that the costs for calculators of Digital Solutions Inc. are as follows:

Variable costs:	
Direct materials	$ 3.00 per unit
Direct labor	10.00
Factory overhead	1.50
Selling and administrative expenses	1.50
Total	$ 16.00 per unit
Fixed costs:	
Factory overhead	$50,000
Selling and administrative expenses	20,000

Digital Solutions Inc. desires a profit equal to a 20% rate of return on assets, $800,000 of assets are devoted to producing calculators, and 100,000 units are expected to be produced and sold. The calculators' total cost is $1,670,000, or $16.70 per unit, computed as follows:

Variable costs ($16.00 × 100,000 units)		$1,600,000
Fixed costs:		
Factory overhead	$50,000	
Selling and administrative expenses	20,000	70,000
Total costs		$1,670,000
Total cost per calculator ($1,670,000/100,000 units)		$16.70

The desired profit is $160,000 (20% × $800,000), and the markup percentage for a calculator is 9.6%, computed as follows:

$$\text{Markup Percentage} = \frac{\text{Desired Profit}}{\text{Total Costs}}$$

$$\text{Markup Percentage} = \frac{\$160,000}{\$1,670,000} = 9.6\% \text{ (rounded)}$$

Based on the total cost per unit and the markup percentage for a calculator, Digital Solutions Inc. would price each calculator at $18.30 per unit, as shown below.

Total cost per calculator	$16.70
Markup ($16.70 × 9.6%)	1.60
Selling price	$18.30

The ability of the selling price of $18.30 to generate the desired profit of $160,000 is shown by the following income statement:

Digital Solutions Inc.		
Income Statement		
For the Year Ended December 31, 2008		
Sales (100,000 units × $18.30)		$1,830,000
Expenses:		
Variable (100,000 units × $16.00)	$1,600,000	
Fixed ($50,000 + $20,000)	70,000	1,670,000
Income from operations		$ 160,000

The total cost concept of applying the cost-plus approach to product pricing is often used by contractors who sell products to government agencies. In many cases, government contractors are required by law to be reimbursed for their products on a total-cost-plus-profit basis.

Example Exercise 24-7

objective 2

Apex Corporation produces and sells Product Z at a total cost of $30 per unit of which $20 is product cost and $10 is selling and administrative expenses. In addition, the total cost of $30 is made up of $18 variable cost and $12 is fixed cost. The desired profit is $3 per unit. Determine the markup percentage on total cost.

Follow My Example 24-7

Markup percentage on total cost: $\dfrac{\$3}{\$30} = 10.0\%$

For Practice: PE 24-7A, PE 24-7B

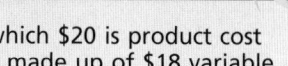

Integrity, Objectivity, and Ethics in Business

ETHICS

PRICE FIXING

Federal law prevents companies competing in similar markets from sharing cost and price information, or what is commonly termed "price fixing." For example, the Federal Trade Commission brought a suit against the major record labels and music retailers for conspiring to set CD prices at a minimum level, or MAP (minimum advertised price). In settling the suit, the major labels ceased their MAP policies and provided $143 million in cash and CDs for consumers.

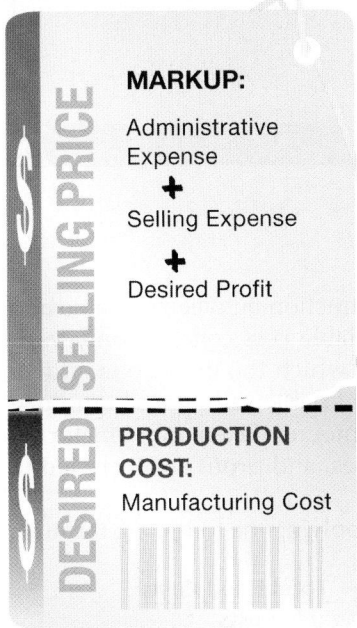

PRODUCT COST CONCEPT

DESIRED SELLING PRICE

MARKUP:

Administrative
Expense

+

Selling Expense

+

Desired Profit

**PRODUCTION
COST:**

Manufacturing Cost

PRODUCT COST CONCEPT

Using the **product cost concept**, only the costs of manufacturing the product, termed the product cost, are included in the cost amount to which the markup is added. Estimated selling expenses, administrative expenses, and profit are included in the markup. The markup percentage is determined by applying the following formula:

$$\text{Markup Percentage} = \frac{\text{Desired Profit} + \text{Total Selling and Administrative Expenses}}{\text{Total Manufacturing Costs}}$$

The numerator of the markup percentage formula is the desired profit plus the total selling and administrative expenses. These expenses must be included in the markup, since they are not included in the cost amount to which the markup is added. The denominator of the formula includes the costs of direct materials, direct labor, and factory overhead.

To illustrate, assume the same data used in the preceding illustration. The manufacturing cost for Digital Solutions Inc.'s calculator is $1,500,000, or $15 per unit, computed as follows:

Direct materials ($3 × 100,000 units)		$ 300,000
Direct labor ($10 × 100,000 units)		1,000,000
Factory overhead:		
Variable ($1.50 × 100,000 units)	$150,000	
Fixed	50,000	200,000
Total manufacturing costs		$1,500,000
Manufacturing cost per calculator		
($1,500,000/100,000 units)		$15

The desired profit is $160,000 (20% × $800,000), and the total selling and administrative expenses are $170,000 [(100,000 units × $1.50 per unit) + $20,000]. The markup percentage for a calculator is 22%, computed as follows:

$$\text{Markup Percentage} = \frac{\text{Desired Profit} + \text{Total Selling and Administrative Expenses}}{\text{Total Manufacturing Costs}}$$

$$\text{Markup Percentage} = \frac{\$160,000 + \$170,000}{\$1,500,000}$$

$$\text{Markup Percentage} = \frac{\$330,000}{\$1,500,000} = 22\%$$

Based on the manufacturing cost per calculator and the markup percentage, Digital Solutions Inc. would price each calculator at $18.30 per unit, as shown below.

Manufacturing cost per calculator	$15.00
Markup ($15 × 22%)	3.30
Selling price	$18.30

Example Exercise 24-8   objective **2**

Apex Corporation produces and sells Product Z at a total cost of $30 per unit of which $20 is product cost and $10 is selling and administrative expenses. In addition, the total cost of $30 is made up of $18 variable cost and $12 is fixed cost. The desired profit is $3 per unit. Determine the markup percentage on product cost.

(continued)

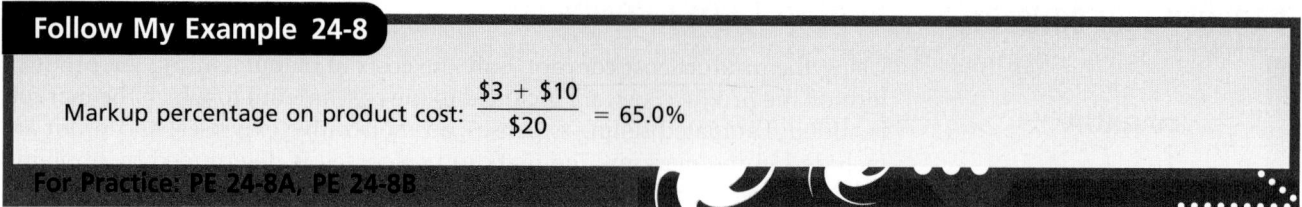

For Practice: PE 24-8A, PE 24-8B

VARIABLE COST CONCEPT

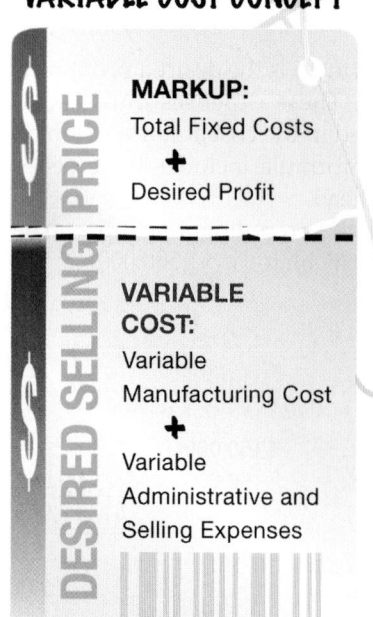

VARIABLE COST CONCEPT

The **variable cost concept** emphasizes the distinction between variable and fixed costs in product pricing. Using the variable cost concept, only variable costs are included in the cost amount to which the markup is added. All variable manufacturing costs, as well as variable selling and administrative expenses, are included in the cost amount. Fixed manufacturing costs, fixed selling and administrative expenses, and profit are included in the markup.

The markup percentage is determined by applying the following formula:

$$\text{Markup Percentage} = \frac{\text{Desired Profit} + \text{Total Fixed Costs}}{\text{Total Variable Costs}}$$

The numerator of the markup percentage formula is the desired profit plus the total fixed manufacturing costs and the total fixed selling and administrative expenses. These costs and expenses must be included in the markup, since they are not included in the cost amount to which the markup is added. The denominator of the formula includes the total variable costs.

To illustrate, assume the same data used in the two preceding illustrations. The calculator variable cost is $1,600,000, or $16.00 per unit, computed as follows:

Variable costs:	
Direct materials ($3 × 100,000 units)	$ 300,000
Direct labor ($10 × 100,000 units)	1,000,000
Factory overhead ($1.50 × 100,000 units)	150,000
Selling and administrative expenses ($1.50 × 100,000 units)	150,000
Total variable costs	$1,600,000
Variable cost per calculator ($1,600,000/100,000 units)	$16.00

The desired profit is $160,000 (20% × $800,000), the total fixed manufacturing costs are $50,000, and the total fixed selling and administrative expenses are $20,000. The markup percentage for a calculator is 14.4%, computed as follows:

$$\text{Markup Percentage} = \frac{\text{Desired Profit} + \text{Total Fixed Costs}}{\text{Total Variable Costs}}$$

$$\text{Markup Percentage} = \frac{\$160,000 + \$50,000 + \$20,000}{\$1,600,000}$$

$$\text{Markup Percentage} = \frac{\$230,000}{\$1,600,000} = 14.4\%$$

Based on the variable cost per calculator and the markup percentage, Digital Solutions Inc. would price each calculator at $18.30 per unit, as shown below.

Variable cost per calculator	$16.00
Markup ($16.00 × 14.4%)	2.30
Selling price	$18.30

Example Exercise 24-9

objective **2**

Apex Corporation produces and sells Product Z at a total cost of $30 per unit of which $20 is product cost and $10 is selling and administrative expenses. In addition, the total cost of $30 is made up of $18 variable cost and $12 is fixed cost. The desired profit is $3 per unit. Determine the markup percentage on variable cost, rounding to one decimal place.

Follow My Example 24-9

Markup percentage on variable cost: $\dfrac{\$3 + \$12}{\$18}$ = 83.3%, rounded to one decimal place

For Practice: PE 24-9A, PE 24-9B

CHOOSING A COST-PLUS APPROACH COST CONCEPT

All three cost concepts produced the same selling price ($18.30) for Digital Solutions Inc. In practice, however, the three cost concepts are usually not viewed as alternatives. Each cost concept requires different estimates of costs and expenses. This difficulty and the complexity of the manufacturing operations should be considered in choosing a cost concept.

To reduce the costs of gathering data, estimated (standard) costs rather than actual costs may be used with any of the three cost concepts. However, management should exercise caution when using estimated costs in applying the cost-plus approach. The estimates should be based on normal (attainable) operating levels and not theoretical (ideal) levels of performance. In product pricing, the use of estimates based on ideal- or maximum-capacity operating levels might lead to setting product prices too low. In this case, the costs of such factors as normal spoilage or normal periods of idle time might not be considered.

The decision-making needs of management are also an important factor in selecting a cost concept for product pricing. For example, managers who often make special pricing decisions are more likely to use the variable cost concept. In contrast, a government defense contractor would be more likely to use the total cost concept.

ACTIVITY-BASED COSTING

As illustrated in the preceding paragraphs, costs are an important consideration in setting product prices. To more accurately measure the costs of producing and selling products, some companies use activity-based costing. **Activity-based costing (ABC)** identifies and traces activities to specific products.

Activity-based costing may be useful in making product pricing decisions where manufacturing operations involve large amounts of factory overhead. In such cases, traditional overhead allocation using activity bases such as units produced or machine hours may yield inaccurate cost allocations. This, in turn, may result in distorted product costs and product prices. By providing more accurate product cost allocations, activity-based costing aids in setting product prices that will cover costs and expenses.[2]

TARGET COSTING

A method that combines market-based pricing with a cost reduction emphasis is **target costing**. Under target costing, a future selling price is anticipated, using the demand-based methods or the competition-based methods discussed previously. The targeted cost is determined by *subtracting* a desired profit from the expected selling price. In contrast, the three cost-plus concepts discussed previously begin with a given cost and *add* a markup to determine the selling price.

---

2 Activity-based costing is further discussed and illustrated in a later chapter.

Target costing is used to motivate cost reduction as shown in Exhibit 11. The bar at the left in Exhibit 11 shows the actual cost and profit that can be earned during the present time period for a particular product. The bar at the right shows that the market price is expected to decline in the future. Thus, to earn a profit, a target cost is estimated as the difference between the expected market price and the desired profit. This target cost establishes a product cost objective that will maintain competitiveness and profitability.

EXHIBIT 11

Target Cost Concept

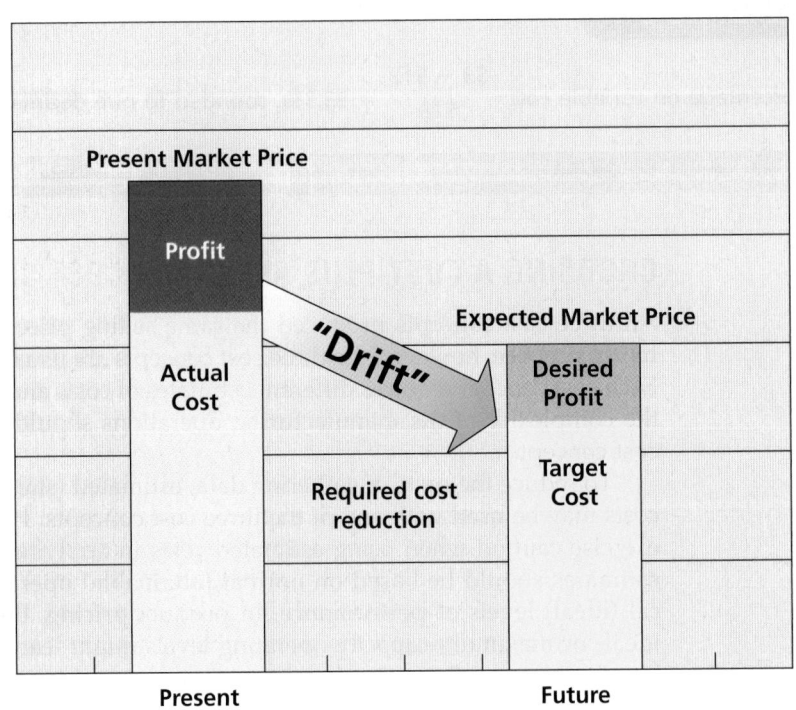

Since the target cost is less than the current cost, managers must plan and remove cost from the design and manufacture of the product. The planned cost reduction is sometimes referred to as the cost "drift." Cost can be removed from a product in a variety of ways, such as by simplifying the design, reducing the cost of direct materials, reducing the direct labor content, or eliminating waste from manufacturing operations. Using the target cost concept in this way provides managers with an improvement goal for gauging the success of their efforts over time. Target costing is especially useful in highly competitive markets that require continual product cost reductions to remain competitive, such as personal computers.

Product Profitability and Pricing Under Production Bottlenecks

objective 3

Compute the relative profitability of products in bottleneck production environments.

An important consideration influencing production volumes and prices is production bottlenecks. A production **bottleneck** (or *constraint*) occurs at the point in the process where the demand for the company's product exceeds the ability to produce the product. The **theory of constraints (TOC)** is a manufacturing strategy that focuses on reducing the influence of bottlenecks on a process.

PRODUCT PROFITABILITY UNDER PRODUCTION BOTTLENECKS

When a company has a bottleneck in its production process, it should attempt to maximize its profitability, subject to the influence of the bottleneck. To illustrate, assume

Business Connections

REAL WORLD

WHAT IS A PRODUCT?

A product is often thought of in terms beyond just its physical attributes. For example, why a customer buys a product usually impacts how a business markets the product. Other considerations, such as warranty needs, servicing needs, and perceived quality, also affect business strategies.

Consider the four different types of products listed below. For these products, the frequency of purchase, the profit per unit, and the number of retailers differ. As a result, the sales and marketing approach for each product differs.

Product	Type of Product	Frequency of Purchase	Profit per Unit	Number of Retailers	Sales/Marketing Approach
Snickers®	Convenience	Often	Low	Many	Mass advertising
Sony® TV	Shopping	Occasional	Moderate	Many	Mass advertising; personal selling
Diamond ring	Specialty	Seldom	High	Few	Personal selling
Prearranged funeral	Unsought	Rare	High	Few	Aggressive selling

The sand in the hourglass can pass only as fast as the narrowest point in the glass will allow.

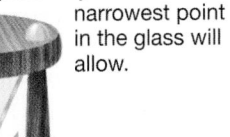

Bottleneck

that PrideCraft Tool Company makes three types of wrenches: small, medium, and large. All three products are processed through a heat treatment operation, which hardens the steel tools. PrideCraft Tool's heat treatment process is operating at full capacity and is a production bottleneck. The product unit contribution margin and the number of hours of heat treatment used by each type of wrench are as follows:

	Small Wrench	Medium Wrench	Large Wrench
Unit selling price	$130	$140	$160
Unit variable cost	40	40	40
Unit contribution margin	$ 90	$100	$120
Heat treatment hours per unit	1	4	8

The large wrench appears to be the most profitable product because its unit contribution margin is the greatest. However, the unit contribution margin can be a misleading indicator of profitability in a bottleneck operation. The correct measure of performance is the value of each bottleneck hour, or the unit contribution margin per bottleneck hour. Using this measure, each product has a much different profitability when compared to the unit contribution margin information, as shown in Exhibit 12.

EXHIBIT 12

Unit Contribution Margin per Bottleneck Hour

	Small Wrench	Medium Wrench	Large Wrench
Unit selling price	$130	$140	$160
Unit variable cost	40	40	40
Unit contribution margin	$ 90	$100	$120
Bottleneck (heat treatment) hours per unit	/ 1	/ 4	/ 8
Unit contribution margin per bottleneck hour	$ 90	$ 25	$ 15

The small wrench produces the most unit contribution margin per bottleneck hour (heat treatment) used, while the large wrench produces the smallest unit contribution margin per bottleneck hour. Thus, the small wrench is the most profitable product. This information is the opposite of that implied by the unit contribution margin.

Example Exercise 24-10   objective 3

Product A has a unit contribution margin of $15. Product B has a unit contribution margin of $20. Product A requires three furnace hours, while Product B requires five furnace hours. Determine the most profitable product assuming the furnace is a constraint.

Follow My Example 24-10

	Product A	Product B
Unit contribution margin	$15	$20
Furnace hours per unit	/ 3	/ 5
Unit contribution margin per bottleneck hour	$ 5	$ 4

Product A is the most profitable in using bottleneck resources.

For Practice: PE 24-10A, PE 24-10B

Latrobe Steel Division of The Timken Company originally used total cost plus a markup to price its steel products. However, Latrobe recalculated the profitability of its products, based on the unit contribution margin per hour of bottleneck. This analysis caused Latrobe management to change the product mix in favor of products with high unit contribution margin per hour of bottleneck. Management estimated that these changes improved income from operations by 20%.

PRODUCT PRICING UNDER PRODUCTION BOTTLENECKS

Each hour of a bottleneck delivers profit to the company. When a company has a production bottleneck, the unit contribution margin per bottleneck hour provides a measure of the product's relative profitability. This information can also be used to adjust the product price to better reflect the value of the product's use of a bottleneck. Products that use a large number of bottleneck hours per unit require more unit contribution margin than products that use few bottleneck hours per unit. For example, PrideCraft Tool Company should increase the price of the large wrench in order to deliver more unit contribution margin per bottleneck hour.

To determine the price of the large wrench that would equate its profitability to the small wrench, we need to solve the following equation:

$$\text{Unit Contribution Margin per Bottleneck Hour for Small Wrench} = \frac{\text{Revised Price of Large Wrench} - \text{Unit Variable Cost for Large Wrench}}{\text{Bottleneck Hours per Unit for Large Wrench}}$$

$$\$90 = \frac{\text{Revised Price of Large Wrench} - \$40}{8}$$

$$\$720 = \text{Revised Price of Large Wrench} - \$40$$
$$\$760 = \text{Revised Price of Large Wrench}$$

The large wrench's price would need to be increased to $760 in order to deliver the same unit contribution margin per bottleneck hour as does the small wrench, as verified below.

Revised price of large wrench	$760
Less: Unit variable cost of large wrench	40
Unit contribution margin of large wrench	$720
Bottleneck hours per unit of large wrench	/ 8
Revised unit contribution margin per bottleneck hour	$ 90

At a price of $760, the company would be indifferent between producing and selling the small wrench or the large wrench, all else being equal. This analysis assumes that there is unlimited demand for the products. If the market were unwilling to purchase the large wrench at this price, then the company should produce the small wrench.

At a Glance

1. Prepare a differential analysis report for decisions involving leasing or selling equipment, discontinuing an unprofitable segment, manufacturing or purchasing a needed part, replacing usable fixed assets, processing further or selling an intermediate product, or accepting additional business at a special price.

Key Points	Key Learning Outcomes	Example Exercises	Practice Exercises
Differential analysis reports for leasing or selling, discontinuing a segment or product, making or buying, replacing equipment, processing or selling, and accepting business at a special price are illustrated in the text. Each analysis focuses on the differential revenues and/or costs of the alternative courses of action.	• Prepare a lease or sell differential analysis.	**24-1**	24-1A, 24-1B
	• Prepare a discontinued segment differential analysis.	**24-2**	24-2A, 24-2B
	• Prepare a make or buy differential analysis.	**24-3**	24-3A, 24-3B
	• Prepare an equipment replacement differential analysis.	**24-4**	24-4A, 24-4B
	• Prepare a process or sell differential analysis.	**24-5**	24-5A, 24-5B
	• Prepare an accept business at a special price differential analysis.	**24-6**	24-6A, 24-6B

2. Determine the selling price of a product, using the total cost, product cost, and variable cost concepts.

Key Points	Key Learning Outcomes	Example Exercises	Practice Exercises
The three cost concepts commonly used in applying the cost-plus approach to product pricing are the total cost, product cost, and variable cost concepts.	• Compute the markup percentage using the total cost concept.	**24-7**	24-7A, 24-7B
	• Compute the markup percentage using the product cost concept.	**24-8**	24-8A, 24-8B
	• Compute the markup percentage using the variable cost concept.	**24-9**	24-9A, 24-9B
Activity-based costing can be used to provide more accurate cost information in applying cost-plus concepts when indirect costs are significant. Target costing combines market-based methods with a cost-reduction emphasis.	• Describe activity-based costing.		
	• Define and describe target costing.		

3. Compute the relative profitability of products in bottleneck production environments.

Key Points	Key Learning Outcomes	Example Exercises	Practice Exercises
The profitability of a product in a bottleneck production environment is determined by dividing the unit contribution margin by the bottleneck hours per unit. The resulting measure indicates the product's profitability per hour of bottleneck use. This information can be used to support product pricing decisions.	• Compute the unit contribution margin per bottleneck hour.	**24-10**	24-10A, 24-10B
	• Compute the indifference price between products using the unit contribution margin per bottleneck hour.		

Key Terms

activity-based costing (ABC) (1077)
bottleneck (1078)
differential analysis (1063)
differential cost (1063)
differential revenue (1062)

markup (1072)
opportunity cost (1069)
product cost concept (1075)
sunk cost (1062)
target costing (1077)

theory of constraints (TOC) (1078)
total cost concept (1073)
variable cost concept (1076)

Illustrative Problem

Inez Company recently began production of a new product, M, which required the investment of $1,600,000 in assets. The costs of producing and selling 80,000 units of Product M are estimated as follows:

Variable costs:		
Direct materials	$	10.00 per unit
Direct labor		6.00
Factory overhead		4.00
Selling and administrative expenses		5.00
Total	$	25.00 per unit
Fixed costs:		
Factory overhead	$800,000	
Selling and administrative expenses	400,000	

Inez Company is currently considering establishing a selling price for Product M. The president of Inez Company has decided to use the cost-plus approach to product pricing and has indicated that Product M must earn a 10% rate of return on invested assets.

Instructions

1. Determine the amount of desired profit from the production and sale of Product M.
2. Assuming that the total cost concept is used, determine (a) the cost amount per unit, (b) the markup percentage, and (c) the selling price of Product M.
3. Assuming that the product cost concept is used, determine (a) the cost amount per unit, (b) the markup percentage, and (c) the selling price of Product M.
4. Assuming that the variable cost concept is used, determine (a) the cost amount per unit, (b) the markup percentage, and (c) the selling price of Product M.
5. Assume that for the current year, the selling price of Product M was $42 per unit. To date, 60,000 units have been produced and sold, and analysis of the domestic market indicates that 15,000 additional units are expected to be sold during the remainder of the year. Recently, Inez Company received an offer from Wong Inc. for 4,000 units of Product M at $28 each. Wong Inc. will market the units in Korea under its own brand name, and no selling and administrative expenses associated with the sale will be incurred by Inez Company. The additional business is not expected to affect the domestic sales of Product M, and the additional units could be produced during the current year, using existing capacity. (a) Prepare a differential analysis report of the proposed sale to Wong Inc. (b) Based upon the differential analysis report in part (a), should the proposal be accepted?

Solution

1. $160,000 ($1,600,000 × 10%)

2. a. Total costs:

Variable ($25 × 80,000 units)	$2,000,000
Fixed ($800,000 + $400,000)	1,200,000
Total	$3,200,000

Cost amount per unit: $3,200,000/80,000 units = $40.00

b. Markup Percentage = $\dfrac{\text{Desired Profit}}{\text{Total Costs}}$

Markup Percentage = $\dfrac{\$160,000}{\$3,200,000}$ = 5%

c.

Cost amount per unit	$40.00
Markup ($40 × 5%)	2.00
Selling price	$42.00

3. a. Total manufacturing costs:

Variable ($20 × 80,000 units)	$1,600,000
Fixed factory overhead	800,000
Total	$2,400,000

Cost amount per unit: $2,400,000/80,000 units = $30.00

b. Markup Percentage = $\dfrac{\text{Desired Profit} + \text{Total Selling and Administrative Expenses}}{\text{Total Manufacturing Costs}}$

Markup Percentage = $\dfrac{\$160,000 + \$400,000 + (\$5 \times 80,000 \text{ units})}{\$2,400,000}$

Markup Percentage = $\dfrac{\$160,000 + \$400,000 + \$400,000}{\$2,400,000}$

Markup Percentage = $\dfrac{\$960,000}{\$2,400,000}$ = 40%

c.

Cost amount per unit	$30.00
Markup ($30 × 40%)	12.00
Selling price	$42.00

4. a. Variable cost amount per unit: $25
Total variable costs: $25 × 80,000 units = $2,000,000

b. Markup Percentage = $\dfrac{\text{Desired Profit} + \text{Total Fixed Costs}}{\text{Total Variable Costs}}$

Markup Percentage = $\dfrac{\$160,000 + \$800,000 + \$400,000}{\$2,000,000}$

Markup Percentage = $\dfrac{\$1,360,000}{\$2,000,000}$ = 68%

c.

Cost amount per unit	$25.00
Markup ($25 × 68%)	17.00
Selling price	$42.00

5. a.

Proposal to Sell to Wong Inc.

Differential revenue from accepting offer:	
Revenue from sale of 4,000 additional units at $28	$112,000
Differential cost from accepting offer:	
Variable production costs of 4,000 additional units at $20	80,000
Differential income from accepting offer	$ 32,000

b. The proposal should be accepted.

Self-Examination Questions

1. Marlo Company is considering discontinuing a product. The costs of the product consist of $20,000 fixed costs and $15,000 variable costs. The variable operating expenses related to the product total $4,000. What is the differential cost?
   A. $19,000   C. $35,000
   B. $15,000   D. $39,000

2. Victor Company is considering disposing of equipment that was originally purchased for $200,000 and has $150,000 of accumulated depreciation to date. The same equipment would cost $310,000 to replace. What is the sunk cost?
   A. $50,000   C. $200,000
   B. $150,000   D. $310,000

3. Henry Company is considering spending $100,000 for a new grinding machine. This amount could be invested to yield a 12% return. What is the opportunity cost?
   A. $112,000   C. $12,000
   B. $88,000   D. $100,000

4. For which cost concept used in applying the cost-plus approach to product pricing are fixed manufacturing costs, fixed selling and administrative expenses, and desired profit allowed for in determining the markup?
   A. Total cost   C. Variable cost
   B. Product cost   D. Standard cost

5. Mendosa Company produces three products. All the products use a furnace operation, which is a production bottleneck. The following information is available:

	Product 1	Product 2	Product 3
Unit volume—March	1,000	1,500	1,000
Per-unit information:			
Sales price	$35	$33	$29
Variable cost	15	15	15
Unit contribution margin	$20	$18	$14
Furnace hours	4	3	2

From a profitability perspective, which product should be emphasized in April's advertising campaign?
A. Product 1   C. Product 3
B. Product 2   D. All three

Eye Openers

1. Explain the meaning of (a) differential revenue, (b) differential cost, and (c) differential income.
2. It was reported that Exabyte Corporation, a fast growing Colorado marketer of backup tape drives, has decided to purchase key components of its product from others. For example, Sony Corporation of America provides Exabyte with mechanical decks, and Solectron Corporation provides circuit boards. A former chief executive officer of Exabyte stated, "If we'd tried to build our own plants, we could never have grown that fast or maybe survived." The decision to purchase key product components is an example of what type of decision illustrated in this chapter?
3. In the long run, the normal selling price must be set high enough to cover what factors?
4. A company could sell a building for $250,000 or lease it for $2,500 per month. What would need to be considered in determining if the lease option would be preferred?
5. A chemical company has a commodity-grade and premium-grade product. Why might the company elect to process the commodity-grade product further to the premium-grade product?
6. A company accepts incremental business at a special price that exceeds the variable cost. What other issues must the company consider in deciding whether to accept the business?
7. A company fabricates a component at a cost of $6.00. A supplier offers to supply the same component for $5.50. Under what circumstances is it reasonable to purchase from the supplier?

8. Many fast food restaurant chains, such as McDonald's, will occasionally discontinue restaurants in their system. What are some financial considerations in deciding to eliminate a store?
9. Why might the use of ideal standards in applying the cost-plus approach to product pricing lead to setting product prices that are too low?

10. Although the cost-plus approach to product pricing may be used by management as a general guideline, what are some examples of other factors that managers should also consider in setting product prices?
11. What method of determining product cost may be appropriate in settings where the manufacturing process is complex?
12. How does the target cost concept differ from cost-plus approaches?
13. Under what circumstances is it appropriate to use the target cost concept?
14. What is a production bottleneck?
15. What is the appropriate measure of a product's value when a firm is operating under production bottlenecks?

Practice Exercises

PE 24-1A
Lease or sell decision
obj. 1

Monroe Company owns equipment with a cost of $235,000 and accumulated depreciation of $185,000 that can be sold for $120,000, less a 4% sales commission. Alternatively, the equipment can be leased by Monroe Company for five years for a total of $135,000 at the end of which there is no salvage value. In addition, repair, insurance, and property tax that would be incurred by Monroe Company on the equipment would total $16,000 over the five years. Determine the differential income or loss from the lease alternative for Monroe Company.

PE 24-1B
Lease or sell decision
obj. 1

Stein Company owns a truck with a cost of $80,000 and accumulated depreciation of $50,000 that can be sold for $25,000, less a 5% sales commission. Alternatively, the truck can be leased by Stein Company for three years for a total of $30,000 at the end of which there is no salvage value. In addition, repair, insurance, and property tax that would be incurred by Stein Company on the truck would total $9,000 over the three years. Determine the differential income or loss from the lease alternative for Stein Company.

PE 24-2A
Discontinue a segment decision
obj. 1

Product J has revenue of $340,000, variable cost of goods sold of $290,000, variable selling expenses of $64,000, and fixed costs of $100,000, creating a loss from operations of $114,000.
a. Determine the differential income or loss from sales of Product J.
b. Should Product J be discontinued?

PE 24-2B
Discontinue a segment decision
obj. 1

Product T has revenue of $56,000, variable cost of goods sold of $40,000, variable selling expenses of $6,000, and fixed costs of $15,000, creating a loss from operations of $5,000.
a. Determine the differential income or loss from sales of Product T.
b. Should Product T be discontinued?

PE 24-3A
Make-or-buy decision
obj. 1

A company manufactures various sized plastic bottles for its medicinal product. The manufacturing cost for small bottles is $45 per unit (1,000 bottles), including fixed costs of $12 per unit. A proposal is offered to purchase small bottles from an outside source for $36 per unit, plus $4 per unit for freight. Provide a differential analysis of the outside purchase proposal.

PE 24-3B
Make-or-buy decision
obj. 1

A restaurant bakes its own bread for $150 per unit (100 loaves), including fixed costs of $25 per unit. A proposal is offered to purchase bread from an outside source for $110 per unit, plus $10 per unit for delivery. Provide a differential analysis of the outside purchase proposal.

PE 24-4A
Replace equipment decision
obj. 1

A machine with a book value of $186,000 has an estimated six-year life. A proposal is offered to sell the old machine for $165,000 and replace it with a new machine at a cost of $320,000. The new machine has a six-year life with no salvage value. The new machine would reduce annual direct labor costs by $24,000. Provide a differential analysis on the proposal to replace the machine.

PE 24-4B
Replace equipment decision
obj. 1

A machine with a book value of $49,000 has an estimated five-year life. A proposal is offered to sell the old machine for $30,000 and replace it with a new machine at a cost of $64,000. The new machine has a five-year life with no salvage value. The new machine would reduce annual direct labor costs by $8,000. Provide a differential analysis on the proposal to replace the machine.

PE 24-5A
Process or sell decision
obj. 1

Product L is produced for $1.85 per gallon including a $0.90 per gallon fixed cost. Product L can be sold without additional processing for $2.20 per gallon, or processed further into Product P at an additional cost of $0.80 per gallon, including a $0.30 per gallon fixed cost. Product P can be sold for $2.80 per gallon. Provide a differential analysis for further processing into Product P.

PE 24-5B
Process or sell decision
obj. 1

Product X is produced for $24 per pound including a $9 per pound fixed cost. Product X can be sold without additional processing for $30 per pound, or processed further into Product Y at an additional cost of $5 per pound, including a $1.50 per pound fixed cost. Product Y can be sold for $33 per pound. Provide a differential analysis for further processing into Product Y.

PE 24-6A
Accept business at a special price
obj. 1

Product N is normally sold for $58 per unit. A special price of $45 is offered for the export market. The variable production cost is $31 per unit. An additional export tariff of 20% of revenue must be paid for all export products. Determine the differential income or loss per unit from selling Product N for export.

PE 24-6B
Accept business at a special price
obj. 1

Product S is normally sold for $13 per unit. A special price of $9 is offered for the export market. The variable production cost is $7 per unit. An additional export tariff of 30% of revenue must be paid for all export products. Determine the differential income or loss per unit from selling Product S for export.

PE 24-7A
Markup percentage on total cost
obj. 2

Green Thumb Inc. produces and sells home and garden tools and equipment. A lawn mower has a total cost of $140 per unit of which $110 is product cost and $30 is selling and administrative expenses. In addition, the total cost of $140 is made up of $125 variable cost and $15 fixed cost. The desired profit is $14 per unit. Determine the markup percentage on total cost.

PE 24-7B
Markup percentage on total cost
obj. 2

Nova Corp. produces and sells lighting fixtures. An entry light has a total cost of $50 per unit of which $36 is product cost and $14 is selling and administrative expenses. In addition, the total cost of $50 is made up of $30 variable cost and $20 fixed cost. The desired profit is $10 per unit. Determine the markup percentage on total cost.

PE 24-8A
Markup percentage on product cost
obj. 2

Green Thumb Inc. produces and sells home and garden tools and equipment. A lawn mower has a total cost of $140 per unit of which $110 is product cost and $30 is selling and administrative expenses. In addition, the total cost of $140 is made up of $125 variable cost and $15 fixed cost. The desired profit is $14 per unit. Determine the markup percentage on product cost.

PE 24-8B
Markup percentage on product cost
obj. 2

Nova Corp. produces and sells lighting fixtures. An entry light has a total cost of $50 per unit of which $36 is product cost and $14 is selling and administrative expenses. In addition, the total cost of $50 is made up of $30 variable cost and $20 fixed cost. The desired profit is $10 per unit. Determine the markup percentage on product cost. Round to one decimal place.

PE 24-9A
Markup percentage on variable cost
obj. 2

Green Thumb Inc. produces and sells home and garden tools and equipment. A lawn mower has a total cost of $140 per unit of which $110 is product cost and $30 is selling and administrative expenses. In addition, the total cost of $140 is made up of $125 variable cost and $15 fixed cost. The desired profit is $14 per unit. Determine the markup percentage on variable cost.

PE 24-9B
Markup percentage on variable cost
obj. 2

Nova Corp. produces and sells lighting fixtures. An entry light has a total cost of $50 per unit of which $36 is product cost and $14 is selling and administrative expenses. In addition, the total cost of $50 is made up of $30 variable cost and $20 fixed cost. The desired profit is $10 per unit. Determine the markup percentage on variable cost.

PE 24-10A
Bottleneck profitability
obj. 3

Product E has a unit contribution margin of $24. Product F has a unit contribution margin of $30. Product E requires three furnace hours, while Product F requires six furnace hours. Determine the most profitable product assuming the furnace is a constraint.

PE 24-10B
Bottleneck profitability
obj. 3

Product S has a unit contribution margin of $100. Product T has a unit contribution margin of $80. Product S requires 10 testing hours, while Product T requires four testing hours. Determine the most profitable product assuming the testing is a constraint.

Exercises

EX 24-1
Lease or sell decision
obj. 1

✓ a. Differential revenue
from lease, $30,000

Vanderhoff Construction Company is considering selling excess machinery with a book value of $260,000 (original cost of $380,000 less accumulated depreciation of $120,000) for $210,000, less a 4% brokerage commission. Alternatively, the machinery can be leased for a total of $240,000 for five years, after which it is expected to have no residual value. During the period of the lease, Vanderhoff Construction Company's costs of repairs, insurance, and property tax expenses are expected to be $28,000.

a. Prepare a differential analysis report, dated January 3, 2008, for the lease or sell decision.
b. ▬▬▶ On the basis of the data presented, would it be advisable to lease or sell the machinery? Explain.

EX 24-2
Differential analysis report for a discontinued product
obj. 1

✓ a. Differential cost of
annual sales, $299,400

A condensed income statement by product line for Canadian Beverage Inc. indicated the following for Lemon Mist for the past year:

Sales	$362,000
Cost of goods sold	185,000
Gross profit	$177,000
Operating expenses	215,000
Loss from operations	$ (38,000)

It is estimated that 23% of the cost of goods sold represents fixed factory overhead costs and that 27% of the operating expenses are fixed. Since Lemon Mist is only one of many products, the fixed costs will not be materially affected if the product is discontinued.

a. Prepare a differential analysis report, dated January 3, 2008, for the proposed discontinuance of Lemon Mist.
b. ▬▬▶ Should Lemon Mist be retained? Explain.

EX 24-3
Differential analysis report for a discontinued product
obj. 1

✓ a. Differential income:
bowls, $46,450

The condensed product-line income statement for Country Ceramics Company for the current year is as follows:

Country Ceramics Company
Product-Line Income Statement
For the Year Ended December 31, 2008

	Bowls	Plates	Cups
Sales	$132,000	$108,000	$83,000
Cost of goods sold	71,000	55,000	49,000
Gross profit	$ 61,000	$ 53,000	$34,000
Selling and administrative expenses	35,000	24,000	38,000
Income from operations	$ 26,000	$ 29,000	$ (4,000)

(continued)

Fixed costs are 15% of the cost of goods sold and 28% of the selling and administrative expenses. Country Ceramics assumes that fixed costs would not be materially affected if the Cups line were discontinued.

a. Prepare a differential analysis report for all three products for 2008.
b. ▬▬▶ Should the Cups line be retained? Explain.

EX 24-4
Segment analysis, Charles Schwab Corporation
obj. 1

The Charles Schwab Corporation is one of the more innovative brokerage and financial service companies in the United States. The company recently provided information about its major business segments as follows (in millions):

	Individual Investor	Institutional Investor	U.S. Trust
Revenues	$2,742	$803	$832
Income from operations	758	317	103
Depreciation	145	29	33

a. ▬▬▶ How do you believe Schwab defines the difference between the "Individual Investor" and "Institutional Investor" segments?
b. Provide a specific example of a variable and fixed cost in the "Individual Investor" segment.
c. Estimate the contribution margin for each segment.
d. If Schwab decided to sell its "Institutional Investor" accounts to another company, estimate how much operating income would decline.

EX 24-5
Decision to discontinue a product
obj. 1

On the basis of the following data, the general manager of Feet to Go Inc. decided to discontinue Children's Shoes because it reduced income from operations by $26,000. What is the flaw in this decision?

Feet to Go Inc.
Product-Line Income Statement
For the Year Ended August 31, 2008

	Children's Shoes	Men's Shoes	Women's Shoes	Total
Sales	$150,000	$300,000	$500,000	$950,000
Costs of goods sold:				
Variable costs	$ 90,000	$150,000	$220,000	$460,000
Fixed costs	40,000	60,000	120,000	220,000
Total cost of goods sold	$130,000	$210,000	$340,000	$680,000
Gross profit	$ 20,000	$ 90,000	$160,000	$270,000
Selling and adminstrative expenses:				
Variable selling and admin. expenses	$ 30,000	$ 45,000	$ 95,000	$170,000
Fixed selling and admin. expenses	16,000	20,000	25,000	61,000
Total selling and admin. expenses	$ 46,000	$ 65,000	$120,000	$231,000
Income (loss) from operations	$ (26,000)	$ 25,000	$ 40,000	$ 39,000

EX 24-6
Make-or-buy decision
obj. 1

✓a. Cost savings from making, $3.00 per case

Hart Computer Company has been purchasing carrying cases for its portable computers at a delivered cost of $68 per unit. The company, which is currently operating below full capacity, charges factory overhead to production at the rate of 35% of direct labor cost. The fully absorbed unit costs to produce comparable carrying cases are expected to be:

Direct materials	$25.00
Direct labor	32.00
Factory overhead (35% of direct labor)	11.20
Total cost per unit	$68.20

If Hart Computer Company manufactures the carrying cases, fixed factory overhead costs will not increase and variable factory overhead costs associated with the cases are expected to be 25% of the direct labor costs.

a. Prepare a differential analysis report, dated June 5, 2008, for the make-or-buy decision.
b. ▬▬▶ On the basis of the data presented, would it be advisable to make the carrying cases or to continue buying them? Explain.

EX 24-7
Make-or-buy decision

obj. 1

The Association of Retired Educators (ARE) employs five people in its Publication Department. These people lay out pages for pamphlets, brochures, and other publications for the ARE membership. The pages are delivered to an outside company for printing. The company is considering an outside publication service for the layout work. The outside service is quoting a price of $18 per layout page. The budget for the Publication Department for 2008 is as follows:

Salaries	$225,000
Benefits	38,000
Supplies	32,000
Office expenses	25,000
Office depreciation	22,000
Computer depreciation	30,000
Total	$372,000

The department expects to lay out 17,500 pages for 2008. The computers used by the department have an estimated salvage value of $5,000. The Publication Department office space would be used for future administrative needs, if the department's function were purchased from the outside.

a. Prepare a differential analysis report, dated December 15, 2007, for the make-or-buy decision, considering the 2008 differential revenues and costs.
b. ▬▬▶ On the basis of your analysis in part (a), should the page layout work be purchased from an outside company?
c. ▬▬▶ What additional considerations might factor into the decision making?

EX 24-8
Machine replacement decision

obj. 1

✓a. Annual differential income, $12,250

A company is considering replacing an old piece of machinery, which cost $560,000 and has $320,000 of accumulated depreciation to date, with a new machine that costs $460,000. The old equipment could be sold for $78,000. The variable production costs associated with the old machine are estimated to be $170,000 for eight years. The variable production costs for the new machine are estimated to be $110,000 for eight years.

a. Determine the total and annualized differential income or loss anticipated from replacing the old machine.
b. What is the sunk cost in this situation?

EX 24-9
Differential analysis report for machine replacement

obj. 1

✓a. Annual differential increase in costs, $2,500

Bay Area Electronics Company assembles circuit boards by using a manually operated machine to insert electronic components. The original cost of the machine is $140,000, the accumulated depreciation is $110,000, its remaining useful life is 15 years, and its salvage value is negligible. On January 20, 2008, a proposal was made to replace the present manufacturing procedure with a fully automatic machine that will cost $270,000. The automatic machine has an estimated useful life of 15 years and no significant salvage value. For use in evaluating the proposal, the accountant accumulated the following annual data on present and proposed operations:

	Present Operations	Proposed Operations
Sales	$275,000	$275,000
Direct materials	$ 80,000	$ 80,000
Direct labor	45,000	—
Power and maintenance	7,500	32,000
Taxes, insurance, etc.	3,500	8,500
Selling and administrative expenses	80,000	80,000
Total expenses	$216,000	$200,500

a. Prepare a differential analysis report for the proposal to replace the machine. Include in the analysis both the net differential change in costs anticipated over the 15 years and the net annual differential change in costs anticipated.
b. Based only on the data presented, should the proposal be accepted?
c. ▬▬▶ What are some of the other factors that should be considered before a final decision is made?

EX 24-10
Sell or process further
obj. 1
✓a. $225

Oregon Lumber Company incurs a cost of $465 per hundred board feet in processing certain "rough-cut" lumber, which it sells for $625 per hundred board feet. An alternative is to produce a "finished cut" at a total processing cost of $545 per hundred board feet, which can be sold for $850 per hundred board feet. What is the amount of (a) the differential revenue, (b) differential cost, and (c) differential income for processing rough-cut lumber into finished cut?

EX 24-11
Sell or process further
obj. 1

Golden Roast Coffee Company produces Columbian coffee in batches of 7,700 pounds. The standard quantity of materials required in the process is 7,700 pounds, which cost $5.00 per pound. Columbian coffee can be sold without further processing for $8.90 per pound. Columbian coffee can also be processed further to yield Decaf Columbian, which can be sold for $11.60 per pound. The processing into Decaf Columbian requires additional processing costs of $18,326 per batch. The additional processing will also cause a 6% loss of product due to evaporation.

a. Prepare a differential analysis report for the decision to sell or process further.
b. Should Golden Roast sell Columbian coffee or process further and sell Decaf Columbian?
c. Determine the price of Decaf Columbian that would cause neither an advantage or disadvantage for processing further and selling Decaf Columbian.

EX 24-12
Decision on accepting additional business
obj. 1
✓a. Differential income, $112,000

Workman's Denim Co. has an annual plant capacity of 65,000 units, and current production is 45,000 units. Monthly fixed costs are $40,000, and variable costs are $24 per unit. The present selling price is $36 per unit. On January 18, 2008, the company received an offer from Marshall Company for 16,000 units of the product at $31 each. Marshall Company will market the units in a foreign country under its own brand name. The additional business is not expected to affect the domestic selling price or quantity of sales of Workman's Denim Co.

a. Prepare a differential analysis report for the proposed sale to Marshall Company.
b. Briefly explain the reason why accepting this additional business will increase operating income.
c. What is the minimum price per unit that would produce a contribution margin?

(handwritten margin note: +operating less than capacity)

EX 24-13
Accepting business at a special price
obj. 1

Jupiter Company expects to operate at 90% of productive capacity during May. The total manufacturing costs for May for the production of 25,000 batteries are budgeted as follows:

Direct materials	$272,000
Direct labor	96,000
Variable factory overhead	32,000
Fixed factory overhead	54,000
Total manufacturing costs	$454,000

The company has an opportunity to submit a bid for 1,000 batteries to be delivered by May 31 to a government agency. If the contract is obtained, it is anticipated that the additional activity will not interfere with normal production during May or increase the selling or administrative expenses. What is the unit cost below which Jupiter Company should not go in bidding on the government contract?

EX 24-14
Decision on accepting additional business
obj. 1

✓a. Differential revenue, $1,500,000

Sure-Grip Tire and Rubber Company has capacity to produce 170,000 tires. Sure-Grip presently produces and sells 130,000 tires for the North American market at a price of $90 per tire. Sure-Grip is evaluating a special order from a European automobile company, Continental Motors. Continental is offering to buy 25,000 tires for $60 per tire. Sure-Grip's accounting system indicates that the total cost per tire is as follows:

Direct materials	$26
Direct labor	9
Factory overhead (35% variable)	22
Selling and administrative expenses (40% variable)	18
Total	$75

Sure-Grip pays a selling commission equal to 5% of the selling price on North American orders, which is included in the variable portion of the selling and administrative expenses. However, this special order would not have a sales commission. If the order was accepted, the tires would be shipped overseas for an additional shipping cost of $6.00 per tire. In addition, Continental has made the order conditional on receiving European safety certification. Sure-Grip estimates that this certification would cost $110,000.

a. Prepare a differential analysis report dated August 4, 2008, for the proposed sale to Continental Motors.
b. What is the minimum price per unit that would be financially acceptable to Sure-Grip?

EX 24-15
Total cost concept of product costing
obj. 2

✓ *d. $340*

Sirrus Phone Company uses the total cost concept of applying the cost-plus approach to product pricing. The costs of producing and selling 3,500 units of mobile phones are as follows:

Variable costs:		Fixed costs:	
Direct materials	$130.00 per unit	Factory overhead	$175,000
Direct labor	50.00	Selling and adm. exp.	70,000
Factory overhead	35.00		
Selling and adm. exp.	25.00		
Total	$240.00 per unit		

Sirrus desires a profit equal to a 30% rate of return on invested assets of $350,000.

a. Determine the amount of desired profit from the production and sale of mobile phones.
b. Determine the total costs and the cost amount per unit for the production and sale of 3,500 units of mobile phones.
c. Determine the markup percentage (rounded to two decimal places) for mobile phones.
d. Determine the selling price of mobile phones. Round to the nearest dollar.

EX 24-16
Product cost concept of product pricing
obj. 2

✓ *b. 28.30%*

Based on the data presented in Exercise 24-15, assume that Sirrus Phone Company uses the product cost concept of applying the cost-plus approach to product pricing.

a. Determine the total manufacturing costs and the cost amount per unit for the production and sale of 3,500 units of mobile phones.
b. Determine the markup percentage (rounded to two decimal places) for mobile phones.
c. Determine the selling price of mobile phones. Round to the nearest dollar.

EX 24-17
Variable cost concept of product pricing
obj. 2

✓ *b. 41.67%*

Based on the data presented in Exercise 24-15, assume that Sirrus Phone Company uses the variable cost concept of applying the cost-plus approach to product pricing.

a. Determine the variable costs and the cost amount per unit for the production and sale of 3,500 units of mobile phones.
b. Determine the markup percentage (rounded to two decimal places) for mobile phones.
c. Determine the selling price of mobile phones. Round to the nearest dollar.

EX 24-18
Target costing
obj. 2

Toyota Motor Corporation uses target costing. Assume that Toyota marketing personnel estimate that the competitive selling price for the Camry in the upcoming model year will need to be $34,000. Assume further that the Camry's total manufacturing cost for the upcoming model year is estimated to be $28,500 and that Toyota requires a 20% profit margin on selling price (which is equivalent to a 25% markup on product cost).

a. What price will Toyota establish for the Camry for the upcoming model year?
b. ⊏⊐➤ What impact will target costing have on Toyota, given the assumed information?

EX 24-19
Target costing
obj. 2

✓ *b. $25*

Spectrum Imaging Company manufactures color laser printers. Model A200 presently sells for $300 and has a total product cost of $250, as follows:

(continued)

Direct materials	$170
Direct labor	50
Factory overhead	30
Total	$250

It is estimated that the competitive selling price for color laser printers of this type will drop to $270 next year. Spectrum Imaging has established a target cost to maintain its historical markup percentage on product cost. Engineers have provided the following cost reduction ideas:

1. Purchase a plastic printer cover with snap-on assembly. This will reduce the amount of direct labor by six minutes per unit.
2. Add an inspection step that will add three minutes per unit of direct labor but reduce the materials cost by $6 per unit.
3. Decrease the cycle time of the injection molding machine from four minutes to three minutes per part. Thirty percent of the direct labor and 42% of the factory overhead is related to running injection molding machines.

The direct labor rate is $32 per hour.

a. Determine the target cost for Model A200 assuming that the historical markup on product cost is maintained.
b. Determine the required cost reduction.
c. Evaluate the three engineering improvements to determine if the required cost reduction (drift) can be achieved.

EX 24-20
Product decisions under bottlenecked operations

obj. **3**

Samson Metals Inc. has three grades of metal product, Type 5, Type 10, and Type 20. Financial data for the three grades are as follows:

	Type 5	Type 10	Type 20
Revenues	$16,000	$20,800	$12,000
Variable cost	$ 6,000	$ 8,000	$ 5,000
Fixed cost	4,000	4,000	4,000
Total cost	$10,000	$12,000	$ 9,000
Income from operations	$ 6,000	$ 8,800	$ 3,000
Number of units	/ 4,000	/ 4,000	/ 4,000
Income from operations per unit	$ 1.50	$ 2.20	$ 0.75

Samson's operations require all three grades to be melted in a furnace before being formed. The furnace runs 24 hours a day, 7 days a week, and is a production bottleneck. The furnace hours required per unit of each product are as follows:

Type 5:   5 hours
Type 10: 10 hours
Type 20:   5 hours

The Marketing Department is considering a new marketing and sales campaign.
Which product should be emphasized in the marketing and sales campaign in order to maximize profitability?

EX 24-21
Product decisions under bottlenecked operations

obj. **3**

✓ a. Total income from operations, $115,000

Gannett Glass Company manufactures three types of safety plate glass: large, medium, and small. All three products have high demand. Thus, Gannett Glass is able to sell all the safety glass that it can make. The production process includes an autoclave operation, which is a pressurized heat treatment. The autoclave is a production bottleneck. Total fixed costs are $550,000. In addition, the following information is available about the three products:

	Large	Medium	Small
Unit selling price	$240	$180	$120
Unit variable cost	126	80	68
Unit contribution margin	$114	$100	$ 52

	Large	Medium	Small
Autoclave hours per unit	6	10	4
Total process hours per unit	20	16	12
Budgeted units of production	2,500	2,500	2,500

a. Determine the contribution margin by glass type and the total company income from operations for the budgeted units of production.

b. Prepare an analysis showing which product is the most profitable per bottleneck hour.

EX 24-22
Product pricing under bottlenecked operations
obj. 3

✓ *Medium, $270*

Based on the data presented in Exercise 24-21, assume that Gannett Glass wanted to price all products so that they produced the same profit potential as the highest profit product. Thus, determine the prices for each of the products so that they would produce a profit equal to the highest profit product.

Problems Series A

PR 24-1A
Differential analysis report involving opportunity costs
obj. 1

On July 1, Daybreak Stores Inc. is considering leasing a building and purchasing the necessary equipment to operate a retail store. Alternatively, the company could use the funds to invest in $280,000 of 5% U.S. Treasury bonds that mature in 20 years. The bonds could be purchased at face value. The following data have been assembled:

Cost of store equipment	$280,000
Life of store equipment	20 years
Estimated residual value of store equipment	$20,000
Yearly costs to operate the store, excluding depreciation of store equipment	$70,000
Yearly expected revenues—years 1–10	$88,000
Yearly expected revenues—years 11–20	$96,000

Instructions

1. Prepare a report as of July 1, 2008, presenting a differential analysis of the proposed operation of the store for the 20 years as compared with present conditions.

2. Based on the results disclosed by the differential analysis, should the proposal be accepted?

3. If the proposal is accepted, what would be the total estimated income from operations of the store for the 20 years?

PR 24-2A
Differential analysis report for machine replacement proposal
obj. 1

Quebec Printing Company is considering replacing a machine that has been used in its factory for four years. Relevant data associated with the operations of the old machine and the new machine, neither of which has any estimated residual value, are as follows:

Old Machine

Cost of machine, 10-year life	$360,000
Annual depreciation (straight-line)	36,000
Annual manufacturing costs, excluding depreciation	325,000
Annual nonmanufacturing operating expenses	215,000
Annual revenue	740,000
Current estimated selling price of machine	210,000

New Machine

Cost of machine, 6-year life	$410,000
Annual depreciation (straight-line)	68,333
Estimated annual manufacturing costs, exclusive of depreciation	284,000

Annual nonmanufacturing operating expenses and revenue are not expected to be affected by purchase of the new machine.

Instructions

1. Prepare a differential analysis report as of October 13, 2008, comparing operations utilizing the new machine with operations using the present equipment. The analysis should indicate the total differential income that would result over the 6-year period if the new machine is acquired.
2. ➤ List other factors that should be considered before a final decision is reached.

PR 24-3A
Differential analysis report for sales promotion proposal

obj. 1

✓1. Moisturizer differential income, $163,000

Cleopatra Cosmetics Company is planning a one-month campaign for May to promote sales of one of its two cosmetics products. A total of $110,000 has been budgeted for advertising, contests, redeemable coupons, and other promotional activities. The following data have been assembled for their possible usefulness in deciding which of the products to select for the campaign:

	Moisturizer	Perfume
Unit selling price	$56	$75
Unit production costs:		
Direct materials	$10	$14
Direct labor	5	8
Variable factory overhead	3	5
Fixed factory overhead	8	8
Total unit production costs	$26	$35
Unit variable selling expenses	12	18
Unit fixed selling expenses	4	2
Total unit costs	$42	$55
Operating income per unit	$14	$20

No increase in facilities would be necessary to produce and sell the increased output. It is anticipated that 10,500 additional units of moisturizer or 8,000 additional units of perfume could be sold without changing the unit selling price of either product.

Instructions

1. Prepare a differential analysis report as of April 15, 2008, presenting the additional revenue and additional costs anticipated from the promotion of moisturizer and perfume.
2. ➤ The sales manager had tentatively decided to promote perfume, estimating that operating income would be increased by $50,000 ($20 operating income per unit for 8,000 units, less promotion expenses of $110,000). The manager also believed that the selection of moisturizer would have less of an impact on operating income, $37,000 ($14 operating income per unit for 10,500 units, less promotion expenses of $110,000). State briefly your reasons for supporting or opposing the tentative decision.

PR 24-4A
Differential analysis report for further processing

obj. 1

✓1. Differential revenue, $9,800

The management of Delta Sugar Company is considering whether to process further raw sugar into refined sugar. Refined sugar can be sold for $1.75 per pound, and raw sugar can be sold without further processing for $1.05 per pound. Raw sugar is produced in batches of 24,000 pounds by processing 90,000 pounds of sugar cane, which costs $0.25 per pound. Refined sugar will require additional processing costs of $0.36 per pound of raw sugar, and 1.2 pounds of raw sugar will produce 1 pound of refined sugar.

Instructions

1. Prepare a report as of August 30, 2008, presenting a differential analysis of the further processing of raw sugar to produce refined sugar.
2. ➤ Briefly report your recommendations.

PR 24-5A
Product pricing using the cost-plus approach concepts; differential analysis report for accepting additional business

objs. 1, 2

Plasma Labs Inc. recently began production of a new product, flat panel displays, which required the investment of $3,000,000 in assets. The costs of producing and selling 20,000 units of flat panel displays are estimated as follows:

✓2. b. Markup
percentage, 6%

Variable costs per unit:		Fixed costs:	
Direct materials	$150	Factory overhead	$2,000,000
Direct labor	30	Selling and administrative expenses	1,000,000
Factory overhead	50		
Selling and administrative expenses	20		
Total	$250		

Plasma Labs Inc. is currently considering establishing a selling price for flat panel displays. The president of Plasma Labs has decided to use the cost-plus approach to product pricing and has indicated that the displays must earn a 16% rate of return on invested assets.

Instructions
1. Determine the amount of desired profit from the production and sale of flat panel displays.
2. Assuming that the total cost concept is used, determine (a) the cost amount per unit, (b) the markup percentage, and (c) the selling price of flat panel displays.
3. Assuming that the product cost concept is used, determine (a) the cost amount per unit, (b) the markup percentage (rounded to two decimal places), and (c) the selling price of flat panel displays (rounded to nearest whole dollar).
4. Assuming that the variable cost concept is used, determine (a) the cost amount per unit, (b) the markup percentage, and (c) the selling price of flat panel displays.
5. ▬▬▶ Comment on any additional considerations that could influence establishing the selling price for flat panel displays.
6. Assume that as of September 1, 2008, 13,000 units of flat panel displays have been produced and sold during the current year. Analysis of the domestic market indicates that 4,400 additional units are expected to be sold during the remainder of the year at the normal product price determined under the total cost concept. On September 3, Plasma Labs Inc. received an offer from Vision Systems Inc. for 2,600 units of flat panel displays at $255 each. Vision Systems Inc. will market the units in Canada under its own brand name, and no selling and administrative expenses associated with the sale will be incurred by Plasma Labs Inc. The additional business is not expected to affect the domestic sales of flat panel displays, and the additional units could be produced using existing capacity.
   a. Prepare a differential analysis report of the proposed sale to Vision Systems Inc.
   b. Based upon the differential analysis report in part (a), should the proposal be accepted?

PR 24-6A
*Product pricing and
profit analysis with
bottleneck operations*

objs. 1, 3

✓1. High Grade,
$125

Atlas Steel Company produces three grades of steel: high, good, and regular grade. Each of these products (grades) has high demand in the market, and Atlas is able to sell as much as it can produce of all three. The furnace operation is a bottleneck in the process and is running at 100% of capacity. Atlas wants to improve steel operation profitability. The variable conversion cost is $6 per process hour. The fixed cost is $1,530,000. In addition, the cost analyst was able to determine the following information about the three products:

	High Grade	Good Grade	Regular Grade
Budgeted units produced	6,000	6,000	6,000
Total process hours per unit	15	15	12
Furnace hours per unit	5	3	2
Unit selling price	$375	$350	$320
Direct materials cost per unit	$160	$140	$130

The furnace operation is part of the total process for each of these three products. Thus, for example, 5 of the 15 hours required to process High Grade steel are associated with the furnace.

Instructions
1. Determine the unit contribution margin for each product.
2. Provide an analysis to determine the relative product profitabilities, assuming that the furnace is a bottleneck.
3. Assume that management wishes to improve profitability by increasing prices on selected products. At what price would High and Good grades need to be offered in order to produce the same relative profitability as Regular Grade steel?

Problems Series B

PR 24-1B
*Differential analysis
report involving
opportunity costs*

obj. 1

On December 1, Open Gate Distribution Company is considering leasing a building and buying the necessary equipment to operate a public warehouse. Alternatively, the company could use the funds to invest in $800,000 of 7% U.S. Treasury bonds that mature in 14 years. The bonds could be purchased at face value. The following data have been assembled:

Cost of equipment	$800,000
Life of equipment	14 years
Estimated residual value of equipment	$170,000
Yearly costs to operate the warehouse, excluding	
depreciation of equipment	$105,000
Yearly expected revenues—years 1–7	$250,000
Yearly expected revenues—years 8–14	$190,000

Instructions

1. Prepare a report as of December 1, 2008, presenting a differential analysis of the proposed operation of the warehouse for the 14 years as compared with present conditions.
2. Based on the results disclosed by the differential analysis, should the proposal be accepted?
3. If the proposal is accepted, what is the total estimated income from operations of the warehouse for the 14 years?

PR 24-2B
*Differential analysis
report for machine
replacement proposal*

obj. 1

Saginaw Tooling Company is considering replacing a machine that has been used in its factory for two years. Relevant data associated with the operations of the old machine and the new machine, neither of which has any estimated residual value, are as follows:

Old Machine	
Cost of machine, 8-year life	$ 96,000
Annual depreciation (straight-line)	12,000
Annual manufacturing costs, excluding depreciation	26,000
Annual nonmanufacturing operating expenses	9,500
Annual revenue	45,000
Current estimated selling price of the machine	58,000

New Machine	
Cost of machine, 6-year life	$126,000
Annual depreciation (straight-line)	21,000
Estimated annual manufacturing costs, exclusive of depreciation	9,000

Annual nonmanufacturing operating expenses and revenue are not expected to be affected by purchase of the new machine.

Instructions

1. Prepare a differential analysis report as of March 22, 2008, comparing operations utilizing the new machine with operations using the present equipment. The analysis should indicate the differential income that would result over the 6-year period if the new machine is acquired.
2. List other factors that should be considered before a final decision is reached.

PR 24-3B
*Differential analysis
report for sales
promotion proposal*

obj. 1

Mercury Athletic Shoe Company is planning a one-month campaign for April to promote sales of one of its two shoe products. A total of $125,000 has been budgeted for advertising, contests, redeemable coupons, and other promotional activities. The following data have been assembled for their possible usefulness in deciding which of the products to select for the campaign.

	Tennis Shoe	Walking Shoe
Unit selling price	$112	$98
Unit production costs:		
Direct materials	$ 22	$17
Direct labor	12	10
Variable factory overhead	5	7
Fixed factory overhead	9	12
Total unit production costs	$ 48	$46
Unit variable selling expenses	9	12
Unit fixed selling expenses	12	16
Total unit costs	$ 69	$74
Operating income per unit	$ 43	$24

No increase in facilities would be necessary to produce and sell the increased output. It is anticipated that 5,000 additional units of tennis shoes or 7,500 additional units of walking shoes could be sold without changing the unit selling price of either product.

Instructions

1. Prepare a differential analysis report as of March 13, 2008, presenting the additional revenue and additional costs anticipated from the promotion of tennis shoes and walking shoes.
2. ▭▭▶ The sales manager had tentatively decided to promote tennis shoes, estimating that operating income would be increased by $90,000 ($43 operating income per unit for 5,000 units, less promotion expenses of $125,000). The manager also believed that the selection of walking shoes would increase operating income by $55,000 ($24 operating income per unit for 7,500 units, less promotion expenses of $125,000). State briefly your reasons for supporting or opposing the tentative decision.

PR 24-4B
Differential analysis report for further processing
obj. 1

✓ 1. Differential revenue, $23,700

The management of Pittsburgh Aluminum Co. is considering whether to process aluminum ingot further into rolled aluminum. Rolled aluminum can be sold for $1,650 per ton, and ingot can be sold without further processing for $980 per ton. Ingot is produced in batches of 60 tons by smelting 400 tons of bauxite, which costs $450 per ton. Rolled aluminum will require additional processing costs of $415 per ton of ingot, and 1.2 tons of ingot will produce 1 ton of rolled aluminum.

Instructions

1. Prepare a report as of December 20, 2008, presenting a differential analysis associated with the further processing of aluminum ingot to produce rolled aluminum.
2. ▭▭▶ Briefly report your recommendations.

PR 24-5B
Product pricing using the cost-plus approach concepts; differential analysis report for accepting additional business
objs. 1, 2

✓ 3. b. Markup percentage, 25%

Stay Glow Company recently began production of a new product, the halogen light, which required the investment of $1,000,000 in assets. The costs of producing and selling 18,000 halogen lights are estimated as follows:

Variable costs per unit:		Fixed costs:	
Direct materials	$23.00	Factory overhead	$216,000
Direct labor	12.00	Selling and administrative expenses	54,000
Factory overhead	5.00		
Selling and administrative expenses	5.00		
Total	$45.00		

Stay Glow Company is currently considering establishing a selling price for the halogen light. The president of Stay Glow Company has decided to use the cost-plus approach to product pricing and has indicated that the halogen light must earn a 9% rate of return on invested assets.

Instructions

1. Determine the amount of desired profit from the production and sale of the halogen light.

(continued)

2. Assuming that the total cost concept is used, determine (a) the cost amount per unit, (b) the markup percentage (rounded to two decimal places), and (c) the selling price of the halogen light (rounded to nearest whole dollar).

3. Assuming that the product cost concept is used, determine (a) the cost amount per unit, (b) the markup percentage, and (c) the selling price of the halogen light.

4. Assuming that the variable cost concept is used, determine (a) the cost amount per unit, (b) the markup percentage (rounded to two decimal places), and (c) the selling price of the halogen light (rounded to nearest whole dollar).

5. ▭➤ Comment on any additional considerations that could influence establishing the selling price for the halogen light.

6. Assume that as of June 1, 2008, 7,000 units of halogen light have been produced and sold during the current year. Analysis of the domestic market indicates that 9,000 additional units of the halogen light are expected to be sold during the remainder of the year at the normal product price determined under the total cost concept. On June 5, Stay Glow Company received an offer from Night Light Inc. for 2,000 units of the halogen light at $46 each. Night Light Inc. will market the units in Japan under its own brand name, and no selling and administrative expenses associated with the sale will be incurred by Stay Glow Company. The additional business is not expected to affect the domestic sales of the halogen light, and the additional units could be produced using existing capacity.

    a. Prepare a differential analysis report of the proposed sale to Night Light Inc.
    b. Based upon the differential analysis report in part (a), should the proposal be accepted?

PR 24-6B
Product pricing and profit analysis with bottleneck operations

objs. **1, 3**

✓1. Ethylene, $34

Gulf Coast Chemical Company produces three products: ethylene, butane, and ester. Each of these products has high demand in the market, and Gulf Coast Chemical is able to sell as much as it can produce of all three. The reaction operation is a bottleneck in the process and is running at 100% of capacity. Gulf Coast wants to improve chemical operation profitability. The variable conversion cost is $8 per process hour. The fixed cost is $990,000. In addition, the cost analyst was able to determine the following information about the three products:

	Ethylene	Butane	Ester
Budgeted units produced	18,000	18,000	18,000
Total process hours per unit	3	3	2
Reactor hours per unit	0.8	0.5	0.4
Unit selling price	$168	$128	$115
Direct materials cost per unit	$110	$75	$85

The reaction operation is part of the total process for each of these three products. Thus, for example, 0.8 of the 3 hours required to process Ethylene are associated with the reactor.

Instructions
1. Determine the unit contribution margin for each product.
2. Provide an analysis to determine the relative product profitabilities, assuming that the reactor is a bottleneck.
3. Assume that management wishes to improve profitability by increasing prices on selected products. At what price would Ethylene and Ester need to be offered in order to produce the same relative profitability as Butane?

Special Activities

SA 24-1
Product pricing

ETHICS

Marcia Martinez is a cost accountant for Ascend Inc. Marcus Todd, vice president of marketing, has asked Marcia to meet with representatives of Ascend's major competitor to discuss product cost data. Marcus indicates that the sharing of these data will enable Ascend to determine a fair and equitable price for its products.

▭➤ Would it be ethical for Marcia to attend the meeting and share the relevant cost data?

SA 24-2
Decision on accepting additional business

A manager of Back Tee Sporting Goods Company is considering accepting an order from an overseas customer. This customer has requested an order for 20,000 dozen golf balls at a price of $20.00 per dozen. The variable cost to manufacture a dozen golf balls is $17.00 per dozen. The full cost is $23.00 per dozen. Back Tee has a normal selling price of $28.00 per dozen. Back Tee's plant has just enough excess capacity on the second shift to make the overseas order.

➤ What are some considerations in accepting or rejecting this order?

SA 24-3
Accept business at a special price

Internet Project

If you are not familiar with Priceline.com Inc., go to its Web site. Assume that an individual bids $60 on Priceline.com for a room in Dallas, Texas, on August 24. Assume that August 24 is a Saturday, with low expected room demand in Dallas at a Marriott International, Inc., hotel, so there is excess room capacity. The fully allocated cost per room per day is assumed from hotel records as follows:

Housekeeping labor cost*	$30
Hotel depreciation expense	42
Cost of room supplies (soap, paper, etc.)	5
Laundry labor and material cost*	10
Cost of desk staff	5
Utility cost (mostly air conditioning)	3
Total cost per room per day	$95

*Both housekeeping and laundry staff include many part-time workers, so that the workload is variable to demand.

➤ Should Marriott accept the customer bid for a night in Dallas on August 24 at a price of $60?

SA 24-4
Make-or-buy decision

The president of Monarch Materials Inc., Todd Bentley, asked the controller, Megan Mayfield, to provide an analysis of a make vs. buy decision for material TS-101. The material is presently processed in Monarch's Roanoke facility. TS-101 is used in processing of final products in the facility. Megan determined the following unit production costs for the material as of March 15, 2008:

Direct materials	$ 7.50
Direct labor	2.70
Variable factory overhead	1.20
Fixed factory overhead	2.00
Total production costs per unit	$13.40

In addition, material TS-101 requires special hazardous material handling. This special handling adds an additional cost of $1.60 for each unit produced.

Material TS-101 can be purchased from an overseas supplier. The supplier does not presently do business with Monarch Materials. This supplier promises monthly delivery of the material at a price of $10.10 per unit, plus transportation cost of $0.40 per unit. In addition, Monarch would need to incur additional administrative costs to satisfy import regulations for hazardous material. These additional administrative costs are estimated to be $0.80 per purchased unit. Each purchased unit would also require special hazardous material handling of $1.60 per unit.

a. Prepare a differential analysis report to support Megan's recommendation on whether to continue making material TS-101 or whether to purchase the material from the overseas supplier.
b. What additional considerations should Megan address in the recommendation?

SA 24-5
Cost-plus and target costing concepts

The following conversation took place between Theo James, vice president of marketing, and Lee Corso, controller of Astor Computer Company:

Theo: I am really excited about our new computer coming out. I think it will be a real market success.
Lee: I'm really glad you think so. I know that our price is one variable that will determine if it's a success. If our price is too high, our competitors will be the ones with the market success.

Theo: Don't worry about it. We'll just mark our product cost up by 25% and it will all work out. I know we'll make money at those markups. By the way, what does the estimated product cost look like?

Lee: Well, there's the rub. The product cost looks as if it's going to come in at around $2,400. With a 25% markup, that will give us a selling price of $3,000.

Theo: I see your concern. That's a little high. Our research indicates that computer prices are dropping by about 20% per year and that this type of computer should be selling for around $2,500 when we release it to the market.

Lee: I'm not sure what to do.

Theo: Let me see if I can help. How much of the $2,400 is fixed cost?

Lee: About $400.

Theo: There you go. The fixed cost is sunk. We don't need to consider it in our pricing decision. If we reduce the product cost by $400, the new price with a 25% markup would be right at $2,500. Boy, I was really worried for a minute there. I knew something wasn't right.

a. If you were Lee, how would you respond to Theo's solution to the pricing problem?

b. How might target costing be used to help solve this pricing dilemma?

SA 24-6
Pricing decisions and markup on variable costs

REAL WORLD

Internet Project

Group Project

Many businesses are offering their products and services over the Internet. Some of these companies and their Internet addresses are listed below.

Company Name	Internet Address (URL)	Product
Delta Air Lines	http://www.delta.com	airline tickets
Amazon.com	http://www.amazon.com	books
Dell Inc.	http://www.dell.com	personal computers

a. In groups of three, assign each person in your group to one of the Internet sites listed above. For each site, determine the following:
   1. A product (or service) description.
   2. A product price.
   3. A list of costs that are required to produce and sell the product selected in part (1) as listed in the annual report on SEC form 10-K.
   4. Whether the costs identified in part (3) are fixed costs or variable costs.

b. Which of the three products do you believe has the largest markup on variable cost?

Answers to Self-Examination Questions

1. **A**   Differential cost is the amount of increase or decrease in cost that is expected from a particular course of action compared with an alternative. For Marlo Company, the differential cost is $19,000 (answer A). This is the total of the variable product costs ($15,000) and the variable operating expenses ($4,000), which would not be incurred if the product is discontinued.

2. **A**   A sunk cost is not affected by later decisions. For Victor Company, the sunk cost is the $50,000 (answer A) book value of the equipment, which is equal to the original cost of $200,000 (answer C) less the accumulated depreciation of $150,000 (answer B).

3. **C**   The amount of income that could have been earned from the best available alternative to a proposed use of cash is the opportunity cost. For Henry Company, the opportunity cost is 12% of $100,000, or $12,000 (answer C).

4. **C**   Under the variable cost concept of product pricing (answer C), fixed manufacturing costs, fixed administrative and selling expenses, and desired profit are allowed for in determining the markup. Only desired profit is allowed for in the markup under the total cost concept (answer A). Under the product cost concept (answer B), total selling and administrative expenses and desired profit are allowed for in determining the markup. Standard cost (answer D) can be used under any of the cost-plus approaches to product pricing.

5. **C**   Product 3 has the highest unit contribution margin per bottleneck hour ($14/2 = $7). Product 1 (answer A) has the largest unit contribution margin, but the lowest unit contribution per bottleneck hour ($20/4 = $5), so it is the least profitable product in the constrained environment. Product 2 (answer B) has the highest total profitability in March (1,500 units × $18), but this does not suggest that it has the highest profit potential. Product 2's unit contribution per bottleneck hour ($18/3 = $6) is between Products 1 and 3. Answer D is not true, since the products all have different profit potential in terms of unit contribution margin per bottleneck hour.

Capital Investment Analysis

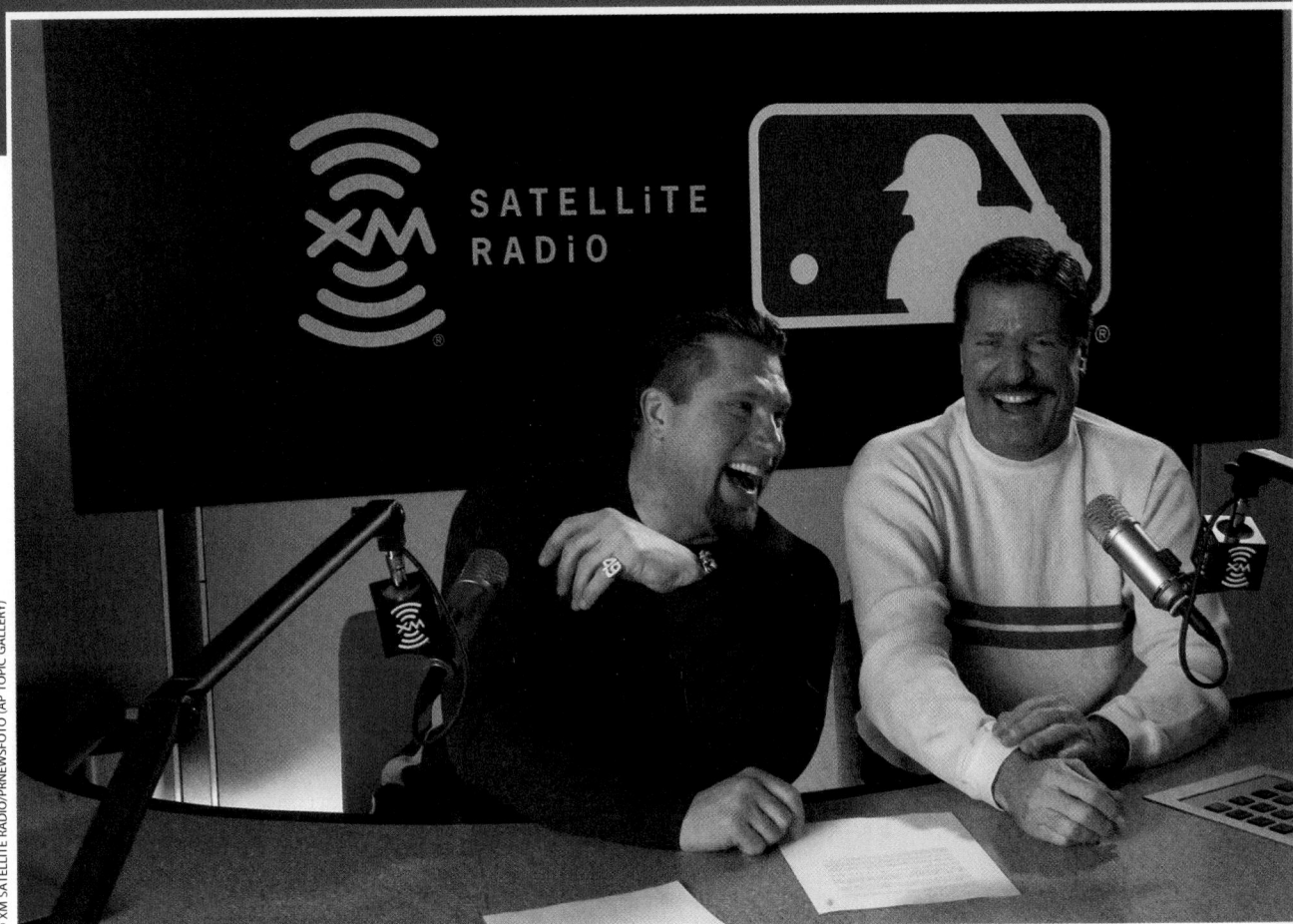

objectives

After studying this chapter, you should be able to:

1 **Explain the nature and importance of capital investment analysis.**

2 **Evaluate capital investment proposals, using the following methods: average rate of return, cash payback, net present value, and internal rate of return.**

3 **List and describe factors that complicate capital investment analysis.**

4 **Diagram the capital rationing process.**

XM Satellite Radio

Why are you paying tuition, studying this text, and spending time and money on a higher education? Most people believe that the money and time spent now will return them more earnings in the future. In other words, the cost of higher education is an investment in your future earning ability. How would you know if this investment is worth it?

One method would be for you to compare the cost of a higher education against the estimated increase in your future earning power. The more your future increased earnings exceed the investment, the more attractive the investment. As you will see in this chapter, the same is true for business investments in fixed assets. Business organizations analyze potential capital investments by using various methods that compare investment costs to future earnings and cash flows.

For example, XM Satellite Radio provides access to music, sports, and special feature radio programming from anywhere in the United States using satel-

lite technology. XM's spacecraft system required an investment of over $600 million. XM Satellite Radio used capital investment analysis to compare this investment with the future earnings ability of this system over its 17-year expected life. XM must be satisfied with its investments, because it will be launching several more satellites during the end of this decade.

In this chapter, we will describe analyses useful for making investment decisions, which may involve thousands, millions, or even billions of dollars. We will emphasize the similarities and differences among the most commonly used methods of evaluating investment proposals, as well as the uses of each method. We will also discuss qualitative considerations affecting investment analyses. Finally, we will discuss considerations complicating investment analyses and the process of allocating available investment funds among competing proposals.

Nature of Capital Investment Analysis

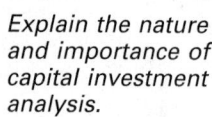

objective 1

Explain the nature and importance of capital investment analysis.

How do companies decide to make significant investments such as the following?

- Yum! Brands, Inc., adds 375 new international Taco Bell, Pizza Hut, and KFC units.
- The Walt Disney Company commits to investing $315 million to build a new theme park in Hong Kong.
- XM Satellite Radio commits to launching its fourth and fifth satellites at a cost of over $300 million by the end of 2007.

Companies use capital investment analysis to help evaluate long-term investments. **Capital investment analysis** (or *capital budgeting*) is the process by which management plans, evaluates, and controls investments in fixed assets. Capital investments involve the long-term commitment of funds and affect operations for many years. Thus, these investments must earn a reasonable rate of return, so that the business can meet its obligations to creditors and provide dividends to stockholders. Because capital investment decisions are some of the most important decisions that management makes, capital investment analysis must be carefully developed and implemented.

A capital investment program should encourage employees to submit proposals for capital investments. It should communicate to employees the long-range goals of the business, so that useful proposals are submitted. All reasonable proposals should be considered and evaluated with respect to economic costs and benefits. The program may reward employees whose proposals are accepted.

Methods of Evaluating Capital Investment Proposals

objective **2**

Evaluate capital investment proposals, using the following methods: average rate of return, cash payback, net present value, and internal rate of return.

Capital investment evaluation methods can be grouped into the following two categories:

1. Methods that do not use present values
2. Methods that use present values

Two methods that do not use present values are (1) the average rate of return method and (2) the cash payback method. Two methods that use present values are (1) the net present value method and (2) the internal rate of return method. These methods consider the time value of money. The **time value of money concept** recognizes that an amount of cash invested today will earn income and therefore has value over time.

Management often uses a combination of methods in evaluating capital investment proposals. Each method has advantages and disadvantages. In addition, some of the computations are complex. Computers, however, can perform the computations quickly and easily. Computers can also be used to analyze the impact of changes in key estimates in evaluating capital investment proposals.

METHODS THAT IGNORE PRESENT VALUE

The average rate of return and the cash payback methods are easy to use. These methods are often initially used to screen proposals. Management normally sets minimum standards for accepting proposals, and those not meeting these standards are dropped from further consideration. If a proposal meets the minimum standards, it is often subject to further analysis.

The methods that ignore present value are often useful in evaluating capital investment proposals that have relatively short useful lives. In such cases, the timing of the cash flows is less important.

Average Rate of Return Method The **average rate of return**, sometimes called the *accounting rate of return*, is a measure of the average income as a percent of the average investment in fixed assets. The average rate of return is determined by using the following equation:

A CFO survey of capital investment analysis methods used by large U.S. companies reported the following:

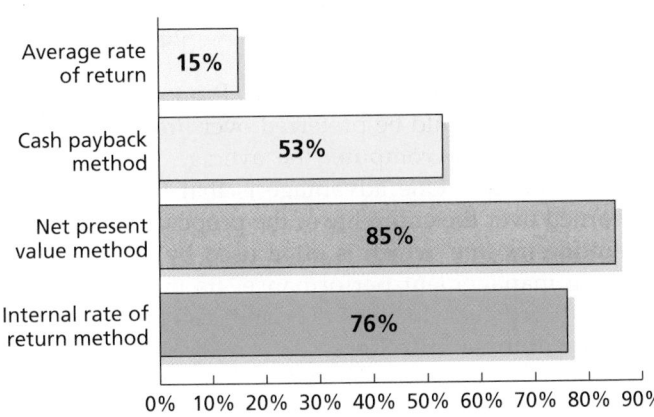

Percentage of Respondents Reporting the Use of the Method as "Always" or "Often"

Average rate of return — 15%
Cash payback method — 53%
Net present value method — 85%
Internal rate of return method — 76%

0% 10% 20% 30% 40% 50% 60% 70% 80% 90%

Source: Patricia A. Ryan and Glenn P. Ryan, "Capital Budgeting Practices of the Fortune 1000: How Have Things Changed?" *Journal of Business and Management* (Winter 2002).

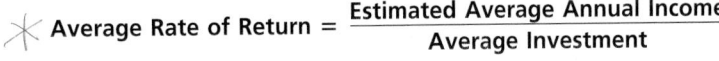

$$\text{Average Rate of Return} = \frac{\text{Estimated Average Annual Income}}{\text{Average Investment}}$$

The numerator is the average of the annual income expected to be earned from the investment over the investment life, after deducting depreciation. The denominator is the average book value over the investment life. Thus, if straight-line depreciation and no residual value are assumed, the average investment over the useful life is equal to one-half of the original cost.[1]

---

1 The average investment is the midpoint of the depreciable cost of the asset. Since a fixed asset is never depreciated below its residual value, this midpoint is determined by adding the original cost of the asset to the estimated residual value and dividing by 2.

To illustrate, assume that management is considering the purchase of a machine at a cost of $500,000. The machine is expected to have a useful life of four years, with no residual value, and to yield total income of $200,000. The estimated average annual income is therefore $50,000 ($200,000/4), and the average investment is $250,000 [($500,000 + $0 residual value)/2]. Thus, the average rate of return on the average investment is 20%, computed as follows:

$$\text{Average Rate of Return} = \frac{\text{Estimated Average Annual Income}}{\text{Average Investment}}$$

$$\text{Average Rate of Return} = \frac{\$200,000/4}{(\$500,000 + \$0)/2} = 20\%$$

The average rate of return of 20% should be compared with the minimum rate for such investments. If the average rate of return equals or exceeds the minimum rate, the machine should be purchased.

When several capital investment proposals are considered, the proposals can be ranked by their average rates of return. The higher the average rate of return, the more desirable the proposal. For example, assume that management is considering two capital investment proposals and has computed the following average rates of return:

	Proposal A	Proposal B
Estimated average annual income	$ 30,000	$ 36,000
Average investment	$120,000	$180,000
Average rate of return:		
$30,000/$120,000	25%	
$36,000/$180,000		20%

If only the average rate of return is considered, Proposal A, with an average rate of return of 25%, would be preferred over Proposal B.

In addition to being easy to compute, the average rate of return method has several advantages. One advantage is that it includes the amount of income earned over the entire life of the proposal. In addition, it emphasizes accounting income, which is often used by investors and creditors in evaluating management performance. Its main disadvantage is that it does not directly consider the expected cash flows from the proposal and the timing of these cash flows.

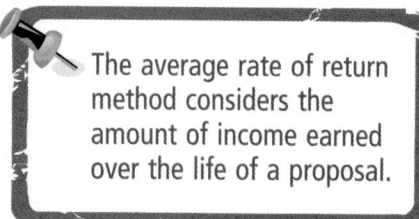

The average rate of return method considers the amount of income earned over the life of a proposal.

Example Exercise 25-1   objective **2**

Determine the average rate of return for a project that is estimated to yield total income of $273,600 over three years, has a cost of $690,000, and has a $70,000 residual value.

Follow My Example 25-1

Estimated average annual income $91,200 ($273,600/3 years)
Average investment $380,000 ($690,000 + $70,000)/2
Average rate of return   24% ($91,200/$380,000)

For Practice: PE 25-1A, PE 25-1B

Cash Payback Method   Cash flows are important because cash can be reinvested. Very simply, the capital investment uses cash and must therefore return cash in the future in order to be successful.

The expected period of time that will pass between the date of an investment and the complete recovery in cash (or equivalent) of the amount invested is the **cash payback period**. To simplify the analysis, the revenues and expenses other than depreciation related to operating fixed assets are assumed to be all in the form of cash. The excess of the cash flowing in from revenue over the cash flowing out for expenses is termed *net cash flow*. The time required for the net cash flow to equal the initial outlay for the fixed asset is the payback period.

To illustrate, assume that the proposed investment in a fixed asset with an eight-year life is $200,000. The annual cash revenues from the investment are $50,000, and the annual cash expenses are $10,000. Thus, the annual net cash flow is expected to be $40,000 ($50,000 − $10,000). The estimated cash payback period for the investment is five years, computed as follows:

$$\frac{\$200,000}{\$40,000} = \text{5-year cash payback period}$$

In this illustration, the annual net cash flows are equal ($40,000 per year). If these annual net cash flows are *not* equal, the cash payback period is determined by adding the annual net cash flows until the cumulative sum equals the amount of the proposed investment. To illustrate, assume that for a proposed investment of $400,000, the annual net cash flows and the cumulative net cash flows over the proposal's six-year life are as follows:

Year	Net Cash Flow	Cumulative Net Cash Flow
1	$ 60,000	$ 60,000
2	80,000	140,000
3	105,000	245,000
4	155,000	400,000
5	100,000	500,000
6	90,000	590,000

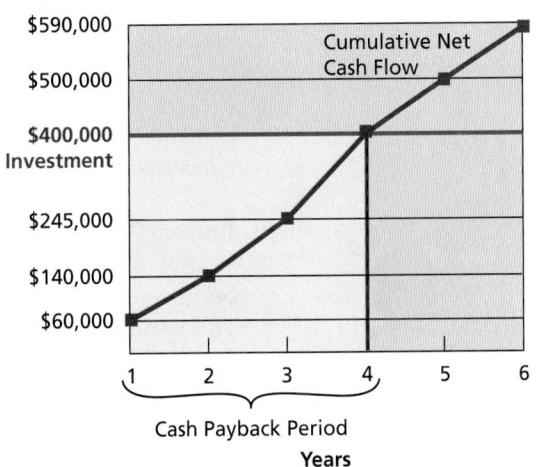

The cumulative net cash flow at the end of the fourth year equals the amount of the investment, $400,000. Thus, the payback period is four years.

If the amount of the proposed investment had been $450,000, the cash payback period would occur during the fifth year. Since $100,000 of net cash flow is expected during the fifth year, the additional $50,000 needed to cover the total investment of $450,000 would occur approximately half way through the fifth year ($50,000/$100,000). Thus, the cash payback period would be 4½ years.[2]

The cash payback method is widely used in evaluating proposals for investments in new projects. A short payback period is desirable, because the sooner the cash is recovered, the sooner it becomes available for reinvestment in other projects. In addition, there is less possibility of losses from economic conditions, out-of-date assets, and other unavoidable risks when the payback period is short. The cash payback period is also important to bankers and other creditors who may be depending upon net cash flow for repaying debt related to the capital investment. The sooner the cash is recovered, the sooner the debt or other liabilities can be paid. Thus, the cash payback method is especially useful to managers whose primary concern is liquidity.

One of the disadvantages of the cash payback method is that it ignores cash flows occurring after the payback period. In addition, the cash payback method does not use present value concepts in valuing cash flows occurring in different periods. In the next section, we will review present value concepts and introduce capital investment methods that use present value.

---

2 Unless otherwise stated, we assume that the net cash flows are received uniformly throughout the year.

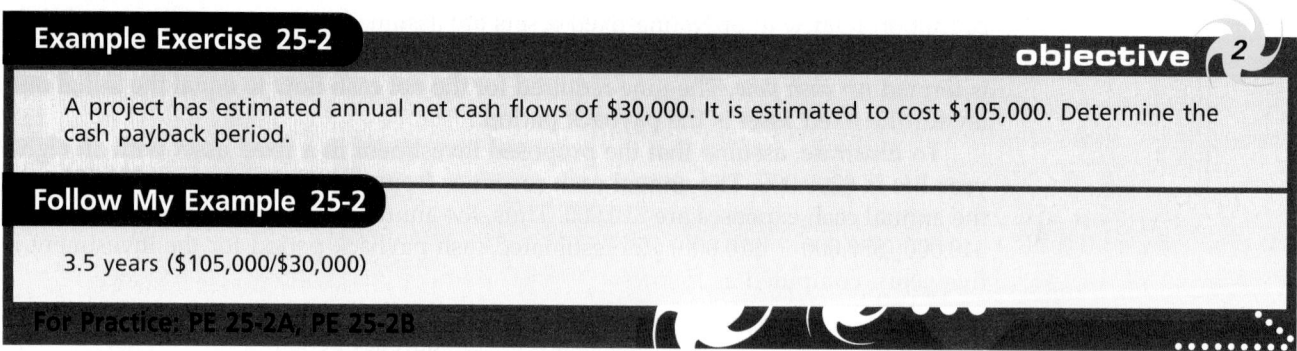

For Practice: PE 25-2A, PE 25-2B

PRESENT VALUE METHODS

An investment in fixed assets may be viewed as acquiring a series of net cash flows over a period of time. The period of time over which these net cash flows will be received may be an important factor in determining the value of an investment. Present value methods use both the amount and the timing of net cash flows in evaluating an investment. Before illustrating how these methods are used in capital investment analysis, we will review basic present value concepts.[3]

Present Value Concepts   **Present value concepts** can be divided into the *present value of an amount* and the *present value of an annuity*. We describe and illustrate these two concepts next.

Present value concepts can also be used to evaluate personal finances. For example, the Heritage Foundation compared the present value of social security contributions of a 35-year-old average earner with the present value of social security benefits. Using an interest rate of 6%, the present value of the social security benefits is $300,000 less than the present value of the contributions. For a younger worker or a higher-salary earner, the difference is even greater.

Present Value of an Amount   If you were given the choice, would you prefer to receive $1 now or $1 three years from now? You should prefer to receive $1 now, because you could invest the $1 and earn interest for three years. As a result, the amount you would have after three years would be greater than $1.

To illustrate, assume that on January 1, 2008, you invest $1 in an account that earns 12% interest compounded annually. After one year, the $1 will grow to $1.12 ($1 × 1.12), because interest of 12¢ is added to the investment. The $1.12 earns 12% interest for the second year. Interest earning interest is called *compounding*. By the end of the second year, the investment has grown to $1.254 ($1.12 × 1.12). By the end of the third year, the investment has grown to $1.404 ($1.254 × 1.12). Thus, if money is worth 12%, you would be equally satisfied with $1 on January 1, 2008, or $1.404 three years later.

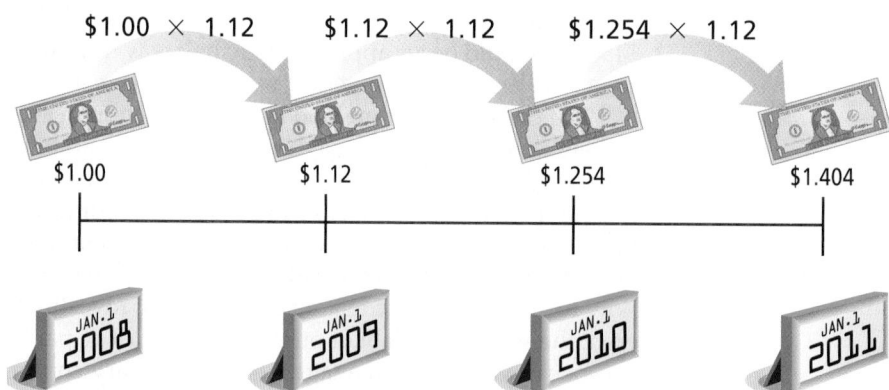

On January 1, 2008, what is the present value of $1.404 to be received on January 1, 2011? This is a present value question. The answer can be determined with the aid

---

3 Present value calculations were introduced in accounting for bond liabilities. Present value concepts are developed again here in order to reinforce that introduction.

of a present value of $1 table. For example, the partial table in Exhibit 1 indicates that the present value of $1 to be received three years hence, with earnings compounded at the rate of 12% a year, is 0.712. Multiplying 0.712 by $1.404 yields $1, which is the present value that started the compounding process.[4]

Present value of an Annti

EXHIBIT 1

Partial Present Value of $1 Table

	Present Value of $1 at Compound Interest				
Year	6%	10%	12%	15%	20%
1	0.943	0.909	0.893	0.870	0.833
2	0.890	0.826	0.797	0.756	0.694
3	0.840	0.751	**0.712**	0.658	0.579
4	0.792	0.683	0.636	0.572	0.482
5	0.747	0.621	0.567	0.497	0.402
6	0.705	0.564	0.507	0.432	0.335
7	0.665	0.513	0.452	0.376	0.279
8	0.627	0.467	0.404	0.327	0.233
9	0.592	0.424	0.361	0.284	0.194
10	0.558	0.386	0.322	0.247	0.162

Present Value of an Annuity   An **annuity** is a series of equal net cash flows at fixed time intervals. Annuities are very common in business. For example, monthly rental, salary, and bond interest cash flows are all examples of annuities. The **present value of an annuity** is the sum of the present values of each cash flow. That is, the present value of an annuity is the amount of cash that is needed today to yield a series of equal net cash flows at fixed time intervals in the future.

To illustrate, the present value of a $100 annuity for five periods at 12% could be determined by using the present value factors in Exhibit 1. Each $100 net cash flow could be multiplied by the present value of $1 at 12% factor for the appropriate period and summed to determine a present value of $360.50, as shown in the following timeline:

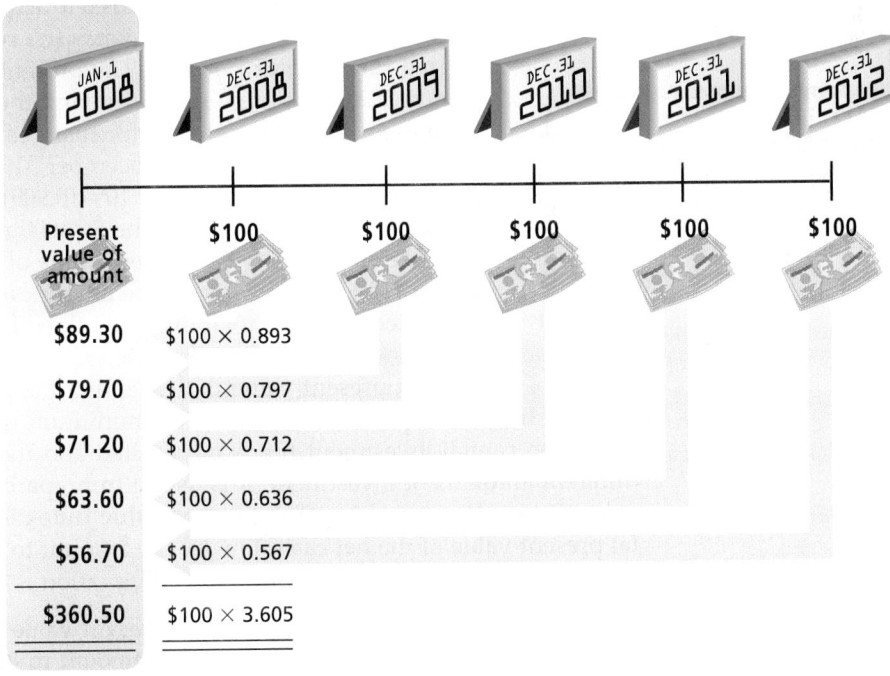

---

4 The present value factors in the table are rounded to three decimal places. More complete tables of present values are in Appendix A.

Using a present value of an annuity table is a simpler approach. Exhibit 2 is a partial table of present value of annuity factors.[5] These factors are merely the sum of the present value of $1 factors in Exhibit 1 for the number of annuity periods. Thus, 3.605 in the annuity table (Exhibit 2) is the sum of the five individual present value of $1 factors at 12%. Multiplying $100 by 3.605 yields the same amount ($360.50) that was determined in the preceding illustration by five successive multiplications.

EXHIBIT 2

Partial Present Value
of an Annuity Table

Present Value of an Annuity of $1 at Compound Interest

Year	6%	10%	12%	15%	20%
1	0.943	0.909	0.893	0.870	0.833
2	1.833	1.736	1.690	1.626	1.528
3	2.673	2.487	2.402	2.283	2.106
4	3.465	3.170	3.037	2.855	2.589
5	4.212	3.791	**3.605**	3.353	2.991
6	4.917	4.355	4.111	3.785	3.326
7	5.582	4.868	4.564	4.160	3.605
8	6.210	5.335	4.968	4.487	3.837
9	6.802	5.759	5.328	4.772	4.031
10	7.360	6.145	5.650	5.019	4.192

A 55-year-old janitor won a $5 million lottery jackpot, payable in 21 annual installments of $240,245. Unfortunately, the janitor died after collecting only one payment. What happens to the remaining unclaimed payments? In this case, the lottery winnings were auctioned off for the benefit of the janitor's estate. The winning bid approximated the present value of the remaining cash flows, or about $2.1 million.

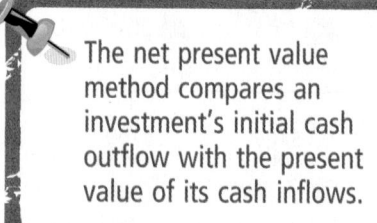

The net present value method compares an investment's initial cash outflow with the present value of its cash inflows.

Net Present Value Method   The **net present value method** analyzes capital investment proposals by comparing the initial cash investment with the present value of the net cash flows. It is sometimes called the *discounted cash flow method*. The interest rate (return) used in net present value analysis is the minimum desired rate of return set by management. This rate, sometimes termed the *hurdle rate*, is often based upon such factors as the nature of the business, the purpose of the investment, and the cost of securing funds for the investment. If the net present value of the cash flows expected from a proposed investment equals or exceeds the amount of the initial investment, the proposal is desirable.

To illustrate, assume a proposal to acquire $200,000 of equipment with an expected useful life of five years (no residual value) and a minimum desired rate of return of 10%. The present value of the net cash flow for each year is computed by multiplying the net cash flow for the year by the present value factor of $1 for that year. For example, the $70,000 net cash flow to be received on December 31, 2008, is multiplied by the present value of $1 for one year at 10% (0.909). Thus, the present value of the $70,000 is $63,630. Likewise, the $60,000 net cash flow on December 31, 2009, is multiplied by the present value of $1 for two years at 10% (0.826) to yield $49,560, and so on. The amount to be invested, $200,000, is then subtracted from the total present value of the net cash flows, $202,900, to determine the net present value, $2,900, as shown at the top of the following page. The net present value indicates that the proposal is expected to recover the investment and provide more than the minimum rate of return of 10%.

When capital investment funds are limited and the alternative proposals involve different amounts of investment, it is useful to prepare a ranking of the proposals by using a present value index. The **present value index** is calculated by dividing the total present value of the net cash flow by the amount to be invested. The present value index for the investment in the previous illustration is calculated as follows:

$$\text{Present Value Index} = \frac{\text{Total Present Value of Net Cash Flow}}{\text{Amount to Be Invested}}$$

$$= \frac{\$202,900}{\$200,000} = 1.0145$$

5 Expanded tables for the present value of an annuity are in Appendix A.

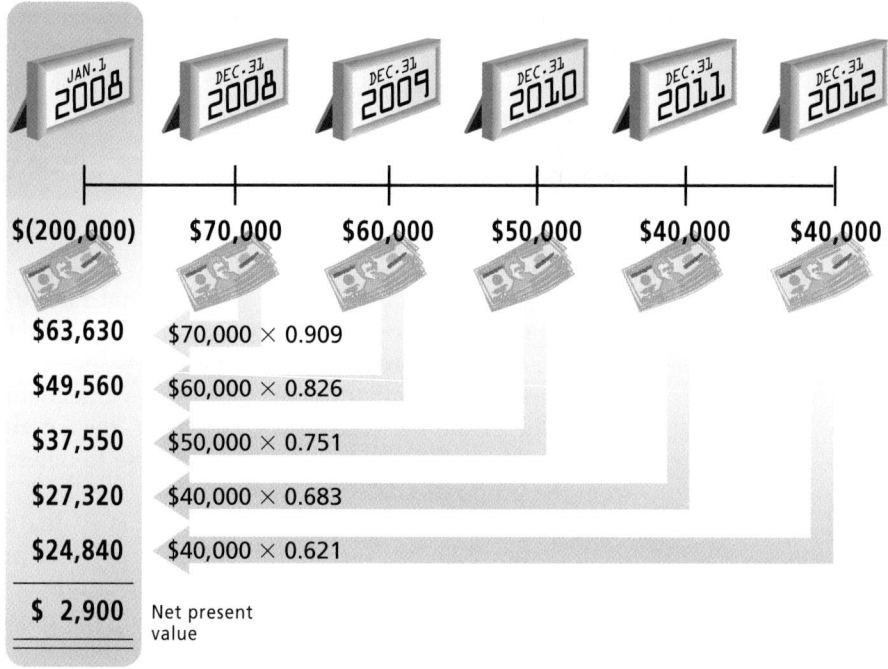

$63,630 $70,000 × 0.909

$49,560 $60,000 × 0.826

$37,550 $50,000 × 0.751

$27,320 $40,000 × 0.683

$24,840 $40,000 × 0.621

$ 2,900   Net present value

If a business is considering three alternative proposals and has determined their net present values, the present value index for each proposal is as follows:

	Proposal A	Proposal B	Proposal C
Total present value of net cash flow ..	$107,000	$86,400	$86,400
Amount to be invested	100,000	80,000	90,000
Net present value	$ 7,000	$ 6,400	$ (3,600)
Present value index	1.07 ($107,000/$100,000)	1.08 ($86,400/$80,000)	0.96 ($86,400/$90,000)

A project will have a present value index greater than one when the net present value is positive. This is the case for Proposals A and B. When the net present value is negative, the present value index will be less than one, as is the case for Proposal C.

Although Proposal A has the largest net present value, the present value indices indicate that it is not as desirable as Proposal B. That is, Proposal B returns $1.08 present value per dollar invested, whereas Proposal A returns only $1.07. Proposal B requires an investment of $80,000, compared to an investment of $100,000 for Proposal A. Management should consider the possible use of the $20,000 difference between Proposal A and Proposal B investments before making a final decision.

An advantage of the net present value method is that it considers the time value of money. A disadvantage is that the computations are more complex than those for the methods that ignore present value. However, the use of spreadsheet software can simplify these computations. In addition, the net present value method assumes that the cash received from the proposal during its useful life can be reinvested at the rate of return used in computing the present value of the proposal. Because of changing economic conditions, this assumption may not always be reasonable.

Example Exercise 25-3   objective 2

A project has estimated annual net cash flows of $50,000 for seven years and is estimated to cost $240,000. Assume a minimum acceptable rate of return of 12%. Using Exhibit 2, determine (a) the net present value of the project and (b) the present value index, rounded to two decimal places.

(continued)

Internal Rate of Return Method   The **internal rate of return (IRR) method** uses present value concepts to compute the rate of return from the net cash flows expected from capital investment proposals. This method is sometimes called the *time-adjusted rate of return method*. It is similar to the net present value method, in that it focuses on the present value of the net cash flows. However, the internal rate of return method starts with the net cash flows and works in reverse to determine the rate of return expected from the proposal.

To illustrate, assume that management is evaluating a proposal to acquire equipment costing $33,530. The equipment is expected to provide annual net cash flows of $10,000 per year for five years. If we assume a rate of return of 12%, we can calculate the present value of the net cash flows, using the present value of an annuity table in Exhibit 2. These calculations are shown in Exhibit 3.

EXHIBIT 3		
Net Present Value Analysis at 12%	Annual net cash flow (at the end of each of five years)	$10,000
	Present value of an annuity of $1 at 12% for 5 years (Exhibit 2)	× 3.605
	Present value of annual net cash flows	$36,050
	Less amount to be invested	33,530
	Net present value	$ 2,520

In Exhibit 3, the $36,050 present value of the cash inflows, based on a 12% rate of return, is greater than the $33,530 to be invested. Therefore, the internal rate of return must be greater than 12%. Through trial-and-error procedures, the rate of return that equates the $33,530 cost of the investment with the present value of the net cash flows is determined to be 15%, as shown below.

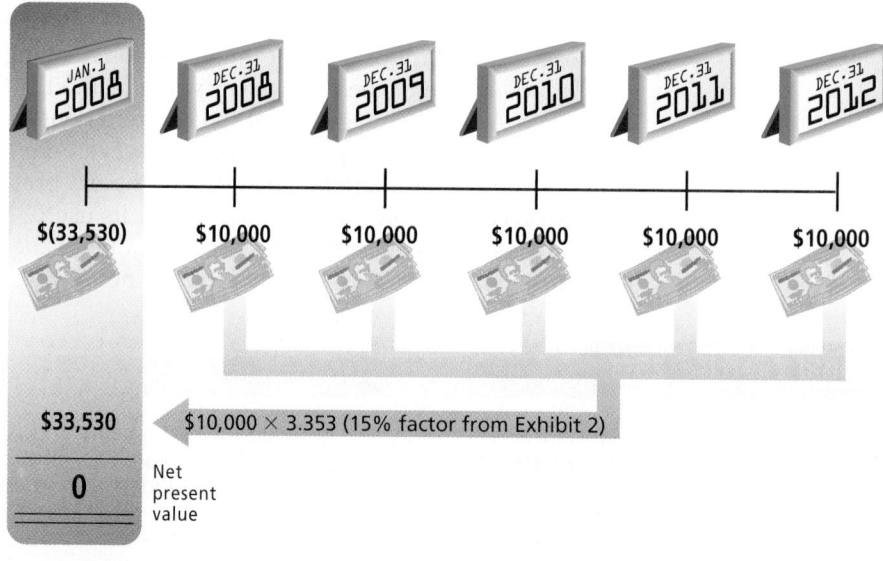

Such trial-and-error procedures are time consuming. However, when equal annual net cash flows are expected from a proposal, as in the illustration, the calculations are simplified by using the following steps:[6]

1. Determine a present value factor for an annuity of $1 by dividing the amount to be invested by the equal annual net cash flows, as follows:

$$\text{Present Value Factor for an Annuity of \$1} = \frac{\text{Amount to Be Invested}}{\text{Equal Annual Net Cash Flows}}$$

2. In the present value of an annuity of $1 table, locate the present value factor determined in step (1). First locate the number of years of expected useful life of the investment in the Year column, and then proceed horizontally across the table until you find the present value factor computed in step (1).
3. Identify the internal rate of return by the heading of the column in which the present value factor in step (2) is located.

To illustrate, assume that management is considering a proposal to acquire equipment costing $97,360. The equipment is expected to provide equal annual net cash flows of $20,000 for seven years. The present value factor for an annuity of $1 is **4.868**, calculated as follows:

Present Value Factor for an Annuity of $1

$$= \frac{\text{Amount to Be Invested}}{\text{Equal Annual Net Cash Flows}}$$

$$= \frac{\$97,360}{\$20,000} = \textbf{4.868}$$

For a period of seven years, the partial present value of an annuity of $1 table indicates that the factor **4.868** is related to a percentage of **10%**, as shown below. Thus, 10% is the internal rate of return for this proposal.

Present Value of an Annuity of $1 at Compound Interest

Year	6%	10% ←	12%
1	0.943	0.909	0.893
2	1.833	1.736	1.690
3	2.673	2.487	2.402
4	3.465	3.170	3.037
5	4.212	3.791	3.605
6	4.917	4.355	4.111
7	5.582	4.868	4.564
8	6.210	5.335	4.968
9	6.802	5.759	5.328
10	7.360	6.145	5.650

If the minimum acceptable rate of return is 10%, then the proposed investment should be considered acceptable. When several proposals are considered, management often ranks the proposals by their internal rates of return. The proposal with the highest rate is considered the most desirable.

---

6 Equal annual net cash flows are assumed in order to simplify the illustration. If the annual net cash flows are not equal, the calculations are more complex, but the basic concepts are the same.

REAL WORLD

The minimum acceptable rate of return for Owens Corning is 18%; for General Electric Company, it is 20%. The CFO of Owens Corning states, "I'm here to challenge anyone—even the CEO—who gets emotionally attached to a project that doesn't reach our benchmark."

The primary advantage of the internal rate of return method is that the present values of the net cash flows over the entire useful life of the proposal are considered. In addition, by determining a rate of return for each proposal, all proposals are compared on a common basis. The primary disadvantage of the internal rate of return method is that the computations are more complex than for some of the other methods. However, spreadsheet software programs have internal rate of return functions that simplify the calculation. Also, like the net present value method, this method assumes that the cash received from a proposal during its useful life will be reinvested at the internal rate of return. Because of changing economic conditions, this assumption may not always be reasonable.

Example Exercise 25-4

objective 2

A project is estimated to cost $208,175 and provide annual net cash flows of $55,000 for six years. Determine the internal rate of return for this project, using Exhibit 2.

Follow My Example 25-4

15%   [($208,175/$55,000) = 3.785, the present value of an annuity factor for six periods at 15%, from Exhibit 2]

For Practice: PE 25-4A, PE 25-4B

Business Connections

REAL WORLD

PANERA BREAD STORE RATE OF RETURN

Panera Bread owns, operates, and franchises bakery-cafes throughout the United States. A recent annual report to the Securities and Exchange Commission (SEC Form 10-K) disclosed the following information about an average company-owned store:

Operating profit	$317,000
Depreciation	75,000
Investment	905,000

Assume that the operating profit and depreciation will remain unchanged for the next 10 years. Assume operating profit plus depreciation approximates annual net cash flows, and that the investment salvage value will be zero. The average rate of return and internal rate of return can then be estimated. The average rate of return on a company-owned store is:

$$\frac{\$317,000}{\$905,000/2} = 70.1\%$$

The internal rate of return is calculated by first determining the present value of an annuity of $1:

$$\text{Present value of an annuity of \$1:} \quad \frac{\$905,000}{\$317,000 + \$75,000} = 2.31$$

For a period of three years, this factor implies an internal rate of return near 15% (from Exhibit 2). However, if we more realistically assumed these cash flows for 10 years, Panera's company-owned stores generate an estimated internal rate of return of approximately 42% (from a spreadsheet calculation). Clearly, both investment evaluation methods indicate a highly successful business.

© PHILLIP NEALY/PHOTODISC/GETTY IMAGES

Factors that Complicate Capital Investment Analysis

objective 3

List and describe factors that complicate capital investment analysis.

In the preceding discussion, we described four widely used methods of evaluating capital investment proposals. In practice, additional factors may have an impact on the outcome of a capital investment decision. In the following paragraphs, we discuss some of the most important of these factors: the federal income tax, unequal lives of alternative proposals, leasing, uncertainty, changes in price levels, and qualitative factors.

INCOME TAX

In many cases, the impact of the federal income tax on capital investment decisions can be material. For example, in determining depreciation for federal income tax purposes, useful lives that are much shorter than the actual useful lives are often used. Also, depreciation can be calculated by methods that approximate the double-declining-balance method. Thus, depreciation for tax purposes often exceeds the depreciation for financial statement purposes in the early years of an asset's use. The tax reduction in these early years is offset by higher taxes in the later years, so that accelerated depreciation does not result in a long-run saving in taxes. However, the timing of the cash outflows for income taxes can have a significant impact on capital investment analysis.[7]

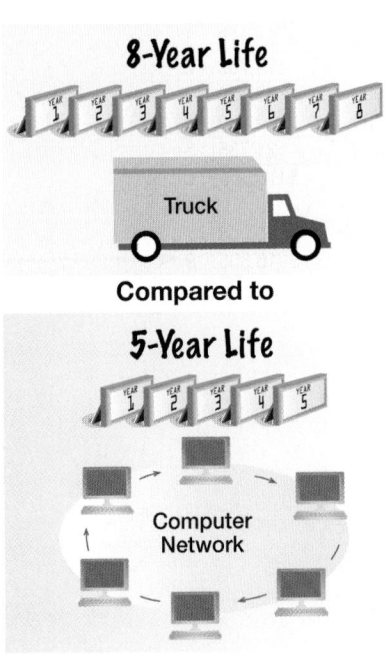

8-Year Life

Truck

Compared to

5-Year Life

Computer Network

for 100,000

UNEQUAL PROPOSAL LIVES

In the preceding discussion, the illustrations of the methods of analyzing capital investment proposals were based on the assumption that alternative proposals had the same useful lives. In practice, however, alternative proposals may have unequal lives. To illustrate, assume that alternative investments, a truck and a computer network, are being compared. The truck has a useful life of eight years, and the computer network has a useful life of five years. Each proposal requires an initial investment of $100,000, and the company desires a rate of return of 10%. The expected cash flows and net present value of each alternative are shown in Exhibit 4. Because of the unequal useful lives of the two proposals, however, the net present values in Exhibit 4 are not comparable.

To make the proposals comparable for the analysis, they can be adjusted to end at the same time. This can be done by assuming that the truck is to be sold at the end of five years. The residual value of the truck must be estimated at the end of five years, and this value must then be included as a cash flow at that date. Both proposals will then cover five years, and net present value analysis can be used to compare the two proposals over the same five-year period. If the truck's estimated residual value is $40,000 at the end of year 5, the net present value for the truck exceeds the net present value for the computers by $1,835 ($18,640 − $16,805), as shown in Exhibit 5. Therefore, the truck may be viewed as the more attractive of the two proposals.

Example Exercise 25-5   **objective 3**

Project 1 requires an original investment of $50,000. The project will yield cash flows of $12,000 per year for seven years. Project 2 has a calculated net present value of $8,900 over a five-year life. Project 1 could be sold at the end of five years for a price of $30,000. (a) Determine the net present value of Project 1 over a five-year life with salvage value assuming a minimum rate of return of 12%. (b) Which project provides the greatest net present value?

(continued)

---

7 The impact of income taxes on capital investment analysis is described and illustrated in advanced textbooks.

Follow My Example 25-5

Project 1

a. Present value of $12,000 per year at 12% for 5 years $43,260 [$12,000 × 3.605 (Exhibit 2, 12%, 5 years)]
    Present value of $30,000 at 12% at the end of 5 years   17,010 [$30,000 × 0.567 (Exhibit 1, 12%, 5 years)]
    Total present value of Project 1 $60,270
    Total cost of Project 1   50,000
    Net present value of Project 1 $10,270

b. Project 1—$10,270 is greater than the net present value of Project 2, $8,900.

For Practice: PE 25-5A, PE 25-5B

EXHIBIT 4

Net Present Value Analysis—Unequal Lives of Proposals

	A	B	C	D	
		Truck			
	Year	Present Value of $1 at 10%	Net Cash Flow	Present Value of Net Cash Flow	
1	1	0.909	$ 30,000	$ 27,270	1
2	2	0.826	30,000	24,780	2
3	3	0.751	25,000	18,775	3
4	4	0.683	20,000	13,660	4
5	5	0.621	15,000	9,315	5
6	6	0.564	15,000	8,460	6
7	7	0.513	10,000	5,130	7
8	8	0.467	10,000	4,670	8
9	Total		$155,000	$112,060	9
10					10
11	Amount to be invested			100,000	11
12	Net present value			$ 12,060	12

	A	B	C	D	
		Computer Network			
	Year	Present Value of $1 at 10%	Net Cash Flow	Present Value of Net Cash Flow	
1	1	0.909	$ 30,000	$ 27,270	1
2	2	0.826	30,000	24,780	2
3	3	0.751	30,000	22,530	3
4	4	0.683	30,000	20,490	4
5	5	0.621	35,000	21,735	5
6	Total		$155,000	$116,805	6
7					7
8	Amount to be invested			100,000	8
9	Net present value			$ 16,805	9

EXHIBIT 5

Net Present Value Analysis—Equalized Lives of Proposals

	A	B	C	D	
		Truck—Revised to 5-Year Life			
	Year	Present Value of $1 at 10%	Net Cash Flow	Present Value of Net Cash Flow	
1	1	0.909	$ 30,000	$ 27,270	1
2	2	0.826	30,000	24,780	2
3	3	0.751	25,000	18,775	3
4	4	0.683	20,000	13,660	4
5	5	0.621	15,000	9,315	5
6	5 (Residual				6
7	value)	0.621	40,000	24,840	7
8	Total		$160,000	$118,640	8
9					9
10	Amount to be invested			100,000	10
11	Net present value			$ 18,640	11

Truck NPV greater than Computer Network NPV by $1,835

LEASE VERSUS CAPITAL INVESTMENT

Leasing fixed assets has become common in many industries. For example, hospitals often lease diagnostic and other medical equipment. Leasing allows a business to use fixed assets without spending large amounts of cash to purchase them. In addition, management may believe that a fixed asset has a high risk of becoming obsolete. This risk may be reduced by leasing rather than purchasing the asset. Also, the *Internal Revenue Code* allows the lessor (the owner of the asset) to pass tax deductions on to the lessee (the party leasing the asset). These provisions of the tax law have made leasing assets more attractive. For example, a company that pays $50,000 per year for leasing a $200,000 fixed asset with a life of eight years is permitted to deduct from taxable income the annual lease payments.

In many cases, before a final decision is made, management should consider leasing assets instead of purchasing them. Normally, leasing assets is more costly than purchasing because the lessor must include in the rental price not only the costs associated with owning the assets but also a profit. Nevertheless, using the methods of evaluating capital investment proposals, management should consider whether it is more profitable to lease rather than purchase an asset.

Merck & Co., Inc., a major pharmaceutical company, includes uncertainty in analyzing drugs under research and development. A single hit would pay for the investment costs of many failures. Management uses a technique in probability theory, called *Monte Carlo analysis*, which shows that the drugs under development could be very profitable.

UNCERTAINTY

All capital investment analyses rely on factors that are uncertain. For example, the estimates related to revenues, expenses, and cash flows are uncertain. The long-term nature of capital investments suggests that some estimates are likely to involve uncertainty. Errors in one or more of the estimates could lead to incorrect decisions.

CHANGES IN PRICE LEVELS

In performing investment analysis, management must be concerned about changes in price levels. Price levels may change due to **inflation**, which occurs when general price levels are rising. Thus, while general prices are rising, the returns on an investment must exceed the rising price level, or else the cash returned on the investment becomes less valuable over time.

Price levels may also change for foreign investments as the result of currency exchange rates. **Currency exchange rates** are the rates at which currency in another country can be exchanged for U.S. dollars. If the amount of local dollars that can be exchanged for one U.S. dollar increases, then the local currency is said to be weakening to the dollar. Thus, if a company made an investment in another country where the local currency was weakening, it would adversely impact the return on that investment as expressed in U.S. dollars. This is because the expected amount of local currency returned on the investment would purchase fewer U.S. dollars.[8]

Management should attempt to anticipate future price levels and consider their effects on the estimates used in capital investment analyses. Changes in anticipated price levels could significantly affect the analyses.

QUALITATIVE CONSIDERATIONS

Some benefits of capital investments are qualitative in nature and cannot be easily estimated in dollar terms. If management does not consider these qualitative considerations, the quantitative analyses may suggest rejecting a worthy investment.

Qualitative considerations in capital investment analysis are most appropriate for strategic investments. Strategic investments are those that are designed to affect a company's long-term ability to generate profits. Strategic investments often have many uncertainties and intangible benefits. Unlike capital investments that are designed to cut costs, strategic investments have very few "hard" savings. Instead, they may affect future revenues, which are difficult to estimate. An example of a strategic investment is IBM's decision to develop molecular and atomic level nanotechnology

---

8 Further discussion on accounting for foreign currency transactions is available on the companion Web site at www.thomsonedu.com/accounting/warren.

Integrity, Objectivity, and Ethics in Business

ETHICS

ASSUMPTION FUDGING

The results of any capital budgeting analysis depend on many subjective estimates, such as the cash flows, discount rate, time period, and total investment amount. The results of the analysis should be used to either support or reject a project. Capital budgeting should not be used to justify an assumed net present value. That is, the analyst should not work backwards, filling in assumed numbers that will produce the desired net present value. Such a reverse approach reduces the credibility of the entire process.

for enhancing information technology. IBM's investment is justified more on the strategic potential of nanotechnology than on any economic analysis of cash flows.

Qualitative considerations that may influence capital investment analysis include product quality, manufacturing flexibility, employee morale, manufacturing productivity, and market opportunity. Many of these qualitative factors may be as important, if not more important, than the results of quantitative analysis.

Capital Rationing

objective 4

Diagram the capital rationing process.

Funding for capital projects may be obtained from issuing bonds or stock or from operating cash. **Capital rationing** is the process by which management allocates these funds among competing capital investment proposals. In this process, management often uses a combination of the methods described in this chapter. Exhibit 6 portrays the capital rationing decision process.

In capital rationing, alternative proposals are initially screened by establishing minimum standards for the cash payback and the average rate of return. The proposals that survive this screening are further analyzed, using the net present value and internal rate of return methods. Throughout the capital rationing process, qualitative factors related to each proposal should also be considered. For example, the acquisition of new, more efficient equipment that eliminates several jobs could lower employee morale to a level that could decrease overall plant productivity. Alternatively, new equipment might improve the quality of the product and thus increase consumer satisfaction and sales.

The final steps in the capital rationing process are ranking the proposals according to management's criteria, comparing the proposals with the funds available, and selecting the proposals to be funded. Funded proposals are included in the *capital expenditures budget* to aid the planning and financing of operations. Unfunded proposals may be reconsidered if funds later become available.

EXHIBIT 6 | Capital Rationing Decision Process

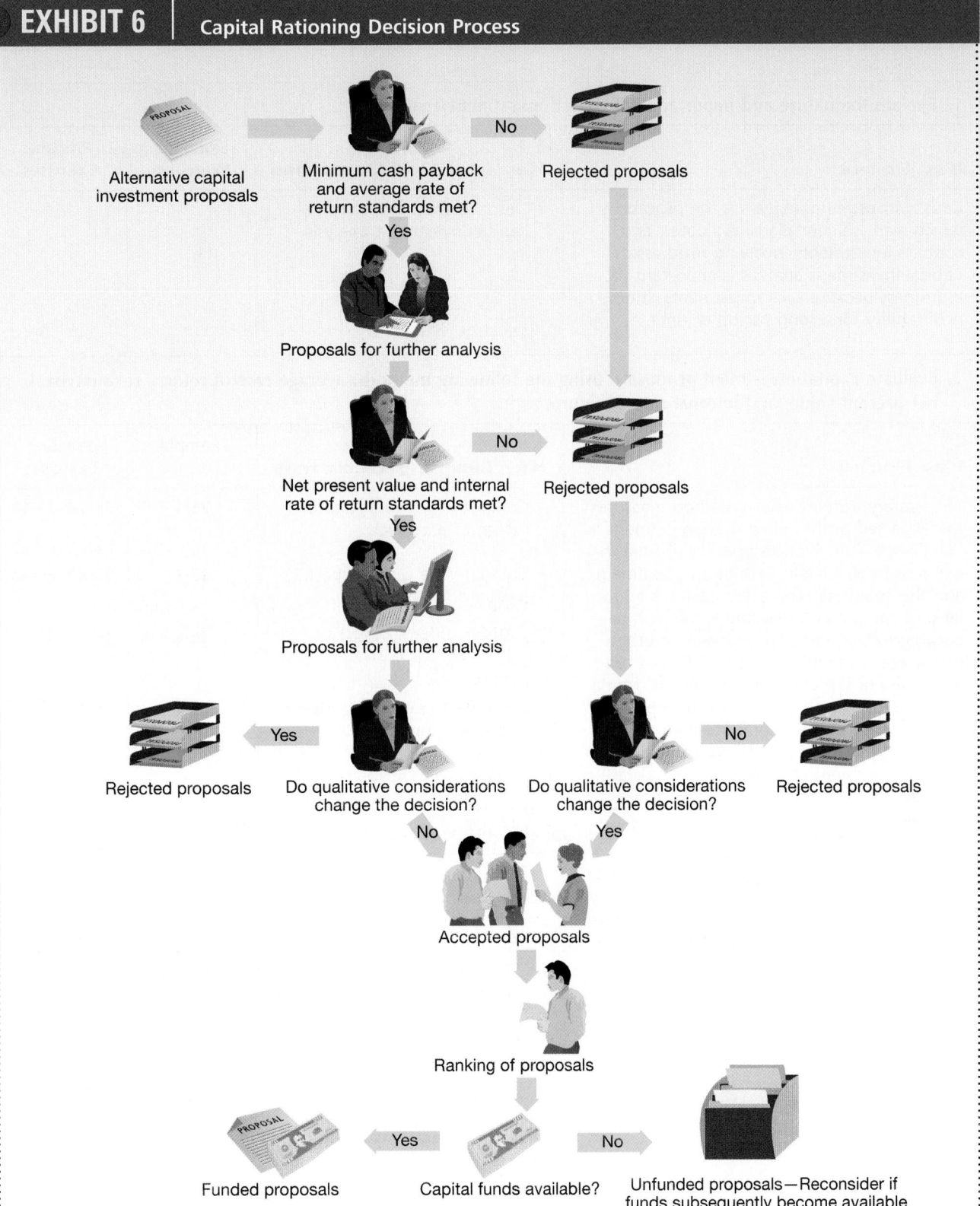

Alternative capital investment proposals

Minimum cash payback and average rate of return standards met?

No → Rejected proposals

Yes

Proposals for further analysis

Net present value and internal rate of return standards met?

No → Rejected proposals

Yes

Proposals for further analysis

Yes → Rejected proposals

Do qualitative considerations change the decision?

Do qualitative considerations change the decision?

No → Rejected proposals

No

Yes

Accepted proposals

Ranking of proposals

Yes → Funded proposals

Capital funds available?

No → Unfunded proposals—Reconsider if funds subsequently become available

At a Glance

1. Explain the nature and importance of capital investment analysis.

Key Points	Key Learning Outcomes	Example Exercises	Practice Exercises
Capital investment analysis is the process by which management plans, evaluates, and controls investments involving fixed assets. Capital investment analysis is important to a business because such investments affect profitability for a long period of time.	• Describe the purpose of capital investment analysis.		

2. Evaluate capital investment proposals, using the following methods: average rate of return, cash payback, net present value, and internal rate of return.

Key Points	Key Learning Outcomes	Example Exercises	Practice Exercises
The average rate of return method measures the expected profitability of an investment in fixed assets. The expected period of time that will pass between the date of an investment and the complete recovery in cash (or equivalent) of the amount invested is the cash payback period. The net present value method uses present values to compute the net present value of the cash flows expected from a proposal. The internal rate of return method uses present values to compute the rate of return from the net cash flows expected from capital investment proposals.	• Compute the average rate of return of a project. • Compute the cash payback period of a project. • Compute the net present value of a project. • Compute the internal rate of return of a project.	25-1 25-2 25-3 25-4	25-1A, 25-1B 25-2A, 25-2B 25-3A, 25-3B 25-4A, 25-4B

3. List and describe factors that complicate capital investment analysis.

Key Points	Key Learning Outcomes	Example Exercises	Practice Exercises
Factors that may complicate capital investment analysis include the impact of the federal income tax, unequal lives of alternative proposals, leasing, uncertainty, changes in price levels, and qualitative considerations.	• Describe the impact of income taxes in capital investment analysis. • Evaluate projects with unequal lives. • Describe leasing versus capital investment. • Describe uncertainty, changes in price levels, and qualitative considerations in capital investment analysis.	25-5	25-5A, 25-5B

4. Diagram the capital rationing process.			
Key Points	**Key Learning Outcomes**	Example Exercises	Practice Exercises
Capital rationing refers to the process by which management allocates available investment funds among competing capital investment proposals. A diagram of the capital rationing process appears in Exhibit 6.	• Define *capital rationing*. • Diagram the capital rationing process.		

Key Terms

annuity (1107)
average rate of return (1103)
capital investment analysis (1102)
capital rationing (1116)
cash payback period (1104)

currency exchange rate (1115)
inflation (1115)
internal rate of return (IRR)
   method (1110)
net present value method (1108)

present value concept (1106)
present value index (1108)
present value of an annuity (1107)
time value of money concept
   (1103)

Illustrative Problem

The capital investment committee of Hopewell Company is currently considering two investments. The estimated income from operations and net cash flows expected from each investment are as follows:

	Truck		Equipment	
Year	Income from Operations	Net Cash Flow	Income from Operations	Net Cash Flow
1	$ 6,000	$ 22,000	$13,000	$ 29,000
2	9,000	25,000	10,000	26,000
3	10,000	26,000	8,000	24,000
4	8,000	24,000	8,000	24,000
5	11,000	27,000	3,000	19,000
	$44,000	$124,000	$42,000	$122,000

Each investment requires $80,000. Straight-line depreciation will be used, and no residual value is expected. The committee has selected a rate of 15% for purposes of the net present value analysis.

Instructions
1. Compute the following:
   a. The average rate of return for each investment.
   b. The net present value for each investment. Use the present value of $1 table appearing in this chapter.
2. Why is the net present value of the equipment greater than the truck, even though its average rate of return is less?
3. Prepare a summary for the capital investment committee, advising it on the relative merits of the two investments.

(continued)

Solution

1. a. Average rate of return for the truck:

$$\frac{\$44,000 \div 5}{(\$80,000 + \$0) \div 2} = 22\%$$

Average rate of return for the equipment:

$$\frac{\$42,000 \div 5}{(\$80,000 + \$0) \div 2} = 21\%$$

b. Net present value analysis:

Year	Present Value of $1 at 15%	Net Cash Flow Truck	Net Cash Flow Equipment	Present Value of Net Cash Flow Truck	Present Value of Net Cash Flow Equipment
1	0.870	$ 22,000	$ 29,000	$19,140	$25,230
2	0.756	25,000	26,000	18,900	19,656
3	0.658	26,000	24,000	17,108	15,792
4	0.572	24,000	24,000	13,728	13,728
5	0.497	27,000	19,000	13,419	9,443
Total		$124,000	$122,000	$82,295	$83,849
Amount to be invested				80,000	80,000
Net present value				$ 2,295	$ 3,849

2. The equipment has a lower average rate of return than the truck because the equipment's total income from operations for the five years is $42,000, which is $2,000 less than the truck's. Even so, the net present value of the equipment is greater than that of the truck, because the equipment has higher cash flows in the early years.

3. Both investments exceed the selected rate established for the net present value analysis. The truck has a higher average rate of return, but the equipment offers a larger net present value. Thus, if only one of the two investments can be accepted, the equipment would be the more attractive.

Self-Examination Questions

(Answers at End of Chapter)

1. Methods of evaluating capital investment proposals that ignore present value include:
   A. average rate of return.
   B. cash payback.
   C. both A and B.
   D. neither A nor B.

2. Management is considering a $100,000 investment in a project with a five-year life and no residual value. If the total income from the project is expected to be $60,000 and recognition is given to the effect of straight-line depreciation on the investment, the average rate of return is:
   A. 12%.   C. 60%.
   B. 24%.   D. 75%.

3. The expected period of time that will elapse between the date of a capital investment and the complete recovery of the amount of cash invested is called the:

   A. average rate of return period.
   B. cash payback period.
   C. net present value period.
   D. internal rate of return period.

4. A project that will cost $120,000 is estimated to generate cash flows of $25,000 per year for eight years. What is the net present value of the project, assuming an 11% required rate of return? (Use the present value tables in Appendix A.)
   A. ($38,214)   C. $55,180
   B. $8,653   D. $75,000

5. A project is estimated to generate cash flows of $40,000 per year for 10 years. The cost of the project is $226,009. What is the internal rate of return for this project?
   A. 8%   C. 12%
   B. 10%   D. 14%

Eye Openers

1. What are the principal objections to the use of the average rate of return method in evaluating capital investment proposals?
2. Discuss the principal limitations of the cash payback method for evaluating capital investment proposals.
3. Why would the average rate of return differ from the internal rate of return on the same project?
4. What information does the cash payback period ignore that is included by the net present value method?
5. Your boss has suggested that a one-year payback period is the same as a 100% average rate of return. Do you agree?
6. Why would the cash payback method understate the attractiveness of a project with a large salvage value?
7. Why would the use of the cash payback period for analyzing the financial performance of theatrical releases from a motion picture production studio be supported over the net present value method?
8. A net present value analysis used to evaluate a proposed equipment acquisition indicated a $7,900 net present value. What is the meaning of the $7,900 as it relates to the desirability of the proposal?
9. Two projects have an identical net present value of $9,000. Are both projects equal in desirability?
10. What are the major disadvantages of the use of the net present value method of analyzing capital investment proposals?
11. What are the major disadvantages of the use of the internal rate of return method of analyzing capital investment proposals?
12. What provision of the Internal Revenue Code is especially important to consider in analyzing capital investment proposals?
13. What method can be used to place two capital investment proposals with unequal useful lives on a comparable basis?
14. What are the major advantages of leasing a fixed asset rather than purchasing it?
15. Give an example of a qualitative factor that should be considered in a capital investment analysis related to acquiring automated factory equipment.
16. Monsanto Company, a large chemical and fibers company, invested $37 million in state-of-the-art systems to improve process control, laboratory automation, and local area network (LAN) communications. The investment was not justified merely on cost savings but was also justified on the basis of qualitative considerations. Monsanto management viewed the investment as a critical element toward achieving its vision of the future. What qualitative and quantitative considerations do you believe Monsanto would have considered in its strategic evaluation of these investments?

Practice Exercises

PE 25-1A
Average rate of return
obj. 2

Determine the average rate of return for a project that is estimated to yield total income of $234,000 over four years, has a cost of $450,000, and has a $50,000 residual value.

PE 25-1B
Average rate of return
obj. 2

Determine the average rate of return for a project that is estimated to yield total income of $72,000 over three years, has a cost of $125,000, and has a $25,000 residual value.

PE 25-2A
Cash payback period
obj. 2

A project has estimated annual net cash flows of $150,000. It is estimated to cost $885,000. Determine the cash payback period.

PE 25-2B
Cash payback period
obj. 2

A project has estimated annual net cash flows of $27,200. It is estimated to cost $68,000. Determine the cash payback period.

PE 25-3A
Net present value
obj. 2

A project has estimated annual net cash flows of $65,000 for six years and is estimated to cost $265,000. Assume a minimum acceptable rate of return of 10%. Using Exhibit 2, determine (1) the net present value of the project and (2) the present value index, rounded to two decimal places.

PE 25-3B
Net present value
obj. 2

A project has estimated annual net cash flows of $22,000 for four years and is estimated to cost $70,000. Assume a minimum acceptable rate of return of 12%. Using Exhibit 2, determine (1) the net present value of the project and (2) the present value index, rounded to two decimal places.

PE 25-4A
Internal rate of return
obj. 2

A project is estimated to cost $175,665 and provide annual net cash flows of $35,000 for 10 years. Determine the internal rate of return for this project, using Exhibit 2.

PE 25-4B
Internal rate of return
obj. 2

A project is estimated to cost $745,200 and provide annual net cash flows of $120,000 for eight years. Determine the internal rate of return for this project, using Exhibit 2.

PE 25-5A
Net present value—unequal lives
obj. 3

Project 1 requires an original investment of $80,000. The project will yield cash flows of $14,000 per year for eight years. Project 2 has a calculated net present value of $5,000 over a five-year life. Project 1 could be sold at the end of five years for a price of $50,000. (a) Determine the net present value of Project 1 over a five-year life with salvage value assuming a minimum rate of return of 10%. (b) Which project provides the greatest net present value?

PE 25-5B
Net present value—unequal lives
obj. 3

Project A requires an original investment of $35,000. The project will yield cash flows of $8,000 per year for seven years. Project B has a calculated net present value of $1,000 over a five-year life. Project A could be sold at the end of five years for a price of $20,000. (a) Determine the net present value of Project A over a five-year life with salvage value assuming a minimum rate of return of 15%. (b) Which project provides the greatest net present value?

Exercises

EX 25-1
Average rate of return
obj. 2

✓ Testing equipment, 10%

The following data are accumulated by Green Mountain Testing Services Inc. in evaluating two competing capital investment proposals:

	Testing Equipment	Centrifuge
Amount of investment	$34,000	$40,000
Useful life	6 years	8 years
Estimated residual value	0	0
Estimated total income over the useful life	$10,200	$14,000

Determine the expected average rate of return for each proposal.

EX 25-2
Average rate of return—cost savings
obj. 2

International Fabricators Inc. is considering an investment in equipment that will replace direct labor. The equipment has a cost of $85,000, with a $5,000 residual value and a 10-year life. The equipment will replace one employee who has an average wage of $23,000 per year. In addition, the equipment will have operating and energy costs of $6,000 per year.

Determine the average rate of return on the equipment, giving effect to straight-line depreciation on the investment.

EX 25-3

Average rate of return—new product

obj. 2

✓ *Average annual income, $216,000*

Airwave Communications Inc. is considering an investment in new equipment that will be used to manufacture a PDA (personal data assistant). The PDA is expected to generate additional annual sales of 4,800 units at $350 per unit. The equipment has a cost of $910,000, residual value of $50,000, and a 10-year life. The equipment can only be used to manufacture the PDA. The cost to manufacture the PDA is shown below.

Cost per unit:	
Direct labor	$ 52.00
Direct materials	195.00
Factory overhead (including depreciation)	58.00
Total cost per unit	$305.00

Determine the average rate of return on the equipment.

EX 25-4

Calculate cash flows

obj. 2

✓ *Year 1: ($62,725)*

Gardeneer Inc. is planning to invest $184,000 in a new garden tool that is expected to generate additional sales of 7,500 units at $38 each. The $184,000 investment includes $54,000 for initial launch-related expenses and $130,000 for equipment that has a 10-year life and a $17,500 residual value. Selling expenses related to the new product are expected to be 6% of sales revenue. The cost to manufacture the product includes the following per-unit costs:

Direct labor	$ 6.00
Direct materials	11.75
Fixed factory overhead—depreciation	1.50
Variable factory overhead	1.80
Total	$21.05

Determine the net cash flows for the first year of the project, years 2–9, and for the last year of the project.

EX 25-5

Cash payback period

obj. 2

✓ *Proposal 1: 5 years*

First Union Bank Corporation is evaluating two capital investment proposals for a drive-up ATM kiosk, each requiring an investment of $300,000 and each with an eight-year life and expected total net cash flows of $480,000. Location 1 is expected to provide equal annual net cash flows of $60,000, and Location 2 is expected to have the following unequal annual net cash flows:

Year 1	$90,000	Year 5	$45,000
Year 2	80,000	Year 6	45,000
Year 3	65,000	Year 7	45,000
Year 4	65,000	Year 8	45,000

Determine the cash payback period for both proposals.

EX 25-6

Cash payback method

obj. 2

✓ *a. Cosmetics: 4 years*

Family Care Products Company is considering an investment in one of two new product lines. The investment required for either product line is $600,000. The net cash flows associated with each product are as follows:

Year	Liquid Soap	Cosmetics
1	$120,000	$165,000
2	120,000	155,000
3	120,000	140,000
4	120,000	140,000
5	120,000	110,000
6	120,000	90,000
7	120,000	80,000
8	120,000	80,000
Total	$960,000	$960,000

a. Recommend a product offering to Family Care Products Company, based on the cash payback period for each product line.

b. ⬛▬▬ Why is one product line preferred over the other, even though they both have the same total net cash flows through eight periods?

EX 25-7
*Net present value
method*

obj. 2

✓ a. NPV ($7,700)

The following data are accumulated by Zadok Company in evaluating the purchase of $370,000 of equipment, having a four-year useful life:

	Net Income	Net Cash Flow
Year 1	$67,500	$160,000
Year 2	47,500	140,000
Year 3	(12,500)	80,000
Year 4	(12,500)	80,000

a. Assuming that the desired rate of return is 12%, determine the net present value for the proposal. Use the table of the present value of $1 appearing in Exhibit 1 of this chapter.
b. ▭▭▶ Would management be likely to look with favor on the proposal? Explain.

EX 25-8
*Net present value
method*

obj. 2

✓ a. $21

Metro-Goldwyn-Mayer Studios Inc. (MGM) is a major producer and distributor of theatrical and television filmed entertainment. Regarding theatrical films, MGM states, "Our feature films are exploited through a series of sequential domestic and international distribution channels, typically beginning with theatrical exhibition. Thereafter, feature films are first made available for home video generally six months after theatrical release; for pay television, one year after theatrical release; and for syndication, approximately three to five years after theatrical release."

Assume that MGM releases a film during early 2009 at a cost of $115 million, and releases it halfway through the year. During the last half of 2009, the film earns revenues of $140 million at the box office. The film requires $45 million of advertising during the release. One year later, by the end of 2010, the film is expected to earn MGM net cash flows from home video sales of $36 million. By the end of 2011, the film is expected to earn MGM $19 million from pay TV; and by the end of 2012, the film is expected to earn $4 million from syndication.

a. Determine the net present value of the film as of the beginning of 2009 if the desired rate of return is 20%. To simplify present value calculations, assume all annual net cash flows occur at the end of each year. Use the table of the present value of $1 appearing in Exhibit 1 of this chapter. Round to the nearest whole million dollars.
b. ▭▭▶ Under the assumptions provided here, is the film expected to be financially successful?

EX 25-9
*Net present value
method—annuity*

obj. 2

✓ a. $50,000

Maddox Excavation Company is planning an investment of $205,000 for a bulldozer. The bulldozer is expected to operate for 1,600 hours per year for five years. Customers will be charged $95 per hour for bulldozer work. The bulldozer operator is paid an hourly wage of $25 per hour. The bulldozer is expected to require annual maintenance costing $14,000. The bulldozer uses fuel that is expected to cost $30 per hour of bulldozer operation.

a. Determine the equal annual net cash flows from operating the bulldozer.
b. Determine the net present value of the investment, assuming that the desired rate of return is 10%. Use the table of present values of an annuity of $1 in the chapter. Round to the nearest dollar.
c. ▭▭▶ Should Maddox invest in the bulldozer, based on this analysis?

EX 25-10
*Net present value—
unequal lives*

objs. 2, 3

✓ Net present value,
Apartment Complex,
$117,500

Blue Ridge Development Company has two competing projects: an apartment complex and an office building. Both projects have an initial investment of $720,000. The net cash flows estimated for the two projects are as follows:

	Net Cash Flow	
Year	Apartment Complex	Office Building
1	$240,000	$280,000
2	210,000	280,000
3	210,000	265,000
4	160,000	265,000
5	150,000	
6	120,000	
7	90,000	
8	60,000	

The estimated residual value of the apartment complex at the end of year 4 is $420,000.

Determine which project should be favored, comparing the net present values of the two projects and assuming a minimum rate of return of 15%. Use the table of present values in the chapter.

EX 25-11
Net present value method

obj. 2

✓ a. Net investment,
$1,693,000

IHOP Corp. franchises breakfast-oriented restaurants throughout North America. The average development costs for a new restaurant were reported by IHOP as follows:

Land	$ 667,000
Building	800,000
Equipment	341,000
Site improvements	185,000
Total	$1,993,000

IHOP develops and owns the restaurant properties. IHOP indicates that the franchisee pays an initial franchise fee of $300,000 for a newly developed restaurant. IHOP also receives revenues from the franchisee as follows: (1) a royalty equal to 4.5% of the restaurant's sales; (2) income from the leasing of the restaurant and related equipment; and (3) revenue from the sale of certain proprietary products, primarily pancake mixes.

IHOP reported that franchise operators earned annual revenues averaging $1,500,000 per restaurant. Assume that the net cash flows received by IHOP for lease payments and sale of proprietary products (items 2 and 3 above) average $200,000 per year per restaurant, for 10 years. Assume further that the franchise operator can purchase the property for $700,000 at the end of the lease term.

Determine IHOP's:

a. Net investment (development cost less initial franchise fee) to develop a restaurant.
b. Net present value for a new restaurant, assuming a 10-year life, no change in annual revenues, and a 12% desired rate of return. Use the present value tables appearing in Exhibits 1 and 2 in this chapter.

EX 25-12
Net present value method

obj. 2

✓ a. $95,950,000

Carnival Corporation has recently placed into service some of the largest cruise ships in the world. One of these ships, the *Carnival Glory*, can hold up to 3,000 passengers and cost $530 million to build. Assume the following additional information:

- The average occupancy rate for the new ship is estimated to be 85% of capacity.
- There will be 300 cruise days per year.
- The variable expenses per passenger are estimated to be $80 per cruise day.
- The revenue per passenger is expected to be $310 per cruise day.
- The fixed expenses for running the ship, other than depreciation, are estimated to be $80,000,000 per year.
- The ship has a service life of 10 years, with a salvage value of $90,000,000 at the end of 10 years.

a. Determine the annual net cash flow from operating the cruise ship.
b. Determine the net present value of this investment, assuming a 12% minimum rate of return. Use the present value tables provided in the chapter in determining your answer.
c. Assume that Carnival Corp. decided to increase its price so that the revenue increased to $320 per passenger per cruise day. Would this allow Carnival Corp. to earn a 15% rate of return on the cruise ship investment, assuming no change in any of the other assumptions? Use the present value tables provided in the chapter in determining your answer.

EX 25-13
Present value index

obj. 2

✓ Location A, 0.95

Drive By Doughnuts has computed the net present value for capital expenditure locations A and B, using the net present value method. Relevant data related to the computation are as follows:

	Location A	Location B
Total present value of net cash flow	$306,280	$177,660
Amount to be invested	322,400	164,500
Net present value	$ (16,120)	$ 13,160

Determine the present value index for each proposal.

EX 25-14
Net present value method and present value index
obj. 2

✓ b. Packing Machine, 1.09

MVP Sporting Goods Company is considering an investment in one of two machines. The sewing machine will increase productivity from sewing 120 baseballs per hour to sewing 180 per hour. The contribution margin is $0.80 per baseball. Assume that any increased production of baseballs can be sold. The second machine is an automatic packing machine for the golf ball line. The packing machine will reduce packing labor cost. The labor cost saved is equivalent to $24 per hour. The sewing machine will cost $354,300, have an eight-year life, and will operate for 1,750 hours per year. The packing machine will cost $148,300, have an eight-year life, and will operate for 1,500 hours per year. MVP seeks a minimum rate of return of 15% on its investments.

a. Determine the net present value for the two machines. Use the table of present values of an annuity of $1 in the chapter. Round to the nearest dollar.
b. Determine the present value index for the two machines. Round to two decimal places.
c. ▭▬► If MVP has sufficient funds for only one of the machines and qualitative factors are equal between the two machines, in which machine should it invest?

EX 25-15
Average rate of return, cash payback period, net present value method
obj. 2

✓ b. 5 years

Southern Rail Inc. is considering acquiring equipment at a cost of $442,500. The equipment has an estimated life of 10 years and no residual value. It is expected to provide yearly net cash flows of $88,500. The company's minimum desired rate of return for net present value analysis is 12%.
    Compute the following:

a. The average rate of return, giving effect to straight-line depreciation on the investment.
b. The cash payback period.
c. The net present value. Use the table of the present value of an annuity of $1 appearing in this chapter. Round to the nearest dollar.

EX 25-16
Payback period, net present value analysis and qualitative considerations
objs. 2, 3

The plant manager of O'Brien Equipment Company is considering the purchase of a new robotic assembly plant. The new robotic line will cost $1,250,000. The manager believes that the new investment will result in direct labor savings of $250,000 per year for 10 years.

a. What is the payback period on this project?
b. What is the net present value, assuming a 10% rate of return?
c. ▭▬► What else should the manager consider in the analysis?

EX 25-17
Internal rate of return method
obj. 2

✓ a. 4.487

The internal rate of return method is used by Timberframe Renovations Inc. in analyzing a capital expenditure proposal that involves an investment of $62,818 and annual net cash flows of $14,000 for each of the eight years of its useful life.

a. Determine a present value factor for an annuity of $1 which can be used in determining the internal rate of return.
b. Using the factor determined in part (a) and the present value of an annuity of $1 table appearing in this chapter, determine the internal rate of return for the proposal.

EX 25-18
Internal rate of return method
obj. 2

REAL WORLD

IBM recently saved $250 million over three years by implementing supply chain software that reduced the cost of components used in its manufacture of computers. If we assume that the savings occurred equally over the three years and the cost of implementing the new software was $175,500,000, what would be the internal rate of return for this investment? Use the present value of an annuity of $1 table found in Exhibit 2 in determining your answer.

EX 25-19
Internal rate of return method—two projects
obj. 2

Southwest Chip Company is considering two possible investments: a delivery truck or a bagging machine. The delivery truck would cost $39,918 and could be used to deliver an additional 36,250 bags of taquitos chips per year. Each bag of chips can be sold for a contribution margin of $0.40. The delivery truck operating expenses, excluding depreciation,

✔ *a. Delivery truck, 10%*   are $0.35 per mile for 18,000 miles per year. The bagging machine would replace an old bagging machine, and its net investment cost would be $49,920. The new machine would require three fewer hours of direct labor per day. Direct labor is $16 per hour. There are 250 operating days in the year. Both the truck and the bagging machine are estimated to have seven-year lives. The minimum rate of return is 11%. However, Southwest has funds to invest in only one of the projects.

    a. Compute the internal rate of return for each investment. Use the table of present values of an annuity of $1 in the chapter.
    b. ➤ Provide a memo to management with a recommendation.

EX 25-20
Net present value method and internal rate of return method
obj. 2

✔ *a. ($6,606)*

Buckeye Healthcare Corp. is proposing to spend $96,030 on an eight-year project that has estimated net cash flows of $18,000 for each of the eight years.

    a. Compute the net present value, using a rate of return of 12%. Use the table of present values of an annuity of $1 in the chapter.
    b. ➤ Based on the analysis prepared in part (a), is the rate of return (1) more than 12%, (2) 12%, or (3) less than 12%? Explain.
    c. Determine the internal rate of return by computing a present value factor for an annuity of $1 and using the table of the present value of an annuity of $1 presented in the text.

EX 25-21
Identify error in capital investment analysis calculations
obj. 2

Integrated Technologies Inc. is considering the purchase of automated machinery that is expected to have a useful life of four years and no residual value. The average rate of return on the average investment has been computed to be 25%, and the cash payback period was computed to be 4.5 years.

    ➤ Do you see any reason to question the validity of the data presented? Explain.

Problems Series A

PR 25-1A
Average rate of return method, net present value method, and analysis
obj. 2

✔ *1. a. 45.7%*

The capital investment committee of Estate Landscaping Company is considering two capital investments. The estimated income from operations and net cash flows from each investment are as follows:

	Greenhouse		Skid Loader	
Year	Income from Operations	Net Cash Flow	Income from Operations	Net Cash Flow
1	$16,000	$ 30,000	$26,000	$ 40,000
2	16,000	30,000	21,000	35,000
3	16,000	30,000	16,000	30,000
4	16,000	30,000	11,000	25,000
5	16,000	30,000	6,000	20,000
	$80,000	$150,000	$80,000	$150,000

    Each project requires an investment of $70,000. Straight-line depreciation will be used, and no residual value is expected. The committee has selected a rate of 12% for purposes of the net present value analysis.

Instructions
1. Compute the following:
    a. The average rate of return for each investment. Round to one decimal place.
    b. The net present value for each investment. Use the present value of $1 table appearing in this chapter.
2. ➤ Prepare a brief report for the capital investment committee, advising it on the relative merits of the two investments.

PR 25-2A

Cash payback period, net present value method, and analysis

obj. 2

✓1. b. Plant Expansion, $104,410

Unique Boutique Inc. is considering two investment projects. The estimated net cash flows from each project are as follows:

Year	Plant Expansion	Retail Store Expansion
1	$ 280,000	$ 260,000
2	260,000	260,000
3	230,000	250,000
4	260,000	250,000
5	270,000	280,000
Total	$1,300,000	$1,300,000

Each project requires an investment of $770,000. A rate of 15% has been selected for the net present value analysis.

Instructions

1. Compute the following for each project:
    a. Cash payback period.
    b. The net present value. Use the present value of $1 table appearing in this chapter.
2. ▭▭▭▶ Prepare a brief report advising management on the relative merits of each project.

PR 25-3A

Net present value method, present value index, and analysis

obj. 2

✓2. Railcars, 0.97

Continental Railroad Company wishes to evaluate three capital investment proposals by using the net present value method. Relevant data related to the proposals are summarized as follows:

	Route Expansion	Acquire Railcars	New Maintenance Yard
Amount to be invested	$830,000	$480,000	$410,000
Annual net cash flows:			
Year 1	450,000	245,000	215,000
Year 2	400,000	220,000	205,000
Year 3	370,000	190,000	200,000

Instructions

1. Assuming that the desired rate of return is 20%, prepare a net present value analysis for each proposal. Use the present value of $1 table appearing in this chapter.
2. Determine a present value index for each proposal. Round to two decimal places.
3. ▭▭▭▶ Which proposal offers the largest amount of present value per dollar of investment? Explain.

PR 25-4A

Net present value method, internal rate of return method, and analysis

obj. 2

✓1. a. Generating unit, $191,750

The management of Genco Utilities Inc. is considering two capital investment projects. The estimated net cash flows from each project are as follows:

Year	Generating Unit	Distribution Network Expansion
1	$650,000	$180,000
2	650,000	180,000
3	650,000	180,000
4	650,000	180,000

The generating unit requires an investment of $2,060,500, while the distribution network expansion requires an investment of $546,660. No residual value is expected from either project.

Instructions

1. Compute the following for each project:
    a. The net present value. Use a rate of 6% and the present value of an annuity of $1 table appearing in this chapter.
    b. A present value index. Round to two decimal places.
2. Determine the internal rate of return for each project by (a) computing a present value factor for an annuity of $1 and (b) using the present value of an annuity of $1 table appearing in this chapter.

3. What advantage does the internal rate of return method have over the net present value method in comparing projects?

PR 25-5A
Evaluate alternative capital investment decisions
objs. **2, 3**

✓1. Project II, $72,626

The investment committee of Safe Hands Insurance Co. is evaluating two projects. The projects have different useful lives, but each requires an investment of $225,000. The estimated net cash flows from each project are as follows:

	Net Cash Flows	
Year	Project I	Project II
1	$70,000	$98,000
2	70,000	98,000
3	70,000	98,000
4	70,000	98,000
5	70,000	
6	70,000	

The committee has selected a rate of 12% for purposes of net present value analysis. It also estimates that the residual value at the end of each project's useful life is $0, but at the end of the fourth year, Project I's residual value would be $150,000.

Instructions
1. For each project, compute the net present value. Use the present value of an annuity of $1 table appearing in this chapter. (Ignore the unequal lives of the projects.)
2. For each project, compute the net present value, assuming that Project I is adjusted to a four-year life for purposes of analysis. Use the present value of $1 table appearing in this chapter.
3. Prepare a report to the investment committee, providing your advice on the relative merits of the two projects.

PR 25-6A
Capital rationing decision involving four proposals
objs. **2, 4**

✓5. Proposal B, 1.18

Madison Capital Group is considering allocating a limited amount of capital investment funds among four proposals. The amount of proposed investment, estimated income from operations, and net cash flow for each proposal are as follows:

	Investment	Year	Income from Operations	Net Cash Flow
Proposal A:	$540,000	1	$ 42,000	$150,000
		2	42,000	150,000
		3	42,000	150,000
		4	(18,000)	90,000
		5	(18,000)	90,000
			$ 90,000	$630,000
Proposal B:	$250,000	1	$ 50,000	$100,000
		2	40,000	90,000
		3	30,000	80,000
		4	15,000	65,000
		5	15,000	65,000
			$150,000	$400,000
Proposal C:	$640,000	1	$ 92,000	$220,000
		2	82,000	210,000
		3	82,000	210,000
		4	62,000	190,000
		5	32,000	160,000
			$350,000	$990,000
Proposal D:	$310,000	1	$ 68,000	$130,000
		2	38,000	100,000
		3	(2,000)	60,000
		4	(2,000)	60,000
		5	(2,000)	60,000
			$100,000	$410,000

The company's capital rationing policy requires a maximum cash payback period of three years. In addition, a minimum average rate of return of 12% is required on all projects. If the preceding standards are met, the net present value method and present value indexes are used to rank the remaining proposals.

Instructions

1. Compute the cash payback period for each of the four proposals.
2. Giving effect to straight-line depreciation on the investments and assuming no estimated residual value, compute the average rate of return for each of the four proposals. Round to one decimal place.
3. Using the following format, summarize the results of your computations in parts (1) and (2). By placing a check mark in the appropriate column at the right, indicate which proposals should be accepted for further analysis and which should be rejected.

Proposal	Cash Payback Period	Average Rate of Return	Accept for Further Analysis	Reject
A				
B				
C				
D				

4. For the proposals accepted for further analysis in part (3), compute the net present value. Use a rate of 12% and the present value of $1 table appearing in this chapter. Round to the nearest dollar.
5. Compute the present value index for each of the proposals in part (4). Round to two decimal places.
6. Rank the proposals from most attractive to least attractive, based on the present values of net cash flows computed in part (4).
7. Rank the proposals from most attractive to least attractive, based on the present value indexes computed in part (5).
8. ▭▭▭▶ Based upon the analyses, comment on the relative attractiveness of the proposals ranked in parts (6) and (7).

Problems Series B

PR 25-1B

Average rate of return method, net present value method, and analysis

obj. 2

✓ 1.a. 15.9%

The capital investment committee of Triple C Trucking Inc. is considering two investment projects. The estimated income from operations and net cash flows from each investment are as follows:

Year	Warehouse Income from Operations	Warehouse Net Cash Flow	Parcel Tracking Technology Income from Operations	Parcel Tracking Technology Net Cash Flow
1	$ 46,000	$162,000	$ 19,000	$135,000
2	46,000	162,000	29,000	145,000
3	46,000	162,000	54,000	170,000
4	46,000	162,000	54,000	170,000
5	46,000	162,000	74,000	190,000
Total	$230,000	$810,000	$230,000	$810,000

Each project requires an investment of $580,000. Straight-line depreciation will be used, and no residual value is expected. The committee has selected a rate of 12% for purposes of the net present value analysis.

Instructions

1. Compute the following:
   a. The average rate of return for each investment. Round to one decimal place.
   b. The net present value for each investment. Use the present value of $1 table appearing in this chapter.
2. ▭▭▭▶ Prepare a brief report for the capital investment committee, advising it on the relative merits of the two projects.

PR 25-2B

Cash payback period, net present value method, and analysis

obj. 2

✓ *1. b. Home & Garden, $92,360*

Family Life Publications Inc. is considering two new magazine products. The estimated net cash flows from each product are as follows:

Year	Home & Garden	Today's Teen
1	$230,000	$160,000
2	210,000	280,000
3	190,000	200,000
4	50,000	40,000
5	40,000	40,000
Total	$720,000	$720,000

Each product requires an investment of $440,000. A rate of 15% has been selected for the net present value analysis.

Instructions

1. Compute the following for each project:
   a. Cash payback period.
   b. The net present value. Use the present value of $1 table appearing in this chapter.
2. ▭▶ Prepare a brief report advising management on the relative merits of each of the two products.

PR 25-3B

Net present value method, present value index, and analysis

obj. 2

✓ *2. Branch office expansion, 0.98*

First Security Bancorp Inc. wishes to evaluate three capital investment projects by using the net present value method. Relevant data related to the projects are summarized as follows:

	Branch Office Expansion	Computer System Upgrade	Install Internet Bill-Pay
Amount to be invested	$505,000	$375,000	$640,000
Annual net cash flows:			
Year 1	250,000	210,000	335,000
Year 2	235,000	190,000	320,000
Year 3	215,000	180,000	315,000

Instructions

1. Assuming that the desired rate of return is 20%, prepare a net present value analysis for each project. Use the present value of $1 table appearing in this chapter.
2. Determine a present value index for each project. Round to two decimal places.
3. ▭▶ Which project offers the largest amount of present value per dollar of investment? Explain.

PR 25-4B

Net present value method, internal rate of return method, and analysis

obj. 2

✓ *1. a. Radio station, $50,400*

The management of Horizon Media Inc. is considering two capital investment projects. The estimated net cash flows from each project are as follows:

Year	Radio Station	TV Station
1	$160,000	$450,000
2	160,000	450,000
3	160,000	450,000
4	160,000	450,000

The radio station requires an investment of $456,800, while the TV station requires an investment of $1,366,650. No residual value is expected from either project.

Instructions

1. Compute the following for each project:
   a. The net present value. Use a rate of 10% and the present value of an annuity of $1 table appearing in this chapter.
   b. A present value index. Round to two decimal places.
2. Determine the internal rate of return for each project by (a) computing a present value factor for an annuity of $1 and (b) using the present value of an annuity of $1 table appearing in this chapter.
3. ▭▶ What advantage does the internal rate of return method have over the net present value method in comparing projects?

PR 25-5B
*Evaluate alternative
capital investment
decisions*

objs. 2, 3

✓ 1. Site B, $150,470

The investment committee of Mr. Bob Restaurants Inc. is evaluating two restaurant sites. The sites have different useful lives, but each requires an investment of $445,000. The estimated net cash flows from each site are as follows:

Net Cash Flows

Year	Site A	Site B
1	$170,000	$230,000
2	170,000	230,000
3	170,000	230,000
4	170,000	230,000
5	170,000	
6	170,000	

The committee has selected a rate of 20% for purposes of net present value analysis. It also estimates that the residual value at the end of each restaurant's useful life is $0, but at the end of the fourth year, Site A's residual value would be $340,000.

Instructions

1. For each site, compute the net present value. Use the present value of an annuity of $1 table appearing in this chapter. (Ignore the unequal lives of the projects.)
2. For each site, compute the net present value, assuming that Site A is adjusted to a four-year life for purposes of analysis. Use the present value of $1 table appearing in this chapter.
3. ▬▬▶ Prepare a report to the investment committee, providing your advice on the relative merits of the two sites.

PR 25-6B
*Capital rationing decision
involving four proposals*

objs. 2, 4

✓ 5. Proposal B, 1.26

Horizon Communications Inc. is considering allocating a limited amount of capital investment funds among four proposals. The amount of proposed investment, estimated income from operations, and net cash flow for each proposal are as follows:

	Investment	Year	Income from Operations	Net Cash Flow
Proposal A:	$680,000	1	$ 74,000	$210,000
		2	74,000	210,000
		3	74,000	210,000
		4	14,000	150,000
		5	14,000	150,000
			$250,000	$930,000
Proposal B:	$155,000	1	$ 29,000	$ 60,000
		2	64,000	95,000
		3	9,000	40,000
		4	(1,000)	30,000
		5	(11,000)	20,000
			$ 90,000	$245,000
Proposal C:	$281,250	1	$ 18,750	$ 75,000
		2	18,750	75,000
		3	18,750	75,000
		4	18,750	75,000
		5	(6,250)	50,000
			$ 68,750	$350,000
Proposal D:	$260,000	1	$ 38,000	$ 90,000
		2	38,000	90,000
		3	28,000	80,000
		4	28,000	80,000
		5	23,000	75,000
			$155,000	$415,000

The company's capital rationing policy requires a maximum cash payback period of three years. In addition, a minimum average rate of return of 12% is required on all projects. If the preceding standards are met, the net present value method and present value indexes are used to rank the remaining proposals.

Instructions

1. Compute the cash payback period for each of the four proposals.
2. Giving effect to straight-line depreciation on the investments and assuming no estimated residual value, compute the average rate of return for each of the four proposals. Round to one decimal place.
3. Using the following format, summarize the results of your computations in parts (1) and (2). By placing a check mark in the appropriate column at the right, indicate which proposals should be accepted for further analysis and which should be rejected.

Proposal	Cash Payback Period	Average Rate of Return	Accept for Further Analysis	Reject
A				
B				
C				
D				

4. For the proposals accepted for further analysis in part (3), compute the net present value. Use a rate of 10% and the present value of $1 table appearing in this chapter. Round to the nearest dollar.
5. Compute the present value index for each of the proposals in part (4). Round to two decimal places.
6. Rank the proposals from most attractive to least attractive, based on the present values of net cash flows computed in part (4).
7. Rank the proposals from most attractive to least attractive, based on the present value indexes computed in part (5). Round to two decimal places.
8. Based upon the analyses, comment on the relative attractiveness of the proposals ranked in parts (6) and (7).

Special Activities

SA 25-1
Ethics and professional conduct in business

ETHICS

Elisa McRae was recently hired as a cost analyst by Medlab Medical Supplies Inc. One of Elisa's first assignments was to perform a net present value analysis for a new warehouse. Elisa performed the analysis and calculated a present value index of 0.75. The plant manager, I. M. Madd, is very intent on purchasing the warehouse because he believes that more storage space is needed. I. M. Madd asks Elisa into his office and the following conversation takes place.

I. M.: Elisa, you're new here, aren't you?

Elisa: Yes, sir.

I. M.: Well, Elisa, let me tell you something. I'm not at all pleased with the capital investment analysis that you performed on this new warehouse. I need that warehouse for my production. If I don't get it, where am I going to place our output?

Elisa: Hopefully with the customer, sir.

I. M.: Now don't get smart with me.

Elisa: No, really, I was being serious. My analysis does not support constructing a new warehouse. The numbers don't lie, the warehouse does not meet our investment return targets. In fact, it seems to me that purchasing a warehouse does not add much value to the business. We need to be producing product to satisfy customer orders, not to fill a warehouse.

I. M.: Listen, you need to understand something. The headquarters people will not allow me to build the warehouse if the numbers don't add up. You know as well as I that many assumptions go into your net present value analysis. Why don't you relax some of your assumptions so that the financial savings will offset the cost?

Elisa: I'm willing to discuss my assumptions with you. Maybe I overlooked something.

I. M.: Good. Here's what I want you to do. I see in your analysis that you don't project greater sales as a result of the warehouse. It seems to me, if we can store more goods, then we will have more to sell. Thus, logically, a larger warehouse translates into more sales. If you incorporate this into your analysis, I think you'll see that the numbers will work out. Why don't you work it through and come back with a new analysis. I'm really counting on you on this one. Let's get off to a good start together and see if we can get this project accepted.

→ What is your advice to Elisa?

SA 25-2
Personal investment analysis

A Masters of Accountancy degree at Mid-State University would cost $15,000 for an additional fifth year of education beyond the bachelor's degree. Assume that all tuition is paid at the beginning of the year. A student considering this investment must evaluate the present value of cash flows from possessing a graduate degree versus holding only the undergraduate degree. Assume that the average student with an undergraduate degree is expected to earn an annual salary of $45,000 per year (assumed to be paid at the end of the year) for 10 years. Assume that the average student with a graduate Masters of Accountancy degree is expected to earn an annual salary of $57,000 per year (assumed to be paid at the end of the year) for nine years after graduation. Assume a minimum rate of return of 10%.

1. Determine the net present value of cash flows from an undergraduate degree. Use the present value tables provided in this chapter.
2. Determine the net present value of cash flows from a Masters of Accountancy degree, assuming no salary is earned during the graduate year of schooling.
3. → What is the net advantage or disadvantage of pursuing a graduate degree under these assumptions?

SA 25-3
Changing prices

Global Products Inc. invested $1,000,000 to build a plant in a foreign country. The labor and materials used in production are purchased locally. The plant expansion was estimated to produce an internal rate of return of 20% in U.S. dollar terms. Due to a currency crisis, the currency exchange rate between the local currency and the U.S. dollar doubled from two local units per U.S. dollar to four local units per U.S. dollar.

a. Assume that the plant produced and sold product in the local economy. Explain what impact this change in the currency exchange rate would have on the project's internal rate of return.
b. Assume that the plant produced product in the local economy but exported the product back to the United States for sale. Explain what impact the change in the currency exchange rate would have on the project's internal rate of return under this assumption.

SA 25-4
Qualitative issues in investment analysis

The following are some selected quotes from senior executives:

CEO, Worthington Industries (a high technology steel company): "We try to find the best technology, stay ahead of the competition, and serve the customer. . . . We'll make any investment that will pay back quickly . . . but if it is something that we really see as a must down the road, payback is not going to be that important."

Chairman of Amgen Inc. (a biotech company): "You cannot really run the numbers, do net present value calculations, because the uncertainties are really gigantic . . . You decide on a project you want to run, and then you run the numbers [as a reality check on your assumptions]. Success in a business like this is much more dependent on tracking rather than on predicting, much more dependent on seeing results over time, tracking and adjusting and readjusting, much more dynamic, much more flexible."

Chief Financial Officer of Merck & Co., Inc. (a pharmaceutical company): ". . . at the individual product level—the development of a successful new product requires on the order of $230 million in R&D, spread over more than a decade—discounted cash flow style analysis does not become a factor until development is near the point of manufacturing scale-up effort. Prior to that point, given the uncertainties associated with new product development, it would be lunacy in our business to decide that we know exactly what's going to happen to a product once it gets out."

→ Explain the role of capital investment analysis for these companies.

SA 25-5
Analyze cash flows

You are considering an investment of $300,000 in either Project A or Project B for West Coast Studios Inc. In discussing the two projects with an advisor, you decided that, for the risk involved, an average rate of return of 12% on the cash investment would be required. For this purpose, you estimated the following economic factors for the projects:

	Project A	Project B
Useful life	4 years	4 years
Residual value	0	0
Net income:		
Year 1	$ 80,000	$ 40,000
2	65,000	55,000
3	55,000	73,000
4	40,000	79,200
	$240,000	$247,200

	Project A	Project B
Net cash flows:		
Year 1	$155,000	$115,000
2	140,000	130,000
3	130,000	148,000
4	115,000	154,200
	$540,000	$547,200

Although the average rate of return exceeded 12% on both projects, you have tentatively decided to invest in Project B because the rate was higher for Project B. You noted that the total cash flow from Project B is $547,200, which exceeds that of Project A by $7,200.

1. Determine the average rate of return for both projects.
2. ▬▬▶ Why is the timing of cash flows important in evaluating capital investments? Calculate the net present value of the two projects at a minimum rate of return of 12% to demonstrate the importance of net cash flows and their timing to these two projects. Round to the nearest dollar.

SA 25-6
Capital investment analysis

Internet Project

Group Project

In one group, find a local business, such as a copy shop, that rents time on desktop computers for an hourly rate. Determine the hourly rate. In the other group, determine the price of a mid-range desktop computer at **http://www.dell.com**. Combine this information from the two groups and perform a capital budgeting analysis. Assume that one student will use the computer for 35 hours per semester for the next three years. Also assume that the minimum rate of return is 10%. Use the interest tables in Appendix A in performing your analysis. (*Hint:* Use the appropriate present value factor for 5% compounded for six semiannual periods.) Does your analysis support the student purchasing the computer?

Answers to Self-Examination Questions

1. **C** Methods of evaluating capital investment proposals that ignore the time value of money are categorized as methods that ignore present value. This category includes the average rate of return method (answer A) and the cash payback method (answer B).

2. **B** The average rate of return is 24% (answer B), determined by dividing the expected average annual earnings by the average investment, as follows:

$$\frac{\$60,000/5}{(\$100,000 + 0)/2} = 24\%$$

3. **B** Of the four methods of analyzing proposals for capital investments, the cash payback period (answer B) refers to the expected period of time required to recover the amount of cash to be invested. The average rate of return (answer A) is a measure of the anticipated profitability of a proposal. The net present value method (answer C) reduces the expected future net cash flows originating from a proposal to their present values. The internal rate of return method (answer D) uses present value concepts to compute the rate of return from the net cash flows expected from the investment.

4. **B** The net present value is determined as follows:

Present value of $25,000 for 8 years at 11%	
($25,000 × 5.14612)	$128,653
Less project cost	120,000
Net present value	$ 8,653

5. **C** The internal rate of return for this project is determined by solving for the present value of an annuity factor that when multiplied by $40,000 will equal $226,009. By division, the factor is:

$$\frac{\$226,009}{\$40,000} = 5.65022$$

In Appendix A on pp. A-4 and A-5, scan along the $n = 10$ years row until finding the 5.65022 factor. The column for this factor is 12%.

Cost Allocation and Activity-Based Costing

© LINDSAY PIERCE/THE DAILY TIMES/ASSOCIATED PRESS

objectives

After studying this chapter, you should be able to:

1 Identify three methods used for allocating factory overhead costs to products.

2 Use a single plantwide factory overhead rate for product costing.

3 Use multiple production department factory overhead rates for product costing.

4 Use activity-based costing for product costing.

5 Use activity-based costing to allocate selling and administrative expenses to products.

6 Use activity-based costing in a service business.

Cold Stone Creamery

Have you ever had to request service repairs on an appliance at your home? The repair person may arrive and take five minutes to replace a part, yet the bill may indicate a charge for a minimum amount that is more than five minutes of work. Why might the service person have a minimum charge just for showing up? The answer is that the service person must charge for the time and expense of coming to your house. In a sense, the bill reflects two elements of service: the cost of coming to your house and the cost of providing the repair. The first portion of the cost reflects the time required to "set up" the job, while the second part of the cost reflects the cost of performing the repair. Notice that the setup charge will be the same, whether the repairs take five minutes or five hours. In contrast, the second portion of the bill reflects the actual repair performed that varies with the time on the job.

Like the repair person, companies must be careful to cost their products and services to reflect the different activities involved in producing the product. Otherwise, the cost of products and services may be distorted and lead to improper management decisions. For example, Cold Stone Creamery, a chain of super premium ice cream shops, uses activity-based costing to determine the cost of its ice cream products, such as cones, mixings, cakes, frozen yogurt, smoothies, and sorbets. The cost of activities, such as scooping and mixing, are added to the cost of the ingredients to determine the total cost to prepare each product. As stated by Cold Stone's president, "it only makes sense to have the price you pay for the product be reflective of the activities involved in making it for you."

In this chapter, we will explain and illustrate three different methods of allocating factory overhead to products. In addition, we will explain how product cost distortions can result from improper factory overhead allocation. We will end the chapter by describing activity-based costing for selling and administrative expenses and illustrating its use in service businesses.

Product Costing Allocation Methods

objective *1*

Identify three methods used for allocating factory overhead costs to products.

How does Nissan Motor Company determine if its *Xterra* SUV is a profitable product? First, it needs to determine the revenues earned from selling the cars. Most companies have accounting systems that trace revenues to individual product lines. In addition, however, Nissan needs to subtract the cost of manufacturing *Xterra* SUVs in order to determine the profit from *Xterra* sales. Nissan's cost accounting system provides this cost information. Determining the cost of the *Xterra*, or any other product, is termed **product costing**.

We introduced product costing in the job order costing chapter. We stated that product costs consist of direct materials, direct labor, and factory overhead. The direct materials and direct labor are direct to the product. However, factory overhead is often indirect to products and must be allocated. In this chapter we will illustrate three different factory overhead allocation approaches: (1) the single plantwide factory overhead rate method, (2) the multiple production department factory overhead rate method, and (3) the activity-based costing method.

Three Factory Overhead Allocation Methods

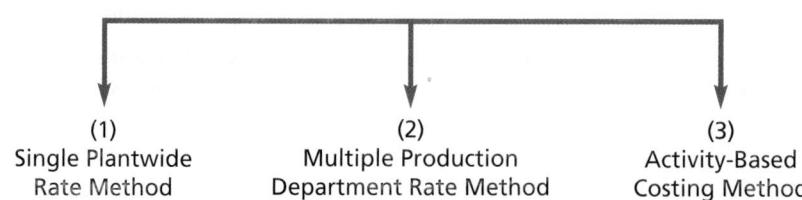

(1)	(2)	(3)
Single Plantwide Rate Method	Multiple Production Department Rate Method	Activity-Based Costing Method

How does an accountant know which method to use? In this chapter we will illustrate each of the three methods and identify the conditions favoring each method. Managers should be concerned about which method is selected because the method of allocation determines the accuracy of the resulting product cost. Accurate product costs support management decisions, such as determining product mix, establishing product price, or determining whether or not to emphasize a product line. For example, after implementing a more accurate factory overhead cost allocation system, a senior manager at Kraft Foods remarked, "I expect to see that there are some products we definitely should not be manufacturing and some other products that we should be committing many more resources to. . . . [The cost system] should affect our long-term decisions on which businesses Kraft should be in."[1] Thus, factory overhead allocation is not just necessary for financial reporting purposes, but it also contributes to management decision making.

Single Plantwide Factory Overhead Rate Method

objective 2

Use a single plantwide factory overhead rate for product costing.

As we discussed in a previous chapter, companies may use a predetermined factory overhead rate to allocate factory overhead costs to products. Under the **single plantwide factory overhead rate method**, all of the factory overhead is allocated to all the products, using only one rate.

To illustrate, assume that Ruiz Company manufactures two products, snowmobiles and lawnmowers. Both products are manufactured in a single factory. In addition, there is $1,600,000 of factory overhead budgeted for the period. The factory overhead consists of factory and equipment depreciation, factory power, factory supplies, and indirect labor.

Under the single plantwide factory overhead rate method, the $1,600,000 budgeted factory overhead is applied to all products by using one rate. This rate is computed by dividing the total budgeted factory overhead cost by the total budgeted (estimated) plantwide allocation base as follows:

$$\text{Single Plantwide Factory Overhead Rate} = \frac{\text{Total Budgeted Factory Overhead Cost}}{\text{Total Budgeted Plantwide Allocation Base}}$$

REAL WORLD

Many professional service companies use a single overhead rate in determining their prices and job profitability. For example, medical, legal, and accounting services develop hourly rates that will provide a profit after covering labor and overhead.

The budgeted allocation base is a measure of operating activity in the factory. Common allocation bases would include direct labor hours, direct labor dollars, and machine hours.

Assume that Ruiz Company allocates factory overhead to the two products on the basis of budgeted direct labor hours. The total budgeted direct labor hours can be determined by multiplying the budgeted manufacturing volume by the direct labor hours per unit. Ruiz Company plans to manufacture 1,000 units of each product. Assume that snowmobiles and lawnmowers both require 10 direct labor hours per unit to manufacture. The total budgeted plantwide direct labor hours is 20,000, as shown below.

Snowmobile:	1,000 units × 10 direct labor hours = 10,000 direct labor hours
Lawnmower:	1,000 units × 10 direct labor hours = 10,000
	20,000 direct labor hours

---

1 R. Cooper, R. S. Kaplan, L. S. Maisel, E. Morrissey, and R. M. Oehm, *Implementing Activity-Based Cost Management: Moving from Analysis to Action* (Institute of Management Accountants, 1992), p. 269.

The single plantwide factory overhead rate is $80 per direct labor hour, determined as follows:

$$\text{Single Plantwide Factory Overhead Rate} = \frac{\$1,600,000}{20,000 \text{ direct labor hours}}$$

$$= \$80 \text{ per direct labor hour}$$

This plantwide rate of $80 per direct labor hour can be used to allocate factory overhead to each product, as shown below.

	Single Plantwide Factory Overhead Rate	×	Direct Labor Hours per Unit	=	Factory Overhead Cost per Unit
Snowmobile:	$80 per direct labor hour	×	10 direct labor hours	=	$800
Lawnmower:	$80 per direct labor hour	×	10 direct labor hours	=	$800

The factory overhead allocated to each unit of product is the same. This is because each product used the same number of direct labor hours.

The effects of using the single plantwide factory overhead rate method are summarized for Ruiz Company in Exhibit 1.

Many military contractors use a single plantwide rate for allocating factory overhead costs to products, such as jet fighters. This approach is satisfactory when all products in the plant are manufactured under cost plus profit margin contracts to a single customer, such as the Department of Defense. However, cost distortions can still occur. This is one reason why government contractors sometimes make "$200 flashlights" that could be purchased at the local hardware store for $5.

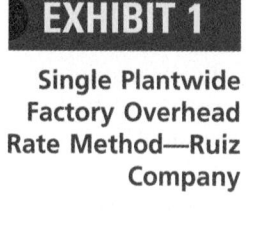

EXHIBIT 1

Single Plantwide Factory Overhead Rate Method—Ruiz Company

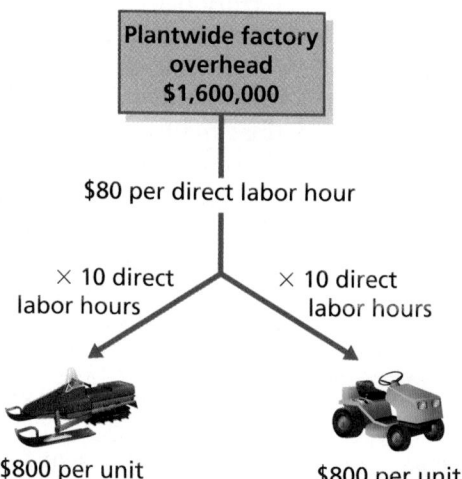

The greatest advantage of the single plantwide overhead rate method is that it is simple and inexpensive to apply in practice. Using a plantwide rate, we assume that the factory overhead costs are consumed in the same way by all products. For example, for Ruiz Company, we assume that all factory overhead can be accurately allocated to the two products based on the total number of direct labor hours consumed by each product. For companies that manufacture one or very few products, this assumption may be true. However, if the company manufactures many different types of products that consume factory overhead costs in different ways, then the assumption may not be true. In such a situation, a single plantwide rate may not accurately allocate factory overhead to the products. A solution may be to use multiple production department factory overhead rates, which we illustrate in the next section.

Example Exercise 26-1

objective 2

The total factory overhead for Morris Company is budgeted for the year at $650,000. Morris manufactures two office furniture products: a credenza and desk. The credenza and desk each require four direct labor hours to manufacture. Each product is budgeted for 5,000 units of production for the year. Determine (a) the total number of budgeted direct labor hours for the year, (b) the single plantwide factory overhead rate, and (c) the factory overhead allocated per unit for each product using the single plantwide factory overhead rate.

Follow My Example 26-1

a.   Credenza: 5,000 units × 4 direct labor hours = 20,000 direct labor hours
    Desk: 5,000 units × 4 direct labor hours =   20,000
                                        40,000 direct labor hours

b.   Single plantwide factory overhead rate: $650,000/40,000 dlh = $16.25 per dlh

c.   Credenza: $16.25 per direct labor hour × 4 dlh per unit = $65/unit
    Desk: $16.25 per direct labor hour × 4 dlh per unit = $65/unit

For Practice: PE 26-1A, PE 26-1B

Integrity, Objectivity, and Ethics in Business

ETHICS

FRAUD AGAINST YOU AND ME

The U.S. government makes a wide variety of purchases. Two of the largest are health care purchases under Medicare and military equipment. The purchase price for these and other items is often determined by the cost plus some profit. The cost is often the sum of direct costs plus allocated overhead. Due to the complexity of determining cost, government agencies review the amount charged for products and services. In the event of disagreement between the contractor and the government, the U.S. gov-ernment may sue the contractor under the False Claims Act, which provides for three times the government's dam-ages plus civil penalties. For example, Serono, a major pharmaceutical company, agreed to pay $704 million to settle a recent fraud case under the False Claims Act in-volving allegations of kickbacks to doctors and pharma-cies for prescribing and recommending *Serostim*®, an AIDS-related drug.

Multiple Production Department Factory Overhead Rate Method

objective 3

Use multiple production department factory overhead rates for product costing.

When production departments *differ significantly* in their manufacturing processes, factory overhead costs are likely to be incurred differently in each department. For example, a fabrication department that uses equipment may require more depreciation, power, and maintenance than would an assembly department that uses people. In addition, different products may consume the factory overhead from each production department in different proportions. For example, some products may use more of the fabrication department, while others use more of the assembly department. Under these conditions, the factory overhead costs may be more accurately allocated using multiple production department factory overhead rates.

The **multiple production department factory overhead rate method** uses different rates for each production department to allocate factory overhead to products. This is in contrast to the single plantwide rate method, which uses only one rate to allocate plantwide factory overhead to the products. Exhibit 2 illustrates how these two methods differ.

EXHIBIT 2

Comparison of Single Plantwide Rate and Multiple Production Department Rate Methods

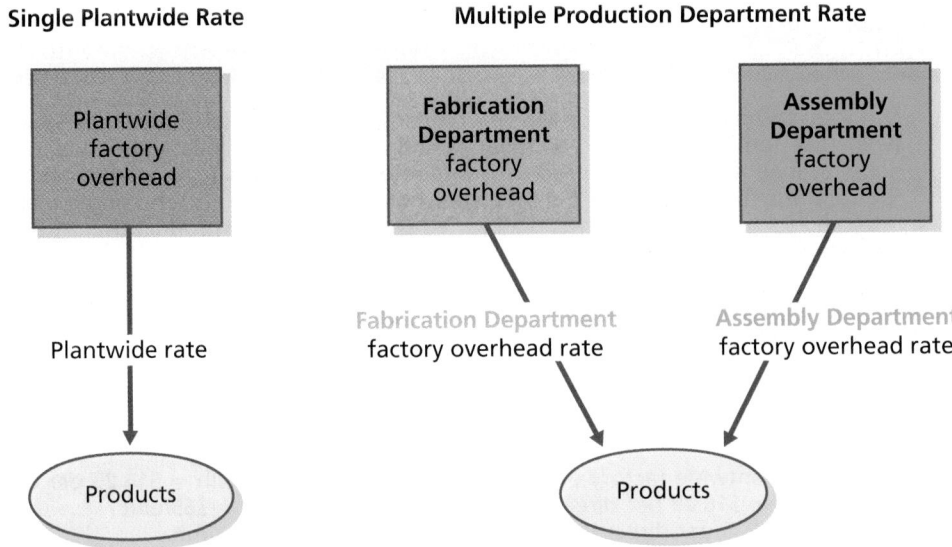

Single Plantwide Rate

Multiple Production Department Rate

To illustrate the multiple production department factory overhead rate method, we will continue with the Ruiz Company example introduced in the previous section. Assume that Ruiz Company has two production departments, Fabrication and Assembly. Also assume that the budgeted factory overhead associated with the Fabrication Department is $1,030,000 and with the Assembly Department is $570,000.[2] The Fabrication Department has nearly twice the factory overhead of the Assembly Department because of the additional machinery-related factory overhead, such as power, equipment depreciation, and factory supplies. Note that the sum of the budgeted factory overhead in the two production departments of $1,600,000 ($1,030,000 + $570,000), equals the budgeted plantwide factory overhead.

Production Department Factory Overhead Rates and Allocation

A company may use different allocation bases for different departments. For example, a machine-intensive department may use machine hours as an allocation base, and a labor-intensive department may use labor hours as an allocation base. However, in situations where one employee operates one machine, machine hours and labor hours will be equal and will yield the same allocation results.

The **production department factory overhead rates** are determined by dividing the budgeted production department factory overhead by the budgeted allocation base for each department. For Ruiz Company, direct labor hours are used as the allocation base for each production department. Each production department uses 10,000 direct labor hours. Thus, the factory overhead rates for the two departments are determined as follows:

$$\text{Fabrication Department Factory Overhead Rate} = \frac{\$1,030,000}{10,000 \text{ dlh}}$$

$$= \$103 \text{ per direct labor hour}$$

$$\text{Assembly Department Factory Overhead Rate} = \frac{\$570,000}{10,000 \text{ dlh}}$$

$$= \$57 \text{ per direct labor hour}$$

---

2 The factory overhead is allocated to production departments by using methods that are discussed in advanced texts.

Recall that each product requires ten direct labor hours. We will now assume some additional information about these hours. The snowmobile requires eight direct labor hours in the Fabrication Department and two direct labor hours in the Assembly Department. The lawnmower requires two direct labor hours in the Fabrication Department and eight in the Assembly Department.

Factory overhead is allocated to each product by multiplying the direct labor hours used by each product in each department by the production department factory overhead rate. Exhibit 3 shows this process for Ruiz Company.

> **EXHIBIT 3**   Allocating Factory Overhead to Products—Ruiz Company

	Allocation-Base Usage per Unit	×	Production Department Factory Overhead Rate	=	Allocated Factory Overhead per Unit of Product
Snowmobile					
Fabrication Department	8 direct labor hours	×	$103 per dlh	=	$824
Assembly Department	2 direct labor hours	×	$ 57 per dlh	=	114
Total factory overhead cost per snowmobile					$938
Lawnmower					
Fabrication Department	2 direct labor hours	×	$103 per dlh	=	$206
Assembly Department	8 direct labor hours	×	$ 57 per dlh	=	456
Total factory overhead cost per lawnmower					$662

The multiple production department rate allocation method for Ruiz Company is summarized in Exhibit 4. You should note that the production department factory overhead rates are not the same for each department. The Fabrication Department is more expensive in terms of factory overhead per direct labor hour than is the Assembly Department. In addition, the snowmobile uses more Fabrication Department direct labor hours than does the lawnmower. As a result, the total overhead allocated to each snowmobile is greater than that allocated to each lawnmower.

> **EXHIBIT 4**
>
> **Multiple Production Department Rate Method—Ruiz Company**

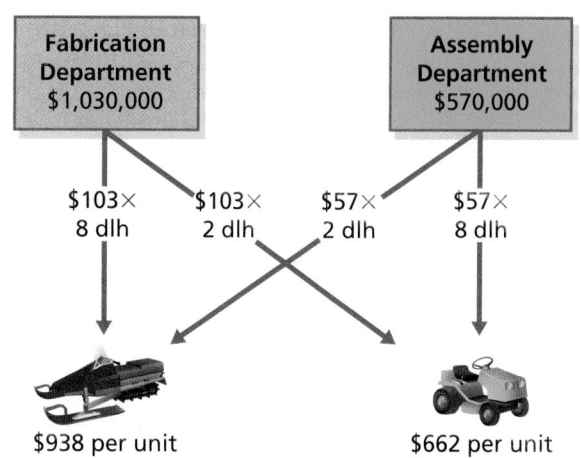

DISTORTION IN PRODUCT COSTS—SINGLE PLANTWIDE VERSUS MULTIPLE PRODUCTION DEPARTMENT FACTORY OVERHEAD RATES

For Ruiz Company, the following table shows the difference in the factory overhead per unit for each product, using the single plantwide and the multiple production department factory overhead rate methods:

	Factory Overhead Cost per Unit	
	Single Plantwide Rate	Multiple Production Department Rates
Snowmobile	$800	$938
Lawnmower	800	662

Which method is correct? In this case, the single plantwide factory overhead rate distorts the product cost by averaging the differences between the high factory overhead costs in the Fabrication Department and the low factory overhead costs in the Assembly Department. Using the single plantwide rate, we assume that all factory overhead is directly related to a single allocation base representing the entire plant. In many plants, this assumption is not realistic. Thus, using a single plantwide rate may result in product cost distortion.

In general, the following conditions may indicate that a single plantwide factory overhead rate will lead to distorted product costs:

> The single plantwide factory overhead rate distorts product cost by averaging high and low factory overhead costs.

Condition 1: Differences in production department factory overhead rates. There are significant differences in the factory overhead rates across different production departments. That is, some departments have high rates, while others have low rates.

and

Condition 2: Differences in the ratios of allocation-base usage. The products require different ratios of allocation base-usage across the departments.

Exhibit 5 illustrates both conditions for Ruiz Company. Condition 1 exists because the factory overhead rate for the Fabrication Department is $103 per direct labor hour, while the rate for the Assembly Department is only $57 per direct labor hour. This condition, by itself, will not cause product cost distortion. However, Condition 2 also exists. The snowmobile consumes 8 direct labor hours in the Fabrication Department, while the lawnmower consumes only 2 direct labor hours (8:2 ratio). The opposite is the case in the Assembly Department (2:8 ratio). Since both conditions exist, the product costs calculated using the single plantwide factory overhead rate are distorted. If Ruiz Company used the $800 product cost to determine its pricing strategy for both products, it would likely *underprice* the snowmobile and *overprice* the lawnmower. Eventually, Ruiz might be shut out of the lawnmower business due to this pricing error. If Ruiz used the multiple production department factory overhead rate approach, however, its product costs would be more accurate, and thus it would have a better starting point for making pricing decisions.

Conditions for Product
Cost Distortion—Ruiz
Company

Fabrication Department	Assembly Department

Condition 1: Differences in production department factory overhead rates

$103 per direct labor hour

$57 per direct labor hour

Condition 2: Differences in the ratios of allocation-base usage

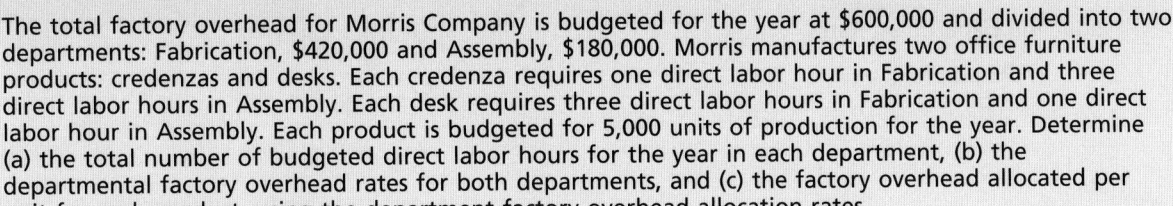

8 direct labor hours	2 direct labor hours
2 direct labor hours	8 direct labor hours

Example Exercise 26-2
objective 3

The total factory overhead for Morris Company is budgeted for the year at $600,000 and divided into two departments: Fabrication, $420,000 and Assembly, $180,000. Morris manufactures two office furniture products: credenzas and desks. Each credenza requires one direct labor hour in Fabrication and three direct labor hours in Assembly. Each desk requires three direct labor hours in Fabrication and one direct labor hour in Assembly. Each product is budgeted for 5,000 units of production for the year. Determine (a) the total number of budgeted direct labor hours for the year in each department, (b) the departmental factory overhead rates for both departments, and (c) the factory overhead allocated per unit for each product, using the department factory overhead allocation rates.

Follow My Example 26-2

a. Fabrication: (5,000 credenzas × 1 dlh) + (5,000 desks × 3 dlh) = 20,000 direct labor hours
    Assembly: (5,000 credenzas × 3 dlh) + (5,000 desks × 1 dlh) = 20,000 direct labor hours
b. Fabrication Department rate: $420,000/20,000 direct labor hours = $21.00 per dlh
    Assembly Department rate: $180,000/20,000 direct labor hours = $9.00 per dlh

c. Credenza:

    Fabrication Department   1 dlh × $21.00 = $21.00
    Assembly Department   3 dlh × $ 9.00 = 27.00
    Total factory overhead per credenza $48.00

    Desk:

    Fabrication Department   3 dlh × $21.00 = $63.00
    Assembly Department   1 dlh × $ 9.00 =   9.00
    Total factory overhead per desk $72.00

For Practice: PE 26-2A, PE 26-2B

Activity-Based Costing Method

In today's more complex manufacturing systems, product costs may still be distorted when multiple production department factory overhead rates are used. One way to avoid this distortion is by using the **activity-based costing (ABC) method**. This approach allocates factory overhead more accurately than does the multiple production department rate method.

The activity-based costing method uses cost of activities to determine product costs. Under this method, factory overhead costs are initially accounted for in **activity cost pools**. These cost pools are related to a given activity, such as machine usage, inspections, moving, production setups, and engineering activities. In contrast, when multiple production department factory overhead rates are used, factory overhead costs are first accounted for in production departments. Exhibit 6 illustrates how these two approaches compare.

EXHIBIT 6   Multiple Production Department Factory Overhead Rate Method vs. Activity-Based Costing

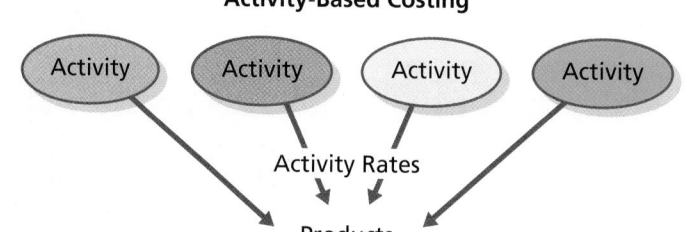

Another term for "setup" is "changeover." This term is often used in continuous process industries. Often, machine characteristics are changed while the process continues running ("on the fly"). Such changeovers are still costly, however, because the machines will make low-quality product for a period of time during the changeover.

To illustrate the activity-based costing method, assume that Ruiz Company has five activities. Two activities are the fabrication and assembly production activities. We now call these *activities*, rather than *departments*, because the factory overhead costs in these pools are more closely related to their activity bases than under the multiple department factory overhead rate method.

Ruiz has three additional activities, which are described below.

- *Setup*—the activity of changing the characteristics of a machine to prepare for manufacturing a different product. Often, a production run requires a **setup**. For example, changing a stamping machine from stamping the body for a snowmobile to stamping the body for a lawnmower would require stopping the machine and changing the die. The work associated with changing the die is a setup activity.

- *Quality control inspection*—the activity of inspecting the product for defects. For example, a snowmobile inspection may require the snowmobile to be run for several hours and then be disassembled to test for component strength, fit, and function.

- *Engineering changes*—the activity of processing changes in product design characteristics. An **engineering change order (ECO)** initiates an administrative process to change the design of a product. For example, to change the type of blade assembled in a lawnmower would require an engineering change order.

We will assume the following budgeted factory overhead associated with each activity:

Activity Cost Pool	Amount
Fabrication	$ 530,000
Assembly	70,000
Setup	480,000
Quality control inspection	312,000
Engineering changes	208,000
Total budgeted factory overhead	$1,600,000

REAL WORLD

The U.S. Postal Service has initiated a new activity-based costing system, called PostalOne!, which will track the real costs associated with processing and delivering each class of mail.

The total budgeted factory overhead to be allocated is still $1,600,000. However, the budgeted factory overhead has now been divided into activity cost pools. The costs in the fabrication and assembly pools are less than the costs in the production departments from the previous section because the production departments included costs that were not closely related to fabrication and assembly activities. These costs, which total $1,000,000 ($480,000 + $312,000 + $208,000), are now related to their own activity pools, namely setup, quality control inspection, and engineering changes.

> Activity rates are determined by dividing the budgeted activity cost pool by the total estimated activity base.

ACTIVITY RATES AND ALLOCATION

The activity cost pools are assigned to products, using factory overhead rates for each activity. These rates are often called **activity rates** because they are related to activities. Activity rates are determined by dividing the cost budgeted for each activity pool by the estimated activity base for that pool. We use the term **activity base**, rather than allocation base, since the base is related to an activity cost pool. For example, the activity rate for the setup activity would be determined by dividing the setup budgeted cost pool by the number of estimated setups. Setup cost would be related to a product by multiplying the setup activity rate by the number of setups used by that particular product.

To determine each activity-base quantity, assume the following additional information about the snowmobiles and lawnmowers for Ruiz Company:

- *Snowmobiles:* Ruiz Company estimates that the total production for snowmobiles will be 1,000 units. Snowmobiles are a new product for Ruiz Company, and the engineers are still tinkering with design changes. Thus, there are 12 engineering change orders estimated for the period. In addition, the snowmobile production run is expected to be set up 100 times during the period, or 10 units per production run (1,000 units total production/100 setups). For quality control purposes, 100 snowmobiles (10% of total production) will be inspected.

- *Lawnmowers:* Ruiz Company estimates that the total production for lawnmowers will also be 1,000 units. Lawnmowers are a mature and stable product that has been produced by Ruiz Company for many years. Thus, Ruiz Company expects the lawnmower to have only four engineering changes for the period. Due to its long history of successful production of lawnmowers, Ruiz expects fewer quality problems; thus, only four lawnmowers (0.4% of production) will be quality-control inspected. In addition, the lawnmower production run is expected to be set up 20 times during the period, or 50 units per production run (1,000 units total production/20 setups).

The estimated **activity-base usage quantities** are the total activity-base quantities related to each product. These quantities reflect differences with respect to using setup, quality control inspection, and engineering change activities, as we noted in the preceding paragraphs. In addition, each product uses different amounts of direct labor hours in the fabrication and assembly activities, as we noted in an earlier section. The estimated activity-base usage quantities for all 1,000 units of production for each product are shown in Exhibit 7.

EXHIBIT 7   Estimated Activity-Base Usage Quantities—Ruiz Company

	Activities				
Products	Fabrication	Assembly	Setup	Quality Control Inspections	Engineering Changes
Snowmobile	8,000 dlh	2,000 dlh	100 setups	100 inspections	12 ECOs
Lawnmower	2,000	8,000	20	4	4
Total activity base	10,000 dlh	10,000 dlh	120 setups	104 inspections	16 ECOs

The activity rates for each activity can now be determined by dividing the budgeted activity cost pool by the total estimated activity base from Exhibit 7. These activity rates are shown in Exhibit 8.

EXHIBIT 8   Activity Rates—Ruiz Company

Activity	Budgeted Activity Cost Pool	/	Estimated Activity Base	=	Activity Rate
Fabrication	$530,000	/	10,000 direct labor hours	=	$53 per direct labor hour
Assembly	$ 70,000	/	10,000 direct labor hours	=	$7 per direct labor hour
Setup	$480,000	/	120 setups	=	$4,000 per setup
Quality control inspections	$312,000	/	104 inspections	=	$3,000 per inspection
Engineering changes	$208,000	/	16 engineering changes	=	$13,000 per engineering change order

The product costs for the snowmobile and lawnmower are computed by multiplying the activity rate by the related activity-base quantity for each product. The total of these costs for each product is the total factory overhead cost for that product. This amount is divided by the total number of units of that product budgeted for manufacture in the period. This result, as shown in Exhibit 9, is the factory overhead cost per unit.

EXHIBIT 9   Activity-Based Product Cost Calculations

	A	B	C	D	E	F	G	H	I	J	K	L	
				Snowmobile						Lawnmower			
	Activity	Activity-Base Usage	×	Activity Rate	=	Activity Cost		Activity-Base Usage	×	Activity Rate	=	Activity Cost	
1	Fabrication	8,000 dlh		$53/dlh		$ 424,000		2,000 dlh		$53/dlh		$106,000	1
2	Assembly	2,000 dlh		$7/dlh		14,000		8,000 dlh		$7/dlh		56,000	2
3	Setup	100 setups		$4,000/setup		400,000		20 setups		$4,000/setup		80,000	3
4	Quality control												4
5	inspections	100 inspections		$3,000/insp.		300,000		4 inspections		$3,000/insp.		12,000	5
6	Engineering												6
7	changes	12 ECOs		$13,000/ECO		156,000		4 ECOs		$13,000/ECO		52,000	7
8	Total factory												8
9	overhead cost					$1,294,000						$306,000	9
10	Budgeted units												10
11	of production					/ 1,000						/ 1,000	11
12	Factory overhead												12
13	cost per unit					$ 1,294						$ 306	13

The activity-based costing method for Ruiz Company is summarized in Exhibit 10. Compare Exhibit 10 with Exhibit 4. In both exhibits, multiple rates are used. In Exhibit 4, production department factory overhead costs were allocated to products on the basis of the production department factory overhead rates. In contrast, under activity-based costing, the activity cost pools are allocated to the products on the basis of each activity's own unique activity rate.

DISTORTION IN PRODUCT COSTS—MULTIPLE PRODUCTION DEPARTMENT FACTORY OVERHEAD RATE METHOD VERSUS ACTIVITY-BASED COSTING

The factory overhead costs per unit for Ruiz Company across all three allocation methods are shown below.

Factory Overhead Cost per Unit— Three Cost Allocation Methods			
	Single Plantwide Rate	Multiple Production Department Rates	Activity-Based Costing
Snowmobile	$800	$938	$1,294
Lawnmower	800	662	306

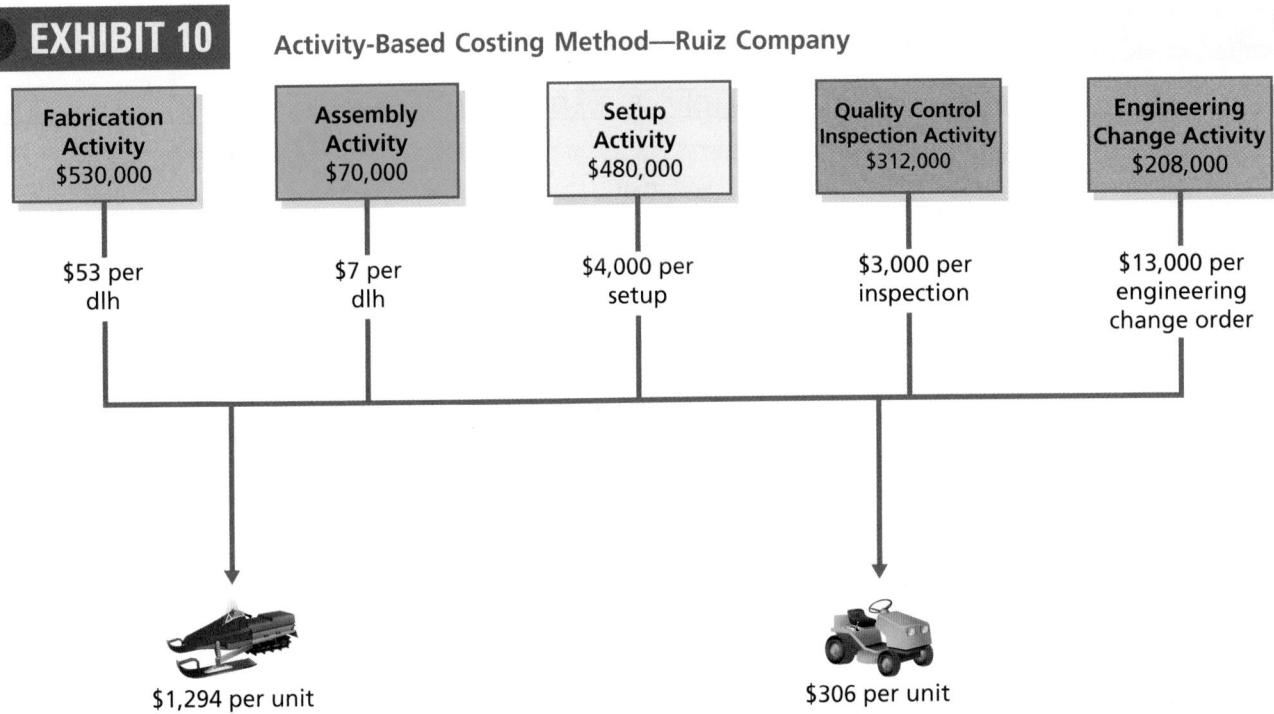

EXHIBIT 10   Activity-Based Costing Method—Ruiz Company

Fabrication Activity $530,000	Assembly Activity $70,000	Setup Activity $480,000	Quality Control Inspection Activity $312,000	Engineering Change Activity $208,000
$53 per dlh	$7 per dlh	$4,000 per setup	$3,000 per inspection	$13,000 per engineering change order

$1,294 per unit $306 per unit

As you can see, the activity-based costing method produced different product costs from the multiple department factory overhead rate method. What caused these differences, and which method is more accurate? The answer lies in how the $1,000,000 of setup, quality control, and engineering change activities were treated. Under the multiple production department factory overhead rate method, this factory overhead was included in the production department factory overhead and allocated to products on the basis of direct labor hours. However, each product did *not* consume *activities* in proportion to its direct labor hours. Namely, the snowmobile consumed a larger portion of the setup, quality control inspection, and engineering change activities, even though each product consumed 10,000 labor hours. As a result, activity-based costing allocates more of this factory overhead cost to the snowmobile and less to the lawnmower than did the multiple production department factory overhead rate method. In summary, the activity-based costing method provided the most accurate product costs because activities were consumed in different proportions than the direct labor used in the two products.

THE DANGERS OF PRODUCT COST DISTORTION

Product cost distortion can lead to bad management decisions, and bad decisions can lead to business disasters. To illustrate, ArvinMeritor, Inc., conducted an activity-based costing study after one of its best-selling axles had begun losing market share. The study found that incorrect factory overhead cost allocations had "overcosted" its highest-volume axle by roughly 20%, while underestimating the cost of low-volume axles by as much as 40%. Since the sales prices were based on these estimated costs, Arvin-Meritor had underpriced its low-volume axles and overpriced its high-volume axles. As a result, competitors had begun to attract customers away from ArvinMeritor's best-selling, high-volume axles. Without the activity-based costing analysis, ArvinMeritor could well have discovered that it was gradually being forced out of the high-volume axle business—not by choice, but because of inaccurate product costing and bad pricing decisions.

REAL WORLD

Procter & Gamble used activity-based costing information to simplify its business by standardizing product formulas and packaging, to reduce promotions, to eliminate marginal brands, and to standardize advertising campaigns.

REAL WORLD

One survey showed that 20% of the surveyed companies had adopted activity-based costing.

Source: "2001 Survey on Cost Management Practices," IMA.

Example Exercise 26-3

The total factory overhead for Morris Company is budgeted for the year at $600,000, divided into four activity pools: fabrication, $300,000; assembly, $120,000; setup, $100,000; and material handling $80,000. Morris manufactures two office furniture products: a credenza and desk. The activity-base usage quantities for each product by each activity are as follows:

	Fabrication	Assembly	Setup	Material Handling
Credenza	5,000 dlh	15,000 dlh	30 setups	50 moves
Desk	15,000	5,000	220	350
	20,000 dlh	20,000 dlh	250 setups	400 moves

Each product is budgeted for 5,000 units of production for the year. Determine (a) the activity rates for each activity and (b) the activity-based factory overhead per unit for each product.

Follow My Example 26-3

a. Fabrication: $300,000/20,000 direct labor hours = $15 per dlh
    Assembly: $120,000/20,000 direct labor hours = $6 per dlh
    Setup: $100,000/250 setups = $400 per setup
    Material handling: $80,000/400 moves = $200 per moveb.

	A	B	C	D	E	F	G	H	I	J	K	L	
				Credenza						Desk			
		Activity-Base		Activity		Activity		Activity-Base		Activity		Activity	
	Activity	Usage	×	Rate	=	Cost		Usage	×	Rate	=	Cost	
1	Fabrication	5,000 dlh		$15 per dlh		$ 75,000		15,000 dlh		$15 per dlh		$225,000	1
2	Assembly	15,000 dlh		$6 per dlh		90,000		5,000 dlh		$6 per dlh		30,000	2
3	Setup	30 setups		$400/setup		12,000		220 setups		$400/setup		88,000	3
4	Moves	50 moves		$200/move		10,000		350 moves		$200/move		70,000	4
5	Total					$187,000						$413,000	5
6	Budgeted units					/ 5,000						/ 5,000	6
7	Factory overhead												7
8	per unit					$ 37.40						$ 82.60	8

For Practice: PE 26-3A, PE 26-3B

Activity-Based Costing for Selling and Administrative Expenses

objective 5

Use activity-based costing to allocate selling and administrative expenses to products.

Generally accepted accounting principles require that selling and administrative expenses be treated as period expenses on the income statement prepared for external users. However, accountants may allocate selling and administrative expenses to products in preparing product profitability reports for management. A traditional method is to allocate selling and administrative expenses to the products based on product sales volumes. However, products may consume activities in ways that are unrelated to their sales volumes. When this occurs, activity-based costing may provide a more accurate allocation approach.

To illustrate, assume that Abacus Company has two products, Ipso and Facto. Both products have the same total sales volume. However, both products are not the same in terms of how they consume selling and administrative activities. Exhibit 11 identifies some of these differences.

EXHIBIT 11

Selling and
Administrative
Activity Product
Differences

Selling and Administrative Activities	Ipso	Facto
Post-sale technical support	Product is easy to use by the customer.	Product requires specialized training in order to be used by the customer.
Order writing	Product requires no technical information from the customer.	Product requires detailed technical information from the customer.
Promotional support	Product requires no promotional effort.	Product requires extensive promotional effort.
Order entry	Product is purchased in large volumes per order.	Product is purchased in small volumes per order.
Customer return processing	Product has few customer returns.	Product has many customer returns.
Shipping document preparation	Product is shipped domestically.	Product is shipped internationally, requiring customs and export documents.
Shipping and handling	Product is not hazardous.	Product is hazardous, requiring specialized shipping and handling.
Field service	Product has few warranty claims.	Product has many warranty claims.

REAL WORLD

ExxonMobil Corporation has analyzed the cost of its selling and administrative activities to better determine the cost of its lubrication products. In addition, the activity information helped ExxonMobil discover the relative costs of serving customers directly versus through distributors. Examples of selling and administrative activities used in its activity-based costing analysis included sales, maintenance, engineering calls, distributor calls, order taking, market research, and advertising.

If the selling and administrative expenses of Abacus Company were allocated on the basis of sales volumes, both products would be allocated the same amount, since they both have the same sales volume. Does this seem correct? Should both products have the same selling and administrative expenses? No, they should not. Ipso is much less complex and hence less expensive than Facto. The activity-based costing approach would allocate the selling and administrative activities to each product based on its individual differences in consuming these activities. For example, assume that the field service activity of Abacus Company had a budgeted cost of $150,000. Additionally, assume that 100 warranty claims were estimated for the period. Using warranty claims as an activity base, the cost per warranty claim would be $1,500 per warranty claim, computed as follows:

$150,000 field service activity cost/100 claims = $1,500 per warranty claim

Assume that Ipso had 10 warranty claims and Facto had 90 warranty claims. The field service activity would be allocated to each product as follows:

Ipso: 10 warranty claims × $1,500 per warranty claim = $15,000
Facto: 90 warranty claims × $1,500 per warranty claim = $135,000

Allocating selling and administrative expenses using activity-based costing would result in more accurate product profitability reports for Abacus Company management.

For some companies, selling and administrative expenses may be more related to *customer* behaviors than to differences in products. That is, some customers may demand more service and selling activities than other customers. In such cases, activity-based cost reports can be developed to show the impact of these differences on customer profitability. For example, a recent survey of manufacturers (suppliers) indicated that Wal-Mart has earned the distinction of being the easiest, and often most profitable, retailer with which to do business.[3] In the next section, we will see how service companies can also use activity-based costing to evaluate their costs in serving customers.

Example Exercise 26-4   objective 5

Converse Company manufactures and sells LCD display products. Converse uses activity-based costing to determine the cost of the customer return processing and the shipping activity. The customer return processing activity has an activity rate of $90 per return, and the shipping activity has an activity rate of $15 per shipment. Converse shipped 4,000 units of LCD Model A1 in 2,200 shipments (some shipments are more than one unit). There were 200 returns. Determine the (a) total and (b) per-unit customer return processing and shipping activity cost for Model A1.

Follow My Example 26-4

a.   Return activity: 200 returns × $90 per return = $18,000
     Shipping activity: 2,200 shipments × $15 per shipment =   33,000

     Total activity cost $51,000

b. $12.75 per unit ($51,000/4,000 units)

For Practice: PE 26-4A, PE 26-4B

Activity-Based Costing in Service Businesses

objective 6

Use activity-based costing in a service business.

REAL WORLD

Owens & Minor, a medical distributor, used activity-based costing information to price distribution services to customers, based on the number of orders and the number of items per order.

Service companies have a need to determine the cost of services in order to make pricing, promoting, and other decisions with regard to service offerings. Many service companies find that single and multiple department overhead rate methods may lead to distortions similar to those of manufacturing firms. Thus, many service companies are now using activity-based costing for determining the cost of providing services to customers.

   To illustrate activity-based costing for a service company, assume that Hopewell Hospital uses an activity-based costing system to determine how hospital overhead is allocated to patients. Hopewell Hospital first determines the activity cost pools and then allocates the activity cost pools to patients, using activity rates. We will assume that the activities of Hopewell Hospital include admitting, radiological testing, operating room, pathological testing, and dietary and laundry. Each activity cost pool has an estimated activity base measuring the output of the activity. The cost of activities is allocated to patients by multiplying the activity rate by the number of activity-base usage quantities consumed by each patient. Exhibit 12 illustrates the activity-based costing method for Hopewell Hospital.

   Each activity rate shown in Exhibit 12 is determined by dividing the budgeted activity cost pool by the estimated activity-base quantity. To illustrate, assume that the radiological testing activity cost pool budget is $960,000, and the total estimated activity-base quantity is 3,000 images. The activity rate of $320 per image is calculated as follows:

$$\text{Radiological Testing Activity Rate} = \frac{\$960,000}{3,000 \text{ images}} = \$320 \text{ per image}$$

---

3 As reported in Jerry Useem, "One Nation Under Wal-Mart" Fortune, February 18, 2003.

Integrity, Objectivity, and Ethics in Business

ETHICS

UNIVERSITY AND COMMUNITY PARTNERSHIP—LEARNING YOUR ABC'S

Students at Harvard's Kennedy School of Government joined with the city of Sommerville, Massachusetts, in building an activity-based cost system for the city. The students volunteered several hours a week in four-person teams, interviewing city officials within 18 departments. The students were able to determine activity costs, such as the cost to fill a pothole, processing a building permit, or responding to a four-alarm fire. Their study will be used by the city in forming the 2006 city budget. As stated by some of the students participating on this project: "It makes sense to use the resources of the university for community building. ...Real-world experience is a tremendous thing to have in your back pocket. We learned from the mayor and the fire chief, who are seasoned professionals in their own right."

Source: Kennedy School Bulletin, Spring 2005, "Easy as A-B-C: Students take on the Sommerville Budget Overhaul."

EXHIBIT 12   Activity-Based Costing Method—Hopewell Hospital

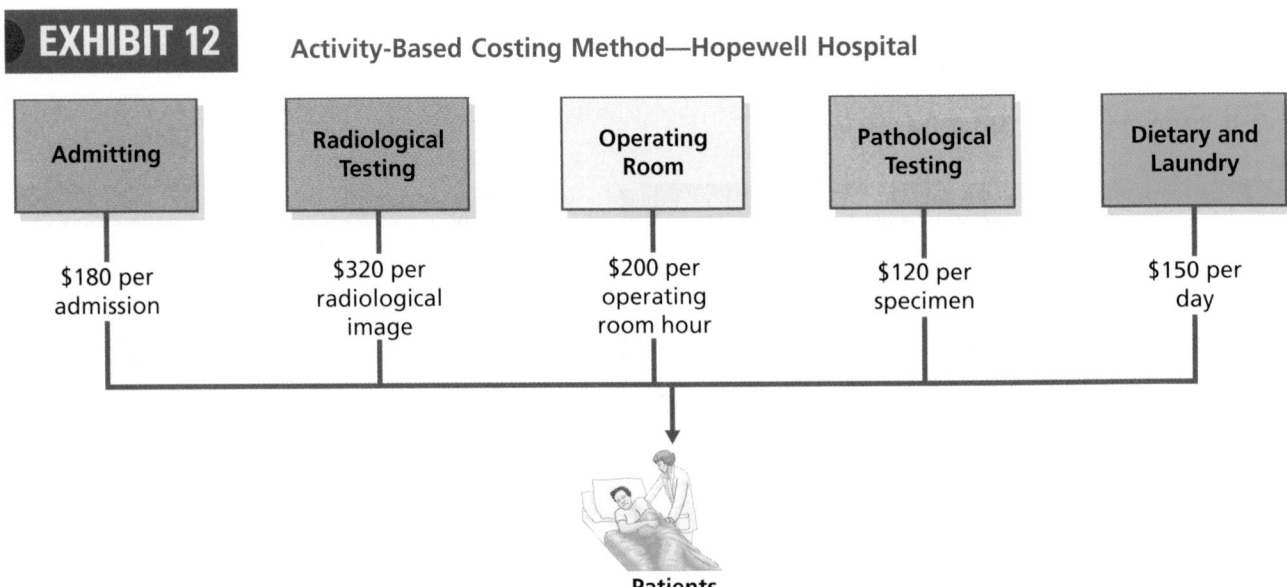

The activity rates for the other activities would be determined in a similar manner. These activity rates are used to allocate costs to patients. To illustrate, assume that Mia Wilson was a patient of the hospital. The hospital overhead cost associated with services (activities) performed for Mia Wilson is determined by multiplying the activity-base quantity for Mia Wilson's stay in the hospital by the activity rate. The sum of the costs across the activities is the total hospital overhead cost of services performed for Mia Wilson. These calculations are shown below.

	A	B	C	D	E	F	
	\multicolumn{6}{c}{Patient Name: Mia Wilson}	
	Activity	Activity-Base Usage	×	Activity Rate	=	Activity Cost	
1	Admitting	1 admission		$180/admission		$ 180	1
2	Radiological testing	2 images		$320/image		640	2
3	Operating room	4 hours		$200/hour		800	3
4	Pathological testing	1 specimen		$120/specimen		120	4
5	Dietary and laundry	7 days		$150/day		1,050	5
6	Total					$2,790	6

The patient activity costs can be combined with the direct costs, such as drugs and supplies, and reported with the revenues earned for each patient in a customer profitability report. A partial customer profitability report for Hopewell Hospital is shown in Exhibit 13.

The report in Exhibit 13 can be used by the administrators to guide decisions on pricing or service delivery. For example, there was a large loss on services provided to Brian Birini. Further investigation might reveal that services provided to Birini were out of line with what would be allowed for reimbursement by the insurance company. As a result, future losses could be avoided by lobbying for a higher insurance reimbursement or aligning the services closer to the revenues allowed by the insurance company.

EXHIBIT 13

Customer Profitability Report

Hopewell Hospital
Customer (Patient) Profitability Report
For the Period Ending December 31, 2008

	Adcock, Kim	Birini, Brian	Conway, Don	Wilson, Mia
Revenues	$9,500	$21,400	$5,050	$3,300
Less: Patient costs:				
Drugs and supplies	$ 400	$ 1,000	$ 300	$ 200
Admitting	180	180	180	180
Radiological testing	1,280	2,560	1,280	640
Operating room	2,400	6,400	1,600	800
Pathological testing	240	600	120	120
Dietary and laundry	4,200	14,700	1,050	1,050
Total patient costs	$8,700	$25,440	$4,530	$2,990
Income from operations	$ 800	$ (4,040)	$ 520	$ 310

Example Exercise 26-5   objective **6**

The Metro Radiology Clinic uses activity-based costing to determine the cost of servicing patients. There are three activity pools: patient administration, imaging, and diagnostic services. The activity rates associated with each activity pool are $45 per patient visit, $320 per X-ray image, and $450 per diagnosis. Julie Campbell went to the clinic and had two X-rays, each of which was read and interpreted by a doctor. Determine the total activity-based cost of Campbell's visit.

Follow My Example 26-5

Imaging	$ 640	(2 images × $320)
Diagnosis	900	(2 diagnoses × $450)
Patient administration	45	(1 visit × $45)
Total activity cost	$1,585	

For Practice: PE 26-5A, PE 26-5B

Business Connections

FINDING THE RIGHT NICHE

Businesses often attempt to divide a market into its unique characteristics, called market segmentation. Once a market segment is identified, product, price, promotion, and location strategies are tailored to fit that market. This is a better approach for many products and services than following a "one size fits all" strategy. Activity-based costing can be used to help tailor organizational effort toward different segments. For example, Fidelity Investments uses activity-based costing to tailor its sales and marketing strategies to different wealth segments. Thus, a higher wealth segment could rely on personal sales activities, while less wealthy segments would rely on less costly sales activities, such as mass mail. The following table lists popular forms of segmentation and their common characteristics:

Form of Segmentation	Characteristics
Demographic	Age, education, gender, income, race
Geographic	Region, city, country
Psychographic	Lifestyle, values, attitudes
Benefit	Benefits provided
Volume	Light vs. heavy use

Examples for each of these forms of segmentation are as follows:

Demographic: Fidelity Investments tailors sales and marketing strategies to different wealth segments.
Geographic: Pro sports teams offer merchandise in their home cities.
Psychographic: The Body Shop markets all-natural beauty products to consumers who value cosmetic products that have not been animal-tested.
Benefit: Cold Stone Creamery sells a premium ice cream product with customized toppings.
Volume: Delta Air Lines provides additional benefits, such as class upgrades, free air travel, and boarding priority, to its frequent fliers.

© PAUL CONNORS/FIDELITY INVESTMENTS/FEATURE PHOTO SERVICE (NEWSCOM)

At a Glance

1. Identify three methods used for allocating factory overhead costs to products.

Key Points	Key Learning Outcomes	Example Exercises	Practice Exercises
There are three basic cost allocation methods used for determining the cost of products: the single plantwide factory overhead rate method, the multiple production department factory overhead rate method, and the activity-based costing method.	• List the three primary methods for allocating factory overhead costs to products.		

2. Use a single plantwide factory overhead rate for product costing.

Key Points	Key Learning Outcomes	Example Exercises	Practice Exercises
A single plantwide factory overhead rate can be used to allocate all plant overhead to all products. The single plantwide factory overhead rate is simple to apply, but it can lead to significant product cost distortions.	• Compute the single plantwide factory overhead rate and use this rate to allocate factory overhead costs to products. • Identify the conditions that favor the use of a single plantwide factory overhead rate for allocating factory overhead costs to products.	26-1	26-1A, 26-1B

3. Use multiple production department factory overhead rates for product costing.

Key Points	Key Learning Outcomes	Example Exercises	Practice Exercises
Product costing using multiple production department factory overhead rates requires identifying the factory overhead associated with the production departments. Using these rates will result in greater accuracy than using single plantwide factory overhead rates when: 1. There are significant differences in the factory overhead rates across different production departments. and 2. The products require different ratios of allocation-base usage in each production department.	• Compute multiple production department overhead rates and use these rates to allocate factory overhead costs to products. • Identify and describe the two conditions that favor the use of multiple production department factory overhead rates for allocating factory overhead costs to products as compared to the single plantwide factory overhead rate method.	26-2	26-2A, 26-2B

(continued)

4. Use activity-based costing for product costing.

Key Points	Key Learning Outcomes	Example Exercises	Practice Exercises
Activity-based costing requires factory overhead to be budgeted to activity cost pools. The activity cost pools are allocated to products by multiplying activity rates by the activity-base quantity consumed for each product. Using activity rates rather than multiple production department factory overhead rates may result in more accurate product costs when products consume activities in ratios that are unrelated to their departmental allocation bases.	• Compute activity rates and use these rates to allocate factory overhead costs to products. • Identify the conditions that favor the use of activity-based rates for allocating factory overhead costs to products, as compared to the other two methods of cost allocation. • Compare the three factory overhead allocation methods and describe the causes of cost allocation distortion.	**26-3**	26-3A, 26-3B

5. Use activity-based costing to allocate selling and administrative expenses to products.

Key Points	Key Learning Outcomes	Example Exercises	Practice Exercises
Selling and administrative expenses can be allocated to products for management profit reporting, using activity-based costing. The traditional approach to allocating selling and administrative expenses is by the relative sales volumes of the products. Activity-based costing would be preferred when the products use selling and administrative activities in ratios that are unrelated to their sales volumes.	• Compute selling and administrative activity rates and use these rates to allocate selling and administrative expenses to either a product or customer. • Identify the conditions that would favor the use of activity-based costing for allocating selling and administrative expenses.	**26-4**	26-4A, 26-4B

6. Use activity-based costing in a service business.

Key Points	Key Learning Outcomes	Example Exercises	Practice Exercises
Activity-based costing may be applied in service settings to determine the cost of individual service offerings. Service costs are determined by multiplying activity rates by the amount of activity-base quantities consumed by the customer using the service offering. Such information can support service pricing and profitability analysis.	• Compute activity rates for service offerings and use these rates to allocate indirect costs to either a service product line or a customer. • Prepare a customer profitability report using the cost of activities. • Describe how activity-based cost information can be used in a service business for improved decision making.	**26-5**	26-5A, 26-5B

Key Terms

activity base (1147)
activity cost pools (1146)
activity rate (1147)
activity-base usage quantity (1147)
activity-based costing (ABC)
method (1146)

engineering change order (ECO)
(1146)
multiple production department
factory overhead rate method
(1141)
product costing (1138)

production department factory
overhead rates (1142)
setup (1146)
single plantwide factory overhead
rate method (1139)

Illustrative Problem

Hammer Company plans to use activity-based costing to determine its product costs. It presently uses a single plantwide factory overhead rate for allocating factory overhead to products, based on direct labor hours. The total factory overhead cost is as follows:

Department	Factory Overhead
Production Support	$1,225,000
Production (factory overhead only)	175,000
Total cost	$1,400,000

The company determined that it performed four major activities in the Production Support Department. These activities, along with their budgeted costs, are as follows:

Production Support Activities	Budgeted Cost
Setup	$ 428,750
Production control	245,000
Quality control	183,750
Materials management	367,500
Total	$1,225,000

Hammer Company estimated the following activity-base usage quantities and units produced for each of its three products:

Products	Number of Units	Direct Labor Hrs.	Setups	Production Orders	Inspections	Material Requisitions
TV	10,000	25,000	80	80	35	320
Computer	2,000	10,000	40	40	40	400
Cell phone	50,000	140,000	5	5	0	30
Total cost	62,000	175,000	125	125	75	750

Instructions

1. Determine the factory overhead cost per unit for the TV, computer, and cell phone under the single plantwide factory overhead rate method. Use direct labor hours as the activity base.
2. Determine the factory overhead cost per unit for the TV, computer, and cell phone under activity-based costing.
3. Which method provides more accurate product costing? Why?

Solution

1. Single Plantwide Factory Overhead Rate = $\dfrac{\$1,400,000}{175,000 \text{ direct labor hours}}$

= $8 per direct labor hour

Factory overhead cost per unit:

	TV	Computer	Cell Phone
Number of direct labor hours	25,000	10,000	140,000
Single plantwide factory overhead rate	× $8/dlh	× $8/dlh	× $8/dlh
Total factory overhead	$200,000	$ 80,000	$1,120,000
Number of units	/ 10,000	/ 2,000	/ 50,000
Cost per unit	$ 20.00	$ 40.00	$ 22.40

2. Under activity-based costing, an activity rate must be determined for each activity pool:

Activity	Activity Cost Pool Budget	/	Estimated Activity Base	=	Activity Rate
Setup	$428,750	/	125 setups	=	$3,430 per setup
Production control	$245,000	/	125 production orders	=	$1,960 per production order

Activity	Activity Cost Pool Budget	/	Estimated Activity Base	=	Activity Rate
Quality control	$183,750	/	75 inspections	=	$2,450 per inspection
Materials management	$367,500	/	750 requisitions	=	$490 per requisition
Production	$175,000	/	175,000 direct labor hours	=	$1 per direct labor hour

These activity rates can be used to determine the activity-based factory overhead cost per unit as follows:

TV

Activity	Activity-Base Usage	×	Activity Rate	=	Activity Cost
Setup	80 setups	×	$3,430	=	$274,400
Production control	80 production orders	×	$1,960	=	156,800
Quality control	35 inspections	×	$2,450	=	85,750
Materials management	320 requisitions	×	$490	=	156,800
Production	25,000 direct labor hrs.	×	$1	=	25,000
Total factory overhead					$698,750
Unit volume					/ 10,000
Factory overhead cost per unit					$ 69.88

Computer

Activity	Activity-Base Usage	×	Activity Rate	=	Activity Cost
Setup	40 setups	×	$3,430	=	$137,200
Production control	40 production orders	×	$1,960	=	78,400
Quality control	40 inspections	×	$2,450	=	98,000
Materials management	400 requisitions	×	$490	=	196,000
Production	10,000 direct labor hrs.	×	$1	=	10,000
Total factory overhead					$519,600
Unit volume					/ 2,000
Factory overhead cost per unit					$ 259.80

Cell phone

Activity	Activity-Base Usage	×	Activity Rate	=	Activity Cost
Setup	5 setups	×	$3,430	=	$ 17,150
Production control	5 production orders	×	$1,960	=	9,800
Quality control	0 inspections	×	$2,450	=	0
Materials management	30 requisitions	×	$490	=	14,700
Production	140,000 direct labor hrs.	×	$1	=	140,000
Total factory overhead					$181,650
Unit volume					/ 50,000
Factory overhead cost per unit					$ 3.63

3. Activity-based costing is more accurate, compared to the single plantwide factory over-head rate method. Activity-based costing properly shows that the cell phone is actually less expensive to make, while the other two products are more expensive to make. The reason is that the single plantwide factory overhead rate method fails to account for activity costs correctly. The setup, production control, quality control, and materials management activities are all performed on products in rates that are different from their volumes. For example, the computer requires many of these activities relative to its actual unit volume. The computer requires 40 setups over a volume of 2,000 units (average production run size = 50 units), while the cell phone has only 5 setups over 50,000 units (average production run size = 10,000 units). Thus, the computer requires greater support costs relative to the cell phone.

The cell phone requires minimum activity support because it is scheduled in large batches and requires no inspections (has high quality) and few requisitions. The other two products exhibit the opposite characteristics.

Self-Examination Questions

(Answers at End of Chapter)

1. Which of the following statements is most accurate?
   A. The single plantwide factory overhead rate method will usually provide management with accurate product costs.
   B. Activity-based costing can be used by management to determine accurate profitability for each product.
   C. The multiple production department factory over-head rate method will usually result in more product cost distortion than the single plantwide factory overhead rate method.
   D. Generally accepted accounting principles require activity-based costing methods for inventory valuation.

2. San Madeo Company had the following factory over-head costs:
   Power $120,000
   Indirect labor 60,000
   Equipment depreciation 500,000

   The factory is budgeted to work 20,000 direct labor hours in the upcoming period. San Madeo uses a single plantwide factory overhead rate based on direct labor hours. What is the overhead cost per unit associated with Product M, if Product M uses 6 direct labor hours per unit in the factory?
   A. $34   C. $204
   B. $54   D. $150

3. Which of the following activity bases would best be used to allocate setup activity to products?
   A. Number of inspections
   B. Direct labor hours
   C. Direct machine hours
   D. Number of production runs

4. Production Department 1 (PD1) and Production Department 2 (PD2) had factory overhead budgets of $26,000 and $48,000, respectively. Each department was budgeted for 5,000 direct labor hours of production activity. Product T required 5 direct labor hours in PD1 and 2 direct labor hours in PD2. What is the factory overhead cost associated with a unit of Product T, assuming that factory overhead is allocated using the multiple production department rate method?
   A. $26.00   C. $45.20
   B. $40.40   D. $58.40

5. The following activity rates are associated with moving rail cars by train:
   $4 per gross ton mile
   $50 per rail car switch
   $200 per rail car

   A train with 20 rail cars traveled 100 miles. Each rail car carried 10 tons of product. Each rail car was switched 2 times. What is the total cost of moving this train?
   A. $5,400   C. $44,100
   B. $10,000   D. $86,000

Eye Openers

1. How does a company use product costing?
2. Why would it be appropriate for a company that builds aircraft carriers for the Navy to use a single overhead rate?
3. Why would management be concerned about the accuracy of product costs?
4. Why is the sum of product costs under alternative factory overhead cost allocation methods equal?
5. Why would a manufacturing company with multiple production departments still prefer to use a single plantwide overhead rate?
6. How do the multiple production department and the single plantwide factory overhead rate methods differ?
7. How are multiple production department factory overhead rates determined?
8. How is the allocation base for a production department selected?
9. Under what two conditions would the multiple production department factory overhead rate method provide more accurate product costs than the single plantwide factory overhead rate method?
10. How does activity-based costing differ from the multiple production department factory overhead rate method?
11. Shipping, selling, marketing, sales order processing, return processing, and advertising activities can be related to products by using activity-based costing. Would allocating these activities to products for financial statement reporting be acceptable according to GAAP?
12. What would happen to net income if the activities noted in Eye Opener 11 were allocated to products for financial statement reporting and the inventory increased?
13. Under what circumstances might the activity-based costing method provide more accurate product costs than the multiple production department factory overhead rate method?
14. When might activity-based costing be preferred over using a relative amount of product sales in allocating selling and administrative expenses to products?
15. How can activity-based costing be used in service companies?
16. How would a telecommunications company use activity-based costing in conducting profit analysis?

Practice Exercises

PE 26-1A
Single plantwide overhead rate and allocation
obj. 2

The total factory overhead for Goldstein Company is budgeted for the year at $270,000. Goldstein manufactures two types of men's pants: jeans and khakis. The jeans and khakis each require 0.2 direct labor hour for manufacture. Each product is budgeted for 15,000 units of production for the year. Determine (a) the total number of budgeted direct labor hours for the year, (b) the single plantwide factory overhead rate, and (c) the factory overhead allocated per unit for each product using the single plantwide factory overhead rate.

PE 26-1B
Single plantwide factory overhead rate and allocation
obj. 2

The total factory overhead for Kell Marine Company is budgeted for the year at $800,000. Kell Marine manufactures two types of boats: a speedboat and bass boat. The speedboat and bass boat each require 5 direct labor hours for manufacture. Each product is budgeted for 200 units of production for the year. Determine (a) the total number of budgeted direct labor hours for the year, (b) the single plantwide factory overhead rate, and (c) the factory overhead allocated per unit for each product using the single plantwide factory overhead rate.

PE 26-2A
Multiple production department factory overhead rates and allocation
obj. 3

The total factory overhead for Goldstein Company is budgeted for the year at $270,000, divided into two departments: Cutting, $90,000, and Sewing, $180,000. Goldstein manufactures two types of men's pants: jeans and khakis. The jeans require 0.04 direct labor hour in Cutting and 0.16 direct labor hour in Sewing. The khakis require 0.16 direct labor hour in Cutting and 0.04 direct labor hour in Sewing. Each product is budgeted for 15,000 units of production for the year. Determine (a) the total number of budgeted direct labor hours for the year in each department, (b) the departmental factory overhead rates for both departments, and (c) the factory overhead allocated per unit for each product using the department factory overhead allocation rates.

PE 26-2B
Multiple production department factory overhead rates and allocation
obj. 3

The total factory overhead for Kell Marine Company is budgeted for the year at $800,000, divided into two departments: Fabrication, $550,000, and Assembly, $250,000. Kell Marine manufactures two types of boats: speedboats and bass boats. The speedboats require 1.5 direct labor hours in Fabrication and 3.5 direct labor hours in Assembly. The bass boat require 3.5 direct labor hours in Fabrication and 1.5 direct labor hours in Assembly. Each product is budgeted for 200 units of production for the year. Determine (a) the total number of budgeted direct labor hours for the year in each department, (b) the departmental factory overhead rates for both departments, and (c) the factory overhead allocated per unit for each product using the department factory overhead allocation rates.

PE 26-3A
Activity-based rates and allocation
obj. 4

The total factory overhead for Goldstein Company is budgeted for the year at $270,000, divided into four activity pools: cutting, $75,000; sewing, $60,000; setup, $85,000; and inspection, $50,000. Goldstein manufactures two types of men's pants: jeans and khakis. The activity-base usage quantities for each product by each activity are as follows:

	Cutting	Sewing	Setup	Inspection
Jeans	600 dlh	2,400 dlh	1,600 setups	3,500 inspections
Khakis	2,400	600	400	500
	3,000 dlh	3,000 dlh	2,000 setups	4,000 inspections

Each product is budgeted for 15,000 units of production for the year. Determine (a) the activity rates for each activity and (b) the activity-based factory overhead per unit for each product.

PE 26-3B
Activity-based rates and allocation
obj. 4

The total factory overhead for Kell Marine Company is budgeted for the year at $800,000, divided into four activity pools: fabrication, $300,000; assembly, $150,000; setup, $140,000; and inspection, $210,000. Kell Marine manufactures two types of boats: a speedboat and bass boat. The activity-base usage quantities for each product by each activity are as follows:

	Fabrication	Assembly	Setup	Inspection
Speedboat	300 dlh	700 dlh	50 setups	100 inspections
Bass boat	700	300	90	400
	1,000 dlh	1,000 dlh	140 setups	500 inspections

Each product is budgeted for 200 units of production for the year. Determine (a) the activity rates for each activity and (b) the activity-based factory overhead per unit for each product.

PE 26-4A
Activity-based costing—selling and administrative expenses
obj. 5

Gemini Company manufactures and sells shoes. Gemini uses activity-based costing to determine the cost of the sales order processing and the shipping activity. The sales order processing activity has an activity rate of $18 per sales order, and the shipping activity has an activity rate of $24 per shipment. Gemini sold 40,000 units of walking shoes, which consisted of 5,000 orders and 3,000 shipments. Determine (a) the total and (b) the per-unit sales order processing and shipping activity cost for walking shoes.

PE 26-4B
Activity-based costing—selling and administrative expenses
obj. 5

Playtyme Company manufactures and sells outdoor play equipment. Playtyme uses activity-based costing to determine the cost of the sales order processing and the customer return activity. The sales order processing activity has an activity rate of $32 per sales order, and the customer return activity has an activity rate of $85 per return. Gemini sold 2,000 swing sets, which consisted of 500 orders and 40 returns. Determine (a) the total and (b) the per-unit sales order processing and customer return activity cost for swing sets.

PE 26-5A
Activity-based costing—service business
obj. 6

National Bancorp uses activity-based costing to determine the cost of servicing customers. There are three activity pools: teller transaction processing, check processing, and ATM transaction processing. The activity rates associated with each activity pool are $2.40 per teller transaction, $0.18 per canceled check, and $0.90 per ATM transaction. Jacob Ferris had 5 teller transactions, 65 canceled checks, and 12 ATM transactions during the month. Determine the total monthly activity-based cost for servicing Ferris during the month.

PE 26-5B
Activity-based costing—service business
obj. 6

Comfort Suites Hotel uses activity-based costing to determine the cost of servicing customers. There are three activity pools: guest check-in, room cleaning, and meal service. The activity rates associated with each activity pool are $5.80 per guest check-in, $18.60 per room cleaning, and $2.75 per served meal (not including food). Maurice Dee visited the hotel for a 3-night stay. Dee had four meals in the hotel during his visit. Determine the total activity-based cost for servicing Dee for this visit.

Exercises

EX 26-1
Single plantwide factory overhead rate
obj. 2

Spacely Company's Fabrication Department incurred $130,000 of factory overhead cost in producing gears and sprockets. The two products consumed a total of 5,000 direct machine hours. Of that amount, sprockets consumed 2,100 direct machine hours.

Determine the total amount of factory overhead that should be allocated to sprockets.

EX 26-2
Single plantwide factory overhead rate
obj. 2

✓ a. $32 per direct labor hour

River City Band Instruments Inc. makes three musical instruments: trumpets, tubas, and trombones. The budgeted factory overhead cost is $156,800. Factory overhead is allocated to the three products on the basis of direct labor hours. The products have the following budgeted production volume and direct labor hours per unit:

	Budgeted Production Volume	Direct Labor Hours per Unit
Trumpets	2,800 units	0.6
Tubas	700	1.8
Trombones	1,400	1.4

a. Determine the single plantwide factory overhead rate.
b. Use the factory overhead rate in (a) to determine the amount of total and per-unit factory overhead allocated to each of the three products.

EX 26-3
Single plantwide factory overhead rate
obj. 2

✓ a. $58 per processing hour

Snappy Snack Food Company manufactures three types of snack foods: tortilla chips, potato chips, and pretzels. The company has budgeted the following costs for the upcoming period:

Factory depreciation	$115,500
Indirect labor	336,600
Factory electricity	43,400
Indirect materials	72,900
Selling expenses	171,000
Administrative expenses	92,800
Total costs	$832,200

Factory overhead is allocated to the three products on the basis of processing hours. The products had the following production budget and processing hours per case:

	Budgeted Production Volume (Cases)	Processing Hours per Case
Tortilla chips	16,000	0.14
Potato chips	34,000	0.18
Pretzels	12,000	0.12
Total	62,000	

a. Determine the single plantwide factory overhead rate.
b. Use the factory overhead rate in (a) to determine the amount of total and per-case factory overhead allocated to each of the three products under generally accepted accounting principles.

EX 26-4
Product costs and product profitability reports, using a single plantwide factory overhead rate

obj. 2

✓ c. Pistons gross profit, $13,500

Flint Engine Parts Inc. (FEP) produces three products—pistons, valves, and cams—for the heavy equipment industry. FEP has a very simple production process and product line and uses a single plantwide factory overhead rate to allocate overhead to the three products. The factory overhead rate is based on direct labor hours. Information about the three products for 2009 is as follows:

	Budgeted Volume (Units)	Direct Labor Hours per Unit	Price per Unit	Direct Materials per Unit
Pistons	5,000	0.40	$45.00	$25.50
Valves	15,000	0.18	12.80	4.60
Cams	2,500	0.14	32.00	18.40

The estimated direct labor rate is $22 per direct labor hour. Beginning and ending inventories are negligible and are, thus, assumed to be zero. The budgeted factory overhead for FEP is $101,000.

a. Determine the plantwide factory overhead rate.
b. Determine the factory overhead and direct labor cost per unit for each product.
c. Use the information above to construct a budgeted gross profit report by product line for the year ended December 31, 2009. Include the gross profit as a percent of sales in the last line of your report, rounded to one decimal place.
d. What does the report in (c) indicate to you?

EX 26-5
Multiple production department factory overhead rate method

obj. 3

✓ b. Small glove, $5.80 per unit

Golden Glove Company produces three types of gloves: small, medium, and large. A glove pattern is first stenciled onto leather in the Pattern Department. The stenciled patterns are then sent to the Cut and Sew Department, where the final glove is cut and sewed together. Golden uses the multiple production department factory overhead rate method of allocating factory overhead costs. Its factory overhead costs were budgeted as follows:

Pattern Department overhead	$100,000
Cut and Sew Department overhead	350,000
Total	$450,000

The direct labor estimated for each production department was as follows:

Pattern Department	2,500 direct labor hours
Cut and Sew Department	5,000
Total	7,500 direct labor hours

Direct labor hours are used to allocate the production department overhead to the products. The direct labor hours per unit for each product for each production department were obtained from the engineering records as follows:

Production Departments	Small Glove	Medium Glove	Large Glove
Pattern Department	0.04	0.05	0.07
Cut and Sew Department	0.06	0.09	0.08
Direct labor hours per unit	0.10	0.14	0.15

a. Determine the two production department factory overhead rates.
b. Use the two production department factory overhead rates to determine the factory overhead per unit for each product.

EX 26-6

Single plantwide and multiple production department factory overhead rate methods and product cost distortion

objs. 2, 3

✓ b. Portable computer, $348 per unit

Orange Computer Company manufactures a desktop and portable computer through two production departments, Assembly and Testing. Presently, the company uses a single plantwide factory overhead rate for allocating factory overhead to the two products. However, management is considering using the multiple production department factory overhead rate method. The following factory overhead was budgeted for Orange:

Assembly Department	$ 420,000
Testing Department	740,000
Total	$1,160,000

Direct machine hours were estimated as follows:

Assembly Department	6,000 hours
Testing Department	4,000
Total	10,000 hours

In addition, the direct machine hours (dmh) used to produce a unit of each product in each department were determined from engineering records, as follows:

	Desktop	Portable
Assembly Department	0.90 dmh	1.80 dmh
Testing Department	0.60	1.20
Total machine hours per unit	1.50 dmh	3.00 dmh

a. Determine the per-unit factory overhead allocated to the desktop and portable computers under the single plantwide factory overhead rate method, using direct machine hours as the allocation base.
b. Determine the per-unit factory overhead allocated to the desktop and portable computers under the multiple production department factory overhead rate method, using direct machine hours as the allocation base for each department.
c. Recommend to management a product costing approach, based on your analyses in (a) and (b). Support your recommendation.

EX 26-7

Single plantwide and multiple production department factory overhead rate methods and product cost distortion

objs. 2, 3

✓ b. Diesel engine, $874 per unit

The management of Power Torque Engines Inc. manufactures gasoline and diesel engines through two production departments, Fabrication and Assembly. Management needs accurate product cost information in order to guide product strategy. Presently, the company uses a single plantwide factory overhead rate for allocating factory overhead to the two products. However, management is considering using the multiple production department factory overhead rate method. The following factory overhead was budgeted for Power Torque:

Fabrication Department factory overhead	$620,000
Assembly Department factory overhead	325,000
Total	$945,000

Direct labor hours were estimated as follows:

Fabrication Department	5,000 hours
Assembly Department	5,000
Total	10,000 hours

In addition, the direct labor hours (dlh) used to produce a unit of each product in each department were determined from engineering records, as follows:

Production Departments	Gasoline Engine	Diesel Engine
Fabrication Department	2 dlh	6 dlh
Assembly Department	6	2
Direct labor hours per unit	8 dlh	8 dlh

a. Determine the per-unit factory overhead allocated to the gasoline and diesel engines under the single plantwide factory overhead rate method, using direct labor hours as the activity base.
b. Determine the per-unit factory overhead allocated to the gasoline and diesel engines under the multiple production department factory overhead rate method, using direct labor hours as the activity base for each department.
c. Recommend to management a product costing approach, based on your analyses in (a) and (b). Support your recommendation.

EX 26-8
Identifying activity bases in an activity-based cost system
obj. 4

Eden Foods Inc. uses activity-based costing to determine product costs. For each activity listed in the left column, match an appropriate activity base from the right column. You may use items in the activity base list more than once or not at all.

Activity	Activity Base
Accounting reports	Engineering change orders
Customer return processing	Kilowatt hours used
Electric power	Number of customer orders
Human resources	Number of customer returns
Inventory control	Number of customers
Invoice and collecting	Number of direct labor hours
Machine depreciation	Number of inventory transactions
Materials handling	Number of inspections
Order shipping	Number of machine hours
Payroll	Number of material moves
Production control	Number of payroll checks processed
Production setup	Number of production orders
Purchasing	Number of purchase orders
Quality control	Number of accounting reports
	Number of setups

EX 26-9
Product costs using activity rates
obj. 4
✓ b. $52,200

E-gift Inc. sells china and flatware over the Internet. For the next period, the budgeted cost of the sales order processing activity is $115,200, and 12,800 sales orders are estimated to be processed.

a. Determine the activity rate of the sales order processing activity.
b. Determine the amount of sales order processing cost that china would receive if it had 5,800 sales orders.

EX 26-10
Product costs using activity rates

obj. **4**

✓ *Treadmill activity cost per unit, $51.98*

Lifeway Equipment Company manufactures stationary bicycles and treadmills. The products are produced in its Fabrication and Assembly production departments. In addition to production activities, several other activities are required to produce the two products. These activities and their associated activity rates are as follows:

Activity	Activity Rate
Fabrication	$28 per machine hour
Assembly	$9 per direct labor hour
Setup	$40 per setup
Inspecting	$26 per inspection
Production scheduling	$19 per production order
Purchasing	$13 per purchase order

The activity-base usage quantities and units produced for each product were as follows:

Activity Base	Stationary Bicycle	Treadmill
Machine hours	1,960	1,120
Direct labor hours	462	184
Setups	59	19
Inspections	683	425
Production orders	64	14
Purchase orders	211	130
Units produced	900	900

Use the activity rate and usage information to calculate the total activity cost and activity cost per unit for each product.

EX 26-11
Activity rates and product costs using activity-based costing

obj. **4**

✓ *b. Dining room lighting fixtures, $56.00 per unit*

Nordic Night Inc. manufactures entry and dining room lighting fixtures. Five activities are used in manufacturing the fixtures. These activities and their associated activity cost pools and activity bases are as follows:

Activity	Activity Cost Pool (Budgeted)	Activity Base
Casting	$286,000	Machine hours
Assembly	161,000	Direct labor hours
Inspecting	27,600	Number of inspections
Setup	78,000	Number of setups
Materials handling	36,000	Number of loads

Corporate records were obtained to estimate the amount of activity to be used by the two products. The estimated activity-base usage quantities and units produced are provided in the table below.

Activity Base	Entry	Dining	Total
Machine hours	6,000	5,000	11,000
Direct labor hours	4,600	6,900	11,500
Number of inspections	1,700	600	2,300
Number of setups	240	60	300
Number of loads	780	220	1,000
Units produced	8,282	4,595	12,877

a. Determine the activity rate for each activity.
b. Use the activity rates in (a) to determine the total and per-unit activity costs associated with each product.

EX 26-12

*Activity cost pools,
activity rates, and
product costs using
activity-based costing*

obj. 4

✓ b. Oven, $74.00 per unit

Master Chef Inc. is estimating the activity cost associated with producing ovens and refrigerators. The indirect labor can be traced into four separate activity pools, based on time
records provided by the employees. The budgeted activity cost and activity base information are provided as follows:

Activity	Activity Pool Cost	Activity Base
Procurement	$159,300	Number of purchase orders
Scheduling	10,000	Number of production orders
Materials handling	32,000	Number of moves
Product development	26,400	Number of engineering changes
Total cost	$227,700	

The estimated activity-base usage and unit information for Master Chef's two product
lines was determined from corporate records as follows:

	Number of Purchase Orders	Number of Production Orders	Number of Moves	Number of Engineering Changes	Units
Ovens	800	260	480	140	1,850
Refrigerators	550	140	320	80	1,816
Totals	1,350	400	800	220	3,666

a. Determine the activity rate for each activity cost pool.
b. Determine the activity-based cost per unit of each product.

EX 26-13

*Activity-based costing
and product cost
distortion*

objs. 2, 4

✓ c. CD, $3.91

Storage Devices Inc. is considering a change to activity-based product costing. The company produces two products, compact disks (CDs) and data cartridges, in a single production department. The production department is estimated to require 5,000 direct labor hours.
The total indirect labor is budgeted to be $460,000.

Time records from indirect labor employees revealed that they spent 40% of their time
setting up production runs and 60% of their time supporting actual production.

The following information about CDs and data cartridges was determined from the
corporate records:

	Number of Setups	Direct Labor Hours	Units
CDs	500	2,500	50,000
Data cartridges	1,100	2,500	50,000
Total	1,600	5,000	100,000

a. Determine the indirect labor cost per unit allocated to CDs and data cartridges under a
single plantwide factory overhead rate system using the direct labor hours as the allocation base.
b. Determine the activity pools and activity rates for the indirect labor under activity-based
costing. Assume two activity pools—one for setup and the other for production support.
c. Determine the activity cost per unit for indirect labor allocated to each product under
activity-based costing.
d. Why are the per-unit allocated costs in (a) different from the per-unit activity cost assigned to the products in (c)?

EX 26-14

*Multiple production
department factory
overhead rate method*

obj. 3

✓ b. Blender, $17.00 per unit

Gourmet Assistant Appliance Company manufactures small kitchen appliances. The product line consists of blenders and toaster ovens. Gourmet Assistant presently uses the multiple production department factory overhead rate method. The factory overhead is as follows:

Assembly Department	$225,000
Test and Pack Department	150,000
Total	$375,000

The direct labor information for the production of 10,000 units of each product is as follows:

	Assembly Department	Test and Pack Department
Blender	400 dlh	1,100 dlh
Toaster oven	1,100	400
Total	1,500 dlh	1,500 dlh

Gourmet Assistant used direct labor hours to allocate production department factory overhead to products.

a. Determine the two production department factory overhead rates.
b. Determine the total factory overhead and the factory overhead per unit allocated to each product.

EX 26-15
Activity-based costing and product cost distortion

obj. 4

✓ *b. Blender, $19.25 per unit*

The management of Gourmet Assistant Appliance Company in Exercise 26-14 has asked you to use activity-based costing to allocate factory overhead costs to the two products. You have determined that $60,000 of factory overhead from each of the production departments can be associated with setup activity ($120,000 in total). Company records indicate that blenders required 330 setups, while the toaster ovens required only 150 setups. Each product has a production volume of 10,000 units.

a. Determine the three activity rates (assembly, test and pack, and setup).
b. Determine the total factory overhead and factory overhead per unit allocated to each product.

EX 26-16
Single plantwide rate and activity-based costing

objs. 2, 4

✓ *a. Low, Col. C., 143.7%*

Whirlpool Corporation conducted an activity-based costing study of its Evansville, Indiana, plant in order to identify its most profitable products. Assume that we select three representative refrigerators (out of 333): one low-, one medium-, and one high-volume refrigerator. Additionally, we assume the following activity-base information for each of the three refrigerators:

Three Representative Refrigerators	Number of Machine Hours	Number of Setups	Number of Sales Orders	Number of Units
Refrigerator—Low Volume	28	21	39	140
Refrigerator—Medium Volume	284	18	145	1,350
Refrigerator—High Volume	865	12	123	4,500

Prior to conducting the study, the factory overhead allocation was based on a single machine hour rate. The machine hour rate was $220 per hour. After conducting the activity-based costing study, assume that three activities were used to allocate the factory overhead. The new activity rate information is assumed to be as follows:

	Machining Activity	Setup Activity	Sales Order Processing Activity
Activity rate	$190	$350	$60

a. Complete the following table, using the single machine hour rate to determine the per-unit factory overhead for each refrigerator (Column A) and the three activity-based rates to determine the activity-based factory overhead per unit (Column B). Finally, compute the percent change in per-unit allocation from the single to activity-based rate methods (Column C). Round to one decimal place.

Product Volume Class	Column A Single Rate Overhead Allocation per Unit	Column B ABC Overhead Allocation per Unit	Column C Percent Change in Allocation (Col. B − Col. A)/Col. A
Low			
Medium			
High			

b. Why is the traditional overhead rate per machine hour greater under the single rate method than under the activity-based method?

c. Interpret Column C in your table from part (a).

EX 26-17
Evaluating selling and administrative cost allocations
obj. 5

Productivity Plus Furniture Company has two major product lines with the following characteristics:

Commercial office furniture: Few large orders, little advertising support, shipments in full truckloads, and low handling complexity

Home office furniture: Many small orders, large advertising support, shipments in partial truckloads, and high handling complexity

The company produced the following profitability report for management:

Productivity Plus Furniture Company
Product Profitability Report
For the Year Ended December 31, 2008

	Commercial Office Furniture	Home Office Furniture	Total
Revenue	$3,600,000	$1,800,000	$5,400,000
Cost of goods sold	1,500,000	700,000	2,200,000
Gross profit	$2,100,000	$1,100,000	$3,200,000
Selling and administrative expenses	1,200,000	600,000	1,800,000
Income from operations	$ 900,000	$ 500,000	$1,400,000

The selling and administrative expenses are allocated to the products on the basis of relative sales dollars.

Evaluate the accuracy of this report and recommend an alternative approach.

EX 26-18
Construct and interpret a product profitability report, allocating selling and administrative expenses
obj. 5

✓ b. Generators operating profit-to-sales, 21%

Portable Power Equipment Company manufactures power equipment. Portable Power has two primary products—generators and air compressors. The following report was prepared by the controller for Portable Power's senior marketing management:

	Generators	Air Compressors	Total
Revenue	$1,750,000	$970,000	$2,720,000
Cost of goods sold	1,312,500	727,500	2,040,000
Gross profit	$ 437,500	$242,500	$ 680,000
Selling and administrative expenses			293,100
Income from operations			$ 386,900

The marketing management team was concerned that the selling and administrative expenses were not traced to the products. Marketing management believed that some products consumed larger amounts of selling and administrative expense than did other products. To verify this, the controller was asked to prepare a complete product profitability report, using activity-based costing.

The controller determined that selling and administrative expenses consisted of two activities: sales order processing and post-sale customer service. The controller was able to determine the activity base and activity rate for each activity, as shown below.

Activity	Activity Base	Activity Rate
Sales order processing	Sales orders	$100 per sales order
Post-sale customer service	Service requests	$320 per customer service request

The controller determined the following additional information about each product:

	Generators	Air Compressors
Number of sales orders	444	791
Number of service requests	80	450

a. Determine the activity cost of each product for sales order processing and post-sale customer service activities.
b. Use the information in (a) to prepare a complete product profitability report dated for the year ended December 31, 2008. Calculate the gross profit to sales and the income from operations to sales percentages for each product.
c. Interpret the product profitability report. How should management respond to the report?

EX 26-19
Activity-based costing and customer profitability

obj. 6

✓ a. Customer 1, $2,308

Square D Company manufactures power distribution equipment for commercial customers, such as hospitals and manufacturers. Activity-based costing was used to determine customer profitability. Customer service activities were assigned to individual customers, using the following assumed customer service activities, activity base, and activity rate:

Customer Service Activity	Activity Base	Activity Rate
Bid preparation	Number of bid requests	$140/request
Shipment	Number of shipments	$26/shipment
Support standard items	Number of standard items ordered	$48/std. item
Support nonstandard items	Number of nonstandard items ordered	$120/nonstd. item

Assume that the company had the following gross profit information for three representative customers:

	Customer 1	Customer 2	Customer 3
Revenue	$17,500	$26,250	$42,000
Cost of goods sold	9,100	12,600	26,040
Gross profit	$ 8,400	$13,650	$15,960
Gross profit as a percent of sales	48%	52%	38%

The administrative records indicated that the activity-base usage quantities for each customer were as follows:

Activity Base	Customer 1	Customer 2	Customer 3
Number of bid requests	6	20	8
Number of shipments	22	34	16
Number of standard items ordered	35	48	52
Number of nonstandard items ordered	25	50	15

a. Prepare a customer profitability report dated for the year ended Decemer 31, 2008, showing (1) the income from operations after customer service activities and (2) the income from operations after customer service activities as a percent of sales. Prepare the report with a column for each customer. Round percentages to the nearest whole percent.
b. Interpret the table in part (a).

EX 26-20
Activity-based costing for a hospital

obj. 6

✓ a. Patient Malone, $6,495

Mercy Hospital plans to use activity-based costing to assign hospital indirect costs to the care of patients. The hospital has identified the following activities and activity rates for the hospital indirect costs:

Activity	Activity Rate
Room and meals	$165 per day
Radiology	$250 per image
Pharmacy	$45 per physician order
Chemistry lab	$85 per test
Operating room	$680 per operating room hour

The records of two representative patients were analyzed, using the activity rates. The activity information associated with the two patients is as follows:

	Patient Malone	Patient Talbot
Number of days	8 days	4 days
Number of images	5 images	3 images
Number of physician orders	6 orders	2 orders
Number of tests	7 tests	3 tests
Number of operating room hours	4.5 hours	2 hours

a. Determine the activity cost associated with each patient.

b. Why is the total activity cost different for the two patients?

EX 26-21
Activity-based costing in an insurance company
objs. 5, 6

✓ a. Auto, $840,375

Sentinel Insurance Company carries three major lines of insurance: auto, workers' compensation, and homeowners. The company has prepared the following report for 2009:

Sentinel Insurance Company
Product Profitability Report
For the Year Ended December 31, 2009

	Auto	Workers' Compensation	Homeowners
Premium revenue	$6,000,000	$5,000,000	$7,000,000
Less estimated claims	4,200,000	3,500,000	4,900,000
Underwriting income	$1,800,000	$1,500,000	$2,100,000
Underwriting income as a percent of premium revenue	30%	30%	30%

Management is concerned that the administrative expenses may make some of the insurance lines unprofitable. However, the administrative expenses have not been allocated to the insurance lines. The controller has suggested that the administrative expenses could be assigned to the insurance lines using activity-based costing. The administrative expenses are comprised of five activities. The activities and their rates are as follows:

	Activity Rates
New policy processing	$170 per new policy
Cancellation processing	$260 per cancellation
Claim audits	$550 per claim audit
Claim disbursements processing	$115 per disbursement
Premium collection processing	$50 per premium collected

Activity-base usage data for each line of insurance was retrieved from the corporate records and is shown below.

	Auto	Workers' Comp.	Homeowners
Number of new policies	1,200	1,400	3,100
Number of canceled policies	500	180	1,650
Number of audited claims	350	120	710
Number of claim disbursements	375	150	740
Number of premiums collected	7,800	1,600	12,000

a. Complete the product profitability report through the administrative activities. Determine the income from operations as a percent of premium revenue, rounded to one decimal place.

b. Interpret the report.

Problems Series A

PR 26-1A
Single plantwide factory overhead rate

obj. 2

✓ *1. b. $166 per machine hour*

Custom Car Accessory Company manufactures three chrome-plated products—automobile bumpers, valve covers, and wheels. These products are manufactured in two production departments (Stamping and Plating). The factory overhead for Custom Car is $996,000.

The three products consume both machine hours and direct labor hours in the two production departments as follows:

	Direct Labor Hours	Machine Hours
Stamping Department		
Automobile bumpers	500	780
Valve covers	460	710
Wheels	740	910
	1,700	2,400
Plating Department		
Automobile bumpers	210	1,100
Valve covers	240	930
Wheels	250	1,570
	700	3,600
Total	2,400	6,000

Instructions

1. Determine the single plantwide factory overhead rate, using each of the following allocation bases: (a) direct labor hours and (b) machine hours.
2. Determine the product factory overhead costs, using (a) the direct labor hour plantwide factory overhead rate and (b) the machine hour plantwide factory overhead rate.

PR 26-2A
Multiple production department factory overhead rates

obj. 3

✓ *2. Wheels, $433,825*

The management of Custom Car Accessory Company, described in Problem 26-1A, now plans to use the multiple production department factory overhead rate method. The total factory overhead associated with each department is as follows:

Stamping Department	$663,000
Plating Department	333,000
Total	$996,000

Instructions

1. Determine the multiple production department factory overhead rates, using direct labor hours for the Stamping Department and machine hours for the Plating Department.
2. Determine the product factory overhead costs, using the multiple production department rates in (1).

PR 26-3A
Activity-based and department rate product costing and product cost distortions

objs. 3, 4

✓ *4. Snowboards, $455,500 and $18.22*

Mountain Jam Sports Inc. manufactures two products: snowboards and skis. The factory overhead incurred is as follows:

Indirect labor	$ 480,000
Cutting Department	350,000
Finishing Department	260,000
Total	$1,090,000

The activity base associated with the two production departments is direct labor hours. The indirect labor can be assigned to two different activities as follows:

Activity	Activity Cost Pool	Activity Base
Production control	$150,000	Number of production runs
Materials handling	330,000	Number of moves
Total	$480,000	

The activity-base usage quantities and units produced for the two products are shown below.

	Number of Production Runs	Number of Moves	Direct Labor Hours—Cutting	Direct Labor Hours—Finishing	Units Produced
Snowboards	60	2,000	3,500	1,500	25,000
Skis	340	4,000	1,500	3,500	25,000
Total	400	6,000	5,000	5,000	50,000

Instructions

1. Determine the factory overhead rates under the multiple production department rate method. Assume that indirect labor is associated with the production departments, so that the total factory overhead is $650,000 and $440,000 for the Cutting and Finishing departments, respectively.
2. Determine the total and per-unit factory overhead costs allocated to each product, using the multiple production department overhead rates in (1).
3. Determine the activity rates, assuming that the indirect labor is associated with activities rather than with the production departments.
4. Determine the total and per-unit cost assigned to each product under activity-based costing.
5. Explain the difference in the per-unit overhead allocated to each product under the multiple production department factory overhead rate and activity-based costing methods.

PR 26-4A
Activity-based product costing

obj. 4

✓ 2. Newsprint total activity cost, $405,595

Georgia Forest Paper Company manufactures three products (computer paper, newsprint, and specialty paper) in a continuous production process. Senior management has asked the controller to conduct an activity-based costing study. The controller identified the amount of factory overhead required by the critical activities of the organization as follows:

Activity	Activity Cost Pool
Production	$ 763,200
Setup	255,000
Moving	27,200
Shipping	90,000
Product engineering	37,000
Total	$1,172,400

The activity bases identified for each activity are as follows:

Activity	Activity Base
Production	Machine hours
Setup	Number of setups
Moving	Number of moves
Shipping	Number of customer orders
Product engineering	Number of test runs

The activity-base usage quantities and units produced for the three products were determined from corporate records and are as follows:

	Machine Hours	Number of Setups	Number of Moves	Number of Customer Orders	Number of Test Runs	Units
Computer paper	1,080	130	290	440	90	1,200
Newsprint	1,350	60	130	135	20	1,500
Specialty paper	450	310	430	625	140	500
Total	2,880	500	850	1,200	250	3,200

Each product requires 0.9 machine hour per unit.

Instructions
1. Determine the activity rate for each activity.
2. Determine the total and per-unit activity cost for all three products. Round to the nearest cent.
3. Why aren't the activity unit costs equal across all three products since they require the same machine time per unit?

PR 26-5A
Allocating selling and administrative expenses using activity-based costing

obj. 5

✓ *3. Mid-States University income from operations, ($58,300)*

Cool Zone Inc. manufactures cooling units for commercial buildings. The price and cost of goods sold for each unit are as follows:

Price	$120,000 per unit
Cost of goods sold	85,000
Gross profit	$ 35,000 per unit

In addition, the company incurs selling and administrative expenses of $477,700. The company wishes to assign these costs to its three major customers, Mid-States University, Celebrity Arena, and Hope Hospital. These expenses are related to three major nonmanufacturing activities: customer service, project bidding, and engineering support. The engineering support is in the form of engineering changes that are placed by the customer to change the design of a product. The activity cost pool and activity bases associated with these activities are:

Activity	Activity Cost Pool	Activity Base
Customer service	$209,000	Number of service requests
Project bidding	147,200	Number of bids
Engineering support	121,500	Number of customer design changes
Total costs	$477,700	

Activity-base usage and unit volume information for the three customers is as follows:

	Mid-States University	Celebrity Arena	Hope Hospital	Total
Number of service requests	110	35	45	190
Number of bids	14	12	20	46
Number of customer design changes	75	25	35	135
Unit volume	5	10	15	30

Instructions
1. Determine the activity rates for each of the three nonmanufacturing activity pools.
2. Determine the activity costs allocated to the three customers, using the activity rates in (1).
3. Construct customer profitability reports for the three customers dated for the year ended December 31, 2009, using the activity costs in (2). The reports should disclose the gross profit and income from operations associated with each customer.
4. Provide recommendations to management, based on the profitability reports in (3).

PR 26-6A
Product costing and decision analysis for a hospital

obj. 6

✓ *3. Procedure B excess, $263,250*

Nightingale Healthcare Inc. wishes to determine its product costs. Nightingale offers a variety of medical procedures (operations) that are considered its "products." The overhead has been separated into three major activities. The annual estimated activity costs and activity bases are provided below.

Activity	Activity Pool Cost	Activity Base
Scheduling and admitting	$ 207,000	Number of patients
Housekeeping	2,064,000	Number of patient days
Nursing	2,310,000	Weighted care unit
Total costs	$4,581,000	

Total "patient days" are determined by multiplying the number of patients by the average length of stay in the hospital. A weighted care unit (wcu) is a measure of nursing effort used to care for patients. There were 140,000 weighted care units estimated for the year. In addition, Mercy estimated 4,600 patients and 17,200 patient days for the year. (The average patient is expected to have a a little less than a four-day stay in the hospital.)

During a portion of the year, Nightingale collected patient information for three selected procedures, as shown below.

	Activity-Base Usage
Procedure A	
Number of patients	210
Average length of stay	× 5 days
Patient days	1,050
Weighted care units	15,000
Procedure B	
Number of patients	500
Average length of stay	× 4 days
Patient days	2,000
Weighted care units	4,500
Procedure C	
Number of patients	900
Average length of stay	× 3 days
Patient days	2,700
Weighted care units	19,000

Private insurance reimburses the hospital for these activities at a fixed daily rate of $300 per patient day for all three procedures.

Instructions
1. Determine the activity rates.
2. Determine the activity cost for each procedure.
3. Determine the excess or deficiency of reimbursements over activity cost.
4. Interpret your results.

Problems Series B

PR 26-1B
Single plantwide factory overhead rate

obj. 2

✓1. b. $228 per machine hour

Morningside Dairy Company manufactures three products—whole milk, skim milk, and cream—in two production departments, Blending and Packing. The factory overhead for Morningside Dairy is $684,000.

The three products consume both machine hours and direct labor hours in the two production departments as follows:

	Direct Labor Hours	Machine Hours
Blending Department		
Whole milk	270	820
Skim milk	290	760
Cream	215	290
	775	1,870
Packing Department		
Whole milk	355	460
Skim milk	520	490
Cream	150	180
	1,025	1,130
Total	1,800	3,000

Instructions

1. Determine the single plantwide factory overhead rate, using each of the following allocation bases: (a) direct labor hours and (b) machine hours.
2. Determine the product factory overhead costs, using (a) the direct labor hour plantwide factory overhead rate and (b) the machine hour plantwide factory overhead rate.

PR 26-2B

Multiple production department factory overhead rates

obj. 3

✓ *2. Cream, $105,000*

The management of Morningside Dairy Company, described in Problem 26-1B, now plans to use the multiple production department factory overhead rate method. The total factory overhead associated with each department is as follows:

Blending Department	$561,000
Packing Department	123,000
Total	$684,000

Instructions

1. Determine the multiple production department factory overhead rates, using machine hours for the Blending Department and direct labor hours for the Packing Department.
2. Determine the product factory overhead costs, using the multiple production department rates in (1).

PR 26-3B

Activity-based and department rate product costing and product cost distortions

objs. 3, 4

✓ *4. CD players, $478,000 and $47.80*

Soundwave Audio Inc. manufactures two products: receivers and CD players. The factory overhead incurred is as follows:

Indirect labor	$ 560,000
Subassembly Department	420,000
Final Assembly Department	350,000
Total	$1,330,000

The activity base associated with the two production departments is direct labor hours. The indirect labor can be assigned to two different activities as follows:

Activity	Activity Cost Pool	Activity Base
Setup	$360,000	Number of setups
Quality control	200,000	Number of inspections
Total	$560,000	

The activity-base usage quantities and units produced for the two products are shown below.

	Number of Setups	Number of Inspections	Direct Labor Hours— Subassembly	Direct Labor Hours— Final Assembly	Units Produced
Receivers	200	1,000	600	400	10,000
CD Players	40	250	400	600	10,000
Total	240	1,250	1,000	1,000	20,000

Instructions

1. Determine the factory overhead rates under the multiple production department rate method. Assume that indirect labor is associated with the production departments, so that the total factory overhead is $700,000 and $630,000 for the Subassembly and Final Assembly Departments, respectively.
2. Determine the total and per-unit factory overhead costs allocated to each product, using the multiple production department overhead rates in (1).
3. Determine the activity rates, assuming that the indirect labor is associated with activities rather than with the production departments.
4. Determine the total and per-unit cost assigned to each product under activity-based costing.
5. Explain the difference in the per-unit overhead allocated to each product under the multiple production department factory overhead rate and activity-based costing methods.

PR 26-4B
Activity-based product costing

obj. 4

✓ *2. Brown sugar total activity cost, $529,600*

Caribbean Sugar Company manufactures three products (white sugar, brown sugar, and powdered sugar) in a continuous production process. Senior management has asked the controller to conduct an activity-based costing study. The controller identified the amount of factory overhead required by the critical activities of the organization as follows:

Activity	Activity Cost Pool
Production	$ 600,000
Setup	450,000
Inspection	172,000
Shipping	260,000
Customer service	74,000
Total	$1,556,000

The activity bases identified for each activity are as follows:

Activity	Activity Base
Production	Machine hours
Setup	Number of setups
Inspection	Number of inspections
Shipping	Number of customer orders
Customer service	Number of customer service requests

The activity-base usage quantities and units produced for the three products were determined from corporate records and are as follows:

	Machine Hours	Number of Setups	Number of Inspections	Number of Customer Orders	Number of Customer Service Requests	Units
White sugar	3,840	100	200	800	40	9,600
Brown sugar	1,600	150	300	2,200	250	4,000
Powdered sugar	2,560	150	500	1,000	110	6,400
Total	8,000	400	1,000	4,000	400	20,000

Each product requires 0.4 machine hour per unit.

Instructions
1. Determine the activity rate for each activity.
2. Determine the total and per-unit activity cost for all three products. Round to the nearest cent.
3. Why aren't the activity unit costs equal across all three products since they require the same machine time per unit?

PR 26-5B
Allocating selling and administrative expenses using activity-based costing

obj. 5

✓ *3. Office Warehouse, income from operations, $119,510*

Z-Rox Inc. manufactures office copiers, which are sold to retailers. The price and cost of goods sold for each copier are as follows:

Price	$450 per unit
Cost of goods sold	365
Gross profit	$ 85 per unit

In addition, the company incurs selling and administrative expenses of $228,160. The company wishes to assign these costs to its three major retail customers, Office Warehouse, General Office Supply, and Office-to-Go. These expenses are related to its three major non-manufacturing activities: customer service, sales order processing, and advertising support. The advertising support is in the form of advertisements that are placed by Z-Rox Inc. to support the retailer's sale of Z-Rox copiers to consumers. The activity cost pool and activity bases associated with these activities are:

Activity	Activity Cost Pool	Activity Base
Customer service	$ 61,200	Number of service requests
Sales order processing	39,560	Number of sales orders
Advertising support	127,400	Number of ads placed
Total activity cost	$228,160	

Activity-base usage and unit volume information for the three customers is as follows:

	Office Warehouse	General Office Supply	Office-to-Go	Total
Number of service requests	50	10	180	240
Number of sales orders	240	100	520	860
Number of ads placed	20	15	105	140
Unit volume	1,900	1,900	1,900	5,700

Instructions
1. Determine the activity rates for each of the three nonmanufacturing activity pools.
2. Determine the activity costs allocated to the three customers, using the activity rates in (1).
3. Construct customer profitability reports for the three customers, dated for the year ended December 31, 2008, using the activity costs in (2). The reports should disclose the gross profit and income from operations associated with each customer.
4. Provide recommendations to management, based on the profitability reports in (3).

PR 26-6B
Product costing and decision analysis for a passenger airline

obj. 6

✓ *3. Flight 102 income from operations, $8,357*

Up and Away Airline provides passenger airline service, using small jets. The airline connects four major cities: Atlanta, Cincinnati, Chicago, and Los Angeles. The company expects to fly 125,000 miles during a month. The following costs are budgeted for a month:

Fuel	$1,040,000
Ground personnel	766,000
Crew salaries	628,000
Depreciation	342,000
Total costs	$2,776,000

Up and Away management wishes to assign these costs to individual flights in order to gauge the profitability of its service offerings. The following activity bases were identified with the budgeted costs:

Airline Cost	Activity Base
Fuel, crew, and depreciation costs	Number of miles flown
Ground personnel	Number of arrivals and departures at an airport

The size of the company's ground operation in each city is determined by the size of the workforce. The following monthly data are available from corporate records for each terminal operation:

Terminal City	Ground Personnel Cost	Number of Arrivals/Departures
Atlanta	$264,000	320
Cincinnati	98,800	130
Chicago	133,500	150
Los Angeles	269,700	290
Total	$766,000	890

Three recent representative flights have been selected for the profitability study. Their characteristics are as follows:

Description	Miles Flown	Number of Passengers	Ticket Price per Passenger
Flight 101	Atlanta to LA	1,850	23	$1,700
Flight 102	Chicago to Atlanta	600	29	680
Flight 103	Atlanta to Cincinnati	350	14	475

Instructions
1. Determine the fuel, crew, and depreciation cost per mile flown.
2. Determine the cost per arrival or departure by terminal city.
3. Use the information in (1) and (2) to construct a profitability report for the three flights.
4. Evaluate flight profitability by determining the break-even number of passengers required for each flight. Round to the nearest whole number.

Special Activities

SA 26-1
Ethics and professional conduct in business

The controller of Accent Systems Inc. devised a new costing system based on tracing the cost of activities to products. The controller was able to measure post-manufacturing activities, such as selling, promotional, and distribution activities, and allocate these activities to products in order to have a more complete view of the company's product costs. This effort produced better strategic information about the relative profitability of product lines. In addition, the controller used the same product cost information for inventory valuation on the financial statements. Surprisingly, the controller discovered that the company's reported net income was larger under this scheme than under the traditional costing approach.

Why was the net income larger, and how would you react to the controller's action?

SA 26-2
Identifying product cost distortion

King Soda Company manufactures soft drinks. Information about two products is as follows:

	Volume	Sales Price per Case	Gross Profit per Case
Jamaican Punch	10,000 cases	$30	$12
King Kola	800,000 cases	30	12

It is known that both products have the same direct materials and direct labor costs per case. King Soda allocates factory overhead to products by using a single plantwide factory overhead rate, based on direct labor cost. Additional information about the two products is as follows:

Jamaican Punch: Requires extensive process preparation and sterilization prior to processing. The ingredients are from Jamaica, requiring complex import controls. The formulation is complex, and it is thus difficult to maintain quality. Lastly, the product is sold in small (less than full truckload) orders.

King Kola: Requires minor process preparation and sterilization prior to processing. The ingredients are acquired locally. The formulation is simple, and it is easy to maintain quality. Lastly, the product is sold in large bulk (full truckload) orders.

Explain the product profitability report in light of the additional data.

SA 26-3
Activity-based costing

Acordia, Inc., is an insurance brokerage company that classified insurance products as either "easy" or "difficult." Easy and difficult products were defined as follows:

Easy: Electronic claims, few inquiries, mature product
Difficult: Paper claims, complex claims to process, many inquiries, a new product with complex options

The company originally allocated processing and service expenses on the basis of revenue. Under this traditional allocation approach, the product profitability report revealed the following:

	Easy Product	Difficult Product	Total
Revenue	$600	$400	$1,000
Processing and service expenses	420	280	700
Income from operations	$180	$120	$ 300
Operating income margin	30%	30%	30%

Acordia decided to use activity-based costing to allocate the processing and service expenses. The following activity-based costing analysis of the same data illustrates a much different profit picture for the two types of products.

	Easy Product	Difficult Product	Total
Revenue	$600	$ 400	$1,000
Processing and service expenses	183	517	700
Income from operations	$417	$(117)	$ 300
Operating income margin	70%	(29%)	30%

Explain why the activity-based profitability report reveals different information from the traditional sales allocation report.

Source: Dan Patras and Kevin Clancy, "ABC in the Service Industry: Product Line Profitability at Acordia, Inc." As Easy as ABC Newsletter, Issue 12, Spring 1993.

SA 26-4
Using a product profitability report to guide strategic decisions

The controller of Audio Eclipse Inc. prepared the following product profitability report for management, using activity-based costing methods for allocating both the factory overhead and the marketing expenses. As such, the controller has confidence in the accuracy of this report. In addition, the controller interviewed the vice president of marketing, who indicated that the floor loudspeakers were an older product that was highly recognized in the marketplace. The ribbon loudspeakers were a new product that was recently launched. The ribbon loudspeakers are a new technology that have no competition in the marketplace, and it is hoped that they will become an important future addition to the company's product portfolio. Initial indications are that the product is well received by customers. The controller believes that the manufacturing costs for all three products are in line with expectations.

	Floor Loudspeakers	Bookshelf Loudspeakers	Ribbon Loudspeakers	Totals
Sales	$8,000,000	$50,000,000	$25,000,000	$83,000,000
Less cost of goods sold	5,200,000	25,000,000	24,000,000	54,200,000
Gross profit	$2,800,000	$25,000,000	$ 1,000,000	$28,800,000
Less marketing expenses	3,200,000	5,000,000	600,000	8,800,000
Income from operations	$ (400,000)	$20,000,000	$ 400,000	$20,000,000

1. Calculate the gross profit and income from operations to sales ratios for each product.
2. Write a memo using the product profitability report and the calculations in (1) to make recommendations to management with respect to strategies for the three products.

SA 26-5
Product cost distortion

Orlando Ortega, president of Tower Tech Inc., was reviewing the product profitability reports with the controller, Tameka Dorr. The following conversation took place:

Orlando: I've been reviewing the product profitability reports. Our high-volume calculator, the T-100, appears to be unprofitable, while some of our lower-volume specialty calculators in the T-900 series appear to be very profitable. These results do not make sense to me. How are the product profits determined?

Tameka: First, we identify the revenues associated with each product line. This information comes directly from our sales order system and is very accurate. Next, we identify the direct materials and direct labor associated with making each of the calculators. Again, this information is very accurate. The final cost that must be considered is the factory overhead. Factory overhead is allocated to the products, based on the direct labor hours used to assemble the calculator.

Orlando: What about distribution, promotion, and other post-manufacturing costs that can be associated with the product?

Tameka: According to generally accepted accounting principles, we expense them in the period that they are incurred and do not treat them as product costs.

Orlando: Another thing, you say that you allocate factory overhead according to direct labor hours. Yet I know that the T-900 series specialty products have very low volumes but require extensive engineering, testing, and materials management effort. They are our newer, more complex products. It seems that these sources of factory overhead will end up being allocated to the T-100 line because it is the high-volume and therefore high direct labor hour product. Yet the T-100 line is easy to make and requires very little support from our engineering, testing, and materials management personnel.

Tameka: I'm not too sure. I do know that our product costing approach is similar to that used by many different types of companies. I don't think we could all be wrong.

Is Orlando Ortega's concern valid, and how might Tameka Dorr redesign the cost allocation system to address Ortega's concern?

SA 26-6
Allocating bank administrative costs

Banks have a variety of products, such as savings accounts, checking accounts, certificates of deposit (CDs), and loans. Assume that you were assigned the task of determining the administrative costs of "savings accounts" as a complete product line. What are some of the activities associated with savings accounts? In answering this question, consider the activities that you might perform with your savings account. For each activity, what would be an activity base that could be used to allocate the activity cost to the savings account product line?

Answers to Self-Examination Questions

1. **B** Activity-based costing provides accurate product costs, which can be used for strategic product profitability analysis. The single plantwide factory overhead rate method (answer A) can distort the individual product costs under a variety of reasonable conditions. The multiple production department factory overhead rate method will lead to less (not more) distortion than the single plantwide factory overhead rate method (answer C). Generally accepted accounting principles do not require activity-based costing for inventory valuation (answer D).

2. **C** The single plantwide factory overhead rate is $34 per hour (answer A), determined as $680,000/20,000 hours. This rate is multiplied by 6 direct labor hours per unit of Product M to determine the correct overhead per unit of $204. The total overhead should be used in the numerator in determining the overhead rate, not just power and indirect labor (answer B) or equipment depreciation (answer D).

3. **D** The number of production runs best relates the activity cost of setup to the products. Number of inspections, direct labor hours, and direct machine hours (answers A , B, and C) will likely have very little logical association with the costs incurred in setting up production runs.

4. **C** PD1 rate: $26,000/5,000 dlh = $5.20 per dlh
   PD2 rate: $48,000/5,000 dlh = $9.60 per dlh
   Product T: (5 dlh × $5.20) + (2 dlh × $9.60) = $45.20

5. **D** (100 miles × 20 cars × 10 tons × $4) + ($200 × 20 cars) + (20 cars × 2 switches × $50) = $80,000 + $4,000 + $2,000 = $86,000

chapter
27

Cost Management for Just-in-Time Environments

© BANANA STOCK/FIRST LIGHT

objectives

After studying this chapter, you should be able to:

1 *Compare and contrast just-in-time (JIT) manufacturing practices with traditional manufacturing practices.*

2 *Apply just-in-time manufacturing practices to a traditional manufacturing illustration.*

3 *Describe the implications of a just-in-time manufacturing philosophy on cost accounting and performance measurement systems.*

4 *Apply just-in-time practices to a nonmanufacturing setting.*

5 *Describe and illustrate activity analysis for improving operations.*

Precor

W hen you order the salad bar at the local restaurant, you are able to serve yourself at your own pace. There is no waiting for the waitress to take the order or for the cook to prepare the meal. You are able to move directly to the salad bar and select from various offerings. You might wish to have salad with lettuce, cole slaw, bacon bits, croutons, and salad dressing. The offerings are arranged in a row so that you can build your salad as you move down the salad bar.

Many manufacturers are producing each product directly to customer needs, in much the same way that the salad bar is designed to satisfy each customer's needs. Like customers at the salad bar, products move through a production process as they are built for each customer's unique needs. Such a process eliminates many sources of waste, which is why it is termed just in time.

Using just in time principles can dramatically improve performance. For example, Precor, a manufacturer of fitness equipment, used just-in-time principles to improve its manufacturing operations. Within three years, Precor improved on-time shipments from near 40% to above 90%, decreased direct labor costs by 30%, cut the number of suppliers from 3,000 to under 250, reduced inventory by 40%, and chiseled warranty claims by near 60%.

In this chapter, we will discuss the just-in-time philosophy and illustrate the managerial accounting principles and tools used in just-in-time environments. We will complete the chapter by discussing and illustrating the accounting for quality costs and process activity analysis.

Just-in-Time Principles

objective   **1**

Compare and contrast just-in-time (JIT) manufacturing practices with traditional manufacturing practices.

The operating methods used by many companies are undergoing significant change. Companies are recognizing the need to produce products and services with high quality, low cost, and instant availability. Achieving these objectives requires a change in the methods of manufacturing products and delivering services. One approach reflecting these changes is the just-in-time philosophy. **Just-in-time (JIT)**, sometimes called *short-cycle* or *lean* **manufacturing**, focuses on reducing time, cost, and poor quality within manufacturing and nonmanufacturing processes.

We will first discuss just-in-time principles within a manufacturing setting. Exhibit 1 lists some of the just-in-time manufacturing principles and the traditional manufacturing principles. In the following paragraphs, we briefly discuss each of the just-in-time principles. We will then address the accounting implications of these principles.

REDUCING INVENTORY

Just-in-time manufacturing views inventory as wasteful and unnecessary, and thus attempts to reduce or eliminate inventory. Under traditional manufacturing, inventory hides underlying production problems. For example, inventory is often used to maintain sales and production levels during various production interruptions, such as machine breakdowns, manufacturing schedule changes, transportation delays, and unexpected scrap and rework. An important focus in just-in-time manufacturing is to remove these production problems so that the materials, work in process, and finished goods inventory levels can be reduced or eliminated.

The role of inventory can be explained by referring to a river. Inventory is the water in a river, while the rocks at the bottom of the river are the production problems. When the water level is high, all the rocks at the

EXHIBIT 1   Operating Principles of Just-in-Time versus Traditional Manufacturing

Issue	Just-in-Time Manufacturing	Traditional Manufacturing
Inventory	Reduces inventory.	Increases inventory to protect against process problems.
Lead time	Reduces lead time.	Increases lead time to protect against uncertainty.
Setup time	Reduces setup time.	Disregards setup time as an improvement priority.
Production layout	Emphasizes product-oriented layout.	Emphasizes process-oriented layout.
Role of the employee	Emphasizes team-oriented employee involvement.	Emphasizes work of individuals, following manager instructions.
Production scheduling policy	Emphasizes pull manufacturing.	Emphasizes push manufacturing.
Quality	Emphasizes zero defects.	Tolerates defects.
Suppliers and customers	Emphasizes supply chain management.	Treats suppliers and customers as "arm's-length," independent entities.

bottom of the river are hidden. That is, inventory hides the production problems. However, as the water level drops, the rocks become exposed, one by one. Reducing inventory reveals production problems. Once these problems are fixed, the "water level" can be reduced even further to expose more "rocks" for elimination until an efficient, effective production process is achieved.

Integrity, Objectivity, and Ethics in Business

THE INVENTORY SHIFT

Some managers take a shortcut to reducing inventory by shifting inventory to their suppliers. With this tactic, the hard work of improving processes is avoided. Enlightened managers realize that such tactics often have short-lived savings. Suppliers will eventually increase their prices to compensate for the additional inventory holding costs, thus resulting in no savings. Therefore, shifting a problem doesn't eliminate a problem.

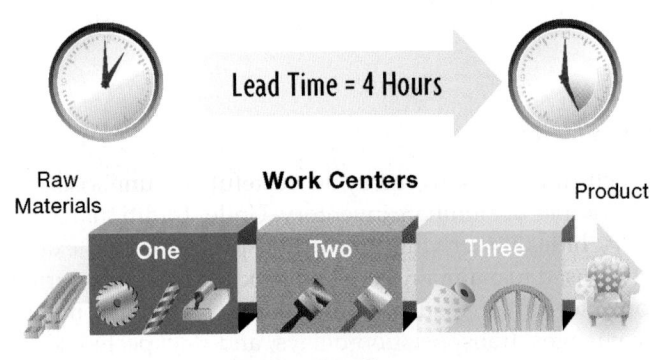

Production Process

REDUCING LEAD TIMES

Lead time, sometimes called *throughput time*, is a measure of the time that elapses between starting a unit of product into the beginning of a process and completing the unit of product. As shown in the illustration, if a product begins the process at 1:00 P.M. and is completed at 5:00 P.M., the lead time is four hours.

Reducing lead times can be an objective for products manufactured in the plant or any other item that is produced through a process. For example, lead times could be reduced for processing sales orders, invoices, insurance applications, or hospital patients.

The total lead time can be divided into value-added and non-value-added time portions, as shown in Exhibit 2. **Value-added lead time** is the time required to actually manufacture a unit of a product. It is the conver-

EXHIBIT 2 | Components of Lead Time

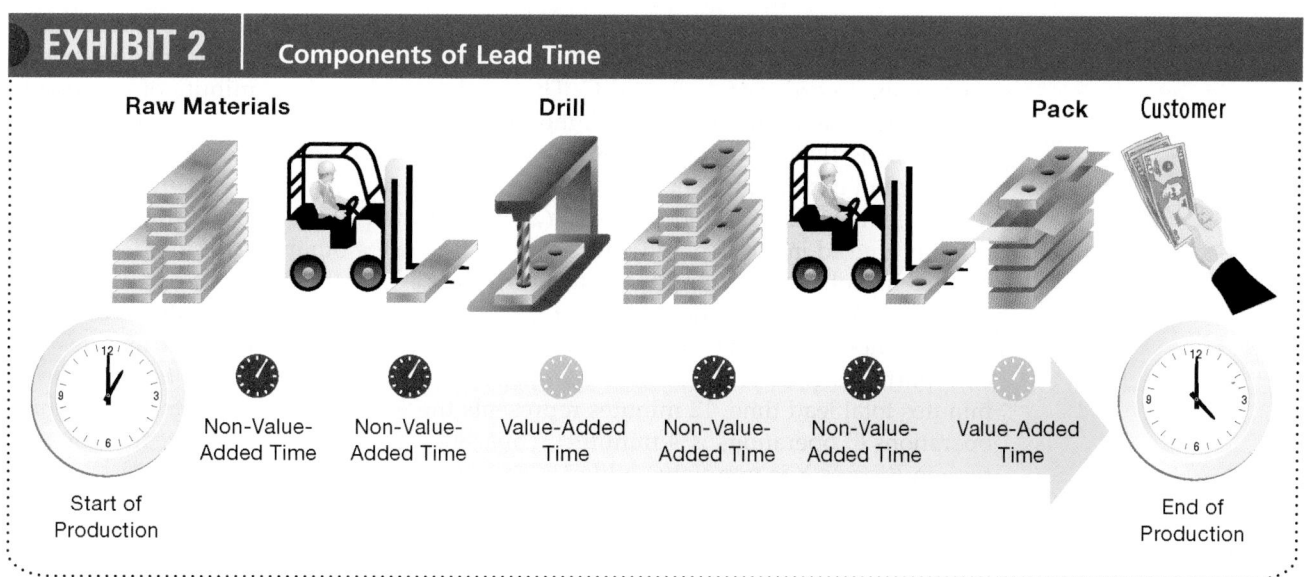

Crown Audio reduced the lead time between receiving a customer order and delivering it from 30 days to 12 hours by using just-in-time principles.

sion time for a unit. For example, value-added lead time would include the time to drill and pack parts for shipment. The **value-added ratio** is the ratio of the value-added lead time to the total lead time. **Non-value-added lead time** is the time that a unit of product sits in inventories or moves unnecessarily. Non-value-added lead time occurs in poor production processes. In a well-functioning process, the product should spend very little time waiting in inventory, because inventory is at a minimum. The product should also spend little time moving, because operations are sequenced closely.

Just-in-time manufacturing reduces or eliminates non-value-added time, thereby reducing the cost and improving the speed of production. Reducing non-value-added lead time is often directly related to reducing inventory. Organizations that use many work in process inventory locations may discover that the value-added ratio can be as little as 5% of the total lead time.

REDUCING SETUP TIME

As we introduced in the previous chapter, a *setup* is the effort required to prepare an operation for a new production run. For example, a beverage company's bottling line would need to be cleaned between flavor changes. If setups are long and expensive, the production run (*batch*) must be large in order to recover the setup cost. Large batches increase inventory, and larger inventories add to lead time. Exhibit 3 is a diagram of the relationship between setup times and lead time.

EXHIBIT 3 | Relationship between Setup Times and Lead Time

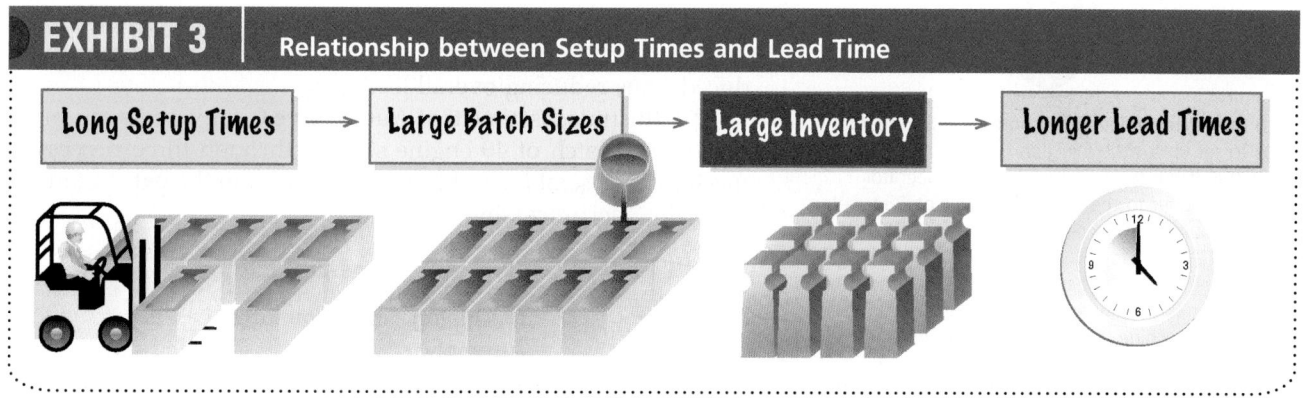

Exhibit 4 illustrates the impact of batch sizes on lead times, using a product that is manufactured in two identical processes (X and Y) that require three operations in each process in the order of A, B, and C. The product requires one minute of processing inside each operation. In Process X, the batch size is one unit, while in Process Y, the batch size is five units. Process X has only three units in process—one unit being produced in each of three operations. The lead time for any particular unit in Process X is three minutes, while for Process Y, it is 15 minutes. In Process Y, three units are being produced in the operating departments, while the other 12 are stored as work in process inventory. Each unit waits its "turn" while other units in the batch are being processed. At each operation, one unit takes five minutes to complete the operation—four minutes waiting its "turn" and one minute in production. The four minutes that each part "waits its turn" at each operation is called *within-batch wait time*. Of the 15 minutes total lead time, 12 minutes represents the within-batch wait time for all three operations (3 operations × 4 minutes). Thus, 80% (12 minutes/15 minutes) of the lead time in Process Y is non-value-added.

EXHIBIT 4   Impact of Batch Sizes on Lead Times

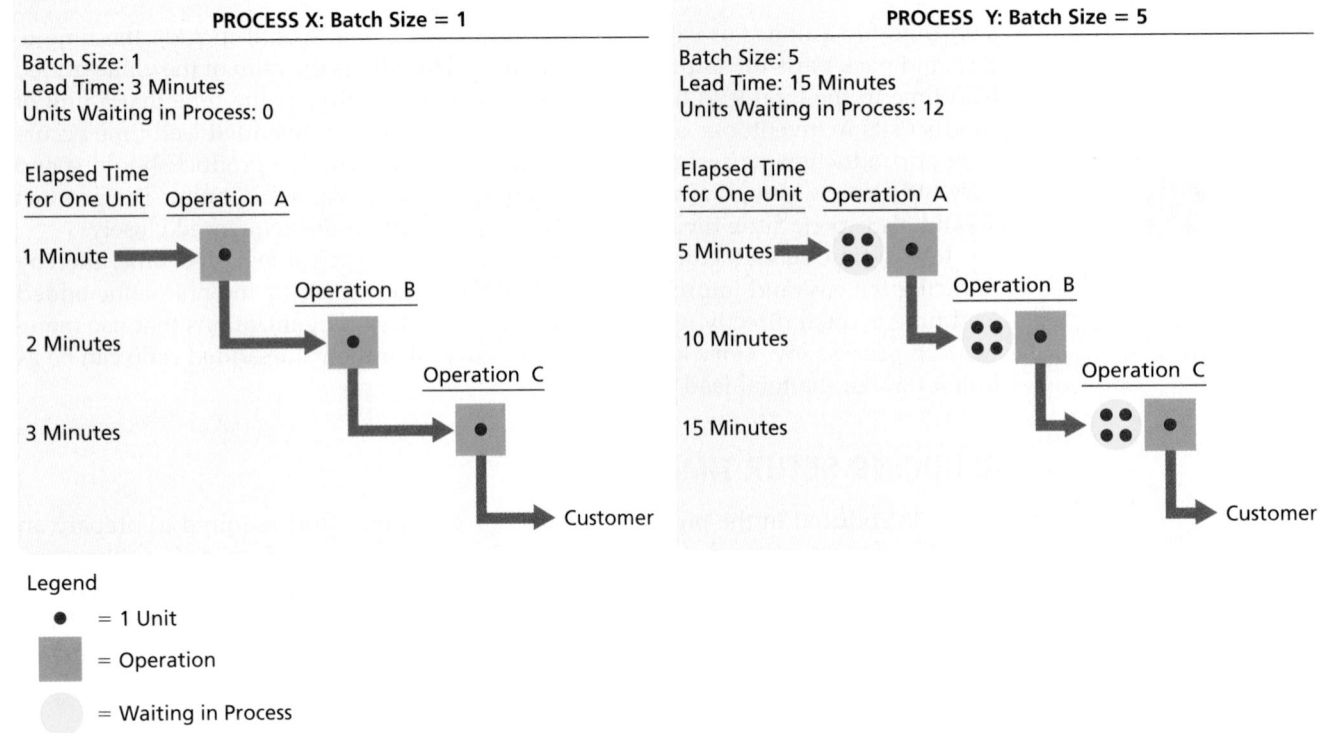

PROCESS X: Batch Size = 1

Batch Size: 1
Lead Time: 3 Minutes
Units Waiting in Process: 0

Elapsed Time
for One Unit   Operation A

1 Minute

Operation B

2 Minutes

Operation C

3 Minutes

→ Customer

PROCESS Y: Batch Size = 5

Batch Size: 5
Lead Time: 15 Minutes
Units Waiting in Process: 12

Elapsed Time
for One Unit   Operation A

5 Minutes

Operation B

10 Minutes

Operation C

15 Minutes

→ Customer

Legend

● = 1 Unit

■ = Operation

○ = Waiting in Process

Tech Industries required five hours and 84 separate steps to set up a large injection molding machine. A videotape of the setup showed that the operator climbed a ladder to the top of the machine 35 times, walked around the machine 37 times, and left the area for tools 12 times, for over 3,000 yards of walking. The improvement team reorganized the setup so that the operator climbed the machine only seven times, walked around the machine 12 times, and never left the area for tools. These improvements reduced the number of process steps from 84 to 19 and the setup time from five hours to one hour.

Organizations that use just-in-time practices try to reduce setup times in order to reduce the batch size. Once batch sizes are reduced, the work in process inventory and wait time are reduced, thus reducing overall lead time.

To illustrate, assume that Automotive Components Inc. manufactures a batch of 40 engine starters through three processes: machining, assembly, and testing. Each unit in the batch requires the following processing times:

Processing Time per Unit	
Machining	6 minutes
Assembly	10
Testing	8
Total	24 minutes

After machining, it takes 10 minutes to move the machined batch to assembly. It then takes 15 minutes to move the assembled batch to testing. The lead time can be analyzed as follows:

	Lead Times	Percent of Total
Value-added lead time	24 minutes	2.5%
Non-value-added lead time:		
Within-batch wait time [24 min. $\times$ (40 $-$ 1)]	936	95.0
Move time (10 min. $+$ 15 min.)	25	2.5
Total lead time	985 minutes	100.0%

The value-added time is the sum of the machining, assembly, and testing processing times per unit, or 24 (6 + 10 + 8) minutes. The within-batch wait time is the time for the units that are not being processed to wait their turn. This is equal to one minus the batch size, or 39 units, multiplied by the amount of processing time per unit, or 936 minutes [(40 − 1) × 24 minutes]. The total non-value-added time of 961 minutes is the sum of the within-batch time of 936 minutes plus the move time of 25 minutes.

Approximately 97.5% of the lead time is consumed by non-value-added waiting and moving. How could Automotive Components improve its lead time performance? First, it could reduce setups so that the batch size could be reduced to one piece, termed *one-piece flow*. Second, it could move the processes closer to each other so that the move time is eliminated. With these two steps, the total lead time would approach the value-added lead time.

Business Connections

ELIMINATING NONVALUE TIME ON THE B-2 STEALTH BOMBER

Northrop Grumman is a defense contractor that designs, develops, and manufactures a wide variety of defense electronics and systems, aerospace management systems, precision weapons, marine systems, logistic systems, and automation and information systems. Along with other projects, Northrop provides systems for the F-16 and F-22 fighter aircraft, the Longbow Apache helicopter, and the B-2 Stealth Bomber.

In an attempt to improve its manufacturing operations, Northrop videotaped a mechanic in its Palmdale, California plant, whose job was to apply approximately 70 feet of tape to the B-2 bomber. The mechanic walked away from the airplane 26 times and took three hours to gather the necessary chemicals, hoses, gauges, and other material needed just to start, and the total job took 8.4 hours. The diagram on the left shows the path of the mechanic in performing this job.

By designing prepackaged kits for the job, the mechanic did not have to leave the plane at all, and the total time to perform the job dropped to 1.62 hours. The diagram on the right shows the path of the mechanic using the prepackaged kits.

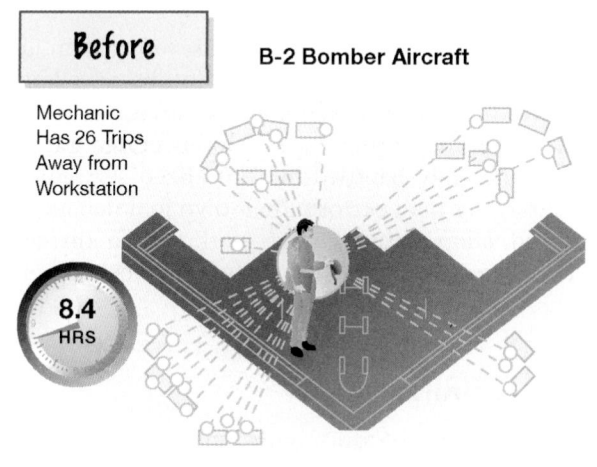

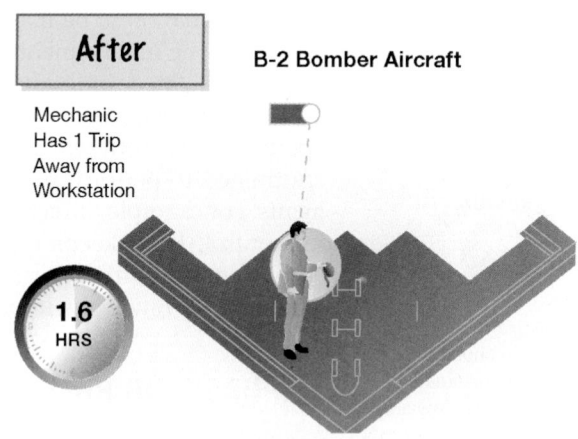

Source: Andrew Pollack, "Aerospace Gets Japan's Message," *The New York Times*, March 9, 1999.

Example Exercise 27-1   objective

The Helping Hands glove company manufactures gloves in the cutting and assembly process. Gloves are manufactured in 50-glove batch sizes. The cutting time is 4 minutes per glove. The assembly time is 6 minutes per glove. It takes 12 minutes to move a batch of gloves from cutting to assembly.

a. Compute the value-added, non-value-added, and total lead time of this process.
b. Compute the value-added ratio. Round to one decimal.

Follow My Example 27-1

a. Value-added lead time: 10 min.   (4 min. + 6 min.)
    Non-value-added lead time:
        Within-batch wait time   490   [10 min. × (50 − 1)]
        Move time   12
    Total lead time   512 min.

b. Value-added ratio: $\dfrac{10 \text{ min.}}{512 \text{ min.}}$ = 2.0%

For Practice: PE 27-1A, PE 27-1B

Sony has organized a small team of four employees to completely assemble a camcorder, doing everything from soldering to testing. The new line reduces assembly time from 70 minutes to 15 minutes per camera. "There is no future in conventional conveyor lines. They are a tool that conforms to the person with the least ability," states a Sony representative.

EMPHASIZING PRODUCT-ORIENTED LAYOUT

Organizing work around products is called a **product-oriented layout** (or *product cells*), while organizing work around processes is called a **process-oriented layout**. Just-in-time methods favor organizing work around products rather than processes. Organizing work around products reduces the amount of materials movement, coordination between operations, and work in process inventory. As a result, lead time and production costs are reduced.

For example, Yamaha manufactures its musical instruments in a product-oriented layout. It has a unique process for trumpets, horns, saxophones, clarinets, and flutes. These processes are broken into subprocesses for each of the unique elements of the product. For a trumpet, Yamaha uses subprocesses to make the bell, valve casings, valve pistons, tubing, and mouthpieces.

EMPHASIZING EMPLOYEE INVOLVEMENT

Employee involvement is a management approach that grants employees the responsibility and authority to make decisions about operations, rather than relying solely on management instructions. This decision-making authority requires accounting and other information to be made available to all employees.

Employee involvement uses teams organized in product cells, rather than just the efforts of isolated, individual employees. Such employee teams can be *cross-trained* to perform any operation within the product cell. For example, employees learn how to operate several different machines within their product cell. Moreover, team members are trained to perform functions traditionally handled by centralized service departments. For example, direct labor employees may perform their own maintenance, quality control, housekeeping, and production improvement work. When direct labor employees perform such indirect functions, the distinction between direct and indirect labor cost becomes less important.

Kenney Manufacturing Company, a manufacturer of window shades, estimated that 50% of its window shade process was non-value-added. By using pull manufacturing and changing the line layout, it was able to reduce inventory by 82% and lead time by 84%.

EMPHASIZING PULL MANUFACTURING

Another important just-in-time principle is to produce items only as they are needed by the customer. This principle is called **pull manufacturing** (or *make to order*). In pull manufacturing, the status of the next operation determines when products are moved or produced. If the next operation is busy, then production stops so that material does not pile up in front of the busy operation. If the next operation is ready, then product can be produced or moved to that operation.

The system that accomplishes pull manufacturing is often called *kanban*, which is Japanese for "cards." Electronic cards or containers signal production quantities to be filled by the feeder operation. The cards link the customer back through each stage of production. When a consumer purchases a product, a card triggers assembly of a replacement product, which in turn triggers cards to manufacture the components required for the assembly. This creates a flow of parts and products that move to the drumbeat of customer demand.

In contrast, the traditional approach is to schedule production based on forecasted customer requirements. This principle is called **push manufacturing** (or *make to stock*). In push manufacturing, product is released for manufacturing without reference to line status but according to a production schedule. The schedule "pushes" product to inventory ahead of known customer demand. As a result, manufacturers using push manufacturing will generally have more inventory than will manufacturers using pull manufacturing. As stated by one consultant, "If your manufacturing operations are still set up around guessing demand, you will forever be in a loop of producing and holding the wrong items and not having enough of what the customer actually wants."[1]

EMPHASIZING ZERO DEFECTS

Ford Motor Company's Cleveland Engine Site earned Ford's best overall warranty results by engaging its employees in a six-sigma system.

Just-in-time manufacturing practices include eliminating poor quality. Poor quality results in scrapped product, fixing product made wrong the first time (termed *rework*), and warranty costs. In addition to these direct costs, poor quality also causes disruptions in the production process, additional recordkeeping for scrap, inspection effort, and bad will from dissatisfied customers. One of the methods used to improve the quality of products and processes is six-sigma. **Six-sigma** is a widely adopted improvement system developed by Motorola Corporation.[2] The system consists of five steps: define, measure, analyze, improve, and control (DMAIC). Motorola has claimed over $17 billion in savings since six-sigma was adopted. Six-sigma is now used by thousands of organizations worldwide.

EMPHASIZING SUPPLY CHAIN MANAGEMENT

Supply chain management is the coordination and control of materials, services, information, and finances as they move in a process from the supplier, through the manufacturer, wholesaler, and retailer to the consumer. Supply chain management involves developing long-term customer/supplier agreements with supply chain partners. Such partnering encourages supply chain partners to commit to delivering products with the right quality, at the right cost, at the right time. Supply chain management often involves improving partner operations by employing just-in-time principles. Thus, the just-in-time approach does not stop within the four walls of the factory but extends to the supply chain partner operations as well. Toyota Motor is famous for its willingness to work with supply chain partners in developing its just-in-time capabilities.

Supply chains that embrace just-in-time principles use electronic data interchange, radio frequency identification devices (RFID), and the Internet to improve the information flows between suppliers and customers. **Electronic data interchange (EDI)** is a method of using computers to electronically communicate orders, relay information, and make or receive payments from one organization to another. **Radio frequency identification devices (RFID)** are electronic tags (chips) placed on or embedded within products that can be read by radio waves that allow instant monitoring of product location. The Internet allows customers and suppliers to link their business planning

---

1 Quoted by David Rucker of TBM Institute in "E-biz Requires Leaner Operations, More Integration," Jennifer Shah, *Electronic Buyer News*, July 31, 2000.
2 The term "six-sigma" refers to a statistical property whereby a process has less than 3.4 defects per one million items.

and control systems through enterprise resource planning systems. **Enterprise resource planning (ERP)** systems are integrated business and information systems used by companies to plan and control both internal and supply chain operations. The result is an effective and efficient supply chain that operates from raw materials to the final consumer.

Applying a Just-in-Time Approach to Anderson Metal Fabricators

objective **2**

Apply just-in-time manufacturing practices to a traditional manufacturing illustration.

To illustrate just-in-time manufacturing principles, we will assume that Anderson Metal Fabricators (AMF) makes two types of metal covers, large and small, for electronic test equipment. Metal covers are made by stamping a pattern of the cover from sheet steel, much like a cookie cutter stamps cookies out of dough. The stamped patterns are then sent through a punching operation, which punches holes on the pattern for fasteners. The last operation is the forming operation, where the pattern is bent into a cover and fasteners are attached.

TRADITIONAL OPERATIONS—AMF

Exhibit 5 illustrates the plant layout of AMF as a traditional manufacturer. The facility is divided into three major production departments: Stamping, Punching, and Forming. This is an example of the process-oriented layout found in many traditional manufacturing operations. AMF has many machines in each department. Within each department, partially completed products are stored in work in process inventory, waiting to be worked on by the next department. The Maintenance and Tooling Department is in a centralized location within the plant. Customers order product from the finished goods inventory. Departments receive their production schedules and work instructions based on forecasted demand, which is an example of push manufacturing.

Following the traditional approach, AMF's purchasing function attempts to supply the correct amount of raw materials according to production schedules. Extra raw materials are ordered "just in case" a shipment is missed, delayed, or incorrect. Likewise, uncertainty about the final output of any department, because of machine break-

EXHIBIT 5

Traditional Operations—AMF

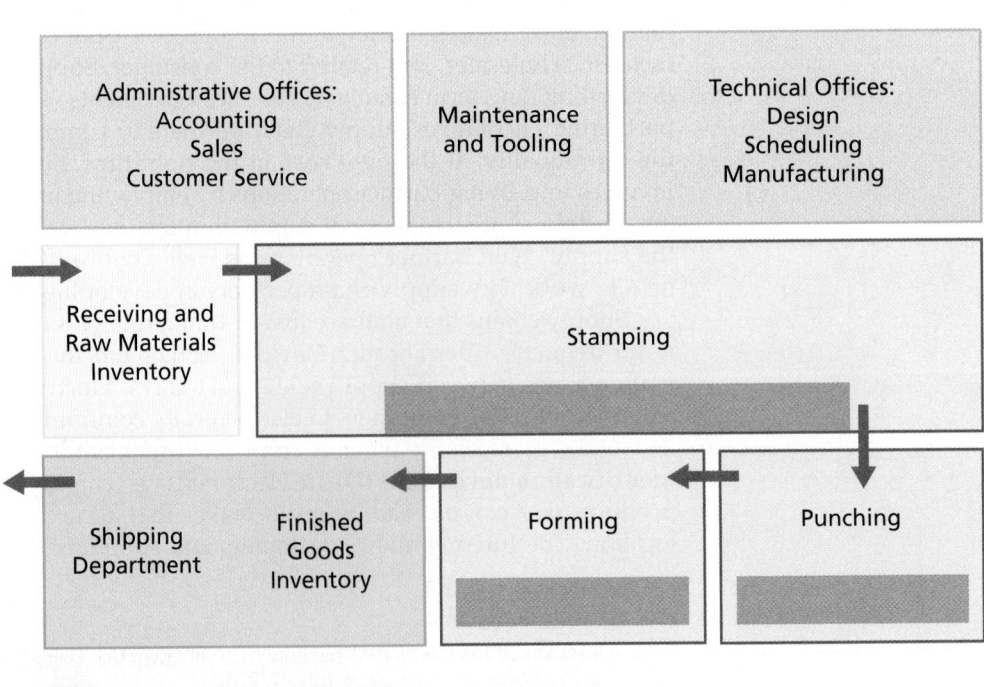

= Work in Process Areas

downs, scrap, rework, or production inefficiency, causes managers to increase work in process inventory. For example, the large work in process inventory in the Stamping Department keeps the Punching Department from running out of stampings when the stamping machines break down. Finally, the machines within AMF's departments must be set up to change production between the small and large covers.

JUST-IN-TIME OPERATIONS—AMF

The management of AMF wishes to introduce a new product, the medium-size metal cover. Unfortunately, the existing production capacity and space will not support the increased production. As a result, AMF management has decided to use just-in-time principles in order to better utilize the existing productive capacity and space.

Exhibit 6 illustrates the just-in-time operations for AMF. To apply just-in-time principles, management revised the department structure. Rather than organizing the production departments around the various operational processes, they are now organized around the three product lines (small, medium, and large covers). This product-oriented layout was accomplished by taking the machines and the people in each of the old departments and separating them into three product production cells. For example, the Stamping Department machines were separated to form the first position in three separate product cells.

EXHIBIT 6

Just-in-Time Operations—AMF

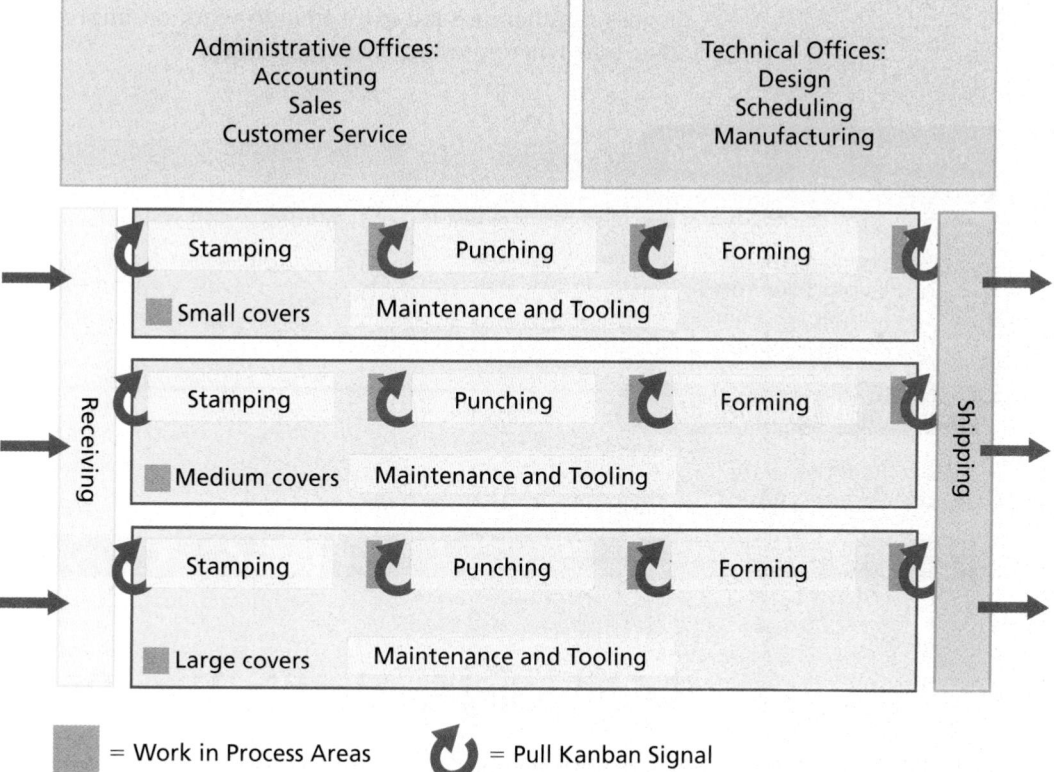

= Work in Process Areas   = Pull Kanban Signal

Since each product has its own product cell, there is no longer any need for setups. For example, the medium cover line has no setups because only medium covers are manufactured in this cell. Eliminating setup time releases productive capacity to make the medium covers. In addition, the operations within a product cell are positioned physically close to each other in order to minimize move time. The close physical distance between each machine allows materials to be transferred between each operation in small batches, using kanban signals.

The Maintenance and Tooling Department was decentralized. Each product cell now includes a maintenance and tooling function. This allows equipment to be repaired more quickly, since the parts, tools, and personnel are physically closer to the problem.

The materials, work in process, and finished goods inventory storage space is reduced significantly. Eliminating the wasted space used for inventory provides room for producing the medium covers. Thus, AMF is able to expand production without investing in new facilities.

AMF orders raw materials only as they are needed for production. In the just-in-time environment, trucks often arrive daily or even more frequently, with just enough raw materials to last until the next shipment arrives. The raw materials are received directly by the various product cells, without inspection, because suppliers guarantee zero defects through supplier partnering.

Minimal work in process inventory exists between the product cells because of employee involvement to reduce the mistakes and errors within the process. Thus, AMF's employees have improved quality, while reducing machine failures, scrap, and rework. Normally, small work in process inventory levels would cause AMF to risk a loss in productivity through unexpected manufacturing stoppages. However, the process improvements will allow AMF's production to continue without risk of shutdown, even with reduced inventory. As a result of these improvements, the non-value-added lead time has been significantly reduced.

Operations do not produce product just to remain busy and improve machine utilization. In pull manufacturing, operations respond only to customer orders. As a result, all operations within a cell operate at the same pace. This practice avoids a buildup of work in process inventory from "out-running" slower operations. If customer demand slows, then the production pace will also be slowed to match the demand. Employees can then use the extra time to work on improving the process or to move to other cells where product demand is high.

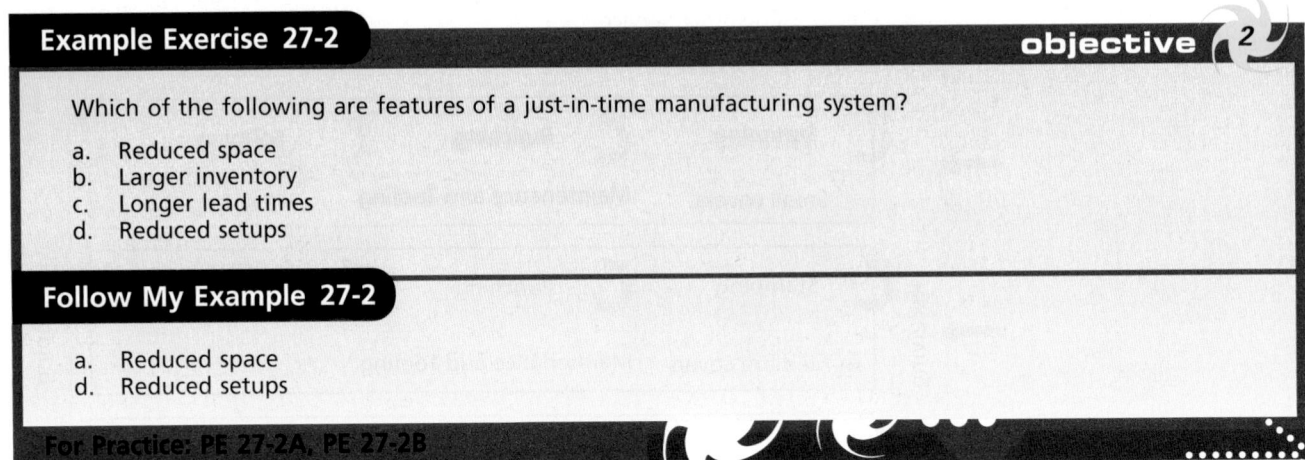

Example Exercise 27-2   objective 2

Which of the following are features of a just-in-time manufacturing system?

a. Reduced space
b. Larger inventory
c. Longer lead times
d. Reduced setups

Follow My Example 27-2

a. Reduced space
d. Reduced setups

For Practice: PE 27-2A, PE 27-2B

Accounting for Just-in-Time Operations

objective 3

Describe the implications of a just-in-time manufacturing philosophy on cost accounting and performance measurement systems.

In just-in-time operations, the accounting system will have the characteristics listed below.[3] Each of these characteristics is described in the following paragraphs.

■ *Fewer transactions.* The accounting system is simpler because there are fewer transactions to record.

■ *Combined accounts.* All in-process work is combined with raw materials to form a new account, **Raw and In Process (RIP) Inventory**, while the direct labor becomes part of the conversion cost.

■ *Nonfinancial performance measures.* There is a greater emphasis on nonfinancial performance measures.

---

3 A good summary of just-in-time implications for accounting can be found in Brian H. Maskell and Bruce L. Baggaley, "Lean Accounting: What's It All About?" *Target* (First Issue, 2006) pp. 35–43.

4. Apply just-in-time practices to a nonmanufacturing setting.

Key Points	Key Learning Outcomes	Example Exercises	Practice Exercises
Just-in-time principles can be used in service businesses and administrative processes. For example, hospitals are removing delays in serving patients by improving admission, testing, and recovery processes. This is accomplished by designing product-focused hospital units that use cross-trained caregivers in the delivery of hospital care.	• Illustrate the use of just-in-time principles in a nonmanufacturing setting, such as a hospital.		

5. Describe and illustrate activity analysis for improving operations.

Key Points	Key Learning Outcomes	Example Exercises	Practice Exercises
Companies use activity analysis to identify the costs of quality, which include prevention, appraisal, internal failure, and external failure costs. The quality cost activities may be reported on a Pareto chart, which visually highlights the most expensive quality cost categories. In addition, the quality costs can be summarized in a quality cost report by each of the four major classifications. An alternative method for categorizing activities is by value-added and non-value-added classifications. An activity analysis can also be used to determine the cost of processes. Process costs can be improved by either improving processing methods or eliminating unnecessary or wasteful work.	• Define the costs of quality. • Define and prepare a Pareto chart. • Prepare a cost of quality report. • Identify value-added and non-value-added activity costs. • Use a process activity analysis to measure process improvement.	27-4 27-5	27-4A, 27-4B 27-5A, 27-5B

Key Terms

activity analysis (1199)
appraisal costs (1200)
backflush accounting (1195)
cost of quality report (1202)
costs of quality (1199)
electronic data interchange (EDI) (1191)
employee involvement (1190)
enterprise resource planning (ERP) (1192)
external failure costs (1200)
internal failure costs (1200)

just-in-time (JIT) manufacturing (1185)
lead time (1186)
nonfinancial measure (1197)
non-value-added activity (1203)
non-value-added lead time (1187)
Pareto chart (1201)
prevention costs (1200)
process (1204)
process-oriented layout (1190)
product-oriented layout (1190)
pull manufacturing (1190)

push manufacturing (1191)
radio frequency identification devices (RFID) (1191)
Raw and In Process (RIP) Inventory (1194)
six-sigma (1191)
supply chain management (1191)
value-added activity (1203)
value-added lead time (1186)
value-added ratio (1187)

Illustrative Problem

Krisco Company operates under the just-in-time philosophy. As such, it has a production cell for its microwave ovens. The conversion cost for 2,400 hours of production is budgeted for the year at $4,800,000.

During January, 2,000 microwave ovens were started and completed. Each oven requires six minutes of cell processing time. The materials cost for each oven is $100.

Instructions

1. Determine the budgeted cell conversion cost per hour.
2. Determine the manufacturing cost per unit.
3. Journalize the entry to record the costs charged to the production cell in January.
4. Journalize the entry to record the costs transferred to finished goods.

Solution

1. Budgeted Cell Conversion Cost Rate $= \dfrac{\$4,800,000}{2,400 \text{ hours}} = \$2,000$ per cell hour

2.

Materials	$100 per unit
Conversion cost [($2,000 per hour/60 min.) × 6 min.]	200
Total	$300 per unit

3.

		Debit	Credit	
1	Raw and In Process Inventory	200 0 0 0 00		1
2	Accounts Payable		200 0 0 0 00	2
3	To record materials costs.			3
4	(2,000 units × $100 per unit).			4
5				5
6	Raw and In Process Inventory	400 0 0 0 00		6
7	Conversion Costs		400 0 0 0 00	7
8	To record conversion costs.			8
9	(2,000 units × $200 per unit).			9
10				10
11	Finished Goods (2,000 × $300 per unit)	600 0 0 0 00		11
12	Raw and In Process Inventory		600 0 0 0 00	12
13	To record finished production.			13

4. (rows 11–13 above)

Self-Examination Questions

(Answers at End of Chapter)

1. Which of the following is not a characteristic of the just-in-time philosophy?
   A. Product-oriented layout
   B. Push manufacturing (make to stock)
   C. Short lead times
   D. Reducing setup time as a critical improvement priority

2. Accounting in a just-in-time environment is best described as:
   A. more complex.
   B. focused on direct labor.
   C. providing detailed variance reports.
   D. providing less transaction control.

3. The product cell for Dynah Company has budgeted conversion costs of $420,000 for the year. The cell is planned to be available 2,100 hours for production. Each unit requires $12.50 of materials cost. The cell started and completed 700 units. The cell process time for the product is 15 minutes per unit. What is the cost debited to finished goods for the period?
   A. $8,750   C. $43,750
   B. $35,000   D. $140,000

4. In-process inspection activities are an example of what type of quality cost?
   A. Prevention
   B. Appraisal
   C. Internal failure
   D. External failure

5. A Pareto chart is used to display:
   A. a ranking of attribute totals, by category, in the form of a bar chart.
   B. important trends in the form of a line chart.
   C. percentage information in the form of a pie chart.
   D. a listing of attribute totals, by category, in a table.

Eye Openers

1. What is the benefit of just-in-time processing?
2. What are some examples of non-value-added lead time?
3. Why is a product-oriented layout preferred by just-in-time manufacturers over a process-oriented layout?
4. How is setup time related to lead time?
5. Why do just-in-time manufacturers favor pull or "make to order" manufacturing?
6. Why would a just-in-time manufacturer strive to produce zero defects?
7. How is supply chain management different from traditional supplier and customer relationships?
8. Why does accounting in a just-in-time environment result in fewer transactions?
9. Why is a "raw and in process inventory" account used by just-in-time manufacturers, rather than separately reporting materials and work in process?
10. Why is the direct labor cost category eliminated in many just-in-time environments?
11. How does accounting under a just-in-time environment provide less transaction control?
12. What are some possible explanations for the actual conversion cost per unit being greater than the budgeted cost per unit in a just-in-time production cell?
13. What just-in-time principles might a hospital use?
14. What is the benefit of an activity analysis?
15. How does a Pareto chart assist management?
16. What is the benefit of identifying non-value-added activities?
17. What ways can the cost of a process be improved?

Practice Exercises

PE 27-1A
Lead time computation and analysis
obj. 1

The Winterscape Ski company manufactures skis in the finishing and assembly process. Skis are manufactured in 35-ski batch sizes. The finishing time is 18 minutes per ski. The assembly time is 12 minutes per ski. It takes 9 minutes to move a batch of skis from finishing to assembly.

a. Compute the value-added, non-value-added, and total lead time of this process.
b. Compute the value-added ratio. Round to one decimal.

PE 27-1B
Lead time computation and analysis
obj. 1

The Fashion Jean company manufactures jeans in the cutting and sewing process. Jeans are manufactured in 60-jean batch sizes. The cutting time is 8 minutes per jean. The sewing time is 15 minutes per jean. It takes 18 minutes to move a batch of jeans from cutting to sewing.

a. Compute the value-added, non-value-added, and total lead time of this process.
b. Compute the value-added ratio. Round to one decimal.

PE 27-2A
Identify just-in-time benefits
obj. 2

Which of the following are features of a just-in-time manufacturing system?

a. Centralized maintenance areas
b. Smaller batch sizes
c. Employee involvement
d. Push scheduling

PE 27-2B
Identify just-in-time benefits
obj. 2

Which of the following are features of a just-in-time manufacturing system?

a. Production pace matches demand
b. Centralized work in process inventory locations
c. Less wasted movement of material and people
d. Receive raw materials directly to manufacturing cells

PE 27-3A
Just-in-time journal entries
obj. 3

The budgeted conversion costs for a just-in-time cell are $1,927,000 for 2,050 production hours. Each unit produced by the cell requires 12 minutes of cell process time. During the month, 850 units are manufactured in the cell. The estimated materials cost are $1,450 per unit. Provide the following journal entries:

a. Materials are purchased to produce 870 units.
b. Conversion costs are applied to 850 units of production.
c. 840 units are placed into finished goods.

PE 27-3B
Just-in-time journal entries
obj. 3

The budgeted conversion costs for a just-in-time cell are $270,000 for 1,800 production hours. Each unit produced by the cell requires 24 minutes of cell process time. During the month, 370 units are manufactured in the cell. The estimated materials cost are $95 per unit. Provide the following journal entries:

a. Materials are purchased to produce 400 units.
b. Conversion costs are applied to 370 units of production.
c. 350 units are placed into finished goods.

PE 27-4A
Cost of quality report
obj. 5

A quality control activity analysis indicated the following four activity costs of a manufacturing department:

Rework	$ 12,000
Inspecting incoming raw materials	30,000
Warranty work	3,000
Process improvement effort	105,000
Total	$150,000

Sales are $1,000,000. Prepare a cost of quality report.

PE 27-4B
Cost of quality report
obj. 5

A quality control activity analysis indicated the following four activity costs of a hotel:

Inspecting cleanliness of rooms	$ 90,000
Processing lost customer reservations	495,000
Rework incorrectly prepared room service meal	45,000
Employee training	270,000
Total	$900,000

Sales are $6,000,000. Prepare a cost of quality report.

PE 27-5A
Process activity analysis
obj. 5

Tudor Company incurred an activity cost of $360,000 for inspecting 60,000 units of production. Management determined that the inspecting objectives could be met without inspecting every unit. Therefore, rather than inspecting 60,000 units of production, the inspection activity was limited to 25% of the production. Determine the inspection activity cost per unit on 60,000 units of total production both before and after the improvement.

PE 27-5B
Process activity analysis
obj. 5

Stuart Company incurred an activity cost of $45,000 for inspecting 5,000 units of production. Management determined that the inspecting objectives could be met without inspecting every unit. Therefore, rather than inspecting 5,000 units of production, the inspection activity was limited to a random selection of 500 units out of the 5,000 units of production. Determine the inspection activity cost per unit on 5,000 units of total production both before and after the improvement.

Exercises

EX 27-1
Just-in-time principles
obj. 1

The chief executive officer (CEO) of Lordsland Inc. has just returned from a management seminar describing the benefits of the just-in-time philosophy. The CEO issued the following statement after returning from the conference:

This company will become a just-in-time manufacturing company. Presently, we have too much inventory. To become just-in-time we need to eliminate the excess inventory. Therefore, I want all employees to begin reducing inventories until we are just-in-time. Thank you for your cooperation.

▶ How would you respond to the CEO's statement?

EX 27-2
Just-in-time as a strategy
obj. 1

The American textile industry has moved much of its operations offshore in the pursuit of lower labor costs. Textile imports have risen from 2% of all textile production in 1962 to over 60% in 2006. Offshore manufacturers make long runs of standard mass-market apparel items. These are then brought to the United States in container ships, requiring significant time between original order and delivery. As a result, retail customers must accurately forecast market demands for imported apparel items.

▶ Assuming that you work for a U.S.-based textile company, how would you recommend responding to the low-cost imports?

EX 27-3
Lead time reduction—service company
objs. 1, 4

Homeguard Insurance Company takes ten days to make payments on insurance claims. Claims are processed through three departments: Data Input, Claims Audit, and Claims Adjustment. The three departments are on different floors, approximately one hour apart from each other. Claims are processed in batches of 100. Each batch of 100 claims moves through the three departments on a wheeled cart. Management is concerned about customer dissatisfaction caused by the long lead time for claim payments.

▶ How might this process be changed so that the lead time could be reduced significantly?

EX 27-4
Just-in-time principles
obj. 1

Celestial Shirt Company manufactures various styles of men's casual wear. Shirts are cut and assembled by a workforce that is paid by piece rate. This means that they are paid according to the amount of work completed during a period of time. To illustrate, if the piece rate is $0.10 per sleeve assembled, and the worker assembles 700 sleeves during the day, then the worker would be paid $70 (700 × $0.10) for the day's work.

The company is considering adopting a just-in-time manufacturing philosophy by organizing work cells around various types of products and employing pull manufacturing. However, no change is expected in the compensation policy. On this point, the manufacturing manager stated the following:

"Piecework compensation provides an incentive to work fast. Without it, the workers will just goof off and expect a full day's pay. We can't pay straight hourly wages—at least not in this industry."

▶ How would you respond to the manufacturing manager's comments?

EX 27-5
Lead time analysis
obj. 1

Kiddie Kuddles Inc. manufactures toy stuffed animals. The direct labor time required to cut, sew, and stuff a toy is 12 minutes per unit. The company makes two types of stuffed toys—a lion and a bear. The lion is assembled in lot sizes of 50 units per batch, while the bear is assembled in lot sizes of 5 units per batch. Since each product has direct labor time of 12 minutes per unit, management has determined that the lead time for each product is 12 minutes.

▶ Is management correct? What are the lead times for each product?

EX 27-6
Reduce setup time
obj. 1

Compressor Inc. has analyzed the setup time on its computer-controlled lathe. The setup requires changing the type of fixture that holds a part. The average setup time has been 200 minutes, consisting of the following steps:

Turn off machine and remove fixture from lathe	10 minutes
Go to tool room with fixture	30
Record replacement of fixture to tool room	15
Return to lathe	30
Clean lathe	25
Return to tool room	30
Record withdrawal of new fixture from tool room	20
Return to lathe	30
Install new fixture and turn on machine	10
Total setup time	200 minutes

a. ➤ Why should management be concerned about improving setup time?

b. ➤ What do you recommend to Compressor Inc. for improving setup time?

c. How much time would be required for a setup, using your suggestion in (b)?

EX 27-7
Calculate lead time
obj. 1

Madison Machining Company machines metal parts for the automotive industry. Under the traditional manufacturing approach, the parts are machined through two processes: milling and finishing. Parts are produced in batch sizes of 90 parts. A part requires 6 minutes in milling and 8 minutes in finishing. The move time between the two operations for a complete batch is 10 minutes.

Under the just-in-time philosophy, the part is produced in a cell that includes both the milling and finishing operations. The operating time is unchanged; however, the batch size is reduced to 5 parts and the move time is eliminated.

Determine the value-added, non-value-added, total lead time, and the value-added ratio under the traditional and just-in-time manufacturing methods. Round whole percentages to one decimal place.

EX 27-8
Calculate lead time
obj. 1

Mercury Memories Inc. is considering a new just-in-time product cell. The present manufacturing approach produces a product in four separate steps. The production batch sizes are 45 units. The process time for each step is as follows:

Process Step 1	6 minutes
Process Step 2	4 minutes
Process Step 3	15 minutes
Process Step 4	9 minutes

The time required to move each batch between steps is 20 minutes. In addition, the time to move raw materials to Process Step 1 is also 20 minutes, and the time to move completed units from Process Step 4 to finished goods inventory is 20 minutes.

The new just-in-time layout will allow the company to reduce the batch sizes from 45 units to 4 units. The time required to move each batch between steps and the inventory locations will be reduced to 3 minutes. The processing time in each step will stay the same.

Determine the value-added, non-value-added, total lead times, and the value-added ratio under the present and proposed production approaches. Round whole percentages to one decimal place.

EX 27-9
Lead time calculation—doctor's office
objs. 1, 4

✓ b. 140 minutes

Mi Chen caught the flu and needed to see the doctor. Chen called to set up an appointment and was told to come in at 1:00 p.m. Chen arrived at the doctor's office promptly at 1:00 p.m. The waiting room had 12 other people in it. Patients were admitted from the waiting room in FIFO (first-in, first-out) order at a rate of five minutes per patient. After waiting until her turn, a nurse finally invited Chen to an examining room. Once in the examining room, Chen waited another 15 minutes before a nurse arrived to take some basic readings (temperature, blood pressure). The nurse needed five minutes to collect the clinical information. After the nurse left, Chen waited 15 additional minutes before the doctor arrived. The doctor arrived and diagnosed the flu and provided a prescription for antibiotics. This took the doctor 10 minutes. Before leaving the doctor's office, Chen waited 10 minutes at the business office to pay for the office visit.

Chen spent 5 minutes walking next door to fill the prescription at the pharmacy. There were five people in front of Chen, each person requiring 8 minutes to fill and purchase his or her prescription. Chen finally arrived home 22 minutes after paying for her prescription.

a. What time does Chen arrive home?
b. How much of the total elapsed time from 1:00 p.m. until when Chen arrived home was non-value-added time?
c. Why does the doctor require patients to wait so long for service?

EX 27-10
Suppy chain management
obj. 1

The following is an excerpt from a recent article discussing supplier relationships with the Big Three North American automakers.

"The Big Three select suppliers on the basis of lowest price and annual price reductions," said Neil De Koker, president of the Original Equipment Suppliers Association. "They look globally for the lowest parts prices from the lowest cost countries," De Koker said. "There is little trust and respect. Collaboration is missing." Japanese auto makers want long-term supplier relationships. They select suppliers as a person would a mate. The Big Three are quick to beat down prices with methods such as electronic auctions or rebidding work to a competitor. The Japanese are equally tough on price but are committed to maintaining supplier continuity. "They work with you to arrive at a competitive price, and they are willing to pay because they want long-term partnering," said Carl Code, a vice president at Ernie Green Industries. "They [Honda and Toyota] want suppliers to make enough money to stay in business, grow and bring them innovation." The Big Three's supply chain model is not much different from the one set by Henry Ford. In 1913, he set up the system of independent supplier firms operating at arm's length on short-term contracts. One consequence of the Big Three's low-price-at-all-costs mentality is that suppliers are reluctant to offer them their cutting-edge technology out of fear the contract will be resourced before the research and development costs are recouped.

a. Contrast the Japanese supply chain model with that of the Big Three.
b. Why might a supplier prefer the Japanese model?
c. What benefits might accrue to the Big Three by adopting the Japanese supply chain practices?

Source: Robert Sherefkin and Amy Wilson, "Suppliers Prefer Japanese Business Model," *Rubber & Plastics News,* March 17, 2003, Vol. 24, No. 11.

EX 27-11
Employee involvement
obj. 1

Quickie Designs Inc. uses teams in the manufacture of lightweight wheelchairs. Two features of its team approach are team hiring and peer reviews. Under team hiring, the team recruits, interviews, and hires new team members from within the organization. Using peer reviews, the team evaluates each member of the team with regard to quality, knowledge, teamwork, goal performance, attendance, and safety. These reviews provide feedback to the team member for improvement.

➤ How do these two team approaches differ from using managers to hire and evaluate employees?

EX 27-12
Accounting issues in a just-in-time environment
obj. 3

Vision Electronics Company has recently implemented a just-in-time manufacturing approach. A production department manager has approached the controller with the following comments:

I am very upset with our accounting system now that we have implemented our new just-in-time manufacturing methods. It seems as if all I'm doing is paperwork. Our product is moving so fast through the manufacturing process that the paperwork can hardly keep up. For example, it just doesn't make sense to me to fill out daily labor reports. The employees are assigned to complete cells, performing many different tasks. I can't keep up with direct labor reports on each individual task. I thought we were trying to eliminate waste. Yet the information requirements of the accounting system are slowing us down and adding to overall lead time. Moreover, I'm still getting my monthly variance reports. I don't think that these are necessary. I have nonfinancial performance measures that are more timely than these reports. Besides, the employees don't really understand accounting variances. How about giving some information that I can really use?

➤ What accounting system changes would you suggest in light of the production department manager's criticisms?

EX 27-13
Just-in-time journal entries
obj. 3
✓ b. $78

Wave Media Inc. uses a just-in-time strategy to manufacture DVD players. The company manufactures DVDs through a single product cell. The budgeted conversion cost for the year is $998,400 for 1,920 production hours. Each unit requires 9 minutes of cell process time. During March, 1,100 DVDs are manufactured in the cell. The materials cost per unit is $70. The following summary transactions took place during March:

1. Materials are purchased for March production.
2. Conversion costs were applied to production.
3. 1,100 DVDs are assembled and placed in finished goods.
4. 1,050 DVDs are sold for $250 per unit.

a. Determine the budgeted cell conversion cost per hour.
b. Determine the budgeted cell conversion cost per unit.
c. Journalize the summary transactions (1)–(4) for March.

EX 27-14
Just-in-time journal entries
obj. 3
✓ a. $60

Glowstream Inc. manufactures lighting fixtures, using just-in-time manufacturing methods. Style BB-01 has a materials cost per unit of $24. The budgeted conversion cost for the year is $120,000 for 2,000 production hours. A unit of Style BB-01 requires 15 minutes of cell production time. The following transactions took place during June:

1. Materials were acquired to assemble 650 Style BB-01 units for June.
2. Conversion costs were applied to 650 Style BB-01 units of production.
3. 640 units of Style BB-01 were completed in June.
4. 630 units of Style BB-01 were sold in June for $65 per unit.

a. Determine the budgeted cell conversion cost per hour.
b. Determine the budgeted cell conversion cost per unit.
c. Journalize the summary transactions (1)–(4) for June.

EX 27-15
Just-in-time journal entries
obj. 3

Allendale Audio Company manufactures audio speakers. Each speaker requires $68 per unit of direct materials. The speaker manufacturing assembly cell includes the following estimated costs for the period:

Speaker assembly cell estimated costs:

Cell labor	$33,100
Cell depreciation	5,900
Cell supplies	2,200
Cell power	1,300
Total cell costs for the period	$42,500

The operating plan calls for 170 operating hours for the period. Each speaker requires 18 minutes of cell process time. The unit selling price for each speaker is $260. During the period, the following transactions occurred:

1. Purchased materials to produce 600 speaker units.
2. Applied conversion costs to production of 570 speaker units.
3. Completed and transferred 560 speaker units to finished goods.
4. Sold 540 speaker units.

There were no inventories at the beginning of the period.

a. Journalize the summary transactions (1)–(4) for the period.
b. Determine the ending balance for raw and in-process inventory and finished goods inventory.

EX 27-16
Just-in-time—fast-food restaurant
obj. 4

The management of Mister Burger fast-food franchise wants to provide hamburgers quickly to customers. It has been using a process by which precooked hamburgers are prepared and placed under hot lamps. These hamburgers are then sold to customers. In this process, every customer receives the same type of hamburger and dressing (ketchup, onions, mustard). If a customer wants something different, then a "special order" must be cooked to the customer's requirements. This requires the customer to wait several minutes, which often slows down the service line. Mister Burger has been receiving more and more special orders from customers, which has been slowing service down considerably.

a. How would you describe the present Mister Burger service delivery system?
b. How might you use just-in-time principles to provide customers quick service, yet still allow them to custom order their burgers?

EX 27-17
Pareto chart
obj. 5

Integrity Memory Circuits Inc. manufactures RAM memory chips for personal computers. An activity analysis was conducted, and the following activity costs were identified with the manufacture and sale of memory chips:

Activities	Activity Cost
Correct shipment errors	$108,000
Disposing of scrap	126,000
Emergency equipment maintenance	81,000
Employee training	27,000
Final inspection	103,500
Inspecting incoming materials	27,000
Preventive equipment maintenance	22,500
Processing customer returns	90,000
Scrap reporting	36,000
Supplier development	18,000
Warranty claims	261,000
Total	$900,000

Prepare a Pareto chart of these activities.

EX 27-18
Cost of quality report
obj. 5

✓ *a. Appraisal, 14.5% of total costs*

a. Using the information in Exercise 27-17, prepare a cost of quality report. Assume that the sales for the period were $4,500,000.
b. Interpret the cost of quality report.

EX 27-19
Pareto chart for a service company
obj. 5

Countrywide Cable Company provides cable TV and Internet service to the local community. The activities and activity costs of Countrywide Cable are identified as follows:

Activities	Activity Cost
Billing error correction	$ 30,000
Cable signal testing	108,000
Reinstalling service (installed incorrectly the first time)	78,000
Repairing satellite equipment	12,000
Repairing underground cable connections to the customer	24,000
Replacing old technology cable with higher quality cable	132,000
Replacing old technology signal switches with higher quality switches	144,000
Responding to customer home repair requests	42,000
Training employees	30,000
Total	$600,000

Prepare a Pareto chart of these activities.

EX 27-20
Cost of quality and value-added/non-value-added reports
obj. 5

✓ *a. External failure, 29% of total costs*

a. Using the activity data in Exercise 27-19, prepare a cost of quality report. Assume that sales are $2,000,000. Round percentages to one decimal place.
b. Using the activity data in Exercise 27-19, prepare a value-added/non-value-added analysis.
c. Interpret the information in (a) and (b).

EX 27-21
Process activity analysis
objs. 4, 5

✓ b. $40 per claim
payment

Metropolitan Insurance Company has a process for making payments on insurance claims as follows:

An activity analysis revealed that the cost of these activities was as follows:

Receiving claim	$ 30,000
Adjusting claim	130,000
Paying claim	40,000
Total	$200,000

This process includes only the cost of processing the claim payments, not the actual amount of the claim payments. The adjusting activity involves verifying and estimating the amount of the claim.

The process received, adjusted, and paid 5,000 claims during the period. All claims were treated identically in this process.

To improve the cost of this process, management has determined that claims should be segregated into two categories. Claims under $1,000 and claims greater than $1,000: claims under $1,000 would not be adjusted but would be accepted upon the insured's evidence of claim. Claims above $1,000 would be adjusted. It is estimated that 65% of the claims are under $1,000 and would thus be paid without adjustment. It is also estimated that the additional effort to segregate claims would add 12% to the "receiving claim" activity cost.

a. Develop a table showing the percent of activity cost to the total process cost for the claim payment activities.
b. Determine the average total process cost per claim payment, assuming 5,000 total claims.
c. Prepare a table showing the changes in the activity costs as a result of the changes proposed by management.
d. Estimate the average cost per claim payment, assuming that the changes proposed by management are enacted for 5,000 total claims.

EX 27-22
Process activity analysis
obj. 5

✓ b. $20 per payment

The procurement process for Baker Company includes a series of activities that transforms a materials requisition into a vendor check. The process begins with a request for materials. The requesting department prepares and sends a materials request form to the Purchasing Department. The Purchasing Department then places a request for a quote to vendors. Vendors prepare bids in response to the request for a quote. A vendor is selected based on the lowest bid. A purchase order to the low-bid vendor is prepared. The vendor delivers the materials to the company, whereupon a receiving ticket is prepared. Payment to the vendor is authorized if the materials request form, receiving ticket, and vendor invoice are in agreement. These three documents fail to agree 45% of the time, initiating effort to reconcile the differences. Once the three documents agree, a check is issued. The process can be diagrammed as follows:

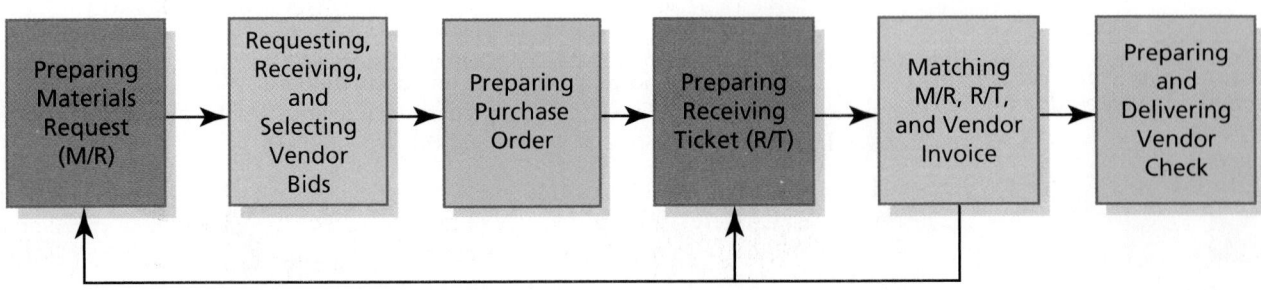

Correcting Reconciliation Differences

An activity analysis indicated the following activity costs with this process:

Preparing materials request	$ 40,000
Requesting, receiving, and selecting vendor bids	120,000
Preparing purchase order	25,000
Preparing receiving ticket	35,000
Matching M/R, R/T, and invoice	50,000
Correcting reconciliation differences	180,000
Preparing and delivering vendor payment	50,000
Total process activity cost	$500,000

On average, the process handles 25,000 individual requests for materials that result in 25,000 individual payments to vendors.

Management proposes to improve this process in two ways. First, the Purchasing Department will develop a preapproved vendor list for which orders can be placed without a request for quote. It is expected that this will reduce the need for requesting and receiving vendor bids by 75%. Second, additional training and standardization will be provided to reduce errors introduced into the materials requisition form and receiving tickets. It is expected that this will reduce the number of reconciliations from 45% to 15%, over an average of 25,000 payments.

a. Develop a table showing the percent of individual activity cost to the total process cost for the procurement activities.
b. Determine the average total process cost per vendor payment, assuming 25,000 payments.
c. Prepare a table showing the improvements in the activity costs as a result of the changes proposed by management.
d. Estimate the average cost per vendor payment, assuming that the changes proposed by management are enacted for 25,000 total payments.

Problems Series A

PR 27-1A
Just-in-time principles
obj. 1
✓ 3. $0.20 per pound

Safety Glow Co. manufactures light bulbs. Safety Glow's purchasing policy requires that the purchasing agents place each quarter's purchasing requirements out for bid. This is because the Purchasing Department is evaluated solely by its ability to get the lowest purchase prices. The lowest cost bidder receives the order for the next quarter (90 working days).

To make its bulb products, Safety Glow requires 24,300 pounds of glass per quarter. Safety Glow received two glass bids for the second quarter, as follows:

• *Continental Glass Company:* $20.00 per pound of glass. Delivery schedule: 27,000 pounds at the beginning of April to last for 3 months.
• *Emory Glass Company:* $20.15 per pound of glass. Delivery schedule: 300 pounds per working day (90 days in the quarter).

Safety Glow accepted Continental Glass Company's bid because it was the low-cost bid.

Instructions
1. Comment on Safety Glow's purchasing policy.
2. What are the additional (hidden) costs, beyond price, of Continental Glass Company's bid? Why weren't these costs considered?
3. Considering just inventory financing costs, what is the additional cost per pound of Continental Glass Company's bid if the cost of money is 8%? (*Hint:* Determine the average value of glass inventory held for the quarter and multiply by the quarterly interest charge.)

PR 27-2A
Lead time
obj. 1

✓ 1. Total wait time,
1,843 minutes

Soundwave Audio Company manufactures electronic stereo equipment. The manufacturing process includes printed circuit (PC) card assembly, final assembly, testing, and shipping. In the PC card assembly operation, a number of individuals are responsible for assembling electronic components into printed circuit boards. Each operator is responsible for soldering components according to a given set of instructions. Operators work on batches of 50 printed circuit boards. Each board requires 6 minutes of assembly time. After each batch is completed, the operator moves the assembled cards to the final assembly area. This move takes 10 minutes to complete.

The final assembly for each stereo unit requires 18 minutes and is also done in batches of 50 units. A batch of 50 stereos is moved into the test building, which is across the street. The move takes 15 minutes. Before conducting the test, the test equipment must be set up for the particular stereo model. The test setup requires 30 minutes. The units wait while the setup is performed. In the final test, the 50-unit batch is tested one at a time. Each test requires 5 minutes. The completed batch, after all testing, is sent to shipping for packaging and final shipment to customers. A complete batch of 50 units is sent from final assembly to shipping. The Shipping Department is located next to final assembly. Thus, there is no move time between these two operations. Packaging and labeling requires 8 minutes per unit.

Instructions
1. Determine the amount of value-added and non-value-added lead time and the value-added ratio in this process for an average stereo unit in a batch of 50 units. Round percentages to one decimal place. Categorize the non-value-added time into wait and move time.
2. ▭▭▭▶ How could this process be improved so as to reduce the amount of waste in the process?

PR 27-3A
Just-in-time accounting
obj. 3

✓ 4. Raw and In Process
Inventory, $4,075

Display Labs Inc. manufactures and assembles automobile instrument panels for both Yamura Motors and Detroit Motors. The process consists of a just-in-time product cell for each customer's instrument assembly. The data that follow concern only the Yamura just-in-time cell.

For the year, Display Labs Inc. budgeted the following costs for the Yamura production cell:

Conversion Cost Categories	Budget
Labor	$610,000
Supplies	84,000
Utilities	26,000
Total	$720,000

Display Labs Inc. plans 2,500 hours of production for the Yamura cell for the year. The materials cost is $115 per instrument assembly. Each assembly requires 25 minutes of cell assembly time. There was no June 1 inventory for either Raw and In Process Inventory or Finished Goods Inventory.

The following summary events took place in the Yamura cell during June:

a. Electronic parts and wiring were purchased to produce 515 instrument assemblies in June.
b. Conversion costs were applied for the production of 500 units in June.
c. 490 units were started and completed and transferred to finished goods in June.
d. 475 units were shipped to customers at a price of $400 per unit.

Instructions
1. Determine the budgeted cell conversion cost per hour.
2. Determine the budgeted cell conversion cost per unit.
3. Journalize the summary transactions (a) through (d).
4. Determine the ending balance in Raw and In Process Inventory and Finished Goods Inventory.
5. ▭▭▭▶ How does the accounting in a JIT environment differ from traditional accounting?

PR 27-4A
Pareto chart and cost of quality report—municipality
objs. 4, 5

✓ 3. Non-value-added, 61.5%

The administrator of elections for the city of Maryville has been asked to perform an activity analysis of its optical scanning center. The optical scanning center reads voter forms into the computer. The result of the activity analysis is summarized as follows:

Activities	Activity Cost
Correcting errors identified by election commission	$ 38,400
Correcting jams	57,600
Correcting scan errors	33,600
Loading	12,000
Logging-in control codes (for later reconciliation)	14,400
Program scanner	7,200
Rerunning job due to scan reading errors	18,000
Scanning	31,200
Verifying scan accuracy via reconciling totals	12,000
Verifying scanner accuracy with test run	15,600
Total	$240,000

Instructions
1. Prepare a Pareto chart of the department activities.
2. Use the activity cost information to determine the percentages of total department costs that are prevention, appraisal, internal failure, external failure, and not costs of quality. Round percentages to one decimal place.
3. Determine the percentages of the total department costs that are value- and non-value-added. Round percentages to one decimal place.
4. ▭▭▶ Interpret the information.

Problems Series B

PR 27-1B
Just-in-time principles
obj. 1

✓ 3. $3.25 per frame

Hawg Wild Motorcycle Company manufactures a variety of motorcycles. Hawg's purchasing policy requires that the purchasing agents place each quarter's purchasing requirements out for bid. This is because the Purchasing Department is evaluated solely by its ability to get the lowest purchase prices. The lowest cost bidder receives the order for the next quarter (90 days). To make its motorcycles, Hawg Wild requires 7,200 frames per quarter. Hawg Wild received two frame bids for the third quarter, as follows:

- *Forever Frames, Inc.:* $262 per frame. Delivery schedule: 80 frames per working day (90 days in the quarter).
- *Iron Horse Frames Inc.:* $260 per frame. Delivery schedule: 7,200 (80 frames × 90 days) frames at the beginning of July to last for three months.

Hawg Wild accepted Iron Horse Frames Inc.'s bid because it was the low-cost bid.

Instructions
1. ▭▭▶ Comment on Hawg Wild's purchasing policy.
2. ▭▭▶ What are the additional (hidden) costs, beyond price, of Iron Horse Frames Inc.'s bid? Why weren't these costs considered?
3. Considering just inventory financing costs, what is the additional cost per frame of Iron Horse Frames Inc.'s bid if the cost of money is 10%? (*Hint:* Determine the average value of frame inventory held for the quarter and multiply by the quarterly interest charge.)

PR 27-2B
Lead time
obj. 1

Kitchenware Appliance Company manufactures home kitchen appliances. The manufacturing process includes stamping, final assembly, testing, and shipping. In the stamping operation, a number of individuals are responsible for stamping the steel outer surface of the appliance. The stamping operation is set up prior to each run. A run of 80 stampings is completed after each setup. A setup requires 100 minutes. The parts wait for the setup to be completed before stamping begins. Each stamping requires 4 minutes of operating time.

✓ 1. Total wait time,
3,418 minutes

After each batch is completed, the operator moves the stamped covers to the final assembly area. This move takes 12 minutes to complete.

The final assembly for each appliance unit requires 20 minutes and is also done in batches of 80 appliance units. The batch of 80 appliance units is moved into the test building, which is across the street. The move takes 24 minutes. In the final test, the 80-unit batch is tested one at a time. Each test requires 6 minutes. The completed units are sent to shipping for packaging and final shipment to customers. A complete batch of 80 units is sent from final assembly to shipping. The Shipping Department is located next to final assembly. Thus, there is no move time between these two operations. Packaging and shipment labeling requires 12 minutes per unit.

Instructions

1. Determine the amount of value-added and non-value-added lead time and the value-added ratio in this process for an average kitchen appliance in a batch of 80 units. Round percentages to one decimal place. Categorize the non-value-added time into wait and move time.

2. ▭▭▭▸ How could this process be improved so as to reduce the amount of waste in the process?

PR 27-3B

Just-in-time accounting

obj. 3

✓ 4. Raw and In Process
Inventory, $2,100

Telecom Technologies Inc. manufactures and assembles two major types of telephone assemblies—a desk phone and a mobile phone. The process consists of a just-in-time cell for each product. The data that follow concern only the mobile phone just-in-time cell.

For the year, Telecom Technologies Inc. budgeted the following costs for the mobile phone production cell:

Conversion Cost Categories	Budget
Labor	$100,000
Supplies	38,000
Utilities	12,000
Total	$150,000

Telecom plans 3,000 hours of production for the mobile phone cell for the year. The materials cost is $75 per unit. Each assembly requires 18 minutes of cell assembly time. There was no October 1 inventory for either Raw and In Process Inventory or Finished Goods Inventory.

The following summary events took place in the mobile phone cell during October:

a. Electronic parts were purchased to produce 840 mobile phone assemblies in October.
b. Conversion costs were applied for 830 units of production in October.
c. 815 units were completed and transferred to finished goods in October.
d. 810 units were shipped to customers at a price of $210 per unit.

Instructions

1. Determine the budgeted cell conversion cost per hour.
2. Determine the budgeted cell conversion cost per unit.
3. Journalize the summary transactions (a) through (d).
4. Determine the ending balance in Raw and In Process Inventory and Finished Goods Inventory.
5. ▭▭▭▸ How does the accounting in a JIT environment differ from traditional accounting?

PR 27-4B

Pareto chart and cost of quality report— manufacturing company

obj. 5

✓ 3. Non-value-added,
38%

The president of Cardio-Care Exercise Equipment Inc. has been concerned about the growth in costs over the last several years. The president asked the controller to perform an activity analysis to gain a better insight into these costs. The activity analysis revealed the following:

Activity	Activity Cost
Correcting invoice errors	$ 18,000
Disposing of incoming materials with poor quality	22,500
Disposing of scrap	49,500
Expediting late production	54,000
Final inspection	31,500
Inspecting incoming materials	9,000
Inspecting work in process	45,000
Preventive machine maintenance	31,500
Producing product	162,000
Responding to customer quality complaints	27,000
Total	$450,000

The production process is complicated by quality problems, requiring the production manager to expedite production and dispose of scrap.

Instructions

1. Prepare a Pareto chart of the company activities.
2. Use the activity cost information to determine the percentages of total costs that are prevention, appraisal, internal failure, external failure, and not costs of quality.
3. Determine the percentages of total costs that are value- and non-value-added.
4. ➤ Interpret the information.

Special Activities

SA 27-1
Ethics and professional conduct in business

ETHICS

In August, Apollo Company introduced a new performance measurement system in manufacturing operations. One of the new performance measures was lead time. The lead time was determined by tagging a random sample of items with a log sheet throughout the month. This log sheet recorded the time that the item started and the time that it ended production, as well as all steps in between. The controller collected the log sheets and calculated the average lead time of the tagged products. This number was reported to central management and was used to evaluate the performance of the plant manager. The plant was under extreme pressure to reduce lead time because of poor lead time results reported in June.

The following memo was intercepted by the controller.

Date: September 1
To: Hourly Employees
From: Plant Manager

During last month, you noticed that some of the products were tagged with a log sheet. This sheet records the time that a product enters production and the time that it leaves production. The difference between these two times is termed the "lead time." Our plant is evaluated on improving lead time. From now on, I ask all of you to keep an eye out for the tagged items. When you receive a tagged item, it is to receive special attention. Work on that item first, and then immediately move it to the next operation. Under no circumstances should tagged items wait on any other work that you have. Naturally, report accurate information. I insist that you record the correct times on the log sheet as the product goes through your operations.

➤ How should the controller respond to this discovery?

SA 27-2
Just-in-time principles

Winter Comfort Inc. manufactures electric space heaters. While the CEO, Kevin Cross, is visiting the production facility, the following conversation takes place with the plant manager, Alicia Alvarez:

Kevin: As I walk around the facility, I can't help noticing all the materials inventories. What's going on?

Alicia: I have found our suppliers to be very unreliable in meeting their delivery commitments. Thus, I keep a lot of materials on hand so as to not risk running out and shutting down production.

Kevin: Not only do I see a lot of materials inventory, but there also seems to be a lot of finished goods inventory on hand. Why is this?

Alicia: As you know, I am evaluated on maintaining a low cost per unit. The one way that I am able to reduce my unit costs is by producing as many space heaters as possible. This allows me to spread my fixed costs over a larger base. When orders are down, the excess production builds up as inventory, as we are seeing now. But don't worry—I'm really keeping our unit costs down this way.

Kevin: I'm not so sure. It seems that this inventory must cost us something.

Alicia: Not really. I'll eventually use the materials and we'll eventually sell the finished goods. By keeping the plant busy, I'm using our plant assets wisely. This is reflected in the low unit costs that I'm able to maintain.

If you were Kevin Cross, how would you respond to Alicia Alvarez? What recommendations would you provide Alicia Alvarez?

SA 27-3
Just-in-time principles

Zenith Concepts Inc. prepared the following performance graphs for the prior year:

Total Manufacturing Lead Time

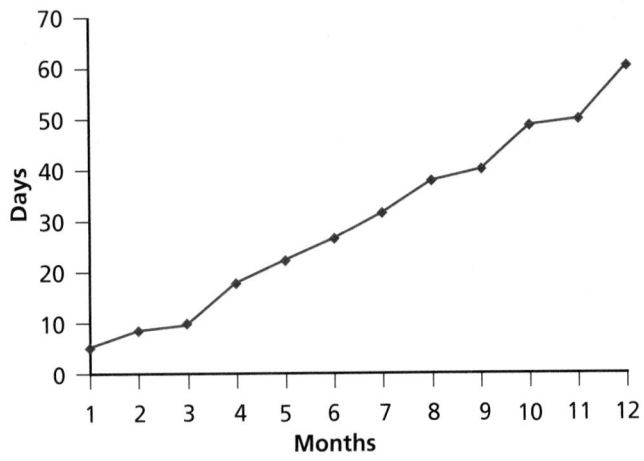

Total Inventory Dollars (in 000s)

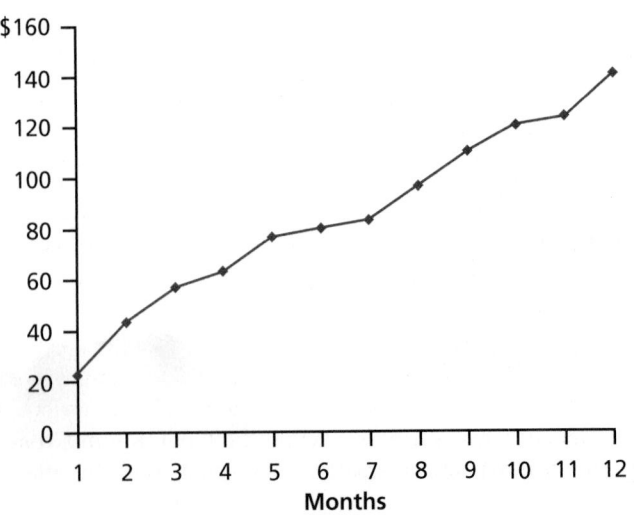

Percent of Sales Orders Filled on Time

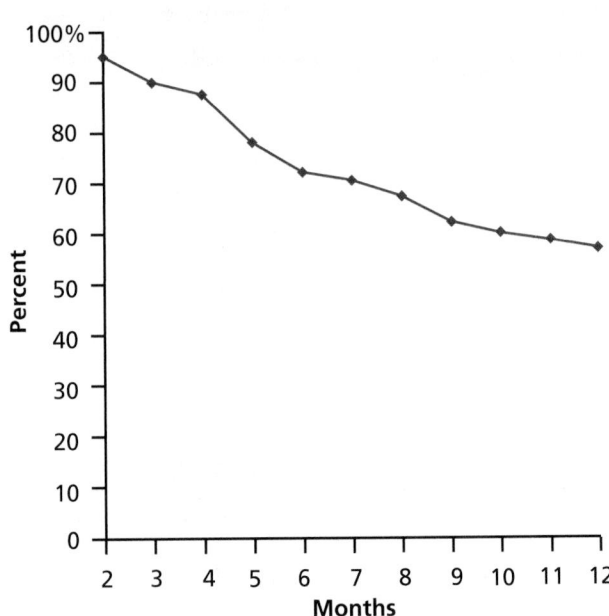

▭▬▸ What do these charts appear to indicate?

SA 27-4
Value-added and non-value-added activity costs

Midland Company prepared the following factory overhead report from its general ledger:

Indirect labor	$500,000
Fringe benefits	60,000
Supplies	110,000
Depreciation	230,000
Total	$900,000

The management of Midland Company was dissatisfied with this report and asked the controller to prepare an activity analysis of the same information. This activity analysis was as follows:

Processing sales orders	$198,000	22%
Disposing scrap	189,000	21
Expediting work orders	153,000	17
Producing parts	135,000	15
Resolving supplier quality problems	108,000	12
Reissuing corrected purchase orders	81,000	9
Expediting customer orders	36,000	4
Total	$900,000	100%

▭▬▸ Interpret the activity analysis by identifying value-added and non-value-added activity costs. How does the activity cost report differ from the general ledger report?

SA 27-5
Lead time

Group Project

In groups of two to four people, visit a sit-down restaurant and do a lead time study. If more than one group chooses to visit the same restaurant, choose different times for your visits. Note the time when you walk in the door of the restaurant and the time when you walk out the door after you have eaten. The difference between these two times is the total lead time of your restaurant experience. While in the restaurant, determine the time spent on non-value-added time, such as wait time, and the time spent on value-added eating time. Note the various activities and the time required to perform each activity during your visit to the restaurant. Compare your analyses, identifying possible reasons for differences in the times recorded by groups that visited the same restaurant.

Answers to Self-Examination Questions

1. **B** The just-in-time philosophy embraces a product-oriented layout (answer A), making lead times short (answer C), and reducing setup times (answer D). Pull manufacturing, the opposite of push manufacturing (answer B), is also a just-in-time principle.

2. **D** Accounting in a just-in-time environment should not be complex (answer A), not focus on direct labor (answer B) because it is combined with other conversion costs, and not provide detailed variance reporting (answer C) because of a higher reliance on nonfinancial performance measures. However, the just-in-time accounting environment will have fewer transaction control features than the traditional system (answer D).

3. **C** $420,000\2,100 hours = $200 per hour
   $200 per hour × 0.25 hour = $50 per unit
   700 units × ($50 + $12.50) = $43,750

4. **B** Appraisal costs (answer B) are the costs of inspecting and testing activities, which include detecting, measuring, evaluating, and auditing products and processes. Prevention (answer A) activities are incurred to prevent defects from occurring during the design and delivery of products or services. Internal failure costs (answer C) are associated with defects that are discovered by the organization before the product or service is delivered to the consumer. External failure costs (answer D) are the costs incurred after defective units or service have been delivered to consumers.

5. **A** A Pareto chart is a bar chart that ranks attribute totals by category (answer A). A line chart (answer B), a pie chart (answer C), and a table listing (answer D) are other ways of displaying information, but they are not Pareto charts.

Appendices

Appendix A • • • • • • • • • • • • • • • • • • •

Interest Tables

Present Value of $1 at Compound Interest Due in n Periods: $p_{\overline{n}|i} = \dfrac{1}{(1 + i)^n}$

$n \backslash i$	5%	5.5%	6%	6.5%	7%	8%
1	0.95238	0.94787	0.94334	0.93897	0.93458	0.92593
2	0.90703	0.89845	0.89000	0.88166	0.87344	0.85734
3	0.86384	0.85161	0.83962	0.82785	0.81630	0.79383
4	0.82270	0.80722	0.79209	0.77732	0.76290	0.73503
5	0.78353	0.76513	0.74726	0.72988	0.71290	0.68058
6	0.74622	0.72525	0.70496	0.68533	0.66634	0.63017
7	0.71068	0.68744	0.66506	0.64351	0.62275	0.58349
8	0.67684	0.65160	0.62741	0.60423	0.58201	0.54027
9	0.64461	0.61763	0.59190	0.56735	0.54393	0.50025
10	0.61391	0.58543	0.55840	0.53273	0.50835	0.46319
11	0.58468	0.55491	0.52679	0.50021	0.47509	0.42888
12	0.55684	0.52598	0.49697	0.46968	0.44401	0.39711
13	0.53032	0.49856	0.46884	0.44102	0.41496	0.36770
14	0.50507	0.47257	0.44230	0.41410	0.38782	0.34046
15	0.48102	0.44793	0.41726	0.38883	0.36245	0.31524
16	0.45811	0.42458	0.39365	0.36510	0.33874	0.29189
17	0.43630	0.40245	0.37136	0.34281	0.31657	0.27027
18	0.41552	0.38147	0.35034	0.32189	0.29586	0.25025
19	0.39573	0.36158	0.33051	0.30224	0.27651	0.23171
20	0.37689	0.34273	0.31180	0.28380	0.25842	0.21455
21	0.35894	0.32486	0.29416	0.26648	0.24151	0.19866
22	0.34185	0.30793	0.27750	0.25021	0.22571	0.18394
23	0.32557	0.29187	0.26180	0.23494	0.21095	0.17032
24	0.31007	0.27666	0.24698	0.22060	0.19715	0.15770
25	0.29530	0.26223	0.23300	0.20714	0.18425	0.14602
26	0.28124	0.24856	0.21981	0.19450	0.17211	0.13520
27	0.26785	0.23560	0.20737	0.18263	0.16093	0.12519
28	0.25509	0.22332	0.19563	0.17148	0.15040	0.11591
29	0.24295	0.21168	0.18456	0.16101	0.14056	0.10733
30	0.23138	0.20064	0.17411	0.15119	0.13137	0.09938
31	0.22036	0.19018	0.16426	0.14196	0.12277	0.09202
32	0.20987	0.18027	0.15496	0.13329	0.11474	0.08520
33	0.19987	0.17087	0.14619	0.12516	0.10724	0.07889
34	0.19036	0.16196	0.13791	0.11752	0.10022	0.07304
35	0.18129	0.15352	0.13010	0.11035	0.09366	0.06764
40	0.14205	0.11746	0.09722	0.08054	0.06678	0.04603
45	0.11130	0.08988	0.07265	0.05879	0.04761	0.03133
50	0.08720	0.06877	0.05429	0.04291	0.03395	0.02132

Present Value of \$1 at Compound Interest Due in *n* Periods: $p_{\bar{n}\backslash i} = \dfrac{1}{(1 + i)^n}$

n \ i	9%	10%	11%	12%	13%	14%
1	0.91743	0.90909	0.90090	0.89286	0.88496	0.87719
2	0.84168	0.82645	0.81162	0.79719	0.78315	0.76947
3	0.77218	0.75132	0.73119	0.71178	0.69305	0.67497
4	0.70842	0.68301	0.65873	0.63552	0.61332	0.59208
5	0.64993	0.62092	0.59345	0.56743	0.54276	0.51937
6	0.59627	0.56447	0.53464	0.50663	0.48032	0.45559
7	0.54703	0.51316	0.48166	0.45235	0.42506	0.39964
8	0.50187	0.46651	0.43393	0.40388	0.37616	0.35056
9	0.46043	0.42410	0.39092	0.36061	0.33288	0.30751
10	0.42241	0.38554	0.35218	0.32197	0.29459	0.26974
11	0.38753	0.35049	0.31728	0.28748	0.26070	0.23662
12	0.35554	0.31863	0.28584	0.25668	0.23071	0.20756
13	0.32618	0.28966	0.25751	0.22917	0.20416	0.18207
14	0.29925	0.26333	0.23199	0.20462	0.18068	0.15971
15	0.27454	0.23939	0.20900	0.18270	0.15989	0.14010
16	0.25187	0.21763	0.18829	0.16312	0.14150	0.12289
17	0.23107	0.19784	0.16963	0.14564	0.12522	0.10780
18	0.21199	0.17986	0.15282	0.13004	0.11081	0.09456
19	0.19449	0.16351	0.13768	0.11611	0.09806	0.08295
20	0.17843	0.14864	0.12403	0.10367	0.08678	0.07276
21	0.16370	0.13513	0.11174	0.09256	0.07680	0.06383
22	0.15018	0.12285	0.10067	0.08264	0.06796	0.05599
23	0.13778	0.11168	0.09069	0.07379	0.06014	0.04911
24	0.12640	0.10153	0.08170	0.06588	0.05323	0.04308
25	0.11597	0.09230	0.07361	0.05882	0.04710	0.03779
26	0.10639	0.08390	0.06631	0.05252	0.04168	0.03315
27	0.09761	0.07628	0.05974	0.04689	0.03689	0.02908
28	0.08955	0.06934	0.05382	0.04187	0.03264	0.02551
29	0.08216	0.06304	0.04849	0.03738	0.02889	0.02237
30	0.07537	0.05731	0.04368	0.03338	0.02557	0.01963
31	0.06915	0.05210	0.03935	0.02980	0.02262	0.01722
32	0.06344	0.04736	0.03545	0.02661	0.02002	0.01510
33	0.05820	0.04306	0.03194	0.02376	0.01772	0.01325
34	0.05331	0.03914	0.02878	0.02121	0.01568	0.01162
35	0.04899	0.03558	0.02592	0.01894	0.01388	0.01019
40	0.03184	0.02210	0.01538	0.01075	0.00753	0.00529
45	0.02069	0.01372	0.00913	0.00610	0.00409	0.00275
50	0.01345	0.00852	0.00542	0.00346	0.00222	0.00143

Present Value of Ordinary Annuity of $1 per Period: $p_{\overline{n}\backslash i} = \dfrac{1 - \dfrac{1}{(1 + i)^n}}{i}$

n \ i	5%	5.5%	6%	6.5%	7%	8%
1	0.95238	0.94787	0.94340	0.93897	0.93458	0.92593
2	1.85941	1.84632	1.83339	1.82063	1.80802	1.78326
3	2.72325	2.69793	2.67301	2.64848	2.62432	2.57710
4	3.54595	3.50515	3.46511	3.42580	3.38721	3.31213
5	4.32948	4.27028	4.21236	4.15568	4.10020	3.99271
6	5.07569	4.99553	4.91732	4.84101	4.76654	4.62288
7	5.78637	5.68297	5.58238	5.48452	5.38923	5.20637
8	6.46321	6.33457	6.20979	6.08875	5.97130	5.74664
9	7.10782	6.95220	6.80169	6.65610	6.51523	6.24689
10	7.72174	7.53763	7.36009	7.18883	7.02358	6.71008
11	8.30641	8.09254	7.88688	7.68904	7.49867	7.13896
12	8.86325	8.61852	8.38384	8.15873	7.94269	7.53608
13	9.39357	9.11708	8.85268	8.59974	8.35765	7.90378
14	9.89864	9.58965	9.29498	9.01384	8.74547	8.22424
15	10.37966	10.03758	9.71225	9.40267	9.10791	8.55948
16	10.83777	10.46216	10.10590	9.76776	9.44665	8.85137
17	11.27407	10.86461	10.47726	10.11058	9.76322	9.12164
18	11.68959	11.24607	10.82760	10.43247	10.05909	9.37189
19	12.08532	11.60765	11.15812	10.73471	10.33560	9.60360
20	12.46221	11.95038	11.46992	11.01851	10.59401	9.81815
21	12.82115	12.27524	11.76408	11.28498	10.83553	10.01680
22	13.16300	12.58317	12.04158	11.53520	11.06124	10.20074
23	13.48857	12.87504	12.30338	11.77014	11.27219	10.37106
24	13.79864	13.15170	12.55036	11.99074	11.46933	10.52876
25	14.09394	13.41393	12.78336	12.19788	11.65358	10.67478
26	14.37518	13.66250	13.00317	12.39237	11.82578	10.80998
27	14.64303	13.89810	13.21053	12.57500	11.98671	10.93516
28	14.89813	14.12142	13.40616	12.74648	12.13711	11.05108
29	15.14107	14.33310	13.59072	12.90749	12.27767	11.15841
30	15.37245	14.53375	13.76483	13.05868	12.40904	11.25778
31	15.59281	14.72393	13.92909	13.20063	12.53181	11.34980
32	15.80268	14.90420	14.08404	13.33393	12.64656	11.43500
33	16.00255	15.07507	14.23023	13.45909	12.75379	11.51389
34	16.19290	15.23703	14.36814	13.57661	12.85401	11.58693
35	16.37420	15.39055	14.49825	13.68696	12.94767	11.65457
40	17.15909	16.04612	15.04630	14.14553	13.33171	11.92461
45	17.77407	16.54773	15.45583	14.48023	13.60552	12.10840
50	18.25592	16.93152	15.76186	14.72452	13.80075	12.23348

Present Value of Ordinary Annuity of \$1 per Period: $p_{\bar{n}|i} = \dfrac{1 - \dfrac{1}{(1+i)^n}}{i}$

$n \backslash i$	9%	10%	11%	12%	13%	14%
1	0.91743	0.90909	0.90090	0.89286	0.88496	0.87719
2	1.75911	1.73554	1.71252	1.69005	1.66810	1.64666
3	2.53130	2.48685	2.44371	2.40183	2.36115	2.32163
4	3.23972	3.16986	3.10245	3.03735	2.97447	2.91371
5	3.88965	3.79079	3.69590	3.60478	3.51723	3.43308
6	4.48592	4.35526	4.23054	4.11141	3.99755	3.88867
7	5.03295	4.86842	4.71220	4.56376	4.42261	4.28830
8	5.53482	5.33493	5.14612	4.96764	4.79677	4.63886
9	5.99525	5.75902	5.53705	5.32825	5.13166	4.94637
10	6.41766	6.14457	5.88923	5.65022	5.42624	5.21612
11	6.80519	6.49506	6.20652	5.93770	5.68694	5.45273
12	7.16072	6.81369	6.49236	6.19437	5.91765	5.66029
13	7.48690	7.10336	6.74987	6.42355	6.12181	5.84236
14	7.78615	7.36669	6.96187	6.62817	6.30249	6.00207
15	8.06069	7.60608	7.19087	6.81086	6.46238	6.14217
16	8.31256	7.82371	7.37916	6.97399	6.60388	6.26506
17	8.54363	8.02155	7.54879	7.11963	6.72909	6.37286
18	8.75562	8.20141	7.70162	7.24967	6.83991	6.46742
19	8.95012	8.36492	7.83929	7.36578	6.93797	6.55037
20	9.12855	8.51356	7.96333	7.46944	7.02475	6.62313
21	9.29224	8.64869	8.07507	7.56200	7.10155	6.68696
22	9.44242	8.77154	8.17574	7.64465	7.16951	6.74294
23	9.58021	8.88322	8.26643	7.71843	7.22966	6.79206
24	9.70661	8.98474	8.34814	7.78432	7.28288	6.83514
25	9.82258	9.07704	8.42174	7.84314	7.32998	6.87293
26	9.92897	9.16094	8.48806	7.89566	7.37167	6.90608
27	10.02658	9.23722	8.54780	7.94255	7.40856	6.93515
28	10.11613	9.30657	8.60162	7.98442	7.44120	6.96066
29	10.19828	9.36961	8.65011	8.02181	7.47009	6.98304
30	10.27365	9.42691	8.69379	8.05518	7.49565	7.00266
31	10.34280	9.47901	8.73315	8.08499	7.51828	7.01988
32	10.40624	9.52638	8.76860	8.11159	7.53830	7.03498
33	10.46444	9.56943	8.80054	8.13535	7.55602	7.04823
34	10.51784	9.60858	8.82932	8.15656	7.57170	7.05985
35	10.56682	9.64416	8.85524	8.17550	7.58557	7.07005
40	10.75736	9.77905	8.95105	8.24378	7.63438	7.10504
45	10.88118	9.86281	9.00791	8.28252	7.66086	7.12322
50	10.96168	9.91481	9.04165	8.30450	7.67524	7.13266

Appendix B ● ● ● ● ● ● ● ● ● ● ● ● ● ● ● ● ● ●

Reversing Entries

Some of the adjusting entries recorded at the end of an accounting period have an important effect on otherwise routine transactions that occur in the following period. A typical example is accrued wages owed to employees at the end of a period. If there has been an adjusting entry for accrued wages expense, the first payment of wages in the following period will include the accrual. In the absence of some special provision, Wages Payable must be debited for the amount owed for the earlier period, and Wages Expense must be debited for the portion of the payroll that represents expense for the later period. However, an *optional* entry—the reversing entry—may be used to simplify the analysis and recording of this first payroll entry in a period. As the term implies, a *reversing entry* is the exact opposite of the adjusting entry to which it relates. The amounts and accounts are the same as the adjusting entry; the debits and credits are reversed.

@netsolutions

We will illustrate the use of reversing entries by using the data for NetSolutions' accrued wages, which were presented in Chapter 3. These data are summarized in Exhibit 1.

EXHIBIT 1

Accrued Wages

1. Wages are paid on the second and fourth Fridays for the two-week periods ending on those Fridays. The payments were $950 on December 13 and $1,200 on December 27.

2. The wages accrued for Monday and Tuesday, December 30 and 31, are $250.

3. Wages paid on Friday, January 10, total $1,275.

December

S	M	T	W	T	F	S
1	2	3	4	5	6	7
8	9	10	11	12	13	14
15	16	17	18	19	20	21
22	23	24	25	26	27	28
29	30	31				

Wages expense (paid), $950

Wages expense (paid), $1,200

Wages expense (accrued), $250

January

S	M	T	W	T	F	S
			1	2	3	4
5	6	7	8	9	10	11

Wages expense (paid), $1,275

The adjusting entry for the accrued wages of December 30 and 31 is as follows:

1							1
2	Dec.	31	Wages Expense	51	2 5 0 00		2
3			Wages Payable	22		2 5 0 00	3
4			Accrued wages.				4

After the adjusting entry has been posted, Wages Expense will have a debit balance of $4,525 ($4,275 + $250), as shown on the top of page B-3. Wages Payable will have a credit balance of $250, as shown at the bottom of this page. After the closing process is completed, Wages Expense will have a zero balance and will be ready for entries in the next period. Wages Payable, on the other hand, has a balance of $250. Without a reversing entry, it is necessary to record the $1,275 payroll on January 10 as follows:

1							1
2	2008 Jan.	10	Wages Payable	22	2 5 0 00		2
3			Wages Expense	51	1 0 2 5 00		3
4			Cash	11		1 2 7 5 00	4

The employee who records the January 10 entry must refer to the prior period's adjusting entry to determine the amount of the debits to Wages Payable and Wages Expense. Because the January 10 payroll is not recorded in the usual manner, there is a greater chance that an error may occur. This chance of error is reduced by recording a reversing entry as of the first day of the fiscal period. For example, the reversing entry for the accrued wages expense is as follows:

1							1
2	2008 Jan.	1	Wages Payable	22	2 5 0 00		2
3			Wages Expense	51		2 5 0 00	3
4			Reversing entry.				4

The reversing entry transfers the $250 liability from Wages Payable to the credit side of Wages Expense. The nature of the $250 is unchanged—it is still a liability. Because of its unusual nature, an explanation is normally written under the journal entry. When the payroll is paid on January 10, the following entry is recorded:

1							1
2	Jan.	31	Wages Expense	51	1 2 7 5 00		2
3			Cash	11		1 2 7 5 00	3

After this entry is posted, Wages Expense has a debit balance of $1,025. This amount is the wages expense for the period January 1–10. The sequence of entries, including adjusting, closing, and reversing entries, is illustrated in the following accounts:

ACCOUNT *Wages Payable*					ACCOUNT NO. *22*		
		Post.				Balance	
Date	Item	Ref.	Debit	Credit		Debit	Credit
2007 Dec. 31	Adjusting	5		2 5 0 00			2 5 0 00
2008 Jan. 1	Reversing	7	2 5 0 00			—	—

ACCOUNT *Wages Expense*						ACCOUNT NO. *51*	
		Post.			Balance		
Date	Item	Ref.	Debit	Credit	Debit	Credit	
2007 Nov. 30		1	2 1 2 5 00		2 1 2 5 00		
Dec. 13		3	9 5 0 00		3 0 7 5 00		
27		3	1 2 0 0 00		4 2 7 5 00		
31	Adjusting	5	2 5 0 00		4 5 2 5 00		
31	Closing	6		4 5 2 5 00	—	—	
2008 Jan. 1	Reversing	7		2 5 0 00		2 5 0 00	
10		7	1 2 7 5 00		1 0 2 5 00		

In addition to accrued expenses (accrued liabilities), reversing entries may be journalized for accrued revenues (accrued assets). For example, the following reversing entry could be recorded for NetSolutions' accrued fees earned:

2	Jan.	1	Fees Earned		41	5 0 0 00		2
3			Accounts Receivable		12		5 0 0 00	3
4			Reversing entry.					4

As we mentioned, the use of reversing entries is optional. However, with the increased use of computerized accounting systems, data entry personnel may be inputting routine accounting entries. In such an environment, reversing entries may be useful, since these individuals may not recognize the impact of adjusting entries on the related transactions in the following period.

Exercises

EX B-1
Adjusting and reversing entries

On the basis of the following data, (a) journalize the adjusting entries at December 31, the end of the current fiscal year, and (b) journalize the reversing entries on January 1, the first day of the following year.

1. Sales salaries are uniformly $14,000 for a five-day workweek, ending on Friday. The last payday of the year was Friday, December 26.
2. Accrued fees earned but not recorded at December 31, $7,975.

EX B-2
Adjusting and reversing entries

On the basis of the following data, (a) journalize the adjusting entries at June 30, the end of the current fiscal year, and (b) journalize the reversing entries on July 1, the first day of the following year.

1. Wages are uniformly $9,375 for a five-day workweek, ending on Friday. The last payday of the year was Friday, June 27.
2. Accrued fees earned but not recorded at June 30, $6,100.

EX B-3
Entries posted to the wages expense account

Portions of the wages expense account of a business are shown at the top of the following page.

ACCOUNT   **Wages Expense**   **ACCOUNT NO. 53**

Date	Item	Post. Ref.	Dr.	Cr.	Balance Dr.	Balance Cr.
2007						
Dec. 26	(1)	49	62,500		1,747,800	
31	(2)	50	12,500		1,760,300	
31	(3)	51		1,760,300	—	—
2008						
Jan. 1	(4)	52		12,500		12,500
2	(5)	53	60,000		47,500	

a. Indicate the nature of the entry (payment, adjusting, closing, reversing) from which each numbered posting was made.

b. Journalize the complete entry from which each numbered posting was made.

EX B-4
Entries posted to the salaries expense account

Portions of the salaries expense account of a business are shown below.

ACCOUNT   **Salaries Expense**   **ACCOUNT NO. 53**

Date	Item	Post. Ref.	Dr.	Cr.	Balance Dr.	Balance Cr.
2007						
Dec. 26	(1)	29	30,000		1,500,000	
31	(2)	30	10,000		1,510,000	
31	(3)	31		1,510,000	—	—
2008						
Jan. 1	(4)	32		10,000		10,000
2	(5)	33	30,000		20,000	

a. Indicate the nature of the entry (payment, adjusting, closing, reversing) from which each numbered posting was made.

b. Journalize the complete entry from which each numbered posting was made.

Appendix C

Special Journals and Subsidiary Ledgers

In the beginning chapters of this text, all transactions for NetSolutions were manually recorded in an all-purpose (two-column) journal. The journal entries were then posted individually to the accounts in the ledger. Such manual accounting systems are simple to use and easy to understand. Manually kept records may serve a business reasonably well when the amount of data collected, stored, and used is relatively small. For a large business, such manual processing is too costly and time consuming; thus, a computerized system is preferred. For example, a large company such as Verizon Communications has millions of telephone fees earned on account with millions of customers daily. Each telephone fee on account requires an entry debiting Accounts Receivable and crediting Fees Earned. In addition, a record of each customer's receivable must be kept. Clearly, a simple manual system would not serve the business needs of Verizon Communications.

When a business has a large number of similar transactions, using an all-purpose journal is inefficient and impractical. In such cases, subsidiary ledgers and special journals are useful. As a business becomes more complex, the manual system can be supplemented or replaced by a computerized system. Although we will illustrate the manual use of subsidiary ledgers and special journals, the basic principles described in the following paragraphs also apply to a computerized accounting system.

SPECIAL JOURNALS

One method of processing data more efficiently in a manual accounting system is to expand the all-purpose two-column journal to a multicolumn journal. Each column in a multicolumn journal is used only for recording transactions that affect a certain account. For example, a special column could be used only for recording debits to the cash account, and another special column could be used only for recording credits to the cash account. The addition of the two special columns would eliminate the writing of *Cash* in the journal for every receipt and every payment of cash. Also, there would be no need to post each individual debit and credit to the cash account. Instead, the *Cash Dr.* and *Cash Cr.* columns could be totaled periodically and only the totals posted. In a similar way, special columns could be added for recording credits to Fees Earned, debits and credits to Accounts Receivable and Accounts Payable, and for other entries that are often repeated.

An all-purpose multicolumn journal may be adequate for a small business that has many transactions of a similar nature. However, a journal that has many columns for recording many different types of transactions is impractical for larger businesses.

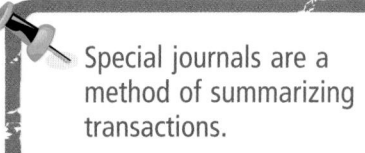

Special journals are a method of summarizing transactions.

The next logical extension of the accounting system is to replace the single multicolumn journal with several **special journals**. Each special journal is designed to be used for recording a single kind of transaction that occurs frequently. For example, since most businesses have many transactions in which cash is paid out, they will likely use a special journal for recording cash payments. Likewise, they will use another special journal for recording cash receipts. Special journals are a method of summarizing transactions, which is a basic feature of any accounting system.

The format and number of special journals that a business uses depends upon the nature of the business. A business that gives credit might use a special journal designed for recording only revenue from services provided on credit. On the other hand, a business that does not give credit would have no need for such a journal. In other cases, record-keeping costs may be reduced by using supporting documents as special journals.

The transactions that occur most often in a small- to medium-size service business and the special journals in which they are recorded are as follows:

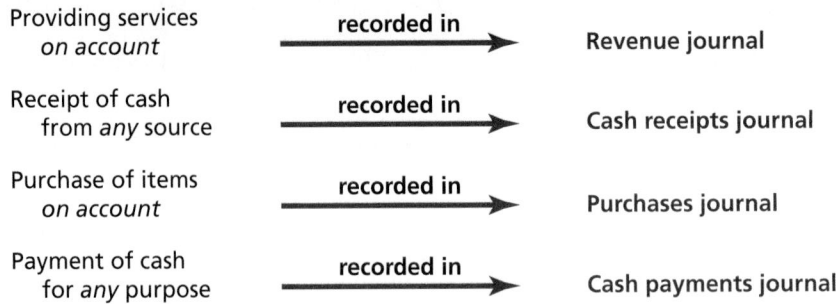

Providing services *on account*	recorded in →	Revenue journal
Receipt of cash from *any* source	recorded in →	Cash receipts journal
Purchase of items *on account*	recorded in →	Purchases journal
Payment of cash for *any* purpose	recorded in →	Cash payments journal

The all-purpose two-column journal, called the **general journal** or simply the *journal*, can be used for entries that do not fit into any of the special journals. For example, adjusting and closing entries are recorded in the general journal.

SUBSIDIARY LEDGERS

An accounting system should be designed to provide information on the amounts due from various customers (accounts receivable) and amounts owed to various creditors (accounts payable). A separate account for each customer and creditor could be added to the ledger. However, as the number of customers and creditors increases, the ledger becomes awkward to use when it includes many customers and creditors.

A large number of individual accounts with a common characteristic can be grouped together in a separate ledger called a **subsidiary ledger**. The primary ledger, which contains all of the balance sheet and income statement accounts, is then called the **general ledger**. Each subsidiary ledger is represented in the general ledger by a summarizing account, called a **controlling account**. The sum of the balances of the accounts in a subsidiary ledger must equal the balance of the related controlling account. Thus, you may think of a subsidiary ledger as a secondary ledger that supports a controlling account in the general ledger.

The individual accounts with customers are arranged in alphabetical order in a subsidiary ledger called the **accounts receivable subsidiary ledger**, or *customers ledger*. The controlling account in the general ledger that summarizes the debits and credits to the individual customer accounts is *Accounts Receivable*. The individual accounts with creditors are arranged in alphabetical order in a subsidiary ledger called the **accounts payable subsidiary ledger**, or *creditors ledger*. The related controlling account in the general ledger is *Accounts Payable*. The relationship between the general ledger and these subsidiary ledgers is illustrated in Exhibit 1.

@netsolutions

In the following paragraphs, we illustrate special journals and subsidiary ledgers in a manual accounting system for NetSolutions. To simplify the illustration, we will use a minimum number of transactions. We will focus our discussion on two common operating cycles: (1) the revenue and collection cycle and (2) the purchase and payment cycle. We will assume that NetSolutions had the following selected general ledger balances on March 1, 2008:

Account Number	Account	Balance
11	Cash	$6,200
12	Accounts Receivable	3,400
14	Supplies	2,500
18	Office Equipment	2,500
21	Accounts Payable	1,230

EXHIBIT 1   General Ledger and Subsidiary Ledgers

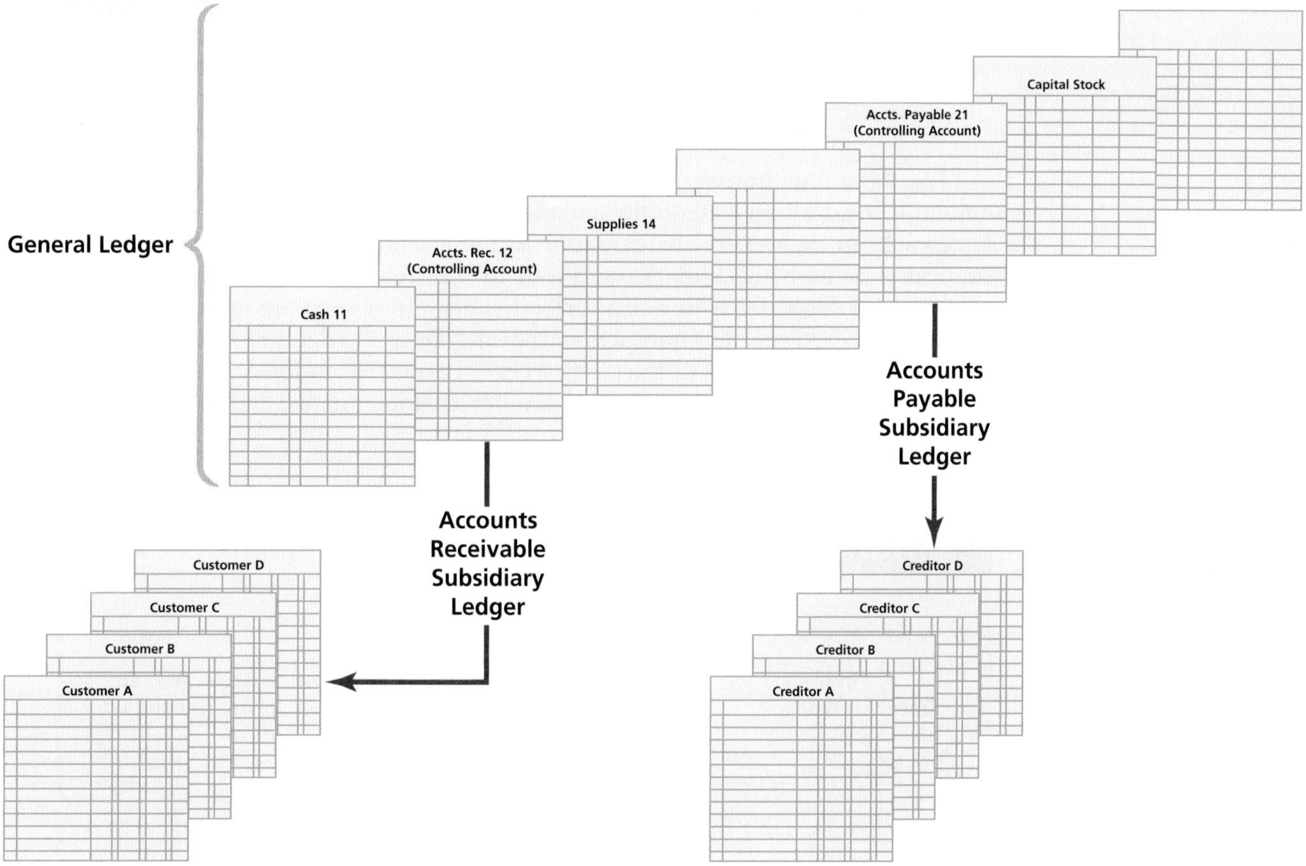

General Ledger

Cash 11

Accts. Rec. 12
(Controlling Account)

Supplies 14

Accts. Payable 21
(Controlling Account)

Capital Stock

**Accounts
Payable
Subsidiary
Ledger**

**Accounts
Receivable
Subsidiary
Ledger**

Customer D
Customer C
Customer B
Customer A

Creditor D
Creditor C
Creditor B
Creditor A

THE REVENUE AND COLLECTION CYCLE

The *revenue and collection cycle* for NetSolutions consists of providing services on account and collecting cash from customers. Revenues earned on account create a customer receivable and will be recorded in a revenue journal. Customers' accounts receivable are collected and will be recorded in a cash receipts journal.

Internal control is enhanced by separating the function of recording revenue transactions in the revenue journal from recording cash collections in the cash receipts journal. For example, if these duties are separated, it is more difficult for one person to embezzle cash collections and manipulate the accounting records.

Revenue Journal   The **revenue journal** is used only for recording *fees earned on account. Cash fees earned would be recorded in the cash receipts journal.* The sale of products is recorded in a sales journal, which is similar to a *revenue journal.* We will compare the efficiency of using a revenue journal with a general journal by assuming that NetSolutions recorded the following revenue transactions in a general journal:

2008					
Mar.	2	Accounts Receivable—Accessories By Claire	12/✔	2 2 0 0 00	
		Fees Earned	41		2 2 0 0 00
	6	Accounts Receivable—RapZone	12/✔	1 7 5 0 00	
		Fees Earned	41		1 7 5 0 00

(continued)

	2008 Mar.	18	Accounts Receivable—Web Cantina	12/✔	2 6 5 0 00	
			Fees Earned	41		2 6 5 0 00
		27	Accounts Receivable—Accessories By Claire	12/✔	3 0 0 0 00	
			Fees Earned	41		3 0 0 0 00

For these four transactions, NetSolutions recorded eight account titles and eight amounts. In addition, NetSolutions made 12 postings to the ledgers—four to Accounts Receivable in the general ledger, four to the accounts receivable subsidiary ledger (indicated by each check mark), and four to Fees Earned in the general ledger. These transactions could be recorded more efficiently in a revenue journal, as shown in Exhibit 2. In each revenue transaction, the amount of the debit to Accounts Receivable is the same as the amount of the credit to Fees Earned. Therefore, only a single amount column is necessary. The date, invoice number, customer name, and amount are entered separately for each transaction.

EXHIBIT 2   Revenue Journal

REVENUE JOURNAL   Page 35

	Date	Invoice No.	Account Debited	Post. Ref.	Accts. Rec. Dr. Fees Earned Cr.	
1	2008 Mar. 2	615	Accessories By Claire		2 2 0 0 00	1
2	6	616	RapZone		1 7 5 0 00	2
3	18	617	Web Cantina		2 6 5 0 00	3
4	27	618	Accessories By Claire		3 0 0 0 00	4
5	31				9 6 0 0 00	5

The basic procedure of posting from a revenue journal is shown in Exhibit 3. A single monthly total is posted to Accounts Receivable and Fees Earned in the general ledger. Each transaction, such as the $2,200 debit to Accessories By Claire, must also be posted individually to a customer account in the accounts receivable subsidiary ledger. These postings to customer accounts should be made frequently. In this way, management has information on the current balance of each customer's account. Since the balances in the customer accounts are usually debit balances, the three-column account form shown in the exhibit is often used.

To provide a trail of the entries posted to the subsidiary ledger, the source of these entries is indicated in the *Posting Reference* column of each account by inserting the letter *R* (for revenue journal) and the page number of the revenue journal. A check mark (✓) instead of a number is then inserted in the *Posting Reference* column of the revenue journal, as shown in Exhibit 3.

If a customer's account has a credit balance, that fact should be indicated by an asterisk or parentheses in the *Balance* column. When an account's balance is zero, a line may be drawn in the *Balance* column.

At the end of each month, the amount column of the revenue journal is totaled. This total is equal to the sum of the month's debits to the individual accounts in the subsidiary ledger. It is posted in the general ledger as a debit to Accounts Receivable and a credit to Fees Earned, as shown in Exhibit 3. The respective account numbers (12 and 41) are then inserted below the total in the revenue journal to indicate that the posting is completed, as shown in Exhibit 3. In this way, all of the transactions for fees earned during the month are posted to the general ledger only once—at the end of the month—greatly simplifying the posting process.

EXHIBIT 3 Revenue Journal Postings to Ledgers

REVENUE JOURNAL   Page 35

	Date	Invoice No.	Account Debited	Post. Ref.	Accts. Rec. Dr. Fees Earned Cr.	
	2008					
1	Mar. 2	615	Accessories By Claire	✔	2,200	1
2	6	616	RapZone	✔	1,750	2
3	18	617	Web Cantina	✔	2,650	3
4	27	618	Accessories By Claire	✔	3,000	4
5	31				9,600	5
6					(12) (41)	6

GENERAL LEDGER

ACCOUNT Accounts Receivable   Account No. 12

Date	Item	Post. Ref.	Dr.	Cr.	Balance Dr.	Balance Cr.
2008						
Mar. 1	Balance	✔			3,400	
31		R35	9,600		13,000	

ACCOUNT Fees Earned   Account No. 41

Date	Item	Post. Ref.	Dr.	Cr.	Balance Dr.	Balance Cr.
2008						
Mar. 31		R35		9,600		9,600

ACCOUNTS RECEIVABLE SUBSIDIARY LEDGER

NAME: Accessories By Claire

Date	Item	Post. Ref.	Dr.	Cr.	Balance
2008					
Mar. 2		R35	2,200		2,200
27		R35	3,000		5,200

NAME: RapZone

Date	Item	Post. Ref.	Dr.	Cr.	Balance
2008					
Mar. 6		R35	1,750		1,750

NAME: Web Cantina

Date	Item	Post. Ref.	Dr.	Cr.	Balance
2008					
Mar. 1	Balance	✔			3,400
18		R35	2,650		6,050

Cash Receipts Journal All transactions that involve the receipt of cash are recorded in a **cash receipts journal**. Thus, the cash receipts journal has a column entitled *Cash Dr.*, as shown in Exhibit 4. All transactions recorded in the cash receipts journal will involve an entry in the *Cash Dr.* column. For example, on March 28 NetSolutions received cash of $2,200 from Accessories by Claire and entered that amount in the *Cash Dr.* column.

The kinds of transactions in which cash is received and how often they occur determine the titles of the other columns. For NetSolutions, the most frequent source of cash is collections from customers. Thus, the cash receipts journal in Exhibit 4 has an *Accounts Receivable Cr.* column. On March 28, when *Accessories By Claire* made a payment on its account, NetSolutions entered *Accessories By Claire* in the *Account Credited* column and entered *2,200* in the *Accounts Receivable Cr.* column.

The *Other Accounts Cr.* column in Exhibit 4 is used for recording credits to any account for which there is no special credit column. For example, NetSolutions received cash on March 1 for rent. Since no special column exists for Rent Revenue, NetSolutions entered *Rent Revenue* in the *Account Credited* column and entered *400* in the *Other Accounts Cr.* column.

EXHIBIT 4   Cash Receipts Journal and Postings

CASH RECEIPTS JOURNAL   Page 14

	Date	Account Credited	Post. Ref.	Other Accounts Cr.	Accounts Receivable Cr.	Cash Dr.	
	2008						
1	Mar. 1	Rent Revenue	42	400		400	1
2	19	Web Cantina	✔		3,400	3,400	2
3	28	Accessories by Claire	✔		2,200	2,200	3
4	30	RapZone	✔		1,750	1,750	4
5	31			400	7,350	7,750	5
6				(✔)	(12)	(11)	6

GENERAL LEDGER

ACCOUNT   Rent Revenue   Account No. 42

Date	Item	Post. Ref.	Dr.	Cr.	Balance Dr.	Balance Cr.
2008						
Mar. 1		CR14		400		400

ACCOUNT   Accounts Receivable   Account No. 12

Date	Item	Post. Ref.	Dr.	Cr.	Balance Dr.	Balance Cr.
2008						
Mar. 1	Balance	✔			3,400	
31		R35	9,600		13,000	
31		CR14		7,350	5,650	

ACCOUNT   Cash   Account No. 11

Date	Item	Post. Ref.	Dr.	Cr.	Balance Dr.	Balance Cr.
2008						
Mar. 1	Balance	✔			6,200	
31		CR14	7,750		13,950	

ACCOUNTS RECEIVABLE SUBSIDIARY LEDGER

NAME: Accessories By Claire

Date	Item	Post. Ref.	Dr.	Cr.	Balance
2008					
Mar. 2		R35	2,200		2,200
27		R35	3,000		5,200
28		CR14		2,200	3,000

NAME: RapZone

Date	Item	Post. Ref.	Dr.	Cr.	Balance
2008					
Mar. 6		R35	1,750		1,750
30		CR14		1,750	—

NAME: Web Cantina

Date	Item	Post. Ref.	Dr.	Cr.	Balance
2008					
Mar. 1	Balance	✔			3,400
18		R35	2,650		6,050
19		CR14		3,400	2,650

Invoices that have yet to be collected are often termed *open invoices.*

Postings from the cash receipts journal to the ledgers of NetSolutions are also shown in Exhibit 4. This posting process is similar to that of the revenue journal. At regular intervals, each amount in the *Other Accounts Cr.* column is posted to the proper account in the general ledger. The posting is indicated by inserting the account number in the *Posting Reference* column of the cash receipts journal. The posting reference CR (for cash receipts journal) and the proper page number are inserted in the *Posting Reference* columns of the accounts.

The amounts in the *Accounts Receivable Cr.* column are posted individually to the customer accounts in the accounts receivable subsidiary ledger. These postings should be made frequently. The posting reference CR and the proper page number are inserted in the *Posting Reference* column of each customer's account. A check mark is placed in the *Posting Reference* column of the cash receipts journal to show that each amount has been posted. None of the individual amounts in the *Cash Dr.* column is posted separately.

At the end of the month, all of the amount columns are totaled. The debits should equal the credits. Because each amount in the *Other Accounts Cr.* column has been posted individually to a general ledger account, a check mark is inserted below the column total to indicate that no further action is needed. The totals of the *Accounts Receivable Cr.* and *Cash Dr.* columns are posted to the proper accounts in the general ledger, and their account numbers are inserted below the totals to show that the postings have been completed.

Accounts Receivable Control and Subsidiary Ledger   After all posting has been completed for the month, the sum of the balances in the accounts receivable subsidiary ledger should be compared with the balance of the accounts receivable controlling account in the general ledger. If the controlling account and the subsidiary ledger do not agree, the error or errors must be located and corrected. The balances of the individual customer accounts may be summarized in a customer balance summary report. The total of NetSolutions' customer balance summary report, $5,650, agrees with the balance of its accounts receivable control account on March 31, 2008, as shown below.

Accounts Receivable (Control)		NetSolutions Customer Balance Summary March 31, 2008	
Balance, March 1, 2008	$ 3,400	Accessories By Claire	$3,000
Total debits (from revenue journal)	9,600	RapZone	0
Total credits (from cash receipts journal)	(7,350)	Web Cantina	2,650
Balance, March 31, 2008	$ 5,650	Total accounts receivable	$5,650

THE PURCHASE AND PAYMENT CYCLE

The *purchase and payment cycle* for NetSolutions consists of purchases on account and payments of cash to suppliers. To make purchases of supplies and other items on account requires establishing a supplier account payable. These transactions will be recorded in a purchases journal. The payments of suppliers' accounts payable will be recorded in the cash payments journal.

Internal control is enhanced by separating the function of recording purchases in the purchases journal from recording cash payments in the cash payments journal. Separating duties in this way prevents an individual from establishing a fictitious supplier and then collecting payments for fictitious purchases from this supplier.

Purchases Journal   The **purchases journal** is designed for recording all *purchases on account. Cash purchases would be recorded in the cash payments journal.* The purchases journal has a column entitled *Accounts Payable Cr.* The purchases journal also has special columns for recording debits to the accounts most often affected. Since NetSolutions makes frequent debits to its supplies account, a *Supplies Dr.* column is included for these transactions. For example, as shown in Exhibit 5, NetSolutions recorded the purchase of supplies on March 3 by entering *600* in the *Supplies Dr.* column, *600* in the *Accounts Payable Cr.* column, and *Howard Supplies* in the *Account Credited* column.

The *Other Accounts Dr.* column in Exhibit 5 is used to record purchases, on account, of any item for which there is no special debit column. The title of the account to be debited is entered in the *Other Accounts Dr.* column, and the amount is entered in the

EXHIBIT 5   Purchases Journal and Postings

PURCHASES JOURNAL   Page 11

	Date	Account Credited	Post. Ref.	Accounts Payable Cr.	Supplies Dr.	Other Accounts Dr.	Post. Ref.	Amount	
	2008								
1	Mar. 3	Howard Supplies	✔	600	600				1
2	7	Donnelly Supplies	✔	420	420				2
3	12	Jewett Business Systems	✔	2,800		Office Equipment	18	2,800	3
4	19	Donnelly Supplies	✔	1,450	1,450				4
5	27	Howard Supplies	✔	960	960				5
6	31			6,230	3,430			2,800	6
7				(21)	(14)			(✔)	7

GENERAL LEDGER

ACCOUNT Accounts Payable   **Account No. 21**

Date	Item	Post. Ref.	Dr.	Cr.	Balance
2008					
Mar. 1	Balance	✔			1,230
31		P11		6,230	7,460

ACCOUNT Supplies   **Account No. 14**

Date	Item	Post. Ref.	Dr.	Cr.	Balance
2008					
Mar. 1	Balance	✔			2,500
31		P11	3,430		5,930

ACCOUNT Office Equipment   **Account No. 18**

Date	Item	Post. Ref.	Dr.	Cr.	Balance
2008					
Mar. 1	Balance	✔			2,500
12		P11	2,800		5,300

ACCOUNTS PAYABLE SUBSIDIARY LEDGER

NAME: Donnelly Supplies

Date	Item	Post. Ref.	Dr.	Cr.	Balance
2008					
Mar. 7		P11		420	420
19		P11		1,450	1,870

NAME: Grayco Supplies

Date	Item	Post. Ref.	Dr.	Cr.	Balance
2008					
Mar. 1	Balance	✔			1,230

NAME: Howard Supplies

Date	Item	Post. Ref.	Dr.	Cr.	Balance
2008					
Mar. 3		P11		600	600
27		P11		960	1,560

NAME: Jewett Business Systems

Date	Item	Post. Ref.	Dr.	Cr.	Balance
2008					
Mar. 12		P11		2,800	2,800

Purchases are often initiated with a request to a vendor, termed a *purchase order*.

Amount column. For example, NetSolutions recorded the purchase of office equipment on account on March 12 by entering *Office Equipment* in the *Other Accounts Dr.* column, *2,800* in the *Amount* column, *2,800* in the *Accounts Payable Cr.* column, and *Jewett Business Systems* in the *Account Credited* column.

Postings from the purchases journal to the ledgers of NetSolutions are also shown in Exhibit 5. The principles used in posting the purchases journal are similar to those used in posting the revenue and cash receipts journals. The source of the entries posted to the subsidiary and general ledgers is indicated in the *Posting Reference* column of each account by inserting the letter *P* (for purchases journal) and the page number of the purchases journal. A check mark (✓) is inserted in the *Posting Reference* column of the purchases journal after each credit is posted to a creditor's account in the accounts payable subsidiary ledger.

At regular intervals, the amounts in the *Other Accounts Dr.* column are posted to the accounts in the general ledger. As each amount is posted, the related general ledger account number is inserted in the *Posting Reference* column of the *Other Accounts* section.

At the end of each month, the amount columns in the purchases journal are totaled. The sum of the two debit column totals should equal the sum of the credit column.

The totals of the *Accounts Payable Cr.* and *Supplies Dr.* columns are posted to the appropriate general ledger accounts in the usual manner, with the related account numbers inserted below the column totals. Because each amount in the *Other Accounts Dr.* column was posted individually, a check mark is placed below the $2,800 total to show that no further action is needed.

Cash Payments Journal   The special columns for the **cash payments journal** are determined in the same manner as for the revenue, cash receipts, and purchases journals. The determining factors are the kinds of transactions to be recorded and how often they occur.

The cash payments journal has a *Cash Cr.* column, as shown in Exhibit 6. All transactions recorded in the cash payments journal will involve an entry in this column. Payments to creditors on account happen often enough to require an *Accounts Payable Dr.* column. Debits to creditor accounts for invoices paid, often called *bills*, are recorded in the *Accounts Payable Dr.* column. For example, on March 15 NetSolutions paid $1,230 on its account with Grayco Supplies. NetSolutions recorded this transaction by entering *1,230* in the *Accounts Payable Dr.* column, *1,230* in the *Cash Cr.* column, and *Grayco Supplies* in the *Account Debited* column.

NetSolutions makes all payments by check. As each transaction is recorded in the cash payments journal, the related check number is entered in the column at the right of the *Date* column. The check numbers are helpful in controlling cash payments, and they provide a useful cross-reference.

The *Other Accounts Dr.* column is used for recording debits to any account for which there is no special column. For example, NetSolutions paid $1,600 on March 2 for rent. The transaction was recorded by entering *Rent Expense* in the space provided and *1,600* in the *Other Accounts Dr.* and *Cash Cr.* columns.

Postings from the cash payments journal to the ledgers of NetSolutions are also shown in Exhibit 6. The amounts entered in the *Accounts Payable Dr.* column are posted to the individual creditor accounts in the accounts payable subsidiary ledger. These postings should be made frequently. After each posting, *CP* (for cash payments journal) and the page number of the journal are inserted in the *Posting Reference* column of the account. A check mark is placed in the *Posting Reference* column of the cash payments journal to indicate that each amount has been posted.

At regular intervals, each item in the *Other Accounts Dr.* column is also posted individually to an account in the general ledger. The posting is indicated by writing the account number in the *Posting Reference* column of the cash payments journal.

At the end of the month, each of the amount columns in the cash payments journal is totaled. The sum of the two debit totals is compared with the credit total to determine their equality. A check mark is placed below the total of the *Other Accounts Dr.* column to indicate that no further action is needed. When each of the totals of the other two columns is posted to the general ledger, an account number is inserted below each column total.

Accounts Payable Control and Subsidiary Ledger   After all posting has been completed for the month, the sum of the balances in the accounts payable subsidiary ledger should be compared with the balance of the accounts payable control account in the general

EXHIBIT 6   Cash Payments Journal and Postings

CASH PAYMENTS JOURNAL

Page 7

	Date	Ck. No.	Account Debited	Post. Ref.	Other Accounts Dr.	Accounts Payable Dr.	Cash Cr.	
	2008							
1	Mar. 2	150	Rent Expense	52	1,600		1,600	1
2	15	151	Grayco Supplies	✔		1,230	1,230	2
3	21	152	Jewett Business Systems	✔		2,800	2,800	3
4	22	153	Donnelly Supplies	✔		420	420	4
5	30	154	Utilities Expense	54	1,050		1,050	5
6	31	155	Howard Supplies	✔		600	600	6
7	31				2,650	5,050	7,700	7
8					(✔)	(21)	(11)	8

GENERAL LEDGER

ACCOUNT   Accounts Payable   Account No. 21

Date	Item	Post. Ref.	Dr.	Cr.	Balance
2008					
Mar. 1	Balance	✔			1,230
31		P11		6,230	7,460
31		CP7	5,050		2,410

ACCOUNT   Cash   Account No. 11

Date	Item	Post. Ref.	Dr.	Cr.	Balance
2008					
Mar. 1	Balance	✔			6,200
31		CR14	7,750		13,950
31		CP7		7,700	6,250

ACCOUNT   Rent Expense   Account No. 52

Date	Item	Post. Ref.	Dr.	Cr.	Balance
2008					
Mar. 2		CP7	1,600		1,600

ACCOUNT   Utilities Expense   Account No. 54

Date	Item	Post. Ref.	Dr.	Cr.	Balance
2008					
Mar. 30		CP7	1,050		1,050

ACCOUNTS PAYABLE SUBSIDIARY LEDGER

NAME: Donnelly Supplies

Date	Item	Post. Ref.	Dr.	Cr.	Balance
2008					
Mar. 7		P11		420	420
19		P11		1,450	1,870
22		CP7	420		1,450

NAME: Grayco Supplies

Date	Item	Post. Ref.	Dr.	Cr.	Balance
2008					
Mar. 1	Balance	✔			1,230
15		CP7	1,230		—

NAME: Howard Supplies

Date	Item	Post. Ref.	Dr.	Cr.	Balance
2008					
Mar. 3		P11		600	600
27		P11		960	1,560
31		CP7	600		960

NAME: Jewett Business Systems

Date	Item	Post. Ref.	Dr.	Cr.	Balance
2008					
Mar. 12		P11		2,800	2,800
21		CP7	2,800		—

ledger. If the controlling account and the subsidiary ledger do not agree, the error or errors must be located and corrected. The balances of the individual creditor (supplier) accounts may be summarized in a supplier balance summary report. The total of NetSolutions' supplier balance summary report, $2,410, agrees with the balance of the accounts payable control account on March 31, 2008, as shown below.

Accounts Payable (Control)		NetSolutions Supplier Balance Summary March 31, 2008	
Balance, March 1, 2008	$ 1,230	Donnelly Supplies	$1,450
Total credits (from purchases journal)	6,230	Grayco Supplies	0
Total debits		Howard Supplies	960
(from cash payments journal)	(5,050)	Jewett Business Systems	0
Balance, March 31, 2008	$ 2,410	Total	$2,410

Exercises

EX C-1
Identify journals

Assuming the use of a two-column (all-purpose) general journal, a revenue journal, and a cash receipts journal as illustrated in this chapter, indicate the journal in which each of the following transactions should be recorded:

a. Receipt of cash for rent.
b. Receipt of cash refund from overpayment of taxes.
c. Closing of dividends account at the end of the year.
d. Sale of office supplies on account, at cost, to a neighboring business.
e. Receipt of cash from sale of office equipment.
f. Providing services for cash.
g. Adjustment to record accrued salaries at the end of the year.
h. Receipt of cash on account from a customer.
i. Providing services on account.
j. Investment of additional cash in the business by issuing capital stock.

EX C-2
Identify journals

Assuming the use of a two-column (all-purpose) general journal, a purchases journal, and a cash payments journal as illustrated in this chapter, indicate the journal in which each of the following transactions should be recorded:

a. Adjustment to prepaid insurance at the end of the month.
b. Adjustment to prepaid rent at the end of the month.
c. Purchase of office supplies for cash.
d. Purchase of office supplies on account.
e. Payment of six months' rent in advance.
f. Purchase of services on account.
g. Adjustment to record depreciation at the end of the month.
h. Adjustment to record accrued salaries at the end of the period.
i. Advance payment of a one-year fire insurance policy on the office.
j. Purchase of an office computer on account.
k. Purchase of office equipment for cash.

EX C-3
Identify postings from revenue journal

Using the following revenue journal for Omega Services Inc., identify each of the posting references, indicated by a letter, as representing (1) posting to general ledger accounts or (2) posting to subsidiary ledger accounts.

REVENUE JOURNAL

Date	Invoice No.	Account Debited	Post. Ref.	Accounts Receivable Dr. Fees Earned Cr.
2008				
Sept. 1	772	Environmental Safety Co.	(a)	$2,625
10	773	Greenberg Co.	(b)	1,050
20	774	Eco-Systems	(c)	1,400
27	775	SSC Corp.	(d)	965
30				$6,040
				(e)

EX C-4
Identify transactions in accounts receivable ledger

The debits and credits from three related transactions are presented in the following customer's account taken from the accounts receivable subsidiary ledger.

NAME   *Impact Graphic Design*
ADDRESS   *1319 Elm Street*

Date	Item	Post. Ref.	Debit	Credit	Balance
2008					
Dec. 3		R50	680		680
9		J9		70	610
13		CR38		610	—

Describe each transaction, and identify the source of each posting.

EX C-5
Identify postings from purchases journal

Using the following purchases journal, identify each of the posting references, indicated by a letter, as representing (1) a posting to a general ledger account, (2) a posting to a subsidiary ledger account, or (3) that no posting is required.

PURCHASES JOURNAL   Page 49

Date	Account Credited	Post. Ref.	Accounts Payable Cr.	Store Supplies Dr.	Office Supplies Dr.	Other Accounts Dr. Account	Post. Ref.	Amount
2008								
June 4	Corter Supply Co.	(a)	4,200		4,200			
6	Coastal Insurance Co.	(b)	5,325			Prepaid Insurance	(c)	5,325
11	Office To Go	(d)	2,000			Office Equipment	(e)	2,000
13	Taylor Products	(f)	1,675	1,400	275			
20	Office To Go	(g)	5,500			Store Equipment	(h)	5,500
27	Miller Supply Co.	(i)	2,740	2,740				
30			21,440	4,140	4,475			12,825
			(j)	(k)	(l)			(m)

EX C-6
Identify postings from cash payments journal

Using the following cash payments journal, identify each of the posting references, indicated by a letter, as representing (1) a posting to a general ledger account, (2) a posting to a subsidiary ledger account, or (3) that no posting is required.

CASH PAYMENTS JOURNAL

Page 46

Date	Ck. No.	Account Debited	Post. Ref.	Other Accounts Dr.	Accounts Payable Dr.	Cash Cr.
2008						
Oct. 3	611	Aquatic Systems Co.	(a)		4,000	4,000
5	612	Utilities Expense	(b)	325		325
10	613	Prepaid Rent	(c)	3,200		3,200
17	614	Advertising Expense	(d)	640		640
20	615	Derby Co.	(e)		1,450	1,450
22	616	Office Equipment	(f)	3,900		3,900
25	617	Office Supplies	(g)	250		250
27	618	Evans Co.	(h)		5,500	5,500
31	619	Salaries Expense	(i)	1,750		1,750
31				10,065	10,950	21,015
				(j)	(k)	(l)

EX C-7

Identify transactions in accounts payable ledger account

The debits and credits from three related transactions are presented in the following creditor's account taken from the accounts payable ledger.

NAME *Moore Co.*
ADDRESS *101 W. Stratford Ave.*

Date	Item	Post. Ref.	Debit	Credit	Balance
2008					
Mar. 6		P34		12,200	12,200
10		J10	300		11,900
16		CP37	11,900		—

Describe each transaction, and identify the source of each posting.

Problems

PR C-1

Revenue journal; accounts receivable and general ledgers

✓ 1. Revenue journal, total fees earned, $1,060

A-Plus Learning Centers was established on March 20, 2008, to provide educational services. The services provided during the remainder of the month are as follows:

Mar. 21. Issued Invoice No. 1 to J. Dunlop for $70 on account.
22. Issued Invoice No. 2 to K. Thorne for $310 on account.
24. Issued Invoice No. 3 to T. Morris for $95 on account.
25. Provided educational services, $125, to K. Thorne in exchange for educational supplies.
27. Issued Invoice No. 4 to F. Mintz for $190 on account.
28. Issued Invoice No. 5 to D. Bennett for $175 on account.
30. Issued Invoice No. 6 to K. Thorne for $105 on account.
31. Issued Invoice No. 7 to T. Morris for $115 on account.

Instructions

1. Journalize the transactions for March, using a single-column revenue journal and a two-column general journal. Post to the following customer accounts in the accounts receivable ledger, and insert the balance immediately after recording each entry: D. Bennett; J. Dunlop; F. Mintz; T. Morris; K. Thorne.

(continued)

2. Post the revenue journal and the general journal to the following accounts in the general ledger, inserting the account balances only after the last postings:

12	Accounts Receivable
13	Supplies
41	Fees Earned

3. a. What is the sum of the balances of the accounts in the subsidiary ledger at March 31?
   b. What is the balance of the controlling account at March 31?
4. Assume that on April 1, the state in which A-Plus operates begins requiring that sales tax be collected on educational services. Briefly explain how the revenue journal may be modified to accommodate sales of services on account that require the collection of a state sales tax.

PR C-2

Revenue and cash receipts journals; accounts receivable and general ledgers

✓ *3. Total cash receipts, $34,680*

Transactions related to revenue and cash receipts completed by Palm Beech Architects Co. during the period September 2–30, 2008, are as follows:

Sept. 2. Issued Invoice No. 793 to Morton Co., $5,400.
    5. Received cash from Mendez Co. for the balance owed on its account.
    6. Issued Invoice No. 794 to Quest Co., $1,980.
    13. Issued Invoice No. 795 to Shilo Co., $2,950.
        Post revenue and collections to the accounts receivable subsidiary ledger.
    15. Received cash from Quest Co. for the balance owed on September 1.
    16. Issued Invoice No. 796 to Quest Co., $6,100.
        Post revenue and collections to the accounts receivable subsidiary ledger.
    19. Received cash from Morton Co. for the balance due on invoice of September 2.
    20. Received cash from Quest Co. for invoice of September 6.
    22. Issued Invoice No. 797 to Mendez Co., $8,020.
    25. Received $2,000 note receivable in partial settlement of the balance due on the Shilo Co. account.
    30. Recorded cash fees earned, $11,930.
        Post revenue and collections to the accounts receivable subsidiary ledger.

Instructions
1. Insert the following balances in the general ledger as of September 1:

11	Cash	$13,650
12	Accounts Receivable	15,370
14	Notes Receivable	5,000
41	Fees Earned	—

2. Insert the following balances in the accounts receivable subsidiary ledger as of September 1:

Mendez Co.	$8,960
Morton Co.	—
Quest Co.	6,410
Shilo Co.	—

3. Prepare a single-column revenue journal and a cash receipts journal. Use the following column headings for the cash receipts journal: Fees Earned, Accounts Receivable, and Cash. The Fees Earned column is used to record cash fees. Insert a check mark (✓) in the Post. Ref. column.
4. Using the two special journals and the two-column general journal, journalize the transactions for September. Post to the accounts receivable subsidiary ledger, and insert the balances at the points indicated in the narrative of transactions. Determine the balance in the customer's account before recording a cash receipt.
5. Total each of the columns of the special journals, and post the individual entries and totals to the general ledger. Insert account balances after the last posting.
6. Determine that the subsidiary ledger agrees with the controlling account in the general ledger.

PR C-3
Purchases, accounts payable account, and accounts payable ledger

✓3. Total accounts payable credit, $16,500

Forever Spring Landscaping designs and installs landscaping. The landscape designers and office staff use office supplies, while field supplies (rock, bark, etc.) are used in the actual landscaping. Purchases on account completed by Forever Spring Landscaping during May 2008 are as follows:

May 2. Purchased office supplies on account from Lawson Co., $360.
     5. Purchased office equipment on account from Peach Computers Co., $5,150.
     9. Purchased office supplies on account from Executive Office Supply Co., $305.
    13. Purchased field supplies on account from Yee Co., $1,360.
    14. Purchased field supplies on account from Nelson Co., $2,940.
    17. Purchased field supplies on account from Yee Co., $1,345.
    24. Purchased field supplies on account from Nelson Co., $3,810.
    29. Purchased office supplies on account from Executive Office Supply Co., $225.
    31. Purchased field supplies on account from Nelson Co., $1,005.

Instructions
1. Insert the following balances in the general ledger as of May 1:

14	Field Supplies	$ 6,310
15	Office Supplies	830
18	Office Equipment	14,300
21	Accounts Payable	1,105

2. Insert the following balances in the accounts payable subsidiary ledger as of May 1:

Executive Office Supply	$365
Lawson Co.	740
Nelson Co.	—
Peach Computers Co.	—
Yee Co.	—

3. Journalize the transactions for May, using a purchases journal similar to the one illustrated in this chapter. Prepare the purchases journal with columns for Accounts Payable, Field Supplies, Office Supplies, and Other Accounts. Post to the creditor accounts in the accounts payable subsidiary ledger immediately after each entry.
4. Post the purchases journal to the accounts in the general ledger.
5. a. What is the sum of the balances in the subsidiary ledger at May 31?
   b. What is the balance of the controlling account at May 31?

PR C-4
Purchases and cash payments journals; accounts payable and general ledgers

✓1. Total cash payments, $81,160

Artesian Springs Water Testing Service was established on September 16, 2008. Artesian uses field equipment and field supplies (chemicals and other supplies) to analyze water for unsafe contaminants in streams, lakes, and ponds. Transactions related to purchases and cash payments during the remainder of September are as follows:

Sept. 16. Issued Check No. 1 in payment of rent for the remainder of September, $1,500.
     16. Purchased field supplies on account from Heath Supply Co., $4,360.
     16. Purchased field equipment on account from Test-Rite Equipment Co., $15,900.
     17. Purchased office supplies on account from Baker Supply Co., $280.
     19. Issued Check No. 2 in payment of field supplies, $2,420, and office supplies, $300.
         Post the journals to the accounts payable subsidiary ledger.
     23. Purchased office supplies on account from Baker Supply Co., $410.
     23. Issued Check No. 3 to purchase land, $35,000.
     24. Issued Check No. 4 to Heath Supply Co. in payment of invoice, $4,360.
     26. Issued Check No. 5 to Test-Rite Equipment Co. in payment of invoice, $15,900.
         Post the journals to the accounts payable subsidiary ledger.
     30. Acquired land in exchange for field equipment having a cost of $7,000.
     30. Purchased field supplies on account from Heath Supply Co., $5,300.
     30. Issued Check No. 6 to Baker Supply Co. in payment of invoice, $280.
     30. Purchased the following from Test-Rite Equipment Co. on account: field supplies, $700, and field equipment, $3,600.
     30. Issued Check No. 7 in payment of salaries, $21,400.
         Post the journals to the accounts payable subsidiary ledger.

Instructions

1. Journalize the transactions for September. Use a purchases journal and a cash payments journal, similar to those illustrated in this chapter, and a two-column general journal. Use debit columns for Field Supplies, Office Supplies, and Other Accounts in the purchases journal. Refer to the following partial chart of accounts:

11	Cash	19	Land
14	Field Supplies	21	Accounts Payable
15	Office Supplies	61	Salary Expense
17	Field Equipment	71	Rent Expense

At the points indicated in the narrative of transactions, post to the following accounts in the accounts payable subsidiary ledger:

> Baker Supply Co.
> Heath Supply Co.
> Test-Rite Equipment Co.

2. Post the individual entries (Other Accounts columns of the purchases journal and the cash payments journal and both columns of the general journal) to the appropriate general ledger accounts.
3. Total each of the columns of the purchases journal and the cash payments journal, and post the appropriate totals to the general ledger. (Because the problem does not include transactions related to cash receipts, the cash account in the ledger will have a credit balance.)
4. Prepare a supplier balance summary report.

PR C-5

All journals and general ledger; trial balance

✓ *2. Total cash receipts, $52,560*

The transactions completed by Lightening Express Delivery Company during July 2008, the first month of the fiscal year, were as follows:

July 1. Issued Check No. 610 for July rent, $6,400.
     2. Issued Invoice No. 940 to Capps Co., $2,420.
     3. Received check for $5,400 from Perkins Co. in payment of account.
     5. Purchased a vehicle on account from Browning Transportation, $31,600.
     6. Purchased office equipment on account from Bell Computer Co., $4,200.
     6. Issued Invoice No. 941 to Darr Co., $5,920.
     9. Issued Check No. 611 for fuel expense, $850.
    10. Received check from Shingo Co. in payment of $4,050 invoice.
    10. Issued Check No. 612 for $905 to Office To Go Inc. in payment of invoice.
    10. Issued Invoice No. 942 to Joy Co., $1,260.
    11. Issued Check No. 613 for $3,605 to Crowne Supply Co. in payment of account.
    11. Issued Check No. 614 for $805 to Porter Co. in payment of account.
    12. Received check from Capps Co. in payment of $2,420 invoice.
    13. Issued Check No. 615 to Browning Transportation in payment of $31,600 balance.
    16. Issued Check No. 616 for $38,900 for cash purchase of a vehicle.
    16. Cash fees earned for July 1–16, $17,800.
    17. Issued Check No. 617 for miscellaneous administrative expense, $260.
    18. Purchased maintenance supplies on account from Crowne Supply Co., $1,730.
    19. Purchased the following on account from McClain Co.: maintenance supplies, $1,980; office supplies, $430.
    20. Issued Check No. 618 in payment of advertising expense, $1,700.
    20. Used $3,500 maintenance supplies to repair delivery vehicles.
    23. Purchased office supplies on account from Office To Go Inc., $600.
    24. Issued Invoice No. 943 to Shingo Co., $5,070.
    24. Issued Check No. 619 as a dividend, $3,000.
    25. Issued Invoice No. 944 to Darr Co., $6,200.
    25. Received check for $3,950 from Perkins Co. in payment of balance.
    26. Issued Check No. 620 to Bell Computer Co. in payment of $4,200 invoice of July 6.
    30. Issued Check No. 621 for monthly salaries as follows: driver salaries, $16,500; office salaries, $8,200.
    31. Cash fees earned for July 17–31, $18,940.
    31. Issued Check No. 622 in payment for office supplies, $800.

Instructions

1. Enter the following account balances in the general ledger as of July 1:

11	Cash	$158,965	32	Retained Earnings	$197,950
12	Accounts Receivable	13,400	33	Dividends	—
14	Maintenance Supplies	9,300	41	Fees Earned	—
15	Office Supplies	4,500	51	Driver Salaries Expense	—
16	Office Equipment	24,300	52	Maintenance Supplies	
17	Accumulated Depreciation			Expense	—
	—Office Equipment	4,500	53	Fuel Expense	—
18	Vehicles	84,600	61	Office Salaries Expense	—
19	Accumulated Depreciation		62	Rent Expense	—
	—Vehicles	12,300	63	Advertising Expense	—
21	Accounts Payable	5,315	64	Miscellaneous Administrative	
31	Capital Stock	75,000		Expense	—

2. Journalize the transactions for July 2008, using the following journals similar to those illustrated in this chapter: cash receipts journal, purchases journal (with columns for Accounts Payable, Maintenance Supplies, Office Supplies, and Other Accounts), single-column revenue journal, cash payments journal, and two-column general journal. Assume that the daily postings to the individual accounts in the accounts payable ledger and the accounts receivable ledger have been made.
3. Post the appropriate individual entries to the general ledger.
4. Total each of the columns of the special journals, and post the appropriate totals to the general ledger; insert the account balances.
5. Prepare an unadjusted trial balance.
6. Verify the agreement of each subsidiary ledger with its control account. The sum of the balances of the accounts in the subsidiary ledgers as of July 31 are:

Accounts Receivable	$18,450
Accounts Payable	4,740

Appendix D ● ● ● ● ● ● ● ● ● ● ● ● ● ● ● ● ● ● ●

End-of-Period Spreadsheet (Work Sheet) for a Merchandising Business

A merchandising business may use an end-of-period spreadsheet (work sheet) in assembling the data for preparing financial statements and adjusting and closing entries. In this appendix, we illustrate such a spreadsheet (work sheet) for the perpetual inventory system.

The end-of-period spreadsheet (work sheet) in Exhibit 1 is for NetSolutions on December 31, 2009. In this spreadsheet (work sheet), we list all of the accounts, including the accounts that have no balances, in the order that they appear in Net-Solutions' ledger.

The data needed for adjusting the accounts of NetSolutions are as follows:

Physical merchandise inventory on December 31, 2009		$62,150
Office supplies on hand on December 31, 2009		480
Insurance expired during 2009		1,910
Depreciation during 2009 on: Store equipment		3,100
Office equipment		2,490
Salaries accrued on December 31, 2009: Sales salaries	$780	
Office salaries	360	1,140
Rent earned during 2009		600

There is no specific order in which to analyze the accounts in the spreadsheet (work sheet), assemble the adjustment data, and make the adjusting entries. However, you can normally save time by selecting the accounts in the order in which they appear on the trial balance. Using this approach, the adjustment for merchandise inventory shrinkage is listed first as entry (a) on the spreadsheet (work sheet), followed by the adjustment for office supplies used as entry (b), and so on.

After all the adjustments have been entered on the spreadsheet (work sheet), the Adjustments columns are totaled to prove the equality of debits and credits. As we illustrated in Chapter 4, the adjusted amounts of the balances in the Trial Balance columns are extended to the Adjusted Trial Balance columns.[1] The Adjusted Trial Balance columns are then totaled to prove the equality of debits and credits.

The balances, as adjusted, are then extended to the statement columns. The four statement columns are totaled, and the net income or net loss is determined. For Net-Solutions, the difference between the credit and debit columns of the Income Statement section is $75,400, the amount of the net income. The difference between the debit and credit columns of the Balance Sheet section is also $75,400, which is the increase in retained earnings as a result of the net income. Agreement between the two balancing amounts is evidence of debit-credit equality and mathematical accuracy.

---

1 Some accountants prefer to eliminate the Adjusted Trial Balance columns and to extend the adjusted balances directly to the statement columns. Such a spreadsheet (work sheet) is often used if there are only a few adjustment items.

EXHIBIT 1 — End-of-Period Spreadsheet (Work Sheet) for Merchandising Business Using Perpetual Inventory System

	A	B	C	D	E	F	G	H	I	J	K	

NetSolutions
End-of-Period Spreadsheet (Work Sheet)
For the Year Ended December 31, 2009

	Account Title	Unadjusted Trial Balance		Adjustments		Adjusted Trial Balance		Income Statement		Balance Sheet		
		Dr.	Cr.	Dr.	Cr.	Dr.	Cr.	Dr.	Cr.	Dr.	Cr.	
1	Cash	52,950				52,950				52,950		1
2	Accounts Receivable	91,080				91,080				91,080		2
3	Merchandise Inventory	63,950			(a)1,800	62,150				62,150		3
4	Office Supplies	1,090			(b) 610	480				480		4
5	Prepaid Insurance	4,560			(c)1,910	2,650				2,650		5
6	Land	20,000				20,000				20,000		6
7	Store Equipment	27,100				27,100				27,100		7
8	Accum. Depr.—Store Equipment		2,600		(d)3,100		5,700				5,700	8
9	Office Equipment	15,570				15,570				15,570		9
10	Accum. Depr.—Office Equipment		2,230		(e)2,490		4,720				4,720	10
11	Accounts Payable		22,420				22,420				22,420	11
12	Salaries Payable				(f)1,140		1,140				1,140	12
13	Unearned Rent		2,400	(g) 600			1,800				1,800	13
14	Notes Payable											14
15	(final payment due 2017)		25,000				25,000				25,000	15
16	Capital Stock		25,000				25,000				25,000	16
17	Retained Earnings		128,800				128,800				128,800	17
18	Dividends	18,000				18,000				18,000		18
19	Sales		720,185				720,185		720,185			19
20	Sales Returns and Allowances	6,140				6,140		6,140				20
21	Sales Discounts	5,790				5,790		5,790				21
22	Cost of Merchandise Sold	523,505		(a)1,800		525,305		525,305				22
23	Sales Salaries Expense	52,650		(f) 780		53,430		53,430				23
24	Advertising Expense	10,860				10,860		10,860				24
25	Depr. Exp.—Store Equipment			(d)3,100		3,100		3,100				25
26	Delivery Expense	2,800				2,800		2,800				26
27	Miscellaneous Selling Expense	630				630		630				27
28	Office Salaries Expense	20,660		(f) 360		21,020		21,020				28
29	Rent Expense	8,100				8,100		8,100				29
30	Depr. Exp.—Office Equipment			(e)2,490		2,490		2,490				30
31	Insurance Expense			(c)1,910		1,910		1,910				31
32	Office Supplies Expense			(b) 610		610		610				32
33	Misc. Administrative Expense	760				760		760				33
34	Rent Revenue				(g) 600		600		600			34
35	Interest Expense	2,440				2,440		2,440				35
36		928,635	928,635	11,650	11,650	935,365	935,365	645,385	720,785	289,980	214,580	36
37	Net income							75,400			75,400	37
38								720,785	720,785	289,980	289,980	38
39												39

(a) Merchandise inventory shrinkage for period, $1,800 ($63,950 − $62,150).

(b) Office supplies used, $610 ($1,090 − $480).

(c) Insurance expired, $1,910.

(d) Depreciation of store equipment, $3,100.

(e) Depreciation of office equipment, $2,490.

(f) Salaries accrued but not paid (sales salaries, $780; office salaries, $360), $1,140.

(g) Rent earned from amount received in advance, $600.

The income statement, retained earnings statement, and balance sheet can be prepared from the spreadsheet (work sheet). These financial statements are shown in Exhibits 1, 3, and 4 in Chapter 5. The Adjustments columns in the spreadsheet (work sheet) may be used as the basis for journalizing the adjusting entries. NetSolutions' adjusting entries at the end of 2009 are shown at the top of the following page.

			JOURNAL			Page 28	
	Date		Description	Post. Ref.	Debit	Credit	
1	2009		Adjusting Entries				1
2	Dec.	31	Cost of Merchandise Sold	510	1 8 0 0 00		2
3			Merchandise Inventory	115		1 8 0 0 00	3
4			Inventory shrinkage.				4
5							5
6		31	Office Supplies Expense	534	6 1 0 00		6
7			Office Supplies	116		6 1 0 00	7
8			Supplies used.				8
9							9
10		31	Insurance Expense	533	1 9 1 0 00		10
11			Prepaid Insurance	117		1 9 1 0 00	11
12			Insurance expired.				12
13							13
14		31	Depr. Expense—Store Equipment	522	3 1 0 0 00		14
15			Accumulated Depr.—Store Equipment	124		3 1 0 0 00	15
16			Store equipment depreciation.				16
17							17
18		31	Depr. Expense—Office Equipment	532	2 4 9 0 00		18
19			Accumulated Depr.—Office Equipment	126		2 4 9 0 00	19
20			Office equipment depreciation.				20
21							21
22		31	Sales Salaries Expense	520	7 8 0 00		22
23			Office Salaries Expense	530	3 6 0 00		23
24			Salaries Payable	211		1 1 4 0 00	24
25			Accrued salaries.				25
26							26
27		31	Unearned Rent	212	6 0 0 00		27
28			Rent Revenue	610		6 0 0 00	28
29			Rent earned.				29

The Income Statement columns of the work sheet may be used as the basis for preparing the closing entries. The closing entries for NetSolutions at the end of 2009 are shown on page 233 of Chapter 5.

After the closing entries have been prepared and posted to the accounts, a post-closing trial balance may be prepared to verify the debit-credit equality. The only accounts that should appear on the post-closing trial balance are the asset, contra asset, liability, and stockholders' equity accounts with balances. These are the same accounts that appear on the end-of-period balance sheet.

Problems

PR D-1
*End-of-period
spreadsheet (work sheet),
financial statements, and
adjusting and closing
entries for perpetual
inventory system*

✓*2. Net income: $107,900*

The accounts and their balances in the ledger of Stones Co. on December 31, 2008, are as follows:

Cash	$ 9,000	Sales	$775,000
Accounts Receivable	72,500	Sales Returns and Allowances	11,900
Merchandise Inventory	165,000	Sales Discounts	7,100
Prepaid Insurance	9,700	Cost of Merchandise Sold	457,200
Store Supplies	4,250	Sales Salaries Expense	76,400
Office Supplies	2,100	Advertising Expense	25,000
Store Equipment	160,000	Depreciation Expense—	
Accumulated Depreciation—		Store Equipment	—
Store Equipment	40,300	Store Supplies Expense	—
Office Equipment	70,000	Miscellaneous Selling Expense	1,600
Accumulated Depreciation—		Office Salaries Expense	34,000
Office Equipment	17,200	Rent Expense	16,000
Accounts Payable	66,700	Insurance Expense	—
Salaries Payable	—	Depreciation Expense—	
Unearned Rent	1,200	Office Equipment	—
Note Payable		Office Supplies Expense	—
(final payment due 2016)	125,000	Miscellaneous Administrative	
Capital Stock	10,000	Expense	1,650
Retained Earnings	124,600	Rent Revenue	—
Dividends	25,000	Interest Expense	11,600
Income Summary	—		

The data needed for year-end adjustments on December 31 are as follows:

Physical merchandise inventory on December 31		$159,000
Insurance expired during the year		3,700
Supplies on hand on December 31:		
Store supplies		1,100
Office supplies		600
Depreciation for the year:		
Store equipment		5,000
Office equipment		2,800
Salaries payable on December 31:		
Sales salaries	$2,600	
Office salaries	500	3,100
Unearned rent on December 31		600

Instructions
1. Prepare an end-of-period spreadsheet (work sheet) for the fiscal year ended December 31, 2008. List all accounts in the order given.
2. Prepare a multiple-step income statement.
3. Prepare a retained earnings statement.
4. Prepare a report form of balance sheet, assuming that the current portion of the note payable is $25,000.
5. Journalize the adjusting entries.
6. Journalize the closing entries.

PR D-2
End-of-period spreadsheet (work sheet), financial statements, and adjusting and closing entries for perpetual inventory system

✓ *1. Net income: $49,750*

The accounts and their balances in the ledger of LeClassic Sports Co. on December 31, 2008, are as follows:

Cash	$ 18,000	Sales Returns and Allowances	$ 13,900
Accounts Receivable	42,500	Sales Discounts	7,100
Merchandise Inventory	215,000	Cost of Merchandise Sold	557,000
Prepaid Insurance	9,700	Sales Salaries Expense	81,400
Store Supplies	4,250	Advertising Expense	45,000
Office Supplies	2,100	Depreciation Expense—	
Store Equipment	182,000	Store Equipment	—
Accumulated Depreciation—		Delivery Expense	6,000
Store Equipment	40,300	Store Supplies Expense	—
Office Equipment	60,000	Miscellaneous Selling Expense	1,600
Accumulated Depreciation—		Office Salaries Expense	44,000
Office Equipment	17,200	Rent Expense	25,200
Accounts Payable	56,700	Insurance Expense	—
Salaries Payable	—	Depreciation Expense—	
Unearned Rent	1,200	Office Equipment	—
Note Payable (final payment due, 2013)	125,000	Office Supplies Expense	—
Capital Stock	40,000	Miscellaneous Administrative	
Retained Earnings	177,600	Expense	1,650
Dividends	5,000	Rent Revenue	—
Income Summary	—	Interest Expense	11,600
Sales	875,000		

The data needed for year-end adjustments on December 31 are as follows:

Merchandise inventory on December 31		$210,000
Insurance expired during the year		6,800
Supplies on hand on December 31:		
Store supplies		1,200
Office supplies		750
Depreciation for the year:		
Store equipment		7,500
Office equipment		3,800
Salaries payable on December 31:		
Sales salaries	$2,600	
Office salaries	1,500	4,100
Unearned rent on December 31		400

Instructions

1. Prepare an end-of-period spreadsheet (work sheet) for the fiscal year ended December 31, listing all accounts in the order given.
2. Prepare a multiple-step income statement.
3. Prepare a retained earnings statement.
4. Prepare a report form of balance sheet, assuming that the current portion of the note payable is $15,000.
5. Journalize the adjusting entries.
6. Journalize the closing entries.

Appendix E

WILLIAMS-SONOMA, INC.

2 0 0 5   A N N U A L   R E P O R T

Annual Meeting of Shareholders
May 23, 2006

ITEM 8. FINANCIAL STATEMENTS AND SUPPLEMENTARY DATA

Williams-Sonoma, Inc.
Consolidated Statements of Earnings

	Fiscal Year Ended		
Dollars and shares in thousands, except per share amounts	Jan. 29, 2006	Jan. 30, 2005	Feb. 1, 2004
Net revenues	$3,538,947	$3,136,931	$2,754,368
Cost of goods sold	2,103,465	1,865,786	1,643,791
Gross margin	1,435,482	1,271,145	1,110,577
Selling, general and administrative expenses	1,090,392	961,176	855,790
Interest income	(5,683)	(1,939)	(873)
Interest expense	1,975	1,703	22
Earnings before income taxes	348,798	310,205	255,638
Income taxes	133,932	118,971	98,427
Net earnings	$ 214,866	$ 191,234	$ 157,211
Basic earnings per share	$ 1.86	$ 1.65	$ 1.36
Diluted earnings per share	$ 1.81	$ 1.60	$ 1.32
Shares used in calculation of earnings per share:			
Basic	115,616	116,159	115,583
Diluted	118,427	119,347	119,016

See Notes to Consolidated Financial Statements.

Williams-Sonoma, Inc.
Consolidated Balance Sheets

Dollars and shares in thousands, except per share amounts	Jan. 29, 2006	Jan. 30, 2005
ASSETS		
Current assets		
Cash and cash equivalents	$ 360,982	$ 239,210
Accounts receivable (less allowance for doubtful accounts of $168 and $217)	51,020	42,520
Merchandise inventories – net	520,292	452,421
Prepaid catalog expenses	53,925	53,520
Prepaid expenses	31,847	38,018
Deferred income taxes	57,267	39,015
Other assets	7,831	9,061
Total current assets	1,083,164	873,765
Property and equipment – net	880,305	852,412
Other assets (less accumulated amortization of $679 and $2,066)	18,151	19,368
Total assets	$1,981,620	$1,745,545
LIABILITIES AND SHAREHOLDERS' EQUITY		
Current liabilities		
Accounts payable	$ 196,074	$ 173,781
Accrued salaries, benefits and other	93,434	86,767
Customer deposits	172,775	148,535
Income taxes payable	83,589	72,052
Current portion of long-term debt	18,864	23,435
Other liabilities	25,656	17,587
Total current liabilities	590,392	522,157
Deferred rent and lease incentives	218,254	212,193
Long-term debt	14,490	19,154
Deferred income tax liabilities	18,455	21,057
Other long-term obligations	14,711	13,322
Total liabilities	856,302	787,883
Commitments and contingencies – See Note L		
Shareholders' equity		
Preferred stock, $.01 par value, 7,500 shares authorized, none issued	—	—
Common stock, $.01 par value, 253,125 shares authorized, 114,779 shares issued and outstanding at January 29, 2006; 115,372 shares issued and outstanding at January 30, 2005	1,148	1,154
Additional paid-in capital	325,146	286,720
Retained earnings	791,329	664,619
Accumulated other comprehensive income	7,695	5,169
Total shareholders' equity	1,125,318	957,662
Total liabilities and shareholders' equity	$1,981,620	$1,745,545

See Notes to Consolidated Financial Statements.

Form 10-K

Williams-Sonoma, Inc.
Consolidated Statements of Shareholders' Equity

Dollars and shares in thousands	Common Stock		Additional Paid-in Capital	Retained Earnings	Accumulated Other Comprehensive Income (Loss)	Deferred Stock-Based Compensation	Total Shareholders' Equity	Comprehensive Income
	Shares	Amount						
Balance at February 2, 2003	114,317	$1,143	$196,259	$446,837	$ (11)	$(250)	$ 643,978	
Net earnings	—	—	—	157,211	—	—	157,211	$157,211
Foreign currency translation adjustment and related tax effect	—	—	—	—	3,298	—	3,298	3,298
Exercise of stock options and related tax effect	3,295	33	59,516	—	—	—	59,549	
Repurchase and retirement of common stock	(1,785)	(18)	(3,450)	(56,227)	—	—	(59,695)	
Amortization of deferred stock-based compensation	—	—	—	—	—	250	250	
Comprehensive income								$160,509
Balance at February 1, 2004	115,827	1,158	252,325	547,821	3,287	—	804,591	
Net earnings	—	—	—	191,234	—	—	191,234	$191,234
Foreign currency translation adjustment	—	—	—	—	1,882	—	1,882	1,882
Exercise of stock options and related tax effect	1,818	18	39,257	—	—	—	39,275	
Repurchase and retirement of common stock	(2,273)	(22)	(4,862)	(74,436)	—	—	(79,320)	
Comprehensive income								$193,116
Balance at January 30, 2005	115,372	1,154	286,720	664,619	5,169	—	957,662	
Net earnings	—	—	—	214,866	—	—	214,866	$214,866
Foreign currency translation adjustment	—	—	—	—	2,526	—	2,526	2,526
Exercise of stock options and related tax effect	1,829	18	43,727	—	—	—	43,745	
Repurchase and retirement of common stock	(2,422)	(24)	(5,741)	(88,156)	—	—	(93,921)	
Stock-based compensation expense	—	—	440	—	—	—	440	
Comprehensive income								$217,392
Balance at January 29, 2006	114,779	$1,148	$325,146	$791,329	$7,695	$ —	$1,125,318	

See Notes to Consolidated Financial Statements.

Williams-Sonoma, Inc.
Consolidated Statements of Cash Flows

	Fiscal Year Ended		
Dollars in thousands	Jan. 29, 2006	Jan. 30, 2005	Feb. 1, 2004
Cash flows from operating activities:			
Net earnings	$ 214,866	$ 191,234	$ 157,211
Adjustments to reconcile net earnings to net cash provided by operating activities:			
Depreciation and amortization	123,199	111,624	99,534
Loss on disposal/impairment of assets	12,050	1,080	2,353
Amortization of deferred lease incentives	(24,909)	(22,530)	(19,513)
Deferred income taxes	(20,791)	(6,254)	(6,472)
Tax benefit from exercise of stock options	15,743	13,085	20,429
Stock-based compensation expense	440	—	250
Other	—	335	—
Changes in:			
Accounts receivable	(6,829)	(10,900)	2,796
Merchandise inventories	(67,474)	(48,017)	(82,196)
Prepaid catalog expenses	(405)	(15,056)	(3,302)
Prepaid expenses and other assets	9,032	(19,702)	(15,161)
Accounts payable	14,365	17,773	(11,358)
Accrued salaries, benefits and other	15,950	9,955	(1,020)
Customer deposits	24,066	32,273	23,014
Deferred rent and lease incentives	27,661	42,080	34,800
Income taxes payable	11,409	7,457	7,986
Net cash provided by operating activities	348,373	304,437	209,351
Cash flows from investing activities:			
Purchases of property and equipment	(151,788)	(181,453)	(211,979)
Net cash used in investing activities	(151,788)	(181,453)	(211,979)
Cash flows from financing activities:			
Proceeds from bond issuance	—	15,000	—
Repayments of long-term obligations	(9,235)	(9,789)	(7,610)
Proceeds from exercise of stock options	28,002	26,190	39,120
Repurchase of common stock	(93,921)	(79,320)	(59,695)
Credit facility costs	(654)	(288)	(41)
Net cash used in financing activities	(75,808)	(48,207)	(28,226)
Effect of exchange rates on cash and cash equivalents	995	523	1,269
Net increase (decrease) in cash and cash equivalents	121,772	75,300	(29,585)
Cash and cash equivalents at beginning of year	239,210	163,910	193,495
Cash and cash equivalents at end of year	$ 360,982	$ 239,210	$ 163,910
Supplemental disclosure of cash flow information:			
Cash paid during the year for:			
Interest[1]	$ 3,352	$ 3,585	$ 2,367
Income taxes	130,766	105,910	79,184
Non-cash investing and financing activities:			
Assets acquired under capital lease obligations	—	—	1,275
Consolidation of Memphis-based distribution facilities:			
Fixed assets assumed	—	—	19,512
Long-term debt assumed	—	—	18,223
Other long-term liabilities assumed	—	—	1,289

[1] *Interest paid, net of capitalized interest, was $2.2 million, $1.9 million and $0.2 million in fiscal 2005, 2004 and 2003, respectively.*

See Notes to Consolidated Financial Statements.

Williams-Sonoma, Inc.
Notes to Consolidated Financial Statements

Note A: Summary of Significant Accounting Policies

We are a specialty retailer of products for the home. The retail segment of our business sells our products through our six retail store concepts (Williams-Sonoma, Pottery Barn, Pottery Barn Kids, Hold Everything, West Elm and Williams-Sonoma Home). The direct-to-customer segment of our business sells similar products through our eight direct-mail catalogs (Williams-Sonoma, Pottery Barn, Pottery Barn Kids, Pottery Barn Bed + Bath, PBteen, Hold Everything, West Elm and Williams-Sonoma Home) and six e-commerce websites (williams-sonoma.com, potterybarn.com, potterybarnkids.com, pbteen.com, westelm.com and holdeverything.com). The catalogs reach customers throughout the U.S., while the six retail concepts currently operate 570 stores in 43 states, Washington, D.C. and Canada.

In January 2006, we decided to transition the merchandising strategies of our Hold Everything brand into our other existing brands by the end of fiscal 2006. In connection with this transition, we incurred a pre-tax charge of approximately $13,500,000, or $0.07 per diluted share, in the fourth quarter of fiscal 2005. These costs primarily included the initial asset impairment and lease termination costs associated with the shutdown of the Hold Everything retail stores, the asset impairment of the e-commerce website, and the write-down of impaired merchandise inventories. Of this pre-tax charge, approximately $4,500,000 is included in cost of goods sold and approximately $9,000,000 is included in selling, general, and administrative expenses. We expect to incur an additional after-tax charge of $0.03 per diluted share in the first half of fiscal 2006.

Significant intercompany transactions and accounts have been eliminated.

Fiscal Year
Our fiscal year ends on the Sunday closest to January 31, based on a 52/53-week year. Fiscal years 2005, 2004 and 2003 ended on January 29, 2006 (52 weeks), January 30, 2005 (52 weeks) and February 1, 2004 (52 weeks), respectively. The Company's next 53-week fiscal year will be fiscal 2007, ending on February 3, 2008.

Use of Estimates
The preparation of financial statements in accordance with accounting principles generally accepted in the United States of America requires us to make estimates and assumptions that affect the reported amounts of assets, liabilities, revenues and expenses and related disclosures of contingent assets and liabilities. These estimates and assumptions are evaluated on an on-going basis and are based on historical experience and various other factors that we believe to be reasonable under the circumstances. Actual results could differ from these estimates.

Cash Equivalents
Cash equivalents include highly liquid investments with an original maturity of three months or less. Our policy is to invest in high-quality, short-term instruments to achieve maximum yield while maintaining a level of liquidity consistent with our needs. Book cash overdrafts issued but not yet presented to the bank for payment are reclassified to accounts payable.

Allowance for Doubtful Accounts
A summary of activity in the allowance for doubtful accounts is as follows:

Dollars in thousands	Fiscal 2005	Fiscal 2004	Fiscal 2003
Balance at beginning of year	$217	$207	$ 64
Provision for loss on accounts receivable	(49)	10	143
Accounts written off	—	—	—
Balance at end of year	$168	$217	$207

Merchandise Inventories

Merchandise inventories, net of an allowance for excess quantities and obsolescence, are stated at the lower of cost (weighted average method) or market. We estimate a provision for damaged, obsolete, excess and slow-moving inventory based on inventory aging reports and specific identification. We generally reserve, based on inventory aging reports, for 50% of the cost of all inventory between one and two years old and 100% of the cost of all inventory over two years old. If actual obsolescence is different from our estimate, we will adjust our provision accordingly. Specific reserves are also recorded in the event the cost of the inventory exceeds the fair market value. In addition, on a monthly basis, we estimate a reserve for expected shrinkage at the concept and channel level based on historical shrinkage factors and our current inventory levels. Actual shrinkage is recorded at year-end based on the results of our physical inventory count and can vary from our estimates due to such factors as changes in operations within our distribution centers, the mix of our inventory (which ranges from large furniture to small tabletop items) and execution against loss prevention initiatives in our stores, off-site storage locations, and our third party transportation providers.

Approximately 63%, 62% and 61% of our merchandise purchases in fiscal 2005, fiscal 2004 and fiscal 2003, respectively, were foreign-sourced, primarily from Asia and Europe.

Prepaid Catalog Expenses

Prepaid catalog expenses consist of third party incremental direct costs, including creative design, paper, printing, postage and mailing costs for all of our direct response catalogs. Such costs are capitalized as prepaid catalog expenses and are amortized over their expected period of future benefit. Such amortization is based upon the ratio of actual revenues to the total of actual and estimated future revenues on an individual catalog basis. Estimated future revenues are based upon various factors such as the total number of catalogs and pages circulated, the probability and magnitude of consumer response and the assortment of merchandise offered. Each catalog is generally fully amortized over a six to nine month period, with the majority of the amortization occurring within the first four to five months. Prepaid catalog expenses are evaluated for realizability on a monthly basis by comparing the carrying amount associated with each catalog to the estimated probable remaining future profitability (remaining net revenues less merchandise cost of goods sold, selling expenses and catalog related-costs) associated with that catalog. If the catalog is not expected to be profitable, the carrying amount of the catalog is impaired accordingly. Catalog advertising expenses were $321,610,000, $278,169,000 and $250,337,000 in fiscal 2005, fiscal 2004 and fiscal 2003, respectively.

Property and Equipment

Property and equipment is stated at cost. Depreciation is computed using the straight-line method over the estimated useful lives of the assets below. Any reduction in the estimated lives would result in higher depreciation expense in a given period for the related assets.

Leasehold improvements	Shorter of estimated useful life or lease term (generally 3 – 22 years)
Fixtures and equipment	2 – 20 years
Buildings and building improvements	12 – 40 years
Capitalized software	2 – 10 years
Corporate aircraft	20 years (20% salvage value)
Capital leases	Shorter of estimated useful life or lease term (generally 4 – 5 years)

Internally developed software costs are capitalized in accordance with the American Institute of Certified Public Accountants Statement of Position 98-1, "Accounting for the Costs of Computer Software Developed or Obtained for Internal Use."

Interest costs related to assets under construction, including software projects, are capitalized during the construction or development period. We capitalized interest costs of $1,200,000, $1,689,000 and $2,142,000 in fiscal 2005, fiscal 2004 and fiscal 2003, respectively.

43

For any store closures where a lease obligation still exists, we record the estimated future liability associated with the rental obligation on the date the store is closed in accordance with Statement of Financial Accounting Standards ("SFAS") No. 146, "Accounting for Costs Associated with Exit or Disposal Activities." However, most store closures occur upon the lease expiration.

We review the carrying value of all long-lived assets for impairment whenever events or changes in circumstances indicate that the carrying value of an asset may not be recoverable. In accordance with SFAS No. 144, "Accounting for the Impairment or Disposal of Long-Lived Assets," we review for impairment all stores for which current cash flows from operations are negative, or the construction costs are significantly in excess of the amount originally expected. Impairment results when the carrying value of the assets exceeds the undiscounted future cash flows over the life of the lease. Our estimate of undiscounted future cash flows over the lease term (typically 5 to 22 years) is based upon our experience, historical operations of the stores and estimates of future store profitability and economic conditions. The future estimates of store profitability and economic conditions require estimating such factors as sales growth, employment rates, lease escalations, inflation on operating expenses and the overall economics of the retail industry for up to 20 years in the future, and are therefore subject to variability and difficult to predict. If a long-lived asset is found to be impaired, the amount recognized for impairment is equal to the difference between the carrying value and the asset's fair value. The fair value is estimated based upon future cash flows (discounted at a rate that approximates our weighted average cost of capital) or other reasonable estimates of fair market value.

Lease Rights and Other Intangible Assets
Lease rights, representing costs incurred to acquire the lease of a specific commercial property, are recorded at cost in other assets and are amortized over the lives of the respective leases. Other intangible assets include fees associated with the acquisition of our credit facility and are recorded at cost in other assets and amortized over the life of the facility.

Self-Insured Liabilities
We are primarily self-insured for workers' compensation, employee health benefits and product and general liability claims. We record self-insurance liabilities based on claims filed, including the development of those claims, and an estimate of claims incurred but not yet reported. Factors affecting this estimate include future inflation rates, changes in severity, benefit level changes, medical costs and claim settlement patterns. Should a different amount of claims occur compared to what was estimated, or costs of the claims increase or decrease beyond what was anticipated, reserves may need to be adjusted accordingly. We determine our workers' compensation liability and general liability claims reserves based on an actuarial analysis. Reserves for self-insurance liabilities are recorded within accrued salaries, benefits and other on our consolidated balance sheet.

Customer Deposits
Customer deposits are primarily comprised of unredeemed gift certificates and merchandise credits and deferred revenue related to undelivered merchandise. We maintain a liability for unredeemed gift certificates and merchandise credits until the earlier of redemption, escheatment or seven years. After seven years, the remaining unredeemed gift certificate or merchandise credit liability is relieved and recorded within selling, general and administrative expenses.

Deferred Rent and Lease Incentives
For leases that contain fixed escalations of the minimum annual lease payment during the original term of the lease, we recognize rental expense on a straight-line basis over the lease term, including the construction period, and record the difference between rent expense and the amount currently payable as deferred rent. Any rental expense incurred during the construction period is capitalized as a leasehold improvement within property and equipment and depreciated over the lease term. Deferred lease incentives include construction allowances received from landlords, which are amortized on a straight-line basis over the lease term, including the construction period. Beginning in fiscal 2006, in accordance with Financial Accounting Standards Board

("FASB") Staff Position ("FSP") FAS 13-1, "Accounting for Rental Costs Incurred During a Construction Period," we will expense any rental costs incurred during the construction period.

Contingent Liabilities
Contingent liabilities are recorded when it is determined that the outcome of an event is expected to result in a loss that is considered probable and reasonably estimable.

Fair Value of Financial Instruments
The carrying values of cash and cash equivalents, accounts receivable, investments, accounts payable and debt approximate their estimated fair values.

Revenue Recognition
We recognize revenues and the related cost of goods sold (including shipping costs) at the time the products are received by customers in accordance with the provisions of Staff Accounting Bulletin ("SAB") No. 101, "Revenue Recognition in Financial Statements" as amended by SAB No. 104, "Revenue Recognition." Revenue is recognized for retail sales (excluding home-delivered merchandise) at the point of sale in the store and for home-delivered merchandise and direct-to-customer sales when the merchandise is delivered to the customer. Discounts provided to customers are accounted for as a reduction of sales. We record a reserve for estimated product returns in each reporting period. Shipping and handling fees charged to the customer are recognized as revenue at the time the products are delivered to the customer.

Sales Returns Reserve
Our customers may return purchased items for an exchange or refund. We record a reserve for estimated product returns, net of cost of goods sold, based on historical return trends together with current product sales performance. If actual returns, net of cost of goods sold, are different than those projected by management, the estimated sales returns reserve will be adjusted accordingly. A summary of activity in the sales returns reserve is as follows:

Dollars in thousands	Fiscal 2005[1]	Fiscal 2004[1]	Fiscal 2003[1]
Balance at beginning of year	$ 13,506	$ 12,281	$ 10,292
Provision for sales returns	243,807	215,715	182,829
Actual sales returns	(243,631)	(214,490)	(180,840)
Balance at end of year	$ 13,682	$ 13,506	$ 12,281

[1]*Amounts are shown net of cost of goods sold.*

Vendor Allowances
We may receive allowances or credits from vendors for volume rebates. In accordance with Emerging Issues Task Force ("EITF") 02-16, "Accounting by a Customer (Including a Reseller) for Certain Consideration Received from a Vendor," our accounting policy is to treat such volume rebates as an offset to the cost of the product or services provided at the time the expense is recorded. These allowances and credits received are primarily recorded in cost of goods sold or in selling, general and administrative expenses.

Foreign Currency Translation
The functional currency of our Canadian subsidiary is the Canadian dollar. Assets and liabilities are translated into U.S. dollars using the current exchange rates in effect at the balance sheet date, while revenues and expenses are translated at the average exchange rates during the period. The resulting translation adjustments are recorded as other comprehensive income within shareholders' equity. Gains and losses resulting from foreign currency transactions have not been significant and are included in selling, general and administrative expenses.

Financial Instruments

As of January 29, 2006, we have 14 retail stores in Canada, which expose us to market risk associated with foreign currency exchange rate fluctuations. As necessary, we have utilized 30-day foreign currency contracts to minimize any currency remeasurement risk associated with intercompany assets and liabilities of our Canadian subsidiary. These contracts are accounted for by adjusting the carrying amount of the contract to market and recognizing any gain or loss in selling, general and administrative expenses in each reporting period. We did not enter into any new foreign currency contracts during fiscal 2005 or fiscal 2004. Any gain or loss associated with these types of contracts in prior years was not material to us.

Income Taxes

Income taxes are accounted for using the asset and liability method. Under this method, deferred income taxes arise from temporary differences between the tax basis of assets and liabilities and their reported amounts in the consolidated financial statements. We record reserves for estimates of probable settlements of foreign and domestic tax audits. At any one time, many tax years are subject to audit by various taxing jurisdictions. The results of these audits and negotiations with taxing authorities may affect the ultimate settlement of these issues. Our effective tax rate in a given financial statement period may be materially impacted by changes in the mix and level of earnings.

Earnings Per Share

Basic earnings per share is computed as net earnings divided by the weighted average number of common shares outstanding for the period. Diluted earnings per share is computed as net earnings divided by the weighted average number of common shares outstanding for the period plus common stock equivalents, consisting of shares subject to stock options and other stock compensation awards.

Stock-Based Compensation

We account for stock options and awards granted to employees using the intrinsic value method in accordance with Accounting Principles Board Opinion No. 25, "Accounting for Stock Issued to Employees." No compensation expense has been recognized in the consolidated financial statements for stock options, as we grant all stock options with an exercise price equal to the market price of our common stock at the date of grant, however, stock compensation expense is recognized in the consolidated financial statements for restricted stock unit awards. SFAS No. 123, "Accounting for Stock-Based Compensation," as amended by SFAS No. 148, "Accounting for Stock-Based Compensation – Transition and Disclosure," however, requires the disclosure of pro forma net earnings and earnings per share as if we had adopted the fair value method. Under SFAS No. 123, the fair value of stock-based awards to employees is calculated through the use of option pricing models. These models require subjective assumptions, including future stock price volatility and expected time to exercise, which affect the calculated values. Our calculations are based on a single option valuation approach, and forfeitures are recognized as they occur.

The following table illustrates the effect on net earnings and earnings per share as if we had applied the fair value recognition provisions of SFAS No. 123, as amended by SFAS No. 148, to all of our stock-based compensation arrangements.

	Fiscal Year Ended		
Dollars in thousands, except per share amounts	Jan. 29, 2006	Jan. 30, 2005	Feb. 1, 2004
Net earnings, as reported	$214,866	$191,234	$157,211
Add: Stock-based employee compensation expense included in reported net earnings, net of related tax effect	273	—	154
Deduct: Total stock-based employee compensation expense determined under fair value method for all awards, net of related tax effect	(16,788)	(17,059)	(16,780)
Pro forma net earnings	$198,351	$174,175	$140,585
Basic earnings per share			
As reported	$ 1.86	$ 1.65	$ 1.36
Pro forma	1.72	1.50	1.22
Diluted earnings per share			
As reported	$ 1.81	$ 1.60	$ 1.32
Pro forma	1.69	1.47	1.16

The fair value of each option grant was estimated on the date of the grant using the Black-Scholes option-pricing model with the following weighted average assumptions:

	Fiscal Year Ended		
	Jan. 29, 2006	Jan. 30, 2005	Feb. 1, 2004
Dividend yield	—	—	—
Volatility	59.2%	60.1%	63.9%
Risk-free interest rate	4.3%	3.9%	3.4%
Expected term (years)	6.5	6.8	6.7

In January 2006, we issued 840,000 restricted stock units of our common stock to certain employees. Fifty percent of the restricted stock units will vest on January 31, 2010, and the remaining fifty percent will vest on January 31, 2011 based upon the employees' continued employment throughout the vesting period. Accordingly, total compensation expense (based upon the fair market value of $42.18 on the issue date) of $35,431,000 will be recognized on a straight-line basis over the vesting period. In fiscal 2005, we recognized approximately $440,000 of compensation expense related to these restricted stock units.

During fiscal 2001, we entered into employment agreements with certain executive officers. All stock-based compensation expense related to these agreements was fully recognized as of our first quarter ended May 4, 2003. We recognized approximately zero, zero and $250,000 of stock-based compensation expense related to these employment agreements in fiscal 2005, fiscal 2004 and fiscal 2003, respectively.

New Accounting Pronouncements
In December 2004, the FASB issued SFAS No. 123R, "Share Based Payment." SFAS No. 123R will require us to measure and record compensation expense in our consolidated financial statements for all employee share-based compensation awards using a fair value method. In addition, the adoption of SFAS No. 123R requires additional accounting and disclosure related to the income tax and cash flow effects resulting from share-based payment arrangements. We expect to adopt this Statement using the modified prospective application transition method beginning in the first quarter of fiscal 2006. We anticipate the adoption of this Statement to result in a reduction to our diluted earnings per share of approximately $0.19 for fiscal 2006.

In March 2005, the FASB issued FASB Interpretation No. ("FIN") No. 47, "Accounting for Conditional Asset Retirement Obligations – An Interpretation of FASB Statement No. 143," which requires an entity to recognize a liability for the fair value of a conditional asset retirement obligation when incurred if the liability's fair value can be reasonably estimated. We adopted the provisions of FIN 47 as of January 29, 2006. The adoption of this Interpretation did not have a material impact on our consolidated financial position, results of operations or cash flows.

In October 2005, the FASB issued FSP No. FAS 13-1, "Accounting for Rental Costs Incurred during a Construction Period," which requires us, beginning on January 30, 2006, to expense all rental costs associated with our operating leases that are incurred during a construction period. Prior to this date, rental costs incurred during the construction period were capitalized until the store opening date. We anticipate the adoption of this Staff Position to result in a reduction to our diluted earnings per share of approximately $0.03 for fiscal 2006.

In September 2005, the EITF issued EITF No. 05-6, "Determining the Amortization Period for Leasehold Improvements Purchased after Lease Inception or Acquired in a Business Combination," which requires us to amortize leasehold improvements that are placed in service significantly after the beginning of a lease term over the shorter of the useful life of the assets, or a term that includes required lease periods and renewals that are deemed to be reasonably assumed at the date the leasehold improvement is purchased. This EITF did not have a material impact on our consolidated financial position, results of operations or cash flows.

Reclassifications
Certain items in the fiscal 2004 and fiscal 2003 consolidated financial statements have been reclassified to conform to the fiscal 2005 presentation.

Note B: Property and Equipment

Property and equipment consists of the following:

Dollars in thousands	Jan. 29, 2006	Jan. 30, 2005
Leasehold improvements	$ 651,498	$ 600,249
Fixtures and equipment	437,243	398,826
Land and buildings	131,484	131,471
Capitalized software	145,407	132,614
Corporate systems projects in progress[1]	98,398	77,077
Corporate aircraft	48,677	48,618
Construction in progress[2]	31,501	8,063
Capital leases	11,920	11,920
Total	1,556,128	1,408,838
Accumulated depreciation and amortization	(675,823)	(556,426)
Property and equipment – net	$ 880,305	$ 852,412

[1]*Corporate systems projects in progress is primarily comprised of a new merchandising, inventory management and order management system currently under development.*
[2]*Construction in progress is primarily comprised of leasehold improvements and furniture and fixtures related to new, unopened retail stores.*

Note C: Borrowing Arrangements

Long-term debt consists of the following:

Dollars in thousands	Jan. 29, 2006	Jan. 30, 2005
Senior notes	—	$ 5,716
Obligations under capital leases	$ 3,458	5,673
Memphis-based distribution facilities obligation	15,696	17,000
Industrial development bonds	14,200	14,200
Total debt	33,354	42,589
Less current maturities	18,864	23,435
Total long-term debt	$14,490	$19,154

Senior Notes

In August, 2005, we repaid the remaining outstanding balance of $5,716,000 on our unsecured senior notes, with interest payable semi-annually at 7.2% per annum.

Capital Leases

Our $3,458,000 of capital lease obligations consist primarily of in-store computer equipment leases with a term of 60 months. The in-store computer equipment leases include an early purchase option at 54 months for $2,496,000, which is approximately 25% of the acquisition cost. We have an end of lease purchase option to acquire the equipment at the greater of fair market value or 15% of the acquisition cost.

Subsequent to year-end, we exercised the early purchase option on three of these leases and expect to exercise this option on the remaining computer equipment leases during fiscal 2006.

See Note F for a discussion on our bond-related debt pertaining to our Memphis-based distribution facilities.

Industrial Development Bonds

In June 2004, in an effort to utilize tax incentives offered to us by the state of Mississippi, we entered into an agreement whereby the Mississippi Business Finance Corporation issued $15,000,000 in long-term variable rate industrial development bonds, the proceeds, net of debt issuance costs, of which were loaned to us to finance the acquisition and installation of leasehold improvements and equipment located in our newly leased Olive Branch distribution center (the "Mississippi Debt Transaction"). The bonds are marketed through a remarketing agent and are secured by a letter of credit issued under our $300,000,000 line of credit facility. The bonds mature on June 1, 2024. The bond rate resets each week based upon current market rates. The rate in effect at January 29, 2006 was 4.5%.

The bond agreement allows for each bondholder to tender their bonds to the trustee for repurchase, on demand, with seven days advance notice. In the event the remarketing agent fails to remarket the bonds, the trustee will draw upon the letter of credit to fund the purchase of the bonds. As of January 29, 2006, $14,200,000 remained outstanding on these bonds and was classified as current debt. The bond proceeds are restricted for use in the acquisition and installation of leasehold improvements and equipment located in our Olive Branch, Mississippi facility. As of January 29, 2006, we had acquired and installed $14,700,000 of leasehold improvements and equipment associated with the facility.

The aggregate maturities of long-term debt at January 29, 2006 were as follows:

Dollars in thousands

Fiscal 2006[1]	$18,864
Fiscal 2007	1,668
Fiscal 2008	1,584
Fiscal 2009	1,438
Fiscal 2010	1,462
Thereafter	8,338
Total	$33,354

[1]*Includes $14.2 million related to the Mississippi Debt Transaction classified as current debt.*

Credit Facility

As of January 29, 2006, we have a credit facility that provides for a $300,000,000 unsecured revolving line of credit that may be used for loans or letters of credit and contains certain financial covenants, including a maximum leverage ratio (funded debt adjusted for lease and rent expense to EBITDAR), and a minimum fixed charge coverage ratio. Prior to August 22, 2009, we may, upon notice to the lenders, request an increase in the credit facility of up to $100,000,000, to provide for a total of $400,000,000 of unsecured revolving credit. The credit facility contains events of default that include, among others, non-payment of principal, interest or fees, inaccuracy of representations and warranties, violation of covenants, bankruptcy and insolvency events, material judgments, cross defaults to certain other indebtedness and events constituting a change of control. The occurrence of an event of default will increase the applicable rate of interest by 2.0% and could result in the acceleration of our obligations under the credit facility, and an obligation of any or all of our U.S. subsidiaries to pay the full amount of our obligations under the credit facility. The credit facility matures on February 22, 2010, at which time all outstanding borrowings must be repaid and all outstanding letters of credit must be cash collateralized.

We may elect interest rates calculated at Bank of America's prime rate (or, if greater, the average rate on overnight federal funds plus one-half of one percent) or LIBOR plus a margin based on our leverage ratio. No amounts were borrowed under the credit facility during fiscal 2005 or fiscal 2004. However, as of January 29, 2006, $36,073,000 in issued but undrawn standby letters of credit were outstanding under the credit facility. The standby letters of credit were issued to secure the liabilities associated with workers' compensation, other insurance programs and certain debt transactions. As of January 29, 2006, we were in compliance with our financial covenants under the credit facility.

Letter of Credit Facilities

We have three unsecured commercial letter of credit reimbursement facilities for an aggregate of $145,000,000, each of which expires on September 9, 2006. As of January 29, 2006, an aggregate of $105,260,000 was outstanding under the letter of credit facilities. Such letters of credit represent only a future commitment to fund inventory purchases to which we had not taken legal title as of January 29, 2006. The latest expiration possible for any future letters of credit issued under the agreements is February 6, 2007.

Interest Expense

Interest expense was $1,975,000 (net of capitalized interest of $1,200,000), $1,703,000 (net of capitalized interest of $1,689,000), and $22,000 (net of capitalized interest of $2,142,000) for fiscal 2005, fiscal 2004 and fiscal 2003, respectively.

Note D: Income Taxes

The components of earnings before income taxes, by tax jurisdiction, are as follows:

	Fiscal Year Ended		
Dollars in thousands	Jan. 29, 2006	Jan. 30, 2005	Feb. 1, 2004
United States	$ 337,468	$ 303,986	$ 252,119
Foreign	11,330	6,219	3,519
Total earnings before income taxes	$ 348,798	$ 310,205	$ 255,638

The provision for income taxes consists of the following:

	Fiscal Year Ended		
Dollars in thousands	Jan. 29, 2006	Jan. 30, 2005	Feb. 1, 2004
Current payable			
Federal	$ 131,242	$ 105,096	$ 87,194
State	19,002	17,642	15,640
Foreign	4,479	2,487	2,065
Total current	154,723	125,225	104,899
Deferred			
Federal	(18,912)	(6,168)	(3,587)
State	(1,538)	(70)	(2,015)
Foreign	(341)	(16)	(870)
Total deferred	(20,791)	(6,254)	(6,472)
Total provision	$ 133,932	$ 118,971	$ 98,427

Except where required by U.S. tax law, no provision was made for U.S. income taxes on the cumulative undistributed earnings of our Canadian subsidiary, as we intend to utilize those earnings in the Canadian operations for an indefinite period of time and do not intend to repatriate such earnings.

Accumulated undistributed earnings of our Canadian subsidiary were approximately $13,440,000 as of January 29, 2006. It is currently not practical to estimate the tax liability that might be payable if these foreign earnings were repatriated.

A reconciliation of income taxes at the federal statutory corporate rate to the effective rate is as follows:

	Fiscal Year Ended		
	Jan. 29, 2006	Jan. 30, 2005	Feb. 1, 2004
Federal income taxes at the statutory rate	35.0%	35.0%	35.0%
State income tax rate, less federal benefit	3.4%	3.4%	3.5%
Total	38.4%	38.4%	38.5%

Significant components of our deferred tax accounts are as follows:

Dollars in thousands	Jan. 29, 2006	Jan. 30, 2005
Deferred tax asset (liability)		
Current:		
Compensation	$ 15,362	$ 14,667
Inventory	11,580	11,357
Accrued liabilities	14,186	13,725
Customer deposits	36,079	19,342
Deferred catalog costs	(20,696)	(20,540)
Other	756	464
Total current	57,267	39,015
Non-current:		
Depreciation	(11,559)	(18,634)
Deferred rent	8,683	8,275
Deferred lease incentives	(16,506)	(11,595)
Other	927	897
Total non-current	(18,455)	(21,057)
Total	$ 38,812	$ 17,958

Note E: Accounting for Leases

Operating Leases

We lease store locations, warehouses, corporate facilities, call centers and certain equipment under operating and capital leases for original terms ranging generally from 3 to 22 years. Certain leases contain renewal options for periods up to 20 years. The rental payment requirements in our store leases are typically structured as either minimum rent, minimum rent plus additional rent based on a percentage of store sales if a specified store sales threshold is exceeded, or rent based on a percentage of store sales if a specified store sales threshold or contractual obligations of the landlord have not been met.

We have an operating lease for a 1,002,000 square foot retail distribution facility located in Olive Branch, Mississippi. The lease has an initial term of 22.5 years, expiring January 2022, with two optional five-year renewals. The lessor, an unrelated party, is a limited liability company. The construction and expansion of the distribution facility was financed by the original lessor through the sale of $39,200,000 Taxable Industrial Development Revenue Bonds, Series 1998 and 1999, issued by the Mississippi Business Finance Corporation. The bonds are collateralized by the distribution facility. As of January 29, 2006, approximately $31,249,000 was outstanding on the bonds. During fiscal 2005, we made annual rental payments of approximately $3,753,000, plus applicable taxes, insurance and maintenance expenses.

We have an operating lease for an additional 1,103,000 square foot retail distribution facility located in Olive Branch, Mississippi. The lease has an initial term of 22.5 years, expiring January 2023, with two optional five-year renewals. The lessor, an unrelated party, is a limited liability company. The construction of the distribution facility was financed by the original lessor through the sale of $42,500,000 Taxable Industrial Development Revenue Bonds, Series 1999, issued by the Mississippi Business Finance Corporation. The bonds are collateralized by the distribution facility. As of January 29, 2006, approximately $34,396,000 was outstanding on the bonds. During fiscal 2005, we made annual rental payments of approximately $4,181,000, plus applicable taxes, insurance and maintenance expenses.

In December 2003, we entered into an agreement to lease 780,000 square feet of a distribution facility located in Olive Branch, Mississippi. The lease has an initial term of six years, with two optional two-year renewals. The agreement includes an option to lease an additional 390,000 square feet of the same distribution center. We exercised this option during fiscal 2005, however, as of January 29, 2006, we had not occupied this space. During fiscal 2005, we made annual rental payments of approximately $1,927,000, plus applicable taxes, insurance and maintenance expenses.

52

On February 2, 2004, we entered into an agreement to lease 781,000 square feet of a distribution center located in Cranbury, New Jersey. The lease has an initial term of seven years, with three optional five-year renewals. The agreement requires us to lease an additional 219,000 square feet of the facility in the event the current tenant vacates the premises. As of January 29, 2006, the current tenant had not yet vacated the premises. During fiscal 2005, we made annual rental payments of approximately $3,339,000, plus applicable taxes, insurance and maintenance expenses.

On August 18, 2004, we entered into an agreement to lease a 500,000 square foot distribution facility located in Memphis, Tennessee. The lease has an initial term of four years, with one optional three-year and nine-month renewal. During fiscal 2005, we made annual rental payments of approximately $913,000, plus applicable taxes, insurance and maintenance expenses.

Total rental expense for all operating leases was as follows:

	Fiscal Year Ended		
Dollars in thousands	Jan. 29, 2006	Jan. 30, 2005	Feb. 1, 2004[1]
Minimum rent expense	$ 119,440	$ 110,618	$ 101,377
Contingent rent expense	33,529	26,724	21,796
Less: Sublease rental income	(62)	(59)	(90)
Total rent expense	$ 152,907	$ 137,283	$ 123,083

[1]Includes rent expense for our Memphis-based distribution facilities which were consolidated by us on February 1, 2004. See Note F.

The aggregate minimum annual rental payments under noncancelable operating leases (excluding the Memphis-based distribution facilities) in effect at January 29, 2006 were as follows:

Dollars in thousands	Minimum Lease Commitments[1]
Fiscal 2006	$ 178,846
Fiscal 2007	176,891
Fiscal 2008	170,041
Fiscal 2009	160,569
Fiscal 2010	149,092
Thereafter	672,358
Total	$ 1,507,797

[1]Projected payments include only those amounts that are fixed and determinable as of the reporting date.

Note F: Consolidation of Memphis-Based Distribution Facilities

Our Memphis-based distribution facilities include an operating lease entered into in July 1983 for a distribution facility in Memphis, Tennessee. The lessor is a general partnership ("Partnership 1") comprised of W. Howard Lester, Chairman of the Board of Directors and a significant shareholder, and James A. McMahan, a Director Emeritus and a significant shareholder. Partnership 1 does not have operations separate from the leasing of this distribution facility and does not have lease agreements with any unrelated third parties.

Partnership 1 financed the construction of this distribution facility through the sale of a total of $9,200,000 of industrial development bonds in 1983 and 1985. Annual principal payments and monthly interest payments are required through maturity in December 2010. The Partnership 1 industrial development bonds are collateralized by the distribution facility and the individual partners guarantee the bond repayments. As of January 29, 2006, $1,887,000 was outstanding under the Partnership 1 industrial development bonds.

During fiscal 2005, we made annual rental payments of approximately $618,000 plus interest on the bonds calculated at a variable rate determined monthly (3.5% in January 2006), applicable taxes, insurance and maintenance expenses. Although the current term of the lease expires in August 2006, we are obligated to renew the operating lease on an annual basis until these bonds are fully repaid.

Our other Memphis-based distribution facility includes an operating lease entered into in August 1990 for another distribution facility that is adjoined to the Partnership 1 facility in Memphis, Tennessee. The lessor is a general partnership ("Partnership 2") comprised of W. Howard Lester, James A. McMahan and two unrelated parties. Partnership 2 does not have operations separate from the leasing of this distribution facility and does not have lease agreements with any unrelated third parties.

Partnership 2 financed the construction of this distribution facility and related addition through the sale of a total of $24,000,000 of industrial development bonds in 1990 and 1994. Quarterly interest and annual principal payments are required through maturity in August 2015. The Partnership 2 industrial development bonds are collateralized by the distribution facility and require us to maintain certain financial covenants. As of January 29, 2006, $13,809,000 was outstanding under the Partnership 2 industrial development bonds.

During fiscal 2005, we made annual rental payments of approximately $2,600,000, plus applicable taxes, insurance and maintenance expenses. This operating lease has an original term of 15 years expiring in August 2006, with three optional five-year renewal periods. We are, however, obligated to renew the operating lease on an annual basis until these bonds are fully repaid.

As of February 1, 2004, the Company adopted FIN 46R, which requires existing unconsolidated variable interest entities to be consolidated by their primary beneficiaries if the entities do not effectively disperse risks among parties involved. The two partnerships described above qualify as variable interest entities under FIN 46R due to their related party relationship and our obligation to renew the leases until the bonds are fully repaid. Accordingly, the two related party variable interest entity partnerships from which we lease our Memphis-based distribution facilities were consolidated by us as of February 1, 2004. As of January 29, 2006, the consolidation resulted in increases to our consolidated balance sheet of $18,250,000 in assets (primarily buildings), $15,696,000 in debt, and $2,554,000 in other long-term liabilities. Consolidation of these partnerships did not have an impact on our net income. However, the interest expense associated with the partnerships' debt, shown as occupancy expense in fiscal 2003, is now recorded as interest expense. In fiscal 2005 and fiscal 2004, this interest expense approximated $1,462,000 and $1,525,000, respectively.

Note G: Earnings Per Share

The following is a reconciliation of net earnings and the number of shares used in the basic and diluted earnings per share computations:

Dollars and amounts in thousands, except per share amounts	Net Earnings	Weighted Average Shares	Per-Share Amount
2005			
Basic	$214,866	115,616	$1.86
Effect of dilutive stock options	—	2,811	
Diluted	$214,866	118,427	$1.81
2004			
Basic	$191,234	116,159	$1.65
Effect of dilutive stock options	—	3,188	
Diluted	$191,234	119,347	$1.60
2003			
Basic	$157,211	115,583	$1.36
Effect of dilutive stock options	—	3,433	
Diluted	$157,211	119,016	$1.32

Options with an exercise price greater than the average market price of common shares for the period were 320,000 in fiscal 2005, 196,000 in fiscal 2004 and 436,000 in fiscal 2003 and were not included in the computation of diluted earnings per share, as their inclusion would be anti-dilutive.

Note H: Common Stock

Authorized preferred stock consists of 7,500,000 shares at $0.01 par value of which none was outstanding during fiscal 2005 or fiscal 2004. Authorized common stock consists of 253,125,000 shares at $0.01 par value. Common stock outstanding at the end of fiscal 2005 and fiscal 2004 was 114,779,000 and 115,372,000 shares, respectively. Our Board of Directors is authorized to issue stock options for up to the total number of shares authorized and remaining available for grant under each plan.

In May 2005, our Board of Directors authorized a stock repurchase program to acquire up to 2,000,000 additional shares of our outstanding common stock. During the fourth quarter of fiscal 2005, we repurchased and retired 780,800 shares at a weighted average cost of $41.70 per share and a total cost of approximately $32,556,000. During fiscal 2005, we repurchased and retired a total of 2,422,300 shares at a weighted average cost of $38.77 per share and a total cost of approximately $93,921,000. As of fiscal year-end, the remaining authorized number of shares eligible for repurchase was 20,000. During the first quarter of fiscal 2006, we repurchased and retired these shares at a weighted average cost of $38.84 per share and a total cost of approximately $777,000, which completed all stock repurchase programs previously authorized by our Board of Directors.

In March 2006, our Board of Directors authorized a stock repurchase program to acquire up to an additional 2,000,000 shares of our outstanding common stock. Stock repurchases under this program may be made through open market and privately negotiated transactions at times and in such amounts as management deems appropriate. The timing and actual number of shares repurchased will depend on a variety of factors, including price, corporate and regulatory requirements, capital availability, and other market conditions. The stock repurchase program does not have an expiration date and may be limited or terminated at any time without prior notice.

Prior to March 2006, we had never declared or paid a cash dividend on our common stock. In March 2006, our Board of Directors authorized the initiation of a quarterly cash dividend. The quarterly dividend will be initiated at $0.10 per common share, payable on May 24, 2006, to shareholders of record as of the close of business on April 26, 2006. The aggregate quarterly dividend is estimated at approximately $11,500,000 based on the current number of common shares outstanding. The indicated annual cash dividend, subject to capital availability, is $0.40 per common share, or approximately $46,000,000 in fiscal 2006 based on the current number of common shares outstanding.

Note I: Stock Compensation

Our 1993 Stock Option Plan, as amended (the "1993 Plan"), provides for grants of incentive and nonqualified stock options up to an aggregate of 17,000,000 shares. Stock options may be granted under the 1993 Plan to key employees and Board members of the company and any parent or subsidiary. Annual grants are limited to options to purchase 200,000 shares on a per person basis under this plan. All stock option grants made under the 1993 Plan have a maximum term of ten years, except incentive stock options issued to shareholders with greater than 10% of the voting power of all of our stock, which have a maximum term of five years. The exercise price of these options is not less than 100% of the fair market value of our stock on the date of the option grant or not less than 110% of such fair market value for an incentive stock option granted to a 10% shareholder. Options granted to employees generally vest over five years. Options granted to non-employee Board members generally vest in one year.

Our 2000 Nonqualified Stock Option Plan, as amended (the "2000 Plan"), provides for grants of nonqualified stock options up to an aggregate of 3,000,000 shares. Stock options may be granted under the 2000 Plan to employees who are not officers or Board members. Annual grants are not limited on a per person basis under this plan. All nonqualified stock option grants under the 2000 Plan have a maximum term of ten years with an exercise price of 100% of the fair value of the stock at the option grant date. Options granted to employees generally vest over five years.

Our Amended and Restated 2001 Long-Term Incentive Plan (the "2001 Plan") provides for grants of incentive stock options, nonqualified stock options, restricted stock awards and deferred stock awards up to an aggregate of 8,500,000 shares. Awards may be granted under the 2001 Plan to officers, employee and non-employee Board

55

members of the company and any parent or subsidiary. Annual grants are limited to options to purchase 1,000,000 shares, 200,000 shares of restricted stock, and deferred stock awards of up to 200,000 shares on a per person basis. All stock option grants made under the 2001 Plan have a maximum term of ten years, except incentive stock options issued to 10% shareholders, which have a maximum term of five years. The exercise price of these stock options is not less than 100% of the fair market value of our stock on the date of the option grant or not less than 110% of such fair market value for an incentive stock option granted to a 10% shareholder. Options granted to employees generally vest over five years. Options granted to non-employee Board members generally vest in one year. Non-employee Board members automatically receive stock options on the date of their initial election to the Board and annually thereafter on the date of the annual meeting of shareholders (so long as they continue to serve as a non-employee Board member).

The following table reflects the aggregate activity under our stock option plans:

	Shares	Weighted Average Exercise Price
Balance at February 2, 2003	14,567,106	$14.77
Granted (weighted average fair value of $15.56)	1,596,075	24.37
Exercised	(3,294,478)	11.87
Canceled	(1,089,045)	18.07
Balance at February 1, 2004	11,779,658	16.58
Granted (weighted average fair value of $20.58)	1,626,811	32.57
Exercised	(1,817,308)	14.41
Canceled	(488,734)	20.81
Balance at January 30, 2005	11,100,427	19.08
Granted (weighted average fair value of $23.77)	1,754,990	39.07
Exercised	(1,829,082)	15.30
Canceled	(716,426)	26.81
Balance at January 29, 2006	10,309,909	22.63
Exercisable, February 1, 2004	5,077,371	$12.83
Exercisable, January 30, 2005	5,461,541	14.26
Exercisable, January 29, 2006	5,704,164	16.00

Options to purchase 2,424,858 shares were available for grant at January 29, 2006.

The following table summarizes information about stock options outstanding at January 29, 2006:

Range of exercise prices	Options Outstanding			Options Exercisable	
	Number Outstanding	Weighted Average Contractual Life (Years)	Weighted Average Exercise Price	Number Exercisable	Weighted Average Exercise Price
$ 4.50 – $ 9.50	1,651,008	2.71	$ 8.17	1,651,008	$ 8.17
$ 9.66 – $14.50	1,880,843	4.07	12.80	1,529,680	12.61
$15.00 – $22.47	2,006,335	5.68	19.56	1,282,100	18.26
$22.48 – $31.58	1,786,723	7.14	26.80	922,126	26.66
$32.01 – $43.85	2,985,000	8.82	36.39	319,250	32.92
$ 4.50 – $43.85	10,309,909	6.07	$22.63	5,704,164	$16.00

In January 2006, we issued 840,000 restricted stock units of our common stock to certain employees. Fifty percent of the restricted stock units will vest on January 31, 2010, and the remaining fifty percent will vest on January 31, 2011 based upon the employees' continued employment throughout the vesting period. As of January 29, 2006, 840,000 restricted stock units were outstanding.

Note J: Associate Stock Incentive Plan and Other Employee Benefits

We have a defined contribution retirement plan, the "Williams-Sonoma, Inc. Associate Stock Incentive Plan" (the "Plan"), for eligible employees, which is intended to be qualified under Internal Revenue Code Sections 401(a), 401(k) and 401(m). The Plan permits eligible employees to make salary deferral contributions in accordance with Internal Revenue Code Section 401(k) up to 15% of eligible compensation each pay period (4% for certain higher paid individuals). Employees designate the funds in which their contributions are invested. Each participant may choose to have his or her salary deferral contributions and earnings thereon invested in one or more investment funds, including investing in our company stock fund. Prior to November 1, 2005, all matching contributions were invested in our company stock fund. Effective November 1, 2005, participants were allowed to reallocate past matching contributions to one or more investment funds. Effective December 1, 2005, company contributions are invested in a similar manner as the participant's salary deferral contributions. Effective August 1, 2003, our matching contribution is equal to 50% of the participant's salary deferral contribution each pay period, taking into account only those contributions that do not exceed 6% of the participant's eligible pay for the pay period (4% for certain higher paid individuals). For the first five years of the participant's employment, all matching contributions generally vest at the rate of 20% per year of service, measuring service from the participant's hire date. Thereafter, all matching contributions vest immediately. Our contributions to the plan were $3,322,000 in fiscal 2005, $2,850,000 in fiscal 2004 and $3,540,000 in fiscal 2003.

We have a nonqualified executive deferred compensation plan that provides supplemental retirement income benefits for a select group of management and other certain highly compensated employees. This plan permits eligible employees to make salary and bonus deferrals that are 100% vested. We have an unsecured obligation to pay in the future the value of the deferred compensation adjusted to reflect the performance, whether positive or negative, of selected investment measurement options, chosen by each participant, during the deferral period. At January 29, 2006, $11,176,000 was included in other long-term obligations. Additionally, we have purchased life insurance policies on certain participants to potentially offset these unsecured obligations. The cash surrender value of these policies was $9,661,000 at January 29, 2006 and was included in other assets.

Note K: Financial Guarantees

We are party to a variety of contractual agreements under which we may be obligated to indemnify the other party for certain matters. These contracts primarily relate to our commercial contracts, operating leases, trademarks, intellectual property, financial agreements and various other agreements. Under these contracts, we may provide certain routine indemnifications relating to representations and warranties or personal injury matters. The terms of these indemnifications range in duration and may not be explicitly defined. Historically, we have not made significant payments for these indemnifications. We believe that if we were to incur a loss in any of these matters, the loss would not have a material effect on our financial condition or results of operations.

Note L: Commitments and Contingencies

On September 30, 2004, we entered into a five-year service agreement with IBM to host and manage certain aspects of our data center information technology infrastructure. The terms of the agreement require the payment of both fixed and variable charges over the life of the agreement. The variable charges are primarily based on CPU hours, storage capacity and support services that are expected to fluctuate throughout the term of the agreement.

Under the terms of the agreement, we are subject to a minimum charge over the five-year term of the agreement. This minimum charge is based on both a fixed and variable component calculated as a percentage of the total estimated service charges over the five-year term of the agreement. As of January 29, 2006, we estimate the remaining minimum charge to be approximately $21,000,000. The fixed component of this minimum charge will be paid annually not to exceed approximately $5,000,000, while the variable component will be based on usage. The agreement can be terminated at any time for cause and after 24 months for convenience. In the event the agreement is terminated for convenience, a graduated termination fee will be assessed based on the time period remaining in the contract term, not to exceed $9,000,000. During fiscal 2005, we recognized expense of approximately $12,000,000 relating to this agreement.

In addition, we are involved in lawsuits, claims and proceedings incident to the ordinary course of our business. These disputes, which are not currently material, are increasing in number as our business expands and our company grows larger. Litigation is inherently unpredictable. Any claims against us, whether meritorious or not, could be time consuming, result in costly litigation, require significant amounts of management time and result in the diversion of significant operational resources. The results of these lawsuits, claims and proceedings cannot be predicted with certainty. However, we believe that the ultimate resolution of these current matters will not have a material adverse effect on our consolidated financial statements taken as a whole.

Note M: Segment Reporting

We have two reportable segments, retail and direct-to-customer. The retail segment has six merchandising concepts which sell products for the home (Williams-Sonoma, Pottery Barn, Pottery Barn Kids, Hold Everything, West Elm and Williams-Sonoma Home). The six retail merchandising concepts are operating segments, which have been aggregated into one reportable segment, retail. The direct-to-customer segment has seven merchandising concepts (Williams-Sonoma, Pottery Barn, Pottery Barn Kids, PBteen, Hold Everything, West Elm and Williams-Sonoma Home) and sells similar products through our eight direct-mail catalogs (Williams-Sonoma, Pottery Barn, Pottery Barn Kids, Pottery Barn Bed + Bath, PBteen, Hold Everything, West Elm and Williams-Sonoma Home) and six e-commerce websites (williams-sonoma.com, potterybarn.com, potterybarnkids.com, pbteen.com, westelm.com and holdeverything.com). Management's expectation is that the overall economics of each of our major concepts within each reportable segment will be similar over time.

These reportable segments are strategic business units that offer similar home-centered products. They are managed separately because the business units utilize two distinct distribution and marketing strategies. It is not practicable for us to report revenue by product group.

We use earnings before unallocated corporate overhead, interest and taxes to evaluate segment profitability. Unallocated costs before income taxes include corporate employee-related costs, depreciation expense, other occupancy expense and administrative costs, primarily in our corporate systems, corporate facilities and other administrative departments. Unallocated assets include corporate cash and cash equivalents, the net book value of corporate facilities and related information systems, deferred income taxes and other corporate long-lived assets.

Income tax information by segment has not been included as taxes are calculated at a company-wide level and are not allocated to each segment.

Segment Information

Dollars in thousands	Retail[1]	Direct-to-Customer	Unallocated	Total
2005				
Net revenues	$2,032,907	$1,506,040	—	$3,538,947
Depreciation and amortization expense	84,045	17,566	$ 21,588	123,199
Earnings (loss) before income taxes[2]	278,057	232,023	(161,282)	348,798
Assets[3]	986,222	295,200	700,198	1,981,620
Capital expenditures	96,918	20,984	33,886	151,788
2004				
Net revenues	$1,810,979	$1,325,952	—	$3,136,931
Depreciation and amortization expense	76,667	16,174	$ 18,783	111,624
Earnings (loss) before income taxes	253,038	210,809	(153,642)	310,205
Assets[3]	910,924	279,579	555,042	1,745,545
Capital expenditures	90,027	40,894	50,532	181,453
2003				
Net revenues	$1,622,383	$1,131,985	—	$2,754,368
Depreciation and amortization expense	68,800	15,472	$ 15,262	99,534
Earnings (loss) before income taxes	231,512	172,266	(148,140)	255,638
Assets[3]	822,340	218,603	429,792	1,470,735
Capital expenditures	121,759	11,845	78,375	211,979

[1]Net revenues include $64.6 million, $50.1 million and $42.7 million in fiscal 2005, 2004 and 2003, respectively, related to our foreign operations.

[2]Includes $11.4 million, $2.0 million, and $0.1 million in the retail, direct-to-customer, and corporate unallocated segments, respectively, related to the transitioning of the merchandising strategies of our Hold Everything brand into our other existing brands.

[3]Includes $26.5 million, $23.1 million and $22.5 million of long-term assets in fiscal 2005, 2004 and 2003, respectively, related to our foreign operations.

Glossary

A

absorption costing The reporting of the costs of manufactured products, normally direct materials, direct labor, and factory overhead, as product costs. (884)

accelerated depreciation method A depreciation method that provides for a higher depreciation amount in the first year of the asset's use, followed by a gradually declining amount of depreciation. (404)

account An accounting form that is used to record the increases and decreases in each financial statement item. (51)

account form The form of balance sheet that resembles the basic format of the accounting equation, with assets on the left side and the liabilities and owner's equity sections on the right side. (21, 219)

account payable The liability created by a purchase on account. (14)

account receivable A claim against the customer created by selling merchandise or services on credit. (15, 65, 354)

accounting An information system that provides reports to stakeholders about the economic activities and condition of a business. (7)

accounting cycle The process that begins with analyzing and journalizing transactions and ends with the post-closing trial balance. (184)

accounting equation Assets = Liabilities + Owner's Equity (12)

accounting period concept The accounting concept that assumes that the economic life of the business can be divided into time periods. (106)

accounts receivable turnover The relationship between net sales and accounts receivable, computed by dividing the net sales by the average net accounts receivable; measures how frequently during the year the accounts receivable are being converted to cash. (369, 669)

accrual basis of accounting Under this basis of accounting, revenues and expenses are reported in the income statement in the period in which they are earned or incurred. (106)

accrued expenses Expenses that have been incurred *but not recorded* in the accounts. (108)

accrued revenues Revenues that have been earned *but not recorded* in the accounts. (108)

accumulated depreciation The contra asset account credited when recording the depreciation of a fixed asset. (117)

accumulated other comprehensive income The cumulative effects of other comprehensive income items reported separately in the stockholders' equity section of the balance sheet. (536)

activity analysis The study of employee effort and other business records to determine the cost of activities. (1199)

activity base (driver) A measure of activity that is related to changes in cost. Used in analyzing and classifying cost behavior. Activity bases are also used in the denominator in calculating the predetermined factory overhead rate to assign overhead costs to cost objects. (757, 840, 1147)

activity cost pools Cost accumulations that are associated with a given activity, such as machine usage, inspections, moving, and production setups. (1146)

activity rate The cost of an activity per unit of activity base, determined by dividing the activity cost pool by the activity base. (1147)

activity-base usage quantity The amount of activity used by a particular product measured in activity-base terms. (1147)

activity-based costing (ABC) A cost allocation method that identifies activities causing the incurrence of costs and allocates these costs to products (or other cost objects), based upon activity drivers (bases). (758, 1077, 1146)

adjusted trial balance The trial balance prepared after all the adjusting entries have been posted. (122)

adjusting entries The journal entries that bring the accounts up to date at the end of the accounting period. (107)

adjusting process An analysis and updating of the accounts when financial statements are prepared. (107)

administrative expenses (general expenses) Expenses incurred in the administration or general operations of the business. (216)

aging the receivables The process of analyzing the accounts receivable and classifying them according to various age groupings, with the due date being the base point for determining age. (361)

Allowance for Doubtful Accounts The contra asset account for accounts receivable. (357)

allowance method The method of accounting for uncollectible accounts that provides an expense for uncollectible receivables in advance of their write-off. (355)

amortization The periodic transfer of the cost of an intangible asset to expense. (413)

annuity A series of equal cash flows at fixed intervals. (571, 1107)

appraisal costs Costs to detect, measure, evaluate, and audit products and processes to ensure that they conform to customer requirements and performance standards. (1200)

assets The resources owned by a business. (12, 53)

available-for-sale securities Securities that management expects to sell in the future but which are not actively traded for profit. (538)

average cost method The method of inventory costing that is based upon the assumption that costs should be charged against revenue by using the weighted average unit cost of the items sold. (270)

average rate of return A method of evaluating capital investment proposals that focuses on the expected profitability of the investment. (1103)

B

backflush accounting Simplification of the accounting system by eliminating accumulation and transfer of costs as products move through production. (1195)

Bad Debt Expense The operating expense incurred because of the failure to collect receivables. (355)

balance of the account The amount of the difference between the debits and the credits that have been entered into an account. (52)

balance sheet A list of the assets, liabilities, and owner's equity *as of a specific date*, usually at the close of the last day of a month or a year. (18)

balanced scorecard A performance evaluation approach that incorporates multiple performance dimensions by combining financial and nonfinancial measures. (1033)

bank reconciliation The analysis that details the items responsible for the difference between the cash balance reported in the bank statement and the balance of the cash account in the ledger. (324)

bank statement A summary of all transactions mailed to the depositor or made available online by the bank each month. (320)

bond A form of an interest-bearing note used by corporations to borrow on a long-term basis. (566)

bond indenture The contract between a corporation issuing bonds and the bondholders. (568)

book value The cost of a fixed asset minus accumulated depreciation on the asset. (403)

book value of the asset (or net book value) The difference between the cost of a fixed asset and its accumulated depreciation. (117)

boot The amount a buyer owes a seller when a fixed asset is traded in on a similar asset. (409)

bottleneck A condition that occurs when product demand exceeds production capacity. (1078)

break-even point The level of business operations at which revenues and expired costs are equal. (848)

budget An accounting device used to plan and control resources of operational departments and divisions. (932)

budget performance report A report comparing actual results with budget figures. (981)

budgetary slack Excess resources set within a budget to provide for uncertain events. (935)

business An organization in which basic resources (inputs), such as materials and labor, are assembled and processed to provide goods or services (outputs) to customers. (2)

business combination A business making an investment in another business by acquiring a controlling share, often greater than 50%, of the outstanding voting stock of another corporation by paying cash or exchanging stock. (543)

business entity concept A concept of accounting that limits the economic data in the accounting system to data related directly to the activities of the business. (11)

business stakeholder A person or entity who has an interest in the economic performance of a business. (4)

business transaction An economic event or condition that directly changes an entity's financial condition or directly affects its results of operations. (12)

C

capital expenditures The costs of acquiring fixed assets, adding to a fixed asset, improving a fixed asset, or extending a fixed asset's useful life. (398)

capital expenditures budget The budget summarizing future plans for acquiring plant facilities and equipment. (950)

capital investment analysis The process by which management plans, evaluates, and controls long-term capital investments involving property, plant, and equipment. (1102)

capital leases Leases that include one or more provisions that result in treating the leased assets as purchased assets in the accounts. (399)

capital rationing The process by which management plans, evaluates, and controls long-term capital investments involving fixed assets. (1116)

capital stock The portion of a corporation's owners' equity contributed by investors (owners) in exchange for shares of stock. (13)

carrying amount The balance of the bonds payable account (face amount of the bonds) less any unamortized discount or plus any unamortized premium. (578)

cash Coins, currency (paper money), checks, money orders, and money on deposit that is available for unrestricted withdrawal from banks and other financial institutions. (317)

cash basis of accounting Under this basis of accounting, revenues and expenses are reported in the income statement in the period in which cash is received or paid. (106)

cash budget A budget of estimated cash receipts and payments. (952)

cash dividend A cash distribution of earnings by a corporation to its shareholders. (495)

cash equivalents Highly liquid investments that are usually reported with cash on the balance sheet. (328)

cash flows from financing activities The section of the statement of cash flows that reports cash flows from transactions affecting the equity and debt of the business. (610)

cash flows from investing activities The section of the statement of cash flows that reports cash flows from transactions affecting investments in noncurrent assets. (610)

cash flows from operating activities The section of the statement of cash flows that reports the cash transactions affecting the determination of net income. (610)

cash payback period The expected period of time that will elapse between the date of a capital expenditure and the complete recovery in cash (or equivalent) of the amount invested. (1104)

cash short and over account An account which has recorded errors in cash sales or errors in making change causing the amount of actual cash on hand to differ from the beginning amount of cash plus the cash sales for the day. (317)

Certified Management Accountant (CMA) A private accountant employed by companies, government, and not-for-profit entities, requiring a college degree, two years of experience, and successful completion of a two-day examination. (9)

Certified Public Accountant (CPA) Public accountants who have met a state's education, experience, and examination requirements. (10)

chart of accounts A list of the accounts in the ledger. (53)

clearing account Another name for the Income Summary account because it has the effect of clearing the revenue and expense accounts of their balances. (154)

closing entries The entries that transfer the balances of the revenue, expense, and drawing accounts to the owner's capital account. (154)

closing process The transfer process of converting temporary account balances to zero by transferring the revenue and expense account balances to Income Summary, transferring the Income Summary account balance to the owner's capital account, and transferring the owner's drawing account to the owner's capital account. (154)

common stock The stock outstanding when a corporation has issued only one class of stock. (490)

common-size statement A financial statement in which all items are expressed only in relative terms. (665)

compensating balance A requirement by some banks requiring depositors to maintain minimum cash balances in their bank accounts. (328)

comprehensive income All changes in stockholders' equity during a period, except those resulting from dividends and stockholders' investments. (536)

consolidated financial statements Financial statements resulting from combining parent and subsidiary statements. (543)

continuous budgeting A method of budgeting that provides for maintaining a twelve-month projection into the future. (936)

continuous process improvement A management approach that is part of the overall total quality management philosophy. The approach requires all employees to constantly improve processes of which they are a part or for which they have managerial responsibility. (718)

contra account (or contra asset account) An account offset against another account. (117)

contract rate The periodic interest to be paid on the bonds that is identified in the bond indenture; expressed as a percentage of the face amount of the bond. (569)

contribution margin Sales less variable costs and variable selling and administrative expenses. (846, 885)

contribution margin analysis The systematic examination of the differences between planned and actual contribution margins. (899)

contribution margin ratio The percentage of each sales dollar that is available to cover the fixed costs and provide an operating income. (846)

controllable cost Cost that can be influenced (increased, decreased, or eliminated) by someone such as a manager or factory worker. (892)

controllable expenses Costs that can be influenced by the decisions of a manager. (1024)

controllable variance The difference between the actual amount of variable factory overhead cost incurred and the amount of variable factory overhead budgeted for the standard product. (988)

controller The chief management accountant of a division or other segment of a business. (716)

controlling A phase in the management process that consists of monitoring the operating results of implemented plans and comparing the actual results with the expected results. (718)

controlling account The account in the general ledger that summarizes the balances of the accounts in a subsidiary ledger. (220)

conversion costs The combination of direct labor and factory overhead costs. (723)

copyright An exclusive right to publish and sell a literary, artistic, or musical composition. (414)

corporation A business organized under state or federal statutes as a separate legal entity. (3)

cost A payment of cash (or a commitment to pay cash in the future) for the purpose of generating revenues. (719)

cost accounting system A branch of managerial accounting concerned with accumulating manufacturing costs for financial reporting and decision-making purposes. (751)

cost allocation The process of assigning indirect cost to a cost object, such as a job. (757)

cost behavior The manner in which a cost changes in relation to its activity base (driver). (840)

cost center A decentralized unit in which the department or division manager has responsibility for the control of costs incurred and the authority to make decisions that affect these costs. (1022)

cost concept A concept of accounting that determines the amount initially entered into the accounting records for purchases. (11)

cost object The object or segment of operations to which costs are related for management's use, such as a product or department. (720)

cost of goods manufactured The total cost of making and finishing a product. (726)

cost of goods sold budget A budget of the estimated direct materials, direct labor, and factory overhead consumed by sold products. (945)

cost of merchandise purchased The cost of net purchases plus transportation costs. (215)

cost of merchandise sold The cost that is reported as an expense when merchandise is sold. (213, 726)

cost of production report A report prepared periodically by a processing department, summarizing (1) the units for which the department is accountable and the disposition of those units and (2) the costs incurred by the department and the allocation of those costs between completed and incomplete production. (804)

cost of quality report A report summarizing the costs, percent of total, and percent of sales by appraisal, prevention, internal failure, and external failure cost of quality categories. (1203)

cost per equivalent unit The rate used to allocate costs between completed and partially completed production. (802)

cost price approach An approach to transfer pricing that uses cost as the basis for setting the transfer price. (1038)

cost variance The difference between actual cost and the flexible budget at actual volumes. (978)

costs of quality The cost associated with controlling quality (prevention and appraisal) and failing to control quality (internal and external failure). (1199)

cost-volume-profit analysis The systematic examination of the relationships among selling prices, volume of sales and production, costs, expenses, and profits. (846)

cost-volume-profit chart A chart used to assist management in understanding the relationships among costs, expenses, sales, and operating profit or loss. (853)

credit memorandum A form used by a seller to inform the buyer of the amount the seller proposes to credit to the account receivable due from the buyer. (223)

credit period The amount of time the buyer is allowed in which to pay the seller. (222)

credit terms Terms for payment on account by the buyer to the seller. (222)

credits Amounts entered on the right side of an account. (52)

currency exchange rate The rate at which currency in another country can be exchanged for local currency. (1115)

current assets Cash and other assets that are expected to be converted to cash or sold or used up, usually within one year or less, through the normal operations of the business. (152)

current liabilities Liabilities that will be due within a short time (usually one year or less) and that are to be paid out of current assets. (152)

current ratio A financial ratio that is computed by dividing current assets by current liabilities. (667)

currently attainable standards Standards that represent levels of operation that can be attained with reasonable effort. (979)

D

debit memorandum A form used by a buyer to inform the seller of the amount the buyer proposes to debit to the account payable due the seller. (226)

debits Amounts entered on the left side of an account. (52)

decentralization The separation of a business into more manageable operating units. (1020)

decision making A component inherent in the other management processes of planning, directing, controlling, and improving. (718)

defined benefit plan A pension plan that promises employees a fixed annual pension benefit at retirement, based on years of service and compensation levels. (457)

defined contribution plan A pension plan that requires a fixed amount of money to be invested for the employee's behalf during the employee's working years. (456)

depletion The process of transferring the cost of natural resources to an expense account. (412)

depreciation The systematic periodic transfer of the cost of a fixed asset to an expense account during its expected useful life. (117, 400)

depreciation expense The portion of the cost of a fixed asset that is recorded as an expense each year of its useful life. (117)

differential analysis The area of accounting concerned with the effect of alternative courses of action on revenues and costs. (1063)

differential cost The amount of increase or decrease in cost expected from a particular course of action compared with an alternative. (1063)

differential revenue The amount of increase or decrease in revenue expected from a particular course of action as compared with an alternative. (1062)

direct costs Costs that can be traced directly to a cost object. (720)

direct labor cost The wages of factory workers who are directly involved in converting materials into a finished product. (722)

direct labor rate variance The cost associated with the difference between the standard rate and the actual rate paid for direct labor used in producing a commodity. (985)

direct labor time variance The cost associated with the difference between the standard hours and the actual hours of direct labor spent producing a commodity. (985)

direct materials cost The cost of materials that are an integral part of the finished product. (721)

direct materials price variance The cost associated with the difference between the standard price and the actual price of direct materials used in producing a commodity. (983)

direct materials purchases budget A budget that uses the production budget as a starting point to budget materials purchases. (942)

direct materials quantity variance The cost associated with the difference between the standard quantity and the actual quantity of direct materials used in producing a commodity. (984)

direct method A method of reporting the cash flows from operating activities as the difference between the operating cash receipts and the operating cash payments. (612)

direct write-off method The method of accounting for uncollectible accounts that recognizes the expense only when accounts are judged to be worthless. (355)

directing The process by which managers, given their assigned level of responsibilities, run day-to-day operations. (717)

discontinued operations Operations of a major line of business or component for a company, such as a division, a department, or a certain class of customer, that have been disposed of. (533)

discount The interest deducted from the maturity value of a note or the excess of the face amount of bonds over their issue price. (441, 492, 569)

discount rate The rate used in computing the interest to be deducted from the maturity value of a note. (441)

dishonored note receivable A note that the maker fails to pay on the due date. (366)

dividend yield A ratio, computed by dividing the annual dividends paid per share of common stock by the market price per share at a specific date, that indicates the rate of return to stockholders in terms of cash dividend distributions. (504, 679)

dividends Distributions to the owners (stockholders) of a corporation. (16, 53)

division A decentralized unit that is structured around a common function, product, customer, or geographical territory. (1020)

double-declining-balance method A method of depreciation that provides periodic depreciation expense based on the declining book value of a fixed asset over its estimated life. (403)

double-entry accounting system A system of accounting for recording transactions, based on recording increases and decreases in accounts so that debits equal credits. (60)

DuPont formula An expanded expression of return on investment determined by multiplying the profit margin by the investment turnover. (1029)

E

earnings per common share (EPS) Net income per share of common stock outstanding during a period. (535)

earnings per share (EPS) on common stock The profitability ratio of net income available to common shareholders to the number of common shares outstanding. (677)

effective interest rate method The method of amortizing discounts and premiums that provides for a constant rate of interest on the carrying amount of the bonds at the beginning of each period; often called simply the "interest method." (575)

effective rate of interest The market rate of interest at the time bonds are issued. (569)

electronic data interchange (EDI) An information technology that allows different business organizations to use computers to communicate orders, relay information, and make or receive payments. (1191)

electronic funds transfer (EFT) A system in which computers rather than paper (money, checks, etc.) are used to effect cash transactions. (318)

elements of internal control The control environment, risk assessment, control activities, information and communication, and monitoring. (311)

employee fraud The intentional act of deceiving an employer for personal gain. (310)

employee involvement A philosophy that grants employees the responsibility and authority to make their own decisions about their operations. (1190)

employee's earnings record A detailed record of each employee's earnings. (451)

engineering change order (ECO) A document that initiates a change in the specification or a product or process. (1146)

enterprise resource planning (ERP) An integrated business and information system used by companies to plan and control both internal and supply chain operations. (1192)

equity method A method of accounting for an investment in common stock by which the investment account is adjusted for the investor's share of periodic net income and cash dividends of the investee. (541)

equity securities The common and preferred stock of a firm. (538)

equivalent units of production The number of production units that could have been completed within a given accounting period, given the resources consumed. (798)

ethics Moral principles that guide the conduct of individuals. (4)

expenses Assets used up or services consumed in the process of generating revenues. (15, 53)

external failure costs The costs incurred after defective units or services have been delivered to consumers. (1200)

extraordinary items Events and transactions that (1) are significantly different (unusual) from the typical or the normal operating activities of a business and (2) occur infrequently. (534)

F

factory burden Another term for manufacturing overhead or factory overhead. (722)

factory overhead cost All of the costs of producing a product except for direct materials and direct labor. (722)

feedback Measures provided to operational employees or managers on the performance of subunits of the organization. These measures are used by employees to adjust a process or a behavior to achieve goals. *See* **management by exception**. (718)

fees earned Revenue from providing services. (14)

FICA tax Federal Insurance Contributions Act tax used to finance federal programs for old-age and disability benefits (social security) and health insurance for the aged (Medicare). (445)

financial accounting The branch of accounting that is concerned with recording transactions using generally accepted accounting principles (GAAP) for a business or other economic unit and with a periodic preparation of various statements from such records. (8, 714)

Financial Accounting Standards Board (FASB) The authoritative body that has the primary responsibility for developing accounting principles. (10)

financial statements Financial reports that summarize the effects of events on a business. (18)

finished goods inventory The direct materials costs, direct labor costs, and factory overhead costs of finished products that have not been sold. (726)

finished goods ledger The subsidiary ledger that contains the individual accounts for each kind of commodity or product produced. (762)

first-in, first-out (FIFO) method The method of inventory costing based on the assumption that the costs of merchandise sold should be charged against revenue in the order in which the costs were incurred. (270, 796)

fiscal year The annual accounting period adopted by a business. (176)

fixed (plant) assets Assets that depreciate over time, such as equipment, machinery, and buildings. (152)

fixed asset impairment A condition when the fair value of a fixed asset falls below its book value and is not expected to recover. (531)

fixed asset turnover ratio The number of dollars of sales that are generated from each dollar of average fixed assets during the year, computed by dividing the net sales by the average net fixed assets. (418)

fixed assets (or plant assets) Long-term or relatively permanent tangible assets that are used in the normal business operations. (117, 395)

fixed costs Costs that tend to remain the same in amount, regardless of variations in the level of activity. (842)

flexible budget A budget that adjusts for varying rates of activity. (938)

FOB (free on board) destination Freight terms in which the seller pays the transportation costs from the shipping point to the final destination. (228)

FOB (free on board) shipping point Freight terms in which the buyer pays the transportation costs from the shipping point to the final destination. (228)

free cash flow The amount of operating cash flow remaining after replacing current productive capacity and maintaining current dividends. (630)

fringe benefits Benefits provided to employees in addition to wages and salaries. (455)

future value The estimated worth in the future of an amount of cash on hand today invested at a fixed rate of interest. (569)

G

general ledger The primary ledger, when used in conjunction with subsidiary ledgers, that contains all of the balance sheet and income statement accounts. (220)

generally accepted accounting principles (GAAP) Generally accepted guidelines for the preparation of financial statements. (10)

goal conflict A condition that occurs when individual objectives conflict with organizational objectives. (935)

goodwill An intangible asset that is created from such favorable factors as location, product quality, reputation, and managerial skill. (414)

gross pay The total earnings of an employee for an employee for a payroll period. (443)

gross profit Sales minus the cost of merchandise sold. (213)

gross profit method A method of estimating inventory cost that is based on the relationship of gross profit to sales. (285)

H

held-to-maturity securities Investments in bonds or other debt securities that management intends to hold to their maturity. (582)

high-low method A technique that uses the highest and lowest total costs as a basis for estimating the variable cost per unit and the fixed cost component of a mixed cost. (844)

horizontal analysis Financial analysis that compares an item in a current statement with the same item in prior statements. (660)

I

ideal standards Standards that can be achieved only under perfect operating conditions, such as no idle time, no machine breakdowns, and no materials spoilage; also called theoretical standards. (979)

income from operations (operating income) Revenues less operating expenses and service department charges for a profit or investment center. (216, 1027)

income statement A summary of the revenue and expenses *for a specific period of time*, such as a month or a year. (18)

Income Summary An account to which the revenue and expense account balances are transferred at the end of a period. (154)

indirect costs Costs that cannot be traced directly to a cost object. (720)

indirect method A method of reporting the cash flows from operating activities as the net income from operations adjusted for all deferrals of past cash receipts and payments and all accruals of expected future cash receipts and payments. (612)

inflation A period when prices in general are rising and the purchasing power of money is declining. (1115)

intangible assets Long-term assets that are useful in the operations of a business, are not held for sale, and are without physical qualities. (413)

interest revenue Money received for interest. (15)

internal controls The policies and procedures used to safeguard assets, ensure accurate business information, and ensure compliance with laws and regulations. (308)

internal failure costs The costs associated with defects that are discovered by the organization before the product or service is delivered to the consumer. (1200)

internal rate of return (IRR) method A method of analysis of proposed capital investments that uses present value concepts to compute the rate of return from the net cash flows expected from the investment. (1110)

inventory shrinkage The amount by which the merchandise for sale, as indicated by the balance of the merchandise inventory account, is larger than the total amount of merchandise counted during the physical inventory. (232)

inventory turnover The relationship between the volume of goods sold and inventory, computed by dividing the cost of goods sold by the average inventory. (286, 670)

investment center A decentralized unit in which the manager has the responsibility and authority to make decisions that affect not only costs and revenues but also the fixed assets available to the center. (1028)

investment turnover A component of the rate of return on investment, computed as the ratio of sales to invested assets. (1029)

investments The balance sheet caption used to report long-term investments in stocks not intended as a source of cash in the normal operations of the business. (541)

invoice The bill that the seller sends to the buyer. (222)

J

job cost sheet An account in the work in process subsidiary ledger in which the costs charged to a particular job order are recorded. (754)

job order cost system A type of cost accounting system that provides for a separate record of the cost of each particular quantity of product that passes through the factory. (751)

journal The initial record in which the effects of a transaction are recorded. (54)

journal entry The form of recording a transaction in a journal. (54)

journalizing The process of recording a transaction in the journal. (54)

just-in-time (JIT) manufacturing A business philosophy that focuses on eliminating time, cost, and poor quality within manufacturing processes. (1185)

just-in-time (JIT) processing A processing approach that focuses on eliminating time, cost, and poor quality within manufacturing and nonmanufacturing processes. (809)

L

last-in, first-out (LIFO) method A method of inventory costing based on the assumption that the most recent merchandise inventory costs should be charged against revenue. (270)

lead time The elapsed time between starting a unit of product into the beginning of a process and its completion. (1186)

ledger A group of accounts for a business. (53)

leverage The amount of debt used by a firm to finance its assets; causes the rate earned on stockholders' equity to vary from the rate earned on total assets because the amount earned on assets acquired through the use of funds provided by creditors varies from the interest paid to these creditors. (675)

liabilities The rights of creditors that represent debts of the business. (12, 53)

limited liability company (LLC) A business form consisting of one or more persons or entities filing an operating agreement with a state to conduct business with limited liability to the owners, yet treated as a partnership for tax purposes. (4)

line department A unit that is directly involved in the basic objectives of an organization. (715)

long-term liabilities Liabilities that usually will not be due for more than one year. (152)

lower-of-cost-or-market (LCM) method A method of valuing inventory that reports the inventory at the lower of its cost or current market value (replacement cost). (280)

M

management (or managerial) accounting The branch of accounting that uses both historical and estimated data in providing information that management uses in conducting daily operations, in planning future operations, and in developing overall business strategies. (9)

management by exception The philosophy of managing which involves monitoring the operating results of implemented plans and comparing the expected results with the actual results. This feedback allows management to isolate significant variations for further investigation and possible remedial action. (718)

management process The five basic management functions of (1) planning, (2) directing, (3) controlling, (4) improving, and (5) decision making. (716)

Management's Discussion and Analysis (MD&A) An annual report disclosure that provides management's analysis of the results of operations and financial condition. (681)

managerial accounting The branch of accounting that uses both historical and estimated data in providing information that management uses in conducting daily

operations, in planning future operations, and in developing overall business strategies. (715)

manufacturing business A type of business that changes basic inputs into products that are sold to individual customers. (3)

manufacturing cells A grouping of processes where employees are cross-trained to perform more than one function. (810)

manufacturing margin The variable cost of goods sold deducted from sales. (885)

manufacturing overhead Costs, other than direct materials and direct labor costs, that are incurred in the manufacturing process. (722)

margin of safety The difference between current sales revenue and the sales at the break-even point. (860)

market price approach An approach to transfer pricing that uses the price at which the product or service transferred could be sold to outside buyers as the transfer price. (1035)

market segment A portion of business that can be assigned to a manager for profit responsibility. (894)

markup An amount that is added to a "cost" amount to determine product price. (1072)

master budget The comprehensive budget plan linking all the individual budgets related to sales, cost of goods sold, operating expenses, projects, capital expenditures, and cash. (940)

matching concept (or matching principle) A concept of accounting in which expenses are matched with the revenue generated during a period by those expenses. (20, 106)

materiality concept A concept of accounting that implies that an error may be treated in the easiest possible way. (75)

materials inventory The cost of materials that have not yet entered into the manufacturing process. (725)

materials ledger The subsidiary ledger containing the individual accounts for each type of material. (754)

materials requisitions The form or electronic transmission used by a manufacturing department to authorize materials issuances from the storeroom. (754)

maturity value The amount that is due at the maturity or due date of a note. (366)

merchandise available for sale The cost of merchandise available for sale to customers. (216)

merchandise inventory Merchandise on hand (not sold) at the end of an accounting period. (213)

merchandising business A type of business that purchases products from other businesses and sells them to customers. (3)

mixed cost A cost with both variable and fixed characteristics, sometimes called a semivariable or semifixed cost. (842)

multiple production department factory overhead rate method A method that allocated factory overhead to product by using factory overhead rates for each production department. (1141)

multiple-step income statement A form of income statement that contains several sections, subsections, and subtotals. (214)

N

natural business year   A fiscal year that ends when business activities have reached the lowest point in an annual operating cycle. (176)

negotiated price approach   An approach to transfer pricing that allows managers of decentralized units to agree (negotiate) among themselves as to the transfer price. (1036)

net income or net profit   The amount by which revenues exceed expenses. (20)

net loss   The amount by which expenses exceed revenues. (20)

net pay   Gross pay less payroll deductions; the amount the employer is obligated to pay the employee. (443)

net present value method   A method of analysis of proposed capital investments that focuses on the present value of the cash flows expected from the investments. (1108)

net purchases   Determined when purchases returns and allowances and the purchases discounts are deducted from the total purchases. (215)

net realizable value   The estimated selling price of an item of inventory less any direct costs of disposal, such as sales commissions. (281, 357)

net sales   Revenue received for merchandise sold to customers less any sales returns and allowances and sales discounts. (214)

noncontrollable costs   Costs that cannot be influenced (increased, decreased, or eliminated) by someone such as a manager or factory worker. (892)

nonfinancial measure   A performance measure that has not been stated in dollar terms. (1197)

nonfinancial performance measure   A performance measure expressed in units rather than dollars. (995)

non-value-added activities   The cost of activities that are perceived as unnecessary from the customer's perspective and are thus candidates for elimination. (1203)

non-value-added lead time   The time that units wait in inventories, move unnecessarily, and wait during machine breakdowns. (1187)

notes receivable   A customer's written promise to pay an amount and possibly interest at an agreed-upon rate. (152, 354)

number of days' sales in inventory   The relationship between the volume of sales and inventory, computed by dividing the inventory at the end of the year by the average daily cost of goods sold. (269, 671)

number of days' sales in receivables   The relationship between sales and accounts receivable, computed by dividing the net accounts receivable at the end of the year by the average daily sales. (369, 672)

number of times interest charges are earned   A ratio that measures creditor margin of safety for interest payments, calculated as income before interest and taxes divided by interest expense. (584)

O

objectives (goals)   Developed in the planning stage, these reflect the direction and desired outcomes of certain courses of action. (717)

objectivity concept   A concept of accounting that requires accounting records and the data reported in financial statements be based on objective evidence. (11)

operating leases   Leases that do not meet the criteria for capital leases and thus are accounted for as operating expenses. (399)

operating leverage   A measure of the relative mix of a business's variable costs and fixed costs, computed as contribution margin divided by operating income. (859)

operational planning   The development of short-term plans to achieve goals identified in a business's strategic plan. Sometimes called tactical planning. (717)

opportunity cost   The amount of income forgone from an alternative to a proposed use of cash or its equivalent. (1069)

other comprehensive income items   Specified items that are reported separately from net income, including foreign currency items, pension liability adjustments, and unrealized gains and losses on investments. (536)

other expense   Expenses that cannot be traced directly to operations. (217)

other income   Revenue from sources other than the primary operating activity of a business. (217)

outstanding stock   The stock in the hands of stockholders. (489)

overapplied factory overhead   The amount of factory overhead applied in excess of the actual factory overhead costs incurred for production during a period. (758)

owner's equity   The owner's right to the assets of the business. (12)

P

par   The monetary amount printed on a stock certificate. (489)

parent company   The corporation owning all or a majority of the voting stock of the other corporation. (543)

Pareto chart   A bar chart that shows the totals of a particular attribute for a number of categories, ranked left to right from the largest to smallest totals. (1201)

partnership   An unincorporated business form consisting of two or more persons conducting business as co-owners for profit. (3)

patents   Exclusive rights to produce and sell goods with one or more unique features. (413)

payroll   The total amount paid to employees for a certain period. (442)

payroll register   A multicolumn report used to assemble and summarize payroll data at the end of each payroll period. (448)

period costs   Those costs that are used up in generating revenue during the current period and that are not involved in manufacturing a product, such as selling, general, and administratvie expenses. (723, 763)

periodic system   The inventory system in which the inventory records do not show the amount available for sale or sold during the period. (216)

permanent differences   Differences between taxable and income (before taxes) reported on the income statement that may arise because certain revenues are exempt from tax and certain expenses are not deductible in determining taxable income. (529)

perpetual system   The inventory system in which each purchase and sale of merchandise is recorded in an inventory account. (216)

petty cash fund A special cash fund to pay relatively small amounts. (327)

physical inventory A detailed listing of merchandise on hand. (269)

planning A phase of the management process whereby objectives are outlined and courses of action determined. (717)

post-closing trial balance A summary listing of the titles and balances of accounts in the ledger after closing entries have been prepared to ensure the ledger is in balance at the beginning of the next period. (157)

posting The process of transferring the debits and credits from the journal entries to the accounts. (61)

predetermined factory overhead rate The rate used to apply factory overhead costs to the goods manufactured. The rate is determined by dividing the budgeted overhead cost by the estimated activity usage at the beginning of the fiscal period. (757)

preferred stock A class of stock with preferential rights over common stock. (490)

premium The excess of the issue price of a stock over its par value or the excess of the issue price of bonds over their face amount. (492, 569)

prepaid expenses Items such as supplies that will be used in the business in the future. *Also see* **deferred expenses**. (14, 108)

present value The estimated worth today of an amount of cash to be received (or paid) in the future. (569)

present value concept Cash to be received (or paid) in the future is not the equivalent of the same amount of money received at an earlier date. (1106)

present value index An index computed by dividing the total present value of the net cash flow to be received from a proposed capital investment by the amount to be invested. (1108)

present value of an annuity The sum of the present values of a series of equal cash flows to be received at fixed intervals. (571, 1107)

prevention costs Costs incurred to prevent defects from occurring during the design and delivery of products or services. (1200)

price factor The effect of a difference in unit sales price or unit cost on the number of units sold. (899)

price-earnings (P/E) ratio The ratio of the market price per share of common stock, at a specific date, to the annual earnings per share. (544, 677)

prime costs The combination of direct materials and direct labor costs. (723)

prior period adjustments Corrections of material errors related to a prior period or periods, excluded from the determination of net income. (502)

private accounting The field of accounting whereby accountants are employed by a business firm or a not-for-profit organization. (9)

proceeds The net amount available from discounting a note payable. (441)

process A sequence of activities linked together for performing a particular task. (995, 1204)

process cost system A type of cost system that accumulates costs for each of the various departments within a manufacturing facility. (752, 793)

process manufacturers Manufacturers that use large machines to process a continuous flow of raw materials through various stages of completion into a finished state. (792)

process-oriented layout Organizing work in a plant or administrative function around processes (tasks). (1190)

product cost concept A concept used in applying the cost-plus approach to product pricing in which only the costs of manufacturing the product, termed the product cost, are included in the cost amount to which the markup is added. (1075)

product costing Determining the cost of a product. (1138)

product costs The three components of manufacturing cost: direct materials, direct labor, and factory overhead costs. (723)

production budget A budget of estimated unit production. (941)

production department factory overhead rates Rates determined by dividing the budgeted production department factory overhead by the budgeted allocation base for each department. (1142)

product-oriented layout Organizing work in a plant or administrative function around products; sometimes referred to as product cells. (1190)

profit center A decentralized unit in which the manager has the responsibility and the authority to make decisions that affect both costs and revenues (and thus profits). (1024)

profit margin A component of the rate of return on investment, computed as the ratio of income from operations to sales. (1029)

profit-volume chart A chart used to assist management in understanding the relationship between profit and volume. (855)

profit The difference between the amounts received from customers for goods or services provided and the amounts paid for the inputs used to provide the goods or services. (2)

profitability The ability of a firm to earn income. (666)

property, plant, and equipment The section of the balance sheet that includes equipment, machinery, buildings, and land. (152)

proprietorship A business owned by one individual. (3)

public accounting The field of accounting where accountants and their staff provide services on a fee basis. (9)

pull manufacturing A just-in-time method wherein customer orders trigger the release of finished goods, which trigger production, which trigger release of materials from suppliers. (1191)

purchase return or allowance From the buyer's perspective, returned merchandise or an adjustment for defective merchandise. (214)

purchases discounts Discounts taken by the buyer for early payment of an invoice. (214)

push manufacturing Materials are released into production and work in process is released into finished goods in anticipation of future sales. (1191)

Q

quantity factor The effect of a difference in the number of units sold, assuming no change in unit sales price or unit cost. (899)

quick assets Cash and other current assets that can be quickly converted to cash, such as marketable securities and receivables. (461, 668)

quick ratio A financial ratio that measures the ability to pay current liabilities with quick assets (cash, marketable securities, accounts receivable). (461, 668)

R

radio frequency identification devices (RFID) Electronic tags (chips) placed on or embedded within products that can be read by radio waves that allow instant monitoring of product location. (1191)

rate earned on common stockholders' equity A measure of profitability computed by dividing net income, reduced by preferred dividend requirements, by common stockholders' equity. (676)

rate earned on stockholders' equity A measure of profitability computed by dividing net income by total stockholders' equity. (675)

rate earned on total assets A measure of the profitability of assets, without regard to the equity of creditors and stockholders in the assets. (674)

rate of return on investment (ROI) A measure of managerial efficiency in the use of investments in assets, computed as income from operations divided by invested assets. (1029)

ratio of fixed assets to long-term liabilities A leverage ratio that measures the margin of safety of long-term creditors, calculated as the net fixed assets divided by the long-term liabilities. (671)

ratio of liabilities to stockholders' equity A comprehensive leverage ratio that measures the relationship of the claims of creditors to that stockholders' equity. (672)

Raw and In Process (RIP) Inventory The capitalized cost of direct materials purchases, labor, and overhead charged to the production cell. (1194)

real accounts Term for balance sheet accounts because they are relatively permanent and carried forward from year to year. (154)

receivables All money claims against other entities, including people, business firms, and other organizations. (354)

receiving report The form or electronic transmission used by the receiving personnel to indicate that materials have been received and inspected. (754)

relevant range The range of activity over which changes in cost are of interest to management. (840)

rent revenue Money received for rent. (15)

report form The form of balance sheet with the liabilities and owner's equity sections presented below the assets section. (21, 219)

residual income The excess of divisional income from operations over a "minimum" acceptable income from operations. (1032)

residual value The estimated value of a fixed asset at the end of its useful life. (400)

responsibility accounting The process of measuring and reporting operating data by areas of responsibility. (1021)

responsibility center An organizational unit for which a manager is assigned responsibility over costs, revenues, or assets. (933)

restrictions Amounts of retained earnings that have been limited for use as dividends. (501)

restructuring charge The costs associated with involuntarily terminating employees, terminating contracts, consolidating facilities, or relocating employees. (532)

retail inventory method A method of estimating inventory cost that is based on the relationship of gross profit to sales. (234)

retained earnings Net income retained in a corporation. (17)

retained earnings statement A summary of the changes in the retained earnings in a corporation for a specific period of time, such as a month or a year. (18, 501)

revenue expenditures Costs that benefit only the current period or costs incurred for normal maintenance and repairs of fixed assets. (398)

revenue recognition concept The accounting concept that supports reporting revenues when the services are provided to customers. (106)

revenues Increases in owner's equity as a result of selling services or products to customers. (14, 53)

S

sales The total amount charged customers for merchandise sold, including cash sales and sales on account. (14, 214)

sales budget One of the major elements of the income statement budget that indicates the quantity of estimated sales and the expected unit selling price. (941)

sales discounts From the seller's perspective, discounts that a seller may offer the buyer for early payment. (214)

sales mix The relative distribution of sales among the various products available for sale. (858, 896)

sales returns and allowances From the seller's perspective, returned merchandise or an adjustment for defective merchandise. (214)

Sarbanes-Oxley Act of 2002 An act passed by Congress to restore public confidence and trust in the financial statements of companies. (308)

selling expenses Expenses that are incurred directly in the selling of merchandise. (216)

service business A business providing services rather than products to customers. (3)

service department charges The costs of services provided by an internal service department and transferred to a responsibility center. (1025)

setup Changing the characteristics of a machine to produce a different product. (1146)

single plantwide factory overhead rate method A method that allocates all factory overhead to products by using a single factory overhead rate. (1139)

single-step income statement A form of income statement in which the total of all expenses is deducted from the total of all revenues. (217)

sinking fund A fund in which cash or assets are set aside for the purpose of paying the face amount of the bonds at maturity. (578)

six-sigma A quality improvement process developed by Motorola Corporation consisting of five steps: define, measure, analyze, improve, and control (DMAIC). (1191)

slide An error in which the entire number is moved one or more spaces to the right or the left, such as writing $542.00 as $54.20 or $5,420.00. (76)

solvency The ability of a firm to pay its debts as they come due. (666)

special-purpose fund A cash fund used for a special business need. (327)

staff department A unit that provides services, assistance, and advice to the departments with line or other staff responsibilities. (716)

standard cost A detailed estimate of what a product should cost. (978)

standard cost systems Accounting systems that use standards for each element of manufacturing cost entering into the finished product. (978)

stated value A value, similar to par value, approved by the board of directors of a corporation for no-par stock. (489)

statement of cost of goods manufactured The income statement of manufacturing companies. (727)

statement of cash flows A summary of the cash receipts and cash payments *for a specific period of time*, such as a month or a year. (18, 610)

statement of stockholders' equity A summary of the changes in the stockholders' equity in a corporation that have occurred during a specific period of time. (502)

static budget A budget that does not adjust to changes in activity levels. (937)

stock Shares of ownership of a corporation. (486)

stock dividend A distribution of shares of stock to its stockholders. (497)

stock split A reduction in the par or stated value of a common stock and the issuance of a proportionate number of additional shares. (503)

stockholders The owners of a corporation. (486)

stockholders' equity The owners' equity in a corporation. (13, 53)

straight-line method A method of depreciation that provides for equal periodic depreciation expense over the estimated life of a fixed asset. (402)

strategic planning The development of a long-range course of action to achieve business goals. (717)

strategies The means by which business goals and objectives will be achieved. (717)

subsidiary company The corporation that is controlled by a parent company. (543)

subsidiary ledger A ledger containing individual accounts with a common characteristic. (220)

sunk cost A cost that is not affected by subsequent decisions. (1062)

supply chain management The coordination and control of materials, services, information, and finances as they move in a process from supplier, through the manufacturer, wholesaler, and retailer to the consumer. (1191)

T

T account The simplest form of an account. (51)

target costing The target cost is determined by subtracting a desired profit from a market method determined price. The resulting target cost is used to motivate cost improvements in design and manufacture. (1077)

taxable income The income according to the tax laws that is used as a base for determining the amount of taxes owed. (527)

temporary (nominal) accounts Accounts that report amounts for only one period. (154)

temporary differences Differences between taxable income and income before income taxes, created because items are recognized in one period for tax purposes and in another period for income statement purposes. Such differences reverse or turn around in later years. (528)

temporary investments The balances sheet caption used to report investments in income-yielding securities that can be quickly sold and converted to cash as needed. (538)

theory of constraints (TOC) A manufacturing strategy that attempts to remove the influence of bottlenecks (constraints) on a process. (1078)

time tickets The form on which the amount of time spent by each employee and the labor cost incurred for each individual job, or for factory overhead, are recorded. (755)

time value of money concept The concept that an amount of money invested today will earn income. (1103)

total cost concept A concept used in applying the cost-plus approach to product pricing in which all the costs of manufacturing the product plus the selling and administrative expenses are included in the cost amount to which the markup is added. (1073)

trade discounts Discounts from the list prices in published catalogs or special discounts offered to certain classes of buyers. (230)

trade-in allowance The amount a seller allows a buyer for a fixed asset that is traded in for a similar asset. (409)

trademark A name, term, or symbol used to identify a business and its products. (414)

trading securities Securities that management intends to actively trade for profit. (538)

transfer price The price charged one decentralized unit by another for the goods or services provided. (1035)

transportation in Costs of transportation. (215)

transposition An error in which the order of the digits is changed, such as writing $542 as $452 or $524. (76)

treasury stock Stock that a corporation has once issued and then reacquires. (498)

trial balance A summary listing of the titles and balances of accounts in the ledger. (74)

two-column journal An all-purpose journal. (61)

U

underapplied factory overhead The amount of actual factory overhead in excess of the factory overhead applied to production during a period. (758)

unearned revenue The liability created by receiving revenue in advance. (63)

unearned revenues *See* **deferred revenues**. (108)

unit contribution margin The dollars available from each unit of sales to cover fixed costs and provide operating profits. (847)

unit of measure concept A concept of accounting requiring that economic data be recorded in dollars. (11)

units-of-production method   A method of depreciation that provides for depreciation expense based on the expected productive capacity of a fixed asset. (402)

unrealized holding gain or loss   The difference between the fair market value of the securities and their cost. (539)

V

value-added activities   The cost of activities that are needed to meet customer requirements. (1203)

value-added lead time   The time required to manufacture a unit of product or other output. (1186)

value-added ratio   The ratio of the value-added lead time to the total lead time. (1187)

variable cost concept   A concept used in applying the cost-plus approach to product pricing in which only the variable costs are included in the cost amount to which the markup is added. (1076)

variable costing   The concept that considers the cost of products manufactured to be composed only of those manufacturing costs that increase or decrease as the volume of production rises or falls (direct materials, direct labor, and variable factory overhead). (845, 884)

variable costs   Costs that vary in total dollar amount as the level of activity changes. (841)

vertical analysis   An analysis that compares each item in a current statement with a total amount within the same statement. (663)

volume variance   The difference between the budgeted fixed overhead at 100% of normal capacity and the standard fixed overhead for the actual production achieved during the period. (989)

voucher   A special form for recording relevant data about a liability and the details of its payment. (319)

voucher system   A set of procedures for authorizing and recording liabilities and cash payments. (319)

W

whole units   The number of units in production during a period, whether completed or not. (798)

work in process inventory   The direct materials costs, the direct labor costs, and the applied factory overhead costs that have entered into the manufacturing process but are associated with products that have not been finished. (725)

Y

yield   A measure of materials usage efficiency. (809)

Z

zero-based budgeting   A concept of budgeting that requires all levels of management to start from zero and estimate budget data as if there had been no previous activities in their units. (936)

Subject Index

Income from operations
  comparing under the two concepts, 889
  def., 216, 1027
  rate of, to total assets, 675
  when units manufactured are less than units sold, 887
  when units manufactured equal units sold, 886
  when units manufactured exceed units sold, 886
Income statement(s), 20, 149
  absorption costing, 884, *illus.*, 886, 890
  accounts, 56
  balance sheet columns and, 180
  balance sheet data for direct method and, *illus.*, 625
  budgeted, *illus.*, 947
  budgets, 941, *illus.*, 940
  by product line report, variable costing, *illus.*, 897
  by salesperson report, variable costing, *illus.*, 897
  columns, spreadsheet with amounts extended to, *illus.*, 181
  common-size, *illus.*, 665
  comparative, *illus.*, 662, 664
  contribution margin, *illus.*, 846
  def., 18
  for a manufacturing company, 726
  for three production levels, variable costing, *illus.*, 891
  for two production levels, absorption costing, *illus.*, 890
  illus., 763, 1036, 1037
  multiple-step, 214, *illus.*, 215
  reporting unusual items on, 530, *illus.*, 531
  single-step, 217, *illus.*, 218
  unusual items affecting current period's, 530
  unusual items affecting prior period's, 534
  unusual items in, *illus.*, 532
  variable costing, 884, *illus.*, 885, 891, 902, 903
  variances from standards in, *illus.*, 994
  with earnings per share, *illus.*, 536
  with statement of costs of goods manufactured, *illus.*, 729
Income Summary, *def.*, 154
Income tax payable, estimated, 527*fn*
Income taxes, 443, 1113
  allocating, 527
  cash payments for, 628
  corporate, 526
  depreciation for federal, 405
  payment of, 526
  provision for, 527*fn*
Incorporation
  application of, 487
  articles of, 488
Indenture
  bond, 568
  trust, 568
Indirect costs
  classifying, *illus.*, 721
  def., 720
Indirect expenses, 1025
Indirect method, 24*fn*
  adjustments to net income (loss), *illus.*, 617

cash flow from operations, *illus.*, 613
cash flows from operating activities, 615, *illus.*, 620
  def., 612
spreadsheet for statement of cash flows, 630, *illus.*, 632
statement of cash flows, 614, *illus.*, 624
Individual character, 5
Industry Norms & Key Business Ratios, 666
Inflation, *def.*, 1105
Information
  and communication, 315
  flow of accounting, 147
  highway, navigating, 731
Information Systems Audit and Control Association, 9
Installments, 440
Institute of Internal Auditors, 9
Institute of Management Accountants (IMA), 9
Intangible assets
  comparison of, *illus.*, 415
  def., 413
  financial reporting for, 416
  frequency of disclosures, *illus.*, 415
  in balance sheet, *illus.*, 417
Interest
  charges, number of times earned, 584, 672
  expense, 628
  market or effective rate, 569
  revenue, *def.*, 15
  tables, A-2–A-5
Interest method, 575
  amortization of discount by, 584
  amortization of premium by, 585
Internal control, 310
  def., 308
  elements of, *illus.*, 311
  for payroll systems, 453
  objectives of, 310
  problems, warning signs of, *illus.*, 316
  procedures, *illus.*, 313
  report on adequacy of, 681
Internal Control—Integrated Framework, 310
Internal failure costs, *def.*, 1200
Internal rate of return (IRR) method, *def.*, 1110
Internal Revenue Code, 405, 1105
Internal stakeholders, 4
International differences in financial statements, 153
Interpretation, financial analysis and, 234, 286, 330, 369, 418, 461, 504, 544, 584, 630
Interpretations, 10
Inventory, 287
  balance sheet presentation of, in manufacturing and merchandising companies, *illus.*, 726
  control of, 268
  determining by retail method, *illus.*, 284
  estimating by gross profit method, *illus.*, 285
  finished goods, 726
  manufacturing costs and, *illus.*, 752
  materials, 725
  merchandise, 213

number of days' sales in, 286, 671
physical, 269
reducing, 1185
work in process, 725
Inventory analysis, 670
Inventory at lower of cost or market, determining, *illus.*, 280
Inventory cost
  estimating, 284
  flow assumptions, 269
Inventory costing methods
  comparing, 278
  illus., 271
  on financial statements, effect of, *illus.*, 270
  retail, 284
  under periodic inventory system, 275
  under perpetual inventory system, 272
Inventory errors on financial statements, effect of, 282
Inventory ledger, 269
Inventory profits, 279
Inventory shift, 1186
Inventory shortage, 232
Inventory shrinkage
  adjusting entry for, 232
  def., 232
Inventory turnover, *def.*, 286, 670
Investing activities
  cash flows from, 22, 610, 612
  net cash flow provided by, 613
  net cash flow used for, 613
  noncash, 613
Investing strategies, 682
Investment center
  def., 1028
  responsibility accounting for, 1028
Investment turnover, *def.*, 1029
Investments, 355, 396
  def., 541
  rate of return on, 1029
  return on, 1031
  temporary, 538
Investments in bonds, 579
  accounting for, 579, 581
Investments in stocks
  accounting for, 538
  long-term, 541
  sale of, 542
  short-term, 538
Investor Protection, Auditor Reform, and Transparency Act of 2002, 10
Invoice
  def., 222
  illus., 222
  open, C-6
  phony scams, 754
  vendor's, 268

J

Job, 751
  assigning factory overhead to, *illus.*, 759
  shops, 751
Job cost sheets
  and work in process controlling account, *illus.*, 761
  comparing data from, *illus.*, 765
  def., 754
Job order cost system
  and process cost system, comparing, 793, *illus.*, 794

Company Index